Webster's New World™

Crossword Puzzle Dictionary

Compiled by
Jane Shaw Whitfield

Prentice Hall
New York • London • Toronto • Sydney • Tokyo • Singapore

Prentice Hall General Reference
15 Columbus Circle
New York, NY 10023

A Webster's New World™ Book

Webster's New World Dictionary and colophon are
registered trademarks of Simon & Schuster, Inc.
Prentice Hall is a registered trademark of Prentice-Hall, Inc.

Library of Congress Catalog Card Number 83-116262

ISBN 0-671-46870-7 (Paper Edition)

Manufactured in the United States of America

18   19   20   21   22   23   24   25

FOREWORD

This reference work has been compiled especially for the millions who enjoy solving crossword puzzles and for those who construct them. But because of its comprehensive coverage of rare, arcane, technical, and dialectal terms, as well as of many proper names from geography, literature, the Bible, and the like, it is also an invaluable aid to those who enjoy solving other kinds of word puzzles or playing word games. And its listings of synonyms and of identifying facts about persons, places, and things make it as well a useful thesaurus and general reference book for the home library.

Unlike some other puzzle dictionaries on the market, this one is not merely a mechanical listing of words of six letters or fewer, offering no clue as to meanings. This list contains answers actually found in a survey of thousands of puzzles, and so you will discover here words from two to fourteen or more letters, as well as phrases and compounds of two or more words, of the kind frequently encountered in puzzles today, such as "in a trice" for "instantly" or "black eye" for "contusion."

A special feature of this book is the arrangement of the materials. All clue words are in bold-face type, alphabetically arranged, with subcategories, where these exist, in italic type, also in alphabetical order. The answer terms for each clue are arranged by the count of letters in each word (or phrase), in numerical order. Each group of answers with the same letter count are then arranged alphabetically to help you find quickly the solution to your problem fill-in.

For example: you need the six-letter name of a Greek sun god. You turn to **Greek god of**, find the subcategory *sun*, and discover after the numeral **6** the two names "Apollo" and "Helios." If you have even one letter of the answer already filled in, you know immediately which is the correct name.

In general, words are shown with their prevailing spellings, but certain rarer variants that commonly appear in puzzles are also given. Although upper-case and lower-case distinctions, and accents on foreign words, are insignificant in crossword puzzle practice, the other uses to which this book will undoubtedly be put made it desirable to observe these orthographic conventions.

So to all enthusiasts of crossword puzzles and to their creators, I hereby dedicate this WEBSTER'S NEW WORLD™ CROSSWORD PUZZLE DICTIONARY.

Jane Shaw Whitfield

ABBREVIATIONS USED IN THIS WORK

Abbr .... Abbreviation
abdom .... abdominal
aborig .... aboriginal
Acad .... Academy
adj .... adjective
adm .... admitted
Afr .... African
Agric .... Agriculture
Alex .... Alexander
Am Ind .... American Indian
Anat .... Anatomy
anc .... ancient
Anglo-Ir .... Anglo-Irish
Anthrop .... Anthropology
Antiq .... Antiquity
Arab .... Arabian
Arch .... Architecture
Archaeol .... Archaeology
Astrol .... Astrology
Astron .... Astronomy
Austral .... Australia(n)

Babyl .... Babylonia
Belg .... Belgium
Bib .... Bible, Biblical
Biol .... Biology
Bot .... Botany
Braz .... Brazil(ian)
Brit .... Britain, British
Brit Col .... British Columbia
Buddh .... Buddhism
Bus .... Business

Can .... Canada, Canadian
Capt .... Captain
Caucas .... Caucasian
Celt .... Celtic
Cent .... Central, Century
Cent Am ...... Central America
Chem .... Chemistry
Chin .... Chinese
Chr .... Christian
coll .... colloquialism
comb form .... combining form
Confed .... Confederation
Constell .... Constellation
contemp .... contemporary
Criminol .... Criminology

Dan .... Danish
Dept .... Department
derog .... derogatory
dial .... dialectal
div .... division
Du .... Dutch

E .... East
East Ch .... Eastern Church
Eccl .... Ecclesiastical
Educ .... Education
Egypt .... Egyptian
Elec .... Electricity
Eng .... England, English
Episcop .... Episcopal
equiv .... equivalent
Esk .... Eskimo
est .... established
Eur .... Europe(an)
exclam .... exclamation
ext .... extinct

FDR .... Franklin D. Roosevelt
Fem .... Feminine
Finan .... Finance, Financial
Flem .... Flemish
Fr .... France, French

Gen .... General
Geog .... Geography
Geol .... Geology
Geom .... Geometry
Ger .... German
Gov .... Governor
Govt .... Government
Gr .... Greek
Gram .... Grammar
Gr Brit .... Great Britain

Haw .... Hawaiian
Heb .... Hebrew
Hem .... Hemisphere
Her .... Heraldry
Hind .... Hinduism
Hindu .... Hindustani
Hist .... Historical
Holl .... Holland
Horol .... Horology
Hung .... Hungarian

illeg .... illegal
Ind .... India, Indian
Indo-Chin .... Indo-China
Ins .... Insurance
Internat .... International
Ir .... Irish
irreg .... irregular
Isl(s) .... Island(s)
It .... Italian

Jap .... Japanese
Jew .... Jewish

L .... Latin
Legislat .... Legislature
Lit .... Literature
Log .... Logic

Maced .... Macedonia
Malay .... Malayan
Math .... Mathematics
MD .... Doctor of Medicine
Med .... Medical
Mex .... Mexican
Mil .... Military
Mohamm .... Mohammedan
Mt(s) .... Mountain(s)
Mus .... Music
Myth .... Mythology

Nat'l .... National
Naut .... Nautical
Nav .... Naval, Navy
neg .... negative
New Test .... New Testament
NZ .... New Zealand
No .... North
No Am .... North American

obs .... obsolete
Old Test .... Old Testament
opp .... opposite
Orient .... Oriental
Oxf Univ .... Oxford University

Penol .... Penology
Pers .... Persian
pert .... pertaining
Petrol .... Petrology
Pg .... Portuguese
Pharm .... Pharmaceutical
Philat .... Philately
Phil I .... Philippine Islands

Philol .... Philology
Philos .... Philosophy
Phonet .... Phonetics
Phys .... Physical
pl .... plural
PO .... Post Office
poet .... poetic
Polit .... Politics, Political
Polyn .... Polynesian
ppty .... property
pref .... prefix
P Rico .... Puerto Rico
Pros .... Prosody

R .... Roman
RCCh ...... Roman Catholic Church
Rd .... Road
ref .... referring
Relig .... Religion
R Estate .... Real Estate
Rev War .... Revolutionary War
Rhet .... Rhetoric
Riv .... River
Rom .... Roman
rr .... railroad
Rum .... Rumania
Russ .... Russian

S .... South
Scot .... Scotland, Scottish
Scand .... Scandinavian
Shakesp .... Shakespeare
sing .... singular
sl .... slang
Slav .... Slavonic
So Afr .... South Africa
So Am .... South America
Sp .... Spanish
Surg .... Surgical
sym .... symbol

Tag .... Tagalog
Tahit .... Tahiti
Terat .... Teratology
terr .... territory
Teut .... Teutonic
Theat .... Theatrical
Theol .... Theology
Theos .... Theosophy
triang .... triangular
TID .... Ter in die
Trop .... Tropical
Turk .... Turkish
TV .... Television

U .... Union
Univ .... University
USS .... United States Ship
USSR .... Union of Soviet
                        Socialist Republics

Vet .... Veterinary

W .... West
WAC ...... Women's Army Corps
W Indies .... West Indies
WWI .... World War I

Yidd .... Yiddish
YMCA ... Young Men's Christian
                        Association
yr .... year

Zool .... Zoology

A

A... 5. alpha, first 7. article
A 1... 5. prime 6. symbol 8. superior
10. first–class
aa (Haw)... 4. lava
aal... 8. morindin (dye), mulberry
aam (Du)... 7. measure (liquid)
11. water bucket
Aani (Egypt)... 3. ape (sacred)
6. baboon 12. cynocephalus
aardvark... 3. pig 6. farrow
8. anteater
aardwolf... 5. hyena 8. Proteles
Aaron (pert to)...
 ally (Bib).. 3. Hur
 brother 5. Moses
 burial place.. 3. Hor
 leader (Jew).. 9. Levitical 10. High
  Priest
 rod.. 4. wand (magic) 7. molding,
  mullein
 sister.. 6. Miriam
 son.. 5. Abihu, Nadab
Aaru (Egypt Relig)... 12. fields of Aaru
14. abode of the dead
aasvogel... 7. vulture
abaca... 4. hemp 5. lupis 6. linaga
abacus... 4. slab 8. cupboard
10. calculator 11. compartment
Abaddon... 3. pit (bottomless) 4. Hell
5. Sheol 8. Apollyon (angel)
11. destruction
abaft... 3. aft 5. after 6. astern,
behind
abalone... 5. awabi, ormer, uhllo (ullo)
6. sea ear 8. ear shell
abandon... 4. quit 5. cease, leave,
remit, waive, yield 6. abjure, depart,
desert, disuse, give up, maroon,
reject, resign, vacate 7. cast off,
discard, forsake, freedom, neglect
8. abdicate, forswear, renounce
9. surrender, turpitude 10. relinquish
11. abandonment, discontinue,
unrestraint 12. carelessness,
heedlessness
abandoned... 4. left, lost 7. disused,
forlorn, given up 8. derelict,
deserted, forsaken 9. desolated,
discarded, neglected 11. surrendered
12. relinquished, unredeemable,
unrestrained
abase... 5. lower, shame 6. bemean,
depose, humble, reduce 7. degrade,
mortify 8. cast down, disgrace
9. humiliate 10. depreciate
abash... 5. shame 6. appall, dismay
7. astound, confuse, disturb, mortify
8. bewilder, confound 9. discomfit,
embarrass, humiliate 10. disconcert,
put to shame
abate... 3. ebb 4. lull, wane 5. let
up, relax, remit 6. deduct, lessen,
reduce 7. abolish, nullify, qualify,
slacken, subside 8. decrease,
diminish, discount, moderate
abatement... 5. letup 6. myosis
(miosis), rebate 8. decrease
9. lessening, reduction
10. diminution, mitigation,
moderation
abb... 4. wool, yarn 6. fleece (pert to)
Abba... 5. abbot, title 6. Father
abbe... 4. monk 6. cleric, curate,
priest
abbess... 4. amma 15. spiritual mother
abbreviate... 7. abridge, curtail,
shorten 8. compress, condense,
contract, simplify 9. epitomize
11. make briefer
abbreviation... 5. brief, lapse 6. digest
8. abstract 9. reduction
10. abridgment, compendium,
shortening 11. contraction
12. condensation
abdicate... 4. cede, quit 5. demit,
leave 6. depose, disown, resign,
retire 7. lay down 8. disclaim,
renounce, withdraw 9. surrender
10. disinherit, relinquish
Abdiel (Heb)... 5. angel 12. servant of
God
abdomen... 3. pot (sl) 4. wame
5. belly, tharm (obs) 6. paunch,
venter 7. stomach 8. potbelly
12. pelvic cavity
abdominal... 7. coeliac, gastric, ventral
11. ventricular
abdominal limb (crustacean)...
7. ploopod
Abel's brother... 4. Cain, Seth
aberration... 5. mania, wrong
6. lunacy, oddity 7. errancy,
madness 8. dementia, insanity
9. departure, deviation, variation,
wandering 10. alienation, digression,
divergence 11. abnormality,
derangement, distraction, peculiarity
12. eccentricity, irregularity
14. disorientation
abet... 3. aid, egg 4. back, help
5. egg on 6. assist, foment, incite,
second, succor, uphold 7. connive,
endorse, support, sustain 8. advocate
9. encourage, instigate
11. countenance
abeyance... 4. rest, stay 5. lapse,
pause 7. waiting 9. inertness
10. expectancy, suspension
abhor... 2. ug 4. hate, shun
6. detest, loathe 7. despise, dislike
8. execrate 9. abominate
abhorrence... 5. odium 6. hatred,
horror 7. dislike 8. aversion, loathing
9. antipathy, disliking, repulsion

10. repugnance

abide... 4. bide, live, stay, wait
5. await, dwell, pause, tarry
6. endure, remain, reside 7. sojourn
8. continue, submit to, tolerate
9. acquiesce, withstand

abide by... 3. own 4. avow, heed
5. admit, allow, yield 6. accept,
follow, regard 7. concede, respect
8. adhere to 9. conform to
11. acknowledge

abiding... 7. durable, lasting
8. constant, enduring 9. permanent,
steadfast 10. continuing, indwelling,
persisting

Abies... 4. firs 5. pines 8. conifers
10. evergreens

abigail... 4. ayah, maid 5. bonne
7. servant 9. soubrette

Abijah's son (Bib)... 3. Asa

ability... 4. gift 5. force, might,
power, skill 6. genius, talent
7. caliber, faculty, fitness, potency
8. aptitude, capacity, strength
10. capability, competence, efficiency
11. proficiency, sufficiency
13. qualification

abiosis... 11. without life

abject... 3. low 4. base, mean, meek,
vile 6. humble, menial, supine
7. hangdog, ignoble, servile, slavish
8. beggarly, contrite, cringing,
degraded, wretched 9. groveling,
miserable 10. despicable, obsequious

abjuration... 6. denial 8. palinode
(song), yielding 9. disavowal,
rejection, surrender 10. abjurement,
retraction, withdrawal
11. abandonment, forswearing,
recantation, repudiation
12. disclamation 14. relinquishment

abjure... 4. deny, wave 6. disown,
recant, reject, revoke 7. abandon,
disavow 8. disclaim, forswear,
renounce 9. disaffirm, repudiate

able... 3. can, fit 5. adept, smart
6. clever, fitted, suited 7. adapted,
capable, learned, solvent 8. adjusted,
literate, powerful, skillful (skilful),
vigorous 9. competent, effective,
efficient, qualified 10. omnipotent,
proficient

able (pert to)...
suffix.. 7. capable, fitness
to pay.. 7. moneyed, solvent
8. affluent 10. prosperous
to read and write.. 8. lettered, literate
10. book taught

ablepsia... 9. blindness

ably... 7. capably 11. competently,
effectively, efficiently

abnormal... 6. albino 7. erratic,
unusual 8. aberrant 9. deviative,
eccentric, irregular, unnatural
11. exceptional 13. extraordinary

aboard... 4. onto 6. across 7. athwart
9. alongside

abode... 3. dar, hut 4. cell, cote,
Eden, home 5. delay, house, lodge
7. habitat, Olympus, sojourn
8. dwelling, tenement 9. apartment,
residence 10. habitation

abode of the dead... 3. Dar 4. Aalu,
Aaru, Hell 5. Aralu, Hades, limbo,
Orcus, Sheol 6. Asgard, heaven,
Naraka 7. Abaddon, Elysium, Nirvana
8. paradise, Valhalla 9. perdition,
purgatory 11. Pandemonium

abolish... 4. undo 5. annul, quash
6. cancel, recall, repeal, revoke,
vacate 7. destroy, nullify, rescind,
retract, reverse 8. abrogate, withdraw
10. annihilate, invalidate
11. countermand

abominable... 4. base, dire, foul, vile
5. awful, gross 6. odious, wicked,
woeful 7. beastly, hateful 8. dreadful,
grievous, infamous, shocking, terrible,
wretched 9. execrable, loathsome,
obnoxious 10. despicable, detestable,
outrageous, unpleasant
12. disagreeable, disreputable

Abominable Snowman... 4. Yeti

abominate... 4. hate 5. abhor
6. detest, loathe 8. execrate

abomination... 3. woe 4. evil
5. odium, wrong 6. hatred, horror,
plague 7. disgust, outrage
8. aversion, loathing, vexation
9. grievance 10. abhorrence,
defilement, odiousness, repugnance

aboriginal... 5. first, natal 6. binghi,
native 7. ancient 8. original
9. beginning, primitive
10. autochthon, indigenous

aborigines... 4. Ainu (Aino), Toda
5. lubra, Sakai, Vedda 7. cave men,
Indians, natives, savages
9. indigenes, old-timers
10. Dravidians 11. preadamites

abortion... 6. arrest 7. failure
11. embryoctomy, miscarriage,
miscreation 13. misconception

abound... 4. flow, teem 5. swarm
8. overflow 9. exuberate, plentiful

abounding... 4. rife 5. ample, flush
7. copious, teeming 8. abundant
9. exuberant, luxuriant, plentiful

abounding in...
blossoms.. 7. flowery
forests.. 6. sylvan
grass.. 6. cressy
snow.. 5. nival

about... 2. of, on, re 3. amb (pref)
5. anent, astir, circa 6. almost,
around, nearly 8. circiter
10. concerning 13. approximately

about to happen... 8. imminent

above... 2. on, up 3. o'er, sur (pref)
4. atop, over, upon 5. aloft, super,
supra (pref)

abrade... 3. rub 4. file, fret, gall
5. chafe, grate 6. scrape
9. excoriate

Abraham (pert to)...
birthplace.. 2. Ur
concubine.. 5. Hagar
father.. 5. Terah
grandfather.. 5. Nahor
grandson.. 4. Esau
nephew.. 3. Lot
son.. 4. Shua (Shuah) 5. Isaac,
Medan 7. Ishmael
wife.. 5. Sarah (Sara, Sarai)

Lewis, Peary 6. Carson (Kit)
9. Ellsworth
musician.. 6. Foster 8. Damrosch,
Gershwin 9. Bernstein, MacDowell,
Stokowski
naturalist.. 4. Muir 5. Beebe
7. Audubon, Burbank
patriot.. 4. Clay, Hale, Otis 5. Dawes,
Henry (Patrick), Paine (Thomas)
6. Revere
physicist.. 6. Teller (H–bomb)
pianist.. 6. Duchin, Levant
8. Horowitz, Liberace, Williams
(Roger) 10. Van Cliburn
pirate.. 4. Kidd (Capt)
poet.. 4. Nash 5. Benet, Eliot, Frost
6. Kilmer, Lowell, Millay 8. Sandburg
10. Longfellow
Red Cross organizer.. 6. Barton (Clara)
Scouts (Girl) organizer.. 3. Low
(Juliette)
sculptor.. 6. Calder 7. Borglum
singer.. 4. Pons 5. Jones, Moore
6. Farrar, Peerce 7. Kirsten, Merrill,
Tibbett 8. Anderson (Marian)
statesman.. 4. Clay, Root 6. Baruch,
Dulles 8. Harriman
suffragette.. 4. Catt (Carrie Chapman)
violinist.. 7. Menuhin
writer, novelist.. 6. Ferber 8. Faulkner
9. Hemingway
American Indian (pert to)...
chief.. 5. brave 6. sachem
child.. 7. papoose
conference.. 8. powwow
girl.. 7. Nokomis (Myth)
9. Minnehaha, Sacagawea
(Sakajawea) 10. Pocahontas
hero (Myth).. 8. Hiawatha
magician.. 6. shaman, wabeno
(Ojibway)
shelter.. 4. tent 5. hogan, tepee
-(teepee) 6. wigwam 7. wickiup
(wikiup)
American Indian tribe... see also
Indian 3. Fox, Oto (Otoe), Ree, Sac,
Ute 4. Cree, Crow, Erie, Hopi, Iowa,
Pima 5. Creek, Kansa, Osage, Piute,
Sioux 6. Cayuga, Dakota, Mohawk,
Oneida, Pueblo, Seneca 7. Arapaho,
Choctaw, Mohican, Ojibway, Siksika
8. Cherokee, Chippewa, Iroquois,
Onondaga, Seminole 9. Algonquin,
Blackfoot, Chickasaw 10. Athapascan,
Muskhogean
ami... 5. lover 6. friend (law)
amiable... 6. kindly 7. lovable
8. charming, friendly, pleasant,
pleasing 9. agreeable, indulgent
10. hospitable
amicable... 4. kind 8. friendly, sociable
9. congenial, peaceable
10. harmonious
amicus curiae... 5. judge 6. deputy,
lawyer 16. friend of the court
amid, amidst... 2. in 5. among
7. amongst, between
amigo... 6. friend 8. neighbor
amiss... 3. ill 5. badly, fault, wrong
6. astray, sinful 8. faultily, improper
10. disorderly 11. erroneously

amity... 4. love 5. peace 7. harmony
10. friendship 11. sociability
12. congeniality, friendliness
amma... 6. abbess, mother (spiritual)
ammonia... 9. hartshorn 10. fertilizer
11. refrigerant
ammoniac plant... 5. oshac
ammunition (pert to)...
box.. 9. bandoleer
chest.. 7. caisson
type.. 4. arms, bomb, shot 7. bullets
8. grenades, missiles, munition,
shrapnel 10. explosives
wagon.. 7. caisson
amnesty... 6. pardon 8. oblivion
9. acquittal 13. forgetfulness
amoeba, ameba... 3. olm 4. cell
7. proteus 10. protoplasm
13. microorganism
among, amongst... 2. in 3. mid
4. amid, with 5. midst 6. amidst,
imelle 7. between
among nations... 13. international
Amor... 4. Eros 5. Cupid
AMORC... 11. Rosicrucian
amorous... 4. fond 6. ardent, erotic,
loving, tender 7. adoring, devoted
8. enamored 10. passionate
12. affectionate
amorous looks... 4. ogle 5. stare
8. coquetry 10. come–hither,
flirtation
amorphous... 8. abnormal, formless
9. deviative, shapeless, subnormal
14. uncrystallized
amorphous mineral... 4. opal
amort... 8. dejected, lifeless
9. inanimate 10. spiritless
amortize... 5. clear 6. convey, payoff,
settle 9. discharge, negotiate
amount... 3. lot, sum 4. cost, rate,
rise, unit 5. chunk, price, ratal,
store, total 6. ascend, degree
7. quantum, signify 8. quantity
amount (pert to)...
due.. 5. price 6. arrear 7. default,
deficit
mean.. 7. average
realized.. 4. take 6. intake
8. proceeds
small.. 6. morsel 7. modicum
smallest.. 5. least
to.. 3. all 4. even 5. equal, match,
total 10. correspond
amour... 6. affair 7. liaison, romance
8. intrigue, triangle 10. flirtation
ampere... 3. amp 4. unit 6. ohmage
7. current, voltage
ampersand... 3. and 4. also
Amphibia... 5. Anura, frogs, toads
7. Aglossa 8. tadpoles 9. Salientia
11. salamanders
amphibious... 5. mixed 9. adaptable
10. fifty–fifty 11. half–and–half, mixed
nature (land and water)
amphibole... 7. edenite, mineral, uralite
8. aluminum, nephrite
amphigory, amphigouri... 5. rhyme
6. jingle, poetry 8. doggerel
9. rigmarole
amphilogism, amphilogy...
9. ambiguity, duplexity (meaning)

10. equivocacy
Amphion (pert to)...
capturer of.. 6. Thebes
husband of.. 5. Niobe
son of.. 4. Zeus
twin of.. 6. Zethus
amphitheater... 4. bowl 5. arena,
cavea, scene, stage 6. circus, cirque
7. stadium 8. coliseum, platform
10. hippodrome
amphora... 3. jar, urn 4. vase
5. diota, prize 7. measure
8. ornament
ample... 4. full, rich, wide 5. broad,
large, roomy 6. enough, plenty
7. liberal 8. abundant 9. bountiful,
capacious, extensive, plenteous,
plentiful, unstinted 10. munificent
12. satisfactory
ampliation... 5. flare 9. expansion,
extension 11. enlargement
12. postponement 13. amplification
14. aggrandizement
amplify... 3. pad 5. widen 6. dilate,
extend 7. develop, enlarge
8. increase 9. aggravate, expatiate
10. exaggerate, overstress
amplitude... 4. size 6. amount
7. breadth 8. fullness 9. greatness,
plenitude 12. spaciousness
amputate... 4. trim 5. prune, sever
6. cut off 8. mutilate, retrench,
truncate
amuck, amok... 3. fit 4. rage
6. attack, frenzy, malady
12. corybantiasm
amulet... 3. gem 5. charm 6. fetish,
scarab, voodoo 7. periapt
8. ornament, talisman 10. protection
amuse... 3. wow 6. divert, please,
regale, tickle 7. beguile, gratify
8. recreate 9. entertain, titillate
10. exhilarate
amusement... 3. fun 4. play 5. farce,
mirth, sport 7. pastime 9. avocation,
diversion 10. recreation, relaxation
13. divertisement, entertainment
amusement place... 4. club, park
6. casino, midway 7. cabaret, theater
ana... 5. books 6. events 8. analecta,
excerpts 9. Americana 10. collection
11. collectanea, compilation,
memorabilia
anachronous... 8. misdated, mistimed
10. beforehand, behindhand
anaglyph... 5. cameo, carve 6. chisel,
plaque, relief 10. embossment
Anak (Eccl)... 5. giant (Canaan)
6. Anakim
analogous... 4. like 7. similar
8. parallel 10. comparable, equivalent
11. correlative
analogue... 8. parallel 11. resemblance
13. correspondent
14. correspondence
analogy... 8. likeness, sameness
9. agreement 10. accordance,
comparison, similarity
14. correspondence
analysis... 5. assay, logic 6. biopsy,
theory 9. breakdown, diagnosis
10. compendium, discussion,

dissection 11. examination
14. classification
analyze... 5. assay, parse, study
7. discuss, dissect, examine
8. classify, describe, diagnose,
separate
Ananias (Bib)... 4. liar 8. disciple
(Damascus), Shadrack (Sidrack)
10. high priest 12. prevaricator
anarch, anarchist... 3. red 7. radical
8. nihilist 9. socialist, terrorist
13. revolutionist
anarchy... 4. riot 5. chaos 6. acracy
7. license, misrule 8. disorder
9. confusion, mobocracy, rebellion
10. ochlocracy
anathema... 3. ban 5. curse
9. damnation 11. abomination,
imprecation, malediction
Anatolian rug... 4. Kurd 5. Tuzla
anatomy... 4. body 5. build, frame
7. carcass 8. analysis, skeleton
9. formation, structure
11. arrangement
anatomy of animals... 7. zootomy
ancestor... 4. Adam, sire 5. elder,
stock 6. atavus, family, parent
8. forebear 9. patriarch, precursor
10. antecedent, forefather,
forerunner, progenitor
11. grandfather, predecessor
ancestral... 4. aval 6. avital, lineal
7. atavism 8. maternal, paternal
9. atavistic, primitive 10. hereditary
11. patrimonial
ancestral spirits... 5. lares, manes
7. lemures, penates
ancestry... 4. race, rank 5. birth,
blood 7. descent, lineage
11. antecedents 14. progenitorship
anchor... 3. fix, tie 4. hook, moor,
rest, stop 5. affix, clamp, kedge
6. attach, batten, fasten, secure
7. grapnel, killick
anchor (pert to)... 3. arm, cat, pee
4. cast, palm, tore (ring) 5. fluke
7. capstan
anchorite, anchoret... 6. hermit,
shut-in 7. ascetic, eremite, recluse,
stylite 8. homebody
anchor-shaped... 8. ankyroid
10. hook-shaped
anchovy... 4. alec 5. sauce, sprat
7. herring
ancienne noblesse... 5. elect, elite
7. royalty 8. nobility 11. aristocracy
ancient... 3. eld, old 4. aged, auld,
wise 5. adept, early, hoary, olden
7. antique 8. historic, obsolete,
outdated, primeval, pristine
9. grandeval, primitive, venerable
10. aboriginal, antiquated, preadamite
12. antediluvian
ancient (pert to)...
chariot.. 5. essed
city.. 4. Elis, Tyre 5. Argos, Sedon
6. Athens, Sparta, Thebes
drink.. 5. morat
empire.. 4. Gaul 5. Roman 6. Lydian
7. Persian 8. Assyrian, Athenian,
Chaldean, Hellenic 10. Babylonian,
Phoenician

god.. 4. Esus (Gaulish)
isles.. 5. Chios, Crete, Samos
  6. Aegina, Ionian, Ithaca, Lemnos,
  Lesbos, Rhodes 7. Salamis
  8. Cyclades
language.. 4. Pali 5. Latin 6. Celtic,
  Gaelic 7. Cornish, Gaulish
mariner.. 4. Rime (of) 5. rover
  6. roamer, sailor, seaman
  8. seafarer, wanderer 9. navigator
soldier.. 7. peltast
theater.. 5. odeum
and... 2. et 4. also, plus 8. et cetera
  9. ampersand, including
  12. additionally
andante... 5. largo, tempo 6. slowly
Andean (pert to)...
camel.. 5. llama
deer.. 4. pudu
region, wind.. 4. puna
term.. 5. grand, lofty
andiron... 3. dog 7. firedog, Hessian
andrenid... 3. bee 10. Andrenidae
androgyny... 9. sissiness
  10. effeminacy 11. unmanliness
  15. hermaphroditism
android... 5. robot 9. automaton
anecdote... 4. tale, yarn 5. story
  7. account 9. chronicle, narrative
anecdotes... 3. ana 7. sayings, stories
anemone... 7. actinia 10. windflower
anent... 2. of, on, re 4. upon, with
  5. about 8. opposite 10. concerning
anesthesia, anaesthesia...
  8. deadness, numbness
  13. insensibility
anesthetic... 3. gas 5. ether
  8. freezing, Novocain, procaine
  9. pentothal 10. chloroform
  13. refrigeration
anesthetize... 4. dull, numb, stun
  6. benumb, deaden, freeze 7. stupefy
  8. etherize, paralyze 9. narcotize
  10. chloroform 11. desensitize
anew... 5. again, newly 6. afresh, de
  novo 8. recently
angel... 6. cherub, genius, seraph
  (seraf) 7. Madonna, prophet
angel (pert to)...
Arab (apostate).. 5. Eblis
archangel.. 5. Uriel 7. Gabriel,
  Michael, Raphael
Biblical.. 6. bishop, pastor
Fallen.. 6. Belial, Mammon
financial.. 6. backer, patron
  7. sponsor 8. promoter
fish.. 5. shark 9. spadefish
Hebrew.. 6. Abdiel 8. cherubim,
  seraphim
Jewish.. 6. Azrael (of death)
  7. Zadkiel (of planet Jupiter)
  8. Metatron
Mohammedan (Mus).. 7. Israfil
  (Israfeel)
Moslem.. 5. Nakir (Repudiating)
  6. Munkar (Unknown)
angelic... 5. godly 7. lovable, saintly
  8. cherubic, heavenly, seraphic,
  virtuous 9. celestial 10. beneficent
angelica... 4. herb 6. lovely 7. liqueur
Angelus... 4. boll, call 6. prayer
  8. devotion

anger... 3. ire, vex 4. fume, rage, rile
  5. annoy, chafe, wrath 6. choler,
  dander, enrage, nettle, offend,
  temper 7. dudgeon, emotion,
  inflame, madness, passion, trouble
  8. vexation 9. infuriate 10. affliction,
  enragement, irritation, resentment
  11. displeasure, indignation
  12. exasperation
angered... 3. mad 5. irate, wroth
  8. incensed, wrathful 9. indignant,
  irascible
angle... 3. ell, tee, zig 4. axil, coin,
  fish, fork, hade, nook 5. acute,
  ancon, arris, right, slant, story
  6. akimbo, distal, epaule, obtuse,
  octant 7. bastion, outlook, ravelin,
  salient 8. attitude 9. incidence,
  rectangle, viewpoint
angler... 6. fisher 7. dibbler, trawler,
  troller 8. piscator 9. fisherman,
  Waltonian
angler's basket... 5. creel
Anglican... 7. English
Anglo–Celtic... 7. British
  10. Anglo–Saxon
Anglo–Indian (pert to)...
Empire founder.. 5. Clive
measure.. 3. ser 4. tola
pageant.. 7. tamasha
peasant.. 4. ryot
princess.. 5. begum
wealthy.. 5. nabob
Anglo–Saxon (pert to)...
armor.. 7. haubork
assembly.. 4. moot 5. gemot
  (gemote)
attendant.. 5. thane
consonant.. 3. edh, eth
council.. 9. heptarchy
councilman.. 5. witan
epic (heroic).. 7. Beowulf
native.. 7. English 11. Anglo–Celtic
prince (heir apparent).. 8. atholing
slave.. 4. esne
tenant.. 6. goneat
warrior.. 5. thane
Angora...
capital of.. 6. Turkey
garment.. 5. shawl
goat.. 6. chamal
wool fabric.. 6. mohair
angry... 3. hot, mad 4. sore 5. cross,
  grame, irate, irked, vexed 6. ireful,
  stormy 7. enraged, painful
  8. inflamed, wrathful 9. indignant,
  irascible, resentful, turbulent
  10. passionate
anguish... 3. woe 4. bale, pain, pang
  5. agony, dolor, grief, throe
  6. misery 7. remorse, sadness,
  torment, torture 8. distress
  9. heartache 10. desolation
  11. lamentation
angular... 4. bent, bony, edgy
  5. gaunt, sharp 6. abrupt, akimbo,
  forked 7. crooked, pointed, scrawny
  8. cornered, crotched
ani... 8. keelbill (keelbird) 9. blackbird
animadversion... 7. censure, comment,
  obloquy 8. judgment, reproach
  9. aspersion, criticism

10. imputation, reflection
12. condemnation
animadvert... 4. note 5. watch
6. notice, regard, remark 7. censure, comment, observe 9. criticize (criticise)
anima humana... 4. mind, self, soul
5. heart, human 6. psyche, spirit
animal (pert to)...
anatomy.. 7. zootomy
back, spine.. 4. nota 5. chine
body.. 4. soma
castrated.. 3. seg (segg)
coat.. 6. pelage
cud.. 5. rumen
disease.. 8. enzootic
enclosure.. 3. pen, sty 4. cage, coop, cote, reem, yard 5. hutch, kraal, stall 6. corral 7. pasture
fabulous.. 7. griffin
group.. 3. gam, pod 4. herd
5. drove, flock, pride 9. menagerie
hairless.. 5. pelon
hindleg part.. 4. crus
hornless.. 7. pollard
hybrid.. 4. mule 5. hinny
hypnosis.. 9. cataplexy
male.. 3. tom 4. bull, jack, stag
5. steer 8. stallion
many–egged.. 5. zooid
many–footed.. 7. polyped
molt.. 8. exuviate
mother.. 3. dam
no feet.. 4. apod
nose.. 5. snout
oar–footed.. 7. remiped
one–egged.. 4. zoon
one–footed.. 6. uniped
pet.. 4. cade
reference to.. 4. wild 6. carnal
7. bestial, fleshly, kingdom 8. domestic 12. ferae naturae 14. domitae naturae
regional.. 5. fauna
small.. 10. animalcule
symbolic.. 5. totem
track, trail.. 4. rack 5. piste, spoor
web–footed.. 8. pinniped
wing–footed.. 6. aliped
worship.. 8. zoolatry
young.. 3. cub, kid, pup 4. calf, colt, fawn, foal, lamb 5. filly, puppy 6. kitten
animal family...
bear.. 6. ursine
cat.. 6. feline
cow.. 6. bovine
deer.. 7. cervine
dog.. 6. canine
fox.. 7. vulpine
horse.. 6. equine
pig.. 7. porcine
sheep.. 5. ovine
wolf.. 6. lupine
animal stomach...
1st.. 5. rumen 6. paunch
2nd.. 5. tripe 9. honeycomb, reticulum
3rd.. 6. omasum 9. manyplies
4th.. 4. read (reed) 8. abomasum
animate... 3. act 4. fire, live, move
5. alive, cheer, imbue, impel, liven

6. arouse, ensoul, spirit, vivify
7. enliven, inspire, organic, refresh
8. energize, vitalize 9. stimulate
10. exhilarate
animated... 3. gay 5. alive, brisk
6. active, lively, living, minded 8. disposed (in mind), prompted 9. energetic, refreshed
animated spirit... 6. animus
animation... 3. pep 4. brio, dash, life
5. ardor 6. energy, gaiety, spirit 8. airiness, buoyancy, vivacity 10. excitement, liveliness, motivation 11. earnestness, inspiration 12. invigoration, vivification 13. sprightliness
animation suspended... 6. apathy, torpor 8. dormancy, lethargy
animé... 6. bright 8. animated
animosity... 5. clash, spite 6. enmity, hatred, rancor 7. ill will 8. conflict 9. antipathy, hostility 10. antagonism, opposition, repugnance
animoso... 6. lively 8. animated
9. energetic
animous... 3. hot 8. resolute, vehement
animus... 4. mind, will 6. desire, spirit, temper 8. attitude, volition 9. intention 10. discretion 11. disposition, inclination
ankh (Egypt)... 3. tau 4. life 5. cross
6. emblem, symbol
ankle... 4. tali (pl) 5. joint, pivot, talus
6. tarsus 8. astragal 9. ginglymus 10. astragalus 11. diarthrosis
ankle cover... 4. spat 6. gaiter
ankylostoma... 7. lockjaw
annalist... 6. writer 8. recorder
9. historian 10. chronicler 11. memorialist 12. chronologist
annals... 5. diary 6. record 7. history, journal 8. register 9. chronicle 11. publication
Annam... 5. Hanoi 6. Tonkin (Tongking)
Annamese... 7. Chinese 8. Buddhist
9. Mongolian
anneal... 4. fuse, heat 6. harden, temper 7. inflame, toughen 8. indurate
Anne Hathaway's home... 8. Shattery
annelid... 3. lug 4. lurg, naid, worm
6. phylum 7. lugworm
annex... 3. add, ell 4. join, wing
5. affix 6. append, attach, fasten 7. acquire, subjoin 8. addition 9. extension
annexation... 7. adjunct 8. addition
9. accession 10. affixation 13. appropriation
Annie Oakley... 4. pass 6. ticket (free)
annihilate... 4. undo, void 5. erase, wreck 6. quench, reduce, stifle 7. abolish, destroy, expunge, nullify, smother 8. decimate 9. extirpate 10. extinguish, obliterate 11. exterminate
annihilation... 5. death 6. demise
7. passing 10. extinction

11. destruction, dissolution
13. extermination 14. extinguishment
anniversary... 5. cycle 6. course
7. jubilee, wedding 8. birthday
10. centennial, regularity
13. commemoration
annotation... 4. note 5. gloss
7. apostil, comment 8. exegesis,
notation, rescript, scholium
9. reference 10. commentary
annotator... 6. critic 7. analyst
9. expositor, expounder, publicist,
scholiast 10. glossarist
11. commentator
announce... 3. bid 4. call, tell 5. bruit
6. affirm, assert, herald, notify
7. declare, forerun, gazette, presage
8. proclaim 9. advertise, broadcast,
pronounce 10. annunciate,
promulgate
announcement... 4. fiat 5. blurb, edict
6. decree, notice 8. bulletin
9. manifesto 10. commercial
11. affirmation, declaration
12. notification, proclamation
13. advertisement
announcer... 4. page 5. crier, emcee
6. nuncio 9. harbinger, informant
10. newscaster, proclaimer
11. broadcaster
annoy... 3. irk, nag, try, vex 4. bore,
rile 5. anger, devil, harry, peeve,
spite, tease 6. bother, harass,
molest, offend, pester, ruffle
7. disturb, trouble 8. irritate
9. displease 13. inconvenience
annoyance.. 4. bore, pest
8. nuisance, vexation 10. resentment
11. molestation 13. inconvenience
annoying... 4. sore 7. galling
9. vexatious 11. distressing
annual... 4. book 5. plant 6. yearly
7. etesian 10. periodical
11. publication
annuity... 5. rente, trust 6. income
(life) 7. pension, subsidy, tontine
9. allotment 10. investment, life
income
annul... 4. cass, undo, void 5. avoid,
blank, quash 6. cancel, repeal,
revoke 7. abolish, nullify, rescind
8. abrogate, derogate, overrule,
withdraw 9. disaffirm 10. invalidate,
neutralize, obliterate 11. countermand
annular... 6. banded, cyclic, ringed
8. cingular, circular
annulet... 4. ring (Her) 6. fillet
7. circlet, ringlet
annulment... 6. repeal 7. erasure,
vacatur 9. abolition 10. abrogation,
defeasance, revocation
12. invalidation 14. neutralization
annunciate... 6. affirm, assert
8. announce, proclaim
annunciation... 11. affirmation
12. announcement, proclamation
13. pronouncement
anoa... 2. ox (wild) 8. sapiutan
anode... 8. terminal (positive)
9. electrode (opp of cathode)
anodic... 12. turned toward
anodyne... 4. balm 6. opiate

7. soother 8. antalgic, narcotic,
pacifier, sedative 9. analgesic
10. depressant, palliative
anoesia... 6. idiocy
anoint... 3. oil 4. balm, cere, nard
5. anele, bribe, smear 6. chrism,
grease, spread 7. moisten
8. medicate 9. embrocate, lubricate
10. consecrate
anoli, anole... 6. lizard
anomalous... 3. odd 7. erratic,
strange, unusual 8. aberrant,
abnormal, peculiar 9. eccentric,
irregular 10. dissimilar
11. exceptional 13. unconformable
anomaly... 6. oddity, rarity
11. abnormality, nondescript
12. irregularity
anomy... 7. miracle
anon... 4. soon 5. again, later
6. mañana, thence 7. by–and–by
8. tomorrow 10. eventually
11. straightway
anonymous (opp of onomatous)...
7. unknown 8. nameless, unavowed
9. undefined
anoöpsia... 10. strabismus (upward)
Anopheles... 10. mosquitoes
anophthalmia... 13. absence of eyes
(congenital)
anopia... 15. defective vision
anorak... 12. hooded jacket (Arctic)
anorexia... 10. no appetite
anorthopia... 15. distorted vision
anosmia... 11. loss of smell
another... 3. new 4. more 5. alias,
extra, other 6. second 7. further
10. additional
another time... 5. again
10. otherwhile
ansa... 4. loop 6. handle
anserine... 6. stupid 9. gooselike
answer... 2. do 3. say 4. echo
5. avail, reply, sauce, serve
6. oracle, retort 7. defense, epistle,
respond, riposte 8. conclude,
reaction, repartee, response, solution
9. rejoinder 10. correspond,
responsory 11. acknowledge
16. counterstatement
answerable... 6. liable 8. amenable,
solvable 11. responsible
12. commensurate 13. proportionate
answer the purpose... 2. so 3. fit
4. suit 5. avail, serve 6. become
7. benefit, satisfy, suffice
ant (pert to)...
family.. 10. Formicidae, Myrmicidae
11. Formicoidea (super),
Hymenoptera
feeding on.. 13. formicivorous
genus.. 6. Eciton, Termes 7. Formica
killer.. 9. formicide
male.. 8. macraner (large), micraner
(small)
nest.. 9. formicary
ref to.. 6. formic
type.. 5. emmet 7. formica, pismire
white.. 4. anay (anai) 7. termite
wingless.. 8. ergatoid
worker.. 6. ergate 9. harvester
antacid... 6. alkali, remedy 8. medicine

9. absorbent 11. neutralizer
  12. counteragent 13. counteractant
Antaeus, Antaios (Gr)... 5. giant
  6. Libyan 8. wrestler
antagonism... 3. war 5. clash
  8. conflict 9. antipathy, hostility
  10. opposition, repugnance
  11. contrariety 12. disagreement
  13. counteraction
antagonist... 3. foe 5. enemy, rival
  6. foeman 8. opponent 9. adversary
antagonistic... 7. hostile, opposed
  8. contrary, converse, inimical,
  opposite 9. repugnant 10. unfriendly
  11. belligerent, disagreeing
  13. counteractive
Antarctic...
  Circle.. 4. Pole 6. region
  continent.. 10. Antarctica
  explorer.. 4. Byrd, Ross
  islands.. 11. Archipelago
  rel to.. 8. subpolar 9. antipodal,
  South Pole
  sea.. 4. Ross 7. Weddell
  seal (brown) discoverer.. 7. Weddell
  volcano.. 6. Erebus
ante... 3. pay, pot 4. bank, fund, pool
  5. kitty, stake 7. jackpot
anteater... 5. Manis 7. echidna
  8. aardvark, edentate, pangolin,
  tamandua
antecede... 4. head 5. front 6. prefix
  7. outrank, precede, preface
antecedent... 4. fore 5. prior, scout
  6. former 7. pioneer 8. ancestor,
  previous 9. foregoing, precedent,
  preceding, precursor 10. forerunner,
  precedence 11. voortrekker (Dutch)
  12. avant–courier
antecedents... 7. fathers 9. ancestors,
  forebears 10. ascendants
  (ascendents) 11. forefathers
  12. predecessors 13. prerequisites
antechamber... 4. hall 5. lobby
  6. lounge 7. chamber 8. anteroom
  9. vestibule
antedate... 7. precede, predate
  8. datemark, pre–exist 10. anticipate
antelope... 3. gau, gnu, kob, nil
  4. guib, koba, oryx, roan 5. addax,
  bovid, eland, goral, oribi, peele,
  saiga, serow 6. cabree, dzeren,
  impala, nilgai, pygarg 7. blaubok,
  blesbok, bubalia, chamois, gazella,
  gazelle, gemsbok, sassaby
  8. agacella, bontebok, steinbok
  9. duikerbok, pronghorn
  10. hartebeest
antenna... 4. horn, mast, palp
  5. clava (Zool), tower 6. aerial, feeler
  7. scanner
antepast... 6. canape, repast
  8. aperitif 9. antipasto, appetizer,
  foretaste 11. hors d'oeuvre,
  prelibation
anteroom... 4. hall 5. lobby 6. lounge
  7. chamber 9. vestibule
  11. antechamber
anthem... 3. lay 4. hymn, song
  5. motet, music, psalm 7. chorale
  8. doxology 9. antiphony, offertory
  10. responsory

anthill... 5. mound 9. formicary
anthology... 3. ana 5. album
  6. corpus 7. omnibus, prayers
  8. analects 9. potpourri
  10. collection 11. collectanea,
  compilation
Anthozoa... 6. corals, polyps
  8. anemones
anthropoid... 3. ape, lar, man
  6. gibbon 7. gorilla, primate,
  siamang 9. orangutan (orangoutang)
  10. chimpanzee, troglodyte
  12. Anthropoidea (suborder)
anthropophagi... 9. cannibals,
  man–eaters
anti... 6. contra 7. adverse, counter,
  opposed 8. contrary, converse
  13. contradictory
antiaircraft artillery... 4. guns
  6. ack–ack, Archie, cannon
  7. weapons 8. cannonry, ordnance
  10. skysweeper
antibiotics... 5. drugs 7. vaccine
  10. penicillin 12. streptomycin
antic... 4. dido 5. caper, prank, stunt
  6. frolic, gambol 7. bizarre, buffoon,
  gambado 9. grotesque
  11. merry–andrew, monkeyshine
anticipate... 4. hope 5. await, dread
  6. expect 7. foresee, obviate,
  portend, prevent 8. preclude
  9. forestall, foretaste, forethink
  11. contemplate
anticipation... 4. hope 9. foresight,
  foretaste, intuition, prolepsis
  10. foreboding 11. expectation,
  forethought 12. presentiment
  13. preoccupation
anticlimax... 6. bathos 8. comedown,
  decrease
antidote... 6. remedy 10. corrective,
  preventive 11. neutralizer
  12. counteragent, prophylactic
  13. counteractant
Antioch... 7. capital (Syria)
antipathy... 6. hatred, nausea
  7. dislike 8. aversion, loathing
  9. disrelish, hostility 10. abhorrence,
  antagonism, opposition, reluctance,
  repugnance 11. contrariety,
  detestation, inimicality
  13. counteraction 14. disinclination
antipodal... 5. polar 7. counter (global)
  8. contrary, opposite
  14. contrapositive
antiquated... 4. aged 5. passé
  6. bygone, voided 7. antique,
  archaic, elderly 8. absolute, medieval
  9. Victorian 10. fossilized
  12. old–fashioned 13. superannuated
antique... 3. old 5. hoary, relic
  7. ageless, ancient 8. dateless,
  outmoded 9. venerable
  12. old–fashioned
antiquities... 5. codex, ruins 6. relics
  7. fossils, papyrus, remains, tablets
  9. archaisms, artifacts, monuments
  11. manuscripts, palimpsests
antiquity... 3. ago, eld 4. past, yore
  7. oldness 9. paleology
  11. ancientness, elderliness
  13. aboriginality, primitiveness

11. perceptibly

apparition . . . 4. bogy, form 5. ghost,
shade, spook 6. shadow, spirit,
sprite, vision, wraith 7. eidolon,
fantasy, phantom, specter (spectre)
8. illusion, phantasm, revenant
9. hobgoblin 10. appearance,
phenomenon, revelation

appassionato . . . 9. emotional
11. impassioned

appeal . . . 3. beg, cry 4. call, cite,
plea, pray, suit 5. charm, plead
6. avouch, invoke, prayer 7. address,
beseech, entreat, implore, request,
solicit 8. entreaty, petition
9. importune 10. lovability,
loveliness, supplicate
11. winsomeness 12. supplication

appealing . . . 4. nice 7. winsome
8. alluring, charming, engaging,
pleasant 9. agreeable, glamorous,
imploring 10. attractive, beseeching,
bewitching, delightful, enchanting,
entreating 11. fascinating, interesting

appear . . . 4. loom, seem 5. occur
6. arrive, attend, emerge
11. materialize

appearance . . . 3. air 4. form, look,
mien 5. front, guise, looks, phase
6. aspect, format, manner, ostent
7. arrival, feature, specter (spectre)
8. illusion, presence, pretense
9. emergence, semblance
10. apparition, disclosure, revelation
11. resemblance 13. manifestation

appearance (pert to) . . .
book . . 6. format
false . . 8. disguise
first . . 4. dawn 5. debut 8. promiere
frontal . . 6. façade
surface . . 6. patina
truth (appearance of) . .
  14. verisimilitude
white . . 6. pallid

appease . . . 4. calm 5. allay, atone,
mease, quiet, salve 6. pacify, soothe
7. content, placate, relieve, satisfy
8. mitigate 10. conciliate
11. tranquilize

appeasement . . . 6. relief 7. salving
8. easement 10. compromise,
mitigation, palliation 12. pacification

appellation . . . 3. tag 4. name 5. label,
style, title 7. calling, epithet
8. cognomen, nickname 10. sobriquet
11. designation 12. denomination,
nomenclature 14. identification

append . . . 3. add 4. hang 5. affix,
annex 6. adjoin, attach 7. subjoin
11. superimpose

appendage . . . 3. arm, awn, cue, tab,
tag 4. barb, flap, lobe, tail 5. cauda,
queue 6. ligule (Bot), palpus
7. adjunct, pigtail 8. addition,
hanger-on, pendicle 9. accessory,
tailpiece 10. dependency
12. appurtenance
13. accompaniment

appendix . . . 6. sequel 7. codicil,
process 8. addendum, addition
9. accessory, appendage
10. dependency 12. augmentation

appertain . . . 4. bear 5. apply 6. affect,
belong, regard, relate 7. involve,
pertain

appetite . . . 4. zest 5. taste 6. desire,
hunger, orexis, thirst 7. longing,
passion 8. cupidity 9. appetency
10. hungriness, propensity

appetizer . . . 4. fish (sauce) 6. canape
8. antepast, aperitif 9. antipasto,
foretaste 11. hors d'oeuvre

appetizing . . . 6. savory 7. piquant
8. tempting 9. appealing, desirable
10. attractive 11. captivating,
provocative, tantalizing

applaud . . . 4. clap, hail, laud, root, yell
5. cheer, extol, shout 6. hurrah,
praise 7. acclaim, approve,
commend, endorse 10. compliment

applauders (paid) . . . 6. claque
8. clappers 9. claqueurs

applause . . . 4. clap, hand 5. bravo,
éclat, huzza 6. encore, praise
7. acclaim, ovation 8. plaudits
11. acclamation 12. commendation

apple . . . 3. May, Spy 4. crab, pome
6. annona, pippin, rennet, russet
7. Baldwin, codling (codlin), costard,
Newtown, Roxbury, winesap
8. Greening, Jonathan, Mandrake,
McIntosh, queening 9. astrachan,
Delicious 10. bellflower, Rome
Beauty 11. Gravenstein, Northern Spy

apple (pert to) . . .
acid . . 5. malic
crushed . . 6. pomace
dessert . . 10. brown betty
disease . . 7. stippen
genus . . 5. Malus
juice . . 5. cider 9. applejack
love . . 6. tomato
seed . . 3. pip
shaped . . 6. pomiform

Apple of Discord (Gr Myth) . . . 4. Eris

apple of one's eye . . 3. pet 4. idol
5. jewel, pupil 7. darling, desired
8. favorite 10. preference

applesauce . . . 4. bunk, pooh 5. tripe
6. phooey 7. baloney, hogwash
8. malarkey, nonsense, tommyrot
12. fiddlesticks 13. horsefeathers

appliance . . . 3. dam (dental) 4. tool
6. device, gadget 7. utensil
8. facility 9. commodity, implement
10. instrument 11. application,
contraption, convenience

applicable . . . 3. apt, fit 6. usable
7. pliable 8. apposite, relative,
relevant 9. compliant, pertinent
11. appropriate

application . . . 3. use 6. appeal, effort
7. bearing, concern, request
8. petition, recourse 9. attention,
constancy, diligence, relevance,
relevancy 10. connection,
employment, pertinence
11. attribution, disposition,
engrossment, persistence, requisition
12. perseverance 14. administration

application (body) . . . 4. balm 5. salve,
stupe (hot) 7. plaster 8. cosmetic,
poultice

apply . . . 3. use 4. suit 6. appose,

bestow, comply, devote, employ, relate 7. solicit, utilize 9. associate, attribute 10. administer 11. appropriate

appoggiature... 9. grace note 13. embellishment

appoint... 3. fix 4. name 5. equip 6. assign, decree, depute, detail, ordain 7. destine, prepare 8. delegate, deputize 9. designate, establish, prescribe 10. constitute

appointment... 4. date 5. order, tryst 7. command 8. position 9. direction, equipment, ordinance 10. engagement 11. designation 13. establishment

appointments... 6. things 8. fittings, fixtures 9. equipment, furniture 10. belongings, upholstery 11. acquirement, furnishings 12. accumulation, conveniences 13. accouterments, paraphernalia

apportion... 3. fix, lot 4. deal, dele, mete, part 5. allot, carve, share 6. assign, budget, divide 7. arrange, dispose 8. allocate 9. collocate, partition 10. distribute

appose... 4. abut 5. audit, liken, place 6. adjoin 7. compare, examine 9. juxtapose

apposite... 3. apt 4. like 5. close, match 6. timely 7. fitting, germane 8. position, relative, relevant 9. pertinent 11. appropriate

appraise... 4. mark, rank, rate 5. assay, gauge, judge, price, value 6. assess, evalue, praise 7. apprise, commend, measure 8. consider, estimate, evaluate 10. adjudicate, appreciate

appraiser (tax)... 5. rater 6. lister 8. assessor

appreciable... 3. any 8. tangible 9. estimable 11. perceptible

appreciate... 4. feel, grow, know 5. enjoy, prize, savor, value 6. admire, esteem 7. advance, amplify, approve, augment, realize, respect 8. estimate, increase, treasure

appreciation... 7. respect 9. appraisal, awareness, gratitude 10. estimation 11. realization, recognition, sensibility 12. gratefulness, thankfulness

apprehend... 3. ken, see 4. know, take 5. dread, grasp, pinch (sl), savvy, sense 6. arrest 7. capture, imagine, realize 8. conceive, perceive 10. anticipate, comprehend, understand

apprehensible... 8. knowable 9. scrutable 10. explicable, fathomable 11. accountable 12. discoverable, intelligible 14. comprehensible, understandable

apprehension... 4. fear, idea 5. alarm, doubt, dread, qualm 6. arrest 7. anxiety, capture, concern, opinion, seizure 8. distress, distrust, suspense 9. misgiving, suspicion 10. foreboding, solicitude, uneasiness 11. fearfulness, premonition

12. intelligence 13. understanding

apprehensive... 5. smart 6. uneasy 7. alarmed, fearful, knowing, nervous, worried 8. troubled 9. cognizant, concerned, conscious, perturbed 10. perceptive, solicitous

apprentice... 4. tyro 6. novice 7. amateur, trainee 8. beginner

apprize, apprise... 4. rate, tell 5. price, value 6. advise, assess, impart, inform, reckon 8. acquaint, appraise 9. enlighten 11. communicate

apprized... 5. aware 8. informed 9. cognizant

approach... 3. way 4. adit, come, near, road 5. stalk, verge 6. access, accost, advent, impend 7. arrival, nearing, sea gate 8. entryway, likeness, nearness, overture, resemble 11. approximate, entranceway

approachable... 4. open 8. gettable, passable 9. reachable 10. accessible, attainable 13. communicative

approbation... 5. favor, proof 6. praise 7. plaudit 8. applause, approval, sanction 10. acceptance, admiration 12. commendation, confirmation

appropriate... 3. apt, fit 4. akin, meet, take 5. allot, steal, usurp 6. borrow, pirate, proper, timely, worthy 7. condign, germane, related, special 8. deserved, relevant, suitable 9. befitting, expedient, favorable, opportune, pertinent 10. assimilate, monopolize, plagiarize 11. conformable

appropriately... 4. duly 5. aptly 6. timely

appropriation... 5. theft 6. corner, taking 8. monopoly 9. allotment 10. assignment, possession, usurpation

approval... 6. assent 7. consent, support 8. sanction 10. admiration 11. approbation, endorsement 12. ratification

approve... 2. OK 4. like, okay, pass, sign, test 6. attest, ratify 7. applaud, betoken, certify, confirm, endorse (indorse), signify 8. accredit, sanction, validate 9. authorize, undersign 10. appreciate 11. countenance 12. authenticate

approve of... 5. favor 6. accept 7. endorse (indorse) 8. sanction 11. countenance

approximate... 4. near 5. about, circa, match 8. approach, draw near, parallel, resemble 10. correspond

approximately... 5. about, circa 6. around, nearly 11. thereabouts

appui... 4. prop, stay 6. bridle (manège) 7. support

appulse... 6. syzygy 7. impinge 8. approach 9. collision 11. conjunction (Astron)

appurtenance... 4. gear 7. adjunct 8. addition 9. accessory, apparatus, appendage, belonging, component

appurtenant... 7. annexed 8. incident, relevant 9. appendant, belonging

11. appropriate
après... 5. after 10. afterwards
apricot (pert to)...
 African.. 6. meebos (dried)
 beverage.. 7. cordial, liqueur, persico
 color.. 9. red–yellow
 confection.. 6. meebos (mebos)
 Japanese.. 3. ume 4. ansu
 vine.. 6. maypop
a priori (opp of posteriori)...
 9. deductive 11. conditional,
 presumptive 12. hypothetical
 13. presumptively
apron... 3. bib 4. boot, brat, tier
 5. smock 6. barvel (barvell), runway
 7. garment, tablier 8. airstrip,
 lambskin (Masonic), pinafore
 9. appendage
apropos, a propos... 3. apt, pat
 7. germane, purpose 8. by the way,
 relevant, suitably 9. pertinent
 10. applicable, seasonable
 11. appurtenant, opportunely
 12. incidentally
apt... 3. fit, pat 4. deft 5. adept,
 prone, ready, smart 6. clever, expert,
 likely, prompt, suited 7. capable,
 elegant, subject 8. apposite,
 disposed, inclined, skillful, suitable
 9. competent, dexterous, ingenious,
 masterful, pertinent, qualified,
 teachable 10. proficient
 11. appropriate
apteral... 8. apterous, wingless
Apteryx... 3. moa (extinct) 4. kiwi
aptitude... 3. art 4. bent, gift, turn
 5. flair, skill 6. genius, talent
 7. ability, aptness, fitness, leaning
 8. penchant, tendency 9. liability
 10. likelihood, proclivity
 11. inclination 12. suitableness
 15. appropriateness
aptly... 7. exactly, readily 8. suitably
 11. pertinently
aptness... 5. skill 7. fitness
 8. tendency 9. smartness
 11. suitability 12. teachability
aqua... 3. eau 4. agua 5. water
aquatic... 6. natant, wading, watery
 8. natatory, swimming 12. grallatorial
 13. water–dwelling
Aquila... 6. eagles 13. constellation
 (Milky Way)
aquiline... 6. hanate, hooked
 7. curving 8. aduncous, unciform
 10. Roman–nosed
ara... 5. macaw 7. goddess
 (vengeance) 8. aracanga 9. screw
 pine 13. constellation
Arab... 4. waif 5. gamin, horse,
 nomad 6. Semite 7. Bedouin,
 Saracen 8. wanderer, Yemenite
 9. Caucasian
araba... 3. cab 5. coach 6. monkey
 (howling)
Arabia... see *Saudi–Arabia*
Arabian (pert to)...
 antelope.. 5. addax
 beverage.. 4. boza (bosa) 5. leban
 (lebban)
 bird.. 7. phoenix
 chief.. 5. sheik

cloth (shoulder).. 6. cabaan (caban)
demon.. 5. Eblis, jinni (jinnee)
 6. afreet
father.. 3. Abu (Ab, Abou) 4. Abba
garment.. 3. aba 4. haik 8. burnoose
gazelle.. 4. cora, oryx 5. ariel
horse.. 4. Kohl 8. kadischi, palomino
jasmine.. 4. bela
judge.. 4. cadi
juniper (Bib).. 5. retem
nomad.. 7. Saracen
peasant.. 6. fellah
physician.. 8. Avicenna
poet.. 5. Antar
prince.. 4. amir (ameer) 5. sheik
 6. sherif, sultan
romance.. 5. Antar (Antara)
ruler.. 6. caliph (calif)
Satan.. 5. Eblis 6. Azazel
scripture.. 7. Alcoran
seaport.. 4. Aden 5. Mocha
state of bliss.. 3. kef (kaif)
street urchin.. 5. gamin
tambourine.. 4. taar
tribe.. 3. Aus (anc)
vessel.. 4. dhow 6. boutre, sambuk
winds (hot).. 6. simoom (simoon)
arable land... 4. farm 5. arada, arado
 6. plowed, tilled 10. cultivated
arachnid... 4. mite, tick 6. spider
 8. scorpion 9. Arachnida
Aralu... 5. Hades
Aram (Bib)... 6. Rimmon (deity)
 7. Aramaic, Semitic 8. language
araneous... 4. thin 7. weblike
 8. delicate 10. cobweblike
arapunga... 8. bellbird 9. campanero
Arawak... 5. Guana 6. Indian
arbeit... 4. work 8. research
arbiter... 3. ump 5. judge 6. umpire
 7. arbiter, referee 8. mediator
 0. moderator 10. arbitrator
arbitrary... 6. thetic 8. absolute,
 despotic, dogmatic 9. imperious,
 unlimited 10. autocratic, capricious,
 high–handed, peremptory, tyrannical
 11. determinate, dictatorial
 13. discretionary
arbitrate... 6. decide 7. bargain,
 mediate 9. determine, intervene,
 negotiate 12. intermediate
arbitrator... 5. judge 6. umpire
 7. arbiter, referee 8. mediator
 9. moderator 11. conciliator
arbor, arbour... 5. bower, kiosk
 6. alcove, garden, pandal 7. pergola,
 retreat, trellis 11. latticework,
 summerhouse
arboreal... 6. ramous 8. branched,
 treelike 10. arboriform
arboreal mammal... 2. ai 4. unau
 5. lemur, sloth 6. aye–aye, monkey
arc... 3. bow 5. curve 6. radian
 7. azimuth, rainbow
arca... 3. box 5. chest, paten
 9. reliquary
arcade... 3. orb 4. arch, hall
 6. arches, avenue 7. gallery, portico
 8. arcature, corridor 9. colonnade,
 peristyle 10. passageway
Arcadia...
 composition.. 4. poem 5. prose

7. romance
district .. 6. Greece
huntress .. 8. Atalanta
pert to .. 5. rural 8. pastoral
poetic .. 6. Arcady
priestess .. 4. Auge
woodland spirit .. 3. Pan
arcanum ... 6. elixir, enigma, remedy,
   secret 7. mystery
arch ... 3. arc, sly 4. ogee 5. chief,
   hance (part), ogive, vault 6. fornix,
   instep 7. cunning, eminent, roguish
   8. greatest, memorial, monument
   9. principal 11. mischievous
arch (pert to) ...
enemy .. 5. devil, Satan 9. adversary
inner curve .. 8. intrados
memorial .. 6. pailou (pailoo)
stone .. 8. keystone
title .. 4. duke 6. bishop, deacon
   7. duchess
archaic ... 3. old 8. obsolete,
   old–world 10. antiquated
   12. old–fashioned
archangel (celestial) ... 5. Uriel
   7. Gabriel, Michael, Raphael
archangel plant ... 4. mint 8. angelica
archbishop ... 6. bishop (chief), exarch
   9. patriarch
arched ... 6. curved 7. embowed
Archer (Astron) ... 11. Sagittarius
archery ... 3. bow 4. vane 5. arrow,
   clout 6. quiver 8. fistmele, shooting
   10. ballistics
archetype ... 4. idea 5. model
   7. pattern 8. standard 9. prototype
Archie (sl) ... 3. gun 12. antiaircraft
Archipelago (pert to) ...
Alaska .. 9. Alexander
Australia .. 8. Bismarck
Indonesia (largest) .. 5. Malay
Italy .. 6. Aegean
architect ... 6. artist, author 7. builder,
   planner 8. designer 9. artificer,
   draftsman 11. constructor, enterpriser
architectural (pert to) ...
arch .. 8. keystone, voussoir
base .. 5. socle 6. plinth
construction .. 8. tectonic
ornament (part) .. 5. gutta 6. bezant,
   finial, frieze 8. acanthus, dosseret,
   fretwork 10. chambranle
pier .. 4. anta
space (triang) .. 8. pediment
style .. 5. Doric, Greek, Ionic, Tudor
   6. Gothic 7. Baroque, Cape Cod,
   Moorish, Spanish 8. Colonial,
   Etruscan, Georgian 9. Byzantine,
   Palladian 10. Corinthian, Romanesque
   11. Renaissance 13. Mediterranean
archives ... 6. annals 7. records
   8. chancery, registry 9. documents,
   registers 10. chronicles
arch traitor ... 6. Arnold (Benedict),
   Brutus 8. Quisling 13. Judas Iscariot
archway ... 6. pailou (pailoo)
arctic ... 5. polar 6. boreal, frigid,
   galosh 7. Alaskan 8. hibernal,
   Northern, Siberian 11. hyperborean
Arctic (pert to) ...
base .. 4. Etah (Greenland)
bird .. 3. auk 4. xema 6. falcon

cetacean .. 7. narwhal
current .. 8. Labrador
dog .. 5. Husky (Siberian) 8. Malemute
food .. 8. pemmican (pemican)
jacket (hooded) .. 5. parka (parkee)
   6. anorak
native .. 5. Aleut 6. Eskimo, Indian
polar .. 6. Circle
sea .. 7. Barents 8. Beaufort
arctoid ... 6. ursine 8. bearlike
Arctoidea ... 4. bear 6. weasel
   7. raccoon
ardent ... 3. hot 4. avid, keen, warm
   5. eager, fiery, rethe 6. fervid, fierce
   7. amorous, cordial, fervent, flaming,
   glowing, intense, shining, violent,
   zealous 8. eloquent, vehement
   10. passionate 12. affectionate,
   enthusiastic
ardilla ... 8. squirrel
ardor ... 4. élan, fire, heat, love, zeal
   5. estro, flame, gusto, verve
   6. fervor, fougue, spirit, warmth
   8. fervency 9. affection, eagerness,
   eloquence, intensity 10. enthusiasm
   11. impetuosity
arduous ... 4. hard 5. steep 6. trying
   7. onerous 8. toilsome 9. difficult,
   laborious, strenuous, wearisome
   10. burdensome, exhausting
area ... 4. belt, loci (pl), size, zone
   5. areal, basin, field, locus, range,
   scope, space, tract 6. extent, locale,
   region, sector, sphere 7. circuit,
   compass, environ, expanse
   8. province, vicinity 9. bailiwick,
   territory 12. neighborhood
Areca ... 4. palm
arena ... 4. bowl, oval, ring, rink
   5. court, field 6. campus, circus
   7. cockpit, stadium, theater
   8. coliseum, platform 9. gymnasium
   10. hippodrome 12. amphitheater
arenose ... 5. sandy 6. grainy, gritty
   8. sabulous
areola ... 4. halo, ring 5. space
   6. armlet, wreath 7. aureole, garland
   10. interstice
Ares (pert to) ...
consort .. 9. Aphrodite
father .. 4. Zeus
god .. 3. war
Roman name .. 4. Mars
argala ... 7. marabou 8. adjutant (bird)
argent ... 5. white 6. silver 7. shining,
   silvery 9. whiteness
Argentina ...
capital .. 11. Buenos Aires (1535)
city .. 5. Lanus 6. Paraná 7. Cordoba,
   Mendoza, Rosario
Indian .. 4. Lule
mountain .. 5. Andes 9. Aconcagua
   (peak) 10. Cordillera (Range)
native .. 7. Mestizo
Plains .. 6. Pampas 9. Gran Chaco
plateau .. 9. Patagonia
poet .. 7. Andrade 10. Echeverria
river .. 5. Plata 6. Chubut, Paraná
Argentine (pert to) ...
color .. 7. silvery 8. art brown
cowboy .. 6. gaucho
dance .. 5. tango

Argonauts (pert to)...
destination.. 7. Colchis (anc)
heroes (50).. 6. Jason's
objective.. 12. Golden Fleece
of '49.. 6. miners (gold)
ship.. 5. Argos
Argos... 3. dog (of Odysseus)
argosy... 4. ship 5. fleet 6. armada,
  vessel 8. flotilla
argot... 4. cant, jive 5. lingo, slang
  6. jargon, patois 7. dialect
  10. vernacular
argue... 3. rap 4. moot, spar
  5. plead, prove 6. bicker, debate,
  evince, reason 7. contend, contest,
  discuss, dispute, wrangle 8. indicate,
  maintain, persuade 10. controvert
  11. expostulate, ratiocinate,
  remonstrate
argument... 4. case, plea, spar
  5. cavil, lemma, proof, theme
  6. debate, hassle 7. defence, dispute,
  fallacy, polemic, premise, sophism
  8. brouhaha, squabble 9. dialectic,
  discourse, enthymeme, pro and con
  10. discussion 11. altercation,
  disputation 13. consideration,
  ratiocination
argumentative... 7. eristic 8. forensic
  10. indicative, rhetorical
  11. belligerent, contentious,
  presumptive, quarrelsome
  12. disputatious 13. controversial
Argus (Gr Myth)... 7. monster (founder
  of Argos)
Argus–eyed... 8. vigilant 9. observant
  11. hundred–eyed 12. sharpsighted
argute... 5. acute, sharp 6. astute,
  shrewd, shrill, subtle 9. sagacious
aria... 3. air, lay 4. nolo, song, tune
  5. canto 6. cantus, melody, strain
  7. ariette, sortita
arid... 3. dry 4. dull 6. barren, jejune,
  vacant 7. parched, sterile, thirsty
  9. anhydrous, waterless
  13. unimaginative
Arid Austral zone... 7. Sonoran
Ariel... 5. angel, sylph 6. spirit
  7. lioness 9. Jerusalem
ariel... 7. gazelle
Aries (Astron)... 3. ram 4. sign
  6. meteor 13. constellation
aries... 12. battering–ram (anc)
aright... 4. fine, well 7. exactly
  8. directly, straight 11. straightway
aril... 3. pod 7. arillus, coating
  8. arillode (false), covering
Arion... 4. poet (of Lesbos) 5. horse
  (talking)
arioso... 7. melodic, tuneful
  9. melodious
arise... 4. lift, rise, soar, stem, zoom
  5. begin, issue, mount, occur, rebel,
  surge, tower, waken 6. appear,
  ascend, emerge, revolt, spring
  7. emanate 9. originate
Aristarch... 6. critic 10. grammarian
Aristides... 7. The Just 9. statesman
  (Athens)
aristocracy... 5. elite 7. peerage,
  royalty 8. nobility 10. government,
  patriciate, upper class

aristocrat... 4. lord, peer 5. noble
  7. aristos, Brahman, Brahmin,
  grandee, parvenu 8. cavalier, eupatrid
  (Athens), nobleman 9. blueblood,
  patrician 12. silk–stocking
aristology, science of... 6. dining
Aristotle (pert to)...
birthplace.. 6. Thrace 7. Stagira
  (Macedonia)
famed as.. 9. scientist
  11. philosopher 12. The Stagirite
school.. 6. Athens
teacher.. 5. Plato
wife.. 7. Pythias
arithmetic... 4. sums 7. numbers
  11. computation, enumeration,
  mathematics
arithmetic terms... 5. prime 6. result
  7. divisor, product 8. dividend,
  multiple, quotient 9. remainder
  10. multiplier 12. multiplicand
Arizona...
capital.. 7. Phoenix
city.. 4. Yuma 5. Tempe 6. Bisbee,
  Tucson
famed site.. 9. Hoover Dam
  11. Grand Canyon 13. Painted
  Desert 15. Petrified Forest
Indian.. 4. Hano, Hopi, Pima
  6. Apache, Navaho (Navajo)
river.. 4. Gila 8. Colorado
State admission.. 11. Forty–eighth
State bird.. 10. cactus wren
State flower.. 6. cactus 7. saguaro
State motto.. 9. Ditat Deus 11. God
  Enriches
State nickname.. 11. Grand Canyon
ark... 3. vat 4. boat, ship 5. chest,
  haven 6. asylum, refuge, vessel
  8. flatboat 9. broadhorn, sanctuary
  (Ararat)
Arkansas...
capital.. 10. Little Rock
city.. 8. El Dorado 9. Fort Smith
famed for.. 8. diamonds (found in
  Murfreesboro)
famed newspaper.. 7. Gazette (1819)
mountain.. 6. Ozarks 9. Ouachitas
Park (Nat).. 10. Hot Springs
river.. 5. White 11. Mississippi
State admission.. 11. Twenty–fifth
State bird.. 11. mockingbird
State flower.. 12. apple blossom
State motto.. 13. Regnat Populus
  16. Let the People Rule
State nickname.. 19. Land of
  Opportunity
arm... 4. limb 5. equip, saber, sword
  6. branch, member, pistol, tappet,
  weapon 7. forearm, fortify, protect,
  quillon (of sword), support 8. revolver
  9. appendage 10. projection
  12. ramification
arm (pert to)...
armpit.. 5. oxter 6. axilla
bone.. 4. ulna 6. radius 7. humerus
hole.. 4. scye (of sleeve)
muscle.. 6. biceps 7. triceps
projection.. 6. tappet
sea.. 4. gulf, mere 5. bayou, firth,
  inlet 7. estuary
sundial.. 6. gnomon

walk arm in arm.. 5. oxter
armada... 5. fleet 6. argosy
  8. armament, flotilla, squadron,
  warships 10. escadrille
Armada (famed)... 7. Spanish (1588)
  10. Invincible
armadillo... 4. apar, peba (peva)
  5. apara, poyou, tatou (tatu)
  6. mulita, peludo (giant) 7. tatouay
  10. pichiciago, Tolypeutes
  11. quirquincho (hairy)
Armageddon... 3. war 7. Megiddo
  (Bib) 8. conflict, world war
armed... 6. fitted, rigged 7. clothed,
  endowed 8. equipped, invested,
  prepared, provided, supplied
  9. furnished, outfitted 10. laquearian
  (with noose)
armed (pert to)...
  conflict.. 3. war 6. combat 7. warfare
  11. hostilities
  forces.. 4. army, host 5. ranks
  6. troops 8. military 9. besiegers
  vessel.. 3. HMS, sub, USS 5. U–boat
  9. destroyer, submarine
  10. battleship 11. battlewagon
Armenia...
  anc name.. 9. Armenenak
  capital.. 6. Erivan
  founder.. 4. Haik
  herb.. 5. cumin 7. caraway
  highlanders.. 5. Gomer
  mountain.. 6. Ararat, Taurus
  river.. 3. Kur 5. Cyrus 6. Araxes,
  Tigris 9. Euphrates
  worshiper.. 7. Yesidio (Yesdi)
  9. Gregorian
armistice... 5. peace, truce
  9. cessation 12. pacification
armoire... 5. ambry 8. cupboard,
  wardrobe 10. repository
armor... 4. arms, bard (barde), egis,
  jamb, mail, tace 5. acton, aegis,
  plate, seton, tasse 6. cuisse, gorget,
  graith, greave, helmet, lorica, sconce,
  shield, tasset, tuille 7. ailette,
  cuirass, hauberk, jambeau, panoply
  8. aventail, brassort, ordnance,
  pallette, solleret 9. cubitiere,
  epauliere, gardebras, mainferre,
  rerebrace 10. cataphract
armor–bearer... 6. squire 7. armiger,
  esquire
armored... 6. mailed 8. equipped,
  ironclad, mailclad 9. cuirassed,
  loricated, panoplied
armpit... 5. oxter 6. axilla
arms... 7. weapons 8. armament,
  ordnance 9. munitions
arms depository... 5. depot 6. armory
  7. arsenal
army... 3. mob 4. host, unit 5. array,
  crowd, horde, posse 6. forces,
  galaxy, legion, rabble, throng, troops
  9. multitude, Salvation
army (pert to)...
  brown.. 7. rosario
  commission (special).. 6. brevet
  trader.. 6. sutler
army unit... 4. ROTC 5. corps, guard
  (Nat), squad 7. brigade, cavalry,
  company, militia, platoon, Sabaoth

  (Bib) 8. division, infantry, Landwehr,
  regiment, reserves 9. artillery,
  minutemen 10. volunteers
Arnold's co–conspirator... 5. Andre
  (Maj)
aroma... 4. musk, odor, tang 5. attar,
  balmy, nidor, savor, scent, smell,
  spice 6. flavor 7. bouquet, feature,
  incense, perfume 9. fragrance,
  muskiness, redolence 11. peculiarity,
  singularity
aromatic... 5. spicy 6. savory
  7. odorous, pungent 8. fragrant,
  redolent 11. fluorescent
aromatic (pert to)...
  gum.. 5. myrrh 12. frankincense
  herb.. 4. mint 5. clary, nondo
  oil.. 4. balm 6. balsam 9. sassafras
  seed.. 4. anis 6. nutmeg 7. aniseed
  tree.. 5. aromo 6. balsam
  7. champac 8. huisache
around... 4. near, peri (pref) 5. about,
  circa 9. bordering, somewhere
  11. thereabouts 13. approximately
arouse... 4. fire, stir, wake 5. alarm,
  anger, evoke, raise, rally, roust
  6. awaken, elicit, excite, incite,
  kindle, summon 7. animate
arpa... 4. harp
arpeggio... 5. chord 7. roulade
  8. division, flourish
arraign... 4. cite 6. accuse, charge,
  indict 7. impeach 8. denounce,
  reproach 9. prosecute
arrange... 3. fix 4. cast, cite, file,
  plan, plot, sort 5. adapt, aline,
  besee, drape, ettle, frame, grade,
  preen, range, stack 6. adjust, deploy,
  design, devise 7. dispose, mediate,
  prepare, provide, seriate 8. classify,
  contract, contrive, laminate, organize,
  tabulate 9. catalogue (catalog),
  negotiate 10. distribute, paniculate
  11. alphabetize, systematize
arranged... 5. fixed, timed 6. ranked,
  sorted 7. aligned, grouped, ordered,
  orderly, planned, settled, uniform
  9. regulated 10. contracted
arranged in...
  fives.. 7. quinate
  fours.. 11. tetramerous
  hours.. 9. staggered
  rays.. 6. radial
  threes.. 7. ternate
arrangement... 3. art, rig (sails)
  4. plan, rank 5. order, setup
  6. series, syntax, system 7. echelon
  (troops), musical 8. disposal,
  neatness, trimness 9. agreement,
  condition, structure 10. adaptation,
  engagement, settlement
  11. collocation, combination,
  permutation, preparation
  12. distribution
arrant... 3. bad 6. wicked 8. rascally
  9. confirmed, shameless
  11. unmitigated 12. disreputable
array... 3. don 4. deci, robe 5. adorn,
  align, dress, order 6. clothe, muster,
  series, throng 7. arrange, dispose,
  envelop, marshal 8. clothing,
  garments 9. adornment

11. arrangement
arrears... 3. due 4. debt 5. short
7. wanting 9. arrearage, deficient
10. behindhand, defaulting
arrest... 4. halt, hold, stop 5. check,
delay, seize 6. detain, hinder,
impede, retard 7. custody, seizure
8. obstruct, restrain, stoppage
9. apprehend, hindrance, intercept,
restraint 11. retardation
arrested... 6. behind 7. checked,
delayed, impeded, stopped
8. detained, retarded 10. restrained
11. intercepted
arrested development... 6. simple
7. dwarfed, idiotic, moronic
8. backward, retarded 10. half–witted
13. unintelligent
arrival... 5. comer (anc) 6. advent,
coming 7. landing 8. approach,
reaching 10. attainment, homecoming
11. achievement
arrive... 4. come 5. debus, reach
6. alight, debark, happen 7. detrain
9. disembark
arrogance... 5. pride 7. conceit,
disdain, hauteur 8. audacity,
rudeness, snobbery 9. brashness,
insolence, loftiness 10. effrontery
11. haughtiness 12. impertinence
arrogant... 4. bold, pert 5. cocky,
lofty, proud 6. lordly, uppish
7. forward 8. impudent, insolent
9. audacious, insulting, masterful,
presuming 10. disdainful
11. domineering, high–falutin,
impertinent, overbearing
12. contemptuous, contumelious,
presumptuous, supercilious
arrogate... 5. seize, usurp, wrest
6. assume 11. appropriate
arrow... 4. barb, dart, reed, vire
(feathered) 5. guide, shaft 6. finger
7. missile, pointer 10. guideboard
arrow (pert to)...
astronomy.. 7. Sagitta
bows.. 6. bowyer (maker, seller)
case.. 6. quiver
end.. 4. nock 9. arrowhead
feather (to).. 6. fletch
handle.. 5. stele
head.. 4. dart
poison.. 4. inee, upas 5. urali
6. curare, uzarin
poisoned.. 6. sumpit 8. sumpitan
propeller.. 3. bow
shape.. 6. beloid 9. cuneiform,
sagittate
stone.. 9. belemnite
variety.. 4. self 6. footed 7. chested
9. bobtailed
arrowroot... 3. pia 5. araru 6. ararao,
starch 7. Maranta
arroyo... 5. brook, creek 6. ravine,
stream 11. watercourse
arroz... 4. rice
arse... 4. butt, rump (vulgar)
8. buttocks 9. posterior
arsenal... 4. dump 5. depot, plant
6. armory 7. factory 8. magazine
10. depository, storehouse
arsis... 5. ictus 6. accent, stress (opp

of thesis), upbeat
arson... 7. burning, cautery
9. pyromania 12. incendiarism
art... 4. wile 5. cameo, craft, knack,
skill, taste, trade 6. design
7. calling, cartoon, cunning, drawing,
science 8. aptitude, artifice, artistry,
business, ceramics, drafting, intaglio,
painting, vocation 9. dexterity,
duplicate, engraving, ingenuity,
readiness, sculpture, sketching
10. adroitness, decoration, profession
11. contrivance, photography,
portraiture 12. architecture
art (pert to)...
addict.. 8. aesthete (esthete)
decoration.. 9. sgraffito
design.. 7. graphic
fancier.. 10. dilettante
gallery.. 5. salon
grotesque.. 11. incongruous
mystic.. 6. cabala
of assaying.. 8. docimasy
of discourse.. 8. rhetoric
of embossing.. 9. toreutics
of government.. 8. politics
of horsemanship.. 6. manège
of imitation.. 7. mimicry
of manual craft.. 5. sloyd
of memory.. 10. mneumonics
of metal inlay.. 6. niello
primitive.. 9. artifacts
realistic.. 5. genre
rhyming.. 5. poesy 6. poetry
self–defense.. 6. boxing 7. fencing,
jujitsu (jiujitsu)
style.. 6. cubism, purism 7. baroque,
Dadaism, Fauvism 8. futurism
9. modernism 10. surrealism
13. impressionism
theme.. 5. motif
tooling.. 10. dieslnking
transmutation.. 7. alchemy
Artemis (pert to)...
brother (twin).. 6. Apollo
epithet (Homeric).. 6. Phoebe
father.. 4. Zeus
goddess of.. 4. moon 6. nature
7. the Hunt 8. Olympian
Mother.. 4. Leto
religion.. 4. Upis
Roman equivalent.. 5. Diana
artery... 4. tube, vein 6. avenue,
street, vessel 7. channel, highway,
passage 8. ligament 10. passageway
artery (Anat)... 4. tube, vein 5. aorta
6. vessel 7. anonyma, carotid,
trachea 9. capillary, pulmonary
10. innominate
artery pulsation... 4. beat 5. ictus
artful... 3. sly 4. foxy, wily 5. cagey
6. adroit, clever, crafty, shrewd,
subtle, tricky 7. crooked, cunning,
knowing, politic 8. skillful, stealthy
9. deceitful, deceptive, designing,
dexterous, imitative 10. artificial
Artful Dodger... 3. fox 6. rascal
7. slicker 8. deceiver 11. John
Dawkins (Dickens tale) 12. crafty
person
artfulness... 5. skill 7. finesse
8. artifice, subtlety, wiliness

9. stratagem 10. cleverness,
refinement, shrewdness
arthron ... 5. hinge, joint, pivot
12. articulation
Arthurian abode ... 6. Avalon
9. Lyonnesse (Leonnoys)
Arthurian character ... 6. Arthur (King),
Elaine, Merlin 7. Geraint 8. Lancelot
9. Percivale
artichoke ... 6. canada, Cynara
7. chorogi, thistle 9. Jerusalem
article .... 3. mat 4. item, news, term
5. scoop, story, thing 6. belief,
clause, detail, gadget, object, treaty
7. camelot, feature (news), grammar,
integer 8. treatise 9. commodity,
editorial 10. particular
11. composition, stipulation
article (Gram) ...
English .. 1. a 2. an 3. the
French .. 2. la, le, un 3. les, une
Spanish .. 2. el, un 3. las, los, una
article (of) ...
agreement .. 8. contract
apparel .. 5. smock, tunic 6. duster,
gaiter, mantle 8. pinafore
faith .. 5. canon, creed, dogma, tenet
6. belief 7. precept
property .. 7. chattel
virtu .. 5. curio, relic 6. rarity
7. antique
articulation ... 4. tone 5. hinge, joint,
sound, voice 7. voicing 8. locution,
sonation 9. phonation, utterance
11. enunciation 12. vocalization
13. pronunciation
artifact ... 5. curio, relic, virtu 6. fossil
7. antique, remains 8. archaism
artifice ... 4. plot, ruse, wile 5. blind,
chest, craft, dodge, fraud, guile,
shift, trick 6. deceit 7. cunning,
evasion, finesse, knavery, sleight
8. intrigue, maneuver, trickery
9. chicanery, collusion, deception,
expedient, imposture, stratagem
10. connivance, imposition,
subterfuge 11. contrivance,
machination, skulduggery
artificer ... 5. smith 6. artist, framer
7. artisan, creator, deviser, workman
8. Daedalus, inventor, mechanic
9. architect, carpenter, craftsman,
goldsmith 11. coppersmith,
silversmith
artificial ... 4. fake, mock, sham
5. bogus, dummy, false, phony
6. ersatz, forged, unreal 7. assumed,
bastard, elegant, feigned 8. affected,
fabulous, spurious 9. imaginary,
imitation, pretended, unnatural
11. adulterated, counterfeit,
unauthentic 12. supposititious
artificial (pert to) ...
butter .. 4. oleo 13. oleomargarine
channel .. 3. gat 4. leat 5. canal,
flume 6. sluice
gum .. 7. dextrin
language .. 2. ro 3. Ido 5. Arulo
7. Volapuk 9. Esperanto
10. Occidental
silk .. 5. nylon, rayon
surface .. 4. rink

voice .. 8. falsetto
artillery ... 4. army, guns 5. bombs
6. cannon, slings 7. cavalry,
gunners, gunnery, mortars
8. ordnance 9. arbalests, catapults
10. ballistics
artillery (pert to) ...
emplacement .. 7. battery
fire .. 5. salvo 6. rafale
man .. 6. gunner 8. rifleman, topechee
9. cannoneer, musketeer
11. artillarist
wagon .. 7. battery
artiodactyl ... (opp of perissodactyl)
2. ox 3. pig 4. deer, goat 5. camel,
sheep 6. artiad 7. giraffe
12. hippopotamus
artisan ... 6. artist, limner 7. painter,
workman 8. mechanic, virtuoso
9. artificer, craftsman
artist ... 5. rapin (Fr pupil) 6. etcher,
limner, potter 7. artisan, painter
8. designer, sculptor 9. architect,
decorator 10. cartoonist, ceramacist
11. illustrator 12. photographer
artist (pert to) ...
equipment .. 5. easel 7. palette
8. maquette
sleight of hand .. 4. mage 5. Magus
8. magician 9. alchemist
artiste ... 5. actor, adept 6. dancer,
singer 7. artisan 8. musician
9. performer
artistic ... 4. pure 6. ornate 7. classic
8. graceful, skillful, tasteful
9. aesthetic (esthetic), art–minded,
beautiful, exquisite
artistic (pert to) ...
ardor .. 5. verve 6. spirit
dance .. 6. ballet
quality .. 6. virtue
symbol of the dead .. 5. orant
temperament .. 7. caprice, emotion
artless ... 4. naif, open, rude 5. frank,
naive 6. candid, simple 7. natural,
sincere 8. ignorant 9. guileness,
ingenuous, unskilled 10. inartistic,
unaffected, uncultured
11. undesigning 15. unsophisticated
artlessness ... 6. candor 7. naiveté
9. frankness, innocence
11. naturalness 13. ungenuousness
arts (pert to) ...
liberal .. 7. trivium 10. quadrivium
quadrivium .. 5. music 8. geometry
9. astronomy 10. arithmetic
trivium .. 5. logic 7. grammar
8. rhetoric
aru ... 6. indeed, really
arui ... 5. oudad, sheep 7. chamois
(Bib)
arum ... 4. taro 5. calla (lily) 6. starch
9. arrowroot
arx ... 7. citadel
Aryan (pert to) ...
God of Fire .. 4. Agni
invader .. 4. Pict
people .. 4. Mede 5. Hindu
9. Caucasian 11. Indo–Iranian
as ... 3. qua 4. como, than, thus
5. since, while 7. because, equally,
similar 9. similarly

Asa... 11. King of Judah
asafetida... 8. medicine
   13. antispasmodic
Asa's son... 11. Jehoshaphat
ascend... 3. fly 4. rise, soar, upgo
   5. arise, climb, mount, scale, tower
   6. aspire, uprise 7. clamber, upsurge
ascendancy... 4. sway 7. control,
   mastery 8. dominion, prestige,
   priority 9. authority, influence,
   supremacy 10. domination
   11. sovereignty, superiority
   12. predominance 13. preponderance
ascendant, ascendent... 5. elder
   6. father 7. supreme 8. ancestor,
   forebear, superior 9. governing,
   patriarch 10. antecedent, decoration
   (Arch)
ascended... 4. rose 5. arose, risen
   6. uprose
ascending... 6. anodic, rising
   7. scaling, sloping 8. mounting,
   racemose 9. emanating
ascending signs... 5. Aries 6. Gemini,
   Pisces, Taurus 8. Aquarius
   9. Capricorn
ascenseur... 8. elevator
Ascension Day... 8. Thursday (Holy),
   (40 days after Easter)
Ascension lily... 7. Madonna
ascertain... 4. find 5. learn, prove,
   solve 6. decide 7. certify
   9. determine
ascetic... 4. yati, yoga, yogi 5. fakir,
   stoic 6. Essene, hermit, strict
   7. austere, eremite, puritan, recluse
   8. anchoret, Diogenes, solitary
   9. abstainer, anchorite, mendicant
   10. abstemious
asceticism... 4. Yoga 9. austerity,
   nephalism 10. abstention, abstinence,
   puritanism 11. anchoritism,
   teetotalism
ascribable... 3. due 9. traceable
   10. assignable 11. attributive
   12. attributable
ascribe... 5. count, refer 6. assign,
   attach, credit, impute, reckon
   7. ascribe 8. accredit 9. attribute
ascus fruit... 8. truffles
asepsis... 6. purity 7. clarity 9. sterility
   13. taintlessness
ash... 4. sorb, tree 5. rowan
   6. samara (fruit) 8. Fraxinus
ashes... 4. dust, lava, lees, slag
   5. dregs, ruins 6. embers
   7. cinders, residue
ash tree symbol (Norse Myth)...
   10. Yggdrasill (horse of Yggr)
Asia... 4. East 6. Orient, region 7. Far
   East 8. Old World 9. continent
Asia Minor...
   city (anc).. 4. Myra, Teos, Troy
   5. Ilium, Issus, Lydia 6. Nicaea,
   Sardes 7. Ephesus
   district.. 4. Aria 5. Ionia, Troad (The
   Troad) 6. Aeolis
   island.. 6. Lesbos
   language (anc).. 6. Lycian, Lydian
   8. Etruscan
   mountain.. 3. Ida
   old name.. 8. Anatolia

sea.. 5. Black 6. Aegean 7. Marmosa
   13. Mediterranean
Asiatic (pert to)...
   barbarian (anc).. 3. Hun 6. Vandal
   desert.. 4. Gobi
   gulf.. 4. Aden, Oman, Siam 6. Tonkin
   7. Persian
   island.. 4. Java 5. Luzon, Malay
   7. Celebes, Diomede (Big), Formosa,
   Sumatra 8. Japanese, Mindanao,
   Sakhalin 11. Philippines
   mountain.. 4. Ural 5. Altai, Sayan
   7. Everest 8. Caucasus, Himalaya
   9. Hindu Kush
   native.. 4. Arab, Turk, Yuit 5. Tatar
   6. Indian, Innuit (Esk), Syrian
   7. Chinese, Malayan 8. Annamese,
   Japanese 9. Mongolian
   nomad.. 4. Arab
   river.. 2. Ob 4. Amur, Lena
   5. Hwang, Indus 6. Ganges
   7. Yangtze, Yenisei 9. Euphrates,
   Irrawaddy 11. Brahmaputra
   sea.. 4. Azov (Azof) 5. Black, China,
   Japan 6. Bering, Yellow 7. Caspian,
   Okhotsk
Asiatic animal...
   antelope.. 5. goral
   ass.. 6. onager
   camel.. 8. Bactrian 9. dromedary
   carnivore.. 5. panda, tiger
   cattle.. 4. zobo
   deer.. 4. axis 10. chevrotain
   elephant.. 7. Elephas
   fox.. 6. corsac
   gazelle.. 3. ahu
   goat.. 5. serow
   lemur.. 5. loris 6. macaco
   lynx.. 7. caracal
   mongoose.. 4. urva
   monkey.. 6. langur (long-tailed)
   ox.. 3. yak
   rodent.. 4. pika
   sheep.. 3. sha 5. uriel 6. argali
   squirrel.. 8. jelerang 10. polatouche
Asiatic bird...
   finch.. 9. brambling
   jay.. 7. sirgang
   owl.. 4. utum
   partridge.. 6. seesee
   plover.. 8. dotterel
   songless.. 5. Pitta
   talking.. 4. myna (mynah)
Asiatic snake... 3. asp 5. cobra
   8. ringhals
Asiatic storm (pert to)...
   sand.. 6. simoom (simoon) 7. tebbard
   snow.. 5. buran
   wind.. 5. buran 7. monsoon
aside... 4. away 5. apart, hence
   6. aslant, astray, beside 7. whisper
   8. sidewise 9. alongside, privately,
   sotto voce 12. interjection
asinine... 4. dumb 5. inane, inept, silly
   6. mulish, stupid 7. doltish, foolish,
   idiotic 9. obstinate
ask... 3. beg 4. quiz 5. claim, exact,
   query, speer 6. assess, demand,
   invite 7. beseech, entreat, implore,
   inquire, request, require, solicit
   8. petition, question 9. catechize,
   obsecrate (Relig) 11. interrogate

askance... 4. awry 5. askew
7. asquint, crooked 8. sideways
9. obliquely
askew... 4. agee, alop, awry 5. agley,
amiss 6. faulty 7. askance, asquint,
crooked 8. deranged 9. distorted,
obliquely 10. catawampus, disorderly
aslant... 5. atilt 6. tilted, tipped
7. athwart, leaning, listing, pitched,
sloping 8. inclined 9. careening,
obliquely
asleep... 4. dead, dull, numb
7. dormant, unaware 8. deadened,
sleeping, unarisen 9. oblivious,
senseless, unruffled 10. motionless
11. inattentive, insensitive,
unconscious
Asoka's Empire (anc Ind)... 5. Patna
asp... 5. cobra, snake, viper 6. uraeus
(sacred sym)
aspect... 3. air 4. look, mien, pose,
side, view 5. angle, decil, facet,
guise, phase, shape, sight, state
6. decile, facies, status, visage
7. bearing, posture, scenery
8. attitude 9. astrology, component,
influence, seaminess, situation
10. appearance 11. countenance
aspen... 4. tree, wood 6. poplar
7. quaking 9. quivering, shivering,
trembling, tremulous, vibrating
asperge... 3. wet 4. damp 5. spray,
water 7. baptize 8. humidify, sprinkle
asperge... 9. asparagus
Asperges... 4. rite 6. anthem
10. sprinkling (altar)
aspergillum... 5. brush 7. sprayer
8. baptizer 9. sprinkler
asperity... 5. rigor 7. raucity
8. acerbity, acrimony, hardship,
severity, tartness 9. bleakness,
roughness 10. causticity, difficulty,
inclemency, moroseness, resentment
asperse... 4. slur 5. abuse, decry, libel
6. defame, malign, revile, vilify
7. blacken, slander, traduce
8. besmirch 9. bespatter, discredit
10. calumniate
aspersion... 4. rite, slur 6. insult
7. affront, baptism, calumny, outrage,
wetting 8. innuendo 9. indignity
10. defamation, sprinkling
12. calumniating, calumniation
13. disparagement
asphalt... 4. pave 5. pitch 7. bitumen,
mineral 8. blacktop, pavement,
uintaite 9. gilsonite 10. macadamize
asphyxia... 5. apnea (apnoea)
7. choking 11. suffocation
12. smotheration
aspic... 3. asp (poet) 5. jelly
6. cannon 8. lavender 9. galantine
aspiration... 3. aim 4. hope, wish
5. ideal 6. breath, desire
7. pumping, sucking, suction
8. ambition, staccato 9. breathing
10. exhalation 11. inspiration
aspire... 4. long, plan, rise, soar
5. tower 6. attain, desire, expect,
intend 7. breathe, propose
ass... 3. ono (comb form) 4. dolt,
dope, fool, jack 5. burro, jenny

assail... 4. pelt 5. beset, stone
6. attack 7. assault 9. implicate
11. incriminate
assailant... 3. foe 5. enemy 7. invader
8. assailer, attacker, opponent
9. adversary, aggressor
10. antagonist, challenger
Assam...
capital.. 8. Shillong
native.. 4. Ahom 8. Assamite
11. Indo–Chinese
province of.. 5. India
river.. 11. Brahmaputra
tribe.. 2. Ao 3. Aka 4. Garo, Naga
assassin... 4. Cain, thug 5. bravo
6. apache, cuttle, gunman, killer,
slayer 7. gorilla, ruffian 8. murderer,
sicarian 9. manslayer 11. slaughterer
assassination... 5. purge 6. murder
7. killing 8. regicide 11. liquidation
12. manslaughter
Assassin Order... 8. Ismalian
10. Mohammedan
assault... 5. onset, storm 6. assail,
attack, charge 7. descent, seizure
8. invasion 9. incursion
13. incrimination
assay... 3. try 4. test 5. prove, trial
6. accost 7. attempt 8. analysis,
docimasy (art), endeavor
10. experiment 12. verification
assay cup... 5. cupel
assemblage... 3. all 4. herd 6. throng
8. assembly, entirety 9. gathering
12. congregation
assemblage (pert to)...
cattle.. 5. drove, rodeo 7. roundup
fashionable.. 5. salon
mob.. 4. rout 6. rabble
splendid.. 6. galaxy
tents.. 4. camp 10. encampment
assemble... 3. pod 4. mass, meet
5. amass, piece, rally, unite
6. couple, gather, muster 7. cluster,
collect, convene, convoke, recruit
10. congregate
assembly... 4. bevy, diet, moot
5. agora, gemot, group, synod, troop
6. assize, sabbat 7. company,
council, landtag, meeting 8. auditory,
conclave (secret), folkmoot (Hist)
9. concourse, gathering
10. collection, convention
11. convocation 12. congregation
assent... 3. aye, nod, yea, yes
4. amen 5. admit, agree, grant
6. accede, accord, concur
7. consent 8. sanction 9. acquiesce,
agreement 10. compliance
12. acquiescence
assert... 3. say 4. aver, pose 5. claim,
plead, posit, state, voice 6. affirm,
allege, avouch, relate, uphold
7. contend, declare, profess, protest,
support 8. advocate 9. pronounce,
vindicate 10. asseverate
assertion... 5. claim 6. remark, thesis
7. premise 8. averment 9. statement
10. assumption, hypothesis
11. affirmation, declaration,
maintenance, proposition, vindication
assertiveness... 10. pragmatism

14. aggressiveness
assertor... 8. affirmer, defender
9. supporter 10. vindicator
assess... 3. ask, tax 4. cess, levy,
mise, rate 5. price, value 6. charge
7. measure 8. appraise, estimate
assessment... 3. fee, tax 4. levy, rate,
scot 5. ratal, stock, value 6. surtax
7. pricing, scutage 8. estimate
9. appraisal, valuation 10. evaluation
11. measurement
assets... 5. funds, means 6. wealth
7. capital 8. accounts, property
9. resources
asseverate... 3. say, vow 4. aver
5. state, swear 6. affirm, allege,
assert 7. contend, declare, profess,
protest 8. maintain 9. pronounce
asseveration... 3. vow 4. oath
(solemn) 8. averment 9. assertion
11. affirmation, declaration
13. pronouncement
assiduity... 8. industry 9. diligence
11. painstaking, persistence
12. perseverance
assiduous... 4. busy 6. active
7. intense, zealous 8. diligent,
sedulous 9. energetic, laborious,
unwearied 11. industrious,
perseverant 13. indefatigable,
unintermitted
assign... 3. fix, set 4. cast, cede, seal
5. allot, refer 6. allege, commit,
detail 7. address, adjudge, appoint,
ascribe, consign, empower
8. accredit, allocate, delegate,
nominate, transfer 9. attribute
10. commission 11. appropriate
assignment... 3. job 4. task 5. chore,
stint 6. lesson 7. mission
8. exercise, transfer 9. allotment
10. allocation, commission,
commitment 11. attribution
13. specification
assimilate... 5. adapt, learn, liken
6. absorb, digest, imbibe 7. convert
10. understand 11. approximate
assimilation... 8. imbibing, learning
9. anabolism, digestion, ingestion,
reduction 10. absorption, adaptation,
comparison, conversion
14. naturalization
assist... 3. aid 4. abet, back, help
5. avail, boost, favor 6. attend,
prompt, second, succor 7. benefit,
relieve, support, sustain 8. befriend
9. accompany, subsidize
assistance... 3. aid 4. help 5. grant
6. relief, succor 7. service, subsidy,
support 10. logrolling (Polit)
11. furtherance
assistant... 4. aide, ally 5. tutor
6. deputy, helper 7. abettor,
famulus, servant, teacher
9. associate, attendant, auxiliary
11. subordinate 12. right–hand man
assize... 3. fix 4. rate 5. edict, trial,
value 6. assess, decree 9. ordinance
10. regulation 11. instruction,
measurement
associate... 3. mix, pal 4. ally, chum,
mate 5. buddy, crony 6. fellow,

friend, hobnob, mingle 7. combine,
comrade, consort, partner
9. colleague, companion
10. accomplice 11. concomitant,
confederate
associated... 6. allied, banded, joined,
united 7. coupled, leagued, related
9. connected 10. affiliated,
concurrent
associates... 4. crew 5. force, staff
7. retinue 9. personnel
12. constituency
association... 4. body, club 5. artel,
cabal, guild, hanse (Hist), union
6. league, lyceum, symbol
7. company, society 8. alliance,
relation, sodality, sorority 9. syndicate
10. fellowship, fraternity
11. affiliation, combination,
comradeship, concurrence, corporation
13. communication, interrelation
assonance... 3. pun 4. rime 5. rhyme
8. paragram 9. agreement
11. paronomasia, resemblance
12. alliteration
assort... 4. sort, suit 5. adapt, class,
grade, group 7. consort (with)
8. classify, separate 9. associate
(with) 10. categorize, distribute
assortment... 3. mix, set 4. hash,
mess, olio 5. class, group 6. jumble,
medley 7. mélange, mixture, sorting
9. potpourri 10. collection,
hodgepodge, miscellany
11. arrangement 14. conglomeration
assuage... 4. calm, ease 5. allay, slake
6. lessen, mellow, pacify, quench,
soften, solace, soothe 7. appease,
comfort, gratify, qualify, relieve,
satisfy 8. mitigate, palliate
9. alleviate
assuasive... 5. balmy 6. easing
8. remedial, soothing 9. relieving,
softening 10. mitigating, palliative
11. alleviative 13. tranquilizing
assume... 3. don 4. deem, sham, take
5. adopt, feign, guess, imply, infer,
judge, think, usurp 6. affect, allege,
betake, borrow, deduce 7. believe,
imagine, premise, presume, pretend,
suppose, surmise 8. arrogate,
conclude, simulate 9. undertake
11. appropriate, counterfeit
assume (pert to)...
character.. 11. impersonate
different forms.. 7. protean
unduly.. 5. usurp 8. arrogate
without proof.. 11. theoretical
12. hypothetical
assumed... 6. deemed 7. alleged,
implied, thought 8. affected, inferred,
presumed, supposed 9. fictional,
pretended 10. fictitious, understood,
undertaken 11. conjectured,
make–believe, presumptive,
presupposed, theoretical
12. appropriated, hypothetical,
suppositious
assuming... 5. lofty 8. arrogant,
superior 9. presuming
10. assumptive 11. overweening,
pretentious 12. presumptuous

assumption ... 8. adoption
  9. arrogance, postulate, reception
  10. usurpation 11. implication,
  proposition, supposition
  13. appropriation, incorporation
  14. presupposition
assurance ... 4. hope, oath 5. poise,
  trust 6. aplomb, belief, pledge,
  surety 7. comfort, courage, promise
  8. security, sureness 9. certainty,
  guarantee, impudence, insurance
  10. confidence, steadiness
  11. assuredness, intrepidity
  12. cocksureness 14. self–confidence
assure ... 4. aver 5. vouch 6. assert,
  avouch, depose, ensure, insure,
  secure 7. confirm, declare, protest,
  satisfy 8. convince, embolden,
  persuade, reassure 9. encourage,
  guarantee 10. asseverate
Assyria ...
  capital .. 7. Nineveh
  city .. 5. Calab (Bib) 9. Khorsabad
  (ruins)
  empire (anc) .. 5. Assur (Ashur)
  language .. 6. Semite 9. cuneiform
  (written)
  people .. 6. Semite 7. Amorite (Bib)
Assyrian god ...
  atmosphere .. 5. Hadad
  fire .. 5. Nusku
  hunt .. 7. Ninurta
  moon .. 3. Sin
  storm .. 2. Zu
  sun .. 7. Shamash
  war .. 6. Nergal 7. Ninurta
  winds .. 4. Adad 5. Hadad
Assyrian goddess ... 5. Nanai
  6. Allatu, Ishtar 9. Sarpanitu
  (Zirbanit)
Assyriology, science of ... 8. language
  11. antiquities
aster ... 4. star 9. asterwort, karyaster
  10. Carduaceae
asterisk ... 4. mark (reference), star
  6. accent, figure (star) 9. highlight
  10. asteriskos (Eccl)
astern ... 3. aft 4. baft, rear 5. abaft,
  after 6. behind 8. hindward,
  rearward, tailward
asteroid ... 5. Ceres (largest) 6. planet
  8. starlike 9. planetoid
Asteroidea ... 8. starfish
astir ... 2. up 5. about, afoot, eager
  6. active, moving 8. stirring
  11. forthcoming
as to ... 7. apropos, suppose
  9. regarding 10. concerning,
  respecting
astonish ... 4. stun 5. amaze, appal
  7. astound, stagger, startle
  8. bewilder, confound, surprise
  9. overwhelm
astonishing ... 7. amazing 8. fabulous
  9. appalling, marvelous, wonderful
  10. incredible, remarkable
astound ... 4. stun 5. abash, amaze,
  shock 6. appall (appal), dismay
  7. stagger, stupefy 8. astonish,
  surprise 10. disconcert
astounding ... 8. horrible, shocking
  9. appalling, frightful 10. horrendous,

horrifying 11. astonishing
astraddle ... 7. astride 9. horseback,
  pickaback (piggyback) 10. straddling
astral ... 6. spirit, starry 7. stellar
  8. sidereal, starlike 9. celestial
  11. star–studded
astray ... 4. lost 5. amiss, wrong
  6. adrift, afield, erring 8. aberrate,
  mistaken 9. erroneous 10. bewildered
astray, to go ... 3. err, sin 4. mang,
  rove 5. drift, lapse, stray 6. wander
  7. deviate, digress 8. miscarry
  9. backslide 10. misbelieve
astriction ... 4. bond 7. binding
  8. thirlage 9. fastening 10. litigation
  11. confinement, contraction
  12. constipation
astride ... 8. straddle 9. astraddle,
  horseback, pickaback (piggyback)
astringent ... 4. acid, alum, sloe, sour
  5. acerb, acrid, harsh, sapan, stern
  6. tannin 7. austere, bitters, caustic,
  pungent, rhatany (root), styptic
  9. vitriolic 10. antiseptic
  11. acrimonious, argentamine
  12. constrictive
astrologer ... 8. Chaldean 9. stargazer
  11. astrologian, astromancer,
  Nostradamus
astrology (pert to) ... 5. house, signs
  6. aspect, zodiac 7. mansion,
  mundane 8. siderism 9. horoscope,
  planetary 11. horoscopist
astronaut ... 7. Martian 8. spaceman
  9. cosmonaut, rocketeer
astronomer ... 9. stargazer
  11. uranologist 12. uranographer
  13. meteorologist, uranographist
astronomer, famed ... 6. Kepler
  7. Galileo 12. Eratosthenes
astronomical ... 4. huge, vast 5. large
  6. cosmic, uranic 7. immense,
  mammoth, Uranian 8. colossal,
  empyreal, heavenly 9. celestial
  10. prodigious, stupendous,
  tremendous
astronomy (pert to) ... 4. coma (the)
  5. apsis, saros (Bab) 6. syzygy
  7. almanac, apsides, azimuth,
  gibbous 8. sidereal 9. idiometer,
  insulated 11. debilissima
astute ... 3. sly 4. keen, wily 5. acute,
  canny, smart 6. artful, clever, crafty,
  shrewd 7. cunning, skilled
  9. insidious, sagacious 10. discerning
  14. discriminating
asunder ... 5. apart, cleft, split
  6. atwain, halved 7. divided
  9. disjoined, separated
as yet ... 8. hitherto
asylum ... 3. ark 4. home, jail, port
  5. haven 6. harbor, refuge
  7. retreat, shelter 9. hospitium,
  infirmary, sanctuary 10. stronghold
  11. institution
asymmetrical ... 6. uneven, warped
  7. twisted, unequal 8. contorted,
  distorted 11. zygomorphic
  16. disproportionate
at ... 2. by, in 4. near, nigh 5. there
  8. location, position 9. direction,
  situation

at (pert to)...
  great length.. 7. on and on
    9. tediously
  home.. 2. in 4. here 9. en famille
  last.. 3. end 7. finally 9. extremely
    10. ultimately
  once.. 3. now 7. readily
  the same time.. 6. coeval
    10. coetaneous 12. contemporary
atabal... 4. drum 5. tabor
  10. kettledrum
atabeg... 5. title 6. vizier
Atalanta (pert to)...
  defeated in romantic race by..
    10. Hippomenes 17. three golden
    apples (Gr Myth)
  famed.. 8. huntress
  foe.. 9. Aphrodite
  husband.. 8. Milanion
  legend.. 8. Arcadian, Boeotian
atalaya... 10. watchtower
atap... 4. nipa, palm
atavism... 8. heredity 9. reversion
  10. regression
ate... 5. dined, fared 6. dieted,
  gnawed, supped
Ate... 7. goddess (of infatuation)
atelier... 5. easel 6. studio
  8. workshop
a tempo... 4. time
Aten (Egypt)... 9. solar disk
ates... 8. sweetsop
athanasia... 8. athanasy
  11. immortality 13. deathlessness
  15. imperishability
athanor (Fr)... 7. furnace (alchemist's)
Athapascan Indian... 5. Tinne
  6. Apache, Navaho (Navajo)
atheist... 5. pagan 7. heathen, Infidel,
  nastika 8. agnostic 10. unbeliever
  11. disbeliever, unchristian
  13. antichristian
Athena (pert to)...
  attributes.. 3. owl 5. aegis 7. serpent
  festival.. 11. Panathenaea
  Rom equivalent.. 7. Minerva
  shrine.. 9. Parthenon (Athens)
Athena, goddess of...
  arts, crafts.. 6. Ergane
  health.. 6. Hygeia
  horses, tamer of.. 6. Hippia
  light.. 4. Alea
  maid of Athens.. 12. Pallas Athene
  poetry.. 6. Pallas
  victory.. 4. Nike
  wisdom.. 8. Palladis
Athenian (pert to)...
  assembly.. 4. Pnyx
  Bee.. 5. Plato
  general.. 8. Xenophon
  lawgiver.. 5. Draco, Solon
  sculptor.. 7. Phidias
  statesman.. 8. Pericles 9. Aristides
  (The Just) 10. Alcibiades
  temple.. 11. Nike Apteros
Athens...
  capital of.. 6. Attica (anc), Greece
  citadel.. 9. Acropolis
  magistrate.. 5. Draco, Solon
  rival.. 6. Sparta (anc)
  senate.. 5. boule
  temple.. 9. Parthenon

Athens of...
  America.. 6. Boston 9. Nashville (The
  South)
  Ireland.. 4. Cork 7. Belfast
  North.. 9. Edinburgh 10. Copenhagen
  Switzerland.. 6. Zurich
  West.. 7. Cordoba
athlete... 7. acrobat, gymnast, tumbler
  11. funambulist, palaestrian,
  pancratiast 13. contortionist
athlete (pert to)...
  foot disease.. 15. dermatophytosis
  of Christendom.. 10. Scanderbeg
  portico (Gr, Rom).. 6. xystus (xyst)
athletic... 5. lusty, thewy, yauld
  6. brawny, robust, sinewy, strong
  8. muscular, stalwart, vigorous
  9. acrobatic, agonistic, gymnastic
  10. palaestral (palestral)
  15. broad–shouldered
athwart... 6. across, aslant
  8. sideways, sidewise, traverse
  9. crosswise, obliquely
  10. crisscross, perversely
atimon... 9. muskmelon
Atlantean... 6. strong 7. titanic
  8. gigantic 9. Atlaslike
  10. Gargantuan
atlantes (opp of caryatids)...
  7. columns (carved men)
  9. telamones
Atlantic Sisters (Gr)... 8. Pleiades
  (stars)
Atlas (pert to)...
  converted into.. 7. Mt Atlas
  daughter.. 7. Calypso 8. Pleiades
  famed as a.. 5. giant, Titan
  king of.. 10. Mauretania
  mother.. 4. Asia 7. Clymene
  supporter of.. 5. earth 10. the
  heavens
Atman (Hind)... 3. ego 4. Self, Soul
  6. Brahma
atmosphere... 3. air 4. aura, mood
  5. ether, ozone 7. climate
  10. aerosphere, background
  11. environment, hydrosphere
atmosphere (pert to)...
  condition.. 9. epedaphic
  density.. 8. isostere, isoteric
  disturbance.. 5. storm 6. static
  9. tornadoes, whirlwind
  pressure.. 10. barometric
  shooting star.. 6. meteor
  spectrum.. 7. rainbow
atole... 5. gruel 8. porridge
atoll... 4. belt, reef (coral) 6. island
atom... 3. ace, bit, ion, jot 4. gram,
  iota, mite, whit 5. monad
  8. molecule, particle 9. corpuscle
atomic... 3. Age, ray 4. beam, bomb,
  tiny 5. power 6. energy, minute,
  number, radius, weight 7. nuclear
  9. atomistic, molecular, radiation
  10. intangible 11. microscopic
  13. infinitesimal
atomic submarine... 5. Skate 6. Triton
  8. Nautilus, Thresher 9. Sea Dragon
atomize... 4. fume 5. smash, spray
  6. aerate, gasify 7. fission, perfume,
  shatter 8. dissolve, fumigate, nucleize
  9. carbonate, decompose, evaporate,

micronize, pulverize 11. disorganize
12. disintegrate
atomy... 4. atom, mote 5. dwarf,
pygmy 6. droich, midget 8. skeleton
10. micromorph
atonement... 6. amends 7. apology,
penance, redress 8. requital
10. recompense, redemption,
reparation 11. reclamation, restitution
12. propitiation 15. indemnification
Atreus (pert to)...
brother.. 8. Thyestes
father.. 6. Pelops
king of.. 7. Mycenae
mother.. 10. Hippodamia
slayer of.. 12. Thyestes' sons
son.. 8. Menelaus 9. Agamemnon
wife.. 6. Aerope
atrium... 4. hall, room 5. court (inner)
6. cavity (Anat) 7. chamber
9. peristyle
atrocious... 4. rank, vile 5. awful,
cruel, grave 6. brutal, savage, sinful,
wicked 7. heinous, vicious, violent
8. dreadful, flagrant, horrible,
infamous, ruthless, shocking, terrible,
wretched 9. monstrous, nefarious
10. abominable, deplorable,
detestable, outrageous
atrociousness... 8. baseness, vileness
12. dreadfulness, shamefulness
13. nefariousness 15. Schrecklichkeit
atrocity... 4. evil, harm 5. abuse,
havoc, wrong 7. misdeed, outrage
8. enormity 9. indignity
12. mistreatment
atrophy... 5. tabes 7. disease
8. marasmus 10. emaciation
11. attenuation
Atropos (Gr)... 7. goddess (Fate)
attach... 3. add, fix, pin, put, tag, tie
4. bind, glue, join, vest 5. affix,
annex, hitch, paste, seize, unite
6. append, assign, fasten 7. ascribe,
connect, postfix, subjoin 9. associate,
attribute 11. superimpose
attached... 4. fond 6. adnate, welded
7. annexed, devoted, engaged,
sessile (Bot), smitten 8. cemented,
enamored
attachment... 4. bond, love 5. fancy
6. liking, regard 7. adjunct, fixture
8. addition, devotion, fidelity,
fondness 9. accession, adherence,
affection, fastening, increment
10. annexation 11. attribution
12. augmentation
attack... 3. fit 4. pang, raid 5. beset,
blitz, drive, feint, ictus, onset, sally,
siege, spasm 6. affret, assail, charge,
onrush, oppugn, sortie 7. aggress,
assault, bowling, descent, offense,
seizure 8. camisado (anc), paroxysm,
sickness 9. offensive, onslaught
10. aggression 11. enunciation
13. incrimination
attain... 2. do 3. get, win 4. earn,
gain 5. enact, reach 6. accede,
arrive, effect, obtain 7. achieve,
acquire, compass, fulfill, perform,
realize 9. discharge 10. accomplish,
consummate

attainable... 8. gettable 9. available
10. achievable
attainment... 5. skill 7. arrival
8. learning 9. accession
11. acquirement, acquisition,
cultivation, edification, realization
14. accomplishment
attar... 4. otto 5. scent 6. parfum
7. essence, perfume, rose oil
attempt... 3. aim, jab (sl), try 4. dare,
seek, stab 5. assay, ensue, essay,
fling, offer, onset, siege, trial
6. attack, effort, result 7. venture
8. endeavor 9. undertake
attend... 4. hark, heed, help, mind,
note, tend, wait 5. ensue, nurse,
serve, treat, visit 6. doctor, escort,
follow, foster, listen, result
7. conduct, hearken, nurture, observe
9. accompany
attendance... 4. draw 5. court
7. service, turnout 8. presence,
tendance 9. following
13. accompaniment
attendant... 4. maid, page 5. nurse,
staff, usher 6. caddie, escort, gillie,
porter, waiter 7. bellboy, orderly
8. follower 9. associate, attending,
companion 10. subsequent
11. concomitant, ministering
attendants, train of... 5. suite
7. cortege, retinue 9. entourage
attention... 3. ear 4. care, heed, hist,
note 6. notice, regard 7. concern,
hearing, respect, thought 8. courtesy
11. mindfulness 13. concentration,
consideration
attentive... 5. alert, awake, eared
6. intent 7. careful, heedful, mindful
8. obedient, vigilant, watchful
9. courteous, listening, observant,
wide–awake 10. meticulous,
respectful 11. circumspect,
considerate, surveillant
attenuated... 3. cut 4. fine, rare, slim,
thin 6. svelte, wasted 7. diluted,
gracile, reduced, slender, thinned,
watered 8. lessened, rarefied,
weakened 9. decreased, emaciated
attest... 4. seal 5. vouch 6. adjure,
affirm, avouch, depose 7. certify,
testify, witness 8. evidence, indicate,
manifest 9. testimony 10. deposition
12. authenticate
attestation... 4. oath (solemn) 5. proof
6. avowal 8. swearing 9. assertion
10. allegation 11. affirmation,
certificate, declaration, testimonial
13. testification 14. authentication
attic... 3. top 4. dome, head, loft,
wall 6. belfry, garret 8. cockloft
Attic... 5. salty, witty 6. simple
7. elegant, refined 8. academic,
Athenian, tasteful 9. classical
10. Ciceronian
Attic (pert to)...
Bee.. 9. Sophocles (poet)
bird.. 11. nightingale (Milton)
Muse.. 8. Xenophon
native.. 8. Athenian
school.. 9. sculpture
Attica (pert to)...

capital of.. 6. Athens
state of.. 6. Greece (anc)
famed as.. 15. world's first city
Attila... 3. Hun (leader) 5. Etzel
  (fabled) 12. Scourge of God
attitude... 3. air, set 4. pose, view
  5. angle, slant, stand 7. bearing,
  feeling, opinion, outlook, posture,
  thought 8. position, reaction
  9. arabesque (dance), sentiment,
  viewpoint 10. estimation, impression
attitude (reverent)... 6. salaam
  8. kneeling 9. obeisance
  12. genuflection (genuflexion)
attorney... 6. lawyer 7. counsel,
  pleader 9. barrister, counselor
  (counsellor) 11. intercessor
attract... 4. bait, draw, lure, pull
  5. charm, tempt 6. appeal, beckon,
  enamor, engage, entice, invite
  0. interest 9. captivate, fascinate,
  influence, magnetize
attraction... 4. lure, pull, star
  6. appeal 7. gravity 8. affinity,
  headline, interest, penchant
  9. magnetism, seduction
  10. allurement 11. fascination
attractive... 4. cute 6. lovely, pretty,
  taking 7. winsome 8. alluring,
  engaging, fetching, graceful, magnetic
  9. allicient, appealing, beauteous,
  beautiful, desirable 10. attracting,
  delightful 11. captivating, interesting
attractive and repellent...
  10. ambivalent
attrahent... 6. magnet 7. drawing
  8. sinapism (Med) 10. attracting
attribute... 3. owe 5. refer, trait
  6. impute, nature, symbol 7. ascribe,
  feature, quality 8. property
  9. adjective, qualifier, specialty
attrition... 4. wear 5. grief (Theol)
  7. massage 8. abrasion, friction,
  limation 9. detrition 10. contrition
attune... 4. tune 5. chime 6. accord,
  adjust 7. concord, harmony, syntony
  9. melodious 10. symphonize
  11. concordance
atwain... 7. asunder
atweel... 5. truly 6. surely
aubade (Fr)... 3. lay 4. poem, song
  6. ballad 7. concert (morning)
  8. serenade
auberge... 3. inn
aubergiste... 9. innkeeper
auction... 3. bid 4. cant, roup, sale
  5. block 6. vendue 7. bidding
auction (game)... 4. pool 5. pitch
  6. bridge, euchre, hearts 8. pinochle
audacious... 4. bold 5. saucy
  6. brazen, daring 7. defiant
  8. impudent, insolent, intrepid,
  spirited 9. barefaced, foolhardy,
  insulting 11. adventurous,
  challenging, impertinent, presumptive,
  venturesome
audacity... 5. cheek, crust, nerve
  6. daring 7. courage 8. defiance,
  temerity 9. assurance, hardihood,
  impudence, insolence, sauciness
  10. effrontery, enterprise
  11. presumption 12. impertinence

13. audaciousness, foolhardiness,
  shamelessness
audible... 5. aloud, clear 8. distinct,
  hearable 10. articulate
audible respiration... 4. sigh
audience... 3. ear 5. house, trial
  6. parley, tryout 7. hearing, theater
  8. audition, auditory, congress
  9. interview, listeners 10. conference
  12. congregation
audit... 5. check 6. reckon, verify
  7. certify, collate 10. accounting
  11. examination
auditor... 5. clerk 6. censor, hearer
  7. actuary, apposer 8. examiner,
  listener 10. accountant, bookkeeper
  11. comptroller
auditorium... 4. hall, nave (anc)
  5. house 7. theater 8. auditory,
  building 9. Guildhall
auditory... 4. otic 5. audio, aural
  6. phonic 7. hearers 8. audience
  9. acoustic, auricular
  12. congregation
au fait... 4. able 6. expert 7. equal to
  8. informed, skillful 9. qualified
  10. conversant (with)
au fond... 9. basically, primarily
  11. essentially 13. fundamentally
auger... 3. bit 4. bore, tool 5. borer,
  drill 6. gimlet, wimble 10. perforator
aught... 3. any 4. none, some, zero
  5. ought 6. cipher 7. nothing
  8. anything
augment... 3. add, eke 5. affix, annex,
  exalt, swell 6. expand, extend
  7. amplify, broaden, develop,
  enhance, enlarge 8. increase
  9. reinforce
Augsburg Church ... 8. Lutheran
augur... 4. bode, omen, seer 5. sibyl,
  vates (Gauls) 6. oracle 7. betoken,
  presage 8. forebode, forecast,
  foretell, forewarn, haruspex (Rom),
  indicate, prophesy 10. anticipate,
  astrologer, conjecture, soothsayer
  13. prognosticate 14. prognosticator
augury... 4. omen, rite 7. auspice,
  portent 8. ceremony
august... 5. awful, grand, novel, regal
  6. sedate, solemn 7. courtly,
  eminent, stately 8. imposing, majestic
  9. dignified, honorable, important,
  venerable 11. magnificent, ritualistic
  12. aristocratic
August... 6. Lammas 8. Sextilis
  10. First month (Rom year)
August meteor (11th of month)...
  7. Perseid
auk... 4. Alca, Alle, bird (sea), falk
  5. murre, noddy 6. auklet, rotche
  (rotch) 7. Alcidae, dovekie
  9. guillemot, razorbill
Auk... 6. Indian 7. Alaskan, Tlingit
  (tribe) 9. Koluschan
aula... 4. hall, room 5. court
  6. emblic (E Ind tree) 9. ventricle
aulos... 5. flute 8. woodwind
  9. woodwinds (collectively)
aura... 3. air 4. halo, ring 6. astral,
  circle, fringe (Psychol), nimbus
  7. aureola 9. effluvium, emanation

10. atmosphere, exhalation
aureole... 4. halo 5. glory 6. circle, nimbus
auricle... 3. ear 4. lobe 5. pinna
 6. atrium (heart) 9. appendage
auricular... 4. otic 5. aural, eared
 6. phonic 8. acoustic, auditory
aurifex... 9. goldsmith
aurochs... 3. tur 4. goat, urus
 5. bison
aurora... 3. eos 4. dawn 5. sunup
 7. sunrise 8. borealis, daybreak, daylight 9. australis 11. polar lights
aurora borealis... 14. northern lights
auroral... 4. dawn, eoan, rosy
 7. eastern, radiant, roseate
auspices... 3. aid 4. care, sign, wing
 5. aegis (egis) 6. charge 7. backing, custody 8. guidance 9. patronage
 10. management, protection
 11. sponsorship, supervision
auspicious... 4. good 6. timely
 9. favorable, fortunate, opportune
 10. convenient, propitious, prosperous, seasonable
 12. advantageous
Aussie... 6. digger 10. Australian
Auster... 9. southland, south wind
austere... 4. dour, hard 5. acrid, harsh, rigid, rough, stern 6. bitter, severe, strict 7. ascetic, pungent
 8. exacting 10. astringent
Australasia... 7. Oceania 15. South Sea Islands
Australasian bird... 8. lorikeet
 9. pardalote
Australia... see also *Australian*
 capital.. 8. Canberra
 desert.. 10. Great Sandy 13. Great Victoria
 First Englishman (1688).. 14. William Dampier
 holiday.. 13. Foundation Day (Jan 26)
 island.. 8. Tasmania
 mountain peak.. 9. Kosciusko
 ocean.. 6. Indian
 river.. 6. Murray
 sea.. 5. Coral 6. Tasman
 Tropic (southern).. 9. Capricorn
Australian (pert to)...
 bee.. 5. karbi
 bedroll.. 6. bindle 7. matilda
 candy.. 5. lolly
 feast.. 10. corroboree
 fish.. 4. mako (shark) 5. yabby
 flag.. 13. Southern Cross
 flower.. 7. waratah (tulip)
 9. rhodanthe
 hut.. 6. miamia
 native.. 5. myall 6. Aussie, binghi
 8. kangaroo, warragal 9. aborigine, Dravidian
 reptile.. 6. elapid, goanna, lizard (barking, frilled)
 soldier.. 5. Anzac 6. digger
Australian animal...
 dog (wild).. 5. dingo
 horse (wild).. 6. brumby
 sheep dog.. 6. kelpie
 mammal.. 7. daysure 8. duckbill, platypus 9. blind mole
 marsupial.. 4. tait 5. koala 6. wombat

7. echidna 8. anteater, kangaroo
 9. phalanger, teddy bear
 10. kookaburra 14. Tasmanian Devil
Australian bird... 3. emu, owl 4. lory, titi 5. arara, ariel, galah 6. leipoa, petrel 7. boobook, bustard, corella (parrot), grinder, rosella (parakeet)
 8. ganggang, lorikeet, lyrebird, morepork, nightjar, paradise
 9. bowerbird, cassowary, pardalote
 10. flycatcher, goatsucker
 11. budgereegah (parakeet)
Australian State capitals... 5. Perth
 6. Darwin, Hobart, Sydney
 8. Adelaide, Brisbane, Canberra (chief) 9. Melbourne
Australian tree... 4. teak, toon
 5. belah, penda 6. jarrah, mallee, marara, she–oak, wattle 7. gunnung (mahogany) 8. Alstonia (dogbane), ironbark (eucalypt) 9. boobyalla (willow)
Austria...
 capital.. 6. Vienna
 city.. 4. Graz, Linz 8. Salzburg
 9. Innsbruck
 forest belt.. 10. Wiener Wald
 monarchy.. 14. Austria–Hungary
 mountain.. 4. Alps 6. Otztal
 9. Dolomites
 mountain peak.. 10. Wildspitze
 13. Gross–Glockner
 Pass (famed).. 7. Brenner
 river.. 3. Inn, Mur 4. Enns
 6. Danube
Austrian (pert to)...
 botanist.. 6. Mendel (Mendel's Law)
 composer.. 6. Mozart 7. Strauss
 inventor.. 8. Welsbach
 pianist.. 8. Kreisler
 ruler (former).. 6. Kaiser
 scientist.. 5. Adler, Freud
 soldier.. 5. jager
 theaterman.. 9. Reinhardt (Max)
autarch... 6. despot, tyrant 8. autocrat
authentic... 4. pure, real, true 5. valid
 6. native 7. certain, correct, genuine, natural 8. bona fide, credible, official, original, orthodox, reliable 9. firsthand
 11. trustworthy 13. authoritative
authenticate... 6. affirm, attest, ratify
 7. certify, confirm, warrant
 8. validate 12. substantiate
authenticity... 11. genuineness, reliability 13. dependability
 15. trustworthiness
author... 4. doer, poet 5. ghost, maker 6. parent, penman, writer
 7. creator, inditer 8. annalist, begetter, compiler, composer, essayist, inventor, novelist, producer
 9. dramatist, scribbler 10. originator
 13. encyclopedist (encyclopaedist)
authoritative... 4. wise 5. valid
 6. potent, ruling, strong 7. weighty
 8. approved, forceful, official, oracular, orthodox, positive, powerful
 9. authentic, imperious
 10. commanding, peremptory
 11. dictatorial, influential
 13. determinative
authoritative (pert to)...

command.. 4. fiat 5. usage
  6. decree, dictum 7. mandate
example.. 9. precedent
  10. antecedent
letter.. 4. writ 5. breve
authority... 5. judge, power, right
  6. critic, expert, oracle, regent
  7. command, warrant, witness
  8. dominion, validity 9. influence,
  testimony 10. commission,
  competency 11. connoisseur,
  prerogative 12. jurisdiction
  13. authorization
authorize... 6. accept, permit, ratify
  7. certify, charter, empower, endorse,
  entitle, justify, license, warrant
  8. accredit, delegate, sanction,
  validate 10. commission
  11. enfranchise 12. legitimatize
authorless... 8. nameless
  9. anonymous
autobiography... 7. journal, letters,
  memoirs 11. memorabilia
autochton... 6. binghi, native
  8. indigene 9. primitive
  10. aboriginal
autocracy... 8. monarchy 9. despotism
  10. absolutism 15. totalitarianism
autocrat... 4. czar (tsar) 5. mogul
  6. despot 7. arbiter, monarch
  8. dictator 9. sovereign
  10. taskmaster
autodidactic... 8. self-made
  10. self-taught 12. self-educated
autograph... 4. seal, sign 5. cross
  9. signature 11. John Hancock
automatic... 7. machine
  10. mechanical, self-acting
  11. instinctive, involuntary,
  spontaneous
automatic device... 3. gun 4. gear
  5. drill, pilot, rifle, robot 6. pistol,
  switch 8. computer, revolver
  10. six-shooter
automaton... 5. golem, robot
  6. puppet 7. android, machine
automobile... 3. cab, car 4. auto, taxi
  5. coupe 6. jalopy 7. autocar,
  flivver, machine, taxicab, vehicle
  8. motorcar
autosuggestion... 7. therapy
  8. hypnosis 9. hypnology, mesmerism
  10. psychology 14. self-suggestion
autumn... 4. fall 6. mature, old age,
  season (yearly) 7. equinox, harvest,
  October 8. maturity, November
  9. September
auxiliary... 4. ally, plus 5. extra
  6. aiding, helper 7. adjunct, helping
  9. accessory, ancillary, assistant,
  attendant, coadjutor, colleague,
  companion, secondary 10. additional,
  subsidiary, supporting
  11. confederate, cooperating,
  subordinate, subservient
  12. nonessential, supplemental
  13. supplementary
auxiliary army... 6. relief 7. support
  8. Landwehr, recruits, reserves
  11. contingents 14. reinforcements
auxiliary verb... 3. can, had, has, may
  4. hast, have, will 5. could, shall,

would 6. should
avail... 3. use 4. good, help 5. value
  6. inform, profit 7. benefit, service,
  utility 9. advantage, expedient
availability... 7. utility 9. usability
  10. usefulness 13. acquirability
  attainability 14. serviceability
available... 4. free, open 5. handy,
  ready, valid 6. on hand, usable,
  vacant 8. unfilled 9. securable
  10. accessible, attainable, convenient,
  obtainable, unoccupied
avalanche... 5. slide 7. descent
  (sudden) 8. slippage
avant-garde... 3. van 8. vanguard
avant-propos... 7. preface
  12. introduction (remarks)
avarice... 4. lust 5. greed 7. avidity
  8. avidness, cupidity, grasping,
  rapacity, voracity 10. greediness
  12. covetousness
avarice demon... 6. Mammon
avaricious... 5. close 6. grabby,
  greedy 7. miserly 8. covetous,
  grasping 9. niggardly, penurious,
  rapacious, voracious 12. parsimonious
avatar... 8. epiphany 10. embodiment
  11. incarnation 14. transmigration
avatars of Vishnu (Hind Relig)...
  11. incarnation (deity to man)
avaunt... 4. away 5. allez, boast,
  scram, vaunt 6. begone, depart
  7. advance, vamoose
ave... 4. hail, viva, vive 8. farewell
Ave Maria... 4. bead (rosary), song
  6. prayer 10. devotional
Avena... 4. oats 7. grasses
avenge... 7. requite 9. retaliate,
  vindicate
Avenging Angels... 8. nickname (Polit
  1858) 10. Danite Band (Mormons)
Avenging Spirit... 4. Fate, Fury
  6. Erinys 7. Alastor, Atropos
avenue... 3. rue 4. land, pike, road,
  vent 5. alley 6. arcade, artery, defile,
  egress, outlet, street 7. channel,
  freeway, highway, opening
  8. corridor, turnpike 9. boulevard,
  concourse 10. passageway
  12. thoroughfare
aver... 3. say 5. state 6. affirm,
  allege, assert 7. declare, profess,
  protect 10. asseverate
average... 2. go 3. par, run 4. mean,
  rule 6. common, medial, medium,
  normal 7. balance 8. mediocre
  10. generality
averment... 6. dictum, remark
  7. witness 9. assertion, statement,
  testimony, utterance 10. allegation
  11. affirmation, attestation
  12. verification 13. pronouncement
Avernus... 4. lake (poison vapors)
  5. Hades
averse... 5. loath 7. adverse
  9. reluctant, unwilling 11. disinclined
aversion... 4. hate 5. odium
  6. hatred, horror 7. disgust, dislike
  9. antipathy, repulsion
  10. abhorrence, repugnance
  11. abomination 12. estrangement
  13. indisposition, unwillingness

aversion to... see also *fear of*
novelty.. 9. neophobia
society.. 14. anthropophobia
strangers.. 10. xenophobia
wine.. 10. oenophobia
avert... 4. fend, save 5. check, deter,
evade, repel 6. forbid, retard, switch,
thwart 7. deflect, prevent 8. alienate,
prohibit 9. forestall, sidetrack
aviary... 4. cage 5. house 7. dovecot
(dovecote) 8. ornithon 9. birdhouse,
columbary, enclosure
11. columbarium
aviation... 6. flight, flying 7. winging
9. skyriding 10. airplaning
11. aeronautics
aviation maneuver... 9. Immelmann
(Ger)
aviator... 3. Ace 5. flier (flyer), pilot
6. airman, Icarus (fabled first)
7. wingman 8. aeronaut, aviatrix,
operator 9. astronaut, birdwoman,
Immelmann
avichi (Buddh)... 4. Hell 5. Hades
9. depravity, perdition 10. underworld
avid... 4. agog, keen 5. eager
6. grabby, greedy 7. anxious,
craving, zestful 8. grasping
9. rapacious, voracious 10. avaricious
avidity... 4. lust 5. greed 7. avarice
8. cupidity, grasping 9. eagerness
10. greediness 12. covetousness
avion... 5. plane 8. airplane
avisa... 4. news 6. advice, caveat
7. tidings, warning 11. information
Avis Indica (Astron)... 4. Apus
13. constellation
avital... 9. ancestral
avoid... 4. shun, snub 5. annul,
dodge, elude, evade 6. escape,
eschew, repeal, revoke, vacate
7. abstain, forbear 10. invalidate
avoidance... 6. outlet 7. evasion,
removal 8. emptying, shunning,
vacating 9. annulment 10. withdrawal
avoirdupois... 4. beef 6. weight
7. gravity, tonnage 8. poundage
9. heaviness
avoirdupois weight... 3. ton 4. dram
5. grain, ounce, pound
13. hundred–weight
avow... 3. own, vow 5. admit, swear,
vouch 6. allege, assert, pledge
7. confess, declare, profess, promise
10. avouchment 11. acknowledge
avulsion... 7. removal 9. severance
10. extraction, separation (ppty),
withdrawal
awabi... 7. abalone
awaft... 6. adrift, afloat, wafted
await... 4. bide, come, heed, loom,
pend, wait 5. abide, tarry, watch
6. ambush, attend, expect, impend,
waylay 8. approach 9. forthcome
awake... 5. alert, alive, astir, rouse
6. arouse, excite, waking
8. open–eyed 9. attentive, conscious,
sleepless, wide–awake
awaken... 5. awake 6. arouse, excite,
stir up 8. roust out
award... 4. gift, give, meed, mete
5. allot, grant, medal, Oscar, prize

6. reward, trophy 7. adjudge,
present, verdict 8. accolade
9. medallion
aware... 3. hep 4. know 5. sense
7. mindful 8. apprized, sensible
9. cognizant, conscious
11. intelligent
awareness... 5. sense 7. feeling
9. sensation 10. impression,
perception 11. mindfulness, sensibility
13. consciousness
away... 2. on 3. awa, far, fro, off, out
4. gone 5. aside, hence 6. abroad,
absent, begone, onward, thence
7. escaped 8. vanished 9. elsewhere
away from...
body center.. 5. ectad 6. distal
mouth.. 6. aborad, aboral
wind.. 4. alee
awe... 3. cow 4. fear 5. dread
6. regard, terror, wonder 7. emotion,
respect 8. astonish, frighten, surprise
9. reverence 10. admiration,
veneration, wonderment
13. consideration
aweather... (opp of alee) 8. windward
11. weatherward
awe–inspiring... 5. eerie (eery)
7. awesome, ghostly 8. glorious,
imposing, splendid, terrific
9. wonderful 10. impressive
11. magnificent
awe–struck... 4. awed 9. terrified
10. astonished, fear–struck,
spellbound 12. wonder–struck
13. thunderstruck
awful... 4. awed, ugly 5. dread, great,
gross 6. sacred, silent, solemn,
woeful 7. awesome, fearful, hideous
8. dreadful, infamous, reverent,
shocking, terrible 9. appalling,
atrocious, deathlike, ludicrous,
venerable, wonderful 10. deplorable,
impressive, outrageous, unpleasant
11. exceedingly
awkward... 5. gawky, inapt, inept
6. clumsy, gauche 7. froward,
loutish, unhandy 8. bungling,
clownish, lubberly, perverse, ungainly,
unwieldy 9. graceless, inelegant,
lumbering, maladroit, ponderous
10. backhanded, blundering,
ungraceful 12. embarrassing,
incommodious, inconvenient
awkward age... 4. teen 5. teens
awkward fellow... 6. galoot
11. hobbledehoy
awless, aweless... 4. bald 6. brazen
8. fearless, unafraid 9. bold–faced,
dauntless 10. irreverent
11. unsurprised 12. unastonished
awn... 4. barb 5. beard (plant)
6. arista, papous 7. bristle
awning... 6. canopy, screen, shield
7. shelter 8. velarium (anc)
AWOL... 5. hooky 7. truancy
9. truantism 11. absenteeism
awry... 4. agee 5. agley, amiss, askew
6. faulty 7. askance, asquint,
crooked, oblique 9. distorted
10. disorderly 11. disarranged
12. disorganized

ax, axe... 3. adz (adze), ask (dial)
   4. tool 6. hammer, poleax (poleaxe)
   7. hatchet (small) 8. axhammer
   9. discharge, dismissal
ax (pert to)...
  ancient.. 4. celt 6. chisel
  blade.. 3. bit
  execution.. 10. guillotine
  handle.. 5. helve
axial... 7. central, midmost, pivotal
axilla... 3. ala 4. axil 5. oxter
   6. armpit 8. shoulder
axiom... 3. law, saw 4. rule 5. adage,
   maxim, motto, truth 6. byword,
   dictum, saying, truism 7. dictate,
   precept, proverb, theorem
   8. aphorism, apothegm 9. principle
   11. proposition
axiomatic... 10. aphoristic, proverbial
   11. self–evident, sententious
   12. epigrammatic
axis... 3. hub 4. axle, bloc, nave,
   stem 5. pivot, stalk 6. caulis, center,
   league 7. fulcrum 8. alliance,
   vertebra 9. coalition
axle... 3. pin 4. axis 5. pivot, shaft
   6. swivel 7. spindle 8. axletree
axle tooth... 5. molar
ayal... 4. amah, maid 5. mammy
   9. governess, nursemaid
   11. maidservant
aye... 2. ay 3. pro, yea, yes 4. ever,
   vote 5. voice 6. always, assent
   8. thumbs up, viva–voce

aye–aye... 5. lemur (Madagascar)
ayes... 10. all in favor
Azazel... 5. Eblis, Satan 9. scapegoat
Azerbaijanian... 4. Turk
   14. Transcaucasian
azimuth... 3. arc 4. dial 6. circle
   7. compass, horizon 8. distance,
   magnetic 10. North point
Azores...
  capital.. 5. Angra
  city.. 5. Horta
  group (islands).. 6. St Mary 8. St
   George 9. St Michael
  locale.. 8. Atlantic (Ocean)
  owner.. 8. Portugal
Aztec (pert to)...
  calendar.. 7. Mexican
  capital (anc).. 12. Tenochtitlan
  emperor.. 9. Montezuma
  god.. 4. Xipe (sowing)
   12. Quetzalcoatl (peace)
  hero.. 4. Nata (Myth) 6. Cortez
  language.. 7. Nahuatl
  locale (anc).. 6. Aztlan
  Noah (Mex).. 6. Coxcox
  stone.. 12. chalchihuitl
  temple.. 8. teocalli
  tribe.. 9. Nahuatlan
azure... 4. blue 7. celeste, sky–blue
   8. bice blue, cerulean 9. blue vault,
   cloudless 11. lapis lazuli
azygous... 3. odd 4. only, sole
   6. single, unique 8. singular
   10. unrepeated
azymous... 10. unleavened

B

B... 4. beta 6. letter (2nd)
ba (Egypt)... 3. khu 4. soul
baa... 5. bleet
baahling... 4. lamb
Baal... 4. idol 5. deity 6. Baalim (pl)
   7. Baalath 8. false god 9. fertility
baba (pert to)...
  India.. 4. baby 5. child
  Malaya.. 4. male
  Slavic.. 5. nurse 7. midwife 8. old
   woman
  Turkey.. 5. title (of respect)
babacoote... 5. lemur (Madagascar)
Babbar... 3. Utu (Utug) 6. sun god
babbo... 5. daddy 6. father
babel... 5. clang 6. jargon, tumult
   7. discord 8. confusion
   11. pandemonium
Babel (pert to)...
  Bible.. 5. Tower 8. ziggurat
  presently.. 14. Temple of Marduk
  site (ancient).. 6. Shinar (land of)
  site (present).. 7. Babylon
babirusa, babiroussa... 9. quadruped
   (hoglike)

Babism (Persia)... 4. sect
baboon... 3. ape 5. Papio 6. chacma
   7. babuina, monster 8. mandrill
babushka... 11. grandmother
baby... 4. babe, doll 6. coward, infant,
   puppet, weanie 7. bambino, chicken
   8. juvenile, weakling 9. miniature,
   youngling, youngster 10. diminutive
baby carriage... 4. pram 5. wagon
   6. go–cart 8. stroller
   12. perambulator
babyish... 6. simple 7. dollish, puerile
   8. childish 9. childlike, infantile
Babylon... see also *Babylonian*
  capital of.. 9. Babylonia
  kingdom.. 4. Elam 5. Akkad (Accad)
  meaning.. 9. Gate of God
  mountain.. 6. Ararat
  river.. 6. Tigris 9. Euphrates
  World Wonder.. 14. Hanging Gardens
Babylonian (pert to)...
  abode of the dead.. 5. Aralu
  chaos.. 4. Apsu
  deity.. 5. Alalu (Alala), Siris
  earth mother.. 6. Ishtar

god .. 2. Ea, Zu 3. Anu, Bel 4. Adad, Apsu, Irra 5. Dagan, Enlil 6. Nergal 7. Shamash
goddess .. 3. Aya 4. Nina 5. Belit (Beltis)
hero (Myth) .. 5. Adapa, Etana 9. Tilgamesh
king .. 6. Sargon 9. Habonidus, Hammurabi 10. Nabonassar 14. Nebuchadnezzar (Nebuchadrezzar)
temple, tower .. 8. ziggurat
bacach ... 6. beggar 7. cripple
bacalao ... 7. codfish, grouper
bacalao bird ... 3. auk 5. murre 9. guillemot
Bacardi ... 3. rum
bacca ... 5. berry
baccalaureate ... 6. degree (college), sermon 8. bachelor
baccate ... 5. pulpy 9. berrylike
bacchanal ... 7. reveler 8. carouser
Bacchanalia ... 4. orgy 5. feast 7. debauch 8. festival (Bacchus)
bacchante ... 6. maenad 7. bacchae
Bacchus ... 4. wine 9. god of wine
baccivorous ... 11. berry–eating
bachelor ... 4. male 6. degree (Acad), garçon 8. benedict, celibate 10. misogamist
bacillus ... 9. bacterium
Bacis ... 2. Ra 4. bull (sacred)
back ... 3. aft, aid, fro 4. abet, hind, past, rear 5. stern 6. behind, second, uphold 7. finance, sponsor, support, sustain 8. extrados, intrados, resource 9. encourage, posterior 10. background
back (Anat) ... 4. loin, nape 5. notum 6. dorsal, dorsum, lumbar, tergal, tergum 7. occiput 8. backbone, notalgia 10. opisthenar (hand)
backbone ... 4. grit, guts 5. nerve, pluck, spunk 6. mettle, spirit 7. courage, stamina, support 8. firmness, gameness, mainstay 10. dependence
backbone (Anat) ... 4. axis 5. brace, chine, spine 6. column, spinal 7. spinule, support 8. ossicles 9. vertebrae
backer ... 5. angel 6. patron 7. abettor, sponsor 8. financer, promoter, upholder 9. supporter, sustainer 10. maintainer
background ... (opp of foreground) 4. rear 5. stage 6. offing 7. horizon, setting 8. backdrop, distance, practice, training 9. education 10. experience 11. savoir–faire
backhanded ... 6. clumsy 7. awkward, devious 9. insincere, insulting, sarcastic 10. circuitous
backslider ... 8. apostate, deserter, recreant 10. unfaithful
back–to–back ... 7. dos–à–dos
backward ... 4. back, dull, late 5. arear, loath, tardy 6. averse, modest, stupid 7. bashful, belated, reverse 8. arrested, dilatory, perverse, rearward, retarded, reticent, retrorse, reversed 9. hindwards, recessive, reluctant, subnormal, unwilling

10. behindhand, hesitating, regressive, retrograde 11. unfavorable 13. retrogressive, retrospective
bacon ... 4. lard, pork, side 5. prize 6. flitch, gammon, rasher 8. Canadian, sowbelly
Bacon's Rebellion ... 6. revolt (Va 1676)
bacteria ... 5. cocci, germs 7. aerobes, aerobia, bacilli 8. microbes, spirilla 9. organisms
bacteriologist culture ... 4. agar
Bactrian camel ... 9. two–humped
bad ... 3. ill, mal (pref) 4. evil, fell, foul, poor, vile 5. drole, fetid, nasty, wrong 6. arrant, in pain, putrid, rotten, sinful, wanton, wicked 7. corrupt, hurtful, naughty, noxious, spoiled, tainted, unlucky, unmoral, unsound, vicious 8. annoying, criminal, improper, inferior, iniquity, sinister 9. dangerous, defective, offensive, perverted, worthless 10. iniquitous, malodorous, unsuitable 11. inexpedient, inopportune 12. disagreeable, inauspicious
bad (pert to) ...
blood .. 4. feud 6. rancor 7. ill will 10. bitterness, resentment
custom .. 9. cacoethes
legislation .. 7. dysnomy
luck .. 5. deuce 7. ambsace
man's oatmeal .. 7. hemlock (poison) 11. wild chervil
badge ... 3. pin 4. mark, sign, star 5. index, token 6. emblem, ensign, plaque, shield, symbol 7. earmark 8. insignia 14. identification
badger ... 3. nag, rag 4. bait 5. harry, tease, worry 6. bother, extort, harass, hawker, heckle, hector, pester 8. huckster
badger (animal) ... 5. Meles (anc), pahmi, ratel 6. bauson, mammal, teledu, wombat 9. bandicoot, mistonusk
Badger State ... 9. Wisconsin
badinage ... 4. fool 5. joker, sport 6. banter 8. raillery 9. badinerie, simpleton 10. persiflage, pleasantry
badly ... 3. bad, ill 4. sick 5. amiss, wrong 6. poorly, unwell 8. faultily, wickedly 9. viciously 11. exceedingly, imperfectly 12. disagreeably, unskillfully 13. unfortunately
badly off ... 3. sad 7. hapless, unblest, unhappy, unlucky 8. luckless 11. impecunious, unfortunate 12. unprosperous 14. unprovidential
baff ... 4. beat, blow, thud 6. strike, stroke (golf)
baffle ... 4. balk, foil 5. cheat, elude, evade, spike 6. defeat, delude, muffle, puzzle, thwart 7. mystify, nonplus 8. bewilder, confound 9. bamboozle, frustrate 10. disconcert
baffling ... 7. elusive, evasive 8. puzzling 9. bothering, confusing, dismaying 10. mystifying, perplexing, perturbing 11. frustrating 13. disconcerting

baft... 3. aft 4. baff 5. abaff, cloth, shaft 6. astern

bag... 3. net, pac, pot, sac, sag 4. etui, grip, load, poke, sack, trap 5. ascus, belly, catch, droop, pouch, purse, seize, snare, steal 6. entrap, sachet, valise 7. bladder, capture, distend, handbag, pannier, satchel 8. reticule, suitcase 9. Gladstone, haversack, sac de nuit 10. pocketbook 11. portmanteau

bag and baggage... 10. completely 11. impedimenta

bagatelle... 3. toy 4. game 6. bauble, geegaw, trifle 7. trinket 10. knickknack, triviality 12. fiddle–faddle

Bagdad, Baghdad...
capital of.. 4. Iraq
character.. 6. Sinbad (The Sailor)
city.. 8. Moslem
founder (762).. 8. Almanzor
kingdom (anc).. 11. Mesopotamia
Oriental term.. 8. lambskin (raw)
river.. 6. Tigris
transportation (famed).. 7. Railway

bagpipe, bagpipes... 5. drone, pipes 7. musette 9. Dudelsack 10. doodlesack, sordellina

bagpipe (pert to)...
music variations.. 7. pibroch
parts.. 4. lill, oboe 5. drone 7. chanter 9. chalumeau
player.. 5. piper
tube.. 6. drones 7. chanter
tune.. 4. port

Bahamas, Bahama Islands...
capital.. 6. Nassau
discoverer.. 8. Columbus
native.. 5. conch
naval base (US).. 9. Mayaguana
San Salvador (now).. 14. Watlings Island (Watling Island)

bahan... 6. poplar, willow (Bib)

bahay... 5. house

bahi... 7. fortune (gypsy)

bail... 3. dip 4. bond, hoop, lade, lave, ring, rynd 5. court, ladle, throw 6. bucket, dipper, handle, pledge, secure, surety 8. replevin, security 9. guarantee

bailiff... 5. agent, bobby, reeve, staff 6. deputy, staves (pl) 7. marshal, officer, sheriff, shrieve, steward 8. bluecoat, gendarme, overseer 9. constable 12. understeward

bailiwick... 6. canton, county, domain 7. commune, diocese 8. precinct, province 12. municipality

bain... 4. near 5. lithe, ready, short 6. direct, limber, supple 7. forward, willing

bairn... 3. kid, tot 4. mite 5. child 6. urchin

bait... 3. fly 4. feed, hook, lure, trap 5. bribe, decoy, snare 6. badger, harass, hockle 7. fulcrum, torment 8. inveigle 9. persecute 10. enticement, exasperate, temptation

bait... 3. dap, dib 4. fish, hook 6. dibble

bakal (Orient)... 9. tradesman 10. shopkeeper

bake... 3. dry 4. cake, cook, fire, kiln 5. roast 6. anneal, harden 8. clambake 9. dehydrate

bakehead... 4. rail 5. guard, shack 6. stoker 7. fireman 8. trainman

baken... 4. buoy 6. beacon 8. landmark

baker's dozen... 4. long 6. devil's 7. inbread 8. thirteen

baksheesh... 3. sop, tip 5. bribe 7. largess (largesse) 8. gratuity 12. compensation

bal... 4. ball, mine, prom

balance... 4. even, rest, rule 5. poise, ratio, scale, weigh 6. adjust, aplomb, normal, offset, reason, rhythm, sanity 7. average, ballast, compare, euphony, measure, remains, surplus 8. equality, equalize, leftover, residual, saneness, serenity, symmetry 9. composure, equipoise, remainder, stability 10. equanimity, neutralize, proportion, symmetrize 11. equilibrium 12. counterpoise

balanced... 4. even, just 6. poised 7. equable 8. measured 9. equitable 10. euphonious 11. symmetrical 13. self–possessed

balancer... 7. acrobat, gymnast 10. ropedancer 11. equilibrist

balcony... 4. dais 5. stage 6. podium 7. estrade, gallery, rostrum 8. brattice, platform

bald... 4. bare, dull, mere, open 5. crude, naked, plain 6. simple 7. epilose 8. depilous, hairless 9. bald–pated 11. unconcealed

baldachin, baldaquin . 6. canopy (St Peter's, Rome), fabric

Balder (pert to)...
father.. 4. Odin
god of.. 5. light, peace
mother.. 5. Frigg
slain by.. 9. mistletoe (dart)
wife.. 5. Nanna

balderdash... 3. rot 4. bosh 5. trash 6. bunkum, jargon 7. bombast 8. buncombe, falderal, nonsense, tommyrot 9. poppycock

baldness... 6. acomia 8. alopecia 11. phalacrosis 12. hairlessness

baldric... 4. belt (ornament) 6. zodiac 7. support (sword)

bale... 3. woe 4. bind, load, pack 5. truss 6. ballot, bundle, burden, misery, packet, seroon 7. anguish, package 11. encumbrance

Balearic Islands... 5. Iviza 7. Cabrera, Majorca, Minorca 10. Formentera

baleful... 3. bad, sad 4. dire 6. woeful 7. baneful, harmful, malific, noisome, noxious 8. damaging 9. ill–omened, malignant 10. pernicious 12. inauspicious

balk... 4. foil 5. check, ridge 6. baffle, defeat, fallow, rafter, signal (fishing), thwart 7. blunder, faux pas, stickle 9. frustrate, hindrance 10. bafflement, disappoint

14. disappointment
Balkan Peninsula ...
native .. 4. Serb
river .. 3. Une 5. Saave 6. Danube
sea .. 5. Black 6. Aegean 7. Marmosa
   8. Adriatic 13. Mediterranean
State .. 6. Greece, Serbia, Turkey (Eur)
   7. Albania, Rumania 8. Bulgaria
balky ... 7. restive 9. faltering,
   obstinate, shrinking, stickling
ball ... 3. bal, fly, hop, lob, orb
   4. bead, clew (yarn), pill, shot
   5. dance, globe, pearl, pinda (rice)
   6. pellet, pelota, sphere 7. rissole
   8. conglobe, snowball 9. eight ball
   10. cannonball 12. medicine ball
ball (of games) ... 4. golf, hand, polo,
   soft 6. basket, tennis, volley
   7. bowling, cricket, croquet, jai alai
   8. baseball, billiard, ping-pong
ballad ... 3. lay 4. lied, poem, song
   5. derry, rhyme, verse 6. sonnet
   7. ballade, canzone
ballast ... 5. poise 6. aplomb, steady,
   weight 7. balance 9. kentledge,
   saburrate, stabilize 10. equanimity,
   equivalent 14. counterbalance
balled up ... 7. complex, mixed up,
   muddled 8. confused, fouled up
   9. befuddled, entangled, snarled up
   10. disordered 11. complicated
ballet (pert to) ...
arrangement .. 12. choreography
dance .. 6. adagio 9. pantomime
dancer .. 8. coryphee, danseuse
   9. ballerina
jump .. 4. jeté 5. coupé
lover .. 11. balletomane
music .. 5. opera 6. comedy
   7. d'action 14. divertissement
balloon ... 3. bag 4. ball, tire 5. barge
   (Siam), blimp, swell 6. aviate, ballon,
   dilate, expand, gasbag 7. distend,
   nacelle 8. aerostat, aircraft
   9. dirigible
balloon (type) ... 4. free, kite 5. pilot
   7. captive 8. sounding
   11. montgolfier, observation
ballot ... 4. bale, poll, vote 5. elect,
   slate, voice 6. select, ticket
   8. suffrage
ballyhoo ... 4. plug 5. boost, noise
   6. fracas, hoopla, hubbub, ruckus,
   rumpus 7. promote 9. advertise,
   publicity 10. hullabaloo
balm ... 3. oil 4. bito, calm 5. cream,
   salve 6. balsam, elixir, lotion, pacify
   7. anodyne, cushion, Melissa,
   perfume, relieve, unction, unguent
   8. liniment, mitigate, ointment
   9. calmative, fragrance, mitigator
   10. palliative
balm (pert to) ... 5. Vicks 6. arnica,
   zachun 7. camphor, lanolin, menthol
   8. glycerin, ointment, vaseline
   10. petrolatum
Balm of ... 6. Gilead
balmy ... 4. mild 5. batty, daffy, dippy,
   drunk, goofy, moony, spicy, sweet
   6. dreamy, insane, savory 7. healing
   8. aromatic, fragrant, lenitive,
   redolent, soothing 9. ambrosial,

assuaging, emollient 10. palliative,
   refreshing 11. odoriferous
   12. sweet-scented
balsam ... 3. fir 4. riga, tolu 5. resin
   6. embalm, poplar, storax
   7. benzoin, perfume 8. bdellium
   (Bib), medicine 9. oleoresin
   12. Balsam of Peru, Balsam of Tolu
Baltimore ...
Belle .. 4. rose
bird .. 6. oriole
butterfly .. 7. phaeton
city of .. 8. Maryland
hemp .. 4. flax
history of .. 18. Star Spangled Banner
   (1814)
baluster ... 4. post 7. support, upright
   8. banister
bam ... 4. fake, hoax, mock, sham
   5. cheat, spoof, trick 6. deceit
   7. wheedle 8. flimflam 9. deception,
   imitation
bambino ... 4. babe, baby, icon
   5. child, Pietà 6. infant (Christ)
bamboo (pert to) ...
curtain .. 8. frontier
English .. 10. Philippine
genus .. 7. Bambuss
sacred .. 6. nandin
sprouts (pickled) .. 5. achar
stems .. 4. cane
sugar .. 6. silica 9. tabasheer
bamboozle ... 4. dupe, hoax 5. trick
   6. baffle, cajole, humbug 7. beguile,
   deceive, mystify, perplex 9. victimize
ban ... 4. coin, tabu, veto 5. curse,
   edict, taboo, title (anc) 6. muslin,
   outlaw 7. embargo, exclude, kokumin
   8. anathema 9. interdict, ostracism,
   ostracize 10. injunction, kokumingun
   11. malediction, prohibition
   12. proscription 15. excommunication
banal ... 4. flat 5. corny, stale, trite
   6. cliché, common, old hat
   11. commonplace, stereotyped
   13. platitudinous
banana ... 4. Musa, saba 6. ensete
   8. Musaceae, plantain
banana (pert to) ...
Bananaland .. 10. Queensland
bananalike .. 8. plantain
bird .. 4. quit 6. oriole
boa .. 5. snake
color .. 7. sunbeam
fish .. 8. ladyfish
freckle .. 7. disease
leaf .. 5. frond
oil .. 7. lacquer
Philippine .. 7. saguing
shrub .. 9. evergreen
band ... 3. bar, tie 4. belt, body, crew,
   hoop, line, pack, ring, sash, zone
   5. bunch, corps, group, patte, strap,
   stria, strip, tribe, unite 6. cohort,
   collar, fascia, fillet, girdle, ligula,
   outfit, pledge, radula (Zool), tether
   7. bandage, company 8. cincture,
   encircle, ensemble, neckband, striping
   9. frequency (radio), orchestra,
   striation
bandage ... 3. gag 4. bind, tape
   5. sling, spica, truss 6. ligate,

swathe 7. wrapper 8. compress,
dressing, ligature 9. accipiter,
blindfold 10. tourniquet
bandicoot... 3. rat 9. Perameles
bandit... 4. thug 5. thief 6. dacoit,
outlaw, robber 7. bandido, brigand,
footpad, ladrone 8. marauder,
picaroon 9. bandolero
10. highwayman
bandmaster... 5. Sousa 6. leader
7. maestro 8. choragus, director
9. conductor 13. Kapellmeister
bandolero... 5. thief 6. robber
10. highwayman
bandy... 4. beat, cart, game 5. bowed
6. curved, strive, stroke (tennis)
7. contend, embowed 8. carriage
(Ind), exchange, to and fro
9. bowlegged 11. bandy–legged,
reciprocate
bandy words... 5. argue 6. bicker,
parley 7. contend, wrangle
8. converse
bane... 3. woe 4. evil, harm, kill, pest,
ruin 5. curse, venom 6. injury,
plague, poison, slayer 7. disease
(sheep), scourge 8. murderer,
vexation 9. grievance 10. affliction,
pestilence, visitation
baneful... 3. ill 4. vile 7. harmful,
noxious 9. injurious 10. pernicious
11. detrimental
bang... 3. hit, rap 4. beat, blow,
dash, drub, kick, lift, shut, slam
5. crack, knock, pound, punch,
smack, thump, verve, whack
6. energy, report, strike, thrash, thrill
7. collide 8. coiffure
bangle... 5. charm 7. circlot
8. bracelet
banish... 3. ban 4. oust 5. exile, expel
6. deport, dispel, outlaw, punish
7. condemn, dismiss, exclude
8. relegate 9. ostracize, proscribe
10. expatriate 13. excommunicate
banister... 4. post, rail 8. baluster
10. balustrade
banjo... 7. samisen
bank... 3. row 4. brae, edge, heap,
quay, ripa 5. brink, flock, hurst
(sandy), marge, shoal, shore, slope,
table 6. aviate, margin, quarry,
rivage, series, stakes, strand
7. anthill, barrier, deposit, incline
8. buttress, treasury 9. acclivity,
riverside 13. fortification
bank account... 5. funds, means
6. assets, moneys 8. finances
9. exchequer
banker... 4. game 6. broker, lender
9. financier 11. moneylender
12. money–changer
bankrupt... 4. bust, ruin 5. broke,
smash 6. failed, quisby (sl) 7. failure
9. destitute, insolvent, moneyless,
penniless 12. impoverished
banner... 4. fane, flag 6. ensign,
poster 7. leading, pennant, placard
8. foremost, headline, standard,
streamer 9. exemplary 10. surpassing
banns, marriage... 6. notice
7. sibrede 12. proclamation

banquet... 4. fete 5. diffa, feast, festa
6. fiesta, junket, regale, repast,
spread 8. festival, jamboree
10. regalement
Banquo... 9. character (Shak)
banshee, banshie... 4. shee 5. fairy,
Geist, sidhe 6. spirit, sprite
bantam (pert to)...
cock.. 4. fop 5. dandy, sport
7. peacock 8. strutter 9. swaggerer
12. swashbuckler
Java.. 4. duck, fowl 5. breed
6. Brahma, Cochin
slang.. 4. runt 6. peewee, shrimp
sports.. 6. weight
bantamweight... 5. boxer (118 lbs)
7. fighter 8. pugilist 9. contender
10. contestant
banter... 4. jest, josh, mock, twit
5. borak, chaff, sport, tease, trick
6. delude, deride, satire 7. asteism,
wheedle 8. badinage, raillery, ridicule
10. persiflage, pleasantry
Bantu, South Africa...
language.. 3. Ila 8. Kongoese
people.. 5. Duala 6. Basuto
tribe.. 4. Vili, Zulu 6. Damara, Kaffir
7. Negroid, Swahili 8. Bechuana
banzai... 4. hail 5. hello, hullo
6. attack, charge 8. greetings
11. salutations
baobab tree (pert to)...
bark.. 4. rope 5. cloth, paper
fruit.. 11. monkey bread
genus.. 9. Adansonia
pulp.. 8. beverage
baptism... 4. rite 6. naming 7. wetting
8. ablution 9. aspersion, immersion,
sacrament 10. initiation, sprinkling
11. christening 12. consecration,
purification, regeneration (spiritual)
baptism (pert to)...
cloth.. 7. chrisom
dead (RCCh).. 5. Blood 6. Desire
fire.. 9. fuertaufe
place.. 4. font 10. baptistery (anc)
receptacle.. 5. basin 7. piscina
water.. 5. laver
bar... 3. ban, dam, fid, pry, rod
4. bolt, deny, fess, joke, line, rack,
rail, sess, type 5. betty
(thieves' slang), block, court, deter,
easer, estop, ingot, lever, shoal,
space, staff 6. except, forbid, hinder,
ripper, saloon, stitch, stripe
7. barrier, barroom, bass–bar,
chevron, counter, crowbar, exclude,
prevent, railing, sandbar, trapeze
8. blockade, disallow, obstacle,
obstruct, preclude, prohibit
9. barricade, hindrance
10. impediment, profession,
singletree 11. obstruction,
whippletree 12. underscoring
barb... 3. jag 4. clip, flue, harl, herl,
seta 5. horse, point, ramus, scarf
(nun's), speed 6. setula, striga
7. bristle, feather, pinnula 8. kingfish
9. arrowhead 10. projection
Barbados Island...
capital.. 10. Bridgetown
drink.. 3. rum

government.. 7. British
location.. 8. Antilles (Lesser) 10. West Indies
native.. 3. Bim (nickname)
barbarian... 3. hun 4. Goth, rude 5. beast, brute 6. savage, vandal 8. cannibal, man–eater 9. untutored, vulgarian 10. extraneous, Philistine, unlettered 11. uncivilized 15. anthropophagite
barbaric... 5. cruel 6. brutal, Gothic, savage 7. foreign, inhuman, vicious 8. non–Greek, non–Latin, ruthless 9. barbarous, primitive 10. extraneous 11. uncivilized 12. non–Christian
barbarism... 6. ferity 8. rudeness, solecism 9. barbarity, crudeness, Gothicism, ignorance, vulgarism 10. coarseness, corruption, foreignism 11. impropriety
Barbarossa... 7. emperor (Rom) 8. red beard
Barbary ape... 5. magot
Barbary State (former)... 5. Tunis 7. Algiers, Morocco 12. Tripolitania
barbate... 7. bearded, stubbly 9. whiskered 11. barbigerous
barbecue... 5. feast, roast 6. animal (whole), picnic 7. brazier, hibachi 9. Dutch oven 10. shish kebab 13. entertainment (out–of–doors)
barber... 5. shave 6. figaro, shaver, tonsor 7. tonsure 10. haircutter 12. tonsorialist
Barber of Seville character... 6. Figaro, Rosina
Barcelona, Spain...
building (famed).. 6. palace (Kings of Aragon) 9. Cathedral (Gothic)
port.. 13. Mediterranean
street (famed).. 6. Rambla
bard... 4. muse, poet, scop (Hist) 5. druid, runer, vates 8. minstrel, musician (wandering) 10. Parnassian
Bard of...
Avon.. 11. Shakespeare
Ayrshire.. 5. Burns
Rydal Mount.. 10. Wordsworth
bare... 3. raw 4. bald, mere, nude, open 5. alone, empty, naked, plain, shear, sheer, stark, strip 6. barren, denude, divest, expose, reveal, simple, vacant 7. exposed, unarmed, uncover 8. desolate, disclose, stripped 9. destitute, unadorned, uncovered 10. stark–naked, threadbare 11. defenseless, unconcealed
barefaced... 4. bare, bold 6. brassy, brazen 8. impudent 9. audacious, shameless 11. undisguised
barely... 4. jimp, only 5. faint 6. hardly, merely, nudely, poorly, simply 7. nakedly 8. narrowly, scantily, scarcely 14. insufficiently
bargain... 3. buy 4. deal, pact, prig, sell 5. trade 6. barter, chisel, dicker, haggle 7. chaffer, compact, mediate 8. contract, covenant, purchase 9. agreement, Bon Marché, cheapness, negotiate 10. engagement

11. stipulation, transaction
barge... 3. ark, hoy 4. raft, scow, ship 5. ferry, float, praam, scold 6. berate, lumber, rebuke, tender 7. birlinn (birling) 9. transport
barge in... 5. enter 6. bungle, butt in, invade, push in 7. blunder, intrude
barghest... 6. goblin
bargoose... 4. duck 9. merganser, sheldrake
bark... 3. bay, yap, yip 4. bang, bast, husk, peel, rind, ross, ship, skin, tapa, yelp 5. cough, niepa, shout, strip, youff 6. bowwow, clamor, cortex, outcry, packet, scrape 7. canella 8. ballyhoo, periderm 9. sassafras
barker... 4. tout 6. pistol 7. spieler 9. solicitor 10. ballyhooer, theaterman
barking... 7. latrant 8. hylactic
Barlaam and Josaphet (Joasaph)... 11. Buddha story (Christian version)
barley... 4. bigg, food, seed 5. grain 6. ptisan, tsamba 7. Hordeum
barley (pert to)...
bird.. 6. siskin 7. wagtail (yellow), wryneck 11. nightingale
bree.. 3. ale 6. liquor
shaped.. 10. hordeiform
barlow... 9. jackknife (one–bladed)
barm... 5. froth, yeast 6. leaven 7. ferment
barn... 3. bay, mow 4. loft
barnacle... 4. bray (Her) 5. acorn, goose, leech 6. animal, sucker 8. adherent, parasite 9. sycophant 10. Cirripedia, crustacean
barnstormer... 5. actor 7. aviator 11. entertainer
baron... 4. peer 5. mogul, noble 6. daimio, tycoon 7. freeman 8. nobleman, somebody 9. financier, personage 10. capitalist 13. industrialist
baroque... 6. ornate, quaint, rococo 7. bizarre 9. irregular 11. extravagant
barracks... 4. camp, huts 6. casern, laager 9. barracoon 10. encampment
barraclade... 7. blanket (homemade)
barracuda... 4. fish, spet 5. barry (Bahamas) 6. sennet
barrage... 3. dam 4. weir 5. blitz 6. strafe 7. barrier, gunfire, milldaw 9. cannonade, roadblock 11. obstruction
barrage (military)... 3. box 5. mines 6. normal 7. balloon 8. creeping, standing 9. emergency 12. anti–aircraft
barranca... 4. bank 5. bluff 6. ravine
barratry... 5. breach, simony 8. bad faith, mala fide 10. infidelity 11. dereliction
barred... 6. cooped, fenced, grated, ribbed 7. striped 8. confined, debarred, excluded, streaked
barrel... 3. box, keg, tun 4. cade, cask, drum, knag 5. quill, speed 6. runlet, tierce 7. calamus (Zool), rundlet 8. cylinder 9. kilderkin
barrel (pert to)...

maker.. 6. cooper
miscellaneous.. 3. gun, pen 4. pipe
　6. pencil
sling.. 9. parbuckle
stopper.. 4. bung
barren... 3. dry 4. arid, bare, dull
　5. blank, empty, heath, inane
　6. desert, effete, jejune, karroo,
　meager, Sahara, stupid 7. sterile
　8. desolate, impotent, unpoetic
　9. infertile 10. unfruitful, unprolific
　12. unproductive, unprofitable
barricade... 3. bar 4. bolt, rail, seal,
　stop 5. block, close, fence 6. abatis
　7. barrier, padlock 8. blockade,
　obstacle, obstruct 11. obstruction
　13. fortification
barrico... 3. keg 4. cask
barrier... 3. Alp, bar, dam 4. clog,
　door, gate, wall, weir 5. block,
　fence, hedge, panel 6. screen
　7. parapet, railing 8. blockade,
　boundary, fortress, obstacle, stockade,
　stoppage 9. partition, restraint
　10. impediment, portcullis
　11. obstruction
barrikin (Eng sl)... 6. jargon
　9. gibberish
barrister... 6. lawyer 7. adviser,
　pleader 8. advocate, attorney
　9. counselor (counsellor), solicitor
barroom... 3. bar, pub, tap 6. saloon,
　tavern 7. cantina, taproom
　8. alehouse 11. rathskeller
barrow... 3. hod, hog (male) 4. brae,
　fell, hill, knap, moor 5. grave (anc),
　mound 7. tumulus 8. mountain
　11. wheelbarrow 12. Reihengräber
bartender... 5. mixer 6. barman, histro
　7. barkeep, tapster 8. publican
barter... 4. deal, sell, swap 5. trade,
　truck 7. bargain, permute, traffic
　8. commerce, exchange
Bartholomew (pert to)... 4. Fair, Play
　(Shak) 5. Saint 6. martyr 7. Apostle
　(one of 12) 8. Massacre
Bartimeus (Bib)... 6. beggar (blind)
barton... 4. farm 5. abode, manor
　6. grange 7. demesne 8. farmyard,
　hacienda 9. homestead
baru... 4. tree (fiber) 7. majagua
base... 3. bed, low 4. dado, evil, foot,
　foul, mean, root, seat, site, sole
　5. basis, basso, cause, petty, radix,
　socle, voice 6. abject, bottom,
　center, factor, patten, plinth, podium,
　singer, sordid, vulgar, wicked
　7. servile, station 8. basement,
　cosmetic, degraded, infamous,
　inferior, pedestal, shameful, standard
　9. principle, worthless
　10. despicable, foundation, villainous
　12. contemptible, dishonorable,
　headquarters
baseball (terms)... 3. bag, bat, box,
　fan, fly, hit, lob, out, RBI, run
　4. ball, base, bunt, deck, foul,
　home, nine, pill, sack, save, walk,
　wild 5. bench, clout, coach, count,
　curve, drive, error, field, first, force,
　glove, homer, liner, mound, pitch,
　plate, pop–up, score, slide, sport,

swing, third 6. assist, batter, bungle,
　double, dugout, fumble, ground,
　putout, rubber, runner, screen,
　second, series, single, sinker, stance,
　strike, string, target, triple, windup
　7. battery, bullpen, diamond, fielder,
　floater, rhubarb (sl), squeeze, stretch
　8. backstop, grounder, keystone,
　knuckler, outfield, pinch–hit,
　powdered, spit ball 9. sacrifice,
　strikeout 10. ballplayer
baseborn... 3. low 4. mean 5. lowly,
　plain 6. common, humble 7. bastard,
　ignoble, lowborn 8. plebeian,
　spurious 11. commonplace
　12. illegitimate
based on...
evidence.. 7. damning 8. decisive
　10. conclusive
experience . 7. empiric 9. empirical
numbers.. 5. hexad 6. nonary, senary
　7. tertial
baseness... 6. infamy 7. badness
　9. servility, vulgarity 10. wickedness
　11. inferiority 13. dastardliness,
　subordination
bash... 3. bat, jab, lam 4. heat, belt,
　biff, blow, conk, mash, slug, sock
　5. clout, paste, punch, smack, whack
　6. bruise, strike, wallop 7. clobber
Basham's King... 2. Og
bashful... 3. coy, shy 5. heloe, mousy,
　timid 6. demure, modest
　8. blushing, retiring, sheepish,
　timorous, verecund 9. diffident
　13. self–conscious
basic... 4. root 5. basal, basis
　7. essence, primary 8. alkaline,
　original 9. essential 10. underlying
　11. fundamental
Basilian... 3. art 4. monk, rule
　6. bishop 7. liturgy, St Basil (The
　Great) 8. precepts 10. Cappadocia
basilica... 5. major, minor, title
　6. canopy, church, shrine, temple
　11. patriarchal
Basilican (pert to)...
books.. 5. sixty 6. Digest
century.. 5. Tenth
empire.. 9. Byzantine
laws.. 9. Justinian
basin... 3. bed (water), cup, pit, tub
　4. bowl, cock, font, hole, sink, tank
　5. laver, plain, playa, stoup 6. cavity,
　chafer, coulee, ground, lavabo,
　marine, valley, vessel 7. lowland,
　piscina 8. curvette 9. washbasin
　10. depression
basis... 4. base, fond, root 5. cause,
　start 6. bottom, factor, motive,
　reason, thesis 7. premise, warrant
　9. assertion, principle 10. foundation,
　groundwork 13. justification
bask... 3. sin, tub 4. warm 5. bathe,
　revel 7. suffuse 8. apricate
　9. luxuriate
basket... 3. bin, box, car (balloon),
　net, ped, pod 4. caba, cage, kish,
　skep, trug 5. cabas 6. dosser,
　gabion, vessel, wisket 7. corbeil,
　hanaper, pannier, scuttle, wattage
　9. container

basket (pert to) . . .
coal mine . . 3. tub 4. corf
fig . . 5. frail 6. tapnet
fire . . 5. grate 7. cresset
fishing . . 3. pot 4. buck (eel), caul,
 weel 5. crail, crate, creel 6. hamper
making . . 5. slath 6. slarth
wicker . . 3. cob 5. cesta, osier
 6. hamper 7. hanaper 8. bassinet
Basque (pert to) . . .
ancestors . . 8. Iberians
cap . . 5. beret
home . . 5. Spain 8. Pyrenees
bas–relief . . . 7. carving, relievo
 12. basso–relievo (basso–rilievo)
bass . . . 4. fish 5. fiber, voice (low)
 6. singer 8. weakfish 13. basso
 profundo
bassoon . . . 4. oboe 6. fagott 7. fagotto
bast . . . 4. bass 5. fiber
Bast (Egypt) . . . 4. Ptah 7. goddess
 10. lady of life
bastard . . . 3. odd 4. heel (sl), sham
 5. false, louse (sl) 7. batarde
 8. abnormal, bantling, spurious
 9. scoundrel 10. adulterate
 12. illegitimate 13. nullius filius
baste . . . 3. hit, sew 4. cook, lard, lash,
 tack, whip 6. stitch, thrash
 7. trounce 8. lambaste
bastion . . . 5. redan 8. fastness
 10. stronghold 13. fortification
bat . . . 3. hit, jag, lam, rap 4. belt,
 blow, clip, club, slug, sock, swat,
 wink 5. binge, clout, paste, smack,
 spree, stick, whack 6. bender,
 cudgel, racket, wallop 7. clobber
bat (mammal) . . . 6. aliped, fox bat,
 kalong 7. noctule, vampire
 8. serotine 9. flying fox, pipistrel
 (pipistrelle), reremouse 10. Chiroptera
batch . . . 3. lot 4. heap, lump, mess,
 slew 5. bunch, group, stack
 6. amount, baking 7. mixture
 8. quantity 10. collection
bath . . . 3. dip, tub 4. sitz 5. steam,
 sweat, vapor 6. plunge, shower,
 sponge 7. Finnish, mineral, sulphur
bath (pert to) . . .
Eccl . . 8. ablution
house . . 6. bagnic, cabana 8. balneary
 10. natatorium
photography . . 5. toner 9. developer
Roman . . 7. balneum 11. Warm
 Springs
sitz . . 5. bidet
warm . . 5. therm
bathe . . . 3. tub, wet 4. bask, lave,
 swim, wash 5. flush 6. drench
 7. immerse, moisten, pervade,
 suffuse 8. medicate, permeate
baton . . . 3. rod 4. mace, wand
 5. staff, stick 6. baston, cudgel,
 fasces 7. scepter, support
 9. truncheon
Batrachia . . . 5. Anura, frogs, toads
 7. Surinam 8. Salienta
Battalion of Death (Russ) . . .
 13. legion of women
batten . . . 5. close, gloat 6. fasten,
 fatten, secure, thrive, timber
battered . . . 6. beaten, pasted

7. bruised 8. impaired 9. shattered,
 weathered
battery . . . 3. set 4. guns, pack
 6. cohort, series 7. assault, platoon
 8. baseball (term) 9. artillery
battery (Elec) . . . 4. cell, grid, pole
 5. anode, plate 6. Leyden
 7. storage, voltaic 9. electrode
battle . . . 3. war 4. fray, meet, tilt
 5. brush, fight, joust, scrap
 6. action, affray, barney, combat,
 tussle 7. contest, scuffle, warfare
 8. conflict, skirmish, struggle
 9. challenge, encounter
 10. engagement
Battle (pert to) . . .
Bib . . 8. Aceldama 12. potter's field
Civil War . . 7. Bull Run 15. Lookout
 Mountain
formation . . 4. line 5. herse, order
Great . . 10. Armageddon
Hundred Years (1346) . . 5. Crecy
Revolution . . 10. Bunker Hill
slogan . . 8. aux–armes 9. battle cry
World War I . . 6. Verdun (1916)
World War II . . 11. Pearl Harbor
 (1941)
battologize . . . 6. repeat 7. iterate,
 recount, restate 9. reiterate
 12. recapitulate
bauble . . . 3. toy 4. gaud 6. doodad,
 geegaw, trifle, trivia 7. bibelot, trinket
 8. falderal (folderol) 9. bagatelle,
 plaything 10. knickknack
Bavaria . . .
capital . . 6. Munich
city . . 8. Augsburg, Wurzburg
 9. Nuremburg 12. Ludwigshafen
freeway . . 8. autobahn
government . . 10. Third Reich
king (former) . . 10. Maximilian
prince . . 6. Rupert
river . . 4. Eger, Isar
bawdry . . . 6. filthy 8. ribaldry, salacity,
 unchaste 9. obscenity
 11. pornography
bawl . . . 3. cry, say, sob 4. bark, howl,
 roar, wail, weep, yell 5. blare, shout
 6. bellow, boohoo, plaint 8. proclaim
 10. vociferate
bay . . . 3. ria 4. cove, howl, roan, wail
 5. bight, horse, inlet, oriel, sinus
 6. recess, window 7. ululate
bay (pert to) . . .
antler . . 9. stag's tine (2nd)
bird . . 5. snipe 6. curlew, godwit,
 plover
color . . 4. roan
tree . . 6. laurel
Bayard . . . 5. horse, steed (Rinaldo's)
bayonet . . . 5. lance, saber, spear,
 sword 6. dagger, weapon 7. poniard
bayou . . . 5. creek, marsh 6. slough,
 stream 7. channel 11. watercourse
Bayou State . . . 11. Mississippi
Bay State . . . 13. Massachusetts
bazaar . . . 4. fair, shop 6. market
 7. canteen (army) 10. exposition
be . . . 2. am 3. are 4. live 5. exist
 7. prevail
beach . . . 5. coast, plage, playa, praya,
 sands, shore 6. shilla, strand

9. waterside
beachcomber... 4. wave 6. loafer
　8. vagabond
beacon... 4. beam, flag, sign, vane
　5. fanal, light, radar, radio
　6. marker, pharos, signal 7. cresset,
　lantern, seamark 10. lighthouse,
　watchtower
bead... 4. ball, drop 5. bugle, pearl,
　sight (firearm) 6. rondel 8. ornament
beads... 5. grain, sewan 6. rosary
　7. chaplet, granose (antennae),
　jewelry, prayers
beak... 3. neb, nib 4. bill, lora, nose,
　peck, prow 5. judge, mouth, spout,
　tutel 10. magistrate 11. stipendiary
beaker... 3. cup 6. vessel (Chem)
beakless... 9. erostrate
beam... 3. ray 4. emit, grin, sile, sill,
　stud 5. caber, gleam, joist, shaft,
　shine, smile, tonka, trave 6. girder,
　mantel, rafter, timber 7. radiate,
　support, trimmer 8. trabeate
bean... 4. buck, faba, gram, lima,
　mung, navy, seed, soya 5. black,
　coral, pinto, Sieva 6. adzuki, castor,
　frijol (frijole), kidney, legume, lentil,
　string 7. calabar 9. Phaseolus
bean (pert to)...
　eye of.. 5. hilum
　game.. 7. beanbag
　licorice seed.. 9. jequirity
　lima.. 4. haba
　seed (string bean).. 7. haricot
　shaped.. 8. fabiform
　slang.. 4. buck, head 5. brain
　6. dollar, noodle, trifle
bear... 3. aim, cub, lug 4. dubb, tote,
　turn, ursa 5. bring, brown, bruin,
　carry, clack, crank, koala, polar,
　press, short, sloth, stand, ursus, yield
　6. animal, endure, grouch, harbor,
　Kodiak, stress, suffer, Syrian, uphold
　7. Ephraim (nickname), furnish,
　grizzly, incline, musquaw, produce,
　support 8. cinnamon, fructify,
　maintain, Melursus, sorehead, tolerate
　10. speculator 11. short seller
　(Finan)
bear (pert to)...
　cat.. 5. panda 9. binturong
　class.. 6. ursine 7. Ursidaw
　color.. 6. yellow
　constellation.. 9. Ursa Major, Ursa
　Minor
　flag.. 10. California (State)
　head.. 4. hure
　The.. 6. Russia
beard... 3. awn 6. arista, goatee
　7. stubble, Vandyke 8. whiskers
bearded... 5. awned 7. barbate,
　pappose 8. aristate 9. whiskered
beards, science of... 10. pogonology
bearer... 3. boy 5. macer, usher
　6. porter, tender 7. carrier
　8. cargador, conveyor, escudero
　9. attendant 10. khidmatgar,
　pallbearer
bearing... 3. air 4. mien, port
　5. poise 6. bel air, regard
　7. concern, conduct, dignity,
　meaning, posture 8. behavior,

carriage, demeanor, relation, tendency
　9. direction, influence, relevance
　10. connection, deportment,
　supporting 12. significance
bearing (Her)... 4. enté, orle 5. bevel,
　pheon 6. billet
bear witness... 6. attest 7. testify
beast... 4. bête, game, lion, pard
　5. brute, camel, demon, fiend, horse,
　spado, tiger 6. animal, cattle,
　dragon, savage 7. carrier, critter,
　leopard, monster 8. behemoth,
　creature 9. dromedary
beastly... 5. gross 6. animal, bloody,
　carnal, odious 7. bestial, brutish,
　hideous, inhuman, leonine, theroid,
　ungodly 8. dreadful 9. execrable
　10. abominable, disgusting
beat... 3. hit, lam, tan, taw, wap
　4. bang, bash, best, cane, drub,
　drum, flog, lace, lash, maul, pelt,
　tund 5. baste, excel, pound, pulse,
　route, scoop, throb, thump 6. bruise,
　cudgel, defeat, larrup, pommel,
　punish, rhythm, strike, stroke, swinge,
　thrash, thresh 7. baffled, belabor,
　cadence, clobber, conquer, flutter,
　musical, pulsate, routine, surpass,
　trounce 8. chastise, fatigued,
　lambskin, overcome, vanquish
　9. exhausted, pulsation
beat (pert to)...
　back.. 7. repulse
　black and blue.. 9. suggilate
　down.. 6. haggle 7. cheapen
　into plate.. 8. malleate
　slang.. 4. blow 5. scoot, scram
　6. beat it, skidoo 7. vamoose
　traverse.. 6. patrol
beatify... 5. bless, cheer, saint
　6. hallow 7. gladden, glorify
　8. unshrine, sanctify
beatnik... 8. Bohemian, maverick,
　sulphite 13. nonconformist
beau... 3. fop 5. blade, dandy, flame,
　lover, spark, swain 6. escort, squire
　7. admirer, courter 9. caballero,
　inamorato 10. beau–garçon
beautiful... 4. fair, fine 5. bonny,
　kalon (Gr) 6. comely, lovely, poetic,
　pretty 7. elegant, Tempean
　8. graceful, handsome, stunning
　9. aesthetic (esthetic), exquisite
　15. pulchritudinous
beautify... 4. deck, trim 5. adorn,
　grace 6. bedeck, doll up, enrich
　8. decorate, prettify 9. embellish,
　glamorize
beauty... 5. belle, charm, glory, grace
　8. elegance 10. loveliness, prettiness
　11. pulchritude
beauty, famed...
　Egypt.. 9. Cleopatra
　Greek.. 4. Hebe 6. Graces
　9. Aphrodite 11. Helen of Troy
　Historical.. 4. Lais
　Persian.. 4. peri 5. houri
　Norse.. 5. Freya
　Roman.. 5. Venus
Becken... 7. cymbals
beckon... 4. beck 5. court 6. invite,
　summon 7. gesture 11. gesticulate

becloud... 5. bedim, cloud, shade, smoke 6. bemist, darken, opaque 7. conceal, encloud, obscure 8. nubilate, overcast 9. adumbrate
become... 2. go 3. fit, get, wax 4. grow, rise, suit 5. befit, grace 6. befall, beseem, mature, mellow 7. behoove, benefit 8. befuddle 9. originate
becoming... 3. fit 6. comely, decent, fitted, likely, proper, seemly, suited 7. decorum, suiting 8. decorous, pleasing, suitable, tasteful 9. befitting, expedient 11. appropriate
bec–scie... 4. duck 9. merganser
becuna... 9. barracuda
bed... 3. cot, kip, tye (feather) 4. bunk, crib, doss, lair, nest 5. basin, berth, couch 6. billet, bottom, flower, litter, pallet 7. channel, feather, stratum 8. bassinet 9. stretcher 10. foundation
bed (pert to)...
canopy.. 4. ceil 6. tester
coverlet.. 5. quilt 6. spread 7. blanket 9. comforter 11. counterpane
famed.. 15. bed of Procrustes
bedaub... 3. dab 4. blur, daub, soil 5. paint, smear, stain 6. belaud, smudge 7. bedizen, besmear 8. besmudge, ornament
bedazzle... 4. daze, stun 5. blind, shine 6. dazzle 7. astound, confuse 8. astonish, bewilder
bedeck... 3. gem 4. trim 5. adorn, array, grace, prink 6. clothe, rag out 7. bedrape 8. ornament
bedevil... 3. hex 4. foul, ride 5. abuse, tease 6. befoul, muddle, needle, pester, plague 7. bewitch, confuse, torment 8. demonize 9. diabolize, tantalize 10. complicate
bedight... 5. adorn, array, equip
bedikah... 6. ritual
bedim... 3. dim, fog 4. blur, fade 5. blear, cloud 6. bemist, darken 8. bedarken
bedlam... 3. din 6. clamor, tumult, uproar 8. madhouse 9. charivari 11. pandemonium
Bedlam (London)... 6. priory (1247) 8. Hospital (St Mary of Bethlehem)
Bedouin... 4. Arab, Moor 5. gypsy, nomad 7. Saracen, vagrant
Bedouin head cord... 4. agal
bedroll... 6. bindle 7. matilda
bee... 3. dor 4. apis 5. drone, karbi, queen 6. insect, worker 8. andrenid, angelito, honeybee 9. bumblebee 12. carpenter bee
bee (pert to)...
fear of.. 9. apiphobia
glue.. 8. propolis
hive.. 4. butt, scap, skep (straw) 6. apiary 7. alveary 8. workshop
keeper.. 8. apiarist, skeppist
sociable.. 7. husking, raising 8. quilting, spelling
study.. 10. apiculture 11. melittology
wax.. 7. beeswax, ceresin, cerotic

9. cera flava
Beebe, William... 13. ichthyologist
beef... 4. heft, kine, thew 5. brawn, sinew, steer 6. buccan (dried), cattle, muscle 8. poundage 10. brawniness 11. muscularity
Beelzebub (pert to)...
Bible.. 5. deity 6. oracle 14. prince of demons
literature.. 5. demon (Prince), devil 11. fallen angel
zoology.. 6. monkey
beer... 3. ale 4. bock, flip, hops, suds 5. lager, weiss 6. liquor, porter, swipes
beer (pert to)...
cask.. 4. butt
inventor.. 9. Gambrinus (Myth king)
mug.. 4. toby 5. stein 8. schooner
vessel.. 6. tanker 9. blackjack
beet... 4. Beta 5. chard 6. mangel 8. beet root 9. sugar beet
Beethoven, Ludwig Van (pert to)...
birthplace.. 4. Bonn (Ger)
composed.. 7. Fidelio 10. symphonies
famed as.. 7. pianist 8. composer
beetle... 3. bat, bug, dor, jut, ram 4. June, rose 5. Amara, gogga, Hispa, meloe, snout 6. chafer, elater, golach, goloch, hammer, masher, sawyer, scarab, weevil 7. ladybug, prionid 8. circulio, sharnbud, skipjack 9. cockroach, dorbeetle 10. cockchafer, Elateridae
beetlehead... 5. stupe 6. plover (bird), stupid 8. bonehead 9. blockhead 10. loggerhead
befall... 3. hap 4. come 5. occur 6. betide, chance, happen 9. eventuate, transpire
befit... 4. suit 5. serve 6. become, beseem, please
befitting... 3. fit 4. meet 6. filial, proper, seemly, timely 7. ethical, fitting, suiting 8. becoming, decorous, suitable 9. expedient 10. seasonable 11. appropriate
befog... 3. dim, fog 5. blind, cloud 6. bemist 7. becloud, conceal, confuse, mystify, obscure
before... 3. ere 5. afore, ahead, avant, early, prior 6. anteal, facing, openly, sooner 7. already, earlier, forward, yestern 8. anterior, foremost, formerly, hitherto 9. foregoing, preceding 10. beforehand, face to face, heretofore, previously 11. theretofore
before (pert to)...
birth.. 8. prenatal
long.. 4. soon
mentioned.. 4. said, same, such 5. named 6. former 10. aforenamed
others.. 5. first
this.. 3. ere 5. prior 6. erenow
before (pref)... 3. pre, pro 4. ante, prae
befoul... 4. soil 5. taint 6. bemire, defile, muddle 7. bedevil 8. entangle 10. complicate 11. contaminate
befriend... 3. aid 4. abet, help 5. favor 6. assist, foster, succor

7. benefit, support, sustain
11. countenance
befuddle... 3. fog 5. addle, besot
6. fuddle, muddle 7. becloud,
confuse 9. inebriate 10. intoxicate
beg... 3. ask, sue, woo 4. pray, sorn
5. cadge, crave, mooch, plead,
touch (sl) 6. appeal 7. beseech,
entreat, implore, solicit 8. petition
9. importune 10. supplicate
beget... 3. ean 4. sire 5. breed,
hatch, spawn 6. father 7. develop
8. engender, generate 9. procreate,
reproduce
begetter... 4. sire 5. pater 6. author,
father, mother, parent 7. creator
10. procreator, progenitor
beggar... 3. bum 4. hobo, waif
5. fakir (Moslem), gamin, lazar, rogue
6. loafer, pauper, wretch
7. almsman, dervish, vagrant, wastral
8. indigent, vagabond 9. mendicant,
suppliant 10. panhandler, ragamuffin
14. tatterdemalion
beggarly... 3. low 4. base, mean,
poor, rank 5. petty 6. abject,
meanly, paltry, vulgar 7. hangdog,
ignoble 8. bankrupt, indigent,
infamous, wretched 9. miserable,
niggardly 10. despicably, obsequious
12. contemptible
Beggars, King of (Eng)... 5. Carew
beggary... 4. want 6. penury
9. indigence, mendicity, pauperism
10. mendicancy 11. destitution,
panhandling
begin... 4. open 5. enter, start
6. attack 8. commence, initiate, take
rise 9. instituto, introduce, originate
10. inaugurate
begin again... 5. renew 6. resume
10. recommence
beginner... 3. dub 4. tyro (tiro)
5. chela 6. infant, novice
7. amateur, entrant, recruit
8. begetter, freshman, neophyte
9. debutante, fledgling, initiator,
novitiate 10. catechumen, originator,
tenderfoot 11. inaugurator
beginning... 4. head, rise, root
5. alpha, birth, debut, onset, start
6. origin, outset, source 7. genesis,
infancy, opening 8. entrance,
inchoate, nascency, outstart, starting
9. inception, threshold 10. derivation,
foundation, incomplete, initiation
12. commencement, introduction
begone... 3. out 4. away, scat, shoo
5. allez, scram 6. aroint, avaunt,
depart 7. vamoose
begrudge... 4. envy 5. covey, stint
6. grudge, refuse 7. grumble
beguile... 4. dupe, lure, vamp
5. amuse, charm, cozen, elude,
spend, trick 6. delude, divert, regale
7. bewitch, deceive, ensnare, mislead
8. enthrall, intrigue 9. bamboozle,
captivate, deception, entertain,
fascinate, victimize 11. double−cross
14. disappointment
begum (Hind)... 5. queen 7. heiress
8. princess

begunk... 4. jilt 5. trick
behalf... 4. gain, good, part, sake,
side 5. avail, stead 6. affair, matter,
profit 7. benefit, defense, service,
support, welfare 8. interest
9. advantage
behalf of... 3. for 6. lieu of, rather
7. defense (of), instead
behave... 2. do 3. act 4. bear
5. carry 6. demean, deport, manage
7. conduct 8. regulate, restrain
behavior, behaviour... 3. air 4. mien
6. action, manner 7. actions,
address, bearing, conduct, decorum,
manners 8. carriage, demeanor,
maintien 10. deportment
11. comportment
behavior (pert to)...
good.. 7. decorum, P's and Q's
riotous.. 7. rampage
wicked.. 10. wrongdoing
behead... 7. execute 9. decollate
10. decapitate, guillotine
Behemoth (Bib)... 5. beast
12. hippopotamus
behest... 3. vow 5. order 7. bidding,
command, mandate, promise
10. injunction 11. commandment
behind... 3. aft 4. late, past, rear,
rump (vulgar), slow, tail 5. abaff,
abaft, after, ahind, arear, later, tardy
6. astern 7. delayed, impeded
8. arrested, backward, retarded 9. in
the past, posterior, remaining
behindhand... 4. late 5. tardy
7. arrears, belated, overdue
8. backward, dilatory, misdated,
mistimed 10. defaulting, delinquent
behind the times... 5. passé
behold... 2. lo 3. see 4. ahoy, ecce,
ecco, espy, look, ocan, view 5. voilà
6. descry, regard, retain 7. discern,
observe, witness 8. maintain,
perceive
beholden... 5. bound 7. bounden,
obliged 8. grateful, indebted, thankful
9. obligated
beholder... 5. gazer 7. watcher,
witness 8. looker−on, observer,
onlooker 9. spectator
beige... 4. ecru, hopi 5. grège
6. dorado 13. reddish−yellow
being... 3. ego, ens, man, one
4. bion, body, esse, home, life, self
5. entia, gnome, human, thing, wight
6. actual, animal, entity, extant,
mortal, person 7. Adamite, essence,
present, reality 8. creature, existent,
existing, organism, presence
9. actuality, existence, personage,
something 10. individual
11. subsistence
being (pert to)...
celestial.. 4. deva 5. angel 6. cherub,
seraph
imaginary.. 4. pixy (pixie) 5. fairy,
sylph
science of.. 8. ontology
supernatural.. 6. Garuda (Hind)
Supreme.. 3. God 7. Creator
belaud... 4. laud 5. extol 6. praise
7. glorify

belay... **4.** halt, quit, stop **5.** beset, cease, cover, halte **6.** fasten, invest, waylay **7.** besiege, silence **8.** encircle

belch... **4.** burp, emit, vent **5.** eject, eruct, erupt, spout, vomit **7.** gush out **8.** disgorge, eructate **9.** small beer (vulgar) **10.** eructation

beldam, beldame... **3.** cat, hag **4.** fury **5.** crone, frump, shrew, vixen, witch **6.** virago **7.** she–wolf, tigress **8.** ancestor (fem), harridan **9.** termagant **11.** grandmother

Belgian (pert to)... see also *Belgium*
anthem.. **13.** La Brabanconne
hare.. **8.** leporide
horse.. **9.** Brabancon
marble.. **5.** rance
resort.. **6.** Ostend
sheep dog.. **8.** Malinois **11.** Groenendael
violinist.. **5.** Ysaye

Belgian Congo... see *Zaire*

Belgium...
capital.. **8.** Brussels
city.. **5.** Ghent, Liege **6.** Bruges **7.** Antwerp, Louvain **9.** Charleroi
commune.. **3.** Ath
forest.. **8.** Ardennes
king.. **6.** Albert **7.** Leopold **8.** Baudouin
native.. **7.** Fleming (of Flanders), Flemish, Walloon
nickname.. **15.** cockpit of Europe
World War II Battle of.. **8.** The Bulge

Belgravia (London)... **8.** district (fashion)

Belial... **5.** devil, Satan (New Test) **10.** wickedness (Old Test) **11.** Fallen Angel

belie... **4.** deny **6.** belong, defame, oppose, oppugn **7.** besiege, falsify, gainsay, pertain, slander **8.** disclaim, disprove, surround **9.** encompass **10.** calumniate **12.** misrepresent

belief... **3.** fay (anc), ism **4.** cult, rule, sect, view **5.** credo, creed, dogma, faith, maxim, tenet **7.** opinion, precept **8.** credence, doctrine, reliance, religion, teaching **9.** assurance, certainty, principle **10.** confidence, conviction, persuasion **13.** Apostles' Creed

believe... **3.** buy **4.** deem, feel, trow, ween **5.** think, trust **6.** accept, credit, reckon **7.** suppose, swallow **8.** conceive, consider

believer (pert to)...
all religions.. **6.** omnist
facts.. **7.** realist
religion.. **5.** deist **6.** theist **9.** Adventist, Calvinist **13.** particularist

Belit (Bab)... **8.** goddess (wife of Bel)

belittle... **4.** slur **5.** decry, dwarf, scoff, scorn **6.** debase, demean, deride, impugn **7.** detract, run down **8.** minimize **9.** discredit, disparage, underrate **10.** depreciate **13.** underestimate

bell... **4.** gong **5.** codon, knell **6.** curfew, tocsin **7.** campana,

cowbell **8.** carillon, doorbell **9.** ship's bell **10.** dinnerbell, schoolbell **12.** glockenspiel **13.** tintinnabulum

bell, bells (pert to)...
bird.. **9.** campanero **10.** wood thrush
botany.. **7.** corolla
evening.. **6.** curfew **7.** Angelus
flat.. **4.** gong **6.** tam–tam (Chin), tom–tom
funeral.. **5.** knell
nautical.. **8.** half hour
ringer.. **6.** toller
ringing.. **7.** peeling **14.** tintinnabulism
science of.. **11.** campanology
set of.. **6.** chimes **8.** carillon
shaped.. **11.** campaniform
specialist.. **9.** campanist **13.** campanologist
tongue.. **7.** clapper
tower.. **6.** belfry **9.** campanile
warning.. **6.** tocsin

belle... **4.** lady (fine) **5.** toast **6.** beauty **7.** charmer **8.** handsome **10.** grande dame

belles–lettres... **8.** classics **10.** humanities (The), literature

bellflower... **8.** daffodil

belligerent... **7.** hostile, scrappy, warlike **8.** choleric, militant **9.** bellicose, irascible, litigious, offensive, wrangling **10.** aggressive, pugnacious **11.** contentious, quarrelsome **12.** disputatious

belligerent's right (Internat law)... **6.** angary

bellow... **3.** cry, low, moo, say **4.** bawl, roar, wail, yawp **5.** blare, shout **6.** clamor **7.** thunder **10.** vociferate

bellows... **4.** fish **5.** gills, lungs **6.** blower, lights (Zool), rotary **8.** ctenidia (Zool)

bellwether... **5.** sheep **6.** leader, wether (with bell)

belly... **3.** bag, pot **4.** crap, wame **5.** bulge, front, tummy **6.** bottom, paunch, venter **7.** abdomen, stomach **8.** potbelly, swell out **9.** ingluvies

belong (to)... **6.** answer, inhere **7.** pertain, related **9.** appendant, ingrained, possessed (by) **10.** correspond

belonging (to)...
collector, hobbyist.. **10.** collection **11.** collectible (collectable)
dean.. **7.** decanal
era.. **7.** epochal
Fall.. **8.** autumnal
pencil (a).. **6.** desmic
people.. **7.** endemic
present (the).. **7.** current
Spring.. **6.** vernal
Summer.. **7.** estival
Winter.. **6.** hiemal

belongings... **4.** duds, gear **5.** goods, traps **6.** family, things **7.** baggage, effects, kinsmen **8.** chattels, property **9.** homefolks, relations, trappings **11.** connections, perquisites, possessions **13.** accouterments, appurtenances

beloved... 3. pet 4. dear 6. prized
7. darling 8. precious, truelove
9. cherished, inamorata
beloved physician... 6. St Luke
below... 4. alow, here, less 5. Hades,
neath, sotto, under 6. aneath, in hell
7. beneath, short of 10. downstairs
11. belowstairs
Belshazzar (Bib)... 11. crown prince
Bel's wife... 5. Belit (Beltis)
belt... 3. bar, bat, hit 4. area, band,
beat, blow, cest, mark, pelt, ring,
sash, sock, whip, zone 5. apron,
Libya, strap, whack, zonar 6. cestus,
cingle, cordon, fascia, fasten, fillet,
girdle, region, strait, streak, stripe
7. baldric, kurbash, sjambok,
stratum, terrain 8. cincture, encircle,
surround 9. encompass
10. cummerbund
Belteshazzar (Bib)... 6. Daniel
belt of heaven... 6. zodiac 7. circuit
beluga... 5. whale (white)
Belus (pert to)...
father of.. 4. Dido
king of.. 4. Tyre 7. Assyria
son of.. 5. Libya
sons.. 7. Cepheus, Phineus
8. Aegyptus
belvedere.. 5. cigar 7. cypress (mock)
10. watchtower 11. summerhouse
bema... 8. platform 9. sanctuary
bemoan... 4. pity, wail 5. mourn
6. bewail, grieve, lament, regret,
repine 7. deplore 10. sympathize
bemuse... 4. daze 5. addle, besot
6. absorb, muddle 7. stupefy
8. befuddle, distract 10. intoxicate
ben... 2. in 3. oil, son 4. tree
(Moringa) 6. within
bench... 3. pew 4. banc (judge's),
seat 5. chair, court, siege, staff,
stand, stool, table 6. exedra, settee,
settle 7. terrace 8. platform,
woolsack 9. committee
bend... 3. bow, nod, ply, sag, sny
4. bias, flex, genu, kink, knot, sway,
turn, warp 5. crimp, crook, curve,
drink, kneel, prone, squat, stoop,
twist, yield 6. buckle, crouch, curtsy,
direct, divert, humble, inflex, kowtow,
pleach, relent, salaam, strain, swerve
7. bendlet (Her), chevron (Her),
incline, refract, retract 9. genuflect,
introvert, sinuosity 10. inflection
bend (pert to)...
an ear.. 4. hear, heed 6. listen
one's will.. 4. bias, move, sway
the elbow.. 5. drink
the knee.. 5. kneel 6. kowtow,
salaam 9. genuflect
the mind.. 5. think
bends... 7. caisson, disease
8. blackout (aeronaut)
beneath... 4. alow 5. below, lower
(than), 'neath, under 6. aneath,
nether 7. in Hades 11. underground
beneath one's dignity... 8. infradig
15. infra dignitatem
benedict... 7. husband
10. bridegroom, married man (newly)
benediction... 4. rite 6. praise, prayer,

thanks 7. benison 8. blessing
10. invocation 12. thanksgiving
benefaction... 4. alms, boon, gift,
good 5. favor 7. benefit, present
8. courtesy, donation, gratuity,
kindness 9. beau geste
11. beneficence, benevolence
benefactor... 5. angel, donor
6. backer, helper, patron 8. promoter
10. befriender
beneficence... 7. charity 8. goodness,
kindness 11. benefaction,
benevolence 12. philanthropy
beneficial... 4. good 6. benign, useful
7. helpful 8. edifying, salutary
9. favorable, healthful, lucrative,
wholesome 10. profitable, salubrious
11. serviceable 12. advantageous,
remunerative
beneficiary... 4. heir 5. donee
6. vassal 7. devisee, feoffee, grantee,
legatee 8. assignee 9. annuitant
benefit... 3. aid, use 4. boon, gift,
good, help, vail 5. avail, favor, trust
6. profit, relief, succor 7. advance,
concert, improve, service, welfare
8. blessing, kindness 9. advantage
11. benefaction, convenience,
performance
benevolence... 3. tax 4. gift, good
6. bounty, giving 7. charity
8. altruism, bestowal, blessing,
donation, kindness 10. generosity,
liberality 11. munificence
12. contribution, philanthropy
14. charitableness
benevolent... 4. free, good, king
6. benign 7. liberal 8. generous,
princely 9. benignant, bountiful
10. altruistic, charitable, munificent
11. magnanimous 13. philanthropic
Bengal, Indian State...
capital.. 8. Calcutta
gentleman.. 5. baboo (babu)
language.. 7. Bengali
native.. 3. Kol (Kohl) 6. banian
7. Bengali
negro.. 3. Ibo (Ebo)
river.. 6. Ganges 11. Brahmaputra
river boat.. 7. bauleah
benign... 4. mild 5. bland 6. genial,
humane, kindly 7. benefic (Astrol),
liberal 8. gracious, salutary
9. benignant, favorable, healthful,
wholesome 10. propitious, salubrious
benignity... 5. favor 7. benefit
8. blessing, goodness, mildness
9. salubrity 10. kindliness
11. benevolence 12. graciousness
benison... 8. blessing 9. beatitude
10. invocation 11. benediction
benjamin... 6. jacket 7. benzoin
8. overcoat 9. spicebush
Benjamin (Bib), (pert to)...
father.. 5. Jacob
history.. 5. tribe
mother.. 6. Rachel
Benjamin's mess... 6. big end
10. lion's share
benjy (Brit sl)... 3. hat (straw)
0. waistcoat
benne... 6. sesame

bennet... 4. herb 5. daisy 7. hemlock
bent... 3. aim, way, wry 4. bias, turn,
 warp 5. drift, grass, slant, tenor,
 trend, twist 6. course, curved,
 desire, minded, nature, swayed
 7. angular, aptness, crooked,
 heather, leaning, stooped 8. aptitude,
 penchant, tendency 9. obliquity,
 prejudice, proneness 10. propensity
 11. disposition, inclination
 12. idiosyncrasy, predilection
 13. prepossession 14. predisposition
Benthamism... 9. welfarism
 14. utilitarianism
benthonic... 7. benthal, deep sea
benthonic plant... 6. enalid
benthos... 5. deeps 6. depths
 8. ocean bed 16. Davy Jones's
 locker
benumb... 3. nip 4. drug, numb, stun
 5. chill 6. deaden, freeze 7. stupefy
 8. paralyze 11. anesthetize,
 desensitize
Beowulf... 4. poem (oldest in Teutonic
 language)
bequeath... 4. give, will 5. endow,
 leave 6. bestow, demise, devise,
 invest, will to 7. bequest 8. transmit
bequest... 4. will 6. devise, legacy
 8. heritage 9. patrimony, testament
 10. birthright 11. inheritance
berate... 3. jaw, nag 4. lash, rail
 5. chide, scold, slate 7. censure,
 reprove, upbraid
Berber... 4. Riff 6. Hamite, Kabyle,
 Taureg
berceau... 4. walk (leaf–covered)
 5. arbor, bower 6. cradle
berceuse... 10. cradlesong
 11. composition
bereave... 3. die, rob 5. leave, strip
 6. divest, orphan, sadden 7. deprive,
 despoil 10. disentitle, dispossess
bereavement... 4. loss 5. death
 9. privation 10. divestment
bereft... 4. lorn 7. denuded, fleeced,
 shorn of, witless 8. bereaved,
 divested, orphaned, stripped
 9. senseless 10. parentless,
 pauperized
Bereshith (Jew)... 7. Genesis
 9. Beginning
beret... 3. cap, tam 7. biretta
bergamot... 4. pear 5. snuff 6. orange
 7. essence 9. fragrance
beriberi... 5. kakke 7. disease
Berkeleianism (pert to)...
 founder.. 8. Berkeley (Bishop)
 science.. 10. philosophy
 system.. 8. idealism 13. immaterialism
Berlin, Germany...
 avenue.. 14. Unter den Linden
 capital.. 7. Germany
 garden (Zool).. 10. Tiergarten
 gate.. 11. Brandenburg
 government.. 9. Reichstag
berm, berme... 4. mall, path 5. prado
 6. runway 7. terrace 8. shoulder
 (road)
Bermuda...
 capital.. 8. Hamilton
 color.. 12. geranium pink

discoverer.. 8. Bermudez
government.. 7. British
grass.. 5. decil
ocean site.. 8. Atlantic
Bernardine Order... 11. Cistercians
Berne, Bern (Switz)... 7. capital
berry... 3. haw 4. buck, seed
 5. bacca, cubeb, fruit, grain, money
 6. acinus, kernel
berry, fruit... 5. grape, salal
 6. banana, tomato 7. currant
 8. bilberry, dewberry, hagberry,
 mulberry 9. bearberry, blueberry,
 cranberry, raspberry 10. blackberry,
 elderberry, gooseberry, loganberry,
 strawberry 11. boysenberry,
 huckleberry 12. checkerberry,
 whortleberry
berserk... 4. amok, bunk, dock, post,
 room 5. house, roost 6. billet,
 marina, office, reside 8. quarters
 9. situation 11. appointment
bertha... 4. cape 6. cannon, collar
 7. Perchta (goddess) 9. Big Bertha
 (Ger gun)
beseech... 3. beg, sue 4. pray
 5. crave, plead 6. obtest 7. entreat,
 implore, solicit 9. obsecrate
 10. supplicate
beset... 3. dun, ply, vex 4. stud
 5. harry, haunt, hem in, siege, worry
 6. attack, harass, infest, invade,
 obsess, plague, ravage 7. besiege
 8. blockade, surround 9. beleaguer,
 importune, infatuate
beset with danger... 5. risky
 6. chancy 8. perilous 9. dangerous
 10. jeopardous
beset with hairs... 7. barbate,
 bearded
beside, besides... 2. by 3. too, yet
 4. also, else, near, nigh, para (pref)
 5. about, along 6. nearby
 8. likewise, moreover 9. other than
 11. furthermore 12. over and above
beside oneself... 3. mad 4. wild
 5. crazy, rabid 6. beserk, raging,
 raving 7. frantic, ranting 8. frenzied
 9. desperate, overjoyed
 10. distracted, distraught
 11. overwrought
besiege... 5. beset 6. attack, harass,
 obsess, plague 7. torment
 8. blockade, surround 9. beleaguer
besmear... 3. dab 4. coat, daub,
 mark, soil, spot 5. paint, smear,
 stain, taint 6. bedaub 7. tarnish
 8. besmudge
besmirch... 4. blot, soil 5. smear, sully
 6. defile, smirch, smudge, vilify
 7. besmear, blacken, tarnish
 8. discolor
besom... 5. broom, hussy
besotted... 4. dull 5. drunk
 7. muddled, sottish 8. obsessed
 9. senseless, stupefied 10. infatuated
 11. intoxicated
bespangled... 5. aglow 7. lighted,
 studded, trimmed 8. spangled
 9. decorated, garnished
 10. glittering, ornamented
 11. embellished, illuminated

bespatter... 3. wet 4. blot, spot
5. dirty, slosh, smear, stain, sully
6. splash, vilify 7. asperse, scatter,
spatter, tarnish 8. besmirch, splatter,
sprinkle 9. denigrate 10. stigmatize
bespeak... 4. mean, show 5. imply
6. ask for, attest, engage, evince
7. address, betoken, connote, exhibit,
suggest, testify 8. foretell, indicate,
manifest 11. demonstrate
best... 4. aces, beat, most, tops
5. cream, elite, queen 6. choice,
finest 7. largest 8. champion,
outstrip 9. nonpareil, overmatch
11. superlative
bestial... 3. low 4. vile 5. cruel
6. brutal, filthy, savage 7. beastly,
brutish, inhuman, sensual
8. depraved, ruthless 9. barbarous
bestow... 4. deal, give 5. allot, apply,
award, grant, spend 6. accord,
confer, convey, demise, devote,
donate, impart, render, tender
7. deposit, present 8. transmit
10. administer
bestow honor upon... 5. adorn, exalt,
grace 7. dignify, ennoble, glorify
10. aggrandize 11. distinguish
bestride... 4. pass 5. mount 7. climb
on, protect, support 8. straddle
10. bestraddle
bet... 3. bas (roulette), pot 4. play
5. stake, wager 6. gamble, hazard,
pledge
beta test (army)... 12. intelligence
bête... 5. beast, silly 6. stupid
7. foolish
betel (pert to)...
loaf.. 3. pan 4. buyo, paun (pan)
palm.. 5. areca
pepper.. 4. itmo (ikmo)
bête noir... 4. ogre 7. bugbear
10. black beast, frightener,
mumbo–jumbo, Mumbo Jumbo
bethel... 4. kirk 6. chapel, church
8. Bethesda (Jerusalem)
12. meetinghouse
bethink... 5. think 6. recall 7. reflect
8. cogitate, remember 9. cerebrate,
recollect
betide... 3. hap 4. fall 5. occur
6. befall, happen 7. betoken,
presage 9. come about, eventuate,
transpire
betimes... 4. anon, soon 5. early
7. ere long, shortly 8. directly,
speedily 9. forthwith, presently
10. beforehand, seasonably
12. occasionally
betise... 5. folly 9. asininity, silliness,
stupidity 11. foolishness
betoken... 4. mark, mean, note
5. augur 6. denote, typify
7. bespeak, connote, express,
portend, presage, purport, signify
8. evidence, indicate 9. foretoken,
symbolize
betray... 4. blab, dupe, hoax, sell
5. bluff, peach, trick 6. reveal,
seduce, tattle 7. beguile, deceive,
divulge, mislead, sell out 8. disclose,

inform on 9. bamboozle, victimize
11. double–cross
betrayal... 4. ruse 5. trick 7. sellout,
treason 8. giveaway 9. Judas kiss,
seduction, treachery 10. disclosure
betrayer... 5. Judas 6. Arnold, Brutus
7. seducer, traitor 8. derelict,
informer, Quisling, turncoat
10. treasonist 13. double–crosser,
Judas Iscariot
betroth... 4. affy, earl 5. tryst
6. engage, pledge, plight
7. espouse, promise 8. affiance,
contract, espousal 10. engagement
better... 3. top 4. more 5. amend,
emend, excel, raise (poker), safer,
wiser 6. bigger, exceed, outwit,
reform 7. advance, choicer, greater,
improve, promote, surpass, victory
8. improved, superior 9. advantage,
meliorate 10. ameliorate, preferable
11. superiority
betting term... 4. ante, odds, tout
6. parlay 7. pyramid 10. parimutuel
11. sweepstakes
between... 5. among, mesne
6. atween 7. average, betwixt
bevel... 4. edge, ream 5. angle, bezel,
slant, slope, snape, splay 6. square
7. incline, oblique 9. obliquity
beverage... 3. ade, opo (comb form),
pop, tea 4. coke, malt, maté, mead,
milk, soda 5. cider, cocoa, drink,
luban, morat (anc), punch, water
6. coffee, eggnog, frappé, nectar
7. Seltzer 8. Adam's ale, Coca–Cola,
lemonade, root beer, sourdook
9. ginger ale, orangeade, phosphate
10. buttermilk, grape juice
12. sorsaparilla
beverage (alcoholic)... 3. ale, gin, rum
4. beer, brow, grog, kava, port, raki
5. booze, cider, hooch, julep, lagor,
negus, punch, smash, vodka
6. arrack, bishop, brandy, cognac,
eggnog, kurniss, kummel, likker,
porter, posset, sherry, tiswin, whisky
(whiskey), zythum (anc) 7. Bacardi,
bootleg, bourbon, cordial, liqueur,
martini, tequila 8. absinthe, aleberry,
Burgundy, cocktail, highball, muscatel,
sauterne, vermouth 9. applejack,
aqua vitae, firewater, Manhattan
10. shandygaff, Tom Collins
11. Benedictine, boilermaker,
grasshopper, mountain dew
bevy... 4. bund, gang, herd, host
5. covey, flock, group, party, troop
6. galaxy, throng 7. company
8. assembly 10. collection
bewail... 3. rue 4. keen, mean
5. mourn 6. bemoan, grieve, lament,
regret, repine, sorrow 7. deplore
bewilder... 3. fog 4. daze 5. addle,
amaze 6. baffle, dazzle, puzzle
7. buffalo, confuse, fluster, mystify,
nonplus, perplex 8. astonish,
confound, distract 9. bamboozle,
embarrass
bewilderment... 3. awe, fog 4. maze
6. wonder 9. confusion
10. perplexity 11. distraction

12. perturbation 13. disconcertion, embarrassment
bewitch ... 3. hex 5. charm, witch
6. enamor, entice, hoodoo, voodoo
7. beguile, delight, enchant
8. enthrall 9. captivate, enrapture, ensorcell, fascinate, infatuate
bewitching ... 5. siren 6. hexing, lovely
7. magical 8. alluring, charming, enticing 10. enchanting
11. captivating, fascinating
bey (Turk) ... 5. title 8. governor
beyond ... 2. by 3. too, yet 4. meta (pref), past, plus, well 5. above, extra, ultra 6. yonder 7. besides, farther, further, yonside 8. moreover
9. exceeding, Hereafter (The)
11. furthermore 12. additionally, ultraliminal
beyond hope ... 9. desperate
bezant (pert to) ...
  architecture .. 4. disc 8. ornament
  coin (anc) .. 7. solidus (gold)
  heraldry .. 4. disc (gold)
  offering (Eng king) .. 4. gold
bezel ... 4. edge 5. crown (gem), facet
6. chaton, flange 8. pavilion, template (templet) 9. obliquity
bezonian ... 6. mucker, wretch
7. budmash, caitiff, recruit
8. blighter 9. pilgarlic, scoundrel
bhikshu ... 6. gelong 7. ascetic
8. sannyasi 9. mendicant
bhut (Dravidian) ... 5. demon, ghost
6. goblin
bias ... 3. ply 4. awry, bent, turn, warp
5. amiss, slant, twist 6. desire
7. leaning, oblique 8. diagonal, slanting, tendency 9. obliquity, prejudice 10. favoritism, partiality, prepossess, transverse 11. disposition
biased ... 4. bent 6. narrow, swayed
7. bigoted, partial 8. diagonal, partisan, slanting 10. prejudiced
bib ... 3. sip, sup 4. swig 5. apron, drink, quaff 6. guzzle, imbibe, tipple, tucker 7. tablier 8. pinafore
bibacious ... 6. toping 7. drunken, sottish 8. bibulous, drinking, tippling
Bible ... 7. The Book, The Word, Vulgate 10. Scriptures, Testaments (Old, New)
Bible (pert to) ...
  battle site .. 10. Armageddon
  city .. 2. Ur 5. Joppa, Sidon, Sodom
  6. Hebron 9. Bethlehem, Jerusalem
  coin .. 6. talent
  Commandments .. 9. Decalogue
  Holy Land .. 9. Palestine
  interpretation .. 7. anagoge
  introduction .. 9. Isagogics
  kingdom .. 4. Elam 6. Basham, Canaan 7. Chaldea
  land of plenty .. 6. Goshen
  language .. 7. Aramaic
  mountain .. 4. Ebol, Zion 5. Horeb, Sinai 6. Ararat, Gilead, Moriah, Olives (Olivet), Pisgah
  pause .. 5. selah
  pool .. 6. Siloam
  precious stone .. 6. ligure (jacinth)
  Promised Land .. 6. Canaan

  sea .. 3. Red 4. Dead 7. Galilee
  Sermon on the Mount ..
  10. Beatitudes
  sheep .. 7. chamois
  town .. 4. Edar 5. Babel
  Wells of .. 5. Hagar, Jacob
Bible character ...
  archangel .. 7. Raphael
  giant .. 4. Anak 7. Goliath
  High Priest .. 3. Eli
  hunter .. 6. Nimrod
  liar .. 7. Ananias
  patriarch .. 5. Jacob 6. Israel
  prophet .. 4. Amos, Joel 5. Hosea, Jonah, Micah, Nahum 6. Daniel, Haggai, Isaiah, Joseph, Joshua, Samuel 7. Ezekiel, Malachi, Obadiah
  8. Habakkuk, Jeremiah 9. Zachariah, Zephaniah
Bible version ... 5. Douay, Reims
6. Geneva 7. Bishop's, Luther's, Revised, Targums, Vulgate
8. Cranmer's, Matthew's, Peshitta, Tyndale's, Wartburg, Wycliffe 9. King James, Maccabees 10. Great Bible, Septuagint 15. American Revised
bicker ... 5. argue, cavil 6. hassle, quiver, strife 7. dispute, flicker, flutter, quarrel, quibble, rhubarb (sl), wrangle 8. argument, pettifog
9. scrimmage, tremulous
10. contention 11. altercation
bicuspid ... 5. bifid, tooth, valve
6. cuspid 8. premolar
10. two–pointed 13. double–pointed
bid ... 3. beg 4. pray 5. offer, order, utter 6. charge, direct, enjoin, invite, reveal, tender 7. command, declare, entreat, offered, summons
8. overture, proclaim 9. quotation
12. presentation
biddy ... 3. hen 4. dame 5. skirt
6. female 7. chicken, Partlet
8. bedmaker 11. maidservant
bide ... 4. bear, stay, wait 5. abide, await, tarry 6. endure, remain, suffer
8. continue, tolerate 9. encounter, withstand
bield ... 3. den 4. cozy 7. comfort, courage, hearten, shelter 8. boldness, embolden 9. sheltered
10. confidence, habitation
bien ... 4. fine, good, snug
bienseance ... 7. decorum, manners
9. propriety 11. correctness, proprieties (the) 12. mannerliness
17. conventionalities
bier ... 6. coffin, litter 10. catafalque
Bier ... 4. beer
biff ... 4. bash, blow, slug, sock
5. paste, punch
bifold ... 4. dual 5. duple 6. binary, binate, double 7. twofold
bifurcate ... 3. wye (letter) 4. fork
7. forking, furcate 8. biforked, branched, forklike 9. two–forked
big ... 4. huge 5. bulky, grand, great, grown, jumbo, large 6. august, famous, mighty 7. massive, pompous, teeming 8. boastful, powerful, pregnant, swelling
9. momentous 10. tremendous

11. magnanimous, pretentious
big (pert to)...
shot.. 3. VIP
stick.. 5. power (T Roosevelt)
toe.. 6. hallux
top.. 6. circus
wig.. 3. VIP (humorous)
Big (pert to)...
Ben.. 5. clock 13. Tower of London
Bend State.. 9. Tennessee
Bertha.. 3. gun 5. Krupp (factory)
Board.. 6. Bourse 8. Exchange
11. stock market 13. stock exchange
House.. 3. pen 6. prison (State)
12. penitentiary
Push (WWI).. 5. Somme
bight... 3. bay 4. bend, gulf, loop
5. angle, noose, point 6. corner,
hollow 7. estuary
bigot... 3. bug, nut 6. zealot
7. fanatic 9. dogmatist, hypocrite,
illiberal 10. enthusiast, opinionist,
positivist
bigoted... 5. petty 6. little, narrow
10. intolerant, prejudiced
12. narrow–minded
bijou... 5. jewel 7. trinket
bilbi, bilby... 8. kangaroo
bilbo... 5. sword 6. rapier
bilingual... 6. diglot 12. linguistical
bilious... 3. ill 8. choleric, liverish
9. dyspeptic, jaundiced
11. ill–tempered
bilk... 2. do 3. gyp 4. balk, hoax, sell
5. cheat, cozen, trick 6. delude,
fleece, illude 7. deceive, defraud,
swindle 8. flimflam 11. hornswoggle
bill... 3. dun, nab, nib, pee, tab, Vee
($5) 4. beak, deed, list, menu, sign
5. carte, money 6. dockot, pickax,
poster, ticket 7. account, invoice,
mattock, placard, program, receipt,
statute, voucher 8. billhook, schedule
9. publicize, statement
10. prospectus 11. legislative
13. advertisement
billet... 3. bar, log 4. note, pass
5. berth, stick, strap 6. assign,
docket, letter, notice, ticket
7. bearing (Her), epistle, missive,
molding 8. dispatch, document,
insignia, position, quarters
11. appointment
billiard shot... 5. carom, masse
6. cannon
Billingsgate... 4. Gate (London)
10. fish market 12. vituperation
billow... 3. sea 4. roll, toss, wave
5. eagre, heave, surge, swell
6. dilate 7. distend 10. undulation
billowy... 4. wavy 5. surgy 7. surging
8. swelling 10. undulating
bin... 3. box 4. crib, loft, vina
5. frame, kench, pungi (Hind flute)
6. manger 8. elevator
binary... 4. dual 6. bifold, binate,
double, duplex 9. duplicate
bind... 3. jam, tie 4. ally, frap, gird,
gyve, hold, lace, lash, rope, tape
5. chain, leash, stick, truss, withe
6. engage, fasten, fetter, pinion,
pledge, secure 7. confine, shackle

8. obligate 10. constipate
binding... 4. tape 5. valid 6. binder,
edging 7. girding, joining, liaison
8. trimming, trussing, wrapping
9. bordering, fastening, stringent
10. astringent, compulsory, obligatory
11. restraining, restrictive
binding (agreement)... 4. bond, pact
7. bargain, promise 8. contract
binding (book)... 4. yapp 5. cover
6. jacket 10. bibliopegy
binge... 4. bout 5. spree 6. bender
8. carousal 11. celebration
bingo... 3. pop 4. bang, keno
5. lotto, socko 6. brandy
biographer... 8. annalist 9. historian
10. chronicler 11. biographist,
memorialist
biography... 4. life 6. memoir
7. history, memoire, recount
8. memorial 11. hagiography
biological... 4. gene 5. class, genus,
order, vital 6. biotic, family
7. animate, organic, paracme,
species
biology, science of... 6. botany
7. ecology, zoology 8. eugenics,
genetics 9. bionomics, organisms
10. embryology, morphology,
physiology
biopsy (Med)... 8. analysis (tissue)
9. diagnosis 11. examination
(microscopic)
biped... 3. man 9. two–legged
birch... 4. flog 5. stick 6. switch
birch tree (pert to)...
family.. 10. Betulaceae
genera.. 5. alder, birch, hazel
order.. 7. Fagales
product.. 16. oil of wintergreen
variety.. 5. paper, river, sweet, white
6. cherry, yellow
bird (pert to)...
best swimmer.. 4. loon 6. gannet
cage.. 6. aviary 7. paddock
8. dovecote
Class.. 4. Aves
crested.. 7. hoatzin 9. stinkbird
fabled, sacred.. 3. roc 4. ibis
fastest flyer.. 4. hawk 5. eagle, swift
6. falcon
fastest runner.. 7. ostrich
feathers.. 5. remix (sing) 7. remiges
first.. 13. archaeopteryx
footless.. 4. apod
greatest traveler.. 4. tern
greatest wingspread.. 9. albatross
halcyon.. 10. kingfisher
highest flyer.. 5. goose
immortal.. 7. phoenix
killing.. 7. avicide
largest.. 6. condor 7. ostrich
13. whooping crane
Latin.. 4. avis
life.. 5. ornis
longest–lived.. 5. macaw
lover.. 12. ornithophile
most dangerous.. 9. cassowary
naked hatched.. 11. gymnogenous
of prey (prized).. 6. falcon
oldest known.. 13. archaeopteryx
one year old.. 8. annotine

Order.. 7. Rasores 8. Raptores
smallest.. 14. bee hummingbird
smartest.. 4. crow
study.. 6. oology
young.. 4. eyas 8. birdikin, nestling
   9. fledgling
bird, anatomy (pert to)...
beak.. 3. neb, nib 4. bill, lora
   5. ceral 7. rostrum
eye process.. 6. pecten
head.. 4. lore 6. pileum
jaw.. 4. mala
leg (featherless).. 9. cnemidium
wing part.. 5. alula
bird, Arctic... 3. auk 4. gull, skua
   5. brant 6. dunlin, fulmar, jaeger
   7. penguin 9. ptarmigan
bird, colorful... 3. kea 5. egret,
   macaw 6. magpie, parrot, trogon
   7. peacock, quetzal (quezal)
   8. lyrebird 10. kingfisher 14. bird of
   paradise
bird, common... 3. ani, daw, owl
   4. chat, dove, lark, pisk, wren
   5. finch, pipit, robin, vireo 6. dunlin,
   linnet, martin, oriole, phoebe, pigeon,
   shrike, siskin, thrush, towhee 7. blue
   jay, bunting, catbird, cowbird, flicker,
   grackle, kinglet, sparrow, swallow,
   tanager, warbler, waxwing
   8. blackcap, bluebird, bobolink,
   cardinal, grosbeak, kingbird, redstart,
   starling, titmouse 9. chickadee,
   goldfinch, nighthawk, sandpiper
   10. flycatcher, meadowlark,
   turtledove, woodpecker
   11. hummingbird, mockingbird,
   nightingale, pyrrhuloxia
   12. whippoorwill, yellowhammer
   14. scarlet tanager
bird, crow family... 4. crow, rook
   5. crake, raven 6. chough, magpie
   7. corvine, jackdaw
bird, duck family... 4. clee, coot,
   lory, smew, teal, wood 5. eider,
   goose 6. scoter 7. gadwall, mallard,
   Muscovy, pintail, pochard
   8. baldpate, redshank, shoveler
   9. merganser 10. bufflehead,
   canvasback
bird, flightless... 3. emu, moa
   4. dodo (ext), kiwi, rhea, weka
   7. apteryx, ostrich, peacock, penguin
   8. Notornis 9. cassowary
bird, foreign...
Africa.. 4. taha 5. crane 6. cuckoo
   7. ostrich 8. umbrette
   10. weaverbird
Arctic.. 3. auk 4. gull, skua 5. brant
   6. dunlin, falcon, jaeger 7. penguin
   8. grayling 9. gyrfalcon, ptarmigan
Asia.. 4. myna 5. pitta 6. bulbul,
   linnet 7. boobook, peacock, sirgang
   8. dotterel, leaf bird 9. brambling,
   muted swan
Australia.. 3. emu 4. kiwi, lory
   5. lowan 6. leipoa 7. boobook,
   grinder 8. ganggang, lorikeet,
   lyrebird, morepork, parakeet, platypus
   9. bowerbird, cassowary, pardalote
Central America.. 6. barbet, toucan
   7. quetzal (quezal) 8. puffbird

Cuba.. 6. trogon 8. tocororo 14. bee
   hummingbird
England.. 4. kite, rook 9. cormorant
   11. carrion crow
Europe.. 4. merl 5. pipit, stilt
   (3–toed), stork (white), swift, tarin
   6. godwit, hoopoe, merlin, roller,
   siskin 7. bittern, ortolan, skylark,
   starnel 8. bee eater, dotterel,
   garganey, nuthatch, redstart
   9. brambling, chaffinch, gallinule,
   sheldrake 10. lammergeir, turtledove
   11. nightingale, wallcreeper
   12. capercaillie (grouse)
Hawaii.. 2. io, o–o 3. ava, iwa, poe
   4. iiwi, mamo 6. parson 7. frigate
India.. 5. shama 8. amadavat,
   pheasant 11. red hornbill
Java.. 7. sparrow 8. rice bird 9. fruit
   dove
New Guinea.. 9. cassowary 14. bird
   of paradise
New Zealand.. 3. ihi, kea, moa, tui
   4. kuku, weka
So America.. 4. guan 5. macaw
   6. barbet, motmot, toucan
   7. jacamar, tinamou, warrior
   8. boatbill, caracara 9. trumpeter
   11. scarlet ibis
bird, game... 4. teal 5. brant, goose,
   quail, snipe 6. grouse, pigeon,
   plover, turkey (wild) 7. bustard,
   gadwall, mallard 8. bobwhite,
   pheasant, woodcock 9. partridge,
   ptarmigan 10. canvasback 14. prairie
   chicken
bird, group...
partridge.. 5. covey
pheasant.. 3. nye 4. nide
quail.. 4. bevy
bird, long–legged... 4. ibis, rail, sora
   5. crane, egret, heron, stilt, stork
   6. avocet, curlew, jacana 7. seriema
   8. flamingo 9. sandpiper
   10. demoiselle
Bird of...
Freedom.. 9. bald eagle
Jove.. 5. eagle
June.. 7. peacock
Minerva.. 3. owl
Wonder.. 7. phoenix
bird, pet... 4. myna (mynah)
   6. canary, parrot 8. cockatoo,
   lovebird, parakeet
bird, poultry... 4. duck 5. goose
   6. pigeon, turkey 7. chicken
   8. pheasant
bird, shore... 4. swan 5. egret, heron,
   stork 6. avocet, curlew, plover, willet
   7. frigate, pelican 8. dotterel, killdeer
   10. demoiselle
bird, sky... 4. erne (ern), gier (Bib),
   hawk, kite 5. Buteo, eagle, saker
   6. condor, falcon, gannet, jaeger,
   merlin, osprey 7. buzzard, harrier,
   kestral, vulture 8. caracara, ringtail
   9. Accipiter 10. lammergeir
bird, water... 3. auk 4. coot, gull,
   ibis, loon, rail, shag, skua, swan
   5. cahow, crane, grebe, heron, stork
   6. curlew, cygnet, gannet, jabiru,
   jacana, petrel, plover 7. bittern,

bustard, dovekie, pelican, seriema,
skimmer 8. dabchick, flamingo,
umbrette 9. albatross, cormorant,
gallinule, guillemot, phalarope,
spoonbill 10. kingfisher, yellowlegs
biretta . . . 8. skullcap 9. headdress
birl . . . 4. spin 6. rattle 7. resolve
birth . . . 3. nee 4. line 5. blood, breed
6. origin 7. descent, genesis, lineage
8. heritage, nativity, nobility
9. beginning 10. derivation,
extraction, renascence
11. inheritance, Renaissance
birthday (pert to) . . .
astrology . . 7. casting, lineage (the
gods)
nativities . . 9. genethlic 10. genethliac
poems . . 12. genethliacon
birth flower (by months) . . .
Jan . . 9. carnation
Feb . . 8. primrose
Mar . . 6. violet
Apr . . 5. daisy
May . . 15. lily of the valley
June . . 4. rose
July . . 8. sweet pea
Aug . . 9. gladiolus
Sept . . 5. aster
Oct . . 6. dahlia
Nov . . 13. chrysanthemum
Dec . . 5. holly 10. poinsettia
birthmark . . . 4. mole 5. nevus (naevus)
birthright . . . 6. rights 8. heritage
9. privilege 10. possession
11. inheritance
birth seniority . . . 9. first–born
13. primogeniture
birthstone (by days) . . .
Sun . . 5. topaz 7. diamond
Mon . . 5. pearl 7. crystal
Tues . . 4. ruby 7. emerald
Wed . . 8. amethyst 9. loadstone
Thurs . . 8. sapphire 9. carnelian
Fri . . 7. cat's eye, emerald
Sat . . 7. diamond 9. turquoise
birthstone (by months) . . .
Jan . . 6. garnet
Feb . . 8. amethyst
Mar . . 6. jasper
Apr . . 7. diamond 8. sapphire
May . . 5. agate 7. emerald
June . . 7. emerald 11. alexandrite
July . . 4. onyx, ruby
Aug . . 8. sardonyx 9. carnelian
Sept . . 8. sapphire 10. chrysolite
Oct . . 4. opal 10. aquamarine
Nov . . 5. topaz
Dec . . 4. ruby 9. turquoise
bis . . . 5. again, ditto, twice 6. encore,
repeat 7. replica 8. repetend
9. duplicate 10. repetition
biscuit . . . 3. bun, doe 4. rusk
5. bread, cooky, scone, wafer
6. pommel 7. cracker 8. biscotin,
zwieback
bise . . . 4. wind (cold) 6. winter
7. Norther
bisect . . . 4. fork 5. cross, halve, split
6. cleave, divide
bishop . . . 4. Abba 7. pontiff, prelate
8. chessman, director, overseer
9. churchman, clergyman, inspector

14. superintendent
bishop (pert to) . . .
Bible . . 10. Great Bible
cap . . 4. hura 5. miter
revenue . . 7. annates
staff . . 7. baculus, crosier (crozier)
throne . . 3. see 4. apse
vestment . . 4. cope 5. stole 6. rochet
7. gremial, pallium 8. dalmatic
10. omophorion
bishopric . . . 3. see 4. seat 7. diocese
10. episcopacy, episcopate
bison . . . 2. ox 4. gaur, urus
7. aurochs, buffalo 9. quadruped
bisque (pert to) . . .
ceramics (unglazed) . . 7. biscuit
color . . 9. red–yellow
food . . 4. soup 8. ice cream
term (sports) . . 4. turn 5. point
6. stroke
bissext (pert to) . . .
calendar . . 6. Julian (Rom)
day . . 5. sixth (intercalary)
year . . 8. Leap Year
bistro . . . 6. tavern 7. barroom 8. wine
shop 10. restaurant
bit . . . 3. ace, jot, ort 4. bite, coin,
iota, mite, mote, part (acting), role,
snip, tool, tube, whit 5. check,
crumb, hitch, money, piece, scrap,
speck 6. morsel, smidge, tittle
7. portion, smidgen, traneen
8. somewhat 9. something
bit (harness) . . . 4. curb 6. bridle,
Pelham 7. snaffle 9. Liverpool
bit (money) . . .
two bits . . 7. quarter 9. ninepence
(Bahamas)
four bits . . 10. half dollar
bitch . . . 6. female (animal) 8. slattern,
strumpet (vulgar)
bite . . . 3. cut, eat, nip, zip 4. food,
gnaw, grip, hold, knap, pang, tang,
zest 5. champ, smart, snack, sting,
taste 6. morsel, nibble, pierce
8. pungency
biting . . . 4. acid, tart 5. acerb, acrid,
sharp 6. bitter, rodent 7. caustic,
cutting, mordant, nipping, painful,
piquant, pungent 8. piercing,
poignant, scathing, stinging
9. sarcastic, trenchant, vitriolic,
withering 10. astringent, irritating
11. acrimonious, penetrating
biting nails . . . 12. phaneromania
bito (pert to) . . .
bark . . 10. fish poison
seeds . . 6. zachun (oil)
tree . . 7. hajilij
bitter . . . 4. acid, cold, keen, sore, sour
5. acerb, acrid, irate, sharp
6. severe 7. cutting, hostile, pungent
8. grievous, stinging, virulent
9. rancorous, resentful
10. embittered, unpleasant
11. acrimonious, distressful,
reproachful
bitter (pert to) . . .
apple (herb) . . 9. colocynth
chemical . . 4. alum
earth . . 8. magnesia
gentian . . 9. baldmoney

grass .. 9. colicroot
herb .. 3. rue 4. aloe 5. aloin
  8. centaury
plant .. 10. bitterroot 11. bittersweet
  (poisonous)
prefix .. 5. picro
salts .. 5. Epsom
suffix .. 6. picrin
vetch .. 3. ers
waters (Bib) .. 5. Marah
wintergreen .. 10. pipsissewa
wormwood .. 8. de Gaulle (said of)
bitterness ... 3. rue 5. venom
  6. rancor 7. remorse 8. acerbity,
  acrimony, tartness, wormwood
  9. animosity, poignancy, virulence
  10. causticity, resentment
bivalve ... 4. clam, spat, Unio 5. pinna
  6. Anomia, mussel, oyster, Teredo
  7. mollusk, pandora, scallop
  10. brachiopod (fossil form)
bivocal ... 9. diphthong (dipthong)
bivouac ... 4. camp 6. encamp, laager
  7. camping, leaguer (Hist)
  10. encampment
biwa ... 6. loquat
bizarre ... 3. odd 5. dedal, outré, queer
  6. absurd, exotic, quaint, rococo
  7. baroque 8. fanciful 9. eccentric,
  fantastic, grotesque, highflown
  11. extravagant, sensational -
Bizen ... 7. pottery (unglazed)
Bizet ... 8. composer (Carmen)
bizzarro (Mus) ... 7. bizarre
  9. whimsical
blab ... 6. gossip, reveal, snitch, tattle,
  tell on 7. blabber, chatter
  8. informer, squealer, telltale
  10. taleteller, tattletale 11. taletelling
blabber ... 4. blab 6. babble, gabber,
  gossip, tattle 7. chatter, twaddle
  8. informer, nonsense
black ... 3. ink, jet 4. ebon, evil, foul,
  inky, noir 5. color, cruel, ebony,
  murky, negro, niger, raven, sable,
  tarry 6. dismal, filthy, gloomy, pitchy,
  somber, sullen, wicked 7. hateful,
  melanic, nigrine, nigrous, ominous,
  unclean 8. atrament, menacing,
  mournful, sinister 9. atrocious,
  lightless, nigricant 10. calamitous,
  disastrous, forbidding
black (pert to) ... see also *Black*
African .. 10. blackamoor
alloy .. 6. niello
and blue .. 5. livid 7. bruised
  10. discolored, ecchymosed,
  ecchymosis 11. bluish–black,
  lead–colored
art .. 5. magic 7. alchemy 8. wizardry
  10. black magic
ball .. 7. exclude 9. ostracize
bird .. 2. Zu (Myth) 3. ani, daw, pie
  4. crow, merl, rook 5. amsel, ouzel,
  raven 6. thrush 7. jackdaw
  10. Melanesian, Polynesian
bottom .. 9. clog dance
coffee .. 8. café noir
diamond .. 4. coal
duck .. 6. Cayuga
earth .. 4. mold 9. Chernozem (Russ)
face .. 4. type 5. sheep 8. minstrel

fish .. 6. tautog
garnet .. 8. melanite
gibbon .. 7. siamang
guard .. 5. drole, gamin, knave, rogue,
  scamp 6. rascal 7. vagrant, villain
  8. criminal, scalawag, scullion,
  vagabond 9. scoundrel
  11. rapscallion
Harry .. 7. sea bass
jack .. 4. flag (pirate) 6. coerce,
  cudgel, hijack 9. strong–arm
  10. Jolly Roger
partridge .. 9. francolin
rhinoceros .. 7. borelle
sheep .. 10. scapegrace
smith .. 5. smith 6. forger, smithy
  7. farrier
spruce .. 7. yewpine
strap .. 8. molasses
widow spider .. 6. pokomo
Black (pert to) ...
Bess .. 4. mare (Dick Turpin's)
Current .. 5. Japan
Death .. 6. Plague (bubonic)
Foot .. 6. Indian (Siksika)
  10. Algonquian
Friar .. 4. monk 9. Dominican
  (mendicant Order)
Friday .. 10. Good Friday 14. public
  disaster (day)
Hand .. 7. anarchy, Camorra, Society
  (secret) 9. blackmail
Hawk .. 3. War (1831) 11. Indian
  Chief
Hole .. 8. Calcutta
Jack (General) .. 5. Logan (Civil War)
  8. Pershing (WWI)
Maria .. 7. vehicle (prisoner's)
  14. explosive shell
Monday .. 12. Easter Monday (1630)
Monk .. 11. Benedictine
Plague .. 7. bubonic
Prince .. 6. Edward
Republic .. 5. Haiti
Rood .. 8. crucifix, Holy Rood (anc)
Sea (Asia) .. 6. Euxine (anc)
Sea (Russia) .. 11. Chernoe More
Shirt .. 7. Fascist 8. Fascisti
Watch .. 16. Royal Highlanders
Water State (nickname) .. 8. Nebraska
blacken ... 5. sully 6. defame
  9. denigrate
bladder ... 3. bag, sac 4. sack
  5. pouch 6. bubble, pocket
  7. blister, globule
blade ... 3. arm, bit, fop 4. beau,
  dude, edge, epee, foil, leaf, vane
  5. blood, dandy, frond, knife, spark,
  spear, spire, sport, sword 6. cutter,
  rafter (roof), runner, Toledo (sword)
  7. gallant, sabreur, scapula, traneen
  9. swordsman
blague ... 6. humbug 8. claptrap
blah ... 4. bunk 8. contempt, nonsense
blain ... 4. bleb, sore 5. bulla
  7. blister, inflame, pustule
  8. swelling 9. chilblain
Blake's symbolic figure ... 3. Zoa
blame ... 5. chide, curse, shend
  6. accuse, charge, revile 7. accusal,
  censure, obloquy, reproof, reprove
  8. denounce, reproach 9. criticism,

damnation, reprehend 10. accusation, imputation 11. attribution, reprobation 12. condemnation, denunciation, reprehension 14. responsibility

blameless... 7. sinless 8. innocent 9. faultless, guiltless 12. sans reproche

blameworthy... 8. culpable 10. censurable, reprovable 11. impeachable 13. reprehensible

blanch... 4. fade, pale 5. gloss, scald 6. whiten 8. etiolate 9. whitewash

blanc mange... 7. dessert, pudding

bland... 4. glib, mild, oily, smug, soft, tame 5. suave 6. gentle, smooth 7. affable 8. soothing (manner), unctuous 9. temperate 10. flattering 12. hypocritical, ingratiating, mealy–mouthed, smooth–spoken

blandishment... 7. amenity, coaxing, palaver 8. cajolery, flattery 9. wheedling 10. allurement, inducement

blank... 4. arid, bare, dash, dull, form, nude, null, void 5. empty, naked, verse 6. closed, hollow, jejune, poetry, stupid, vacant, vacuum 8. bull's–eye, document, spotless (domino) 9. fruitless, unadorned, untrimmed 10. instrument (law), tabula rasa 11. empty–headed, thoughtless 13. unembellished, unintelligent 14. expressionless

blank book... 5. album 6. tablet 8. memo book, notebook 10. memorandum, pocketbook

blanket... 3. rug 4. robe 5. bluey, cloak, cotta, cover, manta, quilt, throw 6. afghan, shroud, spread 7. lap robe 8. covering, coverlet 10. barraclade (homespun)

blankness... 7. vacancy, vacuity 8. negation 9. emptiness

blare... 4. bawl, blow, bray, honk, peal, toot 5. blast, blaze, glare 6. bellow 7. fanfare, tantara 9. tantarara

blarney... 6. bunkum 7. wheedle 8. buncombe, cajolery, flattery, soft–soap 9. adulation

Blarney Stone site... 13. Blarney Castle (Cork, Ir)

blart... 4. blab, roar 5. bleat 6. bellow

blasé... 5. bored, sated 6. casual 9. easygoing, sans souci, surfeited 10. hard–boiled, nonchalant 11. indifferent, self–assured, unconcerned, worldly–wise 12. disenchanted 13. disillusioned, disinterested, lackadaisical

blaspheme... 4. damn 5. abuse, curse, swear 6. revile, vilify 10. calumniate

blasphemy... 7. cursing, impiety 8. anathema, swearing 9. profanity, sacrilege 10. execration 11. desecration, imprecation, irreverence, malediction

blast... 3. jet, pop 4. bang, blow, gust, ruin, shot, toot 5. curse, stunt 6. blight, flurry, onrush, wither 7. blowout, explode 9. discharge,

explosion, explosive, frustrate 10. detonation, propulsion 11. fulmination

blasted... 5. blown 6. blamed, cursed, danged (sl), darned, ruined 7. wrecked 8. blighted 10. confounded

blatant... 5. crude, noisy 6. garish, puling, vulgar 7. flaring, glaring, howling, ululant, wailing 8. brawling 9. clamorous, turbulent 10. blustering, uproarious, vociferous 12. obstreperous

blate... 4. blab, dull, slow 5. bleat, blunt, prate, timid 7. bashful 8. sheepish 9. diffident 10. spiritless

blaw... 4. blow, brag 5. boast

blaze... 4. fire, gash, mark (trail), sign 5. flame, flare 6. luster 7. bonfire, flare–up 8. eruption, outburst, radiance, splendor 9. explosion, firebrand 10. effulgence 11. resplendent

blazer... 6. jacket

blazon... 4. deck, show 5. adorn, blaze, grace, paint 6. enrich, shield 7. display, étalage, exhibit, furbish 8. proclaim 9. embellish 10. coat of arms, exhibition 11. publication

blazoning arms... 8. bearings, heraldry

bleach... 3. lye, sun 4. lime 6. blanch, purify, whiten 7. decolor, lighten 8. chemical, chlorine, etiolate, peroxide 9. whiteness 10. dealbation, decolorant 11. decolorizer

bleaching vat... 4. kier 5. kieve

bleak... 3. dry, raw 4. arid, bare, cold, pale 5. gaunt, sharp 6. bitter, desert, dismal, dreary, frigid, pallid, severe 7. cutting, exposed 8. desolate, rigorous 9. cheerless, wind–blown, wind–swept 10. depressing

blear... 3. dim, fog 4. blur, dull, film 6. bleary 7. blurred 10. indistinct

bleat... 3. baa 4. blat 5. blate, whine 7. blather

bleb... 5. bulge, bulla 6. bubble 7. bladder, blister, globule, pustule, vesicle

bleed... 3. cup, tap 4. milk, soak 5. drain 6. fleece, grieve, let out, suffer 7. agonize, despoil, exploit, overtax 8. let blood, transude 9. surcharge 10. hemorrhage, overcharge

bleeding... 7. cupping 9. hemorrhea 10. hemorrhage, phlebotomy 11. venesection 12. bloodletting

blemish... 3. mar 4. blot, blue, dent, flaw, mole, mote, pock, rift, scar, spot, wart 5. crack, fault, nevus, sully, taint 6. breach, macula, macule, stigma 7. failing, fissure, freckle, lentigo 8. cicatrix, pockmark 9. birthmark, cicatrice, deformity, disfigure 10. defacement, deficiency 12. imperfection 13. disfigurement

blench... 4. duck, pale, wile 5. blink, dodge, quail, trick, wince 6. bleach, cringe, flinch, recoil, shrink, whiten 9. stratagem 10. disconcert

blend ... 3. mix 4. fuse, melt
5. merge, shift, unite 6. fusion,
mingle 7. combine, mixture, scumble
8. coalesce, compound, tincture
9. commingle, composite, harmonize
10. amalgamate 11. combination,
incorporate
blended ... 5. fondu, mixed 6. merged
7. mingled 9. confluent
blending ... 6. crasis 11. inheritance
blessing ... 4. boon, gift, good, luck,
rite 5. favor, grace 7. benefit,
benison, fortune, godsend, service,
welfare 8. good turn, kindness
9. advantage 10. benedicite, good
wishes 11. benediction, benevolence
12. felicitation 13. beatification
blight ... 3. mar, nip 4. dash (hope),
ruin, rust, seer, smut 5. blast, crush,
spoil 6. freeze, mildew, wither
7. destroy, shatter 9. frustrate
10. disappoint
blighter ... 4. chap 6. beggar (anc),
fellow
blimp ... 6. ballon 7. airship, balloon
8. potbelly, zeppelin 9. dirigible
10. bureaucrat 12. Graf Zeppelin,
stuffed shirt
blind ... 3. dim 4. ante (poker), mask,
peed, ruse, seel, slat, veil, wile
5. ciego, guise, trick 6. ambush,
scheme, screen 7. benight, conceal,
dim—eyed, eyeless, gimmick, obscure,
pretext, shutter 8. artifice, hoodwink,
jalousie, purblind, unseeing
9. dead—drunk, senseless, sightless
10. ableptical, dim—sighted,
subterfuge 11. inattentive
12. undiscerning 13. stalking—horse
blind (pert to) ...
alley .. 7. impasse 8. cul—de—sac
fear .. 5. panic
girl (of Pompeii) .. 5. Nydia
gut .. 6. caecum, window
10. persiennes
one eye .. 4. peed
printing for .. 7. braille
blindness ... 7. anopsia, meropia (part)
8. ablepsia 9. achropsia, amaurosis
10. bleariness, nyctalopia 11. gutta
serena, hemeralopia
13. achromatopsia
blink ... 4. wink 5. light, quail, wince
6. cringe, flinch 7. flicker, glimmer,
glimpse, glitter, nictate, shimmer,
twinkle 9. nictitate 10. bat the eyes
blink at ... 6. accept, ignore
7. condone 8. overlook, tolerate
9. be blind to, disregard
bliss ... 3. joy 4. Eden 6. heaven
7. delight, harmony, rapture
8. delight, gladness 9. beatitude,
happiness 11. blessedness
12. spirituality 14. blithesomeness
blissful ... 4. holy 5. seely 6. Edenic
7. blessed, Elysian, Utopian
8. ecstatic 9. beatified, glorified
blister ... 4. bleb, blob, burn, flay
5. blain, bulge, bulla, roast 6. beat
up, bubble, oyster, scorch (with
words), thrash 7. bladder, blemish,
pustule, trounce, vesicle 9. criticize

10. vesicatory
blistered ... 6. seared, singed
7. parched 8. scorched 9. vesicated
blithe ... 4. airy, glad 5. merry
6. cheery, joyous 7. jocular
8. cheerful 10. blithesome
blitz ... 5. shell 6. strafe 7. bombard
10. blitzkrieg
blizzard ... 4. blow, wind 5. purga
7. tornado 9. snowstorm 10. snow
squall 11. white squall
Blizzard State ... 11. South Dakota
bloated ... 5. cured (herring), proud,
tumid 6. sodden, turgid 7. dilated,
pompous, swollen 8. inflated, puffed
up, tumefied 9. distended, flatulent,
plethoric 10. incrassate
13. emphysematous
bloated plutocrat ... 9. bourgeois
10. capitalist
blob ... 3. wen 4. bleb, blot, daub,
drop, lump, mark 5. bulge
6. bubble, pimple 7. blister, globule,
pustule, splotch
bloc (political) ... 4. axis 5. cabal, union
6. league 7. faction 8. alliance
9. coalition 11. combination
block ... 3. bar, dam, set 4. cake,
clog, cube, mass, peck, plot, stop
5. check, parry, shape, solid
6. hamper, hinder, impede, oppose,
shares, stymie 7. auction, barrier,
outline 8. blockage, obstacle,
obstruct 9. barricade 10. impediment
11. obstruction
block (pert to) ...
architecture .. 5. socle 6. dentil,
mutule, plinth 7. tessera
blacksmith's .. 5. anvil
coal (Eng) .. 3. jud
executioner's .. 10. guillotine
falconry .. 5. perch
finance .. 6. shares
football .. 4. clip
glacier .. 5. serac
insulating .. 6. taplet
land .. 4. city 5. tract 7. section
medicine .. 10. anesthesia
railroad .. 6. signal
sandstone (Eng) .. 6. sarsen
blockade ... 3. bar, dam 5. hem in,
siege 6. shut in 7. closure, exclude,
fortify 8. obstacle, obstruct
9. exclusion 11. obstruction
blockhead ... 3. oaf 4. dolt, fool,
mome (anc) 5. dunce, idiot
7. half—wit, tomfool 8. bonehead,
lunkhead 11. knucklehead
blockhouse ... 4. fort 7. shelter 8. log
cabin 10. stronghold
bloke ... 3. man 4. bird, chap, tuff
6. fellow 9. personage
blond, blonde ... 4. fair 5. color, light
6. flaxen 10. goldilocks
blood ... 4. cell, clot, type, vein
5. aorta, fluid, group, grume, hemad
(haemad), hemal, hemic, ichor
(gods'), lymph, serum 6. artery,
factor, fibrin, haemal, plasma, Rhesus
(type) 7. blister, carotid 8. platelet
9. corpuscle, hemamoeba, leucocyte
10. hemachrome, hemoglobin,

hemorrhage, phlebotomy
11. erythrocyte, transfusion
12. bloodletting
blood (pert to)...
clotted.. 4. gore 5. cruor 8. thrombus
color.. 7. crimson, para red 8. blood
red, sanguine 11. sanguineous
13. sanguinaceous
disease.. 6. anemia 8. leukemia
(leukaemia, leucemia)
feud.. 8. vendetta
flower.. 5. hippo 9. blood lily
horse.. 7. blooded 12. thoroughbred
hound.. 4. lyam (lyme)
money (anc).. 3. cro 4. eric
7. galanas, wergild 9. bloodwite
particle (foreign).. 7. embolus
poisoning.. 6. pyemia (pyaemia)
pressure.. 12. hypertension
pudding.. 7. sausage
relationship.. 3. sib 6. agnate
7. cognate, kinship, kinsman, progeny,
sibship
shed.. 6. murder 7. killing, slaying
9. slaughter
stone.. 10. chalcedony
sucker.. 5. leech 8. parasite
10. sanguisuge
thirsty.. 5. cruel 8. sanguine
9. ferocious, murderous
10. sanguinary 11. ensanguined
vessel.. 3. vas 4. vein 6. artery
9. capillary
blood, kinship... 4. race, ties 5. birth,
breed, stock 6. strain 7. descent,
kinsman, lineage, royalty, sibship
8. heredity, nobility, relation 9. blue
blood, lifeblood, life force
10. extraction 13. consanguinity
bloodless... 4. pale 5. ashen, faint
6. anemic (anemic) 7. ghastly,
inhuman 8. lifeless, peaceful
9. unfeeling 11. cold of heart
bloody... 4. gory 5. cruel, wound
6. cruent (obs), cursed 7. smeared
8. infamous 9. murderous
10. sanguinary 11. ensanguined
12. bloodstained, bloodthirsty
Bloody (pert to)...
Angle.. 11. battlefield (Spotsylvania,
1860)
Mary.. 5. Queen (Eng) 8. cocktail
bloom... 3. dew 4. glow, posy
5. blush, flush, youth 6. beauty,
flower, health, heyday, thrive
7. blossom 11. healthiness
bloomer... 5. boner, error 6. bobble,
boo-boo 7. blooper, blunder, failure,
faux pas, mistake, trouser
blossom... 4. bell, blow, grow, posy
5. bloom, ripen 6. floret, flower,
mature, thrive 7. develop, prosper
8. flourish, floweret, progress
10. effloresce 13. efflorescence
blossoming... 4. rise 5. growth
8. anthesis, blooming 9. flowerage,
flowering 10. florescent, unfoldment
11. development, florescence,
flourishing, progressing
13. efflorescence, inflorescence

blot... 3. dry, mar 4. blur, soil, spot
5. erase, error, fleck, smear, speck,
stain, sully 6. absorb, blotch, damage,
impair, smutch, soak up, sponge,
stigma 7. blacken, blemish, erasure,
expunge 9. bespatter 10. obliterate,
stigmatize 12. obliteration
blot out... 3. fix 4. dele, kill 5. purge
6. absorb, cancel, delete, efface,
excise, rub out 7. bump off, destroy,
expunge, obscure, wipe out 8. black
out 10. obliterate
blotch... 4. bleb, mark, soil, spot
5. patch, stain 6. macula, mottle,
stigma 7. blemish
blotched... 4. pied 5. pinto 6. spotty
7. mottled 8. speckled
blouse... 4. blou, sark 5. bluey, middy,
shift, shirt, smock, tunic, waist
6. basque 7. casaque 10. shirtwaist
blow... 3. dab, hit, rap, tap 4. brag,
bump, coup, gust, pant, puff, slap,
toot, waft, wind 5. bloom, devel,
faint, impel, knock, shock, sound, utter
6. expand, puff up 7. beating,
bluster, whiffle 8. calamity, disaster,
disclose, lambskin (obs)
14. disappointment
blow... 4. flee, over, rant, slog
5. boast, clout, scram 6. beat it,
betray, buffet, depart, wallop
8. squander 10. blow me down
blow (pert to)...
hard.. 6. blower 7. windbag
8. braggart 11. braggadocio
hot and cold.. 4. vary 5. shift, waver
6. seesaw 7. quibble 9. fluctuate,
vacillate 12. shilly-shally
out.. 5. douse, snuff 10. extinguish
blower... 4. blow, gale, wind 5. whale
6. puffer (fish), squall 7. bellows,
bloomer, blowgun, boastor, monsoon,
tornado 8. braggart 9. hurricane,
whirlwind, windstorm
11. braggadocio
blow up... 4. fail, rage 5. blast, bloat,
burst, fluff 6. berate, dilate, excite,
expand, forget, praise 7. blow out,
enlarge, explode, inflate 8. demolish,
detonate, disprove 9. fulminate
blowzy... 5. dowdy, ruddy, tacky
6. coarse, frowzy, sloppy, untidy
7. unkempt 8. careless, frumpish,
slovenly 10. disheveled, slatternly
blubber... 3. fat 4. weep 6. bubble
7. whimper 8. whale fat
blubbery... 3. fat 7. swollen
9. quivering 10. gelatinous
bludgeon... 3. bat, hit 4. beat, club,
mace 5. billy, bully, stick 6. coerce,
cudgel, menace 8. browbeat,
bulldoze, threaten 9. truncheon
10. intimidate, shillelagh (shillalah)
blue... 4. anil, baby, bice, bleu, navy
5. azure, beryl, Ching, email, king's,
merle, perse, royal, smalt 6. cobalt,
cyanic, French, indigo, powder
7. aniline, azarite, cesious, Dresden,
Dumont's, gobelin, lobelia, mesange,
peacock, Persian 8. caesious,

calamine, cerulean, Coventry, electric, lavender, midnight, pavonine, sapphire, wisteria 9. turquoise 10. aquamarine, cornflower

blue (pert to)... see also *Blue*
baby.. 8. cyanotic
bonnet.. 3. cap 4. Scot 6. flower (Texas State) 8. Scotsman, titmouse
china.. 7. Nanking
circle (archery).. 6. target
day.. 6. Monday
emblem of.. 6. Oxford 9. Cambridge
grass.. 3. poa
ground.. 10. kimberlite
hero.. 9. Bluebeard
melancholy.. 3. sad 6. gloomy 7. pensive, wistful 8. tristful 9. cheerless, depressed, penseroso 10. atrabiliar 11. atrabilious, melancholic 13. hypochondriac
nose.. 4. snob 5. prude 7. Puritan 10. goody–goody 11. Nova Scotian
pencil.. 4. dele, edit 6. delete, excise, revise
print.. 4. plan, plot 5. graph 6. layout 7. diagram, program 8. schedule 9. cyanotype 10. master plan, photograph, photoprint
ribbon.. 5. award, badge 10. cordon bleu, decoration
skin.. 5. livid
sky.. 5. ether, vault 6. caelum, heaven, welkin 7. the blue 8. empyrean 9. firmament 10. blue yonder, the heavens
stocking.. 4. blue 6. pedant 7. bas bleu 8. Gamaliel (Bib) 9. formalist, pedagogue 10. Parliament

Blue (pert to)...
Boy.. 8. painting (Gainsborough)
Grass State.. 8. Kentucky
Grotto site.. 5. Capri
Law State.. 11. Connecticut

Bluebeard's wife... 6. Fatima
blue–gray... 7. cesious (caesious)
blue–green... 8. calamine
bluff... 4. bank (steep), crag, curt, dupe, fool, rude, wall 5. brash, cliff, frank, gruff, krans, sheer, short 6. abrupt, crusty 7. beguile, blinder, blinker, bluffer, bluster, brusque, deceive, pretend, uncivil 8. impolite 9. bamboozle, blusterer, charlatan, falseness, four–flush, precipice 11. four–flusher 13. unceremonious
bluffer... 5. quack 9. blusterer, charlatan 10. mountebank 11. four–flusher
bluffness... 6. candor 9. bluntness 10. abruptness 11. brusqueness
blunder... 3. err, mix 4. bull, goof, slip 5. boner, botch, error, misdo 6. boo–boo, bungle, fumble 7. faux pas, mistake, stumble 8. flounder, solecism (speech) 9. mismanage
blunt... 4. curt, dull, open 5. bluff, frank, gruff, plain 6. benumb, candid, deaden, obtund, obtuse, snippy, stupid, weaken 7. artless, brusque, sincere 8. hebetate 9. ingenuous 13. unceremonious
blur... 3. bog, dim, hum 4. blob, blot,

film, mist, soil, spot 5. blear, cloud, smear, stain 6. blotch, darken, mackle 7. blemish, dimness, obscure, splotch 9. disfigure
blurb... 2. ad 4. plug 5. boost, brief 6. notice 7. write–up 8. ballyhoo 9. publicity 12. announcement, commendation 13. advertisement
blurt out... 4. blab, bolt 7. blunder 9. ejaculate
blush... 4. glow, look 5. bloom, color, flush 6. glance, mantle, redden 7. modesty, redness 9. suffusion
blushing... 4. meek 5. ruddy 6. modest 7. roseate 8. flushing, sheepish 9. reddening, rubescent 10. erubescent
bluster... 4. blow, bray, fume, rage, rant, roar 5. broil, bully, furor, noise 6. flurry, hoopla, hubbub, squall, tumult 7. roister, swagger, turmoil 8. boasting, bullying, threaten 9. agitation, confusion 10. swaggering, turbulence 11. rodomontade
blusterer... 5. bully 7. boaster 8. blowhard, braggart 9. roisterer, swaggerer 11. braggadocio 12. swashbuckler
bo... 4. hobo 5. buddy, tramp 9. sundowner 10. landlouper 11. bindle stiff
bo, boh (Burma)... 5. chief 6. leader 7. captain
boa... 5. aboma, scarf (feather), snake 8. anaconda
boar... 3. hog, sus 4. apex, hure (head) 5. swine 6. barrow, hogget (2–year) 9. hoggaster (3–year)
board... 4. deal, doll, feed, lath, side, slat, wood 5. curia (anc), enter, forum, meals, plank, table 6. border, lumber, timber 7. binding (book), council, lodging 8. approach, exchange (Finan), tribunal 9. committee, provision 11. accommodate, bed and board, directorate, refreshment 14. accommodations
boast... 4. brag, crow 5. extol, exult, glory, pride, vapor, vaunt 6. menace 7. bluster, swagger 8. braggart, flourish 9. gasconade
boastful... 4. vain 8. bragging 9. conceited, overproud, presuming 11. thrasonical 12. vainglorious 13. self–important
boat... 3. ark, bac, gig, tub, tug 4. brig, dhow, dory, junk, punt, saic, scow, ship, trow, yawl 5. aviso, balsa, barge, canoe, craft, dandy, dhoni, dingy, ferry, kayak, ketch, liner, oolak, praam, scull, skiff, U–boat, umiak, xebec, yacht 6. argosy, baidak, bateau, convoy, cutter, dinghy, dogger, launch, mistic, oomiac, packet, randan, sampan, settee, tanker, vessel, whaler 7. bidarka, caravel, coracle (anc), cruiser, gondola, masoola, piragua, pirogue, rowboat, scooter, shallop, trawler, tugboat, warship

8. dahabeah, man–of–war, palander,
sailboat, seaplane 9. catamaran,
destroyer, steamship, submarine
10. brigantine, windjammer
11. side–wheeler, treckschuyt
boat (pert to)...
boatswain.. 5. bosun 6. serang
captain.. 4. rais (reis) 6. master
7. skipper
deck.. 4. poop 6. flight 9. promenade
man.. 5. rower 6. bargee 7. ferrier,
oarsman 9. gondolier, yachtsman
sail.. 3. jib 4. main, reef 6. lateen,
mizzen
shaped.. 9. navicella, navicular
side.. 7. gunwale
song.. 7. chantey 9. barcarole
bob... 3. bow, cut, nod, rap, tap
4. bend, jeer, jerk, jest 5. cheat,
filch, float, flout, plumb, shake, taunt,
trick 6. bobble, curtsy, delude,
hairdo, kowtow, sinker, weight
7. haircut 8. coiffure, greeting,
shilling 9. obeisance, oscillate
bobac... 6. pahmi 8. marmot
bobber... 4. duck (ruddy) 5. float
6. bobfly 7. dropper 8. deadhead
bobbin... 3. pin 4. coil, cord, pirn,
reel 5. braid, spool 7. spindle
bobble... 3. bob, dib (angling) 4. muff
5. shake 6. boggle, bungle, fumble
7. blunder 9. oscillate
bobby... 6. peeler 9. policeman
Boche... 6. German (a)
bodach... 5. churl, clown 7. bugaboo
bodacious... 4. bold 8. insolent,
reckless 9. audacious, bumptious,
insulting 12. contumelious
bode... 5. augur 6. divine 7. portend,
presage 8. forebode, foreshow,
foretell 13. prognosticate
bodhisattva... 8. Buddhism
13. Enlightenment
bodice... 4. belt 5. stays, waist
6. basque, girdle 7. corsage,
garment
bodily... 6. carnal 7. fleshly, somatic
8. corporal, material, physical
9. corporeal 10. completely
boding... 7. ominous 10. foreboding,
portentous, prediction, prognostic
12. apprehension
bodkin... 3. awl 6. dagger, needle
7. hairpin, poniard 8. stiletto
9. eyeleteer
body... 3. man 4. deha (Theos), homo,
soma 5. being, human, trunk
6. corpse, entity, licham, mortal,
person 7. carcass 8. creature,
organism 9. substance 10. individual
13. corpus delicti 14. substantiality
body (pert to)...
armed.. 5. corps, posse
business.. 7. company
11. cooperation 12. organization
celestial.. 3. sun 4. luna, star
5. comet 6. meteor, planet
church.. 4. nave
dead.. 6. corpse 7. cadaver
division (mollusk).. 7. prosoma
injury.. 6. mayhem, trauma
petrified.. 6. fossil

political.. 4. weal 6. senate 7. cabinet
11. legislature
small.. 6. nanoid 8. dwarfish
body of...
people.. 3. mob 4. band, bevy, gang,
host 5. bunch, crowd, flock, group,
horde 6. rabble, throng 9. multitude
singers.. 5. choir 6. chorus
soldiers.. 4. file 5. corps, squad,
troop 7. brigade, company, platoon
8. division
water.. 3. bay, sea 4. lake, pond,
pool 5. fiord (fjord), inlet, ocean
6. lagoon 9. reservoir
Boeotian (pert to)...
city.. 5. Ionia (Dist) 6. Thebes
figurine.. 7. Tanagra
king (Myth).. 6. Ogyges
Boer (pert to)...
General, statesman.. 5. Botha
language.. 4. Taal 9. Afrikaans
War site.. 9. Ladysmith (S Afr)
bog... 3. bug, fen 4. blei, bold, holm,
mire, moor, moss 5. ooze, quag, sink
6. jheel, marsh, saucy, swamp
6. morass, slough 8. quagmire
9. everglade
bogey, bogie, bogy... 3. par 5. Devil
6. goblin 7. bugaboo, bugbear
boggle... 3. shy 4. foil, quip 5. botch,
cavil, demur, parry, pause, start
6. bicker, bungle, falter, object,
shrink 7. dispute, quibble, scruple
8. hesitate, sidestep 9. dissemble,
objection 10. difficulty, equivocate
bogglebo... 5. bogle 7. bugaboo,
specter 9. hobgoblin, scarecrow
bogus... 4. fake, mock, sham
5. phony, queer 8. spurious
10. apocryphal, factitious, fictitious
11. counterfeit
bohawn... 3. hut 5. cabin 7. cottage
Bohemia...
capital.. 6. Prague
city.. 5. Praha 6. Aussig, Pilsen
7. Budweis, Teplitz 11. Reichenberg
dance.. 6. redowa
measure.. 5. stopa 6. merice
mineral.. 6. egeran
reformer.. 4. Huss
river.. 4. Elbe, Iser 6. Moldau
tribe (anc).. 4. Boii
vagabond.. 5. gypsy (gipsy)
bohunk... 6. Slovak 7. laborer
8. Bohemian, Croatian (formerly)
boil... 3. sty (styr) 4. buck, cook,
fume, stew 5. churn, steam
6. bubble, pimple, seethe 7. bristle
8. furuncle
boiling... 5. angry 7. cooking, flushed,
stewing 8. seething, sizzling
9. agitating, ebullient 10. smoldering
bois (Fr)... 4. wood
boisterous... 4. loud 5. noisy, rough,
rowdy 6. stormy 7. blatant, excited,
furious, roaring, violent 8. brawling
9. clamorous, turbulent
10. blustering, roisterous,
tumultuous, unyielding
12. obstreperous
Bokhara (pert to)...
fur.. 9. astrakhan, broadtail

rug .. 8. Turkoman
sheep .. 7. karakul (caracul)
site .. 4. Asia (Russ)
bola ... 4. tree (fiber) 6. weapon
bold ... 4. deep, pert, rash, rude, snug
5. steep, stout 6. abrupt, brazen,
daring, heroic, raised 7. dashing,
defiant, eminent, forward, salient,
valiant 8. fearless, immodest,
impudent, in relief, intrepid, powerful,
repoussé, stalwart 9. audacious,
confident, dauntless, shameless,
unabashed 10. courageous
11. lionhearted, outstanding,
precipitous, venturesome
12. presumptuous, stouthearted
boldness ... 5. valor 6. defial, virtue
7. bravery, courage 8. audacity,
defiance, salience, temerity
9. assurance, gallantry, hardihood,
immodesty, impudence
10. brazenness, confidence,
effrontery, prominence, resolution
11. forwardness, intrepidity,
obviousness 12. protuberance
13. dauntlessness
14. courageousness
bolero ... 5. dance, music, waist
6. jacket
boliche ... 3. inn 5. bowls
Bolivia ...
capital .. 5. La Paz (Polit), Oruro (anc),
Sucre (law)
hero .. 5. Sucre 7. Bolivar, Pizarro
Indian tribe .. 3. Uro 4. Iten, Moxo
lake .. 8. Titicaca (world's highest)
mountain .. 5. Andes 6. Sorata
8. Illimani
product .. 3. tin 8. tungsten
river . 4. Beni 6. Blanco
bolo ... 5. knife 7. machete 8. pacifist
(Bolo Pasha, traitor) 9. defeatist
Bolshevik, bolshevik ... 7. Marxian,
radical (Bolsheviki) 9. Communist
(1918), Socialist 13. revolutionist
14. Social Democrat 18. Third
International
Bolshevist (Communist) leader ...
5. Lenin 6. Stalin 7. Kosygin
8. Bulganin 9. Krushchev
bolster ... 3. pad 4. bear, hold
5. boost 6. pillow 7. cushion,
support, sustain 8. maintain
bolt ... 3. bar 4. dart, flee, lock, roll,
sift 5. arrow, rivet, scram, screw,
shaft, speed 6. decamp, devour,
faster, flight, pintle, secede, staple,
toggle 7. missile, padlock 8. firebolt,
separate 10. projectile 11. eat
greedily, fulguration, thunderbolt
bolus ... 4. bite, clay, clod, food
(chewed), mass, pill 6. tablet, troche
8. mouthful
bomb ... 3. dud, egg 5. shell 6. petard
7. grenade, missile 8. divebomb,
fireball, surprise 9. bombshell,
pineapple 10. projectile
bomb (type of) ... 4. time 5. stink
6. aerial, atomic, rocket 7. nuclear,
tear gas 8. hydrogen 10. demolition
bombard ... 3. zap 5. blitz, shell
6. assail, attack, strafe 7. atomize,

barrage 9. cannonade
bombardier ... 5. jager 6. bomber,
gunner 9. cannoneer, musketeer
12. artilleryman
bombast ... 4. blow, brag, rage, rant,
rave 5. boast 7. fustian 8. boasting,
inflated, stuffing (hist) 9. bombastic,
turgidity 11. rodomontade
12. magniloquent 13. grandiloquent
bombastic ... 5. tumid 7. orotund,
pompous, stilted 8. boastful, inflated
12. high–sounding 13. grandiloquent
Bombay ...
capital of .. 11. Maharashtra (state)
college .. 11. Elphinstone
duck .. 10. lizard fish
hemp .. 4. sunn 6. ambary
merchant .. 7. Arab
seaport of .. 5. India
bomber ... 5. stuka 10. bombardier
Bombyx ... 4. eria, moth 8. silkworm
bona fide ... 4. real 7. genuine
9. authentic 10. constantly, faithfully,
legitimate
bona mano ... 3. tip 8. gratuity
bon ami ... 5. lover 6. friend
10. good friend, sweetheart
bonanza ... 6. riches 8. El Dorado
(Myth), gold mine (US)
Bonanza State ... 7. Montana
bond ... 3. tie, vow 4. duty, gyve, link,
mise, pact, yoke 5. chain, nexus,
rente 6. fetter, league 7. entente,
manacle, shackle 8. contract,
covenant, relation, security (Finan)
9. agreement, captivity
10. allegiance, connection
11. association, certificate
bondage ... 4. yoke 6. chains
7. serfdom, slavery 9. captivity,
restraint, servitude, thralldom
11. enslavement, subjugation
bondman, bondsman ... 4. esne, serf
5. churl, helot, slave 6. thrall, vassal
7. servant 8. bailsman 9. guarantor
bone ... 2. os 4. chip 5. boner
6. dollar, osteon 7. blunder, counter
(game), ossicle 8. skeleton, wishbone
9. funny bone (humerus), pygostyle
(bird's), whalebone
bone (Anat) ... 3. rib 4. ulna 5. femur,
ilium, incus (ear), malar, skull, spine,
talus, tibia 6. carpus, coccyx, fibula,
tarsus 7. humerus, maxilla, patella,
scapula, sternum 8. astragal, clavicle,
mandible, phalange, vertebra
9. calcaneus, occipital
10. metacarpus, metatarsus
bone (pert to) ...
bonelike .. 6. osteal 7. osteoid
cell .. 10. osteoblast
china .. 7. English
curvature .. 8. lordosis
divination .. 10. osteomancy
fish .. 9. operculum
marrow .. 7. medulla
process .. 7. mastoid 8. alveolar
9. apophysis
science .. 9. osteology
surgery .. 9. osteotomy 11. osteoclasis
12. osteoplastic
tissue .. 6. ossein

tumor.. 7. osteoma
bones... 4. body, dice, form, ossa
  5. cubes, frame, money, torso, trunk
  6. end man, refuse 7. carcass,
  ivories 8. skeleton 11. rattlebones
boneyard... 4. bank (game)
  8. golgotha 9. graveyard
  10. necropolis 11. polyandrium
bonhomie... 8. pleasant 9. good
  humor 10. affability, amiability
Bonhomme Richard... 4. ship
  8. man—of—war (1779), (opponent of
  Serapis)
bonito, bonita... 4. nice 6. pretty
  8. mackerel, skipjack
bon mot... 9. witticism 10. jeu
  d'esprit 11. smart saying
bonne... 5. mammy 9. nursemaid
  10. baby sitter 11. maidservant
bonnet... 3. cap, hat 4. coif, hood,
  poke 5. toque 7. chapeau
  9. headdress
bonnetman... 10. Highlander
bonny, bonnie... 3. bon 4. good
  6. plump 0. comely, lively, pretty
  7. healthy, très bon 8. handsome
  9. beautiful
Bontok... 7. Malayan (Luzon)
  10. Indonesian
bonus... 3. tip 4. cash, gift 5. batta,
  bribe, extra, share, stock (Finan)
  7. cumshaw, douceur, premium,
  rake–off, subsidy 8. dividend, gratuity
  9. Trinkgeld 10. honorarium
bon vivant... 7. epicure, gourmet
  8. gourmand, hedonist, sybarite
  10. boonfellow, good fellow,
  voluptuary 12. Heliogabalus (anc)
bony... 4. hard, thin 6. osteal, skinny
  7. osseous 8. rawboned, skeletal
bonze (Far East)... 2. bo 4. monk
boo... 4. hoot, jeer, razz 7. catcall,
  feather (ostrich) 9. raspberry
  10. Bronx cheer
boob... 4. dupe, fool, goon, jerk
  5. chump, dunce 6. nitwit
  7. fathead 9. schlemiel, simpleton
boobook... 3. owl 8. morepork
booby hatch... 3. can, jug 4. jail
  6. asylum, cooler, prison
  8. hoosegow, madhouse
  11. institution (mental)
boodle... 3. sop 4. loot, swag
  5. booty, bribe, bunch, crowd, graft,
  money (hush) 6. spoils 8. caboodle
  10. pork barrel 11. counterfeit
boohoo... 3. rob 4. bawl, hoot, weep
  5. shout 8. sailfish
book... 2. mo (abbr) 3. day 4. hire,
  opus, tome 5. album, atlas, Bible,
  canto, diary, folio, liber, novel
  6. agenda, engage, ledger, manual,
  missal, primer, record, sign up,
  volume 7. diurnal, journal, mystery
  8. brochure, libretto, register,
  schedule, songbook, whodunit
  9. paperback, storybook
  10. literature, memorandum
  11. publication
book (pert to)...
announcement.. 5. blurb
back.. 5. spine

binder.. 12. bibliopegist
binding devise.. 7. trindle
collector.. 10. bibliothec
  12. bibliomaniac 14. bibliothecaire
cover.. 5. recto 6. jacket
destroyer.. 11. biblioclast
division.. 7. chapter
lore.. 10. bibliology
lover.. 11. bibliophile
one versed in.. 11. bibliognost
page.. 5. folio
seller.. 10. bibliopole (rare books)
sheath.. 5. forel
size.. 6. quarto
stealer.. 11. biblioklept
style.. 6. Aldine 8. Etruscan
  9. Arabesque
treatise.. 8. isagogue
worshiper.. 11. bibliolater
writer.. 13. bibliographer
book (religious)... 4. Ordo 5. Bible,
  Kells, Tobit 6. Esdras, Mormon
  7. Psalter 8. Holy Writ
  9. Apocrypha, Catechism Testament
  10. Pentateuch, Scriptures
Book of
award (Harvard).. 5. detur
Concord.. 8. Lutheran
Discipline.. 12. Presbyterian
Hours.. 5. Horae
Moses (Laws).. 10. Pentateuch
Psalms.. 7. Psalter
the Dead.. 12. Pyramid Texts
boom... 3. hum 4. gain, peal, raft,
  roar, spar, zoom 5. boost, cable,
  speed, sprit, withe 6. thrive, upturn
  7. pontoon, resound, thunder
  8. bowsprit, flourish, increase
  9. cannonade, Golden Age, outrigger
  10. navigation, prosperity
boomerang... 6. rosile 7. rebound
  8. backfire, ricochet
Boomer State... 8. Oklahoma
boon... 3. gay 4. bene, gift, good,
  nice 5. favor, jolly 6. jovial, kindly
  7. benefit, gleeful, godsend, present
  8. blessing 9. convivial
  11. benefaction
boor... 3. cad, oaf 4. hick, lout
  5. churl, clown, yokel 6. rustic
  7. bumpkin, cauboge, peasant, ruffian
  9. roughneck, vulgarian
  10. clodhopper, husbandman
boorish... 4. rude 5. gawky, surly
  6. clumsy, rustic, sullen 7. awkward,
  crabbed, loutish, uncouth 8. churlish,
  inurbane, lubberly, ungainly
  9. farmerish, unrefined
  11. countrified
boost... 4. help, hike, lift, plug, push
  5. heist, raise, shove 6. assist,
  thrust 7. commend, hearten, inspire,
  promote, upswing 8. advocate,
  increase 9. promotion, publicize
  10. assistance 11. advancement
  12. commendation
boot... 3. pac 4. kick, pack, sack,
  shoe 5. armor, bonus, jemmy, kamik,
  wader 6. buskin, fumble, rookie,
  sheath 7. dismiss, recruit, trainee
  8. balmoral, enlistee, inductee,
  napoleon 9. discharge

booth... 3. hut, pew 4. crib, loge
5. stall, stand, store 6. manger
11. compartment
booty... 4. gain, loot, pelf, swag
5. graft, prize, spoil 6. spoils
7. pillage, plunder
booze... 4. bout 5. drink, spree
6. liquor 8. potation
boozer... 3. pub, sot 5. toper
6. barfly, bibber, saloon 7. guzzler,
reveler, tippler 8. drunkard
9. alcoholic, inebriate
11. dipsomaniac
Bordeaux, France...
capital.. 7. Gironde
entrance gate.. 16. Porte de
Bourgogne
Roman name.. 9. Burdigala
wine.. 5. Cotes, Medoc, Palus
6. claret (best–known), Graves
border... 3. hem, rim, tip 4. abut,
brow, dado, edge, line, rand, rund
5. bound, brink, flank, limit, marge,
shore, skirt, touch, verge, wings
6. adjoin, fringe, margin, ruffle
7. bordure, confine, flounce, selvage,
valance 8. boundary, frontier,
neighbor 9. periphery 10. borderland,
sidepieces
border (pert to)...
heraldry.. 4. orle 7. bordure
lace.. 5. picot 9. hemstitch
picture.. 3. mat 4. orle
stamps (PO).. 8. tressure
wall.. 4. dado
Border Country (Russ)... 6. Latvia,
Poland 7. Estonia, Finland, Romania
9. Lithuania
bordering... 4. near 6. edging
7. binding 8. abutting, adjacent,
marginal, skirting, trimming
9. adjoining, immediate
10. contiguous
Border State (Civil War Era)...
8. Arkansas, Delaware, Kentucky,
Maryland, Missouri, Virginia
9. Tennessee 13. North Carolina
bore... 3. irk, tap 4. drip, hole, pest,
pill, ream 5. auger, drill, eagre (tidal
wave), weary 6. bother, cavity, pierce
7. caliber, carried 8. diameter,
nuisance, ordnance (anc), puncture,
terebate 9. penetrate, perforate, tidal
wave, worriment 10. capability
11. perforation
boredom... 5. ennui 6. tedium
boring... 3. dry 5. yawny 6. tiring
7. irksome, tedious 8. piercing,
tiresome, wearying 11. penetrating
boring tool... 3. awl, bit 4. rime (Eng)
5. auger, drill 6. gimlet, reamer,
wimble
born... 3. ean, nee 4. bred, foal, lamb
5. calve, hatch, issue 7. hatched,
quicken 9. originate
born (pert to)...
after father's death.. 10. posthumous
again (Theos).. 7. renewed
high.. 8. imperial 11. to the purple
14. porphyrogenite
in the country.. 10. rurigenous
nature.. 6. inborn

well.. 7. eugenic
borne... 4. held 6. eolian, upheld
7. aeolian, carried, endured
8. produced 9. cherished, supported
10. maintained
borné... 6. narrow 7. limited
12. narrow–minded
Borneo...
aborigine.. 4. Dyak (Dayak), Iban
5. Dusun, Malay
ape.. 9. orangutan (orangoutang)
island of.. 11. Archipelago (Malay)
mountain.. 8. Kinibalu
pirate tribe (anc).. 5. Bajau 9. Samal
Laut
protectorate.. 6. Brunei 7. Sarawak
river.. 6. Rejang
rubber.. 9. gutta susu
sea.. 4. Java, Sulu 10. South China
tree (antproof).. 7. billian
borough... 4. burg, town, ward
5. burgh, manor 6. suffix
8. precinct, township 10. municipium
11. corporation 12. municipality
borrow... 4. copy, take 5. adopt,
steal, touch 8. simulate
10. plagiarize, substitute
11. appropriate
borsch, borscht... 4. soup (beet juice)
6. ragout
borzoi... 9. wolfhound
Bos... 2. ox 3. cow 4. beef, calf, neat
6. cattle 8. ruminant 9. quadruped
bosh... 4. bull, bunk 5. trash
6. humbug, piffle 7. baloney
8. buncombe, falderal, nonsense
9. poppycock 10. balderdash
bosky... 5. braky, bushy, shady, tipsy,
woody 6. woodsy 7. fuddled,
shadowy 11. intoxicated (Eng)
Bosnia...
capital.. 8. Sarajevo
native.. 5. Croat 8. Adriatic, Croatian
race.. 4. tall 14. Slavic–speaking
republic (present).. 10. Yugoslavia
site.. 15. Balkan Peninsula
bosom... 4. bust 5. chest 6. breast,
dickey, spirit 7. cherish, embrace
8. inner man, interior 9. enclosure
(loving), innermost 10. affections
12. heartstrings
boss... 4. dean 6. manage, master
7. foreman 8. director 9. supervise
14. superintendent
boss (pert to)...
architecture.. 4. knob, stud
12. protuberance
politics.. 4. whip 6. leader 7. cacique
(W Indies) 8. dictator
sculpture.. 5. chase, raise 6. emboss,
relief 7. relievo 8. ornament
shield.. 4. umbo
bosthoon (Anglo–Ir)... 4. boor, dolt
5. clout
Boston...
building (Hist).. 11. Faneuil Hall
14. Old North Church
capital of.. 13. Massachusetts
famed names.. 6. Holmes, Lowell
7. Emerson 8. Whittier 9. Hawthorne
10. Longfellow
hero.. 10. Paul Revere

history.. 8. Massacre (1770), Tea
Party (1773)
Puritan leader.. 8. Winthrop (Gov)
river.. 7. Charles
botany (pert to)...
development (plant).. 7. peloria
10. craticular
research terms.. 7. ecology
8. cytology, taxonomy 9. pathology
10. morphology
science.. 7. biology 9. plant life
Botany Bay...
colony (original).. 5. penal
discoverer.. 4. Cook (1770)
settlers.. 8. convicts (Eng)
site.. 9. Australia
botch... 3. fix, mar 4. hash, mend,
mess, mull 5. patch, spoil 6. boggle,
bungle, fiasco, goof up, muddle
7. blunder, failure
both... 3. two 4. duad, pair 5. twain
6. as well 7. equally
bother... 3. ado, ail, nag 4. fuss,
to–do 5. annoy, tease 6. badger,
bustle, harass, molest, pester, pother
7. concern, confuse, fluster, torment,
trouble 8. bewilder, distress, irritate,
nuisance 9. commotion
10. discommode, excitement,
perplexity 11. botheration,
disturbance 13. inconvenience
bothersome... 6. trying 7. galling,
irksome, onerous 8. annoying
9. difficult, worrisome 10. disturbing
11. troublesome
both sexes... 7. epicene, sexless
10. effeminate
bo tree (Buddh)... 5. pipal 6. sacred
(at Buddh Gaya)
bottle... 3. pig 4. lota, vial 5. cruet,
flask, gourd, phial 6. carate, carboy,
flagon, lagena, matara, vacuum
7. ampoule (ampule), ampulla (anc),
costrel, enclose 8. borachio,
calabash, decanter, preserve
9. aryballus (anc)
bottom... 3. bed (water) 4. base, glen,
hulk, less, root, rump, vale, vlei
5. basin, fanny, floor, marsh, nadir
6. coulee, hopper (RR) 7. bedrock,
channel 9. underside 10. nethermost
bottomless... 7. abysmal, abyssal
8. baseless 9. plumbless, soundless
10. fathomless 12. unfathomable
boudoir... 7. bedroom, cabinet,
chamber 10. bedchamber
bouffant... 4. full 7. bulging 9. puffed
out
bough... 4. fork, limb, spur, twig
5. shoot, spray, sprig 6. branch
8. offshoot
bought... 8. boughten (dial)
9. purchased (see also *buy*)
bouillabaisse... 7. chowder (fish)
boulevard... 4. pike 7. highway
8. highroad, turnpike
12. thoroughfare
bounce... 3. hop 4. bang, brag,
bump, jump, kick, leap, snap
5. bound, burst, carom, eject, shake,
thump, verve 6. levity, recoil, spring
7. bluster, bravado, rebound

8. buoyancy, outburst, ricochet
9. discharge, lightness 10. resilience
11. fanfaronade, ostentation,
springiness 16. lightheartedness
bouncer... 4. liar 5. bully 6. fibber,
ouster 7. boaster, chucker, whopper
8. braggart, fanfaron 9. falsehood
bound... 3. hop, run 4. jump, leap,
skip, tied 5. ambit, limit, speed,
taped, tiled (secrecy), vault, verge
6. border, bounce, bourne, domain,
hurdle, spring, sprint 7. barrier,
certain, confine, cramped, limited,
obliged, pledged, rebound, secured,
trussed 8. beholden, boundary,
confined, enclosed, frontier, precinct,
promised, resolved, surround
9. committed, duty–bound,
encompass (incompass)
10. borderland, determined,
restrained, restricted 11. termination
12. circumscribe
boundary... 3. end, rim 4. edge, mere
(obs), mete, term, wall 5. ambit,
bourn, fence, limit, march, verge
7. barrier 8. terminus 9. perimeter
11. conterminal, termination
13. circumference
bounder... 3. cad 4. snob 6. rotter
7. epicier, parvenu, upstart
bounding (Mus)... 8. saltando
boundless... 4. vast 7. endless
8. infinite, termless 9. limitless,
unlimited 10. unconfined
11. illimitable 12. interminable,
unfathomable
bounds... 4. pale 6. frames, limits,
skirts 7. borders, margins
8. confines, outlines 9. outskirts
10. delineated 11. limitations
bounteous... 5. ample 6. freely, lavish
7. liberal 8. generous, prodigal
9. bountiful, plentiful 10. munificent
11. extravagant
bountiful... 4. rich 7. copious, fertile,
liberal, teeming, uberous
8. abundant, fruitful, generous,
prolific 9. bounteous, exuberant,
luxuriant, plentiful
bounty... 3. fee 4. gift 5. bonus
6. reward 7. largess, premium,
subsidy 8. gratuity, solatium, sportula
9. pourboire 10. generosity, liberality
11. beneficence 12. compensation
bouquet... 4. odor, posy 5. aroma,
cigar, spray 7. corsage, flowers,
incense, nosegay, perfume
9. fragrance, redolence
10. compliment
Bourbon, bourbon...
ancient.. 7. Reunion (Isl)
dynasty.. 5. Spain 6. France, Naples
famed personage.. 4. Duke
13. French General
famed ruins.. 7. castles (Dukes')
liquor.. 6. whisky (whiskey)
rose.. 9. Le Phoenix
bourd... 3. fun 4. jest 7. mockery
bourdon... 4. stop (organ) 5. baton,
music (bagpipe), spear, staff
6. burden (Fr), cudgel
bourgeois... 4. type (size)

8. commoner 9. common man,
plutocrat 10. capitalist
11. middle–class, proletarian
bourn, bourne... 3. aim 4. goal, port
5. bound, brook, limit, realm
6. arroyo, stream 7. rivulet
8. boundary 11. destination
bourock... 3. hut 4. heap (stone)
5. crowd, mound 7. cluster
Bourse... 5. Board 8. Exchange
13. Stock Exchange
bouse... 3. cup 4. haul (Naut), swig,
tope 5. booze, drink, heave
6. beaker 7. carouse
bouser... 5. toper 6. boozer, bursar
7. fuddler, swigger
bout... 2. go 3. act, war 4. coup,
fray, game, spar, turn 5. cycle, fight,
match, revel, round, scrap, set–to,
spree, trial 6. fracas, inning, series,
stroke 7. attempt, circuit, contest,
exploit 8. conflict, maneuver, rotation
9. encounter 10. enterprise, prize
fight 11. celebration
boutade... 4. whim 5. dance, prank
7. caprice 8. outbreak
11. composition (Mus)
boutonniere... 6. flower 7. bouquet,
nosegay 8. incision 10. buttonhole
bovine... 2. ox 3. Bos, cow, yak
4. bull, dull, goat, kine, zebu
5. bison, dogie, steer, stirk, zebus
6. catalo, cattle, oxlike, stolid, stupid
7. bullock, cattalo, taurine, vaccine
8. maverick, sluggish 10. complacent
11. beef–brained
bow... 3. arc, bob, nod 4. arch, beak,
bend, knot, node, prow 5. bulge,
curve, debut, embow, kneel, stoop,
yield 6. assent, convex, curtsy,
encore, kowtow, salaam, submit,
weapon 7. curtain (Theat), incline,
rainbow 8. crossbow, greeting
9. obeisance 11. fiddlestick 12. bow
and scrape
bow (out)... 4. exit 6. depart
7. concede, dismiss
Bow Bells (pert to)...
area.. 10. cockneydom
bells of.. 9. Bow Church (St Mary le
Bow)
city.. 6. London
bowels... 3. pit 4. guts 5. abyss,
chasm, depth 7. innards, insides,
viscera 8. entrails, interior (earth)
10. compassion (Shak), tenderness
bower... 5. abode, arbor, cards
(game), kiosk 6. alcove, pandal
7. retreat, shelter 11. summerhouse
bowfin... 4. Amia 7. mudfish
bowhead (Arctic)... 10. Right whale
Bowie, bowie (pert to)...
instrument.. 5. knife
knife inventor.. 5. Bowie (James)
Scottish.. 3. tub 4. cask 8. milk pail
State nickname.. 8. Arkansas
bowkail... 4. kale (kail) 7. cabbage
bowl... 3. cup, jug 4. ball, roll, vase
5. arena, basin, kitty (poker), mazer,
rogan 6. cavity, crater, hollow, patina
(anc), vessel 7. stadium 8. washbowl
9. washbasin 10. hippodrome,

receptacle 12. amphitheater
Bowl (sports)...
Abilene.. 5. Pecan
Atlanta.. 5. Peach
Dallas.. 6. Cotton
El Paso.. 3. Sun
Honolulu.. 4. Hula
Houston.. 10. Bluebonnet
Jacksonville.. 5. Gator
Memphis.. 7. Liberty
Miami.. 6. Orange
Mobile.. 6. Senior
New Orleans.. 5. Sugar
Orlando.. 9. Tangerine
Pasadena.. 4. Rose
Sacramento.. 8. Camellia
bowlegged... 6. valgus
bowler... 3. hat 5. derby 6. kegler
7. trundle
bowling... 4. ball, rink 5. alley, green,
spare 6. strike 7. rolling, tenpins
8. ninepins 10. greensward,
playground
Bowling Green... 4. Park (Ky, NY)
bowsprit... 3. jib 4. boom 6. steeve
box... 2. ro (Jap) 3. bin, pew, pyx
4. arca (alms), cage, case, cist, cuff,
kist, kite, loge, safe, spar, tray
5. brace (faro), caddy (tea), cheat,
crate, stall, vault 6. buffet, carton,
casket, coffin, encase 7. confine,
enclose 8. bungalow 9. fisticuff
11. compartment
box (pert to)...
alms.. 4. arca
bed.. 7. springs
cosmetic.. 4. inro
floating.. 3. car (for fish)
lifesaving.. 9. faking box
railroad.. 6. boxcar 8. box wagon
resistance.. 8. rheostat
sewing.. 5. plait, pleat
sleigh.. 4. pung
sports.. 5. score
tea.. 5. caddy 8. canister
theater.. 4. loge, seat
tree.. 8. Buxaceae
boxer... 3. dog, pug 5. champ
6. miller 7. bruiser, fighter, sparrer
8. derby hat, pugilist 11. fisticuffer
12. prizefighter 13. militia member
(Chin)
boxer weight... 3. fly 5. heavy, light
6. bantam, middle, welter 7. feather
10. light heavy
boxing... 4. bout 5. match, set–to
7. contest, crating 8. pugilism,
sparring 10. encasement, fisticuffs
12. shadowboxing
boy... 2. bo 3. bat, bus, lad, tad, tot
4. nino, page, puer 5. child, gamin,
knave, rogue, water, youth
6. garçon, laddie, master, rascal,
shaver, urchin, varlet 7. callant,
gossoon 8. muchacho
boy (pert to)...
book author.. 5. Alger, Henty
errand.. 4. page 9. messenger
friend.. 4. beau 10. sweetheart
interjection.. 5. Oh boy
organization.. 6. Scouts
Scout founder.. 11. Baden–Powell

street.. 4. Arab 6. urchin
boycott... 3. ban 6. oppose, strike
9. blackball, ostracize
brace... 3. leg, tie, two 4. bind, cord,
gird, pair, prop, span, stay, yoke
5. spale, staff, stave, strut 6. couple
7. bandage, bracket, fulcrum, refresh,
rigging, support 8. encircle
9. reinforce, stimulate 10. invigorate,
recuperate, strengthen
bracelet... 5. armil, armor, chain
6. sankha 7. armilla 8. handcuff,
vambrace 10. calombigas
bracer... 4. prop 5. tonic 7. reviver,
support 8. pick–me–up, roborant
9. stimulant
bracing... 5. crisp, tonic 10. salubrious
11. stimulating 12. invigorating
bracken... 4. fern 5. brake, plaid
bracket... 4. mark 5. ancon, angle,
group, strut 6. corbel, sconce
7. fixture 11. electrolier
brackish... 4. foul 5. salty 7. saltish
8. nauseous 11. distasteful
bract... 4. leaf 5. glume, palea, palet
6. spathe 8. bractlet 9. bracteole
brad... 3. pin 4. nail 5. sprig
brae... 4. bank, down, hill, moor
5. slope 6. valley 8. hillside
brag... 4. crow 5. bluff, boast, vaunt
6. flaunt 7. blow off, bluster,
deceive, roister, swagger 8. braggart
9. gasconade 11. braggadocio
braggart... 4. brag 6. crower
7. boaster 8. boastful, fanfaron
9. blusterer, swaggerer
11. braggadocio 12. swashbuckler
bragging... 11. thrasonical
Brahma... 3. God 4. fowl 5. Hindu
Brahman (pert to)...
learned.. 6. pundit
precept.. 5. sutra 8. netineti
sacred book.. 4. Veda
Sanskrit scholar.. 6. pundit
Supreme soul.. 6. Brahma
title.. 3. Aya
Trinity.. 4. Siva 6. Brahma, Vishnu
woman created by.. 6. Alalya
Brahmin... 4. prig, snob 7. egghead
8. highbrow 10. high–hatter
12. intellectual
braid... 3. cue 4. cord, gimp, hair,
plat, trim 5. lacet, orris, plait, pleat,
queue, tress, twist, weave 6. oxreim,
sennit 7. entwine, outline, pigtail,
topknot 8. ornament, soutache
9. interlace 10. interweave
brain... 4. head, mind, nous
6. psyche, reason 9. intellect,
mentality 10. encephalon, vital organ
brain (pert to)...
canal.. 4. iter
case.. 3. pan 5. skull 7. cranium
division.. 8. cerebrum 10. cerebellum
11. pons Varolii 16. medulla
oblongata
matter.. 4. alba, dura, tela
operation.. 6. trepan 8. trephine
term.. 4. lobe, lura 6. sulcus
7. fissure 9. ventricle
11. convolution
tumor.. 6. glioma

X–ray.. 14. encephalograph
brainless... 4. dumb 5. dizzy, giddy,
silly 6. unwise 7. asinine, foolish,
witless 9. senseless 10. unthinking
11. thoughtless 14. scatterbrained
brainy... 5. smart 6. bright, clever
9. brilliant
brake... 4. cage, curb, drag, fern, reef,
skid, trap 5. check, delay, snare
6. bridle, retard 7. dilemma, thicket
9. canebrake 10. decelerate
bramble... 4. burr 5. berry, brier,
shrub (prickly), thorn 6. nettle
7. prickle, thicket 9. brierbush
10. blackberry 12. brambleberry
branch... 3. arm, set 4. axil, fork,
limb, rame, stem, twig, wing
5. bough, class, frond, ramus, shoot,
spray, sprig, vimen, withe 6. divide,
member, ramify, sprout, stolon,
stream, switch 7. descent, diverge,
lineage 8. category, division, offshoot
9. affiliate, bloodline, filiation
10. department, descendant,
triskelion (three branches)
Branchiata (Group)... 6. fishes
9. Crustacea 10. Amphibians
brand... 4. burn, iron, kind, mark,
sear, smit 5. label, stamp, sword,
torch 6. smirch, stigma 7. earmark,
feature, hot iron, quality 8. gridiron
(Hist), hallmark 9. trademark
10. stigmatize
brandish... 5. shake, swing, wield
6. flaunt 7. flutter, glitter 8. flourish
brandy... 6. cognac 7. rosolio (cordial)
8. rossolis 11. aguardiente
brash... 4. dash, rain, rash 5. gruff,
saucy, storm 6. scurry 7. brittle
(lumber) 8. impudent, tactless
9. impetuous
brass... 4. cash, gall 5. alloy, braze,
cheek, money, nerve, plate 6. latten,
ormolu, platen 8. brass hat, officers,
sisterce (anc coin) 9. impudence
10. instrument (wind)
brass (wind instrument)... 5. bugle
6. cornet, lituus (anc) 7. althorn,
brasses, clarion, saxhorn, trumpet
8. trombone 9. saxophone
10. flügelhorn, French horn
brasserie... 6. saloon 7. brewery
8. beer shop
brassy... 4. bold 6. aerose, brazen
8. impudent
brat... 3. bib, elf, imp 4. film, minx,
scum 5. apron, bairn, child, cloak,
minor 6. mantle 7. garment
8. clothing 9. offspring 14. enfant
terrible, whippersnapper
brattice... 7. support 9. partition
(mining) 10. breastwork
bravado... 6. bounce, daring, defial
7. bluster, bombast, bravery, bravura
8. defiance 11. braggadocio
brave... 4. bold, buck, dare, game,
hero, meet 5. boast, bravo, bully,
front, manly, showy, stout 6. daring,
endure, heroic, Indian 7. Amerind,
gallant, soldier, spartan, valiant,
warrior 8. confront, fearless, intrepid,
valorous 10. courageous, untimorous

12. stouthearted
bravery . . . **5.** valor **7.** bravado, bravura, courage
bravo . . . **3.** mug **4.** good, thug **5.** rough, tough **6.** bandit **7.** gorilla, ruffian **8.** assassin **9.** blusterer, cutthroat, roisterer, roughneck, swaggerer **11.** exclamation
bravura . . . **4.** dash **5.** macho **6.** daring **7.** bravado, bravery **10.** brilliance (Mus), confidence
brawl . . . **3.** row **4.** fray, fury, rage, riot **5.** broil, fight, furor, scold **6.** affray, clamor, fracas, hubbub, rumpus, shindy, tumult, uproar **7.** dispute, quarrel, rampage, turmoil, wrangle **10.** hullabaloo, turbulence **11.** altercation, embroilment
brawny . . . **5.** beefy, burly, lusty, thewy **6.** fleshy, robust, sinewy, strong, sturdy **7.** callous **8.** muscular, powerful, stalwart **9.** corpulent
bray . . . **4.** beat **5.** blare, bleat, grind, neigh **6.** heehaw, powder, thrash, whinny **9.** pulverize, triturate **12.** disintegrate
braze . . . **4.** weld **5.** plate (with metal) **6.** solder
brazen . . . **4.** bold, pert **5.** brass, brave, harsh **6.** brassy, cheeky, harden **7.** aweless, callous **8.** immodest, impudent, indurate, insolent, metallic **9.** bold–faced, shameless, unabashed **10.** unblushing **13.** bronze–colored, harsh–sounding
brazier . . . **5.** grill **6.** brazer **7.** hibachi **8.** barbecue, gridiron **10.** money chest (anc)
brazil . . . **3.** red **4.** wood (hard) **8.** dyestuff
Brazil . . . see also *Brazilian*
capital . . **8.** Brasilia **12.** Rio de Janeiro (old)
city . . **5.** Bahia, Belem **6.** Recife, Santos **8.** Sao Paulo **9.** Horizonte **11.** Porto Alegre, Sao Salvador
discoverer . . **6.** Cabral (1500)
Falls (world wonder) . . **6.** Iguacu
lake . . **12.** Lago dos Patos
product . . **6.** coffee
river . . **5.** Negro **6.** Amazon, Branco, Paraná **7.** Madeira, Orinoco **8.** Paraguay **9.** Tocantins
Brazilian (pert to) . . .
aborigine . . **5.** Carib
ant (powerful) . . **9.** tucandera
bird . . **3.** ani, ara **5.** arara, macaw **6.** cuckoo, darter, tiribo **7.** maracan, sierema
crab (land) . . **8.** horseman
dance . . **5.** samba **6.** maxixe
drink . . **5.** assai
flycatcher . . **6.** yetapa
Indian . . **4.** Anta **5.** Arara, Araua, Guana **6.** Tupian **8.** Araquayu, Arawakan (tribe)
mammal . . **5.** tapir
parrot . . **3.** ara **5.** macaw **6.** tiriba
plant . . **4.** yaje **5.** caroa **7.** ayapana (Med)
tree . . **3.** apa **4.** anda (oil), jara **5.** assai (palm) **6.** embuia, satiné

7. araroba, gomavel, seringa (rubber), wallaba **8.** bakupari **10.** barbatimao
weight . . **4.** onza **5.** libra **6.** arroba **7.** quintal
breach . . . **3.** gap **4.** rent, rift **5.** break, burst, chasm, cleft, split **6.** schism **7.** caesura, dispute, quarrel, rupture **8.** fracture, solecism **9.** violation **10.** disruption, falling–out, infraction, separation **12.** infringement, interruption **16.** misunderstanding
bread . . . **4.** cush, food, gelt, loaf, pain (obs), pita, pone, rusk **5.** azyme, miche, panis, toady, toast, tommy **6.** damper, panada, sippet **7.** chapati, hoecake, matzoth **8.** tortilla **9.** eucharist (part of), sourbread **10.** livelihood
bread (pert to) . . .
basket . . **7.** stomach
bread and butter . . **5.** plate **6.** letter (of thanks), pickle, staple **7.** prosaic **8.** juvenile
fruit . . **3.** nut **4.** tree **7.** castana **8.** chestnut
winner . . **6.** earner, toiler, worker **7.** workman **10.** wage earner
break . . . **3.** gap **4.** dash, knap, luck, lull, rent, rift, ruin, rush, slip, snap, stop **5.** blank, burst, cleft, lapse, letup, pause, smash, train **6.** breach, chance, change, depose, escape, hiatus, injury, lacuna, market (Finan), recess, subdue, weaken **7.** blunder, caesura (cesura), disrupt, getaway, respite, rupture, shatter, violate **8.** bad break, bankrupt, breakage, breather, fracture, interval **9.** interlude, jail break, violation **10.** depreciate, falling–out, infraction, suspension **11.** fragmentize **12.** intermission, interruption **13.** discontinuity
break down . . . **3.** cry, sob **4.** bawl, raze, weep **5.** crush **6.** boohoo, divide, master, reduce, revolt, subdue **7.** analyze, crack up, dissect, resolve, unnerve **8.** classify, collapse, separate **9.** decompose, overwhelm, subdivide
breakdown . . . **7.** debacle, failure **8.** analysis **9.** cataclysm **10.** dissection, impairment, revolution
breakfast . . . **6.** brunch (late) **8.** dejeuner **10.** chota hazri
break in . . . **4.** open, tame **5.** enter, force, train **6.** butt in, subdue **7.** barge in, intrude, prepare **9.** interrupt **10.** housebreak
break up . . . **4.** cure, rift, ruin **5.** decay, leave, smash, spall, split, upset **7.** adjourn, atomize, crumble, disband, relieve, scatter, shatter **8.** disperse, dissolve, separate, unsettle **9.** decompose **10.** demobilize, dispersion, disruption **11.** disorganize, dissolution **12.** disintegrate
breakwater . . . **4.** dike, mole, pier **5.** jetty, jutty **6.** refuge, riprap **7.** sea wall **8.** buttress **10.** embankment **11.** obstruction
bream . . . **4.** fish, scup **5.** clean (Naut)

breast... 4. bust, soul, teat 5. bosom,
cheat, gland (mammary), heart
6. spirit, thorax 8. inner man
9. encounter
breast (pert to)...
absence of.. 7. amastia
bone.. 6. ratite 7. sternum
breastlike.. 7. mastoid
plate.. 4. Urim 5. armor, ephod
6. gorget, lorica 7. poitrel
12. breastsummer
works.. 7. defense, parapet, railing
(Naut), ravelin 8. mantelet
9. banquette
breath... 3. air 4. fume, life, odor,
pant, puff, wind 5. draft, pause,
prana, scent, smell, touch, vapor,
whiff 6. breeze, caress, flatus,
pneuma, spirit 7. halitus, respite,
whisper 8. breather 9. emanation,
ozostomia, utterance 10. exhalation
11. respiration
breathe... 3. say, tip 4. gulp, live,
mean, pneo (comb form), rest, sigh,
tell 5. exist, imbue, imply, scent,
smell, snuff 6. evince, exhale, infuse,
inhale, let out, reveal 7. bespeak,
divulge, emanate, instill (instil),
pervade, respire, suspire, whisper
8. aspirate, indicate
breathe (pert to)...
comb form.. 4. pnea, pneo
convulsively.. 4. sigh
hard.. 4. pant
one's last.. 3. die 6. expire, perish
7. decease, succumb
vengeance.. 9. retaliate
breather... 4. lull, rest 5. break,
pause, truce 6. recess 7. interim,
respite 9. interlude 12. intermission
breathing... 5. alive, vital 6. living,
zoetic 7. animate, panting, respite
8. animated 9. conscious, phonation,
utterance 10. aspiration
11. respiration, respiratory, ventilation
12. articulation
breathing (pert to)...
apertures.. 5. stoma 8. spiracle
morbid.. 4. rale 7. stridor
8. rhonchus
painful.. 8. dyspnoea
pause.. 7. caesura
smooth.. 4. lene
breathless... 4. awed, dead, gone,
keen 5. eager 6. ardent, fervid,
winded 7. airless, demised, fervent
8. deceased, lifeless, windless,
wordless 9. impatient 10. astonished,
speechless, spellbound
bred... 6. hybrid, inbred, reared, tablet
(compressed) 7. lowbred, mongrel
8. exogamic, purebred 9. autogamic,
crossbred, endogamic, half–caste,
interbred 11. half–blooded,
impregnated, inseminated
12. thoroughbred
bree... 4. brow 5. broth, scare
6. liquor 7. eyebrow 9. commotion
11. disturbance
breech... 4. doup, rump, tail 5. fanny,
stern 6. bottom 8. buttocks
9. posterior, underside

breeches... 5. chaps, jeans, pants,
trews 8. britches, jodhpurs, trousers
10. pantaloons 12. galligaskins
(jocular)
breed... 3. ilk 4. kind, race, rear, sort
5. beget, brood, caste, class, mixed,
raise, stock, train, tribe 6. family
7. descent, educate, lineage,
mongrel, produce 8. engender,
generate, instruct 9. originate,
posterity, procreate, propagate
10. crossbreed
breeding... 6. polish 7. culture,
decorum, exogamy, manners, raising,
rearing 8. autogamy, endogamy,
hatching, training 9. education,
fostering, gentility 10. deportment,
upbringing 11. instruction,
procreation, propagation
breeding place... 4. nest 5. nidus
7. brooder 8. hatchery 9. incubator
10. birthplace
breeze... 3. air, row 4. aura, pirr,
snap, stir, wind 5. cinoh, rumor
6. squall, zephyr 7. ill wind, whisper
8. duck soup, pushover
9. commotion 11. disturbance
breezy... 4. airy, spry 5. blowy, brisk,
gusty, windy 6. drafty, jaunty, lively
7. squally 8. animated, blustery,
spirited 9. vivaceous 12. lighthearted
Brehon Law... 4. eric (anc)
10. Senchus Mor 12. Book of Aicill
breve... 4. note (Mus), writ 5. brief,
order 7. compose
brevet... 4. fiat 5. ukase 6. decree
7. warrant 10. commission
11. certificate (teaching)
breveté... 8. patented
breviary... 6. manual, ritual
7. compend, epitome
brevity... 9. briefness, shortness,
terseness 11. conciseness,
transience 12. succinctness
brew... 3. ale, mix 4. grog, plot
5. hatch, steep 6. cook up, foment,
gather, menace, scheme 7. concoct,
distill (distil) 8. contrive, threaten
9. aqua vitae
brewer's grain... 4. corn, malt
6. barley
brewer's yeast... 4. barm 6. leaven
bribe... 3. oil, sop 5. bonus
6. boodle, buy off, grease, suborn
9. hush money
bric–a–brac... 6. curios 7. artware
8. antiques, trinkets 9. artifacts,
objet d'art 11. knickknacks
bric–a–brac cabinet... 7. étagère,
whatnot
brick... 3. bat 4. dobe, tile 5. adobe,
stone 6. pament (pamment)
7. clinker 8. hardness
brick (pert to)...
color.. 3. red 7. Saravan
kiln.. 5. clamp
layer.. 3. cad (helper) 5. mason
laying.. 8. toothing
slang.. 3. pip 4. lulu 5. dilly, peach
6. corker, winner 8. jim–dandy
10. sweetheart 11. crackerjack
12. lollapaloosa

unburned.. 5. samel
brickbat... 4. rock 5. stone 7. affront, missile, offense 9. indignity
bridal (pert to)...
chest.. 9. trousseau
flower.. 13. orange blossom
ode, song.. 9. Brautlied
   11. Epithalamon (anc)
portion.. 3. dot 5. dower, dowry (dowery)
rite.. 7. wedding 8. marriage, nuptials
bridge... 3. tie 4. arch, bond, link, pons, pont, span 5. unite
   7. connect, passage (Mus), pontoon, viaduct 9. structure
   13. steppingstone
bridge (pert to)... 4. deck, game, nose 5. magas, truss 6. phoebe (bird)
   7. bascule, trestle 9. dentistry
   10. ponticello (Mus)
bridge, historic...
Bridge of Boats.. 10. Hellespont
Bridge of Sighs.. 6. Venice (Doge's Palace) 7. Al Sirat (Moslem, over infernal fire)
Norse Myth.. 7. Bifrost (rainbow)
Old Bridge.. 12. Ponte Vecchio (Florence It, 1345)
Bridge game... 3. bid 4. pass, ruff, slam 5. honors, points, renege, tenace 7. finesse 9. part–score
bridle... 3. bit 4. cord (kite), curb, rein 5. check, guide, smirk 6. fetter, govern, halter, master, simper, subdue 7. harness, manacle, repress, shackle, snaffle 8. cavesson, headgear, noseband, restrain, suppress 9. hackamore, headstall, restraint
brief... 4. curt, plan, writ 5. breve, charm, pithy, short, terse 6. report 7. compact, concise, laconic, summary 8. fleeting, instruct, succinct 9. condensed, ephemeral, summarize, transient
   10. compendium, short–lived, transitory 11. compendious
   14. inconsiderable
brier, briar... 4. burr, pipe 5. heath, shrub, spine, thorn 7. bramble, bruyère, clotbur, prickle, sticker, thistle 8. adherent 11. French brier
brig... 4. boat 6. vessel
   10. guardhouse
brigade... 4. unit 6. troops 7. company 8. regiment
brigand... 5. rover, thief 6. bandit, dacoit, pirate, robber 7. bedouin, cateran, ladrone 8. picaroon
   10. highwayman
bright... 3. apt, gay 4. naif, rosy 5. alert, beamy, fresh, lucid, nitid, palmy, sleek, smart, sunny, vivid, witty 6. brainy, clever, florid, garish, golden 7. halcyon, radiant, shining, unfaded 8. cheerful, colorful, flashing, gleaming, luminous, lustrous, splendid 9. brilliant, effulgent, refulgent, sparkling 10. auspicious, epiphanous, glistening, glittering, optimistic
   11. intelligent, resplendent
brightness... 5. sheen 6. luster

7. sparkle 8. radiance, splendor 9. alertness, clearness, smartness
   10. brilliance 12. cheerfulness, colorfulness, pleasantness
brilliance, brilliancy... 5. éclat, glory 6. luster 7. glitter, oriency, success 8. radiance, splendor 9. smartness, vividness 10. brightness, cleverness
brilliant... 5. smart, vivid, witty 6. bright 7. eminent, radiant, shining 8. gorgeous, meteoric, splendid 9. refulgent, sparkling 10. glittering
   11. illustrious
brilliant group... 6. galaxy
brim... 3. hem, lip, rim 4. edge 5. brink, marge, verge 6. border, margin 7. selvage
brine... 3. sea 4. main, salt 5. brack, ocean, tears 6. pickle 7. the deep
   12. preservative
bring... 3. get 4. bear, cost, haul, lead 5. carry, fetch, go get, yield 6. convey, entail, induce, obtain 7. contain, involve, require 8. comprise 9. transport
bring about... 2. do 4. make 5. cause 6. create, effect 7. achieve, produce 8. generate 9. instigate
   10. accomplish, consummate, effectuate
bring around... 4. cure, heal, ween 5. renew, sober 6. revive 7. convert, restore, win over 8. persuade
   10. rejuvenate
bring back... 5. fetch 6. recall, return, revive 7. restore 8. rekindle, remember, retrieve 9. recollect, resurrect
bring forth... 3. ean 4. bear, rise 5. beget, breed, cause, educe, hatch, spawn, yield 6. adduce, elicit, reveal 7. develop, produce 8. disclose, fructify, generate, manifest
bring forward... 4. cite 5. offer 6. adduce, broach, submit 7. advance, improve, promote, propose 8. manifest 9. introduce
bring into...
bondage.. 7. enslave
court.. 7. arraign
harmony.. 6. attune
position.. 5. align, aline
union.. 7. correlate
bring together... 5. amass, group 6. gather 7. cluster, compile, reunite 8. assemble 9. harmonize, reconcile
   10. accumulate
bring to light... 4. find 5. trace 6. elicit, expose, reveal 7. uncover, unearth 8. disclose, discover
bring to mind... 6. recall, remind 8. look like, remember, resemble
bring to pass... 2. do 5. cause 6. author, father 9. originate
   10. accomplish, effectuate
bring up... 4. rear, spew 5. drill, raise, train, vomit 6. foster, muster 7. advance, educate, nurture, propose 9. challenge, condition, cultivate 10. discipline
   11. regurgitate

bring up to date... 4. post 6. update
  9. modernize 10. streamline
brink... 3. lip, rim 4. bank, brow,
  edge, near 5. ditch, marge, skirt,
  verge 6. border, margin
briny... 3. sea 4. salt 5. salty
  6. saline 8. brackish
Brisbane, capital of... 10. Queensland
  (Austral)
Brisbane tree... 3. box 8. quandong
brisk... 3. gay 4. cold, fast, keen,
  racy, spry, yern 5. agile, alert, alive,
  crisp, fresh, peart, quick, sharp,
  tangy, zippy 6. breezy, lively, nimble,
  snappy 7. caustic, pungent
  8. animated, forceful, spirited,
  vigorous 9. energetic, sprightly,
  vivacious 11. stimulating
bristle... 4. barb, hair, seta 5. anger,
  seton 6. chaeta, palpus, ruffle,
  rumple, see red, setula, setule
  7. acicula, prickle, stubble
bristling... 5. angry 6. horrid (anc)
  7. horrent 9. offensive
bristly... 5. rough, setal 6. hispid,
  setose, thorny 7. prickly, scopate,
  unshorn 8. acicular, echinate
  11. bristlelike
Bristol...
  church (England's finest).. 15. St
    Mary Redcliffe
  fashion.. 6. ataunt 9. shipshape
  library.. 6. oldest (British Isles)
  milk.. 6. sherry
Britain...
  name, ancient.. 6. Albion
  name, modern.. 12. British Isles,
    Commonwealth, Great Britain
    13. United Kingdom
  name, Roman.. 9. Brittania
  native 5. Iceni (tribe), Jutoo, Picts,
    Scots 6. Angles 7. Britons, Silures
  native (sl).. 5. limey (limy), tommy
    7. Blighty
  sea.. 5. Irish, North 8. Atlantic,
    Hebrides
British (pert to)... see also *English*
  battle.. 8. Hastings
  boat (anc).. 7. coracle
  cavalry.. 8. yeomanry
  earldom (Egypt).. 7. Khartum (1898)
  emblem.. 4. lion
  fish.. 8. dragonet (gobylike)
  oak.. 5. robur
  Order of.. 9. The Garter
  prison.. 4. gaol
  pudding.. 4. suet 9. Yorkshire
  tavern.. 3. pub 9. beerhouse, jerry
    shop
  thief (wharf).. 6. tosher
  Z (letter).. 3. Zed
British people...
  author.. 6. Austen, Barrie, Jonson
    7. Dickens
  buccaneer.. 4. Kidd 6. Morgan
  explorer.. 4. Cook, Ross 6. Baffin
    7. Stanley 9. Vancouver
    11. Livingstone
  hero (sea).. 6. Nelson
  king (legend, Myth).. 3. Lud 4. Beli,
    Bran, Brut 7. Belenus
  painter.. 8. Rossetti

  philosopher.. 7. Russell (Bertrand)
  physicist.. 5. Boyle
  poet.. 7. Chaucer 8. Browning,
    Tennyson 9. Masefield
  soldier.. 7. Redcoat (Hist)
Brittany... 7. Armoric 8. Bretagne
brittle... 4. weak 5. brash, candy,
  crisp, frail 6. feeble, infirm, slight
  7. fragile, friable 8. delicate, insecure
  9. breakable, frangible
  11. shatterable
broad... 4. free, girl, lake (Eng), wide
  5. ample, large, roomy, thick, wench
  7. breadth, diffuse, general, liberal
  8. spacious, strumpet, sweeping,
  tabulate, tolerant 9. expansive,
  extensive 10. collective, commodious,
  indefinite, voluminous
  13. comprehensive
broad (pert to)...
  arrow.. 5. pheon (Her) 6. stigma
    8. insignia
  footed.. 8. platypod
  hearted.. 8. generous
    11. magnanimous
  minded.. 7. liberal 8. tolerant
    9. receptive
broaden... 5. swell, widen 6. dilate,
  expand, extend, spread 7. augment,
  enlarge, ennoble 8. increase
broadly... 3. far 6. widely 10. far and
  wide 11. extensively 12. indefinitely,
  right and left
broadside... 4. guns, side 6. folder
  7. gunfire, quarter, surface
  8. enfilade, sideways 10. broadsheet,
  floodlight 11. breadthwise
broadsword... 7. cutlass, Ferrara
  8. claymore, scimitar
Brobdingnagian... 5. giant, titan
  8. colossal, gigantic 10. gargantuan
brocade... 6. broché, fabric
  8. baudekin 9. baldachin
brochan... 7. oatmeal 8. porridge
brochure... 5. tract 6. folder
  7. booklet, leaflet 8. chapbook,
  pamphlet
brod... 3. awl 4. goad, pike, urge
  5. thorn 6. sprout 9. incentive
brode, brodee... 11. embroidered
brodyaga... 7. vagrant 8. vagabond
brogan, brogue... 4. shoe
brogue... 4. burr 5. twang 6. accent
  7. dialect
broil... 4. cook, fray, fume 5. brawl,
  grill, melee 6. affray, braise (braize),
  scorch 7. contest, discord, dispute,
  quarrel 8. conflict, grillade, scramble
  10. contention, dissension, turbulence
  11. altercation, embroilment
broke... 4. flat 6. busted, ruined
  8. bankrupt, strapped 9. destitute,
  insolvent, penniless
broken... 4. tame 5. broke, bumpy,
  burst, rough, tamed 6. chined,
  ruined, shaken, uneven, zigzag
  7. crushed, décousu, severed,
  subdued 8. bankrupt, detached,
  impaired, ruptured, sporadic,
  weakened 9. conquered, dispersed,
  irregular, shattered, unsettled
  10. incoherent, incomplete

11. fragmentary, housebroken, interrupted 12. disconnected, domesticated, intermittent 13. discontinuous
broken pottery (anc)... 5. shard (sherd) 8. potsherd
broker... 5. agent 6. dealer, jobber 7. cambist, scalper (ticket) 8. marriage 9. go–between, insurance, middleman, schatchen 10. pawnbroker, real estate 11. internuncio, stockbroker 12. intermediary
brokerage... 3. fee 4. agio 6. charge 8. agiotage, business 9. exactment 10. commission
brolly... 5. chute 8. umbrella 9. brollyhop, parachute
bromide... 4. corn 5. trite 6. Babbit, cliché, halide, old hat 8. banality, sedative 9. conformer, criticism, platitude 10. conformist, Philistine 15. conventionalist
bronco, broncho... 4. pony 5. horse 6. cayuse 7. mustang 10. broomstick
bronco, bucking... 9. estrapade
broncobuster, bronchobuster... 6. cowboy 7. trainer, vaquero
Bronx cheer... 3. boo 4. hiss, razz 9. raspberry
bronze... 3. aes (anc), tan 5. alloy, color 6. ormolu, patina, suntan 9. sculpture
Bronze Age... 9. Neolithic 11. Aeneolithic
Bronze Plaques (pert to)...
called.. 14. Eugubine Tables (Iguvine Tables, 1444)
number.. 5. Seven
site.. 6. Gubbio (It)
brooch... 3. bar, pin 4. boss, ouch 5. cameo, clasp 6. fibula (anc), shield 8. pectoral 9. breastpin
brood... 3. fry, nye, set 4. kind, mope, mull, muse, nide, race 5. breed, covey, folks, hatch, pride (lions), young 6. clutch, family, farrow (pigs), litter, ménage, people, strain 7. lineage, progeny, reflect 8. cogitate, incubate, meditate, ruminate, soredium 9. household, offspring 11. contemplate
brood over... 4. fret, mope 5. hover 6. grieve, ponder 7. agonize 8. remember
brook... 3. run 4. bear, beck, burn, rill, sike 5. abide, bourn, creek, crick 6. arroyo, endure, rillet, runlet, suffer 7. freshet, rivulet 8. brooklet 9. arroyuelo, streamlet
broom... 5. besom, shrub, spart, sweep, whisk
broth... 4. soup 5. stock 6. brewis 8. bouillon, consommé
brother... 3. fra 4. mate, monk 5. friar, title 6. frater, friend, member, oblate 8. alter ego, relative 9. associate 11. counterpart
brotherhood... 5. lodge 7. kinship, society 8. sodality 10. fellowship, fraternity 11. association

12. fraternalism 13. confraternity
brotherly... 4. kind 6. tender 8. friendly 9. fraternal 11. sympathetic 12. affectionate
Brothers... 7. Danites (Mormon) 9. Christian (RCCh)
brothers and sisters (same family)... 8. siblings
brow... 3. cap, rim, tip, top 4. brae 5. brink, crest, crown 6. border, summit, tiptop, visage 7. eyebrow, feature 8. boldness, forehead 9. gangplank 10. effrontery 11. countenance
browbeat... 3. cow 5. bully 7. buffalo, henpeck 8. bulldoze, domineer 10. intimidate
brown... 4. dark 5. cheat, dusky 6. august, braise, tanned 9. red–yellow (class)
brown... 3. bay, dun, nut, tan 4. ecru, faon, fawn, roan, rust, seal 5. acorn, cocoa, hazel, henna, khaki, mocha, olive, otter, sepia, snuff, sumac, tawny, tenné, toast, topaz 6. auburn, bister, bronze, burnet, coffee, copper, loutre, oriole, russet, sienna, sorrel, titian, walnut 7. asphalt (smoke), gazelle, perique, rosario (army) 8. chestnut, cinnamon, mahogany 9. buckthorn, chocolate 10. café au lait, terra cotta
brown (pert to)...
Bess.. 6. musket
betty.. 5. daisy 7. pudding 10. coneflower
earth.. 5. umber
ebony.. 6. wamara 10. coffeewood
browned in deep fat... 7. rissole
Brownian movement (Bot)... 7. pedesis
brownie... 3. elf 4. cake 5. dwarf, gnome, nisse, pixie, Scout, urisk 6. camera, goblin 9. sandpiper
Brownism (Eng)... 17. Congregationalism
browze... 4. brut (obs), read, scan 5. graze 6. nibble
bruckle... 5. frail 7. brittle 9. breakable 10. changeable, inconstant
bruin... 4. bear
bruise... 4. bash, beat, hurt, maul 5. abuse, crush, dinge, pound, wound 6. batter, buffet, injury 7. contuse 8. abrasion, black eye 9. contusion, pulverize, triturate
bruiser... 3. mug, pug 5. boxer, bravo, tough 7. fighter, ruffian, sparrer 8. pugilist 11. fisticuffer
bruit, bruit about... 3. din 4. fame, hawk, tell 5. bandy, noise, rumor 6. clamor, report 9. advertise
brujo... 8. magician, sorcerer 11. witch doctor
brumal... 4. cold 6. hiemal, wintry 8. hibernal 10. winterlike
brune... 6. brunet (brunette) 11. Melanochroi
Brunhild... 5. Queen (wife of Siegfried) 8. Valkyrie (Myth)
brunt... 3. rub 4. crux 5. pinch, shock

6. stress 7. squeeze
brush... 3. art 4. bush, comb, tail
(fox), tuft 5. besom, briar, broom,
clash, graze, groom, sweep, touch
6. artist, forest, pappus, stroke,
teazel 7. painter, scuffle, thicket
8. conflict 9. brushwood, encounter
10. paintbrush 11. undergrowth
brush aside... 5. spurn 6. reject
7. dismiss 8. shrug off 9. disregard
brush wolf... 6. coyote
brusque... 4. curt 5. bluff, blunt,
brash, brusk, frank, gruff, rough,
sharp, short 6. abrupt, candid,
snippy
brutal... 5. cruel, gross 6. animal,
carnal, coarse, savage 7. bestial,
inhuman 8. ruthless 9. barbarous
brutality... 7. cruelty 9. barbarian,
carnality 12. ruthlessness
brute... 5. beast, gross, harsh, rough
6. animal 7. beastly, bestial, sensual,
varment 8. soulless 9. barbarian,
inanimate 10. unpolished
11. uncivilized
brutish... 4. rude 5. cruel, gross
6. brutal, carnal, fierce, savage,
stupid 7. bestial, inhuman, sensual,
vicious 9. barbarous, ferocious,
insensate, unfeeling 10. insensible,
irrational
Brutus... 3. wig 6. hairdo, peruke
7. traitor (Julius Caesar)
13. chrysanthemum
Bryan's speech (1896)... 11. Cross of
Gold 13. Crown of Thorns
bryology, science of... 6. mosses
10. bryophytes, liverworts
Brython... 4. Celt 6. Briton
8. Welshman
Brythonic god... 3. Ler 4. Dran
Brythonic goddess... 9. Arianrhod
bubble... 4. bead, bleb, blob, boil,
foam 5. bulge, empty, fancy, tumor
6. burble, gurgle, murmur, ripple,
scheme, trifle 7. chimera (chimaera),
globule, trickle 8. bubbling, delusive,
illusion 9. ephemeron, intumesce,
lightness 10. effervesce
16. unsubstantiality
buccal... 4. oral 5. cheek, mouth
buccaneer... 4. Kidd (Capt) 5. rover
6. Morgan, pirate, rifler, viking
7. corsair, Lafitte, spoiler
8. marooner, picaroon 9. privateer
10. Blackbeard (Capt Teach),
freebooter
Bucephalus... 5. horse, steed
7. charger 8. war horse (Alex the
Great)
buck... 3. man, ram, rat 4. bunt, butt,
deer, goat, hare, jump, male, sore
(4–yr deer) 5. fight, sasin 6. animal,
combat, dollar, Indian, oppose
7. contest, launder, pricket
8. antelope, sawhorse 10. fallow
deer
buckaroo... 6. cowboy 7. trainer,
vaquero 8. horseman
12. broncobuster (bronchobuster)
bucket... 3. tub 4. bail, bowk, pail,
ship 5. chest, cozen, scoop, skeel

6. bailer, bushel, drench, sityla
10. bucket shop
Buckeye State... 4. Ohio
Buckingham Palace... 9. residence
11. St James Park (London)
buckle... 3. bow 4. bend, curl, kink,
warp 5. tache 6. fasten 8. marriage
9. fastening
buckthorn... 4. tree 5. brown, shrub
7. cascara, Rhamnus
buckwheat... 4. cake, coal, herb,
seed, titi 5. flour
bucolic... 4. idyl, poem, poet 5. idyll,
local, rural 6. farmer, poetic, rustic
7. eclogue, georgic 8. agrestic,
pastoral 9. bucoliast
bud... 3. deb 4. bulb, cion, germ,
grow, knop, stem 5. brier, buddy,
gemma, graft, plant, shoat, youth
6. embryo, sprout 7. blossom,
brother, burgeon, develop
8. rudiment, soredium 9. debutante,
germinate
Buddha (Gautama)... 2. Fo 4. sage
(Shakya) 5. amita, deity 7. ascetic,
teacher 8. Daibutsu 10. Blessed One
Buddhism (pert to)...
church.. 4. tera
city (sacred).. 5. Lassa (Lhasa)
evil spirit.. 4. Mara
fate.. 5. Karma
festival.. 3. Bon
friar, monk.. 2. Bo 5. arbat, bonze
6. bhikku, gelong 7. Mahatma
8. poonghia 9. Dalai Lama
goal.. 13. Enlightenment
hell.. 6. Naraka
language (sacred).. 4. Pali 5. sutra
9. Tripitaka
liberation.. 7. Nirvana
mountain (sacred).. 4. Omei (Chin)
paradise.. 4. Jodo 8. gokuraku
sect.. 3. Zen
shrine (Ind).. 4. tope 5. stupa
6. dagoba
temple.. 4. rath, Tera 6. vihara
temple column.. 3. lat
term.. 6. nidana
buddy... 3. pal 4. chum, mate
5. crony 7. brother, comrade
8. tentmate 9. bedfellow, companion
budge... 3. fur (lambskin) 4. grog,
move, stir 5. booze, brisk, stiff
6. guzzle, jocund, liquor, solemn,
tipple 7. austere, pompous
8. movement 11. nervousness
budget... 3. bag 4. bulk, plan, sack
5. funds, pouch, purse, store
6. agenda, assets, bundle, moneys,
packet, parcel, ration, wallet
7. program, stipend 8. finances,
quantity, schedule 9. allowance,
statement 12. accumulation
Buenos Aires (pert to)...
avenue (famed).. 13. Avenida de
Mayo
bourse.. 5. Bolsa
capital.. 9. Argentina
river.. 7. La Plata
buff... 3. rub 4. hide (animal) 5. color,
scour 6. polish 7. burnish, leather
buffalo (animal)...

American.. **5.** bison
Asian, African.. **2.** ox **4.** arna, Cape,
  gaur **8.** seladang
European.. **7.** aurochs
hybrid.. **7.** cattalo (catalo)
Indian.. **4.** arna
Philippines.. **7.** carabao, timarau
buffalo (pert to)...
grass.. **5.** grama **6.** guinea **11.** St.
  Augustine
pea.. **4.** plum **5.** vetch
  10. bluebonnet
slang.. **3.** cow **5.** bully **7.** perplex
  8. bulldoze, confound
Buffalo Bill... **11.** William Cody
buffer... **4.** buff **5.** guard, wheel
  6. bumper **7.** bulwark, cushion
  8. backstop, polisher
buffet... **3.** bar, box, hit **4.** beat,
  blow, cuff, slap, toss, whip
  5. abuse, smite, stool **6.** bruise,
  oppose, strike **12.** chastisement
  14. disappointment
buffet... **6.** supper **7.** counter, hassock
  8. cupboard **9.** sideboard
buffo... **7.** buffoon **10.** bass singer
  (comic opera), buffo–basso
buffoon... **4.** fool, mima (fem), mime,
  zany **5.** actor, clown, droll, mimer
  6. jester, mummer **8.** humorist,
  ridicule **9.** Hanswurst, harlequin
  12. Eulenspiegel (Tyll)
  13. pickel–herring (pickle–herring)
buffoonery... **6.** japery, pranks
  7. fooling **8.** clownery, drollery,
  trickery **9.** slapstick **10.** buffoonism
  12. harlequinade
bug (insect)... **3.** fly, sow **4.** flea, gnat,
  moth, pill, tick **5.** Anasa, aphid,
  Aphis, cimex, louse **6.** beetle, cicada,
  earwig, locust, mantis, needle,
  scarab, slater, spider, weevil
  7. firefly, hexapod, katydid, ladybug,
  Ranatra, termite **8.** chilipod,
  diplopod, mosquito, myriapod
  9. arthropod (jointed), centipede,
  cockroach, lightning, millipede,
  tarantula **10.** silverfish
  11. grasshopper
bug (slang)... **3.** nut **4.** bogy, flaw,
  rage **5.** craze, fault, manis **6.** defect,
  zealot **7.** bugaboo, bugbear, fanatic,
  passion **9.** energumen
bugaboo... **4.** bogy, ogre, trap (golf)
bugan... **5.** ghost **6.** spirit (evil)
  9. hobgoblin
bugger... **3.** guy, rat **4.** chap, heel
  6. booger, jasper, wretch
buggy... **3.** bus **4.** ga–ga, shay
  5. wagon **6.** cuckoo **7.** caboose,
  foolish, haywire, vehicle **8.** carriage,
  demented, infested, stanhope
  9. insectile **10.** insectlike
bug juice... **6.** liquor (strong), whisky
  (inferior)
bugle... **3.** iva (ragweed) **4.** bead, call
  (mating), honk, horn, nose, toot
  7. clarion, trumpet **9.** schnozzle
  10. instrument
bugle call... **4.** taps **6.** alerte, sennet
  (Hist) **7.** retreat, tantara **8.** last post,
  reveille

build... **4.** form, rear **5.** edify, erect,
  found, frame, raise, shape **6.** create,
  evolve, figure, nidify **7.** fashion,
  stature **8.** increase, physique
  9. construct, establish
building... **4.** barn, casa, crib, shed,
  wing **5.** annex, tower **6.** casino,
  castle, lean–to, making, museum
  7. edifice, factory, forming, rookery,
  rotunda, theater **8.** creation, dwelling,
  erecting, erection, tenement
  9. apartment, structure
  10. fashioning, production,
  skyscraper, storehouse **11.** fabrication
build–up... **5.** boost **9.** promotion
  11. advertising **12.** commendation
built... **4.** made **6.** formed, shaped
  7. crested, erected **9.** fashioned
  10. fabricated **11.** constructed
bulb... **3.** bud **4.** corm, lily, root,
  sego, stem **5.** onion, swell, tuber,
  tulip **6.** bulbil, camass, crocus, dahlia
  7. bulblet, globule, rhizome
  8. earthnut
bulbous... **5.** round **7.** bulbose,
  bulging **8.** swelling, tuberous
Bulgaria...
capital.. **5.** Sofia
city.. **5.** Varna **6.** Plevna, Sliven
  7. Ruschuk
native.. **6.** Bulgar
origin.. **4.** Slav **9.** Mongolian
river.. **6.** Danube, Marica (Maritsa),
  Struma
bulge... **3.** bow **4.** bump, edge, hump,
  jump, knob, odds **5.** bilge, bloat,
  flash, pouch, swell **6.** convex, wallet
  7. vantage **9.** advantage
  10. projection **12.** protuberance
bulk... **3.** sum **4.** loom, mass, most,
  size **5.** extent, staple, volume
  7. bigness, quantum **8.** majority,
  quantity **9.** dimension, largeness,
  substance, thickness **11.** massiveness
  12. accumulation **13.** preponderance
bulky... **5.** heavy, hulky, stout, thick
  6. clumsy **7.** awkward, lumpish,
  massive **8.** unwieldy **9.** corpulent,
  policemen (Eng sl), ponderous
  10. cumbersome, unwielding
  11. substantial
bull... **4.** fiat, seal **5.** edict, error,
  large, ukase **6.** brevet, decree,
  firman, humbug, letter (papal), market
  (Finan), rising, Taurus **7.** blunder
  8. nonsense, solecism **9.** Irish bull,
  policeman **10.** speculator
bull (male animal)... **2.** ox **3.** cow
  4. Apis (sacred), stot, toro, zebu
  5. moose, steer, whale **6.** walrus
  7. bullock **8.** elephant, Minotaur,
  terrapin
bull (slang)... **4.** blah, bosh, bunk
  5. hokum **6.** hot air **7.** baloney
  8. buncombe, flimflam
bulla... **4.** bleb, boss, case (leather),
  knob, seal (papal), stud **6.** button
  7. blister, globule, pendant, vesicle
  8. ornament
bulldog... **3.** ant **4.** pipe **5.** leech
  7. courage, forceps **8.** barnacle,
  stubborn, tenacity **9.** newspaper

(early), tenacious

bulldoze... 3. cow 5. bully, grade, level 6. coerce, harass 7. buffalo 8. browbeat 10. intimidate

bullet... 4. ball (cannon), shot, slug 6. dumdum, pellet, sinker (angling), tracer 7. missile

bulletin... 5. brief, flash 6. notice, record 7. account, message 8. newsbill 9. statement 10. newsletter, periodical 11. publication 12. announcement

bullfighter... 6. torero 7. matador, picador 8. capeador, toreador

bullfinch... 3. alp 4. nope 5. hedge 11. pyrrhuloxia 12. gray grosbeak

Bull Moose... 16. Progressive Party

bullpen (pert to)...
  camp.. 8. barracks 9. enclosure
  ice hockey.. 5. bench (penalty)
  ring cell.. 5. toril
  Western US.. 6. corral

Bull Run (battle)... 8. Manassas

bully... 4. beef 6. hector, jovial 7. gleeful, ruffian 8. browbeat, bulldoze 9. bulldozer, tormentor 10. browbeater, intimidate

bulwark... 4. bank 6. buffer, sconce 7. barrier, parapet, rampart 8. abutment, buttress 10. protection 13. fortification

bum... 3. beg 5. idler, revel, rummy, souse, spree 6. beggar, loafer, tipple, wretch 7. budmash, moocher, wastrel 8. blighter, drunkard, vagabond 9. lazzarone, schnorrer 10. panhandler

bump... 3. hit, jog 4. bang, clop, jolt, lump, meet, push, thud 5. bulge, cahot, crash, crump, knock, lower, plunk, tumor 6. demote, impact, reduce, strike 7. collide 8. demotion, dilation, swelling 9. air pocket, collision, downgrade

bumpkin... 4. boor, clod, gawk, hick, lout, rube, tike 5. yokel 6. farmer, rustic 7. cauboge, hayseed, hoosier, lumpkin 9. chawbacon 10. clodhopper

bumptious... 8. insolent 9. audacious, insulting 12. contumelious

bunch... 3. bob, lot, mop, set 4. pack, tuft, wisp 5. batch, clump, covey, crowd, flock, grist, group 6. bundle 7. cluster, company 8. assemble, quantity 9. multitude 10. congregate

bundle... 3. lot, wad 4. bale, bolt, hank, pack, send 5. bluey, bunch, fagot, sheaf, shook 6. bindle, fardel, fascis, packet, parcel, seroon 7. fascine, package, rouleau 10. collection

bung... 3. tap 4. cork, plug, stop 5. spile 6. bruise 7. contuse, stopper, stopple, tampeon, tampoon 8. bankrupt, bunghole 9. falsehood

bungle... 3. err 4. muff 5. botch, fudge 6. bobble, foozle, fumble, tailor (hunting) 7. blunder

bungling... 5. fudgy 6. clumsy 7. awkward, unhandy 8. botchery

9. unskilled 10. blundering, unskillful

bunion... 12. hallux valgus

bunk... 3. bed, kip, rot 4. blah, brag 5. abide, berth, couch, dwell, hokum, hooey, sleep 6. humbug, kibosh 7. baloney, hogwash 8. nonsense, tommyrot 9. cross–beam (logging)

Bunker Hill (Mass)... 6. battle (1775)

bunkum... see *buncombe*

Bunsen... 4. cell, disk 5. flame, valve 6. burner 9. Professor (Ger)

bunt... 3. bat, dig, jab, jog, tap 4. blow, bump, butt, pike, push, tail (Scot) 5. knock, shove 7. bunting 10. propulsion

bunting... 4. flag, hood 5. flags 6. banner, pennon 7. pennant 8. streamer

bunting (bird)... 3. red 4. cirl, corn, crow, lark, pape (Creole) 5. finch 6. indigo, towhee 7. cowbird, ortolan 8. bobolink 12. yellowhammer

buoy... 3. dan 4. bell 5. float 6. marker 7. can buoy, nunbuoy 8. bell buoy, deadhead, life buoy, spar buoy 11. mooring buoy 12. breeches buoy 13. whistling buoy

buoyance, buoyancy... 4. hope, snap 5. verve 6. bounce 7. flotage 9. lightness 10. levitation, resilience 12. floatability 16. lightheartedness

buoyant... 5. light 7. elastic 8. cheerful, floating, levitate, volatile 11. supernatant 12. lighthearted, recuperative

bur, burr... 3. nut 5. thorn 8. adherent (see also *burr*)

burble... 6. muddle 7. confuse, trouble 8. disorder

burbot... 4. ling, Lota 7. eelpout

burden... 3. key, tax 4. birn, care, cark, clog, lade, load, note, onus, task, tone 5. cargo, cross, music, tenor, voice 6. charge, cumber, hamper, saddle, weight 7. bourdon, freight, oppress, payload, refrain 8. capacity, overload, pressure 10. impediment, imposition 11. encumbrance

burdensome... 5. heavy 7. arduous, massive, onerous, weighty 8. unwieldy 9. difficult, laborious, ponderous 10. cumbersome, oppressive 11. troublesome 12. impedimental

bureau... 4. desk, shop 6. office 7. dresser 8. chambers 10. chiffonier, department

bureaucracy... 10. government 11. directorate, officialdom, officialism

burgeon... 3. bud 4. grow 5. gemma, shoot, sprit 6. sprout

burglar... 4. yegg 5. thief 9. cracksman 11. safecracker 12. housebreaker

burglary... 5. theft 6. burgle 7. larceny, robbery 8. stealage 13. housebreaking

burgle... 3. rob 8. burglary 10. burglarize

burgomaster... 5. mayor 7. alcalde
   10. magistrate 11. burghmaster
burgoo, burgout... 4. stew 5. gruel
   7. pudding (oatmeal) 8. porridge
burial... 5. inurn 7. funeral
   9. interment, sepulture
   10. engulfment, inhumation,
   submersion 11. concealment,
   submergence
burial ground... 4. pyre 5. grave
   6. barrow 7. tumulus 8. bone yard,
   catacomb, cemetery, golgotha
   9. graveyard 10. churchyard,
   necropolis 11. polyandrium
   12. potter's field
burlesque... 3. fun 4. jest 5. farce,
   comic 6. parody, review, satire
   7. mimicry, mockery, overact,
   take–off 8. burletta, doggerel,
   ridicule, travesty 9. charivari,
   imitation, travestie 10. caricatura,
   caricature 13. entertainment
Burlingame Treaty... 11. Immigration
   (Chin 1868)
burly... 3. fat 5. bulky, large, noble,
   obese, stout 6. brawny 7. stately
   8. imposing, stalwart 9. corpulent,
   excellent
Burma, Burmese...
   alphabet.. 4. Pali
   capital (anc).. 3. Ava 4. Pegu
   capital, present.. 7. Rangoon
   city.. 8. Mandalay
   dagger.. 3. dah (dhao)
   gibbon.. 3. lar
   girl.. 4. mima
   monk.. 2. bo
   native.. 3. Lai
   relation.. 5. Thais (Tais) 6. Malays
   7. Chinese 8. Tibetans
   10. Mongolians
   religion.. 8. Buddhism
   robber.. 6. dacoit
   shed (public).. 5. zayat
   tribe.. 3. Mon, Tai 4. Laos, Shan
   7. Siamese
   viol.. 4. turr (3–stringed)
Burma Road... 6. Lashio (to China,
   1938–1942, replaced by Ledo Rd)
burn... 3. dry, tan 4. char, fire, glow,
   hurt, pain, sear, sere 5. blaze,
   brand, brook, cense, flame, scald,
   singe 6. ignite, injury, scorch
   7. cremate, encauma, flicker,
   sunburn, swelter, torrefy 9. cauterize,
   sacrifice 10. incandesce, incinerate
burner... 3. jet 4. lamp 5. torch
   6. Bunsen, candle, censer (incense)
   7. cresset 9. blowtorch
   10. lucubrator 11. incinerator
burning... 3. hot 4. fire, pain, sore
   5. afire, angry, ardor, arson, blaze,
   fiery, flame 6. ablaze, ardent, fervid
   7. blazing, cautery, excited, fervent,
   flaming, glowing, shining, zealous
   8. eloquent, feverish, inustion
   9. cremating, cremation, execution
   10. combustion, ustulation
   13. conflagration
burning place... 4. ghat 9. crematory
   10. cinerarium
burnish... 3. rub 4. buff 5. glaze,

gloss, shine 6. patina, polish
burnt... 3. red 5. dried 6. burned,
   seared, singed 7. charred
   8. hardened, scorched, sunburnt
   9. blistered, sunburned
burnt (pert to)...
   art.. 11. pyrography, pyrogravure
   color.. 4. rose 5. ocher, topaz
   6. almond, orange, russet, sienna
   8. amethyst
   sugar.. 7. caramel
burn with anger, excitement...
   4. fume 5. smoke 6. seethe,
   simmer, sizzle 7. smolder
burp... 5. belch, eruct 8. eructate
burr... 3. cut, hem 4. buzz, whir
   5. brier, drone, gnarl, knurl, thorn
   6. brogue, corona (moon), meatus
   (ear) 7. bramble, clotbur, prickle,
   silique, sticker 8. excavate, follicle
   9. cocklebur, whetstone
burro... 3. ass 4. jack 5. cuddy,
   neddy 6. dickey, donkey 7. jackass
burrow... 3. dig 4. abri, hide, hole,
   lair, mine 5. couch (otter's), lodge
   (beaver's) 6. search, tunnel 7. shelter
burrowing... 9. effodient, fossorial
   11. lithodomous (in rock)
burrowing animal... 4. mole, peba
   5. poyou 6. peludo 8. suricate
   9. armadillo
burst... 3. pop 4. bang, rend 5. blast,
   blaze, break, broke, erupt, flare,
   flash, shots, spurt 6. volley
   7. explode, flare–up, gunfire, implode
   8. outbreak, outburst, ruptured
   9. discharge, explosion, fractured
   10. detonation 11. dissiliency
burst (forth)... 4. grow 5. erupt, sally
   6. sprout
burst (pert to)...
   applause.. 5. éclat, hands 7. ovation,
   plaudit 8. clapping
   cheers.. 5. salvo
   gunfire.. 6. rafale
   laughter.. 3. fit 4. peal, roar
   10. convulsion
   temper.. 4. rage 5. scene, storm
   7. passion 9. explosion
bursting... 4. full 7. brimful, crammed,
   excited, replete 8. overfull, thrilled,
   volcanic 9. explosive, surfeited
   10. detonating 11. impassioned,
   overflowing, overwhelmed
bury... 4. hide, sink 5. cache, cover,
   inter, inurn, plant, stash 6. engulf,
   entomb, inhume 7. conceal,
   embosom, repress, secrete
   8. submerge 9. overwhelm, sepulture
bus... 6. jitney 7. omnibus 10. motor
coach
bush... 3. tod 4. shag (hair) 5. brush,
   plain, shrub, wahoo, wilds 6. branch,
   lining 7. boscage, bushing
   8. bushveld, woodland 10. hinterland
bushed... 4. beat 5. all in 6. pooped
   7. baffled 8. dog–tired 9. exhausted,
   nonplused, perplexed, played out
   10. nonplussed
bushel... 3. foo 4. full 6. basket,
   vessel 7. measure (dry) 8. imperial,
   standard 10. Winchester

Bushido (Jap)... 11. code of honor
bushing... 4. bush 6. lining, sleeve
  (mach) 7. bearing, padding (piano)
Bushman... 3. San 4. Saan 5. nomad,
  pygmy 6. Abatua, rustic
  8. woodsman 9. aborigine
bushmaster... 5. snake
bushwhacker... 7. pioneer 8. guerilla
  10. forerunner 11. bushfighter,
  voortrekker 12. frontiersman
bushy... 5. hairy, thick, woody
  6. dumose, shaggy, woodsy
  7. hirsute, scrubby, shrubby
business... 3. job 4. firm, game, line,
  work 5. craft, house, trade 6. affair,
  career, matter, racket 7. calling,
  company, concern, pursuit
  8. commerce, industry, interest,
  practice, vocation 10. enterprise,
  occupation, proceeding, profession
  11. transaction 13. establishment
business (pert to)...
  agreement.. 6. cartel
  businesslike.. 11. pragmatical
  customer.. 6. patron
  cycle.. 9. recession 10. depression,
  prosperity 11. liquidation
  deal.. 4. turn 9. operation
  11. negotiation, transaction
  Exchange.. 4. bank 5. Bolsa
  6. Bourse 11. stock market
  man.. 6. tycoon 8. salesman
  9. solicitor
  place.. 4. mart, shop 5. store
  6. office, shoppe 8. Exchange
bust... 4. bang, fail, hand (Bridge),
  tame (bronco) 5. burst, chest, crash,
  flunk, spree 6. breast, figure
  7. degrade, explode, failure
  8. collapse, demotion, fracture
  9. sculpture 10. bankruptcy
bustard... 4. bird (Old World), kori,
  Otis 5. goose, paauw 6. curlew
  8. Otididae
busted... 4. flat 5. broke 6. broken,
  failed, ruined 7. severed 8. bankrupt,
  ruptured, strapped 9. insolvent,
  penniless 10. stone–broke
bustle... 3. ado 4. fuss, stir, to–do
  5. haste, whirl 6. flurry, hubbub,
  hustle, pother, scurry, tumult
  7. bluster, ferment, fluster, scamper,
  turmoil 8. activity 9. agitation,
  commotion 10. excitement,
  hurly–burly 11. disturbance
bustling... 6. active 7. hurried, rushing
  8. eventful, stirring
busy... 4. nosy, work 5. drive
  6. active, devote, employ, engage,
  occupy 7. engaged, on the go,
  operose 8. diligent, employed,
  meddling, occupied, on the run,
  sedulous 9. assiduous, attentive,
  laborious, officious 10. meddlesome
  11. industrious, inquisitive,
  persevering
busy... 4. dick 6. gossip 7. gumshoe,
  meddler 8. busybody, flatfoot
  9. detective
busybody... 6. gossip 8. quidnunc
  9. pragmatic
but... 2. ma 3. yet 4. even, just,

mere, save 5. hence, outer, still
  6. except 7. however, without
  10. regardless 12. nevertheless
  15. notwithstanding
butcher... 3. fly (angling), mar 4. kill,
  slay 5. botch, spoil 6. killer, vendor
  7. croaker, meatman 8. merchant,
  train–boy 9. slaughter 11. slaughterer
  12. bloodshedder
butchery... 6. murder 7. carnage
  8. business, massacre, shambles
  9. slaughter 14. slaughterhouse
butt... 3. aim, end, jut, pit, ram, tun,
  tup 4. buck, bunt, cart, cask, goat,
  rump, stub 5. cigar, hinge, joint,
  mound, piece, stump 6. target
  (archery), thrust (fencing) 7. buttock,
  parapet, project 8. flatfish
  9. cigarette 13. laughingstock
butter... 3. pat 4. coat, ghee (ghi),
  oleo 5. smear 6. bedaub, spread
  7. butyric 8. flattery 9. margarine,
  suaveness 10. semiliquid
  13. oleomargarine
butter–and–eggs... 8. flaxweed,
  ranstead, toadflax
buttercup fruit... 6. achene
  7. crowtoe
butterfingered... 6. clumsy
  7. awkward, unhandy 8. bungling,
  careless 9. all thumbs 10. blundering
butterflies (slang)... 6. nerves
  7. fidgets, jitters
butterfly (pert to)...
  American.. 7. viceroy
  family.. 10. Agapetidae
  11. Rhopalocera
  genus.. 7. Lycaena 11. Lepidoptera
  large.. 7. monarch
  larva.. 11. caterpillar
  lily.. 4. sego 8. mariposa
  peacock.. 2. io 7. buckeye
  swallowtail.. 5. black, tiger, zebra
  type.. 4. moth 5. satyr 10. fritillary,
  silverspot
buttocks... 4. butt (vulgar), hips, rear,
  rump, seat 5. fanny, podex
  6. bottom 8. haunches, maneuver
  (wrestling) 9. backsides, posterior
buttress... 4. pier, pile, prop, stay
  5. brace, tower 7. shelter, support
  8. abutment 10. projection,
  strengthen 11. counterfort
  13. fortification
buttress (Arch)... 4. pier 6. flying
  7. hanging
buxom... 3. gay 4. boon, rosy 5. jolly,
  plump 6. blithe, jocund, jovial
  7. gleeful
buy... 5. bribe 6. accept, redeem
  7. bargain, expiate 8. purchase
buy back... 6. redeem
Buyer Beware... 12. Caveat Emptor
buzz... 3. hum, saw 5. rumor, snore
  6. bustle, murmur, rumble
  7. ferment, whisper 9. fricative,
  murmuring 10. sibilation
buzzard... 4. aura (turkey), hawk, pern
  5. buteo 6. osprey, stupid 7. harrier
  9. dorbeetle, senseless
  10. cockchafer
buzz bomb... 9. doodlebug

10. bumblebomb
14. Chase–Me–Charlie
bwana (Afr) ... 4. boss 6. master
by ... 2. at, in, on 3. ago, bei, par,
per, via 4. away, gone, near, over,
pass (bridge), past, with 5. after,
aside 6. beside, beyond, nearby,
toward 7. abreast, close by, through
9. in reserve
by–and–by ... 4. anon, soon 5. later,
sweet 6. mañana 7. betimes,
bientôt, ere long, shortly 8. directly
9. presently 11. tout à l'heure
by birth ... 3. nee
bygone ... 3. ago 4. lost, over, past
6. buried, bypast, gone by, passed
7. elapsed, extinct 8. departed,
preterit (preterite)
byname ... 6. eponym 7. babyism,
epithet, surname 8. cognomen,
monicker, nickname 9. sobriquet
10. patronymic 11. appellation
bypass ... 4. go by, miss 5. byway,
elude 6. byroad, detour, escape
7. deviate, digress 8. side path

10. circumvent, roundabout
By the Grace of God ... 9. Dei Gratia
byword ... 3. mot, saw 5. adage,
maxim 6. byname, phrase, saying,
slogan 7. adagium, parable, proverb
8. aphorism, nickname, reproach
9. catchword, sobriquet
10. shibboleth
by word of mouth ... 4. oral 5. parol
(parole)
Byzantine Empire ...
architecture .. 7. St Marks (Venice)
9. elaborate
bookbinding .. 9. unadorned (earlier)
10. bejewelled (later)
church .. 7. Eastern
city .. 14. Constantinople (Istanbul)
creator .. 11. Constantine (the Great)
historian .. 9. Procopius 11. Anna
Comnena
poetry .. 5. hymns
scepter .. 6. ferula
writer .. 6. Prazes 7. Priscus, Romanus
Byzantium ... 14. Constantinople
(Istanbul)

C

C ... 4. clef 7. cedilla, century,
hundred, keynote
caama ... 3. fox 4. asse 10. hartebeest
cab ... 4. pony, taxi 7. measure,
purloin, shelter, taxicab, vehicle
8. carriage (anc) 9. cabriolet
10. locomotive (part) 11. translation
cabal ... 4. clan, plot 5. group, junta,
party 7. chatter, complot, coterie,
dispute, faction 8. intrigue
9. camarilla, collusion, Committee
10. complicity, conspiracy
cabala ... 7. mystery 9. mystic art,
occultism
cabalessou ... 9. armadillo (giant)
cabalistic ... 6. occult 7. cabalic
8. abstract, anagogic, esoteric,
mystical 10. mysterious
caballeria ... 7. measure (land)
8. chivalry 10. knighthood
caballero ... 5. lover, rider 6. knight
8. cavalier, horseman 9. chevalier,
gentleman 10. equestrian
caballo ... 5. horse
cabaret ... 3. inn 4. cafe 6. hostel,
posado, tavern 7. barroom 9. night
club, roadhouse 11. café dansant
13. entertainment
cabbage ... 3. kos (cos) 4. cole, kale,
palm 5. colza, savoy 7. collard
8. colewort, kohlrabi 11. cauliflower
15. Brussels sprouts
cabbage (pert to) ...
curly leaf .. 5. savoy
daisy .. 11. globeflower

fermented .. 5. kraut
headless .. 4. kale
salad .. 4. slaw
seed .. 5. colza
slang .. 4. crib, fool 6. pilfer
7. fathead, purloin 9. numbskull
11. cabbagehead, knucklehead
species .. 8. Brassica
tree .. 4. palm 7. angelin 8. palmetto
white .. 9. butterfly
yellows .. 7. disease (destructive)
caber ... 4. apar, beam, pole 6. rafter,
timber
cabin ... 3. hut 4. shed 5. booth,
coach (Naut), house, hovel, lodge,
shack 6. cabana, saloon 7. caboose
10. blockhouse
cabinet ... 3. box, den 4. Body, buhl,
case 6. bureau, closet, office
7. almirah, boudoir, council, étagère,
whatnot 8. cellaret, cupboard,
ministry 9. committee
cable ... 4. boom, cord, rope, wire
5. chain, twine 6. fasten, hawser
7. coaxial, measure, molding,
ropeway 8. telegram 9. cablegram
cable (pert to) ...
car .. 7. telpher
holder (Naut) .. 7. wildcat 10. cable
wheel
post .. 4. bitt
cabling ... 9. rudenture
cabochon ... 5. jewel, stone (uncut),
style (convex cut) 8. ornament
caboodle ... 3. all, kit, lot 5. bunch,

whole 10. collection 14. kit and caboodle

caboose... 3. car (RR) 5. buggy 6. galley 7. kitchen 9. deckhouse

cabotin... 5. actor (strolling) 9. charlatan

cachaca... 3. rum (white)

cache... 4. hide, hole 5. stash, store 7. conceal, hide–out, retreat 8. hideaway 10. storehouse

cachet... 4. seal 5. sigil, stamp, wafer 6. signet 7. capsule

cachilla... 8. white man

cachot... 7. dungeon

cackle... 3. gab 4. cank, chat, crow, talk 5. clack, laugh, prate 6. babble, gabble, giggle, gossip, jabber 7. chatter, prattle 8. laughter

cacodemon... 4. deva 5. devil, fiend, Indra 10. evil spirit

cacology... 10. bad diction, corruption (speech) 16. mispronunciation

cacophonous... 7. raucous 8. jangling, strident 9. diaphonic, dissonant 10. discordant 11. unmelodious

cacophony... 5. clash 6. jangle 7. discord 8. diaphony (Mus) 9. harshness 10. dissodence

cactus... 4. bleo 5. agave 6. chaute, cholla, mescal 7. Opuntia, saguaro 8. fishhook 9. Turk's–head 11. prickly pear 12. Echinocactus

cad... 4. boor, chum, heel, hick 5. yokel 6. mucker 7. bounder, servant 8. townsman 9. scoundrel, vulgarian

cadaver... 4. body (dead) 5. stiff 6. corpse 7. carcass 8. skeleton

cadaverous... 4. pale 5. gaunt, lurid 6. sickly, wasted 7. ghastly, haggard 9. emaciated 10. attenuated, corpselike

caddis (pert to)...
bait.. 3. fly 4. worm 5. cadew
material.. 4. yarn 5. twill 6. crewel 7. worsted
worm.. 5. larva (aquatic)

caddle... 4. fuss 5. annoy, worry 6. gossip 7. confuse, trouble 8. disarray 9. confusion

cade... 3. keg, oil (Med), pet 4. cask, lamb (orphan) 6. barrel, coddle, petted

cadeau... 4. gift

cadence... 4. beat, lilt, tone 5. meter 6. rhythm 7. balance 9. free verse, vers libre 10. modulation

cadence... 4. half 6. trill 6. plagal 7. perfect 9. authentic, deceptive, imperfect, suspended 11. interrupted

cadency (Her)... 4. rose 5. label 6. mullet 7. annulet, martlet 8. crescent 10. fleur–de–lis 11. cross moline

cadenza... 7. cadence 8. flourish

cadet... 3. son 4. pleb 5. color (blue), youth 6. junior 10. midshipman

cadge... 3. beg 4. hawk 5. fakir, mooch 6. beggar, hawker, mumper, peddle, sponge, vendor 7. carrier, moocher, sponger 8. huckster, sannyasi

cadgy... 6. wanton 7. lustful 8. cheerful, mirthful

Cadmus (pert to)...
daughter.. 3. Ino 6. Semele
father.. 6. Agenor
founder of.. 6. Thebes (Boetia)
sister.. 6. Europa
wife.. 8. Harmonia

cadre... 4. list, unit 5. frame, panel 6. line–up, roster, scheme 8. cadastre, register, schedule, skeleton 9. framework

caduceus (Gr Antiq)... 4. wand (Hermes') 5. staff 6. symbol 8. insignia (Med Corps)

Caesar (pert to)...
betrayer.. 6. Brutus
colleague.. 7. Bibulus
death site.. 4. Nola
Emperor, Dictator of.. 4. Rome
fatal day.. 4. Ides (of March) 11. Ides of March
language.. 5. Latin
rival.. 6. Pompey
river.. 7. Rubicon
sister.. 4. Atia
uncle.. 11. Caius Marius
wife.. 8. Cornelia

caesura, cesura... 4. rest 5. break, colon, comma, pause 8. interval 12. interruption

cafard... 5. bigot, blues 6. humbug 9. hypocrite 10. depression

café... 5. coffe 6. coffee 10. restaurant 11. coffeehouse

café (pert to)...
au lait.. 5. brown 6. alesan 10. French nude
creme.. 5. suede (color)
noir.. 4. musk (color) 11. black coffee
parfait.. 8. beverage

cafetière... 9. coffeepot 10. percolator

caffeine... 6. coffee, theine (in tea) 8. alkaloid 9. stimulant

cafila... 7. caravan (camel)

cage... 3. mew, pen 4. coop 6. corral 7. confine, goal net, impound 8. goal post

cagey... 3. sly 4. foxy, wary, wily 5. canny, leery 6. artful, crafty, shifty, shrews 7. cunning, evasive, knowing

Cain (pert to)...
brother.. 4. Abel
founder of.. 5. Enoch (1st city)
Land of.. 3. Nod
slayer of.. 4. Abel
son.. 5. Enoch

cairn... 4. heap (stones) 6. menhir 8. catstone (catstane), landmark, memorial, monument

Cairo...
capital.. 5. Egypt
city gate (famed).. 9. Bab–el–Nasr
mosque.. 12. Sultan Hassan
resident.. 7. Cairene
river.. 4. Nile
seaport.. 10. Alexandria
tomb.. 10. Mehemet Ali
warrior.. 9. Rameses II

caisson... 3. box 4. case 5. chest, wagon 7. chamber

C
E

caitiff... 4. base, mean, vile
  6. coward, wicked, wretch
  7. budmash, captive 10. despicable
cajole... 4. coax, urge 5. cheat, jolly
  6. delude 7. flatter, palaver,
  sweeten, wheedle 8. blandish
  9. importune 10. honeyfogle
Cajun (pert to)...
  descent.. 6. French (Canadian)
  dialect.. 5. Cajun
  home (present).. 9. Louisiana
  native of.. 6. Acadia (Nova Scotia)
cake... 3. bun, wig 4. bake, food,
  lump, mass, wigg 5. batty, block,
  crust, solid, torte, wafer 6. gateau,
  harden 7. bannock, congeal, oatcake,
  pancake 8. corn pone, solidify
  9. charlotte, simpleton
  11. griddle–cake
cake (pert to)...
  almond paste.. 7. ratafia
  corn.. 4. pone
  flat.. 7. placent
  fried.. 7. cruller 8. doughnut
  Lenten.. 6. cimbal, simnel
  Scotch.. 4. farl (farle) 5. scone
  unleavened.. 8. tortilla
Cake Day (Scot)... 8. hogmanay (New
  Year's)
calabar bean... 6. myotic, ordeal
  7. eserine 8. alkaloid
  13. physostigmine
calabash... 5. gourd 6. baobab, bronze
  (color)
calaboose... 4. gaol, jail 5. choky,
  clink 6. bagnio, lockup, prison
  8. bastille, calabozo 9. Bridewell
calamitous... 3. sad 4. dire, evil
  5. black 6. tragic, woeful 7. adverse,
  baleful, ruinous, unhappy 8. grievous,
  tragical, wretched 10. afflictive,
  deplorable, disastrous
  11. cataclysmic, destructive,
  distressful, unfortunate
  12. catastrophic
calamity... 4. blow, evil, ruin 5. wrack
  6. mishap 7. tragedy 8. casualty,
  disaster, distress, fatality 9. adversity
  10. affliction, misfortune
  11. catastrophe, direfulness,
  unhappiness 12. wretchedness
calathiform... 9. cup–shaped
calcarea... 5. coral 7. sponges
calceiform... 10. orchidlike
  13. clipper–shaped
calcitrant... 8. stubborn
  12. recalcitrant
calcitrate... 4. boot, kick 6. oppose
calculate... 3. aim 4. deem, rate, tell
  5. allow, count, frame, judge, score,
  tally, think 6. cipher, deduce, figure,
  gather, number, reckon 7. average,
  compute, suppose 8. conclude,
  estimate 9. determine, enumerate
calculated... 7. advised, studied,
  weighed 8. measured
  10. considered, deliberate
  11. intentional 12. contemplated
calculating... 8. plotting, scheming
  9. computing, designing, judicious
  10. estimating, numerative, reflecting,
  thoughtful 11. circumspect,

  considerate 14. discriminative
calculator... 5. table 6. abacus
  7. suan pan (swan pan, Chin)
  8. computer 9. estimator, tabulator
  10. parimutuel 11. Comptometer,
  totalizator
caldron, cauldron... 3. pot, red
  (color), vat 6. boiler, kettle, mortar,
  retort 7. alembic 8. crucible
Caleb (pert to)...
  daughter.. 7. Achsaph
  literally.. 3. dog
  son.. 3. Hur, Iru
  spy of.. 6. Canaan
calèche... 7. vehicle (Quebec)
Caledonia (anc)... 8. Scotland
Caledonia bird... 4. kagu
Caledonian... 5. brown 6. Scotch
  8. Scotsman, Scottish
calefacient... 4. warm 6. remedy
  7. heating 11. calefactory
calendar... 4. list, Ordo 5. index, slate
  6. docket, line–up, record
  7. almanac, calends (kalends),
  program 8. register, schedule
  9. catalogue, ephemeris
  10. chronology, prospectus
calendar (type)... 5. Roman, Swiss
  6. Jewish, Julian 7. Chinese
  9. Cotsworth, Gregorian, perpetual
  13. International (fixed)
calenture... 4. glow 5. ardor, fever
  7. passion, pyrexia 9. febrility,
  sunstroke
calepin... 4. book (ref) 7. lexicon
  10. dictionary
calf... 3. leg (part) 4. dolt, fool, skin
  6. bovine, island, weaner 7. iceberg,
  leather 9. youngling
calf (pert to)...
  flesh.. 4. veal
  hide.. 3. kip
  leg (part).. 5. sural
  motherless.. 5. dogie 8. maverick
  sweetbread.. 9. ris de veau
  time.. 5. youth
Caliban (pert to)...
  character.. 5. brute, slave (The
  Tempest)
  deity.. 7. Setebos
  mother.. 7. Sycorax (witch)
caliber, calibre... 4. bore 7. ability
calico... 4. dame 5. cloth 6. salloo
  8. goldfish 12. multicolored
calico (pert to)...
  bird.. 9. turnstone
  bush.. 6. laurel
  horse, pony.. 5. pinto 7. piebald
  printing.. 4. teer 7. topical
calid... 3. hot 4. mild, warm 6. genial
  7. burning, thermal
California...
  bay.. 8. Monterey
  capital.. 10. Sacramento
  city.. 6. Fresno 7. Oakland 8. San
  Diego, Stockton 9. Long Beach
  10. Los Angeles 12. San Francisco,
  Santa Barbara
  desert.. 6. Mojave 8. Colorado
  discoverer.. 6. Cortez (1535)
  flower.. 5. poppy
  history.. 8. Gold Rush (1848),

Missions 11. Sutter's Mill
lake.. 5. Tahoe 8. Elsinore 9. Salton
Sea
lowest point.. 11. Death Valley
mountain.. 6. Lassen, Shasta
7. Whitney
oldest living thing.. 8. redwoods
14. General Sherman (tree)
15. bristlecone pine
river.. 4. Kern 7. Feather, Russian
10. Sacramento
pageant.. 10. Rose Parade
17. Tournament of Roses
State admission.. 11. thirty–first
State motto.. 6. Eureka
State nickname.. 6. Golden
caliph, calif... 3. Ali (4th) 4. Imam
(Imaum), Omar 6. Othman 7. Abu
Bekr 8. Islamite
Caliph Ali's descendants... 5. Alids
(Alides)
caliphate... 7. Omniads, Shiites
(Sectaries) 8. Idrisids 9. Fatimites
calk, caulk... 4. copy, plug, stop
5. close, sleep (Naut sl) 6. calque,
catnap, chinse, plug up, stop up
7. occlude
call... 3. bid, cry, dub, hip, nod
4. ahoy, beck, dial, name, plea, ring,
soho, sook (hog), taps, term, yell
5. alarm, basis, cause, clepe, rally,
rouse, shout, style, visit, waken
6. appeal, demand, ground, invoke,
motive, muster, option, reason,
sennet, signal, slogan, summon
7. appoint, bidding, collect, convoke,
fanfare, summons, trumpet
8. assemble, nominate, occasion,
reveille 9. battle cry, challenge,
designate, induction, telephone,
watchword 10. denominate, invitation
11. recruitment, requisition
12. conscription 13. justification
call (pert to)...
attention.. 6. direct, remind 8. point
out
back.. 6. recall, recant, repeal, revive,
revoke 7. retract 8. remember
9. recollect
down.. 6. invoke 7. bawl out,
reprove, tell off
evil upon.. 8. execrate
forth.. 5. evoke, rouse 6. elicit,
excite, induce, prompt, summon
names.. 4. cite 5. abuse, curse
6. insult, revile, vilify 8. besmirch
10. vituperate
together.. 6. muster, summon
7. convoke
to mind.. 4. cite 8. remember
9. visualize
callant, callan... 3. boy, lad 4. chap
5. youth 6. fellow, garçon, laddie
8. customer, muchacho
11. hobbledehoy
calle... 6. street
called... 5. named 6. dubbed, y–clept,
yermed 7. y–cleped
calling... 3. art, nod 4. beck, lure,
name, work 5. trade 6. career,
metier, naming, outcry 7. bidding,
mission, pursuit, styling, summons

8. biddance, business, labeling
(labelling), practice, vocation
9. condition, evocation
10. employment, invitation,
occupation, profession
13. circumstances
calling crab... 7. fiddler
calling hare... 4. pika
Calliope... 4. Muse (poet) 5. organ
8. asteroid
Calliope's son... 7. Orpheus
callous, calloused... 4. horn, sear
5. horny, inure 6. harden, seared
8. hardened 9. heartless, indurated,
unfeeling 10. impervious
11. hardhearted 12. thick–skinned
14. pachydermatous
callow... 5. crude, green 6. tender,
unripe, vernal 7. budding
8. immature, unformed 9. unfledged
10. unseasoned 11. undeveloped
15. unsophisticated
callus... 6. tyloma
calm... 3. lay 4. cool, dill, fair, lull,
mild 5. allay, balmy, peace, quiet,
sober, still 6. becalm, hushed, pacify,
placid, sedate, serene, smooth,
soothe, steady 7. appease, compose,
halcyon, orderly, pacific, placate,
restful, unmoved 8. peaceful, tranquil
9. quiescent, unruffled
10. phlegmatic 11. tranquilize,
undisturbed 13. dispassionate,
imperturbable
calmant, calmative... 7. anodyne,
soother 8. lenitive, pacifier, sedative,
soothing 10. depressant, palliative
11. alleviative 12. tranquilizer
calmato (Mus)... 4. calm 8. tranquil
calmness... 4. calm, lull 5. peace,
poise, quiet 6. repose 8. quietude,
serenity 9. composure, placidity
10. equanimity, quiescence
11. restfulness, self–control
calor... 4. heat 5. therm 7. thermal
calorifics... 4. heat 7. heating
calumniate... 4. slur 5. belie, libel
6. accuse, revile 7. asperse, slander,
traduce 9. blaspheme
calumnious... 7. abusive 8. derisive,
insolent, libelous 9. insulting
10. defamatory, derogatory,
slanderous 11. maledictory,
opprobrious
calumny... 5. abuse 7. lampoon,
slander 9. contumely 10. detraction,
scurrility 11. malediction
12. vilification
calvary... 8. crucifix
Calvary (Bib)... 8. Damascus, Golgotha
9. Jerusalem
Calvinism (pert to)...
author.. 6. Calvin
doctrine.. 5. Grace 9. Atonement,
Depravity (total) 12. Perseverance (of
Saints) 14. Predestination
site.. 6. Geneva
Calvinistic Methodist... 5. Welsh
10. Whitefield 14. Lady Huntingdon
Calypso... 6. Ogygia (home)
8. Cytherea, sea nymph (The
Odyssey)

calyx... 3. cup 4. husk 5. galea, sepal
6. corona 7. corolla 8. epicalyx,
perianth
camarada... 7. comrade, partner
9. companion
camaraderie... 8. good will
11. familiarity 14. good–fellowship
camarilla... 5. cabal 6. clique
7. council
camata... 6. acorns 8. oak fruit
cambist... 6. banker, broker
9. financier 11. moneylender
12. money–changer
Cambodia...
capital.. 6. Angkor 8. Pnom–Penh
language.. 5. Khmer 9. Cambodian
religion.. 8. Buddhism
seaport.. 6. Kampot
Cambria... 5. Wales
Cambridge University (pert to)...
English examination.. 6. tripos
English student.. 5. sizar 6. optime
(honor)
Massachusetts.. 3. MIT 7. Harvard
camel... 4. oont 5. llama 6. deloul,
mammal, vicuna 7. Camelus
8. Bactrian (2–humped)
9. Camelidae, dromedary
camel hair shawl... 8. cashmere
camelopard... 7. giraffe
13. constellation
Camelot... 6. legend 10. King Arthur,
palace site, Round Table
cameo... 4. onyx 7. relievo
8. anaglyph
camera type... 5. Kodak 7. Brownie
10. Rollieflex
Cameroon...
capital.. 7. Yaounde (Afr)
native.. 4. Sara
river.. 5. Shari
seaport.. 6. Douala
tribe.. 3. Abo 5. Bantu
Camino Real (Calif)... 9. Royal Road
12. El Camino Real, King's Highway
Camorra (It)... 12. organization (secret)
camouflage... 7. falsify 8. disguise
9. dissemble 10. false front
12. misrepresent
camp... 4. clan, tent 5. abode, etape,
junto, tabor 6. campoo, clique,
laager 7. bivouac, faction
10. encampment
campaign... 5. serve 7. crusade
9. operation
camphorated tincture of opium...
9. paregoric
campus... 4. quad 5. field (academic)
can... 3. jar, may, tin 6. hopper,
vessel 7. capable 8. canister,
conserve 9. competent
10. receptacle
can... 5. skill 7. ability 9. competent
10. receptacle
can (sl)... 3. jug, tin 4. boot, bump,
fire, jail, john, kick 6. bounce,
cooler, toilet 7. dismiss 9. discharge
11. give the gate
Canaan... 9. Palestine 12. Promised
Land
Canada... see also *Canadian*
capital (Federal).. 6. Ottawa

city.. 7. Toronto 8. Hamilton,
Montreal, Winnipeg 9. Vancouver
discoverer.. 9. John Cabot (1497)
Hudson's Bay Co.. 8. fur trade
native.. 6. French 7. English
nickname.. 6. Canuck
park.. 6. Jasper
peninsula.. 5. Gaspé
police.. 8. Mounties 12. Royal
Mounted (7,000)
river.. 5. Peace, Slave 6. Fraser,
Nelson, Ottawa 8. Gatineau
9. Athabasca, Churchill, Mackenzie
10. St Lawrence
Canadian (pert to)...
flour.. 6. Shorts (milling) 8. canaille
jay.. 9. moose bird 10. whisky jack
lynx.. 5. pishu
plum.. 6. cheney
porcupine.. 5. urson 7. cawquaw
squaw.. 6. mahala
canaille... 3. mob 4. ruck 6. rabble,
ragtag, Shorts 8. riffraff
10. roughscuff
canal... 4. duct, iter (brain), pipe, tube
5. drain 6. meatus 7. acequia,
channel 10. waterspout
11. watercourse
Canal... 4. Erie, Kiel, Suez 6. Panama
13. Sault Ste Marie (Soo)
Canal Zone Lock... 5. Gatun
10. Miraflores
canard... 4. duck, hoax 5. rumor
6. humbug 9. falsehood
canary... 6. yellow 8. song–bird,
songster, weakling
Canary Islands...
capital.. 9. Santa Cruz (Teneriffe)
city.. 9. Las Palmas (Grand Canary)
commune.. 4. Icod
owner.. 5. Spain
cancel... 4. blot, dele, kill, omit, undo
5. annul, erase 6. delete, excise,
recall, repeal, revoke 7. abolish,
destroy, nullify, rescind, retract
8. write off 10. invalidate, neutralize,
obliterate 11. countermand
cancellation... 6. repeal 7. erasure
8. deletion, write–off 10. moratorium
12. obliteration
cancer... 4. evil 5. tumor 6. canker,
growth 7. sarcoma 8. neoplasm
9. carcinoma
Cancer... 4. crab 7. mansion (moon)
10. zodiac sign 13. constellation
cancion... 4. song 5. lyric
Candia... 5. Crete (Isl)
candid... 4. fair, just, open, pure
5. frank 6. direct, honest 7. sincere
9. guileless, impartial, ingenuous
10. impersonal 13. dispassionate
15. straightforward
candidate... 6. seeker 7. aspirer,
electee, nominee 8. aspirant, selectee
9. applicant, appointee, postulant
10. solicitant
candidate list... 4. leet 5. slate
6. roster
Candide (pert to)...
hero, title.. 5. novel
novel, author.. 8. Voltaire
philosophy.. 8. optimism

candied... 5. sweet 7. honeyed
  9. congealed, incrusted, preserved
  10. flattering, granulated
  12. crystallized
candied sea holly... 6. eryngo (eringo)
candle... 3. dip, wax 5. light, power,
  taper 6. bougie, cierge, tallow, votive
  7. paschal 8. bayberry 9. chandelle
candlestick (pert to)...
  Bib.. 6. lampad
  branched.. 9. girandole
  ornamental.. 10. candelabra
  Scot.. 6. crusie
  spike.. 7. pricket
  three–branched.. 9. tricerion
  torch type.. 8. flambeau
  wall.. 6. sconce
candlewood... 6. flower 8. ocotillo
candor... 8. fairness, openness
  9. frankness, sincerity, unreserve
  10. directness 11. artlessness,
  unrestraint 13. outspokenness
candy... 5. sweet 6. penide (pulled),
  sweets 7. sweeten 8. crystals
  9. granulate, sweetmeat
  10. confection 11. crystallize
  13. confectionary
candy (type)... 4. mint 5. fudge, taffy
  6. bonbon, nougat, toffee 7. brittle,
  caramel, fondant, panocha, penuche,
  praline 8. licorice, lollipop
  9. chocolate 11. marshmallow
candytuft... 6. iberis
cane... 3. rod 4. beat, club, reed,
  stem, whip 5. crook, sorgo, staff,
  stick, sugar 6. bamboo, rattan
  7. bagasse, bourdon, sorghum,
  sucrose 9. handstaff, truncheon
  12. swagger stick
canescent... 5. hoary, white 7. grizzly,
  silvery, whitish 9. snow–white
Canfield... 9. solitaire
canine... 3. cur, dog, fox, pug, pup
  4. lobo, mutt, tike 5. dingo, pooch,
  puppy, whelp 6. animal, coyote
  7. Canidae, doggish, laniary, mastiff,
  mongrel, reynard 8. dogtooth,
  eyetooth
canis... 3. dog
Canis Majoris... 13. Constellation (with
  Dog Star, Sirius)
cannibalism... 9. barbarity, endophagy
  10. perversion 11. blood thirst
  13. anthropophagy
cannon... 3. gun 5. crash 6. mortar
  7. firearm, robinet 8. dog of war,
  howitzer, ordnance 9. artillery,
  collision
cannon (pert to)...
  ball.. 6. pellet 7. missile
  bore.. 6. breech
  fire.. 7. barrage
  handle.. 4. anse
  nautical.. 5. chase
  part.. 8. cascabel
  pivot.. 8. trunnion
  platform.. 10. terreplein
  plug.. 7. tampion
  shot.. 5. grape
  shoulder part.. 7. rimbase
cannonade... 4. boom, peal, roar
  5. blitz, shell 6. rumble, strafe

  11. bombardment
canny... 3. sly 4. foxy, wary, wily
  6. artful, frugal, shrewd, subtle
  7. cunning, knowing, prudent, thrifty
  8. cautious 9. sagacious
canoe... 4. kiak, pahi, proa, waka
  5. bongo, bungo, kayak, umiak,
  waapa 6. corial, dugout, oomiak,
  pitpan 7. almadia, buckeye (bugeye),
  coracle, piragua, pirogue
  12. pambanmanche
canon... 3. law 4. code, list, rule,
  type 5. model, nodus (Mus)
  6. belief, clergy, decree, ritual
  7. measure, precept 8. decision
  9. catalogue, criterion 10. regulation
  11. composition 12. constitution
canonical... 4. None (hour), Sext
  (hour) 5. Lauds, Prime 6. Matins
  7. creedal 8. dogmatic, orthodox
  9. doctrinal 10. scriptural
  11. theological 14. ecclesiastical
canonization... 8. sainting
  10. ordainment, ordination
  12. consecration, enshrinement
canopy... 3. sky 4. ceil, cope, dais,
  tent 5. cover, shade, vault
  6. awning, testor 7. blanket,
  marquee, shelter 8. caponier
  (caponiere), ciborium, pavilion
  9. baldachin, firmament
canorous... 5. clear 8. sonorous
  9. melodious 10. euphonious
cant... 3. tip 4. lean, list, sing, song,
  sway, tack, tilt 5. angle, argot,
  chant, lingo, pitch, slang, slope,
  whine 6. careen, intone, jargon,
  patois, snivel 7. auction, incline,
  mummery 8. pretense 9. hypocrisy
  10. intonation, sanctimony
  17. sanctimoniousness
cantabank... 6. singer (ballad)
cantador... 6. singer (folk songs)
cantankerous... 8. perverse
  9. malicious 10. contention,
  ill–natured 12. cross–grained
cantata... 5. motet 8. serenata
  9. pastorale
canter... 4. gait, lope 6. gallop
  (Canterbury) 8. vagabond
Canterbury...
  archbishop.. 7. Cranmer, Primate
  13. Thomas à Becket (murdered)
  capital (Eng).. 14. ecclesiastical
  famed building.. 9. Cathedral
  gallop.. 5. aubin 6. canter
  Tales, author.. 7. Chaucer
canticle... 3. lay, ode 4. hymn, lied,
  song 5. carol, ditty 6. Te Deum
Canticle of Canticles (Bib)...
  11. Song of Songs 13. Song of
  Solomon
cantilena... 6. legato, melody
  8. graceful
cantina... 3. bag 6. pocket, saloon
  7. canteen
cantle... 4. nook, part 5. crown, slice
  6. corner, saddle (part) 7. segment
  11. cornerpiece
canto... 4. book, song 5. poems (div
  of), tenor, verse 6. cantus, melody,
  poetry 7. descort

canton... 3. Uri (Switz) 6. county
7. commune, quarter 8. district,
insignia (Her), mofussil (Ind)
9. bailiwick, partition
cantor... 6. leader, singer 7. soloist
8. melodist, vocalist 9. precentor
cantoria... 7. balcony, gallery (choir)
cantrip... 5. charm, magic, spell, trick
canty... 6. lively 7. chipper 8. cheerful
9. sprightly
Canuck... 8. Canadian
canvas... 4. sail, tent, tuke (tewke)
5. cloth 6. circus 7. picture, tentage
8. covering, likeness, pavilion
9. tarpaulin 14. representation
canvasback... 4. duck
canvass... 4. poll 5. study 6. survey
7. examine, inquiry, solicit
8. campaign, consider 10. scrutinize
11. electioneer 12. solicitation
13. questionnaire
canyon, cañon... 4. abra (mouth)
5. chasm, dalle (wall), gorge, gulch
6. arroyo, coulee, ravine, violet
7. couloir
canzone, canzonetta... 4. poem, song
6. ballad, melody 8. canzonet,
madrigal
caoba... 8. mahogany, muskwood
caoutchouc... 3. ule 6. caucho, rubber
cap... 3. fez, hat, lid, taj, tam 4. atef,
coif, hood, kepi 5. beret, boina,
busby, shako, toque 6. barret,
biggin, bonnet, calpac, cloche, pileus,
turban 7. biretta (beretta), calotte,
calpack, chapeau 8. Balmoral,
havelock 9. headdress, headpiece,
shtreimal, sou'wester, zucchetto
10. cervelière 11. mortarboard,
tam–o'–shanter
cap (outer part)... 3. lid, tip, top
4. dome, fuze, peak, type 5. cover,
crown, excel, match, spire, trump
6. summit, top off 7. capital (Arch),
overlie, patella 8. complete
9. copestone, detonator
capa... 5. cloak 6. mantle 7. tobacco
capability... 5. power, skill 6. genius
7. ability, caliber, faculty, potency
8. ableness, adequacy, capacity
10. competence 13. qualification
capable... 3. apt, can, fit 4. able
5. adept 6. expert 7. equal to,
skilled 8. adequate 9. competent,
effective, efficient, qualified
10. proficient 12. accomplished
capable of...
boring.. 10. zylotomous
carrying.. 9. portative
flying.. 6. volant
growing.. 6. viable
living in harmony.. 10. compatible
penetration.. 8. pervious
suffering.. 8. passible 9. sensitive
capable of being...
ascertained.. 12. determinable
cultivated.. 6. arable
cut.. 7. sectile
defended.. 7. tenable
done.. 10. effectible
heard.. 7. audible
prevented.. 9. avertible

proved.. 8. testable 12. demonstrable
regulated.. 12. controllable
separated.. 9. divisible
spread.. 10. infectious
12. communicable
thrown.. 7. missile
uttered.. 7. effable
capacious... 4. full, much, wide
5. ample, broad, large, roomy
8. generous, spacious 9. expansive,
extensive 10. commodious,
voluminous 12. considerable
13. comprehensive
capacity... 4. role, room, size 5. limit,
power, skill, space 6. extent, spread,
status, talent, volume 7. caliber,
content, faculty, fitness, measure
8. adequacy, aptitude, function,
position, relation, strength
9. character 10. capability, efficiency
11. capacitance (Elec)
12. intelligence 13. accommodation
capacity for knowing... 9. intellect
cap and bells... 6. bauble, comedy
(symbol), motley 7. costume, marotti
9. headdress
caparison... 3. rig 4. tack 5. armor,
dress, get–up 6. livery 7. harness,
housing, panoply 10. horsecloth
12. horse blanket
cape... 3. ras 4. hood, mino, naze,
ness, spur 5. amice, cappa, cloak,
fichu, orale, point, sagum, talma
6. mantle, sontag, tippet 8. pelerine
(fur) 9. Inverness
cape (pert to)...
gooseberry.. 4. poha
hen.. 4. skua 6. petrel
pigeon.. 7. pintado
polecat.. 5. zoril
ruby.. 6. garnet, pyrope
sheep.. 9. albatross (Naut term)
Cape Cod turkey... 7. codfish (humor)
Cape Dutch... 9. Afrikaans (language)
Cape of Good Hope discoverer...
4. Diaz (1488)
caper... 3. tea 4. dido, leap, romp,
skip 5. antic, berry, dance, frisk,
prank 6. cavort, frolic, gambol,
prance 8. capriole, marigold
9. privateer (Hist)
capercaille... 6. grouse 13. cock of
the wood
caper herb family... 6. Cleome
8. Capparis 9. Polanisia
10. clammyweed 13. Capparidaceae
Cape Town... 7. capital (U of S Afr)
Cape Verde Island (Afr)... 3. Sal
Cape Verde negro... 5. Serer
capias... 4. writ 6. caveat 7. process,
warrant 8. mandamus 9. nisi prius
capillary... 4. fine, tube 6. minute,
vessel 7. slender 8. hairlike, trichoid
capilliform... 7. thready 8. hairlike
capillus... 4. hair
capistrate... 6. cowled, hooded
capital... 3. top 4. city, main, rare,
seat, type 5. chief, crest, crown,
funds, major, means, prime, vital
6. assets, letter, ruling, supply
7. leading, primary, serious, weighty
8. cardinal, dominant, foremost,

splendid 9. excellent, financial,
important, paramount, principal,
prominent 10. commanding,
preeminent, shoestring
capitalism ... 8. politics
10. government 11. bourgeoisie
14. free enterprise
capitalist ... 5. baron 6. tycoon
7. rich man 8. investor 9. bourgeois,
financier, plutocrat
capital letter ... 6. uncial 9. majuscule
capital punishment ... 5. noose
7. gallows, hanging 8. shooting, the
chair 9. beheading, execution,
fusillade 10. guillotine
12. decapitation 13. electrocution
capitano ... 3. don 4. capo 5. chief
7. captain, headman
capitate ... 7. globose 8. enlarged,
headlike
Capitol (pert to) ...
Federal .. 10. Washington (DC)
State .. 10. Statehouse
capitulate ... 4. cede, fall 9. surrender
capitulation ... 6. résumé, review,
treaty 7. recount, summary
9. agreement, reckoning, rehearsal,
statement, summation, surrender
10. compendium 11. enumeration,
stipulation 14. relinquishment
capon ... 3. hen 4. cock, fowl
6. pullet, rabbit (castrated)
7. chicken, poulard, poultry, rooster
caporal ... 4. boss 7. foreman, tobacco
8. overseer
capote ... 4. hood 5. cloak 6. bonnet,
mantle, piquet 8. overcoat
capped ... 7. crested, pileata, pileate
Capri ...
beverage .. 4. wine (white)
color .. 4. blue 9. blue green
island site .. 11. Bay of Naples
ruins (famed) .. 7. palaces (Tiberius)
8. grottoes 10. Blue Grotto
caprice ... 3. fad, toy 4. kink, mood,
whim 5. fancy, freak, humor, prank,
quirk 6. vagary 7. whimsey (whimsy)
8. crotchet, escapade, flimflam
capricious ... 5. moody 6. fickle, fitful
7. erratic, wayward 8. fanciful,
freakish, humorous, notional, sporadic,
unsteady 9. arbitrary, crotchety,
eccentric, fantastic, whimsical
10. inconstant 12. inconsistent
13. temperamental
Capricorn ... 4. goat 7. mansion (of
Saturn) 10. zodiac sign
13. constellation
capriole ... 4. leap 5. caper 6. cavort,
curvet, gambol
capsicum ... 4. herb 5. chili 6. pepper
capsize ... 5. spill, upset 7. subvert, tip
over 8. overturn 9. overthrow
10. turn turtle
capsule ... 3. sac 4. pill 5. ascus,
brief, theca, wafer 6. précis, sheath
7. enclose, epitome 8. abstract,
envelope, pericarp, seedcase,
synopsis 10. compendium
capsulize ... 5. brief 7. abridge, outline
8. abstract, condense 9. epitomize,
summarize

captain ... 4. skip 5. chief, ruler
6. leader, master, patron, police
7. headman, officer, skipper
8. overlord 9. commander
10. shipmaster
Captain Kidd ... 6. pirate
Captains Courageous (pert to) ...
author .. 7. Kipling
setting .. 9. Grand Bank
(Newfoundland)
tale of .. 7. romance
caption ... 5. title 6. legend, rubric
7. capture, seizure 8. headline,
subtitle
captious ... 6. severe 7. carping,
cynical, peevish 8. caviling, critical
9. bickering, paltering, quibbling
12. equivocatory, faultfinding
13. hypercritical
captivate ... 4. lure, vamp 5. charm,
snare 6. allure, enamor, ravish,
seduce 7. attract, becharm, beguile,
bewitch, capture, delight, enchant
8. enthrall 9. enrapture, fascinate,
infatuate, transport
captive ... 4. bond, serf 5. helot
6. détenu, thrall, unfree, vassal
7. hostage 8. conquest, enslaved,
prisoner 10. subjugated
captivity ... 6. duress 7. bondage,
durance, serfdom, slavery
9. detention, servitude, thralldom
10. internment, subjection
11. confinement, impoundment
12. imprisonment 13. incarceration
captor ... 5. taker 7. catcher
8. capturer
capture ... 3. beg, nab, net, win
4. gain, haul, take 5. catch, pinch,
raven, snare 6. arrest, collar
7. caption, seizure 9. apprehend,
detention 12. apprehension
capuche (Eccl) ... 4. cowl, hood
capuchin ... 3. sai 5. Cebus
6. monkey, pigeon
caput ... 3. cap, top 4. head 5. crest,
crown 7. chapter, section
9. paragraph
car ... 4. auto, cart, jeep, tram
5. coupe, motor, sedan, truck, wagon
6. hot rod, jalopy, wheels (sl)
7. caboose, chariot, clunker (sl),
compact, flivver, machine, Pullman,
vehicle 8. carriage 9. dune buggy,
hatchback 10. automobile,
subcompact
carabao ... 5. mango 7. buffalo
carabinieri ... 9. policeman
10. carabineer
caracal ... 3. fur 4. lynx, pelt
caracara ... 4. hawk 8. carancha
caracole ... 5. caper (manège)
9. staircase
caract ... 5. charm 6. symbol (magic)
carafe ... 6. bottle
carafon ... 8. decanter
carapace ... 5. plate, shell (turtle)
6. chitin, lorica, shield 7. carapax
caravan ... 3. van 5. wagon 6. cafila
(camel) 9. cavalcade, motorcade
10. expedition, procession
caravansary ... 3. inn 4. khan (chan)

5. hotel, serai 6. hostel, imaret, posado 8. hostelry 9. resthouse, roadhouse

carbine... 5. rifle 6. musket 7. escopet

carbohydrate... 5. sugar 6. starch 7. dextrin, glucose, lactose, maltose, sucrose 8. dextrose, glycogen, nutrient 9. cellulose 10. saccharide, saccharose

carbon... 4. coke, copy, fuel, lead, soot 7. diamond, residue 8. graphite

carbonate... 3. ore 5. trona 6. aerate, natron 9. carbonize 11. chemicalize

carbon dioxide... 3. gas 6. dry ice 7. seeding (cloud) 11. refrigerant

Carborundum... 5. emery 8. abrasive 14. silicon carbide

carcass... 4. body 5. bones, kreng (whale) 6. corpse 7. cadaver, remains 8. skeleton

carcer... 5. stall (Rom circus) 6. prison

card... 3. map, tum 4. comb, menu, post, rove 6. docket, domino, oddity, postal, record, ticket 7. calling, program 8. calendar, schedule 9. character 13. communication

card game... 3. gin, hoc, loo, pan 4. bank, faro, keno, skat 5. cinch, comet, monte, pitch, poker, rummy, stuss, tarot, whist 6. bridge, casino, écarté, hearts, piquet, rounce 7. auction, bezique, canasta, cassino, cayenne 8. baccarat, contract, cribbage, pinochle 9. solitaire 10. panguingui

card game term... 3. ace 4. meld, pass, pone, slam, trey, vole 5. joker, pedro, tarot 6. cathop, misère, tenace, tricon 7. declare 9. mistigris

cardinal... 3. red 4. bird, fish, main 5. chief 6. bishop, deacon, number, priest, ruling 8. crowning, dominant, foremost 9. paramount, principal 10. preeminent

cardinal (pert to)...
astrology.. 5. nadir 6. zenith
astronomy.. 10. solstitial 11. equinoctial
biology.. 7. maximum, minimum, optimum
compass point.. 4. east, west 5. north, south
number.. 7. primary (one, two, three)
office.. 6. datary 7. dataria
virtues.. 7. justice 8. prudence 9. fortitude 10. temperance
virtues (Theol).. 4. hope 5. faith 7. charity

cardinal's hat... 3. red 4. rank 6. office

care... 4. duty, fret, heed, reck, task, tend, wish 5. aegis, worry 6. desire, regard 7. anxiety, caution, cherish, concern, custody, keeping 9. attention, patronage 10. affliction, protection, solicitude 11. carefulness, heedfulness, supervision, thriftiness 12. jurisdiction 13. consideration

careen... 3. tip 4. cant, heel, keel, lean, list, tilt 5. slant, slope

career... 3. set 4. flow, flux, line, work 6. course, stream 7. calling, mission,

passage, pursuit 8. business, practice, progress, vocation 10. occupation, profession

care for... 4. help, like, love, mind, reck, tend 5. fancy, guard, nurse, prize, watch 6. attend, dote on, foster, mother, relish, wait on 7. nurture 10. appreciate

carefree... 5. happy 6. jaunty 8. debonair 10. insouciant 12. lighthearted

careful... 4. wary 5. canny, chary, exact 7. anxious, guarded, heedful, mindful, prudent, thrifty 8. cautious, discreet, gingerly, vigilant 9. advertent, attentive 10. meticulous, scrupulous, solicitous, thoughtful 11. circumspect, considerate, painstaking, punctilious

careless... 3. lax 5. loose 6. rakish, remiss, sloppy 8. heedless, mindless, reckless, slipshod, slovenly 9. impulsive, negligent, unheeding, unmindful 10. nonchalant, regardless, unthinking 11. inadvertent, thoughtless, unconcerned 13. inconsiderate

carelessness... 8. bungling, disorder 9. disregard, unconcern 10. blundering, negligence 11. nonchalance 12. heedlessness, indifference, recklessness 13. impulsiveness 15. inconsideration, thoughtlessness

caress... 3. pat, pet 4. bill, kiss 5. touch 6. coddle, cosset, dandle, fondle, pamper, stroke 10. endearment

caressing... 7. hugging, kissing 8. fondling 9. endearing

cargo... 4. load 5. goods 6. burden, charge, lading 7. carload, freight 8. boatload, shipload 9. truckload

cargo (pert to)...
afloat.. 7. flotsam
cast overboard.. 6. jetsam
loader, unloader.. 9. stevedore

Carib... 6. Indian

caribou... 4. deer 8. reindeer

caricature... 5. comic 6. overdo, parody 7. cartoon, picture 8. satirize, travesty 9. burlesque 10. caricatura, distortion 12. exaggeration

caricaturist... 6. artist 8. humorist, parodist 10. burlesquer

caries... 5. decay (Dent) 10. ulceration

carillon... 4. lyra 5. bells (fixed) 6. chimes 12. glockenspiel

cark... 3. vex 4. care, heed, load 5. pains, worry 6. burden, charge, harass 7. trouble 8. distress

carl, carlot... 4. boor 5. churl 6. rustic 7. peasant, villein 8. bondsman 10. husbandman, pinchpenny

Carmelite... 3. nun 4. monk 5. friar 8. White Nun 10. White Friar

carmen... 4. poem, song 11. incantation

Carmen... 5. gypsy, opera (1875) 7. heroine, romance

carmine... 3. red 5. color, stain

7. crimson, scarlet
carnage ... 8. butchery, massacre
9. bloodshed, slaughter
10. decimation
carnal ... 4. lewd 6. bodily, fleshy
7. earthly, mundane, sensual, worldly
9. corporeal 11. unspiritual
12. bloodthirsty
carnation ... 3. red 4. pink, self
7. bizarre, picotee 8. Dianthus
carnelian ... 4. sard 9. copper red
10. chalcedony
carnival ... 4. fair, show 6. circus
7. revelry 8. feasting, festival
9. amusement, Mardi Gras
11. merrymaking 12. masquerading
carnivore ... 3. cat, dog 4. bear, lion,
puma, seal 5. civet, coati, genet,
hyena, otter, panda, ratel, sable,
tiger, ursus 6. badger, mammal,
marten, weasel 7. meerkat, raccoon
8. mongoose 9. ichneumon
10. cacomistle
carnivorous ... 10. meat–eating,
predaceous 11. omophageous
carol ... 3. lay 4. lied, lilt, noel, sing,
song 5. dance (anc) 6. ballad,
warble 7. rejoice
Caroline Islands (coral) ... 3. Yap
5. Parao 6. Ponape
carom ... 4. bump 6. bounce, cannon,
strike 8. ricochet
carousal ... 4. lark, orgy, romp
5. binge, feast, fling, revel, spree
6. frolic 7. banquet, carouse, revelry,
wassail
carouse ... 4. birl 5. bouse, drink,
spree, toast 9. dissipate
carpet ... 3. mat, rug 4. Agra, Kali,
Kuba 5. Herat (Herati), namda, tapis
6. nammad, Wilton 7. drugget
8. Brussels, flooring, moquette
9. Axminster, broadloom
11. Baluchistan
carpetbagger ... 8. swindler
10. politician
carriage ... 3. air 4. mien, pose
7. bearing, posture 8. attitude,
demeanor, presence 10. deportment
carriage (pert to) ...
English.. 6. waggon 7. growler
8. dormeuse, stanhope
French.. 6. fiacre 7. caliche, voiture
general.. 3. bus, cab, car, gig, rig,
van 4. baby, hack, pram, shay, trap
5. buggy, coach, wagon 6. calssh,
chaise, cisium, dennet, go–cart,
hansom, landau, surrey, tandem
7. cariole, chariot, omnibus, phaeton,
tallyho, vehicle 8. carryall, clarence,
dearborn, rockaway, victoria
9. kittereen, landaulet
10. conveyance, shandrydan
12. perambulator
history.. 7. tumbrel, vis–à–vis, whiskey
8. curricle
Indian.. 4. okka 5. tonga 6. gharry
7. hackery
Italian.. 7. vettura
one–horse.. 3. gig 4. shay 5. sulky
Orient.. 4. sado 10. jinrikisha

Philippines.. 9. carromata
Russia.. 5. araba 6. troika 7. droshky
9. tarantass
carried ... 5. borne, giddy, toted
6. carted, lugged 8. conveyed,
ravished 11. transported
carrier ... 3. boy 4. mail, mule, rail,
ship, wave 5. crate 6. bearer, coolie,
pigeon, porter, redcap, runner, vessel
7. courier, drayman, express
8. cargador, conveyor, teamster
9. messenger, stevedore
carrier (pert to) ...
disease.. 3. fly, rat 7. typhoid
8. mosquito
Indian.. 5. Tinne (Brit)
staff.. 5. macer
carrion ... 4. vile 6. corpse, rotten
7. carcass, corrupt 9. loathsome
carrion (pert to) ...
bug.. 6. beetle
buzzard.. 4. hawk 7. vulture
8. caracara
flower.. 5. morel
fungus.. 9. stinkhorn
carrot ... 5. drias (deadly) 6. Daucus
(Old World) 9. Ammiaceae
10. nivernaise (glazed), umbellifer
carrousel ... 9. whirligig
10. roundabout, tournament
12. merry–go–round
carry ... 3. lug 4. bear, cart, hold,
take, tote, wart 5. ferry 6. convey
7. conduct, publish 8. transfer,
transmit 9. transport
carry away, off ... 3. win 6. abduct,
eloign, enamor, remove 7. succeed
9. fascinate 10. accomplish
carry on ... 4. rage, wage 6. endure,
frolic, manage 7. conduct, operate
8. continue 9. misbehave, persevere
carry out, through ... 2. do 5. apply
6. ravish 7. execute, perform, sustain
8. complete, continue, transact
10. accomplish
cart ... 4. dray, wain 5. carry, sulky,
wagon 6. convey, reckla, telega
7. morfrey (morphrey), tumbrel (anc),
vehicle (2–wheeled)
carta, Charta ... 4. deed 5. Magna
(Eng) 7. charter 9. parchment
cartage ... 7. drayage, portage
8. carriage, teamster, truckage
10. expressage 14. transportation
carte ... 3. map 4. card, list, menu
5. chart 7. diagram 10. bill of fare
cartel ... 4. bloc (Polit), defy, pact, pool
5. paper, truce, trust 6. letter
7. compact, entente 8. covenant
9. agreement, challenge, syndicate
10. convention 11. arrangement
Carthage ... see also _Carthaginian_
capital.. 13. Vandal Kingdom
destroyer.. 6. Romans
queen.. 4. Dido
rebuilt by.. 8. Augustus
Carthaginian (pert to) ...
apple.. 11. pomegranate
foe.. 4. Cato
general.. 6. Xerxes 8. Hannibal
god.. 6. Moloch 8. Melkarth
language 5. Punic

Lion .. 8. Hannibal
magistrate .. 7. suffete
name (later) .. 15. Justinianopolis
wars (three) .. 5. Punic
Carthusian Order (pert to) ...
founder .. 7. St Bruno
monastery .. 7. Certosa (It, 1396)
site .. 8. Grenoble (Fr)
cartilage ... 4. bone (ossified) 6. tissue
    7. gristle
cartload ... 6. fother
cartograph ... 3. map 4. plat 5. chart
cartoon ... 6. design, sketch 7. pattern,
    picture 10. caricature
cartoonist ... 4. Arno, Capp, Ding, Nast
    6. Disney
cartouche ... 5. shell 6. corbel, design,
    shield (Her), tablet 7. console
    9. cartridge 10. cantilever (Arch)
cartwheel ... 4. coin 6. dollar
    8. somerset 10. handspring,
    somersault
carve ... 3. cut, hew 4. form, make
    5. chase, grave, sever, shape
    6. chisel, cleave, furrow, incise
    7. engrave, fashion 9. apportion,
    fabricate, sculpture
carving ... 5. cameo 8. diaglyph,
    intaglio 9. anaglyphy, embossing,
    sculpture 11. anaglyptics
caryatid ... 6. column, figure (fem)
    8. pilaster 11. priestesses (temple)
casa ... 5. adobe, cabin, house
    8. building
cascade ... 4. fall, linn 5. Falls, Sault
    7. Niagara 8. cataract 9. waterfall
case ... 3. box 4. etui, file 5. cover,
    crate, crush (sl), event, folio
    6. carton, coffer, pillow, sheath,
    victim 7. attaché, cabinet, example,
    holster, lawsuit 8. argument,
    covering, cupboard, instance
    9. condition, portfolio 10. receptacle
    12. circumstance
case (in any) ... 3. yet 4. even
    6. anyhow, anyway 7. anywise,
    however 8. possibly, provided
    10. regardless 15. notwithstanding
case (pert to) ...
arrow .. 6. quiver
book .. 5. forel
bottle (liquor) .. 8. cellaret
cigar .. 7. humidor
conscience (Sci) .. 9. casuistry
grammar .. 6. dative 8. ablative,
    genitive, vocative 10. nominative
history (disease) .. 6. record
    9. anamnesis
image (Bib) .. 5. ephod
jewel, relics .. 3. tye 4. apse
spore .. 5. ascus
surgeon's .. 7. trousse
cash ... 4. coin, dust (gold) 5. darby,
    funds, money 6. silver, specie
    7. capital, coinage, mintage
    8. currency 9. spondulix
cashmere ... 4. goat, wool 5. shawl
    6. fabric
casino ... 6. tavern 7. cabaret, cassino
    (game) 8. ballroom, gambling
    9. roadhouse 11. summerhouse
cask ... 4. butt, case, drum, pipe

5. terce 6. bareca, barrel, casket,
    firkin, tierce 8. puncheon 9. kilderkin
cask (pert to) ...
amt when not filled .. 6. ullage
bulge .. 5. bilge
oil .. 4. rier
part .. 3. lag 4. hoop 5. stave
rim .. 5. chime (chimb)
support .. 8. stillage
casket ... 3. box, pyx, tye (jewel)
    4. cist, kist, tomb 5. chest
    8. cassette 11. sarcophagus
casserole ... 4. dish, mold 5. brown
    (color) 6. vessel 8. saucepan
cassine ... 4. game (card)
cast ... 3. hue 4. form, hurl, kind, look,
    mold, role, shed, tone, toss, type
    5. eject, fling, heave, model, pitch,
    sling, throw 6. glance, matrix, squint,
    troupe 7. pattern 8. template
    9. facsimile 10. impression,
    strabismus 16. dramatis personae
cast (pert to) ...
aside .. 4. jilt, junk, shed 5. scrap
    6. reject 7. discard
away .. 5. eject, wreck 6. unmoor
    9. shipwreck
blame .. 6. accuse 7. censure
    8. reproach 9. reprehend
off .. 4. doff, knit, molt, shed 5. untie
    6. unmoor 7. discard 9. eliminate
castaway ... 6. pariah 7. outcast
    8. derelict 9. reprobate
caste ... 4. race, rank 5. breed, class,
    stock 6. status 7. lineage, society
    8. standing
caste (Ind) ... 3. Dom, Meo 4. Ahir,
    Jati, Koli, Magi, Mali, Pasi, Teli
    5. Gaddi, Sudra, Varna 6. banian,
    pariah, Vaisya 7. Brahman
    9. Kshatriya
caster, castor ... 4. vial 5. cruet, horse
    (old), wheel 6. roller, vessel
    (condiment)
castigate ... 5. emend 6. punish,
    revise, strafe 7. chasten, correct,
    reprove 8. chastise, penalize
    9. criticize 10. discipline
Castile ... 4. soap 7. kingdom
Castilian ... 7. Iberian, Spanish
castle ... 4. fort, keep 5. house, tower,
    villa 6. donjon 7. chateau, citadel
    8. fortress 10. stronghold
    13. fortification
Castor (pert to) ...
brother (twin) .. 6. Pollux
constellation .. 6. Gemini
mother .. 4. Leda
stars .. 6. Castor, Pollux
castrate ... 4. geld, spay 5. alter,
    prune 10. emasculate
castrated (pert to) ...
bull .. 5. steer
cat .. 3. gib
horse .. 7. gelding
man .. 6. eunoch
rooster .. 5. capon
casual ... 5. stray 6. chance, random
    9. offhanded 10. contingent,
    fortuitous, incidental, occasional,
    unforeseen 11. indifferent
    14. unpremeditated

casual observation... 6. remark
casualty... 6. chance, hazard, injury,
  mishap 7. payment, tragedy
  8. accident, calamity, disaster, fatality
  9. mischance 10. misfortune
  11. contingency, contretemps
  12. misadventure
casus (pert to)...
  act of God.. 14. casus fortuitus
  common law.. 12. casus omissus
  conscience.. 17. casus conscientiae
  Latin.. 4. case 5. event 8. occasion
  treaty.. 13. casus foederis
  war.. 10. casus belli
cat... 3. gib 4. balu, eyra, lynx, pard,
  puma 5. alley, civet, Felid, Felis,
  genet, hyena, manul, ounce, tabby,
  tiger 6. caffre, cougar, feline, jaguar,
  margay, ocelot, pajero, rasset, serval
  7. cheetah, dasyure, leopard,
  panther, wildcat 9. catamount,
  grimalkin
cat (pert to)...
  fear of.. 12. ailurophobia, aleurophobia
  fish.. 4. pout, raad 6. hassar, tandan
  7. eelpout
  game.. 6. tipcat
  gut.. 5. tharm 6. string (violin)
  slang.. 6. hepcat
  term.. 5. kitty, shrew, tabby, vixen
  6. kitten 8. ailuroid 9. chessycat,
  Mehitabel (Mehetabel)
cat (species)... 4. Manx 5. Manul,
  Tibet 6. Angora, Caffre, Margay
  7. Burmese, Maltese, Persian,
  Siamese, Turkish 8. Cheshire,
  Egyptian 10. Abyssinian, Chinchilla
  13. tortoise–shell (black and yellow)
cataclysm... 4. ruin 6. deluge
  7. debacle 8. calamity, disaster, The
  Flood, upheaval 10. convulsion,
  inundation, revolution 11. catastrophe
catacomb... 4. tomb 5. crypt, vault
  6. grotto, locule 8. cemetery
  (underground) 9. Appian Way
catalepsy... 6. trance 8. hypnosis
  9. cataplexy 10. thanatosis
catalogue... 4. book, file, list 5. index,
  tally 6. codify, digest, record
  8. calendar, classify, pamphlet,
  register, schedule, tabulate
  11. enumeration
catamaran... 4. boat, raft 5. balsa,
  float 6. vessel 7. jangada
catamount... 3. cat 6. cougar
  12. catamountain
catapult... 4. hurl 5. shoot, sling
  6. engine, onager 7. robinet
  8. arbalest, ballista, scorpion
  9. slingshot
cataract... 4. fall, linn 5. Falls, flood,
  sault (soo) 6. deluge 7. cascade,
  disease, Niagara, opacity (eye),
  torrent 8. downpour, Victoria
  9. cachoeira, waterfall
cataria... 6. catnip
catasta... 5. stage (slave traffic)
  6. stocks 8. scaffold
catastrophe... 4. doom, ruin 6. finale,
  mishap, payoff 7. tragedy
  8. calamity, disaster 9. cataclysm

  10. denouement, misfortune,
  revolution 11. termination
catastrophic... 4. dire 5. black
  7. ruinous 10. calamitous,
  deplorable, disastrous
catawba... 4. wine 5. color (red),
  grape 6. Indian
catch... 3. get, nab 4. draw, hear,
  hold, hook, take, trap 5. fault, ketch,
  prize, reach, rondo, seize, snare,
  trick, troll 6. detent (clock), engage,
  entrap, ignite 7. attract, capture,
  seizure 8. overtake 9. intercept
catch (pert to)...
  a likeness.. 4. draw 6. depict
  7. portray
  a ride.. 4. hook 5. hitch, thumb
  9. hitchhike
  sight of.. 3. see 4. espy 6. behold,
  descry 7. discern, glimpse
catchword... 3. cry, cue 6. byword,
  phrase, slogan 7. formula
  10. shibboleth
cate... 4. food 6. viando 8. dainties
  10. delicacies, provisions (bought)
catechism... 5. guide 6. belief, manual
  9. questions (set of) 11. instruction
  (oral)
catechumen... 5. chela, pupil
  6. layman, novice 7. convert
  8. disciple, neophyte
categoric, categorical... 6. direct
  7. crucial, logical 8. absolute,
  explicit, positive 9. arbitrary,
  pragmatic 10. convincing
  11. dictatorial, unequivocal,
  unqualified
category... 4. head 5. class, genre,
  genus, group, order, state 6. branch,
  family, specie 7. bracket, species
  8. division 12. denomination
  14. classification
catena... 5. chain 6. series
  8. sequence 10. continuity
catenary... 5. curve (Math) 9. chainlike
cater, cater to... 4. feed 5. favor,
  humor, serve, toady 6. oblige,
  pander, please, purvey 7. indulge,
  procure, provide, satisfy 10. minister
  to 11. diagonalize 13. cater–cornered
caterpillar... 4. grub, weri 5. aweto,
  eruca, larva 7. tractor
caterwaul... 3. woo (derog) 4. meow,
  wail 5. court, miaow 7. screech
cathedral... 3. dom 4. fane (anc)
  5. duomo 6. church 8. official
  10. ex cathedra 13. authoritative
Cathedral...
  England.. 6. Durham 9. Salisbury
  France.. 5. Reims (Rheims) 6. Amiens
  9. Notre Dame
  Istanbul (Constantinople).. 8. St
  Sophia
  Italy.. 7. Lateran, St Mark's
  Rome.. 8. St Peter's
  Scotland.. 7. St Giles
cathedral (pert to)...
  chair (Bishop's).. 8. cathedra
  chapter member.. 10. capitulary
  church.. 3. dom 7. Lateran (Rome)
  city.. 3. Ely (Eng)
  passage.. 5. slype

catholic... 4. wide 5. broad 6. church, global 7. general, liberal 8. orthodox, pandemic 9. Christian, universal 10. ecumenical 12. cosmopolitan
Catholic publication... 4. Ordo
catkin... 5. ament, spike 7. cattail
catlike... 5. catty 6. feline 8. stealthy 9. noiseless
catling... 3. cat (little) 6. kitten, string (violin)
Cato (pert to)...
    author of.. 13. De Agri Cultura
    famed as.. 7. General 9. statesman 10. ambassador (to Carthage)
    nickname.. 8. The Elder 11. Cato of Utica
Catoism... 9. austerity, harshness
cats... 8. Kilkenny
cat's cradle... 3. hei 4. game 7. ribwort
cat's–paw... 4. dupe, gull, loof, pawn, tool 5. cully, hitch (knot) 6. breeze (Naut), puppet, stooge 10. instrument
cattail... 4. musk, reed, tule 5. ament, raupo, teree 6. catkin, totora 7. matreed 9. Typhaceae
cattle... 3. Bos 4. cows, kine, neat, oxen, stot, yaks 5. asses, goats, mules, sheep, stock, swine 6. bovine, camels, horses, llamas, niatas, rabble, Taurus 7. banteng, chattel 8. bullocks, property 9. livestock
cattle (breed)... 4. Zebu 5. Angus, Devon, Kerry, Niata, Welsh 6. Brahma, Durham, Jersey, Sussex 7. Dishley 8. Guernsey, Hereford, Holstein, Longhorn 9. Charolais, Leicester, Shorthorn 14. Santa Gertrudis
cattle (pert to)...
    collection.. 4. herd 5. drove
    disease.. 7. murrain 10. rinderpest
    driver.. 6. drover
    food.. 5. agist 6. forage
    herder.. 6. cowboy, drover
    hybrid.. 4. Zobo 7. cattalo 9. cattleyak
    motherless.. 6. dogies
    pen.. 4. crew 5. barth, reeve
    shed.. 6. hemmel
    stealer.. 7. abactor, abigeus, rustler
    unbranded.. 9. mavericks
catty... 6. feline, weight 7. catlike, cattish 8. spiteful, stealthy 11. treacherous
cauboge... 4. boor 7. bumpkin
Caucasian... 4. race, Slav, Svan, Turk 5. gypsy, Latin, Norse, Osset, Pshav, white 6. Hebrew, Semite, Teuton, Viking 8. Armenian, Bohemian, Georgian, White Man 10. Anglo–Saxon 11. Xanthochroi
Caucasian (pert to)...
    blond.. 6. Teuton 8. Estonian 11. Xanthochroi
    brunette.. 7. Iberian 8. Armenian 11. Melanochroi
    Chinese.. 4. Lolo, Nosu
    dialect.. 4. Andi, Avar, Svan
    European.. 8. Japhetic

goat (wild).. 3. tur
liquor.. 5. kefir
Moslem.. 3. Laz (Laze, Lazi) 7. Sunnite
mountain.. 8. Caucasus
peak.. 6. Elbrus (Elbruz), Kazbek
cauchemar... 9. nightmare
caucus... 7. meeting (Polit), primary 8. assembly
cauda... 4. scut, tail 9. appendage
caudata... 5. newts 8. Amphibia 11. salamanders
caught... see also catch 5. treed 7. latched 8. cornered
caught (pert to)...
    napping.. 7. unready 8. unprimed 10. unprepared
    sight of.. 3. saw 6. espied 8. descried
    up in.. 4. tied 7. engaged, tangled 8. absorbed, intent on, involved 10. implicated
caul... 3. net 6. basket 7. netting, network, omentum 8. membrane
cause... 5. aetio (comb form), agent, basis, drive, greed 6. create, factor, ground, induce, motive, reason, source 7. crusade, produce, provoke 8. campaign, etiology, movement, occasion 9. originate 10. mainspring 13. justification
cause (pert to)...
    approach.. 7. attract
    be done.. 4. writ 11. fieri facias
    bring about.. 6. effect
    buy and sell.. 7. whipsaw
    coagulate.. 4. curd 6. curdle 7. congeal, thicken
    contract unevenly.. 6. pucker
    face East.. 6. orient
    harm.. 4. bane
    irritate.. 6. rankle
    raise in relief.. 6. emboss
    remember.. 6. remind
    roll.. 7. trundle
    speed up.. 10. accelerate
    take root.. 8. radicate
causerie... 4. chat, talk 6. parley 7. article 8. converse, treatise 9. paragraph 10. discussion 12. conversation
causes, science of... 8. etiology
causeuse... 4. sofa 9. tête–à–tête
causeway... 4. dike 7. highway 10. embankment
causing...
    destiny.. 5. fatal
    emotion.. 7. emotive
    forgetfulness.. 8. nepenthe
    laughter.. 8. risorial
    motion.. 6. motile
caustic... 4. acid, tart 5. acrid, curve (optic), sharp 6. biting, bitter, severe 7. burning, cutting, erodent, mordant, pungent, pyrotic 8. snappish, stinging, virulent 9. corrosive, satirical, vitriolic 10. astringent, escharotic 11. acrimonious, penetrating
caustic agent... 3. lye 4. alum, lime 7. erodent 9. quicklime
causticity... 7. acidity 8. acerbity,

acrimony, asperity, pungency, tartness
9. mordacity 10. bitterness
11. astringency 13. corrosiveness
cautel ... 5. trick 7. caution
8. prudence 9. direction (Eccl)
10. precaution
cauterize ... 4. burn, char, sear
5. brand, singe 7. torrefy
cautery ... 7. burning, searing
8. inustion 10. instrument
13. cauterization
caution ... 4. card (coll), care, heed,
warn 5. aviso 6. advice, caveat,
notice, oddity 7. anxiety, counsel,
precept, proviso, warning 8. forecast,
prudence, wariness 9. chariness,
vigilance 10. admonition, providence,
solicitude 11. exhortation,
forethought, mindfulness
12. cautiousness, notification,
watchfulness 14. circumspection
cautious ... 4. wary 5. canny, chary
6. Fabian 7. careful, guarded,
heedful, mindful, prudent
11. circumspect
cautiously ... 6. cagily, warily
7. cannily, charily 8. gingerly
9. carefully, guardedly, heedfully,
mindfully, prudently 10. discreetly
13. circumspectly
cavalcade ... 4. raid, ride 5. march
6. parade, review 7. caravan,
pageant 8. motorcade 10. procession
cavalier ... 3. gay 4. coin (Fr), curt
5. brave, frank, lover, rider 6. escort,
knight, squire 7. admirer, brusque,
esquire, gallant, haughty, soldier
8. horseman, Royalist 9. caballero,
cavaliere, chevalier, Roundhead
10. disdainful, equestrian
12. high–spirited, supercilious
cavalry ... 4. army 6. horses, yellow
(color) 8. horsemen 10. knighthood
cavalry (pert to) ...
horse .. 6. lancer
man .. 5. spahy, uhlan 6. Hussar,
lancer 7. dragoon, trooper
unit .. 5. troop
weapon .. 5. lance, saber 9. demilance
cave ... 3. den, mew 4. abri, cove,
grot, hole, lair 5. antre, cover, lodge
(beaver), speos 6. antrum, cavern,
cellar, covert, dugout, grotto,
subway, tunnel 7. chamber, shelter,
spelunk 10. subterrane
cave (pert to) ...
fish .. 9. blindfish
man .. 11. Paleolithic
nature of .. 9. speluncar
study of .. 10. speleology
cave canem ... 11. Beware of Dog
cave dweller ... 10. troglodyte
Cave of Adullam ... 9. Seceeders
(1866)
caviar, caviare ... 3. roe 5. garum
6. relish 8. delicacy, fish eggs
cavil ... 4. cark, carp, marl, quip
5. dodge, evade, parry, shift
6. bicker, boggle, haggle, palter
7. quibble, shuffle 9. criticize,
pussyfoot 10. equivocate
caviler ... 5. momus 6. critic, hedger

8. frondeur, quibbler 10. criticizer
11. equivocator, faultfinder
cavity ... 3. dip, pit, sac, vug (voog)
4. aula, bore (gun), cava, hole, sink,
well 5. abyss, antra, atria, bursa,
chasm, fossa, fosse, geode, lumen,
shaft, sinus 6. antrum, areole,
atrium, caries, coelom, crater, hollow
7. cochlea, loculus 10. depression
11. compartment
cavort ... 4. dido, romp, skip 5. antic,
caper, cut up, frisk, prank 6. curvet,
gambol, prance 7. flounce, gambade,
gambado
cavy ... 3. pig 4. paca 5. stray
6. agouti, rodent 8. capybara
(capibara) 9. guinea pig
caw ... 3. cry 5. croak, quark, quawk
11. exclamation
cay ... 3. kay 5. islet
cease ... 3. end 4. quit, rest (law),
stop 5. avast, pause, stint 6. desist,
perish 7. abandon, fade out, refrain
8. intermit, leave off, shutdown
9. disappear, pretermit
11. discontinue
ceaseless ... 7. endless, nonstop
8. constant, unbroken, unending
9. continued, incessant, perennial,
perpetual, unceasing 10. continuous
12. interminable 13. round the
clock, uninterrupted
ceaselessness ... 9. constancy
10. continuity, incessancy, perpetuity
11. endlessness 14. successiveness
cease to be ... 3. die 6. expire, perish
8. dissolve 9. disappear
cease to please ... 4. pall
Cebus ... 3. sai 6. monkey 8. capuchin
cecils ... 10. croquettes
cecity ... 0. blindness
Cecrops (pert to) ...
daughter .. 5. Herse 8. Aglauros
founder of (tradition) .. 6. Athens
king of .. 6. Attica
symbol .. 7. half man 10. half dragon
cedar (pert to) ...
bird .. 7. waxwing
class .. 7. conifer
fruit .. 6. cedron
genus .. 5. Thuja, Toona 6. Cedrus
9. Juniperus
green .. 5. cedre
moss .. 8. hornwort
type .. 5. savin 6. deodar, sabine
7. incense, juniper, Lebanon (Bib),
Spanish 10. arborvitae
11. cryptomeria
cede ... 5. grant, waive, yield 6. assign,
confer 7. abandon 8. renounce
9. surrender 10. capitulate, relinquish
cedula ... 3. tax 6. permit 8. schedule,
security (Finan) 10. obligation
11. certificate
ceil ... 4. line 5. cover 7. overlay
8. wainscot
ceiling ... 4. acme, roof 5. astel, limit,
price, trave 6. apogee, lining, screen,
utmost 7. curtain, lacunar, maximum,
plafond 8. covering 9. lacunaria
10. planchment, visibility
12. consummation

celebrant... 6. priest (Eucharist)
  9. worshiper (worshipper)
  11. communicant
celebrate... 4. keep, laud, sing
  5. extol, honor, revel 6. herald,
  praise 7. glorify, maffick, observe,
  roister 8. emblazon, proclaim
  9. solemnize 11. commemorate,
  memorialize
celebrated... 5. famed, noted
  6. famous 7. feasted, honored,
  popular 8. far–famed, observed,
  renowned 9. distingué, well–known
  11. illustrious 13. distinguished
celebration... 4. bout, fete, rite
  5. fling, revel, spree 6. bender
  7. fanfare, jubilee 8. ceremony,
  function 9. epinicion, festivity,
  rejoicing 10. observance
  13. commemoration
celebrity... 3. VIP 4. fame 5. éclat,
  glory 6. notary 7. notable
  8. luminary, somebody
  10. famousness, popularity
  11. recognition
celerity... 5. haste, speed 8. dispatch,
  rapidity, velocity 9. swiftness
  10. speediness
celery... 4. ache 8. smallage (wild)
  9. Ammiacaea
celestial... 6. astral, divine, uranic
  7. angelic, sky blue 8. ethereal,
  heavenly 12. paradisaical
Celestial (pert to)...
  being.. 5. angel 6. cherub, seraph
  body.. 4. star 5. comet 6. nebula
  city.. 6. heaven, utopia 9. Jerusalem
  empire.. 7. Chinese, Tien Chu
  equator.. 8. meridian
  mind elevation.. 7. anagoge
  teacher.. 6. Taoist
celibate... 4. monk 6. single
  8. bachelor, monastic, Platonic,
  spinster 9. abstinent, continent,
  unmarried
cell... 3. egg, kil 4. cyst, germ, ovum
  5. cnida, crypt 6. cytode, prison
  7. alveola, cellule, dungeon
  11. compartment
cell (pert to)...
  animal.. 6. amoeba (ameba) 7. rotifer
  8. protozoa
  biology.. 7. energid, meiosis, mitosis,
  nucleus, spireme
  cell–like.. 9. celliform
  division.. 5. linin 7. spireme
  8. amitosis
  eating.. 9. cytophagy
  Egyptian (tomb).. 6. serdab
  honeycomb.. 8. alveolus
  Irish.. 3. kil (kill)
  locomotive.. 5. sperm, zooid
  Roman.. 4. alla, naos
  study.. 8. cytology
  substance.. 5. linin
  walls.. 9. cellulose
cellaret... 4. case 8. tantalus
  9. sideboard
Celt... 4. Erse, Gael, Manx, Scot
  5. Welsh 6. Breton 7. Cornish
Celtic (pert to)...
  abbot.. 5. coarb

bard.. 6. Ossian
cattle.. 2. ox
church.. 9. Christian
deity.. 7. Taranis
foot soldier.. 4. kern
horse.. 4. pony (Shetland)
Island.. 4. Manx
language.. 4. Erse
minstrel.. 4. bard
Mother of Gods.. 3. Ana (Anu)
mountain.. 3. ben
Neptune.. 3. Ler
nickname.. 10. Turtleback
Order.. 5. Druid
people.. 5. Gauls, Irish, Scots, Welsh
  7. Bretons, Britons
perfume.. 4. nard 9. spikenard
sun god.. 3. Lug (Lugh)
cembalo... 8. dulcimer 11. harpsichord
  12. clavicembalo
cement... 4. bind, fuse, glue, join,
  paar, pave 5. putty, stick, unite
  6. cohere, fasten, mastic, mortar,
  solder 8. adhesive, concrete,
  pavement, solidify
cemetery... 6. litten 7. Calvary
  8. boneyard, catacomb, Golgotha,
  lich gate (entrance), mortuary
  9. graveyard, mausoleum
  10. churchyard, necropolis
  11. polyandrium 12. potter's field
cenobite... 4. Monk 5. Order (anc)
  6. Essene 7. recluse
cenotaph... 4. tomb (empty)
  7. memento 8. memorial, monument
censer bearer... 7. acolyte 8. altar
  boy, thurifer
censor... 5. judge 6. critic 7. monitor
  8. censurer, reviewer, superego
  11. faultfinder
censure... 4. flay 5. blame, chide,
  slate, targe 6. accuse 7. chasten,
  condemn, impeach, inveigh, reprove,
  slating 8. reproach 9. damnation,
  expurgate, reprimand 11. reprobation
  12. condemnation, denunciation,
  reprehension
cent... 4. coin, game (old) 5. penny
  6. copper, trifle 7. hundred, red cent
centaur (Myth)... 4. race (Thessaly)
  6. Nessus 8. Lapithae, man–horse
  (half man) 9. bucentaur, Centaurus
  (Astron)
centennial... 4. game (dice)
  9. hundredth, red–yellow
  11. anniversary
Centennial State... 8. Colorado
center... 3. cor, hub 4. base, core,
  nave 5. axial, focus, heart, midst
  6. kernel, marrow, middle
  7. midmost, nucleus, pivotal, seaport
  8. emporium
center (pert to)...
  away from.. 6. distal
  bull's–eye.. 5. clout 6. target
  line.. 6. axiate, cesura
center of...
  attention.. 8. cynosure
  earth.. 9. epicenter
  gravity.. 6. kernel 7. centrum
  nervous system.. 5. brain
  sail.. 4. bunt

target.. **3**. eye **8**. bull's–eye
centerpiece... **4**. bowl **7**. epergne
centipede... **4**. rope (Naut) **6**. earwig,
  insect **8**. chilipod, myriapod
central... **3**. mid **4**. arch, main
  5. axial, basic, chief, focal, prime
  6. master, middle **7**. capital, centric,
  leading, midmost, pivotal, primary
  8. cardinal, dominant, foremost
  9. principal **11**. equidistant
Central America...
  bird.. **7**. jacamar **8**. puffbird
  boat.. **6**. cayuco, pitpan
  country.. **6**. Panama **8**. Honduras
  9. Costa Rica, Guatemala, Nicaragua
  10. El Salvador
  Indian.. **4**. Maya **5**. Carib
  monkey.. **4**. mono
  rodent.. **4**. paca
  snake.. **10**. bushmaster
  tree.. **3**. ebo, ule **5**. amate
  9. sapodilla
Central Asia (pert to)...
  gazelle.. **3**. ahu
  wild horse.. **6**. tarpan
  wind storm.. **5**. buran
Central State... **6**. Kansas
centuries (ten)... **7**. chiliad
century... **3**. Age **4**. aeon (eon)
  7. centred (anc), hundred **8**. eternity
  9. centenary **10**. centennial
century plant... **4**. aloe **5**. agave
  6. maguey
ceorl (Eng Hist)... **5**. churl, thane
  7. freeman, villein
cepa... **5**. onion
cephalon... **4**. head (Zool)
cephalopod... **3**. ink (secretion)
  5. sepia **6**. cuttle **7**. octopus
  10. cuttlefish
ceramics... **4**. tile **5**. china, delft,
  spode **6**. mosaic **7**. pottery, Satsuma
  8. crockery, majolica, Wedgwood
  9. porcelain
ceramics term... **4**. clay, kiln, laun
  5. adobe, stove, wheel **6**. sleeve (silk)
  7. furnace **8**. ceramist **10**. ceramicist
  12. ceramography
ceratoid... **5**. horny **8**. hornlike
  10. horn–shaped
cere... **3**. wax **4**. wrap (dead body)
  6. anoint **12**. protuberance (bird's)
cereal... **4**. bran, mush, rice **5**. grits,
  gruel, maize, wheat **6**. farina, hominy
  7. granola, oatmeal **8**. porridge
  10. corn flakes
cereal grass... **3**. oat, rye **4**. ragi
  5. grain, maize, wheat **6**. barley,
  raggee
cereal spike... **3**. ear
cerebellum... **5**. brain (part)
cerebral (pert to)... **4**. lobe **5**. brain
  6. speech **8**. arteries, peduncle
  9. consonant (Phonet) **11**. crus
  cerebri, hemispheres
cerebrum... **5**. brain **10**. encephalon
cere cloth... **7**. wrapper (corpse)
  8. cerement, chrismal **12**. grave
  clothes
ceremonial... **4**. prim **5**. stiff
  6. custom, formal, ritual **7**. precise,
  service, studied **8**. ceremony,

function, liturgic **9**. formality
  11. punctilious **12**. conventional
ceremonial (pert to)...
  chamber.. **4**. kiva
  departure.. **6**. congee
  splendor.. **9**. pageantry
ceremonious... **6**. formal, polite
  7. precise **8**. gracious **9**. attentive,
  courteous **10**. ceremonial, respectful
  11. deferential, ritualistic
ceremony... **4**. form, pomp, rite, show
  6. parade, review, ritual **8**. function
  9. formality, solemnity
  10. observance **11**. performance
ceremony, without... **6**. humbly,
  meekly, simply **7**. quietly **8**. casually,
  modestly **9**. sans façon
  10. informally **15**. unceremoniously
Ceres, Rom (pert to)...
  astronomy.. **8**. asteroid (lst found)
  father.. **6**. Saturn
  Feast.. **8**. Cerialia (Apr 19)
  Goddess of.. **4**. Corn **5**. Grain
  9. Fertility **11**. Agriculture
  Greek name.. **7**. Demeter
  mother.. **3**. Ops
Cereus... **6**. cactus **7**. saguaro
  13. night–blooming
cerise... **5**. color **7**. blue–red, fuchsia
  10. cherrylike
ceroplastics... **8**. modeling, waxworks
certain... **3**. one **4**. sure **5**. clear,
  exact, fixed, plain **7**. assured,
  decided, insured, precise **8**. absolute,
  definite, positive **9**. certified,
  confident, exclusive, indubious,
  undoubted, warranted
  10. guaranteed, inevitable,
  undeniable, undoubting
  11. determinate, trustworthy
  14. unquestionable
  16. incontrovertible
certainly... **3**. yea, yes **4**. amen
  5. truly **6**. indeed, really, surely, verily
  7. clearly, in truth, utterly **8**. actually,
  of course **9**. assuredly, precisely
  10. absolutely, by all means,
  definitely, inevitably, positively
certainty... **6**. pledge, shoo–in, surety
  8. sureness **9**. assurance, certitude
  13. inevitability, infallibility
certificate... **5**. check, money
  6. ticket **7**. diploma, voucher
  10. credential **11**. testimonial
certificate (pert to)...
  financial.. **3**. IOU **5**. draft, scrip
  9. debenture
  India.. **5**. hundi
  medical (Eng college).. **8**. aegrotat
certification... **2**. OK **3**. fix **5**. proof
  8. sanction **10**. validation
  11. affirmation, attestation, certificate,
  endorsement **12**. confirmation,
  ratification **13**. ascertainment,
  authorization **14**. substantiation
certify... **5**. prove, swear, vouch
  6. assure, attest, avouch, ratify, verify
  7. approve, confirm, endorse, witness
  8. accredit, validate **9**. ascertain,
  determine, establish, guarantee
  11. acknowledge, corroborate
cerulean... **4**. blue **5**. azure

7. sky—blue
cerumen... 6. earwax
cervine... 8. deerlike
cess... 3. bag, tax 4. cede, duty, levy,
toll 5. yield 6. assess, impost, tariff
7. revenue 9. surrender
10. assessment
cessation... 3. end 4. lull, stay
5. letup, truce 7. respite
8. abeyance, desition 9. interlude
10. suspension 12. intermission,
interruption 14. discontinuance
cetacea, cetacean... 3. orc 4. apod,
orca, susu (blind) 5. whale 6. whales
7. cowfish, finback, grampus, narwhal
(narwal), rorqual
Cete... 5. whale 10. The Cetacea
Cetus... 8. The Whale 13. constellation
(Equator)
Ceylon...
capital.. 7. Colombo
city.. 5. Galle, Kandy (famed Buddhist
Temple) 6. Jaffna
mountain peak.. 14. Pidurutalagala
ocean.. 6. Indian
old name.. 9. Taprobane
people.. 5. Tamil 6. Malays, Veddas
8. Malabars 10. Singhalese
Ceylon (pert to)...
boat.. 5. dhoni (doni)
canoe.. 5. balsa
Festival.. 8. Perahera
garment.. 6. sarong
hill dweller.. 4. Toda
monkey.. 4. maha 6. langur, rillow
moss.. 4. alga 6. Jaffna 7. gulaman
8. agar—agar
palm.. 7. talipot
rat.. 9. bandicoot
sand (sea bottom).. 4. paar
tree.. 4. doon
chabouk, chabuk (Ind)... 4. whip
9. horsewhip
chacma... 6. baboon
chafe... 3. cut, irk, rub, vex 4. fret,
fume, fuss, gall, heat, rage, skin,
warm 5. anger, annoy, grate, grind,
pique, scuff, worry, wound
6. abrade, banter, excite, harass,
injure, nettle, rankle 7. inflame
8. irritate
chaff... 3. hay 4. bran, husk, quiz,
twit 5. dregs, fluff, husks, palea,
straw, trash, waste 6. banter,
cobweb, glumes, refuse, scraps
7. remains, residue, tailing 8. raillery,
ridicule, riffraff
chaffer... 5. trade, wares 6. buying,
dicker, haggle, higgle, market
7. bargain, chaffer, chatter, selling
9. negotiate 11. merchandise
chafing dish... 7. cresset
chagrin... 7. anxiety, mortify
8. distress, troubles, vexation
13. mortification
chain... 4. bind, bond, boom, gyve,
reef, torc 5. cable, range 6. catena,
fasten, fetter, secure, series, tether,
torque 7. creeper, sorites
15. contravallation (fort series)
chair... 4. seat, sill 5. bench, sedan
6. rocker, throne 7. enchair, speaker

chair (pert to)...
back.. 5. splat 7. upright
collegiate.. 10. fellowship
13. professorship
cover.. 4. tidy 12. antimacassar
India.. 6. musnud
Japan.. 4. kago
maker.. 5. caner 6. reeder
chair (type of)... 4. camp, deck, easy,
high, lawn, wing 6. lounge, Morris,
swivel 7. contour, folding, steamer,
Windsor 8. armchair, captain's,
electric, fauteuil, straight
10. ladder—back 11. overstuffed
chairman... 7. officer, speaker
8. director 9. moderator
chalcedony... 4. onyx, opal, sard
5. agate 6. jasper, quartz 7. opaline
9. carnelian 11. chrysoprase
Chaldean (pert to)... 2. Ur 4. seer
6. Semite 10. astrologer, soothsayer
13. Neo—Babylonian (language)
chalice... 3. ama, cup 5. amula (anc),
calix, grail 6. goblet 8. daffodil
chalice pall... 4. veil 8. animetta
chalk... 4. draw, mark, pale, tick
5. score 6. blanch, bleach, crayon,
credit, pastel, whiten 7. account,
drawing 9. limestone, reckoning
chalker... 7. milkman (Eng sl)
chalklike... 10. calcareous
chalky... 5. white 7. crumbly, friable,
powdery 10. cretaceous
challenge... 4. dare, defy, gage
5. claim, doubt, query 6. accost,
cartel, defial, demand, impugn
7. dispute, protest 8. question,
reproach 10. accusation, controvert
11. questioning
chamal... 4. goat (Angora)
chamber... 4. cave, hall, kiva, room
5. court 6. camera, cavity
7. bedroom, boudoir, cabinet,
chambre, cubicle 10. bedchamber
11. compartment
chamber (pert to)...
harem.. 3. oda
heart.. 7. auricle 9. ventricle
King's.. 9. camarilla
music.. 14. sonata da camera
chambers... 4. flat 5. suite 6. office
9. apartment, bicameral (Legis)
14. Inns of Chancery (Eng)
chameleon... 6. lizard 10. vacillator
13. changeability, constellation
chamfer (to)... 5. bevel, carve, flute,
score 6. chisel, groove
chamois... 5. Gemse, izard 8. antelope
champ... 4. bite, chew, mash
5. gnash 6. victor 7. trample
11. battlefield
champagne... 4. wine 9. red—yellow
13. chrysanthemum
champaign... 5. field, plain 7. expanse
11. battlefield
champion... 3. Ace 4. best, hero
5. champ 6. defend, expert, victor,
winner 7. espouse, fighter, titlist
8. advocate, defender 9. combatant,
conqueror 10. unexcelled
champion (pert to)...
Christian (anc).. 3. Cid

constellation.. 7. Perseus
knight (legend).. 7. Paladin
Spanish.. 12. conquistador
chance... 3. die, hap, lot 4. fate, luck,
odds, risk, turn 6. casual, gamble,
happen, mishap, tossup 7. fortune,
lottery, tychism 8. fortuity, Lady
Luck, occasion 9. happening,
mischance 10. likelihood
11. opportunity, possibility, probability
12. happenstance
chancel (pert to)...
part.. 4. bema
screen.. 4. jube
seats.. 7. sedilia
change... 4. flux, move, turn, vary,
veer 5. alter, amend, break, coins,
money, shift 6. modify, mutate,
switch 7. caprice, convert, deviate,
variety 8. transfer 9. diversity,
transform, transmute, variation
10. alteration, fickleness, modulation
11. inconstancy, vicissitude
12. substitution 13. metamorphosis
14. transformation 15. diversification
change (pert to)...
color.. 3. dye, wan 4. fade, pale
5. blush 6. blanch, redden
medicine.. 11. heterotopia
mind.. 6. repent 12. tergiversate
music.. 4. muta
order of.. 9. metabolic, rearrange,
transpose
changeable... 6. fickle, fitful, mobile
7. erratic, flighty, mutable, protean
8. freakish, notional, unstable,
variable, volatile, weathery
9. alterable, chameleon, metabolic,
uncertain, unsettled, whimsical
10. capricious, inconstant
15. interchangeable
changeling... 3. oat 4. dolt 5. idiot
7. waverer 8. imbecile, renegade,
turncoat 9. simpleton 10. substitute
(child)
channel... 3. bed, cut, gat, way
4. dike, duct, gate, gurt, lane, leat,
pass, vein 5. basin, canal, ditch,
drain, flume, flute, fosse, radio, river,
sinus, stria 6. alveus, avenue, coulee,
groove, gutter, outlet, sluice, trench,
trough 7. conduit, tideway
8. aqueduct, tailrace 9. broadcast
10. passageway
Channel Islands... 4. Sark (Sercq)
6. Jersey 8. Alderney
chanson... 4. song 5. lyric 6. ballad
chant... 3. say 4. sing 6. intone,
melody, warble 7. introit, singing
8. canticle 10. intonation
11. composition
chanter... 6. cantor, singer 7. bagpipe
(part), intoner, sparrow (hedge)
8. songster, vocalist 9. chanteuse,
chorister
chanticleer... 4. cock 7. rooster
11. cock–a–doodle
14. cock–a–doodle–doo
chaos... 2. Nu (Egypt) 3. pie (type)
4. gulf, mess 5. abyss, babel, chasm
7. anarchy 8. disorder 9. confusion,
imbroglio 10. unruliness

13. orderlessness
Chaos (pert to)...
daughter.. 3. Nox, Nyx
parent of.. 5. earth 6. heaven
8. Creation
son.. 6. Erebus
chaotic... 6. muddle 8. confused,
formless 12. disorganized
chap... 3. boy, buy, guy, lad, man
4. kibe (sore) 5. buyer, chink, cleft,
crack, scout, split, youth 6. barter,
choose (Scot), fellow, galoot
7. chapman 8. customer
chapeau... 3. cap, hat, lid 5. beret
chapel... 4. cape, cope, cowl, hood
5. altar, choir 6. bethel 7. chantry,
galilee, oratory, service, Sistine
8. sacellum (anc) 9. reliquary
chaperon... 4. hood 6. attend,
duenna, escort 8. guardian
9. attendant 10. gooseberry
chaplet... 4. band 5. beads
6. anadem, wreath 7. garland,
prayers 8. beadroll, insignia, necklace
chappaul... 9. squawfish
chaps... 8. overalls 10. chaparajos
chapter... 4. Sura 5. topic 6. clause
7. council, meeting, passage,
section, Society 8. division
9. capitular 10. fraternity
12. organization
chaptrel... 6. impost
char... 4. burn 5. trout 6. scorch
8. charcoal, sandbank
character... 4. hero, kind, mark, role,
sign, star 5. trait 6. cipher, letter,
nature, repute, status, symbol
7. quality 8. function 9. reference
10. reputation 11. temperament
14. characteristic
character (pert to)...
giver.. 5. toner
Hebrew.. 3. Tav, Taw
Irish.. 5. Ogham
musical.. 3. bar 4. clef, rest
5. neume
of people.. 5. ethos
real.. 7. essence
science of.. 8. ethology
Teutonic.. 4. rune
characteristic... 4. mark 5. habit, trait
7. feature, impress, quality, typical
8. peculiar, symbolic 9. attribute,
character, idiopathy, lineament,
specialty 11. distinctive, peculiarity,
singularity, symptomatic
13. individualism
characteristic (pert to)...
descent.. 6. racial
peculiar.. 9. idiopathy
spirit.. 5. ethos
tone (Mus).. 7. seventh
characterization... 4. role 5. drama
9. depiction, portrayal
11. description, distinction
13. impersonation 14. identification,
representation
characterize... 4. mark, name 5. enact
7. engrave, imprint, portray
8. describe, inscribe 9. delineate,
designate, epitomize, represent
11. distinguish

characterized by...
abstinence.. 7. ascetic
bacteria exclusion.. 7. asepsis
cruelty.. 7. Neronic
exact thinking.. 13. ratiocinative
melody.. 6. ariose
poison (bloodstream).. 6. sepsis
pomposity.. 13. grandiloquent
characterless... 5. inane 9. colorless,
pointless
charcoal... 4. coke, fuel, lave, peat
5. black, chark 6. carbon, fusain
7. drawing, residue 9. boneblack,
briquette
charge... 4. bill, cost, dues, fill, load,
onus, rate, task, toll, ward 5. blame,
chore, debit, onset, order, price,
trust 6. accuse, advice, advise,
allege, amount, attack, client,
commit, credit, demand, dictum,
impute, indict 7. assault, command,
concern, custody, expense, impeach,
keeping, mandate, precept, primage,
protégé 8. guidance, insignia,
instruct, tutelage 9. dependent,
electrify, exactment 10. accusation,
commission, imposition, impregnate,
injunction, management
11. arrangement, attribution,
instruction, supervision
13. incrimination 14. responsibility
charge of affairs... 8. diplomat
15. chargé d'affaires
charge off... 5. debit 6. forget
7. dismiss, forgive 8. discount
charges (law)... 4. dues, fees 5. costs
9. retainers
charge with...
crime.. 6. indict 7. impeach
11. incriminate
debt.. 5. debit
gas.. 6. aerate
offense.. 6. accuse
to.. 5. blame 7. ascribe 9. attribute
charily... 6. cagily, warily 8. frugally
9. carefully, thriftily 10. cautiously
12. economically, suspiciously
chariness... 7. caution 8. caginess,
distrust, wariness 9. frugality
11. heedfulness, thriftiness
chariot... 3. car 4. biga, cart, rath
(ratha), wain 5. essed (anc), wagon
7. vehicle 8. quadriga
charioteer... 6. Auriga (Astron), Ben
Hur
charitable... 3. big 4. kind 6. kindly
7. lenient, liberal 8. generous,
tolerant 9. forgiving, indulgent
10. altruistic, benevolent, bighearted
11. beneficent 12. eleemosynary,
humanitarian 13. compassionate,
philanthropic
charity... 4. alms, dole 6. bounty,
virtue 7. handout, largess
8. lenience, pittance 9. tolerance
10. almsgiving, liberality
11. benevolence 12. philanthropy
charity dispenser... 7. almoner
charivari... 5. babel 6. medley, uproar
8. serenade (mock) 10. callithump
charlatan... 5. faker, fraud, phony,
quack 6. humbug 7. empiric

8. impostor 9. pretender
10. medicaster, mountebank
Charlemagne, Emperor (pert to)...
brother.. 8. Carloman
emperor of.. 7. The West
father.. 5. Pepin (the Short)
name also.. 15. Charles The Great
nephew.. 7. Orlando
charm... 3. obi 4. lure, mojo, play,
song 5. grace, magic, oomph, spell
6. allure, amulet, appeal, beauty,
enamor, entice, fetish, glamor, scarab
7. beguile, bewitch, cantrip, delight,
enchant, glamour, periapt
8. breloque, elegance, entrance,
ornament, talisman 9. captivate,
fascinate, sex appeal, sweetness
10. allurement, attraction, brimborion
(brimborium), lovability
11. captivation, conjuration,
incantation, pulchritude, winsomeness
12. antinganting 14. attractiveness,
delightfulness
charmer... 5. siren 6. beauty
7. enticer 8. exorcist, magician,
sorcerer 9. bewitcher
charming... 7. winsome 8. alluring,
pleasing 10. bewitching, delightful
11. captivating, fascinating
chart... 3. map 4. list, plat, plot
7. diagram
charter... 4. hire 5. carta, grant
6. charta, firman, treaty 7. license
9. privilege (special), purwannah
chartreuse... 4. mold (cookery)
5. color 7. liqueur
Chartreuse... 9. monastery 18. La
Grande Chartreuse (Grenoble)
chary... 4. wary 5. cagey 6. frugal,
skimpy 7. thrifty 8. cautious
10. suspicious 12. parsimonious
Charybdis... 6. Scylla 8. Galofaro
9. whirlpool (Messina)
chase... 3. gun (Naut), set (gem)
4. hunt, park, race 5. chevy (chivy),
raise, sport, track 6. emboss, follow,
furrow, groove, hasten, pursue,
shikar, stroke (tennis) 7. engrave,
pursuit, repulse 8. ornament
12. steeplechase
Chase (The), goddess of... 5. Diana
chasm... 3. gap, pit 4. gulf, hole, rift,
well 5. abyss, cleft, shaft 6. breach,
canyon, cavity, hiatus 7. fissure,
opening 9. crevasse
chasma... 7. yawning
chasse... 4. step (dance) 6. shrine
9. reliquary
chaste... 4. pure 6. modest, simple
8. innocent, virtuous 9. continent,
uncorrupt, undefiled, unmarried
10. immaculate
chasten... 4. rate 5. smote 6. punish,
refine 7. correct 8. chastise,
penalize, restrain 9. castigate
10. discipline
chastened... 4. meek 5. smote
7. subdued 8. punished, purified,
tempered 10. restrained
chastise... 4. beat, slap, whip
5. amend, blame, scold, spank, taunt
6. punish, rebate, rebuke, swinge

7. correct, reprove 9. castigate
10. discipline
chastity... 6. purity, virtue
9. cleanness 10. chasteness
12. virtuousness
chat... 3. gab, rap, yak 4. chin, coze,
jist, talk, tove 5. prate 6. babble,
confab, gabble, gibber, gossip, jabber
7. chatter, prattle 8. causerie,
chitchat, converse 12. conversation
14. chitter–chatter
chatelaine... 3. pin 4. etui, hook
5. clasp, purse, watch 6. brooch,
torque
chattels... 4. naam 5. goods, money,
wares 6. estate 7. effects
8. holdings, property 9. livestock,
principal 11. possessions
chatter... 3. gab, yap 5. clack, prate
7. clatter, prattle
chatterer... 3. jay, mag 4. bird, piet
6. magpie 10. chatterbox
chatty... 3. pot (earthen) 4. glib
5. gabby 7. affable 8. sociable
9. garrulous, prattling, talkative
14. conversational
Chaucer (pert to)...
author of.. 15. Canterbury Tales
Inn.. 9. (The) Tabard
pilgrimage city.. 10. Canterbury
style of work.. 7. novella
chauvinist... 5. jingo 6. Rajput
7. chauvin, patriot 8. jingoist
9. warmonger 10. militarist
cheap... 5. small, tacky, tinny, trade,
value 6. cheesy, paltry, plenty, sleazy
7. abashed, bargain, chintzy, cut–rate,
reduced, schlock 9. niggardly
11. inexpensive
cheat... 2. do 3. ban, con, fob, gyp
4. hilk, fake, flam, hoax, liar, rook,
scam, sell, sham 5. cozen, elude,
guile, phony, sculp 6. deceit, fleece,
humbug, hustle, illude, rip–off
7. deceive, finesse, sharpen, swindle
8. artifice, impostor 9. bamboozle,
overreach, stratagem, victimize
10. thimblerig 12. bait–and–switch
check... 3. nip, tab 4. balk, curb,
damp, mark, rein, stem, stop, test
5. agree, brake, count, delay, limit,
money, plaid, repel, stunt, tally
6. bridle, cheque, detain, detent,
impede, oppose, rebuff, retard, ticket,
verify 7. counter, examine, inhibit,
measure, monitor, pattern, repress
9. hindrance, restraint 12. verification
check (pert to)...
in.. 3. die 6. arrive 8. register
out.. 3. die 5. croak, leave 6. assess
8. withdraw
pattern.. 11. houndstooth
game, term.. 5. chess 8. gambling
checkered... 4. vair 5. diced, plaid
6. mosaic, tartan, varied 7. checked
10. changeable, tesserated,
variegated 11. diversified
checkers, chequers... 4. game
8. draughts (Brit)
cheek... 4. gall, gena, jowl 5. brass,
bucca, crust, malar, nerve 8. audacity,
chutzpah 9. impudence

10. buccinator
cheer... 3. rah 4. yell 5. bravo, elate,
huzza, liven, mirth, salvo 6. gaiety,
hurrah, regale, repast, salute, solace
7. animate, applaud, console, gladden,
hearten, jollity, refresh, rejoice
8. applause, inspirit, pleasure, vivacity
9. encourage, merriment
10. exhilarate 12. conviviality
cheerful... 3. gay 4. gleg (Scot), rosy
5. happy, peart, sunny 6. blithe,
cheery, genial, hearty, jocund, joyful
8. gladsome, homelike 9. contented,
lightsome 12. lighthearted
cheerfulness... 3. joy 4. glee
5. cheer, mirth 6. gaiety 7. jollity
8. gladness, hilarity 9. happiness,
merriment 12. exhilaration
cheerio... 5. adios, aloha, skoal, toast
6. hurrah, prosit 8. au revoir,
farewell, Godspeed 9. greetings
cheerless... 3. sad 4. cold, drab
5. drear 6. dismal, dreary, gloomy
7. forlorn, joyless, unhappy
8. dejected 9. unsmiling
10. depressing, melancholy
11. dispiriting 12. disconsolate
cheese... 3. pot 4. bleu, brie, edam,
feta, jack 5. cream, Gouda, Swiss
6. barrie, Dunlop, mysost, Romano,
zieger 7. Cheddar, cottage, fromage,
Munster, sapsago 8. American,
Monterey (jack), Parmesan
9. Camembert, Limburger, Roquefort
10. Gorgonsola, Neufchatel
cheese dish... 6. fondue, omelet,
quiche, strata 7. rarebit, soufflé
cheesy... 3. bad 6. paltry 8. inferior
9. worthless 12. disreputable
cheetah... 3. cat 5. youse (youze)
7. guepard (gueparde)
cheilos... 3. lip
chela... 4. claw 6. novice 8. disciple
Chelonia... 7. reptile, turtles
9. tortoises
chemical (pert to)...
analysis.. 5. assay
cleanser.. 6. kryton
etching.. 11. chemigraphy
strength.. 5. titer (titre)
term.. 3. gas 4. acid, atom, base, salt
5. imine 6. alkali, eluate 7. hormone,
nonacid, organic, radical, valence
8. catalyst, compound 10. bathoflore
11. bathochrome
vessel.. 4. etna 6. aludel, retort
7. alembic 8. crucible, reductor
chemical suffix... 2. ac, el, yl 3. ane,
ene, ile, ine, ole, ose 4. enol, olic,
osan
chemin de fer... 7. railway
8. baccarat, railroad
chemist... 7. analyst 8. druggist
9. alchemist 10. apothecary,
biochemist 12. iatrochemist (anc)
cherish... 3. aid, hug, pet, woo
4. love 5. adore, cheer, nurse, prize
6. caress, faddle, fondle, foster
7. care for, comfort, nourish, nurture,
protect, support 8. enshrine,
remember, treasure 9. cultivate,
encourage, entertain

cherry . . . 3. pin 4. Bing, bird, gean, ming 5. black 6. egriot, Prunus 7. capulin, marasca, mazzard, Morello, oxheart 8. Napoleon 9. amarelles, bigarreau, Queen Anne 11. chokecherry, Montmorency
cherub . . . 5. angel, child, saint 6. seraph, spirit 7. darling, eudemon 8. cherubim, seraphim
chess (pert to) . . .
chessman . . 4. king, pawn, rook 5. piece, queen 6. bishop, castle, knight
Italian . . 7. scacchi
term . . 4. dual, move 5. debut 6. chassé, fidate, gambit 7. end game, opening, problem 9. checkmate, en passant, rook's tour, stalemate 10. fianchetto
chesslike . . . 8. scacchic
chest . . . 3. ark, box 4. arca, cist, kist 5. bahut 6. breast, cajeta, coffer, coffin, locker 7. highboy, wanigan (wangan) 10. chiffonier 11. gardeviance
chest (pert to) . . .
ammunition . . 7. caisson
animal . . 7. brisket
human . . 6. thorax 7. midriff
sound . . 4. rale
sepulchral . . 6. larnax
Chester (Eng), inhabitant . . . 8. Cestrian
chesterfield . . . 4. sofa 5. divan 8. overcoat 9. cigarette, davenport
chestnut . . . 4. ling, rata 5. horse, water 6. marron 7. buckeye 8. Aesculus, Castanea 10. breadfruit, chinquapin
chestnut . . . 4. joke 6. cliché 7. bromide 8. banality
chestnut color . . . 4. roan 5. brown 6. sorrel 12. reddish–brown
chevalier . . . 5. cadet (nobility), noble 6. knight 7. gallant 8. cavalier, horseman 10. greenshank (bird)
chevron . . . 4. beam 5. glove 6. rafter, stripe, zigzag 8. insignia
chevrotain . . . 4. napu 7. deerlet, kenchil, meminna 9. Tragulina
chevy . . . 3. cry (hunting) 4. game, hunt 5. chase 6. flight, harass, pursue 7. torment
chew . . . 3. cud 4. bite, chaw, gnaw, quid 5. champ, chomp, grind, munch 6. chavel, ponder 8. meditate, ruminate 9. masticate
chiasma . . . 11. decussation 12. intersection
chiasmus . . . 9. inversion (of words)
chib (Gypsy) . . . 6. tongue 8. language
chic . . . 4. trig, trim 5. natty, smart 6. modish, spruce 7. stylish
Chicago's nickname . . . 9. Windy City
chicanery . . . 4. ruse, wile 5. feint, trick 6. deceit 7. knavery 8. artifice, trickery 9. stratagem 11. skulduggery
chickadee . . . 8. titmouse 10. Pebthestes
chicken . . . 3. hen 4. cock, fowl, girl 5. biddy, capon, chick, deedy, fryer, poult, young 6. coward, pullet

7. broiler, rooster 8. cockerel, weakling 9. youngling 11. chanticleer, milquetoast
chickenhearted . . . 5. timid 8. cowardly 12. fainthearted
chicory . . . 6. endive 7. succory 12. Cichoriaceae
chide . . . 4. rate 5. blame, scold 6. berate, rebuke 7. censure, reprove, wrangle 8. admonish, reproach 9. reprimand
chief . . . 3. dux, top 4. arch, head, main, rais (reis) 5. first, forte, major, mogul 6. leader, primal, staple, syndic 7. kingpin, supreme 9. directing, governing, paramount, potentate, principal, prominent 11. predominant
chief (pert to) . . .
African . . 3. dey 4. kaid 5. negus 6. induna
Am Indian . . 6. sachem 7. Osceola 8. sagamore
Arab . . 5. sheik
Chinook . . 4. tyee
Cossack . . 6. ataman, hetman
Egypt . . 3. Min (Panopolis)
Europe . . 6. syndic
Germany . . 6. Führer (Fuehrer), Kaiser
Iran . . 9. ayatollah
Italy . . 4. doge, duce
Japan . . 6. mikado, shogun
Mexico . . 7. cacique
Nepal . . 4. Rais
Oriental . . 4. kahn 6. sirdar
Persia . . 4. shah
Russia . . 4. czar (tsar)
Spain . . 7. alcalde
Tibet . . 9. Dalai Lama
Turkey . . 3. aga (agha) 6. vizier
chilblain . . . 6. pernio
child . . . 3. imp, tad, tot 4. babe, baby, bata, brat, teen, tike 5. bairn, cupid, elfin, fetus 6. cherub, childe (anc), infant, urchin 7. adoptee, nestler, preteen, progeny 9. offspring 10. descendant
childish . . . 4. weak 5. naive, petty, young 6. senile, simple 7. babyish, kiddish, puerile, unmanly 8. immature 9. infantile, kittenish
children (pert to) . . .
doctor . . 12. pediatrician
mythology . . 6. Titans
Patron Saint . . 5. Santa
slain by Herod . . 12. The Innocents
study of . . 8. pedology 10. pediatrics
Chile . . . see also *Chilean*
cape . . 4. Horn
capital . . 8. Santiago (1541)
city . . 4. Lota 5. Arica 8. Valdivia 10. Concepcion, Valparaiso (1543)
conqueror . . 7. Pizarro 8. Valdivia
desert . . 7. Atacama
explorer . . 8. Magellan (1520)
mountain . . 5. Andes
river . . 3. Loa 6. Biobio
settlement (southernmost) . . 8. Navarino (Isl) 14. Puerto Williams
Chilean (pert to) . . .
coconut . . 7. coquito
evergreen . . 6. pepino 10. arborvitae

shrub (poison).. 5. lithi
wind.. 5. sures 11. sures pardos
workman.. 4. rote
chiliad... 8. thousand 9. millenium
　13. thousand years
chill... 3. ice, raw 4. ague, cold,
　damp 5. algor, frost, rigor
　6. damper, formal, shiver 7. malaria
　8. coldness, coolness, dispirit
　10. depressing 11. refrigerate
chilly... 3. raw 4. ague, cold 5. gelid
　6. aguish, freeze, frosty
　12. refrigerated
chiloplasty... 10. lip surgery
　12. mouth surgery
chime... 4. bell, peal, ring, suit
　5. agreé, bells, prate, rhyme
　6. accord, concur, cymbal, jingle
　7. harmony
chimera... 5. dream, fancy, vapor
　6. bubble, utopia 7. monster
　8. illusion, paradise (fool's)
chimerical... 4. vain 7. utopian
　8. delusive, fanciful, romantic
　9. fantastic, imaginary, unfounded
chimney... 3. lum 4. flue 5. cleft,
　stack, tewel 10. smokestack
chimpanzee... 6. gibbon, nchega
　7. gorilla
chin... 4. talk 5. genio (comb form)
　6. mentum, weight (Chin)
　8. converse 10. chew the rag
　11. genioplasty (Surg), mentoplasty
　(Surg)
china... 7. Dresden, pottery
　8. crockery 9. porcelain
　11. earthenware
China... see also *Chinese*
　Buddha.. 2. Fo
　capital.. 7. Nanking
　capital, former.. 7. Peiping (Poking)
　city.. 4. Amoy, Tsin, Wuhu 6. Canton,
　Hankow, Ningpo 7. Foochow,
　Nanking, Soochow 8. Hangchow,
　Shanghai, Tientsin
　dynasty.. 3. Han, Kin, Sui 4. Chou,
　Hsia (BC), Ming, Tsin, Yuan 5. Ching
　6. Mongol (Kublai Khan's)
　island.. 5. Matsu 6. Quemoy, Taiwan
　(Formosa)
　magistrate.. 5. tupan 6. tuchun
　8. mandarin
　Mainland.. 15. People's Republic
　Military Academy.. 7. Whompoa
　Mongol.. 3. Hun
　mountain.. 7. Kuen–lun 9. Himalayas
　nickname.. 14. Flowery Kingdom
　philosopher.. 6. Laotse 9. Confucius
　poet.. 4. Li Po 7. Li Tai Po
　race.. 9. Mongoloid
　religion.. 6. Taoism 8. Buddhism
　9. Confucian 12. Confucianism
　river.. 5. Peibo 7. Hwanglo, Yangtze
　sea.. 5. China 6. Yellow
　treaty port.. 4. Amoy
Chinese (pert to)...
　antelope.. 6. dzeren
　boat.. 4. junk 5. tanka 6. sampan
　cabbage.. 7. pakchoi
　card game.. 6. fantan
　carpet.. 6. Khotan 7. Kashgar,
　Yarkand 9. Samarkand, Turkestan

Catholic Church.. 11. Tien Chu T'ang
　12. Tien Chu Chiao
chestnut.. 4. ling
confection.. 8. chowchow
deer.. 8. elaphure
defense.. 4. Wall (2,000 mi long)
desert.. 4. Gobi 5. Shamo
dragon.. 6. chi–lin
fabric.. 3. sha 7. nankeen
festival (Spring).. 9. Ch'ing Ming
flute.. 4. tche (che)
fruit.. 6. litchi (nut)
ginger.. 9. galingale
God.. 4. Shen (Chr) 7. Shangti, Tien
　Chu (RCCh)
gong.. 6. tam–tam, tom–tom
grass.. 5. ramee
idol.. 4. joss 6. pagoda (pagod)
instrument.. 3. che, kin 4. tche
　5. sheng (cheng)
jade.. 2. yu
jute.. 7. chingma
laborer.. 6. coolie
lily.. 9. narcissus
liquor.. 6. samshu (rice)
literary degree.. 8. hsiu tsai
monkey.. 4. douc
nurse.. 4. amah
officer.. 4. kwan
oil.. 4. tung
ox.. 4. zebu
pagoda.. 3. taa
paradise (Buddh).. 4. Jodo
　7. Ching–tu 8. Gekuraku
philosophy.. 10. Yang and Yin
religion.. 6. Taoism 8. Buddhism
　12. Confucianism
residence (official).. 5. yamen
screen (folding).. 10. Coromandel
silkworm.. 4. sina 9. ailanthus
sky.. 4. tien
society (secret).. 3. hui (hoey) 4. tong
vessel.. 4. junk 6. lorcha
Chinese Wall, Great (pert to)...
　builder.. 15. Ch'in Shih Huang Ti
　composition.. 7. granite (blocks)
　length in miles.. 11. two thousand
　time.. 2. BC
chink... 4. rent, rift, rima, rime, ring
　5. cleft, crack 6. cranny, furrow
　7. bunting (bird), fissure
　10. interstice
chinook... 4. herb, wind 6. salmon
　7. quinnat
Chinook (pert to)...
　chief.. 4. tyee
　tribe.. 8. Flathead
　State (nickname of).. 10. Washington
chinquapin... 3. oak 6. bonnet (water)
　8. chestnut
chip... 3. cut, hew 4. coin 5. break,
　carve, flake, piece, scrap, token
　6. chisel, gallet (stone) 7. counter
chipmunk... 6. hackee
chipped stone (instrument)...
　9. paleolith
chipper... 5. chirp 6. babble, chisel,
　hammer, lively 7. chirrup, twitter
　8. cheerful
chirognomy... 9. palmistry
　10. chiromancy
chironomy... 7. gesture (hands)

9. pantomime

chiropter... 3. bat 6. aliped

chirp... 3. pew (pue) 4. peep
5. cheep, chirl, tweet 7. chirrup, twitter

chisel... 3. cut, gad, hew 4. celt (anc), form, pare 5. bruzz, burin, carve, cheat, drove, gouge, grave 6. furrow, jagger, mallet, peeker, pommel 7. engrave, swindle 9. sculpture

chit... 4. note, runt, wisp 5. child, shoot 6. sprout 10. memorandum 14. recommendation

chitarra, chitarrine... 6. guitar

chiton... 7. garment (anc), mollusk

chivalrous... 5. brave 6. gentle, heroic 7. gallant, valiant 8. knightly 9. courteous 11. magnanimous

chive... 4. stab 5. onion, plant 6. garlic

chloride... 3. ore 4. salt 5. ester 7. calomel

chlorine... 2. Cl 7. bromine, halogen, radical 8. cyanogen, fluorine

chloroform... 4. dope, kill 6. poison 7. stupefy 9. narcotize 11. anesthetize

chlorophyll... 5. ester, green 7. etiolin 9. deodorant

chocolate... 5. brown, cacao, candy, cocoa, color 6. pinole 8. beverage 13. Sterculiaceae

choice... 4. beat, rare, will 5. prime 6. dainty, option, select, tidbit 8. election, free will, uncommon 9. recherché, selection 10. preference, well–chosen 11. alternative

choir... 6. chorus 7. singers

choir leader... 6. cantor 9. precentor

choke... 3. gag, jam, ram 4. clog 5. burke, check 6. hinder, impede, muffle, stifle 7. garrote, repress, smother 8. obstruct, strangle, throttle 9. constrict, suffocate

choler... 3. ire 4. bile, foam, gall, rage 5. anger, wrath 6. spleen 10. resentment 11. biliousness 12. irascibility

choleric... 5. angry, testy 7. bilious, enraged, iracund 8. wrathful 9. dyspeptic, irascible 10. passionate

chololith... 9. gallstone

choose... 3. opt 4. cull, like, list, pick, want 5. elect 6. desire, optate, prefer, select

choosing... 6. optant 8. eclectic, elective 9. selecting

chop... 3. axe, cut, hew, jaw, lop 4. dice, fell, hack, jowl, meat, raze, seal 5. cheek, mince, prune, sever, stamp 7. griskin 8. noisette (eye of)

choppy... 5. bumpy, rough 6. uneven 7. jolting 8. unstable, variable 9. irregular 10. changeable, incoherent 13. discontinuous

chord... 4. rope 6. radius, secant, string, tendon 7. concord, harmony 8. arpeggio, concento, filament

chord (terms)... 5. major, minor, tonic, triad 6. broken, common, tetrad

7. seventh 8. dominant, unbroken 10. enharmonic

chords... 4. tune 7. cadence, cantata

chore... 3. job (odd) 4. task, work 5. stint 10. assignment

chorography... 5. chart 7. diagram 10. topography 11. cartography, description (region), ichnography

chortle... 5. laugh, snort 7. chuckle, snortle

chorus... 4. echo 5. choir 6. accord, outcry, unison 7. refrain, singers 8. chanters 9. unanimity

chorus (pert to)...
girl.. 7. chorine, chorist
leader.. 8. choragus 9. conductor
small.. 7. octette

Chosen (anc)... 5. Korea

Chosen People... 10. Israelites

chrism... 7. unction, unguent 10. anointment 12. confirmation

christen... 4. name 6. launch 7. baptize 10. denominate, inaugurate 12. Christianize

Christian (pert to)...
Eastern.. 5. Uniat
feast.. 5. agape (anc) 8. Epiphany 9. Christmas
martyr (first).. 7. Stephen
philosopher (anc).. 6. Jesuit 9. Schoolman 10. Scholastic
sect.. 7. Docetae
symbol.. 5. orant (fem)

Christmas (pert to)...
bag.. 6. piñata
carol.. 4. Noel
decoration.. 6. crèche
feast.. 4. Yule
mummer.. 6. guiser
plant.. 5. holly 9. evergreen, mistletoe
term.. 4. Noel, Xmas 8. Nativity, Yuletide 11. Weihnachten

Christ's–thorn... 4. nabk

chromosome... 2. id 5. idant 8. biophore, germ cell

chronic... 7. abiding 8. constant, enduring, habitual 9. confirmed 10. continuous, inveterate, persistent 14. valetudinarian

chronicle... 4. sard 5. annal, diary 6. record 7. account, archive, history 8. register 9. narrative 10. chronology

chronicler... 6. writer 8. annalist, compiler, recorder 9. historian 12. chronologist

chronology error... 9. prolepsis

chronometer... 5. clock, timer, watch 6. ghurry 7. sundial 9. hourglass, metronome, timepiece

chrysolite... 5. green (color) 7. olivine, peridot

chthonian... 4. gods (underworld) 7. hellish, worship 9. diabolist 11. demonolater

chub... 4. bass, dace, dolt, fool, lout 6. shiner, tautog 8. fallfish 9. hornyhead, squawfish

chubby... 3. fat 5. plump, pudgy, round 6. stocky, stubby 9. corpulent

chuck... 4. beef, cast, food, hurl, jerk, toss 5. fling, heave, pitch, throw

9. eliminate

chuckle... 5. cluck, laugh 6. cackle,
   wabble 7. chortle

chuff... 3. fat 4. boor 5. churl, clown,
   cross, proud, sulky, surly 6. chubby,
   elated, rustic 9. conceited
   11. ill–tempered

chum... 3. pal 4. bait, pard 5. buddy,
   crony 6. fellow, hobnob 7. company,
   comrade, consort, partner
   8. playmate, roommate 9. associate,
   classmate, colleague, companion

chump... 3. ass 4. dolt, dupe, fool,
   head 5. block, booby 8. endpiece

chunk... 3. dab, gob, pat, wad
   4. hunk, junt, lump, slug (metal)
   5. stick, stump, throw 8. fragment

chunky... 3. fat 4. game (Am Ind),
   junt 5. lumpy, stout, tubby
   6. chubby, portly, stocky, stodgy,
   stubby 8. thickset

church... 3. dom 4. fane (anc), kirk,
   sect 5. abbey 6. bethel, temple
   7. Lateran, minster, templet
   8. basilica, conclave 9. cathedral
   10. House of God, worshipers
   11. Christendom 12. denomination

church (pert to)...
   assistant.. 5. Elder
   attendant.. 6. sexton, verger
   calendar.. 4. Ordo
   Court.. 10. Consistory
   dignitary.. 4. dean 6. bishop, priest
      7. prelate, primate 8. benefice,
      minister
   dissenter.. 7. sectary 10. anti–Nicean,
      anti–Nicene
   doctrine (State, church).. 8. Erastian
   dominion.. 10. sacerdotum
   doorkeeper.. 7. ostiary
   Elder.. 9. Proobyter
   feast.. 4. utas (octave of) 6. Easter
   governing body.. 7. classis
   law.. 5. canon, synod 7. council
   part.. 4. apse, bema, nave 5. altar,
      canon 7. narthex 8. transept
      10. clerestory
   peace device.. 8. irenicon
   property.. 5. glebe
   Roman.. 7. Lateran 8. basilica
   seats.. 4. pews 7. sedilla
   service (part).. 3. pax 4. Mass
      5. crede 7. epistle, introit, sanctus
      8. Agnus Dei, blessing
      9. communion
   stipend.. 7. prebend
   traffic (preferments).. 6. simony
   vessel.. 3. ama, pyx (pix) 6. lavabo
      8. ciborium
   vestry.. 8. sacristy

churl... 3. cad, oaf 4. boor, carl, hind,
   lout, serf 5. ceorl, knave 6. rustic
   7. bondman, freeman, peasant, villain
   9. vulgarian 10. countryman

churlish... 4. mean 5. gruff, rough,
   surly 6. rustic, sordid, sullen, vulgar
   7. boorish, crabbed, knavish
   9. gruffness, niggardly
   10. ill–humored 11. countrified

churn... 4. beat, kirn, stir, whip
   5. mixer, shake 6. beater, seethe,
   vessel 7. agitate 8. agitator, emulsify

chute... 4. tube 5. flume, scarp, slide
   6. trough 7. channel, incline,
   passage 9. parachute

cibel... 5. chive, onion 7. shallot

ciborium... 3. pyx 6. canopy, coffer,
   vessel

cicada... 6. dog–day, locust
   9. Cicadidae

cicatrix... 4. mark, scar 7. blemish

Cid... 3. Ruy 4. hero, poem 5. Chief
   6. leader (Christian) 7. Rodrigo

cider (weak)... 6. perkin

Cid's sword... 6. colada

cienaga... 5. marsh, swamp

cigar... 4. rope, toby 5. claro
   6. concha, corona, Havana, stogie
   7. cheroot, culebra, londres
   8. cigarite, colorado, panatela
   9. belvedere, cigarillo

cigarette... 3. fag 4. pill 5. cubeb
   6. gasper, reefer 9. cigarillo

cilium... 4. hair, lash 7. eyelash
   8. barbicel, ciliolum, filament
   9. eyewinker

cimarron... 6. maroon 7. bighorn, wild
   dog 8. district (Okla)

cimex... 6. bedbug

Cimmerian, Homer Myth... 4. dark
   5. Nomad (anc) 6. gloomy (abode)
   8. Cimmeria

cinch... 4. game (cards), grip, sure
   5. girth 6. fasten 7. harness (part)
   9. certainty, sure thing

cinders... 3. ash 4. lava, slag
   5. ashes, dross 6. embers
   7. residue 8. clinkers

cinerarium... 8. mortuary

cinerator... 7. furnace 9. crematory
   11. crematorium, incinerator

cingular... 7. annular 8. circular

cinnamon... 5. brown, spice 6. cassia
   8. ishpingo (S Am)
   10. Cinnamomum

cinque... 4. dice, five

cipher... 3. nil 4. code, zero 5. aught
   6. figure, nobody, number, symbol
   7. compute 9. calculate, character,
   nonentity

circa... 5. about 6. around
   13. approximately

Circe (pert to)...
   brother.. 6. Aeetes
   father.. 6. Helios
   Island abode.. 5. Aeaea
   role, Odyssey.. 5. siren 7. charmer
      9. sorceress, temptress
   sister.. 5. Medea

circle... 3. orb 4. halo, hoop, loop,
   ring 5. ambit, orbit, rhomb, rigol,
   round, wheel 6. clique, cordon,
   girdle, rotate, sphere 7. annulus,
   aureole, circuit, compass, enclose,
   revolve 9. circulate, encompass
   13. circumference

circle (pert to)...
   astronomy.. 6. tropic
   celestial.. 6. colure 10. almucantar
   Japan.. 4. maru
   luminous.. 6. corona
   of hell (8th).. 9. Malebolge
   of monoliths.. 8. cromlech 9. cyclolith
   part.. 3. arc 6. areola, octant, radius,

sector 7. sextant 8. diameter
circuit... 3. lap, orb 4. bout, gyre,
  loop, tour, zone 5. ambit, cycle,
  orbit, relay, round, route 6. circle,
  detour 7. compass 9. round trip
  10. revolution
circuit court... 4. eyre
circuitous... 4. mazy 6. curved
  7. crooked, devious, sinuous, twisted,
  vagrant, winding 8. circular, flexuous,
  indirect, tortuous 9. deceitful,
  deviating, underhand, wandering
  10. roundabout, serpentine
  12. disingenuous, labyrinthine
  14. circumlocutory
circular... 5. round 6. ringed
  7. annular, discoid, program
  8. cingular, coronary, ringlike
  9. crownlike, orbicular 10. circuitous,
  roundabout 13. advertisement
circular (pert to)...
  enclosure.. 3. lis (liss)
  indicator.. 4. dial
  letter.. 10. encyclical
  ornament.. 6. patera
circulate... 4. pass 5. issue 6. circle,
  rotate, spread 7. diffuse, publish
  8. monetize 9. propagate
  11. disseminate
circumference... 4. girt 5. ambit,
  bound, girth 6. bounds 7. circuit,
  compass 8. encircle, surround
  9. outskirts, perimeter, periphery
circumscribe... 5. bound, fence, limit
  6. define 7. enclose, environ
  8. encircle, restrict 9. encompass
circumscribed... 6. finite, narrow
  9. definable 10. restricted
circumspect... 4. wary 5. chary
  7. careful, politic, prudent
  8. cautious, discreet 9. judicious
  10. thoughtful 11. considerate
circumstance... 4. fact, item, pomp
  5. event, state 7. proviso
  8. incident, occasion, position
  9. condition, provision, situation
  10. occurrence, particular
  11. arrangement, opportunity,
  stipulation
circumstantial... 5. exact 6. minute
  7. precise 8. detailed 10. evidential,
  incidental, particular 11. conditional
  12. nonessential
circumvent... 5. cheat, evade
  6. delude, entrap, outwit, thwart
  7. capture, circuit, deceive
  8. surround 9. encompass, frustrate
circus... 4. hawk, ring, show 5. arena
  6. big top, circle, cirque 7. harrier,
  theater 8. carnival, side show
  12. amphitheater
circus (pert to)...
  concessionaire.. 7. grifter
  hawk.. 15. circus assimilis
  rider.. 8. desultor
  Roman.. 13. Circus Maximus
  sideshow.. 6. freaks
  superintendent.. 10. ringmaster
cirque... 6. circle, corrie 7. circlet
cis (pref)... 8. this side
cist... 3. box, pit 5. chest 7. chamber
  8. cistvaen (kistvaen)

Cistercian... 4. monk, Rule
  (Benedictine) 5. Order 8. Trappist
cistern... 3. bac, sac, tub, vat
  4. back, tank, well 7. cuvette,
  raintub 9. impluvium, reservoir
citadel... 3. arx 4. fort 5. Alamo,
  tower 6. castle 7. bastion, bulwark
  8. fastness, fortress 9. acropolis
  10. stronghold 13. fortification
  14. propungnaculum
citation... 5. honor 6. eulogy, notice
  7. mention, summons 8. subpoena
  9. quotation 11. enumeration
  12. verification
cite... 5. quote 6. adduce, allege,
  repeat, summon 7. extract
  8. indicate
citizen... 3. cit 6. native 7. citoyen,
  denizen (of beasts), dweller
  8. civilian, townsman 10. inhabitant
citizenship... 10. citizenism
  15. enfranchisement
citron... 5. melon 6. cedrat (cedrate),
  citrus, yellow
citrus fruit... 4. lime 5. lemon
  6. orange 7. kumquat 8. citrange,
  shaddock 10. grapefruit
cittern, cithern... 4. lute (anc)
  6. zither 7. cithara, gittern
city... 4. town 8. township
  10. metropolis 12. municipality
city (parts)... 4. ward 5. civic, urban
  8. district, precinct
City of...
  Bells.. 10. Strasbourg
  Bridges.. 6. Bruges
  Brotherly Love.. 12. Philadelphia
  Churches.. 8. Brooklyn
  David.. 9. Jerusalem
  Dead (The).. 8. cemetery
  10. Necropolis
  Elms.. 8. New Haven
  Gods.. 6. Asgard (Asgarth)
  Golden Gate (The).. 12. San Francisco
  Great King.. 9. Jerusalem
  Hundred Towers.. 5. Pavia
  Kings.. 4. Lira
  Lilies.. 8. Florence
  Magnificent Distances..
  10. Washington (DC)
  Masts.. 6. London
  Palms (Bib).. 7. Jericho
  Prophet (The).. 6. Medina
  Rams.. 6. Canton
  Saints.. 8. Montreal
  Seven Hills.. 4. Rome
  Straits.. 7. Detroit
  Sun (the).. 7. Baalbek 10. Heliopolis
  Victory.. 5. Cairo
  Violated Treaty.. 8. Limerick
  Violet Crown.. 6. Athens
civet... 5. fossa, genet, rasse
  6. foussa, musang 7. nandine
  10. paradoxure
civic... 5. civil, urban 6. public
  7. burghal, oppidan 9. municipal
  12. metropolitan
civil... 4. hend (hende) 5. suave
  6. decent, polite, public, urbane
  7. affable, courtly, elegant, secular
  8. discreet, gracious, obliging,
  polished, well-bred 9. courteous,

political 10. respectful
11. complaisant 13. condescending
civil (pert to)...
dress.. 5. mufti 7. civvies
fraud (Rom).. 11. stellionate
process.. 4. writ
strife.. 6. stasis
wrong.. 4. tort
civility... 6. comity 7. amenity
8. courtesy, urbanity 9. attention,
etiquette, gentility 10. affability,
politeness
civilization... 6. kultur, polish
7. culture 10. refinement
11. cultivation
civilize... 4. tame 6. polish
8. humanize, urbanize 9. cultivate
11. domesticate
clad... 5. robed 6. decked, garbed
7. arrayed, attired, clothed, dressed
9. appareled, garmented
claim... 3. hak (hakh) 4. case, lien,
name 5. right, title 6. assert,
demand 7. preempt, profess, require
8. arrogate, maintain, pretense
(pretence), proclaim 9. postulate
10. pretension
claimant... 7. claimer 9. applicant,
plaintiff, pretender 10. solicitant
clairvoyance... 3. ESP 7. insight
8. lucidity, sagacity 9. intuition
10. divination 11. penetration
clairvoyant... 4. seer 7. prophet,
seeress 9. sagacious 12. clearsighted
clam... 3. Mya 5. Chama, razor, Solen
6. gweduc, Mactra, quahog
7. mollusk 10. veneriform (shape)
clam destroyer... 6. winkle
10. periwinkle
clammy... 4. cool, damp, dank, soft
5. moist, mucid 6. sticky, sweaty
clamor... 3. cry, din, hue 4. roar, wail
5. decry, noise, vocal 6. hubbub,
outcry, racket, uproar 10. hullabaloo
clamorous... 4. loud 5. noisy
7. blatant, clamant, excited
8. brawling 9. demanding, insistent,
turbulent 10. blustering, uproarious,
vociferous
clamp... 4. vise 6. fasten 9. appliance
clan... 3. set 4. camp, club, cult,
gens, race, sept 5. group, party,
tribe 6. circle, clique, family
7. coterie, society
clan (quarrel)... 4. feud 8. vendetta
clandestine... 3. sly 5. privy 6. covert,
secret 7. furtive, illicit 8. stealthy
9. concealed, underhand
10. fraudulent, undercover
11. unobtrusive 13. surreptitious
clang... 4. ding, ring 5. clank, sound
6. jangle 7. ringing
clang color... 6. timbre 8. tonality
clangor... 3. din 4. ring 5. clang,
noise 6. fracas, hubbub, jangle,
racket, ruckus, rumpus, tumult,
uproar 7. discord, ringing
clank... 4. ring 5. clang 7. ringing
clapper... 4. bell, clap 5. bones
(minstrel)
claque... 8. chaqueur, opera hat

9. applauder
clarify... 5. clear 6. filter, purify,
refine, render, strain 7. cleanse,
explain, rectify
clash... 3. jar 4. bang, bump 5. crash
6. impact, jangle, tussle 7. collide,
scuffle 8. conflict, disagree, skirmish
9. collision, encounter, hostility
10. dissonance
clasp... 3. hug 4. belt, grip, hasp,
hold, ouch (anc), tach 5. grasp,
morse (priest's), seize, stick, tache
(anc) 6. buckle, enwrap, fasten,
secure 7. agraffe (agrafe), embrace,
tendril 8. fastener 10. chatelaine
class... 3. ilk 4. rank, sect 5. caste,
genus, grade, order, tribe 6. brevet
(mil), status 7. station 8. category,
classify, division 9. catalogue
14. classification
class (learned)... 8. literate, literati
14. intelligentsia
classical... 4. pure 5. Attic 6. chaste
7. classic, elegant 8. academic,
literary, tasteful 10. Ciceronian
classification... 4. rank, sort 5. genus,
grade 6. rating, system 7. species
8. analysis, category, grouping
12. distribution
classify... 4. list, rank, rate, sort, type
5. grade, label, range 6. assort,
digest, ticket 7. aggroup, arrange
8. register 9. catalogue
clatter... 3. din, jar 5. noise, rumor
6. babble, gabble, hubbub, racket,
rattle, rumpus, tattle, uproar
7. chatter, prattle 9. commotion
11. disturbance
clause... 5. rider 6. phrase
7. passage, proviso, section
claustral... 9. cloistral 10. cloistered
claw... 4. hand, nail, unce 5. chela,
cloot, clute, talon 8. nipper, unguis
claw... 3. dig 4. grab, grip, pull, tear
5. grasp, seize 6. clutch, scrape,
snatch 7. grapple, scratch
clay... 3. mud 4. marl, mire, soil
5. argil, earth 6. corpse, kaolin
clay (pert to)...
baked.. 4. tile 5. brick
box.. 6. sagger
covered.. 6. lutose
mix.. 3. pug
mold.. 3. dod
molded.. 7. fictile
nodule.. 10. eaglestone
pipe.. 2. TD 10. meerschaum
plug.. 4. bott
polish.. 5. rabat
softening.. 8. malaxage
variety.. 4. bole, loam, marl 5. gault,
ocher, tasco 8. petuntse
clayey... 4. soft 5. adobe, bolar
6. earthy 12. argillaceous
clean, cleanse... 4. dust, swab, wash,
wipe 5. brush, purge, rinse, scrub
6. kosher, purify, refine 7. cleanse,
deterge, launder 8. absterge,
depurate, renovate 9. disinfect,
elutriate, expurgate
cleanness... 6. purity (of life) 7. clarity
8. chastity, elegance, neatness,

pureness, tidiness 10. immaculacy
13. impeccability
clear... 3. net, rid 4. free, gain, over,
pure 5. clean, lucid, plain 6. acquit,
excuse, exempt, hurdle, limpid,
pardon, purify 7. absolve, concise,
crystal, evident, explain, graphic,
lighten, release 8. apparent, distinct,
incisive, luculent 9. cloudless,
exonerate, extricate, vindicate
clear land... 7. thwaite (Eng)
clearsighted... 4. keen 10. discerning
13. perspicacious
cleat... 4. bitt 5. level, strip, wedge
7. joinery
cleave... 3. cut 4. part, rend, rive,
tear 5. clave, cling, clove, crack,
sever, shear, split 6. adhere, bisect,
cohere, divide, pierce 7. dispart
8. separate
cleek... 5. marry, pluck, seize
6. clutch, snatch
clef... 1. C, F, G 4. alto, bass
6. treble 7. descant, soprano
9. character
cleft... 3. gap 4. reft, rent, rift, rima
5. chasm, chink, crack, notch, riven,
split 6. chappy, cranny, gaping,
recess 7. crevice, fissure 8. scissure
cleft palate operation...
13. staphyloraphy (staphylorrhaphy)
clemency... 5. favor, grace, mercy
6. lenity 7. quarter 8. kindness,
leniency, mildness 10. compassion,
indulgence 11. forbearance
Clemens (Samuel) pen name...
9. Mark Twain
clench... 4. fist, grip, grit, hold
5. grasp 6. clinch, clutch
8. purchase 9. interlock
Cleopatra (pert to)...
attendant.. 4. Iras
downfall.. 3. asp
lover.. 6. Antony (Marc), Caesar
obelisk (two).. 6. Needle
queen of.. 5. Egypt
river.. 4. Nile
clepe... 3. bid 4. call, name 6. invite,
invoke 7. address 8. christen
clergy... 5. cloth 6. pulpit
9. clergymen, clericals 10. priesthood
clergyman... 4. abbé, dean 5. canon,
vicar 6. cleric, curate, divine, parson,
pastor, priest, rector 7. dominie,
prelate 8. minister, preacher, sky
pilot 9. presbyter 12. ecclesiastic
clergywoman... 3. nun 8. minister
9. parsoness, priestess 10. religieuse
cleric, non... 4. laic
clerical... 7. scribal 11. ministerial
clerical (pert to)...
attire.. 3. alb 5. amice, cloth, fanon,
orale, stole
collar.. 5. rabat
hat.. 7. biretta
clerk... 3. nun 4. monk 5. write
6. cleric, hermit, layman, scribe
7. scholar (anc) 8. salesman
9. assistant, clergyman
12. ecclesiastic
cleronomy... 8. heritage
11. inheritancy

clever... 3. apt 4. able, cute, deft
5. handy, slick, smart, witty
6. adroit, astute, brainy, bright,
expert, habile, nimble 7. amiable,
cunning, parlous 8. pleasing, skillful,
talented 9. brilliant, dexterous,
ingenious 11. good–natured
cleverness... 4. tact, wits 5. skill
6. esprit 7. cunning 9. ingenuity,
smartness, wittiness 10. adroitness,
astuteness, shrewdness
clew, clue... 3. key 4. ball, loop
(Naut), rope 5. globe 6. cocoon,
tackle (see also *clue*)
cliché... 4. joke 5. banal, trite 6. old
saw 7. bromide 8. banality, chestnut
9. Joe Miller, platitude
click... 3. rap 4. snap 5. clack 6. go
over 7. prosper, succeed
click beetle... 3. dor (dorr) 6. elater
cliff... 3. gat 4. crag, klip, rock, wall
5. bluff, cleve, crest, scarp, slope
6. rocher 7. clogwyn 8. palisade
9. precipice 10. escarpment
climax... 3. cap, epi (Arch) 4. acme,
near, peak, shut 5. tight 6. apogee,
result, summit 7. heights
11. culmination 12. consummation
climb... 3. fly, gad 4. shin 5. grimp,
scale, speel 6. ascend, ascent
7. clamber, upgrade 9. acclivity
climbing... 7. scaling 8. scandent
10. scansorial
climbing plant... 3. hop, ivy 4. bine,
nito, vine 5. betel, liana 6. bryony
clime... 4. zone 5. realm, tract
6. region 7. climate
clinch... 4. bind, grip, hold, seal
5. grasp, prove, seize 6. clutch,
fasten, secure 7. confirm, grapple
8. conclude, purchase 9. establish
cling... 4. hold 5. stick 6. adhere,
cohere
clingfish... 6. testar
clink... 4. rime, slap 5. rhyme
6. jingle, lockup, prison, strike
9. assonance
clinquant... 4. gold, sham 6. tinsel
8. frippery, tinseled 10. glittering
clip... 3. bob, lop, mow 4. barb,
blow, dock, gaff, snip, trim 5. clasp,
prune, shear 6. clutch, fasten
7. curtail, scissor, shorten
8. ornament 10. instrument
clique... 3. set 4. cell, clan, club, ring
5. group, Junta, junto 6. circle
(people) 7. coterie
Cloaca Maxima (anc Rome)...
5. sewer 10. repository
cloak... 3. aba 4. cape, mask, pall,
wrap 5. cover, grego, jelab, manta,
sagum 6. abolla, capote, dolman,
mantle, mantua, screen, serape,
shield 7. chlamys (anc), conceal,
galabia, manteau, paenula (anc),
paletot, pelisse, pretext, protect
8. disguise 9. dissemble, new–market
10. witzchoura
clobber... 3. hit 4. beat, conk, poke,
swat 5. clout, punch, whack
6. defeat, strike, wallop
clock... 3. nef (ship's) 4. dial, time

5. knock 6. record 7. digital
8. recorder, sidereal 9. clepsydra,
metronome, timepiece 10. isochronon
11. chronometer
clockwise... 6. deasil (dessil)
11. withershins 14. dextrorotation,
dextrorotatory
clog... 4. stop 5. choke, dance
6. daggle, hamper, impede
8. encumber, obstruct, restrain
clog shoe... 4. geta 5. sabot
6. chopin, cobcab (Orient), patten
7. chopine
cloister... 4. stoa 5. abbey 6. arcade,
friary, immure, priory 7. confine,
convent, nunnery, retreat
9. anchorage, hermitage, monastery,
peristyle 10. passageway
cloistered... 7. recluse 8. enclosed,
monastic 11. sequestered
close... 2. at, by 3. end 4. near, nigh,
seal, shut, slam 5. dense, finis, stivy
6. finale, finish, period, secret, stingy,
sultry 7. airless, extreme, occlude,
related 8. complete, conclude,
familiar, imminent, intimate, stifling
9. extremity, secretive, terminate
11. approximate, termination
13. juxtaposition
close (pert to)...
eyes (the).. 4. seel 5. blink
fasten.. 6. batten
of day.. 8. eventide 9. nightfall
poetic.. 4. nigh 5. anear
tightly.. 3. bar 4. bung, seal
6. clench, enseal 8. obturate
closely... 4. just 6. almost, barely,
nearly 8. narrowly
closely allied... 6. chummy
7. germane 8. intimate
closeness... 7. density, secrecy
8. fidelity, intimacy, likeness,
nearness, sameness 9. tightness
10. chumminess, narrowness,
similarity, stinginess, strictness,
sultriness 11. airlessness,
compactness, conciseness, familiarity,
resemblance 14. oppressiveness
closet... 5. ambry, cuddy, emery
6. locker, pantry 7. cabinet
8. cupboard, wardrobe 9. cloakroom,
storeroom
closing device... 3. key 4. lock, snap
5. clasp, hinge, latch 6. Velcro (tm),
zipper
closing measure (Mus)... 4. coda
clot... 4. lump, mass 5. grume
7. thicken 8. coagulum, concrete
9. coagulate 12. crassamentum
cloth... 3. net, tat 4. brin, crea, drap,
felt, lamé, silk, tapa, wool 5. adati,
baize, bezan, bluet, carda, crash,
crepe, denim, khaki, linen, manta,
nylon, orlon, rayon, satin, scrim,
surat, tamis, terry, tulle, twill, voile
6. alpaca, burlap, calico, canvas,
chintz, cotton, damask, dimity,
dowlas, duffel, faille, jersey, madras,
mohair, muslin, nankin, pongee,
poplin, samite (gold), sateen, velour
7. acetate, baracan, brocade,
bunting, cambric, challis, chiffon,

drap d'or, flannel, foulard, gingham,
nankeen, organdy, organza, percale,
sacking, spandex, taffeta, ticking,
worsted 8. cashmere, chambray,
corduroy, cretonne, drilling,
nainsook, Shantung 9. crinoline,
gabardine, polyester, sailcloth,
tarpaulin, tricotine 10. broadcloth,
seersucker 11. cheesecloth, drap
d'argent (silver), marquisette
cloth (pert to)...
checkered.. 5. plaid
finisher.. 7. beetler
piece.. 4. bolt 5. scrap
ridge.. 4. wale
selvage.. 4. roon 6. border 7. listing
twilled.. 5. denim, serge
weaving.. 4. warp, weft, woof
clothe... 3. tog 4. deck, garb, gird,
robe, vest 5. array, drape, dress,
endue, indue 6. afford, enrobe, invest
7. empower, provide, sheathe
8. accouter
clothes... 3. rig 4. duds, garb, togs
5. guise, habit, jeans, Levis 6. attire,
bikini, briefs 7. apparel, costume,
raiment, regalia, threads (sl)
8. clothing, garments, leotards,
swimsuit 9. dungarees
10. bedclothes, garmenture
11. habiliments, investiture
cloud... 3. fog, low 4. dust, film, haze,
mist, rack, scud 5. nepho (comb
form), nubia, stain, sully, taint, vapor
6. cirrus, damage, darken, defame,
defect, nebule, nimbus, shadow,
stigma 7. blacken, blemish, cumulus,
nubilus, obscure, pea–soup, stratus,
tarnish, tornado 8. cat's–tail, cocktail,
overcast 10. horizontal
clouds (pert to)...
astronomy 4. coma 9. nubeculan
kind.. 6. cirrus, nimbus 7. cumulus,
fractus, stratus 9. mare's–tail
luminous.. 5. nimbi
Magellanic.. 5. Major, Minor
photography.. 9. nephogram
science of.. 9. nephology
seeding.. 10. nucleation
vapory.. 4. rack
cloudy... 4. dark, hazy 5. filmy, foggy,
misty, murky, shady, vague 6. gloomy,
lowery, opaque 7. nebular, obscure
8. confused, overcast, vaporous
9. cloudlike 10. indistinct, lackluster
clout... 3. hit, jab, rag 4. blow, bump,
clod, mend, nail, swat 5. patch,
power, shred, smack 9. influence
12. handkerchief
clove... see also *cleave* 5. spice
clover... 3. red 4. bush 5. lotus, snail,
white 6. alsike 7. crimson, melilot,
prairie, spotted 9. Melilotus
clown... 3. oaf 4. boor, fool, lout,
mime, mome, zany 5. comic, Kelly
(Emmet), mimer, yahoo 6. jester,
rustic 7. buffoon 9. harlequin
10. countryman 11. merry–andrew
clownish... 4. rude 5. gawky, rough
6. clumsy, coarse, rustic 7. awkward,
boorish, ill–bred, loutish, uncivil
8. churlish, ungainly

9. untutored 10. buffoonish
11. countrified
cloy . . . 4. clog, glut, pall, sate
5. gorge, stuff 6. accloy 7. satiate,
satisfy, surfeit
club . . . 3. bat, hit 4. beat, join, mace
5. billy, clout, staff, unite, yokel
6. cudgel, league, weapon 7. society
8. bludgeon, spontoon
9. boomerang, espantoon
10. nulla–nulla, pogamoggan
11. association
club (pert to) . . .
actors . . 6. Friars
historic . . 5. Whigs 8. Jacobins
10. Cordeliers
Service . . 7. Kiwanis
Women's (first) . . 7. Sorosis
clubfoot . . . 7. talipes 9. deformity, pes
valgus 13. talipes valgus
club–shaped . . . 7. clavate
clue, clew . . . 3. key, tip 4. data, hint
5. scent 6. thread 7. inkling
8. evidence 9. suspicion
11. fingerprint
clump . . . 3. tod 4. heap, lump, thud,
tuft 5. bunch, chunk, group, motte
(mott), patch, stamp 6. growth,
trudge 7. cluster, thicket
clumsy . . . 4. ugly 5. bulky, gawky,
inapt, inept, unfit 6. gauche, oafish
7. awkward, uncouth, unhandy
8. slipshod, ungainly, unwieldy
9. inelegant, lumbering, maladroit,
misshapen 10. blundering,
cumbersome, left–handed
13. inappropriate
clumsy person . . . 4. gawk 5. jumbo,
staup 7. bungler
clupeoid fish . . . 7. herring
cluster . . . 4. crop, cyme, gang, tuft
5. bunch, clump, group 6. huddle
8. fascicle 9. glomerule
cluster (pert to) . . .
bean . . 4. guar 6. legume
fibers . . 3. nep
flowers . . 6. raceme 7. rosette
8. anthemia, panticle
fruit . . 6. grapes
spores . . 5. sorus
stars . . 8. Globular, Pleiades (The)
clustery . . 8. racemose
clutch . . . 3. nab 4. claw, grip, hold,
nest 5. brood, catch, clasp, grasp,
seize 6. clench, cletch, crisis
clyster . . . 5. enema 6. lavage
9. injection
Clytemnestra's mother . . . 4. Leda
cnemis . . . 4. shin 5. tibia
coach . . . 3. car, rig 5. prime, stage,
train, tutor 6. direct, fiacre, jarvey
7. adviser, prepare, tallyho, teacher
8. carriage, equipage, instruct,
preparer 9. charabanc 10. instructor
coach dog . . . 9. Dalmatian
coachman . . . 3. fly (angling) 4. fish,
jehu, whip 6. driver
coagulate . . . 3. gel, jel, set 4. cake,
clot, curd, lump 6. curdle, posset
7. congeal 8. solidify
coagulator . . . 6. enzyme, rennet
coagulum . . . 4. clot, curd 5. grume

7. clabber
coal . . . 4. fuel 5. black, ember
6. carbon, cinder 7. lignite, residue
coal (pert to) . . .
bin . . 6. bunker
car . . 3. dan 4. corf, tram 6. hopper
dust . . 4. coom (coomb), culm, smut
gas . . 7. Pintsch 9. acetylene
miner . . 7. collier
miner's disease . . 11. anthracosis
oil . . 8. kerosene
tar . . 5. lysol, pitch 6. cresol, decane,
phenol 7. toluene
tunnel . . 4. adit
type . . 3. egg, nut, pea 4. dant, hard,
peat, soft 6. broken, cannel
8. charcoal, chestnut 9. buckwheat
10. anthracite, bituminous
coalition . . . 5. trust, union 6. fusion,
hookup, league, merger 7. society
8. alliance 10. federation
11. affiliation, combination,
confederacy, conjunction
coalition advocate . . . 9. fusionist
coals . . . 5. gleed 6. embers 7. cinders
coarse . . . 3. fat, low 4. dank, lewd,
rude, vile 5. broad, crass, gross,
thick 6. carnal, earthy, impure,
ribald, rustic, vulgar 7. goatish,
obscene, sensual 8. granular,
immodest, indecent, inferior, unchaste
9. inelegant, offensive, unrefined
10. unfinished, unpolished
coarse (pert to) . . .
grain . . 4. meal
grass . . 4. reed 5. sedge 6. quitch
hominy . . 4. corn, samp
coast . . . 4. sail 5. beach, glide, shore,
slide 6. rivage 7. seaside
8. seaboard, seashore
coast (pert to) . . .
dweller . . 7. orarian
live oak . . 6. encina
projection . . 4. cape, ness
coat . . . 4. jupe 5. cloak, frock, parka,
tunic 6. blazer, capote, duster,
jacket, raglan, reefer, trench, tuxedo,
ulster 7. cassock, cutaway, paletot,
slicker 8. gossamer, Mackinaw,
tegument 9. newmarket, redingote
coat (pert to) . . .
fastener . . 4. frog 6. zipper
of animal . . 3. fur 4. pelt, wool
6. pelage 8. feathers
of arms . . 5. crest 8. blazonry
10. escutcheon
of mail . . 6. byrnia 7. hauberk
of the eye (inner) . . 6. retina
coati . . . 5. Nasua 6. narica 7. raccoon
coating (pert to) . . .
cake . . 5. glacé, icing 8. frosting
copper, bronze . . 6. patina
grain . . 4. bran
medical . . 9. collodion
metal . . 5. plate
seed . . 5. testa 6. tegmen
10. endopleura
tin, lead . . 5. terne
vitreous . . 6. enamel
coax . . . 3. beg, ply 4. lure, urge
5. press, tease 6. cajole, entice,
exhort 7. beguile, flatter, implore,

wheedle 8. blandish, inveigle,
persuade 9. importune
10. manipulate

cob... 4. axis, blow, gull, loaf, mole,
pier, swan 5. block, chief, horse
6. basket, leader, muffin, spider
7. beating, corncob 8. dumpling
10. breakwater

cobbler... 3. pie 5. coler, sutor
6. bungle, repair, souter 7. botcher,
crispin 9. fortescue (fortesque),
shoemaker

cobbra... 4. head 5. skull

cobby... 5. stout 6. hearty, lively,
stocky 10. headstrong

cobra... 3. asp 4. Naga (Myth), Naja
5. mamba, snake, viper 8. ringhals

cobweb... 3. net 4. trap 5. snare,
wevet 7. fiction, network 8. filament,
gossamer 9. intricacy

cobweblike... 8. araneous 9. arachnoid

cocaine... 4. coca, snow (sl)
8. narcotic 9. mydriatic
10. anesthetic

coccus... 4. cell 5. spore
9. bacterium, cochineal

cochleate... 6. spiral 11. shell-shaped

cock... 3. nab, tap 4. bird, heap,
kora, pile, vane (weather) 5. strut,
valve 6. faucet, grouse, leader,
muckna 7. rooster, swagger

cockade... 4. knot 7. rosette

Cockade State... 8. Maryland

cockatoo... 3. ara 5. arara (palm),
galah 6. parrot 8. ganggang

cockle... 4. boat, gith, kiln, oast
5. shell, stove 6. pucker 7. mollusk,
wrinkle

cockpit... 3. pit 4. well 5. arena,
cabin (airplane) 7. gallera

cockscomb (ooxoomb)... 5. crest, plant

cocktail... 5. cloud, drink, horse
6. beetle 9. appetizer

cocky... 4. pert 5. saucy 6. jaunty
7. stuck up 9. conceited

cocoa... 5. broma, cacao 8. beverage
9. chocolate 11. theobromine

coconut (pert to)...
fiber.. 4. coir, kyar
India.. 6. nargil (narghile)
meat.. 5. copra

cocoon... 3. pod 4. bave (silk), clew,
kell, pupa 9. chrysalis

cod... 3. bib, cor 4. fish, ling
5. scrod, sprag 6. burbot, cultus,
gadoid 7. bacalao

coddle... 3. pet 4. baby, cook
5. humor, spoil 6. caress, fondle,
pamper 11. mollycoddle

code... 3. law 5. canon, codex, Morse,
salic 6. digest, equity, signal, symbol
7. pandect, precept
12. Commandments

codfish (pert to)...
Alaska.. 6. wachna
genus.. 5. Gadus
ready for cooking.. 5. scrod
type.. 3. cod, red 4. cusk, rock
6. Murray, tomcod 7. buffalo

codger... 5. crank, miser 6. oddity

codicil... 4. will 5. rider 6. sequel
8. addition, appendix 10. instrument

Cody (William)... 11. Buffalo Bill

coerce... 4. curb 5. force 6. compel
7. dragoon, enforce, repress
9. blackjack, strong-arm, terrorize
10. intimidate

coercion... 5. force 6. duress
8. violence 10. compulsion,
constraint

coffee (pert to)...
bean.. 3. nib
container.. 8. canister
cup holder.. 4. zarf
extract.. 8. caffeine
kind.. 3. Rio 4. Java 5. Milds,
Mocha 6. Bogota, Brazil, Santos
7. Sumatra, Turkish 8. Medellin
9. Maracaibo
mix.. 7. chicory
pot.. 6. biggin 10. percolator

coffin... 3. box, urn 4. bier, case, kist,
mold 5. chest, crust 6. basket,
casing, casket 11. sarcophagus

coffin (pert to)...
cloth.. 4. pall 5. cloak
litter.. 4. bier
nail.. 7. cigarette
prehistoric.. 4. cist 5. chest

cog... 3. cam 4. boat (fishing), gear
5. catch, cheat, cozen, tenon, tooth
7. ratchet, wheedle 8. sprocket
9. deception

cogent... 5. valid 6. potent, strong
7. telling 8. powerful 9. effective
10. compelling, conclusive,
convincing, persuasive

cogitate... 4. mull, muse, plan
5. think 6. ponder 8. meditate
9. cerebrate

cognizance... 3. ken 4. heed, plea
5. badge (knight's) 9. knowledge
11. recognition 12. apprehension

cognizant... 5. aware 7. knowing
8. sensible 9. conscious
10. perceptive 11. intelligent

cognomen... 4. name 5. title
6. y-clept 7. surname 8. nickname
10. patronymic 11. appellation

coheir... 5. joint 8. parcener

cohere... 5. agree, cling, serry, stick,
unite 6. adhere, cleave 9. glutinate

coherence... 5. cling 8. adhesion,
cohesion, sticking 9. adherence,
connected 11. consistency

coil... 4. ansa, clew, curl, loop, mesh,
wind 5. querl, twine, twist 6. spiral
7. haycock 8. encircle
11. convolution

coiled... 7. tortile, twirled

coin... 3. rin, sou, yen 4. cash, cent
5. money, penny, stamp 6. specie

coin (pert to)...
Bib.. 6. talent
brass.. 13. Rosa Americana (1722)
gold.. 3. lev 4. ryal (rial) 5. daric,
eagle 6. guinea
minor.. 4. doit
parts of.. 4. flan 5. field, tails, verso
6. legend 7. exergue, obverse (front),
reverse
silver.. 4. batz, obol, ryal (rial)
5. crown, ducat, sceat 6. tester
tester.. 6. shroff (saraf)

coincide . . . 5. agree, check, chime, match, tally 6. concur 7. consent 10. correspond 11. synchronize

coincident . . . 9. consonant 10. concurrent 12. contemporary

coiner . . . 8. inventor 9. neologist (words) 10. fabricator 13. counterfeiter

coins (pert to) . . .
roll of . . 7. rouleau
science of . . 11. numismatics
specialist . . 11. numismatist

colander . . . 5. sieve 6. filter, sorter 8. strainer

Colchis King . . . 6. Aeetes

cold . . . 3. icy, nip, raw 4. dank, dead, drow, dull, frio, sure 5. algid, bland, bleak, frore (anc) 6. chilly, frigid, frosty 7. chilled, cinched 8. chilling, reserved, unheated 9. heartless 10. lackluster 11. indifferent, passionless, unconscious

cold (pert to) . . .
blooded . . 9. heartless, unfeeling 13. dispassionate, heterothermal 14. poikilothermal
feet . . 9. cowardice
infection . . 4. post 5. rheum 6. coryza 7. catarrh
sore . . 6. herpes 7. simplex, vesicle 14. herpes labialis
steel . . 5. sword 7. bayonet, weapons
term . . 8. frigoric
wind . . 4. bise

Coleoptera . . . 7. beetles, insects

Coleridge's sacred river . . . 4. Alph (Kubla Khan)

colewort . . . 4. kale 7. cabbage

colic . . . 4. pain 5. gripe, spasm 7. tormina 10. enteralgia 11. stomachache

coliseum . . . 4. bowl 5. arena 6. circus 7. stadium, theater 9. Colosseum 10. hippodrome 12. amphitheater

collaborate . . . 3. aid 6. co–work 8. coauthor 9. cooperate 10. fraternize

collage . . . 6. gluing 7. montage 8. abstract, adhesive 9. cyclorama

collapse . . . 4. cave, fail, fall 5. crash, slump 6. cave–in, defeat 7. crack–up, debacle, deflate, failure 8. downfall 9. breakdown, shrinking 10. bankruptcy, exhaustion 11. prostration

collar . . . 4. band, grab, ruff 5. chain, rabat, ruche 6. arrest, bertha, rabato, tackle, torque 7. barghan, capture, harness (part), shackle 8. carcanet, neckband 10. pickadilly

collate . . . 5. audit, check 6. verify 7. certify, compare, examine

collateral . . . 5. extra 6. margin 7. related 8. indirect, relation (folks), security 9. accessory, secondary 10. contingent, obligation, subsidiary 11. subordinate 12. nonessential

collation . . . 3. tea 4. meal 5. lunch 6. repast, sermon 7. address, reading 8. luncheon, treatise 10. collection, comparison,

conference 12. consultation, contribution

colleague . . . 6. fellow 7. compeer, comrade, consort, partner 8. camarada, confrere 9. associate, companion 11. confederate

collect . . . 3. bag, tax 4. levy, mass 5. amass, glean, raise, rally 6. deduce, forage, garner, gather, muster, prayer, sheave 7. compile, procure 8. assemble, mobilize 9. aggregate 10. accumulate, congregate

collection . . . 3. ana, bag, set 4. book, olio 5. group, hoard, store 6. rosary, sorite 8. assembly, donation, offering 9. aggregate, congeries, gathering, repertory 10. assemblage, repertoire 11. acquisition

collection (pert to) . . .
anecdotes . . 3. ana 4. data 8. analecta
animals (wild) . . 3. zoo 9. menagerie
bubbles . . 4. foam
curiosities . . 6. museum
documents . . 4. Veda 6. corpus 7. dossier
fruit . . 7. syncarp
implements (Surg) . . 7. trousse
of four . . 6. tetrad
of twenty–four . . 5. quire
poems . . 5. sylva 9. anthology
proper names . . 11. onomasticon
type . . 4. font
writing . . 10. literature

collector (pert to) . . .
bird eggs . . 8. oologist
books . . 10. bibliothec 11. bibliophile 12. bibliomaniac
coins . . 11. numismatist
rent . . 8. landlord
stamps . . 11. philatelist

colleen . . . 4. girl, lass, maid 6. damsel, maiden 7. girleen

college . . . 6. school 7. academy, society 9. Alma Mater, institute 10. université, university 11. corporation, institution

college (pert to) . . .
campus . . 4. lawn, quad 7. grounds
graduate . . 6. alumna 7. alumnus
license for absence . . 5. exeat
official . . 4. dean 5. prexy 6. beadle, bursar, regent 7. proctor

collegiate . . . 8. academic 9. collegian, scholarly 11. college–bred

collide with . . . 3. hit, ram 5. clash, crash 6. hurtle, strike 7. contend 8. conflict, disagree

collier . . . 5. miner 6. plover

collieshangie . . . 3. row 7. quarrel 8. squabble 11. disturbance (noisy)

collision . . . 4. bump 5. clash, crash 6. impact 7. smashup 8. accident 9. hostility 11. composition, impingement 12. interference

colloquial . . . 6. common 8. everyday, familiar, informal 9. unstudied 10. vernacular 11. undignified 14. conversational

colloquy . . . 4. chat, talk 6. parley 9. discourse 10. conference

12. conversation
Cologne Kings (legend)... 4. Magi
  6. Gaspar 8. Melchior 9. Balthasar
Colombia...
  capital.. 6. Bogota (1538)
  city.. 4. Cali 5. Pasto 8. Medellin
    9. Cartagena 10. Santa Marta
  Falls.. 10. Tequendama
  Liberator.. 7. Bolivar (Simon)
  mountain.. 5. Andes 11. Cordilleras
  river.. 9. Magdalena
colonize... 6. gather, people, settle
    8. populate 9. establish
colonizer... 3. ant 6. oecist
    7. planter, settler
colonnade... 3. row (columns) 4. stoa
    6. arcade 7. columns, pillars, portico
    8. cloister 9. peristyle
colony... 4. body 5. group, swarm
    8. dominion 9. community
    10. dependency, settlement
colophon... 4. logo 6. emblem
    9. bookplate 11. inscription (book)
color... 3. dun, dye, hue 4. tint, tone
    5. blush, paint, shade, stain, terne,
    tinge 6. flaxen, nuance, pastel, sallow,
    timbre 7. piebald, pigment 8. tincture
    (Her) 10. complexion
color (pert to)...
  application (paste).. 7. impasto
  blending.. 4. teer 5. fondu
    9. scumbling
  blind.. 13. achromatopsia
  clouded.. 9. nebulated
  colorful.. 9. chromatic
  colorless.. 4. drab, dull, pale 6. pallid
    7. whitish 8. blanched
    10. achromatic
  irregularity.. 5. fleck 6. streak
    10. rivulation
  material.. 5. eosin, morin, smalt
    7. pigment 11. chlorophyll
  off color.. 6. risqué 8. improper
  organ.. 8. clavilux
  paint, rouge.. 6. ruddle 7. blusher
  science of.. 10. chromatics
    11. spectrology
  variegated.. 7. rainbow, The Flag,
    vibgyor 8. spectrum 11. iridescence
Colorado...
  canyon.. 5. Black 10. Royal Gorge
  capital.. 6. Denver
  city.. 5. Aspen, Lamar 6. Pueblo
    7. Boulder, Manassa, Manitou
  Indian.. 7. Arapaho
  lake (highest).. 10. Frozen Lake
  Mt peak.. 6. Elbert 9. Pike's Peak
  park.. 5. Estes 15. Garden of the
    Gods
  river.. 4. Gila 6. Platte 8. Arkansas
  State admission.. 12. Thirty–eighth
  State bird.. 11. lark bunting
  State flower.. 9. columbine
  State motto.. 13. Nil Sine Numine
    (Nothing Without God)
  State nickname.. 10. Centennial
colossal... 4. huge 5. great, large
    6. absurd, superb 7. mammoth
    8. gigantic 9. monstrous
colossal beast... 8. behemoth (Bib)
colt... 3. gun 4. foal 5. filly, horse
    8. yearling

Columbus (pert to)...
  birthplace.. 5. Genoa (It)
  companion.. 5. Ojeda
  discoverer.. 7. America (1492)
  landing site.. 11. San Salvador
  sailing site.. 5. Palos (Sp)
  vessel.. 4. Nina 5. Pinta 10. Santa
    Maria
column... 3. lat (Buddh) 4. anta
    5. pylon, shaft, stele (stela) 6. pillar
    7. telamon 8. baluster, caryatid,
    pilaster
column (pert to)...
  base.. 5. socle 6. plinth 9. stylobate
  military.. 4. unit 9. formation
  Order (Arch).. 5. Doric, Ionic
    6. Tuscan 9. Composite
    10. Corinthian
  ref to.. 5. train 7. cortege
    8. cylinder, memorial, monument
    10. procession
  shaft.. 4. fust 5. scape 8. apophyge
  term.. 5. bague, galbe, shank
    7. capital, entasis
coma... 4. daze, tuft 5. carus, sleep,
    sopor 6. stupor, trance 9. catalepsy
    12. sluggishness 13. insensibility
    15. unconsciousness
comatose... 6. drowsy, torpid
    9. apathetic, lethargic 10. cataleptic,
    insensible 11. unconscious
comb... 4. card, wave 5. cock's, crest,
    curry, groom, scour, tease 6. search
    7. rummage 8. caruncle
combat... 3. war 4. cope, duel, fray,
    tilt 5. fight, joust (anc), repel
    6. action, battle, karate, kung fu,
    oppose, strife 7. contest, jujitsu,
    scuffle 8. argument, conflict
    9. withstand 10. antagonize,
    contention, engagement
combat (pert to)...
  challenge.. 6. cartel 8. gauntlet
  code.. 8. duello
  scene.. 5. arena 8. coliseum
combatant... 6. dueler 7. battler,
    fighter 8. disputer 9. contender
    10. competitor, contestant
combative... 8. militant 9. agonistic,
    bellicose 10. aggressive, pugnacious
    11. belligerent, contentious
combination... 4. gang, pact, pool
    5. blend, combo, party, trust, union
    6. clique, fusion, hookup, league,
    merger 7. amalgam, combine, faction,
    mixture 8. alliance, coalesce,
    ensemble, junction 9. camarilla,
    coalition, synthesis 10. embodiment
    11. aggregation, association,
    confederacy, unification
    12. undergarment 13. incorporation
combine... 3. add, mix 4. join, pool
    5. merge, unite 6. concur, mingle
    7. machine 10. synthesize
combining form...
  above, beyond.. 3. sur 5. ultra
  across.. 4. tran 5. trans
  bad.. 3. dys, mal
  black.. 4. mela
  earth.. 3. geo 5. terra
  equal.. 3. iso 4. homo, pari
  far.. 3. tel 4. tele

good.. 2. eu
hundred.. 4. cent
inner, within.. 4. ento (ent)
kidney.. 4. reni
middle.. 4. medi 5. medio
mountain.. 3. oro
needle.. 3. acu
new.. 3. neo
not.. 2. un 3. non
old, ancient.. 5. paleo
one.. 3. uni 4. mono
outside, without.. 3. ect, ext 4. ecto
personal.. 4. idio
soft.. 4. leni
stone.. 4. lith
thought.. 4. ideo
thrice.. 3. ter
tooth.. 3. odonto
touch.. 3. tac
up, upward.. 3. ano
watery.. 4. sero
comblike... 7. ctenoid 8. pectinal
combustible... 5. fiery, quick
  7. piceous 8. volcanic 9. irascible
  10. accendible 11. hot–tempered,
  inflammable
combustion... 4. fire 6. tumult
  7. blazing, flaming 8. ignition
  9. agitation, confusion, cremation
  12. inflammation 13. conflagration
come... 3. hop 4. near 5. issue, occur
  6. appear, arrive, happen
  8. approach 9. transpire
come (pert to)...
across.. 3. pay 4. meet 7. confess
  10. contribute
back.. 6. answer, retort, return
  7. rebound, recover 8. remember,
  repartee
before.. 4. lead 7. precede, prevene
  8. antecede
between.. 8. estrange, interlie
  9. interpose, intervene
by.. 3. get 4. gain 6. obtain
  7. acquire, inherit, receive
forth.. 3. jet 4. gush, spew 5. hatch,
  issue, occur 6. appear, emerge,
  spring 7. emanate 9. originate
together.. 4. join, knit, meet 5. clash
  7. collide, convene 8. assemble,
  converge
come (to)...
light.. 7. develop
maturity.. 5. ripen
pass.. 5. occur 6. befall, betide,
  happen 9. eventuate
rest.. 3. sit 5. light 6. settle
comedian, comedienne... 4. buff
  5. actor, comic 6. player 7. farcist
  8. funnyman 9. dramatist
comedy... 5. drama, farce, revue
  7. comedie 8. travesty 9. burlesque,
  slapstick
comestibles... 4. food 5. manna
  8. eatables, victuals
comfort... 4. ease 5. cheer, quilt
  6. relief, solace, soothe, succor
  7. confirm, console, enliven, fortify,
  refresh, relieve, support, sustain
  8. inspirit, nepenthe (drug)
  9. enjoyment 10. invigorate,

strengthen 11. consolation
  12. satisfaction
comfortable... 4. cozy, easy, snug
  5. scarf 8. adequate, cheerful,
  homelike, wristlet 9. contented,
  endemonic 10. complacent,
  prosperous 11. consolatory,
  encouraging
comforter... 5. quilt 6. tippet
  7. solacer 8. pacifier 9. Paraclete
comfortless... 7. forlorn 8. desolate
  9. cheerless, heartsick 10. despairing
  11. distressing 12. disconsolate,
  inconsolable
comic, comical... 3. odd 5. cutup,
  droll, funny, queer, witty 6. absurd,
  quaint 7. cartoon, risible
  8. comedian, farcical, humorous
  9. burlesque, laughable, ludicrous,
  quizzical, whimsical 10. capricious,
  outlandish
coming... 3. due 6. access, advent,
  future 7. arrival, forward, looming
  8. eventual, expected, imminent
  9. imminence 11. approaching,
  forthcoming
coming into being... 7. genesis,
  nascent
comity... 7. amenity, suavity 8. civility,
  courtesy, urbanity 10. affability
command... 3. bid, gee, haw, hup
  4. bade, beck, fiat, hest, rule, sway
  5. avast, check, edict, exact, grasp,
  order, power, ukase 6. behest,
  charge, compel, decree, direct,
  enjoin, govern 7. control, dictate,
  mandate, mastery 8. dominion,
  restrain 9. authority, prescribe
  10. domination 11. commandment
  12. jurisdiction
commander... 3. cid 5. chief, ruler
  6. leader 7. admiral, captain, skipper
  8. dictator, governor, myriarch,
  overlord
commander, Eastern... 3. ras 4. amir,
  emir, Imam, khan, rani 5. ameer,
  begum, dewan, emeer, nawab, Nizam
  6. caliph, regent, Sultan
commanding... 8. dominant
  9. imperious 10. imperative
  13. authoritative
commandments... 4. laws 6. orders,
  tables 8. mandates, precepts
  9. Decalogue (Ten)
comme il faut... 8. properly
  9. correctly 10. decorously 12. as it
  should be
commemoration... 7. service
  8. Encaenia (Oxford Univ)
  10. observance 11. anniversary,
  celebration, remembrance
  13. solemnization
commence... 4. open 5. arise, begin,
  start 6. spring 8. initiate 9. originate
commencement... 4. rite 6. source
  8. ceremony, nascency 9. beginning,
  formality, inception, novitiate
  10. initiation
commend... 4. plug 5. boost, extol,
  offer 6. assign, commit, praise,
  remand, resign 7. approve, deliver,
  entrust 8. advocate, delegate

9. recommend 10. compliment
commendation ... 4. hype, plug, puff
5. boost, kudos 8. approval
10. assignment, commitment,
compliment, delegation
11. approbation, consignment,
entrustment
comment ... 4. note, talk 6. gossip,
postil, remark, report 7. descant,
discuss, explain, mention 8. annotate,
critique 9. criticism, discourse
commentary ... 5. gloss 6. memoir
7. remarks 8. treatise 9. memoranda
10. annotation 11. explanation
commerce ... 5. trade 7. traffic
8. dealings 9. communion
11. interchange 13. communication
commis ... 5. agent, clerk 6. deputy
commiserate ... 4. pity 7. condole,
console 10. sympathize
commiseration ... 4. pity, ruth
5. mercy 6. sorrow 7. empathy,
feeling 8. sympathy 10. compassion,
condolence
commission ... 4. duty, task 5. allot,
board, share, trust 6. brevet, depute,
office, ordain 7. empower, mandate,
mission, payment, rake-off, warrant
8. delegate 9. authority
10. assignment, constitute,
delegation, deputation
11. performance 12. perpetration
commissioned ... 8. allotted, assigned,
breveted 9. delegated
10. accredited, authorized
commissioner ... 5. envoy 6. dubash,
legate 7. steward 8. delegate,
emissary, official 9. commissar
commissure ... 4. seam 5. cleft, joint,
mitre, raphe 6. stitch, suture
7. closure 8. juncture 10. interstice
commit ... 2. do 3. con 4. game
(cards) 5. refer 6. remand 7. confide,
consign, entrust promise
8. memorize, relegate
10. commission, perpetrate
commode ... 3. cap 5. chest
8. fontange 9. washstand
10. chiffonier
commodious ... 3. fit 5. ample, roomy
6. proper 8. suitable 9. capacious,
expansive, opportune 10. convenient
11. comfortable, serviceable
13. accommodating
commodity, commodities ... 5. goods,
wares 6. profit 7. staples
common ... 4. park 5. cheap, plain,
stale, trite, usual 6. mutual, paltry,
vulgar 7. average 8. familiar,
frequent, mediocre, ordinary, plebeian
9. customary, household, universal
11. commonplace
common (pert to) ...
ancestor .. 4. Adam 10. progenitor
funds .. 4. pool 7. tontine
gender .. 6. unisex 7. epicene
informer .. 7. delator
people .. 3. mob 5. demos, gente
6. vulgus 7. demotic 8. populace
commonly accepted ... 7. vulgate
commonly thought ... 8. putative
commonplace ... 5. banal, daily, stale,

theme, trite, usual 6. truism
7. humdrum, prosaic 8. ordinary,
workaday 9. platitude
commonwealth ... 5. group, State
7. society 8. Kentucky, Virginia
9. Australia, community
12. Pennsylvania 13. Massachusetts
commotion ... 3. ado 4. fray, riot,
to-do, whir 5. flare, tizzy 6. flurry,
fracas, hubbub, rumpus, tumult, unrest
7. turmoil 8. foofaraw, uprising
9. agitation, confusion
10. concussion (med), excitement,
turbulence 12. perturbation
commune ... 4. area, soil 5. realm,
share 6. confer, impart 7. kibbutz
8. converse 9. communion
10. commonalty 11. intercourse
(spiritual) 12. conversation
Commune of Paris (1871) ...
10. government
communicate ... 3. say 4. give, join
5. share 6. bestow, impart, inform
7. apprize 8. converse, transmit
9. communion
communication ... 4. word 5. radio
6. letter, report 7. account, contact,
epistle, message 8. buzzword,
feedback 9. statement
10. communique, connection
11. computerese, impartation,
information, intercourse 12. body
language 14. word processing
communion ... 5. share 6. church
7. concord, rapport 8. converse
9. agreement 11. intercourse
12. denomination 13. participation
Communion ... 9. Eucharist, Sacrament
10. intinction, Last Supper
communion (pert to) ...
bread (blessed) .. 4. host 5. wafer
7. eulogia 9. antidoron
cloth .. 8. corporal, corporas
plate .. 5. paten 12. processional
table .. 5. altar
vessel .. 3. ama, pyx
communique ... 4. word 7. message
8. dispatch 13. communication
comose ... 5. hairy 6. tufted
compact ... 4. etui, firm, pact, plot,
snug, trim 5. brief, close, dense,
pithy, press, solid, terse, tight
6. treaty, united, vanity 7. concise,
crowded, entente, leagued, serried
8. alliance, compress, contract,
covenant, succinct 9. agreement,
condensed 10. compressed,
conspiracy 11. compendious,
sententious, stipulation
companion ... 3. pal 4. ally, fare, mate,
twin 5. amigo, crony 6. fellow,
shadow 7. Achates, compeer,
comrade, consort 8. alter ego,
co-worker 9. associate
11. confederate, counterpart
companionship ... 5. amity 7. society
10. fellowship, fraternity
11. comradeship, sociability
13. accompaniment
company ... 3. set 4. band, bevy,
body, crew, gang, ging, host
5. crowd, flock, group, party, troop

6. circle, cohort, throng, troupe
9. concourse, gathering
company (pert to)...
detachment.. 5. posse
people, players.. 4. bevy, crew, gang, team 5. troop 6. galaxy, guests, troupe 9. cavalcade
ships.. 5. fleet 6. armada
8. squadron
soldiers.. 5. corps, squad 7. brigade, phalanx, platoon 9. battalion
travelers.. 7. caravan 8. pilgrims, tourists 9. merchants
comparative... 5. equal, rival
8. relative 10. comparable, relational
compare... 4. even 5. liken 6. confer, semble 7. collate, examine
8. contrast
comparison... 6. simile 7. parable
8. likening, metaphor
10. accordance, similarity
11. parallelism
compartment... 3. bin 4. cell, part
5. stall 6. alcove 7. cellule, chamber, quarter 8. district, division
10. department
compass... 3. arc 4. area, plot, ring
5. guide, range (Mus), reach, solar, sweep 6. attain, bounds, circle, curved, degree, extent 7. circuit, divider, enclose, imagine 8. circular, distance, surround
compass (pert to)...
housing.. 8. binnacle
part.. 3. pen 6. needle
point.. 4. airt 5. rhumb 7. azimuth
sight.. 4. vane
suspender.. 6. gimbal
compassion... 4. pity, ruth (anc)
5. mercy 8. humanity, sympathy
10. condolence 13. commiseration
compassionate... 6. gentle, humane
7. clement, pitiful 8. merciful
11. sympathetic, warmhearted
12. sympathizing
compatible... 8. affinity, suitable
9. accordant, agreeable, congruous
10. consistent, harmonious
12. congeniality
compeer... 4. mate, peer 5. equal, match, rival 7. comrade
9. companion
compel... 4. urge 5. drive, force, impel, press 6. coerce, incite, oblige, obsess 7. actuate, dragoon, require
9. constrain, influence, instigate
compelling... 6. urgent 7. driving
8. pressing 9. insistent, necessary, obsessing 10. compulsory, motivating, obligatory, persuasive
compelling assent... 6. cogent
compelling attention... 9. insistent
compendious... 5. brief, short, terse
7. compact, concise 8. abridged, succinct 9. condensed
10. summarized
compendium... 5. brief 6. abrégé, digest 7. capsule, epitome, medulla, pandect, summary 8. abstract, syllabus, synopsis 9. comprisal
10. abridgment 11. compilation, contraction 12. abbreviation

compensate... 3. pay 5. atone, repay
6. reward 7. redress, requite
9. indemnify 10. recompense, remunerate 14. counterbalance
compensation... 3. pay 4. hire
5. bonus, wages 6. manbot (manbote), reward, salary 7. penalty, stipend 8. gratuity, pittance, requital, solatium 9. atonement, indemnity
10. reparation 12. remuneration, satisfaction 15. indemnification
compete... 3. vie 4. cope 5. match
6. outvie, strive 7. contend, contest, emulate
competence... 5. means, skill
7. ability, fitness 8. adequacy, capacity, property 10. capability, efficiency 11. proficiency, sufficiency, suitability 13. effectiveness, qualification
competent... 3. apt, can, fit 4. able
5. capax, smart 7. capable
8. adequate, suitable 9. effective, effectual, efficient, qualified
10. catechumen, sufficient
12. appertaining (to)
competition... 5. match, trial 6. strife
7. contest, rivalry 8. ambition, concours 9. emulation 10. corrivalry
compilation... 5. cento 6. digest
9. Americana 10. collection
compile... 3. add 4. edit 5. amass
6. gather 8. assemble
complacent... 4. smug 6. bovine
7. fatuous 9. contented, satisfied
11. considerate 13. self-satisfied
complain... 4. beef, carp, fret, kick, pule, wail 5. gripe, growl, whine
6. accuse, bewail, grieve, grouse, lament, murmur, mutter, repine, squawk, yammer 7. deplore, grumble, protest 9. bellyache
complaint... 6. charge, lament, malady
7. ailment, disease, illness, protest
8. disorder, repining, reproach
9. grievance, murmuring
10. accusation, imputation
11. declaration, lamentation
complaisance... 6. regard 7. amenity, concern, suavity 8. civility, courtesy, urbanity 10. indulgence, solicitude, submission, toleration
13. consideration
complaisant... 4. easy, kind 5. civil
6. polite 7. lenient 8. gracious, obliging 9. compliant, courteous
complement... 4. crew 7. adjunct
8. addition, complete
10. correspond, supplement
11. counterpart
complete... 3. all, end 4. dead, fill, full, sole 5. stark, total, utter, whole
6. effect, entire, finish, intact, mature
7. achieve, execute, germane, perfect, plenary, realize 8. absolute, conclude, detailed, outright
9. terminate 10. accomplish, complement, consummate
11. unqualified
completely... 3. all 5. fully, quite, stark 7. solidly, totally, utterly
8. entirely

completeness... 9. entelechy, integrity
complex... 4. mazy 5. mixed
  6. knotty 7. twisted 8. involute,
  involved 9. entangled, intricate,
  perplexed 10. interlaced
  11. complicated
complexion... 4. blee, mode, tone
  5. color, guise, tinge 10. appearance
compliance... 6. assent 7. consent
  9. accession, obedience
  10. concession, conformity,
  observance, submission
  11. willingness 12. acquiescence
compliant... 6. docile 7. duteous,
  dutiful, willing 8. obedient
  10. submissive 11. acquiescent,
  complaisant, conformable
complicated... 6. daedal 7. complex,
  Gordian, snarled, tangled 8. involved
  9. difficult, embroiled, intricate
  11. embarrassed 12. labyrinthine
complication... 4. node (drama)
  5. nodus 7. illness 9. complexus
  10. complexity 11. combination
compliment... 6. praise 7. adulate,
  commend, flatter 8. encomium,
  flattery 12. blandishment,
  commendation 14. congratulation
comply... 4. obey 5. agree, yield
  6. accede, accord, assent, submit
  7. conform, observe 9. acquiesce
compone... 6. settle 7. arrange,
  compose 8. compound
component... 3. ion 4. part 5. basis
  6. factor 7. element 8. integral
  10. ingredient 11. constituent
comport... 3. act 6. accord, behave
  7. conduct 10. correspond
comportable... 8. suitable
  10. consistent
compose... 3. pen 4. calm, form,
  make 5. order, score, write
  7. arrange, fashion, prepare
  8. compound, melodize 9. reconcile
  10. constitute 11. orchestrate,
  tranquilize
composed... 4. calm, cool 5. quiet,
  sober, wrote 6. sedate, serene
  7. consist 8. arranged, tranquil
  9. collected 11. unflappable
composed of...
  flat plates.. 9. lamellate
  lobes.. 6. lobate
composer... 6. author 7. idylist
  (idyllist) 10. compositor, typesetter
composer of...
  Aida.. 5. Verdi
  Carmen.. 5. Bizet
  Faust.. 6. Gounod
  La Boheme.. 7. Puccini
  Merry Widow.. 5. Lehar
  Mikado.. 8. Sullivan
  Naughty Marietta.. 7. Herbert
  Stars and Stripes Forever.. 5. Sousa
composition... 4. opus 5. piece,
  theme 6. make–up 7. melange
  9. formation, synthesis
  12. constitution, construction
composition (pert to)...
  literature.. 5. cento, essay, poesy,
  prose 6. poetry, satire, thesis
  8. treatise 10. brainchild

  music.. 2. op 4. aria, glee, hymn,
  opus 5. drama, étude, motet, nonet,
  opera, rondo, suite 6. anthem,
  septet (septuor), sextet (sestet),
  sonata 7. duetino, quartet
  8. concerto, oratorio, postlude,
  symphony
composure... 6. repose 8. calmness,
  coolness, serenity 9. placidity
  10. equanimity, quiescence,
  sedateness 11. tranquility
compound... 3. mix 4. olio 5. agree,
  amide, ester, oxide, pyran, unite
  6. anisil, elixir, iodide, ketone
  7. ammonia, combine, farrago,
  metamer 8. tincture 9. composite
comprehend... 3. see 4. know
  5. grasp, sense 6. embody, fathom
  7. enclose, imagine, include, involve,
  realize 8. comprise, conceive
  10. understand
comprehensible... 8. exoteric,
  included, knowable 9. comprised
  11. conceivable, discernible,
  perceptible 12. intelligible
comprehensive... 4. full, wide
  5. large 7. generic, knowing
  8. thorough 9. extensive, inclusive,
  universal 11. compendious
compress... 4. firm 5. cling, crowd,
  pinch, press, stupe 7. compact,
  densify, embrace, squeeze 8. astringe,
  condense, contract, decrease
comprise, comprize... 5. imply
  6. number 7. contain, embrace,
  enclose, include, involve 8. perceive
  10. comprehend, constitute
compromise... 4. bind 6. adjust
  8. compound, trade–off 9. agreement
  10. adjustment, concession,
  settlement 11. appeasement,
  arbitration
compulsion... 5. drive, force
  6. duress, urging 7. impulse
  8. coaction, coercion 9. necessity,
  obsession 10. compelling
compulsory... 7. driving 9. mandatory,
  necessary 10. compelling, imperative,
  obligatory 11. involuntary
compunction... 3. rue 5. guilt, pangs,
  qualm 6. regret 7. remorse
  8. pricking 9. penitence
  11. impenitence 13. regretfulness
compute... 5. count, score, tally
  6. cipher, figure, number, reckon
  8. estimate 9. calculate, enumerate
computer terms... 3. bit 4. byte,
  GIGO 5. BASIC, COBOL, coder, input,
  modem 6. access, analog, glitch
  7. digital, FORTRAN 8. data base
  (bank), hard copy, printout, software,
  terminal 9. mainframe, videodisc
  10. floppy disc 11. computerese
  12. minicomputer
  13. microcomputer, word processor
  14. cathode–ray tube
comrade... 3. pal 4. ally, chum, mate,
  peer 5. buddy, crony 6. fellow, frater
  7. compeer 8. camarada, sidekick
  9. associate, colleague, companion
con... 2. no 3. nay 4. know, read
  5. cheat, learn, steer, study

6. peruse 7. convict, deceive,
swindle 8. memorize, negative
10. understand 13. confidence man
conceal ... 4. dern, hide, mask, palm,
veil 5. cloak, cover, derne, eloin,
feign 6. eloign, pocket, screen
7. secrete 8. bescreen, disguise,
enshield
concealed ... 5. doggo 6. covert,
hidden, latent, perdue, secret, veiled,
velate 7. covered, larvate, obscure,
unknown, velated 9. disguised,
incognito, insidious 11. clandestine
concede ... 3. own 5. admit, agree,
allow, grant, yield 6. accord
7. confess, consent 8. consider
9. surrender 11. acknowledge
conceit ... 3. ego 4. idea 5. fancy,
pride 6. vagary, vanity 7. caprice,
egotism, foppery, tympany 8. priggery
12. boastfulness
conceited ... 4. smug, vain 5. proud
7. foppish 8. arrogant, boastful,
priggish 9. egotistic, pragmatic
11. egotistical, opinionated
12. stuffed shirt
conceivable ... 7. tenable 8. credible
9. plausible 10. believable,
imaginable 12. intelligible
conceive ... 5. dream, fancy, think
6. create, devise, ideate 7. imagine,
produce, realize, suppose, suspect
9. originate 10. understand
concentrate ... 4. mass 5. focus
6. center 7. compact, densify,
extract 8. condense, converge
9. intensify 10. centralize
11. consolidate
concept ... 4. idea 5. image
7. opinion, thought 8. category
conception ... 4. idea 5. image, savvy
6. notion 7. conceit, opinion
9. pregnancy 12. apprehension
13. comprehension, understanding
concern ... 4. care, firm, sake 5. event,
grief 6. affair, affect, import, matter
7. anxiety, pertain 8. business,
interest, salience 9. relevance
10. importance 11. consequence
12. significance 13. consideration
concerning ... 2. of, on, re 3. for
4. over, upon 5. about, anent
9. regarding 10. respecting
concert ... 6. aubade 7. recital
9. agreement, unanimity
11. co–operation, performance
concert hall ... 5. odeum (odeon)
6. lyceum 7. theater 9. music hall,
playhouse
concession ... 5. grant 6. market
7. consent 8. discount
10. compromise, confession
13. qualification
concierge ... 6. porter, warden
7. ostiary 8. chokidar 10. doorkeeper
conciliate ... 4. ease 6. pacify
7. appease, mollify, placate
9. reconcile 10. propitiate
conciliatory ... 6. assent, irenic
8. irenical 9. appeasing, forgiving
10. mollifying
concise ... 4. curt, neat 5. brief, crisp,

pithy, terse 6. précis 7. laconic,
pointed, serried, summary 8. succinct
11. compendious, sententious
13. comprehensive
conclude ... 3. end 4. rest 5. close,
infer 6. deduce, endeth, finish, settle
7. arrange, presume, resolve,
suppose 8. complete 9. determine,
terminate
conclusion ... 3. end 4. last 5. close,
finis 6. finale, finish, result
8. decision, epilogue 9. deduction,
diagnosis, inference 10. completion
13. determination
conclusive ... 5. final, valid 8. decisive,
ultimate 9. mandatory
10. convincing, evidential
11. irrefutable, sockdologer (answer)
12. unanswerable
concoct ... 3. mix 4. brew, cook, make
6. devise, digest, invent, scheme
7. perfect, prepare 9. fabricate
concoction ... 4. dish, plan, plot
6. device 7. mixture 8. compound
9. falsehood, invention
11. combination, fabrication,
preparation
concomitant ... 9. accessory, attendant,
co–operant 10. coincident, concurrent
11. synchronous 12. accompanying,
simultaneous
concord ... 4. tune 5. chord, peace
6. accord, treaty, unison 7. concert,
harmony, rapport 8. symphony
9. agreement, unanimity
concordant ... 8. agreeing, harmonic,
unisonal 9. consonant, unanimous
10. harmonious 11. conformable
13. correspondent
concrete ... 4. hard, pave 5. béton,
solid 6. cement 7. congeal, plaster
8. hardness, pavement, solidify
11. substantial
concur ... 5. agree, chime, unite
6. accede, assent 7. approve,
combine, consent 9. acquiesce,
co–operate 11. synchronize
concurrence ... 6. united 7. joining
9. adherence, concourse, unanimity
11. coincidence, conjunction,
convergence, co–operation, parallelism
concurrent ... 5. joint 6. united
7. meeting, uniting 8. parallel,
syndrome 9. unanimous
10. associated, coincident, synergetic
11. co–operative, synchronous
12. accompanying, simultaneous
concussion ... 5. clash, shock, smash,
wound 6. injury, trauma 9. collision
condemn ... 3. ban 4. doom 5. blame,
decry 7. adjudge, censure, convict
8. penalize, sentence
condense ... 3. mix 5. unite 6. absorb,
decoct, deepen, harden, lessen,
narrow, reduce 7. abridge, combine,
compact, densify, enhance, shorten,
squeeze, thicken 8. compress,
contract, diminish, heighten, solidify
9. constrict, intensify
11. concentrate, consolidate
condensed ... 7. compact, concise,
cramped, tabloid 9. shortened

10. compressed, contracted
12. concentrated
condenser (anc)... 9. Leyden jar
condescend... 5. deign, stoop
6. submit, unbend 7. concede,
descend 9. patronize, vouchsafe
condign... 3. fit 4. just 6. severe,
worthy 7. fitting 8. adequate,
deserved, suitable
condiment... 3. soy 4. dill, mace,
mint, sage, salt 5. chili, clove, curry,
sauce, spice 6. catsup, garlic,
ginger, nutmeg, pepper, relish
7. cayenne, ketchup, mustard,
paprika, vinegar 9. seasoning
10. peppermint
condition... 2. if 4. case, haze, rank,
term 5. covin, limit, stage, state
6. estate, fettle, health, plight, status
7. posture, proviso, quality, station
8. capacity, position, standing
9. requisite, situation 10. limitation
11. predicament 12. circumstance
condition (pert to)...
favorable.. 4. odds
flushed.. 4. rosy
habitual.. 5. tenor
hypnotic.. 4. daze 6. stupor, trance
7. narcose
made.. 7. premise
murk.. 3. fog 4. haze, mist 5. gloom
proper.. 6. kilter
stipulation.. 7. proviso
conditionally... 2. if 8. provided
11. tentatively 13. provisionally
condone... 5. remit 6. accept, excuse,
pardon 7. absolve, forgive 8. tolerate
11. countenance
condor... 6. falcon 7. vulture
conduce... 4. lend, tend 5. serve
6. effect 7. advance, dispose,
incline, redound 10. contribute
conducive... 6. useful 7. helpful
11. implemental, serviceable
12. instrumental
conduct... 3. act, run 4. lead, mien,
rule 5. guide, usage, usher
6. action, convey, convoy, direct,
escort, govern, manage 7. bearing,
comport, control, manners
8. behavior, demeanor, regulate
9. operation, supervise
10. deportment, management
11. comportment, superintend
conduct (pert to)...
a cause.. 5. plead
breach.. 6. guilty
doctrine of.. 6. morals
one's self.. 6. behave, demean
7. comport
conducting inward... 9. afference
conductor... 5. guide 6. escort, leader
7. cathode, maestro, manager
8. cicerone, director, operator,
trainman
conduit... 3. way 4. adit, duct, pain,
pipe, tube 5. canal, sewer 6. course
7. channel 8. aqueduct
cone (pert to)...
conelike.. 5. conic 6. pineal
7. conical
pine.. 8. strobile

silver.. 4. pina
tree.. 5. larch 7. conifer
confab, confabulation... 4. chat, talk
7. palaver, prattle 8. chinfest, talkfest
12. conversation
confection... 3. jam 5. candy, dulce,
icing, jelly 6. cimbal, comfit, nougat,
sweets 7. caramel, fondant, praline,
succade 8. preserve 9. sweetmeat
11. bittersweet, marshmallow
confederacy... 5. cabal, hanse, union
6. fusion, league 8. alliance,
covenant 9. coalition 10. complicity,
conspiracy, federation 11. affiliation,
association, combination
13. consolidation
confederate... 3. pal, reb 4. ally
5. stall 7. abettor 9. accessory,
assistant, associate, auxiliary
10. accomplice
confer... 4. give 6. advise, bestow,
invest, parley 7. collate, commune,
consign, consult, counsel 8. ordinate
(knighthood) 10. deliberate
conference... 5. trust 6. huddle,
parley, powwow 7. council, palaver
9. interview 10. discussion
12. consultation
conferring respect... 9. honorific
conferring title... 9. ennobling
confess... 3. own, rue 4. avow
5. admit, own up 6. regret, repent,
reveal, shrive 7. concede
11. acknowledge
confession... 5. credo (of faith), creed
6. avowal, shrift 9. admission,
communion 10. profession
14. acknowledgment
(acknowledgement)
confetti... 5. paper 6. ribbon
7. bonbons 9. cascarons (in
eggshells) 10. sweetmeats
11. confections
confidant... 6. friend 8. intimate
confide... 4. hope, rely 5. trust
6. commit, depend, repose
confidence... 5. faith, poise 6. belief,
morals, secret 7. courage
8. credence, sureness 9. assurance,
impudence 10. effrontery
12. impertinence
confident... 4. smug, sure 6. secure
7. assured, certain, hopeful, reliant
8. cocksure, positive, sanguine,
unafraid 9. convinced 10. determined
confidential... 5. privy 6. secret
7. private 8. esoteric, intimate
9. auricular 10. unquotable
11. trustworthy
confidentially... 7. sub rosa
configuration... 4. form 5. shape
6. figure 7. contour, Gestalt, pattern
8. asterism 13. constellation
confine... 3. dam, hem, mew, pen,
sty, tie 4. bind, cage, coop, jail,
lock 5. bound, limit, stint 6. border,
immure, intern, secure, strain
7. compass 8. imprison, restrain
9. enclosure 11. incarcerate,
restriction 12. circumscribe
confined... 4. pent 5. bound, caged
6. shut-in 7. cribbed, endemic,

limited 8. esoteric, impended,
interned 9. bedridden, impounded,
invalided, parochial
confinement... 5. limbo 7. durance,
lying–in 9. detention, isolation,
restraint 10. cabin fever, childbirth
12. accouchement, imprisonment
13. incommunicado
15. circumscription
confirm... 4. seal 5. prove 6. assure,
attest, ratify, settle, verify 7. approve,
fortify, sustain 8. convince, sanction,
validate 9. establish 11. corroborate
12. substantiate
confirmed... 6. proved 7. chronic
8. habitual, ratified 10. encouraged,
inveterate 11. established
confiscate... 5. seize, usurp
7. impound 11. appropriate
conflagrant... 5. afire 6. ablaze,
aflame 7. blazing, burning
conflagration... 4. fire 5. blaze, fever
8. wildfire 9. holocaust
12. inflammation
conflict... 3. war 4. bout, duel, fray
5. clash, fight, run–in 6. action,
battle, combat, oppose, strife, tussle
7. contend, contest, discord
8. clashing, struggle 9. antipathy,
collision, encounter, hostility
10. contention, donnybrook,
opposition 11. competition
confluence... 4. flow 5. crowd
6. stream 7. flowing (together),
meeting 8. junction 10. assemblage
11. concurrence, convergence
12. assimilation
conform... 2. go 3. fit 4. lean, obey,
suit 5. adapt, agree 6. adjust,
concur, settle 7. compose, consent,
observe 8. coincide, fine–tune
9. reconcile 11. accommodate
conformity... 6. dharma 7. harmony
8. legality, symmetry 9. agreement,
congruity 10. compliance
15. conventionality
confound... 3. mix 5. abash, amaze
6. baffle, dismay, puzzle, thwart
7. astound, buffalo, mystify, nonplus,
perplex 8. astonish, bewilder
9. dumbfound, embarrass, frustrate
10. complicate, contradict, disconcert
11. intermingle
confront... 4. face, meet 5. front
6. oppose 7. compare 9. encounter
confrontation... 6. crisis 7. face–off
8. showdown 9. encounter
10. opposition
confuse... 3. mix 4. maze 5. abash,
addle, upset 6. baffle, flurry, jumble,
muddle 7. derange, fluster
8. befuddle, bewilder, disorder,
distract, entangle 9. embrangle
10. complicate, disarrange,
discompose, disconcert
confused... 7. chaotic, jumbled, rattled
8. deranged 9. chagrined, flustered,
perplexed, uncertain 11. indistinct
confusion... 3. ado, din 4. mess, moil
5. babel, chaos 6. jumble, pother,
welter 7. anarchy, clutter, turmoil
8. disarray, disorder 9. abashment,

agitation 10. perplexity
11. derangement 12. bewilderment
13. embarrassment
confute... 4. deny 5. rebut 6. answer,
expose, refute 7. dismiss
8. confound, overcome, redargue
9. overwhelm (by argument)
congeal... 3. gel, ice, set 4. rime
6. freeze 7. pectize, thicken
congenial... 4. boon 7. kindred
8. friendly 9. accordant, agreeable
10. affinitive, compatible
11. sympathetic
congenital... 6. inborn, innate
7. connate, genetic, natural
14. constitutional
conger... 3. eel 8. cucumber
13. Leptocephalus
congeries... 4. heap 9. amassment
10. collection 11. aggregation
congestion... 3. jam 4. heap
8. fullness, stoppage 9. gathering
11. obstruction 12. accumulation
Congo...
  capital.. 11. Brazzaville
  city.. 6. Makoua 7. Louboma
  port.. 11. Pointe Noire
  river.. 5. Congo (Zaire) 6. Sangha
congratulate... 4. laud 5. bless
6. salute 7. rejoice 8. macarize
10. compliment, felicitate
congregate... 4. herd, mass, meet
5. group, troop 6. gather, muster
7. collect 8. assemble 9. forgather
congregation... 4. mass 5. house,
laity 7. council 8. assembly, audience
9. gathering 10. collection
11. churchgoers
congress... 4. diet 5. synod
6. durbar, indaba, soviet 7. council,
meeting 8. assembly, conclave
9. Sanhedrin 10. convention,
parliament 11. convergence,
convocation, legislature
12. congregation
congruous... 3. fit 4. meet 6. proper
7. fitting 8. agreeing, becoming,
suitable 9. consonant
conic, conical... 8. parabola
9. pyramidal 10. cone–shaped,
funnellike
conifers... 4. yews 5. pines 6. cedars
7. larches, Pinales, Sabines, spruces,
Torreys 8. hemlocks, Soledads
9. Coniferae, Corsicans
10. evergreens
conjecture... 3. aim 5. ettle, guess,
opine, think 6. divine 7. conjoin,
imagine, presume, suppose, surmise,
suspect 8. supposal 9. inference
10. assumption, hypothesis
11. supposition
conjoin... 4. join, link, yoke 5. hitch,
unite 6. adjoin, concur 7. combine,
connect 8. corelate 9. correlate
conjoined parts... 6. adnexa
conjointly... 10. hand–in–hand
conjugal... 7. marital, nuptial
9. connubial 11. matrimonial
conjugate... 4. join 5. yoked
6. couple, united 7. coupled, related
8. bijugate, combined

10. paronymous 12. etymological
conjugation... 5. union 6. fusion
7. duality, joining, uniting
10. assemblage 11. combination
13. juxtaposition
conjunct... 6. united 8. combined
9. conjoined, corporate
conjunction... 2. as, et, if, or 3. and,
but, nor 4. than, that 5. since,
union 6. casual, though 7. whether
10. connection 11. adversative,
association, combination, concurrence,
correlative
conjure... 4. pray 5. charm 6. adjure,
enjoin, invoke, juggle, summon
(magic) 7. beseech, enchant, entreat,
implore 10. supplicate
conjure (up)... 5. raise 6. call up
8. exorcise (exorcize), remember
9. visualize
conjurer, conjuror... 4. mage
6. voodoo, wizard 7. juggler
8. exorcist, magician
conk... 4. head, nose 5. decay (tree)
conk out... 4. fade, fail 5. stall
6. fizzle, perish, weaken
connate... 4. akin 6. allied 7. cognate,
related, similar 9. congenial
10. congenital
connect... 3. tie 4. ally, join, link,
meet 5. unite 6. adjoin, attach,
couple, enlink, fasten, relate
7. bracket, succeed 9. associate,
hyphenate
connected... 3. met 5. telic
6. adnate, joined 7. serried, similar
8. coherent, inlinked, syndetic
10. continuous, correlated
Connecticut...
capital.. 8. Hartford
city.. 6. Darien, Mystic 7. Meriden
8. Hartford, New Haven 9. Waterbury
10. Bridgeport
college (famed).. 4. Yale (1701)
historic site.. 10. Charter Oak (1687,
Hartford)
museum.. 6. Barnum (P T)
river.. 6. Thames 9. Naugatuck
10. Hoosatonic 11. Connecticut
State admission.. 5. Fifth
State Motto.. 21. Qui Transtulit
Sustinet (He Who Transplants
Sustains)
State nickname.. 6. Nutmeg
12. Constitution
connecting link... 3. tie 4. bond
6. connex 7. kiaison 8. ligament,
vinculum 11. intermedium
12. intermediary
connection... 4. bond 5. nexus, union
6. clevis, family, series 7. kinship,
passage 8. alliance, commerce,
junction, relation 9. coherence,
go–between, relevance 10. continuity
11. association, intercourse
12. intermediary, relationship
13. communication, juxtaposition
conner... 5. pilot 6. balker, tester
7. peruser 8. examiner 9. inspector
connive... 4. plot, wink 5. blink
6. scheme 7. collude, complot,
finagle 8. conspire, contrive,

maneuver, overlook
conniving... 8. scheming 9. collusive,
deceitful 10. conspiring
11. calculating
connoisseur... 5. judge 6. expert
7. epicure, gourmet 8. gourmand
11. cognoscente, connaisseur
connotation... 5. sense 6. import,
intent 7. meaning, purport
10. denotation 11. implication
12. significance 13. comprehension
connubial... 7. martial, nuptial
8. conjugal 11. matrimonial
12. epithalamium (song)
conquer... 3. win 4. beat, best
5. crush 6. defeat, humble, master,
reduce, subdue 7. subject
8. overcome, overturn, surmount,
vanquish 9. discomfit, overpower,
overthrow, subjugate
conqueror... 4. hero 6. captor, Cortez,
victor, winner 7. subduer
10. subjugator 12. conquistador
conquest... 6. Norman (1066)
7. mastery, triumph, victory
consanguinity... 5. nabob 7. kinship,
sibship 8. affinity, relation (blood)
12. relationship
conscience... 4. mind, self 6. psyche
8. superego 9. casuistry
conscientious... 7. dutiful, servile
8. faithful 10. fastidious, meticulous,
scrupulous 11. punctilious
conscientious objection... 7. scruple
conscious... 4. keen 5. alive, awake,
aware, vital 7. animate, feeling
8. sensible, sentient 9. breathing,
cognizant 13. self–conscious
consecrate... 4. sain 5. bless, exalt
6. anoint, devote, hallow, ordain
7. glorify 8. dedicate, sanctify
consecrated (pert to)...
bread.. 4. host 5. wafer
oil.. 6. chrism
thing.. 6. sacrum
consent... 4. give 5. agree, grant,
yield 6. accede, accord, assent,
concur, permit 8. approval
9. acquiesce 10. compliance,
permission 11. concurrence
13. understanding
consequence... 3. end 5. event
6. course, effect, result, weight
7. dignity, outcome 8. pursuant (in),
sequence 9. aftermath, inference,
influence, loftiness, outgrowth
10. importance, notability
11. distinction
consequential... 7. pompous
8. eventual 9. important
13. self–important
consequently... 2. do 4. ergo, then
5. hence 9. as a result, therefore,
wherefore 12. subsequently
13. consecutively
conservative... 4. Tory 5. staid
7. die–hard, fogyish, old–line
8. moderate 10. long–haired
11. reactionary 12. preservative
13. unprogressive
conserve... 3. jam 4. save 5. guard,
uvate 6. defend, secure, shield,

uphold 7. protect, sustain
8. maintain 9. preserves, sweetmeat
consider ... 3. ain, see 4. care, deem,
heed, muse, rate 5. judge, think,
treat, weigh 6. esteem, intend,
ponder, regard 7. discuss, examine,
reflect, revolve 8. cogitate, meditate,
ruminate 10. deliberate
11. contemplate
considerable ... 5. great, large
7. notable, several 8. numerous
9. important 10. noteworthy,
remarkable 13. authoritative
considerate ... 4. kind 6. gentle
7. careful, heedful, prudent, serious
8. obliging 9. attentive, judicious
10. deliberate, reflective, solicitous,
thoughtful
consideration ... 4. self 5. study
6. esteem, regard 7. respect,
thought 9. attention, deference,
incentive, influence 10. cogitation,
importance, meditation, reflection,
reputation, rumination
11. examination 12. compensation,
deliberation
considering ... 2. if 5. since 8. after
all, inasmuch, in view of
consign ... 5. allot 6. assign, commit,
devote, remand, resign 7. deliver,
entrust 8. transfer 11. subscribe to
consignee ... 6. factor 7. awardee
8. assignee 9. committee
consign to ...
a place .. 8. allocate
prison .. 6. commit, send up
ruin .. 4. doom
unimportance .. 8. relegate
consistent ... 5. equal, solid, stiff
7. equable, logical, uniform
8. coherent 9. agreement,
consonant, steadfast 10. persisting
consisting of ...
cavities .. 9. cellulose
layers (thin) .. 8. laminate
names .. 8. onomatic
one word .. 7. monepic
pages .. 7. paginal
three measures .. 8. trimeter
three spots .. 4. trey
three styles (Bot) .. 10. tristylous
two parts .. 6. binary
consist of ... 5. imply 6. embody
7. contain, embrace, enclose, involve
8. comprise (comprize)
consolation ... 6. solace 7. comfort
10. condolence
console ... 4. desk 5. cheer, organ,
table 6. solace, soothe 7. bracket,
cabinet, comfort, support, sustain
9. alleviate, encourage
consolidate ... 4. knit, mass 5. merge,
unify, unite 7. combine, densify
8. coalesce, compress, organize,
solidify 10. intensify, strengthen
consonant ... 4. lene, surd 5. lenis,
nasal, velar 6. dental, labial
7. lingual, palatal, spirate 8. gutteral
9. accordant, congruous
10. compatible, concordant,
consistent
consonant (pert to) ...

hissing .. 8. sibilant
rustling .. 9. fricative
voiceless (breathed) .. 6. atonic
7. spirate
consort ... 4. Devi (of Siva), mate, wife
5. group, Sakti 6. mingle, spouse
7. husband, partner 9. associate,
colleague, companion, harmonize
11. combination, confederate,
conjunction
conspicuous ... 6. famous, signal
7. eminent, glaring, obvious, salient,
visible 8. distinct, lionized, manifest,
striking 9. important, prominent
10. celebrated, noticeable, remarkable
11. illustrious, outstanding
13. distinguished
conspiracy ... 4. plot 5. cabal, unite
6. scheme 8. intrigue 9. collusion
10. connivance 11. confederacy,
machination
conspire ... 4. plot 5. unite 6. concur,
scheme 7. collude, complot, finagle
9. fainaigue 11. confederate
constable ... 3. cop 5. staff 6. beadle,
keeper, warden 7. bailiff 8. tipstaff
9. policeman
constabulary ... 6. bureau (police)
10. constables
constancy ... 4. zeal 5. ardor, faith,
truth 6. fealty, garnet (symbol)
7. honesty, loyalty 8. devotion,
fidelity 9. adherence, continual,
eagerness, integrity, stability
10. allegiance, attachment,
permanence, perpetuity, uniformity
11. devotedness, earnestness
12. faithfulness
constant ... 4. firm, true 5. fixed
7. regular, uniform 8. faithful,
resolute 9. continual, invariant,
parameter (Math), perpetual, steadfast
10. continuous, invariable, persistent
12. unchangeable
constant desire ... 4. itch 9. hankering
Constantine (pert to) ...
birthplace .. 4. Nish (Nis) 7. Naissus
(now Yugoslavia)
known as .. 8. The Great
title .. 7. Emperor (Rome)
Constantinople ...
official name .. 8. Istanbul
patriarch .. 9. Nestorius
site .. 6. Turkey (Eur)
constellation ... 5. stars 6. galaxy
8. asterism 10. luminaries
13. configuration (stars)
Constellations (partial list) ...
arrow .. 7. Sagitta
bears (Dipper) .. 9. Ursa Major, Ursa
Minor
Bird of Paradise (S Pole) .. 4. Apus
bull .. 6. Taurus
crab .. 6. Cancer
crane .. 4. Grus
dog .. 5. Canis
dragon .. 5. Draco
eagle .. 6. Aquila
fishes .. 6. Pisces
goat .. 9. Capricorn
goldfish .. 6. Dorado
hunter .. 5. Orion (most conspicuous)

lion.. 3. Leo
Noah's Ark.. 4. Argo
Northern Crown.. 14. Corona Borealis, Northern Lights
peacock.. 4. Pava
scorpion.. 7. Scorpio
serpent (sea).. 5. Hydra
Southern Cross.. 4. Crux
swan.. 6. Cygnus
Twins.. 6. Gemini
virgin.. 5. Virgo
water bearer.. 8. Aquarius
whale.. 6. Cestus
winged horse.. 7. Pegasus
wolf.. 5. Lupus
Constellations' brightest star...
　3. Cor
Constellations of the Zodiac...
　3. Leo 5. Aries, Libra, Virgo
　6. Cancer, Gemini, Pisces, Taurus
　7. Scorpio 8. Aquarius
　11. Capricornus, Sagittarius
constituent... 5. voter 6. factor,
　matter 7. elector, element, essence
　8. elective 9. component
　10. ingredient 11. determinant
　(Math)
constituent of...
　blood serum.. 7. opsonin
　coal.. 6. carbon
　coffee, tea.. 8. caffeine
　hair, nails.. 7. keratin
　oil of cloves.. 7. eugenol
constitute... 4. form 5. enact, found
　6. create, depute 7. appoint,
　compose 8. legalize 9. determine,
　establish
constitution... 3. law 6. crasis,
　custom 7. passage 8. creation
　9. enactment, essential, ordinance,
　structure 11. composition, institution
　12. organization
Constitution (ship)... 12. Old Ironsides
constitutional... 5. legal, valid
　6. innate 9. essential, healthful
　12. governmental 13. dispositional
constitutional (pert to)...
　health.. 4. walk 8. exercise
　right.. 9. franchise
　temperament.. 6. crasis
　vigor.. 5. nerve
Constitution State... 11. Connecticut
constrain... 4. curb, urge 5. chain,
　check, drive, force, impel, press
　6. compel, oblige 7. confine, repress
　8. restrain 11. necessitate
constrained... 6. forced, modest
　7. cramped 8. moderate, reserved
　9. obligated
constraint... 4. bond, urge 5. force
　6. duress, stress 7. modesty, reserve
　8. coercion, pressure 9. restraint,
　stiffness 10. compulsion, moderation
　11. confinement
constrict... 3. tie 4. bind 5. cramp
　6. narrow, shrink 7. squeeze, tighten
　8. astringe, condense, contract
　10. constringe
constriction... 9. narrowing, stricture,
　tightness 11. contraction
　13. strangulation
constrictor... 3. boa 5. snake

7. serpent, styptic 9. sphincter
10. compressor
construct... 4. make, rear 5. build,
　erect, frame 6. create 7. compose
　9. establish, fabricate, originate
constructive... 7. virtual 8. creative,
　implicit 9. anabolism 10. suggestive
　14. interpretation, interpretative
construe... 5. parse 6. deduce, render
　7. explain 9. interpret, translate
consuetude... 5. habit, usage
　6. custom
consuetudinary... 6. manual (customs),
　ritual 9. customary
consult (with)... 6. advise, confer, take
　up 7. discuss 10. deliberate
consultation... 7. counsel 8. audition,
　congress 9. interview 10. conference,
　discussion 12. deliberation
consume... 3. eat, use 4. burn
　5. spend, waste 6. absorb, devour,
　expend 7. destroy (fire) 8. squander
　9. dissipate 12. disintegrate
consumed　3. pau
consummate... 3. end, top 4. ripe
　5. ideal 6. finish, utmost 7. achieve,
　perfect 8. complete 10. accomplish
consumption... 3. use 4. loss
　5. decay, waste 6. eating
　7. disease, using up 8. phthisis
　9. decrement 11. destruction
　12. tuberculosis 13. deterioration
contact... 4. meet 5. touch, union
　6. impact, syzygy (Astron)
　7. meeting, oscnode (Math)
　8. junction, tangency, touching
　10. contiguity 13. communication
contain... 4. have, hold, keep 5. cover
　6. embody, number, retain
　7. embrace, enclose, include, involve,
　subsume 8. comprise, restrain
　9. divisible (by) 10. comprehend
container... 3. bag, bin, box, can,
　cup, jug, lug, pan, pod, pot, tin,
　tub, urn, vat 4. case, crib, ewer,
　pail, sack, vase 5. crate, cruet,
　pouch 6. basket, bottle, carboy,
　carton, hamper, hatbox 7. capsule,
　hanaper 8. canister, decanter
containing...
　air.. 9. pneumatic
　antimony.. 8. stibiate
　boron.. 5. boric 7. boracic
　carbon.. 7. organic 13. carboniferous
　copper.. 6. cupric
　fire.. 7. igneous
　gold.. 4. doré 5. auric
　iron.. 6. ferric
　silver.. 5. lunar
　slag.. 6. drossy
　ten.. 6. denary
　tin.. 7. stannic
containing maxims... 6. gnomic
contaminate... 4. slur, soil 5. stain,
　sully, taint 6. befoul, defile, infect,
　poison 7. corrupt, debauch, degrade,
　pollute, vitiate 8. dishonor
　9. desecrate 10. adulterate
contemn... 4. defy, hate 5. scorn,
　spurn 6. reject 7. despise, disdain
contemplate... 4. muse, plan, scan,
　view 5. study 6. design, expect,

intend, ponder 7. examine, foresee,
propose 8. consider, envision,
meditate
contemplation ... 5. study 6. musing
7. theoria, thought 8. scrutiny
9. foresight, intuition 10. expectancy,
reflection 11. examination,
expectation, speculation
contemplative ... 6. sedate 7. pensive
10. meditative, reflective, ruminative,
thoughtful 11. speculative
13. retrospective
contemporary ... 6. coeval 7. present
10. coetaneous, coexistent,
coincident 11. concomitant,
synchronous 12. simultaneous
15. contemporaneous
contempt ... 4. fico, geck 5. scorn,
shame, sneer 7. despect, disdain
8. defiance, derision, ridicule
9. arrogance, contumely
10. disrespect 12. disobedience
contemptible ... 3. low 4. base
5. cheap, petty, sorry 6. abject,
paltry, sordid 7. pitiful 8. beggarly,
inferior, unworthy 9. groveling,
worthless 10. despicable
13. insignificant
contemptuous ... 6. sneery 7. haughty
8. insolent, scornful 10. disdainful
12. contumelious, supercilious
contemptuous action ... 9. indignity
10. incivility
contend ... 3. vie, war 4. cope, deal,
race 5. argue, fight 6. assert, bicker,
insist, strive 7. compete, contest,
grapple, quarrel, wrangle 8. contrive,
maintain, militate
content, contents ... 4. list, room
5. index, space 6. amount, please,
volume 7. filling, gratify, makings,
satisfy, suffice 8. capacity
9. contented, happiness, satisfied
10. components, dimensions
11. ingredients
contention ... 3. war 4. feud
6. combat, debate, strife 7. quarrel,
rivalry 8. argument, conflict, struggle,
variance 9. emulation 10. dissension,
litigation 11. altercation, competition,
controversy 12. disagreement
contentious ... 7. peevish 8. perverse
9. combative, litigious, wrangling
10. pugnacious 11. belligerent,
dissentious, quarrelsome
13. argumentative
contentment ... 4. ease 5. bliss
8. pleasure 11. peace of mind
12. satisfaction 13. contentedness,
gratification
conterminous ... 4. next 8. abutting,
adjacent, proximal 9. adjoining
contest ... 3. sue, vie 4. agon, bout,
cope, deny, game, race, tilt
5. argue, set–to, trial 6. debate,
oppose, strife, strive, tryout
7. contend, dispute, tourney, wrangle
8. argument, disclaim, litigate,
skirmish, struggle 9. emulation
10. engagement 11. altercation,
competition
contest (pert to) ...

art of .. 10. agonistics
draw .. 9. stalemate
log hurling .. 5. roleo
prize .. 5. stake
undecided .. 4. draw
contestant ... 5. rival 6. player
7. athlete, entrant 8. opponent
9. candidate, combatant, contender
10. competitor
contiguous ... 4. near, next
8. adjacent, touching 9. adjoining,
immediate, proximate 11. neighboring
Continent ... 4. Asia 6. Africa, Europe
7. Eurasia, Lemuria 8. Atlantis (lost),
Cascadia 9. Australia, Greenland
10. Antarctica 12. North America,
South America
contingency ... 4. case 5. event
6. chance 8. accident, casualty,
exigency, juncture 9. emergency,
liability 11. eventuality, possibility,
uncertainty
contingent ... 6. casual 8. eventual
9. dependent (law), provisory
10. accidental, fortuitous, incidental
11. conditional, provisional
continual ... 7. endless, eternal, regular,
undying, uniform 8. constant,
enduring, frequent, unbroken
9. ceaseless, connected, continued,
incessant, perennial, permanent,
perpetual, unceasing 10. continuous,
invariable 11. everlasting, intermitted,
unremitting 12. imperishable
13. uninterrupted
continually ... 3. aye 4. ever 5. often
7. eternal 9. eternally 10. constantly
11. perpetually, unceasingly
12. continuously
continuation ... 6. sequel 8. addition,
sequence 10. continuity
11. continuance, propagation,
protraction 12. postponement,
prolongation
continue ... 3. run 4. go on, last, stay
5. abide 6. endure, extend, remain,
resume 7. perdure, persist, proceed,
sustain 8. protract 9. persevere,
steadfast (be)
continuing ... 5. still 7. chronic,
durable, lasting 9. permanent
10. continuous 11. persevering
continuous ... 7. chronic, endless,
uniform 8. unbroken 9. continued,
perpetual 13. uninterrupted
contorted ... 3. wry 4. bent 6. coiled,
warped 7. garbled, gnarled, twisted,
wristed 8. deformed 9. perverted
contour ... 4. form, line 5. curve,
graph 6. figure 7. isobase, outline,
profile 9. lineament, periphery
13. configuration
contra ... 6. offset 7. against, counter,
reverse 8. contrary, opposite 9. vice
versa 10. conversely 12. contrariwise
contraband ... 7. bootleg, illegal, illicit
8. unlawful 9. moonshine
10. prohibited
contract ... 4. hale, knit, pact 5. incur,
lease 6. cartel, engage, pledge,
reduce, shrink 7. bargain, compact,
promise, shorten, shrivel 8. covenant

9. agreement, constrict, indenture
10. convention, obligation, straighten
11. arrangement 13. understanding
contraction... 3. tic 4. coup, fist
5. spasm 7. elision, systole
8. decrease 9. reduction, short–hand,
stricture 11. compression
contrada... 3. way 4. ward 6. street
7. quarter
contradict... 4. deny 5. belie, rebut
6. impugn, negate, oppose, refute
7. gainsay 10. counteract
contradiction... 6. denial 7. paradox
10. opposition, refutation
11. contrariety 13. counteraction
contradictory... 7. denying 8. contrary,
opposite 10. refutatory
12. inconsistent
contrary... 7. adverse, counter,
froward, opposed, reverse
8. captious, inimical, opposite,
perverse, refutive 9. different,
repugnant 10. discordant, unorthodox
12. antagonistic
contrast... 7. compare 8. opposite
11. contrariety
contravene... 4. defy 6. hinder,
oppose, refute, thwart 7. violate
8. infringe 9. disregard
contravention... 6. denial 9. violation
10. opposition, refutation
contribute... 3. aid 4. give 6. donate
7. benefit, conduce, provide
9. subscribe
contribution... 3. tax, tip 4. boon,
gift, scot 6. tariff 7. payment, tribute
8. donation 12. subscription
13. participation
contrite... 6. abject, humble
8. penitent 9. repentant, sorrowful
10. remorseful 11. penitential
contrition... 7. remorse 9. attrition,
penitence 11. compunction
contrivance... 3. art 5. means, shift
6. design, devise 7. coinage,
machine, measure, project 8. artifice,
intrigue 9. expedient, invention,
makeshift 11. contraption
contrive... 4. plan, plot 5. frame,
hatch, weave 6. design, devise,
invent, manage, scheme 7. fashion,
project 9. fabricate
control... 4. hold, rein, rule, sway, test
5. check, gripe, guide, leash, power,
wield 6. direct, govern, manage,
subdue 7. conduct, mastery, preside,
regimen 8. dominate, dominion,
ironhand, regulate, restrain
9. direction, influence, regulator,
restraint 10. management, regulation
11. self–control, superintend
controller, comptroller... 7. auditor
8. governor 9. dominator, regulator
controversial... 7. eristic, polemic
9. eristical, polemical, pro and con
11. contentious 12. disputatious,
questionable 13. argumentative
controversy... 6. debate 7. dispute,
quarrel, wrangle 8. argument
10. contention 11. altercation
12. disagreement, disputatious
controvert... 4. deny, moot 5. argue

6. debate, oppose, refute 7. discuss,
dispute 10. contradict
contumacious... 6. unruly 7. riotous
8. mutinous, perverse 9. seditious
10. headstrong, rebellious, refractory,
unyielding 11. disobedient, intractable
12. ungovernable 13. insubordinate
contumelious... 7. haughty 8. insolent
9. insulting 10. derogatory,
despiteful, disdainful
12. contemptuous
contumely... 5. scorn 8. contempt
9. indignity, insolence 10. revilement
11. humiliation, malediction
contusion... 4. blow 6. bruise, injury
8. black eye 13. discoloration
conundrum... 5. rebus 6. enigma,
puzzle, riddle 7. charade
convalesce... 5. rally 7. recover,
recruit 10. recuperate
convene... 3. sit 4. come, meet
5. unite 6. summon 8. assemble
10. congregate, foregather
convenient... 5. handy, ready 6. fitted,
nearby, suited, timely 7. adapted
8. suitable 9. agreeable, available,
opportune 10. accessible,
commodious, seasonable
11. comfortable
convent... 4. meet 6. concur, friary,
priory 7. convene, nunnery
8. cloister, lamasery 9. monastery,
sanctuary
convention... 4. rule 5. usage
6. accord, custom 7. meeting
8. assembly 9. gathering, tradition
10. assemblage, compliance,
conformity
conventional... 5. fixed, nomic, usual
6. formal, modish 7. correct
8. accepted, orthodox 9. customary
10. ceremonial 11. established,
traditional
converge... 4. meet 5. focus, unite
conversant (with)... 5. adept 6. expert,
versed (in) 7. skilled 8. familiar
9. practiced 10. acquainted,
proficient
conversation... 4. chat, talk 7. trialog
8. causerie, converse, dialogue
9. communion, discourse
10. conference 11. association
13. conversazione, interlocution
conversationalist... 6. talker
9. converser 10. discourser
12. confabulator
convey... 4. cede, deed, pass, send
5. bring, carry, eloin, grant
6. assign, convoy, demise, devise,
impart, import 7. dispone 8. transfer,
transmit 9. transport 10. commission
11. communicate
conveyance... 3. bus, car, van
4. auto, sled, taxi, tram 5. plane,
train 6. demise, litter 7. cession,
norimon, trailer, vehicle 8. airplane,
carriage 10. automobile
conveyer, conveyor... 6. bearer,
coolie, pigeon (homing), porter
7. bheesty, carrier 8. cargador
9. stevedore
convict... 4. damn 5. felon, lifer

6. refute, termer, trusty 7. condemn,
culprit 6. refute 8. criminal, prisoner
10. malefactor
conviction... 4. hope 6. belief
7. opinion 9. certainty
10. persuasion 12. condemnation
convince... 6. assure, subdue
7. confute, jawbone 8. overcome,
persuade 9. overpower
convincing... 5. proof 6. cogent,
potent 7. telling 8. assuring
10. conclusive, persuasive, satisfying
convivial... 3. gay 4. gala 5. jolly,
merry 6. festal, jovial, joyful, joyous,
social 7. festive, jocular 9. hilarious
convocation... 4. diet 5. synod
7. bidding, council, meeting,
summons 8. assembly, congress
10. convention 12. congregation
convoke... 4. call 6. summon
7. convene 8. assemble
convoy... 5. guard, guide 6. attend,
escort 7. conduct 8. navigate
9. accompany, conductor
convulse... 5. amuse, shake 6. regale
7. agitate, disturb, torture
9. entertain 10. discompose
convulsion... 5. cramp, spasm, throe
6. tumult, uproar 8. laughter,
paroxysm 9. agitation, commotion
10. revolution 11. disturbance
cony, coney... 3. das, fur 4. dupe,
hare, pika 5. daman, hyrax 6. burbot,
rabbit
cony catcher... 5. cheat 7. sharper
8. swindler
coo... 4. bill (and), curr 5. chirr
6. murmur, mutter
cook... 4. bake, boil, chef, stew
5. broil, roast, sauté, spoil (chess),
steam, trill 6. braise, seethe
7. parboil, stir–fry 8. barbecue,
magirist 9. charbroil, cuisinier
cookie... 5. scone 7. biscuit, brownie
8. macaroon 10. gingersnap,
ladyfinger, shortbread
cooking (pert to)...
art.. 8. magirics
device.. 3. wok 4. etna, olla 5. grill,
plate, stove 6. spider 7. griddle
9. autoclave, microwave (oven)
room.. 6. galley 7. cuisine, kitchen
8. scullery 11. kitchenette
scent.. 4. reek 5. nidor
cool... 3. fan, ice 4. calm 5. chill,
fresh, nervy, sober, tepid 6. chilly,
freeze, sedate, temper 7. unmoved
8. careless, composed, impudent,
mitigate, reserved, tranquil
9. apathetic, collected, unruffled
10. nonchalant, unfriendly, unsociable
11. indifferent, levelheaded,
unconcerned 13. dispassionate,
imperturbable, self–possessed
cooler... 4. icer, jail 6. icebox, lockup,
prison 7. chiller 10. ventilator
11. refrigerant 12. refrigerator
coolness... 4. cold 5. nerve
6. aplomb 7. reserve
12. indifference 14. unfriendliness
coop... 3. mew, pen 4. cage, cote,
yard 5. court, hutch 6. confine

9. enclosure
cooper... 5. drink 6. vessel
8. grogshop (floating) 11. barrel
maker 12. wine retailer
cooperate... 4. join, tend 5. agree,
coact 6. concur 7. combine,
conduce, connive 8. conspire
9. interface, synergize 10. contribute
11. collaborate
coordinate... 5. talky 6. adjust
7. syntony (radio) 8. classify, equalize,
organize, regulate 9. harmonize,
integrate 10. proportion
11. systematize
copious... 4. full, rich 5. ample
7. diffuse, profuse 8. abundant,
numerous 9. exuberant, plenteous,
plentiful 11. overflowing
copper... 2. Cu 3. aes 4. cent, coin
5. metal, penny 6. cuprum
9. policeman 12. reddish–brown
copper (pert to)...
alloy.. 5. brass 6. bronze, oroide
brass.. 6. chalco
cup.. 3. dop
engraving.. 9. mezzotint
film.. 6. patina
kettle (anc).. 5. lebes
pewter.. 7. rheotan
Copperfield characters... 4. Dora
6. Dartle 8. Micawber 9. Uriah Hee[
11. Little Emily
coppice... 4. bosk, holt 5. copse,
grove 6. growth 7. boscage, thicket
9. brushwood, underwood
Coptic (pert to)...
church.. 8. Egyptian
color.. 7. oxblood
title.. 4. anba
copy... 3. ape 4. news 5. model,
Xerox (tm) 6. ectype, follow
7. edition, estreat, imitate, pattern,
replica, reprint, tracing 8. protocol,
revision 9. duplicate, imitation
10. transcribe, transcript
11. counterfeit 12. reproduction
coquet, coquette... 4. vamp 5. flirt
7. amorous 11. hummingbird
coquille... 5. shell 7. ruching
Coquille... 6. Indian 10. Athapascan
coquin... 5. knave, rogue 6. rascal
coral... 3. red 6. polyps, porite
8. Anthozoa 9. madrepore, millepore
coral (pert to)...
branch.. 7. ramicle
division.. 7. Aporosa
formation.. 5. palus
island.. 3. key 5. atoll
ridge.. 4. reef 5. shoal
snake.. 5. Elaps 6. garter 7. Micurus
worm.. 6. palolo
cord... 3. guy, rib 4. lace, line, rope,
welt, wood 5. sinew, twine 6. lariat,
sennet, spinal, string, tendon
7. measure (cubic), skirreh
8. corduroy, shoelace 9. hamstring
11. clothesline
cordage... 5. ropes 7. rigging
8. ropework
cordelle... 6. hauler 7. towline,
towrope
cordial... 4. real, warm 6. ardent,

elixir, genial, hearty, liquor 7. fervent,
liqueur, sincere, zealous 8. friendly,
vigorous 9. unfeigned 10. hospitable
cordial (liqueur)... 5. shrub 6. kummel
8. anisette, periscot 9. Cointreau
11. Benedictine, crème de moka
13. crème de menthe
cordiality... 4. zeal 5. ardor 6. fervor
7. ardency 8. kindness, warmness
9. geniality 11. hospitality
12. empressement, friendliness
core... 3. ame, hub, nub, nut 4. gist,
nave, pith 5. heart, nowel 6. center,
kernel, matrix 7. nucleus
9. substance
Corinthian (pert to)...
Age.. 5. plush 11. extravagant
color.. 3. red 4. pink 6. purple
Epistles (Bib).. 12. New Testament
General (Rom).. 9. Flaminius
King.. 8. Polybius
Spring.. 14. Pirene Fountain
Temple.. 5. Doric 7. Minerva
cork... 3. ork 4. bark, bung, plug
5. float, shive, suber (oak)
7. blacken, stopgap, stopper, stopple
corm... 4. bulb (flower)
cormorant... 4. bird, shag 5. norie,
scart, urile 8. ravenous 9. snakebird,
voracious 13. Phalacrocorax
corn... 4. joke 5. grain, grist 6. cliché,
kaffir, kernel, liquor
corn (pert to)...
bread.. 4. pone 8. dumpling
10. corndodger
goddess.. 5. Ceres
hulled.. 4. samp 5. hominy
Indian.. 3. Zea 5. maize
lily.. 4. Ixia 8. bindweed
10. wandflower
liquor.. 6. whisky (whiskey)
meal.. 4. masa 7. hoecake
porridge.. 5. atole
salad.. 8. fotticus
Corn Belt... 4. Iowa, Ohio 6. Dakota,
Kansas 7. Indiana 8. Illinois,
Missouri, Nebraska 9. Minnesota
Corncracker State... 8. Kentucky
corner... 2. in 4. nook, pose, trap,
tree 5. angle, coign (coigne), herne,
ingle, niche, quoin
cornered... 5. cater (diagonal), sharp
7. angular, up a tree 10. cornerwise
cornerstone... 4. coin 5. quoin
8. keystone 10. foundation
Cornhusker State... 8. Nebraska
cornice... 4. drip, eave 7. antefix
8. astragal
Cornish... 3. elm 4. fowl 5. heath
7. dialect, diamond (Cornwall)
Cornwallis surrender site... 4. York
(Va)
corolla... 5. galea (Her), petal
8. perianth
corollary... 6. effect, porism, result
7. adjunct 8. addition 9. deduction
11. proposition
corona... 4. coin, halo 5. cigar, crown
6. circle 7. aureole, circlet, garland,
scyphus 8. Borealis 11. corona lucis
Corona Australis... 13. Southern
Crown

Corona Borealis... 13. Northern Crown
coronet... 5. crown, tiara 6. anadem,
circle, diadem, wreath 8. insignia,
ornament
corporate... 5. joint 6. united
7. leagued 8. conjoint
10. associated
corporeal... 5. hylic, somal 6. bodily
7. fleshly, somatic 8. corporal,
material, physical, tangible
corpse... 4. body 7. cadaver, carcass
9. endowment (Eccl)
oorpulent... 3. fat 5. bulky, obese,
stout 6. fleshy
corpuscle... 11. poikilocyte, schistocyte
12. erythroblast
corral... 3. mew, pen, sty 4. coop,
herd 5. atajo, pound, tambo
7. impound 8. stockade
9. enclosure, inclosure
correct... 2. OK 4. edit, okay, true
5. amend, emend, right 6. better,
proper, punish, reform, remedy,
revise, strict 7. chasten, improve,
perfect, rectify, regular, retouch
8. accurate, definite, orthodox,
rigorous 9. faultless 10. particular,
scrupulous 11. grammatical,
punctilious 12. conventional
correlative... 2. or 3. nor 6. mutual
7. similar 8. conjoint 10. reciprocal
11. conjunction, counterpart
13. corresponding
correspond... 3. fit 4. suit 5. agree,
equal, match, tally 6. accord
7. comport 8. assonate (sound),
coincide, parallel 9. analogous,
harmonize 11. parallelize
correspondence... 4. mail 8. homology
(Biol), identity, symmetry
10. conformity, opistolary, similarity
11. equivalence, intercourse
corresponding... 8. balanced
9. analogous, homologic, isometric
10. coinciding 11. paralleling
corridor... 4. hall 5. aisle 6. airway,
arcade 7. gallery 10. passageway
corrige (obs)... 6. punish 7. correct
corrigible... 8. amenable
10. submissive 11. rectifiable
corroborate... 5. prove 7. certify,
confirm, support 8. calidate, roborate
9. establish 12. adminiculate,
substantiate
corroborative... 11. adminicular
corrode... 3. eat 4. bite, etch, gnaw,
rust 5. erode, waste 11. deteriorate
12. disintegrate
corrosive... 4. acid 7. caustic,
erodent, erodine, mordant
9. corroding 10. escharotic
14. disintegrative
corrugate... 5. crimp 6. rugate
7. crumble, wrinkle 8. crumpled,
furrowed, wrinkled
corrupt... 3. rot 5. bribe, taint, venal
6. Augean, debase, putrid, rotten
7. attaint, crooked, defiled, deprave,
putrefy, vitiate 8. polluted
9. dishonest 11. adulterated
12. contaminated
corruption... 5. taint 6. pidgin

(language) 8. impurity 9. chicanery,
pollution 10. debasement, defilement,
distortion 11. depravation,
putrescence 12. adulteration
13. contamination

corsage... 5. waist 6. bodice
7. bouquet (boquet), flowers

corsair... 5. rover 6. pirate
7. Saracen 8. picaroon, rockfish
9. buccaneer, privateer
10. freebooter

Corsica...
capital.. 7. Ajaccio
birthplace of.. 8. Napoleon
feud (blood).. 8. vendetta
seaport.. 6. Bastia

cortege... 5. train 6. parade
7. funeral, retinue 10. procession

Cortes palace site... 8. Coyoacan
(Mexico)

cortex... 4. bark, peel, rind

corundum... 3. gem 5. emery
7. mineral 8. abrasive

corundum colors...
blue.. 5. white 8. sapphire
brown.. 14. adamantine spar
green.. 7. emerald
purple.. 8. amethyst
red.. 4. ruby
topaz.. 6. yellow

coruscate... 5. gleam, shine 7. glitter,
radiate, sparkle 11. scintillate

cosmetic... 5. cream, henna, paint,
rouge 6. enamel, lotion, make–up
7. blusher, mascara 8. lipstick,
toiletry 11. beautifying

cosmic... 4. vast 5. great 7. orderly
8. catholic, infinite 9. grandiose,
universal 10. harmonious

Cosmic Order... 4. Rita (Vedic law)

Cossack (pert to)...
chief.. 6. ataman, hetman
district.. 6. Voisko
native.. 5. Tatar 7. Russian
squadron.. 6. sotnia
village.. 8. stanitsa (stanitza)
whip (knotted).. 5. knout

cosset... 3. pet 4. lamb 6. caress,
coddle, cuddle, fondle, pamper

cost... 4. loss, rate 5. price
6. amount, charge, figure, outlay,
rental 7. expense 9. detriment,
suffering 11. deprivation, expenditure

costa... 3. rib 4. vein (Bot) 5. ridge
6. border, midrib

Costa Rica...
capital.. 7. San José
crater (world's greatest).. 4. Poas
discovered.. 8. Columbus (4th visit)
export.. 6. coffee 8. bananas
port.. 5. Limon 10. Puntarenas

costate... 6. ribbed (Bot)

costermonger... 6. coster, hawker
7. peddler 9. costerman 11. apple
seller

costly... 4. dear, rich 8. gorgeous,
splendid 9. expensive, sumptuous
10. high–priced 11. extravagant

costume... 3. rig 4. garb, suit
5. dress, habit 6. attire, tights
7. apparel, raiment 8. clothing

cot... 3. bed, hut, pen, set 4. boat (Ir),

coop, cote 5. cabin, cover, house
6. cabana 7. charpoy, cottage,
shelter 8. bedstead

cote... 3. hut, pen 4. coop 5. house
7. cottage, shelter 9. sheepfold

coterie... 3. set 4. clan, club, ring
5. cabal, group, junto 6. circle, clique
9. camarilla (secret)

cottage... 3. cot, hut 4. shed
5. cabin, house, villa 6. cabana
7. shelter 8. bungalow

cottager... 6. cottar (cotter) 7. cottier,
laborer, peasant

cotton (pert to)...
cloth.. 4. jean, lawn 5. denim, khaki,
scrim, surat, terry 6. calico, dimity,
madras, nettle 7. batiste, percale
fiber.. 4. lint 6. staple 7. viscose
gin inventor.. 7. Whitney (Eli)
knot.. 3. nep
layer.. 7. batting
medical.. 5. gauze 6. sponge
raw.. 5. bayal
roll.. 4. slub
seed.. 4. bole, boll
seed sugar.. 9. raffinose
staple.. 6. upland (short) 8. Egyptian
(long) 14. Sea Island (long)
twisted.. 5. lisle 6. thread

Cotton State... 7. Alabama

couch... 3. bed, cot 4. lair, sofa
5. divan 6. canapé, canopy, litter,
lounge, pallet, phrase 8. loveseat
9. embroider (with gold), stretcher

cougar... 3. cat 4. lion, puma
7. panther 9. catamount

cough... 4. bark (sl), hack 6. tussis

council... 4. diet, rede 5. cabal, synod
6. senate 7. cabinet 8. assembly,
conclave, tribunal 10. conference,
parliament 12. consultation
15. League of Nations

council table cover... 5. tapis

counsel... 4. rede 6. advice, advise,
confer, lawyer 8. guidance
9. recommend 10. suggestion
11. instruction 12. deliberation

counselor, counsellor... 4. sage
6. lawyer, mentor, nestor 7. adviser,
advisor, counsel 8. attorney
9. barrister, solicitor

count... 3. sum, tot 4. tale, tell
5. check, judge, relay, tally
6. number, reckon, rely on
7. compute, summary 8. nobleman,
quantify 9. calculate, enumerate,
reckoning, summation 12. capitulation

Count (pert to)...
Mayence.. 3. Gan 7. Ganelon
Monte Cristo.. 6. Dantes
Rousillon.. 7. Bertram

countenance... 3. aid 4. abet, brow,
face, mien 6. aspect, permit, visage
7. approve, endorse, support
8. approval, sanction, tolerate
9. composure, encourage
10. appearance, permission

counter... 4. chip 5. table, token
7. adverse 8. computer, contrary,
opposite 9. retaliate 10. calculator

counteract... 6. offset, oppose, thwart
7. nullify 8. antidote 10. neutralize

11. countermand
counter current... 4. eddy 5. swirl
6. vortex 9. whirlpool
12. counterforce
counterfeit... 4. base, fake, mock,
sham 5. bogus, false, feign, forge,
phony, queer 6. assume, forged,
unreal 7. falsify, forgery, imitate
8. simulant, spurious 10. artificial,
fictitious 11. unauthentic
counterirritant... 4. moxa 5. seton
6. arnica, iodine, pepper 7. mustard
countermand... 5. annul 6. cancel,
forbid, recall, revoke 7. abolish,
reverse 8. prohibit 9. frustrate
10. counteract 12. counterorder
counterpane... 5. quilt 8. bedcover,
coverlet 9. comforter 10. counterpin
11. comfortable
counterpart... 4. copy, like, twin
5. image 6. double, eponym (name)
8. parallel 9. duplicate
10. complement, equivalent
counterpoise... 6. offset 8. equalize
10. compensate, counteract
12. counterforce 14. counterbalance
countersign... 4. sign 6. signal
7. tessera 8. password 9. signature,
watchword 10. mot de passé, open
sesame 12. counterstamp
countersink... 4. ream 5. bevel
6. deepen 7. chamfer
countertenor... 4. alto (male)
8. falsetto
counterthrust (fencing)... 7. riposte
(ripost) 12. return thrust
countless... 8. infinite 10. numberless,
unnumbered 11. innumerable
12. incalculable
countrified... 5. rural 7. boorish,
hickish, uncouth 8. inurbane
10. unpolished
country... 4. land, pais (law), vale
5. rural, state, weald 6. nation,
region 9. territory 10. fatherland
12. commonwealth
country (pert to)...
alien.. 7. enclave, exclave
ancient.. 4. Aram, Elis, Gaul
bumpkin.. 4. clod, jake, rube
5. churl, yokel 9. greenhorn
gallant.. 5. swain
mythical.. 2. Oz
native (earliest).. 9. aborigine
Roman.. 8. campagna
term.. 5. rural, urban 6. rustic
8. agrestic, pastoral, praedial (predial)
countryman... 4. rube 5. yokel
6. rustic 7. hayseed, patriot, peasant
10. compatriot, home towner
county... 4. seat 5. shire 6. domain,
parish 8. district
coup... 3. buy 4. blow, move (games)
5. scoop, upset 6. barter, strike,
stroke (master) 8. overturn, strategy
9. trump card
coup de grâce... 9. deathblow
coup de main... 6. attack (sudden)
8. strategy 9. stratagem
coup d'état... 6. stroke (political)
8. strategy
couple... 3. duo, tie, two 4. bond,

dyad, join, link, mate, pair, span,
team, twin, yoke 5. brace, marry,
twain, unite 6. Gemini 7. bracket
coupled... 5. gemel, mated 6. braced,
joined, linked, paired, teamed, united
7. leagued, married
couplet... 3. two 4. pair 5. brace,
verse 7. distich, doublet
coupon... 5. scrip, stock, token
6. ticket 11. certificate (Finan)
courage... 4. grit, sand, will 5. heart,
metal, nerve, pluck, valor 7. bravery,
heroism, prowess 8. audacity,
boldness, firmness 9. fortitude,
gallantry, hardihood 11. intrepidity
12. fearlessness 13. dauntlessness
courageous... 4. bold, game 5. brave,
hardy, manly, stout 6. daring, heroic,
spunky 7. gallant, spartan, valiant
8. fearless, intrepid, knightly,
resolute, stalwart, valorous
11. adventurous 12. enterprising,
stouthearted
courant... 4. romp 5. caper 6. letter
7. gazette, running (Her)
9. messenger, newspaper
courier... 5. guide 8. dragoman,
horseman 9. attendant, messenger
course... 3. run 4. flow, line, mode,
path, road, rote, tack 5. route,
study, trend 6. career, manner,
method, policy, series, stream
8. progress 9. direction, procedure
10. succession
course (pert to)...
college.. 7. seminar
direct.. 7. beeline
regular.. 4. rote 6. regime 7. routine
roundabout.. 6. detour 11. indirection
course of...
action.. 5. habit 7. routine
9. procedure
eating.. 4. diet
instruction.. 6. lesson
procedure.. 4. rule
thought.. 5. tenor
courser... 5. horse, steed 6. hunter,
plover 7. charger 8. war horse
court... 3. see (papal), woo 4. area,
eyre, fawn (upon), rota 5. atria,
curia, dairi, gemot, patio, spark
6. palace, parvis, street 7. council,
tribune 8. tribunal 10. attendance,
curry favor, quadrangle
court (Eng)... 3. soc 4. eyre, leet
8. woodmate 10. court-baron
court (pert to)...
assistant.. 5. staff 6. elisor
crier, cry.. 4. hear, oyez (oyes)
6. beadle
criminal.. 6. assize
exemption, excuse.. 6. essoin
game.. 6. tennis 9. badminton
hearing.. 4. oyer
minutes.. 4. acta
order.. 4. writ 5. arret 6. capias
7. summons 8. subpoena
public.. 5. forum 8. forensic
sitting.. 7. session
courteous... 5. civil 6. gentle, polite,
urbane 7. affable, gallant
8. debonair, gracious 9. attentive

10. respectful
courtly... 4. hend (hende) 5. aulic, civil 7. elegant, gallant, stately 9. dignified 10. obsequious 11. ceremonious
courtship... 4. suit 6. plight, wooing 7. romance 8. courting
covenant... 4. bond, pact 6. engage 7. bargain, compact, entente, promise 8. contract 9. agreement, stipulate, testament 11. undertaking
Covenant of God to Noah... 7. rainbow
cover... 3. cap, lap, lid 4. coat, cozy, hide, mask, pale, pave, roof, span, veil 5. blind, crust, drape, tapis 6. canopy, mantle, purdah, screen, shield, thatch 7. elytron, overlay, shelter 8. chrismal, coverlet 9. tarpaulin 10. overspread
cover (pert to)...
alloy.. 5. terne
cork.. 9. corticate
crumbs.. 5. bread
dots.. 7. stipple
figures (Her).. 4. seme
straw.. 6. thatch
turf.. 3. sod
up.. 4. bury 5. inter 7. conceal 8. submerge 10. camouflage
with wax.. 4. cere
covering... 3. mat, rug 4. caul, film, hull, tile 5. apron, armor, shell, testa 6. awning, carpet, cestus, lorica, pelage, screen, shroud 7. epeiric, shelter, tegumen, wrapper 8. lineolum, pericarp 9. caparison 10. integument, protection 11. smoke screen
covering (head)... 3. cap, hat, wig 4. hood 5. beret, scarf, snood 6. bonnet, peruke, toupee 7. chapeau 10. fascinator
coverlet... 5. quilt 6. afghan, spread 7. blanket, lap robe 11. counterpane
covert... 3. den, lie 4. abri, lair 6. hidden, refuge, secret 7. covered, private, thicket 9. concealed, disguised, insidious, sheltered
covet... 4. envy 5. crave, yisse (obs) 6. aspire, desire, grudge, hanker 7. long for 8. begrudge
covetousness... 5. greed 7. avarice
covey... 4. bevy, pack 5. brood, flock, hatch 6. flight 7. company 9. multitude
cow... 3. awe 5. abash, daunt 7. overawe, terrify 8. browbeat, frighten 10. intimidate
cow (animal)... 3. Bos 4. calf, kine, moil 5. Angus, bossy, brock (obs), Kerry, vache 6. bovine, heifer 7. pollard 8. Ayrshire, maverick, moulleen
cow (pert to)...
barn.. 4. byre, shed 5. reeve, stall 6. stable 7. vaccary, vachery
food (chewed).. 3. cud 5. rumen
hornless.. 6. mulley 7. pollard 8. moulleen
sea.. 6. dugong, walrus 7. manatee, Sirenia 12. hippopotamus

tether.. 4. rope 6. baikie
unbranded.. 8. maverick
young.. 4. calf 6. heifer
coward, cowardly... 3. shy 5. sneak 6. afraid, craven, scared 7. caitiff, chicken, dastard, milksop 8. poltroon, recreant, weakling 9. dastardly, fraidy–cat, jellyfish 12. uncourageous 13. pusillanimous
cowboy... 5. roper 6. herder 7. llamero, puncher, vaquero 8. jackaroo, neatherd 12. broncobuster (sl)
cowboy breeches... 5. chaps 8. jodhpurs
cower... 4. fawn 5. crawl, quail, stoop 6. cringe, crouch, grovel
cowfish... 3. ray 4. toto 7. dolphin, grampus, manatee 8. porpoise
cowled... 9. cucullate
coxcomb... 3. fop 4. dude, fool 5. cleat (Naut), dandy 8. popinjay
coy... 3. shy 4. arch 5. timid 6. demure, modest 7. bashful 10. coquettish 13. self–conscious
coyote... 4. wolf (prairie)
Coyote State... 11. South Dakota
coypu... 6. nutria, rodent
cozen... 5. cheat, trick 7. beguile, deceive, defraud
cozy... 4. easy, snug 6. chatty 8. cheerful, familiar, homelike, sociable 9. contented, talkative 11. comfortable
crab... 3. Uca 4. king, Maia (genus) 5. ayuyu (Guam) 6. partan, spider 7. fiddler, limulus, mollusk, Ocypode 8. Lithodes 9. horseshoe 10. crustacean
crabbed... 5. cross 6. bitter, crusty, morose, trying 7. bilious, peevish 8. abstruse, liverish 9. difficult, fractious, irascible, irregular 10. perplexing
crab claw... 5. chela 6. metope, nipper
crab eater... 4. seal 5. heron 7. opossum, raccoon
crachoir... 8. cuspidor, spittoon
crack... 4. blow, chap, clap, flaw, kibe, leak, quip, rift, rime, snap 5. brack, break, chink, craze, spang, split 6. breach, cleave, cranny 7. crackle, crevice, fissure, rupture 8. fracture
Cracker State... 7. Georgia
crackle... 4. snap 5. craze (art), crink 9. crepitate
crackman... 4. yegg 7. burglar
cradle... 4. slee (ship's) 7. infancy, nursery 8. bassinet, cunabula 10. beginnings, incunabula
cradle book... 11. incunabulum
Cradle of Liberty... 11. Faneuil Hall (Boston)
cradle song... 7. lullaby 8. berceuse 13. Schlummerleid
craft... 3. art 4. boat 5. skill, trade 6. device, tender 7. cunning, finesse, know–how, prowess 8. aptitude, vocation 9. dexterity 10. employment, handicraft,

occupation, watercraft 12. skillfulness
craftsman... 6. artist, writer
  7. artisan, workman 9. artificer
crafty... 3. sly 4. foxy, slim, wily, wise
  6. artful, astute, shifty, shrewd, subtle,
  tricky 7. cunning 8. skillful (skilful)
  9. deceitful, ingenious, underhand
  10. fraudulent 13. Machiavellian
  15. Mephistophelean
crag... 3. tor 4. spur 5. arête, cliff
  7. nunatak 9. precipice
craggy... 5. rough 6. cliffy, clifty,
  jagged, knotty, rugged
cram... 4. fill 5. choke, crowd, drive,
  force, gorge, press, study, stuff
  9. overstuff 10. gluttonize
cramp... 4. pain 5. stunt 6. hamper
  7. confine, seizure 8. compress,
  restrict 9. hindrance, paralysis
  (muscle) 11. restriction
cranberry... 3. red 9. sourberry
cranberry center of trade...
  10. Barnstable (Mass)
crane... 3. gib, jib 6. davit, jenny,
  titan 7. derrick, machine
crane... 4. Grus 6. heron, sarus
  7. Gruidae 9. cormorant
  10. Gruiformes 13. constellation
cranial nerve... 5. radix, vagus
cranium... 5. skull 8. cerebrum
crank... 3. wit 4. bear, crab 5. crook,
  winch 6. griper, grouch, handle
  7. fanatic, growler, hothead
  8. frondeur, grumbler, sorehead
  9. eccentric 10. bellyacher,
  crosspatch, monomaniac
cranny... 4. hole, nook 5. chink, cleft,
  crack 6. corner, furrow 7. crevice,
  fissure 8. crevasse
crash... 4. bank, fail 5. smash
  7. debacle, failure, intrude, shatter
  8. accident 9. collision
  10. bankruptcy
crate... 3. box 4. case 6. basket,
  cradle, encase, hamper 8. airplane
  9. container 10. automobile
crater... 3. pit 6. cavity 7. caldera
  13. constellation (The Cup)
cravat... 3. tie 4. teck 5. ascot, stock
  7. bandage, bolo tie, necktie
  9. neckcloth 10. four-in-hand
crave... 3. ask, beg 4. long, seek
  5. covet, yearn 6. desire, hanker
  7. beseech, entreat, implore, request,
  solicit 10. supplicate
craven... 6. afraid, coward 7. caitiff,
  dastard 8. cowardly, poltroon,
  recreant 12. fainthearted
  13. pusillanimous
craving... 4. pica 6. desire, thirst
  7. longing 8. appetite, yearning
craw... 3. maw 4. crop 6. gebbie
  7. gizzard, stomach 9. ingluvies
crawfish... 5. yabby (yabbie) 7. back
  out, crawdad, lobster, retreat
  8. crayfish
crawl... 4. fawn, inch, shug 5. creep
  6. cringe, grovel, recant
crayon... 5. chalk 6. pastel, pencil
  8. charcoal
craze... 3. fad 4. flaw, maze 5. crack
  (ceramics), crush, furor, mania, vogue

  6. defect, whimsy 7. crackle, fashion
  9. infirmity 11. infatuation
craze (for)... see also *madness, mania*
  foreign customs.. 9. xenomania
  freedom.. 14. eleutheromania
  love (erotic).. 10. erotomania
  music.. 9. melomania
  setting fires.. 9. pyromania
  shopping.. 9. oniomania
  single subject.. 9. monomania
  stamps (postage).. 11. timbromania
  stealing.. 11. kleptomania
  wandering.. 10. dromomania
  wealth.. 10. plutomania
crazed... 4. amok 6. insane, marked
  (with crazes) 7. severed 8. deranged
  10. distraught
crazy... 3. mad 4. amok, loco, luny
  6. dottle, insane 7. damaged, foolish,
  unsound 9. deficient
cream... 4. best, ream 5. elite
  6. lotion 8. sillabub (with wine)
cream of tartar... 5. argol
crease... 4. fold, tuck 5. crimp, pleat
  7. wrinkle 9. plication
create... 4. make 5. build, cause,
  clone, hatch 6. invent 7. fashion,
  produce 8. generate 9. originate
creation... 3. art 5. virtu, world
  6. cosmos, making 7. classic, fantasy,
  forming, product 8. artifact, universe
  9. objet d'art 10. providence
  11. composition, fabrication,
  manufacture, masterpiece
creator... 5. maker 6. author
  8. designer, inventor, producer
  10. originator
Creator... 3. God 5. Maker
  7. Jehovah 8. Almighty, Demiurge
  11. King of Kings
creature (pert to)...
  oivotliko.. 3. cat
  duplicate.. 5. clone
  elflike.. 4. peri 6. hobbit
  evil.. 7. hellcat 8. hellicat
  fire.. 10. salamander
  folklore.. 3. elf 4. Yeti 5. dwarf, fairy,
  pixie 9. sasquatch
  ghost.. 11. poltergeist
  minute.. 10. animalcule
  outer space.. 5. alien
  sentient.. 6. animal
  timid.. 4. deer 5. sheep
  underground.. 5. gnome
  water.. 5. sylph 6. undine
  winged (Myth).. 6. wivern
  10. cockatrice
credence... 5. trust 6. belief, credit
  8. affiance, reliance 10. acceptance,
  confidence, dependence
  15. trustworthiness
credential... 7. voucher
  11. certificate, testimonial
  14. recommendation
credible... 6. likely 7. tenable
  8. probable 9. plausible
  10. believable 11. well-founded
credit... 5. faith, honor, trust 6. belief,
  esteem, impute 7. account, believe
  8. accredit, credence 10. estimation,
  regulation 15. trustworthiness
creditor... 5. agent (collection)

6. debtee, dunner, usurer 7. Shylock (greedy)
creed... 5. credo, dogma, tenet
  6. belief, Nicene 8. Apostles'
  9. Catechism 10. Athanasian, confession
creek... 3. rio 4. burn, slue, wick
  6. arroyo, estero, slough, spruit, stream
creel... 4. rack, trap 6. basket (fish)
creep... 5. crawl, prowl, skulk, slink, sneak, steal (away) 6. grovel
  8. scramble 9. pussyfoot
creeping... 4. slow 7. reptant
  8. crawling 10. slithering
  11. reptatorial
Cremona, famed names... 5. Amati
  6. violin 10. Guarnerius
  12. Stradivarius
crena... 4. gash, kerf, nick 5. cleft, notch 7. scallop 10. depression
  11. indentation
creole... 6. French 7. mestizo
  9. half—breed, janissary
Creole State... 9. Louisiana
crepitate... 4. snap 7. crackly
crescent... 4. cusp, horn, lune
  5. curve 8. meniscus
crescent—shaped... 4. horn, lune
  6. bicorn, lunate 7. lunular
  8. lunulate 9. horseshoe, meniscate, semilunar
crest... 3. top 4. comb, peak, tuft
  5. arête, crown, ridge 6. copple, crista, height, summit 7. panache, topknot, wave top 8. feathers, insignia, pinnacle 9. cockscomb
  11. mountaintop
crested... 6. capped, topped, tufted
  7. coppled, cristed, crowned, pileate
creta... 5. chalk
Crete...
  capital.. 5. Canea
  city.. 6. Candia, Khanis
  civilization (anc).. 6. Aegean, Minoan
  king (anc).. 5. Minos (Gr)
  monster.. 8. Minotaur (man, bull)
  mountain.. 3. Ida 9. Theodoros
  priests.. 7. Curetes
cretin... 5. idiot 8. imbecile
crevice... 3. gap 4. rift 5. chink, cleft
  6. cranny 7. fissure, opening
  8. peephole 10. interstice
crew... 3. men 4. band, body, gang, pack 5. force, staff 7. company
  9. employees, personnel
crib... 3. bed, bin, den (gambling)
  5. cheat, stall, steal 6. Cratch (stars), manger, pilfer 7. brothel
  8. Praesepe
cricket... 4. game, grig 6. acheta, cicada, locust 7. katydid 9. footstool
  10. Orthoptera 11. grasshopper
cricket (pert to)...
  game term.. 3. bye, run 6. yorker
  noise.. 5. chirp 7. stridor
  symbol (Myth).. 4. tice 5. ashes
cried... 4. wept 6. bawled, called, wailed, yelled 7. shouted, uttered
  8. lamented, screamed, shrieked
  9. exclaimed 10. proclaimed
crime... 3. sin 4. evil 5. guilt, wrong

6. delict, felony, mayhem 7. offense
  8. delictum, iniquity 9. violation
  10. illegality, wickedness, wrongdoing
  11. malfeasance
crime (pert to)...
  benefice (Eccl).. 6. simony
  goddess (Myth).. 3. Ate
  of 1873.. 12. Silver Dollar
  scene.. 5. venue
Crimea...
  city.. 5. Kerch, Yalta 10. Sevastopol
  isthmus site.. 8. Black Sea
  Russian.. 4. Krim
  sea (Russ).. 4. Azof
criminal... 4. thug, yegg 5. crook, felon, thief 6. nocent 7. convict, yeggman 8. swindler 9. desperado, dishonest, felonious 10. malefactor, recidivist 11. blameworthy, disgraceful
  13. reprehensible
criminal refuge... 7. Alsatia
  11. Whitefriars (London)
criminology... 8. penology
crimp... 4. curl, fold 5. frizz, notch, plait 6. ruffle, thwart 7. crinkle, wrinkle 8. Shanghai
cringe... 4. fawn 5. cower, quail, sneak, wince 6. flinch, grovel, shrink, submit 7. truckle
crinkle... 4. curl, kink, turn, wind
  5. twist 6. rustle 7. wrinkle
crinose... 5. hairy 7. hirsute
  11. barbigerous
cripple... 4. halt, hock, lame, maim
  6. injure, weaken 7. amputee, disable 8. handicap 9. hamstring
  12. incapacitate
crisis... 5. cycle, peril 8. exigency, juncture 9. criterion, emergency
  11. climacteric
crisp... 4. cold 5. curly, flaky, sharp, short, spalt 7. brittle, concise, crackle, crinkle, friable 8. clear—cut
  9. frangible
criterion... 4. norm, rule, test, type
  5. canon, model 7. measure
  8. standard 9. yardstick
critic... 5. judge, Momus (Myth)
  6. censor, slater, Zoilus 8. collator, reviewer 9. literator 11. connoisseur, criticaster, faultfinder
critical... 4. edgy 7. carping, crucial, cynical, Zoilean 8. captious, caviling, exacting 10. censorious, particular
  12. faultfinding 13. hairsplitting
  14. discriminating
Critical system of philosophy...
  10. Kantianism
criticism... 3. rap 5. cavil, roast
  6. report, review 7. censure, Zoilism
  8. critique, judgment 9. aspersion
  10. commentary
criticize, criticise... 3. pan 4. carp, flay 5. cavil, judge, knock, slate
  6. review 7. censure, comment
  9. castigate 10. animadvert
Croatian... 4. Slav 5. Croat
  11. Yugoslavian
Croatian capital... 6. Zagreb
crock... 3. ewe (old), jug, pot, urn
  4. smut, soil, soot 5. horse (old)
  7. ceramic 8. potsherd

11. earthenware
crocodile ... 3. goa 5. nakoo 6. gavial, mugger 7. reptile, sophism 9. Niloticus 10. Crocodilia, Crocodilus
crocus ... 4. bulb, herb, iris 6. flower, yellow 7. saffron
croft ... 5. crypt, field, vault 6. carafe, cavern 7. hillock
crone ... 3. ewe (old), hag 5. witch 6. beldam (beldame)
Cronus (pert to) ...
god of .. 8. Harvests
father .. 6. Uranus
son .. 4. Zeus
wife .. 4. Rhea
crony ... 3. pal 4. chum 5. buddy 6. friend 9. companion 10. playfellow
crook ... 4. bend, warp 5. angle, curve, staff, thief 6. akimbo 7. crosier 8. criminal, insignia 10. camshachle
crooked ... 3. wry, zag 4. agee, awry, bent 5. agley, askew, false 6. aslant, curved, hooked, zigzag 7. angular, askance, asquint, oblique 8. deformed 9. dishonest, distorted 10. circuitous, fraudulent 12. dishonorable
crooked legs ... 8. rhebosis (rhaebosis) 10. tortuosity
croon ... 3. hum 4. boom, sing, wail 5. whine 6. bellow, lament, murmur 8. complain
crop ... 3. lop, maw 4. clip, craw, dick, reap, whip 5. belly, shear, yield 6. gebbie, growth, sheave 7. harvest, produce, soilage, stomach 11. cultivation
cross ... 2. go 3. tau 4. crux, ford, rood 5. bless, corse, irate, staff 6. oppose, thwart, touchy 7 athwart, fretful, oblique, peevish, pettish 8. crucifix, insignia, monument, obstruct, petulant, snappish, swastika (swastica), traverse 9. hybridize, intersect, irritable 10. disappoint, transverse 11. crucifixion
cross (pert to) ...
archaeology .. 4. ankh
astronomy .. 13. Southern Cross
barred .. 11. trabeculate
beam .. 5. spale, trave 6. girder
bow .. 8. arbalest
breed .. 5. Husky (dog) 6. hybrid
British .. 6. Celtic
Egypt .. 10. life symbol
eye .. 9. esotropia 10. strabismus
heraldry .. 6. pattée 7. erminee, patonce
Latin .. 12. crux commissa
palm .. 5. bribe (gypsy)
St Anthony's .. 3. tau
stroke .. 5. serif
tau–shaped .. 10. crux ansata
crossing ... 6. voyage 7. chiasma, fording, passage 8. cheating, opposing 9. hybridism 10. traversing 13. crossbreeding
crossing (famed) ...
Alps .. 8. Hannibal, Napoleon
Hellespont .. 6. Xerxes

Pyrenees .. 8. Hannibal
Rubicon .. 6. Caesar
crouch ... 4. bend, fawn 5. cower, squat, stoop 6. cringe, grovel, hunker
crow ... 3. daw 4. brag, rook 5. aylet, boast, crake, raven, vaunt 6. chough, Corvus, Indian (Sioux) 7. corvine, jackdaw 8. laughter 13. constellation
crowbar ... 5. jimmy, lever 7. gablock
crowberry ... 5. shrub 8. bilberry 9. cranberry
crowd ... 3. jam, mob 4. bike (Scot), cram, host, pack, push, ruck, urge 5. crush, drive, drove, horde, press, serry, swarm, three, wedge 6. galaxy, hasten, legion, masses, throng 7. squeeze 8. compress 9. multitude 10. assemblage
crowded ... 6. packed 7. compact, crammed, serried, teeming 8. numerous, populous 9. congested, jampacked
crown ... 3. cap, top 4. atef, coin, pate, peak, poll, tiar 5. crest, miter (mitre), tiara 6. anadem, circle, corona, diadem, fillet, reward, summit, trophy, wreath 7. chaplet, coronet, garland, glorify, install 8. coronate, enthrone, ornament, pinnacle, surmount
crowning glory ... 8. last word
crucial ... 5. final 6. severe, trying, urgent 7. crossed 8. critical, decisive 9. cruciform 13. demonstrative
crucible ... 3. pot 4. etna, test 6. retort, vessel 10. conversion
crucifix ... 3. pax 4. rood 5. cross 6. emblem
crucifixion ... 5. death (on a cross) 7. torture 9. execution, suffering 11. persecution
crude ... 3. raw 4. rude 5. crass, green, rough 6. callow, coarse, common, garish, savage, vulgar 8. unseemly 9. inelegant, rough–hewn, tasteless, uncourtly, unrefined 10. outlandish, unpolished 13. inexperienced
crudity ... 7. rawness 9. crassness, harshness, roughness, vulgarity 10. immaturity
cruel ... 4. fell, hard 5. harsh 6. brutal, savage, severe, unkind 7. inhuman, painful, unhuman 8. dreadful, fiendish, pitiless, ruthless, tyrannic 9. ferocious, heartless, merciless, murderous, truculent 11. remorseless
cruelty ... 9. brutality 10. inclemency, inhumanity 12. ruthlessness 13. heartlessness 15. remorselessness
cruelty, lover of ... 6. sadist 9. masochist
cruet ... 3. ama 4. vial 6. bottle, caster (castor), vessel 7. ampulla, urceole
cruller ... 7. olycook (olykoek) 8. doughnut 9. friedcake
crumb ... 3. bit 5. break, piece 6. little 8. fragment
crumble ... 5. decay 6. molder, powder

7. friable 9. pulverize
12. disintegrate
crumple... 4. ruck 6. crease, raffle,
rumple 7. wrinkle 9. corrugate
cruor... 4. gore 5. blood, ichor
crusade... 5. cause, drive, issue, jihad
(jehad) 7. crusado 8. campaign
10. expedition
Crusades... 8. Holy Land 9. Children's
(1212)
crush... 3. jam 4. bray, mash, sink
5. crash, crowd, grind, press, smash
6. bruise, crunch 7. conquer,
mortify, oppress, shatter, squeeze
8. compress, suppress 9. humiliate,
pulverize 11. infatuation
crushed sugar cane... 7. bagasse
crust... 4. rind 5. shell 8. dumpling,
exterior 9. impudence 11. lithosphere
14. aggressiveness
crustacean... 4. crab 5. prawn
6. huitre, isopod, limpet, mussel,
oyster, shrimp 7. limulus, lobster,
scallop 8. barnacle, crawfish, starfish
9. shellfish, trunkfish 10. coquillage,
periwinkle
crustacean (pert to)...
extinct.. 5. Eryon
footless.. 4. apod, apus
fossil.. 9. trilobite
genus.. 5. Hippa 6. Triops 7. Caridea
(Carida) 8. Copepoda, Decapoda
10. Notostraca
larva.. 5. alima
limb.. 6. endite, podite
crutch... 5. brace, staff, stave
6. crotch 7. support
cry... 3. baa, caw, cri, hue, mew, olé,
sob 4. alas, barr, call, evoe, home,
hoot, mewl, pish, pule, wail, weep,
yell, yelp 5. alack, avast, bleat,
crook, miaou, yoick 6. bellow,
boohoo, clamor, outcry, scream,
shriek, slogan, snivel, squawk
7. tantivy (hunting), trumpet, weeping
8. entreaty, jeremiad, lackaday,
proclaim 10. shibboleth
11. lamentation
cry (out)... 5. crake, decry, shout
6. accuse, clamor, object, scream,
suffer 7. censure, exclaim
8. complain, denounce 10. vociferate
crying... 6. puling, urgent 7. clamant,
heinous, howling, sobbing, weeping
9. insistent, notorious
crying bird... 6. Aramus 7. courlan,
limpkin 8. raillike
cryptic... 4. Rite (Freemasonry)
6. hidden, occult, secret 8. puzzling
9. concealed, enigmatic
10. mysterious 11. problematic
12. hieroglyphic
cryptogram... 4. code 5. agama
7. writing (secret) 8. symbolic
crystal... 4. dial 5. clear, glass, lucid
6. argent (Her), quartz 7. diamond
8. pellucid 9. glassware, snowflake
11. crystalline, transparent
crystal (pert to)...
diamond.. 7. glassie
gazer.. 4. seer 7. diviner 8. presager
10. soothsayer 13. fortuneteller

gazing.. 4. scry
twin.. 5. macle
crystalline... 4. pure 8. pellucid
11. transparent 12. crystal–clear
crystalline (pert to)...
colorless.. 7. orcinol
compound.. 5. oscin 6. anisil, dulcin
mineral.. 4. spar 7. apatite
8. elaterin, feldspar
rock.. 7. diorite, greisen
salt.. 5. borax 8. analgene (analgen)
cub... 3. bin, boy, fox, pen, pup
4. bear, coop, crib, lion, shed
5. shark, stall, tiger, whale, whelp
8. boy scout, cupboard 9. youngling
Cuba...
capital.. 6. Havana
castle.. 5. Morro
city.. 8. Santiago 10. Bahia Honda,
Guantánamo
discoverer.. 8. Columbus (1492)
island.. 11. Isle of Pines (Isla de
Pinos)
mountain.. 8. Camaguey 9. Las Villas
12. Pico Turquino
nickname.. 18. Pearl of the Antilles
province.. 7. Oriente
Cuban (pert to)...
asphalt.. 9. chapapote
bird.. 6. trogan 8. tocororo
dance.. 5. rumba
fish.. 4. bobo
rodent.. 5. hutia (jutia) 6. pilori
rum.. 7. Bacardi
cube... 3. die 4. dice 5. solid 6. triple
7. tessera (marble) 10. third power
cubic (pert to)...
body.. 3. die 4. dice
decimeter.. 5. litre
math.. 9. isometric
measure.. 4. cord
meter.. 5. stere
shape.. 6. cuboid 8. cubiform
cubicle... 4. cell, room, tomb
7. bedroom, chamber, roomlet
9. cubiculum
cuckoo... 5. mimic 8. imitator,
songbird
cuckoo (pert to)...
ally.. 3. ani
American.. 8. Coccyzus
bees.. 9. Nomadidae
bird (Orient).. 4. coel (koel)
cap.. 9. monkshood
family.. 9. Cuculidae
fool.. 7. wryneck
pint.. 4. arum 10. cuckoo spit
cucumber... 4. cuke, pepo 6. pedata
(sea), pepino
cucurbit... 5. flask, gourd 7. matrass
cud... 4. bite, quid 5. rumen
8. merycism
cuddle... 3. hug, pet 6. fondle, nestle
7. snuggle
cudgel... 3. bat, hit 4. beat, club,
drub 5. baste, staff, stave, stick
6. alpeen 7. belabor 9. fustigate,
shillalah (shillelagh)
cue... 3. nod, rod, tip 4. ball, clue,
hint, role, tail 5. braid, queue, twist
6. prompt 8. billiard (term), function
9. catchword 10. intimation

cuerpo... 4. body, hulk 5. naked, torso
10. dishabille (in)
cuff... 3. hit 4. band, blow, slap
5. clout 6. strike 8. chastise,
gauntlet, handcuff 12. chastisement
cuirass... 4. mail 5. armor 6. lorica
11. breastplate
cul–de–sac... 5. alley (blind)
7. impasse 14. pouch of Douglas
cull... 4. pick 6. assort, choose, select
8. separate
culmination... 3. end 4. acme, apex,
auge, noon 6. ascent, climax, result,
vertex, zenith 10. perfection
12. consummation
culpability... 5. blame, fault, guilt
11. criminality 15. blameworthiness
culpable... 6. faulty, guilty 7. immoral
8. criminal 9. accusable, imputable
10. censurable, indictable
11. blameworthy 12. reproachable
13. reprehensible
cultivate... 3. ear (dial), hoe 4. farm,
grow, plow, teel, till 5. court, train
6. excite, foster, harrow, plough,
refine 7. educate, improve
8. approach, civilize
cultivated... 4. grew, hoed 6. seeded,
tilled, urbane 7. genteel, refined
8. cultured, polished, well–bred
cultivation... 5. tilth 7. culture,
farming, tillage 9. husbandry
10. refinement 12. civilization
culver... 4. dove 6. pigeon 10. wood
pigeon
cumbersome... 5. bulky 6. clumsy
8. cumbrous, unwieldy
10. burdensome
cummer... 4. lass 5. witch 6. friend
(girl) 7. midwife 9. companion,
godmother
cummerbund... 4. band, belt, sash
6. cestus, girdle
cumshaw... 3. tip 5. bonus 6. thanks
7. present 8. gratuity
cunning... 3. sly 4. cute, foxy, wile,
wily 5. sharp, skill 6. artful, clever,
crafty, dainty, shrewd, subtle, tricky
7. politic, shyness 8. dextrous,
foxiness, skillful, stealthy, trickery
9. designing, dexterity, ingenious,
ingenuity, insidious 13. Machiavellian
cunningly formed... 6. daedal (dedal)
cup... 3. ama, can, dop, mug, tyg
4. tass, teet, Toby 5. calyx, chark,
cruse, cupel, cylix, grail, jorum, ladle,
stein 6. beaker, goblet, noggin,
trophy 7. chalice, tumbler
cupbearer... 4. Hebe, saki
8. Ganymede
cupboard... 3. kas 5. ambry (anc)
6. buffet, closet, larder, pantry
7. armoire, dresser 8. aparador
9. sideboard
Cupid... 3. boy, Dan 4. amor, Eros,
Kama, love 5. Freya 7. Amorino,
cupidon
Cupid (pert to)...
mother.. 5. Venus
sweetheart.. 6. Psyche
title.. 3. Dan
cupidity... 4. lust 5. greed 6. desire

7. avarice, avidity, longing
8. appetite, avidness, rapacity
cuplike (pert to)...
calyx.. 9. calicular
stone.. 5. geode
vessel.. 4. zarf
cupola... 4. dome, kiln 5. tower
6. concha (Arch) 7. ceiling, furnace
(foundry)
cur... 3. dog 4. mutt 7. gurnard (fish),
mongrel 9. goldeneye
curare, curari... 5. urali 7. extract
9. Strychnos 11. arrow poison
curate... 4. abbé 6. cleric, parson,
pastor, priest 7. dominie
9. clergyman
curator... 6. keeper 7. manager,
steward 8. guardian 9. custodian,
librarian, treasurer
curb... 3. bit 4. rein 5. check, limit
6. arrest, border, bridle, market
(Finan) 7. control, inhibit, repress
8. restrict 9. hindrance, restraint
curd... 4. crud 6. casein
curds and whey... 7. clabber
cure... 4. balm, heal, salt 5. smoke
6. elixir, remedy, rizzor 7. nostrum,
panacea, restore, therapy 8. preserve
10. corrective
curio... 8. artifact 9. bric–a–brac,
curiosity
curiosity... 5. curio 6. gabion (rare),
oddity, prying, wonder 8. interest
9. exception, spectacle
14. meddlesomeness
15. inquisitiveness
curious... 3. odd 4. rare 5. nosey
(nosy), outre, queer 6. prying, quaint
7. careful, strange, unusual
8. cautious, meddling, singular
9. inquiring, intrusive 10. meticulous
11. inquisitive
ourl... 4. coil, kink, lock, roll 5. crimp,
crisp, frizz, tress, twirl, twist
6. marcel, spiral 7. crinkle, frizzle,
ringlet 8. curlicue 9. corkscrew
11. convolution
curled... 5. curly, spiry 6. coiled
7. crimped, savoyed, twisted
8. wrinkled (Bot)
curlew... 4. bird, fute 5. kioea, snipe,
whaup 6. marlin 7. bustard
8. whimbrel
curlewlike... 6. godwit 9. sandpiper
curly... 4. wavy 5. kinky, oundy (obs)
6. crispy, frizzy, kinked 8. crinkled
curmudgeon... 4. crab 5. churl, miser
7. niggard 8. tightwad 9. skinflint
currant... 3. red 5. berry, Ribes
6. raisin, rizzar (rizzart)
currency... 5. money, scrip 6. dinero
9. publicity 10. greenbacks,
popularity, prevalence
15. fashionableness
ourrent... 4. eddy, flow, race (water),
rife, tide 5. draft, going, rapid,
trend, usual 6. course, stream
7. present, topical 8. existent
9. direction, prevalent
11. fashionable
current regulator...
electric.. 9. rheometer

12. galvanometer
physiology.. 11. hematometer
curriculum... 7. courses, studies, Three
R's 8. curricle
curry... 4. comb, cook, drub 5. dress,
groom 6. cajole 9. condiment
curry favor... 6. cajole 7. flatter,
smoodge (smooge), wheedle
curse... 3. ban 4. bane, damn, oath
5. swear 7. bewitch, malison
8. anathema, execrate 9. blaspheme
10. affliction 11. imprecation,
malediction 13. excommunicate
cursed... 6. damned, odious, wicked
7. hateful 8. damnable, shrewish
9. execrable 12. cantankerous
Cursores... 5. birds (long–legged)
7. spiders (wolf)
Cursoria... 6. mantes (mantis)
10. Orthoptera 11. cockroaches
cursory... 5. hasty 6. fitful, roving,
slight 7. passing 8. careless,
rambling 9. desultory, irregular
10. evanescent 12. disconnected,
unmethodical
curt... 4. buff 5. bluff, brief, brusk,
gruff, short, terse 6. abrupt
7. brusque, concise, curtate, laconic
9. condensed
curtail... 3. lop 4. crop, dock, pare,
slip 5. short 6. lessen, reduce
7. abridge, shorten 8. compress,
decrease, diminish, retrench
curtain... 4. mask, veil 5. drape,
shade 6. coster (altar), encore,
purdah, riddel, screen, shadow, shield
7. drapery, secrecy, shelter, vitrage
8. portiere
curtsy, curtsey... 3. bow, nod
4. bend 6. kowtow, salaam
12. genuflection
curvature... 3. arc, bow 4. arch, bend
5. plane, sinus 6. camber
7. arching, curving, evolute
8. aduncity, cyrtosis, lordosis,
vaulting 9. curvation 11. convolution
curve... 3. arc, bow, ess 4. arch,
bend, ogee, turn 5. crook, polar
6. spiral, toroid 7. cissoid, evolute,
flexure 8. extrados, parabola, sinusoid
9. curvature, sinuosity
curved (pert to)...
arch.. 8. arciform, arcuated
glass.. 4. lens
inward.. 5. adunc 8. aduncous
molding.. 4. ogee
planking (ship's).. 3. sny
process.. 5. hamus (Zool)
roundabout.. 10. circuitous
staircase.. 8. caracole
wedge.. 3. cam
curvet... 4. leap 5. bound, caper,
frisk, prank 6. frolic, gambol
cush... 3. cow 5. money 7. cookery,
sorghum
Cush (pert to)...
father.. 3. Ham
land of.. 8. Ethiopia 10. land of Cush
son.. 4. Seba 6. Nimrod
cushion... 3. pad 4. mute, seat
6. ignore, pillow, sachet 7. brioche,
conceal, dashpot, muffler 8. plantula,

pulvinus, suppress, swelling (Queen
Mary's) 9. pulvillus 10. pincushion
cusk... 4. fish (codlike), tusk 5. torsk
6. burbot
cusp... 3. end, tip 4. apex, peak
5. crown, point 6. cantle, corner
8. paracone
custard... 4. flan 7. charlet, pudding
custard apple... 4. tree 5. papaw
8. sweetsop
custodian... 5. guard 6. bailee, jailer,
keeper, warden, warder 7. curator,
janitor 8. curatrix, guardian
custody... 4. care, keep 5. trust
6. charge 8. guidance 10. protection
12. guardianship, jurisdiction
custom... 3. fad, law, mos, use
4. mode, wont 5. habit, mores,
usage, vogue 7. fashion 8. practice
9. patronage, tradition
10. consuetude, consuetudo
customary... 5. usual 6. wonted
7. general, usitate 8. habitual,
orthodox 11. traditional
12. conventional
customs... 4. duty 5. mores, taxes
cut... 3. bob, lob, lop, mow, nip, rip
4. blow, chop, crop, dock, edit, fell,
gash, hack, make, mode, nick, open,
pain, pare, reap, slit, snee, snip,
snub, trim 5. canal, carve, cleft,
lance, notch, piece, plate, scarp,
sever, share, shear, shorn, slash,
slice, slish (Shak), snick, split, vogue
6. dilute, furrow, injury, mangle,
reduce, trench 7. affront, curtail,
engrave, offense, sectile, serrate,
truancy, whittle 8. discount, excision,
incision 9. engraving, indignity,
reduction 10. adulterate
cut (pert to)...
and furrow.. 7. chamfer
and polish.. 8. lapidate
and weave.. 5. plash
back.. 6. polled 7. shorten
capable of being.. 7. sectile
down.. 5. razee
fine.. 5. mince
in.. 7. intrude 9. interpose, interrupt,
introduce
in half.. 9. dimidiate
in squares.. 4. dice
into.. 6. incise
jaggedly.. 4. snag
out.. 6. excide, excise
up.. 6. frolic, grieve 9. apportion,
misbehave
vertically.. 5. scarp, slice
with shears.. 4. snip 5. shirl
cutaneous... 4. skin 6. dermal, dermic
cute... 4. keen 5. peart, sharp
6. brainy, clever, dainty, pretty,
shrewd 7. cunning 10. attractive
11. picturesque
cuticle... 4. skin 5. cutin, cutis
8. membrane, pellicle 9. epidermis,
scarfskin 10. integument
cut of beef... 4. loin, ribs, rump
5. chine, roast, steak 6. corned,
cutlet, rosbif, saddle 7. brisket,
icebone 8. shoulder 9. aitchbone,
roundbone

cut off... 3. bob 4. crop, dock, drib,
snip 5. elide, pared, roach (Naut)
6. bereft, bobbed, divest, lopped,
screen 7. abscind, abscise, clipped,
deprive, severed 8. amputate
9. amputated, apocopate, intercept
10. disinherit

cut off (pert to)...
by bits.. 4. drib
edges (coins).. 3. nig
on slant.. 4. bias 5. bevel, miter
short.. 3. bob 4. crop
syllable.. 5. elide
with die.. 4. dink
wool.. 3. dod (dodd)

cut short... 3. bob, lop 4. crop, dock,
halt, stop 5. check 6. arrest
7. clipped, cropped, curtail, shorten
9. terminate

cutter... 4. boat 5. knife, sloop, tooth
6. sleigh, vessel 7. incisor

cutting... 4. cold, slip, tart 5. piece,
scion, sharp 6. biting, secant, severe
7. caustic, incisal, sathic, swulle
8. chilling, piercing 9. sarcastic,
severance, trenchant 10. separating
11. penetrating 12. adulteration

cutting (pert to)...
diamonds (imperfect).. 4. bort
edge.. 5. blade
in two.. 6. secant
last letter of word.. 7. apocope
off.. 7. apocope 10. abscission,
amputation
tool.. 3. axe (ax), bit 4. adze 5. razor
6. chisel
wit.. 6. satire

outtle... 4. thug 5. knife 7. ruffian
8. assassin 9. swaggerer

cuttlebone... 7. osselet

cuttlefish... 5. Sepia, squid
7. mollusk, octopus

cuttlefish secretion... 3. ink (black)

cuttyhunk... 11. fishing line

Cyclades Islands (Gr)... (200 in all)
3. Ios 5. Delos (smallest), Melos,
Naros, Paros, Tenos, Thera 6. Andros
7. Amorgos, Myconus

cycle... 3. Age, eon, era 4. aeon
5. orbit, recur, saros (Astron), wheel
6. course, period, series 7. bicycle,
circuit 8. electric, tricycle
9. Arthurian 10. revolution
12. Carlovingian (Charlemagne)

cyclone... 5. storm 6. baguio
7. tornado, twister, typhoon
9. hurricane

cyclopean... 4. huge, vast 7. massive,
one–eyed 8. gigantic

Cyclops (pert to)...
assistant to.. 6. Vulcan (Fire God)
father.. 6. Uranus
forger of.. 12. thunderbolts
home.. 6. Sicily (Mt Etna)
oddity.. 7. one–eyed
race (Myth).. 6. giants

cygneous... 8. swanlike

cygnet... 4. swan

cylinder... 4. drum, pipe, roll, tube
5. inker, stele 6. barrel, gabion,

platen, record, roller, rounce, terete
10. cylindroid

cylindrical... 5. conic 6. terete
7. tubular

cymbal, cymbals... 3. tal, zel
6. Becken, piatti 7. potlids
8. doughnut

Cymric... 5. Welsh 9. Brythonic

Cymric (pert to)...
bard.. 6. Merlin 7. Aneurin
god of the dead.. 5. Pwyll
god of the sky.. 7. Gwydion
god of the sun.. 4. Lleu
god of the waves.. 5. Dylan

cynic... 5. Timon 7. ascetic, doglike,
egotist, snarler 9. pessimist
11. misanthrope

Cynic (pert to)...
pupil.. 8. Socrates
school.. 10. Philosophy
teacher.. 8. Diogenes
teaching.. 6. virtue

cynical... 7. currish 8. captious,
snarling 9. sardonic 11. pessimistic
12. misanthropic

cynosure... 5. guide 8. lodestar
(loadstar), polestar 9. celebrity, North
Star 13. constellation

cyprinoid (fish)... 2. id 3. ide, orf
(orfe) 4. bass (black), carp, chub,
dace 6. chevin, shiner 7. herring
(lake) 8. fallfish 9. hornyhead,
squawfish

Cyprus...
capital.. 7. Nicosia (Sicily)
colonizer (anc).. 11. Phoenicians
history.. 11. New Stone Age
mountain.. 7. Troodos
port.. 7. Lornaca 8. Limassol
9. Famagusto

Cyrenaic (pert to)...
city.. 6. Cyrene
country.. 9. Cyrenaica (Afr)
division of.. 5. Libya
harbor.. 6. Tobruk 7. Bengazi
philosophy.. 8. hedonism, pleasure

Cyrene... 4. city (anc) 5. nymph
7. goddess

cyrus... 5. crane, sarus

Cyrus the Elder (pert to)...
conqueror of.. 7. Babylon
founder of.. 6. Persia (Empire)
king of.. 5. Lydia, Media
subduer of.. 9. Palestine

cyst... 3. box, sac, wen 5. chest,
pouch 7. vesicle

Czar... 4. Ivan, tsar, tzar 5. Peter
8. Nicholas

Czechoslovakia...
capital.. 6. Prague (Praha)
city.. 5. Praha 6. Pilsen 7. Ostrava
10. Bratislava
empire (anc).. 7. Bohemia, Moravia
8. Slovakia
forest.. 12. Great Bohemia
mountain, peak.. 3. Ore 6. Tatras
11. Carpathians
people.. 6. Czechs 7. Slovaks
river.. 4. Elbe (Labe), Iser, Oder
6. Vltava

czigany... 5. gypsy

D

D ... 3. 500 6. letter (4th)

dab ... 3. hit, tap 4. blow 5. paint, smear 6. expert, lizard, smooth 7. dabster 8. flatfish

dabble ... 4. mass 5. dally 6. befoul, meddle, paddle, potter, splash, tamper, trifle 7. spatter 8. sprinkle

dabbler ... 7. trifler 8. sciolist 10. dilettante

dabchick ... 5. grebe 9. gallinule

dacha (Russ) ... 5. villa 12. country house

dacoit ... 6. bandit, robber

dacry, dacryo (comb form) ... 5. tears

dactyl ... 3. toe 4. foot 6. finger 8. dactylus

dactyliomancy ... 17. divination by rings (finger)

dactylogram ... 11. fingerprint

dactylology ... 12. sign language

Dadaism ... 4. cult 8. negation

daddy–longlegs ... 5. stilt 6. curlew, spider, Tipula 7. spinner

daedal, dedal ... 4. rich 6. varied 8. artistic, skillful (skilful) 9. ingenious, intricate 10. variegated

Daedalus (Gr Myth) ... 9. artificer

daffodil ... 6. yellow 9. narcissus 10. bellflower

daffy, daft ... 3. gay, mad 4. wild 5. batty, crazy, giddy, goofy, loony 6. insane 7. foolish, idiotic

Dagda (pert to) ...
children .. 6. Aengus (Angus), Brigit
famed as .. 7. harpist
Gaelic name .. 7. Jupiter
god of .. 10. pagan Irish

dagger ... 4. dirk, kris, snee 5. kalar 6. anlace, bodkin, creese 7. bayonet, poniard 10. misericord

Daibutsu (pert to) ...
famed image .. 6. Buddha
Japanese Bronze .. 11. Great Buddha
site .. 8. Kamakura (near Tokyo)

daily ... 4. a day 7. diurnal, journal 9. hodiurnal, newspaper, quotidian 11. day in day out

daily food ... 4. fare 5. bread 10. livelihood 11. subsistence, substenance

dainties ... 5. cates, estes 7. titbits (tidbits)

dainty ... 4. fair, fine, rare 5. frail, small 6. choice, pretty, select 8. elegance 9. exquisite, toothsome 10. fastidious

dairy ... 4. farm 8. creamery 9. lactarium

dairymen caste (Ind) ... 4. Ahir

dais ... 5. stage, table 7. estrade 8. platform

daisy ... 5. gowan, oxeye 6. morgan, Shasta 7. Gerbera 9. Whiteweed

dale ... 4. dell, dene, vale 5. spout 6. dingle, ravine, trough, valley

dalles ... 5. dells 11. canyon walls

dalliance ... 4. chat 5. delay 6. gossip, trifle 8. fondling, trifling 10. flirtation

dally ... 3. toy 5. tarry 6. dawdle, linger 13. procrastinate

Dalmatia ...
capital .. 7. Spalato (Yugoslavia)
cherry .. 7. marasca
coast .. 8. Adriatic
dog .. 5. coach 8. carriage
home of .. 10. Diocletian
people .. 5. Serbs 8. Adriatic 9. Yugoslavs
product .. 4. lace

dam ... 4. stay, stem, stop, weir 5. Aswan, block, check, choke, Gatun (CZ) 6. Hoover (Boulder), mother, Norris, parent 7. barrier 8. millpond, obstruct, Oroville, restrain 9. Roosevelt 10. Bull Shoals, Glen Canyon 11. Grand Coulee

damage ... 3. mar 4. harm, hurt, loss, noxa 6. impair, injury, mayhem, scathe, strafe 8. disserve, sabotage 9. detriment, vandalism 10. impairment

daman ... 4. cony (Bib) 5. Hyrax 6. mammal 8. Procavia

Damascus, Syria (pert to) ...
Bib scene .. 20. Street Called Straight
division .. 6. Jewish, Moslem 9. Christian
history .. 16. world's oldest city (inhabited)
mosque (renowned) .. 7. Ommiade
river .. 5. Abana 6. Barada

damask ... 3. red (color) 5. cloth, steel (Damascus) 8. to deface (the Great Seal, Eng)

dame ... 4. lady, Miss 5. Madam, title 6. matron, Nature, parent

damn ... 4. cuss, ruin 5. abuse, curse 6. shucks 7. accurse, condemn, swear at

damsel ... 4. girl, lass 5. Rhoda (Bib), wench 7. colleen 10. damoiselle

dance ... 4. jazz, prom, skip, trip 5. frisk, glide 6. cavort, frolic, gambol 7. flicker, flutter, rejoice, saltate 10. tripudiate

dance (pert to) ...
art .. 12. choreography
clumsily .. 6. balter
mimetic (Rom) .. 5. Salii 7. Luperci

146

8. Curetics
movement.. 6. chassé, gestic
7. saltant 9. pirouette
step.. 3. pas 5. coupe 6. chassé
7. gambado (gambade), shuffle
8. glissade 9. arabesque, grapevine
10. pigeonwing
dance (type)... 3. bal, hop, jig, toe
4. ball, clog, haka, kolo, polo, reel,
shag 5. gavot (gavotte), pavan,
polka, tango, waltz 6. althea, apache,
ballet, bolero, cancan, corant, maxixe,
minuet, morris, redowa, rhumba
(rumba), shimmy, square, watusi
7. beguine, coranto (old), courant,
foxtrot, gavotte, hoedown, mazurka,
one–step, ridotto, tempete, two–step
8. bunny hug, cakewalk, courante,
fandango, halliard (anc), hornpipe,
lanciers, rigadoon 9. allemande (anc),
butterfly, farandole, polonaise,
quadrille 10. Charleston, tarantella
11. schottische (schottish)
dancer... 6. hoofer 7. danseur
8. coryphee, danseuse, stripper
9. ballerina, ecdysiast, jitterbug
11. terpsichore 13. choreographer
dancer (pert to)...
Bib.. 6. Salome
Egyptian.. 4. alme (almeh) 7. ghawazi
8. Baramika
Japanese.. 6. geisha (girl)
Oriental.. 4. hula 6. nautch
8. bayadere
dancing (pert to)...
arrangement.. 12. choreography
Muse of.. 11. Terpsichore
term.. 6. ballet, chassé, gestic
7. hoofing, saltant
dandelion... 4. herb 5. plant 6. yellow
9. Taraxacum
dandified 7. foppish
dandify... 6. spruce 7. adonize,
smarten 8. titivate (tittivate)
dandy... 3. fop 4. beau, dude, good,
toff 5. daisy 6. Adonis 7. coxcomb
9. exquisite 11. Beau Brummel
dangerous... 3. bad 4. dire 5. feral,
risky 6. chancy 7. ominous, parlous
8. alarming, critical, insecure,
perilous 9. hazardous 10. jeopardous,
precarious
dangle... 3. lop 4. hang, loll, yawl
5. droop, swing 6. flaunt, mizzen
Daniel (pert to)...
Bib.. 4. Book (Old Test) 7. prophet
(Heb)
form of verse.. 7. lyrical, sestina
verse adopted by.. 5. Dante
8. Petrarch
Danish... see also Denmark
capital.. 10. Copenhagen
council (anc).. 8. Rigsraad
country.. 7. Denmark
doctor.. 6. Finsen
export.. 8. cryolite
fiord.. 3. Ise
flag.. 9. Dannebrog
island.. 3. Als (Alsen) 5. Faroe
9. Greenland
King (anc).. 6. Canute
native.. 4. Dane 12. Scandinavian

parliament.. 7. Rigsdag
prince (legend).. 6. Hamlet
settlers in Ireland.. 6. Ostmen
dank... 3. wet 4. damp 5. humid,
moist, muggy
Dan McGrew... 11. Hound of Hell
danseuse... 7. danseur 8. coryphee
9. ballerina
Dante (pert to)...
birthplace.. 8. Florence
famed as.. 4. poet 6. lyrist
famed poem.. 12. Divine Comedy
poem's companion.. 6. Vergil (Virgil)
poem's division.. 4. Hell 6. Heaven
9. Purgatory
poem's love.. 8. Beatrice
Danube River (pert to)...
end.. 8. Black Sea
source.. 11. Black Forest
tributary.. 4. Isar, Raab 5. Drava
6. Morava
Danubian (pert to)...
color.. 5. green
fish.. 6. huchen (huch)
goose.. 10. Sevastopol
Danzig...
Polish name.. 6. Gdansk
river site.. 7. Vistula
Sea.. 6. Baltic
territory of (now).. 6. Poland
dap... 3. bob, dab, dib, dip
6. bounce, dibble, guddle 7. rebound
Daphne (pert to)...
Bib.. 4. Park (Antioch, Syria)
father.. 5. Ladon 6. Peneus
lover.. 6. Apollo
transformation.. 10. laurel tree
dapper... 4. braw, neat, pert, trim
5. natty, sleek 6. jaunty, little, lively,
spruce 7. dashing, finical
dappled... 6. dotted 7. flecked,
piebald, spotted
dare... 4. daze, defy, face, osse, risk
5. brave 6. assume, dazzle
7. venture 8. confront, defiance,
paralyze 9. challenge, undertake
daring... 4. bold, rash 5. brave, manly
8. boldness, defiance 9. audacious,
foolhardy 11. adventurous,
venturesome 12. enterprising
dark... 3. dim, mum, sad 4. ebon
5. black, blind, dense, faint, mirky,
murky, night, unlit, vague 6. closed,
gloomy, occult, opaque, secret,
wicked 7. joyless, melanic, obscure,
stygian 8. abstruse, ignorant,
moonless 9. ambiguous, atrocious,
Cimmerian (realm), lightless, nightfall,
tenebrous, uncertain 10. foreboding,
indistinct
dark (pert to)...
Ages.. 6. Middle 8. Medieval
9. Neolithic
Continent.. 6. Africa (formerly)
10. unexplored
horse.. 7. unknown 9. candidate
hue.. 5. dusky, swart 6. somber
7. swarthy
moon area.. 4. mare
darken... 3. dim 4. dull 5. blind,
umber 6. darkle, sadden, shadow
7. becloud, blacken, confuse, eclipse,

enshade 8. bewilder 9. obfuscate

darkness... 4. dark, dusk, mirk, murk
5. shade 6. Erebus, shadow
7. dimness, tenebra 9. blackness,
blindness, ignorance, obscurity
10. opaqueness

darling... 2. jo 3. pet 4. dear, idol,
lief 5. cheri, sweet 6. minion
7. acushla, beloved 8. favorite
9. mavournin 10. mavourneen,
sweetheart 13. cushlamochree
(cushlamachree)

darnel... 4. tare, weed 5. grass
6. Lolium

dart... 4. barb, bolt, flit, leap, vire
5. arrow, bound, lance, scoot, shoot,
start, throw 6. dartle, elance, glance,
spring, weapon 7. javelin, missile,
stinger 8. jaculate

Darwinism... 9. Evolution (theory,
1858) 12. Evolutionism

das, dasse... 6. badger

dash... 4. code, élan, gift, race, ruin,
rush, slam 5. ardor, crash, haste,
onset, plash, smash, speed, swash
6. energy, obelus (anc), spirit, sprint,
strike, stroke 7. bravura, spatter,
splurge 8. confound, gratuity
9. animation 11. punctuation

dashing... 3. gay 4. fast 5. showy
6. dapper, jaunty, sporty 7. stylish

dastardly... 4. base, foul 6. craven
8. cowardly

data... 5. facts, logic 7. grounds (for
facts) 11. information

date... 3. age 4. line (newspaper),
time 5. fruit, tryst 6. person
10. engagement 11. appointment

date (pert to)...
birth.. 5. natal
coin line.. 7. exergue
error.. 11. anachronism
fruit of.. 4. palm
plum.. 6. sapote

daub... 3. dab 4. blob, gaum, soil,
teer 5. paint, smear, stain, sully
6. bedaub 7. besmear, picture (art),
plaster 8. scribble

daughter... 5. child 7. cadette
9. offspring 10. descendant

daughter of...
Inachus (river god).. 2. Io
Night.. 7. Nemesis
the moon.. 7. Nokomis
the Spanish king.. 7. infanta

daunt... 3. awe, cow 4. faze 5. amate
(anc) 6. dismay, subdue 7. overawe,
repress 10. discourage, dishearten,
intimidate

dauntless... 4. bold 7. aweless
(awless) 8. fearless, intrepid, resolute
9. dreadless 11. unfaltering

davenport... 3. bed 4. desk, sofa
5. divan 12. Chesterfield

David (Bib)...
daughter.. 5. Tamar
father.. 5. Jesse
helpers.. 4. Igal 5. Abner
7. Shammah
king of.. 6. Israel (40 years)
slayer of.. 7. Goliath
son.. 7. Solomon

wife.. 7. Abigail

davit... 4. spar 5. crane

dawdle... 3. lag 4. idle, poke, toit
5. dally 6. linger, loiter, potter, trifle
9. vacillate 10. dillydally
13. procrastinate

dawn... 2. eo (comb form) 3. Eos
(goddess), red 4. morn 5. sunup
6. appear, aurora, sink in 7. sunrise
8. daybreak 9. beginning, penetrate

day (pert to)...
Athenians, Jews.. 6. sunset
Babylonians.. 7. sunrise
blindness.. 10. nyctalopia
11. hemeralopia
divisions.. 5. lunar, solar 8. sidereal
dream.. 4. muse 5. fancy 7. fantasy,
reverie 8. phantasy
Egyptians, Romans.. 8. midnight
god.. 5. Horus
nursery.. 6. crèche
scholar.. 7. externe

Day of...
Atonement.. 9. Yom Kippur
Brahma.. 9. Maha Yugas
doom.. 8. Judgment

day's march... 5. étape

day's work... 4. darg (dargue)

daze... 3. fog 4. asea, maze, stun
5. sopor, swoon 6. benumb, dazzle,
stupid, trance 7. confuse, stupefy
8. bewilder 9. dumbfound
12. razzle–dazzle

dazzling... 6. bright, garish 7. glaring
8. blinding, gorgeous 9. beautiful,
brilliant 11. bewildering

dead... 3. fey 4. flat, numb, obit
5. amort, blind, inert, napoo, passé
6. active, barren, lapsed 7. defunct,
expired, insipid, tedious 8. ad patres,
complete, deceased, inactive, lifeless,
obsolete 9. apathetic, inanimate
10. lusterless, motionless, spiritless,
unexciting 11. nonexistent

dead (pert to)...
Dead Sea apple.. 12. Apple of
Sodom
Dead Sea country.. 4. Moab
5. Sodom 8. Gomorrah
language.. 5. Latin
rise from the.. 7. resurge
9. reanimate, resurrect
set (slang).. 8. full tilt, hell–bent
tree.. 7. rampike (rampick)

deaden... 4. damp, dull, mute, numb
6. muffle, obtund, opiate, weaken
7. relieve, repress 8. enfeeble
10. devitalize

deadly... 4. dire, mort 5. fatal
6. lethal, mortal 7. deathly
8. venomous 10. implacable,
lifelessly 11. destructive, internecine

deaf... 4. surd 7. earless
10. intolerant 11. inattentive,
preoccupied

deaf alphabet... 11. dactylology
12. sign language

deaf and dumb... 9. surdomute
10. deaf–mutism 11. surdimutism

deafness... 6. amusia (tone) 7. surdity
13. insensibility

deafness operation... 8. fenestra

deal . . . 3. lot 4. dole, give, mede,
mete, sale, sell 5. allot, share, trade,
treat 6. parcel 7. dispose, portion,
wrestle 8. business, dispense,
quantity 9. apportion, entertain
10. administer, distribute
dealer (pert to) . . .
　cattle . . 6. drover, herder
　cloth . . 6. draper, mercer
　drug . . 8. druggist 10. apothecary,
　pharmacist 14. pharmacopolist
　retail . . 6. grocer, monger 8. merchant
　9. tradesman
　stock exchange . . 6. broker, jobber,
　trader 11. stockbroker
dean, dene . . . 4. dell 6. valley
dean . . . 4. head, Inge 5. decan, doyen
6. fellow (Educ), master, senior,
verger 7. officer 9. churchman,
principal
dear . . . 5. chere, cheri, deary, lover,
sugar, sweet 7. beloved, darling
8. precious 9. expensive
10. sweetheart
dearth . . . 4. want 6. famine, rarity
7. paucity, poverty 8. rareness,
scarcity, sparsity
death . . . 4. doom, mort, obit 5. sleep
(eternal) 6. demise 7. decease,
passing, quietus, release
10. euthanasia (mercy), expiration
11. evanishment
death (pert to) . . .
　after . . 10. posthumous
　eternal . . 9. perdition
　foreboding . . 6. funest 7. doleful
　lawless . . 8. lynching
　notice . . 4. obit 5. orbit 8. obituary
　of a deity . . 4. Mors
　rattle . . 4. rale
　stoning (by) . . 8. lapidate
deathlessness . . . 9. athanasis
11. immortality 15. everlastingness
debacle . . . 4. rout 5. crash, flood
7. washout 8. collapse, stampede
9. breakdown, cataclysm
11. catastrophe, destruction
debar . . . 3. bar 4. deny 5. estop
6. forbid, hinder, refuse 7. exclude
8. obstruct, preclude, prohibit
debark . . . 4. land 8. go ashore
9. disembark
debase . . . 5. abase, alloy, lower
6. demean, demote, reduce
7. corrupt, degrade, deprave
8. disgrace 10. adulterate, depreciate
11. deteriorate
debasement . . . 8. demotion
9. abasement, abjection, reduction,
vitiation 11. degradation
13. deterioration
debatable . . . 4. moot 9. refutable
10. disputable 11. contestable
13. controversial
debate . . . 4. agon (anc), moot
5. argue, forum, plead, weigh
6. reason 7. analyze, closure,
cloture, dispute, wrangle
8. argument, consider, forensic,
militate 9. quodlibet 10. deliberate,
discussion 11. controversy
12. deliberation, dissertation

13. argumentation
debauch . . . 4. bout, orgy 5. broil,
spree, taint 6. defile, seduce, splore
7. mislead 8. carousal, escapade
9. disaffect, dissipate
11. contaminate
debauchee . . . 4. rake, roué 5. satyr
7. rounder 9. libertine 10. profligate
debenture (Finan) . . . 4. bond 5. claim
6. pledge 7. voucher 10. instrument
11. certificate
debilitated 4. weak 5. seedy
6. feeble, infirm, sapped, sickly
7. languid 8. asthenic, impaired,
weakened 9. enfeebled, langorous
11. devitalized
debility . . . 5. atony 7. languor
8. adynamia, asthenia, cachexia,
weakness 9. infirmity, lassitude
10. feebleness, sickliness
debit . . . 4. debt 5. entry 6. charge
debonair, debonaire . . . 4. airy
5. suave 6. breezy, jaunty, urbane
7. affable, buoyant 8. carefree
debris . . . 4. junk 5. attle, ruins, scrap,
talus, trash 6. litter, refuse, rubble
7. deposit, remains, rubbish
8. detritus 10. clamjamfry
debt . . . 3. due, IOU, sin (Bib)
7. arrears, default 8. trespass
9. arrearage, liability 10. obligation
debut . . . 3. bow 8. entrance (formal)
9. coming out 12. introduction,
presentation
debutante . . . 3. bud, deb 6. subdeb
9. socialite
decade . . . 3. ten 9. decennium
decadence . . . 5. decay 7. decline
13. deterioration, retrogression
decamp . . . 4. flee 6. depart
7. abscond, vamoose
12. absquatulate
decanter . . . 4. ewer 5. croft 6. bottle,
carafe, vessel (liquors)
decapod . . . 4. crab 5. prawn 6. shrimp
7. Homarus, lobster 8. Decapoda
10. crustacean
decay . . . 3. rot 4. blet, doty 5. spoil,
waste 6. caries, wither 7. crumble,
mortify, putrefy 8. spoilage
9. decadence, decompose
11. deteriorate, dissolution
13. decomposition, deterioration
deceased . . . 4. dead, gone, late 6. at
rest 7. defunct, demised
8. decedent, departed
deceit . . . 5. covin, craft, fraud, guile,
guise 7. cunning 8. artifice,
cozenage, intrigue, subtlety, trickery,
wiliness 9. chicanery, deception,
duplicity, imposture, mendacity,
sophistry, treachery 10. craftiness,
sneakiness 13. deceitfulness,
dissimulation 14. tergiversation
15. treacherousness
deceitful . . . 4. wily 5. false 6. artful,
crafty, sneaky, tricky 8. guileful,
scheming, trickish 9. deceptive,
gnathonic, insincere 10. fraudulent
11. Machiavellian 13. Machiavellian
deceive . . . 3. cog, lie 4. bilk, dupe,
flam, fool, gull, hoax, sile 5. cheat,

cozen, elude, hocus, trick, troil
6. baffle, delude, illude, seduce
7. beguile, mislead 8. hoodwink
deceiver ... 3. gay 5. cheat 6. hoaxer,
trepan (trapan) 8. betrayer, impostor
9. trickster
decency ... 7. decorum, fitness,
modesty 8. chastity, niceness
9. propriety 10. seemliness
12. tastefulness
decent ... 4. kind 6. comely, kindly,
proper, seemly 7. clothed
8. adequate, gracious, suitable,
tasteful 9. tolerable
deception ... 3. lie 4. hoax, wile
5. cheat, fraud, guile 6. deceit,
misled 7. fallacy 8. artifice, deceived,
flimflam, illusion 9. duplicity,
imposture
deceptive ... 5. vague 8. illusive,
illusory 9. deceiving, sirenical (sirenic)
10. fallacious
decide (upon) ... 3. opt 4. vote
5. adapt, elect, judge 6. choose,
settle 7. referee, resolve 9. arbitrate,
ascertain, determine, influence
decima ... 4. stop (organ) 5. tenth,
tithe 8. interval
decimal ... 3. ten 5. tenth 7. tenfold
8. repetend
decimate ... 3. few 4. kill, slay
5. burke, tenth 6. divide 7. destroy
8. subtract 9. devastate, slaughter
decipher ... 4. read 5. crack
6. decode, detect 7. unravel
8. discover 9. translate
decision ... 4. grit 5. arret, nerve,
pluck 6. mettle, report 7. verdict
8. firmness 10. conclusion,
resolution, settlement
12. announcement 13. determination
decisive ... 3. end 5. final 7. certain,
crucial 8. critical, resolute
9. mandatory 10. conclusive,
convincing
decisive moment ... 6. crisis
deck (ship's) ... 3. gun 4. main, poop
5. orlop, upper 6. bridge 7. scupper
(gutter) 8. hatchway, platform
9. promenade 10. forecastle
deck ... 4. gild 5. adorn, array, cards
(playing), equip 6. blazon, clothe,
enrich 7. bedizen, dress up
8. emblazon
declaim ... 4. rant, rave 5. orate, spiel,
spout 6. herald, recite 8. denounce,
harangue, perorate 9. discourse
11. declamation
declamation ... 7. lecture 9. elocution
10. recitation
declaration ... 3. vow 4. oath
6. avowal, decree, oracle 8. pleading
(law) 9. assertion, manifesto,
testimony 10. confession (of faith)
11. affirmation 12. proclamation
13. pronouncement
declare ... 3. say 4. aver, avow, meld
5. bruit, state 6. affirm, allege,
assert, blazon, herald, spread
7. publish 8. announce, indicate,
maintain 9. advertise
declare (pert to) ...

against .. 6. indict
as fact .. 5. posit
innocent .. 6. acquit
declension ... 4. drop, fall 5. slope
7. decline, descent, refusal
10. inflection 13. deterioration
decline ... 3. dip, ebb, set 4. fade, fail,
fall, flag, sink, wane 5. droop, repel,
slope, slump, stoop 6. refuse, reject,
weaken 7. dwindle 8. decrease,
downhill 9. decadence, declivity,
repudiate 10. retrograde
12. depreciation
declivity ... 3. dip 4. drop, hill
5. scarp, slope 7. descent
8. downgate 9. downgrade
decoction ... 4. sapa (sape) 6. apozem,
cremor, tisane 7. boiling
10. extraction 11. preparation
decompose ... 3. rot 4. frit 5. decay
7. resolve 10. photolysis
12. disintegrate
decorate ... 4. deck, trim 5. adorn,
honor 6. emboss 7. bedizen,
brocade, miniate 8. beautify,
ornament 9. scrimshaw
decorated ... 5. fancy 6. ornate
7. adorned 8. nielloed 9. sigillate
(pottery) 11. embellished
decoration ... 4. buhl 5. gutta (anc)
medal 6. plaque, purfle, ribbon
7. epergne, festoon, garnish 8. gold
star, ornament, trimming
9. adornment, garniture, sgraffito
10. cordon bleu, emblazonry,
embroidery
decorous ... 4. calm, prim 5. grave,
quiet, staid 6. decent, demure,
modest, proper, sedate, seemly,
serene 7. fitting, regular, settled
8. becoming, composed, suitable,
tasteful 9. unruffled 12. conventional
decorticate ... 4. bark, flay, husk, pare,
peel, skin 5. strip 9. excoriate
decoy ... 4. bait, lure, tole 6. capper,
entrap 8. by—bidder 9. come—on man
11. stool pigeon
decrease ... 3. ebb 4. drop, sink, wane
5. abate, waste 6. decess, lessen,
reduce, shrink 7. decline, dwindle,
shorten, slacken, subside
8. compress, diminish, moderate
9. abatement, deduction, deflation,
lessening 10. diminution
11. contraction 12. depreciation
decree ... 3. act, law 4. bull, fiat, rede
(anc), will 5. arret, canon, edict,
enact, irade, order, ukase 6. dictum,
ordain 7. command, mandate, verdict
8. decision, rescript 9. ordinance
decree beforehand ... 7. destine
decree nisi ... 7. divorce
decrepit ... 3. old 4. aged, lame, weak
6. infirm, senile, wasted (with age)
7. worn out 8. unstable, unsturdy
decry ... 3. boo 4. slur 5. lower
7. condemn, degrade, detract
8. belittle, denounce, derogate
9. discredit, disparage, underrate
10. depreciate, undervalue
dedal ... see _daedal_
dedicate ... 6. devote, hallow

7. address 8. inscribe
10. consecrate
deduce... 5. infer 6. deduct, derive, elicit, evolve 7. suppose
deduct... 4. bate, faik, take 6. remove 8. discount, retrench, separate, subtract
deduction... 6. rebate 7. reprise 8. discount, illation 9. allowance, corollary, induction, inference, reasoning, syllogism
deed... 3. act, ado 4. feat, fiat, gest (geste) 5. actum, actus, stunt, title 6. action, doings 7. exploit 8. contract, tenendum 11. achievement, malefaction, performance
deem... 5. judge, opine, think 6. esteem, regard 7. believe, presume, suppose 8. conclude, consider 10. adjudicate
deemed... 7. assumed, reputed 8. adjudged, inferred, presumed, supposed 10. considered
deep... 3. low, pit 4. rich, wide, wise 5. great 6. hidden, remote, solemn 7. learned, obscure, serious 8. immersed, involved, powerful, profound 9. engrossed, entangled, sagacious 10. deep-seated, mysterious
deep (pert to)...
  dish pie.. 7. cobbler
  sea.. 6. depths
  seated.. 8. habitual 9. ingrained 11. established
  sleep.. 5. sopor
  sound.. 6. bell, gong
deepen... 5. lower 6. dredge 7. broaden, enhance 9. aggravate, intensify 10. strengthen
deer... 3. olk, red, roe 4. buck, fawn, hart, hind, maha, stag 5. eland, moose, ratwa 6. fallow, sambar, wapiti 7. caribou, deerlet, roebuck 8. reindeer, ruminant
deer (pert to)...
  antler.. 3. dag 4. snag 8. tres-tine (royal)
  Asiatic.. 6. sambar
  barking.. 7. muntjac (muntjak)
  deerlike.. 10. chevrotain
  female.. 3. doe, roe 4. hind
  genus.. 4. Dama 6. Cervus 8. Cervidae
  Japanese.. 4. sika
  Java.. 4. napu 7. muntjac (muntjak)
  Lapland.. 8. reindeer
  male.. 4. buck, hart, stag 6. havier 7. brocket (brok), pricket
  meat.. 7. venison
  mouse.. 7. plandok
  Oriental.. 4. axis, Rusa 5. kakar 6. chital, rativa, sambar 7. kanchil, muntjac (muntjak)
  Russian.. 4. olen
  S American.. 4. pita 6. guemal (guemul) 7. brocket, spitter
  Tibet.. 4. shou
  tiger.. 6. cougar
  tracks.. 3. run 4. slot
  type.. 3. red, roe 4. mule 6. fallow

11. black–tailed, white–tailed
deface... 3. mar 4. ruin, scar 5. spoil 6. damage, injure 7. blemish, distort 9. discredit, disfigure
defamation... 5. libel 7. calumny, slander, spatter 8. disgrace, dishonor 9. aspersion 10. defilement, detraction
defame... 5. libel 6. accuse, charge, infamy, malign, vilify 7. asperse, blacken, detract, slander, traduce 8. dishonor 10. calumniate
default... 4. fail, lack, loss, mora 7. deficit, failure, neglect 9. deficient, denigrate, oversight 10. nonpayment 11. delinquency 14. nonfulfillment
defeat... 4. beat, best, lose, rout 5. worst 6. baffle, derout, master, refute 7. beating, clobber, confute, conquer, failure, mastery, repulse, triumph (over), undoing 8. Waterloo 9. frustrate, overthrow 10. disappoint 11. subjugation 12. discomfiture 14. disappointment
defeating... 7. beating, routing 10. anatreptic, conquering 11. vanquishing
defeatism... 6. malism 7. Boloism 10. retreatism
defect... 4. flaw, lisp, lock, quit, want 5. fault 7. blemish, forsake 8. withdraw 9. discredit 10. deficiency, inadequacy 12. imperfection, irregularity
defection... 4. loss 7. failing, failure 9. desertion 10. abjuroment 11. abandonment
defective... 3. bad 4. lame 5. idiot 6. cretin, faulty 7. half–wit, lacking 8. crippled 9. deficient, imperfect, subnormal 10. incomplete
defective vision... 6. anopia, myopia
defend... 4. save, ward 5. guard, plead, shend, watch 6. screen, secure, shield, uphold 7. contest, justify, protect, shelter, support, sustain 8. enshield, preserve 10. controvert
defendant... 4. reus 7. accused, libelee, suspect 8. appellee 10. respondent
defender... 8. advocate, champion 9. justifier, protector 10. vindicator
defense... 4. boma, fort, plea 5. alibi, guard 6. abatis (abattis), glacis (slope) 7. bulwark, rampart, ravelin 8. estacade (dike), sepiment, stockade 10. protection 12. counterscarp 13. justification, machicolation
defenseless... 7. aidless, forlorn, unarmed 8. helpless 9. unarmored, unguarded 10. undefended, unshielded 11. unfortified, unprotected
defer... 3. bow 4. wait 5. delay 6. retard 7. adjourn, suspend 8. postpone, protract, stave off 13. procrastinate
defer (to)... 5. yield 6. admire, regard, submit 7. concede, respect

9. recognize 11. acknowledge

deference... 5. honor 6. esteem, fealty, homage, regard 7. respect 8. courtesy 9. reverence 10. politeness, submission 12. complaisance 13. consideration

deferential... 8. obeisant 9. attentive, courteous 10. respectful, submissive 11. ceremonious

defiance... 6. defial 8. audacity, boldness 9. challenge, disregard, insolence

deficiency... 4. lack, want 6. dearth, ullage 7. aneuria, deficit 8. scarcity, shortage 10. inadequacy 13. insufficiency 14. incompleteness

deficient... 5. minus, short 6. faulty, meager (meagre), scarce 7. lacking, missing, wanting 8. inferior 9. defective, imperfect 10. inadequate, incomplete 12. insufficient

defile... 4. file, pass (Mt), soil 5. dirty, gorge, notch, sully, taint 6. befoul, debase, ravine, vilify 7. corrupt, debauch, deprave, pollute, tarnish 8. dishonor 10. passageway

define... 3. fix 4. name 5. bound, limit 6. decide 7. delimit, explain, outline 8. boundary 9. delineate, determine, stipulate 11. distinguish 12. characterize, circumscribe

defined (sharply)... 8. clear–cut 9. trenchant

defined track... 3. rut 4. slot

definite... 4. sure 7. certain, limited, precise 8. absolute, distinct, explicit, manifest, positive 10. undeniable 11. determining, unqualified 12. unmistakable 14. unquestionable

definitely... 10. explicitly, positively 12. conclusively, unmistakably

definition... 6. naming 7. clarity, meaning 9. sharpness 11. description, explanation 12. delimitation, distinctness 14. interpretation

deflation... 7. decline 8. collapse 9. reduction 10. cheapening 11. devaluation, humiliation 12. depreciation

deflect... 4. bend, warp 5. avert 6. divert 7. deviate

deformed... 5. varus 7. taliped 8. formless 9. amorphous, distorted, grotesque, loathsome, malformed, misshapen, monstrous 10. clubfooted

defraud... 3. gyp, rob 4. bilk, gull 5. cheat, cozen 6. fleece 7. swindle

deft... 3. apt, fit, pat 4. meet, trim 5. adept, handy, quick 6. adroit, clever, expert 8. skillful (skilful) 9. dexterous, masterful

defunct... 3. die 4. dead, gone 6. depart, finish 7. extinct 8. deceased 11. nonexistent

defy... 4. dare 5. beard, brave, stump 6. cartel 7. disdain, disobey 9. challenge

degenerate... 6. debase, wicked, worsen 7. atrophy, corrupt, degrade, deprave 8. decadent 10. retrogress

11. deteriorate

degeneration... 7. decline 9. decadence, turpitude 10. degeneracy 11. degradation 13. deterioration, retrogression

degradation... 5. shame 7. censure, decline 8. demotion, disgrace, ignominy 9. reduction, turpitude 10. debasement, punishment 11. humiliation 13. deterioration

degrade... 5. abase, lower 6. debase, demean, demote, depose, humble 7. corrupt 8. disgrace, dishonor 9. humiliate 10. depreciate

degrade (socially)... 8. declassé

degree... 4. rank, step, tate 5. class, grade, order, point, scope, shade, stage, stair 6. extent 7. station 8. capacity, relation 9. intensity

degree (pert to)...
academic.. 8. bachelor 9. doctorate, masterate 11. engineering 13. baccalaureate
highest.. 13. summa cum laude
slight.. 5. shade 9. gradation
to what.. 9. howsoever 10. howsomever

dehydrate... 3. dry 5. dry up 6. wither 8. preserve 9. anhydrate, dessicate, evaporate, exsiccate

deify... 5. exalt 7. ennoble, glorify, idolize 8. enshrine 11. apotheosize, immortalize

deign... 7. consent 9. vouchsafe 10. condescend

deity... 2. El 3. Dea, God 4. Deus, deva 5. numen 6. Elohim 7. goddess, godhead, godhood 8. Almighty, Divinity, Immortal 12. Supreme Being

deity (aboriginal)... 4. mana, Zemi 5. huaca, wakan 6. manito (manitou), nagual, orenda, pokunt 8. tamanoas

deity (pert to)...
avenging.. 6. Erinys 7. Alastor, Anteros
destroying.. 4. Siva (Shiva)
evil.. 5. Sebek (crocodile–headed)
hearth.. 5. Vesta
household.. 3. Lar 7. Penates
human sacrifice.. 6. Moloch
judge of the dead.. 4. Yama
love.. 4. Amor, Eros 5. Cupid
mockery.. 5. Momus
music.. 6. Apollo
solar.. 5. Mentu (Ment, falcon–headed)
sun.. 2. Ra
supreme.. 6. Ormazd
two–faced.. 5. Janus
underworld.. 3. Dis 4. Gwyn 5. Pluto 6. Osiris
war.. 4. Ares
woodland.. 3. Pan 4. faun 5. satyr 7. silenus

dejected... 3. sad 5. amort 6. abased, droopy 7. à la mort, lowered 8. downcast 9. depressed, prostrate 10. despondent 11. downhearted, low–spirited

dejection... 7. lowness, sadness

10. depression, melancholy
11. despondency
Delaware ...
beach .. 8. Rehoboth
capital .. 5. Dover
church (oldest Prot) .. 9. Old Swedes
city .. 5. Lewes 9. New Castle
10. Wilmington (Fort Christina, 1638)
corporation .. 6. DuPont
product .. 9. chemicals 13. Blue Hen chicks
river .. 8. Delaware 10. Brandywine
State admission .. 5. first
State motto .. 22. Liberty and Independence
State nickname .. 5. First 7. Diamond
delay ... 3. lag 4. halt, mora, stay, wait 5. block, check, dally, defer, demur, pause, tarry 6. arrest, detain, hinder, impede, loiter, retard
7. confine, setback 8. lateness, obstruct, postpone, reprieve, slow–down 9. detention, hindrance
10. cunctation, moratorium
13. procrastinate 15. procrastination
delayed ... 4. late, slow 5. tardy
7. belayed, overdue 10. behindhand
delectable ... 6. savory 8. luscious, pleasing 9. ambrosial, delicious
10. delightful 11. scrumptious
delegate ... 4. name, send 6. assign, commit, depute, deputy, legate
7. appoint, consign, entrust
8. deputize 9. authorize
10. commission 12. commissioner
14. representative
delete ... 4. dele 5. erase 6. cut out, excise, remove 7. edit out, expunge
0. eradicate 10. obliterate
deleterious ... 7. harmful, hurtful, noxious 9. injurious 10. pernicious, prejudiced 11. destructive, detrimental, prejudicial
deletion ... 4. stet 7. apocope
8. excision 9. expunging
delf, delft ... 3. pit 4. mine 6. quarry
Delhi ... 7. capital (Ind)
deliberate ... 4. cool, muse, pore, slow
5. study, think, weigh 6. ponder
7. discuss, reflect, studied
8. consider, measured, prepense
9. calculate, leisurely, speculate, unhurried, voluntary 11. contemplate, intentional, premeditate
12. premeditated 13. dispassionate
deliberately ... 6. slowly 7. tardily
8. by design 9. expressly, purposely, willfully 13. intentionally
delicacy ... 4. cate, tact 5. snack, taste
6. caviar, luxury, nicety, tidbit
7. finesse, frailty, tenuity 8. fineness, niceness, softness, subtlety
9. exactness, fragility, precision
10. daintiness, refinement, slightness
11. sensitivity
delicate ... 3. sly 4. fine, lacy, nice, soft 5. frail, light 6. dainty, mignon, petite, pretty, queasy, subtle, tender
7. elegant, fragile, minikin, refined, tenuous 8. araneous, graceful, luscious, tasteful 9. exquisite,

sensitive 10. fastidious, meticulous, scrupulous 11. considerate
delicious ... 5. tasty 8. luscious
9. ambrosial, nectarean
10. delightful, nectareous
delight ... 3. joy 4. glee 5. amuse, bliss, charm, exult, mirth 6. divert, please, ravish, regale, relish
7. enchant, gratify, overjoy
8. pleasure 9. delectate, enrapture, happiness 13. gratification
delightful ... 6. lovely, savory
7. amusing, winsome 8. charming, engaging, pleasant 9. appealing, delicious, enjoyable 10. enchanting
11. fascinating
delineate ... 3. map 4. draw, limn, line
5. trace 6. define, depict 7. outline, picture, portray 8. describe
9. represent
delinquency ... 7. default, failure
8. omission 9. violation
10. nonpayment 11. malfeasance, misdemeanor, misfeasance
13. nonobservance
deliquesce ... 4. give, melt 6. ramify
7. liquefy 8. diminish, dissolve
delirious ... 6. insane, raving 8. frenzied
9. wandering (mental)
14. disorientation
delirium ... 4. fury, rage 6. frenzy, lunacy 7. madness, passion
8. insanity 9. phrenitis
10. aberration, excitement, unsaneness 11. derangement
13. hallucination
deliver ... 4. free, give, save 5. speak
6. commit, impart, ransom, redeem, render, resign 7. consign, release, relieve 8. transfer 9. discharge, enunciate, extradite, surrender
deliver of evil spirits ... 8. exorcise
deliver oration ... 7. declaim
dell ... 4. dale, dene, vale 5. slade
6. dalles (pl), dingle, ravine, valley
Delos ...
famed for .. 5. ruins 10. Stone Lions
island group .. 8. Cyclades
sea .. 6. Aegean
Delphi, Delphoi (Gr) ...
modern name .. 6. Kastri
oracle .. 7. Delphic 8. Delphian
priestess .. 6. Pythia
delude ... 3. jig 4. dupe, flam, fool, hoax 5. elude, trick 6. befool
7. beguile, deceive, mislead
9. bamboozle, frustrate, victimize
11. double–cross
deluge ... 5. flood 6. drench 7. freshet, Niagara, torrent 8. cataract, flooding, inundate, overflow, submerge, The Flood 9. cataclysm, overwhelm
10. oversupply 14. superabundance
delusion ... 4. ruse 6. mirage
7. fallacy, fantasm 8. illusion, phantasm 9. deception
10. misleading 13. hallucination
delve ... 3. dig 4. mine, till 5. gouge, scoop, spade 6. exhume 8. excavate
demand ... 3. ask, COD, cry, dun, fee
4. call, need 5. claim, query 6. elicit
7. require 8. exaction, question

9. requisite, ultimatum
11. requirement, requisition
demeanor, demeanour... 4. mien
7. bearing, conduct, posture
8. behavior, carriage
11. comportment
demented... 3. mad 4. daft, loco, luny
5. crazy, loony 6. crazed, insane
7. cracked 8. deranged
10. unbalanced 11. disoriented
Demeter... 7. goddess (Agric)
demigod... 4. hero 5. satyr (sylvan)
6. Triton 7. godling, half–god
10. semidivine
demise... 5. death, lease 6. convey
7. decease 8. bequeath
10. alienation, conveyance
demit... 4. quit 5. leave 6. resign,
vacate 8. abdicate 10. relinquish
11. resignation
demiurgic... 8. creative 9. formative
demivolt... 4. jump 5. vault (half)
6. curvet 8. capriole
Democrat (Polit slang)... 6. Hunker
demoded... 5. passé 6. passed
10. out of style
demolish... 4. rase, raze, ruin, undo
5. wreck 7. destroy, shatter
9. devastate, dismantle, overthrow
11. disassemble
demon, daemon... 3. hag, imp, nat
4. atua, jinn, Mara, ogre, Rahu
5. asura, devil, Eolis, fiend, genie,
jinni (jinnee), lamia, Satan 6. afreet
7. Amaimon, villain 8. Asmodeus
9. cacodemon (cacodaemon)
demoniac... 8. devilish, fiendish
demons (pert to)...
adjurers.. 9. exorcists
assembly of.. 6. sabbat
charm against.. 10. demonifuge
possessed of.. 8. demoniac
theory of.. 10. demonology
worship of.. 11. demonolatry
demonstrate... 4. show 5. prove
6. evince, typify 7. display, explain,
portray 8. manifest 9. exemplify
demonstrative... 7. gushing 8. effusive
9. emotional 10. indicative
11. explanatory 12. affectionate,
illustrative
Demosthenes (Gr)... 6. orator
(greatest)
demur... 4. stay 5. delay, pause, tarry
6. linger, object (to) 7. scruple
8. demurrer, hesitate 9. objection
12. irresolution
demure... 3. coy, mim, shy 4. prim,
smug 5. grave, staid, timid
6. sedate, solemn, stuffy 7. bashful,
prudish, serious 8. decorous
den... 4. cave, dell, lair, nest, room
5. cavea (anc), group (scouts), haunt,
study 6. cavern, grotto, hollow,
ravine 7. retreat 8. hideaway
denial... 5. cross 7. refusal
8. demurrer, negation 9. disavowal,
disowning, rejection 10. refutation
11. deprivation 12. disallowance
13. disaffirmance
denizen... 3. cit 6. native 7. citizen,
dweller, hellion (of hell) 9. indweller

10. inhabitant 11. cosmopolite
Denmark... see also *Danish*
anc name.. 5. Thule
capital.. 10. Copenhagen
city.. 6. Nyborg (Fyn Isl), Odense
7. Aalborg 8. Elsinore
founder.. 7. Absalon (Axel)
Hamlet's grave.. 8. Elsinore
island possession.. 6. Faroes
9. Greenland
peninsula.. 7. Jutland
river.. 5. Guden
ruler (anc).. 6. Canute (Kanute)
denomination... 3. ism 4. cult, name,
sect 5. class, party, value 6. church,
number, school 7. society
8. category 10. persuasion
11. appellation, designation,
stipulation
denote... 4. mark, mean, note, show
5. imply 6. convey 7. bespeak,
betoken, connote, express, purport,
signify 8. indicate 10. denominate
denoting (pert to)...
equal pressure.. 8. isobaric
final end (Gram).. 5. telic
usual action.. 9. usitative
denouement... 3. end 5. issue
6. result 7. outcome (plot)
8. solution 10. revelation
denounce... 4. damn 6. accuse, assail,
scathe 7. arraign, censure, condemn,
upbraid 9. reprobate 10. denunciate,
stigmatize
de novo... 3. new 4. anew 5. fresh,
newly 6. afresh
dense... 4. dewy, firm 5. close, crass,
gross, heavy, solid, thick 6. opaque,
stupid 7. compact, crowded
8. populous, thickset 11. thickheaded
density... 4. dord (Chem) 8. dumbness
9. stupidity 11. compactness
dent... 3. pit 4. dint 5. dinge, notch,
tooth 6. batter, hollow, indent
7. imprint 10. depression, impression
11. indentation
dentagra... 7. forceps 9. dentalgia,
toothache
dental (pert to)...
appliance.. 3. dam 6. scaler
7. forceps
drill.. 8. cavitron
filling.. 5. inlay
measure.. 10. dentimeter
toothache.. 8. dentagra 9. dentalgia
dentate... 7. serried, toothed
dentine... 5. ivory
dentist... 10. exodontist
12. orthodontist 14. prosthodontist
denude... 4. bate 5. scalp, strip
6. divest, expose, unrobe 7. uncover
denunciation... 6. menace, threat
7. inveigh 8. reproach
10. accusation 11. arraignment
deny... 4. nego 5. debar 6. abjure,
impugn, negate, recant, refuse,
renege 7. confute, disavow, dispute,
gainsay 8. disclaim, forswear,
traverse 9. repudiate 10. contradict,
contravene, controvert
deodar (species)... 5. cedar
depart... 2. go 3. die 4. exit, quit

5. leave, mosey 6. decamp, demise, egress, perish 7. abscond, vamoose 8. separate (Chem), withdraw

depraved ... 4. evil, vile 6. shrewd, wicked 7. corrupt, immoral, vicious 8. vitiated 9. debauched, dissolute, perverted 10. degenerate

depravity ... 8. depraved 9. turpitude 10. corruption, wickedness 15. incorrigibility

depreciate ... 4. fall 5. lower, slump 6. debase, lessen, reduce, shrink 7. cheapen, deflate 8. belittle, discount, pejorate, vilipend 9. disparage 10. undervalue

depreciation ... 8. decrease, discount 9. deflation 10. cheapening, pejoration 12. belittlement 13. disparagement 14. undervaluation

depredator ... 5. thief 6. looter, robber 7. spoiler 8. marauder, ravisher 9. despoiler, plunderer

depress ... 4. dont, sink 5. lower 6. dampen, deepen, deject, indent, reduce, sadden 7. flatten, imprint, oppress 8. dispirit, enfeeble 10. discourage

depressed ... 3. low, sad 4. dire, sunk 6. dismal, oblate 8. dejected, downcast 9. debruised (Her), flattened (vertically) 10. dispirited 11. downhearted 12. disheartened

depressing ... 5. chill 6. dismal, dreary, gloomy, somber 7. joyless 9. saddening 10. melancholy

depression ... 3. col, dip, pit 4. dent, fall 5. blues, fossa (Anat), gloom, gully 6. cavity, crater, ravine, trough, vapors 10. melancholy 11. despondency, humiliation

deprivation ... 4. loss, want 7. deposal, ousting, removal 9. privation, unseating 10. divestment 11. bereavement

deprive ... 3. rob 4. take 5. debar, mulct, strip 6. divest, remove 7. bereave, despoil 10. dispossess

deprived of ...
authority .. 9. dethroned
life .. 5. slain 6. killed 12. exterminated
limb .. 6. maimed
natural qualities .. 9. denatured
possessions .. 12. expropriated
professional standing .. 8. laicized
rank .. 7. deposed
reason .. 8. demented
vigor .. 6. sapped 8. deadened, unnerved 9. enervated, enfeebled

depth ... 5. abyss, midst 6. extent 9. intensity 10. profundity

depths ... 3. sea 5. adyta (spiritual), ocean 16. Davy Jones's locker

depute ... 6. assign, devote 7. appoint 8. delegate, deputize

deputy ... 5. agent, envoy, proxy, vicar 6. legate 8. alter ego 9. alternate 10. substitute

deracinate ... 6. evulse, unroot, uproot 7. extract (forcibly)

deride ... 3. pan 4. dupe, geck, gibe, jeer, mock, razz 5. cheat, fleer, flout, scoff, scorn, trick 6. insult 8. ridicule

derision ... 5. fleer, scorn 7. asteism, mockery 8. contempt, ridicule

derivation ... 6. effect, origin, source 7. descent, lineage 9. deduction, education, evolution 10. derivative 12. transmission

derivation of ...
descent .. 7. lineage 8. pedigree 9. genealogy
name (race, tribe) .. 7. eponymy
word .. 9. etymology

derivative of ...
bauxite .. 8. aluminum
benzine .. 6. phenol
coal tar .. 8. creosote
flax .. 5. linen
mercury .. 11. quicksilver
milk .. 6. lactic
morphine .. 6. heroin
pitchblende .. 6. radium 7. uranium
sorrel .. 10. oxalic acid

derogate ... 5. annul, decry 6. repeal 7. detract 8. restrict, withdraw 9. disparage

derogatory ... 10. detracting, detractory, pejorative 11. deprecatory, disparaging 12. depreciatory

derrick ... 3. rig 4. spar 5. crave, hoist, tower 6. lifter, steeve, tackle 7. hangman, staging

dervish ... 4. monk 5. fakir, friar 6. beggar, fakeer 7. ascetic 11. religionist

dervish cap ... 3. taj 4. atef

dervishes ...
howling .. 8. Rufaiyah
wandering .. 12. Kalandariyah
whirling, dancing .. 10. Maulawiyah

descend ... 4. fall, sink 5. deign, stoop 6. alight, unbend 7. decline 9. gravitate 10. condescend

descendant ... 3. son 5. child, scion 8. daughter, offshoot 9. offspring

descendants ... 5. breed 7. progeny 9. posterity

descent ... 4. drop, fall, root 5. birth, issue, scarp, slope, stock 7. assault, decline, lineage 8. ancestry, downfall, invasion (sea), pedigree 9. declivity, incursion, posterity 10. extraction 11. degradation

describe ... 4. name 5. paint, parse, state 6. define, depict, relate 7. explain, express, narrate, outline 9. delineate, designate, represent 12. characterize

description ... 4. idyl, kind, sort 5. idyll 7. account, version 8. features, relation 9. discourse, narration, narrative, portrayal 10. definition 11. delineation, explanation 14. representation 18. descriptio personae

descry ... 3. see 4. espy, view 6. behold, detect, reveal 7. discern, observe, witness 8. discover 9. determine 11. distinguish

Desdemona's husband ... 7. Othello

desecrate ... 5. abuse 6. misuse 7. profane, violate 8. misapply

Deseret ... 4. Utah (1849)

desert... 3. due 4. bolt, fail 5. merit,
oasis 6. defect, renege, reward
7. abandon, forsake 8. desolate
10. apostatize, relinquish, wilderness
desert (pert to)...
Africa.. 5. El Erg 6. Karroo
Algeria.. 3. Erg
Australia.. 10. Great Sandy 13. Great
Victoria
beast.. 5. camel
dweller.. 4. Arab
Mongolia (Asia).. 4. Gobi
phenomenon.. 6. mirage
prospector.. 3. rat
ship.. 5. camel
shrub.. 5. ratem 6. Alhagi 7. juniper
(Bib)
train, travelers.. 7. caravan
wind (hot).. 6. simoom (simoon)
7. sirocco
deserter... 3. rat 6. bolter 8. apostate,
recreant, renegade, turncoat, turntail
deserved... 3. due 4. fair, just
5. rated 6. earned, worthy
7. condign, merited 8. rightful
9. justified, warranted
11. appropriate
deserving... 6. worthy 8. laudable
10. creditable, entitled to
11. commendable, meritorious
12. praiseworthy
desiccated... 3. dry 4. arid, sere
5. dried 6. seared 7. parched
9. preserved 10. dehydrated,
exsiccated
design... 3. aim, art, end 4. draw,
form, idea, mean, plan, plot 5. ettle
6. intent, layout, motive, object,
scheme, sketch 7. destine, drawing,
meaning, outline, pattern, propose
8. artifice, artistry, contrive
11. arrangement
design (pert to)...
carved.. 4. seme 5. cameo 8. intaglio
metal, glass.. 4. etch 6. niello
ornamental.. 9. medallion
10. needlework
pattern.. 5. batik 6. mosaic
skin.. 6. tattoo
designate... 3. fix, set 4. call, mark,
name, show 5. state, style, title
6. select 7. appoint, entitle, specify
8. describe, indicate, nominate
9. determine, stipulate
10. denominate 11. distinguish
12. characterize
designation... 4. name 7. meaning
9. selection 10. indication
12. denomination 13. signification
desire... 3. yen 4. care, urge, want,
wish 5. covet, crave, yearn 6. aspire,
hunger, prefer, thirst 7. craving,
longing, passion, request 8. appetite
9. appetency, eagerness
10. desiderium 11. inclination
desire (pert to)...
expectant.. 4. hope
greatly.. 6. aspire
liquid.. 6. thirst
ungovernable.. 5. mania
desirous... 4. avid 5. eager 6. ardent
7. envious, lustful, willing

8. covetous, spirited 9. ambitious
10. solicitous
desist... 2. ho 3. end 4. don't, halt,
quit, stay, stop 5. cease 6. lay off
7. forbear, refrain 8. cut it out
11. discontinue
desk... 4. ambo, dais 5. board, table
6. pulpit 7. lectern, rostrum
8. kneehole 9. monocleid
(monocleide), secretary 10. escritoire
desolate... 3. sad 4. arid, lorn, ruin
5. alone, bleak, drear, gaunt
6. barren, dismal, gloomy, lonely,
ravage 7. forlorn 8. deserted,
forsaken, solitary, wretched
9. destitute 10. depopulate
11. comfortless, uninhabited
desolation... 3. woe 4. ruin 5. gloom,
grief, havoc, waste 6. ravage
7. sadness 10. gloominess,
loneliness, melancholy 11. destitution,
destruction, devastation, forlornness
12. depopulation, solitariness,
wretchedness
despair... 11. desperation,
despondency, forlornness
12. hopelessness
desperado... 5. brave 6. outlaw
7. ruffian 8. criminal 10. lawbreaker
desperate... 3. mad 4. rash, wild
7. frantic, furious 8. headlong,
heedless, hopeless, reckless
10. despairing, desponding,
distraught, infuriated 11. extravagant,
precipitate 13. irretrievable
despicable... 4. base, vile 6. odious,
shabby 8. terrible, unworthy,
wretched 9. miserable
12. contemptible, contemptuous,
disreputable, vilipendious
despise... 4. defy, hate 5. scorn,
scout, spurn 6. detest, slight
7. contemn, disdain 8. vilipend
9. disregard
despised being... 6. pariah 7. outcast
despoil... 3. rip, rob 4. riot 5. reave,
rifle, strip 6. divest, fleece, injure,
ravage, ravish 7. bereave, debauch,
deprive, disrobe, pillage, plunder
9. depredate
despondency... 7. despair
10. depression 11. desperation
13. heartlessness
despot... 4. czar (tsar), lord 6. master,
satrap, tyrant 8. autocrat, dictator
9. patriarch
despotic... 8. arrogant 9. arbitrary,
·tyrannous 10. autocratic, tyrannical
11. dictatorial, patriarchal
12. governmental
dessert... 3. ice, pie 4. cake 5. fruit,
glacé, sweet 6. mousse, pastry,
sweets 7. parfait, pudding, sherbet,
strudel 8. ice cream 10. shoofly pie
destination... 3. end 4. goal, port
5. bourn (bourne) 7. address, destiny
9. objective
destine... 4. doom, fate 5. allot
6. design, devote, intend, ordain
7. appoint 8. set apart 9. designate
10. foreordain, predestine
12. predetermine

destiny... 3. end, lot, ure (anc)
4. bahi, doom, eure, fate, goal
5. karma, stars 6. Kismet 7. fortune
11. destination
destitute... 4. void 5. needy 6. bereft,
devoid 7. forlorn, lacking
8. bankrupt, forsaken, homeless
9. abandoned, penniless
10. down–and–out
destitution... 6. penury 7. poverty
11. deprivation 12. helplessness
destroy... 3. end 4. kill, rase, raze,
root, ruin, sack, slay, undo 5. abash,
annul, erase 6. ravage 7. abolish,
consume, nullify, unbuild
8. decimate, demolish, overturn
9. dismantle, eradicate
10. annihilate, neutralize
11. exterminate
destroyer... 3. hun 6. ruiner, vandal
7. marplot, wrecker 8. nihilist,
saboteur 9. iconclast (of images)
11. torpedo boat
destroying angel... 6. Danite
7. Abaddon, Amanita (fungus)
8. Apollyon
destruction... 4. loss, ruin 5. havoc,
waste 7. killing 8. downfall,
genocide, ravaging, sabotage,
shambles 9. holocaust, overthrow,
perdition, ruination 10. decimation,
demolition, desolation, extinction,
subversion 11. devastation,
dissolution, extirpation
13. extermination
destructive... 5. fatal 6. deadly, mortal
7. baleful, fateful, ruinous 8. aneretic
(anaeretic), ravaging 10. calamitous,
catawampus, pernicious, subversive
desuetude... 6. disuse, nonuse
9. cessation 12. obsolescence
13. nonemployment
14. discontinuance
desultory... 4. idle 5. hasty 6. roving,
wanton 7. aimless, cursory, wayward
8. rambling, unsteady, wavering
9. deviative, orderless, unsettled
10. discursive, inconstant
detach... 4. part, wean 5. sever
7. disjoin, isolate 8. disunite,
separate, withdraw 9. disengage
detached... 4. free 5. alone, aloof,
scarp 7. detaché, retired, severed
8. isolated, secluded, separate,
solitary 9. unrelated, withdrawn
11. unconnected 12. disconnected
detachment... 8. disunion
9. aloneness, aloofness, isolation,
seclusion, unconcern 10. separation
11. disjunction 14. demobilization
detail... 4. item, unit 6. assign
7. appoint, itemize, minutia, narrate,
specify 9. enumerate, narrative
10. particular 12. technicality
details... 6. trivia 8. minutiae
11. particulars
detain... 4. hold, keep, stop 5. check,
delay 6. arrest, hinder, intern, retard
8. imprison, restrain, withhold
detect... 3. see, spy 4. show, spot,
tail 6. accuse, descry, reveal
7. discern, find out, uncover

8. discover, perceive 9. recognize
detective... 4. dick 6. beagle, sleuth,
tailer, tracer 7. gumshoe, spotter
8. exposing, flatfoot, Hawkshaw,
mouchard 9. operative
12. investigator
detent... 3. dog 4. pawl 5. catch,
click, fence 6. tongue 7. ratchet
detention... 5. delay 6. duress
7. detinue 9. captivity, hindrance
10. detainment, internment
11. restraining, retardation,
withholding 12. imprisonment
deter... 5. daunt, delay, repel
6. divert, hinder 7. prevent
8. restrain 10. discourage, disincline
deterge... 5. purge 6. purify
7. cleanse 8. depurate 9. elutriate
detergent... 4. soap 7. cleaner,
purging, saponin (saponine), smectic,
solvent 8. cleanser, medicine, purifier
9. cleansing 10. abstergent, lixiviator
deteriorate... 4. wear 6. impair,
weaken, worsen 10. degenerate,
retrogress
deterioration... 5. decay 7. decline
9. decadence 10. debasement,
declension, impairment, perversion
11. degradation 12. degeneration
13. retrogression
determinate... 5. fixed 6. cymose
7. certain, special 8. definite,
resolute, resolved, specific 9. arbitrary
10. definitive, invariable
11. established, unqualified
determination... 4. will 5. limit, proof
6. choice 7. purpose, resolve, verdict
8. decision, firmness, judgment
9. impulsion 10. conclusion,
definition, discussion, resolution,
settlement 11. disputation,
measurement, termination
12. decisiveness, dijudication,
resoluteness 13. specification
determine... 3. end 5. impel, learn,
prove, state 6. assess, choose,
decide, define, direct, ordain, settle
7. delimit, resolve, specify
8. conclude, discover 9. arbitrate,
ascertain, stipulate, terminate,
variously 10. dijudicate, foreordain
determined... 3. set 4. sure 5. fixed
6. mulish 7. assured, cinched,
decided, settled 8. foregone,
perverse, resolute, stubborn
9. obstinate, pigheaded
detest... 4. hate 5. abhor 8. execrate
9. abominate
detestable... 6. odious 7. hateful
8. accursed, terrible 9. abhorrent,
execrable, loathsome, obnoxious
10. abominable 12. contemptible
dethrone... 6. depose, disbar, divest
7. uncrown 8. disbench
detonation... 4. bang, boom 5. blast
7. blowout 8. backfire 9. discharge,
explosion 10. combustion
detract... 6. deduce, deduct, vilify
7. asperse, traduce 8. belittle,
derogate, distract, subtract, withdraw
9. disparage 10. depreciate
detraction... 5. delay 7. calumny,

slander 9. aspersion 10. belittling
11. distraction, subtraction
detriment... 4. hurt, loss 6. damage,
injury 8. mischief, weakness
10. impairment, impediment
12. disadvantage
detrimental... 7. baleful, baneful,
harmful, hurtful, noxious 9. injurious
10. pernicious 11. deleterious,
mischievous, prejudicial
15. disadvantageous
Deus Fidius... 7. Jupiter
Deus vobiscum... 12. God be with
you
Deus vult... 8. God wills (anc cry)
deuterogamy... 6. digamy
Deuteronomy (pert to)...
comprising.. 10. law of Moses
Fifth Book of.. 10. Pentateuch
meaning.. 11. repeated law (of
Moses)
devastate... 4. rape, ruin, sack
5. havoc, strip, waste 6. ravage
7. destroy, pillage, plunder, scourge
8. demolish, desolate 10. depopulate
devastation... 4. ruin 5. havoc, waste
6. ravage 7. scourge
develop... 4. grow 5. arise, ripen,
train 6. appear, detect, evolve,
expand, mature, reveal 7. advance,
convert, enlarge, expound, further,
improve, perfect, promote
8. discover, generate 9. elaborate
(details)
developed... 4. ripe, zoon 5. adult
6. mature, mellow 7. grownup
8. improved 9. perfected
10. precocious
development... 6. growth 7. changes,
endysis 8. increase, maturity
9. evolution, expansion, formation,
unfolding 10. maturation
11. elaboration, improvement,
ontogenesis 12. phylogenesis
devest... 5. strip 6. denude, divest
7. deprive, undress 8. alienate
Devi (Hind)... 3. Uma 4. Kali
5. Durga, Gauri 6. Chandi, Shakti
7. heroine, Parvati 8. divinity
9. Haimavati
deviate... 3. err, yaw 4. hade, miss,
slew, vary, veer 5. sheer, stray
6. change, depart, swerve, wander
7. deflect, digress, diverge
deviation... 3. yaw 5. lapse 6. change
7. circuit, synesis 8. aberrant
9. aberrance, deformity, departure,
diverging, obliquity, variation
10. deflection, difference, digressing,
digression, distortion, divergence
11. abnormality 12. eccentricity
device... 4. plan, tool 5. motto, shift,
trick 6. design, desire, gadget,
scheme 7. adjunct, compass, project,
purpose 8. artifice, insignia
9. appliance, expedient, implement,
invention, stratagem 10. instrument
11. contrivance
device (pert to)...
bark peeling.. 8. stripper
clamping.. 4. vise 7. pincers
distilling.. 7. alembic

fabric stretching.. 7. stenter
heating.. 4. etna 5. stove
hoisting.. 5. crane, davit, lewis
6. garnet 7. derrick 8. elevator
9. parbuckle
leveling.. 6. gimbal
measuring.. 4. gage, tape 5. chain,
gauge, meter, ruler 9. ergometer,
yardstick 10. micrometer
nautical.. 4. bitt 5. cleat, otter
6. becket 8. paravane
regulating.. 5. valve 9. remontoir
spraying.. 8. atomizer 9. sprinkler
steering.. 4. helm 5. wheel 6. rudder,
tiller
stopping.. 5. brake, sprag
devil... 3. imp 4. deil, deva, evil, haze
5. annoy, demon, error, fiend, grill,
ruler (of Hell), Satan, tease
7. hellion, serpent, tempter, torment
8. printer's 9. archenemy, daredevil,
dust devil
devil (pert to)...
dog.. 6. marine
bird.. 3. owl 5. swift 10. goatsucker
fish.. 3. ray 5. manta, whale (gray)
7. octopus
grass.. 7. Bermuda
lore.. 10. demonology
tree.. 4. dita
Devil, the... 5. Deuce, Eblis, Satan
6. Azazel, Belial, Diablo, Teufel
7. Ahriman, Amaimon (Amammion),
diavolo, Evil One, Lucifer, Old Nick,
Sammael, Shaitan (Sheitan)
8. Apollyon, Asmodeus, Diabolos
9. Archenemy, Archfiend, Beelzebub
11. Auld Clootie 14. Mephistopheles
devilish... 5. cruel 6. daring, rakish,
wicked 7. extreme, hellish, satanic
8. fiendish, infernal 9. chthonian
10. demoniacal 11. mischievous
deviltry... 6. malice 7. cruelty, devilry
8. mischief 9. diablerie, diabolism
10. black magic, wickedness
12. fiendishness
devious... 6. errant, erring, roving,
sinful 7. oblique, vagrant, winding
8. rambling, tortuous 9. deviative,
eccentric 10. circuitous
11. out–of–the–way
14. unconventional
devise... 3. aim 4. form, plan
5. array, build, frame 6. create,
divide, evolve, invent, scheme, will to
7. appoint, arrange, bequest,
concoct, fashion 8. bequeath,
contrive 9. fabricate 10. distribute,
excogitate 11. distinguish
deviser of IQ test... 5. Binet
devoid... 4. free, void 5. empty
6. faulty, vacant 7. without
9. destitute 11. nonexistent
devoid of...
feeling.. 9. apathetic, insensate
interest.. 6. jejune
devote... 3. use, vow 5. apply
6. employ, hallow, resign 7. address,
consign, destine 8. dedicate, set
apart 10. consecrate 11. appropriate
devoted... 5. loyal, pious, vowed
6. doomed, loving 7. zealous

8. addicted, constant, faithful,
friendly, obedient 9. dedicated,
engrossed, patriotic
devotee... 3. fan, ist, nun 4. monk
6. votary 7. epicure, fanatic, Pietist
8. aesthete (esthete), partisan
devotion... 4. love, zeal 5. ardor, piety
6. novena, prayer 7. pietism, worship
9. addiction, adoration, constancy
10. attachment, dedication,
devoutness, friendship
11. devotedness, earnestness,
engrossment 12. consecration
13. appropriation, religiousness
devour... 3. eat 4. bolt, gulp, wolf
5. gorge, use up, waste 6. absorb,
engulf 7. consume, engorge, swallow
(up) 8. prey upon 9. devastate
10. annihilate
devout... 4. holy, warm 5. godly,
pious 6. hearty, solemn 7. cordial,
devoted, saintly, sincere, zealous
8. reverent 9. religious, righteous
10. worshipful
dew... 4. rime 5. bedew, bloom, roris
dewy... 5. roral, roric
dexterity... 3. art 5. knack, magic,
skill 7. ability, address, aptness,
finesse, sleight 8. aptitude, deftness,
facility 9. smartness 10. adroitness
15. right–handedness
dexterous... 3. apt 4. deft, yare
5. adept, handy, quick, ready
6. adroit, artful, clever 7. skilful
8. skillful 11. right–handed
dextral... 5. right (to the) 9. favorable
diabolical... 5. cruel 6. wicked
7. beastly, demonic, hellish, satanic,
ungodly 8. damnable, demoniac,
devilish, fiendish, infernal
diacritic... 4. mark 5. point
7. symptom 10. diagnostic
14. distinguishing
diacritical mark... 5. breve, tilde
6. tittle 9. diaeresis (dieresis)
diadem... 5. crown, tiara 6. anadem,
circle, emblem, empire, fillet
7. coronet 8. headband, insignia,
ornament 11. sovereignty
diaeresis, dieresis... 4. mark 5. break
8. division 10. resolution
diagnose... 7. analyze 8. construe
9. interpret
diagnosis... 8. analysis, decision,
nosology 9. prognosis
14. interpretation
diagonal... 4. bias 7. oblique
8. bendwise (Her) 10. transverse
11. cater–corner 13. cater–cornered
diagram... 4. draw, icon, plan, plot,
tree 5. chart, epure, gamut, graph
6. design 7. drawing 9. blueprint
dial... 4. disk 5. plate 8. horologe
9. indicator, timepiece
11. chronometer
dialect... 5. idiom, lingo 6. patois,
speech 7. diction 8. language,
locution, parlance 10. vernacular
dialect (pert to)...
Afrikaans.. 4. Taal
Aramaic.. 6. Syriac

Aryan.. 4. Pali
provincial.. 6. patois
Semitic.. 4. Geez
diameter... 2. pi (3.1416) 4. bore
5. width 6. module, radius
7. breadth, caliber (calibre)
9. thickness
diametric, diametrical... 6. averse
7. adverse 8. antipode, opposite
9. antipodal, diametral
diamond... 3. gem, ice 5. cards, field
(baseball), jager, jewel, plane
6. carbon 7. adamant, infield,
lozenge, rhombus 8. treasure
diamond (pert to)...
crystal.. 7. glassie
cutting.. 4. bort
cutting cups.. 3. dop
famed.. 4. Pitt 5. Sancy 6. Orloff
7. Lesotho (601 carat) 8. Cullinan,
Koh–i–noor 9. Excelsior 10. Great
Mogul 14. Star of the South
surface.. 5. facet
weight.. 5. carat (karat)
Diamond State... 8. Delaware
diaphanous... 4. fine, thin 5. filmy,
gauzy, lucid, sheer 6. flimsy
9. gossamery 11. translucent,
transparent
diaphragm... 4. wall 6. middle,
septum 7. midriff 9. partition
diary... 3. log 6. record 7. journal
8. register 9. chronicle
13. autobiography
diaskeuast... 6. editor 7. reviser
diatribe... 6. screed, tirade 7. lecture
8. berating, harangue 9. invective,
philippic 10. discussion (prolonged)
dice... 3. cog, die (sing) 4. cube,
game, sice (6's) 5. bones, craps,
cubes 7. ivories, tessera
Dickens characters... 3. Tim 4. Dora,
Nell 5. Fagin, Miggs, Sikes 6. Cuttle
7. Barnaby 9. Pecksniff
10. Chuzzlewit 11. Oliver Twist
Dickens pseudonym... 3. Boz
dictate... 3. law 4. rule 5. maxim,
order, utter 6. advise, dictum, enjoin,
impose 7. command, deliver, require,
suggest 9. prescribe 10. injunction
dictatorial... 5. bossy 6. lordly
7. pompous 8. absolute, arrogant,
despotic, dogmatic, oracular, positive
9. imperious, masterful, pragmatic
10. autocratic, dogmatical,
imperative, peremptory
11. categorical, domineering,
magisterial, opinionated, overbearing
13. authoritative
diction... 5. style 8. language,
parlance, phrasing 9. elocution
10. vocabulary 11. enunciation,
phraseology 14. expressiveness
dictionary... 5. words 7. calepin,
lexicon 8. wordbook 9. reference
10. vocabulary 11. terminology
dictionary compiler... 7. Webster
(Noah) 13. lexicographer
dictum... 3. saw 5. adage, maxim
6. saying 7. opinion, precept,
proverb 8. aphorism, apothegm
11. declaration

didactic... 8. teaching 9. mentorial
   10. preceptive 11. instructive
dido... 5. antic, caper, prank, trick
   6. frolic
Dido (also Elissa)... 5. Queen (of
   Carthage) 8. Princess (Tyrian)
die... see also *dice* 4. fade, mold,
   pass, seal, wane 5. stamp 6. expire,
   perish, recede, vanish, wither
   7. decease, succumb 8. languish
   12. extinguished (to be)
die–hard... 4. Tory 11. British Army
   12. Conservative
dies... 3. day
dies atri... 9. black days
dies faustus... 13. favorable omen
   (day of)
diet... 4. fare 5. board 6. Hoftag,
   ration, viands 7. Council, Landtag,
   regimen 8. assembly, Kreistag
   9. allowance, nutrition, Reichstag
   10. Parliament
Diet (of)... 5. Worms (1521)
   6. Speyer (1529), Spires
   8. Augsburg (1530)
dietetics... 8. sitology 9. nutrition
   12. biochemistry, dietotherapy
differ... 4. vary 5. clash 7. dispute,
   dissent, quarrel 8. disagree
difference... 3. sum 5. shade
   6. nuance 8. variance 10. inequality,
   unlikeness 11. contrariety, distinction,
   distinguish 12. disagreement,
   discriminate 13. differentiate,
   dissimilarity
different... 4. many 5. novel, other
   6. divers, sundry, unlike 7. diverse,
   several, unequal, unusual, variant
   8. assorted, contrary, distinct,
   manifold, opposite, separate, variform
   9. divergent, otherwise 10. dissimilar,
   variegated 11. diversified
   13. heterogeneous
different place... 9. elsewhere
   10. otherwhere
difficulty... 3. bar, rub 4. clog, crux,
   knot, snag 5. cavil, check, demur,
   nodus 6. plight, scrape, strait
   7. barrier, problem, trouble
   8. obstacle 9. hindrance
   10. impediment, ruggedness
   11. obstruction 12. disagreement
difficulty in swallowing...
   9. dysphagia
diffidence... 5. doubt, qualm
   7. anxiety, modesty 8. distrust,
   humility, timidity 10. hesitation
   11. bashfulness 12. apprehension
diffident... 3. coy, shy 5. timid
   6. modest 7. anxious 8. doubtful,
   reserved, retiring 9. shrinking,
   unwilling 11. distrustful
   12. apprehensive
diffuse... 4. full, shed 5. strew
   6. expand, extend, prolix 7. copious,
   perplex, pervade, publish, radiate,
   refract, verbose 8. disperse
   9. redundant 10. widespread
diffused... 5. loose 6. sparse
   7. flowing 9. dispersed
diffusion... 7. osmosis 9. pervasion,
   radiation 10. dispersion, refraction

dig... 3. jab 4. find, grub, mine, open,
   pion, prod, root 5. delve, dwell,
   spade 6. exhume, loosen, pierce,
   plunge, search, thrust 7. extract,
   unearth 8. excavate 10. understand
digamy... 11. deuterogamy 12. twice
   married (legally)
digest... 4. code 5. brief 6. abrégé,
   codify 7. epitome, Pandect
   8. abstract, classify, synopsis
   10. assimilate, compendium
digestion... 6. pepsis 8. eupepsia
   9. dyspepsia, ingestion
   10. absorption 12. alimentation,
   assimilation
digestive secretions... 4. bile, gall
   6. pepsin, rennin 7. chalone, gastric,
   glucase, hormone, maltase
   8. salivary, thyroxin 9. endocrine
   10. intestinal, pancreatic
digestive tract... 7. enteron
   15. alimentary canal
digger... 3. loy, pal 4. plow, wasp
   5. spade 6. Indian, sapper
   7. comrade, soldier 8. Levelers
   9. excavator 12. New Zealander
digit... 3. toe 4. unit 5. thumb
   6. finger, number (under 10)
   7. dewclaw, integer, measure
digits repeated... 8. repetend
digitus... 6. finger, tarsus 8. dactylus
dignified... 5. grand, lofty, manly,
   sober, staid 6. august, graced,
   sedate 7. courtly, pompous, togated
   8. decorous, ennobled, imposing,
   majestic 9. venerable
   11. ceremonious 12. aristocratic
dignify... 5. exalt, grace, honor
   7. elevate, ennoble 9. solemnize
   11. distinguish
dignitary... 3. don 4. rank 5. mogul
   6. priest, sachem 7. magnate,
   notable, prelate 9. clergyman
dignity... 4. rank 5. grace, honor
   6. status 7. decorum, majesty
   8. nobility, prestige, standing
   9. loftiness, nobleness
   10. excellence, sedateness
digraph... 8. ligature 9. diphthong
digress... 4. veer 5. shift 6. swerve,
   wander 7. deviate, diverge
   8. divagate 9. turn aside
   10. transgress
digression... 4. loop 6. ecbole
   7. circuit, episode 8. excursus
   9. deviation, excursion, obliquity
   10. discussion
digressive... 8. rambling 9. deviative,
   excursive, wandering 10. circuitous,
   discursive
dike, dyke... 3. bar, dig, gap 4. bank,
   gulf, ha–ha, mole, pond, pool
   5. ditch, levee, mound 7. barrier,
   channel 8. causeway, estacade
   9. earthwork 10. embankment
   11. watercourse 13. fortification
diked land... 6. polder
dike rock... 7. odinite
dilapidation... 4. ruin 5. decay, waste
   7. breakup 9. disrepair
   10. impairment 11. dissolution
   13. decomposition 14. disintegration

dilate... 5. bulge, swell, widen
6. expand 7. distend, enlarge, inflate
9. expatiate
dilation... 7. ectasia, ectasis
8. swelling 9. expansion
10. dilatation, distension
dilatory... 3. lax 4. slow 5. slack,
tardy 6. fabian, remiss 8. backward,
delaying, inactive, sluggish
10. behindhand 13. lackadaisical
15. procrastinating
dilemma... 4. trap 5. brike (obs),
snare 8. argument, quandary
10. perplexity 11. alternative,
predicament
dilettante... 7. amateur, dabbler,
devotee, esthete (aesthete)
diligence... 4. care, heed 6. effort
7. caution 8. industry, sedulity
9. assiduity, attention, constancy
10. stagecoach 11. application,
earnestness, painstaking
12. heedlessness, perseverance,
sedulousness 15. industriousness
diligent... 4. busy 6. active 7. operose
8. sedulous 9. assiduous, attentive,
laborious 11. industrious, persevering
dill, dill seed... 4. anet, herb 5. anise
(Bib) 6. fennel
dillydally... 3. lag 6. linger, loiter,
trifle 9. vacillate 12. shilly–shally
13. procrastinate
dilute... 3. cut 4. thin 6. debase,
rarefy, reduce, weaken 8. lengthen
9. attenuate 10. adulterate
12. denaturalize
diluted... 4. thin, weak 7. reduced,
thinned, watered 10. attenuated
dim... 4. dull, fade, pale 5. bleak,
blear, faint 6. darken 7. darkish,
dimness, eclipse, obscure 8. overcast
10. caliginous, indistinct, mysterious
dimension... 4. size 6. extent, height,
length 7. breadth 9. magnitude,
thickness 11. measurement
13. circumference
diminish... 3. ebb 4. bate, fade, pare,
ploy, wane 5. abase, abate, lower,
peter, taper 6. lessen, recede,
reduce, weaken 7. curtail, dwindle
8. decrease, subtract 9. disparage
diminution... 5. abate, taper 7. litotes
8. decrease, lowering 9. decrement,
lessening, reduction 10. moderation
diminutive... 3. wee 4. runt, slip
5. minny, small 6. bantam, little,
peewee, petite 7. bendlet
diminutive suffix... 2. el, ie 3. ole,
ule 4. ette
dimmer... 8. rheostat
din... 4. ding 5. clang, noise
6. clamor, hubbub, racket, rattle,
tumult, uproar 7. clatter, turmoil
9. commotion
dingle... 4. dale, dell, glen, ring, vale
6. jingle, tingle, tinkle, valley
7. tremble 9. storm door
dining room... 4. hall 5. salon
6. spence 7. cenacle 8. mess hall
9. refectory 12. salle à manger
dining science... 10. aristology
dinosaur... 7. reptile 8. sauropod

9. Sauropoda 10. Diplodocus,
Morosaurus 11. Ornithopoda,
Stegosaurus 12. Brontosaurus,
Ceratosaurus, Megalosaurus,
Palaeosaurus 13. Atlantosaurus,
Tyrannosaurus
diocese... 3. see 6. parish 8. district,
province 9. bishopric 12. jurisdiction
Diocletian martyr (Rome)... 5. Agnes
Dionysus (pert to)...
birthplace.. 6. Thebes
father.. 4. Zeus
festival.. 8. Dionysia
god of (Gr).. 4. wine (Bacchus, later)
10. vegetation
lover.. 6. Selene
mother.. 6. Semele
Dioscuri, The (Gr Myth)... 4. cult
5. twins (Castor and Pollux)
8. Castores 10. Polydeuces
dip... 3. dap, dib, sop 4. bail, dunk,
lade 5. merge, merse, pitch, rinse,
scoop, slope, souse 6. candle,
plunge 7. baptize, immerse
9. declivity 10. pickpocket 11. hors
d'oeuvre
diphthong, dipthong... 5. sound
7. digraph 8. ligature
diploma... 8. testamur 9. sheepskin
10. credential 11. certificate,
testimonial
diplomacy... 4. tact 7. address,
cunning 9. dexterity 10. artfulness,
discretion 11. arbitration
diplomatism, negotiation, savoir–faire
diplomat... 5. doyen (head), envoy
8. consul 7. attaché 8. emissary,
minister 10. ambassador, politician
15. chargé d'affaires, plenipotentiary
diplomatic... 6. crafty 7. cunning
8. consular 11. mediatorial
diplomatic corps, staff... 7. embassy
8. legation 17. corps diplomatique
dipsomania... 9. addiction, oenomania,
potomania 10. alcoholism
15. delirium tremens
dipthong... see *diphthong*
dire... 3. bad 4. base, evil, rank, want
5. awful, fatal, needy 6. deadly,
dismal, funest, odious 7. baneful,
doleful, fearful, ghastly 8. dreadful,
horrible, terrible, ultimate
10. oppressive 12. inauspicious,
overpowering
direct... 3. ain, bid, con 4. bend,
boss, head, lead, turn 5. order,
pilot, refer, steer, teach 6. govern,
manage 7. avigate, command,
conduct, marshal 8. instruct, straight
9. influence
direction... 3. way 4. airt, bent, care,
east, west 5. avast, belay, north,
route, south, trend 6. advice, course
7. address, command, pointer
8. guidance 10. management
11. instruction 15. superintendence
directly... 4. soon 6. pronto 7. shortly
8. as soon as, promptly 9. forthwith,
instantly, presently 15. immediately
directly opposite... 9. antipodal,
diametric 10. intipodean
director... 4. boss 5. aimer (gunner)

6. conner, leader 7. manager, teacher 8. governor, producer 14. superintendent

direful ... 4. dire 6. woeful 8. dreadful, terrible 10. calamitous

dirge ... 4. keen, Mass, song 5. psalm, rites 6. lament 7. requiem 8. coronach

dirigible ... 4. Roma 5. blimp 7. balloon 10. Shenandoah 12. Graf Zeppelin

Dirigo ... 5. I Lead 7. I Direct (Maine motto)

dirk ... 4. snee, stab 5. knife, sword 6. dagger

dirt ... 3. mud 4. dust, foul, land, muck, soil 5. earth, filth, grime, stain 6. gossip, refuse 7. scandal, slander 9. obscenity

dirty ... 4. foul, mean 5. dingy, foggy, gusty, mucky, nasty 6. bemire, filthy, soiled, stormy, untidy 7. clouded, muddied, squalid, sullied

dis (pert to) ...
Greek.. 5. Pluto
Norse.. 5. Freya 7. spirits 9. Valkyries 11. superhumans
prefix.. 5. twice 6. double
Roman.. 3. Dis 8. Dis pater 12. realm of Pluto

disable ... 4. main 5. unfit 6. impair, weaken 7. cripple 9. disparage, hamstring 10. disqualify 12. incapacitate

disadvantage ... 3. out 4. harm, hurt 6. damage, injury 7. penalty, trouble 8. drawback, handicap 9. detriment, liability, prejudice 12. inexpedience 13. inconvenience

disagreeable ... 4. edgy 5. cross, nasty 7. fulsome 8. unsavory 9. dissonant, invidious, irritable, offensive, repugnant 10. ill–humored, unpleasant 11. displeasing, ill–tempered, incongruous 13. uncomfortable

disagreement ... 5. clash 7. detente, discord, dispute, dissent, wrangle 8. variance 9. diversity 10. contention, difference, dissension, unlikeness 11. contrariety, controversy, discrepancy, incongruity 13. nonconformity 16. misunderstanding

disappear ... 3. die 4. face, pass 5. cease 6. be lost, perish, vanish 7. dwindle 8. evanesce 9. evaporate

disappoint ... 4. balk, bilk, fail, fall, foil 6. baffle, thwart 7. let down 9. frustrate 10. disenchant, dissatisfy 11. disillusion

disappointment ... 3. rue 6. defeat 7. failure 10. bafflement 11. frustration 15. dissatisfaction

disapprobation ... 5. odium 11. disapproval 12. condemnation 13. disparagement

disapproval ... 3. boo 4. hiss, veto 7. censure, protest 9. objection, rejection 12. condemnation 14. disapprobation

disarrange ... 4. muss 5. upset 6. foul

up, jumble 7. disturb 8. disorder, unsettle 10. discompose 11. disorganize

disarray ... 5. strip 6. unrobe 7. despoil, undress, unkempt 8. disorder 9. confusion, ungarment 10. disarrange, dishabille 12. discomposure, dishevelment

disaster ... 4. evil, ruin 6. mishap 8. accident, calamity, casualty, fatality 9. cataclysm, mischance 10. misfortune 11. catastrophe 12. misadventure

disastrous ... 4. dire 7. unlucky 8. ill–fated 9. ill–boding 10. calamitous 11. destructive, unfortunate 12. unpropitious

disavow ... 4. deny 6. abjure, disown, recant, refuse 7. decline, retract 8. disclaim, renounce 9. disaffirm, repudiate

disbeliever ... 5. pagan 7. atheist, heathen, heretic, infidel 8. agnostic

disburse ... 5. spend 6. defray, expend, pay out

disbursement ... 5. outgo 6. outlay 7. payment 8. spending 11. expenditure

disc ... see also *disk* 3. man 4. dial, puck 5. medal, plate, quoit, wheel 6. circle, record 7. discoid 8. artifact 9. gyroscope, medallion

discard ... 4. drip, shed 5. scrap, sluff 6. disuse, reject, remove 7. abandon, cast off, dismiss, forsake 9. eliminate, eradicate, throw away

discern ... 3. see, spy 4. espy, know, read, view 5. sight 6. behold, descry, detect 7. witness 8. discover, perceive 10. understand 11. distinguish 12. discriminate 13. differentiate

discernible ... 7. evident, obvious, visible 8. apparent, distinct, knowable, manifest 11. conspicuous, perceptible 15. distinguishable

discerning ... 4. sage 5. acute, sharp 6. astute, shrewd 9. sagacious 14. discriminating, discriminative

discernment ... 4. tact 6. acumen 7. insight 8. sagacity 9. sharpness 10. astuteness, perception, shrewdness 12. perspicacity 14. discrimination

discharge ... 2. do 4. bang, cass, fire, sack, shot 5. blast, egest, eject, erupt, expel, exude, flash, salvo, shoot, speed 6. acquit, bounce, defray, exempt, pay off, report, unload, volley 7. dismiss, execute, explode, payment, quietus, release 8. emission, eruption 9. acquittal, dismissal, excretion, execution, explosion, fusillade 10. accomplish, detonation, observance 11. performance

disciple ... 5. chela, Judas, pupil 7. apostle, convert, learner, scholar, student 8. adherent, believer, follower

disciples (Bib) ... 6. twelve (72, Vulgate) 10. Christians

disciplinarian ... 7. Puritan, teacher,

trainer 8. martinet

discipline . . . 4. rule, whip 6. govern, punish 7. chasten, control, culture, educate, penance, scourge 8. training 9. education, restraint 10. correction, punishment 11. castigation, instruction, self–control 12. chastisement 13. regimentation

disclaim . . . 4. deny 6. abjure, cry out, disown, recant, refuse, reject 7. disavow 8. abnegate, disallow, renounce 9. repudiate

disclose . . . 4. bare, open, show, tell 5. utter 6. expose, impart, reveal, unmask, unveil 7. divulge, uncloak, unclose 8. discover, indicate

disclosure . . . 6. exposé 8. exposure 9. discovery, revealing, unmasking, unveiling 10. appearance, revealment, revelation

discolor . . . 4. spot 5. stain 6. bruise 7. distain (anc), tarnish 9. ecchymose (by blood)

discolored . . . 4. doty (by decay) 5. faded 7. altered 8. ustulate 10. variegated

discomfit . . . 4. balk, rout 5. upset 6. baffle, defeat, dismay 7. confuse 9. embarrass, frustrate, overthrow 10. disconcert

discomfiture . . . 4. rout 6. defeat, flurry 7. letdown 9. confusion, overthrow 10. bafflement 11. frustration 13. embarrassment, inconvenience 14. disappointment

discomfort . . . 4. pain 6. sorrow 7. misease 8. distress 9. annoyance 10. uneasiness 11. displeasure 13. embarrassment, inconvenience

discommode . . . 6. bother, molest, put out 7. trouble 9. incommode 13. inconvenience

discompose . . . 4. fret 5. upset 6. excite, flurry, rubble 7. agitate, confuse, derange, disturb, fluster 8. unsettle 9. embarrass 10. disarrange, disconcert

disconcert . . . 5. abash, alarm 6. rattle, thwart 7. confuse, disturb, fluster, nonplus 8. bewilder 9. discomfit, embarrass 10. disarrange

disconnect . . . 5. sever 6. detach, unyoke 7. disjoin 8. disunite, separate, uncouple

disconnected . . . 6. broken 8. detached, rambling 9. desultory, scattered 10. disjointed, incoherent 11. unconnected

disconsolate . . . 3. sad 6. gloomy, woeful 7. forlorn 8. desolate, hopeless 9. sorrowful 10. despairing, despondent, melancholy 12. inconsolable

discontent . . . 6. misery, unrest 8. disquiet 10. inquietude, uneasiness 11. displeasure, unhappiness 14. discontentment 15. dissatisfaction

discontinue . . . 3. end 4. drop, quit, stop 5. cease 6. desist, give up 7. abandon, refrain 8. intermit 9. terminate

discord . . . 3. din 5. noise 6. strife 7. dissent 8. disunity, variance 9. cacophony, Discordia, harshness 10. antagonism, contention, difference, discordant, disharmony, dissension, dissonance 11. altercation 12. disagreement

discord (goddess of) . . . 3. Ate 4. Eris

discordant . . . 5. harsh 7. grating, jarring 8. contrary, jangling 11. cacophonous, disagreeing, incongruous, quarrelsome, unmelodious 12. inconsistent, inharmonious 14. irreconcilable

discordant (pert to) . . .
  music . . 8. scordato
  serenade . . 9. charivari 10. callithump
  sound . . 6. jangle

discount . . . 3. cut 4. agio 6. rebate 9. abatement, allowance, reduction 10. concession, percentage

discourage . . . 4. damp 5. check, daunt, deter 6. deject, dismay, oppose 7. depress 8. dispirit, dissuade 10. dishearten

discourse . . . 4. talk, tell 5. essay, paper (written), prose, speak, spiel 6. homily, lesson, screed, sermon 7. account, address, article, declaim, discant, dissert, expound, lecture, narrate, oration 8. converse, treatise 9. expatiate, narrative 10. exposition, recitation 12. conversation, dissertation

discourteous . . . 4. rude 7. uncivil 8. impolite, insolent 9. ungallant 10. ungracious 13. disrespectful

discover . . . 3. see 4. espy, find 5. learn 6. descry, detect, expose 7. exhibit, find out, uncover, unearth 9. apprehend, ascertain

discoverer . . . 3. spy 5. scout

discoverer of . . .
  America . . 4. Eric (the Red) 7. Vikings 8. Columbus (1492)
  blood circulation . . 6. Harvey
  electric light . . 6. Edison
  North Pole . . 5. Peary (1909)
  radium . . 5. Curie (Madame)
  South Pole . . 8. Amundsen (1911)
  telegraph . . 5. Morse (Samuel)
  telephone . . 4. Bell (Alexander)
  vaccination . . 6. Jenner

discovery, logic of . . . 8. heuretic

discredit . . . 5. doubt 7. asperse, falsify, scandal 8. disgrace, dishonor, disprove, distrust 9. disbelief, disparage, disrepute, misgiving, suspicion 10. invalidate 11. discredence

discreet . . . 4. wary 5. civil 6. polite 7. careful, mindful, politic, prudent 8. cautious 9. judicious, selective 11. circumspect 12. noncommittal 13. discretionary

discrepancy . . . 8. variance 9. disaccord, disparity, diversity 10. difference 11. contrariety 12. disagreement 13. inconsistency 15. incompatibility

discretion . . . 4. tact, will 6. option 7. caution, reserve 8. judgment, prudence, wariness 11. disjunction

12. cautiousness, discreetness
13. discontinuity, judiciousness, secretiveness 14. circumspection, discrimination
discretionary... 7. politic, prudent 8. discreet 9. arbitrary, judicious, voluntary 10. prudential 11. considerate 14. discriminating
discriminate... 6. divide, screen, secern 8. separate, set apart 11. distinguish 13. differentiate
discrimination... 5. taste 6. acumen, option 9. prejudice 10. discretion 11. discernment, distinction, penetration, segregation
discursive... 6. roving 7. cursory 9. desultory, diffusive, wandering 10. circuitous, digressive
discus... 4. disk 5. plate, quoit
discuss... 3. air, rap 4. moot 5. argue, treat 6. confer, debate, parley 7. bargain, canvass, dispute, dissert, mention 9. discourse
discus thrower... 10. discobolus
disdain... 5. pride, scorn 7. askance, contemn, despise 8. contempt 9. arrogance 11. haughtiness 16. contemptuousness
disease... 6. malady 7. ailment, illness, trouble 8. disorder, sickness 9. affection, infirmity 10. affliction, disability 11. derangement
disease (of)...
animals (Afr).. 5. nenta
apoplexy.. 4. esca
apples.. 7. stippen 9. bitter pit
blood.. 6. anemia 8. leukemia (leukaemia, leucemia)
cattle.. 5. hoose (hooze) 6. nagana, wheeze 7. anthrax
chickens.. 3. pip 4. roup
diet.. 7. rickets 8. pellagra, rachitis
divers.. 5. bends 7. caisson
dog.. 5. lyssa 6. rabies 11. hydrophobia
eye.. 6. caligo 7. pinkeye 8. cataract, glaucoma, trachoma 9. amaurosis 14. conjunctivitis
fungus.. 6. mildew 9. elm blight
Oriental.. 8. beriberi
painful.. 7. lumbago 9. arthritis
plant.. 4. rust, smut 5. ergot, scald 6. Panama (banana) 7. erinose (grape)
potato, tomato.. 8. dartrose
skin.. 5. hives, psora 6. eczema, herpes, tetter 7. scabies 8. impetigo, shingles 9. psoriasis, urticaria 10. erysipelas
stonecutter's.. 9. silicosis
sugar cane.. 5. sereh
disease (pert to)...
classification.. 8. nosology 10. nosography
decline.. 9. catabasis
determination of.. 9. diagnosis
germ transfer.. 7. vection
native to.. 7. endemic
outlook.. 9. prognosis
science of.. 8. etiology, medicine
spread of.. 8. epidemic
suffix.. 4. itis, osis
treatment.. 7. therapy 12. kinesiatrics

disembark... 4. land 6. alight, debark 7. deplane, detrain, pile out (sl)
disembowel... 3. gut 10. eviscerate
disengage... 5. clear 6. detach, loosen 7. release 8. liberate, unfasten 9. extricate 11. disencumber, disentangle 12. disembarrass
disentangle... 4. card, comb 5. clear, loose, ravel, solve 6. evolve, sleave, sleeve 7. unravel, unsnare, untwine, untwist 8. simplify 9. disengage, extricate 10. disinvolve, unscramble
disfavor... 7. dislike 8. distaste 9. detriment, disrepute 10. alienation 11. disapproval, displeasure 14. discountenance
disfigure... 3. mar 4. scar 6. deface, deform, injure, mangle, uglify 7. blemish 8. mutilate
disgorge... 4. barf (sl), spew, vent 5. eject, eruct, erupt, expel, heave, vomit 7. exhaust 9. discharge 10. relinquish 11. regurgitate
disgrace... 5. abase, odium, shame, shend, sully 7. attaint, degrade, distain, obloquy, upbraid 8. dishonor, ignominy, reproach 9. discredit, disesteem, disrepute, humiliate 10. opprobrium 11. abomination, humiliation 13. disparagement
disguise... 3. mum (mumm) 4. mask, veil 5. cloak, feign 6. covert, masque 7. conceal, costume, falsify, pretend 9. dissemble, incognito, inebriate 10. camouflage, masquerade 11. dissimulate 12. misrepresent
disgust... 6. nausea 7. offense, quarrel 8. aversion, loathing, nauseate 9. animosity, annoyance, antipathy, revulsion 10. abhorrence, repugnance 11. abomination
disgusting... 5. nasty 6. filthy, odious 9. loathsome, obnoxious, offensive, repellent, repulsive, revolting, sickening
dish... 3. jar, pot 4. boat (gravy) 5. cruse, nappy, paten, plate 6. patera, saucer, tureen 7. charger (anc), platter, ramekin 9. casserole
dish (food)... 5. kibbe (kibbeh), pilaf, pilau, salmi 6. hachis, haslet, omelet, potage, ragout 7. bok choy, chowder, falafel (felafel), pudding, soufflé 10. egg foo yong, shish kabob 11. ratatouille
dishabille... 6. kimono 7. neglige, undress 8. bathrobe, negligee, peignoir 9. housecoat, nightgown
dishearten... 5. amate (anc), appal, daunt, deter, unman 6. deject, dismay 7. depress, unnerve 8. dispirit 10. disconcert, discourage
disheveled... 5. tousy 6. frowzy, mussed, shaggy, untidy 7. ruffled, tousled, tumbled, unkempt 8. deranged, uncombed 10. disarrayed, disordered 11. disarranged
dishonest... 4. base 5. false 6. crafty, unjust 7. corrupt, crooked, knavish 8. rascally, scheming 9. deceitful, truthless 10. fraudulent, perfidious

untruthful 12. dishonorable
dishonor... 5. shame 6. defame,
  infamy 7. debauch, degrade, obloquy
  8. disgrace, ignominy, reproach
  9. desecrate, disrepute, improbity
  10. disrespect, opprobrium
  13. disparagement
dishonorable... 7. ignoble 8. infamous,
  shameful 9. dishonest 10. inglorious
  11. disesteemed, disgraceful
  12. disreputable
disillusion... 10. disquixote
disillusioned... 8. thwarted
  12. disappointed, disenchanted
disinclination... 7. dislike 8. aversion,
  distaste 10. reluctance, repugnance
  12. disaffection 13. indisposition
disinclined... 6. averse 8. indolent
  9. reluctant, unwilling 10. indisposed
disinfectant... 5. Lysol 6. cresol,
  iodine, phenol 7. alcohol
  9. germicide 10. antiseptic
  12. formaldehyde
disintegrate... 5. decay, erode
  7. break up, corrode, crumble,
  disband, resolve 8. dissolve
  9. decompose 11. disorganize
disjoin... 4. part, undo 5. sever, untie
  6. detach, sunder, unhook 7. unhitch
  8. disunite, separate, unbutton
  9. disengage 10. disconnect,
  dissociate
disk, disc... 4. puck 5. medal, paten,
  plate, quoit, wafer, wheel 6. harrow,
  record, sequin 7. discoid, medalet
  9. faceplate, gyroscope, medallion
dislike... 4. mind 5. odium 6. detest
  8. aversion, distaste 9. antipathy,
  disrelish 12. disaffection
dislike of children... 9. misopedia
dislike of home... 9. ecophobia
disloyal... 5. false 6. fickle, untrue
  9. faithless 10. inconstant,
  perfidious, unfaithful 11. treacherous
dismal... 3. sad, wan 4. dark
  5. black, bleak, drear, lurid
  6. dreary, gloomy, somber 7. doleful,
  joyless, Stygian, unhappy, unlucky
  8. dolorous, dreadful, funereal,
  lonesome, mournful, overcast, sinister
  9. ill—omened, sorrowful
  10. calamitous, depressing,
  lugubrious 11. pessimistic,
  unfortunate
dismantle... 4. raze, undo 5. strip
  6. divest 7. deprive, destroy, disrobe,
  uncloak 8. demolish 11. disassemble
dismay... 4. fear 5. alarm, daunt
  6. appall, fright, terror 8. affright,
  bewilder 9. dejection 10. depression,
  disconcert 12. apprehension
  13. consternation
  14. discouragement
dismiss... 4. drip, fire 5. amand,
  amove, eject, exile, remue 6. acquit,
  bounce, depose, recall, refute, shelve
  7. forgive, release 8. relegate
  9. discharge, disregard 10. relinquish
dismount... 6. alight 7. descend,
  unhorse, unmount 11. disassemble
disobedient... 7. forward, froward,
  wayward 8. mutinous 10. rebellious,

refractory 11. intractable
  12. contumacious
disorder... 3. tic 4. mess, riot
  5. chaos, deray, snarl 6. malady,
  tumult 7. ailment, anarchy, derange,
  illness, misdeed 8. disarray, paranoia,
  sickness 9. confusion, craziness,
  distemper, paranomia
  10. discompose, revolution
  11. lawlessness, misdemeanor
  12. irregularity 13. indisposition
  14. disarrangement
  15. disorganization
disorderly... 3. bad 5. mussy, rowdy
  6. unruly 7. chaotic, naughty, violent
  8. confused, rowdyish, slipshod
  9. irregular, offensive, turbulent
  12. ungovernable, unmanageable
disorganization... 5. decay 7. anarchy,
  breakup, split—up 8. disorder
  10. separation 11. destruction,
  dissolution 13. disbandonment
  14. disarrangement, disintegration
disown... 4. deny 5. expel 6. recant,
  reject 7. disavow 8. disclaim,
  renounce 9. disaffirm, repudiate
  10. disinherit
disparage... 4. slur 5. decry, lower (in
  rank) 6. slight 7. degrade, detract
  8. dishonor, minimize 10. depreciate,
  disapprove, discourage, undervalue
  11. incongruity
disparagement... 7. diasyrm
  8. disgrace 9. indignity
  10. detraction 12. depreciation
disparaging... 8. decaying
  10. defamatory, pejorative
  11. unfavorable
dispart... 4. open, rend, rive 5. break,
  sever, split 6. cleave, divide
dispassionate... 4. cool, fair 0. serene
  8. composed, moderate 9. collected,
  impartial, temperate, unruffled
  11. unemotional 12. unprejudiced
dispatch... 4. kill, mail, post, send,
  slay 5. haste, speed 6. hasten
  7. message 8. celerity, conclude,
  expedite 9. diligence 10. accelerate,
  accomplish, promptness
dispatch boat... 5. aviso 6. packet
Dis pater (Rom)... 3. god (underworld)
  5. Pluto (Gr) 12. realm of Pluto
dispel... 6. vanish 7. scatter
  8. disperse 9. dissipate
dispensation... 6. scheme 7. economy
  9. exemption, remission
  10. dispersion, management,
  misericord (misericorde)
  11. arrangement 12. distribution
  13. apportionment 14. administration
dispense... 4. deal, dole, give, vend
  6. effuse, excuse, exempt 7. absolve
  8. disperse 9. apportion
  10. administer
dispenser of alms... 7. almoner
disperse... 3. sow 4. rout 5. strew
  6. branch, spread, vanish 7. diffuse,
  refract, scatter 9. apportion, dissipate
  10. distribute 11. disseminate
dispirit... 3. cow 4. damp 5. daunt
  6. deject 7. depress 10. discourage,
  dishearten, intimidate

displace... 6. depose, mislay, remove
8. misplace 9. discharge, dislocate,
supersede 10. substitute
display... 3. air 4. pomp, show, wear
5. array 6. evince, flaunt, parade,
set out 7. exhibit, pageant, splurge
8. emblazon 9. advertise
10. appearance 11. demonstrate,
ostentation 13. manifestation
display (pert to)...
case.. 10. show window
in public.. 5. stage
of emotion.. 10. enthusiasm
of force (distant).. 9. telenergy
of temper.. 5. scene 9. spectacle
displease... 3. vex 4. miff 5. anger,
annoy, pique 6. offend 7. provoke
8. irritate 10. dissatisfy
displeasure... 5. anger 7. disgust,
dislike, offense, trouble 8. disfavor,
distaste 10. resentment, uneasiness
11. indignation, unhappiness
14. disapprobation 15. dissatisfaction
dispose (of)... 3. set 4. give, mind,
sell, tend 5. order, place 6. adjust,
assign, bestow, settle 7. arrange,
destroy, discard, testate 8. give
away, regulate 9. eliminate
10. distribute, relinquish
disposed... 5. prone 7. settled, willing
8. arranged, assigned, inclined
11. distributed
disposed (pert to)...
favorably.. 7. propend
to cling together.. 8. clannish
to doubt.. 9. skeptical
to please.. 11. complaisant
disposition... 3. use 4. bent, bias,
mood, turn 6. animus, giving,
morale, nature, temper 7. control
8. tendency 9. character
10. management, settlement
11. arrangement, elimination,
temperament 12. organization
13. apportionment
dispossess... 5. eject, evict 6. divest,
refute 8. disseize
dispossessed... 6. bereft, ousted
7. ejected, evicted 8. deprived,
divested
disproof... 6. answer, denial
8. negation, rebuttal 10. refutation
11. confutation 12. invalidation
disprove... 5. belie, rebut 6. refute
7. confute 9. discredit 10. invalidate
disputation... 6. debate 7. polemic
8. argument 10. contention
11. controversy 12. conversation
disputatious... 7. eristic, polemic
11. contentious, quarrelsome
13. argumentative, controversial
dispute... 4. deny, feud, moot, spar
5. brawl, broil 6. bicker, debate,
haggle, higgle, naggle 7. contest,
dissent, protest, quarrel, wrangle
8. argument, squabble
11. altercation, controversy
disqualify... 5. debar 9. indispose
10. invalidate 12. incapacitate
disquiet... 3. vix 4. fret 5. alarm
6. excite 7. agitate, concern, disturb
8. distress, frighten 12. apprehension

disquisition... 5. essay 10. discussion
12. dissertation
disregard... 4. snub 6. ignore, slight
7. neglect 8. defiance 9. unconcern
11. inattention
disreputable... 3. low 4. base
5. seamy 7. raffish 8. shameful,
unworthy 13. discreditable
15. persona non grata
disrespect... 7. affront 9. disesteem,
insolence 10. incivility
11. discourtesy
disrespectful... 7. uncivil 8. impudent,
insolent 10. irreverent
12. discourteous
disrupt... 4. part (forcibly), rend, tear
5. upset 6. thwart 11. disorganize
dissatisfaction... 8. vexation
10. discontent 11. displeasure,
unsatisfied
dissect... 3. cut 6. divide 7. analyze
8. separate 9. anatomize
disseize (law)... 4. oust 5. evict
6. depose 10. dispossess
11. expropriate
dissemble... 4. hide 5. cloak, feign
7. conceal 8. disguise 9. disregard
11. counterfeit
disseminate... 3. sow 6. effuse,
spread 7. publish, scatter 8. disperse
9. circulate, propagate
dissension... 7. discord 8. brouille,
friction 10. dissidence
12. disagreement
dissent... 3. nay 8. apostasy, disagree
10. separation 12. disagreement,
nonagreement 13. nonconformity
14. nonconcurrence
dissenter... 7. heretic, Sectary
8. apostate, recusant 9. protester
10. Protestant 13. nonconformist
dissertation... 5. essay, tract
6. debate, thesis 7. article, lecture
8. treatise 9. discourse
10. discussion, exposition
12. disquisition
dissidence... 7. dissent 8. variance
9. cacophony 10. difference,
dissension 12. disagreement
dissimilarity... 7. variety 9. disparity,
diversity 10. difference, unlikeness,
unsameness 13. dissimilation,
heterogeneity 17. heterogeneousness
dissipate... 5. spend, waste 6. dispel,
expend 7. consume, scatter, shatter
8. dispense, dissolve, squander
9. disappear
dissipation... 4. loss 9. decrement,
diffusion 10. dispersion, profligacy
11. consumption, prodigality
12. intemperance 13. disappearance,
dissoluteness 14. disintegration
dissolute... 3. lax 4. lewd, wild
5. loose 6. loosed, rakish, wanton,
wicked 7. lawless, vicious
8. reckless, uncurbed 9. abandoned,
debauched, unbridled 10. dissipated,
licentious, profligate 11. demoralized
12. unrestrained
dissolve... 4. fuse, melt 5. solve
7. adjourn, liquefy 9. decompose,
disappear 11. disorganize

12. disintegrate
dissolved... 6. solute 7. soluble
dissonant... 5. harsh 7. grating, jarring
8. jangling 9. deviative, different,
differing 10. discordant, discrepant
11. disagreeing, unmelodious
12. inconsistent, inharmonious
13. contradictory
dissuade... 5. deter 6. advise, dehort,
divert 8. admonish 10. discourage,
disincline 11. expostulate
distaff side... 5. women 6. female
distain... 5. stain, tinge 6. define
7. tarnish 8. discolor
distance... 4. step, yond 5. depth,
range, space 6. offing 7. mileage,
reserve, yardage 8. coldness, outstrip
9. aloofness, antiquity, dimension
10. remoteness
distant... 3. far, tel, yon 4. afar, cold,
tele (pref) 5. aloof 6. remote,
utmost, yonder 7. foreign 8. ulterior
distaste... 7. disgust 8. aversion
9. disrelish 10. repugnance
11. displeasure 14. disinclination
15. dissatisfaction
distasteful... 7. hateful 8. nauseous,
unsavory 9. loathsome, offensive
10. disgusting, unpleasant
11. displeasing, unpalatable
12. disagreeable
distemper... 3. vex 4. soak 5. anger,
color, steep 6. dilute, malady, ruffle
7. ailment, disease, disturb
8. painting (process), sickness
13. indisposition
distend... 4. grow 5. bulge, swell
6. dilate, expand, spread 7. enlarge,
inflate, stretch 8. lengthen
distended... 5. tumid 7. bloated,
swollen 8. inflated, patulous, puffed
up
distich... 7. couplet 8. two lines
distill, distil... 4. leak 6. decoct,
infuse 7. extract, squeeze, trickle
8. vaporize
distilling device... 5. flask 6. retort
7. alembic 10. distillery
distinct... 4. fair 5. clear 7. audible,
obvious, precise, several 8. explicit,
manifest 9. different 10. individual
13. distinguished
distinction... 4. rank 5. honor
6. repute 8. nobility 9. clearness,
greatness, variation 10. difference
14. discrimination 15. differentiation
distinctive... 7. typical 8. peculiar
9. prominent 14. characteristic,
discriminative
distinctive mark... 4. sign 5. badge
6. cachet, emblem, symbol
distinctive quality... 6. genius, talent
9. specialty
distinguish... 6. secern 7. discern
8. perceive, separate 9. recognize
12. discriminate 13. differentiate
distinguished... 5. great, noted
6. famous, marked 7. defined,
eminent, honored, special 8. laureate,
renowned, superior 9. different,
egregious, prominent 10. celebrated
11. conspicuous, illustrious

13. extraordinary 14. characteristic
distort... 4. warp 5. screw, twist,
wrest 6. deform 7. contort, falsify,
pervert 10. camshackle
12. misrepresent
distorted... 4. awry 6. rubato
7. twisted
distortion... 5. loxia 10. perversion
12. malformation
distract... 5. craze 6. divert, harass,
madden, puzzle 7. confuse, perplex
10. distraught
distracted... 3. mad 7. frantic
8. distrait, diverted, rambling
9. disturbed 10. distraught
11. overwrought
distraction... 6. frenzy, tumult
7. despair, madness 8. disorder
9. agitation, confusion, diversion
10. dissension, perplexity
11. derangement, disturbance,
inattention 12. perturbation
distress... 3. ail 4. pain 5. agony,
annoy, grief, worry 6. danger, grieve,
harrow, misery 7. anguish, anxiety,
perplex, poverty, trouble 8. distrain,
vexation 9. necessity 10. affliction,
discomfort
distress call... 3. SOS
distribute... 3. dot, sow 4. deal, dole,
mete 5. allot, share 6. assign,
assort, divide, spread 7. deal out,
prorate, scatter 8. allocate, classify,
dispense, disperse 9. apportion,
broadcast 10. administer
distribution... 8. disposal 9. allotment
10. dispersion 11. arrangement,
disposition 12. dispensation
13. apportionment 14. classification
distribution of favors... 9. patronage
11. benefaction
distributor... 5. agent 6. agency
8. merchant 11. broadcaster
district... 4. pale, slum, ward 5. realm
6. canton, domain, ghetto, region
7. circuit, demesne, quarter
8. province 9. bailiwick, territory
District of Columbia... see
Washington, DC
distrust... 5. doubt, qualm 8. jealousy,
mistrust, wariness 9. misgiving,
suspicion, treachery
disturb... 3. vex 4. riot, roil 5. alarm,
annoy, rouse, roust, upset 6. excite,
molest, ruffle 7. agitate, derange,
fluster, perturb, trouble 8. disorder,
distract 9. interrupt 10. discompose,
disconcert
disturbance... 5. alarm, brawl
6. hubbub, rumpus, static, tumult,
uproar 7. anxiety, clatter 8. stramash
9. agitation, annoyance, commotion,
confusion 10. excitement, turbulence
11. derangement 12. perturbation
disturbed... 6. uneasy 7. annoyed,
excited, inquiet, unquiet 8. agitated
10. bewildered 12. disconcerted
disunion... 9. severance 10. alienation,
detachment, dissension, separation
11. disjunction 13. disconnection
disunite... 3. rip 4. part 5. sever,
untie 6. divide, sunder, unteam,

unyoke 7. discerp, disjoin, unravel
8. alienate, separate 9. dismember
disuse ... 6. misuse, nonuse
7. abandon, discard 8. disusage
9. desuetude 11. antiquation,
discontinue 12. obsolescence
ditch ... 3. sap 4. dike, hole, moat,
rine 5. canal, evade, fossa, fosse,
rhine 6. escarp, furrow, relais, trench
7. abandon, acequia, channel
dithyramb ... 3. ode 4. hymn 6. poetry
7. epithet (of Dionysus)
ditty ... 3. lay 4. poem, sing, song
5. carol 6. saying 7. canzone
8. canticle
diurnal ... 5. daily 8. everyday
9. quotidian
divan ... 4. sofa 5. couch 6. leewan,
settee 9. davenport 12. Chesterfield
dive ... 4. swim 6. plunge, resort,
saloon 7. brothel, descend, descent,
explore 8. submerge
divergence ... 7. theorem 9. deviation,
obliquity 10. difference, separation
12. disagreement, divarication
divers ... 5. cruel 6. sundry 7. several,
various 8. perverse 9. different
diver's disease ... 5. bends 7. caisson
diverse ... 6. sundry, unlike 7. several,
various 8. distinct, separate
9. different, multiform
diver's gear ... 8. flippers
12. respirometer
diversify ... 4. vary 6. change
7. variate 9. variegate 10. distribute
13. differentiate
diversion ... 4. game, play 5. hobby,
sport 6. change 7. pastime
8. apostasy 9. amusement
10. deflection, recreation
11. distraction 13. entertainment
diversity ... 7. variety 10. difference
11. variegation 12. multiformity
divert ... 5. amuse, avert, parry
7. deflect, delight 8. dissuade,
distract, recreate 9. entertain
10. disincline
divest ... 4. doff, reft, tirl 5. strip
6. debunk, depose 8. unclothe
10. dispossess
divide ... 3. lot 4. fork, part 5. cleft,
halve, sever, share, slice, space, split
6. bisect, cleave, septum, sunder
7. prorate 8. alienate, classify,
separate 9. apportion, bifurcate,
calculate, dismember, partition,
segregate, watershed 11. distinguish
divide (pert to) ...
areas (small) .. 8. areolate
feet .. 4. scan
four parts .. 4. paly (Her) 7. quarter
many parts .. 8. fraction 9. multisect
seven parts .. 9. septimole
steps .. 8. graduate
transversely .. 12. cross–section
two parts .. 6. bisect
divided ... 4. enté (Her), reft 5. bifid,
split, zoned 6. halved, parted
7. partial, partite, septate
8. aerolate, bifidate, unjoined
9. alienated, disunited 11. distributed
dividend ... 5. bonus, share 6. number

7. payment
divination ... 3. art (magic) 4. omen,
sors 6. augury, sortes 7. presage
9. intuition
divination by ...
ashes (sacrificial) .. 11. tephromancy
cards .. 10. cartomancy
dead spirits .. 10. necromancy
dreams .. 11. oneiromancy
eggs .. 7. oomancy
fig leaf .. 9. sycomancy
figures .. 8. geomancy
fire .. 9. pyromancy
footprints .. 10. ichnomancy
forehead .. 11. metapomancy
fountains .. 9. pegomancy
letters of a name .. 7. nomancy
8. onomancy
mice .. 8. myomancy
moon .. 10. seleomancy
neighing horse .. 10. hippomancy
oracles .. 9. theomancy
palmistry .. 10. chiromancy
pebbles .. 9. thrioboly
romantic medium .. 5. daisy
salt .. 9. halomancy
serpents .. 10. ophiomancy
smoke (sacrificial) .. 10. capromancy
stars .. 11. sideromancy
straws (burning) .. 11. sideromancy
sword .. 13. machairomancy
verses .. 13. rhapsodomancy
wands, rods .. 11. rhabdomancy
water .. 10. hydromancy
weather .. 9. aeromancy
wild animals .. 11. theriomancy
wine .. 9. oenomancy
divine ... 5. divus, guess, pious
6. priest, sacred, superb 7. foresee,
godlike, predict 8. forebode, foretell,
heavenly, minister, prophecy
9. beautiful, celestial, clergyman,
religious 10. anticipate, superhuman,
theologian 12. supernatural
divine (pert to) ...
being .. 4. deva
breath .. 4. soul
force .. 5. deity, numen 6. spirit
gift .. 8. blessing
inspiration .. 8. afflatus
messenger .. 7. apostle
opinion .. 14. theologoumenon
power .. 7. entheos (obs)
utterance .. 7. prophecy
wisdom .. 8. theogamy
word .. 5. grace, logos
work .. 7. theurgy
divining rod ... 4. wand 6. dowser
9. doodlebug
divinity ... 3. God, Ler 4. Deus, Lord
5. Allah, deity, Khuda, Mazda
6. Brahma, Christ 7. Jehovah,
Saviour, Taranis, Trinity 8. Almighty
division ... 4. part, sect, unit 5. share
6. schism, sector 7. faction, section
8. cleavage, disunion, variance
9. allotment, bisection, partition
10. alienation, department, separation
11. compartment, disjunction
12. distribution 13. apportionment,
disconnection, dismemberment
14. classification

14. classification
division (pert to)...
center (Biol).. 9. centriole
city.. 4. ward 5. block 8. precinct
French.. 6. canton 7. Commune
   10. department 14. arrondissement
mankind.. 4. race
poem.. 5. canto, verse 6. stanza
time.. 3. Age, Eon (Aeon), Era
   6. Eogaea (Zool)
zone (earth).. 6. frigid, torrid, tropic
   9. temperate
divorce, Mohammedan law... 5. talak
divot... 3. sod 4. clod, turf
divulge... 4. tell 6. expose, impart,
   reveal 7. confide, publish, uncover
   8. disclose, discover, proclaim
   11. communicate
Dixie, Dixieland... 4. song 6. utopia
   7. Sunbelt 8. The South (US)
dizziness... 5. whirl 7. vertigo
   9. giddiness 10. fickleness
dizzy... 5. crazy, giddy, tipsy 6. fickle,
   stupid 7. foolish 8. confused,
   swimming, unsteady 9. delirious
   10. capricious 11. vertiginous
Djibouti, east Africa...
city.. 5. Obock 6. Dikkil
gulf.. 4. Aden
do... 2. ut (Mus) 3. act, pay 4. dost,
   fare, make, suit, work 5. avoid, cause,
   cheat, exert, serve, solve 6. answer,
   effect, finish 7. achieve, deceive,
   execute, perform, produce, prosper,
   suffice 8. transact 9. discharge
   10. administer
docile... 4. calm, tame 6. gentle
   7. duteous 9. compliant, teachable,
   tractable
dock... 4. clip, pier, slip 5. basin, jetty,
   plant, wharf 6. cut off, deduct,
   hangar 7. curtail, shorten
   8. waterway 9. anchorage
   12. witness stand
docket... 4. list, mark 6. record, ticket
   8. calendar, schedule 11. certificate
docking post... 7. bollard
dock worker... 6. loader 7. laborer
   9. stevedore 12. longshoreman
doctor... 3. cut, fly (angling) 4. dose
   5. spike, title, treat 6. degree, dilute,
   healer, intern (interne) 7. surgeon,
   teacher 9. physician 10. adulterate,
   veterinary 12. psychiatrist
doctrine... 3. ism, ist 4. rule 5. credo,
   creed, dogma, logic, maxim, tenet
   6. gospel 7. article, opinion, precept
   8. position 9. principle
doctrine (pert to)...
existence (Philos).. 6. henism
finality (Theol).. 11. eschatology
good.. 8. agathism
inevitability.. 8. fatalism
philosophy.. 10. pragmatism
secrecy.. 6. cabala 8. esoteric
selfishness.. 6. egoism
doctus... 7. learned
document... 4. deed, writ 5. paper,
   proof, scrip 6. escrow 7. archive
   11. corroborate
document (pert to)...
copy (true).. 5. Xerox 7. estreat

8. syngraph 9. duplicate, photostat
depository.. 8. archives
file, report.. 7. dossier
hamper.. 7. hanaper
dodecade... 5. dozen 6. twelve (series)
dodge... 4. duck, jouk, snub 5. avoid,
   cheat, elude, evade, parry, trick
   6. escape, palter 7. deceive
   8. artifice 9. expedient
dodger... 7. biscuit, shirker
   8. deceiver, handbill
dodo... 3. moa 4. bird (extinct)
doe... 3. tag, teg 4. deer, hind
doer... 5. actor, agent, maker
   6. author, factor, worker 7. manager
   8. attorney, executor, producer
   9. performer
doff... 4. vail 5. strip 6. divest,
   remove 7. take off, undress
dog... 3. cur, pug 4. foot, lyam (lyme)
   5. canis, hound, pooch, whelp
   6. canine, fallow, shadow, wretch,
   yelper 7. mongrel 9. carnivore
   13. constellation
dog (breed)... 3. pom 4. chow, Dane
   5. boxer, husky 6. basset, beagle,
   collie, lucern, nootka, poodle, Saluki,
   setter, Sussex 7. bulldog, griffon,
   mastiff, pointer, Samoyed, Shih Tzu,
   spaniel, terrier, whippet 8. Airedale,
   Doberman, Keeshong, Labrador,
   Malemute, Pekinese, Sealyham,
   shepherd 9. Chihuahua, dachshund,
   Dalmatian, greyhound, Pekingese,
   retriever, schnauzer, St Bernard,
   wolfhound 10. bloodhound,
   Pomeranian, schipperke 11. Skye
   terrier 12. gazelle hound 13. Boston
   terrier
dog (pert to)...
Buster Brown.. 4. Tige
Cape (hunting).. 8. cynhyena
days.. 8. canicule
F D R's.. 4. Fala (Falla)
ferocious.. 7. agouara
fictional.. 4. Asta, Toby
house.. 6. kennel
howl.. 9. ululation
like.. 6. cynoid
mythical.. 7. Cerebus
part.. 5. flews 7. dewclaw
short-eared (Her).. 4. alan (aland)
star.. 6. Sirius 8. Canicula
Victor records.. 6. Nipper (His
   Master's Voice)
wild.. 5. dhole, dingo 6. bandog,
   kolsun 8. cimarron
Doge's barge... 9. Bucentaur
dogfish... 5. shark 6. burbot
   9. blackfish 10. nursehound
dogma... 4. code 5. tenet 6. belief,
   dictum, ritual 7. precept 8. doctrine
   9. Levitical, principle
dogmatic... 7. certain 8. absolute,
   positive 9. assertive, canonical,
   doctrinal, pragmatic 11. dictatorial,
   doctrinaire, magisterial, opinionated
dogmatism... 10. pragmatism
   11. intolerance
dogwood... 5. osier 6. cornel
   7. boxwood
do it again... 5. itero

dole... 4. alms, mete 5. grief
6. sorrow 8. pittance 9. allotment
10. distribute, misfortune
12. distribution
doleful... 3. sad 4. dree 5. drear
6. dismal, dreary, rueful, woeful
8. doloroso, dolorous, grievous,
jeremiad, mournful 10. lugubrious,
melancholy
doll... 3. toy 4. baby (toy), girl
6. moppet, puppet 9. miniature,
plaything
dolphin... 4. fish, inia 5. bouto
6. dorado, dugong, sea pig
8. Cetacean, porpoise 9. goosebeak
10. bottlenose
dolt... 3. ass, oaf 4. clod, dope, loon,
lout, moke 5. dunce, idiot 7. dullard
8. clodpate, dumbbell, numskull
9. blockhead, dumb bunny
10. ignoramous
domain... 5. realm 6. empery, empire,
sphere 7. country, demesne
8. dominion
dome... 4. arch, head, roof (Astron)
5. spire, tower 6. cupola, turret
Domesday, doomsday... 4. Book (Eng
Hist) 11. Judgment Day 13. Great
Domesday 14. Little Domesday
17. Domesday of St Paul's
domestic... 4. tame 5. domal
7. servant 9. enchorial, home–grown,
intestine (not foreign)
domestic establishment... 6. ménage
9. household
domicile... 5. abode, house 7. habitat
8. dwelling 9. residence
10. habitation
dominant... 5. chief, chord 6. ruling
7. regnant, supreme 8. superior
9. ascendant, governing, imperious,
paramount, principal
10. pre–eminent, prevailing
11. influential, outweighing,
overtopping 12. preponderant
13. authoritative, overbalancing
dominate... 4. boss, rule, sway
5. reign 6. govern 7. command,
control, overtop, possess
11. predominate
domineering... 6. lordly 7. haughty
8. arrogant, blustery 9. imperious,
masterful 10. oppressive
11. overbearing
Dominican Republic...
capital.. 12. Santo Domingo
city.. 14. Ciudad Trujillo
discoverer.. 8. Columbus
island site.. 10. Hispaniola
oldest city (W Hem).. 12. Santo
Domingo (1496)
dominion... 4. rule, sway 5. realm
6. empery, empire, sphere 7. control
9. authority, hierarchy (celestial)
12. jurisdiction
domino... 3. pip (spot) 4. game (in
pl), hood, mask 5. amice, cloak,
ivory 7. costume
dominoes, galloping... 7. ivories
donate... 3. tip 4. give 6. bestow
7. present
done... 4. fini 5. baked, ended, finis

6. agreed, cooked 7. through
8. finished, tired out 9. completed,
concluded, exhausted
done (pert to)...
by stealth.. 13. surreptitious
by word of mouth.. 5. parol
for pay.. 9. mercenary
with effort.. 5. labor
Don Juan's girl (novel)... 6. Haidee
donkey... 3. ass 4. moke 5. burro,
neddy 6. onager
donna... 4. Dona, lady, wife
5. madam, woman 8. mistress
Don Quixote's steed... 9. Rosinante
doom... 3. fey, lot 4. fate, ruin
5. death 7. condemn, destine,
destiny 8. sentence 11. destruction
doomed... 3. fey 5. death, fated,
goner 9. sentenced
doomsday... 8. Ragnarok
11. Judgment Day (see *Domesday*)
door... 4. gate 6. portal 7. doorway,
opening, passage, postern
11. entranceway 12. porte–cochere
doorframe... 3. dar 4. jamb, rail,
sash, sill 5. janua, panel, stile
6. lintel 9. threshold
doorkeeper... 4. hasp 5. tiler 6. porter
7. durwaum, ostiary 8. chokidar
9. concierge
dope... 3. hop, LSD 4. hemp
6. mescal, opiate, peyoti (peyote)
7. fathead 8. narcotic 9. marijuana
Dorian Festival (Sparta)... 6. carnea
(carneia)
Dorian magistrates... 6. ephors
Doric Order (Gr Arch)...
capital.. 6. abacus
frieze fillet.. 6. taenia
frieze space.. 6. metope
history.. 6. oldest 8. simplest
dormant... 5. inert 6. asleep, latent,
torpid 7. resting 8. inactive, sleeping
9. quiescent
dormer window... 5. oriel 6. gablet
7. dormant (obs), lucarne
dormeuse... 5. couch 8. carriage
(sleeping), nightcap
dormouse... 4. Glis, loir 5. lerot
6. rodent
dorsal (pert to)...
back.. 5. notal, notum 6. dorsum,
lumbar, neural, tergal, tergum
column.. 6. spinal
dose... 5. bolus, draft, treat 6. potion
7. portion
dot... 3. jot 4. clot, code, lump
5. dowry, fleck, point, speck, telia
(fungus) 6. period 7. stipple
dote... 3. rot 5. decay, dowry
6. babble, dotage, dotard, drivel,
stupor 7. portion (marriage)
8. imbecile
dotted... 5. pinto 7. piebald, specked,
studded 8. stippled 9. sprinkled
11. diversified
Douay. Bible... 4. Aree
double... 2. di (pref) 4. dual, fold,
twin 5. duple, plait, twice 6. binary,
binate, duplex, folded 7. twofold
8. artifice, two–faced 9. deceitful,
duplicate, insincere, intensify

11. counterpart
double (pert to)...
bars (Her).. 5. gemel
cross.. 7. deceive, two–time
dagger.. 6. diesis
edged.. 9. ancipital
ghost (live person).. 11. counterpart
12. Doppelgänger, doubleganger
meaning.. 9. equivocal
doubt... 5. demur, waver 8. hesitate,
mistrust, question 9. misgiving,
suspicion 10. Pyrrhonism, skepticism
11. uncertainty
doubter... 5. cynic 6. Humist
7. skeptic 10. Pyrrhonist
doubtful... 7. dubious 8. wavering
9. ambiguous, equivocal, uncertain,
undecided 10. hesitating, improbable,
precarious 11. distrustful, vacillating
12. questionable, unbelievable,
undetermined 13. problematical
doubtful authority... 6. mythic, unreal
10. apocryphal
dough... 4. cash, mash 5. money,
paste 6. leaven, noodle
doughnut... 6. sinker 7. cruller, simball
9. friedcake
dour... 5. harsh, stern 6. gloomy,
severe 9. obstinate 10. inflexible
dove... 3. nun 4. blue (color), Inca
5. color 6. culver, pigeon
7. Columba, tumbler
Dove, the... 6. symbol (Relig)
10. Holy Spirit
dovefoot... 8. geranium (wild)
dovekey, dovekie... 3. auk 4. Alle
6. rotche 9. guillemot
dowdy... 3. pig (deep–dish) 6. pastry,
shabby, untidy 7. pudding 8. slovenly
10. slatternly
dowel... 3. pin 4. coak 5. tenon
6. fasten, pintle
dower... 3. dos 5. dowry, endow,
grant 6. dotate 7. bequest
8. dotation, jointure
down... 2. de (pref) 3. nap 4. fuzz,
hair 5. adown, below, floor
7. descent 8. softness
downcast... 3. low, sad 7. lowered
8. dejected 9. bowed down,
depressed 10. despondent, dispirited
11. discouraged, downhearted
downright... 4. flat 5. blunt, plain,
sheer, stark, utter 6. arrant, candid
8. positive, thorough 10. absolutely,
forthright 11. unqualified
13. unceremonious
downy... 4. soft, wary 5. nappy, pilar,
quiet 6. placid 7. villous 8. feathery
10. flocculent, lanuginose, lanuginous
dowry... 3. dos, dot 4. gift 5. dower,
sulka 6. talent 9. endowment
dowser's tool... 4. wand 6. willow
Doxology... 4. hymn 6. praise
7. Kaddish
doze... 3. nap, nod 5. sleep
6. catnap, drowse, snooze 7. stupefy
(obs)
draft, draught... 3. map, nip 4. dose,
dram, draw, plan, pull, swig
5. drink, epure 7. current, diagram,
drawing, outline 8. protocol, recruits,

traction 9. conscript 10. money
order
drag... 3. lag, lug, tow, tug 4. clog,
draw, hale, haul, pull, sing, tump
5. drawl, scent (hunt), smoke, trail
6. drogue, harrow 7. grapnel
8. dragrope, linger on, obstacle
10. conveyance
dragoman... 11. interpreter (official)
dragon... 4. lung 5. drake, Rahab (Bib)
6. animal, duenna, lizard, musket
(anc), pigeon 7. dragoon, monster
(Her), serpent 10. earthdrake
14. Dragon of Komodo
drain... 3. gaw, sap 4. lade, loss,
sink, sump 5. ditch, dreen, empty,
rhine, sewer, siver 6. filter, trench
7. acequia, alberca, channel,
consume, exhaust, outflow
11. watercourse
dram... 3. nip 4. mite, slug 5. draft,
drink 6. drachm 8. potation
11. indifferent
drama (pert to)...
beginning.. 8. Dyonysia (anc)
form.. 4. play 5. opera 6. comedy
7. tragedy 10. peripeteia
11. composition
parts.. 8. epitasis, protasis
12. introduction
scenery.. 7. diorama
dramatic... 4. wild 5. stagy, vivid,
vocal 6. poetic, scenic 8. thespian
10. histrionic, theatrical
11. pretentious, spectacular
12. melodramatic
dramatic piece... 4. skit
drastic... 5. stern 6. fierce, severe
7. intense, radical 8. rigorous
draught... see *draft*
Dravidian (pert to)...
country (anc).. 5. India
ghost.. 4. bhut
language.. 5. Tamil 8. Kanarese
12. Dravido–Munda
native.. 5. Croat 8. Croatian
people.. 4. Nair 6. Slavic
soldier.. 8. Croatian
draw... 3. lug, tie, tow, tug 4. drag,
etch, haul, limn, lure, plot, pull, tole
5. draft, smoke 6. allure, arroyo,
convey, entice 7. attract, conduct,
extract, lottery 9. delineate
10. attraction
draw (pert to)...
away.. 6. abduce, divert 7. detract
close.. 4. loom, near 5. hover
8. approach
forth.. 5. educe 6. elicit, ferret
7. extract
off.. 6. siphon 7. extract 8. abstract,
withdraw
through an eye.. 4. rove
together.. 4. coul, frap, lace, rake
8. assemble
drawback... 5. fault, wince 6. defect,
resile, retire 8. obstacle 9. objection
12. disadvantage
drawing... 3. art 5. draft 7. diagram,
hauling, picture, pulling 8. doodling
9. animation 10. attracting,
extracting

drawing back... 9. retrahent
drayage... 6. charge 7. cartage,
  haulage 8. truckage
  14. transportation
dread... 3. awe 4. fear 5. timor
  6. dismay, horror, terror 7. anxiety
  8. affright, disquiet 9. reverence
  12. apprehension
dreadful... 4. dire 6. horrid
  7. awesome, fearful, hideous
  8. horrible, terrible, terrific 9. frightful
  10. formidable, outrageous
dreadnaught, dreadnought... 5. cloth
  7. garment 8. fearless 10. battleship,
  fearnought
dream... 4. muse, rêve 5. fancy
  6. bubble, vision 7. imagine,
  reverie, romance, suppose
  8. illusion, stargaze
  11. contemplate
dream (pert to)...
  interpretation.. 10. oneirology
  interpreter.. 12. oneirocritic
  tranquility.. 3. kef (keef) 7. reverie
dreamer... 4. seer 7. fantast
  8. idealist, puffbird 9. visionary
  11. romanticist 13. castle–builder
dreamy... 3. kef (keef) 6. poetic
  7. languid 8. soothing 9. visionary
  11. imaginative
dreary... 3. sad 4. dull, gray 5. bleak,
  ourie 6. dismal, elenge, gloomy,
  remote 7. doleful, tedious
  9. cheerless 10. depressing,
  foreboding, melancholy, monotonous
  11. comfortless
dredge... 4. tong (for oysters)
  5. scoop 6. burrow, deepen, grains,
  tunnel 8. excavate
dregs... 4. faex, lees, marc, silt
  5. draff, dross, magma 6. refuse,
  scoria, sludge 7. grounds, hogwash,
  residue 8. riffraff, sediment
  9. settlings 10. faex populi
drench... 4. hose, soak 5. douse,
  draft, imbue, purge, scour, souse
  6. potion 7. immerse 8. inundate,
  permeate, saturate, submerge
drenched... 4. asop 5. asoak
  6. doused, soaked 9. saturated
dress... 3. rig, tog 4. deck, garb,
  gown, suit, trim 5. getup, mufti,
  preen 6. attire, clothe, enrobe, livery,
  toilet 7. apparel, threads (sl)
  8. clothing, decorate, negligee
  10. habiliment 13. mother hubbard
dress (pert to)...
  flax.. 3. ted
  gaudily.. 5. prank 7. bedizen, spangle
  leather.. 3. taw, tew 5. curry
  of Mecca pilgrims.. 5. ihram
  riding.. 5. chaps, habit 7. hacking
  (jacket) 8. jodhpurs 10. chaparajos
  stone.. 3. dab, nig 5. nidge
  surgically.. 5. dight, panse 7. bandage
  8. ligature
  up.. 4. dude 5. preen, primp
  6. spruce 8. titivate
dressed loosely... 8. discinct,
  ungirded
dressing... 4. lint 5. sauce
  7. bandage, pledget, raiment, reproof

8. attiring, scolding 9. condiment,
  neatsfoot (leather) 11. castigation
drew... see *draw*
dried... 4. sere 5. wiped 6. seared,
  wasted 7. drained, parched, wizened
  9. shriveled 10. dehydrated,
  desiccated, exsiccated
dried meat... 7. biltong (biltongue),
  charqui 8. pemmican 10. jerked beef
dried tubers (orchids)... 5. salep
drift... 3. aim, sag 4. idle, pile, sail,
  soar, tide, tool 5. float, stray, tenor,
  trend 6. course, intent 7. deposit,
  impetus, meaning 8. crescent
  (sidewise), movement, seaweeds,
  tendency 9. deviation
drill... 3. gad, row (seeds), tap 4. bore
  5. auger, borer, train 6. baboon,
  pierce 7. machine 8. excavate,
  exercise, practice, rehearse
  9. perforate
drilling... 5. denim 7. nurture
  8. training 11. inculcation
drink... 3. ade, ale, bib, lap, nip, pop,
  rum, sip, tea, tot 4. flip, fram, grog,
  shot, slug, soda, soma, swig, tope
  5. bouse, draft, julep, negus, posca,
  punch, quaff, skink, toast, toddy,
  water 6. caudle, coffee, imbibe,
  liquor, mai tai, mao–tai, posset, potion,
  ptisan, tipple 8. beverage, cocktail,
  highball, sillabub 9. decoction
  10. intoxicant, mixed drink
drink (pert to)...
  ancient.. 5. morat
  Arabian.. 4. boza
  English.. 7. wassail 8. champers
  fond of.. 8. bibulous
  frozen.. 6. frappé
  gods (of the).. 6. nectar
  honey.. 4. mead 5. morat
  hot.. 5. salep, toddy 6. posset, saloop
  Irish.. 10. shandygaff
  Japanese.. 4. sake
  mix.. 5. setup 8. vermouth
  9. grenadine
  rum.. 5. bumbo
  Russian.. 5. vodka 6. kumiss (koumiss)
  Spanish.. 7. tequila
  together.. 9. symposium
  tropical.. 7. sangria 8. sangaree
  Turkish.. 4. raki 5. airan, arrak
drinking salutation... 5. skoal, toast
  6. prosit 7. propine, slainte
drinking vessel... 3. mug 4. bowl,
  tass 5. cylix (anc), glass, gourd, jorum,
  mazer, stein 6. goblet, rhyton
  7. tankard 8. schooner 10. Vaphio
  cups (gold)
drip... 3. bore, drop, leak 5. droop
  7. dribble, falling, trickle
drive... 3. caa 4. herd, ride, slog, urge
  5. force, guide, impel, pilot, press,
  rouse 6. attack, compel, energy,
  propel, thrust 7. crusade, operate
  8. campaign 10. compulsion
drive (pert to)...
  away.. 4. rout 5. chase, exile, expel,
  repel 6. banish, dispel, rebuff
  7. repulse 8. disperse
  down.. 4. tamp
  frantic.. 4. loco 6. madden 7. bedevil

obliquely.. 3. toe 5. slice
stakes.. 4. camp, park 6. locate, settle
drivel... 4. dote 5. drool 6. slaver 7. slobber, twaddle 8. nonsense
driveler... 4. fool 5. doter, idiot 6. dotard, prater 8. jabberer 9. blatherer, chatterer
driver... 4. club (golf), jehu 6. drover, hammer, mahout, sarwan 7. speeder 8. coachman, engineer, motorist, operator, overseer, reinsman 9. propeller 10. charioteer, taskmaster
drizzle... 4. mist, rain, smur 6. mizzle (misle)
droll... 3. odd 4. zany 5. comic, merry, queer, witty 6. jester 7. amusing, buffoon, waggish 8. farcical, humorous 9. diverting, laughable, whimsical 10. ridiculous 11. merry–andrew
drollery... 3. wit 4. jest 5. farce, humor 6. puppet 9. absurdity 10. buffoonery
dromedary... 4. oont 5. camel (one–hump) 6. hageen 7. Camelus 8. Bactrian (two–hump)
drone... 3. bee, dor, hum 4. male (bee) 5. idler, snail 7. bagpipe, humming 8. sluggard 9. non worker, slow mover
drool... 6. drivel, slaver 7. dribble, slabber, slobber
droop... 3. lop, sag 4. flag, hang, loll, pine, sink, tire, wilt 6. nutate, slouch 7. decline 8. languish
drooping... 4. alop, weak 5. loose 7. hanging, nodding, sinking 8. dejected, fatigued 11. languishing
drooping eyelids... 6. ptosis
drop... 4. bead, blob, dose, dram, drib, drip, fall, omit, shed, sink, clot, stop, tear 5. candy, dreep, droop, gutta, lower, minim, remit 6. letter, plunge 7. abandon, descent, distill (distil), earring, globule, pendant, trickle 8. ornament, trapdoor 9. declivity 10. relinquish
drop (pert to)...
anchor.. 4. moor
by drop.. 7. guttate 9. guttation
measure.. 7. pipette 11. stactometer
nautical.. 5. hance
serene.. 9. amaurosis (Med)
vowel.. 5. elide
dropsy... 5. edema 8. hydropsy, swelling
dross... 4. lees, scum, slag 5. chaff, dregs, scobs, sprue, waste 6. refuse, scoria, sinter (iron)
drove... 4. herd 5. crowd, drive, flock
drover... 4. boat 6. dealer (cattle), driver 8. herdsman
drowse... 3. nid, nod 4. doze 5. dover (Eng), sleep 6. snooze
drowsiness... 7. languor 8. dullness, lethargy 9. lassitude, oscitance 10. narcolepsy, sleepiness 12. listlessness, sluggishness
drowsy... 4. logy 6. sleepy 8. oscitant, soothing 9. somnolent, soporific

drudge... 3. fag 4. grub, hack, mail, plod, toil 5. labor, slave 6. toiler 7. plodder
drug... 4. alum, dope, dull, numb 6. opiate 7. stupefy 8. narcotic, sedative 10. medication 11. anesthetize
drug (pert to)...
action.. 7. synergy
addict.. 6. junkie
analgesic.. 6. Anacin 7. aspirin 10. acetanilid, phenacetin
anesthesia.. 3. gas 5. ether 8. Novocain 10. chloroform
dangerous.. 11. thalidomide
emetic.. 6. ipecac 11. ipecacuanha
eye.. 8. atropine 10. belladonna
forgetfulness.. 8. nepenthe
narcotic.. 3. hop, kif 4. hemp 5. bhang, daggo, opium 6. codein 7. cocaine 9. marijuana
sedative.. 7. bromide, Seconal, Veronal 8. barbital, Nembutal 11. scopolamine 13. phenobarbital
drugget... 3. mat, rug 5. cloth
druggist... 8. gallipot 10. apothecary, pharmacist
Druids (anc)... 5. Order (Relig) 9. conjurers 12. philosophers
drum... 4. beat 5. naker, snare, tabor, tombe 6. atabal, barrel, tambor (tambour), tom–tom, tympan 7. taboret, timbrel, timpany 8. cylinder, tympanum (ear)
drum (pert to)...
call.. 4. dian (diana) 6. rappel, tattoo 8. rataplan
Indian.. 6. nagara
nautical term.. 7. capstan
Oriental.. 6. tom–tom 7. anacara
drunkard... 3. sot 4. snek 5. souse, toper 6. addict, barfly, boozer 7. guzzler, tippler 9. alcoholic, inebriate 11. dipsomaniac
dry... 3. sec, ted 4. arid, blot, brut, dull, keen, seco, sere, wipe 5. drain, parch, vapid 6. aerify, barren, jejune, shrewd 7. insipid, sterile, thirsty, xerotic 8. solidify, tiresome 9. dehydrate, fruitless, pointless 12. unprofitable 13. uninteresting
dryad... 5. deity, Napea, nymph, oread
duck... 3. dip 4. flee, fowl 5. dodge, douse 6. plunge 7. bob down
duck (breed)... 4. Anas, coot, pato, skua, smee, smew, teal 5. Anser, eider, scaup 6. Aythya, Nyroca, Peking, scoter 7. mallard, Muscovy, pintail, pochard, Spatula, widgeon 8. Anatinae, bluebill, shoveler (shoveller) 9. harlequin, merganser, sheldrake 10. bufflehead, canvasback, ring–necked
duck (pert to)...
baby.. 8. duckling
class.. 3. sea 5. river 7. Muscovy
disabled.. 4. lame
ducklike.. 5. decoy 8. duckbill
fabric.. 5. cloth
flock (mallards).. 4. sord
flower.. 12. lady's slipper
game.. 6. tenter

hawk . . 6. falcon 7. harrier
litter . . 4. team
male . . 5. drake
ruddy . . 5. noddy
duct . . . 3. vas 4. main, pipe, race,
tube 5. canal 7. channel, passage,
trachea 8. aqueduct
ductile . . . 6. docile, facile, pliant
7. elastic, plastic, tensile 8. flexible,
tractile, yielding 9. compliant,
complying, malleable, tractable
10. manageable
dude . . . 3. fop 5. dandy 7. coxcomb,
Johnnie 10. tenderfoot
dudeen . . . 4. pipe (tobacco)
due . . . 4. debt, duty, just, meed, owed
5. owing 6. charge, lawful 7. exactly
8. adequate, directly, expected,
rightful 9. appointed 10. ascribable,
sufficient
duel . . . 4. tilt 5. fence 6. combat
7. contest 8. conflict 9. monomachy
12. satisfaction
duelist's aide . . . 6. second
duet . . . 3. duo 8. duettino
dug . . . see *dig*
dugong . . . 7. manatee, Sirenia
8. Halicore
dugout . . . 4. abri, cave, shed 5. canoe
6. cavity 7. pirogue, shelter
dulcet . . . 5. sweet 6. ariose 7. tuneful
8. pleasant, soothing 9. agreeable,
melodious 10. harmonious
dulcimer . . . 6. citole 7. bagpipe,
cembalo 8. psaltery 10. instrument
dull . . . 3. dim, dry, dun 4. dead, drab,
gray, logy, poky 6. barren, cloudy,
deaden, dismal, dreary, drowsy,
jejune, leaden, muffle, obtund,
obtuse, sleepy, somber, stupid
7. doltish, irksome, prosaic, tedious
8. lifeless, listless, overcast, sluggish,
stagnant, tiresome 9. apathetic,
inanimate, saturnine, unfeeling
10. insensible, lackluster, melancholy,
slow–witted 13. unimaginative
dull (pert to) . . .
finish . . 3. mat (matte)
heavy . . 4. logy 5. leady 6. stodgy
of cloth . . 6. starry (Eng)
statement . . 9. platitude
dullard . . . 3. oaf 4. dope, mope
5. dunce 8. dumbbell, numskull
9. dumb bunny
dumb . . . 4. mute 6. aphony, silent,
stupid 7. aphonia 8. ignorant,
taciturn 9. inanimate, irregular
10. speechless 12. inarticulate
dumbfounded . . . 6. amazed 7. crabbed
9. staggered, surprised
10. astonished, bewildered
11. overwhelmed 13. flabbergasted
dummy . . . 3. pel 4. copy, dolt, mort
(cards), sham 5. model 6. pontic,
silent 9. imitation, mannequin,
nonentity 10. figurehead, substitute
11. counterfeit
dump . . . 3. tip 4. bump, game (Eng),
jail, sell, thud, tune 5. empty, hovel
6. plunge, unload 7. discard
10. rendezvous

dumpling . . . 7. biscuit, gnocchi
10. appleberry
dupe . . . 3. fox 4. bilk, cull, tool
5. cheat, fraud, trick 6. delude,
sucker 7. cat's–paw, deceive, mislead
duplicate . . . 4. copy, game (cards),
twin 6. double, duplex 7. estreat,
mislead, replica, twofold 8. likeness
9. analogous, facsimile, identical,
replicate 10. transcript
11. counterpart 12. reproduction
duplicated . . . 7. dittoed 8. repeated
10. repetitive
duplicity . . . 5. fraud, guile 6. deceit
7. duality 9. deception, duplexity,
falsehood, treachery
13. dissimulation, double–dealing
durable . . . 4. firm 5. stout, tough
6. staple 7. lasting 8. constant,
enduring 9. permanent
10. continuing, persistent
11. everlasting, substantial
duration . . . 3. age 4. date, span, term,
time 6. period 8. eternity, lifetime
10. durability, permanence
11. continuance
during . . . 4. time 5. while 6. whilst
7. pending, through 10. throughout
dusk . . . 3. dark 5. dusky, gloom, slate
(color) 8. gloaming, twilight
dusky . . . 3. dim, sad 4. dark, dusk
5. murky, tawny, umbra 6. gloomy,
somber 7. swarthy 8. blackish
10. melancholy
dust . . . 4. cash, coom (coomb), dirt,
gold, pilm, soil 5. briss, brush, chaff,
clean, color, earth, money, stive,
stour (dial), trash 6. corpse, pollen,
powder 7. dryness, turmoil
9. commotion, confusion, sweepings
dust (pert to) . . .
flax . . 5. pouce
flour . . 5. stive
glacier . . 10. kryokonite
reduce to . . 4. mull
speck . . 4. mote
Dutch (pert to) . . . see also *Netherlands*
cheese . . 4. Edam 7. cottage
country . . 7. Germany, Holland
11. Netherlands
man . . 10. Hogen–Mogen
news agency . . 5. Aneta
painter . . 4. Hals
poet . . 7. Da Costa
pottery . . 4. delf (delft) 9. delftware
river . . 3. Eem 4. Maas 5. Meuse
scholar . . 7. Erasmus (Humanist)
woman, wife . . 4. frow
uncle . . 3. eme (dial), oom
Dutch East Indies (Indonesia) . . .
capital . . 7. Batavia (former), Jakarta
(Djakarta)
islands (3,000), largest . . 4. Bali, Java
6. Borneo (part) 7. Celebes, Sumatra
8. Malaysia (part) 9. New Guinea
(part)
renamed . . 9. Indonesia
Dutch Guiana (Netherlands Antilles) . . .
capital . . 10. Paramaribo
mountain . . 10. Tumuc Humac
renamed . . 7. Surinam
dutiful . . . 6. devout, docile 7. duteous

8. obedient, reverent 9. compliant
10. respectful, submissive
11. deferential, reverential
duty . . . 3. job, tax 4. care, onus, rite,
task, toll 5. chore, stint, trick
6. devoir, dharma, excise, heriot
(anc), impost, tariff 7. payment,
respect 9. reverence 10. imposition,
obligation
dwale . . . 5. sable (Her) 6. opiate,
potion 9. soporific 10. belladonna,
nightshade
dwarf . . . 3. elf, urf 4. grig, puny, runt
5. crile, gnome, midge, pygmy
(pigmy), small, stunt, troll 6. droich,
durgan, midget 7. manikin, Pacolet,
stunted 9. dandiprat, micrander
10. diminished, homunculus
dwarfish . . . 6. nanoid
dwarfishness . . . 6. nanism
Dwarfs, The Seven . . . 3. Doc
5. Dopey, Happy 6. Grumpy, Sleepy,
Sneezy 7. Bashful
dwell . . . 4. bide, harp, live, stay
5. abide, delay, lodge, pause, tarry
6. linger, remain, reside
dwelling . . . 3. hut 4. flat 5. abode,
hotel, house, hovel 6. duplex, shanty
7. trailer 8. abidance, domicile,
tenement 9. apartment, residence
10. habitation
dwelling (pert to) . . .
house (law) . . 8. messuage
in field . . 10. arvicoline
in groves . . 10. nemoricole
of dead (Bab) . . 5. Aralu
of souls (Polyn) . . 2. Po
Oriental . . 3. dar
dwindle . . . 4. melt, wane 5. taper,
waste 6. lessen, shrink, sicken

8. decrease, diminish 10. degenerate
dyad . . . 3. two 4. duad, pair
6. couple, dyadic
Dyak, Dayak . . . 5. tribe (Borneo)
7. blowgun 8. sumpiter 9. aborigine
dye . . . 4. anil 5. color, imbue, stain,
tinge 7. pigment 8. colorant
dye stuff (pert to) . . .
blue . . 4. woad (wad, wade)
brown . . 5. erika, sumac
indigo . . 4. anil
mulberry . . 3. aal
red . . 4. chay 5. aurin, eosin, henna
6. isatin, madder, relbun 7. annatto,
magenta 8. morindin 9. rhodamine
10. orseilline
violet . . 5. murex 6. archil
yellow . . 7. xanthic 8. luteolin,
orpiment 10. quercitron
dyke . . . see *dike*
dynamic . . . 4. keen 5. acute, vivid
6. potent 7. intense, kinetic
8. forceful, forcible 9. energetic,
strenuous
dynamite inventor . . . 5. Nobel (1866)
dynamo (pert to) . . .
attachment . . 10. commutator
inventor . . 7. Faraday
machine . . 9. generator
part . . 5. rotor 8. armature
dynast . . . 5. ruler 6. prince 8. governor
dynasty . . . 4. race 8. dominion,
lordship 10. succession
11. sovereignty
dynasty (pert to) . . .
Chinese . . 2. Fo 3. Han, Yin 4. Isin,
Ming, Sung, Tang
Spanish . . 6. Ommiad
dysphoria . . . 7. illness 8. debility
dyvour . . . 6. beggar 8. bankrupt
dzeran . . . 8. antelope

E

E . . . 7. Epsilon (Gr)
Ea (Bab) . . . 3. God 5. deity
each . . . 3. all, per 5. alike, every
6. apiece, singly 10. separately
12. individually 14. distributively
eager . . . 3. apt 4. agog, avid, keen,
yare 5. agasp, sharp 6. ardent,
greedy, intent 7. anxious, burning,
excited, thirsty, willing, zealous
8. desirous, spirited 9. strenuous
eager beaver . . . 7. hustler 8. go–getter
10. enthusiast
eagerness . . . 4. élan, zeal 5. ardor
6. fervor 7. avidity 8. alacrity,
cupidity, fervency 9. alertness,
readiness 10. enthusiasm, impatience
13. impetuousness
eagle . . . 4. erne (ern), gier (Bib), seal
6. bergut, eaglet, emblem

8. standard (Rom) 13. constellation
(Milky Way)
eagle (pert to) . . .
American . . 4. bald
brood . . 5. aerie, eyrie
coin . . 4. gold
European . . 3. sea 5. harpy 6. golden
8. imperial
genus . . 6. Aquila
heraldry . . 8. allerion
male . . 6. tercil
sacred to Jupiter . . 9. Jove's bird
S America . . 9. eagle hawk
scout badge . . 5. merit
Eagles . . . 14. Fraternal Order
eagre (acker) . . . 4. bore, flow, wave
5. flood (tidal)
ear . . . 4. head 5. auris 7. auricle,
hearing 8. orillion 9. appendage,

attention, orecchion (obs)
ear (pert to)...
anvil .. 5. incus
bone .. 6. stapes, tegman 7. stirrup
canal .. 7. cochlea 9. labyrinth
  10. Eustachian, scala media
external .. 6. concha
grain .. 3. epi 5. spica 6. mealie,
  rizzom (ressum)
hammer .. 7. malleus
inflammation .. 6. otitis
middle .. 8. tympanum
part .. 5. helix, pinna 6. tragus
science .. 7. otology
shell .. 5. ormer 7. abalone
specialist .. 6. aurist 9. otologist
stone .. 7. otolith
term .. 4. otic 5. aural
wax .. 7. cerumen
earache ... 6. otalgy 7. otalgia
early ... 4. soon 7. ancient, betimes,
  matinal 9. premature, primitive
  10. beforehand, beforetime
earn ... 3. get, win 4. gain 5. ettle,
  merit 7. acquire, deserve
earnest ... 5. arles (pledge), grave,
  sober, staid 6. ardent, hearty, pledge,
  sedate, solemn 7. handsel (money),
  serious, sincere, zealous 8. resolute
  9. heartfelt, important 10. thoughtful
  12. wholehearted
earnestly ... 8. solemnly 9. intensely,
  zealously 10. resolutely
earphone ... 7. trumpet (double)
  8. otoscope 9. auriphone, topophone
  (double) 11. stethescope
earring ... 4. hoop 6. earbob, pendle
  7. earstud, pendant 9. girandole
  (girandola)
earth ... 3. erd 4. clay, clod, dirt, land,
  marl, muck, sand, soil, vale 5. geest,
  loess, sloam, terra 6. ground, planet,
  rideau 7. topsoil 8. alluvium
earth (pert to)...
center .. 10. geocentric
  12. centrosphere
comb form .. 3. geo
deformation .. 10. epeirogeny
formed beneath .. 8. hypogene,
  plutonic
formed by ores .. 9. supergene
formed on surface .. 7. epigene
god (Egypt) .. 3. Geb (Keb)
goddess .. 4. Erda, Gaea (Gaia), Tari
  6. Semele 7. Demeter
produced by .. 6. mortal
  11. terrigenous
satellite .. see *satellite*
volcanic .. 5. trass
earthdrake ... 6. dragon
earthly ... 7. mundane, secular, terrene,
  worldly 8. temporal 11. terrestrial,
  universally, unspiritual
  13. materialistic
earthmover ... 6. digger 7. backhoe,
  leveler 9. bulldozer, excavator
  10. steam shovel
earth pig ... 8. aardvark
earthquake ... 5. quake, seism
  7. temblor 12. diastrophism

earthstar ... 6. fungus 7. Geaster
earthworm ... 7. annalid, dew worm,
  ipokoea 9. Lumbricus
earthy ... 3. low 5. gross 6. coarse
  7. worldly 8. material 9. unrefined
ease ... 4. calm, rest 5. abate, allay,
  peace, quiet, relax 6. pacify, relief,
  repose, soothe 7. assuage, comfort,
  content, leisure, relieve, slacken
  8. facility, mitigate 9. alleviate,
  disburden, enjoyment 10. prosperity,
  relaxation, solicitude 11. informality,
  tranquilize 12. tranquillity (tranquility)
easily ... 4. eath (eith) 6. gently, slowly,
  softly 7. readily 8. smoothly
  11. comfortably, dexterously
  12. effortlessly
easily (pert to)...
broken .. 6. shelly 7. fragile, friable
frightened .. 8. skittish
managed .. 6. docile
moved .. 6. mobile
offended .. 9. sensitive
split .. 8. schistic
understood .. 5. lucid
east ... 4. Asia, dawn 6. Levant, Orient
  7. sunrise 8. eastward
East Africa ...
hartebeest .. 4. tora
house (mud) .. 5. tembe
republic .. 5. Kenya 7. Somalia
island .. 8. Zanzibar
tribes .. 3. Luo 4. Embu, Teso
  5. Bantu, Masai 6. Kikuyu, Mau Mau
  7. Nilotes
vessel .. 4. dhow
East India ... see also *East Indian*
drink .. 4. nipa
fan .. 6. punkah (punka)
gateway (temple) .. 5. toran (torana)
hat, helmet .. 5. topee (topi)
money of account .. 4. anna
mountain pass .. 4. ghat (ghaut)
musical instrument .. 4. vina 5. ruana,
  saron
police station .. 5. thana (tanna)
sailing vessel .. 5. dhoni (doni)
  7. patamar
sugar, molasses .. 3. gur
  10. massecuite
water vessel (brass) .. 4. lota (lotah)
East Indian animal ...
antelope .. 5. bongo, takin 6. impala,
  nilgai 8. axis deer
cattle .. 4. gaur, zebu 5. gayal, tsine
  7. banteng
civet .. 6. musang 10. paradoxure
goat (wild) .. 4. tahr 7. markhor
lemurlike .. 7. tarsier
raccoonlike .. 3. wah 5. panda
rat .. 9. bandicoot
swine .. 8. babirusa (babiroussa)
East Indian bird ...
broadbill .. 4. raya
bulbul .. 4. kala
falcon .. 5. besra
fruit pigeon .. 6. treron
thrush .. 5. shama
weaverbird .. 4. baya
East Indian people ...

boatswain .. **6.** serang
chief .. **6.** sirdar
groom .. **4.** syce
harem .. **6.** zenana
native sailor, soldier .. **5.** sepoy
  6. lascar
nurse .. **4.** amah, ayah
peasant .. **4.** ryot
poet .. **6.** Tagore
princess .. **4.** rani (ranee)
robber .. **6.** dacoit
title .. **4.** raja **5.** rajah, sahib
warrior .. **5.** singh
East Indian tree, plant ...
bark .. **4.** lodh **5.** niepa
cedar .. **6.** deodar
cotton .. **5.** simal
fiber .. **4.** jute
fruit .. **3.** bel **6.** lanseh (lansa)
gum .. **4.** kino
herb .. **5.** tikor **6.** sesame **7.** roselle
mahogany .. **4.** toon
mulberry .. **4.** tapa
palm .. **3.** tal (fiber) **4.** nipa (thatch)
  5. sural (juice), toddy **7.** palmyra
pea .. **4.** dhak **5.** Butea
rubber .. **3.** saj
shade .. **6.** banyan
timber .. **3.** saj, sal (saul) **4.** poon, teak
  5. siris **6.** sissoo
walnut .. **6.** lebbek
east wind ... **5.** Eurus
easy ... **4.** calm, slow **5.** loose, suave
  6. cinchy, facile, gentle, simple
  7. natural **8.** gullible, informal,
  moderate, tranquil, unforced
  9. leisurely, unhurried
  10. manageable, nonchalant,
  unaffected **11.** comfortable,
  complaisant, unconcerned
easy-going ... **4.** calm **11.** unflappable
easy job ... **8.** sinecure
easy mark ... **4.** dupe, gull **6.** sucker,
  victim **7.** cat's-paw
eat ... **3.** sup **4.** dine, etch, feed, gnaw
  5. board, erode **6.** devour, ravage
  7. consume, corrode, destroy
eat (pert to) ...
between meals .. **4.** nosh **5.** bever,
  snack
by rule .. **4.** diet
earth, clay .. **8.** geophagy
  12. chthonophagy
greedily .. **3.** lab **4.** glut **5.** gorge,
  scarf (down) **6.** gobble, pig out (sl)
  7. edacity **8.** voracity
eatable ... **6.** edible **8.** esculent,
  gustable **10.** comestible
eater ... **5.** diner **7.** epicure, glutton,
  gourmet **8.** gourmand
eating (pert to) ...
alone .. **9.** monophagy
comb form .. **7.** phagous
decay .. **12.** saprophagous
fish .. **11.** piscivorous
  13. icthyophagous
flesh, raw .. **9.** omophagia
flesh-eating .. **9.** creophagy
  10. zoophagous **11.** carnivorous
man-eating .. **12.** androphagous
  13. anthropophagy
nuts .. **10.** nucivorous

  11. nuciphagous
plants, herbs .. **11.** herbivorous
  12. phytophagous
roots .. **12.** rhizophagous
eavesdrop ... **3.** bug **4.** drip **6.** harken,
  listen **7.** wiretap **10.** stillicide
  14. listen secretly
ebb ... **3.** low **4.** neap, sink, tide, wane
  5. abate, decay **6.** recede, reflux,
  retire **7.** decline, dwindle, shallow,
  subside **8.** decrease
ebb and flow ... **5.** surge **6.** aestus
  (estus) **11.** alternation
ebb tide ... **8.** low water
ebullition ... **7.** boiling, ferment
  8. bubbling **9.** agitation, commotion
  12. fermentation **13.** effervescence
eccentric ... **3.** cam (shaft), odd
  5. flaky, kinky **6.** weirdo **7.** erratic,
  strange **8.** abnormal **9.** erratical,
  irregular **13.** nonconformist
  15. idiosyncratical
eccentricity ... **6.** oddity **9.** queerness
  10. aberration, erraticism
  11. abnormality, peculiarity,
  strangeness **12.** idiosyncrasy,
  irregularity **13.** nonconformity
  17. unconventionality
Ecclesiastes ... **8.** Koheleth (Gr)
echidna ... **7.** monster (Gr Myth)
  8. anteater
echinoderm ... **8.** starfish **9.** sea urchin
echo ... **4.** mute, stop (organ) **5.** nymph
  (Myth), reply **6.** repeat **7.** imitate,
  resound, respond **8.** resemble,
  response **9.** duplicate **10.** repetition
  13. reverberation
echoism ... **12.** onomatopoeia
Eciton ... **4.** ants (legionary)
eclipse ... **5.** cloud, sully **6.** darken
  7. obscure, surpass **10.** extinguish
ecliptic term ... **5.** lagna, orbit
  6. circle **9.** penumbral
ecology, oecology ... **4.** sere **6.** botany
  7. biology **9.** bionomics, sociology
  10. bioecology
economical ... **5.** canny, chary
  6. frugal, saving **7.** careful, thrifty
  8. domestic **9.** provident
  12. parsimonious
economics terms ... **5.** T-bill
  7. bailout **8.** bankable, cash flow,
  rollover **9.** plutology **10.** monetarism,
  production (wealth)
economize ... **4.** save **5.** skimp, stint
  6. scrimp **7.** husband, utilize
  8. retrench
economy ... **4.** care **6.** saving, thrift
  7. cutback **8.** prudence **9.** canniness,
  husbandry **10.** providence
ecstasy ... **5.** bliss **6.** trance
  7. emotion, rapture **9.** enrapture
ecstatic ... **4.** rapt **7.** rapture
  9. rapturous, rhapsodic
ectad ... **7.** outward
ecto (comb form) ... **7.** outside, without
  8. external
Ecuador (pert to) ...
capital .. **5.** Quito
export .. **7.** bananas
hat .. **6.** Panama **8.** 'Jipijapa'
island .. **9.** Galapagos

mountain.. 5. Andes
reptile.. 6. iguana 8. tortoise
volcano.. 10. Chimborazo
ecumenical... 7. general, liberal
8. catholic, tolerant 9. universal,
world–wide 12. cosmopolitan
eczema... 6. herpes, tetter 8. eruption
9. salt rheum
edacity... 5. greed 7. avarice
8. appetite, gulosity, voracity
10. greediness
eddy... 4. bore, gulf 5. gurge, surge,
swirl, whirl 6. vortex 7. current,
wreathe 9. whirlpool
Edentate (Zool)... 6. sloths
7. mammals 9. aardvarks, anteaters
10. armadillos
edge... 3. hem, jag, lip, rim 4. brim,
brow, side 5. arris, brink, crest,
marge, sharp, sidle (to), splay, verge
6. border, flange, labrum, margin
7. ambitus, selvage 8. acrimony,
pungency, selvedge 9. advantage,
sharpness 10. escarpment
edged... 5. erose 7. crenate
8. bordered, invected (Her)
edging... 3. hem 4. lace, welt 5. frill,
ruche 6. border, fringe, ruffle
7. binding, bordure (Her), flounce,
tatting
edgy... 5. sharp 7. angular, nervous
8. critical, snappish 9. excitable,
impatient 13. sharp–cornered
edict... 3. act, ban 4. Bull (Pope's),
fiat 5. arret, dicta (pl), irade, order,
ukase 6. assize, decree, dictum,
firman 7. command, mandate
8. decretal 9. ordinance
12. proclamation
edification... 8. learning 9. knowledge
11. improvement, instruction
edifice... 5. house 6. church, palace,
temple 7. Capitol 8. building
9. structure 10. tabernacle
edify... 5. build, teach 7. educate,
improve 8. instruct, organize
9. construct, enlighten, establish
Edinburgh...
burgh.. 5. Leith
capital of.. 8. Scotland
county.. 10. Midlothian
famed street.. 9. Royal Mile
Gaelic name.. 7. Dun Edin (Dunedin)
nickname.. 16. Athens of the North
site.. 12. Firth of Forth
edit... 5. emend 6. direct, excise,
redact, revise, reword 7. arrange,
correct, prepare
edition... 4. copy 5. issue 6. number
7. version
editions (Bib)...
eight texts.. 7. octapla
four texts.. 8. tetrapla
six texts.. 7. hexapla
style and type.. 7. Elzevir (1583)
editor... 7. analyst, newsman, reviser
8. arranger, redactor 9. annotator,
gazetteer 10. journalist, supervisor
11. commentator 12. newspaperman
Edom... 5. Teman (Bib) 7. Idumaea
Edomite... 4. Esau 5. Isaac, Jacob
8. Idumaean

educate... 4. rear 5. teach, train
6. inform 7. develop 8. instruct
9. cultivate, enlighten 10. discipline
12. indoctrinate
educated... 6. taught 7. erudite,
learned, trained 8. cultured,
informed, lettered, literate
11. enlightened
education... 8. breeding, literacy,
training 9. opsimathy (late in life),
schooling 10. discipline
educe... 4. draw 6. deduce, elicit,
evolve, obtain, secure
eel (pert to)...
colorful.. 5. moray 7. Muraena
genus.. 8. Anguilla 13. Leptocephalus
marine.. 5. elver 6. conger
mud.. 5. siren
sand.. 4. grig
young.. 5. elver
eellike... 4. lant, ling 7. eelpout,
lamprey 8. Ophidion 10. anguilloid
11. Lepidosiren
eels, fishing for... 7. sniggle
eels, migration of... 7. eelfare
eelworm... 4. nema 8. Nematoda
9. roundworm 10. vinegar eel
eerie, eery... 5. scary, timid, weird
6. gloomy, spooky 7. awesome,
fearful, uncanny 9. deathlike,
unearthly 10. frightened
efface... 5. erase 6. cancel, delete
7. blot out, expunge 10. obliterate
effect... 4. does 5. close, éclat, force,
mneme 6. mirage, obtain, result
7. achieve, compass, conjure,
execute, fulfill, meaning, operate,
outcome, perform, reality, realize
8. complete 9. discharge, execution,
influence 10. accomplish,
appearance, consummate, impression
11. consequence, performance
effective... 4. able 6. active, actual,
cogent 7. capable, telling
8. adequate, eloquent, equipped,
striking 9. brilliant, competent,
effectual, efficient, operative,
trenchant 11. efficacious, influential
effects... 5. goods, wares 8. movables,
property
effeminate... 3. sop 5. sissy
6. female, tender 7. cockney,
epicene, womanly 8. feminine,
womanish 9. Sybaritic
11. mollycoddle 12. overdelicate
13. overemotional
effervescent... 5. fizzy 6. bubbly, lively
7. boiling, hissing 8. bubbling,
mousseux 9. ebullient, sparkling
10. boisterous
effete... 4. aged, idle 5. spent
6. barren 7. worn out 9. exhausted,
fruitless 11. ineffectual
efficacious... 4. able 5. valid
6. potent 9. effective, effectual,
operative 11. influential
efficacy... 4. dint 5. force, power
6. virtue 7. ability, potency
10. efficiency
efficiency... 5. power, skill 7. ability,
utility 8. efficacy 10. capability,
competence 11. proficiency

12. productivity 13. effectiveness
15. efficaciousness
efficient... 4. able 7. capable, operant
9. competent, effective, effectual,
operative 10. productive
12. businesslike
effigy... 4. copy, icon 5. image
8. likeness 9. facsimile, jackstraw,
semblance 11. resemblance
effluvium... 4. aura, fume, odor
9. ectoplasm, emanation
efflux... 3. end 6. expiry, runoff
7. outflow 8. effusion 9. effluence,
emanation
effodient... 9. burrowing, fossorial
effort... 3. try, tug 4. dint, jump, toil,
will, work 5. assay, burst, labor,
nisus, pains, trial 6. strain
7. attempt, conatus, trouble
8. endeavor, exertion, struggle
11. application
effrontery... 5. brass 8. audacity,
boldness 9. arrogance, impudence,
sauciness 11. presumption
effulgence... 5. aglow, glory 6. luster
8. radiance, rutilant, splendor
10. brightness, brilliance
effusive... 7. gushing 9. exuberant,
rhapsodic 13. demonstrative
eft... 4. evet, newt 6. lizard, triton
7. urodele 10. salamander
egest... 4. emit, void 7. excrete
9. discharge, ejaculate, eliminate
egg... 3. nit, ova (pl), ove 4. goad,
ovum, prod, urge 5. ovule 6. incite
9. instigate
egg (pert to)...
bird's.. 7. chalaza (white of), treadle
(embryo)
case.. 6. ovisac
comb form.. 2. oo 3. ovi
part.. 7. latebra
shaped.. 4. ooid, oval 5. ovate, ovoid
6. ooidal 9. ovaliform
shell.. 5. shard 6. ovisac
undeveloped.. 5. addle
white.. 5. glair 7. albumen
yolk, yelk.. 7. liaison 8. lecithin
eggplant... 9. melongena
eggs (pert to)...
feeding on.. 9. ovivorous
fish.. 3. roe 5. berry, spawn
preserved.. 5. pidan
tester of.. 7. candler
two at a time.. 8. ditokous
egis, aegis... 4. care 5. guard
6. shield, symbol (anc) 7. backing,
defense 8. advocacy, auspices,
guidance, tutelage 9. fosterage,
patronage 10. protection
11. sponsorship
ego... 3. man 4. self 5. atman (Hind)
6. psyche, spirit 7. conceit, jivatma
(Hind) 11. selfishness
egress... 4. exit 5. issue 6. outlet
8. issuance 9. departure
egret... 5. heron, plume 8. aigrette
Egypt, UAR... see also *Egyptian*
capital.. 5. Cairo
Christian.. 4. Copt
city (ruined).. 5. Luxor, Tanis
6. Karnak, Thebes

dam.. 5. Aswan
desert.. 5. Dakla
gulf.. 4. Suez 5. Aqaba
language (anc).. 6. Coptic
lighthouse (anc).. 6. Pharos
mother.. 3. Mut
peninsula.. 5. Sinai
philosopher.. 8. Plotinus
port.. 4. Said, Suez 10. Alexandria
queen.. 9. Cleopatra
river.. 4. Nile
ruler.. 5. pasha 6. caliph 7. khedive
ruler.. 6. Farouk 7. Busiris (Myth),
Pharaoh, Ptolemy, Rameses
sea.. 3. Red 13. Mediterranean
Egyptian (pert to)...
abode of dead.. 4. Aaru (fields of)
6. Amenti
antelope.. 7. bubalis
ape (sacred).. 4. Aani
beetle.. 6. scarab
bird (crocodile).. 6. sicsac
bird (sacred).. 4. Benu, ibis
7. phoenix
bull.. 4. apis
cobra.. 4. haje
cross.. 3. tau 4. ankh (emblem of
life) 10. crux ansata
crown.. 4. atef
dancing girl.. 4. alma (alme, Almeh)
7. ghawazi 8. Baramika
dog.. 6. saluki (gazelle hound)
headdress of ruler.. 6. Uraeus
heaven.. 4. Aaru
lizard.. 4. adda 5. skink
lute.. 5. nable
paper.. 7. papyrus
solar disk.. 4. aten
soul.. 2. Ba 4. khet, sahu
stone (famed).. 7. Rosetta
symbol.. 3. asp 6. scarab (beetle)
tomb.. 6. serdab (cell) 7. mastaba
watchman.. 6. ghafir (ghaffir)
writing.. 13. hieroglyphics
Egyptian god of...
day.. 5. Horus
earth.. 3. Geb, Keb
life.. 4. Ptah
pleasure.. 3. Bes
primeval fluid.. 2. Nu
sea.. 5. Aegir
sun.. 2. Ra 3. Tem (Tum) 4. Atmu
5. Mentu (Ment) 7. Khepera
11. Harpocrates
supreme.. 4. Amen (Amon)
underworld.. 6. Osiris 7. Hershef
unknown.. 2. Ka
wisdom.. 5. Thoth 6. Dhouti
Egyptian goddess of...
arms.. 4. Anta
fertility.. 4. Isis
gods.. 4. Sati
motherhood.. 4. Apet
sea.. 3. Ran
truth.. 4. Maat
eidolon... 5. image 7. phantom
8. illusion 10. apparition
eight, eighth (pert to)...
day (every).. 5. octan
feast day.. 4. utas
group.. 5. octad, octet 6. octave
7. octette

heaven.. 5. stars (fixed)
number.. 4. ocho 6. ogdoad
philosophy.. 8. Diagrams
sided.. 9. octagonal
tone, note.. 4. unca 6. quaver (8th)
   8. diatonic
eighteen inches... 5. cubit
Eire... 4. Erin 7. Ireland
ejaculate... 4. emit, oust, void
   5. blurt, eject, evict, expel
   7. exclaim 8. dislodge
eject... 4. emit, oust, spew, void
   5. evict, expel, spout, spurt
   6. banish 7. extrude 9. discharge,
   eliminate
ejection... 6. ouster 8. eviction
   9. expulsion 11. elimination
eke (out)... 3. add, imp, tab 4. also,
   etch 8. addition, appendix (dial),
   increase, piece out 10. postscript
El... 3. God 5. deity
elaborate... 6. ornate, refine
   7. develop, improve, perfect, studied
   9. embellish, perfected, superfine
   11. complicated, high–wrought
Elam capital... 4. Susa (anc)
élan... 4. dash 5. ardor 6. spirit
   9. eagerness 10. enthusiasm
elapse... 2. go 3. die, fly, run 4. flit,
   pass, slip 5. lapse 6. expire
elastic... 6. pliant, rubber 7. buoyant,
   ductile, springy 8. flexible, stretchy
   9. expansive, resilient
   12. recuperative
elasticity... 4. give 6. elater, spring
   7. pliancy, rebound 9. ductility
   10. resilience
elated... 6. jovial 7. gleeful
   8. exultant, jubilant 9. overjoyed
Elbe tributary... 4. Eger, Iser
elbow... 5. ancon, joint, nudge
   6. jostle 8. chelidon (hollow of)
El Camino Real... 9. Royal Road
   12. King's Highway (Pac Hwy)
elder... 3. iva 4. ainé, blue (color)
   5. berry, judge, ruler 6. Mormon,
   senior 7. ancient 8. ancestor
   10. forefather
eldest... 5. eigne 6. oldest 8. earliest
   9. firstborn
eldritch... 4. wild 5. eerie (eery), weird
   9. frightful
elect... 3. ort 4. name 5. elite
   6. choose, select 9. designate
election... 6. choice 11. alternative
   13. determination 14. discrimination
electric (pert to)...
atom.. 8. electron
condenser (anc).. 9. Leyden jar
conductor.. 6. ohmage
current.. 2. AC, DC 7. circuit
force.. 4. elod
generator.. 6. dynamo
light.. 3. arc 4. neon
   12. incandescent
meter.. 7. ammeter 9. voltmeter,
   wattmeter
particle.. 3. ion 6. cation (kation)
power.. 7. wattage
safety device.. 4. fuse
unit.. 3. ohm, rel 4. volt, watt
   5. farad, henry, joule 6. ampere,

proton 7. coulomb, oersted
   8. kilowatt
electrical wonders... 6. Venus V
   9. Surveyor V-11. Oroville Dam
   12. nuclear plant
electricity... 5. juice, power
   10. illuminant
eleemosynary... 4. alms, free
   7. charity 10. almsgiving
elegance... 5. charm, grace, taste
   6. beauty, polish 9. propriety
   10. ornateness, politeness, refinement
   13. sumptuousness
elegant... 4. rich 6. dressy, ornate,
   soigné, urbane 7. courtly, genteel,
   refined 8. graceful, handsome,
   polished, tasteful 9. admirable,
   beautiful, excellent 10. fastidious
   11. fashionable 13. grandiloquent
element... 3. air 4. fire 5. earth,
   water
elementary... 5. basic 6. simple
   7. primary 8. inchoate, original
   9. beginning 11. fundamental
elephant... 3. cow 4. bull, calf
   5. hathi, rogue 6. tusker
   8. behemoth 9. pachyderm
elephant (pert to)...
apple.. 7. Feronia
boy.. 4. Sabu
call, cry.. 4. barr 7. trumpet
enclosure, trap.. 6. keddah
goad.. 5. ankus
keeper.. 6. mahout
seat.. 6. howdah
tusk.. 5. ivory 9. scrivello
young.. 4. calf
elevate... 4. lift, rear 5. elate, exalt,
   raise 6. refine, uplift 7. advance,
   dignify, ennoble, glorify, inspire,
   promote 10. exhilarate
elevated... 2. el 5. lofty, risen
   6. elated 7. exalted, sublime
   8. eminence
elevation... 4. hill 6. height (highth)
   9. promotion 10. exaltation
   11. composition (Eccl), distinction
   13. glorification
elevation of the mind... 7. anagoge
elevator... 3. bin 4. cage, lift, silo
   9. ascenseur
eleven... 7. hendeca (comb form)
elf... 3. fay, hob, imp, nix 4. peri
   5. fairy, gnome, ouphe, pixie
   6. goblin, sprite 7. brownie
elfish... 5. elfin 6. elvish, impish
   7. elflike, tricksy 8. eldritch
   11. mischievous
Elgin Marbles... 10. sculptures (by
   Phidias)
elicit... 3. get 4. draw, pump
   5. claim, educe, evoke, exact, wrest,
   wring 6. deduce, demand, entice,
   extort, induce, obtain 7. extract
elide... 4. dele, omit 5. annul
   6. ignore 7. destroy, nullify, shorten
   8. demolish, suppress 9. eliminate
eligible... 3. apt, fit 4. meet
   6. worthy 8. entitled, suitable
   9. competent, desirable, qualified
   10. acceptable, admissible
Elijah... 7. prophet 8. oratorio

14. John the Baptist (Bib)

eliminate... 3. rid 4. kill 5. erase, expel 6. detach, remove 7. discard, divulge, exclude, excrete, release 8. evacuate, separate 9. segregate 11. exterminate

Elisha... 7. prophet 8. disciple (of Elijah)

elision... 7. syncope 9. severance 10. abridgment, shortening 11. suppression (vowel)

elite... 5. stars 6. flower, galaxy 7. fashion, society 9. beau monde 10. upper crust

elixir... 6. remedy 7. cure–all, essence, extract, heal–all, panacea 8. medicine, tincture 10. catholicon 12. quintessence

elixir of life... 11. elixir vitae

Elixir of Love... 13. L'Elisir d'Amore

elk... 4. deer 5. Alces, eland, moose 6. sambar, wapiti

ellipse, elliptical... 5. curve, ovoid, ovule

elm (pert to)...
borer.. 6. beetle, lamiid
fruit.. 6. samara
genus.. 5. Ulmus
rock, wing (kinds).. 5. wahoo

Elm City... 8. New Haven

Elmo... 11. patron saint (sailors)

elocution... 7. oratory 8. rhetoric 9. eloquence 10. expression

elocutionist... 6. reader 7. reciter 11. elocutioner 13. recitationist

eloge... 6. eulogy 7. address, oration 8. encomium, eulogium

eloign... 6. convey, remove 7. conceal

elongate... 6. extend, remove 7. stretch 8. continue, lengthen, protract

elongated... 4. lank, long 6. linear, oblong 7. prolate, slender 8. extended 9. stretched 10. attenuated

elope... 6. decamp 7. abscond, skip out 8. slip away

eloquence... 7. fluency, oratory 9. discourse, elocution 14. expressiveness

eloquence, teacher of... 6. rhetor

eloquent... 5. vivid 10. Ciceronian, expressive, meaningful, oratorical 11. significant

else... 2. or 4. ense (ens) 5. if not, other 9. otherwise 10. additional 12. accompanying

elsewhere... 4. away 5. alibi (law)

elucidate... 5. clear, lucid 7. clarify, clear up 8. simplify 9. interpret 10. illustrate

elude... 4. flee, foil, mock, shun 5. avoid, dodge, evade 6. baffle, befool, escape 10. circumvent

elusive... 4. eely 6. subtle 7. elusory, evasive 8. baffling 9. equivocal 10. impalpable

elves... see *elf*

Elysium (Myth)... 8. paradise

em... 2. en (half) 4. unit (Elec)

emaciated... 4. lean 5. gaunt 6. peaked, wasted 7. pinched

10. attenuated, cadaverous

emanation... 4. aura, odor 5. light, niton (radium), vapor 7. outcome 8. creation, effluvia 9. ectoplasm, radiation 10. exhalation, generation 11. consequence

emancipation... 6. rescue 7. freedom, release 10. liberation 11. manumission 15. enfranchisement

emasculate... 4. geld, spay 5. unman 6. soften 8. castrate 9. expurgate, sterilize 10. effeminize

embalmer... 5. cerer 9. mortician, preserver 10. undertaker

embankment... 3. dam 4. bund, dike 5. levee, revet, shore 7. barrier, pilapil (rice field) 8. buttress 10. breakwater 13. fortification

embargo... 5. edict, order 7. exclude 8. blockade, prohibit, stoppage 9. exclusion 10. impediment 11. prohibition, requisition

embark... 4. sail, ship 6. depart, invest, unmoor 7. cast off, entrain

embarrass... 5. abash, shame 6. hamper, hinder, impede 7. confuse, fluster, involve, mortify, nonplus 8. bewilder, confound, encumber, handicap 9. discomfit, dumbfound 10. complicate, disconcert

embarrassment... 5. shame 9. abashment, confusion 11. involvement, predicament 12. discomfiture, entanglement 13. inconvenience, mortification

embellish... 3. gem 4. deck, gild 5. adorn, array, dress, gouge, grace 6. bedeck, enrich 7. bedrape, enhance, garnish 8. beautify, emblazon, furbelow, ornament 9. embroider 10. exaggerate

embellishment... 9. garniture 10. decoration, furbishing 12. exaggeration 13. ornamentation

ember... 3. ash 4. coal (live), izle 5. gleed 6. cinder 7. residue

embers... 5. ashes 8. emotions (past), memories

embezzle... 5. steal, swipe 6. lessen, thieve, weaken (obs) 7. purloin 8. peculate, squander 9. dissipate 11. appropriate

embitter... 4. sour 5. anger 7. envenom 8. acerbate 10. antagonize, exacerbate

emblazon... 4. laud 5. color, extol 6. praise 7. display, exhibit, glorify 9. celebrate, embellish

emblem... 3. rue 4. mace, sign, type 5. badge, crown, image, token, totem 6. device, figure, symbol 7. balance (justice), coronet, sceptor 9. prototype

emblematic... 5. typal 7. typical 8. symbolic 10. figurative 14. characteristic

embodiment... 4. Apis 6. avatar, matter 7. epitome 9. inclusion 10. enfoldment 11. combination, composition, incarnation

12. organization 13. incorporation
14. representative 15. personification

embolden... 5. nerve 6. assure
7. hearten 8. reassure 9. encourage

embosom... 6. foster 7. cherish,
embrace, enclose 8. surround

embrace... 3. hug 4. fold, gain, hold,
love, wrap 5. adopt, clasp, cling,
grasp, inarm, seize 6. accoll (obs),
caress, enfold 7. cherish, contain,
enclose, espouse, include, involve,
welcome 8. comprise, encircle,
greeting, surround 9. encompass

embroider... 7. falsify 8. decorate,
ornament 9. embellish
10. exaggerate

embroidery... 8. appliqué 9. hardanger

embroidery frame... 7. taboret
(tabouret)

embroil... 5. upset 6. jumble
7. agitate, disturb, perplex, trouble
8. convulse, disorder, distract
9. commingle, implicate
10. complicate, discompose

eme... 5. uncle 6. friend, gossip

emend... 4. edit, mend 5. amend,
right 6. better, remedy, revise
7. correct, improve, rectify

emerald... 5. beryl, color, green
7. smaragd

Emerald Isle... 4. Erin 7. Ireland

emerge... 3. dip 4. pend, rise
5. hatch, issue 6. appear
7. debouch, emanate
10. disembogue

emergency... 5. pinch 6. clutch, crisis,
strait 8. exigency, juncture
9. extremity, necessity 10. substitute

emery... 6. pumice 8. abradant,
abrasive, corundum 9. sandpaper

emesis... 6. puking 7. spewing
8. vomiting 12. disgorgement
13. regurgitation

emeute... 4. riot 6. Putsch
8. outbreak 10. insurgence
12. insurrection

emigrant... 6. emigré 7. migrant,
outgoer, settler 8. colonist, stranger
9. immigrant, migratory (of birds)

eminence... 4. hill 5. title 6. height,
rideau 7. dignity 9. authority,
elevation, greatness, loftiness
10. famousness, importance,
projection 11. superiority
13. transcendency

eminent... 4. arch, high 5. great,
lofty, noted 6. famous, marked,
signal 8. renowned, superior,
towering 9. important 10. celebrated,
protruding 11. illustrious
13. distinguished

emissary... 3. spy 5. agent, scout
8. delegate, diplomat

emit... 4. glow, reek, shed 5. eject,
eruct, exude, issue, pluff, voice
6. exhale 7. distill (distil), emanate,
publish, radiate 8. opalesce (colors),
transmit 9. discharge, irradiate

emmet... 3. ant 7. pismire 8. formicid

emollient... 4. balm 8. ointment,
soothing 9. lubricant, softening

emolument... 4. fees, gain 5. wages

6. profit, salary 7. stipend, tribute
9. allowance 12. compensation

emotion... 5. agony, stoic 6. pathos
7. feeling, passion 9. agitation,
gratitude, sensation, sentiment
10. excitement 11. disturbance,
sensibility

emotionless... 9. apathetic, impassive,
unfeeling 10. spiritless
11. unemotional 12. unresponsive

emperor... 4. czar, tsar 5. Mogul
7. monarch 9. commander,
imperator, sovereign

emphasis... 6. accent, stress
7. cadence 8. salience
10. insistence 14. impressiveness

emphasize... 6. accent, insist, stress
7. point up 9. punctuate
10. accentuate

emphatic... 7. earnest 8. forcible,
positive, striking 9. energetic,
insistent 10. expressive
11. significant

empire... 4. rule, sway 5. green
(color), reign, state 6. domain
7. control, country

Empire (pert to)...
of the Rising Sun.. 5. Japan
State.. 7. New York
State of the South.. 7. Georgia

empiric... 4. fake 5. cheat, quack
8. impostor 9. charlatan
10. mountebank

employ... 3. use 4. busy, coax, hire
5. apply, exert 6. devote, occupy
7. concern, entrust, service
10. occupation

employees... 4. crew, gang, help
5. force, hands, staff 9. personnel
10. associates

employer... 4. user 5. hirer 6. master
8. consumer 12. entrepreneur

employment... 3. use 4. work
5. trade 7. calling, purpose, service
8. business, vocation 10. occupation,
profession

emporium... 4. fair, mart 5. store
6. bazaar, market 10. exposition

empower... 6. enable 7. entitle
8. delegate, deputize 9. authorize
10. commission

empty... 4. idle, toom, vain, void
5. blank, clear, drain, inane
6. hollow, hungry, jejune, vacant,
vacate 7. deplete, foolish, vacuous
8. evacuate, unfilled 9. insincere
.10. unburdened, unoccupied

empusa (Gr Myth)... 5. fungi
7. specter 9. hobgoblin

empyrean... 3. sky 5. ether 6. Caelus,
welkin 7. heavens, the blue

emulate... 5. equal, outdo, rival
7. compete, imitate, vie with
11. competition

emulsion... 9. demulcent
10. semiliquid, suspension

enable... 5. equip 6. clothe
7. empower, qualify 9. authorize
10. capacitate

enact... 4. pass, play 6. decree,
enjoin, ordain, record 7. actuate,
appoint, perform 9. legislate,

represent 10. constitute
11. impersonate

enactment... 3. law 4. veto 5. canon, edict, usage 6. decree 7. statute 9. ordinance 11. legislation

encamp, encampment... 4. camp, tent 5. siege 7. bivouac, camping

enchant... 5. charm 6. delude 7. bewitch, delight 8. ensorcel 9. captivate, enrapture, fascinate

enchantment... 5. charm, magic, spell 7. sorcery 8. witchery 10. allurement, necromancy, witchcraft 11. bewitchment, fascination, incantation

enchantress... 5. Circe, Medea 7. charmer 9. bewitcher, sorceress, temptress

encina... 7. live oak

encircle... 3. orb 4. gird, ring, zone 5. belay, inorb, twist 6. enfold 7. besiege, circuit, enclose, environ, include, wreathe 8. surround 12. circumscribe

encircled... 4. girt 5. orbed, paled, zoned 6. belted, forded, hooped, ringed 7. enlaced 8. enclosed, enfolded, wreathed 10. surrounded

enclose... 3. hem, mew 5. bound, fence 6. corral, encase, engulf 7. enclave, envelop, harness, include 8. imprison, surround 9. encompass 12. circumscribe

enclosed... 4. pent, sept (area) 7. encased 8. confined 10. surrounded

enclosure... 3. pen 4. bawn, cage, yair (yare), yard 5. carol (cloister), kraal (craal), sekos 6. corral 8. contents, poundage, stockade

encomium... 4. hymn 5. eloge 6. eulogy, praise 7. tribute 8. accolade 9. panegyric

encompass... 4. ring 5. hem in 6. begird, effect 7. besiege, circuit, compass, contain, enclose, environ, include 8. encircle, surround 10. accomplish 12. circumscribe

encompassing... 7. ambient 13. circumambient

encore... 3. bis 4. echo, over 5. again 8. applause, once more

encounter... 4. bout, meet 5. brave, brush, fight, incur, onset 6. attack, breast, oppose 7. collide, meeting 8. conflict 10. engagement, experience

encourage... 4. abet, urge 5. boost, cheer, impel, nerve, rally 6. assure, exhort, foster, incite 7. advance, comfort, console, hearten, inspire, promote 8. embolden, inspirit 9. instigate, stimulate 11. countenance

encouragement... 3. aid 7. comfort 9. fosterage, incentive 10. inducement 11. emboldening

encroach upon... 5. poach 6. invade, trench 7. impinge, intrude 8. infringe, overstep, trespass

encumber... 4. clog, load 5. check 6. burden, hamper, hinder, retard,

saddle 7. involve, oppress 8. entangle, handicap, obstruct, overload 9. embarrass 10. overburden

encumbrance... 5. alien (law), claim 6. burden 9. dependent 10. impediment

encyclic... 6. letter 7. pandect 8. circular, treatise 10. encircling 13. comprehensive

encyclopedic learning, person of... 10. polyhistor 13. encyclopedist

end... 3. aim, neb, tip, toe 4. fate, kill, ruin, tail 5. amend, close, death, finis, limit, omega, point, telos, upend 6. expire, finale, finish, result, thirty 7. destroy, purpose 8. complete, conclude, dissolve 9. cessation, determine, extremity, intention, objective, terminate 10. completion 11. termination

end (pert to)...
arrow.. 4. nock
boundary.. 5. bourn 7. abuttal
cloth.. 7. remnant
game.. 4. goal
man.. 8. minstrel
news.. 6. thirty
timber.. 5. tenon

endanger... 4. risk 6. expose, hazard 7. imperil 10. compromise, jeopardize

endeavor... 3. aim, try, vie 4. seek 5. essay, ettle, nisus, tempt 6. effort, strive 7. attempt 8. struggle

endemic... 6. native 10. indigenous 14. characteristic

ending... 5. death 6. result 9. cessation, desinence 10. completion, conclusion 11. destruction, termination

endless... 4. many 6. eterne 7. eternal, undying 8. eternity, infinite, numerous, unending 9. boundless, continual, incessant, perpetual, unceasing, unstinted 10. continuous 11. everlasting 12. interminable 13. uninterrupted

endorse, indorse... 4. sign 6. attest, second 7. approve, support 8. sanction 9. authorize, guarantee

endorsement... 4. fiat, visa (vise) 8. approval, sanction 9. provision, signature 10. acceptance, validation 12. ratification 14. authentication

endow... 3. dow, due 4. dote, vest 5. dower, endue, indue 6. bestow, clothe, enrich, give to, invest 7. empower, furnish, provide

endowment... 4. gift 5. dower, grant 7. talents 8. appanage (apanage) 9. insurance, provision 11. empowerment, instruction (Mormon)

endue... 5. endow, teach 6. clothe, digest, invest, supply 7. empower

endurable... 8. bearable 9. tolerable 10. sufferable 11. supportable

endurance... 7. stamina 8. patience, strength 9. fortitude, suffering 10. durability, permanence, sufferance

11. continuance, resignation
12. perseverance
endure ... 4. bear, bide, dree, last, live, tide, wear 5. abide, allow, brook, stand 6. afford, remain, suffer 7. condone, persist, sustain, undergo 8. continue, tolerate 9. persevere, withstand
enduring ... 7. durable, lasting, patient 9. permanent 11. persevering, substantial, unforgotten 13. long–suffering
enemy ... 3. foe 5. devil, force, fremd (frenne), hater, rival, Satan 6. foeman 8. opponent 9. adversary 10. antagonist
energetic ... 5. fresh 6. active 8. forceful, forcible, vigorous 9. strenuous 11. industrious
energy ... 2. go 3. erg, pep, vim 4. bent 5. force, nerve, power, vigor 6. spirit 7. potency, sthenia 8. strength 9. animation
energy (pert to) ...
lack of .. 5. atony 6. anergy 7. aneuria, inertia 8. asthenia
mental .. 9. psychurgy
personified .. 6. Shakti
potential .. 5. ergal
unit .. 3. erg 5. ergon
enervate ... 3. sap 5. drain, unman 6. weaken 7. exhaust, unnerve 8. enfeeble 10. debilitate
enfeeble ... 4. numb 6. sicken, soften, weaken 7. depress 8. enervate 9. attenuate 10. debilitate
enfilade ... 4. rake 5. vista 7. barrage 9. broadside 11. arrangement (in rows)
enfold, infold ... 4. fold, wrap 5. clasp, cover 6. infold 7. embrace, envelop 8. surround
enforce ... 5. drive 6. assail, compel 7. execute, inspire 9. constrain, encourage, intensify, reinforce 10. invigorate
enfranchise ... 4. free 5. admit 7. deliver, set free 8. liberate 10. emancipate
engage ... 4. bind, draw, hire, rent 5. lease 6. absorb, embark, employ, enlist, induce, occupy, pledge 7. attract, betroth, engross, involve, promise 8. contract, entangle 9. interlock, intermesh
engaged ... 4. busy 5. hired 6. bonded, meshed 7. earnest, entered, pledged, versant 8. embedded, employed, involved, occupied, promised 9. affianced, betrothed, engrossed 10. contracted
engaged in controversy ... 9. disputant
engagement ... 4. date 6. battle 7. promise 9. betrothal, encounter 10. attachment 11. appointment, involvement
engaging ... 5. sapid 6. taking 8. alluring, duelling 10. attractive, delightful 11. interesting
engender ... 3. sow (seeds) 5. beget, breed, cause 6. excite 7. develop, produce 8. generate, occasion 9. call

forth, procreate, propagate
engine ... 3. gin, ram 5. mogul, motor 6. onager 7. machine, robinet, turbine 10. locomotive
engine (type) ... 3. gas 5. motor, solar, steam 6. Diesel, rocket 8. gasoline 10. combustion
engineer ... 4. plan 7. manager 8. computer, contrive, designer, inventor, maneuver, operator, therblig 9. construct 11. constructor, superintend
engineer (type) ... 5. civil, corps, sales 6. driver, mining 7. planner 8. chemical, geodetic, military, railroad, research, sanitary 9. hydraulic 10. electrical, industrial, mechanical, structural 11. electronics 12. aeronautical, construction 14. administrative
engird ... 6. begird, circle, girdle 7. envelop 8. encircle, ensphere
England ... see also *English*
called .. 6. Albion (anc) 7. Britain 9. Britannia
capital .. 6. London
city .. 3. Ely 4. Hull, York 5. Derby, Leeds 6. Exeter 7. Bristol, Croydon 8. Brighton, Coventry, Hastings, Plymouth 9. Liverpool, Sheffield 10. Birmingham, Epsom Downs, Manchester, Nottingham, Portsmouth 11. Southampton
college (famed) .. 4. Eton 6. Harrow, Oxford 9. Cambridge, Sandhurst (military)
conqueror .. 5. Danes 6. Angles, Saxons 7. Normans
constitution .. 10. Magna Carta (1215) 12. Bill of Rights (1688)
county .. 4. Kent 5. Devon, Essex 6. Dorset, Sussex 9. Yorkshire
emblem .. 4. lion, rose
House of .. 4. York 5. Blois, Tudor 6. Stuart 7. Hanover, Windsor 8. Normandy 9. Lancaster 11. Plantagenet
island .. 5. Wight 6. Scilly, Virgin 7. Bahamas, Bermuda, Solomon 8. Falkland, Windward 9. Isle of Man
king (anc) .. 6. Arthur (legend), Egbert 8. Ethelred 9. Ethelwulf
native (anc) .. 4. Celt, Dane, Jute 5. Saxon 8. Anglican 9. Sassenach 10. Anglo–Saxon
river .. 3. Exe 4. Avon, Ouse 5. Trent 6. Thames
royal residence .. 7. Windsor
street (London) .. 10. Piccadilly 12. Threadneedle
English (pert to) ...
bride's gift .. 3. dos
court .. 4. eyre (circuit), leet (anc)
dislike of .. 11. Anglophobia
district .. 4. Soho
estate (feudal) .. 4. fief
excuse (legal) .. 6. essoin
festival (country) .. 3. ale
field .. 5. croft
forest .. 5. Arden 8. Sherwood
freeman .. 5. ceorl, thane, thegn

hamlet.. 4. dorp
heather.. 4. ling
lawyer.. 9. barrister, solicitor
leave of absence (school).. 5. exeat
lover of.. 10. Anglophile
Marbles.. 6. Oxford 7. Arundel
money of account.. 3. ora
news agency.. 6. Reuter
Parliament process.. 7. Hansard
political party.. 4. Tory, Whig
    8. Laborite 12. Conservative
porcelain.. 5. Spode 8. Wedgwood
prehistoric site.. 8. Piltdown
race course.. 5. Ascot 9. Newmarket
    10. Epsom Downs
races (famed).. 5. Derby 7. The Oaks
sheep (blackface).. 4. Lonk
song (mock).. 12. lillibullero
stolen article (on thief).. 7. mainour
symbol.. 4. bull, lion, rose
thicket.. 5. copse 7. spinney
tract (sandy).. 4. dean (dene)
trolley.. 4. tram
uplands.. 5. downs
wren.. 6. tomtit
English Channel... 8. La Manche
English, famed...
composer.. 6. Handel 7. Stainer
diarist.. 5. Pepys
engraver.. 3. Pye 7. Hogarth
essayist.. 4. Elia (Charles Lamb), Lang
    6. Steele 7. Addison
explorer.. 4. Ross 5. Cabot 6. Baffin,
    Beatty, Hudson 7. Raleigh
    10. Shackleton
financier.. 7. Gresham
historian.. 4. Bede 7. Spelman,
    Toynbee 8. Macaulay
humorist.. 4. Lear (Edward)
mathematician.. 5. Hooke 6. Gunter
murderer (famed).. 4. Aram
navigator.. 4. Cook 5. Drake
    6. Nelson
painter.. 4. Lear 6. Turner
    7. Hogarth, Lutyens, Millais
philosopher.. 7. Spencer
physicist.. 7. Faraday
poet.. 5. Noyes 8. Browning,
    Tennyson 9. Masefield, Swinburne
printer.. 6. Caxton
reformer.. 4. Owen 6. Spence
saint.. 6. George (patron saint)
    7. Alphege, Swithin
scientist.. 6. Newton
spy (in Am Rev).. 5. André
statesman.. 4. Peel, Pitt 7. Baldwin,
    Balfour, Walpole 8. Cromwell,
    Disraeli, Thatcher 9. Churchill
    11. Chamberlain, Lloyd George
surgeon.. 5. Haden, Paget 6. Lister
theologian.. 5. Booth 6. Becket
    7. Tyndall 8. Wycliffe 10. Whitefield
thesaurus compiler.. 5. Roget
engrave... 3. cut 4. etch, rist
    5. carve, chase, hatch, infix 6. chisel,
    incise 7. enchase, impress, imprint,
    stipple 9. sculpture
engraver's tool... 5. burin
engraving... 3. cut 5. print
    7. etching, chasing, tooling
    8. celature, incising, intaglio
    9. stippling 10. xylography (wood)

    11. lithography 12. glyptography
engross... 6. absorb, engage
    10. monopolize 11. concentrate
engrossed... 4. busy, rapt 6. intent
    8. absorbed, employed 10. interested
engulf... 4. gulf, gulp 5. swamp
    6. absorb 7. swallow 8. inundate,
    submerge 9. overwhelm
enhance... 4. lift 5. exalt, extol, raise
    7. advance, augment, elevate, enlarge,
    magnify 8. increase 9. aggravate
    10. exaggerate
enigma... 3. why 5. rebus 6. puzzle,
    riddle 7. charade, mystery
    9. conundrum 11. mind-boggler
enigmatic... 6. arcane, mystic
    8. puzzling 12. inexplicable
enjoin... 3. bid 5. order 6. advise,
    charge, decree, direct, forbid
    7. command 8. admonish, prohibit
enjoy... 4. bask, have 5. savor
    6. relish 10. appreciate
enjoyment... 4. ease, zest 6. relish
    7. delight 8. felicity, fruition, pleasure
    9. amusement, happiness
enlarge... 3. eke 4. ream 5. swell
    6. dilate, expand, extend, spread
    7. amplify, augment, develop, distend
    8. increase 9. expatiate
    10. exaggerate
enlargement... 8. increase
    9. expansion, extension
    12. augmentation 13. amplification
enlighten... 5. teach 6. inform
    7. educate, explain 8. enkindle,
    instruct 10. illuminate 11. disillusion
enlightened person... 10. illuminate
enlist... 4. join, list 6. engage, enroll,
    induce, muster
enliven... 5. amuse, cheer, rouse
    7. animate, comfort, inspire, refresh
    8. brighten, energize, inspirit
    9. encourage, stimulate
    10. exhilarate, invigorate
enmity... 3. war 4. feud 6. hatred,
    malice, rancor 7. discord 8. aversion
    9. antipathy, disaccord, hostility
    10. antagonism, repugnance
    11. malevolence 14. unfriendliness
ennead... 4. gods (nine), nine
    18. Ennead of Heliopolis (famed)
ennoble... 5. exalt, honor, raise
    6. uplift 7. elevate, glorify, promote
ennui... 4. bore 5. bored 6. tedium
    7. boredom, fatigue, languor
    9. weariness 15. dissatisfaction
enormous... 4. huge, vast 5. great
    6. wicked 7. immense, massive,
    titanic 8. abnormal, colossal, gigantic,
    infamous 9. atrocious, excessive,
    monstrous 10. inordinate, prodigious,
    stupendous
Enos' father... 4. Seth
enough... 4. enow 5. ample, basta,
    fully, quite 6. plenty 8. adequate
    9. amplitude 10. sufficient
    12. satisfactory
enounce... 5. state, utter 8. proclaim
    9. enunciate, pronounce
enow... 9. presently
enrage... 5. anger 6. madden
    7. incense, inflame 9. infuriate

enraged... 5. irate 7. angered
8. maddened 10. infuriated
enraptured... 6. enrapt 8. ecstatic
9. delighted, entranced
10. enravished
enravished... 4. rapt 9. enchanted,
entranced, rapturous 10. enraptured
enrich... 4. lard 5. adorn, endow
6. fatten 7. improve 8. increase,
ornament 9. embellish, fertilize
enroll... 4. coil, join, list, roll 5. enter
6. enlist, induct, unfurl, wrap up
7. engross, impanel 8. initiate,
register 11. matriculate
ens... 5. being 6. entity 7. essence
ensconce... 4. hide 5. cover 6. settle
7. conceal, protect, shelter
9. establish
ensemble... 3. all 5. decor, group,
whole 7. costume
enshroud... 4. wrap 6. clothe, swathe
7. conceal, enclose 8. enshrine
ensiform... 12. xiphisternum
ensign... 4. flag 6. banner 7. officer
8. gonfalon, standard 9. oriflamme
(oriflamb, anc)
ensign of Othello... 4. Iago
enslave... 8. enthrall
ensnare... 3. web 4. trap 5. benet,
catch, innet, noose 6. allure,
enmesh, entrap, seduce 7. involve
ensorcell, ensorcel... 7. bewitch,
enchant
ensue... 6. follow, pursue, result
7. imitate, succeed 8. come next
ensuing... 4. next 9. resultant
10. subsequent, succeeding
ensure... 6. assure, insure, secure
7. protect, warrant 9. guarantee
entad... 6. inward (opp of ectad)
ental... 5. inner (opp of ectal)
entangle... 3. mat, web 4. mesh, mire
5. afoul, ravel, snarl, twist 6. enlace,
enmesh, puzzle, raffle 7. confuse,
ensnare, involve, perplex 8. bewilder
9. embarrass 10. interweave
entanglement... 4. knot 5. snare, snarl
6. abatis 8. obstacle 9. barricade,
imbroglio 10. barbed wire, complexity
11. involvement
enter... 4. join, list 5. begin, start,
train 6. engage, enlist, enroll, insert,
record 8. initiate, inscribe, register
9. introduce, penetrate
11. participate
enter (pert to)...
career.. 6. incept
legal objection.. 5. demur
with hostility.. 6. invade
without permission.. 7. intrude
8. encroach, infringe
enterprise... 4. firm 5. essay 6. daring
7. attempt, crusade, exploit, venture
10. initiative 11. undertaking
enterprising... 4. bold 6. daring
9. energetic 11. up–and–coming
entertain... 4. fete 5. amuse, treat
6. divert, regale 7. beguile, cherish
8. interest
entertainer... 5. actor 6. dancer,
singer 7. actress, speaker
8. magician 9. performer

11. pantomimist 12. impersonator
entertainment... 4. play 5. party,
revue, sport 6. kermis (kermess),
repast 7. pastime, ridotto, theater
8. entr´acte, musicale 9. amusement,
diversion, reception, wayzgoose
10. recreation 12. Roman holiday
enthusiasm... 4. élan, fire, zeal, zest
5. ardor, craze, estro, furor (furore),
mania, verve 6. fervor 7. ecstasy
8. interest 9. animation, eagerness,
transport 10. exaltation
enthusiast... 3. fan 5. bigot 6. rooter,
zealot 7. devotee, fanatic
enthusiastic... 5. eager, nutty, rabid
6. active, ardent 7. zealous
10. interested
entice... 4. bait, coax, lure, tole
5. decoy, tempt 6. allure, cajole,
incite, seduce 7. attract, wheedle
8. inveigle, persuade
enticement... 9. seduction
10. allurement, attraction, incitement,
inducement, persuasion, temptation
12. inveiglement
entire... 3. all 5. cover (Philat), sound,
total, utter, whole 6. intact
7. perfect, sincere, upright
8. complete, faithful, stallion
9. integrate, undivided
10. unimpaired 11. unqualified
12. undiminished
entirely... 3. all 5. clean, fully, stark
6. solely, wholly 7. totally 9. every
inch, perfectly, sincerely
10. completely
entitle... 3. dub 4. call, name, term
5. style 6. assign, enable, impute
7. empower, qualify 9. authorize,
designate 10. denominate
entity... 3. ens 4. soul, unit 5. being,
entia, thing 7. integer 8. infinity
(Math) 9. existence
entomb... 4. bury 5. inter, inurn
6. hearse, inhume 7. confine
9. sepulture
entourage... 5. suite, train 7. retinue
10. associates, attendants
12. surroundings
entr'acte... 3. act 5. dance, music
7. interim 9. interlude
entrails... 4. guts 6. bowels
7. insides, viscera 8. interior
10. intestines
entrance... 3. way 4. adit, door, gate
5. entry, inlet 6. access, portal
7. gateway, ingress, postern
9. admission, insertion, threshold,
vestibule 10. admittance
entrance (pert to)...
church (Eastern).. 5. Great 6. Little
formal.. 5. debut 12. introduction
hostile.. 9. incursion
temple (Buddh).. 5. toran (torana)
entranced... 4. rapt 8. dreaming
9. delighted, overjoyed
10. fascinated, hypnotized, spellbound
11. overpowered
entrap... 4. net 5. trap 5. catch,
decoy, noose, snare 6. tangle
7. beguile, ensnare 8. entangle,
inveigle

entreat... 3. ask, beg, woo 4. pray
5. crave, halse (obs), plead
6. adjure, appeal 7. beseech,
implore, solicit 8. petition
9. importune 10. supplicate
entreaty... 4. plea, suit 6. appeal,
prayer 7. request 8. petition
10. invitation 11. importunity
12. solicitation, supplication
entree, entrée... 4. dish 6. access
7. ingress, opening 9. admission
10. permission (to enter)
entrench... 6. invade 7. enter on,
fortify, intrude 8. encroach, trespass
9. establish
entrenchment... 7. defense, parapet
9. intrusion 10. protection
12. encroachment, infringement
13. establishment
entrepot... 5. depot, store
9. warehouse 10. depository
entrepreneur... 7. provost 9. executive
10. impresario 13. administrator
entrust... 6. commit 7. confide,
consign 8. delegate 10. commission
entry... 4. hall, item, lane, post
7. ingress 8. entrance, register
9. admission, vestibule
10. contestant, memorandum
12. introduction
entwine... 4. lace 5. clasp, twine,
twist, weave 6. enlace 7. wreathe
9. interknit
enumerate... 4. list, tell 5. count
6. detail, number, reckon, relate
7. compute 8. estimate, name over,
rehearse 9. calculate, catalogue
(catalog) 12. recapitulate
13. particularize
enumeration... 4. list 5. count
6. census 10. numeration
14. recapitulation
enunciate... 3. say 5. utter 6. affirm
7. declare 8. announce, proclaim
9. postulate, pronounce
10. articulate
enunciation... 9. statement, utterance
11. affirmation, attestation,
declaration 12. announcement
13. pronouncement, pronunciation
envelop... 4. case, wrap 5. cover
6. clothe, encase, enwrap, infold,
invest, sheath, shroud 7. conceal,
enclose, sheathe 8. encircle,
surround 9. encompass, enwreathe
10. integument
envelope... 3. bur (burr) 5. cover,
curve 6. jacket 7. conceal, rampart,
vesicle, wrapper 8. membrane
10. integument
enveloped... 6. amidst 7. covered
10. surrounded
envenom... 5. taint 6. poison
8. embitter
envious... 7. jealous 8. covetous,
grudging, spiteful 9. green–eyed
10. begrudging
environ... 3. hem 6. suburb
7. compass, envelop, hedge in,
involve, purlieu 8. encircle, outskirt,
surround 9. encompass
environment... 4. area 6. medium,

milieu 7. setting, suburbs, terrain
8. environs 10. background
12. neighborhood, surroundings
13. encompassment
envisage... 4. face 8. confront
9. visualize 11. contemplate
12. meet squarely
envision... 5. dream 7. picture
9. visualize 11. contemplate
12. meet squarely
envoy... 5. agent 6. legate, l'envoi,
stanza 7. refrain 8. ablegate,
delegate, diplomat 9. messenger
10. ambassador, postscript
12. commissioner
envy... 5. covet 6. grudge 8. jealousy
12. covetousness
enwrap, inwrap... 4. roll, wrap
6. clothe, enfold, infold 7. engross
8. surround
enzyme... 3. ase (suff) 5. bread (Eccl)
6. lotase, olease, pepsin, rennin,
urease 7. amylase, ferment, laccase,
ptyalin, trypsin 8. diastase, protease
9. digestant
enzyme activator... 11. biocatalyst
eoan... 7. auroral 8. daybreak, easterly
eon, aeon... 3. age, era 4. time
5. cycle 8. eternity 10. generation
ephemeral... 7. diurnal 9. chickweed,
deciduous, transient 10. short–lived
ephemeris... 5. diary 7. almanac,
journal 8. calendar 10. periodical
11. publication
Ephesus (pert to)...
city of.. 6. Greece (anc)
famed for.. 5. ruins 12. Christianity
site.. 9. Aegean Sea
temple.. 7. Artemis
visitor (early).. 6. St Paul
Ephraim... 4. bear (grizzly) 5. tribe
8. fruitful
epi... 6. finial
epic... 3. cid 4. epos, poem, saga
5. epode 6. Aeneid (by Vergil),
epopee, heroic 9. narrative
epicene... 7. neutral, sexless
10. effeminate
epicure... 6. friand (obs) 7. glutton,
gourmet 8. gourmand, Sybarite
10. voluptuary 11. connoisseur
epidemic... 4. pest 6. plague
8. pandemic 9. prevalent, spreading
10. contagious, pestilence
epidermis... 4. skin 7. cuticle
8. ectoderm 9. scarfskin
epigram... 3. mot, saw 4. poem, quip
5. adage, maxim 6. dictum, saying
7. distich 11. inscription (obs)
epigraph... 5. motto, title 9. quotation
11. inscription
Epiphany (Eccl)... 5. Feast (Jan 6)
Epirus, oracle of... 6. Dodona (Mt
Tomarus, Gr)
episode... 5. event, story 8. incident
10. digression (Mus), occurrence
epistle... 4. note, post 6. billet,
lesson, letter 7. message, missive,
writing 8. dispatch, rescript
13. communication
epitaph... 7. writing (monument) 8. hic
jacet 11. inscription

epithet... 4. name, term 5. label
6. byname 7. agnomen 9. sobriquet
11. appellation (significant)
epitome... 6. digest 7. summary
8. abstract 9. comprisal
10. abridgment, compendium
epitomize... 7. abridge, curtail
8. abstract, compress, condense,
contract, diminish 9. capsulize
epoch... 3. age, day, eon, era 4. date,
time 5. event 6. period
epopee... 4. epic, epos, poem
5. genre (epic) 6. poetry (epic)
epoptic... 6. mystic, secret
equable... 4. even 6. steady
7. uniform
equal... 3. iso (pref), par, tie 4. both,
even, fere (obs), just, pari (pref),
peer, same 5. match, rival
7. compeer, emulate, equable,
uniform 8. adequate, parallel
9. equitable, identical 10. coordinate,
equivalent, substitute 11. counterpart
12. commensurate 13. proportionate
equal day and night...
11. equidiurnal, equinoctial
equal density (atmospheric)...
8. isoteric
equality... 3. par, tie 6. equity, owelty
(payment), parity 7. egalite, isonomy
(law) 8. adequacy, evenness, fairness,
identity, sameness 10. uniformity
12. impartiality
Equality State... 7. Wyoming (first
with Woman Suffrage)
equalize... 4. even 5. equal, level,
match 6. equate, smooth 7. balance
10. symmetrize
equally... 2. as 4. equi (pref) 5. alike
6. evenly, justly 11. identically
15. correspondingly
equanimity... 5. poise 6. aplomb
7. balance 8. calmness, evenness,
serenity 9. assurance, composure
10. confidence, equability
11. tranquility 12. tranquillity
equilibrium... 5. poise 7. balance
8. equality 9. stability 10. equanimity
equine... 3. ass 4. colt, foal, mare
5. filly, horse, steed, zebra 6. donkey
equine cry... 5. neigh 6. whinny
equip... 3. arm, fit, imp, rig 4. deck,
gear, gird 5. dress, endow
7. costume, furnish, qualify
8. accouter
equipment... 4. gear 5. armor
6. outfit, tackle, traits (personal)
7. ability, panoply (warriors)
8. equipage 9. apparatus
11. preparation 12. accouterment,
accoutrement
equitable... 4. fair, just 5. right
6. honest 7. upright 9. impartial
10. bonitarian (Rom law), reasonable
equity... 4. laws 6. rights 7. honesty,
justice 8. fairness 9. rectitude
11. uprightness
equivalence... 3. par 7. valence
8. equality, sameness 10. relativity
11. correlation
equivalent... 5. alike, equal
9. identical 10. tantamount

equivocal... 7. dubious, obscure
8. doubtful, puzzling 9. ambiguous,
enigmatic, uncertain 10. amphibolic,
mysterious, perplexing
13. indeterminate, problematical
equivocate... 3. lie 5. dodge, evade,
fence, shift 6. palter, trifle
7. quibble, shuffle 11. prevaricate
12. tergiversate
era... 2. AD, BC 3. age, eon 4. date,
time 5. cycle, epoch 6. period
10. Anno Domini 12. Before Christ
eradicate... 4. dele, root, weed
5. annul, erase 6. remove, uproot
7. abolish, destroy, epilate, extract,
root out 9. eliminate, extirpate
10. annihilate 11. exterminate
erase... 4. dele, kill 5. arase (obs)
6. cancel, delete, efface, excise
7. expunge, relieve 10. obliterate
Erasmus (Dutch)... 6. lovely 7. scholar
Erastus (Swiss)... 9. physician
10. theologian
ere... 4. also, soon 5. early, prior
6. before, erenow, sooner 7. earlier,
ere long 8. erewhile, formerly
10. before long, previously, sooner
than
Erebus (pert to)...
brother.. 3. Nox
father of.. 3. Day 6. Aether
Greek myth.. 8. darkness (nether)
native of.. 5. Hades
son.. 5. Chaos
erect... 4. lift, rear, stay 5. build,
found, raise, stand, upend 6. raised
7. elevate, upright 8. uplifted,
vertical 9. construct, establish,
institute 13. perpendicular
eremite... 6. hermit 7. recluse
8. anchoret, solitary 9. anchorite
erenow... 5. prior 8. erewhile, formerly
10. heretofore
ergo... 5. hence 9. therefore
Erin... 4. Eire 7. Ireland
Eritrea, Africa...
capital.. 6. Asmara
coastline of.. 8. Ethiopia
ruler.. 7. England (formerly It)
site.. 6. Red Sea
ermine... 3. fur 4. robe (emblem)
5. stoat (stot) 6. clothe, lasset,
weasel 7. ermelin
erode... 3. eat 4. gnaw, wear
7. corrode, decline, destroy
11. deteriorate 12. disintegrate
erotic... 6. loving, sexual 7. amative,
amatory, amorous 8. doctrine (of
love)
err... 3. sin 4. miss, slip 5. stray
6. bungle 7. blunder, deviate
10. transgress 12. miscalculate,
misinterpret
Er Rai... 5. stars 8. shepherd
errand... 4. task, trip 7. journey,
mission 8. business (special)
10. commission
errand boy... 4. page 7. bellboy,
bellhop, courier 9. messenger
errant... 6. erring, roving 7. peccant
8. fallible 9. deviating, erroneous,
itinerant, wandering 10. journeying

erratic... 5. queer, rogue 6. whacky
  7. nomadic, strange 8. abnormal
  9. eccentric, irregular, planetary,
  wandering 10. capricious, changeable
erroneous... 5. false, wrong 6. untrue
  7. peccant 8. illusory, mistaken
  9. wandering
error... 3. sin 4. flub, muff, slip
  5. boner, lapse 6. errata (pl), miscue
  7. blunder, falsity, misstep, mistake
  8. iniquity 11. anachronism,
  misjudgment 14. miscalculation
ersatz... 5. proxy, token 9. vicarious
  10. equivalent, substitute
  11. alternative, replacement
  12. substitution
Erse... 5. Irish 6. Celtic, Gaelic
erst, erstwhile... 4. also, once 5. first
  6. former, sooner 8. earliest, formerly
  10. heretofore, previously
erudite... 4. wise 7. learned
  8. cultured, educated, literate
  9. scholarly
erudition... 4. lore 6. finish, wisdom
  7. letters 8. learning, pedantry
  9. knowledge
eruption... 4. rash 6. geyser
  7. volcano 8. ejection, outbreak,
  outburst 9. commotion, exanthema
  10. nettlerash 13. efflorescence
Esau (pert to)...
  Bible ref.. 7. Genesis
  brother.. 5. Jacob
  father.. 5. Isaac
  home.. 4. Seir
  mother.. 7. Rebekah
  name (later).. 4. Edom
escape... 4. flee 5. dodge, elope,
  elude, evade, spill 7. evasion
  9. avolation 13. circumvention
escargot... 5. snail
escarpment... 5. cliff, slope
  9. precipice 13. fortification
eschar... 4. scab, sore 5. crust
  6. slough
escharotic... 7. caustic, mordant
  8. stinging 9. corrosive
escheat... 4. fall 5. lapse 6. revert
  (land) 7. forfeit 9. reversion
  10. forfeiture
eschew... 4. shun 5. avoid 7. abstain,
  refrain
escolar... 4. fish 8. mackerel (like)
escort... 3. see 4. beau 5. guard
  (honor), usher 6. attend, convoy,
  gigolo, squire 7. conduct, retinue
  8. chaperon 9. accompany
  13. accompaniment
escritoire... 4. desk 6. bureau
  7. dresser 9. secretary 10. secretaire
escrow... 4. bond, deed (deposit)
  9. muniments
esculent... 6. edible 7. eatable
  8. gustable 10. comestible
escutcheon... 4. fess (band), orle
  (voided) 5. crest 6. shield
esker, eskar... 2. os 4. osar (pl)
  5. drift, hills, mound, ridge
Eskimo... 3. Ita 4. Yuit 5. Aleut
  6. Innuit 10. skraelling 11. Yikirgaulit
  (Diomede Isles)
Eskimo (pert to)...

boat, canoe.. 5. kayak, umiak
  (oomiac)
boot (sealskin).. 5. kamik
coat (bird skin).. 5. parka 6. temiak
color.. 5. brown (rustic)
dog.. 5. Husky 8. Malemute
family.. 9. Eskimauan
fish.. 4. Atka 8. mackerel
hut, house.. 5. igloo, tupek (tupik)
jacket.. 6. temiak
knife (woman's).. 3. ulu
memorial post.. 3. xat
settlement.. 4. Etah
totem.. 4. pole, post 6. symbol
esne... 4. serf 5. slave 8. hireling
esophagus, oesophagus... 4. crop,
  gula 6. gullet, throat 7. pharynx
esoteric... 5. inner 6. occult, secret
  7. private 8. abstruse, initiate,
  personal 9. recondite 12. confidential
esoteric doctrine... 6. cabala
esoteric wisdom... 6. gnosis
espalier... 7. epaulet, railing, trellis
Español... 7. Spanish
especial... 5. chief 7. special
  8. peculiar, uncommon
Esperanto... 3. Ido 8. language
  (Internat)
espionage... 4. espy 6. spying
  11. observation (secret)
  14. reconnaissance
esplanade... 4. walk 5. drive, level,
  Prado, praya 6. strand 7. walkway
espousal... 7. wedding 8. adoption,
  ceremony 10. acceptance
  11. embracement
espouse... 3. wed 4. bind, mate
  5. adopt, marry 6. defend, pledge
  7. betroth, embrace, support
  8. maintain, plead for
esprit de corps... 3. wit 6. spirit
  8. devotion 10. enthusiasm,
  fellowship 11. partisanism
esprit fort (Relig)... 11. freethinker
espy... 3. see 5. watch 6. behold,
  descry, detect 7. discern 8. discover
  9. look about
esquire... 5. title 6. escort, gentry
  7. armiger 8. escudero, nobleman
  11. armor–bearer 12. shield–bearer
essay... 3. try 4. test 5. assay, chris
  (Rhet), paper, theme, tract, trial
  6. effort, thesis 7. attempt
  8. endeavor, treatise 11. composition
  12. disquisition, dissertation
esse... 5. being (real) 9. existence
essence... 3. ens 4. gist, odor, pith
  5. attar, being, scent 6. nature
  7. element, extract, perfume
  9. principle, substance
  12. quintessence
essential... 5. vital 6. mortal
  7. needful 8. existent, inherent
  9. necessary, necessity
  13. indispensable
essential oil... 8. volatile 12. attar of
  roses
essential part... 4. core, crux, gist,
  pith 7. element 8. inherent
  10. inwardness
establish... 3. fix 4. base, seat
  5. build, enact, erect, found, plant,

prove, set up 6. create, ground, locate, ordain, settle 7. confirm, pre–empt 8. ensconce, legalize, radicate (rare) 9. ascertain, originate

established . . . 5. fixed 6. proved, rested, stable 11. naturalized, traditional 12. conventional

established (pert to) . . .
church . . 9. Episcopal (Eng)
rule . . 8. standard
thing . . 4. fact
truth . . 8. verified

establishment . . . 4. mill 5. plant 6. custom, menage 7. factory 9. structure 12. organization

establishment of cordial relations . . . 13. rapprochement

establishment of new plant home . . . 6. ecesis

estate . . . 4. alod, fief (feudal), rank (social) 5. manor, title 6. assets, equity 7. alodium, demesne, fortune 8. interest, property 9. situation

esteem . . . 4. dear 5. adore, honor, judge, pride, value 6. admire, regard, repute, revere 7. respect 8. appraise, venerate 10. appreciate 13. consideration

ester of . . .
silicic acid . . 8. silicate
stearic acid . . 7. stearin 8. stearate
tropic acid . . 7. tropate
vinegar . . 7. acetate

esthetic, aesthetic . . . 6. essene 8. artistic, tasteful 9. beautiful

estimable . . . 6. worthy 8. valuable 9. admirable, honorable, reputable, venerable 10. measurable 12. praiseworthy

estimate . . . 3. aim, set 4. gage, rank, rate 5. audit, gauge, guess, prize, think 6. assess, repute 7. adjudge, compute, measure, opinion 8. appraise, judgment 9. calculate, statement, valuation

Estonia . . .
capital . . 5. Revel 7. Tallinn
industry . . 3. oil
island . . 5. Oesel
peasant (rich) . . 5. kulak
ruler . . 4. USSR

estop . . . 3. bar 4. fill, halt, plug, stay 6. impede, stop up 7. prevent 8. prohibit

estrange . . . 4. part, wean 6. divert, divide 8. alienate, disunite, separate

estreat . . . 4. copy 6. amerce, sconce 7. extract 9. duplicate, penalties (law)

estuary . . . 3. bay 4. Pará 5. firth, frith, Plata

etch . . . 3. cut 4. bite 5. infix 7. corrode, engrave, impress (upon)

eternal . . . 6. eonian 7. aeonian, ageless, endless, lasting 8. enduring, immortal, timeless 9. boundless, ceaseless, immutable, incessant, unceasing 10. unchanging 11. everlasting 12. imperishable, interminable, unchangeable

Eternal City . . . 4. Rome

eternal death . . . 9. perdition

eternal home . . . 6. heaven 12. The Hereafter

eternity . . . 3. eon 4. aeon, ages, olam 8. Olam haba

etesian . . . 4. wind (Aegean Sea) 6. annual 8. seasonal 10. periodical

ether . . . 3. air, sky 5. ester, space 6. anisol, heaven (anc) 8. empyrean 10. anesthetic

ethereal . . . 4. rare 5. aerie (aery), light 7. fragile, slender, tenuous 8. delicate, heavenly, vaporous 9. celestial 10. atmosphere (earth's), spiritlike 11. phantomlike 13. unsubstantial

ethereal (pert to) . . .
being . . 5. sylph
color . . 7. sky blue
fluid . . 5. ichor (icor)
poetic . . 4. aery
salt . . 5. ester

ethical . . . 5. moral, right 7. upright 8. virtuous

ethics . . . 6. morals 8. hedonics 10. principles (moral) 11. highest good, summum bonum 12. Magna Moralia (Aristotle)

Ethiopia (Abyssinia) . . .
capital . . 10. Addis Ababa
city . . 5. Adowa
colony . . 7. Eritrea
empress . . 7. Zauditu
king (Myth) . . 5. Negus 6. Memnon
native . . 5. Negro 6. Hamite 10. Abyssinian, black–a–moor
river . . 3. Omo 4. Juba 5. Abbai (Blue Nile)
ruler . . 7. Menelik 13. Haile Selassie
tribes (anc) . . 5. Bejas, Galla 7. Hamites, Semites

Ethiopian (pert to) . . .
ape . . 6. gelada
banana . . 6. ensete
dialect . . 4. Geez
lily . . 5. calla
Torah . . 5. tetel

ethnic . . . 5. pagan 6. racial 7. gentile, heathen

ethnology . . . 5. races (Man)

ethology . . . 7. manners 9. bionomics, character

ethos (opp of pathos) . . . 9. attitudes (moral), esthetics

etiquette . . . 4. form 5. label, mores 6. ticket 7. decorum, manners 9. amenities, propriety 10. civilities

etiquette, breach of . . . 8. solecism

Etruria, Italy . . . see *Etruscan*

Etruscan (pert to) . . .
bookbinding (anc) . . 9. classical
deity . . 3. Lar, Uni
pottery . . 8. bucchero (black)
race . . 7. Rasenna 8. Tursenoi, Tyrrheni
soothsayer . . 8. haruspex (a)
soothsayer's function . . 8. extispex

ettle . . . 3. try 4. plan 6. aspire, design, intent 8. consider, endeavor

etui, etwee . . . 4. case 7. trousse

etymology . . . 10. word origin

eucalyptus . . . 4. lerp (laap, juice) 7. gum tree 8. eucalypt

Eucharist (pert to)...
administer to.. 6. housel 8. viaticum
(dying)
plate.. 5. paten
rite.. 9. Communion (Holy) 11. Lord's
Supper
wafer.. 4. host
wafer vessel.. 8. ciborium
wine.. 5. krama
wine vessel.. 3. ama 5. amula
Euclid (Gr)... 8. geometer (BC)
eulogist... 9. encomiast 10. panegyrist
eulogize... 4. laud 5. boost, extol
6. praise 7. commend, glorify
9. celebrate 10. panegyrize
eulogy... 5. eloge 6. hesped (Heb),
praise 7. oration 8. citation,
encomium 9. laudation, panegyric
euphony... 5. meter 6. melody,
rhythm, speech (ease of) 7. harmony
Eurafrica... 5. Egypt 6. Europe
7. Algeria 9. Abyssinia (anc)
Eurasia... 4. Asia 6. Europe 7. Scythia
(anc)
Eurasian (pert to)...
herb.. 6. yarrow 7. gosmore
mint.. 6. Nepeta
people.. 5. Finns 7. Ugrians
9. Armenians, Turanians
eureka... 11. exclamation 12. I Have
Found It (Calif motto)
Euripedes (Gr)... 4. poet (BC)
Europe... see also *European*
basin (coal).. 4. Saar
battlefield.. 5. Marne 6. Verdun
8. Normandy, Waterloo 11. Belleau
Wood
capitals.. 4. Bonn, Oslo, Riga, Rome
5. Berne, Paris, Sofia 6. Athens,
Berlin, Lisbon, Madrid, Moscow,
Prague, Warsaw 8. Belgrade,
Budapest, Helsinki 9. Amsterdam,
Bucharest, Stockholm
10. Copenhagen, Monte Carlo
country (anc).. 4. Elis (Gr) 7. Etruria
(It)
country (modern).. 5. Italy, Spain
6. France, Greece, Latvia, Monaco,
Norway, Poland, Russia, Sweden
7. Denmark, Finland, Germany,
Hungary, Rumania 8. Bulgaria,
Portugal 10. Yugoslavia
11. Netherlands, Switzerland
14. Czechoslovakia
gulf.. 4. Riga 7. Bothnia
health resort.. 5. Baden 10. Baden
Baden (Ger)
invaders.. 4. Huns 5. Arabs, Turks
7. Mongols
kingdom (anc).. 5. Arles 6. Aragon
8. Burgundy
lake.. 9. Zuider Zee (Holland)
lancer.. 5. uhlan 6. hussar
mountain region.. 4. Alps 5. Tyrol
race (anc).. 5. Goths 7. Teutons
9. Visigoths 10. Ostrogoths
river.. 4. Elbe, Isar 5. Loire, Meuse,
Rhine, Rhone, Seine, Volga
6. Danube 7. Dneiper, Moselle
sea.. 4. Aral, Azov 5. North 6. Baltic
strait.. 8. Bosporus
valley.. 4. Ruhr

European (pert to)...
antelope.. 7. chamois
bat.. 8. serotine
bird.. 3. ani, mew (gull) 4. kite, stag
5. glede, mavis, ousel, serin
6. godwit, linnet, marten, merlin
(falcon) 7. bittern, ortolan, starnel
8. dotterel, garganey 9. brambling,
gallinule 10. turtledove
11. lammergeier 12. capercaillie
bison.. 7. aurochs
clover.. 6. alsike
dog.. 7. griffin
fish.. 3. gar 4. dace, rudd, spet, tope
(shark) 5. sprat 6. allice, barbel,
brasse, morgay, turbot
grape.. 6. muscat
linden.. 4. teil
mint.. 6. hyssop 9. horehound
mouse.. 4. loir, vole 5. lerot
polecat.. 7. fitchew
rodent.. 3. erd 4. loir 5. stoat
(ermine) 6. leriot 7. hamster
sandpiper.. 4. ruff 5. terek
squirrel.. 5. sisel 10. polatouche
tree.. 4. cade (juniper), sorb (apple)
5. carob 9. terebinth
wheat.. 5. emmer (speltz) 7. einkorn
evacuant... 6. emetic 8. diuretic
9. cathartic, purgative
evacuate... 4. void 5. empty, expel
6. depart, vacate 7. deprive, exhaust
8. withdraw 9. discharge
evade... 3. gee 4. foil, shun 5. avoid,
dodge, elude, parry, shirk, shunt
6. baffle, escape, illude 7. beguile,
quibble 8. slip away 10. circumvent
evanescent... 8. fleeting 9. ephemeral,
transient, vanishing 11. impermanent
12. disappearing 13. infinitesimal
evangelical... 7. Gospels 8. orthodox
10. Protestant, scriptural
Evangeline (pert to)...
home.. 6. Acadia
lover.. 7. Gabriel
poem by.. 10. Longfellow (1847)
evangelist... 6. Graham, Sunday (Billy)
7. apostle, Roberts 9. McPherson
evaporate... 3. dry 5. steam
6. escape, exhale 7. avolate
8. vaporize 9. cease to be,
dehydrate, disappear
evasion... 5. dodge, shift 6. escape
8. avoiding 9. avoidance, quibbling,
shuffling 12. equivocation
13. circumvention, secretiveness
evasive... 3. sly 4. eely 6. shifty
7. elusive, elusory 9. deceitful,
quibbling, secretive
eve... 3. iva (herb), wet 4. dusk, thaw
6. sunset 12. on the brink of, on
the verge of
even... 3. e'en, tie 4. just, tied
5. equal, exact, level, match, plane
6. placid, smooth, square, steady
7. abreast, balance, equable, neutral,
regular, uniform 8. directly, parallel
9. impartial, precisely
11. symmetrical
even (if)... 8. although
12. nevertheless 15. notwithstanding
even (so)... 3. yes 12. nevertheless

evener... 9. equalizer 10. doubletree
evenglow... 3. red (color) 8. twilight
evening... 5. Abend 6. sunset
evening dress... 4. gown 6. jewels,
  tuxedo 8. slippers (high heel) 9. full
  dress, headdress 10. dinner coat
  11. tie and tails 17. swallow–tailed
  coat
event... 4. fate (obs), game 5. drama,
  issue 6. result 7. contest, episode,
  scandal 8. incident 9. adventure,
  happening, milestone 10. conclusion,
  occurrence 11. consequence,
  termination 12. circumstance
event (pert to)...
  extraordinary.. 10. phenomenon
  supernatural.. 7. miracle
  theater.. 6. opener 8. premiere
  turning point.. 6. crisis 8. decision,
  landmark
eventide... 4. dusk 6. sunset, vesper
  7. evening, sundown 8. twilight
  9. nightfall
eventually... 3. yet 6. lastly 7. finally
  10. ultimately
ever... 3. e'er 4. anon 5. at all
  6. always 7. forever 10. constantly
  11. perpetually
Everest peak... 6. Lhotse (28,100 ft)
evergreen shrub... 4. Ilex, moss, Olax,
  titi 5. heath, holly, savin, toyon
  6. laurel 7. baretta, jasmine
  9. perennial 12. rhododendron
evergreen tree... 3. fir, yew 4. pine
  5. carob, cedar, larch, olive, Taxus
  6. balsam, deodar, spruce, tarata
  7. conifer, hemlock, madrona,
  redwood
everlasting... 6. eterne 7. aeonian,
  agelong, durable, endless, eternal,
  forever, lasting, tedious 8. enduring,
  evermore, immortal, infinite
  9. continual, incessant, perpetual,
  unceasing, wearisome 10. immortelle,
  indefinite 11. never–ending,
  strawflower 12. Eternal Being,
  imperishable 13. unintermitted,
  uninterrupted
every... 3. all, any, ilk 4. each, ilka
  6. entire 8. complete
every one, everyone... 3. all 4. each
  9. everybody 10. individual
everything... 3. all, sum 5. total
evict... 4. oust 5. eject, expel, prove
  6. remove 7. confute 8. force out
eviction... 6. ouster 9. ejectment
  11. dislodgment 13. dispossession
evidence... 4. clue, sign 5. proof,
  token 6. attest, evince 7. constat
  (law), probate, support 8. argument,
  manifest, rebuttal 9. testimony
  10. indication 15. circumstantiate
evident... 5. clear, plain 6. patent
  7. obvious, visible 8. apparent,
  manifest, palpable 9. notorious
  11. indubitable
evil... 3. bad, ill, mal (pref) 4. bane,
  vile 6. injury, sinful, wicked
  7. adverse, baleful, corrupt, hurtful,
  immoral, malefic, misdeed, satanic,
  unsound, vicious 8. depraved,
  iniquity, sinister 9. injurious,

malignant, offensive 10. calamitous,
  malevolent, pernicious, wrongdoing
  12. unpropitious
evil (pert to)...
  child.. 3. imp
  deed.. 3. sin 4. harm
  devil (little).. 9. deevilick (Scot)
  doer.. 5. cheat 9. miscreant,
  wrongdoer 10. malefactor
  omen.. 5. knell
  spirit.. 5. bugan, demon, devil, ghoul,
  Satan 6. Belial 7. Ahriman, Amaimon
  8. Asmodeus 9. cacodemon,
  demonkind, lost souls
evils... 4. ills, mala
evince... 4. show 7. display, exhibit,
  express, provoke 8. convince,
  evidence, indicate, manifest
evoke... 4. call (out) 5. educe, voice
  6. elicit, prompt, summon 7. conjure
evolution... 7. biogeny, cosmism
  8. heredity, maneuver, movement
  9. Darwinism, phylogeny, unfolding,
  unrolling 10. evolvement
  11. development 13. manifestation,
  Spencerianism
evolve... 4. emit 5. educe 6. create,
  deduce, derive, unfold, unroll
  7. develop, grow out 9. disengage,
  expatiate, extricate 11. disentangle
ewe... 3. keb 4. lamb 5. crone (old),
  sheep 6. theave
ewer... 3. jug 5. crock 7. pitcher
exacerbate... 5. anger 6. incite
  8. embitter, irritate 9. aggravate
exact... 4. just, levy, nice 6. assess,
  demand, elicit, extort, formal, minute,
  oblige, strict 7. careful, correct,
  literal, precise, regular, require
  8. accurate 10. methodical,
  meticulous
exact (pert to)...
  opposite of.. 8. antipode 9. antipodal
  penalty.. 4. fine 7. estreat
  thinking.. 13. ratiocination
  vengeance.. 6. avenge
exacting... 6. severe, strict 7. arduous
  8. critical 9. demanding, elicitory
  10. fastidious 12. extortionate
exacting devotion (exclusive)...
  7. jealous
exactly... 3. due 5. spand 6. nicely
  7. quite so 8. as you say
  9. precisely 10. accurately
exaggerated... 5. outré 8. enhanced,
  enlarged, overdone, romanced
  9. excessive, increased, magnified
  10. overstated 11. exceptional
  13. overestimated 14. misrepresented
exaggerated comedy... 5. farce
exalt... 5. elate, extol, raise 6. praise
  7. elevate, ennoble, glorify, inspire,
  promote, worship 8. enthrone,
  increase, sanctify 10. aggrandize
exalted... 5. grand, noble, sheen
  6. elated 7. refined, sublime
  8. elevated, extolled 9. dignified
  11. illustrious
examination... 4. test 5. audit, trial
  7. inquiry 8. research, scrutiny,
  specimen 10. discussion, inspection
  11. inquisition 13. investigation

examine... 3. pry, spy, try (law)
4. pore, scan, sift, test 5. audit,
probe, quest 6. censor, debate,
ponder 7. analyze, collate, discuss,
explore, inspect 8. consider
10. scrutizine 11. interrogate
examiner... 6. censor, conner, tester
7. auditor, officer (court) 9. inspector
example... 4. case, norm, type
5. bysen (obs), model 6. sample
7. pattern, warning 8. instance,
paradigm, specimen 9. exemplify,
precedent 12. illustration
15. exemplification
ex animo... 9. sincerely 12. from the
heart
excavate... 3. dig 4. cave, mine
5. dig up, scoop, stope 6. dredge,
exhume, quarry 9. hollow out
excavation... 3. pit 4. hole, mine
5. stope 6. cavity, dugout 7. digging
8. opencast
exceed... 3. top 4. pass 5. excel,
outdo 6. outvie, overdo 7. eclipse,
outrank, surpass 8. outstrip, overstep
9. overshoot, transcend
11. predominate
exceedingly... 4. many, very
9. extremely 13. extraordinary
excel... 3. cap, top 4. beat, best
5. outdo, outgo, rival 6. better,
exceed, precel 7. surpass
8. dominate, outshine 9. transcend
excellence... 4. meed 5. merit
6. desert, virtue 7. classic, probity
9. supremacy 13. inimitability
excellent... 4. A-one, best, fine, good
5. bravo, prime, super 6. choice,
golect, tiptop, worthy 7. capital,
corking 8. skillful (skllful), stunning,
valuable 9. admirable, exquisite,
first-rate 12. transcendent
except... 3. bar, but 4. omit, save
6. exempt, reject, unless 7. besides
9. eliminate, other than
exception... 4. plea 5. cavil, doubt
6. oddity 7. dissent 8. demurrer
9. condition, exclusion, exemption,
objection, rejection 11. restriction
exceptional... 4. rare 7. notable,
unusual 8. superior, uncommon
9. exclusive, wonderful
10. remarkable 11. outstanding
13. extraordinary
excerpt... 4. cite 5. quote, scrap
6. choice 7. extract, passage
(selected) 9. selection
excess... 3. too 4. over, plus 5. luxus
7. nimiety, overage, profuse, surplus
10. indulgence (undue), redundancy
11. superfluity 12. intemperance
14. immoderateness, superabundance
excess (solar over lunar month)...
5. epact
excessive... 3. too 5. undue 6. overly
7. extreme, profuse 8. overmuch
9. fanatical, plethoric 10. exorbitant,
immoderate, inordinate, redundancy
11. exaggerated, extravagant
12. unreasonable
excessive (pert to)...
development.. 11. hypertrophy

fear.. 5. panic 6. phobia
gushing.. 8. effusion
waste.. 12. extravagance
excessively... 3. too 5. enorm
6. unduly 12. exorbitantly,
inordinately 13. intemperately
exchange... 4. swap 5. bandy, trade
6. barter, resale, rialto 7. dealing,
traffic 9. transpose 10. substitute
11. interchange, reciprocate
exchange (pert to)...
discount.. 4. agio
for money.. 4. cash, sell
letters.. 10. correspond
place.. 4. mart 5. store 6. bourse,
market, shoppe
premium.. 4. agio
visits.. 3. gam
exchequer... 4. fisc (fisk) 5. funds,
purse 8. finances, treasury
11. possessions (money)
excise... 3. tax 4. toll 6. impost
exciseman... 5. gager 7. officer
8. revenuer
excision... 7. erasure, removal
10. cutting off, cutting out, mutilation
11. destruction, extirpation
excite... 4. fire, roil, spur, stir, urge
5. elate, impel, rouse 6. arouse,
awaken, bestir, incite, kindle, prompt,
stir up 7. agitate, animate, inflame,
provoke, psych up 8. energize,
interest 9. electrify, impassion,
instigate, stimulate
excited... 4. agog 6. hoopla
7. aroused, fevered, keyed up
8. agitated, startled 10. interested
11. impassioned
excited, not easily... 6. stolid
7. stoical 9. impassive
excitement... 3. ado 4. stir 5. fever
6. furore 7. emotion, ferment
9. agitation, commotion
10. incitement, irritation
11. disturbance, stimulation
exciting... 5. kicky 6. gung-ho, hectic
7. parlous 8. alluring 9. desirable,
thrilling 10. delightful 11. interesting,
provocative
exciting compassion... 7. piteous
exclamation... 2. ah, lo, oh, so
3. aha, bah, boo, fic, hep, oho, tut,
ugh, yah 4. ahem, alas, drat, egad,
evoe, phew, pish, rats, yech 5. bravo,
humph, pshaw 6. indeed, shezam
7. kerwham 9. alackaday
11. ejaculation 12. interjection
exclude... 3. bar 4. omit 5. debar,
eject, expel 6. banish 7. shut out
8. disallow, preclude, prohibit
9. eliminate 13. excommunicate
exclusive... 5. aloof, ritzy 6. select
7. special 8. limiting, snobbish
9. seclusive 10. definitive, unsociable
11. prohibitive, restrictive
exclusive right... 6. patent
10. concession 11. restriction
excoriate... 4. flay, gall, peel 5. strip
6. abrade 9. criticize
excrescence... 4. boss (Arch), lump
6. growth, nodule 9. appendage,
outgrowth 10. protrusion

excrete . . . 5. egest 9. discharge,
eliminate
excruciating . . . 7. painful, racking
9. agonizing, torturing 11. distressing
excursion . . . 3. row 4. ride, sail, tour,
trek, trip 5. jaunt, sally 6. junket,
outing, ramble 7. circuit, journey,
outlope 8. circuity 10. expedition
excusable . . . 6. venial 9. allowable,
justified 10. defensible, exemptible,
pardonable, remissible 11. justifiable
excuse . . . 4. plea 5. alibi, remit
6. acquit, essoin, pardon 7. absolve,
apology, condone, forgive, pretext
8. overlook 9. exonerate, extenuate
execrable . . . 7. impious 9. nefandous
execute . . . 2. do 3. act 4. hang, kill,
vest 6. direct, effect, finish, manage
7. conduct, enforce, perform 8. carry
out, complete, transact
10. accomplish, administer
execution . . . 4. writ 7. hanging
10. production, punishment
11. achievement, performance,
transaction 14. accomplishment
exegate . . . 6. leader 7. adviser
8. dragoman 11. interpreter
exegesis . . . 7. explain 9. interpret
10. exposition, expounding
exemplar . . . 5. ideal, model
7. example, paragon, pattern
8. specimen 9. archetype
exemplary . . . 8. laudable, monitory
11. commendable 12. exemplifying,
praiseworthy 14. representative
exemplify . . . 4. copy 6. typify
7. explain 10. illustrate, transcribe
exempt . . . 4. exon 5. clear 6. immune
7. absolve, release 8. dispense,
excepted, excluded, released, set
apart 10. privileged
exemption . . . 6. essoin 7. freedom
8. immunity, impunity, navicert
12. dispensation
exercise . . . 3. ply, ure (anc), use
4. task, yoga 5. drill, étude, exert,
train 6. action, employ, lesson,
praxis, school, tai chi 7. display,
jogging, problem, workout
8. activity, aerobics, ceremony,
practice, training 9. athletics
10. exhibition, gymnastics,
isometrics
exertion . . . 5. essay, trial 6. effort
7. attempt 8. endeavor
exhalation . . . 4. aura, fume 5. steam
6. breath 7. halitus 9. effluvium,
emanation 10. expiration
11. evaporation 12. vaporization
exhale . . . 4. emit 6. vanish 7. exhaust,
respite 9. transpire 10. breathe out
exhaust . . . 3. fag, sap 4. emit, jade,
tire 5. drain, empty, spend, waste,
weary 6. exhale, overdo, weaken
7. consume, deplete, fatigue
9. discharge 10. impoverish
exhausted . . . 4. done, worn 5. spent,
tired 6. used up 7. emptied, petered
(out) 8. dog–tired, forspent
exhaustion . . . 6. effete 7. burnout,
fatigue 9. depletion, lassitude
11. prostration 14. impoverishment

exhibit . . . 3. air 4. fair, shew (anc),
show, wear 5. stage, state 6. evince,
expose, flaunt, parade, reveal
7. display 8. disclose, evidence,
manifest 9. spectacle
11. demonstrate 15. circumstantiate
exhibit (pert to) . . .
colors (change of) . . 8. iridesce,
opalesce
pleasure . . 5. gloat, revel (in)
taste (refined) . . 6. ostent 7. elegant
exhibition . . . 4. fair, show 9. spectacle
10. exposition 11. ostentation
13. manifestation
exhibition room . . . 10. panopticon
exhilaration . . . 6. gaiety 7. jollity
8. gladness, hilarity 9. animation,
merriment 10. excitement, joyousness
11. gleefulness, refreshment
12. cheerfulness, invigoration
exhort . . . 4. urge, warn 6. advise,
dehort, incite, preach 7. caution
9. encourage, stimulate
exhume . . . 3. dig 5. delve 7. unearth
8. disinter, exhumate
exigeant . . . 8. exacting
11. importunate
exigency . . . 4. need, urge 6. crisis
7. demands, urgency 8. juncture,
pressure 9. emergency, extremity,
necessity 12. requirements
exigent . . . 4. writ 6. strict, urgent
8. critical, exacting, pressing
9. demanding, necessary
10. compelling 13. indispensable
exile . . . 6. banish, deport 7. outcast
8. outlawry, relegate 9. expulsion
10. banishment, expatriate
12. expatriation, proscription
exist . . . 2. am, be, is 3. are 4. live
5. alive 6. abound 9. be present
existence . . . 3. ens 4. esse, life
5. actus, being, entia 6. extant
7. essence, reality 8. presence
9. actuality 13. manifestation
existing (pert to) . . .
fancifully . . 9. imaginary 10. transitory
name only (in) . . 7. nominal, titular
now . . 6. extant 7. current, present
9. immediate
same time . . 15. contemporaneous
way of . . 9. lifestyle
exit . . . 3. die 4. door, gate, vent
5. going, go out, issue 6. egress,
outlet 7. leaving, passage (out),
walkout 9. departure
exitus . . . 5. death, issue 6. exodus,
outlet 7. outcome
exlex . . . 6. outlaw
ex libris . . . 8. colophon 9. bookplate
exodus . . . 4. Book (Bib), exit 5. going
6. flight, hegira 9. departure
exonerate . . . 4. free 5. clear 6. acquit
7. absolve, release, relieve
9. disburden (obs), exculpate
exorbitant . . . 5. undue 9. excessive
10. high–priced
exorbitant interest . . . 5. usury
exorcism . . . 5. spell 7. formula
9. expulsion (of evil spirits)
11. conjuration, incantation
exordium . . . 5. proem 7. preface,

prelude 8. overture 9. beginning
12. introduction
exoteric... 8. exterior, external, outsider
14. comprehensible
exotic... 5. alien 7. foreign, strange
8. colorful, ulterior 9. not native,
peregrine, unrelated 10. extraneous,
outlandish
expand... 4. grow, open 5. sheet,
splay, tract 6. dilate, spread
7. broaden, develop, distend, enlarge
9. expatiate, intumesce
expanse... 3. sea 4. main (broad)
5. ocean, plain, reach, tract
6. desert, extent, spread 7. stretch
8. eternity (time) 9. expansion
expansion... 4. size 6. extent, growth,
spread 8. dilation, increase
10. distention 11. development,
enlargement, expatiation
expansive... 4. wide 5. broad, large
7. elastic, liberal 8. effusive,
spacious 9. bombastic, grandiose
11. extensional, sympathetic
12. unrestrained 13. comprehensive
expatiate... 5. dwell 6. dilate
7. descant, enlarge 10. widespread
expatriate... 5. exile, expel 6. banish,
outlaw 7. exclude, outcast
9. ostracize 13. excommunicate
expect... 4. deem, hope, wait
5. await, think 6. intend 7. suppose
10. anticipate
expectation... 4. hope 9. imminence,
intention 12. anticipation
expedience... 6. wisdom 7. fitness
10. adaptation, timeliness
11. suitability
expedient... 4. wise 5. shift 6. timely
7. fitting, politic, ressort, stopgap
8. artifice, resource 9. advisable
10. profitable 12. advantageous
expedite... 3. hie 4. easy, free
5. hurry, light, speed 6. hasten
7. further, quicken 8. dispatch
10. accelerate, facilitate
expedition... 5. drave, foray, haste,
speed 6. safari 7. Crusade, entrada,
journey 8. Crusades 9. excursion,
hastening
expel... 4. oust, void 5. eject, evict,
exile 6. banish, exhale 7. extrude
9. discharge, eliminate
10. dispossess
expend... 3. pay, use 5. spend, waste
7. consume 8. disburse
10. distribute
expenditure... 5. outgo, price 6. outlay
7. expense, payment
11. consumption 12. disbursement
expense... 4. cost 5. price 6. outlay
9. allowance 11. consumption
12. disbursement
expensive... 4. dear, high 5. fancy,
steep 6. costly, lavish 7. liberal
10. high-priced 11. extravagant
experience... 3. see, try 4. feel, have,
know, test 5. maxim, sense, skill
6. ordeal, suffer, wisdom 7. emotion,
undergo 8. facility 9. knowledge,
sensation 10. occurrence

experience (pert to)...
pleasure.. 5. enjoy
regret.. 6. repent
suffering.. 7. calvary
worldly.. 14. sophistication
experiment... 3. try 4. test 5. essay,
proof, prove, trial 6. verify
11. observation
expert... 3. ace 4. deft 5. adept
6. adroit, clever, habile, master
7. casuist (in conscience) 8. artistic,
skillful 10. proficient 11. connoisseur,
experienced 12. professional
expiate... 5. atone, purge 6. purify,
shrive (anc)
expiation... 4. rite 6. amends
7. redress 8. piacular 9. atonement
10. redemption 12. compensation,
propitiation
expire... 3. die, end 4. pass 5. cease,
lapse 6. elapse, perish 7. breathe
(out) 9. terminate
explain... 5. clear, solve 6. define
7. expound, premise 8. describe
9. elucidate, interpret
11. demonstrate
explanation... 6. theory 7. meaning
8. exegesis, scholium, solution
10. exposition 11. description,
explication 13. clarification
14. interpretation 15. exemplification
explanatory description... 5. title
7. titulus
expletive... 3. gee 4. egad, gosh,
oath 5. curse, there, voilà 6. behold
8. addition 9. added word
11. exclamation
explicit... 4. open 5. exact, fixed
6. candid 7. express, precise
8. absolute, distinct, implicit,
manifest, positive 9. outspoken
11. unambiguous, unequivocal,
unqualified 13. unconditional
14. discriminating
explode... 3. pop 4. fail 5. blast,
burst 6. blow up 7. implode
8. backfire, detonate
exploit... 3. act (heroic) 4. dare, deed,
feat, gest, milk 5. bleed 7. heroism
9. advantage 10. overcharge
11. achievement
exploration, modern... 10. space
probe
explore... 4. look, view 5. probe
6. search 7. examine 8. discover
9. penetrate 11. investigate
explorer... 5. diver 7. pioneer
10. discoverer
explorer... 4. Byrd, Eric, Gama
7. Johnson (Osa), Wilkins (Hubert)
8. Amundsen, Magellan 9. Ellsworth
explosion... 3. pop 4. bank 5. blast,
noise 6. report 7. failure 8. outburst
10. detonation
explosive... 3. cap, TNT 4. mine
5. niter, shell 6. amatol, petard,
powder, tittle, tonite 7. cordite,
grenade, lyddite 8. dynamite
9. cartridge, cellulose, fulgurite,
guncotton, pyroxylin 11. firecracker
13. nitroglycerin 15. trinitrotoluene
exponent... 4. note 5. index

7. symptom 9. explainer, expounder
10. explaining 11. interpreter
expose... 3. air 4. bare, open
6. divest, reveal, unmask 7. exhibit,
unearth 8. disclose, discover,
endanger 9. ventilate 10. exposition
expose to danger... 11. periclitate
expose to scorn... 6. satire 7. pillory
exposition... 4. fair 6. bazaar, exposé,
lesson 7. display 8. exposure,
treatise 9. discourse, spectacle
10. disclosure, exhibition
11. abandonment, explanation
12. dissertation 14. interpretation
expostulate... 5. orate 6. advise,
demand 7. call for, discuss, protest
8. complain, dissuade
11. remonstrate
exposure... 8. disproof, jeopardy,
openness, snapshot 9. liability
10. appearance, disclosure,
exposition, visibility
express... 3. say 4. mean, show
5. exude, speak, state, train, utter,
voice 6. depict, evince, extort,
phrase 7. betoken, carrier, declare,
exhibit, expound, extract, signify,
testify 8. describe, dispatch, indicate,
intimate, manifest 9. delineate,
messenger, posthaste, utterance
11. declaration
express (pert to)...
censure.. 10. animadvert
disapproval.. 9. deprecate
fervor.. 7. enthuse
gratitude.. 5. thank
indirectly.. 5. imply
in words.. 6. phrase
numerically.. 8. evaluate
regard.. 6. praise 10. compliment
regret.. 9. apologize
sympathy.. 7. condole, console
10. grieve with 11. commiserate
expressing...
doubt.. 10. dubitative
extra phrase (Gram).. 12. periphrastic
feeling.. 7. emotive
past tense.. 11. preteritive
pique.. 5. pouty
praise.. 9. laudatory
expression... 4. grin, show, term
5. scowl, smile 6. aspect, oracle,
phrase 7. diction, meaning
8. locution 9. statement, utterance
10. extraction, indication
11. delineation 13. manifestation
14. representation
expression (pert to)...
mathematics.. 8. equation
of approval.. 4. clap 7. ovation
8. applause
of contempt.. 3. fie 5. pshaw, sneer
of disapproval.. 6. rebuke
of ideas.. 4. mode 5. style 7. fashion
of politics.. 4. vote
of weariness.. 4. sigh
peculiar.. 5. idiom
without.. 7. deadpan
expressive motion... 7. gesture
13. gesticulation
expulsion... 5. exile 10. banishment,
expiration 11. elimination

expunction... 4. blot 7. erasure
10. effacement 12. obliteration
expunge... 4. dele 5. erase 6. cancel,
delete, efface, excise, rub out 7. blot
out, destroy 9. strike out
10. annihilate, obliterate
expurgate... 5. bathe, purge
6. censor, excise, purify 7. cleanse
exquisite... 4. fine, rare 6. dainty,
superb 7. perfect, refined 8. delicate
9. beautiful, delicious, matchless
10. delightful, fastidious
exsanguine... 6. anemic 9. bloodless
exsiccate... 3. dry 4. arid, sear 5. dry
up, parch 7. exhaust 9. evaporate
extant... 5. being 7. in vogue,
present, visible 8. existent, existing
extempore... 5. ad lib 7. offhand
9. impromptu 13. improvisation
14. unpremeditated
extend... 2. go 3. eke, jut, lie, run
4. give, span 5. bulge, reach,
renew, steal, widen 6. deepen,
deploy, expand, spread 7. amplify,
broaden, draw out, proffer, prolong,
radiate, stretch 8. continue, increase,
lengthen, postpone, protract, protrude
10. exaggerate, straighten
extended... 4. open 5. broad
6. valued 7. assured, diffuse
8. expanded, spacious
10. lengthened 12. outstretched
extended view... 8. panorama
extension... 4. area 5. range, scope
6. extent 8. addition, duration,
increase, sequence 9. expansion
10. denotation 11. continuance,
enlargement, lengthening
12. augmentation 13. extensiveness
extension of time... 4. stay 7. respite
extensive... 4. vast, wide 5. broad,
large 7. immense, titanic
8. expanded, spacious 9. expansive,
wholesale 10. widespread
11. far-reaching
extent... 4. area, bulk, room, side, writ
5. areal, range, reach, scope
6. amount, degree, length
7. breadth, compass, expanse,
measure 8. distance, frontage
9. dimension 10. assessment (Hist),
denotation, proportion
extenuate... 4. thin 6. excuse, lessen,
reduce, sicken, weaken 7. justify
8. diminish, palliate 9. attenuate
extenuating... 10. justifying, qualifying
exterior... 5. ectad (toward), ectal,
outer 7. outside 8. external
10. extraneous
exterminate... 4. kill 5. expel
7. abolish, destroy 8. get rid of
9. eradicate, extirpate 10. annihilate
extermination... 9. expulsion
11. destruction, eradication
extern... 7. outward 8. exterior,
external 9. extrinsic
external... 4. ecto 5. outer, outre
6. nonego 7. outside 8. cortical
10. extraneous
external appearance... 5. guise,
image, looks 6. aspect 8. features
9. semblance

extinct... 4. dead, past 5. passé
7. defunct, died out, expired
8. quenched 11. nonexistent
12. extinguished
extinct bird... 3. moa 4. dodo
extinction... 5. death 9. quenching
11. destruction 12. annihilation
extinct reptile... 11. pterodactyl
extinguish... 5. annul, choke, douse,
quell 6. quench, stifle 7. destroy
8. suppress
extirpate... 4. dele, root, stub
5. erase, expel 6. excise, uproot
7. destroy 9. eradicate
11. exterminate
extol... 4. laud 5. exalt, kudos
6. praise 7. applaud, commend,
elevate, glorify 8. emblazon
9. celebrate
extort... 5. bleed, exact, steal, wrest,
wring 6. compel, elicit, wrench
7. extract 10. overcharge
extortion... 7. robbery, seizure
8. exaction, rapacity 10. extraction,
oppression, overcharge
extortionist... 5. harpy 7. vampire,
vulture 9. profiteer 11. blackmailer
extra... 3. bye 4. over 5. added,
spare, super 7. surplus 8. superior
9. accessory 10. additional
extra cache... 5. stock, store
7. reserve 9. reservoir
extract... 4. cite, pull 6. deduce, elicit,
select 7. essence, estreat, excerpt
8. withdraw
extract (pert to)...
balsam.. 7. toluene
Bible.. 7. passage 8. pericope
forcibly.. 6. evulse
newspaper.. 8. clipping
orchid (climbing).. 7. vanilla
extraction... 5. birth, stock 6. origin
7. essence, excerpt 8. tincture
9. parentage 10. withdrawal
extraneous... 5. outer 6. exotic
7. foreign 9. extrinsic, separated,
unrelated 11. unessential
extraordinary... 3. odd 4. rare, unco
5. great 7. notable, special, unusual
8. singular 9. irregular, marvelous,
wonderful 10. noteworthy, remarkable
11. exceptional 13. distinguished
extravagance... 5. waste 6. excess
8. wildness 9. abundance
10. fanaticism, lavishness
11. exorbitance, prodigality
12. exaggeration, intemperance,
recklessness
extravagant... 3. E la 4. ee la (Mus),
high (priced) 5. outré 6. absurd
7. baroque, bizarre, diffuse, fanatic
8. boastful, prodigal, wasteful
9. excessive, fanatical, fantastic,
luxurious, plentiful 10. digressive
11. intemperate 12. unrestrained
extreme... 3. end 4. last, sore
5. final, great, ultra 6. excess,
severe, utmost 7. drastic, intense,
outward, radical 8. farthest, greatest,
ultimate 9. excessive, extremity,
fanatical, outermost 10. conclusive,
immoderate

extreme fear... 5. panic 6. horror
extreme unction... 5. anele 9. last
rites, sacrament
extremist... 7. radical 8. ultraist
extremity... 3. end, tip 4. foot, limb
(body), pole 5. verge 6. border,
crisis, summit 8. terminal
9. necessity 11. termination
extricate... 4. free 5. loose 6. evolve,
rescue, wangle 7. extract 8. liberate
9. disengage 10. disembroil
11. disentangle 12. disembarrass
extrinsic... 7. foreign, outward
8. external 9. objective
10. accidental (Log), contingent,
extraneous, incidental
12. adventitious, nonessential
extrovert... 11. personality (opp of
introvert)
exuberance... 6. excess, plenty
8. overflow, rankness, vivacity
9. abundance, animation, profusion
10. friskiness, liveliness, luxuriance
11. copiousness 14. superabundance
exuberant... 6. frisky, lavish 7. fertile,
profuse 8. effusive, fruitful, thriving
9. luxuriant, plentiful 11. overflowing
13. superabundant
exudation... 3. gum, lac, tar 5. pitch,
resin 6. oozing 8. emission, sweating
9. discharge, excretion
exude... 4. emit, ooze, reek 5. sweat
7. excrete, give out 9. discharge
exult... 3. joy 4. crow, leap (obs), rave
5. boast, elate, ovare, pride
7. rejoice 8. jubilate
exultant... 5. ovant 6. elated
exultation... 3. joy 7. delight
8. boasting 9. jubilance, rejoicing
10. jubilation
exults... 5. leaps 7. glories, springs
9. jubilates
eye... 2. ee 3. orb, see 4. auge, glim,
hole, ogle 5. optic, organ (human),
sight, watch 6. look at, peeper
7. observe, witness 10. scrutinize
eye (pert to)...
absence of pupil.. 6. acorea
black.. 5. mouse 6. shiner
brow.. 4. arch 6. eebree
11. supercilium
cavity.. 5. orbit 6. hippus, socket
disease.. 8. cataract, glaucoma,
hypopyon, trachoma 9. amblyopia
14. conjunctivitis
disorder.. 6. squint 7. walleye
9. exotropia 10. strabismus
dropper.. 7. pipette
glass.. 4. lens 7. lorgnon, monocle
8. pince—nez 10. spectacles
inflammation.. 6. ititis 7. uveitis
lash, lashes.. 5. cilia (pl) 6. cilium
lid.. 8. palpebra
part.. 4. iris, uvea 5. pupil 6. cornea,
retina
to blind (falconry).. 4. seel
eyelet... 7. cringle, grommet, ocellus
8. loophole, peephole
eyetooth... 6. cuspid 8. dogtooth
eyot... 3. ait 4. holm 5. islet
eyra... 7. wildcat
eyrie, eyry... 4. nest 5. aerie, nidus

F

F... 6. letter (6th)
fabes... 10. gooseberry
fabian... 7. caution 8. dilatory, inaction
   15. procrastination
Fabian... 7. General (Rom), Society
fable... 3. lie 4. myth 5. story
   6. legend 7. fabliau, fantasy, fiction,
   Marchen, parable 8. allegory,
   apologue, folk tale 9. falsehood
fable (pert to)...
   being.. 5. troll
   king.. 3. Log
   monster.. 4. ogre 7. centaur
   narrator.. 10. parabolist
   writer.. 5. Aesop
fabric... 5. build, cloth 6. tissue
   7. texture 8. erection, material
   9. framework 11. workmanship
   12. construction
fabric (types of)... 3. rep 4. alma,
   duck, felt, gros, jean, lawn, leno, silk
   5. baize, batik, beige, crash, crepe,
   denim, linen, nylon, pekin, rumal,
   satin, scrim, serge, suede, tulle,
   tweed, twill, voile, wigan 6. agaric,
   alpaca, burlap, calico, canvas, chintz,
   cotton, dimity, étoile, madras,
   mohair, moreen, muslin, penang,
   pongee, poplin, ratiné, sateen, tricot
   7. batiste, brocade, bunting, challis,
   chiffon, delaine, elastic, etamine,
   flannel, galatea, gingham, hernani,
   paisley, percale, satinet, ticking,
   worsted 8. cashmere, chambray,
   chenille, corduroy, cretonne, drilling,
   prunella, sarcenet, Shantung,
   sheeting, whipcord 9. crinoline,
   gabardine, grenadine, lansdowne,
   matelassé, paramatta 10. broadcloth,
   seersucker, terry cloth
fabric (pert to)...
   dealer.. 6. mercer
   ornamental.. 4. lace 8. fagoting
   silk, watered.. 5. moiré
   silk and gold.. 4. acca (anc)
   7. brocade
   twill.. 6. caddis (cadis)
   velvet.. 5. panne, terry 6. velure
   7. velours
   waste.. 5. mungo
   window shade.. 7. Holland
   woven.. 6. tricot
fabricate... 4. coin, form, make, mint
   5. build, frame, weave 6. create,
   devise, invent, scheme 7. falsify,
   fashion, produce, trump up
   9. construct 11. manufacture
fabrication... 3. lie, web 5. guile
   6. cogger, deceit, making 7. fiction,
   forging, untruth 9. falsehood,

invention 12. construction
fabulist... 4. liar 5. Aesop
   11. storyteller
fabulous... 6. absurd 7. feigned
   8. mythical 9. fictional, imaginary,
   legendary 10. fictitious, remarkable
   11. astonishing 12. mythological
fabulous (pert to)...
   animal.. 7. unicorn 9. rosmarine
   (walrus)
   beast.. 4. lung 6. dragon, wivern
   7. griffon, serpent 10. earthdrake
   being.. 6. Lapith, Nessus 7. centaur
   bird.. 3. moa, roc 4. rukh
facade... 4. face 5. facia, front
   7. frontal
face... 3. mug 4. dare, defy, dial, line,
   meet, moue, phiz 5. brave, cover,
   front 6. answer, obvert, oppose,
   phizog, visage 7. grimace
   8. boldness, confront, envisage,
   exterior, features, pretense
   9. encounter, impudence
   10. effrontery 11. countenance,
   physiognomy, self–respect
face (pert to)...
   bone.. 6. zygoma (cheek) 7. maxilla
   (jaw)
   east.. 9. orientate
   gem.. 5. facet
   lifting.. 13. rhytidoplasty
   masonry.. 5. revet
   nose.. 11. rhinoplasty
   pains.. 4. ague 13. tic douloureux
   surgery.. 14. blepharoplasty (eyelid)
   to face.. 6. afront 7. vis–à–vis
   value.. 3. par
faces (twelve)... 12. dodecahedron
facet... 4. face 5. bezel, culet
   6. aspect, collet 8. exterior
facetious... 5. droll, funny, witty
   6. facete, jocose 7. comical, jesting
   8. laughter 9. whimsical
facia... 5. plate 6. tablet
facial pain... 3. tic 4. ague
   9. neuralgia 13. tic douloureux
facient... 4. doer 5. agent
   10. multiplier
facile... 4. easy 5. quick, ready
   6. expert, fluent, gentle, pliant
   7. affable, lenient, pliable
   9. compliant, teachable
facilitate... 3. aid 4. ease, help
   6. assist
facility... 3. art 4. ease, help 5. éclat,
   means, skill 7. address, pliancy
   8. easiness 9. readiness
   10. adroitness, expertness, pliability
   11. convenience, furtherance
   13. accommodation

198

facing... 6. lining, veneer 7. coating, surface 8. opposite
facing (pert to)...
glacier direction.. 5. stoss
inward.. 8. introrse
outward.. 8. extrorse
facsimile... 4. copy 5. match 7. replica 9. duplicate 11. counterpart
fact, facts... 4. data, deed, feat, fiat 5. datum, event, posit, truth 6. really 7. keynote, lowdown, paradox 9. actuality
fact collector... 7. statist 12. statistician
faction... 4. bloc, camp, sect, side 5. cabal, junto, party 6. clique 7. machine (Polit) 11. combination, partisanism
factious... 9. demagogic, seditious, turbulent
factitious... 4. made (by art), mock, sham 5. phony 9. unnatural 10. artificial 11. make—believe
factor... 4. ager, gene 5. agent, cause 6. detail 9. component 11. constituent
factotum... 4. maid 5. do—all 7. servant 8. busybody
faculties... 4. wits 6. senses 7. talents 9. abilities, aptitudes 12. capabilities
faculty... 3. art 4. body, ease, gift 6. talent 7. ability, know—how 8. aptitude, teachers 9. endowment (mental) 12. professorate
fad... 4. rage, whim 5. craze, fancy, hobby 6. custom 7. caprice, fashion
faddist... 10. monomaniac
fade, fade out... 3. ago, dim, dow, wan 4. flat, pale, wilt 5. daver, decay, peter 6. perish, vanish, weaken, wither 7. decline, insipid 8. discolor, dissolve, languish 9. disappear 11. deteriorate
faded... 3. dim 4. dull, pale 5. faint, passé 8. impaired
Faerie Queene (pert to)...
author.. 7. Spenser
character.. 3. Ate, Una 5. Guyon, Truth 7. Acrasia 8. Gloriana
theme.. 8. chivalry 10. knighthood
type work.. 4. poem 8. allegory
fag... 4. flag, hack, jade, tire, toil, work 5. droop, slave, weary 6. drudge, menial 7. exhaust, fatigue, untwist (rope end) 8. drudgery 9. cigarette
fag end... 3. end 4. tail 6. scraps, tag end 7. remnant 8. last part, leavings
Fagin... 3. Jew (Oliver Twist)
Fagin's pupil... 12. Artful Dodger (John Dawkins)
fagot, faggot... 4. bind 5. bunch 6. bundle, emblem (Her) 8. firewood, slattern
fail... 3. ebb, err 4. flop, lack, miss, sink 5. decay, flunk, lapse 6. defect, desert, weaken 7. decline, exhaust 8. unbetide 9. fall short 10. disappoint, go bankrupt

11. deteriorate
failed admission... 11. blackballed
failed to follow suit... 7. reneged
failure... 3. dud 4. flop, foil, lack, lose, miss 5. decay, fault, lapse 6. defeat, fiasco 7. default 10. bankruptcy, deficiency, insolvency, nonsuccess, suspension 11. delinquency
faint... 3. din, ill 4. pale, soft, weak 5. swelt, swoon, timid 6. feeble, sickly 7. languid 8. cowardly, fatigued, listless, timorous 10. indistinct, oppressive
faintness... 5. qualm (sudden) 7. dimness, syncope 8. paleness, weakness 10. feebleness
fair... 4. just, mart 6. bazaar, blonde, comely, honest, kermis 8. festival, mediocre, rainless, unbiased 9. impartial 10. auspicious, reasonable 12. unprejudiced 13. dispassionate
fairy, faery... 3. elf, fay 4. peri, pixy 5. genie, magic, nymph, ouphe, pixie 6. elfkin, sprite 7. brownie, gremlin 8. illusion
fairy (pert to)...
abode (Scot).. 4. shee (sidhe)
death spirit.. 7. banshee
evil.. 4. ogre, puck 9. hobgoblin
fort.. 3. lis (liss)
German.. 6. kobold
Irish.. 10. cluricaune, leprechaun
king.. 6. Oberon
Persian.. 4. peri
queen.. 3. Mab, Una 7. Titania
Scandinavian.. 5. nisse
tale.. 3. fib 7. Marchen 8. allegory 9. narrative
faith... 4. hope 5. creed, piety, troth, trust 6. belief, credit, verily, virtue 7. loyalty 8. credence, fidelity 9. assurance, authority, orthodoxy 10. confidence 11. credibility
faithful... 3. fast, feal, leal, true 5. liege, loyal, pious 6. devout, steady, trusty 7. devoted, sincere, staunch 8. constant, obedient, reliable 9. believers, steadfast, veracious
faithful friend... 7. Achates (Vergil's Aeneid)
faithless... 5. false, punic 6. fickle, untrue 8. apostate, disloyal, shifting 9. deceptive, mercurial, skeptical 10. perfidious, unfaithful 11. incredulous, irreligious, treacherous, unbelieving 12. falsehearted
fake... 3. rob 4. sham 5. cheat, fraud, trick 7. trump up 8. doctor up 9. deception, fabricate, imitation 11. counterfeit
faker... 5. cheat, fraud 7. bluffer 8. impostor 9. hypocrite, pretender
fakir... 4. sect (Moslem, Islam), yogi 7. dervish 9. mendicant
falcon... 4. hawk 5. besra, saker 6. laggar, lanner, luggar, merlin, shahin (shaheen), sorage, tercel 7. kestrel, sakeret 8. lanneret,

Raptores 9. gyrfalcon (gerfalcon), peregrine
falcon, military... 8. ordnance
falconry term... 4. hood, jess, lure, seel 6. rebate 7. hawking
fall... 3. ebb 4. bang, drop, plop, ruin, sink, slip 5. crash, spill 6. autumn, defeat, perish, plunge, tumble 7. descend, descent, devolve, failure, plummet, relapse 8. collapse, commence, downfall, rainfall 9. abatement, overthrow, surrender, waterfall 10. depreciate, subversion 11. degradation, precipitate
fall (pert to)...
back.. 6. recede, recoil 7. relapse, retreat 10. retrogress
behind.. 3. lag 4. lose 7. regress
guy.. 5. patsy
in.. 4. cave 5. agree, lapse 6. concur, line up 8. collapse 9. terminate
rhythmical.. 6. cadent
short.. 4. lack, want 10. disappoint
fallacious... 4. wily 5. false 6. crafty, untrue 8. delusive, guileful 9. deceitful, deceptive, erroneous, illogical, insidious 10. fraudulent, misleading 13. disappointing
fallacy... 5. error 6. idolum 7. sophism 9. deception, falseness, sophistry 13. deceitfulness
false... 4. sham, tale 5. bogus, paste 6. betray, impugn, pseudo, untrue 7. mislead 8. apostate, spurious 9. deceitful, deceptive, erroneous, faithless, incorrect, insincere, pretended, unfounded 10. fictitious, mendacious, traitorous, unfaithful, unreliable, untruthful 11. counterfeit 12. illegitimate
false (pert to)...
friend.. 5. Judas 7. traitor
front.. 8. disguise 11. affectation
fruit.. 10. pseudocarp
god.. 4. idol
hearted.. 9. deceitful 10. perfidious 11. treacherous
items.. 6. spuria
jewelry.. 5. paste 6. strass
reasoning.. 10. paralogism
report.. 5. rumor 6. canard 7. slander
show.. 6. tinsel
wing (bird's).. 5. alula
falsehood... 3. lie 4. tale 7. falsity, fiction, perjury, untruth 9. imposture, mendacity 11. counterfeit, fabrication 12. exaggeration
falseness... 5. error 8. illusion 9. deception, falsehood 10. infidelity
falsetto... 5. voice (false) 10. artificial 11. high–pitched
falsify... 3. lie 5. belie, forge 7. distort, pervert 8. disprove 10. adulterate 11. counterfeit 12. misrepresent
Falstaff... 5. opera (Verdi) 9. character (Shak)
falter... 3. lag 4. fail 5. demur, pause, waver 6. flinch, quaver, totter 7. stagger, stammer, stumble, tremble 8. hesitate, lose hope

fame... 4. note 5. éclat, glory, kudos 6. renown, repute
famed... 7. eminent, honored, popular 8. renowned 9. notorious 10. celebrated
familiar... 4. easy 5. usual 6. common, versed 7. affable 8. domestic, frequent, friendly, habitual, informal 9. companion, customary, well–known 10. accustomed, colloquial, conversant 12. domesticated, presumptuous 13. unconstrained
familiarity... 8. intimacy 9. awareness, knowledge, liberties 10. affability 12. acquaintance (close), friendliness
familiarize... 6. inform 8. accustom 9. habituate
family... 3. ilk, kin 4. clan, line, race 5. class, group, house, tribe 6. stirps 7. kindred, lineage 9. community, household, posterity 10. kith and kin
family (pert to)...
bees.. 5. apina 7. Apoidea
favoritism.. 8. nepotism
herbs.. 7. Ranales
Italians (famed).. 4. Este
kings.. 7. dynasty
name.. 7. surname
famous... 5. named, noted 7. eminent, namable, notable 8. renowned 9. excellent, notorious 10. celebrated, remarkable 13. distinguished
famous murderer... 4. Aram, Cain 9. Bluebeard
famous pirate... 4. Kidd (Capt)
fan... 4. blow, cool, vane, whip 5. punka (punkah) 6. blower, foment, incite, rooter, spread, thresh, winnow 7. admirer, devotee, refresh 9. stimulate, strike out (baseball), ventilate 10. enthusiast
fanatic, fanatical... 3. mad 5. bigot, crank, crazy, rabid 6. maniac, zealot 7. devotee, frantic, lunatic 8. frenzied 9. energumen, phrenetic 10. enthusiast, unbalanced 11. extravagant, overzealous 12. enthusiastic 13. nonconformist, overreligious
fanatical partisan... 6. zealot
fancied... 6. unreal 7. dreamed, ideated 8. favorite, imagined 9. well–liked 10. ornamental
fanciful... 3. odd 5. queer 7. bizarre, strange 9. fantastic, grotesque, visionary, whimsical 10. capricious, chimerical 11. imaginative 13. grandiloquent
fancy... 3. fad 4. idea, like, love, ween, whim 5. dream, freak 6. design, desire, devise, humour, ideate, megrim, notion, ornate, vagary 7. caprice, conceit, fantasy, imagine, impulse, suppose, thought 8. illusion, phantasy, superior 9. expensive 10. conception, impression 11. extravagant, imagination, inclination 12. ostentatious

fandango... 3. hop 4. ball, prom
   5. dance 7. cantico
fandango bird... 7. manakin
Faneuil Hall (1742)... 4. hall
   6. market (Boston) 15. Cradle of
   Liberty
fanion... 4. flag 6. guidon, marker
fanon... 4. cape (Pope's) 5. orale
   6. banner 7. maniple
fan-shaped... 10. flabellate
fan sticks (radiating)... 4. brin
   7. panache
fantastic... 3. odd 5. outré, queer
   6. absurd, rococo, unreal
   7. baroque, bizarre, caprice, foppish,
   unusual 8. fanciful, freakish, illusory
   9. eccentric, grotesque, visionary
   10. capricious, chimerical, irrational
   11. extravagant, imaginative
   12. phantastical
fantastic imitation... 6. parody
   8. travesty
fantasy... 5. dream, fancy, story
   6. vision 7. caprice, phantom,
   romance 8. illusion 10. apparition
   13. hallucination
far... 3. tel (pref) 4. afar, long, tele
   (pref) 6. marked, remote
   9. separated 10. abstracted
farce... 4. mime, play 5. drama
   (humorous), exode, humor, stuff
   6. comedy 7. mockery 8. stuffing
   9. burlesque, forcemeat
farceur... 5. joker 8. comedian
   9. dramatist
fare... 3. eat 4. diet, food, rate
   5. crowd, going, swarm, table
   7. conduct, journey, passage,
   prosper, succeed 9. passenger
   10. expedition
farewell... 3. ave 4. vale 5. adieu,
   adioo, aloha, congé (formal)
   7. good bye, leaving, parting 8. au
   revoir, Godspeed 9. bon voyage
   11. leave-taking
farinaceous drink... 6. ptisan
farinaceous food... 4. sago 5. flour,
   grain, salep, wheat 7. cereals
farm... 4. plot, till, torp 5. croft, ranch
   6. grange, rancho 7. acreage,
   cotland 9. cultivate
farm (pert to)...
   English.. 6. barton
   laborer.. 4. hind 6. farmer, tiller
   prefix.. 4. agro
   repairer.. 10. plowwright
   Spanish.. 8. hacienda
   steward.. 7. granger
   tenant.. 6. cotter
farmer... 4. ryot 5. kulak 6. grower,
   tiller 7. cropper, metaver, peasant,
   planter, rancher 10. agronomist,
   cultivator 13. agriculturist
faro term... 4. bank 5. monte, stuss
   6. cathop, layout
Faroe (Faeroe) Islands...
   called also.. 12. Sheep Islands
   capital.. 9. Thorshavn
   magistrate.. 4. foud
   rule.. 5. Norse (anc) 7. Denmark
   whirlwind.. 2. oe
far-reaching... 4. deep, long 5. scope

   7. intense 9. extensive
farrow... 3. pig 6. litter
farsighted... 6. shrewd 9. provident,
   sagacious 10. presbyopic
   11. foresighted 12. clearsighted
farther, further... 4. also 7. thither
   8. moreover 10. additional
farthest... 5. final 6. inmost, utmost
   7. endmost, extreme, longest
fascia... 4. band, sash 6. fillet, ribbon
   7. bandage
fascinate... 5. charm 6. allure,
   enamor, thrill 7. bewitch, delight,
   enchant 8. entrance, interest
   9. captivate, enrapture
fascinating... 5. siren 8. alluring,
   charming 10. attractive, bewitching,
   delightful 11. interesting
Fascist (1919)... 6. Pareto
   9. Mussolini 10. Black Shirt
fashion... 3. fad, fit, ton, way
   4. make, mode, mold, rage
   5. adapt, carve, craze, feign, forge,
   frame, guise, model, shape, style,
   vogue 6. create, custom, invent
   7. compose 8. contrive 9. construct,
   fabricate, smartness 10. appearance
fashionable... 5. smart 6. formal,
   modish 7. a la mode, in vogue,
   stylish 8. up-to-date 10. conforming
   13. well-appearing
fast... 5. agile, fixed, fleet, hasty,
   quick, rapid, sound, space, stuck,
   swift 6. lively, speedy, staple
   7. abiding, soundly 8. enduring,
   securely 10. profligate, stationary,
   unyielding 11. expeditious
fasten... 3. bar, pin, tie 4. bind, clip,
   lace, lash, moor, nail, rope, seal,
   tack, wire 5. affix, belay, chain,
   clamp, clasp, latch, paste, rivet
   6. attach, secure, solder, staple,
   tether, toggle 7. padlock
fastening... 5. desmo (comb form)
fastest (pert to)...
   animals.. 6. coyote 7. cheetah
   8. antelope
   birds.. 5. eagle, goose 7. ostrich
fast horse... 6. pelter
fastidious... 4. nice 6. dainty
   7. elegant, finical, precise 8. critical,
   delicate, exacting, overnice
   9. squeamish 10. meticulous,
   particular, scrupulous
fastness... 4. fort 6. fixity 7. citadel
   8. celerity, firmness, velocity
   9. stability 10. profligacy, stronghold
fat... 4. lard, oily, suet 5. adeps, fatty,
   lipin, obese, olein, stout 6. axunge
   (goose), grease, portly, steato (pref),
   stocky, tallow 7. adipose, lanolin,
   opulent, paunchy, stearin, wealthy
   9. corpulent, plentiful 10. profitable
fatal... 5. fated 6. deadly, doomed,
   lethal, mortal 7. fateful, ominous
   8. destined 9. condemned, prophetic
   10. calamitous, disastrous
   11. destructive
fatality... 4. fate 5. death 8. disaster
   10. deadliness
fatally... 8. mortally 9. ruinously
fate... 3. end, lot 4. doom, luck, ruin

5. karma 6. chance, kismet
7. destiny, fortune 8. disaster,
downfall 13. inevitability

fateful... 5. fated 6. deadly
9. momentous 10. inevitable,
portentous 11. destructive,
predestined

Fates (Gr)... 6. Clotho, Moirae (group
of Three) 7. Atropos 8. Lachesis

Fates (Norse)... 4. Urth 5. Norns
(group of three), Skuld 9. Verthandi

Fates (Rom)... 4. Fata, Mona 5. Morta
6. Decuma, Parcae (group of three)

father... 2. pa 3. Abu, dad 4. abba,
papa, père, sire 5. adopt, friar,
padre, pater, vater 6. priest, senior
7. creator 8. generate 9. confessor,
procreate 11. acknowledge

Father (of)...
Ajax.. 7. Telamon
Christmas.. 10. Santa Claus
English learning.. 4. Bede
engraving.. 3. Pye
Evil.. 5. Satan
his country.. 6. Cicero (Rom), Medici
(It) 10. Washington (US)
history.. 9. Herodotus
Mankind (Myth).. 7. Iapetus
New York.. 13. Knickerbocker
Ocean.. 7. Neptune
the Gods.. 6. Amen–Ra
Time.. 10. Methuselah
Waters.. 11. Mississippi

father (pert to)...
land.. 6. native
land, love of.. 10. philopater
term.. 6. agnate 8. paternal
wise.. 6. mentor

fatherless... 6. orbate 7. forlorn
8. helpless, orphaned

fathom... 3. try 4. test 5. delve,
plumb, solve, sound 7. measure,
plummet 8. encircle 9. penetrate
10. understand 13. take soundings

fatigued... 5. bored, faint, jaded,
spent, tired, weary 6. fagged
7. languid, wearied 9. exhausted

Fatima (pert to)...
character in.. 14. Arabian Nights
father.. 8. Mohammed
husband.. 9. Bluebeard

fatten... 4. feed 6. batten, enrich
7. improve, prosper 8. pinguefy

fatty... 5. suety 6. greasy 7. adipose
9. aliphatic

fatty (pert to)...
acid.. 6. adipic 7. valeric
degeneration.. 8. adiposis
substance, sheep.. 5. suint
tumor.. 6. lipoma

fatuous... 4. vain 5. inane, silly
6. vacant 7. foolish, idiotic, witless
8. demented, illusory, imbecile
9. insensate 11. thoughtless

faucet... 3. peg, tap 4. cock 6. spigot
7. fixture, hydrant, petcock

fault... 4. hade, lode, slip, vice
5. cavil, cleft, culpa (law), error,
lapse, tache (anc) 6. defect, foible
7. blemish, blunder, demerit, failing,
frailty, misdeed, offense 8. fracture
10. peccadillo 11. delinquency

12. imperfection

faultfinder... 6. carper, nagger
7. caviler 10. complainer, criticizer

faultfinding... 7. carping, nagging
8. captious, caviling, critical
9. censorial

faultless... 4. pure 5. right 7. correct,
paragon, perfect 8. flawless, innocent
9. blameless 10. impeccable
13. unimpeachable 14. irreproachable

faultlessness... 8. accuracy
9. innocence 10. perfection
11. preciseness

faulty... 3. ill 5. amiss, unfit 6. guilty
8. culpable 9. blemished, defective,
deficient, erroneous, imperfect
11. blameworthy

faun... 3. Pan 5. deity, satyr
6. Faunus 10. Praxiteles

Faust... 4. hero 5. drama (Goethe),
opera

faux pas... 5. error, gaffe 6. booboo
7. blunder, misstep, mistake

favor, favour... 3. aid 4. boon, gift,
help 5. bless, grace, token
6. esteem, letter, regard 8. good
will, kindness, leniency, resemble
9. patronage, patronize, privilege
10. assistance, concession,
favoritism, partiality, permission
11. approbation

favorable... 4. good, kind, rosy
6. benign, timely 7. helpful, hopeful,
popular 8. friendly, gracious, pleasing
9. approving, opportune
10. auspicious, beneficial, propitious
11. complaisant 12. advantageous

favorite... 3. pet 4. lamb (pet)
6. minion 7. darling 10. preference

favoritism... 4. bias 7. leaning
8. nepotism 10. partiality
12. predilection

fawn... 3. doe 4. buck, coax, deer,
faon (color) 5. color, cower, crawl,
creep, toady 6. cringe, grovel, shrink
7. truckle 10. ingratiate

fawning... 7. servile 8. toadyish
9. truckling 10. obsequious
11. bootlicking, sycophantic

fawnskin (classic art)... 6. nebris

fay... 3. elf 5. fairy 6. sprite

fealty... 4. duty 6. homage 7. loyalty,
respect 8. fidelity 9. constancy
10. allegiance, obligation

fear... 3. awe 5. alarm, dread, panic
6. dismay, fright, horror, phobia,
terror 7. anxiety 8. venerate
9. apprehend, cowardice, reverence
11. nervousness 13. consternation

fear (of)...
animals.. 9. zoophobia
bees.. 9. apiphobia
being alone.. 10. autophobia,
monophobia
blood.. 10. hemophobia
cats.. 12. aelurophobia
crossing streets.. 11. dromophobia
crowds.. 11. ochlophobia
darkness.. 11. nyctophobia,
scotophobia
death.. 11. necrophobia
disease.. 10. nosophobia

enclosures.. 14. claustrophobia
fire.. 10. pyrophobia
food.. 10. cibophobia
heights.. 10. acrophobia
    11. hypsophobia
holy things.. 11. hagiophobia
men.. 11. androphobia
new things.. 9. neophobia
open spaces.. 11. agoraphobia
pain.. 10. algophobia
places (certain).. 10. topophobia
poison.. 10. toxiphobia
reptiles.. 13. herpetophobia
sea.. 14. thalassophobia
strangers.. 10. xenophobia
sunlight.. 11. heliophobia
thirteen.. 13. tridecaphobia
weeds.. 11. runcophobia
fearful... 4. dino (pref), dire 5. awful,
    pavid, timid 6. afraid, craven
    7. anxious, nervous 8. dreadful,
    horrible, timorous 9. appealing,
    frightful 11. distressing, frightening
    12. apprehensive
fearless... 4. bold 5. brave 6. daring
    7. impavid 8. harmless, intrepid
    9. audacious, confident, dauntless,
    undaunted 10. courageous
feast... 4. fete, meal 5. agape, epulo,
    revel 6. junket, picnic, regale, repast
    7. banquet, gratify 8. carousal,
    festival 9. carrousel
Feast (of)...
Lanterns (Jap).. 3. Bon
Lots.. 5. Purim
Nativity.. 9. Christmas
Pentecost (weeks).. 8. Shabuoth
Tabernacles.. 7. Succoth
feasting... 6. dining 9. epulation
feat... 3. act 4. deed 5. stunt
    7. exploit 11. achievement,
    performance 14. accomplishment
feather... 4. deck, flaw (jewel), tuft
    5. adorn, penna, plume, quill
    6. clotho, fletch, hackle, trifle
    7. plumage 9. lightness
feather (pert to)...
an arrow.. 6. fledge, fletch
barb.. 7. pinnula 8. barbicel
bird (area).. 7. pteryle
featherlike.. 7. pinnate
filament.. 4. dowl
key (machine).. 6. spline
molt.. 3. mew
repair (falconry).. 3. imp
shaft.. 5. scape
feathered... 5. swift 6. plumed,
    winged 7. fledged 8. pennated,
    plumaged 10. ornamented
feature... 4. face 5. motif, trait
    6. aspect 7. special 8. headline,
    resemble 9. component, lineament
    10. appearance, comeliness
    11. countenance 14. characteristic
features... 3. mug 4. face 5. looks
    6. visage 7. outline 9. geography
February birthstone... 8. amethyst
federation... 5. union 6. league
    8. alliance 10. government
    11. affiliation 13. confederation
fed up... 5. bored, jaded 7. wearied
    8. satiated 9. surfeited

fee... 3. feu, tip 4. fief, rate, wage
    5. bribe 6. charge, estate (law)
    8. gratuity, retainer 9. emolument
    10. honorarium
feeble... 4. aged, lame, puny, weak
    5. dotty 6. infirm 10. indistinct
    11. debilitated
feeble–minded... 5. anile 9. infirmity
    10. irresolute, weak–willed
    11. vacillating
feed... 4. dine, meal, sate 5. stoke
    6. fodder, gavage 7. engorge,
    foldage, furnish, indulge, nourish,
    nurture, pannage (swine)
    9. encourage, provision
feel... 3. ail, air 4. palp 5. grope,
    sense, touch 6. handle, suffer
    7. examine, explore, quality, texture
    8. perceive 10. atmosphere,
    experience
feel (pert to)...
compunction.. 6. repent
dejection.. 6. repine
fear.. 2. ug
melancholy.. 6. grieve
worth of.. 10. appreciate
feeler... 4. palp, test 6. barbal, palpus
    7. antenna 8. question, tentacle
feeling... 4. feel, tact, view 5. hunch,
    touch 7. emotion, opinion, passion
    8. attitude 9. sensation, sentiment
    10. atmosphere, experience,
    perception 11. sensibility
    13. consciousness
feeling (pert to)...
capable of.. 5. emote 8. sentient
    9. sensitive
displeasure.. 9. resentful
hostility.. 6. animus 9. animosity
ill.. 7. malaise 10. discomfort
impassive.. 8. stoicism
joyful.. 6. jocund
offense.. 5. pique
superiority.. 9. arrogance
without.. 6. apathy, steely 7. callous
    8. numbness 9. unfeeling
    13. insensibility
feet... see also *foot*
designating.. 5. podal
having.. 6. pedate
number.. 7. footage
two (Pros).. 6. dipody 7. dimeter
    9. ditrochee
without.. 4. apod 6. apodal
    8. footless
feign... 3. act 4. sham 5. fable
    6. affect, assume, gammon, garble,
    invent 7. connive, imagine, pretend
    8. malinger (illness), simulate
    9. dissemble 11. counterfeit,
    make–believe
feint... 5. appel (fencing), blind, shift,
    trick 6. attack (mock), thrust
    7. mislead, pretext 8. artifice,
    pretense
Felicia... 7. thistle 9. happiness
felicitate... 4. laud 5. bless
    8. macarize 10. compliment
    12. congratulate
felicity... 5. bliss, grace 7. aptness,
    success 8. aptitude 9. happiness,
    well–being 11. achievement (happy),

blessedness 12. blissfulness
Felidae... 4. cats, lion, lynx, pard,
puma 5. tiger 6. jaguar 7. cheetah,
leopard, wildcat
feline... 3. sly 5. Felis 6. animal
7. catlike, furtive 8. stealthy
11. treacherous
Felis... 3. cat
fell... 3. cut, hem, hew 4. beat, hill,
kill, pelt, ruin, skin 5. cruel, level
6. fierce, fleece, lay low, mighty,
savage 7. brutish, tumbled
9. barbarous, ferocious, overthrow,
prostrate
fellow... 3. lad, man 4. beau, chap,
peer 5. equal 6. member, person
7. comrade 8. neighbor 9. associate,
companion 10. sweetheart
11. confederate
fellow (pert to)...
accomplice.. 7. abettor 9. accessory
11. confederate
awkward.. 4. boor, gawk
clumsy.. 3. oaf 4. lout, pleb 5. yahoo
7. bumpkin
coward.. 3. cad, fop 4. drip
7. bounder 8. spalpeen
droll.. 3. wag 4. card
old.. 6. geezer 7. callant
small.. 6. shaver
smart.. 5. aleck
young.. 4. chap 5. blade, youth
7. younker 9. stripling
fellowman... 7. brother 11. fellow
being
fellowship... 4. sect 5. guild, union
7. company 8. alliance, sodality
9. communion 10. membership
11. affiliation, comradeship,
partnership, scholarship
12. friendliness 13. companionship
felon... 3. bum 4. wild 5. cruel
6. wicked 7. convict, culprit, outcast,
villain, whitlow 8. criminal, disloyal
9. infection, malignant, murderous
10. malefactor, paronychia, traitorous
felony... 3. sin 5. crime, wrath
6. daring, deceit 8. baseness,
burglary, outlawry 9. treachery
10. illegality, wickedness
11. misdemeanor
female... 4. bibi, dame, doña, girl,
gyne, lady, miss 5. donna, femme,
rhyme, squaw, woman 6. maiden,
matron 7. distaff, dowager, fair sex,
Sahibah 8. mistress 9. weaker sex
female (pert to)...
architecture.. 8. Caryatid
comb form.. 5. gyneo, thely
erudite.. 10. pedantress
fox.. 5. vixen
government.. 8. gynarchy
hormone.. 8. estrogen
monster.. 6. gorgon
prayerful.. 5. orant
spirit.. 7. banshee
suffix.. 4. ette
term.. 8. gynecoid
warrior.. 6. Amazon
feminine... 4. soft, weak 6. female,
gender, tender 7. womanly
8. maidenly 10. effeminate

femme fatale... 4. vamp 5. siren
7. Lorelei, vampire
femur... 3. hip (bone) 4. bone (thigh),
coxa
fen... 3. bog 4. moor, pool 5. marsh,
swale 7. The Fens
fence... 3. aha 4. bank, duel, ha–ha,
pale, rail, wall 5. close, ditch, fight,
hedge, stile 6. paling, picket, secure
7. barrier, confine, enclose, fortify,
protect, railing 8. palisade, prohibit
9. enclosure, swordplay
11. self–defense
fencing (pert to)...
breastplate.. 8. plastron
defense.. 5. carte, parry, prime, sixte
6. octave, quinte, tierce 7. seconds,
septime
master.. 7. lanista
position.. 9. pronation 10. supination
sword.. 4. epee, foil, tuck 5. extoc
6. rapier
term.. 4. volt 7. corrida 8. estocado
thrust.. 6. remise 7. riposte
fend... 4. ward 5. avert, parry, shift
6. defend, resist 7. prevent, repulse,
ward off
fender... 5. guard 6. buffer, bumper,
shield, sluice 7. cushion 9. fireguard
10. firescreen 11. splashboard
fenestra... 6. window 7. foramen,
opening, orifice
Fenian... 5. Irish 11. Brotherhood
fennel... 4. herb 6. Seseli 7. Azorian,
Nigella
feral... 4. wild 6. deadly, ferine,
savage 7. bestial, untamed
8. funereal, unbroken 9. malignant
12. uncultivated
feretory... 4. bier 6. chapel, shrine
(saint's) 8. feretrum
ferment... 4. barm, brew, fret, sour,
stum, zyme 5. anger, fever, yeast
6. enzyme, foment, leaven, rennin,
seethe, uproar 7. glucase, maltase
8. diastase, disorder 9. agitation
10. effervesce, turbulence
fermentation... 6. unrest 9. agitation,
chemistry, leavening 10. ebullition
13. effervescence
fermenting vat... 4. gyle
fern... 4. tara 5. brake, heath, holly
6. osmund, spider 7. bracken
8. polypody 10. maidenhair
11. elephant–ear
fern (pert to)...
family.. 12. pteridophyte
genus.. 6. Anemia
leaf.. 5. frond
scale.. 8. ramentum
ferocious... 4. grim, wild 5. cruel,
feral 6. bloody, brutal, fierce, savage
7. acharne, inhuman 8. pitiless,
ravenous, ruthless 9. barbarous,
malignant, merciless, murderous,
rapacious, truculent 10. implacable,
malevolent, relentless, sanguinary
11. remorseless 12. bloodthirsty
ferret... 3. hob 4. hunt, jill, tape
5. worry 6. badger, harass, search,
weasel 7. polecat
ferrotype... 7. tintype 10. photograph

ferrum... 2. Fe (sym) 4. iron
ferry... 7. traject 9. transport 10. sail across
ferryboat... 3. bac 4. pont 6. wherry
ferryman... 6. Charon (River Styx) 7. ferrier
fertile... 4. rank, rich 7. teeming 8. abundant, fruitful, prolific 9. exuberant, inventive, plenteous, plentiful 10. productive
fertilizer... 4. marl 5. guano 6. pollen 7. compost, nitrate 8. dressing 9. phosphate
ferule... 3. rod 5. ruler 6. fennel 10. punishment
fervency... 4. heat, keen, zeal 5. ardor, eager, fiery, gusto, verve 6. fervor, warmth 7. ardency, passion 9. eloquence, vehemence 12. empressement 15. impassionedness
fervent... 3. hot 4. keen, warm 5. eager, fiery 6. ardent, fervid 7. excited, intense, zealous 8. eloquent, vehement 10. passionate 11. impassioned
fervid... 3. hot 5. fiery 6. ardent, tropic 7. boiling, fervent, zealous 8. vehement 11. impassioned
fervor... 4. rage, zeal, zest 5. ardor 7. ecstasy, passion 11. earnestness
fester... 6. rankle 7. abscess, pustule, putrefy 9. suppurate
festival... 3. ale, bal 4. fete, gala 5. Delia (Apollo), feast, revel, Seder 6. Easter, Kermis 7. holiday, uphelya 8. apodosis (Church) 9. Christmas, Mardi gras 10. Parentalia, Saturnalia
festive... 3. gay 4. gala 5. merry 6. joyous 8. mirthful, sportive 9. convivial
festivity... 3. joy 4. fete, gala 5. mirth, revel 6. gaiety 7. jollity, whoopee 8. festival, jamboree 10. joyfulness 11. celebration, merrymaking 12. conviviality
fetch... 3. get 5. bring, reach 6. attain, deduce, revive 7. achieve 8. go and get, retrieve
fetching... 8. alluring, charming, pleasing 10. attractive, delightful 11. fascinating
fete... 4. gala 5. feast, party 6. fiesta 8. carnival, festival 10. Saturnalia 13. entertainment
fetid... 4. olid, rank 5. fusty 7. noisome 10. maladorous 11. ill–smelling
fetish... 3. obi 4. idol, joss, juju 5. charm, image, totem 6. amulet, avatar, mascot 7. Dahoman 8. talisman
fetter... 4. band, bond, gyve, iron 5. chain 6. hamper, hobble, hopple, thrall 7. enchain, manacle, shackle
feud... 4. fief, fray 5. broil 6. affray, estate, strife 7. contest, dispute, quarrel 8. vendetta 9. hostility
feudal (pert to)...
  estate.. 3. fee 4. fief, soke
  French.. 4. feod

  lord.. 6. tenure 8. overlaid, suzerain
  payment.. 6. socage
  service.. 5. banal
  tenant.. 4. leud 6. vassal
  tribute.. 6. heriot
fever... 4. ague 5. ardor 6. frenzy 8. delirium, sickness 9. calenture 10. excitement
fever (pert to)...
  heat.. 9. sunstroke
  intermittent.. 5. octan 7. quartan
  malarial.. 4. ague
  marsh.. 6. elodes 7. helodes
  subsidence.. 12. defervescent
  term.. 7. febrile, pyretic
  tropical.. 6. dengue 9. calenture
feverish... 5. hasty 7. excited, febrile, fervent, fevered 8. restless 9. delirious, overeager 10. disordered
fey... 4. dead 5. dying, elfin, fatal, spell 9. enfeebled, visionary 12. otherworldly
fez... 3. cap 5. busby, shako 8. tarboosh 9. headdress
fiat... 3. act 5. edict, order 6. decree 7. command 8. decision, sanction
fiber... 3. nap, nep, tal 4. bast, eruc, imbe, lint, pile, pita, silk, yarn 5. datil, istle, kapok, linen, nerve, rayon, sisal 6. fibril, raffia, staple, thread 7. filasse, texture 8. fibrilla, filament
fiber plant... 4. hemp, imbe, palm 5. abaca, agave 6. ambary, cotton, linaga
fibers... 5. hairs 7. strands 9. filaments
fibula... 4. bone (arm) 5. class 6. brooch (anc), buckle 9. safety pin
fickle... 5. false 6. mobile 7. mutable 8. unstable, unsteady, variable, wavering 9. changeful, deceitful, faithless, unsettled 10. capricious, changeable, inconstant, irresolute, unfaithful 11. vacillating
fiction... 4. tale 5. false, fancy, novel, story 6. legend 7. coinage, figment, forgery, romance 9. falsehood, invention 11. fabrication
fictitious... 5. false 6. poetic, pseudo (pref) 7. assumed, feigned 8. chimeric 9. imaginary, imitative, pretended 10. artificial
fictitious name... 5. alias 6. anonym 7. pen name 8. nickname 9. pseudonym, stage name 10. nom de plume 11. nom de guerre
fidelity... 5. topaz, troth, truth 6. fealty 7. honesty 8. accuracy, devotion, veracity 9. adherence, constancy, exactness 10. allegiance 12. faithfulness
fidget... 4. fuss 5. worry 6. twitch 9. dysphoria 10. uneasiness 12. restlessness
fidgety... 5. jerky 6. uneasy 7. nervous, restive, twitchy 8. bustling, restless 9. excitable, impatient
fiducial... 4. firm 5. solid, sound 6. secure, stable 7. trusted 8. trustful 9. confident

fiduciary... 4. held (in trust) 5. trust
7. founded, holding, in trust, trustee
12. confidential

fief... 3. fee 4. feud 6. estate

field... 3. lea, lot 4. acre, ager, land,
mead, rand 5. croft, glebe, range,
tract 6. campus, ground, meadow,
sphere 7. compass, diamond,
expanse, pasture, savanna (savannah),
terrain 8. clearing, gridiron
11. battlefield

field (pert to)...
athletic.. 4. oval 5. arena, court, track
6. course, sphere 7. diamond,
stadium 8. gridiron
bloodshed.. 8. Aceldama (Akeldama)
13. Ager Sanguinis
duck.. 7. bustard
god of.. 4. Faun
mouse.. 4. vole
snow.. 4. neve
stubble.. 5. rowen
term.. 5. agral 8. agrarian
10. campestral

fiend... 3. foe 5. demon, devil, enemy,
Satan 6. addict, wizard 7. Amaimon
(Amamon) 9. archfiend 10. evil spirit

fiendish... 5. cruel 6. wicked
7. Avernal, demonic 8. demoniac,
devilish, diabolic

fierce... 4. grim 5. cruel, eager
6. raging, savage 7. furious, racking,
violent 9. ferocious, impetuous,
truculent 10. catawampus, forbidding,
passionate 11. belligerent,
overwrought 12. overpowering

fierceness... 7. cruelty 8. violence
10. truculence

fiery... 3. hot, red 4. sore 5. angry
6. ardent 7. burning, excited,
fervent, flaming, glowing, igneous,
parched, violent 8. choleric, feverish,
inflamed, spirited, vehement
9. impetuous, irascible
10. mettlesome, passionate
11. hot–tempered, inflammable

fiery cross... 5. alarm 6. emblem,
signal, symbol 8. crantara 10. call to
arms

fiesta... 5. color 7. holiday 8. festival
9. festivity

fifish... 6. cranky 9. half crazy

Fifteenth Amendment... 16. Negro
Citizenship (1870)

fig... 4. fico 5. eleme, gruit 6. Carica,
Fiscus, Smyrna, trifle

fig basket... 5. cabas, seron

fight... 3. row, war 4. bout, duel, fray,
mell, tilt 5. brawl, melee, scrap
6. affray, attack, barney, battle,
combat, oppose, strife, strike, strive
7. contest, quarrel, warfare
8. conflict, struggle 9. pugnacity
13. combativeness

fighter... 7. battler, duelist, soldier,
warrior 8. champion, pugilist,
scrapper 9. combatant

fighting... 3. war 4. game 6. plucky
7. warlike 8. militant 10. contention,
pugnacious 11. belligerent

fig leaf... 6. symbol (modesty)

8. clothing (Bib), covering

figment... 5. fancy 7. fiction
9. falsehood, invention

figurative... 6. florid 7. flowery, typical
8. allusive 9. numerical
12. emblematical, metaphorical

figure... 4. body, dash, dope, form,
nude, rank, type 5. digit, image,
judge, price, shape, solve 6. aspect,
emblem, entail, number, symbol
7. diagram, numeral, outline, pattern
8. ornament, phantasm 9. calculate,
celebrity, character, personage
10. appearance, impression,
similitude 11. distinction

figure (pert to)...
column.. 6. elamon 7. telamon
8. Atlantes, Caryatid, pilaster
geometric.. 4. cone, lune 5. prism,
rhomb 6. isagon, isogen, isogon
(rare) 7. ellipse, rhombus
8. pentagon, triangle
13. parallelogram, quadrilateral
16. parallelepipedon
praying.. 5. orant
repeated digits.. 8. repetend
speech.. 5. trope 6. aporia, simile
8. metaphor
star–shaped.. 8. pentacle

figured... 4. rich 6. ornate 7. façonné
10. ornamented

figurine... 4. doll 7. carving, tanagra
9. sculpture, statuette

Fiji Island, Viti Levu...
capital.. 4. Suva
export.. 5. sugar
mountain.. 8. Victoria
natives.. 9. cannibals (anc)
11. Melanesians
ruler.. 7. British

filament... 4. barb, dowl (dowle), hair
5. fiber (fibre), harle 6. strand,
thread

filament lamp... 12. incandescent

filbert... 3. nut 5. brown, hazel
7. Corylus 8. hazelnut

filch... 3. nim, rob 4. beat 5. steal,
theft 6. pilfer 7. purloin

file... 3. row 4. list, rasp, rate
5. enter, march, store 6. abrade,
smooth 7. sharpen 8. classify
9. catalogue 10. pickpocket
11. triggerfish (filefish)

file (combmaking)... 5. grail (graille)
6. carlet 7. quannet

filibeg... 4. kilt 5. skirt

filibuster... 6. pirate 7. impeder
8. thwarter 9. legislate
10. freebooter, obstructer
14. obstructionist

filicide... 6. murder (child by parent)

filigree... 4. lace 5. adorn (with)
7. pattern 8. fanciful 10. decorative
13. unsubstantial

Filipino, Filipina (pert to)...
homeland (mostly).. 5. Luzon
native of.. 11. Philippines
tribe.. 5. Bikol (Bicol) 7. Malayan
(Christian), Tagalog (Tagal), Visayan
(see also *Philippine*)

fill... 3. pad 5. calk, feed, glut, hold,
plug 5. block, close, gorge, stuff

6. occupy, stop up 7. execute, fulfill, pervade, satiate, satisfy, suffuse 8. complete, compound, permeate 10. accomplish 11. superabound

fille... 4. girl 8. daughter

filled... 5. dated 7. replete 8. suffused 9. saturated

filled with crevices... 7. areolar

fillet... 4. band, orle, ring, tape 5. snood, tiara 6. anadem, border, ribbon, taenia 7. bandage 8. headband, insignia 9. lemniscus, scantling 10. tenderloin

fillet (Arch)... 5. stria 6. cimbia, listel, reglet, regula, taenia 7. chaplet, molding (part)

filly... 4. colt, foal, girl, mare

film... 4. brat, haze, scum, skin, veil 5. cover, layer 6. lamina, patina 7. coating 8. pellicle 10. photograph

filmy... 3. dim 4. fine 5. gauzy, misty 6. cloudy, opaque 7. clouded 9. laminated 10. indistinct

fils... 3. son

filter... 4. ooze 5. clean, drain 6. purify, strain 7. trickle 8. colature 9. percolate

filth... 4. dirt, muck, slut 5. lucre 6. vermin 7. squalor 9. excrement, obscenity, scoundrel

filthiness... 8. cenosity 9. fetidness, obscenity 10. odiousness

filthy... 3. low 4. foul, vile 5. dirty, fetid, gross 6. impure, odious, putrid 7. obscene, squalid, unclean 9. polluting 10. licentious

filthy lucre... 4. gain (shameful) 5. money

fimbriated... 5. edged 7. fringed 8. bordered (Her), margined

fin... 3. arm 4. five, keel

fin (pert to fish)...
median.. 4. anal 6. caudal, dorsal
paired.. 6. pelvic 7. ventral 8. pectoral

final... 3. end 4. last 5. be-all, telic 7. dernier 8. decisive, definite, eventual, ultimate 9. mandatory, ultimatum 10. conclusive, definitive 11. unqualified 13. determinating

final argument... 11. ultima ratio

finale... 3. end 4. coda 5. close 6. result 8. swan song 10. completion, conclusion 11. termination

finality... 5. finis 6. finale, finish, windup 10. conclusion 11. termination 12. decisiveness 14. conclusiveness

finally... 10. eventually, ultimately 12. conclusively

final outcome... 5. issue 6. upshot 10. denouement

financial... 6. fiscal 8. monetary 9. pecuniary

finch... 4. moro 5. Junco, serin, spink, tarin 6. burion, linnet, siskin, towhee 7. chewink, redpoll 9. brambling, chaffinch, Fringilla

find... 3. get 4. gain 5. learn 6. detect, locate, summon, supply

7. procure, provide 8. discover, meet with, perceive 9. determine, discovery, good thing 10. experience 11. acquisition

find fault... 4. beef, carp 5. cavil 8. complain 9. criticize

finding... 7. verdict 8. solution 9. discovery 11. serendipity

find out... 5. learn, solve 6. detect 8. discover 9. ascertain

fine... 3. fit 4. good, lacy, pure, rare, thin 5. dandy, filmy, frail, gaudy, noble, sharp, sheer 6. ornate, slight, smooth 7. elegant, fragile, healthy, perfect, powdery, precise, slender 8. absolute, ethereal, handsome, polished, skillful, superior 9. beautiful, excellent, sensitive 10. fastidious, pulverized, surpassing

finery... 6. beauty 7. clothes, gaudery, gewgaws 8. elegance, fineness, frippery, ornament 10. decoration, lavishness 11. refinements

finesse... 5. skill 6. purity, serene 7. cunning 8. artifice, card play, subtlety, thinness 9. clearness, good taste, stratagem 10. refinement 14. discrimination (subtle)

finger... 3. toy (with) 4. hook 5. digit, touch 6. dactyl, handle, pilfer 7. measure, purloin

finger (pert to)...
alphabet.. 11. dactylology
cymbal.. 8. castanet
fish.. 8. starfish
flower.. 8. foxglove
fore.. 5. index 7. pointer
little.. 6. pinkie 7. minimus 9. auricular
middle.. 6. medius
ring.. 7. annular
stall.. 3. cot
term.. 7. digital

fingernail moon... 6. lunule

fingernail overgrowth... 10. onychauxis

fingerprint (term)... 4. arch, loop 5. whorl 9. composite 11. dactylogram 12. dactyloscopy

finial... 3. epi, tee

finical... 4. nice 5. fussy 6. dainty, dapper, jaunty, spruce 7. finicky, foppish, mincing, prudish 8. delicate 9. finicking, squeamish 10. fastidious, meticulous 11. overprecise 14. overscrupulous

finis... 3. end 4. goal 6. finale 8. finality 10. conclusion 11. culmination

finish... 3. end 4. kill 5. chare, close, matte (mat), style 6. enamel, polish 7. destroy, perfect, surface, texture 8. complete, conclude 9. terminate 10. completion, consummate, perfection

finished... 3. o'er 4. done, fine, over, ripe 5. ended 6. closed 7. refined, stopped 8. climaxed, complete, lustered, polished 9. completed, concluded, perfected 10. terminated

finite... 7. fleshly, limited 9. definable 10. restricted, terminable

11. conditional
fink... 3. spy 4. scab 5. finch
8. informer 13. strikebreaker
Finland... see also *Finnish*
capital.. 8. Helsinki (Helsingfors)
Finnish for Finland.. 5. Suomi
government.. 8. republic
island.. 5. Aland
language.. 6. Magyar 7. Swedish
8. Estonian
legislature.. 9. Eduskunta
port.. 3. Abo 5. Turku 9. Mariehamn
Finnish (pert to)...
bath.. 5. sauna
dramatist.. 4. Kivi 7. Waltari
people.. 5. Finns, Suomi 9. Karelians
10. Tavastians
fire... 4. heat, zeal 5. blaze, fever,
flame 6. excite, fervor, igneus, ignite,
incite, kindle 7. barrage, explode,
inspire 8. detonate, illumine
9. discharge, eloquence
11. inspiration 12. inflammation
13. conflagration
fire (pert to)...
basket.. 5. grate 7. cresset
comb form.. 4. igni
cracker.. 6. petard
dog.. 7. andiron
fear of.. 10. pyrophobia
god.. 6. Vulcan
opal.. 7. girasol (girasole)
power over.. 10. ignipotent
worshiper.. 5. Parsi 9. pyrolater
10. ignicolist
firearm... 3. gat, gun 5. piece, rifle
6. musket 7. demihag, rimbase (part)
8. ordnance, revolver 9. harquebus
(arquebus)
firearms discharge... 9. fusillade
fired... 3. lit 4. shot 5. baked 6. on
fire (Her) 7. excited 8. inspired
10. discharged
fireman... 4. vamp 6. fueler, stoker
8. trainman 9. fire–eater
11. firefighter
fireplace... 5. fogon, forge, ingle
6. hearth 9. inglenook 13. Franklin
stove
fireside (home)... 11. hearthstone
firewood... 6. billet
fireworks... 4. caps, gerb 6. flares
7. fizgigs, gunfire, rip–raps, rockets
8. serpents 9. pinwheels, sparklers,
torpedoes 10. girandoles
12. firecrackers, Roman candles
firm... 4. fast, hard, safe, sure, trig
5. dense, fixed, rigid, solid, sound,
stout, tight 6. secure, stable, stanch,
steady, strict, strong 7. compact,
company, decided, devoted, staunch
8. faithful 9. immovable, steadfast
10. determined, unslipping, unyielding
11. substantial
firmament... 3. sky 5. vault 6. Caelus,
welkin 7. heavens 8. empyrean
firmly set... 5. fixed, solid 6. rooted
10. inveterate
firmness... 8. fidelity, rigidity, solidity,
strength, tenacity 9. constancy,
stability 10. immobility, steadiness
11. reliability 15. indissolubility

firmness, want of... 5. loose 6. laxity
8. weakness 11. instability, vacillation
firn... 3. ice 4. neve, snow
firs... 5. Abies, pines
first... 5. chief, front, prime 6. maiden,
primal, primus 7. highest, initial,
leading, primary 8. earliest, foremost,
original 9. beginning, elemental,
principal 10. primordial
first (pert to)...
appearance.. 5. debut 8. premiere
born.. 5. eigne 6. eldest
Christian martyr.. 7. Stephen
coin (silver).. 8. sesterce
days of Rom month.. 7. calends
(kalends)
fruits (Eccl).. 7. annates
letter.. 4. Alif 5. Aleph
stages.. 8. inchoate 9. rudiments
world navigator.. 8. Magellan
fish... 3. dib 4. food 5. angle, drail,
seine, troll 6. Pisces
13. constellation
fish (types of)... 2. id 3. cat, cod, gar,
ray 4. bass, carp, char, chub, cusk,
dace, goby, hake, ling, opah, parr,
peto, pike, ruff, scup, shad, sisi,
sole, tuna, ulua 5. bream, cisco,
fluke, guppy, perch, porgy, shark,
skate, smelt, snook, sprat, trout,
tunny, wahoo 6. barbel, bonito,
bowfin, burbot, conger, darter,
marlin, minnow, puffer, redfin,
salmon, shiner, sucker, tarpon,
tautog, turbot 7. alewife, anchovy,
catfish, crappie, croaker, dogfish,
garfish, grouper, haddock, halibut,
herring, hogfish, jewfish, lamprey,
mudfish, oquassa, pollack, pompano,
redfish, sardine, sawfish, sunfish,
torpedo, walleye 8. albacore, blue
fish, bluegill, bonefish, bullhead,
chimaera, filefish, flatfish, flounder,
goldfish, grayling, kingfish, lumpfish,
mackerel, menhaden, pickerel,
pilchard, sailfish, sergeant, sting ray,
sturgeon, toadfish, weakfish
9. barracuda, cigarfish, devilfish,
jellyfish, namaycush, sheatfish,
whitefish 10. barramunda, butterfish,
candlefish, hammerhead, yellowtail
11. muskellunge (see also *mammal*)
fish (pert to)...
adhering.. 4. pega 6. remora
ascending rivers.. 7. anadrom
10. anadromous
bait.. 4. chum 5. chack 6. minnow
9. killifish (killy)
basket.. 4. caul 5. creel, slath (slarth)
bivalve, mollusk.. 4. clam, slug
5. snail, whelk 6. limpet, mussel,
oyster 7. abalone, Ocypode (crab),
scallop
caviar–yielding.. 7. sterlet
climbing, jumping.. 5. saury
6. anabas 7. skipper
club.. 6. muckle
codfish.. 4. cusk 5. torsk 7. bacalao,
buffalo
comb form.. 7. ichthyo
crustacean.. 3. Uca 4. crab 6. shrimp
7. lobster 8. Decapoda

devil.. 3. ray 5. manta
eaters.. 12. ichthyophagi
eating.. 11. piscivorous
  14. ichthyophagous
fabled (Pers).. 4. Mahi (Mah)
gaff (through ice).. 5. ching
game.. 4. tuna 5. chiro, sword, trout
  6. marlin, salmon, tarpon 8. grayling
  11. muskellunge
genus.. 4. Amia (bowfin), Mola
  (sunfish) 5. Elops (tarpon), Perca
  (perch) 8. Haliotis (abalone),
  Octopoda (octopus)
hook.. 5. Kirby, snell (part)
  8. Aberdeen, barbless, Carlisle,
  Limerick
largest (freshwater).. 8. arapaima
like.. 8. ichthyic
line.. 6. nossel (norsel) 7. spillet
living by.. 9. piscatory
living on.. 12. ichthyophagy
man–eating.. 6. caribe 7. piranha
mollusk.. see *bivalve*
nest building.. 5. acara
net.. 4. fyke 5. seine, snell, trawl
  7. boulter, spiller
pond.. 7. piscina 8. aquarium
roe.. 6. caviar
salmon.. 3. fog 4. masu, parr
  5. sprod 6. alevin 7. gilling
sauce.. 4. alec
spear.. 3. gig
taboo.. 13. ichthyophobia
treatise.. 11. ichthyology
worship.. 12. ichthyolatry
young brood.. 3. fry
fisherman... 6. angler 8. piscator
fishery... 7. piscary
fishing... 4. chug (through ice)
  8. snelling 9. halieutic, piscation
fishing vessel... 5. smack 6. seiner
  7. trawler
fishy... 4. dull 6. vacant 8. fishlike
  9. deceptive, dishonest
  10. improbable, lusterless, suspicious,
  unreliable 11. extravagant
  14. expressionless
fissure... 3. gap 4. leak, lode, open,
  rent, rift, rima, seam, slit, vein
  5. break, chasm, chine, chink, cleft,
  crack, sever, split 7. crevice
fissured... 5. cleft 6. rimate, rimose
fist... 4. duke, hand (closed) 5. nieve
  6. clench 8. tightwad
  11. handwriting
fit... 3. due, fay, pat 4. able, gear,
  meet, mesh, ripe, suit, whim
  5. adapt, equip, fancy, ready, spasm,
  train 6. attack, enmesh, frenzy,
  proper, stroke, suited 7. adapted,
  caprice, conform, healthy, prepare,
  tantrum 8. disposed, dovetail,
  eligible, outbreak, suitable
  9. competent, qualified
  11. accommodate, appropriate
fit (pert to)...
  an arrow (archery).. 4. nock
  fury.. 4. rage
  groove (Arch).. 4. dado
  resentment.. 4. huff, mood 5. pique
    7. tantrum
  to eat.. 6. edible

to till.. 6. arable
fitchew... 5. skink, zoril 7. foumart,
  polecat
fitful... 8. restless, unstable, variable
  9. impulsive, irregular, orderless,
  spasmodic 10. capricious, convulsive
  12. intermittent
fitly... 4. duly 5. right 6. timely
  8. properly, suitably 10. decorously
fitness... 7. decorum 9. congruity
  10. expedience, timeliness
  11. eligibility, suitability
  12. preparedness
fitting... 3. apt, pat 4. just, meet
  6. proper, seemly, timely
  8. adapting, suitable 9. expedient
  11. appropriate
five (pert to)...
  Books of Moses.. 10. Pentateuch
  children (born at once)..
    11. quintuplets
  Civilized Tribes (Ind).. 5. Creek
    7. Choctaw 8. Cherokee, Seminole
    9. Chickasaw
  comb form.. 5. penta
  cornered.. 11. pentagonous
  divided by.. 11. quinquesect
  dollar bill.. 1. V 3. fin 5. fiver
  feet.. 10. pentameter
  five–year period.. 6. pentad 7. lustrum
    (census) 12. quinquennial
  fold.. 9. quintuple
  group.. 6. pentad 8. fivesome
  lines (nonsense).. 8. limerick
  Nations (Ind Confed).. 7. Cayugas,
    Mohawks, Oneidas, Senecas
    9. Onondagas
  trump card (auction pitch).. 5. pedro
fix... 3. peg, pin, set 4. mend, moor,
  nail 5. amend, brace, bribe, imbed,
  limit, stamp 6. adjust, anchor,
  cement, define, fasten, ossify, punish,
  repair, settle 7. arrange, confirm,
  delimit, dilemma, prepare, rectify
  8. organize, solidify 9. condition,
  establish, stabilize, stipulate
  10. prearrange
fixed... 3. set 4. firm 5. rigid
  6. formal, intent, nailed, static
  7. assured, limited, settled, special
  8. arranged, habitual 9. immovable,
  permanent, unwinking
  11. established, prearranged,
  traditional
fixed (pert to)...
  allowance.. 4. diet 6. ration
    7. stipend 10. remittance
  beforehand.. 13. predetermined
  by choice.. 8. elective
  manner.. 9. immovably
  star.. 4. Veda
  time.. 3. era 4. date, fast
fizgig... 9. fireworks, whirligig
flabellate... 9. fan–shaped
flabrum... 3. fan 9. flabellum
flaccid... 4. limp, weak 6. flabby
  8. yielding
flag... 3. sag 4. fail, fane, iris, pave,
  pine, sign, weak, wilt 5. Roger
  (pirate) 6. banner, burgee, colors,
  cornet, ensign, fanion, flower, guidon,
  pennon, signal 7. bunting, calamus,

decline, pennant 8. gonfalon,
masthead, standard, streamer,
vexillum 9. banderole 16. Quincunx
of Heaven
flagging . . . 4. weak 7. languid
8. pavement 10. flagstones, spiritless
11. languishing
flagging in energy . . . 9. lassitude
flagitious . . . 6. wicked 7. corrupt,
heinous 8. criminal, flagrant
10. scandalous, villainous
flagon . . . 3. jug 4. ewer 5. stoup
6. bottle, carafe 7. canteen
8. demijohn
flagpole standard . . . 7. bracket
9. bracciale
flagrant . . . 4. rank 5. great 6. absurd,
wanton, wicked 7. glaring, hateful,
heinous, obvious, scarlet, violent
8. infamous, terrible 9. abandoned,
atrocious, monstrous, nefarious
10. profligate, villainous
flail . . . 4. beat, flag, whip 6. thrash,
weapon (anc) 7. swingle
flam . . . 4. hoax 5. cheat, spoof, trick
6. cajole 7. pretext 8. drumbeat,
flimflam 9. deception, falsehood
flambeau . . . 5. torch (flaming)
7. cresset 11. candlestick
flamboyant . . . 4. wavy (Arch) 6. florid,
ornate 9. brilliant, flamelike
11. resplendent
flame . . . 3. arc 4. beam, burn, fire,
glow, leye (obs), love, zeal 5. ardor,
blaze, flare, flash, glare, ingle, light,
lover 6. redden 7. scarlet
8. flammule (small) 10. brightness,
sweetheart
flamen . . . 6. priest (anc)
flamenco . . . 5. dance (gypsy)
Flaminian Way . . . 4. Rome
Flanders, Belgium . . .
brick . . 4. Bath
capital . . 5. Ghent (East) 6. Bruges
(West)
city . . 5. Alost 6. Ostend 7. Dixmude
(Dixmuide)
people (anc) . . 5. Celts 6. Franks
11. Burgundians
poppy . . 9. corn poppy
flap . . . 3. tab 4. blow, slap, sway,
wave 5. skirt 6. dangle, lappet,
stroke 7. flapper, flutter
9. appendage
flare . . . 5. blaze, flame, flash, fusee,
glare, light 6. signal, spread
7. display, flicker 8. outburst
10. illuminate
flaring . . . 5. gaudy 6. spread
7. burning, glaring 8. dazzling,
flashing
flash . . . 4. show 5. blaze, burst, gleam,
glint, shine, spark 6. glance, signal
7. display, glimmer, glisten, glitter,
instant, shimmer, sparkle 8. dispatch
9. telegraph
flashing . . . 5. showy 6. flashy
8. meteoric, snapping 9. transient
flashy . . . 3. gay 5. fiery, gaudy, showy
6. frothy, garish, sporty 7. raffish
8. vehement 9. flaunting, impetuous
13. grandiloquent

flask . . . 4. ewer, olpe 5. betty
6. flagon 7. ampulla, canteen
9. aryballus (aryballos, anc)
flask–shaped . . . 10. lageniform
flat . . . 3. low 4. palm 5. banal, blunt,
level, molle, plain, plane, prone,
stale, suite, tract, vapid 6. boring,
dreary, wholly 7. insipid, uniform
8. tenement, unbroken 10. horizontal
flat (pert to) . . .
boat . . 3. ark 4. punt, scow 5. barge
breastbone . . 6. ratite
canopy . . 6. tester
flatfoot . . 9. pes planus 13. talipes
planus
iron . . 7. sadiron
nosed . . 6. simous
piece . . 4. slab
surface . . 4. area 6. pagina 7. tabular
worm . . 9. planarian, trematode
flatfish . . . 3. dab 4. sole 5. brill, fluke
6. acedia, turbot 7. halibut
8. flounder
flatten . . . 4. even 5. level 6. deject,
smooth 7. depress 8. dispirit
9. prostrate 10. discourage,
dishearten
flattened . . . 6. evened, oblate
7. leveled 8. smoothed 9. applanate
flatter . . . 3. oil 4. coax, palp 5. charm,
float 6. cajole, caress, please, praise,
smooge, soothe 7. adulate, beguile,
blarney, flutter 8. blandish
9. encourage 10. compliment,
ingratiate
flatterer . . . 6. flunky, glozer 7. Jenkins
8. adulator, courtier, parasite
9. sycophant
flattering . . . 9. adulatory, gnathonic,
insincere 10. obsequious
13. complimentary
flattery . . . 5. gloze, taffy 6. praise
7. blarney, eyewash, fawning, palaver
8. cajolery 9. adulation
10. compliment, sycophancy
14. obsequiousness
flaunt . . . 4. wave 5. boast, vaunt
6. parade 7. display, flutter
8. brandish
**Flavian, House of Flavius,
Emperors** . . . 5. Titus 8. Domitian
9. Vespasian
Flavian Amphitheater . . . 9. Colosseum
(Rome)
flavor . . . 4. gust, odor, tang, zest
5. aroma, imbue, sapid, sapor,
sauce, savor, scent, taste 6. season
7. perfume 8. piquancy 9. flavoring
14. characteristic
flaw . . . 3. gap, mar 4. rase, rift
5. cleft, fault 6. breach, defect
7. blemish, fissure, sophism
8. fracture 12. imperfection
flax . . . 3. lin, tow 5. linen
flax (pert to) . . .
capsule . . 4. boll
dust . . 5. pouce
filaments . . 4. harl
process plant . . 7. rettery
refuse . . 5. pob, tow 5. hurds
seed . . 7. linseed
soak . . 3. ret

weed.. 8. toadflax
flaxweed... 8. toadflax
flay... 4. peel, skin 6. fleece
  7. censure, reprove, scarify
  9. criticize, excoriate
flea... 4. puce 5. pulex 6. beetle,
  chigoe 7. chigger, cyclops
  8. reminder 13. Ctenocephalus
fleam... 6. lancet, stream
  10. millstream
fleck... 4. flea, mark, spot 5. flake
  6. blotch, dapple, streak, stripe
  7. freckle, speckle, stipple 8. particle
  9. variegate
flection, flexion... 7. bending, turning
flee... 3. fly, run 4. shun 5. avoid,
  elope, evade, speed 6. vanish
  7. abandon, forsake 9. disappear
fleece... 3. abb, nap 4. flay, pile, skin,
  wool 5. fleck, mulct, sheer, strip
  6. divest 7. despoil, swindle
  10. overcharge
fleer... 4. gibe, jeer, mock 5. flout,
  scoff, sheer, taunt
fleet... 4. fast, flit, flow, navy, sail,
  swim 5. drift, group, quick, rapid,
  swift 6. armada, hasten, nimble,
  speedy 9. transient 10. evanescent,
  transitory
fleeting... 7. passing 9. transient
  10. evanescent, transitory
Fleet Street... 5. Fleta (book written
  in prison) 6. prison (London)
  11. London press
Flemish painter... 5. David 6. Rubens
  7. Van Dyke
flesh... 3. kin 4. body, meat, pink,
  pulp, race (human) 6. family, fatten,
  muscle 7. kindred, kinsmen, mankind
  8. humanity 9. mortality
  10. sensuality
flesh (pert to)...
  eating.. 8. omophagy (raw)
  9. omophagia 10. omophagous,
  zoophagous 11. carnivorous,
  creophagous
  fond of.. 12. sarcophilous
  like.. 7. carnose
  lust for.. 9. carnality
  resembling.. 7. sarcoid
  slain animals.. 7. carnage
fleshpots... 6. plenty, wealth 10. high
  living, prosperity 12. fat of the land
fleshy... 3. fat 5. beefy, human,
  obese, plump, pulpy, stout 6. carnal
  7. adipose, carnose 9. corpulent
fleshy fruit... 4. pear, pome 5. bacca,
  berry, drupe
fleur-de-lis... 3. lis (Her) 4. iris, lily,
  luce 6. emblem
flew... see fly
flexible... 4. limp 5. lithe 6. limber,
  pliant, supple 7. elastic, lissome
flexion, flection... 9. anaclasis
flexure... 4. genu 5. crook 7. bending
flicker... 4. burn, flit 5. blaze, glare,
  waver 7. flutter, high-hoe
  10. woodpecker
flickering... 7. burning, lambent
  8. flickery 9. irregular
flier, flyer... 3. ace 4. bird 5. pilot,

train 6. airman, gamble, insect
  7. aviator, speeder, sunfish, venture
  11. speculation
flight... 3. hop 4. rout 5. arrow
  (volley), flock, skein (wild fowl), speed
  6. exodus, fletch (arrows), flying,
  hegira, perron, stairs, throng
  7. soaring 8. escapism, mounting,
  stampede, swarming 9. excursion,
  formation, migration 10. volitation
flighty... 5. barmy, swift 6. fickle, fitful
  7. foolish 8. fanciful, freakish, volatile
  9. frivolous 10. capricious
flimflam... 5. freak, hocus, trick
  6. humbug 7. caprice, swindle
  8. nonsense, trifling 9. deception,
  deceptive 11. nonsensical
flimmer... 7. flicker, glimmer
flimsy... 4. limp, rare, thin, vain, weak
  5. frail 6. feeble, paltry, sleazy,
  slimsy 7. flaccid, shallow, trivial
  9. illogical 11. superficial
  13. unsubstantial
flinch... 4. game 5. quail, start, wince,
  wonde 6. blench, cringe, falter,
  flense, recoil, shrink, swerve
fling... 3. shy 4. dart, dash, gibe,
  hurl, toss 5. cheat, dance, flock
  (sandpipers), revel, sling, sneer, throw
  6. baffle, spirit 7. cast off, sarcasm
  9. prostrate
flint... 5. chert, clint, silex 6. quartz
  7. lighter 8. hardness 9. firestone,
  skinflint
flip... 3. hop, tap 4. flap, glib, snap,
  toss 5. drink (spiced), flick, flirt,
  throw 6. fillip 8. flippant, turn over
  10. somersault 11. impertinent
flippant... 4. flip, glib, pert 5. cocky
  6. chatty, fluent 8. impudent
  10. persiflate 11. impertinent
flipper... 3. arm, fin, paw 4. hand
  5. panel 8. flapjack
flirt... 3. toy 4. dart, fike, flip, jerk,
  jilt, mash, play, toss 5. dally
  6. coquet, fillip, masher, trifle
  7. trifler 8. coquette 11. philanderer
flirtation... 5. dance 8. coquetry,
  trifling 10. love affair
flit... 3. fly 4. dart 5. glide, hover
  6. nimble 7. flicker, flutter, migrate
flitter... 3. rag 5. hover, piece
  6. tatter 7. flicker, flutter, fritter
  8. fragment
flittermouse... 3. bat
float... 4. buoy, cork, hove, lure, raft,
  ride, sail, soar, swim, waft 5. balsa,
  drift, hover, ladle 6. launch
  7. support 8. navigate, undulate
  9. transport 10. inaugurate
floating... 4. free 5. awash, loose
  6. adrift, natant 7. buoyant,
  movable, rumored 8. changing,
  drifting, shifting 9. launching,
  wandering
floating herb... 7. frogbit
  16. Hydrocharitaceae
flock... 4. bevy, fold, herd, pack, raft
  6. flight, hirsel 7. company
  9. multitude 10. assemblage,
  collection 11. aggregation
flock (pert to)...

bees.. 4. hive 5. swarm 6. colony
cattle.. 4. herd
fish.. 5. shoal
geese.. 5. skein 6. gaggle
herons.. 5. sedge
insects.. 6. swarm
like.. 6. gregal
lions.. 5. pride
partridge...5. covey
pheasants.. 4. nide (nid)
sandpipers.. 5. fling
walrus.. 3. pod
flocks, god of... 3. Pan
floe... 3. ice 4. berg
flog... 3. cat, tan 4. beat, cane, goad,
lash, wale, welt, whip 6. larrup,
punish, strike, thrash 8. chastise
flogging... 4. toco (toko) 7. beating
8. whipping 9. thrashing
10. punishment 12. chastisement
flood... 3. sea 5. eagre, spate
6. deluge, drench, excess 7. freshet,
torrent 8. cataract, inundate, overflow
9. cataclysm 10. oversupply
14. superabundance
flood (pert to)...
disaster.. 9. Galveston (1900),
Johnstown (1889)
gate.. 4. gool, lock, slow 6. sluice
8. penstock
lights.. 5. klieg
tidal.. 5. eagre
floor... 4. base, pave, sill 5. chess
(pontoon), story 6. baffle, bottom,
defeat 7. coaming, silence
9. overthrow 10. substratum
floor leader... 4. whip
flora... 6. plants 11. florilegium
flora and fauna... 5. biota
Florence gallery... 5. Pitti 6. Uffizi
Florentine (pert to)...
color.. 7. scarlet
family (famed).. 6. Medici
lily.. 6. giglio
school.. 6. Tuscan
sculptor.. 8. Ammanati, Ghiberti
florid... 3. red 5. ruddy 6. ornate,
rococo 7. flowery, flushed
8. enriched, rubicund 10. figurative,
melismatic, rhetorical 11. embellished
13. grandiloquent
Florida...
capital.. 11. Tallahassee
city.. 5. Miami, Tampa 7. Key West
8. Sarasota 9. Pensacola 11. St
Augustine (1565) 12. St Petersburg
discoverer.. 11. Ponce de Leon
(1513)
fish.. 6. mullet, shrimp, tarpon, testar,
tetard 8. blue crab
flower.. 13. orange blossom
Indian.. 8. Seminole
lake.. 10. Okeechobee
museum.. 10. Circus Hall (Ringling)
plant.. 7. coontie
river.. 8. Suwannee
State admission.. 13. twenty–seventh
State motto.. 22. Liberty and
Independence
State nickname.. 8. Sunshine
swamp, park.. 10. Everglades
trail.. 7. Tamiami

flounce... 4. flap, fold, jerk, trim
5. caper, frill, twist 6. edging, frolic
8. flounder, struggle
flounder... 4. roll 6. bungle, muddle,
welter 7. stumble 8. struggle
9. fluctuate
flounder (fish)... 3. dab 5. fluke
6. plaice, turbot 8. flatfish
flour... 4. bran, meal 6. farina, pinole,
powder 9. middlings, pulverize
flour (pert to)...
diabetic.. 9. aleuronat
gravy.. 4. roux
maker.. 6. miller
pudding.. 4. duff
flourish... 4. grow, show, wave
5. vaunt 6. flaunt, paraph (signature),
thrive 7. display, fanfare, prosper,
roulade 8. arpeggio, brandish,
ornament 9. embellish, luxuriate
11. ostentation
flout... 4. defy, gibe, jeer, mock
5. fleer, scoff, scout, sneer, taunt
6. insult 8. ridicule
flow... 3. jet, run 4. bore, flow, flux,
gush, ooze, pour, roll, teem 5. glide,
issue, river, spout 6. abound, afflux,
course, stream 7. current, fluency,
flutter 9. streaming 10. outpouring
flow (pert to)...
along.. 4. lave
back.. 7. redound
jet.. 4. gush 5. spurt
out.. 5. exude, issue, spill
over.. 5. slosh, spill 6. deluge, engulf
8. inundate 9. overwhelm
tide.. 5. ebb 4. flow, neap
flower... 3. bud 4. best, blow
5. bloom 6. unfold 7. blossom,
develop, essence, produce
8. choicest, ornament 11. Four
Hundred (Society)
flower (types of)... 3. gul (rose) 4. iris,
ixia, lily, pink, rose 5. aster, calla,
canna, daisy, pansy, peony, phlox,
poppy, stock, tulip 6. azalea,
cosmos, crocus, dahlia, lupine,
maypop, orchid, oxalis, violet, zinnia
7. arbutus, begonia, fuchsia, gentian,
passion, petunia, rhodora, verbena
8. amaranth, arethusa, camomile,
cyclamen, daffodil, geranium,
hepatica, hyacinth, larkspur, magnolia,
marigold, Mariposa (lily), primrose,
sweet pea 9. amaryllis, calendula,
carnation, edelweiss, gladiolus,
hollyhock, mayflower, narcissus, water
lily 10. cornflower, delphinium,
fleur–de–lis, marguerite, mignonette,
nasturtium, periwinkle, poinsettia,
snapdragon 11. forget–me–not,
strawflower 13. chrysanthemum
15. lily of the valley
flower (pert to)...
arranging.. 7. ikebana
bed, garden.. 8. floretum, parterre
bloom (full).. 8. anthesis
bud (sauce).. 5. caper
bunch.. 4. posy 7. bouquet, corsage,
nosegay
bursting into.. 12. efflorescent
cluster, clustered.. 4. cyme 5. umbel

8. racemose 9. glomerule
10. paniculate
largest.. 9. rafflesia (3–ft diameter)
like.. 7. anthoid
meadow–grown.. 6. pratal
part.. 4. stem 5. bract, calyx, petal,
sepal, torus 6. carpel, pistil
7. corolla, petiole 8. epicalyx,
peduncle, perianth
poet's.. 8. asphodel 9. narcissus
sacred.. 5. lotus
seed.. 5. ovule
shaped.. 7. fleuron
small.. 7. fleuret
stand.. 7. epergne
flower, shrub... 5. lilac 6. azalea,
laurel 7. dogwood, heather, jasmine,
spiraea, syringa 8. bayberry,
hawthorn 9. jessamine, mistletoe,
sagebrush 10. bitterroot
12. rhododendron
flower, vine... 8. clematis, wisteria
11. honeysuckle 12. morning glory
flower, wild... 5. bluet, daisy
6. cactus, clover, myrtle, pasque
7. anemone, cowslip 8. bluebell,
camellia 9. buttercup, goldenrod,
mayflower, sunflower 10. bluebonnet
12. lady's–slipper
flowering again... 9. remontant
flowers... 9. flowerage
flowers, goddess of... 5. Flora (Rom)
Flowery Kingdom... 5. China
flowing... 5. fluid 6. afflux, fluent
7. copious, cursive, emanant, fluxing
8. coursing, eloquent 9. streaming
10. transitive
flowing (pert to)...
from source.. 6. rising 9. emanating
together.. 9. confluent
veil.. 5. colet (anc)
well.. 6. gusher
fluctuate... 4. roll, vary, veer 5. waver
7. vibrate 8. intermit, undulate,
unsteady 9. oscillate, vacillate
10. irresolute 12. undetermined
flue... 4. barb 5. fluke 6. funnel,
tunnel 7. chimney
fluent... 4. glib 5. fluid, ready
6. facile, smooth, solute 7. copious,
elegant, flowing, gliding, verbose,
voluble 8. eloquent 9. talkative
10. loquacious
fluff... 4. down, girl, lint, yarn 5. floss
6. bungle 8. softness 9. lightness
fluffy... 4. soft 5. downy, drunk, fuzzy,
linty 8. feathery 9. forgetful
12. undependable
fluid... 3. gas, ink, oil 4. bile, milk
5. ichor, serum, water 6. fluent,
liquid, plasma, watery 7. flowing
8. floating, nonsolid
fluke... 4. fish, worm 5. blade (whale)
8. accident, flatfish, flounder
flume... 5. shoot 6. raving, sluice
7. channel, conduit
flunk... 4. fail, miss, slip 5. shirk
6. flinch 7. back out
flunky, flunkey... 4. snob 5. toady
6. cookee, lackey 7. footman,
servant 8. henchman 9. stagehand
flurry... 3. ado 4. fret, gust 5. haste,

hurry 6. bustle, squall 7. bluster,
fluster, flutter 8. snowfall
9. agitation, commotion, confusion
10. excitement
flush... 3. hot, jet 4. full, glow, gush,
rush 5. blush, cards, color, drunk,
fever, rinse, ruddy 6. drench, lavish,
redden, thrill 7. healthy, wealthy
8. abundant, affluent, prodigal,
rosiness, squarely, unbroken
10. prosperous
flushed... 3. hot, red 4. ruby
5. aglow, drunk 6. elated, florid
7. excited, fervent 8. blushing,
exultant, feverish, reddened
fluster... 4. move 5. shake 6. bustle,
excite, flurry, pother 8. distract
10. excitement 11. distraction
flute... 5. crimp, twill 6. furrow,
groove 7. magadis 9. organ stop,
wineglass 10. instrument
flute (pert to)...
bagpipe part.. 7. chanter
nose.. 3. bin 5. pungi
player.. 6. aulete 7. tootler
shrill.. 7. piccolo
stop.. 7. ventage
transverse.. 4. fife
fluting... 5. strix 7. gadroon, shading
10. decoration
flutter... 4. flap, flit, wave 5. float,
haste, hover, waver 6. bustle, ruffle
7. agitate, pitapat 8. disorder
9. agitation, confusion, palpitate
flux... 4. flow, fuse, melt 5. flood,
purge, resin, rosin, smalt, smear
6. course 7. flowing, liquefy, outflow,
solvent
fly... 3. hop 4. flee, flit, leap, melt,
soar, wave, whir, wing 5. alate,
float, glide, speed 6. aviate, elapse,
escape, insect, spring, vanish
7. avigate, avolate 8. fishhook
9. cease to be, disappear
fly (types of)... 3. bot 4. gnat
5. cadew, horse, house, midge
6. Asilus, caddis, gadfly, punkie,
tsetse 7. Diptera, nosee–um
8. dipteron, lacewing, mosquito
11. caterpillar
fly (pert to)...
African.. 4. zimb (zebub) 6. tsetse
agaric.. 8. mushroom (poisonous)
artificial.. 4. harl 5. alder, sedge
6. Cahill, claret 7. grannom
blow.. 4. eggs 5. larva
catcher.. 4. tody 6. peewee (pewit),
phoebe 8. kingbird
flying... 5. a–wing, brief, hasty, yarak
(falcon) 6. volant, waving 7. fleeing
8. fleeting, floating 9. temporary,
transient 12. aeronautical
flying (pert to)...
adder.. 9. dragonfly
boat.. 8. airplane, seaplane
9. amphibian
cat.. 5. lemur 6. marmot
Dutchman.. 5. opera 7. mariner
(fabled) 8. wanderer
fox.. 3. bat 6. kalong
island.. 6. Laputa (Gulliver's Travels)
machine.. 9. gyroplane, orthopter

foal... 4. colt 5. filly 8. Equuleus (Astron) 9. youngling

foam... 4. barm, boil, fume, rage, scum, suds 5. froth, spume, yeast 6. trivia 7. bubbles

foaming... 7. spumous 8. bubbling 10. fermenting, infuriated 11. overwrought

fob... 4. sham 5. cheat, trick 6. impose, pocket 7. palm off 8. ornament

focal point... 8. omphalos

focus... 6. center 8. converge, omphalos 10. adjustment 11. concentrate

fodder... 3. hay 4. corn, feed 5. straw, vetch 6. forage, silage, stover 7. stubble 8. ensilage 9. pasturage, provender

fodder (pert to)...
pit.. 4. silo
storage.. 6. haymow
store.. 6. ensile
stored.. 6. silage

foe... 4. army 5. enemy, rival 8. opponent 9. ill–wisher

fog... 4. blur, daze, haar, haze, mist, roke, smog 5. brume, cloud, vapor 6. nebula, opaque, stupor 7. aerosol, confuse, pogonip (Sierras) 9. confusion

fogdog... 5. stubb 8. fogeater

foggy... 3. dim 4. dull, hazy, roky 5. dense, misty, vague 6. cloudy, opaque 7. muddled, obscure 8. confused, nubilous 9. beclouded, uncertain 10. indistinct 12. muddleheaded

foghorn... 5. siren, voice (hoarse) 6. signal

fogle... 12. handkerchief (thieves')

fogy... 4. dull, slow 6. dotard, fogram, Hunker 8. mossback 10. Barnburner 12. conservative, old–fashioned 16. overconservative

foible... 5. blade (part), fault 7. failing, frailty 8. weakness 9. infirmity 12. imperfection

foil... 4. balk 5. actor, metal, sheet, stump, sword 6. defeat, offset, outwit, stooge, thwart, weapon 7. failure, repulse 9. frustrate 10. disappoint 11. frustration

Foism... 8. Buddhism

foist... 4. palm 5. cheat 7. intrude 9. interpose 11. interpolate

fold... 3. end, lap, pen, ply 4. coil (serpent), fail, furl, loop, pile, reef, ruga, sile, tuck, wrap 5. clasp, close, crimp, drape, laity, plait, pleat, plica 6. crease, dewlap, double, infold, lamina, lappet, rimple, suffix 7. entwine, envelop, plicate (fanlike) 8. collapse 9. plicature 10. go bankrupt

folded, not... 8. eplicate

folder... 7. booklet, leaflet 8. pamphlet 13. advertisement

foliage... 5. spray 6. leaves, ramage 7. bouquet, leafage, umbrage 8. ornament (Arch)

folio... 4. case, leaf 5. paper (folded) 6. folder, number (serial)

folk... 4. race 5. tribe 6. nation, people 8. servants 9. followers, relatives, retainers 11. aggregation

folk (pert to)...
learned.. 7. pedants
lore.. 6. legend 9. mythology, tradition 12. superstition
song.. 4. fado, lied 7. art song, lullaby 9. Kunstlied, Volkslied
tale.. 4. myth, saga 5. fable, Nancy 6. legend, mythos, mythus 7. fantasy, parable

follow... 3. dog, tag 4. heed, heel, next, nose, obey, seek, tail 5. after, ensue, trace, trail 6. pursue, result, shadow 7. conform, draggle, emulate, imitate, observe, replace, succeed 8. come next, practice, supplant 9. persevere, supervene 10. understand

follower... 3. fan, ist (suff), ite (suff), son 4. aper 5. lover (of) 6. copier, ensuer, votary, zealot 7. devotee, pursuer, sequent 8. adherent, believer, disciple, henchman, partisan 9. Christian, dependent, satellite 10. enthusiast 11. cuadrillero

follower of...
Arius.. 5. Arian
Buddha.. 8. Buddhist
Confucius.. 9. Confucian
Falstaff.. 3. Nym
Mohammed.. 6. Moslem 8. Islamite

following... 4. next, sect 5. suant 7. ensuing, pursuit, sequent 8. trailing 9. resultant 10. subsequent, succeeding, successive 13. accompaniment

following (pert to)...
exact words.. 7. literal
one's death.. 10. posthumous
stories.. 6. sequel, series

folly... 3. sin 5. crime 6. levity, lunacy 7. blunder, foolery, madness 8. lewdness, unwisdom 9. silliness 10. desipience, imprudence, wantonness 11. foolishness 12. indiscretion

foment... 3. egg 4. abet, brew, spur 5. bathe, rouse 6. arouse, excite, incite 7. agitate, cherish 9. encourage, instigate

fomentation... 6. lotion, stupes 10. excitement 11. instigation 13. encouragement

Fomoriana (Celt Myth)... 10. sea robbers (race of)

fonda... 3. inn 5. hotel 6. fonduk

fondle... 3. pet 4. neck 5. ingle 6. caress, coddle, cosset, foster, pamper 7. cherish 8. blandish

fondling... 3. pet 4. fool 5. ninny 9. caressing, simpleton 10. love–making

fondly... 6. dearly 8. tenderly 14. affectionately

fondness... 3. gra 4. love 6. desire, doting, liking, relish 8. appetite 9. affection 10. attachment, propensity

fond of...

hunting .. **7.** venatic
sea .. **15.** thalassophilous
wife (overly) .. **8.** uxorious
font ... **3.** jet **4.** fons, lava **5.** stoup
  6. source, spring **7.** piscina
  8. fountain **9.** reservoir
food ... **3.** cud, pap **4.** cate, chow,
  diet, eats, fare, grub, junk (food), meat,
  tofu **5.** bread, manna, scran **6.** bulgur
  (wheat), cereal, gluten, quiche, snacks,
  Tex–Mex, viands **7.** aliment, cuisine,
  edibles, tapioca **8.** chili dog,
  fast–food, kreplach, munchies, victuals
  9. nutriment, nutrition, provender
  10. sustenance **11.** charcuterie,
  comestibles, nourishment
food (pert to) ...
animal .. **6.** forage **9.** provender
bit .. **4.** bite **6.** morsel **7.** munchie
devotee .. **7.** epicure, gourmet
digestant .. **5.** chyle
digested (partly) .. **5.** chyme
dislike of .. **9.** sitomania
  10. cibophobia
element .. **7.** protein, vitamin
fasting (Lenten) .. **7.** xerophagy
gods, the .. **6.** amrita **8.** ambrosia
heavenly .. **5.** manna
impure .. **4.** tref
provide .. **5.** cater, scaff **6.** tucker
room .. **5.** ambry **6.** pantry, spence
  7. butlery, pantler
fool ... **3.** ass, toy **4.** butt, dolt, dupe,
  jerk, nerd, nizy, raca (Bib), simp
  5. clown, idiot, moron, ninny
  6. dotard, jester, noodle, trifle, turkey
  7. buffoon, deceive, dingbat, fathead
  9. ignoramus, simpleton
foolhardy ... **4.** rash **7.** Icarian
  8. reckless **11.** adventurous
fool hen ... **6.** grouse
foolish ... **3.** mad **4.** daft, race, rash,
  zany **5.** inane, inept, silly **6.** absurd,
  harish **5.** palty **6.** simple, stupid,
  unwise **7.** asinine, fatuous, idiotic,
  puerile, witless **9.** brainless, desipient,
  imprudent, ludicrous, senseless
  10. illadvised, irrational, ridiculous
  12. preposterous **13.** insignificant
foolish fancy ... **7.** chimera (chimaera)
foolishness ... **5.** folly **6.** levity
  9. absurdity, stupidity **10.** triviality
fool's bauble ... **7.** marotte
fool's gold ... **6.** pyrite
foot ... **3.** pad **6.** paw pes (pref)
  4. base, hoof, inch (part), sole, step,
  walk **5.** sum up, tread **6.** reckon
  7. residue **9.** calculate, extremity
foot (pert to) ...
bone .. **6.** tarsus **10.** metatarsus
care of .. **8.** pedicure, podiatry
  9. chiropody **11.** chiropodist
lever .. **5.** pedal **7.** treadle
like .. **8.** pediform
measure .. **4.** inch
part .. **3.** toe **4.** arch, heel, sole
prefix .. **4.** pedi
race course (anc) .. **7.** diaulos
reference to .. **5.** pedal, podal
rest .. **4.** rail **7.** cricket, hassock,

ottoman, support **8.** footrail
  9. footstool
sole .. **7.** plantar
unstressed part (Pros) .. **5.** arsis
foot, feet (metric) ... **4.** iamb, mora,
  unit **6.** dactyl, dipody, iambus
  7. anapest, dimeter, pyrrhic, spondee,
  tripody **8.** trimeter **9.** hexameter
  10. heptameter, pentameter
football terms ... **3.** end **4.** trap
  5. guard, slant **6.** center, safety,
  tackle **7.** flanker, lineman **8.** goalpost,
  receiver **9.** touchdown
  10. linebacker, yard marker
  11. quarterback
footed ... **5.** biped **7.** bipedal,
  megapod (large), metered
footing ... **4.** lace, rank **5.** basis,
  dance, tread **6.** status **7.** support
  8. foothold, progress, standing
  9. condition **11.** calculation
footman ... **6.** varlet, walker **7.** servant
  9. attendant **10.** pedestrian
footprint mold ... **7.** moulage
footway ... **7.** catwalk (Naut)
fop ... **3.** nob **4.** Adon, buck, dude
  5. dandy, puppy, sport, swell
  6. Adonis, masher **7.** coxcomb,
  gallant **9.** exquisite, pretender
  12. boulevardier
foppish ... **6.** dapper, spruce **7.** finical,
  foplike **8.** dandyish **9.** conceited,
  dandified
for ... **2.** to **3.** pro **5.** spite
  7. because, instead **8.** behalf of
  9. intending **10.** indicating
  11. preparation
for (pert to) ...
each .. **3.** per
example .. **2.** as, eg **4.** vide
  13. exempli gratia
fear .. **4.** lest
most part .. **6.** mostly **7.** chiefly,
  usually **9.** generally
nothing .. **6.** gratis, naught
  9. lagniappe (lagnappe)
this reason .. **4.** ergo **5.** hence
forage ... **4.** food, mast, raid **5.** spoil
  6. browse, ravage **7.** plunder
  9. pasturage
foramen ... **4.** pore **7.** opening, orifice,
  passage **8.** fenestra
foray ... **4.** raid **6.** ravage, sortie
  7. pillage **9.** incursion
forbear ... **4.** lose, shun **5.** avoid
  6. desist, endure **7.** abstain, decline,
  refrain **8.** part with **9.** be patient
forbearance ... **5.** mercy **6.** disuse,
  lenity **8.** leniency, mildness, patience
  9. tolerance **10.** abstinence,
  temperance **11.** forgiveness,
  placability
forbid ... **3.** ban **4.** deny, tabu, veto
  5. debar, taboo **6.** disbar, hinder,
  impede, oppose **7.** exclude, inhibit,
  prevent **8.** disallow, preclude, prohibit
  9. interdict, proscribe
  11. countermand
forbiddance ... **3.** ban **4.** veto
  11. unallowable **12.** illiberality,

interdiction, proscription
forbidden city . . . 5. Lhasa (Tibet),
Pekin (walled, now Peiping)
forbidden food (Bib) . . . 4. tref
8. terephah
forbidding . . . 4. grim, ugly 5. plain,
stern 6. fierce, odious 9. offensive,
revolting 10. prevention, unpleasant
11. displeasing, prohibitive
force . . . 3. vim, vis 4. dint, make, urge
5. drive, impel, power, press, repel,
staff, vigor 6. coerce, compel, effect,
energy, extort, hasten, strain
7. impetus, meaning 8. eloquent,
momentum, pressure, validity,
violence 9. constrain, influence,
puissance 10. compulsion, constraint
11. necessitate
force (pert to) . . .
alleged . . 2. od
armed . . 4. army 5. posse
by seizure . . 5. usurp
down . . 7. detrude
full . . 5. amain
substance . . 8. catalyst
unit . . 4. dyne 5. staff, tonal
7. poundal
forced . . . 7. labored 9. reluctant,
unwilling 10. artificial, compulsory,
farfetched 11. constrained
forced feeding . . . 6. gavage
forceful . . . 5. valid 6. mighty, potent,
strong 7. dynamic 8. eloquent,
emphatic, vigorous 9. effective,
energetic 10. compulsory
forces . . . 4. army 5. armed 6. troops
forcible . . . 6. cogent, mighty, potent
7. violent, weighty 8. eloquent,
emphatic, positive, puissant
9. energetic 10. compulsory,
impressive 11. influential
forcible entry . . . 10. effraction
forciform . . . 6. forked 7. furcate
11. forficulate 14. scissors–shaped
ford . . . 4. wade 5. cross 6. stream
fore . . . 3. way 5. front, prior, track
6. former 7. journey
forebear . . . 4. sire 5. elder 6. parent
8. ancestor 10. antecedent,
forefather, progenitor
forebode . . . 5. augur 7. betoken,
portend, predict, presage 8. foretell
15. prognostication
foreboding . . . 6. augury 8. croaking,
sinister 11. pessimistic, presagement
12. apprehension, presentiment
forecast . . . 4. bode, plan 6. scheme
7. foresee, fortune, predict
8. foretell, prophecy 9. calculate,
foresight, foretoken 10. foreordain,
prediction 12. predetermine
forecaster . . . 4. seer 5. vates 6. oracle
7. diviner, palmist, prophet
8. dopester, presager 10. astrologer,
soothsayer 11. Nostradamus
13. meteorologist 14. prognosticator
foreclose . . . 5. debar 6. hinder
7. prevent, shut out 8. preclude
10. dispossess
foredoom . . . 4. doom 7. predict
12. predestinate

foredoomed . . . 3. fey 5. fatal
8. accursed
forefather . . . 4. sire 5. elder 6. parent
8. ancestor, forebear 10. progenitor
forefinger . . . 5. index
foregather . . . 4. meet 7. convene
8. assemble 9. encounter
forego, forgo . . . 6. pass by 7. neglect,
precede 8. renounce
foregoing . . . 4. past 5. above
6. former, prefix 7. leading
10. antecedent
foregone . . . 4. past 8. previous
11. predestined, preordained,
preresolved 13. predetermined
foregone conclusion . . . 9. certainty
forehead . . . 4. brow 8. calvaria,
glabella, sinciput 9. assurance
10. effrontery
forehead, divination by . . .
11. metopomancy
forehead, frontal . . . 7. metopic
foreign . . . 4. xeno (comb form)
5. alien, fremd 6. exotic, remote
7. distant, outside (of country),
strange 8. excluded 9. extrinsic,
peregrine, unrelated 10. extraneous,
outlandish 11. incongruous
12. adventitious
foreign (pert to) . . .
accent . . 4. burr 6. brogue, patois
7. dialect
crystals (Geol) . . 7. epigene
disease . . 7. ecdemic
insertion . . 13. interpolation
place . . 6. forane
quarter . . 4. Para 5. Latin 6. French
7. enclave
service residence . . 9. consulate
foreigner . . . 5. alien 6. gringo
8. outsider, stranger 9. outlander,
uitlander 10. tramontane
12. ultramontane
foreland . . . 8. headland 10. promontory
forelock . . . 4. bang 7. cowlick, fetlock
8. linchpin 9. cotter pin, fastening
(armor)
foreman . . . 4. boss 5. chief 6. leader
7. juryman, overman 10. supervisor
14. superintendent
foremost . . . 5. chief, first, front
7. leading, supreme 8. headmost
13. most important
forensic . . . 10. rhetorical
13. argumentative
foreordain . . . 7. destine 9. predicate,
preordain 12. foreordinate,
predestinate, predetermine
forerun . . . 6. herald 7. advance,
prelude, presage 8. announce,
antecede 9. forestall, introduce,
prefigure 10. anticipate, foreshadow
forerunner . . . 4. omen, sign 6. augury,
herald 8. ancestor 9. harbinger,
messenger, precursor 10. forefather,
foreganger, progenitor, prognostic
11. predecessor
foreshadow . . . 6. shadow (beforehand)
7. presage 9. adumbrate, prefigure
foresight . . . 8. sagacity 9. prevision
10. precaution, prediction,
prescience, prevoyance, providence

11. omniscience 13. foreknowledge

forest... 4. wold, wood 5. grove,
woods 6. jungle, timber 8. woodland
9. greenwood 10. timberland,
wilderness

forest (pert to)...
deity.. 3. Pan 7. Aegipan
fire.. 5. crown, stand 6. ground
7. surface
fire–finding instrument.. 7. alidade
glade.. 6. camass (camas, cammas)
love of, lover of.. 9. nemophile,
nemophily
regarding.. 6. sylvan 7. nemoral
tilled.. 7. thwaite
warden.. 6. ranger

forestall... 6. hinder 7. exclude, head
off, prevent 9. intercept
10. anticipate, monopolize

foretell... 4. bode, spae 5. augur,
insee 7. portend, predict, presage
8. forebode, forecast, prophesy
10. vaticinate 13. prognosticate

foretelling... 6. augury 7. fatidic
9. fatidical, prophetic 10. vaticinant

forethought... 8. prepense, prudence
9. foresight, provident 10. deliberate,
precaution 12. aforethought,
anticipation 13. premeditation

foretoken... 4. omen 7. presage
8. foreshow, indicant 10. presignify
13. preindication, prognosticate

foretooth... 5. biter 6. cutter
7. incisor 9. milk tooth

forever... 3. ake (Maori), aye (ay)
4. olam, ever 6. always, eterne
7. endless 8. infinity 9. continual,
perpetual 10. constantly, invariably
11. ceaselessly, continually,
incessantly, perpetually, unceasingly
12. interminably, unchangeably
13. everlastingly

forewarning... 4. omen 7. caution,
portent 9. informing 10. admonition,
foreboding

foreword... 5. proem 7. preface,
prelude 8. exordium, preamble,
prologue 12. introduction

forfeit... 4. fine, lose, loss 5. forgo,
mulct 6. forego, pledge 7. deodand,
penalty

forfeiture... 4. fine, loss 5. dédit,
mulct 7. penalty 10. amercement

forfend... 5. avert 6. forbid 7. prevent,
protect 8. preserve, prohibit

forfex... 6. shears

forgather... 4. meet 7. consort,
convene 8. assemble 9. encounter
10. fraternize

forge... 4. coin, form, mint 5. feign
6. create, smithy, stithy, swinge
7. falsify, imitate 8. bloomery,
smithery 11. counterfeit

forgery... 4. sham 7. fiction
9. falsehood, invention
11. counterfeit, fabrication
13. falsification

forget... 4. omit 5. lapse, remit
6. slight 7. neglect 9. disregard
11. disremember

forgetfulness... 5. Lethe (Myth), lotus
(legend) 7. amnesia, amnesty

8. Manasseh, oblivion
12. carelessness, heedlessness
13. obliviousness

forgive... 5. remit, spare 6. acquit,
excuse, pardon 7. condone

forgiveness... 6. pardon 9. remission
10. absolution 11. condonation,
exoneration, magnanimity

forgiving... 6. humane 8. merciful,
placable 9. remissive
11. magnanimous

forgo... 4. quit 5. leave, waive 6. give
up, resign 7. abstain, forbear, forfeit,
forsake, neglect, refrain 8. overlook,
renounce 9. do without
10. relinquish

forhoo... 7. abandon, despise

fork... 4. tine 5. prong 6. expend, pay
out 7. dilemma, diverge
10. divaricate, divergence,
headstream 11. bifurcation

fork (pert to)...
garden.. 5. graip
pickle.. 13. runcible spoon
table.. 5. salad 6. dinner, oyster
7. dessert 8. ice–cream

forked... 5. bifid 6. horned, ramous
7. divided, furcate 8. branched,
crotched 9. ambiguous, equivocal
10. bifurcated, branchlike

forlorn... 4. reft 5. alone 6. abject,
bereft 8. deserted, desolate, forsaken,
helpless, pitiable 9. abandoned,
destitute, miserable 10. friendless
12. disconsolate

form... 4. body, cast, idea, mold, rite
5. build, guise, model, shape
6. beauty, create, figure, invent,
ritual 7. compose, contour, formula,
outline, pattern, profile, species,
variety 8. ceremony, conceive,
document 9. establish, formality
10. appearance 11. arrangement
12. conformation 13. configuration,
questionnaire 15. conventionality

form (pert to)...
bust.. 6. taille
chainlike.. 8. catenate
deceptive.. 5. ghost 7. specter
8. phantasm
display.. 4. rack
good.. 4. chic 6. fettle
government.. 6. polity
hollow.. 5. shell
into fabric.. 4. knit, spin 5. weave
primitive.. 9. prototype
spiral.. 5. helix
suffix.. 5. shape 10. resembling

formal... 4. prim 5. exact, stiff
6. solemn 7. orderly, outward,
precise, regular, stilted 8. affected,
apparent, starched 9. formative
10. ceremonial, methodical
11. pharisaical, ritualistic, superficial
12. conventional

formal introduction... 5. debut
12. presentation

formalities... 5. rites 9. etiquette
10. ceremonies

formal warning... 5. alarm 6. caveat
12. caveat emptor

format... 4. size 5. shape, style

formation... 4. form 5. order
　9. structure 11. arrangement,
　composition 12. construction
formation (pert to)...
　chain (twisted).. 9. torquated
　geologic.. 7. terrain, terrane
　military.. 4. line 5. herse 7. echelon
　sand.. 4. dene, dune
formed... 4. made 5. built 7. created,
　decided, matured, settled 8. arranged
　9. fashioned, organized
　11. constructed
formed (pert to)...
　by law.. 9. corporate
　by lips.. 6. labial
　mountain foot.. 8. piedmont
　on earth's surface.. 7. epigene
　plates (two).. 11. bilamellate
formed into...
　chain.. 8. catenate 9. torquated
　fabric.. 4. spun 5. woven 7. knitted
　mass (hard).. 4. iced 5. caked
　6. frozen 9. congealed
　mosaic.. 9. tessellar 11. tessellated
former... 2. ex 3. old 4. erst, late,
　once, past 5. front, prior 6. passed,
　whilom 7. ancient, earlier 8. previous
　9. foregoing, preceding
　10. antecedent
former days... 3. eld, old 4. yore
formerly... 3. nee 4. erst, once, then
　6. before, whilom 7. one-time
　8. sometime 9. aforetime, erstwhile
　10. heretofore, previously
formicary... 7. anthill 8. ant's nest
formicid... 3. ant 5. emmet
　7. Formica
formidable... 7. fearful 8. alarming,
　dreadful, menacing, terrible
　9. difficult 11. redoubtable,
　threatening
formless... 5. arupa 7. anidian, chaotic
　9. amorphous, shapeless
　13. indeterminate
Formosa, Taiwan...
　capital.. 6. Taipei
　city.. 6. Tainan 7. Hualien, Keelung
　9. Kaohsiung
　group.. 6. Penghu (64 Isls)
　island.. 5. Matsu 6. Quemoy
formula... 3. law 4. form, rule
　5. axiom, creed, lurry, maxim, model
　6. method, recipe, ritual
　12. prescription
forsake... 4. deny, quit, shun 5. avoid,
　leave 6. depart, desert, refuse, reject
　7. abandon 8. renounce, withdraw
　9. surrender
forsaken... 4. lorn 6. vacant 7. forlorn
　8. deserted, lovelorn, rejected
　9. abandoned
forspeak... 5. curse 6. forbid
　7. asperse, bewitch 8. renounce
　10. relinquish
fort... 5. redan, tower 6. abatis,
　castle, escarp, glacis (bank of)
　7. bastion, bulwark, castlet
　8. bastille, fastness, fortress
　10. stronghold 13. fortification,
　propugnaculum
Fort (Fr Ind War)... 9. Necessity
forth... 3. out 4. away 6. abroad,

onward 7. forward, outward
forthright... 5. ahead 7. frankly
　8. forwards 9. downright
　11. immediately, straightway
　13. straightforth
forthwith... 3. now 6. pronto
　8. promptly 9. summarily
　11. immediately, straightway
fortification... 4. wall 5. redan
　6. abatis 7. bastion, citadel, defense,
　parados, ravelin, redoubt 8. barbette
　(part), fortress 10. stronghold
　13. corroboration, strengthening
fortify... 3. arm, man 4. gird 5. add
　to, spike, stank 6. defend, secure
　7. confirm, refresh 8. embattle
　10. adulterate (drink), invigorate,
　strengthen, vitaminize 11. corroborate
fortitude... 6. virtue 7. bravery,
　courage 8. strength 9. endurance
　10. resolution 12. resoluteness
　14. impregnability
fortress... see *fort*
fortuitous... 3. hap 6. chance
　10. accidental 12. unexpectedly
fortunate... 5. happy, lucky 6. timely
　7. favored 10. auspicious,
　prosperous, successful
　12. providential
fortune... 3. hap, lot 4. doom, fate,
　luck 6. chance, estate, riches, wealth
　7. destiny, success 8. accident
　10. prosperity 13. circumstances
fortune (pert to)...
　gypsy.. 4. bahi
　ill.. 9. mischance
　planet (Astrol).. 5. Venus 7. Jupiter
　teller.. 4. seer 5. sibyl, Tyche
　6. oracle 7. spaeman
forward... 2. on, to 3. aid 4. abet,
　bold, fore, help, pert, send, ship,
　vain 5. ahead, along, eager, front,
　impel, ready, relay, saucy, ultra
　6. active, bright, hasten, onward
　7. deliver, earnest, extreme, further,
　radical, willing 8. advanced,
　immodest, impudent, transmit
　9. audacious, encourage
　10. precocious 11. progressive
　12. presumptuous
forward moving (Zool)... 5. proal
　(digestion) 11. mastication
fosse, foss... 3. pit 4. moat 5. canal,
　ditch, fossa, grave 6. cavity, trench
　10. depression
fossil, fossils... 5. relic, stone
　7. antique, remains
fossil (pert to)...
　egg.. 7. ovulite
　footprint.. 7. ichnite
　resin.. 5. amber
　shell.. 6. dolite 8. ammonite
　site.. 8. Badlands (Dakota, Nebraska)
　study of.. 12. paleontology
　toothlike.. 8. conodont
　worm track.. 7. nereite
foster... 4. rear 5. breed, nurse
　7. cherish, gratify, indulge, promote
　9. cultivate
fosterage... 7. nurture
　11. development
foster child... 4. dalt 5. norry (nurry)

7. stepson 8. nursling
12. stepdaughter
fought... see *fight*
foul... 3. bad 4. olid, ugly 5. dirty,
fetid, grimy, nasty, reeky, spoil, sully
6. defame, filthy, malign, odious,
putrid, rotten, thwart, unfair
7. abusive, confuse, noisome,
obscene, profane, unclean
8. entangle, indecent, infamous,
shameful, stagnant, stinking
9. dishonest, obnoxious
10. complicate, malodorous,
scurrilous 11. contaminate,
ill–smelling, unfavorable
12. inauspicious, unpropitious
foul play... 6. murder, unfair (play)
7. perfidy 8. violence 9. deception,
treachery 10. unfairness
found... 3. fix 4. base, cast 5. endow,
set up 6. attach, create 9. establish,
institute, originate
foundation... 3. bed 4. base, plot, sill
5. basal, basis 6. legacy, riprap
7. bedding, charity, premise, support
8. cosmetic, creation, donation,
pedestal 9. placement
11. corporation 13. justification
found by chance (thing)...
11. serendipity
founded on...
base.. 10. predicated
evidence.. 10. evidential
experience.. 7. empiric 9. empirical
imagination.. 7. Utopian
founder... 4. fail, fall, sink 6. author
7. capsize, creator, stumble
8. miscarry 9. break down, organizer
10. originator
foundling... 3. oaf 4. waif 5. child
(unclaimed) 6. orphan 8. derelict,
nurseling
fountain... 3. jet, spa 4. font, head,
well 6. spring 9. reservoir
11. scuttlebutt (ship's)
12. fountainhead
fountain (pert to)...
god of.. 4. Fons
Muse (Gr).. 8. Aganippe
nymph.. 5. naiad 6. Egeria
of Lions.. 8. Alhambra (Granada, Sp)
four (pert to)...
bits.. 7. quarter (silver)
Books.. 8. Classics (Chin)
footed.. 8. tetrapod
genii, of Amenti.. 13. Horus' children
group.. 6. tetrad
Hundred.. 5. elect, elite 7. society
letters, word of.. 9. tetragram
seas.. 13. Great Britain's
senses (Bib).. 15. interpretations
four–flusher... 5. cheat, fraud
7. bluffer 8. impostor 9. pretender
fourth (pert to)...
Caliph.. 3. Ali
century martyr.. 8. St Blaise
estate.. 5. press 10. newspapers
part.. 6. fardel 7. quarter
stomach (cow).. 8. abomasum
fowl... 3. hen 6. bantam, Gallus
7. Blue Hen, broiler, chicken,
Dorking, leghorn, Minorca, poultry,

rooster, seafowl 8. pheasant
9. guinea hen, waterfowl
11. chanticleer
fox... 3. cub, tod 4. stag 5. vixen
fox (pert to)...
African.. 4. asse
Asian.. 5. adive 6. corsac
female.. 5. vixen
genus.. 6. Vulpes
hedge (hunter's).. 4. oxer
foot.. 3. pad
Indian.. 10. Algonquian
Russian.. 6. corsac 7. karagan
foxglove... 9. digitalis
foxy... 3. sly 6. artful, crafty
7. cunning
foyer... 5. lobby 8. anteroom, entrance
9. greenroom
fracas... 3. row 5. brawl, melee,
set–to 6. uproar 7. quarrel
9. commotion 11. disturbance
fraction... 3. bit 4. part 5. piece,
scrap 6. sector 7. element, ruction
8. division, fragment 9. commotion
fractious... 4. ugly 5. cross 6. unruly
7. peevish, waspish 8. perverse,
snappish 9. irritable 10. ill–humored
11. disobedient
fracture... 4. rend 5. break, cleft,
crack 6. breach, injury 7. rupture
fragile... 4. weak 5. brash, frail
6. frough (obs), infirm, slight
7. brittle 8. delicate, slattery
9. frangible
fragment... 3. bit, ort 4. chip, grot,
part, snip 5. groat, piece, relic,
scrap, shard, sherd, shred, torso (art)
6. morsel, sippet 7. flinder
8. fraction
fragments... 3. ana 6. fardel, groats,
rubble 8. buttlings, excerpts, flinders
10. miscellany 11. smithereens
fragrance... 4. odor 5. aroma, elemi,
smell 7. incense, perfume
9. redolence
fragrant... 4. nard 5. balmy, olent,
spicy, sweet 7. odorous 8. aromatic,
redolent 9. ambrosial 11. odoriferous
12. sweet–scented
13. sweet–smelling
frail... 4. girl, thin, weak 5. woman
6. basket (fig), feeble, sickly, slimsy
7. brittle, fragile 8. strumpet,
unchaste 10. weak–willed
12. destructible
frailty... 5. fault 6. defect 7. failing
8. thinness, weakness 9. fragility,
infirmity 12. imperfection
frame... 4. body, make, plan, rack,
sess, sill 5. build, easel, grate,
herse, knape 6. abacus, border,
charge (falsely), direct, tenter
7. carcass, chassis, cresset (torch),
fashion, prepare, setting, taboret
8. conceive, skeleton 9. construct
10. prearrange
framework... 4. rack, sill 5. cadre,
shell 6. cradle 7. trestle 8. skeleton
11. scaffolding
France... see also *French*
anc name.. 4. Gaul 6. Gallia
Bay.. 6. Biscay

Botanical Gardens.. 16. Jardin des
Plantes
capital.. 5. Paris
city.. 4. Nice 5. Lyons 7. LeHavre
8. Bordeaux, Toulouse 9. Marseille
10. Strasbourg
dread of.. 11. Gallophobia
island.. 6. Comoro (Afr) Tahiti
7. Corsica, Réunion 10. Guadeloupe
(Leeward), Martinique (Windward)
12. New Caledonia
lover of.. 10. Gallophile
mountain.. 4. Alps, Jura 5. Pelat
8. Pyrenees 9. Mont Blanc 11. Pic
Montcalm
port.. 4. Caen 5. Brest, Havre
6. Calais, Toulon 8. Bordeaux
9. Dunkerque (Dunkirk)
resort.. 3. Pau 5. Vichy 6. Cannes,
Menton (Mentone) 7. Riviera
11. Aix–les–Bains (anc)
river.. 3. Lys 4. Yser 5. Aisne, Eiser,
Loire, Meuse, Rhône, Seine
Southern.. 4. Midi
Verdun battle site.. 4. Vaux
franchise... 4. vote 5. right 6. patent
7. freedom, license 8. immunity,
suffrage 9. exemption
frank... 4. free, mail, open 5. blunt,
naive, plain 6. candid, direct, honest
7. artless, liberal, sincere
8. generous 9. ingenuous, outspoken
10. unreserved 11. frankfurter
15. straightforward, unsophisticated
frankincense... 4. thus 8. gum resin,
olibanum 9. fragrance
Frankish (pert to)...
dynasty.. 11. Carolingian, Merovingian
king.. 5. Pepin 6. Clovis
law.. 5. Salic
site.. 4. Gaul
tribe (anc).. 6. Salian
Franklin, Benjamin... 11. Poor
Richard
frantic... 3. mad 4. mang 5. moved,
rabid 7. furious 8. frenetic, frenzied.
9. delirious, desperate, turbulent
10. distracted, distraught
11. overwrought
frappé... 3. ice 5. chill 6. freeze
7. dessert, mixture (sweet)
8. beverage
fraternal... 4. kind 5. order, twins
7. society 8. friendly 9. brotherly
fraud... 4. fake, sham, wile 5. cheat,
covin, craft, guile 6. deceit, ringer
7. defraud, roguery 8. artifice,
cozenage, impostor, subtlety,
swindler, trickery 9. deception,
imposture, stratagem 10. imposition
13. circumvention
fraudulence... 9. improbity
10. subreption
fraudulent... 4. fake, wily 5. snide
6. crafty, quacky 7. cunning, knavish
8. cheating, guileful, spurious
9. deceitful, deceiving, deceptive,
designing, dishonest, insidious
10. fallacious 11. counterfeit,
treacherous
fraught... 4. lade, load 5. cargo,
equip, laden 6. burden, filled

7. freight 9. freighted, transport
fray... 4. fret (cloth), wear 5. broil,
dread, melee, panic, ravel 6. affray,
combat, fright, hassle, terror, tumult
7. contest, frazzle, ruction
9. commotion 12. apprehension
freak... 4. flam, lune, whim 5. fancy,
prank, sport 6. streak, vagary
7. caprice, checker, crochet, monster
9. eccentric, variegate
11. monstrosity 12. whimsicality
freakish... 7. curious 9. eccentric,
fantastic, whimsical 10. capricious,
changeable
freck... 4. bold, hale 5. eager, frack,
lusty, ready, stout 6. strong
7. forward 8. desirous
freckle... 4. mark, spot 7. blemish,
ephelis, lentigo, speckle 10. ferntickle
free... 3. rid 4. easy, open 5. clear,
frank, loose 6. acquit, candid,
exempt, gratis, immune, vacant
7. absolve, inexact, manumit, not
busy, release, relieve, unbound
8. liberate 9. extricate, footloose,
voluntary 10. autonomous, gratuitous,
unconfined, unhampered
11. emancipated 12. uncontrolled,
unrestrained, unrestricted
free (pert to)...
bacteria.. 7. aseptic, sterile
difficulty.. 9. extricate
doubt.. 7. resolve
flesh (dietary).. 6. maigre
knots.. 7. enodate, unravel
reproach.. 9. blameless
slavery.. 7. manumit 10. emancipate
suspicion.. 5. clear, purge 6. acquit
7. absolve 9. exculpate, exonerate
sweetness.. 3. sec
freebooter... 5. rover 6. pirate
8. pillager 9. plunderer 10. filibuster
freed... 3. rid 6. loosed, spared,
untied 8. released 9. delivered,
liberated 10. manumitted
11. emancipated
freedom... 6. candor 7. leisure, liberty,
license 8. latitude 9. exemption,
privilege 11. manumission
12. emancipation, independence
freedom (pert to)...
abused.. 7. liberty (excess), license
from doubt.. 9. assurance, certitude
from sepsis.. 7. asepsis
Freedom Our Rock (motto)...
7. Tammany (1789)
free enterprise... 6. policy
8. commerce 10. capitalism
15. noninterference
freely... 6. gratis 7. largely, readily
9. bountiful, copiously, liberally,
willingly 10. abundantly, generously
11. bounteously, plenteously,
plentifully, voluntarily 12. gratuitously
freeze... 3. ice 5. be–ice, chill
6. steeve 7. congeal, terrify
8. preserve, solidify 9. stabilize
11. anesthetize, refrigerate
freezing, science of... 10. cyrogenics
freight... 4. load, ship 5. cargo, laden,
train 6. burden, charge, lading
7. fraught, rattler 8. shipment

9. transport 14. transportation
freight boat... 5. barge 9. freighter
freit, freet... 4. omen 5. charm
fremd (obs)... 5. alien 7. foreign,
  hostile 9. unrelated
French (people)...
  artist, painter.. 4. Doré 5. Corot,
    David, Monet 6. Gervex, Greuze,
    Renoir 7. Gauguin, Lemoine, Matisse
    8. Daubigny, Rousseau
  author.. 4. Hugo, Loti, Zola
    5. Dumas, Renan, Verne (Jules)
    6. Balzac, Proust
  caricaturist.. 7. Gavarni
  chemist.. 7. Gautier, Holbach, Pasteur
  composer.. 4. Lalo 5. Bizet, Ravel
    6. Gounod 7. Debussy
  conqueror (anc).. 6. Clovis
  crusader.. 7. Godfrey (of Bouillon)
  dramatist.. 6. Favart 8. Quinault
  dynasty.. 5. Caput 6. Valois
  Foreign Legion creator, 1831..
    8. Philippe (Louis)
  impressionist.. 5. Monet 8. Pissarro
  marshal.. 3. Ney 4. Foch, Niel, Saxe
    5. Murat
  naturalist.. 8. Audebert
  navigator.. 9. Freycinet
  pantomimist.. 7. Pierrot
  patron saint.. 5. Denis 6. Martin
  philosopher.. 5. Bayle, Camus
    6. Pascal 7. Abelard 8. Rousseau
    9. Descartes
  physician.. 7. Laveran
  physicist.. 5. Binet 6. Ampere
  poet.. 6. Villon 7. Gilbert, Mistral
    8. Rousseau 9. Deschamps
  radical.. 7. Jacobin
  scientist.. 5. Curie 7. Pasteur
  sculptor.. 4. Etex 5. Barye, Rodin
    6. Gerome, Millet
  statesman.. 4. Coty 5. Laine, Laval,
    Morny 6. Carnot 7. Briande, Herriot
    8. DeGaulle
  therapist.. 4. Coué
French (pert to)...
  academic rank.. 6. agrégé
  Academy.. 12. The Institute
  and.. 2. et
  annuity.. 5. rente
  anthem.. 12. Marseillaise
  article.. 2. la, le, un 3. les, une
  beast.. 4. bête
  calender (Rev).. 6. Nivose 7. Ventose
  champagne.. 2. Ay
  cheese.. 4. Brie 6. Chevre
    9. Camembert
  chorus (male).. 7. orpheon
  coach.. 6. fiacre
  coat–of–arms.. 10. fleur–de–lis
  coffee (black).. 8. café noir
  company (Bus).. 3. cie
  crown (gold coin).. 3. ecu
  cult (art).. 7. Dadaism
  daisy.. 10. marguerite
  dance.. 3. bal 5. gavot 6. cancan
  decree, edict.. 5. arrêt
  dialect.. 6. patois
  dugout.. 4. abri
  father.. 4. père
  fortification.. 7. parados
  fugitive.. 6. émigré

God.. 4. Dieu
hairdresser.. 7. friseur
hat.. 5. beret 7. chapeau
here.. 3. ici
inn.. 6. hostel
lace.. 5. Cluny
language (Provence).. 9. Provençal
laugh.. 3. ris
liquor.. 8. absinthe (banned 1915)
mask.. 4. loup
morning.. 5. matin
mountain peak.. 3. pic
narcissus.. 10. polyanthus
native.. 8. Gallican
nursemaid.. 5. bonne
ornaments (set of).. 6. parure
outcast.. 5. Agote, Cagot 6. pariah
pancake.. 5. crepe
parliament.. 5. Sénat
pastry.. 7. dariole, galette
plane.. 5. avion
poem, poetry.. 3. dit 6. aubade,
  rondel
police.. 6. Sûreté 8. gendarme
political club.. 7. Jacobin
porcelain.. 6. Sèvres 7. Limoges
priest.. 4. abbe, père
racecourse.. 7. Auteuil
restaurant.. 4. café 6. bistro
sauce.. 8. ravigote 9. allemande
school.. 5. école, lycée
school of painting.. 8. Barbizon
securities.. 6. rentes
smoking room.. 9. estaminet
soldier.. 5. poilu 6. Zouave
stable.. 6. écurie
stock exchange.. 6. Bourse
storm.. 5. orage
street.. 3. rue
summer.. 3. été
theater.. 10. Comédie Française
verse.. 3. lai 4. alba 6. rondel
  7. ballade, virelay
wall.. 3. mur
water.. 3. eau
wind.. 7. mistral
wine.. 5. Medoc 6. Barsac, brandy,
  claret, Cognac, masdeu 8. Bordeaux,
  Burgundy, sauterne 10. Beaujolais
world.. 5. monde
Frenchman... 4. frog, Gaul 6. froggy,
  Picard (of Picardy) 8. Parisian
  9. frogeater
Frenchy... 6. Gallic
frenzied... 4. amok 5. rabid
  7. enraged, frantic, madding
  8. maddened 9. turbulent
  11. overwrought
frenzy... 3. mad 5. furor, mania
  7. frantic, madness 8. delirium
  9. agitation 10. excitement,
  turbulence
frequent... 3. oft 5. haunt, often,
  usual 6. common 7. current
  8. familiar, habitual, intimate (with)
  9. recurrent 10. persistent
frequenter... 7. habitué, visitor
  8. attender
frère... 5. friar 7. brother
fresh... 3. new 4. good, lush 5. relay,
  ruddy, sound, sweet 6. florid, lively,
  strong, unused 7. healthy, unfaded,

untried 8. impudent, original
10. additional, refreshing, unimpaired
13. inexperienced
freshen... 4. cool 5. renew 6. revive
7. refresh, sweeten
freshet... 4. gush 5. flood, spate
6. stream 7. outflow, torrent
10. inundation (sudden)
freshman... 5. frosh 6. novice
7. student
freshness... 7. newness, novelty
8. verdancy 9. impudence
11. originality
freshwater fish... 2. id (ide) 4. chub,
dace, inid (porpoise) 6. anabas
7. herring 8. drumfish
fret... 3. eat, nag, orp, rub, vex
4. fray, fume, gall, gnaw, stew
5. adorn, annoy, chafe, grate, tease,
worry 6. abrade, grieve, harass,
plague, strait 7. agitate, consume,
disturb, network, roughen
8. diminish, irritate, ornament
fretful... 5. angry 6. repine 7. peevish,
pettish 8. captious, petulant
9. impatient, irascible, irritable,
plaintive, querulous 10. ill–humored,
ill–natured
friable... 5. crisp, frail, mealy, short
7. brittle 8. fragible
friar... 3. fra 4. fish (small), monk
5. abbot, Minor 6. lister (obs)
7. brother 8. cenobite, Minorite,
Teresian (anc) 9. Carmelite,
Dominican 10. Franciscan
11. Augustinian
friction... 7. erasure, rubbing
8. clashing 9. attrition, disaccord
10. resistance 12. disagreement
13. counteraction
friend... 3. ami, pal 4. ally, amie,
chum, kith, sect 5. amigo, crony
7. comrade 8. promoter
9. associate, attendant, companion,
supporter 10. benefactor, sweetheart,
well–wisher
Friend... 6. Quaker
friendless... 5. alone 7. forlorn
8. helpless 9. destitute (friends)
friendly... 3. sib 4. kind 7. affable
8. amicable, homelike, sociable
9. favorable 10. harmonious,
hospitable 11. comfortable
Friendly Islands... 5. Tonga
friendship... 4. kelt 5. amity
7. harmony 8. good will, relation
9. affection, right hand
10. attachment 12. friendliness
frieze... 4. band (sculptured) 5. adorn,
chase 6. taenia (Doric) 8. ornament,
trimming 10. decoration, embroidery
Frigga, Norse Myth (pert to)...
goddess.. 3. sky
maid.. 5. Fulla
named for.. 6. Friday
wife of.. 4. Odin
fright... 3. awe 4. fear, ogre 5. alarm,
panic, scare, shock 6. terror
7. eyesore 13. consternation
frighten... 3. cow 5. alarm, appal,
scare 7. startle, terrify 10. intimidate
frightened... 3. rad 5. eerie, timid

6. afraid 8. skittish
frightful... 5. awful, great 6. horrid
7. hideous 8. alarming, dreadful,
horrible, shocking, terrible, terrific
11. frightening
frightfulness... 13. atrociousness
15. Schrecklichkeit
frigid... 3. icy 4. cold 5. stiff
6. formal 8. freezing, impotent,
reserved
frijol, frijole... 4. bean
frill... 4. purl 5. jabot, ruche (rouche)
6. border, edging, ruffle 8. furbelow
9. frillback (pigeon) 11. superfluity
fringe... 4. lace, loma, tuft 5. thrum
6. border, edging, margin 8. ciliella,
trimming
frisk... 4. skip 5. brisk, caper 6. frolic,
gambol, lively, search 7. disport,
rejoice
frisky... 3. gay 6. lively 7. playful
8. sportive 10. frolicsome
frisson... 5. chill 6. quiver, shiver, thrill
7. shudder 10. excitement
frivolous... 5. giddy, petty 6. fickle,
slight 7. fatuous, trivial 9. worthless
13. shallow–witted
frock... 4. gown, wrap 5. dress, tunic
6. jersey, kirtle (anc), mantle
7. garment, soutane
frog... 3. pad (horse's) 4. Rana, toad
5. Anura 6. peeper 7. croaker,
paddock, tadpole 8. Amphibia,
pollywog 9. Batrachia, Frenchman,
Salientia 10. hoarseness
froglike... 6. ranine
frogman... 5. diver 6. seaman
7. swimmer 9. Frenchman
frog pond... 8. ranarium
frolic... 3. fun 4. lark, ogle, play,
ramp, romp 5. binge, caper, frisk,
prank, spree, trick 6. gambol, shindy
7. disport, marlock, shindig, wassail
8. carousal
frolicsome... 3. gay 5. merry 6. frisky
7. playful, waggish 8. sportive
from... 2. at, de (pref), of 3. apo
(pref) 4. away 5. above, out of
6. source 8. away from, downward
from (pert to)...
beginning to end.. 4. over 7. through
egg to apple.. 16. ab ovo usque ad
mala
head to foot.. 7. cap–a–pie
slang.. 10. soup to nuts 11. stem to
stern
front... 3. bow, van 4. face, fore
5. aface, afore, blind (false), forne
(obs) 6. before, façade 7. obverse
8. confront, mediator 9. forefront
10. appearance, figurehead
11. affectation 12. intermediary
frontier defense... 11. arcifinious
frontiersman... 5. Boone 6. Carson
(Kit)
frost... 3. ice, mat 4. cold, foam, rime
5. chill 6. freeze, whiten 7. failure
8. severity (manner)
14. unfriendliness
frosty... 3. icy 4. cold, gray, rimy
5. chill, hoary, white 6. frigid
8. freezing, inimical 10. unfriendly

froth... 4. foam, scum, suds 5. spume, yeast 6. lather 7. bubbles

frothy... 5. foamy, light, sudsy 7. spumous 8. sillabub

frow... 4. froe (tool), wife 5. woman 6. maenad 8. slattern

froward... 5. cross 7. peevish, wayward 8. perverse, petulant, scolding, shrewish, untoward 9. obstinate 10. refractory, unyielding 11. disobedient 12. ungovernable

frowl... 9. guillemot

frown... 5. gloom, lower, scowl 6. glower

frowsey, frowzy... 5. musty 7. unkempt 8. slovenly 9. offensive 10. discordant, disordered

frozen... 4. cold 5. frore (anc), froze, gelid, glacé 6. chilly, mousse 7. chilled 9. congealed, terrified, unfeeling, unmovable 10. unyielding 11. coldhearted 12. refrigerated

frugal... 5. chary 6. meager, saving 7. careful, sparing, thrifty 9. provident 10. economical, unwasteful 11. inexpensive 12. parsimonious

frugality... 6. thrift 7. economy 9. parsimony

fruit (types of)... 3. fig 4. lime, pear, plum, pome 5. apple, berry, drupe, grape, guava, lemon, mango, melon, olive, peach, pomum 6. banana, cherry, orange, papaya, pawpaw, pomelo 7. apricot, azarole, genipap, tangelo 8. shaddock 9. persimmon, tangerine 10. grapefruit, watermelon 11. pomegranate

fruit... 4. diet, food 5. yield, young 7. benefit, product 9. offspring, outgrowth, posterity 11. consequence

fruit (pert to)...
aggregate.. 7. etaerio
astringent.. 4. sloe
basket.. 6. pottle
buttercup.. 6. achene 8. achenium
class.. 6. simple 9. aggregate 10. collective
cordial.. 7. ratafia (ratafee)
decay.. 4. blet
dried.. 6. raisin 7. apricot
drink.. 3. ade 6. nectar
Goddess.. 6. Pomona
gourd.. 4. pepo 7. chayote
grapefruit.. 6. pomelo
imperfect.. 6. nubbin
jelly substance.. 6. pectin
Jove's.. 9. persimmon
part.. 7. epicarp 8. mesocarp, pericarp 9. sarcocarp
preserve.. 7. compote 9. marmalade
pulpy.. 3. uva
rose.. 3. hip
study of.. 9. carpology
tree.. 4. date, nuts 5. regma 6. camato, samara (winged)
tropical.. 3. fig 4. date 5. guava, mango, papaw (pawpaw) 6. papaya

fruitful... 7. fertile, uberous 8. abundant, prolific 9. plenteous

fruitfulness, goddess of... 7. Demeter

fruitless... 4. vain 6. barren 7. sterile, useless 10. profitless 11. ineffectual 12. unprofitable, unsuccessful

frump... 3. vex 4. mock, snub 5. crone, flout, shrew 6. gossip, insult 7. provoke 8. irritate

frustrate... 4. balk, bilk, foil 5. block, cross, elude 6. baffle, blight, defeat, outwit, thwart 7. nullify 8. confound 9. checkmate 10. circumvent, disappoint, disconcert

frustrater... 7. marplot 8. thwarter

frustration... 4. balk 6. defeat, fiasco 13. circumvention 14. disappointment 15. disillusionment

fry... 4. cook 5. brood (fish), group, saute, young 7. stir-fry 9. offspring

frying pan... 6. spider 7. skillet

fubsy... 5. plump, short 6. chubby

fuddle... 4. bout (drinking) 5. drink (strong), spree 6. muddle, tipple 7. confuse 9. confusion, inebriate

fudge... 4. fake 5. candy, cheat 6. bungle, humbug 7. trump up 8. nonsense 9. makeshift 10. substitute 11. counterfeit

Fuegian... 3. Ona 5. tribe 6. Indian, Yakgan 8. Alikuluf 14. Tierra del Fuego (pert to)

fuel... 3. gas, log, oil 4. coal, coke, peat 5. diesel, elding 7. gasohol, nuclear, synfuel 8. gasoline 9. petroleum 11. combustible

fugie... 4. cock (nonfighter) 6. coward

fugient... 7. fleeing 8. retiring

fugitive... 5. exile 6. outlaw, roving 7. fleeing, refugee, roaming, runaway 8. fleeting, unstable, vagabond, volatile 9. fugacious, strolling, uncertain 10. evanescent

fugue... 5. theme, tonal 7. amnesia, stretto (stretta) 9. psychosis, ricercare

fulcrum... 4. axis, bait, prop 5. pivot, scale (fish), thole 7. support

fulfill... 4. meet 6. finish, redeem 7. execute, satisfy 8. complete 10. accomplish, effectuate

fulfillment... 8. fruition 9. execution, flowering 10. completion 11. performance 14. accomplishment

full... 3. fat 4. fill 5. drunk, sated 6. entire, filled, rotund 7. perfect, plenary, replete, satiety 8. abundant, adequate, complete, occupied, resonant, satiated, thorough 9. satisfied

full (pert to)...
blooded.. 6. virile 8. rubicund 12. thoroughbred
bloom.. 8. anthesis, blooming, maturity
control.. 7. mastery 10. domination
force.. 5. amain
house.. 3. SRO

full of...
cracks.. 6. rimose
hollows.. 8. lacunose
love.. 7. amative, amatory
meaning.. 5. pithy 10. meaningful
openings (tiny).. 6. porous
sand.. 7. arenose 8. sabulous
substance.. 5. meaty

suffix .. 3. ose
thorns .. 6. briary
vigor .. 5. lusty
fulness, fullness ... 4. much
    7. orotund, pleroma, satiety, surfeit
    9. abundance, greatness, plenitude,
    repletion, resonance 10. perfection
    12. completeness
fulsome ... 3. bad, fat 4. base, foul,
    full 5. nasty, plump, suave
    7. copious, overfed 8. abundant
    9. offensive, overgrown, repulsive
    10. disgusting
Fulton's Folly ... 8. Clermont
fumble ... 5. grope 6. bungle, huddle,
    mumble 7. confuse
fume ... 4. odor, rage, rant, reek
    5. anger, smoke, steam, vapor
    8. outburst 10. excitement,
    exhalation
fun ... 4. gell, jest, joke, play 5. chaff,
    sport 9. amusement, merriment
function ... 3. act, use 4. duty, rite,
    role, work 5. party 6. office
    7. calling, operate, purpose, service
    8. ceremony, province
    10. providence
function (pert to) ...
  math .. 4. sine 6. cosine
  mind .. 8. ideation
  social .. 3. tea
functional ... 8. official 9. operative
    11. ceremonious, utilitarian
fund ... 5. basis, money 6. bottom,
    supply 7. capital, provide, revenue
    10. foundation, groundwork
fundamental ... 4. tone 5. basal, basic,
    vital 7. basilar, organic, primary,
    radical 8. original, rudiment
    9. elemental, essential, principle
    10. elementary
Fundamental Orders (US Hist) ...
    8. document (1639) 12. Constitution
    (first, 1639 Conn)
funds ... 5. means 6. assets, moneys
    8. finances
funeral ... 5. rites 6. burial 8. exequies
    9. obsequies 10. procession
funeral (pert to) ...
  bell .. 5. knell
  ceremony .. 6. exequy
  hymn, song .. 5. dirge, éloge, elogy
    7. requiem 8. threnody
  oration, poem .. 5. elegy
  pile .. 4. pyre
  procession .. 6. exequy 7. cortege
  vase .. 3. urn
funereal ... 3. sad 4. dark 6. dismal,
    solemn 8. exequial, mournful
    9. dirgelike
fungi ... 5. rusts, Uredo 6. mildew
    7. Boletus
fungoid ... 6. fungal, fungus
fungus ... 4. bunt, mold, rust, smut
    5. ergot, morel, uredo 6. agaric,
    mildew 7. aminita, blewits, boletus,
    geaster, truffle 8. mushroom, puffball
    9. toadstool
fungus, edible ... 5. morel 7. truffle
    8. mushroom
funguslike ... 6. agaric
funk ... 4. kick, odor, rage 5. panic,

smell (bad), smoke, spark 6. flinch,
fright, shrink, terror 8. frighten
    9. cowardice, touchwood
funnel ... 4. cone, flue, pipe, tube
    6. hopper 7. channel
funnel–shaped ... 8. choanoid
funny ... 3. odd 5. comic, droll, queer,
    witty 7. comical, rowboat (Eng),
    strange 8. humorous 9. eccentric,
    laughable
fur ... 3. fox 4. mink, pelt, seal, vair
    5. coypu, fitch, genet, otter, sable,
    skunk 6. badger, ermine, martin,
    nutria 7. miniver (anc) 8. squirrel
    10. chinchilla
fur (pert to) ...
  collective .. 6. peltry
  cover .. 4. pelt 6. pelage
  garment .. 4. robe 5. stole 6. tippet
    7. pelisse
  tippet .. 8. palatine
furbish ... 3. rub 4. vamp 5. clean,
    scour 6. polish 7. burnish, touch up
    8. renovate 9. embellish
Furies ... 5. Dirae 6. Alecto, ghosts,
    Semnae 7. Erinyes (Erinys), Magaera,
    spirits (avenging) 9. Eumenides,
    Tisiphone
Furies, The Three ... 6. Alecto
    7. Magaera 9. Tisiphone
furious ... 5. angry, hasty 6. fierce
    7. frantic, violent 8. frenzied,
    vehement 9. impetuous, turbulent
    10. boisterous, passionate,
    tumultuous 11. overwrought
furl ... 4. roll, wrap 6. bundle, inroll
furlough ... 5. leave 14. leave of
    absence
furnace ... 4. etna, kiln, oven 5. forge,
    stove 7. caldron, reactor, rotator,
    smelter
furnish ... 3. fit 4. bear, give, lend
    5. adorn, cater, endow, equip, indue
    6. afford, fit out, render, supply
    7. appoint, provide
furnishing ... 7. fitting 8. fixtures,
    ornament 9. adornment, apparatus,
    furniture, provision 10. enrichment
furnish with ...
  funds .. 5. endow
  meals .. 5. board, cater
  Mil equipment .. 8. accoutre
  tapestry .. 5. arras
  wings .. 3. imp
furniture ... 5. goods 6. Empire, graith,
    outfit 7. Regency (Regence)
    8. hardware, Sheraton, supplies
    9. equipment 10. decoration,
    housewares 11. Chippendale,
    Renaissance
furor ... 4. fury, rage 5. anger, craze
    6. fervor, flurry, frenzy, furore, tumult
    7. madness 10. excitement,
    turbulence
furrow ... 3. rut 4. plow 6. groove,
    gutter, trench 7. channel, wrinkle
furrowed ... 5. rutty 6. rivose
    7. grooved
further ... 3. aid, and, new, yet
    4. abet, more 7. advance, develop,
    improve, promote, remoter, thither
    10. additional

furtherance ... 3. aid 4. help 6. relief, succor 8. progress 9. promotion 11. advancement, development
furtherer ... 7. abettor 8. promoter
furthermore ... 3. and, yet 4. then 5. again 7. au reste, besides 8. moreover 10. in addition 12. additionally
furtive ... 3. sly 4. wary 6. covert, secret, sneaky, stolen 8. skulking, stealthy 9. deceitful 11. clandestine
fury ... 3. ire 4. rage 5. anger, wrath 6. frenzy 7. madness 8. violence 10. excitement, turbulence 13. desperateness
Fury ... 6. Erinys, Spirit (avenging) 7. Atropos
furze ... 4. Ulex, whin 5. gorse, shrub
fuse ... 4. flux, frit (partly), melt 5. blend, smelt, unite 6. anneal, mingle, solder 7. combine, liquefy 8. dissolve 9. detonator
fusee ... 5. flair, torch 6. signal
fusion ... 5. alloy, blend, union 7. melting, mixture, nuclear 8. fluidity

9. coalition
fuss ... 3. ado 4. spat, to–do 5. busle 6. bother, bustle, pother, tumult 7. bombast, dispute, quarrel, trouble 8. brouhaha 9. confusion
fussy ... 7. finical 8. overnice 10. fastidious, meticulous
fustian ... 4. rant 5. cloth, tumid 7. bombast, pompous 8. claptrap, inflated 9. bombastic, worthless
fustic ... 3. dye 5. amber, morin 7. dyewood
futile ... 4. idle, vain 6. otiose 7. trivial 8. hopeless 11. ineffectual
futility ... 8. nugacity 10. invalidity 11. uselessness 12. bootlessness
future ... 3. yet 4. to be 5. later, still, tense 6. fiancé 8. expected, intended 9. hereafter 11. prospective
fuzzy ... 5. downy, hairy 6. fluffy 7. blurred, frizzly 9. imperfect 10. indistinct
fyke ... 3. net 6. bag net
fylfot ... 8. swastika 9. gammadion

G

G ... 4. tone (scale) 6. letter (7th)
gab ... 3. lie 4. mock, talk 5. boast, mouth, prate, scoff, taste 6. tongue 7. chatter, deceive 9. utterance
gabardine ... 6. cotton, woolen
gabble ... 4. chat 6. babble, jabber, mumble 7. chatter 8. nonsense
gabelle ... 3. tax 5. likin (imports) 6. excise, impost
gaberdine ... 4. gown 5. frock 6. mantle 7. garment (loose) 8. covering, pinafore 9. gabardine
gable ... 4. roof (part) 7. aileron (half) 8. pediment
gablock ... 4. gaff, spur 5. spear 6. gaffle 7. crowbar 8. gavelock
Gabon, Africa ...
capital .. 10. Libreville
Gabriel (pert to) ...
astrology .. 10. moon spirit
New Test .. 6. herald 11. good tidings
Old Test .. 5. angel
tradition .. 9. archangel (one of seven), messenger
gaby ... 4. fool 9. simpleton
gad ... 3. bar, God (oath), rod 4. goad, roam, rove, whip 5. ingot, spear, staff 6. billet, chisel, wander 7. on the go, run wild, traipse (trapes) 8. gadabout 9. gallivant
Gad (pert to) ...
Bib .. 7. prophet
deity (Bib) .. 7. Fortune
father .. 5. Jacob
tribe .. 6. Gadite, Israel (one of seven)

gadabout ... 3. gad 6. roving 7. dogcart, gadding, on the go
Gaddang, Gaddan ... 7. Malayan 8. language (Indonesia)
gadfly ... 6. botfly, insect 8. horsefly
gadget ... 6. device, jigger 7. gimmick 8. gimcrack 11. contrivance, thingumajig
Gadsden Purchase (1853) ... 5. tract 7. Arizona 9. New Mexico
gadwall ... 4. duck
Gaea, Gaia ... 12. Earth Goddess
Gael ... 4. Celt, Kelt, Manx, Scot 10. Highlander
Gaelic (pert to) ...
for John .. 3. Ian
hero .. 6. Ossian
language .. 4. Erse
native .. 4. Erse 5. Irish 6. Celtic, Keltic, Scotch
pagan god .. 5. Dagda (harpist)
sea god .. 3. Ler
spirit .. 7. banshee
warriors .. 7. Fenians
gaff ... 4. hoax, hook, scam, spar, spur, talk 5. fraud, spear, trick 6. deceit, fleece, gamble 7. chatter, prating 8. trickery 9. spearhead
gaffer ... 4. hick, rube 6. old man 11. electrician (TV)
gag ... 4. hoax, joke 5. choke, retch 7. closure, prevent, shackle 8. obstruct, one–liner, restrain, silencer 9. imposture 10. instrument 13. interpolation

gage, gauge ... 4. rule, test 5. scale
6. device, pledge 7. measure
8. capacity, defiance, diameter
(firearm), mortgage, security
9. challenge 11. measurement

gaggle ... 5. flock (geese), group
(women) 6. cackle

gaiety, gayety ... 4. gala, glee, show
5. mirth 6. finery 7. jollity
8. vivacity 9. festivity, merriment,
showiness 10. liveliness
12. colorfulness, conviviality

gain ... 3. get, net, win 4. earn, pelf,
reap 5. booty, clear, lucre, reach
6. attain, come by, obtain, profit,
secure, trover 7. acquire, benefit,
procure, realize 8. addition, arrive at,
increase 9. advantage 11. acquisition
12. accumulation 13. amplification

gainsay ... 4. deny 6. forbid, impugn,
oppose, refute 7. dispute
10. contradict, controvert

gait ... 3. run, way 4. lope, pace, trip,
trot, walk 5. amble, order, strut, tread
6. canter, gallop 8. slowness, velocity

gaiter ... 4. boot, spat 5. strad
6. puttee 7. legging 8. overshoe
11. galligaskin

gala ... 4. fete, pomp 6. festal, fiesta,
gaiety 8. festival 9. festivity
11. celebration

Galago ... 5. lemur

Galatea ... 7. heroine 8. sea nymph
9. sculpture (Pygmalion)
11. shepherdess

galaxy ... 6. throng 8. Milky Way
10. assemblage 11. celebrities

gale ... 4. gust, wind 5. storm
8. outburst 9. hurricane

galea ... 6. helmet

galeate ... 12. helmet–shaped

Galen (Gr) ... 9. physician

Galilean (pert to) ...
astronomer .. 7. Galileo
province .. 9. Palestine
religion .. 9. Christian
town .. 4. Cana 8. Tiberias

gall ... 3. vex 4. bile, fret 5. annoy,
chafe, grate, spite 6. bitter, harass,
rancor 8. irritate 9. impudence,
secretion, virulence

gallant ... 4. hero 5. dandy, lover,
noble, spark, swain 6. escort, suitor
7. stately 8. cavalier, cicisbeo
9. attentive, courteous
10. chivalrous, courageous

gallantry ... 7. bravery, courage,
display 8. courtesy 9. courtship
11. intrepidity

galleon ... 6. vessel (sailing)

gallery ... 3. poy 4. hall 5. salon
6. dedans, loggia, museum
7. passage, veranda 8. audience,
corridor, platform 9. promenade
10. ambulatory 11. observatory

galley ... 4. boat, tray 6. vessel
7. caboose, caravel (caravelle),
dromond, kitchen 8. cookroom

galley, Roman ...
one–bank oared .. 7. unireme
two–bank oared .. 6. bireme
three–bank oared .. 7. trireme

six–bank oared .. 7. hexeris
slave .. 5. rower 6. drudge

Gallic ... 4. Gaul 6. French 7. Frenchy

Gallic chariot ... 5. essed

gallimaufry ... 4. hash, olio, stew
6. medley, ragout 9. potpourri
10. hodgepodge

gallipot ... 6. vessel (Medit) 8. druggist

gallo ... 7. rooster 12. fighting cock

gallop ... 3. run 4. lope, ride 6. canter
7. tantivy

gallopade ... 5. dance, galop 6. curvet

gam ... 3. leg 4. herd 5. visit
6. school

Gambia, Africa ...
capital .. 6. Banjul

gambit ... 4. move 7. comment,
opening (chess) 8. maneuver
9. launching 10. concession

gamble ... 3. bet 4. dice, game, risk
5. stake, wager 6. chance, exacta,
hazard, plunge 8. perfecta
9. speculate, totalizer 10. parimutuel,
superfecta 11. daily double,
uncertainty

gambler ... 5. shill 7. sharper

gambol ... 3. hop 5. bound, caper,
prank 6. cavort, curvet, frolic

Gambrinus (King) ... 6. brewer (1st)

game ... 4. lark, play, prey 5. brave,
dodge, prank, sport 6. frolic, gamble,
gritty, plucky, quarry 7. contest,
pastime 8. resolute 9. amusement,
diversion 10. courageous

game, ball ... 4. golf, polo, pool
5. rugby 6. hockey, pelota, soccer,
squash, tennis 7. cricket, croquet
8. baseball, football 11. racquetball

game, beans ... 6. fan–tan
8. beanbags

game, board ... 4. keno 5. bingo,
chess, lotto 7. pachisi (parchesi)
8. checkers, cribbage, Monopoly
10. backgammon

game, card ... 3. gin, pam 4. bank,
faro, skat 5. pitch, poker, rummy,
whist 6. bridge, écarté, flinch, hearts
7. bezique, canasta, cassino, old
maid, seven–up

game, club ... 4. golf 6. hockey
7. cricket

game, court ... 6. pelota, squash,
tennis 7. jai alai 9. badminton

game, parlor ... 5. jacks 7. marbles
8. charades, dominoes
11. tiddlywinks

game plan ... 6. scheme 8. strategy

game, ring ... 6. quoits

gamin ... 3. tad 4. serf 6. urchin
7. mudlark 10. street Arab

gamut ... 5. orbit, range 6. extent
7. compass

gamy ... 4. game 7. lustful 8. sporting
12. high–flavored

gander ... 5. goose 6. stroll
9. simpleton

Gandhi (Hind) ... 6. Indira, leader
7. Mahatma (Mohandus)

gang ... 3. mob, set 4. band, crew,
pack, team, walk (cattle) 5. group,
horde, sheet (Print), shift 6. clique
7. company 9. pasturage

gangling ... 5. lanky 9. spindling
gangrene ... 5. decay 6. slough
   8. necrosis 9. sphacelus
   13. mortification
gangster ... 4. thug 5. thief 6. bandit
   7. mobster 8. criminal, hireling
   9. racketeer
gannet ... 4. ibis, Sula 5. booby,
   goose, solan 6. gander
gap ... 3. col 4. hole, pass 5. break,
   chasm, cleft, fault, meuse, shard,
   space, split 6. breach, hiatus,
   lacuna, lacune, ravine 7. opening
gaping ... 5. agape 6. chappy
   7. ringent, yawning 9. expectant
garb ... 5. array, dress, habit, style
   6. clothe 7. apparel, costume,
   fashion, raiment, uniform 8. clothing
   10. appearance, habiliment
garbed ... 4. clad 7. attired, dressed,
   habited
garble ... 5. alloy 6. mangle 7. distort,
   falsify, pervert 8. mutilate
   12. misinterpret, misrepresent,
   sophisticate
garden ... 3. bed 4. yard 5. hardy,
   patch 6. jardin, verger 7. topiary
   8. outfield 9. arboretum, cultivate,
   enclosure, herbarium
garden (pert to) ...
   Berlin .. 10. Tiergarten
   Bible .. 4. Eden
   city .. 4. Kent 6. Sicily 7. Chicago
   8. Touraine
   colony .. 5. Natal
   Colorado .. 9. of the Gods
   Kansas .. 9. of the West
   kind of .. 5. truck 8. kaleyard
   9. botanical 10. zoological
   State .. 9. New Jersey
garden implement ... 3. hoe 4. fork,
   rake 5. graip, mower 6. scythe,
   sickle, trowel, weeder
Garfield's death site ... 7. Elberon
   (NJ)
Gargantua (pert to) ...
   character .. 4. King (Rabelais romance)
   son .. 10. Pantagruel (giant)
gargantuan ... 4. huge 7. titanic
garish ... 5. gaudy, showy 7. flighty,
   glaring 8. dazzling
garland ... 3. lei 6. anadem, circle,
   corona, fillet, rosary, trophy, wreath
   7. chaplet, coronal, festoon
   8. headband 9. anthology
   11. compilation
garlic ... 4. herb, moly 5. clove
   6. ramson
garment ... 4. cape, coat, gown, robe,
   suit, vest, wrap 5. cloak, dress,
   frock, shift, simar, smock, stole, tunic
   6. coatee, duster 7. pelisse, raiment,
   surcoat, topcoat 8. overcoat,
   vestment
garment (pert to) ...
   African .. 6. kaross
   ancient .. 5. burel
   Arab .. 3. aba
   clerical .. 3. alb 5. amice 6. chimer
   7. cassock, zimarra 8. surplice
   cover .. 5. apron 8. overalls, pinafore
   9. coveralls

   Eskimo .. 5. parka
   Jewish .. 5. ephod
   knight's .. 6. tabard
   patchwork .. 5. cento
   thin .. 8. gossamer
garner ... 4. reap 5. amass, store
   6. gather 7. collect 10. accumulate
garnet ... 3. gem, red 5. color
   6. aplome, pyrope 7. olivine (green)
   8. cinnamon (stone), essonite
   (yellow), melanite (black)
   9. almandine (almandite, dark red),
   uvarovite (green)
garnish ... 4. trim 5. adorn 6. attach,
   bedeck 7. fetters 8. decorate,
   ornament
garnishment ... 4. lien 7. summons
   8. ornament 10. attachment,
   decoration
garret ... 4. loft 5. attic 6. turret
   8. cockloft 10. watchtower
garrot ... 9. goldeneye (duck)
   10. tourniquet
garrote, garrotte ... 8. strangle
   9. execution 10. throttling
   13. strangulation
garrulous ... 5. gabby, wordy 6. chatty
   7. diffuse 9. talkative 10. loquacious
gas ... 4. brag, talk 5. vapor 6. poison
   7. chatter 8. gasoline, nonsense
   10. anesthesia, asphyxiate, illuminant
   11. anesthetize
gas ... 3. air 4. neon 5. argon, ether,
   ozone, radon, xenon 6. arsine,
   butane, ethane, helium, ketene,
   nebula (luminous), oxygen 7. methane
   8. chlorine, cyanogen, etherion,
   hydrogen, nitrogen 9. butadiene
gascon ... 7. boaster 8. braggart
   11. braggadocio 12. swashbuckler
gasconade ... 4. brag 5. boast
   7. bluster, bravado 11. fanfaronade,
   rodomontade
gaseous ... 4. smog, thin 5. smoke
   7. tenuous 8. vaporous
   13. unsubstantial
gash ... 3. cut 5. cleft, notch, sever,
   slash 6. furrow, gossip, injury, tattle
   8. incision
gasp ... 3. say 4. pant, yawn 5. utter
   7. breathe
gasping ... 5. agasp 7. panting
gastropod ... 4. slug 5. Harpa, Murex,
   Oliva, snail, whelk 6. Nerita, volute
   7. abalone, mollusk 8. sea snail
gat ... 3. gun, rod 7. channel, passage
   8. revolver
gate ... 3. dar 4. door, hole, pass
   5. start (racing), toran, valve
   6. defile, portal 7. barrier, opening,
   postern 8. Lion-Gate 9. floodgate,
   turnstile 10. Needle's Eye
   (Jerusalem), portcullis
gateau ... 4. cake
gather ... 4. bale, brew, fold, meet,
   reap 5. amass, glean, pleat, rally,
   shirr 6. bundle, deduce, garner,
   muster, pucker 7. acquire, collect,
   compile, convene, convoke, harvest,
   procure, suppose 8. assemble
   10. accumulate
gatherer, collector of ...

coins .. 11. numismatist
money .. 5. miser
news .. 8. reporter 10. journalist
stamps .. 11. philatelist
gathering ... 3. sum 4. stag 5. crowd,
party, troop 6. galaxy, smoker
7. abscess, meeting 8. swelling
10. assemblage, harvesting
11. contraction 12. accumulation,
congregation 14. conglomeration
gaucho ... 6. cowboy (pampas)
8. herdsman, horseman
gaucho weapon ... 4. bola
gaud ... 4. jest, joke 5. adorn, fraud,
paint, sport, trick 6. finery, flashy,
gewgaw 7. trinket 8. artifice,
ornament
gaudy ... 4. fine, loud 5. cheap, feast,
showy 6. flashy, flimsy, garish,
tawdry, tinsel 7. glaring, trinket
9. flaunting 11. pretentious
12. meretricious, ostentatious
13. overdeveloped
gaufre ... 4. iron (waffle) 6. waffle
gauge, gage ... 4. norm, rate, rule, size
5. judge, scale, value 6. assess
7. measure 8. estimate
gauge (pert to) ...
airplane .. 10. tachometer
distance .. 10. micrometer
miles .. 8. odometer
pointer .. 3. arm
rain .. 8. udometer
velocity .. 11. speedometer
wind .. 10. anemometer
Gaul ... 5. Aedui 6. France, Gallia
9. Frenchman
Gauls ... 4. Remi 5. Celts, Cymry
gaunt ... 4. bony, lank, lean, thin, ugly
5. spare 7. haggard 8. desolate
gauntlet ... 4. cuff 5. armor (part),
glove 7. bandage
gaur ... 5. gayal 7. buffalo
gauss ... 4. unit (Elec)
Gauss ... 13. mathematician
gauze ... 4. haze, leno 5. crape, lisse,
marli (marly) 6. barege, filter, tissue
8. dressing
gauze film on wine ... 8. beeswing
gavage ... 7. feeding
gave ... see *give*
Gavia ... 4. loon
gavial ... 11. crocodilian
gaw ... 4. gape 5. drain 6. trench
gawk ... 4. dolt, gowk, left, lout
5. booby, stare 9. simpleton
gawky ... 6. clumsy, cuckoo, stupid
7. awkward, foolish 8. clownish
gay ... 4. airy, glad 5. drunk, gaudy,
jolly, merry, riant, showy 6. blithe,
cheery, jovial, joyful, joyous, lively
7. dashing, festive, gleeful
8. cheerful, colorful, rory–tory,
sportive 9. convivial, sprightly,
vivacious 10. frolicsome, profligate
12. lighthearted
gay time ... 4. lark 5. spree
8. jamboree
gazabo, gazebo ... 4. cony 6. rabbit,
turret 7. balcony, blunder, whopper
11. summerhouse
gaze ... 3. con, eye 4. gape, look,

moon, peer, pore, scan 5. glare,
gloat, stare 6. glower, regard
gazelle ... 3. ahu, goa 4. admi, cora,
dama, kudu, mohr, oryx 5. ariel,
brown, korin 7. chikara (4–horn),
corinne, dibatag 8. antelope
9. springbok
gazette ... 7. journal, publish
8. announce 9. newspaper
15. Arkansas Gazette (1819)
gazetteer ... 7. newsman 9. newspaper
10. dictionary
gear ... 3. cam, rig 5. equip, goods,
tools, wheel 6. things 7. baggage,
conform, harness, rigging 8. adjust
to, clothing, cogwheel, garments
9. equipment, mechanism, trappings,
vestments 10. appliances, implements
gecko ... 6. lizard 7. tarente
geese ... 5. brant, quink, solan
geese (pert to) ...
fat .. 6. axunge
flock .. 4. raft 6. gaggle
genus .. 4. Chen 5. Anser 6. Branta
Gekko ... 6. lizard
gelatin, gelatine ... 4. agar, food, jell
5. jelly 6. collin 7. protein
8. agar–agar
gelid ... 3. icy 4. cold 6. frozen
gem ... 4. jade, onyx, opal, ruby, sard,
type 5. agate, beryl, jewel, pearl,
stone, topaz 6. garnet, ligure, spinel,
zircon 7. cat's–eye, diamond,
emerald, jacinth 8. amethyst,
hawk's–eye, sapphire 9. carnelian,
moonstone 10. aquamarine
11. alexandrite, lapis lazuli 12. star
sapphire
gem (pert to) ...
artificial .. 5. paste
carver .. 8. lapidary
Egyptian .. 6. scarab
flaw .. 8. gendarme
food .. 6. muffin
imperfect .. 5. loupe
semiprecious .. 5. cameo 8. intaglio
six rays .. 7. asteria
surface .. 5. bezel, facet
weight .. 5. carat
gemel ... 4. bars (Her), twin 6. paired
7. coupled, doubled
gemsbok ... 4. goat, oryx 7. chamois
Gem State ... 5. Idaho
gendarme ... 4. blue, flaw (gem)
5. guard 6. police 7. soldier, trooper
9. policeman 10. cavalryman
gender ... 3. sex 5. breed, genus
7. grammar (term) 8. engender
genealogy ... 4. tree 5. order (of
descent) 6. family 7. account,
history, lineage, peerage, progeny
8. pedigree, register 9. offspring
genealogy of the gods ... 8. theogony
gener ... 8. son–in–law
general ... 5. gross, usual, vague,
whole 6. common, public 7. officer
8. catholic, communal 9. extensive,
prevalent, universal, well–known
10. encyclical, indefinite
11. approximate
general (pert to) ...
agreement .. 5. chief, court

aspect.. **6**. facies
chief.. **6**. Führer, Il Duce **9**. president **10**. Grand Mogul **13**. Generalissimo
court.. **5**. Synod
direction.. **5**. tenor, trend **6**. course
favor.. **7**. popular **10**. popularity
feature.. **5**. motif
group.. **8**. ensemble
orders.. **7**. routine
rule.. **5**. canon
summary.. **8**. synopsis
type.. **7**. average
generalize... **5**. widen **6**. extend, reason, spread **7**. broaden **12**. universalize
General Sherman (pert to)...
Civil War march.. **15**. Atlanta to the Sea
giant trees.. **8**. sequoias
tree.. **10**. eucalyptus
generate... **5**. beget, breed, cause **6**. create **7**. develop, produce **8**. engender **9**. originate, procreate, propagate
generation... **3**. age **7**. descent **8**. lifetime **9**. epigonous (later), formation, genealogy **10**. production **11**. abiogenesis, procreation
generosity... **10**. liberality **11**. hospitality, magnanimity, munificence
generous... **4**. free **5**. large **7**. liberal **8**. tolerant **9**. indulgent, plentiful, unstinted **10**. hospitable **11**. magnanimous
genesis... **4**. Book **5**. birth **6**. origin (of races) **8**. nascency **9**. beginning, ethnology, etymology, inception **10**. generation
genet... **3**. fur **5**. civet
genethliac... **5**. stars (influence) **9**. birthdays
Geneva Cross... **8**. Red Cross
genial... **4**. warm **5**. bland **6**. jovial, kindly **7**. amiable, festive, nuptial **8**. cheerful, friendly, pleasant **9**. expansive **10**. enlivening
geniculate... **5**. kneel
genie... **4**. jinn **6**. genius
genius... **5**. deity, jinni **6**. talent **7**. ability, prodigy **9**. endowment (supreme) **11**. inspiration **12**. intelligence
Genoa lace... **4**. tape **6**. bobbin **7**. macramé **13**. gold and silver
genos... **4**. clan, gens, race
genre... **3**. art (style) **4**. kind, sort **5**. genus **6**. gender **7**. species **8**. category
genteel... **6**. polite **7**. refined **8**. wellborn, well–bred
Gentiles... **6**. goyims **10**. Christians, non–Moslems **14**. non–Mohammedans
gentle... **4**. calm, easy, meek, mild, soft, tame **5**. bland, quiet **6**. docile, humane, kindly, tender **7**. amabile (Mus), clement, genteel, refined, subdued **8**. moderate, peaceful, soothing, tranquil, wellborn **9**. courteous, honorable, temperate, tractable **10**. chivalrous

11. considerate **13**. compassionate
gentleman... **3**. sir **6**. knight **7**. esquire, shoneen (would–be), younker **8**. nobleman
gentleness... **6**. lenity **8**. elegance, leniency, meekness, softness **9**. lightness **10**. kindliness, moderation **11**. genteelness
genuflect... **5**. kneel **6**. curtsy
genuine... **4**. pure, real, true **5**. frank, pucka (pukka) **7**. germane, sincere **8**. existent **9**. authentic, simon–pure, unalloyed, veritable **10**. unaffected **13**. unadulterated
genus... **4**. kind, sort **5**. class, order
genus, animal life...
animals (one–celled).. **6**. Amoeba **8**. Protozoa **9**. Rhizopoda
ants.. **6**. Eciton
apes.. **5**. Simia
armadillos.. **9**. Glyptodon
auks.. **4**. Alle
bears.. **5**. Ursus
bees (honey).. **4**. Apis
beetles.. **10**. Coleoptera
birds.. **7**. Ratitae
bivalve mollusks.. **6**. Anomia **8**. Estheria
bugs (long–legged).. **5**. Emesa
cats.. **5**. Felis
cattle.. **3**. Bos
crabs.. **5**. Maia
dogs.. **5**. Canis
ducks.. **3**. Aix **4**. Anas **7**. Harelda **8**. Clangula
elks.. **5**. Alces
fish.. **6**. Cybium, Remora **7**. Girella, Muraena
flies.. **6**. Asilus **8**. Glossina (tsetse)
frogs.. **4**. Rana **5**. Anura **8**. Amphibia **9**. Batrachia
geese.. **4**. Chen **5**. Anser
goats.. **5**. Capra
gulls.. **4**. Xema
herons.. **7**. Egretta
hogs.. **3**. Sus
horses.. **5**. Equus
insects.. **10**. Coleoptera
lemurs.. **6**. Galago
lizards.. **3**. Uta **5**. Agama
mammals.. **4**. Homo
Man.. **11**. Homo sapiens
marten.. **7**. Mustela
mice.. **3**. Mus
monkeys (spider).. **6**. Ateles
moose.. **5**. Alces
moths.. **5**. Tinea
oysters.. **6**. Ostrea
peacocks.. **4**. Pavo
pigeons (crowned).. **5**. Goura
porcupines.. **7**. Hystrix
porpoise.. **4**. Inia
rats.. **6**. Spalax
roadrunners.. **9**. Geococcyx
scorpions.. **4**. Nepa
seabirds.. **4**. Sula
sloths.. **11**. Megatherium
slugs.. **5**. Arion
snails.. **5**. Mitra **6**. Nerita, Triton **8**. Geophila
snakes.. **4**. Eryx (sand) **7**. Ophidia
spiders.. **7**. Agalena

squirrels.. 7. Sciurus
swans.. 4. Olar 6. Cygnus
ticks.. 6. Ixodes
tortoises.. 4. Emys
turkeys.. 9. Meleagris
wasps.. 5. Vespa
whales.. 4. Orca 5. Areta
  9. Sibbaldus (blue)
genus, plant life...
algae (blue–green).. 10. Gloeocapsa
apple trees.. 5. Malus
cabbage.. 3. Cos
currant.. 5. Ribes
elms.. 5. Ulmus
evergreen, heaths.. 5. Erica
fern.. 6. Anemia
fungi.. 7. Boletus 10. geoglossum
grasses.. 3. Poa (blue) 5. Avena
  6. Elymus 7. Setaria
herbs.. 4. Arum 6. Asarum, Asitis
  (mustard), Cassia, Seseli
  7. Hedeoma, Linaria 8. Solidago
holly.. 4. Ilex
ipecac.. 4. Evea
ivy.. 11. Hedera helix
lily.. 7. Bessera
maples.. 4. Acer
olives.. 4. Olea
orchids.. 5. Vanda 7. Listera
palms.. 5. Areca, Assai 6. Bacaba
poplar.. 5. Alamo
rhubarb.. 5. Rheum
vines (woody).. 6. Hedera
geode... 3. vug (vugg, vugh, voog)
  5. druse 6. nodule
geological (pert to)...
division.. 3. eon, era
era.. 6. Eocene 7. Miocene
  8. Cenozoic, Mesozoic 9. Paleozoic
  11. Archaeozoic
period.. 4. Dyas, Lias 5. Trias
prelife.. 5. Azoic
zone (fossil).. 6. assise
geologist... 6. Strabo (anc Gr)
  8. geognost 12. mineralogist
geometric (pert to)...
angle.. 9. incidence
axis.. 8. abscissa
contact.. 10. osculation
curve.. 6. spiral 7. evolute
pottery.. 7. Dipylon (anc)
geometric figure... 4. cone, cube,
  lune 5. prism 6. gnomon, oblong,
  square 7. hexagon, octagon, polygon,
  rhombus 8. heptagon, pentagon,
  triangle 9. rectangle, trapezoid
  10. quadrangle 13. parallelogram
geometric proposition (pert to)...
ratio.. 2. pi (3.1416)
surface.. 4. tore 5. nappe
term.. 4. sine 5. locus 6. secant
  7. tangent 11. asses' bridge
geometry (pert to)...
figure.. 6. conoid 9. ellipsoid
  10. paraboloid
mathematician.. 6. Euclid, Pascal
proposition.. 6. porism
geoponic... 5. rural 6. rustic
Georgia...
capital.. 7. Atlanta
city.. 5. Macon 7. Augusta

  8. Columbus, Marietta, Savannah
  9. Brunswick
holiday.. 10. Georgia Day (Feb 12)
memorial.. 11. Warm Springs
  16. Little White House (FDR)
mountain.. 7. Lookout 9. Blue Ridge
  11. Alleghenies
peak.. 9. High Point 13. Brasstown
  Bald
river.. 8. Savannah, Suwannee
settler (1st).. 10. Oglethorpe
State admission.. 6. Fourth
State nickname.. 5. Peach 7. Cracker
  16. Empire of the South
swamp.. 10. Okefenokee
Georgian of the Caucasus... 4. Svan
georgic... 4. poem (rural)
geosphere... 5. earth
Geraint, Sir... 6. Knight (Round Table)
germ... 3. bud 4. ovum, seed
  5. spore 6. embryo, origin
  7. microbe 8. bacteria (pl)
  9. bacterium 13. microorganism
germ (free)... 7. aseptic 10. antiseptic
German... 3. Hun 5. Boche, jerry
  6. Almain (Alman), Teuton
  9. Deutscher
German (pert to)... see also *Germany*
air force.. 9. Luftwaffe
airplane.. 5. Gotha, Stuka 7. Dornier,
  Heinkel, Junkers 13. Messerschmitt
article.. 3. das, der, ein
battleship.. 8. Graf Spee (1939)
beverage.. 5. lager
cake.. 5. torte
castle.. 7. schloss
Christmas.. 11. Weihnachten
dance.. 9. allemande
drinking salute.. 6. prosit
folklore.. 5. gnome 6. kobold
gun.. 6. Bertha (Big)
hail.. 4. heil
highway.. 8. autobahn
knight.. 6. Ritter (title)
language.. 7. Deutsch
law.. 5. Salic
league.. 4. Bund 6. Verein
  9. Hanseatic 10. Turnverein
letter.. 4. rune
lyric poems.. 6. lieder
mister.. 4. Herr
ox (wild).. 4. urus
parliament.. 9. Bundestag, Reichstag
people.. 5. Quadi 6. Franks, Saxons
  7. Teutons, Vandals 8. Lombards
  9. Prussians 10. Herminones
police.. 7. Gestapo
prison.. 6. stalag
society.. see *league* (above)
song.. 4. lied
student set.. 7. Kommers
teacher.. 6. docent 12. privatdocent
title.. 3. Von 4. Graf, Herr 6. Ritter
tribal group.. 3. gau
union.. 9. Auschluss
vowel change.. 6. umlaut
wheat.. 5. spelt
wine.. 4. wein 5. Rhine 7. Moselle
woman.. 4. frau 8. fraulein
yes.. 2. ja
germane... 4. akin 6. allied 7. kindred
  8. relevant 11. appropriate

German people (famed) . . .
  actor . . 8. Jannings (Emil)
  astrologer . . 5. Faust
  astronomer . . 5. Gallo 6. Kepler
  author . . 4. Dahn 5. Ebers
    8. Brentano
  bacteriologist . . 4. Koch (Nobel Prize,
    1905)
  biographer . . 6. Ludwig
  chemist . . 6. Bunsen
  composer . . 3. Abt 4. Bach 5. Hasse
    6. Handel, Wagner
  deity . . 5. Donar (thunder)
  educator . . 5. Grimm 6. Beneke
    7. Francke
  Egyptologist . . 5. Ebers
  general . . 6. Rommel
  geographer . . 6. Ritter
  Gestapo chief . . 7. Himmler
  goldsmith (anc) . . 5. Faust
  historian . . 4. Dahn 5. Moser
    7. Neander (Eccl)
  inventor . . 6. Diesel
  metaphysician . . 4. Kant 5. Lange
  mystic . . 7. Eckhart
  naturalist . . 9. Ehrenberg
  neurologist . . 5. Ebing 6. Krafft
  painter . . 5. Durer 7. Lessing
  pathologist . . 6. Eberth
  philologist . . 5. Grimm, Heyne
  philosopher . . 4. Elze 5. Groos, Hegel,
    Weber 6. Ritter 8. Spengler
    9. Feuerbach
  physician . . 8. Hufeland
  physicist . . 3. Ohm 5. Weber
    6. Franck 7. Doppler 10. Fahrenheit
  pianist . . 5. Bauer
  poet . . 4. Elze 5. Heine 6. Goethe,
    Uhland 7. Lessing 8. Schiller
  president (first) . . 5. Ebert
  sculptor . . 5. Begas
  Socialist . . 10. Liebknecht
  theologian . . 5. Bauer 6. Spener
    (Pietist) 7. Francke
Germany . . .
  capital . . 4. Bonn 6. Berlin
  cathedral town . . 5. Essen
  city . . 3. Ulm 4. Bonn, Gera
    5. Baden, Emden, Essen, Gotha
    6. Munich
  coal region . . 4. Ruhr, Saar 6. Aachen
  East . . 10. Third Reich
  empire . . 14. Deutsches Reich
  kingdom . . 6. Saxony 7. Bavaria,
    Hanover
  lake . . 9. Constance
  leader . . 6. Hitler (Fuehrer), Kaiser
    13. von Hindenburg
  mountain . . 4. Harz
  port . . 5. Emden
  river . . 3. Aar 4. Elbe, Iser, Oder,
    Ruhr 5. Rhine, Saale
  steel region . . 5. Essen
  West . . 15. Federal Republic
  wine (white) . . 4. hock
germicide . . . 6. iodine (iodin), phenol
    10. antiseptic 12. disinfectant
germinate . . . 3. bud 4. grow 5. beget
    6. sprout 7. develop 8. vegetate
    10. effloresce
Geronimo . . . 6. Apache (Chief)
gerrymander (Polit) . . . 6. divide (unfairly)

    10. manipulate
gesticulation . . . 6. motion 7. gesture
gesture . . . 3. act 4. gest (geste), sign
    5. sanna 6. beckon, behave, motion
    7. perform, pretext 8. carriage (body)
    11. gesticulate 13. gesticulation
get . . . 3. pen, win 4. earn, hear, pain,
    take, trap 5. beget, fetch, incur,
    learn 6. attain, become, derive,
    induce, obtain, profit, secure
    7. achieve, acquire, capture, prepare,
    procure, receive 8. contract, contrive,
    discover 9. ascertain, determine
    10. understand
get along . . . 3. age 5. hurry
    6. begone, depart, manage, move on
    7. advance, prosper
get around . . . 5. evade 6. cajole,
    outwit, spread 7. deceive 9. circulate
    10. circumvent
get off . . . 5. start, utter 6. alight,
    depart, escape, go free 8. dismount
get out . . . 4. exit 5. scram 6. elicit,
    escape, reveal 7. draw out, leak out,
    publish 8. evacuate 9. extricate
get over . . . 4. move 5. cover
    6. bridge, finish 7. recover
    8. surmount 9. make clear
Ghana, capital of . . . 5. Accra (Gold
    Coast)
ghastly . . . 3. wan 4. grim, pale
    5. lurid 6. dismal, grisly, pallid
    7. deathly, hideous 8. gruesome,
    horrible, shocking, terrible
    9. deathlike, frightful 10. cadaverous
ghost . . . 3. Ker 5. larva (Rom Relig),
    lemur, shade, spook 6. daemon,
    spirit, wraith 7. banshee (banshie),
    eidolon, phantom, specter
    8. phantom, revenant
    10. apparition, glimmering, substitute
    11. ghostwriter, poltergeist
ghostly . . . 5. eerie (eery) 8. spectral
    9. spiritual
giant . . . 4. huge, ogre 5. Titan
    6. afreet, nozzle, thurse 7. monster
    8. colossus 9. monstrous
    10. gargantuan, prodigious,
    tremendous
giant (pert to) . . .
  Biblical . . 7. Goliath, Rephaim
  classic . . 5. Atlas
  crafty . . 5. Cacus
  Greek . . 5. Mimas
  hundred–armed . . 9. Enceladus
  land, country . . 9. Utgarthar
    10. Jotunnheim 11. Brobdingnag
  Norse . . 4. Ymir (Ymer) 5. Mimir
    6. Jotunn (Jotun) 12. Utgartha–Loki
  one–eyed . . 5. Arges 7. Brontes,
    Cyclops 10. Polyphemus
  primeval . . 4. Ymir 5. Titan
    12. Utgartha–Loki
  rock . . 9. Gibraltar 13. Stone Mountain
    (Atlanta)
  sea god . . 5. Aegir
  seer . . 5. Mimir
  strong . . 6. Samson, Targan
    7. Antaeus 8. Hercules
  Teutonic . . 4. Wade 5. Aegir
  thousand–armed . . 4. Bana
  three–hundred handed, many–handed . .

8. Briareus
giantess (Teut Myth)... 4. Norn
gibbed... 9. castrated (cat)
gibber... 4. chat, hump, talk (rapid)
   5. stone (loose) 6. mumble
   7. boulder, chatter 8. swelling
gibberish... 4. talk 5. lingo 6. jargon,
   patois, patter 8. nonsense
gibbet... 3. jib 4. hang 7. gallows
   9. execution
gibbon... 3. ape, lar 6. wou–wou
   7. hoolock, siamang 10. anthropoid
gibe... 4. jape, jeer, jibe, quip 5. fleer,
   flirt, flout, scoff, sneer, taunt
   6. heckle
Gibraltar...
   named for (legend).. 5. Gobir
   ruled by.. 12. Great Britain
   site.. 5. Spain (coast)
giddy... 4. reel 5. dizzy, tipsy, whirl
   6. fickle 7. flighty 8. gyratory,
   heedless 9. delirious
   14. scatterbrained
gift... 4. alms, bent, boon, dole, free
   5. bribe, grant, knack, token
   6. legacy, talent 7. aptness, faculty,
   largess (largesse), present
   8. aptitude, blessing, donation,
   gratuity 9. endowment, lagniappe
   (lagnappe), readiness 11. serendipity
   12. contribution
gifted... 7. endowed 8. talented
gigantic... 4. huge 5. giant, large,
   titan 7. immense, mammoth
   8. colossal, enormous 9. colossean,
   monstrous 10. prodigious
giggle... 5. laugh (silly), te–hee
   6. tee–hee, titter 7. chuckle, snicker,
   snigger
Gila monster... 4. Gila 6. lizard
gild... 4. coat, lure 5. adorn, paint,
   tempt 7. aureate, falsify 8. brighten
   9. embellish
gilding... 4. gilt, gold 6. ormolu
   7. coating 8. ornament, painting
gill... 5. brook, leach, organ, penny
   6. tipple, valley, wattle 7. measure
   10. sweetheart
gimcrackle... 3. fob, toy 5. showy
   6. bauble, gewgaw, paltry, trifle
   7. trinket 8. trumpery, whimwham
   15. Jack–of–all–trades
gimlet... 3. awl 4. tool 5. drink
   (mixed) 6. wimble
gimp... 5. orris (upholstery) 6. fabric,
   thread 7. galloon 8. fishline,
   trimming
gin... 4. game, sloe, tool, trap, whim
   5. snare, trick 6. device, liquor,
   scheme, thresh 7. machine
   8. artifice, schnapps 11. contrivance
ginger... 3. pep 5. color 6. Asarum,
   energy, lively, mettle, spirit
   8. pungency, Zingiber 9. rootstalk
gingerbread... 4. cake 5. money
   6. flimsy, frills, wealth 8. ornament
   (tawdry) 11. superfluity
gingerly... 6. warily 7. charily
   9. carefully, finically, guardedly
   10. cautiously 12. fastidiously
gingham... 5. cloth 8. umbrella
   (cheap)

gipsy... see *gypsy*
giraffe... 5. okapi 6. mammal, spinet
   10. camelopard 13. constellation
girasol, girasole... 4. opal
   9. artichoke, sunflower
gird... 4. belt, bind, gibe, girt, sill
   5. brace, equip, scoff, sneer
   6. fasten, girdle, secure 7. enclose,
   environ 8. surround 10. strengthen
girder... 4. beam 5. truss 6. timber
   7. support
girdle... 3. obi 4. band, belt, cest,
   ring, sash 6. cestus, cingle, circle,
   corset 8. cincture, encircle
   10. cummerbund
girdle bone... 12. sphenethmoid
Girdle of Venus (pert to)...
   bridal.. 11. power of love
   palmistry line.. 8. hysteria
   11. nervousness
girl... 3. sis 4. bint, chit, dame, lass,
   minx, miss 5. filly, sissy, skirt
   6. damsel, female, giglet, hoyden
   (hoiden), lassie, maiden, shiver, thrill,
   tomboy 7. colleen, damosel, fillock,
   ingénue, roebuck 10. sweetheart
   11. maidservant
girlish... 4. pert 5. sissy 7. artless
   8. immature, maidenly 10. flapperish
girt... 4. band 6. fasten, saddle
   7. besiege 9. encircled
girth... 4. band, hoop, size 5. brace,
   strap 6. girdle, saddle 7. measure
   8. encircle 13. circumference
gist... 3. nub 4. core, crux, meat, pith
   5. point (main) 7. essence, meaning
give... 3. gie 4. hand 5. endow,
   grant, yield 6. accord, afford,
   bestow, confer, devote, donate,
   impart, remise, render, supply
   7. present, proffer, provide
   9. attribute, vouchsafe
   10. administer, elasticity
give (pert to)...
   and take.. 11. reciprocity
   authority.. 7. empower
   away.. 5. break, grant, marry, yield
   6. bestow, betray 7. discard, divulge,
   succumb 8. disclose 9. sacrifice
   10. relinquish
   back.. 4. echo 5. remit 6. recede,
   remand, remise, retire, return
   7. replace, restore, retreat
   birth to.. 4. foal 5. calve 6. farrow,
   mother 9. originate
   expectation.. 7. promise
   forth.. 4. emit 5. blaze 6. afford,
   exhale 7. publish
   information.. 4. tell 6. inform, report
   7. divulge, publish 8. disclose
   9. advertise
   out.. 4. deal, emit 5. exude, issue,
   print, utter (publicly) 6. report,
   weaken 7. declare, publish, release
   8. announce 9. apportion, circulate
   prominence.. 4. star 7. feature
   8. headline
   up.. 4. cede, emit, fail, quit 5. demit,
   waive, yield 6. betray, disuse, resign,
   vacate 7. abandon, despair, succumb
   8. abdicate, part with, renounce
   swear off 9. sacrifice, surrender

10. relinquish
given... 5. dated, datum, fixed
  6. stated 7. assumed, granted
  8. accorded, addicted, bestowed,
  inclined, set forth 10. determined,
  disposed to
given (pert to)...
  by word of mouth.. 4. oral 5. parol
  name.. 7. surname
  particularly.. 9. specified
given (to)...
  experiment.. 7. empiric
  expression.. 13. demonstrative
  meditation.. 13. contemplative
  suspicion.. 9. querulent
giving... 6. ceding 7. largess (largesse)
  9. bestowing 10. conferring, liberality
  12. philanthropy, presentation
  13. administering
giving name to a country...
  8. eponymic
giving up... 8. yielding
  10. abandoning, despairing
  11. sacrificing 12. surrendering
  13. relinquishing
glacial (pert to)...
  deposit.. 6. placer 7. moraine
  direction.. 5. stoss (opp to lee)
  drift.. 8. diluvium
  dust.. 10. kryokonite
  erosion wall.. 6. cirque
  mill.. 6. moulin
  ridge.. 4. kame (Scot) 5. esker (eskar)
  snow.. 4. neve
glaciarium... 4. rink (skating)
glacis... 5. slope 7. incline
  13. fortification
glack... 4. fork (road) 6. defile, ravine,
  valley
glad... 3. gay 4. fain 5. merry
  6. elated, joyful, joyous 8. animated,
  cheering, pleasing 9. animating,
  beautiful, delighted, gratified
  11. exhilarated, well–pleased
  12. exhilarating
gladden... 5. cheer, elate 6. please
  7. gratify
gladdy... 12. yellowhammer
glade... 4. dell, nemo (comb form),
  vale 5. laund 6. valley 8. clearing
  9. everglade, open space
gladiator... 6. fencer 7. lanista
gladiator's arena... 4. ludi
gladly... 4. fain, lief 5. fitly 6. freely
  7. eagerly, readily 8. joyfully, properly
  9. willingly 10. cheerfully, preferably
gladsome... 4. glad 6. blithe, joyful
  7. festive, jocular, pleased
  8. cheerful
Gladstone... 3. bag (travel) 4. wine
  7. Liberal (Party) 8. carriage,
  Irishman 11. portmanteau
glad tidings... 3. joy 6. gospel
  7. evangel
glamorous... 8. alluring, charming
  10. bewitching 11. fascinating
glance... 3. eye 4. hint, leer, look,
  ogle, scry, skew 5. flash, gleam,
  glint, touch 6. allude, signal
  7. glimpse
gland... 5. gonad, liver, lymph, ovary
  6. spleen, thymus 7. adrenal,

carotid, parotid, thyroid 8. pancreas,
salivary 9. pituitary 10. suprarenal
gland (pert to)...
  enlargement.. 6. ademia
  full of.. 7. adenose
  glandlike.. 7. adenoid 9. glandular
  inflammation.. 8. adenitis
  secretion.. 7. hormone
  tumor.. 7. adenoma
glaring... 5. clear, plain 6. bright,
  garish 7. evident, flaring, obvious,
  staring, visible, vividly 8. apparent,
  distinct, flagrant, manifest
  9. barefaced 11. conspicuous
glass... 4. lens, pony 5. glaze, purex
  6. goblet, liquor, mirror, seidel
  7. binocle, crystal, reflect, tumbler
  9. barometer, binocular, hourglass,
  telescope 10. microscope, opera
  glass 11. stactometer, thermometer
glass (pert to)...
  blue.. 5. smalt
  device.. 7. ironman
  flask.. 7. matrass (mattrass)
  French for.. 5. verre
  furnace, oven.. 4. lehr (leer) 5. bocca,
  siege, tisar 7. drosser (part)
  like.. 6. vitric 8. vitreous
  material.. 4. frit (fritt)
  mineral.. 7. hyalite 8. feldspar
  molten.. 7. parison
  mosaic.. 7. tessera
  paste (jewelry).. 6. strass
  red.. 7. schmelz (schmelze)
  refuse.. 4. calx
  rod.. 5. punty (pontil)
  sheet.. 4. pane 5. slide 7. platten
  showcase.. 7. vitrine
  volcanic.. 6. pumice 8. obsidian
  worker.. 7. glazier
glass (type of)... 3. cut 4. milk
  6. safety 7. hobnail, Lalique, plastic,
  stained, Swedish 8. Fostoria,
  Sandwich, Venetian 9. Fiberglas,
  Plexiglas, Vitaglass
glass blowing (pert to)...
  annealing term.. 4. fuse, heat
  glass content.. 4. sand, zinc
  6. potash, temper 7. soda ash
  oven.. 4. lehr (leer)
  rod.. 5. punty (pontil)
glazier's diamond... 5. emery (emeril)
glazing machine... 8. calender
gleam... 3. ray 4. glow 5. flash, glint,
  gloze, light 7. glimmer, shimmer
  8. radiance 9. coruscate
  10. brightness
glean... 4. reap 5. sheaf (of hemp)
  6. bundle, deduce, gather 7. collect,
  harvest, procure
glee... 3. joy 4. club, song 5. mirth
  7. delight, temper 8. pleasure 9. merriment
  12. cheerfulness
glen... 4. dale, dell, vale 6. dingle,
  ravine, valley 10. depression
glib... 4. easy, oily 5. suave 6. facile,
  fluent, smooth 8. castrate, flippant,
  slippery 9. talkative 10. loquacious
glide... 4. sail, skid, slip, soar
  5. coast, slide
gliding over... 7. lambent
  10. slithering

glimmer... 3. bit 4. hint, leam
5. blink, flash, gleam, glint
7. glimpse, glitter 10. perception
(slight)
glimpse... 4. view (quick) 5. flash,
tinge, trace 6. glance, luster
7. glimmer, inkling
glisten... 5. flash, shine 7. glister,
sparkle 9. coruscate
glitter... 5. glare, gleam, shine
7. glimmer, glisten, sparkle
9. coruscate, showiness
14. attractiveness
gloaming... 4. dusk 8. twilight
9. darkening 11. candlelight
globe... 3. map, orb 4. ball, moon
5. earth 6. sphere 10. hemisphere
(half)
Globe, The... 7. Theater (London, first
to play Shakespeare)
globular... 5. beady 7. globose
9. orbicular, spherical 10. orbiculate
11. globe–shaped
globule... 4. bead, blob, drop, pill,
tear 5. minim 6. bubble 8. spherule
glochis... 4. hair (barbed) 7. bristle
glockenspiel... 4. lyra, stop (organ)
8. carillon 10. instrument
gloom... 5. cloud, frown, scowl
7. dimness, sadness 8. darkness
9. dejection, heaviness, obscurity
10. cloudiness, depression,
melancholy, sullen look
gloomy... 3. dim, sad, wan 4. dark,
dour, glum 5. drear, eerie, lurid,
moody, murky 6. cloudy, droopy,
lowery, morose 7. obscure
8. darkling, dejected, dolesome,
downcast 9. darkening, depressed,
tenebrous 10. depressing, foreboding,
tenebrific 11. pessimistic
12. disheartened
Gloomy Dean... 4. Inge
gloomy person... 7. killjoy
Gloria... 4. rite 8. doxology
glorification... 6. praise 7. worship
8. doxology, honoring 9. festivity
10. apotheosis 13. jollification
14. sanctification
glorify... 4. laud 5. adore, bless, exalt,
extol, honor 6. praise 7. elevate,
worship 8. beautify, sanctify
9. celebrate
glorious... 3. sri 5. grand, noble
6. elated, superb 7. eminent, radiant
8. ecstatic, renowned, splendid
9. beautiful, hilarious 10. celebrated,
delightful 11. illustrious, magnificent,
resplendent 12. praiseworthy
glory... 4. fame, halo 5. bliss
(celestial), boast, éclat, honor
6. heaven, nimbus (cloud of), praise,
renown 8. grandeur 10. admiration,
brilliancy, effulgence 11. distinction
13. glorification
gloss... 4. glow 5. color, sheen, shine
6. enamel, luster, polish, remark
7. burnish, pretext 8. glossary,
palliate 9. extenuate 10. brightness,
commentary 14. interpretation
gloss over... 4. fard (obs), wink
5. blink, color 6. excuse 8. palliate

glossy... 5. glacé, nitid, shiny, sleek
6. luster, sheeny, smooth 7. radiant,
shining 8. lustrous, polished
10. reflecting
glove... 3. mit 4. mitt 5. trank
(shaped) 6. boxing, ceatus, mitten
7. gantlet 8. gauntlet
12. mousquetaire
glow... 4. burn 5. ardor, flame, flush,
glean, shine 6. beauty, redden
7. redness 9. eloquence
10. luminosity 13. incandescence
glower... 4. gaze 5. glare, scowl, stare
glowing... 3. red 4. warm 5. drunk
6. ardent, cadent 7. burning,
excited, fervent, flushed 8. eloquent,
luminous 9. beautiful 12. enthusiastic
glucose... 5. rutin, sugar 8. dextrose
glue... 3. fix 4. join 5. paste, stick
6. adhere, cement, fasten, sizing
7. gelatin 8. adhesive, fastener
9. viscosity
glum... 3. sad 5. moody 6. dismal,
gloomy, sullen 8. frowning
glut... 4. cloy, fill, sate 5. gorge, stuff
6. pamper 7. engorge, satiate,
satisfy, surfeit 8. overfill, overload,
plethora, saturate
gluten... 3. gum 4. glue 6. fibrin
7. gliadin 8. adhesive
glutinous... 4. sizy 5. gluey 6. viscid
8. adhesive
glutton... 6. rascal, wretch 7. epicure
8. gourmand 9. cormorant,
scoundrel, wolverine 11. gormandizer,
greedy eater
gluttony... 5. greed 7. edacity
8. voracity 12. intemperance
13. voraciousness
glycerine machine man... 8. effetman
gnar, gnarr (of dogs)... 5. growl, snarl
gnarl... 4. knot 5. growl, snarl, twist
6. tangle 7. contort, distort, roughen
10. contortion 12. protuberance
(tree)
gnarled... 5. rough 6. knotty, rugged
7. complex, knotted, twisted
12. cross–grained
gnash... 4. bite 5. grate, grind (teeth)
gnat... 3. fly 5. nidge 6. insect
8. mosquito
gnaw... 3. eat 4. bite, chew 5. grind,
waste 6. rankle 7. corrode 8. wear
away
gnede... 6. scanty 7. lacking, miserly,
sparing
gnib... 5. ready, sharp 6. clever
gnome... 3. elf, imp, saw 5. bodie,
bogey, dwarf, maxim, nisse
6. goblin, kobold, sprite 8. aphorism
gnomic... 8. didactic 10. aphoristic
gnomic poets (Gr)... 5. Solon
8. Theognis (of Megara)
10. Phocylides (of Miletus)
gnostic... 4. wise 6. shrewd
7. knowing 9. sagacious
Gnostic... 6. Ophite 7. Abraxas
(Abrasax), Sethite
gnu... 6. kokoon 8. antelope
go... 3. act, die, gae, run 4. fail, fare,
game, move, pass, turn, walk, wane,
wend, work 5. leave, sally 6. betake,

decamp, depart, elapse, embark,
energy, extend, result, retire, travel,
weaken 7. advance, entrain, journey,
proceed 8. continue, diminish,
withdraw 9. eventuate, harmonize
go (pert to)...
around.. 6. detour 7. circuit
   8. surround
ashore.. 4. land 9. disembark
astray.. 3. err
at.. 6. attack 9. undertake
away.. 4. exit, scat, shoo 5. scoot,
   scram 6. begone, depart
   9. disappear
back.. 3. ebb 6. recede, repass,
   retire, return, revert 7. regress,
   retrace
before.. 7. precede 8. antecede
   11. participate
down, under.. 4. fail, sink 7. capsize,
   descend, founder, succumb, undergo
   8. submerge 11. deteriorate
easily.. 4. lope 5. amble
furtively.. 5. steal 6. tiptoe
over.. 5. renew 6. revise 7. retrace
   8. rehearse, traverse 9. backtrack,
   re–examine
through.. 4. pass 5. spend 6. suffer
   7. exhaust (fortune), persist, undergo
   9. persevere 10. experience
up.. 4. fail, rise 5. arise, raise
   6. ascend
with.. 4. suit 5. agree, court
   6. accord 8. coincide 9. accompany
   10. understand
goa... 5. Tribe (Queensland) 6. mugger
   7. gazelle
goad... 3. egg 4. poke, prod, prog,
   spur, urge 5. ankus (elephant),
   decoy, impel, prick, sting, thorn,
   yalet (manège) 6. incito 7. inflame
   8. irritate, stimulus 9. incentive
goal... 3. aim, end 4. base, fate,
   home, mark 5. bourn (bourne),
   Mecca, reach, sooro, Thule (Myth)
   6. object 7. purpose 9. objective
   11. destination
goanna... 6. iguana, lizard 7. monitor
goat... 4. buck, dupe 5. brown
   6. engine, lecher 9. scapegoat
   13. laughingstock
goat (pert to)...
astronomy.. 9. Capricorn
fig.. 8. caprifig
fish.. 6. mullet
get one's.. 3. irk, vex 4. rile 5. pique
   6. nettle
god.. 3. Pan
haircloth.. 5. Tibet (Thibet) 6. camlet
hair cord (Bedouin).. 4. agal
goat (type of)... 3. kid, ram, tur, zac
   4. ibex, tahr, urus 5. Capra, goral,
   pasan (pasang), serow, takin
   6. Alpine, Angora, chamal, Jemlah,
   mammal 7. aurochs, markhor
   8. Cashmere, ruminant
goatsucker... 4. bird 7. dorhawk,
   grinder 9. nighthawk
   12. whippoorwill
gob... 4. lump, mass 5. choke, mouth
   6. sailor 8. mouthful, quantity
goby... 4. fish, mapo

go–by... 4. snub 7. evasion, passing
   13. circumvention
god (Myth, Relig)...
Babylonian.. 2. Zu 3. Anu, Sin
   4. Adad, Enzu, Nama, Nebo (Nebu)
   5. Aruru, Cirru, Dagan, Nintu
   8. Ningirsu 10. Ninkhursag
   11. Ningishzida
Celtic.. 6. Aengus
Cymric.. 4. Lleu (Llew)
Egyptian.. 2. Ra 3. Bes, Dis, Geb
   (Keb), Min, Seb 4. Amen, Amon,
   Ptah 5. Horus, Thoth 6. Dhouti,
   Osiris
false.. 4. Baal, idol 6. Mammon
Greek.. 4. Ares, Zeus 5. Comus,
   Hymen, Momus, Pluto 6. Hermes,
   Somnus 7. Bacchus 8. Dionysus
Hebrew.. 3. Jah 7. Jehovah
Hindu.. 4. Agni, Deva, Kama, Siva
   (Shiva) 6. Varuna
household.. 3. Lar 5. Lares 6. Penate
Irish.. 5. Dagda (pagan)
love of, for.. 5. piety 6. bhakti
   9. theophile
Norse.. 2. Er, Ve 3. Tyr, Ull, Van
   4. Loki, Odin, Thor, Ymir 5. Aesir,
   Donar, Vanir, Wodin
Roman.. 4. Jove 5. Comus, Janus,
   Orcus 7. Bacchus, Mercury 8. Dis
   · pater
Semitic.. 5. Hadad 6. Nergal
Supreme.. 3. Dei, Deo, Dio 4. Deus,
   Soul, Zeus 6. Elohim, Spirit
   12. Infinite Mind, Supreme Being
Teutonic.. 3. Tiu 4. Hoth
god (of)...
agriculture.. 4. Nebo 6. Faunus
beauty.. 6. Aengus (Oengus)
beginnings, creation.. 4. Ptah, Zeus
   5. Janus 6. Varuna
commerce.. 5. Vanir 7. Mercury
darkness, evil.. 3. Set, Sin 6. Nergal
day.. 5. Horus
dead.. 5. Orcus 6. Osiris
discord.. 4. Loki
earth.. 3. Geb (Keb), Seb 5. Dagan
east wind.. 5. Eurus
evil.. 2. Zu 3. Set, Sin 6. Nergal
fate.. 5. Moira (Moera)
fire.. 4. Agni 5. Girru 6. Vulcan
flocks.. 3. Pan
January.. 5. Janus
joy.. 5. Comus
justice.. 7. Forseti (Forsete)
law.. 4. Zeus
lightning.. 4. Agni
love.. 4. Amor, Ares, Eros, Kama
   5. Bhaga, Cupid 6. Aengus (Oengus)
March.. 4. Mars
marriage.. 5. Hymen
medicine.. 11. Ningishzida
mountains.. 5. Atlas 7. Olympus
music.. 6. Apollo
Northmen.. 5. Aesir
oceans.. 7. Oceanus
poetry.. 5. Bragi
ridicule.. 5. Momus
sea.. 7. Neptune, Proteus
sky.. 3. Anu
sleep, dreams.. 6. Somnus
   8. Morpheus

storm .. 2. Zu 6. Teshup
sun .. 2. Ra (Re) 6. Apollo, Nergal
thunder .. 4. Thor 7. Jupiter
Thursday .. 4. Thor
Tuesday .. 3. Tiu, Tyr
underworld .. 3. Dis 5. Pluto 6. Osiris
   7. Serapis 8. Dis pater
   11. Ningishzida
war .. 3. Ira, Tyr 4. Mars 5. Woden
   8. Ningirau
wealth .. 5. Bhaga 6. Plutus
Wednesday .. 5. Woden
wind .. 4. Adad 5. Eolus, Eurus,
   Hadad 6. Aeolus, zephyr 8. Favonius
wine .. 7. Bacchus 8. Dionysus
wisdom .. 4. Nebo 5. Thoth 6. Dhouti
woods .. 7. Silenus
youth .. 6. Apollo
goddess ... 3. Ate, Dea, Eir, Eos, Nox,
   Nyx, Ops, Pax, Uni 4. Apet, Eris,
   Fury, Gaea, Hera, Isis, Leda, Maat,
   Nike, Nina, Sati 5. Aruru, Damia,
   Diana, Doris, Epona, Freya, Hygea,
   Irene, Pakht, Salus, Venus, Vesta
   6. Allatu, Athena, Aurora, Cybele,
   Hecate, Hestia, Ningal, Pietho,
   Selene, Semele, Tellus, Vacuna
   7. Artemis, Demeter, Minerva, Parvati
   9. Aphrodite, Eumenides, Mnemosyne
   10. Persephone, Proserpina
goddess of ...
agriculture .. 3. Ops 7. Demeter
arts .. 6. Athena, Pallas
beauty .. 3. Sri 5. Freya, Venus
   7. Lakshmi
dawn .. 3. Eos 5. Ushas 6. Aurora,
   Matuta
destiny .. 4. Fate 5. Moira, Parca
discord .. 3. Ate 4. Eris
earth .. 4. Gaea 5. Aruru 6. Ishtar,
   Tellus
Eskimos .. 5. Sedna
fertility .. 7. Demeter
fire .. 6. Hestia
fortune .. 5. Tyche
freedom .. 7. Feronia
fruit .. 6. Pomona
grain, harvest .. 3. Ops 5. Ceres
Hawaiians .. 4. Pele
healing .. 3. Eir 4. Gula
health .. 5. Damia, Hygea, Salus
hearth .. 5. Vesta
history .. 4. Saga
horses .. 5. Epona
hunt .. 5. Diana 6. Vacuna
infatuation .. 3. Ate
justice .. 7. Nemesis
light .. 6. Lucina
love .. 5. Venus 6. Ishtar 9. Aphrodite
magic, witchcraft .. 6. Hecate
marriage .. 4. Hera
maternity .. 4. Apet
mischief .. 3. Ate 4. Eris
moon .. 4. Luna 5. Diana 6. Phoebe,
   Selene (Selena)
mother of the gods .. 4. Rhea
nature .. 4. Rhea 5. Nymph 6. Cybele
night .. 3. Nox, Nyx
peace .. 3. Pax 5. Irene 6. Athena
poetry .. 5. Erato
rainbows .. 4. Iris

sea .. 5. Doris
seasons .. 5. Horae
summer .. 6. Aestus
sun .. 5. Pakht (Pacht)
trees .. 6. Pomona
truth .. 4. Maat
underworld .. 4. Fury 6. Allatu
   10. Persephone, Proserpina
vengeance .. 3. Ara, Ate 7. Nemesis
victory .. 4. Nike
virtue .. 5. Fides
war .. 5. Anath, Bella
wealth .. 3. Sri 7. Lakshmi
wisdom .. 6. Athena 7. Minerva
youth .. 4. Hebe
Godforsaken ... 6. vacant 7. forlorn
   8. desolate, wretched 9. neglected
godly ... 5. pious 6. devout, divine
   7. saintly 9. religious, righteous
godmother ... 6. cummer (kimmer)
   7. sponsor
God's ...
abode .. 7. Olympus
acre .. 10. churchyard
board .. 14. communion table
country .. 4. home 8. homeland
   9. Vaterland 10. fatherland
cupbearer .. 8. Ganymede
fluid (vein) .. 5. ichor (icor)
food .. 8. ambrosia
gods, The (pert to) ...
death of .. 9. theoktony
marriage of .. 8. theogamy
messenger of .. 6. Hermes
mother of .. 4. Rhea
Twilight of .. 8. Ragnarok
worship of .. 9. theolatry
Goetae ... 7. wizards (anc) 9. sorcerers
   14. thaumaturgists
Goethe (pert to) ...
home .. 6. Weimer (Ger)
masterpiece .. 5. Faust
talent .. 4. poet 8. novelist
   9. dramatist
goffer, gauffer ... 5. crimp, flute, plait
   (lace, paper)
gog ... 3. bog 4. stir 9. agitation
Gog (Bib) ... 5. Ruler (of Magog), tribe
goggle ... 3. eye 4. roll 5. state
   6. squint 11. roll the eyes
goggler ... 4. fish (oceanic)
goggles ... 6. screen 7. glasses
   8. blinkers, eyeshade 10. spectacles
going ... 6. moving, travel 7. current,
   working 9. departure 10. obtainable
   11. in operation
gola ... 7. granary 9. storeroom
   11. Indian caste
golach, goloch ... 6. beetle, earwig
   9. centipede
Golconda ... 6. wealth 8. rich mine
gold ... 2. Au 3. oro 4. gelt, gilt
   5. aurum, color, lucre, metal, money
   6. riches, wealth 7. bullion
gold (pert to) ...
alloy .. 4. asem 6. oroide
artificial .. 8. Mannheim
assayer cup .. 5. cupel
bar .. 5. ingot
braid, lace .. 5. orris
brick .. 7. swindle
coin (US) .. 5. eagle

compound.. 6. auride
containing.. 4. doré
discoverer (US).. 6. Sutter (1849)
field (Bib).. 5. Ophir
fish.. 9. shubunkin
fool's.. 6. pyrite
gilding.. 6. ormolu 9. imitation
Heraldry.. 2. or
King (Myth).. 5. Midas
land of (Bib).. 5. Ophir
like.. 5. auric 7. aureate
measure.. 5. carat
Rush.. 8. Klondike (1897)
   10. California (1849)
seekers (Calif).. 9. Argonauts (1849)
   11. Forty–Niners
symbol.. 2. Au
vein.. 4. lode
washing pan.. 5. cupel
gold and silver... 11. noble metals
golden... 4. gilt 5. auric, blest
   6. blonde, yellow 7. aureate,
   aureous, halcyon 8. metallic,
   precious, valuable 9. Pactolian
   10. auspicious 11. flourishing
golden (pert to)...
Age.. 9. Saturnian, siècle d'or
apple.. 3. bel 4. Eris (goddess)
   5. Paris (giver) 6. tomato
bird.. 6. oriole
bough.. 9. mistletoe
Fleece seeker.. 5. Jason 8. Argonaut
Fleece ship.. 5. Argos
rod.. 8. solidago
goldenrod (pert to)...
genus.. 8. Solidago
State Flower of.. 7. Alabama
   8. Kentucky, Nebraska
goldfish... 4. carp 9. shubunkin
Goldfish (Astron)... 6. Dorado
golf (pert to)...
club.. 4. iron 5. baffy, spoon
   6. driver, mashie, putter 7. brassie,
   midiron, niblick
hazard.. 4. trap 5. stymy 6. bunker
   11. restriction
score.. 3. par 4. bogy (bogie)
   5. eagle 6. birdie
stroke.. 4. baff, chip, hook, loft, putt
   5. drive, slice
term.. 3. ace, par, tee 4. baff, fore
   5. bogey, divot, eagle, green, slice
   6. birdie, dormie, sclaff, stymie
   (stimy) 7. gallery
Golgotha... 7. Calvary 8. cemetery
goliath... 4. frog 5. crane, giant,
   heron
Goliath (pert to)...
Bib.. 5. giant (Philistine)
death site.. 4. Elah
home.. 4. Gath
slayer.. 5. David
Gomorrah (Bib)... 5. Sodom
   13. wicked country
Gomuti palm... 5. areng
gondola race (Venice)... 7. regatta
gone... 3. ago, off 4. dead, left, lost,
   past, yore 5. since 6. absent,
   passed, ruined 8. departed, past
   hope, vanished 9. forgotten
   10. infatuated
goober... 6. peanut

good... 2. eu (pref) 3. bon, fit 4. able,
   full, gain, just, kind 5. ample, godly,
   moral, nifty, pious, sound, valid
   6. benign, devout, expert, profit,
   savory 7. genuine, helpful, liberal,
   trained, upright 8. decorous, interest,
   pleasing, salutary, suitable, virtuous
   9. admirable, competent, enjoyable,
   estimable, excellent, favorable,
   honorable, indulgent, reputable
   10. auspicious, beneficial,
   courageous, gratifying, profitable,
   sufficient 11. commendable,
   well–behaved 12. considerable,
   satisfactory, stouthearted
good (pert to)...
bye.. 4. ta–ta 5. adieu, adios, ciaou
   6. so long 7. cheerio 8. farewell
for nothing.. 4. mean 5. idler
   6. wretch 7. useless 8. indolent
   9. worthless 11. rapscallion
health.. 5. skoal 6. prosit
management.. 6. eutaxy
mighty.. 7. skookum
ordinarily.. 8. mediocre
spirit.. 6. daemon 8. Eudaemon
   12. agathodaemon
tidings.. 6. gospel 7. evangel
will.. 5. favor 9. affection, readiness
   11. benevolence 12. friendliness
goodness... 5. piety 6. virtue
   8. kindness, validity 9. godliness,
   propriety 10. excellence, generosity,
   savoriness
goods... 5. wares 7. ability 8. chattels,
   property 11. information, merchandise
goods cast overboard, sunk...
   5. lagan (lagend) 6. jetsam
   7. flotsam 10. contraband
goose... 4. bean, dupe, fool, gull, iron,
   snow, tule 5. Anser, brant, solan
   6. Canada, gander, gannet, goslet
   7. gosling, graylag (greylag)
   8. barnacle 12. white–fringed
goose (pert to)...
grease.. 6. axunge
pygmy.. 6. goslet
relating to.. 8. anserine
story character.. 5. ganza
gooseberry... 5. fabes (color)
   6. escort, groser (groset), thapes
   8. chaperon, feaberry
gopher... 5. snake 6. rodent 7. burglar
   8. squirrel, tortoise 10. salamander
Gopher State... 9. Minnesota
gore... 3. mud 4. dirt, dung, stab
   5. blood, cloth (triang), filth, slime
   6. pierce 8. heraldry 9. bloodshed,
   penetrate
gorge... 3. eat 4. bolt, glut, sate
   5. chasm, gully 6. canyon, coulee,
   defile, nullah, ravine, valley 7. choke
   up, overeat, pitcher, satiate 8. overfill
gorgeous... 5. grand, showy
   8. colorful, dazzling 9. beautiful
   10. delightful 11. magnificent,
   resplendent
gorgon... 4. ogre, ugly 7. Jezebel
   (Bib), monster
Gorgons (Gr Myth)... 6. Medusa,
   Stheno 7. Euryale 9. sentinels
gorilla... 3. ape 4. thug 5. brute

6. monkey 8. assassin
gorilla man... 9. Du Chaillu (brought ape from Africa)
gormandizer... 9. chowhound 11.. trencherman
gorse... 5. furze 7. juniper
goshawk... 5. Astur 6. tercel
gospel... 5. faith, truth 6. belief 7. epistle, evangel 8. doctrine 9. orthodoxy, selection (Bib) 10. revelation 11. glad tidings 12. proclamation
Gospels (Four)... 11. diatessaron
gossip... 3. cat, eme, gup 4. chat, news, talk 5. on–dit 6. claver, gabble, norate, report, tattle 7. clatter 8. idle talk, quidnunc 9. chatterer 10. newsmonger, talebearer
gossoon... 3. boy, lad (serving) 5. youth 6. garçon
got... see *get*
Gotham... 9. Newcastle (Eng) 11. New York City
Gothamite... 9. New Yorker
Gothic (pert to)...
alphabet.. 11. Moeso–Gothic
architecture.. 6. French
design.. 7. writing 12. architecture
era.. 10. Middle Ages
people.. 4. rude 5. Goths 6. fierce 7. Teutons
printing type.. 5. Doric 9. square–cut
gouge... 4. tool 5. cheat 6. chisel, groove 7. defraud, swindle 8. impostor 10. imposition
Gounod's opera... 5. Faust
gourd... 4. pepo 5. color, flask, melon 6. squash 8. calabash, cucurbit 9. Cucurbita 11. calabazella
gourmand... 5. eater (luxurious) 6. taster 7. epicure, glutton, gourmet 10. fastidious, gluttonous, voluptuary 11. connoisseur
gourmet... 7. epicure 8. gourmand 11. connoisseur
gout... 4. clot, drop 6. blotch 7. disease 9. arthritis
govern... 3. run 4. curb, lead, rein, rule 5. reign 6. bridle, direct, manage 7. conduct, control, preside 8. dominate, regulate, restrain 9. influence, supervise
governess... 4. ayah 5. nurse 6. abbess, duenna 8. guardian 12. instructress
government... 4. rule, sway 6. polity 7. control, regimen 10. management 12. jurisdiction 14. administration
government (pert to)...
agent.. see *representative* below
centralized.. 12. totalitarian
church.. 9. hierarchy 10. hierocracy
foe.. 3. Red 9. anarchist, mercenary, terrorist
form.. 6. polity
grant.. 6. patent
in exile.. 7. de facto
lands.. 5. amani
levy.. 3. tax 6. impost
official.. 10. bureaucrat
representative.. 6. consul 8. diplomat,

minister 10. ambassador
science of.. 8. politics
strong.. 5. power
system.. 6. regime
vicarious.. 7. regency
without.. 6. acracy
government by...
church.. 9. hierarchy 10. hierocracy
few.. 9. oligarchy
God.. 8. theonomy
holy body.. 9. hagiarchy 10. hagiocracy
inner control.. 8. endarchy
law.. 9. nomocracy
men.. 9. andocracy
mob.. 10. ochlocracy
no one.. 6. acracy
rich.. 10. plutocracy
seven.. 9. heptarchy
six.. 12. sextumvirate
slaves.. 10. doulocracy
ten.. 8. decarchy (dekarchy)
three.. 8. triarchy 11. triumvirate
women.. 11. gynecocracy
worst men.. 12. kakistocracy
governor... 4. woon 5. chief, nabob, ruler 6. dynast, regent 7. alcalde, decarch (of 10 men), viceroy 8. decurion, director 9. mechanism 10. magistrate
gown... 4. robe, toga 5. cloak, dress, frock 6. chiton, clothe, cyclas, invest, kimono, mantle 7. cassock, college, garment, matinee, soutane (Eccl), sultane 8. negligee, peignoir 9. nightgown
gozell, gozill... 10. gooseberry
gozzard... 9. gooseherd
gra... 4. love 5. agrah 6. liking 8. fondness 10. sweetheart
grab... 3. nab 4. game (cards), take 5. grasp, seize 6. arrest, clutch, snatch, vessel
grabble... 4. feel 5. grope 6. grovel, sprawl 7. harvest 11. appropriate
grace... 4. fate, luck, note, tact 5. adorn, charm, favor, honor, mercy, title 6. beauty, become, bedeck, polish, prayer, virtue 7. dignify, enhance 8. clemency, easiness, elegance, kindness, reprieve 10. comeliness, refinement, seemliness 12. graciousness, thanksgiving
graceful... 4. airy, easy, feat 6. comely, seemly 7. elegant, fitting, tactful 8. charming, debonair 9. beautiful, courteous, sylphlike 11. appropriate
Graces, The Three (Gr Myth)... 5. Aegle (Mother) 6. Aglaia (Brilliance), Thalia (Bloom) 10. Euphrosyne (Joy)
gracile... 4. slim, thin 6. slight 7. slender
gracious... 4. kind 5. suave 6. benign, urbane 7. affable 8. generous 9. courteous, favorable
grackle... 3. daw 4. bird, myna 7. jackdaw 9. blackbird
gradation... 4. step 5. scale, steps 6. ablaut, nuance, series, stages

7. degrees 10. graduation,
   succession
grade... 4. even, rank, rate, size, sort,
   step 5. level, order 6. assort,
   degree, school, smooth 7. arrange,
   incline 8. classify, gradient, graduate
gradual... 4. easy, slow 6. gentle
   9. leisurely
graduate... 4. pass, size 5. grade,
   taper 6. alumna 7. alumnus,
   promote, student 8. shade off
graffito (scratched crudely)...
   7. drawing 10. scratching
   11. inscription
Graf Spee blown up... 7. Uruguay
   (1939)
graft... 3. dig 4. cion (scion), join,
   toil, work 5. ditch, fraud, labor,
   spade, unite 6. boodle, fasten,
   inarch, trench 7. bribery, implant,
   joining
grafted (Her)... 4. enté
Grail... see *Holy Grail*
grain... 3. jot, rye 4. atom, bran,
   corn, dram, food, grit, iota, malt,
   meal, mite, oats, rice, whit 5. fiber,
   maize, scrap, spark, trace, wheat
   6. barley, millet, sesame 8. particle
grain (pert, to)...
   Bible.. 4. ador
   bundle.. 5. sheaf 7. sheaves
   chaff.. 4. bran, grit
   cracked.. 6. groats
   ear of.. 5. spike 6. ressum (rizzom)
   exchange (Finan).. 3. pit
   feeding on.. 11. granivorous
   fungus, disease.. 1. rust, smut
   5. ergot 6. mildew
   goddess of.. 5. Ceres
   ground.. 4. meal 5. flour, grist
   husks.. 4. bran 5. straw
   measure.. 6. thrave
   mill.. 5. quern
   mixture.. 6. fodder 7. farrage
   9. bullimong
   small.. 7. granule
   spike.. 3. ear 6. rizzom
   stack.. 4. rick
   storage, warehouse.. 3. mow 4. silo
   5. hutch 8. elevator
grammar (pert to)... 5. parse
   6. gender, simile, syntax 7. diction,
   parsing, prosody, synesis, wordage
   8. enallage, language, metaphor,
   paradigm 9. accidence, etymology,
   phonology 10. conformity, declension,
   inflection 11. conjugation
grammatical case... 6. dative
   8. ablative, genitive, vocative
   9. objective 10. accusative,
   nominative
grampus... 3. arc 4. orca 5. whale
   6. killer 7. dolphin 8. cetacean
granada... 11. pomegranate
Granada Moorish Castle site...
   8. Alhambra (Sp)
granary... 3. bin 6. grange 8. cornloft
   10. repository, storehouse (grain)
grand... 4. epic 5. great, large, lofty,
   money, noble, piano 6. august,
   epical, famous, superb, swanky
   7. eminent, sublime 8. gorgeous,

majestic, splendid, thousand
   9. dignified, grandiose, important,
   sumptuous 11. illustrious, magnificent
Grand Canyon State... 7. Arizona
grandchild... 2. oe, oy
grandchild, great... 5. ieroe
grandee... 7. magnate 8. nobleman
   10. clarissimo
grandeur... 5. glory 7. dignity, majesty
   8. elegance, eminence, vastness
   9. greatness, immensity, sublimity
   10. augustness 11. stateliness
grandeval... 4. aged 7. ancient
grandfather... 4. aiel (obs), avus
   6. atavus 8. gudesire
grandiloquent... 5. grand, lofty
   6. turgid 7. pompous 9. bombastic
   12. magniloquent
grandiose... 4. epic 5. grand 6. turgid
   8. imposing 9. bombastic, flaunting
   12. ostentatious
Grandma Moses... 17. Anna Mary
   Robertson
grandmother... 6. beldam (beldame),
   granny, gudame 7. grandam
   (grandame), grandma 8. babushka
grandparent (pert to)... 4. aval
grandson... 6. nepote
Grand Teton peak... 7. Wyoming
grange... 4. farm 7. granary
   9. farmhouse 11. association (1867)
   18. Patrons of Husbandry
granite... 4. rock 5. stone 6. aplite,
   marble, quartz 8. feldspar
   9. pegmatite
Gran Quivira... 5. ruins (mission)
   18. National Monument (N M)
grant... 4. cede, deed, enam, gift,
   give, lend, loan, mise 5. admit,
   allow, bonus, jagir (jaghar), spare
   6. accord, bestow, confer, demise,
   permit, remise 7. appease, concede,
   confess, subsidy 8. appanage,
   sanction, transfer 10. conveyance
   11. acknowledge
granulated... 5. rough 6. coarse
   7. grained 8. granular, hardened
   12. crystallized
grape... 3. fox, uva 5. Tokay
   6. Malaga, Muscat 7. Catawba,
   Concord, Hamburg, Mission, Niagara
   8. Delaware, grenache, Isabella,
   Thompson 9. Chasselas, muscadine
   10. sweetwater 11. scuppernong
grape (pert to)...
   cluster.. 6. raceme
   color.. 7. blue–red 9. cathedral
   conserve.. 5. uvate
   cultivation.. 11. viticulture
   dried.. 4. pasa 6. raisin
   family, genus.. 5. Vitus 8. Vitaceae
   juice.. 4. dibs, must, sapa, stum
   military.. 4. shot
   pomace.. 4. marc, rape
   preserve.. 7. raisine
   residue.. 4. marc, rape 6. pomace
   seed.. 6. acinus
   sugar.. 7. maltose 8. dextrose
grapefruit... 6. pomelo 8. shaddock
   12. Citrus Maxima
grapevine... 4. caro 5. rumor
   6. canard, report 8. maneuver

(wrestling), pipeline 9. dance step
11. information, underground
graph... 5. chart 7. contour, diagram,
drawing
graphic... 5. clear, drawn, vivid
7. written 8. engraved 9. pictorial
11. descriptive, picturesque,
significant 12. diagrammatic
grasp... 4. grip, hent (obs), hold, take
5. catch, clasp, gripe, seize
6. clinch, clutch, gowpen (gowpin)
7. control 8. handgrip 9. apprehend
10. comprehend, understand
grasping... 4. avid 5. close 6. greedy
7. holding, miserly 8. covetous
9. rapacious 10. avaricious,
prehensive 11. acquisitive
13. comprehending, understanding
grass... 3. eel, hay, Poa, rye 4. cane,
Coix, crab, gama, herb, oats, reed,
rice, rush, tare, wire 5. ankee,
Avena, Briza, brome, chess, goose,
grain, grama, hedge, otate, spart,
spear 6. bamboo, barley, darnel,
fescue, marram, millet, redtop,
sesame, switch 7. alfalfa, Bermuda,
buffalo, esparto, Hordeum, Poeceae,
timothy 8. mesquite 9. blue–grass,
Boutelous
grasshopper... 4. grig 6. cicada, locust
7. katydid
grassland... 3. lea, sod 4. mead, veld
(veldt) 5. llano, range, sward
7. pasture, prairie, savanna
(savannah)
grate... 3. rub 4. fret, grid, grit, rasp
5. annoy, chafe, grind 6. abrade,
scrape 7. network 8. irritate
grateful... 7. cumshaw (beggar's
phrase), welcome 8. pleasing,
thankful 10. gratifying
12. appreciative
gratification... 6. relish, reward
8. gratuity, pleasure 10. indulgence,
recompense
gratified... 4. glad 7. pleased
gratify... 5. favor, grace, humor
6. arride, foster, pamper, please
7. appease, delight, flatter, indulge,
requite, satisfy 10. remunerate
grating... 4. grid 5. grate, grill, harsh,
raspy 6. grille 7. lattice, network
8. strident 9. partition 10. irritating
11. latticework 12. nerve–racking
gratis... 4. free 6. freely 10. on the
cuff 10. for nothing, gratuitous, on
the house 12. gratuitously
gratitude... 5. grace 6. praise, thanks
12. appreciation, gratefulness,
thankfulness
gratuitous... 4. free 5. given 6. gratis,
wanton 7. assumed 8. baseless,
needless 9. voluntary 10. groundless
11. superfluous, unwarranted
gratuity... 3. fee, tip 4. dole, gift,
give, vail 5. bonus, bribe 6. bounty
7. cumshaw, pension, present
9. baksheesh (bakshish), buonamano,
lagniappe (lagnappe), pourboire
grave... 3. pit, urn 4. bier, tomb
5. fosse (foss), sober, staid
6. sedate, solemn, trench 7. earnest,

engrave, serious 8. sermonic
9. important, momentous, ponderous,
sculpture, sepulcher
grave (pert to)...
cloth.. 6. shroud 8. cerement
9. cerecloth
coffin.. 4. pall
comb form.. 5. serio
mound (anc).. 6. barrow 7. hillock,
tumulus
person.. 10. sobersides
robber.. 5. ghoul
gravel... 5. geest, grain, stone
6. baffle, defeat, refute 7. calculi,
erratic (boulder), pebbles
10. meerschaum (color)
graven... 6. etched 7. infixed
8. engraved 10. sculptured
gravestone... 5. stele (stela) 6. cippus,
marker, pillar 8. monument
9. tombstone 11. sarcophagus
gravitation... 7. descent, gravity
10. attraction
gravity... 6. weight 7. dignity, sadness
8. enormity, grimness, sobriety
9. formality, solemnity 10. attraction,
importance 11. earnestness,
seriousness, weightiness
12. significance 13. momentousness
gravity law, discoverer... 6. Newton
gray, grey... 3. dim, old, sad 4. aged,
dark, dull, gris, obex 5. dingy, hoary,
polio (comb form), sober 6. animal
(gray), dismal, somber 7. hueless,
neutral, silvery 9. cheerless
10. achromatic
gray, grey (color)... 3. ash, bat, dun
4. ashy, dove, iron, lead, mole, zinc
5. acier, ashen, dusty, mouse, pearl,
slate, smoke, steel, taupe 6. French,
Oxford, Quaker, reseda, silver
7. cesious, dappled, grizzle
8. charcoal, cinereal, gunmetal
10. battleship, dapple–gray
13. pepper–and–salt
graze... 3. eat, rub 4. drab, rase, skim
5. brush, shave 6. browse, feed on,
scrape 7. scratch
grease... 3. fat, oil, tip 4. daub, lard,
mort, saim, soil 5. bribe, smear,
suint 6. axunge 7. fatness, fawning,
lanolin 8. flattery 9. lubricate
greasy... 4. oily 5. dirty, gross, thick
6. smooth 8. slippery, unctuous
10. indelicate
great... 3. big 4. good, huge, vast
5. ample, chief, large, major, stout,
whole 6. famous, grande 7. drastic,
eminent, extreme 8. intimate,
numerous 9. elaborate, important
11. magnanimous 12. considerable
13. distinguished
great (comb form)... 5. macro, megal
Great (pert to)...
Barrier (NZ).. 4. Otea (lsl) 9. coral
reef
Beyond.. 5. grave 9. afterlife,
hereafter 10. after world, The
Unknown 11. eternal home
14. beyond the grave
Cham of Literature.. 13. Samuel
Johnson (Dr)

Circle sailing .. **10.** orthodromy
Commoner .. **4.** Clay, Pitt **7.** Stevens
    (Thaddeus) **9.** Gladstone
Divide .. **7.** Rockies **8.** Rocky Mts
    9. watershed (US) **14.** Rocky
    Mountains **17.** Continental Divide
Fire .. **6.** London (1666) **7.** Chicago
    (1871)
Lakes .. **4.** Erie **5.** Huron **7.** Ontario
    8. Michigan, Superior
Mogul .. **5.** Akbar (Hind) **7.** diamond
Names .. **6.** Hector **8.** Hercules,
    Lysander **9.** Alexander
Pyramid .. **6.** Cheops
Spirit (Ind) .. **4.** Mana, Zemi **5.** Wakan
    6. Manito (orenda), Pokunt
White Way .. **8.** Broadway (NY)
Great Britain ... **5.** Wales **7.** England
    8. Scotland **12.** Commonwealth
    13. United Kingdom **15.** Northern
    Ireland
greatest ... **6.** utmost **7.** extreme,
    noblest
greatness ... **9.** largeness
    10. importance **11.** magnanimity
Greco, Graeco (comb form) ... **5.** Greek
    7. Grecian
Greece ... see also *Greek*
ancient .. **4.** Elis **5.** Argos, Doris, Ionia
    6. Attica, Epirus, Hellas **7.** Argolis,
    Boeotia
cape .. **5.** Melea **7.** Matapan
capital .. **4.** Elis (anc) **6.** Athens
citadel .. **9.** Acropolis
city .. **6.** Patras, Sparta **7.** Corinth,
    Piraeus **8.** Salonika, Thessaly
island .. **5.** Chios, Corfu, Crete, Samos
    6. Lesbos **10.** Dodecanese,
    Samothrace
mountain .. **3.** Ida **5.** Athos **6.** Peleon,
    Pindus **7.** Olympus **9.** Parnassus
peninsula .. **6.** Balkan
river .. **4.** Arta **7.** Hellada **9.** Archelous
sea .. **6.** Aegean, Ionian
seaport .. **4.** Enor, Volo **5.** Corpu,
    Pylos **8.** Salonika **9.** Gallipoli
Greek, Grecian (pert to) ...
abbess .. **4.** amma
alphabet .. see *Greek alphabet*
altar .. **7.** eschara
architecture .. **5.** Doric, Ionic **6.** xystus
    (part) **10.** Corinthian
assembly .. **4.** pynx **5.** agora
avenging spirit .. **3.** Ate, Ker **6.** Erinys
boat .. **6.** caique
bowl (golden) .. **5.** depas
breath .. **6.** pneuma
chariot .. **4.** biga
church section .. **6.** andron, bemata
citadel .. **9.** Acropolis
city (Greek for) .. **5.** polis
commander (anc) .. **7.** navarch
commune .. **4.** deme, nome
contest .. **4.** agon (anc) **6.** Delian
    7. Pythian, Olympic **8.** marathon
courtesan (Athen) .. **5.** Thais
culture, literature .. **7.** classic
    9. classical
cup, bowl .. **5.** depas **6.** cotula
cupid .. **4.** Eros
dance (anc) .. **6.** hormos **7.** pyrrhic,
    strophe **9.** dithyramb

department .. **8.** nomarchy
dish .. **5.** gyros **9.** souvlakia
early .. **5.** Arius **6.** oecist
epic .. **5.** Iliad **7.** Odyssey
female worshipper .. **5.** orant
garment .. **5.** tunic **6.** chiton, peplos
gravestone .. **5.** stele
horse (talking) .. **5.** Arion
hospitality .. **5.** zenia
judge .. **6.** dicast
language .. **6.** Romaic
lawgiver .. **5.** Minos, Solon
magistrate .. **6.** archon, eparch
    7. nomarch
mistress .. **7.** hetaera (hetaira)
monster .. **8.** Typhoeus (100–headed)
note .. **4.** nete **5.** neume **6.** pneuma
    9. hexachord **10.** tetrachord
Old Testament .. **10.** Septuagint
platform .. **4.** bema **7.** logeion
poem .. **5.** Iliad **7.** Odyssey
portico .. **4.** stoa, xyst
sacred enclosure .. **5.** sekos
sacred object .. **6.** sacrum
sacrificial offering .. **5.** hiera
    8. sphagion
school .. **7.** Eleatic
serpent .. **4.** seps **6.** Python
slave .. **5.** Baubo, helot, iambe
    6. penest
soldier .. **7.** hoplite
song .. **5.** melos
sorceress .. **5.** Circe
spirit .. **5.** Momus (evil)
temple .. **4.** naos **5.** cella (part)
theater .. **5.** odeon
war cry .. **5.** alala
youth (would–be citizen) .. **7.** ephebus
Greek alphabet ... **2.** Mu, Nu, Pi, Xi
    3. Chi, Eta, Phi, Psi, Rho, Tau
    4. Beta, Iota, Zeta **5.** Alpha, Delta,
    Gamma, Kappa, Omega, Sigma, Theta
    6. Lambda **7.** Digamma (obs), Epsilon,
    Omicron, Upsilon
Greek Furies ... **6.** Alecto, Erinys
    7. Magaero **9.** Tisiphone
Greek god of ...
atmosphere .. **5.** Hadad
chief .. **4.** Zeus
dreams .. **8.** Morpheus
fire .. **6.** Vulcan
flocks .. **3.** Pan
heavens .. **6.** Uranus
love .. **4.** Eros
lower world .. **5.** Hades
ridicule .. **5.** Momus
river .. **8.** Eridanus
sea .. **6.** Nereus
storm .. **6.** Teshup **7.** Hittite
sun .. **6.** Apollo, Helios **7.** Phoebus
vegetation .. **8.** Dionysus
war .. **4.** Ares **8.** Enyalius
winds .. **5.** Eurus **6.** Aeolus
youth .. **6.** Apollo, Pothos (winged)
Greek goddess of ...
agriculture .. **7.** Artemis, Demeter
beauty .. **9.** Aphrodite
chase .. **7.** Artemis
clouds .. **5.** Niobe
dawn .. **3.** Eos **7.** Alcmene, Ariadne
discord .. **4.** Eris
earth .. **2.** Ge **4.** Gaea

fate.. 5. Moira
fortune.. 5. Tyche
heaven.. 4. Hera
infatuation.. 3. Ate
magic.. 6. Hecate (3–headed)
memory.. 9. Mnemosyne
moon.. 2. Io 5. Diana 6. Selene
nature.. 7. Artemis
night.. 3. Nyx 4. Leto 6. Hecate
peace.. 5. Irene
phallus.. 5. Baubo
retribution.. 7. Nemesis
underworld.. 6. Hecate (Hekate)
vengeance.. 3. Ara 7. Nemesis
victory.. 4. Nike
wisdom.. 6. Pallas 7. Minerva
youth.. 4. Hebe
Greek Myth...
  character.. 5. Niobe, Sinon 6. Adonis,
    Gorgon, Rhesus 7. Calchus, Icarius,
    Pandora, Phrixos 8. Atalanta,
    Endymion, Meleager, Tantalus
    12. Erichthonius
  deity.. 5. Satyr, Titan 6. Cronus
  enchantress.. 5. Circe, Medea
  giant.. 7. Antaeus 9. Enceladus
    (100–armed)
  huntress.. 8. Atalanta
  monster.. 8. Typhoeus (100–headed)
  nymph.. 5. Oread 6. Nereid
  serpent.. 6. Python
  spirit (evil).. 5. Momus
Greek personalities...
  astronomer.. 12. Eratosthenes
  author.. 6. Lucian
  biographer.. 8. Plutarch
  counselor.. 6. Nestor
  dramatist.. 9. Aeschylus (Poet),
    Euripedes, Sophocles
    12. Aristophanes
  fabulist.. 5. Aesop
  geographer.. 6. Strabo
  hero.. 4. Ajax 5. Talos 6. Nestor,
    Thesus 7. Cecrops 10. Hippolytus
  historian.. 8. Xenophon 9. Dionysius,
    Herodotus 10. Thucydides
  mathematician.. 6. Euclid
    10. Archimedes
  painter.. 7. Apelles, El Greco
  patriarch.. 5. Arius
  philosopher.. 5. Galen, Plato, Timon
    6. Nestor 8. Diogenes 9. Aristotle
    10. Heraclitus, Parmenides,
    Pythagorus, Xenophanes
    11. Anaximander
  physician.. 5. Galen
  poet.. 5. Arion, Homer 6. Pindar
    7. Thespis 8. Anacreon 9. Aeschylus
  poetess.. 6. Erinna, Sappho
    7. Corinna
  sage.. 6. Thales
  sculptor.. 5. Myron 7. Phidias
  statesman.. 8. Pericles 9. Aristides
green... 3. raw 4. vert 5. fresh, mossy
  6. callow, praseo (comb form),
  unripe 7. emerald, verdant
  9. malachite, unskilled, untrained
  11. flourishing 13. inexperienced
  15. unsophisticated
green (pert to)...
  back.. 4. frog 11. legal tender (US)
  blue.. 4. cyan, saxe 7. sistine

comb form.. 6. praseo
eyed.. 7. jealous
famous.. 6. Gretna (Scot)
film.. 6. patina
gray.. 5. olive 6. reseda
pale.. 7. celadon
pigment.. 10. terre–verte
quartz.. 5. prase
sickness.. 9. chlorosis
tea.. 5. Hyson
green–back herring... 5. cisco
Greenland...
  Bay.. 6. Baffin
  capital.. 8. Godthaab
  Danish word.. 8. Crönland
  explorer.. 9. Frobisher (1576)
    10. Eric the Red
  natives.. 6. Eskimo (mostly)
  settlement.. 4. Etah
  strait.. 5. Davis
  whale.. 5. right
Green Mt Boys' leader... 10. Ethan
  Allen (1775)
Green Mt State... 7. Vermont
greenness... 5. color 8. sourness
  9. ignorance 10. immaturity
  11. gullibility 12. inexperience
Greenwich time (London)...
  8. absolute, standard 16. Royal
  Observatory
Greenwich Village... 9. Manhattan
  11. New York City
greeting... 3. ave, how 4. hail 5. hallo
  6. accoil, halloa, salute 7. address,
  welcome 8. saluting 9. reception
  10. compliment, salutation
  14. correspondence
gregarious... 6. common, social
  7. affable 8. sociable
  12. social–minded 13. communicative
grego... 5. cloak 6. jacket 9. greatcoat
Gregory... 4. Code (Rom law), Pope,
  year 5. chant, staff (Mus) 6. church
  8. calendar
grenier... 5. attic
grey... see *gray*
grid... 5. grill 7. grating, griddle,
  network 8. gridiron 13. football field
grief... 3. rue, woe 4. care, pain, ruth
  5. abuse, dolor, trial 6. mishap,
  sorrow 7. anguish, offense, remorse,
  sadness 8. disaster, distress,
  document 9. grievance, suffering
  10. affliction 11. bereavement,
  lamentation
grieve... 3. cry, rue 4. erme, pain
  5. mourn, wound 6. lament, sorrow
  7. afflict 8. complain, distress
  10. discomfort
grievous... 4. sore 6. bitter, severe
  7. doleful, heinous, intense
  8. terrible 9. sorrowful
  10. disastrous, oppressive
  11. distressing, gravaminous
griff... 4. claw, glen 6. griffe, ravine
griffe... 4. spur (Arch) 7. mulatto
griffin, griffon... 6. charge (Her)
  7. monster 10. decoration
grig... 3. eel 5. annoy, dwarf
  7. cricket, heather 8. irritate
  9. tantalize 11. grasshopper
grill... 4. cook 5. broil 7. griddle,

network, torture 8. gridiron
10. restaurant 11. interrogate
12. cross—examine
grille ... 6. window (ticket) 7. grating,
network
grilse ... 6. salmon 7. botcher
grim ... 4. dour, sour 5. gaunt, harsh,
stern 6. grisly, horrid, savage, sullen
7. ghastly, hideous 8. horrible,
pitiless, ruthless, sinister 9. ferocious,
frightful, merciless, repellent
10. forbidding, inexorable, relentless,
unyielding
grimace ... 3. mop, mow, mug 4. face,
mock, moue, pout, sham 8. pretense
10. distortion 11. affectation
grimalkin ... 3. cat 5. vixen 6. feline
8. old woman
grime ... 4. dirt, smut, soot 5. sully
9. blackness
grin ... 5. fleer, smile, smirk
grind ... 3. dig, rub, vex 4. bray, grit,
mull, whet 5. crush, gnash, grate,
study 6. abrade, drudge, harass,
polish, powder, satire, school, squash
7. operate, routine, sharpen
8. drudgery 9. comminute, masticate,
pulverize, triturate
grinder ... 5. molar, tooth, tutor
8. sideshow 9. announcer
10. flycatcher, goatsucker
grinding ... 6. boning 7. grating
9. attrition 10. burdensome,
irritating, tyrannical 12. excruciating
grinding (pert to) ...
  mental .. 6. boning 8. cramming,
  studying
  stone .. 4. mano 6. metate, muller
  9. millstone
  substance .. 5. emery 8. abrasive
gringo ... 5. alien 8. American
9. foreigner 10. Englishman
grip ... 3. bag 4. hold 5. clasp, cleat,
ditch, drain, grasp, seize, spasm
6. clench, clutch, furrow, grippe,
handle, obsess, trench, valise
7. control, illness 8. gripsack,
handfast
gripe ... 4. grip, hold, pain 5. annoy,
brake, colic, grasp, pinch, spasm
6. clutch, harass 7. afflict, control,
mastery, vulture 8. complain, distress
9. complaint 10. affliction,
oppression
griskin ... 4. chop, loin 5. steak
grisly ... 4. grim 5. harsh 7. ghastly,
hideous 8. gruesome, terrible
9. deathlike 10. forbidding
grist ... 3. lot 4. malt 5. grain, grind
8. quantity (bees)
grit ... 4. sand 5. nerve, pluck
6. gravel 7. bravery, courage, Liberal
9. sandstone 11. persistence
12. perseverance
grivet ... 4. tota, waag 6. monkey
grizzly bear ... 7. Ephraim (hunter's)
15. Ursus horribilis
groats ... 5. grain, wheat (cracked)
6. cereal
grog ... 3. rum 5. rumbo 8. beverage
9. firewater
groggy ... 5. dazed, drunk, shaky, tipsy

8. unsteady, wavering 9. tottering
groin ... 4. lisk 6. inguen
groom ... 4. syce, tidy 5. brush, curry,
dress, preen, train 7. hostler,
servant, shopboy 8. assistant,
stableman 10. bridegroom,
manservant
groove ... 3. rut 4. dado 5. chase,
croze, flute, scarf, stria, track
6. furrow, rabbet, raggle, scrobe,
sulcus 7. channel, rifling, routine
8. philtrum 10. excavation
11. canaliculus
grooved ... 6. fluted 7. striate, sulcate
11. canalicular 12. canaliculate
grope ... 4. feel 6. fumble, search
7. grabble, grubble
groper ... 4. fish 7. grouper
grosbeak ... 5. finch 8. hawfinch
gros point ... 4. lace (Venetian)
6. stitch (Aubusson) 8. tapestry
(Gobelin) 11. cross—stitch
gross ... 3. fat 5. obese 6. brutal,
coarse, earthy, greasy, impure, vulgar
7. brutish, massive, obscene,
sensual, witless 8. flagrant, indecent,
receipts 9. aggregate, unrefined
10. indefinite, indelicate, scurrilous
grotesque ... 3. odd 5. antic, clown,
freak 6. unique 7. awkward, baroque,
bizarre 8. deformed, fanciful
9. fantastic 11. incongruous
grotesque figure (Chin) ... 5. magot
grotto ... 3. den 4. blue, cave, grot
5. crypt, speos, vault 6. cavern,
recess 8. catacomb
ground ... 3. bog 4. acre, area, base,
clay, clod, farm, land, moor, park,
plot, root, soil 5. basis, cause, earth,
field, hurst, march, ridge, solum,
swale, train 6. belief, bottom, milled,
region 7. country, gritted, opinion,
premise, terrain (terrane) 8. initiate,
instruct 9. establish, territory,
viewpoint 10. background,
foundation, substratum
ground (pert to) ...
  beetles .. 5. Amara
  berry .. 9. cranberry 12. checkerberry
  grain .. 4. bran, meal 5. flour, grist
  nut .. 5. chufa, gobbe 6. goober,
  peanut
  squirrel .. 5. Xerus 6. gopher, hackee,
  rodent 8. chipmunk 11. spermophile
groundhog (pert to) ...
  American .. 6. marmot
  day .. 9. Candlemas (Feb 2)
  home .. 8. Puxatori
  termed .. 6. marmot, rodent
  8. aardvark, whistler 9. woodchuck
  10. whistlepig
groundless ... 4. idle 5. false
8. baseless 9. unfounded
11. unwarranted 13. unsubstantial
grounds ... 4. lees, park 5. basis,
dregs 7. residue 8. scruples
group ... 3. set 4. band, bevy, clan,
crew, gang, herd, pack, sect, sept,
team, unit 5. batch, bunch, class,
clump, corps, flock, genus, order,
panel, shift, tribe 6. legion, troupe
7. arrange, bracket, cluster,

company, species 8. assemble,
category, classify, division
10. assemblage 11. aggregation
group (pert to) . . .
actors . . 6. troupe
animals . . 3. gam, nid, nye, pod
4. herd, nide 5. covey, drove, pride
(lions)
birds . . 4. Pici (woodpeckers)
brilliant . . 6. galaxy
far out . . 6. hippie 7. hipster
laymen . . 5. laity
political . . 4. bloc, ring 5. party
7. machine
singer . . 4. duet 5. choir, octet
6. chorus 7. chanter, quartet
(quartette)
students (graduate) . . 7. seminar
trees . . 4. tope 5. copse, grove,
woods 7. alameda, orchard, pinetum
(pines)
group (quota of) . . .
eight . . 5. octad, octet (octette)
five . . 6. pentad
four . . 6. tetrad 7. quartet (quartette)
nine . . 6. ennead
seven . . 6. heptad, septet (septette)
six . . 6. sextet (sextette)
ten . . 5. decad 6. decade
three . . 4. trio 5. triad, trine 7. Trinity
two vowels . . 6. digram 7. digraph
9. diphthong
grouped . . . 7. classed 8. agminate,
arranged, gathered 9. assembled,
collected, organized 10. classified
grouper . . . 4. fish 5. guasa 6. groper
8. rock hind
grouse . . . 4. bird 6. repine 7. grumble
8. complain 9. ptarmigan
12. capercaillie
grouse (pert to) . . .
courtship . . 3. lak
red . . 7. Lagopus
ruffed . . 6. Bonasa
grouty . . . 5. cross, sulky 6. crabby,
grumpy 7. grouchy
grove (pert to) . . .
living in . . 7. nemoral
mango . . 4. tope
pine . . 7. pinetum
poplar . . 7. alameda
sacred . . 5. Altis (Gr), Nemus (to
Diana)
small trees . . 5. copse
grovel . . . 4. fawn, roll 5. crawl, creep
6. cringe, crouch, shrink, tumble,
wallow, welter 7. debauch, truckle
8. flounder
groveling, grovelling . . . 6. abject
7. fawning 9. prostrate, truckling
11. bootlicking
grow . . . 3. bud, wax 4. come 5. raise
6. accrue, expand, mature, thrive
7. augment, develop, enlarge,
improve, produce 8. increase,
vegetate 9. cultivate
grow (pert to) . . .
dark . . 6. darkle
dim . . 5. blear
intense, profound . . 6. deepen
thin . . 8. emaciate
tiresome . . 4. bore, pall

together . . 7. accrete
worse . . 11. deteriorate
growing (pert to) . . .
angry . . 8. irascent
from without . . 9. ectogenic
10. ectogenous
in . . 6. linose
on trees . . 10. epidendral, epidendric
11. xylophilous (fungus)
out from . . 3. bud 4. stem 5. enate
6. sprout
spontaneously . . 9. adventive
together . . 7. accrete, joining
8. adhering
growing in . . .
clusters . . 8. racemose
fields . . 8. agrestal 9. agrestial
10. campestral
ground . . 9. geogenous
mud . . 9. uliginose
pairs . . 6. binate
rubbish . . 7. ruderal
snow . . 5. nival
water . . 7. aquatic
growl . . . 4. girn, gnar, rome 5. snarl
6. mutter 7. grumble 8. complain
growler . . . 3. cab, can 4. bass (black)
7. iceberg, pitcher 8. clarence
growth . . . 3. bud, wen 4. rise 5. felon,
shoot, tumor 6. effect, result
8. increase, swelling 9. expansion
10. vegetation 11. consequence,
development, enlargement
12. augmentation
growth (pert to) . . .
from within . . 8. endogeny
from without . . 9. ectogenic
10. ectogenous
fungus . . 4. mold, moss 6. mildew
marine . . 7. seaweed
of wood . . 5. copse 7. coppice
9. brushwood
premature . . 9. precocity
process of . . 8. nascency
retarding . . 9. paratonic
grub . . . 3. dig 4. food, plod, root,
spud 5. larva, mathe, slave, stump
6. assart, drudge, maggot, search
7. plodder 8. victuals
grubby . . . 5. dirty, grimy, small
8. dwarfish, infested, slovenly,
toadfish
grudge . . . 4. envy 5. covet, spite
6. hatred 7. grumble 8. begrudge
10. resentment
grudging spender . . . 8. tightwad
gruel . . . 4. diet 6. cereal, liquid
7. disable 8. porridge
grueling, gruelling . . . 6. trying
9. demanding, punishing, weakening
10. exhausting
gruesome . . . 4. ugly 6. grisly, horrid,
sordid 7. ghastly, hideous, macabre
9. deathlike
gruff . . . 4. deep, rude, sour 5. bluff,
harsh, surly 6. clumsy, hoarse,
morose, severe 7. austere, bearish,
brusque
grum . . . 4. glum, sour 6. sullen
8. gutteral 13. harsh–sounding
grumble . . . 4. fret, hone, kick 5. growl,
snarl 6. grouse, mumble, mutter,

repine, rumble 7. maunder
8. complain
guacharo... 6. owlish 7. oilbird
10. goatsucker
Guam...
capital.. 5. Agana
discoverer.. 8. Magellan (1521)
idol, fetish.. 5. anito
island.. 7. Mariana
mountain peak.. 6. Lamlam
port.. 4. Apra
guanaco... 5. llama (like) 6. alpaca
guarantee... 6. avouch, ensure, insure,
surety 7. endorse, promise, warrant
8. guaranty, security, warranty
9. agreement
guaranty... 4. bond 6. pledge
8. security, warranty 9. agreement,
assurance, guarantee
guarapucu... 5. wahoo
guard... 3. van 4. care, curb, keep,
tend, tile 5. tiler, watch 6. bantay,
bridle, convoy, defend, escort, fender,
gaoler, jailer, keeper, patrol, picket,
police, shield, warden 7. defense,
protect 8. restrain, sentinel,
watchman 9. attention, protector
10. cowcatcher, precaution,
protection
guarded... 4. wary 7. careful
8. cautious, defended, discreet,
vigilant, watchful 9. protected
10. restrained 11. circumspect,
sentinelled
guardhouse... 4. brig
guardian... 5. angel, tutor 6. helper,
keeper, patron, warden 7. trustee
8. defender, tutelary 9. custodian,
protector 10. mystagogue (Church
relics)
guardian (Gr)... 5. Argus (100—eyed)
8. Cerberus (3—headed)
guardianship... 4. care 6. charge
7. custody, tuition 8. guidance,
tutelage 13. protectorship
Guatemala...
ant.. 5. kelep
bird (sacred).. 7. quetzal (quezal)
capital.. 13. Guatemala City
coin (gold).. 7. quetzal
fruit (avocadolike).. 4. anay
Indian tribe.. 4. Inca
port.. 7. San José 10. Champerico
13. Puerto Barrios
ruins.. 5. Mayan
volcano.. 4. Agua 5. Fuego
gudgeon... 4. bait, dupe, goby
9. killifish 10. allurement
gue... 5. rogue 7. sharper
guenon... 6. monkey (long—tailed)
guerdon... 5. crown, prize 6. reward
8. requital 10. recompense
guereza... 6. monkey
Guernsey... 6. brandy, cattle, Island
(Channel) 7. garment
guess... 5. fancy, think 6. divine
7. imagine, presume, surmise,
suspect 8. estimate 10. conjecture
guest... 6. caller, inmate, lodger,
patron 7. visitor 9. inquiline (insect)
Guiana...
British capital.. 10. Georgetown

Dutch (Surinam) capital..
10. Paramaribo
French capital.. 7. Cayenne
guide... 3. con, key 4. clew, clue,
lead, rein, sign, sley 5. order, pilot,
steer, teach, tutor, usher 6. advise,
direct, dirigo, govern, guidon
7. adviser, conduct, courier, marshal
8. Baedeker (book), cicerone,
director, polestar, regulate
9. regulator
Guido (scale)... 2. ut 3. alt, A re, B
mi, E la (highest) 5. E la mi, gamut
7. alamire
guild... 5. hanse 7. society
10. fellowship 11. association,
brotherhood
Guildhall statue (London)... 3. Gog
5. Magog (1708)
guile... 5. craft 6. deceit 9. duplicity,
falseness, treachery 11. furtiveness
guileless... 5. naive 6. simple
7. artless, natural, sincere
8. innocent
guillemot... 3. auk 4. coot 5. murre
guilt... 3. sin 4. sake 5. culpa
8. iniquity, peccancy 10. guiltiness,
wickedness 11. criminality, culpability
14. impeachability
guilty... 6. nocent 8. culpable
Guinea, W Afr...
capital.. 7. Conakry (Konakri)
city.. 4. Boke, Labe
export.. 7. bananas 10. pineapples
government.. 8. republic
mineral.. 4. gold 7. bauxite
8. diamonds
tree.. 4. akee
tribe.. 6. Fullah 7. Malinke, Soussou
guinea fowl... 3. hen 4. koot
6. turkey 7. pintado 8. pheasant
guinea pig... 4. boar, cavy 5. Cavia
8. capybara
guise... 3. way 4. form, garb, mask,
mien, mode 5. cloak, cover
6. aspect, custom 7. fashion, pretext
8. behavior 9. semblance
10. appearance
guitar (pert to)...
Hindu.. 4. vina
like.. 4. lute 7. bandore
octaves.. 5. three
Oriental.. 5. sitar
pitch (term).. 5. dital
ridge.. 7. samisen
small.. 7. ukulele
strings, number.. 3. six
gula... 4. cyma, neck, ogee 6. gullet
7. cavetto, molding
gulch... 5. cleft, gorge 6. arroyo,
coulee, ravine
gulf... 3. bay, pit, sea (landlocked)
4. eddy 5. abyss, basin, chasm,
cleft, inlet 6. vorago 7. opening
9. whirlpool 10. separation (wide)
gull... 4. dupe, fool, gray 5. brick,
cheat, cully, fraud 7. cheater,
deceive, defraud, mislead 8. impostor
gull (bird)... 3. cob (cobb), mew
4. Lari, pirr, skua, tern, Xema
5. pewit (laughing) 7. Larinae
8. seedbird 9. kittiwake

gullet... 3. maw 4. tube 5. gully
  6. throat 7. channel, harness (part)
  9. esophagus
Gulliver, Lemuel (pert to)...
  brutes.. 6. Yahoos (race of)
  character, story by.. 5. Swift
  romance.. 16. Gulliver's Travels
  voyage.. 6. Laputa 8. Lilliput
  9. Houyhnhnm 11. Brobdingnag
gully... 3. gut 4. wadi (wady) 5. drain,
  gorge, gulch 6. arroyo, gutter, ravine
  7. couloir 11. watercourse
gum... 3. ase 4. chew, lerp (larp,
  laarp) 5. elemi, myrrh, xylan
  6. acacia, arabic, chicle, conima,
  thwart, tupelo 7. camphor, deceive,
  elastic, gingiva 8. bdellium (Bib),
  mucilage 12. frankincense
gum (pert to)...
  Africa.. 4. kino 7. catechy
  Asia.. 6. Storax 8. galbabum
  Australia.. 5. tuart
  Central America.. 6. chicle
  Egypt.. 5. kikar
  India.. 5. amrad
  Philippines.. 8. galagala
  United States.. 5. Nyssa 6. tupelo
gumbo... 3. mud 4. okra (ocra), sail,
  soup 6. patois
gumboil... 7. abscess, parulia
gummy... 5. lumpy 6. viscid
  7. viscous 8. adhesive, resinous
gumption... 8. sagacity 10. enterprise,
  initiative, shrewdness
gums... 3. ula 6. resins 8. gingivae
gun... 3. gat, rod 4. iron, pump, roer
  5. Maxim, rifle, thief, tommy
  6. ack–ack, Archie, barker, Bertha,
  cannon, mortar, pistol, Rodman
  7. bazooka, carbine, firearm, Gatling,
  machine, shotgun 8. amusette,
  ordnance, revolver
gun (pert to)...
  blow.. 8. sumpitan
  caliber.. 4. bore
  case (leather).. 7. holster
  chamber.. 5. gomer
  cleaner.. 6. ramrod
  cotton.. 5. nitro 9. explosive, pyroxylin
  mount.. 6. turret
  platform.. 11. emplacement
gunfire... 5. salvo 6. strafe 8. enfilade
gunner... 10. bombardier
  12. artilleryman
guppy... 6. minnow 8. Lebistes
  9. killifish
gurnard... 4. fish 6. rochet, Trigla
  8. dragonet, sea robin
guru (Ind)... 7. teacher
gush... 3. jet 4. flow, pour 5. emote,
  spurt 7. chatter 10. outpouring
  14. sentimentalize
gushing... 7. flowing 8. diffused,

effusive, spurting 9. exuberant
  11. sentimental 13. demonstrative
gusset... 4. gore 7. bracket
  9. abatement (Her)
gust... 4. blow, gale, scud, wind
  5. berry, blast, storm 6. flurry, squall
  8. outburst 10. excitement
gusto... 4. élan, zest 5. savor, taste
  6. fervor, liking, relish 9. eagerness
  12. appreciation
gut... 3. sac (silkworm) 5. gully
  6. bowels, catgut, defile, strait
  7. destroy, plunder 8. entrails
  9. intestine 10. disembowel,
  eviscerate
guts... 5. belly, force, pluck 6. vitals
  7. courage, insides, stamina,
  stomach 8. backbone, gluttony
  10. intestines
gutta... 4. drop, spot 5. latex
  7. campana, marking 8. ornament
guttate... 7. spotted 8. droplike
gutter... 4. rone 5. brook, ditch, drain,
  eaves, gully, siver 6. cullis, groove
  7. channel, conduit, scupper
  11. watercourse
gutteral... 3. dry 4. burr 5. husky,
  velar 6. hoarse 7. rasping, throaty
guttersnipe... 4. Arab 5. gamin
  6. poster 9. ragpicker, sandpiper,
  vulgarian
guy... 3. rod 4. flee, rope, stay, vang
  5. chaff, chain, guide 6. banter,
  decamp, effigy (Guy Fawkes), fellow,
  person
Guy Fawkes Day... 13. Gunpowder
  Plot (Eng, Nov 5,1605)
guzzle... 3. tun 4. tope 5. drain,
  drink, spree 6. gutter, liquor, throat,
  tipple 7. debauch, swallow
gymnast... 7. acrobat, athlete, teacher
gymnastics... 9. exercises
  10. acrobatics 12. calisthenics
gypsy (pert to)...
  book.. 3. lil
  devil.. 5. theng
  Dutch.. 8. Heidenen
  horse.. 3. gri (gry)
  Hungarian.. 7. Czigany
  husband.. 3. rom
  India.. 7. Bazigar
  language.. 6. Romany
  man.. 4. chal
  sea.. 6. Selung
  Spanish.. 6. gitano 7. Zincalo
  Syrian.. 5. Aptal
  term.. 4. calo 5. nomad
  woman.. 4. chai (chi)
gyrate... 4. spin 5. twirl, whirl
  6. rotate 7. revolve
gyre... 5. demon, whirl 10. revolution
gyves... 5. irons 6. chains 7. fetters
  8. shackles

H

H . . . 5. aitch, zygal (shaped) 6. letter (8th), symbol 8. aspirate
haab . . . 8. calendar (Mayan)
haar . . . 3. fog
haba . . . 4. bean 8. lima bean
Habakkuk . . . 4. Book (Old Test) 7. prophet
habble . . . 5. brawl 6. gabble, hobble, uproar 9. confusion 10. difficulty
habeas corpus . . . 4. writ 7. summons (you have the body)
habile . . . 3. apt, fit 4. able 6. adroit, clever, expert 8. skillful (skilful), suitable 9. dexterous
habiliment . . . 4. garb 5. dress, habit 6. attire 7. apparel, costume, raiment 8. clothing, vestment 11. furnishings
habilitate . . . 5. dress, equip 6. clothe, fit out 7. entitle, qualify (for teaching)
habit . . . 3. rut, use 4. garb, suit, vice, wont 5. array, dress, haunt, usage 6. attire, clothe, custom, joseph (riding), nature 7. costume 8. clothing, habitude, practice 9. mannerism 10. deportment, habiliment
habitat . . . 4. home 5. abode, house, hovel 6. harbor, reside 7. exhibit (museum), lodging, station
habitation . . . 4. ecad, home 5. hovel 6. ghetto, warren (rabbit) 7. lodging 8. domicile, dwelling, tenement 9. occupancy, residence
habitual . . . 5. usual 6. common, wonted 7. orderly, regular 9. customary 10. accustomed, inveterate
habituate . . . 5. enure, inure 6. addict, inborn, season, settle 8. accustom, frequent, inherent 9. acclimate 11. acclimatize, familiarize
habitué . . . 8. attender 10. frequenter
hacendero . . . 6. farmer 10. proprietor
hache . . . 2. ax 7. hatchet
hacienda . . . 4. farm 5. abode, croft 6. estate 7. revenue 13. establishment
hack . . . 3. cut, hew 4. chop, jade, rent 5. coach, cough, devil, horse (rented), sever 6. drudge, mangle, writer 8. carriage, mutilate 9. mercenary 11. chronometer
hackberry . . . 6. Celtis 8. hapberry, oneberry 10. sugarberry
hackee . . . 8. chipmunk
hackle . . . 3. fly (angling) 4. comb, hack 6. shiner, temper 7. feather, hatchel, plumage 11. stickleback
hackneyed . . . 3. saw 5. banal, corny,

trite 6. cliché 8. timeworn 10. threadbare 11. commonplace, stereotyped 13. platitudinous
Hades . . . 3. pit 4. hell 5. abyss, limbo 7. inferno 9. perdition 10. lower world, underworld 11. netherworld
Hades (pert to) . . .
Babylonian . . 5. Aralu
capital . . 11. Pandemonium
god . . 5. Pluto
Greek . . 8. Tartarus
Hebrew . . 5. Sheol 7. Abaddon, Gehenna 8. Apollyon
Hindu . . 6. Naraka
mother . . 4. Rhea
river . . 4. Styx 5. Lethe 7. Acheron
Roman . . 3. Dis 5. Orcus
hadj . . . 10. pilgrimage
haft . . . 4. ansa, grip, hold 6. handle 8. dwelling
hag . . . 4. Fury, goad 5. crone, ghost, Harpy, vixen, witch 6. beldam (beldame), goblin 8. harridan, old woman 9. hobgoblin
hageen, hagein . . . 9. dromedary
hagfish . . . 5. borer 6. Mysine 7. lamprey (lowest existing craniate vertebrate)
haggard . . . 4. bony, lank, lean, pale, thin, wild 5. gaunt, spare 6. wanton 7. anxious, untamed 8. harrowed, unchaste, wild-eyed 9. deathlike, suffering, untrained 10. cadaverous 11. intractable, overwrought
haggle . . . 3. cut, hew 4. hack, prig 5. cavil 6. chisel, dicker, higgle, palter 7. bargain, chaffer, stickle, wrangle
Hague, The . . . 7. capital (Neth)
Haida (pert to) . . .
famed for . . 6. totems 7. carving 10. seamanship
Indian . . 15. British Columbia
tribe . . 11. Skittagetan
hail . . . 3. ave, ice 4. ahoy, call 5. avast, greet, skoal 6. accost, health, signal 7. acclaim, address, graupel, pellets
hair . . . 3. cue, fur, mop 4. lock, mane, seta, shag 5. pilus, plume, tress 6. thread 7. bristle 8. filament 10. narrowness
hair (pert to) . . .
accessory . . 3. net, pin 8. barrette
Angora . . 6. mohair
band . . 5. snood 6. fillet
braid . . 3. cue 4. fall 5. queue 7. pigtail
cell . . 12. Organ of Corti
cloth . . 3. aba 5. shirt 6. cilice

247

comb form . . **4.** pilo
curly . . **10.** cymotrichy
disease . . **8.** dandruff, psilosis
dresser . . **7.** friseur (Fr), stylist
dryness . . **7.** xerasia
excessive growth . . **7.** pilosis
flaxen . . **5.** linus
horse's foot . . **7.** fetlock
intestinal . . **6.** villus
liquid for . . **3.** set **5.** spray **6.** lotion
   7. relaxer
lock . . **5.** tress **7.** earlock, ringlet
   8. lovelock **9.** dreadlock
loss of . . **8.** alopecia, baldness
of the . . **6.** crinal
remover . . **9.** decalvant, epilatory
   10. depilatory
straight . . **10.** leiotrichy
style . . **3.** set **4.** Afro, tete, updo
   6. hairdo **7.** chignon, cornrow
   8. coiffure
tuft . . **4.** coma **5.** beard **6.** goatee
   7. cirrose, Galways, Vandyke
   8. whiskers **9.** sideburns
wave . . **4.** perm **6.** marcel
wig . . **6.** peruke **7.** periwig
wooly . . **9.** ulotrichy
hairiness . . . **7.** villous **9.** villosity
hairless . . . **4.** bald **5.** acoma
   7. acomous, epilose **8.** depilous,
   glabrous
hairpin . . . **6.** bodkin **8.** bobby pin
hairsplitting . . . **9.** quibbling
   11. distinction **13.** hypercritical
   14. hypercriticism, overparticular
hairy . . . **4.** noil **5.** pilar **6.** comate,
   comoid, comose, crinal, pilose, shaggy
   7. bristly, crinose, hirsute **8.** trichoid
Haiti, Haitian . . .
bandit . . **4.** caco
capital . . **12.** Port–au–Prince
dance . . **5.** mambo
discoverer . . **8.** Columbus (1492)
evil spirit . . **4.** baka (boko)
island . . **10.** Hispaniola **15.** Greater
   Antilles
language . . **6.** Creole, French, patois
liberator . . **9.** Toussaint
product . . **6.** coffee
sweet potato . . **6.** batata
hake . . . **4.** fish **5.** idler, tramp **6.** loiter
   7. handgun **8.** kingfish
halberd . . . **4.** bill **5.** frame (flogging)
   6. glaive, weapon (Mil)
halcyon . . . **4.** bird, calm **8.** peaceful,
   tranquil **10.** auspicious, kingfisher
Halcyone (pert to) . . .
changed to . . **10.** kingfisher
daughter of . . **6.** Aeolus
wife of . . **4.** Ceyx (Gr)
hale . . . **3.** tug **4.** drag, draw, haul, pull,
   well **6.** hearty, robust, strong
   7. healthy **8.** vigorous **9.** strapping
half . . . **4.** demi, hemi, part, semi, term
   5. share **6.** moiety **7.** divided, partial
   8. division, semester **9.** equal part,
   bisection **11.** imperfectly
half (pert to) . . .
and half . . **5.** equal, mixed **6.** halved
   7. neutral
boot . . **3.** pac (pack) **6.** buskin
man, half bull . . **8.** minotaur

man, half horse . . **7.** centaur
mask . . **6.** domino
moon–shaped . . **9.** semilunar
nelson (wrestling) . . **4.** hold
stem to stern . . **8.** midships
turn (manège) . . **8.** caracole (caracol)
wit . . **4.** dolt **5.** dunce **9.** blockhead
Half Moon ship (pert to) . . .
captain . . **11.** Henry Hudson
country . . **11.** Netherlands
first to sail . . **11.** Hudson River (1609)
Halicarnassus, famed for . . .
Historians (Gr) . . **9.** Dionysius,
   Herodotus
monument . . **9.** Mausoleum (Tomb of
   Mausolus, 325 BC)
hall . . . **4.** aula, room, sala **5.** entry,
   foyer, odeum (odeon) **6.** atrium,
   lyceum **7.** hallway, passage, theater
   8. corridor **9.** vestibule
   10. auditorium, passageway
hallow . . . **5.** bless **8.** dedicate,
   sanctify, venerate **9.** celebrate
   10. consecrate
hallowed place . . . **4.** fane, holy
   5. altar **6.** bethel, church, shrine,
   temple **8.** cathedral, synagogue
hallucination . . . **6.** mirage **7.** chimera,
   fantasy **8.** delusion **9.** nightmare
hallux . . . **3.** toe **5.** digit
halo . . . **3.** arc **4.** aura, glow, nimb, ring
   5. glory, light **6.** areola, brough,
   circle, corona, nimbus **7.** aureole
   (aureola) **8.** encircle, halation
halt . . . **3.** end **4.** camp, lame, limp,
   stop **5.** cease, check, pause, stand
   6. arrest, hold up, maimed **7.** limping
   8. blockage, crippled, lameness
   9. mutilated **10.** standstill
halter . . . **4.** hang, rope **5.** noose, strap
   6. hamper **7.** shackle **8.** cavesson,
   restrain **9.** hackamore
halting . . . **4.** lame **6.** maimed
   7. limping **8.** spavined
   10. hesitating, stammering
halting place . . . **4.** camp **5.** étape
   7. bivouac **10.** encampment
halved . . . **9.** dimidiate
Hamburg, Germany . . .
color . . **5.** white **6.** yellow **7.** carmine
   11. carmine lake
fowl . . **11.** Leghornlike
fruit . . **5.** grape
lace . . **6.** edging
root (edible) . . **7.** parsley
steak . . **4.** beef
hamiform . . . **6.** curved, hooked
   7. hamulus **8.** aquiline
   10. hook–shaped
Hamilton (pert to) . . .
dynamics . . **8.** equation
famed as . . **9.** statesman
   11. philosopher **13.** mathematician
math . . **10.** quaternion
Hamite (N Afr) . . . **5.** Fulah **6.** Berber,
   Somali (Somal)
hamlet . . . **4.** dorp, vill **5.** aldea (aldee),
   casal (casale), thorp (thorpe)
   7. grouper (fish), village
Hamlet (pert to) . . .
character . . **11.** Shakespeare
country . . **7.** Denmark

friend.. 7. Horatio
site.. 8. Elsinore
hammer... 4. beat, claw, jack, maul,
  peen, tack, tamp 5. gavel, kevel,
  madge, pound 6. beetle, martel,
  oliver, sledge, strike, swinge
  7. belabor 8. malleate
hammer (pert to)...
bird.. 8. umbrette
blacksmith's.. 6. fuller, oliver
bricklayer's.. 6. scutch
end.. 4. poll
face.. 4. trip
head.. 4. peen 5. shark
medical.. 6. plexor 7. plessor
out.. 5. anvil, forge
smite.. 5. skite
stone.. 5. kevel, spall
hamper... 3. ped 4. clog, curb, load,
  slow 5. cramp, crate, maund
  6. basket, burden, fetter, hinder,
  hopple, impede, seroon 7. confine,
  hanaper, manacle, shackle, trammel
  8. encumber, restrain, restrict
  9. container, embarrass
  10. impediment
Ham's son... 4. Cush
hamster... 6. rodent 8. Cricetus
hamus... 4. hook 7. process (Zool)
hanaper... 6. basket, hamper
hand... 3. paw 4. fist, give, mano,
  palm, part, pass, side, till 5. claut,
  grasp, index, manus, power, share,
  skill 6. agency, worker 7. ability,
  pointer, workman 8. applause,
  tendency, transmit 9. craftsman,
  handiwork, signature 10. metacarpus
  11. handwriting, performance
  15. instrumentality
hand (pert to)...
back of.. 10. opisthenar
bag.. 4. etui, grip 5. cabas, purse
  8. reticule
book.. 4. tome 5. codex 6. manual
  9. vade mecum
cuffs.. 7. darbies 8. manacles
  9. bracelets
handful.. 4. kirn 6. gowpen
  7. maniple 8. quantity
measure.. 8. fistmele
me–down.. 4. used, worn 5. cheap
  9. ready–made 10. secondhand
of the.. 6. chiral, manual
palm.. 4. loof 6. thenar
picked.. 5. eleme 6. choice
  8. selected
script.. 6. Neskhi (Neski)
stone (grinding).. 4. mano
without.. 7. amanous
writing.. 11. chirography
writing on walls.. 4. doom, mene
  (Bib), omen 8. graffito
handicap... 4. lisp, race 6. burden,
  hamper, hinder, impede
  8. encumber, equalize, penalize
  9. advantage 10. impediment,
  stuttering 11. encumbrance
  12. disadvantage
handicraftsman... 7. artisan
handkerchief... 7. malabar
  8. mouchoir 9. neckcloth
  11. neckerchief

handle... 3. ear, paw, ply, use
  4. ansa, bail, deal, feel, haft, hilt,
  knob, maul, name, toat, tote
  5. helve, pilot, snath, swipe, title,
  touch, treat, wield 6. deal in, direct,
  manage, rounce, second, sneath,
  tiller 7. control, operate
handle (pert to)...
awkwardly.. 6. fumble, mumble
carelessly.. 6. cajole 7. tweedle
roughly.. 4. maul 6. bruise, injure,
  mangle
shaped.. 6. ansate
skillfully.. 6. manage 7. control
  10. manipulate
hands (pert to)...
nautical.. 4. crew, gang
off.. 4. don't, quit, stop 5. taboo
  6. desist 9. interdict
on hips.. 6. akimbo
without.. 7. amanous
handsome... 5. ample 6. comely,
  heppen (dial) 7. elegant, gallant,
  liberal 8. generous, gracious,
  pleasing, suitable 9. agreeable,
  beautiful 10. jimpricute
  11. appropriate, magnanimous
  12. considerable
handwriting on the wall... 4. mene
  (Bib) 8. graffito, upharsin
handy... 4. deft 5. adept, ready
  6. adroit, heppen, nearby, wieldy
  8. skillful (skilful) 9. dexterous,
  versatile 10. accessible, convenient
hang... 3. sag 4. pend, rest, sway
  5. cling, drape, droop, hover, knack
  6. cleave, dangle, depend
  7. execute, meaning, suspend
hang (pert to)...
around.. 4. loaf, wait 6. loiter
  8. frequent
back.. 3. lag 5. demur, loath 6. falter
  9. reluctant
down.. 3. lop 4. lave 5. droop
  6. depend
loosely.. 3. lop 4. flag, loll 6. bangle,
  dangle
on, onto.. 5. cling 6. adhere, depend
  9. persevere
over.. 6. impend
together.. 4. loin 6. cohere
  9. co–operate
hanger–on... 3. bur 5. toady 6. heeler
  8. follower, loiterer, parasite
  9. appendage, dependent, sycophant,
  toadeater (menial) 10. blackguard
hanging... 5. arras, drape, loose
  7. curtain, pendant (pendent),
  pensile, valance 8. downcast,
  pendency 9. execution, suspended
hanging (pert to)...
Eccl.. 6. dorsal, dossal (dossel)
Gardens of Babylon, builder..
  14. Nebuchadnezzar (Nebuchadrezzar)
ornament.. 6. bangle 7. pendant
stage.. 7. scenery
hangman... 8. carnifex 9. Jack Ketch
  11. executioner
hangman's noose... 4. rope
  6. hempen
hangnail... 6. agnail 7. whitlow
hangout... 5. joint 10. rendezvous

hank... 3. ran (twine) 4. coil 5. skein
hanker after... 5. crave, yearn
  6. aspire, desire, hunger 7. long for
Hannibal (pert to)...
  accomplishment.. 8. Punic War (2nd)
  father.. 13. Hamilcar Barca
  native of.. 8. Carthage
  rank.. 7. General (genius)
  victory at.. 6. Cannae
Hanover, House of... 8. Victoria
Hanukkah, Hanukka... 7. holiday
  (Jew) 16. Festival of Lights (Bib)
  17. Feast of Dedication (Jew)
haphazard... 6. chance, random
  8. accident, careless 9. orderless
haply... 9. perchance
happen... 4. come, fall, fare 5. evene
  (obs), occur 6. arrive, befall, betide,
  chance, mayhap 9. eventuate,
  transpire
happening... 4. fact 5. event (chance)
  6. tiding 7. episode 8. incident,
  periodic, sporadic 10. occurrence
happily... 5. fitly, haply 6. gladly
  9. tactfully, willingly 10. blissfully,
  cheerfully, gracefully 11. contentedly,
  opportunely 12. auspiciously,
  felicitously, prosperously, successfully
  13. appropriately
happiness, science of...
  11. eudaemonics
happy... 3. apt 4. cosh, glad 5. blest,
  faust, lucky, ready, seely, sunny
  6. joyful, timely 7. blessed, content,
  fitting 8. cheerful 9. contented,
  fortunate, pertinent 10. auspicious,
  felicitous, propitious, prosperous
Happy Valley... 8. paradise (of
  Rasselas, Andrew Jackson)
hara–kiri (Jap)... 7. seppuku, suicide
harangue... 3. nag 4. rant 5. orate,
  spiel, spout 6. screed, speech, tirade
  7. address, declaim, expound,
  lecture, oration
harass... 3. din, fag, nag, try, vex
  4. bait, fret, gall, haze, jade, raid,
  tire 5. annoy, beset, bully, chafe,
  grind, harry, tease, weary, worry
  6. badger, bother, heckle, hector,
  molest, pester, plague 7. agitate,
  disturb, hagride, perplex, provoke,
  torment, trouble 8. distress, irritate
  9. persecute, tantalize
harbinger... 4. host, omen 5. usher
  6. herald 7. presage, shelter
  8. fourrier, harborer 9. informant,
  messenger, precursor 10. forerunner
harbinger of Spring... 5. robin
  6. crocus
harbor, harbour... 3. bay 4. cave,
  port 5. haven 6. covert, foster,
  refuge 7. lodging, outport, retreat,
  shelter
hard... 3. fit 4. cold, dour, firm, iron,
  mean 5. close, harsh, rigid, stern,
  stony 6. knotty, robust, steely, stingy,
  strict, strong 7. callous, onerous
  8. diligent, rigorous, toilsome
  9. difficult, heartless, intricate,
  strenuous, stringent, wearisome
  10. inflexible, relentless, unyielding
  12. impenetrable, incorrigible

  13. unsympathetic
hard (pert to)...
  boiled.. 4. hard 5. tough 6. strict
  7. callous 8. hardened 10. solidified
  13. sophisticated
  coal.. 10. anthracite
  money.. 6. silver 8. metallic
  prefix.. 3. dys
  question.. 5. poser
  rubber.. 7. ebonite 9. vulcanite
  shell.. 6. lorica
  stone.. 7. adamant (diamond)
  wood.. 4. mabi, teak 5. maple
  6. walnut 8. mahogany
harden... 3. gel, set 4. cake, kern
  5. enure, inure, steel 6. freeze,
  ossify, temper 7. toughen
  8. indurate, solidify 9. habituate
  10. strengthen
hardened... 4. hard 5. caked
  6. frozen, wicked 7. callous, steeled
  8. indurate, obdurate, ossified
  9. heartless, reprobate, unfeeling
  10. impenitent, impervious,
  inveterate, solidified 12. impenetrable
hardening of the arteries...
  16. arteriosclerosis
hardening of the eyeball...
  8. glaucoma
hardheaded... 5. boche (Boche)
  6. German, shrewd, strict
  9. obstinate, sagacious
hardhearted... 4. mean 5. cruel
  7. callous 8. pitiless 9. unfeeling
  13. unsympathetic
hardship... 5. rigor 6. injury 7. trouble
  8. hardness 9. adversity, privation
hardtack... 5. bread 7. galette
  10. sea biscuit
hardwood... 3. ash, oak 4. ipil, mabi,
  teak 5. maple 6. walnut
  8. mahogany
hardy... 4. bold, hale, rash 5. brave,
  lusty, stout 6. daring, strong
  7. healthy, spartan 8. intrepid,
  resolute 9. audacious, confident
  10. courageous
hare... 3. doe, wat (watt) 4. buck,
  cony, pika (tailless) 5. lapin, Lepus
  6. rabbit, rodent, tapeti 7. leveret
hare (pert to)...
  constellation.. 5. Lepus
  harelike.. 6. agouti 8. leporine
  tail.. 4. scut
  track.. 4. slot
  type.. 10. cottontail, jack rabbit
harem... 5. serai 6. purdah, zenana
  8. seraglio 9. gynaeceum
harem room... 3. oda (odah)
harem slave... 9. odalisque (odalisk)
hark... 4. heed, hist 6. listen
  7. hearken, whisper 9. attention
harkened... 5. heard 6. heeded
  8. listened 9. hearkened
harlequin... 4. duck (sea) 5. clown,
  color 7. buffoon 9. fantastic, trickster
  11. masquerader 12. multi–colored,
  parti–colored
Harlequin (comedy)... 11. pantomimist
harm... 3. mar 4. bane, dere, evil,
  hurt, pain 5. grief, wrong
  6. damage, impair, injure, injury,

scathe (scath), sorrow
10. misfortune, wickedness
12. disadvantage
harmful... 3. bad 4. evil, upas
  6. nocent 7. baneful, hurtful, malefic,
  noisome, noxious 8. damaging,
  sinister 9. injurious 10. pernicious
  11. deleterious, detrimental
  12. insalubrious
harmless... 5. seely 6. unhurt
  8. dehorned, unharmed
  9. innocuous, undamaged, uninjured
  11. unoffending
harmonious... 6. syntax 7. harmony,
  musical, orderly, spheral, tuneful
  9. accordant, agreeable, congruous,
  consonant, eurythmic (eurhythmic),
  melodious 10. compatible,
  concordant, euphonious
  11. conformable, symmetrical
harmonize... 2. go 3. gee 4. tone
  5. agree, blend, chime 6. attune
  7. conform, consist 9. reconcile
  10. correspond, symmetrize,
  sympathize
harmony... 4. tone, tune 5. music,
  order, triad, unity 6. accord, cosmos,
  melody, unison 7. concord, euphony
  8. symmetry 9. agreement,
  harmonics 10. conformity,
  consonance
harness... 4. gear 5. armor, equip
  6. graith, tackle 7. uniform
  8. accouter, ornament 9. caparison,
  parachute
harness part... 3. tug 4. hame, rein
  5. trace 6. collar, halter, terret
  7. apparel 9. hackamore
  10. breastband, martingale
harp... 4. arpa, koto, lyre, Lyra (Astron)
  5. nanga 8. Irishman 11. clairschach
harp (pert to)...
key.. 5. C Flat
octaves (number).. 11. six and a half
pedals.. 5. seven
star.. 12. Harp of Arthur
strings.. 8. forty–six
harping... 7. humdrum, tedious
  9. iterating, repeating 11. repetitious
harpoon... 5. spear 7. javelin 8. lily
iron
harpsichord... 6. spinet 8. clavecin
  9. lyrichord 12. clavicembalo
harpy... 3. bat 5. eagle, fiend
  9. plunderer 12. extortionist
Harpy (Myth)... 5. Aello, ghoul
  7. Celaeno, monster (part bird,
  woman), Ocypete, Podarge (The Iliad)
harridan... 3. hag 5. vixen, witch
  6. virago 7. Jezebel 8. strumpet
  9. termagant
harrier... 3. dog 4. hawk 5. bully,
  hound 7. heckler 8. badgerer
  9. tormentor
harrow... 4. dish, pain 5. harry, herse
  (Hist), wound 7. oppress, torment,
  torture 8. distress, lacerate
  9. cultivate, formation (geese),
  implement
harrowing... 7. painful, racking, tilling
  9. agonizing, torturous

11. cultivating, distressing
12. heart–rending
harry... 3. vex 4. sack 5. annoy,
  hound, worry 6. harass, hector,
  plague, ravage, ravish 7. agitate,
  besiege, pillage, plunder, violate
  8. lay waste 9. persecute
Harry... 5. Devil (Shak)
harsh... 3. raw 4. dure, grim
  5. acerb, acrid, asper, crude, gruff,
  raspy, stern, stiff 6. bitter, coarse,
  severe, unkind 7. drastic, painful,
  pungent, rasping 8. clashing,
  gutteral, jangling, rigorous, strident
  9. inclement, offensive, repellent
  10. discordant, relentless
  11. acrimonious, disagreeing
harshness... 5. rigor 7. raucity
  8. acrimony, pungency, severity
  9. gruffness 11. raucousness
hart... 4. deer, stag 5. spade
hartebeest... 4. asse, tora 5. caama
  (kaama) 6. lecama 7. bubalis
  8. antelope 10. Alcelaphus
Harvard College honor... 4. book
  5. detur 12. let it be given
harvest... 4. crop, gain, rabi, reap
  5. fruit, yield 6. autumn, gather,
  reward 7. acquire, produce
harvest (pert to)...
god.. 6. Cronus, Saturn
goddess.. 3. Ops 5. Ceres
home.. 4. kirn, mell 6. hockey
moon.. 4. full 15. autumnal equinox
second.. 9. aftermath
tick.. 6. acarid
hash... 4. food 5. mince 6. jumble,
  medley, ragout 7. mixture
  10. hodgepodge 11. gallimaufry, olla
  podrida
hashish... 4. hemp 5. bhang (bang)
  8. cannabis, narcotic
hassle... 4. fray 5. brawl, melee
hasten... 3. hie 4. scud, urge
  5. amain, apace, hurry, scamp,
  speed 7. further 8. expedite
  10. accelerate 11. precipitate
hastened... 3. ran 4. hied, sped
  5. raced 6. rushed 7. hurried,
  scooted 8. galloped 9. expedited
  11. accelerated 12. precipitated
hasty... 4. fast, rash 5. brash, eager,
  fleet, quick, swift 6. speedy, sudden,
  urgent 7. cursory, hurried 8. reckless
  9. impetuous, impulsive, premature
  11. expeditious, precipitate
hasty pudding... 4. mush 9. stirabout
hat... 3. fez, tam, top 4. felt, hood,
  silk 5. beret, derby, gibus, opera,
  straw, terai, toque 6. bonnet, cloche,
  cocked, fedora, Panama, sailor,
  topper, turban 7. chapeau, picture,
  pillbox, porkpie, tricorn 8. sombrero
  9. headdress, sou'wester, stovepipe,
  ten–gallon 11. mortarboard
  13. three–cornered
hat (pert to)...
antique.. 7. bycoket (bycockot),
  petasos (petasus)
covering.. 8. havelock
crown.. 4. poll
defensive.. 4. coif

Eccl.. 7. biretta 9. Cardinal's
military.. 5. shako
opera.. 4. tile 5. gibus 6. topper
pass (the hat).. 10. collection
slang.. 4. plug 5. dicer
stovepipe.. 8. caroline
under one's.. 6. secret 9. to oneself
hatch... 4. door, gate, line (art), plot
  5. breed 6. invent 7. concoct,
  produce 8. contrive, hatchway,
  incubate 9. floodgate, originate
  10. bring forth, sluice gate
hatchet... 2. ax (axe) 3. adz (adze)
  4. mogo 8. tomahawk
hate... 4. miso (comb form) 5. abhor,
  odium 6. detest, hatred, loathe,
  rancor 7. despise, dislike
  9. abominate, antipathy
hateful... 6. odious 7. heinous
  8. terrible 9. abhorrent, execrable,
  invidious, loathsome, malicious,
  obnoxious, offensive, revolting
  10. abominable, detestable,
  disgusting 11. distasteful
  12. disagreeable
hater of...
children.. 10. misopedist
mankind.. 11. misanthrope
marriage.. 10. misogynist
mathematics.. 8. misomath
newness.. 9. misoneist
sights.. 11. misoscopist
strangers.. 8. misoxene
work.. 11. ergophobiac
hatred... 5. odium 6. enmity, rancor
  8. aversion 9. animosity, malignity
  10. abhorrence, repugnance
  11. detestation, malevolence
hatred of...
argument.. 8. misology
change.. 9. misoneism
children.. 9. misopedia
God, gods.. 10. misotheism
mankind.. 11. misanthropy
marriage.. 8. misogamy
strangers.. 8. misoxeny
  10. xenophobia
war.. 9. polemical 11. misopolemic
wisdom.. 9. misosophy
women.. 8. misogyny
hauberk... 5. armor 9. habergeon
haughty... 4. airy, bold, high 5. lofty,
  noble, proud 6. snooty 7. fatuous,
  stately 8. arrogant, cavalier, orgulous,
  scornful 10. disdainful, hoity–toity
  11. domineering, highfalutin
  12. contemptuous, supercilious
haul... 3. lug, tow, tug 4. cart, drag,
  draw, pull 5. booty, bouse, catch,
  check, shift 9. reprimand, transport
haul down a flag... 6. strike
haunch... 3. hip 4. huck 10. leg and
  loin 12. hindquarters
haunch bone... 10. innominate
haunt... 3. den 4. dive, nest 5. ghost,
  habit 6. infect, obsess, resort
  7. torment 8. frequent, practice
hautboy... 4. oboe
have... 3. get, hae, own 4. hold,
  keep, know 5. beget, trick 6. accept,
  effect, retain 7. cherish, perform,
  possess, swindle 10. experience,

understand, suffer from
have (pert to)...
ambition.. 6. aspire
charge.. 4. tend
on.. 4. wear
thoughts of.. 6. ideate
to do with.. 4. deal
weight.. 8. militate
haven... 3. bay 4. port 5. hithe
  (small), inlet 6. asylum, harbor,
  recess, refuge 7. shelter 9. sanctuary
havier... 4. deer
having (pert to)...
blind end.. 6. caecal
branches.. 6. ramose
clamp, pincers.. 7. chelate
dignity.. 8. majestic
equal sides.. 9. isosceles
eyes.. 7. oculate
faith.. 8. trusting
featherlike petals.. 7. pinnate
feelers.. 9. antennate
fingers.. 8. digitate
foreknowledge.. 9. prescient
four feet.. 11. quadrupedal
harmful quality.. 9. innocuous
leaves.. 6. foliar 7. foliate
limits.. 6. finite
local designation.. 7. topical
lumps.. 7. noduled
more than one mate.. 9. polyandry
no angles.. 6. agonic
no interest.. 6. supine
no teeth.. 7. edental 8. edentate
nothing to do.. 6. otiose
one foot.. 6. uniped
pits, depressions.. 7. foveate
  9. foveolate
plane surfaces.. 7. faceted
pointed end.. 6. peaked 7. cuspate
  8. aristate
power over fire.. 10. ignipotent
power to believe.. 9. creditive
reflecting surface.. 8. specular
same ending.. 11. conterminal
same parents.. 7. germane
sawlike edge.. 7. serrate
scales.. 8. perulate
scalloped edge.. 7. crenate
taste.. 5. sapid
thorns.. 7. spinate
three broods yearly.. 11. trigoneutic
two feet.. 5. biped 7. bipedal
two horns.. 6. bicorn
two meanings.. 9. ambiguous
unequal sides.. 7. scalene
web feet.. 8. pinniped
wings.. 4. alar
having a...
backbone.. 10. vertebrate
beak.. 8. rostrate
beard.. 8. aristate
handle.. 6. ansate
large nose.. 6. nasute
shield.. 9. clypeated
stem.. 9. petiolate
tail.. 7. caudate
tuft.. 6. comose
veil.. 6. velate
will.. 7. testate
havoc... 4. harm 5. botch, waste
  7. destroy 11. destruction,

devastation 12. annihilation
haw ... 4. sloe 5. fence, hedge
  6. eyelid (3rd) 7. stammer
  8. hawthorn, messuage, turn left
  9. enclosure 11. exclamation
Hawaii ... see also *Hawaiian*
  capital .. 8. Honolulu
  city .. 4. Hilo 7. Wailuku
  district .. 7. Lahaina
  explorer .. 4. Cook (Capt)
  harbor .. 5. Pearl (bombed 12/7/41)
  islands (major) .. 4. Maui, Oahu
  5. Kauai, Lanai 6. Hawaii, Niihau
  7. Molokai 9. Kahoolawe
  lake .. 5. Waiau
  native .. 10. Polynesian
  old name .. 15. Sandwich Islands
  peak .. 8. Mauna Kea, Mauna Loa
  9. Waialeale
  resort .. 7. Waikiki
  Southernmost point (US) .. 5. Ka Lae
  State admission .. 8. Fiftieth
  State bird .. 13. Hawaiian goose
  State flower .. 8. hibiscus
  State nickname .. 5. Aloha
  20. Paradise of the Pacific
  volcano .. 7. Kilauea 8. Mauna Loa
  (largest active)
Hawaiian ... 6. Kanaka
  10. Melanesian, Polynesian
  16. South Sea islander
Hawaiian (pert to) ...
  banquet, feast .. 7. ahaaina
  basket .. 2. ie
  beverage .. 4. kava 8. kavakava
  bird .. 2. io, o–o 3. iwa 4. iiwi, mamo
  (ext), noio, o–o–a–a 6. olomao (thrush)
  8. drepanis
  canoe .. 5. waapa
  chant .. 4. mele
  cloth, clothes .. 4. kapa, tapa
  coffee .. 4. kona
  dance .. 4. hula
  fern .. 4. pulu
  fibre (pine) .. 2. ie
  fish .. 3. awa 4. ulua 5. akule, lania
  flower wreath, garland .. 3. lei
  food .. 3. poi 4. kalo, taro
  garment .. 6. holoku, muumuu
  god .. 5. Wakea 7. Kanaloa (Pantheon)
  goddess .. 4. Pele (volcanoes, fire)
  gooseberry .. 4. poha
  grass .. 6. emoloa
  greeting .. 5. aloha
  herb .. 3. pia (starch root)
  king (first) .. 10. Kamehameha
  lava .. 2. aa 8. pahoehoe
  loincloth, girdle .. 4. malo
  musical instrument .. 7. ukulele
  pepper .. 3. ava 4. kava 8. kavakava
  precipice .. 4. pali
  Queen .. 8. Kamamalu
  royalty .. 4. alii
  seaweed (edible) .. 4. limu
  shampoo, massage .. 8. lomi–lomi
  shrub .. 3. pia 4. akia, pulu 5. olona
  temple .. 5. heiau
  tern .. 4. noio
  veranda .. 5. lanai
  windstorm .. 4. kona
  woman .. 5. haole 6. wahine
  yam .. 3. hoi

hawfinch ... 8. grosbeak
hawk ... 3. cry 4. hunt, sell, vend
  6. peddle 7. canvass 9. plunderer,
  warmonger
hawk (bird) ... 2. io 3. hen 4. eyas,
  kahu, kite, nyas, seel (blind) 5. Astur,
  Buteo 6. falcon, osprey, tercel (tiercel)
  7. buzzard, Cooper's, goshawk,
  harrier, kestrel, puttock, sparrow,
  vulture 8. caracara 9. Accipiter,
  red–tailed
hawker of fruit (Eng) ... 6. coster
  12. costermonger
hawk–eyed deity ... 2. Ra
Hawkeye State ... 4. Iowa
hawking ... 7. hunting, vending
  8. falconry
hawk moth ... 6. sphinx 8. sphingid
hawksbill ... 4. pawl 6. turtle
  8. tortoise
hawkshaw ... 6. sleuth 9. detective
  11. sleuthhound
hawk's nest ... 5. aerie (aery)
hawser ... 4. line, rope
hawser post ... 4. bitt 7. bollard
hawthorn ... 3. may 5. hazel (fruit)
  6. red haw 7. haw tree 9. mayflower
Hawthorne, Nathaniel ... 6. author
  8. novelist
hay ... 6. fodder 7. timothy
hay (pert to) ...
  bird .. 7. hay jack 8. black cap
  9. sandpiper (pectoral)
  bundle .. 3. mow 4. bale, cock, rick
  5. stack
  fork .. 5. pikel (pikle), pitch
  herb .. 8. sainfoin
  mown .. 5. swath
  second cutting .. 5. rowen
  spreader .. 6. tedder
  stack .. 4. rick 7. hayrick
  storage site .. 3. mow 4. barn, loft,
  silo
hazard ... 3. fog 4. dare, game, jump,
  risk 5. peril 6. gamble, sanger, stroke
  7. imperil, jeopard, presume, venture
  8. cabstand, casualty, endanger,
  jeopardy 11. restriction
hazardous ... 5. hairy (sl), jumpy, risky
  6. chancy, queasy, unsafe 7. unsound
  8. perilous 9. uncertain, venturous
  10. fortuitous 11. speculative,
  venturesome
haze ... 3. fog 4. beat, film, glin (at
  sea), mist, smog 5. scold, smoke,
  vapor 7. dimness, drizzle 8. frighten
hazy ... 3. dim 5. filmy, foggy, misty,
  smoky, thick, vague 6. cloudy,
  opaque, stupid 7. muddled, nebular,
  obscure 8. overcast 9. invisible,
  uncertain 10. indistinct
he ... 2. il 3. man 4. ipsi, male 6. any
  one, letter 7. pronoun
head ... 3. aim, nob 4. lead, pate, poll,
  tete 5. caput, chief, skull 6. noggin,
  noodle (sl), source 7. cranium
head (pert to) ...
  abbey .. 5. abbot 6. abbess
  back of .. 7. occiput
  bald .. 6. acomia 9. pilgarlic
  bone .. 8. parietal 9. occipital
  Gorgon .. 6. Medusa (Myth)

hard.. 5. boche
of hair.. 5. crine
pert to.. 8. cephalic
proportion.. 14. mesitacephalic
shaven.. 7. tonsure
shrunken.. 7. tsentsa
headache... 6. megrim 8. migraine
   11. cephalalgia
head covering... 3. cap, hat, tam, wig
   4. hair, hood, veil 5. beret, miter,
   scalp 6. bonnet, peruke, toupee,
   wimple 7. biretta 8. sombrero
   10. fascinator
headdress... 3. wig 4. pouf, tête
   5. busby, miter, shako, tiara
   6. coiffe, diadem, hennin, peruke,
   pinner 7. bandore, buzz wig, coronet,
   periwig 8. coiffure, headtire
headdress (Egypt)... 6. uraeus (with
   sacred asp)
headhunters (Luzon)... 7. Igorots
heading... 3. top 5. front, title, topic
   6. pillow 7. bolster, caption
   8. headline 9. direction
   12. decapitation
headland... 4. cape, mull, ness
   5. morro, ridge 10. promontory
headless... 6. stupid 7. acephal,
   topless 9. acephalus (monster)
   10. acephalous
headline... 6. banner 7. caption,
   display, heading
headliner... 4. star 7. feature
   8. composer
headlong... 4. rash 5. hasty, steep
   6. head–on, sudden 8. reckless
   9. headfirst, impetuous, impulsive
   10. recklessly 11. impulsively,
   precipitate, precipitous
headpiece... 3. cap, hat, top 4. atef
   5. crown 6. halter, helmet, lintel
   7. fitting 8. covering, ornament, skull
   cap 9. headboard, headdress,
   headstall
head–shaped... 8. capitate
headstrong... 4. rash 6. entêté, unruly
   7. violent, wayward 9. obstinate
   11. intractable, opinionated
   12. contumacious, ungovernable
heal... 4. cure, knit, mend 6. doctor,
   pacify, remedy, repair 7. correct,
   restore 9. cicatrize
healing (pert to)...
   agent.. 6. balsam
   compound.. 4. balm
   goddess.. 3. Eir
   magic.. 6. powwow
   process.. 4. scar 8. cicatrix
   remedy.. 8. curative, sanative
   science.. 9. iatrology
   suffix.. 7. iatrics
health (pert to)...
   care.. 7. welfare
   comb form.. 4. sani
   conditions.. 8. sanitary
   goddess.. 5. Salus 6. Hygeia
   7. Minerva
   Latin.. 5. salus
   neurotic.. 13. hypochondriac
   resort.. 3. spa 7. springs
   symbol.. 5. pansy

healthful... 7. healthy 8. curative,
   salutary, sanatory 9. medicinal
   10. salubrious
healthy... 4. hale, sane, well
   6. hearty, robust 8. salutary,
   vigorous 9. healthful, wholesome
   10. salubrious
heap... 3. cop 4. dess, load, lump,
   pile, pyre, raff, raft 5. amass, cairn,
   crowd, stack 6. plenty, sorite, throng
   7. cumulus 9. multitude
   10. accumulate
heaped... 5. piled 7. stacked
   8. acervate 9. collected
hear... 3. see 4. feel, heed, oyez
   (oyes) 5. favor, judge, learn
   6. attend, listen 7. hearken (harken)
   8. listen to, perceive 9. attention
   10. adjudicate
hearer... 7. audient, auditor
   8. disciple, listener 9. hearkener
   (harkener) 12. eavesdropper
hearing (pert to)... 3. act, aid, ear
   4. otic, oyer 5. aural, sense
   (special), sound, trial 6. otosis, tryout
   7. earshot 8. audience, audition,
   auditory 9. attention, auricular,
   interview, knowledge
hearken, harken... 4. hear, heed
   6. attend, listen 7. give ear, inquire
hearsay... 4. talk 5. bruit, rumor
   6. gossip, report 8. evidence
heart... 3. cor 4. card, core, gist, life,
   love, mood, soul 5. cheer, organ
   6. center, depths, kardia, middle,
   spirit, vitals 7. courage, emotion,
   essence, feeling 9. affection,
   substance 10. conscience
   11. temperament
heart (pert to)...
   ache.. 5. grief 6. sorrow 7. anguish
   active.. 7. sthenic
   beat.. 5. pulse, throb 7. systole
   8. diastole 9. pulsation
   10. palmoscopy
   bleeding (flower).. 8. dicentra
   burn.. 4. envy 6. enmity 7. burning,
   pyrosia 8. jealousy 10. cardialgia,
   discontent, heartscald (heart–scaud)
   cavity.. 6. atrium
   chamber.. 6. atrium 7. auricle
   9. ventricle 11. ventriculum
   contraction.. 7. systole
   disease.. 14. angina pectoris
   Egypt.. 2. Ab 4. hati
   expansion.. 8. diastole
   felt.. 4. dear, deep, real, true
   7. genuine, sincere
   shaped.. 7. cordate
   valve.. 6. mitral 8. bicuspid
   9. tricuspid
hearten... 5. cheer 7. comfort
   8. embolden, inspirit, reassure
   9. encourage
hearth... 4. home 5. ingle 6. astrer
   (pert to) 7. fireside 9. fireplace
hearth goddess... 5. Vesta 6. Hestia
hearty... 4. hale, real, rich, warm
   5. heavy, lusty 6. active, robust,
   stanch 7. cordial, earnest, fervent
   8. friendly, vigorous 9. convivial,
   energetic, unfeigned 10. nourishing

11. substantial
heat... 4. fire, race, warm, zeal
5. ardor, calor, cauma, fever, tepor
6. degree, warmth 7. inflame,
passion 10. excitement
11. temperature
heat (pert to)...
heating.. 9. calorific
measure.. 5. therm (therme) 7. calorie
(calory) 10. centigrade, Fahrenheit
pert to.. 7. thermic
plaster.. 4. mull 7. steatin
principle.. 7. caloric
white.. 13. incandescence
heater... 4. etna, kiln, oven 5. forge,
stove, tisar 6. boiler, retort
7. brazier, furnace 8. annealer,
register 12. electron tube
heath... 4. moor 5. Erica, plain, savin,
waste 8. tamarisk 10. underbrush
heathen... 5. pagan 6. ethnic, paynim
7. gentile, godless, infidel
10. unbeliever 11. irreligious
13. unenlightened
heathen deity... 4. idol 5. image
6. symbol
heather... 5. color, Erica, plant
9. crowberry 12. poverty plant
heaume... 6. helmet (armor)
heave... 4. cast, draw, hurl, lift, toss
5. fling, hoist, pitch, raise, retch,
scena, throw 11. rise and fall
heaven... 3. sky 4. ciel, Eden 5. ether
6. utopia, welkin 7. arcadia, Elysium,
Nirvana 8. empyrean, Paradise,
Valhalla (Valhall) 9. firmament
heavenly... 5. godly 6. divine, sacred
7. angelic, blessed, uranian
8. supernal 9. beautiful, celestial
10. delightful
heavenly (pert to)...
being.. 5. angel, saint 6. cherub,
seraph 7. Madonna 8. cherubim, Dei
Mater, seraphim
belt.. 6. galaxy, zodiac
body.. 3. sun 4. luna, moon, star
5. comet 6. planet 8. luminary
city.. 4. Zion 12. New Jerusalem
path.. 5. orbit
solar apparatus.. 6. orrery
sphere.. 8. empyrean
twins (Gemini).. 6. Castor, Pollux
heavens... see *heaven*
heaves... 9. emphysema
heavy... 3. sad 4. deep, dull, hard,
role 5. actor, dense, grave, great,
inert, massy 6. coarse, gloomy,
leaden, sleepy, strong, viscid
7. doleful, onerous, serious, villain,
violent, weighty 8. burdened,
grievous, overcast, pregnant, profound
9. difficult, ponderous 10. afflictive,
burdensome, encumbered, oppressive
11. substantial 13. consequential
heavy (pert to)...
handed.. 6. clumsy 7. awkward,
unhandy 8. bungling 9. maladroit
10. oppressive
headed.. 4. dull, logy 6. drowsy,
stupid
hearted.. 3. sad 10. despondent,

melancholy
laden.. 6. loaded 8. careworn
9. oppressed 12. weighted down
with moisture.. 6. sodden
Hebrew... 3. Jew 4. Zion 6. Habiri,
Habiru, Semite 7. Semitic
Hebrew (pert to)...
abode of the dead.. 5. Sheol
acrostic.. 4. agla
amulet.. 4. agla
demon.. 8. Asmodeus
eternity.. 4. Olam 8. Olam haba
excommunication form.. 5. herem
festival.. 5. Purim, Seder 8. Passover
flute (Bib).. 8. nehiloth
forbidden.. 4. tref
God.. 2. El 5. Eloah 6. Adonai,
Elohim 7. Jehovah
grammar.. 7. stative
greeting.. 6. Shalom
instrument (lyrelike).. 4. asor
kinsman.. 4. goel
law book.. 5. Torah (Tora) 6. Talmud
7. Mishnah (Mishna) 8. Tosephta
10. Pentateuch
lesson (Nebiim).. 9. haphtarah
marriage custom.. 8. levirate
month (Spring).. 4. Abib 5. Nisan
Order (Cenobite).. 6. Essene
plural ending.. 2. im
prayer shawl.. 7. tallith
proselyte.. 3. ger
psalm of praise.. 6. hallel
quarters.. 6. ghetto
rabbis, teachers.. 6. sabora
7. amoraim, tannaim 8. saboraim
sacred objects.. 4. Urim 7. Thummin
school.. 5. heder (cheder)
spice (anc).. 6. stacte
town.. 6. Mizpah (Mizpeh)
trumpet.. 7. shophar (shofar)
underworld.. 5. Sheol
Hebrew alphabet... 2. he, pe
3. mem, nun, sin, tav, vau 4. ayin,
beth, caph, koph, resh, shin, yodh
5. aleph, cheth, gimel, sadhe, zayin
6. daleth, lamedh, samekh
Hebrides, New...
administrators.. 6. French 7. British
church.. 6. Celtic (early)
islands.. 4. Iona, Skye 5. Banks
6. Torres
people.. 10. Melanesian
type rule.. 11. Condominium
hecatomb... 9. sacrifice 11. hundred
oxen
hecco... 8. hickwall 10. woodpecker
heckle... 4. gibe 6. badger, hackle,
harass
hectic... 5. fever, flush 7. excited
8. feverish, restless 9. reddening
11. consumptive
hector... 5. bully, worry 6. harass
7. bluster, swagger 8. browbeat
9. roisterer 10. intimidate
Hector (pert to)...
character in.. 5. (The) Iliad
companion.. 8. Diomedes
father.. 5. Priam
mother.. 6. Hecuba
slain by.. 8. Achilles
wife.. 10. Andromache

heddle ... 4. loom 5. blade (with eyelet) 7. weaving
hedge ... 3. bar, haw, hem, pen 4. boma 5. fence 6. hinder, raddle 7. barrier, enclose, quibble 8. boundary, obstruct, sidestep, surround
hedgehog ... 6. animal, tenrec, urchin 7. dredger, echidna, echinus, pudding (fruit) 8. herisson, hurcheon 9. porcupine 11. transformer
hedge trimmer ... 7. plasher, topiary
hedonism (pert to) ...
advocate .. 8. Cyrenaic 9. Epicurean
doctrine of .. 8. pleasure
heed ... 3. ear 4. care, hear, mind, note, obey 6. attend, listen, notice, regard 7. caution, observe 8. consider 9. attention, be careful, diligence 10. cognizance, solicitude 11. observation
heedful ... 4. wary 5. alert 6. attent 7. careful, mindful 8. cautious, vigilant 9. advertent, attentive 11. considerate
heedless ... 6. remiss 8. careless 9. desperate, impulsive, negligent 10. insouciant, regardless 11. improvident, inadvertent, inattentive, thoughtless, unobservant, without heed 13. inconsiderate
heel ... 3. cad, tip 4. cant, foot (part), knob, tilt 5. stern 6. careen, follow 7. bounder, deviate, incline 9. scoundrel 12. protuberance
Heidi author ... 12. Johanna Spyri
heifer ... 3. cow 4. quey 5. stirk, woman 6. bovine 8. terrapin (fem) 10. colpindach
height ... 3. alt, top 4. apex 5. crest, pitch 6. summit 7. stature 8. altitude, eminence, highness 9. elevation 10. The Heavens
heighten ... 5. raise 7. augment, elevate 8. increase 9. aggravate, intensify 10. exaggerate
height of action, drama ... 10. catastasis
heimlich ... 10. reticently 12. mysteriously
Heimweh ... 9. nostalgia 12. homesickness
heinous ... 3. bad 6. odious, wicked 7. beastly (Brit), hateful 8. flagrant, infamous, terrible 9. atrocious, malicious 10. outrageous
heir ... 5. scion 7. heritor, legatee 8. atheling (apparent), parcener (joint) 9. firstborn, inheritor, successor 11. beneficiary
Hejaz ...
city .. 5. Islam, Mecca 6. Medina
monument .. 14. Tomb of Mohammed (Mosque of the Prophet)
district of .. 11. Saudi Arabia
shrine .. 5. Kaaba
helcos ... 5. ulcer
helcos (pert to) ...
repair .. 11. helcoplasty
science .. 9. helcology
ulceration .. 8. helcosis

held ... see *hold*
Helen of Troy (pert to) ...
abductor, lover .. 5. Paris
brother-in-law .. 9. Agamemnon
famed for .. 6. beauty
husband .. 8. Menelaus (King)
mother .. 4. Leda
sister of .. 11. The Dioscuri
helical ... 5. helix (formed) 6. spiral
helical year ... 6. Sothic
helicoid ... 6. curved, ear rim (like) 10. snail shell (like)
helicon ... 4. tuba
helicopter (pert to) ... 5. rotor 7. chopper 8. autogiro (autogyro), heliport 9. eggbeater 10. whirlybird
helicopter developer ... 8. Sikorsky
heliophobia ... 14. fear of sunlight 16. sensitivity to sun
Heliopolis ... 12. City of the Sun (Egypt)
Helios ... 3. Sol 6. sun god 16. Colossus of Rhodes
helix ... 4. coil 5. snail 6. spiral
hell ... 5. grave, Hades, limbo 7. dungeon, inferno 9. perdition, purgatory 10. underworld
hell (pert to) ...
bottomless pit .. 9. barathrum
capital of .. 11. Pandemonium
Hebrew .. 5. Sheol
Hindu .. 6. Naraka
Iliad .. 8. Tartarus
Jewish .. 6. Tophet 7. Gehenna
Norse .. 7. Niflhel (Neflheim)
Queen .. 3. Hel
Roman .. 3. Dis 5. Orcus
hellbent ... 7. dead set, like mad 8. full tilt, reckless 10. determined, recklessly 12. determinedly
Hellene ... 5. Greek
Hellenistic school (Sculp) ... 9. Pergamene
Hellespont, Turkey ...
ancient name .. 9. Gallipoli (Strait of)
city .. 6. Abydos (legend), Sestos
legend .. 4. Hero 7. Leander (swimmer)
modern name .. 11. Dardanelles (The)
helm ... 5. wheel 6. helmet, rudder, summit, tiller 7. control 10. management 12. steering gear
helmet ... 5. armet, armor, galea, topee (topi) 6. casque, heaume, morion, sallet, sconce 7. basinet, hard hat
helmet (pert to) ...
flap .. 8. aventail
lower part .. 6. beaver
nose guard .. 5. nasal
opening .. 3. vue
part .. 4. bell 5. crest, visor (vizor) 7. ventail 8. aventail
shaped .. 7. galeate
helmet of Hades ... 5. magic 8. Tarnhelm 9. invisible, Tarnkappe
helminth ... 4. worm
helmsman ... 5. pilot 6. conner, guider 8. coxswain 9. steersman
helot ... 4. esne, serf 5. slave 6. thrall, vassal 7. servant
help ... 3. aid 4. abet, back, cure

5. avail, boost, serve, stead 6. assist, relief, remedy, succor 7. benefit, forward, further, improve, prevent, relieve, servant, serving, subsidy, support, sustain
helper ... 3. aid (aide) 8. teammate
  9. assistant, paramedic
  10. apprentice, benefactor
helpful ... 6. useful 7. helping
  8. salutary 10. beneficial, tiding over
  12. contributory, instrumental
helpless ... 4. limp, weak 7. forlorn
  8. impotent, unaiding 9. destitute, powerless, spineless 10. bewildered, unsupplied 11. defenseless, unprotected 12. irremediable
helpmate ... 4. wife 5. spouse
  6. helper 7. husband 8. helpmeet
  9. assistant, companion
Helsinki, Finland ... 7. capital
helter-skelter ... 5. haste, hurry
  7. hastily 8. disorder 9. confusion
  10. carelessly, recklessly
helve ... 5. lever 6. handle
hem, hem in ... 3. pen 4. edge
  5. beset 6. border, margin
  7. environ, stammer 8. hesitate, surround 9. hem and haw
  11. circumscribe, exclamation
hemal, haemal (pert to) ... 5. blood
  12. blood vessels
hemeralopia ... 12. day blindness (opp of nyctalopia)
hemi ... 4. half, semi (pref)
hemiplegia ... 9. paralysis (body half)
hemlock ... 3. kex 5. Tsuga 6. conium (fruit) 9. evergreen, poisoning
hemophilia ... 8. bleeding
  10. hemorrhage (uncontrollable)
hemp ... 3. ife, kef 4. flax, koof, kiof, rine, sunn 5. abaca, bhang, istle, sisal (sizal) 6. fennel, Manila 7. hashish, lhiamba (liamba) 8. cannabis
hemp (pert to) ...
  bagasse .. 6. linaga
  cannabis .. 5. ganja (smoking)
  fabric .. 6. burlap
  filament .. 4. harl
  leaves .. 5. sabzi
  like .. 9. cannabine
  loose .. 5. oakum
  resin (narcotic) .. 6. charas
  seed .. 5. rogue, scamp
  short .. 3. tow
hen ... 4. fowl, wife 6. pullet
hen (pert to) ...
  Chaucer character .. 7. Partlet
  clam .. 4. surf 5. pismo
  hawk .. 7. buzzard, harrier
  heath .. 4. gray 6. grouse (black)
  poison .. 7. hebenon, henbane
  water .. 9. gallinule
hence ... 2. so 4. away, ergo, thus
  8. away from 9. therefore
henchman ... 4. page 5. groom
  6. gillie, squire 7. mafioso
  8. follower, hanger-on 9. attendant, supporter 12. right-hand man
hend, hende ... 4. fair, kind, near
  5. civil 6. clever, comely, gentle, kindly 8. gracious, pleasant, skillful (skilful) 9. dexterous 10. convenient

heortology, science of ... 14. liturgical year
hepar ... 5. liver 8. compound (Chem)
hepatitis ... 12. liver disease
Hephaestus (Gr Relig) ... 9. god of Fire
Hepplewhite ... 9. furniture
heptad ... 5. seven (group of)
Hera (pert to) ...
  husband .. 4. Zeus
  mother of .. 4. Ares, Rhea
  rival .. 2. Io 4. Leto
herald ... 5. crier 6. tabard
  7. presage, usher in 8. announce, point man, proclaim 9. harbinger, messenger 10. forerunner
heraldic (pert to) ...
  balls .. 5. palle (6 balls of Medici)
  band .. 3. bar 4. fess, fill
  barnacle .. 4. brey
  bearing .. 4. ente, gore, orle 5. pheon
  6. charge 8. tressure
  boss .. 5. rumbo
  charge .. 5. fusil, gyron 7. bearing, humetty (humettee)
  circle (gold) .. 6. bezant
  cross .. 4. nowy, paty, urde 6. cleche, pattée (patté), raguly 7. patonce, saltier (saltire)
  decoration .. 4. seme 5. crest
  design (fur) .. 4. pean, vair
  division .. 4. ente, paly 5. barry
  6. canton 7. compone
  11. counterpaly
  embattled .. 8. bretessé
  end (metal) .. 7. boterol (boteroll)
  large .. 5. pavis
  lozenge (voided) .. 6. mascle
  opening .. 6. rustre
  panel .. 9. hatchment (death)
  sardonyx .. 8. sanguine
  scalloped, edged .. 8. invected
  segment .. 6. flanch
  ship .. 7. lymphad
  star .. 6. mullet 7. estoile
  stripe .. 4. pale
  swallow .. 10. hirondelle
  winged .. 4. aile
  wreath .. 5. torse 7. chaplet, garland
heraldic (pert to animals) ...
  head .. 8. caboshed (caboched)
  bear .. 5. grise
  beast, running .. 7. courant
  beast, sitting .. 5. assis 6. sejant
  beasts .. 6. enurny
  beast's leg .. 4. gamb (gambe)
  bird .. 7. issuant (half visible), martlet
  9. half eagle
  duck (footless) .. 6. cannet (cannette)
  fish, swimming .. 6. naiant
  headless .. 5. etète
heraldic (pert to color) ...
  black .. 5. sable
  blue .. 5. azure
  brown .. 5. tenne
  gold, yellow .. 2. or
  green .. 4. vert
  purple .. 7. purpure
  red .. 5. gules
heraldic shield (pert to) ...
  back .. 8. aversant
  back to back .. 8. addorsed
  bent .. 9. debruised

broken.. 5. rompu
Danes.. 5. raven
England.. 14. lilies of France
facing each other.. 8. affronté
savages.. 6. tattoo
toward spectator.. 4. gaze 7. gardant
tribe of Judah.. 4. lion
herb... 3. pia, rue 4. aloe, anet, balm,
dill, hemp, mint, moly, sage, woad,
yamp 5. anise, basil, nondo, sedge,
senna, tansy, thyme 6. arnica,
borage, catnip, cicely, clover, endive,
fennel, hyssop, jacoby, madder,
yarrow 7. boneset, caraway, chervil,
chicory, figwort, gentian, ginseng,
henbane, parsley, ragwort
8. abelmosk, licorice, marjoram,
rosemary, samphire, tarragon
9. coriander, digitalis, spikenard
10. elecampane, pennyroyal,
turtlehead
herb (pert to)...
bitter.. 3. rue 4. aloe 5. tansy
7. boneset 8. centaury 9. snakehead
10. turtlehead
dill.. 4. anet
genus.. 3. Iva 4. Arum, Ruta
5. Galax, Inula, Lemna, Rubia
6. Cassia, Mentha, Oxalis, Sagina
7. Alpenia, Anemone, Freesia,
Hedeoma, Tellima, Tovaria
8. Hepatica, Psorales 9. Grundelia
living on.. 11. herbivorous
12. phytophagous
mythical.. 4. moly
narcotic.. 4. hemp
onionlike.. 5. chive
poisonous.. 4. loco 6. conium
7. hemlock, henbane 9. hellebore
salad.. 6. endive 7. chicory
10. watercress
Hercules (pert to)...
father.. 4. Zeus
hero of.. 8. strength 12. twelve
labors
mother.. 7. Alcmene
statue.. 7. Farnese
stone.. 9. loadstone
sweetheart.. 4. Iole
wife.. 4. Hebe
herd... 3. mob 5. crowd, drive, drove,
flock, guard 6. gregis, rabble
7. shelter 11. aggregation
herd's grass... 7. timothy
herdsman... 4. senn 6. drover
7. vaquero (vaciero) 8. Damoetas,
ranchero, wrangler
herdsman's god... 5. Pales
here... 3. ici, now 6. hereat, hither
7. present 8. vicinity 9. this place
11. in this place
here and now... 8. thisness
9. haecceity 11. specificity
here and there... 5. about 6. passim
10. everywhere
hereditary... 6. inborn, innate, lineal
8. heirship 9. ancestral, descended,
lineality 11. inheritable, inheritance,
patrimonial
heredity... 4. gene 5. birth 7. atavism
8. heritage 10. Mendel's law
11. inheritance

heretic... 9. dissenter, sectarian
10. schismatic 13. nonconformist
heretofore... 6. erenow 7. prior to
8. formerly, hitherto, previous
heritage... 3. lot 9. cleronomy
10. birthright 11. inheritance
heritrix, heretrix... 7. heiress
herl, harl... 3. fly (angling) 4. barb
hermeneutics... 14. interpretation
(Scriptures)
Hermes (pert to)...
birthplace.. 7. Cyllene
character.. 6. herald 9. messenger
father.. 4. Zeus
god of.. 5. youth 7. science
9. eloquence, invention
mother.. 4. Maia
Roman equivalent.. 7. Mercury
shoes (winged).. 7. talaria
hermetic... 6. closed, sealed
7. magical 8. airtight 10. alchemical
hermetic art... 7. alchemy
hermit... 4. monk 5. cooky 7. ascetic,
eremite, recluse, stylite (Hist)
8. headsman 9. anchorite, pillarist
11. hummingbird
hermitary... 3. hut 4. cell
hern, herne... 4. hers, hook 5. heron
6. corner
hero... 4. idol, star 5. model
7. demigod, warrior 8. champion
9. celebrity, conqueror
11. protagonist
hero (pert to)...
American.. 5. Allen (Ethan), Bowie
6. Bonham, Travis 8. Crockett
Babylonian.. 5. Etana
deified.. 7. demigod
genealogy.. 9. heroogony
Greek.. 3. Ion 4. Ajax
legendary.. 6. Amadis, Roland
7. Paladin, Tancred
lore.. 9. heroology
Persian.. 6. Rustam (Rustum)
romantic.. 4. Erec 6. Amadis
7. Leander
Russian.. 4. Igor
heroic... 4. bold, epic, huge 5. brave,
great, noble 6. epical, poetic, viking
7. extreme, gallant, valiant
8. fearless, intrepid, powerful
10. courageous 11. magnanimous,
venturesome
heroic poem, story... 4. epic, epos
6. epopee
heroine... 4. Tess 5. actor 6. Esther,
Europa 8. Atalanta 9. celebrity
11. demigoddess
heroism... 5. valor 7. bravery, courage
9. fortitude 11. magnanimity
13. unselfishness
heron... 5. Ardea, crane, egret, herle
7. Bittern 8. Ardeidae, heronsew
9. Great Blue 10. Great White, Little
Blue
heron flock... 5. sedge
herpes... 6. eczema 8. cold sore,
shingles
herring... 3. cob 4. alec, brit, raun
(fem), sile 5. cisco, matie, sprat
7. alewife, anchovy, shadine
8. scuddawn

herring (pert to)...
  barrel.. 4. cade, cran
  bone.. 7. pattern 11. arrangement
  fry.. 4. sile
  herringlike.. 5. cisco 7. anchovy
  young.. 4. brit 5. sprat (sprot)
Herse (Gr)... 7. goddess (dew)
Hershef (Egypt)... 5. deity (tutelary)
hesitate... 3. haw, hem 4. wait
  5. delay, demur, pause, stall
  6. falter, loiter 7. stammer
  13. procrastinate
hesitation... 5. doubt, pause, waltz
  9. faltering, hesitancy 10. reluctance,
  stammering 11. uncertainty,
  vacillation 15. procrastination
hesped (Heb)... 6. eulogy 7. funeral
Hesperides (pert to)...
  group name.. 10. Atlantides
  guards of.. 12. golden apples (Hera)
  nymph.. 5. Aegle 6. Hestia
  7. Hespera 8. Arethusa, Erytheia
Hesperus... 4. poem (Wreck of the
  Hesperus) 5. Venus 6. Hesper
  11. evening star
Hessian... 3. fly 5. boots, Hesse
  6. German 9. mercenary
  10. adventurer
hest... 6. behest 7. command,
  precept, promise 10. injunction
Hestia (pert to)...
  goddess of.. 6. hearth
  guard of.. 12. golden apples
  mother.. 4. Rhea
hetaera, hetaira (Gr)... 4. Lais
  6. Phryne 8. mistress, paramour
hetaerocracy, governed by...
  8. hetaerae 10. college men
Heterodontus... 5. shark
heterodox... 9. heretical
  10. unorthodox 11. nonorthodox
heterogeneous... (opposed to
  homogeneous) 5. mixed 6. unlike
  7. diverse 9. different 10. dissimilar
  11. diversified 13. miscellaneous
hew... 3. cut 4. chop, fell, hack
  5. carve, sever
hex... 3. hag, six 4. jinx 5. lamia,
  spell 7. bewitch 9. sorceress,
  witchwife
hexad... 3. six 6. sestet
hexameter verse...
  meter.. 7. six feet
  terms.. 4. iams 8. dipodies, trochees
  9. anapaests
hexapod... 7. six feet 9. six-footed
hexarchy... 9. six States (group)
hexastich, poem or stanza... 8. six
  lines 9. six verses
heyday... 3. joy 4. acme 8. wildness
  11. high spirits 12. highest vigor
  14. frolicsomeness
heyrat... 8. kinkajou (obs)
Hezekiah (pert to)...
  Biblical.. 4. King (12th)
  kingdom.. 5. Judah
  mother.. 3. Abi
hiatus... 3. col, gap 5. break, chasm,
  pause, space 6. lacuna 7. fissure,
  opening 8. interval 12. interruption
Hiawatha (pert to)...
  character, poem by.. 10. Longfellow

  grandmother.. 7. Nokomis
  mother.. 7. Wenonah
  tribe (Ind).. 8. Iroquois
hibernate... 6. hole up (summer in
  torpor), winter 8. estivate
  10. latibulize
Hibernia... 4. Erin 7. Ireland
Hibernian (pert to)...
  color.. 5. green
  native.. 8. Irishman
  secret society (US 1832)..
  24. Ancient Order of Hibernians
hickory... 4. cane 5. Carya, pecan
  6. switch 8. kiskatom 9. shellbark
hidalgo... 5. title 8. nobleman (lower
  class)
hidden... 4. dern, lurk 5. inner, perdu
  6. arcane, buried, cached, closed,
  covert, latent, masked, occult, secret
  7. covered, cryptic, obscure,
  unknown 8. abstruse, screened,
  secluded, secreted 9. concealed,
  latescent 10. mysterious
  11. clandestine
hide... 3. kip 4. bury, cyst, dern
  (derne), lurk, mask, pelt, skin, veil
  5. cache, cloak, cover, skulk
  6. screen, shroud 7. conceal,
  eelskin, rawhide, secrete 8. carucate,
  disguise, ensconce, suppress
  9. dissemble 10. camouflage
hidebound... 5. bound, petty 6. little,
  narrow 7. bigoted 9. barkbound
  10. restrained (opinion)
  11. strait-laced 12. conventional,
  narrow-minded 13. hyperorthodox
hideous... 4. grim, ugly 6. grisly,
  horrid, odious 7. ghastly 8. scabrous,
  terrible 9. frightful, revolting
  10. detestable, terrifying
hiding place... 3. mew 4. lair
  5. cache 9. latibulum
hi-fi devotee... 10. audiophile
high... 3. alt, dry, ela (note) 4. tall
  5. aloft, drunk, great, noble, steep
  6. costly, shrill 7. eminent, haughty
  8. elevated, foremost, stranded,
  towering 9. excessive, expensive
high (pert to)...
  and mighty.. 8. arrogant 9. imperious
  brow.. 4. snob 7. Brahmin, egghead,
  high-hat, learned 12. intellectual
  14. intelligentsia
  flown diction.. 8. euphuism
  flying.. 7. Icarian 9. visionary
  11. extravagant, pretentious
  12. ostentatious 13. grandiloquent
  handed.. 9. arbitrary 10. autocratic,
  imperative 11. domineering,
  overbearing
  hat.. 8. snobbish 12. aristocratic
  priest.. 3. Eli (Israel) 11. Melchezedek
  (Mormon)
  sounding.. 4. loud 7. fustian
  9. high-toned 13. grandiloquent
  spirited.. 4. edgy 5. fiery 6. lively
  9. excitable 10. mettlesome
  11. high-mettled
  strung.. 4. taut 5. tense 7. nervous
  9. excitable
  time.. 3. fun 5. binge, spree
  8. carousal 11. opportunity

toned .. **5.** tense **7.** stylish **8.** elevated
9. dignified **11.** fashionable
highest ... **3.** top **4.** best **6.** utmost
7. maximum, supreme, topmost
8. bunemost, dominant **9.** nth
degree, uppermost
highest (pert to) ...
comb form .. **4.** acro
dice number .. **3.** six **4.** sise (sice)
point .. **3.** top **4.** acme, apex **5.** crest
6. apogee, climax, summit, vertex,
zenith **7.** ceiling, noonday
8. meridian, noontide, pinnacle
11. ne plus ultra
highway ... **3.** via, way **4.** bahn, iter,
path, pike, road, toby **6.** artery,
course, street **7.** beltway, freeway,
parkway, thruway, (throughway)
8. arterial, autobahn, turnpike
9. boulevard, concourse
10. expressway **12.** thoroughfare
highwayman ... **5.** thief **6.** bandit,
robber **7.** brigand, footpad, ladrone
8. hijacker **9.** bandolero
10. bushranger, highjacker
hike ... **4.** jerk, toss, walk **5.** hitch,
march, raise, throw, tramp
8. backpack, increase
hilarious ... **3.** mad **5.** merry, noisy
7. festive **8.** mirthful **9.** ludicrous
hilarity ... **4.** glee **5.** mirth **6.** gaiety,
levity **7.** jollity, whoopee **8.** laughter
9. joviality **10.** jocularity, joyousness
12. cheerfulness, exhilaration
hill ... **3.** kop, tor **4.** dene, dune, heap,
holt, kame, knob, loma, mesa, paha,
rath **5.** bargh, butte, esker, morra,
mound **6.** barrow, summit
9. acclivity, elevation, monadnock
hill myna ... **8.** starling
hillside ... **4.** bank, brae, hill, knop,
ramp **5.** cleve (cleeve), cliff, knoll,
scarp, slope **6.** glacia
hilt ... **4.** haft **6.** handle
hilum ... **3.** eye (bean) **5.** hilar, notch
7. opening (kidney)
Himalaya (pert to) ...
antelope .. **5.** goral, serow
bear .. **5.** bhalu
bearcat .. **5.** panda
bird .. **5.** monal (pheasant) **6.** chough
(crow)
cat .. **5.** ounce
dweller .. **8.** Nepalese
formations .. **7.** Siwalik
goat .. **4.** ibex, kail, tahe
kingdom .. **5.** Hunza
mountain peak .. **3.** Api **7.** Everest,
The Hump
pass .. **7.** Nathula
plant .. **4.** nard (Med)
sheep (wild) .. **6.** bharal, nahoor
swamp .. **5.** Terai
tree .. **3.** fir (silver) **5.** Neoza (pine)
6. Bhutan, deodar (cedar)
himself ... **4.** ipse
hind ... **3.** doe **4.** back, deer, rear, stag
6. caudal, haunch, rustic **7.** peasant,
servant **8.** domestic **9.** posterior
11. hindquarter
hind (red fish) ... **7.** grouper **8.** cabrilla
hinder ... **3.** bar **5.** block, check,

cramp, debar, delay, deter, embar
6. cumber, hamper, impede, retard
7. prevent **8.** restrain **9.** posterior
hindrance ... **3.** bar, rub **4.** clog, snag,
stop **5.** check, delay **8.** obstacle
9. deterrent, restraint, stricture
10. impediment **11.** obstruction
12. interruption
Hindu, Hindoo ... **4.** Koli, Sikh
5. Tamil **6.** Indian **9.** Hindustan
Hindu (pert to) ...
alphabet .. **6.** Sarada
apartment .. **5.** mahal
ascetic .. **4.** yati, yogi **5.** sadhu
atheist .. **7.** nastika
author of law .. **4.** Manu (Code)
bird .. **5.** Munia **6.** garuda
Buddha's mother .. **4.** Maya
caravansary .. **8.** choultry
carriage .. **6.** gharry (gharri)
caste .. **4.** Bhil **5.** Palli, Sudra, Tamil
7. Brahman
ceremony .. **7.** sraddha
city (sacred) .. **5.** Mecca **7.** Benares
9. Allahabad
coin .. **4.** anna
cymbals .. **3.** tal
dancing girl .. **8.** bayadere
darkness (spiritual) .. **5.** tamas
deity .. **4.** Deva, Rama, Siva (Shiva),
Yama **5.** Ahura, Asura **6.** Brahma,
Vishnu **7.** Krishna **8.** Trimurti
deity consort .. **5.** sakti
dialect .. **5.** Tamil
division .. **5.** Patti, Taraf **6.** zillah
7. Pargana
Dravidian .. **5.** Tamil
drink (sacrificial) .. **4.** soma
evil spirit .. **4.** Mara **5.** asura
6. yaksha
festival .. **4.** Holi, tali **6.** Dewali, Pongal
9. Dashahara
first mortal to die .. **4.** Yama
flute .. **3.** bin **5.** pungi
garment .. **4.** sari (saree)
Gautama's wife .. **6.** Ahalya
gentleman (Mr) .. **5.** baboo (babu), sahib
giant .. **4.** Bana (thousand–armed)
government .. **6.** sircar
guitar .. **4.** vina **5.** sitar
hero .. **4.** Nala
incarnation .. **4.** Rama **5.** asura
6. yaksha
jackal .. **4.** kola
king .. **5.** Rajah
language (oldest) .. **5.** Tamil
language (sacred) .. **4.** Pali
loincloth .. **5.** dhoti
magic .. **4.** jadu (jadoo), maya
magician .. **4.** yogi **5.** fakir
meal (wheat) .. **4.** atta (ata)
mendicant .. **4.** naga **8.** sannyasi
merchant .. **6.** banian (banya)
7. goladar
mind .. **5.** manas
monkey god .. **7.** Hanuman
mountain .. **4.** Meru
mystic .. **4.** yogi
nursemaid .. **4.** ayah
paradise .. **7.** Nirvana
patriarch .. **5.** Pitri
peasant .. **4.** ryot

philosophy.. **4.** yoga, Yuga **5.** tamas
physicist.. **5.** Raman (Nobel 1930)
pillar.. **3.** lat
poet.. **5.** rishi **6.** Tagore (Nobel
   1913)
reign.. **3.** raj
sage.. **5.** rishi **6.** Dharma
   7. Gautama, Mahatma
savant.. **5.** swami
scarf.. **4.** sari (saree)
serpent (semi–human).. **4.** Naga
servant.. **5.** hamal
slave.. **4.** dasi (fem)
soldier.. **4.** sikh **5.** sepoy
supernatural being.. **6.** Garuda
swan.. **5.** hansa
syllable of assent.. **2.** om
Taraf ruler.. **8.** tarafdar
title.. **3.** Sri **4.** Raja, Rana, Rani
   5. Rajah, Ranee **6.** sirdar
   8. maharaja (maharajah)
tree (sacred).. **5.** pipal **6.** bo tree
tribesman.. **4.** Naga
tunic.. **4.** jama (jamah)
underworld (series).. **6.** Patala
village.. **5.** abadi
virtue.. **6.** sharma
widow (cremation).. **6.** suttee
woman (first).. **6.** Ahalya
Hindu Ages, Yoga...
   1st.. **5.** Krita
   2nd.. **5.** Treta
   3rd.. **7.** Dvapara
   4th.. **4.** Kali
   end.. **7.** Pralaya
   total.. **4.** Maha **10.** Manvantara
Hindu goddess... **3.** Sri, Uma **4.** Devi,
   Kali **5.** Durga, Gauri **6.** Chandi,
   Shakti **7.** Lakshmi, Parvati
   9. Haimavati (Durga)
Hindu god of...
   ancestors.. **5.** Pitri
   dead.. **4.** Yama
   fire.. **4.** Agni
   love.. **4.** Kama
   spirit.. **5.** Asura
   unknown.. **2.** Ka
   wisdom (elephant–headed).. **6.** Ganesa
      (Ganesha)
Hindu religion...
   abode of gods.. **4.** Meru
   call to prayer.. **4.** azan (adan)
   ceremony, rite.. **7.** araddha
   congregation.. **5.** samaj
   convert (to Islam).. **6.** shaikh
   creator.. **6.** Brahma
   cremation.. **4.** sati **6.** suttee
   doctrine, destiny.. **5.** karma
   first human to die (deified).. **4.** Yama
   hell.. **6.** Naraka
   Hinduism.. **5.** Agama **6.** Tantra
      7. Jainism **8.** Buddhism
      10. Brahmanism
   holy man.. **5.** Sadhu (Sadh)
   image worship.. **5.** arati
   incarnation.. **4.** Rama **6.** avatar
      11. Ramachandra
   literature (sacred).. **4.** Veda **7.** Shastra
   lord of the world.. **9.** Jagannath
      (Jagannatha)
   monastery.. **4.** math
   philosophy (life).. **5.** artha, atman,

prana **6.** tattva
prayer, call to.. **4.** azan (adan)
prayer rug.. **5.** asana, Melas
religion.. **5.** Agama **6.** Tantra
   7. Jainism **8.** Buddhism
   10. Brahmanism
scripture.. **4.** Veda **5.** Agama
   6. Tantra **7.** Shastra
sect.. **4.** Jain (Jaina), Sikh **6.** tantra
Shastra (4 parts).. **5.** aruti **6.** purana,
   smriti, tantra
Siva worshiper.. **5.** Saiva
Supreme Spirit.. **5.** atman **7.** jivatma
teacher.. **4.** guru **5.** swami
Trimurti (Triad).. **4.** Siva **6.** Brahma,
   Vishnu
trinity, triad.. **8.** Trimurti (Siva,
   Brahma, Vishnu)
unorthodox.. **7.** Jainism
widow (cremation).. **6.** suttee
Hindustan (pert to)...
dialect.. **4.** Urdu **10.** Hindustani
people.. **9.** Dravidian
poet.. **5.** Siraj (Beng)
rice.. **7.** aghanee
tribesman.. **4.** toda
hinge... **3.** pan (part) **4.** axis, axle,
   hang, knee, turn **5.** joint, pivot,
   stand **6.** depend, fasten, lamina,
   pintle
hint... **3.** cue **5.** imply, refer, tinge,
   trace **6.** allude, glance **7.** eyewink,
   inkling, suggest **8.** allusion, innuendo,
   intimate, reminder **9.** insinuate
   10. intimation, suggestion
   11. insinuation, supposition
hip... **3.** hop, pod **4.** coxa, limp, miss,
   skip **6.** haunch **8.** greeting
hip, hips (pert to)...
   bone.. **4.** coxa **5.** ilium **7.** os coxae
   10. innominate
   muscle.. **9.** iliopsoas
   nerve.. **7.** sciatic (largest)
   rose fruit.. **10.** pseudocarp
Hippocrates (pert to)...
   drug.. **5.** mecon (possibly opium)
   famed as.. **9.** physician (Gr)
   oath.. **11.** Hippocratic
hippopotamus... **5.** hippo **6.** seacow,
   zeekoe **8.** behemoth (Bib)
hippopotamus, thong of hide...
   7. chicote
Hiram... **9.** most noble **10.** King of
   Tyre (Bib)
hire... **3.** let, use **4.** hack, rent
   5. bribe, lease, price, wages
   6. employ, engage, reward, salary
   7. charter, stipend **9.** allowance
   12. compensation
hireling... **4.** esne, serf **5.** slave, venal
   8. employee **9.** mercenary
hirmos... **4.** hymn **8.** canticle
   9. troparion
hirondelle (Her)... **7.** swallow
hirsel... **4.** herd **5.** flock **7.** pasture
hirsute... **5.** hairy, rough **6.** coarse,
   shaggy **7.** boorish, bristly, uncouth
Hispania (anc)... **16.** Spain and
   Portugal
hispid... **5.** rough **7.** grooved
   8. strigose
hiss... **3.** boo, tst **4.** fizz **7.** condemn

8. derision, sibilate 10. effervesce, sibilation

historian ... 5. actor 6. writer 8. annalist 10. chronicler

history ... 5. drama 6. events, memoir 7. account 8. relation, treatise 9. chronicle, narrative

history (pert to) ...
development .. 8. ontogeny
Father of .. 9. Herodotus
muse of (Gr Myth) .. 4. Clio
period .. 3. era
personal .. 7. memoirs 9. biography, genealogy 13. autobiography
study, knowledge of .. 10. historical 12. historiology

histrio ... 5. actor

histrion ... 5. actor

histrionics ... 6. acting, actors 9. theatrics 11. theatricals

hit ... 3. bop, lob, rap, tap 4. blow, bunt, slam, slap, slog, suit, swat 5. flick, knock, shoot, smite 6. buffet, larrup, please, strike 7. succeed, success 9. collision

hitch ... 3. hop, tie, tug 4. halt, jerk, knot, limp, pull, yoke 5. catch, cling, crick, marry, unite 6. enlist, fasten, hobble 8. obstacle 9. hindrance 10. enlistment

hitherto ... 3. ago, yet 5. as yet 7. prior to 8. formerly, until now

hit or miss ... 6. casual 8. at random, by chance, careless 9. haphazard

Hittite (pert to) ...
ancestor (Bib) .. 4. Heth
city .. 6. Hamath, Pteria (ruins)
country .. 6. Khatti (Asia Minor)
people (anc) .. 8. Hittites 10. aborigines
storm god .. 6. Teshup (Teshub)

hoar ... 4. aged, gray, rime 5. hoary, white 7. ancient 9. hoarfrost, venerable

hoard ... 5. amass, lay up, store 6. garner, supply 7. husband 8. treasure, treasury 10. accumulate, collection

hoarder ... 5. miser 6. storer 9. treasurer

hoarfrost ... 3. rag 4. hoar, rime 7. needles (ice) 9. Jack Frost

hoarse ... 3. old 4. aged, gray 6. remote (in time) 7. ancient 9. canescent

hoatzin, hoactzin ... 4. anna 5. hanna 8. pheasant 9. stinkbird 11. Opisthocomi (group)

hoax ... 3. bam 4. bilk, ruse, sham 5. bluff, cheat, trick 6. canard 7. deceive 8. artifice 9. deception

hob ... 3. elf, hub, peg, pin 4. game, mark 5. clown, fairy, havoc 6. ferret, rustic, sprite 7. hobnail 8. mischief 9. fireplace, hobgoblin

hobble ... 4. clog, gait (unequal), halt, limp 5. dance 6. fetter, tether, wabble 7. dilemma, pastern, shackle 11. predicament

hobbledehoy ... 4. gawk 5. youth

hobbler ... 5. pilot 7. boatman, hoveler, laborer, soldier 8. retainer

hobby ... 3. fad, nag 5. dolly, horse 6. falcon 7. bicycle, pastime 9. avocation, plaything 10. hobbyhorse 12. rocking horse

hobgoblin ... 3. elf, imp 4. bogy, pixy, Puck 5. scrat 6. sprite 7. bugaboo 9. coltpixie 10. apparition 15. Robin Goodfellow

hobnob ... 9. associate (with), drink with, hit or miss

hobo ... 3. bum 5. tramp 6. beggar 7. vagrant 8. vagabond

hock ... 3. ham 4. pawn 5. ankle, joint, thigh (man) 6. pledge 7. disable 9. hamstring

hockey (pert to) ...
ball, disk .. 3. nur 4. knur, puck
cup .. 7. Stanley (prize)
goal .. 4. cage
stick .. 6. shinny 7. cammock
team number .. 5. seven

hocus ... 4. drug 5. cheat 6. liquor (drugged) 7. deceive, falsify 8. cheating, trickery 10. adulterate

hocus–pocus ... 5. cheat, trick 6. bunkum, humbug 7. juggler 8. flimflam, nonsense, quackery 9. deception, trickster 11. incantation 12. charlatanism 13. sleight of hand 15. juggler's formula

hod ... 3. tub 4. hide 6. barrow, trough 7. scuttle

hodgepodge ... 4. mess, olio, stew 5. cento 6. medley 7. mélange, mixture 10. miscellany 11. gallimaufry, olla–podrida

hog ... 3. pig, sow, Sus 4. bene, boar, galt, gilt 5. sheep (unshorn), shoat, swine 6. barrow 8. babirusa (babiroussa), javelina 9. boschvark, razorback

hog ... 6. corner (the market) 7. glutton 8. slattern 9. take it all 10. locomotive, monopolist

hog (pert to) ...
breed .. 5. Essex 9. Hampshire
food .. 4. mast
ground .. 6. marmot
hoglike .. 7. porcine
salted side .. 5. bacon 6. flitch
shears (snout) .. 7. snouter
thigh (cured) .. 3. ham

hogfish ... 7. capitan, pigfish 8. scorpene

hoggerel ... 5. sheep 6. hogger

hoggery ... 4. hogs 5. greed 11. beastliness 14. hoggish manners

hoggish ... 6. filthy, greedy 7. porcine, selfish, swinish 10. gluttonous

hogshead ... 4. cask 6. barrel 7. measure

hogwash ... 5. swill, waste

hoi polloi ... 3. mob 5. herde 6. masses, rabble 7. the many 8. populace 9. multitude

hoist ... 4. lift, sail 5. boost, heave, hoise, raise 7. elevate 8. elevator

hoisting device ... 3. gin 4. jack 5. crane, davit, lewis 7. capstan, derrick 8. elevator, windlass 9. parbuckle

hoity–toity ... 5. giddy, proud 6. snooty

7. flighty, haughty 8. arrogant
11. exclamation, harum–scarum,
patronizing, thoughtless
13. irresponsible
hold ... 3. own 4. bind, have, keep,
lien, seat, stow 5. avast, cling,
delay, grasp, judge 6. adhere, arrest,
cleave, clench, defend, detain,
endure, harbor, regard, retain
7. contain, control, custody
8. consider, foothold, maintain,
thurrock (ship's), treasury
9. anchorage, constrain, entertain,
prosecute 11. compartment
hold (pert to) ...
back.. 3. dam 4. last, stem 5. delay,
deter, stint 6. detain, hinder, refuse,
retard 7. abstain, inhibit, repress
8. restrain
belief.. 7. suppose
dear.. 7. cherish
fast.. 5. cling 6. adhere 9. persevere
forth.. 5. offer, speak 7. declaim,
descant, exhibit, expound
8. continue, maintain, propound
off.. 5. avert, delay 7. repulse, ward
off 9. stay aloof, temporize
on.. 4. stop, wait 6. endure, retain
7. forbear 8. continue
opinion.. 4. deem
out.. 4. last 6. endure, refuse, resist
7. exclude 8. continue
session.. 3. sit 7. convene
8. assemble
together.. 6. adhere, cohere 8. be
joined 9. co–operate
up.. 3. rob 4. buoy, halt, lift, rein
5. check, delay, raise 6. hinder,
resist, retard 7. display, exhibit,
pillory (to scorn), robbery, support,
sustain
water.. 5. sound 10. consistent
holder ... 3. cop (yarn) 4. file
5. owner, payee 6. bearer, binder,
lienor, tenant 7. trustee 8. endorsee
9. mortgagor, possessor, recipient
10. receptacle
hold in ...
check.. 4. curb, rein 6. arrest, bridle
7. control 8. restrain
custody.. 4. jail 6. detain, intern
hand.. 6. assure 7. control, promise,
toy with
mind.. 6. harbor 7. cherish
9. entertain
holding ... 5. asset, claim, stake, tenet,
title, trust 6. belief, equity, estate,
tenure 8. interest, property
9. retention 10. possessing,
possession, supporting
holding fast ... 9. tenacious
10. persistent
holding sway ... 7. regnant
8. dominant, reigning
hole ... 3. den, pit 4. bore, cave, cove,
dive, flaw, gulf, lair, nook, slot, vent
5. abyss, chasm, fault, hovel, place,
shaft 6. burrow, cavern, cavity,
cellar, hollow, prison 7. impasse,
opening, orifice, ostiole
10. excavation 11. predicament
hole (pert to) ...

bowling ball.. 4. grip
cable (ship's).. 5. hawse
enlarger.. 6. reamer
implement.. 3. awl, eye 4. bore
5. drill 8. stiletto
metal mold.. 5. sprue
mud.. 6. wallow
wall.. 5. niche
water.. 5. oasis
whirlpool.. 5. gourd (obs)
Holi (or Hoolee) ... 8. festival (Hind)
holia ... 6. salmon (humpback)
holiday ... 4. fete 5. feria, merry
6. fiesta, jovial, outing 7. festive,
playday 8. festival, vacation
9. convivial, festivity 10. recreation
holiness ... 5. piety, title (Pope)
8. sanctity 9. godliness
10. sacredness 11. saintliness
13. righteousness
Holland ... 11. Netherlands (which see)
Holland ...
capital.. 8. The Hague (Court)
9. Amsterdam
city.. 3. Ede 5. Doorn 6. Leyden
9. Amsterdam, Rotterdam
government.. 8. monarchy
liquor.. 3. gin 8. schnapps
oddity.. 5. dikes 6. canals, tulips
painter.. 6. Rubens 7. Van Eyck
people.. 5. Dutch
port.. 4. Edam
pottery.. 5. delft (delf)
province.. 4. Edam 7. Drenthe,
Zeeland
river.. 3. Ems, Lek 5. Meuse, Rhine
7. Scheldt (Schelde)
sea.. 5. North
village.. 3. Ede
hollow ... 3. den, pit 4. thin, void
5. bight, empty, false, gaunt, sinus
6. cavern, cavity, cirque, corrie,
groove, hungry, socket, sunken,
vacant 7. concave, unsound
8. capsular, specious 9. cavernous,
depressed, faithless, insincere,
worthless 10. sepulchral
12. unsatisfying
hollowed ... 6. cavate 7. concave,
glenoid
holly ... 4. holm, hull, Ilex 5. yapon
6. hulver, laurel 8. Eryngium
9. blackjack, Ilicaceae 10. Sapindales
hollyhock ... 5. color 7. Althaea,
blue–red 9. perennial
holm ... 3. oak 5. holly, islet, marsh
7. bottoms, low land
holobaptist ... 12. immersionist
holocaust ... 9. sacrifice (by fire)
11. destruction 13. burnt offering
holy ... 5. godly, pious 6. chaste,
devout, sacred 7. epithet (Relig),
sainted 8. hallowed 9. venerated
Holy, holy (pert to) ...
carpet.. 5. kiswa (kiswah)
comb form.. 5. hagio
Joe.. 8. sky pilot 9. clergyman
oil.. 6. chrism 7. unction
Ones.. 9. Innocents (slain by Herod)
pilgrim.. 6. palmer
receptacle.. 5. cruet, stoup
Rood.. 5. cross 8. crucifix

water sprinkler.. 11. aspergillum
Holy Grail (pert to)...
  castle.. 9. Monsalvat (Mt)
  guardian.. 8. Amfortas
  knight.. 7. Galahad
  legend.. 8. Sangraal (Sangreal)
  quest by.. 4. Bors 7. Galahad
    9. Percivale
  terms.. 7. platter, wine cup
homage... 5. dulia, honor, liege
  6. fealty, latria 7. loyalty, ovation,
  respect, worship 9. deference,
  obeisance, reverence 10. allegiance
  12. commendation
homard... 7. Homarus, lobster
hombre... 3. man 4. homo, male
  6. fellow
home... 4. care, goal (games), kern
  (kirn), nest 5. abode, astre, grave,
  heart 6. asylum, estate, hearth
  7. habitat, village 8. domicile,
  dwelling 9. residence 10. fatherland,
  habitation
home (pert to)...
  base.. 3. den 5. plate
  dislike.. 9. ecophobia
  Home Sweet Home author.. 5. Payne
    (John Howard 1823)
  Irish King's.. 4. Tara
  of the gods.. 7. Olympus
  of the Golden Fleece.. 7. Colchis
homely... 4. ugly 5. plain 6. humble,
  kindly, simple 7. plainly 8. domestic,
  homelike, informal, plebeian,
  uncomely 9. unsightly 10. intimately
  11. comfortable 13. unpretentious
homemade... 5. plain 6. simple
  8. domestic, handmade, homespun
Homer (pert to)...
  birthplace.. 5. Chios (claimed)
  book.. 5. Iliad 7. Odyssey
  burial place.. 3. Ios (Isl)
  hero.. 6. Aeneas
Homer's poems (pert to)...
  rhapsodists.. 9. Homeridae
  student, reciter of.. 7. Homerid
    8. Homerist
  study of.. 10. Homerology
  style.. 7. Homeric
homesickness... 7. Heimweh 9. mal
  du pays, nostalgia
homespun... 5. cloth, plain, rough
  6. coarse, russet 8. domestic,
  homemade 10. not elegant,
  unpolished (person)
homicide... 5. morth 6. murder
  7. killing 12. manslaughter
homily... 5. adage 6. sermon
  8. assembly, converse
  9. communion, discourse
homing pigeon... 13. carrier pigeon
hominy... 4. samp 5. maize 10. hulled
  corn
Homo sapiens... 3. man 4. homo
  9. anthropos
Honduras...
  capital.. 11. Tegucigalpa
  city.. 4. Tela 6. Roatan 8. Trujillo
    12. Puerto Cortes
  discoverer.. 8. Columbus
  gulf.. 7. Fonseca
  Indian tribe.. 5. Lenca

language.. 7. Spanish
people.. 6. Indian 7. Spanish
river.. 4. Ulua 5. Negro 6. Patuca
hone... 4. long, pine 5. delay, dress,
  stone (sharpening), strop, yearn
  6. lament 7. grumble, sharpen
  8. oilstone 9. whetstone
honest... 4. open 5. frank 6. candid,
  chaste 7. genuine, up and up,
  upright 8. faithful, suitable, virtuous
  9. guileless, honorable, ingenuous,
  integrity 10. creditable
  13. unadulterated 15. straightforward
honesty... 5. honor 6. equity
  7. justice 8. fairness 9. integrity,
  rectitude 11. genuineness,
  uprightness 12. truthfulness
  15. trustworthiness
honey... 3. mel 5. melli (comb form),
  sweet 6. nectar 7. sweeten
  10. endearment
honey (pert to)...
  bear (sloth).. 8. Melursus
  bearing.. 11. melliferous
  bee.. 5. Apis 6. dingar 7. deseret
    9. mellifera
  bird.. 3. iao 6. manuao 10. honey
    eater
  buzzard.. 4. kite, pern
  comb.. 4. raat 5. favus 8. alveolus
  drink.. 4. mead 5. morat
  flowing.. 11. mellifluent, mellifluous
  pert to.. 8. melissic
  sucking.. 11. mellisugent, mellivorous
  yellow.. 6. dorado 10. melichrous
Hong Kong...
  capital.. 8. Victoria
  government.. 11. Crown Colony
  island.. 12. Stonecutters
  peninsula.. 7. Kowloon
Honolulu...
  capital of.. 6. Hawaii
  island site.. 4. Oahu
  port.. 11. Pearl Harbor
  suburb.. 3. Ewa
honorable, honourable... 5. moral,
  title 7. upright 8. honorary
  9. estimable, reputable, venerable
  10. creditable 11. commendable,
  illustrious, meritorious, respectable
honorably... 5. nobly 6. fairly, justly
  8. worthily 9. equitably, reputably,
  uprightly
honorarium... 7. douceur
honored... 5. famed, feted 6. graced
  7. awarded, revered 8. knighted
  9. accoladed
hood... 4. corf, cowl, hide, mail
  (armor) 5. amice, blind, cloak
  6. bonnet, camail, capote
  7. capuche (capouch) 8. babushka,
  burnoose (burnous), capsheaf,
  covering, liripipe, mozzetta, tapadera
  12. strong–arm man
hood (suff)... 9. condition
hooded... 9. cucullate
hooded seal... 11. bladdernose
hoodwink... 4. dupe, fool, hide, wile
  5. blear, blind, cheat, cover, cozen
  6. befool, delude 7. deceive, mislead
  9. blindfold
hooey... 4. blah, bunk 5. tripe

7. baloney, hogwash 8. buncombe,
malarkey, nonsense 13. horsefeathers
hoof... 4. clee, frog, walk 5. cloof
(clufe, cluve) 6. ungula 7. pastern
(part) 8. periople (part), pododerm
hoof–paring tool... 8. butteris
hoof–shaped... 8. ungulate
hoof track... 5. piste
hook... 4. gaff, lure 5. catch, chape,
cleek, crome, curve, hamus, snare,
steal 6. anchor, clevis, fasten,
hangle, tenter 7. hamulus
hookah, hooka... 4. pipe 8. narghile
hooked... 6. curved, hamate
7. angular, cleeked 8. aduncous
(adunc), anchoral, aquiline, uncinate
Hooker (Thomas)... 9. clergyman
18. Luther of New England
hooks (group)... 5. Party (Neth)
9. pulldevil, scrodgill 10. Kabbeljaws
(Nobles)
hookworm... 7. Necator 9. Uncinaria
hooligan... 6. loafer 7. gorilla,
hoodlum, ruffian 8. larrikin
hoop... 4. bail, band, ring 5. clasp
6. circle, wicket 7. circlet
8. surround
hoop skirt... 9. crinoline
11. farthingale
Hoosier poet... 5. Riley (J Whitcomb)
Hoosier State... 7. Indiana
hop... 3. fly 4. drug, halt, jump, leap,
limp, trip, vine 5. bound, caper,
dance, frisk, opium 6. flight, gambol,
spring 8. narcotic
hope... 3. bay 4. opal, spes, Spes
(Goddess) 6. haven, inlet, trust
6. aspire, desire, expect 7. cherish,
promise 8. optimism, reliance
11. expectation 12. anticipation
hoped for... 7. sperate
hopeful... 8. probable, sanguine
9. confident, expectant 10. propitious
hopeless... 4. vain 6. futile 7. forlorn,
useless 8. downcast 9. desperate,
incurable 10. despairing, despondent
11. ineffectual 12. disconsolate,
irremediable 13. irrecoverable,
irretrievable
hopelessness... 7. despair 8. futility
13. impossibility
hop kiln... 4. oast (ost)
hoplite... 7. soldier
hopper... 3. box 5. chute 6. dancer,
jumper, leaper 7. penguin (rock)
10. receptacle 11. grasshopper
hopscotch... 6. pebble, peever
7. pallall
Horace... 4. poet 10. Ars Poetica
Horae (Gr Relig)... 4. dike (justice)
6. Eirene (peace) 7. Eunomia
(wisdom) 9. goddesses 11. Book of
Hours
horal... 6. hourly
horde... 4. army, camp, clan, pack
5. crowd, swarm, tribe, troop
Horde, Golden... 6. Tatars (Mongol)
Horde, Great (Anthrop)... 5. Kazak
7. Kirghiz
horizon... 4. blue 5. limit, range
6. circle, sea rim 7. azimuth, sea
line, sky line 8. junction (earth and

sky), boundary
horizon glass... 7. sextant
horizontal... 4. flat 5. level 8. parallel
(to horizon)
hormone... 8. estrogen 9. cortisone
horn... 4. Cape, cusp, gore, peak,
tuba 5. alarm, bugle, cornu, keras,
siren 6. antler, beaker, cornet, vessel
7. buccina, process (animal), trumpet
8. tentacle 9. appendage
horn (pert to)...
blare.. 4. toot 7. fanfare, tantara
9. tantarara
comb form.. 5. kerat 6. kerato
crescent moon.. 4. cusp
drinking (anc).. 6. rhyton
insect's.. 7. antenna
Jewish.. 7. shophar (shofar)
player.. 6. bugler 9. cornetist,
trumpeter
producing.. 11. keratogenic
trumpet.. 6. kerana (kerrana)
unbranched (antler).. 3. dag 7. pricket
hornbill... 4. bird, tock 6. homrai,
toucan 7. Buceros
horned animal (Myth)... 7. Unicorn
9. Monoceros
horned rattlesnake... 3. asp 5. viper
8. cerastes 10. sidewinder
horned toad... 6. lizard 9. Iguanidae
hornet... 4. wasp 5. Vespa 6. crabro
horny tissue... 7. keratin 8. keratoid
(ceratoid), keratose (ceratose)
horologe... 4. dial 5. clock, watch
horoscope... 3. map 5. chart
6. scheme 7. diagram
horrendous... 7. fearful 8. horrible
horrible... 4. dire, grim 6. grisly,
horrid, odious 7. ghastly, hideous
8. dreadful, shocking, terrible
9. atrocious, frightful, revolting
10. detestable, horrendous
horror... 3. awe 4. fear 5. dread
6. aghast, terror 8. aversion, distress
10. abhorrence 11. abomination,
detestation 13. consternation
hors d'oeuvre... 6. canapé, relish
8. aperitif 9. antipasto, appetizer
horse... 3. cob, nag 4. colt, foal,
mare, mule, plug, pony, prad, race,
stud 5. beast, burro, draft, filly,
genet (jennet), hobby, mount, pacer,
steed 6. bronco (broncho), cheval,
dobbin, donkey, equine, garran,
hippos, maiden, pelter, rouncy
7. caballo, cavalry, charger, courser,
Equidae, gelding, hackney, harness,
mustang, prancer, quarter, stepper,
trotter 8. roadster, stallion, trotting
9. broomtail
horse (pert to)...
ankle.. 4. hock
arena.. 10. hippodrome
Australian.. 5. dingo, myall
8. warragal, yarraman
breastplate.. 7. poitrel (peytrel)
broken–down.. 6. garran, gleyde
buyer (of nags).. 5. coper 7. knacker
calico.. 5. pinto
collar.. 7. bargham
comb form.. 4. hipp 5. hippo
6. hippus

command.. 3. gee, haw, hup
4. whoa 6. giddap
covering.. 9. caparison
cry.. 5. neigh 6. whinny
dealer.. 7. chanter, scorser
disease.. 5. surra (surrah) 6. heaves,
lampas, spavin 7. founder, lampers
draft.. 9. Percheron
family.. 7. Equidae 9. Miohippus,
Orohippus
fast.. 6. pelter
feed box.. 6. manger
female.. 4. mare, yaud 5. filly
fly.. 4. cleg (clegg) 6. botfly
foot.. 4. frog, hoof 7. fetlock, pastern
forehead.. 8. chanfrin
gait.. 3. run 4. lope, pace, trot, walk
6. canter, gallop
genus.. 5. Equus
giant (Norse).. 7. Goldfax
goddess.. 5. Epona
gray.. 8. schimmel
hide.. 8. cordovan
hired.. 4. hack
hoof (part).. 7. caltrop 8. periople
laugh.. 5. snort 6. guffaw, heehaw
leap.. 6. curvet, hurdle 9. ballotade
lover.. 10. hippophile
mackerel.. 5. atule, tunny 6. bonita
male.. 4. stud 7. gelding 8. stallion
manège term.. 5. longe, mount
6. pesade 7. piaffer, saccade
8. caracole 9. estrapage
measure.. 4. hand
miracle (Myth).. 5. Arion
monster (fabled).. 11. Hippocampus
old.. 4. jade, yaud 5. skate
8. harridan, old paint
opera.. 7. Western
pace.. 4. lope, trot 5. amble
6. canter
pack.. 7. sumpter
pair.. 4. span, team
pasturage right.. 9. horsegate
piebald.. 5. pinto
pole.. 5. poler, wheel
prehistoric.. 8. Eohippus
10. Mesohippus, Pliohippus
13. Protorohippus
racer.. 4. pony 6. mudder, plater,
staker
ref to.. 6. equine, equoid, hippic
9. caballine
relay (remounts).. 6. remuda
riding.. 3. cob
rope.. 5. longe 6. halter
roundup.. 5. rodeo
saddle.. 3. cob 5. mount 7. palfrey
shoer.. 7. farrier 10. blacksmith
slang.. 3. nag 4. hack, plug
6. dobbin 8. bangtail
small.. 3. cob, tit 4. pony 5. bidet,
genet (jennet) 8. Galloway, Shetland
sorrel.. 4. roan 8. chestnut
spirited.. 4. Arab 5. steed 6. rearer
7. courser
stable of.. 6. string
study of.. 9. hippology
swift.. 6. pelter 7. Pacolet
talking (Myth).. 5. Arion
three (harnessed).. 6. tandem

7. unicorn
track, arena.. 10. hippodrome
trappings.. 5. manta 6. tackle
7. harness 9. caparison
trotting.. 6. Morgan
turn.. 7. passade
war.. 5. steed 7. charger 8. destrier
(anc)
white–streaked face.. 4. shim
wild.. 6. bronco, tarpan 7. mustang
8. warragal (warrigal)
winged.. 7. Pegasus
horse, breed ... 4. Arab, Barb 5. Shire,
Waler 6. Cayuse, Morgan 7. Arabian,
Belgian, Hackney, Mustang, Suffolk
8. Galloway, Normandy, Palomino,
Shetland 9. Appaloosa, Miohippus,
Percheron 10. Clydesdale
horse, color ... 3. bay, tan 4. pied,
roan 5. cream, pinto 6. calico, sorrel
7. brindle, dappled, piebald
8. chestnut, palomino, schimmel,
skewbald 10. flea–bitten
horse, famed (and rider) ... 4. Tony
(Tom Mix) 5. Grani (Sigurd)
6. Bayard (Rinaldo), Rienzi (Gen
Sherman), Silver (Lone Ranger),
Trojan (legend), Whitey (Zachary
Taylor) 7. Alborak (Mohammed),
Morengo (Napoleon), Pegasus (Gr
Myth), Trigger (Roy Rogers), Xanthus
(Achilles) 8. Comanche (Gen Custer),
Sleipnir 8–legged (Odin), Soapsuds
(Will Rogers) 9. Black Bess (Dick
Turpin), Houyhnhnm (Gulliver's
Travels), Incitatus (Caligula), Rosinante
(Don Quixote), Traveller (Gen Robt E
Lee) 10. Bootlegger (Will Rogers),
Bucephalus (Alexander the Great),
Cincinnati (Gen Grant), Copenhagen
(Wellington at Waterloo), King Philip
(Gen Forrest) 11. Black Beauty
(legend), Vegliantino (Orlando)
12. Little Sorrel (Stonewall Jackson)
horseman ... 5. rider 6. cowboy
7. centaur, vaquero 8. buckaroo
10. cavalryman, equestrian
12. broncobuster
horsemanship ... 6. manège
horseradish tree ... 3. ben (oil)
5. behen (behn) 7. Moringa
Horus (pert to) ...
bird.. 6. falcon
father.. 6. Osiris
hawk–headed god of.. 3. day
mother.. 4. Isis
slayer of.. 4. Seth
hospice ... 3. inn 6. asylum, imaret
9. hospitium, infirmary
hospitable ... 6. kindly 7. cordial
8. friendly, gracious 9. receptive,
welcoming 10. neighborly
hospital ... 6. crèche, refuge
9. ambulance (mobile), infirmary
10. nosocomium, sanatorium,
sanitarium 11. institution,
xenodochium 12. ambulatorium
hospitality ... 7. accueil, welcome
8. open door 9. open house,
xenodochy 10. cordiality
13. receptiveness
host ... 3. sum (obs) 4. army 5. swarm

6. legion, throng 8. assemble,
landlord 9. multitude, sacrifice
11. entertainer
hostel... 3. inn 5. hotel, motel
6. tavern 8. lodgings 9. residence
(student)
hostelry... 3. inn 5. hotel 6. hostel,
tavern 11. caravansary
hostile... 5. enemy 7. adverse (law),
opposed 8. contrary, inimical
10. malevolent, unfriendly
11. belligerent 12. antagonistic
13. unsympathetic
hostilities... 3. war 5. feuds, raids
hostility... 5. anger 6. animus, enmity,
hatred, rancor 7. ill will, warfare
8. opponent 9. animosity, antipathy
10. antagonism, bitterness,
opposition, resentment 11. contrariety
13. antisocialism 14. unfriendliness,
vindictiveness
hostler... 5. groom 7. equerry
9. innkeeper, stableboy, stableman
Host vessel... 3. Pyx 5. paten
hot... 3. red 5. calid, eager, fiery
6. fervid, raging, recent, torrid,
urgent 7. burning, calidus, excited,
fervent, glowing, peppery, violent
8. feverish, sizzling, vehement
10. hot–blooded, passionate
hot cakes... 8. kneepads (army sl)
hotel... 3. inn 5. lodge 6. hostel,
tavern 7. albergo 11. caravansary
hot-tempered... 5. angry, breth, fiery
7. enraged, iracund 8. choleric,
wrathful 10. hot–blooded
Hottentot, S Africa (pert to)...
cloak.. 6. kaross
hut.. 5. kraal
mixed native.. 6. Griqua
musical instrument.. 4. gora (gorah)
nickname.. 9. Khoi–Khoin (Koi–Koin)
(men of men)
purest tribe.. 5. Namas 7. Namaqua
race.. 6. Bantus 7. Bushmen
tribe.. 6. Damara, Herero
9. Ovahehero
hound... 4. hunt 5. chase, track
6. follow, pursue 7. devotee
9. scoundrel
hound (animal)... 4. alan 6. Afghan,
basset, beagle, setter 7. harrier,
skirter 8. Cerberus (Myth), elkhound,
foxhound 9. boarhound, dachshund,
deerhound, greyhound, staghound,
wolfhound 10. bloodhound,
otterhound
hounds, relay of... 8. avantlay
hour (pert to)...
astrology.. 7. inequal 9. planetary
by the.. 5. horal 6. horary
Eccl.. 4. sext 9. canonical
Latin.. 4. hora 5. Horae (Book of
Hours)
measure.. 9. hourglass
term.. 4. time 6. period 7. measure
8. interval
houri... 5. nymph (Moham)
Hours, Book of... 5. Horae
house... 3. eco (comb form) 4. casa,
firm, home 5. abode, cover, lodge,
tribe 6. billet, family 7. cottage,

enclose, lineage, mansion, quarter,
shelter, theater 8. audience,
bungalow, Congress, domicile,
dwelling 9. playhouse, residence,
workhouse 10. habitation, Parliament
house (pert to)...
astrology.. 7. mansion, mundane
9. planetary
boarding.. 3. inn 5. hotel 6. tavern
9. dormitory
comb form.. 3. eco 4. oeco, oiko
correction.. 9. Bridewell (Eng)
11. reformatory
dog.. 6. kennel
government.. 5. Lords 7. Commons
15. Representatives
ranch.. 4. casa 6. casita 8. hacienda
roof.. 9. penthouse
small.. 3. hut 4. nest 5. cabin, shack
stately.. 5. villa 6. palace 7. mansion
summer.. 6. casino, gazebo
9. belvedere
warming.. 6. infare
household (pert to)...
deity.. 5. Lares 7. Penates
domestic.. 6. family, menage
fairy.. 4. Puck
linen.. 6. napery
housekeeping... 8. oikology
10. management 11. hospitality
House of... 4. Keys (Isle of Man)
5. David, Lords, Peers 7. Bishops,
Commons, Windsor 11. Seven
Gables
housewarming... 6. infare
11. merrymaking
Houston, Texas...
capital.. 8. Republic (Texas, 1837)
college.. 4. Rice
named for.. 10. Sam Houston (Gen)
nickname.. 12. Space City USA
site.. 11. Ship Channel
site of.. 4. NASA
hovel... 3. den, hut 4. shed 5. cabin,
hutch, shack 6. dugout 7. shelter
hover... 4. flit, soar 5. brood, drift,
float 6. linger 7. shelter 9. hang
about 12. be irresolute
however... 3. but, how, tho, yet
6. anyhow, though 7. at least
8. although 11. at all events
12. nevertheless 15. notwithstanding
howl... 3. bay, cry 4. wail, yell, yowl
6. lament 7. ululate
howling monkey... 5. araba
hoyden, hoiden... 4. rude 5. a romp
6. tomboy 7. ill–bred
Hoyle (Edmond)... 6. writer
12. encyclopedia (of games)
hub... 3. hut 4. axle, nave 6. center
(centre) 7. hummock
12. protuberance (rough)
Hub (The)... 6. Boston
hubbub... 3. ado, din 4. game (US
Ind), stir 6. bustle, clamor, outcry,
racket, rumpus, tumult, uproar
8. rowdy–dow 9. agitation,
commotion, confusion 10. turbulence
hubristic... 8. arrogant, insolent
12. contemptuous
hubshi... 5. Negro
huck... 3. hip 4. hook, howk

6. haunch, higgle, hollow 7. bargain
huckleberry... 5. bacca 9. blueberry
12. Vacciniaceae
huckleberry endocarp... 6. pyrene
huckster... 6. broker, hawker, vendor
7. peddler 8. pitchman, retailer
9. middleman
huddle... 3. hug 5. crowd 6. bustle,
confer, jumble, mingle 7. confuse
8. assemble, disorder, grouping
(football) 9. confusion, skinflint
10. conference 14. conglomeration
Hudson (pert to)...
boat.. 8. Half Moon (Henry Hudson's)
explorer.. 11. Henry Hudson
River School.. 8. Painters (19th Cent)
River seal.. 7. muskrat
hue... 4. form, tint, tone 5. color,
guise, shade, shout, swart, tinge
6. outcry 7. swarthy 8. shouting
10. complexion
huff... 4. puff 5. anger, bully, swell
6. offend 7. inflate
hug... 4. hold 5. clasp, seize
6. adhere 7. embrace, welcome
8. greeting
huge... 3. big 4. vast 5. giant, great,
large 7. immense, mammoth,
massive, monster, titanic 8. colossal,
enormous, gigantic 9. monstrous
10. gargantuan
Huguenot... 10. Protestant
Huguenot leader... 6. Adrets (Baron)
hui (Chin)... 4. firm 5. guild 7. society
(secret) 11. partnership
huisache... 4. wabe (wabi) 5. shrub
7. popinac
huissier... 5. usher 7. bailiff, sheriff
10. doorkeeper
huitre... 6. oyster
hulky... 5. bulky, large 6. clumsy
7. hulking, loutish
hull... 3. pod 4. free, husk 5. calyx,
frame (ship), shell, shoot, strip
8. covering
hullabaloo... 3. din 6. clamor
(clamour), hubbub, outcry, racket,
tumult, uproar 9. confusion
hulled corn... 4. samp 5. maize
6. hominy
hulver... 5. holly
hum... 4. buzz, sing (with closed lips)
5. croon, drone 6. murmur
7. deceive
human... 3. man 4. homo, kind
6. humane, mortal 7. Adamite
8. merciful
human (pert to)...
being.. 3. man 6. mortal, person
7. Adamite 8. creature
bondage.. 7. slavery
race.. 3. man 7. mankind
skull.. 10. death's-head
structure.. 7. anatomy
trunk.. 5. torso
humble... 3. low 4. mean, meek, mild,
poor 5. abase, abash, demit, lower,
lowly, plain 6. modest, simple,
subdue 7. degrade, mortify
8. chastise, deferent, disgrace,
plebeian, reverent 9. humiliate
10. unassuming 12. unpretending

humbug... 4. bosh, fake, flam, guff,
hoax, sham 5. cheat, fraud, guile,
trick 7. deceive, mislead 8. pretense
9. deception, imposture, stratagem
humid... 4. damp, dank 5. moist
6. sultry 8. vaporous
humiliate... 5. abase, abash, shame
6. humble, nither 7. affront, degrade,
mortify 8. disgrace
humiliation... 7. subdual 9. abasement
11. disgraceful 13. mortification
humility... 6. humble (spirit)
7. modesty 8. meekness, mildness
9. lowliness (mind) 10. humbleness
hummingbird... 3. ava 4. star
5. sylph, topaz 6. rufous, Sappho
7. colibri, Lucifer 8. calliope
9. sheartail, thornbill, thorntail
10. rackettail 11. Trochilidae
humor, humour... 3. fun, wit 4. baby,
mood, whim 5. blood, cater, fancy,
fluid, freak, quirk 6. comedy, levity,
nature, please 7. caprice, gratify,
indulge 8. drollery 10. comicality
11. inclination, temperament
humorist... 3. wag 5. comic, droll
8. comedian 11. entertainer
humorous... 5. funny, humid, moist,
witty 6. jocose 7. amusing, jocular
9. facetious, laughable, whimsical
10. capricious
hump... 4. arch, hunk, lump 5. bulge,
exert, hurry, mound, sulks
7. hummock 8. shoulder
12. protuberance
humpbacked... 6. humped, kyphos
8. deformed, kyphosis 9. camel back
11. hunchbacked
humpbacked fish... 5. whale
6. salmon, sucker 9. whitefish
humus... 4. mold, soil 5. humin,
mulch
Hun... 6. Attila, vandal 7. soldier
9. barbarian 10. Ephthalite
hunch... 4. bend, hump, lump
5. crook, fudge, shove 6. chilly,
crouch, frosty, thrust 9. intuition
12. protuberance
Hunchback of Notre Dame (pert to)...
character.. 9. Esmeralda (gypsy),
Quasimodo (The Hunchback)
French name.. 16. Notre Dame de
Paris
literature (famed).. 5. novel
hunched... 7. gibbous
hundred (pert to)...
comb form.. 5. centi, hecto
7. hecaton
eyed being.. 5. Argus
fold.. 8. centuple 12. centuplicate
historian (of centuries)..
11. centuriator
Latin.. 6. centum
men, soldiers.. 7. century
12. centumvirate
number.. 7. ten tens 9. five score
symbol.. 1. C
victim sacrifice.. 8. hecatomb
weight.. 6. cental 7. centner
years.. 7. century 9. centenary,
centurial
Hundred Days (pert to)... 8. Napoleon,

Waterloo (Battle 1815)
hundred percent ... 5. quite 8. entirely
 10. altogether 14. unquestionable
hundredth of a right angle ... 4. grad
Hundred Years War ... 5. Crecy
 (Cressy)
hung ... see *hang*
Hungarian (pert to) ... see also *Hungary*
army .. 6. Honvéd 9. Honvédség
cavalryman .. 6. Hussar
dance .. 7. czardas
gypsy .. 7. tzigane
hash .. 7. goulash
legislature .. 8. Felsohaz
measure .. 5. antal, itcze
partridge .. 6. Perdix
physicist .. 6. Teller
poet .. 5. Arany
Pretender to the throne .. 4. Otto
racial unit .. 3. Hun 6. Magyar
surgeon .. 6. Schick
turnip .. 8. kohlrabi
wine .. 5. Tokay
Hungary (People's Republic of) ...
capital .. 8. Budapest (Budapesth)
city .. 6. Szeged (Szegedin)
 8. Debrecen 9. Kecskemet
government .. 9. Communism
lake .. 7. Balaton 10. Neusiedler
mountain .. 5. Tatra 11. Carpathians
Plain (fertile) .. 6. Alfold
port .. 5. Fiume
river .. 4. Raab 5. Drava (Drave)
 6. Danube, Theiss 7. Vistula
hunger ... 4. long, want 6. acoria,
 desire, famine, thirst 7. craving
 8. appetite, coveting, voracity
 9. esurience
hungry ... 4. avid, poor 5. eager
 6. barron, hollow, jejune 7. starved
 8. esurient, famished, indigent
 10. avaricious
Hung Society (secret) ... 5. Triad (Man,
 Earth, Heaven) 6. Deluge
hunt ... 3. dig 4. seek 5. chase, delve,
 hound, probe, quest, track, trail
 6. ferret, follow, pursue, search,
 shikar
hunter ... 3. dog 5. green, horse,
 jager, Jason, Orion 6. cuckoo,
 Nimrod 7. shikari (shikaree), stalker,
 trapper, venerer 8. huntsman
hunting (pert to) ...
act of .. 6. venery 7. pursuit
 10. cynegetics
coyotes .. 7. wolfing
dog .. 5. dhole 6. basset, beagle,
 setter 7. pointer
Dogs (Astron) .. 13. Canes Venatici
expedition .. 6. safari
fond of .. 7. venatic
horn .. 5. bugle
leopard .. 7. cheetah
hurdy–gurdy ... 4. lire, rota 5. organ
 (street) 7. sambuke 10. instrument
 (lutelike), waterwheel
hurl ... 4. cast, pelt, rush, toss
 5. fling, pitch, sling, throw 6. elance
 (dart), hurtle 9. overthrow
hurlbarrow ... 11. wheelbarrow
hurled ... 4. cast, sent 5. flung, slung,

threw 6. pelted, tossed 7. hurtled,
 twisted 8. betossed
hurly–burly ... 5. storm 6. tumult,
 uproar 9. agitation, confusion
 10. excitement
huron ... 6. grison (animal) 9. black
 bass
Huron ... 4. lake 6. Indian 9. Iroquoian
hurrah ... 3. joy 4. viva 5. cheer,
 huzza, shout 7. triumph 8. applause
 10. hallelujah 11. exclamation
 13. encouragement
hurricane ... 5. storm 6. baguio
 7. cyclone, Hurakan (god), tornado,
 typhoon (in China Sea)
hurry ... 3. hie 4. rush, scud 5. chase,
 haste, impel, sessa, speed 6. hasten,
 scurry, tumult, urge on 7. quicken
 8. dispatch, expedite 9. agitation,
 commotion 10. expedition
 11. disturbance, precipitate
hurst ... 4. hill, wood 5. copse, grove,
 knoll 7. hillock (wooded)
hurt ... 4. harm, maim, pain 5. lesed,
 parry 6. damage, grieve, impair,
 injure, injury, offend 8. distress,
 mischief 9. detriment 10. impairment
hurtful ... 6. malign, nocent 7. baneful,
 harmful, malefic, nocuous, noisome,
 noxious, painful 9. injurious
 10. pernicious 11. destructive,
 detrimental, prejudicial
 15. disadvantageous
hurtle ... 4. dash, push 5. clash, fling
 6. assail, jostle 7. collide, resound
 8. brandish
husband ... 3. eke 4. mate, save
 5. marry, store 6. direct (frugally),
 farmer, spouse, tiller 7. espouse,
 granger, manager, steward
 8. conserve 9. cultivate, economize
 10. husbandman
husbandry ... 6. thrift 7. economy,
 farming, tillage 10. management
 (domestic) 11. agriculture, cultivation
husband's brother ... 5. levir
hush ... 3. tut 4. calm, hist, lull
 5. allay, quiet, still 6. soothe
 7. appease, silence 10. keep secret
husk ... 4. bran, leam, rind 5. shood,
 shuck, straw
husky ... 3. dry 5. burly, harsh
 6. hoarse, strong 7. raucous
 8. powerful
Husky ... 3. dog 6. Eskimo
 8. Malemute
huss ... 7. dogfish
hussar ... 4. fish (banded) 6. dolman
 (jacket) 10. cavalryman, skirmisher
hussy ... 4. girl, jade 8. strumpet
 9. housewife
hustings ... 5. court 8. platform
 (Guildhall)
hut ... 3. cot 4. cote, isba, shed, skeo
 (fisherman's) 5. cabin, hogan, hovel,
 igloo, jacal, scale 6. lean–to, shanty,
 wigwam
hutch ... 3. bin, box, car, hut, pen
 4. coop 5. chest, hoard, hovel
 6. coffer, humped, shanty, warren
hyacinth (pert to) ...
color .. 5. tenne 7. blue–red

genus.. 10. Hyacinthus
mineral.. 6. zircon
myth.. 4. iris, lily (Turk's cap)
of Peru.. 9. Cuban lily
precious stone.. 8. sapphire (legend)
wild.. 6. camass
hybrid... 7. mongrel 9. half–breed
hybrid (pert to)...
  buffalo.. 7. cattalo
  dog.. 5. Husky 7. mongrel
  fruit.. 7. plumcot, tangelo 8. citrange
  horse.. 4. mule 5. hinny, jenny
  vegetable.. 6. pomato
  zebra.. 7. zebrass, zebrula 8. zebrinny
hydra... 4. evil 6. polyps
  11. thermometer
Hydra (Gr)... 6. island 7. serpent
  13. constellation
hydraulic (pert to)...
  brake.. 8. cataract
  element.. 5. water
  engine.. 3. ram 6. tremie
  product.. 5. power
hydria... 3. jar 6. kalpis
hydrocarbon... 5. tolan (tolane)
  6. ethane, octane, pinene, pyrene,
  tolane, toluol 7. benzene, methane,
  terpene 9. acetylene
hydrocarbon radical... 4. amyl
  6. pentyl
hydrocyanic acid... 7. cyanide, prussic
  8. fumigant
hydrogen... 1. H 3. gas 7. element
  (univalent)
hydroid... 9. polyplike
hydrophobia... 5. lyssa 6. rabies
Hydrus... 12. water serpent (fabled)
  13. constellation
hyena... 6. mammal 8. aardwolf
  9. earthwolf 13. Tasmanian wolf
hygienic... 7. sterile 8. sanitary
  9. healthful 10. uninfected
  12. prophylactic
hylophagous... 10. wood–eating
hymenopter, hymenopteron... 3. ant,
  bee, fly 4. wasp 9. ichneumon
hymn... 3. ode 4. song (of praise)
  5. dirge, music, paean (pean)
  6. anthem, hirmos, Te Deum
  7. chorale 8. doxology 9. Trisagion
  11. recessional

hymn (pert to)...
  book.. 6. hymnal
  composer.. 7. hymnist
  12. hymnographer
  science of.. 9. hymnology
  singing of.. 7. hymnody
  victory.. 9. epinicion
hypnotic... 6. opiate, sleepy
  8. mesmeric, narcotic, sedative
  9. soporific 12. somnifacient
  13. sleep–inducing
hypnotist... 6. Mesmer 9. mesmerist
  10. hypnotizer
hypnotize... 5. charm 6. dazzle
  8. entrance 9. fascinate, mesmerize,
  spellbind
hypochondriac... 4. hypo 6. insane
  7. invalid (imaginary) 8. dejected,
  neurotic 9. depressed, psychotic
  10. nosomaniac
hypocrisy... 4. cant 6. deceit
  8. feigning 9. falseness
  10. sanctimony, simulation
  11. outward show
hypocrite... 4. fake 5. cheat 7. tartufe
  (tartuffe) 8. deceiver 10. dissembler
hypocritical... 5. false 8. specious
  9. insincere 11. pharisaical
  13. sanctimonious, self–righteous
hypodermic glass vessel...
  7. ampoule (ampule)
hypodermic injection... 4. shot
  11. inoculation
hypothesis... 3. ism 6. theory
  7. premise, theorem 8. proposal
  9. condition, postulate
  10. assumption 11. proposition,
  supposition
hypothetical... 8. academic
  11. conditional, conjectural,
  speculative, theoretical
hypothetical (pert to)...
  being.. 3. ens 5. entia (pl) 6. entity
  biological unit.. 2. id
  force.. 2. od
  medium.. 5. ether
hyrax... 8. procavia
hyssop... 4. mint 11. aspergillum
hysteria... 7. anxiety 12. emotionalism
hysterical... 7. frantic 8. frenzied,
  wild–eyed 9. emotional
  12. uncontrolled

I

I... **2.** me **3.** eye **4.** iota (Gr), self **6.** letter (9th), myself **7.** pronoun
I (pert to)...
big.. **3.** ego
excessive.. **8.** iotacism
love.. **3.** amo
Iago... **7.** villain (Othello)
iambus... **4.** foot, iamb
iatrics (comb form)... **11.** treatment of
iatrology... **7.** healing **8.** treatise
Iberia... **5.** Spain **7.** Georgia (anc)
ibex... **3.** sac, tur, zac **4.** kail (kyl) **6.** sakeen **8.** antelope
ibid... **6.** lizard **7.** monitor
ibidem... **4.** ibid **9.** same place
ibis... **5.** guara, stork **9.** gourdhead
Ibsen (pert to)...
famed as.. **4.** poet **9.** dramatist
native of.. **6.** Norway
story character.. **3.** Ase **4.** Gynt, Nora
ice... **4.** rime **5.** frost, glacé, glaze **6.** freeze **7.** congeal, diamond, jewelry **11.** refrigerant, refrigerate
ice (pert to)...
bartender's.. **5.** rocks (sl)
cream dish.. **4.** cone, soda **6.** frappé, mousse, sundae **7.** parfait
dessert.. **5.** glacé **6.** frappé **7.** ohorbet
fine, slushy.. **4.** grue, hail, oigh, snow **5.** flake, frost, sleet
fishing.. **4.** chug
glacier.. **4.** neve **5.** serac
mass.. **4.** berg, calf, floe **5.** serac **6.** icecap **7.** glacier, growler
pendent.. **6.** icicle
sea.. **6.** sludge
Iceland...
airport.. **9.** Kopavogur
assembly.. **7.** Althing
bird.. **4.** gull **6.** falcon **10.** gyrofalcon
capital.. **9.** Reykjavik
city.. **3.** Hof **8.** Akureyri
dramatist.. **12.** Siguryonsson
epic.. **4.** Edda
first discoverer.. **8.** Norseman (about 870)
giant.. **4.** Atli
glacier.. **6.** Jökull **11.** Orafajökull
god.. see *Norse god(s), goddess*
government.. **8.** republic (1944)
legends.. **5.** Eddas, Sagas **12.** Volsunga Saga
Parliament.. **7.** Althing (world's oldest)
product.. **7.** herring
sculptor.. **9.** Sveinsson
volcano.. **5.** Askja, Hekla, Katla
ichneumon... **3.** fly **8.** mongoose **9.** Herpestes **12.** hymenopteron
ichor... **5.** fluid (of the gods)

ichthus... **4.** fish **6.** amulet, symbol **8.** talisman
ichthyophagy... **10.** fish eating
icicle... **7.** shoggle **10.** stalactite, stalagmite
icing... **8.** frosting, meringue
icterus... **6.** oriole **7.** disease **8.** jaundice **10.** yellowness
ictus... **4.** beat (rhythm), blow **6.** accent, stress, stroke
icy... **4.** cold **5.** algid, gelid **6.** frigid, frosty, frozen **7.** glacial **8.** chilling
id... **4.** idem, unit **5.** idant **6.** libido, psyche, suffix **7.** the same
Idaean (pert to)...
dweller of.. **5.** Mt Ida
goddess.. **4.** Rhea (Crete) **6.** Cybele (Asia Minor)
nature goddess.. **6.** Cybele **11.** Great Mother
Idaho...
capital.. **5.** Boise
city.. **7.** Orofino **9.** Pocatello
crop (famed).. **8.** potatoes
dam.. **5.** Oxbow **8.** Brownlee
famed citizen.. **5.** Borah (Sen)
monument.. **16.** Craters of the Moon
mountain.. **8.** Sawtooth **11.** Bitterroots
river.. **5.** Snake
salmon (landlocked).. **7.** kokanee
State admission.. **10.** Forty-third
State bird.. **8.** bluebird
State flower.. **7.** syringa
State motto.. **11.** Live Forever **12.** Esto Perpetua
State nickname.. **8.** Gem State
ide (id)... **3.** orf (orfe) **4.** fish **7.** the same
idea... **4.** clue, idée, ideo (comb form) **5.** ethic, motif **6.** belief, notion **7.** concept, meaning, opinion, wrinkle **10.** impression **11.** supposition
ideal... **4.** type **5.** dream, model, Thule (Myth) **6.** unreal **7.** paragon, pattern, perfect, typical, Utopian **8.** complete, exemplar, fanciful **9.** faultless, imaginary, visionary **10.** conceptual, consummate, idealistic **11.** mental image, theoretical **12.** intellectual
idealist... **7.** dreamer **8.** romancer **9.** visionary **11.** illusionist
idealistic... **9.** fictional, visionary **10.** starry-eyed **13.** philosophical
ideate... **5.** think **6.** invent **7.** imagine **8.** conceive **9.** prefigure
identical... **4.** same, self, twin **5.** alike, equal **10.** equivalent, tantamount
identification... **3.** tag **4.** disk, sign

5. badge, brand 6. naming
7. earmark 11. recognition,
unification
identify . . . 4. name 5. place, prove
8. coalesce 9. designate, establish
13. associate with
identity . . . 5. unity 7. oneness
8. equality, sameness 9. exactness
11. homogeneity 13. individuality
ideologist . . . 7. dreamer 8. theorist
9. visionary
idiocy . . . 7. amentia, anoesia, fatuity,
idiotry 10. deficiency (mental)
11. foolishness
idiograph . . . 9. trademark
idiom . . . 6. phrase 7. diction
8. language 11. peculiarity
idiosyncrasy . . . 9. mannerism
11. peculiarity 12. eccentricity
14. characteristic
idiot . . . 3. oaf 4. dolt, fool 5. booby,
dunce, moron 6. cretin, nitwit
7. dullard, half–wit 8. imbecile
9. blockhead, simpleton
idiotic . . . 4. daft 5. crazy 7. foolish
9. senseless 12. feeble–minded
idle . . . 4. laze, lazy, loaf, sorn, vain
5. drone, empty, inert 6. loiter,
otiose, tiffle, truant, unused, vacant
7. leisure, loafing, trivial, useless
8. baseless, inactive, indolent,
slothful, trifling 9. unfounded,
worthless 10. groundless,
unemployed, unoccupied
11. ineffectual, unwarranted
idleness . . . 5. folly, sloth 6. vanity
7. inertia 8. delirium, faniente,
laziness 9. silliness 10. inactivity,
triviality 15. lightheadedness
idler . . . 4. hobo 5. drone 6. loafer
7. dawdler, lounger 8. loiterer
idol . . . 3. god (sacred) 4. Baal, icon,
zemi 5. afgod, deity (heathen), eikon,
satyr 6. effigy, fetish, idolum, statue
7. darling, fallacy, phantom, picture
8. impostor 9. pretender
idolater . . . 5. pagan 6. adorer
7. admirer, Baalist, Baalite, heathen
8. idolizer 9. worshiper
idolize . . . 5. adore 6. esteem, revere
7. worship 10. idolatrize
idyl, idyll . . . 4. poem 5. image
7. bucolic, eclogue, picture
8. pastoral
i. e . . . 5. id est 6. that is
if . . . 2. si 3. gif 8. granting, provided
9. supposing
if ever . . . 4. once
if not . . . 4. else, nisi (law) 6. unless
igneous rock . . . 4. boss, dike, trap
5. magma 6. basalt 7. peridot
10. granophyre 11. molten magma
ignis . . . 4. fire
ignite . . . 4. burn, fire, heat 5. light
6. kindle 7. blaze up, flare up 9. set
fire to
ignoble . . . 3. low 4. base, mean, vile
6. menial 8. plebeian, shameful
11. disgraceful 12. dishonorable,
disreputable
ignoramus . . . 4. dolt, fool 5. dunce
6. nitwit, no bill (law)

11. know–nothing
ignorance . . . 5. tamas (Hind)
9. nescience 12. inexperience
ignorant . . . 7. unaware 8. nescient
9. unknowing, untutored
10. illiterate, unlettered
13. inexperienced, unintelligent
ignore . . . 3. cut 4. omit, snub
7. condone, disobey, neglect
8. overlook 9. disregard, eliminate
Igorot . . . 6. Bontok 7. Nabaloi
8. Kankanai 10. Indonesian
iguana . . . 6. goanna (goana), lizard
7. monitor, tuatara 9. Iguanidae
10. lace lizard
I Have Found It . . . 6. Eureka (Calif
motto)
ihi (Maori) . . . 7. skipper 8. halfbeak
10. stitchbird
IHS . . . 5. Jesus 6. symbol 10. In hoc
signo
iiwi . . . 4. bird
ikbal . . . 7. arrival 8. prestige
10. prosperity
Iknaton . . . 9. Amenhotep, Amenophis
(IV)
ikona . . . 9. greenhorn, simpleton
ileum . . . 9. intestine (small)
ilex . . . 5. holly 7. holm oak
11. Paraguay tea
Iliad (pert to) . . .
  founder (anc) . . 4. Troy 5. Ilium
  poem author . . 5. Homer
  poem character . . 4. Ajax 6. Hector
  7. Stentor 8. Achilles, Brisseis
  9. Agamemnon, Cassandra
ilium . . . 4. bone (pelvic)
Ilium . . . 4. Troy (anc)
ill . . . 3. bad, mal (comb form) 4. evil,
hard, poor, rude, sick 5. badly,
wrong 6. ailing, malice, poorly,
savage, unkind 7. noxious, painful,
unlucky 9. dangerous, difficult
10. disastrous, indisposed, iniquitous,
malevolent, unpolished, unskillful
11. unfavorable, unfortunate,
unwholesome 12. disagreeable,
inauspicious
ill (pert to) . . .
  at ease . . 7. awkward 9. graceless,
  maladroit
  bred . . 4. rude 7. uncivil 8. impolite
  9. bourgeois
  hap . . 10. misfortune
  humored . . 5. cross, moody
  natured . . 4. dour 5. cross, moody,
  surly 6. morose, sullen 7. crabbed
  10. crosspatch
  tempered . . 7. bilious 8. choleric
  timed . . 5. inapt 8. untimely
  9. premature 10. malapropos
  11. inexpedient, inopportune
  will . . 6. enmity, malice
  11. malevolence
illegal . . . 4. foul 7. illicit 8. outlawry,
unlawful, wrongful 10. contraband,
unofficial 12. illegitimate,
unauthorized
illegal entry . . . 6. ringer
illimitable . . . 4. vast 8. infinite
9. boundless 11. measureless
12. immeasurable, unrestricted

Illinois...
airport.. 5. O'Hare
capital.. 8. Vandalia (first)
    11. Springfield
city.. 5. Elgin 6. Peoria 7. Chicago,
    Decatur 8. Evanston, Waukegan
    9. Centralia
lake.. 8. Michigan
slogan.. 13. Land of Lincoln
State admission.. 11. Twenty–first
State nickname.. 7. Prairie
illiterate... 6. unread 8. ignorant,
    untaught 9. inerudite, unlearned,
    unrefined, untutored, unwritten
illness... 6. malady 8. cachexia,
    sickness 9. complaint, distemper
    10. affliction 13. indisposition
illuminant... 3. gas 4. lamp
    9. petroleum 10. Kleig light
illuminate... 5. adorn, color, light
    6. illume 7. explain, lighten, miniate
    8. emblazen, illumine 9. elucidate,
    enlighten, irradiate, rubricate
    10. illustrate
illumination, unit of... 3. lux 4. phot
illusion... 5. fancy 6. mirage
    7. chimera, fallacy, mockery,
    phantom 8. delusion, phantasy
    9. deception, false show
    10. apparition 13. hallucination,
    misconception
illusive... 5. false 6. unreal 8. spectral
    9. deceitful, deceptive, imaginary
    10. phantasmal, transitory
Illusory... 5. false 8. delusory, illusive
    9. deceptive, erroneous, imaginary,
    unfounded 10. fallacious
illustrate... 4. cite, draw 5. adorn
    7. explain, picture 8. beautify
    9. elucidate, exemplify, represent
    10. illuminate
illustrious... 5. noble, noted
    6. famous, heroic 7. eminent,
    exalted, radiant 8. glorious, luminous,
    renowned, splendid 9. brilliant,
    honorable 10. celebrated
image... 3. god 4. copy, icon, idea,
    idol, ikon, type 6. alraun, aspect,
    effigy, idolon, mirror, recept, sphinx,
    statue, typify 7. eidolon, phantom,
    picture, portray 8. illusion, likeness,
    phantasm 9. semblance
    10. apparition, conception,
    simulacrum 11. counterpart
    12. reproduction
imaginary... 5. ideal 7. fancied
    8. fanciful, illusory, mythical
    10. fictitious
imaginary disease... 9. nosomania
imagination... 5. dream, fancy
    8. phantasy, poetical
imagine... 5. dream, fancy, opine,
    think 6. ideate 7. suppose
    8. conceive 10. conjecture
imam... 6. caliph, priest (Moham)
imbecile... 4. dolt, weak 5. anile,
    idiot, inane, moron 6. cretin, dotard,
    feeble, stupid, witlet 7. fatuous,
    idiotic, witling 9. driveling
    10. half–witted 12. feeble–minded
imbed... 5. embed, inset 6. cement
    9. establish

imberbe... 9. beardless
imbibe... 4. soak 5. drink, imbue,
    learn 6. absorb, inhale 8. saturate
    10. assimilate
imbroglio... 5. brawl 11. embroilment,
    predicament 16. misunderstanding
imbrue... 3. fig, wet 4. soak 5. color,
    stain (with blood), steep 6. defile,
    drench 7. moisten 8. saturate
imbue... 3. dye 5. steep, teach, tinge
    6. infuse, leaven 7. ingrain, inspire
    8. permeate, saturate, tincture
    9. inculcate 10. impregnate
imitant... 9. imitation 11. counterfeit
imitate... 3. ape 4. copy, mime, mock
    5. mimic 6. borrow 7. emulate
    8. pastiche, resemble, simulate
    9. dissemble, reproduce
imitation... 4. copy, echo, sham
    5. apery, apism, paste 6. ectype,
    olivet (pearl), parody 7. mimesis,
    mimicry 8. travesty 9. burlesque
    10. caricature, simulation
    12. onomatopoeia
imitative... 5. apish 8. apetetic
    9. emulative, imitation 10. simulative
    11. counterfeit
immaculate... 4. pure 5. clean
    6. chaste 8. spotless, unsoiled
    9. faultless, undefiled, unstained,
    unsullied
immanence... 7. inbeing 9. inherence
    10. indwelling, innateness
immanent... 5. inner 6. inward
    8. internal 9. intrinsic 10. indwelling
immaterial... 6. slight 8. trifling
    9. spiritual 10. impalpable, intangible
    11. disembodied, incorporeal,
    unimportant 12. supernatural
    13. insignificant, unsubstantial
immature... 5. crude, green 6. callow,
    unripe 7. untried 8. untimely,
    youthful 9. premature 10. unfinished
    11. undeveloped
immeasurable... 7. endless 8. infinite
    9. boundless, unlimited 10. indefinite
    11. illimitable, innumerable
    12. immensurable, incalculable,
    unfathomable 13. indeterminate
    16. incomprehensible
immediacy... 9. awareness, closeness
    10. directness 11. punctuality
immediate... 4. next 6. direct, prompt
    7. instant, nearest, present
    10. continuous, succeeding
immediately... 3. now 4. anon
    7. closely 8. directly, promptly
    9. instantly, therewith 11. straightway
    12. without delay
immemorial... 3. old 7. ageless,
    ancient 8. dateless 9. out of mind
    11. prehistoric, traditional
immense... 4. huge, vast 5. grand,
    great 6. superb 7. mammoth, titanic
    8. enormous, infinite 9. monstrous
    10. prodigious, unmeasured
immerge... 3. dip 4. sink 5. merge
    6. engulf, plunge 7. immerse
    8. inundate, submerge
immerse... 3. dip 4. bury, dunk, sink
    5. douse, souse 6. absorb, plunge
    7. baptize, engross 9. overwhelm

imminent... 7. nearing 8. menacing, upcoming 9. impending 10. near at hand 11. approaching, forthcoming, overhanging, threatening

immobile... 3. set 5. fixed, inert 6. stable 8. moveless 9. immovable, obstinate, unfeeling 10. inflexible, motionless, stationary

immoderate... 5. ultra, undue 7. extreme 9. excessive 10. exorbitant, inordinate 11. extravagant, intemperate 12. unreasonable

immolation... 8. oblation, offering 9. sacrifice

immoral... 3. bad 6. wicked 7. corrupt, vicious 8. depraved, indecent 9. dissolute 10. licentious, misconduct

immortal... 6. divine 7. abiding, endless, eternal, godlike, undying 8. enduring 9. ambrosial, ceaseless, celebrity, perpetual 10. superhuman 11. amaranthine, everlasting 12. imperishable 13. incorruptible

Immortal (Taoism)... 8. Chang Kuo

immortality... 4. fame 6. amrita (conferring) 9. anathasia 11. lasting fame 13. deathlessness 15. everlastingness

immovable... 3. pat 4. fast, firm 5. fixed, rigid 6. stable 7. adamant 8. immobile, obdurate 9. obstinate, unfeeling 10. inflexible, stationary

immunity... 7. freedom 8. impunity 9. exemption 10. resistance (power of) 11. unrestraint

immure... 4. wall 6. entomb 7. confine 8. imprison, surround 9. encompass 11. incarcerate

immutable... 4. firm 6. stable 7. eternal 8. constant 9. obstinate 10. inflexible, invariable 12. unchangeable 13. unadulterated

imp... 3. bud, elf, fay 4. brat, cion, pixy, slip 5. child, demon, devil, fairy, graft, rogue, scion, shoot, youth 6. repair (falconry), spirit, sprite 7. progeny 9. offspring

impact... 4. pack, slam 5. brunt, force, shock, wedge 6. effect, stroke 7. contact, impulse, meaning 8. striking 9. collision, fix firmly, impinging

impair... 3. mar 4. harm, hurt, ruin, rust, wear 5. break, spoil 6. damage, debase, injure, lessen, reduce, weaken 7. vitiate 8. decrease, enfeeble 11. deteriorate

impairment of...
capital.. 4. loss 7. deficit
character.. 6. injury 10. defamation 11. degradation 13. deterioration
nerve (a).. 11. anerethisia

impale... 4. edge, gore, join (Her), spit, stab 5. hem in, spike 6. border, pierce, punish 7. confine, torture 8. encircle, surround

impalement... 5. calyx 8. stabbing 10. punishment 11. coats of arms (united)

impalpable... 4. fine 10. immaterial, intangible 13. infinitesimal

impart... 3. say 4. give, lend, tell 5. grant, share, yield 6. confer, convey, inform, reveal 7. divulge 8. disclose, discover 9. partake of 10. distribute 11. communicate

impartial... 4. even, fair, just 7. neutral 8. unbiased 9. equitable 12. unprejudiced 13. disinterested, dispassionate

impartiality... 7. justice 8. fairness 10. neutrality 11. unprejudice 17. disinterestedness

impassable... 6. stolid 9. impassive 10. impervious, unpassable 11. impermeable, unnavigable 12. impenetrable

impasse... 8. cul–de–sac 9. stalemate 10. blind alley

impassible... 9. impassive, unfeeling

impassioned... 6. ardent 7. amorous, zealous 8. eloquent, vehement 10. passionate

impassive... 4. calm 6. serene 7. passive 9. apathetic 10. impassable 12. invulnerable 13. insusceptible

impatient... 5. eager, testy 6. uneasy 7. anxious, fretful, itching, peevish, restive 8. choleric, petulant, restless 9. impetuous, irascible, irritable 10. intolerant

impavid... 8. fearless

impeach... 4. harm 6. accuse, charge, hinder, impair, impede, indict 7. arraign, censure, prevent 9. challenge, criminate, discredit, disparage

impeccable... 8. flawless, innocent 9. faultless 10. immaculate

impede... 3. bar, let 4. clog 5. block, debar, estop 6. hamper, hinder, retard, stymie (stimy) 8. encumber, obstruct, restrict

impediment... 3. bar, rub 4. snag 5. hitch 6. defect, malady 7. baggage, barrier 8. obstacle 9. hindrance 10. difficulty 11. encumbrance, obstruction

impel... 3. put 4. move, urge 5. drive, force, forge 6. compel, incite, induce, obsess, prompt, propel 7. actuate 9. constrain, influence

impel a boat... 3. oar, row 4. pole 5. scull

impelling force... 7. impetus 8. momentum

impending... 7. nearing 8. awaiting, imminent, menacing 9. hindering 11. overhanging, threatening

impenetrable... 5. dense 10. impervious 11. impregnable, inscrutable 12. inaccessible, unfathomable 13. unimpressible 14. unintelligible

impenitent... 8. obdurate 10. uncontrite 11. unrepentant, unrepenting

imperative... 4. mood (Gram) 6. needed, urgent 7. binding 8. pressing 9. directive, imperious, mandatory, necessary

10. compulsory, obligatory,
peremptory 13. authoritative
imperceptible... 6. subtle 9. invisible
10. insensible 13. inappreciable,
indiscernible, infinitesimal
14. unintelligible
imperfect... 3. mal (pref) 4. cull
5. frail 6. faulty, second 7. errable
8. fallible, immature, impaired
9. blemished, defective
10. inadequate, incomplete
imperfection... 4. flaw, vice 5. fault
6. defect 7. blemish, failing
8. fraility, weakness 10. deficiency
11. shortcoming 14. incompleteness
imperfectly... 8. slightly
12. inadequately
imperial... 5. regal, royal 6. kingly,
lordly, purple 8. majestic
9. imperious, masterful, monarchal,
sovereign
imperial (pert to)...
Academy.. 6. Han–lin (Chin)
blue.. 5. smalt
cap.. 5. crown
city (anc).. 4. Rome
domain.. 6. empire
legislature.. 4. Diet (Jap)
officer.. 8. palatine
imperil... 4. risk 6. expose
8. endanger 10. jeopardize
imperious... 6. lordly 7. haughty
8. arrogant, despotic, dominant,
pressing 10. commanding,
compelling, tyrannical 11. dictatorial,
domineering, overbearing
imperishable... 7. eternal, undying
8. enduring, immortal 11. everlasting
14. indestructible
impermanent... 8. fleeting, temporal,
unstable 9. ephemeral, momentary,
temporary, transient 10. evanescent,
short–lived
impersonate... 3. ape 4. pose 6. pose
as, typify 7. portray 9. exemplify,
personate (law), personify, represent,
symbolize
impertinence... 4. sass 9. impudence,
insolence, unfitness 10. incivility
11. impropriety, irrelevance
impertinent... 4. rude 5. saucy
7. ill–bred 8. impudent, insolent
9. frivolous, officious 10. inapposite,
irrelevant 12. inapplicable,
inconsequent 13. disrespectful
imperturbability... 8. ataraxia (ataraxy),
serenity
imperturbable... 4. calm, cool
6. placid, serene, steady 8. tranquil
9. impassive 10. phlegmatic
13. dispassionate
impervious... 5. tight 6. opaque
7. callous 10. impassable
12. impenetrable, inaccessible
impetuosity... 5. ardor 6. fougue
8. rashness
impetuous... 3. hot 4. rash 5. eager,
hasty, heady, sharp 6. ardent, bensel
(motion), fervid, sudden 7. furious,
violent 8. forcible, headlong, reckless,
vehement 9. impulsive
10. passionate 11. precipitate

impetus... 4. birr 7. impulse
8. momentum, stimulus 9. incentive
impi (Zulu)... 8. armed men, warriors
impignorate... 4. pawn 6. pledge
8. mortgage
impious... 7. godless, profane
9. nefandous, undutiful 10. irreverent
11. irreligious
impish... 5. elvan 6. elfish 7. puckish
9. malignant 11. mischievous
implacable... 6. enmity
11. immitigable 12. unappeasable
14. uncompromising
implant... 4. root 5. infix, inset, plant
6. enroot, infuse, insert 7. enforce,
engraft, impress, inspire, instill
9. establish, inculcate, inoculate,
insinuate, introduce
implement... 3. kit 4. peel, tool
5. dolly, knife, means, scoop, tongs
6. pestle, petard 7. fulfill, utensil
8. carry out, complete, material,
scissors 9. equipment
10. accomplish, instrument
implement (pert to)...
ancient.. 4. celt 6. eolith 9. paleolith
(stone)
cleaning.. 3. mop 5. broom, brush
6. vacuum 7. sweeper
hide flesher.. 6. slater
holding.. 5. tongs 6. pliers
8. tweezers
lifting.. 3. pry 5. crane, lever, tongs
lumbering.. 4. tode 6. peavey (peavy)
nap.. 6. teasel
printing.. 5. biron, press 6. brayer
reaping.. 5. mower 6. reaper, scythe,
shears, sickle
surgical.. 7. scalpel 9. tenaculum
threshing.. 5. flail
implicate... 5. imply 7. embroil,
entwine, involve 8. entangle
10. interweave 11. incriminate
implicit... 5. tacit 7. implied, virtual
8. complete, inherent 9. entangled,
potential 11. unqualified
12. constructive 13. unquestioning
implied... 5. tacit 11. inferential
12. not expressed
implore... 3. ask, beg 4. pray 5. crave
7. beseech, entreat, solicit
8. petition 10. supplicate
imply... 4. hint, mean 5. argue
6. infold 7. connote, involve,
suggest, suppose 9. predicate
impolite... 4. rude 5. crude, rough
7. uncivil 10. ill–behaved,
mannerless, ungracious, unmannerly,
unpolished 12. discourteous
13. disrespectful
impolitic... 6. unwise 9. untactful
10. indiscreet 11. inexpedient
12. undiplomatic
import... 5. drift, sense, value
6. denote, weight 7. betoken,
meaning, signify 8. commerce,
indicate 9. introduce, of concern
10. importance 11. consequence,
implication, importation, merchandise
importance... 6. moment, stress,
weight 8. prestige 9. influence
10. famousness 11. consequence,

importunity 12. solicitation

important... 5. grave 6. famous, urgent 7. pompous, weighty 8. material 9. momentous 11. considerate, influential, significant, substantial 12. considerable, ostentatious 13. consequential

import tax... 4. duty 6. tariff

importune... 3. beg, ply, tax, woo 4. coax, push, urge 5. beset, impel, plead, press 6. appeal, cajole 7. entreat, press on

importunity... 11. importunate, pertinacity 12. solicitation

impose... 3. tax 4. duty, levy 6. burden, entail 7. command, confirm (Eccl), exploit, inflict, intrude, obtrude, penalty, presume 10. discommode

imposing... 5. noble, regal 6. august 7. stately 9. dignified, grandiose 10. commanding, impressive 11. ceremonious 13. grandiloquent

impossible... 6. absurd 8. hopeless, terrible 9. insoluble 10. outlandish 11. unthinkable 12. unimaginable 13. contradictory, impracticable

impost... 3. tax 4. levy, task, toll 5. abwab 6. custom, excise, surtax, tariff, weight 7. tribute 8. handicap

impostor... 4. fake 5. fraud, phony, quack 6. humbug 7. empiric 9. charlatan, pretender 10. mountebank

imposture... 5. fraud, trick 8. delusion, quackery 9. deception 10. imposition

impotent... 4. weak 6. barren 7. cripple, sterile 9. deficient, incapable, powerless 13. uninfluential

impound... 5. pen in, seize, store 6. freeze 7. collect 8. imprison 9. reservoir 10. confiscate 11. appropriate

impoverish... 4. ruin 6. beggar 7. despoil, exhaust 8. bankrupt, make poor 11. make sterile

imprecation... 4. oath 8. anathema 10. execration 11. malediction

impregnable... 4. hard 10. inviolable 12. inexpugnable, invulnerable 13. unconquerable

impregnate... 5. imbue 6. infuse 8. fructify 9. fertilize, inculcate

impresa... 5. maxim, motto 6. device, emblem

impresario... 7. manager 9. conductor, projector (opera) 12. entrepreneur

impress... 3. awe, fix 4. bite, dent, levy, mark, seal 5. press, print, stamp 6. affect, effect, enlist, indent 7. engrave, imprint 8. printing, shanghai 9. conscript, engraving, inculcate 10. commandeer, impression 11. indentation 14. characteristic

impressed... 4. awed 7. infixed, stamped 8. affected, engraved 9. imprinted

impression... 4. form, idea, mark 5. hunch, print, stamp 6. macule, signet 7. emotion, opinion 8. printing

9. engraving, sensation 10. appearance 11. inculcation, indentation, supposition

impressionable... 6. pliant 7. plastic 9. sensitive, teachable 10. responsive 11. suggestible, susceptible

impressive... 6. solemn 8. dramatic, eloquent 9. arresting, grandiose 10. convincing

imprint... 3. fix 4. dint 5. infix, press, stamp 6. indent 7. edition, engrave 8. printing 9. engraving

imprison... 4. bond, cage, gaol, jail 5. limit 6. arrest, detain, immure, intern, lock up 7. confine, impound 8. restrain 11. incarcerate

imprisonment... 4. band 6. duress 8. coercion 9. restraint 10. constraint, immurement, internment 11. confinement, impoundment 13. incarceration

impromptu... 6. extemp 7. offhand 11. extemporary 13. improvisation 14. extemporaneous 15. autoschediastic

improper... 3. ill, pah 4. evil 5. amiss, wrong 6. vulgar 7. illegal, naughty 8. indecent, unseemly, unsuited, untoward 9. incorrect, inelegant 10. inaccurate, indecorous, indelicate, unbecoming, unsuitable

impropriety... 5. wrong 8. solecism 9. indecency, vulgarity 11. malapropism, misbehavior

improve... 4. mend 5. amend, edify, emend, moise, train 6. better, employ, uplift 7. advance, augment, correct, enhance, perfect, promote, recover, rectify, upgrade 9. cultivate, get better, intensify, meliorate 10. ameliorate, recuperate

improvident... 4. rash 8. prodigal, wasteful 9. negligent 10. thriftless 11. thoughtless

improvise... 5. ad lib 6. invent 7. ad libit 9. ad libitum 11. extemporize 13. autoschediaze

imprudence... 5. brass 8. rashness 9. hardihood 12. indiscretion, recklessness

impudence... 5. cheek 8. rudeness 9. flippancy, indecency, insolence 10. brazenness, disrespect 12. impertinence 13. shamelessness

impudent... 4. bold, pert, rude 5. brash, saucy 6. brazen 8. flippant, insolent, malapert 9. audacious, shameless 11. impertinent 13. disrespectful

impugn... 4. deny 5. blame 6. assail (by words), oppose, refute 7. asperse, censure, gainsay

impulse... 3. ate 4. rush, urge 5. force 6. motive 7. impetus 8. instinct 9. incentive 11. instigation

impulsive... 5. hasty, quick 6. moving 9. impellent, impetuous 10. motivating 11. instinctive 13. ill–considered

impure... 4. foul, lewd 5. dirty, mixed 6. filthy, unholy 7. bastard, defiled,

obscene, unclean 8. unchaste
10. inaccurate, unhallowed
11. adulterated, unwholesome
impure metal ... 5. alloy, matte
6. speiss
impure rock ... 5. chert 9. flintlike
imputation ... 7. censure 8. charging
9. aspersion, criticism
10. accusation, ascription
11. attribution, insinuation
impute ... 6. accuse, charge, credit,
impart, reckon, regard 7. arraign,
ascribe 8. consider 9. attribute
impy ... 11. mischievous
in ... 2. at 4. amid, into 5. among
6. at home, inside, within
in (pert to) ...
abundance .. 5. store 6. galore
accordance .. 8. pursuant
addition .. 3. too, yet 4. also, more,
plus 11. furthermore
all directions .. 8. everyway
12. everywhither
an undertone .. 9. sotto voce
as much as .. 3. for 5. since
6. seeing 7. because, insofar
back .. 3. aft 5. arear 6. astern
7. postern
behalf of .. 3. for, pro 7. favor of
camera .. 9. in private 10. in
chambers
common .. 4. same 5. alike
concert .. 8. together
contact .. 8. touching 9. attingent
current style .. 3. a la 7. alamode,
popular
existence .. 6. extant
fact .. 5. truly 6. indeed 7. de facto
favor of .. 3. aye, pro, yea
good health .. 3. fit 4. hale 7. healthy
love .. 7. smitten 9. enamoured
need .. 7. straits 8. distress
open air .. 7. outdoor 8. al fresco
passing .. 9. en passant
place of .. 3. tor 5. stead 7. instead
possession .. 5. title 6. seizin
private .. 8. in camera
regard to .. 5. anent
rows .. 4. arow 6. serial 7. aligned
(alined)
so far as .. 3. qua
spite of .. 6. mauger 7. despite,
however 11. nonetheless
standing position .. 7. statant
store .. 5. ready 7. waiting 8. awaiting
straight lines .. 8. e regione
succession .. 6. series 8. serially,
seriatim
the future .. 5. hence, later 6. mañana
12. subsequently
the know .. 3. hep
the same place .. 4. ibid 6. ibidem
the year of .. 4. anno
truth .. 6. certes, indeed, verily
8. forsooth
what way .. 3. how 7. quo modo
inability ... 9. impotence
10. inadequacy, incapacity
12. incapability, incompetence
inability to ...
articulate .. 7. inaudia
chew .. 8. amasesis

comprehend .. 11. acatalepsia
move .. 7. apraxia
name objects .. 9. paranomia
read .. 6. alexia
stand erect .. 7. astasia
swallow .. 7. aphagia
inaccessible ... 8. reserved
10. unsociable 11. out–of–the–way
12. unattainable 14. unapproachable
inaccurate ... 5. loose 6. faulty
7. inexact 9. defective, erroneous,
imperfect, incorrect
13. ungrammatical
inaction ... 6. torpor 7. inertia
8. abeyance, idleness 9. inertness
10. suspension
inactive ... 4. idle 5. inert 7. abeyant,
neutral, not busy 8. sluggish
9. sedentary 10. indisposed
inadequacy ... 9. inability
10. deficiency, inequality
11. inferiority 12. incompetence
13. insufficiency 14. incompleteness
inadvertence ... 5. error 7. neglect
11. inattention 12. carelessness,
heedlessness 15. thoughtlessness
inadvertent ... 9. negligent, unwitting
11. inattentive
inadvertently ... 10. heedlessly
11. unwittingly 12. neglectfully
inane ... 4. vain, void 5. empty, inept,
silly 6. famous 7. fatuous, foolish,
puerile, trivial 8. trifling 9. frivolous
11. ineffectual, thoughtless
13. characterless
inappropriate ... 5. inept, undue
8. untimely 10. irrelevant, unsuitable
11. inexpedient
inapt ... 5. inept 10. unsuitable
inattentive ... 3. lax 6. absent, remiss
8. careless, heedless 9. negligent,
unheeding, unmindful 10. distracted,
regardless 11. inadvertent
inaugurate ... 5. admit, begin, start
6. induct 7. install, instate, usher in
8. initiate 9. auspicate, institute,
introduce 10. consecrate
inauspicious ... 7. adverse, ominous,
unlucky 8. sinister, untimely
9. ill–omened 12. unpropitious
inborn ... 6. allied, inbred, innate,
native 7. cognate, natural 8. inherent
10. connatural
inbred ... 6. inborn, innate
9. endogamic 10. bred within 15. to
the manner born
Inca (pert to) ...
descent .. 6. the sun
empire .. 4. Peru (11th cent)
government .. 11. communistic
king .. 9. Atahualpa (15th cent)
prince .. 7. Huascar (16th cent)
incalculable ... 8. infinite 9. boundless,
uncertain, very great 11. illimitable
12. immeasurable 13. unforeseeable
incandescent ... 5. clear, light, white
7. glowing, shining
incantation ... 5. magic, spell
6. powwow 7. sorcery 8. exorcism
10. hocus–pocus, mumbo jumbo
incapable ... 6. unable 8. impotent
11. incompetent, inefficient,

unqualified 12. disqualified
incapacitate... 7. cripple, disable,
invalid 10. disqualify 11. render unfit
incapacitated... 8. crippled, disabled
9. hamstrung, paralyzed
11. invalidated 12. disqualified
13. superannuated (retired)
incarcerate... 5. hem in 6. immure,
intern, lock up, retire 7. confine,
impound 8. imprison 10. disqualify
incarnate... 4. rosy 6. embody
9. enshrined 11. incorporate,
personified 12. impersonated
incarnation... 6. avatar, Christ
10. embodiment
Incarnation of Vishnu (eight)...
4. Apis, Rama 7. Krishna (8th)
incase... 3. box, can 4. pack 5. box
up, cover, crate 6. carton
7. enclose, package 8. surround
incaution... 4. rash 6. unwary
8. careless, heedless, reckless
9. impolitic, imprudent 10. indiscreet
incendiarism... 5. arson 9. pyromania
incendiary... 5. firer 7. exciter
8. agitator, arsonist, incitive
9. seditious 10. instigator
12. inflammatory
incense... 3. ire 5. anger 6. arouse,
enrage, incite 7. inflame, provoke
8. irritate 9. instigate
incense (pert to)...
burner.. 6. censer 8. thurible
9. incensory
carrier.. 8. thurifer
Hebrew for.. 7. keturah
pert to.. 5. aroma, spice 7. perfume
9. fragrance, redolence
product.. 5. matti, myrrh 6. storax
7. linaloa 8. gum resin, olibanum,
pastille, thurible 9. lignaloes,
tacamahac 12. frankincense
sacrifice.. 8. oblation
spice.. 6. balsam, stacte
tree bearing.. 7. linaloa 8. agalloch,
calambac 9. Boswellia
vessel.. 6. censer 7. navette
incensed... 3. mad 5. angry, irate,
vexed, wroth 6. peeved, piqued
7. angered, enraged, nettled
8. wrathful 11. exasperated
incentive... 4. brod, call, goad, spur,
urge, whet 5. spark 6. motive
7. impulse, rousing 8. inciting,
stimulus 9. influence 10. incitement,
inducement 11. provocation,
stimulative 13. encouragement
inception... 6. origin, source
9. reception 10. inchoation, initiation
12. commencement
15. intussusception
inceptive... 9. beginning 10. inchoative
incessant... 7. endless 8. constant
9. ceaseless, continual, perpetual
10. continuous 11. unremitting
13. unintermitted
inch (pert to)...
barometric.. 6. degree
forward.. 4. edge 7. crowhop
inch by inch.. 9. gradually, piecemeal
meal.. 9. gradually
three parts.. 11. barleycorns (anc)

twelve parts.. 5. lines
twelve seconds.. 6. a prime (anc)
verb.. 5. creep 7. measure
inches... 4. hand (4), nail (2 1/4),
span (9)
inchoate... 6. partly 8. initiate, recently
9. beginning, incipient
10. incomplete
inchpin... 10. sweetbread
incident... 5. event 7. episode, subject
8. accident, casualty 9. befalling,
happening 10. incidental, occurrence
11. contingency 12. circumstance,
slight matter
incidental... 3. bye 6. casual, chance,
liable 8. episodic 9. accessory,
extrinsic 10. accidental, contingent,
fortuitous, occasional 11. subordinate
12. nonessential 13. parenthetical
incidentally... 6. obiter 8. by chance,
by the way 9. en passant, in passing
incinerate... 4. burn 7. consume,
cremate
incipient... 4. seat 6. induct 7. initial
8. inchoate 9. beginning, embryonic
10. commencing, inaugurate
11. rudimentary
incise... 3. cut 4. open 5. carve,
lance, sever 6. furrow 7. engrave
incised... 6. carved 7. notched
8. engraved, furrowed 9. laciniate
10. laciniated
incision... 3. cut 4. gash, slit 5. cleft
6. furrow, injury 7. cutting
9. engraving 10. laceration,
separation 11. penetration
incite... 3. egg, tew 4. abet, fire,
goad, prod, spur, urge 5. impel,
sting 6. arouse, foment, stir up,
suborn 7. agitate, animate, inflame,
provoke 9. encourage, stimulate
inclemency... 4. cold 5. rigor
8. coldness, severity, violence
9. bleakness, frigidity, harshness
13. mercilessness
inclination... 3. dip, nod 4. bent,
bias, love, urge 5. fancy, grade,
slant, slope, taste, trend 6. animus,
bowing, desire, liking, nature
8. aptitude, penchant, tendency
9. affection, attention, deviation,
direction, intention, obeisance,
proneness 10. attachment, proclivity,
propensity 11. disposition
12. predilection 13. prepossession
incline... 3. dip, tip 4. bend, cant,
heel, lean, tend, tilt 5. alist, bevel,
grade, slant, slide, slope, trend 9. be
willing, gravitate
inclined... 3. apt, dip 4. wont
5. prone 6. sloped 7. leaning,
pronate, willing 8. disposed
11. predisposed
inclined (pert to)...
plane.. 4. ramp 7. oblique
to believe.. 9. credulous
to droop.. 3. sag
to sin.. 13. transgressive
inclose... see also *enclose* 3. hem,
pen, pin 4. case, mure 5. embar
6. encase, encave, incase
7. enclose, environ

inclosure... 3. pen, ree, sty 4. cage, cote, sept 5. hutch, kraal 6. corral 8. sepiment 9. enclosure 10. impalement
include... 6. shut up 7. confine, contain, embrace, enclose, inclose, involve 8. comprise 9. encompass
including... 8. covering 10. comprising, containing 12. encompassing 13. comprehensive
incognito... 6. veiled 7. feigned 8. disguise, not known 10. camouflage
incoherent... 5. loose 6. broken 8. detached, inchoate 9. delirious, illogical 11. incongruous 12. disconnected, inconsequent, inconsistent
income... 4. gain 5. rente, wages 6. profit, return, usance 7. annuity, pension, produce, revenue, tontine 8. interest, proceeds, receipts 9. emolument
incommensurate... 7. unequal 12. insufficient 14. unsatisfactory 16. disproportionate
incommode... 3. vex 5. annoy 6. molest, plague, put out 7. disturb, trouble 8. disquiet 13. inconvenience
incomparable... 7. eminent, unalike 8. peerless 9. matchless, unrivaled 10. surpassing 11. superlative 12. transcendent, without equal
incompatible... 9. differing 10. intolerant 11. disagreeing 12. inconsistent, inharmonious 13. contradictory, unsympathetic 14. irreconcilable
incompetence... 9. inability, unfitness 10. disability, inadequacy 13. insufficiency 15. unqualification
incompetent... 5. inept, unfit 7. wanting 8. impotent 9. incapable 10. unskillful 11. inefficient 12. disqualified, insufficient 14. incommensurate
incomplete... 5. crude 6. undone 7. lacking 8. immature, inchoate 9. defective, deficient, imperfect, partially 10. unfinished
incomprehensible... 8. infinite 9. wonderful 10. miraculous, mysterious, unreadable 11. unthinkable 12. unfathomable, unimaginable 13. inconceivable, unconceivable 14. unintelligible
incongruity... 9. inharmony 10. dissonance 11. incoherence 12. disagreement, inexpedience 13. inconsistency 14. unsuitableness
incongruous... 5. alien 6. absurd, motley 8. off-color 9. differing, illogical 10. solecistic, unsuitable 12. disagreeable, inconsistent, inharmonious 13. inappropriate
inconsequent... 7. invalid 8. unproved 9. illogical 10. irrelevant 11. impertinent, unimportant 12. inconsistent 13. inconsecutive
inconsiderate... 4. rash 5. hasty 6. unkind 8. careless, heedless

9. imprudent, impulsive 10. ill-advised, incautious, indiscreet, neglectful 11. improvident, injudicious, thoughtless
inconsistent... 9. differing, dissonant, fanatical, illogical 10. discordant, discrepant, incoherent, inconstant 11. incongruous 12. incompatible, inharmonious 13. contradictory 14. irreconcilable
inconspicuous... 9. unseeable 10. out of sight, unapparent 12. not prominent 13. imperceptible, indiscernible
incontestable... 7. certain 10. undeniable 11. indubitable, irrefutable 13. unimpeachable 14. unquestionable
inconvenience... 6. bother 8. disquiet 9. incommode 10. uneasiness 11. awkwardness, disturbance 12. disadvantage, untimeliness, unwieldiness
inconvenient... 6. unfit 7. unhandy 8. annoying, improper, unwieldy 10. unsuitable 11. inexpedient, inopportune, troublesome 12. unreasonable 15. disadvantageous
incorporate... 3. mix 4. fuse 5. blend, merge, unite 6. embody 7. combine, include 8. embodied 10. assimilate
incorporation... 5. union 9. inclusion 10. embodiment 11. affiliation, association, combination, composition, incarnation 12. assimilation
incorporeal... 7. phantom 8. bodiless 9. spiritual 10. immaterial 13. unsubstantial
incorrect... 5. wrong 6. faulty 8. improper 9. erroneous, inelegant 10. inaccurate, solecistic, unbecoming 13. ungrammatical
incorrect naming of objects... 9. paranomia
incorruptible... 4. just 7. upright 8. immortal 11. trustworthy 14. indestructible
increase... 3. add, eke, wax 4. gain, grow, rise 5. add to, amass, raise, swell 6. accrue, dilate, enrich, expand, extend 7. accrete, advance, augment, enhance (inhance), inflate, promote, upswing 8. heighten, multiply 9. accession, aggravate, crescendo, expansion, extension, increment, intensify 10. accelerate 11. aggravation, enlargement 13. amplification 15. intensification
incredible... 8. fabulous, unlikely 9. fantastic, marvelous, wonderful 10. improbable, remarkable 12. unbelievable
increment... 6. growth 8. addition, increase 11. enlargement 12. augmentation
incriminate... 6. accuse 7. involve 9. implicate, inculpate
incubator... 8. couveuse, isolette
incubus... 4. ogre 5. demon, dream 6. burden 9. nightmare 10. evil spirit 13. hallucination

inculcate... 5. imbue, infix 7. implant, impress, instill (instil) 12. indoctrinate
incumbent... 5. vicar 6. rector 8. resident 9. clergyman, impending, overlying 10. burdensome, obligatory (upon) 11. threatening 12. superimposed
incumbents... 3. ins
incunabula... 7. infancy 10. beginnings
incur... 5. bring 6. accrue, entail 7. bring on 8. be liable, contract, fall into 10. be involved
incurable... 8. hopeless 9. apathetic 11. inattentive, indifferent, unconcerned, uninquiring 12. uninterested 13. uninquisitive
incur hostility... 10. antagonize 11. contend with
incursion... 4. raid 5. foray 6. attack, influx, inroad 8. invasion 9. intrusion
incus... 4. bone (ear) 5. anvil 6. hammer
indecency... 8. impurity 9. immodesty, indecorum, obscenity, vulgarity 10. indelicacy, unchastity
indecent... 5. gross 6. impure, vulgar 7. obscene 8. immodest, improper, uncomely 9. offensive 10. ill–looking, indecorous, indelicate 11. inexpedient
indecision... 5. doubt 10. hesitation 11. uncertainty, vacillation 12. irresolution
indecisive... 7. dubious 8. formless 9. uncertain 10. hesitating, indefinite, indistinct, irresolute 11. unsupported, vacillating 12. inconclusive
indecorous... 4. rude 5. wrong 6. coarse, vulgar 7. uncivil 8. impolite, improper, indecent, unseemly 9. inelegant 10. out of place, unbecoming 11. inexpedient
indefatigable... 6. active 8. sedulous, tireless, untiring 9. unwearied, weariless 10. unwearying 11. persevering
indefinite... 5. loose, vague 7. general, inexact, neutral 8. formless 9. ambiguous, equivocal, uncertain 10. inexplicit, unmeasured 12. undetermined 13. indeterminate
indefinite amount... 3. any 4. some 5. about 10. more or less
indehiscent (pert to)...
fruit.. 3. uva 4. pepo (gourd) 5. apple, grape 6. orange, samara 9. sunflower
legume.. 3. pea 4. bean 6. loment
vegetable.. 5. melon 6. squash, tomato 7. pumpkin 8. cucumber
indelible... 4. fast 5. fixed 6. deepfelt 9. permanent 10. inerasable 12. ineffaceable, ineradicable, inexpungible 13. unforgettable
indelicate... 5. gross 6. coarse, vulgar 7. fulsome 8. impolite, improper, indecent, unseemly 9. offensive, unrefined 10. indecorous, unbecoming
indemnification... 9. atonement 10. recompense 11. restitution 12. compensation 13. reimbursement

indemnify... 3. pay 6. recoup, secure 8. make good 9. reimburse 10. compensate, recompense
indent... 3. cut, jag 4. dent 5. inlay, notch, press, stamp, tooth 6. emboss, furrow, recess, zigzag 7. impress, imprint, press in 8. contract, covenant, draw upon 9. indenture 11. requisition
indentation... 3. jab 4. dint, nick 5. choil, notch 6. crenel, furrow, hollow, recess 7. imprint 8. crenelet 10. depression, impression
indented... 6. dented, jagged, milled 7. notched, sinuous 8. serrated (Her) 9. impressed 10. undulating
indenture... 4. dent 5. notch 8. contract, document 9. agreement 10. depression 11. indentation
independence... 7. freedom 9. exemption 10. competency, neutralism, Urania blue 13. unrelatedness 14. nonpartisanism 15. self–subsistence
independent... 4. free 5. Party (Polit) 7. neutral, wealthy 8. separate 9. competent, exclusive, free–lance, isolative, sovereign, uncoerced, unrelated 12. irrespective, uncontrolled, unrestricted 13. self–governing
independent land... 7. alodium (law)
indescribably... 9. ineffably 11. wonderfully
indeterminate... 5. vague 7. apeiron, general, neutral, obscure 8. formless, infinite
index... 4. face, file, fist, list 5. guide, ratio, table 6. gnomon 7. pointer 8. exponent 9. indicator 10. forefinger, indication
India... see also *Indian*
anc.. 9. Hindustan
Bay.. 6. Bengal
Cape.. 7. Comorin
capital.. 4. Agra (anc) 5. Simla (summer) 8. New Delhi
city.. 4. Agra, Gaya 5. Dacca, Delhi, Poona, Surat 6. Bombay, Jaipur, Lahore, Madras, Madura, Nagpur, Nysore 8. Calcutta, Kolhapur, Mandalay, Mirzapur, Shahpura 10. Darjeeling
city, sacred.. 5. Nasik 7. Benares
kingdom.. 5. Asoka, Nepal
mountain.. 5. Ghats 8. Sulaiman (Throne of Solomon) 9. Himalayas, Hindu Kush 12. Vindhya Hills
Persian name (anc).. 9. Hindustan
region.. 3. Goa 5. Assam, Surat 6. Baroda 7. Benares, Kashmir
relics (famed).. 8. Taj Mahal (Agra) 10. Kutab Minar 11. Ajanta Caves
river.. 6. Kistna
State.. 4. Rewa 5. Delhi 6. Baroda, Indore, Jaipur, Madras, Marwar, Punjab, Rampur, Sakkim 7. Manipur
Indian (pert to)...
aeon.. 5. kalpa
animal.. 4. zebu 5. sasin 6. nilgai
apartment.. 6. zenana
army officer.. 4. naik (naig)

7. jemadar
attorney.. **6**. muktar
bandit.. **6**. dacoit
bard.. **4**. bhat
bird.. **4**. baya, kala, koel, kyak
   5. sarus, shama **6**. seesee, shahin
   8. amadavat
boat.. **5**. dhoni (doni)
book (sacred).. **6**. Avesta
bracelet.. **6**. sankha
bread (unleavened).. **8**. chapatty
breakfast.. **5**. hazri
buffalo.. **4**. arna (arnee)
carpet.. **4**. Agra
carriage.. **4**. ekka **5**. tonga **6**. gharry
   (gharri)
caste.. **3**. Jat, Meo **4**. Ahir **5**. Sudra,
   Varna **6**. Lohana, Rajput, Vaisya
   7. Brahman (Brahmin) **9**. Kahatriya
cavalryman.. **5**. sowar **7**. ressala
charm.. **6**. mantra
chief.. **4**. Raja **5**. Rajah **6**. sirdar
   7. Gaekwar
cigarette (cheap).. **4**. biri
claim (legal).. **3**. hak (hakh)
college (Sanskrit).. **3**. tol
Court, Supreme.. **6**. Sudder
crocodile.. **6**. gavial, mugger (muggar,
   muggur)
cymbal.. **3**. tal
dagger.. **5**. katar
dam.. **6**. anicut (annicut)
dancer (fem).. **8**. bayadere
dancing girls.. **6**. nautch
deer.. **4**. axis **5**. kakar **6**. sambur
deity.. **4**. Deva
demon.. **4**. bhut **5**. asura **6**. daitya
devil's tree.. **4**. dita
dialect.. **4**. Urdu **5**. Hindi, Tamil
   7. Prakrit
disciple.. **5**. chela
dog.. **5**. dhole **6**. pariah
drama.. **6**. nataka
drink.. **4**. soma **5**. bhang (bang)
   6. arrack
dust storm.. **7**. peesash, shaitan
   (sheitan)
elephant.. **5**. hathi
elephant driver.. **6**. mahout
elephant trappings.. **5**. jhool
epic.. **8**. Ramayana **11**. Mahabharata
falcon.. **6**. shahin (shaheen)
father.. **4**. babu
festival.. **4**. Holi, Mela **6**. Dewali
   10. Rathayatra
fig tree (sacred).. **5**. pipal **6**. banian,
   banyan
garment.. **4**. sari **7**. luhinga
gateway.. **5**. toran
ghost.. **4**. bhut
god.. **4**. Deva, Yama **5**. Shiva
goddess.. **4**. Amma
governor.. **5**. nazim
grove.. **5**. Sarna
guard.. **7**. daloyet
hall.. **6**. durbar
handkerchief.. **7**. malabar
harem.. **5**. serai **6**. zenana **8**. seraglio
heiress.. **5**. Begum
herb.. **6**. sesame **7**. curcuma,
   tumeric, zeodary

holy.. **3**. sri (shri)
holy powder.. **4**. abir (perfumed)
hunt.. **6**. shikar
intoxicant.. **4**. soma
jungle.. **5**. shola
king.. **4**. Shah
king of serpents (Myth).. **6**. Shesha
   (Sesha)
king's son.. **8**. shahzada
knife.. **3**. dah **5**. kukri
lady.. **7**. sahibah
language.. **4**. Urdu **5**. Hindu, Tamil
   8. Sanskrit (anc)
leader.. **13**. Mahatma Gandhi
legal claim.. **3**. hak (hakh)
leopard.. **7**. cheetah
licorice.. **9**. jequirity (bean)
loincloth.. **5**. dhoti
lover of.. **9**. Indophile
mahogany.. **4**. toon
mail.. **3**. dak (dawk)
medicine man.. **6**. Shaman
mendicant.. **5**. fakir
merchant.. **8**. soudagar
midwife.. **4**. dhai
Minister of Finance.. **5**. Dewan
mountain pass.. **4**. ghat
musical instrument.. **5**. ruana
narcotic.. **4**. bang **5**. bhang
   7. hashish
native.. **5**. Hindu, Sepoy, Tamil
   8. Assamese **10**. Hindustani
Negro.. **6**. hubshi
palanquin (conveyance).. **6**. palkee
   (palhi)
palm.. **7**. Calamus, malacca
peasant.. **4**. ryot
pheasant.. **5**. monal (monaul)
philosopher.. **4**. Yogi
pillar.. **3**. lot
pipe.. **6**. hookah
police.. **4**. peon **5**. sepoy
police station.. **5**. thana
priest.. **5**. mobed **6**. shaman
prince.. **4**. rana
princess.. **4**. rani (ranee) **5**. Begum
queen.. **4**. rani (ranee) **8**. maharani
religious body.. **5**. samaj **7**. ajivika
   (anc)
resort.. **3**. Abu **5**. Mt Abu
rope dancer.. **3**. nat
rubber.. **10**. caoutchouc
ruler.. **4**. rana **5**. nabob, nawab,
   nizam
sage.. **6**. pundit
sailor.. **6**. lascar
sarsaparilla root.. **7**. nunnari
servant.. **3**. par **4**. amah, maty
sheep.. **5**. urial **6**. nahoor
shrine.. **6**. dagoba
silkworm.. **3**. eri
snake.. **5**. krait **6**. bongar, katuka
soldier.. **4**. peon **5**. sepoy; singh
split pea.. **3**. dal
study of.. **8**. Indology
sugar (crude).. **3**. gur **9**. tabasheer
   (bamboo)
Supreme Court.. **6**. Sudder
sword (short).. **5**. kukri
syllable of assent.. **2**. om
tapir.. **8**. saladang

tariff .. **6.** zabeta
teacher .. **6.** mullah (mulla)
temple .. **4.** rath **12.** Seven Pagodas
(of Madras)
title of respect .. **3.** sri (shri) **4.** mian
tower .. **5.** minar, sikar **7.** sikhara
tree .. **3.** saj **4.** dita, teak **5.** dhava
6. banyan, sissoo
umbrella .. **6.** chatta
water carrier .. **7.** bheesty (bheestie)
wheat .. **4.** suji
wine .. **5.** shrab
yellow (color) .. **5.** piuri **7.** majagua
Indian, American (pert to) ...
chief .. **5.** Logan **6.** Joseph, Philip,
sachem **7.** Cochise, Pontiac
8. Geronimo, Red Cloud, Tecumseh
9. Massasoit **10.** Crazy Horse
11. Sitting Bull, Spotted Tail
dance .. **7.** cantico
festival .. **8.** potlatch
hatchet .. **8.** tomahawk
hero .. **4.** Rama (S Am)
largest tribe .. **6.** Navaho (Navajo)
lodge .. **5.** hogan, igloo, tepee
6. wigwam **7.** wickiup
married .. **5.** squaw (fem) **6.** sannup
(male)
Mexico .. **4.** Maya **5.** Aztec
7. Tehueco
money .. **5.** sewan (beads) **6.** wampum
Newfoundland .. **6.** Micmac
pipe (peace) .. **7.** calumet
pony .. **6.** cayuse
richest tribe .. **5.** Osage
S America .. **3.** Ona **4.** Cara (anc),
Inca, Peru, Tupi **5.** Carib **6.** Arawak,
Aymara **7.** Quechua
Spirit, Great .. **6.** Manito **7.** Manitou
12. Gitchi Manito
squaw .. **6.** mahala
symbol .. **5.** totem
tax, impost .. **5.** abwab
village .. **6.** pueblo
water lily .. **5.** wokas (wocas)
Indiana ...
capital .. **12.** Indianapolis
city .. **4.** Gary **6.** Muncie **7.** Hammond
9. Vincennes **10.** Terre Haute
industrial region .. **7.** Calumet
monument (Hist) .. **7.** Lincoln
12. Indian Mounds **13.** Wyandotte
Cave
post office (famed) .. **10.** Santa Claus
river .. **6.** Maumee, Wabash
10. Tippecanoe
State admission .. **10.** Nineteenth
State bird .. **8.** cardinal
State flower .. **5.** peony
State motto .. **19.** Crossroads of
America
State nickname .. **7.** Hoosier
Indian tribes ... **3.** Aht, Fox, Oto
(Otoe), Ree, Sac, Ute **4.** Cree, Crow,
Erie, Hano, Hopi, Iowa, Maya, Mono,
Sauk, Yuma, Zuni **5.** Aleut, Cadoo,
Carib, Coree, Creek, Haida, Huron,
Miami, Moqui, Omaha, Osage, Piute,
Ponca, Sioux, Sooke, Teton, Yazoo
6. Ahtena (Alaska), Apache, Biloxi,
Cayuga, Dakota, Eskimo, Isleta,
Lenape, Mohawk, Mojave, Navaho,

Nootka, Oneida, Paiute (Piute),
Pawnee, Santee, Seneca, Siwash
7. Amerind, Bannock, Catawba,
Chinook, Ojibway, Tlingit, Yavanai
8. Arapahoe, Cherokee, Chippewa,
Comanche, Iroquois, Kickapoo, Nez
Percé, Onondaga, Sagamore,
Seminole, Shoshone **9.** Algonquin,
Athabasca, Blackfoot, Chickasaw,
Winnebago **10.** Muskhogean
12. Narragansett
indicate ... **4.** cite, hint, mark, mean,
show **5.** point **6.** denote, evince,
reveal, sketch **7.** bespeak, betoken,
connote, declare, display, signify,
specify **8.** disclose, evidence,
intimate, manifest, point out, register
9. designate, foretoken
indicated ... **6.** marked, signed
7. denoted, implied **8.** presumed
9. betokened, portended, suggested
indicating succession ... **7.** ordinal
indication ... **4.** clue, hint, mark, note,
omen, sign **5.** proof, token, trace
6. signal **7.** reading (a) **8.** evidence
10. suggestion **13.** manifestation
indicative ... **7.** ominous
10. evidential, indication, meaningful,
suggestive **11.** connotative
13. significative
indicator ... **4.** dial, hand, sign, vane
5. arrow, gauge, index, level
6. gnomon **7.** indices (pl), pointer
9. grape fern (belief) **10.** instrument
11. annunciator, thermometer
15. telethermometer
indicia (sing **indicium**) ... **5.** marks,
signs **6.** tokens **8.** markings (PO)
11. appearances, indications, metered
mail
indict ... **6.** accuse, charge, decree
7. arraign, impeach **8.** proclaim
indictive ... **8.** declared **9.** appointed
10. proclaimed
indictment ... **6.** charge
10. accusation, imputation
11. arraignment
indifference ... **5.** shrug **6.** apathy
7. inertia **8.** coldness **9.** unconcern
10. mediocrity, negligence, neutrality
12. carelessness, heedlessness,
unimportance **13.** insensibility
14. insignificance
indifferent ... **3.** ill **4.** cold, cool, sick
5. blasé **6.** casual, poorly
7. neutral, stoical, uneager
8. careless, heedless, listless,
mediocre **9.** apathetic
10. nonchalant, regardless
11. adiaphorous, unimportant
12. nonessential, uninterested
indigence ... **4.** lack, need, want
6. penury **7.** poverty **10.** deficiency
indigene ... **6.** native **8.** habitant
9. primitive **10.** autochthon
indigenous ... **6.** inborn, innate, native,
rooted **7.** edaphic, endemic, natural
8. endemism, inherent
13. autochthonous
indigent ... **4.** free, poor, void
5. needy **6.** bereft **7.** lacking,
wanting

8. beggarly 9. destitute, penniless
10. pauperized 11. impecunious,
necessitous 15. poverty–stricken
indigestion... 8. disorder, phthisis
9. dyspepsia 10. immaturity
indignant... 3. hot 5. angry, irate,
wroth 7. annoyed 8. incensed,
wrathful 9. resentful 11. exasperated
indignation... 3. ire 4. base, fury
5. .anger, wrath 7. disdain
8. contempt
indignity... 7. affront, dudgeon
10. uncivility
indlgo... 3. dye 4. anil, blue
indigo (pert to)...
 bale of.. 6. seroon
 compound.. 6. isatin
 plant.. 4. anil
 source.. 7. indican 9. indigotin
 wild.. 8. Baptisia
indirect... 7. devious, oblique
9. deceitful, dishonest 10. circuitous,
contingent, misleading, roundabout
indirect expense... 8. overhead
indiscreet... 4. rash 5. hasty, silly
6. unwise 7. foolish, witless
8. careless, heedless 9. imprudent
10. incautious 11. injudicious
12. undiscerning 13. inconsiderate
indiscriminate... 5. mixed 7. mingled
9. extensive, haphazard, orderless,
wholesale 13. heterogeneous
indispensable... 5. basic, vital
6. needed 7. exigent 8. integral
9. essential, requisite, right–hand
10. imperative 13. irreplaceable
indisposed... 3. ill 4. sick 6. averse
9. unwilling 10. disordered, unfriendly
11. disinclined
indisposition... 7. ailment, illness,
malaise 10. averseness, reluctance
13. unwillingness
indisputable... 4. sure 7. certain,
evident 8. positive 10. undeniable
11. indubitable 12. irrefragable
13. incontestable
indistinct... 3. dim 4. hazy 5. vague
7. blurred, obscure, unclear
8. confused 9. ambiguous, undefined
10. indefinite 16. undiscriminating
17. indistinguishable
indite... 3. pen 5. write 6. phrase
7. compose 8. describe, inscribe
individual... 3. man, one 4. bion, idio
(comb form), self, sole, unit, zoon
6. egoist, person, single 7. special
8. organism, selfsame 9. identical
11. inseparable, personality
individuality... 5. being, seity
6. nature 7. oneness 8. ethology,
identity, selfness
individually... 9. severally
10. personally 12. each by itself
14. distributively
Indo–Aryan (pert to)...
 deity.. 5. Indra
 native of.. 5. India
 speech.. 5. Aryan
 type.. 4. Jats 7. khatris, Rajputs
Indo–Chinese (pert to)...
 language.. 3. Tai (Thai)
 mammal.. 4. zebu

 river.. 6. Mekong
 State (former French).. 4. Laos
 7. Vietnam 8. Cambodia
indoctrinate... 5. coach, edify, imbue,
teach 8. instruct 12. rehabilitate
indolence... 5. scorn, sloth 7. inertia,
languor 8. inaction, laziness
10. ergophobia 11. lotus–eating,
spring fever 13. indisposition
indolent... 4. idle, lazy 5. inert
6. otiose 8. inactive, slothful,
sluggish 10. unemployed
indomitable... 10. invincible
11. intractable, "never say die"
13. unconquerable
Indonesia...
 capital.. 7. Jakarta (Djakarta)
 formation.. 11. archipelago (once
 world's largest)
 former name.. 7. Batavia 15. Dutch
 East Indies
 government.. 8. Republic (1950)
 islands (3,000 in all).. 4. Bali, Java
 7. Sumatra 8. Sulawesi (Celebes)
 9. New Guinea (W half)
 10. Kalimantan (W Borneo)
 president.. 7. Sukarno
 race.. 5. Dyaks (Dayaks) 7. Battaks
 (Bataks), Igorots 8. Balinese,
 Javanese
 religion.. 6. Moslem
 shrine.. 6. dagoba
indorse, endorse... see *endorse*
indorsement, endorsement... 4. visa,
visé (passport)
Indra (Hindu)... 3. God 5. Deity, Sakra
(Sakka)
indubitable... 4. fact, sure 7. evident
10. infallible, undeniable
11. irrefutable 12. irrefragable,
unanswerable 13. incontestable
14. unquestionable
16. incontrovertible
induce... 4. lead, move, urge
5. cause, impel, infer 6. allure, elicit,
entice, incite 8. persuade
9. influence, instigate, prevail on
inducement... 6. motive, reason
8. stimulus 9. incentive, influence
10. persuasion 13. consideration
induct... 6. enroll 7. bring in, install
8. initiate 9. conscript, introduce
inductance unit... 5. henry
inductile... 10. inflexible, unyielding
induction... 5. logic 7. causing
8. entrance 9. accession, beginning,
deduction 10. conclusion, initiation,
production 12. commencement,
conscription, installation, introduction
indue... 5. endow 6. assume, clothe,
draw on, invest, supply (spiritual)
7. furnish
indulge... 3. pet 5. grant, humor, yield
6. pamper 7. cherish, gratify
indulgences... 8. excesses
10. tolerances
indulgent... 4. easy 7. lenient, patient
8. tolerant, yielding 9. compliant
10. permissive 11. considerate,
intemperate
indurate... 6. harden 7. callous
10. solidified

indurated... 3. set 5. fixed
9. calloused 10. solidified
industrial magnate... 6. shogun, tycoon
industrious... 4. busy 6. active
7. zealous 8. diligent, sedulous
9. assiduous 11. intentional,
painstaking 13. indefatigable
industry... 4. toil, work 5. labor, trade
7. concern 8. commerce 9. diligence
12. perseverance, sedulousness
indweller... 6. native 7. denizen
8. indigene
indwelling... 7. inbeing 8. immanent,
inherent 9. immanence, inherence
10. inhabiting
inearth... 5. inter 6. inhume
inebriacy... 11. drunkenness
12. intemperance
inebriate... 3. sot 5. addle, drunk,
toper 7. stupefy, tippler 8. drunkard
10. exhilarate (by liquor), intoxicate
ineffable... 4. surd 6. sacred
9. wonderful 11. unspeakable,
unutterable 13. indescribable,
inexpressible 15. unpronounceable
ineffaceable... 9. indelible
10. inerasable 12. ineradicable
ineffectual... 4. vain, weak 6. futile
7. useless 9. fruitless 10. unavailing
11. inefficient 12. unsuccessful
13. inefficacious, uninfluential
inefficient... 6. unable 10. indisposed
11. incompetent 12. unproficient
inelegant... 6. clumsy, vulgar
8. indecent 9. deficient (in beauty)
11. unbeautiful
inept... 4. null, void 5. silly, unfit
6. absurd 7. foolish 8. unsuited
10. out of place, unbecoming,
unskillful, unsuitable 11. inexpedient
inequality... 9. disparity, diversity
10. inadequacy, unevenness
12. disagreement, variableness
13. disproportion
ineradicable... 7. lasting 9. indelible,
permanent 12. ineffaceable
inerrant... 8. unerring 10. infallible
inert... 4. dead, lazy 6. latent, stupid,
supine, torpid 7. passive 8. inactive,
lifeless, listless, slothful, sluggish
9. apathetic, inanimate, lethargic
10. motionless, phlegmatic
inertia... 9. indolence, inertness
10. immobility
inesculant (rare)... 9. indelible
inestimable... 9. priceless
10. invaluable 12. incalculable
inevitable... 3. due 5. fated
7. nemesis 9. necessary
11. unavoidable
inexorability... 5. rigor 9. obstinacy
10. strictness
inexorable... 6. strict 9. obstinate
10. inflexible, relentless, unyielding
inexpedience, inexpedient... 6. unwise
8. untimely 9. ignorance, impolitic,
imprudent, unfitting 10. indiscreet,
unwiseness 11. inadvisable
15. disadvantageous
inexperience... 6. unwise 9. ignorance,
imprudent 10. immaturity, indiscreet

11. inadvisable 12. unprofitable
14. unskillfulness
15. disadvantageous
inexperienced... 3. raw 4. naif
5. green, naive 6. callow
8. ignorant, immature, prentice
9. unskilled 10. amateurish
11. unpracticed
inexplicable... 11. undefinable
12. supernatural 13. preternatural,
unaccountable, unexplainable
inextricable... 4. mazy 5. stuck
8. involved 9. intricate 10. insolvable
infallible... 4. sure, true 6. gospel
7. certain 8. inerrant, unerring
9. inerrable 11. indubitable
infamous... 4. base 6. odious, wicked
8. shameful, terrible 9. negarious
10. detestable 11. ignominious
12. contemptible, disreputable
infamy... 5. shame 8. disgrace,
dishonor, ignominy, reproach
9. disrepute 10. opprobrium
11. abomination
infancy... 8. babyhood, minority
9. beginning
infant... 4. babe, baby 5. child, minor
6. novice 8. bantling 9. foundling
infantryman... 6. Zouave 7. dog–face
8. chasseur 9. musketeer
11. footslogger, foot soldier
14. gravel agitator
infatuated... 7. foolish, smitten
8. enamored, obsessed 9. bewitched
10. captivated, enraptured
12. enthusiastic
infatuation... 3. ate, mad 4. love
5. craze, folly 10. enthusiasm
11. foolishness
infeasible... 8. unlikely 10. improbable,
unsuitable 13. impracticable
infect... 5. taint 6. defile, excite,
poison 7. corrupt, deprave, pollute
11. contaminate
infection... 7. disease 8. epidemic
9. pollution 11. implication (law),
inspiration 13. contamination
infelicity... 6. misery 9. inaptness
10. misfortune 11. unhappiness
12. inexpedience, untimeliness,
wretchedness
infer... 4. hint 5. drive, guess, imply
6. deduce 7. presume, suppose,
surmise 8. conclude, construe
inference... 5. truth 8. illation
9. corollary, deduction
10. assumption, conclusion
11. implication, proposition
inferential... 8. illative 9. deductive,
inducible 10. deductible, suggestive
15. inconsequential
inferior... 3. bad 4. less, poor
5. baser, lower, minor, petit, petty
6. lesser, menial, nether 7. humbler,
unequal 8. anterior, mediocre
10. inadequate, low–blooded
11. subordinate
inferior lawyer... 9. leguleian
11. pettifogger
infernal... 6. cursed, plaguy, wicked
7. hellish, satanic 8. damnable,
devilish 9. chthonian, execrable,

malignant, Tartarean 10. demoniacal,
detestable, outrageous
inferno (pert to)...
Bib.. 4. Hell 5. abyss, limbo
Buddah.. 6. Naraka
Egypt.. 6. Amenti
ferry to.. 4. Styx
Hebrew.. 5. Sheol 7. Abaddon,
Gehenna
myth.. 5. Aralu, Hades, Orcus
7. Acheron, Niflhel 8. Tartarus
infest... 3. vex 5. annoy, beset
6. assail, molest, plague 7. overrun,
torment 8. frequent
infidel... 5. deist, pagan 6. Kaffir
7. atheist, Saracen, skeptic
8. agnostic 10. unbeliever
11. freethinker 12. non—Christian
13. non—Mohammedan
infidelity... 6. deceit 7. perfidy
8. unbelief 9. misbelief, treachery
10. disloyalty 11. incredulity
13. faithlessness
infinite... 4. vast 5. vague 6. divine
7. endless, eternal, immense, perfect
9. boundless, limitless, unlimited
10. indefinite 11. illimitable,
interminate, omnipresent, The
Absolute 12. all—embracing,
interminable, undetermined
13. inexhaustible, The Omnipotent
16. all—comprehensive
Infinite Being... 3. God
Infinite knowledge... 11. omniscience
infinitesimal... 5. small 7. minimum
9. invisible, molecular 10. evanescent
11. microscopic
infirm... 4. weak 5. anile, frail
6. senile 7. fragile 8. decrepit
9. doddering 10. irresolute
11. vacillating
infirmity... 6. defect, foible, malady,
old age 7. disease, failing, frailty,
illness 8. debility, weakness
10. feebleness
Inflame... 4. burn, fire 5. anger
6. arouse, enrage, excite, ignite,
kindle, madden, rankle, redden
7. incense 8. irritate 10. exasperate
inflammable... 5. fiery 6. tinder
7. piceous 8. burnable 9. excitable,
irascible, irritable 10. accendible
11. combustible
inflammable substance... 6. ethane,
tinder 7. acetone, bitumen
inflammation... 8. ignition, soreness
10. congestion, excitement,
incitement
inflammation (pert to)...
bladder.. 8. cystitis
bone.. 7. rickets 8. osteitis
13. osteomyelitis
ear.. 6. otitis
eye.. 6. iritis 7. uveitis
joints.. 4. gout 9. arthritis
10. rheumatism
spinal cord.. 13. poliomyelitis
stomach.. 9. gastritis
suffix.. 4. itis
vein.. 9. phlebitis
inflect... 3. bow 4. bend 5. curve
7. decline, deflect 8. modulate

inflection, inflexion... 4. tone
5. angle, curve 7. bending
8. paradigm 9. accidence
10. modulation
inflexible... 4. iron 5. rigid, stiff
6. strict 8. obdurate, rigorous
9. immovable, immutable, obstinate,
unbending 10. implacable, inexorable,
relentless, unyielding 11. unalterable
14. uncompromising
inflict... 3. add 4. deal 5. wreak
6. impose, punish
inflorescence... 4. cyme 5. whorl
6. cymose 7. budding, flowers
8. racemose 9. flowerage, flowering
10. unfoldment 13. efflorescence
inflow... 6. influx 9. inpouring
11. inspiration
influence... 3. win 4. lead, move, pull,
sway 5. aegis (egis), bribe, force,
impel, lobby 6. affect, effect, induce,
influx, leaven, obsess 7. control,
inspire, mastery 8. dominate,
effusion, persuade, prestige
9. authority, determine
influence (world—wide)... 8. ecumenic
influenced... 6. biased 7. induced,
pliable (easily) 8. affected
10. prejudiced
influential... 6. potent, strong
7. weighty 8. momentus, powerful
9. effective 13. authoritative
influx... 4. tide 5. firth, mouth (river)
6. import, inflow 7. estuary, illapse
9. influence, inpouring
11. debouchment
infold... see *enfold*
inform... 4. tell 5. teach, train
6. advise, notify, report 7. animate,
apprise, inspire 8. instruct
9. enlighten
informal... 7. offhand 9. irregular
information... 3. air, tip 4. data, lore,
news 5. aviso, datum, facts
6. digest 7. advices, tidings
9. knowledge 10. annotation
11. instruction 12. intelligence
informed... 2. up 3. hep 4. up on,
wise 6. posted 8. apprised,
educated, versed in 10. instructed
11. enlightened
informer... 3. spy 4. tout 6. gossip,
snitch, teller 7. delator 8. affirmer,
betrayer, mouchard, reporter, telltale
9. informant, spokesman
10. talebearer, tattletale
informer (sl)... 4. fink, nark 6. canary,
snitch 7. stoolie 8. snitcher, squealer
9. blabberer 11. stool pigeon
12. blabbermouth
infraction... 6. breach 8. fracture,
trespass 9. intrusion, violation
12. encroachment, infringement,
overstepping 13. transgression
infrequency... 6. rarity 7. fewness
8. rareness, solitude 9. isolation
12. uncommonness
infrequent... 4. rare 6. scarce,
seldom, sparse 8. uncommon
9. spasmodic 10. occasional
infrequently... 6. rarely, seldom 8. not
often, sparsely

infringe... 6. defeat, refute 7. confute, destroy, violate 8. encroach, overstep, trespass 9. frustrate

infringement... 6. breach, piracy (copyright) 9. intrusion, violation 10. infraction 12. overstepping 14. nonfulfillment

infundibulum... 4. cone, lura 10. gray matter (brain)

infuriate... 5. anger 6. enrage, incite, madden 8. irritate 10. antagonize

infuscate... 6. darken 7. obscure

infuse... 4. fill, shed 5. steep 6. drench 7. implant, instill 9. insinuate, introduce

infusion... 3. tea 4. wort 8. affusion, tincture 9. admixture, decoction, inpouring 12. instillation

ingang... 5. porch 8. entrance 10. intestines

ingenious... 5. sharp, smart, witty 6. adroit, clever, daedal, gifted, shrewd, subtle 8. skillful, talented 9. Daedalian, deviceful 11. intelligent, resourceful

ingenuity... 5. skill 6. candor, genius 10. adroitness 11. originality 13. inventiveness

ingenuous... 4. naif, open 5. frank, naive, noble, plain 6. candid, innate 7. artless, sincere 8. freeborn, innocent 9. guileless 10. unreserved 15. unsophisticated

ingest... 3. eat 5. learn 6. take in 7. consume, swallow

ingot... 3. gad, pig 4. mold 5. metal 7. bullion

ingratiate... 4. fawn 7. commend, flatter 9. insinuate, introduce

ingredient... 6. factor 7. element 9. component 11. constituent

ingress... 4. go in 5. entry 6. access, portal 8. entrance 9. reception 11. entranceway

ingrowing nail... 7. acronyx

inhabitant... 3. cit 6. inmate, people, tenant 7. citizen, denizen 8. resident

inhabitant (pert to)...
Alaska.. 9. sourdough
desert.. 4. Arab 5. nomad
earliest.. 9. aborigine
foreign.. 5. alien
Maine.. 10. down–easter
moon.. 8. selenite
northern.. 6. Yankee 11. Septentrion (Lowell)

inhabitants, equator's other side... 8. antiscii 10. antiscians

inhabited... 5. lived 7. dwelled, peopled 8. occupied, tenanted 9. populated

inhabiting (pert to)...
caves.. 8. spelaean (spelean) 10. troglodyte
ground.. 9. terricole 11. terricolous
groves.. 7. nemoral 10. nemoricole
islands.. 7. nesiote
lakes.. 9. lacustral
sea.. 7. pelagic 15. thalassophilous
seashore.. 8. littoral

inhale... 4. suck 5. smell, smoke, sniff 7. breathe, inspire, respire

inharmonious... 7. jarring 9. differing, dissonant, unmusical 10. discordant 11. conflicting, disagreeing

inherent... 6. inborn, innate 7. infixed 8. immanent 9. immanence, intrinsic 10. indwelling, subsistent 11. instinctive 13. indispensable

inheritance... 6. legacy 7. bequest, legitim 8. heirship, heredity, heritage, Salic law 9. cleronomy 10. birthright

inheritance diminisher... 6. abator

inheritor... 4. heir 6. coheir 7. heiress, legatee 10. coparcener 11. beneficiary

inhibit... 5. check 6. forbid, hinder 8. prohibit, restrain 9. interdict

inhibition... 3. ban, bar 4. writ 7. embargo 8. checking 9. hindrance, restraint 10. impediment 11. prohibition 12. interdiction

inhuman... 4. fell 5. cruel 6. brutal, savage 7. bestial, brutish 8. devilish, nonhuman 9. barbarous, ferocious 10. demoniacal, diabolical

inhumation... 6. burial 9. arenation, interment

inhume... 4. bury 5. inter, inurn 7. deposit, inearth

inimical... 7. adverse, hostile, opposed 8. contrary 10. unfriendly 11. belligerent, unfavorable

iniquity... 3. sin 4. evil, vice 5. crime 7. misdeed 9. injustice 10. immorality, wickedness

initial... 6. paraph 9. incipient 11. large letter 12. commencement

initiate... 4. open 5. admit, begin, epopt (anc) 6. induct 7. install, instate 8. inchoate 10. inaugurate 11. preinstruct

initiation... 8. ceremony 9. admission 10. admittance 12. inauguration, introduction

injection... 4. hypo 5. enema 7. clyster 9. immission

injudicious... 4. rash 6. unwise 9. impolitic, imprudent 11. inexpedient

injunction... 3. ado 4. writ 5. order, union 6. behest 7. mandate, precept 9. direction 11. prohibition

injure... 3. mar 4. harm, hurt, lame, maim 5. wound, wrong 6. assail, damage, grieve, impair, scathe 7. affront, slander, tarnish

injurious... 3. bad 4. evil 7. abusive, harmful, hurtful, noxious 10. defamatory, slanderous 11. detrimental, mischievous

injury... 3. ill, mar 4. dere (obs), evil, harm, hurt, loss, pain, tort 5. wound, wrong 6. damage, lesion, mayhem, trauma 7. slander 9. detriment, indignity, injustice 10. impairment

injustice... 5. wrong 6. injury 7. umbrage 8. hardship, inequity, iniquity 10. imposition, unfairness

ink... 3. jet 5. black 7. blacken 8. atrament, blacking

ink (pert to)...

bag.. 3. sac (fish)
berry.. 5. holly 6. indigo
black.. 10. atramental
 11. atramentous
cap.. 8. mushroom
fish.. 5. squid 6. cuttle
pad.. 7. tompion (tampion)
ref to.. 10. atramental
source.. 7. inkweed, oak gall
 8. inkstone, pokeweed 9. gallberry
spreader.. 6. brayer
inkle... 4. hint, tape, yarn 5. braid,
 twist 6. thread 8. intimate
inkling... 4. hint 5. rumor 6. desire,
 report 10. intimation 11. supposition
inlaid... 6. mosaic 7. adorned, set into
 9. champleve, decorated
inlay... 4. buhl, line 5. inset 6. insert,
 mosaic, niello, tarsia 7. filling,
 implant 8. buhlwork, intarsia
 9. champleve
Inlet... 3. bay, ria, voe 4. cove, slew,
 sump 5. admit, bayou, bight, creek,
 fiord (fjord), firth, inlay 6. estero,
 recess, strait 7. estuary, orifice
 8. entrance, waterway
inn... 3. pub 4. khan 5. abode, fonda,
 hotel, motel, serai 6. hostel, imaret,
 posada, tavern 7. albergo, cabaret,
 hospice, locanda, osteria, pension,
 shelter 8. alehouse, hostelry
 9. roadhouse 11. caravansary
innate... 4. born 6. inborn, inbred,
 native 7. natural 9. ingrained,
 inherited, intrinsic 10. congenital,
 hereditary, inveterate 11. instinctive
 14. constitutional
innate ability... 6. genius, talent
innate idea (Philos)... 11. immortality
inn courts... 11. Inner Temple
inner... 4. ento (comb form) 5. ental
 6. inside, inward, secret 7. obscure
 8. esoteric, interior, internal
 9. intestine 10. indistinct
 14. intramolecular
Inner circle... 3. set 4. clan, club,
 ring 5. group, junta, junto 6. clique
inner man... 4. mind, self, soul
 6. psyche 7. stomach
innermost coating... 6. intima
Inner Temple... 11. Inns of Court
Innisfail... 4. Eire, Erin 7. Ireland
 15. Island of Destiny
innocence... 6. purity 7. diamond
 11. sinlessness 12. harmlessness
 13. guiltlessness, innocuousness
innocent... 4. Holy, pure 5. idiot,
 naive, seely 6. benign, lawful
 7. artless, sinless, upright 8. spotless
 9. destitute, guiltless, ingenuous,
 permitted, simpleton, stainless,
 unsullied 10. unblamable
 12. simple–minded 13. free from
 guilt
innocuous... 8. harmless, hurtless,
 innocent 9. innoxious 11. inoffensive,
 unoffending
innovation... 3. new 6. change
 7. novelty 13. prolification
innuendo... 4. hint, slur 6. change
 7. meaning 9. aspersion
 10. intimation 11. implication,

 indirection, insinuation
Innuit... 4. Yuit (Eskimo)
innumerable... 6. legion, myriad
 8. infinite, numerous 9. countless
 10. numberless
inodorous... 8. odorless 9. scentless
inopportune... 8. ill–timed, untimely
 10. malapropos, unsuitable
 11. contretemps, inexpedient
 12. embarrassing, unseasonable
inordinate... 5. undue 9. excessive,
 fanatical 10. disordered, disorderly,
 exorbitant, immoderate
 11. unregulated 12. unrestrained
inorganic... 7. mineral 9. inanimate
 13. nonbiological
inquest... 4. jury 5. quest, trial
 6. assize, search 7. inquiry
 11. examination 13. investigation
inquire... 3. ask 4. seek 5. query
 7. examine 8. question
 11. interrogate, investigate
inquirer... 6. seeker 7. querier,
 student, zetetic 8. searcher
inquiry... 5. query 6. examen, tracer
 7. examine, seeking 8. question,
 research 11. examination
 13. investigation
inquisition... 5. trial 6. search
 7. inquiry 8. tribunal 11. examination
 13. investigation
Inquisition... 6. French (1772)
 7. Spanish (1480–1834)
inquisitive... 4. nosy 5. peery
 6. prying 7. curious 8. meddling
 10. meddlesome
inquisitor... 6. tracer 7. coroner,
 sheriff 8. examiner
in re... 10. concerning 13. in the
 matter of
Inroad... 4. raid 5. foray 8. invasion,
 trespass 9. incursion, intrusion,
 irruption 12. overstepping
 13. transgression
insane... 3. mad 4. daft, loco, luny
 5. batty, crazy, loony 6. crazed
 7. cracked, foolish, frantic, rammish,
 touched, witless 8. demented,
 deranged 9. non compos 15. non
 compos mentis
insane urge to steal...
 11. kleptomania
insanity... 5. mania 6. frenzy, lunacy,
 trance 7. madness 8. delirium,
 dementia 10. alienation
 11. derangement 16. mental
 deficiency
inscribe... 4. draw, etch 5. infix,
 stamp, write 6. blazon, enroll
 7. address, engrave, impress
 8. dedicate, depencil
inscribed... 5. runed 7. written
 8. engraved, recorded 10. registered,
 rupestrian (on rocks)
inscription... 4. text 5. motto, title
 6. legend 7. epitaph, writing
 8. colophon, epigraph, graffito
 9. lettering, sgraffito 10. dedication
 14. superscription
inscrutable... 6. secret 8. abstruse
 10. mysterious 12. impenetrable,
 inexplorable, unfathomable

16. incomprehensible

insect... 3. ant, bee, bug, dor, fly
4. flea, gnat, lerp, lice, mite, moth,
tick, wasp 5. aphid, borer, cadew,
emmet, leech, louse, roach, Vespa
6. acarid, beetle, cicada, earwig,
hornet, locust, mantis, sawfly, scarab,
spider 7. ant lion, chigger, firefly,
gallfly, katydid, ladybug, pismire,
termite 8. bullhead, glowworm,
mosquito, stinkbug, turicata
9. bumblebee, butterfly, caddis fly,
centipede, cockroach, dragonfly,
ichneumon, tsetse fly, tumblebug
10. silverfish 11. caterpillar,
grasshopper 12. yellow jacket

insect (pert to)...
adult.. 5. imago
aquatic.. 7. Ranatra
arboreal.. 7. katydid
back.. 5. notum
Bible.. 7. ant lion
butterfly.. 11. Lepidoptera
egg.. 3. nit
eyes.. 6. ocelli 7. stemmas
feelers.. 5. palps 8. antennas
9. tentacles
fly.. 4. zimb 7. Diptera
hymenopterous.. 3. ant, bee 4. wasp
6. sawfly 7. gallfly
immature.. 4. grub, pupa 5. larva
6. maggot 9. chrysalis
immature covering.. 6. cocoon
leg.. 6. proleg
like.. 8. entomoid
long–legged.. 5. emesa
10. harvestman 13. daddy–longlegs
mature.. 5. imago
molting.. 6. instar 7. ecdysis
parasitic.. 4. lice 5. louse
plant.. 5. aphid, aphis, borer, thrip
plate.. 6. scutum
praying.. 6. mantis
reference to.. 11. entomologic
relationship to host.. 7. metochy
10. parasitism
science.. 10. entomology
sound.. 5. chirr 7. stridor
stage.. 4. pupa 5. imago, larva
6. instar 9. chrysalis
stinging.. 3. ant, bee 4. wasp
6. hornet 7. sciniph (Bib) 12. yellow
jacket
wingless.. 4. flea 6. aptera
wing vein.. 5. media

Insectivora (mammals)... 5. moles
6. shrews 7. desmans, tenrecs
9. hedgehogs

insecure... 5. risky, shaky 6. infirm,
unsafe, unsure 7. dubious, rickety,
unsound 8. unstable 9. dangerous,
hazardous 10. precarious

insensate... 5. blind, harsh 6. brutal,
unwise 7. fatuous, foolish 8. lifeless
9. inanimate, unfeeling, untouched
10. insensible, insentient
11. insensitive 13. unintelligent

insensibility... 4. coma 8. neurosis
9. analgesia 13. lack of feeling

insensible... 4. slow 7. gradual,
unaware 9. apathetic, inanimate,
insensate, senseless 11. indifferent,

unconscious 13. inappreciable

insert... 4. gore 5. foist, graft, immit,
inset, panel, wedge 7. ingraft
8. interact, ornament 9. interface,
interpose, introduce 11. intercalate,
interpolate

insertion... 5. inset 9. injection
10. embroidery, needlework

insertion (pert to)...
cords in cloth.. 5. shirr
day in calendar.. 13. intercalation
newspaper.. 2. ad 13. advertisement
phrases, words.. 11. parenthesis
sound in a word.. 9. anaptyxis
10. epenthesis

inset... 5. panel 6. inflow, influx
10. phenocryst

inside out, turning... 5. evert
8. aversion 9. evertible

insidious... 4. deep, wily 7. cunning
8. guileful 9. deceitful, dishonest
11. full of plots, treacherous

insight... 3. ken 6. acumen
9. intuition 11. discernment,
penetration 12. clairvoyance
13. understanding

insignia... 3. bar 4. ankh, flag
5. badge, cross, crown 6. banner,
emblem, symbol 7. chevron, regalia,
scepter 8. caduceus, swastika
15. hammer and sickle

insignificance... 6. trifle 9. smallness
10. slightness 12. unimportance

insignificant... 4. puny 5. minor,
petit, petty, small, zilch 6. paltry
7. trivial 8. inferior 9. senseless
11. meaningless, unimportant
12. contemptible 13. inconsiderate

insignificant object... 8. molehill

insincere... 5. false 8. affected
9. deceptive 12. hypocritical

insinuate... 4. hint 5. enter, imply
6. allude, infuse 8. intimate
9. penetrate 10. ingratiate

insinuation... 4. hint 5. sneer
8. innuendo 9. aspersion, insertion,
intrusion 10. intimation
12. ingratiation, interjection

insipid... 3. dry 4. dead, dull, flat,
tame 5. heavy, prosy, stale, vapid,
wimpy (sl) 6. jejune 7. prosaic
8. lifeless, mediocre 9. tasteless
10. monotonous, namby–pamby,
spiritless, unanimated, wishy–washy
11. indifferent 13. uninteresting

insisted... 5. urged 6. held to
7. pressed 8. demanded 9. persisted
10. maintained, stipulated

insnare... see *ensare*

insolence... 5. serve 6. insult
8. defiance 9. arrogance, contumely,
impudence 11. haughtiness

insolent... 4. pert, rude 7. abusive,
defiant 8. arrogant, impudent
9. insulting 10. disdainful
11. extravagant, impertinent,
overbearing 12. contemptuous,
contumelious 13. disrespectful

insouciant... 8. carefree
11. indifferent, unconcerned

inspect... 3. pry, spy 4. view
5. grade 7. examine 10. scrutinize

inspector... 4. ager 6. conner, grader, police, sealer, tester 8. examiner, overseer
inspiration... 6. sprite 8. afflatus, hiccough 9. influence, intuition 10. exhalation, inhalation, motivation
inspire... 4. fire 5. cheer, exalt 6. infuse, inhale 7. animate, breathe, enliven 8. motivate 9. encourage, infatuate 11. communicate (to the spirit)
inspired power... 7. entheos
inspiring... 8. cheering, eloquent 11. provocative
inspiring (pert to)...
  awe.. 4. fear 5. awful, eerie
  confidence.. 11. encouraging
  favor.. 13. prepossessing
  horror.. 6. grisly
inspirit... 5. cheer, elate, rouse 7. animate, enliven, hearten, inspire, quicken 9. encourage 10. ingratiate, invigorate
instability... 8. weakness 10. changeable, insecurity, mutability, unsafeness 11. inconstancy 12. irresolution, unsteadiness 13. changeability, unreliability
install... 4. seat 6. induct, ordain 7. instate 8. initiate 9. establish 10. inaugurate
instance... 4. case, suit 6. motive 7. example, request, urgency 8. occasion 10. suggestion 11. instigation
instant... 3. pop 4. time, urge 5. flash, trice 6. direct, minute, moment, second, urgent 7. current, solicit 8. pressing 9. immediate, importune 11. importunate
instantly... 3. now 8. directly, in a flash, in a trice
instate... 5. admit, endow 6. invest 7. install 9. establish
instead of... 4. else 5. stead 6. in lieu, rather 10. equivalent, substitute
instigate... 3. egg 4. abet, goad, move, prod, spur, urge 5. impel 6. foment, incite, suborn 7. provoke 8. motivate 9. stimulate
instigator... 5. urger 7. abettor, exciter, inciter 8. agitator, fomenter, inflamer, provoker 10. ringleader
instill, instil... 5. imbue 6. impart, infuse, pour in 7. pervade 9. inculcate, insinuate
instinct... 5. knack 6. libido, talent 7. impulse 8. aptitude 11. instigation, orientation
instinctive... 6. innate 7. natural 8. inherent, original 9. automatic, intuitive 11. involuntary, spontaneous
institute... 5. erect, found 6. create, ordain, school 7. academy, college, precept, society 8. initiate, organize, seminary 9. originate, principle 10. inaugurate 12. organization
Institute (The)... 5. Gaius 6. France 8. Politics 10. Technology
institute a suit... 3. sue 7. go to law 8. litigate 9. prosecute
Institution, International (maritime)...

7. Veritas 13. Bureau Veritas
instruct... 4. show 5. coach, edify, order, teach, train 6. advise, direct, inform 7. command, confirm, educate, nurture 9. enlighten 10. discipline 12. indoctrinate
instruction... 3. act 4. lore, news 6. lesson, report 7. precept, tuition 8. pedagogy, teaching, tutorage 9. paideutic 11. information 13. propaedeutics
instructive... 8. didactic, sermonic 10. commanding, preceptive 11. educational, informative 12. propaedeutic
instructor... 5. tutor 6. mentor 7. adviser, teacher, trainer 8. lecturer 9. preceptor, professor
instrument... 4. barb, bill, deed, tool, writ 5. agent, means 6. medium 7. utensil, writing 8. document 9. implement 11. contrivance
instrument, musical (pert to)...
  ancient.. 4. asor, lyre 5. rebab, rocta, shawn 7. cithern, theorbo 8. penorcon, psaltery
  brass.. 4. horn 6. cornet 7. helicon
  keyboard.. 5. organ, piano 6. spinet 10. clavichord 11. harpsichord
  percussion.. 4. drum, gong 5. bells 6. chimes 7. cymbals, marimba 8. carillon 9. castanets, xylophone 10. vibraphone 12. glockenspiel
  sacred (Mormon).. 4. Urim 7. Thummim
  stringed.. 4. asor, harp, lute, lyre, rota 5. banjo, cello, ribec (ribeck), viola 6. fiddle, guitar, violin 7. ukulele 8. dulcimer, mandolin 10. hurdy-gurdy
  stringed (anc).. 7. bandora
  supplementary.. 7. ripieno
  wind.. 3. sax 4. horn, oboe, reed, tuba 5. flute, organ 6. cornet 7. althorn, bassoon, ocarina, piccolo, trumpet 8. clarinet, trombone 9. accordion, flageolet, harmonica, saxophone
instrument, others (pert to)...
  astronomical.. 5. armil
  Biblical.. 4. Urim
  butcher's.. 5. steel 7. cleaver
  communication.. 9. telegraph, telephone 10. hydrophone
  cooking (eggs).. 7. oometer
  cutting.. 5. knife, razor 6. scythe, shears, sickle 7. cutlery 8. scissors, strickle
  drawing.. 10. pantograph
  gripping.. 4. vise 5. clamp, tongs 7. pincers 8. tweezers
  legal.. 4. deed, writ 6. escrow
  mathematics.. 6. abacus 8. mesolabe
  measure.. 7. ammeter 8. odometer, otoscope, rheostat 9. barometer, koniscope, rheometer 11. pyronometer
  medical.. 6. trocar (trochar) 7. dilator, levator, ligator, scalpel 8. trephine
  mining.. 6. jumper
  music.. 4. bell 9. ergograph, metronome

navigating.. 7. pelorus, sextant
optical.. 7. alidade (alidad)
  9. periscope, telescope
pointed.. 3. awl 6. stylet, stylus
  8. stiletto
time.. 11. chronometer, chronoscope
two–pronged.. 6. bident
instrumental... 6. useful 7. helpful
  9. conducive, promoting, symphonic
  10. orchestral 11. implemental,
  serviceable
instrumental (pert to)...
composition.. 5. fugue, rondo
  6. sonata 7. cantata 8. symphony
grammar.. 4. case
introduction.. 7. intrada
instrumentality... 5. means 6. agency,
  medium 7. organon 9. mechanism
insubordinate... 8. mutinous
  10. unresigned 11. disobedient
  12. contumacious, unsubmissive
insubstantial... 5. frail 6. flimsy
  9. illogical 10. unreliable
  12. apparitional
insufficient... 5. short 6. scanty,
  scarce 7. unequal, wanting
  9. deficient 10. inadequate
  14. incommensurate, unsatisfactory
insular... 5. alone 6. narrow
  7. nesiote 8. detached, islander,
  isolated, secluded 9. illiberal,
  insulated, sclerosis, separated,
  unrelated 10. contracted 12. Island
  of Reil (Anat)
insulated... 5. isled, taped 8. isolated
  9. separated 10. segregated
insulating material... 4. tape 5. kapok
  6. balata, Kerite 7. okonite 10. fiber
  glass 12. friction tape
insult... 3. cag 4. mock, slur 5. flout
  6. offend, revile 7. affront, assault,
  offense, outrage 8. contempt
  9. contumely, indignity
insulting... 8. arrogant, insolent
  9. offensive 10. affrontive
  13. disrespectful
insurance... 4. risk 7. annuity, promise
  8. guaranty, security, warranty
  9. assurance 10. protection
insurance group... 7. tontine
insurance personnel... 5. agent
  6. broker 7. actuary 8. adjuster
insurgent... 5. rebel 8. agitator,
  mutineer, revolter 10. rebellious
  13. insubordinate
insurmountable... 10. impassable,
  invincible 11. insuperable 13. beyond
  control
insurrection... 4. riot 6. mutiny, revolt
  8. sedition, uprising 9. rebellion
  10. insurgence, revolution
intact... 5. sound, whole
  9. unchanged, undefiled, undivided,
  uninjured, untouched 10. unimpaired
intaglio... 3. die, gem 6. relief
  7. carving 9. engraving
intangible... 5. vague 7. phantom
  10. immaterial, impalpable
  13. imperceptible, insubstantial,
  unsubstantial
integer... 3. one 5. whole 6. entity,
  number 8. integral

integral... 3. all 5. inner, whole
  8. totality 9. component, essential
integration... 5. whole 10. adjustment
  11. unification 12. coordination,
  equalization 13. accommodation
integrity... 5. unity 6. purity, virtue
  7. honesty, probity 9. innocence,
  soundness 12. completeness
integument... 4. aril, coat, derm, skin
  5. testa 8. covering, envelope
  10. investment
intellect... 3. wit 4. mind, nous
  5. inwit, mahat 6. genius, noesis,
  reason 7. noetics, wise man
  9. mentality 12. intelligence
  13. understanding
intellectual... 6. brainy, mental, noetic,
  sophic 7. egghead, learned
  8. highbrow 11. intelligent
intelligence... 4. mind, news 5. sense,
  spies 6. acumen, spirit 8. capacity
  9. intellect, knowledge
  11. information 13. understanding
intelligent... 3. apt 4. sane 5. acute,
  aware, smart 6. astute, bright,
  versed 7. knowing, skilled 8. rational,
  sensible 9. cognizant
  13. understanding
intelligentsia... 8. literati 10. illuminati
  11. the educated 13. intellectuals
intelligible... 5. clear, plain
  8. knowable 10. cognizable,
  conceptual, explicable, fathomable
  11. perspicuous 13. suprasensuous
  14. comprehensible, understandable
intelligibly... 6. simply 7. clearly,
  lucidly, plainly 13. unequivocally
  14. comprehensibly, understandably
intemerate... 4. pure 9. inviolate,
  undefiled
intemperance... 6. excess 8. bibacity,
  gluttony, severity, tippling
  10. debauchery, inclemency
  11. drunkenness 12. inabstinence,
  incontinence
intemperate... 6. Frigid (Zone), severe,
  Torrid (Zone) 7. extreme 8. addicted,
  bibulous 9. excessive, inclement,
  indulgent 10. gluttonous,
  immoderate, inordinate
  12. ungovernable, unrestrained
intend... 3. aim 4. mean, plan
  5. serve 6. design, direct, expect,
  regard, set out, strive 7. proceed,
  propose 8. aspire to, attend to,
  consider
intended... 5. meant 8. designed,
  purposed, remedial 9. affianced,
  betrothed, meditated 10. calculated,
  considered 11. deliberated, intentional
  12. contemplated
intense... 4. deep 5. great, vivid
  6. strong 7. violent 8. powerful
  9. energetic 10. high degree
intensely... 4. very 5. quite 7. acutely
intensify... 6. deepen 7. enhance
  8. condense, heighten, increase
  9. aggravate
intensity... 5. depth 6. deepen,
  degree, energy 7. density
  8. loudness, softness, strength
  9. greatness, vehemence

12. colorfulness

intent... 4. rapt 5. eager, tense
6. design 7. earnest, meaning,
purpose 9. intention

intention... 3. aim, end 4. will
6. animus, design, motive, object
7. concept, healing, meaning,
purpose 8. intentio 13. determination

intentional... 5. aimed, meant
7. knowing 8. designed, intended
9. voluntary 10. calculated, deliberate
12. contemplated

intently... 7. eagerly, fixedly
9. earnestly, zealously 10. diligently,
sedulously 11. attentively, steadfastly

inter (pref)... 5. among, intra
6. mutual, within 7. between
10. reciprocal

inter (verb)... 4. bury 5. inurn
6. entomb, inhume 7. inearth

intercalary month... 6. Veadar 8. leap
year 10. bissextile

intercalate... 6. insert 11. interpolate

intercede... 0. umpire 7. bargain,
mediate, referee 9. arbitrate, go
between, interpose, intervene

intercessor... 5. agent, front
6. bishop, Christ 8. mediator
9. middleman 10. interceder
11. internuncio

interchange... 5. trade 6. barter
7. permute 8. commerce, exchange
9. alternate 10. transposal
11. alternation, reciprocate, retaliation

intercourse... 7. dealing 8. commerce
10. connection, fellowship
12. conversation 13. communication

interdependence... 9. mutuality
13. interrelation 16. interaffiliation

interdict... 3. ban 4. veto 5. debar,
taboo (tabu) 6. forbid 7. inhibit
8. prohibit 9. proscribe

interest... 4. hold, weal 5. savor,
share, usury 6. behalf, engage
7. attract, concern 9. entertain

interested... 4. rapt 7. partial 8. a
party to, involved, partisan
9. attentive 10. prejudiced

interesting... 8. exciting 10. attractive
11. provocative

interfere... 5. clash 6. hinder, meddle,
molest, tamper 7. intrude
9. interpose, intervene
11. intermeddle

interim... 7. respite 8. interval,
meantime 9. interlude, meanwhile
12. intermission

interior... 5. inner 6. center, inland,
inside, secret 8. internal 9. enclosure

interjection... 2. eh, lo 3. bah
4. ahem, alas, egad, haha, whew
7. heavens 11. ejaculation,
exclamation

interlace... 3. mix 5. braid, unite
9. alternate, interlink 10. intertwine,
interweave 11. interpolate, intersperse

interlock... 4. knit, mesh 5. unite,
weave 6. device, engage 7. connect
9. interjoin, interlace 11. interrelate

interlope... 6. insert 7. intrude,
obtrude 9. interfere, intervene
11. intermeddle, interpolate

interloper... 8. intruder 10. trespasser
11. gate crasher

interlude... 5. farce, pause, truce
6. verset 7. interim, respite
8. entr'acte, overture, versicle
10. intermezzo 11. performance
13. entertainment

intermediary... 5. agent 6. medium,
middle 8. mediator 9. go–between
10. interagent 11. intervening,
mediatorial

intermediate... 5. mesne 6. grades,
medial, medium, middle 7. aniline
(dye), mediate 8. mediator
9. naphthols 11. interjacent,
intervening 12. intermediary

interminable... 4. aeon, long
7. endless, eternal 8. infinite,
unending 9. boundless, limitless,
perpetual, unlimited 10. continuous,
protracted

intermission... 4. rest 5. pause
6. recess 7. respite 8. entr'acte,
interval 9. cessation 10. suspension
12. interruption

intermit... 4. stop 5. cease, recur
7. suspend 9. interpose, interrupt
11. discontinue

intermittent... 6. broken, fitful
8. periodic 9. irregular, recurrent,
spasmodic 11. alternating

internal... 5. inner 6. inside, inward,
mental, within 7. revenue
8. domestic, esoteric, interior
9. intrinsic, spiritual

internal organs... 6. vitals 7. viscera

international (port to)...
  agreement.. 4. pact 6. accord, treaty
    7. entente 8. suzerain
  business combine.. 6. cartel
  fixed calendar.. 9. Cotsworth
  language.. 2. Ro 3. Ido 5. Arulo
    7. Volapük 9. Esperanto
    10. Occidental 11. Interlingua

interpolate... 5. alter 6. insert
7. corrupt, implant 11. intercalate

interpose... 7. intrude, mediate
9. intercede, interfere, interject,
intervene, introduce

interpret... 4. read, rede, scan
6. define 7. explain, expound
8. construe, diagnose, exegesis
9. elucidate, translate

interpretation... 5. sense 8. solution
9. rendering 10. definition
11. explanation, translation

interpretation, science of...
7. anagoge (Bib) 8. exegesis
9. dittology 12. hermeneutics

interpreter... 5. ulema 6. gnomon
7. exegete, latiner 8. dragoman,
exponent 9. catechist, exegetist,
explainer, go–between, hermeneut
12. oneirocritic (dreams)

interrogate... 3. ask 4. pump, quiz,
test 5. query 7. examine, inquire
8. question 9. catechize

interrogation... 7. eroteme (question
mark) 8. erotisis, question, quizzing
11. examination, questioning

interrupt... 4. stop 5. break, check
6. arrest, hinder, thwart 7. break in,

intrude 8. obstruct 9. intercept
11. interpolate
interrupter (electric) . . . 8. rheotome
interruption . . . 3. gap 5. pause
6. hiatus 7. interim 8. interval
9. cessation, hindrance
10. suspension 11. obstruction
12. intermission, intervention
13. interposition
intersect . . . 3. cut 4. meet 5. cross
6. divide, pierce 9. decussate
10. intercross
intersperse . . . 6. insert, thread
7. scatter 9. diversify
interstice . . . 4. mesh, pore 5. chink,
crack, space 6. areola 7. crevice
8. interval 10. interspace
intertwine . . . 5. unite, weave
8. entangle 9. interknit, interlace
10. intertwist
interval . . . 3. gap 4. rest 5. break,
lapse, pitch, space 6. degree, period,
recess 7. diastem, interim, respite
8. diastema, distance, half step
10. interspace 12. intermission,
interruption
intervals, at . . . 8. brokenly, fitfully
11. haphazardly, irregularly
12. occasionally 14. intermittently
15. longo intervallo
intervene . . . 7. intrude, mediate
9. interlude, interpose 10. lie
between 11. come between
intervening (pert to) . . .
between, among . . 11. interjacent
law . . 5. mesne
space . . 8. distance
time . . 7. interim 9. interlude
interweave . . . 3. mat 4. plat 5. braid,
plait, plash 6. enlace, raddle, splice,
wattle 8. intermix 9. interlace
13. twist together
intestinal . . . 7. enteric 8. visceral
intestine (pert to) . . .
coating . . 4. caul
comb form . . 6. entero
part . . 5. colon, ilium, large, small
6. caecum, rectum 7. jejunum
8. appendix, duodenum
15. alimentary canal
intestines . . . 4. guts 6. bowels
8. entrails
intimacy . . . 9. closeness
10. connection, friendship
11. association, familiarity, sociability
intimate . . . 3. sib 4. hint, near
6. friend, united 8. familiar, friendly,
informal, personal, sociable
9. confidant, innermost
12. confidential
intimation . . . 3. cue 4. clue, hint
5. trace 7. inkling 9. reference
10. foreboding, indication, suggestion
11. supposition 12. announcement,
notification
intimidate . . . 3. awe, cow 5. abash,
bully, daunt, deter 7. overawe, terrify
8. browbeat, frighten, threaten
intolerance . . . 7. bigotry 9. dogmatism,
prejudice 10. impatience, narrowness
12. illiberality
intolerant . . . 6. narrow 7. bigoted

8. dogmatic 9. impatient
10. prejudiced 11. not enduring
intolerant person . . . 5. bigot 7. fanatic
intone . . . 4. sing 5. chant, croon,
sound 7. introit
intoxicated . . . 3. lit, sot 4. tosy
5. drunk, heady, tipsy 6. boiled
7. fervent, fuddled, maudlin
8. besotted, temulent 9. befuddled
10. inebriated
intractable . . . 5. tough 6. sullen, unruly
7. restive, willful (wilful) 8. indocile,
perverse, stubborn 9. obstinate,
unbending, unpliable 10. headstrong,
inflexible, refractory 11. unteachable
12. ungovernable
intransitive . . . 6. neuter, verbal
8. confined 10. in transitu
intrenchment . . . 2. pa (pah) 4. fort
7. defense, parapet 8. stockade
12. encroachment, infringement
intrepid . . . 4. bold 5. brave 6. heroic
7. doughty, valiant 8. fearless,
resolute 9. dauntless, undaunted
10. courageous
intrepidity . . . 5. nerve, valor
7. courage, prowess 8. boldness,
valiancy 9. gallantry
intricacy . . . 9. sinuosity 10. complexity,
involution, perplexity 11. complexness
12. complication, entanglement
intrigue . . . 4. plot 5. amour, cabal
6. brigue, scheme 8. artifice,
cheating 9. fascinate 10. conspiracy
11. machination
intrinsic . . . 4. real, true 5. inner
6. inborn, inbred, inward, native
7. genuine, natural 8. immanent,
implicit, inherent 9. essential,
necessary 11. inseparable
13. indispensable
intrinsically . . . 5. truly 6. really
10. internally 11. essentially
intrinsic being . . . 7. essence
introduce . . . 5. immit, start, usher
6. broach, herald, infuse, insert,
submit 7. bring in, preface, present,
sponsor 8. acquaint, approach,
initiate, innovate 10. inaugurate
11. preinstruct
introduced from foreign country . . .
6. exotic 10. extraneous
introduced serum . . . 10. inoculated
introduction . . . 5. debut, guide, proem
7. introit, isagoge, preface
8. exordium, foreword, preamble
9. insertion 10. innovation
11. instruction, preparation
12. inauguration, presentation
introduction (pert to) . . .
Biblical . . 9. isagogics
drama (anc) . . 8. protasis
new words . . 7. neology
spurious matter . . 13. interpolation
introductory . . . 9. prefatory, prelusive
11. preliminary
introit . . . 4. hymn, rite 5. psalm
8. entrance 12. introduction
introrse . . . (opp of extrorse) 12. facing
inward
introversion . . . (opp of extroversion)
9. inversion, reticence

intrude... 5. enter 6. invade, meddle
8. encroach, infringe, overstep,
trespass 9. interfere, interlope
intruder... 7. invader 8. outsider
9. buttinsky 10. interloper, trespasser
intrust, entrust... 6. commit
7. confide, consign 8. delegate
10. commission
intuition... 5. hunch 6. noesis, regard
7. insight 9. knowledge, reference
13. contemplation
intuitive... 6. noetic, seeing 7. sensing
10. perceiving 11. instinctive
inulase... 6. enzyme
inunction... 7. unguent 8. inunctum,
ointment
inundate... 3. dip 4. dunk 5. douse,
drunk, flood 6. deluge, engulf
7. baptize, immerse 8. overflow,
submerge 9. overwhelm
10. oversupply
inure... 6. harden, season 7. benefit,
callous, toughen 8. accustom
9. habituate
inurn... 4. bury 5. inter 6. entomb
invade... 4. raid 5. enter (foeman),
usurp 6. attack, infest 7. intrude,
overrun, violate 8. encroach, trespass
invader... 4. Pict 8. attacker, intruder
9. aggressor, assailant 10. trespasser
invalid... 4. null, sick, void, weak
5. frail 6. feeble, infirm, sickly
8. nugatory 11. ineffectual
14. valetudinarian
invalidate... 4. undo 5. annul, quash
7. abolish, nullify, vitiate 8. disprove
10. disqualify, neutralize
invalidism... 13. indisposition
17. valetudinarianism
invaluable... 6. useful 8. precious
9. priceless, worthless
11. inestimable
invariable... 7. uniform 8. constant
10. unchanging 12. unchangeable
invasion... 4. raid 5. foray 6. attack,
breach, inroad 8. entrance (hostile)
9. incursion, intrusion, irruption
10. infraction 11. infestation
invective... 5. abuse, curse 6. tirade
7. inveigh, railing 8. diatribe
10. revilement 11. malediction
12. vituperation
inveigle... 4. lure, rope 5. snare
6. allure, entice, entrap, seduce
7. deceive, wheedle 10. lead astray
invent... 4. coin 5. frame 6. create,
design, devise 7. concoct 8. discover
9. fabricate (mentally), originate
inventive... 6. adroit 7. fertile
8. creative, original 9. ingenious
inventor... 7. creator 8. imaginer
10. discoverer, originator
inventor, discoverer of...
airplane.. 6. Fokker, Wright (Bros)
baseball.. 9. Doubleday
brake (safety).. 4. Otis
cotton gin.. 7. Whitney
dynamite.. 5. Nobel
electric light.. 6. Edison
elevator.. 4. Otis
gun.. 4. Colt 5. Maxim 9. Remington
harp (Bib).. 5. Jubal

lamp (safety).. 4. Davy
phonograph.. 6. Edison
printing.. 9. Gutenberg
radio.. 8. De Forest
sewing machine.. 4. Howe
steamboat.. 5. Fitch 6. Fulton
steam engine.. 4. Watt
telegraph.. 5. Morse
wireless.. 7. Marconi
X–ray.. 8. Roentgen
inventory... 4. list 5. index 7. account
8. register 9. catalogue (catalog)
10. tally sheet
inverse... 8. inverted, opposite,
reversed
inversely club–shaped... 9. obclavate
inversely oval... 7. obovate
inversion... 8. overturn, reversal
9. overthrow, reversion
10. conversion 12. introversion
invert... 7. capsize, convert, pervert
(obs), reverse, tip over 8. overturn
9. transpose 10. turn turtle
invertebrate... 5. polyp 6. insect,
sponge 7. mollusk 9. spineless
10. weak–willed
invest... 3. don 4. vest, wrap
5. array, dress, endow, indue, spend
6. clothe 7. empower, envelop,
instate 8. surround
invest (pert to)...
authority.. 8. accredit, sanction
ministry.. 6. ordain
sovereignty.. 8. enthrone
investigate... 3. pry 4. sift 5. probe,
study, track 6. excuse, search
7. discuss, explore 8. indagate
10. scrutinize
investigation... 6. examen 7. inquiry,
zetetic 8. research 9. discovery,
heuristic 10. discussion
11. examination
investiture... 7. clothes, vesture
8. clothing, covering 9. induction
10. holy orders, investment (money),
ordination 11. instatement
12. installation 15. enfranchisement
investment... 5. siege 7. finance,
garment 8. blockade, clothing,
covering, purchase, vestment
9. endowment 11. empowerment
investment list... 9. portfolio
inveterate... 3. old 6. rooted
7. chronic 8. habitual, hardened
9. confirmed, ingrained
10. deep–rooted 11. established,
traditional 15. long–established
invidious... 6. odious, ornery
7. envious, hateful 9. malignant
14. discriminating (unjustly)
invigorate... 3. pep 5. brace, cheer,
nerve, renew 6. vivify 7. animate,
enliven, fortify, refresh 8. energize
9. stimulate 10. exhilarate,
strengthen
invigorating... 4. cool 5. tonic
8. cheering 10. energizing,
life–giving, refreshing 11. stimulating
invincible... 10. unbeatable
11. indomitable 13. unconquerable
inviolate... 6. sacred, secret
8. faithful, unbroken 9. unchanged,

undefiled, unstained 10. inviolable,
unimpaired, unprofound
13. incorruptible
invisible... 3. hid 6. hidden
10. indistinct, unapparent
13. infinitesimal, undiscernible,
unperceivable
Invisible, The... 3. God
11. Rosicrucian 16. German
Protestant
invisible emanation... 4. aura
invitation... 3. bid 4. call 7. bidding,
summons 10. allurement, inducement
12. solicitation
invite... 3. ask, beg, bid, try 4. bade
5. court, order, tempt 6. allure,
entice, induce 7. request, solicit
9. encourage
invocation... 4. call, plea, rite
6. appeal, prayer, sermon
7. summons 8. entreaty
11. conjuration, incantation
12. supplication
invoice... 4. bill 7. account (written)
8. manifest 9. reckoning 12. bill of
lading
invoke... 3. beg 4. pray 6. appeal
7. address, conjure, entreat, implore,
solicit 8. draw down 10. supplicate
involuntary... 9. not willed, reluctant,
unwilling, unwitting 11. instinctive,
spontaneous 13. unintentional
involve... 3. lap 4. coil, wind, wrap
5. imply 6. employ, entail, evince,
infold 7. concern, ensnare, entwine,
envelop, include 8. interest
9. embarrass, implicate
10. complicate 11. incriminate
involved... 7. complex, implied
8. involute, tortuous 9. engrossed
10. implicated
involving punishment... 8. punitive
invulnerable... 10. invincible
11. impregnable, insuperable
12. impenetrable, unassailable
inward... 4. into 5. entad, inner
6. inside 7. ingoing, muffled
8. interior, internal 9. spiritual
10. internally
inwards... 8. entrails 10. intestines
Io... 7. goddess (Gr) 9. butterfly,
satellite (of Jupiter)
iodine, iodin (pert to)...
comb form.. 3. iod 4. iodo
compound.. 6. iodide
containing.. 5. iodic 6. iodous
poisoning.. 6. iodism 9. iododerma
source.. 4. kelp 8. sea water 9. salt
peter 12. thryoid gland
standard.. 9. idiometry
substitute.. 7. Aristol
ion... 5. anion 6. cation (kation)
8. electron, particle (Elec)
Ionian (pert to)...
city.. 4. Teos (birthplace of Anacreon)
islands.. 5. Greek 9. Asia Minor
mode (Mus).. 6. Lydian
Ionic (pert to)...
architecture.. 5. Order
dialect.. 5. Greek
poetry.. 4. foot 5. meter
printing.. 4. type

iota... 3. ace, jot 4. atom, mite, star
(9th brightest), whit 6. letter (Gr),
tittle 8. particle
Iowa...
capital.. 9. Des Moines
city.. 4. Ames 8. Waterloo
9. Davenport, Fort Dodge,
Marquette, Sioux City 10. West
Branch 11. Cedar Rapids
famed attractions.. 10. Hoover home
12. Effigy Mounds 17. Little Brown
Church
famed first.. 12. apple orchard (1799)
famed names.. 6. Joliet 7. Dubuque
9. Marquette
flower.. 8. wild rose
locale.. 8. farm belt (Midwest)
river.. 8. Missouri 11. Mississippi
State admission.. 11. twenty–ninth
(1846)
State nickname.. 7. Hawkeye
ipecac... 4. evea 6. emetic 7. emetive
9. purgative
irade... 6. decree (Turk)
Iran... see also *Iranian*
capital.. 7. Teheran (Tehran)
city.. 6. Abadan, Shiraz 7. Isfahan
conqueror.. 6. Darius 9. Alexander
founder.. 5. Cyrus (the Great)
lake.. 7. Rezaieh
mountain.. 6. Elburz, Zagros
8. Damavand (peak)
parliament.. 6. Majlis (Mejlis)
people.. 3. Tat 7. Indians
ruins.. 10. Persepolis (Shiraz)
Iranian (pert to)...
almond.. 5. badam
books.. 5. Koran, Yasma 6. Avesta
country.. 4. Elam 5. Media
demigod.. 4. Yima
demon.. 7. Ahriman
diadem.. 3. taj
dynasty.. 6. Safavi, Seljuk
10. Sassanidae
fire worshiper.. 5. Parsi (Parsee)
god.. 6. Ormazd (Supreme) 7. Mithras
Koran student.. 5. hafiz
poet.. 4. Omar 5. Saadi
Relig founder.. 9. Zoroaster
tapestry.. 7. susanee
tentmaker.. 4. Omar
Iraq, Mesopotamia...
capital.. 6. Bagdad (Baghdad)
culture (anc).. 8. Sumerian
historic city.. 2. Ur 5. Eridu
7. Babylon, Nineveh
historic Valley.. 15. Tigris–Euphrates
port.. 5. Basra (Busrah)
product.. 3. oil 4. date 5. sheep
river.. 6. Tigris 9. Euphrates
irascibility... 3. ire 6. choler
9. crossness, testiness 10. perversity
11. waspishness 12. churlishness,
irritability
irate... 3. hot 5. angry, wroth
7. enraged 8. incensed 9. irascible
ire... 5. anger, wrath 7. madness
8. vexation 9. vehemence
10. enragement, resentment
12. exasperation
ireful... 5. angry, wroth 7. iracund
9. irascible 10. passionate

Ireland... 4. Eire, Erin 5. Irena 6. Old
 Sod, Ulster 8. Hibernia 9. Innisfail
 11. Emerald Isle, Erin go brath
 14. Ireland Forever
Ireland (pert to)... see also *Irish*
 Bay.. 6. Bantry, Dingle, Galway
 7. Donegal
 capital.. 4. Tara (old) 6. Dublin
 channel.. 5. North 9. St George's
 city.. 4. Cobh (Queenstown), Cork,
 Tara 6. Galway, Tralee, Ulster
 7. Belfast, Donegal, Kildare, Wexford
 8. Kilkenny, Limerick 9. Tipperary
 island.. 4. Aran
 legislature.. 4. Dail
 mountain.. 7. Errigal 13. Carrantuohill
 river.. 3. Lee 4. Erne, Suir 6. Liffey
 7. Shannon
 sea.. 5. Irish
 seaport.. 4. Cobh 6. Tralee
 seat of archbishops.. 6. Armagh
irenic... 7. henotic 8. peaceful
 11. harmonizing 12. conciliatory
iridescent... 7. opaline 9. prismatic
 10. opalescent
iris... 4. flag 6. flower 7. rainbow
iris (pert to)...
 astronomy.. 8. asteroid (7th)
 color.. 11. reddish–blue
 eye part.. 4. uvea 5. irian
 Florentine.. 5. orris (orrice)
 inflammation.. 6. iritis
 mineral.. 6. quartz (iridescent)
Iris, goddess... 7. rainbow
Irish (pert to)...
 alphabet (early).. 4. ogam (ogham)
 battle cry.. 3. abu (aboo) 9. To
 Victory 11. Erin go brath
 cattle.. 5. Kerry
 churchman.. 7. erenach (herenach)
 club, cudgel.. 10. shillalagh (shillalah)
 convention (anc).. 4. Feis 10. Feis of
 Tara
 cordial.. 10. usquebaugh
 dagger (anc).. 5. skean
 dance.. 3. jig 4. rink 10. rinkafadda
 emblem.. 8. shamrock
 exclamation.. 3. aru 5. arrah
 fairy, spirit.. 4. shee (sidhe)
 7. banshee (banshee) 10. leprechaun
 festival.. 4. feis
 goblin.. 5. pooka
 god.. 3. Ler (sea)
 goddess.. 4. Dana
 king's home.. 4. Tara
 landholding.. 7. rundale
 legislature.. 10. Oireachtas (House)
 11. Dail Eireann (Chamber)
 13. Seanad Eireann (Senate)
 liquor house (illegal).. 7. shebeen
 love, sweetheart.. 3. gra
 moss.. 9. carrageen
 peasant.. 4. kern (lerne)
 pig.. 5. bonav
 policeman.. 8. spalpeen
 potato city.. 7. Youghal
 queen (folklore).. 4. Medb
 Society (secret).. 6. Fenian
 soldier.. 4. kern (kerne) 10. galloglass
 tenant.. 4. saer
 tribal lord.. 6. tanist
 verse.. 4. rann

whisky, whiskey (illegal).. 6. poteen
 (potheen)
Irish (people)...
 ancestor (fabled).. 3. Mil 6. Miledh
 author.. 4. Shaw 5. Wilde
 chemist.. 5. Boyle
 composer.. 7. Herbert
 Irishman.. 4. Aire, Celt, Gael
 6. Teague 8. Milesian 9. Hibernian,
 Orangeman 10. Eireannach
 lawyer.. 6. brehon
 Nuns (Order).. 15. Ladies of Loretto
 patriot.. 5. Emmet, Tandy 6. Oakboy
 poet.. 5. Colum, Moore, Wilde, Yeats
 7. Russell (George)
 refugee.. 7. fuidhir
 saint (patron).. 7. Patrick
 Saxon.. 8. Sasanach
 sea robbers (Myth).. 9. Fomorians
 surgeon.. 6. Colles
 tribe (family).. 4. sept 5. cinel
irk... 3. vex 4. bore, tire 5. annoy,
 weary 6. nettle 7. disgust, trouble
 10. exasperate
irksome... 5. vexed, weary 7. operose,
 painful, tedious 8. annoying
 9. fatiguing, vexatious, wearisome
 10. burdensome, exhausting,
 monotonous 12. disagreeable
iron... 2. Fe (symbol) 6. harsh, metal,
 power, press 6. ferrum, fetter,
 mangle, pistol, severe 7. firearm,
 manacle, shackle, sideros
 8. firmness, handcuff, hardness,
 strength 10. inflexible, unyielding
 11. unrelenting
iron (pert to)...
 casting.. 5. mitis
 comb form.. 5. ferro 6. sidero
 compound.. 5. steel
 containing.. 6. ferric
 dog.. 7. firedog
 droop.. 6. ointor
 herb.. 8. Vernonia 9. ironweeds
 lump.. 3. pig
 magnet.. 8. armature
 meteoric.. 8. siderite
 ore.. 7. turgite 8. hematite, siderite
 11. sesquioxide
 ref to.. 6. ferric 7. ferrous
 8. siderous
 rod.. 5. punty (puntee)
 salts of.. 10. chalybeate
 sand.. 7. iserine
 science of.. 10. siderology
 symbol.. 2. Fe
 tailor's.. 5. goose
 tool.. 6. lifter
 vessel, basket.. 7. cresset
ironclad... 6. severe 7. armored,
 Monitor (ship) 8. exacting, rigorous
 9. stringent
ironic, ironical... 3. dry 7. cynical,
 satiric 9. sarcastic 10. figurative
 11. Rabelaisian
irons... 5. gyves 6. chains 7. fetters
 8. manacles, shackles 9. handcuffs
Ironsides... 7. cavalry (Cromwell's)
 8. Cromwell
ironwood... 4. acle 5. olive 6. colima
 7. breakax 8. hornbeam
 9. stavewood

irony... 6. banter, satire 7. lampoon, sarcasm 8. ridicule
Iroquoian Indian... 4. Erie 5. Huron 6. Cayuga, Mohawk, Oneida, Seneca 7. Wyandot 8. Cherokee, Onondaga 9. Conestoga, Tuscarora
Iroquois (pert to)...
  famed.. 11. Five Nations
  native of.. 7. New York 9. Wisconsin
  tribes (Five).. 6. Cayuga, Mohawk, Oneida, Seneca 8. Onondaga
irrational... 6. stupid 9. fanatical, illogical, senseless 10. ridiculous 11. impractical 12. preposterous, unreasonable 13. unintelligent
irregular... 4. wild 5. erose, rough 6. fitful, rugged, uneven 7. atactic, crooked, devious, erratic, mutable, styptic, unequal 8. aberrent, abnormal, atypical, informal, variable 9. anomalous, desultory, distorted, eccentric, haphazard, orderless, unsettled 10. changeable, immoderate, inconstant 11. intemperate 12. unsystematic
irregularity... 6. ataxia (muscular) 7. anomaly 8. disorder 9. deviation 10. distortion 11. abnormality, informality 12. eccentricity
irrelevant... 7. foreign 9. unrelated 10. extraneous 11. impertinent, unessential 12. inconsequent 13. insignificant
irreligious... 5. pagan 7. godless, impious, profane 11. unreligious
irreparable... 4. gone, lost 6. ruined 11. irrevocable 12. incorrigible, irremediable 13. irrecoverable, irretrievable
irrepressible... 7. Homeric (laughter) 12. ungovernable, unrestrained
irrepressible conflict... 8. civil war
irreproachable... 7. perfect 9. blameless 10. impeccable, inculpable
irresolute... 6. fickle, unsure 8. doubtful, unstable 9. uncertain, undecided 10. capricious, changeable, inconstant 12. undetermined
irresolution... 10. fickleness, indecision 11. fluctuation, uncertainty, vacillation 14. capriciousness
irresponsible... 6. fickle 7. lawless 8. carefree 9. insolvent 12. independable 13. unaccountable, untrustworthy
irretrievable... 8. hopeless 9. incurable 11. irreparable 12. irremediable, unchangeable 13. irrecoverable
irreverence... 7. impiety 8. dishonor 9. profanity 10. disrespect
irrevocable... 3. end 4. past 5. final 10. inevitable, past recall 11. unalterable 12. beyond recall, unchangeable
irrigate... 3. wet 5. water 6. dilute, sluice 7. moisten, refresh
irritable... 4. edgy 5. cross, techy, testy 6. cranky, ornery, touchy 7. fretful, iracund, peevish, tempery, twitchy 8. snappish
irritate... 3. irk, nag, vex 4. fret, gall, rasp, rile 5. anger, annoy, chafe, cross, grate, peeve, pique, rouse, sting, tease 6. excite, incite, madden, needle, nettle, rankle 7. incense, provoke 10. exacerbate, exasperate 14. rub the wrong way
irritated... 4. sore 5. afret, testy 6. peeved 7. annoyed, nettled, rankled 8. provoked
irritation... 4. itch 5. pique 6. temper 9. annoyance 10. resentment 12. exasperation
irruption... 5. foray 6. inroad 8. invasion 9. incursion
Irving pseudonym... 13. Knickerbocker (Diedrich)
is... 6. exists 10. represents 11. personifies
Isaac (pert to)...
  Bib.. 9. patriarch (Heb)
  father of.. 4. Esau 5. Jacob
  grandfather of.. 4. Edom
  husband of.. 7. Rebekah
  son of.. 5. Sarah 7. Abraham
Ishmael (pert to)...
  ancestor.. 11. Ishmaelites
  Bib.. 6. pariah 7. outcast
  father of.. 8. Nebaioth
  son of.. 5. Hagar 7. Abraham
isinglass... 4. huso, mica 7. gelatin 8. agar-agar
Isis (pert to)...
  daughter of.. 3. Geb, Nut
  goddess of.. 9. fertility 10. motherhood
  identified with.. 7. Dog Star
  mother of.. 4. Sept (Horus)
  represented (at times).. 9. cow-headed
  shrine of.. 5. Iseum (Iseium)
  wife of.. 6. Osiris
Islam, religion (pert to)...
  founder.. 7. Mahomet
  God.. 5. Allah
  people.. 7. Moslems
  prophet.. 8. Mohammed
Islamic (pert to)...
  convert.. 5. ansar
  holy city.. 5. Mecca 6. Medina
  mosque.. 6. masjid
  pilgrimage.. 5. Kaaba (Caaba) 10. Black Stone
  Supreme Being.. 5. Allah
  teacher.. 4. alim 5. ulema 6. mullah (mulla)
island... 3. ait, cay, ile, key 4. calf, cayo, eyot, holm, isle, reef 5. atoll, islet 7. isolate 8. insulate
island (pert to)...
  city.. 8. Montreal
  coral.. 5. atoll 8. Zanzibar
  enchanted.. 4. Bali
  fabled.. 4. Meru 6. Avalon, Bimini 8. Atlantis
  fabulous.. 7. Zangbar
  group.. 8. Antilles, Marshall 11. archipelago
  inhabitant, native.. 7. nesiote 8. islander
  universe (Astron).. 6. galaxy

Island of ...
Langerhans .. 8. pancreas
Odysseus .. 6. Ithaca
Reil .. 5. brain
Saints .. 4. Erin
Isle of Man ...
Celtic name .. 4. Manx
city .. 4. Peel 6. Ramsey 7. Douglas
division .. 5. Treen
judge .. 8. deemster (dempster)
legislature .. 7. Tynwald
mountain peak .. 8. Snaefell
Northern point .. 4. Ayre
site .. 8. Irish sea
Isle of Wight ...
Queen's summer home .. 12. Osborne
  House
site .. 10. English Sea
sport (famed) .. 9. yacht race
town .. 7. Newport
watering place .. 4. Ryde
Isles of Galway Bay ... 4. Aran
ism .. 4. cult 5. dogma, ideal, tenet
  6. belief, school, system 8. doctrine,
  practice 11. abnormality
isochromatic ... 9. same color
isochronal ... 9. equal time
  11. uniform time
isocracy ... 9. equal rule 10. equal
  power
isodont (Zool) ... 10. alike teeth
isogonal ... 11. equal angles
isolate ... 4. isle 6. enisle 7. seclude
  8. insulate, separate 9. segregate,
  sequester 10. quarantine
isolation ... 8. escapism, solitude
  9. seclusion 10. insulation, loneliness,
  separation 11. segregation
isomer ... 7. metamer 8. compound
  (Chem)
isonomy ... 11. equal rights
isonym ... 7. paronym 8. same name
isosceles ... 10. equal sides (triangle)
Israel (Bib) ... 4. Jews 5. Jacob, Zions
  13. Hebrew Kingdom
Israel (pert to) ... see also *Israelite*
appellation .. 8. Jeshurun
capital .. 9. Jerusalem
city .. 4. Acre 5. Elath, Haifa, Jaffa
  7. Galilee, Jericho, Tel Aviv
desert .. 5. Negev
dust storm .. 7. khamsin
lawgiver .. 5. Moses
Plain of .. 6. Sharon
priest .. 3. Eli
river .. 6. Jordan
sea .. 4. Dead 7. Galilee
song (Zionist) .. 8. Hatikvah
statesman .. 4. Meir 5. Begin
Israelite (pert to) ...
hero .. 6. Gideon
judge .. 4. Elon 8. Jephthah
king .. 4. Ahab, Jehu, Saul (1st)
  5. David (2nd) 7. Solomon
lawgiver .. 5. Moses
priest .. 3. Eli
tribe .. 3. Dan 5. Asher 6. Reuben
tribe, priestly .. 4. Levi
issue ... 3. son 4. come, emit, flow,
  gush 5. arise, child, sally, spout,
  stock, topic, utter 6. effect, emerge,
  escape, sortie, source, upshot

7. edition, emanate, proceed, product,
  progeny 8. question 9. emergence,
  offspring, posterity 11. consequence,
  publication
Istanbul (Constantinople) ...
ancient name .. 9. Byzantium
capital of .. 6. Turkey (to 1923)
foreign quarter .. 4. Pera
Greek quarter .. 5. Fanar
site .. 8. Bosporus 10. Golden Horn
isthmus (pert to) ...
American .. 6. Panama
anatomy .. 6. fauces
Greek (anc) .. 7. Corinth
Siam .. 3. Kra
it ... 5. charm, thing 6. itself, person
  7. egotist, pronoun
Ita ... 4. Acta 7. Negrito
Italian (pert to) ... see also *Italy*
card game .. 5. tarot
carriage .. 7. vettura
cathedral .. 5. duomo
cheese .. 6. Romano 8. Parmesan
  10. mozzarella
condiment .. 6. tamara (tamarind)
deity .. 4. faun
dish .. 5. pizza 7. calzone 8. braciola
  11. saltimbocca
dome, peak .. 4. cima
entertainment .. 5. festa 7. ridotto
food .. see *pasta*
grape .. 6. verdea
hamlet .. 5. casal
house .. 4. casa 6. casino (summer)
inlay .. 6. tarsia
inn .. 7. locanda
innkeeper .. 7. padrone
lady .. 5. donna 7. signora
lake .. 4. lago
law .. 6. Latium 8. Jus Latii
lover .. 7. amoroso
magistrate (anc) .. 8. podesta
marble .. 4. Neri 7. carrara, cipolin
marsh .. 7. maremma
opera house .. 7. La Scala (1778)
peasant .. 7. paesano 9. contadino
photographers .. 9. paparazzi (press)
pottery .. 8. majolica
secret society .. 6. Maffia (Mafia)
  7. Camorra
sheep .. 6. merino
vessel .. 9. trabacolo
wind (hot) .. 7. sirocco
wine .. 4. Asti 5. Capri 7. Chianti,
  Orvieto 12. Asti Spumante
Italian (pert to people) ...
anti–Fascist .. 6. Sforza
architect .. 8. Bramante
astronomer .. 6. Secchi 7. Galileo
author .. 5. Dante
deity .. 6. Faunus
dictator .. 9. Mussolini
educator .. 10. Montessori
explorer .. 8. Columbus, Vespucci
  9. Marco Polo
family (princely) .. 4. Este 5. Doria
  6. Medici
family (violin) .. 5. Amati
friend (outside) .. 10. Italophile
geographer .. 8. Amoretti
goddess .. 3. Ops 4. Juno 5. Diana
hero .. 7. Orlando

historian.. **4**. Dion **5**. Cantu
king.. **7**. Umberto
musician.. **5**. Guido, Verdi **7**. Puccini, Rossini **9**. Scarlatti
naturalist.. **4**. Poli
noblewoman.. **8**. Marchesa **11**. Marchioness
painter.. **5**. Lippi **6**. Giotti **7**. da Vinci, Raphael **10**. Botticelli **11**. Della Robbia **12**. Michelangelo
patriot.. **7**. Foscolo **9**. Garibaldi
people.. **7**. Italici **8**. Umbrians **9**. Etruscans, Ligurians
philosopher.. **7**. Rosmini
physician.. **5**. Abano **9**. Eustachio
physicist.. **5**. Volta **7**. Galvani, Marconi
poet.. **4**. Redi **5**. Dante, Tasso **7**. Manzoni **8**. Annunzio, Casanova, Petrarch **9**. Boccaccio
saint.. **4**. Neri **7**. Aquinas (Thomas)
sculptor.. **5**. Dupre, Leoni **8**. Ammanati **12**. Michelangelo
singer.. **5**. Patti **6**. Caruso
statesman.. **5**. Rossi **8**. Gioberti **11**. Machiavelli
theologian.. **7**. Peronne
tribe (anc).. **5**. Aequi
Italy...
 Alps.. **5**. Cozie **6**. Carnac, Julian **7**. Atesine, Letiche, Pennine **8**. Maritime **9**. Lepontine
 capital.. **4**. Rome
 city.. **4**. Lodi, Pisa **5**. Anona, Fiume, Genoa, Milan, Padua, Pavia, Trent, Turin **6**. Mantua, Modena, Naples, Spezia, Venice, Verona **7**. Messina, Palermo, Pompeii, Ravenna, Trieste **8**. Brandisi, Florence, Sorrento
 commune.. **6**. Rivoli (Hist) **7**. Trieste
 country (anc).. **7**. Etruria, Lucania, Tuscany
 gulf.. **7**. Salerno
 historical site.. **10**. Blue Grotto **18**. Leaning Tower of Pisa
 island.. **4**. Elba **5**. Capri, Leros **6**. Eschia, Sicily **8**. Sardinia
 lake.. **4**. Como **6**. Albano, Lugano **8**. Maggiore
 mountain.. **4**. Alps, Rosa **5**. Blanc **12**. Gran Paradiso
 port (fishing).. **6**. Amalfi
 resort.. **4**. Lido **5**. Capri **6**. Agnone **7**. Riviera
 river.. **2**. Po **4**. Arno **5**. Tiber
 sea.. **6**. Ionian **8**. Apennine

 10. Tyrrhenian
 strait.. **7**. Messina, Obranto
 volcano.. **4**. Etna **8**. Vesuvius **9**. Stromboli
itch... **4**. reef, riff **5**. mange, psora **6**. desire, eczema **7**. scabies, sycosis **9**. cacoethes, hankering, psoriasis, sensation **10**. irritation
ite... **8**. adherent, disciple, follower
item... **3**. bit **4**. news **5**. asset, entry, scrap, topic **6**. detail **7**. article, integer **9**. commodity **10**. memorandum **11**. information
iter... **4**. eyre, road (Rom) **7**. circuit
iterate... **6**. recite, repeat, retell, review **7**. recount **8**. rehearse
iteration... **5**. recap **10**. repetition **11**. restatement
ithand... **8**. constant, diligent **14**. unintermittent
itinerant... **5**. mover, nomad **6**. roamer **7**. nomadic **8**. gadabout **9**. traveling, unsettled, wandering, wayfaring
itinerary... **4**. gest (royal), plan **5**. route **6**. prayer, record **8**. register, roadbook **9**. directory, guidebook
Ivanhoe (pert to)...
 author.. **5**. Scott
 character.. **5**. Boeuf **6**. Cedric, Rowena, Ulrica
 hero.. **7**. Ivanhoe
ivories (pert to)...
 anatomy.. **5**. teeth
 game.. **4**. dice
 piano.. **4**. keys
ivory (pert to)...
 anatomy.. **5**. tooth **7**. dentine
 block.. **4**. dice **7**. tessera
 carving.. **9**. toreutics
 color.. **5**. white (off)
 Latin.. **4**. ebur
 mixture (dust, cement).. **7**. eburine
 plum.. **11**. wintergreen
 tower.. **7**. retreat
ivy... **5**. Rheus, sumac **11**. Hedera helix
iwa... **11**. frigate bird
IWW... **6**. sab–cat (emblem), wabbly (Chin), wobbly
Izaac Walton... **9**. fisherman
izar (Hind)... **4**. star **7**. garment **9**. loin cloth
izle... **4**. root **5**. ember, spark
Izmir... **6**. Smyrna
izzat... **5**. honor **6**. credit **8**. prestige **10**. reputation

J

J . . . 3. Jay 6. letter (10th)
ja (Ger) . . . 3. yes
jaal goat . . . 4. ibex 5. beden
jab . . . 3. dig, hit, jag 4. poke, prod,
stab 5. punch 6. strike, thrust
jabber . . . 4. chat 5. prate 6. babble,
gabble, jargon 7. chatter, twaddle
8. nonsense 9. gibberish
Jabberwock . . . 6. Jubjub 7. monster
(Through the Looking Glass)
Jabberwocky . . . 4. poem 6. prolix
8. nonsense 10. double talk
jabble . . . 6. splash 7. dashing
8. rippling 9. agitation, confusion,
splashing
jabiru . . . 5. stork
jack . . . 3. can, jug, man 4. card, coat,
flag, male, pump 5. hoist, knave,
money 6. lifter, sailor 7. mariner
8. nickname
jackal . . . 3. dog (wild) 4. dieb, kola,
Thos 7. cat's–paw 8. henchman
jackass . . . 3. ass 4. deer (mule), dolt,
fool, hare, nerd 6. clover, donkey,
rabbit 7. morwong, penguin, witling
9. blockhead
jackdaw . . . 3. daw, kae 4. crow
7. grackle
jacket . . . 4. coat, Eton, pelt 5. cover
(book) 6. blazer, blouse, bolero,
casing, jerkin, jumper, reefer
7. garment, Mae West, wrapper
jacket (pert to) . . .
Arctic . . 6. anorak
armor . . 5. acton
Eskimo . . 6. temiak
horseback riding . . 7. hacking (jacket)
knitted . . 6. jersey, sontag 7. sweater
8. cardigan
Levant . . 5. grego
Scottish . . 4. jupe
Spanish . . 8. chaqueta
Jack Ketch . . . 7. hangman (Eng)
11. executioner (public)
jackknife . . . 6. barlow 8. penknife
11. toadstabber, toadsticker
jackstones . . . 4. dibs, game
7. pebbles
Jacob . . . 6. Israel 9. patriarch
Jacob (pert to) . . .
brother . . 4. Edom, Esau
daughter . . 5. Dinah
father–in–law . . 5. Laban
parents . . 5. Isaac 7. Rebekah
retreat . . 5. Haran
son . . 3. Gad, Dan 4. Levi 5. Asher,
Judah 6. Reuben (oldest)
wife . . 4. Leah 6. Rachel
Jacobin . . . 4. Club 5. Friar (Dominican)
7. plotter, radical, Society

8. Democrat (Fr 1789)
Jacob's ladder . . . 4. herb 8. hyacinth
10. belladonna 11. bittersweet
12. Solomon's seal
jade . . . 4. bore, tire 5. green, horse,
stone, wench 7. fatigue 8. strumpet
jaded . . . 8. fatigued, shopworn
9. dissolute 10. bedraggled
jaeger (jager) . . . 4. gull (like), skua
6. teaser
jager . . . 6. hunter 7. diamond
8. huntsman, rifleman
jagged . . . 5. erose, rough, sharp
6. barbed, pinked, ragged, rugged
7. cutting, notched, pointed, slashed
8. serrated 10. saw–toothed
jagua . . . 4. palm 7. genipap
jaguar . . . 3. cat 4. puma 5. ounce
6. cougar 7. panther 11. snow
leopard
Jah (Heb) . . . 3. God 7. Jehovah
jai alai . . . 4. game 5. cesta 6. pelota
7. fronton
jail . . . 3. jug 4. brig, gaol 5. clink
6. cooler, lockup 7. slammer (sl)
8. hoosegow 9. Bridewell (London),
calaboose 11. incarcerate
jailer, jailor . . . 5. quard 6. gaoler,
keeper, warden 7. alcaide, turnkey
jail sentence . . . 3. rap
jalousie . . . 5. blind 7. shutter
Jamaica . . .
beverage . . 3. rum 4. jake
capital . . 8. Kingston
cucumber . . 7. gherkin
ebony . . 10. crocuswood
island . . 10. West Indies
pepper . . 8. allspice
tree (drug) . . 7. quassia
jangle . . . 5. brawl, chide, noise, prate
6. babble, gossip 7. chatter, grate on,
quarrel, ringing, whimper
Janizary (anc) . . . 5. slave 7. soldier
Janus (Rom) . . . 3. god (two–faced)
Japan . . . 5. Jipun (Chin), Nihon, Nisei
6. Nippon 7. Cipango (of Marco
Polo)
Japan . . . see also *Japanese*
capital . . 4. Nara (anc) 5. Kyoto (anc),
Tokyo
city . . 4. Kobe 7. Sapporo
8. Kawasaki, Kumamoto, Nagasaki,
Yokohama, Yokosuka 9. Hiroshima
10. Kitakyushu
current . . 8. Kuroshio
islands . . 6. Honshu, Kyushu
7. Shikoku 9. Haikkaido (Yezo)
mountain . . 8. Fujiyama
naval base . . 8. Yokosuka
port . . 4. Kobe 5. Osaka 6. Nagoya

J
N

8. Yokohama
protectorate.. 9. Manchukuo
river.. 4. Yalu (Annock)
shrine.. 7. Toshogu (at Nikko)
spring (hot).. 6. Hakone
volcano.. 9. Asamayama
Japanese (pert to)...
airplane.. 4. Zero
annals, chronicles.. 7. Nihongi
apricot.. 3. ume
army (conscription).. 6. geneki
army officer.. 7. samurai
art of self–defense.. 4. judo 7. jujitsu
  (jujutsu, jiujutsu)
badge (family).. 3. mon
banjo.. 7. samisen
battle cry.. 6. banzai
brazier.. 7. hibachi
button (carved).. 7. netsuke
cape.. 4. mino
cedar.. 4. sugi
chess.. 5. shogi
church (Buddhist).. 4. tera
circle, ship (suffix).. 4. maru
deer.. 4. sika
dog.. 6. tanate
drama.. 2. no 6. no–gaku
drink.. 4. sake
entertainer.. 6. geisha
festival.. 3. Bon 15. Feast of Lanterns
fish.. 3. ayu, tai 4. fugu
flower arranging.. 7. ikebano
flower design.. 10. Shin, Soe, Tai
  (Heaven, Man, Earth)
game (forfeits).. 3. ken
gateway.. 5. torii
girdle.. 3. obi
girdle box.. 4. inro
greeting.. 6. banzai
herb (edible).. 3. udo
legislature.. 4. Diet
litter (covered).. 7. norimon
news agency.. 5. domei
newspaper (Tokyo).. 12. Asahi
  Shimbun
outlaw.. 5. ronin
pagoda.. 3. taa
painting school.. 4. Kano
palanquin, litter.. 4. pago 7. norimon
persimmon.. 4. kaki
plant.. 3. udo (edible) 6. sugamo
porgy.. 3. tai (fish)
pottery.. 7. Satsuma
prefecture.. 2. fu
radish.. 6. daikon
religion.. 6. Shinto 8. Buddhism
  9. Shintoism
robe.. 6. kimono
salmon.. 4. masu
screen (partition).. 5. shoji
seaweed.. 4. nori
self–defense, art of.. 4. judo 7. jujitsu
  (jujutsu, jiujutsu)
ship suffix.. 4. maru
shout (greeting).. 6. banzai
shrine.. 7. Toshogu (at Nikko)
silk.. 7. habutai 8. chirimen (crepe)
silkworm.. 4. eria 7. yamamai
sock (separate big toe).. 4. tabi
song.. 3. uta
suicide.. 7. seppuku 8. hara–kiri
  (hari–kari)

tree.. 5. akeki, kiaki 7. camphor,
  hinooki
verse.. 5. hokku, tanka 6. haikai
wrestling.. 4. sumo
Japanese people...
aborigine.. 4. Ainu (Aino)
admiral.. 3. Ito 4. Togo
admirer.. 11. Japanophile
American–born.. 5. Issei, Nisei
army officer.. 7. samurai
baron.. 6. daimio
Buddha, Great.. 8. Daibutsu
caste (nobility).. 7. kwazoku
clan.. 7. Satsuma 8. Fujiwara,
  Minamoto
deity.. 5. Amita (Amida) 8. Amitabba
Emperor.. 8. Hirohito
Emperor, founder.. 5. Jimmu (660
  BC)
Emperor, title.. 5. Tenno 6. Mikado
God of Happiness.. 7. Jurojin
  10. Fuku–roku ju
nobility (caste).. 7. kwazoku
outlaw.. 5. ronin
paradise (of Amita).. 4. Jodo
race.. 4. Ainu
jape... 4. fool, jeer, jest, jipe, mock
  5. fraud, trick 6. banter, deride
japery... 4. jest, joke 7. jesting
  8. trickery 10. buffoonery
jar... 4. jolt 5. grate, shake 6. incase,
  rattle 7. startle, vibrate 8. preserve
  9. vibration
jar... 3. jug, urn 4. ewer, lute
  (rubber), olla 5. cadus (anc), crock,
  cruse 6. dolium, goglet, hydria
  7. amphora, terrine 10. jardiniere
jararaca... 7. serpent 10. fer–de–lance
  11. jararacussu
jardiniere... 3. jar, jug, urn 4. vase
  5. stand (plant) 9. flowerpot
jargon... 4. cant 5. argot, idiom, lingo,
  slang 6. drivel, patois, patter, zircon
  7. Chinook, Yiddish 8. nonsense
  9. gibberish 10. vocabulary (secret)
jasmine, jasmin... 4. bela 5. color,
  papaw 7. jessamy 9. jessamine
Jason (pert to)...
friend, sweetheart.. 5. Medea
heroes.. 9. Argonauts
quest.. 12. Golden Fleece
ship.. 4. Argo
son.. 5. Aeson
uncle.. 6. Pelias
jaundice... 7. disease, icterus
  8. jealousy 9. prejudice
  10. yellowness
jaunt... 4. ride, trip 6. ramble
  7. journey 9. excursion
jaunty... 4. airy 5. perky, showy, smart
  6. dapper, rakish 7. finical, stylish
  12. lighthearted
Java... see also *Javanese*
city.. 7. Batavia, Jakarta (Djakarta)
  8. Samarang, Surabaya 9. Surakarta
island group.. 10. East Indies
Java Man (anc).. 15. Pithecanthropus
  (erectus)
location.. 7. equator 16. Malay
  Archipelago
Javanese (pert to)...
arrow poison.. 4. upas

badger.. 5. ratel 6. teledu
carriage.. 4. sado (sadoo)
cotton.. 5. kapok
dancers.. 6. bedoyo
dog (wild).. 5. adjag
ox (wild).. 7. banteng
pantomime.. 6. topeng
plum.. 5. jambo (jambul) 6. lomboy
puppet show.. 6. wajang (wayang)
rice field.. 5. sawah
squirrel.. 8. jelerang
temple.. 6. chandi (candi)
tree.. 4. upas 5. ligas 7. gondang
javelin ... 3. bat 4. dart, pike 5. lance,
     spear 6. jereed (jirid) 7. assagai
     (assegai)
javelina ... 4. boar 7. peccary
jaw ... 3. maw 4. chop 5. scold
     6. berate, splash 7. chatter, orifice
     8. scolding
jaw (pert to) ...
angle of.. 6. gonion
bone.. 7. maxilla 8. mandible
comb form.. 6. gnatho
disease.. 7. lump jaw
     13. actinomycosis
formation.. 8. gnathism
Greek for.. 7. gnathos
muscle.. 8. masseter
ref to.. 5. malar 7. gnathic
without.. 8. agnathic
jawab ... 5. reply 6. answer, mosque
     (false Arch)
jay ... 3. gae 4. bird, blue, dupe
     9. chatterer
jayhawker ... 6. Kansan, spider
     7. soldier 8. guerilla
Jayhawker State ... 6. Kansas
jazz ... 4. jive 5. dance, music, swing
     8. synoopata 11. synoopation
jealous ... 7. envious, zealous
     8. doubtful, grudging, vigilant,
     watchful 9. jaundiced 10. solicitous
     11. distrustful 12. apprehensive
jealousy ... 4. envy 5. doubt 7. rivalry
     8. distrust, jaundice, mistrust
     12. covetousness
jeans ... 8. overalls, trousers
jeer ... 4. gibe, hoot, jape, mock
     5. flout, scoff, sneer, taunt 6. deride
     8. ridicule
Jehovah ... 3. God, Jah 4. Lord
     6. Yahweh (Yahwe) 8. Almighty (The)
     12. Supreme Being
Jehovah's comfort ... 8. Nehemiah
jehu (humorous) ... 8. coachman
     10. fast driver
Jehu's father (Bib) ... 11. Jehoshaphat
jejune ... 3. dry 4. arid 5. banal,
     empty, stale, trite 6. barren, hungry,
     meager 7. insipid 8. foodless
     12. unproductive
jelly ... 3. jam, rob (rhob) 4. food,
     sapa 5. aspic 6. pectin 7. gelatin
     8. gelatine, Kei Apple 10. semiliquid
jellyfish ... 5. quarl 6. coward, medusa
     7. acaleph 8. weakling 9. Acalephae
jellyfish (pert to) ...
class.. 9. Acalephae
group.. 10. discophora
part.. 6. pileus 8. umbrella
     10. exumbrella

stinging.. 9. sea nettle
swim organ.. 5. stene
jemmy ... 4. boot (riding) 5. jimmy,
     lever 7. crowbar 9. greatcoat
Jena (Ger) ... 5. glass 6. battle (1806)
jenna ... 8. Paradise (Moham)
jennet ... 3. ass 5. horse 6. donkey
jenny ... 3. ass 5. crane (moving)
     6. female 8. airplane 13. spinning
     wheel
jenny (pert to) ...
billiards.. 6. hazard
folklore.. 4. wren
howlet.. 3. owl 5. owlet
machine.. 13. spinning wheel
spinner.. 3. fly (angling)
jeopardize ... 4. risk 6. expose, hazard
     7. imperil 8. endanger
jeopardy ... 4. risk 5. peril 6. hazard,
     menace
jeremiad ... 3. woe 6. lament, plaint,
     tirade 9. complaint
jerk ... 3. tic 4. flip, jolt, push, yank
     5. shake, tweak 6. chorea, thrust,
     twitch 7. charqui
jerkin ... 4. coat 6. jacket, salmon
     9. gyrfalcon, waistcoat
jeroboam ... 4. bowl 6. battle, goblet
Jeroboam ... 4. King (of Israel)
jerry ... 5. aware 6. flimsy, Geremy,
     German 7. knowing 9. beer house,
     conscious
jersey ... 5. cloth 6. cattle, jacket
Jersey Red ... 5. swine
     11. Duroc—Jersey
Jersey tea ... 11. wintergreen
     12. checkerberry
Jerusalem ... 5. Ariel, Salem 8. Holy
     City 11. City of David
Jerusalem (pert to) ...
artichoke.. 7. girasol 10. topinambou
capital of.. 6. Israel
corn.. 5. durra
Garden.. 10. Gethsemane
haddock.. 4. opah
hill.. 6. Olivet 13. Mount of Olives
historic site.. 11. Wailing Wall
     12. Mosque of Omar 13. Mount of
     Olives (Olivet) 18. Garden of
     Gethsemane
mosque.. 4. Omar
pool.. 6. Siloam 8. Bethesda
region.. 5. Perea 6. Gilead
Relig.. 7. Judaism 12. Christianity
     13. Mohammedanism
spring.. 5. Gihon 6. Siloam
star.. 7. salsify
Sunday.. 11. Refreshment
thorn.. 7. catechu 12. Christ's—thorn
willow.. 8. oleaster
jess ... 5. strap (hawk's leg) 6. ribbon
jessamy ... 3. fop 5. dandy 7. jasmine
jessant (Her) ... 7. issuing 9. lying over
jessur ... 5. viper (Russell's)
jest ... 3. fun, mot, wit 4. fool, jape,
     jeer, joke, quip 5. droll, prank, sport,
     taunt, trick 6. banter, rail at, trifle
     8. ridicule
jester ... 4. fool, mime 5. clown
     7. buffoon, goliard 8. humorist
     11. merry—andrew
jester's cap ... 7. coxcomb

Jesuit... 5. Order 7. casuist, sectary 8. explorer 9. intriguer 10. missionary 14. Society of Jesus (S J)

jet... 3. jut 4. gush, spew 5. black, ebony, ladle, raven, spout, spray, spurt 6. burner, nozzle, stream 7. mineral, outpour 8. spouting 9. black onyx

jet coal... 6. cannel

jetty... 4. mole, pier 5. wharf 8. buttress

Jew... 6. Essene, Hebrew, Semite 9. Israelite

jewel... 3. gem 4. naif, opal, ruby 5. beryl, stone 6. garnet 7. bearing, diamond, emerald 8. ornament 9. bespangle, brilliant 10. rhinestone 13. precious stone, precious thing

jewel cutter... 10. lapidarist

jeweler's glass... 5. loupe

jeweler's weight... 4. tola 5. carat (karat, kerat)

jewelry... 3. ice 4. ring 5. paste 6. parure, strass 7. costume 10. bijouterie

Jewish... 6. Hebrew 7. Yiddish 9. Israelite

Jewish (pert to)...
academy (Talmudic).. 8. Yeshinah
adherent.. 7. Zionist
benediction.. 5. Shema
Bible.. 5. Torah (Tora) 6. Gemara, Talmud 7. Haggada, Halakah 10. Pentateuch
calendar.. 4. Adar, Ahab, Elul, Iyar 5. Nisan, Sivan, Tebet 6. Kislev, Shebat, Tammuz, Tishri, Veadar (leap year) 7. Heshvan
Day of Atonement.. 9. Yom Kippur
Dispersion.. 8. Diaspora
divorce.. 3. get (gett)
doctrine.. 7. Mishnah (Mishna)
enemy (Bib).. 5. Haman
faction.. 7. Zealots
father, patriarch.. 7. Abraham
festival.. 5. Purim, Seder (Sedar) 7. Sukkoth
greeting, peace.. 6. Shalom
high priest.. 3. Eli 4. Ezra 5. Aaron, Annas 8. Caiaphas
high priest costume.. 4. urim 5. abnet 7. petalon, tallith, yamilke
historian.. 8. Josephus
holiday.. 7. Sukkoth 8. Hanukkah (Hannukka), Tishabov 11. Rosh Hashana (Rosh Hashonoh)
horn.. 7. shophar (shofar)
lawgiver.. 5. Moses
leader.. 8. Nehemiah
liturgy.. 6. minhah (PM) 9. shaharith (AM)
loaves (unleavened).. 9. shewbread (showbread)
mystical writing.. 6. atbash
patriots.. 9. Maccabees
prayer book.. 6. siddur
prophet.. 6. Elijah
psalms of praise.. 6. hallel
quarter (living).. 6. ghetto
ram's horn.. 7. shophar (shofar)
slaughter (Relig).. 8. shehitah

song (Zionist anthem).. 8. Hatikvah (Hattikvah)

jew's harp... 8. guimbard 9. crembalum

Jezebel (pert to)...
epithet.. 5. vixen 6. virago 8. strumpet
father.. 7. Ethbaal
husband.. 4. Ahab (King)
murdered (caused to be).. 6. Naboth

jib... 3. gib, jaw 4. balk, boom, sail, spar, tack 5. crane, shift 6. fleece 8. underlip

jibe... 3. fit 4. gibe 5. agree, shift 9. harmonize

jiff, jiffy... 5. trice 6. moment 7. instant, quickly 9. instantly, twinkling

jig... 4. jerk, jolt 5. dance 6. ballad, twitch 8. fishhook

jigger... 4. club, dram

jiggle... 5. sauce, shake

jimmy... 3. pry 5. handy, smart 6. spruce 7. coal car, crowbar, pry open 10. sheep's head

jimson weed... 6. dature 10. stramonium, thorn apple 11. apple of Peru

jingle... 4. poem, rime 5. clink, rhyme 6. tinkle 13. two–wheeled car

jinn, jinnee... 5. demon, Eblis, genie 6. afreet 8. jenniyeh

jinx... 3. hex 5. Jonah 6. hoodoo, whammy

jitters... 6. nerves 7. dithers, fidgets 8. trembles

jittery... 4. edgy 5. jumpy 7. nervous

jivatma (Hind)... 4. soul 9. life force 10. life energy 11. human spirit

Joan of Arc's appellation...
7. pucelle 13. Maid of Orleans

job... 3. act 4. hire, task 5. chare, chore, stint 8. position, sinecure

Job (pert to)...
Book.. 9. patriarch 12. Old Testament
friend.. 6. Zophar
home.. 2. Uz
literally.. 9. afflicted 10. persecuted

jockey... 3. pad 5. cheat, racer, rider 6. outwit 7. cushion 8. cavalier, horseman, minstrel, vagabond 9. Earl Sande (famed)

jocose... 3. dry 5. droll, lepid, merry 7. jocular 8. humorous 9. facetious

jocular... 3. gay 4. airy, loco 5. droll, funny, merry, witty 6. elated, jocund, lively, ribald 7. comical, festive, gleeful, jesting, playful, waggish 8. animated, mirthful 9. convivial, facetious, hilarious, laughable, vivacious 10. frolicsome

jocund... 3. gay 4. airy 5. merry 6. lively 7. jocular 8. cheerful, sportive

jog... 4. gait, jolt, lope, plod, push, trot, walk 6. canter, notify, remind, trudge 8. slow pace 9. suggest to

John... 3. Ian 4. Ivan, Jack, Juan 8. Chinaman, Johannes 9. policeman

John (pert to)...
Bull.. 10. Englishman
Company.. 9. East India

Crow.. **7.** buzzard (turkey)
Doe (law).. **7.** a nobody **9.** false name
Hancock.. **9.** autograph, signature
Q Public.. **6.** people **8.** populace
johnnycake... **4.** pone **7.** hoecake
9. corn bread
join... **3.** add, mix, pin, tie, wed
4. ally, fuse, link, lock, meet, pair,
seam, team, weld, yoke **5.** annex,
blend, enter, graft, group, hitch, marry,
merge, unite **6.** adjoin, attach,
cement, concur, couple, engage,
enlist, fasten, mingle, solder, splice,
suture, syzygy **7.** combine, conjoin,
connect **8.** assemble, coalesce,
compound **9.** associate
11. incorporate
joint... **3.** ell, hip **4.** dive (sl), knee,
node, seam **5.** alula, elbow, hinge,
miter, nexus, tenon, wrist **6.** rabbet,
resort **7.** hangout, pastern
8. coupling, dovetail **12.** articulation
joint (pert to)...
cavity.. **5.** bursa
firs.. **7.** ephedra
fluid.. **7.** synovia **8.** synovial
grass stem.. **4.** culm
pert to.. **5.** nodal **9.** articular
put out of.. **6.** lucate **9.** dislocate
without.. **10.** acondylous
Joke... **3.** fun, gag, pun **4.** fool, hoax,
jape, jest, quip **5.** prank, rally, sport
6. banter, humbug **7.** bromide
8. chestnut, one–liner
joker... **3.** dor, wag, wit **4.** card
7. buffoon, farceur, gagster
8. humorist **9.** mistigris
jollity... **4.** jest **5.** mirth **6.** gaiety
8. hilarity **9.** enjoyment, festivity,
joviality, merriment **12.** conviviality
jolly... **6.** banter, jovial, joyful, mellow
7. flatter, jocular **9.** make merry
Jolly Roger... **5.** Roger **10.** pirate flag
jolt... **3.** jar, jig, jut **4.** blow, butt, stun
5. shake, shock **6.** jostle, jounce
7. startle **8.** astonish, jail term
(thieves')
Jonah (pert to)...
Bib.. **7.** prophet (Heb)
Book.. **12.** Old Testament
slang.. **4.** jinx
swallowed by.. **5.** whale
Jordan...
capital.. **5.** Amman
city.. **7.** Jericho, Samaria
9. Bethlehem
historic trove.. **14.** Dead Sea Scrolls
official name.. **9.** Hashemite (The)
people (anc).. **7.** Essenes
region.. **5.** Perea **6.** Basham
river.. **6.** Jordan
Jorth (pert to)...
goddess.. **5.** Earth
husband.. **4.** Odin
named also.. **6.** Forgyn
son.. **4.** Thor
Joseph (pert to)...
Bib.. **9.** patriarch
buyer of.. **8.** Potiphar
called also.. **17.** Joseph of Arimathea
coat of.. **10.** many colors
father.. **5.** Jacob

mother.. **6.** Rachel
son.. **5.** Jesus **7.** Ephraim
josh... **3.** guy, kid **5.** chaff, spoof,
tease **6.** banter
Joshi (Ind)... **10.** astrologer,
astronomer
Joshua (pert to)...
associate.. **5.** Caleb
Book.. **12.** Old Testament
burial place.. **5.** Gaash
successor to.. **5.** Moses
tree.. **5.** yucca
jostle... **4.** jolt, push, rush **5.** crowd,
elbow, joust, shake, shove **6.** hustle,
joggle, jounce, thrust
jot... **3.** ace, bit **4.** atom, iota, item,
mite, whit **5.** minim, point, speck
6. tittle **7.** smidgen **8.** particle
jouk... **4.** dart, duck, fawn, hide
5. cheat, dodge, evade, perch, roost,
skulk **6.** cringe **9.** obeisance
Joule, James P... **9.** physicist
journal... **3.** log **5.** diary, paper
6. record **7.** daybook, diurnal,
logbook, support **8.** magazine, register
9. chronicle **10.** periodical
11. account book
journalist... **6.** editor, legman
7. newsman **8.** reporter **9.** columnist,
gazetteer **11.** interviewer
13. correspondent
journey... **3.** run **4.** fare, iter, ride,
tour, trek, trip, wend **5.** jaunt
6. travel, voyage **7.** odyssey
8. traverse **9.** excursion
10. expedition, pilgrimage
13. peregrination
journey (pert to)... **4.** eyre (circuit)
6. viatic **8.** anabasis (upward)
9. itinerary, itinerary, traveling
10. travelling
joust... **4.** bout, spar, tilt **6.** combat
10. tournament
Jove... **7.** Jupiter
jovial... **5.** jolly, merry **6.** elated,
joyous **7.** festive, jocular **8.** Jovelike
9. convivial, hilarious
14. mirth–inspiring
jowl... **3.** jaw **4.** chop **5.** cheek
6. dewlap, wattle **7.** jawbone
joy... **4.** glee **5.** bliss, exult, gelid
6. gaiety **7.** delight, ecstasy, rapture,
rejoice **8.** felicity, gladness, hilarity,
pleasure **9.** beatitude, happiness,
merriment, transport **10.** exultation
12. exhilaration
joyous... **3.** gay **4.** glad **5.** happy,
merry **6.** blithe, elated, festal, joyful
7. festive, gleeful, jocular **8.** cheerful,
mirthful
jubilant... **6.** elated **8.** exultant,
exulting **9.** overjoyed, rejoicing
10. triumphant
Judah (pert to)...
ancestry.. **12.** tribe of Judah
brother.. **4.** Levi **6.** Reuben, Simeon
father.. **5.** Jacob
kingdom.. **9.** Palestine
son.. **2.** Er **6.** Shelah
translation (Heb).. **10.** celebrated
Judas (pert to)...
Bible.. **7.** apostle, traitor **8.** betrayer,

deceiver, disciple
called .. **8.** Iscariot
historic .. **13.** Paschal candle
kiss .. **8.** betrayal **11.** double–cross,
treacherous
priest .. **4.** oath
suicide site .. **8.** Aceldama
Judea (pert to) ...
governor .. **6.** Pilate
king .. **3.** Asa **5.** Herod **7.** Jehoram
11. Jehoshaphat
location .. **5.** Berea
people .. **4.** Jews
province of .. **9.** Palestine
judge ... **3.** try **4.** deem, rate **5.** opine,
think **6.** critic, puisne **7.** arbiter,
referee, suppose **8.** deemster,
estimate, mediator, sentence
9. arbitrate, criticize **10.** adjudicate,
magistrate **11.** connoisseur
judge (pert to) ...
bench .. **4.** banc (bancus)
chamber .. **6.** camera
circuit .. **4.** iter
gavel .. **4.** mace
group .. **5.** bench **9.** judiciary
of the dead .. **6.** Osiris
opinion .. **12.** obiter dictum
sittings .. **7.** assizes
summary .. **6.** postea
judgment ... **4.** doom **5.** arrêt, award,
sense, taste **7.** censure, opinion
8. decision, judicium, sentence
9. criticism **10.** conclusion,
discretion, persuasion (Relig),
punishment **11.** arbitration, sensibility
judgment (pert to) ...
creditor .. **13.** quasi contract
day .. **7.** last day **8.** Dies Irae,
doomsday
left to one's .. **13.** discretionary
note .. **10.** promissory
seat .. **3.** bar **5.** mercy **8.** tribunal,
woolsack
judicial ... **5.** legal **8.** critical
9. judicious **10.** judicatory
judicial (pert to) ...
council .. **5.** cabal, junta, junto
7. coterie
hearing .. **5.** trial
order .. **4.** writ **6.** elegit, venire
7. precept
security .. **7.** custody
judicious ... **4.** wise **7.** politic, prudent
8. cautious, discreet **9.** sagacious
10. discerning **11.** circumspect,
well–advised
jug ... **4.** ewer, jail, olpe, toby
5. askos, buire, cruse, gotch
6. flagon, gomlah, lockup, prison,
tinaja, urceus **7.** pitcher
13. Schnabelkanne
Juggernaut ... **6.** Vishnu (Hind)
juggler ... **5.** cheat, trick **7.** buffoon
8. deceiver **13.** sleight of hand
14. legerdemainist
Jugoslavia, Yugoslavia ...
area .. **6.** Kosovo **8.** Dalmatia
brandy .. **5.** rakia **9.** slivovitz
capital .. **8.** Belgrade
language .. **7.** Slovene
10. Macedonian, Serbo–Croat

leader .. **4.** Tito
monarch .. **5.** Peter
money .. **5.** dinar
organization .. **9.** Comitadji
people .. **4.** Cerb **5.** Croat **7.** Slovene
juice ... **3.** rob, sap **4.** milk (plant),
must, stum **5.** fluid, latex, syrup
(sirup) **7.** essence, hebenon, moisten
10. succulence **11.** electricity
jujitsu, jiujitsu ... **11.** self–defense
juju ... **5.** charm, magic **6.** amulet,
belief, fetish, voodoo
jujube ... **3.** ber **5.** fruit, jelly
7. lozenge **8.** Zizyphus
Jules Verne's captain ... **4.** Nemo (the
Nautilus)
Julian Emperors (first Five) ... **4.** Nero
8. Augustus, Caligula, Claudius,
Tiberius
jumble ... **2.** pi **3.** mix **4.** cake, hash,
heap, mess, raff, stir **5.** blend,
botch, chaos, shake **6.** medley,
muddle **7.** agitate, confuse, mixture
8. disorder, riffraff
jumble type ... **3.** pie (pi)
jump ... **3.** hop, lep **4.** leap, move
(checkers) **5.** bound, caper, halma,
salto, scold, start, vault **6.** chorea,
escape, hurdle, spring, twitch
7. saltary, saltate **8.** increase
9. advantage **10.** transition
jumping (pert to) ...
adjective .. **7.** saltant
Frog, tale by .. **9.** Mark Twain
music .. **7.** saltato
rodent .. **5.** mouse **6.** jerboa
11. kangaroo rat
stick .. **4.** pogo, pole
junction ... **4.** axil, seam **5.** union
6. suture **7.** joining, meeting
11. combination, concurrence
juncture ... **4.** pass **5.** joint, pinch
6. crisis, strait **8.** exigency, quandary
9. emergency **10.** connection
11. conjuncture, predicament
12. articulation
June bug ... **3.** dor **6.** beetle, May bug
8. figeater
jungle ... **4.** camp **7.** thicket
8. woodland **11.** dense growth
12. complication
jungle (pert to) ...
dweller .. **5.** beast **6.** savage
fever .. **7.** malaria
grass .. **3.** poa
ox .. **4.** gaur **5.** gayal **7.** timarau
sheep .. **7.** muntjac
junior ... **5.** cadet, petty **6.** puisne,
recent **7.** student, younger **8.** inferior
9. unskilled
juniper ... **4.** cade, puny **5.** cedar,
gorse, retem (raetem), savin
junket ... **4.** dish (milk), food, meal
5. feast **7.** banquet **8.** festival
9. excursion, sweetmeat
Juno (pert to) ...
consort .. **7.** Jupiter
goddess (Rom) .. **3.** sky **5.** light
identified with .. **4.** Hera
messenger .. **4.** Iris
junta, junto ... **5.** cabal **6.** circle,
clique **7.** coterie, council, faction

8. intrigue 11. combination
jupe... 4. coat 5. jupon, shirt, skirt,
   tunic 6. bodice, jacket
Jupiter (pert to)...
   angel.. 7. Zadkiel
   astronomy.. 6. planet (largest)
   daughter.. 4. Bura
   deity.. 4. Jove 9. Father Sky
   festival.. 14. Vinalis sustica
   god of.. 7. Heavens
   heraldry.. 5. azure
   lover.. 2. Io
   son.. 6. Castor, Pollux
   triad.. 4. Juno 7. Minerva
   wife.. 4. Juno
Jupiter, god of...
   law.. 6. Fidius 10. Dius Fidius
   lightning.. 6. Fulgur
   rain.. 7. Pluvius
   thunder.. 6. Tonans
jurat... 5. juror 8. recorder
   10. magistrate (Channel Isls)
jure... 3. jus (ius), law 5. right
   13. jurisprudence
jurisprudence... 3. law, soc 4. soke
   5. power (legal) 6. charge, sphere
   7. control, custody, emirate
   9. authority, consulate
   10. government, judicature, patriarchy
juror... 6. dicast 7. assizer, juryman
   9. venireman
jury... 5. panel, tales (additions)
   6. venire
jus... 3. law 5. gravy, juice 10. legal
   power, legal right
just... 4. fair, tilt 5. equal, exact, valid
   7. logical, upright 8. provided,
   unbiased 9. equitable, righteous
   10. legitimate

just begun... 8. inchoate
justice... 4. doom 5. right 6. equity,
   virtue 8. fairness, fair play, justness
   9. rectitude 10. judicature 11. give
   and take 12. rightfulness
justice of the peace... 6. squire
   10. magistrate
justification... 7. apology, defense
   11. vindication
justify... 5. clear 6. defend, excuse
   7. absolve, support, warrant
   8. maintain, sanction, underpin
   9. authorize, exculpate, vindicate
   12. substantiate
justly... 5. truly 6. fairly 7. equally
   8. honestly 9. equitably
   10. deservedly
justness... 7. fitness, justice
   8. accuracy, validity 9. exactness
   11. correctness
Justus... 4. just
jute... 5. fiber, gunny 6. burlap
   7. sacking
Jute... 4. Dane 9. Jutlander
jutty... 4. mole, pier 5. jetty
   7. project 8. buttress, protrude
juvenile... 5. actor, young, youth
   8. immature, youthful 9. youngling,
   youthlike 11. undeveloped
juvia... 9. Brazil nut
juxta... 4. near 6. nearby
juxtaposition... 5. touch 7. contact
   8. nearness 9. proximity
   10. contiguity, side by side
jynx... 5. charm, spell 7. wryneck
   10. woodpecker
Jynx... 11. woodpeckers
J'y suis, j'y reste... 18. I am here;
   here I remain

K

K... 5. kappa (Gr) 6. letter (11th)
Ka... 3. God (Hind)
Kaaba, Caaba (pert to)...
   content.. 10. Black Stone (of Mecca)
   location.. 11. Great Mosque (Mecca)
   pilgrimage.. 7. Islamic
   praying direction.. 6. Kiblah
   shape.. 7. cubical
kaama... 10. hartebeest
Kaddish... 8. Doxology
Kadiak, Kodiak, bear... 5. brown
   7. Alaskan
Kaffir (pert to)...
   club weapon.. 10. knobkerrie
   country.. 11. South Africa
   creed.. 10. unbeliever
   13. non—Mohammedan
   race.. 5. Bantu
   servant.. 6. umfaan
   tribes (world's tallest).. 4. Xosa, Zulu
   5. Pondo, Temby

   warriors.. 4. impi
   weapon.. 4. keri 10. knobkerrie
Kaiser brown... 6. ginger
Kaiser's residence... 5. Doorn
kaka... 6. parrot
kakapo... 6. parrot 9. owl parrot
kakar... 7. muntjac
kakariki... 6. lizard
kaki... 5. stilt (bird) 9. persimmon
kakkak... 5. heron 7. bittern
kakke... 8. beriberi
kala... 6. bulbul (bird)
kale... 4. cole 5. money 7. cabbage,
   collard 8. colewort, corecole
kaleidoscopic... 7. varying
   10. changeable, variegated
Kali (pert to)...
   Hindu.. 10. evil genius
   Persian.. 6. carpet
   Vedic Myth.. 12. tongue of Agni
   (fire—god)

kallah... 5. bride (Jew)
kamavachara... 6. heaven (Buddh)
Kamchatka...
  capital.. 13. Petropavlovsk
  peninsula.. 7. Siberia
  people.. 7. Russian 9. Mongolian
  sea.. 6. Bering 7. Okhotsk
Kamehameha Day... 7. holiday (Haw)
Kamerad... 7. comrade 9. surrender
kamik... 12. sealskin boot
Kammerspiel... 5. drama 7. theater
Kanaka... 3. man 8. Hawaiian
  10. Melanesian, Polynesian
  16. South Sea islander
Kanaloa... 3. God (Pantheon)
kangaroo (pert to)...
  class.. 9. marsupial
  family.. 12. Macropodidae
  female.. 3. doe, gin, 'roo
  giant.. 8. forester
  leaping.. 6. jeroba 7. bettong
  (bettonga)
  male.. 5. bilby (bilbi)
  rat.. 7. pototoo
  reference to.. 7. wallaby
  11. macropodine
  small.. 7. wallaby
  young.. 4. joey
kangaroo court... 9. mock court, moot
  court 14. irregular court
Kansas...
  capital.. 6. Topeka
  city.. 5. Dodge 7. Abilene, Wichita
  10. Hutchinson, Kansas City
  11. Leavenworth
  Eisenhower home.. 7. Abilene
  military post.. 9. Fort Riley
  penitentiary.. 11. Leavenworth
  State admission.. 12. Thirty–fourth
  State motto.. 16. Ad Astra per
  Aspera (To the Stars Through
  Difficulties)
  State nickname.. 9. Sunflower
kapok tree... 7. God tree 9. Ceiba
  tree 10. silk–cotton
kappa... 1. K (Gr) 4. star 6. letter
  (10th)
karakul, karakule... 5. sheep
  9. astrakhan, broadtail
karma... 4. fate 7. destiny 8. casualty
Kartvelian people... 4. Svan (Svane)
  9. Georgians 10. Imeritians,
  Svanetians
kasha... 4. mush (Russ)
Kashmir, India...
  alphabet.. 6. Sarada
  capital.. 8. Srinagar
  deer.. 6. hangul
  official.. 6. pundit
Kashyapa (Vedic Myth)... 8. tortoise
Kaskaskia... 5. epoch 6. Indian
  10. Algonquian
kat... 5. shrub 8. narcotic
katar... 6. dagger
katchung... 6. peanut
katogle... 8. eagle owl
kava, kavakava... 6. Kawaka, pepper
kayak... 5. canoe
kea... 6. parrot
Keat's poem... 8. Endymion, Hyperion
keek... 3. spy (of rival fashions)
  6. peeper

keel... 4. cool, seel, ship, skeg, tilt
  6. careen, ruddle, timber (ship's)
  7. capsize 8. overturn, red ocher,
  turn over 10. guinea fowl
keelbill, keelbird... 3. ani
keeling... 7. codfish
keel–shaped... 6. carina 7. carinal
keen... 4. avid, cute, gare, good, nice,
  tart 5. acute, alert, eager, sharp,
  smart, snell, vivid, witty 6. astute,
  bitter, clever, shrewd, shrill
  7. caustic, fervent 9. sensitive,
  trenchant 11. acrimonious,
  penetrating
keenness... 4. edge 5. acies (of sight),
  nifty 6. acumen 8. acrimony,
  pungency 9. acuteness, eagerness,
  sharpness, smartness, wittiness
keep... 4. save 6. detain, retain
  7. confine, custody, fulfill, husband,
  reserve 8. conserve, maintain,
  preserve, restrain, withhold
  14. accommodations
keep (pert to)...
  account.. 5. score
  afloat.. 4. buoy
  apart.. 7. seclude 8. separate
  back, out.. 3. bar, dam 4. save
  5. debar, delay 6. detain, except,
  hinder, retard 7. exclude, reserve
  8. restrain, withhold
  from.. 5. avoid, delay 7. abstain,
  boycott, prevent
  hidden.. 7. secrete
  in.. 6. retain
  off.. 4. fend 7. prevent, repulse, ward
  off
  on.. 6. endure 9. persevere
keeper... 5. guard 6. warden
  9. constable, custodian, possessor
  10. maintainer
keeper of...
  birds.. 8. aviarist
  borders.. 8. margrave
  door.. 5. tiler
  elephant.. 6. mahout
  golden apples (Myth).. 6. Ithunn
  (Ithun)
  parks.. 6. ranger
  prison.. 6. gaoler, jailer, jailor, warden
  7. turnkey
keeping... 4. care 5. board, guard,
  trust 7. custody 8. tutelage
  9. retention 10. caretaking,
  conformity, possession, preserving,
  protection 11. maintenance
  12. guardianship
keeve... 3. tub 4. tuft 5. knoll, plume
  8. haystack
kef... 6. dreamy 7. languor
  12. tranquillity (tranquility)
keg... 3. tun, vat 4. cade, cask
  6. firkin
kelly... 5. derby, killy (fish)
kelp... 4. game 5. sight, wrack
  7. insight, seaweed 9. water lily
ken... 4. lore 9. recognize
  10. cognizance, prescience
  13. understanding
Kentish freedman... 4. laet
Kentucky...
  bluegrass.. 3. poa

capital.. **9.** Frankfort
city.. **7.** Paducah **9.** Lexington
 10. Louisville **12.** Bowling Green
famed road.. **15.** Wilderness Trail
famed sights.. **7.** Obelisk (J Davis)
 8. Fort Knox, Log Cabin (Lincoln)
 11. Federal Hill (My Old Ky Home),
 Mammoth Cave
famed sport.. **13.** Kentucky Derby
 (Churchill Downs)
mountain.. **4.** Pine **10.** Cumberland
pioneer.. **11.** Daniel Boone
river.. **4.** Ohio **10.** Cumberland
State admission.. **9.** Fifteenth
State name meaning (Indian)..
 8. tomorrow
State nickname.. **9.** Bluegrass
Kenya, E Africa...
 capital.. **7.** Nairobi
 product.. **3.** tea
 tribe.. **4.** Embu
kept... see *keep*
Ker (Gr)... **4.** doom, fate **5.** ghost
 6. spirit
kermis, kermess... **4.** fair **8.** festival
kernel... **3.** nut **4.** core, gist, meat,
 pith, seed **5.** grain, heart **6.** acinus,
 nutmeg **7.** nucleus
ketch... **4.** Jack, saic, ship **6.** vessel
ketone... **5.** irone **6.** carone
 7. acetone, camphor **8.** deguelin
kettle... **3.** pot **4.** drum, pail **6.** kibble
 7. caldron **8.** cauldron **9.** teakettle
 10. kettledrum
kettledrum... **4.** drum **5.** naker, tabor
 6. atabal **7.** anacara **8.** tympanon
key... **4.** clue, crib, isle, quay, reef,
 tone **5.** islet, pitch, tasto **6.** clavis,
 cotter, fasten, island, opener, switch,
 tapper **7.** digital **8.** mainstay, solution
 11. explanation, fundamental,
 translation
keyed up... **4.** agog **5.** eager, fired
 7. aroused, stirred **8.** hopped up,
 worked up **10.** stimulated
Keys, House of... **9.** Isle of Man,
 officials
Keystone State... **12.** Pennsylvania
khan... **3.** inn **4.** lord **6.** prince
 9. resthouse **11.** caravansary
kiang... **5.** diver **6.** onager **7.** wild ass
kick... **4.** blow, boot, funk, punt
 6. energy, object, thrill **7.** grumble,
 protest **8.** complain, pungency,
 sixpence **9.** complaint **10.** calcitrate,
 enthusiasm
Kickapoo... **6.** Indian **10.** Algonquian
kickshaw... **3.** toy **6.** trifle **7.** trinket
 8. delicacy
kid... **3.** guy **4.** fool, goat, hoax, joke,
 josh, twit **5.** child, jolly, suede
 6. banter, humbug **8.** antelope
 (young), yeanling **9.** youngling
kidang... **4.** deer **7.** muntjac
kidney... **4.** neer **5.** gland, reins
 7. nephros
kidney (pert to)...
 comb form.. **6.** nephro
 disease.. **7.** nephria **9.** nephritis
 pyramid.. **9.** reniculus
 reference to.. **4.** reni **5.** renal
 6. vitals **7.** nephric

shaped.. **8.** reniform
stone.. **6.** pebble **8.** nephrite
kiki... **14.** castor oil plant
kill... **4.** slay, veto **5.** blast, creek
 6. defeat, murder **7.** channel,
 destroy, execute, silence **8.** dispatch,
 immolate, lapidate, massacre,
 overbeat **9.** slaughter
 11. assassinate, exterminate
killer... **4.** Cain **6.** gunman, slayer
 7. butcher **8.** cannibal, man–eater,
 mongoose, murderer **9.** cutthroat
 12. assassinator
killer whale... **3.** orc **4.** orca
 7. grampus
killing... **5.** fatal **6.** deadly, murder
 7. amusing, carnage, cleanup
 (speculation), garrote **8.** homicide
 9. execution **10.** euthanasia
 11. captivating **12.** overpowering
killing of...
 brother.. **10.** fratricide
 cats.. **8.** felicide
 father.. **9.** patricide
 man.. **8.** homicide
 mother.. **9.** matricide
 old men (tribal).. **8.** senicide
 self.. **7.** suicide **9.** martyrdom
 sister.. **10.** sororicide
 wolf.. **8.** lupicide
kiln... **4.** oast, oven **5.** clamp, stove,
 tiler **7.** furnace
kilo (pref)... **8.** thousand
kind... **3.** ilk **4.** good, race, sort, type
 5. class, genre, genus, order, seely,
 style **6.** benign, gender, humane,
 loving, strain **7.** kindred, lenient,
 species **8.** gracious **9.** benignant
 10. benevolent **11.** sympathetic
 12. well disposed
kindle... **4.** burn, fire **5.** brood, light,
 rouse, young **6.** excite, ignite, incite,
 litter **7.** animate, inflame, provoke
kindly... **4.** mild **6.** benign, blithe,
 genial, humane **7.** natural
 8. benignly, heartily **9.** agreeably,
 benignant, indulgent **10.** beneficent,
 legitimate, pleasantly **11.** sympathetic
kindness... **5.** favor **8.** clemency,
 goodness, humanity, mildness
 9. benignity **10.** compassion,
 generosity, gentleness, indulgency,
 tenderness
kindred... **3.** sib, tie **4.** akin, clan, kith
 5. blood **6.** allied, family **7.** cognate,
 descent, kinship, kinsmen, related
 8. kinsfolk **9.** relations
 12. relationship **14.** consanguineous
kine... **4.** cows **6.** cattle
kinetic... **6.** active, moving
king... **3.** rex, rey, roi **4.** rank **5.** chief,
 ruler **6.** master **7.** regulus
 8. chessman **9.** potentate, sovereign
king (pert to)...
 beasts.. **4.** lion
 birds.. **5.** eagle
 chamber.. **9.** camarilla
 cheeses.. **4.** Brie
 child.. **6.** prince **8.** princess
 dwarfs.. **8.** Alberich (Ger)
 fairies.. **6.** Oberon
 family.. **7.** dynasty

gods.. 7. Jupiter
heaven.. 3. God 6. Christ
herrings.. 4. opah 7. oarfish
  8. chimaera
mackerel.. 4. cero
March (The).. 5. Sousa
metals.. 4. gold
monkeys.. 7. guereza
murder of.. 8. regicide
myth.. 4. Atli 5. Midas
myth (classical).. 4. Zeus 7. Jupiter
rivers.. 6. Amazon
serpents (race of).. 6. Shesha (Sesha)
symbol.. 7. scepter (sceptre)
vultures.. 4. papa
waters.. 7. Neptune, Pacific
Woods (The).. 13. Rex Nemorensis
King Arthur (pert to)...
abode.. 6. Avalon 7. Camelot
battleground (fatal).. 6. Camlan
home.. 8. Caerleon (on the Usk)
Knights of the Round Table..
  6. Gawain 7. Galahad 8. Lancelot,
  Tristran 9. Percivale
Queen.. 9. Guinevere
quest of.. 9. Holy Grail (The)
shield.. 7. Pridwin
sword.. 9. Excalibur
kingdom.. 5. realm 6. empire, estate
  8. dominion, kingship, monarchy
kingdom (pert to)...
ancient.. 4. Elam, Moab
Asia.. 5. Nepal
between Spain, France.. 7. Navarra
  (Navarre)
confusion.. 5. Babel
divisions.. 6. animal 7. mineral
  9. vegetable
Indo–China.. 5. Annam (Anam)
kingfish... 4. cero, haku, opah
  7. kingpin, pintado 8. big wheel
  9. threadfin
kingly... 5. grand, noble, regal, royal
  6. august 7. leonine 8. imperial,
  majestic, princely 9. dignified,
  sovereign 11. monarchical
King of...
Albania.. 3. Zog
Bashan.. 2. Og
Bulgaria.. 5. Boris
Greece (anc).. 9. Agamemnon
Israel.. 4. Ahab, Jehy, Saul 5. David
  7. Solomon 8. Jeroboam
Judea.. 3. Asa
Kings.. 3. God 6. Christ
Men.. 4. Odin, Zeus 7. Jupiter
Oriental.. 11. King of Kings
Persia (Iran).. 5. Cyrus 6. Xerxes
Troy.. 5. Priam
Tyre.. 5. Hiram
Visigoths.. 6. Alaric
Kipling, Rudyard (pert to)...
award.. 10. Nobel Prize (1907)
birthplace.. 6. Bombay
poem (for Queen Victoria)..
  11. Recessional
kissing, science... 13. philematology
knee (pert to)...
bend.. 9. genuflect
bent.. 10. geniculate
bone.. 6. rotula 7. kneepan, patella
britches.. 6. smalls 8. knickers

on bended.. 7. humbled 8. obeisant
  10. submissive, worshipful
  12. supplicatory
kneeling desk... 8. prie–dieu
knew... see *know*
Knickerbocker, Father... 9. New
  Yorker (Hist)
knickknack... 3. toy 6. bauble,
  gewgaw, trifle 7. trinket 8. gimcrack
knife... 4. bolo, snee, stab 5. corer,
  prune 6. cutter, weapon
knife (pert to)...
Burmese.. 3. dah
Hindu.. 5. kukri
Irish.. 5. skean 8. skean dhu
Malay.. 4. kris 6. barong, creese
New Zealand.. 4. patu
one–bladed.. 6. barlow
Scottish.. 4. dirk
Spanish.. 7. machete
surgical.. 7. scalpel 10. greffotome
Turkish.. 8. yataghan (yatagan)
US Navy.. 7. cutlass
knife maker... 6. cutler
knife–throwing game...
  11. mumbletypeg
  12. mumble–the–peg
knight (pert to)...
adventure.. 8. errantry
adventurer.. 8. cavalier 9. caballero,
  chevalier
cloak.. 6. tabard
combat.. 5. joust
ensign.. 8. gonfalon, gonfanon
errant.. 7. Paladin
hero.. 7. Paladin
servant.. 4. page 6. varlet
title.. 3. Sir 8. banneret
wife.. 4. Dame, Lady
wreath (with crest).. 4. orle
Knight of the Round Table... 3. Kay
  6. Gawain 7. Galahad, Paladin
  8. Lancelot, Tristram 9. Percivale
Knight of the Rueful Countenance...
  10. Don Quixote
knit... 4. bind, heal, join, seam
  5. plait, unite, woven 6. cement,
  couple, fasten 7. conjoin, connect,
  wrinkle 8. contract 9. interlace
  11. consolidate
knitting machine guide... 4. sley
knitting stitch... 4. knit, purl
knob... 3. nub 4. boss, head, hill,
  lump, node, stud, umbo 5. bulge,
  knurl 6. croche (antler), pommel
  8. tubercle 12. protuberance
knobkerrie... 4. club, kiri 5. stick
knock... 3. hit, rap, tap 4. bang,
  bash, beat, bump, dash, glow, hill,
  pass, slay, snop 5. pound, thump
  6. hammer, jostle, strike 7. collide
  9. criticism, criticize, disparage
  12. faultfinding
knock (pert to)...
about.. 6. travel, wander
down.. 4. fell, raze 6. deject, strike
  8. vanquish
off.. 3. die 6. deduct, recess
  9. improvise
out.. 2. KO 4. kayo
knocking... 6. rat-tat 7. rapping,
  tapping 9. rat-tat-tat

knock–knee ... 6. in–knee
knoll ... 4. bank, clod, hill, knap, knob, lump 5. bunch, hurst, knell, mound 7. hillock
knot ... 3. bow, nep, tie 4. burl, knar, knob, knur, lump, node, noil, snag 5. gnarl, noose 6. clique, nodule, tangle 7. dilemma, lanyard, problem, rosette 9. sandpiper 10. sheepshank 12. complication, protuberance
knotted ... 3. nep 5. noded, nowed (Her) 6. knotty 7. clotted, complex, gnarled, knitted, nodated 8. abstruse, puzzling 9. difficult, entangled
knotty ... 5. nodal, rough 7. gnarled, knarred, knobbed, knurled, nodular 9. difficult, entangled, intricate 10. perplexing
know ... 3. ken, wis, wot 5. sense 6. regard, reveal 8. perceive 9. apprehend, be certain, recognize 11. be cognizant, distinguish
knowing ... 3. hep 6. artful, crafty, scient, shrewd 7. cunning 8. informed 9. cognitive, conscious, wide–awake 10. perceptive 11. intelligent, intentional 12. familiar with 13. comprehension
know–it–all ... 6. gossip 8. quidnunc, wiseacre
knowledge ... 3. ken 4. kith, lore 5. ology 6. wisdom 7. science 8. learning, scientia 9. erudition 11. familiarity, information, instruction 12. acquaintance
knowledge (pert to) ...
acquisition of .. 7. organon
ancestral .. 9. tradition
epithet of Muses .. 7. Pierian
exhibition of .. 6. pedant
instrument .. 7. organon
lack of .. 9. ignorance, nescience
object of .. 7. scibile
pert to .. 7. gnostic 8. instinct 9. epistemic, intuition, sciential 12. epistemology
pretender to .. 7. aeolist (eolist) 8. sciolist
seeker of .. 10. philonoist
slight .. 7. inkling, smatter 10. smattering
summarized .. 12. encyclopedia

(encyclopaedia)
superficial .. 9. sociology
system .. 7. science
universal .. 9. pantology
without .. 8. atechnic
know–nothing ... 5. dunce 8. agnostic 9. ignoramus
kobird ... 6. cuckoo
kobold ... 3. elf, imp 5. gnome 8. folklore 9. hobgoblin
Kodiak, Kadiak bear ... 7. Alaskan
Kohinoor ... 7. diamond (700 carats)
kohl ... 5. horse 8. antimony, cosmetic
kola ... 3. nut 6. jackal
kooky ... 7. offbeat
kopje ... 5. mound 7. hillock
Koran, Alcoran (pert to) ...
author .. 8. Mohammed
division .. 4. Sura (chapter)
learned man .. 5. ulema
recording angel .. 6. sijill (sijil)
scriptures .. 10. Mohammedan
teacher .. 5. ulema 7. alfaqui (alfaquin)
Korea ...
capital .. 5. Keijo, Seoul
city .. 6. Gensan
mountain peak .. 6. Paekdu
old name .. 6. Chosen 13. Hermit Kingdom
peninsula .. 6. Ongjin
province .. 5. Fusan (Fuzan)
river .. 4. Yalu 5. Tuman 7. Naktong
kosher ... 5. clean 8. kashruth 10. sanctioned
kra ... 3. ape (long–tailed)
krimmer ... 8. lambskin
Krishna (Hind) ... 5. deity (of Vishnu) 6. avatar (8th), Goloka
Krupp steel works, site ... 5. Essen (Gor)
kudu ... 8. antelope 9. gray–brown
kusimansel ... 6. mangue 8. mongoose
Kwantung capital ... 6. Dairen
kwazoku (Jap) ... 8. nobility (modern)
kyah ... 9. partridge
kyaung ... 9. monastery
kymatology, science of ... 5. waves 10. wave motion
kyphosis ... 8. humpback 9. hunchback 15. spinal curvature
kyte ... 5. belly 7. stomach
Kyushu (Jap) ... 6. Island (southernmost)

L

L... 5. fifty (Rom num) 6. lambda, letter (12th) 7. lammedh
laager, lager... 4. camp
laagte... 6. bottom, valley 8. riverbed
Laban (pert to)...
daughter.. 4. Leah 6. Rachel
father.. 7. Bethuel
son–in–law.. 5. Jacob
label... 3. tab, tag 4. band, name 6. fillet, lappet, tassel, ticket 8. insignia 9. designate
labellum... 3. lip 6. labium, labrum
labia... 4. lips
labial stop... 9. organ stop
labial teeth... 6. canine 7. incisor
labile... 8. shifting, unstable
labium... 3. lip
La Boheme... 4. Mimi 7. Puccini
labor, labour... 4. moil, task, toil, work 5. sweat 6. strive 7. travail, work for 8. drudgery, endeavor, exertion, industry
labored... 5. heavy 6. forced, strove 7. not easy, operose 8. strained 9. difficult, elaborate, laborious 11. painstaking
laborer... 4. hind, peon, toty 5. navvy 6. coolie, toiler, worker 7. bracero, wetback, workman
laborious... 4. hard 7. arduous, operose 8. toilsome 9. difficult 11. hard working, industrious, painstaking
labor leader... 5. Hoffa, Lewis, Meany 7. Gompers (1st), Reuther 8. Petrillo
Labrador (pert to)...
Arctic flow.. 7. Current
dog.. 9. retriever 12. Newfoundland
missionary.. 8. Grenfell (Dr)
part.. 12. Newfoundland
tea.. 5. Ledum 8. gowiddie
labyrinth... 4. maze 7. circuit, cochlea 10. perplexity 12. complication
labyrinthe... 7. complex 8. involved 9. intricate 10. circuitous 11. complicated
lac... 4. milk 5. resin 7. lacquer, shellac
lace... 3. net, tat, tie, web 4. band, beat, cord, flog, lash, line, trim 5. braid, filet, lacis, snare 6. fasten, string, tissue 7. network 9. embroider 10. intertwine, shoestring 13. dash of spirits
lace (pert to)...
Antwerp.. 7. pot lace
bobbin.. 3. val 12. Valenciennes
cape, scarf.. 8. mantilla
edge.. 5. picot
Flemish.. 7. malines, Mechlin
French.. 5. filet 7. guipure
frill.. 5. ruche
front.. 5. jabot
gold, silver.. 5. orris
make.. 3. tat 5. weave 7. crochet, entwine
needlepoint.. 7. Alençon
opening.. 6. eyelet
patterned.. 7. guipure
lacerate... 3. cut, rip 4. pain, rend, tear 6. harrow, injure, mangle 7. afflict, torture
lachryma... 4. tear 5. fluid 8. teardrop
lachrymal, lachrymose... 5. teary, weepy 7. tearful 8. tearlike
lack... 4. need, want 6. dearth 7. absence, lacking, missing, require 8. have need, scarcity 9. fall short, neediness 10. deficiency
lack (pert to)...
blood cells (red).. 6. anemia
correspondence.. 13. nonconformity
energy.. 5. atony, tepid 6. energy 7. aimless, sapless
feeling.. 10. insensible 13. insensibility
firmness.. 4. limp 8. boneless 9. spineless
interest.. 6. apathy 9. apathetic
knowledge.. 9. ignorance, nescience
melody.. 6. atonic 9. atonality
preparation.. 8. unfitted
reasoning.. 7. idiotic
refinement.. 5. gross 9. grossness, inelegant 10. inelegance
vigilance.. 6. unwary
lackadaisical... 7. languid 8. listless 10. spiritless
Laconia (anc)...
capital.. 6. Sparta
clan.. 3. obe
inhabitant.. 5. Lacon
location.. 12. Peloponnesus
race.. 6. Dorian
laconic... 5. brief, pithy, short, terse 7. concise, pointed, summary 8. succinct, taciturn
lacquer... 3. lac, red (color) 5. japan, resin 6. enamel 7. shellac, varnish
lacrimando... 9. lamenting, plaintive
lactarium... 5. dairy
lacteal... 5. milky
lacune, lacuna... 3. gap, pit 5. break 6. hiatus 7. opening (small) 10. depression
ladder... 3. run, sty 5. scale 7. scalade 8. escalade 10. stepladder
lade... 3. dip 4. bail, draw, fill, load, ship 5. drain, ladle 6. burden
laden... 6. loaded 8. burdened

9. freighted
lading... 4. load 5. cargo 6. burden
  7. freight
ladle... 3. dip 4. bowl 5. scoop,
  spoon 6. dipper
lady... 4. burd (anc), dame 5. donna
  6. domina, female, senora 7. signora
  8. ladylove 13. harlequin duck
lady (pert to)...
  bird.. 6. beetle 7. Vedalia
  fish.. 6. wrasse
  killer.. 4. wolf 5. shiek 7. Don Juan
   8. Casanova
  like.. 6. female, polite 7. genteel
   8. feminine
Lady Godiva's town... 8. Coventry
Lady of the Lake character
  (legend)... 6. Merlin, Vivian
Lady's Book author... 5. Godey
lady's–slipper... 6. balsam, orchid
  8. Noah's ark 9. nerveroot
lady's–thumb... 9. peachwort, persicary
lag... 4. slow 5. delay, tardy
  6. dawdle, linger, loiter 7. belated
  10. dillydally, fall behind
lagarto... 9. alligator 10. lizard fish
laggard... 4. slow 5. idler 7. lagging
  8. backward, dilatory, indolent,
  loiterer, sluggish 9. loitering, straggler
La Gioconda... 8. Mona Lisa
lagniappe, lagnappe... 5. pilon
  7. largess (largesse), present (trifling)
  8. gratuity
lagoon... 4. lake, pond, pool 5. atoll
laic... 3. lay 5. civil 6. layman
  7. secular 8. temporal
lair... 3. bed, den, pen 4. cave, shed,
  trap 5. abode, couch 6. cavern
  7. retreat
Lais (Gr)... 7. hetaera (of Corinth)
  8. mistress 14. beautiful woman
laissez faire, laisser faire... 5. let go
  7. let pass 8. inaction, inactive
  9. do–nothing, passivism, unconcern
  12. indifference 15. noninterference
Laius' son... 7. Oedipus (of Thebes)
lake... 4. loch, mere, pond, pool, tarn
  5. lacus 6. lagoon 7. carmine (color)
lake (pert to)...
  bass.. 4. rock 6. calico
  deposit.. 5. trona
  duck.. 5. scaup 7. mallard
  dweller.. 10. lacustrian
  dwelling.. 7. crannog
  growing in.. 10. lacustrine
  Hades (of).. 7. Avernus
  highest.. 8. Titicaca
  pert to.. 9. lacustral
  poet (Eng).. 6. lakist 7. Southey
   9. Coleridge 10. Wordsworth
  State.. 8. Michigan
lama... 4. monk 5. Dalai
Lamaism... 8. Buddhism
Lamaism, Buddhism (pert to)...
  convent.. 8. lamasery
  dignitary.. 8. hutukhtu
  palace site.. 5. Lhasa
  priest, monk.. 4. lama 6. Getsul
   9. Dalai Lama, Grand Lama
  reliquary, stupa.. 7. chorten
lamb... 3. ean, ewe 4. cade, yean
  5. gigot, sheep 6. cosset 7. eanling,

lambkin 8. yearling 9. youngling
  10. endearment
Lamb, Charles... 4. Elia (pen name)
lambaste... 4. beat, whip 6. thrash
  7. reprove
lambent... 7. glowing, radiant
  8. wavering 10. flickering 11. gliding
  over
Lambeth (London)... 6. palace (of
  Archbishops) 15. religious center
Lamb of God... 7. paschal 8. Agnus
  Dei
lame... 4. halt 7. halting, limping
  8. crippled, disabled, hobbling
  9. defective 11. inefficient
lame (pert to)...
  brains.. 9. balminess, daffiness,
  goofiness, wackiness
  duck.. 7. session 9. insolvent
   10. politician, speculator
Lamech (pert to)...
  descendant of.. 4. Cain
  father of.. 5. Jabal, Jubal
   9. Tubal–cain
lament... 3. rue 4. keen, moan, sigh,
  wail, weep 5. mourn 6. bemoan,
  bewail, grieve, plaint, regret, repine,
  yammer 7. condole, deplore, elegize,
  weeping 8. jeremiad
lamentation... 3. cry, woe 5. dolor,
  grief, tears 6. sorrow 7. anguish,
  wailing
Lamentations... 4. Book (Old Test)
lamia... 5. witch 7. monster, vampire
  (Myth) 8. cub shark 9. sorceress
lamina... 4. obex (brain) 5. blade,
  flake, hinge, layer
lamp... 4. davy, etna 5. light, torch
  6. crusie 7. lantern, lucigen
  9. veilleuse
lamp (pert to)...
  black.. 4. soot
  holder.. 11. candelabrum
  lighter.. 5. spill
  safety.. 4. davy 7. Geordie
  slang.. 6. look at
  waving of.. 5. arati
lampadedromy (Gr)... 8. foot race
  (with torch)
lampoon... 4. skit 5. squib 6. iambic
  8. ridicule, satirize 10. pasquinade
lampoon writer... 8. satirist
lamprey... 3. eel 6. ramper
Lamps of the Lord... 5. yucca
  (blooms)
Lancashire (Eng)... 6. Eccles
lance... 3. cut 4. dart, hurl, stab
  5. blade, spear 6. incise, launch,
  pierce, weapon 7. javelin
lance (pert to)...
  battle.. 5. joust
  head.. 5. morne
  knight.. 10. lansquenet (Hist)
  officer.. 4. Jack
  surgical.. 6. lancet
Lancelot... 6. Knight 13. Lancelot du
  Lac
Lancelot's beloved... 6. Elaine
lancer... 5. uhlan 6. Hussar
  7. cossack, soldier, spearer
land... 3. lot 4. acre, farm 5. arada,
  downs, field, range, tilth 6. alight,

debark, ground, region 7. country,
pasture 9. disembark
land (pert to)...
absolute ppty.. 4. alod 7. alodium
alluvial.. 5. delta
ancestral.. 5. ethel
assessor.. 8. cadastre (cadaster)
church.. 5. glebe
heritable.. 4. odal, udal
holding.. 6. tenure 9. leasehold
leasehold.. 5. feoff
locked in.. 13. mediterranean
mythical.. 4. Eden 6. Utopia
   9. Shangri–La
northernmost.. 5. Thule (Greenland)
open.. 4. moor, wold 5. heath
pile.. 5. cairn
prefix.. 4. agro
reversion.. 7. escheat
sandy.. 4. dene
surveyor.. 9. arpenteur
Sussex tract (Eng).. 5. laine
treeless.. 5. llano 6. steppe 7. prairie
verb.. 3. win 4. gain 5. catch
   6. secure 7. capture
waste.. 5. heath
landed estate... 5. manor 7. demesne
landing place... 4. deck, dock, pier,
   quay 5. field, levee, strip, wharf
   7. airport 8. platform 9. staircase
landmark... 4. copa, tree 5. senal
Land of (the)...
bondage.. 5. Egypt
Cush.. 8. Ethiopia
Eden (East of).. 3. Nod
Enchantment.. 9. New Mexico
Leal.. 6. Heaven
Little Sticks (Canada).. 19. Barren
   Islands border
Midnight Sun.. 6. Alaska, Norway
O'Cakes.. 8. Scotland
Opportunity.. 8. Arkansas
Plenty.. 6. Goshen
Promise.. 6. Canaan
Regrets.. 5. India
Rising Sun.. 5. Japan
Rose.. 7. England
Shamrock.. 4. Eire 7. Ireland
sleep.. 3. Nod
Steady Habits.. 11. Connecticut
Thistle.. 8. Scotland
Thousand Lakes.. 7. Finland
White Elephant.. 4. Siam
landscape... 7. paysage, scenery,
   topiary
landslide... 9. avalanche
   10. éboulement
Landsmaal, Landsmal... 8. language
   (Norway)
Landstag... 4. Diet 8. assembly
   11. legislature
lane... 4. path, road 5. alley, route,
   track 6. airway, course, gullet, throat
   7. channel, red land 8. footpath
   10. passageway
language... 6. langue, speech, tongue
   7. dialect, diction 8. parlance
   9. utterance 11. linguistics
language (pert to)...
acquiring.. 12. chrestomathy
ancient.. 4. Pali 5. Aryan, Greek,
   Latin 6. Hebrew 7. Chinese

   8. Sanskrit
artificial.. 2. Od, Ro 3. Ido
   7. Volapük 9. Esperanto
classical.. 5. Greek, Latin
conversant in.. 9. pantoglot
dead.. 4. Pali
deaf–mute.. 11. dactylology
expression, peculiar.. 5. idiom, lingo
   6. jargon 7. dialect 13. colloquialism
international.. 2. Od, Ro 3. Ido
   7. Volapük 9. Esperanto
pert to.. 8. semantic
pretentious.. 7. bombast
   11. highfalutin'
Romance.. 5. Latin 6. French
   7. Catalan, Italian, Spanish
   9. Provençal 10. Portuguese
sacred.. 4. Pali
sign.. 11. dactylology
thieves'.. 5. argot
languid... 4. slow, weak 5. faint, inert,
   weary 6. dreamy, feeble, sickly,
   supine, torpid 7. passive 8. careless,
   drooping, flagging, heedless, indolent,
   sluggish 9. apathetic 10. spiritless
languish... 3. die 4. fade, fail, flag,
   pine, wilt 5. droop, faint 6. repine,
   sicken, weaken, wither 7. decline
languor... 3. kef (kief) 7. fatigue
   8. dullness, weakness 9. indolence,
   lassitude 10. dreaminess, drowsiness,
   stagnation 12. listlessness,
   sluggishness
lanky... 4. lean, tall, thin 5. gaunt,
   spare 12. loose–jointed
lanner... 6. falcon
Lanterns, Feast of (Jap)... 3. Bon
Laodicean... 8. lukewarm 9. apathetic
   11. indifferent
Laos...
aborigine.. 3. Kah
capital.. 9. Vientiane 12. Luang
   Prabang
native.. 7. Chinese
   14. Thai–Indonesian
religion.. 8. Buddhism
river.. 6. Mekong
tribesman.. 3. Yun
lap... 3. sip 4. fold, lick, wrap 5. drink
   6. ripple, tipple 7. circuit
lapel... 4. fold 5. rever 6. facing,
   lappet
lapicide... 11. stonecutter
lapidate... 4. kill (by stoning), pelt
   5. stone
lapin... 6. rabbit
lapis lazuli... 4. blue 5. stone
   8. lazurite, sapphire 10. azure stone
Lapland...
people.. 5. Lapps 10. Laplanders
   11. Ural–Altaics 12. tent–dwellers
sledge (traveling).. 5. pulka (pukk)
sledge puller.. 8. reindeer
town.. 6. Kiruna
waterfalls.. 11. Harspranget
lappet... 4. flap, fold, lobe 5. lapel
   6. wattle 9. appendage
lapse... 3. err 4. fall, slip 5. error,
   fault, pause 6. expiry 7. decline,
   misstep, relapse 8. apostasy
   9. reversion
lapsus... 4. slip 5. error

12. inadvertence
lapsus calami... 10. lipography
    12. slip of the pen
lapsus linguae... 15. slip of the
    tongue
lapwing... 4. gull 5. pewee, pewit
    6. plover
larceny... 5. theft 7. robbery
    8. burglary, stealage 10. scrounging
larch... 5. Larix 8. tamarack
lard... 3. fat 4. line, pork 5. adeps,
    bacon, baste, enarm 6. axunge,
    cerate, enrich, fatten, grease
    7. garnish 8. saindoux 9. lubricate
larder... 6. pantry 7. buttery
    8. cupboard 12. commissariat
lares (Rom)... 4. gods (household)
    7. spirits
large... 3. big, nth 4. bold, huge,
    much, vast 5. ample, bulky, burly,
    giant, great, loose, scads 7. copious,
    immense, leonine, liberal, massive,
    titanic, weighty 8. colossal,
    enormous, gigantic, spacious
    9. excessive, extensive, plentiful
    11. exaggerated 12. considerable
    13. comprehensive
large (pert to)...
    artory.. 5. aorta
    comb form.. 5. macro
    fish.. 4. opah, tuna 9. swordfish
    intestine.. 5. colon 6. caecum, rectum
    knife.. 4. bolo, snee
    lettered.. 6. uncial
    number.. 4. slew 6. myriad
    pulpit.. 4. ambo
    volume.. 4. tome
largess, largesse... 4. gift 6. bounty
    7. charity, present 10. generosity,
    liberality 11. beneficence
largest bird... 6. condor 7. ostrich
    13. whooping crane
largest fish (freshwater)... 8. arapaima
larghetto... 9. slow tempo
larghissimo... 8. very slow
lariat... 4. rope 5. honda (part), lasso,
    noose, reata, riata
lark... 5. ghost (anc), prank, revel
    6. frolic 7. skylark, titlark 8. songbird
    9. adventure, Alaudidae, parchment
    (color)
larrigan... 8. moccasin
larrikin... 5. rough, rowdy 6. loafer
    10. street Arab
larrup... 3. hit 4. beat, blow, flog,
    whip
larva... 3. bot (bott) 4. grub, pupa
    5. redia 6. embryo, maggot
    7. atrocha 8. cercaria 9. chrysalis,
    doodlebug 11. caterpillar
lascivious... 4. lewd 5. bawdy
    6. erotic, wanton 7. lustful, sensual
    9. lecherous, salacious 10. libidinous,
    licentious
laser... 9. light beam
lash... 3. tie 4. beat, bind, flag, whip
    5. scold, smite 6. splice, strike
    7. scourge
lass... 4. girl 6. lassie, maiden
    7. colleen 11. maidservant
lassitude... 7. languor 8. debility,

lethargy, weakness 9. weariness
lasso... 4. lash, rope 5. noose, reata
    (riata), snare 6. lariat 8. cabestro
last... 3. end 5. final, omega
    6. endure, latest, lowest, newest,
    penult, ultima, utmost 7. extreme,
    supreme 8. eventual, rearmost,
    terminal, ultimate 9. penultima
    10. antepenult, conclusive, most
    recent
last (pert to)...
    at last.. 6. Eureka
    but one.. 6. penult
    cry.. 10. dernier cri
    evening.. 9. yesterday
    long.. 7. outwear, perdure
        9. perendure
    month.. 3. ult 6. ultimo
    offer.. 9. ultimatum
    person in contest.. 4. mell
    shoe.. 5. block
    syllable but one.. 6. penult
    syllable but two.. 10. antepenult
Last (pert to)...
    Assize.. 11. Last Inquest 12. Last
        Judgment
    Days of Pompeii character.. 4. Ione
        5. Nydia 7. Glaucus
    Gospel.. 4. Mass
    of the Gothic Kings.. 8. Roderick
    of the Mohicans.. 5. Uncas (Chief)
    Supper.. 6. Christ 9. disciples
lasting... 4. long 6. stable 7. abiding,
    durable, eternal 8. constant
    9. continual, lingering, permanent,
    steadfast 11. substantial, unforgotten
lasting briefly... 9. ephemeral,
    temporary
lat... 6. column, pillar
latchet... 3. tap 4. lace (leather)
    5. strap, thong 9. fastening
late... 3. neo (comb form), new
    4. sero 5. tardy 6. former, recent
    7. belated, overdue 8. neoteric
    10. behindhand
latent... 5. inert 6. hidden 7. dormant
    9. disguised, potential, quiescent,
    suspended 10. underlying
later... 4. anon, soon 5. after
    6. future, mañana, puisne
    9. posterior, presently
    12. subsequently
lateral... 5. flank, raphe 8. indirect,
    sideward
lath... 4. slat 9. wood strip
lathe... 4. tool 7. mandrel
lather... 4. foam, suds 5. froth
Latin (pert to)...
    alphabet letters.. 9. twenty—one
    and.. 2. et
    bath.. 7. balneum
    behold.. 4. ecce
    booth.. 7. taberna
    bowl.. 6. patina
    bronze.. 3. aes
    church.. 8. Catholic
    couch.. 9. accibutum
    country.. 6. French 7. Italian, Spanish
    dish.. 4. lanx 6. patina
    foot.. 3. pes
    God.. 3. Dei, Deo 4. Deus
        7. Mercury

goddess .. 3. Dea
grammar (case) .. 6. dative 8. ablative, genitive, vocative 10. accusative, nominative
historian .. 6. Justin
holidays .. 5. feria
hymn .. 13. Adesti Fideles
javelin .. 5. aclys, pilum
land .. 4. ager
law .. 6. Latium
life .. 4. vita
people .. 6. Romans
poet .. 4. Ovid 6. Horace
pronoun .. 2. tu 3. ego, hic 4. ille, ipse, iste
quarter (section) .. 5. Paris 10. New Orleans
ram .. 5. aries
rite .. 4. orgy 5. sacra
seat .. 5. sella
trumpet .. 4. tuba 7. buccina
Way .. 9. Via Latina
latite ... 4. lava
latitude ... 4. zone 5. scope, width 6. extent 7. breadth, freedom 8. distance 10. liberality
latrant ... 7. barking
latter ... 4. last 5. final 6. latest 9. foregoing 10. more recent
Latter–day Saint ... 6. Mormon
lattice ... 6. grille 7. trellis 8. cancelli 9. crossbars, framework 12. crossed slats
latticelike ... 7. grating 8. espalier 9. clathrate 10. cancellate
Latvia ...
capital .. 4. Riga
city .. 6. Dvinsk, Libava (Libau)
money unit .. 3. lat (gold)
people .. 5. Letts
river .. 2. Aa
laud ... 4. sing 5. extol 6. praise 7. applaud, commend, glorify, magnify 8. eulogize
laudable ... 9. admirable, estimable 11. commendable, meritorious 12. praiseworthy
laudatory ... 9. panegyric 10. flattering 11. approbatory, encomiastic 12. commendatory
laugh ... 4. roar 5. fleer, smile, snort 6. cackle, deride, giggle, guffaw, hawhaw, tee–hee 7. chortle, chuckle 8. ridicule 10. cachinnate
laughable ... 3. odd 5. droll, funny, merry, queer, witty 7. amusing, comical, jocular, risible, strange, waggish 8. humorous, sportive 9. burlesque, diverting, facetious, ludicrous 10. ridiculous
laughing ... 3. gay 5. merry, riant 6. rident
laughing (pert to) ...
bird .. 4. loon 10. woodpecker
falcon .. 4. hawk
gas .. 12. nitrous oxide
jackass .. 10. kingfisher, kookaburra
pert to .. 8. gelastic
laughter ... 4. gelo (comb form) 5. gelos, mirth, risus 6. guffaw 12. cachinnation
launch ... 4. hurl 5. begin, float, lance,

shove, start, throw 6. plunge 7. descant 9. undertake 10. inaugurate
laureate ... 4. poet 6. decked (with laurel) 7. drowned, honored 13. distinguished
laurel ... 3. bay, ivy, oak, oil 6. daphne, Kalmia, salmon 8. magnolia 9. sassafras, spoonwood
laurel wreath ... 7. Iresine
lava ... 2. aa, oo 3. ash 5. ashes 6. coulee, latite, scoria 8. lapillus, pahoehoe
lava field ... 8. pedregal
lavaliere, lavalier ... 7. pendant 8. ornament
lavatory ... 5. basin 7. piscina 8. washroom 9. washbasin
lave ... 4. lade, pour, wash 5. bathe, rinse 6. drench 8. absterge
lavender ... 4. mint 6. purple 7. blue–red, perfume 9. fragrance
laver ... 4. bowl 5. basin 6. trough, vessel 7. cistern, seaweed
Lavinia (pert to) ...
father .. 7. Latinus
husband .. 6. Aeneas
mother .. 5. Amata
myth .. 5. Roman
lavish ... 4. free, lush, rank, wild 5. spend 7. profuse 8. abundant, generous, prodigal, reckless, squander 9. bountiful, exuberant, impetuous, luxuriant, plentiful, unstinted 10. immoderate 11. extravagant 12. unrestrained 13. superabundant
law ... 3. act, jus, lex 4. bill, code, jure, nisi, rule 5. axiom, canon, droit, edict, mercy, mesne 6. decree, equity, Latium, police 7. justice, precept, statute 9. enactment 12. constitution 13. jurisprudence
law (pert to) ...
action .. 3. res 4. suit 5. actus 6. trover 7. impeach, implead 8. gravamen, replevin 9. ademption
Bible .. 6. Mosaic 12. Old Testament
claim .. 4. lien
code .. 9. Hammurabi 10. codex juris 16. Codex Justinianus
decree .. 4. nisi 5. edict
degree .. 3. LLD
divine .. 11. commandment
document .. 4. deed, writ 6. capias, elegit
drafting .. 10. nomography
evidence .. 7. constat
expert (US) .. 5. Moore (John B)
for fourth offender (NY) .. 6. Baumes
German Franks .. 5. Salic
goddess .. 4. Maat (Egypt)
heredity .. 8. Gresham's
Manu .. 5. sutra
mathematics .. 7. formula
morals .. 5. conduct
Moses .. 5. Torah (Tora) 10. Pentateuch
offender .. 5. felon 6. sinner 8. criminal 9. wrongdoer
offense .. 4. tort 5. crime, malum 6. delict
pert to .. 3. res 9. judiciary

philology.. 6. Grimm's
science.. 8. nomology
  13. jurisprudence
student.. 8. stagiary
thought.. 7. noetics
warning.. 6. caveat
within the.. 5. licit 8. judicial
wrong.. 4. tort
lawful... 3. due 5. legal, licit, valid
  9. permitted 10. legitimate
  11. permissible
lawgiver... 5. Moses
lawless... 4. lewd 6. unruly 7. illegal
  10. anarchical, disorderly
lawlessness... 4. riot 6. mutiny
  7. anarchy, license 12. disobedience
lawmaker... 5. solon 7. senator
  10. legislator 11. congressman
lawn... 5. green 7. batiste 9. grassplot
  12. village green
lawyer... 5. agent 6. jurist, legist
  7. abogado, shyster 8. advocate,
  attorney, lawgiver 9. barrister,
  counselor (counsellor), legulian,
  solicitor 11. intercessor, pettifogger
lax... 4. dull, free, limp, open, slow
  5. loose, slack, tardy 6. remiss
  7. lenient 8. backward, dilatory,
  inactive, indolent, not tense
  9. dissolute, scattered 10. licentious,
  unconfined 12. unrestrained
lay... 3. bet, put 4. lair, pave, poem,
  song 5. allay, ditty, place, quiet,
  stake, still 6. ballad, hazard, impose,
  impute, pacify 7. appease, ascribe,
  deposit, relieve, store up 9. direction
  10. profession
lay (pert to)...
aside.. 5. table 6. remove, shelve
  7. dismiss, reserve 8. postpone
  9. segregate
away.. 4. heap, hive 5. amass,
  cache, hoard, store 7. husband
  8. treasure 10. accumulate
bare.. 5. strip 6. denude, expose,
  reveal 7. uncover
down.. 3. bet, set 5. level 6. give up
  7. declare, deposit 9. postulate,
  prescribe, stipulate, surrender
off.. 4. don't, stop 5. cease
  6. recess 7. dismiss, measure
out.. 4. plan 5. set up 6. design
  7. pattern
waste.. 6. ravage 7. destroy
  8. desolate 9. depredate, devastate
layer... 3. bed 4. coat, derm, tier,
  uvea 5. sloam (earth) 6. lamina
  7. stratum (strata, pl)
  10. substratum
lazar... 5. leper 9. loathsome
lazaretto, lazaret... 8. hospital 9. pest
  house 10. lazar house
laziness... 7. inertia 8. oisivity,
  vagrancy 9. indolence
  10. ergophobia, remissness
  12. slothfulness 13. shiftlessness
lazy... 3. lax 4. idle, slow 5. slack
  6. otiose, remiss 7. dronish, laggard
  8. dilatory, inactive, indolent, slothful,
  sluggish 9. shiftless 13. lackadaisical
lazy man... 3. bum 4. lusk 5. drone,
  idler 6. rotter 9. lazybones

11. Weary Willie
lea... 4. mead 5. haugh 6. meadow
  7. pasture 9. grassland
leach... 3. wet 7. moisten 9. lixiviate,
  percolate
lead... 3. cue, key, van 4. cart, clue,
  head, lode 5. begin, guide, pilot,
  plumb, usher 6. direct, entice,
  escort, govern, induce 7. conduct,
  pioneer, precede 8. antecede,
  guidance 9. direction, influence,
  precedent 10. precedence
lead (mineral)... 4. carne (rod), gray,
  shot 6. ceruse, fother, galena,
  leaden, strass (glass) 7. bullets,
  plummet 8. graphite, litharge,
  plumbago
lead astray... 4. lure, mang 6. allure,
  delude, entice, induce 7. deceive,
  pervert 8. inveigle
leader... 4. head 5. chief, guide,
  sinew 6. cantor, tendon 7. special
  8. choragus, director 9. chieftain,
  conductor 10. forerunner
leader (Eccl)... 3. fra 4. pope 5. rabbi
  6. bishop, priest 8. cardinal,
  minister, preacher 10. evangelist
leading... 5. chief, first 6. ruling
  7. guiding 8. foremost, in the van
  9. directing, governing
  11. controlling
leaf... 3. ola 4. gear, page 5. blade,
  frond, petal, sepal 6. areola, ligula,
  spathe 7. tendril
leaf (pert to)...
hook.. 5. folio
bud.. 5. gemma
curvature.. 8. epinasty (down)
  9. hyponasty (upward)
floating.. 3. pad
green.. 11. chlorophyll
heart-shaped.. 9. obcordate
mold.. 5. humus
network.. 6. areola
part.. 5. bract, costa, stoma
  6. pagina, stipel 7. petiole
  9. petiolule
point, pointed.. 5. mucro
  9. mucronate 13. mucroniferous
pore.. 8. lenticel
secretion.. 4. lerp
stalk.. 7. petiole 8. petiolus
vein.. 3. rib 5. costa
leafless... 9. aphyllous
leaflet... 5. pinna, tract 6. folder
  7. booklet 8. pamphlet
  13. advertisement
league... 4. band, Bund 5. Hanse,
  union 7. combine 8. alliance
  9. coalition 10. federation
  11. affiliation, combination
  13. confederation
League of Nations site... 5. Paris
  (1920) 6. Geneva (Secretariat)
League of the Iroquois... 11. Five
  Nations
Leah's sister... 6. Rachel
leak... 4. drip, hole, seep 5. crack
  6. escape, run out 7. crevice, fissure
  10. be revealed
leal... 4. just, real, true 5. legal, loyal
  6. lawful 7. correct, genuine

8. accurate, faithful
lean... 4. bare, cant, lank, poor, rely,
    slim, tend 5. gaunt, slope, spare
    6. barren, meager 7. scraggy,
    slender 8. not plump 9. deficient,
    gravitate
lean (pert to)...
    animal, person.. 4. ribe (Scot)
    emaciated.. 6. marcid
    make.. 8. macerate
    towards.. 6. prefer
Leander's love... 4. Hero
leaning... 5. slope 6. desire
    7. pronate, tending 8. aptitude,
    enclitic, penchant, tendency
    9. prejudice 10. partiality
Leaning Tower... 4. Pisa 6. Venice
    7. Bologna 8. Zaragoza
lean–to... 4. roof, shed, wing 5. shack
    9. extension (bldg)
leap... 4. dive, jump, ramp, skip
    5. bound, caper, lunge, salto, spang,
    vault 6. spring 7. saltary 8. capriole
leaping... 7. jumping, salient, saltant
    8. bounding, salience 9. saltation
learn... 4. lere (anc) 6. master
    8. memorize 9. ascertain, determine
learned... 3. wot 4. read, sage
    6. legist 7. erudite 8. lettered,
    literate, schooled 9. scholarly
    12. well–informed
learned man... 6. pundit 7. scholar,
    teacher 8. mastered 9. professor
learning... 3. art, ken, wit 4. lore
    7. culture 8. pedantry 9. education,
    erudition, knowledge, philology (love
    of), philomath 11. scholarship
lease... 3. let 4. hire, rent 5. weave
    6. demise, remise, tenure 8. contract
leasehold... 6. rental, tenure
leash... 4. bind, cord, lash, lune
    (hawking) 5. reins, three 6. fasten,
    string, tierce 9. restraint
    11. subjugation
leash hound... 5. limer
least... 5. grain 6. little, lowest,
    merest 7. minimum 8. minority,
    shortest, simplest, smallest
    9. slightest
leather... 4. hide, skin 5. aluta, leder
    (old spelling) 6. vellum 7. canepin
    8. cheveril (cheverel) 9. toughness
leather (kinds)... 3. kid, kip 4. calf,
    napa, vici 5. Mocha, suede
    6. patent, saddle, skiver 7. chamois,
    Morocco 8. cordovan 9. sheepskin
leather (pert to)...
    artificial.. 7. keratol
    bookbinding.. 4. roan 6. levant
    bottle.. 4. olpe 6. matara
    cuirass.. 6. lorica
    glove.. 5. suede, trank 8. capeskin
    pare.. 5. skive
    patch.. 5. clout
    piece of.. 5. strap, thong 6. latigo
    pouch (Highlander's).. 7. sporran
    process.. 3. tan, taw
    strap.. 5. thong 6. latigo
    term.. 8. efflower
    tool.. 6. skiver
    worker.. 6. chamar, tanner 8. chuckler
leatherneck... 6. marine

leave... 2. go 4. quit 6. depart, retire,
    vacate 7. liberty 9. allowance
    10. permission
leave (pert to)...
    desolate.. 7. bereave
    empty.. 6. vacate
    isolated.. 6. desert, maroon
    of absence.. 5. exeat 8. furlough
    off.. 4. don't, stay 5. cease 6. desist
    out.. 4. omit, skip 8. pass over
    taking.. 5. adieu 6. congee
    7. vamoose 9. departure
leaven... 4. barm 5. imbue, yeast
    6. enzyme 7. corrupt (implied),
    ferment, pervade 10. impregnate
leaves... 5. pages, shaws 6. sepals
    7. foliage
leaves, feeding on...
    13. phyllophagous
leavings... 4. left, orts, rest 5. culls,
    dregs, dross, waste 6. refuse
    7. remains, residue 8. remnants
leban, lebban... 5. drink 8. beverage,
    sour milk
Lebanon capital... 6. Beirut
Lebanon city... 7. Tripoli
lech (anc)... 4. slab 8. capstone,
    monument
lecher... 7. glutton 8. gourmand,
    parasite 9. debauchee, libertine
lectern... 4. ambo, desk 6. pulpit
    10. escritoire
lecture... 4. jobe, rate 5. scold
    6. lesson 7. declaim, expound,
    lection, reproof, reprove 8. instruct,
    scolding 9. discourse 10. admonition
lecturer... 6. docent, reader 7. teacher
    9. prelector
Leda (pert to)...
    geology.. 4. clay (marine)
    husband.. 4. Zeus
    mother of.. 6. Castor, Pollux
    11. Helen of Troy
    zoology.. 7. mollusk
ledge... 4. berm, edge, lode, reef, sill
    5. shelf 7. retable, stratum
leechlike... 8. bdelloid
lees... 5. draff, dregs 8. sediment
leeward... (opp of windward)
    9. protected, sheltered
Leeward Islands... 5. Nevis
    7. Antigua, Barbuda, Redonda
    8. Anguilla, Sombrero 10. Montserrat
    13. St Christopher
Leeward Islands group... 6. Virgin
    7. Society
leeway... 10. enough rope
left... see also *leave* 3. haw, kay
    8. departed, larboard 9. abandoned,
    remaining
left (pert to)...
    aground.. 6. neaped 8. beneaped
    animal (motherless).. 4. cade 5. dogie
    comb form.. 8. sinistro
    hand (Mus).. 8. sinistra
    hand page.. 5. verso
    hand pitcher.. 8. southpaw
    out.. 7. omitted 8. excluded
    10. eliminated
    spirally.. 11. sinistrally
    to one's judgment.. 13. discretionary
    toward the.. 5. aport 9. sinistrad,

sinistral 12. levorotatory (Chem)
left–handed... 6. clumsy, gauche
   7. oblique 8. southpaw 9. insincere,
   insulting 14. sinistromanual
   16. counterclockwise
left–handed marriage...
   10. morganatic
leftist... 7. liberal, radical
   10. left–winger, liberalist
   11. progressive
leg (pert to)...
   armor.. 4. jamb 6. greave 7. jambeau
   bone.. 4. shin 5. tibia 6. fibula
   calf.. 5. sural
   insect.. 4. coxa
   joint.. 4. hock, knee 5. thigh
   longest bone.. 5. femur
   of lamb (cooked).. 5. gigot
   term.. 4. crus 5. jambe 6. crural
legacy... 4. gift, will 6. devise
   7. bequest, codicil 9. testament
   10. bequeathal
legal... 4. leal 5. licit, valid 6. lawful
   10. authorized, legitimate
legal (pert to)...
   abstract.. 6. précis
   act, thing.. 5. actus
   action.. 3. res 4. case 7. detinet,
   lawsuit, summons
   case, postponed.. 7. remanet
   claim.. 4. lien
   confirmation.. 10. validation
   contestant.. 6. suitor 8. litigant
   9. plaintiff
   critic.. 6. censor
   decree, divorce.. 10. decree nisi
   defense.. 5. alibi
   delay.. 4. mora
   denial, stoppage.. 8. estoppel
   extract.. 7. estreat
   order.. 4. writ
   paper.. 4. deed, writ 5. lease
   6. escrow
   possession.. 6. seizin (seisin)
   power (to take).. 7. prender (prendre)
   process.. 6. caveat 7. detinet
   right, by.. 6. ex jure
   security.. 4. bond
   surrender.. 6. remise
legally competent... 5. capax
legate... 5. envoy 8. bequeath,
   delegate 10. ambassador, diplomatic
legend... 4. Edda, myth, saga, tale
   5. fable 7. history 9. narrative,
   tradition 11. inscription
legendary... 8. fabulous 9. imaginary,
   narrative 11. traditional
   12. mythological
legendary (pert to)...
   goddess (slave).. 5. Baube, lambe
   primate.. 6. Dubric
   water sprite.. 6. undine
legendry... 7. legends (collectively)
leggings... 5. chaps, spats 6. strads
   7. gaiters, greaves, puttees
   8. gamashes, gambados
   12. galligaskins
legislate... 3. act 5. elect, enact
   8. pass laws 10. put through
legislative (pert to)...
   agent.. 8. lobbyist
   assembly.. 4. diet 6. assize, senate

8. congress 10. parliament
   group.. 4. bloc
legislator... 5. solon 7. senator
   8. lawgiver, lawmaker 9. statesman
   11. congressman 14. representative
legislature... 4. Diet 5. House
   6. Senate 8. Congress 9. bicameral
   (2 branches)
legitimate... 4. real, true 5. legal, licit,
   valid 6. cogent, lawful 7. genuine
   9. permitted 11. efficacious,
   justifiable
legman... 8. newshawk
legume... 3. pea, pod, uva 4. bean,
   soya 6. clover, lentil, loment
   7. alfalfa
leisure... 4. ease, time, toom 5. otium
   6. otiose 7. freedom 9. spare time
   11. convenience, opportunity
lemming... 4. maki, vari 5. mouse
   6. rodent
lemur... 5. indri, loris, makis, potto
   6. anguid, aye–aye, colugo, galago,
   macaco, monkey 7. tarsier
   8. Anguidae, mongoose
   10. angwantibo
Lenape... 6. Indian (Del)
lend... 4. loan 5. grant 6. devote (to)
   7. advance
length (pert to)...
   measure.. 4. area 5. gauge 6. linear,
   volume
   ten meters.. 9. decameter
   three–quarters inch.. 5. digit
   time.. 3. age, eon, era 6. moment,
   period
   two and 1/4 inches.. 4. nail
   unit.. 6. micron, parsec (Astron)
lengthen out... 7. prolong, stretch
   8. continue, elongate, protract
lengthwise... 5. along 12. horizontally
   14. longitudinally
lenient... 3. lax 4. easy, mild
   7. clement, patient 8. merciful,
   relaxing, tolerant 9. assuasive,
   emollient, softening
Lenin (pert to)...
   birthplace.. 9. Ulyanovsk
   famed as.. 8. Dictator (Russ)
   real name.. 7. Ulianov
Leningrad (Russ)... 9. Petrograd
   12. St Petersburg 15. Window on
   the West
lenis... 4. soft 6. gentle, smooth
lenitive... 4. mild 6. gentle
   8. mitigant, ointment, remedial
   9. assuasive, emollient, mitigator,
   relieving, softening 10. palliative,
   qualifying
lens... 5. toric 7. bifocal, lentoid
   8. meniscus, sunglass 9. lenticula
   10. anastigmat 13. apochromatism
Lent... 6. carême 9. Forty days, Great
   Fast 12. Quadragesima
lentamento... 6. slowly
lentando... 9. retarding 14. becoming
   slower
lenticula... 7. freckle, lentigo (frockly)
lento... 4. slow
Leo constellation star... 7. Regulus,
   the Lion
leopard... 4. pard 5. ounce 6. jaguar,

ocelot 7. cheetah, panther
leper... 5. lazar, mesel 6. Naaman
(Bib)
Lepontine Alps... 10. Monte Leone
(peak)
lepra... 7. leprosy 14. Hansen's
disease
Lesbos... 5. Assos (Aristotle's)
6. Island (Sappho's) 8. Mytilene
Les Miserables author... 4. Hugo
(Victor)
lessen... 4. bate, wane 5. abate,
lower, peter, relax 6. impair, minify,
narrow, reduce, shrink, weaken
7. cut down, relieve 8. decrease,
diminish, mitigate, moderate, palliate
11. deteriorate
lesser... 4. less 5. minor (Mus)
7. smaller 8. inferior
Lesser Bear (Astron)... 9. Ursa Minor
Lesser Dog (Astron)... 10. Canis Minor
Lesser Lion (Astron)... 8. Leo Minor
let... 4. hire, rent 5. allow, lease,
leave 6. hinder, impede, permit
7. prevent
let (pert to)...
down.. 5. lower 8. comedown,
drawback, relaxing 10. slackening
14. disappointment
fall.. 4. drop, slip 5. spill 7. mention
in.. 5. admit, enter 6. insert
it be given.. 5. detur
it stand.. 3. sta (Mus) 4. stet
up.. 4. rest 5. cease, pause, relax
6. slow up 7. slacken 8. decrease
lethal... 5. fatal, feral 6. deadly, mortal
7. deathly, killing 11. destructive
12. death-dealing
lethargic... 4. dull 5. heavy, inert
6. drowsy, sleepy, torpid
8. comatose, listless 9. apathetic
lethargy... 4. coma 5. sleep, sopor
6. apathy, stupor, torpor 7. languor
8. hebetude, neurosis 9. lassitude
10. drowsiness (morbid)
Lethe... 5. abyss, Hades, river
8. oblivion 13. forgetfulness
lethiferous... 6. deadly 11. destructive
Leto (pert to)...
mother of.. 6. Apollo 7. Artemis
Roman name.. 6. Latona
wife of.. 4. Zeus
letter... 4. note, type 7. epistle,
message 9. character
13. communication
letter (pert to)...
bright star.. 4. Beta
carrier.. 6. correo 7. mailman,
postman
cross stroke.. 5. serif
first.. 7. initial
letter for letter.. 9. literatim
marks.. 5. breve
of advice.. 11. lettre d'avis
of challenge.. 6. cartel
representation.. 10. literation
short.. 4. line, note 6. billet
sloping.. 6. italic
sound loss (last).. 7. apocope
two letters (one sound).. 7. digraph
9. diphthong

writer.. 13. correspondent
letters (pert to)...
decorate with.. 7. miniate
10. illuminate
man of.. 9. literatus
ref to.. 8. literary
lettuce... 3. cos 4. head 7. Lactuca,
romaine
leukocyte... 9. corpuscle (white)
Levant... 4. East 6. Orient 7. leather
(Morocco) 8. East wind
Levantine (pert to)...
country.. 13. Mediterranean
garment.. 6. caftan
herb.. 6. madder
ketch.. 3. bum 4. jerm, saic 5. xebec
6. settee 8. levanter
valley.. 4. wadi (wady)
wind.. 7. Morocco
levee... 4. bank, dike, pier, quay
5. ridge 6. durbar, trench
8. assembly 9. reception
10. embankment
level... 4. even, fell, flat, just, raze
5. equal, grade, plane, plani (comb
form), point 6. peavey (peavy)
smooth, steady, topple 7. flatten,
terrace, uniform 8. demolish,
equalize, parterre 12. well-balanced
lever... 3. bar, lam, pry 5. crank,
jimmy, pedal, prise 6. peavey
(peavy), tappet, tiller 7. crowbar,
treadle
leviathan (pert to)...
animal (Bib).. 5. whale 6. dragon
9. crocodile
embroidery.. 6. canvas
11. cross-stitch
political.. 12. (the) commonwealth
size.. 4. huge 7. titanic
10. formidable
Levi's father (Bib)... 5. Jacob
Levite... 5. tribe 10. descendant
Levitical... 7. Aaronic 9. Aaronical
10. priesthood (Mormon)
Leviticus... 10. Pentateuch
levity... 6. gaiety 8. buoyancy
9. frivolity, lightness 10. triviality,
volatility
levy... 3. tax 4. fine, wage (war)
5. rally, stent 6. assess, impose
7. collect, estreat 9. recruital
lex... 3. law 7. statute
lexicon... 4. book (of words)
10. dictionary, vocabulary
lex loci... 13. law of the place
lex non scripta... 12. unwritten law
liability... 4. debt 5. debit 8. cessavit
9. proneness 10. likelihood,
obligation 11. possibility
14. responsibility
liable... 3. apt 5. bound 6. likely
7. exposed, subject 10. answerable,
chargeable 11. responsible
liable (pert to)...
likely to.. 3. apt 5. prone
11. predisposed
not liable.. 6. exempt
to objection.. 13. exceptionable
to penalty.. 6. guilty
Lia Fail... 12. Stone of Scone
15. Coronation Stone (Ir)

liaison... 4. link 7. joining 8. intimacy, intrigue 11. co–operation 18. intercommunication

llana... 4. cipo 5. vines (woody) 9. wild grape

liar... 5. cheat 6. fibber 7. Ananias, wernard (obs) 8. deceiver, fabulist, perjurer 12. prevaricator

Lias system... 8. Jurassic

libation... 5. drink 8. oblation, offering, potation

libel... 4. bill 6. defame 7. lampoon, request, slander 8. circular (obs), handbill, roorback 10. defamation 11. certificate, declaration 12. supplication

liberal... 4. free, Whig 5. ample, frank 7. copious, profuse 8. eclectic, generous 9. bountiful, extensive, plentiful 10. hospitable, munificent 11. broad–minded, magnanimous 12. uncontrolled

liberate... 4. flee, free 5. loose 6. redeem 7. deliver, manumit, release 8. separate, unfetter 9. disengage 10. emancipate

Liberia...
capital.. 8. Monrovia
city.. 8. Buchanan 10. Greenville
gulf.. 5. Sidra
language.. 3. Kru 7. English
people.. 3. Vai (Vei) 5. Negro

liberty... 4. ease, free 5. leave 7. freedom, license 9. exemption, privilege 10. permission 11. opportunity

librarian... 7. bookman 10. bibliosoph, bibliothec 13. bibliothecary

Libya, Africa...
astronomy.. 4. Mars (portion)
capital.. 7. Tripoli 8. Benghazi
district.. 6. Fezzan 9. Cyrenaica 12. Tripolitania
language.. 7. Hamitic
oasis (saline).. 6. Sebkha (Sebka)
people.. 6. Arabs
sea.. 13. Mediterranean

Libya, Gr (pert to)...
children.. 5. Belus 6. Agenor
heroine of.. 5. Libya
husband.. 8. Poseidon

license... 5. right 6. bandon, permit 7. dismiss, freedom, liberty 8. sanction 9. approbate, authority, authorize, privilege 10. permission 11. lawlessness 13. authorization

licentious... 3. lax 4. lewd 5. loose 7. immoral, lawless 9. debauched, dissolute 10. lascivious, profligate 12. uncontrolled, unrestrained

licet... 6. lawful 7. granted 12. it is conceded

lichens (pert to)...
abounding in.. 9. lichenose
derivative.. 4. moss 5. usnic 6. litmus
genus.. 5. Usnea 7. Evernia
study of.. 11. lichenology

licit... 3. sue 4. just 5. legal 6. lawful 9. permitted

lick... 3. lap, win 4. flog, whip 5. lap up, taste 6. baffle, defeat, thrash

7. conquer 8. overcome, vanquish

licorice... 5. abrin 9. jequirity

lid... 3. cap, hat 4. bred, case, roof 5. cover 6. eyelid 7. stopper 9. operculum

lid, put on the... 3. end 6. hush up 7. license 8. complete, suppress

lie... 3. fib 4. rest 7. falsify, falsity, recline, untruth 9. deception, falsehood, mendacity 10. equivocate 13. prevarication

lie (pert to)...
at ease.. 4. loll 5. droop 6. dangle
face down.. 7. pronate
hidden, in ambush.. 4. lurk, plot 6. in wait 9. insidiate 11. concealment
in warmth.. 4. bask 9. luxuriate
low.. 6. abased 9. prostrate
prostrate.. 4. flat 5. creep 6. grovel

Liebestraum composer... 5. Liszt

Liechtenstein, Europe...
capital.. 5. Vaduz
government.. 12. principality
language.. 6. German
religion.. 8. Catholic

lief (anc)... 4. dear, fain, glad 7. willing 8. disposed 9. agreeably, favorably

lieutenant... 6. deputy 10. substitute 11. locum tenens

life... 3. vie 4. bios 5. being 6. always, energy, spirit 8. vitality, vivacity 9. animation, existence

life (pert to)...
after death.. 8. Olam–haba
animal.. 4. bios 5. biota (flora, fauna)
biology.. 4. bios
comb form.. 3. bio
giving.. 9. animative 11. procreative
god of.. 6. Faunus
insurance.. 7. tontine
jacket (sl).. 7. Mae West
later, older.. 8. autumnal
lifelike.. 5. alike, vital 6. biotic 9. realistic
plant.. 4. bios 5. biota
principle.. 5. atman, prana, tenet 6. spirit
prolonger.. 6. elixir
science of.. 7. anatomy, biology, zoology 12. paleontology
sea.. 5. coral 8. plankton
staff of.. 5. bread
without.. 4. dead 5. azoic 8. lifeless 9. inanimate

lifeless... 4. abio (comb form), dead, dull, flat 5. amort, azoic, heavy, inert, vapid 6. jejune, torpid 8. inactive, listless 9. bloodless, exanimate, inanimate, powerless, tasteless 10. lackluster, spiritless, unanimated

lifetime... 3. age, day, eon (aeon) 6. always 8. duration 10. generation

lift... 3. aid, pry 4. jack, perk 5. boost, exalt, heave, hoist, raise, steal, theft 6. puff up, thrill 7. derrick, elevate, improve, inspire 8. elevator 11. inspiration

lifting device... 4. jack, pump

5. crane, davit, lever, tongs
7. capstan, derrick, erector
8. elevator, heighten, windlass
lifting muscle ... 7. erector, levator
ligament ... 4. bond, cord 6. tendon
7. bandage
ligan, lagan ... 6. debris, jetsam
7. flotsam
ligature ... 3. tie 4. band, bond, cord,
note 6. amulet, binder, taenia
7. bandage
light ... 3. arc, gay, sun 4. dawn, easy,
glim, lamp, lume, mild, pale, soft
5. flare, flood, klieg, laser, taper
6. alight, aspect, blonde, bright,
candle, gentle, ignite, illume, medium,
window 7. cresset, fragile, glimmer,
glowing, trivial 8. buoyancy, daylight,
delicate, illumine, lambency, radiance,
trifling 9. effulgent 10. brightness,
luminosity, weightless 11. information
12. incandescent
light (pert to) ...
apparatus .. 9. holophote
circle .. 4. halo, nimb 6. corona,
nimbus 7. aureola, aureole
cloud .. 6. nimbus
coating .. 4. film
footed .. 4. fast 5. agile
globe .. 4. bulb
god .. 6. Balder (Baldr)
handed .. 4. deft
headed .. 5. dizzy 6. fickle
9. beeheaded
image .. 8. spectrum
leading .. 8. luminary
reflector .. 4. lens 6. mirror
refractor .. 5. prism
science .. 6. optics
source .. 3. sun
touch .. 3. dab
unit .. 3. lux, pyr 4. phot, watt
5. lumen 6. carcel, Hefner
without .. 4. dark 7. aphotic, obscure
8. starless 9. pitch–dark
10. caliginous
yellow .. 5. amber
light and airy ... 7. tenuous
8. delicate, ethereal
light and quick ... 6. nimble, volent
light dress fabric ... 6. merino
8. cashmere 9. bombazine, paramatta
(parramatta)
lighten ... 4. ease 5. allay, cheer, clear
6. reduce 7. gladden, relieve
8. brighten, illumine, jettison
9. alleviate, disburden 10. illuminate
lighter ... see also *light* 4. scow
5. barge 7. gabbard, igniter, pontoon
8. chopboat (Chin)
lighthearted ... 3. gay 6. upbeat
7. buoyant 8. carefree, cheerful,
jubilant 9. vivacious
Light Horse Harry ... 3. Lee (Gen
Henry Lee)
lighthouse ... 5. tower 6. beacon,
pharos 7. seamark 10. watchtower
lightness ... 6. gaiety, levity
8. airiness, buoyancy, sobriety
9. flippancy, frivolity, giddiness
10. fickleness, triviality, volatility,
wantonness 11. flightiness,

inconstancy, instability
12. unsteadiness 14. weightlessness
15. thoughtlessness
lightning ... 4. lait 5. flash, levin
6. stroke 8. flashing 9. discharge
lightning (pert to) ...
bug .. 6. beetle 7. firefly
discharge .. 4. bolt 11. thunderbolt
form .. 4. fork 5. chain, sheet
reference to .. 8. fulgural
rod .. 8. arrester
stone .. 9. fulgurite
war .. 10. blitzkrieg
lightsome ... 3. gay 4. airy 5. agile,
clear, light, lucid, merry 6. fickle,
nimble 7. lighted 8. cheerful,
cheering, graceful, luminous, unsteady
9. frivolous 12. lighthearted
lights out ... 4. taps
ligneous ... 5. woody 6. wooden,
xyloid 8. firewood
lignite ... 4. coal
like ... 2. as 4. copy, love 5. enjoy,
equal, liken, savor 6. admire, desire
7. similar 10. comparable
11. counterpart, homogeneous
like (pert to) ...
bone .. 6. osteal
fern .. 8. frondose, frondous
gland .. 7. adenose
gold .. 7. aureate
house, dome .. 5. domal
kneecap .. 7. rotular 10. rotuliform
sea lion .. 7. otarian, otarine
suffix .. 2. ar, ic 3. ine, oid, ose
likeable, likable ... 6. genial
8. charming, pleasant
likelihood ... 8. prospect 10. good
chance 11. possibility, probability
14. apparently true
likely ... 3. apt, fit 5. prone 6. comely
8. credible, feasible, probable, suitable
9. promising 11. verisimilar
likeness ... 4. copy, icon, twin
5. clone, guise, image 6. effigy,
statue 7. parable, picture, replica
8. parallel, portrait 9. imitation,
semblance 10. comparison,
photograph, similarity 11. counterfeit
12. reproduction 14. representation
likewise ... 3. too 4. also 5. ditto
8. moreover 11. furthermore
liking ... 4. like, love, lust 5. fancy
6. comely 7. delight 8. pleasing
10. preference 12. predilection
lilac ... 5. lilas, mauve 6. purple
7. syringa
lilac throat ... 11. hummingbird
Lilliputian ... 4. tiny 5. dwarf, minim
6. midget 7. dwarfed 10. diminutive
lilt ... 3. air 5. song, tune 6. swing
6. poetic, rhythm 7. rejoice
lily ... 2. ti 3. lis 4. aloe, ixia, sego
5. calla, lotus, onion, water, wokas
(wocas), yucca 6. Allium, Nuphar
8. daffodil, mariposa, martagon,
soaproot 9. narcissus
lily (pert to) ...
family, genus .. 4. aloe 6. Tulipa
7. Bessera 9. Liliaceae
10. Hyacinthus
grass .. 10. cuckoopint

iron . . 7. harpoon
of France . . 10. fleur–de–lis
shaped . . 7. crinoid 9. crinoidal
water . . 8. Castalia, Nymphaea
lily of the valley (pert to) . . .
bud . . 3. pip
Cape Cod . . 13. barney–clapper
English . . 6. mugget
family . . 15. Convallariaceae
liliaceous plant . . 5. yucca
shrub . . 10. fetterbush
tree . . 6. sorrel
lima bean disease . . . 6. mildew
　9. yeast spot
liman . . . 5. marsh 6. lagoon
limb . . . 3. arm, fin, imp, leg 4. wing
　5. bough, scamp 6. branch, member
　7. flipper 9. anaclasis
limber . . . 4. limp, weak 5. agile, lithe,
　loose 6. flabby, pliant, supple
　7. flaccid, lissome 8. flexible, yielding
limbo . . . 4. hell, jail 6. prison
　9. purgatory
limbs, absence of . . . 6. amelia
　7. acolous
lime . . . 4. calx 5. color, fruit
　8. chlorine, fumigant 9. deodorant,
　quicklime 11. green–yellow
　12. linden yellow
limen . . . 9. threshold
limestone . . . 4. calp, malm 5. chalk
　6. marble, oolite 8. pisolite
lime tree . . . 6. linden, tupelo
limey . . . 6. sailor 7. soldier
limit . . . 3. end, fix, ori (comb form)
　4. term 5. allot, bourn 6. summit
　7. confine 8. boundary, capacity,
　restrain, restrict, terminal
　11. restriction, termination
　12. consummation
limited . . . 3. few 5. local, scant
　6. finite, narrow, scanty 7. bounded,
　topical 8. confined, reserved
　9. astricted, parochial 10. restricted
　11. conditional, topopolitan
　13. circumscribed
limiting . . . 7. hedging 10. qualifying,
　relational 11. restraining, restricting,
　restrictive
limn . . . 4. draw 5. paint 6. depict
　7. portray 8. decorate 9. delineate
　10. illuminate
limp . . . 3. hop, lax 4. halt, soft, thin,
　weak 5. loose 6. flabby, limber
　7. flaccid 8. drooping, flexible
　9. inelastic 13. unsubstantial
limpid . . . 4. pure 5. lucid 6. bright
　7. crystal 8. pellucid 11. translucent,
　transparent 12. intelligible
Lincoln, Abraham (pert to) . . .
assassin . . 15. John Wilkes Booth
birthplace . . 8. Kentucky (1809)
debater . . 7. Douglas (Stephen A)
dog . . 4. Fido
mother . . 10. Nancy Hanks
Secy of State . . 6. Seward
Secy of War . . 7. Stanton
son . . 10. Robert Todd
wife . . 8. Mary Todd
Lincoln (pert to) . . .
color . . 9. Carthamus 11. yellow–green
sheep (breed) . . 7. English

Lindbergh, Charles A (pert to) . . .
birthplace . . 7. Detroit (1902)
flight field . . 9. Roosevelt (LI)
flight to (1927) . . 5. Paris (1st)
retreat . . 10. Illiec Isle (Fr)
wife . . 10. Anne Morrow
linden . . . 3. lin 4. lime, teil 5. Tilia
line . . . 3. row 4. arow, axis, cant, ceil,
　clew, cord, face, mark, race, rail,
　rein, rule, seam, side 5. agone,
　align, raphe, ridge, route, stria, track
　6. crease, isobar, policy, series,
　streak, stripe 7. engrave, outline
　8. boundary, vocation, wainscot
　9. delineate
line (pert to) . . .
adjusting . . 9. alinement
central . . 4. axis
comb form . . 4. lino
conceptual, geological . . 6. agonic,
　isotac, tropic 7. equator 8. isothere,
　isotherm, latitude, meridian
　9. longitude
equidistant . . 8. parallel
fine (type) . . 5. leger, serif
fishing . . 5. snell 7. ratline (ratlin)
imaginary . . 7. equator, Maginot
mathematics . . 4. sine 5. agone
　6. secant 7. tangent
measure . . 3. gry 4. rule
meteoric . . 6. isobar
nautical . . 6. earing 7. halyard,
　hawsing
poetic . . 5. stich, verse
racing . . 4. wire
raised . . 4. weal, welt 5. ridge
selling . . 11. merchandise
soldiers . . 4. file, rank 6. cordon
transport . . 5. stage 7. carrier
　8. carriage
type . . 5. agate, serif
up, lineup . . 4. plan 5. align
　6. muster 7. arrange 8. schedule
　9. formation 11. arrangement,
　parallelize
lineage . . . 3. kin 4. race 5. birth,
　blood, stock, tribe 6. family, strain
　7. descent 8. pedigree 9. offspring
　10. extraction, progenitor
lineal . . . 6. racial 10. continuous,
　delineated 12. genealogical
lineman . . . 3. end 5. guard 6. center,
　tackle 7. wireman 11. electrician
linen . . . 4. crea, duck, lawn, lint
　5. crash, gulix, inkle (tape), toile
　6. barras, damask, dowlas, napery,
　sheets 7. cambric, Holland, lockram
ling . . . 4. fish, hake 5. heath 6. burbot
　7. eelpout, Gidadae, heather
　8. chestnut
linger . . . 3. lag 4. drag, idle, wait
　5. dally, defer, delay, dwell, hover,
　tarry 6. dawdle, go slow, loiter,
　remain 8. continue, hesitate
　13. procrastinate
lingerie . . . 9. underwear 10. underlinen
　11. underthings 14. unmentionables
lingering . . . 5. delay 7. chronic
　8. dilatory, slowness 10. protracted
lingo . . . 4. cant 6. jargon, lingua,
　patois, patter, tongue 8. language
lingua . . . 5. lingo 6. jargon, tongue

11. hypopharynx
lingual... 7. glossal 9. lingulate
  10. linguiform, tonguelike
linguistics... 6. syntax 7. grammar
  8. language 9. phonology, semantics
  10. lexicology
link... 3. tie 4. bond, join, loop, yoke
  5. annex, nexus, torch, unite
  6. couple, member, relate
  7. connect, liaison, passage
  8. catenate 12. intermediary
linkage... 5. tie–up, union 6. hookup
  7. joinder, joining 8. junction
  11. conjunction
linking... 7. liaison 9. annectent
links in a chain... 7. hundred
lion... 3. cat, cub, leo 4. puma
  5. simba 6. cougar, Lionel, lionet
  8. Felis leo 9. celebrity 12. King of
  Beasts
Lion (pert to)...
  England.. 8. heraldry
  God.. 3. Ali
  Lucerne.. 11. Switzerland (Sculpture)
  St Mark.. 6. Venice (winged)
  the North.. 6. Sweden (King
  Adolphus)
lionlike... 6. feline 7. catlike, leonine
lip... 3. jib, rim 4. edge, kiss, talk
  5. cheil, words 6. flange, labium,
  labrum, speech 7. cheilos
  8. labellum 10. mouthpiece
  12. impertinence
lip (pert to)...
  comb form.. 5. chilo, labio
  formed.. 6. labial
  inflammation.. 9. cheilitis
  ornament.. 6. labret
  service.. 9. hypocrisy 10. sanctimony
  12. unctuousness
  surgery.. 9. chilotomy 11. chiloplasty
  tumor.. 7. chiloma
lipped... 6. labial 7. labiate
liquefy... 4. fuse, melt, thaw
  6. reduce 8. dissolve, fluidify
  10. deliquesce
liqueur... 5. crème, noyau, sirup
  6. cognac, genepi, kummel
  7. cordial, curaçao, ratafia
  8. absinthe, anisette 9. Cointreau
  11. Benedictine
liquid... 5. clear, fluid 6. watery
  7. flowing 8. beverage, manifest, not
  solid
liquid (pert to)...
  assets.. 4. cash 5. money
  9. resources
  chemical.. 7. acetone 8. furfural
  inflammable.. 3. gas 5. ether
  7. alcohol 8. gasoline
  oily.. 5. olein 7. aniline, picamar
  soap.. 6. napalm
  thick.. 3. tar 4. dope 5. syrup (sirup)
  weak.. 5. blash
liquidate... 4. kill 6. depose, pay off,
  settle 8. amortize 9. discharge
  11. exterminate
liquor... 3. ale, dew, gin, rum, rye
  4. beer, brew, grog, lush, sake, wine
  5. hooch, kefir, punch, stout, vodka
  6. arrack (arak), arrope, elixir, whisky
  (whiskey) 8. cocktail, highball

  9. applejack, moonshine
  10. chasse–café
liquor container... 3. keg 5. flask
  6. barrel, bottle 8. cellaret, decanter
liquor maker... 6. abkari (Ind), brewer
  7. vintner 9. distiller
liquor server... 6. barman 7. barmaid,
  skinker (anc), tapster
liquor shop... 3. bar 6. saloon, tavern
  7. barroom, cabaret, shebeen (Scot),
  taproom 8. alehouse 9. groghouse,
  honky–tonk 11. rathskeller (ratskeller)
liripipe, liripoop (Hist)... 4. hood
  5. scarf 6. dotard, tippet
lissom... 5. layer 7. stratum
  8. platform 12. strand of rope
lissome... 5. agile, lithe 6. limber,
  nimble, supple 7. willowy 8. flexible
list... 3. tip 4. edge, file, roll, rota,
  rote 5. index, limit, panel, table
  6. careen, edging, enlist, record,
  roster, stripe 7. catalog, incline
  8. calendar, classify, manifest,
  register, schedule, tabulate
  9. catalogue, enclosure, inventory,
  repertory 10. repertoire
  11. enumeration
list (pert to)...
  actors.. 4. cast
  competitors.. 5. entry, slate
  foods.. 4. menu 5. carte
  investments.. 9. portfolio
  memoranda.. 5. scrip
  officers.. 6. roster
  references.. 5. index
listen... 3. ear 4. hear, heed 6. attend
  7. give ear, hearken (harken)
  8. overhear 9. eavesdrop
listening... 7. audient 9. attentive
listing... 4. list 6. strips 7. selvage
  10. enlistment, enrollment
listless... 4. dull 6. abject, drowsy,
  moping, supine 7. languid
  8. careless, heedless, sluggish
  9. apathetic 10. spiritless
  11. unconcerned 13. uninteresting
litchi nut... 8. rambutan
literary... 6. versed 8. lettered
  9. classical 11. book–learned
literary (pert to)...
  composition.. 5. cento, essay, opera
  8. rhetoric
  criticism.. 9. epicrisis
  drudge.. 4. grub, hack
  extracts.. 9. anthology
  fragments.. 3. ana 5. notes
  8. analecta, analects
  laws.. 9. copyright
  piracy.. 10. plagiarism
  selection.. 7. excerpt
  style.. 5. prose 6. purism 8. pedantic
literature... 4. book, epic, Veda
  5. drama, lyric, novel 6. ballad,
  poetry 7. fiction, writing
  10. nonfiction 13. belles–lettres
lithe... 4. slim 6. limber, supple, svelte
  7. lissome, slender 8. flexible
Lithuania...
  capital.. 5. Vilna (Vilnius) 6. Kaunas
  (Kovno)
  Jew.. 6. Litvak
  people.. 5. Balts, Letts 6. Aestii

port.. 8. Klaipeda (Memel)
river.. 6. Niemen
litigant... 6. suitor 9. defendant,
disputant, litigator, plaintiff
litigation... 4. suit 7. contest, dispute,
lawsuit 10. contention, discussion
litigious... 10. disputable
11. belligerent, contentious
litten... 7. lighted 8. cemetery
10. churchyard
litter... 3. bed, hay 4. bier, mess
5. couch, dooly (doolie), mulch,
straw, young 6. coffin, jumble
7. clutter, rubbish 9. palanquin,
stretcher
litter of pigs... 6. farrow
little... 3. sma, wee 4. puny, tiny,
weak 5. brief, petit, petty, scant,
short, small 6. dapper, petite, slight
7. not much 8. trifling 9. niggardly
11. unimportant 12. narrow–minded
14. inconsiderable
little (pert to)...
bethel.. 6. chapel (seaman's), church
by little.. 6. slowly 7. peu à peu
9. piecemeal, poco a poco
comb form.. 5. steno
devil.. 3. imp 4. minx 5. rogue
7. ruffian 13. mischief–maker
fellow.. 6. shaver
finger, toe.. 7. minimus
flag.. 9. banderole
music term.. 4. poco
ring.. 7. annulet
Little Rhody... 11. Rhode Island
Little Women, author... 6. Alcott
(Louisa)
littoral... 4. zone (marine) 5. shore
7. coastal 9. bordering
liturgical... 10. ceremonial
11. ritualistic
liturgy... 4. rite 6. ritual 8. ceremony
14. consuetudinary
live... 5. dwell, exist 6. reside
7. breathe 8. continue, have life
live (pert to)...
by sponging.. 5. cadge
by stratagems.. 5. shark
by wits.. 5. cheat 7. deceive, falsify
13. Machiavellize
earlier.. 8. pre–exist
in.. 7. inhabit
in tents.. 5. nomad 7. scenite
in the country.. 9. rusticate
live... 5. alert, alive, vital, vivid
6. bright, lively, living, virgin (mineral)
7. charged, not dead 8. vigorous
9. energetic 11. electrified
lively... 3. gay, vif 4. airy, grig, keen,
pert, spry, yare 6. active, blithe,
bright, snappy 7. animate, buoyant,
pungent, tittupy (tittuppy) 8. spirited
9. energetic, sprightly, vivacious
10. enlivening, rebounding
11. interesting 12. effervescent
liver (pert to)...
comb form.. 6. hepato
disease.. 9. cirrhosis, hepatitis
duct.. 4. bile
pert to.. 5. hepar 7. hepatic
resembling.. 8. hepatoid
Liverpool native... 12. Liverpudlian

liverwort... 6. Riccia 8. agrimony,
hepatica 9. bryophyte
living... 4. life 5. alive, being, quick
6. extant 7. animate, organic, topical
8. benefice, existent, lifelike
10. livelihood 11. subsistence
living (in, on, near)...
currents.. 5. lotic
ground.. 7. epigeal
holes.. 11. latebricole
leaves.. 13. phyllophagous
oxygen.. 7. aerobic
plane (same).. 8. coplanar
poverty.. 11. necessitous
river bank.. 9. riparious
rivers, streams.. 9. rheophile
seas (deep).. 8. bathybic
shores.. 8. littoral
solitude, seclusion.. 10. eremitical
11. eremiticism
tents.. 7. scenite
together.. 11. contubernal
living (pert to)...
again.. 6. Buddha 7. revived
8. Hutukhtu 9. redivivus
being.. 5. wight 6. animal
8. organism
capable of.. 6. viable
dull.. 10. vegetation
individual.. 4. bion
near the ground.. 7. epigeal
together.. 8. intimate 11. contubernal
(contubernial)
lixivium... 3. lye 6. bleach 8. cleanser
lizard... 3. dab, eft 4. adda, gila,
newt, seps, uran 5. agama, anoli,
gooko, skink, varan 6. dragon,
hardim, iguana, moloch 7. monitor,
saurian, tuatera 8. basilisk
9. chameleon 10. chuckwalla,
salamander
llama... 6. alpaca, vicuna 7. guanaco
load... 3. jag 4. fill, lade, onus
5. cargo 6. burden, charge, weight
7. fraught, freight, oppress, prepare
8. contents, encumber 10. imposition
11. encumbrance
loaded... 5. drunk, flush, laden, ready
7. charged, fraught 8. burdened,
weighted 10. in the chips
loader of vessels... 9. stevedore
loadstone, lodestone... 6. magnet
8. terrella 9. magnetite
loaf... 4. idle, lump 5. bread 6. loiter,
lounge 9. Eucharist
loafer... 5. idler 6. beggar 7. lounger
8. vagabond
loam... 3. rab 4. clay, lime, silt, soil
5. chalk, loess, regur
loan... 4. lend 6. borrow 7. advance
10. provisions 13. accommodation
loath... 6. averse 7. hostile
9. disliking, reluctant, unwilling
loathe... 4. hate 5. abhor 6. detest
7. despise, dislike 9. abominate
loathsome... 4. foul, vile 5. nasty
6. odious 7. cloying, hateful
9. abhorrent, offensive, repellant
10. abominable, disgusting
lob... 3. box, cop 4. step, till, toss,
vein 5. stair, throw 7. lugworm,
pollack 9. chandelle

lobby... 4. hall, room 5. foyer
  8. anteroom, corridor, coulisse
  9. enclosure, vestibule 10. wirepuller
  13. pressure group
lobe... 5. alula 6. earlap, lappet, lobule
  7. pendant
lobster (pert to)...
  claw.. 5. chela 6. nipper, pincer
  eggs.. 3. roe 5. coral
  French.. 6. homard
  genus.. 7. Homarus, Macrura
  8. Nephrops
  part.. 6. thorax
  tail.. 6. telson
  trap.. 3. pot 4. corf 5. creel 6. bow
  net
local... 7. edaphic, topical 8. regional
  9. parochial 10. epichorial (epichoric)
  13. autochthonous
local court.. 5. gemot (gemote)
locale... 4. site 5. place, scene, venue
locality... 4. area, spot 5. place, situs
  7. endemic, habitat 8. position
locate... 4. find, spot 6. settle
  7. situate 9. establish
locatio... 7. leasing, letting
location... 4. seat, site, spot 5. locus,
  place, situs 6. ubiety 7. habitat
  8. district 9. situation
  12. neighborhood
locator of forest fires... 7. alidade
loch... 3. bay 4. lake, pond 5. inlet,
  lough
lock... 4. bolt, hasp, hold 5. Gatun,
  latch 6. cotter, detent, fasten, fetter
  8. fastener 9. floodgate
lockjaw... 7. tetanus, trismus
  11. ankylostoma
lockman... 8. summoner (Isle of Man)
  11. executioner
lock of hair... 4. curl 5. tress
  6. berger 7. daglock, ringlet
  8. lovelock, spit curl
lockup... 3. jug 4. jail 5. clink
  6. cooler 8. hoosegow (hoosgow)
  9. calaboose
loco... 3. mad 4. daft 5. craze, crazy
  6. crazed 7. disease 10. moonstruck
  15. non compos mentis
locomotion... 6. lation (Astrol), moving,
  travel 7. transit 8. progress
locomotive... 3. hog 5. dolly, mogul
  6. diesel, dinkey, engine, mikado
  9. iron horse
locomotive cowcatcher... 5. pilot
locus... 4. area, drug, site 5. place
  8. locality
locus (pert to)...
  in quo.. 5. where 12. place in which
  sigilli.. 14. place of the seal
locust... 4. weta 6. beetle, cicada,
  cicala, kowhai 7. Locusta
  9. wetapunga 11. grasshopper
locust (pert to)...
  berry.. 5. drupe 9. glamberry
  bird.. 4. dial 7. grackle 8. starling
  10. white stork
  like.. 6. mantis
  plant.. 5. senna
  sound.. 7. stridor 10. stridulate
  tree.. 5. carob, honey 6. acacia
lode... 3. vug (vugg) 4. path, road,

vein 5. canal, drain, ledge 6. course
  7. deposit 8. waterway
lodestar... 8. cynosure, polestar
  11. guiding star
lodestone, loadstone... 6. magnet
  8. terrella 9. magnetite
lodge... 3. hut, lie 4. camp, tent
  5. cabin, hovel 6. billet, encamp,
  reside 7. deposit, quarter
  11. brotherhood
lodge doorkeeper... 5. tiler
lodging... 3. inn 4. gite, room
  5. abode, hotel, roost 6. billet,
  harbor (harbour), tavern 8. barracks,
  dwelling, hostelry, quarters
  9. dormitory, harborage (harbourage)
  10. habitation
loess... 4. loam, silt, soil
lof... 6. praise 7. measure
loft... 3. bin 4. balk 5. attic
loftiness... 6. height 7. dignity
  8. eminence 9. eloquence
  11. distinction, magnanimity
lofty... 4. high, tall 5. proud 6. aerial,
  Alpine, Andean 7. eminent, exalted,
  haughty, stately, sublime 8. arrogant,
  elevated, eloquent, majestic, towering
  9. dignified 11. magisterial,
  magnanimous 13. distinguished
lofty place... 4. peak 5. aerie, eyrie
  (eyry) 6. summit 8. eminence,
  pinnacle
log... 3. birl, slab 5. diary 6. record
  8. firewood, mountain, puncheon,
  register 11. speedometer
log (pert to)...
  cock.. 10. woodpecker
  gin.. 6. jammer
  hauler (sled).. 4. tode
  implement.. 6. nigger, peavey (peavy),
  rosser
  measure.. 7. scalage
  noser.. 6. sniper
  rolling.. 7. birling
  section.. 5. spalt
  support.. 3. nog
logarithmic terms... 3. bel 5. curve
  6. spiral 7. ellipse, tangent
  9. decrement
logarithm inventor... 6. Napier
loge... 3. box 5. booth, stall
loggerhead... 4. tool 6. turtle
  7. fathead 8. bonehead, numskull
  9. blockhead 10. thickskull
loggia... 7. gallery
logging (pert to)...
  boots.. 4. pacs
  rock.. 6. loggan
  sled.. 4. tode 7. travois (travoise)
  wheels.. 7. katydid
logic... 9. reasoning 13. argumentation
logic (pert to)...
  fallacy.. 6. idolum
  induction.. 7. epagoge
  proposition.. 5. lemma 7. ferison
  9. enthymeme, obvertend
  specious.. 7. sophism
  term.. 5. Darii, Ferio 8. Celarent
logical... 4. sane 5. sound, valid
  8. coherent, credible, rational
  9. plausible 10. consistent,
  reasonable

logician... 8. reasoner
logogriph... 5. rebus 6. riddle
  7. anagram 8. logogram
logy... 4. dull 6. drowsy 8. sluggish
Lohengrin (pert to)...
  character.. 4. Elsa 8. Parsifal
  composer.. 6. Wagner (1850)
  Knight.. 15. Knight of the Swan
loin (pert to)...
  beef.. 10. tenderloin
  mutton.. 4. rack 5. chump
  pork.. 7. griskin
loincloth... 5. dhoti, pagne 7. G-string
  11. breechcloth
loir... 8. dormouse
Loire, France...
  Dept capital.. 12. Saint Etienne
  river's old name.. 5. Liger
  town.. 6. Nantes
  tributary.. 5. Indre
loiter... 3. lag 5. dally, delay, tarry
  6. dawdle, linger 7. saunter
loiterer... 4. slug 5. drone, idler
  6. lagger 7. dawdler, laggard
  8. sluggard
Loki (pert to)...
  god.. 7. Discord 8. Mischief
  wife.. 5. Sigyn
loll... 4. hang 5. droop 6. dangle,
  frowst (froust), lounge, repose, sprawl
  7. recline
loma, lomita... 4. hill
Lombard (pert to)...
  ancient.. 6. cannon
  historic.. 4. bank, loan
  Italy.. 5. tribe
  King.. 6. Alboin (legend)
  school.. 11. Renaissance
  street.. 6. London
Lombardy province... 4. Como
lomboy... 0. Java plum
lomilomi (Haw)... 3. rub 7. massage,
  shampoo
London, England...
  art gallery.. 4. Tate
  bank.. 27. Old Lady of Threadneedle
  Street
  borough.. 6. Ealing
  bridge.. 6. Thames
  bridle path.. 9. Rotten Row
  brown.. 9. carbuncle
  clock.. 6. Big Ben
  club (Whigs).. 6. Kit-Kat
  district.. 4. Soho 7. Alsatia, Lambeth,
  Mayfair (fashion) 9. Wimbledon
  10. Marylebone
  hawker.. 6. coster
  monument (Guildhall).. 3. Gog
  5. Magog
  Opera Company.. 12. Sadler's Wells
  porter.. 6. George
  prison.. 7. Newgate 9. Bridewell
  quarter.. 8. Vauxhall
  roisterer (Hist).. 3. mum
  Roman name.. 6. Agusta
  stables.. 4. mews
  stock exchange.. 17. Throgmorton
  Street
  street.. 9. Cheapside, Whitehall
  10. Piccadilly 11. Throgmorton
  12. Threadneedle
Londoner... 7. Cockney

Londres... 5. cigar
lone... 3. one 5. alone 6. lonely,
  single 7. forlorn 8. solitary
  9. unmarried 12. unfrequented
loneliness... 8. loneness, solitude
  9. aloneness, dejection, isolation
  10. depression, desolation
  12. lonesomeness
lonely... 4. lorn 6. dreary 8. desolate,
  lonesome, secluded, solitary
  10. friendless 11. sequestered
  12. unfrequented
Lone Star State... 5. Texas
long... 3. yen 4. pine 5. crave, wordy,
  yearn 6. aspire, prolix, thirst
  7. lengthy, tedious 8. tiresome
  9. prolonged, wearisome
  10. protracted
long (pert to)...
  ago, since.. 3. eld 4. yore
  beard.. 9. graybeard 10. bellarmine
  (jug)
  discourse, speech.. 6. screed, tirade
  7. descant 9. philippic, rigmarole
  dog.. 9. dachshund, greyhound
  dozen.. 8. thirteen
  established.. 8. habitual 10. inveterate
  11. traditional
  for.. 4. hope, pine 5. covet, crave
  horn.. 6. cattle (Tex)
  inlet.. 3. ria
  journey.. 4. trek 7. odyssey
  jump.. 5. halmo
  letters.. 7. screeds
  life.. 9. longevity
  limbed.. 5. rangy
  lived.. 9. macrobian
  periods.. 4. ages, eons
  scarf.. 4. sari
  suffering.. 7. patient 10. forbearing
  Tom.. 3. gun 8. titmouse
  windedness.. 9. garrulity, prolixity
  13. longiloquence
longing... 3. yen 6. desire, pining
  7. craving, wistful 8. yearning
  9. hankering, nostalgia
longitudinal... 10. euthytatic (stress),
  lengthwise
longshoreman... 6. docker, loader,
  lumper, stower 9. stevedore
  10. roustabout
loo... 3. pam 4. game
look... 3. con, ken, pry, see 4. haze,
  heed, leer, peep, scry, seek, seem
  5. point, stare, watch 6. appear,
  expect 7. examine, inspect, observe
  8. indicate, perceive 9. search for
look (pert to)...
  after.. 4. tend 5. serve 6. follow
  7. care for 9. keep vigil, supervise
  at.. 3. eye 4. face, scan, upon
  6. regard 7. examine
  back.. 6. recall 7. retrace
  8. remember 9. recollect 10. call to
  mind
  down upon.. 4. leer, snub 5. fleer,
  gloat 7. askance, despise
  forward to.. 5. await 6. expect
  7. foresee 10. anticipate
  like.. 8. resemble
  obliquely.. 4. skew
  slyly.. 4. leer, ogle, peer

sullen.. 5. frown, lower 6. glower
toward.. 4. face
upon.. 2. at 4. deem 6. behold
   11. contemplate
lookout... 4. view 5. guard, watch
   6. conner 7. outlook 9. vigilance
looks... 4. cons, face, kens, sees
   5. peers, pores, pries, seeks, seems
   6. visage 8. features 9. resembles
   10. appearance 11. countenance
loom... 3. auk 4. loon, tool 6. appear,
   puffin, vessel, weaver 7. machine
   9. guillemot, implement
   10. receptacle
loom part... 3. lam 4. caam, leaf, sley
   5. easer, lathe, lever 6. heddle
loon... 5. diver (great Northern), Gavia,
   grebe, wabby 10. Gavia immer
loon... 4. dolt 6. menial (anc), rascal
   7. lunatic
loop... 3. eye, tab 4. ansa, clew, kink
   5. bight, bride, honda, noose, picot,
   sling, wootz (iron) 6. becket
   7. folding 8. doubling
loophole... 4. hole, plea 5. mense,
   oilet 6. escape, eyelet, outlet
   7. opening, pretext 8. aperture
loop–shaped... 9. fundiform
   11. sling–shaped
loose... 3. lax 4. free, limp 5. slack
   6. detach, remiss, unlash, wanton,
   wobbly 7. escaped, immoral,
   movable, relaxed, slacken, unbound,
   unleash 8. insecure, unstable
   9. discharge (gun, arrow)
   10. unconfined 11. improvident
   12. loose–moraled
   14. unconventional
loose (pert to)...
   ends.. 4. dags 5. slack 7. tagrags
      8. restless
   garment.. 5. simar 6. banion, chimar,
      kimono 7. zimarra 8. peignoir
   jointed.. 5. lanky, rangy 6. wobbly
      7. rickety 10. ramshackle
loosely dressed... 8. discinct
loosen... 4. ease, free, undo 5. pried,
   relax 6. soften 7. slacken
looseness... 7. laxness 8. limpness
   9. slackness, vagueness
   10. remissness, wantonness
loot... 3. rob 4. gelt, haul, sack, swag
   5. booty 6. spoils 7. pillage,
   plunder, seizure 10. contraband
looter... 6. rifler, sacker 7. ravager,
   spoiler 8. marauder, pillager
lop (off)... 3. bob, cut 4. oche, sned,
   trim 5. droop, prune 6. cut off,
   snathe 8. truncate
lopsided... 4. alop 7. leaning
   8. top–heavy 10. unbalanced
   13. unsymmetrical
loquacious... 4. glib 6. chatty
   7. voluble 9. garrulous, talkative
   10. chattering
loquacity... 7. fluency, leresis
   8. glibness 9. gabbiness, garrulity
   12. effusiveness
lord... 3. aga (agha), bey, God 4. earl,
   peer, rule, tsar 5. liege, ruler, title
   6. master, prince 7. Jehovah,
   marquis, Saviour 8. governor,

nobleman, seignior, suzerain, viscount
   10. proprietor 11. Jesus Christ
Lord (pert to)...
   Buddhism.. 6. Buddha
   Jacobite.. 3. Mar
   of Heaven.. 7. Tien Chu (Chin)
   of Lords.. 8. Demiurge (Plato)
      11. King of Kings 13. Prince of
      Peace
   of Wisdom.. 5. Mazda 6. Ormazd
Lord have mercy upon us...
   12. Kyrie eleison 14. Christe eleison
lordly... 6. uppish 8. arrogant,
   despotic 9. dignified, masterful
   10. tyrannical 11. domineering,
   overbearing
Lord's Prayer... 11. Pater Noster
lore... 4. lear 6. advice, wisdom
   7. counsel 8. learning 9. erudition,
   mythology, tradition 12. superstition
lorgnette... 7. lorgnon 8. eyeglass
   10. opera glass
lorica... 5. shell 7. cuirass
   11. Breastplate (St Patrick's)
lorikeet... 6. lories, parrot
loris... 5. lemur
lorn... 6. bereft 7. forlorn 8. deserted,
   desolate, forsaken 9. abandoned
   11. Godforsaken
loro... 10. monk parrot, parrot fish
lose... 4. fail, miss, omit 5. leese
   (obs), spill, waste 6. forget, mislay,
   perish 7. forfeit, let slip 8. estrange,
   squander 9. incur loss 10. wander
   from
lose (pert to)...
   balance.. 4. trip 7. stumble
   courage.. 7. despair, despond
   flesh.. 8. emaciate
   freshness.. 4. fade, wilt 6. wither
   ground.. 7. regress 8. slow down
      9. fall short 10. fall behind
   luster.. 7. tarnish
   vigor.. 3. fag, sag 4. fail, flag, pine
      6. weaken 7. decline
loser... 6. victim 7. also ran
   8. defeatee, underdog
loss... 4. ruin, weak 6. damage, injury
   9. decrement, detriment, privation
   10. forfeiture 11. bereavement,
   destruction
loss of...
   commodities.. 6. ullage
   eyebrows, lashes.. 9. madarosis
   feeling.. 7. agnosia 10. anesthesia
      (anaesthesia)
   hair.. 8. alopecia
   loved one.. 11. bereavement
   memory.. 7. amnesia
   reason.. 7. amentia
   smell.. 7. anosmia
   speech.. 4. mute 6. alalia 7. aphasia
      10. laloplegia
   voice.. 7. aphonia
   willpower.. 6. abulia
lost... 4. asea, gone, lorn 5. unwon
   6. hidden, ruined, sinful, wasted
   7. mislaid 8. absorbed, confused,
   defeated, obscured, vanished
   9. abandoned, forfeited, forgotten,
   perplexed, reprobate, subverted
   10. abstracted, bewildered,

dissipated, overthrown, parted with 11. preoccupied 13. irreclaimable, irretrievable

lost (pert to)...
cause.. 8. Civil War
color.. 5. faded, paled
consciousness.. 7. fainted, swooned
life fluid.. 4. bled
to view.. 5. perdu
tribes (ten).. 10. Israelites

lot... 3. tax 4. doom, fate, luck, much, plat 5. share 6. chance, hazard, studio 7. destiny, fortune, portion 9. allotment, great deal 13. apportionment

Lot (pert to)...
father.. 5. Haran
penalty.. 12. pillar of salt
sister.. 6. Milcah
son.. 4. Moab
uncle.. 7. Abraham

lots, divination by... 9. sortilege

lottery... 4. game 5. bingo, lotto 6. chance, raffle 7. Genoese, grab bag 11. sweepstakes

lottery prize... 4. tern (from three numbers)

lotus... 7. nelumbo 10. chinquapin

lotus (pert to)...
bird.. 6. jacana
eaters.. 9. indolents, Lotophagi 11. daydreamers
tree.. 4. sadr 6. jujube, nettle 9. persimmon

loud... 5. crass, gaudy, noisy, showy 6. coarse, flashy, garish, vulgar 7. blatant, booming 8. vehement 9. clamorous, turbulent, unrefined 10. blustering, boisterous, tumultuous, vociferous 11. stentorious 12. obstreperous

loudmouthed... 10. courrilous, stentorian 11. thersitical

Louise de la Ramée (novelist)... 5. Ouida (pen name)

Louisiana...
bird.. 7. pelican
capital.. 10. Baton Rouge
city.. 10. New Orleans, Shreveport
county.. 6. parish
dialect.. 6. Creole
dish (cooked).. 9. jumbalaya
flower.. 8. magnolia
hero.. 6. De Soto, de Vaca, Pineda 7. La Salle
native.. 5. Cajun 6. Creole, French 7. Acadian, Spanish
purchased from.. 8. Napoleon (1803)
river.. 5. Pearl 6. Sabine 11. Mississippi
State admission.. 10. Eighteenth
State motto.. 22. Union, Justice, Confidence
State nickname.. 7. Pelican
tradition.. 10. pirate lore

Louis Viaud (author)... 10. Pierre Loti (pen name)

lounge... 4. loaf, loll, sofa 5. divan 6. frowst, repose 7. recline

louse... 5. aphis 6. cootie, insect, slater 8. Anoplura, arachnid 9. Hemiptera, scoundrel

lout... 3. oaf 4. boor, clod, dolt 6. lubber, rustic 7. bumpkin

loutish... 4. rude 7. awkward, boorish, ill-bred 8. clownish 11. countrified

lovable... 7. amiable 8. adorable, charming 9. desirable, endearing

love... 3. amo, gra, woo 4. like 5. adore, amore, fancy 6. liking 7. charity 8. fondness, good will 9. affection 10. endearment, sweetheart

love (pert to)...
affair.. 7. liaison, romance 10. flirtation
apple.. 6. tomato
bird.. 6. parrot
call.. 3. coo
feast.. 5. agape
flower.. 4. lily
full of.. 4. dote 6. doting, erotic 7. amative 9. idolizing
god of.. 4. Amor, Ares, Eros, Kama 5. Bhaga, Cupid
goddess of.. 5. Athor, Freya (Freyja), Venus 6. Ishtar 9. Aphrodite
intrigue.. 5. amour
knot, token of.. 6. amoret
meeting.. 5. tryst 10. rendezvous
of.. 5. phile (comb form)
parental.. 6. storge
potion.. 7. philter
science.. 9. erotology
song.. 6. serena (evening) 8. madrigal

lover... 4. beau 5. amant, Romeo 6. minion 7. amorist, Don Juan 8. paramour 9. enamorato 10. sweetheart

lover of... see also *craze for*
animals.. 10. zoophilist
beauty.. 8. aesthete (esthete)
wealth.. 9. plutocrat
work.. 9. ergophile

Lover's Leap... 10. Cape Ducato

Lovers' Quarrels... 12. amantium Irae

loving... 4. fond 5. phile (comb form) 6. ardent, erotic 7. adoring, amative, amatory, amorous, devoted 8. charming, enamored, romantic 11. sentimental 12. affectionate

loving cup... 3. tyg (tig)

low... 3. bas, moo 4. base, deep, neap, orra 5. faint 6. humble, menial, sneaky, vulgar, wicked 8. dejected, indecent, infamous, inferior, plebeian 9. inelegant 11. unfavorable

low (pert to)...
born.. 4. rude 5. lowly 6. common 7. lowbred 8. plebeian
bred.. 5. crude 6. coarse, vulgar
brow.. 9. ignoramus
church.. 11. evangelical
comedy.. 8. travesty
country.. 7. Belgium, Holland 9. Luxemburg 11. Netherlands
German.. 5. Saxon 8. Frankish 12. Plattdeutsch
in spirits.. 4. blue 6. megrim 8. dejected, downcast 10. dispirited, melancholy 11. crestfallen
Roman wall.. 5. spina
shrubs, plants.. 4. moss 5. Erica

syllable (Mus).. 2. ut
tide.. 3. ebb 4. neap 8. low water
lower... 3. dip 4. vail, vase 5. abase,
demit, frown, neath 6. bemean,
debase, deepen, demean, demote,
humble, lessen, meaner, nether,
reduce 7. cheapen, degrade, depress,
descent 8. diminish, inferior
10. depreciate
lower (pert to)...
case letter.. 5. small
Empire.. 9. Byzantine
geology.. 5. Chalk (Eng) 6. strata
7. stratum
most.. 6. bottom, lowest 7. bedrock
10. nethermost
world.. 4. hell 5. earth, Hades, limbo,
orcus, Sheol 7. Abaddon, Gehenna
8. Cerberus 9. perdition, purgatory
lowering... 4. dark 6. gloomy, sullen
7. ominous 8. frowning 9. deepening
10. cheapening 11. threatening
lowery... 6. cloudy, gloomy 8. lowering
lowest (pert to)...
animal life.. 6. amoeba (ameba)
deck.. 5. orlop
least.. 5. minim 6. bottom
7. minimum
pedestal member (Arch).. 6. plinth,
quadra
peer (ranking).. 5. baron
point.. 5. depth, nadir 6. bottom
10. nethermost
point, planet.. 7. perigee
lowing... 6. mooing 7. mugient
9. bellowing
lowland... 4. flat, holm, spit 5. plain,
terai 6. bottom 8. molehill
lowly... 4. mean, meek 6. humble,
humbly, meekly, menial, modest
8. inferior, modestly, plebeian
12. unpretending
loxia... 7. wryneck 9. crossbill
loy... 5. slick (tool), spade
loyal... 4. feal, leal, true 5. liege
6. stanch 7. staunch 8. constant,
faithful, obedient
loyalty... 5. faith 6. fealty, homage
8. devotion, fidelity 9. constancy
10. allegiance, stanchness
(staunchness) 12. faithfulness
13. steadfastness
Loyolite... 6. Jesuit
lozenge... 5. candy, facet 6. jujube,
tablet, troche 7. diamond, molding
8. pastille (pastil, pastile)
11. perforation
lubber... 4. boor, dolt, gawk, lout
5. churl, drone, idler, thick 6. sailor
8. landsman 11. grasshopper
lubricity... 8. lewdness
10. smoothness 12. slipperiness
lubricous... 4. lewd 6. tricky, wanton
7. elusive 8. unstable 10. lascivious
lucban... 8. shaddock
luce... 4. pike 10. fleur—de—lis
lucent... 5. clear 6. bright 7. shining
11. translucent, transparent
lucern... 3. dog 4. lynx
lucerne... 4. herb 6. fodder 7. alfalfa
11. purple medic
lucet, luce... 6. pike (fish)

Lucia's home... 10. Lammermoor
lucid... 4. sane 5. clear, vivid
6. bright, lucent 7. shining
8. luminous, pellucid 11. translucent
12. intelligible
luck... 3. hap 4. cess 5. deuce
6. chance 7. ambsace 8. fortuity
11. good fortune
lucky... 5. canny, happy 6. timely
9. fortunate 10. auspicious 11. good
fortune
lucky animal... 6. mascot
lucky token... 4. mojo 5. charm
6. amulet 7. periapt 8. talisman
9. alectoria 10. rabbit foot
12. antinganting
lucrative... 3. fat 6. paying 7. gainful
10. productive, profitable, worthwhile
12. remunerative
lucre... 4. gain, pelf 6. profit, riches
9. emolument 11. acquisition
lucubrate... 18. burn the midnight oil
ludicrous... 5. antic, comic, droll,
funny 6. absurd 7. amusing, comical,
jesting, risible 9. burlesque, laughable
10. ridiculous
Ludolphian... 2. pi (3.14159)
14. Ludolph's number
Luftpost... 7. airmail, air post
lug... 3. box, ear, hug 4. drag, hale,
haul, loop, pull, tote 5. carry
6. basket 9. container
lugs... 4. airs 7. clothes (showy),
tobacco 10. affections
lugubrious... 3. sad 6. woeful
7. doleful 8. grievous, mournful
9. plaintive 10. lamentable
lugworm... 3. lob 7. annelid
9. Arenicola
luhinga... 9. petticoat
lukewarm... 4. cool 5. tepid 6. tepefy
8. tepidity 9. not ardent
10. irresolute 11. indifferent
lumber... 4. wood 6. bungle, litter,
refuse, rumble, timber, trudge
7. lombard 9. rough wood
10. pawnbroker 11. impedimenta
lumberman... 6. logger, sawyer, scorer
9. timberman 10. lumberjack,
woodcutter
lumberman's half boot... 3. pac
lumberman's sled... 4. tode
7. go—devil, travois (travoise)
luminary... 3. sun 4. fire, star 5. light
7. wise man 9. celebrity
12. illumination, leading light
luminescence... 7. foxfire
12. fluorescence
15. phosphorescence
luminous... 5. clear, lucid 6. bright
7. shining 9. brilliant
11. enlightened, illuminated,
intelligent, transparent
14. phosphorescent
luminous circle... 4. halo
luminous impression... 9. phosphene
10. afterimage
lummox... 4. boor, dolt, lout 5. yahoo
7. bumpkin, bungler 12. clumsy
fellow
lump... 3. gob, lob, wad 4. beat,
blob, clot, hunk, loaf, mass 5. bulge

6. nodule, nubble, nugget, thresh
7. cluster 8. swelling
12. protuberance
lump (pert to) . . .
butter . . 3. pat
clay . . 4. clag, clod
metal . . 3. pig 5. ingot
lumpish . . . 4. dull 5. bulky, inert
6. clumsy, stolid, stupid 7. boorish
8. sluggish 9. heaviness, inertness,
ponderous 11. countrified
13. shapelessness
lumpy . . . 5. drunk, rough 6. choppy
7. gnarled, nodular
lumpy jaw . . . 6. big jaw
13. actinomycosis
luna . . . 6. silver 11. moon goddess
lunacy . . . 4. moon 5. mania
7. madness 8. insanity 9. craziness
11. derangement, foolishness
lunar . . . 5. orbed 6. lunate
8. crescent, moonlike 9. celestial,
satellite 10. moon-shaped
lunar (pert to) . . .
appulse . . 7. eclipse
bone . . 7. lunatum
cycle . . 7. Metonic 9. Callippic
deity . . 6. Selene (Selena)
halo . . 6. corona, nimbus 7. aureola
lunatic . . . 3. mad 5. crazy, idiot, loony
6. insane, madman 8. demoniac
9. moonstruck
lunatic asylum . . . 9. Bethlehem
(London)
lunch . . . 5. snack 6. brunch, repast,
tiffin 8. brown bag, luncheon,
nuncheon 9. collation
11. refreshment
lunchroom . . . 6. eatery 10. coffee
chop, restaurant 12. luncheonette
lundyfoot . . . 5. snuff (by Lundy Foot)
lunge . . . 3. cut, jab 4. grab, pass, stab
5. feint, swing 6. thrust
lungs (pert to) . . .
ailment . . 9. emphysema 10. chalicosis
12. tuberculosis
having . . 9. pulmonate
part . . 5. lobes 6. lights 7. bronchi,
trachea
sound . . 4. rale 6. rattle
lurch . . . 4. joll, roll, sway 5. lunge
6. careen, topple 7. deceive
8. flounder 10. disappoint
lure . . . 4. bait, trap 5. decoy, snare,
tempt 6. allure, entice, invite
7. attract, beguile, trumpet, tweedle
10. enticement
lurid . . . 3. wan 4. dark, pale 5. color,
vivid 6. dismal, gloomy 7. ghastly,
obscene 9. deathlike 11. sensational
lurk . . . 4. hide, lote (obs) 5. creep,
prowl, skulk, slink, sneak 9. lie in
wait, pussyfoot
luscious . . . 4. rich 5. sweet
6. creamy, wanton 7. cloying,
honeyed 8. sensuous 9. delicious
10. lascivious, voluptuous
lush . . . 4. soft 5. drink, drunk, juicy
6. lavish, limber, liquor, mellow
7. verdant 8. flexible 9. luxuriant,
succulent 11. intoxicated
lusory . . . 7. playful 8. sportive

lust . . . 5. greed 6. desire, libido
7. craving, longing, passion 8. virility
14. lasciviousness
luster, lustre . . . 4. naif 5. glory, gloss,
sheen, shine 6. beauty, polish
7. glitter, lustrum 8. radiance,
schiller, splendor 10. brightness
11. distinction, iridescence
lusterless . . . 3. dim, mat 4. dead, dull,
flat 14. expressionless
lustful . . . 4. lewd 5. randy
9. lecherous 10. lascivious
lustrous . . . 4. naif 5. nitid 6. agleam,
bright 7. radiant, shining
11. illustrious, transparent
lustrous mineral . . . 4. spar
lustrum (Roman) . . . 6. census, luster
12. purification (5 yrs), quinquennium
lusty . . . 6. active, robust, strong, sturdy
7. healthy 8. vigorous 9. corpulent
lute . . . 4. clay, ring (rubber), seal
6. cement
lute, lutelike . . . 4. asor 6. guitar
7. bandore, pandore, theorbo, ukulele
8. archlute (archilute)
lute tablature . . . 7. lyraway
lutjanoid fish . . . 4. sesi 7. snapper
Luxembourg . . .
capital . . 10. Luxembourg
government . . 10. Grand Duchy
language . . 6. French, German
13. Letzeburgesch
river . . 7. Moselle
luxuriant . . . 4. lush, rank, rich
6. ornate, uberty 7. fertile, opulent,
profuse, teeming 8. abundant, prolific
9. bounteous, Sybaritic
luxuriate . . . 4. bask 5. revel
8. flourish
luxurious . . . 5. plush, ritzy 6. ornate,
superb 8. imposing 9. expensive,
grandiose, sumptuous 10. impressive
11. extravagant
luxury . . . 4. lust 7. lechery
8. elegance, pleasure, richness
10. prosperity, sensuality
11. superfluity 12. extravagance
13. gratification, sumptuousness
14. voluptuousness
luxury lover . . . 7. reveler 8. Sybarite
Luzon . . .
dialect . . 6. Itaves
mountain . . 3. Iba 6. Pagsan (Sicapoo)
people . . 5. Malay 7. Tagalog
8. Tinggian (Tinguian)
savage . . 6. Igorot (Igorrote)
seaport . . 5. Vigan 6. Aparri, Cavite
volcano . . 5. Mayon
lyam . . . 5. leash (Her) 10. bloodhound
lycanthrope . . . 8. werewolf
9. loup-garou
Lycia (pert to) . . .
citizen . . 6. Lycian
city . . 4. Myra
district of . . 9. Asia Minor
language . . 5. Greek 6. Lycian
Lydia . . .
capital . . 6. Sardis
dynasty of . . 5. Gyges 7. Croesus
13. Cyrus the Great
name, later . . 6. Persia
name, old . . 5. Ionia

queen.. 7. Omphale
river.. 8. Pactolus
ruins.. 6. temple
lye... 4. buck 6. bleach, potash
   8. lixivium
lying... 5. false 6. deceit 7. fudging
   9. decumbent, mendacity, reclining,
   recumbent 10. untruthful
lying (pert to)...
across.. 10. transverse
at mountain base.. 8. piedmont
hidden.. 6. latent 11. delitescent
in.. 12. accouchement
near earth's axis.. 5. polar
on the back.. 5. prone 6. supine
   7. passive
lymph... 3. sap 5. chyle, fluid, serum,
   water 6. plasma 7. cassein
lynch... 4. hang 6. murder, punish
   (lawlessly) 7. execute
lynx... 6. bobcat, lucern 7. caracal,
   wildcat 8. carcajou 13. constellation

lynx–eyed... 7. oxyopia
lyre... 4. asor, harp 6. kissar, sabeca,
   trigon, zither 7. cithara, cittern,
   testudo 8. phorminx
lyre (pert to)...
bird.. 6. Menura 8. lyretail, pheasant
shaped.. 6. lyrate
tree.. 5. tulip
turtle.. 11. leatherback
lyric (pert to)...
Arabic.. 5. gazel
Muse.. 5. Erato 10. Polyhymnia
music, poetry.. 3. lay, ode 4. epic,
   poem 5. epode, melic, rhyme (rime),
   verse, vocal 6. epopee, poetic
   7. canzone, musical, rondeau
   8. operatic, palinode 9. dithyramb
poet.. 5. odist
lyrical... 6. epodic
lyrichord... 11. harpsichord
lyssa... 6. rabies 11. hydrophobia
lyssophobia... 17. fear of hydrophobia

M

M... 2. Mu (Gr) 6. letter (13th)
   8. thousand
Ma (Ma Bellona)... 7. goddess
   (fertility)
maarib (Jew)... 7. liturgy
Maat (Egypt)... 7. goddess (justice)
Mab (Queen Mab)... 4. poem 10. fairy
   queen
mabolo... 4. plum 7. camagon
macabre... 4. grim 5. lurid, weird
   6. grisly 7. ghastly 8. gruesome
   12. Dance of Death
macaco... 5. lemur 6. Macaca
   7. macaque 10. Barbary ape
macan... 4. rice
macao... 4. game (gambling)
Macao... 6. Island 7. seaport
macaque... 6. machin, monkey
Macassar... 7. seaport (Celebes)
macaw... 3. ara 5. arara 6. parrot
   7. maracan 8. aracanga (blue and
   red), ararauna (blue and yellow)
Macbeth (pert to)...
author.. 11. Shakespeare (1605)
character.. 4. Duff, Ross 5. Angus
   6. Hecate, Lennox 7. Macduff
murder victim.. 6. Duncan
play type.. 7. tragedy
rival.. 7. Macduff
McBurney's Point (Med)...
   13. abdominal wall
Maccabees... 11. Hasmonaeans
   14. fraternal order, Jewish patriots
maccaboy... 5. snuff
mace... 4. maul 5. baton, gavel, spice
   (nutmeg), staff 6. ensign, mallet
   7. scepter (sceptre)
mace bearer... 5. macer 6. beadle

Macedonia, Balkans...
capital (anc).. 5. Pella
city.. 5. Berea 6. Edessa 8. Salonika
people.. 6. Greeks 8. Serbians
   9. Albanians 10. Bulgarians
ruler.. 6. Philip 9. Alexander (the
   Great)
site.. 15. Balkan Peninsula
macerate... 3. ret, vex 4. soak
   5. steep 6. soften 7. mortify,
   oppress, torture 8. emaciate
   9. waste away
machete... 4. bolo, fish 5. knife
   6. guitar 11. cutlass fish
Machiavellian, Machiavelian... 4. wily
   6. crafty 7. cunning 8. guileful,
   scheming 9. deceitful
   12. falsehearted
machila... 7. hammock
machin... 6. monkey 7. macaque
machinate... 4. plan, plot 6. scheme
   8. contrive, maneuver
machination... 6. design, device,
   scheme 7. machine 8. intrigue
   9. stratagem 10. conspiracy
machine... 3. car 4. auto 6. device,
   engine 7. vehicle 9. apparatus,
   automaton 10. automobile
   11. association, standardize
machine (pert to)...
cloth maturing.. 4. ager
cloth stretching.. 6. tenter
cotton.. 3. gin 4. mule 5. baler
glazing.. 8. calender
hay.. 5. baler 6. tedder
hoisting.. 3. gin, pry 4. pump
   5. crane, davit, lever, tongs
   7. derrick
hummeling.. 5. awner

hydraulic . . 9. telemotor
imitating . . 9. automaton
military . . 3. ram 6. onager
mixing . . 9. malaxator
ore . . 6. vanner
planing . . 8. surfacer
planting . . 6. seeder
political . . 5. party 6. system
  7. faction
reckoning . . 6. abacus 9. tabulator
  10. calculator
rubber shaping . . 8. extruder
stage effect . . 13. deus ex machina
tool . . 5. drill, lathe
machine gun . . . 4. nest (hidden place)
  5. Maxim 6. cannon 7. Gatling
  9. Hotchkiss 10. chatterbox
machine—made . . . 11. stereotyped
machine power, energy . . . 5. input
  6. output
machinist . . . 7. artisan 8. mechanic
mackerel . . . 5. atule, spike, tunny
  6. sierra, tinker
mackerel (pert to) . . .
bait . . 9. jellyfish
bird . . 7. wryneck 9. kittiwake
genus . . 7. Scomber
goose . . 9. phalarope
like . . 4. cero 6. bonito 7. escolar
net . . 7. spiller
shark . . 9. porbeagle
sky . . 6. clouds 9. striation
small (allowable size) . . 5. spike
  6. tinker 7. blinker
mackle . . . 4. blur, spot 6. blotch,
  macule
macrobiotic . . . 9. long—lived
mad . . . 4. vain, wild 5. angry, crazy,
  irate, rabid, vexed 6. insane, maniac
  7. enraged, foolish, frantic, furious
  8. demented, frenetic, maniacal,
  reckless 9. hilarious, turbulent
  10. distraught, infatuated, infuriated
  12. arreptitious
Madagascar, Malagasy . . .
animal . . 5. indri, lemur 6. aye—aye,
  tenrec (tendrac) 9. babacoote
capital . . 10. Tananarive
cattle . . 4. zebu (humped)
city . . 7. Majanga 8. Tamatave
civet . . 7. fossane
govenment . . 8. Republic (1960)
language . . 16. Malayo—Polynesian
native . . 4. Hova 8. Sakalava
palm . . 6. raffia
religion . . 7. Animist 9. Christian
Madam . . . 3. Mrs 4. Frau, lady,
  Ma'am 5. donna, hussy 6. Madame,
  Señora 8. goodwife, mistress
  9. courtesan
madcap . . . 3. wag 4. rash, wild
  5. blood 6. madman 7. hotspur,
  violent 8. reckless 9. daredevil,
  foolhardy
madden . . . 3. vex 5. craze 6. enrage,
  incite 7. incense 9. infuriate
  10. antagonize
madder . . . 2. al 3. aal, red 4. herb,
  rose (color) 5. brown, Rubia
  6. orange, violet, yellow 7. crimson,
  xanthin 9. turkey—red
made . . . 5. built 7. created, trained

  8. invented, prepared, produced,
  rendered 10. artificial, successful
  11. constructed 12. enfranchised,
  manufactured
made (pert to) . . .
accurate . . 5. trued
believe . . 7. feigned 9. pretended,
  simulated
blind . . 6. seeled
clear . . 9. explained 10. elucidated
destitute . . 6. bereft
fun of . . 6. jeered, mocked 7. derided
  9. ridiculed
hard, obdurate . . 7. steeled
light of . . 7. dwarfed 9. belittled
  10. disparaged
over . . 8. reformed, revamped
  9. remodeled
plain . . 9. evidenced, exhibited
  10. manifested
public . . 5. aired 7. accused, delated
  8. reported
scalloped edges . . 6. pinked
sound . . 7. bleated, rumbled, swished
tart . . 7. euchred
up . . 9. composite 10. artificial,
  fabricated 12. manufactured
up mind . . 7. decided
valid . . 6. proved 9. confirmed
  13. authenticated
whole again . . 7. renewed
  10. reconciled 13. redintegrated,
  re—established
Madeira Islands . . .
capital . . 7. Funchal
embroidery . . 6. eyelet
nut . . 6. walnut
owner of Islands . . 8. Portugal
wind . . 5. leste
wine . . 4. bual 5. tinta (red)
  7. malmsey, sercial 8. verdelho
wood . . 8. ironwood (white), mahogany
madhouse . . . 5. chaos 6. asylum,
  bedlam 8. nuthouse
madman . . . 3. nut 4. coot, loon
  6. maniac 7. lunatic 9. phrenetic
madness . . . 3. ire 4. fury, rage
  5. anger, mania 6. frenzy, lunacy
  8. insanity 9. agitation, theomania
  (Relig) 11. foolishness, inspiration
Mad Parliament (1258) . . .
  18. Provisions of Oxford
Madras, India . . .
capital . . 6. Madras
city . . 5. Adoni, Arcot 7. Calicut
export . . 4. lace 7. fabrics 9. kerchiefs
  (for turbans)
government . . 10. presidency
madrepore . . . 5. coral 6. fossil, marble
  8. Acropora 12. Madreporaria
Madrid, Spain . . .
architecture . . 7. Moorish
boulevard . . 5. Prado 12. Salon de
  Prado
noted buildings . . 7. Armeria
  11. Prado Museum, Royal Palace
madrigal . . . 3. ode 4. glee, poem
  5. lyric, music 6. verses
maduro . . . 5. cigar 6. mature
  11. dark—colored
maelstrom . . . 5. churn 6. foment
  7. turmoil 9. whirlpool (Norway)

maestro ... 6. master 7. teacher
  8. composer, musician 9. conductor
  13. Kapellmeister
maestro—di—cappela ... 11. choirmaster
Mae West ... 8. life belt
Maffia ... 9. syndicate 10. underworld
  12. organization (Sicilian)
maffle ... 6. muddle, mumble
  7. confuse, stammer 8. squander
mafoo, mafu (Chin) ... 5. groom
  9. stable boy
mag ... 6. magpie 7. chatter
  8. titmouse 9. halfpenny
magadis ... 5. flute 9. monochord
magazine ... 4. shop 5. depot, store
  6. review 7. arsenal, chamber (gun),
  tabloid 9. ephemeris, reservoir,
  warehouse 10. periodical, repository,
  storehouse
magazine rifle ... 6. Mauser
  8. repeater
mage ... 5. Magus 6. Merlin 7. Houdini
  8. conjurer, magician
magenta ... 3. dye 7. fuchsia
maggot ... 4. grub, mawk 5. larva,
  mathe 6. notion 7. caprice, Diptera
  12. eccentricity
Magi (Three Wise Men) ... 6. Gaspar
  8. Melchior 9. Balthasar
magic ... 3. art 4. juju, mana, maya,
  rune, show 5. charm, fairy, spell
  6. voodoo 10. necromancy
  11. conjuration, enchantment,
  legerdemain
magic (pert to) ...
  art (black) .. 7. demonry 9. diablerie,
  diabolism
  art (white) .. 5. turgy 7. theurgy
  ejaculation .. 2. om (um) 6. sesame
  goddess .. 5. Circe 6. Hecate
  image .. 5. sigil 8. sigillum
  lantern .. 11. epidiascope
  12. stereopticon
  lantern slide .. 6. tinter
  staff, wand .. 6. rhabdo 8. caduceus
  symbol .. 5. charm 6. caract, fetish
  8. pentacle 9. pentalpha
  word .. 2. om (um) 6. presto, sesame
  10. abacadabra
magical ... 6. goetic (goety)
  8. charming
magician ... 4. mage 5. magus
  6. Merlin, wizard 7. Houdini, juggler
  8. conjurer, mandrake, sorcerer
  9. archimage, charlatan, enchanter
  11. entertainer, necromancer,
  thaumaturge 13. thaumaturgist
  15. prestidigitator
magician (pert to) ...
  attendant .. 7. famulus
  command .. 6. presto 11. abracadabra
  manual .. 8. grimoire
magirics ... 7. cookery
magirist ... 4. cook
magisterial ... 5. lofty, proud
  6. august, lordly 7. haughty, stately
  8. arrogant, dogmatic, judicial, official
  9. dignified, imperious, masterful
  10. commanding 11. dictatorial,
  domineering, overbearing
  13. authoritative
magistrate ... 4. doge 5. ephor, judge

  6. aedile (edile), archon, bailli,
  puisne, syndic 7. alcaide (alcaid),
  alcalde, bailiff
magistrate's orders ... 4. acta
magma ... 5. dregs 8. sediment
  10. molten rock, suspension (Pharm)
magna cum laude ... 14. with great
  honor
magnanimous ... 4. free 5. lofty, noble
  7. exalted, liberal 8. generous
  9. honorable, unselfish, unstinted
  10. high—minded 11. great of mind
  13. disinterested
magnate ... 4. lord 5. baron, mogul,
  noble 6. bashaw, bigwig, tycoon
  7. grandee, richman 9. personage
  11. millionaire
magnesium (pert to) ...
  limestone .. 8. dolomite
  nitrate .. 9. saltpeter
  silicate .. 4. talc
  sulphate .. 10. Epsom salts
magnet ... 7. terella 8. solenoid
  9. loadstone, lodestone
magnet (type) ... 3. bar 9. horseshoe
  10. artificial
magnetic ... 10. attractive, electrical
  14. attractiveness
magnetism ... 5. oomph 8. polarity
magnificence ... 5. glory 8. grandeur,
  splendor 15. superexcellence
magnificent ... 5. grand, regal
  6. lavish, superb 7. exalted,
  pompous, sublime 8. imposing,
  palatial, splendid, striking 9. brilliant,
  grandiose, sumptuous 10. munificent
magnify ... 4. laud 5. exalt, extol
  6. expand, praise 7. enlarge, glorify,
  worship 8. increase 9. intensify,
  overstate 10. exaggerate
magnitude ... 4. size 6. extent
  7. bigness 8. grandeur, nobility
  9. extension, greatness
Magnolia State ... 11. Mississippi
magnum ... 4. bone (wrist) 6. bottle
  9. capitatum
magnum opus ... 9. great work
  11. achievement
magpie ... 3. daw, mag, pie 4. Pica,
  piet (pyet) 5. madge, scold
  6. pigeon, talker 9. chatterer
  10. chattermag
magpie type ...
  diver .. 4. smew
  shrike .. 7. tanager
maguari ... 5. stork
magus ... 8. magician 9. one of Magi
Magyar ... 3. Hun 9. Hungarian
Mah (Persian) ... 9. moon angel
maha ... 10. sambar deer
Mahabharata (blind king, Hind) ...
  13. Dhritarashtra
mahajan, mahajun (Ind) ... 8. great
  man 11. moneylender
mahal ... 8. Taj Mahal 9. residence
  (summer) 10. apartments, Natal
  brown
mahala ... 5. squaw
maharaja, maharajah ... 5. ruler
  6. prince
maharani, maharanee ... 5. queen
mahatma ... 4. sage 7. wise man

9. great soul, occultist 21. Great
White Brotherhood (member)
mahogany . . . 3. roe (burl) 4. toon,
wood 5. brown 6. totara 7. ratteen
maholi . . . 5. lemur
Mahomet . . . see *Mohammedan*
Mahound . . . 5. Devil 8. Mohammed
mahout . . . 6. driver (elephant), keeper
Mah to Mahi . . . 10. Fish to Moon
Maia (pert to) . . .
　mountain nymph . . 7. Arcadia
　son . . 6. Hermes
　star . . 8. Pleiades
maid . . . 4. girl, lass 5. bonne, woman
6. damsel, maiden, virgin 7. abigail,
servant 8. spinster 9. tirewoman
Maid (of) . . .
　Astolat . . 6. Elaine
　Athens . . 12. Theresa Macri
　Lydia . . 7. Arachne (changed to a
　　spider)
　Orléans . . 9. Joan of Arc
　Zeus . . 2. Io (changed to heifer)
maidenhair . . . 4. fern 8. Adiantum
10. Venus's hair
maidenhair tree . . . 6. gingko
maidenly . . . 6. gentle, modest 7. girlish
9. unmarried
maigre . . . 4. diet, fish
mail . . . 3. dak (dawk) 4. post 5. armor
7. consign, letters, plumage
8. dispatch
mail, coat of . . . 5. armor 6. byrnie
(brinie) 7. broigne, cuirass (part),
hauberk, panoply
mail boat . . . 6. packet
maim . . . 6. injure, mangle, mayhem
7. disable 8. mutilate 9. tear apart
main . . . 3. ooo 4. duct 5. chief, first,
great, prime, sheer, utter 6. mighty,
potent 7. chiefly, conduit, leading
8. foremost 9. conductor, essential,
principal 10. on the whole
11. essentially 13. most important
main (pert to) . . .
　act (drama) . . 8. epitasis
　beam . . 6. girder 7. walking
　part . . 4. body
　point . . 3. jet, nub 4. crux, gist, pith
　post . . 9. sternpost
　sea (poet) . . 11. Spanish Main
　　(Caribbean Sea)
Maine . . .
　bay . . 5. Casco 13. Passamaquoddy
　capital . . 7. Augusta
　city . . 4. Saco 5. Hiram, Orono
　　6. Bangor 8. Lewiston, Portland
　　11. Millinocket
　college . . 5. Bates, Colby 7. Bowdoin
　Easternmost city . . 8. Eastport
　Easternmost point . . 19. West Quoddy
　　Head Light
　Easternmost town . . 5. Lubec
　lake . . 6. Sebago 9. Moosehead
　mountain . . 5. Kineo 8. Cadillac,
　　Katahdin
　resort . . 9. Bar Harbor
　resort island . . 8. Mt Desert
　river . . 8. Kennebec 9. Penobscot
　State admission . . 11. Twenty-third
　State motto . . 6. Dirigo 7. I Direct
　State nickname . . 8. Pine Tree

　trout . . 7. oquassa
Maine, The . . . 10. battleship (Sp–Am
War)
maintain . . . 4. aver, hold, keep
5. claim 6. affirm, allege, assert,
avouch, defend, endure, insist, retain
7. justify, support, sustain
8. continue, preserve
maintainable . . . 7. tenable
maintenance . . . 3. aid 6. upkeep
7. alimony, defense, support
9. retention 10. livelihood,
sustenance 11. continuance
12. conservation, preservation,
sustentation
maison . . . 5. house
Maison Carrée . . . 12. Norman Temple
(Nimes)
maison de santé . . . 6. asylum
8. hospital 10. sanatorium
maître d'hôtel (famed) . . . 5. Oscar
maize . . . 3. Zea 4. corn 7. mealies
maja, majo . . . 5. belle, dandy
majestic . . . 5. grand, great, lofty,
noble, regal, royal 6. august, kingly
7. stately, sublime 8. elevated,
eloquent, imperial, splendid
9. dignified, grandiose
11. ceremonious, magnificent
majesty . . . 5. title 7. crowned (Her),
dignity 8. grandeur 9. eloquence,
greatness, loftiness, sceptered (Her)
major . . . 3. dur (Mus) 6. course
(study), ditone 7. greater, officer
8. legal age, majority
major–domo . . . 6. butler 7. bailiff,
steward 9. seneschal
majority . . . 3. age 4. most 6. quorum
7. greater 8. maturity 9. majorship,
plurality, seniority 12. more than half
make . . . 2. do 4. earn, form, gain,
kind 5. shape 6. compel, create,
induce, render 7. compose, execute,
produce 8. contrive, generate
9. structure 10. accomplish
11. composition, manufacture
make (pert to) . . .
　affidavit . . 4. affy
　allowance . . 5. abate, admit
　　7. concede
　allusion to . . 7. mention
　amends . . 5. atone 7. redress
　as if . . 7. pretend 8. as though
　bare . . 5. strip 6. balden, denude
　believe . . 4. sham 5. feign 7. pretend
　　8. pretense
　better . . 5. widen 6. soften
　　7. broaden, improve 9. meliorate
　　10. ameliorate
　book . . 10. record bets
　buoyant . . 8. levitate
　calm . . 5. allay, quiet 6. serene
　　7. appease, compose
　certain . . 6. assure, ensure
　cheerful . . 6. solace 7. comfort,
　　console
　choice . . 3. opt 4. cull 5. choose,
　　select 7. pick out
　clean breast of . . 7. confess
　　8. disclose
　clear . . 7. explain 9. elucidate
　coins . . 4. mint

countercharge.. 11. recriminate
crisp.. 9. embrittle
deduction.. 6. rebate
desolate.. 5. strip 7. bereave
diminutive.. 9. bantamize
do.. 3. eke 5. get by 8. piece out
  9. improvise
eccentric.. 8. decenter
edging.. 3. tat 7. crochet
effective.. 6. compel 7. enforce
enduring.. 6. anneal, temper
equal.. 6. equate
evident.. 6. evince
familiar.. 8. accustom
famous.. 8. eternize 11. immortalize
fast.. 4. snub 5. belay 6. batten,
  secure
faulty.. 6. impair 7. vitiate
  11. contaminate
firm.. 3. fix 5. brace 6. cement
fit.. 4. suit 5. adapt 6. adjust
  7. conform
foolish, stupid.. 4. daff 8. stultify
  10. ridiculous
fun of.. 3. rib 5. scoff 8. ridicule
glass.. 7. platten
good.. 7. absolve, justify, succeed
  9. indemnify, vindicate
happy.. 5. elate 7. beatify 8. felicify
  (obs)
hard, harsh.. 5. steel 6. freeze
  7. roughen
harmonious.. 6. attune
headway.. 4. gain 7. advance
  8. progress
holy.. 5. bless 6. hallow
  10. consecrate
honorable.. 5. exalt 6. uplift
  7. ennoble
ineffective.. 4. void 5. annul
insensible to pain.. 11. anesthetize
  (anaesthetize)
into law.. 5. enact 9. legislate
known.. 6. impart, reveal 7. divulge,
  publish, uncover 8. disclose,
  discover, proclaim
lace.. 3. tat 7. crochet
less dense.. 4. thin 6. rarefy
less smooth.. 7. roughen
level.. 4. true
light.. 4. jetsam 8. illumine, jettison
lively.. 8. energize
love.. 3. coo, woo 5. court
merry.. 5. laugh 6. banter 7. disport
mild.. 8. mitigate, modulate
moral.. 8. ethicize
much of.. 6. praise 7. enthuse, lionize
  10. exaggerate
muddy.. 4. roil
notes.. 8. annotate
out.. 4. know 5. solve 6. decode,
  draw up 7. analyze, discern
  8. contrive, decipher 10. understand
over.. 4. redo 6. revamp 7. convert
  9. refashion, reproduce
pale, sickly.. 8. etiolate
possible.. 6. enable
pottery.. 7. spattle
precious.. 6. endear
pretentious.. 7. buckram
public.. 3. air 5. bruit, noise
  6. delate 7. publish 9. divulgate

  11. acknowledge
ready.. 4. gear 5. coach, prime
  7. prepare
reparation.. 5. atone
resistance.. 5. rebel 6. mutiny, revolt
secure.. 3. fix, pin 4. nail, snub
  5. belay 6. batten, fasten
shift.. 9. temporary
short work of.. 6. hasten 7. destroy
  10. accomplish
shrill noise.. 10. stridulate
smooth.. 4. buff, iron 5. sleek, slick
  6. scrape
spruce.. 4. perk 7. smarten
strong.. 7. stouten
thin.. 9. attenuate
three–cornered.. 11. triangulate
unhappy.. 8. embitter 10. exacerbate
up.. 5. atone, build 6. invent, settle
  7. compose, concoct, prepare
  8. assemble, cosmetic 9. construct,
  improvise, reconcile 10. compensate
use of.. 5. apply 6. borrow, employ
  7. utilize 11. appropriate
waste (law).. 7. estrepe
watertight.. 4. calk, seal
white.. 6. blanch, bleach
worse.. 9. aggravate
zealous.. 7. enthuse
maker of ...
arrows.. 8. fletcher
barrels.. 6. cooper
bundles.. 5. baler
infusion.. 7. steeper
knives.. 6. cutler
pottery.. 6. potter 8. ceramist
makeshift ... 7. stopgap
maki ... 5. lemur
mal (comb form) ... 3. bad, ill 5. badly
  7. disease 8. sickness
Malabar (pert to) ...
bark.. 5. ochna
nutmeg.. 10. Bombay mace
palm.. 7. talipot
rat.. 9. bandicoot
Malacca ... 7. seaport (Malaya)
Malachi ... 4. Book (Old Test)
  7. prophet
malachite ... 4. bice 5. green
  6. copper 7. pigment
maladroit ... 6. clumsy 7. awkward,
  unhandy 8. bungling 9. all thumbs,
  graceless 10. blundering, left–handed,
  ungraceful
maladventure ... 6. mishap
  8. escapade 12. ill adventure
malady ... 4. amok 7. ailment, disease,
  illness 8. disorder, sickness
  9. complaint, distemper
  13. indisposition
mala fide ... 10. in bad faith
Malaga ... 4. city (Sp), wine
  10. oxblood red
Malagasy lemur ... 6. aye–aye
Malagasy region ... 10. Madagascar
malaise ... 4. pain 10. discomfort,
  uneasiness
malapert ... 4. bold, pert 5. saucy
  8. impudent
malaria ... 5. miasm 6. miasma
  10. strophulus
malaxation ... 7. massage 9. softening

Malay Archipelago . . .
animal . . 4. mias 5. tapir, tsine
  6. gibbon, taguan 7. banteng
apparel . . 4. baju 5. banju 6. sarong
buffalo . . 4. gaur 7. carabao, seldang
canoe . . 4. proa 5. prahu
chief (tribal) . . 4. dato (datto)
crane . . 5. sarus
dagger, knife . . 6. creese (kris), parong
disease (jumping) . . 4. Lata (Latah)
gentleman . . 3. sir 4. tuan
island . . 4. Bali, Java 5. Timor
  7. Celebes, Sumatra 9. New Guinea
  11. Philippines
isthmus . . 3. Kra
language . . 7. Tagalog
native . . 5. Bajau 6. Ifugao 8. Filipino
  9. Samal Laut 10. sea gypsies
palm . . 6. Arenga, gomuti (gomuto)
  8. Saguerus
pygmy . . 4. Aeta
rice field . . 5. sawah
seaport . . 7. Malacca
state . . 5. Kedah, Perak 6. Jahore
tree . . 4. upas 5. kapur, niepa, terap
  6. durian (fruit)
vessel . . 4. toup 6. lugger
Malaysia . . .
capital . . 11. Kuala Lumpur
malcontent . . . 5. rebel 6. Fenian,
  uneasy 7. repiner 8. agitator,
  grumbler 10. rebellious
  12. discontented
male . . . 2. he 3. cob, him, tom 4. bull,
  dude, galt, jack, stud 5. andro (comb
  form), macho, manly 6. tercel, virile
  7. rooster 8. stallion 9. masculine
male (pert to) . . .
column (Arch) . . 7. Tolamon
  8. Atlantes
One Hundred eyes . . 5. Argus
malediction . . . 5. curse 6. threat
  7. malison, slander 8. anathema
  11. imprecation 12. denunciation
malefaction . . . 5. crime 7. offense
  9. malum in se
malefactor . . . 5. felon 7. culprit
  8. criminal, evildoer 9. wrongdoer
malevolence . . . 4. hate 5. pique, spite
  6. grudge, malice, rancor 7. ill will
  8. inimical 9. animosity, malignity
  10. bitterness
malevolent . . . 4. evil 6. hating
  7. envious, hateful 8. spiteful
  9. malicious, rancorous
  11. ill–disposed
malfeasance . . . 7. misrule 8. impolicy
  10. wrongdoing 11. evil conduct,
  illegal deed
malfeasant . . . 8. criminal, evildoer
malgré . . . 9. in spite of
  15. notwithstanding
malheur . . . 10. misfortune
Mali, Africa . . .
capital . . 6. Bamako
malice . . . 4. envy, evil 5. malum,
  pique, spite, wrong 6. rancor 7. ill
  will 9. animosity, malignity, malintent
  10. bitterness 11. malevolence
malicious . . . 4. evil, mean 6. bitter,
  malign, ornery 7. hateful 8. sinister,
  spiteful 9. rancorous, resentful,

  vitriolic 11. ill–disposed
  12. cantankerous, unpropitious
malicious (pert to) . . .
destruction . . 5. arson 8. sabotage
  9. vandalism
gossip . . 4. dirt 7. scandal, slander
intention . . 6. animus
maliform . . . 11. apple–shaped
malign . . . 4. evil 5. abuse, libel
  6. deadly, defame, revile, vilify
  7. asperse, baleful, harmful, slander,
  traduce 8. badmouth, virulent
  10. calumniate 12. unpropitious
malignancy . . . 6. malice 9. virulence
  10. deadliness 11. harmfulness,
  noxiousness
malignant . . . 3. ill 4. evil 5. felon
  6. deadly, wicked 7. harmful,
  heinous, vicious 8. spiteful, virulent
  9. felonious, invidious, malicious,
  poisonous, rancorous 10. rebellious
  11. deleterious
maligner . . . 8. libelist 9. slanderer
malignity . . . 4. evil, hate 5. spite,
  venom 11. harmfulness, heinousness
maline(s) . . . 3. net 11. Mechlin lace
malingerer . . . 6. truant 7. quitter,
  shirker, slacker, welsher
malison . . . 5. curse 11. malediction
malkin . . . 3. cat, mop 4. drab, hare
  6. sponge 8. slattern 9. scarecrow
mall . . . 4. gull, walk 5. alley, plaza,
  prado 6. arcade, mallet 7. alameda
  8. assembly 9. esplanade, promenade
  14. shopping center
mallangong . . . 8. duckbill
mallard . . . 4. Anas, duck 5. drake
malleable . . . 4. soft 6. pliant
  7. ductile, plastic 9. teachable
mallemuck . . . 6. fulmar, petrel
  9. albatross
mallet . . . 3. tup 4. club, mace, maul
  5. gavel, madge 6. beater, beetle,
  driver, hammer
malm . . . 4. marl 5. chalk
malmsey . . . 4. wine
malodorous . . . 4. rank 5. fetid
  6. rotten 7. noisome, odorous
  11. ill–smelling, odoriferous
malt (pert to) . . .
froth . . 4. barm
ground . . 5. grist
infusion . . 4. wort 9. sweetwort
liquor . . 4. beer, suds 6. swipes
material . . 5. grain 6. barley
mixture . . 6. zythum 7. maltate
vinegar . . 4. wort 6. alegar
Malta, Mediterranean Isle . . .
capital . . 8. Valletta
fever . . 8. undulent
group island . . 4. Gozo 6. Comino
Maltese . . . 3. cat 5. cross 6. Knight,
  native (of Malta)
maltreat . . . 5. abuse 6. misuse 8. ill
  treat 9. do wrong by
malty . . . 5. drunk
malum . . . 4. evil 5. wrong 7. offense
malversation . . . 9. extortion (in office)
  10. corruption 11. evil conduct,
  fraudulence, misbehavior
mammal . . . 3. ape, man 4. homo
  5. whale 10. vertebrate

mammal... 2. ai, ox 3. ape, bat, cat,
cow, dog, hog, orc, pig, rat, yak
4. bear, bull, deer, lion, mink, mole,
paca, seal, tait, zebu 5. camel, coati,
daman, koala, lemur, llama, moose,
mouse, okapi, otter, ounce, panda,
ratel, rhino, sable, shark, sheep,
swine, tapir, tayra, whale 6. alpaca,
badger, desman, dugong, marten,
monkey, ocelot, rytina (ext), tenrec
(tendrac), walrus, weasel 7. dolphin,
manatee, opossum, peccary, raccoon
8. aardvark, anteater, antelope,
elephant, kangaroo, mongoose,
reindeer 10. chevrotain, rhinoceros
12. hippopotamus

mammal (pert to)...
coat.. 4. hide, skin 6. pelage
cud—chewing.. 8. ruminant
edentate.. 8. anteater, pangolin,
tamandua (anteater)
extinct.. 6. rytina 8. mastodon
9. Glyptodon
flying.. 3. bat
largest.. 5. whale
man.. 6. Bimana (group)
meat—eating.. 9. carnivore
nipple.. 4. teat 8. mammilla
omnivorous.. 3. hog, pig 5. swine
Order.. 7. Cetacea 8. Edentata,
Rodentia
Order, highest.. 7. Primata
8. Mammalia
Order, lowest.. 9. Marsupial
plantigrade.. 7. raccoon
primate (except Man)..
10. Quadrumana
scaled.. 8. pangolin
shelled.. 9. armadillo
smallest.. 5. shrew
snake—eating.. 8. mongoose
toothless.. 8. edentate
web—footed.. 6. aliped
wing—footed.. 6. aliped
zebralike.. 6. quagga

mammock... 4. tear 5. break, scrap
8. fragment

mammon... 5. money 6. riches, wealth
11. fallen angel (Bib) 15. demon of
cupidity

mammoth... 5. giant, large (very)
7. titanic 8. behemoth, elephant,
gigantic, mastodon 9. pachyderm
11. Dinotherium 12. hippopotamus

man... 3. arm, fit, rig 4. homo, male
5. adult, equip, fit up, human, staff
6. outfit, person 7. fortify, furnish,
mankind, prepare, someone
9. human race 10. human being

man (of)...
all work.. 4. mozo 6. Friday
8. factotum 9. assistant
Blood and Iron.. 8. Bismarck
Destiny.. 9. Bonaparte (Napoleon)
Galilee.. 11. Jesus Christ
God.. 5. saint 6. priest 9. clergyman
12. ecclesiastic
law.. 6. lawyer 7. counsel 8. attorney
9. counselor (counsellor)
learning.. 6. pundit, savant 7. scholar
9. literatus 11. litterateur
quackery.. 7. buffoon 9. trickster

10. mountebank
the sea.. 3. tar 6. merman, sailor
the signs.. 12. homo signorum
the woods.. 6. rustic 8. silvanus,
woodsman 9. orangutan
the world.. 6. layman 11. cosmopolite
12. sophisticate
war.. 7. frigate, soldier, warrior

man (pert to)...
aged.. 3. vet 9. patriarch
12. octogenarian
bachelor.. 4. stag 8. celibate
bald.. 9. pilgarlic
conceited.. 7. coxcomb
cunning.. 5. rogue 6. rascal
7. shyster 10. mountebank
dissolute.. 4. roué
eccentric, elderly.. 4. sire 5. uncle
6. codger, gaffer 11. grandfather
effeminate.. 9. androgyne
entire (soul and body).. 3. ego
fashionable.. 3. fop 4. dude 5. dandy
11. Beau Brummel 12. boulevardier
fungus.. 9. earthstar (the)
handsome.. 6. Adonis
hardheaded.. 5. Boche
hard—pressed.. 3. Job
important.. 4. hero, lion 5. chief,
nabob 6. tycoon 7. mugwump
Isle of, capital.. 7. Douglas
lady's.. 4. beau 6. fiancé
lawless.. 7. ruffian
learned.. 6. pundit, savant 7. erudite,
scholar 9. literatus 11. philologist
like.. 7. android 10. anthropoid
little.. 6. mankin, shrimp, squirt
10. homunculus
loud—voiced.. 7. stentor
lowbred.. 4. serf 5. churl 6. rustic
7. peasant 8. plebeian
medicine, magic.. 6. shaman
millionaire.. 7. Croesus 10. capitalist,
Corinthian
newspaper.. 6. editor 8. reporter
10. journalist
old.. 5. elder 7. veteran
12. octogenarian
prehistoric.. 4. cave 6. Ice Age
8. eolithic, Grimaldi, Piltdown
9. neolithic 11. paleolithic
red.. 6. Indian
strong.. 6. Samson 8. ironside
wise.. 4. sage, seer 5. solon
6. nestor 7. Solomon
without a country.. 5. Nolan (Philip)

manacle... 4. gyve, iron 5. chain
6. fetter 7. shackle 8. handcuff
9. restraint

manada... 4. herd 5. drove, flock

manage... 3. man, run 4. boss, head,
lead, tend 5. cater, dight, guide,
pilot, wield 6. direct, govern
7. control, husband, operate
8. contrive, engineer 10. administer,
manipulate

manageable... 4. easy, tame, yare
6. docile, wieldy 7. ductile
9. compliant, tractable
10. governable 12. controllable

management... 4. care 5. charge,
menage 7. conduct, control, gestion
9. direction 10. government

11. negotiation
manager... 4. boss 6. gerent
7. steward 8. director, governor,
operator, overseer 9. economist
12. entrepreneur 13. administrator
managery... 7. cunning 8. artifice
9. frugality, husbandry
10. management 12. manipulation
14. administration
mañana... 8. tomorrow 10. before
long
manas (Hind)... 3. ego 4. mind
Manasseh... 5. tribe (Israel) 11. King
of Judah
Manchuria...
capital.. 6. Mukden (old)
9. Changchun
government.. 9. Communist (Chin)
Japanese name.. 9. Manchukuo
native.. 9. Mongolian
river.. 4. Amur, Liao, Yalu
manciple... 5. slave 7. servant,
steward 8. purveyor
mandarin (pert to)...
bird.. 4. duck
city.. 9. Chungking
color.. 3. red
dialect.. 7. Chinese
figure in Chiness dress, seated..
9. grotesque
fruit.. 6. orange 9. tangerine
official.. 8. governor 10. bureaucrat
residence.. 5. yamen
ware.. 9. porcelain
mandate... 5. edict, order 6. behest,
charge, decree, mandat 7. bidding,
command, precept 9. direction
10. injunction, referendum
mandatory... 10. imperative, obligatory,
preceptive
mandible... 3. jaw 4. beak 5. chops,
molar (part) 9. chelicera
mandrel, mandril... 3. hob 4. axle,
pick (miner's) 5. arbor 7. spindle
mandriarch... 9. monk ruler
mandrill... 6. baboon
mane... 4. hair, juba, shag 6. thatch
manege... 6. school (riding)
7. academy (riding) 8. cavesson
(halter)
manes (Rom)... 4. gods (lower world)
7. spirits
maneuver, manoeuvre... 4. ruse
5. trick 6. device, jockey, scheme,
tactic 7. operate 8. artifice, intrigue,
strategy 9. stratagem 10. manipulate
13. Immelmann turn
mangabey... 6. monkey
manger... 3. bin 4. crib, meal, rack
6. bunker, trough 7. banquet
mangle... 3. cut, mar 4. hack
5. press 6. bruise, injure, ironer
8. calender, demolish, lacerate,
mutilate 9. dismember
mango (pert to)...
bird.. 6. oriole 11. hummingbird
fish.. 9. threadfin
fruit.. 5. amini, bauno, drupe, melon
9. muskmelon
grove.. 4. tope
mangy... 4. mean 5. itchy, seedy

6. ronyon, scurvy, shabby 7. squalid
12. contemptible
manhandle... 4. maul 5. abuse
7. rough up 8. maltreat, mistreat
mania... 4. rage 5. craze, furor
6. frenzy, furore, lunacy 7. madness,
passion 8. delirium 10. alienation
11. fascination, infatuation
mania (for)...
buying.. 9. oniomania
drink.. 9. potomania 10. dipsomania
foreign customs.. 9. xenomania
narcotics.. 10. narcomania
religion.. 9. theomania
stealing.. 10. erotomania
11. kleptomania
wandering.. 10. dromomania
work.. 9. ergomania
manifest... 4. list, open, show
5. clear, index, overt 6. evince,
liquet, patent 7. declare, evident,
express, obvious, visible 8. apparent,
disclose 11. indubitable
12. indisputable, unmistakable
manifestation... 4. aura 5. phase
7. display 8. evidence
10. appearance, disclosure,
exhibition, indication, revelation
13. demonstration
manifestation of...
deity.. 4. Apis 7. serapis
divinity.. 6. Christ 8. Epiphany
Vishnu.. 6. avatar
manifesto... 5. edict 6. decree
8. evidence, rescript 11. declaration
(public) 12. announcement
13. demonstration
manikin... 5. dwarf, model, pygmy
6. figure 7. phantom 9. mannequin
Manila...
boat.. 6. bilalo
capital of.. 11. Philippines
hemp.. 5. abaca
hero.. 5. Dewey (Adm)
island site.. 5. Luzon
native.. 7. Chinese, Tagalog
9. Filipinos
maniple... 5. fanon, orale 7. handful,
phalanx, platoon
manipulate... 3. rig, use 4. work
5. pilot, treat, wield 6. handle,
manage 7. operate
manipulation... 5. using 8. handling,
intrigue 9. operation, stratagem
10. management, use of hands
Manitoba, Canada...
capital.. 8. Winnipeg
Indian.. 4. Cree
lake.. 8. Manitoba
river.. 3. Red
mankind... 3. man 4. Adam, folk
7. menfolk 8. humanity 9. human
race
mankind (pert to)...
division.. 4. race 5. tribe
group (kindred).. 6. ethnos, socius
hater.. 11. misanthrope
science.. 9. ethnogony, ethnology
12. anthropology
manly... 4. bold 5. adult, brave, hardy,
noble 6. daring 8. resolute
9. honorable, masculine, undaunted

10. courageous
manna... 4. food (miracle), lerp (laap, laarp) 7. godsend 10. gazangabin
manner... 3. air, way 4. kind, mien, mode, sort 5. guise, style 6. aspect, custom, method 7. fashion 8. behavior 10. appearance, deportment
manner (pert to)...
frenzied.. 4. amok 5. amuck, huffy 7. haughty
law.. 5. modus
like.. 4. thus 6. in kind 8. parallel
meddlesome.. 9. officious
meditative.. 13. contemplative
rough.. 7. brusque 10. irreverent
mannerism... 4. mode 8. elegance 11. affectation
mannerly... 4. nice 5. moral, suave 6. seemly 8. decorous, politely 9. courteous 10. well–spoken 12. ingratiating
manner of...
making something.. 7. facture
pronouncing.. 6. accent, brogue
speaking.. 7. grammar
manners... 5. mores 8. behavior 9. amenities, etiquette
Mannheim gold... 5. brass
mano (comb form)... 4. hand
manoc... 4. fowl (jungle) 7. chicken, rooster
manor... 4. hall 5. abode 6. estate 7. demesne, mansion
manred... 6. homage 9. vassalage 10. leadership (in war)
mansion... 4. seat 5. house, manor, manse 8. dwelling 9. astrology
manta... 3. ray (fish) 4. wrap 5. cloak, cloth 7. blanket 8. mantelet (mantlet) 9. devilfish
mantilla... 4. cape, veil 5. cloak
mantis... 4. Cagn (deity) 6. insect 7. mantoid 9. rearhorse
mantis crab... 7. squilla
mantle... 4. cape, cope, robe 5. cloak, cover 6. capote, kittel 7. garment 8. filament, insignia, mantelet, mantling (Her), vestment 10. witzchoura 11. mantelletta
manto... 3. ore 4. gown 5. cloak 6. mantle, mantua
mantoid... 6. mantis
Mantua (pert to)...
birthplace of.. 6. Vergil (Virgil)
capital.. 7. Mantova
walled by.. 11. Charlemagne
Manu (Myth)...
laws.. 8. creation, religion
progenitors of.. 3. Man
Seventh Age, author of.. 10. Code of Manu (Hind laws)
manual... 4. book 7. clavier (Mus), didache 8. exercise, handbook 14. consuetudinary
manual (pert to)...
alphabet (deaf).. 11. dactylology
arts.. 6. crafts
crafts.. 5. sloyd (sloid, slojd) 10. handicraft
digit.. 3. toe 5. thumb 6. finger 8. dactylar

ritual.. 7. rituale 8. breviary 9. formulary
manufacture... 4. make 6. invent 7. produce, trump up 9. fabricate
manufacturer of drugs, liquors... 6. abkari (abkary)
manumission... 7. freeing 10. liberation (slave) 12. emancipation
manumit... 4. free 5. let go 6. unhand 7. dismiss, release 8. liberate
manuscript (Ms, Mss)... 4. copy (author's), opus 5. codex, folio 7. writing 8. document 11. composition, handwriting 13. written by hand
manuscript (pert to)...
back.. 5. dorso
blank space.. 6. lacuna
copier.. 6. scribe
mark (old).. 6. obelus
many... 6. divers 7. diverse, several, various 8. frequent, manifold, numerous 9. different, multitude 10. multiplied
many (pert to)...
footed.. 8. multiped
prefix.. 4. poly, vari 5. multi
sided.. 9. versatile 12. multilateral
times.. 5. often 10. frequently
manyplies... 12. third stomach (ruminant)
mao... 7. peacock
Maori (pert to)...
Adam, ancestor.. 4. Tiki
bird.. 3. tui 4. weka (flightless)
canoe, raft.. 4. moki, waka
charm (grotesque).. 7. heitiki
compensation.. 3. utu
fish.. 4. hiku 7. rainbow 9. trumpeter
hero.. 4. Maui
people.. 9. cannibals (anc) 10. aborigines
priest.. 7. tuhunga
sect.. 7. Ringatu
tatooing.. 4. moko
tree.. 5. mapau
tribe.. 3. Ati 4. Hapu
village.. 4. kaik (kaika)
weapon.. 4. mere, patu, rata 6. marree
Maoriland... 10. New Zealand
map... 4. plat 5. chart, image 6. charte, design, isobar (weather line), sketch, survey 7. diagram, epitome, explore, picture 9. delineate 10. embodiment 14. representation
maple (pert to)...
bowl.. 5. mazer, rogan (sap)
flowering.. 8. abutilon
genus.. 4. Acer 9. Aceraceae
insect scale.. 10. pulvinaria
seed.. 6. samara
sugar tube.. 5. stile
tree.. 8. box elder 9. moosewood
map maker... 4. Eric (Father) 7. charter 8. Mercator 12. cartographer
mapo... 4. goby (fish)
mar... 4. ruin, scar 5. botch, spoil 6. damage, deface, impair, mangle

7. blemish 8. mutilate 9. disfigure
Mar... 4. Lord (Jacobite)
marabou, marabout... 5. stork
  6. argala, covert 8. adjutant
maracan... 5. macaw
maranon... 6. cashew
marasca, maraschino... 6. cherry
marasma... 5. waste 7. disease
  10. emaciation 12. malnutrition
maraud... 3. rob 4. loot, raid, rove,
  sack 6. forage 7. brigand, cateran,
  pillage, plunder 10. plundering
marble... 3. mib, mig, taw 4. cold,
  hard 5. agate, white 6. basalt,
  marmor 7. pattern (mottled)
  8. dolomite 9. limestone, sculpture,
  unfeeling
marble (pert to)...
  Belgian.. 5. rance
  Catalonia.. 8. brocatel (brocatelle)
  cork (tree).. 9. tambookie
  famous.. 6. Parian 7. Carrara
    8. Pentelec
  game.. 3. taw 5. alley
  group (famed).. 5. Elgin (Marbles)
  made of.. 9. marmoreal
  mosaic.. 7. tessera
  Roman.. 7. cipolin
  slab.. 5. dalle
marbled... 9. marmorate
Marbles... 5. Elgin 7. Arundel
marc... 6. refuse, spirit 7. residue
  14. eau de vie de marc
marcato (Mus)... 6. marked
  8. accented, emphatic
march... 4. fill, hike, step, trek
  5. troop 6. border, parade
  7. advance, proceed 8. boundary,
  drumbeat, frontier, lockstep,
  movement, progress, smallage
  9. cavalcade, quickstep
March King... 5. Sousa (John Philip)
marcid... 4. weak 7. decayed, tabetic
  8. withered 9. exhausted
  10. emaciating
Marcobrunner... 4. wine (White Rhine)
Mardi Gras... 8. carnival 10. fat
  Tuesday (literal) 13. Shrove Tuesday
Mardi Gras King... 3. Rex
mare... 4. yaud 5. filly, horse
  6. goblin, grasni (gypsy) 7. incubus,
  specter, trestle 8. the blues
  9. nightmare 10. blue devils,
  melancholy
marge, margent... 3. rim 4. brim,
  edge, side 5. brink, shore 6. border,
  fringe, margin 8. marginal
margin... 3. rim 4. brim, edge, rand,
  room, side 5. brink, limit 6. amount,
  border, reward 10. collateral
margin (pert to)...
  business.. 5. gross
  notched.. 5. erose
  note.. 7. apostil 8. scholium
    10. annotation
  scalloped.. 7. crenate
  set in.. 6. indent
  straighten (to).. 5. align
marginal note... 4. kere (kri, keri)
  7. apostil 8. scholium 10. annotation
marigold... 5. aster, boots, caper,
  finch 6. orange (cadmium)

7. cowslip, Tagetes
marijuana... 3. hay 4. hemp 6. reefer
  7. tobacco (wild) 8. locoweed
  9. cigarette
marikina... 7. tamarin 8. marmoset
marimba... 9. xylophone
marina... 4. dock 5. basin
  9. esplanade, promenade (seaside)
marinal... 6. marine, sailor, saline
marine... 3. tar 5. jolly, naval
  7. mariner, oceanic, pelagic
  8. maritime, nautical 11. leatherneck
marine (pert to)...
  animal.. 3. orc 4. brit, seal 5. coral,
  polyp 6. dugong, Otaria, teredo,
  walrus 7. manatee, mollusk, octopus
  clam.. 8. shipworm
  crustacean.. 4. brit 8. barnacle
  fauna, flora.. 7. benthos
  fish.. 5. shark 8. menhaden
  gastropod.. 5. conus (snail), murex
    7. terebra
  growth.. 4. kelp 5. algae 6. enalid
    7. seaweed 10. ditch grass
  individual.. 6. merman 7. mermaid
  skeleton.. 5. coral
  slogan.. 6. gung-ho
mariner... 3. gob, tar 4. salt 5. Jacky
  6. sailor, seaman 8. waterman
mariner's card... 5. chart
mariner's compass points...
  6. rhumba
marionette... 4. doll, duck 6. figure,
  puppet
maritime... 5. naval 6. marine
  7. oceanic 8. nautical
marjoram... 3. dot 4. mint 6. origin
  8. origanum 9. flavoring
mark... 3. aim, tee 4. heed, line,
  note, rist, seal, sign 5. brand, label,
  notch, score, stain, stamp, trait
  6. denote, symbol, target
  7. betoken, blemish, earmark,
  engrave, impress, imprint, insigne
  8. evidence, identify, insignia,
  landmark 9. emphasize, objective,
  punctuate, signature, trademark
  10. indication 11. distinction,
  distinguish 14. characteristic
mark (pert to)...
  bad.. 7. demerit
  bounds.. 7. delimit 9. demarcate
  contest (in a).. 5. bogey (bogie)
  critical.. 6. obelus
  diacritical.. 5. tilde 6. tittle 7. cedilla
  disgrace.. 6. stigma
  fingerprint.. 5. whorl
  logic.. 11. differentia
  misconduct.. 7. demerit
  off.. 4. plot 6. assign 7. measure
    12. characterize, circumscribe
  of homage.. 7. ovation
  of whip.. 4. wale, welt
  out.. 6. cancel 10. obliterate
  possessive.. 10. apostrophe
  printing.. 4. dele, stet 5. caret
    6. dagger, diesis, obelus 7. obelisk
    10. apostrophe
  pronunciation.. 5. breve 6. macron
  proofreading.. 4. dele 5. caret
  prosody.. 7. caesura, triseme
    9. diaeresis, tetraseme

punctuation.. 4. dash 5. colon,
  comma 6. period 9. diaeresis
  (dieresis), semicolon 10. apostrophe
question.. 7. eroteme (erotema)
reference.. 4. star 6. dagger, diesis
  8. asterisk
with bars.. 5. grill
with dots, spots.. 6. dapple 7. stipple
with pointed instrument.. 6. scrive
with ridges.. 3. rib
marked by...
dispute.. 13. controversial
maneuvering.. 8. tactical
nicety.. 7. elegant
small areas.. 9. areolated
time.. 5. dated
marked with...
colors.. 7. mottled 10. variegated
  11. psychedelic
depressions.. 7. dimpled
furrows.. 6. rivose
grooves.. 6. lirate
lines.. 5. ruled 6. linear, notate
sables (Her).. 8. pelleted
spots.. 6. notate 7. mottled
stripes.. 7. lineate
zones.. 6. zonate
marker... 4. buoy 5. pylon 6. scorer,
  signal 7. brander, counter, monitor
  8. bookmark, marksman, monument,
  recorder 9. indicator
market... 4. mart, sale, sell, shop
  5. forum, trade 6. rialto, square
  9. clientele
market (pert to)...
bonds.. 5. float
day (Rom).. 7. nundine
French.. 8. débouché
place.. 4. sook 5. agora, plaza, store
  6. bazaar, rialto 8. emporium,
  exchange
marketable... 6. staple 7. salable
  8. in demand, vendible
  12. merchantable
markhor... 4. goat
marking (crescent)... 6. lunula, lunule
  7. lunulet 9. engraving
markings... 7. rasceta
marksman... 4. shot 6. gunner, sniper
  7. shooter 9. Orangeman
Mark Twain (pert to)...
category.. 8. humorist
character.. 9. Tom Sawyer
  15. Huckleberry Finn
name.. 13. Samuel Clemens
tale.. 9. Gilded Age 10. Roughing It
  15. Innocents Abroad
marl... 4. malm 5. earth, fiber
  6. manure 7. deposit (earthy), marlite
  9. greensand 10. fertilizer,
  overspread
marli... 4. lace 5. gauze, tulle
  6. border (raised on dish)
marlin... 6. curlew, godwit 8. sailfish
  9. spearfish
marlinspike... 3. fid 4. bird, tool
  6. jaeger 8. skua gull
marmalade... 3. jam 6. Achras, sapote
  8. plum tree, preserve 12. mammee
  sapota
marmit... 6. kettle 7. soup pot
marmite (Mil)... 4. bomb (soup kettle)

  5. shell
marmor... 6. marble
marmoset... 4. mico (black–tailed)
  6. monkey, sagoin 7. tamarin
marmot... 5. bobac 6. rodent
  7. Marmota 8. Arctomys, whistler
  9. ground hog, woodchuck
maroon... 5. slave 7. abandon, cast
  off, forsake, isolate 8. chestnut
  13. leave helpless
marquee... 4. tent 6. canopy
marriage... 5. union 7. wedding,
  wedlock 9. matrimony 10. nuptiality
  11. espousement
marriage (pert to)...
absence of.. 5. agamy
age.. 6. mature, nubile
broker.. 9. schatchen 10. matchmaker
forswearer.. 8. celibate
god.. 5. Hymen
goddess.. 4. Hera
hater.. 10. misogamist
intermarriage.. 13. miscegenation
late in life.. 8. opsigamy
more than one.. 6. bigamy, digamy
  8. polygamy 9. polyandry, tetragamy
  (4th) 11. deuterogamy
notice.. 5. banns
of the gods.. 8. theogamy
outside the tribe.. 7. exogamy
pert to.. 7. marital, spousal
  8. hymeneal 9. connubial, endogamic
portion.. 3. dot 5. dotal, dowry
promise.. 7. betroth 8. affiance
secret.. 9. elopement
married... 5. wived 6. wedded
  8. espoused 9. connubial
married (pert to)...
more than once at a time..
  9. polyandry (woman)
once at a time.. 8. monandry
person.. 4. wife 6. spouse
  7. husband 8. benedict
twice.. 6. bigamy, digamy
  11. deuterogamy
marrow... 4. pith 6. center
  7. essence, medulla 9. substance
Mars... 3. god (of War) 4. Ares
  6. planet, war–god
Mars (pert to)...
altar.. 13. Campus Martius (field of
  Mars)
constellation.. 3. Ara
festival.. 5. March 7. October
pert to.. 5. Arean 7. Martian
priests.. 5. Salii
red.. 5. totem
satellites.. 6. Deimos, Phobos
ship.. 8. moon ship 9. spaceship
sons (twin).. 5. Remus 7. Romulus
spot.. 5. oasis
Marseillaise... 4. song (1792)
Marseille, France...
capital of Dept.. 14. Bouches du
  Rhone
church.. 9. Notre Dame
fort.. 11. Rue Noailles 13. Rue
  Cannebière
old name.. 8. Massilia
seaport site.. 13. Mediterranean
marsh... 3. bog, fen 4. meer, mire,
  moor, slue 5. liman, swale, swamp

6. morass, saline, slough
7. maremma
marsh (pert to)...
bird.. 4. sora 5. snipe, stilt
crocodile.. 3. goa
elder.. 3. Iva
fever.. 7. helodes
gas.. 7. methane 8. firedamp
grass.. 5. sedge, spart
hawk.. 5. harpy 7. harrier
hen.. 4. rail
inhabiting.. 12. limnophilous
mallow.. 5. altea
marigold.. 5. boots, calla 7. cowslip
pert to.. 8. paludine
shrub.. 4. reed 5. sedge 7. bulrush,
   cattail 8. moorwort 12. pickerelweed
marshal... 3. Ney (Fr) 4. lead 5. align,
   aline, array, groom, guide, range,
   usher 6. direct, parade 7. farrier,
   officer 8. official
Marshall Islands...
chains (two).. 6. Ralick (eleven isls)
   7. Rattach (13 isls)
government.. 11. trusteeship
WWII scene.. 6. Bikini 8. Eniwetok
   9. Kwajalein
marshberry, marshwort... 9. cranberry
marshy... 3. wet 5. boggy, fenny,
   liman 7. moorish 8. morassey,
   paludine
marsupial... 4. frog, tait 5. kaola
   6. wombat 7. opossum, wallaby
   8. kangaroo 9. bandicoot, phalanger,
   tapoatafa 10. Diprotodon
   11. Marsupialia
marsupium... 5. pouch
martel (Hist)... 6. hammer
martel-de-fer... 6. weapon
   12. hammer of iron
marten... 3. fur 4. pelt 5. sable
   6. mammal 7. Mustela
martial... 4. Mars (pert to) 5. brave
   7. warlike 8. fighting, militant,
   military
Martinique...
capital.. 8. St Pierre (former) 12. Fort
   de France
formation.. 8. volcanic
mountain peak.. 9. Mont Pelée
martyr... 4. kill 5. title 7. Stephen
   (Christian), torture 8. sufferer
marvel... 4. gape 6. wonder
   7. miracle, portent, prodigy
   8. astonish
marvelous... 6. superb 7. strange
   9. wonderful 10. improbable,
   incredible, remarkable 11. astonishing
   13. extraordinary
Maryland...
bay.. 10. Chesapeake
capital.. 9. Annapolis
city.. 9. Baltimore
Hist site.. 8. Antietam 10. State
   House (nation's oldest) 11. Fort Mc
   Henry
mountain.. 8. Backbone, Piedmont
   11. Appalachian
race (famed).. 9. Preakness
   12. Steeplechase
race track.. 5. Bowie 6. Butler, Laurel
   7. Pimlico

school.. 9. Annapolis (Acad)
   12. Johns Hopkins
settler.. 7. Calvert (Leonard)
State admission.. 7. Seventh
State motto.. 22. Manly Deeds,
   Womanly Words
State nickname.. 4. Free 7. Old Line
mash... 4. feed, ogle, pulp 5. crush,
   flirt, press, smash, steep 6. jumble,
   soften 7. mixture 9. pulverize
   11. infatuation
mashal... 7. parable, proverb
masher... 5. dandy, flirt, ricer
   7. utensil 10. pulverizer
   11. philanderer
masjid... 6. mosque
mask... 4. ball, loup, veil 5. cloak,
   cover, dance, drama, onkos
   6. domino, screen 7. conceal,
   pretext 8. disguise 10. subterfuge
masked... 6. comedy, cowled, hidden,
   veiled 7. larvate, obscure
   8. shrouded 9. concealed, disguised
masker... 5. mimer 6. mummer
   11. masquerader
maslin... 5. brass 6. kettle 7. mixture
   (grain) 9. potpourri
Masonic doorkeeper... 5. tiler
masonry... 6. ashlar 9. revetment
mass... 3. cob, dab, gob, mop, pat,
   wad 4. blob, body, bulk, load, loaf,
   lump, roll, size 5. solid 8. quantity
   9. large part, magnitude 11. large
   amount 12. accumulation,
   congregation
mass (pert to)...
book.. 6. missal
collection.. 9. aggregate
directory (RCCh).. 4. ordo
for dead.. 7. requiem
matter.. 5. molar
molten glass.. 7. parison
nerve tissue.. 8. ganglion
tangled.. 3. mop 4. shag
vestment (Eccl).. 5. amice
Massachusetts...
capital.. 6. Boston (1630)
city.. 5. Salem 7. Concord
   8. Plymouth 9. Cambridge, Lexington
   10. Gloucester, New Bedford
   12. Provincetown
college (oldest, US).. 7. Harvard
explorer.. 5. Cabot 7. Gosnold
   9. Capt Smith (John)
hero.. 10. Paul Revere
island.. 9. Nantucket 15. Martha's
   Vineyard
mountain.. 3. Tom 8. Greylock
   10. Berkshires
river.. 10. Housatonic 11. Connecticut
school (first free).. 6. Dedham (1649)
settlers.. 8. Pilgrims, Puritans
State admission.. 5. Sixth
State nickname.. 8. Bay State 9. Old
   Colony
massacre... 5. havoc 6. pogrom
   7. carnage 8. butchery, decimate,
   genocide 9. slaughter
massage... 3. rub 5. knead 6. stroke
   7. therapy
massive... 3. big 4. bold 5. bulky,
   large, massy 7. weighty 8. imposing

9. ponderous 10. impressive
11. substantial
mast... 3. cue, fid 4. pole, spar
5. stick, stuff (oneself)
master... 3. man, rab 4. lord, mian,
rule 5. chief, judge, rabbi, tutor
6. expert, humble, subdue
7. captain, conquer, maestro,
padrone, subject, teacher
8. dominate, overcome, regulate,
surmount, vanquish 9. commander,
conqueror, craftsman, preceptor,
subjugate
master (pert to)...
African.. 5. bwana
Eton.. 4. beak
fencing.. 7. lanista
hard.. 6. despot
Indian.. 5. sahib
music.. 7. maestro
of a house.. 13. paterfamilias
of ceremonies.. 2. M C 5. emcee
of Heaven.. 16. Celestial Teacher
of the horse.. 7. equerry
stroke.. 4. coup
masterful... 6. lordly 7. haughty
8. arrogant, skillful 9. arbitrary,
imperious 10. commanding
11. dictatorial, domineering,
magisterial, overbearing
13. authoritative
mastery... 4. gree 5. power, skill
7. control, victory 8. dominion
10. ascendancy 11. proficiency
12. vanquishment
mastic... 3. asa, gum 5. resin
6. liquor 8. adhesive 9. red–yellow
masticate... 4. chew 5. crush, grind
8. macerate
mastiff... 3. dog 5. burly, matin
7. massive
mastodon... 5. giant 6. animal,
Mammut 7. mammoth 8. behemoth
9. dinothere 10. Dinotheres,
Mammutidae 11. Dinotherium
mat... 3. rug 4. dull (finish) 5. doily,
platt, twist 7. webbing 8. entangle,
material 10. interweave, lusterless
matador (pert to)...
garment.. 4. cape
staff.. 6. muleta (with red flag)
sword.. 7. estoque
matagasse... 11. butcherbird
match... 3. pit 4. copy, game, mate,
pair, peer, sort 5. equal, fusee,
marry, tally, vesta 7. compare,
contest, lighter, lucifer 8. coincide,
marriage, parallel 10. correspond
11. counterpart
matched... 5. mated 6. paired, pitted,
teamed 7. equaled (equalled)
matchless... 5. alone 6. unlike
7. unequal 8. peerless 9. unequaled
10. inimitable 12. incomparable
matchlock... 3. gun 7. gunlock
mate... 4. pair, wife 5. equal, marry,
match 6. seaman, spouse
7. comrade, husband, mariner,
partner 9. companion
11. confederate, counterpart
matelassé... 6. fabric 8. quilting
(imitation) 13. ornamentation

material, materiel... 4. data 5. goods,
stuff 6. fabric, matter, plasma,
staple, swatch 7. weighty
8. relevant, supplies, tangible
9. apparatus, corporeal, equipment,
essential 11. substantial
12. nonspiritual 13. materialistic
material (pert to)...
building.. 4. frit, lime, tile, wood
5. adobe, brick, rabat, tapia
6. cement, thatch 7. plywood
8. asbestos, Masonite 9. wallboard
discard.. 4. slag 5. scrap 6. refuse
7. rubbish
dress.. 4. silk, wool 5. crepe, linen,
satin, surah, tulle, tweed 6. baleen,
faille, sennit, tricot, velvet
8. corduroy
household.. 5. scrim 6. carpet,
damask, lampas, mohair, napery
7. drapery 8. tapestry
needlework.. 4. lace, yarn 6. thread
8. arrasene, chenille
paper.. 3. wax 4. bond, news, note,
rice 6. letter, tissue, vellum
7. drawing, writing 8. wrapping
9. cardboard, onionskin, parchment
11. papier–mâché
polishing.. 11. rottenstone
materia medica... 7. acology
10. leechcraft
maternal... 7. enation 8. motherly
10. motherlike
math... 6. mowing 9. aftermath,
monastery
mathematician... 6. Euclid 7. actuary
9. physicist, Whitehead
mathematics (pert to)...
abbreviation.. 3. QED
arbitrary.. 5. radix 9. parameter
deduction.. 8. analysis
diagram.. 5. graph
element.. 4. cube, root 6. factor
7. decimal, divisor, formula, minuend
8. dividend, fraction, quotient,
repetend 10. multiplier, subtrahend
12. multiplicand
equation.. 2. pi 4. cosh, sine, surd
6. cosine
factor.. 10. quaternion
instrument.. 6. sector 7. compass
8. arbalest
number.. 5. digit
operation, operator.. 5. nabla
6. scalar 7. operand 10. quaternion
proposition.. 7. theorem
quantity.. 6. addend, augend, scalar
sheets of.. 4. cone 5. nappe
symbol.. 5. digit 7. facient, operand
12. multiplicand
type.. 4. pure 6. higher 7. algebra,
physics 8. abstract, calculus,
geometry 10. arithmetic, elementary,
quadratics 12. trigonometry
mathemeg... 7. catfish
matie... 7. herring
matin... 6. aubade (song) 7. morning,
service 8. watchdog 11. morning
song 13. morning prayer
matinee... 5. levee, party, salon
6. soiree 8. negligee 9. reception
13. conversazione, entertainment

matipo... 4. wood (fuel) 5. napau
matka, matkab... 4. seal
matlow... 6. sailor
matrass... 4. tube 5. flask 6. bottle,
carafe 8. bolthead
matriculate... 4. list 5. admit, adopt,
enter 6. enroll 8. register
10. naturalize
matrimonial... 7. marital, nuptial,
spousal 8. conjugal, hymeneal
9. connubial
matrimony... 7. wedlock 8. marriage
matrix... 3. bed 4. cast, form, mold,
womb 5. cutis 6. gangue
10. foundation, impression
matron... 4. dame, wife 5. widow
11. housekeeper
matter... 3. gas, pus 4. body, gear,
malm, pith 5. atoms, fluid, vapor
6. affair, amount, solids 7. problem,
trouble 8. business, elements,
material 10. importance
11. constituent 12. circumstance
matter (pert to)...
alluvial.. 5. geest
celestial.. 6. nebula
coloring.. 5. eosin 10. endochrome
fatty.. 5. sebum
noxious.. 6. miasma
of doubt.. 7. dubiety
of fact.. 7. literal, prosaic 9. practical,
pragmatic
of law.. 3. res
of note.. 8. notandum
particle.. 4. atom
perfume 7. essence
spinal cord.. 4. alba
uniform (physics).. 7. inertia
volcanic.. 2. aa, oo 4. lava
mature... 3. ago, duo, old 4. ripe
5. adult, grown, ripen 6. digest,
mellow, season 7. develop, fall due,
grow old, perfect 8. complete
9. full–grown, perfected, ratheripe
maturity... 8. ripeness 9. adulthood,
readiness 10. falling due
11. development
matutinal... 5. early, matin 7. morning
12. antemeridian
maty... 7. servant
maud... 3. rug 5. plaid, shawl
maudlin... 5. beery, drunk, silly, tipsy
7. tearful, weeping 10. lachrymose
11. sentimental (overly)
maul, mall... 4. beat, bung, club,
mace, mall, moth 5. abuse, gavel,
staff 6. beetle, bruise, mallet
maumet... 3. god (false), guy 4. doll,
idol 5. image 6. puppet
9. scarecrow
maund, maun... 3. beg 6. basket,
hamper 7. begging, measure
Maundy... 4. alms 8. ceremony
10. Last Supper
Maundy Thursday (Bib)... 8. Holy
Week 13. washing of feet
Mauritius, Ile de France...
capital.. 9. Port Louis
government.. 7. British
product.. 5. coral, sugar
site.. 11. Indian Ocean
Mauser... 5. rifle 7. firearm

mauve... 5. lilac 6. mallow, purple,
violet 10. atmosphere (color)
maverick... 4. calf (orphan) 5. dogie
6. animal 8. newcomer
13. nonconformist
mavis, mavie... 6. thrush
maw... 4. craw, crop 6. gullet, mallow
7. gizzard, stomach
mawk... 6. maggot
mawkish... 5. vapid 6. sickly
8. nauseous 9. squeamish
10. disgusting 11. sentimental
maxilla... 7. jawbone
maxim... 3. saw 4. dict, rule
5. adage, axiom, gnome, motto,
tenet, truth 6. saying 7. precept,
proverb 8. aphorism, apothegm
10. apophthegm
maxims... 5. logia 9. moralisms
maximum... 4. most 5. limit
7. highest, supreme 8. greatest
12. consummation
maximus 7. largest
may... 3. can 6. be able 9. be
allowed 11. in one's power,
opportunity
May (pert to)...
apple.. 8. mandrake
bird.. 6. thrush
cock.. 5. melon 6. plover
curlew.. 8. whimbrel
Duke.. 6. cherry
festival.. 7. Beltane (anc)
First.. 7. Beltane 14. May–day festival
fish.. 9. killifish
flower.. 7. arbutus 8. hawthorn,
marigold 9. calla lily 10. stitchwort
12. cuckooflower
fly.. 3. dun 7. shad fly 9. ephemerid
goddess 4. Maia
gowan.. 5. daisy
Maya... 3. Mam (tribe) 6. Indian
8. Pokonchi
Mayan calendar...
five added days.. 5. uayeb
no leap year.. 5. solar
twenty–day month.. 5. uinal
year.. 4. haab
Mayan underworld... 7. xibalba
maybe... 2. if 7. perhaps 8. possibly
9. perchance 11. conceivably,
possibility, uncertainty
Mayfair... 6. London (fashionable)
Mayflower (pert to)...
boat of.. 8. Pilgrims (1620)
Compact.. 9. agreement (1620)
sister ship.. 9. Speedwell
mayhap... 7. perhaps 12. peradventure
mayor... 5. maire 7. alcalde
10. magistrate 11. burgomaster
mazarine... 4. blue (color from Cardinal
Mazarin)
maze... 5. fancy 7. stupefy
8. confound, delirium, delusion
9. confusion, deception, labyrinth
12. bewilderment, complication
mazed... 4. lost 7. in a maze
9. stupefied 10. bewildered
mazuma... 5. money
mead... 5. drink 6. meadow
8. hydromel 9. metheglin
meadow... 3. lea 4. mead 5. field,

haugh, pampa, swale 7. pasture,
savanna (savannah) 9. grassland
10. agostadero
meadow (pert to) . . .
chicken . . 8. sora rail
crocus . . 7. saffron
crowfoot . . 9. buttercup
hen . . 4. coot, rail 7. bittern
mouse . . 4. vole 8. arvicole
part . . 5. swale
sage . . 6. salvia
saxifrage . . 6. seseli
sweet . . 7. Spiraea
meager, meagre . . . 4. arid, bare, lank,
poor, slim 5. gaunt, scant, spare
6. barren, jejune, lenten, narrow,
sparse 7. starved, sterile, trivial
9. emaciated 10. inadequate
meal . . . 3. tub 4. bran, dune, mess
5. feast, grout, salep, snack
6. bucket, fodder, powder, ration,
repast, tiffin 7. banquet 8. sandbank
9. collation, pulverize
mealy . . . 4. pale 7. friable, powdery
10. soft–spoken 11. farinaceous
12. mealymouthed
mealy (pert to) . . .
Amazon . . 6. parrot
back . . 6. cicada
bird, duck . . 5. squaw
bug . . 4. pest 5. scale 10. pear blight
mouth . . 7. warbler
tree . . 9. arrowwood, wayfaring
mealy–mouthed . . . 5. suave
10. flattering 12. hypocritical
13. sanctimonious
mean . . . 3. low 4. base 5. petty,
small, snide, solar (time), sorry
6. common, denote, design, humble,
intend, medium, menial, middle,
midway, paltry, shabby, sordid, stingy
7. average, ignoble, purport, purpose,
servile, squalid 8. beggarly, ordinary,
plebeian, shameful, wretched
9. difficult, malicious, niggardly,
penurious 10. despicable,
ill–humored, spiritless 11. closefisted,
disgraceful 12. contemptible,
dishonorable, narrow–minded,
parsimonious
mean clef (Mus) . . . 5. C clef
meaning . . . 4. null (without) 5. sense
6. import, intent, spirit 7. purport
8. semantic 9. intending, intention,
knowledge 10. understand
12. significance 13. signification
14. interpretation
meaningless . . . 4. rote 5. banal, derry
7. aimless 9. senseless
10. designless 11. purposeless
13. insignificant
meanness . . . 6. infamy, malice
8. baseness, ill–humor 9. servility
10. humbleness, paltriness,
sordidness, stinginess 11. inferiority
means . . . 5. funds 7. capital
8. averages 9. resources
11. wherewithal
means of . . .
access . . 4. adit 5. inlet 7. ingress
8. aperture
communication . . 4. note 5. flags,

phone, radio, smoke 6. letter, postal,
tom–tom 8. telegram 9. telegraph,
telephone
livelihood . . 4. work 5. labor, trade
8. vocation 10. profession
outlet . . 4. door, exit 6. egress
8. aperture
support . . 5. funds 6. assets
7. aliment 11. maintenance
meantime . . . 5. while 7. interim
8. interval, same time 9. meanwhile
measles . . . 7. rubella, rubeola
8. morbilli
measure (pert to) . . .
area . . 2. ar 3. are, rod 4. acre, area,
mile, rood 6. square 7. geodesy,
hectare, section 8. township
Bible . . 3. cab (kab), kor, log 4. epha
5. cubit, homer
gauge . . 3. erg, lea (yarn) 5. ergon,
level, plumb, scale, stone 6. denier,
square 7. calorie (calory), compass,
sextant 8. calipers, quadrant
length . . 3. ell, mil, rod 4. foot, hand,
inch, knot, mile, nail, pace, rule,
tape, yard 5. chain, cubit, meter
6. league 7. furlong 9. kilometer,
yardstick 10. centimeter, micrometer,
millimeter
nautical . . 4. knot 6. fathom, league
paper . . 4. page, ream 5. quire, sheet
poetry . . 6. dipody, iambic, rhythm,
sestet 7. anapest, couplet, distich,
tripody 8. quatrain 9. hexameter
10. ottava rima, pentastich,
tetrameter, tetrastich 11. Alexandrine
printer . . 2. em, en 4. pica 5. agate
volume, weight . . 3. ton, tun (wine)
4. bale, butt, cord 5. carat, liter,
minim, ounce, pound, quart
6. barrel, bushel, finger, gallon,
magnum, pottle 8. hogshead,
teaspoon 9. kiloliter 10. tablespoon
measurement . . . 4. size 6. amount,
alnage, extent, metage 7. azimuth
8. abscissa, capacity, quantity
9. substance 11. calculation,
mensuration
measuring instrument . . . 6. stadia
7. alidade, caliper 8. odometer
12. perambulator (surveyor)
meat . . . 4. beef, fish, food, lamb, pork
5. flesh 6. fillet, kernel, mutton,
quarry 7. brisket 9. aitchbone
(icebone), spareribs
meat (pert to) . . .
ball . . 7. rissole 9. croquette,
hamburger
cured, dried . . 3. ham 5. bacon
6. flitch, jerked 7. biltong (biltongue)
8. pemmican
jellied . . 5. aspic
minced, roll . . 7. rissole
roasted . . 5. cabob (kabob)
9. barbecued
slaughterhouse . . 8. abattoir
smoking place . . 6. buccan (bucan)
stew . . 8. mulligan 9. lobscouse
meatus . . . 4. burr (ear) 5. canal
7. opening, passage
meaty . . . 5. pithy, solid 11. substantial
Mecca, Arabia . . . 8. Holy City 16. City

of the Prophet
Mecca (pert to)...
birthplace of.. 8. Mohammed
capital.. 5. Hejaz
color.. 11. Tuscan brown
famed for.. 5. Kaaba (Caaba, Kaabeth)
  10. Black Stone 11. Great Mosque
governor.. 6. sherif (shereef)
pilgrimage.. 4. hadj
pilgrim's dress.. 5. ihram
rug.. 6. Shiraz
mechanic... 7. artisan, workman
  8. operator 9. artificer, craftsman,
  machinist, operative
mechanical... 8. machinal
  9. automatic, practical, technical
  11. involuntary, stereotyped
mechanical (pert to)...
adjustment.. 9. tentation
drawing.. 8. drafting
law, motion.. 8. dynamics, kinetics
lever.. 6. tappet
part.. 5. rotor 6. stator
mechanics... 9. technique
  11. mechanology
mechanism... 4. gear, tool 5. means
  6. tackle 7. control, rigging
  9. apparatus, machinery, technique
medal... 4. coin, disk (disc) 5. badge
  6. plaque 9. medallion
  10. decoration
medallion... 4. coin 5. cameo, medal,
  panel 6. tablet 8. ornament
meddle... 3. pry 4. nose 6. dabble,
  tamper 7. obtrude 9. interfere
meddler... 8. busybody 9. pragmatic
meddlesome... 7. Paul Fry 8. meddling
  9. officious 11. inquisitive,
  pragmatical
Mede... 6. Median 7. Persian
medial, median... 4. mean 5. mesne,
  raphe (valve) 6. medium, middle
  7. average 11. intervening
  12. intermediate
Median... 4. Magi, Mede 5. Medic
mediate... 5. opine 9. intercede,
  interpose, reconcile
mediator... 5. muser 7. arbiter
  9. go–between 10. interagent
  11. intercessor
medic... 3. doc 6. clover, doctor,
  median, medico 9. physician
medical (pert to)...
comb form.. 3. oma 4. itis 6. iatric
  7. iatrics
compound.. 5. hepar
fluid.. 5. blood, lymph, serum
man.. 5. medic 6. shaman, voodoo
monster.. 5. teras
officer.. 7. coroner
practitioner.. 2. MD 6. doctor, intern
  (interne) 7. surgeon 8. sawbones
system.. 7. therapy 9. allopathy
  10. homeopathy, psychiatry
term.. 8. curative 9. medicinal
medical terms...
chicken pox.. 9. varicella
flat feet.. 9. pes planus
headache.. 11. cephalalgia
heartburn.. 7. pyrosis
hives.. 9. urticaria
measles.. 7. rubella, rubeola

mumps.. 9. parotitis
whooping cough.. 9. pertussis
medicinal (pert to)...
agent.. 3. tea 6. tisane 9. decoction
bark.. 6. cartex
dropper.. 7. pipette
equal parts.. 3. ana
herb, plant.. 3. rue 4. aloe 5. ergot,
  jalap, orris, senna, tansy 6. arnica,
  cohosh, ipecac 7. boneset, chirata,
  comfrey 8. licorice, valerian
pain allaying.. 7. anodyne 8. sedative
  9. goofballs, paregoric
  11. barbiturate
patent.. 7. nostrum
remedy.. 5. drops, salve 6. elixir,
  iodine 7. panacea 8. antidote,
  ointment
science.. 7. biology 10. physiology,
  psychology
tablet.. 4. pill 6. troche 7. lozenge
term.. 4. drug 11. therapeutic
mediety... 6. loiety 10. moderation,
  temperance
medieval, mediaeval... 7. archaic
  10. Middle Ages
medieval (pert to)...
galley (ship's).. 3. nef 5. xebec
  6. bireme, galiot (galliot) 7. dromone
  (dromon), trireme, unireme
garment.. 6. tabard
headdress.. 6. abacot
helmet.. 5. armet
instrument (stringed).. 5. rebec
  (rebeck)
money of account.. 3. ora
monster.. 5. golem 9. automaton
  12. Frankenstein
shield.. 3. ecu 6. scutum
title, teacher.. 8. magister
weapon, club.. 4. mace 5. oncin
Medina, Saudi Arabia (pert to)...
anc name.. 9. Lathrippa
Mohammed supporters.. 6. ansars
sacred city of.. 5. Islam
tombs.. 4. Omar 6. Fatima
  8. Mohammed
mediocre... 4. mean, so–so 6. medium
  7. average 8. middling, ordinary,
  passable 9. tolerable 11. indifferent
meditate... 4. muse, plan, pore
  5. brood, study, watch, weigh
  6. ponder 7. purpose, reflect, revolve
  8. cogitate, consider 11. contemplate
meditation... 4. yoga 7. thought
  8. devotion 10. rumination
  11. thanatopsis 13. contemplation
  14. omphaloskepsis
mediterranean... 6. inland 7. midland
  10. landlocked
Mediterranean (pert to)...
boat.. 3. nef 4. saic 5. xebec (zebec)
  6. galiot (galliot), mistic (mistico)
  settee (setee) 7. felucca, hexeris
cat.. 5. genet
coast.. 7. Riviera
falcon.. 6. lanner
fish.. 6. remora
fowl.. 7. leghorn
fruit.. 5. olive 7. azarole
gulf.. 5. Tunis
herb.. 4. Ammi

inland.. 3. sea
island.. 4. Elba, Gozo 5. Crete, Malta
  6. Candia, Cyprus, Ebusis, Sicily
  7. Majorca 8. Belearic (group),
  Sardinia
island, volcanic.. 6. Lipari, Salina
  7. Vulcano 9. Stromboli
port.. 5. Tunis 7. Tunisia
storm.. 7. borasca (borasco, borasque)
tree.. 5. carob 7. azarole
wind.. 6. solano 7. etesian, gregale,
  mistral, sirocco 8. levanter
  10. euroclyden
medium... 4. agar (cultured), doer,
  mean 5. color, organ 6. degree,
  medial, oracle 7. average, psychic
  8. mediator, mediocre
  10. instrument, interagent
  11. environment 12. intermediary,
  spiritualist
medley... 4. olio 5. relay 6. jumble
  7. ferrago, mélange, mixture
  8. fantasia, mingling 9. potpourri
  10. hodgepodge, salmagundi
medrick... 4. gull (Bonaparte's), tern
  (Wilson's)
medulla... 4. pith 6. marrow
  7. summary 9. oblongata
  10. compendium
Medusa (Myth)... 6. Gorgon, Stheno
  (sister) 9. gorgoneum
Medusa's head (pert to)...
constellation (cluster).. 7. Perseus
star.. 5. Algol
vegetable.. 8. mushroom
Zool.. 10. basket fish
meed... 5. bribe, merit, repay, share
  6. desert, reward 7. bribery
  10. recompense
meek... 4. mild 6. docile, gentle,
  humble, modest 7. pacific, patient
  8. moderate, yielding 10. spiritless,
  submissive
meerkat... 6. monkey
meerschaum... 4. pipe 6. gravel
  (color) 7. seafoam 9. sepiolite
meet... 3. fit 4. face, game, join
  5. equal, match, touch 6. battle,
  combat, concur 7. collide, conform,
  contact, contest, convene, fulfill,
  satisfy 8. assemble, confront
  9. encounter 10. congregate,
  experience, rendezvous
meet halfway... 7. mediate
  10. compromise
meeting... 4. mall, race 5. court,
  gemot (gemote), joint, synod, tryst,
  union 6. caucus, powwow, séance
  7. contact, joining 8. assembly,
  conclave, junction 9. encounter,
  gathering, in contact 10. conference,
  convention, converging, rendezvous
  11. convergence 12. congregation,
  intersection
mega, meg (comb form)... 5. great
  6. mighty
megalith... 5. stone (huge) 6. dolman
  7. boulder 8. monument (Prehist)
megapode, megapod... 6. leipoa
  9. mound bird 10. jungle fowl
  11. brush turkey
megascope... 12. magic lantern

megaseism... 10. earthquake
megrim, megrims... 4. whim 5. fancy,
  freak, humor 8. headache
  9. dizziness 12. hypochondria
Mehitabel, Mehetabel... 3. cat
Mekong River tribe... 3. Moi (Asian)
mel... 5. honey
melancholia... 7. sadness 8. neurosis
  9. nostalgia, psychosis
  10. depression
melancholy... 3. sad 4. blue, dark,
  glum 5. drear, gloom 6. sombre,
  sorrow 7. doleful, sadness
  8. atrabile, liverish, tristful
  9. dejection 10. depressing,
  depression, dispirited, lamentable
  11. despondency, downhearted,
  pensiveness 12. hypochondria,
  mournfulness
Melanesia... 14. Pacific Islands
Melanesian (pert to)...
island.. 4. Fiji 7. Solomon 11. New
  Hebrides
native.. 4. Fiji 6. Papuan
  10. Polynesian
superbeing.. 5. adaro
mélange... 4. olio 6. jumble, medley
  7. mixture 9. pasticcio
  10. miscellany 14. conglomeration
melee... 3. row 4. fray 5. fight
  6. affray 7. contest, diamond (small
  cut) 8. skirmish 9. commotion
melicocca... 5. genip 9. soapberry
melicratum... 4. mead 8. beverage,
  hydromel
melilotus... 6. clover
meliorate... 6. soften 7. improve
  10. ameliorate
melisma... 6. melody 7. cadenza
Melissa... 4. balm 12. Old World mint
mell... 3. mix 4. maul 5. grain (last
  cut), honey 6. beetle, hammer,
  mallet, meddle, mingle
mellow... 4. rich, ripe, soft 5. drunk
  6. genial, jovial, mature, tender
  7. amiable, matured 9. melodious
melodic... 6. ariose 7. cadenza,
  melisma 9. melodious
melodious... 6. ariose, arioso, dulcet
  7. musical, tunable, tuneful
  10. harmonious
melodist... 6. singer 8. composer,
  musician 9. harmonist
melodramatic... 8. dramatic, romantic
  11. sensational
melody... 3. air 4. aria, tune 5. canto,
  charm, dirge, melos, music
  6. rhythm, strain 7. harmony,
  melisma, rosalia 9. cantilena,
  cantilene 11. tunefulness
melon... 4. musk, pepo 6. casaba
  7. Persian 8. honeydew
  9. muskmelon, red–yellow
  10. cantaloupe, paddymelon,
  watermelon
melon (pert to)...
financial.. 4. plum 8. dividend
like.. 5. gourd
pear.. 6. pepino
political.. 5. graft 6. spoils
melongena... 7. brinjal (brinjaul)
  8. eggplant

melos... 4. song 6. melody
melt... 3. run 4. frit, fuse, thaw
  5. smelt, swale 6. render, soften
  7. liquefy 8. diminish, dissolve
  9. disappear 12. disintegrate
member... 4. limb, part 5. organ
  6. branch, fellow, joiner 7. section
  8. belonger, district, enlistee, enroller
  9. associate
member (pert to)...
  boy's club.. 3. cub 5. scout
  Caliph dynasty.. 6. Omniad
  chapter (Eccl).. 9. capitular
  crew.. 4. hand
  diplomatic staff.. 6. consul 7. attaché
   8. minister 10. ambassador
  Jewish brotherhood.. 6. Essene
  laity.. 6. layman
  literary club.. 9. academist
   11. academician
  oldest.. 4. dean
  regiment.. 8. legioner 9. grenadier,
   legionary 11. legionnaire
  religious sect.. 5. Amish 6. Quaker,
   Shaker
  Roman Catholic society.. 6. Jesuit
  State.. 7. citizen
  swing band.. 6. hepcat 7. swinger
membrane... 4. caul, skin, tela
  5. lemma 6. lamina 8. ectoderm,
  striffin
membrane (pert to)...
  brain.. 13. meninges mater
  diffusion.. 7. osmosis
  ear.. 7. eardrum
  fold.. 5. plica
  optical.. 6. retina
  weblike.. 4. tela
memento... 5. relic, token 6. trophy
  8. keepsake, memorial, souvenir
  11. remembrance
Memnon (pert to)...
  famed statue.. 11. vocal Memnon
  father.. 8. Tithonus
  Greek name.. 9. Amenhotep
  king of.. 8. Ethiopia
  mother.. 3. Eos (Aurora)
  war hero.. 6. Trojan
memoir... 4. hint, note 5. éloge, essay
  6. record, report 7. account, history
  9. biography, narrative, reminding
  10. memorandum 12. dissertation
  13. autobiography
memorabilia... 3. ana 5. notes
  6. record 7. memoirs 8. memories
memorable... 7. namable, notable
  9. reminding 11. reminiscent
memorandum... 4. chit, note 5. diary
  6. minute, record 7. tickler
  8. protocol, reminder
memoria... 4. tomb 6. chapel, church,
  shrine 8. monument 9. reliquary
memorial... 6. memoir, memory,
  record, trophy 8. mnemonic,
  monument 10. memorandum
  11. celebrative, remembrance
  12. recollection 13. commemorative
memorial mound... 5. cairn (stone),
  totem (carved)
memory... 4. mind 6. recall
  9. retention 11. remembrance
  12. recollection, reminiscence

  13. commemoration
memory (pert to)...
  aid.. 10. anamnestic
  book.. 5. diary 9. scrapbook
  jog.. 6. remind
  loss of.. 5. lethe 7. amnesia, aphasia
   (partial) 13. forgetfulness
  term.. 6. mnesic 8. mnemonic
Memphis, Egypt (pert to)...
  deity.. 2. Ra (Re) 3. Shu, Tem
  dynasty.. 8. Memphite
  god, chief.. 4. Ptah
men (pert to)...
  armed body.. 5. posse
  gymnasts.. 8. acrobats
  learned.. 8. erudites, literati
  mechanical.. 6. robots
  of same tongue.. 6. langue
  old.. 7. gaffers 10. patriarchs
  party of.. 4. stag 6. smoker
  section, Gr Church.. 6. andron
  single.. 5. stags 9. bachelors,
   celibates
  slang.. 6. blokes
  Three Wise.. 4. Magi (Gaspar,
   Melchior, Balthazar)
  wild.. 7. savages 9. cannibals
menace... 6. threat 8. forebode,
  threaten 10. intimidate
  11. fulmination
menacing... 7. ominous 8. imminent
  11. threatening
menage... 4. club 7. society
  9. homestead, household, husbandry
  10. management 12. housekeeping
menagerie... 3. zoo 10. collection,
  Tiergarten
menald (said of horses)... 8. speckled
  10. variegated
Menaspis... 5. shark (crescent-shaped)
mend... 3. fix, sew 4. cure, darn,
  heal, knit 5. alter, amend, botch,
  emend, moise, patch 6. better,
  cobble, reform, repair 7. correct,
  improve 9. reconcile 10. ameliorate
mendacious... 5. false, lying 6. untrue
  7. in error 9. truthless 10. fallacious
mendacity... 3. lie 5. lying 6. deceit
  7. falsity, fibbery, untruth
mendicant... 5. fakir 6. beggar
  7. begging
mendicant order... 10. Carmelites,
  Dominicans 11. Franciscans
  12. Augustinians
mendole... 4. fish 8. cackerel
Menelaus' wife... 11. Helen of Troy
menhaden... 4. pogy 7. sardine
  8. bonyfish 10. mossbunker
menhir... 5. stone (standing)
  8. monolith
menial... 6. flunky, varlet 7. servant,
  servile, serving, slavish
meninges membrane... 8. pia mater
  9. arachnoid, dura mater
meniscus... 4. lens 8. crescent
  12. crescent moon
Mennonite leader... 11. Menno
  Simons
Mennonite sect... 5. Amish
meno... 4. less 5. month (comb form)
menology (Eccl)... 8. calendar, register
Menominee, Menomini... 5. Falls

(Wis), river 6. Indian 9. whitefish
Menorah... 11. candelabrum (Jew)
    12. organization
mensk... 5. adorn, favor, grace, honor
    6. credit 8. ornament 9. reverence
    12. graciousness
mental... 7. phrenic 9. of the mind,
    psychotic 11. intelligent
    12. intellectual
mental (pert to)...
    alienation.. 8. insanity
    deficiency, deficient.. 5. ament, idiot,
    moron 6. idiocy 8. imbecile
    discipline.. 8. mathesis
    disorder.. 7. aphasia 8. insanity,
    neurosis, paranoia 9. psychosis
    11. megalomania 12. hypochondria
    13. forgetfulness, schizophrenia
    faculties.. 4. mind, wits
    feeling.. 7. emotion
    image, picture.. 4. idea 6. idolus
    8. phantasm 10. conception
    peculiarity.. 12. idiosyncracy
    science, study.. 10. New Thought,
    psychiatry
    state.. 6. morale 7. doldrum
    (doldrums) 8. euphoria
    strain.. 7. tension
mentality... 4. mind 5. sense
    6. acumen, sanity 9. endowment,
    intellect 11. mental power
    12. intelligence
mention... 4. cite, mind, name
    5. refer, speak, trace 6. denote,
    notice, record, remark 7. specify,
    vestige 8. citation, indicate 9. make
    known, statement 10. indication
mentor... 7. adviser, teacher, wise
    man 10. instructor
mentum... 4. chin
menu... 4. card, list 5. carte
    8. schedule 10. bill of fare
Mephistopheles... 5. devil, Faust,
    Satan
mephitis... 4. odor 5. skunk, smell
    6. stench 7. polecat 10. exhilation
    (earth)
mercantile... 5. trade 7. trading
    10. commercial, industrial
mercenary... 4. hack 5. hired, venal
    6. sordid 7. Hessian 8. hireling,
    salaried, vendible
merchandise... 4. ware 5. goods,
    wares 7. effects 9. vendibles
    10. emporeutic (pert to)
    11. commodities 12. stock in trade
merchant... 5. buyer 6. trader
    7. vintner 10. shopkeeper, trafficker
    11. storekeeper
merchant (pert to)...
    group.. 5. guild, hanse 6. cartel
    Indian.. 4. seth
    League.. 9. Hanseatic
    ship.. 6. argosy 8. Indiaman
    wine.. 7. vintner
Merchant of Bagdad... 7. Sindbad
Merchant of Venice character...
    6. Portia 7. Antonio, Shylock
merci... 6. thanks
merciful... 4. kind, mild 6. humane,
    tender 7. clement, lenient
    9. benignant 10. charitable

13. compassionate
merciless... 5. cruel 8. pitiless
    9. unsparing 10. relentless
    13. unsympathetic
mercurial (pert to God Mercury)...
    4. fast 5. swift 6. active, clever,
    fickle 8. metallic 9. saturnine
    11. money–making
mercurous chloride... 7. calomel
mercury... 5. azoth, guide, metal
    7. chibrit, element 9. barometer
    11. quicksilver, temperature,
    thermometer
Mercury (pert to)...
    astronomy.. 6. planet (smallest)
    god of.. 8. commerce
    Greek name.. 6. Hermes
    staff.. 8. caduceus
    statue, image.. 5. herma
    winged cap.. 7. petasos (petasus)
    winged shoes.. 7. talaria
mercy... 4. pity, ruth 5. grace
    6. blithe, lenity 7. charity
    8. clemency, lenience, leniency
    9. tolerance 10. compassion,
    indulgence 11. forbearance
mercy killing... 10. euthanasia
mercy seat... 5. bench 11. golden
    plate (on the Ark), Throne of God
    12. judgment seat 13. seat of
    justice
mere... 3. sea 4. bare, lake, only,
    pool, sole, such, wisp 5. bound,
    limit, sheer, small 6. divide, simple
    8. absolute, boundary, landmark, only
    this
mère... 6. mother
merely... 4. also, just, only 5. quite
    6. barely, purely, simply, singly,
    solely 7. utterly 8. entirely, scarcely
    9. unmixedly 10. absolutely
mere show... 4. airs 5. front
    8. pretense 9. formality
    10. pretension 11. affectation
mere taste... 3. nip, sip 4. gulp
    7. draught
merganser... 3. nun 4. duck, smee,
    smew 6. Mergus 7. bec–scie
    8. Merginae 9. goosander
merge... 4. sink 5. blend, unite
    6. mingle 7. combine, immerse
    8. coalesce 11. consolidate
merger... 4. pool 5. union 6. cartel,
    fusion 8. monopoly 10. absorption
    12. amalgamation
meridian... 3. top 4. apex, noon
    5. plane 6. midday, summit, zenith
    8. latitude, southern 9. celestial
    11. culmination 12. highest point
meringue... 5. icing 8. egg white,
    frosting
Merino... 4. wool, yarn 5. sheep
merit... 4. earn, meed 5. worth
    6. desert, reward 7. deserve
    10. excellence
merited... 3. fit 4. just 6. worthy
    8. adequate, deserved, suitable
    9. warranted
meritorious... 5. valid 6. worthy
    7. merited 9. deserving, honorable
    12. praiseworthy
merlin... 6. falcon

Merlin . . . 7. prophet, romance
  8. magician
mermaid . . . 5. siren 6. merrow
  7. Oceanid, swimmer 8. sea nymph
  9. sea spirit 14. marine creature
mermaid's hair . . . 4. alga
mero . . . 4. fish 5. guasa 7. grouper
  8. rock hind
merogenesis . . . 12. segmentation
meropia . . . 9. blindness (partial)
meros . . . 5. thigh 10. meropodite
merriment . . . 3. fun 4. glee 5. mirth
  6. gaiety (gayety) 8. laughter
  9. amusement, diversion
  11. merrymaking
merrow . . . 7. mermaid
merry . . . 3. gai, gay 4. glad 5. funny,
  happy 6. blithe, bonnie, jocose,
  jovial, joyous 7. comical, festive,
  gleeful, jocular 8. cheerful, mirthful,
  sportive 9. favorable, hilarious,
  sprightly 13. sweet–sounding
merry–andrew . . . 4. mime, zany
  5. antic, clown, joker 6. jester
  7. buffoon 8. merryman
merry–go–round . . . 9. carrousel
  (carousal) 17. revolving platform
merrymaking . . . 4. reel 5. momus,
  revel 7. festive, wassail 9. festivity,
  merriment 12. conviviality
merrythought . . . 8. wishbone
merrytrotter . . . 5. swing 6. seesaw
merrywing . . . 4. duck 9. goldeneye
  10. bufflehead
merse . . . 3. dip 5. marsh 6. plunge
  7. immerse
merycism . . . 7. chewing 10. rumination
mesa . . . 7. mesilla, oakwood (color),
  terrace 14. flat–topped hill
mesel . . . 5. leper
mesh . . . 3. net, web 5. catch 6. areola
  7. complex, ensnare, netting, network
  10. crisscross 11. interaction
mesial plane . . . 5. meson (Zool)
  6. median, middle
mesmeric . . . 11. fascinating, hypnotizing
  12. irresistible, spellbinding
mesmeric force . . . 2. od
Mesopotamia . . .
  ancient city . . 2. Ur 5. Eridu
  7. Babylon, Ninevah
  city . . 5. Basra, Mosul 6. Edessa
  colloquialism . . 6. Mespot
  culture . . 8. Sumerian
  export . . 3. oil
  language . . 6. Arabic
  people (anc) . . 8. Aramaean (Aramean)
  river . . 6. Tigris 9. Euphrates
  wind . . 6. shamal
Mesopotamian . . . 5. Iraqi
Mesozoic era . . . 7. reptile 8. dinosaur
  10. evergreens, ganoid fish
mesquin . . . 4. mean 6. shabby, sordid
mesquita . . . 6. mosque
mesquite . . . 5. pacay 7. thicket
  8. Prosopis 9. algarroba
mesquite bean flour . . . 6. pinole
mess . . . 4. meal 5. batch, share, spoil
  6. bungle, jumble, litter 7. eyesore,
  failure, mixture 8. disorder
  9. confusion 11. predicament
  12. kettle of fish

mess (up) . . . 5. botch, spoil 6. muss
  up 7. clutter, derange, shuffle
  10. disarrange
message . . . 4. news, note, wire, word
  5. cable 6. brevet, letter, notice
  7. epistle, evangel, tidings
  8. dispatch, telegram
  10. communiqué 13. communication
message medium . . . 5. Ouija
messenger . . . 4. Iris, page, sand, toty
  5. angel, envoy 6. herald, nuncio,
  Revere (Paul) 7. apostle, carrier,
  courier, prophet, totyman
  8. delegate, minister 9. estafette
  (estafet) 10. forerunner
messenger bird . . . 9. secretary
Messenger of the Gods . . . 6. Hermes
  (Gr) 7. Mercury (Rom)
Messiah . . . 6. Christ 7. Saviour (Savior)
  8. Oratorio (Handel) 9. deliverer
Messina Rock . . . 6. Scylla
messy . . . 5. dirty 6. untidy 7. jumbled
  8. slovenly 10. disordered
mestive . . . 8. mournful
mesto . . . 3. sad 7. pensive
met . . . 3. sat 7. equaled, measure
  11. measurement (see also *meet*)
metabolism . . . 9. anabolism
  10. catabolism 12. assimilation
  13. dissimilation, metamorphosis
  14. transformation
metacarpus . . . 4. bone
metad . . . 3. rat
metagnomy . . . 10. divination
metagnostic . . . 10. unknowable
metal . . . 3. tin 4. gold, iron, lead, zinc
  5. steel 6. cobalt, copper, erbium,
  nickel, radium, silver, sodium
  7. cadmium, calcium, element,
  gallium, iridium, lithium, mercury,
  terbium 8. cast iron 9. potassium
  11. quicksilver
metal . . . 6. mettle, spirit 8. material
  9. substance
metal (pert to) . . .
  bar . . 3. gad 5. ingot
  cake . . 4. slag
  casting . . 3. pig
  cement . . 6. solder
  clippings . . 7. scissil
  coarse . . 5. matte
  coat . . 6. patina
  color . . 9. pearl blue
  content . . 3. ory
  crude . . 5. matte
  deposit . . 4. lode
  disc . . 5. paten
  dross . . 4. slag
  electric . . 6. magnet
  filings . . 5. lemel
  forging term . . 5. sprue
  goldlike . . 6. oroide
  impurity . . 7. regulus
  layer . . 4. seam, vein 5. stope
  lightest . . 7. lithium
  lump . . 3. pig 4. slug 6. nugget
  patch . . 6. solder
  plate . . 4. foil, shim
  rare . . 6. erbium 7. iridium, terbium,
  yttrium 8. platinum
  refuse . . 4. slag 5. dross 6. scoria
  rock . . 3. ore

science of .. 10. metallurgy
tag .. 5. aglet (aiglet)
test .. 5. assay
tool .. 5. swage 7. stemmer
ware .. 4. tole 6. Revere
worker .. 6. welder 7. riveter
   9. goldsmith 11. silversmith
metamerism ... 12. segmentation (Zool)
metamorphosis ... 6. change
   9. oxidation 10. hydrolysis
   12. degeneration, ossification
   14. transformation
metaphor ... 5. trope 6. simile
   10. comparison 11. tralalition
metaphysics ... 5. being 6. nature
   8. ontology, theology 9. cosmology
   10. psychology
mete ... 4. give, goal 5. award
   7. measure 8. boundary 9. apportion
   10. distribute
meteor ... 5. bolis 6. Bielid, bolide,
   Leonid, Lyraid 7. Arietid, Perseid
   8. fireball 9. Andromede
meteorite (pert to) ...
iron .. 10. siderolite
shower .. 6. Leonid 9. Andromede
   (Andromedid)
stony .. 8. aerolite
meteor mark ... 6. crater
meteorology ... 9. astronomy
   10. atmosphere 11. climatology
meter, metre ... 5. gauge 6. rhythm
   7. cadence, measure 8. measurer
meter (pert to) ...
cubic .. 5. stere
measure .. 5. litre
millionth .. 6. micron
prosody .. 4. mora
square .. 7. centare
ton .. 5. tonne
unit term .. 3. are 6. decare
   9. decameter, decastere
weight .. 4. gram
methane ... 8. paraffin
metheglin ... 4. mead 8. beverage
mether ... 3. cup
method ... 3. way 4. mode, plan, rule
   5. means, order, usage 6. course,
   manner, system 7. fashion, process
   9. procedure 11. arrangement
   14. classification
methodic, methodical ... 6. formal
   7. orderly, regular 10. systematic
Methuselah (pert to) ...
Bib .. 7. aged man 9. Patriarch
father .. 7. Enoch
metic ... 5. alien 7. settler
   9. immigrant
meticulous ... 4. nice, prim 5. fussy
   7. careful, fearful, precise 8. exacting
   9. selective 10. fastidious, scrupulous
   14. discriminating
métier ... 4. line 7. calling 8. business
   10. occupation, profession
metis, metisse ... 7. mulatto
   8. octoroon 9. half-breed
Metis ... 8. asteroid 9. Zeus's wife
metrical ... 8. measured, poetical,
   rhythmic
metrical composition ... 4. poem
   5. poesy 6. poetry

metrical foot ... 4. iamb 6. iambus
   7. anapest, spondee, trochee
   8. choriamb
metrical stress ... 4. scan 5. arsis,
   ictus 6. thesis
metronome (Maelzel's) ... 5. timer
metropolis ... 4. city, seat, town
   6. center 8. district 9. metropole
metropolitan ... 5. chief, urban
   6. bishop, center 7. leading
   9. principal
mettle ... 5. ardor, honor, nerve, pluck,
   spunk 6. spirit 7. courage
   9. fortitude 11. temperament
meuse, muse ... 3. gap 4. hole
   7. opening 8. loophole
Meuse River ... 4. Maas
mew ... 3. cob, den 4. cage, cast,
   coop, gull, molt, shed 5. miaow,
   miaul 6. change 7. seagull, stables
   8. spicknel 11. concealment,
   confinement
mewl ... 3. cry, mew 6. squall
   7. whimper
Mexican (pert to) ... see also *Mexico*
agave .. 5. datil 6. zapupe
   8. henequen
almond .. 7. Malabar
American .. 6. gringo
ancient .. 4. Maya 5. Aztec, Nahua
   6. Mixtec, Toltec 7. Zapotec
antelope .. 9. pronghorn
asphalt .. 9. chapapote
bean .. 6. frijol 7. frijole
bedbug .. 8. conenose
beverage (alcoholic) .. 6. mescal,
   pulque 7. tepache
bird .. 6. jacana, towhee 7. jacamar,
   tinamou 8. zopilote
blanket .. 6. serape
brigand .. 7. ladrone
bull .. 4. toro
cactus .. 6. chaute, mescal
cape .. 6. serape
cat .. 6. margay
cherry tree .. 7. capulin
chief .. 4. jefe 12. jefe politico
cloak .. 5. manta
cockroach .. 9. cucaracha
common land (law) .. 6. ejidos
coral drops (lily) .. 7. Bessera
cottonwood .. 5. alamo
dance (solo) .. 8. guaracha
dish .. 5. atole, chili (chile), tacos
   6. tamale 8. frijoles, tortilla
   9. enchilada 13. chili con carne
dog .. 9. Chihuahua
dollar .. 4. peso 5. adobe
dove .. 4. Inca
drug .. 7. damiana
elm .. 6. mezcal 8. Ulmaceae
estate, farm .. 8. hacienda
fever .. 10. tabardillo
fish (food) .. 6. salema 7. totuava
game (card) .. 4. frog
grass .. 3. mat 5. otate 6. petate
   8. henequen
herdsman .. 8. ranchero
hog .. 7. peccary
hut, house .. 5. jacal
insect .. 8. turicata
labor system .. 7. peonage

landmark.. 5. senal
masonry.. 5. adobe
moon god (Aztec).. 6. Meztli
mullet.. 4. bobo
musical instrument.. 6. clarin (anc)
    7. maracas
Noah.. 6. Coxcox
onyx.. 6. tecali
orange.. 7. Choisya
peasant.. 4. peon
persimmon.. 7. chapote
phlox.. 6. cobaea
plant, shrub.. 4. pita 5. agave,
    amole, datil, istle, sisal, sotol, yucca
    6. maguey 8. ocotillo
    10. candlewood, Dasylirion
rose.. 9. portulaca
saloon.. 7. cantina
sandal.. 8. huaracho (huarache)
sauce.. 7. Tabasco
scarf.. 6. tapalo
shawl.. 6. serape
stirrup.. 7. estribo
stirrup hood.. 8. tapadera (tapadero)
sugar.. 7. panocha
tea.. 6. basote 7. apasote
thong.. 5. romal
throwing stick.. 6. atlatl
tree.. 3. ule 5. alamo, ocote
    6. colima, poplar 7. capulin
    10. cottonwood
war god.. 7. Mexitli
yucca.. 5. izote (isote)
Mexican people...
composer.. 6. Chavez
conqueror.. 6. Cortez
Dictator.. 4. Diaz
historian.. 6. Orozco
painter.. 6. Rivera
Mexico...
battleground.. 6. Puebla
capital.. 10. Mexico City
city.. 6. Merida, Puebla 7. Durango,
    Tampico 8. Mazatlan, Monterey, Vera
    Cruz 11. Guadalajara
conqueror.. 6. Cortes (Cortez)
hero.. 6. Juarez 11. Poncho Villa
lake.. 7. Chapala
mountain.. 12. Popocatepetl
peninsula.. 4. Baja 7. Yucatan
people.. 5. Mayas 6. Aztecs
    7. Toltecs 10. Cuitlateco
river.. 9. Rio Grande
volcano.. 6. Colima 7. Jorullo, Orizaba
    12. Ixtaccihuatl, Popocatepetl
mezzanine... 8. entresol, low story
miaow, miaou... 3. mew
mias... 9. orangutan
miasma... 4. fume 6. poison
    7. malaria, malodor 9. contagion
mib... 7. a marble
mica... 4. talc 5. glist 7. biotite
    8. chlorite, silicate 9. damourite,
    hydromica, isinglass, muscovite
    10. lepidolite
Micah... 4. Book (Old Test) 7. prophet
mice... 3. Mus 5. voles 7. rodents
miche... 5. skulk, sneak 6. lie hid
    7. conceal
micher... 5. sneak, thief 6. truant
Michigan...
capital.. 7. Lansing

city.. 5. Flint 7. Detroit, Lansing
    8. Ann Arbor 9. Marquette
explorer.. 7. Jolliet, Nicolet
    9. Marquette 13. Sault Ste Marie
river.. 4. Cass 5. Huron
State admission.. 11. Twenty–sixth
State motto.. 6. Tuebor 11. I Will
    Defend
State nickname.. 9. Wolverine
mickey finn... 5. drink 8. narcotic
Micky... 8. Irishman
mico... 6. monkey 8. marmoset
micraner... 3. ant (small)
micro (comb form)... 4. moth 5. petty,
    small
microbe... 4. germ 5. virus
    8. organism 9. bacterium
    13. microorganism
microcosm... 4. body (humerous)
    5. world (small) 8. universe
microscopic (pert to)...
algae.. 6. amoeba, diatom
anatomy.. 9. histology
size.. 5. small 6. minute 9. very
    small 13. infinitesimal
miorospores... 6. pollen
Midas (Gr)... 13. King of Phrygia
midday... 4. noon 7. noonday
    8. meridian, noontide
midday nap... 6. siesta
middle... 5. mesne, midst 6. center,
    centry, median, medium, mesial
    7. central 8. interior 11. intervening
    13. intermediator
middle (pert to)...
Age.. 8. Medieval
class.. 9. bourgeois 11. proletarian
comb form.. 3. mes 4. medi, meso
finger.. 6. medius 10. third digit
ground.. 4. mean 7. average
    9. mid–course
man.. 5. agent 6. broker, medium
    8. mediator 9. go–between
    11. intercessor 12. intermediary
middling... 4. fair 6. medium, middle
    7. average, between, midland
    8. mediocre, moderate, ordinary
    10. middle–aged
midge... 3. fly 4. gnat 6. midget,
    punkie 7. minutia
Midi... 8. The South (France)
Midian king... 3. Evi 4. Reba
Midian priest... 6. Jethro
midriff... 9. diaphragm
midshipman... 5. cadet 6. reefer
    8. toadfish
Midsummer Night's Dream (play)...
    4. Puck, Snug 6. Bottom, Oberon
    7. Titania
midwife... 4. baba, dhai 6. cummer
    (kimmer) 11. accoucheuse
mien... 3. air, eye 4. look 5. guise
    6. aspect, manner, ostent
    7. bearing, posture 8. behavior,
    carriage, demeanor 10. appearance,
    deportment
miff... 3. vix 4. tiff 5. anger 6. offend
    7. dudgeon, quarrel 9. displease,
    sulkiness 10. sullenness
mig... 4. duck 7. a marble
might... 3. arm 5. force, power
    7. ability 8. efficacy, strength

9. greatness
mighty ... 4. huge, vast, very
  6. potent, strong 7. eminent, violent
  8. enormous, forcible, powerful,
  puissant 9. extremely 10. omnipotent
  11. efficacious 13. authoritative
migniard ... 6. dainty, minion
  7. mincing 8. delicate, mistress
mignon ... 5. small 6. dainty, petite
  7. blue–red 8. delicate, graceful
mignonette (pert to) ...
color .. 5. green 6. reseda
emblem of .. 6. Saxony
herb .. 6. reseda
tree .. 5. henna
vine .. 7. Madeira, tarweed
migraine ... 6. megrim 8. headache
  10. hemicrania
migrate ... 4. move, trek 8. resettle,
  transfer 12. transmigrate
migration ... 4. trek 5. exode
  6. exodus 7. passage 8. shifting
  (Chem) 10. relocation
migratory ... 6. moving, roving
  7. nomadic 9. peregrine, wandering
migratory (pert to) ...
ant .. 6. driver
cell .. 9. leucocyte
thrush .. 5. robin
mihrab ... 4. slab 5. niche 7. chamber
  (mosque)
Mikado ... 5. dairi, opera, title
  9. red–yellow, sovereign
Mikado character ... 4. Ko–Ko
  6. Yum–Yum 7. Pooh–Bah
Mikania ... 7. dogbane, thistle
  11. Willugbaeya (Willugheia)
  12. Ancylocladus
mike ... 4. loaf 6. loiter
  10. microphone
mil ... 5. mille 8. thousand
milady ... 5. woman 6. madame
  10. noblewoman 11. gentlewoman
Milan (pert to) ...
hat .. 5. straw
opera house .. 5. Scala
point .. 10. bobbin lace 12. point de
  Milan
mild ... 4. calm, kind, meek, soft, warm
  5. bland 6. benign, gentle
  7. clement, insipid, lenient
  8. benedict, gracious, lenitive,
  moderate, soothing, tranquil
  9. assuasive, indulgent, temperate
  10. mollifying 11. considerate
mildew ... 4. mold, must, rust, smut
  6. blight, fungus 8. honeydew
mild expression ... 9. euphemism
mild offense ... 6. delict
mile (term) ... 3. sea 7. statute
  8. nautical 9. Admiralty
  12. geographical
Miledh ... 8. ancestor (fabled)
Milesian ... 4. Celt 8. Irishman
  10. Miledh's son
milestone ... 5. stele 7. waymark
  8. landmark, milepost
milfoil ... 4. herb 6. yarrow
milieu ... 7. ecology 8. ambience
  11. environment 12. surroundings
militant ... 7. hawkish, warlike
  8. battling, fighting 9. combating,

combative 11. contentious
military ... 7. martial 8. soldiers
military (pert to) ...
advance .. 8. anabasis
aide .. 7. attaché
base .. 4. camp 5. depot, field
  7. billets 8. barracks, firebase,
  quarters 10. encampment
call .. 6. tattoo 8. reveille
cap .. 4. kepi 5. busby, shako
cap, hat cover .. 8. havelock
cloak .. 5. sagum (anc)
commission .. 6. brevet
defense .. 4. fort 6. abatis
depot .. 4. base
division .. 4. unit 5. corps, squad
  7. company, platoon 8. regiment
engine .. 6. onager 7. robinet
expedition to Holy Land .. 7. Crusade
force .. 4. army 5. ranks, troop
  6. legion 7. reserve 8. soldiery
guard .. 6. patrol
horsemen .. 7. cavalry, hussars
infraction .. 4. AWOL
inspection .. 5. drill 6. parade, review
instrument .. 5. bugle 7. althorn
landing point .. 9. beachhead
maneuver .. 6. tactic
messenger .. 7. estafet
night attack .. 8. camisade
obstruction .. 6. abatis
officer .. 5. major 7. captain, colonel,
  general 8. corporal, sergeant
  9. brigadier, subaltern 10. lieutenant
operations .. 8. campaign, strategy
order .. 7. command
organization .. 5. cadre
pit .. 10. trou–de–loup
police .. 2. MP 9. gendarmes
  12. constabulary
punishment .. 4. brig 9. strappado
quarters .. 4. camp 7. billets
  8. barracks 10. cantonment
salute (artillery) .. 5. salvo
science .. 3. war 7. war game
  8. warcraft 9. logistics
service stripes .. 9. hashmarks
signal .. 7. chamade (anc)
staff .. 5. cadre
storehouse .. 5. étape 7. arsenal
supplies .. 8. materiel, ordnance
survey .. 11. reconnoiter
testament, will .. 11. nuncupative
tool (hook–shaped) .. 4. croc (anc)
truck (cannon) .. 6. camion
vehicle .. 4. jeep, tank 6. camion
  7. caisson
militate ... 5. fight 6. debate, rebuff
  7. contend 8. conflict
milk ... 3. lac 5. cream, drain, fluid
  6. elicit, suckle 7. despoil, draw out,
  exploit, extract 8. beverage
milk (pert to) ...
beverage .. 4. whig 10. buttermilk
coagulator .. 4. ruen 6. rennet
curd .. 5. zeiga 6. casein
curdled .. 6. yogurt 7. clabber
fermented .. 5. kefir 6. kumiss
  (koumiss) 7. matzoon
fish .. 3. awa 6. Chanos, sabalo
food (fasting) .. 10. lacticinia
glass .. 7. opaline 8. cryolite

mouse.. 6. spurge
pail.. 5. bowie, eshin
pert to.. 6. lactic 7. lactary, lacteal
product.. 6. cheese, yogurt
sap.. 5. latex
sop.. 5. sissy 11. mollycoddle
sour.. 4. curd, whey, whig 6. blinky
store.. 5. dairy 9. lactarium
strainer.. 6. milsey (milsie)
sugar.. 7. lactose
watery part.. 4. whey
with (milk).. 6. au lait
milkweed... 6. spurge 7. dogbane
   10. sow thistle 14. Asclepiadaceae
milkwood... 8. Moraceae 9. paperbark
milky... 4. mild, tame, weak 5. timid,
   white 6. gentle, liquid 7. lacteal
   8. emulsion, emulsive, lactesce (to
   become), timorous 10. effeminate
Milky Way... 6. Galaxy 9. Via Lactea
   14. galactic circle
Milky Way black spaces...
   9. Coalsacks
mill... 3. box 4. beat, coin (to)
   5. crush, dress, fight, grind, knurl,
   quern, shape 6. finish, powder,
   thrash 7. factory, machine, serrate
   8. arrastra, snuffbox, vanquish,
   workshop 9. comminute, pulverize,
   transform 10. move around
   12. housebreaker
mill (pert to)...
beetle.. 9. cockroach
bill.. 3. adz
clapper.. 10. chatterbox
course.. 4. lade 8. millrace, tailrace
end.. 7. remnant
run of.. 4. average 8. millrace,
  ordinary
millefleurs... 7. perfume
millenarian... 8. chiliast
millennium... 6. period, utopia
   9. millenary 13. thousand years
millepede... 6. insect 8. myriapod
millepore... 5. coral 9. madrepore
miller... 3. ray 4. moth 5. boxer
   7. harrier 8. pugilist 10. flycatcher
miller's thumb... 4. bird, fish
   7. warbler 8. titmouse (long-tailed)
   9. goldcrest
millesimal... 10. thousandth
millet... 4. moha 5. bajra, grass,
   hirse, milly 8. cenchrus
   9. broomcorn 10. hirse grass
   14. non-Moslem group
millimeter... 6. micron 14. thousandth
   part
millions, one thousand... 7. billion
millions of millions... 9. trillions
Mills grenade... 4. bomb
milo... 5. durra 12. grain sorghum
Milvus... 4. kite
Milwaukee... 21. German Athens of
   America
mime... 3. ape 4. aper, copy 5. actor,
   clown, mimic 6. jester, mummer
   7. buffoon, imitate
mimesis... 7. mimicry 9. imitation
mimic... 3. ape 4. aper, copy, mime,
   mimo, mock 5. actor 6. mummer,
   parrot 7. buffoon, copying, imitate,
   mimetic 8. imitator 9. imitative

   11. counterfeit
mimicry... 5. apery, apism 7. mimesis,
   mockery 8. parrotry
mimic thrush... 11. mockingbird
Mimidae, Miminae... 7. catbird
   8. thrasher 11. mockingbird
Mimir... 5. giant
mimsey... 4. prim 7. prudish
min... 5. ruler 6. memory, prince,
   remind 8. remember
   11. remembrance
Min (Egypt)... 3. god (procreation)
   5. deity
Minar... 4. myna 5. Kutab (Delhi),
   tower
minaret... 4. lamp 5. tower
   10. lighthouse
minaway... 6. minuet
mince... 3. cut 4. chop, dice, hash
   5. slash 8. diminish, prim step
   9. subdivide 10. short steps
minced meat... 7. rissole
minced oath... 4. drat, egad
minchen... 3. nun
minchery... 7. nunnery
minchiate... 5. tarot
mind... 4. care, heed, mens, obey,
   reck, tend, will 6. desire, memory,
   psyche 7. opinion 9. intellect,
   intention 11. remembrance
   12. intelligence
mind (pert to)...
development.. 13. psychogenesis
jubilant.. 7. elation
peace of.. 8. ataraxia, calmness
  16. imperturbability
pert to.. 6. mental 7. phrenic
picture.. 4. idea 5. image
split.. 13. schizophrenic
Mindanao...
language.. 3. Ata
site.. 11. Philippines
town.. 4. Dapa 5. Davao
  9. Zamboanga
tribe.. 3. Ata 4. Moro 5. Lutao
  6. Bagobo, Illano
volcano.. 3. Apo 9. Malindany
mindful... 8. disposed 9. observant,
   regardful 11. remembering
mine... 2. my 3. bal, dig, mio, pit,
   sap 4. meum 5. stope 6. cavity,
   quarry 7. gallery, passage
   10. excavation 12. entrenchment
mine (pert to)...
basket, tub.. 4. corf
ceiling.. 5. astel
coal.. 3. rob
deviation (lode).. 4. hade
device (sweeper).. 3. gad 8. paravane
entrance, passage.. 4. adit 5. stulm
excavation.. 5. stope
floor.. 4. sill
guardian (Myth).. 5. gnome
holes.. 7. gophers
prop.. 5. sprag, stull
reservoir.. 4. sump 8. standage
shack.. 3. doe
shaft.. 4. sump 6. upcast
signalman.. 5. cager 7. cageman
step.. 7. stemple (stempel)
surface.. 6. placer
thrower.. 6. minnie 11. minenwerfer

tunnel .. 5. stulm
vein .. 4. lode
waste .. 3. gob 4. goaf
worker .. 5. cager, miner 8. onsetter
miner (pert to) ...
disease .. 8. phthisis
instrument .. 4. dial
lamp .. 4. davy
pick .. 3. gad 7. mandrel
sieve .. 6. dillue
worm .. 8. hookworm
mineral .. 3. ore, tin 4. alum, iron
  5. pitch 6. barite, egeran, gangue,
  iolite, pinite, quartz 7. apatite,
  asphalt, ataxite, bullion, epidote,
  felsite, felspar 8. danalite, edentite,
  misenite 9. uraninite
mineral (ore) ...
black .. 3. jet 6. cerine, yenite (Elba)
  7. niobite 8. graphite 10. minguetite
blue–green .. 5. beryl
brittle .. 7. euclase
brown .. 6. cerine, egeran, rutile
  9. elaterite
calcium, plus .. 7. calcite 8. calespar,
  diopside
crosslike .. 10. staurolite
dark .. 7. minette
fibrous .. 8. asbestos (abeston)
flaky .. 4. mica
gray white .. 5. trona
green .. 7. alalite, erinite 9. malachite
gunpowder .. 5. niter 7. thorite
hard .. 4. ruby 6. spinel (spinelle)
  7. adamant
jelly .. 8. vaseline
jewelry .. 8. diopside
lustrous .. 4. spar 7. blendes
magnetic .. 9. lodestone (loadstone)
nonmetallic .. 5. boron 6. iodine
plaster of Paris .. 6. gypsum
rare, brittle .. 7. euclase, thorite
red .. 4. ruby 6. garnet
soft .. 4. talc
waxlike .. 9. ozocerite 11. hatchettine
white, colorless .. 6. barite, gypsum
yellow .. 5. topaz 6. pyrite 7. epidote
mineral (pert to) ...
cavity .. 3. vug (vugg, vugh, voog)
dark spot .. 5. macle
deposit .. 4. lode 6. placer
greasy .. 7. atopite
oil .. 5. colza
pitch .. 7. asphalt
pocket .. 4. nest
salt .. 4. alum
spring .. 3. spa 4. well
tallow, wax .. 9. ozocerite
  11. hatchettine
tar .. 6. maltha
water .. 6. lithia 7. Seltzer 8. alkaline
Minerva (pert to) ...
feast .. 11. Quinquatrus
flower, plant .. 6. azalea
goddess of .. 5. civic 6. health
  11. handicrafts
shield .. 5. aegis (egis)
temple site .. 8. Aventine (Rome)
ming ... 6. remind 7. mention, recount
  8. remember
Ming (Chin) ... 7. dynasty
mingle ... 3. mix 4. fuse, meld

  5. admix, blend, merge, unite
  7. combine, concoct 8. coalesce,
  intermix 9. associate 10. amalgamate
  11. consolidate
mingle–mangle ... 6. jumble, medley
  7. mixture 9. potpourri
  10. hodgepodge, miscellany
minhag (Jew) ... 6. custom, manner
  7. liturgy
miniate ... 5. paint 8. decorate,
  luminate 9. rubricate
minikin ... 4. type 5. baize 6. dainty
  7. elegant, mincing 8. affected,
  delicate 10. diminutive
minim ... 3. jot 4. drop 5. Order
  (RCCh) 6. minute 8. smallest
  11. small amount
minimize ... 6. reduce 7. detract
  8. belittle 9. disparage
  10. depreciate 13. underestimate
minimum ... 3. jot 5. least 6. lowest
minion, minionette ... 4. idol, neat
  5. lover 6. dainty, pretty 7. darling,
  elegant 8. delicate, favorite, ladylove,
  mistress, paramour
minister ... 4. tend 5. angel, cater,
  serve 6. afford, attend, curate,
  parson, pastor, priest, supply
  7. furnish 8. diplomat, executor,
  preacher 9. clergyman, officiate
ministerial ... 7. serving 9. executive
  12. instrumental 14. administrative,
  ecclesiastical
minister's home ... 5. manse
  9. parsonage
Minnesota ...
capital .. 6. St Paul
city .. 6. Duluth 11. Minneapolis
hero .. 14. Father Hennepin
lake .. 3. Red 10. Minnewaska
land of .. 16. Ten Thousand Lakes
mountain .. 6. Cayuna, Mesabe
  9. Vermilion
river .. 3. Red 10. St Lawrence
  11. Mississippi
State admission .. 12. Thirty–second
State motto .. 13. L'Etoile du Nord
  14. Star of the North
State nickname .. 6. Gopher 9. North
  Star
Minoan ... 6. Cretan 7. culture (Prehist)
  8. language
minor ... 3. key 4. less, mode 5. friar
  (Franciscan), petit, petty, scale, youth
  6. course, infant, league, lesser
  7. smaller 8. inferior, interval,
  underage 9. youngling
minority ... 3. few 6. nonage
  7. smaller 8. underage
  10. immaturity 11. inferiority
Minos (pert to) ...
daughter .. 7. Ariadne
father .. 4. Zeus
king of .. 5. Crete
mother .. 6. Europa
Minotaur (Gr) ... 7. monster (half man,
  half bull)
minster ... 6. church 9. monastery
minstrel ... 3. lay 4. bard, poet, show
  6. end man, troupe 7. gleeman,
  goliard 8. jongleur, musician
  9. troubador 11. entertainer

minstrel show (pert to)...
  end man.. 5. bones
  middleman.. 12. interlocutor
  part.. 4. olio
mint... 3. aim 4. blow, coin, sage
  5. basil, feint, money 6. hyssop,
  intend, invent, mentha, ramona
  7. attempt, purpose, venture
  8. endeavor 9. fabricate
mint (pert to)...
  charge, levy.. 8. brassage
  11. seigniorage
  drink.. 5. julep
  family.. 5. basil 6. catnip 8. calamint
  9. Lamiaceae
  genus.. 6. Ramona 7. Melissa
  geranium.. 8. costmary
  hog.. 8. shilling
  sauce.. 5. money
minuet... 5. dance 7. scherzo
minus... 4. lack, less 6. absent, bereft,
  defect 7. short of, without
  8. subtract 10. deficiency
minuscule... 4. type 5. petty, small
  6. letter (lower case) 10. diminutive
minute... 3. jot, wee 4. mite, note,
  tiny 5. draft, petty, small 6. atomic,
  little, moment, period, record, slight,
  tittle 7. instant 8. atomical, trifling
  10. memorandum 11. unimportant
  12. sixty seconds 14. circumstantial
minute (pert to)...
  animal.. 10. animalcule
  details.. 11. particulars
  difference.. 5. shade
  glass.. 9. hourglass
  Jack.. 10. timeserver
  opening.. 4. pore 5. stoma
  organism.. 5. monad, spore
  8. zoospore
  part.. 8. tittle
  particle.. 4. atom, iota, mote
  record.. 8. protocol
minutely... 9. continual, unceasing
  11. every minute
minutes... 4. acta 6. record
minutia... 6. detail, minute 11. minor
  detail, petty matter
minx... 4. brat, doll, miss 6. pet dog
  7. colleen 8. pert girl 9. saucy girl,
  saucy jade 13. mischief–maker
minyan... 6. quorum 7. pottery
Miohippus... 5. horse
miqra... 9. Bible text (Heb)
mir (Pers)... 4. head 5. chief, title
  9. president
miracle... 4. feat, play 5. anomy
  6. marvel, wonder 10. occurrence,
  phenomenon 17. supernatural event
miracle scene... 4. Cana
miracle wheat... 7. poulard
miracle worker... 8. magician
  11. thermaturge
miraculous... 9. marvelous, wonderful
  12. supernatural 13. wonder–working
mirador... 5. brown, oriel 6. loggia,
  turret 7. balcony 9. bay window
  10. watchtower
mirage... 5. serab 7. chimera, reflect
  8. illusion 10. phenomenon
mire... 3. bog, mud, wet 4. glar, moil,
  ooze, slud 5. addle, dirty, marsh,

slush, stall 7. sludder
mirror... 5. glass 7. crystal, paragon,
  pattern, reflect 8. exemplar,
  speculum 9. reflector 11. image
  worker 12. looking glass
mirror iron... 12. spiegeleisen
mirth... 3. fun, joy 4. glee 6. gaiety
  (gayety), levity, spleen 7. delight,
  jollity 8. gladness, hilarity
  9. happiness, merriment, rejoicing
  10. joyousness 12. cheerfulness
mirthful... 3. gay 5. happy, jolly
miry... 4. oozy 5. boggy, muddy, slimy
  6. filthy, lutose
mis (comb form)... 5. amiss, wrong
misadventure... 6. mishap 8. accident,
  calamity, casualty, disaster
  9. mischance 10. misfortune
misandry (opp of misogyny)...
  12. dislike of man (by woman)
misanthrope... 5. cynic, Timon (Shak)
  8. man hater 9. pessimist
  12. mankind hater
misapply... 5. misdo 6. misuse
  12. misinterpret
misapprehend... 7. mistake
  8. misapply 11. misconceive
  13. misunderstand
misbegotten... 8. deformed
  12. illegitimate
miscalculate... 3. err 8. misjudge
  9. misreckon, overshoot
miscall... 5. abuse 6. revile
  7. misname 9. read amiss
  12. mispronounce
miscarriage... 5. lapse 6. mishap
  7. failure, misdeed, mistake
  8. abortion 9. mischance
  11. misdemeanor
  13. mismanagement 14. premature
  birth
miscegenation... 8. marriage
  13. interbreeding, intermarriage
miscellaneous... 5. mixed 6. medley,
  varied 7. blended, diverse, mingled
  8. combined 12. conglomerate
  13. heterogeneous 14. indiscriminate
miscellany... 6. medley 7. mixture
  8. excerpts 9. anthology
  10. collection 11. odds and ends
mischance... 6. mishap 8. calamity,
  disaster 10. misfortune
  12. misadventure
mischief... 3. ill 4. evil, harm
  5. wrack 6. damage 7. trouble
mischief (pert to)...
  god.. 4. Loki
  goddess.. 3. Ate 4. Eris
  maker.. 8. agitator 12. troublemaker
mischievous... 4. arch 6. elfish
  (elvish), impish 7. harmful, mocking,
  naughty, parlous, roguish, waggish
  8. sportive
misconduct... 7. offense
  10. wrongdoing 11. delinquency,
  misbehavior, misdemeanor
  13. mismanagement
miscreant... 6. rascal, wretch
  7. heretic, villain 8. polisson
  9. reprobate 10. unbeliever, villainous
  11. fallen angel, misbeliever
  12. unscrupulous

miscue . . . 3. err 4. miss, slip 5. error
6. bungle 7. mistake
misdeed . . . 5. crime, wrong 7. offense
8. wrongful 11. misdemeanor
misdemeanor . . . 3. sin 4. tort
5. crime 7. misdeed, offense
10. illegality, wrongdoing
11. misbehavior
mise . . . 4. levy 5. grant 6. layout,
treaty 8. expenses (law), immunity
9. privilege
miser . . . 5. hunks, Nabal (Bib)
6. nipper, wretch 7. boarder, niggard
miserable . . . 3. sad 6. abject, paltry
7. forlorn, pitiful, unhappy
12. disconsolate, disreputable
misericord, misericorde . . . 4. hall, pity
5. mercy 6. dagger 9. refectory
10. compassion 12. dispensation
miserly . . . 4. mean 5. close, tight
6. stingy 7. chintzy (sl) 8. churlish,
covetous 9. niggardly, penurious
10. avaricious 12. parsimonious
misery . . . 3. woe 5. grief 7. anguish,
avarice, poverty, sadness 8. calamity,
distress 9. heartache, privation
10. affliction, misfortune
11. despondency, Pandora's box,
unhappiness 12. covetousness,
wretchedness 13. niggardliness
misfeasance . . . 5. wrong 8. trespass
10. wrongdoing
misfortune . . . 3. ill 4. evil, harm
6. mishap 7. bad luck, reverse,
setback 8. calamity, disaster
9. adversity, holocaust, mischance
11. catastrophe 12. misadventure
misgiving . . . 5. doubt, qualm
7. anxiety 10. foreboding
12. apprehension
mishap . . . 4. slip 8. accident, casualty
10. misfortune 11. contretemps,
miscarriage 12. misadventure
Mishnah, Mishna . . . 4. Moed 5. tenet
6. Nashim 7. Nezikim 8. doctrine,
Halakoth, Kodashim, Tohoroth
9. tradition
misinterpret . . . 3. err 4. warp
7. distort, misread 8. misjudge
misjudge . . . 3. err 11. misconstrue
12. miscalculate
misky . . . 5. foggy, misty
mislay . . . 4. lose 8. displace, misplace
misle . . . 4. mist, rain 6. mizzle
7. drizzle
mislead . . . 4. fool 5. blear 6. delude,
seduce 7. deceive 8. misguide
9. deception, misbehave, misinform
misleading . . . 5. false 7. crooked
8. illusory 9. deceptive
10. fallacious, fraudulent
12. misinforming 14. misinformation
mislippen . . . 6. delude 7. neglect,
suspect 10. disappoint
mismanage . . . 5. blunk, misdo
6. bungle, misuse 9. mishandle
misogynist . . . 8. celibate 10. woman
hater
misplace . . . 4. lose 6. mislay, misset
8. displace 9. dislocate, mislocate
11. anachronism

misplay . . . 3. err 5. error 6. renege
7. mismove 9. wrong play
misprise, misprize . . . 5. scorn
6. slight 7. despise, disdain, mistake
8. contempt 9. underrate
10. misprision, undervalue
13. underestimate
misprision . . . 5. scorn 7. mistake
8. contempt, misprize
10. misconduct 11. misdemeanor
12. depreciation
16. misunderstanding
mispronunciation . . . 8. cacology
10. bad diction
misrepresent . . . 5. belie 7. deceive,
distort, falsify 8. disserve
miss . . . 2. Ms. 3. err 4. chit, fail, girl,
lack, lose, omit, skip 5. evade, lapse,
title 7. failure, mistake 8. mistress
9. fall short 10. prostitute
12. mademoiselle
missal . . . 4. book (Eccl) 8. breviary
missel . . . 9. mistletoe
misshapen . . . 4. ugly 8. deformed
9. distorted, monstrous, unshapely
missile . . . 2. MX 4. ICBM, Nike, Thor
5. Atlas, Snark, Titan 6. rocket
7. grenade, matador 8. Redstone
9. Minuteman
missing . . . 3. out 4. gone, lost
6. absent 7. lacking, wanting
8. vanished 11. nonexistent
mission . . . 3. job 4. body, duty, task
5. Alamo 6. charge, church, errand
7. calling, embassy 8. legation,
outreach 10. assignment, commission,
delegation, deputation, missionary
missionary . . . 7. apostle 8. emissary,
preacher 10. evangelist
Missionary Ridge . . . 11. Chattanooga
(Tenn)
Mississippi . . .
capital . . 7. Jackson
city . . 6. Biloxi 7. Natchez 8. Gulfport
9. Vicksburg 13. Pass Christian
explorer, colonizer . . 6. De Soto
9. Iberville
festival . . 9. Mardi gras (Biloxi)
king crop . . 6. cotton
kite (bird) . . 9. everglade
mountain . . 6. Woodal
river . . 5. Yazoo 11. Mississippi
State admission . . 9. Twentieth
State bird . . 11. mockingbird
State flower . . 8. magnolia
State motto . . 14. Virtute et Armis (By
Valor and Arms)
State nickname . . 5. Bayou
Mississippian (Geol) . . .
15. Eocarboniferous (system)
Mississippi River head . . . 10. Lake
Itasca (Minn)
Mississippi River nickname . . .
10. Great River 14. Father of Waters
missive . . . 4. note 6. billet, letter
7. message, missile 8. document
Missouri . . .
capital . . 13. Jefferson City
city . . 7. Sedalia, St Louis 8. Hannibal,
St Joseph
famed native . . 6. Carver (G W),

Truman (Pres) 9. Mark Twain
10. Jesse James
gourd .. 11. calabazilla
mountains .. 6. Ozarks
river .. 8. Big Muddy, Missouri
11. Mississippi
skylark .. 13. Sprague's pipit
State admission .. 12. Twenty–fourth
State bird .. 8. bluebird
State flower .. 8. hawthorn
State nickname .. 6. Show Me
sucker (fish) .. 10. black horse
misspelling ... 10. cacography
misspend ... 4. lose 5. waste
8. squander 10. spend amiss
misstep ... 4. slip, trip 7. faux pas
mist ... 3. dim, fog 4. blur, film, gray,
haze, rain, smur 5. bedim, brume,
cloud 7. droplet 9. obscurity
11. uncertainty
mistake ... 3. err 4. bull, goof, slip
5. boner, botch, error, fault, folly
7. blooper, blunder, erratum, violate
8. miscount, solecism
11. anachronism 12. inadvertence
13. misconception
15. misapprehension
mistaken ... 5. wrong 9. erroneous
12. misconceived 13. misunderstood
14. judging wrongly
mistletoe ... 6. emblem (Okla), missel,
Viscum 9. Loranthus
mistonusk ... 6. badger
mistress ... 4. bibi (beebee) 5. title,
woman 6. matron 7. control, teacher
8. Dulcinia, ladylove 9. concubine,
governess, patroness 10. proprietor,
sweetheart
Mistress of ...
Adriatic .. 6. Venice
Charles II .. 4. Nell
Seas .. 12. Great Britain
World .. 4. Rome (anc)
misty ... 3. dim 4. hazy, roky 5. foggy,
rouky, vague 6. blurry, cloudy, hoarse
7. obscure, shadowy 10. indistinct
13. unenlightened, unilluminated
misuse ... 5. abuse 6. revile 7. pervert
8. maltreat, misapply, wrong use
9. misemploy 12. misrepresent
misuse of words in speech ...
11. heterophemy, malapropism
mite ... 3. bit, jot 4. atom, coin, mote
5. child, speck 6. acarus, insect
7. bdellid, chigger, smidgen (smidge)
8. acaridan, particle
miter, mitre ... 4. belt 5. frank, joint,
tiara 6. fillet, girdle, gusset, tavern
7. petalon (Eccl) 8. dovetail,
headband, insignia 9. headdress
mithridate ... 8. antidote 9. electuary
12. alexipharmic
mitigate ... 4. ease, tone 5. abate,
allay, mease, relax, remit, slake
6. lessen, reduce, soften, temper
7. appease, mollify, qualify, relieve
8. diminish, lenitive, moderate, palliate
9. alleviate, extenuate, meliorate
mitigation ... 6. relief 9. abatement
10. diminution, moderation
11. extenuation 13. mollification
mix ... 3. pug (clay) 4. ease, join,

meng, stir 5. addle, blend, cross,
knead, unite 6. jumble, mingle,
muddle 7. combine, fluster
8. coalesce 9. associate
10. complicate
mixable ... 8. miscible
mixed (pert to) ...
breed .. 7. mongrel
type .. 2. pi
with water .. 6. slaked
with yeast .. 6. barmed, frothy
mixer ... 5. whisk 6. beater 7. mingler
9. eggbeater, (food) processor
mixture ... 4. hash, mash, olio
5. blend, chaos, mixed 6. batter,
medley, miscue 7. amalgam, mélange
8. compound, solution
9. admixture, potpourri
10. hodgepodge 11. combination,
preparation
mixture (pert to) ...
beverage .. 5. clary 10. shandygaff
cement .. 5. putty
medicinal .. 5. hepar 6. potion
12. prescription
metallic .. 6. speiss
sand and clay .. 4. loam
mix–up ... 5. melee, snafu 6. muddle,
tangle 8. conflict 9. confusion
Mizar ... 4. Zeta (Great Dipper)
mizmaze ... 9. confusion
12. bewilderment
mizzenmast ... 9. aftermast, third mast
mizzle ... 4. mist, rain 5. misle
6. decamp 9. slink away
mizzy ... 3. bog 8. quagmire
Mnenosyne (pert to) ...
ancestor .. 5. Titan
goddess .. 6. memory
mother of .. 8. The Muses
moa ... 6. ratite (flightless) 8. Dinornis
moab ... 3. hat (anc)
Moabite (pert to) ...
dwelling (Bib) .. 7. Dead Sea
language .. 7. Semitic
mountain .. 4. Nebo
people .. 4. Emim
stone (Bib) .. 11. black basalt
moan ... 3. cry 4. suum, wail
5. groan, sough 6. bemoan, bewail,
grieve, lament, suffer 9. complaint
11. lamentation
moat ... 4. foss (fosse) 5. ditch
6. trench 13. fortification
mob ... 3. set 4. gang, herd, mass
5. crowd, drove, flock, group, Mafia,
taunt 6. clique, rabble, throng
7. company 8. canaille, populace
mobile ... 7. movable 8. not fixed
9. versatile 16. changeable
Mobile Bay hero ... 8. Farragut (Adm)
mobile home ... 3. van 6. camper
7. caravan (Brit), trailer
mob member ... 6. rioter 7. Mafioso
8. criminal, mobocrat 9. roisterer
mobocracy ... 7. mob rule
Moby Dick (pert to) ...
author .. 8. Melville (Herman)
character .. 4. Ahab 5. Peleg
theme .. 7. whaling 10. White Whale
moccasin ... 3. pac 4. shoe 5. snake
6. Flower (Minn State), orchid

8. larrigan 10. argus brown
11. cottonmouth

moch... 4. moth

mocha... 4. bark, town (Arab)
6. coffee, dollar 7. leather 9. moss
agate

mock... 3. ape 4. defy, gibe, jape,
jibe, sham 5. feign, fleer, flout,
mimic, scoff, sneer, taunt 6. delude,
deride 7. imitate, mockery, pretend
8. ridicule 10. disappoint
11. counterfeit

mock (pert to)...
brawn.. 10. headcheese
cucumber.. 11. balsam apple
duck.. 4. meat 8. pork chop
hero.. 5. comic
jewelry.. 5. logie, paste 9. imitation
lead, ore.. 10. sphalerite
moon.. 10. paraselene
nightingale.. 7. warbler 8. blackcap
olive.. 9. axbreaker 12. cherry laurel
orange.. 7. syringa (seringa)
plane.. 8. sycamore
sun.. 9. parhelion
turtle.. 9. calf's head

mockage... 7. mimicry, mockery
9. imitation

mocker... 5. mimic 7. scoffer
8. deceiver 11. mockingbird

mockernut... 7. hickory

mockery... 5. farce 6. satire
7. mimicry, sarcasm 8. derision
9. imitation 11. counterfeit

mockingbird... 5. Mimus

mode... 3. fad, way 4. form 5. flair,
style, vogue 6. manner, method
7. fashion, variety

mode (pert to)...
expression.. 10. vernacular
government.. 6. regime, system
logic.. 7. Ferison (3rd figure)
procedure.. 5. order 6. system
speech.. 8. parlance 11. phraseology
standing.. 4. pose 6. stance
7. posture 8. position

model... 3. act 4. form, idea, mold,
norm, plan, plat, pose 5. ideal,
image, shape 7. example, manikin,
measure, paragon, pattern, templet
8. ensample, paradigm, standard,
template 9. archetype, mannequin,
precedent 11. meritorious
12. reproduction

model (of)...
a word.. 8. paradigm
a work.. 9. archetype
excellence.. 7. paragon 8. exemplar
solar system.. 6. orrery
11. planetarium

moderate... 4. bate, ease, slow, some
5. abate, lower, slake 6. frugal,
lessen, soften, temper 7. control,
lenient, mediate, modesto
8. mediocre, modulate, slow down
9. temperate 10. reasonable
11. inexpensive 12. conservative
14. inconsiderable

moderation... 7. control 9. abatement,
restraint 10. diminution, governance,
limitation, mitigation 11. restriction
13. temperateness

moderator... 5. judge 6. umpire
7. arbiter 8. mediator 10. arbitrator,
controller

modern... 3. neo (pref), new 4. late
6. latter 7. present 8. neoteric

modernize... 6. update 10. streamline

Modern School of Art... 4. Dada
7. Dadaism (1920)

modern Syriac script... 5. serta
8. peshitta

modest... 3. coy, mim, shy 6. chaste,
demure, humble, seemly 8. reserved,
retiring, virtuous 9. diffident
11. well–behaved 13. unpretentious
14. inconsiderable

modesty... 7. decency, reserve,
shyness 8. chastity, humility, pudicity
10. diffidence, humbleness
11. self–control

modicum... 3. bit 4. drop 5. minim,
share 6. little 11. small amount
12. small portion

modification... 4. tone 6. change,
umlaut 9. variation 10. adaptation,
alteration, limitation 13. qualification
15. differentiation

modify... 4. vary 5. alter, limit
6. change, master, temper
7. assuage, qualify 8. attemper,
mitigate, moderate, quantify
9. influence 13. differentiate

modish... 4. chic, trim 5. smart 7. in
vogue, stylish 8. vogueish (voguish)
11. fashionable

modiste... 8. milliner 9. couturier
10. couturière, dressmaker

modulated... 5. toned 6. merged
7. adapted, attuned, changed,
intoned 8. softened, tempered
9. inflected, regulated

modulation... 4. tone 6. change
8. shifting 9. tempering
10. alteration, inflection, moderation

moggan... 8. stocking 10. knit sleeve

moggy... 3. cat, cow 4. calf 7. pet
name 8. slattern 9. scarecrow

mogo... 7. hatchet

mogul... 4. lord 5. nabob 6. tycoon
7. magnate 8. autocrat 9. dignitary
10. locomotive, panjandrum
14. great personage

Mogul... 6. Empire, Mongol 7. dynasty
9. Mongolian

Mohammed (pert to)...
birthplace.. 5. Mecca
daughter.. 6. Fatima
flight to Mecca.. 6. hegira
horse.. 5. Fadda (white mule)
7. Alborak
names.. 7. Mahomet, Mahound
son–in–law.. 3. Ali

Mohammedan (pert to)...
angel of death.. 6. Azrael
ascetic.. 4. Sufi 5. fakir (fakeer)
8. Marabout
caliph.. 3. Ali 4. Omar 6. Othman
7. Abu Bekr
chief.. 3. aga (agha) 4. dato (datto)
5. sayid 6. Caliph
crier (for prayer).. 7. muezzin
crusader's enemy (Moslem)..
7. Saracen

deity.. 5. Allah 9. Termagant
demon.. 5. afrit, eblis, jinni (jinnee)
7. Shaitan (Sheitan)
Malay (Javanese).. 6. Sassak
Moslem.. 5. hanif 9. Mussulman
noble.. 4. amir (ameer), emir
nymph.. 5. houri
officer.. 3. aga 5. diwan 6. vizier
(vizir)
princess, queen.. 5. begum
saint.. 3. pir 6. santon
scholars, body of.. 5. ulema
sect.. 6. Wahabi (Wahabee, Wahhabi)
student (Theol).. 5. softa
successor.. 6. Caliph (Calif)
teacher.. 5. mufti 6. mullah (mollah)
unbeliever.. 6. Kaffir (Kafir)
Mohammedanism (pert to)...
Bible, book.. 5. Koran 7. Alcoran
bier, tomb.. 5. tabut
cap.. 3. taj
caravansary.. 6. imaret
crusade.. 5. jihad (jehad)
custom, tradition.. 6. sunnah
divorce.. 5. talak 7. mubarat
dome, over tomb.. 6. turbeh
Easter.. 3. Eed
Fast (annual).. 7. Ramadan
festival.. 6. Bairam
garment.. 4. izar 6. jubbah
house (men's part).. 8. selamlik
instrument.. 5. rebab
marriage custom.. 5. iddat
marriage settlement.. 4. mahr
Messiah, priest.. 4. Imam (Imaum)
6. Mahdi
monastery.. 5. ribat
platform, porch.. 7. mastaba
prayer.. 4. azan (adan) 5. namaz
property (law).. 6. mushaa
religion.. 6. Moslem 8. Islamism
saber.. 8. yataghan (yatagan)
salutation.. 6. salaam (salam)
shrine (Mecca).. 5. Kaaba (Caaba,
Kaabeh) 10. Black Stone
veil.. 7. yashmak (yashmac)
war (Relig).. 5. jihad (jehad)
moho... 4. rail 9. gallinule 10. honey
eater
mohr... 7. gazelle
moider... 4. toil 5. crowd, worry
6. wander 7. smother 8. bewilder,
encumber
moiety... 4. half, part (small)
7. portion
moil... 4. spot, tire, toil 5. labor, taint
6. seethe 7. torment, trouble,
turmoil 8. drudgery 9. confusion
10. defilement
moiré... 7. clouded, watered
moist... 3. wet 4. damp, dank, dewy,
uvid 5. humid, rainy 7. tearful
moisten... 3. wet 4. hose, moil
5. bedew, spray 6. anoint, dampen,
sparge 8. humidify, sprinkle
moisture... 3. dew, fog 5. vapor,
water 6. liquid 8. dampness,
dankness, dewdrops, humidity
moisture (pert to)...
body.. 6. humors 9. exudation
condensed.. 4. drip, drop
excess, swelling.. 5. edema

expose to.. 3. ret
remove.. 4. wipe 5. wring
mojo... 4. Moxo 5. charm (voodoo)
6. amulet 7. majagua
moke... 4. dolt, mesh 5. horse
6. donkey 7. network 8. minstrel
9. performer
moki... 4. raft
moko... 9. tattooing
moky... 5. foggy, misty
molar... 5. tooth 6. molary
7. chopper, grinder 8. grinding
molarimeter... 11. thermometer
molasses... 5. sirup 7. treacle
8. theriaca
mold, mould... 3. die 4. cast, form,
must 5. humus, knead, nowel,
plasm, sprue 6. blight, growth
(fungus), matrix, mildew 7. moulage
9. sculpture 12. reproduction
Moldavia, Rumania...
balm.. 4. mint
capital.. 5. Balta 8. Tiraspol
govt.. 9. Socialist
molding... 3. ess 4. bead, beak,
cyma, ogee, reed, tori 5. conge,
gulla, ovolo, splay, torus 6. fascia,
fillet, listel, reglet, scotia 7. cavetto,
cornice, reeding, shaping 8. astragal,
bezantee 12. reproduction
molding (pert to)...
convex.. 5. torus
decoration.. 4. dado
egg and dart.. 9. arrowhead
series.. 7. surbase
suit of.. 8. ledgment (ledgement)
moldy, mouldy... 5. fusty, mucid,
musty, stale 8. mildewed
mole (rat)... 4. gray 5. fault, nevus
(naevus), shrew, snake, Talpa, taupe
6. rodent 7. blemish, Nesokia
8. birthmark 12. imperfection
molecule... 3. ion 4. atom, unit
6. steric 8. particle
molest... 4. harm 5. annoy, tease
6. bother, harass, pester 7. disturb
8. mistreat 9. incommode
13. interfere with
Molière (pert to)...
author of.. 5. drama, plays
6. comedy, L'Avare, satire 8. Tartuffe
character (story).. 5. Damis 6. Eraste,
Scapin 7. Dorante
mollify... 4. calm 5. allay, relax, sleek
6. pacify, relent, soften, temper
7. appease, lighten, qualify, relieve
9. alleviate 10. conciliate
mollitious... 8. sensuous 9. luxurious,
softening
mollusk... 3. asi 4. clam, pipi, slug,
spat 5. chama, snail, squid, whelk
6. cockle, limpet, mussel, oyster
7. abalone, bivalve, octopus, scallop,
veliger 8. univalve 10. cuttlefish
mollusk... 5. Anoma, Chama, Murex
6. Chiton 7. Astarte, Etheria
8. Buccinum, Mollusca, Nautilus
mollusk (pert to)...
bait.. 6. limpet
eight-armed.. 7. octopus
freshwater.. 7. etheria
marine.. 7. abalone, scallop

8. nautilus
shell.. 4. test 5. testa 6. cockle,
cowrie (cowry)
shell, without.. 4. slug
shell concretion.. 5. pearl
teeth.. 6. radula
ten–armed.. 5. squid
young.. 4. spat
mollycoddle... 6. coddle, pamper
8. weakling 12. spoiled child
13. effeminate boy
Moloch (pert to)...
Bible.. 5. deity
doctrine.. 4. evil
zoology.. 6. agamid, lizard
Molotov cocktail... 4. bomb
molt, moult... 3. mew 4. cast, mute,
shed 7. ecdysis 8. exuviate
molten rock... 2. aa
Moluccas, Spice Islands...
capital.. 7. Amboina
island.. 5. Banda
product.. 5. spice
site.. 9. Indonesia
moly... 4. herb (fabled) 6. garlic
momble... 6. jumble, tangle
mome (anc)... 4. fool 7. buffoon
9. blockhead
moment... 4. time 5. avail, flash,
nonce, point, trice, value 6. crisis,
minute, second, weight 7. impetus,
instant 9. influence, twinkling
10. importance 11. consequence
13. consideration, signification
momentary... 9. ephemeral, transient
10. transitory 13. instantaneous
momentous... 7. weighty 8. eventful
9. important 11. influential
13. authoritative
momo... 3. owl
Momus (Gr)... 3. god (of ridicule)
6. critic 11. faultfinder
mon... 5. badge (imperial) 7. kikumon
13. chrysanthemum
monachal... 8. celibate, monastic
9. claustral
monad... 3. one 4. atom, unit
5. deity, monas 8. particle
10. individual 12. Supreme Being
monadnock... 4. hill 8. mountain (NH)
Mona Lisa (pert to)...
famed for.. 5. smile (subtle)
named also.. 10. La Gioconda
painter.. 7. da Vinci
site (of picture).. 6. Louvre (The)
monandry... 10. one husband (at a
time)
monarch... 4. czar, king, shah
5. chief, queen, ruler 6. dynast,
kaiser, sultan 7. czarina, emperor
9. potentate, sovereign 13. royal
highness
monarch... 9. butterfly
13. constellation
monastery... 5. abbey 6. friary, priory
7. convent, hospice, nunnery
8. cloister
monastery (pert to)...
head.. 3. dom 5. abbot
Pavia.. 10. Carthusian
room.. 4. cell
Tibet.. 8. lamasery

monastic... 4. monk 5. friar
7. monkish 8. celibate 9. claustral
monde... 5. globe, world (fashion)
6. circle (fashion) 7. coterie, société,
society 9. beau monde
monetary... 7. coinage 8. currency
9. financial, pecuniary
money... 3. wad 4. cash, coin, grig,
mina, pelf 5. frank, funds, lucre,
maneh, uhllo (ullo) 6. mazuma,
talent, wampum, wealth 8. currency
10. spondulics (spondulix) 11. legal
tender
money (pert to)...
ancient.. 3. aes
bank (Eur).. 5. banco
box, chest.. 4. arca, safe, till, tray
5. chest 6. drawer 7. brazier
8. register
changer.. 6. banker, broker, shroff
(saraf), usurer 7. cambist
coinage.. 4. mint
English slang.. 7. ooftish (oof)
found.. 5. trove
gamblers'.. 6. barato
gift.. 4. alms 7. bequest
9. endowment
lender.. 6. banker, usurer 7. Shylock
10. pawnbroker
luck.. 6. barato 7. handsel
maker.. 6. coiner, minter
13. counterfeiter
manual.. 7. cambist
matters.. 6. fiscal 9. economics
of account.. 3. ora
paper.. 4. bill, kale 7. lettuce
pledge.. 5. arles
premium.. 4. agio
roll (coins).. 7. rouleau
shell.. 5. uhllo (ullo) 6. cowrie (cowry)
slang.. 4. gilt, jack, lour 5. rhino
6. boodle, wampum
spinner.. 6. usurer 10. speculator
to coin.. 4. mint
wildcat.. 9. yellow dog
worthless.. 4. pelf
moneyed... 4. rich 5. flush 7. opulent,
wealthy 8. affluent, well–to–do
10. prosperous, well–heeled
monger... 6. dealer, mercer, trader,
vendor 7. peddler 8. merchant
9. tradesman
mongler... 9. sandpiper
Mongol... see also *Mongolian*
5. Asian, Tatar 9. yellow man
Mongolian (pert to)...
ass (wild).. 8. chigetai
capital.. 4. Urga
conjurer.. 6. shaman
conqueror.. 9. Tamerlane
desert.. 4. Gobi
dynasty.. 4. Yuan
monk, priest.. 4. lama
religion.. 9. Shamanism, Shintoism
12. Confucianism
river.. 3. Pei 4. Onon
tribe.. 3. Lai 4. Lapp 5. Ordos
7. Khalkas, Tsaktar 9. Ouryantai
mongoose... 4. urva 5. lemur
9. ichneumon
mongrel... 3. cur 5. mixed 6. hybrid
10. crossbreed 14. stilt sandpiper

mongrel fish... 5. skate (angelfish)
8. tullibee (whitefish)
monial... 3. nun
moniker... 4. name 8. nickname
monition... 6. advice, notice
7. summons, warning
10. admonition, dissuasion, intimation
11. forewarning
monitor... 4. ship (Civil War), uran
5. varan 6. lizard, manual, mentor,
nozzle 7. adviser, student, warning
8. conenose (bug), director, recorder,
reminder 9. informant
monk... 3. fra 4. bede, lama, saki
5. fakir, friar, padre 6. ferret,
monkey 7. ascetic, caloyer, dervish
8. anchoret, capuchin, celibate,
cenobite 9. anchorite, bullfinch,
touchwood
monkey (pert to)...
African.. 4. waag 5. potto 6. grivet,
vernet
American.. 4. saki 5. acari 7. ouakari
8. marmoset 9. beelzebub
bearded.. 8. entellus
bonnet.. 4. zati 5. toque
bread.. 6. baobab
chimpanzee.. 6. nchega
crying.. 4. kaha
cups.. 9. nepenthes 12. pitcher plant
family.. 10. Catarrhina
flower.. 7. mimulus (herb)
genus.. 5. Cebus 6. Ateles
7. Colobus, Saimiri, Tarsius
8. Alouatta
handsome.. 4. mona
house.. 5. apery
howling.. 4. mono 5. araba 7. stentor
8. alouatte
large.. 5. sajou
Madagascar.. 8. mangabey (mangaby)
organ grinder.. 5. Cebus 8. capuchin
Oriental.. 7. macaque
puzzle.. 5. piñon
small.. 8. marmoset
South American.. 4. titi 6. grison
9. beelzebub
spider.. 7. sapajou
squirrel.. 7. saimiri
tailless.. 3. ape
wrench.. 7. spanner
monk's hood... 4. cowl
monkshood... 4. atis 7. aconite
9. dandelion
monoceros... 4. fish (one–horned)
7. sawfish, Unicorn 9. swordfish
13. Constellation
monochord... 7. concord, harmony
9. sonometer 10. clavichord,
instrument
monocle... 8. eyeglass
monocleid, monocleide... 4. desk (one
key) 7. cabinet
monocracy... 9. autocracy
13. undivided rule
Monodelphia... 7. mammals
8. Eutheria
monody... 3. ode 4. poem (lament),
song 5. dirge 6. melody
9. homophony
monogamy... 11. one marriage
monogram... 6. cipher, sketch

7. outline 8. initials 9. character
monolith... 5. stone 6. menhir, pillar,
statue 8. monument
monologue... 6. speech 9. soliloquy
monomachy... 4. duel 6. combat
monopoly... 5. grant, right, trust
6. corner 7. charter, control
9. privilege, syndicate 10. possession
(exclusive)
monotonous... 4. dead, drab, dull
5. drone, thrum 6. dreary, samely
7. humdrum, tedious 8. singsong
9. wearisome 11. repetitious
monotony... 6. tedium 8. sameness
9. wearisome 10. sameliness,
uniformity 15. repetitiousness
monoxylon, monoxyle... 4. boat
5. canoe
monseigneur... 5. title 6. My Lord
monster... 4. ogre 5. fiend, harpy,
teras 6. dragon, ellops, geryon,
gorgon, sphinx 8. behemoth,
Cerberus 11. monstrosity
monster (pert to)...
classic.. 8. minotaur
comb form.. 6. terato
eight–headed.. 6. Scylla
fabled.. 5. harpy 6. kraken, sphinx
7. centaur 9. bucentaur
flame–breathing.. 7. chimera
(chimaera)
half man, half bull.. 8. minotaur
headless.. 9. acephalus
like.. 8. teratoid.
man–eating.. 4. ogre 5. lamia
medical.. 5. teras
three–bodied.. 6. Geryon (slain by
Hercules)
twin.. 10. xiphopagus
two–bodied.. 7. disomus
two–headed.. 10. dicephalus,
opodidymus
winged.. 5. harpy
monstrous... 4. huge, ugly, vast
5. enorm (anc) 6. absurd, wicked
7. strange, titanic 8. deformed,
gigantic, infamous 9. fantastic,
monstrous, unnatural 10. prodigious,
stupendous 12. overpowering,
overwhelming 13. extraordinary
Montana...
capital.. 6. Helena
city.. 5. Butte 8. Anaconda, Billings
10. Great Falls
Historic site.. 14. Custer Cemetery
lake.. 8. Flathead
mountain.. 7. Rockies 17. Continental
Divide
park.. 7. Glacier 11. Yellowstone
peak.. 7. Granite
reservation (Ind).. 4. Cree, Crow
5. Sioux 8. Cheyenne, Chippewa
9. Blackfeet
State admission.. 10. Forty–first
State motto.. 13. Gold and Silver
State nickname.. 8. Treasure
montanto... 6. rising 10. broadsword
Monte Cristo, Count of (pert to)...
author.. 5. Dumas (Alexandre)
hero.. 6. Dantès
Montenegro... 10. Yugoslavia
montero... 3. cap (hunter's) 6. ranger

8. forester, huntsman, mountain
Montezuma (pert to)...
Chief of.. 6. Aztecs
cypress.. 9. ahuehuete
hero of.. 6. Mexico
prisoner of.. 6. Cortez
ruins, site of.. 6. Pueblo
month (pert to)...
astronomy.. 5. lunar, solar
half.. 9. fortnight
revolution.. 8. sidereal 9. synodical
term.. 5. epact 6. ultimo 7. proximo
twelfth part.. 8. calendar
monticule... 4. cone (volcano)
  5. mount 7. hillock 10. prominence
  (small)
montilla... 6. sherry
Montmorency... 6. cherry
monture... 5. frame, horse (saddle),
  mount
monument... 4. tomb 5. cairn, stele
  (stela), tower, vault 6. bilith, dolmen
  7. obelisk 8. cenotaph, cromlech,
  monolith 9. sepulcher 10. gravestone
  11. commemorate, remembrance
monumental... 4. high 5. great
  7. mammoth, massive, notable
  8. colossal 10. impressive, sculptural,
  stupendous
Monumental City... 9. Baltimore
moo... 3. low (of a cow) 6. lowing
mooch... 4. loaf 5. skulk, sneak, steal
  6. loiter, pilfer 7. vagrant
moocha... 6. girdle 10. loincloth
mood... 3. tid 4. tone, vein, whim
  5. freak, humor 6. nature 7. caprice
  11. disposition
moody... 3. sad 4. glum 5. sulky
  6. gloomy, sullen 7. pensive
  9. whimsical 10. capricious
mool... 4. bury, mold, soil 5. earth,
  grave 6. mingle 7. crumble
mools... 10. chilblains
moon... 4. idle, Luna 5. Diana
  6. Phoebe, wander 7. Cynthia
  8. crescent 9. satellite 13. celestial
  body
moon (pert to)...
age (first of year).. 5. epact
area.. 4. mare
Astrol.. 6. Cancer (mansion), planet
autumn.. 7. harvest
beam.. 3. ray 9. pearl blue
bird.. 11. goldencrest
blindness.. 10. nyctalopia
calf.. 4. dolt 7. monster 8. born fool,
  imbecile
comb form.. 5. selen
fern.. 8. moonwort
festival.. 8. neomenia
fish.. 4. opah 6. minnow 7. sunfish
  9. spadefish
flower.. 10. oxeye daisy
gazing.. 16. absent–mindedness
geographer.. 13. selenographer
god.. 3. Sin 6. Nannar
heraldry.. 6. argent
inhabitant.. 8. Selenite
instrument.. 11. selenoscope
lighter.. 9. serenader 10. moonshiner
  11. night worker
lily.. 10. moonflower

mad.. 7. lunatic
mock.. 10. paraselene
month.. 5. lunar
new.. 6. phasis
phase.. 7. gibbous, horning
picture of.. 11. selenograph
point.. 4. cusp, horn 5. apsis
  6. apogee 7. perigee
position.. 6. octant
raker.. 10. stupid lout
  12. woolgatherer
stone.. 3. gem 8. feldspar
  10. hecatolite
struck.. 7. lunatic 8. obsessed
Uranus's.. 5. Ariel
valley.. 4. rill (rille) 5. cleft
moon goddess...
Greek.. 6. Hecate, Phoebe 7. Artemis,
  Cynthia
Italian.. 5. Diana
Phoenician.. 6. Tanith (Tanit)
  7. Astarte
Roman.. 3. Dea 5. Virgo 9. Caelestis
moonish... 7. flighty 10. capricious
moonshine... 5. empty 6. liquor,
  poteen, whisky (whiskey) 7. bootleg
  8. egg sauce, nonsense
  10. balsamweed
moony... 5. round 6. dreamy
  9. moonlight 10. abstracted
  14. crescent–shaped
moor... 3. bog, fen 4. hill, root
  5. heath, marsh, swale 6. anchor,
  fasten, secure 9. fix firmly
Moor... 6. Berber, Moslem
  7. Moorman, Saracen 8. goldfish
  (black), Moroccan
moor (pert to)...
berry.. 9. cranberry
bird.. 6. grouse
blackbird.. 5. ouzel
buzzard.. 5. harpy 7. harrier
cock.. 9. blackcock
dance.. 7. morisco
grass.. 5. heath 6. sundew
hen.. 4. coot 9. gallinule
monkey.. 7. macaque
stone.. 7. granite
Moorish... 6. Moslem 8. Moresque
Moorish (pert to)...
garment.. 5. jupon
horse.. 4. barb (Barbary)
judge.. 4. cadi
kettledrum.. 5. tabor 6. atabal
Order.. 7. Alcazar 8. Alhambra
  9. horseshoe, Saracenic
palace.. 7. Alcazar
moose... 3. elk 4. alce 5. eland
  7. society (Loyal Order)
moose bird... 9. Canada jay
moot... 4. pose 5. argue, plead, speak
  6. debate 7. discuss, propose
mop... 4. swab, wipe 5. scrub
  6. merkin 7. drink up, grimace
  9. blindfold, implement
mope... 4. sulk 5. dumps, idler
  6. grieve
moppet... 3. tot 4. baby, doll, tike
  7. darling, toddler 9. youngster
mora... 4. tree (Trinidad) 5. delay,
  stool 7. default 8. syllable
  9. footstool 11. Spartan army

12. postponement
moral . . . 4. good, pure 5. maxim
6. lesson 7. epimyth, ethical,
upright, virtual 8. likeness, virtuous
9. righteous
moral (pert to) . . .
excellence . . 6. virtue
fault . . 4. vice
law . . 9. Decalogue
obligation . . 4. duty
poem . . 3. dit
principle . . 7. precept
story . . 5. fable 7. parable
8. apologue
morale . . . 4. hope, zeal 6. morals,
spirit 8. morality 10. confidence
moralist . . . 4. prig 7. teacher
9. moralizer 10. sermonizer
morality . . . 6. amoral, ethics, virtue
13. righteousness
morals . . . 8. morality 10. ethography
morass . . . 3. bog, fen 4. moor
5. marsh, swamp 6. slough
8. quagmire 9. everglade
moratorium . . . 5. delay 10. suspension
Moravia, capital . . . 5. Brünn (Brno)
Moravian . . . 9. Christian 10. Herrnhuter
13. Unitas Fratrum 19. Church of
the Brethren
moray . . . 3. eel 6. hamlet 7. Muraena
8. food fish 10. Muraenidae
morbid . . . 4. sick 6. gloomy 7. ghastly,
unsound 8. diseased 9. unhealthy
11. unwholesome
morbid (pert to) . . .
appetite . . 10. adephagous
complex . . 11. inferiority
condition . . 8. ochlesis
desire for music . . 9. melomania
displacement . . 7. ectopia
morbus . . . 7. disease, illness
morceau . . . 3. bit (Mus) 6. morsel
mordant . . . 4. acid, keen 6. biting
7. burning, caustic, pungent
8. scathing 9. corrosive, sarcastic
11. acrimonious
more . . . 3. yea 4. also, mair, plus,
some 5. again, extra 6. plural
7. greater 10. additional
13. approximately
more (pert to) . . .
cunning . . 5. slyer 6. tricky
difficult . . 6. harder
distant . . 8. ulterior
mature . . 5. older, riper
miserly . . 6. closer, meaner, nearer
not any . . 4. dead, past 8. vanished
11. nonexistent
or less . . 4. some 8. somewhat
13. approximately
over . . 3. and 4. also, else
7. besides, further, thereto
precious . . 6. dearer
relative . . 11. comparative
severe . . 7. sterner
so . . 3. yea
than . . 4. over 5. above 6. beyond
9. exceeding 10. in excess of
than enough . . 3. too
than one . . 4. many 6. plural
7. several
than this . . 3. yes

unusual . . 5. rarer
vapid . . 6. staler
morel . . . 6. fungus 8. mushroom
morello . . . 4. ruru 6. cherry
7. boobook 8. morepork, mulberry
(color)
morena . . . 8. brunette
mores . . . 7. customs, manners
9. etiquette 11. conventions
Moreton Bay . . . 9. Australia
Morgan . . . 5. horse 10. sea dweller
morganatic marriage . . .
10. left–handed (royal)
morgay . . . 7. dogfish
morglay . . . 5. sword
morgue . . . 8. mortuary 9. deadhouse,
stolidity 11. haughtiness, impassivity
Morgue (The) . . . 17. Library of
Congress
moribund . . . 4. sick 5. dying 9. near
death
moriform . . . 14. mulberry–shaped
morindin dye . . . ?. al
morion . . . 6. helmet, quartz 8. cabasset
Mormon Church (pert to) . . .
Band (Polit) . . 6. Danite (1837)
cricket . . 11. grasshopper
emblem . . 3. bee
Indian . . 8. Lamanite
instrument . . 4. Urim 7. Thummin
officer . . 5. Elder
official name . . 36. Church of Jesus
Christ of Latter Day Saints
patriarch . . 11. Joseph Smith
12. Brigham Young
prophet . . 6. Moroni
State . . 4. Utah
tea plant . . 7. Brigham
tree . . 11. black poplar
morning (pert to)
clouds . . 4. velo
coat . . 7. cutaway
concert . . 6. aubade
glory . . 3. nil 7. ipomoea
14. Convolvulaceae
goddess . . 3. Eos
performance . . 7. matinee
prayer . . 5. matin
reception . . 5. levee
star . . 4. Mars 5. Venus 6. Saturn
7. Daystar, Jupiter, Lucifer, Mercury
8. Phosphor
term . . 4. dawn 5. matin, wight
6. Aurora 7. sunrise 9. matutinal
moro . . . 5. finch
moro (comb form) . . . 6. stupid
Moro . . . 6. Moslem
Morocco . . .
capital . . 5. Rabat
city . . 7. Tangier 10. Casablanca
color . . 3. red
enclave . . 4. Ifni
famed site . . 5. Casba
hat . . 3. fez
island . . 7. Madeira
Jewish quarter . . 8. El Millah
language . . 6. Arabic
leather imitation . . 4. roan
military expedition . . 5. harka
millet . . 12. Johnson grass
people . . 4. Arab, Moor 6. Berber
plateau . . 6. mesata

ruler.. 4. king 5. malek 6. sultan
soldier.. 5. askar
morology... 5. folly 8. nonsense
moron... 4. dull 5. ament, idiot, zombi
  6. nitwit, stupid 8. imbecile, sluggish
  12. stupid person
morose... 4. blue, dour, glum, grum,
  sour 5. moody, surly 6. crusty,
  gloomy, sullen 7. crabbed, unhappy
  9. splenetic 10. embittered
Morpheus (Gr)... 10. god of Sleep
  11. god of Dreams
morphine... 6. heroin 8. hypnotic
  9. analgesic, calmative
morphology... 7. anatomy 8. cytology
  9. histology 10. embryology
  12. organography
morris... 4. game 5. chair, dance
morro... 4. hill 6. Castle (Havana)
  7. hillock 11. point of land
Mors (Rom)... 5. Death, deity
Morse... 4. code, lamp 8. alphabet
morsel... 3. ort 4. bite, chip 5. piece,
  scran (sl), scrap, snack 6. tidbit,
  titbit 7. morceau 8. delicacy,
  fragment 11. small amount
mort... 4. dead, lard 5. death, fatal
  6. deadly, grease, salmon
  9. abundance
mortacious... 4. very 9. extremely
mortal... 5. fatal, human 6. deadly,
  lethal 10. perishable
mortally... 5. amort 6. deadly 7. à la
  mort, deathly, fatally 9. extremely
  10. grievously
mortar... 3. rab 4. bowl 5. putty
  6. cannon 7. mortier 10. night light
  (Hist)
mortarboard... 3. cap (Acad)
mortgage... 4. bond, pawn 6. pledge
mortician... 8. embalmer
  10. undertaker 15. funeral director
mortification... 5. decay, shame
  7. chagrin 8. gangrene, vexation
  11. humiliation
mortify... 5. abase, abash, abuse,
  shame, spite 6. ashame, deaden,
  humble 7. chagrin 9. embarrass,
  humiliate
mortis causa... 15. by reason of
  death
mortise, mortice... 6. cavity, insert
  8. amortize 10. foundation
mortuary... 4. gift (burial) 6. morgue
  7. funeral 8. funereal 9. deadhouse,
  sepulcher 10. cinerarium
  12. corsepresent (offering, Hist)
mosaic... 5. virus 6. design
  7. ceramic, picture 10. decoration,
  variegated 11. tessellated
mosaic (pert to)...
apply.. 7. incrust
gold.. 6. ormolu
law.. 5. Torah (Moses)
piece.. 7. tessera
Moscow...
capital of.. 6. Russia
citadel.. 7. Kremlin
river.. 6. Moskva
shrine.. 9. Lenin Tomb, Red Square
Third Internat.. 9. Comintern
Moselle... 4. Saar, wine 5. river,

Ruwer 9. Rhine wine
Moses (pert to)...
Bible.. 7. prophet 8. lawgiver
brother.. 5. Aaron
emissary.. 5. Caleb
father.. 5. Amram
father–in–law.. 6. Jethro
law.. 5. Torah (Tora) 10. Pentateuch
mother.. 8. Jochebed
mountain.. 4. Nebo
sister.. 6. Miriam
successor.. 6. Joshua
wife.. 8. Zipporah
mosey... 6. depart, stroll 7. shuffle
Moslem... 5. Hanif, Islam, Salar
  7. Saracen 9. Mussulman
  10. Mohammedan
Moslem (pert to)...
ablution.. 4. wudu (widu, wuzu)
cap.. 3. fez, taj
capturer of Jerusalem.. 4. Omar
caste.. 5. mopla (moplah)
chief.. 4. dato (datto), rais
city (holy).. 5. Mecca
college, school.. 8. madrasah
  (madrasa, madrasseh)
dagger.. 7. khanjar
deity.. 5. Allah, Eblis
devil.. 5. Eblis
devotee.. 6. santon 7. dervish
Easter.. 3. Eed
guide (spiritual).. 3. pir
interpreter.. 5. ulema
invocation.. 9. bismillah
javelin.. 6. jereed
judge.. 4. cadi
lawyer.. 5. mufti
market, booth.. 4. sook
monastery.. 5. ribat 7. khankah
mosque.. 6. masjid
noble.. 4. amir (ameer), emir
officer.. 5. dewan (diwan)
pilgrimage to Mecca.. 4. hadj
prayer.. 4. azan (adan)
priest.. 4. imam (imaum)
saint.. 3. pir 6. santon 8. Marabout
sect.. 6. Senusi (Senousi, Senussite)
shrine, Mecca.. 5. Kaaba (Caaba,
  Kaabeh)
teacher.. 4. Alim 8. mujtahid
title.. 3. Sid 5. Sayid (Said)
tradition.. 7. Al Sirat (Bridge to
  Paradise)
tribesman.. 4. Moro
Turkish.. 5. Salar
university.. 8. madrasah (madrasa)
viceroy.. 7. Saracen
mosque... 4. Omar 5. Kaaba (Caaba)
  6. masjid 11. Great Mosque
mosque tower... 7. minaret
mosque warden... 5. nazir
mosquito (pert to)...
bite preventive.. 10. culicifuge
coast.. 8. Honduras 9. Nicaragua
comb form.. 6. culici
destroyer.. 8. culicide
disease.. 7. malaria 11. yellow fever
family.. 9. Culicidae
fish.. 8. gambusia
genus.. 5. Aedes, Culex 7. Diptera
  8. Mansonia 9. Anopheles, Culicidae
  10. Psorophora

hawk .. **9**. dragonfly, nighthawk
Indian drink .. **6**. mushla
larvae .. **8**. wigglers
plant .. **4**. mint **10**. pennyroyal
shaped .. **10**. culiciform
term .. **7**. culicid **11**. gallinipper
moss ... **3**. bog, rag **4**. agar **5**. Maium,
money, Musci, swamp **6**. lichen,
morass **7**. skeeter **8**. agar–agar
9. treebeard
moss (pert to) ...
back .. **4**. dodo, fogy (fogey) **9**. old
turtle **10**. fuddy–duddy, Southerner
(1861) **12**. conservative
berry .. **9**. cranberry
capsule .. **9**. operculum
color .. **5**. green
coral .. **8**. bryozoan
duck .. **7**. mallard **8**. moss–head
9. merganser
fish .. **8**. menhaden **10**. mossbunker
grown .. **10**. antiquated
kind .. **4**. peat **7**. Spanish
like .. **6**. mnioid
mossy ... **4**. dull **5**. boggy, downy
6. marshy, stupid **9**. crumbling
most ... **7**. highest, maximum
8. greatest, main part, majority
9. nearly all
most favorable ... **7**. optimum
Most High ... **3**. God **12**. Supreme
Being
most northerly land ... **5**. Thule
mot ... **5**. adage, maxim, motto
7. opinion **9**. witticism
mote ... **4**. atom, hill, iota **5**. match,
speck, squib **6**. barrow, height, trifle
7. tumulus **8**. eminence, particle
mote nut ... **5**. carap
motet ... **4**. hymn **6**. anthem, choral
moth ... **2**. io **5**. egger, tinea
6. lappet, millor **7**. noctuid, Tineina
8. forester (8–spotted), Tineidae
9. Tineoidea **11**. Lepidoptera
moth (pert to) ...
hawk .. **10**. goatsucker
kind .. **5**. gypsy **6**. carpet **9**. browntail
spot (Med) .. **8**. chloasma
spot (wing) .. **8**. fenestra
mother ... **2**. ma **3**. dam **4**. amma
5. adopt, mamma, mater **6**. abbess,
parent **7**. care for, creator
8. ancestor, begetter, genetrix,
producer **10**. procreator
mother (pert to) ...
church .. **9**. cathedral **16**. Christian
Science
goddess .. **6**. matris **7**. Shaktis
10. sapta–matri (7 mothers)
goddess of motherhood (Egypt) ..
4. Isis
godmother .. **4**. Rhea **6**. cummer
(kimmer) **9**. Brigantia
Goose character .. **5**. Simon, Sprat
6. Bo–peep
Govt .. **10**. matriarchy, metrocracy
house .. **7**. convent **9**. monastery
Hubbard .. **4**. gown **6**. dress
Maid .. **10**. Virgin Mary
Mother Carey's chickens .. **7**. petrels
(stormy)
Myth (Gr) .. **5**. Niobe

related .. **6**. enatic
spiritual .. **4**. amma
Tagalog .. **3**. Ina
motherly ... **8**. maternal
mother of ...
Castor .. **4**. Leda
gods .. **4**. Rhea **9**. Brigantia
Graces .. **5**. Aegle
Nature .. **6**. Cybele
Night .. **3**. Nox, Nyx
pearl .. **5**. nacre **7**. abalone
presidents .. **8**. Virginia
States .. **8**. Virginia
the month .. **4**. Moon
motif ... **5**. theme, topic **6**. edging
7. subject
motion ... **3**. bob **4**. lipe, move
5. impel, trend **6**. seesaw, travel,
tremor, unrest **7**. gesture, propose,
request, suggest **8**. kinetics, mobility,
movement, petition
motionless ... **5**. inert, rigid, still
6. static **8**. immobile, stagnant
10. stationary, stock–still
motion picture terms ... **4**. film, show
5. flick, klieg (light), movie, rerun
6. cinema **7**. cartoon, feature
9. filmstrip, videotape **11**. golden
oldie **12**. silver screen
motivate ... **4**. move **5**. force, impel
6. compel, incite, induce, propel
7. actuate, animate, promote, trigger
9. stimulate
motive ... **4**. sake, spur **5**. cause,
motif, topic **6**. reason **7**. pretext
8. stimulus **9**. incentive, influence,
intention **10**. incitement, inducement
11. instigation **13**. consideration
motley ... **5**. mixed **6**. fabric
7. diverse, mixture, mottled
9. checkered, diversity **10**. variegated
12. parti–colored **13**. heterogeneous
motor ... **5**. mover, rotor **6**. Diesel,
dynamo, engine **7**. turbine **8**. motor
car **9**. locomotor **10**. automobile
motor speed control ... **8**. governor,
rheocrat
mottled ... **3**. roe **4**. pied **5**. pinto
6. calico **7**. dappled, marbled,
piebald, spotted **13**. pepper–and–salt
mottled soap ... **7**. castile
motto ... **3**. mot **5**. adage, axiom,
gnome, maxim **6**. advice **7**. empresa
(impresa), precept **8**. aphorism
9. principle **11**. inscription
motto of ...
Boy Scouts .. **10**. Be Prepared
Coast Guard .. **11**. Always Ready
13. Semper paratus
Order of the Garter .. **20**. Honi soit qui
mal y pense
Queen Elizabeth .. **11**. Semper Eadem
13. Always the Same
mouche ... **5**. patch (black)
mouchoir ... **12**. handkerchief
mouflon, moufflon ... **5**. sheep
mould, mold ... **5**. knead **6**. matrix
moulrush ... **7**. pollack (food fish)
mound ... **3**. dam, dun, tee **4**. bank,
dene, doon, dune, heap, hill, terp,
tomb, tump **5**. knoll **6**. bounds
7. barrier, bulwark, rampart, tumulus

8. boundary 9. elevation
10. embankment 13. fortification
mound (pert to)...
bird.. 8. megapode
City.. 7. St Louis
lily.. 5. yucca
memorial.. 5. cairn
of light.. 8. Kohinoor (diamond)
Polynesian.. 3. ahu
prehistoric.. 5. matte
Scottish.. 5. toman
mount... 3. fly, set (jewel) 4. glue,
hill, lift, pony (polo), rise 5. arise,
climb, horse, paste 6. ascent
7. elevate 8. increase, mountain
10. promontory
Mount (pert to)...
Etna city.. 7. Catania
Everest peak.. 6. Lhotse
Parnassus fountain, spring.. 8. Castalia
mountain...
Africa.. 11. Kilimanjaro
Alaska.. 8. McKinley
Asia.. 7. Everest
Babylonia.. 6. Ararat
California.. 6. Shasta 7. Whitney
Crete.. 3. Ida
Europe.. 4. Ural 8. Pyrenees
fabled.. 4. Meru
Greek (Myth).. 7. Helicon
Japan.. 8. Fujiyama
legendary.. 3. Kaf, Qaf (Moslem)
4. Meru
Mexico.. 12. Popocatepetl
Montana.. 6. Tetons
Switzerland.. 4. Alps 10. Matterhorn
Thessaly.. 4. Ossa 6. Pelion
U S Chain.. 5. Rocky 7. Sawback,
Sierras 9. Blue Ridge
11. Appalachian
Yukon.. 5. Logan
mountain (pert to)...
ash.. 5. rowan
badger.. 6. marmot
balsam.. 3. fit
banana.. 3. fei
barometer.. 8. orometer
beaver.. 8. sewellel
blackbird.. 5. ouzel
cat.. 4. lynx 6. bobcat, cougar
10. cacomistle
comb form.. 3. oro
cowslip.. 8. auricula
crest, spur.. 6. arête
curassow (pheasant).. 10. oreophasis
defile.. 3. gap 4. gate, ghat (ghaut),
pass 5. gorge
depression.. 3. col
dew.. 6. whisky
eagle.. 6. golden
goat.. 4. ibex
highest.. 7. Everest
ice.. 4. berg 7. glacier
ivy.. 6. laurel
lake.. 4. tarn
lion.. 4. puma 6. cougar
lodge.. 4. gite
low.. 5. butte
nymph.. 5. oread
oak.. 8. chestnut
peak.. 3. tor
raspberry.. 10. cloudberry

rose.. 6. laurel
sheep.. 7. bighorn 13. Rocky
Mountain
shrub.. 10. fetterbush
sickness.. 7. soroche
State.. 7. Montana
sunset.. 9. alpenglow
Tatars.. 5. Tauli
witch.. 9. quail dove
mountaineer... 7. climber
11. backsettler
mountains, science of... 7. orology
9. orography
mountant... 6. raised, rising
8. mounting 9. ascendant
mountebank... 4. gull 5. cheat, quack
7. buffoon, empiric 8. impostor
9. charlatan, pretender 11. quack
doctor
mounted men... 7. knights
mounting... 6. ascent 7. rimbase,
seating, setting 9. adjusting,
equipment 13. embellishment
mourn... 3. rue 4. erme, long, sigh,
wail, weep 6. bemoan, bewail,
grieve, lament, murmur, repine,
sorrow 7. deplore
mourner... 6. keener, wailer 7. griever
8. lamenter
mournful... 3. sad 6. repine 7. elegiac
8. grievous 9. elegiacal, plaintive,
saddening, sorrowful, threnodic,
woebegone
mournful poem... 5. elegy
mourning... 3. sad 4. garb 5. crape,
weeds (dress) 6. lament, sorrow
7. drapery 9. sorrowing 10. black
badge 11. lamentation
mourning dress... 5. weeds 6. sables
mouse... 3. erd, Mus 4. buck, vole
5. prowl, shrew 6. jerboa, migale
7. harvest, toy with
mouse (pert to)...
bird.. 4. coly 6. shrike
color.. 4. gray
deer.. 7. plandok 10. chevrotain
ear.. 8. hawkweed 9. bloodwort,
chickweed 11. forget–me–not
fish.. 9. sargassum
hare.. 4. pika
hound.. 6. weasel
kind.. 6. pocket 7. harvest, jumping
leaping.. 6. jerboa
milk.. 6. spurge
mouselike.. 6. murine
web.. 6. cobweb, phlegm
8. gossamer
mousse... 7. dessert 9. moss green
12. gelatine dish
moutan... 5. peony
mouth... 2. os 3. mow, mun 4. boca,
dupe, lade, lick 5. inlet, stoma
6. cavity, rictus 7. declaim, opening,
orifice 8. aperture, lorriker
9. impudence
mouth (pert to)...
away from.. 6. aboral
deformity.. 7. harelip
disease.. 6. canker 10. stomatitis
furnace.. 5. bocca
glands.. 8. salivary
muscle.. 7. caninus

organ.. 4. harp 7. Pandean
   8. jew's–harp 9. crembalum,
   harmonica
part.. 3. lip 5. uvula 6. palate
   7. pharynx
pert to.. 4. oral 6. rictal, stomal
   8. stomatic
piece (Mus).. 10. embouchure
through the.. 7. peroral
tissue.. 3. gum
toward.. 4. orad
wide, gaping.. 6. rictus
mouthed, loud... 11. thersitical
mouton... 5. sheep 9. prison spy
movable... 6. mobile 10. changeable
   12. transferable
movable property... 8. chattels
move... 3. act, gee, mog, say
   4. goad, sell, spur, stir 5. budge,
   cause, impel, rouse, shift 6. excite,
   incite, induce, kindle, motion,
   prompt, travel 7. actuate, advance,
   animate, propose, provoke
   9. instigate, recommend, stimulate
move (pert to)...
about.. 8. locomote
along.. 5. mosey, scram 7. maunder
back.. 3. ebb 6. recede, retire, revert
   7. retreat 10. retrogress
back and forth.. 6. teeter, wigwag
   7. shuttle 9. oscillate
clumsily.. 4. joll
false.. 4. balk 5. feint
forward.. 4. edge, scud 5. drive
   7. advance 8. progress
furtively.. 5. slink, sneak
heavily.. 3. lug 6. fidget, lumber,
   trudge
in circles.. 4. purl
place to place.. 7. migrate
   8. emigrate
quickly.. 3. ply 4. dart, dash, scud,
   shot 5. scoot, spank 6. bustle,
   gallop, hurtle
restlessly.. 6. kelter
rhythmically.. 5. dance
sideways, sidewise.. 4. slue 5. sidle
slowly.. 3. jog, lag 4. edge, inch,
   pant
smoothly.. 4. slip 5. glide, skate,
   slide
spasmodically.. 6. twitch
to and fro.. 3. wag 4. flap, sway
together.. 5. unite 8. converge
towards each other.. 8. converge
towards the east.. 9. orientate
unsteadily.. 4. reel 6. wabble
   7. stagger
up and down.. 3. bob 6. teeter
with exertion.. 5. heave
with measured tread.. 5. march
moved by entreaty... 8. exorable
moved easily... 5. loped 6. mobile
   8. affected 9. emotional
movement... 5. cause, trend 6. action,
   motion, rhythm, travel 7. emotion,
   gesture, impulse 8. activity,
   maneuver, progress
movement (pert to)...
backwards.. 13. retrogression
dance step.. 4. lilt 6. chassé
   9. pirouette

music.. 4. moto 7. con moto
of ships.. 5. heave, pitch, scend
of waves.. 4. roll, toss 5. surge
   6. tumble, welter
vibratory.. 6. tremor
moving... 6. active, motile 7. nomadic
   8. eloquent, exciting, pathetic
   9. affecting, impelling, traveling
   10. motivating
moving stairway... 9. escalator
mow... 3. cut, lay, mew 4. dess, fell,
   heap, mass, math, mock, raze, stow
   5. mouth, stack 6. garner, smooth
   7. cut down, grimace, harvest,
   shorten 10. cornfield
mowana... 6. baobab
mowing... 7. cutting, mockery
   8. derision 9. grimacing
   10. harvesting, meadowland
mowing machine... 5. mower
   6. scythe, sickle
moxieberry... 9. snowberry
moy... 4. mild 6. demure, gentle
   8. affected
moyen... 3. way 5. means 6. agency,
   course 8. property 9. influence
Mozambique...
Bay.. 8. Mossuril
capital.. 15. Lourenco Marques
native.. 3. Yao
port.. 10. Mozambique
mozo... 10. manservant
Mrs... 5. madam 8. goodwife, Mistress
mucaro... 3. owl
much... 3. lot 4. high, many 5. great
   7. greatly 8. abundant, uncommon
   9. great deal 10. indefinite
   12. considerable
muchacha... 4. girl, lass
muchacho... 3. boy, lad 7. servant
mucid... 5. musty, slimy 6. clammy,
   mucous 8. muculent
mucilage... 3. gum 5. paste
   6. mucago 8. adhesive 9. lubricant
mucilaginous... 5. moist 6. sticky,
   viscid
muckender... 12. handkerchief
mucker... 4. fall (from a horse), mess
   6. muddle, wretch 8. disorder
   9. confusion, vulgarian
muckle... 4. club, fret 6. bother,
   putter
muckraker... 7. defamer 8. vilifier
   9. slanderer
mud... 4. mire, muck, silt, slop
   5. abuse, gumbo, limus, shine
   6. gobbet, sludge 12. offscourings
   14. abusive charges
mud (pert to)...
bath.. 10. illutation
dab.. 8. flounder
dauber.. 4. wasp
devil.. 10. hellbender
eel.. 5. siren
hole.. 6. puddle 8. quagmire
lark.. 5. gamin, horse 6. magpie,
   urchin
like.. 7. luteous
living in.. 10. limicolous
peep.. 9. sandpiper 11. meadow pipit
pike.. 5. saury
puppy.. 10. hellbender, salamander

rake .. **5.** claut
shoveler .. **13.** spoonbill duck
snipe .. **8.** woodcock
sunfish .. **4.** bass **8.** warmouth
teal .. **9.** greenwing
volcano .. **5.** salse
Mudcat State ... **11.** Mississippi
muddle ... **3.** mix **4.** daze, mess, soss,
 stir **5.** addle, botch, snafu **6.** bemuse,
 bollix, jumble **7.** confuse, perplex,
 stupefy **8.** befuddle, bewilder,
 confound, disorder, squander
 10. intoxicate **11.** predicament
muddled ... **3.** ree **6.** drunk, muzzy,
 tipsy **7.** burbled, fuddled **8.** confused
 9. befuddled, entangled
muddlehead ... **4.** dolt **9.** blockhead
muddy ... **4.** base, miry **5.** dingy, dirty,
 roily, slaky **6.** lutose, opaque, slushy,
 turbid **7.** clouded, obscure
 8. confused **9.** besmeared
muddy places ... **7.** wallows
muezzin ... **4.** azan (adan) **5.** crier
 (Moham)
muff ... **5.** beard, cover **6.** bungle
 7. bungler, failure **8.** feathers
 11. mollycoddle, whitethroat
muffed ... **5.** vexed **7.** crested
 9. irritated
muffet ... **11.** whitethroat
muffetee ... **7.** muffler **8.** wristlet
muffin ... **3.** cob, gem **5.** bread, hazel,
 plate, scone **7.** biscuit, crumpet,
 English, popover
muffle ... **3.** gag **4.** damp, dull, mute,
 wrap **6.** deaden, mumble, shroud,
 stifle **7.** conceal **8.** decorate,
 envelope **9.** blindfold, soft–pedal
muffler ... **3.** gag **4.** mute **5.** scarf
 6. muzzle, tippet **8.** silencer
 10. suppressor
mufflin ... **8.** titmouse
mufti ... **5.** dress (civilian)
mufti (Moham) ... **4.** alim **5.** judge
 6. priest **8.** assessor, official
mug ... **3.** cup **4.** cram, dupe, face,
 fool, Toby **5.** mungo, pulse, sheep,
 study **6.** noggin **7.** drizzle, grimace
 8. quantity **10.** photograph
muga ... **4.** moth, silk **11.** caterpillar
mugger ... **3.** goa **6.** robber, tinker
 7. peddler **9.** crocodile
mugget ... **8.** woodruff **15.** lily of the
 valley
muggins (game) ... **5.** cards **7.** penalty
 8. dominoes
muggy ... **4.** damp, warm **5.** humid,
 moist, moldy **6.** sticky, stuffy, sultry
 10. sweltering **11.** whitethroat
mug house ... **6.** tavern **7.** barroom
 8. alehouse, pothouse
mugient ... **6.** lowing **9.** bellowing
mugwump ... **5.** chief **8.** apostate,
 objector **11.** independent, nonpartisan
 16. Republican bolter
Muhammed ... see *Mohammed*
muir ... **4.** wall
muirfowl ... **9.** red grouse
muishond ... **5.** zoril **6.** weasel
mujer ... **4.** wife **5.** woman
mulberry ... **2.** al **5.** Morus **6.** murrey
 10. blackberry **12.** thimbleberry

mulberry (pert to) ...
bark (paper) .. **4.** tapa (tappa)
beverage .. **5.** morat
bird .. **8.** starling
dye .. **3.** aal **8.** morindin
fig .. **8.** sycamore
purple .. **7.** blue–red **8.** camerier
tree .. **5.** Morus
wild .. **7.** yawweed
mulch ... **5.** straw **6.** ground, leaves
 7. sawdust
mulct ... **4.** fine, scot **6.** amerce,
 defect, punish **7.** blemish, deceive,
 penalty, swindle **10.** amercement
mulcter ... **7.** amercer
mule ... **4.** mewl, mool, mute **5.** coble,
 hinny, jenny **6.** acemia, hybrid
 7. slipper, tractor **9.** chilblain
 10. crossbreed, locomotive
 15. obstinate person
mule (pert to) ...
chair .. **7.** cacolet
driver .. **7.** skinner **8.** muleteer
drove .. **5.** atajo
killer .. **6.** mantis
leading .. **8.** cencerro
skinner .. **6.** driver
untrained .. **9.** shavetail
muleteer ... **4.** peon **6.** driver
mulga ... **6.** acacia, shield
muliebria ... **8.** feminine
muliebriety ... **9.** womanhood
 10. femininity **11.** womanliness
mulier ... **4.** wife **5.** woman **6.** mother
mulish ... **6.** hybrid, sullen **7.** asinine,
 sterile **8.** stubborn **9.** obstinate
mull ... **3.** cow **4.** crag, dust, heat,
 mess, mold **5.** crush, grind, snout,
 spice **6.** fumble, muddle, muslin,
 muzzle, ponder **7.** failure, rubbish,
 squeeze, steatin, sweeten **8.** cogitate,
 consider, ointment, ruminate, snuffbox
 9. pulverize **10.** promontory
 11. contemplate
mullah ... **6.** priest **7.** teacher (Moham)
mullet ... **4.** bobo, fish, star **6.** puffin
mullet hawk ... **6.** osprey
mulligan ... **4.** stew
mulligatawny ... **4.** soup
mulligrubs ... **5.** blues, colic, sulks
mullock ... **5.** spoil, waste **6.** refuse
 (mine) **7.** rubbish
mulloway ... **7.** jewfish
multi (comb form) ... **4.** many
multifarious ... **8.** manifold
 9. multifold, multiplex **10.** multiphase
multifold ... **7.** diverse **8.** manifold,
 multiple, numerous
multilingual ... **8.** polyglot
multiped ... **10.** many–footed
multiplier ... **6.** bulbil **7.** facient
 8. operator
multiply ... **5.** breed **6.** spread
 7. amplify, magnify **8.** increase
 9. calculate, pluralize, procreate
multitude ... **3.** mob **4.** host, many,
 mass, much **5.** crowd, horde, shoal,
 swarm **6.** legion, throng **7.** myriads
 8. populace **9.** profusion
 11. bourgeoisie **12.** numerousness
multitudinous ... **6.** myriad
mum ... **3.** ale **4.** mute **6.** silent

8. taciturn 11. not speaking
mumble... 4. chew, mump 6. chavel,
fumble, mutter, patter
mumbo jumbo... 6. genius
7. bugaboo 12. superstition
13. awesome person
mummer... 5. actor 6. guiser
7. buffoon 9. performer
mummy... 5. brown, Congo (color),
relic 6. corpse, mother 7. cadaver,
carcass
mummy apple... 6. papaya
mump... 3. beg 5. cheat, sulks
6. mumble, sponge 7. deceive,
grimace 10. impose upon
mumpish... 4. dull, glum 5. sulky
6. sullen
mumruffin... 8. titmouse
mundane... 6. cosmic 7. earthly,
horizon, secular, terrene, worldly
8. temporal 11. unspiritual
mundatory... 9. cleansing
11. purificator
mundil... 6. turban (embroidered)
mungo... 4. herb, wool (reclaimed)
8. mongoose, mung bean
13. mongoose plant
municipal... 5. civic, urban 7. oppidan
9. political 10. municipium
munificence... 6. bounty 7. largess
(largesse) 10. generosity, liberality
13. bounteousness, unselfishness
muniment... 6. record 7. defense
8. evidence, writings 9. valuables
10. furnishing 13. fortification
munity... see _immunity_ 9. privilege
munshi (Hind)... 6. writer 7. teacher
9. secretary 11. interpreter
muntjac, muntjak... 5. kakar, ratwa
6. kidang
mura (Jap)... 7. village 9. community
Mura... 6. Indian
mural... 4. wall (pert to) 5. crown
8. painting
murder... 4. kill, slay 7. carnage
8. homicide 9. slaughter
11. assassinate 12. manslaughter
murder of...
brother.. 10. fratricide
father.. 9. patricide
king.. 8. regicide
mother.. 9. matricide
own child.. 9. prolicide
parent.. 9. parricide
prophet.. 8. vaticide
sister.. 10. sororicide
spouse (by the other).. 10. mariticide
wife.. 9. uxoricide
woman.. 8. femicide
murderous... 4. gory 5. cruel
6. bloody, deadly, savage 7. killing
10. sanguinary 12. bloodthirsty
mure... 4. meek, soft, wall 6. gentle,
immure, modest 8. imprison
murk, mirk... 3. fog 4. dark, mist
5. gloom 6. opaque 7. blacken
8. darkness 9. dark color
11. dark-colored
murky, mirky... 4. dark 5. dense,
foggy, thick 6. gloomy, opaque
7. obscure, stained 11. dark-colored
12. impenetrable

murmur... 3. coo, hum 4. blow, curr,
fret, purl 6. babble, mutter, repine
7. trickle, whisper 8. complain
muscle... 4. beef, thew 5. brawn,
sinew, teres 6. flexor, lacert, tensor
8. lacertus, retentor
muscle (pert to)...
affection.. 5. crick 6. ataxia
bending.. 6. flexor
chemistry.. 6. inosic 8. inosinic
column.. 10. sarcostyle
contracting.. 7. agonist
expander.. 7. dilator
extending.. 8. extensor
eyeball.. 6. rectus
lifting.. 7. levator
loin, tenderloin.. 5. psoas
lower.. 9. depressor
raising.. 7. deltoid, erector, levator
recording.. 8. ergogram 9. ergograph
round.. 5. teres
segment.. 8. myocomma
sense.. 11. kinesthesia
separating.. 11. divaricator
spasm.. 6. tonus
stretching.. 6. tensor
sugar.. 8. inositol
trapezius.. 10. cucullaris
triangular.. 7. deltoid
turning.. 7. evertor, rotator
two-headed.. 6. biceps
muscovite... 4. mica 11. yellow-green
Muscovite... 7. Russian
muscular... 4. wiry 5. beefy, thewy
6. brawny, mighty, sinewy, strong,
torose 8. athletic, stalwart, vigorous
muscular (pert to)...
contraction (involuntary).. 3. tic
5. spasm
co-ordination.. 7. synergy
in-co-ordination.. 6. ataxia
15. locomotor ataxia
non-co-ordination in walking..
6. abasia
spasm.. 5. tonus
stomach.. 7. gizzard
muse... 4. mull, poet, rune 5. dream
6. ponder 7. bagpipe, reverie
8. cogitate, consider, meditate,
ruminate
Muse of...
astronomy.. 6. Urania
choral song.. 11. Terpsichore
comedy.. 6. Thalia
dancing.. 11. Terpsichore
eloquence.. 8. Calliope
history.. 4. Clio
joy.. 4. Tara
music.. 7. Euterpe
poetry.. 5. Erato (lyric) 6. Thalia
(bucolic) 8. Calliope (heroic)
tragedy.. 9. Melpomene
Muses... 4. Clio 5. Erato 6. Thalia,
Urania 7. Euterpe 8. Calliope,
Polymnia (Polyhymnia) 9. Melpomene
11. Terpsichore
Muses (pert to)...
epithet.. 7. Pierian
fountain.. 8. Aganippe (near Thebes)
mother of.. 9. Mnemosyne
mountain.. 6. Pierus 7. Helicon
9. Parnassus

number.. 4. nine
sacred place.. 5. Aonia (Boeotia)
spring.. 7. Pierian
The Muses (Gr).. 8. Pierides
musette... 3. air, bag 4. oboe
  7. bagpipe, gavotte
museum... 6. Louvre 7. gallery
  8. Ptolemy I 10. Pinakothek
  11. glyptotheca, pinakotheke
  14. Madame Tussaud's
museum keeper... 7. curator
  9. custodian
mush... 3. cut 4. call, face, pulp
  5. atole, march (over snow), notch
  6. cereal, indent, sepawn 8. flattery,
  umbrella 12. hasty pudding
  14. sentimentality
mushroom... 5. morel, plant 6. agaric,
  anchor, fungus 7. parvenu, upstart
  8. umbrella 11. beaver brown
mushroom (pert to)...
  disease.. 5. flock
  edible.. 5. morel 11. chanterelle
  poisoning.. 8. mycetism
  poisonous.. 7. amanita 9. toadstool
  stem.. 5. stipe
  umbrella top.. 6. pileus
music (pert to)...
  abridgment.. 7. ridotto
  accompaniment.. 9. obbligato
  aftersong.. 5. epode
  all voices.. 5. tutti
  as written.. 3. sta
  chapel.. 9. a cappella
  character.. 3. bar, key 4. clef, rest,
  slur 5. cleft, neume, segno
  chord.. 8. arpeggio
  clear–cut.. 8. staccato
  closing measure.. 4. coda
  comic.. 6. bouffe
  do.. 2. ut
  drama.. 5. opera
  duet.. 3. duo
  encore.. 3. bis
  flourish.. 7. cadenza
  half note.. 5. minim
  half tone.. 8. semitone
  impassioned, emotional..
  12. appassionato
  interlude.. 6. verset
  interval.. 6. octave 7. tritone
  introduction.. 7. prelude
  it proceeds.. 2. va
  knowledge.. 10. musicology
  lead cue.. 5. presa
  left–handed.. 8. sinistra
  light notes.. 8. ottava
  low pitch.. 5. grave
  lutelike.. 10. hurdy–gurdy
  major.. 3. dur
  major third.. 6. ditone
  melodious.. 6. arioso
  melody.. 5. melos
  nine–piece composition.. 5. nonet
  one performer (choral).. 4. soli
  opera (comic).. 6. bouffe
  organization.. 4. band 5. Ascap, choir
  6. chorus 8. symphony 9. orchestra
  organ stop.. 6. dulcet, tromba
  7. celesta
  performance.. 7. recital
  phrase.. 9. leitmotiv (leitmotif)

pick.. 8. plectrum
pitch C.. 2. du
pompous.. 7. orotund
refrain.. 5. epode 8. repetend
repetition.. 5. rondo
scale.. 5. gamut
sestet.. 7. sestuor
sextuplet.. 7. sestole (sestolet)
soprano part.. 5. canto
speaking part.. 8. parlando
study.. 5. étude
tenor part.. 5. canto (original)
theme.. 4. tema
third.. 6. tierce
three–chord note.. 5. triad
thrice.. 3. ter
time.. 4. temp 6. giusto
timing device.. 9. metronome
twice.. 3. bis
variations, set of.. 7. partita
whimsical.. 8. bizzarro 9. capriccio
musical direction (pert to)...
  accented.. 8. sforzato 9. sforzando
  bold.. 6. audace
  brisk.. 5. tanto 7. animato
  detached.. 8. spiccato, staccato
  dying away.. 7. calendo
  emphatic.. 7. marcato
  evenly.. 10. egualmente
  fantastic.. 11. carpiccioso
  fast.. 4. vivo 5. tosto 6. presto,
  vivace 10. tostamente
  faster.. 7. stretto
  fluctuating.. 6. rubato
  gay.. 7. giocoso 10. brilliante
  gentle.. 5. dolce
  half.. 5. mezzo
  held firmly.. 6. tenuto
  high.. 3. alt
  hurried.. 7. agitato
  less.. 4. meno
  let it stand.. 3. sta
  lightly.. 10. con agilita
  little by little.. 9. poco a poco
  lively.. 6. vivace 7. allegro, animato
  loud.. 5. forte 10. fortissimo
  louder.. 9. crescendo
  lutelike.. 10. hurdy–gurdy
  more rapid.. 7. stretto (stretta)
  movement (with).. 7. con moto
  muted.. 5. sorda, sordo
  narrating.. 8. narrante
  one by one.. 7. uno a uno
  quick.. 6. presto
  quickening.. 11. affrettando
  quicker than.. 7. andante 9. andantino
  repeat.. 3. bis 6. da capo 7. ripresa
  sadly.. 7. dolente 8. doloroso
  shake.. 5. trill
  silent.. 5. tacet
  sliding.. 9. glissando
  slow.. 5. largo, lento, molto, tardo
  6. adagio 7. andante
  slow (very).. 5. molto
  slowing.. 9. allentato 10. ritardando
  11. rallentando
  smooth.. 6. legato
  soft.. 5. dolce, piano
  softer.. 10. diminuendo
  spirited.. 7. con moto
  strict tempo.. 6. giusto
  sustained.. 6. tenuto 9. sustenuto

tenderly . . **10.** affettuoso, con affetto
turn . . **5.** verte **9.** gruppetto
vivacious . . **7.** con brio
musical form . . . **3.** jig, ode **4.** aria,
jazz, jive, olio, opus, punk (rock), scat,
song, soul **5.** derry, dirge, disco,
elegy, fugue, melos, motet, opera,
salsa **6.** arioso, ballad, medley,
melody, minuet, reggae, sonata
7. ragtime, toccata **8.** carillon (bells),
hornpipe, operetta, oratorio, serenade,
symphony **9.** barcarole, bluegrass,
interlude, polonaise **11.** rock and roll
12. boogie woogie
musical instruments . . . **3.** sax
4. asor, drum, fife, harp, horn, lute,
lyre, oboe, pipe, reed, tuba, viol
5. banjo, bugle, cello, Dobro, flute,
organ, piano, rebec (rebeck), rocta,
tabor, viola **6.** atabal, cither, citole,
cornet, fiddle, guitar, spinet, tabret,
violin, zither **7.** althorn, bagpipe,
bandore, bassoon, celesta, clarion,
clavier, gittern, helicon, marimba,
musette, ocarina, pandora, theorbo,
trumpet, ukulele **8.** castanet, clarinet,
dulcimer, keyboard, mandolin,
trombone **9.** flageolet, saxophone
10. concertina, sousaphone (tuba),
tambourine **11.** harpsichord,
synthesizer, violoncello
musical instruments (foreign) . . .
Africa . . **5.** nanga **7.** kalimba (thumb
piano), sistrum
China . . **3.** kin
E Indies . . **4.** bina
Egypt . . **7.** sistrum
Greece . . **7.** cithara (anc)
Hindu . . **4.** vina (anc)
India . . **5.** ruana
Italy . . **6.** tromba
Japan . . **7.** samisen (shamisen)
10. shakuhachi
Java . . **8.** gamelang (gamelan)
Mexico . . **6.** clarin **7.** maracas
Spain . . **6.** atabal **9.** castanets
musician . . . **4.** bard **5.** piper
6. hepcat, lyrist, singer **7.** chorist,
crooner, drummer, fiddler, flutist,
pianist, yodeler **8.** bandsman,
composer, minstrel, organist
9. conductor, serenader, troubador,
violinist **10.** prima donna, trombonist
11. clarinetist, keyboardist,
minnesinger, saxophonist
12. interlocutor **13.** Kapellmeister
musicians' group . . . **4.** band, duet, trio
5. nonet **6.** septet, sextet **7.** nonetto,
quartet **8.** ensemble, septette,
sextette, symphony **9.** orchestra,
quartette
musicians' patron saint . . . **7.** Cecilia
musk . . . **4.** deer **7.** perfume
musk (pert to) . . .
beaver . . **7.** muskrat
cat . . **5.** civet
cattle . . **4.** oxen
cucumber . . **11.** cassabanana
deer . . **10.** chevrotain
duck . . **7.** Muscovy
hog . . **7.** peccary
melon . . **10.** cantaloupe

okra . . **8.** abelmosk
shrew . . **6.** desman
weasel . . **5.** civet
muskellunge . . . **4.** fish, pike
musket . . . **4.** hawk **5.** rifle **7.** firearm
9. flintlock
Musketeers, Three . . . **5.** Athos
6. Aramis **7.** Porthos **9.** D'Artagnon
muskmelon . . . **6.** atimon, casaba
10. cantaloupe
muskrat . . . **5.** shrew **6.** desman
7. ondatra
Muslim . . . see *Moslem*
muslin . . . **3.** ban, cap **4.** mull **5.** doria,
shela **6.** canvas, gurrah **7.** organdy
8. nainsook, sheeting, tarlatan
muss . . . **4.** mess, soil **5.** chaos, dirty
6. bitter, muddle, rumple, tousle
7. confuse, wrinkle **8.** dishevel,
scramble, squabble **10.** disarrange
mussel . . . **4.** food, naid, unio **5.** horse,
moule, naiad **6.** byssus, mucket, nerita
7. mollusk, Mytilus
Musselman . . . **6.** Moslem **7.** Saracen
10. Mohammedan
must . . . **4.** mold, musk, sapa, stum
5. juice, ought, shall **6.** blight,
mildew, refuse **7.** malodor
9. necessity **10.** obligation
mustang . . . **5.** horse, pinto **6.** bronco,
sphinx
mustard . . . **5.** nigra, senvy **7.** sinapis
8. charlock
mustard (pert to) . . .
chemistry . . **8.** sinapine
gas . . **7.** yperite
genus . . **7.** Sinapis **8.** Brassica
plaster . . **8.** sinapism
Mustelidae . . . **5.** minks **7.** badgers,
martens, weasels
muster . . . **4.** levy **5.** erect **6.** gather,
summon **7.** collect, marshal
8. assemble, comprise
10. assemblage
muster out . . . **7.** disband
musty . . . **3.** bad, old **4.** damp, hoar,
rank **5.** fetid, fusty, moist, moldy,
rafty, stale, trite **6.** rancid **7.** pungent
mutable . . . **6.** fickle **7.** erratic
8. variable **9.** alterable, changeful
mute . . . **3.** mum **4.** dumb, lene, surd
6. muffle, silent **8.** deadener, silencer,
taciturn **9.** voiceless **10.** speechless
mutilate . . . **3.** mar **4.** geld, hack, maim
6. deface, deform, garble, injure,
mangle **7.** cripple, destroy **8.** castrate
9. dismember, tear apart
mutinous . . . **6.** unruly **9.** seditious,
turbulent **10.** rebellious, refractory
11. intractable
mutiny . . . **6.** Putsch (Swiss), revolt,
strife, tumult **9.** commotion, rebellion
12. insurrection **15.** insubordination
mutter . . . **5.** growl **6.** murmur, patter,
plaint **7.** grumble, maunder
8. complain **9.** mussitate
mutton . . . **4.** meat **5.** cabob (kabob),
gigot, sheep **6.** candle
muttonfish . . . **4.** sama **5.** pargo
7. abalone, eelpout, mojarra, snapper
mutual . . . **4.** plan **5.** joint **6.** common

8. intimate 9. symbiotic
10. reciprocal, responsive
15. interchangeable
mutual understanding... 9. agreement, unanimity 12. consentience, co–ordination 13. interrelation
17. interrelationship
mux... 4. mess 5. batch
muy... 4. very 7. greatly
muzhik, muzjik... 7. peasant
muzzle... 3. gag 4. cope, maul, nose
5. mouth, snout 6. clevis, thrash
7. shackle, sheathe, silence
8. restrain 10. respirator
my... 3. mes, mon 4. mine 7. due to me 11. exclamation
myall... 4. wild, wood (fragrant)
6. acacia 11. uncivilized
mycoderma... 5. fungi 6. mother (formed on wine) 8. membrane (ferment)
mycophagy... 11. eating fungi
15. eating mushrooms
myna, mynah... 4. bird 7. grackle
8. starling
Mynheer... 8. Dutchman
myo (comb form)... 6. muscle
myomancy, divination by...
14. muscle movement
myopic... 11. nearsighted
myriad... 11. innumerable, ten thousand 13. multitudinous
myriapod... 9. centipede
myrmicid... 3. ant
myrtle... 8. ramarama 10. periwinkle
11. candleberry
mysterious... 4. dark 6. arcane, mystic, occult, secret 7. cryptic
8. abstruse, esoteric 9. recondite, sphinxian 10. cabalistic
12. inexplicable, unfathomable
mystery... 4. cult, rune 6. arcane, cabala, enigma, puzzle, secret
7. arcanum, esotery, miracle
8. whodunit 9. sacrament
13. inexplainable
19. incomprehensibility
mystic... 4. seer, yogi 5. magic, runic
6. occult, orphic, secret 7. cryptic,

Mahatma 8. cabalist, esoteric, symbolic 9. enigmatic, recondite
10. cabalistic, mysterious
mystic (pert to)...
cry.. 4. evoe
doctrine.. 5. cabal 7. esotery
8. esoteric
initiate.. 5. epopt (Gr Antiq)
ocean isle.. 6. Avalon
theosophy.. 6. cabala
word.. 2. om 7. abraxas
11. abracadabra
mystical... 6. muddle, puzzle
7. confuse, cryptic, furtive, obscure
9. enigmatic, obfuscate
mystical (pert to)...
character (Teut Myth).. 8. Eckehart
meaning.. 7. anagoge
word.. 11. abracadabra
mystify... 5. befog 6. muddle, puzzle
7. becloud, confuse, perplex
8. befuddle, bewilder 9. bamboozle, obfuscate
myth... 4. tale 5. fable, fancy, story
6. legend 7. figment, parable
9. apocrypha, falsehood
mythical... 7. fancied 8. fabulous
9. fictional, imaginary, legendary
10. fictitious 12. mythological
mythical (pert to)...
being.. 6. Garuda, Icarus 7. centaur, griffin
bird.. 3. roc
deity.. 6. Moloch (tyrant)
demon.. 4. Rahu (tail called Kehu)
hero.. 4. Ajax 8. Achilles
heroine.. 4. Leda 6. Europa
8. Atalanta
hunter.. 5. Orion
island.. 8. Atlantis
king (Hind).. 4. Nala
monster.. 4. ogre 7. chimera
mother.. 5. Niobe
river.. 4. Styx
serpent.. 5. Apepi
winged creature.. 7. Alborak
woman.. 6. Gorgon, Medusa, Stheno
7. Euryale
mythogony, science of... 5. myths
mythologist... 9. mythmaker

N

N... 2. en, Nu 8. nitrogen (symbol)
nab... 4. grab 5. catch, seize
6. arrest, nibble, snatch 7. capture
9. apprehend
Nabal's wife (Bib)... 7. Abigail
nabob... 5. nawab 6. bigwig, tycoon
7. viceroy 8. governor 9. plutocrat
10. viceregent
nacelle... 4. boat 7. shelter
nacket... 3. boy 4. cake 5. lunch

6. caddie 8. saucy boy
nacre... 9. shellfish 10. conchiolin
13. mother–of–pearl
Nadab (Bib)... 12. King of Israel
nadir... 4. pole 11. lowest point (opp zenith)
nag... 4. pony, twit 5. annoy, cobra, horse, scold, snake, tease 6. heckle, hector, peck on, pester, plague
7. henpeck 8. harangue

nagor... 8. antelope, reedbuck
nahoor... 5. sheep 6. bharal
naiad... 5. nymph 6. mussel, Nereid
7. limniad, Oceanid
nail... 3. cut, hob 4. brad, claw, spad,
stud, tack, wire 5. clout, spike,
sprig, talon 6. fasten, secure, unguis,
ungula 7. capture, measure
8. sparable 9. finishing, intercept
12. upholstering
nail (pert to)...
headless.. 5. sprig
ingrowing.. 7. acronyx
marking, fingernail.. 6. lunule
size.. 8. tenpenny
slanted.. 4. toed
naissance... 5. birth 6. origin
naive... 5. frank 6. simple 7. artless,
ingenue 8. childish, gullible, untaught
9. guileless, ingenuous, unworldly
10. simplicity 13. unphilosophic
15. unsophisticated
naked... 4. bald, bare, mere, nude,
open 5. clear, plain 6. barren,
meager 7. exposed, literal, obvious
8. manifest, stripped 9. unadorned,
uncovered 11. defenseless,
unprotected, unsupported
nakoo... 6. gavial 9. crocodile
namaycush... 5. togue, trout
namby–pamby... 5. inane, silly, vapid
7. insipid 10. wishy–washy
11. sentimental
name... 3. dub, nom 4. call, cite,
term 5. clepe, nomen, style, title
6. y–clepe 7. appoint, entitle,
mention 8. cognomen, identify
9. celebrity, enumerate, personage
10. denominate, reputation
11. appellation, designation
12. denomination
name (pert to)...
added.. 7. agnomen
assumed.. 3. pen 5. alias 7. John
Doe 9. incognito, pseudonym,
sobriquet 10. nom de plume
bad.. 7. caconym
binomial.. 8. teutonym
by location.. 7. toponym
derivation.. 7. eponymy
family (father's).. 7. eponymy
9. patronymy
fictitious.. 9. pseudonym
first.. 9. baptismal, Christian,
praenomen
Japanese.. 4. maru
known.. 9. onomatous
nickname.. 7. moniker (monicker)
8. cognomen
nominate.. 8. designate
secret.. 9. cryptonym
spelled backwards (real name)..
6. ananym
surname.. 7. eponymy
technical.. 4. onym
unknown.. 9. anonymous
wrong.. 8. misnomer
name as agent... 6. depute
named... 5. cited 6. called, y–clept
(y–cleped)
named for a god... 10. theophorous

nameless... 7. bastard, obscure 8. not
known 9. aforesaid, anonymous,
unnamable 10. unrenowned
12. illegitimate 13. indescribable,
inexpressible 15. undistinguished
namelessness... 9. anonymity
namely... 5. to wit 9. expressly,
nominally, videlicet (viz)
names, divination by... 8. onomancy
names, science of... 11. onomatology
namesake... 6. eponym 7. homonym
nanga... 4. harp
nanism... 12. dwarfishness (opp of
gigantism)
Nanking...
capital.. 5. China (1932–1937)
color.. 12. Naples yellow
province.. 7. Kiangsu
river site.. 7. Yangtze
nanoid... 8. dwarfish
nanpie... 6. magpie
naos... 5. cella 6. shrine, temple
Naos... 4. star
nap... 3. nod 4. doze, pile, shag, wink
5. fluff, grasp, seize, sleep, steal
6. duffel, siesta, snooze
nape... 5. nucha, nuque, scrag
6. scruff, turnip 7. niddick
9. auchenium
napellus... 9. monkshood
napery... 5. linen (table)
napiform... 12. turnip–shaped
napkin... 5. doily, towel 6. diaper
8. kerchief 9. serviette
11. neckerchief
Naples...
biscuit.. 10. ladyfinger
famed building.. 9. Cathedral (Gothic,
1272)
red.. 5. ochre 6. Indian
site.. 11. Bay of Naples
napoleon... 4. game 6. pastry 7. top
boot 11. reddish–blue, sweet cherry
13. crimson clover
Napoleon I (pert to)...
birthplace.. 7. Ajaccio (Corsica)
brother–in–law.. 5. Murat
death site.. 8. St Helena
exiled to.. 4. Elba
father... 7. Charles
island.. 5. Capri
marshal.. 3. Ney (executed)
title.. 7. Emperor (of France)
warfare site.. 5. Ligny, Malta
7. Marengo 8. Waterloo
10. Alexandria
napped (short)... 3. ras
nappy... 3. ale 4. dish 5. downy,
heady, wooly 6. liquor, shaggy,
sleepy 7. foaming 10. inebriated
napu... 10. chevrotain
Naraka (Hind)... 4. hell
Narcissus (Gr)... 6. egoist 14. beautiful
youth
narcosis... 5. sleep 10. drowsiness
narcotic... 4. dope, drug, hemp, junk
5. bhang (bang), ether, opium
6. heroin 7. anodyne, cocaine,
hashish 8. hypnotic, mandrake,
morphine 9. soporific 10. belladonna,
hyoscyamus, stramonium
narcotic (pert to)...

dose.. 3. fix 5. locus
package.. 6. bindle
seller.. 6. pusher 7. peddler
user (group).. 6. love–in 9. snow
party
nard... 6. anoint 8. matgrass,
ointment, rhizomes
nardoo, nardu... 6. clover
nares... 8. nostrils
narghile, nargile, nargileh... 4. pipe
6. hookah
nargil... 7. coconut
nark... 3. spy 5. annoy 8. informer
11. stool pigeon
Narragansett... 3. Bay 5. horse
6. Indian, turkey
narrate... 4. tell 6. detail, recite, relate
7. recount 8. describe
narration... 4. tale 5. drama (acted),
story 6. detail 7. account, recital
8. relation 9. discourse, narrative,
rehearsal
narrative... 4. epic, epos, myth, poem,
saga, tale 5. conte, drama, fable,
story 6. legend 7. account, episode,
history, parable 8. allegory, anecdote
9. narration, statement
narrator... 9. raconteur 11. storyteller
narrow... 4. mean, poor 5. inlet,
scant, taper 6. linear, strait
7. closely, slender 8. strictly
9. confining, illiberal, niggardly
10. restricted, straighten
11. reactionary 12. parsimonious
13. circumscribed
narrow (pert to)...
comb form.. 4. sten 5. steno
leather strip.. 5. thong
minded.. 5. petty 6. biased
7. bigoted 10. intolerant, prejudiced
opening.. 4. rima, slot 9. stenopaic
souled.. 10. ungenerous
narrowly incised... 9. laciniate
narrows... 5. sound 6. strait
narthex... 7. portico 9. asafetida
(asafoetida)
narwhal, narwal... 5. whale
8. cetacean
nasab (Moham Law)... 7. kinship
13. consanguinity
nasal... 4. nose 5. sound 6. narine,
rhinal, twangy 11. inspiratory
nascency... 5. birth 6. origin
7. genesis 9. beginning
naseberry... 9. sapodilla
Nasi... 6. prince 8. Gamaliel
9. patriarch
Nasicornia... 10. rhinoceros
nasology... 9. nose study
Nassau...
capital.. 7. Bahamas
hamlet.. 7. grouper
sports.. 4. golf
nastika... 7. atheist
nasty... 4. foul, mean 5. dirty 6. filthy,
odious 7. obscene 8. indecent,
unsavory 9. offensive
12. disagreeable, dishonorable
Nasua... 5. coati 6. coatis
nasute... 10. large–nosed
nasutiform... 8. noselike
natal... 6. inborn, native 7. gluteal,

nascent 9. from birth
Natal... 7. seaport (Braz) 8. Province
(S Afr)
natator... 7. swimmer
natatorium... 4. pool 6. plunge
12. swimming hole
natchbone... 9. aitchbone
Natchez... 4. city (La) 6. Indian
nation... 4. host, race 5. caste, class,
state 6. people, polity 7. country
9. community, multitude
national... 4. blue 6. racial 7. citizen,
federal
nationality... 4. race 6. nation
8. nativity 9. statehood
11. nationalism
national salute... 13. Twenty–one
guns
native... 3. ite, son 5. natal 6. innate,
normal, simple 7. genuine, natural,
primary 8. inherent, original, primeval
9. unbranded 10. aboriginal,
indigenous, unaffected 11. not
acquired
native (pert to)...
agent.. 9. comprador (compradore)
bear.. 5. koala
cat.. 7. dasyure
dog.. 5. dingo
Indian.. 4. Arab
juniper.. 9. blueberry
Madagascan.. 4. Hova
naturalized person.. 7. denizen
plant, animal.. 8. indigene
salt.. 6. halite
nativity... 5. birth 9. beginning,
horoscope, sculpture
Nativity, The... 8. festival
9. Christmas 13. birth of Christ
natterjack... 4. toad
natty... 4. chic, neat, tidy, trim
6. spruce 10. fastidious
Natty Bumppo's alias... 7. Hawkeye
15. Leatherstocking
natural... 3. raw 4. born 5. flesh,
usual 6. common, cretin, expert,
inborn, inbred, innate, normal
7. genuine, regular, typical
8. informal, inherent, lifelike, ordinary
9. character (Mus), dice throw,
unassumed, unfeigned 10. unaffected
natural (pert to)...
capacity.. 9. endowment
condition.. 4. norm
group.. 4. race 6. ethnic, family
location, position.. 4. site 5. situs
not (natural).. 5. alien 8. acquired
10. artificial
philosophy.. 7. physics
science.. 10. physiology
voice (Mus).. 7. dipetto
naturalist... 4. Muir (John) 7. animist,
Burbank (Luther) 9. biologist, scientist
11. taxidermist
naturalize... 5. adapt 8. accustom
9. acclimate 11. domesticate,
familiarize
nature... 4. kind, self, sort, soul, type
6. cosmos 7. essence 8. tendency,
universe 11. naturalness,
temperament 14. characteristic
nature (pert to)...

concealed.. 7. latency
divinity of.. 5. dryad, naiad, nymph
god.. 3. Pan
goddess.. 6. Cybele 7. Artemis
in the raw.. 6. nudity
of the case.. 9. ipso facto
worship.. 11. physiolatry
natus... 4. born
nausea... 4. pall 5. qualm 8. loathing,
    mal de mer 10. queasiness
    11. seasickness
nauseous... 7. fulsome, mawkish
    9. loathsome, offensive, sickening,
    squeamish 10. disgusting
nautical... 5. naval 6. marine
    7. oceanic 8. maritime
nautical (pert to)...
    almanac.. 9. ephemeris
    direction.. 5. avast, belay
    hail.. 4. ahoy
    instrument.. 3. aba 7. compass,
    pelorus, sextant
    measure.. 3. ton 4. knot 6. fathom
    7. sea mile
nautilus... 7. mollusk 8. argonaut
    9. submarine 10. diving bell
Navaho, Navajo... 5. hogan 6. Indian
    7. blanket 9. red–yellow
naval... 6. marine 8. nautical
naval (pert to)...
    brigade.. 7. militia
    commander.. 7. navarch
    depot.. 4. base
    device.. 6. dolter
    officer.. 5. bosun 6. ensign, yeoman
    7. admiral, captain 9. boatswain
    (bosun), commander 10. lieutenant
nave... 3. hob, hub, nef 4. apse, fist
    5. nieve 7. apsidal
navel... 6. middle, orange 8. omphalos
    9. umbilicus 10. depression
navigate... 4. keel, sail 7. avigate
    11. ship science
navigator... 5. navvy 12. third
    command (or 4th)
navy (fleet)... 7. tankers 8. cruisers,
    flattops, gunboats 10. destroyers,
    submarines 11. battleships 12. mine
    sweepers 13. hospital ships
    16. aircraft carriers
navy (pert to)...
    bean.. 6. kidney
    coffee.. 3. mud
    color.. 4. blue 10. marine blue
    drinking fountain.. 11. scuttlebutt
    fleet.. 6. armada 13. combat vessels
    plug.. 7. tobacco
    ships, collectively.. 5. fleet 6. armada
    song.. 13. Anchors Aweigh
    training camp.. 8. boot camp
    underwear.. 8. skivvies
nawab, nabob... 5. ruler, title
    7. viceroy
nay... 2. no 4. deny 5. flute, never
    6. denial, naysay, refuse 7. refusal
    8. negative 11. prohibition
nayaur... 5. sheep
nayword... 6. byword 7. proverb (of
    reproach) 9. watchword
Nazarene (pert to)...
    artist.. 8. Overbeck (of Rome)
    disciple.. 9. Christian

native.. 11. Jesus Christ
native of.. 8. Nazareth
Nazi... 9. Hitlerite
Nazi emblem... 6. fylfot 8. swastika
nchega... 6. monkey 10. chimpanzee
neanic... 8. immature, youthful
neap... 4. tide 6. tongue (vehicle)
    7. low tide 8. low water
Neapolitan (pert to)...
    dance.. 10. tarantella
    fever.. 8. undulent
    Italian.. 6. Naples
    medlar.. 5. fruit 7. azarole
    music.. 5. chord (6th)
    ointment.. 9. mercurial
    yellow.. 6. Naples
near... 2. at 4. nigh 5. about, close,
    handy 6. around, within 7. closely,
    related 8. adjacent, approach,
    imminent, intimate 11. approximate
    13. propinquitous
nearby, near–by... 3. gin 4. nigh
    5. anent, handy 6. beside, nearly
    7. close by, close to, vicinal
    8. adjacent 9. adjoining
    10. convenient
Nearctic... 9. Greenland, Holarctic
    11. Palaearctic 13. Arctic America
Near East... 7. Balkans 12. Balkan
    States
Near East valley... 4. wadi (wady)
    5. oasis 6. ravine
nearest... 4. next 7. closest
    9. proximate
nearly... 5. about 6. almost 7. closely
    8. narrowly 10. similarity
    13. approximately
nearness... 8. affinity, intimacy,
    likeness, relation 9. closeness
    11. propinquity
near of kin... 7. germane
nearsighted... 6. myopic 8. purblind
    12. narrow–minded, shortsighted,
    undiscerning
neat... 3. pat 4. prim, smug, snod,
    tidy, trig, trim 5. natty 6. adroit,
    dapper, spruce 7. orderly, perjink,
    precise 9. shipshape 10. meticulous,
    perjinkety 12. spick–and–span
neatherd... 7. cowherd 8. herdsman
neathmost... 6. lowest
neb... 3. tip 4. beak, bill, face, kiss,
    nose 5. point, snout
Nebo, Nebu... 8. mountain (Bib)
    11. god of wisdom
Nebraska...
    capital.. 7. Lincoln
    city.. 5. Omaha 8. Hastings
    11. Scottsbluff
    Indian.. 4. Otoe 5. Omaha 6. Pawnee
    meaning.. 11. water valley
    railroad (1865).. 12. Union Pacific
    river.. 6. Nemaha, Platte 8. Missouri
    State admission.. 13. Thirty–seventh
    State motto.. 20. Equality Before the
    Law
    State nickname.. 4. Beef
    10. Cornhusker
nebula... 3. sky 4. mist 5. cloud,
    vapor 10. atmosphere
Nebula of... 4. Lyra 5. Orion
    9. Andromeda

nebulous... 4. hazy 5. misty, vague
  6. cloudy 7. clouded, nebular
  8. nebulose
nebulous envelope... 4. coma
  9. chevelure
necessarily... 8. perforce
  11. unavoidably 12. consequently
  13. indispensably
necessary... 5. vital 7. needful
  9. essential, mandatory, requisite
  11. requirement, unavoidable
  13. indispensable
necessitate... 5. force, impel
  6. compel, entail, oblige 7. require
  9. constrain
necessity... 4. food, need, want
  5. drink 7. aliment, poverty, urgency
  9. neediness 10. constraint
  14. inevitableness
neck... 4. hals (halse) 5. crane, scrag,
  swire 6. cervix, fondle, strag
  7. channel, embrace, isthmus
neck (pert to)...
  armor.. 6. gorget 8. gorgerin
  artery.. 7. carotid
  back of.. 4. nape 5. nucha, nuque
  6. scruff
  frill.. 5. jabot, ruche 6. wimple
  land.. 6. strake 9. peninsula
  muscle.. 8. scalenus
  pendant.. 6. locket 9. lavaliere
  piece.. 3. boa 5. amice, rabat, scarf,
  stole 6. collar
  water.. 6. strait
  zoology.. 4. gula 6. wattle 7. withers
neckcloth... 6. cravat 7. muffler
  9. barcelona 11. neckerchief
neckerchief... 7. belcher 8. kerchief
  12. handkerchief
necklace... 5. beads 6. torque
  7. baldric, chaplet, rivière
  11. shark's-teeth
neckpiece... 3. boa 5. ascot, rabat,
  scarf, stole 6. collar 8. kerchief
necktie... 3. tie 4. band 5. ascot,
  scarf 6. cravat 10. four-in-hand
necrology... 9. death roll 13. death
  register 14. obituary notice
necromancy... 5. goety, magic
  7. sorcery 9. sortilege
  11. conjuration, enchantment
necropolis... 8. cemetery
necropsy... 7. autopsy
  10. post-mortem
nectar... 3. red 5. drink, honey
  8. beverage
nectar of the gods... 8. ambrosia
neddy... 6. donkey 13. life preserver
need... 4. lack, poor, thar, want
  7. poverty, require, urgency
  8. exigency 9. extremity, necessity
  10. compulsion, deficiency
  11. requirement
needle... 3. sew 4. acus, goad, sail
  5. tease, thorn 6. bodkin, pierce
  7. darning, obelisk 9. astatizer
  10. upholstery
needle (pert to)...
  bath.. 3. jet 9. sprinkler
  bird.. 9. phalarope 10. needlebill
  bug.. 4. Nepa 7. Ranatra
  case.. 4. etui (etwee)

fish.. 3. gar 8. pipefish
gun.. 11. Dreyse rifle
kind.. 5. blunt, sharp 7. between,
  crochet, darning 8. knitting
long-eyed.. 10. embroidery
medical.. 10. hypodermic
needlelike body.. 7. spicule
needlework.. 7. crochet, sampler
  8. knitting 10. embroidery
record.. 10. phonograph
shaped.. 6. acuate 7. acerose
  8. acicular
under the skin.. 5. seton
needy... 4. poor 7. almoner
  8. indigent 9. necessary, penniless,
  requisite 10. distressed
neel-bhunder... 8. wanderoo 10. blue
  monkey
neep... 6. turnip
ne'er-do-well... 5. idler 6. wretch
  8. poltroon 9. schlemiel
  14. good-for-nothing
nef... 4. nave 5. clock (ship-shaped)
nefarious... 6. wicked 7. heinous,
  impious 8. horrible, infamous, terrible
  9. atrocious 10. detestable,
  iniquitous, villainous
nefas... 6. sinful
negate... 4. deny 6. refuse, refute
  7. nullify 8. disprove 10. counteract
negative... 2. ir, ne, no 3. nay, non,
  nor, not 4. deny, film, veto 5. minus
  6. refuse 7. neutral 8. disprove,
  negation 9. privative
  13. contradiction
negative (pert to)...
  electrode, pole.. 7. cathode (kathode)
  eyepiece.. 8. Campani's 9. Huygenian
  ion.. 5. anion
  sign.. 5. minus
neglect... 4. fail, omit, slip, snub
  5. shirk 6. slight 7. failure
  8. omission 9. disregard, negligent,
  pretermit 11. inattention
negligee... 4. gown, robe 6. attire
  8. peignoir
negligence... 7. laxness 9. oversight,
  unconcern 10. remissness
  11. inattention 12. carelessness,
  inadvertence
negligent... 3. lax 4. lash 6. remiss,
  supine 8. careless, heedless
  10. neglectful 11. unconcerned
negotiate... 4. deal, pass 5. treat
  6. manage, treaty 7. bargain,
  mediate 8. transact
Negrito (pert to)...
  African.. 4. Akka 5. Batwa, Pygmy
  7. Bambute, Bushman
  Dutch New Guinea.. 6. Tapiro
  Indonesian.. 3. Ata 4. Aeta (Ita)
  Malay.. 6. Semang
Negro (pert to)...
  dance.. 4. juba
  dish.. 9. jambalaya
  Egyptian.. 6. Nubian
  friend of.. 10. negrophile
  magic (anc).. 6. voodoo
  spiritual.. 8. Swing Low
neigh... 4. akin 6. whinny 7. whicker
neighborhood... 7. purlieu 8. environs,
  vicinity 9. proximity 10. thereabout

neighborhood law... 5. venue
neither masculine nor feminine...
  6. neuter 7. sexless
neither right nor wrong...
  11. adiaphorous, indifferent
Nemesis... 7. avenger, goddess,
  penalty
nemoral... 6. sylvan 14. living in a
  grove
neology... 8. new words 9. neologism
  11. new doctrine 14. new
  expressions
neonatus... 7. new baby, newborn
neophobia *(fear of)*... 6. the new
neophyte... 4. tyro 6. novice
  7. convert 8. beginner 9. proselyte
  10. catechumen
neosology *(study of)*... 10. young birds
neoteric... 3. new 4. late 6. modern,
  recent
nep... 6. catnip
Nepal...
  aborigines.. 10. Mongolians
  capital.. 8. Katmandu
  district.. 7. Mustang
  mountain.. 7. Everest 9. Himalayas
  ruler.. 9. Maharajah
nepesh... 4. soul 10. animal soul
  12. divine breath
nephew... 4. neve 6. nepote
nephrite... 4. jade 7. mineral
  11. kidney stone
nephroid... 8. reniform
  12. kidney-shaped
nephros... 6. kidney
nepote... 6. nephew 8. grandson
nepotism... 9. patronage
  10. favoritism, preference
Neptune... 3. sea 5. ocean 6. sea
  god
Neptune *(pert to)*...
  Astron.. 6. planet (3rd largest)
  Celtic.. 3. Ler
  consort.. 7. Salacia
  emblem.. 7. trident
  Greek.. 8. Poseidon
  Roman.. 6. sea god
  son.. 6. Triton
  wife.. 6. Medusa
Nereid *(Gr)*... 8. sea nymph
Nero *(pert to)*...
  excesses.. 7. cruelty 13. burning of
  Rome (64 AD)
  mother.. 9. Agrippina
  Roman title.. 7. Emperor
  wife.. 6. Sabina 7. Octavia
nerve... 4. pulp 5. cheek, fiber, pluck,
  sinew 6. aplomb, energy, tendon,
  tissue 7. courage, nervure
  8. audacity, coolness, strength
  10. resolution
nerve *(pert to)*...
  action.. 9. neurergic
  cell.. 4. axon 6. neuron
  center.. 8. ganglion
  comb form.. 5. neuro
  fiber.. 5. motor 7. sensory
  8. afferent, efferent
  force.. 7. neurism
  gray matter.. 7. cinerea
  inflammation, medical.. 8. neuritis,

neurosis 9. neurotomy
  10. neurectasy, neurolysis, neuropathy
  11. neurologist 13. tic douloureux
network.. 4. rete 6. plexus
of Wrisberg.. 6. facial
operation.. 10. neurolysis
passage.. 4. rete 5. hilum 8. ganglion
ref to.. 6. neural, neuric 7. neuroid
  8. neurotic
root.. 5. radix
science.. 9. neurology
sheath.. 9. medullary
tissue.. 7. cinerea, neurine
  9. neuroglia
tumor.. 6. glioma 7. neuroma
nerveless... 4. dead 5. inert
  9. foolhardy, powerless
  10. courageous
nervous... 5. tense, timid 6. neural,
  touchy 7. fearful, jittery 8. eloquent,
  neurotic, timorous 9. excitable,
  sensitive 10. high-strung
  12. apprehensive
nervous *(pert to)*...
  affliction.. 3. tic 6. ataxia, chorea
  7. aphasia 8. neurosis
  energy deficiency.. 7. aneuria
  seizure.. 4. amok (amuck)
  system, center.. 5. brain, spine
  system, description.. 11. neurography
  system, name.. 9. neuronymy
  system, science.. 9. neurology
  system, specialist.. 12. neuropathist,
  psychiatrist
  tissue tumor.. 11. neurocytoma
ness... 4. cape 8. headland
  10. promontory
nest... 3. bed, den, nye, web 4. inro
  5. abode, aerie, eyrie, group, haunt,
  nidus 6. cuddle, series (graduated)
  7. lodging, retreat 9. residence
  10. nidificate 13. breeding place
nest *(pert to)*...
  boxes.. 4. inro
  eagle's.. 5. aerie, eyrie (eyry)
  pheasant's.. 4. nide
  spider's.. 3. web
  squirrel's.. 4. dray (drey)
  swallow's.. 9. nidus avis
  to build.. 6. nidify
nestle... 3. pet 4. nest 6. cuddle,
  pettle, settle 7. protect, shelter,
  snuggle
nestling... 4. bird 5. child 9. fledgling,
  youngling
Nestor *(pert to)*...
  famed for.. 6. wisdom
  King of.. 5. Pylos
  known as.. 4. sage 7. adviser 8. The
  Elder 9. Patriarch
net... 3. gin, web 4. mesh, toil, trap,
  weir 5. clear, lacis, score, seine,
  snare, weave 6. profit 7. enclose,
  network, trammel 8. receipts
  9. reticulum
net *(pert to)*...
  fishing.. 4. fyke 5. seine, trawl
  7. trammel
  hair.. 5. snood
  lacemaking.. 5. lacis
  silk.. 5. tulle 6. maline
  winged (lacy).. 12. neuropteroid

Netherlands... see also *Dutch, Holland*
capital.. 9. Amsterdam
cheese.. 4. Edam
city.. 5. Delft 7. Utrecht
  9. Eindhoven, Rotterdam
gin.. 8. schnapps
government.. 8. monarchy
government seat.. 8. The Hague
inhabitant.. 5. Dutch 7. Flemish
lake.. 7. Haarlem
legislative body.. 4. Raad
low land.. 6. polder
port.. 9. Rotterdam
possession.. 7. Surinam (Dutch
  Guiana) 8. Antilles (W Ind)
river.. 3. Eem 5. Meuse, Rhine
  6. Ijssel (Yssel), Kromme
sea (inland).. 9. Wadden Sea, Zuider
  Zee 10. Ijssel Lake, Ijsselmeer
nettle... 3. vex 4. fret, herb, line,
  whip 5. anger, annoy, pique, rouse
  6. incite, Urtica 8. provoke 8. irritate
  10. Parietaria, Urticaceae
nettle (pert to)...
bird.. 11. whitethroat
geranium.. 6. coleus
rash.. 5. hives, uredo 9. urticaria
sea.. 5. cnida
network... 3. web 4. caul, fret, kell,
  lace, mesh, moke, rete 5. chain
  6. cobweb, plexus, reseau, sagene
  7. webwork
neume... 5. neuma 6. pneuma
neurad... 12. to neural side
neural... 6. dorsal, nerval 7. ventral
  9. posterial
neuralgia... 3. tic 4. pain 8. face
  ague 13. tic douloureux
neuter... 6. gender 7. neither, neutral,
  sexless 9. impartial
neutral... 7. antacid 8. mediocre,
  middling, negative, unbiased
  10. achromatic 11. indifferent,
  nonpartisan 12. noncombatant,
  noncommittal
neutral equilibrium... 7. astatic
neutralize... 5. annul 6. offset
  7. nullify, vitiate 9. frustrate
  10. counteract 11. countervail
  14. counterbalance
Nevada...
capital.. 10. Carson City
city.. 3. Ely 4. Elko 6. Sparks
  7. Boulder 8. Las Vegas
lake .. 4. Mead 6. Mohave
  7. Pyramid
mine (famed).. 12. Comstock Lode
  (1859)
mountain.. 7. Rockies, Wasatch
  13. Sierra Nevadas
native Indian.. 6. Digger
resort.. 4. Reno 8. Las Vegas (The
  Meadows) 9. Lake Tahoe
State admission.. 11. Thirty–sixth
State motto.. 16. All For Our Country
State nickname.. 6. Silver
  9. Sagebrush
neve... 4. firn, snow 6. nephew
  7. glacier
nevel, nevell... 9. fisticuff
never... 4. nary 6. nowise 7. not ever
  8. at no time, not at all 9. by no

means, nevermore
nevertheless... 3. but, yet 5. still
  6. anyhow 7. however
  15. notwithstanding
nevus... 4. mark, mole 5. tumor
  7. blemish 9. birthmark
new... 3. neo (pref) 4. anew, late,
  nova (star) 5. fresh, novel 6. growth,
  modern, recent 8. neoteric, original,
  untested 9. recreated, renovated
  12. unaccustomed 13. inexperienced
New Brunswick...
capital.. 11. Fredericton
city.. 6. St John
gulf.. 10. St Lawrence
new but yet old... 10. novantique
New England (pert to)...
book.. 6. Primer
explorer.. 13. Capt John Smith
native.. 6. Yankee
theology.. 9. Calvinism
Newfoundland...
city.. 7. St John's 9. Grand Bank
discoverer.. 9. John Cabot (1497)
gulf.. 10. St Lawrence
New Guinea, Papua Island...
capital.. 6. Rabaul
hog (wild).. 4. bene
island size (world).. 5. third
native.. 6. Papuan
parrot.. 4. lory
port.. 4. Daru 7. Moresby
region.. 10. Melanesian
river.. 3. Fly
New Hampshire...
capital.. 7. Concord
city.. 6. Durham 7. Hanover
  8. Merrimac 10. Manchester,
  Portsmouth
cog rail (first).. 12. Mt Washington
lake.. 13. Winnipesaukee
mountains.. 5. White
Our Town.. 13. Grover's Corner
park.. 13. Crawford Notch, Dixville
  Notch
range.. 12. Presidential
river.. 8. Merrimac 11. Connecticut
sculpture.. 14. Great Stone Face
  (Profile Peak)
State admission.. 5. Ninth
State motto.. 13. Live Free or Die
State nickname.. 7. Granite
New Jersey...
capital.. 7. Trenton
city.. 6. Camden, Newark 7. Raritan
  9. Montclair 12. Fort Monmouth,
  New Brunswick
college.. 9. Princeton (1746)
inventor.. 6. Edison
naval air station.. 9. Lakehurst
poet.. 11. Walt Whitman
resort.. 7. Cape May 8. Wildwood
  9. Ocean City 10. Asbury Park
  12. Atlantic City
river.. 7. Raritan
State admission.. 5. Third
State motto.. 20. Liberty and
  Prosperity
State nickname.. 6. Garden
New Mexico...
capital.. 7. Santa Fe
city.. 4. Taos 7. Roswell
  11. Albuquerque

Fort .. 5. Tejon
Indian Reservation .. 5. Acoma (Sky
City) 11. Chaco Canyon
peak .. 7. Wheeler
river .. 4. Gila 5. Pecos 8. Canadian
space center .. 6. Sandia 8. Holloman,
Kirtland 9. Los Alamos 10. White
Sands
State admission .. 12. Forty–seventh
State bird .. 10. road runner
State flower .. 5. yucca
State motto .. 12. Crescit Eundo
15. It Grows as It Goes
State nickname .. 17. Land of
Enchantment
State wonder .. 15. Carlsbad Caverns
new moon festival ... 8. neomenia
news ... 5. flash, scoop 6. report
7. courier, evangel, tidings
news agency ... 2. AP 3. DNB, UPI
4. Tass 5. Aneta, Domei 7. Reuters
9. syndicate
newspaper (pert to) ...
editor .. 7. reviser 8. redactor
file .. 6. morgue
popular name .. 7. gazette
writer .. 8. reporter 9. columnist
10. newscaster 13. correspondent
newsstand ... 5. booth, kiosk, stall
new star ... 4. nova
newt ... 3. eft 6. lizard, triton
10. salamander
New Testament ... 6. Gospel
8. Epistles 15. Pauline Epistles
new wine ... 4. must
new word, usage ... 7. neology
9. neologism, neoterism
New York ...
borough .. 5. Bronx 6. Queens
8. Brooklyn, Richmond 9. Manhattan
buyer (for $24) .. 11. Peter Minuit
capital .. 6. Albany
city .. 5. Utica 7. Buffalo, New York
8. Saratoga 9. Rochester
11. Schenectady 12. Poughkeepsie
college .. 7. Colgate, Cornell
8. Columbia 9. West Point
Falls .. 7. Niagara
Indian .. 6. Oneida, Seneca 8. Iroquois
Irving's home .. 9. Tarrytown
island .. 6. Staten 9. Manhattan
monument .. 7. Obelisk 10. Grant's
Tomb 15. Statue of Liberty
mountains .. 9. Catskills
name, old .. 12. New Amsterdam
nickname .. 6. Gotham 8. Big Apple
river .. 4. East 6. Harlem, Hudson
river channel .. 8. Hell Gate
section (famed) .. 4. SoHo
16. Greenwich Village
State admission .. 8. Eleventh
State bird .. 8. bluebird
State flower .. 4. rose
State motto .. 9. Excelsior 10. Ever
Upward
State nickname .. 6. Empire
New Yorker ... 8. Dutchman
9. Gothamite 13. Knickerbocker
New Zealand ...
capital .. 10. Wellington
city .. 7. Dunedin 8. Auckland,
Hamilton 12. Christchurch

discoverer .. 6. Tasman
explorer .. 4. Cook (Captain James)
location .. 12. South Pacific
native .. 5. Maori 10. Polynesian
peak .. 6. Mt Cook
sect .. 7. Ringatu
soldier .. 5. Anzac
tribe .. 3. Ati 5. Maori
volcano .. 7. Ruapehu
New Zealand (pert to) ...
bird ... 3. kea, moa, poe 4. titi, weka,
kiwi 7. apteryx, boobook, wrybill,
Xenicus
caterpillar .. 5. aweto
club, weapon .. 4. mere
mahogany .. 6. totara
mollusk .. 4. pipi
myrtle .. 8. ramarama
morepork .. 4. peho, ruru
palm .. 5. nikau
parrot .. 6. kakapo 9. owl parrot
pigeon .. 4. kuku
reptile .. 7. tuatara
white pine .. 5. kauri (kaury)
next ... 4. then 5. aware, neist
7. closest, nearest, proximo
9. adjoining, immediate
10. contiguous, succeeding
next to ... 6. almost, beside, nearly
8. adjacent
next to last syllable ... 6. penult
11. penultimate
nexus ... 3. tie 4. bond, link 5. group
6. series 10. connection
15. interconnection
Nez Percé ... 6. Indian 11. pierced
nose
Niagara ... 5. flood, grape (green)
Niagara Falls (pert to) ...
cataract .. 8. American, Canadian
9. Horseshoe
division between .. 10. Bridal Veil,
Goat Island
point of interest .. 14. Cave of the
Winds
nib ... 3. end 4. beak, bill 5. point
(pen), prong 6. tongue
nibble ... 3. eat, nab, nip 4. gnaw,
peck 5. champ, munch 6. browse
Nicaragua ...
capital .. 7. Managua
city .. 7. Granada
lake .. 7. Managua
mountain range .. 10. Cordillera
river .. 4. Coco, Tuma 7. San Juan
nice ... 4. fine, good, kind, neat
6. dainty, proper, queasy, subtle,
tickle 7. elegant, finical, genteel,
prudish, refined 8. exacting, pleasant,
pleasing, suitable 9. agreeable,
squeamish 10. appetizing, delightful,
fastidious, particular, scrupulous
11. considerate, punctilious,
well–behaved 13. hypercritical
14. discriminating, discriminative
Nicene Creed ... 10. Confession
nicety ... 7. finesse, modesty
8. accuracy, delicacy 9. precision
11. preciseness 13. squeamishness
niche ... 4. apse, nook 5. space
(recessed) 6. alcove, covert, recess
7. retreat, secrete 10. tabernacle

nick ... 3. gap 4. dent, dint, slit
  5. notch, steal 7. swindle
nickel (pert to) ...
  alloy .. 5. Invar
  bronze .. 11. cupranickel
  coin .. 13. five–cent piece
  color .. 4. gray 6. nimbus
  compound .. 8. argenton
    11. maillechort
  silver .. 6. German
  symbol .. 2. Ni
nickelodeon ... 4. juke 7. jukebox,
  theater (5–cent)
nickname ... 3. pun 6. monica
  7. agnomen, epithet, misname,
  moniker (monicker), pet name
  8. cognomen, misapply
  10. soubriquet
nicknaming pun ... 12. prosonomasia
nictate ... 4. wink 5. blink 7. twinkle
  9. nictitate
nid ... 3. nod 10. bend and bob
nide ... 4. nest 5. brood
nidge ... 3. nig 5. shake 6. quiver
nidificant ... 12. nestbuilding
nidology, science ... 10. birds' nests
nidor ... 5. aroma, scent
nidus ... 4. nest 5. abode 7. nucleus
  13. breeding place
Nietzsche ... 11. philosopher
nieve ... 4. fist, hand
niffer ... 7. bargain 8. exchange
niffy–naffy ... 7. finical 8. trifling
Niflheim, Nifelheim (Norse Myth) ...
  8. Universe (division of) 10. Nine
  Worlds
nifty ... 5. smart 7. stylish 8. very
  good
Nigeria ...
  capital .. 5. Lagos
  city .. 3. Ede 6. Ibadan
  export .. 5. cocoa
  plains .. 5. Bornu
  tribe .. 4. Eboe 5. Benin
niggardly ... 5. scant 6. paltry, sordid,
  stingy 9. penurious, scrimping
  10. avaricious 12. parsimonious
nigh ... 2. at 3. nei 4. left, near
  5. about, anear, close 6. almost,
  direct, nearly 8. adjacent
  10. contiguous 11. neighboring
night ... 4. nuit 5. death 7. evening
  8. darkness, wee hours 9. adversity,
  nightfall 11. concealment
night (pert to) ...
  bird .. 5. potoo 8. nightjar
    9. nighthawk 10. goatsucker,
    nightchurr, owl swallow, shearwater
    11. nightingale
  blindness .. 10. nyctalopia
  cap .. 6. biggin
  club .. 4. café 5. disco 6. bistro
    7. cabaret 11. discotheque
  goddess .. 3. Nox, Nyx
  jasmine .. 10. hursinghar
  Norse .. 4. Nott
  sight (only) .. 11. hemeralopia
  wandering .. 11. noctivagant
nightfall, at ... 6. sunset 9. acronical
  (achronical) (opp of cosmical)
nightingale ... 6. thrush 8. philomel
  9. bed jacket

night jar ... 5. potoo 10. goatsucker
nightmare ... 3. alp 4. Mara, ogre
  5. dream 7. incubus 9. cauchemar
  13. hallucination
nightshade ... 5. morel (moril)
  7. henbane 10. belladonna
  11. bittersweet
nigrescent ... 8. blackish
nihil ... 7. nothing, no value
nihil debet ... 13. he owes nothing
nihil ex nihilo ... 7. nothing (comes)
  11. from nothing
Nihilist ... 9. anarchist, Socialist
Nile (pert to) ...
  bird .. 4. ibis 7. wryneck
  boat .. 5. baris 6. nuggar 8. dahabeah
  city .. 7. Rosetta
  color .. 3. boa 5. green
  dam .. 5. Aswan
  Falls .. 5. Ripon
  fish .. 5. bagre 8. mormyrid (sacred)
  god .. 4. Hapi
  headstream .. 6. Kagera
  houseboat .. 8. dahabeah
  island .. 4. Roda (Rhoda)
  waste .. 4. sudd
nilgai ... 8. antelope
nimble ... 4. deft, fast, flit, gleg, lish,
  spry 5. agile, alert, brisk, fleet, quick,
  smart, swift 6. active, adroit, clever,
  lively, prompt, volant
nimbose ... 6. cloudy, stormy
  7. clouded 8. nebulous, nubilous,
  overcast
nimbus ... 4. disk, halo 5. cloud, vapor
  6. fabric, gloria, nickel 7. aureole
  10. atmosphere
nimiety ... 6. excess 10. redundancy
niminy–piminy ... 7. mincing, refined
  10. effeminate
nimmer ... 5. thief
Nimrod (Bib) ... 5. ruler 6. hunter
  8. Cush's son
nimshi ... 4. fool 7. half–wit 11. silly
  person
Nimshi's son (Bib) ... 11. Jehoshaphat
nine (pert to) ...
  angles .. 7. nonagon
  banded armadillo .. 4. peba
  based on .. 8. novenary
  Books of nine chapters .. 7. Enneads
  comb form .. 6. ennead
  composition for nine .. 5. nonet
  days' devotion .. 6. novena
  eyes .. 7. lamprey
  gems .. 7. Vikrama
  gods .. 9. Etruscans
  group .. 6. ennead, nonary 18. Ennead
    of Heliopolis
  headed monster .. 5. Hydra
  inches .. 4. span
  number .. 5. ennea, nueve
  pert to .. 8. enneadic
  players .. 8. baseball
  poetic .. 8. ninefold
Nineteenth amendment ...
  14. Woman's Suffrage
Nineveh (Bib) ...
  capital .. 7. Assyria
  famed for .. 11. excavations (1814)
Nine Worlds (Norse) ... 3. Hel
  6. Asgard 7. Alfheim, Midgard

8. Niflheim, Vanaheim
10. Jotunnheim 12. Muspellsheim
13. Svartalfaheim
Nine Worthies ... 5. David, Judas
6. Arthur, Caesar, Hector, Joshua
7. Godfrey 9. Alexander
11. Charlemagne
ninny ... 4. clod, dolt, fool, nerd
9. blockhead, simpleton
ninth ... 5. nones (day before Ides)
8. enneatic, ninefold
11. ennea–eteric (year)
Ninth of Ab (Jew) ... 7. fast day
ninut ... 6. magpie
Niobe (pert to) ...
changed by Zeus to .. 5. stone
father .. 8. Tantalus
husband .. 12. King of Thebes
nip ... 3. bit, cut, sip 4. bite, clip,
dram, peck 5. blast, cheat, check,
chill, clamp, draft, drink, hurry, pinch,
seize, sever, steal, thief 6. benumb,
blight, catnip, cut off, freeze, snatch,
tipple 7. shorten, squeeze
8. compress 10. pickpocket
nipa (pert to) ...
drink .. 9. alcoholic
mat .. 6. thatch
palm .. 4. atap
palm sap .. 5. sugar 7. alcohol
nipcheese ... 5. miser 6. purser
nipper ... 3. boy, lad 4. claw, grab
5. biter, drink, miser, thief 6. cunner,
mitten, urchin 7. gripper, incisor,
pincers 12. costermonger
nippers ... 6. pliers 7. pincers 8. leg
irons, pince–nez 9. handcuffs
nipple ... 3. pap 4. teat 7. mamelon,
papilla 8. mammilla 10. projection
12. protuberance
nippy ... 4. cold 5. brisk 6. active,
biting 7. nipping, pungent
8. grasping, vigorous
Nirvana ... 4. rags 6. heaven
8. oblivion 12. emancipation
Nisan (Jew calendar) ... 10. first month
(Mar–Apr)
nisi ... 5. if not 6. unless
nissen ... 6. goblin, kobold 7. brownie
nisus ... 7. impulse 8. endeavor,
striving
nit ... 3. egg 4. mite 8. parasite
nitency ... 6. luster 10. brightness
niter, nitre ... 6. natron 9. saltpeter
13. sodium nitrate 16. potassium
nitrate
nither ... 5. blast 6. debase, shiver
7. oppress, tremble 9. humiliate
nithing (anc) ... 6. coward 7. niggard
nitid ... 3. gay 6. bright 8. lustrous
nitric acid ... 10. aqua fortis
nitrogen ... 3. azo (comb form), gas
5. azote 7. element 10. atmosphere
nitrogen compound ... 7. ammonia
nitroglycerin, nitroglycerine ...
8. dynamite (1846) 9. explosive,
guncotton
nitrous oxide ... 3. gas 10. anesthetic
11. laughing gas
nitty–gritty ... 4. base, crux, gist
7. essence
Niue, Pacific island ...

territory of .. 10. New Zealand
niveau ... 5. level
niveous ... 5. snowy, white (shining)
nix ... 2. no 5. no one 6. forbid,
nobody, sprite 7. nothing
Njorth, Njord (Norse) ... 3. god
(fertility) 5. Vanir
Njorth's daughter ... 5. Freya (Freyja)
7. goddess (love and beauty)
Njorth's son ... 3. god 4. Frey
no ... 3. naw, nay, nit 4. baal, dead,
gone, none 5. not so 6. denial,
no–gaki, not any 8. not at all
Noah, Bib (pert to) ...
boat .. 3. Ark
dove .. 7. Columba
father .. 6. Lamech
flood .. 6. Deluge
Genesis .. 9. patriarch
grandson .. 4. Aram
landing, the Ark .. 6. Ararat
raven 6. Corvus
son .. 3. Ham 4. Shem 7. Japheth
nob ... 4. head, nave 6. hobnob
8. nobleman 9. personage
nobby ... 4. boat 5. smart 7. stylish
Nobel powder ... 10. Ballistite
noble ... 4. epic, fine, peer 5. ducal,
grand, lofty, manly 6. epical
7. eminent, grandee, liberal, stately,
sublime 8. elevated, generous,
imposing, renowned, splendid
9. dignified, high birth, honorable
10. impressive 11. illustrious,
magnanimous, magnificent
12. aristocratic
nobleman ... 3. sir 4. duke, earl, lord,
peer 5. baron 6. barony, flaith, thakur
7. baronet, grandee, marquis
8. margrave, optimate, viscount
9. blueblood, patrician 10. aristocrat,
chess piece
nobleness of birth ... 6. eugony
noblewoman ... 4. lady 5. begum
7. duchess, peeress 8. baroness,
contessa, countess, marquise
11. marchioness
nobody ... 4. none 5. no one
7. nebbish 8. no person
9. jackstraw, nonentity 10. not
anybody
nocent ... 6. guilty 7. harmful, hurtful
8. criminal (opp of innocent)
nocturnal ... 5. night 7. nightly
8. darkness, nocturne
nocturnal (pert to) ...
animal .. 3. bat 4. coon 5. lemur, ratel
6. possum 7. opossum
astronomy .. 9. astrolabe
bird .. 3. owl
signs .. 8. zodiacal
nocturne ... 7. lullaby 8. serenade
10. night scene (art)
nocuous ... 7. hurtful, noxious
nod ... 3. bow 4. bend, bock, doze,
tend, wink 6. beckon, signal
7. bidding 8. greeting
Nod (Bib) ... 9. Land of Nod 10. East
of Eden
nodding ... 6. nutant 7. annuent,
weeping (as a willow) 8. cernuous,
drooping

noddy... 3. auk 4. fool 6. drowsy, fulmar, noodle, sleepy 7. foolish, hackney 9. simpleton
node... 4. knob, knot, knur, plot 5. joint, nodus 7. dilemma 8. swelling 10. difficulty 12. complication, protuberance
nodule... 4. auge, bump, knot, lump, mass 5. geode 7. granule, nablock 8. tubercle 12. complication
nodus... 4. knot, node 10. difficulty 12. complication
noel... 5. carol (Xmas), shout 9. sign of joy
Noel... 6. Natale 9. Christmas
noeud... 3. bow 4. knot
nog... 3. peg, pin 5. block 6. eggnog, noggin 8. treenail 9. brickwork
nogada... 10. pecan candy
nogal... 5. pecan
noggin... 3. cup, mug 4. head, pate
noise... 3. din, pop, rap 4. bang, boom, klop, roar, rout 5. blare, blast, bruit, chang, clang, click, rumor, sound 6. clamor, outcry, racket, report, strife, uproar 7. brattle, chortle, discord, quarrel, rapping 9. shoutings
noise (pert to)...
  ghost.. 11. poltergeist
  harsh.. 4. bray 7. stridor 9. caterwaul
  respiration.. 4. rale
  rustling.. 5. swish
  Scotch.. 5. chang
  water.. 5. plash 6. ripple, splash
  whirring.. 4. burr
noised... 6. dinned 7. rumored 8. reported
noisemaker... 4. horn 5. siren 6. rattle 7. clacker, whistle 8. whiz–bang
noisome... 3. bad 4. foul 5. fetid, nasty 7. harmful, noxious 8. stinking 9. offensive 10. malodorous, pernicious 11. destructive, unwholesome 12. insalubrious
noisy... 4. loud 7. blatant 8. brawling, clattery 9. clamorous, turbulent 10. blustering, boisterous, vociferous 12. obstreperous, rattley–bang
nom... 4. name
nomad... 4. arab 5. gypsy 6. roamer, Romany 7. Bedouin, Saracen, scenite, zingaro 8. wanderer
nomadic... 9. itinerant
nomarchy (Gr)... 4. nome 8. province 10. department
nom de plume... 7. pen name 9. pseudonym
nomen... 4. gens, name 7. agnomen 8. cognomen 9. praenomen
nomenclature... 4. name 5. onymy 8. glossary, onymatic, register 10. dictionary, Latin names, vocabulary 11. designation, terminology
nominal... 3. par 6. unreal 7. not real, titular, topical 8. so–called
nominal recognizance (law)... 3. Doe
nonage... 6. neanic 8. immature, minority, pupilage, youthful
nonary... 9. nine group 10. base of nine 11. group of nine

nonbeliever... 5. pagan 7. atheist, heathen, infidel 8. agnostic 11. disbeliever 12. non–Christian
nonce... 3. now 8. meantime 11. temporarily
nonchalant... 4. cool 6. casual 8. careless 10. insouciant 11. indifferent, unconcerned 13. imperturbable
noncompliance... 7. refusal 12. disobedience 13. recalcitrance
non compos mentis... 7. unsound 8. demented, deranged 11. disoriented
nonconformist... 7. heretic, sectary 8. objector, recusant 9. dissenter, protester
nondescript... 11. exceptional 13. indescribable 14. indeterminable
none... 2. no 4. nary 5. nones, no one 6. nobody, not any, not one 10. nobody else
nonentity... 7. a nobody, nullity 8. nihility, nonbeing 9. res nihili 11. nothingness 12. nonexistence
nonessential... 8. needless 9. extrinsic 10. adiaphoron, incidental, irrelevant 11. superfluous 12. adventitious
non licit... 8. unlawful
non–Mahometan... 5. Kafir 6. giaour 9. non–Moslem
nonmetallic... 4. spar 5. argon, boron 6. carbon, helium, iodine, oxygen 7. bromine 8. chlorine, nitrogen
nonpareil... 4. type 7. paragon 8. nonesuch, peerless 9. unrivaled 11. unsurpassed 14. painted bunting
nonplus... 4. stop 5. blank, stump 6. baffle, puzzle, thwart 7. mystify, perplex 8. quandary
nonproductive... 6. barren 7. sterile 9. fruitless
nonprofessional... 3. ham, lay 4. laic 5. laity 7. amateur 10. apprentice
nonsense... 3. bah 4. bosh, bunk, tosh 5. folly, stite 6. drivel, humbug, jargon 7. blarney, foolery, trifles, twaddle 8. falderal, flimflam, trumpery 9. absurdity, frivolity, poppycock, senseless, silliness 10. balderdash, tomfoolery, triviality 11. monkeyshine 12. fiddle–dee–dee
nonsense verse... 9. amphigory (amphigouri), rigmarole
non tanto (Mus)... 9. non troppo, not as much
noodle... 4. fool, head 5. brain, ninny 9. blockhead, simpleton 12. stupid person
nook... 4. cant, cove 5. angle, herne, niche 6. corner, cranny, recess 7. crevice 10. promontory
noon... 6. midday, summit 8. meridian, noontide 9. ninth hour 11. noon of night (poet)
noonday rest... 6. siesta
noose... 3. tie 4. bond, hang, loop 5. snare 6. circle, halter 7. laniard (lanyard) 12. hangman's rope
Nootka... 3. Aht, dog 6. Indian
norati... 5. noise 6. gossip

Norbertine ... 12. Premonstrant
Nordic ... 8. Germanic
　　12. Scandinavian
norie ... 9. cormorant
norm ... 4. rule, type 5. model, norma
　　7. average, measure, pattern
　　8. standard, template
norma ... 4. rule 5. gauge, model
　　6. square 7. pattern 8. standard,
　　template 13. constellation
normal ... 3. par 4. just, mean, sane
　　5. usual 6. common 7. average,
　　logical, natural, orderly, regular, typical
　　8. everyday, ordinary 9. customary
Norman ... 6. French 7. crimson
　　8. Northman 10. Romanesque
　　17. conquest of England (1066)
Normandy ...
　　beach .. 5. Omaha
　　capital .. 4. Caen 5. Rouen (old)
　　city .. 5. Havre 6. Dieppe 7. Alençon
　　9. Cherbourg
　　conqueror .. 5. Rollo 8. William I
　　governed by .. 6. France (1940)
　　Viking duke (anc) .. 5. Rollo
Norn (Teut Myth) ... 4. Urth, Wyrd
　　5. Skuld 9. Verthandi
Norse ... 9. Norwegian
　　12. Scandinavian
Norse (pert to) ...
　　abode of gods .. 6. Asgard 8. Valhalla
　　alphabet .. 6. runics
　　ash tree, universe .. 10. Yddgrasill
　　bard .. 5. scald (skald) 7. sagaman
　　collected songs, myths .. 4. Edda
　　demon (Fire) .. 4. Surt (Surtr)
　　earth .. 7. Midgard
　　epic .. 4. saga
　　explorer .. 11. Leif Ericson
　　first man .. 4. Askr
　　giant .. 4. Loki, Ymir (Ymer) 5. Jotun
　　6. Fafnir
　　horse .. 8. Brimfaxi 9. Skinfaksi
　　horse (Odin's) .. 10. Yggdrasill
　　king .. 4. Atli
　　language (old) .. 9. Icelandic
　　maidens (Odin's) .. 8. Valkyrie
　　man .. 8. Northman
　　monster .. 6. kraken 7. Midgard
　　patron saint .. 4. Olaf
　　poem .. 4. rune
　　toast .. 5. skoal
　　warrior .. 8. berserker
　　watchdog (Hel's) .. 4. Garm (Garmr)
　　wolf .. 6. Fenrir
Norse goddess of ...
　　death, underworld .. 3. Hel, Ran
　　fate .. 4. Norn, Urth, Wyrd
　　flowers .. 5. Nanna
　　giantess .. 4. Nott
　　love, beauty .. 5. Freya
　　peace, healing .. 3. Eir
　　sky .. 5. Frigg (Frigga)
Norse God of ...
　　day .. 3. Dag
　　evil .. 4. Loki
　　fertility .. 4. Frey (Freyr) 6. Njorth
　　(Njord)
　　giants .. 4. Ymir
　　justice .. 4. Frey 7. Forseti
　　light .. 6. Balder
　　night .. 4. Nott

　　poetry .. 4. Odin 5. Bragi
　　primeval (the world) .. 4. Ymir (Ymer)
　　sea .. 5. Aegir
　　thunder .. 4. Thor
　　war, wisdom .. 4. Odin (Wodin)
　　watchfulness .. 8. Heimdall
Norse gods, chief ... 3. Tyr (Tiu)
　　4. Frey, Jarl, Loki, Odin (Othin,
　　Wodin), Thor (Donar), Vali, Ymir
　　5. Aesir (group) 6. Balder, Njorth
　　7. Asynjur (group), Forseti
　　8. Heimdall
North (far) ... 6. Arctic
North Africa ... see also *Africa*
　　country .. 7. Algeria, Tunisia
　　fruit .. 3. fig 4. date
　　people .. 4. Moor 6. Berber, Hamite,
　　Libyan
　　port .. 4. Sfax
North America ... see also *America*
　　Indian blanket .. 6. stroud
　　mountain, highest .. 8. McKinley
　　orchid .. 8. arethusa
　　owl .. 7. wapacut
　　rail .. 4. sora
　　reindeer .. 7. caribou
　　river, longest .. 5. Yukon 8. Missouri
　　11. Mississippi
　　snake .. 5. adder
North Atlantic (pert to) ...
　　cape .. 5. Sable
　　island .. 7. Britain, Iceland, Ireland
　　9. Greenland, Manhattan
　　sea gull .. 4. skua
North Carolina ...
　　cape .. 4. Fear 7. Lookout 8. Hatteras
　　capital .. 7. Raleigh
　　city .. 6. Durham 9. Asheville
　　explorer .. 6. De Soto 9. Verrazano
　　famed person .. 12. Virginia Dare
　　　19. Sir Walter Raleigh
　　first flight .. 9. Kitty Hawk
　　mountain .. 10. Mt Mitchell
　　pine .. 8. loblolly
　　river .. 3. Tar 5. Neuse 6. Peedee
　　(Yadkin)
　　State admission .. 7. Twelfth
　　State bird .. 8. cardinal
　　State flower .. 7. dogwood
　　State motto .. 14. Esse Quam Videri
　　20. To Be Rather Than To Seem
　　State nickname .. 7. Tarheel 8. Old
　　North
North Dakota ...
　　capital .. 8. Bismarck
　　city .. 5. Fargo, Minot
　　fort .. 6. Mandan 7. Lincoln
　　11. Abercrombie
　　historic site .. 24. International Peace
　　Garden
　　mountain .. 10. White Butte
　　reservoir .. 8. Garrison
　　State admission .. 8. Fortieth (or
　　Thirty–ninth)
　　State bird .. 10. meadowlark
　　State flower .. 11. prairie rose
　　State nickname .. 5. Sioux
　　11. Flickertail
northeaster ... 4. gale, wind 5. storm
Northern ... 6. boreal 11. hyperborean
　　13. septentrional
Northern constellation ... 3. Cor

9. Andromeda
northernmost world (inhabitable)...
  5. Thule 9. Trondheim
North Pole... 10. boreal pole
North Sea... 6. Baltic, German
North Sea arm... 8. Kattegat
  9. Skagerrak (Skager–Rak)
North Sea canal... 4. Kiel
North Star... 7. Polaris 8. Cynosure,
  lodestar (loadstar), polestar
north wind... 6. Boreas
  10. tramontane
Norway... see also *Norwegian*
  capital.. 4. Oslo 11. Christiania (old)
  city.. 6. Bergen 7. Drammen
    9. Trondheim
  county.. 5. fylke
  inlet.. 5. fiord (fjord)
  mountain.. 6. Kjolen
  parliament.. 8. Storting (Storthing)
  patron saint.. 4. Olaf (Olaus)
  phenomenon.. 11. midnight sun
    14. Northern Lights
  plateau.. 5. fjeld
  river.. 2. Oi 4. Tana 7. Glommen
Norwegian (pert to)...
  bird.. 4. rype 9. ptarmigan
  cart.. 11. stolkjaerre
  dance.. 7. halling
  duck.. 7. widgeon
  embroidery.. 9. hardanger
  goblin.. 5. Nisse 6. kobold
  guardian spirit.. 6. fylgja 8. hamingja
  haddock.. 8. rosefish
  language.. 5. Norse 8. Rigsmaal
    9. Landsmaal
  liquor.. 7. akevitt
  sea monster.. 6. kraken
  tales.. 4. Edda
Norwegian people...
  author, explorer.. 8. Sverdrup
  composer.. 5. Grieg
  dramatist.. 5. Ibsen
  explorer.. 6. Nansen (Nobel Prize)
  king.. 6. Harold (The Fairhaired)
    15. Harold Hardraade
  philologist.. 5. Assen
  raiders.. 7. Vikings
  saint.. 4. Olaf (Olaus)
  violinist.. 7. Ole Bull
  zoologist.. 4. Sars
nose... 3. neb, pry 4. conk, prow
  5. nasus, scent, smell, snout
  6. meddle, muzzle, nuzzle 8. olfactor
  9. detective, proboscis
  11. investigate
nose (pert to)...
  ailment.. 6. coryza 8. rhinitis
  bees, birds.. 4. lore 5. lorum
  bleeding.. 9. epistaxis
  cartilage.. 6. septum
  glasses.. 8. pince–nez
  large.. 6. nasute
  muscle.. 7. nasalis
  opening.. 5. naris (nares, pl) 7. nostril
  partition.. 5. vomer
  plug.. 12. rhineurynter
  relating to.. 5. nasal 6. narial, rhinal
  snub.. 6. simous
  surgery.. 11. rhinoplasty
noseband (bridle)... 6. misrol
nosegay... 4. posy 7. bouquet,

perfume 9. fragrance 10. frangipani
(tree)
nosocomium... 8. hospital
nosography, nosology *(science of)*...
  7. disease
nostalgia... 8. yearning 11. wistfulness
  12. homesickness 14. sentimentality
nostology *(study of)*... 8. senility
  10. geriatrics 11. gerontology
Nostradamus... 4. seer 7. prophet
  10. astrologer
nostril... 5. naris (nares, pl) 6. narial
  9. olfactory
nostril–shaped... 8. nariform
nosy... 5. nasal 6. prying 7. curious
  8. fragrant 10. malodorous
  11. inquisitive
Nosy, Old (nickname)... 16. Duke of
  Wellington
not (pert to)...
  any.. 2. no 4. nane, nary, none
    7. no trace
  at all.. 5. nohow 6. nowise
  easy.. 7. labored
  either.. 7. neither
  feral.. 4. tame
  harmed.. 9. unscathed
  having a will.. 9. intestate
  hollow.. 5. solid
  in motion.. 5. fixed 6. stable, static
    7. stabile 10. stationary
  in the least.. 6. nowhit
  moral.. 6. amoral 7. immoral
  open (fruit).. 11. indehiscent
  prefix.. 2. il, im, in, ir, un 3. non
  professional.. 4. laic 7. amateur
  qualified.. 5. unfit
  running (stream).. 8. stagnant
  separable.. 11. indivisible
  settled.. 4. moot
  subjugated.. 7. unbowed
  suitable.. 5. inept
  the same.. 5. other 9. different
  to know.. 5. unken 10. unfamiliar
notable... 6. famous 8. historic
  9. celebrity, important, memorable,
  notorious 10. noteworthy, remarkable
  13. distinguished, extraordinary
notandum... 4. note 5. entry
  10. memorandum
notary... 5. notar 8. attestor,
  notebook, official 9. scrivener
  12. notary public, stenographer
notation... 4. memo, note 5. entry
  7. comment, marking 9. etymology
  10. annotation
notator... 5. noter 8. recorder
  9. annotator
notch... 3. gap, jap 4. dent, dint,
  kerf, nick, nock 5. cleft, crena, score
  6. defile, dentil (Her), indent
  7. passage 8. undercut 9. indenture
  11. indentation
notched bar (door)... 4. risp
notched opening (Anat)... 5. hilum
note... 2. ut 3. jot 4. chit, heed,
  mark, memo, sign, sole, song, tone,
  tune 5. breve, gloss, sound, token
  6. billet, notice, postil, record,
  remark, report 7. apostil (apostille),
  comment, epistle 8. dispatch,
  eminence, indicate, marginal,

scholium 9. character 10. annotation, importance, indication, memorandum, reputation 11. certificate, observation

note (pert to)...
death sound.. 4. mort
explanatory.. 5. gloss 8. scholium
half.. 5. minim
high.. 3. alt, E la
marginal.. 6. postil 7. apostil (apostille)
musical.. 5. breve 6. ecbole 7. punctus
stem of.. 5. filum

notebook... 6. street 7. estreat 8. ratebook 10. adversaria, memorandum

noted... 4. seen 5. famed 6. famous, marked 7. eminent, notable 8. far–famed, renowned 9. distingué, prominent, well–known 10. celebrated

notes... 5. duole 6. strain 7. tiralee 11. solmization

nothing... 3. nil, nox 4. luke, rien, void, zero 5. nihil 6. naught, nichil, nought, trifle 7. a nobody 9. nonentity 11. empty–handed 12. nonexistence

nothing doing... 4. calm 6. hushed, no dice, no soap, placid 7. I refuse 9. by no means, God forbid, quiescent

notice... 2. ad 3. see 4. heed, idea, mark, mind, news, note, sign 5. blurb, edict, quote 6. advice, espial, notion, regard, remark 7. affiche, mention, observe, warning 8. bulletin, citation 9. attention 10. commentary 11. information, observation 12. announcement, intelligence 13. advertisement

notice (pert to)...
advance.. 8. ballyhoo
death.. 4. obit 8. obituary
marriage.. 4. bans 5. banns

notify... 4. cite, page, tell, warn 6. inform, remind 7. apprise, declare, publish 8. announce

notion... 4. idea, view, whim 5. freit 6. belief, theory, vagary 7. caprice, impulse, opinion 9. intention 10. conception, denotation, knickknack 11. supposition

notionable... 8. fanciful 9. whimsical

notional... 6. unreal 9. imaginary, visionary, whimsical

notions... 5. goods, wares 11. commodities, merchandise

notoriety... 4. fame, plug 5. éclat 8. ballyhoo 9. limelight, publicity, spotlight

notorious... 5. known, noted 6. arrant, famous, notour 8. flagrant, infamous, talked of 10. recognized 11. conspicuous

notorious character... 5. James (Jesse) 7. Cochise, Younger 8. Geronimo, Jennings, Murietta 9. Jack Ketch, Wyatt Earp 11. Billy the Kid, Poncho Villa, Sitting Bull 12. Calamity Jane 13. John Dillinger 14. Wild Bill Hickok

notum... 4. back

notus... 4. back (comb form)

notwithstanding... 3. but, yet 5. still 6. mauger (maugre), though 7. despite, however 8. although 9. in spite of 12. nevertheless

nought, naught... 3. bad, nil 4. zero 5. wrong 7. nothing, useless 9. worthless

noughty... 3. bad 9. worthless

noumenal... 4. real 5. ontal (opp of phenomenal)

noun... 7. subject

noun (pert to)...
gender, common.. 7. epicene
indeclinable.. 6. aptote
irregular.. 5. pecus 11. heteroclite
suffix.. 2. et, ia 3. ent, ery, ier, ion, ior, ist, ite 4. ence
verbal.. 6. gerund

nourish... 4. feed, grow 5. nurse 6. foster, suckle, supply 7. support, sustain 9. cultivate 13. promote growth

nourishing... 6. alible 8. nutrient 9. nutritive 10. alimentary

nourishment... 3. aid 4. food 5. manna, meats 7. aliment, pabulum 9. nutriment, nutrition 10. sustenance 13. nutritiveness 14. nutritiousness

nous... 4. mind 8. ready wit 9. intellect 11. world spirit

Nova... 4. star

Nova Scotia...
bay.. 5. Fundy 10. Chedabucto
cape.. 6. Canso
capital.. 7. Halifax
greens.. 11. sea plantain
island.. 10. Cape Breton
lake, salt.. 7. Bras d'Or
native.. 7. Acadian 8. Bluenose
poetic name.. 6. Acadia (Acadie)
settlement, first.. 9. Port Royal

novel... 3. new 4. book, rare 5. fresh, story 7. fiction, romance, strange, unusual 8. original

novelty... 3. fad 7. newness 9. freshness 10. innovation, recentness 11. originality

novice... 3. nun 4. puny, tyro (tiro) 5. chela, rooky 6. tyrone 7. amateur, convert, learner 8. beginner, freshman, initiate, neophyte, newcomer 9. fledgling, greenhorn, postulant 10. apprentice, catechumen 11. abecedarian 13. alphabetarian

novitiate... 6. novice 9. probation 14. apprenticeship

now... 3. noo 4. here 6. at once 7. present 9. at present, forthwith, instantly 10. very lately 12. at this moment

nowhere... 5. limbo 6. absent 7. no place 8. oblivion 9. nowhither 11. nonexistent, not anywhere, nullibicity

nowhere else... 5. there

nowise... 8. not at all

Nox (pert to)...
brother.. 6. Erebus
daughter.. 10. Hesperides
goddess (Rom).. 5. Night

husband.. 5. Chaos
noxious... 4. evil 5. nasty, yucky (sl)
6. nocent, odious 7. baneful, harmful,
hurtful, noisome 9. injurious,
miasmatic 10. corruptive, pernicious
11. destructive, unwholesome
12. insalubrious
nozzle... 3. tew 4. nose, vent
5. giant, snout 6. nuzzle, outlet,
tuyère 7. conduit 9. sprinkler
nuance... 5. shade 9. gradation,
variation 10. refinement
nub... 4. gist, knob, knot, knub, lump,
neck, snag 9. main point
12. protuberance
Nubia (pert to)...
afterglow.. 14. second twilight
animal.. 4. goat 5. horse
autonym.. 6. Berber 7. Barabra
harp.. 5. nanga
tribe.. 4. Nuba
nubia... 4. wrap 5. cloud
nucha... 4. nape, neck
nuclear complex... 7. Oedipus
nuclear energy (terms)... 4. mass
6. fusion, ionize 7. fission, neutron,
reactor, tokamak 8. hydrogen,
meltdown
nuclear network fiber... 5. linin
nucleus... 4. core 5. cadre, focus,
umbra 6. center, kernel 8. rudiment
nude... 4. bare 5. color, naked
6. Season (color) 7. denuded
8. stripped, undraped 9. unadorned,
unclothed, undressed
nudge... 3. jog, nog 4. knub, lump,
poke, prod, push 5. block, elbow
6. jostle, remind, signal
nudibranch... 7. mollusk
nugatory... 4. vain 7. invalid, trivial
8. trifling 9. worthless
11. ineffectual
nuisance... 4. bane, bore, harm, hurt,
pest 6. injury 9. annoyance
nuit... 5. night
null... 4. void 6. vacant 7. invalid
8. nugatory 11. nonexistent
13. inefficacious, insignificant
nullifidian... 7. skeptic 9. nullibist,
skeptical 10. unbeliever
11. disbeliever
nullify... 4. undo, void 5. annul
6. cancel, negate 7. abolish, destroy
8. abrogate 10. counteract, neutralize
numb... 6. clumsy, freeze, stupid,
torpid 8. benumbed, deadened,
helpless 9. apathetic, incapable,
rigescent 10. insensible
12. anesthetized
number... 3. sum 5. count, digit, limit
7. integer, numeral 8. quantity
9. aggregate, enumerate
10. complement 11. information
number (pert to)...
added.. 6. encore
again.. 10. renumerate
by tens.. 7. decimal
cardinal.. 7. primary (one, two)
consecutively.. 5. folio
copies (printed).. 7. edition
describable.. 6. scalar
irrational.. 4. surd

least whole.. 4. unit
lucky.. 5. seven
many.. 4. herd 6. myriad 7. several
9. multitude 12. considerable
ordinal.. 5. first 6. second (etc)
third power.. 4. cube
votes.. 4. poll
whole.. 7. integer
numbles, nombles... 6. umbles
7. inwards 8. entrails
numbness... 6. torpor 10. rigescence
numeral... 5. Roman 6. Arabic, figure
9. character
numerous... 4. lots, many 7. copious,
crowded 8. abundant, measured,
thronged 9. plentiful
Numidia (pert to)...
city.. 5. Hippo
crane.. 10. demoiselle
language (written).. 5. Punic 6. Tuareg
7. Hamitic
modern kingdom.. 7. Algeria
numskull... 4. dolt, nerd 5. dunce
nun... 4. moth, smew 5. Clare
(Franciscan), Vesta 6. monial, pigeon,
sister 8. titmouse, votaress
9. priestess 13. Lady of Loretto
nun bird... 6. Monasa 8. puffbird
nunciate... 9. announcer, messenger
nuncio... 6. legate 8. delegate
9. messenger 11. internuncio
nuncupate... 7. declare 8. dedicate,
inscribe, proclaim 9. designate
nuncupative... 4. oral 9. unwritten
(will) 11. designative
nun headdress... 6. wimple
nunnari root... 12. sarsaparilla
nunnery... 5. abbey 7. convent
8. cloister
nunnery head... 6. abbess
nunni... 7. blesbok (blesbuck)
8. antelope
Nuphar... 12. spatterdocks 16. yellow
pond lilies
nuptial... 6. bridal 7. marital
9. connubial 11. matrimonial
nurse... 4. amah, ayah, feed, rear, tend
5. bonne, mammy 6. caress, suckle
7. care for, cherish, nourish, nurture,
nutrice 9. nursemaid
nursed... 3. fed 6. tended 7. cradled,
suckled 8. nurtured 9. nourished
nursery... 6. crèche, school 7. day
care (center)
nurse shark... 4. gata
nurture... 3. aid 4. feed, rear
5. nurse 6. foster 7. care for,
cherish 8. breeding, training
9. education, encourage, nutriment
nut... 4. anta, kola (cola) 5. acorn,
betel, pecan, piñon 6. almond, Brazil,
cashew, litchi, peanut, walnut
7. filbert, hickory, maranon
8. beechnut, chestnut 9. butternut
nut (pert to)...
bearing.. 10. nuciferous
brown.. 5. hazel 6. walnut
8. chestnut
coal.. 10. anthracite
collectively.. 4. food 5. shack
9. beechnuts
confection.. 8. marzipan

cracker.. 4. crow
eating.. 10. nucivorous
   11. nuciphagous
edible part.. 6. kernel
grass.. 5. sedge
Med.. 4. kola 5. bichy 9. gourounut
odd.. 9. eccentric
palm.. 5. betel, lichi 7. coconut
ref to.. 5. nucal
shell.. 4. case, hull 6. trifle
Nut (pert to)...
consort of.. 3. Geb
daughter.. 4. Isis 8. Nephthys
goddess of.. 5. earth
son.. 2. Ra
nutation... 3. nod 7. nodding
nuthatch... 4. bird 5. sitta 6. xenops
   8. titmouse 9. nutpecker
nutmeg... 4. mace 5. drupe 6. beaver
   (color)
nutmeg (pert to)...
bird, finch.. 5. cowry 10. weaverbird
family.. 13. Myristicaceae
tree.. 6. camara
Nutmeg State... 11. Connecticut
nutpecker... 8. nuthatch
nut quad... 6. en quad
nutria... 3. fur 5. grège 10. beaverlike
nutria fur bearer... 5. coypu
nutrice... 5. nurse
nutriment... 4. food 7. aliment,
   pabulum 9. nutrition 11. nourishment
nutritious... 9. alimental
   10. alimentary, nourishing
nuts... 4. food, mast 5. shack
   9. beechnuts
nutty... 4. gaga, zest 5. queer, smart,
   spicy 7. amorous, piquant
   10. unbalanced 11. fascinating
   14. cracker–brained
nuzzle... 5. nurse 6. burrow, cuddle,
   foster, nestle 7. cherish 8. make
   snug
nyctalopia... 14. night blindness

nye... 4. eyas, nest, nide 5. brood
nymph... 4. nais 5. deity, dryad,
   naiad, oroad, siren, sylph 6. Nereid
   7. Oceanid 9. hamadryad
nymph (pert to)...
Arcadian.. 6. Syrinx
beloved of Narcissus.. 4. Echo
color.. 4. pink
Cretan.. 8. Cynosura
fountain, river.. 4. nais 5. naiad
   6. Egeria
German legend.. 7. Lorelei
Greek.. 4. Echo 6. Daphne
   8. Arethusa
Hesperides (one of).. 5. Aegle
   7. Hespera
hills, mountain.. 5. oread
laurel tree.. 6. Daphne
Messina Strait.. 6. Scylla
Mohamm paradise.. 5. houri
monster.. 6. Scylla
Mt Ida.. 6. Oenone
ocean.. 5. siren 6. Nereid 7. Galatea,
   Oceanid 10. Callirrhoe
pursued by Apollo.. 6. Daphne, Syrinx
   8. Arethusa
Queen.. 3. Mab
sea bird.. 6. Scylla
tree.. 5. Dryad 9. Hamadryad
water.. 5. Naiad 6. Undine 7. Hydriad
woods.. 5. Dryad 8. Arethusa
   9. Hamadryad
young.. 7. nymphet
Nymphaea... 8. Castalia 11. water
   lilies
nymphs... 10. Atlantides, Hesperides
nystagmus... 14. eyeball disease
Nyx, Nox (pert to)...
daughter.. 4. Eris
father.. 5. Chaos
goddess of.. 5. Night
mother of.. 11. Day and Night
Nzambi... 7. goddess (Afr) 11. earth
   mother

O

O
Q

O (pert to)...
interjection.. 11. exclamation
letter.. 5. tenth
mathematics.. 4. zero 6. cipher
pref (family).. 5. Irish
oaf... 4. boor, dolt, lout 5. idiot,
   ouphe, yokel 9. blockhead, simpleton
   10. changeling
oafish... 6. simple, stupid
oak... 4. club 5. brave, color, oaken,
   stout 6. strong 7. Quercus
   8. hardness, strength 13. artificial fly
oak (pert to)...
apple.. 4. gall 10. she–oak cone
beauty.. 4. moth
California.. 5. roble 6. encina

comb form.. 6. querci
evergreen.. 4. holm, ilex 5. holly
family.. 8. Fagaceae
fern.. 8. polypody
fruit.. 5. acorn 6. camata
fungus.. 10. armillaria
gall.. 8. oak apple
Jerusalem.. 7. ambrose
kinds.. 3. bur, red 5. black, white
   6. ground, poison, willow
   8. chestnut 10. canyon live
plantation.. 9. quercetum
resembling.. 9. roboreous
tannin.. 7. quercic 9. quercinic
thicket.. 9. chaparral
Turkey.. 6. cerris

web.. 10. cockchafer
young.. 8. flittern
oam... 5. steam 7. warm air
Oannes (Bab)... 5. deity (part man, part fish)
oar... 3. row 5. blade, remus, rower, scull 6. paddle, propel 7. oarsman
oar (pert to)...
 blade.. 4. palm, peel
 feather.. 5. remex
 fulcrum, lock.. 5. pivot, thole
 lop.. 6. rabbit
 shaft.. 4. loom
 shaped.. 7. remiped 8. remiform
oars (pert to)...
 collective.. 6. oarage, sculls
 one bank.. 7. unireme
 reverse.. 6. sheave
 three banks.. 7. trireme
 two banks.. 6. bireme
oasis... 3. ojo 4. wadi (wady) 5. Gafsa 6. Dakhla 11. fertile spot
oast... 4. kiln, oven
oat (pert to)...
 cake.. 5. caper
 ear (Old World).. 4. bird 7. wagtail
 fowl.. 11. snow bunting
 genus.. 5. Avena 6. oathay
 grass.. 4. ulla 9. chaparral
 husks.. 5. shood (shude)
 like.. 10. avenaceous
 rent (paid as).. 7. avenage
oath... 3. God 4. aith, drat, egad 5. bedad, curse 6. pledge 7. serment 9. affidavit, holy smoke, profanity 10. deposition 11. affirmation
Obadiah (Bib)... 6. Quaker 7. prophet
obbligato... 8. required 13. accompaniment, indispensable
obduction... 7. autopsy 8. covering
obdurate... 4. firm, hard 5. rough, stony 6. mulish, rugged 7. adamant, callous 8. stubborn 9. heartless, obstinate, unbending, unfeeling 10. impenitent, inflexible, insensible, unyielding 11. hardhearted, intractable
obedient... 6. docile 7. duteous, dutiful, orderly 8. amenable, yielding 9. attentive, compliant 10. submissive 11. conformable
obeisance... 3. bow 5. binge, congé 6. curtsy, fealty, homage 9. deference 10. respectful 14. obsequiousness
obeisance, to make... 3. bow 6. congee, curtsy, salaam
obelisk... 5. pylon 6. guglia (guglio), needle, obelus, pillar 16. Cleopatra's Needle
Oberon (pert to)...
 Astron.. 9. satellite
 character of.. 11. Shakespeare
 classic.. 4. poem 5. opera
 husband of.. 7. Titania
 Myth.. 13. King of Fairies
obese... 3. fat 5. puffy, pursy, squab, stout 6. fleshy, turgid 8. liparous 9. corpulent
obey... 3. ear 4. hear, mind 5. yield 6. comply, submit

obfuscate... 3. dim 6. darken, opaque 7. confuse, perplex 8. bewilder
obi... 4. sash 6. girdle
obit... 4. rest 5. death 6. notice 7. decease, release 8. obituary 9. obsequies 10. necrologue 11. Requiem Mass 12. mortuary roll
obiter... 9. in passing 12. incidentally
obiter dictum... 7. opinion (of judge)
object... 3. aim, end 4. goal, hulk 5. cavil, demur, scoff, thing 6. appose, expose, motive, oppose 7. article, grammar, protest, purpose 9. intention
object (pert to)...
 bulky.. 4. hulk
 circular.. 7. trundle
 cloudlike.. 6. nebula
 illustrative.. 6. realia (pl)
 rare.. 5. curio 7. antique
 rational.. 8. noumenon
 sacred.. 4. Urim 7. Thummim
 small.. 4. mite
object for...
 devotion, worship.. 4. icon, idol 5. totem 6. fetish
 dread.. 5. bogey (bogie) 6. goblin 8. the Devil
 going and coming.. 6. errand
 greed.. 5. lucre, money 6. wealth
 knowledge.. 7. scibile
objection... 3. bar 5. cavil 7. protest, quarrel 8. demurrer, obstacle 9. exception 11. disapproval
objectionable... 9. offensive 11. exceptional, inexpedient 13. uncommendable
objective... 3. aim, end 4. goal 6. motive, target 7. purpose
objector, conscientious... 6. conchy
objects (Bib)... 4. Urim 7. Thummim
objects (floating)... 7. flotsam
objurgate... 5. abuse, chide, scold 6. rebuke 7. reprove, upbraid 9. reprimand
oblate... 5. oblat 7. devoted 9. dedicated, flattened (opp of prolate)
obligated... 5. bound 6. in debt 7. obliged 8. beholden 9. obstringe
obligation... 3. tie, vow 4. bond, debt, duty, oath, onus 7. promise 8. civility, contract 9. agreement, necessity 10. compulsion 11. obstriction
obligatory... 7. binding 8. imposing, required 9. mandatory, necessary 10. compulsory
oblige... 4. bind, pawn 5. favor 6. compel, engage 7. gratify 8. obligate 9. constrain, obstringe 11. accommodate
obliged... 7. favored 8. beholden, grateful 9. duty bound
obliging... 4. kind 7. helpful 9. agreeable, courteous, indulgent 11. complaisant, considerate 13. accommodating
oblique... 4. cant, skew 5. bevel, slant, slope 7. obscure, scalene 8. inclined, perverse, sidelong, sidewise, sinister, slanting

9. underhand 10. circuitous,
collateral, transverse 12. disingenuous
oblique angle... 5. acute 6. obtuse
obliquely... 4. skew 6. aslant
7. askance 8. sideways, sidewise
9. on the bias 10. slantingly
obliterate... 4. blot, dele 5. erase
6. cancel, delete, efface, sponge
7. expunge
obliteration... 6. rasure 7. erasure
8. deletion 10. extinction
oblivion... 7. nirvana, silence
9. unfeeling 13. forgetfulness
15. unconsciousness
oblivion, producing... 8. nepenthe
oblivion, river of... 5. Lethe
oblivious... 6. asleep 8. heedless
9. forgetful, unfeeling 10. abstracted
11. unconscious
oblong... 8. elliptic 9. elongated
11. rectangular 12. quadrangular
obloquy... 5. abuse 6. infamy
7. calumny 9. criticism
11. malediction 12. reprehension
obnoxious... 4. vile 5. nasty
6. odious, rancid 7. hateful
8. amenable, infamous, terrible
9. offensive 13. objectionable
oboe... 4. reed 5. shawm (anc)
7. hautboy, musette 8. schalmei
(schalmey) 9. chalumeau
obscuration... 7. eclipse 9. darkening,
vagueness
obscure... 3. dim, fog 4. dark, hazy,
slur 5. bedim, blind, mirky, misty,
murky 6. cloudy, darken, delude,
mystic, opaque, remote 7. becloud,
conceal, eclipse, shadowy, unknown
8. darkling, formless, nameless,
nubilous, obstruse, oversile (obs)
9. enigmatic, undefined
10. indistinct, unrenowned
obscurity... 3. fog 5. gloom
7. dimness, opacity, unknown
8. darkness 9. nonentity, vagueness
12. formlessness 13. imperspicuous
14. insignificancy, uncomprehended
obsecrate... 7. beseech, entreat
10. supplicate
obsequies... 5. wakes 8. funerals
9. last rites
obsequious... 5. slick 6. abject
7. devoted, dutiful, fawning, servile,
slavish 8. cringing, funereal,
obedient, toadying 9. attentive,
compliant 11. subservient
observance... 3. act 4. form, rite
6. custom 8. behavior, ceremony,
practice 9. attention, deference,
sacrament, vigilance 10. conformity
11. celebration
observant... 7. careful, heedful, mindful
8. faithful, vigilant, watchful
9. attentive, regardant, regardful
observation... 4. idea 6. espial, remark
7. opinion 9. attention
observatory... 4. Lick 6. Yerkes
7. lookout, Palomar 8. Mt Wilson
11. planetarium
observe... 2. lo! 3. eye, see, spy
4. espy, heed, keep, nark, note,
obey, tout 6. behold, notice, remark

7. conform, examine, witness
8. preserve 9. celebrate, solemnize
observed, to be... 8. notandum
10. memorandum
observer... 4. eyer, nark 7. aviator,
student, witness 8. beholder,
informer, looker–on, onlooker
9. spectator 11. stool pigeon
obsess... 5. beset, haunt 6. harass
7. bewitch, possess 8. demonize
9. influence, preoccupy
obsession... 5. mania 8. impelled
11. bewitchment 13. spirit control
obsignate... 4. seal 5. stamp 6. ratify
obsolete... 3. old 5. passé 6. effete
7. archaic, disused, effaced, outworn,
worn out 9. out of date
10. antiquated 12. old–fashioned
obstacle... 3. dam 4. snag 6. hurdle
9. hindrance 10. difficulty,
impediment 11. obstruction
obstetrician... 6. doctor
10. accoucheur
obstetrix... 7. midwife
obstinate... 3. set 5. balky, tough
6. dogged, mulish, sullen 7. willful
8. perverse, stubborn 9. pigheaded
10. determined, headstrong,
self–willed 11. opinionated
obstreperous... 5. noisy 6. unruly
7. blatant 9. clamorous, turbulent
10. vociferous 11. disobedient
12. ungovernable
obstruct... 3. bar, dam, dit 4. clog,
ditt, stop 5. beset, block, check,
choke, delay 6. arrest, hamper,
oppose, stop up 7. occlude
9. barricade, embarrass, interfere,
interrupt
obstruction... 3. ban, dam 4. clog,
reef, snag 7. barrier 8. obstacle
9. hindrance 10. difficulty, filibuster,
impediment 11. retardation
obtain... 3. buy, eke, get, win
4. earn, fang, gain 5. fetch, reach
6. attain, derive, elicit, secure
7. achieve, acquire, capture, prevail,
procure, receive
obtain (pert to)...
by intimidation.. 9. blackmail
by threats.. 6. extort
control of.. 6. corner 8. overcome
equivalent.. 6. recoup
obtest... 6. beg for 7. beseech
10. supplicate
obtrude... 5. eject, expel 6. impose
7. intrude
obtrusive... 7. forward, pushing
9. intrusive, officious
obtund... 4. dull 5. blunt, quell
6. deaden 8. moderate
obtuse... 4. dull 5. blunt, crass, dense
6. stupid 9. unfeeling 11. insensitive
obvelation... 7. veiling 10. concealing
obverse... 5. front 8. converse
10. complement 11. counterpart
obviate... 7. head off, rule out
8. preclude 9. forestall 10. anticipate
obvious... 5. clear, gross, plain
7. evident, patient 8. apparent,
distinct, manifest, palpable
11. conspicuous, open and shut

obvolute ... 7. twisted 9. contorted, convolute 11. overlapping
occasion ... 4. sele, time 5. cause, event, nonce 6. excuse, motive 7. pretext 8. ceremony, exigency, function, incident 9. condition, happening 11. opportunity 12. circumstance
occasional ... 3. odd 4. orra 5. stray 6. casual 10. incidental, infrequent
occasionally ... 7. at times 9. sometimes 10. now and then 11. at intervals 12. sporadically
occasive ... 8. westward 10. setting sun
Occident ... 4. West 6. sunset 17. Western Hemisphere (opp of Orient)
Occidental ... 6. ponent 7. The West, Western 9. Hesperian
occiput ... 10. back of head 11. back of skull
occlude ... 3. dam 4. shut 5. close 6. shut up 8. obstruct
occult ... 5. magic 6. hidden, mystic 7. alchemy, cryptic 8. esoteric 9. concealed, recondite 10. mysterious, necromancy 11. supernormal 12. supernatural
occultation ... 4. gone, lost 7. eclipse 11. concealment
occultism ... 6. cabala 7. mystery
occult science ... 9. esoterics
occupant ... 6. inmate, tenant 10. inhabitant
occupation ... 3. job 4. call, note, work 5. hobby, trade 6. career, tenure 7. calling, pursuit 8. business, vocation 9. avocation 10. employment, habitation, possession, profession 11. engrossment
occupied ... 3. sat 4. busy, held 6. filled 7. engaged 8. employed, pervaded 9. engrossed, inhabited
occupy ... 3. use 4. fill, hold 6. employ, engage, expend, invest 7. engross, inhabit, oversit, pervade, possess 8. interest
occur ... 4. come, fall, meet 5. clash 6. appear, befall, betide, happen
occurrence ... 3. hap 5. event 8. incident, presence, scenario 9. existence, happening 10. appearance 11. eventuality 12. circumstance
occurring (pert to) ...
after death .. 10. posthumous
at nightfall .. 9. acronical
often .. 8. frequent 10. frequently
ocean ... 3. sea 4. brim, deep, main 5. brine 6. depths, pelago 8. great sea
ocean (pert to) . .
approach .. 7. sea gate
bottom .. 3. bed
crop cultivation .. 11. mariculture
deep .. 7. bathyal
deepest, lowest .. 5. hadal 8. bathybic 12. bathypelagic
division .. 6. Arctic, Indian 7. Pacific 8. Atlantic 9. Antarctic

floating matter .. 5. algae 7. flotsam
geography .. 12. oceanography
mammal .. 4. seal 5. whale
on (the ocean) .. 4. asea
periodic motion .. 4. tide
person .. 8. aquanaut, oceanaut 9. skin diver 10. scuba diver
ref to .. 7. pelagic 9. Neptunian
route .. 4. lane
sealing .. 7. pelagic
vessel .. 6. Sealab 9. submarine 10. bathyscaph 11. bathysphere
Oceania, Oceanica ... 9. Melanesia, Polynesia 10. Micronesia 12. Pacific lands
Oceanids (Gr Myth, pert to) ...
father .. 7. Oceanus
mother .. 6. Tethys
nymphs .. 13. three thousand
Oceanus (Gr Myth, per to) ...
children .. 5. Doris 8. Eurynome (goddess), Oceanids
god of .. 6. rivers
wife .. 6. Tethys
ocellus ... 3. eye 6. stemma 7. eyespot
ocelot ... 3. cat 7. leopard
ocher, ochre (pert to) ...
red .. 5. tiver 7. almagra 8. hematite 9. faded rose
yellow .. 3. sil 7. Chinese 8. limonite 9. ochrolite
ochlocracy ... 7. mob rule
ochlophobia (fear of) ... 6. crowds
ocotillo ... 5. shrub 10. candlewood
ocracy ... 9. group rule
octad ... 5. eight (group)
octaemeron ... 12. eight–day fast
octagon ... 8. octangle 11. eight angles
octahedron ... 10. eight faces
octameter ... 8. octapody 9. eight feet
octarchy ... 11. rule by eight
octastich ... 6. octave 10. eight lines 11. eight verses
Octateuch (Old Test) ... 10. Eight Books (1st)
octave ... 4. utas 5. eight 6. eighth 8. wine cask 10. eight notes
Octavia (pert to) ...
sister of .. 8. Augustus
wife of .. 10. Mark Antony
Octavian ... 7. Library (Rome's 1st) 16. committee of eight (one of)
octet, octette ... 7. huitain 12. group of eight
October (pert to) ...
bird .. 8. bobolink
birthstone .. 4. opal 5. beryl
Club .. 9. political
drink .. 3. ale
month .. 5. tenth
octogenarian ... 13. eighty–year–old
octopod ... 9. eight arms, eight legs
Octopoda (Roder) ... 8. mollusks (8–armed) 9. argonauts, octopuses
octopus ... 5. poulp (poulpe)
octroi, octroy ... 3. tax 9. privilege 10. concession
ocular ... 3. eye (pert to) 5. optic, sight 6. visual 10. ophthalmic
oculus ... 3. eye 14. Corona Borealis

odd... 4. orra, rare 5. droll, extra,
outré, queer 6. uneven, unique
7. azygous, bizarre, strange, unequal,
unusual 8. unpaired 9. eccentric,
remaining, unmatched 10. occasional
oddity... 9. queerness 11. peculiarity,
singularity 12. eccentricity,
idiosyncrasy
odds... 6. gamble 7. dispute, quarrel
8. gambling, variance 9. advantage
10. difference, dissension, inequality
11. probability 12. disagreement
13. probabilities
odds and ends... 4. orts 6. refuse,
scraps 7. mixture, remains
8. remnants 10. miscellany
ode... 4. like (suff), poem 5. psalm
8. canticle, serenata
ode (type)... 7. Lesbian, regular
8. Horatian, Pindaric 9. irregular
odeon... 4. hall 7. gallery, theater
Odin (pert to)...
attendants.. 9. Valkyries
god of.. 3. war 6. poetry, wisdom
hall.. 8. Valhalla
horse.. 8. Sleipner
son.. 4. Tyre, Vali 6. Balder
Teutonic name.. 5. Woden
wife.. 5. Frigg
odious... 4. foul, vile 5. nasty
7. hateful 8. infamous, terrible
odium... 6. hatred, infamy 9. antipathy
10. abhorrence, opprobrium
11. detestation
odontist... 7. dentist
odontology (science of)... 5. teeth
9. dentistry
odor, odour... 4. fume, funk, nose
5. aroma, fetor, nidor, scent, smell
6. flavor 7. essence, malodor,
perfume 9. fragrance, redolence
odor, meat cooking... 5. fumet
(fumette)
odorous... 8. aromatic, fragrant,
redolent, smelling
Odysseus (pert to)...
chieftain.. 9. Trojan War
dog.. 5. Argos
father.. 7. Laertes
hero of.. 10. The Odyssey (Homer)
king of.. 6. Ithaca (Gr)
magic herb.. 4. moly
modern name.. 7. Ulysses
wife.. 8. Penelope
oecist... 9. colonizer
oecodomic... 13. architectural
Oedipus (pert to)...
daughter.. 8. Antigone
father.. 5. Laius (King of Thebes)
mother.. 7. Jocasta
oeno (comb form)... 4. wine
oenomancy... 12. wine prophecy
oenophilist... 9. wine lover
oenopoetic... 10. wine making
oestrus... 4. fury 5. sting 6. desire,
frenzy 7. impulse 8. stimulus
of... 2. in, on 4. over, upon, with
5. about, avent 10. indication
of (pert to)...
a chamber.. 7. cameral
a class (related).. 7. generic
a father.. 6. agnate

a flock.. 6. gregal
a forefather.. 9. ancestral
a grandfather.. 4. aval
all.. 3. ava
a mother.. 7. cognate
an epoch.. 4. eral
an order.. 7. ordinal
a wife.. 7. uxorial
common gender.. 7. epicene
each.. 3. ana
earth.. 4. geal
equal value.. 10. comparable
French.. 2. du 3. des
great importance.. 7. capital
9. momentous
high standing.. 8. sterling
little importance.. 5. petty 7. trivial
morning.. 5. matin 7. matinal
New Stone Age.. 9. Neolithic
no avail.. 6. futile
nostrils.. 6. narine
old age.. 8. gerontal
planet's path.. 7. orbital
recent times.. 6. lately 9. latter-day
reign.. 6. regnal
river banks.. 8. riparian
same family.. 7. cognate, germane
sound.. 5. tonal
summer.. 7. estival
tears.. 8. lacrimal
the country.. 5. rural
the mouth.. 4. oral
the third degree.. 7. cubical
the throat.. 5. gular
the tongue.. 7. glossal
the wrist.. 6. carpal
this day.. 9. hodiernal
thread color.. 7. ficelle
winter.. 6. hiemal
yore.. 5. olden
off... 3. ill 4. agee, away, doff
6. aside 8. begone, insane, remote
7. distant, tainted 9. dissonant,
erroneous, imperfect, right-hand
10. unemployed
offal... 5. filth 6. ordure, refuse
7. carrion, garbage, rubbish
offbeat... 14. unconventional
off-color... 6. risqué 7. dubious
8. inferior
offend... 3. cag, sin, vex 4. miff
5. anger, annoy, pique, wound
6. assail, insult, revolt 7. affront, do
wrong, mortify 9. displease
offender... 6. sinner 8. criminal
9. wrongdoer 10. malefactor
12. transgressor
offense... 3. sin 5. crime, delit, fault,
grief, malum 6. delict, felony, insult
7. outrage, umbrage 8. trespass
9. indignity 10. resentment
11. delinquency, misdemeanor,
stellionate
offensive... 4. foul, ugly 6. attack,
odious, ribald, vulgar 7. abusive,
eyesore, fulsome, harmful, obscene
8. invading, shocking 9. assailant,
attacking, insulting, obnoxious,
repugnant, revolting 10. aggressive,
malodorous, scurrilous
11. approbrious, displeasing,
distasteful 12. disagreeable

13. transgressive
offer... 3. bid 6. adduce, tender
   7. proffer, propine, propose
   8. immolate, overture 9. ultimatum
offered for sale... 6. vended
   9. auctioned
offering... 4. gift 6. corban
   7. deodate, present 8. oblation
   9. sacrifice
offering resistance... 8. renitent
offhand... 8. careless, informal,
   slapdash 9. extempore, impromptu
   10. carelessly, nonchalant
   11. extemporary 12. nonchalantly
   15. autoschediastic
office... 4. duty, post, rite, wike (obs)
   5. place, trust 7. station
   8. ceremony, function, position
   9. situation 11. appointment
office (pert to)...
   chief.. 7. manager
   divine.. 9. akoluthia
   for the dead.. 7. trental
   holder.. 8. placeman
   of a datary (Roman Curia).. 7. dataria
   of a ruler.. 7. regency
   relinquish (to).. 5. demit
   third hour.. 6. tierce
officer... 6. tindal 7. bailiff, command,
   conduct, general, manager, marshal,
   sheriff 8. adjutant, avigator, director
   9. constable, policeman, president
officer (pert to)...
   assistant.. 4. aide
   Brit Royal Guard.. 4. exon
   chief executive.. 3. dey 4. czar
   5. mayor 7. emperor, monarch,
   premier 8. governor 9. president
   10. chancellor
   church.. 5. elder 6. sexton
   civil law.. 6. notary, police 7. bailiff,
   marshal, sheriff 9. constable,
   policeman 10. magistrate
   club.. 7. steward
   corrupt.. 7. grafter
   despotic.. 6. satrap
   diplomatic.. 7. attaché
   Jewish Relig.. 6. parnas
   King's stables.. 6. avener
   monastic.. 5. prior
   naval.. 6. ensign, yeoman
   parish.. 6. beadle, bedral
   ship's.. 9. boatswain (boson)
   weights, measures.. 6. sealer
official... 6. formal 9. authentic
   10. functional 13. authoritative
official (pert to)...
   command.. 5. edict
   despotic.. 6. satrap
   game.. 5. judge 6. umpire 7. referee
   government.. 10. bureaucrat
   insurance.. 7. actuary 8. adjuster
   itinerant (Hist).. 6. missus
   mark.. 5. stamp
   order (RCCh).. 8. rescript
   proclamation.. 5. ukase 6. decree
   record.. 5. actum
   state.. 8. governor 9. secretary
officious... 4. cool, pert 5. saucy
   6. formal 8. arrogant, impudent,
   official 9. pragmatic 10. meddlesome
   11. efficacious, impertinent,

pragmatical 12. contemptuous
officiousness... 10. pragmatism
offing... 10. background
offshoot... 3. rod 5. scion 6. branch,
   member 8. addition 9. by–product
   10. descendant 12. organization
offspring... 3. son 4. brat, seed
   5. child, fruit, issue, sprig 6. origin,
   result 7. produce, product, progeny
   8. fountain 9. posterity
   10. descendant
oficina... 5. works 6. office 7. factory
   10. laboratory
often... 3. oft 9. many times
   10. frequently, repeatedly 11. over
   and over 13. time after time
ogdoad... 5. eight 10. eight group
ogee... 4. gula 5. talon 7. molding
   9. cyma recta 11. cyma reversa
ogle... 3. eye 4. gaze, leer 5. stare
   7. examine
Ogpu... 8. Gay–Pay–Oo (Russ secret
   service)
O Henry... 6. Porter (Wm Sydney)
Ohio...
   capital.. 8. Columbus
   city.. 5. Akron 6. Dayton, Toledo
   9. Cleveland 10. Cincinnati
   first settlement.. 8. Marietta
   hero.. 12. Anthony Wayne (Gen)
   lake.. 4. Erie
   name meaning (Indian).. 14. Beautiful
   River
   State admission.. 11. Seventeenth
   State motto.. 27. With God All Things
   are Possible
   State nickname.. 7. Buckeye
oil... 3. ben, fat 4. balm, ghee
   5. bribe, oleum 6. aceite, anoint,
   asarum, grease, olanin 8. flattery,
   medicate, painting 9. lubricant,
   lubricate, petroleum 10. illuminant
oil (pert to)...
   beetle.. 5. meloe
   berry.. 5. olive
   bird.. 8. guachare
   cask.. 4. rier
   class.. 5. fatty, fixed 6. animal
   7. mineral 8. volatile 9. essential,
   vegetable
   cloth.. 8. linoleum
   coal.. 8. photogen
   comb form.. 2. ol 3. ole
   fish.. 7. escolar
   flask.. 4. olpe
   gauge.. 9. oleometer
   glands (birds).. 9. uropygial
   11. elaeodochon
   lamp.. 7. lucigen
   mineral.. 7. naphtha
   plant.. 6. sesame 9. castor–oil
   prefix.. 2. ol
   rock.. 5. shale 9. limestone
   seed.. 3. til (teel) 6. sesame
   7. linseed 8. rapeseed 10. castor
   bean, cottonseed
   skin.. 5. sebum
   stone.. 4. hone 9. whetstone
   term.. 5. oleic
   tree.. 4. eboe (ebo), tung 5. mahua
   6. illupi 7. oil palm 9. candlenut,
   castor–oil

tube .. **5.** vitta
whale .. **5.** sperm
oil of ...
cloves .. **7.** eugenol
myrcia .. **6.** bay oil
orange blossoms .. **6.** neroil
roses .. **4.** otto **5.** attar (atar)
salt .. **7.** bittern
oils ... **10.** elaeoptene (elaeopten) (opp
of stearoptene)
oily ... **3.** fat **4.** glib **5.** bland, oleic,
suave **6.** olease, supple **7.** pinguid
8. unctuous **9.** compliant, plausible
10. flattering, oleaginous
11. insinuating, subservient
12. hypocritical
oily liquids ... **3.** tar **6.** cresol, octane
7. aniline, picamar **8.** creosote
oily tissue ... **3.** fat
ointment ... **4.** balm, cere, lard, nard
5. salve **6.** balsam, carron, cerate,
ceroma, grease **7.** pomatum, unguent
8. liniment **9.** spikenard, veromyron
10. petrolatum **11.** embrocation
Oise (France) ... **5.** Aisne (tributary),
river **10.** department
Ojibway secret order ... **4.** mide
(meda) **9.** midewiwin
ojo ... **5.** oasis
OK ... **6.** righto **7.** correct
Okinawa ...
capital .. **4.** Naha
island group (64) .. **6.** Ryukyu
prefecture of .. **5.** Japan
Oklahoma ...
capital .. **12.** Oklahoma City
city .. **3.** Ada **4.** Enid **5.** Tulsa
6. Lawton **8.** Muskogee
9. Claremore **12.** Bartlesville
Five Civilized Tribes .. **5.** Creek
7. Choctaw **8.** Cherokee, Seminole
9. Chickasaw
lake .. **6.** Texoma
migrant from .. **4.** Okie
mountain .. **5.** Ozark **8.** Ouachita
museum .. **6.** Indian **8.** Woolaroc
native son (famed) .. **10.** Will Rogers
old name .. **15.** Indian Territory
State admission .. **11.** Thirty–third
State bird .. **10.** flycatcher
State flower .. **9.** mistletoe
State motto .. **16.** Labor Omnia Vincit
(Labor Conquers All)
State nickname .. **6.** Sooner
okra ... **5.** bendy, gumbo **6.** mallow
old ... **3.** ald, eld **4.** aged **5.** anile
6. infirm, senile **7.** ancient, antique,
archaic **8.** obsolete **9.** doddering,
senescent, venerable **10.** antiquated
old (pert to) ...
age .. **6.** senile **7.** geratic **8.** gerontic,
senility **10.** geriatrics (Med),
senescence **11.** gerontology
ancient (very) .. **7.** Ogygian
billy, granny .. **5.** squaw
fashioned .. **4.** fogy **7.** antique
9. primitive **12.** conservative
hat .. **5.** trite **9.** out-of-date
maid .. **5.** prude **10.** fussbudget
man .. **5.** elder, timer **6.** codger,
gaffer, geezer, Nestor **8.** kangaroo
10. fuddy–duddy

sailor .. **3.** tar **4.** salt
saying .. **3.** saw **5.** adage, maxim
time .. **3.** eld **4.** syne
woman .. **3.** hag **4.** fogy **5.** crone
6. dotard, gammar
womanish .. **5.** anile **6.** senile
10. effeminate
Old (pert to) ...
Bailey .. **12.** English court
Bay State .. **13.** Massachusetts
Dominion .. **8.** Virginia
Empire .. **4.** Maya
English alphabet .. **10.** Anglo–Saxon
Faithful .. **6.** geyser
Franklin State .. **9.** Tennessee
Gentleman Harry .. **5.** Devil
Gooseberry .. **5.** Devil, Satan
Glory .. **15.** Stars and Stripes
Guard (Waterloo) .. **9.** Napoleon's
Hickory .. **13.** Andrew Jackson
Ironsides .. **15.** USS Constitution
Kingdom .. **7.** Memphis (Egypt)
Lady of Threadneedle Street ..
13. Bank of England
Line State .. **8.** Maryland
Man of the Mountain .. **7.** Profile (The)
Noll .. **14.** Oliver Cromwell
North Church .. **12.** Christ Church
North State .. **13.** North Carolina
Rough and Ready .. **16.** (Gen) Zachary
Taylor
Serpent .. **5.** Satan
Sod .. **4.** Erin **7.** Ireland
Sol .. **3.** sun
Stone Age .. **11.** Paleolithic
Three Stars .. **8.** (Gen) Grant
World .. **7.** Eastern
olden ... **6.** bygone
older ... **5.** elder **6.** senior **8.** ancestor
oldest ... **4.** dean **6.** eldest **7.** stalest
Old Testament (pert to) ...
Books (number) .. **10.** Thirty–nine
Elohim .. **3.** God (The Hexateuch)
Hexateuch .. **13.** first Six Books
Land of riches .. **5.** Ophir
objects (sacred) .. **4.** Urim
7. Thummim
Pentateuch .. **10.** Law of Moses
14. first Five Books
writer .. **7.** Elohist (The Hexateuch)
Old World (pert to) ...
ape .. **7.** Primate **10.** Catarrhina
carnivore .. **5.** genet
falcon .. **5.** saker
herb .. **5.** tansy
lizard .. **5.** Agama
shrub .. **4.** Olax
oleaginous ... **4.** oily **5.** oleic
8. unctuous
oleander ... **6.** Nerium
11. rhododaphne **12.** rhododendron
oleoresin ... **5.** anime, elemi **6.** balsam
7. copaiba
oleum ... **3.** oil
olfaction ... **7.** osmesis **8.** smelling
12. sense of smell
olfactory organ ... **4.** nose **8.** olfactor
olid ... **4.** foul **5.** fetid **6.** rancid, smelly
. malodorous **11.** strong smell
oligarchy ... **10.** rule by a few
olinda bug ... **6.** weevil
olio ... **4.** olla, stem **6.** medley

7. mixture 8. chowchow
9. burlesque, potpourri
10. collection, hodgepodge
11. olla–podrida
oliphant... 8. elephant 9. ivory horn
oliprance... 4. romp, show 7. jollity
11. merrymaking, ostentation
olive (pert to)...
  branch.. 5. child, peace 6. symbol
  (peace)
  color.. 11. yellow–green
  dun.. 3. fly (fishing)
  enzyme.. 6. olease
  family.. 8. Oleaceae
  fly.. 3. dun 4. gnat 5. quill
  gray.. 10. Scotch gray
  gum.. 6. olivil
  overripe.. 5. drupe
  stuffed.. 6. pimola
  true.. 4. Olea
  wild.. 8. oleaster
  yard.. 6. olivet
  yellow.. 9. moss green 10. chartreuse
olla... 3. jug, pot 4. olio 8. palm leaf
(palmyra) 11. olla–podrida
olla–podrida... 4. hash, olio 6. medley
10. hodgepodge
oloroso... 6. sherry
olpe... 5. flask 8. oenochoë 11. wine
pitcher
olycook, olykoek... 7. cruller
8. doughnut
Olympia... 4. ship 7. capital (Wash)
8. heavenly 9. sanctuary (anc)
Olympiad... 14. four–year period
Olympian god... 4. Ares, Zeus
6. Apollo, Hermes 8. Dionysus,
Hercules, Poseidon 10. Hephaestus
Olympian goddess... 4. Hera
6. Athena, Hestia 7. Artemis,
Demeter 9. Aphrodite
Olympic cupbearer... 8. Ganymede
Olympic Games (pert to)...
  honor of.. 4. Zeus
  period.. 14. four years apart
  revival site.. 6. Athens (1896)
  site (first).. 4. Elis 7. Olympia
  time of games.. 8. four days
Olympieion, Olympium... 6. temple
(Athens)
Olympus (Gr)... 3. sky 5. Mount
6. heaven 8. mountain
Olympus (Hind)... 4. Meru
Omaha... 4. city (Neb) 5. Sioux
6. Indian
Omar Khayyam (pert to)...
  country.. 4. Iran 6. Persia
  fish (fabled).. 3. mah
  poem.. 8. Rubaiyat
omasum... 9. manyplies 10. psalterium
12. third stomach
ombro (comb form)... 4. rain
ombrometer... 9. rain gauge
omega... 3. end 4. last 5. final
6. letter (Gr)
omen... 4. bode, sign 5. abode, knell,
token 6. augury 7. auspice, portent,
presage 8. forebode, foreshow
9. abodement 10. divination
15. prognostication
omer... 5. ephah, sheaf 9. fifty days
(Passover to Pentecost)

ominous... 4. dour, trim 8. sinister
9. ferocious 10. inexorable,
portentous 12. inauspicious
omission... 4. want 5. caret, error
7. neglect 9. oversight
10. deficiency, leaving out
13. nonobservance
omission of end syllables...
7. apocope
omission of words... 8. ellipsis
omit... 4. dele, pass, skip 5. elide
6. delete, ignore 7. exclude
11. leave undone
omitting... 7. elision 9. excepting,
excluding 10. precluding
omneity... 7. allness
16. all–comprehensive
omnipotent... 6. divine 8. almighty
9. unequaled, unlimited
11. all–powerful
omniscient... 4. wise 6. divine
7. learned 10. all–knowing
omnitude... 7. allness 8. totality
12. universality
omnivorous... 6. greedy 9. all–eating
10. gluttonous
omoplate... 7. scapula
omphalos... 3. hut 4. knob 5. altar,
navel 6. center 9. umbilicus
on... 2. at 4. atop, upon 5. above,
ahead, along 6. toward 7. against,
forward 10. concerning
13. juxtaposition
On (Bib)... 7. Baalbek 8. holy city
10. Heliopolis (Egypt) 12. City of the
Sun
on (pert to)...
  account of.. 3. for
  all sides.. 5. about 6. around
  and on.. 7. forever, tedious
  9. tediously
  behalf of.. 3. for
  dit.. 5. rumor 6. report
  going.. 7. forward 10. proceeding
  grand scale.. 4. epic
  hand.. 4. here 7. present 9. available
  high.. 5. aloft
  other side.. 4. over 6. across
  sheltered side.. 4. alee
  this side.. 3. cis (pref) 9. cisalpine
  10. cismontane, cispontine
  windward side.. 8. aweather
onager... 3. ass 5. kiang 8. catapult
once in a while... 9. erstwhile
10. now and then 12. occasionally
once upon a time... 6. one day
7. the past, time was 8. formerly
10. the long ago
Oncorhynchus... 6. salmon
ondoyant... 4. wavy (art)
one... 2. an, un 3. ace, ain, ein
4. unit 5. alone, unity, whole
6. person, single 9. unmarried
10. individual
one (pert to)...
  after the other.. 8. serially, seriatim
  12. successfully
  bearing heraldic arms.. 7. armiger
  behind the other.. 6. tandem
  born in serfdom.. 4. neif
  bringing good luck.. 6. mascot
  by one.. 6. apiece, singly 10. one at

a time 12. individually
comb form.. 3. uni 4. mono
curious.. 6. gossip 8. quidnunc
despondent in views.. 9. pessimist
fond of women.. 11. philogynist
footed.. 6. uniped
frantic for freedom..
  15. eleutheromaniac
gigantic in size.. 5. giant, titan
happy in views.. 8. optimist
horse.. 5. petty 6. little 8. inferior
  10. second-rate 13. insignificant
in a thousand.. 6. oddity 7. paragon,
  prodigy
in second childhood.. 6. dotard
instructed in secret system.. 5. epopt
  8. initiate
living on another.. 8. parasite
moving stealthily.. 7. prowler
sided.. 5. askew 7. partial
  10. prejudiced, unilateral
thousand.. 3. mil
time.. 7. quondam 8. formerly
undergoing change.. 6. mutant
oneberry... 9. hackberry
  14. partridgeberry
one devoted to...
deviltry.. 7. hellion
fast driving.. 4. jehu 7. speeder
indolence.. 10. daydreamer,
  lotus-eater
own opinion.. 5. bigot
physical feats.. 7. athlete
pursuit.. 3. ist (suff)
table delicacies.. 7. epicure
onefold... 6. simple, single 7. sincere
  9. guileless
onegite... 8. amethyst
Oneida... 6. Indian 8. Iroquois
  9. Community (NY)
oneiros... 5. dream
oneirotic... 8. dreams (pert to)
enoism... 8. egoism, monism
oneness... 5. union, unity 7. concord
  8. identity, sameness 9. agreement,
  aloneness, constancy 10. loneliness,
  singleness, uniformity, uniqueness
  11. singularity 13. undividedness
one of...
ancient race.. 4. Mede 7. Iberian
Buddhist precepts.. 6. nidana
Persian dynasty.. 8. Sassanid
religious sect.. 10. Anabaptist
the Bears.. 4. Ursa
the Greek Wise Men.. 6. Thales
the initiated.. 5. epopt
twins.. 5. gemel (Her)
onerous... 4. load 5. heavy 6. burden
  7. onerose 9. difficult, laborious,
  ponderous 10. burdensome,
  oppressive 12. impedimental
one versed in...
children's diseases.. 12. pediatrician
law.. 6. legist
literature.. 6. savant 9. literatus
memory.. 9. mnemonist
politics.. 9. statesman
religious law.. 8. canonist
resources, wealth.. 9. economist
one who...
absconds.. 6. eloper 8. decamper,

deserter
appropriates.. 9. pre-emptor
attacks.. 9. aggressor
believes in all religions.. 6. omnist
believes in personal God.. 5. deist
believes in self.. 9. solipsist
beseeches.. 7. pleader
brings meat to royal table.. 7. dapifer,
  steward
cherishes.. 8. fosterer
collects voluntary taxes.. 6. tither
conveys property.. 7. alienor
dies for a cause.. 6. martyr
differs.. 4. anti 9. dissenter, dissident
disowns.. 10. repudiator
displays learning.. 6. pedant
disposes by will.. 7. devisor
edits.. 7. reviser
feigns illness.. 10. malingerer
fights for cause.. 8. crusader
forsakes faith principles.. 8. apostate
frustrates a plan.. 7. marplot
gives up.. 9. abnegator
grants by deed.. 7. remiser
hates argument.. 10. misologist
hates people.. 11. misanthrope
holds office.. 2. in 9. incumbent
inculcates.. 7. infuser 9. instiller
inflicts retribution.. 7. nemesis
misuses authority.. 6. satrap
plunders.. 6. sacker 8. pillager
practises palmistry.. 11. chiromancer
prevents entrance.. 5. hajib
quarrels.. 5. rowdy
removes nuisance.. 6. abator
rules, manages.. 6. gorent
sells provisions to troops.. 6. sutler
shoots from ambush.. 6. sniper
sponges.. 6. cadger 8. parasite
slays.. 6. bidei
summons spirits   8. evocator
testifies.. 8. deponent
transfers property.. 7. alienor
ongall... 5. onset 6. attack
onion... 3. set (bulbs) 4. boll, bulb,
  cepa, leek 5. chive, cibol, pearl,
  reeve 6. Allium 7. Bermuda, onionet,
  shallot 8. eschalot, rareripe, scallion
onkos (Gr)... 7. topknot
only... 4. just, lone, mere, sole
  5. chief 6. lonely, merely, simple,
  simply, single, singly, solely
  8. uniquely 11. exclusively
  13. companionless 14. above all
  others
onocentaur... 3. ape 5. demon
  (fabled)
onomasticon... 7. lexicon
  10. dictionary, vocabulary (Gr)
onomatology (science of)... 5. names
  11. terminology
onomatopoeic... 6. echoic 9. imitative
  (of natural sound)
onset, onslaught... 6. attack
  7. assault 11. rushing upon, setting
  upon
Ontario...
Bay.. 6. Hudson
capital.. 7. Toronto
city.. 6. Ottawa 7. Timmins
  8. Hamilton
lake.. 9. Great Lake (one of five)

province.. 6. Canada
river.. 6. Ottawa, Thames 7. Niagara
  10. St Lawrence
ontogeny... 9. evolution
ontology *(science of)*... 5. being
  7. reality
onus... 4. duty, load 6. burden, charge
  10. impediment, imposition,
  obligation
onus probandi... 13. burden of proof
onward, onwards... 5. ahead, forth
  6. future, moving 7. forward
  8. forwards, progress 9. in advance
onychauxis... 14. nail overgrowth
onyx... 6. nicolo (niccolo), tecali
ooid... 9. egg–shaped
oology *(science of)*... 8. bird eggs
oomancy *(divination by)*... 4. eggs
oont... 5. camel 13. beast of burden
oop... 4. join 5. unite
oopak, oopack... 3. tea (black)
oorial... 3. sha 5. sheep, urial
ooze... 3. bog 4. drip, leak, seep,
  sipe, soak 5. exude, marsh 6. be
  damp 7. leather 8. transude
  9. percolate
oozy... 4. miry 5. muddy, slimy
opah... 4. fish, soko 8. kingfish
  9. Lampridae
opal... 3. gem 4. blue 5. stone
  7. hyalite 10. pearliness
opal, variety of... 4. wood 5. black,
  noble, pitch, resin 6. common
  7. girasol, hyalite 8. menilite,
  precious 9. cacholong, geyserite,
  harlequin 10. chalcedony
opalescent... 6. pearly 7. opaline
  8. irisated 10. iridescent
opaque... 4. dark 6. obtuse, stupid
  7. obscure 8. eyeshade 10. not
  shining 13. unilluminated 14. not
  transparent
open... 3. ope 4. ajar, bare, free,
  undo 5. agape, begin, clear, frank,
  overt, plain, start, untie 6. candid,
  honest, patent, public, reveal, unbolt,
  unfold, unfurl, unlock, unseal, unstop,
  vacant 7. artless, evident, exposed,
  natural, obvious, sincere, unbosom,
  unclose 8. apparent, commence,
  disclose, expanded, initiate, patulous,
  revealed, unclosed, unfasten
  9. spreading, uncertain, uncovered,
  unfeigned 10. accessible, unreserved
  11. unprotected 12. questionable
open (pert to)...
acknowledgment.. 6. avowal
air.. 8. alfresco
and shut.. 7. assured, obvious
  11. prearranged
bursting.. 10. dehiscence
cabinet.. 7. étagère
country.. 5. veldt, weald
court.. 4. area 5. patio
door.. 6. policy 11. hospitality
eyed.. 7. curious 8. vigilant
  9. attentive, expectant
for discussion.. 4. moot
fully.. 4. wide 9. dehiscent, full–blown
land.. 4. moor 5. heath 6. desert,
  plains
out.. 6. deploy (Mil)

partly.. 3. mid 4. ajar
passage in forests.. 5. glade
to scorn.. 9. derisible
to view.. 5. overt
opening... 2. os 3. bay, gap 4. door,
  gate, hole, loop, pore, rift, slot, vent
  5. cleft, mouth, sinus, start
  6. breach, eyelet, hiatus, outlet,
  portal 7. display, foramen, initial,
  orifice, vacancy 8. aperture, fenestra,
  position 9. admission, beginning
  10. passageway, unfoldment
  11. entranceway, opportunity
opening (pert to)...
chess.. 6. gambit
ear.. 4. burr
enlarge.. 4. ream
from 3rd ventricle (Anat).. 4. pila
having.. 10. fenestrate
in a mold.. 6. ingate
minute.. 5. stoma
narrow.. 4. rima, slot 7. crevice
  9. stenopaic
nasal.. 4. nare
small.. 4. pore 5. chink 6. cranny,
  eyelet, lacuna 7. foramen, orifice,
  pinhole
wide (Bot).. 9. dehiscent
openings... 3. ora 7. stomata
openwork... 6. eyelet 7. Madeira,
  tracery 10. decoration
opera (pert to)...
comic (singer).. 5. buffa, buffo
  7. buffoon
glass.. 7. binocle 9. binocular,
  lorgnette
hat.. 5. crush, gibus 6. topper
kind.. 4. soap 5. horse 8. burletta
singer.. 4. bass, diva 5. buffa, buffo,
  tenor 7. buffoon, soprano 10. basso
  buffo, coloratura
solo.. 4. aria 5. scena
star.. 4. diva 10. prima donna
text.. 8. libretto
opera, composer... 5. Bizet, Gluck,
  Verdi 6. Glinka, Gounod, Handel,
  Hayden, Mozart, Wagner 7. Puccini,
  Rossini 9. Donizetti 11. Deems
  Taylor 14. Rimski–Korsakov (Korsakoff)
opera, drama... 4. Aida 5. Boris,
  Faust, Orfeo, Thais, Tosca
  6. Bohême, Carmen, Coq d'or,
  Daphne, Isolde 7. Alceste
  9. Lohengrin, Pagliacci, Rigoletto
  10. Magic Flute, Prince Igor,
  Tannhäuser 11. Don Giovanni, Il
  Travatore 13. Peter Ibbetson
  14. Tales of Hoffman 15. Hansel
  and Gretel, Madame Butterfly
  16. Marriage of Figaro
operation... 6. action, agency
  7. surgery 8. creation 9. influence
  11. functioning, transaction
operation, surgical... 5. major, minor
  6. trepan 8. excision 9. resection
  10. amputation, castration
  11. exploratory 12. appendectomy,
  hysterectomy 13. tonsillectomy
operative... 6. worker 7. artisan,
  working 8. mechanic 9. detective
operative, become... 5. inure (enure)
operator... 5. agent, quack 6. dealer,

worker 7. creator, handler, surgeon
10. mountebank, speculator
operculum (Bot)... 3. cap, lid
7. stopper 8. covering
operose... 4. busy 8. diligent
9. difficult, laborious 11. painstaking
Ophidia... 6. snakes 8. reptiles,
serpents 9. Serpentes
ophidian... 5. snake, viper 7. serpent
ophiolatry... 12. snake worship
ophthalmic... 6. ocular 7. optical
9. eye region
ophthalmology, science... 6. the eye
opiate... 4. drug, hemp, snow
5. opium 6. heroin 7. anodyne,
cocaine, hashish (hasheesh), soother
8. narcotic 9. analgesic, paregoric
11. somniferous 12. somnifacient
opine... 4. deem 5. judge, think
6. remark 7. opinion, suppose
10. conjecture
opinion... 4. idea, view 6. belief,
esteem, notion, report 7. feeling
8. judgment 9. sentiment
10. estimation, impression, ober
dictum, reputation
opinion (pert to)...
expert.. 9. expertise
expression, common.. 5. theme
expression, formal.. 4. vote
religious, unorthodox.. 6. heresy
opinions (pert to)...
collection.. 9. anthology, symposium
professed.. 5. credo
opium... 4. drug 8. narcotic
10. intoxicant
opium (pert to)...
concentrate.. 6. heroin
derivative (Chem).. 7. meconic
Egyptian.. 8. thebaine
extract.. 7. chandoo (chandu), codeine
8. morphine 9. narcotine
10. papaverine
overuse.. 8. opiumism
poppy seed.. 3. maw
source.. 5. poppy
tincture.. 9. paregoric
variety.. 6. Indian, Smyrna, Turkey
7. Chinese, Persian
opodeldoc... 7. plaster 8. liniment
opodidymus... 7. monster (two–headed)
opossum... 7. Marmosa 9. didelphid,
marsupial, phalanger
opossum (pert to)...
S America.. 5. quica 7. sarigue
variety.. 5. mouse, water, wooly
water.. 5. yapok (yapock)
wood.. 10. silver bell
opponent... 3. foe 4. anti 5. enemy,
rival 7. adverse 8. opposite
9. adversary, combatant
10. antagonist
opportune... 3. fit, pat 5. ready
6. timely 7. apropos 8. suitable
9. expedient, well–timed
10. convenient 11. appropriate
opportunist... 10. politician, vacillator
opportunity... 4. turn 6. chance
7. opening 8. occasion
12. circumstance 16. suitable
occasion
oppose... 3. pit 4. deny, face 5. fight,

rebel 6. expose, oppugn, refute,
resist 7. contest, exhibit, gainsay
8. confront 10. antagonize,
contradict, contravene, counteract
opposed... 3. met 4. anti, vied
5. coped 6. averse, pitted
7. adverse, fronted 8. contrary,
renitent, resisted 9. contested,
withstood 12. oppositional
opposed (pert to)...
against.. 6. pitted
lee.. 5. stoss
to change.. 7. die–hard
11. reactionary 12. conservative
to entad (inward).. 5. ectad
zenith.. 5. nadir
opposite... 5. polar 6. facing
7. adverse, antonym, hostile,
opposed, reverse 8. contrary,
converse 9. different, repugnant
10. opposition 12. antagonistic
13. contradictory 14. contrapositive
opposite (pert to)...
directly.. 10. antipodean
exact.. 8. antipode
in action, in nature.. 5. polar
7. inverse
prefix.. 6. contra
science.. 3. art
to spring tide.. 4. neap
opposition... 9. hostility, opponency
10. antagonism, antithesis, refutation,
resistance 11. contrariety, disapproval
13. contradiction
oppress... 4. rape 5. crush 6. burden,
harass, nither (Scot), ravish
7. depress, swelter 8. distress,
macerate, suppress 9. overpower,
overwhelm, persecute, tyrannize
10. extinguish
oppressive... 5. harsh 6. severe,
stuffy, sultry 7. onerous 8. rigorous
9. ponderous 10. burdensome,
depressing, tyrannical
oppressor... 4. czar (tsar), Nero
6. despot, tyrant 8. autocrat,
burdener 11. Simon Legree
opprobrious... 7. abusive 8. despised,
infamous 9. insulting, offensive
10. scurrilous 11. disgraceful
12. contumelious
opprobrium... 5. odium 6. infamy
8. disgrace 11. malediction
oppugn... 6. assail, oppose
10. controvert, counteract
oppugnant... 7. hostile, opposed
8. contrary 12. antagonistic
13. counteractive
Ops (pert to)...
called also.. 10. Ops Consiva
consort of.. 6. Consus, Saturn
Festival.. 6. Opalia
Greek counterpart.. 4. Rhea
Roman goddess of.. 7. Harvest
opsigamy... 14. old–age marriage
opt... 4. pick 5. elect 6. choose
11. make a choice
optic... 6. ocular, visual 11. optological
optical (pert to)...
device.. 9. stenopaic
glass.. 4. lens
illusion.. 6. mirage

instrument.. 5. prism 7. alidade,
reticle 9. eriometer, optometer
10. microscope
membrane.. 6. retina
organ.. 3. eye
optic defect... 6. myopia
optimistic... 4. rosy 7. hopeful,
roseate 8. cheerful, sanguine
9. expectant 10. auspicious
optimum... 4. best 7. maximum
13. most favorable
option... 6. choice, future (Finan)
7. refusal 8. free will 11. alternative
13. right to choose
optional... 8. elective 9. voluntary
10. permissive 13. not compulsory
opulence... 6. plenty, riches, wealth
9. abundance, affluence, amplitude,
profusion
opulent... 4. rich 6. lavish 7. profuse,
wealthy 8. abundant, affluent
9. luxuriant
opulus... 11. guelder–rose
13. cranberry tree
opus... 4. work 5. étude
10. embroidery, needlework
11. composition
oquassa... 5. trout
oracle... 4. seer 5. sibyl 6. Dodona,
medium, mentor 7. prophet, wise
man 8. Delphian (Delphic)
10. revelation
oracular... 4. wise 5. vatic (vatical)
9. prophetic 10. predictive
11. forecasting
orage... 5. storm 7. tempest
oral... 5. parol, vocal 6. spoken, verbal
10. not written 11. nuncupative
orang... 9. orangutan (orangutang)
orange (pert to)...
Bowl site.. 5. Miami
bird.. 7. tanager
color.. 5. ocher, peach 6. carrot
7. apricot 8. mandarin
flower oil.. 6. meroli
genus.. 5. Citrus
heraldry.. 5. tenné
kind.. 4. mock 5. hedge, navel,
Osage 8. bergamot, mandarin,
Valencia 9. tangerine
leaf.. 6. karamu
marigold.. 9. tangerine
membrane.. 4. zest
mock.. 7. seringa
seed.. 3. pip
Orangeman... 14. North Irelander
orangutan... 4. mias 5. orang, Pongo,
satyr, Simia
orate... 5. plead, speak, spiel
8. harangue
oration... 5. éloge 6. eulogy, prayer,
sermon, speech 7. lecture
8. encomium, petition 9. discourse
orator... 6. rhetor 7. speaker
9. perorator 10. petitioner
11. rhetorician, spellbinder
orator, famed... 5. Bryan (Wm
Jennings) 6. Cicero 9. Churchill
11. Demosthenes
oratory... 6. chapel 7. chantry
9. elocution, eloquence
orb... 3. eye, sun 4. ball, moon, star

5. earth, globe, world 6. bereft,
circle, planet, sphere 7. enclose
8. encircle, insignia, surround
orbed... 5. lunar, round
orbit... 4. path 5. globe, route
6. sphere 7. circuit 10. trajectory
orbit (pert to)...
cavity.. 9. eye socket
curve.. 10. trajectory
of a planet.. 7. ellipse
point.. 5. apsis
point, farthest.. 6. apogee
orc, Orca... 5. whale 7. grampus
orchestra (pert to)...
bells.. 12. glockenspiel
circle.. 7. parquet 8. parterre
small.. 11. symphonette
orchestra instrument group...
brass.. 4. horn, tuba 6. cornet
7. trumpet 8. trombone
percussion.. 4. drum 7. cymbals,
timpani (tympani) 8. triangle
strings.. 5. cello, viola 6. violin
10. contrabass 11. violoncello
wind.. 4. oboe 5. flute 7. bassoon
8. clarinet
orchid... 4. Disa 5. vanda 6. Ophrys
7. Listera, lycaste, pogonia
8. arethusa, Cattleya, Oncidium
9. cymbidium, puttyroot 10. letterleaf
orchid (pert to)...
appendage.. 8. caudicle
handsomest.. 4. Disa
largest.. 10. letterleaf
meal.. 5. salep
petal.. 8. labellum
tuber, root.. 5. salep 7. cullion
Orcus... 3. God (Rom) 5. Hades, Pluto
(Gr) 10. lower world
ordain... 4. plan 5. allot, enact, equip
6. decree 7. appoint, arrange,
command, destine, install 8. canonize
9. institute 10. predestine
ordeal... 4. gaff, test 5. trial
7. sorcery 8. judgment
10. experience (painful)
order... 3. bid 4. fiat, ordo, rank, rule,
sect, will 5. array, class, edict,
genus, money 6. cosmos, decree,
direct, enjoin, genera (pl), manage,
system 7. arrange, command,
dispose, mandate, prepare, verdict
8. regulate, sequence 9. condition,
procedure 10. injunction
11. arrangement
order (pert to)...
back.. 6. remand
connecting.. 6. in turn 8. seriatim
cosmic.. 3. tao 4. rita
for writ.. 7. precipe
good.. 6. eutaxy
grammar.. 5. taxis
judicial.. 4. fiat, writ 7. summons
proper.. 6. kilter
written.. 6. billet
Order, architecture... 5. Doric, Ionic
6. Tuscan 8. Etruscan 10. Corinthian
Order, association... 4. Club 5. Guild
7. DeMolay, Society, St Clare
8. Sodality, Sorority 9. The Garter,
Trappists 10. Fellowship, Fraternity,
Sisterhood 11. Brotherhood, Eastern

Star, Purple Heart **12.** The Rising
Sun
ordered ... **4.** bade, trim **7.** regular
   8. arranged, measured, ordained
   9. regulated
orderly ... **4.** neat, tidy, trim **7.** regular,
   uniform **8.** obedient, peaceful
   9. attendant, regularly, shipshape
   10. methodical, systematic
order of ...
   amphibians .. **5.** Anura
   aquatic animals .. **7.** Cetacea
   holy beings .. **9.** hierarchy
   insects .. **7.** Diptera
   mammals .. **8.** Edentata, Primates
   mites .. **6.** acarid
   the day .. **8.** schedule **12.** instructions
   whales .. **4.** Cete
ordinal ... **6.** number, ritual, serial
   10. succession **11.** Book of Rules
   (Eccl), categorical
ordinance ... **3.** law **4.** rite **5.** bylaw,
   edict **6.** assize, decree **7.** control,
   statute **8.** decretum **9.** allotment,
   direction, enactment, sacrament
   10. management, regulation
ordinarily ... **7.** plainly, usually
   8. commonly **9.** generally, naturally
   11. customarily
ordinary ... **4.** ruck, so–so **5.** judge,
   nomic, plain, prosy, usual
   6. common, normal, tavern
   7. average, natural, prosaic, vulgate
   8. everyday, habitual, mediocre,
   plebeian, workaday **9.** of the Mass
   10. table d'hôte
ordinate ... **6.** ordain **7.** appoint,
   orderly, regular **8.** moderate
   9. harmonize **10.** co–ordinate
ordination ... **5.** order **11.** appointment,
   arrangement, disposition
   12. organization
ordnance ... **4.** guns **5.** armor, orgue
   7. petards, rabinet, weapons
   8. armament, firearms, supplies
   9. artillery, torpedoes
   10. ammunition **14.** apparatus belli
ordo ... **5.** order **11.** publication
ore ... **3.** tin **4.** gold, iron, lead, paco
   5. brass, metal, ochre **6.** copper,
   silver, speiss **7.** mercury, mineral,
   seaweed, uranium **8.** cinnabar,
   tungsten **9.** loadstone (lodestone)
   11. quicksilver
ore (pert to) ...
   box .. **6.** sluice
   deposit .. **4.** lode, mine **7.** bonanza
   fuser .. **7.** smelter
   horizontal layer .. **5.** stope
   impure .. **6.** speiss
   iron .. **5.** ocher **8.** hematite
      9. magnetite
   lead .. **6.** galena
   loading platform .. **4.** plat
   machine separator .. **6.** vanner
   refuse .. **6.** scoria **8.** tailings
   roller .. **9.** edgestone
   silver .. **5.** noble (metal)
   sluice .. **5.** trunk
   stirrer .. **5.** dolly
   tin .. **5.** scove
   trough .. **6.** strake

vein .. **4.** lode **5.** scrin, stope
worthless .. **5.** matte
oread ... **5.** nymph **7.** seamaid
Oregon ...
   capital .. **5.** Salem
   caves .. **11.** Marble Halls
   city .. **6.** Eugene **7.** Astoria, Medford
      8. Portland **12.** Klamath Falls
   crab apple .. **7.** powitch
   emigrant route .. **11.** Oregon Trail
   famed persons .. **4.** Gray (Capt)
      5. Astor, Clark, Lewis
   Indian .. **5.** Modoc **7.** Chinook,
      Klamath **8.** Nez Percé
   mountain .. **4.** Hood **5.** Coast
      8. Cascades
   native nickname .. **7.** webfoot
   river .. **5.** Rogue **7.** Klamath
      8. Columbia **10.** Willamette
   State admission .. **11.** Thirty–third
   State motto .. **8.** The Union
   State nickname .. **6.** Beaver
      13. Sawdust Empire
   wind .. **7.** chinook
oremus ... **9.** let us pray
Oreortyx ... **5.** quail
Orestes (pert to) ...
   father .. **9.** Agamemnon
   friend .. **7.** Pylades
   mother .. **12.** Clytemnestra
   sister .. **7.** Electra
   wife .. **8.** Hermione
orf, orfe ... **3.** ide **4.** fish
orfevrerie ... **7.** jewelry **9.** gold plate
organ (pert to) ...
   anatomy .. **3.** ear, eye **4.** lung, nose
      5. brain, heart, liver **6.** kidney,
      syrinx, tongue, tonsil **7.** viscera (pl)
   bristleliko .. **4.** seta
   deck .. **7.** console
   fish .. **8.** drumfish
   honey-secreting .. **7.** nectary
   plant .. **5.** stoma **7.** tendril
   motion .. **6.** muscle
   respiratory .. **4.** lung
   secretion .. **5.** gland
   spider's spinner .. **9.** spinneret
   stop (music) .. **8.** register
   tactile .. **6.** feeler **8.** tentacle
organic ... **5.** state, vital **6.** innate
   8. inherent **9.** organized
   10. structural **11.** fundamental
   14. constitutional
organic (pert to) ...
   compound .. **5.** amine **6.** enzyme,
      ketone
   disease .. **11.** organopathy
   memory .. **5.** mneme
   radical .. **5.** ethyl
   remains .. **5.** azoic
   soil .. **5.** humus
organism (pert to) ...
   bacterial .. **4.** germ **7.** microbe
   body of .. **4.** soma
   elementary .. **5.** monad
   minute .. **5.** spore **6.** amoeba
   pelagic .. **6.** nekton
   plant .. **5.** spore
   potential .. **7.** idorgan
   sea .. **6.** nekton **7.** benthos
      8. plankton
   type .. **5.** plant **6.** animal **9.** vegetable

vegetable.. 4. tree 5. plant
organization... 4. bloc, sect, unit
   5. cadre, guild, party, setup
   6. empire 11. association,
   corporation 12. constitution
   13. establishment 14. classification
organized body... 5. corps, posse
organized matter... 5. fauna, flora
   6. living, nekton 7. animate, benthos
   8. plankton
organology, science... 10. phrenology
   13. splanchnology
organoscopy... 10. phrenology
orgueil... 5. pride 11. haughtiness
orgy... 4. lark, romp 5. binge, revel,
   rites (anc), spree 6. frolic, ritual,
   shindy 7. debauch, revelry, shindig,
   wassail 8. carousal 11. celebration,
   merrymaking
oribi... 7. bleebok, Ourebia 8. antelope
oriel... 3. bay 6. recess, window
   7. balcony, gallery, portion
   8. corridor 10. moucharaby
   11. meshrabiyeh (Moham)
orient... 4. dawn 7. eastern, shining,
   sunrise 8. oriental, pellucid
   11. resplendent
Orient... 4. Asia, East 6. Levant
oriental (pert to)...
   abode, gateway.. 3. dar
   animal.. 4. zebu
   archangel.. 5. Uriel
   beverage.. 6. arrack
   building.. 6. pagoda
   burden bearer.. 5. hamal
   cap (sheepskin).. 6. calpac (calpack)
   caravansary.. 4. khan 5. serai
   6. imaret
   carpet.. 4. kali
   carriage.. 10. jinrikisha (jinricksha)
   cart, wagon.. 5. araba
   chief.. 4. Khan 6. Mikado
   Christian.. 5. Uniat
   corn.. 4. para
   cosmetic.. 4. kohl
   council.. 5. Divan
   cymbals.. 4. zels
   deity.. 3. Bel
   destiny.. 6. Kismet
   disease.. 8. beriberi
   dish.. 4. rice 5. pilau (pilaw) 6. pilaff
   8. chop suey, chow mein
   drug.. 5. opium 6. heroin 7. hashish
   (hasheesh)
   drum.. 6. tom–tom
   dulcimer.. 6. santir
   fan.. 3. ogi
   food.. 4. rice 5. salep
   garment.. 3. aba 6. sarong
   guitar.. 5. sitar
   head cover.. 6. turban
   hospice.. 6. imaret
   inn.. 5. serai
   instrument (Mus).. 7. samisen
   laborer.. 6. coolie (cooly)
   leader.. 4. amir (ameer)
   liquor.. 4. sake, saki
   litter.. 5. dooly (doolie) 9. palanquin
   lute.. 3. tar
   maid.. 4. amah, ayah, eyah
   manservant.. 5. hamal 6. coolie
   marketplace.. 6. bazaar

   monkey.. 7. macaque
   nurse.. 4. amah, ayah (governess)
   obeisance.. 6. salaam (salam)
   pagoda.. 3. taa
   people.. 4. Sere (anc) 5. Asian, Malay
   6. Indian 7. Chinese, Eastern, Tartars
   (Tatars) 8. Japanese
   10. Mohammedan
   pipe.. 8. narghile
   rice paste.. 3. ame
   rug.. 8. sedjadeh 11. Baluchistan
   ruler.. 4. Khan, Shah 5. sahib (saheb)
   6. caliph (calif), sultan
   sabre.. 8. scimitar
   sailor.. 6. lascar
   sash.. 3. obi
   tambourine.. 5. daira
   taxi.. 7. ricksha (rickshaw)
   10. jinrikisha
   trousers (women).. 9. shaksheer
   vessel (sailing).. 4. dhow, saic
   wagon.. 5. araba
   warehouse.. 6. godown
   wind.. 7. monsoon
   worker.. 6. coolie (cooly)
orifice... 4. hole, lura, pore, vent
   5. inlet, mouth, porus, stoma
   6. outlet, porule 7. chimney,
   opening, ostiole 8. aperture,
   bunghole, spiracle
origin... 3. nee 4. rise, root, seed
   5. alpha, birth, cause, start
   6. nature, parent, source 7. genesis
   9. beginning, etymology, inception,
   parentage 10. inconabula, provenance
   11. provenience 12. commencement,
   fountainhead
original... 3. new 5. basic, first, novel
   6. fontal, native, primal, primer,
   unused 7. genuine, pattern, primary
   8. pristine 9. aborigine, beginning,
   inventive, primitive 10. inimitable
   11. fundamental, origination
   12. commencement
original copy... 6. ectype
originate... 4. coin, open, rise, stem
   5. arise, begin, breed, start
   6. author, create, derive, invent
   7. emanate, produce 8. generate,
   initiate 11. etymologize
originator... 5. cause, maker
   7. creator 8. inventor, producer
   9. contriver 10. discoverer
oriole... 5. pirol 6. golden, hooded,
   loriot, Mimeta 7. orchard
   8. Bullock's 9. Baltimore, Icteridae
Orion (pert to)...
   Astron.. 7. Dog Star 10. Canis Major
   11. Orion's Hound 13. constellation
   color.. 11. Holland blue
   Gr Myth.. 6. hunter
   Jacob's Staff.. 10. Yard and Ell
   13. Golden Yardarm
   slain by.. 7. Artemis
   star.. 5. Rigel
orison... 6. prayer
Orkney Islands, Scotland...
   capital.. 8. Kirkwall
   Firth.. 8. Pentland
   fishing grounds.. 4. haaf
   island, largest.. 6. Pomona
   President, Supreme Court.. 4. foud

stone tower (Prehist).. 5. broch
orle (Her)... 6. border, fillet, wreath
   7. bearing, chaplet 10. escutcheon
   (voided)
Orloff... 5. horse 7. diamond (Russ,
   194 3/4 carats)
orlop... 4. deck (lowest)
Ormazd (Pers)... 5. deity (supreme)
ormer... 7. abalone 8. ear shell
ornament... 4. ouch, semé 5. adorn,
   decor, gutta, honor 6. amulet,
   brooch, emboss, finery, sequin
   7. antefix 8. appliqué, decorate
   9. embellish 10. decoration
   13. embellishment
ornament (pert to)...
   apex.. 6. finial
   ball.. 6. pompon
   bell–shaped.. 9. clochette
   Bible.. 4. Urim
   boat–shaped.. 3. nef
   brilliant.. 4. gaud 5. spang 6. sequin,
   tinsel 7. spangle
   circular.. 7. rosette
   delicate.. 7. tracery
   diamond–shaped.. 11. epigonation
   dress.. 5. jabot 9. stomacher
   10. embroidery
   egg–shaped.. 3. ove
   hair, head.. 4. comb 5. tiara
   8. barrette
   indented.. 5. chase
   Japanese girdle.. 4. inro
   leaves and grapes.. 6. pampre
   magical.. 6. amulet
   mantel.. 7. bibelot, trinket
   pendant.. 6. bangle, tassel 7. earring
   9. lavaliere (lavalier)
   pretentious.. 6. rococo
   protuberant.. 4. boss
   raised design.. 7. brocade
   scroll–like.. 6. voluto
   set of.. 6. parure
   setting in.. 5. inlay 7. emblema
   silverware.. 7. gadroon
   spiral.. 5. helix
   terminal.. 6. finial
   wall.. 6. plaque, sconce
ornamental (pert to)...
   bottle.. 8. decanter
   button.. 4. stud
   description.. 5. fancy 10. decorative
   lace edge.. 5. picot 7. tatting
   metal.. 6. niello
   raised.. 7. brocade
   stand.. 7. étagère
   vase.. 3. urn
ornamented... 6. chased, etched,
   tooled 8. engraved
ornate... 3. gay 5. fancy 6. florid,
   tawdry 7. adorned 9. decorated
ornery... 8. perverse, stubborn
   9. malicious 11. ill–tempered
ornithoid... 8. birdlike
ornithology (study of)... 5. birds
ornithon... 6. aviary
oro... 4. gold 5. money
Oro... 3. God (Tahiti)
oro (comb form)... 5. month, serum
   8. mountain
orology (science of)... 9. mountains
orotund... 7. pompous 9. bombastic

orp... 4. fret, weep
Orpheus (pert to)...
   astronomy.. 6. Cygnus
   eighteenth century.. 6. Handel
   father.. 6. Apollo
   mother.. 8. Calliope
   poet.. 8. Thracian
   reference.. 6. Orphic
   river.. 6. Hebrus
   wife.. 8. Eurydice
Orphic... 3. egg (Creation's) 5. hymns
   7. tablets (gold) 13. Book of the
   Dead (rites)
orphrey... 10. embroidery (gold)
orpit (Scot)... 7. fretful
orra... 3. odd 5. oddly 10. not
   matched, occasional, unemployed
   13. miscellaneous
ort... 3. end 4. bits 5. scrap
   6. refuse, scraps 7. remnant
   8. leavings, leftover
orthodox... 7. Trinity 8. accepted,
   approved, believer, standard
   9. canonical, customary
   12. conventional
Orthodox Moslem... 5. hanif
orthography... 8. spelling
ortolan... 7. bunting 8. bobolink, sora
   rail, wheatear
Oryx... 5. beisa 7. gazelle, gemsbok
   8. antelope, leucoryx
os... 4. bone 5. mouth, osker (Geol)
   7. opening
Osage... 5. river 6. Indian (Sioux)
   10. orange tree
Osaka, Japan... 7. capital
   10. prefecture
oscillate... 3. wag 4. rock, sway, vary
   5. swing, waver, weave 7. vibrate
   9. fluctuate
Oscines... 12. singing birds
oscitancy... 6. gaping 7. yawning
   8. dullness, lethargy 10. drowsiness
oscitant... 4. dull 6. drowsy, gaping,
   sleepy 7. yawning 8. careless,
   sluggish 9. apathetic
osculate... 4. buss, kiss
osculation... 4. kiss 7. contact, kissing
osier... 3. rod 4. wand 6. sallow,
   willow 7. dogwood
Osiris, Egypt (pert to)...
   brother.. 3. Set (Seth)
   crown.. 4. atef
   enemy.. 3. Set 7. brother
   father.. 3. Geb
   god.. 9. fertility 10. underworld
   god (Gr).. 8. Dionysus
   husband of.. 4. Isis
   king of.. 5. Egypt
   mother.. 3. Nut
   seat.. 6. Abydos
   son.. 5. Horus 6. Anubis
Osmanli... 4. Turk 8. language
osmesis... 8. smelling 9. olfaction
osmosis... 10. absorption
   12. infiltration
osprey... 4. hawk 7. feather (hat)
   8. fish hawk 9. ossifrage
   10. breakbones
ossature... 8. skeleton 9. framework
   (Arch)
osse... 4. dare 7. attempt, presage,

promise 8. prophecy
osseous... 4. bony, hard 10. ossiferous
ossifrage... 5. eagle 6. osprey
　11. lammergeier
ossuary... 3. urn 4. tomb
　10. depository 12. charnel house
　13. burial chamber
ostend... 6. reveal 7. exhibit
　8. manifest 11. demonstrate
ostensible... 5. shown 6. avowed
　7. alleged, seeming 8. apparent,
　declared, specious 9. exhibited,
　plausible, professed
ostent... 3. air 4. mien 5. token
　7. portent 10. appearance
ostentatious... 4. arty, vain 5. dashy
　6. sporty 7. pompous
　11. conspicuous, pretentious
ostiole... 4. pore 5. stoma 7. orifice
　8. aperture
ostler... 7. hostler 9. stableman
ostracize... 5. exile, expel 6. banish,
　deport 7. cast out, exclude
　9. extradite 10. expatriate
ostrich... 3. emu 4. Rhea 5. nandu
　8. Struthio 9. cassowary
ostrichlike... 11. struthiform
ostrich tail feather... 3. boo
Otaheite... 6. Tahiti
otalgia... 7. earache
Othello (pert to)...
　opera by.. 5. Verdi
　tragedy by.. 11. Shakespeare
　villain.. 4. Iago
　wife.. 9. Desdemona
other... 2. or 5. alter, ither 6. either,
　second 8. one of two 9. different
　10. additional
others... 7. the rest 9. remaining
otherwise... 2. or 5. alias, ossia, other
　6. or else 9. different 10. contrarily
　11. differently
Othman... 4. Turk 5. Osman 6. sultan
　7. Osmanli, Ottoman, Turkish
Othman's successor... 3. Ali
otiant... 4. idle 8. in repose
　10. unemployed
otiose... 4. idle 6. at ease, futile
　7. sterile, useless 8. indolent
　12. functionless
otium... 7. leisure
otkon... 4. okee (oki) 5. demon
　(Iroquois)
otologist... 6. aurist 9. ear doctor
ottava... 6. eighth, octave
ottava rima... 15. eight–line stanza
ottavino... 7. piccolo
ottoman... 4. seat 5. couch, stool
　7. cricket 9. footstool
Ottoman (pert to)... see also *Othman*
　color.. 9. vermilion
　court.. 5. Porte 12. Sublime Porte
　Empire.. 7. Turkish
　fabric.. 6. ribbed 10. corded silk
　governor.. 3. bey, dey 5. pasha
　leader.. 5. Osman
　native.. 4. Turk
　poetry (couplet).. 4. beyt
　province.. 6. eyalet (former) 7. vilayet
　Turkish.. 7. Osmanli
oubliette... 7. dungeon (top opening)

ouch... 5. bezel, clasp, jewel
　6. brooch 8. ornament
　11. exclamation
ought... 4. duty, must, zero 5. at all,
　aught, owned 6. cipher, should
　7. behoove, nothing 8. anything, in
　need of 9. possessed 10. obligation
Ouija board... 10. planchette
ouk... 4. week
ouphe... 3. elf 6. goblin
Our (pert to)...
　Father.. 11. Lord's Prayer
　French.. 5. notre
　Lady.. 10. Virgin Mary
　Lady's–mint.. 9. spearmint
　Lady's Wand (Astron).. 10. Orion's
　Belt
　Lady's Way.. 6. Zodiac
ourie... 4. cold 5. dingy 6. dreary
ousia... 6. nature 7. essence
　9. substance, true being
oust... 3. bar 5. eject, evict
　6. depose, remove 7. turn out
out... 3. odd 4. away 5. drunk
　6. absent, beyond, excuse, issued,
　outlet 9. published 10. dislocated,
　extinguish 11. unconscious
　12. extinguished, not available
out and out... 8. absolute, complete,
　outright, thorough 9. downright
　13. thoroughgoing
outbreak... 4. rash, riot 5. burst, spurt
　6. emeute, tumult 7. outcrop,
　ruction 8. eruption, hysteria, outburst
　12. insurrection 13. recrudescence
outburst... 4. gale 5. blast, flare, flash
　8. ejection, eruption 9. explosion
　10. ebullition
outcast... 5. exile, leper, ronin
　6. pariah 7. quarrel 8. castaway,
　derelict, vagabond 10. expatriate
outclass... 5. excel, outdo 6. outvie
　7. outrank, surpass 8. outshine
　10. outperform
outcome... 5. issue 6. effect, outlet,
　result, sequel, upshot 7. emanate,
　product 8. solution 10. denouement
　11. consequence
outcry... 4. wail, yell 5. alarm, shout
　6. clamor, plaint 7. suction
　8. proclaim 11. exclamation
outdo... 5. excel 6. defeat, exceed,
　outwit
outdoor game... 4. polo 6. hockey,
　tennis 7. cricket, croquet
outer... 5. ectad, ectal 7. outside,
　outward 8. exterior, external
　9. objective 10. extraneous
outer (pert to)...
　boundary.. 9. perimeter
　coat.. 4. coat, hull 5. testa 6. extine,
　jacket 8. tegument
　garment.. 4. suit, wrap 5. cloak,
　dress 7. paletot, sweater
　8. mackinaw, mantilla, overcoat,
　raincoat
　layer of roots.. 7. exoderm
　opposed to.. 5. ental
　shell.. 4. test
　skin.. 9. epidermis
Outer Mongolia...
　capital.. 4. Urga 14. Ulan Bator

Khoto
desert .. **4.** Gobi
outermost ... **6.** utmost **7.** extreme,
   outmost **8.** far–flung, farthest
outfit ... **3.** kit, rig **4.** gear, suit, unit
   5. equip, group **7.** company, costume
   8. wardrobe **12.** organization
   13. paraphernalia
outflow ... **4.** gush, teem **6.** deluge,
   efflux **7.** freshet, outflux, outpour
   8. effusion **10.** ebullience
outgate ... **4.** exit, vent **6.** egress,
   outlet **7.** outcome
outknee ... **6.** bowleg
outlander ... see *outsider*
outlandish ... **3.** odd **6.** remote
   7. bizarre, foreign, strange, uncouth
   8. freakish **9.** barbarous, inelegant,
   unrelated **10.** extraneous, impossible,
   tramontane
outlaw ... **5.** horse, ronin **6.** bandit,
   banish **7.** brigand, outcast
   8. criminal, fugitive **0.** ostracize,
   proscribe
outlet ... **4.** exit, vent **5.** bayou
   6. stream **7.** culvert, opening,
   outcast, passage
outline ... **3.** map **5.** chart, draft,
   frame, shape **6.** sketch **7.** contour,
   drawing, summary **8.** scenario
   9. adumbrate, delineate, lineament,
   perimeter, summarize
   10. compendium **11.** delineation
   13. configuration
outlook ... **5.** scope, vista, watch
   7. purview **8.** frontage, prospect
   9. viewpoint **10.** perception
   11. probability **12.** watchfulness
outmoded ... **5.** passé **7.** offbeat
   8. outdated **10.** superseded
outmost **5** final, utter **6.** remote,
   utmost **8.** farthest **9.** extremest,
   outermost, uttermost **15.** farthest
   outward
out of ...
   agreement .. **6.** dehors
   danger .. **4.** safe
   date, style .. **3.** old **5.** passé
      10. antiquated
   place .. **5.** inept
   sorts .. **5.** nohow **7.** peevish
   the ordinary .. **7.** unusual
   the question .. **10.** impossible
   the way .. **5.** aside **6.** afield
outpeer ... **5.** excel **7.** surpass
output ... **3.** cut **5.** expel, power, yield
   6. amount, energy **7.** turnout
   10. production
outraged ... **6.** abused, harmed
   8. insulted, offended **9.** affronted
   10. infuriated, mistreated
outrageous ... **6.** absurd **7.** furious,
   heinous, obscene **8.** flagrant
   9. atrocious, excessive, monstrous
   10. exorbitant, scandalous
   11. disgraceful, unwarranted
outré ... **3.** odd **6.** absurd **7.** bizarre
   10. immoderate **11.** extravagant
Outre–Mer ... **13.** Book of Travels
   (Longfellow, 1835)
outremer ... **12.** beyond the sea,

foreign parts
outrigger ... **4.** proa, spar **5.** canoe
outright ... **8.** thorough **10.** completely
   11. unqualified **12.** unreservedly
outrival ... **5.** excel **6.** outvie
   7. eclipse, outrank **8.** outclass,
   outshine, outsmart, outstrip
outside ... **3.** exo (pref) **4.** ecto (comb
   form) **8.** exterior, external, outdoors
   10. extraneous **11.** superficial
outsider ... **5.** alien **8.** stranger
   9. auslander, foreigner, Uitlander
outspoken ... **4.** free **5.** blunt, frank
   6. candid, direct **10.** unreserved
   13. communicative
outstanding ... **3.** due **5.** famed, noted
   6. famous, unpaid **7.** eminent,
   obvious **8.** exterior **9.** important,
   principal, prominent **10.** projecting
   11. conspicuous, uncollected
outstrip ... **4.** best, lead **5.** excel,
   outdo **7.** surpass **8.** outrival
outward ... **5.** eclad, evert, outer, overt
   6. formal, spiral **8.** apparent, exterior,
   external, manifest **9.** extrinsic
   11. superficial
outwit ... **4.** balk, best, foil **5.** block,
   check, cross **6.** baffle, thwart
   9. checkmate, frustrate
   10. circumvent, disappoint
outwork (Fort) ... **7.** ravelin **8.** tenaille
   (tenail)
ouvrage ... **4.** work
ouzel, ousel ... **4.** piet **6.** thrush
   8. whistler **9.** blackbird
oval ... **5.** ovate, ovoid **6.** circle
   7. ellipse **10.** elliptical **11.** ellipsoidal
ovale ... **3.** egg
ovate ... **4.** bard, oval **7.** obovate
   (inversely)
oven ... **3.** umu **4.** kiln, oast (oste)
   7. furnace **8.** hot place
   9. microwave **12.** brick chamber
oven (pert to) ...
   glass annealing .. **4.** lehr (leer)
   hop drying .. **4.** oast
   mop .. **6.** scovel
over ... **3.** o'er, too **4.** also, anew, atop
   5. above, again, ended, super, supra
   8. finished
overact ... **3.** haw **5.** emote, spout
overalls ... **5.** chaps **8.** trousers
   10. chaparajos
overbearing ... **7.** haughty **8.** arrogant,
   cavalier, snobbish, subduing
   9. imperious **10.** highhanded
   11. domineering **12.** overpowering
overcast ... **3.** dim **4.** dark **6.** cloudy,
   darken, gloomy **10.** overturned (Geol)
overcoat ... **5.** benny, parka **6.** capote,
   raglan, slip–on, ulster **7.** paletot,
   surtout, topcoat **9.** greatcoat,
   inverness (sleeveless)
overcome ... **3.** awe, win **4.** beat
   5. crush **6.** beaten, defeat, exceed
   7. conquer **8.** outstrip, overbear,
   overturn, persuade, surmount,
   unnerved, vanquish **9.** overpower,
   overthrow, overwhelm, prostrate
overcrowded ... **9.** congested
overdue ... **4.** late **5.** tardy **7.** belated

8. mistimed

overfeed... 4. glut 6. agrote, pamper
7. satiate, surfeit 8. overfill
9. crapulate, overstuff

overflow... 4. teem 5. spate
6. abound, deluge, outlet 7. copious,
overrun 8. inundate, opulence,
overload, plethora, teem with
9. abundance, pour forth
10. ebullience

overfond of... 4. dote 5. silly

overfull... 8. inflated, satiated
9. plethoric 10. overloaded

overhang... 3. jut 6. beetle 7. project,
suspend 9. advantage 11. over and
over

overlapping... 8. obvolute 9. imbricate,
syphering

overloaded... 6. turgic 8. inflated,
overfill 9. bombastic, plethoric

overlook... 4. face, miss, scan, skip,
snub 6. acquit, excuse, ignore,
slight, survey 7. absolve, condone,
forgive, neglect, overtop 9. disregard,
oversight, rise above, supervise

overlord... 6. master 8. domineer,
governor 9. tyrannize

overly... 3. too 8. careless
9. negligent 11. overbearing,
superficial 12. supercilious

overmodest... 7. prudish 8. priggish
11. puritanical, strait-laced

overnice... 5. fussy 6. purist
7. elegant, finicky 8. affected
10. fastidious

overpower... 3. awe 4. rout, stun
5. crush 6. dazzle, defeat, master,
subdue 7. conquer 8. overbear,
overcome, vanquish 9. overthrow,
overwhelm

overpowering... 6. fierce 8. exciting
12. overwhelming

overreach... 4. dupe 5. cheat
6. exceed, nobble, outwit, overgo,
strain 7. deceive 10. circumvent

overrun... 5. crush, swarm 6. abound,
desert, exceed, infest, outrun, ravage,
spread 7. destroy, pervade, run over,
trample 8. overflow 9. overwhelm
11. superabound

overscrupulous... 7. prudish
9. overexact 10. overstrict
14. overfastidious

overshadow... 5. excel 6. darken
7. eclipse, obscure, shelter
8. dominate 9. overcloud

overshoe... 3. gum 6. arctic, galosh
(galoshe)

oversight... 4. care 5. error, lapse,
watch 6. charge 7. control, neglect
8. omission 9. direction
10. inspection 11. supervision
12. guardianship, surveillance
13. nonobservance

overskirt... 7. pannier (anc) 10. upper
skirt

oversleeve... 6. armlet

overspread... 5. cover 6. infest
7. overrun, pervade 8. disperse,
suffused

overt... 4. open 6. patent, public
7. obvious 8. apparent, manifest

10. open to view

overtake... 5. catch, reach, seize
6. detect, rejoin 7. ensnare
9. apprehend, captivate

overthrow... 4. down, rout, ruin
5. worst 6. defeat, depose, refute,
unseat 7. conquer, deposal, destroy,
ruinate, unhorse 8. demolish,
disprove, overcome, overturn,
vanquish 9. prostrate 10. revolution

overthrown... 6. fallen, ruined
8. defeated 9. disproved

overtones... 5. tones 8. partials
9. harmonics

overtop... 5. dwarf, excel 7. obscure,
surpass 8. go beyond, overhead,
override 9. transcend 10. tower
above

overture... 5. offer, proem 7. opening,
prelude 8. aperture, proposal
11. composition, proposition
13. peace offering

overturn... 3. tip 4. tilt 5. throw,
upset 6. topple 7. capsize, conquer,
destroy, overset, reverse, subvert
9. overthrow, overwhelm

overweight... 7. obesity
11. overbalance 13. preponderance

overwhelm... 4. bury, rout 5. crush
6. defeat, deluge, engulf 7. confute,
conquer, engross, immerse, oppress
8. overturn, submerge 9. overpower,
overthrow

Ovidae, Ovinae... 5. goats, sheep

oviparous... 11. ovoviparous 12. egg
producing (opp of viviparous)

ovoid, ovoidal... 7. egglike
9. egg-shaped

ovule... 3. egg 4. seed 6. embryo,
ovulum

ovum... 3. egg 4. seed 5. spore
6. gamete 8. germ cell

owe... 3. due, own 7. possess 9. be
obliged 10. be indebted

ower... 6. debtor

owl (pert to)...
barn.. 4. lulu 5. padge
breed.. 6. pigeon
eagle.. 7. katogle 14. Tiger of the
Wood
eye.. 4. disc
family.. 9. Strigidae
female.. 3. hen
genus.. 4. Bubo 5. Ninox, Strix
7. Syrnium
horned.. 4. Bubo 6. aziola (small)
8. Hush-wing
light.. 4. dusk
like.. 4. owly 8. strigine
parrot.. 6. kakapo
Puerto Rican.. 6. mucaro
short-eared.. 8. marsh owl
tawny.. 8. billywix
term.. 4. hoot 11. bird of night
13. bird of Minerva
white.. 7. wapacut
young.. 4. utum 5. owlet

own... 4. have 5. admit 7. confess,
possess 11. acknowledge

owner... 6. master 7. planter
(plantation) 8. landlady, landlord
10. proprietor

ownership... **4.** oadl (anc law)
 5. claim **7.** tenancy **8.** dominium,
 interest, property **10.** possession
 11. seigniorage **12.** seignioralty
 14. proprietorship
ox... **5.** beeve, steer **6.** bovine
 8. strength **13.** beast of burden
ox (pert to)...
 Celebes.. **4.** anoa
 genus.. **3.** Bos
 harness.. **4.** yoke
 horned.. **4.** reem
 India.. **4.** gaur
 like.. **5.** bison **6.** bovine **7.** taurine
 stall.. **5.** boose
 Tibetan.. **3.** yak
 type.. **4.** zebu
 wild.. **4.** urus **7.** banteng
 working.. **4.** aver
 yoke.. **4.** span
oxeye... **4.** boce (fish) **5.** daisy
 6. dunlin, plover
oxford... **4.** gray, shoe **5.** cloth
Oxford (pert to)...
 college accts.. **6.** battel
 color.. **4.** blue, gray

 Marbles.. **7.** Arundel
 Museum.. **9.** Ashmolean (1683)
 officer.. **6.** beadle (bedel at Oxford)
  (bedell at Cambridge)
 scholarship.. **6.** Rhodes
 school.. **10.** University (1570)
 sheep (hornless).. **4.** Down
oxide of iron... **4.** rust
oxide of sodium... **4.** soda
oxidize... **4.** rust **5.** erode **9.** sulphuret
 (Philat)
oxter... **3.** arm **6.** armpit **7.** embrace
oxtongue... **5.** plant **7.** biltong,
 bugloss
oxwort... **9.** butterbur
oxygen... **3.** gas **5.** oxide, ozone
 7. element
oxyopia... **10.** extra sight
oyster... **6.** huitre **7.** bivalve, mollusk
oyster (pert to)...
 gatherer.. **7.** tongman
 rake.. **5.** tongs
 shell.. **4.** husk, test **5.** shuck
 spawn.. **6.** cultch
 young.. **4.** spat
Ozark State... **8.** Missouri
ozone... **3.** air **6.** oxygen

P

P... **2.** Pi **6.** letter (16th)
pa... **4.** Papa **6.** father
pa, pah... **4.** fort **7.** village
 10. settlement (fortified)
paauw... **7.** bustard
pabulum... **4.** food, fuel **7.** aliment,
 support **9.** nutriment **10.** sustenance
 11. nourishment
pac, pack... **8.** half boot, moccasin
paca... **6.** rodent **9.** Cuniculus
pace... **3.** run **4.** gait, lope, rate, step,
 trot, walk **5.** speed **7.** measure
 8. movement, velocity
pace (L)... **5.** peace
Pace... **5.** Pasch **6.** Easter
pachyderm... **8.** elephant
 10. rhinoceros **12.** hippopotamus,
 Pachydermata
pachydermous... **11.** thick–walled
 12. thick–skinned
pacific... **4.** calm **6.** irenic, serene
 8. irenical, peaceful, tranquil
 9. peaceable, quiescent
 12. conciliatory
Pacific (pert to)...
 Coast tree.. **7.** madrona **8.** knob pine
 Highway.. **10.** Camino Real
 island bird.. **4.** kagu
 island shark.. **4.** mako **11.** blue
  pointer
 island tree.. **4.** ipil
 islands.. **4.** Guam, Wake **5.** Samos
  7. Oceania **8.** Caroline, Tasmania

 9. Melanesia, Polynesia
  10. Micronesia
 shrub.. **5.** salal
 States.. **6.** Oregon **10.** California,
  Washington
 stepping stones.. **9.** Aleutians (Russia
  to America)
Pacific Ocean discoverer... **6.** Balboa
pacifier... **3.** sop **4.** ring (baby's)
 6. nipple **7.** soother **8.** sedative
 10. peacemaker
pacify... **4.** calm, ease, lull **5.** abate,
 allay **6.** soften, soothe **7.** appease,
 assuage, mollify, placate **8.** mitigate,
 palliate **9.** alleviate **10.** conciliate,
 propitiate **11.** tranquilize (tranquillize)
pack... **3.** ram, set, wad **4.** cram, fill,
 load, stow, tamp **5.** carry, flock,
 horde, steve, truss **6.** bundle, embale
 8. assemble, encumber, quantity,
 send away
pack (pert to)...
 animal.. **3.** ass **5.** burro, camel, llama
  6. donkey
 back.. **8.** knapsack
 horse.. **7.** sumpter
 horse bag.. **5.** kyack **7.** pannier
 of hounds.. **6.** kennel
package... **3.** pad **4.** bale **5.** fadge
 6. bundle, packet, parcel, robbin
 (peppers), seroon **11.** combination
packing... **4.** lute, seal **7.** stowage
 9. packaging **10.** rubber ring

paco... 3. ore 6. alpaca
Pacolet... 10. swift horse
pact... 6. pactum 7. bargain
    8. contract 9. agreement
Pactolian... 6. golden
Pactolus, Myth (pert to)...
   famed for.. 5. Midas 11. gold-bearing
   river (Asia Minor).. 5. Lydia
pad... 3. mat, paw 4. fill, foot, frog,
   line, path, walk 5. quilt, stuff, track,
   tramp 6. tablet, trudge 7. bedding,
   bolster, cushion, footpad
   8. notebook, protract, saturate
   9. footprint, pulvillus 10. highwayman
pad (pert to)...
   cloth.. 7. housing 11. saddlecloth
   hair.. 3. rat
   harness, part.. 5. panel 6. terret
   7. housing 10. horsecloth
   perfume.. 6. sachet
padding... 6. lining 7. wadding
   8. softness, stuffing 11. superfluity
paddle... 3. oar, row 4. beat, stir,
   wade, whip 5. blade, board, scull,
   spank, spoon 6. dabble, propel
   7. flipper 8. lumpfish
paddle (pert to)...
   English.. 7. trample 8. lumpfish
   9. tread upon 10. paddlecock
   Scotch.. 3. hoe 4. spud
paddock (pert to)...
   paddockstool.. 9. toadstool
   piper.. 9. horsetail
   stone.. 10. greenstone
paddy... 4. rice, soft 7. padlike
   8. cushiony 9. rice field 10. hod
   carrier
Paddy... 7. Patrick 8. Irishman
paddymelon... 7. wallaby
Paddy's hurricane (Naut)... 4. calm
paddywhack... 4. beat, blow
   6. temper 9. ruddy duck, thrashing
padge... 7. barn owl
padmasana... 11. cross-legged
   (Buddha style), lotus-shaped
padre... 4. monk 6. Father, priest
   8. chaplain, minister
padrona... 8. landlady, mistress
padrone... 6. master, patron
   8. landlord 9. innkeeper
paedarchy... 14. rule by children
pagan... 6. ethnic, paynim 7. heathen
   10. heathenism, idolatrous, unbeliever
   11. irreligious
Paganalia... 8. festival (Rom)
pagan god... 4. idol
page... 3. boy 4. leaf 5. child, folio
   6. summon 9. attendant, messenger
page (pert to)...
   beginning.. 7. flyleaf
   book.. 5. folio 6. cahier, sheets
   lady's.. 7. esquire 8. escudero
   left-hand.. 5. verso
   number.. 5. folio
   right-hand.. 5. recto
   title.. 5. unwan 6. rubric
   12. frontispiece
pageant... 4. pomp, show 5. drama
   6. parade 7. tableau 8. aquacade
   9. spectacle 10. exhibition
   11. ostentation
pages... 7. paginal 8. paginate

Pagliacci... 5. opera 9. character
pagne... 9. loincloth, petticoat
pagoda... 2. ta 3. taa 4. idol
   5. booth 6. temple
   11. summerhouse
pagoda (pert to)...
   finial.. 3. tee
   sleeve.. 12. funnel-shaped
   stone.. 12. Agalmatolite
   tree.. 6. banyan 10. frangipani
paha... 4. hill 5. ridge (glacial)
pahi... 4. ship 5. canoe (seagoing)
pahmi... 5. bobac 6. marmot
paho... 7. pahutan 11. prayer stick
pahutan... 5. mango
paid... 5. hired 6. cashed 7. content,
   settled, yielded 9. satisfied
   10. discharged
paideutics... 8. pedagogy, teaching
paid office (without work)...
   8. sinecure
paid out... 5. spent 8. expended
   9. disbursed
paigle... 7. cowslip 8. crowfoot
   10. stitchwort 12. cuckooflower
pail... 3. can, pan 4. beat 6. bucket,
   harass, situla, thrash, vessel
   8. cannikin
paillasse, palliasse... 3. bed (masonry)
   8. mattress (straw)
pailles... 6. straws (cookery)
paillou, pailoo... 7. archway
   (memorial)
pain... 3. ail 4. ache, agra, pang
   5. agony, labor, thraw, throb, wound
   6. grieve, stitch 7. afflict, ailment,
   gnawing, torture, trouble 8. disquiet,
   distress 9. suffering 10. affliction,
   punishment
painful... 4. sore 7. careful 8. diligent
   9. difficult, laborious 10. afflictive,
   unpleasant 11. industrious,
   painstaking
painkiller... 7. anodyne 8. medicine,
   sedative 9. analgesic, calmative
   10. depressant
painstaking... 5. fussy 7. careful,
   labored 8. diligent, thorough
   9. assiduity, assiduous, laborious
paint... 4. coat, draw, limn 5. adorn,
   color, rouge, stain 6. depict, parget,
   sketch 7. picture, pigment, portray
   8. cosmetic, describe 9. delineate,
   embellish 11. application (Med)
paint (pert to)...
   blue, green.. 4. bice
   comb form.. 5. picto
   face.. 4. fard
   glossy.. 6. enamel
   Latin.. 6. pinxit
   spreader.. 7. spatula
   through pattern.. 7. stencil
   with vermilion.. 7. miniate
paintbrush... 8. hawkweed 10. painted
   cup 11. St John's wort
painted... 6. coated 7. colored,
   feigned 9. disguised, portrayed
   10. artificial, variegated
painted (pert to)...
   bat.. 11. Vespertilio
   beauty.. 9. butterfly
   bunting.. 5. finch

duck.. 8. mandarin 9. harlequin
enamel.. 7. Limoges
hyena.. 14. Cape hunting dog
lady.. 7. thistle 8. sweet pea
   9. butterfly
process.. 7. scumble
trillium.. 9. wake–robin
turtle.. 8. carapace
painter... 4. puma 6. cougar
   7. panther
painter... 4. Dali 5. Monet 6. Millet,
   Rubens 7. da Vinci, El Greco,
   Picasso, van Gogh 8. Reynolds,
   Whistler 9. Rembrandt
   12. Gainsborough, Grandma Moses,
   Michelangelo
Painter's Easel... 6. Pictor
   (constellation)
painting... 3. oil 5. genre, mural, Pietà
   (sacred), secco 6. fresco, marine
   7. impasto, tempera 9. encaustic,
   grisaille, landscape 10. cerography
   11. portraiture 12. illustration
pair... 3. duo, two 4. dyad, mate,
   span, team, yoke 5. brace, unite
   6. couple
paired... 5. gemel (Her) 7. coupled,
   leagued
pairs, growing in... 6. binate, double
paisano... 7. peasant 10. countryman,
   road runner
pal... 4. chum, pard 5. buddy, crony
   6. cobber 7. partner 9. companion
   10. accomplice
palace... 5. court, Doges, house
   (Astrol) 6. palais 7. palazzo
   10. praetorium (pretorium)
paladin... 4. hero 6. knight (Round
   Table)
Paladins of France... 9. The Twelve
palais... 6. palace 10. courthouse
Palamedes... 4. hero (Trojan War)
palampore... 7. hanging (cotton)
   8. bedcover
palanquin, palankeen... 4. kago
   5. dooly (doolie), palki 6. litter,
   palkee 10. conveyance
palanquin bearer... 5. hamal 6. sirdar
palas... 4. dhak, tree (yellow dye)
palatable... 5. sapid, tasty 6. savory
   8. pleading, seasoned 10. acceptable
palate... 4. cion 5. taste, uvula, velum
   6. relish 10. epipharynx
palatine... 4. bone 6. artery, county
   8. palatial
Palatine Confession... 10. Heidelberg
palaver... 4. talk 6. confer 7. chatter
   8. converse, flattery 10. conference
   12. conversation
pale... 3. dim, wan 4. ashy, fade, lily
   5. ashen, fence, lurid, pasty, stake,
   white 6. blanch, bounds, paling,
   pallid, pallor, sallow, sickly, sphere
   7. haggard, obscure, whitish
   8. palisade 9. deathlike 10. indistinct
palea, palet... 4. fold 5. bract, scale
   6. dewlap 8. ramentum
paleo (comb form)... 3. old 7. ancient
paleolithic culture... 8. Stone Age
Paleozoic... 10. Appalachia
Palestine (pert to)...
   ancient name.. 6. Canaan

animal.. 4. cony (Bib) 5. daman
conqueror.. 5. David, Turks
   11. Constantine
country (anc).. 4. Edom 5. Endor
   (Indur) 8. Nazareth 9. Philistia
lake.. 7. Dead Sea, Galilee
language.. 7. Aramaic
mountain (Bib).. 4. Zion 6. Carmel,
   Gilead, Hermon 13. Mount of Olives
plain, steppe.. 5. Negeb 6. Sharon
river.. 6. Jordan
town, district.. 4. Gaza 5. Haifa
   7. Samaria 9. Jerusalem
paletot... 4. coat 8. overcoat
pali... 9. precipice 10. steep slope
pali (comb form)... 5. again
   8. backward
Pali... 7. dialect (anc) 12. dead
   language
palimpsest... 9. parchment, rewritten
   10. re–engraved 15. codex rescriptus
palindrome (same backward, forward)...
   8. wordplay 9. inversion
paling... 5. fence, limit, palis, stake
   6. fading, picket 7. fencing
   9. enclosure
palisade... 5. cliff, fence, stake
   6. picket 7. defense, enclose, fortify
   8. espalier, palisado, surround
   9. precipice 10. impalement
   13. fortification
pall... 4. pale 5. cloak, cover, faint,
   qualm 6. coffin, mantle, nausea
   7. secrecy 12. graveclothes
pallall... 9. hopscotch
palle... 5. balls 8. six balls (Medici)
pallet... 3. bed 4. pate 5. quilt
   7. blanket 8. mattress 9. headpiece,
   paillasse
palliard... 6. beggar, lecher, rascal
   8. vagabond
palliate... 4. hide 5. abate, cloak,
   cover, gloss 6. excuse, lessen, soften
   7. conceal, qualify, relieve, shelter
   8. disguise, mitigate, moderate
   9. alleviate, extenuate
pallid... 3. wan 4. gray, pale 5. pasty,
   white 6. anemic, sallow
Pallu... 10. Reuben's son (Bib)
palm... 4. hand (part) 5. areca, bribe,
   steal 6. bacaba, handle, rattan,
   stroke, trophy
palm (pert to)...
   civet.. 6. musang
   cockatoo.. 5. arara
   down.. 7. pronate
   drink.. 5. assai
   drink (alcoholic).. 4. beno, nipa
   hand.. 6. palmus, thenar
   handlike.. 7. palmate
   house.. 8. palmetum
   lily.. 2. ti
   mat.. 6. petate
   off.. 5. foist
   ref to.. 10. palmaceous
   sap (fermented).. 5. toddy
   starch.. 4. sago
   sugar.. 7. jaggery
   thatch.. 4. nipa
palm (tree)...
   African.. 7. palmyra (sugar, wine)
   Arab.. 4. doum (doom)

Asiatic.. **4**. atap, nipa
betel.. **5**. areca, bonga **6**. pinang
book.. **4**. tara **7**. taliera
Brazil.. **7**. urucuri (urucury)
bussu, thatching.. **7**. troolie (trooly)
cabbage.. **5**. Sabal **8**. palmetto
Ceylon.. **4**. tala **7**. talipot (fanleaf)
climbing, flexible.. **6**. rattan
dwarf.. **5**. Sabal
E Indies.. **4**. atap, nipa **7**. jaggery
  (sugar), tokopat (hat)
fan.. **7**. talipot **8**. palmetto
fiber.. **3**. tal **6**. raffia **8**. piassava
  (piassaba)
Florida.. **5**. royal
gingerbread tasting.. **4**. doum (doom)
leaf.. **3**. tal **4**. olla (ola)
  12. chiquichiqui
Malayan, feather.. **4**. irok **6**. gomuti
palmyra.. **4**. brab, olla **6**. ronier
Philippine (coconut).. **4**. niog
pinnate.. **5**. assai, nikau **7**. calamus,
  feather
S America.. **5**. bussu, datil **6**. tooroo
  12. chiquichiqui
spiny.. **6**. grugru
palmate... **6**. antler, webbed
  10. hand–shaped
palmer... **6**. ferule **7**. pilgrim (Holy
  Land) **8**. date palm
  15. prestidigitator
Palmetto State... **13**. South Carolina
palmistry... **10**. chirognomy,
  chiromancy
palmodic (Med)... **5**. jerky
palp... **6**. feeler, palpus **8**. tentacle
palpable... **5**. plain **6**. patent
  8. manifest, tangible **9**. touchable
  10. noticeable, ponderable
palpebra... **6**. eyelid
palpebrate... **4**. wink
palpitate... **4**. beat, drum **5**. throb
  7. flutter, pulsate
palpitation... **7**. flutter, tremble
  9. pulsation, quivering, throbbing
  10. excitement
palsied... **5**. shaky **9**. paralyzed,
  tottering
palter...`5`. shift **6**. babble, haggle,
  mumble, parley **7**. bargain, chatter,
  quibble **9**. vacillate **10**. equivocate
  11. prevaricate
paltry... **4**. mean, vile **5**. petty, trash
  6. trashy **7**. pitiful, rubbish
  8. picayune, trifling **9**. worthless
  10. despicable **12**. contemptible
pampas... **5**. Pampa **6**. plains (treeless)
pamper... **3**. pet **4**. cram, glut
  5. humor, spoil **6**. caress, coddle,
  cosset, cuddle, dandle, posset
  7. gratify, indulge **11**. mollycoddle
pamphagous... **10**. omnivorous
pamphlet... **5**. tract **6**. folder
  7. booklet, leaflet **8**. brochure
pan... **3**. tab **4**. part, tina (mining),
  wash **5**. basin, roast, title (nobility)
  6. frying, lappet, spider, vessel
  7. cranium, hardpan, portion, skillet,
  subsoil **8**. ridicule, saucepan
  9. criticize **10**. acetabulum
pan (comb form)... **3**. all **5**. every

Pan (pert to)...
animal.. **3**. ape **10**. chimpanzee
god (Gr).. **6**. flocks
instrument.. **4**. pipe, reed
music.. **9**. Pan's pipes
Pipes of.. **6**. syrinx **8**. Panpipes
Roman identity.. **6**. Faunus
seat of worship.. **7**. Arcadia
son.. **7**. Silenus
panacea... **4**. cure **6**. elixir, remedy
  7. allheal (plant), cure–all
  8. nepenthe **10**. catholicon
  11. panchreston
panache... **4**. tuft (feathered) **5**. plume
  7. swagger
Panama...
bay.. **5**. Limon
capital.. **10**. Panama City
city.. **5**. Colon **6**. Balboa **9**. Cristobal
engineer.. **8**. Goethals
gulf.. **6**. Darien
Indian.. **4**. Cuna
isthmus of.. **6**. Darien (old name),
  Panama **7**. San Blas
redwood.. **5**. quira
river.. **7**. Chagres
Panama Canal Lock... **5**. Gatun
  10. Miraflores
panarchy... **13**. universal rule
panaris... **5**. felon **7**. whitlow
  10. paronychia
panary... **5**. bread **11**. breadmaking
panatela... **5**. cigar
pancake... **6**. froise (fraise) **7**. fritter
  11. griddlecake
Pancake Day... **13**. Shrove Tuesday
pancreas... **5**. gland **10**. sweetbread
  16. Isle of Langerhans
panda... **7**. bearcat
pandemonium... **4**. hell **5**. noise
  6. tumult, uproar
Pandemonium (pert to)...
abode of.. **6**. demons
capital of.. **4**. Hell
palace of.. **5**. Satan
pert to.. **15**. infernal regions
pander... **4**. bawd, pimp **5**. cater,
  serve **7**. toady to **12**. administer to
pandle... **7**. a shrimp
Pandora's Box... **6**. plague **9**. human
  ills
Pandora's husband... **10**. Epimetheus
panegyric... **5**. éloge, elogy **6**. eulogy
  7. oration, writing **8**. encomium
  9. discourse, laudation
pang... **3**. fit **4**. pain **5**. throe
  6. twinge **8**. paroxysm
pangolin... **5**. Manis **8**. anteater
  9. Pholidota
panhandle... **3**. beg
Panhellenic... **5**. games (Isthmian)
  6. Greece **10**. fraternity (Greek–letter)
panic... **4**. fear, fray **5**. alarm, chaos,
  scare **6**. fright **8**. stampede
pannier... **6**. basket, dosser (dorser)
  7. corbeit **9**. overskirt
panoply... **7**. defense **11**. suit of
  armor
panorama... **4**. view **5**. scene
  7. picture, scenery **9**. cyclorama
pant... **4**. beat, gasp **5**. heave, throb
  7. breathe, pulsate **11**. palpitation

Pantagruel (pert to)...
  character (romantic).. 5. giant
  companion.. 7. Panurge
  father.. 9. Gargantua
pantaloon, pantaloons... 5. pants
  6. dotard, old man 8. breeches,
  trousers 11. Patron Saint (Venice)
Pantheon (pert to)...
  aggregate.. 4. gods 7. deities
  builder.. 7. Hadrian (120 AD)
  building.. 6. shrine, temple 10. le
  Pantheon (Paris) 16. Westminster
  Abbey
  Rome.. 15. Temple of the Gods
panther, painter... 4. pard, puma
  6. cougar, jaguar, ocelot 7. leopard
pantler... 6. butler 7. servant
pantry... 5. ambry 6. larder 7. buttery,
  pannier, pantler 8. cupboard
pants... 5. chaps 7. drawers
  8. trousers 10. chaparajos
  (chaparejos), pantaloons
panuelo... 6. collar 8. kerchief
  9. neckcloth
pap... 4. teat 6. nipple 8. mammilla,
  soft diet
papa... 3. dad 4. clay, Pope
  6. baboon, father, potato, priest
  7. vulture
papal... 9. apostolic 10. pontifical
papal (pert to)...
  book of decrees.. 8. decretal
  chancery.. 6. datary
  Court.. 3. See 5. Curia
  envoy.. 8. ablegate
  letter.. 4. bull
  reformer.. 7. Gregory
  seal.. 5. bulla
  vestment.. 5. fanon, orale
paper (pert to)...
  absorbent.. 7. blotter
  broken.. 5. casse
  brown.. 6. manila
  coated.. 6. charta
  collection.. 7. dossier
  copy.. 6. carbon
  crinkled.. 5. crepe
  crisp.. 6. pelure
  currency.. 5. scrip
  cutlet wrap.. 8. papilote
  damaged.. 5. casse, salle 6. retree
  design.. 9. watermark
  fine.. 5. linen 6. vellum 9. parchment
  flower.. 11. strawflower
  folded.. 5. folio
  for pounding gold sheets.. 7. cutches
  gummed.. 5. label, stamp 7. plaster,
  sticker
  legal.. 4. writ 5. title
  measure.. 4. page, ream 5. quire,
  sheet
  nautilus.. 8. argonaut
  official.. 5. targe 8. document
  pad.. 6. tablet
  postage stamp.. 6. pelure
  size.. 3. cap 4. copy, demy, pott,
  quad 5. atlas, crown, folio, legal
  6. octavo 8. foolscap, imperial
  9. colombier
  small piece.. 5. scrip
  thin.. 4. rice 6. pelure, tissue
  9. onionskin

transfer.. 12. decalcomania
untrimmed.. 6. deckle (deckel)
  10. deckle edge 11. deckle–edged
writing size.. 3. cap
paper chase... 13. hare and hounds
papilla... 6. nipple 10. projection
papule... 6. papula, pimple
papyra (comb form)... 5. paper
papyrus... 4. pith, reed 5. paper,
  sedge 6. scroll
par... 2. by 5. value 7. average, by
  way of, strokes, through 8. equality,
  superior
parable... 4. myth, tale 5. fable, story
  8. allegory, apologue
  10. comparison, similitude
parabola... 5. curve
parade... 4. pomp, show 5. march
  6. flaunt 8. flourish, grandeur,
  splendor 9. pageantry, promenade,
  spectacle 10. pretension, procession
  11. ostentation 12. magnificence
  13. formal display
paradigm... 5. model 7. example,
  pattern
paradisaic... 6. Edenic
Paradise... 4. Eden 5. Jenna
  6. Aidenn, heaven, Utopia 7. Elysium
Paradise (pert to)...
  apple.. 5. dwarf
  Arabic form.. 6. Aidenn
  Buddhist, Western.. 4. Jodo
  fool's.. 5. limbo
  grosbeak.. 9. cutthroat (bird)
  Mohammedan.. 5. Jenna
  plumage.. 14. bird of paradise
  poem (Milton).. 12. Paradise Lost
  16. Paradise Regained
  river.. 5. Gihon (Bib)
  tree.. 9. China tree
paragon... 4. type 5. ideal, match,
  model 7. diamond (100 carats),
  paladin, pattern 8. parallel
  9. nonpareil
paragram... 3. pun
Paraguay...
  capital.. 8. Asunción
  city.. 9. Paraguari 10. Concepcion,
  Villarrica
  language.. 7. Guarani, Spanish
  river.. 6. Paraná 8. Paraguay
  tea.. 4. maté 5. yerba 11. yerba de
  maté
parakeet... 5. green 6. parrot, puffin
  11. budgereegah (budgerygah)
paralysis... 5. palsy 7. paresis
  10. hemiplegia, paraplegia 11. loss
  of power
paralyze... 5. scram 6. benumb,
  deaden 7. astound, terrify, unnerve
paramount... 3. top 5. chief, liege
  6. ruling 7. supreme 8. dominant,
  superior 9. principal 10. preeminent
  13. most important
paramour... 5. amour, leman, lover,
  wooer 8. mistress 9. gallantry
  10. sweetheart
paranoia... 9. catatonia, monomania,
  nosomania
parapet... 5. redan 7. barrier, bulwark,
  rampart
parasite... 3. bur, sug 5. drone, toady

6. Gnatho, insect, sponge 7. entozoa
8. hanger–on 9. entophyte,
sycophant
parasite (pert to) ...
animal .. 6. cuckoo 7. cowbird,
entozoa
external .. 12. ectoparasite
internal .. 7. entozoa
marine .. 6. remora, sponge
plant .. 9. entophyte
slang .. 6. flunky
trout .. 3. sug
parasitic (pert to) ...
fish .. 6. remora
fungus .. 4. rust 6. lichen
worm .. 8. trichina (larva)
parcel ... 3. lot 4. mete, part 5. piece,
solum (law) 6. bundle, packet
7. package, portion 8. fragment
parch ... 3. dry 4. burn 5. dry up,
roast, toast 6. scorch 7. shrivel,
torrefy
parched ... 4. sere 5. burnt, dried
7. thirsty 8. withered
parchment (pert to) ...
bookcover .. 5. forel (forrel)
fine .. 6. vellum
manuscript .. 10. palimpsest
roll .. 4. pell 6. scroll
school .. 7. diploma
pard ... 4. chum 5. tiger 7. comrade,
leopard, panther, partner
10. camelopard 11. confederate
pardesi (Hind) ... 9. foreigner, outlander
pardie, parde, pardi (anc) ... 4. oath
6. indeed, surely, verily 9. certainly
pardon ... 5. mercy, remit, spare
6. acquit, excuse 7. absolve,
amnesty, condone, forgive 8. tolerate
9. acquittal, remission
10. absolution, indulgence (Eccl)
11. forgiveness
pardonable ... 6. venial 8. expiable
9. excusable 10. forgivable
pardon chair, stall ... 12. confessional
pare ... 3. cut 4. peel, skin 5. shave
6. cut off, remove, resect
parent ... 3. dad 4. sire 5. pater
6. father, mother, source 7. genitor
8. begetter 9. progenitor
parental affection (animal) ... 6. storge
parget ... 4. coat 5. paint 7. plaster
8. decorate, ornament 9. whitewash
parhelion ... 3. sun (mock)
pariah ... 3. dog (half–wild) 7. outcast
8. commoner, low caste
parian ... 6. marble, market
Parian ... 5. Paros 6. marble
(sculptural) 9. porcelain
parimutuel machine ... 9. totalizer
11. totalizator
Paris (pert to) ...
blue .. 6. cobalt 8. Prussian
daisy .. 10. marguerite
Garden (London) .. 10. bear garden
green .. 11. insecticide
Paris, France ...
anc name .. 7. Lutetia (Lutice)
capital of .. 6. France
criminal .. 6. apache
famed sites .. 6. Louvre 8. Pantheon
9. Notre Dame 10. Montmartre

11. Eiffel Tower 13. Champs Elysées,
Napoleon's Tomb
native .. 8. Parisian
patron saint .. 5. Denis (Denys)
racecourse .. 7. Auteuil
river .. 5. Seine
subway .. 5. Metro
Paris, Gr legend ...
brought about .. 9. Trojan War
10. Fall of Troy
father .. 5. Priam (King of Troy)
killer of .. 8. Achilles
mother .. 6. Hecuba
wife .. 6. Oenone
parish ... 5. laity 7. diocese 8. district
9. parochial
paristhmion ... 6. tonsil
park ... 4. area (enclosed) 5. place,
tract 6. claire, common, settle
7. pasture (Eng) 8. woodland
9. grassland, pleasance
10. playground 11. reservation, set
and leave
Park, Highway ...
Avenue .. 9. Manhattan
Lane .. 6. London
Row .. 9. Manhattan
Park, Historical ... 6. Shiloh 8. Pea
Ridge, Saratoga 9. Minute Man
10. Gettysburg, Morristown
12. Harper's Ferry, Independence
Park, US ... 4. Zion 7. Glacier,
Olympic (rain forests) 8. Sequoyah
(Sequoja), Yosemite (Sequoja) 9. Haleakala,
Mesa Verde 10. Everglades, Mt
McKinley, Shenandoah 11. Grand
Canyon, Kings Canyon, Yellowstone
12. Harper's Ferry 15. Petrified
Forest
parlay, parley ... 4. chat 5. parle, treat
6. confer 7. discuss 8. converse
10. conference, discussion
11. arbitration
parliament ... 4. Diet 8. Congress
11. legislature
parlous ... 4. keen 5. risky 6. shrewd
7. cunning 8. shocking 9. dangerous
Parnassian ... 4. muse, poet
9. butterfly 10. Parnassius
Parnassus, Greece ...
mountain .. 6. Phocis
site of .. 6. Delphi 8. Castalia
(fountain) 13. Delphic Apollo
symbol of .. 6. poetry
parody ... 5. farce 6. satire 7. mockery,
take–off 9. burlesque, imitation
10. caricature
paroemia ... 7. proverb
parol, parole ... 4. oral, word
6. speech 7. freedom, promise,
release 8. pleading 11. word of
mouth
paronomasia ... 3. pun 7. punning
8. wordplay 9. assonance
12. agnomination
paroxysm ... 3. fit 4. pang 5. throe
6. access, attack, frenzy 7. illness
9. agitation 10. fit of anger
12. exacerbation
paroxysm of grief ... 5. agony
parricide *(murder of)* ... 7. kinsman
parrot ... 3. ara, hia, kea 4. jako, kaka,

loro, lory 5. arara, cagit, macaw, polly
6. kakapo, tiriba 7. corella, lorilet
8. cockatoo, lorikeet, lovebird,
parakeet 9. Psittacus (Old World)
14. Psittaciformes
parrot (pert to) . . .
disease . . 11. psittacosis
genus . . 6. Nestor 9. Psittacus
gray . . 4. jako
green . . 5. cagit
hawk . . 3. hia
long–tailed . . 5. macaw
monk . . 4. loro
New Zealand . . 4. kaka
owl . . 6. kakapo
parrot fish . . 4. loro, scar 5. lauia
6. scarid 7. labroid 8. Labridae,
Scaridae
parrotlike (tongued) . . 12. anthropoglot
sheep–killing . . 3. kea
short–tailed . . 7. lorilet
parry . . . 4. fend, ward 5. avert, avoid,
elude, evade, shift 6. refute, thwart
pars . . . 4. part
Parsee Bible . . . 10. Zend Avesta
Parsei, Parsi . . . 6. Gheber (Ghebre)
11. Zoroastrian 13. fire worshiper
Parsifal (pert to) . . .
character . . 6. Knight
healer of . . 8. Amfortas
son . . 9. Lohengrin
parsimonious . . . 4. near 5. close
6. frugal, meager, skimpy, sordid,
stingy 7. miserly, sparing
8. covetous, grasping 9. illiberal,
mercenary, penurious 10. avaricious
parsley . . . 4. herb 5. cumin 7. garnish
9. Ammiaceae, flavoring
parsley camphor . . . 6. apiolo
parson . . . 6. rector 8. minister,
preacher, reverend 9. clergyman
parsonage . . . 5. gleve, manse, tithe
7. rectory 8. benefice, vicarage
9. pastorate 10. presbytery
parson bird . . . 3. tui
part . . . 3. cut, die 4. open, role, twin
5. allot, break, piece, sever, share
6. depart, divide, member, sunder
7. analyze, disband, disjoin, divorce,
portion, section, segment 8. dissever,
disunite, division, fragment, function,
separate 9. component
part (pert to) . . .
basic . . 4. core, pith 7. essence,
nucleus
choice . . 5. cream, elite 6. marrow
coarse . . 5. dregs
composite . . 7. section
corresponding . . 7. isomere
essential . . 4. core, gist, pith 5. heart
extra . . 5. spare
greater . . 4. bulk
hardest . . 5. brunt
infinitesimal . . 4. atom, mite
insignificant . . 3. bit 4. iota 6. trifle
kept . . 6. retent
main . . 4. body 5. trunk
narrow . . 4. neck
proportional . . 5. quota
rootlike . . 7. radicle
sawlike . . 5. serra
segment . . 5. tmema

small . . 3. bit, jot 4. iota 6. detail
7. snippet
smallest . . 4. whit 5. minim
solo accompaniment . . 8. obbligato
tenth . . 5. tithe
unpaid . . 6. arrear 9. arrearage
uppermost . . 3. top 4. peak 6. upside
7. topside
winglike . . 3. ala
with . . 7. discard 10. relinquish
partage . . . 4. part 5. share 7. portion
8. division
partake . . . 3. eat 5. share 7. receive
11. participate
partan . . . 4. crab
parted . . . 5. cleft 6. cloven 7. divided,
severed 9. separated
11. apportioned
parterre . . . 10. level space 12. theater
boxes, theater space 17. ornamental
gardens
parthogenesis . . . 7. apogamy
10. thelyotoky 12. reproduction
partial . . . 6. biased, unfair, unjust
7. limited 8. not total, one–sided,
partisan 9. imperfect 10. fractional,
incomplete, prejudiced
11. predisposed 13. foolishly fond
partiality . . . 4. bias 6. desire
9. injustice, prejudice 10. preference
11. inclination, partisanism
12. partisanship, predilection
participant . . . 6. sharer 7. entrant
8. partaker 9. accessory, colleague
12. participator
particle . . . 3. ace, bit, ion, jot 4. atom,
drop, iota, mite, mote, whit 5. grain,
piece, shred, spark 6. tittle
7. globule, granule, smidgen
particle (pert to) . . .
electric . . 3. ion 5. anion 6. proton
least possible . . 5. minim
minute . . 3. jot, ray 4. atom, iota
5. grain, speck 7. granule
negative . . 3. nor, not
nuclear . . 5. gluon, meson, quark
6. baryon, hadron
parti–colored . . . 4. pied, roan 5. pinto
6. motley 7. piebald 9. harlequin
10. variegated 11. polychromic
particular . . . 4. item, nice, part, sole
5. event, fussy 6. detail 7. precise,
special, topical 8. detailed, especial,
peculiar, separate, specific
9. attentive 10. fastidious, individual,
overminute 11. persnickety
12. circumstance, technicality
partisan, partizan . . . 4. pike 5. staff
6. zealot 7. partial 8. adherent,
advocate, follower 9. supporter
10. fractional, prejudiced
partition . . . 4. wall 5. allot 6. divide,
screen, septum 7. scantle 8. set
apart 9. apportion, severance
10. distribute, separation
13. apportionment
partitioned . . . 7. septate
partly . . . 6. in part 9. partially
partly illuminated . . . 6. shaded
8. adumbral 9. penumbral
partly open . . . 4. ajar
partner . . . 3. pal 4. ally, mate, wife

6. sharer, spouse **7.** comrade,
husband **9.** associate, coadjutor,
colleague **10.** accomplice
11. confederate, participant
partnership . . . **4.** firm **7.** cahoots,
co—mated **8.** business, contract
10. fellowship **11.** affiliation
13. participation
part of . . .
　anchor . . **4.** palm
　bird wing . . **5.** alula
　cannon . . **5.** chase
　church . . **4.** apse, nave **5.** altar
　　7. chancel **8.** transept
　circle . . **3.** arc **6.** degree **7.** segment
　compass . . **6.** needle
　ear . . **4.** lobe **5.** pinna **6.** tragus
　　8. tympanum **9.** labyrinth
　eye . . **4.** iris, uvea **5.** pupil **6.** cornea,
　　retina
　flower . . **4.** stem **5.** calyx, petal, sepal
　foot lever . . **5.** pedal **7.** treadle
　fort . . **5.** redan **7.** bastion
　head . . **4.** pate **5.** scalp, skull
　　7. cranium
　minstrel show . . **4.** olio **5.** bones
　　6. end man **12.** interlocutor
　newspaper . . **3.** ear **4.** item, page
　　6. by—line **9.** editorial
　optical measure . . **7.** alidade
　printing press . . **6.** platen
　rifle (anc) . . **4.** tige
　ship . . **3.** bow **4.** brig, deck, helm,
　　keel, mast **5.** stern, wheel **6.** anchor,
　　bridge, rudder **8.** steerage
　step . . **5.** riser, tread **6.** nosing
　theater . . **3.** box **4.** loge **5.** foyer,
　　stage **7.** balcony, curtain, gallery,
　　parquet **8.** parterre **9.** orchestra
　turtle . . **7.** calipee **8.** calipash
partridge . . . **4.** hill, snow, yutu
　5. covey (flock) **6.** bamboo, chukar
　(chukor), Perdix, seesee **7.** cinerea,
　tinamou **8.** raw umber **9.** francolin
　11. Francolinus **12.** ruffed grouse
party . . . **3.** tea **4.** ball, drum, sect,
　side **6.** clique, fiesta, person
　7. company, faction **8.** sociable
　9. reception **10.** detachment
　11. association, combination
　12. participator
party (pert to) . . .
　deserter . . **6.** bolter
　evening . . **6.** soiree
　lawn . . **4.** fete
　man . . **8.** partisan
　member . . **8.** Democrat, Federate
　　9. Communist, Dixiecrat, Greenback
　　(Hist), Socialist **10.** Republican
　　11. Independent
　men's . . **4.** stag **6.** smoker
Parvati (pert to) . . .
　consort . . **4.** Siva
　father . . **7.** Himavat
　goddess . . **8.** mountain
parvenu . . . **4.** snob **7.** upstart
　12. nouveau riche
Pasch, pasch . . . **4.** lamb, moon
　6. candle, Easter, supper **8.** Passover
　10. Good Friday **11.** candlestick,
　celebration
pascual . . . **8.** pascuage, pastures

pasear . . . **4.** walk **6.** parade, stroll
　9. promenade **11.** perambulate
pasha, pacha . . . **3.** dey **4.** emir **5.** title
　6. bashaw (early) **8.** nobleman
　10. magistrate
pashalik (pashalic) . . . **9.** territory
　(pasha's) **12.** jurisdiction
pashm . . . **6.** fleece (Tibetan goat)
pasigraphy . . . **6.** system (Universal)
　7. symbols **8.** language
Pasiphae (pert to) . . .
　mother of . . **7.** Ariadne
　son . . **8.** minotaur (monster)
　wife of . . **5.** Minos
pasquinade . . . **5.** squib **6.** satire
　7. lampoon, pasquil
pass . . . **2.** go **3.** die, end, gap
　4. ghat, hand, lane, pace, step
　5. canto, enact, gorge, lapse, occur,
　relay, spend, throw **6.** convey, crisis,
　defile, elapse, exceed, happen,
　passus, perish, permit, ratify, ticket
　7. excrete, passage **8.** hand over,
　passport, surmount, transfer
　10. permission **11.** Annie Oakley
　13. complimentary
pass (pert to) . . .
　Alpine . . **3.** col
　around . . **5.** skirt **6.** detour
　as genuine . . **5.** cheat, foist
　　11. interpolate
　away . . **3.** die, end **6.** perish, vanish
　　9. cease to be, disappear, obsolesce
　by . . **4.** cote, omit, skip, snub
　　6. elapse, forego, ignore **7.** proceed
　　8. overlook **9.** disregard
　hurriedly . . **7.** scamper, skitter **9.** skim
　　along
　into . . **5.** glide, merge **6.** become
　　7. get to be **9.** penetrate
　judgment . . **4.** rule **6.** decree, ordain
　　8. sentence
　on . . **3.** die **6.** confer, ratify
　　7. advance **8.** bequeath, continue
　out . . **3.** die **4.** exit **5.** faint **7.** be
　　dazed **9.** disappear **11.** be dead
　　drunk **13.** be unconscious
　over . . **4.** omit, skip **5.** cross
　　6. elapse, excuse, exempt, ignore,
　　slight **7.** condone, exclude, neglect
　　8. overlook, transfer, traverse
　sudden . . **5.** lunge
　through . . **5.** cross, reeve (cringle)
　　6. pierce **7.** pervade, undergo
　　8. traverse **9.** penetrate
　　10. comprehend, experience
　up . . **4.** snub **5.** evade **6.** reject
　　7. decline **9.** disregard
　without touching . . **5.** clear
passable . . . **4.** so—so **7.** current
　8. mediocre, moderate, traveled
　9. navigable, tolerable, traversed
　10. acceptable, accessible, admissible
　12. satisfactory
passado (fencing) . . . **6.** thrust
passage . . . **4.** adit, exit, flue, ford,
　gang, hall, iter **5.** aisle, allay, allée,
　canal, death **6.** atrium, avenue,
　egress, travel, voyage **7.** channel,
　excerpt, journey, transit **8.** corridor,
　incident, progress, sanction
　9. enactment, migration

10. transition 11. altercation, negotiation, preterition
12. thoroughfare
passage (pert to) . . .
book . . 7. excerpt
brain . . 4. iter
closed end . . 7. impasse 8. cul-de-sac
covered . . 4. pawn
history . . 5. alure
mine . . 4. sill 5. stope
narrow . . 3. gut 5. aisle, alley, gully, slype 6. defile, strait
river . . 7. estuary
passageway . . . 4. hall, lane, ramp, slip 5. aisle, alley, lumen 6. access, arcade, avenue, defile, outlet, strait, tunnel 7. gangway 8. corridor
passant . . . 7. cursory, walking (Her) 8. passer-by 9. ephemeral, excelling 10. surpassing, transitory
passé . . . 4. aged, past, worn 5. faded 6. gone by 8. obsolete 10. antiquated 13. superannuated
passed (pert to) . . .
by . . 6. bygone, former 8. preterit (preterite)
over . . 7. fleeted 11. preterition
through pores . . 7. osmosed 8. dialyzed 9. permeated, transuded
passenger . . . 4. fare 6. pigeon, trekku 7. pilgrim, tourist 8. commuter, traveler, wayfarer 9. sightseer, transient
passerine bird . . . 5. finch 7. sparrow 8. songbird
passing . . . 7. cursory 8. elapsing, fleeting 9. departing, enactment, ephemeral, exceeding, happening, transient, vanishing 10. surpassing, transitory 11. preterition
passion . . . 3. ire, yen 4. love, lust, rage, zeal 5. anger, craze, wrath 6. desire 7. emotion, feeling 9. eloquence, martyrdom 10. enthusiasm, excitement
passion (pert to) . . .
flower . . 6. maypop 11. passionwort
flower family . . 10. Passiflora
for doing great things . . 11. megalomania
music . . 8. oratorio
Play . . 14. Christ's Passion (Oberammergau)
Week . . 8. Holy Week
passionate . . . 3. sad 5. angry 6. ardent 7. amorous, excited, fervent, pitiful, violent 8. agitated, eloquent, vehement 9. emotional, irascible 10. passionato 11. hot-tempered, impassioned
passionless . . . 4. calm 8. painless 9. heartless, unfeeling 10. spiritless 11. unemotional 13. dispassionate
passive . . . 5. inert, quiet, stoic 6. stolid 7. languid, patient 8. inactive 9. apathetic 10. submissive 11. acquiescent, indifferent, unresisting
Passover (pert to) . . .
festival . . 5. Seder 6. Jewish
lamb . . 7. paschal
psalm . . 6. hallel 14. Egyptian Hallel

sacrifice . . 11. paschal lamb
The (Passover) . . 5. Pasch
passport . . . 4. pass, visa (vise) 5. congé 6. congee, permit 8. document 11. safe conduct
passus . . . 5. canto
password . . . 9. watchword 10. mot de passé, open sesame 11. countersign
past . . . 2. by 3. ago 4. date, dead, gone, over, yore 5. after, since 6. beyond, ultimo 7. elapsed, outworn 9. foregoing, yesterday
pasta . . . 7. gnocchi, lasagna, ravioli 8. linguini, macaroni 9. fettucini, manicotti, spaghetti 10. vermicelli
paste . . . 3. pap, poi 4. glue, sham 5. dough, stick 6. mastic, strass 8. adhesive, frippery, mucilage 10. confection 13. stick together
pastel . . . 5. light 6. crayon, sketch 9. pale color
pastille . . . 6. troche 7. lozenge
pastime . . . 4. game 5. hobby, sport 9. amusement, diversion 10. recreation 13. entertainment
pastor . . . 5. rabbi 6. curate, divine, keeper, parson, priest, rector 8. chaplain, guardian, minister, Reverend, shepherd
pastoral . . . 4. poem 5. drama, rural 6. poetic 7. romance 14. ecclesiastical
pastoral (pert to) . . .
cantata . . 8. serenata
crook, staff . . 5. pedum 7. crosier
god . . 3. Pan
oboe . . 7. musette
pert to . . 6. rustic 8. agrestic, herdsman, shepherd
pipe . . 3. oat 4. reed
poem . . 4. idyl 7. bucolic, eclogue
pastry . . . 3. pie 4. tart 6. Danish, éclair 7. dariole, strudel 8. napoleon, pandowdy, turnover 9. cream puff, shortcake 10. pâtisserie
past tense . . . 8. preterit (preterite)
pasturage, right of . . . 9. horsegate
pasture . . . 3. ham, lea 4. feed, food 5. agist, grama, grass, graze 6. meadow 9. grassland 10. agostadero
pasture bird . . . 6. plover 7. sparrow
pat . . . 3. dab, fit, paw, tap 4. blow, lump 5. fixed, impel, known, throw 6. caress, smooth, stroke 7. flatten 9. immovable 10. seasonable
Patagonia (S Am) . . .
city . . 11. Punta Arenas
deity . . 7. Setebos
Indian tribe . . 9. Tehuelche
nearby island . . 14. Tierra del Fuego
race (said of) . . 6. giants 7. Big Feet, tallest 9. Patagones
rodent . . 4. cavy 8. capybara, Caviidae
strait . . 8. Magellan (Magallanes)
patamar (pattamar) . . . 6. vessel (Naut) 7. courier 9. messenger
patata . . . 6. potato 11. sweet potato
patch . . . 4. mend, vamp 5. bodge, botch, clump, cover, field 6. blotch 8. appliqué

cobble, parcel 8. addition
9. reconcile
patch (pert to)...
cloth.. 5. clout
imprinting.. 5. friar
metal.. 6. solder
of trees.. 4. mott
patcher (humorous)... 6. sartor
patchwork... 5. quilt 6. jumble, pillow,
scraps 7. mixture 9. checkered,
fancywork, fragments
10. hodgepodge
pate... 3. pie, top 4. head 5. brain,
crown, pasty, patty 6. badger
pâté de foie gras... 5. patty (goose
liver and truffles)
patella... 3. pan 4. bone, dish, vase
7. kneecap, kneepan
paten... 4. disc, dish, disk 5. plate
7. patener (bearer of)
patent... 4. open 5. berat (Turk), right
7. license, warrant 8. document,
manifest 9. available, copyright,
privilege, trademark 10. accessible,
protection, university
12. unobstructed
pater... 6. father, priest
Pater Noster... 11. Lord's Prayer
Paternoster Row... 6. street (London)
Pater Patriae... 18. Father of his
country (Cicero, Marius, Trajan,
Washington, etc)
path... 3. way 4. lane, line 5. piste,
route, swath, track, trail 6. course
7. footway
path (pert to)...
along a slope.. 4. berm (berme)
animal.. 5. piste, spoor 6. roddin
7. rodding
of energy.. 7. ergodic
of moving parts.. 5. locus
of planets.. 5. orbit
Spanish.. 6. camino, comino
pathetic... 3. sad 5. teary 8. dolorous,
grievous, stirring 9. affecting
10. lamentable
pathological... 6. morbid 9. unhealthy
pathological reaction... 7. allergy
patience... 9. endurance, fortitude,
solitaire, tolerance 10. submission,
sufferance 11. forbearance,
resignation 12. acquiescence,
perseverance
patient... 4. calm, meek 6. client
8. tolerant 9. unsettled
11. persevering 13. long–suffering
patio... 5. court 9. courtyard
patriarch... 4. Noah, sire 5. elder,
pater 6. bishop, father 7. aged man,
veteran 9. churchman
10. Methuselah 13. paterfamilias
patrimonial... 9. inherited
10. hereditary
patrimony... 8. heritage 10. birthright
11. ancient rite, inheritance
patriot... 4. Cato (Rom), Otis (Am)
5. jingo 7. chauvin 9. flag–waver
10. chauvinist, countryman
patriotism... 10. chauvinism
11. nationalism 13. love of country
patrol... 5. guard 7. protect
8. traverse 9. keep guard

13. perambulation
patron... 5. buyer, guest 6. backer,
seller, trader 8. customer, guardian
9. financier, protector, supporter
10. benefactor
patronage... 5. aegis (egis), favor
6. defend 7. support 8. auspices
9. clientele, fosterage 10. assistance
13. condescension, encouragement
patronizing... 8. deigning 9. financing,
revealing 10. sponsoring
13. condescending
patrons (group)... 7. backers, masters
9. clientele, customers
Patron Saint of...
beggars.. 5. Giles
boys.. 8. Nicholas
England.. 4. Anne 6. George
fishermen.. 5. Peter
France.. 5. Denis
Ireland.. 7. Patrick
lawyers.. 4. Ives
motherhood.. 6. Gerard
musicians.. 7. Cecilia
Pueblo Indians.. 7. Stephen
sailors.. 4. Elmo
Scotland.. 6. Andrew
shoemakers.. 7. Crispin
swineherds.. 7. Anthony
Venice.. 4. Mark 9. Pantalone
Wales.. 5. David
patten... 4. clog 5. skate 8. footgear,
overshoe, snowshoe
pattern... 4. norm, seme 5. habit,
model 6. design, format 7. diagram,
paragon 8. paradigm, parterre,
template
pavilion... 4. tent 5. cover, kiosk
6. canopy 8. covering 9. gloriette
10. tabernacle
pavis... 5. cover 6. screen, shield
7. protect
paw... 3. pad, pud 4. foot, hand
5. patté, pedal 6. handle, stroke
7. foreleg (Her) 8. forefoot
10. manipulate
pawl... 4. bolt, sear, trip 5. click
6. detent, pallet, tongue 7. ratchet
9. mechanism
pawn... 4. gage, hock, tool 6. pledge
7. counter, peacock 8. chessman,
guaranty, hockshop 9. put in pawn
10. pawnbroker
Pawnee... 6. Indian
pawnie... 7. peacock
pay... 3. aby (abye), fee, tip 4. ante,
meet, wage 5. remit, repay
6. defray, reward, salary, suffer
7. requite, satisfy 9. indemnify,
reimburse, retaliate 10. compensate,
punishment, recompense, remunerate
11. retribution 12. compensation
pay (pert to)...
attention.. 4. heed 6. listen
back.. 6. rebate, refund 9. reimburse,
retaliate
dirt.. 3. ore
envelope.. 5. wages 6. salary
7. stipend
extra.. 5. bonus 8. kickback
for.. 3. aby (abye) 5. atone 6. suffer
off.. 6. punish 7. requite 9. pay in

full, retribute 10. compensate
out.. 5. spend 6. expend, settle
7. hand out 8. disburse
10. distribute 12. exorbitantly
14. through the nose
up.. 4. ante 6. settle 9. liquidate
paymaster... 6. burser, purser
7. cashier
payment... 3. cro, fee 4. dues, mail
6. return 8. defrayal, requital
10. punishment, recompense
12. chastisement, compensation
payment (pert to)...
for homicide, murder.. 3. cro 4. eric
(Brehon Law) 7. galanas (Welsh),
wergild (weregild)
immediate.. 4. cash
upon delivery.. 3. COD 14. cash on
delivery
paynim... 5. pagan 7. heathen, infidel
8. Pagandom 10. Mohammedan
payong... 8. umbrella (golden)
paysage... 7. picture (landscape)
9. landscape
pea (pert to)...
bird.. 6. oriole
chick.. 4. gram 5. Cicer
everlasting (Bib).. 9. vetchling
family.. 8. Fabaceae
flour (seasoned).. 9. Erbswurst
heath.. 7. carmele
pigeon.. 3. dal 5. arhar
sausage.. 9. Erbswurst
shaped.. 8. pisiform
soup.. 3. fog (dull yellow)
split.. 3. dal
tree.. 8. laburnum
tropical.. 4. dove 7. Zenaida
12. mourning dove
vine.. 8. earthpea
peace... 3. pax 5. amity, quiet, truce
6. accord, repose 7. harmony,
Nirvana, silence 8. ataraxia (ataraxy),
serenity 9. stillness 10. quiescence
11. tranquility
peaceable... 5. quiet, still 6. irenic,
silent 7. henotic, pacific 8. amicable,
tranquil 9. quiescent 10. concordant,
harmonious 11. undisturbed
peaceful... 4. calm 5. irene 6. irenic,
placid, serene 7. halcyon, pacific
8. tranquil 11. comfortable
peace pipe... 7. calumet
peach... 5. fruit 6. accuse, betray,
brandy, indict, inform 7. impeach
8. quandong 9. red–yellow
peach (pert to)...
cordial.. 7. persico 8. persicot
family.. 12. Amygdalaceae
French.. 8. persicot
grafted (quince).. 9. melocoton
like.. 6. almond
origin.. 5. China
stone.. 7. putamen
variety.. 7. Elberta 8. Crawford
9. freestone, nectarine 10. clingstone
peacock... 3. mao 4. Pavo (Astron),
pawn, pose 5. strut 9. swaggerer
peacock (pert to)...
blue (color).. 4. paon
butterfly.. 2. io
fan.. 9. flabellum

feather part.. 4. marl
female.. 6. peahen
fish.. 6. wrasse
flower.. 9. poinciana
heron.. 7. bittern
ref to.. 7. peafowl 8. pavonine
tail spot.. 3. eye
peak... 3. alp, epi, pic, top, tor
4. acme, apex, cone, crag, cusp,
dent, dolt 5. crown, piton, slink,
sneak, steal 6. finial, shrink, summit
8. headland, mountain 9. simpleton
10. promontory
Peak... 5. Borah, Logan 7. Everest, St
Elias 8. McKinley 9. Mont Blanc
10. Matterhorn 11. Kilimanjaro
12. Popocatepetl
peal... 4. boom, clap, echo, ring, toll
6. appeal, shovel 7. resound,
summons, thunder 8. carillon
peanut... 5. pinda (pindal, pindar)
6. goober, trifle 8. earthnut,
earthpea, katchung
pear (pert to)...
alligator.. 7. avocado
cider.. 5. perry
Latin.. 5. pirum
prickly.. 4. tuna 5. nopal 7. Opuntia
shaped.. 8. pyriform
shaped vessel.. 6. aludel
squash.. 7. chayote
type.. 4. Bosc 8. Bartlett
pearl... 3. gem 4. drop 5. nacre,
tooth, white 9. margarite
pearl (pert to)...
bird.. 10. guinea fowl
color.. 4. blue 13. mother–of–pearl
eye.. 8. cataract
imitation.. 6. olivet
of great luster.. 6. orient
opal.. 9. cacholong (opaque)
oyster.. 7. Avicula
seed.. 7. aliofar (obs)
vegetable.. 5. onion
pearly... 5. milky, quick, smart
7. opaline, whitish 8. pellucid
10. opalescent 11. flourishing
Pearly Gates (Bib)... 6. heaven, twelve
peasant... 4. boor, hind, peon, serf
5. clown, knave, swain 6. carlot,
cotman, cottar, rascal, rustic
10. countryman
peasant (pert to)...
Arab, Syria.. 6. fellah
cropsharer.. 7. metayer
English.. 4. hind 5. churl
Indian.. 4. ryot
Irish.. 4. kern (kerne) 7. cottier
like.. 4. base, rude 8. clownish
Russian.. 5. kulak (rich)
Scottish.. 4. tyke (tike) 6. cotter
(cottar)
pease... 5. quiet 6. pacify 7. appease
9. reconcile
peasecrow... 4. tern
peat... 3. bog, pet 4. coal, fuel, moor,
moss, turf 6. minion 7. darling
8. favorite 11. combustible
peat (pert to)...
cutter.. 5. piner
moss.. 8. sphagnum
turf spade.. 5. slave

wood.. 11. loosestrife
peau... 4. skin (silks) 6. fabric
peba... 9. armadillo
pebble... 5. scree, stone, talus
6. quartz 7. chuckie (chucky), crystal,
psephos 11. gravelstone, pebblestone
peccadillo... 4. slip 5. error, fault,
lapse 12. indiscretion
peccant... 3. bad 5. wrong 6. guilty,
morbid, wicked 7. corrupt, sinning,
spoiled 9. incorrect, unhealthy
12. insalubrious
peccary... 6. mammal (piglike)
7. Tagassu, Tayassu 8. javelina
pech... 4. pant 11. breathe hard
pecht (Scot)... 5. fairy, gnome, pygmy
peck... 3. dab, dot, eat, nag 4. food,
hole, jerk, kiss 5. pitch, prick, throw
6. peggle, stroke 7. measure
8. quantity 11. large amount
peck at... 3. nag 4. carp, twit
5. tease 6. attack, harass
pectase... 6. enzyme
peculiar... 3. odd 4. idio (comb form)
5. queer 6. oddish, unique
7. curious, special, strange, typical
8. distinct, separate, singular
9. different, eccentric 10. particular
14. characteristic
peculiar expression... 5. idiom
peculiarity... 4. kink 5. quirk, trait
6. oddity 7. oddness 9. mannerism
10. partiality 11. singularity
12. eccentricity 14. characteristic
peculiar to a district... 7. endemic
pecuniary... 6. fiscal 8. monetary
9. financial
pedagogue... 5. tutor 6. pedant
7. teacher 12. schoolmaster
pedal... 4. foot 5. lever 6. driver
7. treadle 9. propeller
pedant... 4. prig 5. tutor 6. dorbel,
purist 9. formalist, pedagogue
10. conformist 12. bluestocking,
precisionist, schoolmaster
peddle... 4. hawk, sell, vend 6. piddle,
retail 11. disseminate
peddler, pedlar... 6. cadger, coster,
hawker, mugger, sutler 7. chapman
8. huckster 9. vivandier
12. costermonger
peddler's French... 6. jargon (thieves')
9. gibberish
pedestal... 7. support 10. foundation
pedestal part... 3. die 4. base, dado
5. socle 6. plinth, quadra
pedestrian... 3. ped 4. dull, slow
5. hiker 6. hoofer, walker
11. commonplace 12. foot traveler
13. unimaginative
pedicel... 3. ray (of an umbel) 4. stem
5. stalk 8. peduncle
pediculosis... 9. lousiness
Pediculus... 4. lice
pedigree... 6. stemma 7. descent,
lineage 8. ancestry, register
9. genealogy 10. family tree
pedio (comb form)... 4. sole 6. instep
pedology... 9. soil study 10. child
study
pedometer... 5. watch 8. odograph
10. instrument, passometer

pedregal... 9. lava field
pedum... 5. crook, staff (pastoral)
peduncle... 4. stem 5. scape, stalk
7. pedicel, pedicle, sessile
peek... 3. pry 4. peep 5. chirp, flash
6. glance 7. glimpse 9. look slyly
peekaboo... 4. game 6. bopeep
peel... 4. bark, pare, rind, skin
5. slipe, stake, strip 6. cut off,
lamina, shovel 8. car blade, palisade,
stockade
peel (off)... 4. harl, pare, tear 7. come
off 8. get loose 11. decorticate
peeler... 4. crab (shedding), yarn
5. corer 7. hustler 8. pillager
9. policeman
peep... 3. pry 4. peek, peer, pule,
skeg 5. cheep, chirp, pipit, sight
(firearms) 6. glance, squeak
7. crevice 8. peephole 9. sandpiper
peephole... 4. hole 6. eyelet
8. aperture 9. sighthole
peer... 4. duke, earl, fere, gaze, mate
5. baron, equal, match, noble, stare,
stime (styme) 7. marquis
8. nobleman, superior, viscount
Peer Gynt (pert to)...
drama, poem by.. 5. Ibsen
mother.. 3. Ase
music suite by.. 5. Grieg
peerless... 9. matchless, nonpareil,
paper size, unequaled, unmatched
10. unexcelled 11. ne plus ultra,
superlative
peesweep, peeseweep... 7. lapwing
10. greenfinch
peetweep... 9. sandpiper (spotted)
peeved... 4. sore 7. annoyed, nettled
9. irritated
peevish... 3. coy 4. sour 5. cross,
sulky, techy, testy 6. crusty, morose,
touchy 7. fretful, pettish, spleeny,
waspish 8. captious, choleric,
contrary, perverse, petulant, snappish
9. irascible, irritable, querulous,
splenetic
peg... 3. hob, leg, nob, nog, pin
4. dram, skeg 5. drink, stake, tooth
6. drudge, fasten, reason 7. pretext,
support 9. persevere, recognize
peg (pert to)...
cribbage.. 4. game
iron.. 5. piton
out.. 7. croquet
shoe.. 5. cleat
wood.. 5. spill, thole 8. treenail
pega... 5. shark 6. remora
Pegasus... 5. horse (winged), steed
13. constellation
Pegasus's rider... 11. Bellerophon
pegomancy, divination by...
7. springs 9. fountains
peho... 8. morepork
peignoir... 8. negligee 12. dressing
gown, dressing sack
pejorative... 11. disparaging
12. depreciatory
Peking, Pekin... 4. blue, city, duck
7. spaniel
pelagic... 6. marine 7. oceanic
9. underseas
pelagic organism... 6. nekton

7. benthos 8. plankton
Pele... 7. goddess (volcanoes)
pêle–mêle... 8. pellmell
Peleus (pert to)...
  father.. 6. Aeacus
  King of.. 9. Myrmidons
  son.. 8. Achilles
  wife.. 6. Thetis
pelf... 3. fur, rob 4. gain 5. booty,
  lucre, money, spoil, trash 6. pilfer,
  profit, refuse, riches, wealth
  7. rubbish 10. ne'er–do–well
Pelias (pert to)...
  daughter.. 5. Medes
  King of.. 6. Iolcus
  nephew.. 5. Jason
  son.. 7. Acastus
pelican (pert to)...
  heraldry.. 10. in her piety
  symbolic of.. 6. Christ 7. charity
Pelican State... 9. Louisiana
pell... 3. fur 4. hide, pelt, skin
  5. hurry 6. hasten 13. parchment
  roll
pellagra... 5. zeism
pellar, peller... 6. wizard 8. conjurer
pellet... 4. ball, pill 6. bullet
  7. granule, missile, pallion
pellicle... 4. film, scum 6. lamina
  7. coating 8. membrane
pell–mell, pellmell... 10. vehemently
  12. furious haste 13. helter–skelter
pellock... 8. porpoise
pellucid... 5. clear 6. bright, limpid
  8. luminous 11. translucent,
  transparent 12. intelligible
pelmet... 7. valance (short)
Peloponnesus...
  capital.. 7. Corinth
  city.. 7. Argolis
  League.. 11. Confederacy
  peninsula (Gr).. 5. Morea
  12. Peloponnesos (old), Peloponnesus
  (modern)
  race (anc).. 6. Dorian 7. Spartan
  School.. 6. Dorian 9. Sculpture
  War.. 12. Athens–Sparta (BC)
Pelops (pert to)...
  father.. 8. Tantalus
  son.. 6. Atreus 8. Thyestes
  wife.. 10. Hippodamia
pelota... 4. ball, game 5. cesta
  7. fronton, jai alai
pelt... 3. fur 4. blow, fell, hide, push,
  skin 5. stone 6. hurl at, pelage,
  refuse, strike, thrust 7. apparel (of
  skins), rubbish 8. woolfell
peltry... 4. furs, pelt 5. skins
peludo... 9. armadillo (six–banded)
pelvic bone... 5. ilium 7. ischium
  8. seat bone
pelvic–shaped... 11. basin–shaped
pemmican... 4. meat (dried) 7. buffalo,
  venison
pen... 3. cot, sty 4. bolt, coop, gaol
  5. abode, hutch, quill, write
  6. fasten, indite 7. confine
  9. enclosure 12. penitentiary
pen (pert to)...
  like.. 7. styloid
  name.. 6. anonym 9. pseudonym
  10. nom de plume

point.. 3. neb, nib 4. stub
text.. 5. ronde
penalize... 4. fine 5. mulct 6. punish
  8. handicap
penalty... 4. fine, loss 7. forfeit
  8. handicap, hardship
  10. punishment, repentance
Penang Islands capital...
  10. Georgetown
penchant... 4. bent 6. desire, liking
  7. leaning 8. tendency 10. attraction
  11. inclination 12. decided taste
pendant... 3. bob, tag 4. tail 5. aglet
  (aiglet), queue 6. tassel 7. eardrop,
  earring, hanging 8. appendix,
  pendulum 9. lavaliere 10. chandelier
pendent... 3. lop 4. pend 7. hanging
  8. appended 9. impending,
  pendulous 11. jutting over,
  overhanging
pendent cone (limestone)...
  10. stalactite
pendulous fold, skin... 6. dewlap
Penelope (pert to)...
  father.. 7. Icarius
  husband.. 7. Ulysses 8. Odysseus
  island.. 6. Ithaca
  suitor.. 7. Agelaus
penetrate... 4. bore, gore, stab
  5. delve, elbow, enter 6. pierce
  7. pervade 8. permeate 9. perforate
  10. move deeply
penetrating... 4. cold, deep 5. acute,
  sharp 6. shrill, subtle 7. caustic,
  odorous 8. incisive 9. pervading,
  sagacious, searching
penetration... 6. acumen 7. ingress,
  insight 9. acuteness, sharpness
  11. discernment, perforation
  14. discrimination
Peneus (pert to)...
  father of.. 6. Daphne
  genus of.. 6. prawns
  god of.. 11. Peneus River (Thessalia)
penguin... 3. auk 6. Johnny 10. rock
  hopper
penguin (pert to)...
  aviation.. 13. training plane
  duck.. 12. Indian Runner (duck)
  genus.. 8. Eudyptes
  nest.. 7. rookery 10. penguinery
  type.. 4. king 6. Adelie 7. emperor,
  jackass
peninsula... 4. neck 6. penile
  10. chersonese
Peninsula...
  Asia.. 5. Malay
  Cimbrian, Cimbric.. 7. Jutland
  Iberia.. 5. Spain
  Seward.. 6. Alaska
  Tauric.. 6. Crimea
  Thracian.. 9. Gallipoli
penitent... 5. sorry 8. contrite
  9. repentant
penitential discipline... 7. penance
penitential period... 4. Lent
pennant... 4. fane, flag, whip
  6. banner, burgee (yacht), ensign,
  pennon, pinion 9. banderole
pennant fish... 11. cobblerfish
pennate... 6. winged 7. pinnate
  9. feathered, penniform

pennon... 4. flag, wing 6. banner, pinion 8. streamer

Pennsylvania...
capital.. 10. Harrisburg
city.. 4. Erie 7. Reading 8. Scranton 10. Pittsburgh 12. Philadelphia
famed site.. 10. Gettysburg 11. Liberty Bell, Valley Forge 16. Independence Hall
founder.. 11. William Penn
mountain.. 5. Davis 11. Alleghenies
named, first.. 10. Penn's Woods
river.. 4. Ohio 8. Delaware 10. Schuylkill 11. Susquehanna
State admission.. 6. second
State motto.. 28. Virtue, Liberty and Independence
State nickname.. 8. Keystone

penny... 4. cent, coin 5. pence 6. copper, stiver 8. denarius (Bib)

penologist, famed... 5. Lawes

penology, study of... 11. criminology 18. punishment for crime

pensive... 3. sad 5. mesto, sober 6. dreamy, musing 7. wistful 10. meditative, melancholy, reflective, thoughtful 13. contemplative

pentastich... 4. poem 6. stanza 7. strophe 10. five verses

Pentateuch... 5. Torah (Tora) 10. Law of Moses 14. First Five Books (Old Test) 16. Five Books of Moses

Pentecost... 8. festival 10. Whitsunday

Pentheus (pert to)...
grandson of.. 6. Cadmus
King of.. 6. Thebes
mother.. 5. Agave

penthouse... 6. lean–to 7. leaning, pentice 9. apartment (roof) 11. overhanging

penury... 4. want 7. poverty 9. indigence, privation 10. scantiness 11. destitution, miserliness

peon... 4. pawn (chess), serf 7. laborer, peasant, soldier 9. attendant, constable, messenger, policeman

peony... 4. piny 6. moutan 7. Paeonia 11. Burmese ruby

people... 3. kin, men 4. folk, ones, race, Rais 5. demos, laity 6. family, nation, public 7. kinsmen, persons 8. populace, subjects 9. citizenry 10. population

people (pert to)...
Am Indian, Eskimo.. 7. Amerind
ancient.. 5. Medes 6. Greeks, Romans 7. Sabines 9. Egyptians, Etruscans
class, lowest.. 8. canaille
common.. 6. vulgar 7. tilikum (tilicum)
headless (Myth).. 8. Acephali
old–fashioned.. 6. prudes 7. squares 13. antediluvians
ref to.. 4. laic 6. ethnic 7. demotic
Spanish.. 5. gente
wild young.. 10. rantipoles

people (of)...
culture (earliest).. 8. Grecians
gentle birth.. 6. gentry
one government.. 6. nation
rank.. 11. aristocracy, aristocrats

the people.. 6. ethnic

peopled... 5. abadi (Ind village) 8. occupied, populous 9. populated

pep... 2. go 3. vim 4. dash 6. energy 7. quicken 9. stimulate 10. initiative, liveliness

pepper... 4. pelt 5. shoot 6. energy 7. bombard 8. sprinkle 9. condiment

pepper (pert to)...
betel.. 4. siri (sirih)
black.. 11. Piper nigrum
box.. 5. tower 8. spitfire
Capsicum, source of.. 7. cayenne, chilies (chili), paprika
climbing.. 5. betel 6. nigrum
condiment.. 7. cayenne, paprika
dulse.. 7. seaweed (red)
genus.. 8. Capsicum
grass.. 5. crass 8. pillwort
sauce.. 7. Tabasco
turnip.. 15. jack–in–the–pulpit

pepper (pert to country)...
Australia.. 4. kava (cava) 8. kavakava
Borneo.. 4. kava (cava)
Guinea.. 5. chili 8. Capsicum
Malay.. 4. siri (sirih)
Spain.. 7. paprika, pimento 8. allspice, pimiento

pepper–and–salt... 4. gray 17. harbinger–of–spring

peppermint... 3. oil 4. herb 6. spirit 7. essence, gum tree, lozenge, menthol (camphor)

peppery... 5. fiery 7. piquant, pungent 8. choleric, spirited, stinging 10. passionate 11. hot–tempered

per... 2. by 7. for each, through 9. by means of 11. according to

peradventure... 3. hap 5. doubt 7. it may be 8. possibly 11. uncertainty

perambulate... 4. walk 6. ramble, stroll 8. traverse 9. promenade, walk about

perceive... 3. see 4. hear, know, note 5. sense 6. behold, descry, detect, divine, notice, remark 7. discern, observe, sensate 9. apprehend 10. comprehend, understand 11. distinguish 12. discriminate

perceptible... 5. faint 7. tactile, visible 8. knowable, manifest, tangible 10. cognizable 11. appreciable, discernible, perceivable

perception... 3. ear 4. tact 5. sense, taste 6. acumen, seeing 8. sagacity 9. awareness, sensation 10. cognizance 11. discernment 13. consciousness 14. discrimination

perceptive... 7. knowing 8. sensible 9. sagacious 14. discriminative

perch... 3. bar, peg, rod, sit 4. fish, pole 5. aerie, barse, roost, sit on, staff 6. alight, aviary, sauger, settle, weapon 7. measure 9. trumpeter

Percheron... 5. horse 15. Percheron Norman

perchers... 5. birds 7. candles 8. Passeres 10. Insessores

percolate... 4. ooze, seep, sift, silt, sipe 5. exude, leach, steep 6. filter, strain 7. trickle 8. permeate, transude

percussion... 9. collision
  10. concussion, detonation
percussion instrument... 4. drum,
  gong 5. bells, bones, traps
  6. Becken, chimes, tom–tom
  7. celesta, cymbals, marimba, potlids
  8. carillon, clappers, triangle
  9. castanets, xylophone
  10. tambourine, vibraphone
  12. glockenspiel
perdition... 4. hell, loss (soul), ruin
  5. wreck 9. damnation
  11. destruction
peregrinate... 6. travel, wander 7. go
  about, sojourn
peregrine... 5. alien 6. exotic, falcon
  7. foreign, pilgrim, strange
  9. foreigner
perempt... 5. quash 6. defeat
  7. destroy
peremptory... 5. final 7. express
  8. absolute, arrogant, decisive,
  dogmatic, positive, resolute
  9. arbitrary, mandatory
  10. compulsory, conclusive,
  imperative, obligatory 11. dictatorial
  13. authoritative 16. incontrovertible
perennial... 7. lasting 8. constant,
  enduring 9. continual, evergreen,
  permanent, perpetual, unceasing
  10. continuous 12. never–failing
perennial (pert to)...
  climbing.. 5. liana (liane)
  grass.. 4. lyme 6. Elymus (genus)
  7. wild rye
  herb.. 4. Geum 5. avens
  weed.. 8. toadflax
perfect... 4. holy, pure, sole 5. ideal,
  model, teleo (comb form), whole
  6. entire 7. correct, develop, improve
  8. finished 9. blameless, faultless,
  inviolate, righteous 10. consummate,
  satisfying 11. unqualified
perfection... 4. acme 5. ideal
  7. paragon 8. accuracy, maturity
  10. completion, excellence
  13. faultlessness
perfectly... 5. quite 7. ideally, rightly,
  utterly 9. correctly 10. absolutely,
  accurately, altogether, completely,
  flawlessly, thoroughly
perfecto... 5. cigar (tapering)
perficient... 6. actual 9. effective,
  effectual
perfidious... 6. shifty 8. disloyal
  9. faithless 11. disaffected,
  treacherous 12. falsehearted
perfidy... 7. treason 8. apostasy
  9. duplicity, treachery 10. disloyalty
  13. faithlessness
perforate... 4. bore, dock 5. drill,
  punch 6. pierce, pounce, riddle
  9. penetrate 10. umbilicate
perforated...
  block.. 3. nut
  initials (Philat).. 10. stamp marks
  nozzle.. 4. rose
  space.. 5. brain
  sphere.. 4. bead
perforation... 4. bore, hole 6. eyelet
  8. aperture, piercing, punching
perform... 2. do 3. act 4. play

  5. enact, exert 6. effect 7. execute,
  fulfill, produce 8. complete, transact
  9. officiate 10. accomplish, bring
  about, perpetrate
performance... 3. act 4. test, work
  6. action 7. exploit 8. ceremony
  9. operation 10. completion,
  exhibition, observance, production
  12. consummation
  14. accomplishment
performance (pert to)...
  clumsy.. 6. bungle
  daytime.. 7. matinee
  for one.. 4. solo
  notable.. 4. feat
  of duty.. 8. feasance
performer... 4. doer 5. actor
  6. dancer, worker 8. magician,
  musician, thespian 9. pretender
  15. prestidigitator
perfume... 4. balm, odor 5. aroma,
  attar, orris, savor, scent, smell
  7. bouquet, cologne, essence, rose
  oil 9. fragrance, redolence
  10. frangipani
perfume (pert to)...
  base.. 4. musk 9. ambergris
  cherry.. 7. mahaleb
  essence.. 8. bergamot
  medicated.. 8. pastille (pastil)
  musky.. 5. civet
  oriental.. 5. myrrh 7. incense
  12. frankincense
  scent.. 7. jasmine 8. lavender
  10. heliotrope
  toilet.. 6. bay rum 12. eau de
  Cologne
  unguent.. 6. pomade
  violet.. 5. irone
pergola... 5. arbor, bower, kiosk
  6. pandal 7. balcony, trellis
  9. colonnade 11. summerhouse
perhaps... 5. maybe 6. ablins (Scot)
  boliko, mayhap 8. doubtful, possibly,
  probably 9. perchance 10. contingent
peri... 3. elf 5. about (pref), fairy
  6. beauty
periapt... 5. charm 6. amulet
pericarp... 3. pod 5. berry, shell
  8. seedcase
Pericles (Gr)... 9. statesman
periculum (Rom law)... 4. risk 5. peril
  6. danger
perigee (Astron)... 12. nearest earth
  (opp of apogee)
peril... 4. risk 6. danger, hazard,
  menace 8. jeopardy
perilously high... 7. Icarian (flying)
perimeter... 5. ambit 6. border
  7. outline 8. boundary 9. periphery
period... 3. age, day, dot, end, eon,
  era, eve 4. stop, term, time, year
  5. cycle, epoch, limit, spell
  6. degree, moment, season
  8. duration, sentence 10. conclusion
  11. termination
period (pert to)...
  historical.. 4. eral 6. Eocene
  7. Neocene
  penitential.. 4. Lent
  statutory.. 10. limitation
  Tertiary.. 6. Eocene 7. Miocene,

Neocene 8. Pliocene
periodic... 4. eral 6. annual 7. etesian
8. seasonal 9. recurrent
10. rhythmical 12. intermittent
periodic (pert to)...
sea motion.. 4. tide
wind.. 2. oe 7. chinook, etesian,
monsoon
windstorm.. 2. oe 7. tornado
9. whirlwind
periodical... 5. paper 6. review
7. etesian, journal 8. magazine
9. recurring 11. publication
periodical cicada... 6. locust (17 yrs)
period of...
delay.. 10. moratorium
dryness.. 7. drought
evolution.. 6. hemera
fifty days.. 13. quinquagesima
five years.. 6. pentad
holding.. 6. tenure
instruction.. 7. session
possession.. 5. lease
probation.. 6. parole
prosperity.. 4. boom 6. golden
recovery.. 13. convalescence
14. reconstruction
sleep.. 11. hibernation
ten years.. 6. decade
time.. 3. age, day, eon 4. span
work.. 4. turn 5. shift, spell, watch
youth.. 6. nonage
peripatetic... 7. walking 8. rambling
Peripatetic (pert to Aristotle)...
6. school 8. disciple 10. Philosophy
peripheral... 6. distal 7. outmost
8. external 9. outlinear 10. round
about
periphery... 3. lip, rim 4. brim
5. ambit 6. areola, border
8. confines 9. perimeter
10. borderland 13. circumference
perique... 7. tobacco (strong) 10. otter
brown
perish... 3. die, rot 4. fade 5. decay,
waste 8. pass away, squander
9. cease to be, disappear 11. be
destroyed
perissodactyl... 15. odd–numbered
toes
peristyle... 7. columns (range of)
8. corridor 9. colonnade
10. peripteral
peritoneum fold... 7. omentum
periwig... 3. wig 6. frizzy, peruke
9. shellfish 10. periwinkle
periwinkle... 4. blue 5. snail
6. mussel, myrtle 9. evergreen
perjink... 4. neat, nice 7. precise
perjure... 7. violate 8. forswear
perjury... 9. violation 12. breech of
~ oath 13. false swearing
perk... 5. preen, prink 7. smarten
9. percolate 10. perquisite
perkin... 5. cider
perk up... 7. cheer up, improve, raise
up, refresh 10. recuperate
permanent... 5. fixed 6. innate, stable
7. abiding, durable, lasting
8. constant, enduring, inherent
9. perpetual 10. changeless,
continuing 12. unchangeable

permeate... 5. imbue 7. pervade
8. saturate
permission... 5. grace, leave
7. consent, license 9. allowance
10. sufferance 13. authorization
permissive... 8. optional 9. allowable,
permitted, tolerated 10. consenting,
permitting 13. power of choice
permit... 3. let 4. leve 5. allow, grant,
leave 6. suffer 7. consent, license,
warrant 8. tolerate 9. authorize
10. permission
permit to live... 5. spare 8. reprieve
permutate... 6. change 9. rearrange
11. interchange
permutation... 6. barter
11. interchange 13. transmutation
14. transformation
pern... 6. Pernis 7. buzzard (honey)
pernicious... 4. bane 5. fatal
6. anemia, deadly, malign, wicked
7. baleful, baneful, harmful, hurtful,
noisome, noxious, ruinous, vicious
10. villainous 11. deleterious
pernio... 9. chilblain
perorate... 5. speak (at length)
7. declaim 8. harangue 9. expatiate
perpendicular... 4. sine 5. erect,
plumb, sheer, steep 7. apothem,
upright 8. binormal, vertical
9. rectitude 10. standing up
11. precipitous
perpetrate... 6. commit 7. perform
12. carry through
perpetual... 7. endless, eternal
8. constant, unending 9. continual,
perennial, permanent, unceasing
10. continuous 11. everlasting
perpetually... 9. endlessly, eternally
11. ceaselessly 12. interminably
perpetuity... 7. annuity 8. eternity
11. endless time
perplex... 3. vex 4. cark 5. amaze
6. puzzle, riddle 7. confuse
8. bewilder, entangle 9. obfuscate
10. complicate
perplexity... 3. fog 6. tangle
7. anxiety, dilemma, problem
8. question 9. confusion, situation
10. complexity 11. distraction
12. bewilderment, complication
perquisite... 3. tip 4. gain 6. boodle
8. appanage, gratuity
perquod... 7. whereby
per se... 6. itself 8. directly
11. essentially 13. intrinsically
perse... 4. blue
persecute... 5. annoy, harry, hound
6. harass 7. afflict, oppress, torment
8. hunt down 9. martyrize
persecution... 9. treatment
10. harassment, oppression
12. mistreatment
Persephone (pert to)...
abductor.. 5. Hades
Attica, name.. 4. Kore (Cora)
deity of.. 11. agriculture
father.. 4. Zeus
Greek name.. 11. Persephassa
mother.. 7. Demeter
Orphic literary name.. 8. Despoina
queen of.. 15. infernal regions

Roman name.. 10. Proserpine
(Proserpina)
Perseus (pert to)...
Astron.. 13. Constellation
father.. 4. Zeus
mother.. 5. Danae
slayer of.. 6. Medusa
perseverance... 8. patience
9. constancy 10. resolution,
steadiness 11. persistence, pertinacity
13. steadfastness
persevere... 5. abide 6. endure, insist,
keep on 7. carry on, persist
8. continue
Persia (Iran, Irani)... see also *Persian*
capital.. 7. Teheran (Tehran)
city.. 5. Niriz 6. Abadan, Shiraz,
Tabriz 7. Hamadan, Ispahan
country (anc).. 4. Elam 7. Chaldea
gulf.. 4. Oman 7. Persian
gulf port.. 7. Bushire 9. Mohamerah
gulf province.. 6. Kuwait
gulf wind.. 6. shamal
lake.. 7. Rezaieh, Urumidh (Salt)
mountain.. 6. Ararat, Elburz, Zagros
9. Hindu Kush
pert to.. 0. Persic
river.. 5. Safid 9. Euphrates
ruins.. 10. Persepolis (Shiraz)
Persian (pert to)... see also *Iranian*
blue.. 10. regimental
calendar reformer.. 9. Jalalaean
(Jalalian)
carpet, rug.. 4. kali 5. Herat (Herati),
Senna 6. Kerman, Tabriz
11. Baluchistan
cushion.. 6. musnud
diadem.. 3. taj
door.. 3. dar
evergreen.. 4. olax
grass.. 6. millet
gum.. 10. tragacanth
hat.. 3. fez 6. turban
idiom.. 7. persism
javelin.. 6. jereed (jerid)
robe.. 3. gul
rug.. see *carpet* (above)
screen.. 6. purdah
Persian animals, birds, fruit...
apple.. 6. citron
bird.. 6. bulbul
cat.. 6. Angora
deer.. 5. maral 6. fallow
gazelle.. 4. cora
lamb.. 9. astrakhan, broadtail
lynx.. 7. caracul
tick (venomous).. 8. Miana bug
Persian Myth, Religion...
angel.. 3. Mah
deity.. 6. Ormazd (Supreme)
demigod, hero.. 4. Yima
demon.. 7. Apaosha
fairy.. 3. elf, fay 4. peri
fire worshiper.. 5. Parsi (Parsee)
god of light.. 7. Mithras
mystic.. 4. sufi
nymph.. 5. houri
religion founder.. 9. Zoroaster
religious doctrine.. 6. Babism
(Babiism)
sacred books (Zoroastrian).. 6. Avesta

scriptures (Moham).. 5. Koran
spirit.. 7. Ahriman
Persian people, government...
assembly (1906).. 6. Majlis (Mejlis)
caste (priestly).. 4. Magi 7. Wise Men
chief.. 3. mir 4. Shah
chief's wife, lady.. 4. bibi
civil officer.. 4. khan
dynasty.. 5. Kajar 7. Arsacid
8. Selencid 10. Sassanidae
(Sassanid)
governor (anc).. 6. satrap
King.. 4. Shah 5. Cyrus 6. Darius,
Xerxes
language (anc).. 4. Zend 7. Pahlavi
(Pahlevi)
natives.. 5. Kurds, Medes, Mukri,
Perse 6. Aryans
New Year's Day.. 7. Nowroze
people.. 7. Hadjemi, Iranics
8. Iranians
poet.. 4. Omar 5. Hafiz, Saadi
ruler.. 4. Shah 6. atabeg (atabek),
Sultan
student (Koran).. 5. hafiz
trader.. 4. Sart
tribe.. 4. Leks, Lurs 5. Arabs, Kurds,
Turks 7. Gypsies 8. Baluchis
Wise Men.. 4. Magi
persiflage... 6. banter 8. raillery
persimmon... 4. kaki 7. chapote
persist... 4. last, urge 6. endure
7. prevail 9. persevere
persistent... 7. durable 8. constant,
habitual 10. determined, inveterate
11. persevering 13. indefatigable
persistently opposed... 8. renitent
9. obstinate 12. recalcitrant
person... 3. one 4. body, soul
5. being, wight 6. figure 8. creature
9. character 10. Individual
person (pert to)...
accuser, challenger.. 9. appellant
acting for another.. 5. proxy
9. alternate
baptized (anc).. 11. illuminatus
base.. 7. caitiff, hangdog
bringing bad luck.. 4. jinx 5. Jonah
bringing good luck.. 6. mascot
canonized.. 5. saint
careless.. 7. trifler 11. pococurante
charged with high mission.. 7. apostle
charitable.. 9. samaritan
cheerful.. 8. optimist
clumsy.. 3. oaf 5. staup 6. lummox
7. bungler
common.. 3. lay 8. roturier
conceited.. 4. prig
contemptible.. 3. cad 4. heel, toad
7. bauchle (Scot)
crazed.. 6. maniac 10. monomaniac,
psychopath
credulous.. 5. Simon
cruel.. 5. fiend
dishonorable.. 6. rotter
dissolute.. 4. roué
drunken.. 4. lush
dull.. 4. dolt 5. dunce, moron, stock
6. dorbel 9. blockhead
dwarf.. 5. shurf
educated.. 6. pedant, pundit, savant
7. erudite, learned, student

8. cultured, highbrow 9. literatus
12. intellectual
emitting smoke .. 7. whiffer
enterprising .. 8. go–getter
fabulously rich .. 5. Midas
foolish .. 3. sop 4. zany 5. clown,
idiot, nutty 6. dotard 7. bonkers,
buffoon 9. simpleton
gigantic .. 5. giant, titan 7. monster
gloomy .. 7. killjoy 10. crosspatch
good luck .. 6. mascot
grotesque .. 9. golliwogg
guilty .. 7. culprit, transgressor
held as pledge .. 7. hostage
image of .. 4. doll, idol 5. clone
6. poppet, puppet
impatient .. 6. fidget 7. hotspur
important .. 3. VIP 5. mogul
7. magnate, notable 9. personage
indifferent .. 5. stoic
inexperienced .. 9. greenhorn
insignificant .. 5. sprat 6. little, nobody
lazy .. 5. drone 8. sluggard
learned .. see *educated* (above)
left–handed .. 6. clumsy 8. sinister
9. portsider
loud–voiced .. 7. stentor 8. blowhard
low–bred ., 3. cad 6. vulgar
miserly .. 9. skinflint 10. curmudgeon
non–Jewish .. 5. Aryan 7. Gentile
overmodest .. 5. prude 8. bluenose
perfidious .. 5. snake 7. traitor
9. faithless
rapacious .. 4. wolf 5. harpy
relaxed .. 4. calm 8. laid–back
representing another .. 5. proxy
7. stand–in 9. alternate
respondent to appeal .. 8. appellee
rich .. 7. wealthy 9. plutocrat
10. capitalist 11. millionaire
rude, ill–mannered .. 4. boor 5. yahoo
scatterbrained .. 6. madcap
self–centered .. 6. egoist 7. egotist
9. extrovert, introvert
self–righteous .. 8. pharisee
sharp–eyed .. 5. alert, Argus
sick .. 9. aegrotant, bedridden
skilled .. 6. artist, master 7. artisan
8. mechanic
staff (Mil) .. 10. aide–de–camp
stupid .. 3. ass 4. dolt, gump, nerd
5. moron, stock
supercilious .. 4. snob 9. conceited
thankless .. 7. ingrate
unclassified .. 11. nondescript
unique .. 4. oner
unknown .. 7. inconnu 8. inconnue
unmarried .. 6. maiden, single
8. bachelor, celibate, spinster
untidy .. 5. messy 6. grungy
8. slipshod, slovenly 9. litterbug
valorous .. 4. hero 8. champion
violent–tempered .. 6. tartar
wealthy .. 5. nabob, pluto (comb form)
10. capitalist 11. millionaire
who reads, writes .. 8. literate
witty .. 3. wag 7. punster
8. comedian 10. comedienne
worthless .. 5. lorel, losel
writ serving .. 6. elisor
young .. 9. stripling
14. whippersnapper

personage ... 5. image, mogul
7. bearing, stature 8. great man,
one's body, portrait
13. impersonation
persona grata ... 13. welcome person
16. acceptable person
personal (pert to) ...
appearance .. 8. presence
comb form .. 4. idio
history .. 6. memoir
ornament .. 6. parure
ownership, land .. 6. estate
7. demesne 8. chattels, property
personality ... 3. ego 5. being
6. person 8. identity 13. individuality
15. distinctiveness
persona non grata ...
18. unacceptable person
personate ... 5. enact 7. feigned
9. represent 10. personated
11. counterfeit
personification ... 3. Una (truth)
10. embodiment 11. attribution
14. representation
person of ...
age .. 5. major
courage .. 7. Spartan
eighty years .. 12. octogenarian
encyclopedic learning .. 10. polyhistor
fifty years .. 15. quinquagenarian
forty years .. 14. quadragenarian
great intellect .. 6. genius
nervous disorders .. 8. neurotic
ninety years .. 12. nonagenarian
one hundred years .. 11. centenarian
seventy years .. 14. septuagenarian
sixty years .. 12. sexagenarian
skill .. 6. master, talent 7. magnate
persons of ...
a familiar set .. 7. coterie
a family tree .. 6. stirps
groups .. 4. army, band, team
6. chorus, troupe 7. company
8. assembly 9. orchestra
organized bodies .. 5. corps, posse
perspicacity ... 6. acumen, vision
8. sagacity 9. acuteness
11. discernment, penetration
perspicuity ... 8. lucidity, sagacity
12. translucency, transparency
perspiration ... 5. sudor, sweat
7. sudoric 8. hard work
11. evaporation, saline fluid
13. transpiration
persuade ... 4. coax, sway, urge
6. entice, induce, reason 7. convert,
suasion 8. convince, inveigle
9. influence, plead with, stonewall
persuasible ... 6. pliant
11. persuadable
14. open–mindedness
persuasive ... 8. eloquent 9. impelling
10. convincing, persuading
pert ... 3. gay 4. bold, keen 5. brash,
sassy, saucy 6. clever, comely,
dapper, daring, lively, nimble
7. forward 8. handsome, skillful
9. exquisite, officious, sprightly
11. impertinent 12. presumptuous
pert (girl) ... 4. chit, minx
pertain ... 5. belie 6. belong, relate
7. adjunct 8. function, peculiar

9. accessory, appendage, appertain, attribute

pertaining to . . .
act of rising . . 6. ortive 7. eastern
agriculture . . 7. georgic
ancestral type . . 9. atavistic
ancient Nile city . . 4. Sais (Saite)
ancient Troy . . 5. Iliac
anything remote . . 6. forane
apostles . . 7. Petrine
Asiatic (old) . . 8. Chaldean
Asiatic mountain . . 6. Altaic
Athens . . 5. Attic
authorized doctrine . . 8. dogmatic
    10. dogmatical
birthmark . . 6. nevoid (naevoid)
body . . 5. somal
body of land . . 11. continental
book description . . 13. bibliographic
both ears . . 8. binaural
both sexes . . 6. unisex 7. epicene
breadmaking . . 6. panary
breastbone . . 7. sternal
bristles . . 5. setal
bunch . . 5. comal
canonical hours . . 7. matinal
carving . . 6. glypic 7. glyptic
cheek . . 5. malar
church, part . . 7. apsidal
city . . 5. civic, urban
cod family . . 6. gadoid
coins . . 12. numismatical
colors . . 9. chromatic
construction . . 8. geodesic, tectonic
cork . . 7. suberic
cough . . 7. tussine
court . . 5. aulic 9. judiciary
crown . . 7. coronal
dance . . 6. gestic 13. terpsichorean
daughter . . 6. filial
dawn . . 4. eoan
day (ordinary) . . 6. forial
desert wastes . . 6. eremic
diaphragm   7. phrenic
dogma . . 9. levitical
doves . . 9. columbine
downward air . . 9. katabatic
downy . . 5. dotal
dreams . . 7. oneiric 9. oneirotic
ducks . . 7. anatine
early church . . 9. patristic
early culture . . 8. eolithic
earth . . 4. geal 5. terra 7. teluric
    9. planetary
earthquake . . 7. seismic
east . . 4. dawn, eoan 7. auroral
elms . . 9. ulmaceous
engraving . . 7. glyptic
equal rights . . 3. ERA 6. libber
essence . . 5. basic
exhaustion . . 7. burnout 9. tiredness
fallow deer . . 6. damine
fashion . . 5. modal 6. preppy, trendy
fasting . . 8. anorexic 9. abstinent
fats . . 6. adipic, sebaic 9. cellulite
feet . . 5. pedal
fields . . 8. agrarian
fine arts . . 9. aesthetic (esthetic)
fingers . . 7. digital
first principles . . 9. elemental
fissure . . 5. rimal
flood . . 7. diluvian

flowers . . 9. floscular 10. florescent
forehead . . 7. metopic
frogs . . 6. anuran, ranine
funeral music . . 10. threnodial
funerals . . 8. exequial
gospel . . 9. evangelic
gulls . . 6. larine
gums (Anat) . . 8. gingival
hair . . 5. pilar 7. blow–dry
hands . . 6. chiral, manual
head . . 8. cephalic
heaths . . 8. ericotal
holiday . . 6. ferial (Eccl), festal
honey . . 10. melaginous
horse . . 6. equine
house . . 5. domal (Astrol)
hypothetical force . . 4. odic
infernal regions . . 7. avernal
ink . . 10. atramental
insects . . 11. entomologic
intellect . . 6. noetic
iron . . 6. ferric
islands . . 7. insular
jaw . . 10. mandibular
kidney . . 5. renal
knots . . 5. nodal
land . . 8. praedial (predial)
language meaning . . 8. semantic
laughter . . 8. risorial
leg . . 6. crural 7. fibular
lips . . 6. labial
liver . . 7. hepatic
living organism . . 13. parasitologic
lockjaw . . 7. tetanic
love . . 6. erotic 7. amatory 8. erotical
male . . 5. macho, manly 7. agnatic
marriage . 7. marital 8. hymeneal
marsh . . 8. paludine
meaning, in language . . 8. semantic
medicine . . 6. latric 8. iatrical
medulla oblongata (brain) . . 6. bulbar
memory . . 6. mnesic 7. mnestic
    8. mnemonic 13. retrospective
midday . . 8. meridian
milk . . 7. lactary, lacteal
mind . . 6. mental 7. phrenic
money matters . . 5. T–bill 7. bailout
    8. economic
morning . . 6. matin, sunup 7. matinal
    9. matutinal
motion . . 7. kinetic
mouth . . 4. oral 7. oscular, palatal
    8. stomatic
mustard family . . 11. cruciferous
nephew . . 7. nepotal
north wind . . 6. boreal
nose . . 5. nasal 6. narial, rhinal
nut . . 5. nucal
ocean . . 7. pelagic
old age . . 6. senile 7. geratic
    8. gerontic 9. geriatric
Old World . . 13. gerontogenous
peacock . . 8. pavonine
people . . 4. laic 7. demotic
pigs . . 7. porcine
pleasure . . 7. hedonic
priests . . 10. sacerdotal
prophecy . . 9. vaticinal
public . . 7. cameral
public prayer . . 8. liturgic 10. liturgical
punishment . . 5. penal 8. punitive
queen . . 7. reginal

rainbow.. 6. iridal
reason.. 6. noetic
region without earthquakes..
  11. peneseismic
rhubarb.. 7. rheumic
river.. 5. amnic
river bank.. 8. riparian
rock.. 7. petrean
royal court.. 5. aulic
salvation.. 8. soterial 9. soterical
sarcasm.. 8. ironical
school of philosophy.. 7. Eleatic
sea.. 6. marine 7. oceanic, pelagic
  9. thelassic
seacoast.. 8. littoral
sense of taste.. 9. gustatory
sepulchral mound.. 7. tumular
shin, shinbone.. 7. cnemial
ship's sails.. 5. velic
singing birds.. 6. oscine
skull.. 5. inial
sole of foot.. 7. plantar
spring.. 6. vernal
stars.. 6. astral 7. stellar 8. sidereal
state affairs.. 9. pragmatic
stepmothers.. 8. novercal
storks.. 7. pelagic
summer.. 7. estival (aestival)
  8. festival
sun.. 5. solar 6. heliac
tail.. 6. caudal
teaching.. 9. pedagogic
tears.. 8. lacrimal
tempo.. 6. agogic
the plague.. 6. loimic
the skin.. 5. deric 6. dermic
thread.. 5. filar
tile.. 7. tegular
time.. 7. chronic
tin.. 7. stranic
tissue.. 5. telar
tongue.. 7. glossal, lingual
tortoises.. 9. chelonian
touch.. 7. tactile
travel.. 6. viatic
trees.. 8. arboreal
verse stress.. 5. ictic
walls.. 5. mural 8. parietal
wax.. 5. ceral
weight.. 5. baric 8. ponderal
whales.. 5. rotal
wife.. 7. uxorial
wine.. 5. vinic
wine making.. 10. oenopoetic
wings.. 5. alary
winter.. 6. hiemal
womanhood.. 9. muliebral
woods.. 6. sylvan
wrist.. 6. carpal
pertaining to country...
  Asiatic.. 8. Chaldean
  Asiatic mountain.. 6. Altaic
  Athens.. 5. Attic
  Carthage.. 5. Punic
  Celts.. 4. Erse
  Cretan language.. 6. Minoan
  Dissenters' meeting house.. 7. pantile
    (from the roofing)
  England.. 8. Anglican
  Ethiopian religion.. 6. Coptic
  France.. 6. Gallic
  Franks.. 5. Salic

Gentiles.. 6. ethnic
German State.. 8. Bavarian
Greek epic.. 9. Homerical
Greek philosophy.. 7. Eleatic
  8. Platonic
Greek race (anc).. 6. Aeolic
Greek valley.. 6. Nemean 8. Argolian
Hindu books, writing.. 5. Vedic
  7. Tantric
Hindu philosophy, inertia.. 5. tamas
Irish.. 6. Celtic, Gaelic
Isle of Man.. 4. Manx
Mars.. 5. Arean
Mediterranean.. 6. Levant
Moses.. 6. Mosaic
Nile city (anc).. 4. Sais (Saite)
Norse poem.. 5. runic
Passover.. 7. Paschal
Red Sea colony.. 8. Eritrean
Rhine.. 7. Rhenish
Scotch Highlander.. 6. Gaelic
Spice Islands.. 7. Molucca
Troy (anc).. 5. Iliac 6. Trojan
Vulcan.. 11. Mulcibirian
West Indies.. 9. Antillean
pertenencia... 10. concession
  11. mining claim
Perth... 6. Atholl (Athole) 7. Ontario
  9. Australia
pertinacious... 4. firm 8. adhering,
  resolute 9. tenacious 10. determined,
  inflexible, persistent, unyielding
  11. persevering
pertinacity... 9. obstinacy
  11. persistency
pertinence... 7. fitness 9. relevancy
  10. timeliness 12. appositeness
perturb... 5. alarm 6. excite
  7. agitate, derange, disturb, fluster,
  trouble 8. bewilder, disorder, distress
  9. confusion
perturbation... 5. alarm 7. anxiety,
  fluster 9. agitation, confusion
  10. excitement 11. fearfulness
  12. bewilderment, irregularity
pertusion... 8. piercing, punching
  11. perforation, punched hole
pertussis... 5. cough 13. whooping
  cough
Peru... see also Peruvian
  capital.. 4. Lima 5. Cuzco (Inca)
  14. City of the Kings
  hero.. 7. Bolivar, Pizarro
  lake.. 8. Titicaca
  mountain.. 5. Andes 10. Cordillera
  port.. 6. Callao 7. Iquitos
  8. Mollendo
  river.. 4. Sama 5. Santa 6. Amazon
  7. Maranon, Ucayali 8. Urubamba
  ruins.. 4. Inca 5. huaco (relics)
Peruvian (pert to)...
  animal.. 4. paco 5. llama 6. alpaca
  bark.. 8. cinchona
  goddess of fertility.. 4. Mama
  inn, tavern.. 5. tambo
  king (petty).. 7. cacique
  plant.. 3. oca
  rodent.. 10. chinchilla
  tinamou.. 4. yutu
  tree.. 8. cinchona
  university.. 9. San Marcos
  volcano.. 7. El Misti

wind (cold).. **4.** puna
pervade... **4.** fill **5.** imbue **6.** extend
  8. permeate, traverse **9.** penetrate
pervading... **9.** prevalent, universal
perverse... **3.** awk **4.** awry, wogh
  5. wrong **6.** cranky, erring
  7. corrupt, forward, froward,
  wayward, willful (wilful) **8.** contrary,
  petulant **9.** obstinate **10.** ill–humored
perversion... **5.** error **6.** misuse
  8. apostasy **9.** sophistry
  10. corruption, distortion
  13. falsification **17.** misinterpretation,
  misrepresentation
perversion of taste... **7.** malacia
pervert... **4.** ruin **5.** upset **6.** divert,
  misuse **7.** corrupt, distort, falsify,
  heretic **8.** apostate, overturn,
  renegade **9.** turn aside
  10. degenerate, lead astray
  12. misinterpret, misrepresent
pervulgate... **7.** publish
Pesach, Pesah... **8.** Passover (Feast)
pesante... **5.** heavy **10.** impressive
peshkash... **3.** tax **7.** present, tribute
  8. offering
peskar... **5.** agent **7.** steward
  8. minister **10.** accountant
pesky... **6.** plaguy **7.** teasing
  9. harassing **10.** tormenting
pes planus... **8.** flatfoot **13.** talipes
  planus
pess... **7.** hassock (church)
pessimist... **5.** cynic **6.** malist
  9. defeatist, worrywart
pessimistic... **6.** gloomy **7.** cynical
  8. cowardly, hopeless **10.** despairing,
  foreboding, uncheerful
pest... **3.** nag **4.** bane **6.** plague
  7. ragweed **8.** epidemic, nuisance
  9. annoyance **10.** pestilence
pester... **3.** nag, rib **5.** annoy, tease,
  worry **6.** badger, harass, impede,
  infuot **7.** torment **8.** entangle
  9. importune **10.** overburden
pestilence... **4.** bane **7.** disease,
  scourge **8.** epidemic **13.** bubonic
  plague
pestilent... **6.** deadly **7.** noxious
  8. annoying **9.** pestering, poisonous
  10. contagious, infectious, pernicious
  11. mischievous, troublesome
pestle... **4.** club **6.** muller **7.** crusher,
  pounder
pes valgus... **9.** bowlegged **13.** talipes
  valgus
pet... **4.** dear, tiff **5.** humor **6.** caress,
  coddle, cosset, dandle, fondle,
  pamper **7.** darling, dudgeon, indulge
  8. cade lamb, favorite
  10. endearment
petals (pert to)...
  flower.. **7.** corolla
  having.. **8.** petalous
  orchid.. **8.** labellum
  ref to.. **5.** whorl **8.** petaline, petaloid
  without.. **9.** apetalous
petard... **9.** explosive **11.** firecracker
peteman (thieves' sl)... **5.** thief
  7. burglar **8.** peterman
  9. cracksman, fisherman (Hist)
  10. safeblower

Peter (pert to)...
  Bell.. **4.** poem
  Bible.. **5.** Simon (also called)
  7. epistle (New Test)
  Ibbetson.. **5.** novel
  Pan.. **3.** boy **4.** play
  Pan dog.. **4.** Nana
  the Great.. **4.** Czar
  the Great's father.. **6.** Alexis
  the Hermit.. **8.** Crusader (1st)
peter out... **4.** fade, fail, tire, wane
  6. weaken **7.** dwindle **9.** cease to
  be
petiole... **4.** stem **5.** stalk **8.** peduncle
  9. leafstalk **10.** mesopodium
petit... **4.** mean **5.** petty, small
  6. little **13.** insignificant
petite... **5.** small **6.** demure, little
petite (pert to)...
  bourse.. **6.** Market (Finan)
  marmite.. **4.** soup
  noblesse.. **8.** nobility (lesser)
petition... **3.** ask, beg, sue **4.** plea,
  pray **5.** apply, plead **6.** prayer
  7. entreat, relator, request, solicit
  8. entreaty **10.** supplicate
peto... **5.** wahoo
petrified... **8.** hardened **9.** terrified
  15. carved from stone
petrified body... **6.** fossil
petrify... **4.** numb **6.** deaden, harden
  7. astound, stupefy **8.** paralyze
  11. become stone
petroglyph... **11.** rock carving **15.** rock
  inscription
Petrograd... **9.** Leningrad
petroleum product... **6.** butane, diesel
  7. naphtha, propane **8.** gasoline
petrology (science of)... **5.** rocks
petrosal... **4.** bone **5.** sinus, stony
  7. petrous **8.** ganglion
petticoat... **4.** girl, kilt **5.** jupon,
  pagne, woman **6.** kirtle **8.** basquine
  9. undercoat, waistcoat
  10. fustanella, underskirt
petticoat tails... **7.** teacake
  9. shortcake
pettifogger... **4.** tyro **5.** quack
  6. lawyer **7.** shyster **8.** attorney
pettish... **7.** fretful, peevish **9.** irritable
pettle... **6.** cuddle, nestle, potter
  7. cherish
petto... **12.** in one's breast **15.** in
  contemplation
petty... **4.** mean, orra **5.** minor, small
  6. paltry **7.** trivial **8.** childish,
  inferior, nugatory, trifling **9.** miniscule
  10. diminutive **11.** small–minded,
  subordinate, unimportant
  12. narrow–minded **13.** insignificant
  14. inconsiderable
petty (pert to)...
  captain.. **9.** centurion
  fault.. **10.** peccadillo
  larceny.. **10.** scrounging
  mullein.. **7.** cowslip
  objection.. **5.** cavil
  prince.. **6.** satrap
petulance... **8.** ill humor, pertness
  9. insolence, sauciness
  10. wantonness **11.** peevishness,
  pettishness

petulant... 4. pert 5. cross, huffy,
saucy, testy 6. wanton 7. forward,
fretful, peevish, wayward, willful
8. contrary, immodest, insolent
9. querulous
peu à peu... 9. by degrees 14. little
by little
pewee... 5. pewit 6. phoebe
8. woodcock 10. flycatcher
pewit... 5. pewee 7. lapwing
12. laughing gull
Pfefferkuchen... 11. gingerbread
Phaëthon, Class Myth (pert to)...
bird.. 4. swan
car.. 3. sun
father.. 6. Helios
sun god.. 6. Helios
phagomania... 8. insanity
16. insatiable hunger
Phalacrocorax... 5. coots
10. cormorants
phalacrosis... 8. alopecia, baldness
phalanger... 5. tapoa 9. marsupial
phalanx... 4. bone 5. pawns 6. troops
7. company (Mil) 8. infantry
phalera... 4. boss 5. cameo
phantasm... 5. dream, fancy, ghost
6. idolum, spirit 7. eidolon, fantasy,
phantom, specter (spectre)
8. delusion, illusion 10. apparition
phantasy, fantasy... 5. fancy, image
6. autism 8. daydream
11. imagination
phantom... 5. fairy, ghost 7. eidolon,
specter (spectre) 10. simulacrum
Pharaoh (Bib)... 4. faro, king
Pharaoh (pert to)...
ancestor.. 2. Ra
chicken, hen.. 7. vulture (Egypt)
fig.. 8. sycamore
mouse.. 9. ichneumon
phare... 6. beacon, pharos
10. lighthouse
pharisee... 7. pietist 9. hypocrite
pharmacology... 5. drugs 13. materia
medica
pharos... 5. cloak 6. beacon
10. chandelier (Eccl), lighthouse,
watchtower
phase... 5. facet, stage 6. aspect
7. caprice, chapter, horning (moon)
phases, having many...
11. Hydra–headed
phasm... 6. meteor 7. phantom
pheasant... 5. cheer, monal 6. pukras
7. kallege 8. tragopan 12. ruffed
grouse
pheasant (pert to)...
brood.. 3. nye 4. nide (nid) 5. flock
cuckoo.. 6. coucal
duck.. 7. pintail 9. merganser
finch.. 7. waxbill
genus.. 10. Oreophasis
wren.. 7. emu wren
pheasant species... 5. argus, blood
6. golden, silver 7. kallege
8. curassow 9. Mongolian
10. ring–necked 12. Lady Amherst's
phenomenal... 7. unusual 8. eventful,
sensible 9. objective, wonderful
13. extraordinary
phenomenon... 4. fact 5. event

(unusual) 7. prodigy
phial... 3. cup 4. bowl, vial 6. bottle,
vessel
phiale... 5. laver 6. vessel 8. fountain
(Eccl)
Phi Beta Kappa (pert to)...
badge.. 8. watch key
founding.. 21. William and Mary
College (1776)
meaning.. 24. Philosophy the guide of
life
society.. 11. Greek–letter (oldest)
philabeg (filibeg)... 4. kilt
Philadelphia...
city.. 12. Pennsylvania
fleabane.. 7. skevish
lawyer.. 6. shrewd
meaning.. 13. brother–loving
ref to.. 12. Philadelphus (Ptolemy II)
philander... 5. flirt, lover 7. opossum
10. flirtation, love–making, lover of
men
philanthropic... 6. humane
10. benevolent 12. eleemosynary
philanthropist... 5. donor 8. altruist,
do–gooder 9. Robin Hood
10. benefactor, benevolist,
Montefiore, Rothschild
12. humanitarian
philanthropy... 7. charity 8. good will
10. almsgiving 11. beneficence,
benevolence (opp of misanthropy)
Philippic... 6. screed, tirade 7. oration
8. diatribe 9. Philippus
Philippine, Philippines...
archipelago.. 4. Sulu 5. Malay
bay.. 6. Manila
capital.. 6. Baguio (summer), Manila
10. Quezon City
city.. 5. Albay, Davao 6. Cavite
7. Dagupan
district.. 7. Lepanto
fort.. 4. Gota 10. Corregidor
island.. 4. Cebu 5. Leyte, Luzon,
Panay, Samar, Ticao 6. Negros
7. Palawan, Paragua 8. Mindanao
mountain.. 3. Apo, Iba 5. Mayon
river.. 4. Abra, Agno 5. Pasig
8. Mindanao, Pampanga
university.. 10. Santo Tomas (1611)
volcano.. 3. Apo 5. Mayon
Philippine (pert to)...
animal.. 5. civet, lemur
ant, termite.. 4. anay (anai)
barracks.. 7. cuartel
boat, canoe, raft.. 5. balsa, banca
breadfruit.. 7. camansi
buffalo.. 7. carabao, timarau (timerau)
chair (on poles).. 7. talabon
dagger.. 4. itac
drink.. 4. beno 5. bubud
fabric.. 4. pina 9. pineapple
fetish, idol.. 5. anito
food.. 3. poi 4. Musa, saba, taro
hemp.. 5. abaca 6. Manila
house.. 5. bahay
knife.. 4. bolo
litter, pole chair.. 7. talabon
lizard.. 4. ibid (monitor)
mango.. 5. bauno 7. pahutan
market day.. 7. tiangue
melon.. 6. atimon

mudfish.. **5.** dalag
palm.. **4.** nipa **6.** anahau (anahao)
parrot (green).. **5.** cagit
reptile.. **6.** python
rice.. **4.** paga **5.** macan
rice field bank.. **7.** pilapil
river.. **4.** ilog
shrub.. **4.** alem
sweetsop.. **4.** ates
town.. **4.** agoa
tree.. **3.** tui **4.** ipil (ypil) **5.** asana,
　ligas, narra, yacal **6.** molavo
　7. Eugenia, tindalo **8.** macaasim
turnip.. **7.** cincoma
vehicle (public).. **9.** carromata
water jar.. **5.** banga
wood.. **4.** teak **5.** ebony **6.** sandal
　8. mahogany
Philippine people (pert to)...
discoverer.. **8.** Magellan (1521)
farmer.. **3.** tao
headman.. **4.** datu
language.. **4.** Moro **7.** Tagalog (Taqal)
　9. Pilipino
Luzon savage.. **4.** Aeta **6.** Igorot
　(Igorrote)
Muslim, Moslem.. **4.** Moro
native.. **3.** tao **4.** Moro, Sulu
native race.. **3.** Lao **4.** Aeta (dwarf)
　7. Tagalog, Visayan
native worker.. **7.** polista
Negrito.. **3.** Ati **4.** Aeta
patriot.. **5.** rizal
peasant.. **3.** tao
priest (Moro).. **7.** pandita
servant.. **4.** bata **5.** alila
tribe (Chr).. **5.** Bikol (Bico, Vicol)
tribe (pagan).. **6.** Italon
Philistine... **5.** enemy **7.** prosaic
　9. philister **10.** conformist,
　uncultured **12.** antagonistic
　13. prosaic person, unenlightened
Philistine (pert to)...
anc name.. **9.** Palestine, Philistia
assimilated by.. **7.** Semites
city.. **4.** Gaza **5.** Ekron (Bib)
god.. **4.** Baal **5.** Dagon
philo (comb form)... **6.** fond of, loving
philogeant... **12.** lover of earth
philogyny... **11.** love of women
philology... **11.** linguistics **14.** love of
　learning
Philomela (pert to)...
father.. **7.** Pandion (King of Athens)
sister.. **6.** Procne
turned into.. **7.** swallow
　11. nightingale
philosopher...
American.. **7.** Emerson **9.** Santayana
Chinese.. **9.** Confucius
Dutch.. **7.** Spinoza
English.. **5.** Bacon
French.. **5.** Renan **8.** Rousseau,
　Voltaire
German.. **4.** Kant **9.** Nietzsche
　12. Schopenhauer
Greek.. **4.** Zeno **8.** Socrates
Scottish.. **4.** Hume
Seven Sages (7 Wise Men of Greece)..
　4. Bias **5.** Solon **6.** Chilon, Thales
　8. Pittacus **9.** Cleobulus
　10. Epimenides (or Periander)

Philosopher of...
Farney.. **8.** Voltaire
Malmesbury.. **6.** Hobbes
Sans Souci.. **17.** Frederick the Great
Syracuse.. **4.** Dion
Wimbledon.. **14.** John Horne Tooke
philosopher's school... **7.** Eleatic
philosophical... **4.** wise **7.** erudite,
　logical, sapient **8.** rational
　9. temperate, unruffled
philosophical being... **6.** entity
philosophy (pert to)...
choice of.. **11.** eclecticism
of law.. **13.** jurisprudence
of pantheists.. **5.** Stoic
sublimated.. **17.** Transcendentalism
theory.. **4.** yoga **9.** pantheism,
　Platonism, solipsism **12.** epistemology
phlegmatic... **4.** calm, dull, slow
　5. inert **6.** mucous, watery
　7. viscous **8.** sluggish **9.** apathetic
phlogistic... **5.** fiery **6.** heated
　7. burning **11.** impassioned
　12. inflammatory
Phoebad... **7.** seeress **9.** priestess
　(Delphian) **10.** prophetess
Phoebe (pert to)...
daughter.. **4.** Leto
epithet of.. **7.** Artemis
mother.. **4.** Gaea (earth goddess)
poetic.. **4.** moon
phoebe... **4.** fish **5.** craps, pewit
　6. peewee **9.** satellite (Saturn)
　10. flycatcher
Phoebus... **3.** Sol **6.** sun god
Phoenicia...
capital city.. **4.** Tyre **5.** Sidon
Colony.. **5.** Hippo **8.** Carthage
deity.. **4.** Baal
famed for.. **9.** purple dye
　10. navigation
goddess of fertility.. **6.** Baltis
　7. Astarte
god of healing.. **6.** Eshmun (Eshmoun)
king.. **6.** Agenor
region.. **5.** Syria
Phoenix... **4.** bird (fabled), palm
　7. capital (Ariz)
phonetic (pert to)...
science.. **9.** phonology
sound.. **7.** phoneme
stop.. **9.** occlusive
system.. **5.** romic
phonic... **6.** spoken, voiced
　7. sounded **8.** auditory **9.** accoustic,
　vibration
phony (comb form)... **5.** sound, voice
phony... **4.** fake **9.** contrived,
　simulated **11.** counterfeit
photograph... **4.** film **5.** image, photo
　7. picture **8.** likeness, portrait
　9. ferrotype, pictorial, portrayal
　10. centerfold, heliograph
　12. photogravure
photographic bath... **5.** toner
　7. reducer **9.** developer
photography, science of... **5.** light
　6. optics **8.** photics
photography inventors... **4.** Land
　6. Niepce, Talbot **8.** Daguerre
photometric unit... **3.** pyr, rad
phrase... **5.** idiom **6.** remark, saying,

slogan 7. diction, epigram, epithet, passage 8. flattery 9. catchword 10. expression 11. phraseology
phraseology... 5. style 6. jargon 7. diction, wording 8. parlance
phratry (Hist)... 4. clan 5. group
phrenetic... 3. mad 5. crazy 6. madman 7. fanatic, frantic, violent 9. delirious 10. passionate
phrenology, science of... 5. skull 10. craniology
Phrygia, Asia Minor...
  cap (comical).. 10. liberty cap
  deity.. 5. Attis
  Eccl Hist.. 9. Montanist
  founder.. 7. Gordius (800 BC)
  King.. 5. Midas
  marble (anc).. 9. pavonazzo (pavonazzetto)
  music.. 4. mode
  river.. 7. Meander
phylactery (Eccl)... 4. case 5. charm, chest, miter 6. amulet, infula, record, scroll
phylarchy... 12. rule by tribes
phyletic... 6. racial 7. descent, species 12. phylogenetic
phyllophagous... 15. feeding on leaves
physical... 6. bodily 7. natural, somatic 8. material 9. corporeal
physical force... 10. attraction
physical unit... 3. erg
physician... 5. medic 6. doctor, healer, intern 7. coroner 8. restorer
physician (pert to)...
  ancient.. 5. Galen
  comb form.. 5. iatro
  French Nobel Prize.. 7. Laveran
  Greek (anc).. 5. Galen 11. Asclepiades
  quack.. 10. medicaster
  symbol.. 8. caduceus
physicist... 7. Faraday, Galvani, Marconi 10. naturalist
physiognomy... 3. mug 4. face 11. countenance 14. external aspect, interpretation
physique... 4. body 6. figure
physis (Gr)... 6. nature
phytology, science of... 6. botany, plants
piacle... 3. sin 5. crime, guilt 7. offense 15. sacrificial rite 17. expiatory offering
pian... 5. tumor 9. frambesia
piano (pert to)...
  direction.. 10. pianissimo (softly)
  duet, upper part.. 5. primo
  dumb keyboard.. 10. digitorium
  early.. 6. spinet
  Italian.. 10. Cristofori
  keyboard.. 7. clavier 8. pedalier
  pedal.. 7. celeste
  pianolike.. 7. celesta
  player.. 7. pianola
  slang.. 11. eighty–eight
  small.. 8. pianette
piatti... 7. cymbals
piazza... 5. campo, porch 6. square 7. gallery, portico, veranda
pic... 4. peak 8. picayune
picacho... 4. hill 5. butte

picador... 3. wit 6. jester 7. debater 8. horseman (with lance), toreador 11. bullfighter
picaro... 5. knave, rogue 7. sharper 8. vagabond 10. picaresque
picaroon... 5. rogue, thief 6. pirate, rascal 7. brigand, corsair 8. prey upon
pick... 4. cull, gaff, peck, sort 5. elect, pluck, strum 6. assort, choose, indent, pickax, pierce, select 7. diamond (card), harvest, the best 8. plectrum, the elite 9. toothpick
pick (pert to)...
  flaws.. 5. cavil
  out.. 6. pilfer, select 7. acquire, procure, specify 9. eliminate, segregate 11. distinguish
  pick–me–up.. 5. tonic 6. bracer 9. kittiwake, stimulate 11. restorative
  up.. 4. tidy 6. arrest 7. improve 9. stimulant 10. recuperate
picked... 4. trim 5. piked, spiny 6. choice, chosen, culled, dainty, peaked, spruce 7. adorned, plucked, pointed 8. stripped 10. fastidious
pickerel... 4. fish, pike 9. Esox niger 12. walleyed pike
picket... 3. peg 4. pale, post, tern 5. fence, guard, stake 6. bullet, fasten, paling, sentry, tether 7. enclose, fortify, shackle 8. sentinel 10. go on strike
pickle... 4. alec, peck 5. achar, brine 6. dawdle, nibble, piddle, pilfer, trifle 7. chutney, vitrial
pickled... 5. drunk 6. soused 9. marinated
pickled pig's feet... 5. souse
pickle fork... 8. runcible
pickle–herring... 7. buffoon 11. merry–andrew 12. Pickelhering
pickpocket... 4. wire 5. thief 6. bulker
picnic... 3. fun 4. camp, play 6. junket, outing 9. festivity
Pict (anc)... 4. Scot 5. Aryan 9. aborigine
Pictland... 8. Scotland
pictorial... 8. painting 11. illustrated, picturesque
Pict's house (Archaeol)... 8. dwelling (subterranean)
picture... 3. oil 4. copy, draw, icon 5. image, print, scene 6. chromo, depict, pastel 7. diorama, etching, portray, porture, tableau 8. describe, likeness, painting, portrait 9. engraving, paintings, represent, visualize 10. photograph 11. description 14. representation
picture (pert to)...
  mounting, border.. 3. mat 5. frame 8. kakemono, makimono (scroll)
  moving.. 4. film 5. movie 6. cinema
  positive.. 5. print
  puzzle.. 5. rebus
  small.. 5. cameo 9. miniature
  stand.. 5. easel
  viewer.. 11. alethoscope, stereoscope 12. magic lantern, stereopticon
picturesque... 5. vivid 6. scenic 7. graphic 9. pictorial

picuda... 9. barracuda (great), picudilla (small)
picudo... 6. weevil 10. boll weevil
piddle... 3. toy 4. pick, play 6. putter, trifle 9. waste time
pie... 4. food, mess 5. chaos, patty 6. jumble, magpie, pastry 7. cobbler, dessert, measure 9. confusion
piebald... 4. pied 5. mixed, pinto 6. motley 7. mongrel, mottled, pintado 10. variegated 13. heterogeneous
piece... 3. bit 4. join, part, role 5. crumb, drama, piece, scrap, shred 6. sample 7. measure, portion, writing 8. chessman, fragment, specimen, treatise
piece (pert to)...
armor.. 5. tasse (tace) 8. corselet
de résistance.. 6. entrée 8. main dish
door, jamb.. 6. lintel
eccentric.. 3. cam
fastening.. 3. gib
fitted.. 4. shim 5. tenon
flat.. 4. slab, slat 5. flake, strip
meal.. 9. by degrees, fragments 12. piece by piece 14. little by little
metal.. 3. sow
neck.. 3. boa 5. rabat, scarf, stole 8. kerchief
of one's mind.. 6. rebuke 7. reproof 13. candid opinion
out.. 3. eke 6. cantle
preventing slippage.. 5. cleat
short.. 4. skit
side.. 3. rib 5. stave
split off.. 6. sliver, splint 8. splinter
tapering.. 4. gore 6. gusset
work (art).. 4. pavé 6. mosaic, niello
pieces of...
eight.. 6. dollar, escudo
meat.. 5. cabob
silk waste.. 4. noil
pied... 4. foot 5. pinto 7. colored (2 or more colors), dappled, piebald 10. variegated 12. parti–colored
pied (pert to)...
blackbird.. 6. thrush
brant.. 5. goose
diver.. 4. smew
duck.. 8. Labrador
Friar (Eccl Hist).. 9. mendicant
monk.. 10. Bernardine, Cistercian
Piper of Hamelin.. 8. musician 10. rat charmer
widgeon.. 8. garganey 9. goldeneye
Piedmont, Italy... 7. capital (Turin)
pieplant... 7. rhubarb
pier... 4. anta, dock, mole, quay 5. groin, wharf 6. pillar 7. landing 8. buttress, gatepost 9. promenade 10. breakwater
pierce... 4. bore, cold, gore, pain, tart 5. enter, gride, lance, probe, spear, spike, sting, wound 6. riddle, tunnel 7. discern 8. puncture 9. penetrate, perforate 10. comprehend
piercing... 4. keen, loud 5. acute 6. shrill 7. caustic, clearly, painful, piteous, pungent, sharply, shrilly, spiking, violent 8. deep–felt, poignant, spearing, stabbing

9. searching
Pieria, Macedonia (pert to)...
epithet of.. 5. Muses
native.. 7. Pierian
reference to.. 6. poetry 9. knowledge
seat of.. 5. Muses
piet... 5. ouzel 6. magpie 7. piebald 10. chatterbox, chattering 11. saucy person
Pietà (It)... 9. sculpture 10. Virgin Mary
pietose (Mus)... 11. sympathetic 13. compassionate
piety... 4. pity, zeal (worship) 6. filial 8. devotion, holiness, religion 9. reverence 10. compassion, devoutness, sanctimony 11. dutifulness
pig... 3. car (RR), ham, hog, sow 4. boar, pork 5. bacon, crosk, flask, swine 6. farrow 7. casting, dogboat, glutton 8. pressman, sixpence, slattern 9. policeman 11. stoolpigeon
pig (pert to)...
bed.. 3. pen, sty 5. reeve 6. pigsty
female.. 3. sow 4. gilt
guinea.. 4. cavy
headed.. 6. stupid 9. obstinate
iron.. 5. ingot
iron, ballast (Naut).. 9. kentledge
iron, cast.. 9. kentledge (Mil)
last of litter.. 4. runt
lead, weight.. 6. fother
litter.. 6. farrow
piglike.. 7. hoglike, porcine, suiform
piglike animal.. 7. peccary 8. babirusa
potato.. 7. cowbane
rat.. 9. bandicoot
skin.. 6. saddle 8. football
yoke.. 7. oxtant 8. quadrant
young.. 5. grice, shoat 6. farrow, piglet 9. gruntling
pigdan... 8. spittoon
pigeon... 3. nun 4. barb, dove, dupe, fowl, girl, gull, ruff 5. heart, piper, pluck, sweet 6. coward, fleece, pouter, roller, turbit 7. fantail, jacobin, pintail, tumbler 9. trumpeter
pigeon, pidgin (pert to)...
Australia.. 5. wonga 10. wonga–wonga
berry.. 7. dogwood 9. Juneberry, wild elder
blood.. 6. garnet
carrier.. 5. homer 6. homing 10. scandaroon
extinct.. 4. dodo
food.. 7. saltcat
genus.. 5. Goura 7. Columba
hawk.. 6. falcon, merlin
house.. 7. dovecot 9. columbary
ref to.. 12. peristeronic
short–beaked.. 4. barb
wood.. 6. cushat 8. ringdove
young.. 5. piper
pigment... 3. red 4. blue, gray, pink 5. black, brown, color, green, ocher (ochre), paint, white 6. orange, purple, yellow 8. colorant
pigment (pert to)...
arsenic, yellow.. 8. orpiment
black.. 3. tar 5. sepia 7. melanin

blue.. 5. smalt
blue–green.. 4. bice
brown.. 5. sepia, umber 6. bister
(bistre), sienna (burnt) 7. cypress
brownish yellow.. 6. sienna
calico yellow.. 7. canarin (canarine)
coal tar.. 7. aniline
cuttlefish.. 5. sepia
madder root.. 7. rubiate
orange red.. 7. realgar
oxide of lead.. 8. massicot
red.. 7. turacin
yellow.. 5. ocher (ochre) 7. etiolin
pigmy... see *pygmy*
pignus... 4. pawn 6. pledge
pig's feet... 9. pettitoes
pigtail... 5. braid, queue 7. tobacco
(rolled) 8. rope's end (Naut)
pika... 6. rodent
pike... 3. ged (gedd) 4. fish, luce, pick
6. beacon, pickax
pike (pert to)...
North American.. 11. muskellunge
perch.. 6. sauger
pikelike.. 3. gar 4. luce 5. lucet
6. robalo 8. robalito 9. barracuda
walleyed.. 4. doré
pikel, pikle... 7. hayfork 9. pitchfork
pikelet... 7. crumpet
piker... 5. thief, tramp 6. coward
7. gambler, quitter, shirker, vagrant
8. tightwad
pilar... 5. downy, hairy
pilaster... 4. anta 6. alette (part),
column
Pilate (Bib)... 10. procurator (Judean)
pilchard... 7. sardine
pile... 3. awn, mow, nap 4. heap,
load, mole, pier, rick, shag
5. amass, slack, spile, stake 6. heap
up, pillar, wealth 7. fortune, store
up, texture
pile (pert to)...
burning.. 4. pyre
defense.. 8. estacade
driver.. 7. fistuca
of hay.. 3. mow 4. dess, rick
5. stack
up.. 4. heap 7. smashup, store up
9. shipwreck 10. exaggerate
pilfer... 3. rob 4. lift, loot 5. filch,
steal, swipe 6. rustle (cattle), snitch
7. purloin
pilgrim... 5. exile (Relig) 6. palmer
8. crusader, newcomer, traveler,
wanderer, wayfarer 9. immigrant,
sojourner 10. tenderfoot
12. peregrinator
Pilgrim (pert to)...
father.. 9. John Alden
Fathers.. 11. Separatists (1620)
garment.. 5. ihram (Mecca)
landing.. 12. Plymouth Rock (1620)
Scotch.. 6. palmer
ship.. 9. Mayflower, Speedwell
pilgrimage to Mecca... 4. hadj
Pilgrim's bottle... 7. ampulla, costrel
Pilgrim's Progress... 8. allegory
(Bunyan)
pill... 3. rob 4. ball, bore, pare, pell,
pool 5. bolus, creek 6. bullet, pellet,
pilule 8. medicine 9. cigarette

11. decorticate
pillage... 4. flay, loot, prey, sack
5. booty, harry, spoil, strip 6. rapine,
ravage 7. despoil, plunder, robbery
9. depredate, extortion 10. spoliation
pillar... 4. post, slab 5. shaft, stele
(stela), tower 6. column 7. support
8. mainstay, monument, pedestal
pillar (pert to)...
airfield.. 5. pylon
Buddhist.. 3. lat
carved.. 9. totem pole
little.. 8. pillaret
of society.. 9. personage
pillarlike.. 6. stelar
saint.. 7. recluse, stylite
tall, slender.. 7. obelisk
with front figure.. 7. osiride
Pillars of Hercules site... 5. Abila,
Calpe 17. Strait of Gibralter
pillbox... 3. cap, hat 8. brougham,
fortress 13. fortification
pillory... 4. yoke 5. stock, trone
6. cangue, punish
pillow... 3. pad 5. block 7. cushion,
support
pillow (pert to)...
case, cover.. 4. sham, slip
long.. 7. bolster
stuffing.. 5. kapok 8. feathers
pilose... 5. hairy 6. pilous
pilot... 4. lead 5. flyer, guide, steer
6. aviate, direct, leader 8. director,
helmsman, preacher 9. clergyman,
navigator 10. cowcatcher
pilot (pert to)...
bird.. 6. plover
expert.. 3. ace
fish.. 6. remora 9. amberfish,
whitefish
house.. 10. wheelhouse
jacket.. 9. pea jacket
sky.. 8. preacher 9. clergyman
snake.. 10. copperhead
weed.. 9. rosinweed
whale.. 9. blackfish
Piltdown, England (pert to)...
Hist yield.. 7. Dawn Man, fossils
Prehist station.. 6. Sussex
piltock... 8. coalfish
pilum... 6. pestle 7. javelin
pilus... 4. hair
Pima... 5. Opata 11. Indian tribe
pimento... 6. pepper 7. paprika
8. allspice, pimiento
pin... 3. hob, peg, pen 4. axle, bolt,
coak (coag), join 5. affix, badge,
dowel, rivet, thole 6. brooch, cotter,
fasten, secure, trifle 7. confine,
enclose, gudgeon, jewelry, spindle,
stopper, trenail 8. linchpin, ornament,
transfix 10. chatelaine
pin (pert to)...
axle.. 8. linchpin
dial.. 5. style
fish.. 11. stickleback
game.. 7. skittle
grass.. 9. alfilaria (forage)
jackstraw (game).. 8. spilikin (spillikin)
meat fastener.. 6. skewer
quoits.. 3. hob
sailmaker's.. 3. fid

small.. 3. peg 4. lill
with looped head.. 7. eyebolt
pinafore... 5. apron, smock 7. tablier
　8. sun dress
Pinafore... 5. opera (Gilbert & Sullivan)
pinag... 4. lake (rain season)
piñata... 5. globe (swinging, with gifts)
pinax... 4. dish 5. table 6. plaque,
　scheme, tablet 7. picture
　9. catalogue
pinbone... 7. hipbone
pince–nez... 7. glasses, nippers
　10. eyeglasses
pincers... 3. tew 5. chela, tongs
　6. pliers 7. forceps, pinette
pinch... 3. nip, rob 4. pain, raid
　5. cramp, gripe, pugil (anc), steal,
　stint, tweak 6. arrest, crisis, extort,
　scrimp, snatch, snitch, strait, twinge
　7. afflict, confine, squeeze, urgency
　8. compress, contract, exigency,
　straiten
pinchbeck... 4. sham 5. alloy (cheap
　jewelry) 8. frippery, spurious
　11. counterfeit
pinched... 4. poor, thin 8. squeezed
　10. compressed, contracted,
　distressed, straitened
pinchem... 8. titmouse
pinda... 6. peanut
Pindar... 4. poet (lyric)
pindaric... 3. ode 9. irregular
　12. unrestrained
pine... 4. flag 5. waste, yearn
　6. grieve, lament, needle, repine,
　sicken, weaken, wither 8. languish
　11. deteriorate
pine (pert to)...
Brazil.. 6. paraná
chemical.. 5. pinic
exudation.. 5. resin, rosin
family.. 3. fir 5. larch, piñon
　6. spruce
finch.. 6. siskin
fir.. 6. balsam 12. Balm of Gilead
fruit.. 4. cone
genus.. 5. Pinus
gum.. 8. sandarac
knot.. 7. dovekie
leaf.. 6. needle
low–growing.. 5. piñon
mahogany.. 6. totara
New Zealand.. 5. kauri (kaury)
Pacific coast.. 8. knobpine
Philippine.. 7. Amboina 8. galagala
screw.. 3. ara 6. pandan
tar extract.. 6. retene
tulip.. 10. pipsissewa
pineal... 5. brain, gland 8. pine cone
pineapple... 4. bomb, pina 5. fiber,
　fruit 6. ananas 8. pine cone
　12. Bromeliaceae
pineapple (pert to)...
cheese.. 7. Cheddar
cloth.. 4. pina
segment.. 3. pip
weed.. 8. marigold
Pine Tree State... 5. Maine
pinguescent... 9. fattening
pinguid... 3. fat 4. oily, rich 5. fatty
　8. unctuous
pinguitude... 7. fatness, obesity

　8. oiliness 10. greasiness
pink... 3. cut, Red 4. deck, rose, stab
　5. adorn, blink, color, coral, smart,
　wound 6. flower, indent, minnow,
　pierce, salmon, vessel 7. radical,
　serrate 8. decorate, grayling
　9. carnation 11. fashionable
pink (pert to)...
coat.. 10. foxhunter's
eye.. 4. duck 14. conjunctivitis
family.. 7. Campion 9. Carnation
　15. Caryophyllaceae
fish.. 8. gobylike
genus.. 6. Silene
lady.. 3. fly (fishing) 8. cocktail
needle.. 9. alfilaria
Pearl.. 6. azalea
pill.. 7. cure–all
root.. 8. wormroot
pinkeen... 6. minnow 19. insignificant
　person
pinna... 3. fin 4. wing 7. auricle,
　feather, leaflet
pinnace... 4. boat 5. woman 6. tender
　(Naut) 9. procuress 10. prostitute
pinnacle... 3. epi, tee, tor 4. acme,
　apex, peak 5. crest, crown, serac,
　spire 6. finial, needle, summit
pinnate... 11. featherlike
pinniped... 4. seal 6. walrus
pinochle term... 3. dix 4. meld
piñon... 4. pine, seed 8. pignolia
　12. monkey puzzle
pintado... 4. cero, fish, sier (fish)
　5. pinto 6. chintz, pigeon, sierra
pintail (pert to)...
duck.. 4. smee 5. river, ruddy
grouse.. 4. sand 11. sharp–tailed
pinto (horse)... 4. pied 6. calico
　7. mottled, painted, piebald, spotted
Pinto... 6. Indian (Pokowa tribe)
pinwing... 7. penguin
pioneer... 4. lead 5. guide, miner
　6. digger, open up 7. settler
　8. colonist, explorer 9. excavator
　10. forerunner
Pioneer's Day... 4. Utah (July 24)
　5. Idaho (June 15)
pious... 5. godly, loyal 6. devout,
　worthy 9. excellent, religious
　11. reverential 13. sanctimonious
pip... 3. ace 4. paip, peep, roup,
　seed, spot, trey 7. disease
　12. officer's star
pipe... 2. TD 3. see, tee 4. blow,
　clay, duct, reed, tube 5. spout, voice
　6. convey, dudeen, hookah (hooka),
　outlet 7. channel 9. brierwood
pipe (pert to)...
connection.. 3. ell, tee 5. cross,
　elbow
dream.. 8. illusion 10. bemusement
end.. 4. taft 6. nozzle
line.. 9. grapevine
Oriental.. 8. narghile (nargile)
pastoral, shepherd's.. 3. oat 4. reed
　7. larigot 8. flageolet
peace.. 7. calumet
player.. 5. fifer 8. shepherd
short.. 6. dudeen
smoke.. 5. tewel
steam.. 5. riser

tobacco.. 10. meerschaum
wood.. 5. brier (briar) 9. brierwood
wrench.. 8. Stillson
pipette... 6. taster, tubule 7. dripper
pipit... 7. titlark
piquancy... 4. zest 5. spice
   8. pungency, raciness, tartness
   11. conciseness
piquant... 4. racy, tart 5. salty, sharp,
   spicy, zesty 7. concise, cutting,
   pungent 11. interesting, provocative
pique... 4. dive, fret, goad 5. anger,
   annoy, sting, tempt 6. grudge, incite,
   nettle, offend 7. dudgeon, offense,
   provoke, umbrage 8. irritate
   9. displease 10. irritation, resentment
   11. displeasure
pir (Moham)... 4. tomb 5. guide, saint
pirate... 6. robber 7. corsair, mariner
   8. marauder, picaroon 9. buccaneer
   10. freebooter 11. appropriate
pirate (famed)... 4. Kidd 6. Morgan
   7. Lafitte 10. Blackbeard (Capt
   Teach)
pirate (pert to)...
   bird.. 10. jaeger gull
   flag.. 5. Roger
   gallows.. 7. yardarm
   perch.. 8. Xenarchi
   weapon.. 4. snee
piraya... 6. caribe (fish) 7. piranha
pirogue... 5. canoe 7. piragua
pirol... 6. oriole
Pisa, Italy...
   capital of.. 7. Tuscany
   famed for.. 9. campanile 12. Leaning
   Tower
   river.. 4. Arno
pis aller... 10. last resort
piscary... 7. fishery 12. fishing place
   13. fishing rights
piscatology *(science of)*... 7. angling,
   fishing 10. halieutics
Pisces... 4. fish 6. fishes
   13. constellation
piscina... 4. tank 5. basin (Eccl)
   8. fishpond 9. reservoir
Piscis Volans... 10. flying fish
   13. constellation
Pisgah (pert to)...
   site.. 4. Nebo 8. mountain (top)
   view.. 12. Land of Canaan 13. Land
   of Promise
   viewer.. 5. Moses
pismire... 3. ant 5. emmet
pistachio... 3. nut 5. green
piste... 4. path 5. spoor, track, trail
   10. racecourse
pisteology, pistiology... 5. faith
   6. belief
pistil... 5. ovary 6. carpel
   9. gynoecium
pistol... 3. dag 7. firearm 9. derringer
pistol (pert to)...
   case.. 7. holster
   lock.. 5. rowet
   slang.. 3. gat, rod 6. barker, cannon,
   heater
pistology (Theol)... 5. faith
piston... 7. plunger
pit... 4. cave, hole, mine, pool, sump,
   tomb, trap, well 5. abyss, arena,

grave, sluig, snare 6. cavity, slough
   7. alveola, cockpit, dungeon
   8. audience 9. waterhole
   10. excavation 13. Stock Exchange
pit (pert to)...
   anatomy.. 5. fossa, fovea
   botany.. 7. alveola, pitamen
   8. endocarp
   bottomless.. 7. Abaddon
   fodder.. 4. silo
   Hades.. 4. hell
   Hawaiian.. 3. imu
   theater.. 7. parquet
   viper.. 9. Viperidae 11. rattlesnake
pitch... 3. key, tar 4. camp, hurl, tilt,
   tone, toss 5. black, color, erect,
   fling, heave, lurch, resin, sense,
   slope, throw 6. degree, encamp,
   plunge, settle, topple 7. incline
   8. flounder 9. sales talk
pitch (pert to)...
   high.. 6. shrill
   identity.. 6. unison
   inflammable.. 7. piceous
   mineral.. 7. asphalt, bitumen
   music.. 4. flat 6. accent, stress
   8. paranete 9. tonometer
   pitchlike.. 7. piceous
pitchblende... 6. radium 7. uranium
pitched ball, curving away...
   8. outshoot
pitcher... 3. jug 4. ewer, olla, olpe,
   toby 5. gorge 8. cruisken (cruiskeen),
   oenochoe (wine), southpaw
   (left–handed)
pitcher (pert to)...
   plant, genus.. 9. Nepenthes
   10. Cephalotus, Sarracenia
   plus catcher.. 7. battery
   shaped.. 9. urceolate
   shaped vessel.. 8. aiguière
piteous... 5. pious 6. devout, paltry,
   tender 7. pitiful, pitying 8. pitiable
   13. compassionate
pitfall... 3. pit 4. lure, trap 5. decoy,
   snare 6. danger 10. difficulty
pith... 3. jet, nub 4. gist, meat, pulp
   6. center, kernel, marrow
   7. essence, meaning, nucleus
   9. substance
pith helmet... 3. cap, hat 5. topee
   (topi)
pith tree (Nile)... 7. ambatch (ambash)
pithy... 4. soft 5. crisp, meaty, pulpy,
   terse 7. laconic 10. meaningful
   12. epigrammatic
pithy (pert to)...
   expression.. 7. epigram
   saying.. 3. mot
   sentence.. 5. motto
pitiable... 3. sad 6. woeful 7. piteous
   8. grievous, terrible 9. miserable,
   sorrowful 10. lamentable
pitiful... 4. mean 6. paltry 7. piteous
   8. pathetic, shameful 10. despicable
   12. contemptible 13. compassionate,
   tenderhearted
pitiless... 5. cruel 8. ruthless
   9. merciless 10. relentless
   13. unsympathetic
pitpit... 8. guitguit 12. honey creeper
Pitri, Hindu (pert to)...

ancestor of . . **4**. gods **6**. demons
  10. four castes
Prajapatis, one of . . **10**. progenitor
  (human race)
semidivine . . **6**. father **9**. patriarch
  10. forefather
pittance . . . **4**. alms, dole, gift, scat
  7. bequest **8**. donation **9**. allowance
  11. small amount
pity . . . **4**. ruth **5**. mercy, yearn
  7. remorse **8**. clemency, sympathy
  10. compassion, condolence,
  repentance **13**. commiseration
pivot . . . **3**. toe **4**. slew, slue, turn
  5. hinge **6**. pintle, swivel
pivotal . . . **4**. crux **5**. polar **7**. turning
pixy, pixie . . . **3**. elf, imp **5**. fairy
  6. goblin, sprite **13**. mischief–maker
Pizarro (pert to) . . .
  adventurer . . **7**. Spanish
  conqueror of . . **4**. Peru
  founder of . . **4**. Lima (capital)
placable . . . **8**. peaceful **9**. agreeable,
  forgiving, peaceable **10**. appeasable
placard . . . **4**. bill, post **5**. edict
  6. notice, poster **7**. affiché
  9. manifesto, stomacher
  12. proclamation
placate . . . **4**. calm **6**. pacify, soothe
  7. appease **10**. conciliate
  11. tranquilize
place . . . **3**. put **4**. lieu, site, spot
  5. abode, locus, posit, situs, stead
  6. locale, locate, region, street
  7. arrange, demesne, deposit
  8. classify, location, position
  9. recognize, situation
place (of) . . .
  amusement . . **4**. park **6**. casino,
  midway
  bliss . . **4**. Eden **8**. paradise
  confinement . . **3**. pen **4**. brig, cage,
  coop, gaol, jail, stir **6**. asylum,
  corral, prison **7**. dungeon
  9. calaboose **12**. penitentiary
  confusion . . **5**. Babel
  content . . **7**. Arcadia
  darkness . . **6**. Erebus
  exit . . **6**. egress
  honor . . **9**. right hand
  origin . . **6**. cradle, source
  refuge . . **3**. ark **4**. port **5**. haven
  resort . . **7**. purlieu
  rest . . **3**. bed, den **4**. lair, nook
  5. chair, couch, grave, niche
  sleep . . **3**. bed **4**. doss **5**. berth,
  couch **6**. pallet **7**. hammock
  suffering . . **10**. Armageddon,
  Gethsemane
  trial . . **5**. venue
place (pert to) . . .
  apart . . **6**. enisle **7**. isolate
  9. sequester
  beneath . . **9**. infrapose
  between . . **9**. interpose
  burial . . **5**. grave **8**. catacomb,
  cemetery **9**. graveyard **10**. necropolis
  by itself . . **7**. isolate
  camping . . **5**. étape
  confidence in . . **7**. entrust
  different . . **10**. otherwhere
  for boats . . **7**. portage

for candles . . **9**. chandlery
forest (open) . . **5**. glade
for keeping animals . . **3**. zoo **4**. barn
  7. pasture **9**. menagerie
frequented . . **4**. dive **5**. haunt
  6. resort
from which jury is taken . . **5**. venue
hallowed . . see *sacred* below
hiding . . **3**. mew **4**. lair **5**. niche
high . . **7**. eminent **8**. eminence
horse training . . **4**. ring **5**. longe
in a row . . **5**. align, aline
in bondage . . **7**. enslave
in order . . **7**. arrange **11**. systematize
in statu quo . . **7**. put back, replace,
  restore
interpretation on . . **8**. construe
landing . . **4**. dock, pier **5**. wharf
  7. airport
market . . **4**. mart **5**. agora **6**. rialto
meeting . . **5**. tryst
of . . **4**. lieu **5**. stead
on mound . . **3**. tee
opposite . . **6**. appose
over . . **11**. superimpose
sacred . . **4**. fane **5**. altar **6**. chapel,
  church, shrine, temple **9**. synagogue
  10. tabernacle
side–by–side . . **9**. collocate, juxtapose
sleeping . . **3**. bed **4**. bunk **5**. berth,
  couch **6**. pallet **7**. hammock
under . . **9**. infrapose
under restraint . . **6**. arrest, intern
value upon . . **5**. price **6**. assess
  8. appraise, estimate
wet . . **4**. slew **5**. marsh **6**. slough
wrestling . . **5**. arena **9**. palaestra
  (palestra)
placed . . . **3**. put **7**. located
  8. arranged, situated **10**. classified
placed in lodgings . . . **6**. roomed
  8. billeted
placid . . . **4**. calm **5**. quiet, suant
  6. demure, gentle, serene
  8. composed, peaceful **9**. agreeable,
  quiescent, unruffled **11**. undisturbed
pladaroma . . . **5**. tumor (eyelid)
plafond . . . **7**. ceiling **14**. contract
  bridge
plage . . . **5**. beach
plagiarism . . . **6**. piracy **8**. cribbing,
  stealing **10**. purloining
  13. appropriation
plague . . . **3**. dun, vex **4**. bane, pest,
  twit **5**. harry, tease, worry **6**. harass,
  hector, infest **7**. scourge, torment
  8. epidemic, nuisance **10**. Black
  Death, pestilence **11**. infestation
plaguy . . . **6**. vexing **8**. annoying
  9. difficult, harassing **10**. tormenting
  11. troublesome
plaice . . . **8**. flatfish, flounder
plaid . . . **4**. maud **6**. tartan
plain . . . **3**. lea **4**. chol, mesa, moor,
  wold **5**. blunt, camas, clear, frank,
  heath **6**. lenten **7**. artless, evident,
  genuine, legible, obvious, prairie
  8. apparent, distinct, explicit, ordinary
  9. downright, primitive, unadorned
  10. unaffected
plain (pert to) . . .
  clothes . . **10**. unofficial

dealing.. 4. open 5. frank
knitting.. 12. garter stitch
of Mars.. 9. palmistry
spoken.. 15. straightforward
Plains (pert to)...
Arctic.. 6. tundra
Europe.. 6. steppe
Florida.. 7. savanna (savannah)
Italy.. 8. campagna
Russia.. 6. steppe, tundra
S African.. 6. pampas
Sp American.. 4. vega 5. llano
6. salada (salt–covered)
Plains Indians... 6. Kiowan, Siouan
7. Caddoan 10. Algonquian,
Athapascan, Uto–Aztecan
plainsman... 6. cowboy 7. llanero
8. herdsman
Plains of Abraham... 10. Quebec City
plaint... 6. bewail, lament 9. complaint
11. lamentation
plaintiff... 4. suer 6. orator 7. accuser
8. claimant, libelant (libellant)
10. complainer 11. complainant
plaintive... 3. sad 5. cross 7. elegiac,
fretful, peevish, pettish, wailful,
wistful 8. mournful, petulant, repining
9. lamenting, sorrowful
10. melancholy 11. complaining
12. discontented
plait... 4. fold, hair, knit, lace, plat
5. braid, pleat, weave 6. pleach,
wimple 9. corrugate, interlace
10. interweave
plaited... 5. Milan (straw) 6. folded,
kilted, sennit (palm leaves)
8. pleached 10. interlaced
11. intertwined
plan... 3. map, way 4. form, idea,
line, plat, plot 5. chart, draft, ettle,
frame, setup 6. design, devise,
intend, layout, method, scheme
7. arrange, diagram, outline, pattern,
project 8. engineer, strategy
9. calculate, procedure
11. arrangement, contemplate,
preconceive, premeditate
plan (pert to)...
architecture.. 5. draft, épure
frustrator of.. 7. marplot
preliminary.. 4. idea 6. map out
8. proposal
secretly.. 4. plot 7. connive
8. conspire
planate... 5. plane 9. flattened
plancher... 3. bed 5. board (occult),
floor, plank 6. pallet 8. planking,
platform
plancier... 6. soffit 7. cornice
plandok... 9. mouse deer
plane... 3. fly 4. even, flat, ramp,
scar, tool 5. level 6. degree, smooth
7. jointer, surface 8. airplane
10. smoothness
plane (pert to)...
block.. 5. stock
boundary.. 9. perimeter
four–angled.. 6. square 7. rhombus
8. tetragon 10. quadrangle
handle.. 4. tote (bench plane)
inclined.. 4. ramp 5. chute
iron.. 5. blade

kind.. 3. mig 5. stuka 6. router
measure.. 10. planimeter
smoothing, chamfering.. 5. howel
tree.. 6. chinar (Orient) 8. Platanus
type.. 5. bench, block, stock
6. trowel 7. jointer, routing
planet... 4. Mars, star 5. Earth, Pluto,
Venus 6. Saturn, Uranus 7. Jupiter,
Mercury, Neptune 8. wanderer
planet (pert to)...
astrology.. 9. alfridary
brightest.. 5. Venus
cone.. 8. strobile
course.. 5. orbit
minor.. 9. satellite
nearest sun.. 7. Mercury
orbit.. 7. ellipse
red.. 4. Mars
remotest.. 5. Pluto (1930)
resembling.. 8. asteroid
ringed.. 6. Saturn
satellite.. 4. moon
shadow.. 5. umbra
small.. 8. asteroid
sphere.. 6. oblate
planet (solar system) *by size*...
7. Jupiter 6. Saturn 7. Neptune
6. Uranus 5. Earth, Venus, Pluto
4. Mars 7. Mercury
planetarium... 5. Zeiss 6. orrery
planetary... 7. earthly, erratic
9. celestial, wandering, worldwide
planetology (study of)... 7. planets
10. satellites
plangor... 4. wail 11. lamentation
planisphere... 7. sextant 9. astrolabe
plank... 3. sny 4. deal, slab 5. board,
shole, stone 6. timber 7. pay down
8. planking 10. gravestone
plank down... 3. pay 7. advance,
deposit
planner... 8. designer, engineer,
gardener 9. architect, projector
plant... 3. fix, sow, spy 4. ache, bury,
herb, seed, trap 5. cache, decoy,
shrub 6. clover 7. falsify 8. colonize,
workshop 9. deception, detective,
equipment, vegetable
plant (pert to)...
abnormal environs.. 4. ecad
adjustment.. 6. ecesis
air.. 8. epiphyte
appendage.. 7. stipula
biggest.. 10. Aspidistra
body.. 6. cormus 7. thallus
bud.. 4. cion 5. scion
climbing.. 4. vine 5. liana
coloring matter.. 11. chlorophyll
crossbred.. 6. hybrid
cross–fertilization.. 9. phytogamy
disease.. 4. gall, rust, smut 5. ergot
7. blister 8. ramentum
embryo.. 8. plantule
enchantment–proof.. 7. haemony
(Milton's Comus)
flowerless.. 4. fern 6. lichen
9. cryptogam 11. Cryptogamia (opp
of phanerogam)
growing on rock.. 6. lichen
growing on sea bottom.. 6. enalid
growing wild.. 9. agrestial
history.. 12. phytogenesis

legendary, forgetfulness.. 5. lotus
male.. 3. mas
mosslike.. 6. orpine
mushroom type.. 6. fungus
native.. 8. indigene
orifice.. 5. stoma
pigment lacking.. 6. albino
poisonous.. 4. atis 6. datura
  7. amanita 8. oleander
poisonous to cattle.. 4. loco
  8. locoweed
pore.. 8. lenticel
round–leaved.. 9. pennywort
science of.. 6. botany
seedless.. 6. agamic
stem, stalk.. 4. bine 5. haulm
  6. caulis
tequila–yielding.. 5. agave
tissue.. 7. tapetum
without chlorophyll.. 6. albino
without petals.. 9. apetulous
woody.. 6. xyloid
plant (type of)...
  aconite.. 4. bikh
  agave, century plant.. 4. aloe, pita
    9. amaryllis
  ammoniac.. 5. oshac
  anise.. 4. dill
  aquatic.. 6. sugamo 7. frogbit
    8. plankton
  aromatic.. 4. mint, nard 5. basil,
    tansy, thyme 8. tarragon
  arum.. 4. sago 6. starch 9. arrowroot
  aster family.. 5. daisy 8. fleabane
  bitter.. 3. rue
  bitter vetch.. 3. ers
  box.. 5. Buxus 7. boxwood
  broom.. 5. spart 6. Canary 7. genista
  bryophytic.. 4. moss
  burdock.. 5. elite 8. Xanthium
  burning bush.. 5. wahoo
  butter–and–eggs.. 8. ranstead
  cactus.. 5. dildo 6. cereus, chaute,
    mescal 7. saguaro 9. xerophyte
  century.. 4. aloe 5. agave 6. maguey
  dill.. 4. anot
  evergreen.. 3. ivy 5. holly 6. laurel
    8. conifers 9. mistletoe
  everlasting.. 6. orpine 11. live–forever
  furze.. 4. ulex 5. gorse
  garlic (wild).. 4. moly
  leguminous.. 3. pea 4. bean
    6. Cassia, clover, lentil
  lilaceous.. 4. aloe, iris, leek 5. lotus,
    onion, tulip, yucca
  linen.. 4. flax
  medicinal.. 4. alem, aloe 5. anise,
    wahoo 6. arnica, cacoon, catnip,
    ipecac 7. aconite, boneset, gentian,
    lobelia, rhatany 8. camomile
  pea family.. 7. Cytisus
  perennial.. 4. Geum 5. avens
    10. sneezewort
  poisonous.. 6. datura 8. oleander
  poisonous to cattle.. 8. locoweed
  poisonous to fowl.. 7. henbane
  prickly, thorny.. 5. brier 6. cactus,
    nettle, teasel 7. thistle
  satinpod (transparent).. 7. honesty
  soap.. 5. amole
  tapioca.. 7. cassava
  thorny.. see *prickly* 6. fatsia

  trifoliate.. 6. clover 8. shamrock
plant, typical of...
  Africa.. 5. argel (arghel)
  Alps.. 9. edelweiss
  Arabia.. 3. kat (stimulant)
  Australia.. 5. Hakes, lilac 6. Correa
    7. columba, fuchsia 8. Rutaceae
  China.. 5. ramie
  Egypt.. 5. anise, cumin 7. aniseed
    8. nepenthe
  Hawaii.. 5. olona
  Japan.. 3. tea 5. acuba 6. quince
    7. cydonia 8. japonica
  Japan (vine).. 8. Bignonia 14. trumpet
    creeper
  Mexico.. 4. chia 5. datil 6. salvia
    9. sabadilla
  Peru.. 3. oca 7. rhatany
  Philippines.. 4. alem (Med) 6. agamid
  Spain.. 3. aji 6. pepper 8. Capsicum
  Syria.. 5. cumin
  tropical vine.. 8. redwithe
    10. tillandsia
  tropics.. 4. arum, palm, taro
    5. agave, zamia 7. dasheen, hamelia
    8. mangrove
plantain... 6. banana
plantation pines... 7. pinetum
plantation trees... 4. holt 6. forest
  7. nopalry (cactus), orchard
planters, Govt of... 11. plantocracy
plantigrade mammal... 5. panda
plaque... 5. medal, patch 6. brooch,
  tablet 8. ornament, platelet (Anat)
plash... 4. plop, pool 5. swash
  6. puddle, ripple, splash
plasm... 4. mold 6. matrix
plasma... 4. cell, whey 5. blood (fluid)
  10. protoplasm
plaster... 4. teer 5. gesso, grout, salve
  6. gypsum, parget, stucco
  8. adhesive, poultice 9. inebriate
plastered... 5. drunk 7. crocked,
  smeared 8. mortared
plasterer... 5. mason
plaster of Paris... 5. gesso
  6. gypsum 15. calcium sulphate
plastic... 3. pug 5. gesso, vinyl
  6. slurry 7. ductile, fictile, pliable,
  viscose 8. creative 9. compliant,
  formative, teachable
  14. impressionable
plastic, commercial... 6. Lucite
  7. Formica 8. Bakelite, Vinylite
  9. Plexiglas
plasty (pert to)...
  comb form.. 7. molding
  eyelid.. 14. blepharoplasty
  face lift.. 13. rhytidoplasty
  nose.. 11. rhinoplasty
plat... 3. map 4. flat, plan, plot
  5. braid, chart, field, level, plain,
  plait, pleat 6. flatly, scheme
  7. outline, plateau 8. absolute,
  directly, straight 9. tableland
  10. interweave 15. straightforward
platanist... 4. fish, susu
plate... 3. gib 4. disc, dish, shoo
  (horse) 5. paten 6. lamina, patera
  7. coating, denture, overlay
  9. bookplate, engraving
  10. receptacle

plate (pert to)...
armor.. 6. cuisse (cuish)
battery.. 4. grid
bone (Anat).. 7. scapula
cooking.. 4. grid
culture.. 8. bacteria
Eccl.. 5. paten 6. patina
graduated.. 4. dial
holder.. 8. cassette
horny.. 5. scute
horse.. 6. plater
insect (bony).. 6. scutum
mark.. 8. hallmark 9. engraving
numbered.. 4. disc
of glass.. 5. slide
perforated metal.. 3. dod
ship–shaped.. 3. nef
plateau... 4. dish, mesa, puna 5. plain
6. plaque, salver 9. tableland
platform... 3. map 4. dais, deck,
k'ang, plan 5. arena, chart, plank,
stage 6. lissom, lyceum, podium,
policy, pulpit, scheme 7. estrade,
outline, rostrum, soapbox, tribune
8. hustings 9. bandstand 14. public
speaking
platform (pert to)...
fort.. 8. barbette
gun.. 11. emplacement
mining.. 6. sollar (soller)
nautical.. 7. foretop, maintop
9. gangplank
scaffold (funeral).. 10. catafalque
wheeled.. 5. float
platic (Astrol)... 8. not exact
9. imperfect
plating... 5. armor 6. lamina
7. shoeing
platinum wire... 4. oese
platitude... 6. cliché, old hat, truism
7. bromide 8. banality 9. staleness,
triteness 11. commonplace
15. commonplaceness
Plato (pert to)...
famed for.. 9. Dialogues
10. philosophy
founder of.. 7. Academe, academy
name, real.. 10. Aristocles
pupil of.. 8. Socrates
platoid... 4. flat 5. broad
Platonic (pert to)...
idea.. 5. eidos
love.. 4. pure 5. ideal 6. chaste
8. virtuous 10. idealistic
11. comradeship
philosophy.. 8. idealism 9. Platonism
11. theoretical
solids.. 10. hexahedron, octahedron
11. icosahedron, tetrahedron
12. dodecahedron
platoon... 3. set 4. unit 5. squad
7. company, coterie 11. subdivision
platoon school... 4. Gary (Ind)
platter... 4. dish, lanx 5. grail, plate
6. record 9. scutellum
platter–shaped... 10. scutellate
platyfish... 8. moonfish
platypus... 8. duckbill
plaudit... 5. cheer, éclat 6. encore
8. applause, approval, clapping,
encomium 10. plaudation
11. acclamation, approbation

plausible... 8. credible, probable,
specious 10. applausive, believable,
ostensible, plauditory, reasonable
11. conceivable
plausible excuse... 5. alibi
play... 3. act, fun, toy 4. game, jest,
romp 5. dally, drama, enact, feign,
sport, wager 6. affect, frolic
7. disport, operate, pretend
9. amusement, diversion, melodrama,
pantomime 10. recreation
11. impersonate 13. entertainment
play (pert to)...
exhibit a.. 5. stage
for time.. 5. stall
house.. 5. movie 6. cinema
7. theater 9. dollhouse
musical.. 5. opera 8. burletta,
operetta
outline.. 8. scenario
part.. 4. role 7. prelude 8. epilogue,
epitasis, prologue
pranks.. 4. haze
silent.. 9. pantomime
story.. 8. scenario
stupid.. 5. boner
the bagpipe.. 5. skirl 6. doodle
the buffoon.. 5. droll
the coquette.. 5. flirt
tricks.. 4. hoax, shab
truant.. 5. miche
unskillfully.. 5. strum
upon words.. 3. pun 11. paronomasia
playa... 5. beach, shore 7. salt pan
playboy... 4. fool 5. clown, cutup
7. buffoon, reveler 8. carouser
10. merrymaker 12. Jack of Trumps
(Spoilfive)
player... 3. dub 4. star 5. actor, idler,
piper 7. gambler, trifler 8. gamester,
musician, stroller, thespian
9. frolicker, performer
11. barnstormer
player on words... 7. punster
playful... 3. gay 6. lusory 7. jocular
8. humorous, playsome, sportive
9. facetious, kittenish
11. mischievous
playing cards... 4. deck, pack
6. tarots
playlet... 4. skit 9. short play
plaything... 3. die, toy 4. dupe
6. bauble 8. cat's–paw
plea... 4. suit 5. claim 6. abater,
appeal, excuse, prayer 7. apology,
defense, pretext 8. argument,
entreaty, pretense 10. advocation,
allegation 13. nolo contendere
plead... 3. beg, sue 5. argue
6. adduce, allege 7. entreat, implore
plead (for)... 7. entreat, justify, solicit
10. supplicate
pleader... 4. suer 6. lawyer
8. advocate 9. entreater, justifier
11. intercessor
pleading... 4. oyer 8. advocacy,
demurrer, entreaty 9. imploring,
objection 10. litigation
12. intercession, supplication
pleasant... 3. fun, gay 4. nice
5. merry, sweet 6. genial 7. affable,
amusing, leesome, winsome

8. cheerful, friendly, humorous,
   pleasing, sportive 9. agreeable,
   diverting, laughable, sprightly
pleasant (pert to)...
   manners.. 9. amenities
   sound.. 6. dulcet 8. euphonic
   9. melodious 10. harmonious
   to peruse.. 8. readable
   weather.. 4. fair, fine 6. bright
   8. rainless 9. cloudless
please... 4. like, suit 5. fancy 6. arride
   7. appease, content, delight, gratify,
   indulge, placate, satisfy 9. vouchsafe
pleased... 4. fain, game, glad
   5. happy 9. contented, gratified
pleasing... 4. cool, lief, nice 5. sooth
   6. comely, eesome, savory
   7. amiable, roseate, welcome
   8. pleasant 9. agreeable, desirable
   10. delectable 11. pleasureful
pleasurable... 7. hedonic 8. pleasant
   10. gratifying
pleasure... 3. joy 4. gree, will, wish
   5. mirth, sport 6. choice, gaiety
   7. delight, purpose 8. gladness,
   hedonism, hilarity 9. amusement,
   diversion, enjoyment, happiness,
   merriment 11. delectation
   12. satisfaction 13. gratification
pleasure (pert to)...
   god.. 3. Bes
   ground.. 4. park 9. pleasance
   pert to.. 7. hedonic
   philosophy.. 8. Hedonism
   seeker.. 5. sport 7. epicure, playboy
   8. hedonist
pleat... 4. fold 5. braid, plait
pleater... 8. plicator
plebeian... 4. pleb (Rom) 6. common,
   vulgar 7. ignoble, ill bred, lowborn
   8. ordinary
plebiscite... 4. vote 6. decree
   10. referendum
pleck... 4. plot (ground), spot
   5. speck, stain 9. enclosure
plectrum... 4. pick 5. uvula 6. tongue
   7. malleus 8. plectron
pledge... 3. bet, vas, vow 4. bond,
   gage, gate, oath, pawn, seal, wage
   5. swear, toast, troth 6. engage,
   parole, plight 7. chattel, earnest,
   promise 8. guaranty, mortgage,
   obligate, security 9. assurance
   10. collateral 11. impignorate
pledget... 4. swab 8. compress
Pleiad (pert to)...
   Alexandria.. 10. Seven Poets
   French.. 10. The Pléiade
   lost Pleiad.. 6. Merope 7. Electra
   philosophical (Gr).. 12. Seven Wise
   Men
Pleiades (pert to)...
   Seven Daughters of Atlas..
   10. Atlantides
   star.. 4. Maia 7. Sterope 8. Asterope
   star cluster.. 8. in Taurus
   (Constellation)
plenary... 4. full 5. great 6. entire
   7. perfect 8. absolute, complete
   9. unlimited 11. unqualified
plenipotentiary... 5. envoy
   8. diplomat, minister 10. ambassador

plenteous... 6. plenty 7. copious,
   fertile, liberal 8. abundant, fruitful,
   generous 9. bounteous, bountiful,
   plentiful 10. productive
plentiful... 4. full, rich, rife 5. ample
   6. lavish 7. copious, fertile, liberal,
   opulent, profuse 9. abounding,
   bounteous, bountiful
   13. superabundant
plentifully... 6. galore 9. abounding,
   abundance
plenty... 4. enow 6. enough, galore,
   uberty 8. fullness 9. abundance,
   plenitude 10. perfection
   11. copiousness 12. completeness,
   considerable 14. superabundance
plenum... 5. space 8. assembly,
   fullness (of space) (opp of vacuum)
pleon... 6. telson 7. abdomen
pleonasm... 8. fullness 10. redundancy
   11. diffuseness, reiteration
plethora... 4. glut 6. excess
   9. repletion 14. superabundance
plethoric... 6. turgid 8. inflated,
   overfull 9. bombastic 10. overloaded
plexiform... 4. rete 7. network
   11. complicated
plexus... 4. rete 5. solar 7. network
pliable... 4. limp 6. limber, pliant,
   supple 7. plastic 8. flexible, suitable
   9. compliant, teachable
pliant... 7. bending, pliable, tensile,
   willowy 8. flexible, workable, yielding
   9. adaptable, compliant
plicate... 4. fold 5. pleat 6. folded
   7. plaited
plight... 4. fold 5. braid, plait
   6. status 7. embrace, promise
   8. position 9. condition, situation
   (bad) 11. predicament
plinth... 4. orlo 7. subbase
Pliosaurus (extinct)... 7. reptile
plod... 3. dig, mog 4. slog, toil, tore
   6. drudge, trudge
plodder... 3. fag 4. grub, hack
   5. slave 6. drudge
plot... 3. lot, map 4. acre, area, brew,
   burn, pack, plan, plat 5. cabal,
   frame, tract, trick 6. design, scheme,
   scorch, secret 7. diagram, project
   8. conspire, intrigue 10. conspiracy,
   prearrange 11. machination
plot (of ground)... 3. lot 4. acre, area,
   plat 5. grave, tract 7. terrain
Plotinus... 11. philosopher (Alexandrian
   School)
plotted... 7. charted, hatched
   8. lineated 9. conspired
   10. delineated 11. prearranged
plotter... 5. Haman 7. Jacobin,
   planner, schemer 8. agitator
   9. contriver 11. conspirator
ploughshare (plowshare) part...
   6. colter (coulter)
plover... 4. dupe 5. piper, sandy
   7. lapwing 9. courtesan, sandpiper,
   shorebird
plover (pert to)...
   crab.. 5. drome
   crested.. 7. lapwing
   egg.. 11. darning ball
   genus.. 12. Charadriidae

Old World.. 8. dotterel, killdeer
page.. 6. dunlin 9. sandpiper
quail.. 13. plain wanderer
ring.. 5. pandy
plow... 4. rove, till 5. break, miner,
scaut 6. furrow, turn up 7. break up
8. reinvest 9. cultivate
plow (pert to)...
fish.. 3. ray
gang.. 6. oxgang 7. measure
light.. 10. Plow Monday 13. hoggler's
light
man.. 6. rustic 10. countryman,
husbandman
part.. 4. buck, chip, hale 5. share,
slade, stilt 6. clevis, colter
type.. 5. sulky 8. mole plow
plowed land... 5. arada, arado
pluck... 3. pug, rob, tug 4. grab, jerk,
pick, pull 5. nerve, spunk, steal,
strip, strum 6. avulse, divest, fleece,
gather, twitch 7. courage, harvest,
pick off, plunder, strip of, swindle
10. resolution, straighten (wool)
plucky... 4. game 5. brave, nervy
6. spunky, sticky 8. adhesive,
resolute, spirited 10. courageous
plug... 3. peg, tap, top 4. blow, bung
5. horse, knock, punch, shoot, spile,
wedge 7. commend, hydrant,
stopper, stopple, tobacco
9. persevere, publicity, publicize
12. commendation
plug (pert to)...
board.. 11. switchboard
cannon muzzle.. 7. tampion (tampeon,
tampoon)
dentristy.. 7. filling
hat.. 4. tile 5. gibus 6. topper
medical.. 4. clot 6. fibrin, tampon
7. embolus
slender.. 5. spill
up.. 4. calk (caulk)
plum... 5. drupe, money, prune
6. Prunus 8. dividend 9. good thing,
sugarplum
plum (pert to)...
beetle.. 8. curculio
bitter.. 4. sloe
California (wild).. 5. islay
coco.. 5. icaco
England.. 6. damson
Europe.. 7. bullace
hybrid.. 7. plumcot
India.. 7. hog plum
Java.. 7. jambool (jambul)
8. jambolan
type.. 5. gage 6. damson
9. greengage, wild–goose 11. Reine
Claude
plumage... 4. down 6. hackle
7. floccus (first down) 8. feathers,
ornament
plumb... 4. seal, true 5. delve, gauge,
sound, utter 6. adjust, fathom,
sinker, weight (lead) 7. examine,
measure, plummet 8. absolute,
complete, vertical 9. downright
13. perpendicular
plumbage... 8. leadwork
plumbog... 9. raspberry (dwarf)
plumcot... 6. hybrid 11. plum apricot

plume... 5. crest, egret, preen, pride
6. plumet 7. feather, panache
8. decorate, plumelet
plummet... 4. dive, drop, fall, lead,
plop, test 5. pitch, sound, swoop
6. fathom, plunge, weight
9. criterion
plump... 3. fat 4. drop, dull, fall, plop,
rude, sink, tidy 5. blunt, buxom,
flock, fubsy, obese 6. chubby, dilate,
fatten, flatly 7. distend 8. blurt out,
straight 9. corpulent, filled out
10. vertically 11. well–rounded
plumpness of person... 9. stoutness
10. embonpoint
plunder... 3. rob 4. boot, loot, pelf,
prey, raid, rape, sack 5. booty,
poach, raven, reave, rifle, strip
6. boodle, fleece, maraud, profit,
rapine, ravage, spoils 7. despoil,
pillage 8. spoliate 9. depredate
plundered... 4. reft 6. looted, robbed
plunderer... 5. thief 6. looter, pirate,
preyer, raider, robber 7. spoiler,
stealer 8. pillager 10. freebooter
plunge... 3. bet, dip 4. dash, dive,
fall, pool, risk, sink 5. douse, drive,
lunge, plumb, souse 6. gamble,
thrust 7. baptize, immerse
8. flounder 9. gravitate, overwhelm,
speculate
plunge (into)... 4. clap, dive 5. begin
7. immerge, immerse 9. set to work,
undertake
plunger... 5. diver 6. risker 7. gambler
10. speculator
plunk... 4. blow, drop, pull, push,
sink, thud 5. drive, plump, strum,
throw 7. a dollar 10. play truant
plurality... 8. majority 9. multitude
11. greater part, large number
plural marriage... 8. polygamy
Plutarch (Gr)... 10. biographer
Pluto (pert to)...
Astron.. 6. planet (most remote)
god of.. 10. lower world
Greek name.. 5. Hades
kingdom.. 5. Hades
Roman name.. 3. Dis 5. Orcus
wife.. 10. Proserpina
plutocracy... 13. rule by wealthy
17. dominion of the rich
Plutus (pert to)...
god of.. 6. wealth
son of.. 6. lasion 7. Demeter
pluvia... 4. rain 9. pluviosus
pluviometer, pluvioscope... 9. rain
gauge
pluvious... 5. rainy 7. pluvial
ply... 4. bend, fold, mold, sail, urge
5. exert, plait, wield 6. employ,
handle, lamina 8. navigate
9. importune, thickness
pneuma... 4. soul 5. neume 6. breath,
spirit 9. breathing, life force, vital
soul
pneumology *(science of)*... 5. lungs
17. respiratory organs
poach... 3. mix, ram 4. poke, push,
sock, stir 5. drive, force, shirr (egg),
steal 6. thrust 7. trample
8. encroach, trespass

poacher... 7. lurcher, stalker, widgeon
Poblacht... 8. Republic
Pocahontas (pert to)...
  father.. 8. Powhatan (Chief)
  husband.. 9. John Rolfe
  Indian title.. 8. Princess
  name.. 12. Rebecca Rolfe
  rescuer of.. 9. John Smith (Capt)
pocket... 3. bag, bin, cly, fob, sac
  4. poke, sack, take 5. money,
  pouch, purse 6. cavity, hollow
  7. conceal, confine, enclose
  8. envelope
pocketbook... 3. bag, lil 5. pouch,
  purse 6. income, wallet 8. notebook
  9. resources
pod... 3. bag, kid, sac 4. aril, boll
  5. belly, carob, chili, pouch, shuck
  6. legume
poem... 3. dit, lay, ode 4. Edda, epic,
  epos, hymn, rune, saga 5. elegy,
  epode, idyll, psalm, verse 6. ballad
  (ballade), jingle, rondel (roundelle),
  sonnet 7. eclogue, erotics, rondeau
  8. limerick, rondelet 9. dithyramb
  10. villanelle 11. acatalectic
poem (pert to)...
  division.. 5. canto, epode, verse
    6. stanza 7. refrain
  eight lines.. 7. triolet
  famed.. 5. Iliad 7. Odyssey
  foot.. 6. iambic 7. anapest, pyrrhic
  imitation.. 6. parody
  line.. 5. stich 6. octave, septet,
    sestet, tercet 7. couplet, triplet
    8. cinquain, quatrain
  meter.. 6. iambic 8. spondaic,
    trochaic 9. dactyllic, hexameter
    10. anaepestic (anapestic),
    pentameter
  ref to.. 5. meter, rhyme, verse
    7. cadence, helicon 8. feminine,
    scansion 9. masculine
  religious.. 4. hymn 5. psalm
  rhythmic break.. 7. caesura
  satirical.. 3. dit 6. parody
poem, famed...
  Homer.. 5. Iliad 7. Odyssey
  Khayyám.. 8. Rubáiyát
  Milton.. 12. Paradise Lost
  Ovid.. 13. Metamorphoses
  Poe.. 8. The Raven
  Poem in Marble.. 8. Taj Mahal
  poem of declaration.. 8. Invictus
  Shakespeare.. 7. Macbeth
  Spenser.. 12. Faerie Queene
poems... 5. poesy, sylva 6. poetry
poet... 4. bard 5. odist, rimer 6. lyrist
  7. dreamer 8. laureate 9. poetaster,
  rhymester, versifier
poet (famed)...
  German.. 5. Heine
  mythology.. 6. Ossian
  Negro.. 11. Braithwaite
  Persian.. 7. Khayyám
  Sierra.. 13. Joaquin Miller
Poet Laureate (a few)... 6. Dryden
  7. Spenser 8. Tennyson 9. Ben
  Jonson, Masefield 10. Wordsworth
poetry (pert to)...
  Muse of.. 5. Erato 6. Thalia
    8. Calliope

Norse god of.. 5. Bragi
School of (anc).. 9. Parnassus
type.. 4. epic 5. lyric 6. ballad
  8. didactic 9. free verse, narrative
  10. blank verse
pogoniate... 7. bearded
pogonip... 3. fog (Sierras)
pogonology (study of)... 6. beards
pogrom... 8. massacre
poi... 4. food, taro, then (Mus)
poignant... 4. keen 5. acute 6. biting,
  bitter 7. cutting, pungent
point... 3. aim, dot, jab, jot, neb, nib,
  pin 4. apex, barb, cape, gaff, gist,
  node, peak, stop, tack 5. focus,
  prong, quill, spike 6. bodkin, direct,
  needle, period, summit, zenith
  7. apicula, punctum 10. breakwater,
  promontory
point (pert to)...
  antler, branch.. 4. snag
  astronomy.. 5. apsis 6. syzygy
  central, pivotal.. 4. crux
  farthest from earth.. 6. apogee
  focal.. 9. epicenter
  geometry.. 6. acnode 7. crunode
  highest.. 4. acme, apex, peak
    6. summit, zenith 8. meridian,
    pinnacle
  lace.. 10. petit point 11. needlepoint
  law.. 3. res 5. locus
  lowest.. 5. nadir 6. bottom
  mathematics.. 5. unode
  nearest earth.. 7. perigee
  of contact.. 5. focus
  of debate.. 6. issue, topic
  of honor.. 7. scruple
  of view.. 5. angle, slant 8. attitude
  opposite zenith.. 5. nadir
  reference to.. 6. apical
  salient.. 7. feature
  starting, golf.. 3. tee
  strong.. 5. forte
  utmost.. 7. extreme
  weak.. 4. flaw 5. fault 6. foible
pointed... 5. aimed, noded, piked,
  sharp, terse 6. acuate, marked,
  peaked 7. angular, concise, conical
  8. aculeate, piercing, poignant,
  spicated, stinging 9. acuminate,
  pertinate, spiculate 10. emphasized
  11. conspicuous, significant
  12. epigrammatic
pointed (pert to)...
  architecture.. 5. ogive 6. Gothic
  end.. 4. cusp
  fox.. 3. red
  instrument.. 3. awl, gad 4. prod
    6. gimlet, stylet
  rod.. 4. goad
pointer... 3. arm, dog, tip 4. sign
  5. index 6. fescue, gnomon
pointless... 4. dull 5. blunt, inane,
  silly, vapid 6. stupid 7. insipid,
  witless
poise... 6. aplomb 7. balance, ballast
  8. carriage 9. composure, equipoise,
  stability
poison (pert to)...
  arrow.. 4. inee, upas 5. urari
    6. curare (curari)
  deadly.. 4. bane, upas 5. arrow

7. arsenic, cyanide, hemlock
10. strychnine
study of.. 10. toxicology
poissarde... 8. fishwife, low woman
poisson... 4. fish
poisson bleu... 7. catfish 8. bluefish, grayling
poitrel... 5. armor, plate 9. stomacher
11. breastplate
poke... 3. bag, jab, jog, pry 4. bore, goad, prod, root, sack 5. grope, nudge, probe, purse 6. dawdle, potter, search, thrust, wallet
7. project, tobacco
poker... 3. rod 6. beadle 7. bugbear, pochard 9. hobgoblin
poker (pert to)...
face.. 8. immobile
form of.. 4. draw, stud
painting.. 10. pyrography
picture.. 11. pyrogravure
stake.. 3. pot 4. ante 6. roodle
poky, pokey... 4. dull, mean, slow
5. dowdy, small 6. bonnet, narrow, shabby 7. cramped, tedious
Poland... see also *Polish*
ancestors.. 5. Lakha, Slavs
ancient name.. 7. Polonia
capital.. 6. Warsaw
city.. 4. Lodz 6. Gdynia, Krakow, Lublin
river.. 7. Dnieper, Vistula
Poland China... 5. swine
polar... 5. curve 6. Arctic 7. guiding
8. opposite 9. Antarctic, magnetism
Polar base (exploration)... 4. Etah
Polaris... 5. Alpha 9. North Star
11. guiding star
pole... 3. bar, oar, pew, poy, rod, xat
4. axle, beam, mast, prop, spar
5. shaft, sprit, staff, stool, totem
pole (pert to)...
bad end.. 7. raw deal
burn.. 7. disease (tobacco)
cat.. 5. skunk, zoril 6. ferret, musang
7. fitchew 8. Putorius 9. scoundrel
cat weed.. 12. skunk cabbage
electric.. 5. anode, pitch 7. cathode
8. magnetic 9. electrode
Gaelic.. 5. caber
head.. 7. tadpole
Spanish.. 4. pale, palo
star.. 5. guide 7. polaris 8. lodestar
9. North Star 13. l'Etoile du Nord
vehicle.. 4. cope, crab 5. thill
well.. 5. sweep
polemic... 9. disputant 11. contentious
13. argumentative, controversial
polenta... 8. porridge
poles of cold... 7. Siberia (Verkhoyansk) 12. Grinnell Land (Fort Conger)
police (pert to)...
badge.. 6. buzzer, shield
club.. 8. spontoon
man.. 3. cop 5. guard 6. bobbie, copper, peeler, Ranger 7. officer, sheriff, trooper 9. constable, detective, N W Mounted
11. carabinière (carabineer)
station.. 5. thana 6. lockup
8. bargello

policy... 3. wit 4. plan 6. wisdom
8. regulate, sagacity 9. insurance
10. government, management, shrewdness 11. contrivance
13. judiciousness 14. administration
policy of segregation... 9. apartheid
polish... 3. rub 4. buff 5. glaze, gloss, rabat, scour, shine 6. finish, luster, smooth 7. burnish, culture, furbish
8. brighten, civilize, elegance, lapidate, levigate, urbanity
10. refinement
Polish (pert to)...
Bull.. 13. Constellation
cake.. 4. baba
carriage.. 7. britska
composer, pianist.. 6. Chopin
10. Paderewski
dance.. 7. mazurka 9. polonaise
11. cracovienne (krakowiak)
nobleman.. 7. starost
premier.. 10. Paderewski (pianist)
president (1st).. 10. Philsudski
scientist.. 5. Curie (Madame)
polishing material... 5. emery, rabat, rouge 6. pumice 11. rottenstone
polite... 4. neat, tidy 5. civil, suave, urban 6. gentle, smooth, urbane
7. gallant, genteel, refined
8. polished 9. courteous, debonaire (debonair, debonnaire) 10. cultivated
11. complaisant
politesse... 10. politeness (formal)
11. cleanliness, courtliness·
12. decorousness
politic... 4. wary 7. cunning, tactful
8. cautious, discreet 9. judicious, political, politique, provident
10. diplomatic
political (pert to)...
boss.. 7. cacique
district.. 4. city, ward 5. State
6. canton, county, parish 7. borough
10. palatinate
economy.. 9. economics
faction.. 4. bloc, ring 5. junta, party
7. machine
hanger–on.. 6. heeler 10. ward heeler
influence.. 5. lobby, rally 6. caucus
party (old).. 4. Tory, Whig 9. Politique
politician... 7. schemer 9. intriguer, statesman 11. gerrymander
12. politicaster
politics... 7. cunning 8. scheming
10. government, profession
15. partisan rivalry 16. political affairs
Polizei... 9. the police
poll... 3. cut, tax 4. clip, head, roll, vote 5. shear, skull 6. fleece, survey
7. despoil 8. election, schedule
pollan... 9. whitefish
polled... 5. shorn 6. shaved
8. hornless
pollen... 4. seed 6. anther 8. fine dust 11. microspores 13. fertilization
pollen brush (bee's)... 5. scopa
pollenization... 5. xenia 13. fertilization
pollent... 6. strong 8. powerful
poller... 5. voter 6. barber
9. plunderer 11. extortioner, taxgatherer

pollex... 5. thumb 11. bastard wing
  (bird) 13. dactylopodite
pollex impression... 10. thumbprint
polliwog... 7. tadpole
pollute... 4. soil 5. taint 6. befoul,
  defile, ravish 7. corrupt, debauch,
  profane 9. desecrate, inebriate
  11. contaminate
pollution... 8. impurity 9. infection
  10. corruption, defilement
  13. contamination
Pollux (pert to)...
  brother (twin).. 6. Castor
  father.. 4. Zeus
  mother.. 4. Leda
  protector of.. 7. sailors
  star.. 13. Beta Geminorum
Polonius... 8. courtier (Shak)
polony... 7. sausage
poltergeist (folklore)... 5. ghost
  6. spirit
poltfoot... 8. clubfoot
poltroon... 4. idle, lazy 6. coward,
  craven, wretch 7. buffoon, dastard
  8. cowardly 9. dastardly
  10. ne'er-do-well, scaramouch
polverine... 6. potash (of Levant)
  8. pearlash
polyandrium (Gr)... 8. cemetery
polyandry... 8. polygamy 14. plural
  husbands (Tibet)
polychromatic... 10. variegated
polyglot... 6. jargon 9. languages
  (confusion of) 10. dictionary
  11. philologist 21. Complutensian
  Polyglot (Bib)
polygon... 6. isagon 7. decagon,
  hexagon, nonagon, octagon
  8. heptagon 9. dodecagon
polygyny... 8. polygamy 11. plural
  wives
polyhedron... 5. solid 6. figure
  14. trisoctahedron
  17. triakisoctahedron
polymny... 10. sacred song
Polynesia...
  native.. 5. Maori 6. Kanaka
  8. Hawaiian 10. Melanesian
  ocean.. 7. Pacific
  origin (probable).. 7. Savaiki (Isl)
  South Sea Island group.. 5. Samoa
  6. Hawaii, Tahiti 7. Savaiki 10. New
  Zealand
Polynesian (pert to)...
  butterfly.. 2. io
  chestnut.. 4. rata
  cloth.. 4. tapa
  demon.. 4. atua
  dragon.. 3. ati
  goddess of volcanoes.. 4. Pele
  god of forests.. 4. Tane
  hero.. 4. Maui
  homeland (fabled).. 7. Havaiki
  loincloth.. 5. pareu
  memorial.. 3. ahu
  oven.. 3. umu
  social tradition.. 6. tattoo
  tribe.. 3. Ati
  wages, reward.. 3. utu
polyp... 5. coral, Hydra, tumor 10. sea
  anemone 12. invertebrate
polyphone... 4. lute

polytropic... 9. versatile
pomade... 6. anoint 7. pomatum,
  unguent 8. ointment
pome... 4. pear 5. apple, fruit
  6. quince 11. pomegranate
pomelo... 8. shaddock 10. grapefruit
Pomerania (pert to)...
  animal.. 3. dog
  capital.. 7. Stettin
  formerly.. 5. duchy (Prussia)
  river.. 4. Oder
pomme de terre... 6. potato
Pomona... 4. city (Calif) 7. college,
  goddess (of fruit)
pomp... 5. pride, state 6. parade
  7. cortege, display, pageant
  8. grandeur 9. pageantry, spectacle
  10. ceremonial 11. ostentation
  12. magnificence
pompano... 7. alewife
Pompeii, Italy (pert to)...
  10. earthquake, excavation, Mt
  Vesuvius (site)
pompous... 5. budge 6. august, stilty
  7. Podsnap (Dickens), stilted
  9. bombastic, grandiose
  11. ceremonious 12. high-sounding,
  ostentatious, stuffed shirt
Ponce de Leon (pert to)...
  discoverer of.. 7. Florida 15. Fountain
  of Youth
  famed as.. 8. explorer
  landing site, America.. 11. St
  Augustine
pond... 4. pool 5. ocean (humorous)
  6. lagoon 7. lakelet
pond (pert to)...
  apple.. 9. evergreen
  crow, hen.. 4. coot
  dogwood.. 10. buttonbush
  duck.. 7. mallard
  fish.. 7. sunfish
  frog.. 8. ranarium
  glass.. 8. aquarium
ponder... 4. mull, muse, pore
  5. brood, opine, weigh 7. perpend,
  reflect 8. appraise, cogitate, consider,
  evaluate, meditate, ruminate
ponderous... 4. dull, huge 5. bulky,
  heavy 7. weighty 8. ungainly
  9. important, momentous
  11. elephantine
pongee... 4. silk 6. tussah
  8. shantung
poniard... 4. dirk, kill 5. sword
  6. dagger, pierce
ponica... 8. gardener
pont... 5. ferry, float 6. bridge
  7. caisson, pontoon 9. ferryboat
Pontiac... 4. city (Mich) 5. Chief
  (Ottawa Indian) 6. Indian
pontiff... 4. pope 6. bishop 8. pontifex
pony... 3. cab, nag 4. crib 5. glass,
  horse, pinto 6. bronco 7. Express
  (mail, 1860), piebald 8. Shetland
  11. translation
pooch... 3. dog 5. pouch
pooka... 6. goblin 7. specter
pool... 3. lin, pot 4. carr, fund, game,
  linn, mere, pond, tank, tarn 5. kitty,
  stake 6. cartel, lagoon, league,
  puddle

7. alberca, plashet 9. billiards,
reservoir, resources 10. natatorium
11. aggregation

pool ball ... 3. cue 4. spot 6. ringer

poon tree ... 5. domba, keena

poor ... 3. bad 4. mean, thin 5. needy
6. feeble, humble, meager, paltry,
shabby, sickly 7. hapless, unlucky
8. indigent, inferior 9. destitute,
illogical, imperfect, infertile
10. unskillful (unskilful)
11. impecunious, unfavorable,
unfortunate 12. impoverished,
inauspicious, insufficient
14. unsatisfactory

poor (pert to) ...
creature.. 9. pilgarlic
joe.. 5. heron
John.. 3. cod 4. hake 8. mean fare
man's remedy.. 8. valerian
Richard.. 8. Saunders (Richard)
section of city.. 4. slum 6. ghetto
7. skid row 10. shantytown
soldier.. 9. friarbird

poorly ... 3. ill 5. badly 8. abjectly,
meagerly, shabbily 10. indisposed
11. defectively 13. disparagingly

pop ... 4. bang, snap, soda 5. bulge,
burst, crack 6. bubble 7. concert
8. beverage

popadam ... 5. wafer (fried) 10. popper
cake

popdock ... 8. foxglove

pope ... 3. fin 4. ruff 6. bishop, puffin,
shrike, weevil 8. beverage
9. bullfinch 14. painted bunting

Pope (pert to) ...
cathedral.. 7. Lateran
collar.. 5. orale
court officer.. 6. datary
crown.. 5. tiara 6. triple
first.. 5. Peter
headdress.. 5. miter (mitre)
name.. 4. Pius 5. Ratti 7. Gregory
palace.. 7. Vatican
poetry.. 10. Essay on Man
scarf.. 5. fanon

popeler ... 7. sea gull 9. spoonbill

popinac ... 8. huisache

popinjay ... 6. parrot

poplar ... 5. abele, alamo, aspen,
bahan, white 10. cottonwood
12. balm of Gilead

poplar (pert to) ...
Arabic.. 5. bahan, garab
balsam.. 9. tacamahac
Fr black.. 4. liar 10. cottonwood
N American.. 7. Populus 8. Lombardy
white.. 5. abele, bolle

poppy ... 3. maw 7. Papaver (opium),
ponceau 8. foxglove

poppycock ... 3. rot 4. bosh
8. nonsense

populace ... 3. mob 4. mass
5. demos, plebs 6. people
11. inhabitants 12. common people

popular ... 3. lay, pop 5. cheap, liked,
usual 6. famous, simple, vulgar
7. crowded, demotic, secular
8. accepted, epidemic, favorite,
populous 9. prevalent, well-known,
well-liked 11. fashionable, proletarian

12. nontechnical

popular belief ... 4. lore 7. opinion
9. tradition 12. old wives' tale,
superstition

popularity ... 4. fame 5. vogue
10. reputation 15. fashionableness

popular success ... 3. hit

population study ... 10. larithmics

porcelain ... 4. frit 5. china 6. kaolin
7. ramekin (mold)

porcelain (kind) ... 5. Spode 6. Sèvres
7. celadon, Dresden, Limoges
8. Haviland

porch ... 4. door, stoa 5. stoop
6. harbor, loggia 7. galilee, gallery,
portico, veranda 8. entrance
9. colonnade

porcine animal ... 3. hog, pig, sow
5. shoat, swine 6. porker 7. peccary
8. babirusa (babiroussa) 9. razorback

porcupine (pert to) ...
anteater.. 7. echidna
Canada.. 5. urson 7. cawquaw
disease.. 10. ichthyosis
grass.. 5. stipa
species.. 6. rodent, tenrec (tendrac)
8. hedgehog, quill pig

pore ... 3. con 4. duct, gaze, vent
5. stare, stoma, study 6. ponder
7. eporose (without), opening, orifice,
ostiole 8. lenticel

porgy ... 4. fish, scup 5. bream, pargo
6. pagrus, red tai

pork (pert to) ...
barrel.. 4. fund (Polit) 6. boodle
chop.. 7. griskin
fish.. 4. sisi

porker ... 3. hog, pig 5. swine, sword
(obs)

porpoise ... 4. Inia 6. seahog
7. dolphin, pellock 8. cetacean,
Phocaena

porr ... 4. cram, kick, poke, push, stir
5. poker 6. thrust

porrect ... 6. tender 7. present

porridge ... 3. pob 4. pobs, samp
5. atole, brose, grout, gruel
6. cereal 7. oatmeal, polenta,
pottage 9. stirabout

port ... 4. gate, left, mien, wine
5. armor, haven 6. harbor, portal
7. airport, bearing, opening, posture
8. carriage, demeanor, larboard,
porthole, portside 10. deportment
11. destruction

portable ... 6. mobile 7. movable

portable altar ... 10. altar stone,
superaltar (Hist)

portal ... 4. door, gate 5. porch
7. gateway 8. entrance 9. vestibule
12. porte-cochere

portcullis ... 3. bar 4. shut 5. herse
7. barrier, grating, lattice (Her)
13. fortification

Porte ... 12. Ottoman court (anc),
Sublime Porte

porte-bonheur ... 5. charm 6. amulet

porte-cochere ... 5. porch (carriage)
7. gateway

portefeuille ... 9. portfolio

portend ... 4. bode 5. augur
7. betoken, predict, presage

8. forebode, foreshow, foretell,
prophecy 9. foretoken
portent... 4. omen, sign 6. marvel,
ostent 7. prodigy 11. forewarning
portentous... 4. dire 5. fatal, grave
6. solemn 7. fateful, ominous
8. sinister 9. monstrous, wonderful
10. impressive 13. extraordinary
porter... 3. ale 4. beer 5. hamal
(hammal), stout (drink) 6. bearer
7. carrier, janitor 9. attendant
10. doorkeeper
Porter's pseudonym... 6. O Henry
Portia (pert to)...
character (Merchant of Venice)..
7. heiress
husband.. 8. Bassanio
husband's friend.. 7. Antonio
maid.. 7. Nerissa
portico... 4. stoa 6. atrium, xystus
(xyst) 7. pteroma, veranda
9. colonnade, peristyle, vestibule
portion... 3. bit, cut, dab, lot 4. dole,
dose, dunt, fate, half, mete, part,
some 5. piece, share, whack
6. moiety, parcel 7. section,
segment 8. quantity 9. allotment,
apportion, partition
portion (pert to)...
curve.. 3. arc 7. segment
detached.. 6. coupon
inheritance.. 7. legitim 9. dead's part
marriage.. 5. dowry
sectional.. 5. curve
widow's.. 5. dower
Portland (pert to)...
arrowroot, sago.. 4. arum
beds (Eng).. 11. Upper Oolite
13. Upper Jurassic
city of.. 5. Maine 6. Oregon
stone.. 6. cement 8. concrete
vase.. 9. Barberini (Rom palace)
10. cameo glass
portmanteau... 3. bag 4. word
(blended) 5. cloak 6. mantle, valise
portoise... 7. gunwale 8. portlast
Porto Rico... see Puerto Rico
portrait... 4. copy 5. image 7. picture
8. likeness, painting 10. similitude
11. description, portraiture
12. lifelikeness 14. representation
portrait on dollars...
fifty.. 5. Grant
five.. 7. Lincoln
five hundred.. 8. McKinley
five thousand.. 7. Madison
one.. 10. Washington
one hundred.. 8. Franklin
one hundred thousand.. 6. Wilson
one thousand.. 9. Cleveland
ten.. 8. Hamilton
ten thousand.. 5. Chase
twenty.. 7. Jackson
two.. 9. Jefferson
portray... 3. act 4. draw, form, limn
5. enact, frame, image, paint
6. depict 7. fashion, picture
8. describe 9. delineate, represent
portrayal... 3. act 5. drama
7. process 8. portrait 9. depiction
11. delineation, description
portreeve... 5. mayor 7. bailiff

Port Royal... 15. Cistercian abbey
(Versailles)
Portugal... see also Portuguese
bridge.. 7. Salazar
capital.. 6. Lisbon
city.. 5. Braga 6. Aveiro, Guarda,
Oporto 7. Granada
island.. 6. Azores 7. Madeira
8. Principe
mountain.. 15. Serra da Estrella
peninsula.. 7. Iberian
port.. 6. Aveiro
province.. 3. Goa 5. Macao, Timor
9. Cape Verde 10. Mozambique
resort.. 7. Estoril
river.. 5. Tagus (Tajo)
Portuguese (pert to)...
author.. 9. de Lobeira
bird, fish.. 8. man-of-war
ceremonial (Inquisition).. 8. auto de fe
coin (gold).. 6. escudo 7. milreis (old)
lady.. 4. dona
legislature.. 6. Cortes 12. Cortes
Geraes
money of account.. 4. reis
navigator.. 6. da Gama 8. Magellan
wine.. 5. porto
Portunus (Rom Relig)... 10. god of
gates
posada... 3. inn 5. hotel
Posaune... 8. trombone 9. organ stop
posca... 5. drink (Hist)
pose... 3. put, sit 5. model 6. baffle,
puzzle, stance 7. nonplus, posture,
pretend, propose 8. attitude,
position, pretense, propound
9. postulate 11. affectation,
impersonate
Poseidon (pert to)...
attributes.. 5. horse 7. dolphin,
trident
cult site.. 7. Corinth
father.. 6. Cronus
god of.. 3. sea 6. waters
mother.. 4. Rhea
wife.. 10. Amphitrite
poser... 5. facer 6. puzzle 7. problem,
sticker 14. attitudinarian
posh... 5. smart 6. spruce 7. elegant
9. luxurious
position... 3. job, lie 4. pose, rank,
seat, site 5. coign (coigne), place,
situs, stand, state 6. manner, stance,
ubiety 7. opinion, posture, premise
8. attitude, location, prestige,
proposal 9. viewpoint 11. affirmation,
supposition
position (pert to)...
anchorlike.. 5. apeak
fencing.. 7. septime
finder (gun).. 13. triangulation
golf.. 6. stance
inescapable.. 7. impasse
of affairs.. 6. status
relative.. 8. standing
secure.. 7. footing
with no responsibility.. 8. sinecure
positive... 4. plus, sure 5. exact
6. actual, thetic 7. certain
8. dogmatic, emphatic 9. assertive,
convinced, downright 11. dictatorial
positive (pert to)...

charge (Elec).. 8. positron
evidence.. 7. constat
pole.. 5. anode
saying.. 6. dictum
school, criminology.. 10. Lombrosian
(by Lombroso)
positivism... 7. Comtism 9. certainty,
dogmatism 10. confidence
11. materialism
positure... 7. posture 11. arrangement,
disposition 13. configuration
posnet... 3. pot (3–footed)
8. saucepan
poss... 4. beat, dash, push 5. drive,
knock, pound, stamp 6. thrust
posse... 5. crowd 6. throng
7. company 9. armed band
10. detachment (police)
possess... 3. own 4. have, know, take
5. haunt 6. inform, occupy
7. bewitch, inhabit 8. convince,
demonize, persuade
possessed... 5. hadst, owned
6. insane 7. haunted 8. demoniac,
obsessed 9. bewitched
possessing (pert to)...
feeling.. 6. souled
flavor.. 5. sapid, tasty
land.. 5. acred
pincer claws.. 8. chelated
power.. 11. plenipotent
sensation.. 8. sentient
special ability.. 6. gifted 8. talented
possession... 4. hold 5. asset
6. taking, wealth 7. control, country,
mastery 8. dominion, property
9. obsession, ownership
10. equanimity 11. bewitchment
possession (pert to)...
again.. 6. revest
law.. 6. seizin (seisin)
not in (possession).. 6. devoid
suffix.. 3. ose
possessions... 6. assets, estate, wealth
7. effects 8. property
posset... 4. turn 6. curdle, pamper
8. beverage, infusion 9. coagulate
possibility... 4. bare 7. latency
9. liability, potential 10. good
chance, likelihood 11. contingency
13. improbability 16. prospective
value
possible... 6. latent, liable, likely
8. feasible 9. plausible, potential
11. practicable
possibly... 5. maybe 7. perhaps
9. perchance 11. conceivably
post... 3. bet, dak (dawk), xat 4. bitt,
fort, list, mail, trot 5. enter, newel,
opium, place, stake, totem 6. alette,
assign, hasten, marker, office,
pillar, pledge 7. bollard, placard,
station, upright 8. dispatch, position
9. messenger, sternpost 12. enter
account
post (pert to)...
adverb.. 5. after, later 9. afterward
boat.. 4. mail 5. stage 6. packet
boy.. 7. courier 9. postilion (postillion)
dance (army sl).. 8. struggle
goal (anc).. 4. meta
Indian memorial.. 3. xat 5. totem

meridian.. 9. afternoon
mortem.. 7. autopsy 8. necropsy
10. after death
office.. 6. correo
prefix.. 5. after 6. behind
10. subsequent
stair.. 5. newel
postage stamp paper (pert to)...
design.. 8. spandrel
paper.. 6. pelure
pattern.. 6. burele 8. burelage
poster... 4. bill, card 7. placard,
sticker 8. bulletin 9. messenger
10. billposter
posthumous... 5. after 10. after death,
post–mortem
postiche... 9. false hair 10. artificial
11. counterfeit
postilion... 5. guide 7. postboy
9. postrider
postimpressionist... 6. cubist, Derain
7. Cezanne, Matisse
postpone... 4. wait 5. defer, delay,
remit, table 6. put off, shelve
7. adjourn, reserve, suspend 8. hold
over, prorogue 10. pigeonhole
11. subordinate 13. procrastinate
postponement... 7. remanet, respite
8. deferral, reprieve 9. deferment
11. prorogation
postprandial... 11. after dinner
postulate... 6. assume 7. prelude,
premise 9. condition, predicate,
stipulate 10. hypothesis
11. stipulation, supposition
posture... 4. pose 6. stance
8. attitude, position, pretense
9. viewpoint 11. frame of mind
pot... 3. jug, pan 4. olla 5. belly,
crock, cruse 6. aludel, kettle, liquor,
teapot 7. amphora (anc), caldron
9. flowerpot 10. jardiniere
potash... 6. potass, saline 7. potassa
8. pearlash 18. potassium carbonate
potassium (pert to)...
bitartrate.. 13. cream of tartar
bromide.. 8. sedative
carbonate.. 6. potash
compound.. 4. alum
dichromatic.. 6. chrome
iodide.. 8. medicine
nitrate.. 5. niter 9. saltpeter
permanganate.. 8. oxidizer
12. disinfectant
sulphate.. 4. alum
potate... 9. liquefied
potation... 5. draft, drink 6. liquor
8. beverage, tippling 12. drinking
bout
potato... 3. oca, yam 4. papa, spud
5. tuber
potato (pert to)...
beetle.. 8. hardback
bogle.. 9. scarecrow
French.. 12. pomme de terre
French style.. 9. lyonnaise
genus.. 10. Solanaceae
Indian.. 4. yamp
moss.. 7. pondgrass
S Am.. 7. Uruguay
sweet.. 6. patata
potator... 5. poter 7. tippler

potboiler... 4. book 6. writer
8. painting (for quick money)
9. potwaller
potdar... 7. assayer, cashier, weigher
potence, potency... 3. vis 4. élan
5. cross, power 6. energy, gibbet
7. gallows 8. virility 9. authority,
influence
potent... 4. able 6. cogent, mighty,
strong, virile 7. dynamic, warrant
(Mil) 8. forcible, heraldry, powerful,
puissant, virulent 9. effective, efficient
11. efficacious, influential
13. authoritative
potentate... 4. amir (ameer), emir
(emeer) 5. mogul, ruler 6. dynast,
prince 7. emperor, monarch
8. syzerain 9. sovereign
potential... 4. mood (Gram) 5. ergal
6. latent, mighty 8. possible
11. influential, in the making,
possibility, undeveloped
potentiality... 5. power 7. latency
11. possibility
poter... 5. toper 7. drinker
potgun... 5. rumor 6. cannon, mortar,
pistol 8. braggart
pothead... 7. dullard 8. terminal (Elec)
9. blackfish
pother... 3. ado, row 4. fuss, stir
5. worry 6. bother, bustle, harass
7. fluster, perplex, trouble
9. commotion 10. excitement,
perplexity 11. disturbance
12. perturbation
potherb... 4. mint 6. greens
7. spinach
pothook... 3. rod 4. hook (S–shaped)
5. crook 6. scrawl, stroke (S–like)
9. pot lifter 10. iron collar (penalty)
pothouse... 3. bar, low 6. saloon,
tavern, vulgar 7. barroom
8. alehouse, grogshop, mughouse
11. public house
potiche... 4. vase 7. ceramic
potion... 4. dose, dram, drug 5. draft,
drink 7. draught, philter 8. nepenthe
potlatch... 4. gift 5. feast 8. Festival
potomania... 10. dipsomania
15. delirium tremens
potong... 5. crown 6. wreath 9. head
cloth
potoroo... 11. rat kangaroo
potpourri... 4. olio, stew 6. medley
7. mixture, perfume 9. anthology
11. olla–podrida, salamagundi
potrero... 4. farm 7. pasture
10. cattle farm
pottage... 4. soup 6. brewis
8. porridge
pottah... 5. lease 6. tenure 9. title
deed
potter... 3. pry 4. mess, poke, push
6. dawdle, doodle, meddle, putter,
tamper, trifle 7. saunter 8. ceramist
potter's clay, earth... 4. slip 5. argil
6. galena, kaolin 8. alquifou
10. terra cotta
potter's wheel... 4. disk 5. lathe,
throw 6. jigger, pallet (palet)
pottery... 5. Delft 6. Samian
7. celadon (Chin), keramos (Gr)

8. Arretine (It), ceramics, Majolica (It)
9. delftware (Holland), keramikos (Gr)
11. earthenware 14. terra sigillata
(anc)
pottery (pert to)...
black.. 6. basalt
broken.. 5. shard (sherd)
decorate.. 6. stamps 9. sigillate
decoration.. 11. sigillation
firing box.. 6. sagger
glasslike.. 8. vitreous
glaze.. 6. enamel
mineral.. 8. feldspar
paste.. 9. barbotine
red.. 7. aretine
pottle... 3. pot 6. basket, vessel
7. tankard
potty... 3. pot 5. crazy 7. foolish,
haughty 8. trifling 12. supercilious
13. insignificant
pot–valiant... 10. courageous (when
drunk)
pouch... 3. bag, pod, sac 4. cyst,
poke, sack 5. bulge, bursa, purse
6. gipser (Hist), pocket 7. bladder,
mailbag, silicle, sporran (sporan)
10. pocketbook
pouch bone... 9. marsupial
pouched (pert to)...
dog.. 9. thylacine 13. Tasmanian wolf
frog.. 9. marsupial
gopher.. 6. pocket
mouse.. 9. marsupial
rat.. 8. kangaroo
rodent (cheek–pouched)..
11. spermophile
stork.. 8. adjutant
poultry... 4. fowl, hens 5. cocks,
ducks, geese 6. capons 7. Bantams,
peahens, pigeons, turkeys
8. chickens, pooooolo, roosters,
volaille 9. cockerels, pheasants
10. guinea fowl
poultry (breeds)... 6. Ancona, Bantam,
Brahma 7. Cornish, Dorking,
Hamburg, Leghorn, Minorca
9. Wyandotte 12. Plymouth Rock
14. Rhode Island Red
poultry (pert to)...
disease.. 3. pip 4. roup, tick
dish.. 9. galantine
farm.. 7. hennery
pounamu... 4. jade 6. weapon
8. nephrite 10. greenstone
pound... 3. hit, ram 4. beat, ding,
drum, maul, pond, tamp 5. money,
pen up, thump 6. bruise, hammer,
kennel, prison 7. impound
9. enclosure, pulverize
pounding instrument... 6. hammer,
pestle
pounds (100)... 6. cental
13. hundredweight
pour... 4. flow, gush, rain, teem, vent,
well 5. flood 6. abound, effuse,
stream 7. niagara, radiate, torrent
8. downpour 9. discharge
11. extravasate
pour (pert to)...
molten glass.. 7. dagrade
molten steel.. 4. teem
off.. 5. drain 6. decant

oil upon.. **6.** anoint, pacify
out.. **11.** extravasate
sacrificial liquid.. **6.** libate
pouring hole (mold)... **5.** sprue
pout... **3.** bib, mop **4.** fish, moue, sulk
  5. pique **7.** catfish, eelpout, grimace
  9. sulkiness
poverty... **4.** lack, need, want **5.** illth
  (opp of wealth) **6.** dearth, penury
  8. leanness, poorness, scarcity
  9. indigence, pearlweed
  11. destitution
powder... **4.** dust, talc **5.** boral
  6. pollen, yttria **7.** crumble
  8. cosmetic, sprinkle **9.** explosive,
  pulverize
powder (pert to)...
antiseptic.. **6.** formin **7.** aristol
bag.. **6.** sachet
festival (Ind).. **4.** abir (perfumed)
goa.. **7.** araroba
heater, melter.. **6.** sinter
insecticide.. **9.** hellebore
medical.. **8.** tannigen
perfumed.. **6.** empasm
polishing.. **5.** emery **7.** tripoli
smokeless.. **6.** poudre **8.** amberite
stamping.. **6.** pounce
powdered (Her)... **4.** semé
power... **3.** arm, art, can, jet, vis
  4. dint, gift, iron, sway, will
  5. force, magic, might, steam, vigor
  6. degree, energy **7.** control, faculty,
  magnate, potency **8.** capacity,
  efficacy, strength **9.** authority,
  eloquence, influence, magnetism,
  puissance **10.** efficiency, government
  11. mathematics (term)
power (pert to)...
creative.. **6.** Shakti
device.. **9.** telemotor
hammer.. **4.** trip
inherent.. **6.** energy
of attorney.. **5.** agent **10.** procurator
of feeling.. **7.** sensate
of mind.. **4.** wits
of resistance.. **7.** stamina
persuasive.. **8.** rhetoric **9.** political
sovereign.. **6.** throne
spiritual.. **8.** divinity
superior.. **10.** prepotency
under one's.. **10.** subjugated
unit.. **3.** erg **4.** dyne **8.** kilowatt
powerful... **4.** loud **5.** great **6.** cogent,
  mighty, potent, strong **7.** drastic,
  intense, leonine, skookum
  8. eloquent, forcible, puissant
  9. effective, effectual, efficient
  10. armipotent, convincing
  11. efficacious, influential
  13. authoritative
powerful force... **6.** libido
powerful man, businessman...
  5. titan **6.** tycoon **7.** magnate
powerless... **4.** weak **8.** impotent
pownie... **7.** peacock
powwow... **6.** frolic, priest **7.** meeting
  8. assembly, ceremony, congress,
  conjurer **9.** gathering **10.** conference,
  convention
poyou... **9.** armadillo
prabble... **7.** chatter, quarrel

  8. squabble
practic... **6.** artful, shrews **7.** cunning,
  skilled **9.** difficult, practical, practiced
  11. experienced
practicable, practical... **5.** utile
  6. usable, useful **7.** virtual, working
  8. feasible, possible, workable
  9. available, expedient, operative,
  pragmatic, realistic **11.** pragmatical,
  utilitarian
practical (pert to)...
Christianity.. **10.** New Thought
example.. **6.** praxis
joke.. **4.** hoax **5.** trick **6.** humbug
judgment.. **7.** ethical (Kant)
practically... **9.** virtually **11.** essentially
  13. approximately
practice, practise... **2.** do **3.** ply, ure,
  use **4.** plot, rite **5.** drill, habit, train,
  usage **6.** action, addict, custom,
  scheme, tryout **7.** perform
  8. ceremony, exercise, intrigue,
  rehearse, training, vocation
  9. procedure **10.** experience,
  experiment, observance
practice (pert to)...
corrupt.. **5.** abuse
established.. **5.** canon **6.** custom
fraud.. **5.** cheat, shark **8.** trickery
specific.. **6.** praxis
voice.. **8.** intonate
witchcraft.. **3.** hex
practicer of evasions...
  13. tergiversator
practicer of palmistry...
  11. chiromancer
prad... **5.** horse
pragmatic... **7.** meddler, skilled
  8. busybody, dogmatic, meddling
  9. conceited, officious, practical
  10. systematic **11.** opinionated
pragmatical... **8.** dogmatic **9.** officious,
  practical **10.** meddlesome
  11. commonplace
Prague, Praha...
capital of.. **14.** Czechoslovakia
famed bldg.. **10.** University (1st in
  Cent Eur, 1348)
famed teachers (anc).. **4.** Huss
  6. Jerome
founder.. **14.** Duchess Libussa (722)
prairie... **3.** bay **5.** llano, plain
  6. camass (camas, cammas),
  meadow, steppe **7.** quamash
  (camass) **9.** grassland **10.** prairillon
prairie (pert to)...
anemone, crocus.. **12.** pasque flower
antelope.. **9.** pronghorn
apple.. **9.** breadroot
artichoke.. **9.** sunflower
berry.. **9.** trompillo
chicken.. **6.** grouse
dog.. **6.** marmot
mud.. **5.** gumbo
pigeon.. **6.** plover **9.** sandpiper
rose.. **14.** Baltimore belle
schooner.. **12.** covered wagon
squirrel.. **11.** spermophile
tree (clump).. **5.** motte
weed.. **10.** cinquefoil
wolf.. **6.** coyote
Prairie State... **8.** Illinois

praise... 4. laud 5. bless, extol, honor,
kudos 6. eulogy 7. acclaim, applaud,
commend, glorify, magnify, plaudit
8. applause, encomium, eulogize,
macarize 9. adulation, celebrate,
panegyric 11. approbation
12. commendation
praise (pert to)...
continual.. 5. chant
high.. 5. extol 8. encomium
hymn of.. 8. doxology
insincere.. 4. bull 7. flatter 8. flattery
of another's blessing.. 8. macarism
9. Beatitude
to God.. 7. Laus Deo
Ye The Lord.. 8. Alleluia (Alleluiah)
10. Hallelujah (Halleluiah)
praiseworthy... 8. laudable
11. commendable, meritorious
prana (Hind)... 6. spirit 9. life force
10. life breath
prance... 4. gait 5. caper, dance
6. cavort, spring 7. swagger
prank... 3. jig 4. fold, joke, prat
5. antic, caper, pleat, shine, trick
6. frolic, prance 7. caprice, dress up
8. escapade 11. monkeyshine
prankish... 9. facetious 10. frolicsome
11. mischievous
prate... 3. gab 4. chat, talk 6. gossip
7. chatter, twaddle 8. nonsense
prattle... 3. gab 4. chat, talk 5. clack,
prate 6. babble 7. blather
12. impudent talk, trifling talk
prawn... 6. shrimp 10. crustacean,
shrimp pink
pray... 3. ask, beg, sue 7. entreat,
implore, request, worship 8. devotion
10. supplicate
praya... 4. bund, road 5. beach
6. strand
prayer... 3. ave 4. bead, bene, plea,
suit 5. credo, grace, matin 6. litany,
orison, vesper 7. request, worship
8. petition 12. intercession,
supplication
prayer (pert to)...
book.. 4. ordo 6. missal 7. portass
(portas) 8. breviary
call (Moham).. 4. azan (adan)
call tower.. 7. minaret
cloak.. 6. zizith (fringed) 7. tallith
evening.. 7. complin (compline)
9. night song
figure.. 5. orant
Incarnation.. 7. Angelus 11. Angelus
Bell
liturgical.. 6. litany 7. complin
Lord's (prayer).. 11. Paternoster
morning.. 5. matin
nine days' devotional.. 6. novena
response.. 8. antiphon
short.. 5. grace
stick.. 4. paho
praying... 8. entreaty 9. precation
12. supplication
praying cricket... 6. mantis
praying figure... 5. orant
preach... 6. exhort 7. expound, lecture
8. advocate, homilize 9. discourse,
sermonize
preacher... 6. parson, rector

7. evangel, teacher 8. homilist,
lecturer, minister 9. clergyman,
pulpiteer
preaching... 6. sermon 7. kerygma
(kerugma) 10. preachment
11. exhortation
preaching friar... 9. Dominican
Preaching of Peter... 9. Apocrypha
preamble... 5. proem 7. preface,
prelude 11. preliminary
12. introduction
prebellum... 7. antewar 12. before the
war
prebend... 7. stipend 8. benefice
9. allowance
precarious... 7. assumed, dubious
8. insecure, unstable 9. hazardous,
uncertain, unsettled 10. unreliable
preceded... 3. led 8. prefaced, was
prior 9. anteceded, antedated
10. introduced, went before 13. had
precedence, occurred first
precedence... 3. pas 4. lead, rank
8. priority 12. anteposition
precedent... 4. sign 5. model, usage
7. example, leading 8. anterior,
decision, standard 10. antecedent,
forerunner 11. going before
preceding others... 5. first 7. leading,
ternary (by threes) 10. antecedent
precept... 4. rule, writ 5. adage,
axiom, maxim, order, sutra (sutta),
torah (tora) 6. belief 7. command
8. doctrine 9. direction
11. commandment, instruction
preceptor... 4. guru 5. guide, tutor
6. master, mentor, mullah, pundit
7. teacher 8. educator 10. instructor
precinct... 5. ambit, space 6. region
8. boundary, district, environs
precious... 4. dear, rare 5. great
6. costly, valued 7. beloved, elegant,
perfect 8. complete, esteemed,
overnice, valuable 9. downright
10. beloved one, fastidious, particular
precious (pert to)...
Blood (RCCh).. 5. Feast (July 1)
garnet.. 6. pyrope
stone.. 3. gem 4. opal, ruby 5. pearl,
topaz 6. garnet, ligure 7. diamond,
emerald, jacinth (Bib) 8. hyacinth,
sapphire
stone, sometimes.. 7. cat's—eye
11. alexandrite
precipice... 4. crag, linn, pali 5. bluff,
cliff 9. declivity
precipitancy... 5. haste 8. rashness
precipitation... 3. gel 4. fall, hail,
mist, rain, snow 5. haste, sleet
8. downpour 9. hastening
11. prematurity 12. acceleration,
condensation, recklessness
precipitous... 4. rash 5. hasty, steep
6. abrupt, sudden 7. rushing
(headlong) 9. very rapid
11. precipitate
précis... 6. sketch 7. epitome,
pandect, summary 8. abstract,
synopsis 9. summarize
precise... 4. prim 5. exact 7. correct,
literal, special 8. accurate, definite,
detailed, overnice 10. meticulous,

overminute, particular, scrupulous
11. ceremonious, punctilious
preciseness... 9. exactness
10. strictness 12. definiteness
14. fastidiousness
precision... 6. nicety 8. accuracy
9. exactness, formality
11. preciseness 12. definiteness
preclude... 3. bar 4. omit, stop
5. avert, debar, estop 6. hinder,
impede 7. head off, prevent, shut
out 8. prohibit
precocious... 7. forward 8. advanced
9. premature
preconceive... 6. ideate, precox
7. presume 8. foreknow, prejudge
9. predecide 10. presuppose
predatory... 7. looting 9. marauding,
pillaging, piratical 10. plundering,
predaceous (predacious)
11. destructive
predatory bird... 3. owl 4. hawk, kite
6. falcon
predatory raid... 5. foray
predestine... 4. doom, fate 6. decree,
ordain 7. appoint 9. determine,
foretoken 10. foreordain
predetermine... 4. bias 7. destine
8. prejudge 9. prejudice, preordain
10. prepossess 11. premeditate
predicament... 3. fix 4. pass 5. state
6. plight, scrape 7. dilemma,
impasse 8. quandary 9. condition,
situation
predicator... 4. seer 5. friar
7. prophet 8. preacher 9. predicter
predict... 4. bode, dope, omen
7. foresee, portend, presage
8. forecast, foretell, prophecy
13. prognosticate
prediction... 6. augury 8. prophecy
9. foresight 10. foreboding
11. foretelling 15. prognostication
predilection... 4. bias 6. desire
8. tendency 9. prejudice
10. favoritism, partiality, preference,
propensity 11. disposition
13. preconception 14. predisposition
predominant... 5. chief 6. ruling
8. reigning, superior 9. hegemonic
11. controlling, influential,
outstanding
predominate... 5. excel 7. prevail
8. dominate 10. be superior
12. preponderate
pre—eminent... 3. top 4. only, star
5. chief 7. palmary, ranking
8. superior 9. excellent, principal
11. outstanding
pre—emption... 8. monopoly, purchase
10. prior right 13. appropriation
preen... 3. pin, sew 4. perk 5. clasp,
dress, groom, plume, primp
6. bodkin, brooch, stitch 9. make
sleek
preface... 5. front, proem 6. herald,
prayer 7. prelude, problem
8. exordium, foreword, preamble,
prologue 10. paraphrase
12. introduction
prefect, praefect... 4. dean (Jesuit)
6. chih fu 7. monitor, officer

8. director, minister, official
9. president 10. magistrate
prefecture... 7. eparchy
prefer... 5. elect, offer 6. choose,
select 7. outrank, present, proffer,
promote 9. be partial 12. give
priority
preference... 6. choice 8. favorite,
priority 9. advantage 10. favoritism
11. alternative, prior choice
12. predilection
prefiguration... 4. omen 9. foretoken,
prototype 12. typification
13. preindication
prefigure... 7. imagine, suggest
8. foretell 10. foreshadow
prefix for...
about.. 3. amb 4. peri
above.. 3. epi, sur 5. hyper, super,
supra
across.. 3. dia 4. tran 5. trans
again.. 2. re
against.. 4. anti
ahead.. 3. pre
all.. 4. omni
alongside.. 3. par 4. para
an.. 2. al
apart.. 2. se 3. dia, dis
appearing to.. 5. quasi
around.. 4. peri
away.. 3. aph, apo
back.. 2. re 3. ana
backward.. 5. retro
bad.. 3. dys, mal
badly.. 3. mis
beauty.. 5. calli (kalli)
before.. 2. ob 3. pre, pro 4. ante,
prae
beside.. 3. par 4. para
between.. 3. dia 4. meta 5. inter
black.. 4. atra
blood.. 4. haem, hemo
bone.. 4. oste 5. osteo
both.. 4. ambi
Chinese.. 4. sino 5. chino
clear.. 4. delo
dawn.. 2. eo
difficult.. 3. dys
distant.. 3. tel 4. tele
double.. 2. di
down.. 2. de 4. cata
earnest.. 5. serio
earth.. 3. geo
eight.. 3. oct 4. octa, octo
equal.. 3. iso
equally.. 4. equi
evil.. 3. mal
far.. 3. tel 4. tele
faulty.. 3. mis
fictitious.. 6. pseudo
fire.. 3. pyr
for.. 3. pro
former.. 2. ex
four.. 5. tetra
from.. 2. ab, de, ec
from away.. 3. apo
gas.. 4. aero
good.. 2. eu
half.. 4. demi, hemi, semi
hard.. 3. dys 6. stereo
ill.. 3. mal, mis
in, into.. 2. en

lizard .. **5.** saura, sauro
many .. **4.** mult, poly **5.** multi
modern .. **3.** neo
mountain .. **3.** oro
nail .. **4.** helo
negative .. **2.** il, ir, un **3.** mon
new .. **3.** neo
not .. **2.** il, im, ir, un **3.** non
numerical .. **3.** uni
one .. **3.** uni **4.** mono
out of, outer .. **2.** ec, ex **3.** ect, exo
　4. ecto
over .. **3.** epi, sur **5.** super, supra
possession .. **3.** ose
pray .. **3.** ora
priority .. **3.** pre
recent .. **3.** neo
release .. **2.** un
reversed .. **2.** di
same, equal .. **3.** iso **4.** equi, homo
separation .. **2.** di **3.** dis
shoulder .. **6.** humero
single .. **4.** mono
son of .. **3.** Mac
ten .. **3.** dec **4.** deca
this side of .. **3.** cis
three, thrice .. **3.** ter, tri **4.** tris
through .. **3.** dia, per
to .. **2.** ap
together .. **3.** com, con, cor, syn
toward .. **2.** ob, oc
turning .. **4.** roto
twice .. **2.** bi, di
twofold .. **2.** bi, di **3.** dua
under .. **3.** sub
upon .. **2.** ep **3.** epi
upward .. **3.** ana, ano
very much .. **3.** eri
well .. **2.** eu
with .. **3.** col, com, pro, syl, syn
within .. **3.** eso **4.** endo **5.** intra
without .. **2.** se **3.** ect **4.** ecto
wood .. **4.** xylo
wrong .. **3.** mis
pregnancy ... **6.** cyesis **10.** cyesiology
prehistoric (pert to) ...
animal .. **7.** reptile **8.** dinosaur,
　mastodon **9.** phytosaur
continent .. **8.** Atlantis (Atalantis)
man .. **4.** cave, Dawn **11.** lake dweller
ref to .. **9.** primitive
tool .. **6.** eolith
prejudiced ... **6.** biased **7.** partial
　8. partisan **11.** opinionated
　12. prepossessed
prejudicial ... **9.** injurious
　11. detrimental **15.** disadvantageous
prelate ... **4.** head, pope **5.** abbot,
　chief **6.** bishop, priest **7.** primate,
　red–blue **8.** minister, superior
　9. Monsignor (Monsignore)
prelector, praelector ... **6.** reader
　7. teacher **8.** lecturer **9.** professor
preliminary ... **5.** prior **7.** preface,
　prelude **8.** entrance, previous,
　proemial **9.** precedent, prefatory,
　threshold **10.** antecedent
　11. preparatory **12.** introduction,
　introductory
preliminary memo ... **8.** protocol
preliminary plan ... **4.** idea
prelude ... **5.** proem **6.** verset

7. preface **8.** overture, ritornel
(ritornelle)
premature ... **6.** infant **8.** too early,
　untimely **10.** precocious
premier ... **3.** bet (gambling) **5.** chief
　7. leading **8.** earliest **9.** principal
　13. prime minister
premiere ... **4.** show **10.** first night
　12. presentation **16.** first
　performance
premium ... **4.** agio **5.** bonus, prize,
　stake **6.** reward **8.** gratuity, interest
　10. recompense
premonition ... **5.** hunch **6.** notice
　7. warning **8.** forecast
　10. foreboding **11.** forewarning,
　information **12.** presentiment
preoccupied ... **4.** lost **6.** absent, filled
　8. absorbed, observed **9.** engrossed
　10. abstracted, pre–engaged **13.** lost
　in thought
preparation ... **8.** training **9.** equipment,
　study hour **10.** groundwork
　11. making ready **12.** introduction
preparation (pert to) ...
of a dress .. **7.** fitting
place .. **10.** laboratory, paratorium
sugar, for candy .. **7.** fondant
without .. **5.** ad lib **9.** impromptu
prepare ... **3.** fit, fix, get **4.** cook, gird,
　make, pave, yark **5.** adapt, equip,
　ready, train **6.** adjust **7.** arrange
prepare (pert to) ...
by boiling .. **6.** decoct
for golf game .. **3.** tee
for melting glass .. **4.** frit
for publication .. **4.** edit
for seasoning .. **8.** marinate
skins .. **3.** taw
prepared ... **5.** armed, ready
　7. adapted, groomed, skilled, trained
　8. equipped, provided
prepared instruction ...
　13. propaedeutics
preponderance ... **6.** weight
　8. dominion, majority **9.** influence
　11. outweighing, superiority
prepose ... **6.** prefix **7.** preface
　11. place before
preposition ... **2.** at, by, ex, in, of, on,
　to, up **3.** off, out, tae **4.** into, onto,
　over, unto, upon, with
prepossession ... **4.** bent, bias
　9. obsession, prejudice
　10. preference **11.** inclination
　12. predilection **13.** appropriation,
　preconception **14.** predisposition
presage ... **4.** bode, omen, osse, sign
　5. token **6.** augury, betide, divine
　7. portend, predict **8.** forebode,
　foretell **10.** prediction, prognostic
　11. preindicate **13.** foreknowledge
presager ... **7.** prophet **9.** foreboder
presbytery ... **6.** church, clergy
　7. council **8.** ministry **9.** parsonage
　10. presbyters
prescribe ... **3.** set **5.** allot, guide,
　limit, order **6.** advise, bestow, direct,
　ordain **7.** control, dictate
　9. designate
presence ... **4.** mien, port **7.** bearing,
　posture, specter **8.** phantasm

9. existence, proximity
10. apparition, appearance, attendance 11. personality
present... 3. now 4. boon, gift, give
5. grant, nonce, offer 6. bestow, bounty, donate 7. largess (largesse)
8. donation, gratuity 9. introduce
10. contribute 11. benefaction
present (pert to)...
for acceptance.. 6. tender
pupil to teacher.. 8. minerval
time.. 3. now 5. nonce, today
7. current 8. juncture
to customers.. 7. freebie, premium
8. giveaway 9. lagniappe (lagnappe)
to foreign ambassador.. 6. xenium
presentation... 4. gift, plan 5. debut, offer 7. present 8. bestowal, donation, offering 10. appearance, exhibition 12. introduction
presently... 4. anon, soon 6. at once
7. shortly 8. nowadays 9. forthwith
10. before long 11. immediately
preservation... 6. saving 9. retention, safeguard 10. protection
11. maintenance, safekeeping
12. conservation, perpetuation
preservative... 4. salt 5. spice
7. alcohol, vinegar 10. protective
14. sodium benzoate
preserve... 3. can, jam, tin 4. corn, cure, keep, salt, save 5. guard, jelly, spare, store 6. defend, pickle, retain, secure, shield, uphold 7. compote, protect, sustain 8. conserve, maintain
9. freeze–dry, safeguard
preserve (pert to)...
by drying.. 9. desiccate
fruit.. 7. compote 9. marmalade
grape.. 5. uvate (conserve)
in brine.. 4. corn, cure, salt
in oil.. 8. marinate
president... 4. head 5. ruler
8. governor 14. chief executive
President (US)... 4. Ford, Polk, Taft
5. Adams (John), Adams (John Q), Grant, Hayes, Nixon, Tyler 6. Arthur (Chester), Carter, Hoover, Monroe, Pierce, Reagan, Taylor, Truman, Wilson 7. Harding, Jackson, Johnson (Andrew), Johnson (L B), Kennedy, Lincoln, Madison 8. Buchanan, Coolidge, Fillmore, Garfield, Harrison (Benj), Harrison (Wm Henry), McKinley, Van Buren 9. Cleveland, Jefferson, Roosevelt (Theo), Roosevelt (F D)
10. Eisenhower, Washington
President (pert to)...
place.. 10. Oval Office, White House
power.. 4. veto
press... 3. dun 4. cram, iron, urge
5. crowd, force, wedge 6. compel, hasten, smooth, throng, thrust
7. impress, squeeze 8. compress, condense, insist on 9. extractor, importune 10. compulsion, journalism, newspapers 12. conscription
press (pert to)...
ancient.. 6. Aldine
bookbinder.. 7. smasher
corrector.. 11. proofreader

critic.. 6. censor 8. reviewer
ranks.. 5. serry
pressed (pert to)...
amber.. 8. amberoid
cheese.. 7. cheddar
grapes, residue.. 4. marc (mark)
into a mass.. 7. kneaded
together.. 5. dense 6. mashed
7. compact, crowded, serried
pressing... 6. urgent, urging
7. exigent 9. insistent
10. compelling, extraction, motivating
11. importunity
pressure... 4. urge 5. force
6. compel, stress, weight 7. squeeze, urgency 8. exigency, instancy
9. authority, influence
10. compulsion, constraint, harassment 11. compression
pressure (pert to)...
barometer.. 7. mesobar
boiler, cooker.. 9. autoclave
instrument (for liquids).. 9. manometer
10. piezometer 11. Bourdon tube
of necessity.. 7. urgency
resisting.. 8. renitent
unit.. 5. barad
prestidigitation... 8. juggling
11. legerdemain 13. sleight of hand
prestige... 4. bias, face, sway 5. clout, éclat 6. renown, repute 7. sorcery
8. illusion 9. authority, deception, influence 10. importance
11. superiority
presto... 5. magic 7. command, passing, quickly 8. suddenly
9. instantly 10. rapid tempo
11. immediately 13. instantaneous
presumably... 7. no doubt 8. probably
10. ostensibly, supposedly
presume... 4. dare, hope 5. imply, judge, think 6. assure, impose
7. suppose, venture 10. presuppose
11. preconceive 14. take for granted
presumption... 4. hope 6. daring
7. opinion 8. audacity 9. arrogance, impudence, insolence 10. effrontery
11. implication, probability, supposition
presumptive... 5. brash 7. assumed, Icarian 8. arrogant, inferred, probable
10. evidential
presumptuous... 5. undue 7. forward, haughty 8. arrogant, insolent
9. foolhardy 11. venturesome
pretend... 3. act, aim 4. fake, sham
5. claim, feign, feint 6. affect, allege, assume, pose as 7. presume, pretext, profess 8. disguise, simulate
11. impersonate, make believe
pretended... 4. sham 7. alleged
8. affected, intended, proposed, so–called 10. ostensible
pretended omission (Rhet)...
9. apophasis 11. paraleipsis (paralepsis)
pretender... 4. idol, snob 5. cowan, quack 6. seemer 7. Aeolist (Eolist)
8. claimant, impostor 9. charlatan
10. mountebank 11. fourflusher
pretense, pretence... 3. act 4. flam,

ruse, sham, show 5. claim, cloak,
cover, feint, horse, study 6. excuse,
tinsel 7. pretext 8. artifice, stalking
10. appearance, masquerade,
subterfuge 11. affectation, fabrication,
ostentation
pretentious... 4. arty 5. showy
6. rococo 7. elegant, pompous
8. affected, boastful 9. high–flown
12. ostentatious 13. grandiloquent
pretentious words, use of...
9. bombastic 10. lexiphanic
pretermit... 4. omit 6. pass by
7. neglect, suspend 8. intermit, pass
over 9. interrupt
pretext... 4. flam, plea 5. cloak, cover,
trick 6. excuse 8. pretense (pretence)
9. deception, semblance
pretty... 3. toy 4. cute, fair, joli, very
5. bonny (bonnie) 6. clever, comely,
lovely, rather 7. dollish, finical,
foppish 8. handsome 9. ingenious,
tolerably 10. attractive, knickknack
11. good looking, interesting
15. pulchritudinous
prevail... 3. win 5. exist 6. induce,
subdue 7. succeed, triumph
8. dominate, frequent 9. prevalent
11. predominate
prevailed... 3. got, won 5. urged
9. succeeded, triumphed
prevailing... 4. rife 5. chief, usual
6. common 7. current, general
8. abundant, dominant 9. prevalent
10. widespread 11. predominant
prevail upon... 4. urge 6. induce
8. persuade
prevalent... 4. rife 6. potent
7. current 8. dominant, powerful
9. extensive 10. prevailing,
successful, victorious, widespread
11. efficacious, influential
prevaricate... 3. lie 5. evade
7. deviate, quibble, shuffle
prevene... 7. prevent 9. forestall
10. anticipate
prevent... 4. warn 5. avert, debar,
deter, estop 7. ward off 8. preclude
9. forestall, frustrate 10. circumvent
preventive, preventive... 8. antidote
9. deterrant 12. prophylactic
previous... 4. past 5. prior 6. before,
former 7. earlier 8. untimely
9. foregoing, preceding, premature
11. unwarranted
previously... 4. erst 6. before
7. earlier 8. formerly 9. aforesaid
10. heretofore
prey... 3. rob 5. booty, spoil
6. quarry, victim 7. plunder
prey (to seize)... 9. raptorial
prey upon... 3. eat 4. feed 5. ravin
(raven) 7. plunder, torment
9. predacity
Priam (pert to)...
daughter.. 8. Polyxena 9. Cassandra
grandfather.. 4. Ilus
King of.. 4. Troy
servant.. 7. Agelaus
son.. 5. Paris 6. Hector 7. Troilus
wife.. 6. Hecuba
price... 3. sum 4. cost, fare, odds,

rate 5. offer, value, worth 6. charge
7. expense 10. estimation,
excellence, recompense
12. preciousness
priceless... 7. amusing 8. precious
10. high–priced, invaluable, not
salable
prick... 4. goad, pain, pang 5. sting,
wound 6. pierce 7. prickle, remorse
8. distress
pricked... 6. dotted, pinked 7. pointed
9. punctured
prickle... 4. burr, prod, seta 5. spike,
thorn 6. pierce, tingle 7. acantha
8. stinging
prickly... 6. tingly 7. pointed
8. echinate
prickly (pert to)...
flower.. 4. burr
pear.. 4. tuna 5. nopal 6. cactus
7. Opuntia
plant.. 3. ash 5. briar, elder 6. teasel
7. juniper, lettuce, thistle
12. Hercules'–club
pride... 6. vanity 7. conceit, egotism
9. arrogance, proudness
11. self–respect
priest... 3. Eli, fra 4. abbé, curé,
lama, père 5. clerk, druid, padre
6. cleric, father 7. prester
9. oratorian
priest (pert to)...
assistant.. 7. acolyte
Brit order (anc).. 5. Druid
cap.. 5. miter (mitre) 7. biretta
collar.. 5. amice, stole
fish.. 8. rockfish
mantle.. 4. cope
newly ordained.. 9. priesteen
priest in–the–pulpit.. 10. cuckoopint
relating to.. 10. sacerdotal
tribe (Israel).. 4. Levi
vestment.. 3. alb 5. ephod
8. scapular
priestly caste... 4. Magi 7. wise men
prig... 3. beg, fog, pan 4. buck, snob
5. dandy, filch, plead, prink, prude,
steal, thief 6. haggle, pilfer, purist,
tinker 7. bargain, entreat, pitcher
8. pilferer
priggish, prim... 7. prudish
8. snobbish, thievish
prim... 4. fish, neat, smug 5. primp,
smelt 6. demure, formal 7. precise,
prudish 8. decorous
prima donna... 4. diva 6. singer
prima facie... 7. at sight 9. first view
10. apparently
primal... 5. basic, chief, first
7. primary 8. original 9. elemental,
primitive
primary... 5. basic, color, first
6. primal 7. initial 8. election,
primeval, pristine 9. elemental,
essential, firsthand, primitive, principal
10. elementary 11. fundamental
primary (pert to)...
armament.. 6. cannon
circles.. 7. equator, horizon
8. ecliptic, galactic
colors.. 3. red 4. blue 6. yellow
primate, bishop... 10. Archbishop

Primates (Order of)... 3. ape, man
  5. lemur 6. mammal, monkey
  8. marmoset 9. orangutan
  (orangoutang)
prime... 4. best, dawn 5. first, paint
  7. primary, the best 8. original,
  primeval 9. primitive
prime minister... 7. premier
primer... 5. paint 8. hornbook,
  textbook, type size 9. detonator
  10. battledore
primeval... 6. primal 7. primary
  8. original, pristine
primeval deity... 5. Titan
primitive... 5. basic, first 6. embryo,
  native, quaint 7. ancient, priscan
  8. pristine 10. aboriginal, antiquated
  11. fundamental
primitive (pert to)...
  area.. 5. Idaho 8. Colorado
  art objects.. 9. artifacts
  group.. 6. ethnos
  self.. 2. id 8. instinct
primness... 8. neatness, niceness
  9. stiffness 11. preciseness
primo... 5. chief, first 12. leading
  tenor
primordial... 7. primary 8. original
  9. elemental, primitive 10. prototypal
  11. rudimentary 12. first created
primrose (pert to)...
  called.. 10. an innocent 13. flower of
  youth
  color.. 6. yellow 10. snapdragon
  genus.. 7. Primula 11. Primulaceae
  green.. 5. color
  League.. 13. Conservatives (Eng)
  path.. 7. sensual
prince... 4. knez 5. prinz 7. dynasty,
  monarch 8. archduke 9. potentate,
  princekin, sovereign 10. princeling
prince (pert to)...
  Albert.. 9. frock coat
  allowance.. 8. appenage
  petty.. 6. satrap
princely... 5. noble, regal, royal
  6. kingly 10. munificent
  11. magnificent
princely Italian family... 4. Este
Prince of...
  Afghanistan.. 4. amir
  apostate angels.. 5. Eblis
  Apostles.. 6. St Paul 7. St Peter
  darkness.. 5. devil, Satan 7. Ahriman
  demons.. 5. devil 9. Beelzebub
  destruction.. 9. Tamerlane
  evil spirits.. 7. Sammael
  liars.. 5. Pinto
  Peace.. 7. Messiah 11. Jesus Christ
  Spanish poetry.. 4. Vega
  the Church.. 8. cardinal
  the ode.. 7. Ronsard
  the sonnet.. 6. Bellay 15. Joachim du
  Bellay
  this world (Bib).. 5. Satan
  Tunis.. 3. bey
princess (pert to)...
  literally.. 5. Sarah
  loved by Cupid.. 6. Psyche
  loved by Zeus.. 6. Europa
  Mohammed.. 5. begum
  mythical.. 5. Danae 8. Atalanta

  royal.. 14. eldest daughter
  Tyrian.. 4. Dido (Elissa)
principal... 3. top 4. arch, head, main
  5. chief, major, prime 6. Führer,
  leader, master, origin, source
  7. captain, leading, palmary, primary
  8. foremost 9. important, organ
  stop, preceptor 10. capital sum
  11. outstanding
principality... 6. Monaco
principal meal (Rom)... 4. cena
principle... 4. rule 5. axiom, canon,
  prana, tenet 6. dictum 7. precept,
  theorem 9. essential 10. foundation
principle (pert to)...
  active in tobacco.. 8. nicotine
  distance.. 11. perspective
  Hindu.. 5. Sakti
  life, theosophy.. 5. prana, tenet
  musical.. 8. tonality
  vital.. 4. soul 5. anima
principles... 5. creed 9. generalia
  10. essentials 12. generalities
princox, princock... 7. coxcomb
  9. pert youth
prink... 4. deck, wink 5. adorn, preen,
  primp 6. bedeck, glance 7. dress up
print... 5. stamp 7. edition, engrave,
  impress, picture, publish
  11. indentation
printed (pert to)...
  defamation.. 5. libel
  fabric.. 4. silk 6. calico 7. percale
  sheets.. 8. pamphlet
printer... 8. pressman 9. publisher
  11. typographer 12. lithographer
printer (pert to)...
  aid.. 5. devil 10. apprentice
  dauber.. 5. biron
  direction.. 4. stet
  hand ink roller.. 6. brayer
  ink pad.. 6. dabber
  manuscript.. 4. copy
  mark.. 4. dash, stet 5. caret, serif,
  tilde 8. asterisk
  measure.. 2. em, en 4. pica
  type, mixed.. 3. pie (pi)
printing (pert to)...
  blur.. 6. mackle, macule
  cylinder.. 6. rounce
  error.. 7. erratum
  form.. 3. die
  for the blind.. 7. braille
  mark.. 4. dele 6. diesis 8. ellipsis
  measure.. 2. em, en 5. agate
  metal block.. 4. quad
  press part.. 6. platen, rounce
  7. frisket
prion... 6. petrel 7. sea bird
prior... 3. ere 4. fore, past 6. before,
  former 8. previous, priorate
  9. preceding 10. antecedent
priority... 10. precedence 11. order of
  time
priory... 5. abbey 8. cloister
priscan... 9. primitive
Priscian... 7. grammar 10. grammarian
Priscilla (pert to)...
  Bib.. 16. Christian convert
  color.. 7. fog blue
  Hist.. 7. Puritan
  husband.. 9. John Alden

tale .. 24. Courtship of Myles Standish
prism (optical device) ... 5. Porro
prismatic ... 10. iridescent, variegated
prison ... 3. jug 4. brig, gaol, jail, keep,
    quod 5. clink 6. carcer
    10. guardhouse 12. penitentiary
prison (pert to) ...
    courtyard .. 4. quad
    English (old) .. 7. Newgate 9. Bridewell
    French .. 8. Bastille
    guarded .. 10. panopticon
    keeper .. 5. quard 6. gaoler, jailer,
    keeper, warden 7. turnkey
    Russian .. 5. gulag
    slang .. 3. jug 4. quod, rock 5. clink,
    limbo 6. cooler 7. slammer 8. big
    house, hoosegow
    spy .. 6. canary, mouton
Prisoner of ...
    Chillon .. 16. Francois Bonivard
    Vatican .. 4. Pope
prisoner's release ... 6. parole
pristine ... 7. primary 8. original
    9. primitive
prittle–prattle ... 7. chatter, prattle
    8. chitchat 9. chatterer, empty talk
privacy ... 7. privity, retreat, secrecy
    8. solitude 9. seclusion
private ... 5. privy 6. covert, secret
    7. one's own 8. esoteric, eyes–only,
    hush–hush, personal, secluded,
    separate, solitary 11. sequestered
    12. confidential
    15. uncommunicative
privateer ... 4. Kidd (Capt) 5. caper
    6. pirate 7. corsair, soldier (not
    enlisted) 9. freelance
privately ... 5. aside 6. secret 8. in
    secret 10. personally, unofficial
    12. unofficially
privation ... 4. loss, want 6. misery
    7. poverty 8. hardship
    10. divestment 11. destitution
privilege ... 3. soc, use 5. favor, right
    7. charter 8. easement 9. advantage
    10. concession 12. carte bianche
privileged ... 6. exempt 8. licensed
prix ... 5. prize
prize ... 3. cup 5. award, booty, Detur
    (Harvard), medal, plate, price, purse,
    stake, value 6. assess, esteem, ribbon,
    trophy 7. premium, respect
    8. treasure
prize fight ... 2. go, KO 3. TKO
    4. bout, spar 6. boxing 7. contest
    8. knockout, pugilism 10. fisticuffs
pro ... 3. aye, for 6. before 8. behalf
    of 9. in front of 12. professional
probability ... 4. odds 6. chance,
    shoo–in (sl) 7. vantage 9. liability
    10. conclusion, good chance,
    likelihood, likeliness 11. credibility
probe ... 3. dig 4. prod, tent 5. sound
    6. feeler, pierce, search, stylet
    7. examine, explore, feel out, inquiry
    10. instrument, scrutinize
probity ... 6. virtue 7. honesty
    9. integrity, rectitude 11. uprightness
problem ... 3. nut 4. crux, knot
    6. enigma, riddle 7. theorem
    8. question 9. situation

pro bono publico ... 16. for the public
    good
proboscis ... 4. nose 5. snout, trunk
procaccia ... 4. cart (carrier's)
    7. carrier
procacious ... 4. pert 8. insolent,
    petulant
procacity ... 8. pertness 9. insolence,
    petulance
Procavis ... 4. cony 5. hyrax 6. rabbit
procedure ... 4. step 5. order
    6. custom, method, policy, system
    7. process 8. behavior
    11. continuance
proceed ... 2. go 4. fare, move, pass,
    wend 5. arise, issue 6. derive
    7. emanate 8. continue, progress
    9. originate
proceed (pert to) ...
    hastily .. 5. speed
    leisurely .. 5. amble, mosey (mosy)
    on one's way .. 4. wend
    rapidly .. 4. zoom 6. gallop
proceeding ... 4. step 5. actum
    6. course 7. conduct, measure,
    process 8. activity, behavior
    9. procedure 11. transaction
proceeding (pert to) ...
    by threes .. 7. ternary
    from earth .. 8. telluric
    from the sun .. 5. polar
proceedings ... 4. acta 5. trial
    6. doings 7. affairs, lawsuit, minutes
    8. activity
proceeds ... 4. gain, ones 6. income
    7. marches, profits, returns
procerity ... 6. height 8. tallness
process ... 4. cook, writ 5. lapse (of
    time), order 6. course, notice
    7. advance, mandate, summons
    8. progress 9. emanation, operation,
    outgrowth, procedure, sterilize
process (pert to) ...
    beak (small) .. 9. rostrulum
    electroplating, steeling .. 8. acierage
    fabric coloring .. 5. batik
    fish (winglike) .. 3. fin
    in organisms .. 6. moisis
    of development .. 7. nascent
    pointed .. 3. awn
    steel making .. 8. Bessemer
    11. cementation
    surveying .. 13. triangulation
    transferring pictures .. 5. decal
    12. decalcomania
procession ... 4. file 5. train 6. parade
    7. cortege 8. sequence 9. formation
prochein, prochain ... 4. next
    7. nearest
proclaim ... 4. hype (sl), tout 5. blaze,
    voice 6. herald 7. declare, enounce,
    presage, publish 8. announce
    10. promulgate
proclamation ... 4. fiat 5. bando,
    banns (bans), blaze, edict, ukase
    6. decree, notice 9. manifesto
    12. announcement, promulgation
proclivity ... 4. bent 6. desire
    7. leaning 8. tendency
    10. propensity 11. disposition,
    inclination

procrastinate... 5. defer, delay, stall
7. soldier 8. postpone
procrastination... 5. delay, stall
7. laxness 10. hesitation
11. vacillation 12. dilatoriness
procrastinator... 7. delayer, trifler
8. deferrer
procreant... 8. fruitful 9. producing
10. generating 11. propagative
Procrustes (Gr legend)...
10. highwayman (Attica)
14. Procrustean bed
procurator... 5. agent 6. lawyer
7. proctor, steward
procure... 3. get 4. gain 5. bring,
fetch 6. effect, elicit, induce, obtain
7. acquire 8. contrive, purchase
prod... 3. egg, jab 4. goad, poke,
urge 6. thrust
prodigal... 4. cloy 6. lavish 7. spender
9. plentiful 10. squanderer
11. extravagant, intemperate,
spendthrift, squandering
prodigality... 5. waste 9. abundance
12. extravagance, intemperance
13. superabundant
prodigious... 4. huge 5. great
7. amazing, immense 8. enormous
9. marvelous, monstrous, wonderful
10. miraculous, portentous,
tremendous 11. astonishing
13. extraordinary
prodigy... 4. omen, sign 6. genius,
marvel, oddity, wonder 7. miracle
prodition... 7. treason 8. betrayal
produce... 2. do 4. bear, make, show,
wage 5. carry, cause, stage, yield
6. author, create, effect 7. exhibit,
product 8. engender, generate,
receipts 9. originate 10. accomplish
11. merchandise
produce (pert to)...
copy of.. 4. type
effect.. 3. act
ideas.. 6. ideate
noise.. 5. sound
produced... 8. extended 9. elongated,
prolonged
produced (pert to)...
by heat.. 7. igneous 8. volcanic
by kitchen gardens.. 7. olitory
8. potherbs
by wind.. 7. aeolian
regularly.. 6. staple
producer... 4. doer 6. farmer, parent
7. creator 10. theaterman
12. manufacturer
producing (pert to)...
cold.. 7. algific
fire.. 8. sparking
illusions.. 15. phantasmagorial
poison.. 6. septic
product... 3. sum 4. crop 5. fruit
6. result 7. hormone 8. artifact,
creation 9. commodity, outgrowth
production... 3. hit 4. book, work
5. fruit 7. produce 8. creation
9. execution, extension
14. accomplishment
productive... 4. rich 7. fertile, gainful
8. creative, fruitful 9. inventive
10. generative

proem... 7. preface, prelude
8. foreword, preamble
12. introduction
profane... 6. misuse, unholy, wicked
7. godless, impious, ungodly, worldly
8. temporal 9. desecrate
10. unhallowed 11. blasphemous,
unspiritual 12. unsanctified
profess... 4. avow 5. claim, feign
6. affirm, allege 7. declare
11. acknowledge
profession... 5. claim, faith, trade
6. avowal, career, metier 7. calling,
pretext 8. vocation 9. testimony
10. occupation 11. affirmation
14. acknowledgment
professional... 4. paid 5. hired
6. expert 7. skilled, trained
8. finished
professional, non... 3. lay 4. laic
7. amateur 9. unskilled
proffer... 3. bid 4. give 5. offer
6. tender
proficient... 3. apt 5. adept 6. expert,
versed 7. skilled 12. accomplished
profile... 4. draw, form 7. contour,
diagram, outline, picture 9. biography
14. representation
profit... 3. net 4. boot, gain, good,
mend 5. avail 6. return 7. benefit,
rake–off, results 8. interest
9. advantage 11. share of gain
12. remuneration
profitable... 6. paying, useful
7. helpful 8. repaying 9. expedient,
lucrative 10. beneficial
12. remunerative
profligate... 6. wicked 7. corrupt,
spender, vicious 8. depraved,
prodigal, wasteful 9. abandoned,
dissolute, reprobate 10. overthrown
11. extravagant
profound... 4. deep, wise 5. heavy
7. abysmal, intense, learned
8. abstruse, complete, deep–felt,
poignant 9. downright, recondite,
sagacious 11. far–reaching
12. encompassing, unfathomable
13. thoroughgoing
profundity... 5. depth 6. wisdom
8. deepness 12. abstruseness
profuse... 6. galore, lavish 7. diffuse,
liberal, palaver 8. abundant,
generous, numerous, prodigal,
wasteful 9. bountiful 10. munificent
11. extravagant, overflowing
profusion... 6. plenty 9. abundance
11. diffuseness, prodigality
12. extravagance, lavish supply
progenitor... 4. sire 6. parent
8. ancestor 9. precursor
10. forefather
progenitor of giants (Norse Myth)...
4. Ymir 8. rime–cold
progeny... 3. son 4. race 5. issue
6. family 7. outcome 8. children,
daughter, outbirth 9. offspring,
parentage, resultant 11. descendants
prognosis... 7. outlook 8. forecast
9. diagnosis 10. prediction
14. interpretation
prognosticate... 4. bode, omen

7. betoken, predict, presage
8. forebode, foreshow, foretell,
prophecy 9. foretoken
program, programme... 4. bill
(printed), card, plan 5. edict
6. notice, policy 7. outline
8. bulletin, platform, schedule,
syllabus 9. broadcast, catalogue,
programma 10. prospectus
12. proclamation, prolegomenon
13. advertisement
programma... 5. edict 6. decree,
notice 7. preface 12. prolegomenon
progress... 4. fare, tour, wend
5. march 6. course, travel
7. advance, journey 10. expedition
11. progression
progress (pert to)...
chart.. 5. Gantt
clumsily.. 8. scramble
intelligently.. 6. egress 7. telesis
(telesia)
laborious.. 4. plod, wade
outward.. 6. egress
weakly.. 6. feebly
progressive... 6. modern, onward
7. forward, gradual, liberal
9. advancing, improving
11. consecutive 12. enterprising
prohibit... 3. ban, bar, bid 5. debar,
estop, taboo (tabu) 6. enjoin, forbid,
hinder 7. prevent 9. interdict
prohibited... 7. illegal, illicit
8. unlawful
prohibition... 3. ban 7. embargo
8. estoppel 9. exclusion
10. prevention, temperance
11. forbiddance 12. interdicting
project... 3. jet, jut 4. abut, cast,
idea, plan 5. shoot 6. beetle,
design, device, scheme 7. pattern,
problem 8. contrive, proposal
protrude 9. intention 10. conception
11. undertaking
projectile... 4. bomb 5. shell 6. bullet,
rocket 7. missile, torpedo
8. parabola 9. cartridge
projection... 3. arm, ear, fin, jag, toe
4. barb, cape, lobe, ness, prop,
snag 5. apsis, bulge, ledge, prong,
redan, socle, tenon 6. lobule, tappet
8. headland
projet... 4. plan 6. design
prolific... 6. fecund 7. fertile, teeming
8. fruitful 9. inventive 10. generative
11. propagative 12. reproductive
prolix... 5. wordy 7. diffuse, verbose
8. tiresome 9. prolonged, rigmarole,
wearisome 10. long–winded,
pleonastic, protracted
prolocutor... 6. orator 7. speaker,
teacher 8. chairman 9. spokesman
10. mouthpiece 11. Lord Speaker
(Eng)
prolong... 4. spin 7. draw out
8. continue, lengthen, postpone,
protract
prolonged... 7. chronic, delayed
8. extended 9. continued, postponed
10. lengthened, protracted
promenade... 4. mall, walk 6. airing,
marina, pasear 7. alameda, gallery

Prometheus (pert to)...
famed as.. 5. Titan (a)
poem (Shelley).. 17. Prometheus
Unbound
tale, tragedy.. 15. Prometheus Bound
16. Prometheus Loosed
24. Prometheus the Fire Bringer
prominence... 4. cusp 6. height
8. eminence, prestige, salience
9. greatness 10. famousness,
importance 11. distinction,
obviousness, prosiliency
12. distinctness, protuberance
prominent... 4. high, star 5. great
6. famous, marked 7. obvious,
salient 8. distinct, manifest
9. important 10. celebrated,
noticeable, prosilient, protruding
11. conspicuous, distinctive,
outstanding 13. distinguished
promiscuous... 5. mixed 8. careless
9. haphazard, orderless
14. indiscriminate
promise... 3. vow 4. hope, oath
5. swear 6. engage, parole, pledge,
plight, votive (by vow) 7. betroth,
predict 8. affiance, contract, give
hope 9. assurance, ray of hope
11. declaration
Promised Land... 6. heaven, utopia
8. Paradise 9. millenium, Shangri–La
11. Happy Valley 13. Celestial City
promontory... 3. tor 4. cape, naze
(nase), ness, scaw 5. mount, point
8. headland 10. projection
promote... 4. help 5. exalt, nurse
6. extend, prefer 7. actuate,
advance, dignify, elevate, finance,
further, improve 8. increase
9. advertise, encourage, patronize
promoter... 5. agent 6. backer
7. planner 8. lobbyist 9. financier,
publicist
promotion... 6. brevet 7. advance
10. preferment 11. advertising,
furtherance, improvement
prompt... 3. cue 4. easy, hint, soon,
tell, yare (anc) 5. alert, early, quick,
ready 6. advise, remind 7. animate,
suggest 8. punctual 11. expeditious
prompter... 3. aid 4. cuer 6. pit man,
reader 7. inducer, reciter 8. reminder
promptly... 4. tite (anc) 6. at once
7. quickly 9. willingly
promulgate... 7. declare, publish
8. proclaim 9. make known
prone... 3. apt 4. bent, flat 5. apish
6. supine 7. willing 8. downward
9. prostrate, recumbent
13. ventricumbent
prone to sin... 8. peccable
prong... 3. nib, peg 4. fang, fork, tine
5. spike, tooth 6. branch
pronghorn... 6. cabree (cabrie)
9. prong buck, springbok
prong key... 7. spanner
pronoun... 2. he, it, me, my, us, we,
ye 3. her, him, one, she, thy, who,
you 4. that, thee, them, they, thou,
what, your 5. these, those 6. itself,
myself 7. herself, himself, oneself,
ourself 8. one's self, yourself

9. ourselves 10. themselves
pronoun (possessive)... 2. my 3. her,
his, its, our 4. hers, mine, one's,
ours, your 5. their, yours 6. theirs
pronounce... 3. say 5. bless (holy),
speak, utter 6. affirm, assert
7. adjudge, declare, deliver
8. announce 9. enunciate
10. adjudicate, articulate, assibilate
pronouncement... 6. decree
8. judgment 9. manifesto
11. affirmation, declaration
12. announcement
pronto... 5. quick 7. quickly
8. promptly 11. immediately
pronunciation... 4. burr 8. orthoepy
9. utterance (clear) 11. enunciation
pronunciation mark... 5. tilde
7. cedilla 8. dieresis
proof... 4. test 5. trial 6. result
7. outcome 8. evidence 9. testimony
11. galley proof 12. confirmation,
verification 13. certification
proofreader's mark... 4. dele, stet
5. caret, space
prop... 3. beg, gib, nog 5. brace,
shore, sprag, staff, stell 6. shorer
7. fulcrum, support 9. stanchion
propagate... 5. breed 6. extend,
spread 7. diffuse, publish
8. disperse, engender, generate,
increase, multiply, transmit
propel... 3. row 4. pole, push, urge
5. drive, impel 7. project
propeller... 3. fan, gun, oar 4. vane
5. screw 6. driver 9. plane part
propensity... 4. bent 6. desire
7. leaning 8. aptitude, tendency
9. proneness 10. proclivity
11. disposition, inclination
proper... 3. fit 4. fine, just, meet,
prim, smug 5. exact, right 6. chaste,
decent, goodly, honest, kilter
7. correct 8. decorous, inherent,
orthodox, suitable 9. excellent,
expedient 11. appropriate,
grammatical, respectable
12. conventional
properly... 5. fitly 7. rightly, utterly
8. decently, strictly, suitably
9. correctly 11. expediently
14. conventionally
proper sense of worth... 5. pride
property... 3. res 4. bona, gear
5. asset, goods, trait 6. estate,
nature, realty, wealth 8. holdings
9. attribute, copyright, ownership
10. real estate 11. peculiarity,
possessions 14. characteristic
property (pert to)...
act to regain.. 8. replevin (repleven)
destruction of.. 8. sabotage
9. vandalism
landed property.. 9. cadastral
light without heat..
15. phosphorescence
movable.. 4. gear 8. chattels
no private ownership..
11. aspheterism
of matter.. 7. inertia
one's own.. 7. alodium
right.. 4. lien

stolen.. 4. loot, pelf 5. lucre, spoil
suit for recovery.. 6. trover
transferrer.. 7. alienor, grantor
wife to husband.. 3. dos
woman's (Hindu).. 9. stridhana
(stridhan)
prophecy... 6. oracle 9. utterance
10. prediction 11. foretelling
prophesy... 4. osse 5. augur
7. predict, presage 8. forecast,
foreshow, foretell 10. vaticinate
11. preindicate 13. prognosticate
prophet... 4. seer 6. medium, oracle
7. psychic 8. Mohammed, preacher,
presager 9. John Smith, predictor
10. soothsayer 11. Joseph Smith
(Mormon)
prophet (Bib)... 4. Amos 5. Cyrus,
Hosea 6. Elijah (Elias) 7. Malachi,
Obadiah
prophet, murder of... 8. vaticide
prophetess... 5. sibyl 7. seeress
9. Cassandra (of evil)
prophetic, prophetical... 5. vatic
6. mantic 7. fateful, vatical
8. oracular 9. vaticinal
10. divinatory, presageful
11. predicative
propinquity... 7. kinship 8. nearness
9. proximity 12. neighborhood,
relationship 13. consanguinity
propitiate... 5. atone 6. pacify
8. atone for 10. conciliate
propitiation... 9. atonement, expiation
12. pacification, satisfaction
14. reconciliation
propitious... 4. rosy 5. happy, lucky
6. benign, timely 7. helpful
9. favorable, opportune, promising
10. auspicious, benevolent,
prosperous 12. advantageous,
well–disposed
proponent... 8. advocate
10. propounder
proportion... 4. part, rate 5. quota,
ratio, share 6. adjust, extent
7. analogy, compare, euphony,
prorate 8. equalize, symmetry
9. apportion
proportional... 4. rate 8. relative
10. comparable, respective
11. dimensional
proportionate... 5. equal 8. adequate,
relative 9. analogous 10. respective
11. comparative 13. corresponding
proposal... 3. bid 4. plan 5. offer
6. feeler, motion 8. marriage
9. intention 10. nomination,
suggestion 11. proposition,
supposition
propose... 5. image, offer, state, toast
6. intend, submit 7. purpose
8. nominate, propound 9. postulate
proposed (pert to)...
for consideration.. 9. suggested
for debate.. 6. mooted
international language.. 2. Ro 3. Ido
9. Esperanto
proposition... 4. plan 5. axiom, lemma
6. porism, thesis 7. project
8. empirema, proposal 9. corollary
11. supposition, undertaking

proposition, proof of ... 18. reductio ad absurdum
propound ... 6. submit 7. propose 8. set forth 9. postulate
proprietary ... 5. owner, title 8. interest, medicine (secret) 9. ownership 10. proprietor 12. landed estate
propriety ... 7. decency, decorum, fitness 8. standard 9. ownership 10. convention, expedience, properness 11. correctness, suitability 12. tastefulness 13. possessorship
propugnaculum ... 7. bulwark, defense 8. fortress
prorogue ... 5. defer 6. extend 7. adjourn, prolong 8. postpone, protract
prosaic ... 4. drab, dull, flat 5. plain, prosy 6. prolix, stupid 7. humdrum, insipid, tedious 8. ordinary, tiresome 10. unexciting 11. commonplace 12. matter-of-fact 13. unimaginative
proscribe ... 3. ban 6. forbid, outlaw 7. condemn (to death) 8. prohibit, restrain 9. interdict, ostracize
proscription ... 5. exile 8. outlawry 11. prohibition 12. interdiction
prosecute ... 3. sue 4. urge 5. chase 6. intend (law), pursue 7. carry on, enforce, execute
prosecutor ... 6. lawyer 7. accuser, relator 8. attorney
proselyte ... 3. ger (to Judaism) 7. convert
proseuche, proseucha ... 7. oratory 9. synagogue 13. place of prayer
prosody ... 13. versification
prospect ... 4. view 5. buyer, scene, vista 6. survey 7. explore, foresee, outlook 8. customer 9. applicant, candidate, foresight, intention 10. contestant 11. probability 12. anticipation
prosper ... 4. fare 5. cheve, speed 6. thrive 7. succeed 8. flourish
prosperity ... 3. hap, ups 4. boom, weal 6. thrift 7. success, welfare 9. well-being 11. good fortune
Prospero (pert to) ...
character .. 9. Ferdinand
daughter .. 7. Miranda
servant .. 5. Ariel
slave .. 7. Caliban
The Tempest .. 11. Duke of Milan
prosperous ... 4. weal 5. lucky, palmy, sonsy (sonsie) 7. wealthy 8. thriving 9. favorable, fortunate 10. auspicious, successful 11. flourishing
prostitute ... 4. drab 5. venal 6. harlot 7. corrupt 8. infamous 12. street walker
prostrate ... 4. flat, raze 5. abase, prone 6. fallen, grieve, supine 7. exhaust 8. helpless, supinate 9. flattened, recumbent 10. obsequious, submissive
prosy ... 3. dry 4. dull 6. jejune 7. prosaic, tedious 11. commonplace 13. plain-speaking
protagonist ... 4. hero, lead (theater)

5. actor 6. leader 8. advocate, champion, defender 9. contender, principal, spokesman 11. participant
Protagoras (Gr) ... 7. Sophist, teacher 11. philosopher
protasis ... 5. maxim 9. drama part 11. proposition 12. introduction
protect ... 3. arm 4. save 5. guard 6. defend, insure, police, screen, sheath, shield 7. cherish, shelter 8. enshield, preserve 9. safeguard
protected ... 5. armed 6. shaded 7. aproned, guarded 8. shielded 12. invulnerable
protection ... 3. bib, lee 4. coat, fort, moat 5. aegis (egis), apron, armor, guard, shade, shell, smock 6. glacis, refuge, safety 7. defense, parapet, shelter 8. havelock, passport, security 11. safekeeping 12. preservation
protector ... 6. patron, regent 8. defender, guardian 10. safekeeper
protector of vineyards (Gr) ... 7. Priapus
protégé ... 4. ward 6. charge 9. dependent
Proteida ... 7. Proteus 10. amphibians 11. salamanders
protein ... 6. casein 7. albumin, mucedin, peptone 8. globulin, lecithin, nutrient 9. protamine 11. chlorophyll
protein (pert to) ...
blood .. 6. fibrin 8. globulin
castor oil bean .. 5. ricin (poison)
egg .. 7. albumin
milk .. 6. casein
muscles .. 8. creatine
seeds .. 7. odontin 8. aleurone, prolamin
Proteles ... 8. aardwolf
protest ... 4. aver, beef, deny 6. assert 7. declare 9. objection, stipulate 10. asseverate 11. expostulate 13. expostulation
protestation ... 6. avowal (public) 7. protest 11. affirmation, obtestation 12. asseveration, supplication
Proteus (pert to) ...
biology .. 3. olm 6. amoeba 8. bacteria 10. salamander
Gr Myth .. 6. sea god
Shakespeare .. 17. Gentleman of Verona
protocol ... 5. rules (official) 7. compact 8. schedule 9. agreement, etiquette 10. memorandum (diplomatic) 12. original copy
protograph ... 9. holograph 12. illustration (of species)
protoplasm ... 5. spore 7. nucleus 9. archetype, cytoplasm 10. primordium 11. basis of life
protoplasmic (pert to) ...
body .. 8. ectosark 9. ectoplasm, endoplasm
cell .. 6. amoeba (ameba)
cell contents .. 9. metaplasm
substance .. 3. gel
Protozoa ... 6. amoeba (ameba), Lobosa, phylum 11. unicellular
protract ... 4. spin 5. defer, delay

6. extend 7. prolong, stretch
8. continue, elongate, lengthen,
postpone, protrude 9. expatiate
protrude... 3. jut 5. bulge 6. exsert
7. project 9. thrust out
protuberance... 3. jag, nub, wen
4. boss, bump, cere, hump, knob,
knot, lobe, lump, node, snag, wart
5. bulge, caput, inion, knurl, torus
8. eminence, swelling 9. extrusion
10. projection
proud... 4. vain 5. grand, lofty, noble
6. elated, lordly 7. haughty, pleased,
stately, valiant 8. arrogant, boastful,
imposing, splendid 9. conceited,
gratified 10. impressive
11. independent, magisterial,
magnificent 12. presumptuous,
supercilious
prove... 3. try 4. test 5. check, nurse
6. evince, try out, verify 7. confirm,
justify, probate 8. identify, manifest
9. ascertain, establish
11. corroborate, demonstrate
prove false... 6. refute
Provençal dialect... 9. langue d'oc
provender... 3. hay 4. food 5. grain
6. fodder 8. ensilage
proverb... 3. saw 5. adage, axiom
6. byword, enigma, saying
8. aphorism, link verb, paroemia
proverbial... 10. aphoristic
11. sententious 12. epigrammatic
provide... 4. give 5. cater, endow,
endue, equip, stock, treat, yield
6. afford, ration, supply 7. care for,
finance 9. make ready 10. contribute
provided... 2. if, so 5. boden
6. sobeit 8. afforded, equipped,
prepared, supplied 11. on condition
13. conditionally
Providence founder... 13. Roger
Williams (1636)
provident... 4. wise 6. frugal, saving
7. prudent, thrifty 9. judicious
10. economical 11. precautious,
preparatory
providential... 5. lucky 7. prudent
9. opportune, provident
10. miraculous 11. foresighted
province... 4. area, beat, nome
5. arena, range, shire, tract
6. colony, domain, empire, eparch,
region, sphere 7. circuit, diocese,
kingdom 8. district 9. territory
10. palatinate (royal) 12. jurisdiction
provincial... 4. rude 5. crude, local,
rural 6. narrow 7. insular, limited
8. suburban 10. restricted,
uncultured 11. countrified
12. narrow–minded
15. unsophisticated
provincialism (diction)... 6. patois
10. patavinity
provision... 4. fare, food 5. board,
stock, store 6. vivres 7. proviso
9. condition 11. preparation
provisional... 9. makeshift, temporary,
tentative 10. promissory, substitute
11. conditional, preparatory
12. experimental 14. circumstantial
provision seller (Mil)... 6. sutler

proviso... 5. salvo 6. clause
provocative... 9. desirable, provoking
10. appetizing, stirring up, suggestive
11. interesting
provoke... 3. ire, vex 4. bate, goad,
move, rile, spur, stir 5. anger,
annoy, start 6. arouse, incite, induce,
invite, invoke, nettle, offend, stir up,
summon 7. incense 8. irritate
9. challenge 10. antagonize,
exasperate
provoking... 8. annoying, exciting
10. suggestive 11. interesting
12. antagonizing
provoking laughter... 7. risible
prow... 3. bow 4. beak, duty, good,
proa, stem 5. brave, honor, prore
6. steven 7. courage, gallant, gun
deck
prowess... 5. valor 9. gallantry
proximal... 9. immediate (opp of distal)
proximate... 4. next 6. direct
7. closest, nearest 9. immediate
10. succeeding
proximity... 8. nearness, nighness,
relation, vicinity 9. adjacence,
closeness 11. propinquity
proxy... 5. agent, power 6. agency,
ballot, deputy 7. proctor 9. authority
10. procurator, substitute
prudence... 6. virtue, wisdom
7. caution, economy 8. sagacity
9. foresight 11. calculation,
forethought 13. judiciousness
14. circumspection
prudent... 4. wary, wise 5. canny
6. frugal 8. cautious, discreet
9. judicious, penny–wise, provident
10. economical 11. circumspect,
considerate
prudish... 4. prim 8. priggish
prune... 3. cut, lop 4. clip, food, frog,
plum, trim, weed 5. dress, plume,
preen, purge, shape 6. anoint 7. cut
down, tonsure 9. simpleton
prunelike fruit... 9. myrobalan
pruning knife... 8. serpette
prurient... 7. itching, longing, lustful
10. lascivious
Prussia...
  bay.. 4. Kiel 6. Danzig
    10. Pomeranian
  cathedral city.. 5. Essen 7. Cologne
    10. Düsseldorf
  city.. 6. Aachen
  color.. 4. blue 12. gold pheasant
  Knight.. 8. Noachite
  lagoon.. 4. haff 12. Frisches Haff
  lancer.. 5. Uhlan
  land aristocracy.. 6. Junker
  legislature.. 7. Landtag
  mountain.. 4. Harz
  resort.. 3. Ems
  river.. 3. Ems 4. Elbe, Oder, Saar
  seaport.. 4. Kiel 5. Emden 7. Stettin
  State.. 6. German
pry... 4. nose, peek 5. lever, mouse,
snoop 6. meddle, search
prying... 7. curious, peeking, peeping,
peering 8. snooping 9. searching
10. meddlesome 11. inquisitive
psalm (pert to)...

book.. 7. Psalter
Fiftieth, Vulgate.. 8. Miserere
Mass opening.. 7. introit
Ninety–fourth, Vulgate.. 6. Venite
Psalms (Old Test)... 7. Psalter
psalterium... 4. lyra 6. omasum
   7. stomach 9. manyplies
psammite... 4. rock 9. sandstone
psephology... 7. pebbles (study of)
psephomancy... 19. divination by
   pebbles
pseudatoll... 9. coral reef
pseudo... 4. sham 5. bogus, false
   6. untrue 7. feigned 8. spurious
   9. deceptive, imitation, pretender
pseudologist... 4. liar (humorous)
pseudology... 5. lying 9. falsehood
pseudonym... 5. alias 6. anonym
   7. pen name 10. nom de plume
pseudonym (famed)...
C L Dodgson.. 12. Lewis Carroll
Mary Ann Evans.. 11. George Eliot
Samuel Clemens.. 9. Mark Twain
W S Porter.. 6. O Henry
psychagogic... 9. inspiring
   10. attractive, persuasive
psyche... 4. mind, self, soul 6. spirit
psychic... 6. mental 9. spiritual
   10. Gnosticism 11. incorporeal
   12. spiritualist, supernatural
   13. psychological
psychic (pert to)...
emanation.. 4. aura
devotion.. 6. autism
monism.. 10. one reality
psychotic... 3. mad 6. insane
   8. neurotic 12. psychopathic
Ptah (pert to)...
Egypt Relig.. 8. chief god (of
   Memphis)
father of.. 3. men 4. gods
representation.. 5. mummy
symbolic of.. 4. life 8. strength
ptarmigan... 4. rype 6. grouse
pterodactyl... 7. reptile (extinct)
   9. pterosaur 11. ornithosaur
ptorography *(description of)*...
   8. feathers
pteroid... 8. fernlike, winglike
pteropod... 6. Clione (Arctic)
   7. mollusk
ptilosis... 7. plumage 9. madarosis
   10. loss of hair 15. loss of
   eyelashes
ptisan... 3. tea 5. drink 6. coddle
   9. decoction
Ptolemy (pert to)...
author of.. 8. Almagest
birthplace.. 5. Egypt (130 AD)
famed as.. 10. astronomer,
   geographer
public... 3. inn 4. open 5. state
   6. people, vulgar 8. communal
   9. clientele, community
public (pert to)...
assembly.. 4. Diet
conveyance.. 3. bus, cab, car 4. taxi,
   tram 5. train 10. jinrikisha (jinricksha)
display.. 10. exhibition
   13. exhibitionism
edict.. 3. ban 12. proclamation

entertainment.. 7. ridotto
hangman (Eng).. 9. Jack Ketch
lands.. 4. ager (Hist) 6. domain
official.. 6. notary
position.. 8. official
storehouse.. 5. étape
walk.. 4. mall 7. alameda
   9. esplanade, promenade
publication... 4. book 8. pamphlet,
   printing 12. notification, proclamation,
   promulgation
publication (pert to)...
article.. 7. feature
condensed.. 7. tabloid
make–up.. 6. format
prelim.. 9. prodromus
publicist... 5. solon 6. Gallup, lawyer,
   writer 10. journalist, publicizer
   11. commentator
publish... 4. edit, vent 5. issue, print
   6. blazon, delate 7. divulge
   8. proclaim 10. promulgate
   11. disseminate
publish (pert to)...
abroad.. 8. promulge
after death.. 10. posthumous
banns.. 7. betroth 8. marriage
far and wide.. 6. blazon
without authority.. 6. pirate
   10. plagiarize
publisher's description (book)...
   5. blurb 13. advertisement
publisher's inscription (book)...
   5. facts 8. colophon
Puccini heroine... 4. Mimi
pucker... 4. fold 5. bulge, purse
   6. crease 7. anxiety, fluster, wrinkle
   8. contract
puckered... 7. bullate 8. wrinkled
   10. contracted
puckish... 6. impish 8. Pucklike
   10. mysterious 11. mischievous
pud... 3. paw 4. hand 8. forefoot
pudding... 4. duff, mush, plum, sago
   6. junket 7. custard, dessert, tapioca
   8. roly–poly, softness, stuffing (game)
   9. Yorkshire
puddle... 3. mud 4. mess, pond, pool
   5. plash, swamp 6. muddle
   7. plashet, pollute
puddle duck... 7. mallard
puddock... 4. kite,· toad 7. buzzard
   9. enclosure (paddock)
pueblo... 4. town 7. village
Pueblo (pert to)...
ceremonial chamber.. 4. kiva
Indian (American).. 4. Hopi, Piro,
   Tano, Zuni 5. Acoma 7. Keresan
   12. cliff dweller
water jar.. 4. olla
puerile... 4. weak 5. young
   7. babyish, trivial 8. childish,
   juvenile, youthful 12. simple–minded
Puerto Rican (pert to)...
bark, beverage.. 4. mabi
dove.. 4. rola
fish.. 4. sama, sisi 8. porkfish
Puerto Rico... see also *Puerto Rico*
capital.. 7. San Juan
city.. 5. Ponce 7. Arecibo
discoverer.. 8. Columbus
first settlement.. 7. Caparra

government.. 12. Commonwealth
Indian name.. 9. Borinquen
island (off shore).. 4. Mona
  7. Culebra
island group.. 15. Greater Antilles
politically.. 12. Commonwealth
program (Polit).. 18. Operation
  Bootstrap
sea.. 9. Caribbean
puff... 4. blow, blub, chug, flam, pant,
  pegh (Scot), pouf, waff 5. elate
  7. efflate
puffbird... 6. barbet 8. barbacou
pug... 3. dog, elf 4. moth, puck, snub
  5. chaff, dwarf 6. harlot, refuse
  (grain), sprite 8. bargeman, mistress,
  pugilist 9. footprint, hobgoblin
pugging... 8. grasping, thieving
pugilistic... 6. fistic 10. pugnacious
pugnacious... 9. combative
  11. belligerent, quarrelsome
pugnacious man... 12. fighting cock
pug–nosed... 5. camus (camuse)
puisne... 4. puny 5. judge, later, petty
  6. feeble, junior 9. associate,
  unskilled 10. law student, subsequent
  11. subordinate
puissance... 5. force, might, power
  8. strength 9. authority
puissant... 6. mighty, potent
  7. mastery 8. forcible, powerful
  13. authoritative
pulchritude... 5. grace 6. beauty
  10. comeliness, loveliness
pule... 4. peep 5. cheep, whine
  7. ululate, whimper
pulicat... 8. bandanna (bandana)
puling... 6. sickly 7. babyish, howling,
  whining 8. childish, delicate
Pulitzer prizes... 6. awards
  10. journalism, literature
pull... 2. pu 3. lug, tow, tug 4. drag,
  draw, haul, yank 5. bouse, drink,
  tweak 6. effort, strain 7. attract,
  extract 9. influence 10. attraction
pull (pert to)...
apart.. 4. rend, tear 7. destroy
  8. demolish, enfeeble, separate
back.. 5. demur 6. recoil 7. retract
  8. withdraw
down.. 4. fell, raze 8. dismantle
off.. 3. pug 6. avulse, commit
  8. carry out 10. accomplish
one's leg.. 4. hoax, joke 7. deceive,
  flatter 8. hoodwink 9. make fun of
out.. 5. leave 6. secede 7. extract
  9. eradicate
up.. 4. stop 5. elate 6. aviate
  7. arraign, extract
pullet... 4. fowl 5. child 7. bivalve
  8. poullard
pulley (pert to)...
groove.. 5. gorge
grooved.. 5. fusee (fuzee)
part.. 4. arse
wheel.. 6. sheave (grooved)
pulp... 3. pap 4. marc, mash, mass
  5. chyme 8. magazine 10. fleshy
  part
pulpit... 4. ambo, bema, dais, desk
  5. stage 6. clergy 7. rostrum
  8. platform, scaffold

pulpy... 5. mushy 7. squashy
pulpy (pert to)...
dregs.. 5. magma
fruit.. 3. uva 4. pome 6. sidder
  (siddow)
state.. 4. mash, soft 6. fleshy
pulsate... 4. beat, drum 5. throb
  7. vibrate
pulsation... 5. ictus 6. moving, rhythm
  7. impulse, systole 8. acrotism
  (failure), vitality 9. throbbing, vibrating
pulsatory... 8. rhythmic, systolic
  9. throbbing
pulse... 3. dal (split) 5. seeds (edible),
  throb 6. rhythm 7. beating
  8. resonate 9. pulsation, throbbing
pulse family... 3. pea 8. Fabaceae
pulverize... 4. bray, mull 5. crush,
  grind 6. abrade, powder 7. atomize
  8. levigate 9. triturate
  12. disintegrate
pulverulent... 5. dusty 7. crumbly
  8. powdered
puma... 6. cougar 7. Quechua
  (Kochua)
pummel... 4. beat, maul 5. thump
  6. batter, buffet, hammer, pommel,
  strike
pump... 3. gin, ram 4. draw, emit,
  quiz 5. eject 6. elicit, propel
  7. extract 8. pulsometer
  11. interrogate
pumpernickel... 5. bread (Westphalian)
pump handle... 5. sweep, swipe
pumpkin (pert to)...
head.. 4. dolt 7. Puritan
  9. blockhead, Roundhead
seed.. 7. sunfish 8. sailboat
yam.. 11. sweet potato
pun... 4. yoke 8. paragram
  9. assonance, equivoque (equivoke),
  witticism 11. paronomasia
punch... 3. die 4. blow, poke, prod,
  tool 5. douse, drink, negus, paste
  6. liquor, pierce 7. mattoir (etcher's)
  8. beverage, puncture 9. perforate
  11. punch cattle
Punch and Judy dog... 4. Toby
Punch Bowl... 6. crater 9. graveyard
  (Honolulu), hot spring (Yellowstone)
puncheon... 3. die 4. cask 5. punch,
  stamp 6. dagger
puncher... 6. cowboy 10. cowpuncher,
  perforator
punching... 8. piercing 9. pertusion
punctilious... 4. nice 5. exact
  6. formal, strict 7. correct, precise
  8. exacting 9. observant
  10. meticulous, scrupulous
punctuation mark... 3. dot 4. dash,
  star 5. brace, breve, colon, comma,
  tilde 6. dagger, hyphen, period, tittle,
  umlaut 8. brackets, ellipsis
  9. ampersand, semicolon
  10. apostrophe, circumflex
  11. exclamation 12. question mark
pundit... 6. nestor, savant 7. Brahmin,
  scholar, teacher 10. learned man
pung... 4. sled 6. sleigh
pungent... 4. keen, racy, sour, tart
  5. acrid, acute, sharp, smart, snell
  6. biting, bitter 7. caustic, odorous,

painful, peppery, piquant 8. piercing,
poignant, stabbing 11. stimulating
pungent herb... 6. Asarum
punish... 4. fine 5. mulct, spank,
wreak 6. amerce 7. chasten, correct
8. chastise, penalize 9. castigate
10. discipline
punishment (pert to)...
Brehon law.. 4. eric
by torture.. 9. strappado
church.. 15. excommunication
condign.. 11. retributive
law.. 5. peine
term.. 5. penal 7. penalty, revenge
8. punitive
Turk, Chin.. 9. bastinade
Welsh law (anc).. 3. cro 7. galanas
punitive... 5. penal 10. revengeful,
vindictive 11. castigatory
Punjab, India...
capital.. 6. Lahore (West) 8. Amritsar
(East)
language.. 7. Panjabi
name meaning.. 10. Five Rivers
soldier.. 4. Sikh
summer capital.. 5. Simla
punk... 3. bad 5. child 6. amadou
7. lighter 8. inferior 9. touchwood
punto... 3. hit 5. joint (fencing)
6. stitch (needle)
puny... 4. weak 5. frail, petty 6. little,
meager, puisne, sickly 8. delicate
14. inconsiderable
pupa... 5. shell 9. chrysalis
pupil... 3. eye, son 4. tyro 5. élève,
youth 7. écolier, learner, scholar
8. disciple, neophyte
puppet... 3. guy 4. doll 5. image
6. maumet 9. miniature, nonentity
10. figurehead, marionette
puppeteer, famed... 4. Sarg
puppy... 3. dog, fop 5. shark, whelp
purblind... 10. dim-sighted 11. partly
blind 12. narrow-minded,
undiscerning
purchasable... 5. venal 8. bribable,
hireling 9. mercenary 11. corruptible
purchase... 3. buy, win 4. earn, hold
5. bribe 6. buying, obtain
7. acquire, bribery, procure
8. barratry, foothold, leverage
purchaser... 5. buyer 6. patron,
vendee 8. customer 9. acquéreur
13. adjudicataire
purdah (Ind)... 4. veil 6. screen
7. curtain
pure... 4. neat, real 5. clean, fresh,
godly, sheer, utter 6. candid, chaste,
simple, vestal 7. genuine, perfect,
refined, unmixed 8. absolute, filtered,
innocent 9. downright, faultless,
inviolate, stainless, undefiled, unsullied
11. pure-blooded, uncorrupted,
unqualified 13. unadulterated
purga (Russ)... 8. blizzard
9. snowstorm
purgative... 5. jalap 6. physic
8. absterge 9. catharsis, cathartic,
cleansing
purgatory... 4. hell 5. limbo 6. erebus
7. torment
purified... 10. elutriated

purified wool fat... 7. lanolin (lanoline)
purify... 5. clean, purge 6. filter,
refine, spurge 7. cleanse, epurate
8. lustrate, renovate, sanctify
9. elutriate
purifying... 7. smectic 8. depurant
9. cathartic, cleansing 10. distilling
Purim... 7. holiday 8. festival (Jew)
11. Feast of Lots
puritan... 5. prude 7. ascetic
9. precisian 10. Separatist
puritan clergyman... 10. Cartwright
puritanical... 6. strict 7. ascetic
11. strait-laced 13. hyperorthodox
purity... 8. chastity 9. innocence
purl... 4. eddy 5. frill 6. murmur,
ripple 7. trickle
purloin... 5. filch, steal, swipe
6. finger 11. appropriate
purple... 4. bice, lake, plum, puce
5. lilac, mauve, pansy, regal, showy
6. damson, orchid, ornate, Tyrian,
violet 7. Cassius, magenta, mollusk,
pigment 8. amaranth, Burgundy,
imperial, mulberry 9. brilliant,
cathedral 11. sovereignty
purple (pert to)...
bottle.. 4. moss
cactus.. 8. Missouri
death adder.. 10. black snake
emperor.. 9. butterfly
Forbidden City.. 5. Lhasa
granadilla.. 13. passion flower
haw.. 7. capulin (Mex) 8. bluewood
Heart, Order of.. 5. medal (Mil) (est
by Washington, re-est.1932)
laurel.. 12. rhododendron
lily.. 8. Turk's cap
martin.. 7. swallow
navy.. 10. marine blue
nightshade.. 9. trompillo
purport... 4. feck, gist, mean
5. sense, tenor 6. allege, import,
intent 7. meaning 9. substance
purpose... 3. aim, end 4. goal, idly,
main, plan, sake 5. avail 6. design,
intend, intent, motive 7. meaning,
resolve 8. function 9. determine,
discourse, intention, objective,
predesign
purposive... 5. telic
purse... 3. bag, cly 5. pouch
6. pucker, wallet 7. wrinkle
8. crumenal (obs) 10. pocketbook
12. porte-monnaie
purser... 5. clerk (ship's) 6. bursar
7. boucher, cashier 9. paymaster
purse rat... 12. pocket gopher
pursue... 3. run 4. hunt, seek, tack
5. chase, court 6. follow 7. carry
on, proceed 9. persecute
10. specialize
pursuit... 5. chase, quest, scent
9. objective 10. occupation
purvey... 5. cater 6. supply 7. foresee,
provide
purveyor of untruth (Bib)...
7. Ananias
purview... 4. body (statute) 5. field
(law), range, scope 7. compass
8. province
push... 2. go 4. bunt, butt, gang,

ping, pole, prod, urge 5. crowd, elbow, impel, nudge, press, shove 6. attack, energy, propel, thrust 9. importune, offensive (Mil) 10. forge ahead, propulsion 12. press forward

pusillanimous... 4. base, weak 5. timid 6. craven 8. cowardly 12. fainthearted, mean–spirited

put... 3. set 4. butt, dupe, fool, sail 5. place, throw 6. impose, option, phrase, repose, rustic 7. deposit 8. invest in 9. attribute

put (pert to)...
an end to.. 5. quash (law)
away.. 4. kill 5. store 6. murder
back.. 6. demote 7. replace, restore
before.. 6. appose
down.. 6. humble 7. degrade, deposit, depress 8. suppress
forth.. 5. exert 7. propose 9. circulate
off.. 4. doff, haft, sail 5. defer, delay, evade 8. postpone
on alert.. 5. alarm 6. alarum
out.. 3. vex 4. oust 5. eject 9. ostracize 10. expatriate
over.. 4. bilk 5. cheat, trick 7. deceive

put in, into...
action.. 6. excite
holy place.. 8. enshrine
motion.. 6. arouse
opposition.. 3. pit
order.. 4. trim 5. mense 6. settle 7. arrange 8. organize 11. systematize
rapture.. 8. entrance
relation to.. 9. correlate 10. coordinate, co–ordinate
rhythm.. 5. meter
scabbard.. 7. sheathe

putrefaction... 3. rot 5. decay 13. decomposition 14. disintegration

puttee... 6. gaiter 7. legging

put to...
flight.. 4. rout
strain.. 3. tax
trouble.. 10. discommode
use.. 5. apply
wrong use.. 8. misapply

put up... 3. pay 4. ante, hang 5. build, offer 6. pledge 7. install 8. nominate 9. construct

put up with... 4. bear 5. stand 6. endure, permit 7. stomach 8. tolerate

puzzle... 3. cap 4. crux, pose 5. griph (griphus), poser, rebus 6. enigma, riddle 7. anagram, confuse, mystify, nonplus, paradox, perplex, problem 8. entangle 9. conundrum 10. complicate, disconcert

puzzle (pert to)...
monkey.. 5. piñon
picture.. 5. rebus
word.. 7. charade 9. crossword 10. anacrostic

puzzling... 6. knotty 10. perplexing 11. enigmatical, paradoxical

pygarg, pygargus... 5. addax 8. sea eagle 9. quadruped (Bib)

Pygmalion (pert to)...

color.. 5. brown
endowed with life.. 7. Galatea (statue)
king of.. 6. Cyprus
sister.. 4. Dido
talented as.. 8. sculptor

pygmy, pigmy... 3. elf 4. Akka, Doko, pixy 5. atomy, Batwa, dwarf, gnome, minim, short 6. Abongo, Achuas 7. manikin 9. dandiprat

pygmy (pert to)...
hog.. 7. Porcula
musk deer.. 10. chevrotain
owl.. 8. gnome owl
rattlesnake.. 10. massasauga
squirrel (smallest known).. 9. Sciuridae

pyic... 8. purulent, virulent

pyknic... 3. fat 5. round, stout

pylon... 4. post 5. tower 6. marker 7. gateway 14. monumental mass

pyosis... 3. pus 4. boil 11. suppuration

pyramid... 4. cone, heap, pile, tomb 5. tower 8. monument 9. speculate

pyramid (pert to)...
builder, largest.. 6. Cheops (khufu)
Egypt.. 9. The Sphinx 12. Great Pyramid, Tomb of Cheops
group.. 5. Gizeh 7. Menkare 8. Chephren 9. Mycerinus
kidney (Anat).. 7. Perrein 10. Malpighian
Mexico.. 7. Benares
site of Cheops.. 4. Giza (Gizeh)
texts.. 12. inscriptions 13. Book of the Dead
world wonder.. 12. Great Pyramid, Tomb of Cheops

pyramidal... 4. huge 7. angular, conical 8. enormous, imposing

pyre... 4. bier, heap, pile 9. cremation, death fire

Pyrenees (pert to)...
bandit.. 8. Miquelet
mountain chain.. 11. France–Spain
peak.. 9. Pic d'Aneto 11. Pic de Méthou
resort.. 3. Pau
State.. 7. Andorra (Fr)

pyriform... 10. pear–shaped

pyrology (study of)... 4. heat

pyromaniac... 7. firebug 8. arsonist 10. incendiary

pyrope... 3. red 6. garnet 7. mineral

pyrophobia... 11. dread of fire

pyrotechnics... 7. oratory, science 9. fireworks

pyrrhic... 4. foot (Pros) 5. dance

Pyrrhic victory... 11. at great cost

pyrrho (comb form)... 3. red 5. tawny

Pyrrho (Gr)... 7. teacher (Pyrrhonism)

pyrrhotist... 7. redhead

Pyrrhulexia... 5. finch 8. grosbeak

Pythagorus (Gr)...
birthplace.. 5. Samos
daughter.. 4. Camo
famed as.. 11. philosopher
friend.. 5. Damon
teacher of.. 8. theorems 18. influence of numbers

Pythian (pert to)...
contests.. 6. Delphi
Festival.. 11. Panhellenic

patron.. 6. Apollo
term.. 8. ecstatic 9. phrenetic
python... 3. boa 8. anaconda
Python (pert to)...
  home.. 11. Mt Parnassus
  myth.. 14. monster serpent
  slaver.. 6. Apollo
  survivor of.. 10. muddy earth (anc)
pythonic... 4. huge 6. Pythia (Delphi),

python 8. oracular 9. monstrous
pythonism, art of... 8. prophecy
  10. divination
pyx, pix... 3. box 4. test, veil
  5. chest 6. coffer, vessel (Eccl)
  8. binnacle, ciborium 10. tabernacle
pyxie... 5. shrub 9. evergreen
pyxis... 3. box 4. Argo (Astron), vase
  9. jewel case

Q

Q... 5. queue 6. letter (17th)
QED... 21. Quod Erat Demonstrandum
Q–ship (Eng)... 11. mystery ship
qua, quabird... 10. night heron
quachil... 12. pocket gopher
quack... 3. cry (duck) 5. faker
  7. empiric 8. impostor 9. charlatan,
  pretender 10. medicaster,
  mountebank
quack medicine... 6. patent
  7. nostrum
quad (pert to)...
  printing.. 5. crown 7. quadrat
  school.. 4. yard 6. campus
  10. quadrangle
  slang (Brit).. 5. horse
quadra... 6. fillet, listel, plinth
quadragenarian... 12. forty–year–old
  (person)
Quadragesima... 4. Foot, Lent
  6. Sunday (1st in Lent) 7. Holy Day
  9. Forty Days
quadrangle... 5. plane (four–angles)
  6. square 7. rhombus 8. tetragon
quadrant... 4. gill 6. fourth
  7. measure, quarter 8. farthing, six
  hours 10. instrument, semicircle
quadrate... 4. suit 5. adapt, agree,
  ideal 6. square 7. conform, perfect,
  squared 8. balanced 10. correspond
  13. correspondent
quadriga... 3. car 7. chariot (4–horse)
  10. four horses
quadrumane... 3. ape 6. mammal
  7. gorilla, Primate (except Man)
  10. chimpanzee 13. feetlike hands
quadruped... 3. ass, cat, cow, dog
  4. bull, calf, colt, foal, lion, mule
  5. burro, horse, jenny, panda, tiger
  6. badger, donkey, mammal
  7. bullock 10. four–footed
quaff... 5. draft, drink 6. tipple
quag... 5. quake 6. quiver 8. quagmire
quagga... 5. zebra 7. wild ass
quaggy... 5. boggy, fenny 6. spongy
  7. queachy 8. yielding
quagmire... 3. bay, fen 4. lair
  5. marsh, swamp 6. morass
  11. predicament
quahog... 4. clam
quail... 3. cow 4. bird 5. colin, cower,

quake, shake 6. blench, curdle,
  flinch, shrink, tremor, Turnix
  7. massena, tremble 8. bobwhite,
  Coturnix 9. coagulate, courtesan,
  eddish hen
quail (pert to)...
  button.. 6. Turnix
  call.. 4. pipe
  color.. 9. hair brown
  flock.. 4. bevy
  French.. 6. caille
  hawk.. 6. falcon
  quailhead.. 11. lark sparrow
  snipe.. 9. dowitcher
quaint... 3. odd 4. wise 5. proud
  6. expert, pretty, proper 7. curious,
  prudent, refined, strange, uncouth
  8. fanciful, peculiar
quake... 5. shake 6. quiver, shiver,
  tremor 7. shudder, tremble, vibrate
  10. earthquake
Quaker (pert to)...
  bird.. 9. albatross (sooty)
  city.. 12. Philadelphia
  colonizer.. 4. Penn (Wm)
  color.. 4. drab, gray 5. acier
  poet.. 6. Barton 8. Whittier
  sect.. 16. Society of Friends
  sect founder.. 9. George Fox
  State.. 12. Pennsylvania
qualified... 3. fit 4. able 6. fitted
  7. adapted, capable, enabled, limited
  8. eligible, entitled, equipped,
  modified, prepared, tempered
  9. competent 10. restrained,
  restricted 11. conditional
qualify... 3. fit 4. name 5. abate,
  adapt, be fit, equip, limit, train
  6. enable, modify, soften, temper
  7. assuage, prepare 8. diminish,
  mitigate, modulate, quantify, regulate,
  restrain, restrict
quality... 5. prime, trait, value
  6. nature, pathos, strain 7. caliber,
  texture 8. accident, capacity, inferior,
  nobility, property 9. attribute,
  character, specialty 10. difference,
  excellence 11. characteristic
quality of heredity... 9. lineality
qualm... 4. pall 5. demur, doubt,
  spasm 6. nausea, regret 7. scruple

9. faintness, misgiving
11. compunction 12. apprehension
quandary... 3. fix 6. pickle, plight,
strait 7. dilemma 10. perplexity
11. predicament
quandy... 9. squaw duck
quant... 11. punting pole
quantity... 3. ace, any, gob, lot, sea,
sum 4. bulk, dose, drop, mass, much,
raff, raft, scad, size, some 5. batch,
scads, store 6. amount, cupful,
degree, extent, hatful, number, oceans
7. handful
quantity (pert to)...
fixed.. 5. quota 8. constant
mathematics.. 4. surd 5. graph
6. scalar, vector
minute.. 4. atom, dram, iota, mill
standard.. 4. unit 9. allotment
time unit.. 4. rate
quantum... 4. body 5. share
6. amount, energy, theory 7. atomics,
portion 8. quantity
quap... 5. heave, throb 6. quaver
9. palpitate
Quapaw... 5. Sioux 8. Arkansas
11. Indian tribe
quarantine... 7. confine, isolate
8. pratique (marine) 9. forty days
(law), isolation, segregate
11. confinement
quarantine flag... 6. yellow
7. warning 10. yellow jack
quarenden... 5. apple (deep red)
quarentene... 4. rood 7. furlong
quark... 3. caw 5. croak, quawk
quarl, quarle... 4. sour, tile 5. brick
6. cundle, medusa 9. jellyfish
quarred... 6. soured 7. curdled (beer)
quarrel... 3. row 4. spat, tiff, tile
5. arrow, brawl, broil, cavil, flite
(flyte), gnarr, scene, scrap 6. affray,
bicker, chisel, dustup, hassle
7. diamond, wrangle 8. argument,
squabble 9. complaint
10. accusation, Donnybrook,
free–for–all 11. altercation
12. disagreement
16. misunderstanding
quarrel (pert to)...
hereditary.. 4. feud 8. vendetta
noisy.. 6. fracas, jangle, uproar
over.. 6. bicker 7. contend, dispute
petty.. 4. miff, spat, tiff
quarrelsome... 8. choleric, petulant
9. irascible, irritable, litigious
10. discordant, pugnacious
11. belliferent, contentious
13. argumentative
quarry... 4. delf, game, heap, mine,
prey 6. victim 8. entrails, excavate
12. object hunted
quart... 5. gills (eight) 6. fourth
7. measure 8. schooner
quarter... 4. coin, side 5. house
6. fourth, region 7. measure, two bits
8. insignia, semester 9. direction,
dismember 10. quadrature (Astron),
quadrisect
quarter (pert to)...
acre.. 4. rood
animal.. 5. horse

astronomy.. 10. quadrature
fathom.. 6. fourth
military.. 8. clemency (to enemy)
music.. 4. note 8. crotchet
nautical.. 4. deck, lift 6. galley
pint.. 4. gill
sports.. 4. back 11. quarterback
quartered... 8. billeted
12. quartersawed (wood)
quarters (living)... 4. camp, room
5. abode 7. housing, lodging, shelter
8. barracks, diggings, lodgings,
lodgment 9. dormitory
Quartodeciman... 10. paschalist
quartz... 4. onyx, sard 5. flint 6. silica
7. mineral
quartz (pert to)...
banded, spotted.. 4. onyx 5. agate
6. jasper 8. sardonyx
blue–red.. 10. bloodstone, heliotrope
brown.. 5. smoky 9. cairngorm
brownish–red.. 7. sinople
chalcedony.. 4. sard 9. carnelian
11. chrysoprase
flint.. 9. hornstone 10. touchstone
glass.. 6. silica
green.. 5. prase (dull) 6. plasma
(bright) 11. chrysoprase
hard.. 5. flint
opaque.. 6. jasper
purple.. 8. amethyst
red.. 4. sard 9. carnelian
ruby–red.. 7. rubasse
silica.. 5. silex
transparent.. 11. rock crystal
violet.. 8. amethyst
yellow.. 5. topaz (false) 7. citrine
quash... 4. cass, void 5. abate, annul,
crush, quell, shake 6. hush up,
subdue 7. shatter 8. suppress
9. overthrow 10. extinguish
quasi... 4. as if 6. pseudo 8. as it
were, as though 9. seemingly
Quasimodo... 9. Low Sunday (1st
after Easter)
quatern... 8. fourfold 10. quadrangle
12. four quarters (having)
quaver... 5. shake, trill 6. quiver
7. tremble, tremolo, vibrate
11. trepidation 13. tremulousness
quawk... 3. caw 5. heron (night)
7. screech 8. quagmire
quay, key... 4. pier 5. levee, wharf
7. landing
queachy... 5. boggy, bushy, fenny
6. marshy, swampy
quean... 4. girl, jade, slut 5. vixen,
wench 6. harlot
queasy... 4. sick 8. delicate, qualmish,
ticklish, troubled 9. hazardous, ill at
ease, nauseated, squeamish, uncertain,
unsettled
Quebec...
battle site.. 15. Plains of Abraham
capital.. 6. Quebec (province)
city.. 6. Verdun 8. Montreal
11. Three Rivers
founder.. 9. Champlain (1608)
river.. 10. St Lawrence
vehicle.. 7. calèche (2–wheeled)
quebrada... 3. gap 5. brook, gorge
7. fissure

qued, quede ... 3. bad 4. evil 8. The Devil

queen ... 3. ant, bee, cat 7. empress, goddess, monarch 8. chessman, honeybee 9. sovereign 10. chess piece 11. playing card

queen (pert to) ...
- bee .. 8. honeybee
- cactus .. 7. Mexican 10. ornamental
- conch .. 5. shell
- fern .. 5. royal
- pigeon .. 7. crowned

Queen (pert to) ...
- Bernice's Hair (Astron) .. 13. Coma Berenices
- City of the Lakes .. 7. Buffalo
- City of the West .. 10. Cincinnati
- Mab .. 11. Fairie Queen (Rom/Juliet)
- Victoria .. 14. Widow of Windsor (nickname by Kipling)

Queen Anne's ...
- lace .. 6. carrot (wild)
- melon .. 6. dudaim
- War .. 17. Spanish Succession
- War treaty .. 14. Peace of Utrecht

queen of ...
- chess .. 4. fers
- fairies .. 3. Mab 7. Titania 8. Gloriana
- gods .. 4. Hera (Gr), Juno (Rom)
- Hearts .. 9. Elizabeth
- heaven .. 10. Virgin Mary
- Isles (Brit) .. 6. Albion
- night .. 4. moon
- Sheba .. 6. Balkis (Koran)
- Spades (solo) .. 5. basta
- the Adriatic .. 6. Venice
- the Antilles .. 4. Cuba
- the East .. 7. Antioch (Syria), Batavia (Java), Zenobia
- the tides .. 7. the moon
- the underworld .. 3. Hel

queen's (pert to)
- arm .. 6. musket
- flower .. 9. bloodwood
- hub .. 7. tobacco
- July flower .. 8. damewort
- ware .. 9. Wedgewood

Queensland (Austral) ...
- animal .. 8. kangaroo 9. koala bear (teddy bear)
- bean .. 8. snuffbox
- capital .. 8. Brisbane
- fire tree .. 5. tulip
- fish .. 9. trumpeter
- hemp .. 4. sida 6. lucern 9. jellyleaf 11. paddy lucern
- plum .. 8. Burdekin
- tree (timber) .. 3. box 4. pine 5. beech, ebony 10. sandalwood 12. Dundathu pine

queer ... 3. odd, rum 4. sham 5. false, funny 6. insane, thwart 7. strange 8. peculiar, singular, spurious 9. eccentric, fantastic, interfere 10. disconcert, suspicious 11. counterfeit 12. questionable

queer fellow ... 4. coot, goop 6. galoot, geezer 9. character

queersome ... 3. odd 7. strange 8. abnormal

Queer Street ... 9. imaginary

queest ... 8. ringdove

queet ... 4. coot 5. ankle

quell ... 3. end 4. calm 5. allay, crush, quash, quiet 6. pacify, reduce, soothe, stifle, subdue 7. destroy, repress 8. suppress 9. overpower 10. extinguish

quench ... 4. cool, damp, sate 5. allay, check, slake, still 6. stifle, subdue 7. assuage, gratify 8. suppress 10. discourage, extinguish 11. clamp down on

quenelle ... 8. meatball

Quercus ... 4. oaks

queriman ... 4. fish 6. mullet

quern ... 4. mill (grain)

quernal ... 5. crown (oak leaves)

querulous ... 7. fretful, peevish 9. plaintive 11. complaining 12. faultfinding

query ... 5. doubt 6. murmur 7. inquire, inquiry, whining 8. question

quest ... 3. bay (dog's) 4. hunt, seek 6. desire, pursue, search 7. inquest, request 8. seek alms 9. adventure 12. solicitation

question ... 3. ask 4. quiz 5. cavil, doubt, grill, poser, query, scout, topic 6. riddle 7. dispute, inquire, inquiry, problem 8. erotesis 9. catechize (catechise) 11. interrogate, uncertainty 12. interpellate (formally) 13. interrogation

question, out of the ... 6. absurd 7. refused 8. hopeless, rejected 10. impossible, prohibited 11. unthinkable

questionable ... 4. moot 7. dubious 8. doubtful 9. debatable, dishonest, uncertain 10. disputable, improbable 12. unbelievable 13. problematical

questioning (prolonged) ... 11. inquisition

question mark ... 7. erotema, eroteme

quet ... 3. auk 5. murre 9. guillemot

quethe ... 3. say 4. call, tell, will 5. quoth, speak 6. clamor 8. bequeath 9. testament

quetzal, quezal ... 6. trogon 14. national emblem (Guatemala)

Quetzalcoatl ... 10. god of winds (Aztec)

queue ... 3. cue 4. hair, line (waiting), tail 7. pigtail 9. lance rest

quey ... 6. heifer

quia–quia ... 9. cigarfish

quib, quibble ... 3. pun 4. carp, quip 5. argue, cavil, cheta, evade 7. shuffle

Quiche, Indian ... 5. Mayan

quick ... 3. apt 4. deft, fast, yare 5. agile, alert, brisk, fiery, fleet, hasty, rapid, ready, smart, swift 6. lively, nimble, presto, prompt, pronto, speedy, sudden 7. animate 9. dexterous, impatient, impulsive, sprightly, vital part 10. passionate 11. expeditious, hot-tempered

quicken ... 5. hurry, rouse, speed 6. excite, hasten, incite, revive, vivify 7. animate, further, refresh, sharpen

8. energize, expedite 9. stimulate 10. accelerate 11. resuscitate 12. reinvigorate

quickly... 4. cito, fast, soon 5. apace 6. presto, pronto 7. briefly, hastily, rapidly 8. promptly, speedily, vigorous

quickness... 4. nous (humor) 5. haste 6. acumen 7. acidity, agility 8. alacrity, celerity, dispatch, pungency, rapidity 9. acuteness, briskness, fleetness, sharpness, smartness 10. expedition, promptness 13. impulsiveness

quicksand... 3. bog 4. syrt 6. Syrtis

quickset... 5. hedge 7. thicket 8. hawthorn

quicksilver... 5. metal 7. mercury

quid... 3. cud, fid 6. guinea 7. essence, tobacco 9. sovereign

quidam... 8. somebody 10. one unknown

quidnunc... 6. gossip 7. what now 11. inquisitive

quid pro quo... 9. tit for tat 10. equivalent, substitute 11. interchange

quiescent... 5. quiet, still 6. at rest, latent, silent, static 8. sleeping 10. motionless

quiet... 2. sh 3. pet 4. calm, ease, hush, lull, mild 5. peace, sober, still 6. gentle, hushed, modest, placid, smooth, soothe 7. halcyon, restful, silence 8. peaceful, tranquil 9. contented, peaceable, quiescent, reposeful, unruffled 10. unmolested 11. undisturbed

quietist... 6. mystic (Quietism)

quietive... 8. sedative

quietly... 6. calmly, gently, simply 8. modestly, silently 9. patiently, peaceably, privately 10. composedly 11. noiselessly 16. unostentatiously

quietude... 4. rest 5. peace 6. repose 7. silence 10. quiescence 12. tranquillity (tranquility)

quietus... 4. mort, obit 5. death 6. defeat 7. release 9. acquittal, deathblow, discharge (of debt)

quiff... 4. coif, puff 5. whiff

quilkin... 4. frog, toad

quill... 3. cop, pen 5. remex 6. bobbin 7. spindle

quilt... 3. pad 4. flog, gulp 5. duvet 6. caddow 7. swallow 8. coverlet 9. patchwork 11. comfortable, counterpane

quin... 7. scallop

quincentenary... 11. anniversary 13. commemoration 16. five hundred years

quindecemvir (Rom)... 10. custodians (Sibylline Books), fifteen men

quink... 5. brant, goose

quinoa... 6. cereal 7. pigweed

Quinquagesima Sunday... 10. before Lent 12. Shrove Sunday

quinque (comb form)... 4. five

quinsy... 10. sore throat 11. tonsillitis

quint... 3. tax (one 5th) 7. E string 8. interval, schooner (5–masted) 9. organ stop

quintal... 13. hundredweight

quintessence... 3. col 5. elite 6. elixir 7. essence, the best 10. perfection

quip... 3. mot 4. gibe, jest 5. sally, taunt 6. oddity 7. caprice, quibble 8. gimcrack 9. witticism 12. equivocation

quires, twenty... 4. ream 6. sheets (20)

quirk... 4. quip, turn 5. clock, shift, twist 7. caprice, evasion, quibble 8. flourish 9. deviation, mannerism, witticism 12. eccentricity

quirt... 4. whip 5. romal

quis... 8. woodcock

quisby... 5. idler, queer 8. bankrupt 10. down and out

quit... 3. rid 4. free, stop 5. cease, clear, leave, pay up, repay, yield 6. depart, resign 7. abandon, discard, forsake, release, relieve, requite 8. abdicate, liberate, renounce 9. surrender 10. relinquish 11. discontinue

quitclaim... 6. acquit 7. release 12. convey a claim 13. deed of release 14. relinquishment

quite... 3. all, yes 4. very 5. stark, truly 6. really, wholly 7. totally 8. entirely, somewhat 10. absolutely, completely, positively

quite so... 8. that is so, very true, very well

quite some... 12. considerable

quittance... 5. repay 6. return 7. requite 8. reprisal, requital 9. atonement, departure, repayment 10. recompense 11. acquittance

quitter... 5. piker 6. coward, truant 7. shirker, welsher

quiver... 4. case 5. quake, shake 6. quaver, sheath, shiver, tremor 7. flicker, tremble, tremolo, vibrate 11. trepidation

quiver leaf... 5. aspen

Quivira (pert to)...
famous for.. 6. wealth
sought by.. 6. Coronado (1541)
town site.. 6. Kansas

Quivira, Gran... 12. mission ruins 16. National Monument (N Mex)

qui vive... 5. alert 7. excited 9. challenge 12. who goes there

quixotic... 7. utopian 9. visionary 10. Don Quixote (like) 11. impractical

quiz... 4. hoax, jest, joke, mock 5. coach 6. banter 8. ridicule 11. examination, inquisitive, interrogate, questioning

quizzical... 3. odd 7. amusing, teasing 9. bantering, eccentric, inquiring, perplexed

quizzing... 6. banter 11. questioning

quizzing glass... 7. monocle 8. eyeglass

quod... 3. jug 6. prison 8. imprison

quoddies... 7. herring

quod erat demonstrandum... 3. QED 24. which was to be demonstrated

quodlibet... 6. medley 8. fantasia, subtlety 13. what you please

quoit... 4. disc 6. discus
quoit pin... 3. hob
quoits... 4. game 8. cromlech
   10. stone cover
quo modo... 5. means 6. manner,
   method
quondam... 6. former 8. formerly,
   sometime
quorum... 7. council 8. majority
   10. select body
quota... 4. part 5. share 6. ration
   10. proportion
quotable... 7. citable
quotation... 5. chria, cital, motto,
   price, stock 7. passage 8. citation

   10. memorandum, repetition
quotation mark... 9. guillemet
quote... 4. cite, name 5. price
   6. adduce, repeat 7. extract
   9. quotation, reference
quoth... 4. said 5. spoke
quotha... 6. indeed 8. forsooth
quotidian... 5. daily 8. day by day,
   every day, ordinary 9. recurring
   11. commonplace
quotient... 6. number, result
quotity... 5. group, quota 7. integer
   10. collection
quotum... 5. quota, ratio
quo vadis... 16. whither goest thou
Quo Vadis tyrant... 4. Nero

R

R... 3. rho (Gr) 6. letter (18th)
Ra, Egypt Relig (pert to)...
   atmosphere.. 3. Shu
   god of.. 3. sun
   morning sun.. 7. Chepera, Khepera
   night sun.. 7. Sokaris
   representation.. 3. cat 4. lion
      5. Bacis (bull) 6. falcon 9. solar disk
   rising sun.. 5. Horus 9. Marmachis
   setting sun.. 3. Tem
   solar disk.. 4. Aten
   son.. 6. Khonsu
   son of.. 3. Nut (the sky)
   wife.. 3. Mut
raad... 15. electric catfish
raad... 7. council (S Afr) 9. volksraad
raadzaal... 11. council hall (S Afr)
rab... 5. mixer (mortar) 6. beater
Rab... 5. title 6. master, rabban
   7. teacher 8. Gamaliel
rabato, rebato... 4. ruff 6. collar
   9. piccadill
rabbet... 4. weld 5. miter 6. groove,
   recess 7. channel 8. dovetail
rabbi... 4. lord 5. rabat, title
   6. master 7. teacher 9. clergyman
   11. breastpiece
rabbi (pert to)...
   examiners.. 8. sabaraim (saboraim)
   interpreters.. 7. amoraim
   teachers.. 7. tannaim
rabbit... 4. cony (coney), hare, tyro
   5. bunny, lapin 6. animal, novice,
   rodent 10. cottontail 11. Belgian
   hare
rabbit (pert to)...
   breeding ground.. 6. warren
      8. rabbitry
   ear.. 7. antenna 8. toadflax
   female.. 3. doe
   fever.. 9. tularemia
   fiction.. 6. Harvey
   fish.. 8. chimaera 9. globefish,
      porcupine

   foot.. 5. charm 8. talisman
   fur.. 4. cony (coney) 5. lapin
   genus.. 5. Lepus
   male.. 4. buck
   mouthed.. 10. harelipped
   rat.. 9. bandicoot
   S America.. 6. tapeti
   shelter.. 5. hutch
   stew.. 12. hasenpfeffer
   tail.. 3. fud 4. scut
rabbitry... 5. hutch 6. warren
rabble... 3. mob 4. herd, raff, rout,
   skim, stir 5. crowd 6. ragtag, tumult
   7. bobtail 8. canaille, riffraff
   9. confusion, rigmarole, the masses
   12. accumulation (chaotic)
rabble rouser... 6. ragtag
Rabelais (Fr)... 6. author 8. satirist
   9. Gargantua (1st work)
rabid... 3. mad 6. raging 7. frantic,
   furious, rampant, violent 8. frenzied
   9. fanatical 10. infuriated
rabies... 5. lyssa 11. hydrophobia
raccoon, ally of... 5. coati, panda
race... 3. cut, hie, run 4. flow, lane,
   line, rush, slit, sort, stem 5. breed,
   caste, flume, relay, speed 6. course,
   family, nation, people, strain
   7. contest, regatta, running, scratch
   10. passageway 11. competition,
   watercourse
race (pert to ethnos)...
   ancient.. 4. Mede 6. Belgae, Sabine
      7. Hittite, Iberian, Walloon
   comb form.. 4. geno
   family.. 3. ilk 6. stirpo
   human.. 3. Man
   mythical.. 7. centaur
   prehistoric.. 5. Aryan, Brunn
   rule by.. 10. ethnocracy
   science of.. 9. ethnology
   undivided.. 9. holethnos
   wandering.. 5. gypsy (gipsy)
race (pert to horses)...

chariot .. 13. Circus Maximus
gait .. 4. lope, pace, trot
horse .. 4. pony 5. racer 6. maiden,
  mantis, plater 8. bangtail
handicap .. 6. impost
open .. 10. Donnybrook, free–for–all
racecourse, racetrack (pert to) . . .
  3. lap 4. heat, oval, tout, turf
  5. track 6. circus (anc), colors
  7. raceway, tipster 8. dopester
Rachel (pert to) . . .
  daughter of .. 5. Laban
  mother of .. 6. Joseph 8. Benjamin
  sister of .. 4. Leah
  wife of .. 5. Jacob
racing colors . . . 5. silks
rack . . . 3. gin 4. gait, gear, pain, ruin
  5. agony, frame 6. punish, strain,
  wrench 7. agonize, support, torment,
  torture 9. framework 10. excruciate
rack (pert to) . . .
  barrel .. 3. job
  comb .. 9. toothcomb
  corn .. 4. crib
  floating .. 5. vapor
  plate .. 5. creel
  skin of .. 6. rabbit
racket . . . 3. bat, din 5. fraud, noise,
  revel 6. bustle, clamor, crosse, outcry,
  scheme 8. vocation 9. commotion
  15. illicit business
rackety . . . 5. noisy 8. clattery, exciting
  9. turbulent 10. boisterous
racy . . . 5. brisk, fresh, naive, smart,
  spicy 6. lively, risqué 7. piquant,
  pungent, zestful 8. eloquent,
  spirited, stirring 11. interesting
  12. exhilarating, full–flavored
rad . . . 4. unit 5. eager, quick, ready
  6. afraid, elated 11. exhilarated
radar (pert to) . . .
  beacon .. 4. buoy 5. racon 6. ramark
  navigation .. 5. navar
  range (Navig) .. 5. loran 6. shoran
  sight .. 5. scope 6. radome, screen
  7. display
  signal .. 3. pip 4. beam, blip 5. pulse
  11. transceiver, transponder
  sounding .. 5. rawin 9. ionosonde
  television .. 7. teleran
raddle . . . 3. rod 4. beat, twig
  5. cheat, color, fence, hedge
  6. branch, hurdle, ruddle, thrash
  7. wheedle 10. interweave
radeau . . . 4. raft 5. gloat
radial . . . 3. ray 8. quadrant
  9. diverging
radiance . . . 5. beamy, glare, light, nitor,
  sheen 6. beauty, luster 7. beaming,
  glitter, glowing, lambent, shining
  8. splendor 9. brilliant, radiation
  10. brilliancy, effulgence
  12. cheerfulness
radiant . . . 5. aglow, beamy, sheen
  7. beaming, glowing, lambent, shining
  8. glorious 9. beautiful, diverging,
  effulgent 11. resplendent
radiate . . . 4. beam, emit, shed
  5. gleam, shine 7. diffuse, diverge,
  emanate 9. irradiate 10. illuminate
radiation . . . 5. alpha (particle), light,

polar (point) 10. divergence
  12. illumination 13. radiant energy
radiation unit . . . 3. rad, rem
  8. roentgen
radical . . . 3. red 4. atom, left, root,
  surd 5. basic, radix, ultra, vital
  7. capital, drastic, extreme
  8. cardinal, reformer 9. extremist
  10. foundation 11. fundamental
radicated . . . 6. rooted 11. established
radicle . . . 4. root 5. radix 6. etymon
  7. rootlet
radio (pert to) . . .
  activity .. 7. fallout 9. radiation
  antenna .. 6. aerial
  detector .. 5. radar 11. transceiver
  frequency .. 5. audio
  interference .. 6. static
  operator .. 2. CB 3. ham (amateur)
  11. dit–da–artist 12. citizens' band
  rays .. 5. beams
  receiver, interfering .. 7. blooper
  tube .. 4. grid 5. diode
radium (pert to) . . .
  discoverer .. 5. Curie (1898)
  emanation .. 5. niton, radon
  paint .. 8. luminous
  source of .. 7. uranite 9. carnotite
radius . . . 4. area, bone 5. spoke
  6. circle, extent 8. diameter
radix . . . 4. root 6. etymon, source
  7. radical, radicle
raff . . . 4. heap, rake, scum 5. sweep,
  trash 6. jumble, litter 7. rubbish
  8. leavings, riffraff
raffia . . . 4. palm 5. fiber 6. jupati
raffish . . . 3. low 6. common, flashy,
  frowsy 7. unkempt 9. worthless
  12. disreputable
raffle . . . 6. chance, rabble, tangle
  7. confuse, crumple, lottery, perplex,
  serrate 8. entangle, plucking, riffraff
  9. stripping 10. plundering
raft . . . 3. lot 4. spar 5. balsa, float
  6. rafter 7. to flock 10. collection
  (large)
raft–breasted (Ornith) . . . 6. ratite
raft duck . . . 5. scoup 7. redhead
  8. bluebill
rag . . . 3. fog 4. mist, sail 5. cloth,
  scold, shred 6. berate, catkin, lichen,
  tatter 7. ragtime, remnant 8. farthing
  9. hoarfrost 11. syncopation
rag (pert to) . . .
  bag .. 10. depository
  doll .. 3. toy 6. moppet, puppet
  10. marionette
  fish .. 10. Icosteidae
  rag picker .. 5. tramp
  weed .. 3. Iva
  wool .. 5. mungo 6. shoddy
ragamuffin . . . 8. titmouse 9. ragged
  boy 14. tatterdemalion
rage . . . 3. fad 4. fume, fury, gret,
  ramp, rant, tear 5. anger, chafe,
  craze, furor (furore), storm, wrath
  6. fervor, frenzy 7. bluster, passion
  8. violence 9. vehemence
  10. excitement
ragged . . . 5. harsh, rough 6. jagged,
  raguly (Her), scoury, shabby, uneven

7. shreddy 9. defective, dissonant, irregular 10. straggling
11. dilapidated

raging... 4. grim 5. rabid 7. acharne
8. storming 9. ferocious, turbulent
10. blustering, infuriated
11. overwrought

raglan... 8. overcoat 11. sleeve style

Ragnarok, Norse (pert to)...
  leader.. 4. Loki
  meaning.. 16. world destruction
  repeopler of the world.. 3. Lif
    10. Lifthrasir

ragout... 4. beef 5. civet, salmi
6. mutton 7. goulash, haricot

rahdar... 14. tollroad keeper

raid... 4. tata 5. foray, seize 6. inroad
8. invasion 9. incursion

rail... 3. bar, jaw 4. coot, jest, rant,
sora 5. cloak, crake, dress, scoff,
scold 6. banter, revile, septum (altar)
7. courlan, garment, inveigh, limpkin,
ortolan 8. reproach

railbird... 4. bird, weka 5. crake
7. clocker, wood hen 9. spectator
12. horse watcher

railing... 5. fence, rails 7. barrier,
parapet 10. balustrade

raillery... 5. chaff, sport 6. banter
7. asteism (Rhet) 8. badinage,
ridicule 10. persiflage

railroad (pert to)...
  flare.. 5. fusee
  signal.. 9. semaphore
  sleeper.. 3. tie 7. pullman
  switch.. 4. frog
  torpedo.. 9. detonator
  worker.. 6. dinger 8. strapper
    11. gandy dancer

Rail Splitter... 14. Abraham Lincoln

raiment... 4. garb 5. amice, dress
7. apparel, clothes, vesture
8. clothing, garments

rain (pert to)...
  cloud.. 6. nimbus
  coat.. 4. mino 6. poncho 7. slicker
  comb form.. 5. hyeto, ombro
    6. pluvio
  fine.. 4. mist 6. serein
  fowl.. 6. cuckoo 10. woodpecker
    11. channelbill
  gauge.. 8. udometer 10. hyetometer
  glass.. 9. barometer
  icy.. 4. hail 5. sleet
  protection.. 9. ombrifuge
  short.. 6. shower
  storm.. 5. spate 13. precipitation
  study.. 9. hyetology, ombrology
  sudden.. 5. plash, spate 6. deluge
    7. torrent 8. downpour

rainbow... 3. arc 4. arch, iris, omen

rainbow (pert to)...
  bridge (Norse Myth).. 7. Bifrost (to
    Asgarth)
  chaser.. 9. visionary 11. doctrinaire
  flower.. 4. iris
  goddess.. 4. Iris
  term.. 6. iridal
  tree.. 5. saman 8. genisaro
  unit.. 4. inch
  worm.. 8. nematode 9. earthworm

rainy... 3. wet 7. showery

rais, reis (Moslem)... 5. chief, title
7. captain (ship's)

Rais... 10. Mongoloids

raise... 3. end 4. grow, levy, lift, rear,
stir 5. boost, breed, erect, exalt,
heave, hoist, rouse 6. awaken,
excite, gather, leaven, muster,
remove, uplift 7. collect, elevate,
enhance, lighten, present, produce,
provoke, recruit 8. heighten, increase
9. construct, cultivate, promotion,
propagate 10. aggrandize

raise (pert to)...
  a nap.. 5. tease 6. teasel
  Cain.. 3. Ned 4. hell 5. cut up 7. be
    noisy 10. vociferate
  the dead.. 13. lift the anchor
  vegetables.. 12. olericulture

raised... 4. bred, hove 6. buoyed,
enlève, hefted, lifted, reared
7. hoisted 8. elevated, leavened,
produced, promoted

raised (pert to)...
  spirits.. 6. elated
  to 3rd power.. 5. cubed
  troops.. 6. levied 7. drafted
    11. conscripted
  type.. 7. braille
  uproar.. 6. rioted
  with a bar.. 7. levered

raisin... 4. pasa 5. grape, lexia

raja, rajah... 4. king, rana 5. title
6. prince 9. dignitary

raja's consort... 4. rani (ranee)
8. princess

Rajmahal hemp... 5. fiber 9. jiti fiber

Rajput... 5. caste 9. Kshatrya

rake... 3. rut 4. comb, path, raff, roué
5. slope, teeth, track 6. lecher
7. debauch, seducer 8. enfilado,
Lothario 9. cultivate, implement,
libertine

rakehell... 4. free, rake 9. debauched,
debauchee, dissolute 10. dissipated,
licentious, profligate

rakh... 3. hay 8. hayfield 9. grassland

raki, rakee... 7. spirits (distilled)

rale... 6. rattle 8. rhonchus
11. morbid sound

rallentando... 9. direction (Mus)
10. ritardando, slackening

Rallidae... 5. birds, coots, rails, wekas
6. crakes 10. gallinules

rally... 6. banter 7. recover, reunite
8. assemble, recovery, ridicule
10. assemblage, call to arms

rallying cry... 4. call 6. slogan
9. battle cry, bugle call

ralph... 5. raven

ram... 3. hit, pun, tup 4. buck, butt,
tamp 5. Aries, crash, sheep
6. rancid, wether 7. collide

Rama... 11. Ramachandra (7th of
fame) 19. incarnation of Vishnu

ramada... 5. arbor 7. pergola

Ramadan (Moham)... 7. fasting
10. ninth month (for fasting)

ramage... 4. wild 5. rough 6. branch
(tree), unruly 7. untamed 8. frenzied

ramage hawk... 8. brancher

ramass... 6. gather 7. collect

ramberge... 6. galley (swift)

ramble... 3. gad 4. roam, rove, walk
5. jaunt, prowl, range 6. stroll,
wander 7. deviate, digress, saunter
8. straggle
rambling... 7. devious 9. desultory,
deviation, deviative, wandering
10. circuitous, discursive, distracted
14. discursiveness
rambunctious... 4. wild 6. unruly
10. rampageous 12. obstreperous
14. uncontrollable
ramentum... 5. palea (palet) 6. scales
8. a shaving, particle (minute)
Rameses Dynasties (pert to)...
famed for.. 5. ruins 7. papyrus
kings.. 6. twelve
site.. 5. Egypt
ramex... 6. hernia 10. varicocele
ram–headed goat... 5. Ammon
ramie... 4. hemp, rhea 5. plant (fiber)
7. garment 9. Boehmeria 10. China
grass
ramification... 3. arm 5. ramus
6. branch 8. offshoot 9. branching
10. divergence 12. embranchment
rammack... 4. gawk, romp 5. scamp
rammel... 4. hard 6. coarse 7. new
milk, raw milk 9. brushwood
11. undergrowth
Ramona (pert to)...
heroine.. 9. half–breed (Ind)
novel by.. 7. Jackson (Helen Hunt)
shrub.. 4. mint
ramp... 3. rob 4. rage, romp, walk
5. bound, climb, crawl, creep, storm
6. dupery, unruly 7. incline,
rampage, swindle 8. gradient,
platform 9. helicline, impetuous
10. cuckoopint
rampant... 6. fierce, unruly, vallum
(anc) 7. ramping 8. abundant, reared
up (Her) 9. exuberant, prevalent,
unchecked 10. rampageous
12. high–spirited, unrestrained
13. perpendicular
rampart... 4. wall 5. agger, mound,
redan 6. escarp 7. barrier, bulwark,
defense, parapet, ravelin 8. buttress
9. earthwork 10. embankment
13. fortification
ram's horn (Heb)... 7. shophar (shofar)
ran... 4. fled, sped 6. flowed
7. coursed, managed, trotted
8. operated
ran (pert to)...
aground.. 8. decamped, levanted,
stranded
away.. 4. fled 6. eloped
9. absconded
out.. 5. spilt 7. petered, spilled
rana (Ind)... 5. title 6. prince
Rana... 5. frogs 10. amphibians
(tailless)
ranarium... 8. frog pond
rance... 4. prop 6. marble 7. support
ranch... 4. casa, farm 6. estate
8. estancia, hacienda
ranchero... 6. cowman 7. vaquero
8. herdsman 9. cattleman
rancid... 4. rank 5. musty, stale
6. reechy 9. obnoxious, offensive

10. unpleasant
rancor, rancour... 3. ire 4. gall
5. spite 6. enmity, hatred, malice,
rankle 7. ill will 9. animosity
10. resentment
rand... 4. edge, rant 5. ridge, storm
6. border, margin
random... 5. stray 6. casual, chance
7. aimless 8. casually 9. at liberty,
haphazard, orderless 10. accidental,
fortuitous 11. haphazardly
randy... 4. wild 5. revel, spree
6. beggar, coarse, frolic, virago
7. canvass 8. carousal 9. festivity
10. disorderly 11. ill–mannered
12. unmanageable
rang (pert to)... see also *ring*
loudly.. 7. clanged
mournfully.. 6. tolled 7. knelled
slowly.. 6. tolled
range... 3. row 4. ally, area, line,
rank, roam, size 5. align, gamut,
orbit, scope 6. limits, ramble, region,
series, wander 7. arrange, compass,
earshot, habitat, pasture 8. classify,
mountain 9. cookstove
range (pert to)...
finder.. 9. mekometer, telemeter
10. trekometer
man.. 5. rider 6. warden
of hills.. 5. ridge
of knowledge.. 3. ken
of stables.. 4. mews
rangle... 5. stray 6. wander
8. entangle, straggle
rani, ranee (Hind)... 4. wife 5. queen
7. empress 8. princess
rani (Romany)... 4. lady, wife
Ranier, Mt... 10. Washington (State)
ranine... 5. frogs 7. Raninae 8. mink
frog
rank... 3. bad, row 4. file, foul, line,
rate, size, tier 5. caste, class, grade,
gross, order, range 6. degree,
estate, rancid, status, wicked
7. arrange, glaring, tainted
8. absolute, abundant, classify,
eminence, flagrant, indecent,
infamous, nobility, palpable, position,
prestige, unsavory 9. downright,
formation, luxuriant, plentiful
10. malodorous 11. distinction
rank (pert to)...
and file.. 4. army 8. regulars
10. commonalty 11. third estate
celestial.. 9. hierarchy
exalted.. 8. eminence
military (old).. 8. banneret
noble.. 10. patriciate
rider.. 8. reckless 10. highwayman
social.. 5. caste
rankle... 5. chafe 6. fester 7. putrefy
8. make sore 9. suppurate 10. be
inflamed
rann... 5. verse 6. stanza, strain
ransack... 4. rake, sack 5. rifle
6. search 7. plunder, rummage
ransom... 4. fine 6. redeem, rescue
7. expiate 8. recovery
ranstead... 8. toadflax (yellow)
13. butter–and–eggs
rant... 4. rage, rail, rave 5. boast

6. steven 7. bluster, bombast,
declaim 9. gay frolic 10. get excited
rantipole ... 4. wild 6. rakish, unruly
9. termagant
ranula ... 4. cyst
Ranunculaceae ... 7. anemone
8. aconitum, clematis, crowfoot
10. delphinium, ranunculus
rap ... 3. bop, hit 4. bang, blow, gibe,
grab, knap, tirl 5. knock, steal
6. rascal, snatch, trifle 8. betrayal,
sentence (prison) 9. criticism,
reprimand 10. punishment 11. skein
of yarn
rapacious ... 6. greedy, rapine
8. grasping, ravenous 9. devouring,
voracious 10. avaricious, predacious
rapacity ... 5. greed, ravin (raven)
6. rapine 8. appetite 9. predacity
rapid ... 4. fast 5. fleet, quick, swift
7. stretto (stretta)
rapidity ... 5. haste, speed 8. celerity,
velocity 9. fleetness, quickness
rapidly   5. amain, apace 7. quickly,
swiftly 8. snappily
rapids ... 5. rifts 6. dalles
rapier ... 5. bilbo, sword 6. verdun
7. ricasso (part)
rapine ... 7. pillage, plunder 8. spoiling
10. ravishment, spoliation
rapport ... 6. accord 7. empathy,
harmony 8. relation 9. agreement
11. co–operation (hypnotism)
rapt ... 8. absorbed, ecstatic
10. enraptured, interested
11. preoccupied, transported
rapture ... 3. joy 4. love 5. bliss
6. trance 7. delight, ecstasy
8. rhapsody 9. transport
10. exultation
rapturous ... 8. ecstatic
rare ... 3. odd, raw 4. thin 6. scarce,
seldom, sparse 7. notable, unusual
8. rarefied, uncommon 10. infrequent
11. undercooked
rare (pert to) ...
  bird .. 8. rara avis
  earth .. 6. cerium 7. terbium, yttrium
  metallic element .. 7. yttrium
  object .. 5. curio 6. oddity 7. antique
Rare Ben, inscription ... 15. tomb of
Ben Jonson (Westminster Abbey)
rarebit ... 10. cheese dish 11. Welsh
rabbit
rarefy ... 4. thin 6. dilute, expand
9. attenuate
rarely ... 6. finely, seldom 8. not often,
scarcely 9. extremely, unusually
11. beautifully 12. infrequently
rarity ... 6. oddity 7. fewness, tenuity
8. scarcity, thinness 11. infrequency
ras ... 4. cape 6. prince
11. ·short–napped 13. Fascist leader
rasa ... 3. sap (tree) 5. fluid, taste
6. amrita, flavor 7. essence
11. living water
rascal ... 3. cad, imp 5. knave, rogue,
scamp 6. varlet 7. miscreant
rascally ... 4. mean 6. impish
7. knavish, roguish 8. scampish
11. mischievous
rase ... 3. cut, rub 4. tear 5. graze,

level 6. scrape 7. scratch
rash ... 3. mad 4. wild 5. giddy, hasty,
heady, hives, scamp 6. unwary,
wanton 7. Icarian 8. careless,
eruption, heedless 9. desperate,
exanthema, impetuous
10. headstrong, incautious, indiscreet
11. temerarious, thoughtless
rasher ... 5. piece, slice 7. portion
9. thin slice
rashness ... 6. acrisy 7. acrisia
8. temerity 9. hastiness
rasion ... 6. filing 7. erasing, rasping,
shaving 8. scraping
Rasores ... 4. fowl 5. birds 6. quails
7. turkeys 8. Columbae, Gallinae
9. pheasants 10. partridges
rasp ... 3. rub 4. file 5. belch, chafe,
erupt, grate 6. abrade, offend,
scrape 8. irritate 9. raspberry
raspberry ... 3. red 5. apple, Rubus
6. raspis 7. plumbog 8. blackcap
rasping ... 5. harsh 7. chafing, grating,
raucous 8. grinding, scraping, very
fast 9. offensive 10. irritating
raspings ... 6. refuse 7. filings, remains
rasse ... 5. civet
rasure ... 3. cut 5. shave 7. erasure,
polling, scratch, tonsure 8. scraping
12. obliteration
rat ... 3. rut 4. scab, snob, wart
5. track 6. desert, ratton, rodent
7. scratch, traitor 8. deserter
9. hairpiece, scoundrel
rat (pert to) ...
  fish .. 8. chimaera
  goose .. 11. common brant
  hare .. 4. pika
  kangaroo .. 7. Potorus 9. marsupial
  pineapple .. 7. pinguin
  poison .. 8. ratsbane
  ratlike .. 4. vole
  rhyme .. 6. jargon 13. doggerel verse
ratafia ... 7. biscuit (almond), curacao,
liqueur (Danzig)
ratchet ... 4. pawl 5. click 6. bobbin,
detent
rate ... 4. fare, pace 5. price, ratio,
style, tempo, value 6. assess, berate,
charge, reckon, regard 7. account,
deserve, premium, reprove
8. appraise, classify, estimate,
evaluate, interest
rate (of exchange) ... 4. agio 5. batta
rath (anc) ... 4. hill, home (walled)
rath, ratha ... 3. car 6. temple (Seven
Pagodas, Madras) 7. chariot
Rathaus ... 8. town hall
rathe, rath ... 4. soon 5. eager, quick,
speed 7. betimes, quickly 8. speedily
rather ... 3. ere, yes 6. before
7. earlier, however, instead
8. somewhat 9. more truly, tolerably
10. especially, preferably
11. immediately 14. on the other
hand
ratification ... 4. amen 5. logic
8. sanction 9. reasoning
11. endorsement 12. confirmation
ratify ... 4. amen, pass, seal 6. enseal,
verify 7. approve, confirm, consent,
endorse 8. roborate, sanction

9. authorize

ratio... 2. pi 4. rate, sine 5. share
6. cosine, ration 7. portion
10. proportion

ratiocination... 5. logic 7. thought
9. reasoning

ration... 5. share 6. budget 8. relation
9. allotment, allowance, provision
11. calculation

rational... 4. sane, wise 5. sober
7. logical 8. sensible 9. reasoning
10. reasonable 11. philosophic

rationale... 6. reason 11. explanation
12. the how and why

ratio scripta... 13. written reason

ratite... (opp of carinate) 7. Ratitae
8. unkeeled 14. flat breastbone

ratite bird... 3. emu (emeu), moa
7. ostrich 9. cassowary

ratoon... 5. shoot, stalk 6. spring,
sprout

rattan, ratan... 4. cane, palm, sega,
whip 6. switch 7. calamus

ratteen... 8. mahogany

rattle... 3. toy 4. herb, rale, rick, tirl
5. annoy, clack 6. assail, prison
(Nav), racket, uproar 7. agitate,
chatter, clapper, clatter, confuse,
fluster, maracas, prattle 8. nonsense
9. chatterer, rapid talk
10. disconcert, noisemaker

rattle (pert to)...
bones.. 8. clappers, snappers
9. castanets
headed.. 8. confused
11. empty–headed 13. rattlebrained
mouse.. 3. bat
nut.. 10. chinquapin
pate.. 3. ass
root.. 7. bugbane

rattlesnake... 7. rattler 8. belltail,
Crotalus, pit viper 9. Sistrurus

rattlesnake (pert to)...
bean.. 6. cedron
bite.. 9. meadow rue
fern.. 9. chain fern, sporangia
flag (Maine).. 13. Don't Tread on Me
(Hist)
herb.. 9. baneberry
leaf.. 8. plantain
pilot.. 10. copperhead
plantain.. 6. orchid
variety.. 3. red 6. banded, timber
7. prairie 11. diamondback
venom.. 8. crotalus

rattletrap... 6. gewgaw 7. rickety
8. claptrap, the mouth
10. knickknack, ramshackle

ratton... 3. rat

ratwa... 7. muntjac

raucous... 3. dry 4. bray, loud
5. harsh, noisy 6. hoarse, raucid,
rauque 8. strident 11. cacophonous

rauk, roke... 4. poke, stir 5. vapor
7. scratch

raun... 3. roe 4. fish 5. spawn

ravage... 4. loot, ruin, sack 5. havoc,
spoil, waste 6. damage, infest
7. debauch, destroy, overrun, pillage,
plunder 9. devastate 10. desolation
11. despoilment, devastation,
infestation

ravages of time... 13. deterioration
14. disintegration

rave... 4. rage, rant 5. crush, storm
7. bluster, declaim, enthuse 8. be
insane, harangue

ravel... 4. fray 6. runner, slough,
unwind, 7. involve, unravel, untwist,
unweave 8. entangle, separate
11. disentangle, loose thread

ravelin... 7. railing 8. demilune,
half–moon 13. fortification

raven... 4. bird, crow 6. Corvus
8. standard (vikings) 10. raven–black
11. Corvus corax

Raven (The)... 4. poem (Edgar Allen
Poe)

ravening... 3. mad 5. rabid 6. greedy,
prying 8. desirous 9. rapacious,
turbulent

ravenous... 6. greedy 8. edacious
9. rapacious, voracious
10. gluttonous 11. catawampous

ravine... 3. gap 4. dell, linn (lin), wadi
(wady) 5. chine, gorge, gulch, slade,
strid 6. arroyo, clough, gulley, nullah
8. barranca

ravish... 3. rob 4. rape 5. seize
7. corrupt, debauch, delight, despoil,
plunder, violate 8. deflower, entrance
9. enrapture, transport

raw... 4. cold, sore 5. bleak, crude,
naked 6. chilly, unripe, vulgar
7. natural, not spun, untried
8. immature, indecent, uncooked
9. inclement, unskilled, wind–swept
10. unprepared 11. undeveloped,
unprocessed 13. inexperienced

rawboned... 4. lank 5. gaunt
7. angular 8. skeletal

rawbones... 5. Death 8. skeleton

raw–flesh–eating... 9. omophagia

rawhide... 4. skin (untanned), whip

rawhide whip... 5. knout, quirt, thong
7. sjambok

raw sugar... 9. cassonade

rax... 5. reach 6. become, strain
7. stretch

ray... 4. beam, dorn, soil, X–ray
5. array, dress, gamma, order, skate
(fish) 6. defile, radius, stripe, vision
7. besmear, raiment 8. particle,
radiance, stingray 11. arrangement,
irradiation

raya... 9. broadbill

rayless... 4. dark 5. blind

rayon... 3. ray 5. fiber 6. radius
14. postal district (Switz)

raze, rase... 3. cut 4. fell, ruin
5. erase, graze, level, shave
6. efface, scrape 7. destroy
8. demolish 9. dismantle, prostrate
10. obliterate

razee... 3. cut (Naut) 5. prune
7. abridge

razor (pert to)...
back.. 3. hog 4. boar 5. ridge
10. roustabout (circus)
bill.. 3. auk 7. skimmer
billed auk.. 4. falk 5. murre, noddy
clam.. 5. Solen 11. chopa blanca
grinder.. 10. goatsucker
sharpen.. 4. hone 5. strop

stone.. 9. whetstone 10. novaculite
strap.. 5. strop
type.. 6. safety 7. rattler
razz... 5. chaff, tease 6. banter, deride
   8. ridicule 9. raspberry
razzle–dazzle... 5. cinch (game), spree
   6. dazzle 7. confuse 8. bewilder
   9. commotion 10. noisemaker
re... 4. back (pref) 5. about, again,
   anent, tone D (Mus) 8. syllable
   (Mus) 10. concerning
Re... 2. Ra (Egypt) see also *Ra*
reach... 4. come, gain, hawk, ryke,
   spar, spit 5. equal, retch 6. advene,
   arrive, attain, extend, length
   7. achieve, compass, earshot,
   expanse, possess, stretch
   8. distance, overtake 9. influence
   10. understand
reach (pert to)...
  across.. 4. span
  for applause.. 9. captation
  high point.. 9. culminate
  out.. 6. extend 7. stretch
  under.. 7. subtend
  up.. 6. aspire
reaction... 4. kick 6. change (Chem)
   7. tropism 8. response 9. influence
   10. opposition
reactionary... 4. Tory 10. malcontent
   12. conservative, recalcitrant
read... 3. con 4. pore, scan, skim, tell
   5. guess, solve 6. advise, browse,
   peruse, recite, relate 7. counsel,
   declare, discern, foresee, prelect
   (praelect), stomach 8. decipher,
   describe, foretell 9. interpret
   10. understand
readable   7. legible 12. decipherable
reader... 6. lector, lister, primer
   (McGuffey) 7. browser, license,
   reciter, speaker, teacher 8. anagnost
   (anagnostes), literate, textbook
   9. churchman, prelector (praelector)
   10. pocketbook 11. proofreader
   12. elocutionist
readily... 6. at once, easily 7. quickly
   8. probably 9. willingly 10. very
   likely
readjust... 7. readapt, restore
   9. rearrange 11. reconstruct
   12. rehabilitate
ready... 3. apt, fit, fix 4. bain, free,
   here, ripe, yare 5. alert, apert,
   eager, handy, point, quick 6. facile,
   fitted, prompt 7. willing 8. cheerful,
   disposed, inclined, prepared, skillful
   9. dexterous 12. unhesitating
ready acceptance... 11. embracement
ready for... 6. awaits 8. liable to
   10. in store for 11. prepared for
ready–to–wear... 12. haute couture
real... 4. true, very 5. pucka (pukka)
   6. actual 7. factual, genuine, sincere
   8. absolute, existent, handmade,
   tangible 9. authentic, veritable
   10. unaffected 11. substantial
real (pert to)...
  being.. 6. entity
  estate.. 5. lands 6. domain, houses,
   realty 7. demesne 8. easement,

freehold, property 9. tenements
   13. hereditaments
  map.. 4. plot
  name (backwards).. 6. ananym
  school.. 10. Realschule
realistic... 5. vivid 8. lifelike
   9. practical 11. descriptive
reality... 5. truth 7. realism
   11. genuineness
reality, non–existent... 8. nihilism
realize... 3. get, win 4. gain, know
   5. sense 7. convert 8. conceive
   10. accomplish
realm... 6. domain, empire, region,
   sphere 7. country, demesne, kingdom
   8. division, province 10. department
   12. jurisdiction
realm (of)...
  darkness (Myth).. 2. po
  Jamshid.. 6. Persia
  perfection.. 6. Utopia
ream... 4. bore, foam, scum 5. widen
   6. bundle 7. enlarge 8. bevel out
   11. countersink 14. enormous
   amount
reanimate... 5. rally 6. revive
   7. refresh 11. resuscitate
   12. reinvigorate
rear... 3. aft 4. back, grow, lift, loom,
   rise, rump 5. breed, build, erect,
   raise, stern, train 6. behind, foster
   7. arriere, educate, elevate, produce
   8. instruct 9. construct, establish,
   posterior 10. background
rear (pert to)...
  admiral.. 7. two bars (silver)
  commodore, yacht club.. 7. officer
  end.. 6. breech 7. hind end
   9. afterpart, posterior
  horse (Insect).. 6. mantle
  most.. 4. last
  toward.. 3. aft 5. abaft 6. astern
   8. backward, rearward
rearing up (horse)... 5. stend
   6. pesade
rearrange... 4. sort 8. readjust
   10. reordinate, reorganize
reason... 5. argue, cause, logic, sense,
   think 6. deduce, ground, motive,
   sanity 7. discuss 8. argument,
   conclude, judgment, question,
   solution 9. discourse, intellect
   11. explanation, ratiocinate, rationalize
   13. justification, understanding
reason (pert to)...
  discursively.. 11. ratiocinate
  doctrine of, author.. 10. Anaxagoras
  higher.. 4. mind, nous 5. logic
  Latin.. 5. causa
  ostensible.. 7. pretext
  pert to.. 6. noetic
  proof of.. 8. argument
  want of.. 7. amentia
  why.. 5. cause 6. motive
reasonable... 4. fair, just, sane
   6. proper 7. logical 8. rational
   9. equitable, plausible, practical
   10. fair–minded 11. inexpensive,
   intelligent, justifiable
reasoning (pert to)...
  basis of.. 7. premise
  delusive.. 7. fallacy

exact.. 5. logic
harmonize.. 11. rationalize
plausible.. 8. specious
reassure... 6. assure, solace
7. comfort, console, hearten
8. embolden, give hope
reata... 4. rope 5. lasso, riata 6. lariat
reave... 3. rob 4. rend, tear 5. break,
burst, seize, split 7. plunder
reb... 5. rebel
rebate... 5. check 6. reduce, weaken
8. diminish, discount 9. abatement,
deduction, remission
rebato (Hist)... 4. ruff 6. collar, rabato
9. piccadill
Rebekah (pert to)...
husband.. 5. Isaac
sister.. 5. Laban
son.. 4. Esau 5. Jacob
rebel... 3. reb 4. rise 6. resist, revolt
8. renounce, turncoat 9. insurgent
13. revolutionist
rebellion... 5. Great (Eng 1642–49)
6. mutiny, revolt 8. American (Civil
War 1861–65) 10. resistance,
revolution 12. insurrection,
renunciation
rebellious... 8. mutinous 9. insurgent
10. refractory 12. contumacious
13. insubordinate, revolutionary
rebirth... 7. revival 9. salvation
10. conversion 11. renaissance
13. reincarnation
rebound... 4. stot 5. carom
6. bounce, recoil, re–echo, spring
7. resound 8. rebounce, ricochet
11. reverberate
rebuff... 4. slap, snub 5. chide, scold
6. defeat, lesson, recoil, refuse,
reject, resist 7. censure, refusal
(brusque), reprove, repulse
9. reprimand
rebuke... 3. nip 4. slap 5. check,
chide 6. rebuff 7. repress, reproof,
reprove 8. admonish, reproach,
restrain 9. criticize, reprehend,
reprimand 11. comeuppance
recalcitrant... 5. rebel 8. renitent
9. obstinate, recoiling, resistant
10. rebellious, refractory
11. disobedient 12. ungovernable
recall... 5. annul 6. encore, recant,
remind, repeal, revoke, summon
7. retract 8. remember, withdraw
9. recollect, reminisce
11. recantation 12. recollection
recant... 6. abjure, revoke 7. disavow,
retract 8. renounce, withdraw
9. repudiate 10. contradict
recapitulate... 5. essay, sum up
6. repeat, review 7. restate
8. argument 9. reiterate, summarize
recapture... 6. recall, regain, retake
7. recover
recede... 3. ebb 4. wane 6. depart,
retire 7. deviate, regress, retreat
8. withdraw 10. retrograde
receipt... 5. axiom 6. acquit, answer,
recipe 7. formula 12. prescription
14. acknowledgment
receipts... 7. the take

receive... 3. get 4. hold, take
5. admit, greet, learn, reset
6. accept, assent, derive, obtain,
take in 7. acquire, contain, procure
9. apprehend
receive (pert to)...
a confession.. 6. shrive
a reward.. 4. reap
stolen property.. 5. reset
receiver... 5. donee, fence 7. catcher
8. believer 9. recipient, treasurer
10. receptacle
receiver (pert to)...
fixed income.. 7. rentier
profits (law).. 6. pernor
property in trust.. 6. bailee
stolen property.. 5. fence
recension... 6. review 8. revising,
revision 9. reviewing
11. enumeration, examination
recent... 3. new 4. late, past 5. fresh
6. former, modern 7. current,
newborn 8. neonatal, neoteric
receptacle... 3. bag, bin, box, can,
cup, pan 4. case, cask, cyst (anc),
etui, pail, tank, tray, vase 5. basin,
crock 6. basket, bottle, bucket,
carton, holder, hopper 7. compote,
hanaper, platter 8. canister, catchall
9. container 10. repository
receptacle (pert to)...
assayer's, stonecutter's.. 7. sebilla
botany.. 5. torus
coal.. 3. bin
corporal (RCCh).. 5. burse
grain.. 3. bin 8. elevator
holy water.. 5. stoup
vote.. 6. situla
reception... 3. tea 5. levee, salon
6. infare, soiree 7. accueil, ovation,
receipt, welcome 8. ceremony,
sociable 9. admission, interview,
intuition 12. housewarming
13. entertainment
reception hall, room... 5. salon
6. atrium, parlor 9. vestibule
receptionist... 4. host 7. hostess
8. landlord
receptive... 6. pliant 8. sensible
9. acceptant, admissive, teachable
10. hospitable, open–minded
11. persuasible
receptor... 5. basin 8. receiver
10. dispositor (Astron), sense organ
recess... 3. ala, bay, pan (leaf)
4. apse, nook, rest 5. crypt, niche,
pause, sinus, space 7. adjourn,
respite, retreat 9. recession, seclusion
11. indentation 12. intermission
recipe... 5. axiom 7. formula, receipt
12. prescription
recipient... 4. heir 5. donee 7. legatee
8. receiver
reciprocal... 5. joint 6. mutual, shared
8. exchange 9. alternate
11. convertible, correlative, retaliatory
15. interchangeable
reciprocate... 5. bandy 6. accord,
concur 8. exchange 9. alternate,
retaliate 10. correspond
11. interchange
recision... 6. repeal 7. pruning

9. canceling (cancelling)
10. rescinding
recital . . . 4. tale 5. story 6. lesson, speech 7. account, concert (exhibition) 8. musicale 9. narration, narrative, rehearsal 10. recitation, repetition 11. enumeration, reiteration
recitation . . . 6. lesson, speech 7. reading 10. exhibition
recite . . . 4. tell 5. quote, speak, state 6. relate, repeat 7. declaim, narrate, recount 8. rehearse, tell over 9. enumerate, pronounce 12. recapitulate
recite (pert to) . . .
in monotone . . 6. intone
metrically . . 4. scan
rhetorically . . 7. declaim
to music . . 5. chant 10. cantillate
reciter . . . 4. book (of extracts) 5. roter 7. relator, speaker 8. narrator
reck . . . 4. care, deem, heed, mind 6. regard 7. concern 8. estimate
reckless . . . 4. rash 5. perdu (perdue) 6. madcap 7. hotspur 8. careless, heedless 9. desperate, hotheaded, imprudent 10. neglectful, regardless 11. indifferent, thoughtless, unconcerned 13. inconsiderate
reckon . . . 4. aret (arette) date, deem, tell 5. class, count, judge, tally, think 6. impute, number, regard, repute 7. account, compute, include, suppose 8. consider, estimate, evaluate 9. calculate, enumerate
reckoning . . . 3. sum 4. bill, shot 5. score, tally 6. esteem 7. account, verdict 8. counting 9. summation 10. estimation 11. calculation
reckoning instrument . . . 6. abacus 9. tabulator 10. calculator
reclaim . . . 4. tame 5. renew, train 6. ransom, recall, redeem, revoke 7. convert, recover, restore 8. civilize 10. regenerate 12. rehabilitate
recline . . . 3. lay, lie, sit 4. lean, loll, rest 6. repose 7. incline, lie down
reclining . . . 4. flat 5. prone 6. supine 7. lolling 8. couchant, reposing 9. prostrate, recumbent
recluse . . . 3. fra, nun 4. monk 6. hermit, hidden, secret, shut up 7. ascetic, eremite, retired (from world) 8. anchoret, isolated, solitary 9. anchorite 10. cloistered 11. sequestered
recognition . . . 4. fame 6. recall 9. detection 10. cognizance 11. discernment 14. acknowledgment
recognize . . . 3. see 4. know 5. admit 6. detect 7. consent 8. identify, perceive 10. appreciate, recognosce 11. acknowledge
recoil . . . 3. shy 4. funk 5. quail 6. flinch, resile, shrink 7. rebound, retreat 8. reaction, withdraw
recollect . . . 6. recall, revive 7. think of 8. remember 10. call to mind
recollection . . . 4. mind 6. memory 9. anamnesis 11. remembrance 12. reminiscence

recommence . . . 5. renew 6. resume 8. return to 9. begin anew
recommend . . . 4. tout, urge 6. advise, commit, denote, praise 7. commend, consign, entrust 8. advocate
recompense . . . 3. fee, pay 4. meed 5. repay 6. reward 8. requital 9. indemnify, reimburse 10. compensate, remunerate 11. reciprocate
recompense (pert to) . . .
Brehon Law . . 4. eric
Germanic law . . 7. wergild
Scot law . . 3. cro
Welsh law . . 7. galanas
reconcile . . . 4. suit, wean 5. atone 6. adjust, pacify, settle 7. cleanse (Eccl), conform, reunite 9. harmonize 10. conciliate, propitiate
reconciliation . . . 7. harmony, reunion 10. adjustment, conformity 12. pacification 13. reconcilement
reconciliator . . . 10. arbitrator, reconciler 13. intermediator
recondite . . . 4. dark, deep 6. hidden, mystic, occult 7. cryptic 8. abstract, abstruse, esoteric 9. concealed
reconnaissance . . . 6. survey 8. scouting 11. examination
reconnoiter . . . 5. scout 6. survey
reconstruct . . . 6. recast, remake 7. rebuild, remodel 9. reproduce 11. reestablish
record . . . 3. log, tab 4. disc, file, list, memo 5. annal, diary, enter, entry, score 6. agenda, legend, memoir, postea 7. archive, estreat, history 8. memorial, register 9. chronicle 10. chronology, transcribe, transcript
record (pert to) . . .
criminal investigation . . 7. dossier
document . . 8. protocol
earth tremor . . 11. seismograph
formal . . 4. vita 8. register
historic . . 6. annals 7. rotulet
keeper . . 9. registrar 10. chartulary
of events . . 5. annal, fasti 7. history
official . . 5. actum
pictorial . . 5. graph
ship's voyage . . 3. log
year's . . 5. diary 8. calendar
recording terms . . . 2. LP 4. reel, tape 5. album, Dolby 6. needle, stereo, stylus 7. capstan 8. cassette 9. cartridge, videotape
recount . . . 3. min 4. tell 5. sum up 6. reckon, relate, repeat, retail 7. narrate 8. rehearse 9. enumerate, reiterate 12. recapitulate
recoup . . . 4. gain 7. recover 8. retrieve 9. indemnity, reimburse 10. compensate
recourse . . . 3. use 5. recur 6. access, betake, refuge, resort, return, revert 7. retreat
recover . . . 3. get 4. cure, gain, heal 5. rally, reach, upset 6. recoup, redeem, regain, rescue, resume 7. get well, reclaim, recruit 8. overcome, retrieve 9. repossess 10. convalesce, recuperate
recovery . . . 6. return 7. salvage

9. retrieval 11. reclamation,
reformation, restoration
recreant... 6. coward, wretch
7. dastard, knavish 8. apostate,
betrayer, cowardly, deserter
9. reprobate 10. unfaithful
recreation... 4. food, game, meal, play
5. sport 7. holiday, renewal
8. vacation 9. amusement, diversion
11. refreshment 12. reproduction
14. reconstruction
recrement... 5. dross 6. refuse, scoria
recruit... 5. raise 6. enlist, gather,
muster, novice, revive, rookie
7. recover, refresh, restore
8. assemble, inductee, newcomer
9. conscript, reinforce, replenish
12. reinvigorate
rectangle... 10. quadrangle
13. parallelogram
rectangular... 6. oblong
12. quadrangular
rectify... 5. amend, emend, right
6. adjust, better, reform, remedy
7. correct, justify 8. emendate,
regulate, set right 10. straighten
rector... 5. chief 6. leader, master
(Oxford), pastor 8. director, governor
9. churchman, clergyman
10. headmaster
rectory... 8. benefice 9. personage
recumbent... 4. idle 5. lying, prone
7. leaning, resting 8. inactive,
reposing 9. reclining
recuperate... 4. rest 6. recoup, regain
7. improve, recover, restore 9. get
better, reimburse
recur... 5. again 6. repeat, return
7. persist, reoccur 8. reappear
recurrent... 10. repetitive
recurring (pert to)...
continually.. 8. constant
10. habitually, repeatedly
ninth day.. 5. nonan
seventh day.. 6. septan
third day.. 7. tertian
red... 4. rosy 5. color, ruddy 7. radical
8. blushing, inflamed, rutilant,
sanguine 9. bloodshot
12. bloodstained 13. revolutionary
red (color)... 4. fire, lake, pink, puce,
rose, ruby, tile, wine 5. blood, brick,
canna, coral, flame, flesh, henna,
poppy 6. auburn, cerise, cherry,
claret, damask, maroon, minium,
raddle, salmon, titian, Turkey
7. anemone, annatto, carmine,
Chinese, crimson, lobster, magenta,
nacarat, scarlet, stammel 8. cardinal,
cinnabar 9. carnation, carnelian,
vermilion
red (pert to)...
cap (Turk).. 8. tarboosh
cell.. 11. erythrocite
corpuscle.. 10. hemoglobin (source of)
dog.. 4. game 8. banknote
dye.. 3. aal, lac 4. chay (choy)
5. aurin (aurine), eosin (eosine)
8. morindin
gum.. 10. strophulus
hair.. 6. titian
herring.. 4. ruse 9. diversion

minded.. 7. radical
planet.. 4. Mars
race.. 7. Indians
robbin.. 14. scarlet tanager
truffle.. 12. melanogaster
viper.. 10. copperhead
Red (pert to)...
Book.. 7. Austria 13. Royal Kalendar
Crescent.. 8. Red Cross (Turk)
Cross.. 9. St George's (Eng)
Friar.. 13. Knight Templar
Guard.. 4. Army 7. Russian
Hand.. 13. Badge of Ulster
Horse.. 10. Kentuckian
Planet.. 4. Mars
Polled.. 6. cattle (hornless)
Prince.. 7. Russian (Frederick Charles)
Ribbon.. 14. Order of the Bath
Rose.. 16. House of Lancaster
Russian.. 9. Bolshevik
Sea.. 14. Erythraean main
Sea city.. 9. Leningrad
Sea colony.. 7. Eritrea
Sea gulf.. 5. Aqaba
Square.. 6. Moscow
The Red.. 4. Eric (Scand)
Triangle.. 4. YMCA (symbol)
redact... 4. edit 5. draft, frame
6. revise
redactor... 6. editor 7. reviser
9. redacteur
reddish (pert to)...
blue.. 5. smalt 9. damascene
brown.. 3. bay 4. roan 5. henna
6. auburn, russet, sorrel 8. chestnut
dye.. 7. annatto
yellow.. 5. amber 6. orange
rede... 6. advice, relate 7. counsel,
explain, predict 9. interpret
redeem... 3. pay 6. ransom, regain,
rescue 7. convert, fulfill, reclaim,
recover 8. liberate 10. repurchase,
substitute
redeemer... 4. goel (Heb) 7. saviour
(savior) 9. deliverer, liberator
11. emancipator
Redeemer, The... 8. Son of God
10. The Messiah, The Saviour
11. Jesus Christ
redintegrate... 5. renew, unite
7. restore 9. reconcile
11. re—establish
redness... 4. glow 8. blushing
10. erubescent, rubescence
redolence... 4. odor 5. aroma, scent
9. fragrance, sweetness
redolent... 5. balmy 7. odorous,
scented 8. aromatic, fragrant
11. impregnated, reminiscent
redouble... 6. re—echo, repeat
7. reflect, reprise (fencing)
9. intensify 10. ingeminate, repetition
11. reduplicate
redoubt... 4. fear 5. doubt 6. reduit
7. defense, ravelin
redound... 5. surge 6. abound, return
7. conduce, resound 8. flow back,
overflow 10. contribute (to)
11. reverberate
redpoll... 5. finch 6. linnet 7. warbler
Red Polled cattle... 8. hornless
redress... 4. help 5. amend, emend

6. reform, remedy 7. correct, relieve
8. atone for, reprisal 9. atonement
10. correction, recompense,
reparation 11. reformation, restitution
reduce... 3. cut 4. bant, bate, pare,
thin 5. abase, abate, lower, razee
6. demote, derate, humble, lessen,
subdue, weaken 7. abridge, analyze,
cheapen, conquer, curtail, deplete,
qualify, relieve, shorten 8. decrease,
diminish, discount, minimize,
moderate 9. subjugate
10. impoverish, slenderize
reduce in flesh... 8. emaciate
reduce in rank... 6. demote
reduce to...
ashes.. 7. cremate
average.. 4. mean 6. equate
bondage.. 7. enslave
common measure.. 12. commensurate
half.. 9. dimidiate
lower grade.. 6. demote 7. degrade
mean time.. 6. equate
spray.. 7. atomize
reduction... 6. rebate 7. subdual
8. decrease, demotion, discount,
lowering 9. weakening
10. abridgment, cheapening,
conversion, moderation
reduction (pert to)...
in value.. 12. depreciation
to absurdity.. 18. reductio ad
absurdum
to common level.. 15. standardization
to compactness.. 12. condensation
to standard.. 15. standardization
redundancy... 6. excess 7. profuse
8. pleonasm, verbiage 9. prolixity,
talkative, tautology, verbosity
10. repetition 11. periphrasis
13. diffusiveness 14. circumlocution
redundant... 6. lavish 7. copious,
diffuse, verbose 9. excessive,
exuberant, plethoric 10. pleonastic
11. overflowing, repetitious,
superfluous 13. superabundant
ree... 3. dam 4. sift, wild 5. crazy,
drunk, river 6. harbor, riddle
7. channel, fuddled 8. coalyard
9. enclosure, sheepfold
re–echo... 7. resound 11. reverberate
reechy... 5. fetid 6. rancid
reed... 4. stem, tube 5. arrow, straw
6. thatch 10. instrument
reed (pert to)...
bird.. 4. wren 7. babbler, warbler
8. bobolink
buck.. 5. bohor, nagar 8. antelope
bunting.. 7. sparrow 8. reedling
loom.. 4. sley
mace.. 7. cattail, matreed
measure (Jew).. 9. six cubits
pipe.. 5. kazoo 8. mirliton
reef... 3. bar, cay (cayo), key (quay)
4. itch, lode, sail, vein 5. islet,
mange, shoal 6. island 7. shorten
8. eruption
reef (pert to)...
coral.. 3. key
knot.. 6. square
mining.. 4. lode, vein
nautical.. 5. sails

sand.. 3. bar
reefer... 5. miner 6. jacket, oyster
9. cigarette 10. midshipman
reek... 3. fug, rig 4. fume 5. equip,
exude, smell, smoke, steam
7. malodor, seaweed 8. fetid air,
smell bad, vaporize 10. exhalation
reel... 4. eddy, pirn, rock, sail, sway,
wind 5. dance, lurch, spool, swift
(yarn), swing, waver, wince 6. tatter
7. scrieve, stagger 8. flounder,
titubate, windlass 12. Virginia reel
reeling... 5. drunk 7. swaying, winding
8. rotating
reem (Bib)... 6. animal (horned), wild
ox 7. unicorn
re–embody... 7. combine, reshape
10. reorganize 11. reincarnate
13. reincorporate
reeve... 3. pen 4. ruff 5. strip
6. thread 8. official (Eng Hist)
9. enclosure, sheepfold
refect... 7. refresh, restore
refectory... 6. frater (monastery)
8. mess hall 10. dining hall
refer... 4. cite 5. apply, recur
6. allude, appeal, charge, impute,
relate, return 7. ascribe 9. appertain,
attribute
refer (to)... 4. harp 6. advert
7. consult, mention
referee... 5. judge 6. umpire 7. arbiter
8. attorney 9. moderator
10. arbitrator
reference... 6. regard 7. respect
8. allusion, relation 9. character,
relevance 10. connection, pertinence
14. recommendation
reference (pert to)...
book.. 5. atlas 8. handbook, syllabus
9. thesaurus 10. dictionary
12. encyclopedia
referendum... 4. vote 7. mandate
8. politics 10. plebiscite
refine... 5. smelt 6. rarefy 7. clarify,
elevate, improve, sublime
9. elaborate, sensitize, sublimate
refined... 4. fine, nice, pure, rare
5. urban 6. chaste 7. elegant,
smelted 8. cleansed, highbred,
purified, well–bred 9. clarified,
courteous, perfected 10. cultivated,
fastidious, meticulous
refined spirit... 5. grace 6. elixir
refinement... 5. taste 6. polish
7. finesse 8. delicacy, elegance,
fineness 9. gentility 11. cultivation,
rarefaction 13. clarification
refinery (ore)... 7. smelter
refining cup... 5. cupel
reflect... 3. say 4. muse, pore
5. radar, think 6. divert, mirror,
ponder 7. deflect 8. cogitate,
consider, meditate, ruminate, turn
back 9. reproduce 11. reverberate
reflecting... 6. musing 9. judicious
10. reflective, ruminating, thoughtful
11. insinuating 13. reverberatory
15. casting reproach
reflection... 4. idea 5. image, light
6. musing 7. bending, thought
8. reaction, thinking 10. cogitation,

meditation, rumination
12. afterthought, recollection
13. consideration, contemplation
reflex... 4. bent 6. turned 8. allusion,
reaction, reversed 9. duplicate,
reflected 13. introspection
reflux... 3. ebb 6. ebbing, reflow
8. backflow, reaction 9. refluence,
returning
reform... 4. mend 5. amend, emend,
renew 6. better, remake, remass,
repair 7. convert, rebuild, reclaim,
rectify, restore 9. amendment
10. regenerate 11. reformation
reformation... 7. rebirth
10. conversion, emendation
12. regeneration, reproduction
15. re–establishment
Reformation leaders (Hist)... 4. Knox
6. Calvin, Luther, Ridley 7. Cranmer,
Latimer, Zwingli 8. Campbell
11. Melanchthon
reformer... 7. amender, reviser
9. reformado, reformist 10. politician
refraction... 7. rebound 9. dioptrics
10. deflection, dispersion
11. anaclastics
refractor... 5. prism 9. telescope
refractory... 7. restive 8. indocile,
stubborn 11. disobedient
12. ungovernable
refrain... 4. curb, shun 5. avoid,
cease, derry, epode 6. chorus,
govern 7. abstain, forbear
8. response, restrain
refrain from using... 5. spare
7. boycott
refresco... 4. food 5. drink
11. refreshment
refresh... 3. air, dew 4. cool 5. cheer,
renew, slake 6. repose, revive
7. freshen, relieve 8. recreate,
renovate 9. reanimate, replenish
10. invigorate, strengthen
11. refreshment 12. reinvigorate
refreshing... 5. balmy 7. bracing
8. regaling 10. heartening
11. stimulating 12. exhilarating
refrigerant... 3. ice 6. cooler
7. ammonia, coolant, cryogen
refrigeration... 7. cooling 8. cryogeny
10. anesthetic, cryogenics
12. preservation
refuge... 3. ark 4. plea 5. haven
6. asylum, covert, excuse 7. retreat,
shelter 8. hospital, recourse, resource
9. sanctuary 10. protection, safety
zone
refugee... 5. exile, fleer 6. émigré
7. escapee, evacuee 8. fugitive,
renegade
refulgence... 6. luster 8. radiance,
splendor 10. brilliancy
refund... 5. repay 6. rebate
9. reimburse
refurbish... 4. vamp 5. renew
8. brighten, renovate 11. recondition
refusal... 3. nay 6. denial 9. rejection
11. declination
refuse... 3. cot (wool), ort 4. balk,
coom (coomb), culm, deny, junk,
marc, scum 5. attle, chaff, dregs,

dross, repel, scrap, trash, waste,
weeds 6. debris, give up, litter,
midden, naysay, reject, renege,
scoria, scraps 7. abandon, bagasse,
cast off, decline, garbage, hogwash,
repulse 8. disclaim, leavings,
oddments, renounce, withhold
9. excrement, repudiate 11. odds
and ends
refuse to...
accept.. 6. reject
acknowledge.. 7. disavow 9. repudiate
comply.. 12. recalcitrant
proceed.. 4. balk
refutation... 6. answer 8. disproof,
elenchus, rebuttal 11. confutation
refute... 4. deny, meet 5. rebut, refel
6. assoil 8. disprove, elenctic,
redargue 9. overthrow 10. contradict
regain... 6. recoup 7. get back,
recover 8. retrieve 9. get back to
10. reach again
regal... 5. royal 6. groove, kingly
7. channel, stately 8. imperial,
majestic, splendid 9. dignified,
sovereign
regale... 4. dine, fete 5. amuse, feast,
treat 7. gratify, refresh 9. entertain
11. refreshment
regalia... 6. finery 7. costume,
emblems, symbols 8. insignia
11. decorations 12. special dress
13. paraphernalia
regard... 3. air, awe 4. care, deem,
gaze, heed, hold, look, love, mind,
obey (law), rate, sake, view 5. honor,
judge, think, treat 6. aspect, behold,
esteem, remark, repute 8. attitude,
consider, estimate, hold dear, listen
to 9. attention, relevance, viewpoint
10. appearance, estimation
11. contemplate, observation
13. consideration
regard (pert to)...
for others.. 8. altruism
for other's wish.. 9. deference
highly.. 6. admire 7. lionize
with approval.. 6. admire
with deference.. 5. honor 7. respect
with veneration.. 6. revere
regardful... 7. careful, mindful
8. cautious 9. attentive, observant
10. altruistic, respectful, thoughtful
11. considerate
regarding... 2. re 5. anent
10. concerning, respecting
regardless... 6. anyhow 8. careless,
heedless, slighted 9. negligent
10. neglectful 11. inattentive,
indifferent, unconcerned, unobservant
15. notwithstanding
regards... 8. respects 9. greetings
11. compliments
regatta cup... 5. Platt 8. Carnegie,
Grimoldi
regency... 4. rule 8. dominion
10. government
regenerate... 5. shape 6. redeem,
reform, revive 7. convert, restore
8. re–create 9. reproduce
11. fashion anew
regeneration... 7. renewal, revival

9. reversion 10. re–creation
11. reformation 12. reproduction
14. divine function
regent... 5. ruler 6. deputy, ruling
7. regnant 8. governor
Regent diamond, 137 carats (pert
to)...
included in.. 11. State jewels (France)
named for.. 14. Regent of France
placed in.. 6. Louvre
sold (1717) to.. 4. Pitt (Gov of
Madras, Ind)
regime, regimen... 4. diet, rule
6. system 7. therapy
10. government, regulation
14. administration
regiment... 4. unit, wing 6. outfit
8. organize 11. systematize
regiment, framework of... 5. cadre
regina... 5. queen
region... 4. area, belt, zone 5. clime,
place, realm, space, tract 6. sphere
7. climate, cockpit, country,
demesne, kingdom, section
8. district, province
region (pert to)...
beyond Jordan.. 5. Perea 6. Basham
blissful.. 4. Eden
comb form.. 5. nesia
desert.. 3. erg 5. waste
indefinite.. 5. tract
infernal.. 7. Avernal 8. Tartarus
meteorological.. 6. pleion
wooded.. 4. wold
woodless.. 5. weald
region of...
contentment.. 6. Arcady
dead (Egypt Myth).. 6. Amenti
fabled wealth.. 8. Eldorado
nether darkness.. 6. Erebus
opposite side earth.. 9. Antipodes
Solomon's gold (Bib).. 5. Ophir
register... 3. act 4. list, roll 5. annal,
entry, index 6. docket, enlist, enroll,
record 7. rotulet 8. archives,
recorder, schedule 9. catalogue,
chronicle, necrology, registrar
11. account book, matriculate
registrar... 8. recorder 9. accounter
regius... 5. royal 13. professorship
regret... 3. rue 4. ruth 5. grief, sorry
6. repent, repine, sorrow 7. deplore,
remorse 9. penitence 10. repentance
11. compunction 12. self–reproach
regretful... 5. sorry 8. repining
9. repentant
regular... 4. even 5. usual 6. formal,
normal, smooth, stated 7. correct,
orderly, typical, uniform 8. constant,
habitual, ordinary, ordinate, rhythmic,
standard 9. isometric 10. systematic
regularity... 5. order 8. symmetry
9. constancy 10. smoothness,
uniformity
regularly... 6. always 7. usually
8. properly, smoothly 9. correctly
10. constantly, habitually
12. methodically, periodically
13. symmetrically
regulate... 3. set 4. rule 6. adjust,
direct, govern, manage, ordain,
remedy 7. arrange, control, dispose

8. organize 9. influence, methodize
11. standardize
regulation... 3. law 4. rule 5. bylaw,
order 6. system 7. control, precept
9. direction, principle
regulator... 7. control 8. governor,
rheostat 9. rheometer
Regulus... 4. king, star 5. Alpha
8. warblers 9. Cor Leonis (star)
rehabilitate... 7. restore 9. reeducate,
reinstall
rehash... 7. restate 9. réchauffé
rehearse... 3. say 4. tell 5. speak,
sum up, train 6. detail, recite, relate,
repeat, try out 7. mention, narrate,
recount 8. describe 9. enumerate,
reiterate 12. recapitulate
rehoboam... 3. hat 4. bowl 6. flagon
8. jeroboam
Rehoboam (Bib)... 11. King of Judah
(1st) 12. King of Israel (last)
reif... 7. plunder, robbery
reign... 3. raj 4. rule, sway 5. guide,
realm 6. empire 7. kingdom, prevail
8. dominion, flourish 11. sovereignty
12. supreme power
Reign of Terror (Fr Hist)... 7. anarchy
9. bloodshed, despotism
12. confiscation
reimburse... 3. pay 5. repay 6. refund
7. pay back, replace 9. indemnify
10. recompense
Reims, Rheims (pert to)...
capital (anc).. 4. Remi
famed building.. 9. Cathedral (Gothic)
famed site.. 15. crowning of kings
(Fr)
rein... 4. curb, stop 5. check, leash
6. direct, retard 7. control
8. reindeer, restrain 9. hindrance
10. bridle part
reina... 8. rockfish
reindeer... 6. tarand 7. caribou
13. constellation
reindeer (pert to)...
age, epoch.. 11. Paleolithic
flower.. 9. buttercup (white)
genus.. 8. Rangifer
reinforce... 4. back 5. add to, brace,
reman 7. restore, support
9. intensify, replenish 10. strengthen
reinforcement... 7. adjunct, support
8. addition 13. replenishment,
strengthening
reins... 5. loins 7. harness, kidneys
9. restraint
reis... 6. escudo 7. milreis 14. money
of account
reit... 5. sedge 7. seaweed
reiterate... 4. drum, harp 6. repeat
8. rehearse 12. recapitulate
reject... 5. repel, spurn 6. disown,
recuse (law), refuse 7. decline,
discard, dismiss 8. athetize, disallow
9. repudiate
rejectamenta... 5. wrack 6. refuse,
reject 7. rubbish 9. excrement
rejection... 6. heresy 7. discard,
refusal 8. ejection 9. exclusion,
objection 11. disapproval, repudiation
rejoice... 5. cheer, elate 7. delight,
gladden 8. jubilate

rejoinder . . . **5.** reply (law) **6.** answer, retort, return **8.** comeback

rejuvenate . . . **6.** revive **7.** restore **9.** stimulate **12.** reinvigorate

relâche . . . **10.** relaxation **12.** intermission **13.** no performance (Theat)

relapse . . . **4.** sink **5.** lapse **7.** subside **8.** slip back **9.** backslide, reversion **10.** recurrence, regression **11.** falling back **12.** recidivation

relate . . . **4.** tell **5.** state **6.** assert, detail, recite, report **7.** narrate, pertain, recount **8.** describe, rehearse **9.** appertain, associate

related (pert to) . . .
by blood . . **3.** sib **4.** akin **7.** cognate
on father's side . . **6.** agnate **7.** cognate **8.** agnation
on mother's side . . **5.** enate **6.** enatic **7.** cognate, enation **9.** umbilical
to land . . **8.** praedial (predial)

relating to . . .
bread . . **6.** panary
Chinese . . **7.** Sinitic
dancing . . **6.** gestic **13.** choreographic
fruit jelly . . **7.** pectous
grandparents . . **4.** aval
Hindu literature . . **5.** Vedic
life . . **5.** vital
morn . . **7.** matinal **8.** forenoon
motion . . **7.** kinetic **9.** kinematic
realities . . **7.** factual **9.** entelechy
soft palate . . **5.** velar
vascular fluid . . **5.** hemic

relation . . . **3.** kin **4.** mode, tale **6.** status, ubiety **7.** account, analogy, kinship, kinsman, recital, telling **8.** relative **9.** character, narration, reference, rehearsal, rishtadar (Hind law) **10.** connection **13.** consanguinity

relationship . . . **4.** outs **7.** kinship, kinsman, metochy **8.** affinity, relative **13.** consanguinity

relative . . . **3.** eme, kin, sib, son **4.** aunt **5.** niece, uncle **6.** allied, cousin, father, mother, nephew, sister **7.** brother, kindred **8.** apposite, daughter, kinsfolk **9.** pertinent **11.** comparative, correlative **13.** corresponding, proportionate

relative (pert to) . . .
favor to . . **8.** nepotism
rank . . **6.** degree
to . . **7.** apropos **12.** in proportion

relax . . . **4.** ease, open, rest **5.** abate, loose, remit **6.** divert, loosen, soften, unbend **7.** detente, slacken **8.** mitigate, slow down

relaxed . . . **4.** calm, cool **5.** casual **8.** laid-back **9.** easygoing

relay . . . **3.** dak (dawk) **4.** race **5.** shift **6.** remuda **7.** relieve **8.** avantlay **10.** television (station)

release . . . **4.** drop, free, trip, undo **5.** death, let go, loose, undam, unpen, untie **6.** acquit, escape, exempt, loosen, parole, remise **7.** deliver, freedom, manumit, receipt, relieve, unleash, unloose **8.** liberate **9.** discharge **10.** liberation, relinquish

11. acquittance, deliverance

relegate . . . **5.** exile, refer **6.** assign, banish, commit, deport, depute, remove **7.** ascribe, consign, discard, dismiss, exclude **8.** delegate

relent . . . **5.** abate, yield **6.** regret, soften, submit **7.** slacken

relentless . . . **6.** strict **9.** merciless **10.** inflexible, unyielding **11.** persevering, unremitting

relevant . . . **7.** germane **9.** pertinent **10.** sufficient **11.** referential

reliable . . . **4.** safe, sure **5.** tried **6.** stable, trusty **7.** solvent **8.** true-blue **11.** trustworthy

reliance . . . **4.** hope **5.** trust **6.** belief **8.** mainstay **10.** confidence, conviction, dependence

relic . . . **5.** curio, huaca, huaco, ruins **7.** antique, memento, remains **8.** artifact, fragment, memorial, souvenir, survival **9.** antiquity

relic cabinet . . . **7.** étagère, whatnot

relict . . . **5.** widow **7.** widower **8.** survivor

relied . . . **6.** banked **7.** counted, reposed, trusted **8.** confided, depended, reckoned

relief . . . **3.** aid **4.** bote (bot), dole, ease, fret (Arch), help **5.** spell **6.** remedy, succor **7.** comfort, outline, redress, relieve, welfare **8.** easement **10.** assistance, embossment, mitigation, substitute, sustenance **11.** alleviation, deliverance **15.** indemnification

relieve . . . **3.** aid **4.** cure, ease, free, help **5.** abate, allay, clear, raise, spell **6.** assist, remedy, remove, succor **7.** assuage, lighten, redress, refresh, support, sustain, unloose **8.** diminish **10.** substitute

religion (pert to) . . . **4.** sect **5.** creed, deism, faith, piety, trust **6.** belief, hermit, schism, theism, voodoo **8.** monastic, theology **9.** solipsism **10.** conformity, persuasion

religion, type . . . **5.** Islam **6.** Taoism **7.** Jainism, Judaism **8.** Buddhism, Hinduism **9.** Mormonism, Moslemism, Muslimism, Shintoism **11.** Anglicanism, Catholicism **12.** Christianity, Confucianism **13.** Mohammedanism, Protestantism

religious . . . **4.** holy **5.** exact, godly, pious, rigid **6.** devout, sacred **7.** devoted, fervent, zealous **9.** born-again, pharasaic, spiritual **10.** devotional, meticulous, scrupulous **11.** theological **13.** conscientious

religious (pert to) . . .
assembly . . **12.** congregation
belief . . **5.** deism **6.** omnist **10.** monotheism
brotherhood . . **8.** sodality **9.** ecumenism **10.** fellowship **11.** ecumenicism
center . . **7.** Lambeth (Eng)
composition . . **5.** motet
cult, sect . . **5.** fakir **6.** Shaker, Shinto **7.** Pietism, Sikhism **8.** cenobite **9.** anchorite **11.** Hare Krishna

devotee.. 5. fakir
devotion.. 6. novena
division.. 6. schism
expedition (Mil).. 7. crusade
fasting.. 4. Lent 9. Ember Days
  10. Ember Weeks
festival.. 4. mela (Ind) 5. Purim (Jew)
madness, mania.. 9. theomania
metaphysics.. 7. gnostic
musical.. 6. anthem
offering.. 7. deodate 8. oblation
Order member.. 6. Marist 7. Templar
poem.. 5. psalm
primitive.. 6. voodoo
psalm.. 4. hymn, poem, song
publication (RCCh).. 4. ordo
relinquish... 3. let 4. cede, quit
  5. forgo, leave, waive, yield
  6. desert, desist, forego, give up,
  remise, resign 7. abandon, forsake,
  release 8. abdicate, renounce
  9. surrender 11. leave behind
  12. withdraw from
relinquishment... 9. surrender
  11. abandonment 12. renunciation
reliquary, reliquiae (pl)... 3. box
  4. arca, tomb 5. chest 6. casket,
  chasse, shrine 8. monument
relish... 4. gust, tang, zest 5. achar,
  enjoy, gusto, sauce, taste 6. canape,
  caviar, degust, flavor, liking
  8. pleasure 9. condiment, degustate,
  enjoyment, flavoring, seasoning
  11. hors d'oeuvre 13. gratification
relucent... 6. lucid 6. lucent
  7. radiant, shining 8. lightish
  9. refulgent
reluctance... 8. aversion
  10. repugnance 12. indisposition,
  unwillingness 14. disinclination
reluctance unit (Elec)... 3. rel
reluctant... 5. chary, loath 6. averse
  8. hesitant, not ready 9. resisting,
  unwilling 11. disinclined
reluctate... 5. repel 6. oppose
  9. repudiate
rely... 4. hold, lean, rest 5. count,
  trust 6. cleave, depend, reckon,
  repose 7. confide
rely on, upon... 4. hope 5. trust
  6. depend, lippen 7. believe
remain... 3. lie 4. bide, last, rest, stay
  5. abide, tarry 6. endure, reside
  8. continue
remainder... 4. rest, stub 5. relic,
  stump 6. estate 7. balance, remnant,
  residue, surplus 8. fragment,
  leavings, residual, residuum
remaining... 4. left, over 6. ledger
  (leger) 7. durable, remnant, staying,
  surplus 8. residual 9. permanent
remaining stationary... 6. static
  7. waiting 8. awaiting
remains... 5. ashes, ruins, stays
  6. corpse, relics 7. cadaver, fossils
  9. remainder
remanent... 4. left 7. further, lasting,
  remains, remnant, residue
  8. enduring, leftover, residual
  9. permanent, remainder
  10. additional 13. supplementary
remark... 3. say, see 4. heed, note

  5. gloss, state 6. notice, regard
  7. comment, observe 8. perceive,
  point out 9. statement
  10. annotation, commentary,
  indication 11. observation
  12. interjection
remark (pert to)...
amusing, witty.. 3. gag 4. quip
clever.. 3. mot
commonplace.. 9. platitude
smarting.. 7. sarcasm, stinger
upon.. 7. explain
witless.. 5. boner
remarkable... 5. great 7. notable,
  strange, unusual 8. uncommon
  9. wonderful 10. noteworthy,
  noticeable, observable
  11. conspicuous 13. extraordinary
Rembrandt (pert to)...
birthplace.. 6. Leyden (Neth)
color.. 5. brown
famed as.. 6. etcher (Dutch)
  7. painter
style.. 14. Rembrandtesque
remedial... 6. remedy (pert to)
  7. healing 8. curative, panacean
  10. corrective 11. therapeutic
remedy... 3. aid, fix 4. bote (bot),
  cure, gain, help 5. amend 6. doctor,
  relief 8. antidote, medicine
  10. assistance, reparation
remedy (pert to)...
cure–all.. 6. elixir
mysterious (of Paracelsus)..
  7. arcanum
quack.. 7. nostrum
soothing.. 4. balm 6. balsam
universal.. 7. panacea
remember... 3. min 9. recollect,
  reminisce 10. keep in mind
remembrance... 4. fame 5. token
  6. memory, Minnie, trophy
  7. memento 8. allusion, memorial,
  reminder, souvenir 12. recollection
  13. commemoration
remex... 12. quill feather
remind... 6. prompt, recall
  8. remember 13. call attention
reminder... 4. memo, twit 7. memento
  8. souvenir 10. memorandum
  11. remembrance
reminiscence... 3. act 4. fact
  5. power 6. memory 8. anecdote
  10. experience 11. memorabilia
  12. recollection
remise... 6. giving, return 7. release,
  replace, respite 8. granting
  9. remission, surrender
remiss... 3. lax 5. slack 7. lenient
  8. careless, dilatory, heedless
  9. negligent 10. neglectful
  11. inattentive, thoughtless
remissness... 7. neglect 9. indolence
  10. negligence 12. improvidence
remit... 3. pay 5. relax 6. acquit,
  assign, cancel, excuse, pardon,
  reduce, resign 7. absolve, forgive,
  release, restore, suspend 8. abrogate,
  liberate, mitigate, recommit
  9. surrender
remnant... 3. ash, end, ort, rag
  4. dreg, left, rest, stub 5. piece,

relic, scrap, shred, trace 7. oddment, remains, yet left 8. fragment 9. remainder, remaining 10. suggestion

remolade... 5. sauce 8. dressing, ointment

remonstrate... 5. plead 7. protest 8. point out 11. expostulate

remontant... 14. flowering again

remora... 4. fish, pega (pegora)

remord... 5. taint 6. ponder, rebuke 7. afflict, censure, remorse

remorse... 4. pity 6. regret, sorrow 8. distress 9. penitence, repentent 10. compassion 11. compunction

remorseful... 5. sorry 7. pitiful 8. contrite, merciful, penitent, pitiable 9. regretful 13. compassionate

remorseless... 8. pitiless 9. merciless, unpitying 10. implacable, inflexible, relentless, unmerciful 11. unregretful

remote... 3. far, off 5. alien, vague 6. elenge, forane, ultima 7. distant, foreign 8. abstruse, reserved, secluded, ulterior 10. farfetched, unsociable 11. out-of-the-way

remote control... 10. pushbutton, tele-action

remote region... 5. Thule (Greenland)

remotest... 7. endmost, very end 8. farthest 14. ghost of a chance

removal... 8. ejection 9. deduction 10. divestment, evacuation, extraction 11. elimination 12. transference

remove... 3. rid 4. dele, doff, move, void, weed 5. erase, evict, expel, strip 6. change, debunk, delete, depose, divest, eloign (law) 7. dismiss, extract, relieve 8. abstract, displace, evacuate, put aside, transfer 9. eliminate, eradicate, translate 11. assassinate

remove (pert to)...
cover.. 5. uncap
from office.. 4. oust 6. depose, recall
moisture.. 3. dry 5. wring 9. dehydrate
point of origin.. 6. distal
seed from flax.. 6. ribble
seeds.. 3. gin, pit
stalk.. 5. strig
to another place.. 8. transfer 9. translate
whole blubber.. 6. flense

removed... 4. took 5. apart 6. betook, remote 7. distant, far away 8. reserved, secluded 9. separated, unrelated 10. unsociable

remover... 6. porter 7. carrier, drayman, solvent 9. scavenger 10. contractor, eradicator

remunerate... 3. pay 5. repay 6. reward 7. require, satisfy 9. reimburse 10. compensate, recompense

remuneration... 3. pay 6. reward 7. payment 8. pittance, requital 9. emolument 10. recompense 12. compensation, satisfaction 13. reimbursement

Remus (pert to)...
brother.. 7. Romulus

father.. 4. Mars
legendary founder of.. 4. Rome (with brother)
slayer.. 7. Romulus

renable... 4. glib 5. ready 6. fluent 8. eloquent

renaissance... 7. rebirth, revival

Renaissance (pert to)...
Archit.. 12. Roman classic
art.. 10. neoclassic
associated with.. 8. Petrarch
furniture.. 6. carved 7. English, Flemish
Italian reference.. 12. Resorgimento (new arising)
lace.. 10. Battenburg

renal... 6. kidney 7. nephric

renascence... 7. rebirth, revival 14. The Renaissance

rencounter... 4. duel 5. clash 6. action, combat, flight 7. contest, meeting 8. conflict 9. collision

rend... 3. rip 4. rive, tear 5. break, burst, sever, split, wrest 7. extract, rupture 8. fracture

render... 3. pay, put 4. give, make, melt 6. return 7. clarify, convert, deliver, execute, extract, narrate, present, requite 8. transmit 9. translate 10. understand 11. communicate

render (pert to)...
accessible.. 4. open
agreeable.. 7. dulcify
angry, choleric.. 6. enrage
conformable to Eng.. 7. Anglify 9. Anglicize
divine.. 5. deify
dull.. 8. hebetate
enduring.. 6. anneal
fat.. 3. try 6. try out
fertile.. 6. enrich
free from bacteria.. 9. sterilize
ineffective.. 4. void 5. annul 10. invalidate
intelligible.. 9. elucidate
less pliant.. 7. stiffen
muddy, turgid.. 4. roil
oblique.. 5. splay
obscure.. 6. darkle 9. obfuscate
sharp.. 9. acuminate
unconscious.. 4. stun

rendezvous... 5. tryst 6. refuge 7. meeting, retreat 11. appointment

rendition... 7. account 8. delivery 9. surrender 10. extraction 11. performance, translation 14. interpretation

renegade... 3. rat 5. rebel 7. pervert, traitor 8. apostate, deserter, fugitive, turncoat

renege... 4. deny 6. desert, revoke 7. decline 8. renounce

renew... 6. resume, revamp, revive 7. convert, refresh, restore 8. renovate 10. invigorate, regenerate 12. redintegrate

renewal... 10. conversion, renovation, resumption 11. restoration

renitent... 7. opposed 9. reluctant, resistant 12. recalcitrant

rennet... 3. lab 5. apple 6. curdle,

rennin 7. extract 9. coagulate
rennin... 6. enzyme
renommé... 8. renowned
   10. celebrated
Renommist... 8. braggart, renowner
   9. swaggerer
renounce... 4. cede, deny 5. forgo
   (forego), waive 6. abjure, desert,
   disown, recant, reject, renege, resign
   7. abandon, forsake, retract
   8. abnegate, forswear, swear off
   9. repudiate, surrender 10. relinquish
   12. abrenunciate
renouncement... 9. rejection
   10. temperance 11. abandonment,
   recantation
renovate... 5. renew 6. repair, resume,
   revive 7. restore 10. regenerate
renown... 4. fame, note 5. éclat, glory
   10. reputation
renowned... 5. famed, noted
   6. famous 10. celebrated
   11. illustrious 13. distinguished
rent... 3. let, pay 4. dues, hire, hole,
   slit, tear, toll, tore, torn 5. break,
   cleft, lease, share, split 6. reward
   7. revenue, rupture, slitted, tribute
   8. tattered
rent (pert to)...
   asunder.. 5. rived
   harvest.. 7. onstand
   in oats.. 7. avenage
   paid.. 3. tac
renter... 6. lessee, lodger, tenant
renunciation... 6. denial 9. disavowal,
   rejection, surrender 10. abjuration,
   disclaimer, temperance
   11. abandonment, recantation
   14. relinquishment
repaid in kind... 10. retaliated
repair... 3. fix 4. darn, heal, mend
   5. amend, patch, renew 6. doctor,
   remedy, resort 7. correct, rebuild,
   restore 8. atone for 9. condition
   13. betake oneself
reparation... 6. amende, amends,
   remedy, repair, reward 7. damages,
   redress 8. reprisal, requital
   9. atonement, indemnity
   10. recompense 11. restitution
   12. compensation, satisfaction
repartee... 3. wit 5. reply 6. retort
   7. riposte
repast... 3. tea 4. feed, meal 5. feast,
   lunch, treat 6. tiffin 8. mealtime,
   prandial 9. collation
repatriate... 5. exile 6. banish
   10. expatriate
repay... 4. meed 6. answer, avenge,
   refund, return 7. requite, restore
   9. reimburse, retaliate
   10. compensate, recompense,
   remunerate
repeal... 5. annul, emend, forgo
   (forego) 6. appeal, cancel, recall
   7. abandon, abolish, rescind, retract,
   reverse 8. abrogate, renounce,
   withdraw
repeat... 4. copy, echo, rame 5. recur
   7. iterate, restate 8. remember
   9. duplicate, reiterate
repeat (pert to)...

mathematics.. 8. repetend
mechanically.. 6. parrot
noisily.. 3. din
performance.. 6. encore
twice (pref).. 3. bis
repeating... 4. rote 10. repetitive
   11. repetitious
repel... 5. avert, check 6. offend,
   oppose, rebuff, refuse, reject, resist,
   revolt 7. disgust, repulse 9. drive
   back, force back
repellent... 5. harsh 6. odious
   9. repulsive, resistant, revolting
repent... 3. rue 6. reform, regret
   9. do penance
repentance... 4. ruth 5. shame
   6. regret 9. penitence 10. contrition
   11. compunction
repercussion... 4. blow 6. impact
   9. afterclap, aftermath 10. reflection
repertory... 4. list 5. index, store
   8. calendar, magazine, treasure
   9. catalogue 10. collection,
   repertoire, storehouse
repetition... 4. rote 5. troll 6. encore
   8. iterance 9. iteration 11. reiteration
   14. recapitulation
repetition (pert to)...
   biology.. 6. merism
   music.. 5. rondo 7. tremolo
   rhetoric.. 8. anaphora 9. tautology
   sound.. 4. echo
   sounds (slight).. 6. patter
repetitive... 8. habitual 9. redundant
   11. repetitious
repine... 4. fret 6. lament, regret
   7. grumble 8. complain
replace... 4. stet 5. reset, stead
   6. repone 7. restore 8. supplant
   9. discharge, supersede
   10. substitute
replaceable... 10. expendable
replenish... 4. feed, fill 5. store
   6. refill 7. perfect, provide
   8. complete
replete... 3. fat 4. full 5. sated
   6. filled, gorged 7. bloated
   8. abundant 9. surfeited
replevin... 4. bail, writ 8. recovery
replica... 3. bis 4. copy 6. repeat
   9. duplicate, facsimile
reply... 4. echo 5. rebut 6. answer,
   oracle, rejoin, retort 7. defense,
   epistle, respond 8. reaction, repartee,
   response 9. rejoinder 11. retaliation
report... 3. cry, pop 4. bang, note
   5. bruit, rumor, sound, state, story
   6. delate, recite, relate, repute
   7. account, hearsay, recital, verdict
   8. describe 9. narration, narrative,
   statement 10. accounting,
   commentary, responsory
   11. information, publication
report (pert to)...
   common.. 6. gossip
   false, absurd.. 5. rumor 6. canard
   7. slander
   following lightning.. 7. thunder
   for duty.. 14. present oneself
   official.. 7. hansard
   of proceedings.. 6. cahier
reporter... 3. cub 6. legman, pistol

7. newsman 8. newshawk
9. informant 12. newspaperman
reporter's rounds... 8. newsbeat
reporter's sign off... 6. thirty
repose... 3. lie, sit 4. ease, rely, rest
5. peace, place, sleep 7. deposit,
recline 9. quiescent, quietness
10. quiescence, relaxation
repository... 3. ark 4. file 5. vault
6. chapel (RCCh), museum
8. treasury 9. confidant, sepulcher
10. depository, storehouse
11. auction room
reposoir... 5. altar
repoussé... 7. art work
reprehensible... 8. blamable, culpable
9. accusable, obnoxious
10. censurable, reprovable
11. blameworthy
reprehension... 5. blame 7. censure,
reproof 9. reprimand 11. reprobation
12. condemnation, denunciation
represent... 5. enact 6. denote,
depict, typify 7. betoken, exhibit,
portray, produce 8. describe
9. delineate
representation... 3. art 4. copy, icon,
idea, idol, show 5. drama 6. avowal,
symbol 7. picture 9. depiction,
enactment, portrayal, spectacle
10. exhibition, profession
11. delineation, description,
portraiture 12. reproduction
representation (pert to)...
by characters (Mus).. 8. notation
graphic.. 5. chart
Medusa's head.. 9. gorgoneum
mental.. 5. image 7. eidolon,
phantom
of scene.. 7. tableau
of solar system.. 6. orrery
of star.. 7. estoile
small.. 5. model 9. miniature
representative... 4. heir, type
5. agent, envoy 6. deputy, legate
7. example, tribune, typical
8. delegate, exponent, symbolic
9. successor 10. ambassador,
legislator, lieutenant, substitute
12. illustrative
repress... 4. curb, rein, stop 5. check,
crush, quell 6. hush up, muffle, stifle
7. put down 8. restrain, suppress
9. overpower
reprieve... 5. delay 6. pardon, relief
7. relieve, respite 8. postpone
reprimand... 5. chide, scold, slate
6. rebuke 7. censure, reprove
reprisal... 7. revenge, revenue
8. requital 11. retaliation
reproach... 4. taca, twit 5. abuse,
blame, chide, shend, taunt
6. accuse, revile, vilify 7. censure,
condemn, reproof, sarcasm, upbraid
8. disgrace, dishonor 9. disrepute,
invective 10. accusation, opprobrium
12. vilification
reproach, free of... 9. blameless
reprobate... 6. disown, reject, wicked
7. abandon, corrupt, knavish, vicious
8. depraved, hardened, recreant
9. condemned, miscreant, reprehend,

scoundrel 10. black sheep
12. unprincipled 13. reprehensible
reproduce... 4. copy 6. recite, remake,
repeat 8. multiply 9. duplicate,
propagate
reproduction... 4. copy 6. ectype,
recall 7. picture, replica 8. likeness
10. repetition 11. counterpart,
duplication 14. representation
reproductive... 5. gamic, spore
10. recreative 12. regenerative
reproof... 5. roast 6. rebuke
7. chiding 8. disgrace, reproach
9. reprimand 10. admonition,
censurable, refutation
11. blameworthy, confutation
12. reprehension 13. reprehensible
reprove... 4. rate 5. blame, chide,
scold 6. berate, rebuke 7. censure,
correct, upbraid 8. admonish,
reproach 9. objurgate, reprehend,
reprimand
reproving... 10. admonitive
reptile... 4. toad, worm 5. snake,
viper 6. dragon, iguana, lizard, turtle
7. monitor, serpent 8. creeping,
Reptilia 9. scoundrel
reptile (pert to)...
class.. 8. Reptilia
crocodile.. 6. mugger
extinct.. 9. pterosaur 10. diplodocus
11. pterodactyl, Pterosauria
group.. 6. Sauria
hard–shelled.. 6. iguana, turtle
8. terrapin, tortoise
iguanalike.. 7. tuatara
large.. 3. boa 9. alligator, crocodile
10. salamander
lizard.. 3. eft 4. adda, newt, seps
5. skink (scink) 6. Anolis, iguana,
moloch 7. monitor 9. chameleon
10. chuckwalla 11. Gila monster
Mesozoic.. 8. dinosaur
myth.. 6. dragon 8. basilisk
10. cockatrice, salamander
oldest.. 9. sea turtle
salamander.. 3. eft 4. newt
scale.. 5. scute
snake.. 3. asp 5. adder, cobra, krait
6. garter, python 8. anaconda,
Squamata 10. copperhead
reptilian... 7. saurian
Reptilian Age... 8. Mesozoic
Republic... 5. State 6. France
7. Andorra (Andorre) 9. San Marino
10. commonweal, government
12. United States
Republican Party... 3. GOP
7. mugwump (bolter 1884)
Republic of Plato... 4. Book (famed)
8. dialogue 10. ideal State
repudiate... 4. deny 6. abjure, disown,
recant, reject 7. disavow, discard,
exclude 8. renounce
repugnance... 4. hate 5. odium
6. nausea 7. disgust, opposed
8. aversion, loathing 9. antipathy,
hostility 10. abhorrence, antagonism,
opposition, reluctance
12. disagreement
repugnant... 6. odious 7. adverse,
hostile, opposed 8. inimical

9. offensive, repellent, repulsive
10. refractory 11. distasteful
12. incompatible 14. irreconcilable
repulse... 5. repel 6. denial, rebuff
7. refusal 9. rejection
repulsive... 4. ugly, vile 5. nasty
6. odious 7. fulsome 9. offensive,
repellent, resistant, revolting
10. disgusting, forbidding,
malodorous
repurchase... 6. redeem
reputable... 6. worthy 9. estimable,
honorable 10. creditable
11. respectable
reputation... 4. fame, name, note
5. glory, honor 9. celebrity, notoriety
11. distinction 13. consideration
repute... 4. hold, word 5. éclat, honor
6. credit, esteem, regard, report,
revere 8. prestige 9. reputable
10. popularity, reputation
reputed... 6. deemed 7. assumed
8. accepted, presumed, putative,
supposed 10. understood
request... 3. ask, beg 4. plea, pray,
suit 6. appeal, behest, demand
7. entreat, solicit 8. entreaty,
petition, rogation 12. supplication
requiescat in pace... 11. rest in
peace
requiescence... 6. repose
requin... 5. shark 8. man-eater
require... 3. ask 4. need 5. claim,
exact, force 6. charge, compel,
demand, enjoin, entail, oblige
8. obligate 11. necessitate
requisition... 5. order 6. demand
11. application, requirement
requital... 7. payment, revenge
8. reprisal 10. recompense
11. retaliation, retribution
12. compensation
requite... 3. pay 5. atone, repay
6. avenge, return, reward
7. revenge, satisfy 9. retaliate
10. compensate, recompense
11. interchange
reredos... 4. wall 6. screen
9. back-plate (armor), partition
reremouse... 3. bat
res... 5. point, thing 6. matter
rescind... 5. annul 6. cancel, recall,
recant, repeal, revoke 7. abolish
8. abrogate
rescue... 3. aid 4. free, save
6. ransom, redeem, regain 7. deliver,
reclaim, recover, release 8. delivery,
liberate 9. extricate 11. deliverance
rese... 4. rage, rush 5. hurry, onset,
quake, shake 7. impulse, tremble
8. rashness
resemblance... 6. ringer 7. analogy
8. affinity, likeness 9. agreement,
semblance 10. similarity, similitude
resembling (pert to)...
bark.. 11. corticiform
comb.. 8. pectinal
goose.. 8. anserine
gypsum.. 11. alabastrine
horse.. 6. equoid
man.. 7. android
minute animals.. 11. animalcular

rind.. 8. cortical
salt.. 6. haloid
seed.. 6. ovular
snakes.. 7. elapine 8. viperine
star.. 7. stellar 8. stellate 9. stellated
turf.. 5. soddy
wall.. 5. mural
resentment... 3. ire 5. pique, spite
6. choler, enmity, hatred, malice,
rancor 7. dudgeon, umbrage
9. animosity, malignity
11. displeasure, indignation
reservation... 5. tract 8. preserve
9. reticence 10. engagement,
limitation 11. withholding
13. qualification
reserve... 4. bank, fund, keep, save
5. allot, spare, stock, store
6. engage, refuge 7. backlog,
modesty, shyness 8. coldness,
distance, postpone, withhold
9. exception, restraint, retention,
reticence, sanctuary 10. constraint,
diffidence, limitation, substitute
11. self-control, taciturnity
reserved... 3. coy 4. cool, kept, unco
5. aloof, saved, staid, taken
6. modest, sedate 7. distant
8. reticent 15. uncommunicative
reservoir... 4. font, pool, sump
5. store 6. cavity, cenote, supply
7. piscina, reserve 8. fountain
reservoir of Pecquet (Anat)...
12. lymph channel 13. cisterna chyli
res gestae... 5. deeds, facts
8. exploits 10. things done
resiant... 7. present 8. resident
reside... 4. bide, live, room, stay
5. abide, dwell, lodge 6. remain
7. sojourn 8. habitate
residence... 4. home, seat, stay
5. abode 6. palace 7. deanery
8. domicile, dwelling 9. consulate,
residency 10. habitation
residencia... 5. court, trial
resident... 3. cit 6. intern, tenant
7. burgess, citizen 8. diplomat,
occupant 10. inhabitant
residual... 7. remnant 8. residuum
9. remainder
residue... 3. ash, ort 4. coke, dreg,
marc, rest, silt, slag 5. ashes
6. pomace, relics 7. balance,
remains, remnant 8. leavings,
sediment 9. remainder
residuum... 7. residue 8. hangover,
leavings 9. remainder
resign... 4. cede, quit 5. demit, waive,
yield 6. give up, submit 7. abandon,
consign 8. abdicate, renounce
9. surrender 10. relinquish
resignation... 5. demit 8. patience
9. demission, endurance
10. abdication, submission
12. renunciation 14. relinquishment
resigned... 9. contented
10. submissive 11. acquiescent
13. uncomplaining
resilient... 7. buoyant, elastic
8. cheerful 9. recoiling
10. rebounding 11. returning to
12. recuperative

resin . . . 3. gum, lac 4. aloe, tolu
5. amber, anime, copal, jalap, rosin
6. dammar, mastic
resin (pert to) . . .
  aromatic . . 4. balm 5. elemi, myrrh
  6. balsam 7. acouchi, camphor,
  copaiba 8. sandarac 12. frankincense
  Bib . . 8. bdellium
  bitter . . 8. labdanum (ladanum)
  brown (mineral) . . 9. elaterite
  Chian turpentine . . 3. alk
  fossil . . 5. amber 8. retinite
  gum . . 5. gugal (googul)
  hard . . 5. rosin
  medicinal . . 7. aroeira 9. asafetida
  (asafoetida)
  narcotic . . 6. charas
  pine . . 7. galipot
  soft . . 5. animé, copal, elemi
  translucent . . 8. sandarac
  tropical . . 5. copal
  varnish ingredient . . 6. dammar
  yellowish . . 5. amber 7. gamboge
resinous substance . . . 3. gum, lac
  5. copal 7. shellac
resist . . . 4. fend, stem 5. rebel, repel
  6. defeat, oppose 7. prevent, ward
  off 8. outstand 9. withstand
  10. counteract
resistance . . . 6. rebuff 7. defense
  8. rheostat 9. hostility 10. opposition
resistant . . . 5. tough 8. obdurate
  9. resisting 10. unyielding
  13. counteractive
resisting . . . 7. hostile 8. opposing
  9. oppugnant, tenacious
  12. antagonistic
resisting (pert to) . . .
  description . . 11. indefinable
  power . . 4. wiry
  pressure . . 8. renitent
  pressure bar . . 5. strut
resolute . . . 4. bold, firm 5. fixed, stern
  6. gritty, steady 7. decided
  8. constant, positive, resolved,
  unshaken 9. desperado, obstinate,
  steadfast 10. determined, inflexible,
  unyielding 11. perseverant,
  persevering
resolution . . . 4. firm 5. nerve
  6. motion, steady 7. courage,
  purpose, resolve, verdict 8. analysis,
  decision, resolved, strength
  9. assurance, constancy, fortitude
  10. conversion, conviction, relaxation,
  separation 11. persevering
  12. perseverance 13. determination,
  steadfastness 15. disentanglement
resolve . . . 4. melt 5. lapse (law),
  parse, relax, solve 6. assure, decide,
  dispel, inform, reduce, settle
  7. analyze, explain, purpose, unravel
  8. convince, dissolve, separate
  9. determine, transform
  11. disentangle
resonance . . . 8. sonority, vibrance
  10. resounding
resonant . . . 7. echoing, ringing, vibrant
  8. sonorous, sounding
  10. resounding 11. reverberant
resort . . . 3. spa 4. dive 5. haunt
  6. betake, casino, refuge 7. finagle,

purlieu 8. frequent, recourse,
  resource 9. expedient, fainaigue,
  honky–tonk
resound . . . 4. echo, peal, ring 6. be
  loud, re–echo 8. proclaim
  11. reverberate
resounding . . . 4. loud 13. reverberating
resource . . . 5. means, skill 6. refuge,
  resort, supply 9. expedient
  10. capability 11. contrivance
resourceful . . . 5. sharp 9. Daedalian,
  ingenious
resources . . . 5. funds, means, money
  6. assets, supply 7. resorts
  10. expedients 12. contrivances
respect . . . 3. awe 4. heed 5. defer,
  favor, honor 6. aspect, detail,
  esteem, homage, regard, repute,
  revere 7. concern, observe, regards
  8. attitude, venerate 9. attention,
  deference, relevance, reverence,
  viewpoint 10. politeness
  13. consideration
respectable . . . 6. decent 9. estimable,
  honorable, reputable, tolerable
  11. presentable
respectful . . . 5. civil 6. polite
  7. careful, duteous, heedful
  8. reverent 11. deferential
respective . . . 6. mutual 7. careful,
  heedful, several, special 9. attentive,
  regardful 10. particular
  12. distributive
respiration . . . 4. rale, sigh 7. eupnoea
  9. breathing
respire . . . 7. breathe
respite . . . 4. rest 5. delay, frist, pause
  6. breath 7. leisure 8. postpone,
  reprieve 9. extension (time)
  10. suspension 11. opportunity,
  short shrift 12. intermission
resplendent . . . 5. grand 7. aureate,
  radiant, shining 8. lustrous, splendid
  9. beautiful, brilliant, refulgent
  10. epiphanous 11. illustrious
respond . . . 4. echo 5. react, reply
  6. accord, answer, retort 8. response
  10. correspond 11. reciprocate
response . . . 4. echo 5. reply
  6. answer, anthem, chorus
  7. rapport, refrain 8. antiphon (Mus),
  reaction
responsibility . . . 4. care, duty, onus
  6. charge 8. solvency 11. reliability
  14. accountability 15. trustworthiness
responsible . . . 6. liable 7. solvent
  8. amenable, reliable 10. answerable
  11. accountable, respectable,
  trustworthy
responsive . . . 6. pliant 7. elastic
  8. reactive 9. answering, sensitive,
  teachable 10. open–minded
  11. persuasible, sympathetic
res publica . . . 5. state 8. republic
  10. commonweal 12. commonwealth
rest . . . 3. lay, set, sit 4. base, calm,
  ease, lair, lean, prop, seat, slip, stay,
  stop 5. cease, death, found, pause,
  peace, quiet, relax, renew 6. depend,
  desist, ground, repose, settle
  7. balance, leisure, recline, refresh,
  remains, remnant, reposal, respite,

silence, support, surplus **8.** at anchor,
interval, lodgment, residuum
9. cessation, quietness, remainder,
stillness **10.** quiescence, remain idle
12. intermission, peacefulness,
tranquillity
rest (pert to) . . .
assured . . **9.** be certain, believe me
at rest . . **4.** abed, dead **6.** otiose
11. comfortable
day . . **7.** Sabbath
foot . . **4.** rail **7.** hassock, ottoman
house (Orient) . . **5.** serai
reading . . **7.** caesura (cesura)
restaurant . . . **4.** café, deli (sl) **5.** diner
6. eatery **7.** automat, beanery,
tearoom **8.** fast-food, pizzeria, snack
bar **9.** cafeteria **10.** coffee shop
11. rathskeller **12.** luncheonette
resting . . . **4.** abed **7.** dormant
8. drowsing **9.** quiescent
resting place . . . **4.** tomb **5.** étape,
roost **6.** hearth **7.** lairage, landing,
support **8.** quarters
restitution . . . **6.** return **9.** atonement,
repayment **10.** recompense,
reparation **12.** compensation
13. reinstatement
restless . . . **5.** antsy, hyper, itchy
6. roving, uneasy **7.** agitato, fidgety,
fretful, unquiet, restive, wakeful
8. agitated **9.** impatient, sleepless,
unceasing, unrestful, unsettled,
wandering **10.** changeable, reposeless
12. discontented
restoration . . . **6.** repair, return
7. renewal, revival **8.** recovery
10. renovation, reparation
11. improvement, restitution
14. redintegration
15. reestablishment
restorative . . . **6.** asceptin **7.** anodyne
8. remedial **10.** reparative
restore . . . **4.** cure, heal **5.** renew,
repay **6.** redeem, refund, repone,
revive **7.** rebuild, recover, replace
8. renovate **9.** reinstate
11. reconstruct, reestablish
12. redintegrate, rehabilitate
restore (pert to) . . .
after cancelling . . **4.** stet
certainty, confidence . . **8.** reassure
to former position . . **9.** reinstate
to original condition . . **9.** refurbish
to proper position . . **5.** right
restrain . . . **3.** dam **4.** bate, bind, curb,
rein, stay **5.** check, cramp, deter,
limit, stint **6.** arrest, bridle, fetter,
halter, hinder, tether **7.** abridge,
confine, control, inhibit, overawe,
qualify, repress **8.** restrict, suppress,
withhold **9.** constrain, detention
restraint . . . **3.** bit **4.** curb, stop
5. check, force **7.** durance, modesty,
reserve **9.** condition, hindrance,
reticence **10.** abridgment, constraint,
inhibition, limitation, moderation,
repression, temperance
11. confinement, deprivation,
self-control **12.** tastefulness
restraint, lack of . . . **9.** looseness
restrict . . . **3.** tie **4.** bind, curb

5. bound, cramp, limit, scant, stint
6. censor, coerce, modify **7.** confine,
qualify, repress **10.** specialize
12. circumscribe
restricted . . . **5.** local **6.** narrow
7. limited, topical **9.** exclusive
10. restrained **11.** specialized
restriction . . . **5.** stint **9.** restraint
10. limitation, narrowness, regulation,
tightening **11.** reservation
12. constriction **13.** qualification
resty . . . **5.** quiet **7.** restive **8.** sluggish
result . . . **3.** end, sum **4.** rise **5.** arise,
ensue, event, fruit, issue, total
6. accrue, answer, effect, follow,
sequel, spring, upshot **7.** proceed,
product **8.** solution **9.** aftermath,
deduction, eventuate, terminate
10. conclusion **11.** achievement,
consequence, termination
resume . . . **5.** recur, renew **6.** reopen
7. recover **8.** reoccupy **9.** epitomize,
reiterate, summarize **10.** recommence
résumé . . . **8.** abstract
10. compendium **11.** work history
resurrection . . . **6.** rising **7.** revival
10. apotheosis **11.** restoration
resuscitate . . . **6.** revive **7.** restore
8. revivify
ret . . . **3.** rot **4.** soak **5.** steep
6. expose, impute **7.** ascribe
retable . . . **5.** ledge, shelf **6.** gradin
(gradine) **8.** predella
retail . . . **4.** sale, sell **6.** repeat
8. dispense, disperse
retain . . . **4.** hold, keep, save, stet
6. employ **8.** maintain, preserve,
remember **9.** recollect
rotainer . . . **3.** fee **4.** gage **6.** menial,
minion, vassal, yeoman **7.** servant
9. attendant, bodyguard
retaining wall . . . **9.** revetment
retaliate . . . **5.** repay **6.** avenge
7. requite **12.** make requital
retaliation . . . **6.** talion (Mosaic law, eye
for eye, tooth for tooth) **7.** revenge
8. reprisal, requital **10.** punishment
11. comeuppance, retribution
retard . . . **4.** clog, drag, slow **5.** defer,
delay, laten **6.** belate, deaden, detain,
hinder, impede **8.** keep back,
obstruct, postpone, slow down
retardant . . . **4.** clog, drag **6.** remora
8. obstacle
retardate . . . **6.** impede **8.** retarded
retch . . . **3.** gag **4.** barf (sl), hawk, spit
5. reach, vomit **6.** expand, extend,
strain **7.** stretch, upchuck
rete . . . **3.** net **6.** plexus **7.** network
retention . . . **6.** memory **7.** custody,
holding, keeping **8.** tenacity
11. maintenance, self-control
retentive . . . **6.** memory **7.** keeping
9. tenacious **12.** recollective
retenue . . . **7.** reserve **10.** discretion
11. self-control **13.** self-restraint
rethe . . . **5.** cruel **6.** ardent, fierce,
severe
retiary . . . **6.** spider **7.** netlike
9. gladiator, retiarius
reticence . . . **7.** reserve, silence
9. restraint **13.** secretiveness

reticulated... 3. web 6. meshed, netted 7. network 12. intercrossed
reticule... 3. bag 4. etui 5. cabas (caba) 7. handbag, reticle, workbag
reticulum... 7. network, stomach (2nd) 9. neuroglia
retinue... 4. crew 5. harem, suite, train 6. escort 7. cortege, service 8. equipage 9. entourage, retainers 10. attendants
retire... 6. depart, depose, pay off, recede, vanish 7. go to bed, retreat 8. withdraw 9. disappear, discharge
retired... 4. abed, left, lone, paid 7. receded 8. departed, emeritus, recessed, resigned, secluded, solitary, vanished, withdrew 9. pensioned 10. disengaged 11. disappeared, sequestered
retirement... 7. deposal, payment, privacy, retreat 8. solitude 9. departure, recession, reticence 10. withdrawal 11. resignation 13. disemployment
retiring... 3. shy 6. modest 8. reserved, reticent 9. diffident 10. not forward, retreating 11. unobtrusive
retort... 3. mot 4. quip 5. reply 6. answer 7. riposte (ripost) 8. repartee 9. retaliate 11. retaliation
retract... 6. abjure, disown, draw in, recent, repeal 7. disavow, rescind, swallow 8. take back 9. repudiate
retraction... 6. repeal 8. palinode 10. revocation, withdrawal 11. recantation
retrad... 8. backward 11. posteriorly
retral... 8. backward 9. posterior 10. retrograde
retreat... 3. den 4. abri, lair, nest, nook, rout 6. asylum, recede, recoil, refuge, retire 7. privacy, retiral, sanctum, shelter 8. fallback, solitude 9. departure, katabasis, seclusion 10. retirement, withdrawal
retrench... 6. cut off, excise, lessen, reduce 7. abridge, curtail, cut down 8. decrease, diminish 9. economize, intercept
retrenchment... 3. cut 8. excision 9. lessening, reduction 10. abridgment 11. curtailment, economizing
retribution... 3. pay 6. return, reward 7. nemesis 8. reprisal, requital 9. vengeance 10. punishment 11. restitution 12. Last Judgment
retrieve... 5. fetch 6. redeem, regain, rescue, revive 8. make good
retrograde... 4. slow 6. recede, retral, revert 7. regress 8. backward, decadent, rearward 10. regressive 11. deteriorate 12. reversionary
retroussé... 6. pugged (nose) 8. turned up
retund... 4. beat, dull 5. blunt 6. refute, subdue 9. attenuate, drive back 10. render weak
return... 5. recur, repay, reply 6. answer, render, repeat, report, revert 7. regress, relapse, requiet,

respond, restore 9. repayment 11. restitution, retaliation
return (pert to)...
day.. 12. answer to writ
evil for evil.. 7. revenge 9. retaliate
tennis term.. 3. lob
thrust (fencing).. 7. riposte (ripost)
to.. 6. resume 7. relapse, revisit
to 1st theme (Mus).. 7. reprise
returns... 5. gains, polls 8. receipts
reune... 4. join 7. reunite 10. reassemble
reunion... 7. joining 8. sociable 14. reconciliation
re–up... 8. re–enlist
reus... 9. defendant
Reuter's News Agency... 6. London
reveal... 3. bid 4. bare, jamb, open, tell, wray 6. impart, unveil 7. divulge, exhibit, uncover 8. disclose, discover, evidence, indicate, manifest 11. communicate
reveal (in trust)... 7. confide
reveal intentionally... 4. tell 6. betray, expose 7. divulge, mislead
reveille... 4. call 5. levet 6. signal (sunrise)
revel... 3. joy 4. orgy, riot, wake 5. feast, spree, watch 6. frolic 7. carouse, delight, rejoice, revelry, wassail 8. carousal, festival 11. celebration, merrymaking 12. conviviality
revelant... 5. clear 8. manifest 12. intelligible
revelation... 6. oracle, vision 8. The Bible 9. discovery 10. appearance, disclosure 13. communication, manifestation
Revelation (Bib)... 10. Apocalypse
revelry... 3. joy 4. evoe, orgy, riot 6. revels 8. carnival, carousal 9. revelment, revelrout 11. merrymaking
revenant... 5. ghost 7. eidolon, specter (spectre) 9. recurring 10. apparition
revendicate... 7. reclaim, recover 10. real action
revenge... 6. avenge 7. requite 8. reprisal, requital 9. retaliate, vengeance 10. punishment 11. retribution
revenue... 3. tax 5. yield 6. income, profit 7. annates
reverberate... 4. echo, ring 5. repel, reply 6. return 7. rebound, reflect, resound
reverberation... 4. echo 9. reboation 10. reflection, resounding
revere... 4. love 5. adore, honor 6. esteem, regard, repute 7. respect, worship 8. venerate
reverence... 3. awe 5. dread, honor, piety 7. respect, worship 8. venerate 9. adoration, deference 10. veneration
reverent... 5. pious 6. devout 7. dutiful 10. respectful, worshipful
reverie... 4. muse 5. dream 6. notion, trance, vision 7. fantasy
reversal... 6. defeat, repeal

9. inversion, reversion
14. tergiversation
reverse... 4. back 5. upset 6. back
up, defeat, invert, repeal, revert,
revoke 7. relapse 8. contrary,
converse, opposite, overturn
9. transpose 10. misfortune
reversion... 6. estate 7. revival
8. transfer 9. inversion
10. regression 11. inheritance
reversion (pert to)...
ancestral.. 7. atavism 9. atavistic
insurance.. 7. annuity
land.. 7. escheat
revert... 5. react, recur 6. advert,
return 7. regress, relapse
11. antistrophe
revest... 4. robe 5. dress 6. attire,
clothe 8. reinvest 9. reinstate
review... 4. edit 6. parade, relate,
survey 8. critique, remember
9. criticism, criticize, re–examine
10. certiorati, commentary,
compendium, discussion, inspection,
periodical, reconsider
11. examination, reiteration
12. recollection 15. reconsideration
reviewer... 6. critic, writer
11. commentator
revile... 4. rail 5. abuse, curse
6. berate, debase, vilify 7. asperse
8. reproach, ridicule
revise... 4. edit 5. amend, emend
6. redact 7. correct, rewrite
8. readjust
revision... 7. revisal 10. correction,
emendation 11. rebeholding
13. re–examination
revival... 7. rebirth, renewal
10. quickening 11. reanimation,
renaissance, restoration
12. resurrection
revive... 4. stum (wine) 5. rally,
renew, rouse 6. come to 7. enliven,
recover, refresh, respire, restore
8. rekindle, remember 11. resuscitate
revocate... 6. recall, revoke 7. repress
revocation... 6. repeal 8. reversal
10. retraction, withdrawal
11. recantation
revoke... 5. adeem, annul 6. abjure,
cancel, recall, recant, renege, repeal,
revive 7. abolish, retract 8. abrogate
9. fainaigue 11. countermand
revolt... 5. rebel 6. mutiny, offend,
strike 8. nauseate, sedition, uprising
9. rebellion 10. revolution
12. insurrection
revolting... 4. ugly 7. hideous
8. shocking 9. offensive, repellent
10. disgusting, nauseating
revolution... 4. gyre, turn 5. cycle,
epoch, round 6. revolt 7. circuit
8. disorder, rotation 9. rebellion
revolutionary... 3. new 7. radical
12. catastrophic 15. insurrectionary
Revolutionary hero... 5. Allen (Ethan),
Gates 6. Revere 8. Burgoyne
10. Cornwallis, Washington
15. Lighthorse Harry (Gen Lee)
revolve... 4. pirl, roll, spin, turn
5. recur, wheel, whirl 6. circle,

gyrate, ponder, rotate 7. trundle
8. meditate 9. circulate
10. deliberate
revolver... 3. gat, gun, rod 6. pistol
7. firearm 10. six–shooter
revolving... 3. orb 4. cowl (metal cap)
6. rotary
revolving (pert to)...
in thought.. 8. perusing
light.. 10. lighthouse
part.. 3. cam 5. rotor
storm.. 7. cyclone
revue... 6. medley, review 9. burlesque
13. musical comedy
reward... 3. pay, utu 4. meed
5. award, bonus, merit, Oscar, yield
6. hallow (to hounds) 7. guerdon
8. reprisal 10. recompense,
remunerate 11. retribution
12. compensation, remuneration
reword... 5. alter 7. restate
8. rephrase 9. reiterate
10. paraphrase
rex... 4. king
rey... 4. king
Reynard... 3. fox (epic character)
rezai... 8. coverlet (quilted)
rhamn... 7. Rhamnus 9. buckthorn
rhapontic... 7. rhubarb 8. knapweed,
pieplant
rhapsodic... 6. poetic 8. ecstatic
rhapsodist... 4. poet 8. minstrel
9. visionary 10. enthusiast
rhapsody... 6. jumble, medley
9. utterance (ecstatic) 10. recitation
11. composition
rhea... 3. emu (emeu) 5. nandu
7. ostrich
Rhea (pert to)...
called.. 16. Mother of the Gods
father.. 6. Uranus
home.. 5. Mt Ida (Crete)
mother.. 4. Gaea
mother of.. 4. Hera, Zeus 5. Hades
8. Poseidon
wife of.. 6. Cronus
rhebok... 5. peele 8. antelope
Rheims... see *Reims*
rhema... 4. term, verb, word
rheophile... 15. living in streams
rhetoric... 7. diction, oratory
9. eloquence 11. composition
rhetorical term... 6. aporia, simile
10. antithesis, oratorical
11. catachresis
rhetoric digression... 6. ecbole
rheumatism root... 7. wild yam
rheumatism weed... 10. Indian hemp,
pepsissewa
rhexis... 7. rupture
rhinal... 5. nasal 6. narial
rhine... 5. ditch, drain 6. runnel
Rhine (pert to)...
breed.. 7. rabbits
native.. 11. Rhinelander
nymph.. 7. Lorelei
ref to.. 7. Rhenish
tributary.. 4. Ruhr 6. Neckar
wine.. 7. Moselle
rhino... 4. cash, nose (comb form)
5. money 10. rhinoceros
rhinoceros (pert to)...

Bib .. **4.** reem
bird .. **8.** hornbill **9.** beefeater
black .. **6.** borele **7.** keitlos
Malay .. **5.** abada
viper .. **5.** snake (poisonous)
rhizopod ... **6.** amoeba **8.** Protozoa
Rhoda ... **4.** rose
Rhode Island ...
  bay .. **12.** Narragansett
  capital .. **10.** Providence
  city .. **7.** Newport **9.** Pawtucket
    10. Woonsocket
  famed cotton mill .. **6.** Slater
  first U.S. synagogue .. **5.** Touro
  founder .. **13.** Roger Williams (1636)
  Rebellion .. **5.** Dorr's (1842)
  resort .. **7.** Newport **11.** Block Island
  river .. **9.** Pawtucket **10.** Blackstone
  settlers .. **8.** Puritans
  State admission .. **10.** Thirteenth
  State motto .. **4.** Hope
  State nickname .. **11.** Little Rhody
Rhode Island Red ... **4.** fowl
Rhodesia ... see *Zimbabwe*
rhododaphne ... **8.** oleander
Rhoeadales ... **5.** poppy
    11. Papaverales
rhomb ... **7.** rhombus **10.** magic wheel
    11. spinning top
rhomboid ... **13.** parallelogram
rhombus ... **5.** rhomb
    13. parallelogram (equilateral)
Rhone tributary ... **5.** Isere
rhubarb ... **5.** clash, Rheum **6.** hassle
    7. citrine, dispute, yawweed
    8. argument, pieplant **9.** rhapontic
    10. discussion
Rhus ... **5.** sumac **7.** wax tree
rhyme, rime ... **4.** poem **6.** poetry,
    rhythm **7.** measure **9.** assonance
rhythm ... **4.** beat, lilt **5.** meter, pulse,
    swing, tempo **6.** poetry **7.** cadence,
    euphony, measure, pattern
    8. movement, rhythmus, symmetry
rhythmical break ... **7.** caesura
ria ... **5.** creek, inlet
rial ... **4.** coin, king **5.** great, noble,
    royal **6.** prince **8.** splendid
    9. excellent, stag's horn
    11. magnificent
rialto ... **4.** mart **6.** Bridge (Venice),
    market **7.** theater **8.** exchange
riant ... **3.** gay **6.** blithe, bright
    7. smiling **8.** laughing
riata ... **4.** rope **5.** lasso **6.** lariat
rib ... **4.** bone, meat, vein **5.** costa,
    ridge **6.** lierne
ribald ... **3.** low **4.** lewd. **6.** coarse,
    erotic, harlot, risqué, vulgar
    7. obscene **10.** scurrilous
    11. blasphemous **12.** ribble–rabble
riband ... **6.** ribbon
ribbed ... **3.** rep **5.** piqué **6.** corded,
    ridged **7.** costate
ribble–rabble ... **6.** gabble, rabble,
    ribald **7.** chatter **10.** incoherent
ribbon ... **3.** bow **4.** band, sash
    5. strip **6.** cestus, fillet, riband
    10. decoration
ribbon (pert to) ...
  badge .. **6.** cordon
  band .. **5.** corse **9.** banderole

fish .. **7.** oarfish **8.** dealfish
inked .. **10.** typewriter
knot .. **7.** rosette
ribbonlike .. **8.** taenioid
snake .. **6.** garter
Society .. **7.** Ireland
worm .. **8.** tapeworm **9.** nemertine
ribwort ... **8.** plantain
rice (pert to) ...
  bird .. **4.** rail, sora **8.** bobolink
  dish .. **5.** pilaf (pilau, pilaw) **7.** risotto
    8. kedgeree **9.** jambalaya, ricetable
  drink .. **5.** bubud
  feeding on .. **11.** oryzivorous
  field .. **5.** paddy
  hen .. **9.** gallinule
  inferior .. **4.** chit, pago
  paste .. **3.** ame
  rat .. **8.** Oryzomys
  refuse .. **5.** shood (shud)
  Spanish .. **5.** arroz
  wild .. **4.** reed
  wine .. **4.** sake
rich ... **3.** fat **5.** opime **6.** creamy,
    fecund, fruity, mighty, ornate, potent
    7. copious, fertile, moneyed, opulent,
    wealthy **8.** abundant, affluent,
    colorful, powerful, resonant, valuable
    9. bountiful, expensive, luxuriant,
    sumptuous **10.** in the chips
    13. grandiloquent
rich (pert to) ...
  English slang .. **4.** oofy **6.** oofier
  man .. **5.** Dives (Bib), Midas, nabob
    7. Croesus **9.** plutocrat **10.** capitalist
    11. millionaire
richard ... **9.** plutocrat
riches ... **5.** lucre, means **6.** mammon
    (Bib), wealth **7.** bonanza, big bucks (sl)
    8. opulence **9.** affluence, megabucks
    (sl) **10.** prosperity
riches, demon of ... **6.** Mammon
rick ... **4.** heap, pile **5.** noise, scold,
    stack, twist **6.** pile up, rattle, sprain,
    wrench **7.** chatter
rickets ... **7.** disease **8.** rachitis
rickety ... **4.** weak **5.** crazy, shaky
    6. senile **7.** unsound **8.** unstable,
    unsteady **9.** tottering **10.** ramshackle
rickle ... **4.** heap, pile, rick **5.** stack
    6. jingle, rattle
rickrack ... **5.** braid **6.** edging
    9. insertion
ricksha, rickshaw ... **10.** jinrikisha
ricochet ... **5.** carom **7.** rebound
    10. bounce back
rid ... **4.** doff, free, kill **5.** clear, empty
    6. remove, rescue **7.** deliver, destroy,
    discard **9.** dispose of, drive away,
    eliminate **11.** disencumber
riddance ... **6.** escape **7.** discard
    11. elimination **14.** relinquishment
riddle ... **3.** ree **4.** crux, sift **5.** rebus,
    sieve **6.** enigma, pierce **7.** perplex
    8. separate **9.** conundrum, perforate
ride ... **4.** twit **5.** drive, float **6.** pester,
    travel **7.** be borne, journey, overlap
    8. domineer, ridicule **9.** carrousel
    (carousel), cavalcade, excursion
    10. forest road **12.** merry-go-round
    13. roller coaster
ride (pert to) ...

herd.. 9. guard over
off.. 4. polo (term)
roughshod over.. 9. tyrannize
shank's mare.. 4. walk
to hog, pig.. 11. boar hunting
to line.. 4. herd
rident... 5. riant 7. smiling 8. laughing
rider... 5. ryder 6. clause, knight
   7. allonge, codicil 8. addition,
   horseman 9. performer
   10. freebooter, highwayman
   11. endorsement, mosstrooper
Rider Haggard's novel... 3. She
ridge... 3. aas, rib 4. hill, rand, wale,
   weal, welt 5. arête, bulge, chine,
   crest 7. wrinkle
ridge (pert to)...
anatomy.. 4. ruga 6. carina
barrier.. 5. parma
between furrows.. 7. porcate
   8. porcated
coral.. 4. reef
glacial.. 2. os 5. esker (eskar)
military.. 6. rideau
mountain.. 4. loma 5. arête 6. sierra
narrow, raised.. 4. wale
oak.. 9. blackjack
raised by stroke.. 5. wheal, whelk
short.. 4. kame
sloping.. 6. cuesta
steep.. 7. hogback
stony.. 4. rand
zoology term.. 5. varix
ridicule... 3. guy, pan 4. butt, gibe,
   jeer, mock, quiz, twit 5. chaff, irony,
   sneer, taunt 6. banter, deride, satire
   7. astoism, mockery, sarcasm
   8. derision, raillery 9. burlesque
ridiculous... 5. funny 6. absurd
   7. amusing 8. farcical 9. grotesque,
   laughable, ludicrous 10. impossible,
   outrageous 12. preposterous,
   unbelievable
ridiculous failure... 6. fiasco
riding (pert to)...
bitts.. 11. anchor cable
breeches.. 8. jodhpurs
dress, costume.. 5. habit
knot.. 8. slipknot
rhyme.. 7. couplet
school.. 6. manège
whip.. 4. crop 5. quirt
rife... 7. replete, rumored 8. abundant
   9. abounding, plentiful, prevalent
   10. prevailing, widespread
riff... 6. rapids, riffle, ripple 7. midriff
   9. diaphragm 13. improvisation
riffle... 7. shallow, shuffle, wavelet
riffraff... 3. mob 4. mean 5. offal
   6. rabble, refuse, trashy 7. rubbish
   9. sweepings
rifle... 3. rob 5. reeve, steal, strip
   6. Mauser, search, snider 7. carbine,
   despoil, firearm, pillage, plunder,
   ransack
rifle (pert to)...
accessory.. 6. ramrod
ball.. 5. Minié 6. bullet
bird.. 14. bird of paradise
bomb.. 7. grenade
French.. 9. chassepot
old form.. 4. tige

rifler... 4. hawk 6. robber
rift... 3. gap, lag 4. rima, rive
   5. break, cleft, split 6. cleave, divide
   10. falling out
rig... 3. fit 4. gear, suit 5. dress,
   equip 6. lateen 7. bedizen, costume,
   rigging, vehicle 9. Bermudian (Naut)
Riga (pert to)...
balsam.. 5. resin (Swiss pine)
capital of.. 6. Latvia
native.. 4. Lett 7. Latvian
rine.. 4. hemp
rigging (ship)... 4. gear, rope, spar
   6. tackle 9. equipment
right... 3. fit, pat 4. fair, true
   6. adjust, dexter, proper, remedy
   7. correct, justice, upright
   8. becoming, suitable 9. equitable,
   faultless, franchise, privilege, propriety
   10. put in order 11. appropriate,
   prerogative 13. justification
right (pert to)...
angled.. 10. orthogonal
comb form.. 6. dextro
exclusive.. 6. patent 10. concession
hand.. 6. dexter
hand page.. 5. recto
law.. 5. droit
neither right nor wrong..
   11. adiaphorous
of belligerent (Naut).. 6. angary
of ownership.. 5. title
of procedure.. 3. pas
real estate.. 8. easement
royal.. 7. regalia
time.. 3. tid
to choice.. 6. option
to pasture.. 6. eatage
turn.. 3. gee
righteous... 4. holy, just 5. godly,
   moral, pious 6. worthy 7. upright
   8. virtuous 9. believers, blameless,
   equitable, guiltless
righteousness... 6. equity, virtue
   8. holiness 9. godliness, rectitude
   11. uprightness
rightful... 4. just, true 5. legal, right
   6. honest, lawful, proper 7. fitting,
   genuine 9. equitable 11. appropriate
rigid... 3. set 4. firm, hard 5. exact,
   stern, stiff, tense 6. formal, narrow,
   not lax, severe, strict 7. ascetic,
   austere 8. rigorous 9. obstinate,
   stringent, unbending 10. inflexible,
   meticulous, unyielding
rigidity... 7. tensity 8. hardness,
   severity 9. exactness, obstinacy,
   stiffness
rigol... 4. ring 6. circle, groove
   7. channel
Rigoletto... 5. dance, opera (Verdi)
rigor, rigour... 4. cold, fury 7. cruelty
   8. asperity, rigidity, severity, violence
   9. exactness, harshness, rigidness
   10. shuddering, strictness
   13. inflexibility
rigor mortis... 10. stiffening (death)
   12. rigor of death
rigorous... 4. cold 5. exact, harsh,
   rigid, stern, stiff 6. severe, strict
   7. austere, drastic, violent
   8. accurate 9. inclement, obstinate,

puritanic 10. inexorable, inflexible, relentless
rikk... 10. tambourine
rile... 3. vex 4. roil 5. anger, muddy 6. offend 7. agitate 8. irritate 9. turbidity
rill... 5. brook 6. course, runnel 7. rillock, rivulet 9. streamlet
rim... 3. lip, web 4. band, brim, edge, orle, tire 5. bezel, brink, felly (felloe), verge 6. border, flange, margin, shield 7. enclose, horizon, rimrock 8. boundary 9. perimeter
rima... 5. cleft 7. fissure 8. aperture 10. breadfruit
rima oris... 16. space between lips
rim ash... 9. hackberry
rimate... 8. fissured
rime... 4. hoar, poem, rent 5. chink, cleft, crack, frost, rhyme 6. poetry 7. fissure 8. aperture 9. assonance, hoarfrost 10. ladder step
rime—cold giant (Norse)... 4. Ymir (Ymer)
rimple... 4. fold 6. ripple, rumple 7. wrinkle
rimption... 3. lot 9. abundance
Rinaldo's steed... 6. Bayard
rind... 4. bark, husk, peel, skin 5. crust 6. cortex 7. epicarp 9. hoarfrost
rindle... 5. brook 6. runnel 7. rivulet
ring... 3. rim, set 4. band, halo, hoop, peal, toll 5. arena, bague, chime, group, knell 6. circle, clique, collar 7. annulus, circlet, coterie, resound 8. encircle, insignia, ornament, surround 9. encompass 11. association
ring (pert to)...
around.. 7. environ
around the sun.. 6. corona
barrel.. 4. hoop
bill.. 4. duck
bird.. 11. reed bunting
comb form.. 4. gyro
dove.. 6. cushat
finger.. 5. third
fruit jar.. 4. lute
gem crown.. 5. bezel
gem setting.. 6. chaton
gun carriage.. 7. lunette (lunet)
harness part.. 6. terret
horse training.. 5. longe
Latin.. 7. annulus
leader.. 6. rouser 9. demagogue 12. rabble—rouser
little.. 7. annulet, circlet
ornament (metal).. 3. bee (angling)
ouzel.. 6. thrush
rope.. 7. grommet
sail.. 4. hank 8. ringtail
tail.. 3. cat 4. coon 5. lemur 6. godwit, marlin 10. cacomistle 11. golden eagle (young)
ringed boa... 5. aboma
ringed worm... 7. annelid
ringhals... 5. snake (spitting)
ringing... 7. clangor, orotund, pealing, tolling 8. clanging, resonant 10. resounding
ringle—eye... 7. walleye

ringlet... 4. curl, lock 5. tress 6. circle 7. circlet 9. fairy ring
ringworm... 5. tinea 6. tetter 7. disease, serpigo 9. millepede
rink... 4. hero, race, ring 6. circle, course 7. warrior 8. encircle, ice sheet (skating) 9. encounter
rinse... 4. lave, sind, wash 5. flush 6. sluice 7. cleanse 8. absterge
rintherout, rintherout (Scot)... 5. tramp 7. vagrant 8. vagabond
rio... 5. river 6. coffee, stream
Rio de Janeiro... 7. capital (old, Braz)
Rio Grande... 5. river 7. disease (lettuce)
riot... 3. din 5. brawl, melee 6. clamor, excess, pogrom, revolt, tumult, uproar 7. dispute, quarrel, revelry 8. carousal, disorder, violence 9. commotion
riotous... 4. raid 5. aroar 6. wanton 7. violent 9. dissolute, luxuriant, seditious 10. profligate, tumultuous 12. unrestrained
riotous jollity... 9. dissolute 11. saturnalian
rip... 3. cut 4. rend, rent, tear 5. break, horse (old) 7. riptide 9. debauchee, libertine, reprobate 10. fish basket, laceration
ripe... 3. fit 5. ready, rife 6. mature, mellow 7. plunder 8. finished, prepared, rareripe 9. developed, full—grown, perfected 10. consummate
ripen... 3. age 5. addle 6. digest, mellow, nature 7. develop, perfect, prepare 8. complete, grow ripe
riposte, ripost... 5. reply 6. answer, retort, thrust 8. repartee
ripping... 5. bully, grand, swell 9. admirable, hunky—dory 12. fine and dandy
rippit... 9. fist fight
ripple... 3. cut, lap 4. fret, purl, riff, tear, wave 5. acker, eagre, graze 6. dimple, murmur 7. crinkle, disturb, scratch, trickle, wavelet 11. corrugation
ripple grass plantain... 7. ribwort
ris de veau... 10. sweetbread
rise... 4. grow, soar, well 5. arise, begin, climb, get up, mount, raise, reach, rebel, start, surge, tower 6. ascend, ascent, attain, be high, emerge, growth, height, revolt, spring, thrive 7. succeed 8. eminence, flourish, increase, levitate, reaction 9. acclivity, ascension, beginning, elevation, originate 11. development
rise (pert to)...
above.. 4. loom 8. surmount 11. triumph over
again.. 7. resurge 11. resurrected
and fall of the sea.. 5. scend, tidal 6. welter
by buoyancy.. 8. levitate
gradually.. 4. loom
hawk's.. 6. mounty
high.. 5. tower
risible... 5. funny 6. absurd

9. laughable

rising... 6. ascent, ortive, revolt
7. growing, montant, sloping, surgent
8. elevated, emergent, gradient (by degrees), swelling 9. acclivity, advancing, ascending, ascension

rising and falling... 5. tidal 7. surging
8. undulant

risk... 4. dare 5. peril 6. chance, danger, expose, gamble, hazard, injury, plight 7. venture 8. endanger
10. investment 12. disadvantage

risky... 6. risqué 9. hazardous
11. venturesome

risp... 3. rub 4. file, rasp, tirl 5. stalk
7. bulrush, scratch

risper... 11. caterpillar

risqué... 4. racy 5. risky, salty
8. off–color 9. hazardous
10. suggestive

rissle... 4. pole 5. staff, stick

risus... 5. laugh 8. laughter

rit (rare)... 3. cut, rip 4. slit, tear
5. split 6. pierce 7. scratch

ritardando... 9. direction, retarding
10. slackening 11. rallentando

rite... 4. cult, form 6. ritual, sacrum
7. formula, liturgy, tonsure
8. ceremony 9. solemnity
10. ceremonial, initiation, observance
12. patriarchate

ritratto... 7. picture 8. portrait

Ritter... 6. knight

ritual... 4. book, code, cult, form, rite
5. feast, salat 6. novena, prayer
7. liturgy 8. ceremony
10. ceremonial

ritus... 5. usage 6. custom

ritzy... 5. smart (vulgarly), swank
6. swanky 11. pretentious
16. ultra–fashionable

rivage... 4. bank, duty 5. coast, green, shore

rival... 3. foe, vie 4. even, peer
5. excel, match 7. compete, emulate
8. emulator, opponent
10. antagonist, competitor
11. compete with

rivalry... 4. feud 9. emulation
11. competition

rive... 3. rip 4. bank, open, rent, rift, tear 5. cleft, sever, shore, split
6. cleave 8. lacerate

rive droite... 9. Right Bank (Seine)

rive gauche... 8. Left Bank (Seine, Paris, including Latin Qtr)

rivel... 6. shrink 7. shrivel, wrinkle

river... 2. ea 3. ria, rio, run 4. ilog
5. amnis, brook, creek 6. stream
7. rivulet, torrent 8. riverlet
9. streamlet

river (pert to)...
arm (of sea).. 7. estuary
bank.. 4. ripa 5. levee
bank, pert to.. 8. riparian
bed.. 4. holm 6. alveus, bottom
7. channel
bend.. 5. oxbow
boat.. 3. ark
delta branch.. 5. bayou
dog.. 10. hellbender
dragon.. 9. crocodile

duck.. 4. teal
fish (spawning, from sea)..
10. anadromous
horse.. 5. hippo 12. hippopotamus
inlet.. 4. slew 5. fiord (fjord)
6. slough
islet.. 3. ait 4. holm
mouth.. 4. lade 5. delta 7. estuary
mussel.. 4. unio
Near East.. 4. wadi (wady)
Nile measure.. 9. Nilometer
nymph.. 4. nais 5. naiad
rat.. 5. thief
ref to.. 5. amnic
region (near).. 8. riverine
siren.. 7. Lorelei
thief.. 3. rat 6. ackman
winding.. 3. ess

river in...
Africa.. 4. Nile, Tana 5. Niger
Austria.. 4. Iser 5. Drava
Bavaria.. 4. Eger, Isar
Belgium.. 4. Yser
Bohemia.. 4. Elbe, Iser
Brazil.. 3. Rio
Bulgaria.. 5. Mesta
China.. 3. Wei 6. Yellow 7. Hwang Ho
England.. 4. Isis 6. Thames
France.. 5. Seine
Germany.. 6. Danube
Italy.. 4. Arno 5. Tiber
Netherlands.. 3. Eem 4. Maas (Meuse)
S America.. 6. Amazon
Siberia.. 2. Ob 4. Lena
Switzerland.. 3. Aar 5. Reuss

river of...
Annie Laurie.. 4. Nith
Caesar.. 7. Rubicon
lower regions.. 4. Styx 5. Lethe
7. Acheron
woe.. 7. Acheron

rixy... 4. tern

road... 3. via, way 4. iter, path, raid
5. agger 7. estrada, highway, journey, passage 8. pavement
9. incursion, roadstead
10. expedition

road (pert to)...
block.. 3. dam 4. weir
goose.. 5. brant
hog.. 8. motorist 10. monopolist
horse.. 6. saddle (horse)
impassable.. 7. impasse
man.. 7. drummer, peddler
8. salesman 9. canvasser
map.. 5. chart, globe 9. directory
master.. 10. supervisor
11. trackmaster
nautical.. 9. roadstead
no outlet.. 8. cul–de–sac
paving.. 6. Tarmac 7. ballast, macadam
runner.. 6. cuckoo
scraper.. 4. harl
weed.. 8. plantain

roam... 2. go 3. err, gad 4. rove
5. prowl, range 6. ramble, stroll, wander 7. meander 9. gallivant

roan... 5. horse (bay, gray, chestnut)
8. antelope 9. sheepskin, yellow–red

roanoke ... 6. wampum
Roanoke ...
  city .. 8. Virginia
  famed as .. 11. First Colony (1584)
  famed for .. 12. Virginia Dare (1st
    white child, 1587)
  settler .. 16. Sir Walter Raleigh
    19. Sir Richard Grenville
roar ... 4. bell, blow, boom, rote (surf)
  5. brool, laugh, shout 6. bellow,
  steven 7. ululate 8. cry aloud
  9. loud sound
roaring ... 5. aroar, great 7. booming,
  riotous 10. disorderly
Roaring (pert to) ...
  Forties .. 8. Broadway (NYC)
  game .. 7. curling (Scot)
  Twenties .. 14. Golden Twenties
    16. Age of Red Hot Mamas
roast ... 4. beef, cook 5. cabob, parch
  6. assate, banter 7. torrefy
  8. ridicule 9. criticize
roasting (pert to) ...
  ear .. 4. corn
  jack .. 9. smokejack
  stick .. 4. spit
rob ... 4. loot, pelf 5. pinch (sl), reave,
  rifle, steal, touch 6. pilfer, ravish,
  snatch, snitch 7. despoil, pillage,
  plunder 10. plagiarize
robbed ... 5. stole 6. rubato (Mus)
  8. snatched, snitched
robber ... 4. yegg 5. crook (sl), thief
  6. bandit, reaver, rifler 7. brigand,
  burglar, yeggman 8. pillager
  9. despoiler, embezzler, larcenist,
  peculator 10. depredator,
  highwayman, shoplifter
robber (pert to) ...
  grave .. 5. ghoul
  high seas .. 6. pirate 7. corsair
    9. privateer
  highway .. 7. footpad, ladrone
  Indian .. 6. dacoit
robbery ... 4. reif 5. theft 6. burgle,
  piracy 7. larceny, pillage, plunder
  8. burglary 10. spoliation
  11. depredation
robe ... 5. array, cover, dress, tunic
  6. invest, mantle 7. costume,
  garment 8. clerical, vestment
robe (pert to) ...
  bishop's .. 6. chimer
  camel's hair .. 3. aba
  long .. 5. talar
  loose .. 5. cymar (symar)
  royal .. 6. ermine, purple
robin ... 4. bird, lout, tody 6. thrush
  7. bumpkin 8. trimming 9. redbreast
  10. toxalbumin
robin (pert to) ...
  dipper .. 14. bufflehead duck
  runaway .. 7. dewdrop
  sandpiper .. 4. knot 5. snipe
    9. dowitcher
  songbird .. 8. accentor
Robin Bluestring ... 13. Robert
  Walpole
robinet ... 6. cannon 9. chaffinch
Robin Goodfellow ... 4. Puck 6. sprite
  9. hobgoblin
Robin Hood (pert to) ...

  famed as .. 6. archer, outlaw, yeoman
  followers .. 9. Friar Tuck 10. Little
    John, Maid Marian
  forest .. 8. Sherwood (Eng)
  habit .. 11. robbing rich (for the poor)
Robinson Crusoe's man ... 6. Friday
roborant ... 4. drug 5. tonic 6. bracer
  8. pick–me–up 9. stimulant
roborean ... 5. oaken, stout 6. strong
robot ... 9. automaton
Rob Roy ... 5. canoe 6. outlaw (Scot)
  15. Robert MacGregor
robust ... 4. hale 5. hardy, lusty,
  rough, sound, stout, wally 6. hearty,
  sinewy, strong, sturdy 7. healthy
  8. muscular, vigorous
roc ... 4. bird (Arabian Nights)
  7. simurgh (simurg)
rocca ... 4. hold 6. donjon 8. fortress
rock ... 3. orc 4. lull, peak, sway, trap,
  tufa, tuff 5. agate, chert, cliff, quiet,
  shake, slate, stone 6. basalt, egeran,
  gneiss, refuge, schist, teeter
  7. diamond, missile 8. dolomite,
  porphyry, strength 9. whinstone
  10. promontory
rock (pert to) ...
  black .. 6. basalt
  brittle .. 5. shale
  broken .. 4. sand 5. attle
  cavity .. 5. druse
  chain .. 4. reef
  coarse .. 8. psammite, psephite
  crystal .. 6. silica
  crystalline .. 6. gneiss, schist
  decomposed .. 6. gossan
  fluid .. 4. lava
  fragments .. 5. scree 8. detritus,
    xenolith
  geyser deposit .. 6. sinter
  glacial .. 7. moraine
  granitelike .. 6. gneiss
  granular .. 6. oolite, quartz 7. diorite
    10. rockallite
  gray .. 5. slate 8. andesite
  igneous .. 4. boss, trap 6. basalt
    7. peridot
  jutting .. 3. tor 4. crag
  nodule .. 5. geode
  pinnacle .. 4. scar 6. needle
  porous .. 5. tufa, tuff
  rounded .. 6. rognon
  science .. 9. petrology
  Sicilian .. 6. Scylla (opp Charybdis)
  stratified .. 5. shale
  suffix .. 3. ite, yte
  volcanic .. 4. tufa 6. basalt, domite,
    latite
rock, animal ...
  badger .. 4. cony
  cavy .. 6. rodent
  dassie .. 6. rabbit
  goat .. 4. ibex
  kangaroo .. 7. wallaby
  squirrel .. 11. spermophile
rock, bird ...
  blackbird .. 9. ring ouzel
  dove .. 9. guillemot 10. rockpigeon
  duck .. 9. harlequin
  goose .. 9. kelp goose
  grouse .. 9. ptarmigan
  hawk .. 6. falcon, merlin

hopper.. 7. penguin
lark.. 5. pipit
pigeon.. 10. sand grouse
sandpiper.. 5. pipit, snipe
shrike.. 10. rock thrush
starling.. 5. ouzel
swallow.. 10. rock martin
rock, fish...
bass.. 5. black 7. striped
clam.. 5. borer
cod.. 7. grouper
cook.. 6. wrasse 7. whiting
eel.. 6. gunnel
gurnet.. 9. fortescue
hind.. 7. grouper (spotted)
lobster.. 8. crayfish
salmon.. 7. codfish 9. amberfish
sucker.. 7. lamprey
trout.. 9. greenling
rock, flora...
bell.. 9. columbine
brake.. 8. polypody
candytuft.. 8. gold dust
cedar.. 7. juniper
cranberry.. 8. mountain
elm.. 11. slippery elm
garden.. 6. alpine
geranium.. 8. alumroot
hair.. 6. lichen
lily.. 9. columbine 12. pasqueflower
maple.. 5. sugar
melon.. 10. cantaloupe
shrub.. 9. buckthorn
rocket... 5. lance 6. ascend, ascent,
fire at 8. aircraft, firework
9. skyrocket, spaceship
rocket (famed)... 5. Titan 6. Apollo,
Gemini, Saturn 7. Jupiter, Mercury
8. Redstone
Rock of Chickamauga... 6. Thomas
(Gen), (Civil War)
rocks... 5. money
rocks, on the... 7. aground
8. bankrupt, stranded 10. saxicoline
rocky... 4. hard 5. stony 6. rugged
7. sickish 8. obdurate, unsteady
9. unfeeling
Rocky Ford... 9. muskmelon
Rocky Mountain...
group.. 5. Coast 8. Cascades
12. Sierra Nevada
park.. 5. Estes
peak.. 6. Elbert 8. McKinley
popular name.. 7. Rockies
range.. 5. Teton, Uinta
rococo... 6. florid 7. baroque, bizarre
9. fantastic, grotesque
13. ornamentation
rod... 3. gat, gun 4. pole, wand, whip
5. baton, perch, power, scion, staff
7. measure, scepter
rod (pert to)...
comb form.. 5. rhabd 6. rhabdo
fibrous.. 5. lytta
flat.. 6. ferula, ferule
grooved.. 4. came (stained glass)
knitting.. 6. needle
meat–holding.. 4. spit
mechanical.. 5. piston
metal.. 7. stemmer
mixing.. 3. rab
pointed.. 4. goat, spit

rodlike.. 9. vergiform
rotating.. 7. spindle
short.. 6. toggle
spinning.. 7. spindle
rodd... 8. crossbow, stonebow
rodent... 4. cony, hare, paca 5. hutia
(jutia), mouse, stoat 6. agouti
(agouty), beaver, gerbil, gopher,
marmot, murine 7. lemming, leveret
8. chipmunk, hedgehog, mongoose,
squirrel 9. guinea pig, porcupine
rodent (pert to)...
Andes.. 8. abrocome
aquatic.. 6. beaver 7. muskrat
Belgian.. 8. leporide
burrowing.. 6. marmot 8. sewellel
disease.. 9. tularemia
European.. 4. cony 5. lerot
fur–bearing.. 6. beaver
genus.. 3. Mus 5. Lepus
gnawing.. 3. rat 4. mole
hare.. 6. rabbit
jumping.. 6. jerboa
largest.. 8. capybara (capibara)
migrating.. 7. lemming
Mongoloid.. 3. rat 6. gopher
12. pocket gopher
mouselike.. 4. vole
rabbitlike.. 4. pika
reference to.. 7. gnawing 8. rosorial
S American.. 4. degu 5. coypu
6. agouti 8. capybara 10. chinchilla
spiny.. 9. porcupine
rodeo... 4. show 7. roundup
9. spectacle 11. performance (public)
rodomontade... 4. brag, rant 5. boast
7. bluster 8. boastful, boasting,
braggart, bragging
roe... 2. ra 3. doo 4. door, hind, roun
6. coral (lobster) 8. fish eggs
Roentgen, Röntgen (Wilhelm)...
famed as.. 9. physicist
famed for.. 5. X–rays 10. Nobel Prize
(1901) 12. Roentgen rays
rogan... 4. bowl (wooden)
10. receptacle (maple sap)
Roger's plane (Will)... 9. Winnie May
rogue... 3. imp, wag 4. kite 5. cheat,
knave, scamp, shark, tramp
6. beggar, pirate, rascal 7. corsair,
vagrant, villain 8. elephant, picaroon,
vagabond 13. mischief–maker
roguish... 3. sly 4. arch 5. pawky
7. knavish 8. espiegle, rascally
10. frolicsome, picaresque
11. mischievous
roguishly... 5. slyly 8. impishly, trickily
10. prankishly
roid... 5. rough 6. severe 7. riotous
10. frolicsome 12. unmanageable
roil... 3. vex 4. foul, roam, romp
5. anger, annoy, horse (Flemish),
muddy 6. fidget, ruffle, wander
7. agitate, disturb 8. irritate
roister... 4. brag, rude 5. bully
7. bluster, boorish, swagger, violent
9. gilravage
roisterer (Hist)... 3. mun
rojo... 3. Red 6. Indian (Mex)
7. Redskin
roke... 3. fog 4. stir 5. moist, smoke,
steam, vapor 8. moisture

roker... 3. ray 8. rockling 9. thornback
roky... 4. damp 5. foggy, misty, smoky
  6. hoarse
role... 4. duty, part 6. office
  8. capacity, function 9. character
  13. impersonation
roll... 3. bun, rob 4. coil, film, food,
  furl, list, pell, rota, sway, wind, wrap
  5. trill, troll 6. billow, bundle, rotate,
  rumble, scroll 8. bankroll, cylinder,
  rotation
roll (pert to)...
  along.. 7. trundle
  back.. 6. reduce 8. retrench
  bread.. 3. bap
  butter.. 3. pat
  cloth.. 4. bolt
  coins.. 7. rouleau
  fish.. 7. rissole
  hair.. 3. rat 7. chignon
  military.. 5. cadre 6. roster
  the bones.. 4. dice 10. shoot craps
  tobacco.. 5. cigar
  to one side.. 5. lurch
  up.. 4. furl 6. bundle 10. accumulate
roller... 4. wave 5. inker, skate, towel
  6. canary, caster, fillet, pigeon,
  platen 7. bandage, rotator, sirgang
  8. cylinder 10. Holy Roller, pulverizer
rolling (pert to)...
  movement.. 6. welter
  pin.. 6. roller 8. cylinder
  stock.. 7. coaches, engines
  8. cabooses, Pullmans 9. motor cars
  11. locomotives
  stone.. 8. wanderer
  weed.. 10. tumbleweed
rollix... 4. play 6. frolic 7. rollick
romaine... 10. cos lettuce
romal... 5. quirt, thong
Roman... 5. brave, Latin 6. frugal,
  honest, simple 7. Italian
Roman (pert to)... see also *Rome*
  afterpiece (theater).. 5. exode, farce
  8. travesty
  alcove.. 8. tablinum
  apostle (Bib).. 4. Neri
  assembly.. 5. forum 7. comitia
  augur.. 6. auspex
  awning.. 8. velarium
  barrack, hut.. 6. canaba (cannaba)
  basilica.. 7. Lateran
  booth, shelter.. 7. taberna
  bowl.. 6. patina
  boxing glove.. 6. cestus
  breastplate.. 6. lorica
  bronze.. 3. aes
  building.. 5. aedes (worship)
  case.. 5. bulla (for amulets)
  cathedral.. 7. Lateran
  chariot.. 5. essed (esseda)
  chest.. 4. cist
  circus post.. 4. meta
  circus wall.. 5. spina
  cistern.. 9. impluvium
  citadel.. 3. arx
  citizen (nonvoting).. 8. aerarian
  clan.. 4. gens
  cloak.. 5. sagum (Mil) 6. abolla
  7. planeta
  concert hall.. 5. odeum
  court (Pope's).. 5. Curia

  cuirass.. 6. lorica
Curia office.. 6. datary 7. dataria
date.. 4. ides 5. nones 7. calends
dish.. 6. patera
division (Polit).. 5. curia
earthwork (Mil).. 5. agger
Empire district.. 5. Pagus
era.. 5. Varro
farce.. 5. exode
festival days.. 5. feria 10. feriae Jovi
  (festivals of Jupiter)
fish sauce.. 4. alec 5. garum
foot coverage, sock.. 3. udo
galley.. 6. bireme 7. trireme
garment.. 4. toga 5. palla, stole,
  tunic
general's cloak.. 12. paludamentum
  (paludament)
Govt of two men.. 10. duumvirate
Hades.. 5. Orcus 10. lower world
hairpin.. 4. acus
hall (concert).. 5. odeum
helmet.. 5. galea
highway.. 3. via 4. iter
highway, famed.. 9. Appian Way
hills.. 7. Viminal 8. Aventine, Palatine,
  Quirinal 9. Esquiline 10. Capitoline
javelin.. 5. pilum
land (public).. 4. ager
language.. 5. Latin
law.. 3. jus 4. cern
law, divine.. 3. fas
market day.. 7. nundine
marriage.. 13. confarreation
matron's garment.. 5. stola, stole
meal (chief).. 4. cena (coena)
military cloak.. 5. sagum
military machine.. 7. terebra
military unit.. 6. legion 7. maniple
money.. 3. aes
ornament (neck).. 5. bulla
palace.. 7. Lateran
peace.. 3. pax
provisions (free).. 6. annona
ram (battery).. 5. aries
religious law.. 3. fas
religious rite.. 5. sacra
road.. 4. iter 6. Appian (paved)
robe.. 4. toga
room.. 3. ala 6. atrium 8. tablinum
seat.. 5. sella
shelter, shop.. 7. taberna
shield.. 6. scutum
soldier's protection.. 7. testudo
spirits (group).. 5. manes 7. lemures
tablet (writing).. 7. diptych
temple.. 4. naos 5. cella
tent.. 7. taberna
theater.. 5. odeum
travesty.. 5. exode
vase.. 7. amphora (wine) 8. murrhine
warship.. 6. bireme 7. trireme
Way (famed).. 6. Appian
wine shop.. 7. taberna
romance... 5. fancy, novel, story
  7. fantasy, fiction, romanza, romaunt
  8. idealize 9. falsehood, sentiment
  11. imagination
romance (pert to)...
  language.. 6. French 7. Catalan,
  Italian, Spanish 9. Provençal
  10. Portuguese

ref to.. 8. knightly 10. chivalrous
verse.. 7. sestina
Roman god (of)...
chief.. 4. Jove 7. Jupiter
dead.. 5. Orcus
fire.. 6. Vulcan
Hades.. 3. Dis 5. Pluto 8. Dispater
households.. 5. Lares 7. Penates
husbandry, animals.. 6. Faunus
love.. 4. Amor 5. Cupid
mirth.. 5. Comus
sun.. 3. Sol
Supreme.. 4. Jove 7. Jupiter
two–faced.. 5. Janus
underworld.. 3. Dis 5. Pluto
   8. Dispater
war.. 4. Mars 8. Quirinus
Roman goddess (of)...
agriculture.. 3. Ops 5. Ceres
beauty.. 5. Venus
burials.. 8. Libitina
childbirth.. 6. Lucina
crops.. 6. Annona
dawn.. 6. Aurora
earth.. 6. Tellus
fertility.. 6. Annona
handicrafts.. 7. Minerva
harvests.. 3. Ops
health.. 7. Minerva
hearth.. 5. Vesta
horses.. 5. Epona
love.. 5. Venus
moon.. 4. Luna 7. Phoebus
mothers, nursing.. 6. Rumina
night.. 3. Nox
peace.. 3. Pax 5. Irene
religion.. 4. Maia
strife.. 9. Discordia
victory (war) 6. Vacuna
womanhood.. 4. Juno
Roman people...
author.. 5. Pliny, Varro
biographer.. 5. Nepos
Bishop.. 4. Pope
boy (free birth).. 8. camillus
Catholic priest.. 8. sacerdos
Catholic Society.. 6. Jesuit
consul.. 6. Scipio
Cupid.. 4. Eros
deity.. 4. faun
Diana.. 7. Artemis
dictator.. 5. Sulla 11. Cincinnatus
diviner.. 5. augur 6. auspex
divinity (chief).. 4. Jove
Emperor.. 4. Nero, Otto 5. Titus
   7. Maximus 8. Tiberius
   11. Constantine 12. Heliogabalus
Eros.. 5. Cupid
farmer.. 7. colonus
Fates.. 4. Nona 5. Morta 6. Decuma
General.. 5. Sulla, Titus 6. Antony,
   Marius, Scipio
ghosts.. 7. lemures
gladiator.. 7. Samnite 9. retiarius
gladiator trainer.. 7. lanista
governor.. 9. proconsul
guard.. 6. lictor
historian.. 4. Livy 5. Nepos 7. Sallust
   8. Appianus (Appian)
judge.. 6. aedile (edile)
king (1st).. 7. Romulus
king's adviser (Myth).. 6. Egeria

magistrate, official.. 5. augur 6. aedile
   (edile), censor, consul 7. praetor
   (pretor), tribune
maiden, betrayer to Sabrines..
   7. Tarpeia
military officer.. 9. proconsul
Naturalist.. 5. Pliny
nun.. 6. vestal
nymph (fountain).. 6. Egeria
officer.. 6. lictor 8. triumvir (one of
   three)
official of public games.. 7. Asiarch
orator.. 5. Pliny 6. Cicero
palace officer.. 8. palatine
patriot.. 4. Cato
people (anc).. 7. Sabines 8. Samnites
   9. plebeians 10. patricians
philosopher.. 4. Cato 6. Seneca
   7. Rosmini
physician.. 11. Aesculapius
poet.. 4. Ovid 5. Lucan 6. Horace,
   Vergil 7. Juvenal (satirical)
politician, courtier.. 7. Sejanus
priest.. 5. epulo 8. tresviri (10 in all)
   9. decemviri 10. septemviri
priest, serving a god.. 6. flamen
priestess.. 6. vestal
priests of Faunus.. 7. Luperci
race (conquered).. 6. Sabine
saint.. 4. Neri
scholar.. 5. Varro
serf.. 6. colona (fem) 7. colonus
   (male)
slave (befriended lion).. 9. Androcles
soldiers (body of).. 6. cohort
statesman.. 4. Cato 6. Caesar, Cicero,
   Seneca
Tarquin rulers.. 9. Etruscans
tenant farmer.. 7. colonus
triumvirate, first.. 6. Caesar, Pompey
   7. Crassus
triumvirate, second.. 6. Antony
   7. Lepidus 8. Octavius
troops.. 6. alares
tyrant.. 4. Nero
virgin.. 6. vestal
writer (comic).. 7. Terence
Romany, Rommany... 5. gypsy
   10. mascot blue
Rome...
cathedral (world's largest).. 8. St
   Peter's
churches.. 7. Lateran 8. Castello,
   Gandolfo
conqueror.. 6. Alaric
founder (legendary).. 7. Romulus
hills.. 5. Seven 6. Sabine 7. Viminal
   8. Aventine, Palatine, Quirinal
lake.. 4. Nemi
original city.. 12. Roma Quadrata
palace (world's largest).. 7. Vatican
peak (Capitoline).. 8. Tarpeian
port (anc).. 5. Ostia
prairie.. 8. Campagna
river.. 5. Tiber
seat of.. 7. Holy See 11. Vatican City
site, ancient.. 13. Campus Martius
site, founding.. 12. Palatine Hill
street (famed).. 6. Corso
Romulus (pert to)...
brother.. 5. Remus
city site.. 12. Palatine Hill

father.. **4.** Mars
founder (Myth).. **4.** Rome
king (1st).. **4.** Rome
mother.. **6.** Sylvia
rescued from.. **5.** Tiber
suckled by.. **7.** she–wolf
ronde... **6.** script (heavy) **9.** round
   hand
rondeau... **4.** game, poem **5.** rondo
   6. rondel
rondel, rondelle... **4.** poem **5.** tower
   (Fort) **8.** round gem
rondure... **9.** plumpness, roundness
ronier... **7.** palmyra
ronin... **6.** outlaw **7.** outcast, samurai
rood... **5.** cross (holy), goose
   7. measure **8.** crucifix
roodebok... **6.** impala **9.** duikerbok
roof... **3.** hip **4.** dome, eave, flat,
   nave, tile **5.** cover, gable, slate, spire
   6. cupola, lean–to **7.** chopper,
   gambrel, mansard, pitched, shingle
   8. housetop, thatched **9.** penthouse
   10. jerkinhead
roof (pert to)...
boards (thin).. **4.** sark
brain cover.. **4.** tela **14.** telachorioidea
frame (raised).. **7.** coaming
material.. **3.** tin **4.** tile **5.** paper, slate
   6. copper, shakes **7.** roofage
   8. shingles
mouth.. **6.** palate
ornament.. **3.** epi
tile.. **7.** pantile
timber.. **6.** rafter
tin (coating).. **5.** terne
tool.. **3.** zax
Roof of the World, Asia... **6.** Pamirs
   (The) **9.** Bam i Dunya
rook... **4.** bird, crow, dupe **5.** cheat
   6. castle **7.** defraud, sharper
   8. chessman **9.** ruddy duck
rookery... **4.** slum **9.** confusion
   13. breeding place (rooks, herons,
   penguins) **14.** breeding ground (seals)
rookie, rooky... **6.** novice **7.** recruit
   8. beginner, newcomer
rooky... **4.** roky **5.** foggy
room... **3.** ala (anc), den **4.** aula, cell,
   hall, sala, seat, shed **5.** attic, lodge,
   place, salon, scope, space **6.** cellar,
   leeway, pantry, parlor, reside
   7. chamber, drawing, laundry,
   nursery, quarter **8.** capacity
   9. apartment, storeroom
   11. opportunity
room (pert to)...
church (bishop's).. **4.** apse
convent.. **9.** parlatory
dining.. **7.** cenacle, dinette
   9. refectory
harem.. **3.** oda
household.. **5.** ewery
inner.. **3.** ben
large.. **4.** aula, hall **7.** rotunda,
   theater **10.** auditorium
monastery.. **4.** cell
outer.. **3.** but
pantry.. **6.** larder **8.** cupboard
prayer.. **7.** oratory
Pueblo Ind ceremonial.. **4.** kiva
Roman.. **6.** atrium

ship's.. **4.** brig **5.** cabin, salon
sleeping.. **5.** lodge **6.** dormer
   7. barrack, bedroom, chamber
   9. dormitory
tower (bell).. **6.** belfry
roomy... **4.** airy **5.** ample **8.** spacious
   9. capacious, expansive
   10. commodious **11.** large–framed
roon... **5.** shred **6.** border **7.** darling
   8. treasure
roorback, roorbach... **3.** lie **6.** canard
   7. lampoon **9.** falsehood
roose... **5.** boast, vaunt **6.** praise
Roosevelt...
president, 26th.. **8.** Theodore
president, 32nd.. **8.** Franklin
roost... **3.** bed, sit **4.** jouk, pole, rest
   5. perch **6.** settle **7.** lodging,
   support
rooster... **4.** cock, male (animal)
   5. gallo **7.** percher **11.** chanticleer
   12. fighting cock
root... **4.** bulb, word **5.** cheer, plant,
   radix, tuber **6.** source **7.** radical
   8. take root **9.** establish
root (pert to)...
aromatic.. **9.** sassafras
edible.. **3.** oca, yam **4.** beet, eddo,
   taro **6.** carrot, potato, radish, turnip
   7. parsnip **8.** rutabaga
food (Maori).. **3.** roi
medicinal.. **4.** atis **5.** jalep **6.** ipecac,
   senega **7.** Senegal
out.. **4.** seek **7.** extract **9.** eliminate,
   eradicate
perfume.. **5.** orris
pungent.. **6.** ginger
starch.. **7.** cassava
stock.. **7.** rhizome
stringy.. **5.** watap (watape)
taro.. **4.** eddo
word.. **4.** etym **6.** etymon
rooted... **8.** habitual **9.** implanted
   10. deep–seated **11.** established,
   traditional
rootlet... **7.** radicel, rhizoid, taproot
rope... **3.** tew, tie, tye **4.** bind, cord,
   line, rood **5.** cable, cigar, lasso,
   longe, noose, reata, wanty **6.** fasten,
   halter, hawser, lariat, string, tether
   7. cordage, lanyard, measure
   8. hangman's, inveigle
rope (pert to)...
boat's.. **4.** rode **6.** hawser **7.** painter
chain.. **3.** tye **9.** stern fast
dancer, walker.. **8.** balancer
   11. equilibrist, funambulist
flag raising.. **7.** halyard
gun carriage.. **8.** prolonge
guy.. **4.** stay, vang
nautical.. **3.** tye **4.** vang, wapp
   6. parrel (parral) **7.** snotter
of onions.. **5.** reeve
security device.. **4.** butt **5.** cleat
ship's.. **3.** tye **4.** stay, vang
   6. hawser, shroud **7.** painter, ratline,
   snotter
splicer's tool.. **3.** fid
straw, twisted.. **5.** sugan (soogan)
two strand.. **7.** marline
walker.. **11.** funambulist
ropery... **6.** banter **7.** roguery

roral... 4. dewy, rory 5. roric
rorqual... 5. whale 7. finback
Ros... 10. Slav rulers (Russ),
   Varangians
rosary... 4. aves 5. beads (prayer)
   7. chaplet (of roses), garland
   8. devotion
rose... 3. cut (jewelry) 5. color, flush,
   Rhoda 6. emblem, flower, nozzle,
   symbol, window 7. fixture
rose (pert to)...
   apple.. 4. plum 6. cherry 7. jambool
      8. poma rosa
   beetle.. 6. chafer, weevil
   City.. 8. Portland (Oreg)
   colored.. 8. alluring 10. auspicious,
      optimistic
   cross.. 6. symbol 11. Rosicrucian
      14. cross in a circle
   genus.. 4. Rosa 6. Acaena
      8. Rosaceae
   hiller.. 7. rosella 8. parakeet
   moss.. 9. portulaca
   of Sharon.. 6. Althea
   petal oil.. 4. otto 5. attar
   rash.. 7. roseola
   under the rose.. 6. secret 7. sub
      rosa
   wild.. 9. eglantine
Rosetta Stone (pert to)...
   decipherer.. 11. Champollion
   famed for.. 11. inscription
      13. hieroglyphics
   site found.. 4. Nile (1799)
   type.. 11. black basalt
roster... 4. list, roll, rota 5. slate
   8. schedule
rostrum... 4. beak, dais, prow
   5. snout, stage 6. pulpit 8. platform
   9. proboscis
rosy... 3. red 4. pink 7. flushed,
   roseate 8. blooming, blushing
   9. rosaceous 10. auspicious,
   optimistic
rot... 3. die 5. decay, spoil 6. blight
   7. corrupt, disease, putrefy
   8. nonsense 9. decompose
   10. degenerate 12. putrefaction
   13. decomposition
rota... 4. Club (Eng), list, roll 5. court,
   round (Mus) 6. roster 15. Sacra
   Romana Rota
rotate... 4. roll, spin, turn, whiz
   5. recur, wheel 6. gyrate 7. rabatte,
   revolve, trundle 8. rotiform
rotation... 4. spin, turn 5. round
   7. turning 8. sequence
   10. revolution, succession
rotator... 5. rotor 6. muscle 7. whirler
   9. carrousel 12. merry–go–round
rotche, rotch... 5. goose, rotge
   7. dovekie
rote... 6. course, custom, system
   7. by heart, routine 8. par coeur,
   practice 9. condition
roti... 5. roast 7. roasted
rotor... 5. wheel 6. roller, stator
   7. rotator, turbine 8. impeller
rotten... 3. bad 4. foul, punk
   5. doted, fetid 6. putrid, wicked
   7. decayed, tainted, unsound
   8. depraved, unstable 9. dishonest,

offensive, putrefied 10. putrescent,
   undermined 13. disintegrated
Rotten Row (Hyde Park, London)...
   12. thoroughfare (equestrian)
rottenstone... 6. polish 7. tripoli
rotter... 3. cad 7. bounder, shirker,
   slacker 10. blackguard
rottgoose... 5. brant
rotund... 5. plump, round, stout
   6. chubby 7. rounded 8. roly–poly
   9. corpulent, spherical
Rotwelsch... 5. argot, slang 6. jargon
   14. secret language
roué... 4. rake, wolf 7. rounder
   9. debauchee, libertine
rouge... 5. blush, flush 6. polish,
   redden 7. radical 8. cosmetic
rough... 4. hard, rude 5. crude, draft,
   harsh, raspy, rowdy, seamy, stern
   6. broken, choppy, coarse, hoarse,
   rugged, severe, shaggy 7. boorish,
   inexact, jarring, jolting, ruffled
   8. scabrous, unsmooth 9. imperfect,
   turbulent 10. incomplete, tumultuous,
   unfinished 11. approximate
rough (pert to)...
   avens.. 6. bennet (herb)
   cloth.. 5. terry
   footed (bird) 9. feathered
   hair.. 4. shag
   hewn.. 6. brutal 10. unpolished
      12. uncultivated
   house.. 5. cut up 9. rowdiness
      10. disorderly, noisy sport
   jest (Mus).. 9. charivari
   neck.. 4. boor 5. rowdy, tough
   rider.. 9. Roosevelt (Teddy)
      10. cavalryman
   rock.. 4. crag
   shod (to ride).. 7. trample
      8. dominate 9. tyrannize
rough and...
   hoarse.. 7. raucous
   loan.. 6. craggy
   ready.. 4. rude 10. unpolished
   Ready.. 6. Taylor (Gen Zachary)
roughen... 4. chap, shag 8. asperate
roughly... 6. rudely 7. harshly
   8. coarsely, severely, unevenly,
   vulgarly 9. brusquely 10. unsmoothly
   13. approximately
roughness... 6. lipper (of the sea)
   8. acrimony, asperity, pungency,
   unfinish 9. gruffness, harshness,
   vulgarity 10. hoarseness
roughsome... 5. rough 6. rustic
   7. uncouth
roulade... 3. run 8. arpeggio, division,
   flourish 13. vocal flourish
roulette... 3. bas (bet) 4. disk, game
   5. wheel 6. roller 8. wagering
rounceval... 5. giant, large 6. strong,
   virago 9. termagant
round... 4. beat, bout, rota, rung, turn
   5. cycle, orbed, rondo 6. circle,
   curved, rotate, rotund, series, sphere
   7. circuit, routine 8. circular, globular
   9. in a circle, spherical
   11. cylindrical
round (pert to)...
   bone.. 3. hip
   building.. 7. rotunda

clam.. 6. quahog
fish.. 9. whitefish
head.. 5. Swede 7. Puritan
house.. 5. cabin, coach 6. lockup,
　prison 10. watch house
of applause.. 7. plaudit
regular.. 4. beat
robin.. 6. angler, letter 7. pancake,
　request 9. cigarfish
worm.. 4. nema 7. ascarid, Ascaris,
　eelworm
roundabout... 5. about, dance
　6. detour, jacket 7. ambient, devious
　8. indirect 10. circuitous
　13. approximately 14. circumlocution
rounded (pert to)...
heap of stone.. 5. cairn
irregularly.. 7. gibbous
leaf.. 6. retuse
molding.. 5. ovolo
projection.. 4. lobe 5. tooth
scalloped.. 7. crenate
Round Table (pert to)...
knight.. 7. Galahad 8. Lancelot
seating.. 7. knights (King Arthur's)
site.. 7. Camelot
type.. 6. marble
roundup... 5. rodeo
roup... 4. cold 6. clamor 7. auction
　8. shouting 10. hoarseness
rouse... 3. hie 4. stir, wake 5. alarm,
　raise, start, upset, waken 6. awaken,
　bestir, elicit, excite, kindle 7. disturb
　9. stimulate
rouser... 7. stirrer 8. surprise
　9. demagogue (demagog)
　10. instigator
roussette... 5. shark 7. dogfish 8. fruit
　bat
roust... 4. roar, stir 5. rouse
　6. bellow, tumult 7. current (tidal),
　roaring 9. bellowing
roustabout... 6. lumper 7. laborer
　8. handy man 12. longshoreman
rout... 3. low, mob 4. bray, roar
　5. crowd, snort 6. bellow, defeat,
　rabble 7. debacle, scatter
　8. disperse, stampede, vanquish
　9. agitation, discomfit, overpower,
　overthrow 11. put to flight
route... 3. way 4. line, path 5. march
　6. detour 7. circuit
routh... 6. plenty 8. abundant
　9. abundance, plentiful
routier... 6. robber 7. brigand 9. free
　lance, plunderer
routine... 3. rut 5. grind, habit, order,
　round, troll 6. course, system
　7. regular 8. everyday 9. treadmill
rove... 3. gad 4. flit, part, roam
　5. range, stray 6. maraud, ramble,
　stroll, swerve, wander, washer
　7. deviate 8. straggle
rover... 5. nomad 6. bandit, pirate,
　viking 7. corsair, pilgrim, vagrant
　8. marauder, wanderer
roving... 8. errantry 9. desultory,
　deviative 10. discursive
row... 3. air, oar 4. file, fuss, live,
　spat, tier 5. align, brawl, broil
　6. lineup, paddle, propel, series
　7. quarrel, ruction 9. commotion

rowboat... 3. cog, gig 4. dory
　5. canoe, coble, skiff 6. randan
rowdy... 5. cutup, rough, tough
　7. boorish, ruffian 8. larrikin,
　plug–ugly 10. boisterous, disorderly
rowdy contention... 10. donnybrook
rowel... 4. spur 5. wheel
rowen... 4. crop (secondary) 5. field
　7. stubble 9. aftermath
rowing... 5. sport 6. randan 7. regatta
　8. sculling
rox... 3. rot 5. decay
royal... 4. real, rial, stag, true 5. basil,
　noble, regal 6. august, kingly
　7. stately 8. imperial, majestic,
　princely, splendid 9. dignified,
　sovereign 11. magnificent
royal (pert to)...
agaric.. 8. mushroom
bay.. 6. laurel
color.. 4. blue 5. smalt
court.. 5. aulic 6. ermine
crest.. 10. fleur–de–lis (Fr)
deer's antler.. 8. tres–tine
fur.. 6. ermine
mace.. 7. scepter (sceptre)
martyr.. 8. Charles I (Eng, 1649)
maundy.. 4. alms
officer.. 7. naperer
rights.. 7. regalia
rock snake.. 6. python
stables.. 4. mews
stars (Astrol).. 7. Antares, Regulus
　9. Aldebaran, Fomalhaut
Royal (pert to)...
Academy.. 4. Arts (1768)
Arcanum.. 7. Society (1877)
Canadian Mounted Police..
　8. Mounties 16. Northwest Mounted
Castle.. 8. Balmoral
Crown.. 5. tiara
Highlanders.. 10. Black Watch
Highness.. 5. title 6. prince
　8. princess
House.. 5. Tudor 6. Stuart, Valois
　7. Bourbon, Hanover, Windsor
Oak (Eng Hist).. 7. lottery
　10. Shropshire
Psalmist.. 9. King David
Scot.. 16. Lothian Regiments
royet... 4. wild 6. unruly 7. romping
　11. mischievous
rub... 4. crux, fret, wipe 6. abrade,
　polish, scrape, smooth, stroke
　7. burnish, massage 8. friction,
　irritate 9. hindrance, triturate
rub (pert to)...
away.. 6. abrade
down.. 4. comb 5. curry, groom
　7. massage
elbows.. 9. associate 10. fraternize
off.. 5. erase 6. abrade, remove
　10. obliterate
out.. 4. kill 5. erase 6. cancel,
　efface, excise 7. expunge, wipe out
　10. obliterate
wrong way.. 6. ruffle 8. irritate
　9. displease 10. antagonize
rub–a–dub... 6. clamor 7. clatter,
　pit–a–pat, rat–a–tat 8. rattatoo
　9. drumbeats
Rubáiyát (pert to)...

author.. 11. Omar Khayyám
stanza form.. 8. quatrain
translator.. 10. Fitzgerald (1859)
rubber... 4. para 5. stare 6. eraser
7. ebonite, elastic 8. massager,
sight–see 10. caoutchouc
rubber (pert to)...
city.. 5. Akron
hard.. 7. ebonite
India (pure).. 10. caoutchouc
plant.. 5. Ficus
ring.. 4. lute 6. gasket
sap.. 5. latex
shoe.. 6. galosh (galoshe)
tree.. 3. ule 7. guayule
wild.. 5. Ceara 6. caucho
rubbish... 4. junk, ross 5. attle, dross,
stent, trash, waste 6. debris, refuse,
rubble, trashy 8. nonsense, riffraff,
trumpery 9. worthless
rubble... 5. brash, chalk, stone, trash
7. rubbish 8. nonsense
11. foolishness
rube... 4. dolt 6. rustic 7. hayseed
rubedity... 7. redness 9. ruddiness
rubella... 7. measles, rubeola
rubescent... 3. red 8. flushing
9. reddening 10. erubescent
rubiator... 4. rake 5. bully 6. rascal
Rubicon... 5. river (Caesar's)
9. Fiumicino (modern)
rubicund... 3. red 4. ruby 5. ruddy
6. florid 7. redness
rubric... 3. rod 6. paraph, ritual
8. category, red chalk 14. title page
in red
rubrics (book of)... 4. ordo
ruby (pert to)...
bird.. 11. hummingbird
horaldry.. 6. gules
stained quartz (red).. 6. Ancona
7. rubasse 9. Mont Blanc
stone.. 3. gem 5. balas 6. spinel
type.. 4. size
ruck... 3. rut, sit (on eggs) 4. heap,
pile, rick 5. cower, crowd, squat,
stack 6. crease, crouch, furrow,
horses (race), pucker 7. wrinkle
9. multitude 10. generality
ruckus... 3. ado, row 5. fight
6. rumpus, uproar 7. quarrel, ruction
8. outbreak 9. commotion
rudd... 3. hue 4. carp, fish 6. redden
7. azurine, redness 10. complexion
rudder... 4. helm 5. guide
rudder part... 8. bearding 9. whipstaff
rude... 3. raw 4. curt 5. rough, rowdy
6. clumsy, coarse, rugged, simple,
vulgar 7. boorish, uncouth
8. ignorant, insolent 9. barbarous,
inclement, makeshift, turbulent,
unlearned, unskilled, untrained
10. boisterous, unpolished
11. impertinent, uncivilized
12. discourteous
rudeness....6. ferity 8. curtness
9. impudence, insolence, vulgarity
11. raucousness 12. impertinence
rudiment... 5. first 6. anlage, embryo,
origin 7. element 9. first step
rudimentary... 5. basic 7. initial

8. original 9. beginning, elemental,
embryonic, vestigial 11. undeveloped
rudimentary digit... 7. dewclaw
rue... 4. rake, Ruta 6. grieve, regret,
repent, sorrow 7. afflict, deplore
10. bitterness, compassion,
repentance 14. disappointment
ruff... 3. ree 5. pride, reeve, ruche,
trump 6. collar, fringe, rebato
7. sunfish 8. drumbeat 9. sandpiper,
vainglory
ruffian... 4. fish, pimp, thug 5. rowdy,
tough 6. brutal, cuttle, pander
8. assassin, paramour, the Devil
9. cutthroat, desperado, murderous,
vulgarian
ruffle... 3. vex 4. fret, roil 5. anger,
annoy, frill, jabot 6. edging, muddle,
nettle, rumple, tousle 7. agitate,
disturb, flounce, fluster, shuffle
8. dishevel, disorder, drumbeat,
irritate 9. balayeuse 10. disarrange,
discompose
ruffler... 5. bully 7. boaster, ruffian
8. braggart 9. swaggerer
10. attachment (sewing)
rug... 3. mat 4. maud, shag
5. Senna, throw 6. carpet, hooked,
petate 7. Chinese, drugget, steamer
8. coverlet, Oriental 9. Samarkand
ruga... 4. fold 7. wrinkle 8. membrane
Rugby... 5. Fives 6. Rugger, school
(Eng) 8. football
Rugby term... 9. scrum half,
scrummage
rugged... 4 rude 5. asper, hardy,
harsh, rough, surly 6. craggy, fierce,
robust, seamed, shaggy, strong,
sturdy 7. austere, crabbed, healthy,
uncivil 8. vigorous, wrinkled
9. irregular, not smooth, turbulent
11. substantial
rugged mountain crest... 5. arête
ruin... 4. bane, doom, fate, loss
5. blast, havoc, spoil, wrack, wreck
6. defeat 7. debauch, destroy,
subvert 8. bankrupt, demolish,
downfall 9. perdition 10. desolation,
subversion 11. destruction,
devastation
ruined... 4. gone 7. spoiled, wrecked
8. bankrupt, defeated 9. destroyed
11. dilapidated 12. irremediable
ruinous... 6. deadly 7. baneful,
decayed 10. demolished, disastrous,
pernicious, submersive, tumbledown
11. destructive
ruins... 5. relic, wreck 7. remains
rukh... 6. forest, jungle
rule... 3. law 4. norm, sway 5. axiom,
guide, habit, order, regle, reign
6. decree, govern, manage, method,
regime, screed 7. counsel, measure,
precept, prevail, regency, regimen
8. dominate, persuade, standard
9. criterion, direction, influence,
principle 12. jurisdiction
15. totalitarianism
rule by...
children.. 9. paedarchy
ecclesiasts.. 9. hierarchy
one.. 8. monarchy

race.. 10. ethnocracy
ten.. 8. decarchy
the mob.. 9. mobocracy
the people.. 9. democracy
tribes.. 9. phylarchy
rule out... 6. cancel, excise 7. obviate
ruler... 3. min 4. amir (ameer), czar,
emir, lord 5. queen 6. despot,
dynast, ferule, gerent, prince, regent,
satrap, sultan, tyrant 7. emperor,
monarch 8. autocrat, governor,
hierarch, measurer 9. potentate
ruling... 3. law 6. decree 7. average,
regnant, statute, verdict 8. decision,
reigning 9. governing, prevalent
11. predominant 12. drawing lines
rullion... 4. shoe 6. sandal
rum... 3. dye (blue), odd 4. good
5. queer, tafia (taffia) 6. liquor
8. Demon rum
rumal... 6. fabric 8. kerchief (man's)
Rumania...
capital.. 9. Bucharest
city.. 4. Cluj, Iasi 7. Ploesti
king.. 5. Carol (former)
mountains.. 10. Carpathian
port.. 6. Galati (Galatz)
privileged class.. 5. boyar (boyard)
river.. 6. Danube
rumble... 4. boom, seat (back)
5. rumor 6. murmur, ripple, stir up
9. complaint 11. rolling tone
rumen... 3. cud 5. tripe 6. gullet,
paunch 7. stomach (1st)
ruminant... 2. ox 3. cow, yak 4. bull,
deer, gaur, goat, oryx, zebu
5. bison, camel, eland, gayal, llama,
moose, okapi, sheep, steer
6. alpaca, nilgai, vicuna, wapiti
7. banteng, buffalo, caribou,
chamois, gemsbok, giraffe
8. antelope, elephant, reindeer,
seladang 9. dromedary, nannygoat,
pronghorn 10. cud–chewing,
hartebeest, meditative, rhinoceros,
thoughtful
ruminant (pert to)...
division.. 8. Ungulata 10. Ruminantia
first stomach.. 5. rumen 6. paunch
fourth stomach.. 8. abomasum
9. rennet bag
second stomach.. 9. reticulum
third stomach.. 6. omasum
9. manyplies 10. psalterium
ruminate... 4. chew, muse 6. ponder
7. reflect 8. consider, meditate
rummage... 4. junk 6. litter, search
7. collect (by search), ransack
rumor, rumour... 4. Fama, talk
5. bruit, noise, story 6. norate,
report 7. hearsay, tidings
11. scuttlebutt
rump... 4. bone 6. breech, sacrum
7. meat cut 8. bankrupt, buttocks
9. remainder
rumpade... 3. rob 6. hold up
rumple... 4. muss 5. touse 6. crease,
ruffle, tousle 7. crinkle, crumple,
wrinkle 8. dishevel 10. disarrange
rumpus... 3. row 6. fracas, hubbub,
uproar 9. commotion, confusion
11. disturbance

rumtytoo... 8. ordinary
11. commonplace
run... 2. go 3. fly, gad, hie 4. dart,
flee, flow, lope, melt, race, scud,
tend, trot 5. blend, hurry, speed,
trend 6. charge, course, elapse,
endure, extend, manage, pursue,
sprint, stream 7. average, liquefy,
operate, proceed, roulade, routine,
smuggle, stretch, trickle 8. continue
9. discharge, suppurate
run (pert to)...
about.. 5. wagon 6. gadder
8. roadster, runagate, vagabond
after.. 5. chase, fetch, toady
6. pursue 7. lionize
aground.. 6. strand 7. founder
along the edge.. 5. skirt
away.. 4. bolt, flee 5. elope
6. decamp, escape 8. stampede
before the wind.. 4. scud
between ports.. 3. ply
down.. 3. hit 4. find 5. trace 7. run
over 9. exhausted 11. dilapidated
12. deteriorated
out.. 3. end 5. lapse, waste
6. elapse, emerge, escape
7. exhaust 8. squander
over.. 6. browse, exceed, ponder
7. trample 8. overflow 9. reiterate
quickly, swiftly.. 4. dart, race, scud
5. scoot 6. gallop, sprint 7. scuttle
stocking.. 6. ladder
through.. 5. stab 6. pierce 7. inspect,
pervade 8. rehearse, squander,
transfix 11. superabound
up against.. 4. find 9. encounter,
stumble on 10. experience
runagate... 7. runaway 8. apostate,
fugitive, renegade, vagabond,
wanderer
rundle... 4. ball, coil, rung, step
5. round 6. circle, roller, sphere,
stream
rune... 5. magic 6. secret, symbol
7. mystery 9. character (anc)
rung... 4. step 5. round, spoke, stair,
tread 6. degree, rundle 7. girdled,
ratline
runic... 5. verse 6. poetic 7. writing
8. alphabet (anc), Norsemen
runner... 3. ski (skee) 4. sled 5. miler,
racer, stolo 6. stolon 7. tendril
8. operator, procurer, salesman,
smuggler, sprinter 9. messenger,
solicitor
running... 7. current, cursive, fleeing,
flowing, melting 9. advancing,
prevalent, smuggling 10. continuous
running knot... 5. noose
running race... 5. relay 6. sprint
running toad... 10. natterjack
runt... 3. elf 4. chit (letter), wrig
5. dwarf, pygmy 6. pigeon
10. diminutive
runway... 4. file, ramp 8. airstrip
rupa... 4. body, form (visual)
rupee... 4. anna, coin 14. money of
account
rupestrian... 14. composed of rock
15. inscribed on rock
ruption... 7. ruction, rupture

8. bursting
rupture... 4. rent 5. break, burst
  6. hernia, injury, rhexis 7. quarrel
  9. hostility 10. disruption, falling out,
  separating
rural... 6. rustic 7. bucolic 8. agrestic,
  pastoral 12. agricultural
rural (pert to)...
  deity.. 3. Pan 6. Faunus
  genus.. 6. potato
  life.. 8. pastoral
  poem.. 7. eclogue, georgic
  Spanish.. 9. policeman
  term.. 8. agrestic
Rusa... 4. deer 6. sambar
ruse... 4. fall, slip, wile 5. fraud, trick
  6. deceit 8. artifice 9. stratagem
  10. subterfuge
rush... 3. jet 4. dart, dash, flow, scud
  5. brook, haste, hurry, plant, press,
  scoot, spate, speed, surge 6. charge,
  course, defeat, demand, hasten,
  runlet, sortie 7. cattail, repulse
  8. outburst, reed mace, stampede
  9. attention, thronging
rush (pert to)...
  forth.. 5. sally
  hour.. 4. peak
  light.. 6. candle, feeble
  nut.. 5. chufa
  Scot.. 5. sprat (herb) 6. Juncus
  toad.. 10. natterjack
  wheat.. 10. couch grass
rusk... 5. bread 7. biscuit
rusma... 9. quicklime 10. depilatory
Russia... see also *Russian*
  capital.. 6. Moscow 9. Petrograd (old)
  citadel.. 7. Kremlin
  city.. 4. Baku, Kiev, Omsk 5. Minsk
  6. Rostov 7. Kharkov 8. Smolensk
  9. Leningrad (St Petersburg),
  Petrograd 10. Sevastopol (Sebastopol)
  11. Vladivostok
  coal fields.. 6. Donets (Ukraine)
  fleet base.. 10. Sevastopol, Stalingrad
  former name.. 7. Muscovy
  founder.. 4. Ivan 15. Ivan the Terrible
  gulf.. 4. Azov
  isthmus.. 7. Karelia
  lake.. 5. Onega 6. Baykal 7. Aral Sea
  10. Caspian Sea
  mountains.. 4. Ural 8. Caucasus
  peninsula.. 4. Kola 6. Crimea
  resort.. 5. Yalta 6. Crimea
  river.. 2. Ob 4. Amur, Lena, Neva,
  Ural 5. Volga 6. Donets 7. Dneiper,
  Yenisei
  sea.. 4. Azov 5. Black, White
  6. Baltic 7. Caspian
  strait.. 6. Bering
Russian (pert to)...
  antelope.. 5. saiga
  aristocratic order.. 4. knez 5. Boyar
  assembly.. 4. duma, rada 7. zemstoo
  association, guild.. 5. artel
  bank.. 4. game
  beer, beverage.. 5. kvass, vodka
  boat.. 6. baidak (baydak)
  braid (trim).. 8. soutache
  calendar (to 1918).. 6. Julian
  cap (peasant).. 4. aska
  carriage.. 6. drosky, troika

9. tarantass (tarantas)
  cart, wagon.. 6. telega
  cathedral.. 5. sober
  cloak (fur).. 5. shuba
  council.. 4. duma, rada 6. soviet
  dance (rustic).. 7. ziganka
  decree.. 5. ukase
  dog (wolfhound).. 6. borzoi
  7. owtchah
  dress (peasant).. 7. sarafan
  duke, prince.. 4. knez (kniaz)
  edict.. 5. ukase
  fur (lamb).. 7. karakul (karakule)
  9. astrakhan
  guild.. 5. artel
  hemp.. 4. rine
  hut.. 4. isba
  leather.. 5. jufti (jufts) 6. Bulgar
  8. shagreen
  marsh, lagoon.. 5. liman
  massacre.. 6. pogrom
  musical instrument.. 5. gudok, gusla
  9. balalaika
  naval academy.. 6. Frunze
  news agency.. 4. Tass
  parliament.. 4. duma
  peasant.. 4. Slav 5. kulak 6. muzhik
  (muzjik)
  plain (treeless).. 6. steppe, tundra
  police (secret).. 5. Cheka
  pound.. 4. pood
  prince, duke.. 4. knez (kniaz)
  satellite.. 7. sputnik
  soup (cabbage).. 5. stchi (shchi)
  6. borsch
  stockade.. 5. etape
  synod.. 5. sobor
  tea urn.. 7. samovar
  turnip.. 8. rutabaga
  villa.. 5. dacha
  wagon (springless).. 6. telega
  wheat.. 5. emmer
  whip.. 4. plet (plete) 5. knout
  wolfhound.. 6. borzoi
  yes.. 2. da
Russian people...
  chess champ (1892).. 8. Alekhine
  composer.. 3. Cui 10. Rubenstein,
  Stravinsky 12. Tschaikovsky
  14. Rimsky–Korsakov
  conqueror.. 6. Tatars 7. Mongols
  Cossack.. 5. Tatar
  czar.. 4. Ivan 13. Peter the Great
  duke.. 5. kniaz (knez, knyoz)
  empress.. 7. Czarina, Tsarina
  General.. 10. Timoshenko
  grand duke.. 8. Nicholas
  language deviser.. 8. Zamenhof
  9. Esperanto (pseudonym)
  leader.. 5. Lenin 6. Stalin 7. Molotov
  8. Brezhnev
  little Russian.. 7. Russene (Ruthene)
  monk.. 8. Rasputin
  novelist.. 7. Tolstoy
  people.. 4. Lett, Slav 7. Cossack
  8. Russniak 9. Muscovite, Ruthenian
  poet.. 7. Pushkin, Yesenin
  9. Pasternak
  premier.. 5. Lenin 7. Kosygin,
  Molotov 8. Bulganin 10. Kruschchev
  saint.. 4. Olga
  teacher, monk.. 7. starets

  Youth Union.. 8. Comsomol
rust... 3. eat 5. erode 6. aerugo,
  patina 7. erosion, oxidize
  9. corrosion
rustic... 4. boor, carl, rube, rude
  5. churl, clown, Damon, rough, rural,
  swain, yokel 6. coarse, simple,
  sturdy, sylvan 7. artless, awkward,
  boorish, bucolic, Corydon, plowboy
  8. agrestic, pastoral 9. agrestian
  10. clodhopper, countryman,
  unpolished
rustic (pert to)...
  lover.. 5. swain
  maiden.. 9. Thestylis
  peasant.. 4. boor
  pipe.. 4. reed
  poetic.. 4. carl
  verse.. 4. idyl (idyll)

rustle... 4. flow 5. steal, swish, whisk
  7. crinkle 11. sound softly
rut... 5. ditch, track 6. furrow, groove,
  strake 7. routine, wrinkle
Ruth (pert to)...
  Book.. 12. Old Testament
  country.. 4. Moab
  husband.. 4. Boaz
  mother–in–law.. 5. Naomi
ruthless... 5. cruel 8. pitiless
  9. merciless 10. ironfisted
rye... 5. bread, grain, grass 6. cereal,
  whisky 9. gentleman (gypsy)
rye bread... 5. black 10. knackebrod
  12. pumpernickel
ryot... 6. farmer, tenant 7. peasant
Rytina... 6. dugong, sea cow
  7. manatee 12. Hydrodamalis
  14. Steller's sea cow
Ryukyu Islands... 7. Okinawa

S

S (pert to)...
  curve.. 4. ogee
  letter.. 10. nineteenth
  shaped.. 7. sigmate, sigmoid
  suffix.. 6. plural
Saal... 4. hall, room (large)
sabalo... 6. tarpon 8. milkfish
sabana... 5. plain 7. plateau, savanna
  (savannah)
sabbat... 8. assembly (demons), festival
  (orgies)
Sabbatarian... 9. ritualist 11. Russian
  sect
Sabbath... 6. Sunday 7. holy day
sabbatical year... 7. seventh
  8. vacation 14. leave of absence
sabbatism... 4. rest 9. ritualism
  12. intermission (labor)
Sabbatist (pert to)...
  devotee of.. 4. cult (Oriental)
  member.. 6. Semite
  named for.. 5. Sabbe (goddess)
  8. Sambathe
saber, sabre (pert to)...
  bean.. 4. jack
  bill.. 6. curlew
  fish.. 7. cutlass
  knot.. 8. military
  legged (horse).. 12. sickle–hocked
  Mohammedan.. 8. yataghan (yatagan)
  oriental.. 8. scimiter
  toothed.. 3. cat 5. tiger
  12. machairodont
  wing.. 11. hummingbird
sabino... 9. ahuehuete, rock cedar
sabio... 4. sage 6. priest 7. wise man
sable... 4. ebon, pelt 5. black, brush
  6. mammal, marten 8. antelope
  10. mysterious, Russia iron
sabotage... 6. damage, mayhem

  9. undermine 11. destruction
  (malicious)
Sabrina... 10. river nymph 11. River
  Severn
sabuline, sabulous... 5. sandy
  6. gritty 8. psammous
  10. arenaceous
sabutan... 5. fibre, straw
sac... 3. bag 4. cyst, sack 5. ascus,
  bursa, pouch, purse, theca 6. cavity,
  pocket, saccus 7. saccule, vesicle
  8. sacculus
Sac, Sauk... 11. Indian tribe
sacalait... 7. crappie 8. warmouth
  9. killifish
saccadic... 5. jerky 9. twitching
  11. eye movement
saccharine... 5. sweet 7. honeyed
  10. sweetening
saccos... 7. tunicle 8. vestment
sacerdocy... 10. priesthood 13. priestly
  order
sacerdos... 6. priest
sachem... 5. chief (Indian) 8. governor
  (Tammany)
sachet... 3. bag 5. pouch 6. powder
  7. perfume 8. reticule 11. perfumed
  pad
sack... 3. bag 4. loot, poke, wine
  5. ascus, bursa, catch, pouch, purse
  6. defeat, ravage, secure 7. pillage,
  plunder 8. desolate 9. discharge,
  dismissal
sack (pert to)...
  baseball.. 3. bag 4. base
  Bible.. 8. mourning
  but.. 4. butt, cask 8. trombone (anc)
  cloth.. 7. penance, sacking 15. garb
  of penitence
  dress.. 4. robe 6. jacket, sacque

sacrament... 3. act 4. oath 5. token
　6. pledge, symbol 7. mystery
　8. ceremony, covenant, practice
　9. communion, Eucharist
　10. intinction (to administer)
Sacramento (pert to)...
　capital, river.. 10. California
　cat.. 10. horned pout
　pike.. 9. squawfish
　salmon.. 7. quinnat
sacrarium (anc)... 6. chapel, shrine
　7. oratory 8. sacristy 9. sanctuary,
　synsacrum
sacred... 4. holy 6. divine 7. blessed
　8. hallowed, reverend 9. dedicated,
　inviolate, religious, venerable
　10. inviolable, sacrosanct
　11. consecrated 13. sanctimonious
sacred (pert to)...
　bark.. 7. cascara 14. cascara sagrada
　bean.. 11. Indian lotus
　beetle.. 10. scarabaeus
　bird.. 4. ibis
　book.. 5. Bible, Koran
　bo tree.. 3. fig 5. pipal
　bull.. 4. apis, zebu
　chest.. 4. arca 9. reliquary
　comb form.. 5. hagio, hiero
　dialect (Buddh writings).. 4. Pali
　grove.. 5. Altis (Olympia)
　image.. 4. icon (ikon) 5. Pietà
　instrument.. 4. Urim 7. Thummim
　malady.. 8. epilepsy
　monkey.. 6. baboon, rhesus
　8. entellus
　most.. 10. sacrosanct
　music.. 4. hymn 5. chant, motet
　8. oratorio
　river (Ind).. 6. Ganges (Ganga)
　room.. 8. sacristy
　traffic (in sacred things).. 6. simony
　weed.. 7. vervain
　wine vessel.. 3. ama
　writ.. 10. Scriptures
sacrifice... 4. lose, loss 5. offer
　6. give up, victim 8. chiliomb
　(1,000 oxen), hecatomb (100 oxen),
　immolate, libation, oblation, offering
　9. atonement, holocaust, martyrdom,
　privation, surrender 11. crucifixion,
　destruction
sacrificer... 6. martyr
sacrificial fire... 5. ignis
sacrilege... 7. robbery (church)
　9. blasphemy 11. desecration,
　profanation
sacrilegious... 7. impious
　10. irreverent 11. blasphemous,
　irreligious
sacrosanct... 4. holy 6. sacred
　8. ironical, most holy
sad... 3. bad 4. blue, dark, dire, dull
　5. dusky, sorry 6. solemn, somber,
　triste, wicked 7. doleful, pensive,
　unhappy 8. dejected, downcast,
　grievous, pathetic, shameful, terrible
　9. cheerless, depressed, sorrowful
　10. calamitous, deplorable,
　depressing, melancholy
　11. distressing, unfortunate
saddle... 4. meat (cut of), ride, seat
　5. ridge 6. burden 7. harness (part)

　8. encumber, straddle
saddle (pert to)...
　back.. 4. hill 5. ridge
　bag.. 7. alforja, pannier
　blanket.. 6. corona, tilpah
　boot.. 7. gambado
　cloth.. 5. cover 7. housing
　8. shabrack 9. appendage
　10. horsecloth
　elephant.. 6. howdah
　girth.. 5. cinch
　horse.. 5. mount 6. remuda 7. palfrey
　light.. 5. pilch 7. pillion
　pack.. 7. aparejo
　part.. 6. cantle, crutch, pommel
　8. tapadera (tapadero) 9. saddlebow
　place behind.. 5. croup
　rock.. 6. oyster
　strap.. 5. girth 6. latigo
saddler... 4. seal 5. horse 6. cozier
　7. cobbler, lorimer 8. merchant
　9. shoemaker
sadness... 5. dolor 6. pathos, sorrow
　9. dejection 10. gloominess,
　melancholy 11. unhappiness
　13. sorrowfulness
sad tree... 10. hursinghar (dye yield)
safari... 4. tour, trip 6. junket
　7. caravan, journey 10. expedition,
　pilgrimage
safe... 4. pete (thieves' sl), sane, sure
　5. chest, vault 6. closet, secure,
　unhurt 8. cautious, cupboard,
　unharmed 9. protected, strongbox
　11. trustworthy
safeblower... 7. burglar, peteman
　8. peteman
safe conduct... 4. pass 5. cowle,
　guard 6. convoy, escort 8. passport
　10. precaution, protection
safekeeping... 4. care 7. custody,
　storage 10. protection
　12. preservation
safety lamp (miner's)... 4. Davy
safety rail... 9. guardrail
saffron... 6. crocus, yellow
　10. colchicine
sag... 4. bend, hang, reed, rush, sink,
　wilt 5. drift, droop, sedge, slump
　6. weaken 10. depreciate
saga... 4. Edda, epic, tale 5. story,
　witch 6. legend 7. recital, sagaman
　9. narrative
Saga... 7. goddess, seeress
sagacious... 4. sage, wise 5. aware,
　witty 6. argute, astute, shrewd
　7. politic, sapient 9. judicious
　10. discerning, farsighted
　11. penetrative 13. perspicacious
sagacity... 3. ken 6. acumen, wisdom
　9. acuteness, quickness
　10. shrewdness 11. discernment,
　penetration 13. judiciousness
sage... 4. mint, wise 5. solon
　6. astute, Salvia, shrewd 7. sapient
　9. counselor, judicious, sagebrush
　10. discerning 11. philosopher
Sage (of)...
　Chelsea.. 7. Carlyle (Thomas)
　Concord.. 7. Emerson (Ralph W)
　Emporia.. 5. White (Wm Allen)
　Ferney.. 8. Voltaire

Monticello . . **9.** Jefferson (Thomas)
Pylos . . **6.** Nestor
sage (pert to) . . .
Bethlehem . . **9.** spearmint
cheese . . **7.** Cheddar
chippy . . **14.** Brewer's sparrow
cock, hen . . **6.** grouse
family . . **4.** mint
rose . . **5.** alder (yellow)
tea . . **5.** tonic
Sagebrush State . . . **6.** Nevada
sagene . . . **5.** seine **7.** measure,
network
sagitta . . . **7.** otolith **8.** keystone (Arch),
The Arrow
Sagittarius . . . **6.** bowman **9.** The
Archer **13.** constellation
sago (pert to) . . .
palm . . **6.** gebang, gomuti
plant . . **10.** cuckoopint
product . . **6.** starch
tree . . **7.** coontie
sagoin . . . **8.** marmoset
saguaro . . . **6.** cactus, flower
saguing . . . **6.** banana
Sahara . . . **5.** cocoa (color), leste (wind)
6. desert
sahib . . . **5.** title **6.** master
9. gentleman
sai . . . **6.** monkey **8.** capuchin
said . . . **6.** stated **7.** uttered
9. aforesaid **15.** before–mentioned
said to be . . . **7.** reputed, rumored
8. reported
saiga . . . **8.** antelope
Saigon nickname . . . **14.** Paris of the
East
sail . . . **3.** jib, lug **4.** luff, tack **5.** craft,
float **6.** vessel, voyage **8.** navigate
sail (pert to) . . .
around . . **14.** circumnavigate
close to wind . . **4.** luff
end . . **7.** yardarm
fish . . **12.** basking shark **15.** quillback
sucker
fore and aft . . **7.** spanker
foresail . . **9.** spinnaker
part . . **4.** clew, yard **5.** leech
rope . . **5.** sheet **6.** earing
secure, lash . . **7.** trice up
strings . . **10.** reef points
type . . **3.** jib, lug, top, try **4.** main,
reef, stay **6.** lateen, mizzen, square
7. topsail **8.** mainsail, save–alls
12. mutton–legger
sailboat . . . **4.** yawl **5.** ketch, skiff,
sloop, yacht **7.** caravel (caravelle)
sailing term . . . **3.** leg, run **4.** asea,
beat, jibe, scud, tack **5.** hoist (sail),
point, reach **7.** gliding
sailing vessel . . . **4.** bark (barque), brig,
saic, yawl **5.** sloop **7.** frigate
8. schooner **10.** barkentine
(barquentine), windjammer
sailor . . . **3.** gob, tar **4.** salt, wave
5. middy **6.** lascar, matlow
7. mariner, voyager **8.** seafarer
10. bluejacket, lobscouser (sl)
sailor (pert to) . . .
associate at meals . . **8.** messmate
clothes . . **11.** bell–bottoms
kit . . **8.** ditty bag **9.** housewife

knot . . **8.** geranium
mess tub . . **3.** kid
patron saint . . **4.** Elmo
song . . **7.** chantey **9.** barcarole
Saimiri . . . **4.** titi **6.** monkey **8.** squirrel
sain doux . . . **4.** lard **6.** grease
saint . . . **3.** Ste **5.** angel **7.** apostle,
pietist **8.** canonize, enshrine, sanctify
10. holy person **11.** godly person
Saint (pert to) . . .
Anthony's fire . . **10.** erysipelas
Buddhist . . **5.** arhat
Elmo's fire (or light) . . **6.** corona,
Helena **9.** corposant
Esprit . . **9.** holy ghost
Francis of Assisi . . **11.** il Poverello
13. little poor man
Gaudens . . **8.** sculptor
George's flag . . **14.** national emblem
Helena's hemlock . . **7.** jellica
John Lateran . . **12.** Mother Church
John's bread . . **5.** carob **9.** algarroba
Leger (Eng) . . **9.** horse race
Luke's summer . . **12.** Indian summer
Martin . . **13.** Bishop of Tours
Martin's feast . . **9.** Martinmas
Mary–le–Bow . . **15.** Cheapside Church
(Cockney area)
Mohammedan . . **3.** pir
Patrick's breastplate . . **6.** lorica
Paul . . **12.** Saul of Tarsus
Paul's Church (London), designer . .
18. Sir Christopher Wren
Peter's dome architect . .
12. Michelangelo
Vitus' dance . . **6.** chorea
Saint, patron . . .
children's . . **8.** Nicholas (Santa Claus)
English . . **6.** George
French . . **5.** Denis
hospitals . . **9.** John of God **10.** Juan
Ciudad
Irish . . **7.** Patrick
Italian . . **7.** Anthony
lawyer's . . **4.** Ives
lover's . . **9.** Valentine
sailor's . . **4.** Elmo
Scottish . . **6.** Andrew
Spanish . . **5.** James
Welsh . . **5.** David
saints (pert to) . . .
biography . . **9.** hagiology
11. hagiography
tomb . . **6.** shrine
worship of . . **10.** hagiolatry
sajou . . . **6.** monkey **7.** sapajou
sake . . . **4.** beer **6.** motive, reason
7. purpose **8.** beverage (rice)
salacious . . . **4.** lewd **5.** horny (sl)
7. lustful, obscene **8.** unchaste
9. lecherous
salad plant, vegetable . . . **4.** bibb
5. cress **6.** celery, endive
7. cabbage, lettuce, romaine
10. watercress
salamander . . . **3.** eft **4.** newt **5.** poker
6. triton **7.** axolotl, Caudata, urodela
9. fire–eater **10.** hellbender
12. pocket gopher
salary . . . **3.** fee, pay **4.** hire, wage
5. wages **6.** reward **7.** stipend
8. pittance **9.** allowance, emolument,

salt money (anc) 10. honorarium
12. compensation, remuneration
salat... 6. prayer (facing Mecca)
sale... 4. deal, vend 6. barter,
demand, market 7. auction, handsel
(1st in morning) 8. contract
11. black market
salesman... 5. agent 6. vendor
7. drummer 9. solicitor
14. representative 18. commercial
traveler
salient... 4. bold 6. trench 7. eminent,
jetting, jumping, leaping, obvious
8. bounding, extended 9. prominent
10. noticeable, protruding
11. conspicuous
salient angle... 5. arris, Doric
Salientia... 5. Anura, frogs, toads
8. Amphibia (tailless)
salient point... 7. feature (detail)
saline... 5. salty 6. salina 8. solution
10. saliferous
saliva... 7. spittle 8. digester, ptyalism
salivary gland... 8. racemose
sallow... 3. wan 4. gray, pale
5. muddy, pasty 6. pallid
9. yellowish
sally... 4. jest, leap, trip 5. issue,
jaunt, start 6. sortie 7. journey
8. escapade, outburst 9. witticism
salmagundi... 4. hash, olio, stew
6. medley 7. mixture 9. potpourri
10. periodical (old)
salmon... 4. fish 5. color 6. orlean,
sauqui 7. annatto, saumont
salmon (pert to)...
adult.. 7. gilling
after spawning.. 4. kelt
cured.. 6. kipper
dog.. 4. keta
family.. 10. Salmonidae
female.. 4. raun 6. baggit
genus.. 12. Oncorhynchus
herring.. 8. milkfish
humpbacked.. 5. haddo, holia
kind.. 7. quinnat
landlocked.. 7. kokanee
male.. 3. gib 6. kipper
newly hatched.. 4. pink
second year.. 6. hepper
silver.. 4. coho
small.. 4. peal 6. grilse
third year.. 4. mort
trout.. 5. sewen
young.. 3. fog 4. parr 5. smolt
6. grilse, samlet 7. essling
Salome (pert to)...
Bib.. 6. dancer
father.. 8. Herodias
grandfather.. 5. Herod
opera, by.. 7. Strauss
salon... 7. gallery 8. New Salon
(Paris), Old Salon 9. reception
10. assemblage, exhibition
11. drawing room
Salon del Prado (Madrid)...
9. promenade
saloon... 3. bar 4. deck 6. tavern
7. barroom, cantina, gallery
8. dramshop, groggery 11. drawing
room
saloop... 8. hot drink 9. sassafras

salt... 3. sal 4. cure 5. brine, taste
6. flavor, halite, sailor, saline
8. piquancy 9. seasoning
10. antiseptic, corrective 14. sodium
chloride
salt (pert to)...
acetic acid.. 7. acetate
alkaline.. 5. borax
astringent.. 4. alum
block, rock.. 3. pig
boric acid.. 6. borate
cat.. 4. lump 10. pigeon food
comb form.. 4. sali
cracker.. 7. saltine
dish for.. 10. saltcellar
ethereal.. 5. ester
flat.. 5. playa
lake.. 5. shott (chott)
marsh, pond.. 6. salina
native.. 6. halite
nature of, like.. 6. haloid
of the earth.. 7. the best
10. commonalty
peter, petre.. 5. niter
rock, block.. 3. pig
spring.. 4. lick
tax.. 7. gabelle
tree.. 4. atle (atlee) 5. cedar
7. tamarix 8. tamarisk
working.. 7. halurgy
works.. 7. saltern, saltery 9. salthouse
saltant... 7. dancing, jumping, leaping
8. bouncing, bounding
salted... 5. briny, cured 6. corned
7. treated 8. brackish, hardened,
seasoned 11. experienced
salty... 3. reh 5. briny, salic, witty
6. risqué, saline
salubrious... 4. good 8. salutary
9. healthful, wholesome
10. beneficial
salutary... 7. healthy 8. curative
9. medicinal 10. salubrious
11. restorative
salutation... 2. hi 3. ave 4. hail
5. aloha, hello, howdy, skoal
6. curtsy, homage, kowtow, Mizpah
(Mizpeh), prosit, salaam (salam)
7. Dear Sir 8. greeting, serenade
salute... 4. hail, kiss 5. greet
6. homage, signal 7. address
salvage... 4. save 6. redeem, rescue
10. redemption 11. reclamation
salvation... 8. soterial 10. liberation,
redemption 11. deliverance,
soteriology 12. preservation
salve... 3. tip 4. balm, cure 5. allay,
quiet 6. anoint, cerate 7. assuage,
relieve 8. flattery, medicate, ointment
9. gloss over, lubricate, mitigator
10. medication
salver... 4. tray 9. flatterer 11. serving
dish
salvo... 6. excuse 7. gunfire, pretext,
proviso, quibble, rockets 8. applause
9. discharge, exception
11. projectiles, reservation
Samaria (pert to)...
capital (anc).. 6. Israel
deity.. 6. Nibhaz
destroyer.. 6. Romans
founder.. 4. Omri (925 BC)

people.. 9. Assyrians
province of.. 9. Palestine
rebuilder.. 5. Herod (the Great)
Samaritan, good... 5. aider 6. helper
 10. befriender, benefactor
 11. helping hand
Sambal (Zambal) language... 4. Tino
sambar (sambur)... 4. deer, maha,
 rusa
same... 2. id 3. ilk, one 4. ibid, idem,
 self 5. alike, ditto 7. cognate, identic
 8. selfsame 9. identical
 10. equivalent
sameness... 6. parity, tedium
 7. analogy, oneness 8. identity,
 monotony 9. alikeness 10. similarity,
 uniformity 11. equivalence
 14. correspondence
Samian (pert to)...
island.. 5. Samos
Sage.. 10. Pythagoras
sea.. 6. Aegean
ware.. 8. Arretine
samlet... 4. parr 6. salmon (young)
Samoa...
capital.. 4. Apia
councilor.. 7. faipule
islands.. 8. American
islands, main.. 5. Manua, Upolu
 6. Savaii 7. Tutuila
natives.. 10. Polynesian
owl (barn).. 4. lulu
political council.. 4. fono
town.. 8. Pago Pago
warrior.. 3. toa
samovar... 3. urn 6. teapot
Samoyed, Samoyede... 3. dog (Arctic)
 8. Siberian
sample... 4. test 5. model, taste
 6. swatch 7. example, pattern
 8. specimen
sampler... 8. original 9. archetype
 10. needlework
Samson (pert to)...
Bib.. 5. judge (Israelite)
death site.. 4. Gaza (Syria)
famed as.. 9. strong man
opera.. 16. Samson and Delilah
tribe.. 3. Dan
wife.. 7. Delilah (betrayer)
Samuel... 4. Book (Old Test) 5. judge
 7. prophet
samurai... 6. vassal 7. officer
Sana native... 8. Yemenite
San Andreas rift... 15. earthquake
 fault (Calif)
San Antonio mission... 5. Alamo
sanative... 7. healing 8. curative,
 sanatory
Sancta Sanctis... 20. Holy things for
 the holy
sanctify... 5. honor 6. hallow
 10. consecrate 11. free from sin
sanctimonious... 4. holy 6. sacred
 7. saintly 8. affected 12. hypocritical
sanction... 4. abet, amen, fiat
 6. assent, permit, ratify 7. approve,
 endorse, support 8. approval
 9. approbate, authority, authorize
 11. countenance, endorsement
 12. ratification 13. authorization
sanctity... 8. holiness 9. godliness,

solemnity 10. sacredness
 11. saintliness 13. inviolability
sanctuary... 4. bema, fane, holy, naos
 5. abbey, bamah, cella, haven
 6. priory, refuge, temple 7. Alsatia,
 convent, retreat, shelter 8. cloister
 9. monastery 10. penetralia
sanctum... 3. den 5. study 6. adytum,
 office 7. retreat
sand... 4. grit 5. arena, nerve, pluck,
 stone
sand (pert to)...
applied to body.. 9. arenation
bog.. 4. syrt 9. quicksand
eel.. 4. grig 6. launce
flea.. 6. chigoe, red bug 7. chigger,
 sandboy
fluke.. 7. sand dab 8. flounder
hill, mound.. 4. dene, dune
hog.. 7. laborer (in compressed air)
 8. tunneler (tunneller)
inhabiting.. 11. arenicolous
like (sand).. 9. arenulous
 10. arenaceous
man.. 5. genie
mixture (clay).. 4. loam 9. sandstone
pear.. 5. Pyrus
submerged bank.. 3. bar 5. hurst,
 shoal
sugar.. 5. niter
widgeon.. 7. gadwall
sandal... 4. boat, shoe, sock 7. talaria
sandpiper... 3. ree 4. knot, pume,
 ruff, stib 5. stint (long–toed)
 6. dunlin 8. pectoral, triddler
sandstone... 7. sarsens 8. ganister
Sandwich Islands... 6. Hawaii
 8. Hawaiian
sandy... 6. desert, gritty 7. arenose
 8. granular, sabulous, Scotsman
 9. sandpiper 10. arenaceous, ring
 plover
sane... 5. lucid, sound 7. logical
 8. rational, sensible 9. practical
 10. reasonable
San Francisco Mil Post... 8. Presidio
sang... 5. blood, sheng 7. chanted,
 ginseng, Society
sang–froid... 8. coolness 9. cold
 blood, composure 11. insouciance
sanguinary... 3. ant (slave) 4. gory
 5. cruel 6. bloody, yarrow
 8. sanguine 9. bloodroot, murderous
 12. bloodthirsty
sanguine... 4. warm 5. ruddy
 6. ardent 7. hopeful 8. blood–red
 9. confident 10. optimistic
 12. bloodthirsty
sanity... 6. reason 8. lucidity, saneness
 9. soundness 13. wholesomeness
San Juan Hill... 4. Cuba (Battle,
 1898)
San Juan Indian... 4. Tewa
San Kuo... 13. Three Kingdoms (Shu,
 Wei, Wu)
San Marino, Europe (pert to)...
famed as.. 11. oldest State (Eur)
government.. 8. Republic (smallest)
mountains.. 8. Appenine
site.. 8. Mt Titano
sannup... 6. Indian (married male) (opp
 of squaw)

Sanskrit (pert to)...
college . 3. tol
dialect .. 4. Pali
drama .. 9. Sakuntala (Shakuntala)
epic .. 8. Ramayana
god .. 4. Kama (Cupid), Vayu (wind)
　5. Indra (Great) 6. Aditya
goddess .. 3. Uma (Splendor) 4. Devi
　(Mother) 5. Aditi, Gauri
human spirit .. 7. jivatma
literature .. 5. sruti (shruti)
period .. 5. Vedic
Phonet (sounds) .. 6. sandhi
poem (epic) .. 11. Race of Raghu,
　Raghuvamsha
poet .. 8. Kalidasa
sacred books .. 4. Veda
soul .. 5. atman
treatise .. 9. Upanishad
Santo Domingo ... 7. capital
　(Dominican Republic)
sap 　　3 gum 4. hoob, dupe, fool,
　mine, seve, upas 5. drain, fluid,
　lymph, sapor 6. juices, trench,
　weaken 7. essence, schnook
　8. unsettle 9. simpleton, undermine
sapid ... 5. tasty 7. zestful 8. flavored
　9. palatable, toothsome
sapient ... 4. sage, wise 6. shrewd
　7. knowing 8. profound 9. sagacious
　10. discerning
sapiutan ... 4. anoa 6. wild ox
sapodilla ... 5. chico 6. chicle, zapote
　7. nispero 9. naseberry
sapor ... 5. savor, taste 6. flavor, relish
sapper ... 5. miner 6. digger
　9. excavator
Saracen ... 4. Arab 5. nomad, pagan
　6. Muslim (Moslem) 7. heathen,
　infidel, ragwort 9. Moor's head (Her)
Saracen Knight ... 8. Ruggiero
Sarah (pert to)...
bird .. 9. wake–robin
husband .. 7. Abraham
mother of .. 5. Isaac
slave of .. 5. Hagar
sarcasm ... 4. gibe 5. irony, taunt
　6. satire 8. ironical, ridicule
sarcastic ... 3. dry 6. biting, ironic
　7. caustic, cutting, satiric 8. ironical,
　sardonic 9. malicious 10. mordacious
sarcophagic ... 10. sarcophagy
　11. flesh–eating 13. sarcophageous
sarcophagus ... 5. chest 6. coffin
　9. limestone 11. Assian stone, lapis
　Assius
sardine ... 4. bang 7. alewife, anchovy,
　herring (young) 8. pilchard
Sardinia, Italy ...
capital .. 8. Cagliari
island .. 13. Mediterranean
sheep .. 7. mouflon (moufflon)
tower (Prehist) .. 6. nuragh
sardonic ... 3. dry 6. ironic, morose
　7. cynical, satiric 8. derisive
　9. sarcastic 11. Rabelaisian
sartor ... 6. tailor
sash ... 3. obi 4. band, belt, benn, tobe
　6. girdle 8. casement
　10. cummerbund
sash pulley weight ... 5. mouse

Saskatchewan, Canada ...
capital . 6. Regina
city .. 8. Moose Jaw 9. Saskatoon
sassaby ... 8. antelope
sassafras (pert to)...
nut .. 8. pichurim
oil of (part) .. 6. safrol
tea .. 6. saloop
tree .. 4. ague
Satan ... 5. Demon, Devil, Eblis, fiend
　6. Belial 7. Lucifer, Tempter
　9. archfiend 14. Mephistopheles
　16. Prince of Darkness
Satan (pert to)...
angel (bottomless pit) .. 8. Apollyon
associate .. 6. Azazel 9. Beelzebub
before his fall .. 7. Lucifer
Jewish .. 8. Asmodeus
Scottish .. 4. deil
son .. 3. Imp (jocular)
satanic ... 5. cruel 6. wicked
　8. devilish, infernal 10. diabolical
satchel ... 3. bag 4. case, etui, grip,
　sack 5. cabas 6. valise
sate ... 4. cloy, glut 5. gorge
　7. gratify, satiate, satisfy, surfeit
　8. saturate
sated ... 4. full 5. blasé 6. gorged
satellite ... 4. Echo, luna, moon
　5. Atlas 6. comsat, planet
　7. aerosat, Landsat, Sputnik, Telstar
　8. Explorer, follower, Vanguard
　9. companion, dependent
satellite of Jupiter ... 2. Io (1st)
　6. Europa (2nd) 8. Callisto,
　Ganymede
satellite of Saturn ... 4. Rhea
　5. Dione, Mimas, Titan 6. Phoebe,
　Tethys 8. Hyperion 9. Enceladus
satellite of Uranus ... 5. Ariel
　6. Oberon 7. Titania, Umbriel
satellite's orbit ... 4. path
　14. geosynchronous
Sati (Egypt) ... 5. Queen
satiate ... 4. cloy, glut, pall, sate
　5. gorge 7. gratify, satisfy, surfeit
satin ... 4. silk 6. étoile, fabric,
　sateen, satiny 9. satinette
　10. smoothness
satire ... 3. wit 5. irony, spoof
　6. parody 7. lampoon
satiric, satirical ... 3. dry 6. bitter,
　ironic 7. abusive, caustic, cutting
　8. ironical, poignant 9. burlesque,
　sarcastic 11. reproachful
satisfaction ... 3. cro 4. duel
　6. amends 7. comfort, content,
　payment, satiety 8. adequacy,
　pleasure, reprisal 9. atonement
　10. recompense, reparation
　11. contentment, fulfillment
　12. compensation, propitiation,
　remuneration 15. indemnification
satisfied ... 5. proud, sated 7. content,
　pleased 8. satiated 9. contented,
　convinced, gratified 10. paid in full
satisfy ... 2. do 3. pay 4. fill, sate,
　suit 5. atone, solve 6. pay off,
　please, supply 7. assuage, content,
　fulfill, gratify, indulge, requite, satiate
　8. atone for, convince

satrap (anc)... 5. ruler 6. despot,
   prince 8. governor, overlord
saturate... 3. ret, sop, wet 4. fill, soak
   5. imbue, souse, steep 6. drench,
   seethe 7. satiate 8. overfill, permeate
   10. impregnate
saturated... 4. full 6. soaked, sodden
Saturday... 6. Samedi 9. sabbatine
   13. Jewish Sabbath
Saturn (pert to)...
   Astron.. 6. planet
   consort.. 3. Ops
   god of.. 4. seed
   Latin.. 8. Saturnus
   rings.. 7. moonlet 9. particles
   rings, part.. 4. ansa
   satellite.. 4. Rhea 5. Dione, Titan
   7. Iapetus 8. Hyperion
   Temple treasury (State).. 8. aerarium
saturnalia... 4. orgy 7. debauch
   8. Festival (of Saturn)
   11. pandemonium
saturnine... 6. dismal, gloomy, somber
   8. funereal
satyr... 4. faun 5. deity 7. demigod,
   silenus 9. butterfly, capripede,
   orangutan
sauce... 3. soy 4. alec, pulp 5. caper,
   curry, garum, gravy, pesto 6. gansel,
   tahini 7. catchup (catsup), soubise,
   Tabasco, veloute 8. amandine,
   dressing, marinara 9. espagnole,
   insolence, seasoning 11. beurre blanc
   12. impertinence
saucy... 4. bold, pert, vain 5. brash,
   cocky, sassy, smart 7. forward
   8. impudent, malapert 9. officious
   11. impertinent 13. disrespectful
Saudi Arabia...
   city.. 5. Islam
   founder.. 7. Ibn Saud (1913)
   gulf.. 7. Persian
   Mohammed's tomb.. 6. Medina
   mosque.. 5. Kaaba
   peninsula.. 7. Arabian
   provinces.. 4. Asir, Nejd 5. Hejaz
   6. El Hasa
   sea.. 3. Red
   sect.. 6. Wahabi (Wahabee, Wahhabi)
sauerbraten... 8. pot roast
sauger... 9. pike perch
Saul (pert to)...
   concubine.. 6. Rizpah
   daughter.. 6. Michal
   father.. 4. Kish
   herdsman.. 4. Doeg
   of Tarsus.. 4. Paul
   uncle.. 3. Ner
   wife.. 7. Ahinoam
   witch of.. 5. Endor
Sault Ste Marie... 3. Soo 6. rapids
   9. ship canal
saumont... 6. salmon
sauna... 4. bath (Finnish)
saunter... 3. jog, lag, mog 4. roam,
   rove, walk 5. range, stray 6. dawdle,
   loiter, lounge, potter, ramble, stroll,
   wander 8. ruminate
sauqui... 6. salmon
saurian... 6. lizard, Sauria 7. reptile,
   crocodile

sausage... 6. banger, salami
   7. bologna, chorizo, saveloy
   8. kielbasa (kolbasi), rolliche
   9. bratwurst, pepperoni
   10. knackwurst
sausage–shaped... 9. allantoid
   10. botuliform
savage... 3. att 4. rude, wild 5. brute,
   cruel, feral, yahoo 6. ferine, fierce,
   Indian 7. brutish, howling 8. cannibal,
   pitiless 9. atrocious, barbarian,
   ferocious, merciless, primitive
   11. uncivilized 12. uncultivated
savanna, savannah... 5. plain
   9. grassland 11. level region
savant... 4. sage 6. pundit 7. scholar
   9. scientist 10. classicist
   12. intellectual, man of letters
save... 3. but 4. keep 5. catch,
   hoard, lay by 6. except, redeem,
   rescue, scrimp 7. prevent, protect,
   reserve, salvage 8. conserve
   9. economize, excepting, safeguard
   10. accumulate
savin, savine... 5. cedar 7. juniper
   9. evergreen
savior, Saviour... 8. Redeemer
   9. deliverer, liberator
   11. emancipator, Jesus Christ
savoir–faire... 4. tact 5. poise, savvy
   (sl) 7. culture 9. gentility 12. ease of
   manner, mannerliness
savor, savour... 4. odor, zest 5. nidor,
   sapor, scent, smack, smell, taste
   6. flavor, relish 9. degustate
savory, savoury... 5. sapid, tasty
   7. piquant 8. gustable 9. agreeable
   10. appetizing, delightful
saw... 3. cut 4. dict 5. adage, maxim
   6. cliché, saying, truism 7. noticed,
   proverb 9. platitude, serration
saw (kind)... 3. jig, rip 4. band, buzz,
   hack, whip 5. crown, power
   7. keyhole 8. crosscut
saw (pert to)...
   back.. 6. sierra
   bill.. 6. motmot 9. merganser
   buck.. 8. sawhorse 13. ten–dollar bill
   crosscut.. 5. briar
   fish.. 3. ray
   grass.. 5. sedge
   horse.. 4. buck, rack 7. sawbuck
   log.. 5. edger
   of sawfish.. 5. serra
   surgeon's.. 6. trepan (trephine)
   teeth.. 5. tines
   two–bladed.. 6. stadda
sawmill gate... 4. sash
saw–whet... 10. Acadian owl
saxhorn... 4. tuba 7. althorn 8. bass
   tuba 9. saxcornet
saxifrage... 6. Seseli
Saxon (pert to)...
   color.. 5. smalt 8. Saxe blue
   10. Bremen blue 13. indigo carmine
   king.. 6. Egbert 8. Ethelred
   14. Alfred the Great
   language.. 10. Anglo–Saxon
   12. Plattdeutsch
   people.. 7. English 9. Sassenach
   10. Anglo–Saxon 11. Lowland Scot

serf.. 4. esne
swineherd.. 5. Gurth (Ivanhoe)
warrior.. 5. thane
Saxony capital... 7. Dresden
   10. Wittenburg (anc)
say... 4. aver, cite, tell 5. gnome,
   speak, state, utter 6. affirm, answer,
   assert, assume, recite, remark,
   speech 9. authority 11. declaration
   12. conversation
say (pert to)...
   a blessing.. 5. bensh
   again.. 6. repeat 7. restate
      9. reiterate
   further.. 3. add
   no (to).. 6. negate, refuse 8. prohibit
      10. disapprove
   one thing, mean another.. 6. palter
      7. falsify 9. fluctuate 10. equivocate
      12. be capricious
   uncle.. 4. cede 9. surrender
      10. capitulate 15. throw in the
   towel
saying... 3. dit, mot, saw 4. quip
   5. adage, axiom, maxim 6. byword,
   enigma, phrase, remark 7. proverb
   8. aphorism, apothegm
   11. declaration
saying, sayings (pert to)...
   collection of.. 9. gnomology
   criterion, party cry.. 10. shibboleth
   dogmatic.. 6. dictum
   religious.. 5. logia
scab... 3. rat 4. sore 5. crust, mange
   6. rotter 7. blemish 8. deserter
   9. scoundrel 12. incrustation
   13. strikebreaker
scabbard... 6. sheath 7. holster,
   pilcher 13. emblem of peace
scabbard fish... 7. cutlass 9. frostfish
scaddle... 5. cruel, timid 6. fierce
   7. nervous 8. skittish, thievish
   11. mischievous
scads... 4. gobs, wads 5. heaps,
   money, piles 6. oodles 11. great
   number 12. considerable
scaffold, scaffolding... 5. easel, stage
   7. staging, support 8. platform
   9. grain loft
scalawag, scallawag... 5. scamp
   6. rascal 7. sculpin 10. scapegrace
scale... 3. hut 4. husk, peel, rate,
   shed, size 5. climb, crust, flake,
   gamut 6. ascend, degree, ladder,
   lamina, rustre (anc armor), series,
   weight 7. compare, measure
   12. incrustation
scale (pert to)...
   botany.. 5. palea
   color.. 10. tintometer
   comb form.. 4. cten 5. cteno, lepis
   duck.. 9. merganser, sheldrake
   fish.. 6. ganoid 8. scabbard
   grand.. 4. epic
   music.. 3. E la (highest note)
      5. gamut, minor 9. chromatic,
      hexachord 10. tetrachord
   slide.. 7. vernier
   tail.. 6. rodent
   Zool.. 6. scutum
scallop... 4. quin 5. crena, notch
   7. mollusk 9. serration, shellfish

   12. summer squash
scalloped... 6. cooked 7. notched
   8. invected (Her) 9. crenulate
scalpel... 5. knife 6. lancet 7. dissect
   8. bistoury
scaly... 5. flaky 6. crusty, scabby,
   scurfy 7. leprose 8. squamous
scamp... 3. imp 5. cheat, knave,
   rogue 6. rascal, slight 7. bacalao,
   codfish 8. scalawag, spalpeen
   9. scoundrel 15. worthless fellow
scamper... 3. hie, run 4. dash, race,
   scud 5. haste 6. hasten 7. brattle
   9. hasten off, skedaddle 11. hasty
   flight
scan... 3. eye 6. browse, peruse
   7. examine 10. scrutinize
   11. contemplate 16. recite metrically
scance... 5. blame, shine 6. glance
   7. comment, glitter
scandal... 5. odium, shame 6. gossip
   7. calumny, offense, slander
   8. disgrace, ignominy
   10. defamation, detraction,
   opprobrium 11. abomination
scandalous... 6. wicked 8. libelous,
   terrible 10. defamatory, slanderous
   11. disgraceful, opprobrious
Scandinavia, countries... see also
   Scandinavian 6. Norway, Sweden
   7. Denmark, Iceland
Scandinavian (pert to)...
   alphabetical character.. 4. rune
   ash tree.. 10. Yggdrasill
   author.. 8. Andersen (Hans C)
   bay.. 5. fjord
   explorer.. 4. Eric
   goblin, brownie.. 5. nisse 6. kobold
   god.. 4. Lake, Thor
   goose.. 5. nisso
   hall of Odin (heroes' souls)..
      8. Valhalln
   legend.. 4. Edda, saga
   maiden of Odin.. 8. Valkyrie
   navigator.. 4. Eric
   people.. 4. Dane, Lapp 5. Swede
      8. Norseman 9. Norwegian
   people, type.. 8. Teutonic
   pert to.. 5. runic
   plateau.. 5. fjeld
   rulers.. 10. Varangians
   saga narrator.. 7. sagaman
   sea monster (fabled).. 6. kraken
   supernatural being (dwarf or giant)..
      5. troll
scant... 3. few 5. chary 6. meager,
   narrow, scarce, slight, sparse
   7. slender, sparing 12. parsimonious
scanty... 4. rare 6. meager (meagre),
   narrow, scarce, sparse 7. scrimpy
   12. insufficient 14. inconsiderable
scapegoat... 4. goat (Bib) 9. sacrifice
   10. substitute
scapegrace... 5. scamp 8. scalawag
   (scallawag) 9. reprobate
   10. profligate 12. incorrigible
scar... 3. arr, shy 4. seam, sear
   5. cliff, mound 7. blemish 8. cicatrix
scarce... 4. rare 5. short 6. scanty
   7. sparing 8. uncommon 9. deficient
   10. infrequent
scarcely... 6. barely, hardly 7. but just

12. infrequently

scarcity... 4. lack, want 6. dearth, famine, rarity 7. paucity 8. rareness 11. infrequency 13. insufficiency

scare... 3. cow 5. alarm, panic 7. startle, terrify 8. affright, frighten

scarecrow... 4. ogre 5. bogle 6. effigy, goblin, malkin, shewel (sewel) 9. jackstraw 10. frightener 11. hide–and–seek

scarf... 3. boa, tie 4. sash 5. ascot, cloud, nubia 6. tippet 7. muffler 9. rigolette 10. fascinator

scarf (pert to)...
bird.. 9. cormorant
broad.. 5. shawl
clerical.. 5. fanon, orale, rabat, stole
feather.. 3. boa
head.. 10. fascinator
Hindu.. 4. sari
India.. 7. dopatta
Mexico.. 6. tapalo
skin.. 7. cuticle 9. epidermis

Scarlet Letter... 5. novel (Hawthorne)
Scarlet O'Hara's home... 4. Tara

scarp... 5. cliff, pitch 7. descent, incline 9. declivity

scary... 5. eerie, timid, weird 7. ghostly, uncanny 8. alarming 12. easily scared

scat... 4. hiss 5. burst, smash 6. buffet 7. scatter

scat, scatt (Orkney Isls)... 3. tax 7. tribute

scathe... 4. flay, harm, hurt 6. assail, damage, injury, scorch 7. scarify 9. excoriate 10. misfortune

scatter... 3. sow, ted 4. deal, rout 5. spray, strew 6. dispel, litter, shower, splash, spread 7. bestrew, diffuse, radiate 8. disperse, separate, squander 9. circulate, dissipate 10. disarrange, strew about

scattered... 4. semé 5. dealt 6. sparse, strewn 8. confused, sparsile, sporadic 9. broadcast, dispersed, separated, sprinkled 10. widespread 11. distributed

scattering... 3. few 8. Diaspora 10. dispersion, separating 13. dissemination

scatty... 7. showery

scaup... 4. duck 8. bluebill 9. blackhead, broadbill

scavenger... 4. bird 8. organism 10. saprophyte 16. garbage collector

scaw... 8. headland 10. promontory

scene... 4. site, view 5. anger, sight, vista 6. locale 7. diorama, picture, tableau

scene (pert to)...
behind the.. 8. secretly 9. backstage, invisible
inside.. 7. neorama
last.. 6. finale
of action.. 5. arena, stage 6. sphere
of confusion.. 5. babel
of miracle (Bib).. 4. Cana
opera.. 5. scena
wright.. 6. artist 8. designer (scenery), stageman

scenic... 8. dramatic 9. panoramic

11. picturesque

scenic (pert to)...
enigma.. 7. charade
pert to.. 5. stage 7. episode, scenery
representation.. 7. diorama
13. motion picture

scent... 4. aura, clue, nose, odor 5. aroma, flair, nairn, nidar, smell, spoor 6. detect 7. perfume 9. fragrance

scented... 5. olent 6. odored 8. perfumed, smelling 11. odoriferous

scepter, sceptre... 3. rod 4. mace 5. baton, staff 6. emblem (royal) 8. insignia 11. sovereignty

schedule... 4. card, list 5. slate 7. program 8. calendar, document 9. catalogue, inventory

scheme... 3. aim 4. lark, plan, plot 5. cabal 6. device, devise, racket, system 7. complot, concoct, diagram, epitome, outline, project, purpose 8. artifice, contrive 9. boomerang 10. conspiracy, enterprise 11. machination

schemer... 7. plotter 8. conniver, finagler 9. intriguer

schism... 4. rent, sect 5. split 6. breach 7. dissent, faction 8. division 10. falling–out, separation

schismatic... 7. heretic, sectary 8. apostate 9. dissenter, sectarian 10. factionist

schist... 4. mica, rock 5. slate 10. hornblende

scholar... 6. pedant, savant 7. learner, student 8. disciple 11. philologist

scholarly... 7. erudite, learned 8. academic, studious 9. philomath 10. scholastic

scholarship... 5. burse 8. learning 9. education, erudition, knowledge 10. foundation 11. instruction

school... 4. cult, sect 5. class, drill, flock, order, teach, train 7. convent, educate, seminar 8. instruct, seminary 9. institute

school (pert to)...
book.. 6. primer, reader 7. speller
English.. 4. Eton 6. Oxford 9. Cambridge
French.. 5. école, lycée
German.. 6. schule
head, inspector.. 9. scholarch
master.. 7. dominie 9. pedagogue (pedagog)
ref to.. 10. scholastic
riding.. 6. manège
teacher.. 4. marm
term.. 8. semester
wrestling.. 9. gymnasium, palaestra (palestra)

school of...
art.. 4. Dada
Fine Arts.. 9. Wagnerian
fishes.. 5. shoal
philosophers.. 7. Eleatic
philosophy.. 7. Gnostic
seals.. 3. pod
thieves.. 4. gang
whales.. 3. gam, pod

schooner... 4. boat, brig, tern 5. glass

6. vessel 7. measure, prairie (Hist)
schuit, schuyt... 5. sloop 6. vessel
  7. eelboat
science... 3. art 5. ology, skill
  9. knowledge 11. proficiency
science of...
  agriculture.. 8. agronomy
  better living.. 9. euthenics
  breeding.. 8. eugenics
  character.. 8. ethology
  children's diseases.. 10. pediatrics
    (paediatrics)
  controversy.. 8. polemics
  creatures.. 10. entomology
  dining.. 10. aristology
  doctrines.. 9. esoterics
  ears.. 7. otology
  family symbols.. 8. heraldry
  forest trees.. 7. silvics (sylvics)
  good.. 6. ethics 9. euthenics
    10.. agathology
  government.. 8. politics
  happiness.. 11. eudaemonics
  healing.. 0. iatrology
  health.. 7. hygiene
  kissing.. 13. philematology
  language.. 9. philology, semantics
    11. linguistics
  life.. 7. biology 10. entomology
  light.. 6. optics
  mind.. 10. psychology
  moral conduct.. 8. ethics
  organism behavior.. 7. ecology
    (oecology) 9. bionomics
  philosophy.. 6. noesia
  reality.. 10. philosophy
  reasoning.. 5. logic
  rocks.. 9. petrology
  sea (the).. 12. oceanography
  self-defense.. 4 judo 7. jujitsu
  sound.. 9. acoustics
  theology interpretation.. 8. exegesis
    12. hermeneutics
  verse.. 7. prosody
  virtue.. 8. aretaics
  words.. 9. semantics
scientific... 5. exact 9. realistic,
  technical 16. precise knowledge
scimitar, scimiter... 4. snee 5. saber
  8. billhook
scintilla... 4. atom, iota, whit
  5. spark, trace 7. modicum
scintillate... 5. flash, gleam, spark
  7. be witty, glitter, twinkle
  9. coruscate 10. be eloquent
scion, cion... 3. son 4. slip 5. graft,
  shoot 10. descendant
scold... 3. jaw, nag 4. carp, rail, rate
  5. chide, shrew 6. berate, chider,
  rebuke 7. reprove, upbraid
  8. admonish 9. reprimand
scolding... 7. froward 8. reproach,
  shrewish 10. upbraiding
  12. admonishment, reprimanding
sconce... 3. top 4. head 5. brain,
  mulct, skull 6. screen 7. bulwark,
  lantern, redoubt, skelter
  11. candlestick, counterfort
scoop... 4. bail, beat, lade, news
  5. empty, ladle, spoon 6. bucket,
  hollow, shovel 8. excavate, gather in

scoop out... 3. dig 5. gouge
  6. chisel, hollow 7. fashion
scope... 4. area, room 5. ambit,
  arena, range, reach 6. degree,
  domain 7. compass, freedom, liberty
  8. latitude 9. gyroscope, intention,
  periscope, telescope 10. microscope
  11. stethoscope 12. kaleidoscope,
  spectroscope
scorch... 4. burn, char, sear, sere
  5. parch, singe, speed 7. shrivel
  9. criticize
scordato... 9. out of tune 14. made
  discordant
score... 3. peg, run, sum, tab 4. debt,
  gain, goal, rate 5. corge, judge,
  notch, scold, slash, tally 6. berate,
  furrow, groove, points, reason, twenty
  7. account, arrange, scratch
  8. incision 9. calculate, tally mark
  10. obligation 11. arrangement,
  composition, orchestrate
  12. indebtedness
scoria (volcano)... 4. lava, slag
  5. dross 6. refuse 7. residue
scorn... 4. defy, geck, mock 5. spurn
  6. deride, reject 7. contemn,
  despise, disdain 8. contempt,
  derision, disgrace 9. contumely
scornful... 8. derisive, insolent
  10. disdainful 12. contemptuous,
  contumelious
Scorpio (pert to)...
  constellation in.. 8. Milky Way
  genus.. 8. Scorpius
  night mansion of.. 4. Mars
  pictured as.. 8. scorpion
  star (brightest).. 7. Antares
  zodiac sign.. 6. eighth
scorpion... 4. nopa 7. alacran, scourge
  (Bib) 8. arachnid, catapult 10. pine
  lizard, vinaigrier 11. vinegarroon
  (vinagron) 15. blue-tailed skink
Scot... 3. Mac 4. Celt, Gael 5. Saxon
  6. Sawney 7. bluecap 8. Scotsman
  10. Caledonian, Highlander
Scotland... see also *Scottish*
  capital.. 9. Edinburgh
  city.. 3. Ayr 5. Perth 6. Atholl
    (Athole), Dundee 7. Glasgow
    (largest), Renfrew 8. Aberdeen
    9. Inverness
  congress (musical).. 3. Mod
  district.. 6. Argyll, Atholl
    10. Midlothian
  famed site.. 9. Trossachs (Lady of the
    Lake) 10. Loch Lomond 11. Loch
    Katrine
  firth.. 3. Tay 4. Loch 5. Clyde, Forth,
    Moray, Tweed
  islands.. 6. Orkney 8. Hebrides,
    Shetland
  Latin name (anc).. 9. Caledonia
  moors.. 10. Lochar Moss
  mountain.. 9. Grampians
  poetic name.. 6. Scotia 9. Caledonia
  resort.. 4. Oban
  river.. 3. Ayr, Dee, Tay 5. Afton,
    Clyde, North, Tweed 6. Teviot
    7. Deveron
  seaport.. 4. Leth 6. Dundee
Scotland Yard headquarters... '

6. London 18. Metropolitan Police
Scott, Sir Walter (pert to)...
  estate.. 10. Abbotsford (Scot)
  famed as.. 4. poet 8. novelist
  novel.. 7. Ivanhoe
  poem.. 13. Lady of the Lake
Scottish (pert to)...
  accent.. 4. birr
  alder.. 3. arn
  attendant (hunter's).. 6. gillie (gilly)
  bagpipe music.. 7. pibroch
  beret.. 3. tam 11. tam–o'–shanter
  bird.. 3. gae (blue) 6. grouse
    7. snabbie (snabby) 9. swinepipe
  blessing.. 6. rebuke 8. scolding
  blood money.. 3. cro 7. galanas
  blue.. 6. homage 8. infernal
    11. reddish–blue
  bluebell.. 8. harebell
  boat.. 4. zulu 7. coracle, skaffie
  bonnets.. 8. mushroom
  brandy.. 6. Athole
  breeches.. 5. trews
  brier, briar.. 4. rose
  broth.. 5. brose
  bull, ox.. 4. stot
  cake (tea).. 5. scone
  cap.. 3. tam 8. Balmoral 9. Glengarry
    11. tam–o'–shanter
  carpet.. 13. Kidderminster
  cattle.. 8. Aberdeen 9. Ayreshire
  celebration.. 4. kirn (harvest)
  child.. 5. bairn 6. scuddy (naked)
  church.. 4. kirk
  cloth.. 4. kelt 6. tartan
  coalfish.. 7. glashan, sillock
  court officer.. 5. macer
  cup.. 4. tass
  dagger (anc).. 4. dirk
  dagger, knife.. 8. skean dhu
  dance.. 4. reel 5. fling 9. ecossaise
    10. strathspey 13. Highland fling
  devil.. 4. deil 6. Hornie
  dirge.. 8. coronach (as on bagpipes)
  duck.. 4. coot 6. scoter
  earth.. 4. eard
  elder.. 7. tobacco
  elm.. 7. wych–elm
  excuse.. 6. sunyie
  eye.. 2. ee
  family (same).. 3. ilk
  festival.. 3. Mod 7. uphelya (Epiphany)
  fish.. 4. sile 7. sillock 8. spalding
  fog.. 4. haar
  Gaelic.. 4. Erse
  ghost.. 6. taisch
  girl.. 4. lass 6. lassie, towdie
    7. winklot
  goblin.. 8. barghest
  godmother.. 6. cummer (kimmer)
  grandchild.. 2. oy (oye)
  grandfather.. 8. gudesire
  hill, hillside.. 4. brae 6. strone
  icicle.. 7. shoggle
  kilt.. 7. filibeg
  kiss (stolen).. 8. smoorich
  lake.. 4. loch
  language.. 4. Erse 6. Lallan (Lalland)
  liquor.. 5. scour 6. Athole 7. whitter
  lovage.. 10. sea parsley
  money, silver.. 5. siller
  nephew.. 6. nepote

New Year's Day.. 7. Cake Day
    8. hogmanay
nightingale.. 7. warbler
ox, bullock.. 4. nowt
plaid.. 4. maud 6. tartan
porridge.. 5. brose
pouch, purse (kilt front).. 7. sporran
pudding.. 6. haggis
reel (fishing).. 4. pirn
rod, over the door.. 10. willow wand
sausage.. 9. whitehass (whitehawse)
schoolmaster.. 3. dux
shawl (plaid).. 4. maud
stream, brook.. 4. sike
sweetheart.. 2. jo
sword.. 8. claymore
toad.. 3. ted 4. taed
tobacco.. 5. elder
topaz.. 9. cairngorm
townhall.. 8. tolbooth (tollbooth)
uncle.. 3. eme
village.. 3. rew
waistcoat (under).. 6. fecket
whirlpool.. 7. swilkie
whisky.. 9. Glenlivet (Glenlivat)
    10. usquebaugh
window.. 7. winnock
youth.. 6. chield (chiel) 7. callant
    (callan)
scoundrel... 3. cad 5. cheat, knave,
    scamp 6. varlet 7. villain
    8. scalawag 9. miscreant
    10. blackguard 11. rapscallion
scoup... 3. run 4. leap, skip
    7. scamper
scourge... 4. bane, flog, lash, whip
    6. punish, swinge, switch 8. chastise
    10. affliction, infliction, punishment
Scourge of God... 6. Attila (King of
    Huns)
Scourge of Princes... 7. Aretino (It
    satirist)
scout... 3. spy 5. flout, scoff
    7. lookout, servant 8. emissary,
    watchman 9. guillemot
    11. reconnoiter 14. razor–billed auk
scow... 4. acon 6. garvey 7. lighter
scowl... 5. frown, lower 6. aspect
    (gloomy), glower 7. wrinkle (brow)
    10. sullen look
scraggly... 5. rough 6. ragged
    7. unkempt 9. irregular
scraggy... 4. bony 5. rough
    6. meager, rugged, skinny
    7. knotted, scrawny, stunted
scram... 6. begone, benumb, decamp
    7. vamoose
scramble... 4. push 5. climb, crowd,
    crush 6. jostle, strive 7. clamber,
    scatter 8. struggle
scrap... 3. bit, end, ort, rag 4. chip,
    junk 5. fight, melee, piece, waste
    6. morsel, refuse 7. cutting, discard,
    excerpt, extract, quarrel, remnant
    8. fragment, ramentum
scrape... 3. row, rub 4. rake, rasp
    5. grate, graze, shave 6. abrade, eke
    out, injure, sclaff 7. collect, scratch
    9. economize, obeisance 10. difficulty
    11. predicament
scraper... 4. harl (wool), tool
    6. barber, rasper 7. abrader, fiddler,

strigil 8. grattoir
scrappy... 9. irregular 10. pugnacious
11. contentious, fragmentary,
quarrelsome
scratch... 3. mar, rit, rub 4. claw,
draw, itch, mark, rake, rist, tear
5. erase 6. cancel, injury, scrape
7. blemish, roughen, scarify
8. scribble, withdraw
scrawl... 6. doodle 7. scratch
8. scribble
scrawny... 4. lean, poor, thin 5. spare
6. skinny 7. scranny 8. rawboned
scream... 3. cry 4. wail, yell 6. shriek,
squeal 7. screech
screamer... 5. swift (bird) 7. blunder
8. headline
scree... 5. stone, talus 6. debris,
pebble
screech... 3. cry, say 6. outcry,
scream, shriek, squeal 7. ululate
screech (pert to)...
hawk.. 10. goatsucker
martin 5. swift
owl.. 4. barn 5. Scops
screed... 4. list, rend, tear 5. shred
6. tirade 7. lecture 8. fragment
12. dissertation
screen... 3. net 4. hide, laun, mask,
sift, sort, veil 5. arras, blind, cloak,
pavis, shade, sieve, spier 6. defend,
grille, riddle, sifter, sorter 7. conceal,
curtain, protect, reredos, shelter
8. parclose 9. partition, safeguard
10. protection 12. discriminate
screw... 3. key 4. coil, turn 5. horse,
twist 6. fasten, gimlet, rotate, spiral
7. contort, distort, tighten, turnkey
9. bargainer, propeller, skinflint
10. contortion, thumbscrew
screwlike... 8. spiral 7. spiroid
scribble... 6. doodle, scrawl 7. scratch
8. scrabble
scribe... 5. clerk 6. author, jurist,
lawyer, penman, writer 8. recorder
10. amanuensis, cuttlefish, journalist
13. bibliographer
scriggle... 5. twist 6. squirm
7. wriggle 8. curlicue
scrimmage... 3. row 5. fight 6. tussle
8. football (term), practice, skirmish,
struggle
scrimp... 4. save 5. scant, stint
6. scanty, scrape, sparse 7. sparing
9. economize
scrip... 3. bag 4. list 5. money
6. wallet 7. writing 8. document,
schedule
script... 5. ronde 6. letter 7. writing
8. scenario 10. manuscript,
typescript 11. handwriting
scriptural... 7. written 8. Biblical,
orthodox
scriptural interpreter... 7. exegete
scripture... 4. writ 5. motto, truth
7. passage, writing 8. document
10. manuscript 11. inscription
13. sacred writing
Scripture, Scriptures... 4. text
5. Bible 6. lesson 7. Oracles,
passage, Vulgate
Scripture interpretation... 8. exegesis

12. hermeneutics
scrivello... 4. tusk (elephant's)
scrivener... 6. notary, scribe, writer
8. recorder 10. amanuensis
scroll... 4. list, roll 5. draft 6. record,
spiral, volute 7. engross, writing
8. document, inscribe, schedule,
streamer 9. parchment
scroll roll... 8. makimono
scrub... 3. mop, rub 4. mean, runt,
tree, wash 5. clean, dwarf, scour
6. drudge, paltry 7. cleanse
8. inferior 10. undersized
scrubby... 4. base 6. paltry, shabby,
stubby 7. bristly, shrubby, stunted
10. underbrush 13. insignificant
scruff... 4. nape, scum, slur 5. crust,
dross, scuff 6. refuse 7. surface
8. dandruff
scruple... 4. coin 5. demur, qualm
6. object, weight 9. small part
10. hesitation 13. unwillingness
scrupulous... 4. nice 5. exact
6. formal, proper, strict 8. qualmish
10. fastidious, meticulous
11. punctilious 13. conscientious
scrutinize... 3. eye, pry 4. scan
5. probe 7. examine, inspect,
observe
scud... 4. dash, foam, gust, rain, sail,
skim 5. speed 6. clouds, shower
scuffle... 4. fray 5. melee 6. strive,
tussle 7. contend, contest, shamble,
shuffle 8. struggle
sculduddery... 9. grossness, obscenity
scull... 3. oar 4. gull 5. shoal, skate
6. basket, paddle, propel 7. rowboat
scullion... 4. base 6. menial
7. servant 10. dishwasher,
kitchenman
scullog, scullogue... 6. farmer, rustic
7. laborer
sculp... 5. carve 7. engrave 8. seal
skin 9. engraving, sculpture
sculptor... 6. artist, carver, imager,
molder 8. chiseler 13. constellation
19. Apparatus Sculptoris
(constellation)
sculptor (famed)... 5. Rodin 7. Cellini,
Phidias 10. Praxiteles
12. Michelangelo, Saint Gaudens
sculptor's tool... 6. chisel, graver
9. ébauchoir
sculpture... 4. form 5. carve, model
6. figure, statue 9. engraving
11. alto-relievo
scum... 4. film, foam 5. cover, dross,
froth, scurf, spume 6. refuse, scoria
7. coating 8. riffraff 10. impurities
scup... 5. bream, porgy
scurrility... 5. abuse 9. indignity,
obscenity
scurrilous... 3. low 4. vile 5. gross
6. vulgar 7. abusive 8. indecent,
scurrile 9. insulting 11. foulmouthed,
opprobrious
scurry... 3. hie 4. dash 5. scoot,
speed 6. flurry, hasten 7. scamper,
scuttle 9. skedaddle
scurvy... 4. base, mean 7. disease
12. contemptible, discourteous
scuttle... 3. hod, run 4. dish, sink

5. haste, scoot 6. basket, hasten,
scurry, shovel 7. octopus, platter
8. hatchway 10. cuttlefish
scutum . . . 5. scute 6. shield
13. constellation (Milky Way)
15. Scutum Sobieskii
Scylla (pert to) . . .
  father . . 5. Nisus
  home . . 4. rock (coast of Italy)
  lover . . 5. Minos
  menace to . . 9. seafarers
  Myth . . 7. monster
  transformed to . . 7. sea bird
scythe . . . 2. sy (sye) 5. swath
scythe handle . . . 5. snath, snead
sea . . . 3. Red 4. Aral, Azov, Ross,
  wave 5. Black, brine, China, ocean,
  swell, water 6. aequor 7. Caspian
  8. seashore 9. Caribbean
sea (pert to) . . .
  adder . . 8. pipefish 11. stickleback
  anemone . . 5. polyp
  Antarctic . . 4. Ross
  arm . . 4. gulf, meer, mere 5. bayou,
  firth 7. estuary
  bird . . 3. auk 4. erne (ern), gull,
  smew, tern 5. booby, cahow, solan
  6. gannet, petrel, puffin 9. albatross
  10. shearwater
  comb form . . 3. mer
  cow . . 6. dugong, rytina (Steller's),
  walrus 7. manatee 8. sirenian
  12. hippopotamus
  cucumber . . 7. trepang
  devil . . 9. angelfish, devilfish
  dog . . 4. seal (Her) 6. fogdog, sailor
  dragon . . 8. dragonet, sea horse
  dread of . . 14. thalassophobia
  duck . . 5. eider, scaup 6. scoter
  eagle . . 4. erne (ern) 6. osprey
  ear . . 7. abalone
  eel . . 6. conger
  farer . . 3. tar 6. sailor, seaman
  7. mariner
  foam . . 5. froth 9. sepiolite
  10. meerschaum
  fowl . . 3. auk 4. gull, tern 6. gannet,
  petrel
  fox . . 5. shark
  god, deity . . 3. Lar 5. Aegir 6. Triton
  7. Neptune, Phorcus, Proteus
  8. Poseidon
  goddess . . 4. Nina 5. Doris
  10. Amphitrite
  gull . . 3. cob, mew 9. kittiwake
  hare . . 7. mollusk
  hen . . 4. skua 9. guillemot
  hog . . 8. porpoise
  holly root . . 6. eryngo (eringo)
  ladder . . 6. Jacob's
  lion . . 4. seal
  mammal . . 4. seal 5. whale 6. dugong
  7. manatee 11. bladdernose
  mouse . . 4. duck (harlequin) 6. dunlin
  7. annelid
  nymph . . 5. naiad, siren 6. nereid
  7. oceanid
  onion . . 6. squill
  otter . . 5. kalan
  owl . . 6. puffin 8. lumpfish
  pig . . 6. dugong 7. dolphin

  8. porpoise
  pumpkin . . 8. cucumber
  quail . . 6. auklet 9. turnstone
  raven . . 7. sculpin 9. cormorant
  10. squaretail
  reference to . . 5. naval 6. marine
  7. oceanic, pelagic 8. maritime
  9. Neptunian, thalassic
  robber . . 6. jaeger, pirate 7. corsair
  9. buccaneer, privateer
  serpent . . 5. Hydra 8. snake eel
  shell . . 5. conch
  sickness . . 8. mal de mer 9. naupathia
  spider . . 10. spider crab
  turtle . . 5. green 9. hawksbill
  10. loggerhead, thalassian
  11. leatherback
  unicorn . . 7. narwhal
  urchin . . 5. heart 10. echinoderm,
  Spatangina 13. cushionflower
  wolf . . 4. seal 6. pirate 9. privateer,
  submarine
sea king . . . 3. Ler 5. chief 6. pirate,
  Viking 7. Neptune
seal (pert to) . . .
  bearded . . 5. ursuk 6. makluk
  breeding ground . . 7. rookery
  eared . . 5. otary
  flock . . 3. pod
  fur (fem) . . 5. matka (matkah)
  harp (male) . . 7. saddler
  leather . . 3. pin
  limb . . 7. flipper
  skin . . 5. sculp
  type . . 3. fur 7. sea lion 8. elephant,
  pinniped
  young . . 3. pup
sealed instrument . . . 6. escrow
seam . . . 4. line, load, scar 5. joint,
  ridge, strip 6. burden, groove, stitch,
  streak, suture 7. crevice, stratum
  9. horseload 10. interstice,
  packsaddle
seaman . . . 3. gob, tar 6. sailor,
  Seabee 7. mariner
seaman's chapel . . . 6. bethel, church
seamark . . . 6. beacon 10. lighthouse
seamy . . . 5. rough 8. wrinkled
  12. disreputable
séance . . . 7. session, sitting
  9. treatment
séance holder . . . 6. medium
sear, sere . . . 3. dry 4. burn, cook
  5. parch 6. braise, scorch, wither
  7. dried up, shrivel 8. deadened,
  withered 9. cauterize 10. threadbare
  11. deteriorate
search . . . 4. comb, fish, hunt, look,
  seek 5. frisk, ghoom, grope, probe,
  quest 6. ferret, forage, survey
  7. inquire, ransack, rummage, zetetic
  9. expiscate 10. scrutinize
  11. investigate
searchlight . . . 4. beam 10. flashlight
seashell . . . 4. clam 5. conch, snail
  7. scallop
season . . . 3. age 4. fall, salt, tide, time
  5. devil, inure, spice 6. flavor,
  mature 7. qualify 8. accustom,
  preserve 11. acclimatize
season (pert to) . . .

Astron .. **5.** Aries, Libra **6.** Cancer
  11. Capricornus
Eccl .. **4.** Lent **6.** Advent, Easter
  7. Trinity **8.** Epiphany **9.** Christr
  11. Whitsuntide
Lent .. **6.** carême
Scot .. **4.** sele
yearly .. **6.** Autumn, Spring
  Winter
seasonable ... **6.** timely **7.**
seasoning ... **4.** sage, salt **5.**
  thyme **6.** cloves, garlic, peppe
  7. mustard, paprika **8.** allspice,
  estragon, marjoram, rosemary,
  turmeric **9.** condiment
Seasons, goddesses of ...
  justice .. **4.** Dike
  order (Universe) .. **5.** Horae
  peace .. **6.** Eirene
  wise laws .. **7.** Eunomia
seat ... **3.** pew **4.** root, site **5.** bench,
  chair, embed, sella, stool **6.** settee,
  settle **7.** install **9.** establish
seat (pert to) ...
  church .. **3.** pew **6.** sedile
  of justice .. **4.** banc
  of self .. **3.** ego
  on elephant .. **6.** howdah
  outdoor .. **6.** exedra
  privileged .. **6.** curule
  series (one of) .. **6.** gradin (gradine)
seaweed ... **4.** kelp **5.** algae, dulse,
  laver, varec, wrack **6.** Alaria
  8. agar–agar
secco ... **3.** dry
secern ... **7.** secrete **8.** separate
  11. distinguish **12.** discriminate
Secessionist (S Carolina) ... **5.** Rhett
secluded ... **5.** aloof, apart **6.** hidden,
  lonely, remote, secret **7.** private,
  retired **8.** debarred, expelled, isolated,
  recessed, retiring, screened, solitary
  9. cloistral, concealed
seclusion ... **7.** privacy, retreat
  8. solitude **9.** aloofness, exclusion
  10. quarantine, retirement, separation
second ... **3.** aid **4.** abet, back, echo,
  time **5.** jiffy, trice **6.** assist, attend,
  backer, double, moment **7.** instant,
  support, sustain **8.** inferior
  9. assistant, encourage, imperfect,
  prototype, reinforce **11.** corroborate,
  subordinate
second (pert to) ...
  childhood .. **6.** dotage, dotard
  8. senility
  crop .. **5.** rowen
  lieutenant .. **9.** shavetail
  number .. **6.** addend
  rate .. **8.** inferior, mediocre
  Republic .. **6.** French (1848–52)
  sight .. **6.** myopia **7.** psychic
  9. intuition **12.** clairvoyance
  team .. **5.** scrub **9.** Yannigans
  thought .. **6.** sequel **12.** afterthought
  15. reconsideration
secondary ... **4.** less **5.** minor
  6. deputy **8.** inferior, offshoot
  9. auxiliary, dependent, satellite
  10. contingent, derivative,
  second–rate, subsequent, substitute
  11. subordinate, unessential

security / seize

7. acquire, assured,
receive **8.** make fas
guarantee **10.** dep
11. undisturbed
security ... **4.** bail
  shelter .. **8.** guar
  insurance .. **4.** stai
sedate ... **4.** staid
  sober, serene, sol
  8. compos
  unruffled
  13. con
sedative ...
  bromi
  barbit
  9. o
sed

secret ...
  agent ..
  7. spotte
  13. underc
  council .. **5.** by
  language .. **5.** arg
  meeting .. **5.** tryst
  movement .. **7.** stealth
  name .. **9.** cryptonym
  place .. **5.** cache **6.** adytun
  7. sanctum **9.** sanctuary
  society .. **3.** hui (Chin) **4.** tong
  7. Camorra (It)
secretary ... **4.** bird, desk **5.** agent
  6. scribe **7.** officer **8.** recorder
  9. confidant **10.** amanuensis,
  escritoire
secrete ... **4.** bury, hide, stow **5.** exude
  7. conceal
secretion (pert to) ...
  gland .. **7.** hormone
  inflammation .. **3.** pus
  liver .. **4.** bile
  mammal gland .. **9.** lactation
  mouth .. **6.** saliva
  nasal .. **10.** secernment
  scale, insect .. **3.** lac
  shrubs .. **4.** lerp
  whale .. **9.** ambergris
secretly ... **5.** aside, slyly **7.** sub rosa
  8. covertly **9.** not openly
  13. clandestinely
sect ... **4.** clan, cult, part **5.** Alogi
  (Hist), class, group, order, party
  6. essene, school, Yezidi (Kurdish)
  9. following, Mennonite
  10. shibboleth (Bib)
  12. denomination
sectarian ... **7.** heretic **8.** partisan
  9. dissenter, heterodox
  13. nonconformist
  14. denominational
section ... **4.** area, part, plot **5.** panel,
  piece, slice, tmema, torso **6.** region
  7. portion, segment, ternion
  8. parabola, surgical **9.** paragraph,
  signature **11.** subdivision
secular ... **3.** lay **4.** laic **5.** civil
  6. laical **7.** earthly, profane, worldly
  8. temporal **9.** centuried, temporary
secure ... **3.** fix, get, pin **4.** bind, easy,
  fast, firm, moor, nail, safe, tape
  5. fetch, spike, trice (sail) **6.** elicit,
  ensure, fasten, obtain, stable

certain, procure,
9. confident,
ndable

gage 5. guard
, vadium 7. defense,
nty 9. guarantee,
ility 10. protection
m 5. douce, quiet,
6. demure, proper,
mn 7. serious, settled
ed, decorous 9. dignified,
11. unobtrusive
emplative, dispassionate
6. remedy 7. anodyne,
e, chloral, veronal 8. atropine,
al, lenitive, soothing
lmative, mitigator, paregoric
palliative, phenacetin
tranquilizer (tranquillizer)
phenobarbital
nt ... 7. sitting (statue)
iment ... 4. lees, silt 5. dregs
7. deposit, grounds, siltage
9. settlings
sedition ... 6. revolt, strife, tumult
7. treason 9. commotion
10. dissension, turbulence
seditious ... 7. riotous 8. factious
9. turbulent 11. treasonable
15. insurrectionary
seduce ... 4. lure 5. decoy, tempt
6. allure, enamor, entice 7. corrupt,
mislead 8. inveigle
seducer ... 7. enticer, tempter
8. Lothario 9. debaucher
seduction ... 5. charm 10. allurement,
corruption, temptation
11. debauchment
sedulous ... 4. busy 6. steady
8. diligent, untiring 9. assiduous,
laborious, unwearied 10. persistent
11. persevering, unremitting
see ... 3. spy 4. espy, heed, know,
look, scry, seat, view 5. visit
6. behold, descry, detect 7. diocese,
discern, witness 8. discover, perceive
9. apprehend, interview, visualize
10. comprehend, understand
11. contemplate
seed ... 3. egg, pip, pit, sow 4. germ
5. grain, ovule, plant, sperm, spore
6. kernel, origin 7. lineage, progeny
8. rudiment 9. beginning
11. descendants
seed (pert to) ...
apple .. 3. pip
aromatic .. 5. anise 7. aniseed,
caraway
coat .. 3. pod 4. aril, burr, husk
5. testa 6. carpel 8. pericarp
container, envelope .. 3. bur (burr),
pod 6. loment, vessel 7. capsule
edible .. 3. pea 4. bean 5. grain
6. lentil
enclosing soft fruit .. 5. drupe
flower .. 6. pistil
immature .. 5. ovule
lemon, orange, apple .. 3. pip
licorice .. 9. jequerity
medicinal .. 8. flaxseed
Moringa, tropical .. 3. ben

naked (one—seeded fruit) .. 6. achene
(akene)
oak .. 5. acorn
one—celled .. 6. carpel
part .. 6. tunica
poppy, opium .. 3. maw
underground .. 6. peanut
winged .. 6. samara
seeds (pert to) ...
cocoa .. 5. cacao
feeding on .. 11. granivorous
perfume .. 8. abelmosk
rudiments .. 3. ova 4. eggs, pips, pits
6. ovules, sperms
seedy ... 5. dingy, lousy, tacky
6. shabby 7. worn out 8. slovenly
10. spiritless 11. spawn—filled
12. bearing seeds
seek ... 3. beg 4. hunt 5. essay
6. pursue, search 7. explore, solicit
8. endeavor 9. neologize (new words)
11. investigate
seeker ... 6. prober, tracer 7. pursuer,
zetetic 8. aspirant, searcher
9. applicant 10. petitioner
seeker of ...
knowledge .. 10. philonoist
new words .. 9. neologist
pleasure .. 7. epicure 8. hedonist
seem ... 4. look 6. appear 7. pretend
8. resemble
seeming ... 5. guise, quasi 8. apparent,
illusion, illusory, pretense, specious
9. befitting
seeming contradiction ... 7. paradox
seeming truth ... 14. verisimilitude
seemly ... 3. fit 4. meet 6. comely,
decent, proper, suited 7. elegant,
fitting 8. decorous, tasteful
9. expedient
seep ... 4. leak, ooze 5. exude 6. filter
8. transude 9. percolate
seer, seeress ... 5. sibyl 6. oracle,
coryer 7. Phoebad, prophet
9. predictor, visionary 10. forecaster,
prophetess, soothsayer
11. Nostradamus 14. prognosticator
seesaw ... 6. teeter, tilter 7. pastime
9. alternate, crossruff, fluctuate,
vacillate 11. oscillation
12. teeter—totter
seethe ... 4. boil, stew, teem 5. be
hot, steep 6. bubble 7. be angry
segment ... 3. pip 4. part 5. tmema
6. cantle 7. portion, section
8. fragment 12. cross section
segment (pert to) ...
botany .. 5. tmema 7. lacinia
corresponding part .. 7. isomere
curve .. 3. arc
shaped .. 5. toric
Zool .. 6. somite, telson 8. metamere,
somatome
seine ... 3. net 5. trawl 6. sagene
7. dragnet, network
seism ... 10. earthquake
seize ... 3. bag, cly, cop, nab, net
4. bind, bite, grab, grip, take, trap
5. annex, catch, grasp, ravin, reave,
usurp, wrest 6. arrest, clutch, collar,
fasten, ravish, snatch 7. capture,
embargo, grapple 8. distrain

9. apprehend, lay hold of
10. confiscate, understand
11. appropriate
seizin... 9. occupancy 10. possession
seizing... 4. cord 7. lashing
9. arresting, raptorial
seizure... 3. fit 4. grip, hold 5. spasm
6. arrest, attack, frenzy, seizin
9. ownership 10. convulsion,
occupation 11. manucapture
seladang... 4. gaur 7. buffalo
selah (Bib)... 4. sign 5. pause
select... 4. cull, name, pick, take
5. elect, elite 6. choice, choose,
picked 7. appoint, pick out, specify
9. exclusive, segregate 10. registrate
11. distinguish, outstanding
selection... 5. piece 6. choice
7. analect, excerpt, passage
10. collection 11. appointment
selective... 5. draft 8. eclectic
9. exclusive 10. particular
14. discriminative
self... 3. ego, own 4. same 5. being
6. person, psyche 7. oneself
10. individual 11. personality
self (pert to)...
acting.. 9. automatic, voluntary
assertion.. 6. egoism, vanity
centered.. 7. selfish 9. egotistic
10. egocentric 11. independent
12. self-absorbed
comb form.. 4. auto
complacent.. 13. self-satisfied
confidence.. 5. poise 6. aplomb
9. assurance 11. self-reliant
contained.. 8. reserved 10. controlled,
sufficient (in itself) 11. independent
15. uncommunicative
control.. 8. stoicism 9. restraint
10. automation, discipline,
equanimity, temperance
defense.. 6. karate, jung fu 7. jujitsu
determination.. 8. autonomy
12. independence
enjoyment.. 13. gratification
esteem.. 5. pride 6. vanity
7. concept, ego-trip
evident.. 6. clear 9. axiomatic
examination.. 13. introspection,
introspective
French.. 3. soi
love of.. 6. egoism
ref to.. 8. personal
reproach.. 7. remorse
righteous.. 5. pious 9. Pharisaic
13. sanctimonious
14. holier-than-thou
same.. 9. identical
satisfied.. 4. smug 6. jaunty
Scottish.. 3. sel (sell)
worship.. 8. idolatry 9. autolatry
selfish... 5. grabby (sl) 11. egotistical,
self-seeking 12. self-centered
sell... 4. vend 5. scalp, trade
6. barter, market, retail 7. auction,
bargain 8. convince, exchange,
persuade 9. negotiate
sell (out)... 6. betray, desert 8. inform
on 9. victimize
seller... 6. dealer, vender, vendor

7. peddler 8. merchant, salesman
9. tradesman 10. saleswoman
semantics... 8. meanings
11. semasiology
semblable... 4. like 5. alike
7. seeming, similar 8. apparent,
suitable 10. ostensible, resembling
11. conformable
semblance... 4. copy, face, form
5. guise, image 6. aspect, figure
7. pretext, umbrage 8. illusion
10. appearance, similarity
11. countenance, presumption,
resemblance
semeiology, semeiotics... 5. signs
(signaling) 11. diagnostics
14. interpretation, symptomatology
semester... 4. term 6. course, period
Seminole chief... 7. Osceola
(1804–38)
Semitic (pert to)...
deity.. 4. Baal
dialect.. 4. Geez
god (evil) 6. Moloch
language.. 5. Iraqi 6. Syrian
7. Arabian, Aramaic 8. Egyptian
11. Palestinian
people.. 6. Harari 8. Moabites
tribe (nomadic).. 6. Shagia (Shaikiyeh)
semper eadem... 13. always the same
(motto of Queen Elizabeth)
semper fidelis... 13. always faithful
semper idem... 13. always the same
semper paratus... 11. always ready
senate... 5. boule 7. council (Rom)
8. assembly 11. legislature
18. administrative body
send... 4. mail, ship 5. drive, grant,
issue, speed 6. bestow, convey,
export, launch, propel 7. forward
8. dispatch, transmit 10. commission
send (pert to)...
back.. 5. remit 6. remand, return
11. reverberate
by different person.. 5. relay
off.. 5. start 6. launch 7. impulse
8. dispatch 11. consignment
13. demonstration
out.. 4. emit, spew 5. shoot
out rays.. 7. radiate
payment.. 5. remit
to an address.. 7. deliver
Seneca... 6. Indian 9. Iroquoian
Senegal, Africa...
capital.. 5. Dakar
ebony.. 9. blackwood
gazell.. 5. korin
gum.. 9. gum arabic
mahogany.. 9. cailcedra
native.. 10. Senegalese
senescence... 5. aging 10. growing
old
senicide... 13. killing old men (tribal)
senility... 6. dotage, old age
8. caducity, dementia 10. feebleness
senior... 4. aine, dean 5. chief, elder
7. ancient, student 8. superior
sensation... 5. sense 6. thrill, uproar,
wonder 7. emotion 8. rhigosis (cold)
10. perception 12. great success
sensational... 5. lurid 6. superb

8. dramatic, exciting 9. emotional
12. melodramatic
sense... 4. feel, mind, sane 5. flair,
sight, smell 7. feeling, meaning
8. sapience 9. awareness, intuition,
sensation, sentience 10. perception,
understand 11. discernment,
recognition 12. intelligence
senseless... 5. inept 6. insane, stupid,
unwise 7. fatuous, foolish, idiotic,
inanity 9. illogical, inanimate,
insensate, unfeeling 10. irrational
11. meaningless, purposeless,
unconscious 12. unreasonable
13. unintelligent
sense of...
beauty.. 8. aesthete (esthete), tasteful
9. aesthetic
dignity.. 5. pride
distance.. 11. telesthetic
hearing.. 8. audition 12. auscultation
humor.. 10. risibility
sight.. 6. vision
smell.. 7. osmatic 9. olfaction
taste.. 6. palate
sense organ... 3. ear, eye 4. nose,
skin 6. tongue 8. receptor, sensilla
senses... 4. wits 6. sanity 7. sensory
9. sensation
sensible... 4. sane 5. aware, privy,
sound 7. logical, prudent 8. rational
9. cognizant, practical, sensitive
10. reasonable, responsive
11. intelligent, susceptible
sensitive... 4. nice, sore 5. acute
6. pliant, tender, touchy 7. sensory
8. sensible 9. receptive
10. responsive 11. susceptible
14. discriminating, impressionable
sensitivity... 9. emotional, hebetated
(blunted) 11. sensibility 12. irritability
14. discrimination
sentence... 4. doom 5. maxim, motto
6. phrase, remark, saying
7. condemn, passage, thought,
verdict 8. decision, judgment,
proposal 9. statement
12. condemnation
sentence (pert to)...
balance.. 7. parison
clause (concluding).. 8. apodosis
concluding.. 8. epilogue (epilog)
construction.. 6. syntax
difficult articulation.. 13. tongue
twister
introductory.. 8. protasis
judicial.. 5. futwa
pithy.. 5. motto 8. aphorism
punishment.. 11. year and a day
subordinate part.. 6. clause, phrase
sententious... 5. pithy, terse
7. concise, laconic 10. aphoristic
13. grandiloquent
sentient... 4. mind 5. aware 7. feeling
8. sensible 9. conscious, sensitive
10. perceptive 13. consciousness
sentiment... 5. toast 7. emotion,
feeling, opinion 8. attitude
10. perception, sentimento
11. sensibility 14. sentimentality
sentimental... 6. loving 7. maudlin,
mawkish 8. romantic 9. emotional

13. lackadaisical
sentimental song... 11. strephonade
sentinel... 5. guard 6. picket, sentry
7. vedette (mounted) 8. watchman
10. lookout man, watchtower
sepad... 5. think 7. believe, suppose
sepal... 4. leaf 5. petal
separate... 4. open, part, shed, sift,
sort 5. alone, apart, sever, space
6. cleave, detach, divide, secern,
single, sleave, sunder, winnow
7. disband, diverge, diverse, divided,
divorce, isolate 8. alienate, discrete,
distinct, peculiar, secluded
9. disjoined, partition, segregate,
sequester, unrelated 10. dissociate,
particular, respective
11. disembodied, unconnected
separate (pert to)...
Chem.. 11. fractionate
from others.. 5. aloof 8. isolated
metal from ore.. 5. smelt
thread.. 6. sleave
separation... 6. tmesis 7. divorce
8. autotomy 9. partition, secession,
seclusion 10. alienation
11. disjunction, segregation
13. sequestration 14. discontinuance,
discrimination
separatist... 7. heretic, seceder
8. apostate 9. dissenter
12. secessionist 13. nonconformist
sepia... 3. dun, ink 5. color
7. pigment 10. cuttlebone, cuttlefish
sepiment... 5. hedge 7. defense
9. enclosure
Sepiola... 10. cuttlefish
sepiolite... 10. meerschaum
sepoy... 7. soldier 9. policeman
seps... 6. lizard 7. serpent
sept... 4. clan 5. class, seven, tribe
7. lineage
septic... 6. morbid, pyemia (pyaemia)
8. diseased, infected, poisoned
9. gangrened, mortified, poisonous
10. septicemia (blood poison)
sepulcher, sepulchre... 4. bury, tomb
5. crypt, grave, vault 6. entomb
9. sepulture 10. repository
sepulchral... 5. urnal 6. gloomy,
hollow 7. charnel 8. funereal
9. deep–toned
sepulchral (pert to)...
chest.. 4. cist
mound.. 7. tumulus
vault.. 6. burial 8. catacomb,
monument 9. interview
sequel... 5. issue 6. effect, series,
upshot 7. outcome 8. follow up,
sequence, sequitur 9. posterity
10. succession
sequela... 7. disease (resulting)
8. adherent 9. inference
10. conclusion 11. concomitant,
consequence 15. morbid condition
sequence... 5. gamut 6. course
(usual), series, tierce (three cards)
8. straight 10. succession
sequential... 9. deducible, resultant
10. continuous, succeeding
11. consecutive
sequestered... 6. lonely, secret

7. private, recluse, retired
8. isolated, secluded, solitary,
withdraw 9. concealed, separated
12. unfrequented
sequitur . . . 9. inference, influence, it
follows 14. natural sequent
sequoia, Sequoia . . . 4. Park (Calif)
6. Indian (famed for alphabet) 7. big
tree, conifer, redwood
seraglio . . . 5. harem, serai 6. zenana
9. enclosure
serape . . . 5. shawl 7. blanket
seraph . . . 5. angel 6. cherub
seraphic . . . 7. angelic, sublime
8. cherubic 9. unworldly
Serb . . . 4. Slav 7. Serbian (Servian)
Serbia, Yugoslavia . . .
church . . 8. Orthodox
conqueror . . 5. Turks
hero . . 6. Dushan, Nemaya (1159)
queen . . 7. Natalie
Revolutionary . . 7. Chetnik
sere . . . 4. claw, sear, worn 5. talon
6. effete, yellow 8. withered
10. desiccated
serenade . . . 4. sing 5. music
8. serenata 9. charivari, entertain
10. callithump 11. celebration
serene . . . 4. calm, cool 5. clear, quiet
6. placid 8. peaceful, serenity,
tranquil 9. collected, unruffled
11. undisturbed 12. tranquillity
(tranquility)
serenity . . . 5. peace 6. repose
8. calmness, coolness 9. composure
10. quiescence
serf . . . 4. esne, noif (fem), peon
5. helot, slave 6. thrall, vassal
7. captive, villein
series . . . 3. set 4. nest 5. class,
gamut, group 8. sequence
9. seriation 10. succession
series, connected . . . 5. chain, suite
6. catena
series of . . .
discussions . . 9. symposium
heroic events . . 4. epos
meetings . . 7. session
pictures . . 8. panorama
races . . 7. regatta
rings . . 4. coil
six . . 5. hexad
steps . . 5. scale
syllogisms . . 7. sorites
travels . . 7. odyssey
serious . . . 4. keen 5. grave, serio
(comb form), sober, staid 6. demure,
sedate, solemn 7. capital, earnest,
weighty, zealous 8. resolute
9. important 10. thoughtful
seriousness . . . 4. zeal 7. gravity
10. importance 11. earnestness
sermon . . . 4. talk, text 5. psalm
6. homily, lesson, preach 7. address,
lecture, reproof 8. harangue
9. discourse, preaching
10. admonition
seron . . . 5. crate 6. hamper
7. boxwood, spanner
serotine . . . 3. bat 4. adda 9. late
bloom
serpent . . . 3. asp 4. seps (anc)

5. cobra, krait, racer, snake
serpent (pert to) . . .
deity, of good . . 12. agathodaemon
13. agathos daemon
fabulous . . 5. Hydra 6. dragon
8. basilisk 11. amphisbaena
large . . 3. boa 5. aboma 6. python
8. jararaca
monster . . 6. ellops
Old . . 5. Satan
semihuman (Hind Myth) . . 4. Naga
sky (Vedic Myth) . . 3. Ahi
worshipers (Gnostic) . . 7. Ophites
serpentine . . . 4. wily 5. snaky
6. subtle, zigzag 7. sinuous, winding
8. diabolic, tempting 9. snakelike
10. circuitous, meandering
serpigo . . . 8. ringworm 11. skin disease
serrano . . . 12. squirrelfish
serrate . . . 7. notched, toothed
8. indented 10. saw–toothed
serried . . . 5. dense 7. compact,
concise, crowded
serum . . . 4. whey 5. blood, fluid
6. serous 9. antitoxin
servant . . . 3. gyp 4. bata, cook, maid,
maty, mozo, serf, syce 5. agent,
boots, chela, nurse, slave, valet
6. bildar, butler, flunky, garçon, gillie
(gilly), menial, servus, vassal, wallah
(walla) 7. equerry (nobleman's)
8. coistrel, domestic, handmaid
9. assistant 11. chamberlain
servant of God . . . 6. bishop
serve . . . 2. do 3. act, aid 4. deal,
help, wait 5. avail, cater 6. assist,
succor 7. advance, bestead, forward,
further, suffice, work for 8. bear
arms, fight for 9. officiate
10. administer, distribute
serve (pert to) . . .
as accomplice . . 4. abet
as escort . . 6. squire
food . . 4. wait 5. cater 7. dish out
religion . . 4. obey 7. worship
tennis . . 7. deliver
server . . . 4. tray 6. player, salver
7. acolyte
Servia . . . see *Serbia*
service . . . 3. aid, use 4. help, mail,
Mass, rite 5. favor, matin 6. employ,
ritual 7. benefit, nocturn, utility
8. ceremony, evensong, kindness,
ministry 9. servitude 10. attendance,
employment 12. ministration
service tree . . . 4. sorb 5. rowan
servile . . . 4. mean 6. abject, menial,
minion 7. fawning, slavish
8. cringing, faithful 9. dependent,
parasitic, truckling 10. obsequious,
submissive 11. subservient,
sycophantic
Servite . . . 9. mendicant 13. Order of
Friars (1233)
servitude . . . 7. bondage, serfdom,
service, slavery 8. servitus
9. vassalage 14. apprenticeship
sesame . . . 3. oil 4. herb 5. benne
7. gingili (seed), teel oil 8. ajonjoli,
sesamine
Sesame, Open . . . 10. magical key
12. magic command (Arab Nights)

sess... 4. heap, pile 9. soap frame
session... 5. court 6. séance
  8. assembly 11. legislature
set... 3. lay 4. form, heal, laid, pose,
  post 5. brood, class, fixed, group,
  place, posit, ready, staid, stand
  6. adjust, clique, define, fasten,
  formal, ossify, series, settle
  7. confirm, congeal, coterie, station,
  stiffen 8. regulate, solidify
  9. coagulate, designate, direction,
  obstinate, stabilize 10. collection,
  determined, solidified 11. established,
  prepared for
set (pert to)...
  afloat.. 6. launch
  against.. 6. oppose 10. antagonize
  apart.. 5. allot, elect, taboo
  6. exempt 7. isolate, reserve,
  seclude 8. allocate, separate
  9. segregate, sequester
  11. distinguish 13. differentiate
  aside.. 4. void 5. annul 6. except,
  reject 7. abolish, discard, dismiss,
  earmark, exclude 8. overrule,
  postpone
  at an angle.. 4. cant
  back.. 4. loss 5. check 6. demote,
  hinder, recess 7. relapse 8. restrain,
  slow down
  exclusive.. 5. elect, taboo 6. clique
  fire to.. 6. ignite, kindle 7. emblaze,
  inflame 8. irritate
  firmly.. 5. embed, plant, posit
  6. cement, ossify
  forth.. 5. adorn 6. depart, expose, lay
  out 7. arrange, commend, display,
  enounce, exhibit, explain, expound,
  present, promote, propone, publish
  8. announce, decorate, indicate,
  manifest 9. translate 10. promulgate
  11. demonstrate
  free.. 6. acquit 7. absolve, release,
  unloose 8. liberate 10. emancipate
  11. disillusion
  off.. 6. incite, offset 7. measure
  8. beautify, detonate 9. demarcate,
  embellish 11. distinguish
  on firm basis.. 9. establish
  out.. 4. plot 5. allot, begin
  7. arrange
  right.. 5. teach 6. adjust, direct,
  remedy 11. disillusion
  up.. 3. rig 4. plan 5. build, cause,
  erect, exalt, hoist, print, raise
  7. elevate, finance, install
  9. construct, establish
  10. inaugurate, prearrange
set (pert to in)...
  a groove.. 5. dadoe
  a row.. 4. tier 5. align, aline, range
  columns.. 7. tabular 8. tabulate
  from margin.. 6. indent
  operation.. 4. move 5. start 6. launch
  opposition.. 3. pit
  order.. 5. align 6. adjust 7. arrange
set (pert to of)...
  eight.. 6. ogdoad
  friends.. 7. coterie
  jeweled ornaments.. 6. parure
  laws.. 4. code 8. statutes
  on end.. 5. upend 10. topsy–turvy

  opinions.. 5. credo
  organ pipes.. 5. stops
  rules.. 4. code
  sheets (paper).. 5. quire
seta... 4. hair 5. spine 7. bristle,
  feather
Seth (pert to)...
  brother.. 4. Abel, Cain
  father.. 4. Adam
  son.. 4. Enos
  wife.. 8. Nephthys
setting... 5. scene 6. locale
  8. mounting, planting
  10. background
settle... 3. fix, pay 4. nest, root, seat,
  sink 5. agree, clear, lodge, order,
  prove, quiet, solve 6. assign, assure,
  decide, locate, pay off, purify, secure,
  soothe 7. arrange, clarify, confirm,
  mediate, resolve 8. colonize,
  ensconce, regulate 9. designate,
  determine, establish, reconcile
  10. strengthen 11. tranquilize
settled... 4. paid 5. ended, fixed
  6. proved, sedate 7. assured,
  decided, located 9. steadfast
  10. unchanging 11. established
settled in advance...
  13. predetermined
settled in mind... 10. equanimity
settlement... 3. dos 4. camp
  6. colony, hamlet 7. payment
  8. fixation, sediment, showdown
  9. community, endowment
  10. adjustment 12. colonization,
  conciliation, satisfaction
  13. determination, establishment
Settlement House... 9. Hull House
  (Chicago) 10. University (NY)
  11. Toynbee Hall (London)
settler... 6. Sooner (Okla) 7. pioneer,
  planter, Puritan 8. colonist
  9. immigrant
settlings... 4. lees 5. dregs
  8. sediment 10. settlement
  12. precipitates
seven (pert to)...
  angles.. 8. heptagon 9. septangle
  arts.. 5. logic, music 7. grammar
  8. geometry, rhetoric 9. astronomy
  10. arithmetic
  comb form.. 5. hepta, septi
  days and nights.. 8. sennight
  fold.. 8. septuple
  gods of happiness.. 5. Ebisu, Hotei
  6. Benten 7. Daikoku, Jurojin
  8. Bishamon 10. Fuku–roku–ju
  group.. 6. heptad, septet 8. septuple
  12. septemvirate
  Hills.. 4. Rome
  languages.. 9. heptaglot
  Latin.. 6. septum
  number.. 8. hebdomad 9. septenary
  Old Test Books (1st seven)..
  10. Heptateuch
  Seas.. 11. world oceans
  Stars.. 8. Pleiades
  tones.. 10. heptachord, heptatonic
seventy... 12. septuagenary
seventy–day period...
  12. septuagesima
seventy–year–old... 14. septuagenarian

sever ... 3. cut, lop 4. part, rend
5. break 6. behead, cleave, detach,
divide, except, exempt 7. disjoin
8. accurate, disunite, separate
9. interpose, segregate
10. decapitate, disconnect, dissociate
12. disassociate
several ... 4. many 6. divers, sundry
7. diverse, various 8. distinct
9. different 10. respective
severe ... 3. bad 4. dure, hard, keen,
sore, tart 5. acute, cruel, exact, grave,
harsh, rigid, snell, sober, stern
6. biting, bitter, chaste, sedate,
simple, solemn, strict, taxing, trying
7. arduous, austere, condign, drastic,
extreme, intense, painful, serious,
violent 8. accurate, rigorous
9. draconian, strenuous, stringent
10. censorious, restrained
severe critic (of Alexandria) ...
9. Aristarch
severity ... 5. rigor 7. cruelty
8. hardness, pungency, violence
9. austerity, exactness, gruffness,
harshness, solemnity, sternness,
stiffness 10. bitterness, difficulty,
inclemency, simplicity, strictness
12. rigorousness
Seville cathedral tower ... 7. Giralda
Seville orange ... 9. red–yellow
12. bitter orange
Sèvres blue ... 5. color 9. bleu de
roi, porcelain 11. bleu céleste
sew ... 4. mend 5. baste, unite
6. fasten, needle, secure, stitch
sewan ... 5. beads, money 6. wampum
sewing ... 6. sutile 8. suturing
9. stitching 10. needlework
sewing case ... 4. etui
sewing machine inventor ... 9. Elias
Howe
sexagenarian ... 13. a sixty-year-old
sexagesimal ... 5. sixty
sexes, common to both ... 6. unisex
7. epicene
sexless ... 6. neuter 7. epicene
sextet, sextette ... 6. sestet 8. six
parts 10. group of six 13. six–line
stanza
sexton ... 6. beetle 7. sacrist
9. sacristan 12. underofficer
sextuplet ... 7. sestole (sestolet) 8. six
notes
sha ... 5. sheep, urial (oorial)
shabbash ... 5. bravo 8. well done
Shabbath ... 7. Sabbath (Jew)
shabbiness ... 8. baseness, slovenry
9. seediness
shabby ... 4. base, mean, worn
5. dowdy, faded, ratty, seedy, tacky,
yucky 6. grungy, paltry, ragged,
scurvy, scuzzy, sleazy 7. outworn,
shagrag, squalid 10. despicable,
ragamuffin, threadbare
12. contemptible
shack ... 3. coe, hut 4. husk, plug
5. chase, hutch, tramp 6. shanty
7. stubble 8. vagabond 9. hibernate
shackle ... 3. tie 4. band, bind, bond,
gyve, iron, ring 5. chain 6. fetter,

hobble, hogtie, impede, pinion
7. manacle, trammel 8. restrain
shackled ... 4. tied 5. bound, gyved
6. curbed, ironed 7. hobbled
8. fettered, hampered, hindered,
manacled 10. restrained
shad ... 4. fish 5. Alosa 7. crappie,
mojarra
shade ... 3. hue 4. dull, roof, tint, tone,
veil 5. ghost, tinge, visor 6. awning,
canopy, darken, degree, follow,
nuance, screen, shadow, shield, sprite
7. eclipse, foliage, parasol, protect,
shelter, umbrage 10. overshadow,
protection 11. adumbration
shade, affording ... 9. umbratile
shadow ... 3. dim, dog, spy 4. hide,
tail 5. cloud, image, umbra 6. attend,
screen 7. blacken, conceal, protect,
remains 8. follower, hanger–on,
illusion, penumbra 9. adumbrate,
detective 10. protection
shadow fighting ... 9. sciamachy
shadowless ... 6. asclan
Shadrach (pert to) ...
enemy .. 14. Nebuchadnezzar
name once .. 7. Ananias 9. Hannaniah
one of three Hebrew youths ..
7. Meshach 8. Abednago, Shadrach
shady ... 4. dark 5. faint, fishy
6. umbral 7. shadowy 8. deceitful,
dishonest, underhand 10. indistinct,
unreliable 12. questionable
shaft ... 3. pit, rod 4. axle, fust, mine,
orlo (part), stem, tige, tole 5. arrow,
scape, shank, spire, stalk, thill, tower,
trunk 6. column, tongue 7. feather,
missile, obelisk 8. monument
9. flagstaff
shag ... 3. nap 4. hair, mane, pile
5. chase, dance 6. follow, rascal
7. tobacco 9. cormorant, make rough
10. blackguard
shaggy ... 5. bushy, furry, nappy, rough
6. ragged 7. hirsute, unkempt, villous
8. confused (of thought), uncombed
10. unpolished
shagrag ... 6. ragged, tagrag
7. unkempt 8. rascally
shake ... 3. jar, jog, wag 4. jolt, rock,
stir, sway, toze 5. swing, trill
6. dither, dodder, quiver, shimmy,
shiner, weaken 7. agitate, flutter,
shingle, shudder, tremble, tremolo
8. enfeeble 10. earthquake
Shakespeare (pert to) ...
actor .. 4. Ward 7. Gielgud, Olivier,
Sothern 8. Modjeska
called .. 10. Bard of Avon
character, female .. 6. Juliet, Portia
7. Ophelia 9. Cleopatra
character, male .. 5. Romeo, Timon
6. Antony, Hamlet 7. Macbeth,
Othello 8. Falstaff
forest .. 5. Arden
river .. 4. Avon
site .. 6. Verona 8. Elsinore
villain .. 4. Iago
wife .. 11. Anne Hathaway
shaky ... 6. infirm, wabbly, wobbly
7. fearful, nervous, unsound

8. agitated, unsecure 9. tottering, trembling, uncertain, unsettled
10. precarious, unreliable
12. questionable
shale... 4. rock 5. flake, scale
8. dandruff
Shalimar Gardens... 6. Lahore
shallow... 5. shoal 6. lagoon (lagune)
7. cursory, trivial 9. depthless, frivolous, insincere 11. superficial
sham... 3. ape 4. fake, hoax, mock
5. dummy, false, fraud, trick
6. deceit, humbug 7. feigned
8. pretense 9. imitation, imposture, pretended
Shamash (pert to)...
  centers of worship.. 5. Larsa
  6. Sippar
  consort.. 3. Aya (Ai)
  deity (Babylon).. 6. sun god
  messenger.. 6. Bunene
  Sumerian equivalent.. 3. Utu (Utug)
  6. Babbar
shame... 5. abash 7. mortify
8. disgrace, dishonor 9. humiliate
11. abomination, humiliation, impropriety
shameful... 4. mean, vile 5. gross
6. wicked 8. flagrant, improper, indecent, infamous, terrible
9. degrading 10. outrageous, scandalous 11. disgraceful, ignominious 12. dishonorable, disreputable, vituperative
shameless... 6. arrant, brazen
8. immodest, impudent 9. audacious
10. unblushing 11. brazenfaced
shammer... 8. impostor
shanghai... 6. abduct, to drug
9. slingshot
shank... 3. leg 4. crus, gamb (gambe)
7. meat cut 12. travel on foot
shape... 4. bend, form, mold (mould), plan 5. frame, model 6. adjust, create, cut out, design, devise, figure
7. arrange, conform, contour, develop, fashion, incline 8. phantasm
10. appearance, figuration
11. arrangement
shaped like a...
  comb.. 9. pectinate
  shield.. 7. peltate, scutate
  strap, thong.. 6. lorate
  urn.. 9. urceolate
shapeless... 7. lumpish 8. deformed, formless 9. amorphous, contorted, distorted, unshapely
shapely... 3. fit 4. neat, trim
6. comely, gainly 10. well–formed
11. symmetrical
16. well–proportioned
shapes (ornamental, garden)... 5. topia
7. topiary
share... 3. cut, lot 4. dole, part
5. enter, quota 6. ration 7. partake, portion 8. take part 9. allowance, apportion 11. co–operative, participate
sharecropper... 7. metayer
shark... 5. fraud 6. lawyer 8. parasite, swindler 9. trickster
shark (fish)... 4. gata, mako, tope

5. lamia (cub), Rhina 6. Galeos, Galeus, requin 7. dogfish, tiburon
8. man–eater, Mustelus, Selachii, sharklet, Squatina 9. porbeagle
10. Carcharias, hammerhead
11. Carcharodon, Galeorhinus
shark–clinger... 4. pega 6. remora
sharp... 4. acid, curt, edgy, keen, tart
5. acerb, acrid, acute, alert, brisk, crisp, edged, harsh, quick, smart, steep, witty 6. abrupt, astute, bitter, crafty, shrill 7. angular, caustic, cutting, nipping, painful, pointed, pungent, sharper 8. incisive, poignant
9. penetrant, sagacious, sarcastic, trenchant 10. discerning, proficient
11. acrimonious, penetrating, well–dressed
sharp (pert to)...
  answer.. 6. retort
  blow.. 4. slap
  cornered.. 7. angular
  edged.. 5. arris
  flavor.. 4. tang
  make.. 10. cacuminate
  pointed.. 5. acute
  saw.. 8. titmouse
  Scot.. 5. snell 6. snelly
  sighted.. 4. keen 6. astute 7. lyncean
  sound.. 4. ping
  Tuesday.. 13. Shrove Tuesday
  witted.. 6. shrewd 10. discerning
  11. intelligent
sharpen... 3. nib, ted 4. edge, hone, whet 5. grind, point, strop 6. acuate
7. enhance, quicken 9. intensify
10. cacuminate
sharper... 5. cheat, knave, rogue
6. keener 8. deceiver, swindler
9. trickster
shatter... 5. blast, break, crash, smash, split 8. splinter
shave... 3. cut 4. pare 5. cheat, strip
6. cut off 7. swindle, tonsure 9. cut prices, thin slice
shaver... 3. boy, lad 4. tool 5. cheat
6. barber 8. swindler 9. youngster
11. extortioner
shavetail... 4. mule 6. ensign
10. lieutenant
shawl... 5. manta 6. serape 7. paisley
8. cashmere
Shawnee (pert to)...
  chief.. 8. Tecumseh
  Indian tribe.. 9. Algonquin
  location (present).. 8. Oklahoma
sheaf... 4. kern, omer 6. bundle
7. cluster 11. hyperpencil
shear... 3. cut 4. clip, snip, trim
5. sever 6. fleece, remove
7. scissor, whittle
shears... 5. lewis 6. forfex 8. secateur
sheatfish... 4. wels 7. catfish
sheath... 4. case 5. forel (book), glove, ocrea, theca 6. sleeve, spathe
7. stipule 8. scabbard
sheathe... 4. wrap 5. cover, drape
6. encase 7. envelop 8. enshroud
sheave... 5. wheel 6. pulley 9. back water, eccentric
shebang... 6. affair, boodle, outfit
7. concern 11. contrivance

13. establishment 14. kit and caboodle

she–cat . . . 4. elle 9. grimalkin

shed . . . 3. hut 4. abri, cote, lair, molt 5. hovel, scale, spill 6. effuse, hangar, lean–to, slough 7. cottage, diffuse, radiate, shelter

shed (light) . . . 4. glow 7. explain, radiate 10. illuminate

shedding . . . 7. ecdysis (Zool), molting

sheen . . . 5. glint, gloss, shine 6. luster 7. glitter, shimmer 8. splendor 9. shininess 10. brightness

sheep . . . 3. ewe, ram, sha, teg, tup 4. buck, lamb, Ovis, zenu 5. bidet, dumba, oudad 6. argali, cosset, gimmer, hogget, mutton, sheder, wether 8. ruminant, shearhog, yeanling 9. blackface

sheep (pert to) . . .
cry . . 3. baa 5. bleat
disease . . 3. coe, gid, rot 4. bane 5. braxy 7. anthrax
faced . . 3. shy 7. hashful 8. sheepish
female . . 3. ewe, teg 6. sheder
flock leader . . 10. bellwether
fold . . 3. ree 4. cote 5. kraal, reeve, stell 6. church
head . . 5. jimmy 8. powsowdy
headed . . 5. silly 6. stupid 12. simple–minded
kidney extract . . 5. renes
laurel . . 6. Kalmia
leg wool . . 4. gare
male . . 3. ram, tup 4. buck 5. heder 6. wether
owner's mark . . 4. smit 6. ruddle
pet . . 6. cosset
sheeplike . . 5. ovine 9. tractable
skin, leather . . 4. pelt, roan 5. basil 7. chamois, diploma 8. woolfell
stealing . . 7. abigest
tick . . 3. ked
wild . . 3. sha 4. Ovis 5. urial 6. aoudad, argali, bharal, nayaur 7. mouflon (moufflon) 9. Thian Shan (Marco Polo's)

sheep, breeds . . . 6. Merino, Romney 7. Cheviot, Delaine, Dishley, Karakul, Suffolk, Targhee 8. Cotswold, Dartmoor 9. Kerry Hill, Leicester, Southdown, Teeswater 10. Corriedale, Dorset Horn, Oxford Down, Shropshire 13. Hampshire Down

sheer . . . 4. mere, pure, thin, turn 5. brant, steep, utter 6. abrupt, swerve 7. deviate, unmixed 8. absolute 9. deviation, downright, undiluted 10. completely, diaphonous 11. transparent 13. perpendicular

sheet . . . 4. leaf, rope, sail 5. paper 6. shroud 9. cover with, duodecimo (12–fold), newspaper, sheathing

sheik, sheikh . . . 4. Arab 5. chief 6. prince

shelf . . . 4. berm (berme), reef, sell 5. ledge, shoal 6. mantel 7. stratum 8. postpone, put aside

shell . . . 3. pod 4. boat, bomb, husk 5. conch, crust, shard, shuck 6. cowrie (cowry) 7. bombard,

---

capsule, grenade, missile 8. carapace, exterior, shrapnel 9. cartridge 10. projectile

shell (pert to) . . .
button source . . 5. troca 6. lorica, mucket
cone . . 7. admiral
ear . . 7. abalone
explosive . . 3. dud 4. bomb 7. grenade
fish . . 4. clam, pipi 6. cockle, limpet, mussel, oyster 7. abalone, lobster, mollusk, scallop 8. barnacle 9. trunkfish
fossil . . 8. ammonite
game . . 10. thimblerig 13. sleight of hand
marine . . 6. cowrie (cowry)
money . . 5. hawok, sewan, uhllo (ulo) 6. cowrie, wampum
out . . 4. give 6. expend, pay out
protective . . 6. lorica
ridge . , 4. lira 5. varix
seaweed . . 8. frustule
spiral . . 5. chank, whelk 8. caracole
trumpet (Triton's) . . 5. conch

shelter . . . 3. lee, pad 4. abri, camp, cote, digs, port, roof, shed, skug, tent 5. condo, cover, haven, house, hutch, shack, shade 6. asylum, burrow, dugout, hangar, harbor, refuge, screen, shield 7. defense, hospice, pillbox, protect, retreat 8. mantelet (mantlet), quarters, security 9. coverture, sanctuary 10. protection

sheltered side . . . 3. lee 4. alee 7. leeward

shelve . . . 5. slope, table, waive 6. retire 7. dismiss, incline 8. postpone, put aside 10. pigeonhole

Shem (pert to) . . .
brother . . 3. Ham
descendant . . 6. Semite
father . . 4. Noah
son . . 3. Lud 4. Aram, Elam

shenanigan . . . 7. foolery 8. trickery, zaniness 9. horseplay 10. hanky–panky 11. monkeyshine

shend . . . 3. mar 4. harm, ruin 5. spoil 6. injure, revile 7. destroy, stupefy 8. confound, disgrace, reproach

Sheol . . . 4. Hell 5. Aralu, grave, Hades 6. the pit, Toppet 7. Abaddon, Gehenna 10. underworld 11. nether world 14. abode of the dead

shepherd . . . 5. guide 6. direct, escort, feeder, herder, pastor, shadow 8. guardian, herdsman 9. clergyman

shepherd, shepherds (pert to) . . .
band of . . 10. pastoureau
dog . . 5. sheep 6. collie
flute . . 7. musette 9. flageolet
god . . 3. Pan
pipe . . 3. oat 4. reed 7. larigot
spider . . 13. daddy longlegs
staff . . 4. Kent 5. crook

sheriff (pert to) . . .
aide . . 5. posse
deputy . . 6. elisor 7. bailiff
jurisdiction . . 9. bailiwick
sheriffdom . . 10. shrievalty

sherry ... **5.** jerez, Xeres **7.** oloroso
　8. montilla
Shetland Islands (pert to) ...
　fishing grounds (deep–sea) .. **4.** haaf
　kingdom of .. **8.** Scotland
　land, fee simple .. **4.** udal
　promontory .. **4.** noup
　Supreme Court Pres .. **4.** foud
　viol .. **3.** gue
shewbread, showbread (Bib) ...
　6. ritual **10.** unleavened
shibboleth (Bib) ... **4.** mode **5.** habit
　6. saying, slogan **9.** criterion,
　watchword **11.** peculiarity (speech)
shield ... **3.** écu **4.** boss, umbo
　5. aegis (egis), armor, cover, pavis,
　pelta, scute, shade, shell, targe (anc)
　6. defend, scutum, target
　7. defense, protect, shelter
　8. insignia **9.** protector
　10. escutcheon, protection
shield (pert to) ...
　Athena's .. **5.** aegis (egis)
　bearer .. **8.** escudero
　border .. **4.** orle **7.** bordure
　emblem .. **7.** impresa
　French (anc) .. **8.** rondache
　heraldry .. **4.** enté **6.** points
　part .. **4.** enté, orle, umbo
　Roman .. **6.** scutum
　sacred .. **6.** ancile (Rom)
　shaped .. **7.** peltate, scutate
　8. aspidate
shift ... **4.** eddy, fend, jibe, move, ruse,
　stir, tack, veer **5.** shunt, smock, trick
　6. baffle, change, device, rustle
　7. deviate, pretext, quibble **8.** artifice,
　mutation, transfer **9.** deviation,
　expedient, fluctuate, vacillate
　10. conversion, subterfuge
　12. redistribute **13.** transposition
shifty ... **6.** crafty, tricky **7.** devious,
　evasive, furtive **9.** deceitful, makeshift
　10. changeable **11.** treacherous
shill, shillaber (circus term) ... **5.** decoy
　8. employer, hanger–on
　10. accomplice
shillalagh, shillalah ... **4.** club
　6. cudgel **7.** sapling
shilly–shally ... **8.** hesitate **9.** vacillate
　10. hestation, indecision
　11. vacillation
Shiloh ... **4.** town (anc) **6.** Seilun
　(modern) **9.** sanctuary (the ark)
　10. battle site (Tenn)
shimmy ... **5.** quake **6.** quiver
　7. chemise, tremble, vibrate **9.** jazz
　dance, vibration
shin ... **5.** climb, tibia **6.** cnemis
　7. foreleg
shindy ... **3.** row **4.** lark, orgy, riot,
　romp **5.** dance, party, revel, spree,
　wince **6.** frolic, uproar **7.** wassail
　8. carousal **9.** commotion, festivity
　11. merrymaking
shine ... **3.** ray **4.** beam, beek, star
　5. excel, gloss, prank **6.** polish
　7. furbish, glisten, glister, glitter,
　radiate, splurge **8.** rutilate **9.** irradiate
shiner ... **6.** bruise **8.** black eye
　9. bootblack **10.** dollarfish
shingle ... **4.** sign, wood **6.** hairdo

　7. haircut, overlap **8.** chastise,
　coiffure, detritus **9.** signboard
shining ... **5.** aglow, lucid, nitid, shiny
　6. glossy, lucent **7.** beaming,
　glowing, radiant **8.** luminous, lustrous,
　nitidous, rutilant, splendid **9.** refulgent
　10. glistening, glittering
　11. illustrious, irradiating, resplendent
Shinto (pert to) ...
　adherent .. **9.** Shintoist
　cult .. **8.** Japanese
　deity .. **8.** Hachiman
　temple .. **3.** sha **5.** jinja (jinsha)
　　7. yashiro
　temple gateway .. **5.** torii
　temple deity .. **5.** Jinja (Jinsha)
shiny ... **5.** nitid, sleek **6.** bright
　7. radiant, shining **8.** luminous,
　nitidous **9.** unclouded
ship ... **3.** ark **4.** lade, load, send
　5. liner, tramp **6.** argosy, vessel
　7. freight, steamer **9.** freighter,
　transport **10.** watercraft
ship (pert to) ...
　abandoned .. **8.** derelict
　apparatus .. **5.** crane, davit, winch
　　7. bollard, capstan **8.** windlass
　Argonaut's .. **4.** Argo
　armored .. **7.** carrack, cruiser
　　9. destroyer, submarine
　attendant .. **7.** steward
　auxiliary .. **4.** dory, life **6.** dinghy
　　(dingy), tender
　biscuit .. **8.** hardtack **10.** pilot bread
　cabin .. **6.** saloon **9.** stateroom
　cargo .. **5.** oiler **6.** tanker **7.** oreboat
　　11. supertanker
　deck .. **4.** main, poop **5.** orlop, upper
　deck, cut down .. **5.** razee
　deserter .. **3.** rat
　duck shooting .. **4.** skag
　flat bottom .. **4.** keel **5.** barge
　fleet .. **6.** armada
　invoice .. **8.** manifest
　jail .. **4.** brig
　kitchen .. **6.** galley **7.** caboose
　Levantine .. **4.** saic
　loader .. **9.** stevedore
　　12. longshoreman
　Mediterranean .. **5.** xebec **6.** galiot
　　(galliot) **7.** polacre
　officer .. **4.** mate **6.** purser **7.** steward
　　9. boatswain (bosun)
　one–masted .. **5.** sloop
　part .. **4.** brig, keel, skeg **5.** stern,
　　waist **6.** bridge, rudder **8.** binnacle,
　　taffrail
　permit to enter .. **8.** pratique
　platform (boarding) .. **9.** gangplank
　privateer .. **10.** brigantine
　prow .. **5.** prore (Poet)
　quarters .. **5.** berth **8.** steerage
　　10. forecastle (fo'c's'le)
　record .. **3.** log
　rope .. **4.** line **6.** hawser **7.** halyard,
　　lanyard, painter, ratline
　sailing .. **4.** bark (barque), dhow, proa,
　　saic **5.** ketch, sloop, xebec **6.** caique,
　　cutter, galley, lugger **7.** Geordie,
　　pinnace, polacre
　side .. **3.** lee **4.** port **9.** starboard
　three–oar bank .. **7.** trireme

twin–hulled.. 9. catamaran
two–oar bank.. 6. bireme
Venetian.. 9. frigatoon
voyage record.. 3. log
war.. 3. sub 7. cruiser, flattop
9. destroyer, submarine
11. dreadnaught
window.. 4. port 8. porthole
worm.. 5. borer 6. teredo
ship, famed... 4. Nina 5. Maine, Pinta
6. Bounty 7. Monitor, Titanic
8. Clermont, Half Moon, Merrimac
9. Mayflower 10. Golden Hind, Santa
Maria 12. Constitution (Old Ironsides)
15. Bonhomme Richard
shipment... 5. cargo 7. carload
shippage... 3. fee 4. levy 8. shipping
shipshape... 3. nef (clock) 4. neat,
tidy, trim 7. orderly
shipwreck, cargo overboard...
6. jetsam 7. flotsam
shire... 5. horse 6. county 8. district,
province 11. subdivision
shirk... 4. duck, pike 5. avoid, dodge,
evade, slink 7. goof off 9. tainaigue
(finagle)
shirker... 5. piker 6. truant 7. quitter,
slacker 8. embusqué 10. malingerer
shirt... 4. polo, sark 6. blouse,
camisa, cilice, skivvy, T–shirt
8. pullover
shiver... 5. quake, shake 6. be cold
7. shatter, shudder, tremble, vibrate
8. fragment 11. trepidation
shivering... 4. cold 6. creepy
7. nervous, shaking 8. fragment
9. agitation, twitching 10. chilliness
shoal... 3. bar 4. bank, reef, spit
5. crowd, flock 6. throng 8. sand
bank (shallow) 9. multitude
shock... 3. jar 4. blow, heap (grain),
jolt, stun 5. appal, brunt, bushy
(hair), shake, stook, start 6. appall,
impact, offend, stroke, trauma
7. disgust, horrify, startle, terrify
8. calamity, frighten, paralyze
9. collision, electrify 10. concussion
shock absorber... 7. cushion, snubber
shocking... 3. bad 5. awful, lurid
6. horrid 7. ghastly, hideous
8. horrible, terrible 9. appalling,
frightful, offensive, revolting, startling
10. abominable
shoe (pert to)... 4. boot, clog, geta,
mule, pump 5. horse, moyle, sabot,
scuff 6. ballet, bootee, brogan,
buskin, gillie, loafer, Oxford, patten,
planch (planche), sandal, secque
7. chopine, rullion, slipper, sneaker,
talaria 8. moccasin, sabotine, solleret
10. clodhopper
shoe (pert to)...
form.. 4. last, tree
grip.. 5. cleat
lace.. 3. tie 5. aglet (aiglet), lacet
6. lacing 7. latchet 8. bootlace
10. shoestring
maker.. 5. sutor 7. cobbler, Crispin
(patron saint) 8. zapatero
part.. 3. cap 4. rand, vamp, welt
6. insole 7. counter 9. inner sole
shoebill, shoebird... 5. stork

shoemaker's patron saint... 7. Crispin
shogun... 5. chief, title (Jap) 6. tycoon
7. shikken
shoneen... 4. snob 5. toady
shoot... 3. rod 4. bine, dart, film, fine,
hunt, kill, plug, twig, weft 5. bough,
craps, eject, gemma, plant, scion,
snipe, spear, sprig, throw, tuber,
vimen 6. branch, sprout, stolon
7. execute, project 9. discharge
10. descendant, photograph
shooting (pert to)...
fish.. 10. archer fish
iron.. 6. pistol 7. firearm 8. revolver
match.. 3. tir 5. skeet
objective.. 6. target
star.. 5. comet 6. meteor 7. cowslip
shop... 4. mart 5. burse, store
6. market, saloon 7. atelier
8. boutique, emporium
shopping mania... 9. oniomania
shore... 4. bank, prop 5. beach, coast,
marge, playa 6. rivage, strand
7. support 9. foreshore, waterside
10. run aground, waterfront
shore (pert to)...
bird.. 3. ree 5. snipe 6. avocet,
curlew, plover, wading 9. Limicolae
inhabiting.. 8. littoral
pine.. 4. sand 8. tamarack
9. lodgepole 10. hack–me–tack
recess.. 3. bay 4. cove 5. bayou,
inlet
short... 4. curt, rude 5. brief, brusk,
scant, terse 6. abrupt, scanty
7. curtate, friable, summary
8. abridged, succinct 12. insufficient
short (pert to)...
and pointed.. 5. terse
and stout.. 5. dumpy 6. stocky,
stodgy 8. roly–poly, thickset
assay.. 6. tract
legged.. 8. breviped
letter.. 4. chit
lived.. 9. ephemeral
stop.. 5. delay, pause 7. respite
8. interval 9. cessation
shortage... 4. want 6. ullage
10. deficiency 13. insufficiency
shorten... 3. bob, cut, lop 4. clip,
dele, dock 5. elide 6. lessen,
reduce, reef in 7. abridge, curtail
8. condense, contract, decrease, hold
back 9. decurtate 10. abbreviate
shortening a syllable... 7. systole
shorthand... 5. Gregg 6. Pitman
8. Tironian (Rom) 11. stenography
12. brachygraphy, speed writing
shortly... 4. soon 6. curtly, not far
7. harshly, quickly 8. abruptly
9. presently
shortsighted... 4. dull 6. myopic,
obtuse 8. purblind 11. nearsighted
Shoshone Indian... 3. Ute 4. Hopi
5. Piute 7. Bannock 8. Comanche
shot... 4. dram 5. carom, speed
6. birdie, bullet, gamble, pellet,
ruined 7. gunfire, missile, worn out
8. marksman, unnerved 9. discharge
10. detonation, photograph, projectile
11. dilapidated, vaccination
shoulder... 5. carry, shelf 6. épaule

7. meat cut, scapula, support
8. buttress, omoplate
shoulder (pert to)...
armor.. 9. épaulière
badge, ornament.. 7. epaulet
blade.. 7. scapula 8. omoplate
comb form.. 3. omo 6. humero
inflammation.. 6. omitis 7. omalgia
of a road.. 4. berm (berme)
reference.. 7. humeral 8. scapular
shout... 3. cry 4. call, hoop, hoot,
root, yell 5. cheer 7. acclaim
8. applause, laughter
shouting... 6. clamor, crying 7. calling,
hooting, yelling 9. bellowing
shove... 4. push 5. drive, eject, elbow
6. propel, thrust
shovel... 4. peel, spud 5. scoop,
skeet, spade 7. scooper 8. strockle
10. antler part
show... 4. lead 5. movie, prove, revue,
teach 6. cinema, escort, evince,
reveal 7. betoken, display, divulge,
exhibit 8. evidence, indicate, instruct,
manifest 11. demonstrate
13. demonstration
show (pert to)...
case (glass).. 7. vitrine
deference.. 3. bow 6. salaam
disapproval.. 3. boo 4. hiss, pout
house.. 4. hall 5. odeum, opera
6. circus 8. coliseum, showboat
musical.. 5. revue
off.. 6. flaunt 10. grandstand
of learning.. 6. pedant
pompous.. 6. parade 7. display,
pageant 9. cavalcade 10. exhibition
to a seat.. 5. guide, usher 6. escort
7. conduct
up.. 6. appear, arrive, attend, expose
shower... 4. bath, give, rain 6. abound
8. sprinkle
shower of meteorites... 6. Leonid
(from Leo) 9. Andromede
showing...
animal remains.. 6. zootic
care.. 9. attentive, regardful
11. considerate
display.. 10. exhibition
12. presentation
envy.. 9. invidious
first.. 8. premiere
good judgment.. 6. astute 8. sensible
showy... 3. gay 4. arty, loud 5. gaudy
6. flashy, garish, sporty, tinsel
7. pompous 8. gorgeous, splendid,
striking 9. sumptuous
12. ostentatious 13. grandiloquent
shred... 3. rag 4. snip 5. piece, strip
6. sliver, tatter 7. vestige
8. fragment, particle
shrew... 3. erd 4. tana 5. satan,
scold, Sorex, vixen 6. mammal,
migale, tartar 7. Blarina, outcast,
villain 9. scoundrel, termagant,
Xanthippe
shrewd... 3. sly 4. cagy, foxy, sage,
wily 5. acute, canny, harsh, sharp,
smart, stern 6. artful, astute, biting,
clever, crafty 7. cunning, knowing,
practic, sapient, subtile 8. shrewish

9. sagacious 10. discerning
11. penetrating, sharp—witted
13. perspicacious
shrewdness... 6. acumen 9. smartness
10. craftiness
shriek... 3. cry, yip 4. yell 5. laugh
6. holler, outcry, scream 7. screech
shrievalty... 7. sheriff (office of)
shrill... 4. keen, pipy 5. acute, clear,
sharp 6. biting, squeak 7. screech
8. piercing, strident
11. high—pitched, penetrating
shrimp... 4. pink 5. dwarf, prawn
7. artemia 8. crevette
10. crustacean
shrine... 3. box 4. case, tomb
5. altar, chest 6. chapel, temple
8. monument 9. holy place, reliquary
10. receptacle
shrine (pert to)...
ancient.. 4. naos
Buddhist.. 4. tope 5. stupa
9. Amaravati
India.. 6. dagoba (dagaba) 7. chaitya
Mecca.. 5. Kaaba (Caaba) 11. Great
Mosque
secret, of goddesses.. 9. anaktoron
shrink... 5. cower, parch, quail, rivel,
wince 6. blench, cringe, flinch,
huddle, recoil 7. dwindle, shrivel
8. contract, draw back 9. constrict
10. depreciate
shrinking... 3. coy, shy 5. timid
6. afraid 9. recoiling, sensitive
10. withdrawal 11. contraction
shrivel... 3. age, dry 5. parch, wizen
6. shrink, wither 11. deteriorate
shroud... 4. cowl, hide, mask, veil,
wrap 5. cloak, cover, sheet
6. clothe, screen 7. conceal, curtain,
foliage, protect 8. cerement
9. cerecloth 12. graveclothes
Shrove (pert to)...
cake.. 7. pancake
Sunday.. 13. Quinquagesima
tide.. 9. pre—Lenten (3 days)
Tuesday.. 9. Mardi gras 10. Pancake
Day
shrub... 4. bush 5. plant (woody)
6. frutex 8. beverage
shrub (pert to)...
Adam's needle.. 5. yucca 9. lady's
comb
Arabian tea, narcotic.. 3. kat
aromatic.. 3. tea 4. mint, sage
5. thyme 6. Aralia 7. jasmine
(jasmin) 8. lavender, rosemary
Asian.. 5. musky 8. abelmosk
cherry.. 6. Prunus 7. Cerasus
12. laurocerasus
Chinese.. 6. Kerria
climbing.. 5. grape, liana, Vitis
8. Bignonia, clematis 14. trumpet
creeper
creeping.. 5. pyxie
dogwood.. 6. aucuba, Cornus
evergreen.. 3. box, yew 4. ilex, moss,
titi 5. erica, heath, pyxie, salal, savin
6. laurel, myrtle 7. jasmine, juniper
8. camellia, oleander 9. mistletoe
flowering.. 5. lilac 6. azalea, laurel
7. spiraea, syringa 10. mignonette

fragrant .. see *aromatic* (above)
Hawaiian .. **5**. akala
Mexican .. **7**. guayule **9**. coyotillo
New Zealand .. **4**. tutu **6**. myrtle
　8. ramarama
ornamental .. **8**. hawthorn
parasitic .. **9**. mistletoe
pea .. **5**. broom
pepper .. **4**. kava **8**. kavakava
poisonous .. **4**. tutu **5**. sumac
prickly .. **5**. Rubus **6**. smilax
　8. barberry, dewberry **9**. raspberry
　10. blackberry
S America .. **5**. ceibo
tropical .. **4**. sida, titi **5**. henna
　7. lantana **8**. Oacaceae, tamarisk
　10. frangipani (frangipane)
shrunken ... **4**. lank, thin **5**. dried
　6. shrunk, wasted **8**. puckered,
　withered **9**. atrophied, shriveled
shudder ... **4**. grue **5**. abhor, dread,
　quake **6**. agrise, loathe, quiver, shiver,
　tremor **7**. frisson, tremble
shuffle ... **3**. mix **5**. scuff, shift
　6. huddle, juggle, riffle **7**. confuse,
　evasion, quibble, scuffle
　10. equivocate **12**. walk slovenly
shuffle off ... **5**. evade, shirk **6**. put
　off **7**. push off **10**. mosey along (sl)
shun ... **5**. avoid, evade, evite
　6. eschew **10**. escape from
　11. keep clear of **12**. cold shoulder
shut ... **3**. bar **4**. stop **5**. close
　7. close in, exclude **8**. prohibit
shut (pert to) ...
in .. **3**. hem **5**. embar **6**. fenced,
　hemmed **7**. bottled, confine, impound,
　invalid, recluse **8**. confined, enclosed
　10. surrounded
out .. **3**. ban, bar **6**. defeat
　7. exclude, lockout, occlude
　8. obstruct preclude, prohibit
up .. **3**. dam, end **4**. cage, pent
　5. close, mewed, pen in **6**. refute
　7. confine, enclose **8**. conclude,
　imprison **9**. terminate
shutter ... **3**. lid **4**. gate **5**. blind
　6. screen **7**. seclude **8**. jalousie
　9. diaphragm
shuttle ... **5**. train **6**. looper, weaver
　7. type bar **9**. alternate, vacillate
　10. oscillator **11**. money drawer
shy ... **3**. coy, mim **4**. wary **5**. aloof,
　dodge, throw, timid **6**. demure,
　modest, recoil, shrink **7**. bashful,
　evasive, fearful, quibble, rabbity
　8. hesitant, reserved, retiring,
　secluded, sheepish, skittish
　9. diffident, reluctant, shrinking
　10. shamefaced, unassuming
　11. distrustful, unobtrusive
Shylock (pert to) ...
character in .. **16**. Merchant of Venice
coin .. **5**. ducat
daughter .. **7**. Jessica
famed as .. **6**. usurer **11**. money
　lender **12**. extortionist
friend .. **5**. Tubal
shyness ... **7**. coyness, reserve
　8. timidity **10**. diffidence
　11. bashfulness
Siam ... **8**. Thailand

Siamese (pert to) ...
group .. **3**. Kui, Lao
temple .. **3**. wat
twins .. **9**. pygopagus (joined at spine)
　11. Chang and Eng
sib ... **4**. akin **6**. allied **7**. kinsman,
　related (by blood)
Siberia ... see also *Siberian*
city .. **7**. Irkutsk **11**. Novosibirsk
conqueror .. **9**. Timafeyev **11**. Genghis
　Khan
government .. **7**. Russian
gulf .. **2**. Ob (Arctic)
Mongoloid .. **6**. Tartar
mountains .. **4**. Ural **5**. Altai
people .. **5**. Yakut **6**. Tartar (Tatar)
　9. Mongolian
plain .. **6**. steppe, tundra
river .. **2**. Ob, Om **4**. Lena **5**. Vitim
　6. Abakan **7**. Yenisei
squirrel .. **7**. miniver
storm .. **5**. buran
Siberian (pert to) ...
antelope .. **5**. saiga
hunters, fishers (tribe) .. **6**. Giliak
　(Gilyak)
mammal .. **5**. sable
squirrel fur .. **7**. calaber (calabar)
swamp .. **5**. urman
tent .. **4**. yurt (yurta)
windstorm .. **5**. buran (bura)
sibilate ... **4**. hiss, lisp **8**. aspirate
sibling ... **5**. child
Sibyl (Gr) ... **6**. oracle **7**. seeress
　10. prophetess **13**. fortuneteller
Sibylline Books (3) ... **7**. oracles
　16. prophetic sayings (BC)
sic ... **4**. thus
siccity ... **7**. aridity, drought, dryness
sice ... **3**. six (dice) **8**. sixpence
Sicilian Vespers (pert to) ...
Bull (anc) .. **8**. Phalaris
massacre of .. **6**. French (1282)
Sicily ...
aborigines .. **6**. Sicani
anc name .. **9**. Trinacria
capital .. **7**. Palermo **8**. Syracuse (anc)
composer .. **7**. Bellini
harbor .. **7**. Palermo
island .. **6**. Lipari (group)
　11. Pantelleria
river .. **4**. Acis
secret society .. **5**. Mafia
volcano .. **4**. Etna **7**. Vulcano
　9. Stromboli
whirlpool .. **9**. Charybdis
sick ... **3**. ill, sad, wan **4**. pale
　5. weary **6**. sickly, unwell
　9. disgusted, nauseated
　10. indisposed
sick (pert to) ...
be .. **3**. ail
deathly .. **5**. amort **7**. à la mort,
　fatally **10**. terminally
flag .. **6**. yellow **10**. quarantine
headache .. **8**. migraine
of .. **7**. tired of **8**. satiated
　9. disgusted
person .. **7**. patient **9**. aegrotant
terms .. **3**. bay **7**. hospice
　8. syndrome **9**. infirmary
　10. dispensary **13**. intensive care

worker.. 5. nurse 11. nursekeeper
sicken... 4. tire 5. weary 6. impair,
  weaken 7. afflict, depress, surfeit
  8. languish 10. impoverish
sickly... 4. pale, sick, weak 5. faint
  6. ailing, feeble, infirm, weakly
  7. languid, mawkish 8. diseased
  9. unhealthy
Siddhartha, Siddhattha... 6. Buddha
side... 4. face, team, wall 6. behalf,
  border, region 7. faction, lateral,
  support, surface 9. declivity
side (pert to)...
  board.. 5. table 6. buffet 8. dressoir,
    whiskers
  by side.. 8. parallel
  ditch.. 6. escarp
  drum.. 5. snare
  hog (salted).. 6. flitch
  kick.. 3. pal 7. comrade, partner
    9. assistant 11. confederate
  left.. 4. port 8. larboard
  long.. 7. lateral, oblique, sloping
    8. indirect, slanting
  meat.. 5. bacon 8. salt pork
  of head.. 6. temple
  of triangle.. 3. leg
  on the side.. 5. apart
  sheltered.. 3. lee 4. alee 8. windless
  sidewalk salesman.. 8. pitchman
  step.. 4. duck 5. dodge, evade,
    hedge 6. astral, starry 7. quibble
  view.. 7. profile
  ways, wise.. 7. athwart, lateral
    9. laterally, obliquely
  whiskers.. 9. sideburns 10. sideboards
  windy.. 4. port 9. starboard
sidereal... 6. astral, starry 7. stellar
  9. celestial
sidero (comb form)... 4. iron
siderography... 14. steel engraving
siderology (science of)... 4. iron
sides, unequal... 7. scalene
sidle... 4. cant, edge, skew, tilt
  7. advance (furtive)
siècle... 3. age 7. century
siècle d'or... 9. Golden Age
siege... 7. besiege 8. assièger
  9. besetting 11. besiegement
  12. wearying time 13. beleaguerment
Siegfried (pert to)...
  hero of.. 5. opera (Wagner's)
  slayer.. 5. Hagen
  sword.. 7. Balmung
  wife.. 9. Kriemhild
Sierra Nevada fog... 7. pogonip
Sierra poet... 13. Joaquin Miller
siesta... 3. nap 4. lull, rest 6. cat
  nap, midday, snooze 10. forty winks
sieve... 3. lue 4. bolt, sift, sile
  5. purée 6. bolter, filter, riddle,
  semmet, sifter, sorter, strain
  7. dilluer 8. strainer 9. segregate,
  separator
sievelike... 8. cribrate
Sif (Norse), (pert to)...
  goddess of.. 4. home
  wife of.. 4. Thor
sift... 3. lue 4. bolt 5. sieve
  6. dredge, filter, riddle, screen,
  sorter, winnow 7. refiner 8. cribrate
sigh... 3. sob 5. mourn, sithe, yearn

  6. bemoan, bewail, exhale, grieve,
  lament 7. deplore 10. lament over
  11. suspiration
sight... 3. see 4. espy, gaze, view
  5. scene, sense 6. behold, descry,
  vision 7. discern, display 8. aperture
  10. exhibition 11. observation
sight (pert to)...
  acuteness of.. 7. oxyopia
  come into.. 4. loom 5. issue
  disorder.. 7. anopsia 8. paropsis
  imaginary.. 6. vision
  offensive.. 7. eyesore
  out of.. 5. range 6. absent
    8. vanished 9. invisible
    10. exorbitant 11. disappeared
  second.. 3. ESP 7. psychic
sigil... 4. seal 5. image (magic), stamp
  8. sigillum 9. signature
  11. endorsement
sigmoid... 3. ess 5. curve 9. intestine
sign... 3. cue, nod 4. code, hire,
  mark, neon, omen 5. token, trace
  6. emblem, engage, intone, motion,
  notice, signal, symbol 7. endorse,
  execute, insigne, portent, presage,
  symptom, vestige, warning
  8. evidence, password 9. semaphore,
  subscribe, watchword 10. forerunner,
  indication, underwrite 11. countersign
  13. advertisement, constellation
sign (pert to)...
  astrological.. 5. Aries 6. Gemini,
    Pisces, Taurus 8. Aquarius
    9. Capricorn 11. Sagittarius
  briefly.. 7. initial
  by the same.. 8. likewise, moreover
    11. accordingly
  diacritical.. 5. tilde 7. cedilla
  language.. 11. dactylology
  music.. 5. presa
  off.. 8. withdraw 10. Yours truly
    11. discontinue
  ref to.. 5. semic 7. semeion
  representing a word.. 8. logogram
  spiritual.. 9. sacrament
  up.. 4. join 6. enlist
  zodiac.. see astrological (above)
signal... 3. cue 4. code, fire, flag,
  sign 5. alarm, flare, token
  6. beacon, emblem, notify, wigwag
  7. eminent, lantern, notable, warning
  8. striking 9. memorable, prominent,
  semaphore, watchword
  10. lighthouse, remarkable
  11. communicate, conspicuous
  13. extraordinary
signal (pert to)...
  aviator's.. 5. roger
  danger, warning.. 4. bell 5. alert,
    fusee
  flag.. 6. ensign, wigwag
  night.. 6. beacon, curlew, pharos
    10. lighthouse
  preceding taps.. 6. tattoo
  railroad.. 5. fusee 9. semaphore
signature... 4. mark, sign, visa (vise)
  5. prima, sigil, stamp 6. signum
  9. autograph 11. endorsement
signed by writer... 9. onomatous (opp
  of anonymous)
signet... 4. mark, seal 5. sigil, stamp

9. signature 10. impression
11. endorsement
significance... 6. import, moment,
weight 7. anagoge, meaning
significant... 4. sign 5. token
6. symbol 7. ominous 8. sinister
9. important, momentous
10. expressive, indicative, meaningful,
portentous, suggestive
13. consequential
signification... 6. import 7. meaning
10. indication 11. consequence
12. notification 13. comprehension,
specification
signify... 4. hint, mean, sign 5. imply,
utter 6. denote, import, matter,
signal 7. betoken, connote, declare,
specify 8. announce, evidence,
foreshow, indicate, intimate, manifest
11. communicate
signum... 4. bell (tower), mark, sign
5. cross 9. signature
sika... 4. deer
sike... 4. rill 5. brook, ditch, gully
6. ravine, stream, trench
sikhara, sikhra... 5. tower (pyramidal)
silage... 4. feed 6. fodder
9. pasturage, provender
Silas (pert to)...
Bib.. 7. prophet 8. Silvanus
character.. 4. Wegg
companion of.. 4. Paul (Bib)
novel.. 11. Silas Marner
sile... 3. fry 4. beam, drip, drop, fall,
flow, pass, pour, sink, skim 5. cheat,
cover, glide, sieve, spawn 6. betray,
filter, strain, stream 7. conceal,
deceive, herring (young), subside
8. strainer
silence... 3. gag 4. hush, kill, lull,
mute, rest 5. quiet, shush, still,
tacet 6. defeat, muffle 7. confute,
repress, secrecy 8. oblivion, preclude,
restrain, suppress 9. eliminate,
stillness 10. silentness 11. taciturnity
13. noiselessness, tacit omission
silent... 3. mum 4. mute, tace
5. quiet, still, tacet, tacit
8. reserved, reticent, taciturn
9. soundless 10. speechless
11. unexpressed
15. uncommunicative
silhouette... 6. shadow 7. contour,
outline, picture, profile 9. delineate,
hourglass
silica... 4. opal 5. silex
silicate... 4. mica 8. calamine, wellsite
silk (pert to)...
ancient.. 6. Mantua, sendal
artificial.. 5. nylon, rayon
Assam.. 4. eria
black.. 5. crape (mourning), crepe
brown.. 4. muga 6. tussah
corded.. 6. faille 7. Ottoman
embroidery thread.. 5. floss
8. arrasene
fiber.. 5. floss
gland.. 9. serictery
gland of.. 7. spiders 9. silkworms
11. insect larva 12. caterpillars
gold.. 4. tash 6. samite 7. brocade
heavy.. 4. crin

kind of.. 5. China, crepe, moiré,
ninon, satin, surah, tabby, tulle
6. pongee, tobine, tussah 7. taffeta
lining.. 8. sarcenet (sarsenet)
muslin.. 16. mousseline de soie
raw.. 8. marabout
rustle of.. 6. scroop
source.. 6. cocoon
thin, glossy.. 7. alamode
thread (for velvets).. 4. tram (trame)
unspun.. 6. sleave
upholstery.. 7. tabaret
waste.. 4. noil 6. strass
watered.. 5. moiré
yarn.. 4. tram 7. schappe
yarn size.. 6. denier
silken... 5. seric, silby, sleek, suave
6. gentle, smooth, tender 7. elegant
8. delicate, lustrous, silklike
9. luxurious 10. effeminate
12. ingratiating
silkworm (pert to)...
Assam.. 3. eri 4. eria
China.. 6. pernyi 9. Ailanthus
cocoon.. 4. clew
disease.. 7. pebrine
genus (moth).. 6. Bombyx
India.. 6. tussah
Japan.. 7. yamamai
silky... 4. soft 5. quiet 6. glossy,
smooth 8. delicate 9. sericeous
11. filamentary 12. ingratiating
silky fabric... 6. barège
sill... 4. base, beam, seat, sile
5. basis 6. timber 9. threshold
10. foundation
silly... 3. mad 4. daft, fond 5. anile,
apish, dazed, dense, inane 6. dottle,
simple 7. asinine, fatuous, foolish,
shallow, trivial 9. brainless
10. indiscreet 12. simple–minded
silver... 2. Ag 4. gray 5. metal,
money, plate, white 6. argent
7. bullion 8. argentum, eloquent,
metallic, sterling
silver (pert to)...
alchemy.. 4. luna 6. occamy
alloy.. 6. billon
ball.. 4. pome
coin.. 6. tester
containing.. 5. lunar
German.. 6. albata
gilded.. 7. vermeil
ingots.. 6. sycee
jackal.. 9. silver fox
lace (with gold).. 5. orris 8. filigree
leaf.. 4. foil 8. hardhack
9. hydrangea, jewelweed 12. buffalo
berry
oak.. 11. flannelbush
tongued.. 7. musical 8. eloquent
uncoined.. 7. bullion
silversides... 5. smelt 6. minnow
12. silver salmon
Silver State... 6. Nevada
silverware... 5. vases 6. dishes
8. flatware 9. ornaments, tableware
silvery... 7. frosted, musical
8. lustrous, metallic 9. argentine
simian... 3. ape 6. monkey 7. apelike
similar... 4. akin, like, such 5. alike
7. uniform 8. analogic 9. analogous

11. homogeneous
similarity... 7. analogy 8. likeness
  11. homogeneity, resemblance
  13. approximation
simile... 8. allegory, metaphor
simper... 5. smirk 10. silly smile
  13. affected smile
simple... 4. easy, mere 5. naive
  6. dorian, oafish 7. artless
  8. innocent 9. ingenuous
  10. elementary 11. open and shut
  15. unsophisticated
simpleton... 3. ass, daw, oaf 4. boob,
  dolt, dupe, fool, gaby, gawk, gump,
  simp, zang 5. dunce, goose, idiot,
  ikona, moron, Simon, yokel, zombi
  6. dawkin, gander, nitwit 7. half–wit
  8. Abderite 9. greenhorn
  10. nincompoop 11. Simple Simon
simplicity... 6. purity 7. modesty,
  naiveté 9. clearness, ignorance,
  innocence, plainness, rusticity
  10. homeliness, humbleness,
  simpleness 11. gullibility, informality
  13. ingenuousness
  14. unaffectedness
simplify... 7. clarify, explain, expound
  9. elucidate, interpret
simply... 5. alone, truly 6. barely,
  easily, merely, purely, really, solely
  7. plainly 10. informally
simulate... 3. act, ape 4. sham
  5. feign 6. affect, assume 7. imitate
  11. counterfeit
simulated... 4. aped, sham 5. acted
  7. assumed, feigned, shammed
  9. pretended 10. fictitious
simurgh, simurg (Myth)... 3. roc
  12. gigantic bird
sin... 3. err 4. evil, vice 5. crime,
  error, guilt, wrong 6. felony, heresy
  7. offense 8. iniquity, peccancy
  9. deviation 10. immorality,
  wickedness 11. misdemeanor
  13. transgression
Sinai (pert to)...
  famed for.. 5. Moses 15. Ten
  Commandments
  location.. 6. Red Sea 11. Gulf of
  Aqaba (Akaba)
  mountain (Bib).. 5. Horeb 6. Serbal
  9. Catharine, Umm Shomer
sinapis... 7. mustard
sinawa... 10. Ceylon hemp
sinay bean... 8. rice bean
since... 2. as 3. ago, for 4. ergo,
  gone, past, syne 5. hence, later
  7. already, because, whereas
  8. inasmuch, until now 9. therefore,
  thereupon 10. seeing that
  11. considering 12. subsequently
sincere... 4. open, pure 5. frank
  6. candid 7. correct, earnest,
  genuine, intense, unmixed, upright,
  zealous 6. authentic, unfeigned,
  veracious 10. unaffected
  11. unvarnished 13. unadulterated
  15. straightforward
sincerity... 4. zeal 6. candor
  7. honesty 10. heartiness
  11. genuineness, sincereness
sincerity symbol... 8. amethyst

sind... 5. rinse 6. drench, quench
  7. rinsing
Sind (Ind)...
  capital.. 7. Karachi
  ibex.. 8. wild goat
  prince.. 5. ameer
Sindbad's bird... 3. roc
Sindbad the Sailor... 9. character
  (Arabian Nights)
sindico... 7. trustee 8. assignee,
  receiver
sine... 7. without
sinew... 4. thew 5. nerve, power
  6. muscle, string, tendon
sinewy... 4. firm, wiry 5. thewy, tough
  6. brawny, strong 7. fibrose, stringy
  8. powerful, vigorous
sinful... 3. bad 4. evil 5. wrong
  6. wicked 7. vicious 10. iniquitous
  11. unrighteous
sing... 3. hum, say 4. hymn, lilt
  5. carol, chant, croon, yodel
  6. intone, warble 7. rejoice
  8. proclaim, vocalize 9. celebrate
sing (pert to)...
  exultantly.. 4. lilt 7. chortle
  10. cheerfully
  jovially.. 5. troll
  off key.. 4. flat
  or whistle.. 7. tweedle
  shrilly.. 4. pipe
  softly.. 5. croon
  sorrowfully.. 7. despond 8. complain
  Swisslike.. 5. yodel
  with trills.. 6. warble 7. roulade
singe... 4. burn, sear 6. scorch
  8. discolor
singer... 4. bard, bird, diva, poet
  5. blues, siren, tenor, torch
  6. cantor, hymner 7. caroler,
  crooner, warbler, yodeler 8. minstrel,
  songster, vocalist 9. chanteuse,
  descanter 10. cantatrice, prima
  donna 11. minnesinger
Singhalese tree... 4. poon 5. domba
singing (pert to)...
  birds.. 6. Oscine
  canary.. 10. white whale
  fish.. 8. toadfish
  group.. 5. choir 6. chorus
  Memnon.. 9. Amenhotep (statue)
  ref to.. 5. melic
single... 3. ace, odd, one 4. lone,
  only, sole, unit 6. simple, unique
  8. sporadic 9. unmarried
single (pert to)...
  algebra.. 6. nomial
  comb form.. 3. uni
  odd.. 7. azygous
  racing term.. 4. heat
  tones (one of two).. 10. monotonous
singleness... 5. unity 8. celibacy
  9. sincerity, unmarried
singly... 4. once, only, solo 5. alone,
  apart 6. simply 8. uniquely
  9. severally 12. individually,
  particularly, single–handed
singular... 3. odd 4. each, rare, sole,
  unit 5. queer 6. unique 7. eminent,
  special, strange, unusual 8. peculiar,
  separate, uncommon 9. eccentric,
  fantastic, whimsical 10. individual,

remarkable, unexampled
11. exceptional 12. unparalleled
13. extraordinary, unprecedented
14. characteristic
singularity... 6. oddity 7. oddness,
oneness 8. peculiar 11. peculiarity
12. eccentricity 13. individuality
15. distinctiveness
Sinic... 7. Chinese, Sinitic
sinister... 4. evil, grim, left 7. adverse,
corrupt, ominous 9. dishonest,
injurious, malicious, underhand
10. disastrous, portentous
11. unfortunate
sinistral... 7. baneful 10. left–handed
12. illegitimate, inauspicious (opp of
dextral)
sink... 3. age, bog, dip, ebb, sag
4. cave, drop, fall, mire, sump
5. drain, droop, lapse, lower, quail
6. cavity, deject, engulf, go down,
recede, settle, sicken, weaken
7. decline, depress, descend,
despond 8. decrease, diminish,
submerge 10. degenerate
sinuous... 4. wavy 7. winding
9. deviating, intricate 10. circuitous
Sioux (pert to)...
division.. 5. Teton 6. Santee
famed as.. 8. warriors
tribe.. 3. Oto (Otoe) 4. Crow, Iowa
5. Omaha, Osage 6. Dakota, Plains
9. Winnebago
sip... 3. lap, sup 4. gulp 5. drink,
quaff, taste 6. tipple
sircar... 5. ruler 6. master 7. servant
8. province (Mogul) 10. government
siren... 5. alarm, Circe, deity, lurer,
vixen 7. charmer, enticer, foghorn,
Lorelei, mermaid 9. bewitcher,
Cleopatra, temptress
Sirenia... 6. dugong, mammal
7. manatee 14. Steller's sea cow
siriasis... 9. sunstroke
Sirius... 4. star 7. Dog Star 10. Canis
Major, dog of Orion (Gr Myth)
sissy... 5. softy 6. prissy, sister
10. effeminate, pantywaist
11. mollycoddle
sister... 3. kin, nun, sib 5. nurse,
soror
sisterhood... 4. nuns 8. sorority
Sistrurus... 11. rattlesnake
sit... 3. fit 4. isle, loll, pose, rest
5. brood, perch, press, roost, squat
6. repose 7. convene 8. incubate
site... 4. ruin, seat 5. place, scene,
venue 6. locale, locate 8. location,
position
site of Taj Mahal... 4. Agra (Ind)
sitting... 4. seat 6. séance, sedent
7. posture, sessile, session
10. incubation 11. convocation
situated... 3. lie, set 4. case, seat
5. fixed 6. clutch, placed, plight
9. ensconced, stationed
11. established
situated (pert to)...
at back.. 6. astern 7. postern
9. posterior
at base.. 5. basal
between folds.. 11. interplical

in middle.. 6. medial, median
on left hand.. 9. sinistrad
on right hand.. 6. dexter
situation... 3. job 4. case, post
5. place, situs, state 6. office, plight
7. station 8. locality, location,
position 9. condition, placement
situation (pert to)...
approximate.. 11. whereabouts
difficult.. 6. scrape 7. dilemma
8. quandary 9. imbroglio
11. predicament 12. circumstance
doomed.. 7. rattrap
favorable.. 7. vantage
Latin.. 5. situs
perplexing.. 6. strait
three choices.. 8. trilemma
Siva, Shiva (pert to)...
consort.. 3. Uma 4. Devi
dancer.. 8. Natajara
god, deity.. 8. Hinduism 9. Destroyer
title.. 8. Mahadeva
trident.. 6. trisul (trisula)
six (pert to)
balls (Medici).. 5. palle
dice number.. 4. sice
eyed.. 9. senocular
feet of earth.. 5. grave
fold.. 8. sextuple
footed.. 7. hexaped 9. hexapodal
group.. 5. hexad
lines.. 6. sestet 7. sextain
pence.. 6. bender 7. fiddler
pert to.. 6. senary
pointed figure.. 4. star
square.. 9. hexagonal
sixty, sixties... 5. cycle, saros
7. numeral
size... 3. cap 4. area, bulk, pica,
pope, pott 5. agate, grade 6. adjust
7. arrange, measure, portion
8. classify 9. magnitude
10. gargantuan 11. measurement
sizzle... 3. fry 4. hiss 5. speed 7. be
angry 10. effervesce
sjambok... 4. flog, whip
skate... 3. jag, ray (fish) 4. plug, skim
5. glide, horse, scull, spree
skean... 4. dirk 6. dagger
skedaddle... 4. bolt, flee, flit 6. scurry
7. run away, scamper
skein... 3. rap (120 yds), web
4. hank, yarn 6. thread 7. spireme
12. flight of fowl
skelder... 5. cheat 7. vagrant
9. panhandle
skeleton... 4. cage 5. bones, frame,
mummy 6. sketch 7. contour,
diagram, outline 8. thinness
9. framework
skeleton (pert to)...
at the feast.. 7. kill–joy 10. wet
blanket 11. crapehanger
English dialect.. 4. reme
framework.. 5. cadre
in the closet.. 4. evil 6. secret
13. mortification
key.. 6. master
marine animal.. 6. sponge
polyp.. 5. coral
skeptic, sceptic... 7. doubter, infidel
8. aporetic 10. Pyrrhonist, unbeliever

11. freethinker, irreligious, nullifidian
skeptical, sceptical ... 8. doubtful,
doubting 11. incredulous, unbelieving
sketch ... 3. jap, jot 4. draw, idea,
limn, plan, skit 5. draft, trace
6. aperçu, design 7. diagram,
drawing, outline 8. esquisse, treatise
9. delineate 11. delineation,
description
sketchy ... 5. rough, vague
10. unfinished
skewer ... 3. pin, rod 5. truss
6. fasten, pierce 9. brochette
skid ... 4. clog, shoe, slip, trig
5. brake, check, slide 7. travois
8. sideslip
skiff ... 4. boat, skim 5. canoe, glide,
graze 6. caique 7. rowboat
11. slight touch
skill ... 3. art 5. craft, knack 6. gifted,
talent 7. ability, address, aptness,
cunning, finesse, mastery 8. aptitude,
deftness, facility 9. adeptness,
dexterity, expertise, readiness,
smartness 10. adroitness, cleverness,
proficient 11. proficiency
skilled ... 5. adept 6. expert
7. endowed, trained 8. talented
10. conversant, proficient
skilled (pert to) ...
in government .. 9. statesman
in mechanics .. 5. sloyd
in strategy .. 7. finesse
skillful, skilful ... 3. apt 4. able, deft,
fine 6. adroit, clever, crafty, daedal,
expert 7. capable 8. artistic,
dextrous, tactical 9. daedalian,
dexterous, ingenious 10. proficient,
well–versed 12. accomplished
skim ... 4. flit, sail, scan, scud
5. glide, graze, scoon, skirr 6. slight
8. pass over
skin ... 4. bark, derm, fell, flay, hide,
pare, peel, pelt, rind, scum 5. cheat,
cutis, derma, fraud, scalp 6. fleece,
lamina, scrape 7. callous, cuticle,
defraud, swindle 8. covering,
tegument 9. epidermis
10. integument 11. decorticate
skin (pert to) ...
animal .. 4. coat, hide, pelt 7. pellage
animal's neck fold .. 6. dewlap
beaver .. 4. plew
comb form .. 4. derm 5. derma
decoration .. 6. tattoo
destitute of .. 8. apellous
disease .. 4. acne 5. hives, mange,
uredo 6. eczema, herpes, tetter
8. ringworm 9. urticaria
drying frame .. 5. herse
dryness .. 7. xerosis
fawnskin (of Dionysus) .. 6. nebris
fold .. 5. plica 6. dewlap
fruit .. 7. epicarp
gobbler's throat .. 3. tar
layer .. 5. cutis, derma
layer, outer .. 7. epicarp
opening .. 4. pore
pert to .. 6. dermal 7. dermoid
piece .. 5. blype
pigment, excess .. 8. melanism
protuberance .. 4. mole, wart

salting bin .. 5. kench
squirrel .. 4. vair
tan .. 3. taw
tanned .. 5. suede
unsheared .. 8. woolfell
skinflint ... 5. cheat, miser 9. bargainer
skink ... 4. adda 6. lizard
skinned ... 6. bested 7. euchred,
fleeced
skinned (pert to) ...
dark .. 7. melanic, swarthy
pert to .. 5. bared 7. denuded
8. stripped
slang .. 7. euchred, fleeced
thick .. 9. pachyderm 11. pachydermic
skinny ... 4. lean, thin 5. scant
6. stingy 8. skinlike 9. emaciated,
niggardly
skip ... 3. dap 4. gait, jump, leap,
omit 5. bound, caper, elide, frisk,
salto, vault 6. gambol, lackey, spring
7. abscond 8. ricochet
skipjack ... 3. fop 4. pike 5. saury
6. bonito 7. bounder, parvenu,
upstart 8. bluefish, sailboat
9. stripling (conceited) 10. butterfish
14. snapping beetle
skipper ... 5. saury 6. locust, maggot,
master, serang 8. skipjack
9. butterfly 11. grasshopper
ski race (obstacle) ... 6. slalom
skirling ... 5. trout 6. salmon
skirmish ... 4. fray 5. brush, clash,
melee 6. combat 8. conflict, flourish
9. encounter 10. velitation
skirt ... 5. dress, evade, woman
6. border, edging, fringe
9. appendage, baseboard, periphery,
petticoat 10. pass around, saddle
part
skirt (pert to) ...
armor .. 5. tasse (tace) 7. lamboys
attached to blouse .. 6. peplum
chaser .. 9. libertine 11. philanderer
dance .. 6. ballet
short .. 4. kilt
skit ... 4. joke, play 5. caper
6. parody, shower, sketch
skittish ... 3. coy, shy 5. jumpy
6. fickle, frisky, tricky 7. bashful
8. unstable, volatile 9. excitable
10. capricious 13. irresponsible
skittles ... 4. game, play 8. ninepins
9. enjoyment (not all beer and
skittles)
skoal ... 5. toast 10. salutation
11. exclamation 14. pledge of health
skulk ... 4. lurk 5. cower, dodge,
hedge, sneak 8. malinger
skull ... 4. bean, head, mind 5. brain
7. cranium, harnpan 8. brain box
skull (pert to) ...
cap .. 6. beanie 7. calotte
9. zucchetto 10. berrettino
cavity .. 5. fossa
measure .. 11. craniometer
monk's .. 6. pileus
operation .. 6. trepan
part .. 5. inion 6. bregma 7. calotte,
occiput
ref to .. 5. inial 6. cranic 7. cranial
science of .. 10. craniology

skull and crossbones... 5. death
  (symb) 10. danger sign
skunk... 5. zoril 6. defeat 7. fitchew,
  polecat, stinker 8. conepate
  (conepati), zorrillo 9. scoundrel
sky... 4. blue 5. ether, vault
  6. caelum, canopy, heaven, welkin
  7. heavens, the blue 8. empyrean
  9. firmament 10. blue yonder
sky (pert to)...
  color.. 4. blue 5. azure 7. celeste
    8. cerulean
  god.. 3. Anu
  lark.. 5. pipit 6. Alauda, frolic
    7. titlark
  light.. 6. window 8. abatjour
  lure.. 7. horizon
  parlor.. 5. attic 6. garret
  pilot.. 8. chaplain 9. clergyman
    10. missionary
  serpent.. 3. Ahi
slab... 3. mud 4. tile 5. board, dalle,
  plank, slime 6. lamina, ledger, pillar
  (stone), puddle 7. portion
  8. monument 9. flagstone
slab (pert to)...
  grave.. 5. stele (stela)
  marble.. 5. dalle 6. tablet
  slablike.. 6. stelar
slack... 3. lax 4. lull, slow 5. chaff,
  inert, let up, loose, shirk, tardy
  6. abated, remiss 7. relaxed
  8. careless, dilatory, inactive,
  indolent, sluggish 9. reluctant,
  secondary 10. diminished, inadequate
  11. inattentive
slacken... 5. abate, delay, relax
  6. loosen, reduce, repose, retard
  7. let down, relieve 8. hold back
slackening of strained relations...
  7. detente (Internat)
slag... 4. lava 5. dross 6. cinder,
  scoria 7. residue 9. recrement
  11. agglomerate
slain... 4. dead 6. fallen, killed
  8. murdered 12. assassinated
slake... 4. cool, sate 5. abate, allay,
  slack 6. quench 7. assuage,
  crumble, hydrate, refresh, relieve,
  satisfy, slacken 8. decrease, mitigate,
  moderate 10. extinguish
  12. disintegrate
slam... 4. bang, blow, give, shut, vole
  5. abuse, score 6. impact
  9. criticism, criticize
slander... 5. belie, libel 6. defame,
  malign, vilify 7. asperse, blacken,
  distort, traduce 8. derogate, disgrace,
  reproach 10. defamation, scandalize
  12. misrepresent
slang... 4. cant 5. argot 6. jargon,
  patois 7. hep talk 10. vernacular
slant... 4. bend, cant, skew 5. angle,
  bevel, slope 6. aslant, aspect,
  biased, glance 7. incline, opinion
  8. attitude, occasion 9. obliquely,
  viewpoint 10. hypotenuse
  11. inclination, opportunity
slap... 3. hit 4. blow, clap, cuff, snub
  5. crack, skelp, sound, twank
  6. buffet, rebuff, slight, strike
  8. chastise 12. chastisement

slash... 3. cut 4. gash, lash, slit
  5. marsh, sever 6. attack, reduce,
  stripe 7. censure, scourge 8. price
  cut 9. criticize, reduction
slate... 4. list, rock 5. color, scold,
  sculp 6. ballot, enroll, record, roster,
  tablet, thrash 7. censure, roofing,
  writing 8. register, schedule, slattern
  9. criticize, reprimand
slate (pert to)...
  ax.. 7. mattock
  black.. 4. gray
  blue.. 9. Swiss blue
  gray.. 7. Russian 9. red–yellow
    10. sandy beige 13. oriental pearl
  roof.. 3. rag
  tool.. 3. zax 7. scantle
slater... 6. critic 7. hellier
slattern... 4. slut 5. frump, idler,
  mopsy 6. sloppy 7. trifler, trollop
  8. careless, slovenly 9. litterbug
slaughter... 4. kill, slay 6. battue,
  murder, pogrom 7. butcher, carnage,
  killing 8. butchery, hecatomb,
  massacre, occision 9. bloodshed
  10. butchering 11. destruction
slaughterhouse... 8. abattoir,
  Aceldama, butchery, matadero,
  shambles 9. stockyard 12. field of
  blood
Slav... 4. Pole, Slav, Sorb, Wend
  5. Croat, Czech 6. Slovak
  7. Russian, Serbian, Servian
  8. Bohemian, Croatian, Moravian
  9. Bulgarian
slave... 4. boor, esne, peon, serf
  5. chela, helot, thane 6. drudge,
  lascar, minion, thrall, vassal
  7. bondman, captive, chattel,
  enslave, odalisk, servant 8. slave ant
  9. bondslave
slave (pert to)...
  block (selling).. 7. catasta
  born.. 4. neif
  comedy (stock name).. 5. Davus
  dealer.. 5. bichy, mango (obs)
  Eleusinian (Gr Relig).. 5. Baubo,
    lambe
  female.. 9. concubine, odalisque
    (odalisk)
  free.. 5. thane (thegn)
  fugitive.. 8. marooner
  Indian.. 10. Athapascan
  The Tempest.. 7. Caliban
slavery... 4. bond 7. bondage, service
  8. drudgery 9. captivity, servitude,
  thralldom, vassalage 11. enslavement
  12. enthrallment
Slave States... 5. Texas 7. Alabama,
  Florida, Georgia 8. Arkansas,
  Delaware, Kentucky, Maryland,
  Missouri, Virginia 9. Louisiana,
  Tennessee 11. Mississippi 13. North
  Carolina, South Carolina
slay... 4. kill 5. amuse, burke, knock,
  lynch, smite 6. murder, strike
  7. butcher, destroy 9. slaughter
  10. annihilate 11. assassinate,
  destroy life, exterminate
slayer... 6. killer 8. criminal, murderer,
  regicide, vaticide 9. matricide,
  patricide 10. fratricide, sororicide

sleave... 4. sley 5. floss 6. tangle
   8. separate 9. floss silk
   11. disentangle 13. untwisted silk
sled... 4. pung 6. sledge, sleigh,
   travoy, troika 8. toboggan
sledge... 4. sled 6. hammer, sleigh,
   strike 7. seven–up (game), vehicle
sleep... 3. nap, nod 4. dorm, doss,
   doze, wink 5. death, sopor
   6. drowse, snooze, somnus
   7. slumber 10. narcolepsy,
   somnipathy 11. hibernation
sleep (pert to)...
   comb form.. 5. somni
   deep.. 6. stupor 8. lethargy
   10. narcolepsy
   hypnotic.. 10. somnipathy
   inducing.. 5. dwale 6. opiate, potion
   8. sedative 9. soporific
   10. anesthesia, belladonna
   insensible.. 4. coma
   midday.. 6. siesta
   prolonged.. 5. sopor
   upon.. 8. consider, postpone
sleeper... 3. tie 4. beam 6. rafter,
   rester, timber 7. Pullman, reposer,
   support 8. dormouse 9. slumberer
   10. slow seller 11. sleeping car
sleeping... 4. dead 5. inert 6. asleep,
   latent 7. dormant 8. dormient,
   inactive 9. quiescent 10. quiescence
   11. inattentive
sleeping (pert to)...
   pill.. 9. soporific
   place.. 3. bed, cot 4. bunk, doss
   5. berth, couch 6. pallet 7. cubicle
   9. dormitory
   sickness.. 6. nagana, tsetse
   9. lethargus
sleepwalking... 8. neurosis
   12. nightwalking, somnambulism
sleepy... 4. dull 5. tired 6. drowsy
   8. soporose 9. lethargic, somnolent
   11. somniferous
sleeve... 3. arm 5. gigot
   (leg-o'–mutton) 10. copper tube
   14. British channel
sleigh... 4. pung 6. cutter
sleight of hand performer... 4. mage
   8. magician 14. legerdemainist
   15. prestidigitator
slender... 4. lank, lean, slim, thin
   5. gaunt, lanky, leger, reedy
   6. lissom, narrow, svelte 8. gracile,
   tenuous, trivial, willowy 9. elongated
slender pinnacle... 3. epi
sleuth... 6. tracer 8. hawkshaw
   9. detective, sleuthdog
   11. sleuthhound 12. investigator
slice... 3. cut, saw 4. gash, slab
   5. piece, share, shave 6. rasher,
   sliver, stroke 7. portion 8. golf term,
   splinter 12. cross section
slick... 4. neat, tidy 5. alert, sleek,
   smart 6. clever, smooth 8. slippery,
   unctuous 9. first–rate, lubricate
   10. glistening 12. accomplished
slide... 3. ski 4. rule, skid, slip, slue
   5. chute, clasp, glide, plane
   (sloping), scoot, skate 6. elapse
   7. lantern, slither 8. toboggan
   9. avalanche 11. deteriorate

slight... 3. cut 4. defy, rare, snub,
   thin 5. faint, frail, leger, minor, oligo
   (comb form), scorn, small 6. flimsy,
   ignore, little, meager 7. disdain,
   fragile, neglect, nominal, scantly,
   shallow, trivial 8. contempt, delicate
   9. disregard, indignity 10. immaterial
   11. unimportant 13. imperceptible,
   unsubstantial 14. inconsiderable
slight (pert to)...
   convexity.. 6. camber
   sound.. 4. peep
   variation.. 6. nuance 7. shading
slightest... 5. least 6. barest
slightly (pert to)...
   damaged paper.. 6. retree
   sour.. 8. acescent
   tapering.. 6. terete
slim... 3. sly 4. lean, mean, thin
   5. small, spare 6. adroit, scanty,
   sparse, svelte 7. slender, tenuous
   9. worthless
slime... 3. mud 4. ooze 5. filth, gleet
   6. mucous
slip... 3. err, pew, sin 4. dock, fail,
   pier, skid, slue 5. boner, cover,
   error, fault, glide, lapse, slide, strip
   6. bungle, elapse 7. blunder, cutting,
   failure, faux pas, misdeed, mistake,
   slither 9. youngling 10. pillowslip
   12. undergarment 13. transgression
slipknot... 5. noose
slipper... 4. mule, neap, shoe
   5. apron, moyle, Romeo 6. pinson,
   sandal 7. scuffer 8. babouche
   (baboosh), covering
slippery... 3. sly 4. eely, glib 5. slick
   6. crafty, fickle, shifty, tricky, wanton
   7. cunning, elusive, evasive
   8. unctuous, unstable 9. deceitful,
   uncertain 10. intangible, precarious,
   unreliable 11. treacherous
   13. untrustworthy
slit... 4. kerf 5. cleft, slash, split
   6. furrow 7. severed
slither... 5. crawl, glide, sidle, slide
sliver... 3. cut 5. shred, slice, split
   8. fragment, splinter
sloe... 3. haw 4. plum
sloe (pert to)...
   berry.. 7. juniper
   bush.. 10. blackthorn
   color.. 9. blue–black
   fruit (blackthorn).. 3. haw 4. sloe
   gin.. 12. sloe–flavored
slogan... 3. cry 5. motto 6. phrase
   9. catchword, watchword
   10. shibboleth (Bib)
sloop... 5. yacht 6. cutter, schuit
   (schuyt) 7. eelboat
slope... 3. dip, lie 4. bank, hade,
   ramp 5. bevel, scarp, slant, talus
   6. calade, decamp, escarp, glacis
   7. terrace 9. declivity 10. declension
   11. inclination
sloping bank... 4. brae 7. terrace
sloth... 2. ai 4. pack (bears), pazy,
   unau 6. acedia, mammal 7. inertia
   8. idleness, slowness 9. indolence
slothful... 4. lazy 8. inactive, indolent,
   sluggish
sloth monkey... 5. lemur, loris

slough . . . 3. bog 4. husk, mire, molt,
shed, skin 5. bayou, swamp
7. channel, discard
sloughing . . . 7. ecdysis, molting
8. shedding 10. discarding
slovenly . . . 5. dowdy, messy, tacky
6. frowzy, sloppy, untidy 8. careless,
slattern, slipshod 9. negligent
10. disheveled, disorderly, slatternly
slow . . . 4. dull, late, poky 5. delay,
inert, relax 6. boring, hinder, retard,
stupid 7. slacken 8. boresome,
dilatory, inactive, moderate
9. lingering 20. inch by inch
phlegmatic 13. unprogressive
slow (pert to) . . .
action . . 6. dawdle 10. deliberate
adverb . . 10. behindhand
down . . 4. idle 6. retard 8. wind
down 10. decelerate
music . . 5. largo, lento, molto, tardo
6. adagio 7. andante 8. lentando
10. lentamento
poke . . 5. snail 7. dawdler
up . . 3. lag 6. retard 7. decline
witted . . 4. dull 6. stupid
sludge . . 3. mud 4. gunk, mire, ooze
5. slime 8. sediment
slug . . . 3. hit 4. blow, dose 5. Arion,
drink, drone, idler, Limax, space, token
6. bullet, loiter, nugget 7. trepang
8. sluggard 9. gastropod
sluggish . . . 4. logy, slow 5. dopey,
inert 6. drowsy, stupid, supine
7. dronish, languid 8. dilatory,
inactive, indolent, listless, stagnant
9. stagnancy, stupidity, torpidity
sluice . . . 4. race 5. flush 6. drench,
stream 7. channel 9. floodgate
slumber . . . 4. doze 5. sleep 6. catnap,
drowse, repose, snooze, somnus
14. arms of Morpheus
slump . . . 4. drop, fall 7. decline,
descend, dessert, sinkage 9. fall short
10. depreciate, depression
slur . . . 4. blur 5. elide 6. defame,
insult, mackle, slight, stigma
7. calumny, traduce 8. disgrace,
innuendo, reproach, skim over
9. aspersion, disparage
10. calumniate, stigmatize
slush . . . 3. mud 4. mire, snow
5. slime 14. sentimentality
sly . . . 4. arch, foxy, wary, wily, wink
5. cagey, catty, snaky 6. covert,
crafty, feline, shrewd, sneaky, subtle
7. cunning, furtive 8. craftily
9. underhand 11. mischievous,
underhanded 15. surreptitiously
smack . . . 3. bit, bop 4. bang, belt,
buss, glow, kiss, tang 5. clout, taste
6. strike, vessel, wallop 8. chastise,
sailboat
smacking . . . 5. brisk 6. lively
7. dashing 8. spanking, vigorous
9. energetic
small . . . 3. tot, wee 4. thin, tiny, wisp
5. dwarf, petty 6. humble, little,
meager, minute, modest, petite
7. faintly, trivial 8. picayune, trifling
9. miniature, minuscule, thumbnail
10. diminutive, undersized

11. unimportant 13. insignificant
14. contemptuously, inconsiderable
small (pert to) . . .
amount . . 3. dab 4. dram 5. minim
6. morsel 7. modicum 8. pittance
anvil . . 5. teest
area . . 6. areola (areole)
armadillo . . 4. peba
arms . . 3. bow 5. rifle, sword 6. pistol
7. carbine, grenade
attractive . . 4. cute 6. dainty
bomb . . 6. petard 7. grenade
bottle . . 4. vial 5. phial
case, handbag . . 4. etui
comb form . . 5. lepto, micro
dab . . 3. pat, wad 5. chunk
deer . . 4. fawn, napu
delicately . . 6. mignon
distance . . 3. hop 4. step
drink . . 3. nip 4. pony, swig
drum . . 5. bongo, tabor
field . . 5. croft
fish . . 3. ide
flag . . 6. fanion
fruits . . 10. low growing
fry . . 4. fish, kids, tots 8. children
10. youngsters
insect . . 4. flea 5. midge
island . . 3. ait 4. isle
lake . . 4. mere, pond
law . . 5. petit
minded . . 4. mean 5. petty 6. biased
10. prejudiced, vindictive
neat . . 6. dapper
number . . 3. few 7. paucity
opening . . 4. poro 5. stoma 7. orifice
ox . . 4. anoa
part . . 4. iota 6. detail 7. snippet
particle . . 4. atom, mote 8. molecule
people . . 5. elves 6. common
7. fairies, midgets, Pygmies
piece . . 3. mot 4. chip, tate 5. speck
7. driblet, morceau
post . . 9. paper size
quantity . . 4. drop, mite 5. trace
7. handful
rope (Naut) . . 7. marline (marling)
Scot . . 3. sma, wee
shield . . 3. écu 9. scutellum
stream . . 3. run 4. rill 6. rillet
surface . . 5. facet
talk . . 6. babble 7. prattle 8. chitchat
task . . 5. chore 6. odd job
things . . 3. fry
tower . . 6. turret 7. minaret
very . . 3. wee 8. picayune
11. Lilliputian
world . . 9. microcosm
smallpox . . . 7. variola
smaragd . . . 7. emerald
smart . . . 3. apt 4. chic, perk, posh,
trig, trim, wise 5. acute, alert, natty,
nifty, quick, sting 6. astute, clever,
shrewd, spruce, trendy 7. dashing,
painful, pungent, stylish 8. impudent,
poignant, pricking 9. competent,
ingenious 10. precocious
11. fashionable, intelligent
smash . . . 4. blow, mash, pulp, ruin
5. break, crush, drink (spirits), stave,
wreck 6. defeat 7. collide, debacle,
destroy, failure, shatter, success

8. accident, beverage 9. collision, pulverize
smear... 3. dab, rub 4. daub, gaum 5. slake, stain, sully 6. anoint, bedaub, defame, defile, grease, malign, smirch, smudge 7. besmear, plaster, pollute, slander 8. besmirch
smear with...
  egg white.. 5. glair 8. meringue
  mud.. 5. slime
  ointment.. 6. anoint
smell... 4. odor, olid, reek 5. aroma, fetor, scent, sense, sniff, stink 6. detect 7. perfume 9. fragrance, redolence 10. atmosphere
smell (pert to)...
  acute.. 8. oxyrhine
  loss of sense of.. 7. anosmia
  offensive.. 3. bad 4. foul, olid 5. fetor 6. stench
  sense of.. 6. osmics 7. osmesis 9. olfaction
smelling salts... 9. hartshorn 17. ammonium carbonate
smelt... 4. fish, fuse, melt 6. tomcod 7. scorify 10. silverside
smilax... 8. catbrier 10. greenbrier
smile... 4. grin 5. laugh, smirk, sneer 6. simper 8. greeting
smiling... 5. agrin, merry, riant 6. rident 8. gleaming, grinning
smirch... 4. blot 5. smear, stain, sully, taint 6. blotch, smutch, stigma, vilify 7. begrime, blacken, blemish, tarnish 8. discolor 10. blackening
smirk... 4. grin, leer 6. simper
smite... 4. kill, slap 6. lay low, strike 7. chasten, impress, inflict, trouble 8. chastise
smithy... 6. forger, stithy 7. farrier 8. smithery 10. blacksmith
smock... 5. kamis, shift, tunic, woman (obs) 7. chemise 9. philander 11. overgarment
smoke... 4. burn, cure, floc, fume, pipe 5. cigar, cloud, cubeb, flume, smook, vapor 6. smudge 7. incense, tobacco 8. fumigate, preserve 9. cigarette
smokestack... 6. funnel 7. chimney 8. fumiduct
smoking apparatus (Orient)... 7. tabagie 8. narghile (nargile)
smolder, smoulder... 4. burn 5. choke, smoke 6. smudge 7. smother 9. suffocate
smooth... 4. comb, ease, even, iron, lene, pave 5. bland, clear, level, plane, press, sleek, slick, suave 6. glossy, mangle, pacify, urbane 7. uniform 8. hairless, unctuous 10. facilitate, flattering 12. frictionless, ingratiating
smooth (pert to)...
  breathing.. 13. spiritus lenis
  comb form.. 3. lio
  feathers, hair.. 5. preen
  hard, transparent.. 6. glassy
  phonetically.. 4. lene
  tare.. 12. slender vetch
  tongued.. 4. glib 5. suave 12. hypocritical

smooth and...
  soft.. 5. furry, silky, soapy 7. velvety
  soothing.. 5. bland
  sweet.. 11. mellifluent
  white.. 11. alabastrine
smother... 4. daub, kill 5. befog, choke, cover 6. deaden, hush up, muffle, stifle, welter 7. overlie, smolder 8. suppress 9. suffocate, to blanket 11. exterminate
smudge... 4. blot, smut, soil, spot 5. smear, smoke, stain 6. smutch 7. begrime, smolder
smug... 4. neat, tidy, trim 5. smart, suave 6. pilfer 7. correct 9. confident 10. complacent 13. self–satisfied
smuggler... 6. runner 9. rumrunner 13. contrabandist
smur... 4. mist 5. cloud, smurr 7. drizzle
Smyrna... 5. Izmir (present name)
Smyrna fig... 5. eleme (elemi)
Smyrna melon... 6. casaba
snail... 4. slug 5. drone, Helix, Mitra, whelk 6. Nerita, Triton 7. mollusk 9. gastropod 10. periwinkle
snake... 3. asp, ess 4. tree, worm 5. adder, cobra, coral, racer, viper 6. garter, gopher 7. hognose, rattler, reptile 8. Micrurus, moccasin 9. Heterodon 10. bushmaster, copperhead, sidewinder 11. cottonmouth, diamondback, rattlesnake 12. schaapsteker
snake (pert to)...
  African.. 5. mamba
  bird.. 6. darter
  black.. 5. racer
  cobra.. 3. nag (naga)
  comb form.. 5. ophio, ophis 6. herpes
  crusher.. 6. python 8. anaconda 14. boa constrictor
  dance.. 4. Hopi 6. ophism
  division (serpents).. 7. Ophidia 9. Serpentes
  expert.. 13. herpetologist
  fear of.. 13. herpetophobia
  Florida.. 8. moccasin
  front–fanged.. 5. cobra, mamba 6. elapid 8. Elapinne
  garter.. 5. Elaps
  genus.. 7. Ophidia
  heraldic.. 5. bisse
  horned.. 8. cerastes
  India.. 5. krait 6. bongar
  killer.. 8. mongoose
  like.. 7. ophioid 9. colubrine
  mouth.. 6. orchid
  movement.. 4. coil, drag, wind 5. crawl, sneak, twist
  mythical.. 6. Python (on Mt Parnassus)
  nonpoisonous.. 4. king 6. garter, gopher 9. Colubrina
  pert to.. 5. ophic 7. anguine 8. viperine 9. colubrine, scoundrel
  poisonous.. 3. asp 5. adder, coral 7. rattler 8. moccasin 10. copperhead 11. cottonmouth 13. thanatophidia

python.. **8.** anaconda
python deity.. **5.** zombi (zombie)
reptilelike.. **9.** herpetoid
Russell's viper.. **6.** daboia, jessur
sacred.. **6.** Shesha
S America.. **5.** aboma
sand snake.. **4.** Eryx
semihuman, race of.. **4.** Naga
shaped.. **9.** anguiform
skin.. **6.** exuvia
spitting.. **8.** ringhals
snaky... **3.** sly **4.** wavy **7.** anguine,
sinuous, wriggly **8.** spiteful, twisting,
venomous **9.** snakelike **10.** perfidious,
serpentine **11.** treacherous
snaky sisters... **6.** Erinys
17. snaky–haired Furies
snap... **3.** bit **4.** bite, flip **5.** break,
crack, flick, quick, snarl, thump
6. energy, fasten, fillip (fingers)
7. bargain, crackle **8.** easy task,
handcuff, snapshot **9.** crispness,
fastening, smartness **10.** gingersnap,
photograph, resilience **11.** sharp
retort
snapper... **4.** bean, sesi **5.** error,
pargo **6.** beetle, bonbon, tamure,
turtle **7.** cracker, grouper **8.** fastener,
rosefish **9.** countfish **10.** stitchwort,
stringbean, woodpecker
11. firecracker
snappy... **4.** cold, fast **5.** quick
6. lively, sudden **7.** pungent
8. snappish **9.** crackling, energetic
snare... **3.** beg, gin, net, web **4.** lure,
mesh, trap **5.** benet, catch, noose,
steal **6.** entoil, trepan **7.** pitfall
9. deception
snark... **3.** nag **5.** snort **6.** boojum
8. creature (fabled)
snarl... **4.** gnar, knot **5.** gnarr, growl,
scold, snare **6.** tangle **7.** confuse,
ensnare, grumble, quarrel
8. complain, entangle **9.** confusion
10. complicate **12.** complication
snatch... **4.** grab, jerk, take **5.** catch,
erept, grasp, gripe, pluck, seize,
steal, wrest **6.** clutch, kidnap, rescue
7. seizure
sneak... **4.** lead (game), lurk **5.** cower,
creep, knave, slink, snoop **6.** coward,
cringe, tattle **7.** smuggle **11.** furtive
move
sneaking... **3.** sly **4.** mean, poor
6. craven, hidden, paltry, secret
7. furtive **8.** cowardly, stealthy
9. dastardly, niggardly, underhand
12. contemptible **13.** surreptitious
sneer... **4.** gibe, jeer, mock **5.** fleer,
flout, laugh, scoff, scorn
sneer, expressive... **8.** sardonic
snell... **4.** keen **5.** acute, eager, quick,
sharp, snood, swift **6.** active, biting,
severe **7.** caustic, pungent
8. piercing
snicker... **5.** laugh, neigh, sneer
6. giggle, nicker, tittle, whinny
7. snigger **8.** laughter
sniff... **4.** nose **5.** scent, smell, snuff
6. detect, inhale **7.** sniffle **8.** sibilate,
smell out **14.** show of contempt
snifter... **3.** nip **4.** dram, good

5. drink, sniff, snort **6.** snivel
9. excellent
snip... **3.** bit, cut **4.** clip, snap
5. notch, piece, shred **8.** fragment,
particle
snipe (pert to)...
eel.. **6.** thread
flock.. **4.** wisp
game.. **6.** godwit
hawk.. **7.** harrier
verb.. **7.** shoot at **10.** sharpshoot
snippy... **4.** curt, tart **5.** brief, sharp
8. snippety, snobbish
11. fragmentary **12.** supercilious
snirl... **5.** gnarl, snare **6.** tangle
7. wrinkle
snitch... **5.** pinch, steal **6.** betray,
inform, pilfer, snatch, tattle
8. informer, particle
snob... **4.** prig **7.** cobbler, parvenu
8. bluenose, commoner, courtier
9. sycophant
snobby, snobbish... **5.** proud
6. uppish **7.** haughty **8.** arrogant
9. exclusive **11.** overbearing
snood... **5.** snell **6.** fillet **7.** hairnet
snook... **4.** fish **5.** smell **6.** robalo,
search **9.** barracuda
snoop... **3.** pry **4.** nose **5.** prowl,
sneak **6.** meddle **7.** meddler
8. busybody **10.** sneak thief
snooze... **3.** nap **4.** doze **5.** sleep
6. cuddle, nuzzle, siesta **7.** snoozle,
snuggle
snore, snoring... **4.** rale **5.** sleep
7. stertor **8.** rhonchus, sibilate
10. sibilation, stertorous **15.** hoarse
breathing
snort... **5.** drink, grunt, laugh, snore
snotty... **5.** dirty, nasty **6.** offish,
snooty **7.** high–hat **9.** offensive
12. contemptible, supercilious
snow... **4.** firn, neve **5.** opium
8. narcotic **12.** interference
snow (pert to)...
bunting.. **5.** finch **9.** snowflake
glacial.. **4.** firn, neve
grouse, quail.. **9.** ptarmigan
house.. **5.** igloo
leopard.. **5.** ounce
lily.. **6.** violet (white)
living in.. **5.** nival
mouse.. **4.** vole **7.** lemming
ref to.. **5.** nival
ridges.. **8.** sastrugi (zastrugi)
runner.. **3.** ski **4.** sled
shoe.. **3.** pac **7.** webfoot
sliding.. **9.** avalanche
slope.. **8.** glissade
snub... **3.** cut **5.** check, quell, scold
6. cut off, ignore, rebuff, rebuke,
slight **7.** neglect, shorten **8.** restrain
9. reprimand **10.** inhalation
snuff... **5.** scent, smell, sniff **6.** draw
in, inhale, snoose **7.** tobacco
(pulverized), umbrage **10.** extinguish,
inhalation
snuff (pert to)...
a candle.. **4.** snot
box.. **4.** mull **9.** tabatière
color.. **10.** mummy brown
type.. **6.** rappee **8.** Maccaboy

10. Copenhagen
snug... 4. cozy, neat, safe, trim
  5. close, tight 6. secure 7. compact
  8. homelike, reticent 9. concealed,
  secretive 10. prosperous
  11. comfortable
snuggle... 6. cuddle, nestle
sny (shipbuilding)... 5. curve (of plank)
so... 2. as 3. how 4. ergo, thus, very
  5. hence 6. if only 7. because
  8. likewise, provided 9. therefore
  11. accordingly, in order that
  12. consequently
so (pert to)...
  far.. 3. yet 7. thus far 8. until now
  Latin.. 3. sic
  so be it.. 4. Amen
  to speak.. 8. as it were
  12. figuratively
soak... 3. dip, sog, sop, wet 4. sock
  5. souse, steep 6. drench, imbrue,
  strike, tipple 7. extract, immerse
  8. drunkard, macerate, marinate,
  permeate, saturate 9. percolate
  10. overcharge
soap... 3. sapo, suds, wash 5. bribe
  6. lather 7. bribery 8. cleanser,
  flattery 9. slush fund
soap (pert to)...
  box.. 4. dais 5. stage 8. platform
  convert to.. 8. saponify
  fish.. 10. lizard fish
  frame bar.. 4. sess
  ingredient.. 3. lye
  liniment (camphorated).. 9. opodeldoc
  making.. 14. saponification
  mottled.. 8. Eschwege (Eschweg)
  opera.. 6. serial 9. broadcast
  13. network serial
  plant.. 5. amole
  soft.. 8. flattery
soar... 3. fly 4. flit, rise, wing 5. float,
  plane 6. ascend, aspire, be high
  9. transcend
soaring... 6. flight 7. gliding, planing,
  winging 8. essorant 9. skyriding
  10. ballooning
sob... 3. cry 4. bawl, weep
  6. boohoo, simper 7. whimper
  9. shed tears
sobeit... 4. amen 8. provided
sober... 4. calm, cool, dark, sane
  5. grave, quiet, staid 6. gentle,
  sedate, solemn, somber, subdue,
  temper 7. chasten, earnest, regular,
  serious 8. composed, moderate,
  sensible 9. abstinent, collected,
  dignified, temperate 10. abstemious,
  thoughtful 11. impassioned
  13. unintoxicated
sobriety... 6. sanity 9. composure,
  restraint, soberness 10. abstinence,
  moderation, temperance
  11. seriousness
sobriquet... 5. alias, title 6. byname
  7. epithet 8. cognomen, nickname
  11. appellation
sociable... 5. party 7. affable
  8. familiar, friendly, informal
  9. reception 10. accessible,
  gregarious 13. communicative,
  companionable

social... 3. tea 5. party 6. smoker
  9. convivial, gathering
  13. companionable
social (pert to)...
  career.. 5. debut
  class.. 4. clan, sept 5. caste
  6. estate
  ethics.. 6. morals 9. standards
  10. principles
  function.. 3. bee, tea 4. ball 5. party
  6. soiree 7. reunion 9. reception
  gathering, men.. 4. stag 6. smoker
  group.. 4. sept 5. tribe 6. ethnos
  8. smart set 10. upper crust
  11. cafe society 13. kaffeeklatsch
  insect.. 3. ant, bee
  outcast.. 5. leper 6. pariah
  standing.. 6. estate
  system.. 6. regime
socialist... 3. Red 8. Nihilist
  9. anarchist, communist
  10. Bolshevist 12. collectivist
society... 5. union 7. company
  8. alliance, populace 9. community
  10. fellowship 11. association,
  partnership 13. companionship,
  confederation, participation
society (pert to)...
  bud.. 3. deb
  Chinese.. 4. Tong
  German.. 6. Verein
  high.. 5. elite 10. upper crust
  Italian.. 6. maffia (mafia)
  of Friends.. 7. Quakers
  secret.. 5. lodge, Order
Society Islands...
  capital.. 7. Papeete
  chief island.. 6. Tahiti
  site.. 12. South Pacific
Socrates (pert to)...
  birthplace.. 6. Athens
  disciple of.. 5. Plato
  famed as.. 7. teacher 11. Grecian
  sage
  wife.. 9. Xanthippe (Xantippe)
sod... 4. soil, turf 5. divot, glebe,
  sward 7. stratum 10. greensward
soda... 3. sal 8. beverage 9. saleratus,
  saltpeter
sodden... 5. drunk, moist, soggy
  6. soaked, stewed, stupid
  7. drunken, steeped 9. saturated
  11. intoxicated
sodium (pert to)...
  carbonate.. 4. soda 5. borax, trona
  7. sal soda, saltcat
  chloride.. 3. sal, tar 4. NaCl, salt
  nitrate.. 5. niter
  salicylate.. 8. medicine
  symbol.. 2. Na
sofa... 5. couch, divan 6. lounge,
  settee 7. dos–à–dos 8. causeuse,
  love seat 9. davenport, tête–à–tête
  12. chesterfield
soft... 4. easy, limp, weak 5. bland,
  downy, mushy, pulpy 6. dreamy,
  gentle, placid, silken, supple, tender
  7. clement, ductile, lenient, lightly,
  quietly, squashy, velvety 8. flexible,
  gullible, merciful, tranquil
  9. temperate, tractable
  10. effeminate, peacefully

11. comfortable, sentimental, sympathetic 13. compassionate

soft (pert to) . . .
cancer . . 11. encephaloma
coal . . 10. bituminous
food . . 3. pap
head . . 9. simpleton
job . . 4. snap 8. sinecure
mass . . 4. pulp
music . . 5. dulce, piano
palate . . 4. cion 5. uvula, velum
pedal . . 3. ban 4. curb 6. subdue 8. tone down
soap . . 7. blarney 8. blandish, flattery 9. wheedling
spoken . . 4. mild 5. suave

soften . . . 4. melt, thaw 5. allay, malax, relax 6. affect, lenify, pacify, relent, soothe, temper, weaken 7. appease, assuage, cushion, mollify, relieve 8. emoliate, enervate, enfeeble, macerate, mitigate, modulate 9. alleviate, meliorate 11. tranquilize

soften (pert to) . . .
by kneading . . 5. malax
by soaking . . 8. macerate
leather . . 5. sammy (sam)
skins . . 3. taw
temper . . 6. relent

softening . . . 7. lenient 8. emulsive 9. relenting, relieving, tempering 10. lightening, mitigating

softening of the brain . . . 8. dementia
softhearted . . . 4. kind 6. tender 8. merciful

softly . . . 3. low 5. sotto 6. easily, gently 10. delicately 13. unobtrusively

soggy . . . 3. wet 4. damp 5. heavy 6. soaked, sodden, watery 9. saturated

soil . . . 4. clay, daub, dirt, land, loam, sand, spot 5. adobe, dirty, earth, glebe, gumbo, humus, stain, sully 6. bedaub, bemire, ground, region, smirch, vilify 7. begrime, besmear, corrupt, debauch, pollute, tarnish 8. alluvium 9. bedraggle, bespatter 11. contaminate 12. fuller's earth

soil (pert to) . . .
barren . . 4. arid, gall 8. lifeless
goddess of . . 7. Demeter
kind of . . 4. clay, lair, loam, malm 5. adobe, humus
oneself . . 4. moil
poetic . . 5. glebe

sojourn . . . 4. bide, stay, stop 5. abide 6. reside 8. abidance, stop over 11. peregrinate

solace . . . 5. allay, amuse, cheer 6. soothe 7. assuage, comfort, console 9. alleviate, entertain 10. relaxation 11. consolation

solan . . . 5. goose 6. gannet

solar (pert to) . . .
deity . . 2. Ra 3. Shu (Su) 6. Helios
disk . . 4. aten
exposure . . 9. sunstroke 10. heatstroke
halo . . 6. nimbus 7. aureole 12. vesica piscis
plexus . . 10. stomach pit
system . . 6. bodies, planet

15. celestial bodies
system apparatus . . 6. orrery
year . . 5. epact

soldier . . . 3. ant 5. cadet, poilu 6. galoot 7. fighter, private, regular, trooper, veteran, warrior 8. gendarme, servitor 9. combatant, grenadier, musketeer 11. enlisted man

soldier (pert to) . . .
Algeria . . 6. Zouave
cavalryman . . 6. lancer 7. dragoon, trooper
Croatian . . 5. Croat
field worker . . 6. sapper
flask . . 7. canteen
French . . 5. poilu
Gaelic . . 4. Kern
girl . . 3. WAC (Army)
Gr Myth . . 8. Myrmidon
hireling . . 9. mercenary
Ind (Brit) . . 5. sepoy
Ind (Brit), with own horse . . 8. silladar
Moroccan . . 5. askar
of fortune . . 7. Hessian 10. adventurer
Prussian . . 5. uhlan
slang . . 6. galoot 7. chicken 8. shackman

soldiers, soldier's . . .
body of . . 5. troop 6. cohort 7. brigade, company, platoon
captured, wounded . . 6. losses
flask . . 7. canteen
Maryland (Rev War) . . 10. macaronies
overcoat . . 6. capote
quarters . . 7. billets 8. barracks
Three . . 5. tales (by Kipling)
vacation . . 4. pass 5. leave 8. furlough

sole . . . 3. one 4. base, fish, only 5. alone, slade 6. entire, lonely, single, unique 8. desolate, isolated, solitary, unshared 9. exclusive, unmarried, unmatched 10. underframe

sole (pert to) . . .
cookery . . 8. Marguéry
foot . . 4. vola 6. planta
hand (palm) . . 4. vola
pert to . . 7. plantar
plow . . 5. slade
toward the sole . . 7. plantad

solecism . . . 5. error 7. blunder 9. barbarism, deviation 11. impropriety

solemn . . . 3. sad 5. grave, pious, sober 6. august, devout, formal, gloomy, ritual, silent 7. earnest, serious, stately, sublime 8. funereal 9. dignified 10. ceremonial, devotional 11. ceremonious, reverential 12. awe–inspiring

solemnity . . . 4. pomp 7. dignity, sadness 8. ceremony 9. formality 10. importance

solicit . . . 3. ask, beg 4. lure, seek, tout 5. claim, court, crave, plead 6. accost, demand, invite, obtain 7. beseech, canvass, entreat, implore, request 8. campaign, petition 9. challenge, importune, panhandle, prosecute 10. supplicate

solicitor... 6. barker, lawyer
  8. attorney 9. canvasser
  10. petitioner
solicitude... 4. care, coda, heed
  7. anxiety, caution, concern
  9. attention 11. carefulness
  12. apprehension
  15. considerateness
solid... 4. cone, cube, firm, full, good,
  hard 5. dense, level, sound, stiff
  6. stable, strong 7. uniform
  8. complete, resolute, sensible,
  sterling 9. estimable, unanimous
  10. dependable, inflexible
  11. homogeneous, responsible,
  substantial, trustworthy
solid (pert to)...
comb form .. 6. stereo
geometrical .. 5. prism
seven–faced .. 11. heptahedron
six–faced .. 4. cube
tapering .. 4. cone 7. pyramid
solidarity... 5. unity 10. correality
  11. nationality 12. completeness
solidity... 5. unity 6. volume
  7. density 8. firmness, hardness,
  solvency, strength 9. solidness,
  stability 11. compactness
  12. completeness 13. dependability
  14. substantiality
solidum... 4. dado 9. entire sum
soliloquy... 4. poem 9. discourse,
  monologue 16. talking to oneself
solitaire... 8. Canfield
solitary... 3. one 4. lone, only, sole
  5. alone, eremo (comb form)
  6. hermit, lonely, single 7. recluse
  8. deserted, desolate, lonesome
  10. individual 12. unfrequented
solitude... 6. desert 7. privacy, retreat
  9. aloneness, isolation, seclusion
  10. loneliness, wilderness
solo accompaniment... 9. obbligato
Solomon (pert to)...
author of (reputed) .. 8. Proverbs
  9. Canticles 12. Ecclesiastes
  15. Wisdom of Solomon
called also .. 8. Koheleth 11. The
  Preacher
famed as .. 4. sage 7. wise man
  12. King of Israel
father .. 5. David
literally .. 9. peaceable
mother .. 9. Bathsheba
Solomon Islands site... 9. South Seas
solon... 4. sage 8. lawmaker
  9. statesman
solstice... 5. limit 13. farthest point
  (from equator)
solution... 3. key 6. answer 7. solving
  8. analysis 10. denouement,
  resolution 11. explanation
  15. disentanglement
solution (pert to)...
alkaline .. 3. lye
saline .. 5. brine
strength .. 5. titer (titre)
Somalia...
capital .. 9. Mogadishu
people .. 6. Somali 7. Hamitic
port .. 5. Zeila 6. Bulhar

somber, sombre... 3. sad 4. dark
  5. grave 6. solemn 7. austere
  9. depressed 10. depressing,
  foreboding, lackluster, melancholy
  11. dark–colored, dispiriting
some... 3. any, one 5. about
  6. plural, suffix 7. several
  10. indefinite, more or less
  13. approximately
somebody... 6. person 7. big name
  8. luminary 9. celebrity, personage
somersault... 4. flip, leap 8. somerset
  9. cartwheel 10. end over end
something... 6. object 8. somewhat
  9. personage 12. in some degree
something (pert to)...
abnormal .. 5. freak 6. mutant
  11. monstrosity 12. malformation
else .. 10. irrelevant
extra .. 5. bonus 6. bounty
  7. premium 9. lagniappe
found .. 5. cache, trove
  11. serendipity 13. treasure–trove
frightening .. 7. bugbear
heavy .. 4. onus 9. ponderant
illogical .. 7. alogism
imagined .. 5. story 7. figment
inserted .. 4. gore 5. inset, wedge
like .. 7. related, similar 8. somewhat
similar .. 8. analogue 11. counterpart
small .. 3. dot, jot 4. atom, iota, whit
  5. speck 6. sliver, tittle
soothing .. 7. unction
superfluous .. 5. luxus 6. luxury
unexplained .. 5. poser 7. mystery
unfinished .. 4. quab
somewhat... 4. part 6. little, partly,
  rather 12. in some degree
somnifacient... 4. drug 8. hypnotic,
  sedative 9. soporific
somniloquy... 12. sleep talking
somnolence... 8. dormancy
  10. drowsiness, sleepiness
somnus... 5. sleep
Somnus (pert to)...
brother .. 4. Mors (Death)
known also as .. 6. Hypnos
son of .. 3. Nox (Night)
son, son of (pert to)...
a gun .. 5. rogue 6. fellow, wretch
Anak .. 5. giant
a Scot .. 3. Mac
God .. 11. Jesus Christ
Heaven (China) .. 7. Emperor
in–law .. 5. gener
in Trinity .. 6. second (person)
Jacob .. 4. Levi
man .. 4. male 6. mortal
Odin .. 2. Ve
Odysseus .. 9. Telegonus
Priam .. 5. Paris
reference to .. 3. ben 4. fils 5. scion
  6. filial 9. offspring 10. descendant
Seth .. 4. Enos
the soil .. 6. farmer 7. peasant
youngest .. 5. cadet
sonance... 4. tune 5. sound
  7. sonancy
sonant... 5. sound, tonic, vocal
  6. voiced 8. sounding 9. intonated
song... 3. air, lay, ode 4. aria, leed,

lilt, noel, poem, tune 5. carol, chant, ditty, melos, troll, verse 6. ballad, melody, strain, trifle 7. chantey (chanty), descant 8. canticle, pittance 9. cabaletta

song (pert to)...
after.. 5. epode
Bib.. 8. canticle 11. Song of Songs 13. Song of Solomon
boat, gondolier.. 7. chantey (chanty)
choral Muse.. 11. Terpsichore
collection.. 9. anthology 10. cancionero
college.. 4. glee
depressing.. 5. blues
evening.. 6. vesper 8. evensong, serenade
French.. 7. chanson
funeral.. 5. dirge, elegy 6. lament 8. threnody 9. epicedium
gay.. 4. lilt
German.. 4. lied 9. Kunstlied
gypsy.. 10. zingaresca
Italian.. 7. canzone
lament.. 8. threnody
love.. 5. lyric 6. ballad 8. madrigal, serenade
merry.. 4. lilt
morning.. 5. matin
mountaineer.. 5. yodel
pert to.. 5. melic
praise.. 5. carol, paean (pean)
sacred.. 4. hymn 5. chant, motet, psalm 6. anthem
sailor's.. 7. chantey (chanty) 9. barcarole
short.. 7. arietta
simple.. 6. ballad
words.. 6. lyrics
songbird 4. lark 5. mavis, robin, veery 6. canary, oriole, thrush 8. throstle 11. mockingbird
sonic recorder... 9. echograph
sonnet... 4. poem, song 5. verse
sonnet (pert to)...
first eight lines.. 5. octet
last six lines.. 6. sestet
two quatrains.. 10. Petrarchan
sonorous... 4. loud 6. tonous 7. ringing 8. resonant 9. melodious 10. impressive, resounding
sonsy, sonsie... 5. buxom, happy 6. comely 11. good-natured
sontag... 4. cape 6. jacket
soon... 3. ere 4. anon 5. early, later 6. at once 7. betimes, erelong, quickly, readily, shortly 8. promptly, speedily 9. certainly, presently 11. immediately
Sooner State... 8. Oklahoma
sooner than... 3. ere 6. before
soot... 4. smut, stup 5. black, grime, smoke 6. carbon, smudge 7. residue 9. lampblack
soothe... 3. pet 4. calm, lull 5. allay, quiet 6. pacify, please, solace 7. assuage, compose, mollify, relieve, satisfy 8. mitigate, palliate 9. alleviate 11. tranquilize
soother... 4. balm 6. luller 7. anodyne, placebo 8. lenitive, pacifier, sedative 9. flatterer

soothing... 5. balmy, sirup (syrup) 6. dulcet, gentle 7. calming 8. lenitive, sedative 9. appeasing, demulcent 13. tranquilizing
soothsayer... 4. seer 5. augur, vatis 6. mantis 7. diviner, prophet 8. Chaldean, haruspex 9. Cassandra 13. praying insect 14. prognosticator
sooty (pert to)...
brown.. 6. bister 8. teakwood
color.. 5. black
mangabey.. 6. monkey
pert to.. 9. albatross 10. fuliginous
petrel.. 7. skimmer 10. shearwater
sophistical... 8. captious 9. deceptive, sophistic
sophistication... 9. sophistry 10. corruption, experience 11. worldliness 13. ungullibility
soporific... 4. drug 6. drowsy, opiate 7. anodyne 8. hypnotic, narcotic, sedative 11. somniferous 12. sleep inducer, somnifacient
soprano (operatic)... 4. Alda, Bori, Lind, Pons 5. Calvé, Eames 6. Callas, Steber
sora... 4. rail 5. crake
sorcerer... 4. mage 5. Magus 6. wizard 7. diviner 8. conjurer, magician 11. necromancer
sorceress... 3. hex 5. Circe, lamia, Medea, witch 6. Gorgon 7. vampire 12. Witch of Endor
sorcery... 5. magic, obeah, spell 6. voodoo 8. pishogue 9. diablerie, diabolism 10. black magic, necromancy, witchcraft
sordid... 3. low 4. base, mean, vile 5. gross 6. filthy, menial 7. ignoble, servile, squalid 8. sluttish, wretched 10. despicable, slatternly 12. contemptible
sore... 4. pain, sair 5. angry, vexed, wound 6. tender 7. painful 8. abrasion, inflamed, offended 9. irritated, vexatious 11. distressing 12. inflammation
soreness... 4. ache 5. anger 8. vexation 10. bitterness, tenderness 11. painfulness 12. irritability
sorghum... 4. milo 5. durra (dari), grain, sorgo 6. imphee, shallu 8. feterita
sorority... 4. club 7. society 10. fellowship, sisterhood
sorrel... 3. oca 4. buck, herb 5. color (horse), Rumex 7. roselle
Sorrento, Italy (pert to)...
anc name.. 9. Sorrentum
famed as.. 6. resort
famed for.. 9. cathedral
site.. 11. Bay of Naples
sorrow... 3. rue, woe 4. sigh, teen, weal 5. dolor, grief, mourn 6. grieve, lament, misery, repent 7. remorse, trouble 8. calamity, distress, egrimony, mourning 9. adversity, penitence 10. affliction, contrition 11. lamentation, tribulation 12. disconsolate, wretchedness
sorrowful... 3. sad 4. blue 5. drear, sadly 6. dismal, dolent, dreary, rueful

7. doleful, grieved, tearful, unhappy
8. mournful 9. plaintive
10. afflictive, melancholy
11. distressing 12. disconsolate
sorry ... 3. sad 4. hurt 5. vexed
6. dismal, gloomy, rueful 7. painful,
pitiful, unhappy 8. contrite, grievous,
mournful, penitent, shameful, wretched
9. afflicted, chagrined, mortified,
regretful, repentant, worthless
10. displeased, melancholy
12. disappointed
sort ... 3. ilk, way 4. cull, kind, rank
5. blend, class, grade, group
6. assort, manner, nature, strain
7. quality, species, variety 8. classify,
separate 9. character 11. description
sortie ... 4. raid 5. foray, onset, sally
6. attack, thrust
sottish ... 4. dull 6. stupid 7. doltish,
drunken, foolish 8. bibulous
9. senseless
sotto (It) ... 5. below, under
sotto voce ... 5. aside 8. secretly
9. privately, undertone 14. under the
breath
soubrette ... 9. lady's maid
10. intrigante 11. maidservant
soudagur ... 8. merchant
10. shopkeeper
soul ... 2. ba, ka 3. ego, God 4. life
5. anima 6. pneuma, spirit
7. essence 8. inspirer 9. substance
10. embodiment 15. exemplification,
personification
soul (pert to) ...
beatified .. 5. saint
destiny of .. 8. theodicy
dwelling place .. 2. Po 6. heaven
Egypt .. 2. Ba
Hindu .. 5. atman 7. jivatma
lost .. 9. âme damnée, the damned
maligners .. 7. Harpies
music .. 14. rhythm and blues
personified .. 6. Psyche
transmigration .. 7. rebirth
13. reincarnation
sound ... 3. bam, cry, hum 4. beep,
bong, hale, honk, rale, ring, sane, test,
tone, toot 5. drone, noise, plumb,
probe, snore, valid, whole 6. intact,
jingle, report, robust, stable, sturdy
7. feel out, perfect, resound
8. flawless, reliable, susurrus
9. undamaged 10. scrutinize
11. trustworthy
sound (pert to) ...
addition to word end .. 8. paragoge
atonic .. 4. surd
dashing .. 5. swash 6. splash
discordant .. 6. jangle 9. cacophony
drum, beating .. 8. rataplan
explosion .. 4. boom 6. report
fixed .. 5. toned
harsh .. 3. caw 4. bray 5. creak,
twang 7. stridor 9. cacophony
insect's .. 5. chirr
loud .. 4. peal 5. blare, clang
low .. 3. hum 4. moan 5. drone
metallic .. 4. ping, ting 5. clank, clink,
twank 6. tinkle
pert to .. 5. tonal 6. sonant

10. acoustical
prosody .. 4. rime (rhyme)
reflected .. 4. echo
sharp .. 3. pop 7. rat-a-tat, tapping
shrill .. 5. reedy
sibilant .. 4. hiss
similar .. 8. assonant
small .. 4. peep 6. rustle
surf .. 4. rote 5. swish
throwing .. 8. abat-sons
trumpet .. 7. clarion
warning .. 5. alarm, siren 6. tocsin
whispering .. 8. susurrus
with rhythm .. 5. music
sounding ... 5. depth, rawin 6. sonant
7. ringing 8. sonation
10. resounding
soundness ... 5. truth 6. sanity
8. solidity, solvency, strength
9. integrity, rectitude, stability
10. heartiness 11. healthiness
soup ... 3. fog 5. broth, chili, purée
6. bisque, potage, won ton
7. borscht, chowder, pottage
8. bouillon, consommé, gazpacho,
julienne 10. oyster stew
11. vichyssoise 12. mulligatawny
soupçon ... 5. taste 7. portion
9. suspicion 10. suggestion
soup dish ... 6. tureen
sour ... 3. wry 4. acid, tart 5. acerb,
acrid 6. acetic, bitter, morose, off
key, rancid 7. acetose, acidify,
crabbed, pungent, tainted
8. acescent, embitter 9. acidulous
10. astringent, unpleasant
sour (pert to) ...
apple .. 9. crab apple
aspect .. 4. dour, hard 6. sullen
berry .. 9. cranberry
bread .. 8. leavened
cherry .. 7. morello
stomach .. 4. acor
turn sour .. 5. prill 6. bleeze
source ... 4. font, germ, mine, rise,
root, seed 5. cause, fount 6. origin,
parent, quarry 8. fountain
9. beginning 10. wellspring
12. fountainhead
source (pert to) ...
income .. 7. revenue
insecticides .. 9. sabadilla
iodine .. 4. kelp
ipecac .. 4. evea
metal .. 3. ore 7. bonanza
opium .. 5. poppy
rubber .. 5. ule
South Africa ... see also *South African*
capital .. 8. Cape Town, Pretoria
city .. 6. Durban 9. Germiston
12. Johannesburg
division .. 5. Natal 9. Transvaal
14. Cape of Good Hope 15. Orange
Free State
exports .. 4. gold 8. diamonds
legislature seat location .. 8. Cape
Town
people .. 5. Boers 7. British, Kaffirs
10. Hottentots 11. Afrikanders
(Dutch)
river .. 4. Vaal 6. Orange
South African (pert to) ...

antelope .. **3.** gnu **5.** eland, oribi, peele
  6. rhebok **7.** sassaby
armadillo .. **4.** para
ass (wild) .. **6.** quagga
bird .. **4.** taha
camp .. **6.** laager
Cape ash .. **9.** essenhout
cocktail .. **9.** sundowner
cony .. **3.** das
council .. **4.** Raad
dialect .. **4.** Taal **9.** Afrikaans
diamond (blue–white) .. **5.** jager
fox .. **4.** asse **5.** caama
grass hut .. **8.** rondawel (rondavel)
grassland .. **4.** veld (veldt) **8.** bushveld
mountain, hill .. **3.** kop
snake .. **8.** eggeater
tableland .. **5.** karoo
tree (dogwood) .. **7.** assagai (assegai)
tribe .. **4.** Zulu **5.** Bantu
village .. **5.** kraal
war .. **4.** Boer
warrior .. **4.** impi
weaverbird .. **4.** taha
whip .. **7.** sjambok
South American (pert to) ...
animal .. **2.** ai **4.** paca **5.** llama, sloth,
  tapir **6.** jaguar, tapeti **7.** agouara
  (dog) **8.** anteater **9.** armadillo
armadillo .. **4.** apar (apara)
  10. pichiciago (burrowing)
arrow poison .. **6.** curare (curari)
balsam .. **4.** tolu
bellbird .. **8.** arapunga **9.** campanero
bird .. **4.** rara, taha **5.** agami, arara,
  chaja, macaw **6.** barbet **7.** oilbird,
  seriema, tinamou **8.** bellbird, boatbill,
  caracara, guacharo, puffbird
blanket .. **6.** serape
city section .. **6.** barrio
cloth .. **4.** orea
drink .. **5.** assai
fiber .. **6.** yachan
fish .. **4.** paru **7.** piranha, scalare
  8. arapaima
Indian .. **2.** Ge (Gesan) **3.** Ona **4.** Inca
  5. Carib **6.** Tapuya (50 tribes)
knife .. **7.** machete
leader .. **6.** Franko **7.** Pizarro
liberator .. **7.** Bolivar
mammal .. **5.** llama, tapir **6.** alpaca
  8. kinkajou **10.** chinchilla
marmoset .. **7.** tamarin
monkey .. **3.** sai **4.** saki, titi **5.** araba
  8. orabassu **9.** barrigudo
native .. **5.** Carib **6.** Arawak
ostrich .. **4.** rhea
palm .. **5.** assai **12.** chiquichiqui
parrot .. **5.** macaw
plains .. **6.** llanos, pampas
plainsman .. **7.** llanero
plant .. **6.** ipecac **11.** ipecacuanha
poison .. **6.** curare
river .. **3.** Apa **4.** Acre, Pará **5.** Plata
  6. Paraná
rodent .. **5.** coypu **6.** agouti (agouty)
  8. capibara, viscacha **10.** chinchilla
snake .. **4.** lora **5.** aboma **8.** anaconda
  10. bushmaster
stork .. **7.** maguari
tinamou .. **7.** tataupa
toucan .. **7.** aracari

trumpeter .. **5.** agami
tuber .. **3.** oca
vulture .. **6.** condor
weapon .. **4.** bola
wild cat .. **4.** eyra
wind .. **7.** pampero
South Carolina ...
capital .. **8.** Columbia
city .. **8.** Beaufort **10.** Charleston
  11. Spartanburg
monument .. **10.** Fort Sumter
mountain .. **9.** Blue Ridge, Sassafras
resort .. **11.** Myrtle Beach
State admission .. **6.** Eighth
State bird .. **4.** wren
State flower .. **9.** jessamine
State motto .. **8.** Dum Spiro, Spero
  (While I Breathe, I Hope)
State nickname .. **8.** Palmetto
State secession .. **5.** First (1860)
South Dakota ...
capital .. **6.** Pierre
city .. **5.** Huron **8.** Deadwood
  9. Rapid City **10.** Sioux Falls
Indians .. **5.** Brule, Sioux
mine (US largest) .. **9.** Homestake
monument .. **10.** Crazy Horse, Mt
  Rushmore
mountain .. **10.** Black Hills, Harney
  Peak
river .. **5.** White **8.** Cheyenne, Missouri
State admission .. **8.** Fortieth (or
  Thirty–ninth)
State bird .. **8.** pheasant
State flower .. **12.** pasqueflower
State motto .. **21.** Under God the
  People Rule
State nickname .. **6.** Coyote
  8. Sunshine
topography .. **8.** Bad Lands **10.** Black
  Hills
southeast wind ... **5.** Eurus
southern ... **7.** austral
Southern (pert to) ...
Buddhism .. **8.** Hinayana
Cross .. **4.** Crux **12.** Stars and Bars
Crown .. **15.** Corona Australis
dish .. **3.** yam **4.** okra, pone **5.** gumbo
  7. catfish, hoecake **8.** chess pie, ham
  hocks **9.** cornbread **11.** hush puppies
  12. chitterlings, turnip greens
shrub .. **8.** magnolia, oleander
States .. **5.** Dixie **7.** Sunbelt
southernmost city ... **12.** Puerto
  Arenas (Chile)
South Pole bird ... **4.** skua **7.** penguin
South Pole constellation ... **4.** Pavo
South Sea ... **12.** Pacific Ocean
South Sea Bubble ... **6.** scheme
  (1720) **10.** stock fraud (Eng)
South Wales people ... **7.** Silures
southwest wind ... **4.** afer
south wind ... **5.** Notus
souvenir ... **5.** relic, token **6.** memory,
  trophy **7.** memento **8.** keepsake,
  memorial, reminder **11.** remembrance
  12. recollection, remembrancer
sovereign ... **5.** chief, liege, regal, ruler
  6. divine, prince, ruling **7.** empress,
  monarch, supreme **8.** princely,
  superior, suzerain **9.** effectual, gold
  piece, paramount, potentate

11. controlling, independent
sovereign (pert to)...
claim.. 11. seigniorage
coin.. 4. skiv
decree.. 5. arrêt
pardon.. 7. amnesty
petty.. 8. tetrarch
power.. 6. throne
sovereignty... 5. realm 6. diadem,
   empery, empire 7. dynasty, scepter
   (sceptre) 8. dominion 9. supremacy
Soviet, Russian (pert to)...
committee.. 9. presidium
farm.. 7. sovkhoz (sovkhose)
government.. 9. Communism,
   Sovietism 10. Bolshevism
hero.. 5. Lenin
newspaper.. 6. Pravda 8. Izvestia
police, secret service.. 3. KGB
sow... 3. pig 4. gilt, seed 5. plant
   7. implant, scatter 8. disperse,
   squander 9. broadcast
   10. salamander 11. disseminate
sow bug... 6. slater
sow thistle... 7. Sonchus
soybean... 4. Soja 8. soya bean
soybean enzyme... 6. urease
spa... 3. Ems 4. Bath 5. Baden
   6. Bilina (Bilin), hot tub 7. Jacuzzi (tm)
space... 3. gap 4. area, rank, room,
   time, void 5. blank, inane, niche,
   place, range 6. areola, areole, degree,
   extent, vacuum 7. arrange, expanse
   8. capacity, distance, interval
   9. concourse, elbow room
space (pert to)...
architectural.. 6. metope 8. pediment
blank.. 5. chasm 6. hiatus, lacuna
botany (leaves).. 6. areola
environment.. 5. ambit 8. ambiance
larynx.. 7. glottis
occupied.. 6. volume
ref to.. 5. areal, outer 6. cosmos,
   galaxy, pulsar 7. heavens, lacunal,
   spatial 8. galactic, infinity 9. black
   hole, deep space
storage.. 4. shed 5. attic, depot
   6. cellar, garage 9. storeroom,
   warehouse
theory.. 7. plenism
time.. 8. interval
travel.. 4. NASA 7. reentry, swingby
   8. time warp
traveler.. 5. alien 6. cyborg
   8. aeronaut 9. astronaut, cosmonaut
vehicle.. 6. rocket, Skylab 7. shuttle,
   sputnik
void.. 5. chasm 7. inanity
wall.. 5. niche
spacious... 5. ample, broad, roomy
   9. capacious, expansive, extensive
   10. commodious, far and wide,
   widespread 13. comprehensive
spadassin... 5. bravo 7. duelist
   9. swordsman
spade... 3. dig, loy 4. spud, stag (3–yr
   old), suit (cards) 5. slade 6. shovel
   11. playing card
spade (pert to)...
bone.. 13. shoulder blade
fish.. 5. porgy 10. paddlefish
foot.. 4. toad

grass.. 4. rush
Irish.. 5. slane
money.. 7. Chinese (early)
peat.. 5. slade
triangular.. 5. didle
spae... 6. divine 8. foretell
Spain... see also *Spanish*
cape.. 9. Trafalgar
capital.. 6. Madrid
city.. 4. Irun 5. Cadiz, Lorca
   6. Malaga 7. Cordoba, Granada,
   Seville 8. Valencia
city cathedral.. 9. Saragossa
islands.. 5. Ceuta 6. Canary 7. Melilla
   8. Balearic
mountain.. 8. Asturias, Pyrenees
old name.. 6. Iberia
palace.. 8. Escorial
river.. 4. Ebro, Muga 5. Tagus
span... 3. two 4. arch, join, pair, team
   6. bridge, extend, length, period (time)
   7. breadth, measure, stretch
   8. overarch 9. encompass
spangle... 6. aiglet, sequin 7. glitter,
   sparkle 8. ornament, zecchino
spaniel... 5. trasy 6. cocker
   8. Brittany, springer
Spanish (pert to)...
arbor.. 6. ramada
battle.. 6. Armada (1588)
bayonet.. 5. yucca
boat.. 5. aviso 7. galleon (ship)
Christmas.. 7. Navidad
cloak.. 4. capa 5. manta 6. mantle
   7. zamarra (zamarro)
corral.. 5. atajo
dance.. 5. tango 6. bolero, gitano
   8. fandango, saraband
fabric.. 4. crea (cotton) 5. tiraz (silk)
fortress chief.. 4. caid 7. alcaide
friend.. 5. amigo
fruit.. 8. pimiento
game.. 6. pelota 7. jai alai
garment.. 6. serape 8. mantilla
gift holder.. 6. piñata
gold.. 3. oro 8. El Dorado
governor.. 10. gobernador
grass.. 5. spart 7. esparto
gruel.. 5. atole
gypsy.. 7. zincalo
holiday.. 6. fiesta
horse.. 5. genet 6. jennet 7. caballo
hotel.. 6. posada
house.. 4. casa 6. casita
jar.. 4. olla, tina 6. tinaja
knight.. 8. cavalier 9. caballero
lake.. 4. lago
language.. 6. Basque 7. Catalan,
   Spanish 8. Galician 9. Castilian
mausoleum.. 8. Escorial
musical instrument.. 6. atabel, guitar
   8. castanet
plant.. 3. aji 8. capsicum
porridge.. 5. atole
promenade.. 5. paseo
raisin.. 4. pasa
river.. 3. ria, rio
road.. 6. camino
room.. 5. sala
shawl.. 5. manta 6. serape
sheep.. 6. merino
sherry.. 5. Xeres 7. oloroso

sorcerer.. 5. brujo
street.. 5. calle
three.. 4. tres
title.. 3. don 5. señor 6. señora
   7. hidalgo 8. señorita
trail.. 6. camino
vehicle.. 7. tartana
watch.. 5. reloj
watchtower.. 7. atalaya
watchword.. 6. alerta
watercourse.. 6. arroyo
wind.. 6. solano
window.. 7. ventana
witchcraft.. 8. brujeria
year.. 3. ano
Spanish people ...
chaperone.. 6. duenna
conqueror.. 7. Pizarro
dramatist.. 9. Echegaray (Nobel Prize
   1904)
explorer.. 7. Mendoza
gentleman.. 5. señor 8. cavalier
   9. caballero
God.. 4. Dios
herdsman.. 7. llanero 8. ranchero
hero.. 3. Cid
justice of the peace.. 7. entrada
king.. 6. Aragon 8. Alphonso
lady.. 4. doña 6. señora 8. señorita
letter carrier.. 6. correo
man.. 3. don 6. hombre
monk.. 5. padre
painter.. 4. Dali, Goya 9. Velasquez
peasant.. 7. paisano
people.. 5. genta
pianist.. 6. Iturbi
soldier.. 8. miquelet
soprano.. 4. Bori (Lucrezia)
spar ... 3. box 4. beam, boom, gaff,
   mast, rung, yard 5. sprit, steve
   6. timber 7. dispute, quarrel,
   topmast, yardarm
spare ... 4. lean, thin 5. chary, lanky
   6. afford, exempt, frugal, meager,
   scanty 7. sparing, surplus
   8. preserve 9. duplicate, parsimony
   10. economical, occasional
   11. superfluous 12. parsimonious
spare time ... 7. leisure
sparing ... 5. chary 6. frugal, meager,
   saving, scanty 7. scrimpy, thrifty
   8. merciful, reticent, stinting
   9. scrimping 12. parsimonious
spark ... 4. beau, fire, funk 5. aizle,
   court, dandy, lover 6. incite
   7. diamond, gallant, glitter, modicum,
   sparkle 8. humorist 10. sweetheart
   11. scintillate
sparkle ... 5. flash, gleam, glint, shine,
   trace 7. be smart, be witty, glisten,
   glister, glitter, radiate, reflect,
   spangle, twinkle 8. be lively
   9. coruscate 10. effervesce,
   illuminate 11. scintillate
   13. scintillation
sparkling ... 4. dewy 5. crisp, witty
   6. bright, starry 7. shining
   8. cheerful, eloquent, glittery,
   gorgeous, mousseux (wine)
   9. twinkling 10. glittering, reflecting
   12. effervescent
sparoid fish ... 4. scup 5. porgy

   8. sea bream 10. sheepshead
Sparta, Greece ... see also *Spartan*
   capital.. 7. Laconia (anc)
   kingdom.. 12. Peloponnesus
   river.. 7. Eurotas
spartan ... 5. hardy, stoic
   10. courageous 13. uncomplaining
Spartan (pert to) ...
   army division.. 4. mora 6. lochus
   cipher writing.. 7. scytale
   class (anc).. 8. perioeci
   commander.. 7. lochage
   dog.. 10. bloodhound
   festival.. 6. Carnea 7. Carneia
   king.. 8. Leonidas, Menelaus
   lawgiver.. 8. Lycurgus
   magistrate.. 5. ephor
   native.. 8. Laconian 9. Spartiate
   serf.. 5. helot
spasmodic ... 6. fitful 7. snatchy
   9. excitable, irregular 10. convulsive
   12. intermittent 13. highly wrought
spasmodic (pert to) ...
   disease.. 5. croup 7. tetanus
   inspiration.. 8. hiccough
   twitch.. 3. tic
spat ... 3. row 4. slap, tiff 5. spawn
   6. gaiter, oyster, strike 7. dispute,
   legging, quarrel 10. oysterseed
spate ... 4. gush 5. flood 7. freshet,
   torrent 9. overwhelm, rainstorm
   10. waterspout
spatial ... 5. areal 8. sterical
   11. dimensional
spatter ... 3. wet 4. soil, spot 5. spurt
   6. dabble, splash 7. sputter
   8. splutter, sprinkle
spawn ... 3. ova, roe 4. eggs, germ,
   seed 7. lay eggs 8. generate
   13. numerous issue
speak ... 3. say 4. chat, lisp, talk, toll
   5. orate, utter 6. reveal 7. address,
   chatter, declaim, sputter 8. converse,
   proclaim 9. discourse, pronounce
   10. articulate 11. tell in words
speak (pert to) ...
   affectedly.. 4. mime 5. mince
   against.. 6. oppose
   boastfully.. 4. brag 5. vaunt
      7. enlarge 10. exaggerate
   from memory.. 6. recite
   ill of.. 5. decry 8. backbite
      9. disparage
   noisily.. 4. rant, rime 8. harangue
   offhand.. 11. extemporize
   slowly.. 5. drawl
   softly.. 7. whisper
   under breath.. 5. mouth 6. mumble,
      murmur, mutter 7. grumble
speaker ... 5. sayer 6. lisper, orator,
   proser 8. lecturer 9. demagogue
   10. mouthpiece, prolocutor
   11. spellbinder
speaker of languages ... 8. linguist,
   polyglot
speaking (pert to) ...
   generally.. 7. as a rule, roughly
      12. in the long run
      13. approximately
   of.. 7. apropos 12. incidentally
   offhand.. 13. extemporizing
   privately.. 7. whisper 9. in one's ear

11. into one's ear
publicly.. 7. oratory 11. declamation
style.. 8. fluently
spear... 4. dart, pike, stab 5. catch,
lance 6. pierce, weapon 7. javelin,
missile 9. penetrate
spear (pert to)...
anc Teutons.. 6. framea (fram)
fish.. 3. gig 4. gaff
iron–tipped.. 7. assagai
shaped.. 7. hastate
three–pronged.. 7. trident
two–pronged.. 6. bident
spearfish... 6. marlin 9. quillback
special... 4. rare 5. extra 6. unique
7. notable, unusual 8. concrete,
detailed, favorite, specific, uncommon
10. individual, noteworthy, particular,
restricted 11. distinctive, exceptional
13. extraordinary
special (pert to)...
ability.. 5. forte 6. talent 7. charism
8. charisma
commodity.. 6. leader 7. feature
10. best seller
edition.. 5. extra
favor.. 9. influence, privilege
train.. 5. flier 7. express
10. cannonball
specialist (pert to)...
atomic.. 9. physicist
ear.. 6. aurist 9. otologist
eye.. 7. oculist 15. ophthalmologist
medical.. 6. doctor 7. surgeon
money.. 9. economist
specialty... 5. skill 8. aptitude,
contract 13. particularity
14. characteristic
specie... 4. cash, coin 5. money (hard)
species... 4. kind, sort, type 5. class,
genre, genus, group 7. general,
isotope, mankind, variety 8. category,
humanity 11. Homo sapiens
12. nomenclature
specific... 5. exact, virus 6. remedy
7. limited, precise, special
8. definite, detailed, explicit, peculiar
specificity... 9. haecceity
specify... 4. name 5. limit, state
6. define, detail 8. indicate 9. be
precise, designate, enumerate,
stipulate
specimen... 4. copy 5. model, piece,
taste, token 6. person, sample,
swatch 7. example, pattern
14. representative
specious... 4. fair 5. showy 7. alleged
8. illusory, pleasing 9. plausible
10. ostensible 12. hypocritical
speck... 3. bit, dot, jot, nit 4. blot,
iota, mark, mite, mote, spot, whit
5. fleck, stain 7. blemish 8. particle
10. sand darter
speckled... 6. menald 7. mottled
9. sprinkled 10. variegated
spectacle... 4. show, view 5. scene,
sight 6. wonder 7. diorama, display,
pageant 8. panorama, spyglass
10. exhibition 14. representation
spectacles... 7. glasses
spectator... 6. espier, viewer
7. watcher, witness 8. audience,

beholder, kibitzer, looker–on, observer,
onlooker 9. bystander
specter, spectre... 4. bogy (bogey,
bogie) 5. ghost, shade, spook
6. idolum, spirit, wraith 7. eidolon,
phantom 8. illusion, phantasm,
revenant 10. apparition
spectral... 5. eerie (eery) 6. ghosty,
spooky 7. ghostly, phantom
12. apparitional
speculate... 5. guess, think 6. gamble,
ponder, wonder 8. consider,
meditate, ruminate, theorize
10. deliberate, doctrinize, philosophy
11. contemplate
speculative... 5. risky 9. uncertain
10. thoughtful 11. inquisitive,
theoretical 12. experimental
13. contemplative
speculator... 7. lookout, scalper
8. explorer, observer, theorist
12. investigator
speculum... 7. diopter 9. reflector
sped... 4. hied 5. raced 6. darted,
dashed, let fly 8. galloped, hastened
10. discharged
speech... 5. spiel 6. dilogy, orison
7. address, chatter, diction, oration
8. colloquy, harangue, language
9. elocution, utterance
12. conversation
speech (pert to)...
abusive.. 6. tirade
blunder.. 8. improper, solecism
comb form.. 4. logo
conclusion.. 10. peroration
conversational.. 13. colloquialism
defective.. 10. disphrasia
difficulty.. 9. baryphony
10. baryphonia
famous.. 9. Philippic (Demosthenes)
goddess.. 3. Vac
hasty.. 7. stammer, stumble, stutter
impediment.. 4. lisp 8. betacism,
mytacism
intemperate.. 6. tirade
loss of.. 6. alalia 7. aphasia
movements.. 9. vocimotor
parts.. 4. verb 6. adverb 9. adjective
11. conjunction, preposition
12. interjection
pompous.. 12. magniloquent
provincial.. 6. patois 7. dialect
set speech (drama).. 6. rhesis
term.. 6. zeugma 9. syllepsis
understatement.. 7. litotes
vitriolic.. 6. tirade
voiceless.. 7. spirate
without.. 4. mute 6. alogia
world.. 7. Volapük 9. Esperanto
speechless... 4. dumb, mute 6. silent
7. aphasic 8. taciturn 9. voiceless
speed... 3. fly, hie, run 4. flit, race,
zoom 5. haste, hurry, spurt 6. assist,
go fast, hasten 8. celerity, dispatch,
expedite, promptly, rapidity, velocity
9. posthaste, quickness, swiftness
10. accelerate, expedition, facilitate
12. precipitance
speedily... 4. soon 5. apace 6. presto
7. betimes, quickly, rapidly, swiftly
8. promptly 13. expeditiously

speedy... 4. fast 5. apace, fleet, hasty, quick, rapid, swift 6. prompt, racing, sudden
spell... 4. bout, mean, snap, tell, turn 5. charm, magic, relay, shift 6. glamor, relate, relief, trance 7. explain, relieve, sorcery, syncope 9. take turns 11. abracadabra 12. entrancement 13. substitute for
spell (pert to)...
　binder.. 6. orator 7. charmer, spieler
　bound.. 10. astonished, interested 11. under a spell
　brief.. 4. snap
　in another alphabet.. 13. transliterate
　out.. 7. explain, itemize
　pretended.. 11. abracadabra
　under a spell.. 9. in a trance 10. hypnotized, mesmerized
　with loss of letter.. 7. syncope
spend... 3. use 4. pass 5. waste 6. employ, expend, lavish, weaken 7. consume, exhaust 8. disburse, squander 9. dissipate, sacrifice 10. distribute
spend the summer... 8. estivate (aestivate)
spendthrift... 4. daft 6. waster 7. spender, wastrel 8. prodigal 10. profligate, squanderer
Spenser, Edmund (pert to)...
　character.. 3. Una
　famed as.. 4. poet
　famed work.. 12. Faerie Queene
　poetic stanza.. 10. Spenserian
Spenser's Ireland personified... 5. Irene
spent... 4. paid 5. weary 6. effete, used up, wasted 7. worn out 8. consumed, lavished, tired out 9. exhausted 10. squandered
speos... 4. cave, tomb 6. grotto
sphenoid. 11. wedge-shaped
sphere... 3. orb 4. ball, star 5. arena, earth, field, glove, orbit, realm, scope 6. extent, planet 7. circuit, heavens 8. terrible 10. atmosphere 12. jurisdiction
sphere of...
　action.. 6. domain
　life.. 5. world
　making.. 7. orbific
spherical (pert to)...
　aberration, free from.. 9. aplanatic
　geometry.. 10. magnitudes
　lune.. 7. portion
　magnet.. 8. terrella (terella)
　nearly.. 8. obrotund
　reference to.. 6. rotund 7. globose 9. orbicular 15. celestial bodies
　ungula.. 5. wedge
sphericity... 9. globosity, rotundity, roundness
sphinx (pert to)...
　builder (Great Sphinx).. 6. Khafre (IV Dynasty)
　Great Sphinx site.. 4. Gaza (Egypt)
　Greek myth.. 7. monster (sphinxlike)
　reference to.. 9. enigmatic 11. inscrutable
　Zool.. 8. hawk moth
spice... 4. dill, herb, mace, sage

5. chili, clove 6. cassia, nutmeg, pepper, season, stacte 7. mustard 8. marjoram, pungency 9. condiment, flavoring, fragrance, seasoning
spicy... 3. hot 4. keen, racy, sexy 5. balmy, natty, smart 6. risqué 7. gingery, peppery, piquant, pungent 8. aromatic, fragrant, spirited
spider... 3. cob, pan 5. arain 6. Epeira, katipo, tripod, trivet 7. pokomoo, retiary, skillet, spinner 8. arachnid, attercop, telarian 9. tarantula 10. black widow
spider (pert to)...
　comb form.. 7. arachno
　crab.. 4. Maia (genus)
　fly.. 4. tick
　genus.. 4. Maia 6. Aranea 7. Agalena, Attidae, Pholcus 9. Drassidae
　Gr Myth.. 7. Arachne (Lydian girl)
　Latin.. 6. aranea
　leaping.. 10. saltigrade
　monkey.. 6. ateles, coaita
　nest.. 5. nidus
　scorpion.. 8. pedipalp
　scorpion appendage.. 10. pedipalpus
　study of.. 10. araneology
　web (anc).. 8. attercop
　weblike.. 9. arachnoid
　web-spinning organ.. 9. spinneret
spieler... 5. crier 6. barker, talker 7. sharper, speaker 8. lecturer 9. solicitor 10. ballyhooer
spiffy... 4. fine, neat 5. smart 8. splendid 9. excellent
spigot... 3. peg, tap 5. spile, spout 6. dossil, faucet 7. stopper
spike... 3. cob, ear 4. brob, stab, tine, umbo 5. ament, prong, thorn 6. antler, flower, pierce, spadix 7. amentum, disable, spinule, trenail 10. adulterate 12. tenpenny nail
spikenard... 3. phu (Cretan) 4. herb, nard 8. ointment
spile... 3. pin, rod 4. plug, tube 5. spill, spout, stake 6. Aralia, spigot
spill... 4. blab, fall, shed, slop 5. flosh, waste 6. let out, splash, tumble 7. divulge, scatter 8. downpour, overflow, overture 11. tell secrets
spin... 4. birl, fish, reel, ride, turn 5. swirl, twirl, twist, whirl 6. extend, gyrate, rotate 7. prolong, revolve
spinach (wrinkled)... 5. savoy
spinal (pert to)...
　column.. 9. vertebrae
　cord.. 4. alba 6. myelon (marrow) 16. medulla oblongata
　disease.. 8. myelitis 10. meningitis
　muscle (attached).. 5. psoas
spindle... 3. pin, rod 4. axis, axle, hasp 5. pivot, xeres 6. swivel 7. mandrel
spindle-legged... 4. lean 5. lanky 14. spindle-shanked
spindling... 4. long 5. gawky, leggy 6. skinny 7. slender 11. ineffectual
spine... 3. awn 4. axis, seta 5. chine, ridge, thorn 6. spirit 7. acicula,

courage, process 8. backbone,
spiculum 9. scoliosis (curvature)
12. spinal column

spinel . . . 5. balas (ruby) 7. mineral
8. spinelle

spineless . . . 4. limp, weak 5. frail
10. weak–willed 12. invertebrate

spinet . . . 5. piano 7. giraffe 8. virginal
10. clavichord 11. couched harp,
harpsichord

spinnaker . . . 4. sail

spinner . . . 3. top 4. liar 6. spider,
weaver 8. narrator 9. nighthawk
10. goatsucker 11. storyteller
12. whippoorwill

spinning . . . 6. rotary 7. strobic
8. telarian, whirling 9. revolving

spinning device . . . 5. jenny 7. distaff,
spindle 8. throstle

spiracle . . . 4. pore, vent 7. orifice
8. aperture, blowhole

spiral . . . 4. coil, curl 5. helix 6. galaxy,
volute 7. helical, winding 8. circling,
helicoid 9. corkscrew

spire . . . 4. coil, surl 5. tower, twist,
whorl 6. ascend, finial, summit
7. steeple

spire finial . . . 3. épi

spirit . . . 3. imp, pep, vim 4. dash,
élan, fire, life, mood, pixy, soul
5. demon, devil, fairy, genie, ghost,
heart, metal, pluck, Satan, shade,
spook, verve 6. animus, breath,
energy, fervor, goblin, intent, morale,
pneuma, sprite 7. bravery, courage,
essence, extract, gremlin, specter
8. spiritus 9. animation
10. enterprise, individual 11. real
meaning 12. cheerfulness
13. consciousness

spirit, spirit of (pert to) . . .
avarice . . 6. Mammon
bad . . 6. afreet 7. Amaimon
(Amaymon)
Egypt . . 2. ba, ka 3. akh
English folklore . . 2. po
evil . . 4. jinn 5. Aecto, jinni (jinnel)
6. Azazel, Belial, Erinys 7. Tempter
(The) 9. Beelzebub
female . . 6. undine 7. banshee
good . . 8. Eudaemon
household . . 5. Lares 15. Lares and
Penates
infatuation . . 3. Ate
knights . . 8. errantry
malignant . . 3. Ker
mockery . . 5. Momus
people . . 5. ethos
refined . . 6. elixir
tapping (theory) . . 9. typtology
the air . . 5. Ariel
the sea . . 5. siren 6. Triton
7. mermaid, Neptune 9. Davy Jones

spirited . . . 3. gay 4. gamy, racy
5. brisk, eager, fiery 6. lively, plucky,
spunky 7. dashing, fervent
8. eloquent, generous, vigorous
9. audacious, energetic, spiritoso,
sprightly 10. mettlesome

spiritless . . . 4. dead, dull, meek
5. amort, vapid 6. gloomy
8. dejected, lifeless, listless

9. depressed, heartless
10. despondent, dispirited

spirits (pert to) . . .
Babylonian . . 5. Igigi
dwelling . . 2. po 5. Hades 7. Elysium
low . . 5. blues, dumps, gloom
8. doldrums
of the dead . . 5. Manes (Rom)
7. lemures 9. chthonian (Gr)

spiritual . . . 4. holy, pure, song
5. pious 6. devout, divine, sacred
7. psychic 8. churchly, internal,
platonic, spectral 9. unworldly
10. immaterial 11. disembodied,
incorporeal 12. supernatural
14. ecclesiastical, heavenly minded

spiritual (pert to) . . .
affinity . . 8. soul mate
apathy . . 6. acedia
being . . 3. ens 5. angel 6. seraph
darkness . . 4. Hell 5. tamas
director . . 9. confessor
meaning of words . . 7. anagoge
meeting . . 6. séance
shrine . . 6. adytum 7. sanctum

spirt . . . 3. jet 4. gush 5. flare, spurt
6. squirt

spit . . . 3. rod 4. rain 5. eject, image,
stick 6. impale, pierce, saliva,
skewer, sputum 7. hissing, spindle,
sputter 8. likeness, sprinkle, turnspit
9. exsputory 11. expectorate

spite . . . 3. vex 4. hate 5. pique,
shame, venom 6. enmity, malice,
offend, thwart 7. dislike, ill will
8. disgrace, dishonor 9. animosity,
cattiness, humiliate 10. resentment
11. malevolence 12. spitefulness

spiteful . . . 4. mean 5. catty 7. cattish
8. annoying 9. malicious, malignant
10. irritating, vindictive

spittoon . . . 6. pigdan 8. crachoir,
cuspidor

splash . . . 3. lap, wet 4. spot 5. spray,
swash 6. blotch, flouse (floush),
ripple 7. scatter, spatter, splurge
8. cut a dash, splatter 9. dashingly
14. ostentatiously

splashboard . . . 4. gate (false) 5. plank
6. fender, screen 9. dashboard
10. flashboard, flushboard

splay . . . 3. hem 4. turn 5. adorn,
carve, slant, slope 6. clumsy,
expand, spread 7. awkward, display
9. dislocate, displayed, expansion

spleen . . . 3. fit 4. fire, mood, whim
5. anger, ardor, freak, gland
6. malice, temper 7. impulse 8. ill
humor 10. low spirits, melancholy,
resentment 11. impetuosity

spleen (pert to) . . .
amarinth . . 4. weed
excision . . 13. splenectomize
reference to . . 6. lienal 7. splenic

splendid . . . 4. braw, fine 5. grand,
regal, showy 6. costly, superb
7. gallant, shining, sublime
8. glorious, gorgeous 9. beautiful,
brilliant, excellent, sumptuous
10. brilliance, effulgence
11. illustrious, magnificent

splendor . . . 4. gite, pomp 5. éclat,

glory 6. beauty, luster 7. display
8. grandeur, radiance, richness
9. pageantry, showiness 10. brilliance
12. gorgeousness, magnificence,
resplendence

splint . . . 4. scob, tace 5. brace, plate,
strip 6. fasten, tasset 7. confine

splinter . . . 4. chip 5. break, broom
6. shiver, sliver 7. shatter
8. fragment 9. matchwood

split . . . 3. cut, rit 4. chap, open, rend,
rent, rive, tear 5. break, burst, cleft,
crack, laugh, leave (sl), riven, wedge
6. bisect, cleave, cloven, depart (sl),
divide, sunder 7. dispart, divided,
rupture, shatter 8. separate
9. apportion, partition 10. separation

split (pert to) . . .
hairs . . 7. quibble 12. discriminate
13. differentiate
into two parts . . 5. bifid 6. cloven
pea . . 3. dal 5. dahll
the difference . . 5. share 7. average
10. compromise 12. go fifty–fifty
up . . 5. cleft 7. disband, divorce
8. separate 9. apportion, partition

spoil . . . 3. mar, rot 4. loot, prey, ruin,
sack 5. botch, decay, harry
6. coddle, impair, injure, pamper
7. destroy, estrepe, louse up (sl),
pillage, plunder, vitiate 9. frustrate

spoilation . . . 6. rapine 7. pillage
10. plundering, spoliation

spoiled . . . 3. bad 5. moldy, musty
6. addled, marred, molded, preyed,
wasted 7. botched, bungled, decayed,
tainted 8. pampered, pillaged
9. plundered 12. deteriorated

spoiler . . . 6. robber 7. marplot
8. pillager 9. despoiler, plunderer

spoils . . . 4. loot, prey, swag 5. booty,
perks (sl) 11. perquisites

spoilsport . . . 7. marplot 10. wet
blanket 11. party–pooper

spoke . . . 3. bar, pin, ray, rod 4. rung,
said 5. check, round, spake, stake
6. radius, speech 7. uttered
9. hindrance 10. impediment

spoke monotonously . . . 6. droned

spoken . . . 4. oral 5. parol
9. declaimed, ideophone (word)

spoliation . . . 6. rapine 7. pillage
8. ravaging 10. spoilation

sponge . . . 3. dry, wet 4. bath, swab
5. erase, mooch 6. absorb, animal,
efface, eraser, extort 7. badiaga,
cleanse, sponger, zimocca
8. drunkard, parasite 9. absorbent,
sycophant 10. obliterate, porousness

sponge (pert to) . . .
Europe . . 7. badiaga
fruit . . 5. luffa (loofah)
Mediterranean . . 7. zimocca
opening . . 7. apopyle
orifice . . 7. osculum
young . . 5. ascon 6. rhagon

sponger . . . 4. sorn 5. leech 6. cadger
7. moocher 8. parasite 9. scrounger
10. freeloader

sponsor . . . 5. angel 6. backer, patron
7. finance 9. financier, godparent,
guarantee, guarantor, patronize

sponsorship . . . 5. aegis (egis)
7. subsidy 8. auspices

spontaneous . . . 4. free 6. native
8. untaught 9. automatic, voluntary
10. self–acting 11. instinctive,
involuntary

spontoon . . . 4. club, pike 7. halberd,
pantoon 9. espantoon, truncheon

spoof . . . 3. guy 4. fool, hoax, joke
5. trick 7. deceive, swindle
8. nonsense 9. deception

spook . . . 5. ghost 6. spirit, zombie
(zombi) 7. specter 8. frighten
9. hobgoblin 10. apparition

spooky . . . 5. eerie, weird 7. ghostly,
haunted, uncanny 8. spectral

spool . . . 4. reel, wind 6. bobbin
7. spindle 8. cylinder

spoon . . . 4. club 5. labis, ladle
6. shovel 7. fish for 8. cochlear,
make love, runcible

spoonbill . . . 5. ajaja (ayaya)
9. sandpiper

Spoon River poet . . . 7. Masters (E L)

spore (pert to) . . .
capsule, sac . . 5. ascus, theca
10. sporangium
cluster . . 5. sorus
formation . . 6. tetrad
fruit . . 7. asocarp

sport . . . 3. fun, toy 4. game, hunt, jest,
joke, play, romp, wear 5. dandy,
mirth 6. banter, flaunt, frolic, gamble,
racing, skiing 7. contest, gambler,
jesting, mockery, pastime 8. raillery
9. amusement, bon vivant, diversion,
good loser, plaything, sportsman
10. pleasantry, recreation
13. entertainment

sport (pert to) . . .
art of (contests) . . 10. agonistics
cheap . . 5. piker
of kings . . 6. racing 7. the turf

sportive . . . 3. gay 5. merry 7. jocular,
playful 8. frolicky, playsome
9. facetious 10. frolicsome

sports . . . 5. Rugby, track 6. hockey, jai
lai, soccer, squash, tennis 7. cricket
8. baseball, football, la crosse, softball
9. athletics, palaestra 10. acrobatics,
gymnastics 11. racquetball

sports attendance . . . 4. gate

sports official . . . 5. coach, judge
6. umpire 7. referee 8. linesman
10. timekeeper

sporty . . . 5. rorty, showy 6. dressy,
flashy

spot . . . 3. dot 4. blet, blot, espy, flaw,
mark, site, soil 5. fleck, place, point,
speck, stain, taint 6. detect, locate,
macula, macule, stigma 7. asperse,
blemish, freckle, observe, speckle,
splotch 8. discolor, disgrace, locality,
location, position 9. bespatter,
limelight, recognize 11. predicament,
small amount

spot (pert to) . . .
cards . . 3. pip
fertile . . 5. oasis
fish . . 7. pinfish
high . . 4. apex 5. climax
mineral . . 5. macle

on the spot.. 3. now 4. here
7. imperil, present 8. promptly
payment.. 4. cash
secluded.. 6. alcove
sun.. 6. lucule 7. granule
wood.. 3. wem
spotless... 4. pure 5. clean 6. chaste
8. innocent 9. blameless, faultless,
unsullied 10. immaculate
11. unblemished, untarnished
14. irreproachable
spotted... 6. espied, marked, soiled
7. dappled, guttate (droplike),
mottled, stained, sullied 8. speckled
9. blemished, sprinkled, tarnished
11. diversified
spouse... 4. mate, wife 5. bride
7. consort, partner 9. companion
10. better half
spout... 3. jet, jut, lip 4. dale, gush,
pawn, rant, spew 5. erupt, spile,
spurt 6. pledge, recite, spigot, squirt,
trough 7. chatter, conduit, declaim
8. downpour, gargoyle (carved)
9. discharge, waterfall
10. waterspout
spouter... 5. whale 6. geyser 7. oil
well, speaker 9. declaimer
11. speechifier
sprat... 6. garvie 7. herring
8. sixpence
spray... 3. jet 4. foam 5. stour, water
6. squirt 7. atomize, flowers, gunfire
8. perfumer, sprinkle 9. spindrift
10. spoondrift
spread... 3. ted 4. meal 5. bruit,
feast, flare, strew, widen 6. expand,
extent, sprawl, unfurl 7. divulge,
radiate, scatter 8. disperse
9. broadcast 11. disseminate
13. advertisement
spread (pert to)...
by defamation.. 5. libel
by report.. 6. norate
by rumor.. 5. noise
eagle.. 8. boastful, insignia
9. patriotic 12. exaggeration
out.. 3. fan 4. open, span 5. flare
6. deploy
over.. 5. cover, smear
thickly.. 7. slather
thin.. 4. bray
spree... 4. lark, orgy, romp 5. binge,
revel 6. bender, frolic, shindy
7. wassail 8. carousal
sprig... 4. trim, twig 5. scion, shoot,
smart 6. active, spruce 8. ornament
9. youngling
sprightly... 3. gay 4. airy, pert
5. alive, brisk, peart 6. blithe, lively
7. briskly, ghostly 8. vigorous
10. enlivening, spiritedly
11. incorporeal
spring... 3. fly, hop, spa 4. dart, font,
jump, leap, well 5. shoot, spurt,
vault, vigor 6. bounce, energy,
geyser, origin, season, source
9. saltation 10. elasticity, resilience
spring (pert to)...
back.. 6. recoil, resile 7. rebound
of the Muses.. 7. Pierian
ref to.. 6. vernal

up.. 4. grow 5. arise, occur
6. appear, ascend 9. originate
springing into being..: 9. renascent
springs... 4. spas 5. baths, fonts
6. resort (health) 7. thermae
sprinkle... 3. deg, dot, wet 4. rain
5. bedew, spray, strew, water
6. bedrop, sparge, spreng 7. baptize,
scatter 9. bespatter
sprinkler... 11. aspergillum (Eccl)
sprinkle with...
flour.. 6. dredge
grit.. 4. sand
heraldic.. 4. semé
powder.. 4. dust
water.. 3. deg
sprint... 3. run 4. dash, race
sprite... 3. elf, fay, hob, imp, nix
4. peri 5. fairy, ghost, gnome, pixie,
sylph 6. goblin, spirit 7. brownie
9. hobgoblin 10. apparition
sprite (pert to)...
fiction.. 5. Ariel
Irish.. 10. leprechaun
mischievous.. 4. Puck
ref to.. 6. elfish
sprocket... 5. tooth, wheel 8. cylinder
(toothed) 10. projection
sprout... 3. bud, son 4. cion, grow
5. scion, shoot, spire, sprit
6. branch, ratoon, tiller 7. burgeon,
upstart 8. offshoot 9. germinate
10. descendant
spruce... 4. chic, neat, posh, smug,
tree, trig, trim 5. adorn, natty, smart
6. dapper 7. finical, smarten
8. titivate
spruce (pert to)...
beverage.. 4. beer
black.. 7. yew pine
fir.. 6. Norway
genus.. 5. Abies, Picea
Japanese.. 6. Alcock
type.. 7. Douglas, hemlock
white.. 8. épinette
sprue... 5. dross, waste 6. thrush
7. disease 8. psilosis 9. asparagus
spry... 5. agile, brisk, quick, smart
6. active, nimble 8. vigorous
9. sprightly
spud... 5. drill, knife, spade 6. dagger,
paddle, potato, reamer, shovel
spume... 4. foam, scum 5. froth
spunky... 4. game 5. quick 6. plucky,
touchy 8. spirited 10. courageous,
mettlesome 13. quick–tempered
spur... 3. egg 4. goad, move, urge
5. drive, press, ridge, rowel, spine
6. calcar, excite, griffe, incite, needle
7. provoke 8. stimulus 9. instigate,
stimulate 10. incitement
spur (pert to)...
badge.. 10. knighthood
fowl.. 5. quail 9. partridge
gamecock's.. 4. gaff 7. gablock
mountain.. 5. arête
pert to.. 7. spicate
railroad.. 5. track
wheel.. 5. rowel
spurious... 4. fake, sham 5. false
6. pseudo 7. bastard 10. adulterate,
apocryphal, artificial, fictitious,

fraudulent 11. counterfeit
12. illegitimate 14. supposititious
spurious (pert to)...
  fruit.. 10. pseudocarp
  olive... 9. heartwood
  rainbow.. 8. faint arc
  wing.. 7. bastard
spurn... 4. defy 5. scorn 6. reject,
  strike 7. contemn, disdain
spurt... 3. jet, jut 4. dash, gush, spew
  5. burst, spout 7. outpour, upsurge
  8. outbreak
spy... 3. pry, see 4. espy, note, tout
  5. scout, sneak, snoop, watch
  6. behold, descry, detect, search
  7. examine, snooper 8. discover,
  emissary, informer, perceive
  10. scrutinize 11. reconnoiter
spy (pert to)...
  city.. 7. Belgium
  in clothing circles.. 4. keek
  Man of.. 14. paleolithic man
  prison.. 6. mouton
squab... 3. fat 4. fowl, sofa 5. piper,
  plump 6. fat man, pigeon 7. cushion
  8. nestling 9. fledgling
squabble... 5. brawl 6. bicker, jangle
  7. contend, quarrel, wrangle
  10. disarrange (Print)
  13. collieshangie
squad... 4. team, unit 5. posse
  7. company
squalid... 4. foul, mean, poor 5. dirty
  6. filthy, sordid 7. unclean
  8. slovenly 9. repellent, repulsive
  11. squalidness 15. poverty–stricken
squall... 3. cry, row 4. blow, gale,
  gust, wail, wind, yell 6. squawk,
  squeal 9. commotion 11. disturbance
squalor... 4. dirt, mire 5. filth
  8. slovenry 9. dirtiness 10. filthiness
  11. squalidness 16. unkempt
  condition
squander... 5. waste 6. lavish
  7. scatter 8. disperse, misspend
  9. dissipate, throw away 10. run
  through
squanderer... 5. loser 7. wastrel
square... 4. even, meal 5. bribe, plaza
  6. common, honest, settle 7. exactly,
  obelisk, old fogy 8. absolute, cube
  face, directly, equalize, quadrate
  9. city block, divergent
  11. unequivocal 13. parallelogram
  14. unsophisticate
  15. straightforward
squash... 4. mash, pepo, pulp
  5. crush, gourd, press 6. cushaw,
  refute, simlin, simnel, soften
  7. cymling (cymbling), Hubbard,
  squeeze 8. pattypan, suppress
  9. crookneck 10. extinguish
  11. calabazilla
squat... 3. low 5. dumpy, pudgy,
  quash, stoop 6. crouch, hunker,
  settle, stubby 7. sit down
  8. squatter, thickset
squatter... 6. nester (illegal) 7. pioneer
  9. sandpiper 11. homesteader
Squatter State... 6. Kansas
squaw... 6. coween, Indian, mahala
  (mahaly)

squeal... 6. betray, inform 7. protest,
  quarrel
squealer... 4. fink 6. grouse, pigeon,
  plover 7. traitor 8. informer
squeamish... 4. nice 5. dizzy
  6. dainty, queasy 7. prudish
  8. overnice, qualmish 9. nauseated
  10. fastidious, scrupulous
squeeze... 3. hug, jam, nip 4. cram,
  crux 5. crowd, crush, pinch, press,
  wring 6. crisis, extort 7. embrace
  8. compress 9. constrict, influence
  10. constraint 11. compression
squeezer, fruit... 6. juicer, reamer
squelch... 5. crush, quash, quell
  6. rebuke, refute, subdue 7. repress,
  silence 8. suppress 10. disconcert
squib... 4. bomb, fuse, pipe, skit, tube
  6. speech, squirt 7. explode,
  lampoon, writing 9. bespatter
  10. pasquinade 11. firecracker
squire... 4. beau 5. court, lover
  6. escort 7. gallant 8. henchman,
  nobleman 9. attendant, gentleman,
  landowner
squirm... 5. twist 6. wiggle, writhe
  7. wriggle
squirrel (pert to)...
  African.. 5. xerus
  American.. 5. bunny 7. assapan
    8. chipmunk 9. chickaree
  American, flying.. 7. assapan
  Asian.. 5. sisel 6. suslik
  Austral, flying.. 9. phalanger
  burrowing.. 6. gopher
  cage.. 9. treadmill
  color.. 4. lead
  E Ind, flying.. 6. taguan
  fish.. 7. serrano
  fur (Her).. 4. vair
  genus.. 6. Tamias 7. Sciurus
  Java.. 8. jelerong
  like.. 8. sciuroid
  nest.. 4. dray, drey
  shrew.. 4. tana 6. Tupaia
  skin.. 4. vair
  Spanish.. 7. ardilla
squirrellike mammal... 8. banxring,
  dormouse
stab... 4. gore, pang, pink 5. knife,
  knive, lunge, wound 6. attack, injury,
  pierce, thrust 7. poniard, slander
  8. puncture, stoccado
stability... 5. poise 7. balance
  8. firmness, strength 9. constancy
  10. permanence, stableness,
  steadiness 11. reliability
  12. immovability, immutability
  13. steadfastness
stabilize... 3. set 5. poise 6. steady
  7. ballast 8. regulate
stable... 3. mew (Royal) 4. barn, byre,
  firm, safe 5. fixed, solid, sound, stall
  6. steady, strong 7. durable, lasting,
  paddock, support 8. constant, reliable
  9. confirmed, permanent, steadfast
  10. stationary, unwavering
  11. established, trustworthy
stableman... 5. groom 7. hostler
  (ostler)
staccato... 7. détaché 8. ricochet
  12. disconnected

stack... 4. heap, load, pile, rick
5. mound, shock 6. pile up
7. chimney, conduit 8. quantity
stacked... 11. accumulated,
prearranged
stacked pack, cards... 8. cold deck
stadium... 5. stage 6. course, dromos
8. foot race (anc)
stadium race, start... 7. aphesis
staff... 3. rod 4. club, mace, pole
5. baton, music, stave 7. scepter,
support 8. caduceus, insignia,
pastoral 9. personnel 10. assistants,
associates
staff (pert to)...
Bacchus.. 7. thyrsus
bearer.. 5. macer
magician's.. 7. rhabdos
marshal's.. 5. baton
member, officer.. 4. aide 7. attaché
mountain climbing.. 10. alpenstock
pastoral.. 5. pedum 7. baculus,
crosier (crozier)
shepherd's.. 5. crook, pedum
sovereign's.. 7. scepter (sceptre)
stag... 4. colt, deer (red), hart
5. party, royal, spade 7. male fox,
pollard 8. gamecock, informer
stage... 4. dais, tier 5. arena, phase,
scene 6. degree 7. display, estrade,
perform, rostrum 8. platform, scaffold
9. dramatize, gradation
10. proscenium, stagecoach
stage (pert to)...
call (trumpet).. 6. sennet
direction.. 5. aside, manet 6. sennet
of disease.. 9. catabasis
of insects.. 5. imago, larva
part.. 5. stair 8. dutchman (patch)
10. proscenium
scene (side).. 8. coulisse
scenery.. 3. set
stagger... 4. reel, stot, stun, sway,
walk 5. lurch 6. excite, totter, zigzag
7. be drunk, tremble, vibrate
8. astonish, flounder, frighten,
titubate, unsettle 9. alternate,
fluctuate
staggering... 5. areel 9. startling
10. astounding 11. the staggers
12. unbelievable
Stagirite, The... 9. Aristotle
stagnant... 4. dull, foul 5. inert, stale,
still 8. inactive, sluggish, standing
10. motionless, not flowing
13. unprogressive
stagnate... 3. rot 4. dull 5. inert
8. stagnant, vegetate 10. motionless
staid... 5. grave, sober 6. demure,
sedate, solemn 7. serious, settled
8. composed, decorous, sensible
9. steadfast
stain... 3. dye 4. blot, soil, spot, tint
5. color, paint, smear, sully
6. infamy, smudge, stigma
7. blemish, corrupt, pigment, tarnish
8. discolor, disgrace, dishonor,
maculate 9. pollution 10. stigmatize
11. contaminate 13. discoloration
stained by decay... 4. doty
stained glass rod (lead)... 4. came
stair... 4. step 5. riser, stage, tread

6. degree, flight (series)
staircase (pert to)...
French.. 8. escalier
moving.. 9. escalator
outdoor.. 6. perron
post.. 5. newel
ship's.. 12. companionway
spiral.. 8. caracole
stairs to bath (Ind)... 4. ghat (ghaut)
stake... 3. bet, peg, pel, pin 4. ante,
pale, pile, post, risk, spit 5. sowel,
teest, wager 6. chance, estate,
gamble, hazard, picket, pledge
7. finance, venture
stale... 3. old 5. banal, fusty, trite,
vapid 7. insipid, spoiled
9. hackneyed, tasteless 10. flavorless
11. commonplace
stalemate... 6. corner 7. impasse
8. cul–de–sac, deadlock 10. blind
alley, standstill
stalk... 4. axis, hunt, risp, stem, walk
6. pursue, stride 7. pedicel
8. peduncle 11. reconnoiter
stalk (pert to)...
cotton, sugar cane.. 6. ratoon
dry.. 3. hay, kex 5. haulm (halm)
flower.. 7. petiole
grain, grass.. 4. culm 5. straw
6. ressum
strawberry.. 4. risp
stalkless... 7. sessile
stall... 3. cot, pew 4. crib, fail, loge,
mire, stop 5. booth, check, choir,
stick 6. hinder, manger, stable
7. disgust 9. temporize 10. dillydally
11. compartment 12. parking space
13. procrastinate
stalwart... 5. brave, stout 6. strong,
sturdy 7. valiant 8. partisan, resolute
9. corpulent 10. courageous,
unyielding
stamina... 5. pluck, vigor 7. courage
8. backbone, strength 9. endurance,
fortitude 12. staying power
stammer... 3. haw, hem 4. mant
6. falter 7. stumble, stutter
8. hesitate
stammering... 8. psellism
stamp... 3. die 4. date, dink, form,
mark, seal, sign, tool 5. brand, infix,
label 6. signet 7. engrave, impress,
imprint, postage, trading 8. tressure
(tressour) 11. endorsement
14. characteristic
stamp (pert to)...
border.. 8. tressure (tressour)
collecting.. 9. philately
collector.. 11. philatelist
madness.. 11. timbromania
paper.. 6. pelure
postage.. 6. timbre
space.. 8. spandrel
stampede... 3. run 4. rout, rush
5. panic 6. flight 7. debacle
11. wild scamper
stance... 4. pose 7. posture, station
8. position
stanch... 5. allay, check, quell
6. steady, strong 7. zealous
8. faithful 9. steadfast 10. extinguish
11. substantial

stanchion... 3. bar 4. post, prop
  5. brace, piton 6. secure 7. support,
  upright
stand... 4. bear, bier, halt, rack, stop,
  zarf 5. abide, arise, booth, easel,
  store, table 6. endure, tripod
  7. coaster, étagère, footing, impasse,
  sustain, taboret 8. attitude, foothold,
  pedestal, position, tolerate
  9. withstand 10. standstill
stand (pert to)...
  against.. 6. resist
  by.. 3. aid 6. defend 7. support
    9. be present
  cost of.. 5. treat
  Eccl.. 4. ambo
  for.. 6. permit, typify 9. represent,
    symbolize
  for candles.. 7. epergne
    10. candelabra
  in.. 6. deputy 10. substitute
  it.. 4. bear 5. brook 6. suffer
  offish.. 4. cold 5. aloof 8. reserved
    10. not cordial
  opposite.. 4. face
  three–legged.. 6. teapoy, tripod, trivot
  up to.. 5. brave 6. resist
standard... 3. par 4. flag, norm
  5. grade, model, usual 6. ensign
  7. average, classic, paragon, precept
  8. orthodox 9. customary, principle
  13. authoritative
standard (pert to)...
  battle.. 9. oriflamme (oriflamb)
  bearer.. 6. leader 7. officer
    10. politician
  chem test.. 5. titer (titre)
  ensign.. 8. gonfalon, gonfanon
  flag (Rom).. 8. vexillum
  of excellence.. 4. idea
  of intelligence.. 5. Binet
  of light.. 6. carcel
  of quantity.. 4. unit
  Ottoman Emp.. 4. alem
standardize... 9. calibrate, normalize
standing... 4. rank 5. fixed, state
  6. at rest, status 7. footing, settled,
  station, upright 8. duration, prestige
  9. permanent 10. durability,
  reputation
standing (pert to)...
  long.. 7. durable 8. duration
    11. traditional
  mode of.. 6. stance
  out.. 7. eminent, salient
  room only.. 3. SRO
  social.. 6. estate, status 8. prestige
  upright.. 11. orthostatic
stannum... 2. Sn 3. tin
stanza... 4. rann, unit 5. stave, verse
  6. octave, sestet 7. strophe, triolet
  (8–lined)
stanza scheme... 6. ballad 10. Gray's
  Elegy, Spenserian
star... 3. sun 4. hero, lead 5. actor,
  shine 6. étoile 7. destiny, fortune
  8. asterisk, insignia, ornament
  9. emphasize, principal
  11. hummingbird 12. heavenly body,
  luminous body
star (pert to)... see also *Stars*
  brightest.. 3. Cor, sun 5. Deneb

  6. Altair, Lucida, Sirius
Bull's Eye.. 9. Aldebaran
divination.. 9. astrology
Dog.. 4. Sept 6. Sirius 8. Canicula
  12. Canis Majoris
evening.. 5. Venus 6. Hesper, Vesper
  7. evestar 8. Hesperus
feather.. 9. comatulid
five–pointed.. 9. pentagram, pentalpha
French.. 6. étoile
gazer.. 4. fish 10. astronomer
giant.. 10. Betelgeuse (Betelgeux)
group (fixed).. 13. constellation
guiding.. 5. Alpha, North 7. Polaris
  8. Cynosure, loadstar, lodestar,
  polestar
large.. 5. Rigel
morning.. 4. Mars 5. Venus 6. Saturn
  7. daystar, Jupiter, Mercury
  8. Phosphor
new.. 4. Nova
North.. 7. Polaris 8. loadstar, lodestar
of Africa.. 15. Cullinan diamond
of Bethlehem (Bib).. 11. guide of
  Magi
of the sea.. 11. Maris Stella (Stella
  Maris)
ornament.. 4. semé
path.. 5. orbit
ref to.. 6. astral, starry 7. sideral,
  stellar 8. sidereal 9. planatoid
representation.. 6. étoile
shooting.. 5. comet 6. Leonid, meteor
starch... 3. vim 4. sago 5. hilum,
  vigor 6. amidin, energy, farina, fecula
  7. cassava 8. glycogen 9. arrowroot,
  formality, stiffness
starchy... 5. stiff 6. formal, viscid
  7. amyloid, precise 9. unbending
stare... 4. gape, gawk, gaze, look,
  ogle, peer 5. glare 6. glower,
  goggle, wonder
starfish... 7. asteria 10. echinoderm
stark... 4. bare, mere 5. rigid, tense
  6. barren, wholly 7. violent
  8. absolute, complete, entirely
  9. downright, unadorned
  10. absolutely
starling... 4. myna, sali 6. pastor
Stars (pert to)...
  and Bars.. 15. Confederate flag
  belt, tract (luminous).. 6. Galaxy
    8. Milky Way
  circumpolar group.. 5. Draco
    6. Dragon
  four (famed).. 4. Crux 13. Southern
    Cross
  North Pole group.. 9. Great Bear
    10. Little Bear 11. Septentrion
  Ursa Major.. 9. Big Dipper, Great
    Bear
  Ursa Minor.. 10. Little Bear 12. Little
    Dipper
start... 4. dart, dash, jerk, rush
  5. begin, enter, sally 6. broach,
  origin, twitch 7. get away, startle
  8. commence 9. advantage,
  beginning, departure, originate
  10. inaugurate
starting point... 4. text (sermon)
  7. scratch 9. departure
startle... 5. alarm, rouse, scare, shock

6. excite, fright 8. astonish
9. electrify
starve... 3. die 4. kill 5. crave
6. famish, perish, scrimp 7. atrophy,
destroy 10. be indigent
starved... 4. thin 5. empty 6. frozen,
hungry 8. famished, ravenous
starwort... 5. aster 9. colicroot
stash... 5. cache, plant, store 7. lay
away 8. hide away
state... 3. say 4. aver, case, état,
mode, tell 5. utter 6. affirm, allege,
assert, plight, recite, remark, report
7. country, declare, expound,
express, narrate 8. announce,
propound 9. condition, enunciate,
postulate, pronounce, territory
10. government, possession
11. body politic 12. circumstance,
commonwealth
state (pert to)...
a fact.. 4. aver 5. posit 6. avouch
7. declare
agitated.. 9. disturbed, perturbed
disordered.. 9. cluttered
formally.. 8. propound 9. enunciate,
pronounce
French.. 4. état
hypnotic.. 6. trance
ideal.. 6. Utopia
office.. 8. governor 11. secretariat
on oath.. 6. depose
police.. 7. trooper
reference.. 6. statal
secret.. 7. arcanum
specifically.. 6. define 7. itemize
13. particularize
treasury.. 4. fisc 6. fiscus
ultimate.. 3. end
under foreign control..
12. protectorate
without proof.. 6. allege
stately... 5. grand, largo, lofty, regal,
royal 6. august, coldly, kingly
7. haughty, queenly, togated
8. eloquent, imperial, imposing,
majestic 9. dignified, grandiose
11. magnificent
statement... 4. bill, list 5. audit, dixit
6. dictum, remark, report, resumé
7. account, invoice, premise
8. abstract, proposal, schedule
9. affidavit, assertion, manifesto
10. accounting, expression, recitation
11. declaration 12. announcement,
presentation
statement (pert to)...
abridged.. 6. précis, resumé
7. summary 10. abridgment
11. abridgement
assumed true.. 7. premise
contradictory.. 7. paradox
defamatory.. 5. libel
detailed.. 8. schedule
dogmatic.. 6. dictum
introductory.. 5. proem 7. preface,
prelude 8. foreword, prologue
legal.. 11. declaration
mathematical.. 7. theorem
of belief.. 5. credo, creed
of introduction.. 8. prologue
precise.. 8. aphorism

self–evident.. 6. truism
sworn.. 9. affidavit
State nicknames...
Alabama.. 6. Cotton 12. Heart of
Dixie, Yellowhammer
Alaska.. (no official)
Arizona.. 11. Grand Canyon
Arkansas.. 17. Land of Opportunity
California.. 6. Golden
Colorado.. 10. Centennial
Connecticut.. 6. Nutmeg
Delaware.. 5. First
Florida.. 8. Sunshine
Georgia.. 5. Peach
Hawaii.. 5. Aloha
Idaho.. 3. Gem
Illinois.. 7. Prairie
Indiana.. 7. Hoosier
Iowa.. 7. Hawkeye
Kansas.. 9. Sunflower
Kentucky.. 9. Bluegrass
Louisiana.. 7. Pelican
Maine.. 8. Pine Tree
Maryland.. 4. Free 7. Old Line
Massachusetts.. 3. Bay 9. Old Colony
Michigan.. 9. Wolverine
Minnesota.. 6. Gopher 9. North Star
Mississippi.. 8. Magnolia
Missouri.. 6. Show Me
Montana.. 8. Treasure
Nebraska.. 4. Beef 10. Cornhusker
Nevada.. 6. Silver 9. Sagebrush
New Hampshire.. 7. Granite
New Jersey.. 6. Garden
New Mexico.. 17. Land of
Enchantment
New York.. 6. Empire
North Carolina.. 7. Tarheel 8. Old
North
North Dakota.. 5. Sioux 11. Flickertail
Ohio.. 7. Buckeye
Oklahoma.. 6. Sooner
Oregon.. 6. Beaver
Pennsylvania.. 8. Keystone
Rhode Island.. 11. Little Rhody
South Carolina.. 8. Palmetto
South Dakota.. 6. Coyote 8. Sunshine
Tennessee.. 9. Volunteer
Texas.. 8. Lone Star
Utah.. 7. Beehive
Vermont.. 13. Green Mountain
Virginia.. 11. Old Dominion
Washington.. 9. Evergreen
West Virginia.. 8. Mountain
Wisconsin.. 6. Badger
Wyoming.. 8. Equality
state of...
dissension.. 8. scission
disuse.. 9. desuetude
ecstasy.. 6. trance 7. rapture
8. paradise
hostility.. 6. feudal
mind.. 4. mood 5. humor 6. morale
8. attitude
unconsciousness.. 4. coma 5. faint
state of being...
a layman.. 9. laicality
artless.. 7. naiveté
a son.. 7. sonship
a woman.. 10. muliebrity
behindhand.. 9. in arrears
beyond natural laws.. 12. supernatural

complete.. 9. plenitude
confined.. 10. internment
free from error.. 9. inerrancy
married twice, illegally.. 6. bigamy
married twice, legally.. 6. digamy
overfull.. 8. plethora
passive.. 9. stolidity
poison.. 5. toxic 8. toxicity
voiced.. 7. sonancy
worse.. 8. pejority
wrong.. 7. errancy
static... 5. inert, noise 6. stable
7. resting 8. electric, inactive
9. quiescent 10. stationary
12. atmospherics, interference
station... 4. fire, post, rank, seat, stop
5. berth, depot, place, radio, serai
6. health, police 7. calling, dignity
8. location, position, prestige
9. situation 11. institution
stationary... 3. set 5. fixed, still
6. stable, static, stator 8. immobile
9. immovable 10. motionless,
unchanging
stationery... 3. pen 5. paper 6. pencil
9. onionskin, papeterie 12. writing
paper
statue... 4. bust 5. image 8. acrolith,
figurine, monument 9. sculpture,
statuette
statue (pert to)...
at Thebes.. 6. Memnon
gigantic.. 8. Colossus
Guildhall (London).. 3. Gog 5. Magog
holy.. 4. icon (ikon)
male figure (support).. 7. telamon
part.. 5. socle, trunk 6. plinth
primitive.. 6. xoanon
Pygmalion's.. 7. Galatea
world wonder.. 6. Helios (Rhodes)
status... 4. rank 5. class, state
7. station 8. position, prestige,
standing
status symbol... 11. swivel chair
statute... 3. act, jus, law, lex
5. bylaw, canon, edict, title
6. decree, rubric, treaty 8. statutum
9. enactment, ordinance
10. regulation 11. legislation
staunch, stanch... 4. firm, true
6. hearty 7. devoted 8. faithful,
resolute 9. steadfast 10. dependable
11. trustworthy
stave... 3. bar, leg 4. fend, pole,
rung, slat 5. staff, stick 6. cudgel,
lathee, letter, stanza 7. baculus,
support, ward off 8. overcome
11. set of verses
stave off... 4. fend 7. prevent
8. postpone
staves, bundle of... 5. shook
stay... 3. guy, leg, rib 4. prop, rely,
stop, wait 5. abide, brace, cease,
check, pause, tarry 6. adhere, arrest,
linger, remain, retard, status
7. prevent, respite 8. postpone,
restrain 9. cessation, hindrance
10. impediment 12. postponement
stead... 4. help, lieu 5. place
6. assist, behalf 7. replace, service,
support 9. advantage, farmstead,
homestead

steadfast... 4. firm, true 5. fixed
6. stable 7. durable, staunch
8. constant, faithful, reliable
9. unwinking 10. unchanging,
unswerving 11. unalterable
steadiness... 5. nerve 7. balance
9. constancy, stability 10. uniformity
11. reliability
steady... 4. firm 5. fixed, grave, sober,
staid 6. stable, sturdy 7. assured,
equable, regular, uniform 8. constant,
resolute 9. incessant, steadfast
10. invariable, unswerving
11. unfaltering, unmitigated
13. uninterrupted
steal... 3. cly, cop, gyp, nim, rap, rob
4. crib, lift, loot 5. filch, pinch,
poach, swipe 6. finger, kidnap, pilfer,
snitch 7. purloin 8. embezzle,
peculate 10. plagiarize
11. appropriate
steal (pert to)...
a march on.. 5. evade 7. precede
10. anticipate 13. gain advantage
away.. 5. creep, slink, sneak
cattle.. 6. rustle
feloniously.. 6. ratten
game.. 5. poach 8. trespass
insane desire to.. 11. kleptomania
nautical.. 7. manavel
stealer... 5. crook, thief 6. lifter, pirate
7. abactor, abigens, filcher, rustler
8. pilferer 9. embezzler, peculator,
purloiner 10. pickpocket, plagiarist
11. biblioklept 12. kleptomaniac
stealthy... 3. sly 6. artful, feline,
secret 7. catlike, cunning, furtive
11. clandestine
steam... 4. boil, fume, heat, mist, reek
5. force, power, smoke, stufa, vapor
6. energy, pother (puther) 8. vaporize
9. evaporate
steam (pert to)...
boat.. 5. liner 7. steamer
9. steamship 11. side–wheeler
jet of.. 5. stufa 8. suffione
organ.. 8. calliope
steamboat cabin (officer's)... 5. texas
steamy... 5. misty 7. excited
8. vaporous 9. steamed up
steatite... 4. talc 9. soapstone
steed... 3. nag 5. horse 7. charger,
courser, Pegasus (winged)
steel... 5. inure 6. harden, smooth
10. strengthen
steel (pert to)...
armor plate.. 4. tace 5. tasse
color.. 4. gray 9. steel blue
12. Prussian blue
conversion to.. 10. acieration
India.. 5. wootz 10. wootz steel
metallurgy of.. 9. siderurgy
process.. 8. Bessemer
11. cementation
type.. 6. damask, Toledo
8. Damascus
steep... 3. ret, sop 4. brae, buck,
high, soak, stew, tall 5. cleve
(cleeve), hilly, lofty, scarp, sharp,
sheer 6. abrupt, clifty, escarp,
imbrue, infuse, seethe 7. extract,
extreme 8. elevated, headlong,

macerate 9. difficult, excessive, expensive, precipice 10. exorbitant 11. precipitous 13. perpendicular

steeple... 5. spire, tower 6. flèche 7. minaret 8. pinnacle

steer... 2. ox 3. cow, ply, yaw 4. helm, luff, stot 5. guide, pilot 6. bovina, direct, govern, manage 7. bullock, control, operate

steer clear of... 4. snub 5. avert, avoid 9. sidetrack, step aside 14. be inhospitable

steer close to wind... 4. luff

steeve... 4. lade, pack, spar (a) 5. store, stuff 6. freeze

stein... 3. mug 4. Toby

stellar... 6. astral, starry 7. leading, starlit 8. starlike, stellate 10. theatrical

Steller's sea cow... 6. Rytina

stem... 3. dam 4. axis, base, cion, corm, prow, root, stop, tige 5. check, shaft, stalk, tuber 6. branch, breast, oppose, scapel, stanch 7. lineage, petiole 8. ancestry, peduncle 9. originate

stem (pert to)...
bulblike.. 4. corm, drub
cylinder.. 5. stele
grass.. 4. culm
joint.. 4. cane, node
mushroom.. 5. stipe
plant.. 4. bine
seedling.. 7. tigella (tigelle) 9. hypocotyl
strawberry.. 4. risp
twining.. 7. tendril
underground.. 5. tuber

stemless herb (evergreen)... 5. Galax 11. acaulescent

stench... 4. odor 5. fetor, smell, stink

stenographer of Cicero... 4. Tiro

step... 3. pas, way 4. gait, pace, rung 5. dance, grise, phase, riser, stair, stalk, strut, tread 6. degree, stride 7. advance, imprint, measure, process 8. distance, footstep 9. footprint, gradation 10. stepladder

step (pert to)...
arrangement of troops.. 7. echelon
clumsy.. 5. stamp
dance.. 3. pas 6. chassé
mincingly.. 6. sashay
mother.. 7. noverca
stately.. 5. stalk
up.. 8. approach 9. intensify 10. accelerate

steppe... 5. plain 9. grassland

steps (outdoor flight)... 6. perron

stereotyped... 5. banal, corny, trite 6. common, old hat 9. hackneyed 11. cut and dried

sterile... 5. arid 6. barren 7. useless 8. impotent 9. fruitless 10. unfruitful 11. ineffective, ineffectual 12. unproductive

stern... 4. dour, grim, hard, rear, rump 5. harsh 6. gloomy, severe, strict, sullen, unkind 7. austere 8. buttocks, hind part, rigorous 9. harshness, unfeeling 10. strictness, unyielding 11. hardhearted 14. uncompromising

sternutation... 8. sneezing

sternutative... 7. errhine

stertorous... 7. snoring 15. hoarse breathing

stevedore... 5. lader 6. loader, stower 7. carrier 8. unloader 12. longshoreman

stew... 3. pot 4. boil, cook, food, fret, fume, mess, olio, olla 5. anger, imbue, steep, worry 6. bustle, ragout, seethe, simmer 7. haricot, swelter 8. meat dish 9. Brunswick 10. excitement, hodgepodge 11. predicament

steward... 5. agent, reeve 6. seaman, waiter 7. dapifer, erenach, foreman, granger, manager, servant 8. manciple 9. custodian, major–domo, seneschal, treasurer 10. magistrate 11. chamberlain, fiscal agent

Stewart, Stuart sovereigns (last)... 4. Anne 5. Henry

stewed fruit... 7. compote

stick... 3. bar, bat, bow, gad, gum, rod 4. cane, dolt, glue, mast, pogo, ship, stab, wand, wood 5. baton, cling, fagot, paste, shaft, staff, stall, stave, stilt 6. adhere, baffle, ballow, cleave, cohere, mallet, pierce, puzzle, thrust 7. defraud 8. chatwood, revolver, transfix 9. drumstick, persevere 10. matchstick, overcharge 13. stick–in–the–mud

stick (pert to)...
bamboo.. 6. lathee (lathi)
bundle.. 5. fagot 6. fasces
crooked.. 5. caman 7. cammock, gambrel
insects.. 5. Emesa
mountain climbing.. 10. alpenstock

sticker... 4. burr 5. label, poser, thorn 6. poster, puzzle, weapon 7. bramble 8. adherent

sticky... 3. goo 5. gluey, humid, moist, woody 6. clammy, slushy, viscid 7. viscous 8. adhesive 9. difficult, glutinous, tenacious 10. saccharine

stiff... 4. dead, hard, hobo, limp, taut 5. harsh, horse, idler, rigid, stark, tense 6. corpse, formal, proper, severe, strict 7. awkward, cadaver, starchy 8. resolute, rigorous, starched 9. dead–drunk, obstinate, unbending 14. uncompromising

stiff–necked... 8. stubborn 9. ankylotic, obstinate 11. strait–laced 12. contumacious

stiffness... 8. rigidity 9. formality, toughness 10. strictness 11. starchiness

stifle... 3. gag 4. stop 5. choke 6. deaden, muffle, quench 7. repress, smother 8. strangle, throttle 9. suffocate 10. extinguish

stigma... 4. blot, mark, scar, slur 5. brand, odium, stain, stamp, taint 6. defect 7. blemish 8. disgrace, reproach

stigmatism... 7. blemish 10. refraction (eye)

stigmatize... 5. brand 0, fathom
8. denounce
still... 3. but, mum, yet 4. calm,
even, lull, moot 5. allay, check, inert,
quiet 6. always, hushed, pacify,
silent, soothe, subdue 7. silence,
subdued 8. inactive, restrain,
suppress, tranquil, until now
9. quiescent 10. distillery,
motionless, photograph
11. continually 12. nevertheless
15. notwithstanding
still water... 4. pond, pool 6. lagoon
stilt... 6. crutch 7. yeguita
(black–necked)
stilted... 6. formal 7. pompous
8. elevated, inflated, on stilts
9. bombastic, inelegant
stimulant... 3. tea 5. salts, tonic
6. bracer, coffee 7. alcohol
8. caffeine, stimulus 9. digitalis,
sassafras 10. adrenaline, strychnine
11. epinephrine
stimulate... 3. jog, pep 4. goad, stir,
urge, whet 5. elate, impel, rouse,
sting 6. excite, fillip (filip), incite,
spur on 7. animate, enliven, quicken,
refresh 8. energize, motivate
9. encourage, instigate, sensitize
10. exhilarate, invigorate
stimulating... 4. cool 7. piquant
8. exciting 10. energizing, refreshing
stimulus... 4. spur 5. sting 6. motive
7. impetus 9. incentive, stimulant
sting... 4. bite, pain 5. smart
6. offend, tingle 8. irritate
sting of conscience... 5. pangs, voice
6. qualms, twinge 11. compunction
sting organ... 10. nematocyst
stingy... 4. dree, mean, near 5. close
6. scanty 7. miserly, selfish
8. covetous 9. niggardly
10. avaricious 11. closefisted
12. parsimonious
stinkbird... 7. hoatzin
stint... 4. duty, task 5. limit 6. scrimp
7. confine 8. be frugal, restrict
9. be sparing
stipend... 3. ann, fee, pay 5. annat,
wages 6. salary 7. annates, pension,
subsidy 9. allowance
12. compensation, remuneration
stipulate... 5. agree 6. demand
7. bargain, specify 8. contract,
indicate 9. designate, guarantee,
postulate
stipulation... 4. bond 6. clause,
demand, detail 7. compact, proviso
8. contract, covenant 9. agreement,
condition 11. arrangement
13. specification
stir... 3. ado, mix 4. fuss, jail, move,
poke, roil, to–do 5. budge, churn,
rally, rouse, shake, stoke, waken
6. arouse, awaken, bestir, bustle,
excite, flurry, hubbub, pother, prison,
rustle, tumult 7. agitate, animate,
disturb, inflame, provoke 8. activity,
movement 9. commotion
12. penitentiary
stir (pert to)...
  colors (calico).. 4. teer

  fire.. 5. stoke
  together.. 3. mix 6. stodge
  up.. 3. mix 4. rile, roil 5. anger,
  awake, rouse 6. arouse, foment,
  incite
stirring... 6. moving 7. rousing
8. bustling, eventful, exciting
9. animating, inspiring
11. stimulating
stirrup... 4. ring 5. strap 6. saddle
(part), stapes 7. support 8. footrest,
tapadera
stitch... 3. bit, hem, sew 4. mend,
pain 5. baste, piece, ridge 6. suture,
tailor 8. particle 9. embroider
stitch (type)... 3. hem 5. chain, coral,
cross 6. carpet, damask, suture
7. glover's 11. needlepoint,
over–and–over
stitchbird... 3. ihi 10. honey eater
stithy... 5. anvil, forge 6. smithy
8. smithery
stoa... 7. portico 9. colonnade
stoat... 6. ermine, weasel
stob... 4. post, stab, stub 5. stake
6. gibbet, pierce
stoccado, stoccata... 4. stab 6. thrust
(rapier)
stock... 4. fund, line, race, stem
5. breed, broth, hoard, store, trunk
6. assets, cravat, pillar, strain, supply
7. capital, lineage, provide, rhizome
8. credence, original 9. livestock,
provision, replenish 10. progenitor
stock (pert to)...
  book.. 6. ledger
  breeding.. 5. brood
  certificate.. 5. scrip 8. document
  flower.. 11. gillyflower
  hawk.. 15. peregrine falcon
  in trade.. 6. assets, supply
    11. merchandise
  market.. 6. Bourse 8. Exchange
    10. Wall Street
  of goods.. 4. line
  owl.. 8. eagle owl
  pile.. 7. reserve 12. accumulation
  theater.. 5. plays
stockade... 3. pen 5. étape, pound
6. corral, kennel, laager 7. barrier,
bulwark, parapet, rampart, redoubt
8. palisade 9. barricade, earthwork,
enclosure
stocking... 4. hose, sock 6. anklet,
argyle 7. bandage, fortune, hosiery
8. seamless 9. livestock
12. bluestocking 15. Leatherstocking
(Natty Bumppo)
stocks... 7. pillory, shackle
10. securities
stoic, stoical... 7. passive, Spartan
8. enduring 9. impassive
11. unflinching
Stoic School founder... 4. Zeno
stoker... 5. firer 6. seaman, teaser
7. fireman, greaser 8. trainman
stolen (pert to)...
  goods receiver.. 5. fence 7. smasher,
  swagman
  property.. 4. pelf 5. booty, spoil
stolid... 4. dull, slow 5. beefy
6. stupid 7. adamant, passive

9. impassive, inanimate
11. inexcitable, unexcitable
stoma . . . 4. pore 5. mouth 7. opening, orifice
stomach . . . 3. gut, maw 4. craw, crop, vell 5. belly, rumen, taste 6. desire, endure, gaster, paunch 7. abdomen, gizzard 8. tolerate 10. resentment
stomach (pert to) . . .
ache . . 5. colic, cramp 7. gullion
8. rumbling 11. borborygmus
acidity . . 4. acor
animal . . 3. maw
bird . . 4. craw, crop
comb form . . 6. gaster 7. gastero
ref to . . 7. gastric, pyloric
ruminant . . 5. rumen 6. omasum
8. abomasum, roddikin 9. manyplies, reticulum 10. psalterium
stone . . . 3. gem, pit 4. kill, pelt, rock, seed 5. agate, block, geode, jewel, lapis, shale, slate, spall 6. attack, pebble 7. diamond, peridot, sharpen 8. monument, pavement 9. hailstone, sculpture, whetstone 10. gravestone, grindstone 12. philosopher's
stone (pert to) . . .
abrasive . . 5. emery
Age . . 8. Eolithic 9. Neolithic
11. Paleolithic
alchemy . . 6. carmot 12. philosopher's
arch (top stone) . . 8. keystone
Bib . . 4. ezel
broke . . 4. flat 8. strapped
broken . . 6. rubble
carved . . 5. cameo 8. intaglio
chisel . . 4. celt
cutters' disease . . 9. silicosis
10. chalicosis
famed . . 4. Hope, Pitt 5. Mogul, Sancy 6. Jonker, Orloff, Regent 7. Blarney, Rosetta 8. Cullinan, Kohinoor (Kohinur) 9. Excelsior 10. Great Mogul 12. Plymouth Rock, Star of Africa
flat . . 4. flag, slab 5. slate
fruit . . 3. pip 4. paip, seed 5. cling 7. putamen 8. endocarp
gem . . 4. jade, opal, ruby, sard 5. agate, pearl, topaz 6. garnet, ligure, spinel 7. diamond, emerald, peridot 8. amethyst, sapphire 9. turquoise 11. alexandrite
gem cutting . . 6. adamas
hammer . . 5. kevel
hard . . 7. adamant 9. chatoyant (cat's–eye)
heap . . 5. cairn
instrument . . 8. lapideon
masonry . . 6. ashlar
medical . . 4. gall 5. renal 7. biliary, otolith 8. calculus
oil . . 4. hone
ornamental . . 9. scagliola
pert to . . 7. lithoid
pillar . . 8. monolith
pyramid . . 6. benben
quarry . . 6. latomy
small . . 6. pebble 8. lapillus
special . . 3. key, lap, oil, rub 4. curb, flag, head, lime, lode, mile, tomb, whet 5. birth, flint, grave, grind

6. cobble, corner 8. stepping
statue (part wood) . . 8. acrolith
to dress . . 3. nig
uncut . . 4. naif
woman turned to stone by Zeus . . 5. Niobe
stonecutter (pert to) . . .
disease of . . 9. silicosis 10. chalicosis
receptacle . . 7. sebilla
tool . . 6. eolith
type . . 6. jadder 7. jeweler 8. lapidary
worker . . 5. mason
stonecutting art . . . 10. stereotomy
stoning, death by . . . 10. lapidation
stony . . . 4. cold, hard 5. rigid, rocky 6. rugged 7. adamant 8. lapidose, obdurate, pitiless 9. petrified 10. inflexible, relentless, unyielding 15. uncompassionate
stooge . . . 4. foil 5. toady 6. flunky 7. cat's–paw 8. henchman
stool . . . 4. seat 5. bench 6. pigeon, tripod 7. taboret 8. informer
stop . . . 2. ho 3. bar, dam, end 4. balk, foil, halt, kill, quit, stay, stem, whoa 5. avast, block, cease, check, choke, close, delay 6. arrest, desist, detain 7. impasse, prevent, silence 9. preclude, swear off 10. standstill 11. discontinue, obstruction, punctuation 12. lower the boom
stop (pert to) . . .
close . . 8. obturate
debate . . 7. cloture
fermentation . . 4. stum
gap . . 7. stopper 9. expedient, makeshift
momentarily . . 5. pause
nautical . . 5. avast
organ . . 4. viola 7. gemsbok 8. dulsiana
seams (boat) . . 4. calk
short . . 5. pause 7. respite 8. interval 12. intermission
unintentional . . 5. stall
watch . . 5. timer
with clay . . 3. pug
stopper . . . 4. bung, cork, plug 5. spile 7. bouchon
storage (pert to) . . .
bin . . 3. mow 4. loft, shed, silo 7. granary 8. elevator
fodder (in silo) . . 6. ensile
hidden . . 5. cache
place . . 3. bin 4. barn 5. attic, depot, étape 6. cellar, closet 7. arsenal, granary 8. cupboard, elevator, magazine 10. promptuary, repository
stork . . . 4. ibis 6. jabiru 7. Maguari, marabou 8. adjutant
storklike . . . 8. pelargic
storm . . . 4. blow, fume, fury, rage, rain, rave, snow, wind 5. orage 6. attack, shower, simoom (simoon), tumult 7. bluster, disturb, tempest, trouble 8. calamity, eruption, outbreak, upheaval, violence 9. agitation 11. disturbance
storm (pert to) . . .
cold . . 11. northeaster
evil storm god . . 2. Zu 9. blackbird

(symb), Hlorrithi

extreme.. 4. gale 7. cyclone, monsoon, tempest, tornado 9. hurricane

occidental.. 6. wester

recorder (thunder).. 11. brontometer

sand.. 6. tebbad

snow.. 5. buran

stormy... 5. rainy 7. furious, riotous, violent 8. agitated 9. inclement, turbulent 10. tumultuous 11. tempestuous

story... 3. fib, lie 4. hoax, joke, lore, saga, tale, tier, yarn 5. fable, floor 6. gossip, legend, serial 7. mystery, narrate, parable, romance 8. anecdote 9. chronicle, falsehood, tradition

story (pert to)...

absurd.. 4. hoax, yarn 6. canard

doleful.. 8. jeremiad

exclusive.. 4. beat, news 5. scoop

part.. 6. serial

short.. 5. conte 7. novella

storyteller... 4. liar 5. Aesop 6. fibber 7. relater 9. raconteur

stot... 2. ox 4. bull 5. steer 6. bounce 7. paunchy, stammer, stumble, stutter

stout... 3. fat 4. bold 5. brave, bulky, burly, hardy, obese, plump 6. fleshy, rotund, stocky, strong 7. haughty, violent 8. forcible, powerful, resolute, thickset 9. corpulent, undaunted 10. courageous, persistent

stoutness... 7. courage 8. strength 10. corpulence, embonpoint

stove... 4. etna, kiln, oven 5. grate, plate, range 6. heater 7. Coleman, furnace, smelter

stove part... 4. oven, pipe 6. burner 7. firebox, griddle

stow... 4. cram, hide, mass, pack 5. crowd, lodge, store, stuff 6. steeve 7. arrange, secrete

straddle... 5. salvo 6. option 7. astride 8. bestride 9. be neutral, go halfway

straggle... 4. rove 6. wander 7. deviate, meander

straight... 5. cards, erect, exact, rigid, stern 6. candid, direct, honest 7. correct, exactly, unmixed 8. directly, reliable, sequence, unbroken, vertical 9. authentic 10. horizontal, racing term 11. straightway, undeviating 13. uninterrupted 15. straightforward

straight (pert to)...

baseball.. 5. liner

course.. 7. beeline

edge.. 5. ruler

line.. 6. secant 8. enfilade 9. asymptote

Math.. 8. vinculum

out.. 6. candid 9. downright 11. unqualified 13. thoroughgoing 14. uncompromising

shooter.. 11. on the square

way.. 4. anon 8. directly 9. forthwith 11. immediately

straighten... 5. align, aline, level,

order, plumb 6. tidy up 7. rectify, unravel 11. disentangle

straightforward... 5. frank 6. candid, direct, honest 7. sincere 8. outright 9. outspoken 10. forthright 11. undeviating

straightway... 4. anon 8. directly 9. downright, forthwith 10. forthright 11. immediately

strain... 3. sye, tax, try, tug 4. bend, dash, kind, mood, ooze, race, sort, tone, vein 5. breed, shade, stock, tense, touch 6. filter, melody, overdo, poetry, refine, sprain, streak, stress, strive 7. descent, fatigue, lineage, progeny, stretch, tension, variety 8. ancestry, endeavor, exertion 9. constrain, overheave, percolate 10. generation

strained... 4. taut 5. tense 6. forced 7. intense, labored 8. wrenched 9. stretched 10. farfetched

strainer... 4. sile 5. sieve, tamis 6. filter, screen, sifter 8. colander, filterer 17. Hippocrates' sleeve

strait... 3. gut 4. neck, need 5. inlet 6. angust, narrow, strict 7. channel, limited 8. rigorous 9. difficult 10. restricted, scrupulous 11. distressful, predicament

Strait... 6. Bering 7. Surigao 8. Bosporus 9. Belleisle

Strait of Gibraltar... 17. Pillars of Hercules

Straits Settlements...

capital, Penang.. 10. Georgetown

capital, Singapore.. 9. Singapore

city.. 7. Malacca

peninsula.. 5. Malay

port.. 4. Prai

strand... 3. sea 4. bank, quay 5. beach, shore 6. maroon, thread 7. channel, current 8. filament

strange... 3. coy, new, odd, shy 4. rare, xeno (comb form) 5. alien, eerie, novel, queer, timid 6. exotic, quaint 7. curious, erratic, unknown, unusual 8. peculiar, singular, uncommon 9. eccentric, unrelated 10. extraneous, outlandish, tramontane, unfamiliar 12. unaccustomed, unacquainted 13. extraordinary, preternatural

stranger... 3. ger 5. alien, guest 7. visitor 8. intruder 9. foreigner, outlander

strangle... 5. choke 6. stifle 7. execute, garrote, repress, squeeze 8. suppress, throttle 9. suffocate

strap... 3. tie 4. belt, bind, hang, jess, rein, riem, whip 5. leash, strop, thong 6. enarme, latigo, oxreim 7. lanyard (laniard) 8. chastise

strap-shaped... 6. lorate 8. ligulate

strass... 5. glass, paste 10. silk refuse

strata... 6. layers 7. classes 10. formations

stratagem... 4. coup, ruse, trap, wile 5. trick 6. device 7. finesse 8. artifice

strategy... 7. tactics 8. artifice, intrigue, maneuver

stratum ... 3. bed 4. coat 5. layer

straw ... 4. stem 5. mulch 6. fodder, sennit, trifle 7. remains, sabutan

straw (pert to) ...
bid .. 5. fraud 7. auction 9. worthless
coat (Jap peasant) .. 4. mino
color .. 6. flaxen
flower .. 11. everlasting
hat .. 4. baku 5. milan 6. panama
like .. 6. chaffy 11. stramineous
vote .. 5. Roper 6. Gallup

stray ... 3. err, gad, sin 4. cavy, roam, rove, waif 5. range 6. swerve, wander 7. deviate, digress 8. aberrant, aberrate, go astray 9. wandering 10. occasional

streak ... 3. roe 4. line, seam, vein 5. fleck, layer, stria 6. groove, strain, strake, stripe

streaked ... 4. liny 6. banded 7. brindle, striped 8. brindled, striated

stream ... 3. run 4. burn, flow, rill, sike (syke) 5. brook, creek, river 6. abound, course, rillet, runlet, runnel, throng 7. current, rivulet, torrent 9. streamlet 11. watercourse

stream (pert to) ...
dry .. 6. arroyo, spruit
gold .. 6. placer
of consciousness .. 8. thoughts 10. psychology 11. abstraction
of forgetfulness .. 5. Lethe
underground .. 3. aar

street ... 4. road 5. calle 6. avenue 7. highway, roadway 8. chaussée 9. boulevard 12. thoroughfare

street (pert to) ...
car .. 4. tram
famed .. 4. Beal, Main, Wall 5. Canal 6. Beacon 7. Downing 8. Broadway 9. Peachtree 12. Threadneedle
French .. 3. rue
narrow .. 4. lane 5. alley
show .. 4. peep 5. raree
Spanish .. 5. calle
urchin .. 4. Arab 5. gamin 7. outcast 8. vagabond 11. guttersnipe

Street called Straight (Bib) ... 8. Damascus

strength ... 3. vis 4. iron, thew 5. brawn, force, might, nerve, power, rally, sinew, titer, vigor 6. energy, health 7. potency, stamina, sthenia, support 8. firmness 9. endurance, lustiness, stoutness, toughness, vehemence, willpower 10. robustness, stronghold

strengthen ... 4. grow, prop 5. brace, nerve 6. deepen 7. confirm, fortify, nourish, toughen 8. increase, roborate 9. encourage, intensify, reinforce 10. invigorate 11. consolidate

strengthening ... 7. bracing 8. roborant 12. invigorating, invigoration

strenuous ... 6. ardent, severe 7. zealous 8. vigorous 9. difficult, energetic, laborious 11. industrious

strepent ... 4. loud 5. noisy

streperous ... 4. loud 5. harsh 7. noisily 9. turbulent 10. boisterous

strepor ... 5. noise

stress ... 5. arsis, ictus, labor 6. accent, insist, strain, weight 7. urgency 8. emphasis, exigency, pressure 9. emphasize 10. elasticity, exaggerate 12. exaggeration

stretcher ... 3. bar, lie 6. litter, racker 9. falsehood

stretch out ... 6. be long, extend 9. expatiate

strew ... 3. ted 6. spread 7. diffuse, overlay, scatter 8. disperse 10. distribute 11. disseminate

strewn ... 4. semé 8. littered 9. scattered 12. disseminated

stria ... 4. line 5. ridge, strip 6. fillet, furrow, groove, hollow, streak, stripe 7. channel 9. striation

stricken ... 7. smitten, worn out, wounded 8. unnerved 13. incapacitated

strickle ... 5. rifle 7. pattern 8. template 10. sweepboard 13. striking board

strict ... 4. hard 5. exact, harsh, rigid, stern 6. severe 7. ascetic, austere, precise 8. accurate, rigorous 9. puritanic, stringent 10. forbidding, inexorable, inflexible, meticulous, relentless, scrupulous 11. strait-laced, undeviating 13. conscientious 14. uncompromising

strict disciplinarian ... 8. martinet

strict discipline ... 13. regimentation

stricture ... 7. binding, censure 9. criticism, narrowing 11. contraction 12. constriction

stride ... 4. gait, pace, step, walk 8. bestride, progress, straddle, velocity

strident ... 6. shrill 7. grating, raucous 11. cacophonous

strife ... 3. war 4. feud 5. fight 6. battle, combat, stasis 7. contest, quarrel 8. conflict, exertion, struggle 9. logomachy 11. altercation

strike ... 3. hit, pat, rap 4. bump, bunt, slap, swat 5. clout, labor, smite, whack 6. attack, revolt 7. impinge 9. discovery

strike (pert to) ...
a balance .. 5. weigh 7. average 8. equalize 10. compromise
against .. 7. collide 8. illision
and rebound .. 5. carom (carrom) 9. carambole
breaker .. 4. fink, scab
dumb .. 4. stun
heavily .. 3. lam, ram 4. bash, slam, slog, sock, wham 5. punch, smite
obliquely .. 5. carom 6. glance
out .. 3. fan 4. dele 5. elide, erase 6. cancel, delete 9. eliminate
to and fro .. 5. bandy
with beak .. 4. peck
with fist .. 5. pound, punch
with head .. 4. butt
with weapon .. 5. crunt
with wonder .. 3. awe 7. astound

striking ... 7. salient 8. dramatic, eloquent, exciting 9. arresting,

wonderful 10. noticeable, remarkable, surprising
striking effect... 5. éclat
striking part... 7. clapper
string... 3. ran, set 4. bind, cord
  5. lacet, snare, twine 6. fasten,
  series, thread 10. succession
string (pert to)...
alphabet.. 5. knots (for blind)
of beads.. 6. rosary 8. necklace
of horses.. 6. stable
out.. 6. line up 8. lengthen
  9. expatiate
pottery.. 13. Schnurkeramik (neolithic)
stringed instrument... 4. harp, lute,
  lyre 5. banjo, piano, recta, viola
  6. fiddle, guitar, violin, zither
  7. bandore, mandore, ukulele
  8. mandolin, psaltery 9. mandolute
  11. harpsichord
stringed instrument bridge...
  5. magas
stringent... 4. ropy 5. rigid, tight
  6. cogent, severe, strict
  10. convincing 11. acrimonious,
  restrictive
stringy... 4. ropy 5. gluey, tough
  6. sinewy, viscid 7. fibrous
  10. threadlike 11. filamentous
strip... 4. bare, belt, live, pare, peel,
  skin, slat 5. cleat, shred, unrig
  6. denude, divest, remove, strake
  7. deprive, plunder, pull off, uncloak,
  uncover, undress 9. dismantle
  10. dispossess, impoverish
  11. decorticate
strip (pert to)...
blubber.. 6. flense
curved.. 5. stave
lead (stained glass).. 4. came
leather.. 4. welt 5. thong 6. latido
  7. belting
narrow.. 4. lath, slat, tape, welt
  5. reeve, stave, strap
off skin.. 4. flay
of possessions.. 4. milk 5. bleed,
  bunko (bunco), shear 6. fleece
  7. despoil, swindle 10. dispossess
raised.. 5. ridge
tease dancer.. 8. stripper 9. ecdysiast
wood.. 5. stave 6. reglet, spline
stripe... 3. bar, pin 4. band, beat,
  line, mark, sort, type, wale, weal,
  welt, whip 5. chalk, strip, vitta
  6. streak 7. chevron 8. insignia
  9. striation
striped (pert to)...
alder.. 11. winterberry
antelope.. 5. bongo
gillyflower.. 9. carnation
longitudinally.. 7. vittate
stripling... 3. boy, lad 5. youth
  8. juvenile 9. youngster
strive... 3. aim, try, tug 4. toil
  5. labor 6. battle, buffet, strain
  7. compete, contend, emulate
  8. endeavor, struggle
strive (pert to)...
for.. 3. aim 4. seek
to equal.. 5. rival 6. strain
  7. emulate
to overtake.. 5. ensue

with.. 3. vie 7. compete
strobile... 4. cone 8. pine cone
strockle... 6. shovel
stroke... 3. fit, pat, pet, rub 4. beat,
  blow, coup, flip, line, putt, shot
  5. ictus, serif, spasm, trait, whisk
  6. caress, fondle 7. illness, solidus
stroll... 4. roam, walk 5. range, stray
  6. go slow, ramble, wander
  7. meander, saunter 8. ambulate
  9. promenade 11. perambulate
stroller... 5. actor, tramp 6. beggar
  7. peddler, vagrant 8. wanderer
  9. saunterer 12. perambulator
strolling... 7. nomadic 8. rambling
  10. meandering 13. perambulation
strong... 3. fit, hot 4. able, firm, hale,
  hard, wiry 5. fetid, hardy, lusty,
  solid, sound, stout, tough 6. potent,
  robust, sinewy, stable, sturdy, virile
  7. healthy, intense, odorous, tainted
  8. accented, forceful, forcible,
  muscular, resonant, stalwart, vigorous
  9. effective, energetic
  10. outrageous, persuasive,
  pronounced, remarkable
  11. substantial 12. concentrated
strong (pert to)...
drink.. 6. liquor 7. spirits 9. distilled
flavor.. 4. racy 5. acrid 7. pungent
hold.. 4. fort 7. citadel 8. fastness,
  Fort Knox, fortress, muniment,
  treasury
man.. 5. Atlas 6. Samson (Sampson)
muscles.. 5. brawn, thewy
music.. 4. loud 5. forte 7. saccade
willed.. 8. resolute 9. obstinate
  10. determined
wind.. 7. pampero
stroygood... 7. wastrel 11. spendthrift
strubbly... 6. untidy 7. unkempt
struck... 4. smit 5. smote 7. smitten,
  swatted 8. shutdown (see also *strike*)
struck (pert to)...
an attitude.. 5. posed
out.. 5. deled 6. elided, erased,
  fanned 7. deleted
with fear.. 6. aghast 7. alarmed
with missiles.. 6. pelted
structure... 3. dam 4. dais, form, pier
  5. frame, house, jetty, kiosk, stage,
  tower 6. bridge, make–up, pagoda
  7. edifice 8. building, platform
  9. formation 10. tabernacle
  11. composition 12. constitution,
  construction
structure (pert to)...
calcareous.. 5. coral
conical.. 7. pyramid
crownlike.. 6. corona
filamentous.. 4. hair
human.. 8. physique
monumental.. 5. pylon
roof.. 6. cupola, dormer
tall.. 5. tower 7. steeple 9. campanile
tentlike.. 10. tabernacle
struggle... 3. tug, vie 4. cope, wade
  5. labor 6. effort, Peniel (Bib), strife,
  strike, strive, tussle 7. contend,
  contest, scuffle, wrestle 8. endeavor,
  flounder, scramble 10. contention,
  difficulty

strumpet . . . 5. belie 6. harlot
8. harridan 10. prostitute
stub . . . 3. end 4. dock, tail 5. squat,
stump 6. coupon, stocky 7. remnant
8. thickset 11. counterfoil
stubble . . . 5. beard, stump 6. arrish
7. bristle 8. eelgrass
stubborn . . . 3. set 4. rude 5. fixed,
hardy, rough, tough 6. coarse, mulish,
sturdy 7. restive 8. perverse,
resolute, starkish, vigorous
9. obstinate, pigheaded
10. determined, headstrong, inflexible,
refractory, unyielding 11. intractable
12. recalcitrant
stuck . . . 4. fast 7. baffled, cohered
8. coherent, stranded (see also *stick)*
stuck–up . . . 4. vain 8. arrogant
9. conceited 10. egocentric
12. supercilious 13. self–important
stud . . . 3. dot, pin 4. boss, knob
5. haras 6. enstar 7. hobnail
8. ornament, stallion 9. studhorse
student . . . 4. co–ed 5. cadet, eleve,
plebe, pupil 6. tosher 7. learner,
scholar 8. disciple 9. collegian
student of . . .
behavior (human) . . 12. psychologist
birds . . 13. ornithologist
birds' eggs . . 8. oologist
Eton . . 7. Etonian
law . . 8. stagiary
medical . . 6. intern (interne)
military . . 5. cadet, plebe
natural history . . 10. naturalist
navy . . 5. cadet 10. midshipman
Oxford . . 8. commoner
proverbs . . 14. paroemiologist
punishment . . 10. penologist
reptiles . . 13. herpetologist
spiders . . 13. arachnologist
students, advanced group . . .
7. seminar 13. upperclassmen
studied . . . 5. boned, pored 6. formal
7. learned, planned, weighed
8. designed, measured, reasoned
10. well–versed 11. intentional
12. premeditated
studio . . . 4. shop 7. atelier, bottega
8. workshop 11. working room
study . . . 3. con, den 4. bone, muse,
pore, scan 5. étude, grind, learn,
weigh 7. discuss 6. peruse, ponder
7. analyze, examine, pegging,
reverie, science, subject, thought
8. endeavor, learning, treatise
10. discussion, inspection
11. contemplate 13. contemplation
study of . . .
animals . . 7. zoology 9. zoography
bees . . 8. apiology
birds' eggs . . 6. oology
disease . . 8. nosology
fingerprints . . 13. dactylography
handwriting . . 10. graphology
insects . . 10. entomology
man . . 12. anthropology
mountains . . 7. orology
old age . . 9. nostology 10. geriatrics
11. gerontology
population . . 10. demography,
larithmics 12. demographics

punishment . . 8. penology
sacred images . . 9. iconology
temples . . 7. naology
words . . 9. etymology
12. lexicography
stuff . . . 3. goo, pad, ram, wad
4. cram, fill, stow 5. gorge, trash
6. fabric, matter, potion 7. content,
element, rubbish, satiate 8. marinate,
material, nonsense, overfill, trumpery
9. principle, substance 10. gluttonize
stuffiness . . . 7. prudery 8. dullness
9. obstinacy 10. sullenness, sultriness
11. pompousness
stuffing . . . 6. lining 7. padding
8. contents, dressing 9. forcemeat
stuffy . . . 3. fat 4. dull, prim 5. close,
stout 6. stodgy, sullen, sultry
7. airless, pompous, prudish
8. resolute 9. bombastic, obstinate
10. old–fogyish 11. strait–laced
12. conservative 13. ill–ventilated
stulm . . . 4. adit 7. passage
8. entrance
stumble . . . 3. err 4. fall, trip 5. lurch
6. boggle, bungle, chance, falter,
happen 7. blunder, perplex, stagger,
stammer 8. confound, flounder
stump . . . 4. butt, dare, skeg, snag,
stab, stub 5. clump, scrab 6. baffle,
trudge 7. declaim, nonplus
8. platform 9. challenge, remainder,
tortillon 11. electioneer
stun . . . 4. bowl, daze 5. amaze, daunt
6. benumb, bruise, deaden
7. astound, stupefy, terrify
8. astonish, bewilder 9. overpower,
overwhelm
stunning . . . 8. striking 9. beautiful
10. astounding, stupefying, terrifying
stunt . . . 4. feat 5. blunt, check, cramp,
crowl, dwarf, whale (2–yr) 6. hinder
7. curtail, exploit, shorten
10. tomfoolery
stunted . . . 7. blunted, checked,
dwarfed 9. curtailed, shortened
stupa . . . 4. tomb 5. mound, tower
6. shrine 8. monument
stupefied . . . 5. doped 6. aghast,
sotted 7. drugged, shocked, stunned
8. benumbed 9. petrified
stupefy . . . 4. daze, dope, drug, numb,
pall, stun 5. besot, blunt, shock
6. bedaze, bemuse, muddle
7. astound, confuse, petrify, terrify
8. bewilder, confound 10. incrassate,
make stupid 11. flabbergast (sl)
stupid . . . 4. clod, dull, dumb 5. blunt,
crass, dense, inane 6. oafish, obtuse,
simple, stolid 7. asinine, doltish,
foolish, witless 8. blockish, Boeotian,
gullible 9. brainless, senseless
11. heavywitted 13. unintelligent
stupid (pert to) . . .
grossly . . 7. asinine 9. imbecilic
person . . 3. ass, oaf 4. clod, coot,
dolt, loon, lout, nerd 5. goose, klutz,
stirk 7. tomfool 11. gillygaupus
render . . 8. hebetate
stupidity . . . 7. fatuity 8. dullness,
hebetude 11. foolishness
12. indifference 13. foolish remark

stupor... 4. coma, daze 5. sleep,
sopor 6. apathy, torpor, trance
8. lethargy, neurosis, numbness
9. lassitude 15. unconsciousness
sturdy... 4. firm 5. burly, hardy, lusty,
stout 6. robust, stable, steady, strong
8. resolute, stalwart, stubborn,
vigorous 10. courageous, determined,
unyielding 11. substantial
sturgeon... 6. beluga, caviar 7. sterlet
9. Acipenser 10. hackleback
stutter... 6. falter 7. stammer
sty... 3. pen 4. boil 5. hovel, stair,
steps, stile 6. ladder, pimple
7. pustule 8. swelling 9. enclosure
style... 3. air, pen, way 4. form, kind,
mode, name 5. get–up, gusto, trend,
vogue 6. gnomon, graver, phrase,
stylus 7. alamode, diction, fashion
8. elegance 9. execution
10. appearance 12. characterize,
presentation
style (pert to)...
architecture.. 5. Doric, Greek, Ionic,
Roman 6. Gothic, Norman 7. Italian
8. Colonial, Georgian 9. Byzantine
10. Corinthian, Romanesque
11. Renaissance
painting.. 5. genre 11. Renaissance
type.. 5. roman, runic 6. italic
styled... 5. named 6. called, termed,
y–clept (y–cleped) 7. phrased
stylet... 5. probe 6. trocar 7. poniard
8. stiletto 9. specillum
stylish... 3. mod 4. chic, cool, neat,
tony 5. nifty, ritzy, sharp, smart,
swank 6. chi–chi, dressy, jaunty,
modish, preppy, snazzy, trendy
7. alamode, voguish 11. fashionable
styptic... 4. alum 10. astringent,
tannic acid 12. constringent
Styx (pert to)...
ferryman.. 6. Charon
suant... 4. even 6. demure, smooth,
steady 7. equable, regular
suave... 4. oily, smug 5. bland
6. urbane 7. fulsome 8. unctuous
9. agreeable 12. ingratiating,
mealy–mouthed 13. smooth–talking
suavity... 7. amenity 8. civility,
courtesy, urbanity 10. gentleness
subdue... 3. cow 4. calm, tame
5. allay, crush, lower, quash, quell,
sober 6. disarm, muffle, reduce,
soften 7. conquer, repress, squelch
8. mitigate, overcome, suppress,
surmount, vanquish 9. overpower,
subjugate 11. subordinate
subdued... 4. meek, soft 7. muffled,
quelled 8. disarmed, relieved,
tempered 9. conquered, toned down
10. made gentle, subjugated 11. soft
colored, unperturbed
subject... 4. text, word 5. cause,
prone, theme, topic 6. matter, motive,
submit, vassal 7. citizen, servant
8. inferior 9. subjugate, substance
10. predispose 11. subordinate
12. part of speech
subjective... 6. mental 7. topical
8. fanciful, illusory 9. of the mind

10. nominative 11. introverted
subject of...
discourse.. 5. theme, topic
disease.. 4. case 7. patient
lawsuit.. 3. res 7. grounds
sentence.. 4. noun
subject to...
abuse.. 6. revile
analysis.. 7. titrate
argument.. 4. moot
change.. 7. mutable 8. amenable
choice.. 8. elective
control.. 7. rulable
death.. 6. mortal
depression.. 5. moody
dislike.. 8. aversion
mistakes.. 7. erratic
outbursts.. 9. irritable
tension.. 8. strained
vassalage.. 5. feoff
sublimation... 9. underling
12. underscoring
sublime... 4. high 6. grand, great,
lofty, noble, proud 6. refine
7. exalted, haughty 8. elevated,
eloquent, empyreal, majestic, splendid,
upraised, vaporize 9. beautiful,
expletive 11. magnanimous
Sublime Porte... 12. Ottoman Court
17. Turkish government
sublimity... 4. acme 5. glory
6. beauty 7. majesty 8. grandeur
9. greatness 10. excellence
11. distinction 12. magnificence
submarine... 3. sub 4. boat, ship
8. Nautilus, Scorpion, Thresher
11. submersible
submarine eye... 9. periscope
submission... 5. kneel 8. fatalism,
meekness, patience, yielding
9. deference, obedience, surrender
10. compliance, confession
11. resignation 13. nonresistance
submissive... 4. meek, tame
6. humble 7. dutiful, patient
8. obedient, resigned, uxorious (to
wife), yielding 9. compliant
11. acquiescent, conformable
submit... 3. bow 4. obey 5. defer,
remit, stoop, yield 6. soften, temper
7. succumb 8. moderate
9. acquiesce, postulate, surrender
10. condescend
submit to... 4. obey 6. endure
11. acknowledge
subordinate... 4. exon 5. minor
6. subdue 7. servant, subject
8. inferior, parergon 9. appendage,
assistant, dependent, secondary
10. collateral, incidental, submissive
11. subservient
subsequent... 5. later 7. ensuing
9. following, postnatal
10. succeeding 11. consecutive
subservient... 6. vassal 7. servile,
subject 9. assistant, truckling
10. obsequious, submissive
11. subordinate 12. instrumental
subside... 3. ebb 4. bate, fall, lull,
sink, wane 5. abate 6. settle
7. descend, relapse 8. decrease,

languish 9. gravitate 11. deteriorate

subsidiary... 8. inferior 9. assistant, auxiliary, extrinsic, tributary 10. collateral 11. stipendiary 12. nonessential 13. supplementary

subsist... 2. be 4. live 5. abide, exist 6. endure, remain 7. prevail, survive 8. continue

subsist on prey... 9. rapacious

substance... 3. sum 4. gist, meat 5. stuff 6. import, matter, wealth 7. aliment, element, essence, meaning, purport, summary 8. hardness, material 9. actuality, affluence, solidness 11. consistency

substance (pert to)...
absorbent.. 5. fomes
aeriform.. 3. gas 5. argon
amorphous.. 7. ferrite
antitoxic.. 5. serum
aromatic.. 5. myrrh, spice 6. balsam
basic.. 7. element
bitter.. 5. aloes, aloin, linin 7. amarine, emetine 8. elaterin
brittle.. 5. glass
cleansing, purifying.. 8. depurant 10. abstergent, clarifiant
corrosive.. 4. acid 7. caustic
dissolved.. 6. solute
dissolving.. 9. resolvent
electrical.. 3. ion
elemental.. 5. metal
expanding.. 8. dilatant
fatty.. 5. lipin, suint
ferment.. 9. activator
flocculent.. 4. wool
food.. 7. protein
fruit jellying.. 6. pectin
gelatinous.. 4. agar
hard.. 4. bone 5. ivory 7. adamant
hypnotic.. 4. ural
inflammable.. 6. tinder 7. bitumen
inorganic.. 7. mineral
ipecac root.. 7. emetine
light.. 4. cork
milk curdling.. 6. rennet
moss (Ceylon).. 4. agar 8. agar-agar
neutralizing.. 6. alkali
resinous.. 3. gum, lac 5. copal 7. shellac
rubberlike.. 5. gutta
soapmaking.. 3. lye
stabilizing.. 7. ballast
sulphur.. 5. hepar
tar.. 6. cresol
unctuous.. 3. fat, oil 7. pinguid
vegetable.. 5. resin, rosin
wax, waxy.. 5. cerin 7. suberin 8. paraffin
whale (perfume).. 9. ambergris
wood ash.. 6. potash

substantial... 4. firm, real, true 5. pucka (pukka), solid, stout 6. actual, bodily, hearty, stable, strong, sturdy 7. genuine 8. abundant, tangible 9. corporeal, essential, important 10. nourishing 12. considerable

substantiate... 6. embody, verify 7. confirm, justify 8. underpin 9. establish 11. corroborate

substantive... 4. firm, noun 5. sound

6. actual, entity 7. pronoun 9. essential 11. substantial 13. self-contained

substitute... 5. proxy, vicar 6. deputy, ersatz 7. apology, replace 8. exchange, nominate 9. alternate, surrogate 10. understudy, viceregent 11. replacement

subterfuge... 4. ruse 5. blind, trick 6. refuge 7. evasion, pretext 8. artifice, pretense 9. expedient 13. prevarication

subterranean... 6. hidden, secret 8. hypogeal, plutonic 10. in the earth 11. underground

subtile... 3. sly 4. rare, wily 6. crafty, subtle 7. cunning, elusive 9. beguiling

subtle... 3. sly 4. fine, nice, rare, thin 6. artful, clever, crafty, shrewd 7. cunning, refined, subtile 8. analytic, delicate 9. beguiling, designing, ingenious 10. mysterious 14. discriminating

subtle (pert to)...
emanation (invisible).. 4. aura 10. atmosphere
sarcasm.. 5. irony
variation.. 6. nuance

subtlety... 5. guile 7. cunning, finesse, slyness 8. delicacy, fineness 9. quodlibet 10. shrewdness

subtraction, terms... 7. minuend 9. deduction 10. difference, subtrahend

subversion... 4. ruin (utter) 9. overthrow 10. corruption, revolution 11. destruction

subvert... 4. ruin 5. evert, upset 6. refute, uproot 7. corrupt, destroy, pervert 8. alienate, overturn 9. overthrow, undermine

subvertive... 8. eversive

subway... 4. tube 5. train 6. tunnel 11. underground 18. underground railway

succade... 8. preserve 10. confection

succeed... 5. ensue, occur 6. attain, follow, thrive 7. achieve, devolve, prosper, replace, triumph 8. come next, flourish, supplant 10. accomplish

succeeding... 4. next 7. ensuing, sequent 9. following 10. subsequent, successful 11. in the wake of

success... 2. go 3. hit 4. luck 5. elate 7. fortune, outcome 8. accolade, smash hit 10. prosperity 11. consequence

successful... 5. lucky 8. thriving 9. fortunate 10. prosperous, succeeding, triumphant 11. flourishing

succession... 3. row, run 5. music (rhythmic) 6. series 7. dynasty, lineage 8. sequence 9. posterity

succin... 5. amber

succinct... 4. curt 5. brief, hasty, short, terse 7. compact, concise, laconic, summary 10. compressed 11. compendious, sententious

succor, succour... 3. aid 4. abet, help

6. brandy (Alpine), relief, rescue
7. comfort, deliver, relieve, sustain
8. befriend, mitigate 10. assistance
succulent ... 3. uva 4. lush 5. juicy,
pappy, tasty 6. cactus, tender
succumb ... 3. die 5. faint, yield
6. perish, submit 7. give way 8. get
tired
such (as) ... 3. sic 4. like 7. certain,
similar 8. analogue 9. analogous
suction (as in clicks of Bantu) ...
9. implosive
Sudan, Africa ...
capital .. 8. Khartoum
desert .. 6. Libyan, Nubian
export .. 9. gum arabic
gazelle .. 4. dama
gum forests .. 8. Kordofan
lake .. 4. Chad
language .. 2. Ga 6. Arabic
people .. 4. Arab, Sere 5. Fulah
(Fula), Negro 6. Nubian
Plain .. 6. Gezira
river .. 8. Blue Nile 9. White Nile
town .. 5. Segou
sudden ... 4. rash 5. hasty, swift
6. abrupt, prompt, speedy 7. violent
8. headlong 9. impetuous,
impromptu, impulsive
10. unexpected, unforeseen
11. precipitate, precipitous
sudden (pert to) ...
all of a .. 5. short 6. presto
8. suddenly
and brilliant .. 8. meteoric
fear .. 13. consternation
sally .. 6. sortie
shock .. 4. jolt
stroke .. 4. coup, dash
thrust .. 3. jab 5. lunge
sudor ... 5. sweat 8. sudation
9. exudation 12. perspiration
Sudra caste ... 3. mal (low) 5. palli
sue ... 3. beg, woo 4. plea, urge
5. court, plead 6. appeal, pursue
7. entreat, request 8. continue,
petition 9. prosecute, seek after
suet ... 6. tallow 8. leaf lard
Suez Canal builder ... 9. de Lesseps
(Ferdinand)
suffer ... 3. let 4. bear, dree 5. admit,
allow 6. endure, permit, submit
7. undergo 8. tolerate
10. experience
suffer (pert to) ...
distress .. 5. gripe, groan, smart
6. starve
from heat .. 7. swelter
remorse .. 3. rue
ruin .. 5. wreck
sufferance ... 4. pain 6. misery
9. endurance, passivity
10. permission 11. forbearance
suffering, scene of ... 10. Gethsemane
suffice ... 2. do 5. avail, serve
6. answer 7. appease, content,
satisfy 11. sufficiency
sufficiency ... 4. fill 7. ability, conceit
8. adequacy, capacity, validity
9. abundance 10. competency
14. self–confidence
sufficient ... 3. due, fit 4. enow, full,

good 5. ample, valid 6. enough,
plenty 7. suffice 8. adequate
9. qualified 11. responsible
12. satisfactory
suffix, for or denoting ...
abounding in .. 5. ulent
abundant .. 3. ose
act of .. 3. ure 4. ance, tion
advocate .. 3. ite
alcohol .. 2. ol
being .. 3. ure
capable of .. 3. ile
chemical .. 2. ac 3. ane, ene, ile, ine,
iol, ole, ose 4. alic, idin, itol
diminutive .. 2. el 3. cle, ole, ule
4. ette
disease .. 4. itis
doer .. 4. ator
enzyme .. 3. ase
feminine .. 3. ess
follower .. 3. ist, ite
full of .. 3. ose
geological age .. 4. cene
inflammation .. 4. itis
inhabitants of .. 3. ese 4. ites
jurisdiction .. 3. ric
law .. 2. ee
medicine .. 2. ia 3. oma 4. itis
profession .. 3. eer
suffocate ... 5. burke, choke 6. stifle
7. smother 8. strangle, suppress,
throttle 10. asphyxiate, extinguish
12. deprive of air
suffrage ... 4. vote 5. voice 6. assent,
ballot, prayer 7. witness 8. petition
9. franchise 10. assistance 11. right
to vote 12. intercession, supplication
sugar ... 4. cane 5. biose, bribe,
candy, maple, money 6. doctor,
season 7. sucrose, sweeten
9. sugarcoat 10. endearment,
saccharose, sweetening
12. carbohydrate 13. dissaccharide
14. monosaccharide
sugar (pert to) ...
and molasses .. 6. melada
burnt .. 7. caramel
chemical .. 6. acrose 7. osamine,
sucrose 8. fructose 10. saccharose
crude .. 3. gur 5. maple
10. massecuite, piloncillo
fruit, honey .. 8. levulose
plant .. 7. sorghum
raw .. 9. cassonade, muscovado
sand .. 5. niter
simple .. 6. ketose, triose 7. glucide
substitute .. 5. honey
syrup .. 7. treacle 8. molasses
tree .. 5. maple
without .. 3. sec
wood .. 6. xylose
sugar cane (pert to) ...
disease .. 5. sereh
pulp, refuse .. 4. marc 7. bagasse
stalk .. 6. ratoon
sugared ... 5. sweet 7. honeyed
9. sweetened 11. mellifluous,
sugarcoated
suggest ... 4. hint, mean, move
5. imply 6. advise, allude, prompt
7. connote, inspire, propose
8. indicate, intimate 9. insinuate

suggestion... 4. clue, hint, idea, plan
  5. tinge, trace 6. advice, symbol
  7. soupçon 8. proposal 9. hypnotism
  10. indication, intimation 11. small
  amount, supposition
Suidae... 5. swine
suit... 3. fit 4. plea 5. befit, cards,
  dress, habit, match, serve, tally
  6. adjust, answer, attire, become,
  prayer, wooing 7. clothes, comport,
  conform, costume, lawsuit, retinue
  8. petition, sequence 9. courtship
  10. litigation 11. accommodate
suit (pert to)...
  at law.. 10. litigation
  for property.. 6. trover
  maker.. 6. sartor, tailor
  starter.. 7. relator
  the occasion.. 6. timely
suitability... 7. fitness 9. propriety
  10. expedience, timeliness
  11. eligibility 13. qualification
suitable... 3. apt, due, fit, pat
  4. meet 6. proper, timely
  8. adequate, apposite, eligible,
  idoneous 9. accordant, agreeable,
  competent, congruent, congruous,
  consonant, expedient 10. compatible,
  consistent 11. appropriate
  12. commensurate 13. correspondent
suitably proportioned...
  13. commensurable
suite... 3. set 5. music, staff
  7. retinue 8. sequence 9. apartment
  10. attendance, succession
  11. consequence
suitor... 5. swain, wooer 7. amoroso
  10. petitioner 12. party to a suit
sulk... 3. pet 4. mope, plow, pout
  6. furrow
sulky... 3. gig 4. dull, glum, plow
  5. moody, pouty, surly 6. gloomy,
  go–cart, sullen 8. carriage
  9. obstinate
sullen... 4. dour, glum, grim, sour
  5. cross, gruff, harsh, moody, pouty,
  sulky, surly 6. crusty, gloomy,
  morose 7. austere, cynical, fretful,
  peevish, pettish 8. chumpish,
  churlish, petulant, spiteful
  9. obstinate, saturnine
sully... 4. foul 5. dirty, smear, stain,
  taint 6. defile, smirch, vilify
  7. blemish, corrupt, debauch,
  disdain, pollute 9. bespatter,
  denigrate 10. stigmatize
  11. contaminate
sulphur (pert to)...
  alchemy.. 7. chibrit
  alloy.. 6. niello
  butterfly.. 7. clouded 9. cloudless
  color.. 6. yellow
  comb form.. 5. thion
  element.. 11. nonmetallic
  reference to.. 7. thionic 9. brimstone
sultan (pert to)...
  decree.. 5. irade
  fowls.. 5. breed
  home.. 5. serai
  Mohammedan State.. 5. ruler
    6. prince 9. sovereign
  Turkish ruler.. 6. Caliph 8. Padishah

  13. Grand Seignior
  wife.. 7. sultana
sultana... 4. roll (dessert), wife
  5. grape 8. mistress 9. gallinule
sultry... 3. hot 5. humid, lurid
  6. torrid 7. dog days, sensual
  10. oppressive, sweltering
sum... 3. add, tot 4. loot 5. count,
  gross, total, whole 6. amount,
  number, result 7. summary
  8. addition, quantity 9. aggregate,
  summarize, summation
  12. recapitulate
sum (pert to)...
  forfeited.. 5. dédit
  of money.. 6. budget
  total.. 8. entirety
  unexpended.. 7. savings
  up.. 3. tot 5. count 8. perorate
sumac... 5. Rheus 7. dogwood
  8. shadbush 9. squawbush
  13. Toxicodendron 14. buckthorn
  brown
Sumatra...
  harbor.. 6. Padang 9. Palembang
  island of.. 16. Malay Archipelago
  kingdom.. 5. Achin, Jambi
  mountain.. 12. Bukit Barisan
  raft (bamboo).. 5. rakit
  river.. 4. Musi 5. Jambi, Rokan
    6. Asahan
  squirrel shrew.. 4. tana
  wildcat.. 4. balu
sumless... 11. inestimable
  12. incalculable 13. unaccountable
summary... 5. brief, short 6. digest,
  prompt, resume 7. epitome
  8. abstract 10. compendium
  11. abridgement, enumeration,
  reiteration 14. recapitulation
summary (pert to)...
  book.. 5. blurb
  concise.. 6. précis
  of facts.. 7. roundup
  of knowledge.. 12. encyclopedia
    (encyclopaedia)
  of principles.. 5. creed
  of speech.. 5. notes
summer... 3. été 6. season
summer (pert to)...
  bird.. 7. cuckold, sparrow, tanager,
    wryneck
  coot.. 9. gallinule
  house.. 6. gazebo 9. belvedere
  lilac.. 8. damewort
  pert to.. 7. estival
  rash.. 11. prickly heat
  resort.. 4. camp
  squash.. 7. cymling, scallop
    9. crookneck
summit... 3. top 4. acme, apex, knap,
  peak 5. crest, crown, knoll, spire
  6. height 7. Everest 8. pinnacle
  9. fastigium 10. perfection
  11. culmination, mountaintop
summon... 4. call, cite, page, sist
  5. evoke 6. call up, demand, elicit,
  invite, muster 7. conjure, evocate
  8. remember 9. conscript
sumpter... 4. mule 9. pack horse
sun... 3. orb, Sol 4. bask 6. Helios
  7. Phoebus 12. heavenly body

13. celestial body
sun (pert to)...
clock.. 6. gnomon (part) 7. sundial
comb form.. 5. helio
crossing the equator.. 7. equinox
disk.. 4. aten
down.. 3. eve 8. twilight
farthest from.. 8. aphelion
fish.. 4. mola, opah 5. bream
god.. 2. Ra 4. Amen, Baal, Lier
   (Llew) 6. Apollo, Helios 7. Khepera
   (Chepera), Shamash, Sokaris
   8. Hyperion
mock.. 9. parhelion
nearest to.. 10. perihelion
outer layer.. 6. corona
over the equator.. 7. equinox
path.. 4. halo 6. circle 8. ecliptic
pert to.. 5. solar 6. heliac
   9. heliology
poetic.. 5. glory, power 6. sunset
   7. daystar, sunrise 8. splendor
satellite.. 6. planet
spot.. 6. facula 7. freckle
squall.. 9. jellyfish
stroke.. 8. siriasis 9. calenture
sundang... 4. bolo 5. knife
sunder... 4. part, rend, rive 5. sever,
   split 6. cleave, divide 7. divorce
   8. dissever, disunite, sejugate
sundry... 6. divers 7. several, various
   8. frequent, manifold, numerous
   9. different 10. multiplied
   12. multifarious 13. miscellaneous
sunflower... 8. marigold, rockrose
   10. heliotrope
Sunflower State... 6. Kansas
sunk... 4. turf 7. baffled, concave,
   lowered 8. dejected, overcome
   9. depressed (see also *sink*)
sunk fence... 4. ha–ha (haw–haw)
sunny... 4. warm 5. clear, merry
   6. bright, sunlit 8. cheerful
   9. sparkling, vivacious
sunrise... 4. dawn
sunset... 3. eve 4. dusk 7. evening,
   sundown 8. twilight
Sunset State... 6. Oregon 7. Arizona
Sunshine State... 9. New Mexico
   11. South Dakota
supawn... 4. mush 12. hasty pudding
superabundance... 5. flood 6. excess,
   plenty 7. surplus 8. plethora
   10. exuberance 11. superfluity
superabundant... 4. rank 6. lavish
   7. profuse 9. excessive, exuberant,
   luxuriant, plentiful 11. overflowing
   14. oversufficient
superannuate... 6. retire 9. antiquate
   10. pension off 13. prove obsolete
superb... 4. rich 5. grand, noble
   6. lordly 7. elegant, stately
   8. majestic, splendid 9. sumptuous
   11. magnificent 13. extraordinary
   14. superexcellent
supercilious... 5. proud 7. haughty
   8. arrogant 9. arbitrary
   11. overbearing 12. contemptuous
   13. hypercritical
supercilious person... 4. snob
superficial... 4. glib 6. slight, square
   7. cursory, shallow, smatter, surface,

trivial 8. apparent, external
   9. frivolous, insincere
superfluity... 6. excess, luxury, wealth
   7. overset 8. frippery 10. redundancy
   11. prodigality 14. superabundance
superfluous... 4. over 5. luxus, spare
   6. excess 7. surplus, useless
   8. needless, wasteful 9. redundant
   10. inordinate 11. extravagant
   12. nonessential 13. superabundant
   14. supererogatory
superhuman... 6. divine 9. Herculean
   12. supernatural 13. extraordinary
superimposed... 4. over, upon
   5. above 7. covered, layered
   8. overlaid 9. overlying
superintend... 4. boss 5. guide
   6. direct, manage 7. oversee
   8. overlook 9. look after, supervise
   10. administer, have charge
superintendent... 4. boss 7. curator,
   manager 8. director, overseer
   9. inspector, straw boss
   10. supervisor 11. chamberlain
superior... 4. over, peer 5. above,
   chief, upper 6. higher, senior
   7. exalted, mastery, ranking
   8. goodness, priority 9. advantage,
   paramount, seniority 10. ascendancy,
   excellence, pre–eminent, surpassing
   11. pre–eminence 12. predominancy
superlative... 4. acme, best, peak
   6. utmost 7. elative, extreme,
   supreme, the best 8. peerless
   9. hyperbole 12. exaggeration
supernatural... 5. eerie, magic
   6. divine 10. miraculous,
   superhuman 13. hyperphysical,
   preternatural
supernatural (pert to)...
being.. 3. God 4. atua 5. jinni
   (jinnee) 7. banshee (banshie), specter
   (spectre)
event.. 7. miracle
power.. 4. ngai 6. fetish 8. talisman
   11. incantation
superscribe... 6. direct 7. address (a
   letter), engrave 8. inscribe
supersede... 4. omit 7. replace,
   succeed 8. displace, make void,
   supplant
superstition... 6. notion, voodoo
   8. folklore, idolatry 9. tradition
   10. Aberglaube 12. old wives' tale
superstitious... 6. goetic 7. magical
   10. idolatrous 11. fetishistic
   (fetichistic)
supervene... 5. occur 6. accrue,
   happen 7. be added 12. be
   subsequent
supervise... 4. boss, read, scan
   5. check 6. direct, govern, peruse,
   revise 7. inspect, oversee
   11. superintend
supervisor... 4. boss 7. foreman,
   proctor 9. inspector, straw boss
supine... 5. inert, prone 6. abject,
   drowsy 7. servile, unalert 8. careless,
   inclined, indolent, listless, sluggish
   9. apathetic, lethargic, recumbent
   11. inattentive, indifferent,
   thoughtless

supplant... 5. upset, usurp 6. remove, uproot 7. replace 8. displace, drive out 9. eradicate, extirpate, overthrow, supersede

supple... 3. sly 4. bent 5. agile, lithe 6. limber, nimble, pliant 7. fawning, lissome 8. flexible, yielding 9. compliant, resilient 10. obsequious, responsive 11. complaisant

supplement... 3. add, eke 5. add to 6. sequel 7. ripieno 8. addition, appendix, complete 9. accessory 10. complement 12. nonessential 13. reinforcement

supplementary, music... 7. ripieno

supplicate... 3. beg 4. pray 5. crave, plead 6. appeal, obtest 7. beseech, conjure, entreat, implore, solicit 8. petition 9. importune, obsecrate

supplication... 4. plea 6. litany, prayer 7. craving 8. entreaty, petition, rogative 11. obtestation 12. solicitation

supplies... 6. hoards, relays, stocks, stores 8. estovers, ordnance 9. provender

supply... 4. fund, give 5. cache, cater, hoard, relay, stock, store, yield 6. purvey, remuda 7. provide, reserve 9. provision, reservoir 10. administer, contribute

supply (pert to)...
food.. 4. feed 5. cater 9. alimental
fuel.. 5. stoke
funds.. 5. endow
horses.. 5. relay
provisions.. 6. purvey

support... 3. aid, arm, fid, guy, leg, peg, rib 4. abet, ally, back, base, buoy, limb, mast, prop 5. brace, cleat, shore, spile, stell, strut, tenon 6. backer, pillar, second, uphold 7. bolster, fulcrum, trestle 8. buttress, underlie 9. auxiliary, encourage, reinforce, stanchion 10. assistance, foundation 11. corroborate 12. substantiate 13. corroboration

support (pert to)...
anatomy.. 3. rib 5. spine
cannon.. 8. trunnion
coffin.. 4. bier
mast.. 4. bibb
resilient.. 6. spring
three–legged.. 5. easel 6. tripod, trivot
upright.. 8. baluster 9. stanchion
wedge–shaped.. 5. cleat

supporters... 6. allies, braces 7. backers, bracers, garters 10. suspenders 15. ministerialists

suppose... 3. wis 4. deem, trow 5. allow, imply, judge, opine, think 6. assume, expect, repute 7. presume 8. conclude, consider 9. apprehend, intention 10. conjecture 11. supposition

supposed... 8. putative

supposition... 2. if 6. theory 7. surmise 8. supposed 9. postulate 10. assumption, conjecture,

hypothesis 11. connotation, implication

suppress... 4. kill, stop 5. check, crush, elide, quash, quell 6. hush up, muffle, retard, stifle 7. abolish, exclude, oppress, smother 8. hold back, prohibit, restrain, withhold 9. interdict, overpower 10. extinguish

suppression... 6. hush up 7. reserve 8. hush–hush 9. overthrow, restraint 10. inhibition

supremacy... 5. power 7. control, mastery, primacy 8. dominion 9. influence 10. ascendancy, domination, first place 11. sovereignty 12. championship

supreme... 3. top 4. last 5. chief, final 6. divine, ruling 7. crucial, highest 8. foremost, greatest, peerless 9. paramount 10. preeminent

supreme being... 3. God 4. Lord 5. Allah, Deity, monad 6. Brahma, Buddha 7. Creator, Jehovah 8. autocrat

surcease... 3. end 4. rest, stop 5. defer, delay 6. desist, relief 7. respite 8. drop work, postpone 9. cessation

surd... 4. deaf, mute 7. aphonic, radical 9. voiceless

sure... 3. yes 4. fast, firm, safe, true 5. bound 6. indeed, secure, stable, steady, strong 7. assured, certain 8. positive, reliable 9. confident, steadfast, unfailing 10. guaranteed, inevitable, infallible 11. trustworthy 12. indisputable 13. incontestable 14. unquestionable

surety... 4. bail, bond, fact 6. backer, pledge, safety 7. sponsor 8. security, sureness 9. certainty 10. confidence, engagement

surf... 4. foam, rote, wave 5. bathe, spray, surge, swell 7. breaker

surface... 4. area, face, orlo, pave, plat, skin 5. facet, meros 6. facing, patina 7. outside 8. exterior 9. periphery

surface (pert to)...
artificial.. 4. rink
front (coin).. 7. obverse
gem.. 5. facet
geometric.. 6. toroid
medical.. 7. acrotic
toward.. 5. ectad
under.. 6. latent 10. internally
water.. 4. ryme

surfeit... 4. cloy, feed, glut, jade, sate 6. excess 7. replete, satiate, satisfy 9. satiation 11. overindulge, superfluity

surge... 4. eddy, flow, rush, wave 5. swarm, swell, whirl 6. billow, thrill 7. estuate 9. gurgitate 11. rise and fall

surgeon (pert to)...
ancient.. 10. chirurgeon
case (instrument).. 6. tweeze (tweese)
slang.. 8. sawbones

surgery... 7. aciurgy 8. medicine 9. operation, resection

surgery (pert to)...
chin .. 11. mentoplasty
ears .. 9. otoplasty
face lift .. 13. rhytidoplasty
  14. blepharoplasty (eyelids)
fractures .. 10. agmatology
mouth, lip .. 12. cheiloplasty
  (chiloplasty)
nose .. 7. nose job 11. rhinoplasty
organ .. 10. transplant
skin .. 12. dermabrasion
vein .. 10. phlebotomy
vertebra .. 11. laminectomy
surgical (pert to)...
compress .. 4. swab 5. stupe
counterirritant .. 5. seton
equpment .. 4. X–ray 6. splint 7. CAT
  scan, scanner 8. iron lung
  10. respirator, tomography, tourniquet
  11. stethoscope 12. resuscitator
hook .. 9. tenaculum
instrument .. 3. saw 5. fleam, lance,
  probe 6. catlin, lancet, stylet, trepan,
  xyster 7. forceps 8. hemostat,
  keratome, speculum, tweezers
knife .. 7. scalpel
puncture .. 8. centesis
saw .. 6. trepan
stitch .. 5. seton 6. suture
Suriname (pert to)...
capital .. 10. Paramaribo
former name .. 11. Dutch Guiana
mountain .. 10. Tumuc–Humac
toad .. 4. pipa
surly ... 4. glum, grum, rude 5. gruff
  6. abrupt, grumpy, morose, sullen
  7. crabbed 8. arrogant, growling
  10. ill–natured 11. intractable
surmise ... 4. deem 5. fancy, guess,
  judge, opine, think 7. imagine,
  presume 8. mistrust 9. suspicion
  10. assumption, conclusion,
  conjecture 11. supposition
surmount ... 3. top 4. pass, rise
  5. climb, excel, mount 6. subdue
  7. conquer, surpass 8. overcome
  9. transcend
surname ... 6. eponym, family, maiden
  7. agnomen 8. cognomen
  10. patronymic 11. appellation
surpass ... 3. cap, top 4. best
  5. excel, outdo 6. better, exceed,
  outvie, outwit 7. outrank, outride
  8. go beyond, outrange, outreach,
  outshine, outsmart, outstrip, surmount
  9. transcend
surpassing ... 12. transcendent
surplice ... 3. fee 5. cotta, ephod
  6. collar 7. pelisse
surplus ... 4. over, rest 5. epact
  6. excess 7. overage, reserve
  8. overplus 9. remaining
  10. additional, redundancy
  11. superfluous
surprise ... 3. awe 5. alarm, amaze,
  seize, shock 6. wonder 7. astound,
  capture, perplex, startle 8. astonish,
  bewilder, confound, dumfound
  9. amazement, dumbfound,
  overwhelm, surprisal 10. wonderment
  11. flabbergast 12. astonishment
surprising ... 7. amazing 8. striking

  9. startling 10. unexpected
  11. astonishing, unlooked for
  13. extraordinary
surrender ... 4. cede, give 5. yield
  6. give up, remise, resign
  7. abandon, cession, deliver
  8. dedition, remittal 9. extradite
  10. relinquish, submission
  11. abandonment, divestiture
  12. cancellation 14. relinquishment
surreptitious ... 3. sly 6. hidden,
  secret 8. stealthy 9. concealed,
  deceitful 10. fraudulent
  11. clandestine
surround ... 4. gird, isle, wrap
  5. beset, hem in, inarm 6. circle,
  encase, incase, invest 7. besiege,
  enclave, enclose, envelop, environ
  8. encircle, inundate, overflow
  9. encompass 12. circumscribe
  14. circumnavigate
surrounding ... 5. about, beset, midst
  7. ambient, setting 9. hemming in,
  perioptic 10. encircling, enveloping
  11. circumpolar 12. circumjacent
survey ... 4. plan, poll, scan 5. study,
  vista 6. regard, review 7. examine,
  inspect, oversee 8. traverse
  9. delineate, determine 10. scrutinize
  11. examination, reconnoiter,
  superintend 14. reconnaissance
surveying (pert to)...
instrument .. 7. alidade (alidad), transit
  9. stadia rod 10. throdolite
mathematics .. 7. geodesy
process .. 13. triangulation
surveyor (pert to)...
helper .. 6. rodman 7. lineman,
  poleman
land .. 8. measurer, overseer
  9. arpenteur
measure .. 5. chain
mine .. 6. dialer
survival ... 5. relic 9. endurance,
  outliving 10. durability
survivor ... 6. relict 8. outliver,
  remainer, survival 11. joint tenant
susceptibility ... 5. sense 7. emotion,
  feeling, pliancy 11. sensibility
  12. teachability 13. affectibility,
  vulnerability 14. sentimentality
susceptible ... 4. easy 6. liable, pliant
  7. exposed, subject 8. sensible
  9. receptive, sensitive, teachable
  10. responsive, vulnerable
  11. softhearted 13. tenderhearted
  14. impressionable
suslik ... 5. sisel 8. squirrel
  11. spermophile
suspect ... 4. fear 5. doubt, fancy,
  guess 7. imagine, presume, suppose
  8. distrust, mistrust 9. discredit
  10. disbelieve, suspicious
suspecting ... 4. wary 8. doubtful,
  doubting 11. incredulous, mistrusting
suspend ... 4. hang, oust, stay, stop
  5. cease, debar, defer, expel, remit
  6. dangle, depose, recess 7. adjourn,
  pensile 8. intermit, postpone, set
  aside, withhold 9. pretermit
suspended ... 4. hung 5. inert
  6. barred, latent 7. abeyant, pendent

8. inactive 9. pendulous
11. inoperative, interrupted
suspenders... 4. pegs 5. belts, hooks,
rings 6. braces, straps 7. gallows,
garters 8. galluses 9. bretelles
10. supporters 11. clothespins
suspense... 5. pause 7. anxiety
10. expectancy 11. uncertainty
12. apprehension, irresolution
14. indecisiveness
suspension... 4. stop 5. delay
7. deposal, failure, hanging, respite
8. abeyance, buoyancy
11. withholding 12. intermission,
interruption
suspicious... 4. fear, hint 5. doubt,
hunch, trace 7. askance, inkling,
soupçon 8. distrust, jealousy,
mistrust, wariness 9. mere trace,
misgiving 10. diffidence, intimation,
skepticism, suggestion 11. incredulity,
supposition 12. apprehension
Sussex (pert to)...
breed (Eng).. 4. fowl 6. cattle
kingdom (anc).. 7. English
land measure.. 4. wist
land tract (Downs).. 5. laine
man.. 8. Piltdown (Prehist)
spaniel.. 6. gun dog
sustain... 4. bear, buoy, feed, prop
5. abide, carry 6. endure, foster,
keep up, uphold 7. confirm, justify,
nourish, prolong, support, undergo
8. continue, maintain, preserve
9. encourage, establish
10. strengthen 11. corroborate
sustained... 6. tenuto, upheld
9. permanent, prolonged, supported
10. unflagging
Susu... 5. tribe (Afr)
suttee... 5. widow 9. cremation,
sacrifice 14. self–immolation
suture... 5. unite 6. stitch 7. pterion
12. synarthrosis
swagger... 4. brag, gait, walk 5. bluff,
boast, bully, strut, swell 6. prance
7. bluster, dashing, roister, stagger,
stylish 8. domineer 11. braggadocio,
ostentation 16. ultrafashionable
swain... 3. boy, lad 4. beau 5. lover
6. suitor 7. admirer, gallant, peasant
8. shepherd 10. countryman
swallow... 3. sip 4. gulp 5. drink
6. absorb, englut, engulf, imbibe,
ingest, recant 7. consume, engorge,
retract 8. tolerate 10. bear meekly
swallow (pert to)...
chimney.. 5. swift
European.. 6. martin
hawk.. 4. kite
plover.. 10. pratincole
sea.. 4. tern
tail.. 4. coat 9. butterfly
the anchor.. 10. quit the sea
swamp... 3. bog, fen 4. mire, muck,
sink, slue, sump 5. flood, marsh
6. deluge, engulf, morass, slough
7. cienaga, pocosin 8. quagmire,
submerge 9. everglade, overwhelm
swamp (pert to)...
boggy.. 7. queachy 8. muskeggy
earth.. 4. muck

gas.. 6. miasma
grass.. 5. sedge
marsh.. 5. slash 8. paludine
tract.. 10. Everglades
swan... 3. cob, pen 4. Olor 5. swear
6. cygnet, cygnus 7. declare
9. trumpeter
swan (pert to)...
astronomy.. 6. Cygnus
flower.. 6. orchid
goose.. 7. Bewick's, Chinese
myth (Hind).. 5. hansa
poem.. 12. Swan of Thames (Pope)
15. Sweet Swan of Avon (Jonson)
star (brightest).. 5. Deneb
trumpeter.. 4. wild
type.. 4. mute 5. black 8. whooping
11. black–necked
swap... 4. beat 5. trade 6. barter,
thrash 8. exchange
11. give–and–take
sward... 3. sod 4. lawn, turf 5. grass
10. greensward
swarm... 3. fry 5. crowd, flock, horde
6. abound, infest, throng 7. pervade
9. migration, multitude
10. congregate 11. aggregation
swarthy... 3. dun 4. dark 5. dusky
8. bistered (bistred), blackish
swashbuckler... 5. bravo 6. gascon
7. ruffian 8. Almanzor 9. blusterer,
daredevil, swaggerer 10. Drawcansir
swastika (swastica)... 6. fylfot, symbol
(since 1918) 9. gammadion
10. hakenkreuz
swat... 3. bat, hit 5. clout 6. strike
7. hit hard
swathe... 4. band, bind, wrap
6. enfold 7. envelop, swaddle
sway... 4. bend, bias, rock, rule, veer,
wave 5. lurch, power, shake, swing,
waver, wield 6. direct, empire,
govern, induce, totter, waddle
7. command, control, deflect, incline
8. flounder 9. fluctuate, influence,
oscillate, vacillate 10. ascendancy
11. fluctuation
swayback... 8. lordosis
swaying... 7. pensile, sagging
8. swinging, waddling 11. influential,
oscillating
swear... 3. vow 4. oath 5. curse,
vouch 6. adjure, pledge (sacred)
7. confirm, declare, promise
10. asseverate, deposition 11. bear
witness
swear (pert to)...
at.. 5. clash (colors), curse
8. disagree
by.. 5. bet on 7. count on 8. take
oath
falsely.. 7. perjure
off.. 4. stop 6. eschew, give up
7. abandon 8. renounce
sweat... 4. work 5. exude, grill, sudor
6. drudge 7. excrete, ferment
8. perspire, transude 9. exudation
10. impatience 11. nervousness
Sweden... see also *Swedish*
capital.. 9. Stockholm
city.. 7. Uppsala (Upsala)
dynasty (1st).. 8. Ynglings

gulf .. **7.** Bothnia
lake .. **6.** Vanern **7.** Vattern
mountain .. **5.** Kölen (Kjölen)
parliament .. **7.** Riksdag
peninsula .. **11.** Scandinavia
port .. **8.** Göteborg **9.** Stockholm
river .. **4.** Klar **7.** Götaalv
sea .. **6.** Baltic
university (oldest) .. **7.** Uppsula (Upsula, 1477)
Swedish (pert to) . . .
artist .. **4.** Zorn
bread .. **10.** knäckebröd
clover .. **6.** alsike
dance .. **6.** polska
explorer .. **5.** Hedin
fir .. **10.** Scotch pine
idiom .. **7.** Suecism
manual training .. **5.** sloyd (slojd)
novelist .. **8.** Lagerlöf (Pulitzer prize, 1909)
philosopher .. **10.** Swedenborg
religion (State) .. **8.** Lutheran
soprano .. **10.** Jennie Lind
    18. Swedish Nightingale
turnip .. **8.** rutabaga
sweep . . . **3.** oar **4.** scan **5.** clean, clear, cover, curve, glide, strip, surge, swish, trail **6.** course, vision **7.** contour **8.** traverse
sweeping . . . **8.** complete, thorough **9.** extensive **12.** all–embracing **13.** comprehensive
sweet . . . **5.** bonny, candy **10.** dolce douce **5.** fresh, spicy **6.** dulcet, gentle, sugary, syrupy **7.** caramel, honeyed, lovable **8.** aromatic, fragrant, luscious, pleasant, preserve **9.** agreeable, ambrosial, melodious, nectarine **10.** confection, saccharine **11.** mellifluous, mellisonant
sweet (pert to) . . .
and fair .. **5.** bonny
bread .. **4.** food **6.** thymus **8.** pancreas **9.** ris de veau
brier .. **4.** rose **9.** eglantine
drink .. **6.** nectar
meat .. **4.** cake **5.** candy **6.** comfit, éclair, pastry **7.** caramel, dessert **8.** marzipan **10.** confection
potato .. **3.** yam **6.** batata
potato, musical .. **7.** ocarina
sop .. **4.** ates, atta **6.** Annone **14.** Annona squamosa
sounding .. **11.** mellisonant
wine .. **4.** port **5.** Lunel
sweetheart . . . **2.** jo **3.** gra **4.** beau, lass **5.** flame, leman, lover, spark, swain **7.** darling **8.** dowsabel, honeybun (sl) **9.** Amaryllis, inamorata, valentine
swell . . . **3.** fob, nob **4.** grow, rise, surf, wave **5.** bulge, dandy, grand, heave, mound, surge **6.** billow, dilate, expand, growth, puff up, tiptop **7.** distend, inflate, stylish **8.** increase, protrude **9.** sumptuous **10.** aristocrat, prominence **11.** enlargement **12.** augmentation
swell (pert to) . . .
ocean .. **4.** surf **6.** billow, expand, roller

rolling .. **7.** seagate
slang .. **3.** nob **5.** dandy, grand **9.** first–rate
swelled (pert to) . . .
head .. **3.** ego **7.** conceit **9.** cockiness **14.** self–importance
out .. **4.** lump, node **5.** tumid **6.** bulged, podded, turgid **9.** grandiose
swelling . . . **4.** sore **5.** bulge, edema **6.** dropsy **9.** bombastic **10.** distention, increasing **12.** protuberance
swelter . . . **4.** fret **5.** exude, roast, sweat **8.** perspire **10.** sultry heat
swerve . . . **4.** veer **5.** dodge, sheer, shift **6.** recoil **7.** deflect, deviate **9.** deviation, turn aside
swift . . . **4.** bird, fast, racy, reel **5.** alert, fleet, hasty, quick, rapid, ready **6.** lizard, prompt, speedy, sudden, winged **8.** headlong
swift (pert to) . . .
astronomer .. **5.** Lewis (Swift)
bird .. **4.** crin **7.** chimney
boat .. **7.** flyboat **10.** Hovercraft
footed .. **5.** ariel (gazelle) **7.** Mercury
satirist .. **8.** Jonathan (Swift)
swiftness . . . **5.** haste, speed **8.** celerity, velocity **9.** quickness **10.** promptness
swimmer . . . **5.** diver **6.** bather **7.** Cloelia (Tiber Riv), Leander (Hellespont), natator
swimming . . . **5.** crawl **6.** natant **7.** vertigo **9.** dizziness, freestyle, skinny–dip **10.** sidestroke **12.** breast stroke
swimming (pert to) . . .
birds .. **9.** natatores
bladder .. **10.** air bladder (fish)
pert to .. **5.** dizzy **7.** aquatic **8.** natatory
pool .. **4.** hole, tank **10.** natatorium
sandpiper .. **9.** phalarope
swindle . . . **3.** con, gyp **4.** dupe, fake, sell **5.** bunco, cheat **6.** trepan **7.** defraud **8.** flimflam **9.** gold brick
swindler . . . **3.** gyp **5.** biter, cheat, crook, knave, rogue, shark **6.** gypper **7.** sharper **9.** defrauder
swindling . . . **6.** estafa
swine . . . **3.** hog, pig, sow, Sus **4.** boar **7.** Anthony (smallest), peccary **8.** slattern **9.** scoundrel
swine, breed of . . . **8.** Cheshire, Tamworth **9.** Berkshire, Hampshire, razorback, Yorkshire **11.** Duroc–Jersey, Poland China **12.** Chester–White
swineherd (pert to) . . .
patron saint .. **7.** Anthony
reference to .. **7.** sybotic
swinelike . . . **7.** porcine
swing . . . **4.** hang, jazz, jive, lilt, sway **5.** shake, trend, waver, wield **6.** dangle, manage, rhythm, totter **7.** suspend, trapeze, vibrate **8.** pendulum, undulate **9.** fluctuate, oscillate
swingtree . . . **11.** whippletree
swinish . . . **5.** gross **6.** carnal, filthy,

greedy **7.** beastly, porcine, sensual **8.** gluttony
swipe... **4.** gulp **5.** draft, drink, lever, steal, swape, swath, sweep **6.** handle, pilfer, snatch **7.** purloin
swipes... **4.** beer (Eng sl)
swirl... **4.** curl, eddy **5.** curve, gurge, surge, twist, whirl, whorl
swirly... **7.** knotted, tangled, twisted
Swiss (pert to)... see also *Switzerland*
ax (ice).. **6.** piolet
bell.. **9.** alpenhorn (alphorn)
cabin.. **6.** chalet
composer.. **4.** Raff
flower, emblem.. **9.** edelweiss
herdsman.. **4.** senn
hero.. **11.** William Tell
language.. **6.** French, German **7.** Italian **8.** Romansch
legislature.. **9.** Bundesrat (Bundesrath), Grosse Rat (Grossrat)
mathematician.. **5.** Euler
pine.. **6.** arolla
scientist.. **6.** Haller (von)
surgeon.. **6.** Kocher (Nobel Prize)
theologian.. **5.** Vinet
warble.. **5.** yodel
warbler.. **7.** yodeler (yodeller)
wind.. **4.** bise
wine.. **7.** Dezaley
Switzerland (pert to)...
ancient.. **8.** Helvetia
canton.. **5.** Aarau
capital.. **5.** Berne (Bern)
city.. **5.** Basel **6.** Geneva, Zurich **7.** Locarno, Lucerne **8.** Lausanne **9.** Constance
famed for.. **5.** banks (Finan)
lake.. **3.** Uri **6.** Brienz, Geneva, Zurich **7.** Lucerne **8.** Maggiore **9.** Constance, Neuchâtel **10.** Stattersee
mountain.. **4.** Alps, Jura **5.** Blanc **8.** Jungfrau **9.** Monte Rosa (peak) **10.** Matterhorn
resort.. **7.** Urseren, Yverdon
river.. **3.** Aar **5.** Reuss, Rhine, Rhone
tunnel.. **5.** Cenis **7.** Gothard, Simplon **11.** Loetschberg
university (oldest).. **5.** Basel
valley.. **3.** Aar
swollen... **5.** pursy, tumid **6.** turgid **7.** bloated, bulbous, bulging, pompous **8.** enlarged, inflated, puffed up, varicose **9.** bombastic, distended, plethoric, tumescent **11.** protuberant
swoon... **3.** fit **5.** faint, spell **7.** ecstasy, syncope **8.** languish **10.** heavy sleep
swoop... **5.** seize, sweep **6.** attack, pounce **7.** descend
sword (pert to)...
ancient.. **5.** estoc **6.** glaive
cavalry.. **5.** saber (sabre)
curved.. **7.** cutlass, Ferrara **8.** Claymore, scimitar
fencing.. **4.** foil, epee **6.** rapier
fine.. **6.** Toledo **8.** Damascus
handle.. **4.** haft, hilt
India.. **5.** kukri
like.. **7.** xiphoid

Mohammedan's.. **8.** scimitar
part.. **5.** forte, talon **6.** foible
practice.. **5.** fence
scabbard tip.. **7.** crampit
Scot Highlander's.. **4.** dirk
seaman's.. **6.** hanger
shaped.. **6.** ensate **7.** xiphoid (xyphoid) **8.** ensiform, gladiate
sheik's.. **4.** pata
Siegfried's.. **4.** Gram **7.** Balmung
Sir Bevis'.. **7.** Morglay
Spanish.. **5.** bilbo
support.. **7.** baldric
two–handed.. **7.** espadon
type.. **4.** epee, pata **5.** blade, degen, estoc, gully, saber **6.** barong, creese, parang, rapier **7.** cutlass **9.** gladiolus
swordfish... **6.** dorado, Dorado (constellation), espada **7.** espadon, Xiphias **9.** broadbill
sword of...
Damocles.. **12.** fateful thing
God.. **6.** Khaled (Moslem hero)
mercy.. **7.** Curtana (pointless)
Sir Bevis.. **7.** Morglay (death)
St George.. **7.** Askelon
the Cid.. **6.** Colada
swordsman... **6.** fencer **7.** duelist, epeeist, saberer, sabreur **9.** gladiator **11.** Beau Sabreur
sworn statement... **9.** affidavit
sworn to secrecy... **5.** tiled
sybarite... **7.** epicure **10.** voluptuary **11.** luxury lover
sybil (sibil)... **4.** seer **5.** witch **7.** seeress **10.** prophetess **13.** fortuneteller
syce... **5.** groom
sycophant... **5.** toady **7.** fawning, spaniel **8.** hanger–on, informer, parasite **9.** charlatan, flatterer, toadeater **10.** talebearer
sycophantic... **7.** fawning, servile, slavish **8.** obedient, toadying **10.** obsequious **11.** bootlicking
syllable...
accented.. **5.** arsis
by syllable.. **11.** syllabation
charm.. **2.** om **6.** mantra
last.. **6.** ultima
last, omission of.. **7.** apocope
last but one.. **6.** penult
last but two.. **10.** antepenult
lengthening of.. **7.** ectasis
ref to.. **5.** affix **6.** prefix, suffix **8.** dactylic, syllabic
short.. **4.** mora
shortening.. **7.** systole
stress.. **5.** ictus
table.. **9.** syllabary
unaccented.. **4.** lene **6.** thesis
syllabled, three... **7.** triseme (3 moras) **11.** trisyllabic
syllabus... **6.** aperçu, digest **8.** abstract, synopsis **10.** compendium, conspectus
syllogism... **7.** premise, sorites **9.** deduction, reasoning **11.** epicheirema (epichirema) **18.** deductive reasoning
sylvan, silvan... **5.** woody **6.** groved, rustic, wooded **8.** forested

10. forestlike
sylvan deity... 3. Pan 4. faun
5. Satyr, Vidar 6. Faunus
symbol... 2. om 4. icon, palm, sign,
type 5. badge, crest, cross, image,
token, totem 6. emblem, ensign,
figure, letter, number 9. character
(graphic), prototype, trademark
12. abbreviation
symbol (pert to)...
authority.. 4. mace
bondage.. 4. yoke
ecclesiastic.. 4. ring
England.. 4. lion
France.. 4. lily
mathematics.. 7. operand
military.. 3. bar 4. star 5. eagle,
wings 6. stripe 7. chevron, epaulet
(epaulette) 8. caduceus
peace.. 4. dove
power.. 4. mace
prayer figure (anc).. 5. orant
royal.. 3. rod 5. crown, tiara
6. corona 7. scepter (sceptre)
Tammany Hall.. 5. tiger
tribal.. 5. totem (pole)
victory.. 4. palm
symbol for...
arsenic.. 2. As
calcium.. 2. Ca
chromium.. 2. Cr
copper.. 2. Cu
gold.. 2. Au
iron.. 2. Fe
lead.. 2. Pb
neon.. 2. Ne
nickel.. 2. Ni
radium.. 2. Ra
silver.. 2. Ag, Ar
sodium.. 2. Na
tin.. 2. Sn
symbolic, symbolical... 7. typical
9. imagerial 10. figurative, relational
11. allegorical, significant
12. emblematical 14. representative
symbolism... 7. mystery, writing
9. mysticism, ritualism, symbolics
10. figuration 11. hieroglyphy
14. representation
symmetric, symmetrical... 7. orderly,
regular, spheral, uniform 8. balanced
10. euphonious
symmetry... 5. order 7. balance,
euphony, harmony 8. equality
9. congruity 10. conformity,
proportion 11. consistency
sympathetic... 4. kind 6. humane,
tender 7. empathy, pitying
8. dewy–eyed 10. responsive
13. compassionate, understanding
sympathy... 4. pity 5. favor
7. consent, harmony, support
8. affinity, interest 9. agreeable,
agreement, tolerance 11. sensitivity
13. commiseration, understanding
sympathy, lack of... 8. dyspathy
9. antipathy
symphony... 6. accord 7. concert,
harmony 8. ritornel 9. orchestra
10. consonance 11. composition
symposium... 4. book, talk 7. banquet
8. dialogue, tippling 10. collection,

discussion 11. compotation
symptom... 4. mark, note, omen, sign
5. alarm, token 7. warning
10. indication
synagogue... 6. temple 10. tabernacle
12. congregation
synagogue (pert to)...
founder (anc).. 4. Ezra
platform.. 7. almemar
singer.. 6. cantor, chazan (chazzan)
synchronize... 5. agree 6. concur
8. coincide 9. harmonize
12. contemporize
syncopation... 5. tempo 7. ragtime,
syncope
syncope... 5. faint, swoon 7. elision
8. fainting, swooning 9. haplology
11. contraction, hyphaeresis
syndicate... 5. chain (journalistic),
group, trust 6. cartel, school
7. combine, council 9. committee
10. underworld 11. association
12. organization
synonym... 7. antonym, homonym,
metonym 8. identity 9. heteronym
synonymous... 4. like 5. alike
7. similar 10. equivalent,
homonymous
synopsis... 6. digest, manual
7. epitome, summary 8. abstract,
syllabus 9. statement 10. abridgment
(abridgement), compendium,
conspectus, tabulation
synthesis... 5. logic 11. combination,
composition 13. incorporation
14. identification
Syracuse (pert to)...
ancient name.. 8. Siracusa
city of.. 6. Sicily
famed for.. 6. battle (BC)
founded by.. 6. Greeks
tyrant of.. 9. Dionysius
Syria, Arab Republic... see also
Syrian
ancient name.. 4. Aram
capital.. 8. Damascus
city.. 4. Hama, Homs 6. Aleppo,
Beirut 7. Antioch, Latakia
8. Damascus
language.. 6. Arabic
organization, party.. 5. Baath
river.. 6. Barada, Jordan 7. Orontes
9. Euphrates
Syrian (pert to)...
antiquarian.. 11. Syriologist
deity.. 2. El 4. Baal 6. Mammon
7. Resheph
goat.. 6. Angora
grass.. 7. Johnson
mallow.. 4. okra
script.. 8. Peshitta (Peshito)
10. estrangelo 11. Syro–Chaldee
sect.. 5. Druse
tribe.. 7. Ansarie (Ansarieh)
wind (hot).. 6. simoom (simoon)
syrinx... 4. tomb 6. larynx 7. Panpipe
10. mouthpiece (anc lute)
13. Arcadian nymph
syrup, sirup... 4. Karo, sapa 5. maple
6. orgeat 7. dhebbus, glucose,
sorghum, treacle 8. molasses
9. grenadine

system... 3. ism, way 4. code, plan
  5. order 6. regime, theory
  8. religion, universe 9. procedure
  10. hypothesis, regularity
  11. arrangement, orderliness
system (pert to)...
  conduct.. 4. code
  eating.. 4. diet 7. dietary
  geological.. 5. Trias
  management.. 6. regime
  manual training.. 5. sloyd
  mystic.. 6. cabala
  numbering.. 7. decimal
  pitch (Mus).. 5. neume
  religious.. 4. cult 6. cultus
  solar.. 6. planet
  weights.. 4. long, troy 5. cubic
    6. liquid 11. avoirdupois
    12. apothecaries'
systematic... 4. neat 6. formal
  7. orderly, regular 9. organized,

schematic 10. methodical
systematics... 8. taxonomy
  14. classification
systematize... 4. code 6. codify
  7. arrange 8. classify, organize,
  regiment 9. catalogue (catalog),
  formulate
systematized knowledge... 7. science
systole (pert to)...
  correlative.. 8. diastole
  medical.. 11. contraction (heart)
    14. coming and going
  rhyme.. 10. shortening (syllable)
syzygy (pert to)...
  astronomy.. 7. appulse
    11. conjunction
  Gnosticism.. 5. aeons (pair)
  rhyme.. 11. coupled feet (group)
  zoology.. 5. union 7. segment
szlachta... 8. nobility (Poland)
szopelka... 4. oboe (Russ)

T

T... 3. tau (Gr) 6. letter (20th)
taa... 6. pagoda
Taal... 8. language 9. Afrikaans
taar... 10. tambourine
Taaroa... 3. God
tab... 3. pan, tag 4. bill, cost, flap,
  loop 5. aglet (aiglet), label, strip
  6. eartab, record 7. account, latchet,
  pendant (pendent) 9. afterpart,
  appendage, reckoning 10. accounting
tabac... 5. brown, snuff 7. tobacco
tabard... 4. cape 5. cloak 6. chimer,
  jacket, mantle
Tabard... 3. Inn (Canterbury Tales)
tabatière... 8. snuffbox
tabby... 3. cat 4. gown, silk 5. dress
  6. fabric, gossip 7. old maid, taffeta
tabernacle... 4. tent 5. abode, niche
  6. church, temple 7. shelter, support
  8. enshrine 9. sanctuary
  10. habitation
table... 4. fare, list, slab 5. board,
  panel, plate, stand 6. lamina, repast,
  tablet, teapoy 7. console, plateau,
  weights 8. postpone, put aside,
  synopsis, tabulate 9. reference
  10. collection 14. multiplication
table (pert to)...
  calculating.. 6. abacus
  centerpiece.. 7. epergne
  communion.. 5. altar 8. credence,
    credenza
  contents.. 5. index
  cover.. 5. baize, tapis
  dish.. 6. tureen
  land.. 4. mesa 6. karroo (karoo),
    plains 7. plateau
  linen.. 6. napery
  philosophy.. 13. deipnosophism

talk (versed in).. 13. deipnosophist
type.. 3. tea 4. turn 6. coffee,
  gaming 7. dinette, dresser, gate–leg,
  kitchen, taboret 8. captain's,
  drop–leaf
tableau... 5. drama, scene 7. picture
  8. schedule 14. representation
tablet... 3. pad 4. pill, slab 5. facia,
  slate, stele 6. troche 7. lozenge
  8. monument, notebook
taboo, tabu... 3. ban 4. deny
  5. debar 6. forbid 7. embargo
  8. disallow, prohibit 9. forbidden,
  interdict, proscribe 11. prohibition
  12. interdiction
tabulate... 4. list 6. record 7. tabular
  8. classify, schedule
tabulation... 7. listing 8. calendar,
  paradigm 12. registration
taccada... 9. fanflower
tacit... 6. silent 7. implied
  8. unspoken, wordless 9. indicated,
  noiseless 10. understood
taciturn... 6. silent 8. reserved,
  reticent 9. saturnine
tack... 4. brad, gear, jibe, join, rope,
  sail, trip 5. baste, lease, route
  6. course, fasten, secure, staple,
  tackle 7. clothes 9. fastening
  10. supplement
tackle... 3. cat, rig 4. gear, tack
  5. davit, seize 6. burton, collar,
  garnet 7. cordage, grapple, harness,
  rigging 8. football (term)
  9. encounter, equipment, undertake
tacky... 5. crude, dowdy, seedy
  6. shabby, sticky, untidy 8. adhesive,
  slovenly
tact... 5. grace, poise, taste

7. address, finesse 8. delicacy
9. diplomacy 10. adroitness,
cleverness, discretion
11. discernment, savoir-faire
14. discrimination
tadpole ... 4. frog, toad 8. polliwog,
porwigle 9. youngling
tag ... 3. add, end, rag, tab 4. flap,
game, loop, name 5. aglet (aiglet),
label, sheep, strip 6. fasten, follow
7. earmark, frazzle, pendant, taglock
9. appendage 11. aiguillette
(ornamental)
Tagalog, Tagal (pert to) ...
child, servant .. 4. anac, bata
deity .. 6. Batala
game (gambling) .. 10. panguingui
native of .. 5. Luzon 11. Philippines
peasant .. 3. tao
race .. 4. Aeta (dwarf) 7. Malayan
Tahiti ...
arrowroot .. 3. pia
boat .. 4. pahi
capital .. 7. Papeete (of all Society
Isles)
food plant .. 4. taro
god .. 3. oro 6. Taaroa (Supreme)
old name .. 8. Otaheite
robe (coronation) .. 4. malo
woman .. 6. wahine (vahine)
Tai, Thai tribes ... 4. Laos, Shan
7. Siamese
tail ... 3. bun, cue, end 4. arse, back,
hair, last, rear 5. cauda, stern
6. follow, shadow 7. pendant
8. entailed, streamer 9. afterpart,
appendage, extremity
tail (pert to) ...
aircraft's .. 9. empennage
boar's .. 6. wreath
coin .. 5. verso 7. reverse
dog's .. 5. plume, stern, twist
having a .. 7. caudate
peacock's .. 5. train
pert to .. 6. caudal 9. coccygeal
rabbit's .. 4. scut
rudimentary .. 6. coccyx
tailrace .. 5. flume 7. channel
tailing ... 5. chaff, waste 6. refuse
tailless ... 6. tenrec (mammal)
7. acaudal, anurous, Ranidae
8. acaudate, ecaudate
tailor ... 3. cut, fit 4. form 6. darzee,
draper, sartor 7. fashion 8. tailleur
tailor (pert to) ...
goose .. 4. iron 12. pressing iron
made .. 6. fitted 9. fashioned
reference to .. 9. sartorial
twist .. 10. silk thread (stout)
taint ... 3. due, hue 5. color, imbue,
spoil, stain, sully, tinge 6. defile,
infect, poison, stigma 7. blemish,
corrupt, deprave, pollute, vitiate
8. disgrace 9. denigrate, infection
10. corruption, stigmatize
11. contaminate
tainted ... 3. bad 6. soiled 7. stained
8. diseased 9. corrupted
taintless ... 4. good 5. clean
6. chaste 8. flawless, innocent
Taiwan ...
capital .. 6. Taipai

Taj Mahal (pert to) ...
architecture .. 9. Saracenic
builder .. 9. Shah-Jahan
mausolem site .. 4. Agra
named for .. 4. wife
take ... 2. go 3. get, win 4. deem,
doff, gain, shut 5. atone, booty, carry,
catch, seize, snare, steal, usurp
6. accept, borrow, deduce, endure,
obtain 7. capture, conduct, control,
detract, receive 8. proceeds, receipts,
subtract, tolerate 9. apprehend
11. appropriate
take (pert to) ...
a chair .. 3. sit
a direction .. 5. steer
advantage of .. 5. abuse 6. misuse
apart .. 8. demolish 11. disassemble
as one's own .. 5. adopt 6. borrow
away .. 5. adeem, clear, reave, steal,
wrest 6. adempt, deduct, remove
7. deprive, detract, retract
8. derogate, subtract, withdraw
11. expropriate
back .. 6. recant, repeal, return
by storm .. 5. seize 6. attack
by stratagem .. 5. trap 8. outsmart
care of .. 4. mind 5. guard, nurse,
serve, watch 6. beware 7. support
10. provide for
charge of .. 8. attend to 9. look after
down .. 4. fell, raze 5. lower, write
6. humble, record 7. reprove,
swallow 8. emaciate
first .. 7. pre-empt
for granted .. 5. infer 6. assume,
expect 7. believe, presume, suppose
in .. 3. eat, see 4. hear 5. admit,
annex, learn 6. absorb, attend
7. embrace, include, involve, receive,
shorten 9. encompass
notice .. 2. NB 3. see
out .. 4. dele 5. elide 6. delete, efface
7. expunge
place of .. 8. supplant 9. supersede
the floor .. 5. speak 7. address
9. legislate
to flight .. 4. flee 7. run away,
scamper 9. skedaddle
up .. 4. fill, lift 5. adopt, begin, raise
6. absorb, assume, gather, occupy
8. engage in 9. undertake
without authority .. 5. usurp
talapoin ... 6. monkey (guenon)
8. poonghie 12. Buddhist monk
talc ... 6. powder, talcum 7. agalite
8. steatite 9. soapstone
tale ... 3. lai, lay, lie 4. myth, saga,
yarn 5. conte, fable, story 6. gossip,
legend 7. romance 8. anecdote
9. discourse, falsehood, narration,
narrative 11. declaration
12. conversation
tale (pert to) ...
adventure .. 4. gest
bearer .. 6. gossip 7. blabber, tattler
8. informer 13. scandalmonger
chivalry .. 7. romance
doleful .. 8. jeremiad
fatality .. 5. drama 7. tragedy
symbolic .. 8. allegory
traditional .. 4. saga 8. folktale

talent... 4. gift 5. dower, flair, forte, money (anc), skill 6. genius 7. ability, faculty 8. aptitude, artistry 9. attribute 11. disposition 14. accomplishment

talesman... 5. juror 8. narrator

talisman... 4. juju, mojo, tara 5. charm, karma 6. amulet, fetish, grigri (greegree), scarab 7. periapt 12. antinganting

talk... 3. gab, gas, rap, yak, yap 4. blab, blat, chat, chin, harp, rant, rave 5. lingo, orate, parle, prate, rumor, speak, spiel, utter 6. babble, confab, confer, gabble, gossip, jargon, lesson, speech 7. address, blabber, chatter, declaim, discuss 8. causerie, chitchat, colloquy, converse, language, parlance 9. dalliance, discourse 11. communicate 12. conversation

talk (pert to)...
about.. 5. rumor 6. gossip
affected, pretentious.. 4. cant, rant
ancient.. 5. parle
back.. 4. sass 6. retort 7. riposte 8. feedback, repartee
flattering.. 7. palaver
fluent.. 7. verbose, voluble
idiotically.. 6. drivel
long.. 9. gibberish, rigmarole
loud.. 5. blate
promoting.. 4. hype 8. ballyhoo
running.. 6. patter
silly.. 5. drool 6. drivel, footle 7. blather, prattle, twaddle
slang.. 3. gab, gas 4. sass 5. spiel
slowly.. 5. drawl
small.. 3. gab 4. chat, chin 7. prattle 8. chitchat
Spanish.. 7. palabra

talkative... 4. glib 6. fluent 7. verbose, voluble 9. garrulous 10. loquacious 13. communicative

talker... 6. gasser, proser, ranter 7. speaker, spieler 10. chatterbox 17. conversationalist

tall... 4. high, long 5. lofty 6. seemly 7. procere, sky–high 8. towering, yielding 10. incredible, statuesque 11. exaggerated

tall (pert to)...
order.. 9. falsehood 10. difficulty
person.. 10. hypermeter
structure.. 7. steeple
talk.. 4. brag 12. exaggeration 14. grandiloquence

tallest known race... 10. Patagonian

tally... 3. run, sum, tab 4. goal, list, mark 5. agree, check, count, match, notch, score 6. accord, reckon, record 7. account, compare, count up 8. coincide, estimate 9. reckoning 10. bottom line, correspond

Talmud... 9. Jewish law

Talmud (pert to)...
academy.. 8. Yeshivah (Yeshiva)
commentary.. 6. Gemara
student.. 5. bahur
text.. 7. Mishnah

talon... 3. paw 4. claw, fang, nail 6. clutch, finger, pincer

talus... 5. ankle 8. clubfoot

tamarisk... 4. atle (atlee) 8. salt tree

tambo... 3. inn 6. corral, stable, tavern 10. tambourine

tambor... 6. puffer 8. rockfish

tambour... 4. desk, drum, lace 5. frame 6. stitch 7. drummer 8. ornament, stockade 9. embroider

tambourine... 4. dove, drum, taar 5. daira 7. timbrel 8. minstrel

tambourine effect (Mus)... 7. travale

tambreet... 8. duckbill

tamburone... 4. drum 8. bass drum

tame... 4. dull, meek, mild 5. inert 6. docile, gentle, humble, subdue 7. crushed, insipid, subdued 8. tone down 9. tractable 10. cultivated 11. domesticate 12. domesticated

Tamil... 5. Hindu 8. language (oldest Dravidian) 9. Dravidian

tamis... 5. sieve, tammy 8. strainer

Tammany (pert to)...
Hall.. 14. Democratic Club
man.. 10. politician
officer.. 8. Wiskinky (Wiskinkie)
scandal.. 9. Tweed Ring
Society site.. 11. New York City (1789)
symbol.. 5. tiger

tamper with... 4. plot 5. alter, bribe 6. meddle, monkey, scheme, tinker 7. falsify 9. influence, interfere

tampion, tampon... 4. plug 6. tympan 7. stopper, turnpin 9. rhynobyon

tan... 3. dun, taw 4. buff, ecru, tent, whip 5. beige, brown, color, tawny 6. rabbit, suntan, thrash 7. sunburn

tanager... 4. yeni 5. lindo 7. Piranga, redbird

tanbark... 3. oak 7. hemlock

Tancred... 6. leader (1st crusade)

Tanganyika... see *Tanzania*

tangible... 4. real 7. tactile 8. palpable 9. objective, touchable 11. perceptible, substantial

tangle... 3. mat, mop 4. kink, shag 5. ravel, snare, snarl, weave 6. entrap, medley, muddle, sleave, tousle 7. ensnare, involve 8. quandary 9. interlock 10. complicate, interweave

tank... 3. vat 4. lake, pond, pool 5. basin 6. hot tub 7. cistern, stomach 9. reservoir 11. army vehicle, hard drinker

tanker... 4. ship 5. oiler 8. fuel ship

tanning shrub... 5. alder, sumac (sumach)

tantalize... 3. vex 5. taunt, tease 6. harass, plague 7. torment

tantalum symbol... 2. Ta

Tantalus (pert to)...
father.. 4. Zeus
father of.. 5. Niobe 6. Pelops
genus of.. 4. ibis
king (rich).. 6. Greece

tantamount... 5. equal 9. identical 10. equivalent 13. corresponding

tantara... 7. fanfare 9. tantarara 12. trumpet blare

tantrum... 3. fit 4. rage 7. caprice 8. tirrivee (tirrivie) 10. conniption

Tanzania, Africa ...
  capital .. 11. Dar es Salaam (Haven of
    Peace)
  famed Mt .. 11. Kilimanjaro
  famed plains .. 9. Serengeti
  famed town .. 5. Ujiji (Stanley found
    Livingstone, 1871)
  formerly .. 8. Zanzibar 10. Tanganyika
  language .. 7. Swahili
  natives .. 5. Bantu
Taoism, names ... 6. Kwanti, Laotze
  7. Yu Hwang
tap ... 3. dum, hit, hob, rap 4. plug,
  tamp 5. sound, spile 6. faucet,
  liquor, siphon, spigot, strike
  7. censure, petcock, reprove
tape ... 3. gin, tie 4. band, wick
  5. strip 6. fillet, ribbon, secure
  7. bandage, measure 9. recording
taper ... 4. ream, wick 5. point, snape,
  spire 6. candle, cierge, narrow
  7. conical 8. decrease, diminish
  9. acuminate 11. pyramidical
tapering (pert to) ...
  blades . 6. opiles
  pert to .. 6. spired, terete 7. conical,
    pointed 8. fusiform 9. narrowing
  piece .. 4. gore 5. miter 6. gusset
  pillar .. 7. obelisk
  solid .. 4. cone
tapestry ... 5. arras, tapis 6. Bayeux,
  dosser 7. Gobelin
tapeworm ... 6. Taenia
tapeworm (pert to) ...
  embryonic .. 10. oncosphere
  like .. 8. taenioid
  segment .. 8. strobila
tapioca, source ... 5. salep 7. cassava
  (casava)
Tapirus ... 6. tapirs
tapster ... 7. barmald, okinker
tar ... 3. gob 4. brea, pave, salt
  5. black, pitch 6. cresol, maltha,
  sailor, seaman 7. mariner 8. telegram
  10. bluejacket
tarantula ... 6. spider 7. mygalid
  10. wolf spider
tarboosh ... 3. fez 6. red cap
tardy ... 3. lag, lax 4. late, slow
  5. slack 6. remiss 7. belated,
  lagging, overdue 8. dilatory
  10. behindhand 11. cunctatious
tare ... 4. weed (Bib) 5. vetch
  8. discount 9. allowance, deduction
target ... 3. aim, tee 4. butt, goal,
  goat, mark, prey 5. sight 6. object,
  shield, tassel 8. bull's–eye, ridicule
  9. objective
tariff ... 4. duty, list, rate 6. charge
  7. tribute 8. schedule
tariffist ... 8. advocate
  13. protectionist
tarnish ... 3. dim 4. dull, soil, spot
  5. cloud, stain, sully, taint 6. smirch,
  stigma, vilify 7. blemish, destroy,
  obscure 8. besmirch, discolor
  10. lose luster, stigmatize
taro ... 3. poi 4. eddo, food, gabi
  (gabe) 5. cocco, tania (tanier)
  12. elephant's–ear
tarot ... 14. fortunetelling (cards)
tarried ... 6. waited 7. dallied

  8. lingered, remained
tarry ... 3. lag 4. bide, stay, wait
  5. abide, await, dally, delay, pause,
  stall 6. dawdle, linger, loiter, retard
  7. outstay
tarsus ... 5. ankle 7. segment
tart ... 4. acid, sour 5. acrid, sharp
  6. pastry, severe 7. caustic, pungent,
  waspish 8. poignant, turnover
  10. astringent 11. acrimonious
tartan ... 4. wool 5. plaid 7. pattern
  (plaid) 10. Highlander
tartar ... 5. argol (argal), shrew, valet
  12. incrustation
Tartar, Tatar ... 4. Turk 6. Mongol
Tartar, Tatar (pert to) ...
  domain .. 7. Khanate
  horseman .. 7. Cossack
  lancer .. 5. uhlan
  nobleman .. 5. murza
  people of .. 6. Turkey 8. Mongolia
  title .. 4. Khan
  tribe .. 2. Hu 3. Hun 6. Mongol
tartarean ... 5. cruel 7. hellish
  8. infernal
Tartarus (Myth) ... 4. hell 5. Hades
  15. infernal regions (Iliad)
task ... 3. job 4. duty, snap, test, toil
  5. chore, labor, stent, stint 6. burden,
  dargue, impost, strain 10. assignment,
  employment 11. undertaking
Tasmania (pert to) ...
  animal (burrowing) .. 6. wombat
  discoverer .. 6. Tasman (1642)
  marsupial .. 9. phalanger
  mountain .. 6. Cradle 9. Ben Lomond
  strait .. 4. Bass
taste ... 3. sip, sup 4. tang 5. flair,
  sapor, savor, sense, smack, style
  6. liking, palate, relish, sample
  7. soupçon 8. delicacy, elegance,
  fondness, judgment 9. gustation
  10. experience 14. discrimination
  15. aesthetic liking
taste (pert to) ...
  bite .. 4. nosh 5. snack
  decided .. 8. fondness, penchant
  French .. 7. soupçon
  fundamental .. 4. acid, salt 5. sweet
    6. bitter
  lacking .. 4. rude 5. bland, gross, stale
    10. unpolished
  ref to .. 7. palatal 9. gustatory
  sharp .. 4. acid, tang
tasteless ... 4. dull, flat 5. vapid
  6. vulgar, watery 7. insipid 8. lifeless
  9. savorless 10. inartistic
tasty ... 6. savory 8. saporous, tasteful
  9. delicious, palatable, toothsome
Tatar ... see *Tartar*
tatouay ... 9. armadillo
tatter ... 3. rag 4. tags, tear 5. patch,
  piece, shred 6. ribbon
tatterdemalion ... 5. gamin
  9. ragpicker 10. ragamuffin
tattle ... 4. blab, tell 5. prate 6. gossip
  7. chatter, divulge, prattle 8. idle
  talk, inform on
tattler ... 6. gossip, willet 8. quidnunc,
  redshank, telltale 10. alarm clock,
  talebearer, yellowlegs
tattoo ... 4. call (drum, bugle), pony,

scar 13. entertainment
tau... 4. ankh, crux, rood 5. cross
　6. letter (Gr) 7. T–shaped
tau cross... 4. ankh 6. symbol
　8. crucifix, insignia 10. St Anthony's
taunt... 4. gibe, jeer, mock, twit
　5. sneer, tease 6. deride 7. provoke
　8. reproach, ridicule 9. aggravate
Taurus... 4. bull 8. Pleiades
　13. constellation
taut... 4. firm, snug, tidy 5. tense,
　tight 6. severe, strict 7. nervous
　9. distended
tautology... 8. pleonasm
　10. redundancy, repetition
tavern... 3. inn, pub 5. hotel
　7. barroom, cabaret, Gasthof, taberna
　8. alehouse, Gasthaus, hostelry
taw... 4. game, whip 6. marble
　7. tanning
tawdry... 4. loud 5. cheap, gaudy,
　showy 6. garish 7. blatant
tawny, tawney... 3. tan 5. dusky,
　olive, tenne 6. tanned 7. jacinth
　8. brindled 9. bullfinch
tax... 4. cess, duty, geld, levy, scat
　(scatt), task, toll 5. stent 6. assess,
　burden, custom, excise, impose,
　income, octroi, strain 7. doomage,
　license, tribute 8. exaction, overtire
　9. prescribe 10. assessment
tax (pert to)...
　ancient.. 3. cro 4. geld 7. galanas
　assessment.. 4. rate 5. ratal
　　7. doomage
　church.. 5. tithe
　commodity.. 6. octroi
　French history.. 6. taille
　kind.. 5. tithe 6. excise, surtax, taille
　　7. boscage 8. auxilium, carucage
　　9. surcharge
　liquor.. 6. abkari (abkary)
　pasturage (Shetland Isls).. 4. scat
　　(scatt)
tea... 5. dance, party, shrub 6. supper
　8. beverage, function, sociable
　9. collation, reception
tea (pert to)...
　chemical content.. 6. tannin, theine
　　(thein) 8. caffeine
　Chinese.. 5. black, hyson
　Formosa.. 6. oolong
　Ind Ceylon.. 5. pekoe
　infusion.. 6. ptisan, tisane
　Labrador.. 5. Ledum 8. gowiddie
　Paraguay.. 5. yerba
　receptacle.. 5. caddy 8. canister
　table.. 6. teapoy (tepoy)
　type.. 3. cha 4. tsia 5. Assam, black,
　　green, hyson, Ledum, oopak, pekoe
　　6. oolong 7. cambric 8. gowiddie
　urn.. 3. pot 7. samovar
　weak.. 7. cambric
teach... 4. show 5. coach, drill, edify,
　guide, prime, train, tutor 6. direct,
　impart, preach, school 7. educate,
　show how 8. instruct 9. enlighten
　11. demonstrate
teacher... 5. coach, guide, rabbi, tutor
　6. doctor, mentor, pastor, pedant,
　priest, pundit, reader, regent, rhetor,
　scribe 7. edifier, starets 8. educator,

preacher 9. pedagogue, preceptor
　10. instructor
teacher (pert to)...
　Alexandrian.. 6. Origen
　Indian.. 4. guru
　Jewish.. 5. rabbi
　Mohammedan.. 3. pir 4. imam
　　6. mullah
　of the deaf.. 7. oralist
　Russian.. 7. starets
teaching... 5. moral 6. docent
　7. precept 8. doctrine 11. instruction
Teaching of the Twelve... 10. The
　Didache
team... 3. two 4. haul, join, pain,
　span, yoke 5. brood, chain, wagon
　7. vehicle 8. carriage 9. yannigans
teamster... 6. carter, driver 7. carrier
Teapot Dome (pert to)...
　known as.. 8. Scandals (Teapot
　　Dome)
　leased by.. 4. Fall (Sec'y of Interior)
　lease of.. 8. oil field
　site.. 8. Elk Hills (Wyo)
tear... 3. rip 4. rend, rent, rive
　5. revel, sever, speed, split, spree
　6. cleave, hasten 7. destroy, shatter,
　torment 8. lacerate, separate
　10. dilacerate
tear (pert to)...
　apart.. 7. disjoin 8. demolish
　asunder.. 10. dilacerate
　down.. 4. rase, raze
　limb from limb.. 6. punish
　　9. dismember
　to shreds.. 6. tatter
　up.. 3. rip 6. damage
　up the roots.. 6. arache
teardrop lace design... 5. larme
tearful... 3. sad 7. maudlin, weeping
　9. lachrymal (lacrimal)
tears... 5. drops (lachrymal), grief,
　rheum 6. lament 9. teardrops
tease... 3. guy, nag, rag, vex 4. twit
　5. annoy, devil, taunt 6. bother,
　harass, heckle, needle, pester, plague
　7. provoke, torment 8. irritate
　9. aggravate, tantalize
teaser... 4. gull 6. carder, curler,
　sniper, stoker 7. curtain, fireman,
　problem 8. pesterer, willower
　9. tormentor 13. advertisement
technical... 7. skilled, trained
　8. specific 11. specialized
　12. professional
technocracy... 12. organization
　17. rule by technicians
technology... 3. art 7. science
　9. technique 10. agrotechny,
　virtuosity 11. terminology
　12. nomenclature 13. ethnotechnics
techy... 6. touchy, vexing 7. fretful,
　peevish 9. irascible, irritable, sensitive
tedious... 3. dry 4. dull 5. bored,
　prosy 6. boring, prolix 7. irksome,
　noxious 11. displeasing, repetitious
　13. uninteresting
tedium... 5. ennui 7. boredom
　10. melancholy 11. tediousness
teeming... 4. full 6. aswarm
　7. pouring, replete 8. crowding,
　numerous, prolific 9. abounding

10. productive 11. overflowing

teeter ... 4. rock 5. waver 6. jiggle, seesaw 9. alternate, fluctuate, sandpiper, vacillate 12. teeter–totter

teeth ... 5. bucks, fangs 6. molars, tushes 7. canines, ivories 8. grinders, incisors

teeth (pert to) ...
all alike .. 7. isodont
cleaning .. 5. brush, floss
  10. dentrifice, toothpaste
covering .. 6. enamel
crustation .. 6. tartar
destitute of .. 5. morné (Her)
  8. edentate 10. edentulous
elephant's .. 9. scrivello 11. scrivelloes
false .. 8. choppers (sl), dentures
few .. 12. oligodontous
large .. 8. megadont 9. macrodont
pointed .. 5. fangs, tusks 6. tushes
ref to .. 4. pulp 5. molar 6. dental
  7. dentine 8. odontoid
science .. 10. odontology

teething ... 6. growth 9. dentition, odontosis 10. odontogeny

teetotaller ... 3. dry 7. non–user 9. abstainer, nephalist, Rechabite (Bib) 11. teetotalist

teg, tag ... 3. doe 5. sheep (young), woman 6. fleece (sheep's)

teguexin ... 4. teju 6. lizard

tegument ... 4. bark, coat, skin 5. cover 6. cortex 10. integument

tekke ... 3. rug 6. carpet 7. convent 9. monastery

tela ... 6. tissue 8. membrane

Telamon (Gr Myth, pert to) ...
brother .. 6. Peleus
companion .. 8. Hercules
expedition .. 8. boar hunt
  10. Argonautic
male figure .. 6. column 7. support
son .. 4. Ajax 6. Teucer

telegraph (pert to) ...
code, inventor .. 5. Morse (Samuel F)
key .. 6. tapper
service .. 5. cable 8. dispatch

telephone (pert to) ...
inventor .. 4. Bell (Alexander)
term .. 3. PBX 4. buzz, call, dial, hold, horn (sl), ring, toll 5. trunk 6. call up 7. collect, hotline 8. exchange, intercom 10. videophone 11. push–button, switchboard 12. speakerphone 14. radiotelephone

telescope ... 4. Lick 6. Yerkes 7. Palomar 8. Galilean (1609) 9. Gregorian (Scot 1663)

telescopic ... 9. farseeing

television ... 2. TV 3. box, set 4. tube 5. telly (Brit) 8. boob tube, idiot box 11. small screen

television (pert to) ...
person .. 6. anchor, viewer 7. sponsor 9. superstar 10. newscaster
program .. 4. show 6. sitcom 7. variety 8. newscast 9. docudrama, soap opera
term .. 3. air 5. audio, bleep, cable, rerun 7. channel, minicam 8. telecast 10. commercial, laugh track

tell ... 3. say 4. talk 5. count, peach,

utter 6. assail, impart, inform, recite, reckon, relate, repeat, report, reveal 7. divulge, narrate, recount 8. acquaint, disclose, rehearse 9. recognize 11. communicate

teller ... 6. banker 8. informer, narrator 9. describer, informant

telling ... 6. cogent, potent 8. forceful, striking 9. affective, narration, pertinent 11. influential, significant

telltale ... 4. blab, clue, hint 6. bearer, device, gossip 7. tattler 8. informer 9. indicator, informing 10. indication, talebearer

tellurian ... 2. Te 7. earthly 11. terrestrial 12. earth dweller

temeritous, temerarious ... 4. rash 8. heedless, reckless 10. headstrong

temerity ... 4. gall 5. cheek, nerve 8. audacity, rashness 10. effrontery 12. recklessness

temper ... 4. mood 5. humor 6. adjust, animus, anneal, attune, dander, harden, nature, season, soften 7. assuage, mollify, tantrum 8. hardness, mitigate, moderate 9. composure 10. equanimity, irritation 11. disposition, temperament

temper (pert to) ...
bad .. 5. angry, rabid 6. fuming, savage 7. furious, ranting
clay .. 6. puddle
even .. 4. calm 5. staid 6. sedate
heat of .. 6. choler
in a .. 4. huff, rage, stew 5. tizzy
metal .. 6. anneal, harden 7. toughen

temperament ... 4. mood 6. crasis, nature 8. artistic 11. disposition

temperance ... 6. virtue 8. calmness, sobriety 10. abstinence, moderation 11. self–control 13. self–restraint 14. abstemiousness

temperate ... 4. calm, cool 5. sober 8. moderate 10. abstemious, restrained 14. self–controlled

tempered ... 5. angry 6. sedate 8. annealed, disposed, moderate 9. moderated, mollified, qualified

tempest ... 4. gale, wind 5. blast, orage, storm 6. tumult 7. turmoil 9. agitation, commotion, windstorm 10. excitement 12. thunderstorm

Tempest (pert to) ...
Cuban .. 6. bayamo
in a teapot .. 10. triviality 12. exaggeration
The (character) .. 5. Ariel (spirit) 7. Caliban, Miranda 8. Prospero

tempestuous ... 5. windy 6. stormy 7. excited, violent 9. turbulent

temple ... 4. fane, naos 5. cella, ratha, speos 6. aedile, church, pagoda 7. edifice

temple (pert to) ...
Anglo–Ind .. 5. kovil (covil)
approach .. 5. toran (torana)
Assyrian .. 8. ziggurat (anc)
Aztec temple site .. 12. Tenochtitlan
Chinese .. 6. pagoda
Hawaiian .. 5. heiau
Mexico .. 8. teocalli
Mohammedan .. 6. mosque

part.. 4. naos 5. cella 6. adytum
  7. narthex, sanctum 10. penetralia
ref to.. 6. hieron
sanctuary.. 10. penetralia
Shinto.. 3. Sha 5. jinja (jinsha)
  7. yashiro
Temple Bar (London)... 7. gateway
Temple Butte site... 11. Grand
  Canyon
Temple of Heaven... 7. Peiping
Temple of Onias... 5. Egypt
Temple of Reason... 9. Notre Dame
Temple of the Sphinx... 5. Egypt
tempo... 4. pace, time 5. grave, largo,
  speed 6. adagio, presto, rhythm
  7. allegro, andante 8. moderato
  11. synchronism
temporal... 4. bene, laic 5. civil
  7. earthly, secular, worldly
  9. ephemeral, temporary
  10. transitory 11. present time
  13. chronological
temporize... 5. delay 6. demand,
  parley 9. negotiate 13. procrastinate
tempt... 4. lead, lure 5. decoy
  6. allure, entice, induce, seduce
  7. attract 8. persuade 9. seduction
  10. inducement
Tempter, The... 5. Devil, Satan 7. Evil
  One 10. Evil Spirit, Old Serpent
  14. Prince of Devils
temptress... 5. siren 7. Delilah (Bib),
  mermaid 11. enchantress
ten (pert to)...
ace.. 10. bridge game
Commandments.. 9. Decalogue
dollars.. 7. sawbuck
fold.. 6. denary 7. decuple
footed.. 7. decapod
gallon hat.. 7. Stetson 8. sombrero
geometric figure.. 7. decagon
  10. decahedron
measure.. 4. acre, bath 6. decare
number.. 5. decad 7. several
physics.. 3. bel
poetic.. 9. decameter (decametre)
prefix.. 4. deca (deka)
stringed.. 9. decachord
thousand.. 6. myriad
year period.. 6. decade 9. decenniad,
  decennium
tenable... 10. defensible
  12. maintainable
tenacious... 5. tough 6. dogged, viscid
  7. viscous 8. adhesive, cohesive,
  sticking, stubborn 9. glutinous,
  obstinate, retentive 10. persistent
  12. pertinacious
tenant... 4. saer 5. ceile, dreng
  (drengh) 6. holder, leaser, lessee,
  renter, vassal 7. cottier, dweller,
  villein 8. occupant 10. inhabitant
tenant's tribute... 4. cens
tend... 4. care, heed, lean, mind, wait
  5. nurse, offer, serve, watch
  6. attend, manage 7. incline, oversee
  8. converge, minister 9. cultivate,
  gravitate, look after
tendency... 4. bent, bias, tide 5. drift,
  drive, trend 6. course, object
  7. bearing, leaning 8. aptitude,
  relation 9. direction, proneness

10. proclivity, propensity
11. disposition, inclination
tender... 3. bed, pay 4. boat, fond,
  gift, give, kind, soft, sore 5. offer,
  young 6. extend, gentle, humane,
  waiter 7. pitiful, present, rail car
  8. delicate, merciful 9. attendant,
  sensitive 10. effeminate
  11. softhearted, sympathetic,
  warmhearted 12. affectionate
  13. compassionate
tender (pert to)...
animal.. 6. cowboy, herder
farm.. 10. husbandman
feeling.. 9. sentiment
foot.. 4. dude 6. novice 8. newcomer
  10. raw recruit
hearted.. 4. kind 8. merciful
horse.. 5. groom 6. ostler 7. hostler
regard.. 4. love 6. tendre
ship.. 7. pinnace
style.. 7. amoroso
tenderloin... 4. meat 7. brothel
  12. city district, vice district
tenderness... 4. love, pity 8. sympathy
  9. affection 10. compassion,
  gentleness
tending to...
arouse.. 7. emotive
assist memory.. 8. mnemonic
check.. 10. repressive
clear of guilt.. 11. exculpatory
control.. 10. regulating
drive away.. 9. repellant
evade.. 7. elusory
lateness.. 7. tardive
separate.. 8. divisive
tear.. 10. lacerative
wear away.. 8. abrasive
tendon... 4. cord, thew 5. sinew
  8. ligament 11. aponeurosis
tendril... 4. coil, curl 5. shoot, sprig
  6. branch, cirrus 7. stipule
  8. filament
tenet... 3. ism 4. rule 5. canon,
  creed, dogma, maxim 6. belief
  7. precept 8. doctrine 9. principle
tenne... 5. brown, color
Tennessee...
battle.. 11. Chattanooga 14. Above
  the Clouds
capital.. 9. Nashville (Athens of the
  South)
city.. 7. Memphis 8. Oak Ridge
  9. Knoxville 11. Chattanooga
first State.. 8. Franklin
Mts.. 7. Lookout 10. Cumberland,
  Great Smoky 13. Clingman's Dome
museum.. 9. Hermitage, Parthenon
  12. Atomic Energy (Oak Ridge)
  13. Ancestral Home (Pres Polk)
park.. 6. Shiloh
river.. 9. Tennessee
State admission.. 9. Sixteenth
State motto.. 16. America At Its Best
State nickname.. 9. Volunteer
tennis (pert to)...
four persons.. 7. doubles
player.. 6. netman
score.. 3. ace 4. love 5. deuce
series.. 3. set
site.. 5. court

stroke.. 3. cut, lob
term.. 3. ace, lob, net, set 5. serve
  6. hazard 7. receive
two persons.. 7. singles
tenon... 3. cog 4. tusk 5. tooth
  7. mortise
tenor... 4. alto (violin), copy, mode,
  tone 5. drift, trend 6. course, intent,
  singer 7. meaning, purport
  8. tenoreno 9. male voice, procedure
  10. transcript
tense... 4. rapt, taut 5. rigid, tight
  6. intent 7. intense, nervous, stretch
  8. strained 9. stretched
  10. breathless
tense (grammar)... 4. past 6. future
  7. perfect, present 9. preterite
  10. pluperfect 11. past perfect,
  progressive
tensile... 6. pliant 7. ductile
  8. tensible
tension... 6. strain, stress 7. detente,
  nervous 9. disaccord, stiffness
tent... 3. hut 4. camp, show 5. cover,
  lodge 6. dossil 7. marquee
  8. pavilion
tent (pert to)...
covering.. 4. tilt
Eskimo.. 5. tubik (skin)
general's.. 10. praetorium (pretorium)
India.. 4. pawl
Indian.. 5. tepee 6. teepee, wigwam
occupant.. 5. nomad 6. camper
  7. tourist
Russian.. 7. kibitka
Scottish.. 6. pulpit
surgical.. 6. screen
tribe (Arab).. 5. Kedar
type.. 3. fly, pup 4. bell, wall
  6. Sibley 8. pavilion
tentacle... 4. hair, palp 6. feeler
  7. tendril
tentative... 7. feeling, testing
  9. makeshift, temporary
  10. substitute 11. making trial,
  provisional 12. experimental
tenterhooks... 6. strain 8. suspense
  10. uneasiness
tenth... 5. decim, tithe 6. decima
  9. organ stop
tenth Muse... 6. Sappho
Tent Maker... 4. Omar
tenuity... 6. rarity 7. poverty
  8. delicacy, subtlety, thinness
  9. indigence, unreality
tenuous... 4. rare, thin 7. slender,
  subtile 8. delicate, ethereal
  13. unsubstantial
tenure... 4. term 5. lease 6. socage
  7. holding 10. possession
tepee, teepee... 4. tent 6. wigwam
tepid... 4. mild, warm 8. lukewarm
tequila... 6. liquor 12. century plant
teraphim... 5. idols 6. images
teras... 7. monster
tergiversate... 3. lie 5. evade, shift
  10. apostasize, equivocate
term... 3. age, end, era 4. date,
  name, time, word 5. epoch, limit,
  style 6. estate, period, tenure
  7. premise 8. duration, semester,
  terminus 12. nomenclature

term (pert to)...
connotation.. 6. intent 11. designation
death.. 4. doom, mort
for years.. 10. real estate
glacial.. 3. stoss
golf.. 4. hook 5. bogey (bogie), divot,
  eagle, slice 6. birdie
grammar.. 6. phrase, syntax
  11. phraseology
logic.. 4. mode 5. major, minor
of life.. 3. age 5. sands (hourglass)
Rugby.. 5. scrum
sea.. 4. ahoy 5. avast, belay
tennis.. 4. love 5. deuce, serve
termagant... 5. scold, shrew, vixen
  6. Amazon, virigo 7. furious
  8. scolding 9. turbulent
  10. boisterous, tumultuous
  11. quarrelsome
Termagant... 5. deity 14. imaginary
  being
terminal... 3. end 4. goal 5. anode,
  depot, final, limit 6. finish 7. limital,
  station 8. desinent, terminus,
  ultimate 9. end of life, extremity
  10. concluding 11. desinential,
  destination, termination
terminal (pert to)...
battery.. 5. anode 7. cathode
  9. electrode
leaf.. 8. apiculus
ornament.. 6. finial
town (end of line).. 8. terminus
terminate... 3. end 4. halt 5. cease,
  close, limit 6. expire, result 7. end
  with 8. complete, conclude .
termination... 3. end 4. amen
  5. close, limit 6. ending, result
  7. outcome 8. terminus 9. desinence
  10. completion, conclusion, expiration
termite... 3. ant (white) 4. anay (anai)
  8. Isoptera (Order)
tern... 4. darr (black), gull 6. Sterna
  (genus) 8. schooner (Naut)
  9. threefold 10. sea swallow
ternary... 5. three, triad 6. tercet
  (Poet), triple 7. ternion, trinity
  9. threefold
ternate... 4. tern 9. threefold
  12. trifoliolate
terpsichore... 5. dance 6. dancer
  7. dancing
Terpsichore (Myth)... 13. Muse of
  dancing
terra... 5. earth 10. terra firma
terrace... 4. flaw (marble), mesa, step
  7. balcony, gallery, plateau, portico
  8. platform (earth) 9. colonnade
terrain, terrane... 4. land 5. tract
  6. region 11. environment
terrapin... 4. Emys 6. turtle
  8. Chelonia, Emydinae, tortoise
  9. cheloniid
terrapin, turtle (pert to)...
color.. 9. grapenuts
type.. 6. potter, slider 10. red–bellied
  11. diamondback 13. yellow–bellied
War.. 14. Eighteen Twelve (1812)
terrene, terrestrial... 4. land 5. earth,
  realm 6. earthy, mortal 7. earthly,
  mundane, worldly
terrestrial planets... 4. Mars 5. Venus

7. Mercury

terrible... 3. bad 4. dire 5. awful
6. tragic 7. fearful, ghastly, hideous,
painful 8. dreadful, horrible, terrific
9. appalling, frightful 10. formidable,
terrifying, unpleasant

Terrible, The... 4. Ivan (Russ Czar)

terrier... 3. fox 4. bull, Skye 5. Cairn,
Irish, Welsh 6. Boston 8. Airedale,
Scottish, Sealyham 9. Kerry blue,
schnauzer 10. Bedlington, Clydesdale
13. Dandie Dinmont

terrific... 5. great 6. superb
7. extreme 8. dreadful, exciting,
terrible 9. appalling, excessive,
frightful 10. tremendous

terrify... 3. awe, cow 4. stun
5. alarm, appal, haunt, scare, shock
6. appall, freeze 7. horrify, petrify
8. affright, frighten

territory... 4. area, land 5. banat, field
6. canton, region 7. country
8. district, environs, Pashalic
(Pasha's), province 10. palatinate

terror... 3. awe 4. fear 5. alarm,
dread, panic 6. fright, horror
7. hellion, Reign of (Hist)
13. consternation

terrorism... 11. subjugation
12. intimidation

terse... 4. curt, neat 5. pithy
6. smooth 7. compact, concise,
laconic, pointed, refined 8. succinct
11. sententious 12. accomplished,
epigrammatic

Tertiary period... 6. Eocene
7. Miocene 8. Pliocene 9. Oligocene
12. Age of Mammals

tertium quid... 12. third someone
13. third somewhat

tertulia... 4. club 5. party 7. meeting

tessellated... 6. mosaic 9. checkered

tessera... 3. die 4. cube, tile 5. token
6. marble, ticket 8. password
11. certificate

test... 3. try 4. exam, feel 5. assay,
proof, prove, taste, tempt, trial
6. ordeal, sample 7. examine,
witness 8. evidence, standard
9. criterion, testimony
10. experience, experiment
11. examination, performance
12. authenticate

test (pert to)...
fineness.. 3. pyx
orally.. 7. examine
ore, value.. 5. assay
pot.. 8. crucible
severe.. 6. ordeal

testa... 7. coating 8. covering,
tegument

testament... 3. New, Old 4. will
8. covenant

testator... 7. legator, witness
9. testatrix

tester... 6. canopy, helmet, prover,
taster 7. assayer, candler, sampler

testify... 4. avow 6. affirm, depone,
depose 7. declare, profess, protest
8. indicate, manifest 11. bear
witness

testimonial... 5. token 7. tribute,

warrant 8. evidence 9. reference
10. compliment 11. certificate

testimony... 7. witness 8. evidence
10. Scriptures 11. affirmation,
attestation, declaration

testy, tetchy... 6. touchy 7. fretful,
peevish 8. petulant, snappish
9. irascible, obstinate 10. headstrong

tetched in the head... 9. pixilated

tetrad... 4. four 7. quartet (quartette),
quatern 8. foursome 10. quaternion

tetragon... 4. park 6. square
7. rhombus 9. courtyard
10. quadrangle

Tetragrammaton... 7. Jehovah
12. Supreme Being 14. four
consonants (unpronounced)

Teuton... 4. Goth 6. German

Teutonic (pert to)...
alphabet character.. 4. rune
deity.. 2. Er 3. Tiu (Tiwaz), Tyr
4. Frea, Odin, Thor 5. Aesir, Bragi,
Wodin 6. Balder, Frigga 7. Forseti
8. Heimdall
demon.. 3. alp
giantess.. 4. Norn 11. demigoddess
goddess.. 3. Eir, Hel, Ran 4. Norn,
Urth (Urthr), Wyrd
homicide (tribal).. 5. morth
land.. 4. odal
law.. 5. Salic
nymph (water).. 3. nis
race.. 5. Goths, Jutes 6. Franks,
Saxons 7. Vandals 8. Lombards
10. Norwegians 13. Scandinavians
supernatural being.. 5. troll

Teutonic goddess of...
death.. 3. Hel, Ran
healing.. 3. Eir
peace.. 7. Nerthus

Teutonic god of...
justice.. 7. Forseti (Forsete)
pantheon.. 5. Aesir (group)
peace.. 6. Balder
sea.. 5. Aegir
skill.. 3. Ull (Ullr)
sky.. 2. Er 3. Tiu (Tiwaz), Tyr
thunder.. 4. Thor 5. Donar
war.. 3. Tiu (Tiwaz), Tyr

Texas...
birthplace of Pres.. 10. Eisenhower
capital.. 6. Austin
cattle.. 8. longhorn
city.. 4. Waco 6. Dallas, El Paso
7. Abilene, Denison, Houston 9. Fort
Worth, Galveston 10. San Antonio
flags (six).. 5. Spain 6. France,
Mexico 8. Republic (of Texas)
11. Confederate 12. United States
flower.. 10. bluebonnet, yellow rose
Indian tribe.. 5. Caddo
monument (Battle).. 10. San Jacinto
police.. 7. Rangers
river.. 3. Red 5. Pecos 9. Rio Grande
shrine, mission.. 5. Alamo
State admission.. 12. Twenty–eighth
State motto.. 5. Tejas 10. Friendship
State nickname.. 8. Lone Star

text... 4. book 5. topic, verse
7. passage 8. libretto, textbook
11. letterpress

textile screw pine... 3. ara

textile shop... 7. mercery
texture... 3. web 4. wale, warp, wooz
   5. grain, weave 6. cobweb, fabric
   7. textile 9. roughness, structure
   10. smoothness
Thailand (Siam), capital... 7. Bangkok
Thames River town... 4. Eton
thana... 13. police station
thanador... 7. officer (Hind)
thanatology doctrine... 5. death
thane... 5. baron (anc) 7. servant,
   warrior 9. Scots peer
thankless... 7. ingrate 10. ungrateful
   13. unappreciated
thanks... 5. grace 6. prayer
   8. gramercy 9. gratitude
   12. appreciation 14. acknowledgment
Thanks to God... 10. Deo gratias
that (pert to)...
   is.. 2. ie 5. id est
   is to say.. 3. viz 5. to wit 6. namely
   9. videlicit
   pronoun.. 3. who 4. what
thatch (pert to)...
   grass.. 4. rope 6. slough
   hair.. 3. mop 4. crop, mane
   palm.. 5. Sabal 7. Thrinax
   roofing.. 5. reeds, straw 6. rushes
   support.. 6. wattle
thatcher... 7. hellier
thaumaturgy... 5. magic 7. sorcery
   8. wizardry 11. legerdemain
the (pert to)...
   end.. 5. omega 6. thirty
   French.. 2. la, le 3. les
   German.. 3. das, der, die
   Italian.. 2. il, la, le 4. ella
   same.. 4. idem 5. ditto
   Spanish.. 2. el, la 3. las, los
theater, theatre... 5. arena, drama,
   odeum, stage 6. lyceum 8. coliseum
   9. playhouse 12. amphitheater
theater (pert to)...
   actress.. 7. heroine, ingénue
   box.. 4. loge
   curtain.. 4. drop 6. teaser
   district.. 6. Rialto 8. Broadway
   floor (lower).. 7. parquet
   full house.. 3. SRO
   Greek.. 5. odeum (odeon)
   part.. 3. box, pit 4. loge 5. foyer,
   stage 7. balcony, gallery, parquet
   8. parterre 9. orchestra
   10. proscenium
theatrical... 5. showy, stagy
   8. affected, dramatic 10. artificial,
   histrionic 12. melodramatic
theatrical (pert to)...
   art.. 10. histrionic
   company.. 6. troupe
   machine.. 9. eccyclema
   spectacle.. 5. revue 7. pageant
   star.. 4. hero, lead 7. heroine
Theban (pert to)...
   bard.. 6. Pindar
   deity.. 4. Amen (Amon) 6. Amen–Ra
   god.. 5. Ammon (Zeus)
   king.. 5. Laius 7. Amphion, Oedipus
   8. Pentheus
   queen.. 5. Niobe 7. Jocasta
   soothsayer (blind).. 8. Tiresias
   triad.. 3. Mut 6. Amen–Ra, Khonsu

Thebes...
   capital of.. 10. Upper Egypt (anc)
   famed avenue.. 8. Sphinxes
   famed for.. 5. ruins
   location.. 4. Nile
   ruined temple.. 5. Ammon 6. Karnak
   Seven against (one of).. 6. Tydeus
theca... 3. pod 4. case, cell
   7. capsule
theft... 6. holdup, piracy 7. larceny,
   robbery 8. burglary, stealing
   10. plagiarism 12. embezzlement
theftlike... 7. piratic 9. piratical
theme... 4. text 5. essay, lemma,
   motif, thema, topic 6. matter, thesis
   7. subject 9. discourse, leitmotiv
then... 3. poi (Mus) 4. also, next,
   when 5. hence 7. besides
   8. formerly 9. therefore
   12. subsequently
thence... 4. away 5. hence 9. after
   that, elsewhere, therefore
   10. henceforth, thereafter
theogamy... 14. marriage of gods
theologian... 5. Arius (Bib) 6. Luther
   7. a divine 8. canonist
theology... 7. irenics 8. canonics,
   religion 9. depositum 10. doctrinism
theorem... 3. law 4. rule 5. axiom,
   topic 7. premise 9. principle,
   statement 11. proposition
theoretical... 5. ideal 8. academic,
   platonic 11. conjectural, impractical,
   speculative 12. hypothetical, not
   practical
theorize... 6. reason 9. postulate,
   speculate
theory... 3. ism 4. plan 6. scheme
   7. formula, opinion 8. analysis,
   doctrine 10. hypothesis
   11. speculation, supposition
   13. contemplation
theory of...
   evolution.. 9. Darwinism
   10. Lamarckism 13. Spencerianism
   knowledge.. 12. epistemology
   language.. 6. bowwow 8. ding–dong,
   pooh–pooh
   philosophy.. 13. phenomenalism
   relativity.. 8. Einstein
theosophist... 7. Mahatma
theosophy... 4. yoga 6. cabala
   7. Nirvana 8. kamarupa (Kama)
therapeutic... 7. healing 8. curative,
   remedies
therapy... 4. cure 5. faith 9. dietetics,
   medicines, treatment
   12. hydrotherapy, therapeutics
   13. psychotherapy
there... 3. yon 5. ready 6. yonder
   7. thereat, thither 11. at that place
therefore... 2. as, so 4. ergo
   5. hence, since 6. thence
   9. thereupon, to that end, wherefore
   11. accordingly 12. consequently
thermometer... 5. Hydra 7. Reaumur
   10. Centigrade, Fahrenheit
Thesaurus compiler... 5. Roget
thesis... 5. essay, theme, topic
   6. accent 7. premise 8. treatise
   9. postulate 10. assumption
   11. affirmation 12. dissertation

thespian... 3. art 5. actor 6. player,
   tragic 7. actress, Thespis (founder)
   8. dramatic
Thessaly, Greece...
   ancient name.. 9. Thessalia
   famed for.. 6. horses 8. horsemen
   mountain.. 4. Ossa 6. Pelion
   native.. 5. Greek 10. Thessalian
   town.. 7. Larissa
thew... 5. brawn, sinew 6. manner,
   muscle, virtue 8. strength
they go out... 6. exeunt
thick... 4. burr, dull, hazy 5. broad,
   bushy, close, crass, dense, gross,
   husky, plump, solid, squat 6. coarse,
   espeso, stodgy, stupid 7. crowded,
   grumous, muffled 8. familiar, friendly,
   intimate, numerous, thickset
   9. luxuriant 10. indistinct
   11. inspissated 12. impenetrable
thicken... 3. gel 4. clot, curd
   5. cloud, flock 6. curdle, deepen,
   harden 7. congeal, stiffen
   8. increase, solidify 9. intensify
   10. incrassate, inspissate, strengthen
thicket... 4. bosk, rone 5. copse,
   grove, hedge, shola 6. bosket
   (bosquet) 7. boscage, coppice,
   spinney 9. brushwood, chaparral
   10. underbrush
thickheaded... 4. dull 5. dense
   6. stupid 7. doltish
thickness... 3. ply 5. layer 7. density
   8. diameter, intimacy
   10. opaqueness 11. consistency,
   measurement
thickset... 5. squat, stout 6. stocky,
   stodgy, stubby 14. closely planted
thick–skinned... 7. callous
   11. hardhearted, insensitive,
   pachydermic 14. pachydermatous
thick soup... 5. purée
thief... 5. scamp 6. ackman, bandit,
   looter, pirate, rascal, robber
   7. burglar, filcher, rustler, stealer
   8. gangster, larcener 9. larcenist,
   scoundrel 10. freebooter, pickpocket,
   plagiarist
thieves (famed)... 5. Fagin 9. Robin
   Hood 10. Dick Turpin, Jesse James
   11. Claude Duval 12. Jonathan Wild
   13. Thief of Bagdad
thieves' Latin... 4. cant 5. slang
   12. secret jargon
thigh (pert to)...
   animal's.. 3. ham 4. hock 5. flank
   armor plate.. 6. cuisse (cuish)
   bone.. 5. femur, ilium
   ref to.. 5. groin, meros (merus)
   6. crural
thimble... 3. cap 4. ring 5. cover,
   watch
thimble (pert to)...
   berry.. 9. raspberry 10. blackberry
   eye.. 12. chub mackerel
   flower.. 8. foxglove
   rig.. 5. cheat 7. swindle 13. sleight
   of hand
   weed.. 6. clover
thin... 4. bony, lank, lean, poor, rare,
   slim, weak 5. gaunt, lanky, lathy,
   reedy, sheer, spare, washy 6. dilute,

meager, rarefy, shrill, sleazy, slinky,
   sparse, watery 7. haggard, insipid,
   scraggy, scrawny, slender
   8. araneous, rarefied 10. attenuated,
   diaphanous 11. transparent
thin (pert to)...
   air.. 5. smoke, vapor 6. bubble
   and delicate.. 8. araneous
   10. diaphanous
   and haggard.. 5. gaunt
   and withered.. 7. wizened 9. shriveled
   fabric.. 8. gossamer
   out.. 5. peter
   plate, bone.. 6. tegmen
   plate, metal.. 4. leaf
   plate, Zool.. 6. lamina 7. lamella
   skinned.. 6. gentle, tender, touchy
   Thin Man's dog.. 4. Asta
thine... 4. tuum
thing... 3. act, res 4. deed, fact, idea,
   unit 5. being, event 6. affair, entity,
   gadget, object 7. article, reality
   8. anything, creature 9. happening,
   situation, something
thing (pert to)...
   added.. 6. insert 8. addendum
   9. insertion 10. supplement
   assumed.. 7. premise 11. implication
   complete.. 4. unit
   cursed.. 8. anathema
   done.. 5. actum
   following.. 6. sequel
   found.. 5. trove
   hard to classify.. 11. nondescript
   huge.. 7. monster
   indefinite.. 7. so–and–so
   10. thingumbob (thingumabob)
   12. what's–its–name
   nonexisting.. 9. nonentity
   of little worth.. 6. stiver, trifle
   7. trinket
   the (thing).. 7. the rage
   unique.. 4. sole
things (pert to)...
   added.. 7. addenda 11. additaments
   brought into being.. 9. creations
   found, surprise.. 11. serendipity
   intricate.. 9. involutes
   little.. 16. inconsequentials
   moving to and fro.. 7. wigwags
   of like nature.. 8. cognates
   suitable to eat.. 9. esculents
   theoretical.. 7. noumena
   to be done.. 6. agenda
   to be learned.. 7. lessons
   to follow.. 7. sequels 8. sequelae
   to sharpen.. 10. whetstones
   widely separated.. 8. extremes
think... 3. wis 4. deem, muse, trow
   5. opine 6. reason 7. believe,
   imagine, reflect, suppose 8. cogitate,
   conceive, meditate 11. contemplate
think (pert to)...
   better of.. 6. repent 10. reconsider
   bring to mind.. 6. recall 7. imagine
   10. conjecture
   logically.. 6. reason
   of.. 5. judge 6. intend, recall
   8. consider, remember 9. recollect
   10. call to mind
   over.. 3. wis 4. mull, muse 5. brood
   6. ponder 8. meditate

up.. 6. devise, scheme 7. concoct
thinker, Relig freedom...
  14. latitudinarian
thinness... 6. rarity 7. tenuity
  8. rareness 11. slenderness
third (pert to)...
  comb form.. 3. tri 4. trit
  day (Quakers).. 7. Tuesday
  estate.. 6. people
  figure.. 7. ferison
  in number.. 8. tertiary
  music.. 6. tierce
  ordinal of.. 5. three
  person.. 6. escort 7. grammar
  8. chaperon
  power.. 4. cube
  Republic.. 6. French (1871)
thirst... 6. desire, hunger 7. craving,
  dryness, longing
this... 4. near 9. the nearer
Thisbe's lover (Bab)... 7. Paramus
thisness... 9. haecceity
thistle (pert to)...
  bird.. 9. goldfinch
  color.. 6. violet (cobalt)
  emblem.. 8. Scotland
  genus.. 6. Arnica, Cosmos 7. Carlina
  star.. 7. caltrop (caltrap)
thistledown... 6. pappus
  12. thistlebeard
thither... 3. yon 5. hence 6. yonder
thong... 4. lash, riem, whip 5. knout,
  lorum, quirt, romal, strap 6. lorate
  7. amentum, lanyard (laniard)
Thor (pert to)...
  father.. 4. Odin
  German.. 5. Donar
  god of.. 7. thunder
  other name.. 9. Hlorrithi
  stepson.. 3. Ull (Ullr)
  wife.. 3. Sif
thorax... 5. chest 6. cavity 7. cuirass
  8. pectoral 11. breastplate
thorn... 4. bane 5. briar (brier), spine
  7. acantha, bramble, prickle
thorn (pert to)...
  apple.. 3. haw 6. Datura
  back.. 3. ray 4. dorn 5. skate
  10. spider crab 11. stickleback
  bill.. 11. hummingbird
  comb form.. 5. spini
  full of.. 6. briary
  letters.. 2. th 3. edh
  lizard.. 6. moloch
  pert to.. 6. spinal
  small.. 7. spinule
thornless... 5. inerm 8. inermous
thorny... 5. sharp, spiny 7. brambly,
  prickly 9. acanthoid, bristling, difficult
thorough... 4. full 8. absolute,
  complete 9. downright, intensive
  10. exhaustive 11. painstaking
thoroughfare... 4. road 6. artery,
  street 7. highway, parkway, passage,
  roadway, thruway 8. arterial,
  autobahn, highroad, pent road,
  turnpike, waterway 9. boulevard,
  concourse 10. autostrada
thoroughgoing... 4. zeal 7. extreme
  9. downright 11. painstaking
thoroughly... 3. all 9. intensive,
  out-and-out 11. intensively

13. letter-perfect
thorp, thorpe... 4. dorp, town
  6. hamlet 7. village
those (pert to)...
  adept at table talk..
  14. deipnosophists
  brought to terms.. 11. transients
  in office.. 3. ins
  in the stock market.. 5. bears, bulls
  7. traders 9. investors
  of a habit.. 7. addicts
  of the same goal.. 6. rivals
  outside a profession.. 5. laity
those who...
  read and write.. 9. literates
  ridicule.. 8. deriders
  verify.. 13. corroborators
  work together.. 13. collaborators
thou... 3. tha 7. pronoun 8. thousand
thought... 4. care, heed, idea, view
  5. logic 6. deemed, opined
  7. anxiety, opinion 9. attention,
  cogitated, reasoning 10. cogitation,
  meditation, reflection 11. cerebration
  12. deliberation, recollection
  13. consideration, ratiocination
thought (pert to)...
  continuous.. 10. meditation
  deep in.. 10. cogitabund
  form.. 6. ideate
  laws of.. 7. noetics
  reader.. 11. telepathist
thoughtful... 4. kind 5. moody
  7. mindful, museful, pensive,
  prudent, serious 9. attentive
  10. cogitative, meditative, reflective,
  ruminative, solicitous
  11. circumspect, considerate
  13. contemplative
thoughtless... 4. rash 6. stupid
  7. foolish 8. careless, heedless,
  reckless 9. brainless, impulsive
  11. harum-scarum, inattentive,
  thought-free 12. unreflecting
  13. inconsiderate
thousand... 3. mil 5. mille 7. chiliad
  10. ten hundred
Thousand and One Nights...
  13. Arabian Nights
thousand men, command of...
  11. chiliarchia
thousandth... 9. chiliadal
  10. millesimal
thousand years... 7. chiliad
  9. millenary 10. millennium
thrall... 4. esne, serf 5. slave
  7. bondage, bondman, captive,
  slavery 9. thralldom 10. oppression
thrash... 3. lam, tan 4. beat, cave,
  drub, flog, whip 5. flail, pound, twist
  6. defeat, punish, strike, swinge,
  thresh 7. belabor, trounce
  8. urticate, vanquish 9. pulverize,
  toss about
thrashing... 7. beating, milling
  8. drubbing, flogging, whipping
  10. punishment
thread... 4. flax, jute, line, silk, vein,
  wire, yarn 5. fiber, floss, linen, lisle,
  rayon 6. cotton, dacron, sleave
  8. arrasene, filament
thread (pert to)...

ancient.. 4. byss
a needle.. 5. reeve
ball.. 4. clew (clue)
cell.. 5. cnida
coiled.. 3. cop
comb form.. 3. nem 4. nema
  5. nemat 6. nemato
fish.. 7. cutlass 9. threadfin
  11. cobblerfish
herring.. 11. gizzard shad
like.. 5. filar 6. filose
loose.. 4. lint 7. raveled
medical.. 5. seton
metal.. 4. wire
mystery lead.. 4. clue
shoemaker's (obs).. 6. lingel (lingle)
silk.. 5. floss 9. filoselle
tangle.. 6. sleave
tape, braid (thread).. 5. inkle
tester.. 9. serimeter
weaving term.. 4. warp, weft, woof
  5. leash
threadbare... 4. sere, worn 5. trite
  6. shabby
threaten... 4. warn 5. curse
  6. menace 7. portend 8. forebode
  9. comminate 10. intimidate
  12. anathematize
threatening... 4. dark 7. ominous
  8. imminent, lowering, menacing
three (pert to)...
banded armadillo.. 4. apar 5. apara
comb form.. 3. ter
dimensional.. 5. bruit, cubic
  12. stereoscopic
fold.. 4. tern 6. ternal, treble, triple
  7. ternate
group of.. 4. trio 5. triad 7. triplet
  8. triplets
hundredth anniversary..
  13. tercentennial
in one.. 6. triune 7. trinity 10. The
  Godhead
legged stand.. 6. teapoy, tripod, trivet
lined.. 9. trilinear
masted vessel.. 5. xebec 7. frigate
  8. schooner
math term.. 2. pi (3.1416)
prefix.. 3. tri
R's.. 7. reading, writing
  10. arithmetic
seeded.. 11. trispermous
sided figure.. 6. trigon 8. triangle
spot.. 4. trey
styled.. 10. trystylous
toed sloth.. 2. ai
Three Kingdoms (Chin)... 2. Wu
  3. Shu, Wei
Three Kings of Cologne... 6. Gaspar
  8. Melchior 9. Balthasar 12. Three
  Wise Men
Three Musketeers... 5. Athos
  6. Aramis 7. Porthos 9. D'Artagnan
  (friend)
Three Sisters (Myth)... 5. Fates
  6. Clotho 7. Atropos 8. Lachesis
Three Wise Men (Kings of Cologne)...
  6. Gaspar 8. Melchior 9. Balthasar
threnody... 5. dirge 7. requiem
  8. coronach
threshold... 3. eve 4. gate, sill
  5. limen 6. portal 8. doorsill

threw... see also *throw* 4. cast
  5. flung, slung 6. bunged, heaved,
  hurled, pelted, tossed 7. pitched
thrice... 3. ter, tri 5. fully 6. highly
  10. repeatedly, three times
thrift... 7. economy 8. prudence
  9. husbandry 10. providence
  11. thriftiness
thriftless... 6. lavish 8. prodigal,
  wasteful 11. extravagant, improvident
thrifty... 6. frugal, saving 7. careful,
  prudent, sparing 9. provident
  10. economical, forehanded,
  prosperous 11. flourishing
thrill... 4. tirl 6. dindle, thrush, tingle,
  tremor 7. delight 9. electrify
  10. excitement
thrive... 4. grow 5. moise (Eng)
  6. batten 7. prosper, succeed
  8. flourish, increase
throat... 3. maw 4. crop, neck
  5. gular, halse, mouth, voice
  6. groove, gullet, larynx, mutter
  7. channel, glottis, jugular, orifice,
  pharynx, trachea 9. esophagus
  10. passageway 12. constriction
throb... 4. ache, beat, drum, pant
  5. pulse 7. pulsate, vibrate
  9. palpitate
throe... 4. pang 5. agony 7. anguish
  8. struggle
Throgmorton Street... 13. Stock
  Exchange (London)
throne... 3. see 4. apse 5. exalt
  8. enthrone 9. royal seat
  11. sovereignty, supreme rank
  12. Chair of State
throng... 4. crew, host, push
  5. crowd, horde, press, swarm
  6. bustle, stress 7. hurried
  9. confusion, multitude
throttle... 5. choke, lever, seize
  6. throat 7. garrote 8. strangle,
  suppress, windpipe
through... 2. by 3. dia, per 4. into,
  thru 5. ended 7. perpend 8. finished
  9. because of, by means of,
  completed
throughout... 5. about 6. during
  8. thorough 10. completely,
  everywhere
throw... 3. cob, don, lob, peg, shy
  4. bear, cast, hurl, kist, pelt, toss,
  yerk 5. chuck, fling, heave, pitch,
  sling, twist, whirl 6. baffle, strike,
  thwart 7. discard, project
  9. prostrate
throw (pert to)...
a scare.. 7. terrify
away.. 7. discard 8. handbill,
  squander
back.. 5. repel 6. reject, revert
dice (term).. 4. sise 7. ambsace
in the towel.. 4. cede, quit
  9. surrender
into confusion.. 7. disturb, perturb,
  trouble 8. stampede 10. demoralize
into ecstasy.. 9. enrapture
into shade.. 7. eclipse
off.. 4. cast, shed 6. derail, reject
  7. abandon, discard
out.. 4. emit, lade 5. egest, eject,

expel 6. bounce 7. discard, project
9. eliminate
over.. 4. jilt 5. build 6. give up,
refute 7. abandon, discard
9. eliminate
overboard.. 8. jettison
water upon.. 5. douse
throwback... 7. setback 9. reversion
10. misfortune, regression
throwing (pert to)...
rope.. 5. lasso, reata, riata 6. lariat
science.. 10. ballistics
stick (anc).. 6. womera (woomera)
thrum... 3. bit, hum 4. drum, tuft
5. strum 6. fringe, repeat
thrush... 5. brown, mavis, robin, veery
7. disease 8. shagbark, songbird
9. blackbird
thrush (pert to)...
American.. 5. robin, veery 12. hermit
thrush
European.. 5. ouzel (ousel) 6. missel
7. redwing 11. nightingale
golden.. 6. oriole
Hawaiian.. 4. omao
Ind.. 5. shama
Scot.. 8. throstle
thrust... 3. dig, jab 4. gird, poke,
push, stab 5. lunge 6. extend,
pierce 7. intrude, obtrude, riposte
8. protrude 9. interject, interpose
thrust (pert to)...
aside.. 5. shove 7. dismiss 8. brush
off
down.. 7. detrude
fencing term.. 5. lunge 7. allonge,
riposte 8. estocade
one's self in.. 5. enter 7. intrude
out.. 5. eject 6. extend 8. protrude
thug... 4. goon, yegg 6. cuttle,
gunman 7. ruffian 8. assassin
9. cutthroat, roughneck
thumb... 6. pollex, thenar
thumb (pert to)...
a ride.. 9. hitchhike
bird.. 9. goldcrest
lady's (herb).. 9. peachwort, persicary
mark.. 4. soil 10. impression
11. fingerprint 14. identification
nail.. 5. small 8. complete
over.. 4. skim 6. browse
part.. 6. thenar
thump... 4. bang, beat, blow, drum,
thud, whip, yerk 5. knock, pound
6. hammer, pummel, strike, thrash
8. chastise 10. pound along
thunder... 4. boom, peal, roar
5. storm 9. fulminate
thunder (pert to)...
bolt.. 5. speed 6. Caesar 8. surprise
9. lightning 11. fulmination
fish.. 4. raad 5. loach 7. catfish
(electric)
god.. 4. Thor 6. Manito
of applause.. 5. cheer 7. ovation
peal.. 4. clap 5. crash
smitten goddess.. 6. Semele
8. Keraunia
thurible... 6. censer
thurifer... 12. censer bearer
Thursday... 4. Thor 8. fifth day
12. god of thunder

thus... 2. so 3. sic 5. hence 7. this
way 9. therefore 11. for instance
12. consequently
thwack... 3. rap 4. bang, blow, club
5. crush, knock, whack 6. defeat,
pommel, strike, thrash 7. belabor
thwart... 4. balk, foil 5. block, clash,
cross, parry, spite 6. defeat, gaffle,
oppose, outwit 7. oblique, prevent
8. obstruct, stubborn 9. frustrate,
interpose 10. across from, disappoint
thymus... 5. gland 10. sweetbread
(lambs, calves)
tiara... 5. crown 6. diadem 7. coronet
8. ornament
Tibbett opera... 12. Emperor Jones
(1932)
tibert... 3. cat
Tibet, Asia... see also *Tibetan*
animal.. 3. goa, sus 5. panda
capital.. 5. Lhasa
dialect.. 9. Bhutanese
kingdom.. 5. Nepal
Mts.. 8. Himalaya 9. Karakoram
religion.. 7. Lamaism
river.. 5. Hwang, Indus 7. Yangtze
11. Brahmaputra
ruler.. 9. Dalai Lama
Tibetan (pert to)...
beer (barley).. 5. chang
deer.. 4. shou
food (barley).. 6. tsamba
gazelle.. 3. goa
monk, priest.. 4. lama
ox.. 3. yak
sheep.. 3. sha 5. urial 6. bharal,
nahoor, nayaur
wild ass.. 5. kiang
wildcat.. 5. manul
tibia... 4. bone, shin 5. flute
6. cnemis
Tibur (anc)... 6. Tivoli
tiburon... 5. shark
Tiburtine... 12. Sibyl of Tibur
tick... 3. ked, tap 4. beat, mark, mite,
pest 5. Argas 6. acarid, Ixodes
7. instant 8. carapato, function,
ticktock 10. pajahuello (pajaroello)
ticket... 3. tag 4. note, pass, slip
5. check, ducat, label, token
6. ballot, billet, permit, record
7. license, voucher 8. document
11. certificate
ticket dealer... 7. scalper
tickle... 5. amuse 6. thrill, tingle
7. delight 9. titillate, vellicate
ticklish... 5. risky 6. fickle, queasy,
touchy 7. comical 8. unstable,
unsteady 9. uncertain 10. precarious,
unreliable
tidal (pert to)...
creek.. 6. estero 7. estuary
current.. 8. tiderace
flood.. 5. eagre
flow.. 3. ebb 4. bore, neap 5. surge
tidbit, titbit... 5. goody 6. morsel
7. saynete 8. delicacy
tide... 3. ebb, rip 4. high, neap, time
5. drift 6. period, stream 7. current
8. low water 9. be carried
tide (pert to)...
gate.. 9. floodgate

go with.. **5.** drift, float **7.** proceed
13. be fashionable
out with.. **3.** ebb **6.** recede
8. diminish, fade away
over.. **6.** endure **8.** surmount **11.** live
through
tidings... **4.** news, word **6.** gospel,
report, rumors **7.** message
10. evangelist **11.** information
tidy... **4.** neat, trig, trim **5.** groom,
natty, plump **6.** spruce **7.** orderly
9. shipshape **10.** put in order
12. antimacassar, considerable
tie... **4.** bind, bond, draw, even, knot,
lash, link **5.** ascot, equal, nexus,
noose, trice, truss **6.** cravat, enlace,
fasten, relate, tether **7.** confine,
necktie, sleeper **8.** equality, fastener,
restrain, shoelace **10.** allegiance,
obligation
tie (pert to)...
off.. **5.** belay
ornament.. **3.** pin
ready–made.. **4.** teck
securely.. **7.** trammel
sports.. **8.** dead heat
uniting.. **4.** bond **5.** tache
up.. **4.** bind, wrap **5.** truss **6.** fasten
8. restrain
tier... **3.** row **5.** grade, layer **6.** series
Tiergarten... **4.** park **16.** Zoological
Garden
tiff... **3.** sip **4.** huff, spat **5.** drink
7. dudgeon, quarrel **8.** outburst
10. fit of anger
tiffin... **3.** tea **5.** brown, lunch
6. repast **8.** luncheon
tiger... **5.** bully **6.** emblem, savage
9. swaggerer
tiger (pert to)...
American.. **6.** jaguar
bird.. **5.** finch **8.** amadavat
family.. **3.** cat **6.** mammal **11.** Felis
tigris
hunting dog.. **5.** dhole
S African.. **7.** leopard
Tasmania.. **9.** thylacine **13.** Tasmanian
wolf
wolf.. **5.** hyena
young.. **3.** cub
tight... **4.** fast, snug, taut, trim
5. alert, close, drunk, tense
6. narrow, stingy **7.** exactly, shapely
9. condensed **11.** closefisted
12. close–fitting, parsimonious
tight (pert to)...
fisted.. **6.** stingy **12.** parsimonious
lipped.. **5.** terse **9.** secretive
wad.. **5.** miser **10.** curmudgeon
tighten... **4.** frap, lace **5.** brace, tense
6. fasten, tauten **7.** squeeze
9. constrict
Tigris River city of ruins...
7. Nineveh (anc)
til... **4.** tree **6.** sesame
tilde... **4.** dash, mark, sign **6.** accent,
tittle **15.** diacritical mark
tile... **3.** red **5.** slate **6.** domino,
mosaic, pament (pamment), tegula
7. ceramic, pantile, tessera
8. pavement
tiler... **5.** thief **6.** slater **7.** hellier

10. doorkeeper
till... **3.** box **4.** farm, plow, tray, when
5. labor, while **6.** before, casket,
drawer, whilst **7.** develop **9.** cultivate
tillable... **6.** arable
tiller... **4.** helm **5.** stalk **6.** farmer,
sprout **7.** plowman, rancher
8. harrower **10.** cultivator,
husbandman
tilt... **3.** tip **4.** cant, heel, list **5.** joust,
pitch, slant, slope **6.** careen, oliver
(hammer), seesaw, unload **7.** incline
8. log house **10.** tournament
11. altercation
timber... **3.** log **4.** beam, tree, wood
6. forest, lumber **7.** support
9. underpier
timber (pert to)...
bend.. **3.** sny
building.. **4.** sill, stud **5.** joist
6. purlin, rafter **8.** stringer
convex.. **6.** camber
cribs (logging).. **4.** dram
cut.. **6.** lumber **7.** fallage
decay.. **4.** doty (doaty)
end.. **5.** tenon
hard, heartwood.. **7.** duramen
Naut.. **3.** rib **4.** bitt, keel, mast, spar,
wale **8.** sternson
support.. **6.** corbel
upright.. **8.** puncheon
wolf.. **4.** lobo
timbre... **4.** tone **5.** clang, crest (Her),
miter **7.** coronet **9.** resonance, tone
color
timbrel... **4.** drum **5.** tabor **7.** sistrum
10. tambourine
time... **3.** age, day, eon, era **4.** aeon,
date, hour, term, turn, week, year
5. clock, epoch, shift, tempo
6. decade, minute, moment, period,
season, second **7.** century
8. duration, occasion, schedule
9. fortnight
time (pert to)...
accurate.. **10.** isochronon
equal.. **10.** isochronal
Fast.. **4.** Lent
geologic.. **5.** azoic
granted.. **4.** stay **5.** delay **8.** reprieve
legal.. **6.** usance **11.** year and a day
long ago.. **4.** once, yore **8.** formerly
medical.. **3.** tid **8.** ter in die (three
times a day)
of vigor.. **6.** heyday
one.. **4.** once
present.. **5.** nonce **12.** contemporary
prior.. **9.** antedated **11.** retroactive
right.. **3.** tid
same.. **7.** however **9.** meanwhile
10. concurrent **11.** synchronous
14. simultaneously
spare.. **7.** leisure
waste.. **4.** idle, loaf **5.** dally **6.** loiter
wrong.. **11.** anachronism
13. anachronistic
timeless... **7.** ageless, eternal, undated
8. dateless, unending, untimely
9. premature **11.** everlasting
12. interminable
timely... **3.** apt, pat **4.** soon **5.** early
6. prompt **9.** opportune

10. seasonably 11. opportunity
timepiece... 4. dial 5. clock, watch
6. gnomon 8. egg glass, horologe
9. clepsydra, hourglass, metronome
10. isochronon, wristwatch
11. chronometer
times... 3. ago, eld 4. yore 5. often
10. frequently, yesterdays 11. ups
and downs
timid... 3. shy 5. eerie, henny, mousy,
pavid, scary 6. afraid, trepid
7. bashful, fearful, nervous, not bold
8. cowardly, retiring, timorous
9. diffident, shrinking 12. fainthearted
13. pusillanimous
timocracy (pert to)...
defined by.. 5. Plato
principle.. 11. love of honor
State.. 6. Sparta (anc)
Timon of Athens... 5. Cynic (The)
11. misanthrope
timorous... 5. timid 6. afraid
7. bashful, fearful 8. hesitant
9. shrinking
Timothy (pert to)...
Bib.. 7. convert 8. Epistles
grass.. 3. hay 10. herd's grass
timpani... 11. kettledrums
tin... 3. can, pan 5. money, plate
7. element, stannum 8. preserve
10. not genuine
tin (pert to)...
alloy (copper).. 6. pewter
box.. 7. trummel
coat with.. 5. terne 10. terneplate
comb form.. 6. stanni
extract.. 8. prillion
foil, plate.. 4. tain
mine.. 8. stannary
ref to.. 7. stannic
sheet.. 6. latten
symbol.. 2. Sn
tinamou... 4. yutu 7. tataupa
9. partridge
tincture... 4. dash 5. color, imbue,
myrrh, tinge, trace 6. iodine
7. extract, vestige 8. solution
9. paregoric, suspicion 10. extraction
tinder... 4. punk 5. spunk 6. amadou
9. touchwood
tine... 3. nib 5. prong, spike, tooth
tinea... 7. sycosis 8. ringworm
tinge... 3. dye 4. tint 5. color, imbue,
shade, stain, taint 6. flavor
8. coloring, tincture 10. suggestion
tingle... 4. ring 5. sting 6. dingle,
thrill 7. prickle 9. sensation,
stimulate
tinkle... 5. clink 6. dingle, tingle
tint... 3. due, hue 4. tone 5. blush,
color, tinge 6. nuance
tintinnabulum... 4. bell 6. tinkle
9. rhymester
tintype... 9. ferrotype
12. old–fashioned
tiny... 3. wee 5. small, teeny
6. atomic, infant, minute, petite
9. miniature 10. diminutive
13. infinitesimal
tip... 3. cue, end, fee, neb, top
4. apex, cant, heel, hint, lean, list,
tilt 5. crown, point, slant, spire,

upset 6. careen, inform, summit,
tiptop 7. cumshaw, incline
8. bonamano, gratuity, overturn
9. extremity, overthrow
tip (pert to)...
end.. 3. neb
French.. 9. pourboire
Italian.. 8. bonamano
near.. 6. apical
Near East.. 9. baksheesh (bakshish)
scabbard.. 5. chape 7. crampet
(crampette)
slender.. 6. arista
to one side.. 4. list, tile 5. alist
6. careen
up and over.. 4. cant
tippet... 4. cape, hood 5. amice, scarf
6. almuce 7. muffler 8. liripipe,
palatine 9. comforter
tipple... 3. bib, nip, pot, sip 4. suck
5. drink, quaff 6. fuddle, guzzle,
liquor, tumble 7. spirits 8. beverage,
overturn
tippler... 3. sot 5. souse, toper
7. drinker 9. draftsman
tipster... 4. tout 8. dopester
9. informant, predictor
10. forecaster, speculator
tipsy... 4. awry 5. drunk, shaky
6. groggy 7. fuddled, muddled
10. staggering 11. intoxicated
tiptoe... 5. alert 6. warily 7. eagerly,
quietly 8. cautious, stealthy
10. cautiously
tirade... 6. screed, speech 8. berating
9. philippic
tire... 3. fag, lag, rim 4. bore, jade
5. dress, weary 6. attire 7. exhaust,
fatigue
tired... 5. bored, jaded, spent, weary
6. aweary
tireless... 8. untiring 9. unwearied
10. unwearying 13. indefatigable
tiresome... 3. dry 4. dull, tame
6. boring, prolix 7. irksome, tedious
8. annoying 9. fatiguing, vexatious,
wearisome 10. irritating
tissue... 3. web 4. bast, tela 5. fiber,
paper 6. fabric 7. culture
8. meshwork
tissue (pert to)...
Biol.. 4. bone 5. nerve 6. muscle
8. ganglion 10. epithelium
cell.. 8. meristem
cellular.. 10. epithelium
connecting.. 6. stroma, tendon
8. ligament
decay.. 6. caries
fatty.. 3. fat 4. suet
hardening of.. 9. sclerosis
horny.. 7. keratin
layer.. 7. stratum
lymphoid.. 7. tonsils
nerve.. 8. ganglion
ref to.. 4. tela 5. telar
spinal.. 4. alba
vegetable.. 4. bast 7. endarch
8. meristem
wood.. 6. lignin, lignum
Titan... 4. Rhea, Thea 5. Coeus,
Creus, deity, Dione, giant, Theia
6. Phoebe, Tethys, Themis

7. Cronius, Iapetus, Oceanus
8. Hyperion 9. Mnemosyne
titanic... 4. huge 5. great 7. immense
8. colossal, enormous, gigantic
Titan War (Thessaly)...
11. Titanomachy
tithe... 3. tax 4. part 5. teind, tenth
11. frank pledge
titi... 6. monkey 7. sea bird
8. ironwood 9. buckwheat
Titian... 3. red 6. artist 7. red hair
9. red–haired
titillate... 5. amuse 6. thrill, tickle
7. delight 8. interest
titlark... 5. pipit
title... 3. sir 4. dame, deed, earl, lord,
name, sire, term, type 5. claim, right
6. knight, madame, squire
7. caption, epithet, esquire, heading
8. muniment 9. designate
11. appellation, designation
titled member, Stock Exchange...
6. orchid (sl)
titmouse... 3. mag, tit 4. wren
5. Parus 6. parine, tomtit 7. jacksaw
9. mumruffin
titter... 5. laugh, te–hee 6. giggle,
tee–hee 7. snicker
tittle... 3. dot, jot 4. iota, mark, whit
5. tilde 6. gossip, tattle 8. particle
tittle–tattle... 6. gossip 8. idle talk
16. scandalmongering
tittupy... 3. gay 5. shaky 6. lively
8. prancing, unsteady
titubate... 4. reel 6. totter 7. stagger,
stammer
titular... 7. nominal 9. incumbent (of a
title)
Tlingit... 6. Indian (Alaska)
TNT... 6. trotol 9. explosive
15. trinitrotoluene
to... 2. at 4. into, till, unto 5. until
6. toward 7. as far as, thither
11. preposition
to (pert to)...
to be.. 4. esse, être
to–do.. 3. ado 4. fuss, stir 6. bustle
9. commotion
to each his own.. 10. suum cuique
to which.. 7. whereto
to wit.. 3. viz 6. namely 8. scilicet
9. videlicet
toad... 4. agua, Bufo, frog, pipa
6. anuran, peeper 7. crapaud
9. amphibian, Batrachia, spadefoot
10. natterjack
toad (pert to)...
eater.. 5. toady 8. hanger–on,
parasite
fish.. 6. puffer, slimer 8. frogfish
head.. 6. plover (golden)
lily.. 9. waterlily
stabber.. 9. jackknife
tree.. 4. Hyla
toadflax... 8. flaxweed, ranstead
13. butter–and–eggs
toadstool... 5. morel 6. fungus
8. mushroom, puffball
toady... 4. ugly 8. parasite, truckler
9. repulsive, sycophant, toadeater
toast... 3. tan 4. cook, leep 5. bread,
brede, brown, parch, roast, skoal

6. pledge, sippet 7. drink to
8. cinnamon
tobacco (pert to)...
ash.. 6. dottle (dottel)
Cuban.. 4. capa 6. Vuelta (leaf)
disease.. 6. calico, mosaic 7. walloon
English.. 8. bird's–eye
epithet.. 12. Lady Nicotine
French.. 7. caporal
Greek.. 7. Knaster
hookah smoking.. 7. goracco
Indian.. 7. uppowoc
introduced by.. 7. Raleigh (Sir Walter)
Kentucky.. 6. Burley
kind.. 4. capa, shag 5. tabac
6. Burley, Vuelta 7. caporal,
henbane, Latakia, perique, Turkish
8. Virginia 9. salvadora
paste.. 7. goracco
Persian.. 6. tumbak (tumbaki)
pipe.. 7. calumet, chibouk (chibouque)
principle (active).. 8. nicotine
receptacle.. 4. pipe 7. humidor
S American.. 8. canaster
small cut.. 3. cud 4. plug, quid
6. dottle (dottel) 7. carotte
Turkish.. 7. Latakia
wrapping.. 9. broadleaf
toboggan... 4. sled 5. coast, glide
7. coaster 12. sharp decline
14. downhill course
toby... 3. dog (Punch's), jug, mug, rob
5. cigar 7. highway, pitcher
tocsin... 5. alarm 9. alarm bell
13. warning signal
toe... 3. tae, tip 5. digit 6. dactyl,
hallux 7. minimus
toehold... 7. footing 8. foothold,
purchase
toes, odd–numbered...
13. perissodactyl
together... 3. com, con, syn 4. mass,
with 5. union 10. conjointly
11. unanimously 12. coincidently,
concurrently, continuously
toggery... 3. set 4. garb, togs
5. dress 7. clothes, harness
9. trappings 12. haberdashery
tolerable... 4. so–so 8. bearable,
passable 9. endurable
10. acceptable, fairly well, sufferable
11. supportable
tolerance... 8. patience
10. indulgence, permission
tolerant... 7. lenient, patient
9. indulgent 10. forbearing,
permissive
tolerate... 4. bear, bide 5. abide,
allow, brook, stand 6. endure,
permit, suffer 9. put up with
toll... 3. due, tax 4. call, duty, peal,
ring 5. knell 6. allure, charge,
custom, entice, impost, invite, strike
7. ringing 8. exaction
10. assessment 12. compensation
Tolypeutes... 4. apar 9. armadillo
Tom, Dick and Harry... 8. everyone,
humanity 15. persons at random
tomahawk... 3. axe 4. kill 6. attack
7. hatchet
tomb... 4. cist, lair 5. crypt, grave,
speos, vault 6. shrine 7. mastaba

(mastabah), orruary, tritaph
  8. catacomb, cenotaph
  9. mausoleum, sepulcher
tombé... 4. drum
tomboy... 3. meg 4. romp 5. rowdy
  6. hoyden (hoiden), tomrig
tomcat... 3. gib
tomcod... 8. bocaccio
tome... 4. book, opus 5. atlas
  6. volume 11. papal letter,
  publication
tomorrow... 5. later 6. mañana 9. the
  morrow
tonant... 7. blatant 10. thundering
tone... 4. mode, mood, note, tang,
  tune 5. pitch, reedy, sound, trend,
  twang, vigor 6. accent, energy,
  melody, nuance, timbre 7. cadence
  8. modulate, monotone, tonology
  9. harmonize 10. inflection,
  intonation, modulation
tone (pert to)...
  down.. 3. dim 6. mellow, modify,
  soften 8. moderate
  lacking.. 5. atony 6. atonal
  quality, color.. 6. timbre
  series.. 5. scale
  single.. 8. monotone
  succession.. 5. melos
  thin.. 7. sfogato
  vibrant.. 5. twang
toneless... 4. weal 5. stony 6. silent
  9. colorless
tonga... 7. vehicle (2-wheeled)
Tonga... 15. Friendly Islands
tongue... 3. gab 4. meat 5. lingo,
  speak 6. speech 7. clapper, lingula
  8. language, lorriker, parlance
  9. utterance
tongue (pert to)...
  classical.. 5. Greek, Latin 6. Hebrew
  fish.. 4. sole
  Jesus.. 7. Aramaic
  lash.. 5. scold 8. scolding
  pivoted.. 4. pawl
  reference to.. 7. glossal, lingual
  sacred.. 4. Pali
  shaped.. 9. lingulate
  tied.. 4. mute 8. taciturn
  wagon.. 4. neap, pole
tongueless... 4. dumb, mute
  10. speechless
tonic... 6. bracer, catnip, liquor
  7. bracing 8. medicine, remedial,
  roborant 9. stimulant 10. refreshing
  11. corroborant 12. invigorating
tonsil... 8. amygdala
tonsorialist... 6. barber
tonsured... 4. bald 5. shorn 6. shaven
  7. clipped 10. baldheaded
too... 3. and 4. also, over, very
  6. overly 7. besides 8. likewise
  9. extremely 11. excessively
  12. additionally
too (pert to)...
  bad.. 4. alas
  much.. 4. trop 6. excess 7. nimiety
  small.. 13. unappreciable
  soon.. 9. premature
tool... 3. axe, saw 4. dupe, file
  5. agent 6. device, gadget, puppet
  7. engrave, gimmick, utensil, utility

  9. appliance 11. contrivance
tool (type)... 2. ax (axe) 3. adz (adze),
  awl, bit, hob, hoe, saw, sax, tap
  4. file, jack, pick, tong, vise
  5. brush, burin, drill, knife, lathe,
  level, plane, punch, razor, spade
  6. chisel, gimlet, hammer, lifter,
  peavey (peavy), pliers, reamer, shears,
  slater, slicer, square, trepan, wrench
  7. cleaver, mattock, mattoir, scalpel,
  spatula 11. screwdriver
tools (pert to)...
  category.. 5. power, speed 7. cutlery,
  machine, medical 9. precision
  11. labor-saving 12. straightedge
  prehistoric.. 4. celt 6. eolith
  9. paleolith
  stone.. 6. banner
  theft of.. 6. ratten
toosh... 4. gown (short), robe
  9. nightgown
toot... 3. pry, spy 4. fool, gaze, peep
  5. blare, drink, revel, shout, spree
  6. sprout 7. whistle 8. carousal,
  eminence, proclaim 9. blow a horn,
  elevation
tooth... 3. cog 4. dent, fang, snag,
  tine, tusk 5. ivory, molar, point,
  prong, taste 6. canine, cuspid,
  wisdom 7. grinder, incisor
  8. bicuspid, eyetooth 10. projection
tooth, teeth (pert to)...
  ache.. 8. dentagra 9. dentalgia
  comb form.. 5. denti, odont
  6. odonto 7. odontia
  cutting of.. 8. teething 9. dentition
  decay.. 6. caries, cavity
  11. saprodontia
  destitute of.. 8. edentate
  irregularity. 11. odontoloxia
  molar.. 4. wang
  ref to. 6. dental 7. odontic
  science.. 10. odontology
  Scot.. 3. gam
  socket.. 8. alveolus
  toothlike.. 8. odontoid 9. dentiform
toothless... 8. decrepid, edentate
toothsome... 5. tasty 9. delicious,
  palatable
top... 3. cap, fid, lid, tip, toy
  4. acme, apex, pate, roof 5. crest,
  criss, crown, excel, mensa, outdo,
  ridge, scalp 6. finial, summit, vertex,
  zenith 7. highest, supreme, surpass,
  topmost 8. dominate, pinnacle,
  teetotum 9. uppermost
topaz... 3. gem 5. color 7. mineral
  11. hummingbird 13. precious stone
tope... 4. tomb, wren 5. drink, grove,
  shark, stupa, tower 6. guzzle, shrine
  7. dogfish
toper... 3. sot 4. tope 5. shark
  6. barfly, boozer 7. guzzler, tippler,
  tosspot 8. drunkard 9. alcoholic,
  inebriate 12. bacchanalian
tophet, topheth... 4. hell 5. chaos
  8. darkness
topi, topee... 3. cap, hat 8. antelope
topiary... 6. garden 9. gardening
topic... 4. plot, text 5. theme
  6. reason, remedy 7. subject
  8. argument 11. application

topical... 5. local 9. temporary
  10. thematical
topknot... 5. crest, onkos 6. pigeon ‘
  8. flounder 9. headdress
topmost... 6. apical 7. highest,
  supreme 8. foremost 9. uppermost
topnotcher... 3. ace 4. hero, star
  6. tiptop 7. supreme 9. first–rate
  11. unsurpassed
topography... 7. mapping 8. location
  9. surveying 11. description
  15. regional anatomy
topple... 3. tip 4. fall, tilt 5. pitch,
  upset 6. totter, tumble 8. overturn
  9. overthrow 10. somersault
topsail... 5. raffe (raffee)
topsy–turvy... 8. confused
  10. contrarily, disordered
  11. withershins
toque... 3. hat 6. monkey (bonnet)
  9. headdress
tor... 4. crag, peak 5. mound
  8. pinnacle
torah, tora... 3. law 7. precept
  10. Law of Moses, Pentateuch,
  revelation
torch... 4. lamp 5. blaze, flare, fusee
  (fuzee), light 7. lighter, lucigen
  8. flambeau 10. flashlight
torero... 11. bullfighter
torment... 3. rib, vex 4. bait, pain,
  rack 5. agony, devil, harry, tease,
  worry 6. badger, harass, harrow,
  hector, pester, plague, stir up
  7. afflict, anguish, bedevil, torture
  8. distress, vexation 9. suffering,
  tantalize 10. punishment
  11. persecution
torn... 4. rent 5. riven, split 6. ripped
  7. severed 8. tattered 9. alienated,
  lacerated (see also *tear*)
tornado... 4. wind 7. cyclone, twister
  8. blizzard, outburst 9. hurricane,
  whirlwind, windstorm
  12. thunderstorm
toro... 4. bull 7. cavalla, cowfish
torpedo... 3. ray 4. boat, mine
  5. shoot 6. attack, gunman
  7. explode 8. fire upon, firework,
  numbfish 9. crampfish, detonator,
  submarine
torpid... 4. dull, numb 5. inert
  6. stupid 7. dormant 8. benumbed,
  inactive, lifeless, listless, sluggish
  9. apathetic, lethargic
torpor... 4. coma 6. acedia, apathy,
  stupor 7. languor 8. dormancy,
  lethargy 9. inertness 10. inactivity
  12. sluggishness 13. insensibility
torque... 5. chain 6. collar 7. torsion
  8. necklace, ornament
torrefy... 5. parch, roast 6. scorch
torrent... 5. flood, spate 6. stream
  7. current, roaring 8. downpour,
  outburst
torrential... 12. overwhelming
torrid... 3. hot 4. arid 7. burning,
  parched 8. scorched, tropical
  10. oppressive, passionate
tortilla cooking dish... 5. comal
tortoise... 4. emyd, Emys 6. gopher,
  turtle 7. hicatee 8. Chelonia,

matamata 9. ellachick
tortuous... 6. spiral 7. devious,
  sinuous, winding 8. twisting
  10. circuitous, roundabout
  12. labyrinthine
torture... 4. flay, pain, rack 5. agony,
  twist 6. impale, punish, wrench
  7. crucify, distort, torment
  10. punishment
tory, Tory... 6. bandit, outlaw, Papist
  8. loyalist, marauder, partisan,
  Royalist 11. reactionary
  12. Conservative
toss... 3. lob 4. cast, flip, hurl
  5. bandy, chuck, fling, flirt, heave,
  pitch, throw 6. billow, thrash
  7. disturb 8. flounder, scramble
  9. commotion 10. excitement
toss (pert to)...
  a coin.. 4. flip
  and turn.. 6. thrash 8. flounder
  9. vacillate
  off.. 5. drink 6. tipple 9. dispose of,
  improvise
  out.. 5. eject 8. trick out
  together.. 8. scramble
tosspot... 3. sot 5. drunk, toper
  6. flagon 8. drunkard
tossup... 6. gamble 10. even chance
  11. uncertainty
tota... 6. grivet, monkey
total... 3. add, all; sum, tot 5. gross,
  utter, whole 6. amount, entire
  7. perfect, summary 8. absolute,
  complete, entirety 9. aggregate
totally... 5. quite 6. wholly 8. entirely
  10. completely
totem... 4. pole, post 6. fetish, pillar,
  symbol
totem pole... 3. xat
toto... 3. all 4. baby 5. totum
totter... 4. reel, rock, sway 5. pitch,
  shake, waver 6. falter, seesaw
  7. stagger 8. titubate 9. fluctuate,
  vacillate
toucan... 4. toco 7. aracari 8. hornbill
  13. constellation (opp Southern
  Cross)
touch... 3. dab, tag, tap, tig 4. abut,
  feel, meet 5. taste, trait 6. adjoin,
  border 7. contact 9. acuteness
touch (pert to)...
  acuteness of.. 8. oxyaphia
  bound.. 4. abut
  closely.. 7. impinge 8. osculate
  examine.. 7. palpate
  light, lightly.. 3. pat 5. brush
  7. attinge, lambent
  off.. 4. fire 6. incite
  ref to.. 7. tactile, tactual
  stone.. 8. basanite 9. criterion
  11. Lydian stone
  wood.. 4. punk 6. amadou, tinder
touching... 6. moving 7. contact,
  feeling, tangent 8. pathetic
  9. affecting, attingent 10. concerning
  11. interesting
touchy... 4. sore 5. cross, testy
  7. peevish 8. ticklish 9. irascible,
  irritable, sensitive 10. precarious
  13. oversensitive
tough... 4. hard, wiry 5. hardy, rowdy,

stiff 6. robust, sinewy, strong
7. ruffian 8. adhesive, hardened,
leathery, stubborn 9. difficult,
obstinate, resistant, tenacious
10. unyielding
toupee... 3. wig 6. peruke 7. periwig
9. false hair
tour... 4. trip 5. shift 6. travel
7. circuit, journey 9. barnstorm,
excursion
tourmaline... 3. gem 6. schorl
9. rubellite 10. indicolite
tournament... 4. tilt 5. games, joust,
trial 6. battle 7. contest, regatta,
tourney 8. Olympics 9. encounter
11. Turnierfest
tourniquet... 6. binder, garrot
7. bandage
tousle, tousel... 4. pull, tear
6. rumple, tussle 8. dishevel
tout... 3. spy 5. scout, watch
6. praise 7. canvass, lookout, tipster
8. give a tip, informer, smuggler
9. predictor, solicitor
tow... 3. tew, tug 4. drag, draw, haul,
pull, rope 5. chain 6. hawser
8. cordelle
toward... 2. ad, at, to 4. near
5. anent 6. facing 7. forward,
towards, willing 8. imminent
9. compliant, headed for
11. approaching
toward (pert to)...
blood vessels.. 5. hemad (haemad)
center.. 5. entad 6. inward
direction.. 7. leeward, seaward
  8. homeward, landward, windward
  9. earthward 10. heavenward
exterior.. 5. ectad
front.. 8. anterior
left.. 3. haw 5. aport 9. sinistrad,
sinistral
mouth.. 4. orad
right.. 7. dextrad 9. dextrally
stern.. 5. aft 5. abaft 6. astern
towards... 7. ynesche
tower... 3. tor 4. boom, silo, soar
5. exalt, pylon, spire, stupa 6. belfry,
height, turret, uplift 7. bulwark,
defense, elevate, steeple, surpass
8. domineer, fortress 9. campanile
10. stronghold, watchtower
tower (pert to)...
astrology.. 7. mansion 14. planetary
house
bell.. 9. campanile
chess.. 6. castle
church.. 5. spire 6. belfry, cupola
glacial.. 5. serac
India.. 5. minar 7. sikhara
marker.. 5. pylon
of.. 4. Pisa 5. Babel, Minar 6. Eiffel,
Hunger, London 7. silence (dakhma)
10. Kutab Minar
Oriental.. 7. minaret
watch.. 7. mirador
towering... 4. high, huge, tall
5. great, lofty 6. Alpine 7. eminent,
soaring 11. overweening
towhee... 5. finch 7. bunting, chewink
town... 4. burg, deme 6. ciudad,
hamlet, Podunk, suburb 7. borough,

commune, village 8. boom town,
township 9. ghost town
townsman... 3. cit 7. citizen, oppidan
(Eton student) 8. resident
9. selectman
toxic... 7. noxious 8. poisoned,
venomous, virulent 9. poisonous
toxicology (*science of*)... 7. poisons
9. antidotes
toxology... 7. archery
toxophilite... 6. archer
toy... 3. pet, top 4. doll, hoop, play,
whim 5. dally, fancy, flirt 6. bauble,
gewgaw, hoople, rattle, trifle 7. cat's
paw, trinket 8. flirting 9. plaything
10. knickknack
trace... 4. clew (clue), copy, find, hint,
mark, nose, seek, sign 5. refer,
shade, tinge, track, trail 6. deduce,
derive, detect, follow, sketch
7. glimpse, outline, thought, vestige
8. evidence, traverse 9. delineate,
footprint 11. investigate, small
amount
trachea... 4. duct 8. windpipe
tracing... 4. copy 6. record
8. ergogram 10. cardiogram
12. reproduction
track... 3. rut, way 4. path, rail, slot,
spur, wake 5. route, spoor, trail,
tread 6. follow, pursue 7. noreite
(worm), vestige 8. traverse
9. footprint, spectacle
tract... 4. area, plot, zone 5. essay,
range 6. estate, region 7. booklet,
country, expanse, leaflet, quarter,
stretch 8. brochure, district,
pamphlet, treatise 9. territory
10. exposition 11. subdivision
12. dissertation
tract (pert to)...
arid.. 4. dene 6. desert
boggy, swampy.. 6. morass
  10. Everglades
grassland.. 7. prairie
lava.. 8. pedregal
treeless.. 5. llano 6. steppe 7. prairie
tractable... 4. easy 6. docile, gentle,
pliant 7. ductile 8. amenable, flexible
9. adaptable, compliant, malleable
10. governable 11. conformable
trade... 3. buy 4. deal, sell, swap,
wind 5. craft 6. barter, merger,
metier 7. bargain, calling, dealing,
pursuit, traffic 8. business,
commerce, exchange, practice,
purchase, vocation 10. handicraft,
occupation, profession 11. intercourse
trade—mark, trademark... 5. brand,
label
trader... 6. dealer, monger, sutler
8. merchant 9. tradesman
10. shopkeeper
trading association... 5. hanse (hansa)
trading station (Mil)... 2. PX 4. fort,
post
tradition... 4. lore, myth 5. usage
6. custom, legend 7. culture
8. folklore 10. convention
(established) 12. superstition
traditional... 3. old 9. legendary
10. historical 12. conventional,

long–standing 15. long–established
traditional tale... 4. saga 6. legend
traduce... 4. slur 5. abuse, belie
6. debase, defame, malign, vilify
7. asperse, pervert, slander
8. disgrace 10. calumniate
traffic... 3. buy 4. sell 5. trade
6. barter, simony (sacred)
8. business, carriage, commerce,
dealings 11. familiarity, intercourse
tragedy... 6. misery 8. calamity,
disaster 10. misfortune
tragic... 3. sad 4. dire 5. fatal
8. dramatic, pathetic 10. calamitous,
disastrous, fatal event
tragopan... 8. pheasant
trail... 3. lag 4. drag, hunt, path, slot,
spur 5. blaze, piste, route, scent,
spoor, trace, track 6. camino, follow
7. draggle 8. be behind, footpath
9. lag behind
Trail (famed)... 6. Mormon, Oregon
7. Santa Fe, Spanish 8. Chisholm, El
Camino, Heritage 10. Lewis–Clark,
Wilderness 11. Appalachian
12. Natchez Trace, Pacific Crest
trail (pert to)...
blazer.. 7. pioneer
deer.. 4. slot
mark a.. 5. blaze
marker.. 5. cairn
mountain.. 4. pass
Spanish.. 6. camino
train... 2. el 4. line, load, tail
5. breed, chain, coach, drill, flier,
focus, shape, suite 6. direct, school,
series 7. caravan, cortege, educate,
retinue 8. accustom, instruct,
railroad, rehearse 9. afterpart,
entourage, following 10. attendants,
conveyance, discipline, line of cars,
procession 11. progression,
streamliner 13. accommodation
trained mechanic... 7. artisan
trainee... 6. rookie 7. recruit, student
8. enrollee
traipse... 3. gad 5. trail, tramp
6. trudge, wander 8. gadabout
trait... 5. habit, touch 6. streak
7. feature, quality 9. lineament,
mannerism 11. peculiarity
13. individuality 14. characteristic
traitor... 3. rat 8. informer, Quisling,
turncoat 10. treasonist
13. double–crosser, Judas Iscariot
14. Benedict Arnold
traject... 3. way 4. sage 5. ferry,
route 6. course 7. passage
8. crossing
trajectory... 5. route 6. rocket
9. celestial 10. fixed orbit
tram... 3. car 4. limb 5. wagon
7. carrier, railway, tramcar, trolley,
vehicle 9. streetcar 10. conveyance
tramontane... 5. alien 8. polestar
9. foreigner, North Star
11. transalpine
tramp... 3. bum 4. hike, hobo, hoof,
step, walk 5. jaunt, nomad, tread
6. beggar, trudge, wander
7. sponger, traipse, trample, vagrant
8. vagabond 9. sundowner

10. landlouper (landloper), pedestrian
11. bindle stiff 12. foot traveler
trample... 5. crush, tread 6. bruise,
subdue 7. conquer, destroy, run over
9. press down
trance... 4. coma, doze 5. dream,
spell, swoon 6. raptus, stupor
7. amentia, ecstasy, rapture
8. hypnosis 9. catalepsy, enrapture,
hypnotize, spellbind
tranchant... 5. sharp 7. cutting
9. trenchant
tranquil... 4. calm, cool, easy, mild
5. quiet, still 6. gentle, placid,
serene 7. pacific, restful
8. composed, peaceful 9. quiescent
11. undisturbed 13. imperturbable
tranquility... 3. keg 5. peace, quiet
8. calmness, serenity 9. composure
10. quiescence 12. peacefulness
tranquilize... 4. calm, lull 5. allay,
quiet, still 6. pacify, settle, soothe
7. appease, assuage, compose
transaction... 4. deal, sale 6. action,
affair 7. bargain 8. business
9. discharge, execution
10. proceeding 11. negotiation,
performance, proposition 16. buying
and selling
transcend... 3. cap 5. excel, mount
6. ascend, exceed 7. surpass 8. go
beyond, outstrip, surmount
transcendent... 5. above 8. ethereal,
heavenly, superior 9. recondite
10. superhuman, surpassing
12. metaphysical, supernatural,
transmundane 13. extraordinary
14. transcendental 15. beyond
knowledge
transcribe... 4. copy 5. write
6. record 9. reproduce, translate
10. paraphrase
transcript... 4. copy 6. record
8. apograph 9. duplicate, imitation
12. reproduction
transfer... 4. cede, deed, pass, sale
5. grant, shift 6. assign, attorn,
change, convey, depute, remove
7. removal 8. alienate, delivery
9. transport 10. conveyance,
transcript
transfer (pert to)...
conveyance (estate).. 5. lease
6. demise
crown to successor.. 6. demise
design.. 5. decal 12. decalcomania
medical.. 10. transplant
of ownership.. 6. attorn
10. abalienate, alienation, conveyance
of property.. 8. disposal
transfigure... 5. exalt 6. change
7. glorify 8. idealize 9. irradiate,
transform, transmute
12. metamorphose
transfix... 3. pin 4. hold 5. spear
6. fasten, impale, pierce 9. hold
fixed 11. transpierce 14. hold
motionless
transform... 4. turn 5. alter
6. change, revamp 7. convert
9. transmute 10. assimilate
11. transfigure 12. metamorphose,

transmogrify 16. transubstantiate
transformation... 3. wig 6. change
  8. mutation 10. conversion, false
  front 13. metamorphosis,
  transmutation 17. anthropomorphosis
transgress... 3. err, sin 5. cross
  6. exceed, offend, thwart 7. disobey,
  infract, violate 8. overstep, trespass
  9. break a law
transgression... 3. sin 5. crime, fault
  7. misdeed, offense 8. trespass
  9. violation 10. effrontery, infraction
  11. lawbreaking 12. infringement
  13. nonconformity
transgressor... 6. sinner 8. offender
  9. wrongdoer 10. delinquent,
  malefactor
transient... 5. brief 6. lodger 7. flighty
  8. fleeting, fugitive, traveler
  9. ephemeral, migratory, momentary
  10. evanescent, short–lived, transitory
transit... 6. travel 7. passage
  9. metabasis 10. conveyance
  12. transference
transition... 5. shift 7. passage
  9. anabolism, evolution, metabasis
  10. catabolism (katabolism),
  conversion, metabolism, modulation
  11. transfusion
transitory... 5. brief, fleet 8. fleeting,
  temporal 9. ephemeral, temporary,
  transient 10. evanescent 11. not
  enduring
transitory things... 8. ephemera
translate... 4. read, rede 6. decode,
  render 7. convert 8. construe,
  transfer 9. interpret 10. paraphrase
translation... 4. pony, trot 7. version
  9. rendition 10. paraphrase
  12. transference 14. interpretation
  15. transliteration
translucent... 6. limpid 8. luminous
  11. transparent 14. shining through
transmit... 4. send 6. convey, render
  7. devolve, forward 8. bequeath,
  hand down, transfer
  11. communicate
transmutation... 9. evolution
transmute... 6. change 7. convert,
  resolve 9. transform 11. transfigure
  12. metamorphose
  16. transubstantiate
transparent... 4. open 5. clear, gauzy,
  lucid, sheer 6. bright, candid, glassy,
  lucent 7. crystal, pelucid, shining
  8. luminous, lustrous 9. guileless
  10. diaphanous 11. crystalline,
  perspicuous, translucent, unconcealed
transparent thing... 4. mica, silk, veil
  5. beryl, water 6. quartz, tissue
  7. crystal, diamond 8. gossamer
  9. isinglass
transport... 3. dak 4. boat, move, raft,
  send, ship 5. bring, carry, truck
  6. banish, convey, deport, vessel
  7. ecstasy, freight, passion, rapture,
  smuggle 8. carriage, emigrate,
  entrance, palander, transfer
  9. enrapture, troopship
transpose... 5. shift 6. change,
  convey, invert 7. convert, reverse
  8. transfer 9. rearrange, translate,

transmute 11. interchange
transposition of sounds, words...
  10. metathesis, spoonerism
Transvaal (pert to)...
  capital.. 8. Pretoria
  city.. 12. Johannesburg
  daisy.. 7. gerbera
  discovery.. 4. gold, Rand (The)
  famed emigration.. 9. great trek
  (1836)
  legislature.. 4. raad
  policeman.. 4. zarp
  settlers.. 5. Boers
  War.. 4. Boer (1899–1902)
transverse... 6. across 7. oblique,
  transom 8. diagonal 9. crosswise
  10. crosspiece
trap... 3. gin, net, pat, web 4. cage,
  door, lure, rock, tipe, tree, weir
  5. catch, creel, mouth, snare
  6. ambush, corner, device, eelpot,
  enmesh, recess 7. dragnet, ensnare,
  pitfall, springe 8. carrlage, deadfall,
  trapping, trickery 9. caparison, road
  block, stratagem
trapper... 5. lurer 6. hunter, netter,
  snarer 7. decoyer
trappings... 4. gear, tack 5. props
  7. scenery 8. wardrobe 9. apparatus,
  caparison, ornaments 10. horse cloth
  13. paraphernalia
trash... 4. bosh, dirt, junk 5. waste
  6. debris, refuse, rubble 7. rubbish
  8. nonsense, riffraff, trumpery
  10. balderdash
trashy... 5. cheap, toshy 6. paltry
  7. useless 8. rubbishy 9. worthless
  11. nonsensical
trauma 5. shock, wound 6. injury
travail... 4. pain, toil 5. agony, labor
  7. journey, trouble 9. suffering
  11. parturition
trave... 9. crossbeam
travel... 2. go 4. fare, move, mush,
  post, ride, taxi, tour, trek, wend
  5. coast 6. motion 7. commute,
  journey, migrate, sojourn 8. progress,
  traverse 9. gallivant 11. peregrinate
travel (pert to)...
  equipment.. 7. baggage 9. viaticals
  expense.. 8. viaticum
  group.. 7. caravan
  over obstacles.. 9. roughshod
  pert to.. 6. viatic
  place to place.. 9. itinerate
traveler, travelers... 5. farer 6. viator
  7. caravan, tourist 8. salesman,
  wayfarer 9. journeyer
travels... 7. odyssey 8. journeys
  14. peregrinations
traverse... 4. deny, pass 5. cross
  6. refute, thwart 7. athwart, oblique,
  parados 8. navigate 10. counteract
travesty... 5. drama 6. parody, satire
  7. lampoon 8. disguise 9. burlesque
  10. caricature 11. incongruity
tray... 6. salver, server 7. ashtray,
  coaster
treacherous... 5. false, Judas, punic,
  snaky 8. disloyal, plotting, unstable
  9. deceitful, faithless, insidious
  10. perfidious, traitorous, unreliable

11. disaffected 13. Machiavellian (Machiavelian), untrustworthy

treachery... 5. guile 6. deceit
7. perfidy, treason 8. betrayal
10. disloyalty

treacle... 4. cure 6. remedy
7. claggum, sweeten 8. molasses
10. sweetening

treacle water... 7. cordial

tread... 3. rut 4. gait, mark, pace, step, volt, walk 5. crush, stair
6. course 7. conquer, set foot, trample 8. footstep, shoe sole
9. footprint

treadle... 5. lever, pedal 7. chalaza

tread underfoot... 5. crush 6. subdue
7. oppress, run over 8. domineer
9. tyrannize

treason... 7. perfidy 8. betrayal, sedition 9. treachery

treasonable, treasonous...
10. perfidious, traitorous
11. treacherous

treasure... 4. fisc (fisk), fund, roon
5. cache, chest, hoard, prize, purse, store, trove, value 6. coffer, fiscus, riches, wealth 7. cherish 8. hold dear 9. exchequer, thesaurus
10. appreciate, depository, repository, storehouse

treasurer... 6. bursar, purser
7. cashier, curator, officer 8. receiver
9. paymaster 11. chamberlain

Treasure State... 7. Montana

treasure–trove... 5. money (hidden)
7. bullion 9. discovery 14. buried treasure

treat... 4. dose 5. Dutch, feast
6. doctor, handle, regale, repast
7. delight, discuss, process
8. consider 9. discourse, entertain, negotiate 10. manipulate

treat (pert to)...
improperly.. 4. snub 5. flout, spite
6. insult, misuse, offend 9. humiliate
maliciously.. 5. frame, spite
of morals.. 6. ethics
royally.. 6. regale 9. with honor
silk (for rustle).. 6. scroop
snobbishly.. 7. high hat, high–hat
surgically.. 7. operate
tenderly.. 6. coddle, pamper
with contempt.. 5. flout, scorn, scout, spurn 7. contemn
with deference.. 7. respect

treatise... 5. essay, study, tract
6. thesis 7. article 9. discourse
10. discussion 12. dissertation

treatise on...
forests.. 5. silva
fruit trees.. 6. pomona
language.. 7. grammar
pines.. 7. pinetum

treatment (pert to)...
application (Med).. 5. stupe
compassionate.. 5. mercy
harsh.. 5. abuse 8. misusage, severity
ill.. 5. abuse
preparatory.. 8. training 10. ground work, processing
term.. 5. usage 8. addition (to soil), handling

treaty... 4. mise, pact 6. cartel
7. compact, entente 8. contract
9. agreement 10. convention
11. arrangement, negotiation
12. capitulation 13. understanding

treaty (pert to)...
bound nations.. 6. allies
Elm.. 12. Philadelphia (1682)
first draft.. 8. protocol
peace.. 5. truce 6. Pax Dei
9. armistice 10. pax in bella
secret.. 13. the Engagement (1647)

treble... 5. three, voice 6. latten, triple
7. soprano 9. threefold
11. high–pitched

treble clef... 3. Gee 5. G clef, staff (G clef)

tree... 5. plant 6. corner, timber
7. gallows 9. genealogy

tree (pert to)... see also *trees*
antidote for snakebite.. 6. cedron
aromatic.. 9. sassafras
bear.. 7. raccoon
cactus.. 7. saguaro
camphor.. 5. kapur
cat.. 9. palm civet
cobra.. 6. mambra
cone–bearing.. 3. fir, yew 5. alder, cedar, larch 7. conifer
evergreen fruit.. 5. lemon 6. orange
exudation.. 3. gum, lac, sap
India.. 4. dita 10. devil's tree
lotus.. 4. sadr
mineral (formed on).. 8. dendrite
of Buddha.. 2. bo
of chastity.. 11. agnus castus
of life.. 10. arbor vitae
of strength.. 3. oak
rain.. 5. saman (zaman) 8. genisaro
resin.. 3. fir 4. pine 6. balsam
sacred (Bib).. 7. asherah
salt.. 4. atle (atlee) 8. tamarisk
snake.. 4. gimp, lora
sprout.. 5. copse, sprig 7. coppice
sugar.. 5. maple
Texas.. 5. alamo 6. poplar
tiger.. 7. leopard
toad.. 4. hyla
trunk.. 4. bole 5. caber, stock
umbrella.. 5. wahoo
victor's crown.. 6. laurel
worshiper.. 5. dryad, nymph (wood)

trees (pert to)...
grove.. 5. copse
plantation.. 6. forest 7. orchard, pinetum
poem.. 6. Kilmer (Joyce)
ref to.. 8. arboreal 9. cacuminal
science.. 7. silvics 12. silviculture
service (rowan).. 5. sorbs

trefoil... 6. clover 8. shamrock
10. black medic, clover leaf (Her)

tregetour (anc)... 7. juggler
8. magician

trek... 6. travel 7. journey, migrate
10. expedition

trellis... 5. arbor 7. lattice, pergola
8. espalier 11. latticework

tremble... 5. quake, shake 6. doddle, falter, quaver, quiver, shiver, tatter, thrill, tremor 7. shudder, tremolo, twitter, vibrate 8. be afraid 9. be

excited, trepidate
trembling... 5. aspen 6. dither, trepid
  7. fearful, nervous, quaking, quavery,
  shaking 9. vibrating
tremendous... 3. big 4. huge
  5. awful, giant, great 6. superb
  8. horrible, powerful, terrific
  9. frightful, momentous, monstrous
  10. terrifying 13. extraordinary
tremolo... 6. quaver 10. fluttering
tremor... 5. palsy, quake, shake
  6. quiver, thrill 7. tremble
  9. vibration
tremulous... 5. aspen, quaky, timid
  7. excited, fearful, nervous, palsied,
  shaking, shivery 9. quavering,
  sensitive, trembling, vibratory
  11. palpitating
trench... 3. gaw 4. bury, gash, leat,
  moat 5. canal, carve, ditch, drain,
  fosse 6. furrow, groove, gutter
  7. acequia, intrude 8. aqueduct,
  encroach, entrench, infringe, trespass
  10. excavation 12. entrenchment
trenchant... 4. keen 5. acute, sharp
  6. biting 7. cutting 8. clear–cut,
  incisive 11. penetrating
trencherman... 5. eator 7. sponger
  8. gourmand 9. chowhound
  11. gormandizer
trend... 4. tone, turn, vein 5. drift,
  skirt, swing, tenor 6. strike
  7. deviate, revolve 8. movement,
  tendency 9. direction 11. inclination
trepan... 3. saw 4. lure, tool 5. snare,
  trick 6. entrap 7. deceive, swindle
  8. deceiver, trephine 9. stratagem,
  trickster
trepang... 10. bêche–de–mer 11. sea
  cucumber 14. sea caterpillar
tropid... 7. quaking 8. timorous
  9. trembling
trepidation... 4. fear 5. alarm
  6. dismay 7. quaking 9. agitation,
  confusion 10. excitement
  11. disturbance, oscillation
  12. perturbation 13. consternation
trespass... 3. sin 4. tort 5. poach
  6. breach, invade, trench 7. intrude,
  offense 8. encroach, entrench,
  infringe, overstep 10. infraction,
  transgress 11. misfeasance
  12. infringement 13. transgression
tress... 4. curl, hair 5. braid, plait
  7. ringlet 10. lock of hair
tressure... 4. band 6. border, fillet,
  ribbon 9. headdress
trestle... 5. bench 7. support, viaduct
tret... 9. allowance
triad... 5. chord, three, trine 7. trinary,
  trinity 9. trivalent 12. ternary group
trial... 2. go 4. bout, case, test
  5. venue 6. assize, ordeal
  7. attempt, contest, empiric
  8. evidence, hardship 9. prolusion,
  trying out 10. experiment
  11. examination, tribulation
triangle... 6. trigon 8. virginal
  13. constellation
triangle (pert to)...
  connection.. 5. delta

draw circle within.. 7. escribe
military.. 10. punishment
music instrument.. 10. percussion,
  triquetrum (anc)
side.. 3. leg
three acute angles.. 6. oxygon
two equal sides.. 9. isosceles
unequal sides.. 7. scalene
triangular (pert to)...
  decoration.. 8. pediment, triqueta
  muscle.. 7. deltoid
  pert to.. 10. trilateral
  piece.. 4. gore 5. miter, wedge
  6. gusset
  sail.. 6. lateen 9. spinnaker
  shaped.. 7. deltoid 8. oxygonal
tribal custom... 7. couvade (childbirth)
tribal symbol... 5. totem 9. totem
  pole
tribe... 4. clan, kind, race, sept
  5. class, group 6. family 7. company
  11. aggregation 14. classification
tribe (pert to)...
  birds.. 5. flock
  head of.. 5. chief 6. sachem
  9. patriarch
  Israel.. 3. Dan 4. Levi 6. Reuben
  migrated.. 5. Aryan
  New Zealand.. 3. ati
  of Ben.. 5. poets (Ben Jonson)
Tribes, Five Civilized... 5. Creek
  7. Choctaw 8. Cherokee, Seminole
  9. Chickasaw
Tribes, Five Nations (Iroquois)...
  6. Cayuga, Mohawk, Oneida, Seneca
  8. Onondaga
tribulation... 5. trial 6. ordeal, sorrow
  8. distress 9. suffering
tribunal... 3. bar 4. banc, seat
  5. bench, court, curia, forum
  9. Areopagus (anc)
tributary... 4. lurk, vein 6. branch,
  feeder 8. affluent, effluent, influent
  9. auxiliary 11. subordinate
  12. contributary
tribute... 3. fee, pay, tax 4. cain,
  duty, levy, scat 5. allow, grant
  6. assign, bestow, homage, impost,
  praise, rental 7. chevage (Hist),
  ovation, payment, pension, respect
  8. encomium 9. attribute, gratitude
  10. allegiance, contribute, obligation
  11. retribution
tricar... 8. tricycle 10. motorcycle (with
  extra car)
trice... 5. jiffy 6. moment 7. instant
  9. twinkling
trick... 3. fob, gag 4. dido, dupe,
  feat, flam, gull, jest, ruse, wile
  5. cheat, child, dodge, fraud, guile,
  knack, prank, shift, stunt 6. deceit,
  delude 7. deceive, defraud, finesse,
  pretext 8. artifice, delusion, flimflam,
  illusion 9. chicanery, deception,
  imposture 10. subterfuge
  11. contrivance, legerdemain
trickery... 5. fraud, hocus 6. deceit
  7. roguery 8. artifice, cheating,
  trumpery 9. chicanery, deception,
  duplicity 10. hanky–panky
  11. amenability, legerdemain
trickle... 4. drip, drop, flow, leak

7. distill (distil), dribble, dripple, leakage

tricks... 4. shab 5. ruses 7. roguery 10. deceptions

trickster... 3. fox 5. cheat, rogue 6. rascal 7. slicker 8. deceiver 12. Artful Dodger

tricky... 3. sly 5. snide 6. artful, clever, crafty, shrewd 7. cunning, devious 8. rascally 9. deceitful 13. Machiavellian

trident... 5. curve, spear 6. symbol 7. leister

tried... 4. true 6. proved, tested 7. devoted 8. faithful, reliable 11. trustworthy

tries... 5. tests 6. assays 8. attempts, contests

trifle... 3. ace, bit, fig, toy 4. doit, fico, fool, jest 5. dally, fable, straw 6. bauble, dabble, dawdle, doodle, fiddle, gewgaw, palter, pewter, potter, wanton 7. dessert, nothing, traneen 8. flimflam, gimcrack, make love 9. bagatelle 10. knickknack, peccadillo, triviality 11. small amount 12. treat lightly

trifler... 7. dallier, flaneur 8. palterer, putterer 10. dilettante

trifles... 4. toys 6. trivia 7. gewgaws, palters 8. minutiae, trumpery

trifling... 4. idle, mere 5. inane, petty 6. little 7. trivial 8. badinage, frippery 9. nugacious 10. immaterial 13. insignificant

trifolium... 6. clover 8. shamrock

trig... 4. chic, neat, prim, tidy, trim 5. natty, smart 6. lively, spruce 7. precise 10. methodical

trigo... 5. wheat

trigon... 4. game, harp, lyre (anc) 8. triangle

trigonometry term... 4. sine 6. cosine, secant 7. tangent 8. spherics 10. goniometry

trihoral... 11. three-hourly 15. every three hours

trill... 4. move, sing 5. shake, twirl 6. quaver, ripple, warble 7. mordent, tremolo, trickle, vibrate 8. grupetto 12. pralltriller

trillion... 5. trega (comb form) 14. million million

trim... 3. bob, cut, lop 4. chic, clip, crop, neat, perk, snod, tidy, whip 5. adorn, natty, nifty, panel, preen, prune, shear, shrag 6. border, dapper, defeat, punish, reduce 7. compact, orderly 9. decorate, ornament 9. embellish, shipshape 10. decoration

trimming... 4. gimp, lace 5. braid, jabot, ruche 6. edging, frieze, fringe, piping 7. falbala, ruching 8. furbelow, ornament 9. chicanery, garniture 10. decoration 11. accessories 13. passementerie

trinity... 5. three, triad 6. triune

Trinity (Eccl)... 7. Godhead (Father, Son, Holy Ghost) 8. Trimurti

trinket... 3. toy 4. gaud, tali (tahli) 5. bijou, jewel 6. bangle, gewgaw,

trifle 7. bibelot 8. ornament 10. knickknack

trip... 3. err, run 4. halt, skip, slip, trap 5. caper, dance, jaunt, speed 6. bungle, cruise, errand, flight, frolic, voyage 7. journey, misstep, stumble 8. obstruct 9. excursion 10. expedition

triple... 3. tri 5. trine 6. tercet, treble 9. intensify, threefold 12. three-base hit

triple crown... 5. tiara (Pope's)

triplet (one of)... 4. trin-

tripletail... 4. fish, sama 9. berrugate, spadefish

tripod... 3. cat (6-legged) 5. easel, stand, three 6. trivet

Tripoli, Libya...
capital of.. 12. Tripolitania
caravan route to.. 5. Wadai 8. Lake Chad, Timbuktu
famed arch to.. 14. Marcus Aurelius
people.. 4. Arab, Turk 5. Negro 6. Berber
ruler.. 3. bey, dey

triptych... 5. volet (part) 10. altarpiece, writing pad 13. writing tablet (3-part)

trismus... 7. lockjaw, tetanus 16. gnashing the teeth

trist... see *tryst*

Tristan and Isolde... 5. opera (Wagner)

triste... 3. sad 4. full 6. dismal 10. depressing

tristful... 3. sad 10. melancholy

tristich group... 10. three lines 11. three verses (stanza)

Tristram & Iseult... 4. poem (Arnold)

trite... 5. banal, corny, petty, stale, vapid 6. betide, cliché, common, jejune 7. bromide 9. hackneyed, well-known 10. threadbare, unoriginal 11. commonplace, stereotyped 13. platitudinous

triton... 3. eft 4. newt 5. shell, snail 10. salamander

Triton (pert to)...
art figure.. 7. demigod
Gr Myth.. 10. sea demigod
symbol.. 7. trumpet

triumph... 3. win 5. exult, glory 6. defeat 8. ceremony (anc), conquest 10. exultation 11. achievement

trivia... 5. trash 7. trifles 8. trumpery

trivial... 5. banal, petty, small, trite 6. common, paltry, slight 7. nominal, piperly, shallow 8. doggerel, ordinary, trifling 9. frivolous, nugacious 11. commonplace, unimportant 13. insignificant

triviality... 3. toy 6. bauble, gewgaw, trifle 8. falderal, nugacity 9. bagatelle, frivolity 10. knickknack 14. insignificance

troche... 4. pill 6. button, rotula, tablet 7. lozenge 8. pastille (pastil) 9. cough drop 10. deer's tines

trochee... 4. foot (2-syllable) 5. meter 7. choreus

trod... see *tread*

trogger... 7. peddler, vagrant
trogon... 7. quetzal
Troilus (pert to)...
  butterfly genus.. 7. Papilio
  legendary hero of.. 7. Chaucer
  son of.. 5. Priam
Trojan (pert to)...
  astronomy.. 9. asteroids
  epic.. 5. Iliad 6. Aeneid 7. Odyssey
  expedition hero.. 4. Ajax 8. Achilles
  founder of.. 4. Troy
  hero.. 5. Paris 6. Hector
    9. Palamedes
  horse.. 6. wooden
  horse builder.. 5. Epeus
  king.. 5. Priam
  native.. 6. Dardan
  soothsayer.. 7. Helenus
  war cause.. 5. Helen (of Troy)
  war leader.. 9. Agamemnon
  warrior.. 6. Agenor
troll (Myth)... 5. dwarf, giant, gnome
troll... 4. bowl, fish, roll, sing 5. angle
  (fishing), rondo 6. allure, entice,
  propel 7. revolve, trundle 9. circulate
trolley... 4. cart, tram 5. truck
  6. barrow, sledge 7. tramcar
  8. handcart 9. streetcar
trolley, off his... 4. nuts 5. balmy,
  batty, daffy, dippy, dotty, goofy
  6. cuckoo
trollop... 5. slump 6. slouch
  8. slattern
trombone (pert to)...
  ancient.. 7. sackbut, sambuke
  instrument.. 5. brass
  mouthpiece.. 5. bocal
  popular size.. 5. tenor
troop... 4. army, band, unit 5. crowd
  7. company, march on, ressala
  8. quantity, soldiers 9. go forward
  10. armed force
troop (pert to)...
  arrangement.. 7. echelon
  encampment.. 5. étape
  formation.. 4. line
  one of.. 7. peltast 8. chasseur
  ship.. 9. transport
troops (pert to)...
  assemble.. 6. muster
  German.. 6. Panzer
  hidden.. 6. ambush
  Hungary.. 7. Hussars
  mounted.. 7. cavalry
  sally.. 6. sortie
  term for.. 4. army 5. squad 6. forces
  7. battery, militia, phalanx
  9. commandos 11. armed forces
trophy... 3. cup 4. palm 5. award,
  medal, Oscar, prize 6. reward
  7. laurels, memento 8. memorial
tropical (pert to)...
  animal.. 4. eyra 5. araba, coati, potto
  6. agouti 7. peccary
  bird.. 3. ani 4. tody 5. jalap
  6. motmot 7. jacamar
  dolphin.. 4. inia
  fish.. 4. toro 6. remora, salema
  fruit.. 3. fig 4. date 5. guava,
  mango, papaw 6. banana, papaya
  lizard.. 5. agama
  rodent.. 6. agouti

tree.. 4. coco, palm 5. balsa, seron
  6. sapota 8. tamarind
vine.. 7. cowhage, lantana
  14. trumpet creeper
trot... 3. jog, run 4. gait, pony
  5. hurry 7. routine 11. translation
trotting horse... 6. Morgan
  7. Hackney 12. Hambletonian
trottoir (rare)... 8. footpath, pavement,
  sidewalk
troubadour... 4. bard, poet
  8. jongleur, minstrel, musician
  9. trovatore
trouble... 3. ado, ail, irk 4. fuss,
  harm, stir 5. annoy, grief, worry
  6. bother, effort, grieve, harass,
  pester, plague, sorrow 7. agitate,
  anxiety, concern, disturb, perturb,
  torment 8. calamity, disorder,
  disquiet, distress, mischief
  9. adversity, annoyance, commotion
  10. affliction, difficulty, misfortune
  11. disturbance 13. inconvenience,
  interfere with
troubled... 6. queasy 7. annoyed,
  anxious 8. agitated 9. disturbed
  10. distressed
troublemaker... 8. agitator, gossiper
  13. mischief–maker
troublesome... 5. pesky 8. annoying,
  perverse 9. difficult, laborious,
  turbulent, vexatious, wearisome
  10. bothersome, burdensome,
  disturbing, oppressing 11. distressing
  12. inconvenient
trough... 3. bin 4. bosh, bowl, dale,
  tank 5. basin, chute, drain, toper
  6. coffin, gutter, manger, sluice,
  trench 7. channel, conduit
trounce... 4. beat, flog 5. scald
  6. indict, punish, thrash 7. censure,
  journey
trout... 4. char, peal 7. oquassa
  9. namaycush 11. Dolly Varden
trout (pert to)...
  genus.. 5. Salmo 6. Trutta
  lake.. 9. namaycush
  Maine.. 7. oquassa
  parasite (external).. 3. sug
  ref to.. 11. truttaceous
  type.. 3. sea 4. rock 5. brook,
  brown, river 7. oquassa, rainbow
  8. speckled 9. cutthroat
trovatore... 10. troubadour
trove... 4. find 8. treasure (buried)
  9. discovery 10. thing found
  13. treasure–trove
trow... 4. boat, hope 5. barge, think,
  trust 6. expect 7. believe, suppose
  9. catamaran
trowing... 5. creed 6. belief 7. opinion
Troy, or Ilium...
  capital of.. 5. Troad (anc)
  defender.. 6. Aeneas
  famed for.. 5. ruins
  founder (Myth).. 4. Ilus (son of Tros),
  Tros
  king.. 5. Priam 9. Agamemnon
  king's wife.. 5. Helen
  mountain.. 3. Ida
  name, present.. 9. Hissarlik
  pert to.. 5. Iliac 6. Trojan

site.. 9. Asia Minor
troy weight... 5. grain, ounce, pound
  11. pennyweight
truant... 4. idle 7. shirker, trivant,
  vagrant 8. absentee
truant, to play... 5. miche
truce... 5. pause, peace, trêve
  9. armistice, cessation 10. brief
  quiet 12. intermission
truck... 3. van 4. deal, dray, haul
  5. bogie, dance, lorry, trade
  6. barter, peddle 7. flatcar, traffic
  8. commerce, exchange, nonsense
  9. groceries
truckle... 4. fawn 5. toady 6. cringe,
  submit 7. knuckle
truculent... 4. base, mean 5. cruel
  6. fierce, savage 8. ruthless,
  scathing 9. barbarous, ferocious
  11. destructive
trudge... 4. pace, plod, slog, walk
  5. tramp 6. go slow 7. traipse
true... 2. so 4. fact, leal, pure, real
  6. gospel, honest, lawful 7. certain,
  devoted, germane, precise, sincere,
  upright 8. faithful, orthodox, reliable,
  straight, unerring 9. authentic,
  steadfast, veracious, veritable
  10. legitimate 11. trustworthy,
  unfaltering
true (pert to)...
blue.. 5. loyal 8. faithful, orthodox
  10. man of honor
copy.. 7. estreat
not.. 5. false 10. figurative
poetic.. 4. leal
skin.. 4. derm (suff) 5. derma
to fact.. 7. literal
to life.. 8. lifelike 11. descriptive
truffle... 5. fungi, tuber 8. earthnut
  10. ascus fruit
truism... 5. axiom, truth 9. platitude
  11. commonplace
trull... 4. girl, lass 5. demon, fiend,
  giant, wench 7. trollop 8. strumpet
truly... 3. yea 4. amen 5. sooth
  6. indeed, justly, verily 7. exactly,
  rightly 8. properly 9. certainly
  10. accurately, positively, truthfully
trump... 3. pam 4. card, ruff (cards),
  suit 7. surpass 10. good fellow
  12. masterstroke
trumpery... 5. fraud, trash 6. deceit
  7. rubbish 8. nonsense
trumpet... 4. horn 5. blare
  6. summon 7. clarion 8. proclaim
  9. organ stop 12. elephant's cry
  14. wind instrument
trumpet (pert to)...
blare.. 7. fanfare, tantara
call (stage).. 6. sennet
creeper.. 6. tecoma
fish.. 7. bellows 10. flutemouth
lily.. 5. calla 7. Bermuda
trumpeter... 4. bird, fish, swan
  5. agami, perch 6. pigeon 7. whiting
  8. musician 9. messenger
truncheon... 4. club 5. baton, staff
  6. cudgel 8. splinter
trunk... 3. box, log 4. body, bole,
  pool, soma, tank 5. chest, stalk,
  torso 6. coffer 7. railway 8. main

stem 9. proboscis 10. lobster pot
trunkfish... 4. toro 7. cowfish
truss... 3. tie 4. bind, gird, pack
  6. bundle, fasten 7. support
  10. strengthen
trust... 4. hope, rely, task 5. faith
  6. belief, commit, credit, dartle,
  depend, estate 7. believe, confide,
  consign, custody, entrust, loyalty
  8. credence, reliance, security
  9. assurance, syndicate
  10. confidence, dependence, give
  credit, investment 12. organization
trustee... 6. bailee 7. sindico
  9. fiduciary, treasurer 10. depository
  13. administrator
trustful... 5. liege 7. reliant 8. trusting
  9. confiding, credulous
  13. unquestioning
trustworthiness... 9. axiopisty
  12. trustability 13. dependability
trustworthy... 4. safe 5. solid
  6. honest 7. certain 8. reliable
  9. authentic 10. dependable
trusty... 7. convict 8. faithful, prisoner
  10. dependable 11. trustworthy
truth... 3. tao 4. fact, real 5. sooth
  (anc) 6. verity 7. honesty, reality
  8. fidelity, veracity 9. constancy,
  exactness, orthodoxy, sincerity
  11. correctness 14. verisimilitude
truth (pert to)...
ancient term.. 5. sooth 6. certes
Chinese Philos.. 3. tao
goddess.. 4. Maat
personified.. 3. Una 4. Maat
ref to.. 6. verily 11. verisimilar
  14. verisimilitude
self–evident.. 5. axiom 6. truism
truthful... 6. honest 7. veridic
  9. veracious, veridical
truthfulness... 5. truth 7. honesty
  8. accuracy, veracity
  13. veraciousness
try... 2. do 3. say 4. test 5. annoy,
  assay, ettle, prove, taste, trial
  6. purify, refine, render, sample,
  strive 7. attempt, contest, torment
  8. audition, endeavor, irritate
  9. prosecute, undertake
  10. experiment 11. demonstrate,
  investigate
trying... 7. irksome, painful, tasting
  8. annoying, sampling 10. attempting
  12. exasperating 13. experimenting
tryst... 6. invite, market 7. beguile,
  meeting 9. agreement, betrothal
  10. engagement, rendezvous
  11. appointment 12. meeting place
tsamba... 5. flour 6. barley
tsar... 4. czar, tzar 6. despot
  8. autocrat
tsetse, tsetse fly... 4. kivu
  8. Glossina, parasite
tsetse fly disease... 6. nagana
  16. sleeping sickness
T–shaped... 3. tau
tsine... 6. wild ox 7. banteng
tuatara, tuatera... 7. reptile
  (iguanalike)
tub... 3. hod, keg, kid, soe, tun, vat
  4. cask, ship, wash 5. barge, bathe,

bowie, keeve 6. barrel, firkin, piggin,
vessel 7. bathtub, cistern, washtub
9. container, fat person
tuba... 6. liquor (palm) 7. helicon,
trumpet (anc) 9. bombardon
10. contrabass 11. bass saxhorn
12. mythical tree
Tubal–cain's father... 6. Lamech
Tubal's father... 7. Japheth
tube... 3. cop 4. bulb, duct, hose,
pipe 5. auget, chute, diode
6. siphon, tunnel 7. burette, cannula,
conduit, fistula, matrass, railway,
salpinx 8. cylinder, electron, stenosis
9. spaghetti, telescope
tuber... 3. oca, yam 4. beet, bulb,
eddo, root, taro 5. jalap, salep
6. potato 12. protuberance
tubular... 4. pipy 5. round 6. tubate
8. cannular, fistular, tubiform
11. cylindrical
tuck... 3. eat, nip 4. cram, fold, poke
5. feast, pinch, pleat, press
7. shorten, tighten 9. appendage
tucker... 3. bib 4. food, meal
5. board 6. ration
Tuesday (pert to)...
French.. 5. Mardi
Norse god.. 3. Tyr (Tiu)
Shrove.. 9. Mardi gras
Teutonic.. 10. Martis dies
tufa... 4. rock, toph, tuff 5. trass
tuft... 4. coma, doss, hair 5. beard,
bunch, clump, crest 6. button,
goatee, pompon, tassel 7. cluster,
fetlock 8. aigrette, feathers
tug... 3. tow 4. drag, draw, haul, pull,
toil 5. labor 6. drudge, effort, strain,
tussle 7. contend, contest, wrestle
8. struggle
tulip (pert to)...
center (World).. 7. Holland
color.. 6. auburn 9. tulipwood
genus.. 6. Tulipa
Mexican.. 6. orchid
military slang.. 9. explosive
tree.. 6. timber 7. majagua, waratah
type.. 6. Darwin, parrot 7. breeder,
cottage
tumble... 4. fall, flop, trip, veer
5. pitch, spill 6. jumble, rumple,
topple, tousle, wallow 7. stumble
8. collapse, disorder, flounder, roll
over 9. break down, confusing
10. handspring, somersault
11. precipitate
tumbler... 3. dog 4. cart, drum
5. glass 6. Dunker, pigeon, vessel
7. acrobat, gymnast, tippler, tumbrel
8. lock part 13. contortionist
tumbleweed... 6. indigo 7. bugseed,
pigweed, thistle 10. amaranthus
tumbrel, tumbril... 4. cart 5. wagon
8. dumpcart 12. cucking stool (Hist)
tumescent, tumid... 6. turgid
7. bloated, bulging, pompous
8. inflated 9. bombastic, disturbed,
plethoric 11. protuberant
tumor... 3. wen 4. cyst, wart
6. cancer, goiter, growth, lipoma,
struma 7. adenoma, sarcoma
8. ganglion, swelling 11. excrescence

12. protuberance
tumor, eyelid... 9. pladaroma
tumult... 3. din, mob 4. fray, riot
5. Babel, brawl, noise 6. affray,
babble, bustle, émeute, hubbub,
uproar 7. bluster, ferment, turmoil
8. disorder, outbreak, uprising
9. agitation, commotion, confusion
10. excitement, turbulence
11. disturbance
tumultuous... 4. wild 5. noisy, rough
7. lawless, riotous, violent
8. agitated, confused 9. disturbed,
turbulent 10. boisterous, disorderly,
hurly–burly
tumulus... 5. mound, stump 6. barrow
7. hillock
tun... 3. cup (anc), jar, tub, vat
4. cask, year (Mayan, 360 day)
5. drink 6. guzzle, vessel 7. measure
tuna... 5. tunny 8. albacore
tune... 3. air, key 4. aria, lilt, port,
song 5. pitch 6. adjust, melody
7. chorale, harmony, sonance
9. harmonize 10. adjustment,
intonation
tune (pert to)...
correctly.. 3. key
down.. 6. reduce, soften 8. moderate
musical instrument.. 6. string
out of.. 9. dissonant 11. inaccordant
12. unconforming
tungsten... 7. wolfram
Tunisia...
cape.. 3. Bon
capital.. 5. Tunis
famed ruins.. 8. Carthage
gulf.. 5. Gabes
oasis.. 5. Gafsa
people.. 5. Arabs 7. Berbers
resort island.. 6. Djerba
river.. 8. Medjerda
ruler.. 3. dey 5. pasha
seaport.. 4. Sfax 7. Bizerte
tunnel... 4. adit, bore, cave, tube
5. drift 6. burrow, dig out, funnel,
subway 10. excavation, smokestack
tunny... 4. tuna 8. albacore
tup... 3. ram 4. beat, butt 5. sheep
6. mallet 7. cuckold
turban... 6. entrée, fillet, Moslem,
mundil, squash 8. bandanna,
seerband 9. headdress
turbid... 4. dark, dull 5. dense,
muddy, roily 6. cloudy, impure,
opaque 7. clouded, muddled
8. confused, feculent, polluted
turbot... 5. brill 8. flatfish
turbulence... 4. fury 6. tumult, uproar
7. bluster, rioting, turmoil
9. agitation, commotion
10. excitement, unruliness
11. disturbance, impetuosity
14. tumultuousness
turbulent... 4. loud, wild 5. noisy,
rough 6. stormy 7. excited, furious
8. virulent 10. tumultuous
turf... 3. sod 4. peat, slab 5. divot,
glebe, grass, sward, track 10. race
course
turgid... 5. tumid 7. bloated,
pompous, swollen 8. inflated

9. bombastic, distended, grandiose,
redundant 12. magniloquent,
ostentatious 13. grandiloquent
Turk ... 5. Tatar 6. Tartar 7. Osmanli,
Ottoman 9. Kizilbash
Turkestan people ... 5. Uzbek (Uzbeg)
turkey ... 4. fowl 5. poult 7. bustard,
gobbler, vulture
Turkey ... see also *Turkish*
capital .. 6. Angora (anc), Ankara
city .. 5. Adana, Izmir (Smyrna)
6. Edessa, Samsun 7. Scutari
8. Istanbul (Constantinople)
10. Adrianople
founder .. 6. Othman
mountain .. 6. Ararat
peninsula .. 9. Anatolian
river .. 5. Mesta 6. Seyhan
Turkish (pert to) ...
army corps .. 4. ordu 8. seraglio
commander, ruler .. 3. aga (agha), bey
4. wali 5. pasha 6. atabeg (atabek)
court (Ottoman) .. 5. Porte
12. Sublime Porte
dignitary .. 5. pasha
dish (food) .. 5. cabob 6. pilaff (pilau)
drink .. 4. boza (bozah), raki 5. airan
6. mastic 9. lion's milk
dynasty .. 6. seljuk
emblem .. 8. crescent
Empire .. 7. Ottoman
flag .. 4. alem, toug (former)
harem girl .. 6. kadein (kadine)
hat, cap .. 3. fez 6. calpac (calpack)
hospice, inn .. 6. imaret
infidel .. 6. giaour
javelin .. 6. jereed (jerid)
judge .. 4. cadi (kadi)
minister of state .. 6. vizier
money of account .. 5. asper
mosque .. 4. jami
music .. 8. janizary
native .. 6. Edesan (anc)
palace .. 5. serai
pavilion .. 5. kiosk
pipe (long–stemmed) .. 7. chibouk
(chibouque)
regiment .. 4. alai
religious war .. 5. jihad (jehad)
rug .. 5. Melas, Tekke, Yomud, Yuruk
6. Afghan 8. Turkoman 9. Kurdistan
ruler .. 3. bey, dey 4. khan 6. sultan
7. chambul
sailing vessel .. 4. saic 6. mahone
sailor .. 9. galiongee (galionji)
soldier .. 5. nizan, redif 6. Arnaut
(Arnaout) 8. Janizary
11. bashi–bazouk
statute .. 8. Tanzimat (1839)
sultan .. 5. Ahmed, Selim 7. Ilderim,
Saladin
sultan's title .. 6. caliph (calif)
sword .. 8. yataghan (yatagan)
tambourine .. 5. daira
tax (from Christians) .. 6. avania
title .. 3. aga (agha), ali 4. amir
(ameer)
tobacco .. 7. chibouk (chibouque),
Latakia
tribe .. 5. Ersar, Tatar 7. Bashkir,
Viddhal
Turkoman .. 11. tribal group

veil (double) .. 7. yashmak (yashmac)
vest .. 6. jelick
whip, lash .. 7. kurbash
turmeric ... 3. rea 4. ango, herb
5. olena 8. curcumin
turmoil ... 3. ado, din 5. upset, worry
6. tumult, unrest 7. ferment,
tempest, trouble 8. disquiet
9. agitation, commotion, confusion
10. excitement, turbulence
12. perturbation
turn ... 3. bow, lap 4. bend, deed,
gyre, roll, slew, slue, spin, tour,
veer, vert 5. curve, lathe, pivot,
quirk, round, shift, spell, wheel,
whirl, whorl 6. abvert, change, crisis,
gyrate, rotate, swivel, zigzag
7. deflect, deviate, reverse, revolve
8. aptitude, circuity, maneuver,
persuade, rotation, tendency
9. deviation, pirouette, reversion
11. convolution 12. metamorphose
turn (pert to) ...
about .. 9. alternate
aside, away .. 4. slew, slue 5. avert,
deter, repel, shunt 6. divert, swerve
7. deflect, deviate, digress, diverge
back .. 5. repel 6. coward, revert
7. evolute, head off, reflect
coat .. 7. traitor 8. apostate, deserter,
renegade
comb form .. 5. tropo
down .. 4. veto 6. refuse, reject
7. decline
gate .. 5. stile 9. turnstile
inside out .. 5. evert 6. invert
7. ransack
inward .. 8. introrse 9. introvert
left .. 3. haw 4. port
of duty .. 5. spell, trick
off .. 5. shunt 7. dismiss, execute
10. extinguish
on axis .. 6. obvert, rotate
one's back upon .. 4. flee, snub
5. avoid 6. ignore, oppose, refuse,
reject
on pivot .. 6. swivel
out .. 4. fare, oust 5. array, evert,
expel, track 6. detour, output, siding
7. dismiss 8. assemble, clearing
9. eventuate, gathering
10. accomplish, extinguish
outward .. 5. evert, splay 8. extrorse
9. extrovert
over .. 3. pie 4. keel, tart 5. sales,
shift, spill 6. assign, pastry
7. capsize 8. hand over, overturn
over a new leaf .. 6. change, reform
over pages .. 4. leaf 5. thumb
over to others .. 4. farm 7. farm out
to left .. 3. haw 4. port
to right .. 3. gee 9. starboard
up .. 4. find, keel 5. occur 6. appear,
arrive 7. be found
upside down .. 4. roll 6. invert, whelve
7. ransack 8. overturn
turned up (nose) ... 9. retroussé
turning ... 6. rotary 7. bending,
crooked, winding 8. rotation,
twisting, whirling 9. deviating,
deviation 10. circuitous, revolution
11. convolution, sinistrorse

turning (pert to)...
left to right.. 9. dextrorse
machine.. 5. lathe
point.. 6. crisis 8. decision, landmark
  11. climacteric 13. crucial period
right to left.. 11. sinistrorse
turnip... 4. neep, rape, root
  8. rutabaga
turnip (pert to)...
large.. 7. Russian, Swedish
  8. rutabaga
shaped.. 8. napiform
wild.. 5. navew
Turnix... 4. bird (3–toed) 5. quail
  10. Hemipodius
Turpentine State... 13. North Carolina
turpentine tree... 4. pine 6. tarata
  9. terebinth
turpid... 3. low 4. base, vile
  8. cowardly
turpitude... 6. fedity 8. baseness,
  vileness 9. decadence, depravity
  10. corruption
turquoise... 3. gem 4. blue
  7. mineral, Turkish
turret... 4. loom, soar 5. tower
  6. cupola (revolving), height
  9. structure 10. stronghold,
  watchtower
turtle (pert to)...
edible.. 8. terrapin
freshwater.. 4. emyd 8. tortoise
genus.. 4. Emys
hawklike.. 5. carat 9. hawk's–bill
large.. 5. arrau 6. jurara, mamata
largest.. 11. leatherback
ref to.. 9. chelonian
sea.. 10. thalassian
shell.. 8. carapace
snapping.. 6. cooter 8. shagtail
Tuscany...
birthplace of.. 7. Galileo (Astronomer)
capital.. 8. Florence
city., 4. Pisa 7. Leghorn
color.. 9. colcothar
famed tower.. 4. Pisa (1174)
island.. 4. Elba (1st exile, Napoleon)
native.. 6. Tuscan
marble.. 7. Carrara
province.. 4. Pisa
river.. 4. Arno 6. Cecina 7. Ombrone
wine.. 7. chianti
tusk... 4. fang 5. ivory, tooth
  6. canine 7. incisor 9. scrivello
  (elephant's)
Tussaud, Madame's London district...
  8. Waxworks (Museum)
  10. Marylebone
tussis... 5. cough
tussle... 7. contend, contest, scuffle,
  wrestle 8. struggle
tutelage... 7. nurture 8. teaching,
  tutorage 9. oversight, tutorship
  11. instruction 12. guardianship
tutelary gods (Rom)... 5. lares
  7. penates
tutor... 5. coach, teach 6. docent,
  ground, mentor, school 7. teacher
  8. instruct 9. pedagogue (pedagog),
  preceptor
twaddle... 3. rot 6. drivel, gabble
  7. chatter, fustian, prattle

8. claptrap, nonsense 9. absurdity,
  silly talk 10. flapdoodle 16. trash
  and nonsense
twang... 4. tang 5. strum 6. accent
  7. dialect 8. pungency
tweak... 4. jerk, pain 5. pinch
  6. snatch, twitch
tweeg... 10. hellbender, salamander
tweezers... 7. pincers 10. instrument
twelfth... 5. twait, uncia 8. duodenal
  9. duodenary
Twelfth Night character... 5. Viola
  6. Olivia, Orsino 7. Sir Toby
  8. Malvolio 12. Sir Toby Belch
Twelfthtide... 8. Epiphany
  10. Twelfth–day
twelve (pert to)...
amount.. 5. dozen
angles.. 9. dodecagon
prefix.. 5. dodec 6. dodeca
rule of.. 9. dodecarch
series.. 8. dodecade
Twelve, The... 8. Apostles
twenty (pert to)...
Anglo–Ind.. 5. carge, score
comb form.. 4. icos 5. icosa, icosi
faces.. 11. icosahedron
pert to.. 7. icosian 8. vicenary
quires.. 4. ream
symbol.. 2. XX
years.. 9. vicennial
twenty–fourth part (gold alloy)...
  5. carat (karat)
twibil (twibill)... 2. ax (axe) 6. pickax
  (pickaxe) 7. mattock 8. battle–ax
  (battle–axe)
twice... 2. bi, di 6. doubly 7. twofold
  8. two times
twig... 4. reis 5. besom, birch, bough
  6. branch, sallow, switch, twitch,
  wattle
twigs, bundle of.. 5. layot 6. barsom
  (sacred)
twilight... 3. dim 4. blue, dusk
  6. shaded 7. obscure 8. foredawn,
  gloaming 9. cocklight 10. crepuscule
Twilight of the Gods... 8. Ragnarok
twill... 3. rib 5. flute, weave 6. fabric
  9. tricotine
twilled... 3. rep 5. reedy, ridgy, sedgy,
  serge 6. corded, fluted
twin... 3. two 4. dual, mate, pair
  5. gemel, macle 6. couple, double
  7. didymus, Siamese 8. didymous,
  matching 9. duplicate, identical
  11. counterpart 12. accompanying
Twin Cities (Minn)... 6. St Paul
  11. Minneapolis
twine... 4. bend, coil, turn, wind, wrap
  5. braid, snarl, twist, weave
  6. enfold, enlace, tangle 7. embrace,
  enclasp, entwine, wreathe
  8. convolve, encircle 9. interlace
  10. intertwine, interweave
  11. intermingle
twine (pert to)...
color.. 4. dune 7. anamite
hank of.. 3. ran
left to right.. 9. dextrorse
right to left.. 11. sinistrorse
Scot.. 4. part
twinge... 4. ache, pain, pang

5. pinch, qualm 6. twitch
twin stars ... 6. Castor, Pollux
twin stock ... 4. bees 7. beehive (two colonies)
twirl ... 4. coil, eddy, gyre, spin
   5. pitch, querl, twist, whirl 6. gyrate, writhe 7. revolve 8. flourish, rotation 11. convolution
twist ... 3. cue, ply 4. coil, curl, slew, slub, slue, spin, turn, warp, wind
   5. braid, quirk, tweak, wrest 7. contort, deflect, distort, falsify, meander, pervert, wreathe, wriggle 8. convolve 9. insinuate, interlace, prejudice 10. distortion 12. eccentricity, misrepresent
twisted ... 3. wry 4. awry, cued
   5. askew, kinky, torse, wrung 6. warped 7. complex, torqued, tortile, wrested, writhed
twisted cord ... 7. torsade
twister ... 3. lie 7. cruller, tornado 8. doughnut 9. dust whirl 10. sand column, somersault, waterspout
twit ... 4. gibe, josh 5. blame, taunt, tease, tweet 6. banter 7. upbraid 8. reproach, ridicule
twitch ... 3. nip, tic, tug 4. hurt, jerk, yank 5. pluck, shake, tweak 6. snatch 9. be excited, quick pull, vellicate 11. contraction
twitter ... 5. chirp 6. giggle, titter 7. chatter, tremble 9. agitation
two (pert to) ...
   chambered .. 9. bicameral
   colored .. 9. dichromic
   edged .. 9. ancipital
   faced .. 5. false 6. double 9. deceitful 11. treacherous 12. falsehearted
   fisted .. 6. virile
   fold .. 4. dual, twin 6. binary, double, duplex 8. didymous
   forked .. 6. bident 9. bifurcate 11. dichotomous
   handed .. 7. bimanal 8. bimanous 10. secondhand 12. ambidextrous
   headed .. 9. ancipital 11. dicephalous
   masted ship .. 4. yawl, zulu
   parts .. 3. duo 4. duad, dyad 7. duality
   poetic .. 5. twain
   prefix .. 2. bi, di
   Scot .. 3. twa
   Spanish .. 3. dos
   spot .. 5. deuce
   time .. 7. deceive
   wheeled carriage, chariot .. 3. gig 6. esseda 10. jinrikisha (jinriksha)
Tyche ... 7. Fortuna 16. goddess of Fortune
tycoon ... 6. shogun 7. magnate 9. financier 13. industrialist
tylopod ... 5. camel
tympanum ... 7. eardrum 9. middle ear 10. water wheel
tympany ... 6. tympan 7. bombast 9. inflation 10. distention
typal ... 7. typical 8. symbolic
type ... 2. pi 4. font, form, kind, norm, sign, sort 5. genre, genus, model, print, Roman, token 6. emblem, italic, minion, symbol 7. measure,

pattern, species 8. boldface, classify, standard 9. archetype, character 10. transcribe 11. Baskerville 14. characteristic, representative
type (pert to) ...
   assortment .. 4. font, kern
   block of .. 4. quad 7. quadrat
   bold style .. 4. text
   bridge .. 7. bascule
   classic .. 5. Roman 6. italic 11. black letter (Gothic)
   line .. 4. slug
   measure .. 2. em, en
   mixed .. 2. pi
   mold .. 6. matrix
   perfection .. 7. paragon
   set .. 7. compose
   setter .. 8. linotype, monotype 10. compositor
   size .. 4. norm, pica, ruby 5. agate, canon, pearl 6. minion 7. diamond
   stroke .. 5. serif
   tray .. 6. galley
typewriter (pert to) ...
   bar .. 6. spacer
   cylinder .. 6. platen, spacer
   type .. 4. pica 5. elite
   type of .. 6. ticker 8. teletype 9. stenotype
typhoon ... 4. wind 5. storm 7. cyclone
typhus fever ... 10. tabardillo
typical ... 4. norm 5. typal 6. normal 7. regular 10. conforming, emblematic, figurative 11. precedental 14. characteristic, representative
typify ... 6. embody 9. prefigure, represent, symbolize
Tyr (Norse) ... 3. Tiu 6. sky–god, war–god
tyrannical ... 5. cruel 6. lordly 8. despotic 9. imperious 10. oppressive 11. domineering
tyrannize ... 7. oppress 8. domineer
tyranny ... 8. severity 9. despotism
tyrant ... 4. czar, Ivan, Nero, tsar, tzar 6. despot 7. monarch
Tyre ... see also *Tyrian*
   capital of .. 9. Phoenicia (anc)
   famed for .. 9. purple dye
   seaport of .. 7. Lebanon
   site .. 9. peninsula 13. Mediterranean
Tyrian (pert to) ...
   alphabet .. 7. Moabite
   Cynosure .. 9. Ursa Minor
   god (Teut) .. 2. Er
   king .. 5. Hiram
   princess .. 4. Dido (Elissa)
tyro, tiro ... 5. pupil 6. novice 7. amateur 8. beginner, neophyte 9. commencer, fledgling, greenhorn 10. apprentice 11. abecedarian
Tyrol ...
   capital .. 9. Innsbruck
   dialect .. 5. Ladin
   district .. 8. Trentino
   mountain .. 4. Alps 9. Dolomites
   province of .. 7. Austria
   river .. 4. Isar
tzar, tsar, czar ... 4. king 5. ruler 6. tyrant
tzigane ... 5. gypsy

U

U... 6. letter (21st)
uang... 6. beetle
uberous... 7. copious 8. abundant, fruitful 9. plentiful
uberty... 6. plenty 12. fruitfulness
ubiety... 8. location, position, relation 9. whereness
ubiquity... 8. doctrine (Luther) 10. everywhere 12. omnipresence
U–boat... 3. sub 9. submarine
base.. 4. Kiel
Uca... 11. fiddler crab
Uchean Indian... 5. Yuchi (Uchee)
udometer... 9. rain gauge
Uffizi Gallery... 8. Florence
Uganda (pert to)...
capital.. 7. Kampala
Falls.. 4. Owen 9. Murchison
lake.. 8. Victoria
lake explorer.. 7. Stanley
mountain.. 9. Ruwenzori 18. Mountains of the Moon
tribe.. 5. pygmy
ugly... 5. cross, surly 6. cranky, homely 7. crabbed, hideous, vicious 8. gruesome, uncomely, unlovely 9. frightful, loathsome, offensive, repulsive, unsightly 10. ill–favored, ill–natured, unpleasant 11. ill–tempered, quarrelsome 12. disagreeable
uhlan... 6. lancer 7. militia, soldier 10. cavalryman
uhllo... 6. wampum 8. currency (shell)
uitlander... 9. foreigner, outlander
ukase... 5. edict, order 12. proclamation
Ukraine (pert to)...
capital.. 4. Kiev 7. Kharkov
legislature.. 4. rada
official name.. 12. Ukrainian SSR
Relig.. 9. Ruthenian 13. Little Russian
scientist.. 10. Bogomolets
sea.. 5. Black
seaport.. 6. Odessa
statesman.. 7. Mazeppa
writer.. 6. Franko
ullage... 5. dregs 7. deficit, wantage 8. shortage 9. shrinkage 10. deficiency
Ulmas... 3. elm
ulna... 4. bone 5. elbow 7. cubitus
ulster... 8. overcoat
ulterior... 6. future 7. further, remoter, thither 10. additional, extraneous, subsequent, succeeding 11. undisclosed
ultima... 4. last 5. final 8. farthest 10. most remote 12. last syllable
ultimate... 3. end 4. dire, last

5. final, telus 6. future, latest, result 7. extreme, maximum 8. eventful, eventual, farthest, terminal 9. elemental 10. conclusive, end product
ultimatum... 5. offer 6. demand 13. ultimate point 14. final objective
ultimo... 3. ult 9. past month (opp of proximo)
ultra... 6. beyond 7. extreme, radical 9. excessive, extremist, fanatical 11. extravagant 14. uncompromising
ultramarine... 11. blue pigment, lapis lazuli 12. beyond the sea
ultramontane... 5. alien 6. beyond 9. foreigner 10. tramontane 13. beyond the Alps, Roman Catholic
ulu (Esk)... 5. knife
ululate... 4. hoot, howl, wail, yelp 6. bellow, lament
Ulysses (pert to)...
antagonist.. 4. Irus
dog.. 5. Argos
enchantress.. 5. Circe
father.. 7. Laertes
Greek name.. 8. Odysseus
hero.. 7. Odyssey (Homer's)
literally.. 5. hater
son.. 9. Telegonus
wife.. 8. Penelope
umber... 3. raw 5. brown, burnt 6. shadow, Turkey 8. grayling, umbrette 10. brown earth
umbilicus (pert to)...
anatomy.. 5. navel
botany.. 5. hilum
geometry.. 5. focus
paleology.. 5. stick (papyrus)
zoology.. 3. pit 10. depression
umbra... 4. fish 5. ghost, shade 6. shadow 7. phantom, vestige
umbrage... 5. doubt, pique, shade, trace 6. offend, resent 7. foliage, offense, shelter 8. disfavor 9. semblance, suspicion 10. overshadow, resentment 11. displeasure
umbrella... 4. gamp 5. cover, guard, shade 6. chatta, payong, pileus (of a jellyfish) 7. parasol, shelter 9. parachute, sea anchor 11. bumbershoot
umbrella tree... 5. bendy 7. dogwood, ginseng 8. magnolia
umbrette... 4. bird, fish 5. omber (ombre) 9. hammerkop
umpire... 5. judge 7. arbiter, referee 8. mediator 9. moderator 10. arbitrator, negotiator
Umpqua... 6. Indian 10. Athapascan

607

unable... 6. cannot 8. helpless,
  impotent 9. incapable
  11. incompetent, inefficient,
  unqualified 13. incapacitated
Una boat... 7. catboat
unabridged... 8. complete
  11. uncondensed
unaccented... 4. lene 6. atonic
unaccountable... 7. lawless, strange
  9. fantastic 10. mysterious
  12. inexplicable, unfathomable
  13. irresponsible, unpredictable
unacknowledged... 9. anonymous,
  forgotten, unthanked 10. unrewarded
unadorned... 4. bald, bare, form
  5. grace, naked, stark 7. austere
  13. plain–speaking
unadulterated... 4. pure 5. naked
  6. honest 7. unmixed 9. unalloyed,
  undiluted 11. uncorrupted
unaffected... 4. naif, real 5. naive,
  plain 6. simple 7. artless, genuine,
  natural, sincere 8. informal
  9. unaltered, untouched
  12. uninfluenced 13. plain–speaking
Unalaska... 5. Aleut, tribe
  9. Eskimauan
unanimous... 5. solid 6. agreed,
  mutual, united 8. agreeing 9. of one
  mind 10. concordant 11. consentient
  12. with one voice
unanimously... 7. una voce 12. with
  one voice
unapproachable... 8. reserved
  10. unsociable 12. inaccessible
unapt... 4. dull, slow 5. inapt
  8. backward 10. unskillful, unsuitable
  13. inappropriate
unaroused... 6. latent 7. dormant
  8. inactive 9. unstirred
unaspirated... 4. lene 6. smooth
unassuming... 3. shy 6. modest
  7. genuine, natural 8. informal,
  retiring 9. diffident 11. undeceptive
  14. unostentatious
unau... 5. sloth (2–toed)
unavailing... 6. futile 8. gainless
unbalanced... 6. insane, uneven,
  unjust 7. unequal 8. deranged,
  lopsided, one–sided 9. off center
  10. disordered
unbecoming... 4. rude 5. inept
  8. unseemly 10. indecorous,
  unsuitable 12. unattractive
unbelievable... 9. fantastic, untenable
  10. incredible, unreliable
  11. implausible, unthinkable
  13. inconceivable
unbeliever... 5. pagan 6. Kaffir (Kafir)
  7. atheist, doubter, heretic, infidel,
  skeptic 8. agnostic
unbend... 4. rest, thaw 5. frese, relax,
  yield 6. loosen 7. slacken 8. be
  pliant, unfasten 10. condescend,
  straighten
unbending... 5. rigid, stern, stiff
  8. resolute 10. inexorable, inflexible,
  unyielding
unbiased... 4. fair, just 9. impartial
  12. free from bias, unprejudiced
unbind... 4. free, undo 5. loose, untie
  6. loosen 7. absolve, deliver, release

  8. dissolve, unfasten
unbound... 4. free 5. loose
  10. unconfined
unbounded... 8. infinite 9. limitless,
  unchecked, unlimited 10. unconfined
  11. measureless 12. uncontrolled,
  unrestrained
unbridled... 4. free 5. loose
  7. lawless, violent 10. licentious
  12. uncontrolled, unrestrained
unbroken... 4. even 5. undug, whole
  6. direct, entire, intact, smooth
  7. untamed 8. constant, straight,
  unplowed 10. continuous
  13. uninterrupted
uncanny... 5. eerie (eery), weird
  6. spooky 7. ghostly, strange
  8. careless 9. unnatural
  10. mysterious
unceasing... 6. eterne 7. endless,
  eternal 9. continual, incessant
  11. everlasting
unceremonious... 4. curt 5. blunt
  6. abrupt, casual 7. offhand
  8. informal 14. unconventional
uncertain... 4. hazy 5. vague
  6. chancy, fickle, fitful, shifty, unsure
  7. dubious 8. doubtful, unsteady,
  variable 9. ambiguous, irregular,
  undecided 10. changeable, indefinite,
  irresolute, precarious 11. unequivocal
  12. questionable 13. indeterminate,
  problematical, untrustworthy
uncertainty... 5. doubt 6. wonder
  7. dubiety 8. suspense 9. dubiosity
  10. fickleness, skepticism
  12. irresolution 14. precariousness
unchanging... 7. eternal, settled,
  uniform 9. immutable, unvarying
  10. invariable, stationary
unchaste... 4. lewd 5. bawdy
  6. impure 7. obscene 8. immodest
unchecked... 4. free 5. loose
  7. rampant 9. permanent, unbridled
unchristian... 5. pagan 7. heathen,
  infidel, ungodly 9. barbarous,
  excessive 11. irreligious, uncivilized
uncivil... 4. rude 6. savage 7. ill–bred
  8. impolite 9. barbarous
  10. indecorous, ungracious
  11. ill–mannered, uncivilized
  12. discourteous 13. disrespectful
uncivilized... 4. rude, wild 5. feral
  6. brutal, ferine, savage 8. barbaric
  9. primitive, unrefined
uncle... 3. eme (yeme), oom
unclean... 4. foul, tref, vile 5. dirty
  6. filthy, immund, impure
  8. polluted, unchaste
  11. unwholesome
Uncle Tom's Cabin (pert to)...
  author.. 5. Stowe (Harriet Beecher)
  character.. 5. Topsy 6. Legree
    8. Uncle Tom 9. Little Eva
  subject.. 7. slavery
unclose... 3. ope 4. open 6. reveal
  7. expound 8. disclose
uncolored... 7. genuine 9. colorless
  10. achromatic
uncommon... 3. odd 4. nice, rare
  5. novel 6. scarce, unique
  7. special, strange, unusual

8. unwonted 10. infrequent,
remarkable 11. exceptional
12. unaccustomed 13. extraordinary
uncommunicative... 6. silent
8. reserved, reticent 9. secretive
10. unsociable
uncomplaining... 5. stoic 7. stoical
uncompromising... 4. firm 5. rigid
6. strict 9. obstinate, unbending
10. inflexible, unyielding
12. conservative, intransigent
unconcerned... 4. cool, free
8. careless 9. apathetic
10. insouciant 11. indifferent, not
involved 13. disinterested
unconditional... 4. free 8. absolute,
explicit 10. unreserved
unconfined... 5. loose 9. boundless,
limitless, unlimited 12. unrestrained
unconscious... 3. out 6. asleep
7. unaware 8. heedless, ignorant,
mindless 9. inanimate, senseless,
unfeeling 10. abstracted, insensible
11. involuntary 12. subconscious
unconstrained... 4. easy, free
6. candid 7. natural 8. informal
11. spontaneous 12. unrestrained
uncontrolled... 4. free, wild 5. loose
7. lawless 9. impulsive, irregular,
unmanaged 10. capricious,
changeable, licentious, ungoverned
11. not governed, unregulated
12. unrestrained
unconventional... 4. easy 5. outré
6. casual 7. devious, offbeat
8. Bohemian, informal
10. unorthodox 13. unceremonious
uncorrupted... 8. pristine
uncouth... 3. odd 4. rude 5. crude
6. clumsy, rustic 7. awkward,
boorish, strange 9. inelegant,
unrefined, untrained 10. outlandish,
uncultured, unpolished
uncover... 4. bare, open 6. detect,
divest, expose, remove, reveal, unveil
7. divulge, lay bare, take off,
undrape 8. disclose, discover
uncovered... 4. bald, bare, nude, open
7. exposed 8. divested, revealed,
stripped, unveiled 9. décolleté
10. bareheaded 11. unprotected
unction... 4. balm, rite 6. fervor
7. lanolin, unguent 8. flattery,
function (divine), ointment
10. anointment
unctuous... 4. oily, smug 5. bland,
fatty, salvy, suave 6. fervid, greasy
7. gushing, pinguid, plastic
10. flattering, oleaginous
12. hypocritical 13. sanctimonious
uncultured... 7. artless, boorish,
uncouth 8. Bohemian 9. unlearned,
unrefined 10. Philistine
11. countrified, undeveloped
undaunted... 4. bold 5. brave
7. Spartan, untamed 8. fearless,
intrepid, unafraid 9. confident,
dauntless 10. courageous,
undismayed 11. persevering,
unconquered
undecided... 4. moot 7. pending
8. doubtful, wavering 9. uncertain,

unsettled 10. inconstant, irresolute,
unresolved 13. problematical
undependable... 6. fickle 7. erratic
9. uncertain 13. irresponsible,
untrustworthy
under... 3. sub 4. alow 5. below,
least, neath, sotto 6. nether
7. beneath 8. guidance 9. lower
than 10. subjection, underneath
11. subordinate
undercover... 6. secret 7. furtive
11. clandestine, underground
13. surreptitious
underestimate... 8. belittle, minimize
9. set too low, underrate
10. undervalue
underfong... 6. entrap 7. ensnare,
receive, sustain 9. undertake
10. circumvent
undergo... 4. bear, dree, pass 5. shirt
6. endure, suffer 7. sustain
9. undermine 10. experience
underhanded... 3. oly 4. dern, mean
5. shady 6. covert, crafty, secret,
sneaky 8. sneaking, unfairly
9. deceitful, dishonest 10. fraudulent
11. clandestine, short-handed
13. unobtrusively 15. surreptitiously
underling... 6. menial, minion
7. servant 8. inferior 11. subordinate
underlying... 5. basic 8. cardinal
11. fundamental
undermine... 3. sap 4. ruin 5. drain,
erode 6. weaken 7. subvert
8. enfeeble, excavate
understand... 3. ken, see 4. know
5. grasp, infer, savvy, sense
6. follow, reason 7. discern, explain,
realize, signify 8. conceive, perceive
9. apprehend, interpret
10. comprehend
understandable... 5. clear, lucid
12. intelligible
understanding... 5. amity, sense
6. accord, reason, treaty 7. compact,
concept, entente, knowing
8. sympathy, Verstand 9. agreement,
intellect, knowledge, tolerance,
unanimity 10. acceptance,
accordance, perception
11. discernment, penetration
12. intelligence 13. comprehension
understatement... 7. litotes
understood... 5. clear, known, lucid,
tacit 7. assumed, implied, settled
8. implicit 11. traditional
undertake... 3. try 4. dare 6. accept,
assume, pledge 7. attempt, promise,
reprove 8. contract, covenant,
endeavor, engage in, set about
9. guarantee, underfong
undertaker... 5. cerer 6. surety
7. manager, rebuker, sponsor
8. embalmer 9. godfather, mortician
12. entrepreneur
undertaking... 3. act 4. task 6. cautio
7. calling, project, promise, venture
8. business 9. adventure, guarantee
10. enterprise
undertone... 4. tone (low) 5. aside
6. murmur 12. subdued color
undertow... 7. riptide

underworld... 3. Dis 4. hell 5. Hades,
   limbo, Mafia, Orcus, Sheol
   6. Erebus, Tophet 7. Abaddon,
   Xibalba 8. Dis pater, gangland
   9. Black Hand, chthonian, perdition,
   purgatory
underwrite... 6. assure, insure
   7. finance, sponsor 8. submit to
underwriter... 7. insurer 8. endorser
   9. financier 10. underclerk 13. Stock
   Exchange 14. Lloyd's of London
undesirable condition... 6. malady
undetermined... 5. vague 7. dubious
   8. not fixed, unproved 9. uncertain,
   undecided 10. irresolute
undeveloped... 5. crude 6. embryo,
   latent 8. immature 10. unprepared
   11. rudimentary
undignified... 6. vulgar 8. informal,
   infra dig, unworthy 9. inelegant
undine... 3. nix 5. gnome, sylph
   6. vessel (glass) 9. planetoid
   10. salamander
undivided... 3. one 5. total, whole
   6. entire, intact, joined 7. unitary
   8. unbroken 9. not shared
   10. continuous
undo... 4. open 5. annul, loose
   6. cancel, defeat, foredo, unlash,
   unwrap 7. destroy, disjoin, nullify,
   release, uncover, unravel 8. unfasten
   10. disconnect, invalidate
undoing... 4. ruin 6. defeat
   8. downfall 9. annulment, overthrow
   11. destruction, disassembly
undomesticated... 4. wild 5. feral
   6. ferine
undone... 3. raw 9. neglected
   10. defeasible
undue... 5. wrong 6. unjust
   7. extreme 8. improper, not owing
   9. excessive 10. exorbitant,
   immoderate, inordinate, undeserved,
   unsuitable 11. unwarranted
   13. inappropriate
undulating... 4. wavy 6. waving
   7. aripple, rolling 8. rippling
   11. fluctuating 16. rising and falling
undulation... 4. beat, wave 5. heave,
   surge, swell 6. motion, waving
   7. tremolo, vibrato 8. waviness
   9. pulsation 11. convolution
undying... 6. eterne 7. ageless,
   endless, eternal 8. immortal,
   unending 9. deathless
   11. amaranthine 12. imperishable
   14. indestructible
unearth... 4. find 5. dig up
   6. exhume, expose 7. uncover
   8. disclose, discover, disinter
   12. bring to light
unearthly... 5. eerie (eery), godly,
   weird 7. awesome, ghostly, strange,
   uncanny 8. heavenly, terrific
   9. appalling, deathlike
   10. mysterious, outlandish
   12. preposterous, supernatural
   13. preternatural
uneasiness... 5. worry 6. unrest
   7. anxiety, malaise 8. disquiet
   10. impatience 11. displeasure,
   disquietude, disturbance

12. apprehension
uneasy... 5. stiff 7. anxious, awkward,
   inquiet, restive, worried 8. agitated,
   cramping, restless 9. difficult,
   impatient, perturbed 10. disquieted,
   distressed 11. constrained,
   troublesome
unemotional... 4. cold 5. stoic
   7. stoical 10. phlegmatic
unemployed... 4. idle, lazy 6. otiose,
   unused 7. not used 8. inactive,
   leisured 11. not invested
unencumbered... 4. free
unending... 7. endless, eternal
   8. termless, timeless 9. boundless,
   perpetual 10. continuous
   12. interminable
unequal... 3. odd 4. odds 5. aniso
   (comb form) 6. uneven, unfair, unjust
   8. variable 9. disparate, irregular
   11. fluctuating, not adequate
   12. asymmetrical 16. disproportionate
unequaled... 7. supreme 8. peerless
   9. matchless, nonpareil, unmatched,
   unrivaled 10. inimitable, surpassing,
   unbeatable, unexcelled
   12. unparalleled
unequivocal... 5. clear, plain 6. candid
   7. sincere 8. explicit 9. downright
   11. categorical, indubitable
unerring... 4. sure, true 5. exact
   7. certain 8. accurate, virtuous
   9. unfailing 10. infallible
unessential... 8. needless 9. extrinsic
   10. irrelevant 11. superfluous,
   unimportant 13. insignificant, void of
   essence
unethical... 6. amoral
uneven... 3. odd 5. erose, rough
   6. rugged, unfair, unjust 7. erratic,
   unequal, varying 8. not level
   10. ill-matched 11. fluctuating
unexamined... 7. a priori
unexampled... 8. peerless
   10. unimitated 12. unparalleled
   13. extraordinary, unprecedented
unexpected... 6. abrupt, sudden
   7. unusual 9. inopinate
   10. unforeseen 14. not anticipated
unfair... 4. foul 5. wrong 6. biased,
   uneven, unjust 8. unseemly
   9. dishonest, unethical 10. not
   cricket, unsporting 11. inequitable,
   unfavorable 12. disingenuous, not
   equitable
unfaithful... 6. betray 7. infidel, traitor
   8. apostate, recreant, turncoat
   9. faithless 10. inaccurate
   12. nonobservant 13. untrustworthy
unfamiliar... 3. new 7. strange,
   unknown 8. not known
   12. unaccustomed, unconversant
unfasten... 4. free, open, undo
   5. unbar, unfix, unpin, untie
   6. detach, loosen, unhook, unlock
   7. unloose 8. unbutton 9. disengage
unfavorable... 3. bad, ill 6. averse
   7. adverse, opposed 8. contrary,
   untimely 9. repulsive 12. inauspicious
unfeeling... 4. dull 5. cruel, stoic,
   stony 6. brutal, steely, stolid, unkind
   7. callous 8. numbness, obdurate

9. apathetic, bloodless, heartless, inanimate, insensate 10. insensible 11. hardhearted 13. unsusceptible 16. unimpressionable
unfeigned ... 4. real 7. genuine, natural, sincere 11. undeceptive 14. not counterfeit 15. not hypocritical
unfermented grape juice ... 4. stum
unfertile ... 4. arid 6. barren
unfettered ... 4. free 5. broad 9. liberated, unchained 10. unshackled
unfinished ... 5. crude, rough 7. sketchy 9. imperfect 10. incomplete 11. uncompleted
unfit ... 5. inept 6. faulty, not fit, unable 8. disabled 9. untenable 11. handicapped, incompetent, unqualified 12. disqualified
unfledged ... 4. eyas 5. green 6. callow 8. immature 11. undeveloped 12. not feathered
unflinching ... 7. staunch 8. resolute, unafraid 9. steadfast 10. unwavering, unyielding 12. not shrinking
unfold ... 3. ope 4. open 6. evolve, expand, flower, reveal, spread, unfurl 7. develop, display, divulge, evolute, explain, release 8. disclose
unfortunate ... 3. ill 4. poor 6. wretch 7. hapless, unlucky 8. luckless, untimely 10. calamitous 12. inauspicious, unsuccessful
unfounded ... 4. idle, vain 8. baseless 9. untenable 10. chimerical 11. unsupported, unwarranted
unfriendly ... 3. icy 4. cool 7. asocial, hostile, not kind, opposed 8. inimical, unsocial 10. unsociable 12. inhospitable
unfruitful ... 6. barren, wasted 7. sterile, useless 9. fruitless, infertile 12. unproductive unprofitable 13. not productive
unfurl ... 4. open 6. expand, spread, unfold, unroll
ungainly ... 5. gawky, lanky 6. clumsy, gauche 7. awkward, uncouth 8. bungling 10. cumbersome, ungraceful
ungenteel ... 6. vulgar 7. ill-bred 8. plebeian 9. inelegant 10. unmannerly
ungentle ... 4. rude 5. harsh, rough 7. ill-bred 12. discourteous
ungodly ... 6. sinful, wicked 7. impious 9. atheistic 11. unbelieving
ungovernable ... 4. wild 6. unruly 9. unbridled 10. disorderly, licentious, rebellious, refractory 12. incorrigible, obstreperous, recalcitrant 13. irrepressible 14. uncontrollable
unguent ... 4. balm 5. salve 6. cerate, chrism, pomade 7. unction 8. ointment 9. lubricant, unguentum
ungula ... 4. claw, hoof, nail 6. unguis
ungulate ... 3. pig 4. deer 5. horse, swine, tapir 6. hoofed 8. elephant, Ungulata 10. rhinoceros 15. hoofed quadruped

unhallowed ... 6. unholy, wicked 10. desecrated
unhappy ... 3. sad 6. dismal, woeful 8. dejected, ill-fated, wretched 9. miserable, sorrowful 10. calamitous, displeased 11. melancholic, unfortunate 12. discontented, unsuccessful
unhealthy ... 3. ill 4. sick 6. sickly, unsafe 11. unwholesome
unhesitating ... 4. sure 5. ready 8. implicit, resolute 10. undoubting
unholy ... 6. wicked 7. impious, profane 8. shocking 10. scandalous, unhallowed
unicorn ... 4. reem (Bib), unie 7. monster 8. narwhale 9. monoceros, spike team 10. pursuivant (Her), rhinoceros (one-horned)
uniform ... 4. even 5. equal 6. livery, outfit, simple, smooth 7. equable, orderly, regular 8. constant, equiform 9. unvarying 10. consistent, invariable, unchanging 11. symmetrical
uniformity ... 5. order 8. equality, evenness, sameness, symmetry 10. compliance, conformity, smoothness 11. consistency, homogeneity 13. invariability
unify ... 5. merge, unite 7. combine, make one 8. coalesce 9. integrate 11. consolidate
unimaginative ... 4. dull 7. literal, prosaic 10. unfanciful
unimpaired ... 4. free 6. entire, intact 8. unmarred 9. undamaged, unspoiled
unimpressed ... 6. unawed 7. unmoved 9. unstirred 10. unaffected
uninformed ... 8. ignorant, nescient 9. unknowing 10. unapprized 13. unenlightened, unintelligent
uninhabited ... 5. empty 6. vacant 8. deserted, desolate, forsaken 9. abandoned, unpeopled 10. unoccupied, untenanted
uninspired ... 4. dull 6. stodgy 9. uninhaled
unintelligent ... 4. dumb 5. brute 6. stupid, unwise 7. foolish 8. ignorant 9. senseless
unintentional ... 7. unmeant 9. unwitting 10. accidental, unintended 11. inadvertent, involuntary, unmeditated 14. unpremeditated
uninterested ... 5. bored 9. apathetic, impartial, incurious 11. unconcerned 13. disinterested
uninteresting ... 3. dry 4. arid, drab, dull 6. boring, prolix, stupid 7. humdrum, insipid, prosaic, tedious 8. tiresome 9. colorless 10. unexciting
union ... 3. one 4. bond 5. joint, unity 6. accord, fusion, league, merger 7. amalgam, entente, liaison, oneness 8. alliance, junction, marriage 9. coalition 10. federation

11. affiliation, association,
combination, concurrence,
confederacy, conjunction
13. juxtaposition
Union (pert to)...
ensign, British.. 12. three crosses (St
Andrew, St George, St Patrick)
General.. 7. Sherman (Civil War)
of States.. 6. Empire 12. United
States
of workers.. 5. artel, guild
Union of So Africa...
capital.. 8. Cape Town (Legis),
Pretoria (Admin)
city.. 6. Durban 9. Germiston
12. Johannesburg
famed Park.. 6. Kruger
**Union of Soviet Socialist
Republics**... see also *Russia*
anc citadel.. 7. Kremlin
capital.. 6. Moscow
city.. 9. Leningrad
Republics (number).. 7. fifteen
resort.. 5. Yalta 6. Crimea
river.. 2. Ob 3. Don 4. Lena, Neva,
Ural 5. Volga 7. Dnieper
sea.. 4. Aral, Azov 5. Black, White
6. Baltic 7. Caspian
strait.. 6. Bering
unique... 3. odd, one 4. rare, sole
5. alone, novel 6. single 7. notable,
special, unusual 8. original, peculiar,
peerless, singular 9. matchless
12. single–valued 13. extraordinary
unison... 5. union 6. accord, assent
7. concord, harmony 9. agreement,
unanimity 10. concordant,
consonance
unit... 3. ace, ane, one 4. item, word
5. digit, group 6. entity 7. measure
8. syllable
unit (pert to)...
astronomy.. 6. parsec
biology.. 5. idant
electrical.. 3. amp, mho, ohm, rel
4. volt, watt 5. farad, henry, joule
6. ampere, proton 7. coulomb
energy.. 3. erg, rad 5. ergon 6. kilerg
7. quantum
fluidity.. 3. rhe
force.. 4. dyne 5. tonal 7. kinetic
heat.. 5. therm (therme) 7. calorie
(calory)
induction.. 5. henry
light.. 3. lux, pyr, rad 5. lumen
6. Hefner
linear.. 3. ell 4. foot, inch, mile, yard
7. furlong
magnetic.. 5. gauss, weber
7. maxwell, oersted
matter.. 5. monad
measure.. 3. are, rod 4. pint
5. maund, meter, stere
military.. 7. brigade, platoon
8. regiment
power.. 2. HP 3. bel 5. dynam,
horse
pressure.. 5. barad, barie
reluctance.. 3. rel
resistance.. 3. ohm
speed.. 4. velo

telegraphic.. 4. baud
thermal.. 7. calorie (calory)
velocity.. 4. velo
volume.. 3. ton 4. cord, peck, pint
5. ounce, pound 6. barrel, bushel,
gallon 8. hogshead
weight.. 3. ton 5. carat (karat),
ounce, pound
wire.. 3. mil
work.. 3. erg 5. ergon, joule 6. kilerg
yarn.. 6. denier
unite... 3. fay, tie, wed 4. ally, bind,
fuse, join, knit, link, meld, weld
5. annex, graft, marry, merge
6. adhere, cement, concur, mingle,
solder 7. combine, connect
8. coalesce, condense, converge,
federate, side with 9. affiliate,
associate 10. amalgamate, federalize
11. consolidate, incorporate
unite (pert to)...
by freezing.. 8. regelate
by interweaving.. 5. plash 6. pleach,
splice
by joints.. 10. articulate
closely.. 11. concentrate
in concordance.. 9. harmonize
timbers.. 6. rabbet
united... 3. one, wed 4. knit, tied
5. added 6. allied, banded, joined,
linked, merged, welded 7. cohered,
grafted, rallied, spliced 8. cemented,
clannish 9. concerted, corporate
10. concurrent, corporated
United Provinces... 11. (The)
Netherlands 13. Dutch Republic
United States... 9. Etats–Unis
United States... see also *American*
artist.. 4. Pyle, Wood 5. Flagg,
Moses (Grandma), Peale, Ryder,
Sloan 6. Eakins, Stuart
author.. 3. Ade, Poe 4. Pyle, Ward
5. Alger, Barth, Beach, Davis, Field,
Harte, James, Lewis, Stowe
6. Alcott, Bryant, Cooper, Ferber,
Hersey, Holmes, Irving, London,
Lowell, O'Henry, Porter 7. Clemens,
Dreiser, Emerson, Stewart, Thoreau,
Whitman 8. Faulkner, Sinclair,
Whittier 9. Hawthorne, Hemingway
10. Longfellow, Tarkington
canal.. 4. Erie 6. Panama
capital.. see separate States
composer.. 4. Kern 5. Foote, Nevin
6. Berlin, Foster 7. Rodgers
8. Gershwin 9. Bernstein
emblem.. 5. eagle
explorer.. 4. Byrd, Long, Pike
5. Boone, Clark, Lewis, Logan, Perry
Falls.. 7. Niagara 8. Yosemite
9. Multnomah
Indian.. see under *Indian (Am)*
inventor.. 3. Hoe 4. Bell, Howe
5. Fiske, Fitch, Morse 6. Edison,
Fulton 7. Whitney
mountain.. 4. Hood 6. Elbert, Helena,
Shasta 7. Rainier, Whitney
8. Katahdin, McKinley
naturalist.. 4. Muir 5. Beebe, Seton
7. Thoreau
ornithologist.. 7. Audubon

philosopher.. **5**. James
pirate.. **4**. Kidd
poet.. **3**. Poe **4**. Nash **5**. Benét,
Field, Moore, Wylie **6**. Bryant,
Holmes, Kilmer, Lanier, Lowell, Millay
7. Whitman **8**. Whittier
10. Longfellow
unity... **3**. one **5**. union **6**. accord
7. concord, harmony, oneness
8. alliance **9**. agreement
10. singleness, uniformity
11. conjunction, unification
12. completeness
universal... **3**. all **5**. local, total, usual,
whole **6**. cosmic, entire, public
7. general **8**. catholic **9**. prevalent,
unlimited, well–known **11**. widely
known
universal (pert to)...
knowledge.. **9**. pantology
language.. **2**. Ro **3**. Ido **9**. Esperanto
language, written.. **10**. pasigraphy
remedy.. **7**. panacea
solvent.. **8**. alkahest
successor, heir.. **5**. heres (haeres)
universe... **4**. olam **5**. world
6. cosmos, system **9**. macrocosm
10. Great World
universe, controlling principle...
5. logos
unkempt... **5**. messy, rough **6**. frowsy,
shaggy, untidy **7**. ruffled, squalid,
tousled, uncouth **9**. unrefined
10. disarrayed, disheveled, unpolished
unkind... **3**. ill **5**. cruel, harsh, stern
6. brutal, severe **8**. ungenial
9. inclement **10**. ungracious,
ungrateful **13**. unsympathetic
15. uncompassionate
unknowable... **6**. mystic **8**. mystical,
noumenon **9**. enigmatic
13. indiscernible **14**. unintelligible
15. absolute reality (Kant), ultimate
reality (Spencer)
unknowable object... **3**. God **7**. the
soul **8**. noumenon
unknown... **7**. inconnu, strange
8. stranger **9**. anonymous, hereafter,
incognito, unheard of **10**. unfamiliar,
unrenowned **12**. incalculable
unlawful... **7**. bastard, illegal, illicit,
lawless **9**. irregular **10**. contraband
11. unwarranted **12**. illegitimate,
unauthorized
unlearned... **4**. lewd **5**. gross
8. ignorant, untaught **10**. illiterate,
uneducated **11**. instinctive
unleashed... **4**. free **5**. loose **6**. untied
8. released **10**. unfettered,
unshackled, untethered
unleavened... **7**. azymous
unleavened bread... **4**. azym **5**. azyme
7. matzoth
unless... **4**. nisi, save **6**. except
7. without **9**. except for, excepting
10. except that
unlettered... **8**. ignorant **10**. illiterate,
uneducated
unlike... **6**. sundry, uneven **7**. dislike,
diverse **9**. different, irregular
10. dissimilar, improbable
11. unpromising **12**. disagreeable

13. heterogeneous
unlikelihood... **11**. small chance
13. improbability
unlikeness... **8**. contrast
13. dissimilarity
unlimited... **4**. vast **9**. boundless,
unbounded, universal **10**. unconfined
11. illimitable **12**. immeasurable,
unrestricted **13**. indeterminate
unload... **3**. rid **4**. dump, sell
5. empty **7**. discard, lighten
9. disburden, discharge, liquidate
unlucky... **3**. bad, fey, ill **7**. infaust
8. ill–fated, untimely **9**. ill–omened
11. unfortunate **12**. inauspicious, not
favorable
unmannerly... **4**. rude **7**. boorish,
uncivil **8**. impolite **10**. mannerless
12. discourteous
unmelodious... **9**. dissonant
11. cacophonous
unmerciful... **5**. cruel **6**. unkind
7. extreme, inhuman **8**. pitiless,
ruthless **9**. heartless, merciless
10. relentless
unmistakable... **4**. open **5**. clear, plain
6. patent **7**. certain, evident, obvious
8. apparent, distinct, manifest
11. unqualified
unmitigated... **4**. mere **5**. sheer
6. arrant **8**. clear–cut, thorough
9. downright **11**. not softened,
unqualified
unmoved... **4**. calm, dead, firm
5. inert **6**. serene **8**. obdurate,
unshaken **9**. apathetic
unnatural... **5**. eerie (eery) **7**. labored,
strange, uncanny **8**. abnormal,
affected **9**. eccentric, irregular
10. artificial, factitious
unnecessary... **4**. fuss **7**. useless
8. needless **11**. not required,
superfluous, uncalled–for
12. nonessential
unobtrusive... **6**. modest **8**. retiring
11. clandestine
unoccupied... **4**. idle, void **5**. empty
7. not busy **8**. deserted
10. unemployed, untenanted
11. empty–headed, uninhabited
unorthodox... **9**. heretical
10. fallacious, left–handed
14. unconventional
unostentatious... **5**. quiet **6**. lenten,
modest **10**. restrained
unparalleled... **5**. alone **6**. unique
8. peerless **9**. matchless, unequaled,
unmatched **10**. inimitable
13. extraordinary
unpleasant... **8**. unsavory **9**. offensive
10. not amiable, ungracious
11. displeasing, distasteful
12. disagreeable
unpolished... **5**. bruit, crude, rough
6. coarse, rugged **7**. uncouth
8. agrestic, unpolite **9**. inelegant
10. agrestical **11**. countrified
unprecedented... **3**. new **5**. novel
10. unexampled, unimitated
13. extraordinary
unprejudiced... **4**. fair **7**. neutral
8. unbiased **9**. impartial

10. impersonal 13. dispassionate
unprepared ... 3. raw 5. unfit
6. unwary 7. unready 9. premature,
unskilled
unprepossessing ... 4. grim, ugly
9. grim–faced 10. ill–looking
unpretentious ... 6. humble, modest,
simple 7. natural 10. unaffected
11. in good taste
unprincipled ... 7. corrupt 9. dishonest
10. fraudulent, perfidious
12. dishonorable, unscrupulous
unprofessional ... 3. lay 6. laical
7. amateur 9. unskilled
10. amateurish 14. unbusinesslike
unprofitable ... 6. barren 7. useless
8. gainless 9. fruitless 10. unfruitful
unpropitious ... 7. adverse, ominous,
opposed 8. untimely 10. disastrous
12. inauspicious
unqualified ... 5. unfit 6. unable
7. genuine, plenary 8. absolute,
complete, unfitted 9. incapable
10. ineligible 11. incompetent
12. not qualified 13. unconditional
unquestionable ... 7. certain, decided,
evident 8. positive 10. undeniable
11. indubitable, irrefutable
12. indisputable 13. unimpeachable
unravel ... 4. undo 5. feaze, solve
6. unfold, unlace 8. separate
9. disengage 10. disinvolve
11. disentangle
unreal ... 5. false, ideal 7. fancied
8. fanciful, illusory, spurious
9. fantastic, imaginary, visionary
10. artificial, fictitious 11. imaginative
13. unsubstantial
unreasonable ... 3. mad 6. absurd,
unwise 9. excessive, fanatical,
illogical, senseless 10. capricious,
exorbitant, immoderate, irrational
11. extravagant, impractical
13. unjustifiable
unrecognizable ... 3. dim 5. vague
7. blurred, obscure, unclear
9. undefined 10. indistinct
14. unintelligible
unrecognized ... 6. unsung 7. unknown
13. unappreciated
unrefined ... 3. raw 4. loud, rude
5. crass, crude, gross, rough
6. coarse, common, earthy, vulgar
7. uncouth 9. inelegant
11. countrified 12. uncultivated
unrefuted ... 4. true 6. proved
8. undenied 10. unanswered
unrelaxed ... 4. taut 5. rigid, tense
7. nervous
unrelenting ... 4. grim, hard, iron
5. stern 6. severe, strict 8. rigorous
9. merciless 10. inexorable,
relentless, unyielding
unreliable ... 6. fickle, unsafe
9. uncertain 10. capricious,
changeable 12. undependable
13. irresponsible, untrustworthy
14. tergiversating
unremitting ... 4. busy 8. constant
9. continual, incessant, perpetual
10. continuous, persistent
11. persevering

unrequited ... 6. unpaid 9. forgotten,
unthanked 10. ungrateful, unrewarded
unreserved, unreservedly ... 4. free,
open 5. frank 6. openly 7. frankly
8. candidly, outright, thorough
9. outspoken 12. unrestricted
unrest ... 6. bustle 8. disquiet
9. commotion 12. restlessness
unrestrained ... 3. lax 4. free, wild
5. loose 6. candid, wanton
7. lawless, riotous 9. unbridled,
unlimited 10. capricious
unrestricted ... 4. free, open
9. unlimited 11. extravagant
12. undiminished 13. communicative
unruffled ... 4. calm, cool 5. still
6. placid, poised, sedate, serene,
smooth 9. quiescent, unexcited
10. unaffected 11. undisturbed
unruly ... 7. lawless 9. fractious,
obstinate, turbulent 10. disorderly,
licentious, refractory 11. disobedient
12. recalcitrant, ungovernable,
unmanageable
unsafe ... 7. dubious, exposed, unsound
8. insecure, perilous 9. dangerous
10. unreliable 12. undependable
unsatisfactory ... 8. inferior
10. inadequate, unbearable
11. intolerable 12. insufficient,
ungratiating 13. disheartening,
unsupportable
unsavory ... 7. insipid 9. offensive,
tasteless 10. unpleasant
11. unpalatable 12. disagreeable
unscrupulous ... 7. devious
9. dishonest 12. unparticular,
unprincipled 13. untrustworthy
16. indiscriminating
unseasonable ... 8. untimely
9. premature 11. inopportune
unseemly ... 5. inapt, wrong 6. vulgar
8. improper, indecent 9. inelegant
10. indecorous, solecistic,
unbecoming 11. undignified
13. ungrammatical
unseen ... 6. hidden 8. unheeded,
viewless 9. invisible, unnoticed
12. undiscovered
unsettled ... 4. moot 6. fickle, queasy
8. confused, deranged, restless,
unplaced, unproved, unstable
9. ambiguous, disturbed, irregular,
uncertain, unquieted 10. irresolute,
unoccupied, up in the air
11. unpopulated
unshorn ... 5. hairy, whole 6. shaggy
unshorn sheep (2nd year) ... 3. tag,
teg
unsightly ... 4. ugly 8. uncomely,
unlovely 9. inelegant, not comely
12. unattractive
unskilled ... 5. green 6. puisne
8. ignorant, malapert
unskillful ... 5. inept 7. artless,
awkward 9. maladroit
12. unproficient 13. inexperienced
unsophisticated ... 4. naif, pure, soft
5. green, naive 6. simple 7. artless,
genuine 8. gullible, innocent
9. ingenuous 11. uncorrupted
unsound ... 4. weak 5. crazy, dotty,

risky, shaky 6. addled, fickle
8. impaired, insecure 9. defective,
imperfect
unspoken ... 5. tacit 6. silent
7. implied 9. ineffable, unuttered
unstable ... 4. weak 6. fickle, fitful,
labile, scanty 7. astatic, erratic,
flighty, plastic 8. insecure, not solid,
ticklish, unsteady 9. ephemeral,
irregular, unsettled 10. inconstant,
precarious, unreliable 11. fluctuating,
vacillating
unsteady ... 5. dizzy, shaky 6. groggy,
wobbly 7. quavery, rickety, unsound
8. titubate, unstable, wavering
9. irregular, uncertain 10. capricious,
changeable, flickering, inconstant,
precarious 11. fluctuating,
ill–balanced, lightheaded, vacillating
unsubstantial ... 4. airy, rare, slim
5. filmy, light 6. aerial, flimsy,
papery 8. illusory 9. illogical,
visionary 10. immaterial, intangible,
unreliable
unsuitable ... 5. inept, undue, unfit
8. untimely 10. unbecoming
11. inexpedient 13. inappropriate
14. unsatisfactory
unsullied ... 4. pure 5. clean 6. chaste
8. innocent, spotless, virginal
10. immaculate
unsure ... 4. weak 5. timid 6. infirm
8. doubtful 10. precarious
11. vacillating
unsweetened ... 3. dry, sec 4. sour,
tart 10. unpleasant
unsympathetic ... 6. unkind 7. hostile
8. pitiless 9. heartless 10. intolerant
11. hardhearted 12. unresponsive
untamed ... 4. wild 5. feral 6. savage
9. unsubdued 11. uncivilized
untangle ... 4. free 5. loose, solve
6. sleave 9. extricate 11. disentangle
untenable ... 10. incredible
11. implausible 12. unbelievable,
unreasonable 13. inconceivable
unthinking ... 4. rash 7. puerile
8. careless, heedless 9. impetuous,
impulsive 11. injudicious, instinctive,
involuntary, thoughtless
13. inconsiderate
untidy ... 5. dowdy, messy 6. frowzy,
shabby 8. careless, frumpish,
slipshod, slovenly, unsuited, untimely
10. disheveled
untie ... 4. free 5. loose 6. loosen,
unbind, unknot, unlash 8. unfasten
9. disengage
until now ... 8. hitherto
untiring ... 8. sedulous, tireless
9. unwearied 10. unflagging
13. indefatigable
untold ... 4. vast 8. infinite
9. boundless, countless
10. uninformed, unrevealed
11. innumerable, unexpressed
12. immeasurable, incalculable,
undetermined
untouched ... 3. new 4. pure 6. intact,
unused 8. pristine, virginal
10. impenitent, unaffected
untoward ... 6. unruly 7. unlucky

8. perverse, stubborn, unseemly
10. indecorous, ungraceful
11. unfavorable, unfortunate
12. unpropitious
untrained ... 4. soft, wild 5. green
8. indocile 9. unskilled, untutored
10. amateurish 11. unpracticed
14. unaccomplished
untrammeled ... 4. free 5. loose 8. not
bound 9. unimpeded, unlimited
10. unfettered, unhampered,
unhindered
untransferable ... 11. inalienable
untried ... 3. new 5. fresh, green
8. unproved 9. unhandled
13. inexperienced
untrue ... 5. false, wrong 8. disloyal
9. dishonest, erroneous, incorrect,
not honest 10. fallacious, unfaithful
untrustworthy ... 6. tricky, unsafe
8. slippery 9. deceitful, dishonest,
uncertain 10. perfidious
untruth ... 3. lie 5. error, fable
7. falsity 9. falsehood, treachery
10. disloyalty 11. fabrication
13. faithlessness
unusual ... 3. odd 4. rare 5. novel,
queer 6. exotic, quaint, unique
7. strange 8. terrific, uncommon
9. anomalous 10. infrequent,
remarkable 11. exceptional
13. extraordinary
unutterable ... 6. sacred, secret
9. ineffable, wonderful
11. unspeakable 13. inexpressible
unvarnished ... 5. plain 6. simple
7. genuine 9. unadorned, unglossed
11. undeceptive 13. unembellished
unvarying ... 7. uniform 8. constant
9. permanent 10. monotonous
unwarranted ... 4. idle, vain 5. undue
7. illegal 8. baseless 9. excessive,
unfounded, untenable 10. exorbitant,
unentitled 11. unjustified
unwary ... 4. rash 7. unaware
8. heedless, off guard 9. unguarded
10. unwatchful
unwavering ... 4. firm, sure 5. solid
8. constant 9. steadfast
10. unweakened 11. not yielding,
persevering
unwelcome ... 8. non grata, unwanted
9. intrusive, uninvited
unwholesome ... 4. evil, sick 6. impure
7. corrupt, immoral, noisome,
noxious 9. unhealthy 12. insalubrious
unwieldy ... 5. bulky 6. clumsy
7. awkward, restive 8. ungainly
9. ponderous 10. cumbersome
12. unmanageable 13. insubordinate
unwilling ... 5. loath (loth) 6. averse
9. reluctant 11. disinclined,
involuntary
unwilling to prosecute ... 7. nol–pros
13. nolle prosequi
unwise ... 7. foolish 9. impolitic,
imprudent, senseless 10. irrational
11. inexpedient, injudicious
unwonted ... 4. rare 6. unused
7. unusual 8. uncommon 9. not
wonted 10. infrequent
12. unaccustomed

unworldly... 5. eerie (eery), godly,
naive, weird 8. heavenly 9. spiritual,
unearthly 10. immaterial
12. supernatural
unyielding... 3. set 4. firm, hard, iron
5. rigid, stern, stiff 6. strict
7. adamant 8. obdurate, stubborn
9. immovable, obstinate
10. adamantine, determined,
inexorable, inflexible
14. uncompromising
up (pert to)...
and coming.. 7. go–ahead 8. hustling
and down.. 6. seesaw, uneven
8. vertical 10. undulating
13. perpendicular
in arms.. 6. at odds 8. prepared
9. resistant
ref to.. 10. at the plate (game)
to.. 4. able, till, unto 5. until
9. cognizant, competent
to date.. 3. new 6. modern 7. stylish
11. fashionable
upas tree, arrow poison... 6. antiar
upbraid... 4. twit 5. blame, chide,
scold, score 6. rebuke 7. reprove
8. admonish, reproach 9. reprimand
10. put to shame
upheaval... 5. storm 6. revolt
9. agitation, cataclysm, elevation
10. convulsion
upheld... 5. aided 6. backed
7. abetted 8. defended 9. supported,
sustained 10. encouraged, maintained
uphill... 6. upward 7. upgrade
9. ascending, difficult, laborious
10. slantingly
uphold... 3. aid 4. abet, back, buoy
5. favor, raise 6. defend 7. confirm,
support, sustain 8. maintain, preserve
9. encourage 11. corroborate,
countenance, lend support
upkeep... 4. cost 6. repair 7. support
11. maintenance
upland... 4. wold 5. weald 6. coteau,
inland 7. country, plateau 8. highland
uplands... 7. country 9. highlands
10. the country
uplift... 5. elate, erect, raise
7. elevate, ennoble, glorify, improve
8. upheaval 9. elevation
11. inspiration
upon... 2. on 3. sur 4. atop, onto
5. about, above 7. against 9. by
means of 10. after which
upon (pert to)...
law.. 3. sur
prefix.. 3. epi, sur
that.. 7. whereat 9. whereupon
which.. 7. whereat
upper... 6. higher 8. superior
upper (pert to)...
bed.. 4. bunk
crust.. 7. society 11. aristocracy
13. highest circle
end.. 3. tip 4. apex, head
hand.. 7. mastery 8. dominion
9. advantage, influence
10. preference
House of Congress.. 6. Senate
shoe part.. 4. vamp
uppermost... 3. top 6. upmost

7. highest, supreme, topmost
8. farthest, foremost 9. outermost
uppish... 5. drunk, proud 6. uppity
7. haughty, peevish, stuck–up
8. arrogant, assuming, snobbish
9. high–flown
upright... 4. good, just, true 5. erect,
moral, piano 6. honest, square
7. endwise, sincere 8. vertical,
virtuous 9. equitable, honorable,
righteous 13. perpendicular
upright (pert to)...
chair part.. 4. slat
comb form.. 5. ortho
posture.. 8. orthotic 11. orthostatic
slab.. 5. stela
timber.. 4. jamb, stud
uprising... 4. riot 6. ascent, mutiny,
revolt 7. sloping 9. acclivity,
ascending, rebellion 12. insurrection
uproar... 3. din 4. riot, rout 5. noise
6. bedlam, bustle, clamor, fracas,
hubbub, outcry, tumult 7. turmoil
8. outbreak 9. commotion, confusion
10. donnybrook, hurly–burly,
tintamarre, turbulence
11. pandemonium 12. insurrection
upset... 3. irk 4. rile, ruin, stir
6. defeat, refute, topple 7. agitate,
capsize, confuse, disturb, fluster,
startle, subvert, unnerve 8. distress,
overturn, startled, unnerved
9. embarrass, overthrow
10. discompose, disconcert,
distressed, frustrated, overturned,
refutation, revolution 11. frustration,
overwrought
upshot... 3. end 5. fruit, issue
6. result, sequel 7. outcome
10. conclusion 11. consequence,
eventuality, termination
12. consummation
upside down... 8. confused, disorder
9. confusion 10. resupinate,
topsy–turvy
upsilon (Gr)... 5. hyoid, vowel
7. Y–shaped
upstart... 4. snob 7. bounder, parvenu
13. social climber
up–to–date... 6. modern 7. alamode,
topical 8. informed 11. fashionable
upward... 2. up 3. ano (comb form)
4. over 5. above, aloft 6. onward
7. skyward 8. upstream 9. ascending
upward movement of vessels...
5. scend
uraeus (Egypt Relig)... 3. asp
6. symbol 8. symbolic
Ural... 5. river 9. mountains
Urania (pert to)...
blue.. 12. independence
epithet of.. 9. Aphrodite
genus of.. 5. moths
Gr Myth.. 4. Muse (Astron)
uranology (*study of*)... 7. heavens
15. celestial bodies
Uranus (pert to)...
astronomy.. 6. planet
daughter.. 4. Rhea
father of.. 9. The Titans (12)
personification of.. 6. heaven
satellite.. 5. Ariel 6. Oberon

7. Titania, Umbriel
son.. 6. Cronus
urare, urari... 6. curare
urban... 5. civic 6. ghetto, polite,
uptown 7. oppidan, refined
8. downtown, polished 9. courteous,
municipal 12. metropolitan
13. sophisticated
urbane... 5. civil, suave 6. polish,
polite 7. affable 8. gracious
9. courteous 11. deferential
urbanity... 7. amenity 8. civility,
courtesy 9. deference
urchin... 3. boy, elf, imp, tad 4. arab,
brat 5. gamin 6. elfish 8. hedgehog
9. dandiprat, sea urchin, youngster
urge... 3. dun, egg, hie, ply, yen
4. abet, coax, goad, prod, push,
spur 5. drive, egg on, impel, press
6. advise, compel, dehort, desire,
exhort, fillip, hasten, incite, induce
7. animate, entreat, solicit
8. persuade 9. constrain, importune,
influence, instigate 10. inducement
urgent... 3. hot 5. grave 7. clamant,
exigent, instant 8. critical, pressing
9. impelling, important, insistent,
necessary 11. importunate
urial... 3. sha 5. sheep 6. oorial
Uriel... 9. archangel 10. flame of God
(Bib)
Urim and Thummim (Bib)...
11. instruments 12. interpreters
(Mormon)
urn... 3. jar 4. ewer, urna (anc), vase
5. grave, steen 6. vessel 7. pitcher,
samovar, vaselet 10. jardiniere
urn–shaped... 8. urceolus 9. urceolate
Ursa... 4. bear 9. Ursa Major (Great
Bear), Ursa Minor (Little Bear)
ursal... 7. fur seal
ursuk... 11. bearded seal
Ursula... 5. Saint 7. she–bear
9. butterfly 15. British princess
(legend)
urubu... 7. vulture
Uruguay...
capital.. 10. Montevideo
city.. 4. Melo 5. Minar 9. Maldonado
estuary.. 5. Plata 12. Rio de la Plata
lake.. 5. Merim
river.. 7. Uruguay
settler.. 5. Cabot (Sebastian, 1527)
university.. 10. Montevideo (1849)
windstorm.. 7. pampero
urus... 2. ox 3. tur 7. aurochs
usable... 3. fit 9. practical
10. functional 11. serviceable,
utilitarian
usage... 3. use 4. wont 5. habit, ritus
6. custom, method 7. utility
8. behavior, practice 9. treatment
10. convention
use... 3. try 5. apply, avail, exert,
spend, treat, wield 6. employ,
expend, occupy 7. consume, exploit,
utilize 8. function 10. manipulate
11. consumption, utilization
use (pert to)...
abusive language.. 4. rail
divining rod.. 5. dowse
frugally.. 5. stint

pert to words.. 7. neology, verbose
8. enallage, pleonasm 9. verbosity
poetry.. 4. vail
refrain from.. 7. boycott
subterfuge.. 7. chicane
up.. 3. eat 7. consume, deplete,
exhaust, fatigue
useful... 4. good 5. utile 7. helpful
9. practical 10. beneficial,
commodious 11. serviceable,
subservient 12. advantageous,
instrumental
usefulness... 5. avail, value 6. profit
7. utility 13. conduciveness
useless... 4. idle, null, vain 6. futile,
otiose 7. of no use 8. bootless,
hopeless 9. fruitless, worthless
10. fifth wheel 11. ineffectual,
superfluous 12. unprofitable
13. unserviceable 14. good for
nothing
uselessness... 8. futility 9. inutility
10. inefficacy
usher... 4. lead, page 5. guide
6. escort 7. chobdar, teacher
9. attendant, harbinger, precursor
10. doorkeeper, forerunner,
inaugurate
usquebaugh... 6. whisky 7. cordial
ustion... 7. burning 13. cauterization
ustulate... 8. scorched 10. discolored
usual... 7. average, typical, usitate
8. everyday, frequent 11. status in
quo
usuer... 5. shark 6. loaner 7. Shylock
11. moneylender
usurp... 4. take 5. seize 6. assume
8. arrogate 11. appropriate
Utah...
capital.. 12. Salt Lake City
city.. 5. Logan, Ogden, Provo
7. Bingham
dam.. 10. Glen Canyon 12. Flaming
Gorge
lake.. 6. Powell 9. Great Salt
mountain.. 5. Uinta 7. Wasatch
9. King's Peak
name desired.. 7. Deseret
natural wonder.. 4. Zion 5. Bryce
13. Rainbow Bridge
settled by.. 7. Mormons 12. Brigham
Young 15. Latter–day Saints
State admission.. 10. Forty–fifth
State motto.. 8. Industry
State nickname.. 7. Beehive
utensil... 3. mop, pan, pot 4. tool
5. broom, brush 6. device, ramrod
7. skillet, sweeper 9. apparatus,
appliance, implement 10. instrument
utilitarian... 5. plain 6. useful
8. economic 9. practical
10. functional 12. matter–of–fact
utility... 3. use 4. tool 5. avail
6. profit 7. benefit, service
9. appliance, happiness, implement
10. usefulness
utmost... 4. best, last 5. final
7. extreme, maximum, supreme
8. farthest, greatest 9. uttermost
11. most distant
Utopia... 4. Eden 6. heaven, island
(imaginary) 7. Erewhon 8. paradise

9. fairyland, Shangri–La
10. millennium
utopian ... 5. ideal 6. Edenic
   8. Quixotic, romantic 9. visionary
   10. chimerical, idealistic, millennial
utter ... 3. say 4. emit, pass, tell, vent
   5. issue, sheer, speak, total, voice
   6. assert, entire, mumble, reveal
   7. deliver, divulge, express, extreme,
   publish, unusual 8. abnormal,
   absolute, complete, disclose,
   disperse, intonate 9. downright,
   enunciate, out–and–out, pronounce
   10. peremptory 11. unqualified
   13. unconditional
utter (pert to) ...
   harshly .. 3. rap 4. bray
   heedlessly .. 4. blat
   in devotion .. 4. pray
   in slow tone .. 5. drawl
   musically .. 6. warble
   publicly .. 4. tell 5. voice 7. enounce
   softly .. 6. murmur 7. whisper
   want .. 9. indigency 11. destitution

with effort .. 5. heave
with impulse .. 9. ejaculate
without voice .. 4. surd 7. spirate
utterance (pert to) ...
   dogmatic .. 6. dictum
   gushing .. 8. effusion
   rhythmic .. 7. cadence
   voice .. 8. phonesis, speaking
      9. phonation 12. articulation
   wise .. 6. oracle
utterer of pithy remarks ... 8. aphorist
utterly ... 5. fully, stark 7. totally
   8. entirely 10. absolutely, completely
   17. straightforwardly
uttermost ... 5. final 6. utmost
   7. extreme
utu ... 6. reward 12. compensation,
   satisfaction
uva ... 5. fruit, grape
uvate ... 8. conserve (grape)
uvea ... 4. iris
uxor ... 4. wife
uxoricide ... 10. wife murder
Uz (Bib) ... 8. Job's home
Uzziel ... 5. angel (Paradise Lost)

V

V ... 5. notch 6. letter (22nd), symbol
   14. five–dollar bill
vaagmer ... 8. dealfish (mare of the
   sea)
Vac (Hind) ... 7. goddess (of speech)
vacant ... 4. free, idle, void 5. blank,
   empty, inane 6. barren, devoid
   7. leisure, vacuous 8. unfilled
   10. disengaged, untenanted
   11. thoughtless 12. unencumbered
   14. expressionless
vacate ... 4. free, quit, void 5. annul,
   empty, leave 6. depart 7. abandon
   8. abdicate, abrogate, evacuate,
   withdraw
vacation ... 4. rest 5. leave 6. outing,
   recess, repeal 7. nonterm, respite
   8. furlough, justitum 10. recreation
   12. intermission 14. leave of
   absence
vacation place ... 3. spa 4. lake, park
   5. beach 6. forest, resort
   9. mountains
vaccination ... 11. inoculation
vaccine (pert to) ...
   discoverer .. 4. Salk 6. Jenner
   protection for .. 5. virus 6. cowpox
   term .. 5. lymph, serum, virus
vacillate ... 4. sway 5. waver 6. dacker
   (daiker), seesaw, teeter, totter
   7. flutter, stagger 8. hesitate,
   titubate 9. fluctuate, oscillate
   13. procrastinate
vacillation ... 5. doubt 8. wavering
   9. faltering, hesitancy 10. fickleness,

indecision, titubation 11. oscillation,
   uncertainty 12. irresolution
   14. changeableness
   15. procrastination
vacuate ... 5. empty 8. evacuate
vacuous ... 4. dull, void 5. blank,
   empty 6. stupid 8. unfilled
   9. senseless 11. empty–headed,
   thoughtless 13. unintelligent
vacuum ... 3. gap 4. void 9. emptiness
   11. rarefaction
vagabond ... 3. bum, vag 4. hobo
   5. lorel, scamp, tramp 6. beggar,
   picaro, rascal, rodney 7. vagrant,
   wastrel 8. Bohemian, brodyaga,
   wanderer 10. ne'er–do–well
vagary ... 4. whim 5. caper, fancy,
   jaunt, prank, trick 6. notion, ramble
   7. caprice, whimsey (whimsy)
   9. excursion, wandering
   10. digression 13. manifestation
vagrant ... 3. bum 4. hobo 5. rogue,
   tramp 6. roving, truant 7. nomadic,
   prowler, wayward 8. brodyaga,
   vagabond, wanderer 9. desultory,
   deviative, itinerant 10. capricious
vague ... 3. dim 4. dark, hazy 5. loose,
   misty 6. dreamy 7. obscure,
   shadowy, unfixed 8. confused,
   formless, nebulous, not clear
   9. ambiguous, unsettled, wandering
   10. indefinite, indistinct, intangible
   13. indeterminate
vail ... 3. tip 4. doff (a hat), dole
   5. avail, bribe, yield 6. humble,

submit 7. descend 8. gratuity
10. beneficial 12. advantageous
vain... 4. idle 5. empty, proud
6. devoid, futile, otiose, snooty
7. foolish, trivial, useless 8. arrogant,
boastful, nugatory 9. conceited,
fruitless, worthless 10. unavailing,
unrewarded 11. empty—headed,
overweening, unimportant
12. vainglorious
vain boasting... 11. fanfaronade
vainglorious... 4. vain 7. heroics
8. boastful 9. gasconade
vair... 3. fur
vajra (Buddh)... 7. diamond, trident
(Indra's) 10. adamantine
11. thunderbolt
valance... 5. drape 6. border, pelmet,
ruffle 7. curtain, drapery, hanging
vale... 4. dale, dell, glen 5. earth,
glade, world 6. valley
valediction... 5. adieu 7. address
8. farewell 11. valedictory
valedictory... 7. address, oration
10. apopemptic 11. leave—taking,
valediction
Valentine (pert to)...
romance.. 5. Orson 8. love song
Saint.. 6. martyr (Rom) 7. holiday
8. feast day
State.. 7. Arizona (adm 2/14/1912)
sweetheart.. 11. one's beloved
valerian... 4. drug 5. plant 7. panacea
valet... 3. man 7. Crispin
9. attendant, cameriere, chamberer
10. manservant 11. body servant
14. valet de chambre
valetudinarian... 6. infirm, shut—in,
sickly, weakly 7. invalid
11. languishing
Valhalla (Valhall)... 8. Pantheon
(Bavaria) 10. hall of Odin (Norse
Myth)
valiant... 4. bold, fine 5. brave
6. heroic, strong, sturdy 7. doughty
8. intrepid, stalwart, vigorous,
virtuous 9. steadfast 10. chivalrous,
courageous 11. meritorious
12. stouthearted
valid... 4. good, just, true 5. legal,
sound 6. cogent, lawful, proved
7. binding, weighty 9. authentic,
effective 10. sufficient 11. efficacious
12. well—grounded
validate... 6. affirm, attest 7. confirm
8. legalize 12. substantiate
validity... 5. force 7. cogency
9. authority, soundness
14. substantiality
Valjean (pert to)...
discoverer.. 6. Javert
friend.. 6. Marius
hero of.. 13. Les Miserables (Victor
Hugo)
protégé.. 7. Cosette
valley... 4. dale, dell, dene, glen, vale,
wady 5. glade, gully 6. coulee,
dingle, ravine, trough 10. depression
valley (pert to)...
anatomy.. 9. vallecula
circular.. 6. rincon
deep.. 6. canyon

geology.. 5. atrio
India.. 5. dhoon
Jerusalem (near).. 6. Hinnom
7. Gehenna, Rephaim
moon.. 5. rille
open.. 6. canada
where David killed Goliath.. 4. Elah
(Bib)
valonia oak... 6. camata (fruit)
9. evergreen
valor... 5. merit, worth 6. virtue
7. bravery, courage, heroism,
prowess 8. boldness, chivalry
9. gallantry 11. distinction
12. fearlessness
valuable... 4. dear 5. asset 6. prized,
useful, worthy 8. precious
9. estimable, treasured
10. worthwhile
value... 3. par, use 4. rate 5. price,
prize, worth 6. assess, esteem,
parity, status 7. apprize (apprise)
cherish, compute, meaning, respect,
utility 8. appraise, estimate, evaluate
9. valuation 10. estimation,
excellence, importance
value (pert to)...
equal.. 6. parity
least possible.. 5. plack
nominal.. 3. par
reduction.. 12. depreciation
valueless... 4. baff 9. worthless
10. threepenny 14. good-for-nothing
valve... 3. tap 4. cock, door, gate
6. faucet, piston, spigot 7. petcock
vamoose... 2. go 4. blow, scat
5. leave, scram 6. beat it, decamp
7. skiddoo 9. skedaddle
vamp... 4. hose, sock 5. flirt, patch,
upper 6. recoct, repair, seduce
7. beguile, bewitch, concoct, touch
up 9. improvise, temptress, transform
vampire... 3. bat 5. fiend, ghost,
lamia, witch 6. Alukah 9. bewitcher,
sorceress, temptress 11. bloodsucker,
extortioner 12. extortionist
van... 4. lead, wing 5. front, wagon
6. shovel, summit, winnow 7. vehicle
9. forefront 10. baggage car
12. advance guard
vandal... 3. Hun 7. wrecker
9. destroyer, mutilator, plunderer
10. iconoclast
vandalize... 3. mar 5. wreck 6. deface
Vandyke... 5. beard, brown 6. artist,
collar 7. picture
vane... 4. cock 11. weathercock,
weathervane
vanish... 3. die 4. fade, flee, melt,
pass 6. perish 8. evanesce 9. cease
to be, disappear
vanity... 5. pride 6. egoism
7. conceit, egotism, falsity 8. futility
9. arrogance, emptiness, vainglory
10. hollowness 11. fatuousness,
self—conceit 12. boastfulness
13. dressing table
vanity case... 4. etui 6. make—up
7. compact 9. cosmetics
vanquish... 3. win 4. beat, best, rout
5. expel 6. defeat, subdue
7. conquer 8. confound, overcome,

suppress, surmount 9. overthrow
vantage . . . 4. gain 9. advantage
  10. perquisite 11. opportunity,
  superiority
vapid . . . 3. dry 4. dead, dull, flat
  5. inane, stale 7. insipid, prosaic
  8. lifeless 9. pointless, tasteless
  10. spiritless, unanimated
  11. indifferent 13. uninteresting
vapor . . . 3. air, fog, gas 4. fume, haze,
  mist 5. brume, cloud, fancy, humor,
  smoke, steam 6. breath, bubble
  7. halitus 8. humidity, illusion,
  phantasm 9. evaporate 10. exhalation
vaporous . . . 4. vain 5. foggy, misty
  6. cloudy, steamy 7. gaseous
  8. ethereal, fanciful, fleeting
  13. unsubstantial
variable . . . 6. fickle, fitful, mobile
  7. protean, unequal 8. shifting,
  unstable, unsteady 10. capricious,
  changeable, inconstant
variance . . . 3. out 7. dissent
  9. deviation, disaccord
  10. contention, difference
  11. discrepancy 12. disagreement
varied . . . 5. mixed 6. daedal, motley
  7. changed, dappled, diverse,
  mottled, piebald, several, various
  8. speckled 9. different
  10. variegated 11. diversified
variegated . . . 5. pinto 6. daedal,
  motley, varied 7. dappled, diverse,
  mottled, painted 9. different
  11. diversified, many–colored
variegation . . . 7. variety 9. diversity
  10. multicolor
variety . . . 4. kind, mode, sort 5. class
  6. change 7. species 9. diversity,
  variation 10. assortment, difference
  13. entertainment
variola . . . 6. cowpox 8. smallpox
various . . . 4. many 6. divers, sundry
  7. diverse, several 8. manifold,
  variable 9. different, many–sided,
  uncertain 10. changeable, inconstant,
  variegated 11. diversified
varnish . . . 4. spar 5. adorn, gloss,
  japan, paint 7. distort, falsify, furbish,
  lacquer, pretext 8. coat over
  9. embellish
Varuna (pert to) . . .
  art consorts . . 5. Jumna 6. Ganges
  deity . . 6. cosmic (supreme)
  god . . 3. sea
  Vedic equiv . . 13. Avestan Ormazd
  Vedic Relig . . 5. Aditi (fem deity)
vary . . . 5. alter, range, shift 6. change,
  differ, modify 7. deviate, dissent,
  diverge 8. disagree 9. alternate,
  diversify, fluctuate, vacillate, variegate
  13. differentiate
vas . . . 4. duct 6. pledge, surety, vessel
vascular (pert to) . . . 5. hemic (haemic)
  6. vessel (blood, lymph) 7. tubular
  9. vesicular 10. hot–blooded
vase . . . 3. jar, urn 4. bowl 5. ascus
  6. vessel 8. ornament
  10. cassolette, jardiniere
vase (pert to) . . .
  covered . . 7. potiche
  Etruscan . . 7. canopic

Greek . . 5. askos, diota 6. deinos
  (dinos) 7. amphora
Roman . . 8. murrhine
vassal . . . 3. man 4. esne, serf
  5. helot, liege, slave 6. varlet
  7. bondman, servant, servile, subject
  9. dependent, feudatory
  11. subordinate, subservient
  12. feudal tenant
vassalage . . . 5. valor 6. fealty
  7. courage, enfeoff, prowess, slavery
  8. dominion 9. servitude
  10. subjection
vast . . . 4. huge 5. broad, great, large
  6. cosmic, mighty, untold
  7. immense, mammoth 8. colossal,
  enormous, gigantic, spacious
  9. cyclopean, extensive
  11. far–reaching
vast (pert to) . . .
  expanse . . 5. ocean 6. desert, empire,
  region
  numbers . . 6. myriad
  period . . 3. eon, era 5. cycle
  space . . 5. waste 9. boundless,
  immensity, limitless
vastness . . . 6. extent 7. expanse
  9. greatness, magnitude
vat . . . 3. bac, pit, tub, tun 4. cask,
  gyle, kier, tank 6. barrel, vessel
  7. caldron (cauldron), chessel,
  cistern, measure, salt pit 8. chessart
Vatican (pert to) . . .
  chapel . . 7. Sistine
  church . . 8. St Peter's
  city . . 10. Papal State (Rome)
  palace of . . 4. Pope
  statuary group . . 7. Laocoon
vatication . . . 8. prophecy
  10. prediction 11. prophesying
vault . . . 3. sky 4. arch, dome, leap,
  over, tomb 5. bound, crypt, enbow,
  groin 6. canopy (of heaven), coffer,
  curvet, grotto, welkin 10. depository
  11. testudinate
vaunt . . . 4. brag 5. boast
Vauxhall . . . 6. resort 13. London
  Quarter (Thames) 14. Lambeth
  Gardens
Veda (pert to) . . .
  hymns . . 8. Sama–Veda
  language . . 13. Vedic Sanskrit
  literature . . 6. sacred (most anc)
  oldest . . 7. Rig–Veda
  prose, poetry (popular) . .
  11. Atharva–Veda
  ritualistic . . 9. Yajur–Veda
Vedic (pert to) . . .
  cosmic order . . 4. Rita
  dialect . . 4. Pali
  god . . 4. Agni 5. Dyaus 6. Aditya,
  Varuna 7. Savitar
  goddess . . 5. Aditi
  hymn . . 6. mantra
  language . . 4. Pali 8. Sanskrit
  sky serpent . . 3. Ahi
  text, treatise . . 6. shakha (sakha)
  9. Upanishad
veer . . . 3. shy, yaw 4. slue, sway, turn
  5. alter, shift, sidle 6. careen,
  change, swerve 7. deviate, digress
  9. fluctuate

veery ... **6.** thrush **13.** Wilson's thrush
vegetable ... **3.** pea, yam **4.** bean,
beet, corn, leek, okra **5.** onion
6. carrot, celery, lentil, potato, radish,
squash, tomato, turnip **7.** cabbage,
lettuce, parsnip, rhubarb, shallot,
spinach (spinage) **8.** broccoli,
eggplant, rutabaga, scallion
9. artichoke **11.** cauliflower
vegetable (pert to) ...
and meat dish .. **4.** stew **6.** ragout
caterpillar .. **5.** aweto
dealer .. **8.** huckster **11.** greengrocer
12. costermonger
green .. **5.** sabzi
herb .. **7.** salsify
leafy, salad .. **5.** chard **6.** endive
7. lettuce, romaine, spinach
oil .. **7.** soybean **8.** macassar
poison .. **5.** abrin
stew .. **11.** ratatouille
sugar yielding .. **4.** beet
vegetate ... **4.** grow, rest **5.** exist
vegetation, goddess of ... **5.** Ceres
vehemence ... **3.** ire **4.** fire, fury, rage,
zeal **5.** anger, ardor **8.** violence
9. eloquence **11.** impetuosity
vehement ... **3.** hot **5.** angry, eager,
fiery **6.** ardent, fervid, heated
7. animose, furious, intense, violent,
zealous **8.** forceful, vigorous
9. impetuous **10.** passionate
vehicle ... **3.** ark, bus, cab, car, van,
wag **4.** auto, cart, dray, hack, jeep,
limo (sl), semi, shay, sled, tank
5. buggy, coach, lorry, moped, sulky,
tonga, truck, wagon **6.** go–cart,
hansom, hot rod, jalopy, landau,
sleigh, travoy, troika, wheels (sl)
7. caleche, caravan, chariot, clunker
(sl), kibitka, minibus, omnibus, phaeton,
scooter **8.** brougham, carriage,
dragster **9.** buckboard, dune buggy,
limousine **10.** automobile,
conveyance, jinrikisha (jinriksha),
motorcycle **11.** convertible
vehicle for oil colors ... **6.** megilp
(meguilp)
veil ... **3.** dim **4.** caul, film, mask
5. cloak, cover, orale, shade, velum,
volet **6.** fannel, masque, screen,
shroud, soften **7.** conceal, curtain,
garment, pretext, secrecy **8.** disguise
9. incognito **11.** superimpose
veiled ... **5.** vague **6.** masked, shaded,
velate **7.** covered **8.** shrouded
9. curtained
veiling ... **5.** tulle, voile **7.** curtain
8. covering **10.** obvelation
vein ... **3.** rib **4.** dash, hilo, lode, mood,
tang, vena, wave **5.** costa, shade,
smack, spice, tinge, touch **6.** cavity,
streak **7.** bonanza, channel, crevice,
fissure, mineral, stratum
vein (pert to) ...
arrangement .. **9.** neuration
inflammation .. **9.** phlebitis
leaf .. **3.** rib
ref to .. **5.** veiny **6.** veinal, venous
7. marbled **8.** venulose
small .. **6.** venule **7.** veinlet
stone .. **6.** gangue, matrix **9.** lodestuff

without a .. **7.** avenous
velar ... **7.** palatal, throaty **8.** gutteral
veld, veldt ... **6.** meadow **8.** bushveld
9. grassland, grassveld
velleity ... **4.** hope **6.** desire
8. volition **9.** faint hope **10.** slight
wish
vellicate ... **3.** nip **5.** pinch **6.** tickle,
twitch **9.** titillate
vellum ... **9.** parchment **10.** manuscript
(on parchment)
velocity ... **4.** pace **5.** speed
8. celerity, rapidity **9.** quickness,
swiftness **10.** speediness
velocity measure ... **4.** velo
velum ... **6.** palate (soft) **8.** membrane
velvet (pert to) ...
breast .. **9.** merganser
cotton .. **9.** velveteen
fabric .. **5.** panne **6.** velure
Japanese .. **6.** birodo
knife .. **6.** trevet
leaf .. **6.** mallow **7.** mullein
return .. **4.** gain **6.** profit
texture .. **4.** soft **5.** nappy **6.** smooth
venal ... **5.** hired **6.** venous **7.** corrupt,
salable (saleable), vedible **8.** hireling,
vendible **9.** mercenary
11. corruptible
vend ... **4.** hawk, sell **5.** trade
6. market, peddle **8.** dispense
13. publish abroad
vender, vendor ... **6.** seller **7.** alienor
vendetta ... **4.** feud **8.** bad blood
vendue ... **4.** sale **7.** auction
venerable ... **3.** old **4.** aged, hoar,
sage **5.** hoary, olden, title **6.** august,
sacred **7.** ancient, antique, classic,
elderly, revered **9.** dignified
11. reverential
venerate ... **4.** love **5.** adore **6.** revere
7. worship
veneration ... **3.** awe **4.** fear **5.** dulia,
piety **6.** esteem, latria **7.** respect,
worship **8.** devotion **9.** adoration,
reverence
Venetian (pert to) ...
barge .. **9.** bucentaur
beach, resort .. **4.** Lido
boat .. **4.** topo (toppo) **7.** gondola
bridge (famed) .. **6.** Rialto
magistrate .. **4.** doge **7.** podesta
medal (New Year's) .. **5.** osela (osella)
painter .. **6.** Titian **7.** Bellini (family),
Vecchio **10.** Tintoretto
school of .. **8.** painting
song .. **9.** barcarole
window (Arch) .. **9.** Palladian
Venezuela ...
anc name .. **12.** Little Venice
capital .. **7.** Caracas
city .. **8.** LaGuaira, Valencia
9. Maracaibo **6.** Ciudad, Guyana
13. Cuidad Bolivar
copper center .. **4.** Aroa
Falls (world's tallest) .. **5.** Angel (found
1937)
hero, liberator .. **7.** Bolivar
lake .. **9.** Maracaibo, Tacarigua
Mt .. **5.** Andes **6.** Concha, Parima,
Sierra **9.** Pacaraima
plains .. **6.** llanos

river.. 6. Caroni 7. Orinoco
sea.. 9. Caribbean
snake.. 4. lora
vengeance... 4. harm 7. revenge
  8. reprisal, requital 10. avengement,
  punishment 11. retaliation, retribution
Vengeance, goddess of (Gr)... 3. Ara,
  Ate 7. Nemesis
Vengeance, god of (Gr)... 6. Erinys
  7. Alastor
veni, vidi, vici... 19. I came, I saw, I
  conquered (Caesar)
venial... 7. trivial 9. excusable,
  tolerable 10. pardonable
  13. insignificant
Venice... see also *Venetian*
beach.. 4. Lido
bridge.. 6. Rialto
canal.. 5. Grand 8. Merceria, San
  Marco
capital of.. 7. Venetia (province)
color.. 4. blue
island.. 6. Rialto
landmark.. 9. Campanile 12. Doges'
  Palaces 13. Bridge of Sighs
of the North.. 9. Stockholm
river.. 6. Brenta
venison... 8. pemmican (pemican)
vennel... 4. lane 5. alley, sewer
  6. gutter
venom... 4. gall 5. spite, virus
  6. malice, poison 9. animosity,
  malignity, virulence
venomous... 5. toxic 6. deadly
  7. baneful, noxious 8. spiteful,
  virulent 9. envenomed, malicious,
  malignant, poisonous, rancorous
vent... 3. say 4. exit, hole, slit
  5. eject, utter 6. egress, escape,
  outlet 7. air hole, fissure, opening,
  publish, release, ventage, volcano
  8. aperture, let loose
  10. escapement
venta... 3. inn
ventilate... 3. air, fan 5. utter
  6. aerate 7. discuss, publish, refresh
  9. oxygenate
ventose... 5. windy 9. flatulent
  12. cupping glass
ventral... 7. sternal 9. abdominal
venture... 3. hap, try 4. dare, risk,
  wage 5. brave, guess, stake 6. be
  bold, chance, danger, gamble, hazard
  7. attempt, presume 8. run a risk
  9. adventure, haphazard, speculate
  10. enterprise, investment
  11. speculation, undertaking
venturesome... 4. bold, rash 5. brave,
  risky 6. daring, heroic 8. fearless,
  reckless 9. dangerous, foolhardy,
  venturous 11. adventurous,
  temerarious 12. enterprising
venturous... 4. bold, rash 5. hardy,
  risky 6. daring 8. fearless
  9. dangerous, hazardous
  11. temerarious, venturesome
venue... 4. bout, site 5. match, onset
  6. thrust 7. arrival, assault
  9. encounter
Venus (pert to)...
astronomy.. 6. planet
church.. 11. Verticordia

goddess.. 7. Victrix 9. Aphrodite
goddess of (Rom).. 6. Beauty
son.. 5. Cupid
sweetheart.. 6. Adonis
zoology.. 7. mollusk
Venus statue (marble)...
Florence.. 8. de Medici
Louvre.. 7. of Arles 8. Genetrix
Melos.. 6. de Milo
Naples.. 7. of Capua
Rome.. 8. Borghese 12. of the
  Capitol
veracity... 5. truth 7. honesty
  8. accuracy, trueness 11. correctness
  12. truthfulness
veranda, verandah... 4. pyal, stoa
  5. lanai, porch, stoep 6. loggia,
  piazza 7. gallery, portico
verb (Gram)... 5. rhema 6. action
verbal... 4. oral 5. wordy 7. literal,
  verbose 8. verbatim 9. talkative,
  vocabular
verbal noun... 6. gerund
verbatim... 6. orally 7. literal
  8. verbally 11. word for word
verbiage... 4. talk 7. chatter, diction,
  fustian, wording 8. claptrap
  9. prolixity, verbosity, wordiness
  10. redundancy
verbose... 5. wordy 6. prolix 7. diffuse
  9. redundant
verbosity... 10. redundancy
verboten... 5. taboo (tabu)
  9. forbidden 10. prohibited
verdant... 3. raw 5. color, green
  6. unripe 9. evergreen
  13. inexperienced 15. unsophisticated
verdelho... 4. wine (white)
verdict... 4. word 7. finding, opinion
  8. decision, judgment
  13. consideration
verdigris... 4. drug 5. green 6. aerugo
  7. deposit (on copper)
verecund... 6. modest 7. bashful
verge... 3. lip, rim, top 4. edge, tend,
  wand 5. brink, limit, marge, range,
  scope 6. border, emblem, extend,
  margin 7. incline 9. extremity
  10. contiguous 13. circumference
Vergil (pert to)...
birthplace.. 6. Mantua (It)
called.. 10. Roman Homer
famed as.. 4. poet
friend.. 8. Maecenas
name (last).. 4. Maro
poem.. 6. Aeneid 8. Eclogues,
  Georgics
poetic form.. 4. epic 15. heroic
  hexameter (Aeneid)
verification... 4. oath, test
  8. averment 9. collation
  12. confirmation 13. ascertainment
verify... 4. back, test 5. check, prove
  6. affirm, attest, second 7. confirm,
  support 8. maintain 12. authenticate,
  substantiate
verily... 3. yea 4. amen 5. truly
  6. certes, indeed, in fact, really
  9. certainly 10. positively
  11. confidently
verisimilitude... 5. truth 10. likelihood
  11. probability, verisimilar

veritable . . . 4. real, true 6. actual,
gospel, honest 7. genuine
9. authentic
verity . . . 4. fact 5. truth 7. honesty,
reality 8. veracity
vermilion . . . 3. dye, red 7. pigment,
vermeil 8. cinnabar
vermin . . . 4. lice, mice, rats 5. filth,
fleas, flies, moths, worms
7. bedbugs, beetles, insects, spiders,
weasels, weevils 8. riffraff, termites
9. parasites 10. centipedes,
mosquitoes 11. cockroaches
Vermont . . .
   capital . . 10. Montpelier
   city . . 5. Barre 7. Rutland
      10. Burlington 11. Brattleboro
   first town . . 10. Fort Dummer
   hero . . 10. Ethan Allen
   historic group . . 17. Green Mountain
      Boys
   lake . . 9. Champlain
   mountain . . 5. Green 7. Taconic
      9. Mansfield
   museum . . 9. Shelburne
      10. Bennington
   product . . 6. marble 10. maple sugar
   river . . 5. Otter 11. Connecticut
   State admission . . 10. Fourteenth
   State motto . . 15. Freedom and Unity
   State nickname . . 13. Green Mountain
vernacular . . . 5. lingo, local
   6. common, jargon, native, patois,
   vulgar 7. dialect 10. colloquial,
   indigenous
vernal . . . 4. mild, warm 5. fresh
   10. springlike
verse . . . 4. epic, poem, rime 5. canto,
   lyric, rhyme, stave, stich 6. poetry,
   rondel, sonnet, stanza 7. measure,
   strophe, triolet, trochee 8. limerick
verse (pert to) . . .
   art . . 10. orthometry
   book of . . 5. poesy 9. anthology
   devotion . . 8. antiphon
   form . . 7. virelay 10. villanelle
   Homeric . . 4. epic 6. epopee
   Irish . . 4. rann
   pause . . 6. cesura 9. diaeresis
      (dieresis)
   romantic . . 7. sestina
   satiric . . 6. iambic
   scripture . . 4. text
   stress . . 5. ictus
   term . . 5. ictic, meter 6. accent,
      poetic, rhythm, scheme 7. cadence
      8. eye rhyme, scansion
      10. synaeresis (syneresis)
      12. alliteration
   trivial . . 6. jingle 8. doggerel, limerick
verse (pert to feet) . . .
   eight . . 9. octameter
   four . . 10. tetrameter
   one . . 9. monometer
   three . . 7. tripody
   two . . 7. dimeter
versed . . . 5. adept 7. erudite, learned,
   skilled 8. familiar 9. practiced
   10. acquainted, conversant, proficient
versification . . . 7. prosody
   10. orthometry
versifier . . . 4. bard, muse, poet

5. rimer 6. rhymer 7. poetess
8. ballader, eulogist 9. poetaster,
rhymester
version . . . 7. edition 9. rendition
10. paraphrase 11. translation
version, Bible . . . 5. Douay, Greek,
Latin 6. Coptic, Geneva, Gothic, Italic
(Itala) 7. Aramaic, Bishops', Luther's,
Revised, Targums, Vulgate
8. Cranmer's, Georgian, Matthew's,
Peshitta, Slavonic 9. Apocrypha, King
James, Serampore 10. Pentateuch,
Septuagint 11. Alexandrian
vers libra . . . 9. free verse
verso (opp of recto) . . . 7. reverse
9. back cover 12. left-hand side
versus . . . 3. con 7. against 8. contrast,
opposite 11. alternative
vertebra, vertebrae . . . 4. axis
8. backbone 12. spinal column
vertebrate . . 6. linked 8. well-knit
9. backboned
vertebrates (pert to) . .
   division . . 6. somite 10. Vertebrata
   feathered . . 5. birds
   group . . 4. Aves 7. Amniota
vertex . . . 3. top 4. apex 6. summit
11. culmination
vertical . . . 5. apeak, erect, plumb,
sheer 6. height 7. upright
10. upstanding 13. perpendicular
vertical panel . . . 5. stile
verticil . . . 5. whorl 6. circle
vertigo . . . 5. dinus 6. megrim
9. confusion, dizziness, giddiness
11. disturbance 12. bewilderment
verve . . . 3. pep 4. dash, élan 5. vigor
6. energy, fervor, spirit 8. vivacity
9. animation 10. liveliness
vervet . . . 6. monkey
very . . 3. erl (comb form) 4. much,
real, très, true 5. truly, utter
6. actual, in tact, really 7. exactly,
genuine 8. absolute, especial,
peculiar, truthful 9. extremely,
precisely, veracious, veritable
10. legitimate 11. exceedingly
Very light . . . 5. flare 6. signal (Very
system)
vesica . . . 7. bladder
vesicate . . . 7. blister
vesicle . . . 3. sac 4. cyst 5. bulla
6. bubble, cavity, vessel 7. bladder,
blemish, blister
Vespa . . . 4. wasp 6. hornet
vespers . . . 6. prayer 7. service
8. ceremony, evensong
vessel . . . 3. ark, can, cup, jar, jug,
mug, pod, pot, tub, urn, vas, vat
4. boat, bowl, dhow, drum, duct,
ewer, junk, olla, olpe, proa, said,
seed, ship, tank, vase, yawl 5. bocal,
craft, crock, cupel, glass, gourd,
jorum, ketch, stein 6. aftaba, aludel,
ampule, barrel, bottle, bucket, caster,
cutter, dipper, firkin, goblet, kettle,
picard, retort, trader, trough
7. catboat, cistern, coracle, cruiser,
frigate, pitcher, psykter, steamer,
tankard, utensil 8. aiguière, ciborium,
decanter, demijohn, hogshead,
schooner 9. alcarraza, catamaran,

privateer, washbasin 10. receptacle
11. earthenware
vessel (pert to)...
  anc.. 3. nef 5. yanky 6. bireme
    7. caravel, galleon, trireme
  Arab.. 4. dhow
  baptismal.. 4. font 7. piscina
  chemist.. 4. etna 6. aludel, beaker,
    retort
  Columbus.. 7. caravel
  cooking.. 9. autoclave
  druggist.. 4. vial 5. phial 8. gallipot
  Dutch.. 4. koff 5. yanky 6. galiot
    (galliot)
  Eccl.. 3. ama, pyx 4. wine 5. amula
    7. stamnos
  Hebrides.. 7. birlinn (birling)
  heraldry.. 7. lymphad
  India.. 6. shibar
  Mediterranean.. 5. xebec 6. settee
    (setee), tartan 7. polacre
  merchant.. 6. argosy 7. baggala
  Nile houseboat.. 8. dahabeah
  oil–burning.. 7. cresset
  part.. 4. deck, keel, prow, skeg
    5. brail 8. steerage
  sacred.. 3. ama
  Scottish.. 6. pourie
  Thames (fishing).. 6. bawley
  Venice.. 9. bucentaur
  war.. 3. sub 5. Maine 6. corvet
    7. carrier, cruiser, felucca, flattop,
    Monitor 9. submarine
    11. dreadnaught 12. Old Ironsides
vessel (sailing)... 3. hoy 4. bark, brig,
  koff, proa, saic, ship, yawl 5. ketch,
  sloop, smack, xebec
vest... 4. robe 5. endow, gilet
  6. invest, jerkin, linder, weskit
  7. furnish, garment 9. waistcoat
vesta... 5. match
Vesta (Rom)... 7. goddess (Hearth)
  8. asteroid
vestal... 4. pure 6. chaste 8. virginal
vestige... 4. mark, sign 5. relic, shred,
  tinge, trace, track 7. remains
  8. footstep 9. vestigium
vestiture... 4. garb 5. dress
  8. clothing, covering
vestment... 3. alb 4. cope, garb,
  gown, hood, robe 5. amice, cotta,
  dress, ephod, miter, orale, tunic
  6. saccos, tippet 7. cassock,
  garment, maniple 8. chasuble,
  crucifix, dalmatic, scapular, surplice
  10. habiliment, omophorion
vestry... 4. room 5. group (Eccl)
  8. sacristy, wardrobe 10. repository
Vesuvius (pert to)...
  Great Eruption (79 AD).. 6. buried
  city.. 7. Pompeii 11. Herculaneum
  mountain.. 8. volcanic
  site.. 6. Naples
veteran... 4. long 7. old hand, soldier
  8. seasoned 9. practiced
  11. experienced
veterinarian... 7. farrier, surgeon
veto... 6. forbid 8. negative, prohibit
  10. disapprove 12. interdiction
vex... 3. irk 4. cark, fret, fuss, gall,
  miff, rile, roil 5. anger, annoy, harry,
  spite, tease, worry 6. bother, harass,

nettle, plague, pother, ruffle
  7. agitate, chagrin, despite, dispute,
  disturb, pervert, provoke, torment
  8. disquiet, irritate 9. displease
vexation... 7. anxiety, chagrin, fatigue,
  trouble 8. disquiet, irritate
  9. annoyance, weariness
  10. affliction, foreboding, harassment,
  irritation 11. disturbance
  13. mortification
vexatious... 5. pesky 6. thorny
  7. irksome 8. annoying 9. disturbed,
  pestilent, provoking, worrisome
  10. afflictive 11. troublesome
vexillum... 3. web 4. flag 5. cross
  6. banner, colors, ensign 7. labarum,
  pennant 8. standard 10. Jolly Roger
via... 2. by 3. way 4. away, road
  6. begone 7. by way of, passage,
  through
viaduct... 4. span 6. bridge 7. trestle
vial... 5. cruet, phial 6. bottle, caster,
  castor, vessel 7. ampoule (ampul),
  ampulla 9. container
viameter... 7. measure 8. odometer
  12. perambulator
viander... 4. host 6. vendor
viands... 4. cate, fare, food 7. viandry
  8. victuals 10. provisions
viaticum... 5. money 8. supplies
  9. allowance, last rites 10. provisions
  14. Extreme Unction
viator... 8. traveler, wayfarer
vibrant... 5. alive 7. pulsing, travale
  8. resonant, sonorous, vigorous
  9. energetic, thrilling, vibrating
  10. resounding
vibrate... 4. beat, rock, tirl, whir
  5. pulse, quake, swing, throb, waver
  6. dindle, quaver, quiver, shimmy,
  shiver, thrill 7. agitate, resound,
  tremble 8. brandish, flichter, resonate
  9. fluctuate, oscillate
vibration... 6. quiver, thrill, tremor
  7. flutter, pulsing 9. resonance,
  throbbing 11. oscillation
vibration, music... 5. trill 7. sonance,
  tremolo, vibrato
vibration measure... 9. tonometer
vicar... 5. proxy 6. curate, deputy,
  priest 9. churchman, clergyman
  10. substitute, vicegerent
vice... 3. sin 4. evil 5. crime, fault,
  taint 6. defect 7. blemish, stopper
  8. iniquity 9. depravity, in place of,
  instead of 10. corruption, substitute,
  succeeding, wickedness, wrongdoing
  11. viciousness
viceroy... 5. nabob 6. satrap
  8. governor 9. butterfly
vicinity... 6. region 9. proximity
  11. propinquity 12. neighborhood
vicious... 3. bad, ill 4. evil, foul, lewd,
  mean, ugly, vile 6. faulty, impure,
  wicked 7. corrupt, immoral, noxious
  8. depraved, spiteful 9. dangerous,
  malicious, nefarious, obstinate,
  perverted 10. iniquitous, profligate
  11. ill–tempered
vicissitude... 6. change 8. mutation,
  shifting 9. variation 10. revolution
  11. fluctuation

victim... 4. dupe, gull, prey 5. cully
6. sucker 7. patient 8. sufferer
victor... 6. captor, master, winner
8. unbeaten 9. conqueror
10. vanquisher
victor fish... 3. aku 6. bonito
Victoria, victoria... 4. plum 5. cross
(Maltese) 7. goddess 8. asteroid,
carriage 10. automobile
Victorian... 3. era 4. prim 6. stuffy
7. antique, archaic, prudish
10. antiquated 11. puritanical,
strait-laced
victorious... 7. winning 8. unbeaten
9. defeating 10. conquering,
triumphant
victory... 7. mastery, success, triumph
8. conquest 9. supremacy
victory (pert to)...
at too great cost.. 7. Pyrrhic
Day.. 9. Armistice
goddess.. 4. Nike
hymn.. 9. epinicion (epinikion)
memorial.. 6. trophy
symbol.. 4. palm
Victrola dog (symbol)... 6. Nipper
victuals... 4. food, grub 6. viands
8. supplies 11. nourishment
videlicet... 3. viz 5. to wit 6. namely
8. scilicet
vie... 3. bet 4. cope, life 5. bandy,
stake, wager 6. endure, oppose,
strive 7. compare, compete, contend,
contest, emulate 8. struggle
9. challenge
Vienna...
artist.. 4. Lieb, Pilz 6. Makart, Zauner
7. Kisling
boulevard (famed).. 11. Ringstrasse
capital of.. 7. Austria
Ger name.. 4 Wien
musician.. 5. Gluck, Haydn 6. Czorny,
Mozart 7. Strauss 8. Schubert,
Schumann 9. Beethoven
palace.. 10. Schönbrunn
park.. 6. Prater
river.. 6. Danube
Vietnam road... 14. Ho Chi Minh Trail
view... 3. aim, end, eye, ken, see
4. look, scan 5. scene, vista
6. aperçu, aspect, object, regard,
survey 7. examine, glimpse, opinion,
outlook, picture 8. attitude,
judgment, panorama, prospect
9. intention 10. appearance,
perception, scrutinize
11. contemplate, expectation
13. contemplation
vigil... 3. eve 4. wake 5. guard,
watch 6. patrol 8. watchman
9. keep guard 11. wakefulness
13. sleeplessness
vigilant... 4. agog, wary 5. alert,
awake, aware 6. awatch 7. wakeful
8. cautious, open-eyed, watchful
9. attentive, observant, sleepless
11. circumspect
vigilantes... 5. posse 9. committee
(vigilance)
vigor, vigour... 3. pep, vim, vir
4. life, zeal 5. force, power, verve
6. energy, health 7. potency,

stamina, sthenia 8. strength, validity,
virility 9. animation, fraîcheur,
vehemence 10. liveliness
vigorous... 4. able, hale, racy, spry
5. eager, frank, fresh, hardy, lusty,
tough 6. potent, robust, strong
7. healthy, zealous 8. athletic,
forceful, spirited, vehement
9. effective, energetic, sprightly,
strenuous 11. efficacious, flourishing
Viking... 4. Eric 5. rover 6. pirate
8. Norseman, Northman, sea rover
9. plunderer 12. Scandinavian
vile... 3. bad 4. base, evil, foul, mean
5. cheap, lowly, nasty 6. coarse,
filthy, impure, odious, sinful, sordid,
wicked 7. corrupt, debased, ignoble,
obscene, unclean, vicious
8. depraved, infamous 9. degrading,
loathsome, nefarious, repulsive
10. abominable, disgusting
12. contaminated
vilify... 5. abuse, curse, libel
6. debase, defame, malign, revile
7. asperse, cheapen, degrade,
slander, traduce 8. belittle, disgrace,
reproach, vilipend 9. blaspheme,
disparage 10. calumniate, stigmatize
vilipend... 6. slight 7. despise
8. belittle 9. disparage
10. depreciate, slanderous
12. calumniatory
villa... 5. aldea, dacha 9. residence,
villaette 10. villanette
village... 3. mir 4. dorp, stad 5. thorp
(thorpe), tract 6. aldeia, castle,
hamlet, pueblo
Village Blacksmith author...
10. Longfellow
villain... 4. boor, lout, ogre, serf
5. demon, heavy, knave, rogue
6. rascal 7. caitiff 9. miscreant,
scoundrel
villainous... 3. bad, low 4. base, evil,
mean, vile 6. vulgar, wicked
7. boorish, knavish 8. criminal,
rascally, terrible, wretched
9. dastardly 10. detestable, iniquitous
11. scoundrelly 13. objectionable
villous... 5. nappy 6. napped, shaggy
vim... 3. pep, zip 4. dash, élan, fire,
gimp, kick 5. drive, force, verve,
vigor 6. energy, esprit, spirit
8. strength
vinaigre... 7. vinegar
vindicate... 4. free 5. claim, clear
6. acquit, assert, avenge, defend,
excuse, uphold 7. absolve, justify,
support, sustain 8. maintain
9. exculpate, exonerate
vindication... 7. defense
vindictive... 7. hostile 8. punitive,
spiteful, vengeful 10. revengeful
11. retaliatory, retributive
vine... 3. hop, ivy 4. bine, odal
5. betel, grape, liana (liane), Vitis
7. cupseed, trailer 8. clematis,
wisteria 9. grapevine 10. chilicothe
11. honeysuckle 12. morning glory
vinegar... 4. acid, sour 6. acetum,
alegar 8. vinaigre
vinegar (pert to)...

acid.. **6.** acetic
comb form.. **5.** aceto
dregs.. **6.** mother
eel.. **4.** worm
ester.. **7.** acetate
fly.. **5.** fruit
preserve in.. **6.** pickle **8.** marinate
salt.. **7.** acetate
spice.. **8.** tarragon
tree.. **13.** staghorn sumac
Vinegar Joe (Army)... **9.** Stillwell (Gen)
vinegarroon... **8.** scorpion, vinagron
vinegary... **4.** sour, tart **7.** acetose,
   crabbed, pungent **9.** unamiable
vineyard... **3.** cru **7.** Priapus (god of)
   10. plantation
vinology *(science of)*... **5.** vines
   10. grapevines
vinous... **4.** winy **5.** color
vintner... **8.** merchant (wine)
viol... **3.** gue **4.** rope **5.** rebec, ruana
   6. vielle **7.** quinton, sarinda **9.** organ
   stop
viola... **5.** gamba **7.** sarangi **9.** organ
   stop **11.** tenor violin
violate... **5.** abuse, break, wrong
   6. defile, invade, ravage, ravish
   7. debauch, outrage, pollute, profane
   8. deflower, dishonor, mistreat
   9. desecrate **10.** transgress
violation... **7.** offense **10.** infraction
   11. anacoluthon, disturbance,
   profanation **12.** infringement,
   interruption **13.** nonobservance,
   transgression
violence... **5.** anger, force **6.** unjust
   7. assault, cruelty, outrage
   8. coercion **9.** vehemence
   10. roughhouse **11.** profanation
   12. infringement
violent... **4.** loud **5.** acute, great,
   rabid, sharp, vivid **6.** fierce, savage,
   stormy **7.** extreme, furious, intense
   8. coercive, vehement **9.** turbulent
   10. passionate **11.** tempestuous
violent (pert to)...
Norse folklore.. **8.** warriors
   9. beserkers
outbreak.. **4.** riot **6.** tumult, uproar
   8. eruption
pain.. **4.** pang **5.** throe **6.** fierce
violet (pert to)...
color.. **5.** mauve **6.** purple
   7. blue–red
dye.. **6.** archil (orchil)
emblem of.. **7.** gravity **8.** chastity
genus.. **9.** Violaceae
perfume.. **5.** irone **6.** ionone
   9. orrisroot
tip.. **9.** butterfly
violin (pert to)...
ancient.. **5.** rebab, rebec, rocta
   12. viola de gamba
bar.. **4.** fret
bass.. **11.** violoncello
bow.. **5.** arcus
city (famed).. **7.** Cremona (It)
make.. **5.** Amati **7.** Cremona
   10. Guarnerius **12.** Stradivarius
maker.. **5.** Amati **9.** Guarnieri
   10. Stradivari
reference to.. **4.** pins **5.** belly

Scot.. **6.** fiddle
small.. **3.** kit
tenor.. **4.** alto
violinist (famed)... **5.** Elman, Stern
   7. Heifitz, Menuhin
violinist, first... **13.** concertmaster
viper... **3.** asp **5.** adder, Echis, snake
   6. kupper **7.** serpent **8.** cerastes,
   ophidian **9.** scoundrel
   10. bushmaster
vir... **5.** vigor
virage... **5.** scold, shrew, vixen, woman
   7. beldame, rullion **9.** termagant
Virgil... see *Vergil*
virgin... **3.** new **4.** maid, pure
   6. chaste, maiden, vestal **8.** spinster
   9. undefiled, unsullied, untouched
   13. unadulterated
virginal... **3.** new **5.** piano (spinet)
   6. chaste, ritual **7.** natural
   8. maidenly **9.** unmarried, unsullied
Virginia...
bay.. **10.** Chesapeake
capital.. **8.** Richmond
city.. **7.** Norfolk, Roanoke
   9. Arlington, Lexington, Lynchburg
   11. Newport News **12.** Hampton
   Roads
famed sites.. **8.** Mt Vernon
   10. Monticello **12.** Williamsburg
   13. Stratford Hall
first white child born.. **12.** Virginia
   Dare
historic town.. **8.** Yorktown
   9. Jamestown **10.** Appomattox
Indian sachem.. **8.** Powhatan
mountain.. **9.** Blue Ridge
   11. Alleghenies
resort.. **13.** Virginia Beach
river.. **4.** York **5.** James **7.** Potomac,
   Rapidan **12.** Rappahannock
settlement (first).. **9.** Jamestown
State admission.. **5.** Tenth
State motto.. **17.** Sic Semper
   Tyrannis **19.** Thus Always to Tyrants
State nickname.. **11.** Old Dominion
Virgin Islands, British...
capital.. **8.** Road Town
crop.. **9.** sugar cane
group.. **7.** Leeward
number islands.. **6.** thirty
Virgin Islands, United States...
capital.. **8.** St Thomas **15.** Charlotte
   Amalia (former)
discoverer.. **8.** Columbus (1493)
largest.. **6.** St John **7.** St Croix **8.** St
   Thomas
virginity... **8.** celibacy, chastity
   10. maidenhood **12.** spinsterhood
Virgin Mary... **5.** Pietà (image) **7.** Our
   Lady **11.** Maris Stella, Mother of
   God **12.** Star of the Sea **13.** Mother
   of Jesus
viridity... **5.** youth **7.** verdure
   9. freshness, greenness **10.** grass
   color
virile... **4.** male **5.** manly **8.** forceful,
   powerful, vigorous **9.** masculine,
   masterful
virose... **5.** fetid **8.** virulent
   9. poisonous **10.** malodorous
virtu... **5.** curio **7.** antique **8.** artistry

12. love of curios 15. artistic quality, study of fine arts
virtual... 9. essential, potential 10. energizing 12. constructive
virtually... 7. morally 11. potentially, practically
virtue... 5. valor, value, worth 6. energy, purity 7. potency, probity 8. chastity, efficacy, goodness, morality 9. godliness, innocence, integrity, rectitude 11. uprightness 13. righteousness
virtue, logic... 8. aretaics
virtues, cardinal... 4. hope 5. faith 7. charity
virtuoso... 6. expert 7. scholar 11. connoisseur, philosopher
virtuous... 4. good, pure 5. brave, godly, moral 6. chaste, honest, potent 7. upright, valiant 8. valorous 9. righteous 11. efficacious
virulent... 5. acrid, rabid 6. deadly, potent 7. noxious 8. venomous 9. animosity, malignant, poisonous 10. infectious, resentment 11. acrimonious
visa, visé... 7. endorse 9. signature 11. certificate, endorsement (passport)
visage... 4. face, look 5. image 11. countenance 14. visible surface
vis-à-vis... 4. seat, sofa 8. carriage, opposite 9. encounter 10. face to face
viscera... 4. guts 6. bowels, vitals 7. insides 8. entrails 10. intestines 11. inside parts
visceral... 7. enteric 10. intestinal, splanchnic
viscid... 4. ropy, waxy 5. slimy 6. sticky 7. viscous 8. adhering, adhesive 9. glutinous
viscosity... 8. tenacity 10. stickiness
viscous... 4. ropy, sizy 5. gluey, gummy, tarry 6. mucous, sticky, viscid 7. stringy 9. glutinous 10. stickiness
vise... 3. jaw 4. tool 5. clamp, winch 6. device 7. squeeze
Vishnu (pert to)...
consort.. 3. Sri 7. Lakshim
deity (supreme).. 6. bhakti 9. preserver
eighth.. 7. Krishna
epithet.. 8. bhagavat
seventh.. 4. Rama
tenth, last incarnation.. 5. Kalki
vehicle.. 6. Garuda
visible... 4. open, seen 5. clear 6. extant, in view 7. evident, in sight, obvious 8. apparent, manifest 10. noticeable 11. discernible, perceivable, perceptible
Visigoth king... 6. Alaric
vision... 3. eye 5. dream, fancy, image, sight 6. glance, mirage 7. glimpse, imagine, specter 8. eyesight 10. apparition
vision (pert to)...
comb form.. 4. opto
daylight.. 8. photopia
defect.. 6. anopia, myopia

double.. 8. diplopia
illusory.. 5. image
lacking.. 8. purblind
measure.. 9. optometer
night.. 8. scotopia
science of.. 9. optometry
term.. 5. optic 6. ocular 9. binocular, monocular
visionary... 4. aery, airy, seer, wild 5. ideal 6. dreamy, unreal 7. dreamer, Laputan, utopian 8. delusive, idealist, quixotic, romantic 9. fantastic, imaginary 10. chimerical, rhapsodist 11. imaginative, impractical
visit... 3. see, vis 4. call, chat, go to, slum 5. haunt 6. attend, call on 10. inspection, visitation 12. conversation
visitor... 5. guest 6. caller 7. company 8. visitant
visne... 5. venue 8. neighbor, vicinage
vison... 4. mink
visor, vizor.. 4. mask 6. vizard 8. disguise 10. camouflage
vista.. 4. view 5. scene, visto 7. outlook 8. corridor, panorama, prospect
visual... 5. optic 6. ocular 11. perceptible
visualize... 7. imagine, picture 8. envisage, envision 9. objectify
vital... 4. live 5. basic 6. living, mortal, viable 7. animate, exigent, needful, organic 8. inherent, vigorous 9. essential, important, necessary, requisite 10. imperative 11. fundamental 13. indispensable
vital (pert to)...
air.. 6. oxygen
force.. 6. energy, spirit 7. neurism 8. bathmism, phrenism 9. theosophy
impulse.. 6. libido 8. instinct
organs.. 6. vitals 7. viscera
records.. 10. demography, statistics
strength.. 7. stamina
vitality... 3. sap, vim 4. life 5. vigor 8. strength 9. animation, lustiness 10. liveliness
vitals... 7. insides, viscera 9. internals 11. vital organs (heart, liver, lungs, brain)
vitamin... 6. biotin, niacin 7. carotin, thiamin 10. riboflavin 11. lactoflavin 12. ascorbic acid
vitellus... 4. yolk 7. egg yolk
vitiate... 5. spoil, taint 6. debase, impair, poison, weaken 7. corrupt, deprave, pervert, pollute 10. adulterate, demoralize, invalidate 11. contaminate
vitiated... 5. pical 6. wicked 7. corrupt, debased, spoiled 9. defective 11. ineffective, invalidated
vitiosity... 4. vice 6. defect 9. depravity 11. viciousness
vitium... 5. fault 6. defect
vitric... 9. glasslike
vitrics... 9. glassware, glasswork
vitrify... 5. glaze 13. make into glass
vitriolic... 4. acid 5. sharp 6. biting,

bitter 7. caustic 8. scathing, virulent
11. acrimonious
vituperate ... 5. abuse, curse, scold
6. berate, revile 7. censure
vituperative ... 7. abusive, railing
8. reviling, scolding 10. scurrilous
11. maledictory, opprobrious
vivacious ... 3. gay 4. airy 5. merry
6. active, lively 8. animated,
gamesome, spirited, sportive
9. energetic 12. lighthearted
vivacity ... 4. dash, élan, fire, keen,
zeal, zest 5. ardor, verve, vigor
6. energy, gaiety (gayety)
9. animation 10. liveliness
Viverra ... 6. civets 9. civet cats
vivers ... 4. food 8. victuals
vix ... 8. scarcely
vixen ... 3. cat, fox 5. scold, shrew,
witch 6. virago 9. termagant
12. female animal
viz ... 5. to wit 6. namely 9. videlicet
vizard ... 4. mask 5. guise, visor
8. disguise
vlei (vley) ... 5. creek, marsh, swamp
voar ... 6. spring (of the year)
vocabulary ... 5. words 6. jargon
7. diction, lexicon 8. glossary,
wordbook 10. dictionary
vocabulist ... 6. writer
13. lexicographer
vocal (pert to) ...
chink .. 7. glottis
composition .. 4. aria, song 5. motet
7. cantata
expression .. 4. oral 9. utterance
flourish .. 7. roulade
handicap .. 4. lisp 7. stutter
sound .. 5. vowel 6. sonant
statue .. 6. Memnon
vocalist ... 4. alto 5. basso, tenor
6. artist, cantor, singer 7. caroler,
crooner, soprano, yodeler 8. songster
10. coloratura, prima donna,
songstress
vocalization ... 11. melismatics
vocalize ... 4. sing 5. sound, utter
6. phrase
vocation ... 4. call 5. trade 6. career
7. calling 8. business
10. employment, occupation,
profession
vociferous ... 4. loud 5. noisy
7. blatant 8. brawling, strident
9. clamorous, turbulent
11. loudmouthed 12. obstreperous
vogue ... 3. ton 4. mode 5. style
6. custom 7. fashion 8. practice
10. popularity
voice ... 3. say, vox 4. alto, bass,
tone, vote, wish 5. rumor, tenor,
utter 7. divulge, opinion, soprano
8. announce, falsetto 9. utterance
10. expression 12. articulation
voice (pert to) ...
box .. 6. larynx
Greek .. 9. phthongos
handicap .. 4. lisp 7. stammer, stutter
loss of .. 7. anaudia, aphonia
loud .. 12. megalophonic
phonetics .. 9. affricate

quality .. 6. timbre (timber)
quiet .. 5. sotto
raise .. 6. insist 10. supplicate
raise against .. 5. decry 6. accuse,
object
singing, above natural .. 8. falsetto
singing, natural .. 7. dipetto
stress .. 5. arsis
with one .. 9. unanimous
12. concurrently
voiced ... 6. sonant, spoken 7. sounded
9. phthongal 11. articulated
voiceless ... 4. dumb, mute, surd
6. atonic, silent 7. spirate 9. not
voiced 12. not expressed
void ... 4. idle, lack, null, want
5. abyss, annul, egest, empty
6. devoid, hollow, vacant, vacuum
7. abolish, nothing, nullify, useless
8. evacuate 9. destitute, emptiness
10. unoccupied 11. ineffectual,
nonexistent
void of ...
interest .. 6. jejune 7. insipid
sense .. 5. inane, silly
space .. 5. blank 6. vacuum
volaille ... 4. fowl 7. poultry
volant ... 5. agile, light, quick 6. flying,
nimble 7. current 8. volatile, volitant
volatile ... 4. airy 5. light 6. fickle,
flying, lively, volant 7. alcohol,
ammonia, buoyant, flighty, gaseous
8. fleeting, vaporous 9. ephemeral,
mercurial 10. capricious, changeable,
transitory 11. vaporizable
12. lighthearted
volatile (pert to) ...
alkali .. 7. ammonia
flux .. 5. smear
liquid .. 5. ether 7. alcohol
oil .. 7. essence, perfume
volcanic (pert to) ...
glass .. 6. pumice 7. perlite
8. obsidian
matter .. 2. aa 4. lava, slag, tufa
5. trass 6. pumice 8. lapillus,
pahoehoe
mud .. 5. salse
orifice of gas issue .. 8. fumarole
ref to .. 9. excitable, explosive
11. hot-tempered
rock .. 5. trass 6. dacite 8. tephrite
saucer .. 6. crater
volcano (pert to) ...
Africa .. 11. Kilimanjaro
Alaska .. 6. Katmai 8. Wrangell
Chile .. 6. Lascar
Ecuador .. 8. Cotopaxi
goddess .. 4. Pele (Hawaii)
Guatemala .. 5. Fuego 7. Atitlan
Hawaii .. 8. Mauna Loa
Iceland .. 5. Askja, Hekla
Italy .. 4. Etna 8. Vesuvius
9. Stromboli
Japan .. 4. Fuji 9. Asamayama
Java .. 4. Gede
Mexico .. 12. Popocatepetl
Philippines .. 3. Apo (Mindanao)
Sumatra .. 6. Merapi
United States (mainland) .. 6. Lassen,
Shasta 7. Rainier
West Indies .. 5. Pelée

vole... 6. craber, rodent 8. water rat
10. field mouse 11. meadow mouse
volée... 6. flight, volley
volery (volary)... 6. aviary 8. bird
cage
volition... 4. will 6. choice
11. voluntarily 13. determination
volley... 4. fire 5. blast, salvo, shots
Voltaire... 11. philosopher (of Ferney)
voluble... 4. glib 6. fluent 8. rotating,
unstable 9. garrulous, revolving,
talkative 10. loquacious
volume... 4. book, bulk, mass, size,
tome 6. amount 7. compass
8. capacity, fullness (fulness)
9. aggregate, Decameron
10. crassitude 14. fullness of tone
voluntary... 4. free 7. prelude, willing
8. elective, intended, purposed
9. volunteer, willingly 10. deliberate,
volitional 11. intentional, spontaneous
13. not accidental
volunteer... 5. offer 6. enlist 7. proffer
9. be willing, voluntary 11. be of
service
Volunteer State... 9. Tennessee
volute... 4. turn 5. whorl 6. cilery
(cillery) 8. rolled up 10. scroll–like
voodoo... 5. magic, obeah 6. fetish
8. sorcerer
voracious... 6. greedy, hungry
8. edacious, esurient, ravening,
ravenous 9. devouring, rapacious
10. gluttonous, immoderate,
unsatiable
voracity... 5. greed 7. edacity
8. gluttony, rapacity 9. esurience
vorago... 4. gulf 5. abyss
vortex... 4. apex, eddy 5. whirl
7. tornado 8. flatworm 9. whirlpool,
whirlwind 10. waterspout
votary... 6. zealot 7. devotee
8. adherent, aesthete, follower
9. supporter 10. enthusiast
vote... 3. vow 5. elect, straw
6. ballot, choice, ticket 7. declare
8. suffrage 9. designate
10. plebescite, referendum
vote (pert to)...
group.. 4. bloc
in.. 5. elect
of assent.. 6. placet
plump.. 14. straight ticket
receptacle.. 6. situla
voter... 6. poller 7. elector 8. balloter
11. constituent
voters... 10. electorate
votive... 7. devoted 11. consecrated
vouch... 4. back 6. affirm, attest,
depose 7. confirm, declare, promise,
sponsor, support 8. accredit
9. assertion 11. attestation, bear
witness
vouchsafe... 4. give 5. deign
6. accept, assure, bestow, permit
7. concede 9. guarantee
10. condescend
voussoir... 8. keystone
vow... 3. vum 4. oath 5. swear,
vouch 6. behest, devote, pledge
7. declare, promise 8. dedicate

9. assertion 10. consecrate,
obligation 11. asseveration
12. supplication
vowel (pert to)...
change of.. 6. umlaut
contradiction.. 6. crasis 7. digraph
9. diphthong
loss of.. 7. aphesis
mark.. 6. macron
point (Heb).. 4. sere (tsere)
separate syllables.. 9. diaeresis
(dieresis)
short.. 5. breve
two, contracted.. 6. crasis
two, group.. 6. digram 7. digraph
9. diphthong (dipthong)
unaspirated.. 4. lene
vowels, none... 6. syzygy
vowels in sequence... 8. caesious
vox (pert to)...
clandestina.. 7. whisper
Dei.. 10. Voice of God
Latin for.. 5. voice
populi.. 16. voice of the people
voyage... 4. trip 6. cruise, travel
7. journey, passage, passing (sea)
9. excursion 10. expedition,
pilgrimage 11. undertaking
Vulcan (pert to)...
consort.. 4. Maia
epithet.. 8. Mulciber
feast of.. 10. Vulcanalia
god of.. 4. fire
Greek.. 10. Hephaestus
work site.. 4. Etna
vulcanite... 7. ebonite
vulcanize... 9. rubberize
vulgar... 3. low 4. lewd 5. crude,
gross 6. coarse, common, garish,
public, ribald 7. boorish, general,
obscene, profane 8. indecent,
ordinary, plebeian 9. inelegant,
offensive, unrefined 10. boisterous, in
bad taste, rowdydowdy
vulgarian... 4. snob 9. pretender
Vulgate... 10. Scriptures
vulnerable... 6. liable 7. exposed
8. beatable 9. pregnable, subject to
10. expugnable 11. conquerable,
defenseless, susceptible
vulpine... 4. foxy 6. artful, crafty,
tricky 7. cunning, foxlike 9. alopecoid
10. vulpecular
vult... 4. mien 6. aspect
10. expression 11. countenance
vulture (pert to)...
African.. 8. aasvogel
American.. 4. aura 5. urubu
6. condor 13. turkey buzzard
European.. 7. griffin 11. lammergeier
(lammergeir)
king.. 4. papa
large.. 6. condor 11. lammergeier
Mexican.. 8. zopilote
raven.. 9. Corvultur
Spanish.. 9. gallinazo
term.. 5. harpy 9. raptorial 10. bird
of prey, predacious
vulturous... 6. lupine 7. wolfish
8. ravenous 9. rapacious
vying... 7. emulous 8. rivaling
9. competing 11. competitive

W

W... 6. letter (23rd) 7. double U
WAAC... 24. Women's Auxiliary Army
Corps
waag... 6. grivet, monkey
waapa... 5. canoe
wabber... 4. cony 5. daman
wabble... see *wobble*
wabby... 4. loon (red–throated)
wabe, wabi... 5. shrub 8. huisache
wachna... 7. codfish
wad... 3. pad, ram 4. cram, lump,
mass, plug, roll, tuft 5. money, stuff,
track 6. bundle, pledge, wealth
7. stopper 8. bankroll
wadding... 4. wads 6. lining
7. padding 8. compress, stopping,
stuffing
waddle... 4. sway 5. mince 6. toddle,
wabble, wamble, wobble 10. clumsy
gait
waddy, waddie... 3. peg 4. beat, club
5. stick 6. attack, cowboy
wade... 4. ford, pass 5. study
6. attack, drudge, paddle, plodge
8. struggle
wader... 4. coot, ibis, rail 5. crane,
heron, snipe, stork 6. jaçana
9. sandpiper, shore bird
11. Grallatores
wadi, wady... 5. oasis, river 6. ravine,
valley 7. channel 11. watercourse
waeg... 9. kittiwake
wafer... 4. cake, disk, ring, seal, snap
5. bread 7. biscuit, cracker 10. altar
bread
waff... 3. wag 4. flap, wave 5. ghost
7. lowborn, vagrant 8. inferior
9. worthless 12. disreputable
waft... 4. gust, puff, wave 5. carry,
float, whiff 6. beckon, convey,
convoy, signal 7. glimpse, pennant
9. beckoning, transport
wag... 3. wit 4. card, wave 5. joker,
rogue, shake 6. signal, waddle,
wiggle 7. farceur, vibrate
8. humorist, jokester 9. oscillate
wagang... 5. death 9. departure
11. leave–taking
wage, wages... 3. bet, fee, pay, utu
4. hire, levy, pawn, risk 5. fight,
incur, stake, yield 6. employ, engage,
pledge, reward, salary 7. attempt,
contend, hire out, stipend, venture
9. emolument 10. recompense
12. compensation, remuneration
wage insurance... 7. chômage
wager... 3. bet, bid, vie 4. risk
5. sport, stake 6. gamble, hazard,
parlay, pledge 7. venture
waggish... 5. droll, merry 7. jesting,

jocular, parlous, roguish
8. humorous, sportive 9. facetious
10. frolicsome 11. mischievous
Wagnerian opera... 6. Rienzi
8. Parsifal 9. Lohengrin
10. Tannhauser
15. Gotterdammerung
wagon... 3. car, van 4. cart, dray,
tram, wain 5. araba, coach, lorry,
tonga 6. telega 7. caisson, chariot,
vehicle 8. carryall, schooner (prairie)
12. perambulator
wagon (pert to)...
canvas–covered.. 15. prairie schooner
lit.. 7. Pullman 11. sleeping car
load.. 6. fother
maker.. 10. wagonsmith, wainwright
on the (wagon).. 8. sworn off, teetotal
part.. 4. neap 5. blade, thill
police.. 3. van 10. Black Maria
sideless.. 6. rolley
wah... 5. panda
wahine... 4. wife 5. woman
8. mistress 10. sweetheart
wahoo... 4. bark, fish, peto 5. shrub
7. rock elm 8. nonsense, tommyrot
9. buckthorn, guarapucu
12. umbrella tree
waif... 4. Arab, flag 5. gamin, stray
7. vagrant, wastrel 8. castaway,
homeless, wanderer 9. lost sheep
wail... 3. cry, sob 4. howl, moan,
weep 5. mourn 6. bemoan, grieve,
lament 7. deplore, screech, ululate
11. lamentation 14. mournful outcry
wainscot... 4. base, ceil, line 5. panel
6. lining 8. paneling (panelling)
9. partition
waist... 4. wasp 5. shirt 6. basque,
blouse, bodice, dickey, middle, taille
7. corsage, garment 9. garibaldi
12. undergarment
waistcoat... 4. vest 5. benjy 6. jacket,
jerkin, weskit
wait... 4. bide, rest, stay, stop
5. dally, defer, delay, hover, serve,
tarry, watch 6. attend, expect, linger,
remain 7. observe 8. hesitate,
postpone 11. expectation
12. watchfulness
waiter... 4. tray 6. garçon, salver,
server 7. messboy, messman,
servant, steward 8. servitor
9. attendant
wait on... 4. help 5. await, cater,
serve 6. escort 7. toady to
9. accompany
waive... 5. defer, forgo (forego)
6. desert, give up, reject, vacate
7. abandon, cast off, forsake

630

8. postpone 9. disregard
10. condescend, relinquish
waka... 5. canoe
Wakashan Indian... 6. Nootka
8. Kwakiutl
wake... 4. call, stir 5. rouse, track,
vigil, waken, watch 6. arouse,
awaken, excite, revive 10. death
watch
wakeful... 5. alert 8. restless, vigilant,
watchful 9. sleepless, wide–awake
Wake Island... 6. Ottori (Jap name)
wake–robin... 4. Arum 8. Trillium
9. Anthurium 10. cuckoopint
12. philodendron
wale... 3. rib 4. welt 5. ridge, wheal
6. stripe
Wales... see also *Welsh*
anc.. 7. Cambria
city.. 7. Rhondda, Swansea
8. Hereford, Pembroke 9. Carnarvon
congress of literati.. 10. eisteddfod
deity.. 4. Bran
emblem (floral).. 4. leek
language.. 7. Cymraeg
mountain.. 7. Snowdon
native.. 5. Cymry (Kymry)
patron saint.. 5. David
port.. 7. Cardiff
river.. 3. Dee, Wye 6. Severn
sea.. 5. Irish
walk... 3. mog, pad 4. foot, gait,
hike, hoof, pace, path, plod, ramp,
step 5. allee, amble, scuff, strut,
tramp, tread 6. ramble, sphere,
stride, stroll, toddle, travel, trudge
7. conduct, shuffle, traipse
8. ambulate, behavior, frescade,
province, sidewalk 9. esplanade,
promenade, wandering
10. passageway 11. base on balls,
perambulate 13. peregrination
walk (pert to)...
a beat.. 6. patrol
about.. 11. perambulate
clumsily.. 5. mince 6. lumber, totter
health.. 14. constitutional
lime–bordered.. 9. tilicetum
proudly.. 5. strut 6. prance
public.. 4. mall 6. arcade 7. alameda
9. esplanade, promenade
wearily.. 4. limp, plod 5. tramp
6. hobble, trudge
with speed.. 10. heel and toe
walking (pert to)...
about.. 7. passant (Her)
11. peripatetic
bearlike.. 11. plantigrade
meter.. 9. pedometer
papers.. 7. deposal, the sack
8. mittimus, pink slip 9. discharge,
dismissal 10. retirement
wall... 4. dado, dike, ha–ha, mure,
pier 5. fence, levee, panel, redan
6. escarp, hinder, immure, paries,
podium, septum, shut in 7. barrier,
defense, enclose, fortify, parapet,
rampart 8. espalier, palisade, restrain,
stockade 9. barricade, enclosure,
encompass, partition, precipice,
revetment 13. fortification
wall (pert to)...

bracket.. 6. corbel, sconce
creeper.. 4. bird
go to the (wall).. 4. fail 10. go
bankrupt
lining.. 8. wainscot
lizard.. 4. newt 5. gecko
masonry.. 9. revetment
pert to.. 5. mural 8. parietal
recess.. 5. niche 6. alcove
Street.. 9. Manhattan 11. money
market, stock market
up.. 6. immure
wallaby... 8. kangaroo, Macropus,
wallaroo 10. paddymelon
wallah, walla... 5. agent 6. master,
person 7. servant
waller... 4. wels 9. saltmaker,
sheatfish
wallet... 3. bag 4. pack, poke, sack
5. purse 8. billfold, knapsack
10. pocketbook 12. porte–monnaie
walleye... 9. exotropia 10. strabismus
wallow... 4. fade, sail 5. surge
6. grovel, welter, wither 7. debauch,
founder, insipid 8. flounder,
kommetje, nauseous 9. tasteless
walnut... 6. bannut
walrus... 3. pod (group) 5. morse
6. mammal, sea cat 8. pinniped
9. rosmarine (fable) 10. pinnipedia
Waltonian... 6. angler 16. disciple of
Walton (Izaak)
wamble... 5. twist 6. quiver, ramble,
rumble, totter, writhe 7. revolve,
stagger, wriggle
wame... 4. room, womb 5. belly
7. stomach
wampum... 4. peag 5. beads, money,
uhllo 6. shells 7. jewelry, roanoke
8. ornament 10. wampumpeag
wan... 3. dim, sad 4. ashy, dark, pale,
sick 5. ashen, black, dusky, faint,
lurid 6. dismal, gloomy, pallid, sickly
7. ghastly, languid 9. deathlike,
sorrowful 10. lusterless
11. lead–colored
wand... 3. rod 4. mace, pole
5. baton, osier, staff, stick (magic)
6. switch, wattle 7. pointer, rhabdos
(magic), scepter (sceptre)
8. caduceus 9. horsewhip
wander... 3. err, gad 4. moon, rave,
roam, rove 5. drift, prowl, range,
stray 6. cruise, depart, ramble, stroll,
travel 7. digress, meander, saunter,
traipse 8. divagate, traverse
9. circulate, itinerate, scamander
11. peregrinate
wanderer... 4. Arab, waif 5. gypsy,
nomad, rover 6. ranger, roamer,
truant 7. migrant, pilgrim, vagrant
9. butterfly, itinerant, straggler
10. covenanter 12. peregrinator
wandering... 5. vague 6. astray,
errant, roving, vagary 8. aberrant,
delirium, straying 9. delirious,
deviating, deviation, itinerant
10. circuitous, discursive, journeying
11. noctivigant, perambulant
13. peregrination
wandering (pert to)...
bird.. 9. albatross

long .. 7. odyssey
minstrel .. 4. bard 10. troubadour
stars .. 12. seven planets
tattler .. 9. shore bird
votary .. 6. palmer
wanderoo ... 6. langur, monkey
   7. macaque
wand–shaped ... 7. virgate
wane ... 3. age, ebb 4. fail, sink, want
   5. abate, peter 6. defect, lessen,
   recede, repine 7. decline, grow dim,
   subside 8. decrease, diminish
   10. defervesce 13. deterioration
wanga ... 5. charm, spell 6. voodoo
   7. philter, sorcery
wangle ... 4. fake, plot 6. adjust,
   juggle, obtain, totter, wiggle
   7. finagle (finaigue), wriggle
   8. contrive, maneuver (manoeuvre)
   9. extricate 10. manipulate
want ... 4. lack, miss, need, wish
   5. crave 6. dearth, desire, hunger,
   penury 7. absence, craving, lacking,
   poverty 8. scarcity, shortage
   9. deficient, indigence, privation
   10. inadequacy 11. destitution,
   requirement
want (of) ...
appetite .. 6. asitia
desire .. 11. inappetence
lacking .. 4. sans 5. out of 7. empty
   of, scant of, short of 8. bereft of
   10. deprived of
power .. 5. atony
sense (good) .. 5. folly
wanting ... 4. void 5. minus, needy
   6. absent, bereft, devoid 7. lacking,
   missing, short of, without
   9. deficient, destitute, imperfect
wanting (pert to) ...
be found .. 9. fall short 10. be inferior
confidence .. 11. distrustful
in energy .. 6. atonic
in firmness .. 7. flaccid
in intelligence .. 12. feebleminded
wanton ... 3. gay 4. lewd 5. merry
   6. frisky, harlot, unruly 7. immoral,
   lustful, wayward 8. flagrant, insolent,
   sportive, unchaste 9. dissolute,
   merciless 10. capricious, frolicsome,
   licentious 11. extravagant
   13. undisciplined
wapiti ... 3. elk 4. deer, stag
war ... 5. fight 6. attack, battle
   8. conflict
war (pert to) ...
agreement .. 6. cartel
cause of .. 10. casus belli
club .. 4. mace
fleet .. 6. armada
gas .. 8. adamsite
German .. 5. krieg 10. blitzkrieg
god .. 3. Ira, Tyr 4. Ares
goddess .. 5. Bella 6. Ishtar
hating .. 13. misopolemical
hawk .. 5. jingo 7. bailiff
horse .. 5. steed 7. charger
   8. partisan 10. campaigner, politician
of words .. 9. logomachy
religious .. 5. jihad (jehad)
vessel, ship .. 3. sub 7. cruiser, frigate
   8. corvette (corvet) 9. destroyer,

   submarine 11. dreadnought
   (dreadnaught)
war bird ... 7. aviator, tanager (scarlet)
warble ... 4. sing 5. carol, trill, yodel
   6. quaver 7. twitter, vibrate
warbler ... 4. wren 6. singer
   8. blackcap, grosbeak, redstart,
   songster 9. beccafico 10. bluethroat
   11. whitethroat
ward ... 4. jail, part, rule 5. watch
   6. govern, prison 7. custody, keeping
   8. district, garrison, guardian,
   watchman 9. dependent
   10. stronghold 12. guardianship
ward (pert to) ...
division .. 4. army, jail 6. forest
   8. hospital
French .. 14. arrondissement
heeler .. 8. henchman 10. politician
off .. 4. fend 5. fence, parry, repel,
   stave 7. expiate, forfend, prevent
warden ... 5. guard, nazir 6. dizdar
   (disdar), jailer, keeper, ranger, sexton
   7. alcaide (alcaid), turnkey
   8. director, guardian, official,
   watchman 9. concierge, custodian
   10. gatekeeper
warder ... 6. warden 7. turnkey
wardrobe ... 4. room 6. closet
   7. almirah, apparel, cabinet, clothes
   8. costumes 12. clothespress
ware ... 4. sage, wary, wise 5. aware,
   china, goods, spend 6. shrewd
   7. careful, heedful, pottery, prudent,
   seaweed 8. cautious, vigilant
   9. cognizant, commodity, conscious,
   porcelain 11. commodities,
   earthenware, merchandise
warehouse ... 4. silo 5. depot, étape
   6. fonduk (fondouk), godown
   7. storage 8. entrepôt
warfare ... 7. contest 8. conflict,
   struggle 11. hostilities 12. armed
   contest
wariness ... 7. stealth 8. distrust
   9. chariness, suspicion
warlock ... 6. wizard 7. monster (Myth)
   8. conjuror, magician, sorcerer
warm ... 3. red 4. heat, keen, mild
   5. angry, calid, eager, humid,
   muggy, tepid, toast 6. ardent, excite,
   genial, hearty, heated, torrid
   7. clement, cordial, fervent
   8. friendly, generous 10. responsive
   11. sympathetic 12. affectionate,
   enthusiastic 13. near discovery, near
   the object (see also *hot*)
warm (pert to) ...
bath .. 5. therm
growing .. 9. calescent
hearted .. 4. kind 6. hearty, kindly,
   tender 7. cordial 8. friendly,
   generous 11. sympathetic
   12. affectionate
pert to .. 7. thermal
praise .. 8. encomium
room .. 10. tepidarium
springs (Rom) .. 7. thermae
warmblooded ... 6. ardent 9. irascible
   13. homoiothermic, quick–tempered
   14. haematothermal (hematothermal)
warmed over ... 5. stale, trite

8. rehashed, reheated 9. rechauffé, twice–told

warmth . . . 4. élan, glow, heat, zeal 5. ardor 7. ardency, thermal 8. fervency 9. animation, eloquency, geniality, vehemence 10. enthusiasm, excitement 11. calefaction, earnestness

warn . . . 4. flag 5. alarm, alert 6. advise, exhort, inform, notify, remind, signal 7. apprise (apprize), caution, counsel, previse 8. admonish, forebode, threaten 9. reprehend

warning . . . 4. bell, omen 5. alarm, alert, radar, siren 6. alarum, beacon, beware, caveat, signal, threat, tocsin 7. blinker, sematic, summons 10. admonition, admonitive 12. caveat emptor

warp . . . 4. bend, bias, hurl, sway, turn, woof 5. fling, throw, twist, weave 6. buckle, swerve 7. contort, deflect, distort, pervert 9. fabricate 10. aberration, distortion 12. misinterpret

warp (pert to) . . . cross threads . . 4. woof threads . . 5. lease 6. stamen yarn . . 3. abb

warragal, warrigal . . . 5. dingo, horse, myall

warrant . . . 4. earn, writ 5. order 6. attest, ensure, permit, secure 7. defense, justify, precept, promise, voucher 8. document, guaranty, sanction, security 9. authorize, guarantee, safeguard 10. credential, instrument, protection 11. acknowledge, certificate 13. authorization

warranty . . . 4. writ 5. proof 7. promise, warrant 8. guaranty, sanction, security 13. authorization

warrior . . . 4. hero, impi 5. brave 6. Amazon 7. fighter, martial, soldier 10. halberdier

warrior (pert to) . . . Bib . . 4. Ehud female . . 6. Amazon Indian . . 6. sannup Roman . . 9. gladiator Trojan . . 6. Agenor, Hector Zulu . . 4. impi 7. Kaffirs

Warsaw (pert to) . . . capital . . 6. Poland river . . 7. Vistula suburb . . 5. Praga

wary . . . 3. shy 5. alert, canny, chary, leery 7. careful, guarded, prudent 8. cautious, discreet, watchful 10. economical 11. circumspect

wash . . . 3. lap, pan 4. lave 5. bathe, clean, elute, flush, leach, marsh, paint, purge, rinse, slosh, swash 6. debris, drench, dry bed (river), purify, splash 7. cleanse, immerse, launder, overlay, shampoo 8. ablution 9. lixiviate

wash (pert to) . . . basin . . 4. bowl 6. lavabo bear . . 7. raccoon

dish . . 11. pied wagtail for gold . . 3. pan one's hands of . . 6. give up, refuse 10. relinquish out . . 4. fade 5. elute, flunk 7. failure, freshet sale (finance) . . 10. fictitious

washing . . . 7. coating 8. ablution 9. drenching

Washington, DC (famed sites) . . . 7. Capitol (Bldg), The Mall 8. Pentagon, Treasury 10. Blair House, White House 11. Mount Vernon 12. Ford's Theater (Lincoln Museum), Supreme Court 14. cherry blossoms 15. Iwo Jima Monument, Lincoln Memorial 16. National Archives, Naval Observatory 17. Jefferson Memorial, Library of Congress 18. Walter Reed Hospital, Washington Monument 19. Unknown Soldier's Tomb 22. Smithsonian Institution 25. Arlington National Cemetery

Washington (State of) . . . capital . . 7. Olympia city . . 6. Tacoma, Yakima 7. Everett, Seattle, Spokane 10. Bellingham, Walla Walla dam . . 10. Bonneville 11. Grand Coulee discoverer . . 4. Gray 9. Vancouver explorer . . 5. Clark, Lewis 6. Wilkes 7. Fremont Falls . . 10. Snoqualmie Fort . . 5. Lewis lake . . 5. Union 6. Chelan 8. Crescent mountain . . 7. Rainier 8. Cascades, Olympics river . . 5. Snake, White 7. Spokane 8. Columbia Sound . . 5. Puget 7. Rosario State admission . . 11. Forty–second State motto . . 4. Al-Ki (By and By) State nickname . . 9. Evergreen wind (SW) . . 7. chinook

wasp . . . 5. Sphex, vespa, whamp 6. dauber, hornet, Tiphia, vespid 8. Vespidae 12. Hymenopteron, yellow jacket

waspish . . . 4. mean 5. cross, testy 6. cranky 7. bearish, peevish, slender 8. choleric, churlish, petulant, snappish, spiteful 9. fractious, irascible, irritable 12. cantankerous

wasp's nest . . . 8. vespiary

wassail . . . 4. lark, orgy, romp 5. toast 6. frolic, shindy 7. carouse 8. beverage, carousal 9. festivity 10. salutation 11. celebration 12. drinking bout

waste . . . 3. eat 4. idle, junk, loss, rind, ross, sack, slag, vain, wear, wild 5. chaff, chips, dross, havoc, spill, trash 6. barren, desert, expend, lavish, ravage, refuse 7. atrophy, exhaust, fritter, rubbish 8. clinkers, demolish, desolate, squander 9. dissipate 10. desolation, diminution 11. destruction, devastation, dissipation, prodigality, uninhabited 12. uncultivated,

unproductive 13. unserviceable
waste (pert to)...
  allowance.. 4. tret
  away.. 3. age 6. shrink, sicken
    7. decline 8. marasmus
    11. deteriorate
  lay waste.. 4. sack 6. ravage
    7. destroy 8. decimate
  matter.. 3. ort 4. slag 5. dross
    7. clinker
  mine.. 3. gob
  silk.. 4. knob, noil 6. frison
  time.. 4. idle, lazy 5. dally 6. daddle,
    footle, loiter 10. dillydally
wasted... 7. haggard 8. phthisic
wasteful... 6. lavish 10. thriftless
    11. extravagant, improvident
wasteland... 5. heath, marsh, swamp
    6. desert, morass 8. badlands
    10. barren land, everglades
wasting... 5. aging 6. awaste
    8. marasmic 10. enfeebling
    11. consumption, devastating
    13. deteriorating
wastrel... 4. waif 5. idler 8. vagabond
    10. profligate 11. spendthrift
watch... 3. eye, spy 4. espy, heed,
    mark, mind, tend, time, wake
    (funeral) 5. guard, vigil 6. ambush,
    patrol, police, sentry 7. bivouac,
    lookout, observe 8. horologe, sentinel
    9. ambuscade, timepiece, vigilance
    11. chronometer, observation,
    wakefulness
watch (pert to)...
  chain.. 3. fob 6. Albert
  face.. 5. bezel
  maker.. 10. horologist
  military.. 5. perdu (perdue) 6. sentry
    7. vedette
  stop.. 5. timer
  tower.. 6. beacon 7. atalaya, mirador
    10. lighthouse
  word.. 6. signal 10. shibboleth (Bib)
    11. countersign
  works.. 10. escapement
watchful... 3. Ira (Heb) 4. wary
    5. alert, aware 7. careful, heedful
    8. cautious, open–eyed, vigilant
    9. observant, regardful
    11. circumspect
watchman... 5. guard 6. sentry,
    warder 8. sentinel, watchdog
    10. gatekeeper
watchword... 4. hint, word 6. signal
    8. party cry 10. intimation,
    shibboleth (Bib) 11. countersign
watchworks... 10. escapement
water... 3. eau, ice, wet 4. aqua, rain
    5. fluid, flume, spray 6. dilute,
    lagoon, liquid 7. moisten
    8. beverage, calendar, irrigate,
    sprinkle 10. adulterate
water (pert to)...
  baptismal.. 5. laver
  bath.. 7. balneum
  bird.. 4. coot, loon 5. diver, ouzel
    6. dipper 7. pintail, swimmer
    9. merganser
  bottle.. 4. olla 6. carafe
  buffalo.. 2. ox 7. carabao
  channel.. 5. canal, flume 6. strait

    8. tailrace
  chart.. 10. hydrograph
  color (art).. 9. aquarelle
  comb form.. 5. hydro 6. hydato
  congealed.. 3. ice 4. snow 5. glacé
    6. icicle
  course.. 4. clow 5. bayou, gorge,
    gully 6. nullah, ravine, sluice
    9. watergate
  cow.. 6. sea cow 7. buffalo, manatee
  cure.. 10. hydropathy
    12. hydrotherapy
  deer.. 10. chevrotain
  destitute of.. 9. anhydrous
  divination by.. 10. hydromancy
  eagle.. 6. osprey
  element.. 6. oxygen 8. hydrogen
  elephant.. 12. hippopotamus
  exhibition.. 8. aquacade
  fowl.. 7. pelican
  gauge (rain).. 8. udometer
  goddess.. 4. Nina 7. Anahita, Anaitis
  hare.. 11. swamp rabbit
  heater.. 4. etna
  history.. 10. hydrognosy
  hog.. 8. capybara
  hole.. 5. oasis 6. tinaja 7. alberca
  jug.. 4. lota (lotah), olla 5. banga
    6. hydria, kalpis
  lava.. 12. hellgrammite
  lily.. 5. lotus 6. Nuphar 7. Nelumbo
    8. Nymphaea, Victoria
    11. spatterdock
  measure.. 10. hydrometer
  meter.. 7. Venturi
  mineral.. 5. Vichy 6. Shasta
    7. Seltzer
  monster.. 6. nicker (fabled)
  nymph.. 5. naiad 6. undine
    7. Oceanid
  of oblivion.. 5. Lethe 12. river of
    Hades
  opossum.. 5. yapok (yapock)
  pert to.. 7. aqueous 8. hydatoid
  plug.. 3. tap 4. cock, cork 6. faucet,
    spigot 7. hydrant
  pocket.. 6. tinaja
  rat.. 4. vole 8. vagabond
  reddish (with iron).. 6. riddam
  reservoir (underground).. 6. cenote
  rough.. 4. eddy 5. ocean 6. rapids
    7. riptide 8. undertow
  sapphire.. 6. iolite 10. saphir d'eau
  scorpion.. 4. Nepa 7. Ranatra
  search for.. 5. dowse
  sheet of.. 5. nappe
  spirit.. 3. Nix 5. Ariel, Nixie 6. kelpie,
    nicker, sprite
  spout.. 5. spate 8. gargoyle
  sprite.. 3. Nix 5. Nixie
  stratum.. 7. aquifer
  study, science of.. 9. hydrology
    11. hydrography
  surface.. 4. ryme
  swelling.. 5. edema
  turkey.. 9. snakebird
  vessel.. 3. jug 4. ewer, lota (lotah),
    pail 5. cruse, flask 6. bottle, bucket,
    tinaja 7. pitcher, stamnos
    8. decanter
  wheel.. 5. noria 6. sakieh (sakiyeh)
    7. turbine 8. tympanum

without .. 9. anhydrous
watery ... 8. ichorous
Watling Street (London) ... 6. Galaxy
  8. Milky Way 9. Roman road
wattle ... 3. rod 4. beat, flog, plat,
  wand 5. fence, twist, weave, withe
  6. barbel, dewlap, hurdle, lappet
  8. caruncle 9. boobyalla, loose flap
  10. intertwine, interweave 11. skin
  process 12. native willow
wattlebird ... 4. crow 10. honey eater
  11. brush turkey
Wattle Day ... 7. holiday
wave ... 3. ola, sea, wag 4. flap, tide
  5. crest, eagre, flood, ridge, surge,
  swell, tilde 6. beckon, billow,
  comber, flaunt, hairdo, marcel, ripple,
  roller, signal 7. breaker, decuman,
  flutter, tsunami, vibrate 8. brandish,
  coiffure, flourish, greeting, undulate
  9. fluctuate, vibration 10. undulation
waver ... 4. reel, sway, veer 5. demur,
  quake 6. falter, quiver, totter
  7. flicker, flutter, stagger, tremble,
  vibrate 8. hesitate 9. fluctuate,
  oscillate, vacillate 12. be indecisive
wavering ... 6. fickle 8. doubtful,
  unsteady 9. desultory 10. irresolute
wavy ... 4. onde, ondé (undee)
  5. curly, snaky 6. repand, undate
  7. billowy, rolling, sinuous
  8. undulant 9. undulated
  10. undulatory
wax ... 4. cere, grow 6. candle, cerate,
  polish 7. beeswax, cerumen
  8. increase, paraffin 9. lubricant,
  lubricate 12. zietrisikite (mineral)
wax (pert to) ...
beeswax cells .. 9. honeycomb
beeswax substitute .. 7. ceresin
candle .. 6. cierge
chemical .. 9. adipocere
Chinese .. 4. pela
molded in .. 7. fictile 9. ceroplast
ref to .. 5. ceral
substance .. 5. cerin
way ... 3. via 4. lane, mode, path,
  plan, ramp, road 5. alley, habit,
  means, Milky, route, track 6. avenue,
  course, manner, method, street
  7. highway, passage 8. causeway,
  distance, sidewalk 9. banquette,
  direction, procedure
way (pert to) ...
astronomy .. 6. Galaxy 8. Milky Way
give .. 5. break, yield 6. weaken
  7. despair 10. depreciate
god of .. 6. Hermes
in .. 7. ingress 8. entrance
in a way .. 8. as it were, somewhat
  13. theoretically
inclined .. 4. ramp
out .. 4. exit 6. egress, escape
roundabout .. 6. detour
waylay ... 3. rob 5. await, seize
  6. ambush, lay for 8. surprise
  9. ambuscade
wayward ... 6. unruly 7. erratic, willful
  8. perverse, stubborn, untoward
  10. capricious, headstrong, refractory
  11. disobedient, intractable
weak ... 3. dim, lax, wan 4. pale,

puny, thin, worn 5. faint, frail, washy
  6. dotish, feeble, infirm, sickly,
  simple, unwise, watery 7. flaccid,
  foolish, fragile, insipid 8. cowardly,
  decrepit, fatigued, impotent, wavering
  9. enfeebled, exhausted, nerveless,
  powerless 10. effeminate
  11. debilitated, ineffective
  12. unconvincing
weak (pert to) ...
fish .. 7. totuava 9. gray trout
  10. squeteague
hearted .. 6. afraid 7. fearful
  12. fainthearted
kneed .. 8. cowardly, yielding
  10. irresolute
sister .. 6. coward 8. weakling
  11. mollycoddle
weaken ... 3. sap 4. tire 5. break
  6. dilute, impair, lessen, reduce
  7. cripple, disable, exhaust, unnerve
  8. enervate 9. undermine
  10. debilitate
weakness ... 4. flaw 5. atony, fault
  6. defect, foible, liking 7. failing,
  fatigue, frailty 8. asthenia, debility
  9. cowardice, impotence, infirmity
  10. feebleness, infirmness
  11. decrepitude 12. imperfection
  13. powerlessness
weal ... 4. mark, wale, welt 5. ridge,
  wheal 6. riches, wealth 7. welfare
  9. happiness, well–being
  10. commonweal
wealth ... 4. good, weal 5. money
  6. assets, mammon, riches
  7. capital, fortune, welfare
  8. opulence, property, treasure
  9. abundance, affluence, well–being
  10. prosperity 11. possessions
wealth (pert to) ...
god of .. 6. Plutus
person of .. 6. monied 7. magnate,
  opulent 9. plutocrat
pursuit of .. 10. plutomania
study of .. 9. economics, plutology
worship of .. 10. plutolatry
wealthy ... 4. rich 5. ample
  8. abundant, affluent
wealthy (pert to) ...
English slang .. 4. oofy
man .. 5. nabob 10. capitalist
rule by .. 10. plutocracy
wean ... 6. detach 8. alienate, estrange
  9. reconcile
weapon ... 3. arm, gat, gun 4. bola,
  bolo, celt, club, dart, epee, snee
  5. arrow, knife, lance, rifle, saber
  (sabre), spear, sword 6. dagger,
  musket, pistol, poleax (poleaxe),
  rapier 7. bayonet, bazooka, carbine,
  gisarme, halberd, machete, trident
  8. battle–ax (battle–axe), catapult,
  crossbow, revolver, stiletto, tomahawk
  9. derringer, Excalibur
  11. blunderbuss
wear ... 3. use 4. bear, fray, fret, show
  5. chafe, weary 7. fatigue
  12. disintegrate
wear (pert to) ...
away .. 3. eat, end 5. erode
  6. abrade 7. corrode, decline

down.. 4. tire 8. persuade
  9. influence
out.. 4. tire 5. waste 7. fatigue
weariness... 5. ennui 6. tedium
  7. boredom, fatigue 9. lassitude
wearisome... 4. hard 6. boring,
  dismal, dreary, tiring 7. irksome,
  tedious 8. tiresome, toilsome
  9. fatiguing, laborious, vexatious
  10. monotonous
weary... 3. fag, irk, sad 4. bore, jade,
  pall, tire, weak 5. bored, spent, tired
  6. plague 7. fatigue, languid
  9. forjesket
weasel... 4. stot, vare 5. ratel, stoat
  6. ermine, ferret
weasellike... 4. mink 5. otter, tayra
  9. musteline, musteloid
weather (pert to)...
  cock.. 4. vane
  glass.. 9. barometer, baroscope
  man.. 13. meteorologist
  map.. 6. isobar
weave... 3. mat 4. knit, lace, reel,
  spin, sway 5. plait, unite 6. devise,
  wattle 7. canelle, entwine, fashion
  8. contrive 9. fabricate, interlace,
  interwind 10. intertwine, intertwist
  11. push one's way
weaver bird... 4. baya, maya, taha
  5. Munia
weaving (pert to)...
  art of.. 4. loom
  fabric (rich).. 3. web 7. brocade,
  webbing
  French.. 5. lisse 8. Jacquard
  material.. 5. reeds, twigs 6. raffia
  term.. 4. beam, dent, loom, sley
  7. shuttle
  together.. 7. plexure
weazen (wizen)... 6. shrink, wither
  7. shrivel
web... 3. net, ply 4. caul, tela, trap,
  veil, warp 5. snare 6. tissue
  7. network, texture 8. filament,
  gossamer, membrane, vexillum
  12. entanglement
web (pert to)...
  footed.. 7. palmate
  like.. 4. lacy 5. telar 7. spidery
  spinning.. 6. telary 7. retiary
  term.. 5. telar
  toed.. 11. totipalmate
  winged.. 3. bat
  work.. 4. maze, mesh 6. tangle
  11. Gordian knot
wed... 4. join, mate 5. marry, mated,
  unite 6. joined 7. espouse, pledged,
  spliced 13. give in wedlock
wedding... 8. ceremony, espousal,
  marriage, nuptials
wedding (anniversary)...
  1st.. 5. paper
  2nd.. 5. straw
  3rd.. 5. candy
  4th.. 7. leather
  5th.. 6. wooden
  7th.. 6. floral
  10th.. 3. tin
  12th.. 5. linen
  13th.. 4. lace
  15th.. 7. crystal

  20th.. 5. china
  25th.. 6. silver
  30th.. 5. pearl
  35th.. 5. coral
  40th.. 7. emerald
  45th.. 4. ruby
  50th.. 6. golden
  75th.. 7. diamond
wedding (pert to)...
  flower.. 13. orange blossom
  proclamation.. 5. banns (bans)
  snow.. 4. rice
  term.. 7. marital, wedlock
  8. marriage, nuptials 9. matrimony
  11. espousement
wedge... 3. jam 4. club, shoe
  5. cleat, ingot, split 6. sector,
  wedgie 7. niblick 8. triangle, voussoir
  9. machinery
wedge–shaped... 7. cuneate
  9. cuneiform (cuniform)
Wednesday... 5. Woden (wise god)
  9. fourth day, Woden's Day
wee... 3. bit 4. dock, fine, tiny
  5. small, teeny 6. little, minute
  10. diminutive, teeny–weeny
weed... 3. bur (burr), hoe, rag 4. loco,
  milk, sida, tare 5. cigar, flesh, vetch
  6. darnel, excise, Jimson, knawel,
  spurge, tumble 7. allseed, mallows,
  mustard, ragweed, tobacco
  8. plantain, purslane, toadflax
  9. cultivate, dandelion
  11. undergrowth
weeds... 8. garments (mourning)
week... 8. hebdomad 9. seven days
week (pert to)...
  day.. 6. ferial
  Eccl.. 4. Holy 7. Passion
  of Sundays.. 5. seven 8. hebdomad
  of years.. 5. seven
  past.. 10. yesterweek
weekly... 5. aweek 10. hebdomadal,
  periodical 11. publication
weeks, two... 9. fortnight
weel... 4. pool, trap 6. basket 8. fish
  trap
ween... 5. think 6. expect 7. believe,
  imagine, suppose 8. conceive
weep... 3. cry, orp, sob 4. drip, rain,
  wail 5. exude, mourn 7. blubber,
  lapwing 9. percolate, shed tears
weeping... 6. crying 7. sobbing
  9. festering
weeping (pert to)...
  monkey.. 8. capuchin
  queen.. 5. Niobe
  tree.. 5. cedar 6. spruce, willow
Weeping Philosopher (anc)...
  10. Heraclitus
weevil (pert to)...
  cotton.. 4. boll
  malt.. 4. boud
  snout.. 8. curculio
  type (other).. 3. pea 4. palm, pine,
  rice, seed 5. flour
weigh... 4. tare, test 5. hoist, poise,
  scale 6. ponder, regard 7. balance,
  be heavy, compare, measure
  8. consider, encumber, estimate,
  ruminate 9. apportion, press hard
weigh down... 4. lade, load

6. burden, hamper 7. ballast,
depress, oppress 11. overbalance
weight... 4. load, mass 5. force,
power 6. burden, import, moment
7. gravity, tonnage 8. encumber,
pressure 9. authority, heaviness,
influence 10. importance
11. consequence 12. significance
weight (pert to)...
allowance.. 4. tare, tret 7. scalage
comb form.. 4. baro
gem.. 5. carat (karat)
light.. 6. suttle
system.. 3. net 4. troy 6. metric
10. apothecary 11. avoirdupois
total.. 5. gross
weighty... 3. fat 5. bulky, heavy, hefty,
large, obese 6. solemn 7. massive,
onerous, serious 8. forcible, powerful
9. corpulent, important, momentous,
ponderous 10. burdensome,
cumbersome, impressive, oppressive
11. influential 13. authoritative
weir... 3. dam, net 4. bank 5. fence,
levee, seine 7. barrier, milldam
9. floodgate
weird... 3. odd 4. omen, wild 5. eerie
(eery), queer, scary 6. creepy, spooky
7. awesome, curious, ghostly,
macabre, strange, uncanny 8. eldritch
9. deathlike, frightful 10. mysterious,
prediction
Weird Sisters (Scot)... 5. Fates
welcome... 4. hail 5. adopt, greet
7. acclaim, accueil 8. grateful,
greeting, pleasing 9. agreeable,
bienvenue, desirable 10. acceptable,
salutation
weld... 5. unite 11. consolidate
welfare... 4. good, weal 5. Salus
(goddess) 9. good cheer
10. prosperity 14. material plenty
welkin... 3. air, sky 6. heaven
10. atmosphere
well... 3. fit, gay, pit 4. gush, hale,
pool 5. aweel, fount, fully 6. easily,
gusher, hearty, justly, kindly, source
7. cistern, closely 8. artesian,
expertly, fountain, friendly 10. full
degree, intimately 11. excellently
12. satisfactory
well (pert to)...
being.. 4. weal 7. comfort 8. eucrasia
9. happiness
Bib.. 4. Esek
born.. 5. noble 7. eugenic
bred.. 6. polite 7. genteel, refined
8. cultured, wellborn 9. pedigreed
10. cultivated 11. gentlemanly
12. thoroughbred
comb form.. 4. mene
defined.. 8. distinct 11. distinctive
groomed.. 4. neat 5. sleek 6. soigné
(soignée)
grounded.. 5. valid 7. logical
9. plausible 11. established,
substantial 12. well–informed
gushing.. 8. artesian
heeled.. 4. rich 5. armed
7. moneyed, wealthy, well–off
8. well–to–do
known.. 6. famous 7. eminent

12. acknowledged
land drain.. 4. sump
lining.. 5. steen
off.. 5. lucky 10. prosperous
oil.. 6. gusher
pole.. 5. sweep
prefix.. 2. eu
timed.. 6. timely 9. opportune
versed.. 7. erudite
watered.. 9. irrigated, irriguous
welsh (welch)... 5. cheat 6. not pay,
renege 7. swindle 10. shirk out of
Welsh (pert to)... see also Wales
boat.. 7. coracle
congress of literati.. 10. eisteddfod
fine, for murder.. 7. galanas
god, underworld.. 4. Bran
instrument (reed).. 7. pibcorn
man.. 5. Taffy 8. Cambrian
onion.. 5. cibal
population.. 6. Cymric
rabbit.. 7. ramekin (ramequin), rarebit
romance collection.. 10. Mabinogion
(Mabinogi)
welt... 4. mark, wale 5. ridge
6. stripe, thrash
welter... 4. reel, roll, soil, toss
6. grovel, tumble, wallow 7. stagger
8. flounder, overturn 9. confusion
wen... 4. cyst, rune 5. tumor
7. blemish 11. excrescence
12. protuberance
wench... 4. doxy, gill, girl 5. child,
squaw, trull, woman 6. damsel,
maiden 7. consort, servant
8. strumpet 11. maidservant
wend... 2. go 4. fare, pass 6. depart,
direct, travel 7. circuit, proceed
8. progress
went (pert to)... see also go
astray.. 6. failed 10. miscarried
away.. 4. left 8. departed
before.. 3. led 8. preceded
9. anteceded
swiftly.. 3. ran 4. sped 6. darted
7. scooted, scudded 8. decamped
wenzel... 4. jack (card game) 5. knave
werewolf... 6. jaguar 8. uturuncu,
werefolk 11. lycanthrope
wergild... 3. cro 4. eric 7. galanas
9. Brehon Law
Wesleyan... 9. Methodist 14. Wesley
follower
West African (pert to)...
baboon.. 5. drill 8. mandrill
city.. 5. Accra, Dakar
gazelle.. 4. kudu, mohr (mhorr), oryx
lemur.. 5. potto 8. kinkajou
monkey.. 4. mona 6. guenon
native.. 7. Ashanti (Ashantee)
pepper.. 5. cubeb
tree.. 5. iroko, odoom
tribe.. 5. Igara
West End, London... 7. Mayfair
9. Belgravia 11. fashionable
12. aristocratic
Western... 9. Hesperian 10. Occidental
Westernmost US... 9. Aleutians
11. Attu Islands 12. Cape Wrangell
West Indies...
bird.. 4. tody 6. mucaro
boat.. 7. drogher (droger)

chief.. 7. cacique
clingfish.. 6. testar
crop.. 5. sugar 7. bananas
ebony.. 9. cocuswood
fish.. 4. cero, paru, sesi 6. testar
flea.. 6. chigoe
fruit.. 5. papaw (pawpaw)
islands.. 4. Cuba 5. Haiti 6. Cayman,
    Virgin 7. Antigua, Bahamas, Leeward
    8. Antilles, Windward
liquor.. 5. mobby (mobbie), tafia
    (taffia)
lizard.. 6. arbalo
magic.. 5. obeah
music.. 7. calypso
owl.. 6. mucaro
resident.. 9. Antillean
rodent.. 6. agouti (agouty)
snuff.. 8. Maccaboy
tea.. 8. goatweed
tortoise.. 7. hicatee
tree.. 4. ausu 5. ebony, papaw
    6. bonduc 8. bayberry 9. sapodilla,
    satinwood
volcano.. 5. Pelée
wood.. 9. cocuswood, sapodilla
    10. granadilla
Westminster clock (London)... 6. Big
    Ben
West Pointer... 5. cadet, plebe
    8. yearling
West Point motto... 16. Duty, Honor,
    Country
West Virginia...
capital.. 10. Charleston
city.. 5. Logan 8. Wheeling
    11. Parkersburg
crop.. 4. coal
mountain.. 10. Spruce Knob
    11. Alleghenies
park (famed).. 12. Harpers Ferry
river.. 4. Ohio 7. Kanawha
    11. Monongahela
Springs (resort).. 8. Berkeley
    12. White Sulphur
State admission.. 11. Thirty–fifth
State motto.. 19. Montani Semper
    Liberi 22. Mountaineers Always Free
State nickname.. 8. Mountain
West wind... 8. Favonius, Zephyrus
wet... 4. asop, damp, dank, dewy, rain
    5. foggy, humid, leach, misty, moist,
    mushy, rainy, soggy, soppy
    6. dampen, drench, soaked, sodden,
    watery 7. moisten 8. sprinkle
wet blanket... 7. kill–joy 8. deadhead
    10. discourage, spoilsport
whale... 3. orc 4. cete, lash, whip
    5. whack 6. beluga, blower, thrash
    7. grampus, ripsack 8. hardhead
    9. zeuglodon 13. sulphur–bottom
whale (pert to)...
Arctic.. 7. narwhal
bird.. 4. gull 6. petrel 9. phalarope
blubber pot.. 6. try–pot
blue.. 9. Sibbaldus
bone.. 6. baleen
carcass.. 5. kreng
constellation.. 5. Cetus
fat.. 7. blubber
food.. 4. brit
gray.. 7. ripsack 8. hardhead

killer.. 4. orca
killer of.. 8. ceticide
legendary.. 9. Mysticeti
monster.. 4. Cete
mustache (legend).. 9. Mysticeti
Order.. 7. Cetacea
ref to.. 5. cetic, sperm 6. baleen
    7. blubber 8. cetacean
school of.. 3. gam, pod
secretion (perfume).. 9. ambergris
small.. 7. grampus
sperm type.. 8. cachalot
study of.. 8. cetology
toothed.. 10. odontocete, zeuglodont
type.. 3. orc 4. blue, orca 5. right,
    sperm 6. killer 7. dolphin, rorqual
    8. cachalot, humpback, porpoise
    9. whalebone
wax.. 10. spermaceti
whalebone.. 6. baleen 10. stiffening
young.. 4. calf 9. shorthead
wharf... 4. dock, pier, quay 5. jetty
    6. staith 7. landing
wharf (pert to)...
fish.. 6. cunner
master.. 10. wharfinger
worker.. 9. stevedore
whatnot... 5. thing 6. object
    (nondescript) 7. étagère
    10. miscellany
what's what... 4. fact 5. truth
    7. reality 10. what's right
what wonders has God wrought
    (Arabic exclamation)... 9. mashallah
whaup... 6. curlew, outcry
    9. scoundrel
wheal... 4. wale, weal, welt 5. whelk
    6. stripe 7. pustule
wheat (pert to)...
beard.. 3. awn
beverage.. 6. zythem
bird.. 4. lark 8. wheatear 9. chaffinch
chaff.. 4. bran
duck.. 7. widgeon 8. baldpate
Europe.. 5. emmer, spelt (speltz)
flour.. 4. atta 5. Hovis
hard.. 5. durum
India.. 4. suji 8. semolina
storage bin.. 4. silo 8. elevator
wheedle... 4. coax, gain 5. tease
    6. banter, cajole, entice 7. blarney,
    flatter 8. blandish, inveigle, persuade
    9. influence
wheel... 3. cam, cog 4. bike, disc,
    helm, ride, roll, rota 5. drive, pivot,
    rotor, rowel, whirl 6. caster, roller,
    rotate 7. bicycle, revolve, rotator,
    torture, vehicle 8. tricycle 10. water
    wheel
wheel (pert to)...
gem–grinding.. 5. skive
hub.. 4. nave
man.. 5. pilot 7. cyclist 8. helmsman,
    pedalist 9. bicyclist
monkey.. 3. gin
part.. 3. rim 5. felly (felloe), spoke
    6. hubcap
pulley.. 6. sheave
shaped.. 8. circular, rotiform
spoke.. 6. radius
spur.. 5. rowel
stopper.. 4. grig 5. sprag

swiveled.. 6. caster
toothed.. 3. cog 4. gear 6. pinion
turbine.. 5. rotor
type.. 3. cog, fly, pin 4. cart, mill,
  spur 5. wagon 6. Ferris, paddle
  7. balance, potter's 9. of fortune
water.. 5. noria 6. sakieh (sakiyeh)
wheels, logging... 7. katydid
wheen... 3. few 5. group 7. several
  8. division, quantity
wheerikins... 10. posteriors
wheetle... 5. chirp 7. whistle
wheeze... 3. gag 4. joke 5. hoose
  (hooze) 6. cliché, saying 7. breathe
  8. sibilate 9. witticism 10. sibilation
whelk... 4. acne 5. snail 6. papule,
  pimple 7. pustule
whelp... 3. boy, cub, pup 5. child,
  puppy, tiger, youth 9. give birth,
  youngling
when... 2. as 3. tho 5. until
  6. though 7. how soon, whereas
  8. although, whenever 10. how long
  ago 11. at which time
where... 4. here, spot 5. place, there
  7. whither 10. inasmuch as 11. at
  what place, whereabouts
whereas... 5. since
whereby... 7. perquod
whereness... 6. ubiety
whereupon... 4. when 7. on which
  9. upon which 10. after which
wherewithal... 5. means, money
  9. resources
whet... 4. hone 5. grind, point, rouse
  6. excite 7. quicken, sharpen
  9. intensify, stimulate
whether... 2. if 6. either
whey... 4. curd 5. serum
whiff... 4. blow, fish, gust, odor, puff,
  waft 6. breath, exhale, stanch
  7. puff out 8. blow away
  10. inhalation
while... 2. as 3. yet 4. time 5. until
  7. beguile, interim, whereas
  11. space of time
whilom... 4. erst, once 5. of old
  6. former 8. sometime 9. erstwhile
whim... 3. fad, pun, toy 4. idea
  5. fancy, freak 6. megrim, notion,
  vagary 7. boutade, caprice, whimsey
  (whimsy), widgeon 8. migraine
whimper... 3. cry, sob 4. mewl,
  moan, pule, weep 5. whine 7. sniffle
whimsey, whimsy... 3. wit 4. whim
  5. craze, fancy, freak 7. caprice
whimsical... 3. fad, odd 4. dish
  5. droll, queer, witty 7. amusing
  8. fanciful, freakish, notional
  9. crotchety, eccentric, fantastic,
  grotesque 10. capricious
whine... 4. moan, pule, wail 6. snivel
  7. screech, ululate, whimper
  8. complain 12. moaning sound
whinny... 4. bray 5. neigh, whine
whip... 3. cat, tan 4. beat, crop, flag,
  flog, goad, lace, lash, wale 5. birch,
  froth, quirt, seize, spank, strap
  6. defeat, incite, punish, strike,
  swinge, thrash 7. agitate, chabouk
  (chabuk), conquer, scourge
  8. emulsify, lambaste 9. bullwhack

10. discipline 11. congressman
whip (pert to)...
hand.. 8. dominion 9. advantage,
  influence
mark.. 4. wale, weal, welt
political.. 5. party 11. floor leader
riding.. 4. crop 5. quirt
Russian.. 4. plet (plete) 5. knout
sewing.. 8. overcast
socket.. 5. snead
whir... 3. fly 4. burr, buzz, whiz
  5. hurry, swirl, whizz 6. hurtle
  7. revolve, vibrate 9. commotion
whirl... 4. eddy, reel, spin, tirl, turn
  5. twirl 6. circle, gyrate, rotate
  7. revelry, revolve 9. commotion,
  pirouette, turn about 10. excitement
whirlpool... 4. eddy 6. gurges (Her),
  vortex 7. sea puss (sea purse)
  9. maelstrom
whirlwind... 2. oe (Faroes) 7. cyclone,
  tornado, twister, typhoon
  9. hurricane, maelstrom
  10. willy–willy
whisk... 4. tuft, whip, wist 5. froth,
  sweep, swish 6. convey 7. agitate
whiskers... 4. chin 5. beard
  8. vibrissa 9. sideburns
whisky, whiskey... 3. rye 4. corn
  6. poteen, redeye 9. moonshine
  10. usquebaugh
whisky (pert to)...
base.. 3. rye 5. wheat 6. barley
drink.. 4. soda, sour 5. punch, smash
  7. stinger
Insurrection.. 12. Pennsylvania (1794)
Ring.. 10. Conspiracy (1875)
term.. 6. lively 7. flighty
whisper... 3. tip 4. blow, buzz
  5. rumor 6. breeze, murmur
  7. divulge 14. vox clandestina
whist, game... 9. Cavendish
  10. Yarborough
whistle... 4. hiss, pipe, sing, toot
  5. alarm 6. rustle, warble, wheeze
  12. interference
whistle (pert to)...
duck.. 9. goldeneye
fish.. 8. rockling
pig.. 9. woodchuck
stop.. 12. one–horse town
tree (for boys' whistles).. 5. maple
  6. willow
Whistler painting... 15. Little White
  Girl, Whistler's Mother
whistling (pert to)...
coot.. 6. scoter
dick.. 6. thrush
duck.. 6. scoter 9. goldeneye
hawk.. 5. eagle
snipe.. 8. woodcock
sound.. 7. stridor
teal.. 6. scoter 8. tree duck
whit... 3. bit, jot 4. atom, iota
  5. bodle, speck 8. particle
white... 3. wan 4. milk, pale, snow
  5. ashen, chalk, color, happy, ivory,
  snowy 6. albino, chalky, chaste,
  honest, pallid 7. ivorine, silvery
  8. innocent, platinum 9. alabaster,
  albescent, Caucasian, favorable,
  fortunate, honorable

11. snow–covered
white (pert to)...
admiral.. 9. butterfly
ant.. 4. anay (anai) 7. termite
belly.. 6. pigeon 7. widgeon
  14. prairie chicken
cat.. 7. catfish
cell.. 9. leucocyte
chub.. 10. spawneater
cloud.. 6. cirrus 7. tendril
coal.. 10. water power
crow.. 7. vulture
curlew.. 4. ibis
devil.. 7. nailrod
elephant.. 6. burden 8. Oriental
ensign.. 12. British naval
fish.. 5. cisco 6. atinga, beluga
  8. menhaden 9. Coregonus
  10. white whale
grouse.. 9. ptarmigan
growing (hoary).. 9. canescent
head.. 6. pigeon 9. blue goose
  10. surf scoter
heat.. 5. anger 13. incandescence
livered.. 6. feeble 8. cowardly
  13. pusillanimous
matter (nerve).. 4. alba
merganser.. 4. smew
miller.. 11. clothes moth
monk.. 10. Cistercian
mule.. 3. gin 6. whisky (illicit)
  9. moonshine
oak.. 5. roble
of egg.. 5. glair
partridge.. 9. ptarmigan
plague.. 7. disease 8. phthisis
  11. consumption 12. tuberculosis
plantain.. 8. pussytoe
poplar.. 5. aspen
pot.. 7. pudding
pudding.. 7. sausage 9. whitehass
pyrite.. 9. marcasite
shark.. 8. man–eater
throat.. 6. muffet (Eng) 7. warbler
whale.. 6. beluga
White (pert to)...
Chapel (Jewish).. 13. London Quarter
Holland.. 6. turkey
Horse.. 6. emblem (Saxons) 7. carving
House designer.. 5. Hoban
Relig.. 6. Friars 7. Fathers, Sisters
  8. Brethren
Rose (Eng).. 6. emblem (House of
  York)
Sands (N Mex).. 13. proving ground
Squadron.. 4. Navy (US Navy 1883)
Tower.. 13. Tower of London
whiten... 6. blanch, bleach 8. etiolate
  9. whitewash
whitewash... 5. paint 6. defeat,
  whiten 7. conceal 9. disinfect,
  exculpate, gloss over
whither... 5. where 7. whereto 11. to
  what place, whereabouts
whiting... 4. fish 5. chalk 6. tomcod
  10. butterfish
whitish... 4. pale 5. white
  9. albescent
whitlow... 4. herb, sore 5. felon
  6. agnail, fetlow 8. hangnail
  9. saxifrage 10. paronychia
  12. inflammation

Whitsunday... 9. Pentacost
Whittington, Dick... 9. Lord Mayor
  (London)
whittle... 3. cut, hew 4. gash, hack,
  pare, trim 5. knife 6. reduce
  7. blanket
whiz, whizz... 3. hum 4. buzz, hiss,
  pirr, whir, zizz 5. whirr 6. corker,
  rotate 8. sibilate 10. speed along
  12. clever person
who... 3. wer, wha 5. which
  6. person 7. one that, pronoun
whole... 3. all, sum 4. pure, sole, unit
  5. gross, total, uncut, unity
  6. entire, intact, mostly, system
  7. healthy, perfect 8. absolute,
  complete, entirety, totality
  9. aggregate, generally, unanimous,
  undivided
whole (pert to)...
comb form.. 4. toti, toto
footed.. 5. frank 8. intimate
  9. ingenuous 10. flat–footed
hearted.. 7. devoted, earnest, sincere
  8. complete 10. unreserved
  11. unmitigated
hog.. 8. whole way 12. all or nothing
note.. 9. semibreve
number.. 7. integer
skinned.. 6. unhurt 9. unscathed
souled.. 5. noble 7. devoted, sincere,
  zealous 11. noble–minded
  12. wholehearted
wholesome... 4. sane 5. sound
  6. hearty, robust 7. healthy
  8. salutary, vigorous 9. favorable,
  healthful 10. beneficial, propitious,
  salubrious
wholly... 3. all 4. toto (comb form)
  5. fully, quite 6. solely 7. totally
  8. entirely, entirety 9. perfectly
  10. altogether, completely, thoroughly
  11. exclusively
whoop... 4. call, hoot, urge, yell
  5. cheer, shout 6. halloo, hoopee
  10. enthusiasm
whooping cough... 9. pertussis
whoop it up... 7. be noisy 8. energize
  9. make merry 12. create gaiety
whop... 4. bang, beat, bump, fall,
  flop, whip 5. knock 6. strike, stroke
whopper... 3. lie (monstrous) 5. story
  (false)
whorl... 4. curl 5. helix, spire
  8. flywheel, verticil, volution (shell)
  11. fingerprint
wicked... 3. bad, ill 4. evil, vile
  6. guilty, sinful, unjust 7. heinous,
  hellish, profane, roguish, ungodly,
  vicious 8. criminal, depraved, devilish,
  diabolic, flagrant 9. abandoned,
  atrocious, malicious, nefarious,
  perverted 10. diabolical, flagitious,
  iniquitous, villainous 11. irreligious,
  mischievous, unrighteous
wickedness... 3. sin 4. evil 6. Belial
  (Bib) 7. badness 8. baseness, iniquity
  10. sinfulness 13. maliciousness
wicked one... 5. Demon, Satan 7. Evil
  One 8. The Devil
wicker (pert to)...
basket.. 5. cesta 6. hamper, kipsey

7. pannier
cradle.. 8. bassinet
material.. 5. twigs 6. osiers, willow, withes
ware.. 8. basketry, plaiting
wicket... 4. arch, door, gate, hoop 6. grille, window 7. grating, guichet, lattice 8. loophole 12. grated window, ticket window
wickiup, wikiup... 3. hut 7. shelter
Widal's, Widal reaction... 16. typhoid fever test
widbin... 7. dogwood 8. woodbine 11. honeysuckle
widdy... 4. rope (twig) 5. noose, widow, withy 6. halter 7. gallows 11. gallows bird
wide... 5. ample, broad, large, loose, roomy 6. opened 7. liberal 8. expanded, spacious 9. capacious, distended 13. comprehensive
wide–awake... 3. hat 4. keen, tern (sooty) 5. alert 7. knowing 8. watchful
widemouthed... 4. loud 5. noisy 6. greedy 7. barking 9. devouring
widen... 4. ream 6. dilate, expand, extend, spread 7. amplify, broaden, enlarge
widespread... 4. rife 5. broad 7. diffuse, general 8. not local, sweeping 9. dispersed, extensive, prevalent, scattered, universal 13. comprehensive
widgeon... 4. duck, smee 5. goose 6. Mareca, zuisin 7. poacher 8. baldpate 9. simpleton
widow... 6. relict 7. bereave, dowager, viduate
widow (pert to)...
bird.. 5. finch, Vidua 6. whidah
cremated.. 6. suttee
fish.. 5. viuva
monkey.. 4. titi
suicide.. 6. suttee
widower... 6. relict
widow's (pert to)...
lock.. 8. hairline 10. widow's peak
mite.. 4. coin 6. lepton
portion.. 5. dower
right.. 5. terce
weeds.. 8. mourning 9. black veil, widowhood
width... 5. girth 7. breadth 8. diameter, latitude, wideness
wield... 3. ply, use 4. cope, deal, rule 5. power, swing 6. direct, employ, handle, manage 7. control 8. brandish 10. manipulate
wife... 4. frau, mate, rani, uxor 5. bride, mujer 6. matron, spouse 7. consort 8. gudewife (guidwife), helpmate, helpmeet 10. better half 12. married woman
wife (pert to)...
French.. 5. femme
killing.. 9. uxoricide
of a rajah.. 4. Rani (Ranee)
one.. 8. monogamy
pert to.. 7. uxorial
slave's.. 9. broadwife
wig... 4. tête 5. jasey 6. peruke,

toupee 7. censure, periwig 8. seal hood 9. dignitary
wight... 3. man 4. loud 5. brave, fairy, swift, witch 6. active, nimble 7. valiant 8. creature, powerful 11. living being
wigwag... 6. signal 8. to and fro 11. oscillation
wigwam... 4. tent 5. hogan, tepee 6. teepee
wild... 3. mad 5. feral, myall, waste, weird 6. ferine, savage, stormy, unruly 7. bestial, howling, riotous 8. aberrant, desolate, dramatic, frenetic, reckless, untilled, wildwood 9. barbarian, barbarous, ferocious, imprudent, primitive, unbridled, uncertain 10. boisterous, chimerical, irrational, profligate, tumultuous, unexplored, wilderness 11. harum–scarum, uncivilized, uninhabited 12. obstreperous, uncontrolled, uncultivated 14. uncontrollable
wild (pert to)...
alder.. 8. goutweed
animal.. 3. gnu 4. bear, deer, lion, lynx 5. klang, moose, tiger 6. dragon, onager 7. polecat 8. antelope 10. wildebeest
banana.. 5. papaw (pawpaw)
beasts.. 4. ziim
buffalo.. 4. arna 5. arnee
carrot.. 8. hilltrot
cat.. 4. balm, eyra 6. ocelot 7. panther
coffee.. 9. feverroot
crocus.. 12. pasqueflower
fancy.. 6. vagary
fowl.. 4. duck 5. goose, quail 8. pheasant 9. partridge
garlic.. 4. moly
goat.. 3. tur 4. tahr 7. markhor (markhor)
gourd.. 7. pumpkin 11. calabazilla
growing.. 8. agrarian
hog.. 4. boar 9. razorback 10. babiroussa
hop.. 6. bryony
horse.. 6. tarpan
ibex.. 5. Capra
Irishman (shrub).. 10. tumatakuru
jalap.. 8. mayapple
mustard.. 8. charlock
ox.. 3. yak 4. anoa
pieplant.. 7. rhubarb
pineapple.. 7. pinguin
plum.. 4. sloe 5. islay
sheep.. 3. sha 5. urial (oorial) 6. argali
sweet potato.. 7. manroot
West show.. 5. rodeo
wildebeest... 3. gnu
wilderness... 5. waste, wilds 6. forest 8. wildwood 9. confusion 12. complication
wile... 3. art, toy 4. lure, ruse 5. fraud, guile, trick 6. deceit 7. cunning 8. artifice, trickery 9. stratagem
will... 4. wish 6. behest, choice, decree, demise, desire 7. bequest,

command 8. volition 9. intention,
testament 10. resolution
11. disposition, inclination
13. determination
will (pert to)...
appendix.. 7. codicil
convey.. 6. demise 7. bequest
having made.. 7. testate
maker of.. 8. testator
power.. 7. purpose 10. resolution
13. determination 14. strength of
mind
proof of.. 7. probate
to live (Buddh).. 5. tanha
willful, wilful... 3. mad 4. rash
5. heady 7. wayward 8. perverse,
stubborn 9. impetuous, obstinate,
voluntary 11. intentional
14. self–determined
willing... 4. free 5. prone, ready
6. minded 8. desirous, disposed,
unforced 9. agreeable, voluntary
10. consenting, deliberate, ready to
act, volitional 11. intentional
12. well–disposed
willingly... 4. fain, lief 6. freely, gladly
7. happily, readily 10. cheerfully
12. with pleasure
willow... 3. iva 4. Itea 5. osier, salix
6. sallow, teaser
willow (pert to)...
basket.. 7. prickle
genus.. 5. Salix
green.. 6. reseda
lark.. 12. sedge warbler
pattern.. 7. Nanking 11. earthenware
twig.. 5. withe 6. sallow
wren.. 10. chiffchaff
willowy... 5. lithe 6. pliant, supple,
svelte 7. slender 8. flexible, graceful
15. tall and graceful
Will Rogers' plane... 9. Winnie May
wilsome... 4. wild 6. astray, dreary
7. violent, willful (wilful) 8. desolate
10. bewildered
wilt... 3. sag 4. flag, tire 5. droop,
quail 6. sicken, wither 8. languish
11. deteriorate, lose courage, make
flaccid
Wilton... 3. rug 6. carpet
wily... 3. sly 4. foxy 5. canny, smart
6. artful, astute, crafty, shrews,
subtle 9. cunning 9. cautelous
wimble... 3. awl 4. bore 5. auger,
brace, scoop, twist 6. gimlet, pierce
9. sprightly, whimsical
wimick... 3. cry 7. whimper
wimple... 4. fold, veil 7. meander
8. covering (head)
win... 3. get 4. earn, gain 5. to get
6. attain, defeat, obtain, secure
7. achieve, acquire, succeed, triumph
8. be victor, endeavor, vanquish
9. captivate 10. accomplish
win (pert to)...
all tricks (game).. 4. slam
by guile.. 8. inveigle
one's spurs.. 10. knighthood
over.. 7. convert 8. convince
persuade.. 10. conciliate
wince... 4. reel 5. start 6. cringe,
flinch, recoil, shrink 8. draw back,

windlass 10. shrink from
wind... 2. oe 3. air 4. bora, coil,
gale, gust, talk, turn, wrap 5. blast,
buran, crank, trade 6. boreal, breath,
breeze, simoom, zephyr 7. chinook,
conceit, cyclone, deviate, etesian,
meander, monsoon, sinuate, sirocco,
tempest, tornado, typhoon
8. convolve, williwaw 9. hurricane,
idle words, windstorm 10. instrument
wind (pert to)...
action on land.. 8. eolation
around.. 6. master 8. dominate
9. influence 13. lead by the nose
cloud.. 4. scud
comb form.. 5. anemo
fall.. 7. godsend 8. buckshee, gratuity
flower.. 7. anemone
gauge.. 4. vane 10. anemometer
god.. 4. Adad 6. Aeolus
god of north wind.. 6. Boreas
god of SE wind.. 5. Eurus
instrument.. 3. sax 4. fife, horn
5. flute, organ 6. cornet 7. bassoon,
hautboy, helicon, ocarina 8. clarinet
9. harmonica, saxophone
in the (wind).. 5. drunk 7. sailing
8. imminent 9. happening
into a ball.. 11. agglomerate
personified.. 6. Caurus 7. Caecias
8. Favonius, Zephyrus
ref to.. 7. Aeolian (Eolian)
rose.. 5. poppy
science.. 9. anemology
storm.. 4. gale 7. cyclone, typhoon
9. hurricane
up.. 3. end 7. prepare 8. complete,
conclude
yarn.. 6. windle
wind (type)...
Adriatic (cold).. 4. bora
cold.. 4. bise, bora, puna 7. mistral
8. williwaw
desert.. 6. simoom 7. sirocco
dry.. 9. harmattan
East.. 8. levanter
Egypt.. 7. khamsin (kamsin)
equator.. 5. trade
fierce.. 4. gale 6. buster, squall
7. monsoon 8. blizzard 9. hurricane
gentle.. 4. aura 6. zephyr
Malta (cold).. 7. gregale
Mediterranean.. 6. solano 7. etesian
8. levanter
North.. 6. Boreas
Northwest.. 6. Caurus 7. etesian
Oriental.. 7. monsoon
Peru.. 4. puna
S America.. 4. puna 7. pampero
South.. 6. Auster
Southeast.. 5. Eurus
Southwest.. 7. chinook
Spain.. 6. solano
West (personified).. 8. Favonius
whirl.. 2. oe
windiness... 7. conceit
12. boastfulness
winding... 5. curve, snaky 6. spiral
7. sinuous, twining 8. rambling,
tortuous 9. deviative, meandrous
10. circuitous
windjammer... 6. bugler, talker, vessel

(sailing) 8. bandsman 9. trumpeter
windlass . . . 4. reel 5. winch 6. windle
   7. capstan, machine (hoisting)
windle . . . 4. reel 5. winch 6. basket
   7. measure, redwing
window (pert to) . . .
arrangement . . 8. fanlight
   12. fenestration
bay . . 5. oriel
dormer, roof . . 5. gable 7. lucarne
   8. skylight
frame . . 4. sash
Latin . . 8. fenestra
leading . . 4. came
nautical . . 8. porthole
oval . . 5. oxeye
part . . 4. pane, sash, sill 5. glass
   7. shutter
recess . . 6. exedra 9. embrasure
ship's . . 4. port 8. porthole
ticket . . 6. wicket 7. guichet
type . . 4. port 5. gable, oriel
   7. eucarne 8. casement, skylight
windpipe . . . 6. gullet, throat
   7. trachea, weasand
windrow . . . 5. swath (swathe) 6. furrow
Winds, Father of (Gr) . . . 8. Astraeus
windward . . . 5. aloof 8. aweather
   9. weatherly
Windy City . . . 7. Chicago
wine (pert to) . . .
and honey . . 5. clary, mulse
   7. oenomel
Baden . . 8. Ruländer
bag . . 8. wineskin
bibber . . 3. sot 5. toper 7. tippler
   8. drunkard
Bordeaux . . 6. claret
bottle . . 6. magnum 8. decanter
cask . . 3. tun
cellar . . 6. bodega
comb form . . 4. oeno
cruet . . 7. burette
cup . . 3. ama 6. goblet 7. chalice
divination by . . 9. oenomancy
dry . . 3. sec
film . . 8. beeswing
French . . 6. Masden, Pontac (Pontacq)
   8. muscatel 9. Hermitage
   10. Montrachet 12. Saint–Emilion,
   Saint–Estèphe
glass . . 6. rummer (Rom)
grower . . 8. vigneron
hater of . . 11. oenophobist
Italian . . 7. Orvieto 8. muscatel
kind . . 4. port 5. Medoc, Rhine, tinta,
   Tokay 6. canary, claret, Malaga,
   sherry 7. Chablis, Madeira
   8. Burgundy, muscatel, sauterne,
   vermouth 9. champagne
lover of . . 11. oenophilist
maker . . 6. abkari (abkary)
making . . 10. oenopoetic
merchant . . 5. abkar
miracle scene . . 4. Cana (Bib)
palm . . 5. taree
Persian . . 6. Shiraz
pitcher . . 4. olpe 8. oenochoe
reference to . . 5. vinic
residue . . 4. marc
sherry . . 5. Xeres 7. Catawba, Moselle,
   oloroso

shop . . 3. bar 6. bistro, bodega
Spain . . 6. Malaga
sparkling . . 8. mousseux
study of . . 8. oenology
sweet . . 5. lunel
taster . . 10. oenologist
Tuscan . . 7. Chianti
white . . 6. Malaga 8. Riesling,
   sauterne, verdelho 12. Marcobrunner
year . . 7. vintage
wing . . . 3. ala, arm, fly 6. convoy,
   flight, member, pinion 7. faction
   8. addition, dispatch
wing (pert to) . . .
anterior . . 7. elytron
comb form . . 7. pterygo
false . . 5. alula
fish . . 8. sea robin
footed . . 6. aliped
Greek . . 6. pteryx
quill . . 7. remiges
shaped . . 7. aliform
tip . . 7. aileron
winglike . . 4. alar 7. pteroid
   9. pterygoid
winged . . . 4. aile (Her), fast 5. alate,
   lofty, rapid, swift 7. pennate, sublime
   9. aliferous, aligerous
winged (pert to) . . .
boots (of Hermes) . . 7. talaria
child . . 6. cherub
fruit . . 6. samara
monster . . 5. harpy
Winged Horse (Gr Myth) . . . 7. Pegasus
Winged Victory . . . 4. Nike
wingless . . . 7. apteral, Apteryx, exalate
   8. dealated (dealate)
wink . . . 3. nap, nod 4. hint 5. blink,
   flash 6. glance, signal, twitch
   7. flicker, instant, nictate, twinkle
   9. nictation, nictitate, twinkling
   10. palpebrate, periwinkle
winker . . . 3. eye 7. blinker, eyelash
   8. blinkard
winking . . . 13. blepharospasm
winks, forty . . . 3. nap 6. catnap
   10. light sleep
winner . . . 3. ace 6. earner, reaper,
   victor 7. sleeper 8. bangster
   9. conqueror 11. breadwinner
winning . . . 7. gaining, lovable, victory,
   winsome 8. alluring, charming
   10. attractive, successful, victorious
   11. acquisition, captivating
winninish, winnonish . . . 6. salmon
   (landlocked) 10. ouananiche
winnock . . . 6. window
winnow . . . 3. fan 5. sift, stir 6. assort,
   select, thresh 8. disperse, separate
   9. eliminate
winsome . . . 3. gay 5. bonny, merry
   7. lovable, winning 8. alluring,
   charming, cheerful, pleasant
   10. attractive 11. captivating
   12. lighthearted
winter . . . 4. bise, snow 5. hiems
   6. old age, season 8. coldness
winter (pert to) . . .
beer . . 6. Schenk
berry . . 4. Ilex 5. holly
bloom . . 6. azalea 10. witch hazel
bonnet . . 4. gull

duck.. 7. pintail 8. old squaw
fever.. 9. pneumonia
god.. 5. Hiems
lettuce.. 6. endive
mew.. 4. gull
pert to.. 6. brumal, hiemal
quarters.. 10. hibernacle
  12. hibernaculum
sleep.. 11. hibernation
teal.. 9. greenwing
Winter Palace (Leningrad)...
  6. museum
wipe... 3. dry, mop, rub 5. cheat,
clean, erase 6. cancel, remove
7. abolish, defraud 10. obliterate
11. exterminate
wire... 4. coil, cord, line, whip
5. cable, snare 6. thread 7. fencing,
lametta (gold), netting, reticle
8. telegram, wirework 9. cablegram,
telegraph 10. pickpocket 14. knitting
needle
wirepuller... 10. influencer, machinator,
politician, strategist
wiry... 4. lean 5. hardy, stiff, tough
6. sinewy, strong 7. stringy
8. enduring, muscular
wis... 5. think 7. imagine, suppose
Wisconsin...
capital.. 7. Madison
city.. 6. Racine 7. Kenosha, Oshkosh
  8. Green Bay 9. Fond du Lac,
Milwaukee
famed as.. 17. America's Dairyland
first white man.. 7. Nicolet (Jean)
lake.. 8. Michigan, Superior
  9. Winnebago
river.. 7. St Croix 11. Mississippi
State admission.. 9. Thirtieth
State motto.. 7. Forward
State nickname.. 6. Badger
wisdom... 5. logos 8. judgment,
learning, sagacity, sapience
9. erudition, knowledge
10. discretion, profundity
wisdom god... 4. Nebo (Nabu)
  6. Ganesa (Ganesha)
wisdom goddess... 6. Athena
  7. Minerva (Gr)
wise... 3. hep 4. sage, sane, wary
5. aware 6. shrewd, subtle, versed
7. erudite, knowing, learned, politic,
sapient 8. discreet, informed,
profound 9. cognizant, expedient,
judicious, provident 10. omniscient
11. circumspect, enlightened,
philosophic 13. sophisticated
wise (pert to)...
councilor.. 6. mentor, nestor
man.. 4. sage 5. solon, witan
  6. nestor, wizard 7. Solomon
saying.. 4. rede 5. adage
Wise Men (three)... 6. Gaspar
  8. Melchior 9. Balthasar
Wise Men of Greece... 5. Seven
Wise Men of the East... 19. Three
Kings of Cologne
wish... 4. care, hope, will, wuss
5. yearn 6. aspire, desire, invoke
7. longing, request 8. optative,
petition 10. aspiration
11. imprecation

wishbone... 7. furcula 8. furculum
10. fourchette 12. merry thought
wisp... 4. floc 5. brush, flock, shred
6. bundle 7. handful 8. fragment
wistful... 7. longing, pensive
8. desirous, yearning 9. nostalgic
10. melancholy
wit... 3. pun, wag 5. humor, sense
6. acumen, esprit, satire, wisdom
7. punster 8. comedian, humorist,
repartee 9. alertness 11. philosopher,
savoir-faire 12. intelligence
13. understanding
wit (to)... 3. viz 5. truly 6. indeed,
namely, that is 8. scilicet 9. videlicet
witch... 3. hag, hex 4. baba 5. Circe,
crone, lamia, shrew, vixen
6. cummer, Hecate (Hekate), Lilith
(Lilis), wizard 7. warlock 8. old
woman 9. grimalkin, sorceress
11. witch doctor 12. ugly old
woman
witchcraft... 5. charm, magic, wanga
7. cunning, hexerei, sorcery
8. brujeria 9. sortilege, voodooism
10. bewitchery, black magic
11. enchantment 12. invultuation
witch doctor... 3. hex 6. shaman
9. voodooist, wangator
witchery... 5. charm, spell 7. sorcery
8. wizardry 10. allurement,
necromancy 11. enchantment,
fascination
with (pref)... 2. co 3. com, con, cum,
mit, syn 4. avec
with... 5. among 7. jointly 8. together
9. alongside, including 10. hand in
hand 11. association
12. concurrently 13. co-operatively
withal... 5. still 9. thereupon 10. for
all that
withdraw... 6. absent, deduct, recall,
recant, recede, remove, repeal, retire,
secede 7. abandon, detract, disavow,
forsake, refrain, regress, retract,
retreat, subside 8. alienate, evacuate,
renounce 9. disengage 10. relinquish
withdrawal... 6. repeal 7. regress,
retiral, retreat 8. escapism
9. departure, recession, seclusion
10. detachment, extraction,
retraction, separation
11. abandonment, recantation,
resignation
withdrawn... 7. ingrown 8. detached,
secluded
withe... 4. band, rope 5. snare
6. halter, wattle, willow
wither... 3. age, die, dry 4. fade,
sear, sere, wilt 5. decay, droop, dry
up, wizen 6. blight, shrink 7. shrivel,
wrinkle 8. languish 11. deteriorate
withered... 4. sere 8. shrunken
9. shriveled
withering... 7. caustic 9. shrinking
10. marcescent 12. contemptuous
13. deteriorating
withhold... 4. curb, deny 5. check
6. detain, refuse, retain 7. abstain,
prevent, refrain, repress, reserve
8. hold back, postpone, restrain
within.., 6. at home, during, inside

7. indoors 8. inside of, inwardly
9. inner side
without... 4. sans, sine 5. minus
6. beyond, except, lack of, unless
7. lacking, not with 9. absence of,
outwardly 10. externally, out-of-doors
without (pert to)... see also *absence of*
action.. 8. deedless
animation.. 5. amort
appointment (of day).. 7. sine die
beginning, or end.. 7. eternal
cause.. 10. unprovoked
connections.. 7. tieless
delay.. 9. summarily
doubt.. 9. sine dubio
ethics.. 6. amoral
exception.. 11. universally
feet.. 4. apod 6. apodal
foliage.. 8. aphylous
friends.. 4. lorn 7. forlorn 8. forsaken
knowledge.. 8. ignorant
mate.. 3. odd
prefix.. 4. ecto
rule.. 8. anarchic
substance.. 5. inane
support.. 7. legless 9. dependent
teeth.. 8. edentate 9. toothless
this.. 7. sine hoc
warning.. 12. out of the blue
wings.. 7. apteral
withstand... 4. bear, bide, defy, last
5. abide 6. endure, oppose, resist
8. confront 10. contradict
witless... 3. mad 5. crazy, dazed
6. stupid 7. foolish, unaware
8. heedless 9. brainless, unknowing
10. indiscreet 13. unintelligent
witness... 3. eye, see 4. know
5. swear, testo, vouch 6. attend,
attest, beheld, behold, testor
7. observe, testify 8. beholder,
deponent, evidence, observer,
onlooker 9. informant, spectator,
subscribe, testimony 11. attestation
witticism... 3. mot, pun 4. jest, joke,
quip 5. droll, sally, slent 8. repartee
9. wisecrack 10. pleasantry
11. gauloiserie, witty saying
wittingly... 8. by design 9. knowingly
13. intentionally
witty... 4. wise 5. comic, droll, sharp
6. clever, facete, jocose, jocund
7. amusing, comical, jocular, knowing
8. humorous 9. facetious, whimsical
wivern, wyvern (Her)... 6. dragon
(2-legged)
wizard... 4. mage, sage 6. expert,
genius, Merlin, pellar, shaman
7. magical, prodigy 8. conjurer,
magician, sorcerer 10. Wizard of Oz
11. necromancer, thaumaturge, witch
doctor 13. thaumaturgist
Wizard of the North... 14. Sir Walter
Scott
wizen... 3. age, dry 4. thin 6. gullet,
shrink, weazen, wither 7. shrivel
8. windpipe 11. deteriorate
wlo (obs)... 3. hem 6. fringe
woad... 3. dye 4. herb 5. tinge
8. dyestuff 10. pastel blue
wobble, wabble... 4. walk 5. shake,

waver 7. stagger, tremble
8. hobbling 9. fluctuate, oscillate,
vacillate
Woden, Wodan (Myth)... 3. god
(chief) 4. Odin 9. Wednesday (named
for Woden)
woe... 4. bale, bane 5. grief
6. misery, sorrow 7. anguish, trouble
8. anathema, calamity 10. affliction,
melancholy, misfortune
woebegone... 3. sad 6. woeful
7. unhappy 8. dejected, desolate
10. dispirited, melancholy
woeful... 3. sad 6. paltry 7. direful,
pitiful 8. grievous, mournful, wretched
9. afflicted, miserable, sorrowful,
woebegone 10. deplorable
12. disconsolate
wold... 3. lea 4. wood 5. downs,
plain, weald 6. forest, meadow
7. low hill
wolf... 4. lobo 5. lupus 6. coyote,
mammal 7. Isegrim 8. werewolf
9. libertine 11. philanderer
wolf fish... 6. blenny
wolfhound... 6. borzoi
wolflike... 6. lupine, thooid
wolverine... 4. Gulo 11. Michigander,
Michiganite
Wolverine State... 8. Michigan
woman... 4. dame, girl, lady, rani, wife
5. adult, begum, gemme, madam,
squaw 6. female 7. distaff
8. feminine, paramour, senorita
9. weaker sex, womankind
10. sweetheart
woman (pert to)...
adviser.. 6. Egeria (Rom Myth)
apartment of.. 3. oda (harem)
8. thalamus
beautiful.. 4. doll 5. filly, pin-up,
siren, sylph, Venus 7. charmer,
Zenobia 8. Musidora
bewitching.. 4. peri 5. siren, vixen
7. charmer
celibate.. 7. agapeta
chaser.. 9. libertine 11. philanderer
club (of women).. 7. sorosis
8. sorority
comb form.. 3. gyn
dignified, elderly.. 7. dowager
dowdy.. 5. frump 6. untidy 8. slattern
gossipy.. 3. cat 15. flibbertigibbet
graceful.. 5. sylph 7. slender
gypsy.. 5. romni
hater.. 10. misogynist
hatred of.. 8. misogyny
kept.. 8. mistress 9. concubine
12. demimondaine
killer.. 8. femicide
learned.. 12. bluestocking
loose.. 4. drab 5. whore 6. harlot
7. trollop 10. prostitute
12. streetwalker
lover of.. 11. philogynist
modest (affectedly).. 5. prude
mythical (ugly).. 6. Gorgon
noisy.. 9. termagant
of rank.. 4. dame
old.. 5. crone, frump 6. granny
7. carline, dowager 8. grandame
9. cailleach

ruler.. 9. matriarch
scolding.. 5. shrew 6. virago
socialite.. 3. deb 6. subdeb
　　9. debutante 13. fashion leader
stately.. 4. lady 6. matron
suffragist.. 8. feminist
vixenish.. 5. shrew 6. virago
　　8. harridan
weeping.. 5. Niobe
will maker.. 9. testatrix
young, unmarried.. 4. lass 6. damsel
　　8. spinster 10. demoiselle
womanhood... 4. Emer 10. femininity
woman's property (free)...
　　10. parapherna
wonder... 3. awe 6. marvel, rarity
　　7. miracle, prodigy 8. surprise
　　9. amazement 10. admiration,
　　wonderment 12. astonishment
wonderful... 6. superb, unique
　　7. amazing, corking, mirific, strange
　　8. wondrous 9. admirable,
　　marvelous, mirifical 10. remarkable,
　　surprising 11. astonishing
　　13. extraordinary
wont... 3. use 5. habit, usage
　　6. custom
woo... 3. sue 6. invite 7. beseech,
　　entreat, solicit
wood... 4. tree 5. xylon 6. lignum,
　　lumber, timber 8. firewood
wood (pert to)...
aromatic.. 5. aloes, cedar 8. agalloch
ash.. 6. potash
black.. 5. ebony
block.. 3. nog 4. dook
boring (of insects).. 8. xylotomy
bundles.. 6. fagots
carving.. 10. xyloglyphy
clearing.. 5. glade
color.. 7. biscuit
comb form.. 4. hylo, xylo 5. ligni,
　　ligno, xylon
core.. 3. ame
curved strip.. 5. stave
dealer.. 10. xylopolist
deity.. 3. Pan 4. faun 5. Diana, Satyr
　　7. Silenus 8. Silvanus
eating.. 11. xylophagous
goddess.. 5. Diana
growing on.. 6. fungus
　　11. xylophilous
growth.. 7. boscage, coppice, thicket
hard.. 3. ash, elm 4. rate, teak
　　5. ebony, maple 6. walnut
　　8. mahogany
inlay.. 9. marquetry
nymph.. 4. moth 5. dryad
overlay.. 6. veneer
resembling.. 6. xyloid
stork.. 4. ibis
strip.. 4. lath, slat 5. sprag, stave
　　6. batten
touch.. 4. punk 5. spunk (sponk)
　　9. touchwood
tough, elastic.. 3. ash
tract.. 5. grove 6. forest
woodchuck... 6. marmot 9. ground
　　hog
Woodchuck Day... 9. Candlemas
woodcock... 5. pewee 6. peewee,
　　shrubs 10. woodpecker

wooden (pert to)...
container.. 3. box 4. case 6. barrel
horse.. 6. Trojan
Indian.. 15. cigar–store brave
joint.. 5. tenon
made of.. 5. treen
pert to.. 4. dull 6. clumsy, stolid,
　　stupid 8. lifeless 14. expressionless
pin.. 3. fid, nog, peg 5. dowel, spile
pole.. 4. palo
shoe.. 5. sabot 6. patten
stand.. 5. criss
tub.. 3. soe
woodpecker... 4. chab 5. Picus
　　6. yaffle, yukkel (yuckle) 7. flicker,
　　wryneck 8. hickwall 9. sapsucker
　　10. carpintero, pickerwood
　　11. woodknacker
woods (pert to)...
inhabiting.. 7. nemoral
lover of.. 11. nemophilist
pert to.. 6. sylvan (silvan)
　　10. sylvestral
sacred (grove).. 10. Nemorensis
woodwind... 4. oboe 5. flute
　　7. bassoon, piccolo 8. clarinet
　　9. saxophone
woody... 6. sylvan, xyloid 8. ligneous
woof... 3. abb 4. weft 6. fabric
　　7. filling, texture
wool... 3. fur 4. down, hair 5. cloth,
　　llama, sheep 6. fleece 8. barragan
　　(barragon)
wool (pert to)...
card.. 3. tum 4. comb 5. tease
clean.. 7. garnett
cloth.. 5. serge, tweed, yerga
　　6. angora, duffel, kersey, satara,
　　tartan, tricot, vicuña 7. doeskin,
　　flannel, ratteen 8. cashmere
　　10. broadcloth
comb form.. 4. lani
dead sheep's.. 8. mortling
dryer.. 5. fugal
fat.. 7. lanolin (lanoline)
fatty substance.. 5. suint
garment.. 6. alpaca, linder
implement.. 6. carder, shears, teaser
　　7. distaff, spindle
inferior, dirty.. 7. cleamer
kind.. 6. alpaca, angora, merino
　　8. picklock
leg.. 4. gare
reclaimed.. 5. mungo 6. shoddy
reference to.. 5. wooly 6. lanate
　　lanose 10. flocculent
spun.. 4. yarn
tuft.. 8. floccule 9. flocculus
undyed, natural.. 5. beige
waste.. 3. fud 4. noil
yarn.. 3. abb 7. eis wool
wooly (woolly)... 5. downy, fuzzy
　　6. fleecy, lanate 7. blurred
　　8. confused, floccose, peronate
word... 4. news, oath 5. adage,
　　maxim, parol 6. avowal, remark,
　　report 7. command, dispute,
　　message, promise, tidings, vocable
　　8. acrostic, password 9. discourse,
　　statement 11. declaration, information
　　13. communication
word, words (pert to)...

action .. **4.** verb
battle of .. **9.** logomachy
blindness .. **6.** alexia
book .. **6.** Gradus **7.** lexicon, speller
8. glossary **9.** thesaurus
10. dictionary
contraction .. **9.** haplology
deletion at end .. **7.** apocope
derivation .. **6.** etymon **8.** etymology
distinguishing (Bib) .. **10.** shibboleth
divine .. **5.** Logos
excessive interest .. **10.** verbomania
figurative use .. **5.** trope
figure of speech .. **7.** metonym,
paronym
first on walls (Bib) .. **21.** mene, mene,
tekel, upharsin
for word .. **8.** verbatim **9.** literally
hard to pronounce .. **10.** jawbreaker
inventor of .. **6.** coiner **9.** neologist
last syllable .. **6.** ultima
last syllable but one .. **6.** penult
last syllable omitted .. **7.** apocope
law .. **7.** by parol **11.** word of mouth
letter .. **8.** logogram **9.** logogriph
11. grammalogue
longest in dictionary ..
28. antidisestablishmentarianism
loss from middle .. **7.** syncope
magical **6.** presto, sesame
meaning .. **9.** semantics
misuse .. **11.** catachresis, heterophemy,
malapropism
mysterious (Bib) .. **5.** selah
new .. **9.** neologism
new usage .. **7.** neology
of different name for same thing ..
9. heteronym
of honor .. **6.** parole **7.** promise
of opposite meaning .. **7.** antonym
of same derivation .. **7.** paronym
of same meaning .. **7.** synonym
of same sound .. **7.** homonym
of imitation .. **6.** echoic **9.** onomatope
12. onomatopoeia
popular .. **5.** cliché **8.** buzzword
pretentious use .. **10.** lexiphanic
puzzle .. **5.** rebus **7.** anagram
8. acrostic **9.** crossword
repetition .. **5.** ploce
root .. **6.** etymon
same back to front .. **10.** palindrome
science .. **10.** lexicology
scrambled .. **7.** anagram
song hits .. **6.** lyrics
substitution .. **5.** trope **7.** metonym
theory .. **6.** bowwow **8.** pooh-pooh
The Word (Bib) .. **5.** Logos
with loss of vowel at beginning ..
7. aphasia
without vowels .. **6.** rhythm, syzygy
with vowels (all) .. **7.** eulogia, miaoued,
sequoia **12.** ambidextrous
with vowels in sequence .. **8.** caesious
wordiness ... **8.** pleonasm, verbiage
9. prolixity, verbacity **10.** redundance
wording ... **8.** phrasing **10.** expression
wordless ... **5.** tacit **6.** silent
wordy ... **6.** prolix **7.** verbose
9. garrulous **10.** long-winded
12. long-drawn-out
work ... **3.** gig, job, mix **4.** book, deed,

duty, make, opus, plan, task, to-do,
toil **5.** chore, ergon, labor, solve,
trade **6.** action, Arbeit, create, effect,
effort **7.** ferment, operate, perform,
product, travail **8.** business, drudgery,
endeavor, function, industry, struggle
10. accomplish, employment,
engagement, management,
occupation, profession
11. achievement, performance,
undertaking
work (pert to) ...
agreement .. **4.** code, pact **8.** contract
bag .. **7.** tote bag **8.** reticule
carelessly .. **5.** scamp
clothes .. **8.** overalls **9.** blue jeans,
coveralls, dungarees
comb form .. **3.** erg **4.** ergo
divine .. **7.** miracle, theurgy **9.** occult
art
hard .. **3.** peg, tew **4.** char, moil, plug,
toil **5.** labor, sweat **6.** drudge
7. travail **9.** lucubrate **18.** burn the
midnight oil
hate of .. **10.** ergophobia
helper .. **3.** aid (aide) **9.** assistant,
paralegal, paramedic
horse .. **4.** mule **5.** burro
hours .. **9.** flexitime (flextime)
household .. **4.** char **5.** chare
incomplete art .. **7.** ébauche
inlay .. **6.** mosaic, niello
lover of .. **9.** ergophile
measure of .. **9.** ergometer
of excellence .. **4.** opus **7.** classic
out .. **5.** solve **7.** arrange, develop
9. calculate
over .. **6.** recast, rehash, revamp
9. brainwash, influence
shift .. **5.** swing **9.** graveyard,
moonlight
slowly .. **6.** potter, putter **7.** ca'canny
study of .. **8.** ergology
together .. **4.** team **9.** cooperate
11. collaborate
unit of .. **3.** erg **5.** ergon, joule
up .. **4.** plan **5.** rouse **6.** excite, incite
7. advance, agitate, develop
10. manipulate
workable ... **6.** pliant **7.** operant
8. feasible, operable, solvable
9. practical **11.** practicable
worker ... **3.** CPA **5.** diver, mason,
miner **6.** barman, cooper, slater,
smithy, tanner, warper, wright
7. analyst, cobbler, glazier, plumber,
riveter, sandhog, servant, spinner
8. honeybee, mechanic, strapper
9. carpenter, clinician, machinist,
stevedore **10.** accountant
11. breadwinner
worker (pert to) ...
fellow .. **5.** buddy **8.** confrere
group .. **4.** crew, gang, team **5.** corps,
staff **9.** personnel
hard .. **6.** beaver, drudge, fagger
10. workaholic
head .. **4.** boss **7.** foreman
8. employer, overseer
14. superintendent
indifferent .. **4.** scab **11.** scissorbill
migrant .. **4.** hobo **6.** boomer

7. floater, wetback
workhouse ... 6. prison 9. almshouse, poorhouse
workman ... 4. peon 6. coolie, earner 7. artisan, laborer 8. operator, opificer 9. artificer, craftsman, performer
workshop ... 3. lab 4. mill 5. plant 6. studio 7. atelier, factory 10. laboratory 11. ergasterion
world ... 5. globe, realm 6. cosmos, domain 7. kingdom, society 8. creation, humanity, universe 9. multitude, the public
world (pert to) ...
external .. 6. nonego
great .. 9. macrocosm
lower .. 5. Hades, Orcus
miniature .. 9. microcosm
of fairies .. 6. faerie (faery)
precreation .. 10. premundane 11. antemundane
reference to .. 7. mundane 11. terrestrial
worldly ... 7. earthly, mundane, secular, terrene 11. terrestrial 13. materialistic, sophisticated
world's oldest city, still inhabited ... 8. Damascus
world's speech ... 7. Volapuk 9. universal
worm ... 3. ess 4. coil, grub, wind 5. borer, tinea 6. blight, insect, maggot, vermin, wretch 8. helminth 9. trematode, vermicule 10. Nemertinea (Nemertina)
worm (pert to) ...
Africa .. 3. loa 6. Guinea
aquatic, marine .. 7. eunicid, lugworm 8. flatworm 9. planarian 13. platyhelminth
arrow .. 7. sagitta
bait .. 9. angleworm, earthworm
bloodsucking .. 5. leech
caddie .. 5. cadew
cotton .. 8. bollworm 10. boll weevil
edible .. 6. palolo
eye-infecting .. 3. loa
genus .. 6. Virmes 7. Ascaris, Filaria 8. Annelida 10. Nemertinea (Nemertina)
grublike .. 5. larva
killer .. 9. vermicide
larva .. 4. army, slug 5. cadew 6. caddis, looper 8. wireworm 11. caterpillar
luminous .. 8. glowworm
marine .. 7. eunicid
measuring .. 6. looper 8. inchworm
parasitic .. 7. Ascaris, Filaria 8. trichina, woodworm 9. trematode 10. Guinea worm 12. enthelmintha
ref to .. 8. anneloid 9. nemertean, nemertine, nemertoid, trematoid
ring .. 5. tinea 7. annelid
round .. 7. ascarid, Ascaris
segmented .. 8. Annelida
ship .. 5. borer 6. teredo
silk .. 4. eria
soft .. 4. grub
study of .. 10. vermeology 13. helminthology

tape .. 6. taenia
track .. 7. nereite 11. helminthite
wire .. 4. lava 9. millepede
worm (type) ... 3. cut, dew, lug, pin 4. army, boll, eria, flat, glow, inch, ring, ship, silk, slug, tape, wire, wood 5. angle, earth, larva, leech, round, tinea 6. marine 9. measuring, parasitic
wormlike ... 7. vermian 11. helminthoid
wormy ... 6. earthy, humble, rotten 8. crawling 9. groveling
worn ... 3. old 4. sere, used 5. stale, trite 7. abraded, haggard 8. attrited, tattered, weakened 9. exhausted, hackneyed 10. secondhand 11. commonplace
worn-out ... 4. used 5. jaded, passé, seedy, spent, trite 6. shabby, used up 7. haggard 8. consumed, fatigued, impaired, tired out 9. enfeebled, exhausted 10. threadbare
worried ... 5. cared, fazed 6. stewed 7. annoyed, anxious, fearful, fretted 8. troubled 9. perturbed
worry ... 3. nag, rux, vex 4. care, cark, faze, fret, stew 5. annoy, brood, harry 6. bother, harass, pester, plague, pother 7. anxiety, bedevil, concern, perturb, torment, trouble 8. distress 9. annoyance 10. harassment, uneasiness
worship ... 5. adore, honor, serve 6. bhakti, homage, revere 7. idolize, liturgy, respect 8. blessing, devotion, idolatry, venerate 9. adoration, deference, reverence 10. veneration
worship (pert to) ...
form of .. 6. preces, ritual 7. liturgy
house of .. 6. chapel, church, mosque, shrine 9. cathedral, synagogue 10. tabernacle
object of .. 4. icon, idol 5. totem 6. fetish
place of .. 5. altar
system of .. 4. cult 6. cultus, fetish, ritual 8. doctrine
worshiper ... 6. adorer, bhakti, votary 8. disciple, idolater 10. ignicolist 12. iconomachist
worshipful ... 6. devout 7. notable 8. esteemed 9. honorable, venerable 13. distinguished
worship of ...
a god .. 9. theolatry
angels .. 5. dulia
genii .. 10. geniolatry
god .. 6. latria (RCCh)
idols .. 8. idolatry
images .. 10. iconolatry
nature .. 11. physiolatry
one god .. 9. monolatry
snakes .. 10. ophiolatry
soul .. 7. animism
sun .. 10. heliolatry
the mob .. 9. mobolatry
worst ... 3. bad 4. beat, evil 6. defeat, wicked 7. harmful 8. inferior 10. calamitous, pernicious, unpleasant 12. disagreeable
worsted ... 4. yarn 6. crewel

7. genappe

worth ... 5. merit, price, value
6. desert, repute, riches, stiver,
wealth 8. eminence, meriting,
property 9. deserving 10. excellence,
importance, usefulness

worthless ... 3. bad, ort 4. base, evil,
mean, raca (Bib), vile 6. futile,
nought (naught), paltry 7. fustian,
useless 8. nugatory, rubbishy,
unworthy 9. valueless
11. undeserving
14. good–for–nothing

worthwhile ... 6. useful 7. gainful
9. expedient, well–spent
10. invaluable, profitable

worthy ... 3. fit 7. merited 8. eligible,
valuable 9. celebrity, competent,
deserving, estimable, excellent,
honorable, qualified, reputable
11. meritorious

worthy of ... 8. credible, meriting
9. deserving 10. entitled to

wound ... 3. cut 4. gore, harm, hurt,
pain, rist, scar, sore, stab 5. sting
6. breach, damage, grieve, injury,
lesion, offend, trauma 8. distress
9. detriment

wound (pert to) ...
discharge .. 5. ichor 6. sanies
dressing .. 7. bandage, pledget
mark .. 4. scab, scar, welt 7. blister

woven ... 4. spun 10. fabricated

wow ... 4. howl, rave, wail 5. whine

wrack ... 4. kelp, rack, ruin 5. tease,
trash, weeds, wreck 6. refuse
7. seaweed 8. eelgrass, wreckage
9. shipwreck 11. destruction

wraith ... 4. food 5. ghost, spook
8. illusion 10. apparition
12. Doppelgänger, doubleganger

wrangle ... 4. herd, spar 5. argue,
brawl 6. bicker, debate 7. contend,
dispute, quarrel 8. haggling
9. altercate, bickering 11. altercation,
controversy 12. disagreement

wrangler ... 6. cowboy 7. debater,
student (Cambridge, Eng)
8. herdsman, opponent
9. combatant, disputant
10. antagonist

wrangling ... 11. belligerent,
contentious

wrap ... 3. rug 4. cape, cere, furl, roll,
wind 5. cloak, gange 6. afghan,
encowl, enfold, swathe 7. blanket,
conceal, package 8. covering,
enshroud, enswathe, envelope
9. encompass

wrapped up ... 7. bound up, selfish
8. absorbed, included, involved
9. dependent, devoted to, engrossed
11. inseparable

wrapper ... 4. gown 5. cerer 6. fardel,
kimono, tillot 7. garment, pelisse
8. envelope, peignoir

wrapping ... 6. charta 7. wrapper
8. cerement, covering 9. parchment

wrasse ... 4. fish 6. ballan, cunner,
Labrus 7. seawife 11. peacock fish

wrath ... 3. ire 4. fury, grim, rage
5. anger 6. choler 7. passion

8. violence 10. turbulence
11. indignation 12. exasperation

wrathful ... 3. mad 5. angry, irate
6. ireful, raging 7. angered
8. incensed 9. indignant, malignant
10. passionate

wreak ... 4. do to 6. avenge 7. gratify,
indulge, inflict 13. bring down upon

wreath ... 3. lei 4. band, orle
5. crown, torse (Her), whorl
6. anadem, circle, corona, laurel,
trophy 7. coronet, festoon, garland,
Iresine 8. encircle

wreathe ... 4. coil, wind 5. crown,
twine, twist 7. entwine 8. decorate,
encircle 9. interlace 10. twist about

wreck ... 4. raze, ruin, undo 5. crash,
smash 6. jalopy 7. destroy, disable
8. accident, demolish, derelict
9. shipwreck 10. broken form
11. disassemble, The Hesperus

wreckage ... 5. ruins 6. jetsam
7. flotsam 8. driftage

wrench ... 4. jerk, pipe, pull, tear
5. twist, wrest 6. sprain, twinge
7. distort 8. crescent, distress

wrench, type of ... 3. box, pin
5. wramp 6. monkey 7. spanner
8. carriage, Stillson 9. alligator

wrest ... 4. rend, turn 5. exact, force,
seize, twist, wring 6. elicit, extort,
wrench 7. distort, extract, pervert,
wrestle 8. misapply

wrestle ... 3. tug 6. squirm, tussle
7. contend, grapple, scuffle, wriggle
8. struggle 9. throw down 10. twist
about 11. come to grips

wrestling school ... 9. palaestra
(palestra)

wretch ... 3. dog 5. miser, ronin
6. outlaw, pariah 7. caitiff, cullion,
outcast 8. derelict, sufferer
9. miscreant 10. base person
11. offscouring, rapscallion
14. good–for–nothing 16. pitiable
creature

wretched ... 3. sad 4. base, mean
6. dismal, paltry, woeful 7. baleful,
forlorn, squalid, unhappy, very bad
8. grievous 9. execrable, miserable
10. despicable, distressed
12. contemptible, disreputable

wretchedness ... 6. misery 8. distress,
meanness, poorness 10. paltriness
11. unhappiness 13. penuriousness

wriggle ... 5. twist 6. squirm, writhe
7. meander

wriggle out of ... 4. turn, wind
5. dodge, snake, twist 6. squirm,
writhe 8. slip away 10. crawl out of
11. squirm out of 13. find a
loophole

wring ... 5. twist, wrest 6. extort,
wrench 7. extract, torture, wrestle
8. compress, convolve 9. cause pain
10. contortion, extraction

wrinkle ... 3. fad 4. fold, idea, ruga,
seam 5. crimp, knack, ridge, rivel
6. crease, furrow, pucker, rimple,
ripple, rumple 7. crinkle, novelty
8. contract 9. corrugate
11. corrugation 12. clever notion

wrinkled... 4. aged 5. savoy
  6. rugate, rugose, rugous 7. creased
  8. crinkled, crumpled, furrowed,
  puckered, rugulose 9. shriveled
  10. contracted, corrugated
wrinkles... 5. rugae
wrist... 5. joint 6. carpal, carpus
  8. os magnum 9. capitatum
writ... 5. breve, tales 6. capias, elegit,
  venire 7. process 8. detainer,
  document, mittimus, replevin,
  subpoena 10. certiorari, instrument
  11. fieri facias
writ (pert to)...
  common law.. 11. fieri facias
  court.. 7. summons 8. subpoena
  execution.. 6. elegit
  jury.. 5. tales 6. venire
  law.. 4. capo, pone 5. breve, error
  6. capias, elegit 7. mandate,
  process, warrant 8. citation
  10. certiorari
write... 3. pen 5. draft, trace
  6. decree, depict, draw up, enroll,
  indite, record, scrive 7. compose,
  scriven 8. inscribe, scribble
  11. communicate
write (pert to)...
  carelessly.. 6. scrawl 8. scrabble,
  scribble
  in large hand.. 7. engross
  off.. 4. drop 6. cancel, deduct, repeal
  out.. 6. record 8. spill out 12. put in
  writing
  poetry.. 7. versify
  up.. 6. record, report 7. article
  9. publicize 11. press report
writer... 4. hack, poet 6. author,
  penman, penner, scribe 7. elegist,
  glosser, hymnist 8. annalist,
  composer, lyricist, novelist, parodist,
  scriptor 9. annotator, columnist,
  scrivener 10. chronicler, journalist
  13. correspondent
writer's afterthoughts... 7. addenda
writhe... 4. bend, coil, curl, wind
  5. twist, wring 6. squirm 7. contort,
  distort, wriggle
writing... 4. book, poem 6. script
  7. article, epistle 8. covenant,
  document, makimono 10. expression,
  penmanship, profession
  11. chirography, composition,
  handwriting, inscription, publication
writing (pert to)...
  alternate.. 13. boustrophedon
  ancient characters.. 9. cuneiform
  ancient manuscript.. 6. uncial
  cipher.. 12. cryptography
  instrument.. 3. pen 5. quill 6. stylus
  italic.. 7. cursive
  mania for.. 11. graphomania
  material.. 3. pad 5. paper, slate
  6. tablet 9. parchment 10. stationery
  omission of a letter.. 8. lipogram
  10. lipography
  pert to.. 7. scribal
  record.. 3. log 5. album, diary
  script.. 5. ronde
  scroll.. 8. makimono
  scroll hanging.. 8. kakemono
  secret.. 4. code 10. cryptogram

  12. cryptography
  unrhymed.. 5. prose
writings, sacred... 5. Bible, Koran
  6. Psalms, Talmud 9. Testament
  (Old, New) 10. Scriptures
written (pert to)...
  agreement.. 6. cartel
  characters.. 6. script
  it is.. 8. it must be 10. in the
  books, in the cards 12. the die is
  cast
  law.. 10. legislated
  law, unwritten.. 6. common
  memo.. 5. scrip
wrong... 3. bad, off, out, sin 4. awry,
  evil, harm, side, tort, vice 5. amiss,
  cheat, crime, false, malum, unfit
  6. faulty, injure, injury, seduce,
  sinful, unjust, wicked 7. defraud,
  immoral, misdeed, offense
  8. improper, iniquity, mistaken
  9. erroneous, incorrect, injustice,
  violation 10. inaccurate, iniquitous
  11. impropriety, inexpedient,
  malfeasance, misfeasance
  12. illegitimate
wrong (pert to)...
  go (wrong).. 3. err 4. fail 5. lapse
  8. go astray, go to ruin 9. backslide
  10. misbelieve 11. go to the dogs
  in the.. 6. guilty 7. at fault, in error
  8. mistaken 9. violation
  law.. 4. tort 5. crime, malum
  name.. 8. misnomer
  nor right (neither).. 7. neutral
  11. adiaphorous
  prefix.. 3. mis
  side of.. 5. shady
  way.. 5. amiss 6. astray 10. out of
  place
wrongdoer... 6. sinner 8. criminal,
  evildoer, violator 10. malefactor,
  trespasser 12. transgressor
wroth... 3. mad 5. angry, irate
  7. violent 8. incensed, wrathful
  9. turbulent, wrought up
  11. exasperated
wrought... 4. made 6. formed,
  shaped, worked 9. decorated,
  fashioned, processed 10. elaborated,
  ornamented 11. embroidered
  12. manufactured
wrought up... 4. agog 5. angry, eager
  7. excited 9. disturbed, stirred up
wry... 4. awry 6. biased, swerve,
  turned 7. crooked, twisted
  9. contorted
wryneck... 4. Jynx, weet 5. loxia
  9. snakebird 11. torticollis
Württemberg, Germany...
  capital.. 9. Stuttgart
  city.. 3. Ulm 9. Esslingen, Heilbronn,
  Hohenheim
  lake.. 9. Constance
  river.. 6. Danube, Neckar
Wyandot... 6. Indian (Iroquois)
Wyandotte... 4. cave, city, fowl
Wycliff (Wyclif), John (pert to)...
  birthplace.. 9. Yorkshire (Eng)
  disciple.. 4. Huss
  remains cast into.. 10. Swift River
  translator of.. 5. Bible

Wyoming . . .
capital . . 8. Cheyenne
city . . 4. Cody 6. Casper 7. Big Horn,
  Laramie 8. Cheyenne, Sheridan
historic site . . 11. Fort Laramie
  17. Buffalo Bill Center
mountain . . 6. Tetons 7. Rockies
  11. Gannett Peak
park . . 10. Grand Teton

  11. Yellowstone
river . . 4. Wind 6. Platte 7. Big Horn
river source . . 8. Colorado, Columbia,
  Missouri
State admission . . 11. Forty–fourth
State bird . . 10. meadowlark
State flower . . 16. Indian paintbrush
State motto . . 11. Equal Rights
Woman Suffrage . . 10. First State

X

X . . . 3. ten 5. error 6. letter (24th),
  symbol 7. unknown
xanthic . . . 6. cyanic, yellow
Xanthippe, wife of . . . 8. Socrates
xanthoma . . . 9. xanthosis 11. skin
  disease 13. yellow patches
xanthos . . . 6. yellow
Xanthus (pert to) . . .
  ancient site . . 7. marbles (Xanthian)
  placed now . . 13. British Museum
xebec . . . 6. vessel 7. corsair
xen, xeno (comb form) . . . 7. foreign
  8. stranger
xenium . . . 4. gift 7. present (official)
Xenocrates (Gr) . . . 11. philosopher
xenogamy . . . 18. cross–fertilization
xenophobic . . . 9. strangers (afraid of)
  12. chauvinistic
Xenophon's historic tale . . .
  8. Anabasis
xenophthalmia . . . 11. foreign body
  (eye) 14. conjunctivitis
Xenopus . . . 5. toads
Xenorhynchus . . . 6. storks
Xenurus . . . 7. tatouay 10. armadillos
Xeres . . . 5. jerez 6. sherry
xerophagy . . . 4. Fast (Lenten)
xerotes . . . 7. dryness (body)
Xerox (tm) . . . 4. copy 9. duplicate,
  replicate, reproduce
Xerus . . . 9. squirrels
Xerxes (pert to) . . .

crossing of . . 10. Hellespont
destroyer of . . 6. Athens (BC)
king of . . 6. Persia
xibalba . . . 10. underworld
Xinca . . . 6. Indian, Jincan
Xipe, Xipe-totec . . . 11. god of sowing
Xiphias . . . 5. comet (sword–shaped)
  6. Dorado (constellation) 9. swordfish
xiphoid . . . 4. bone 8. ensiform
  9. swordlike 12. xiphisternum
Xiphopagus . . . 7. monster (twinlike)
Xiphosura . . . 8. king crab
Xiuhtocutli . . . 7. fire god (Aztec)
Xmas . . . 9. Christmas
X ray (pert to) . . .
  measure . . 3. rad 11. quantimeter
  named . . 12. Roentgen rays
  type . . 7. CAT scan 8. tomogram
  9. myelogram 11. arteriogram
xyloglyphy . . . 11. wood carving (art)
xylography . . . 13. wood engraving
xyloid . . . 5. woody 8. ligneous,
  woodlike
xylomancy, divination by . . . 4. wood
  10. wood pieces
xylophone . . . 5. saron 7. gambang,
  marimba 8. gamelang (gamelan),
  gigelira, sticcado
xyrid . . . 4. iris 5. Xyris
xystus, xyst (Gr) . . . 16. portico
  colonnade

Y

Y . . . 4. tube 5. curve, track 6. letter
  (25th), prefix, suffix
yabber . . . 4. talk 6. jabber
yabby, yabbie . . . 8. crayfish
yaboa . . . 10. night heron
yabu, yaboo . . . 4. pony
yacht . . . 4. boat, race, sail, ship

yaffle . . . 6. armful 7. handful
  10. woodpecker
yahoo . . . 4. lout, rube 5. brute
Yahoo (pert to) . . .
  represented by . . 10. Houyhnhnms
  (horses of reason)
  tale . . 16. Gulliver's Travels

yakalo, yakattalo... 8. creature 10. crossbreed (yak, cattle)
yakka... 4. work 5. labor
yaksha... 4. ogre 5. demon, dryad, fairy, gnome, jinni 6. Kubera (Chief), spirit 7. tree–god 13. guardian angel
Yale (pert to)...
college.. 8. New Haven
color.. 4. blue 7. Rameses
founded at.. 8. Saybrook
founder.. 9. Elihu Yale
graduate.. 9. Yalensian
Yalta Conference... 6. Crimea (1945)
yam (pert to)...
Fiji.. 6. uviyam 8. white yam
Hawaiian.. 3. hoi
reference to.. 5. tuber 6. igname
Scot.. 6. potato
tropical.. 8. cush–cush
US.. 11. sweet potato
yamstchik... 7. postboy 8. coachman 9. postilion
yang... 4. good, male 6. bright (opp of yin)
yang–kin... 8. dulcimer
yank... 4. jerk, pull 6. Yankee
Yankee... 12. New Englander
Yannigans... 9. scrub team (baseball)
Yao... 6. Indian 9. aborigine
yap... 3. cur, dog, gab 4. bark, talk, yell, yelp 6. jabber 7. bumpkin, hoodlum 8. easy mark 9. greenhorn
yapok, yapock... 6. monkey 7. opossum
yapp... 11. bookbinding
yapster... 3. dog
Yaqui... 6. Indian
yard... 3. rae (sail) 4. lawn, spar, wand 5. garth, stick, verge 6. campus 7. confine, enclose, measure 9. courtyard, curtilage, enclosure, yardstick 10. playground
yarn... 3. abb, cop 4. hank, joke, tale 5. fiber, skein, story 6. caddis, crewel, spinel, thread 7. genappe 9. falsehood
yarn (pert to)...
clew.. 4. ball
holder.. 3. cop
measure.. 4. hank, hasp 5. skein 7. spangle
size.. 6. denier
winder.. 10. yarnwindle
yashiro... 3. sha 6. temple (Shinto)
yashmak... 4. veil (double)
yati... 7. ascetic, devotee
yaw... 4. sail, tack 5. steer, tumor 7. deviate 9. deviation
yawl... 4. boat, howl, wail, yell, yowl 5. ketch 9. jolly boat
yawn... 3. gap 4. gape 5. chasm, mouth 7. opening, stretch 8. open wide, oscitate 12. seek greedily
yaws... 9. frambesia
yawweed... 5. shrub 7. rhubarb 12. wild mulberry
Yazoo (pert to)...
Fraud.. 9. land grant (1795)
Indian.. 11. Mississippi
river.. 11. Mississippi
yclept, ycleped... 5. named 6. called, styled

year (pert to)...
after year.. 10. constantly, repeatedly 11. over and over
book.. 7. almanac
division of.. 6. season 8. semester 9. trimester
Latin.. 5. annus
of mourning.. 11. annus luctus
of our Lord.. 10. Anno Domini 11. annus Domini, year of grace
of thirteen months (384 days).. 10. embolismic
of travel.. 10. sabbatical, Wanderjahr 14. leave of absence
old (Zool).. 10. annotinous
pert to.. 5. epact
quarter.. 5. raith
record.. 5. annal 8. calendar
yearly (pert to)...
church income.. 7. annates
payment.. 4. cens
recurring.. 6. annual 7. etesian 8. annually
yearn for... 3. yen 4. ache, hope, itch, long, pine, sigh, wish 6. desire, hanker
yearning... 3. yen 4. wish 5. eager 7. anxious, longing 9. hankering, nostalgia 10. tenderness 11. languishing 12. homesickness
years (pert to)...
adolescent.. 4. teen
ago.. 4. ages 9. long since 10. days of yore, yesteryear
eight.. 9. octennial
fifteen.. 9. indiction
five.. 6. pentad 7. lustrum
hundred.. 9. centenary 10. centennial
ten.. 6. decade 9. decennary
thousand.. 7. chiliad 10. millennium
two.. 8. biennial, biennium
yeast... 4. barm, foam, koji 5. froth 6. leaven 7. anamite, ferment 9. agitation
yeasty... 5. foamy, light, spumy 6. frothy 8. restless 9. frivolous, leavening
yegg... 5. thief, tramp 6. robber 7. burglar, yeggman 8. criminal 10. safeblower 11. safebreaker, safecracker
yell... 3. cry 4. howl, roar, wail, yowl 5. cheer, shout 6. outcry, scream, shriek
yelling... 7. bawling 8. shouting, strident 9. clamorous 11. full of yells
yellow... 3. dun, sil 4. buff, cuir, deer, ecru, flax, gull, mean, nude, yolk 5. amber, beige, color, cream, grège, jaune, lemon, maize, ocher (ochre), straw, taupe, topaz, twine 6. bisque, butter, canary, Cassel, chrome, citron, creamy, flaxen, golden, mimosa, sallow, Seasan 7. anamite, annatto, aureate, egg yolk, envious, etiolin, jealous, jonquil, saffron, sulphur, xanthic, xanthin 8. cowardly, ocherous, primrose, recreant 9. champagne, dandelion, flavicant, goldenrod, jaundiced, lutescent, sunflower 10. flavescent, melancholy 11. treacherous

yellow (pert to) . . .
brown . . 3. dun 5. straw 6. manila
coloring . . 7. xanthic 8. xanthine
comb form . . 5. luteo
dyestuff . . 5. morin 7. annatto
  8. luteolin
golden . . 2. or (Her) 4. gild, gilt
green . . 5. olive 8. tarragon
  10. chartreuse, serpentine
herb . . 3. iva
jacket . . 4. wasp
medical . . 7. icterus 8. jaundice
  11. xanthoderma
mustard . . 8. charlock
ocher, ochre . . 3. sil
pert to . . 7. xanthic
pigment . . 7. etiolin 8. orpiment
race . . 9. Mongolian
red . . 4. roan 5. aloma, sandy
  6. bisque, dorado, orange
  7. annatto, nacarat
sensational . . 5. press 7. journal
yellow fever mosquito . . 12. Aëdes
  aegypti
yellowhammer . . . 4. yite 5. ammer,
  finch, skite 6. gladdy 7. flicker
  10. woodpecker 13. yellow bunting
Yellowhammer State . . . 7. Alabama
yellow jacket . . . 4. wasp 8. eucalypt
Yellowstone Park geyser . . . 11. Old
  Faithful
yelp . . . 3. cry, yip 4. bark, yell
  5. shout 6. outcry, shriek, squeal
  7. ululate 8. complain 9. criticize
yelper . . . 8. redshank 10. yellowlegs
  11. hunting call
yeme . . . 4. heed 5. guard 6. govern,
  regard
Yemen (pert to) . . .
archeology site . . 4. Sana 5. Marib
Bib kingdom . . 5. Sheba (Saba)
capital . . 4. Sana
citadel . . 5. Damar
division of . . 6. Arabia
plateau . . 7. El Jebel
port . . 5. Mocha 7. Hodeida, Loheiya
ruler . . 4. Imam
sea . . 3. Red
yemochik . . . see *yamstchik*
yen . . . 4. coin, urge 5. yearn 6. desire,
  hanker 7. longing
yeoman . . . 4. exon 5. clerk 6. butler,
  seaman 8. retainer 9. assistant,
  attendant 10. freeholder
  11. subordinate 12. petty officer
yep . . . 3. yes 4. bold 5. alert, smart
  6. active 8. vigorous
yerba . . . 4. herb, maté 5. plant
  11. Paraguay tea
yes . . .
English . . 3. aye, yea, yep 5. uh–huh
  6. assent 11. affirmation
French . . 3. oui
German . . 2. ja
Italian, Spanish . . 2. si
Russian . . 2. da
yesterday . . . 6. yester 7. the past
  10. days gone by, heretofore,
  yesteryear 11. bygone times
yet . . . 3. but 5. still 6. algate
  7. besides, however 10. eventually

  11. nonetheless 15. notwithstanding
yew . . . 5. green, Taxus 7. conifer,
  hemlock 9. evergreen
Yiddish . . . 6. Jewish
  12. Judaeo–German (Judeo–German)
yield . . . 3. bow, net 4. bear, bend,
  cede, crop, give, lose, obey, vail
  5. admit, allow, defer, grant, stoop,
  waive 6. accede, afford, comply, give
  up, relent, render, reward, soften,
  submit 7. concede, consent,
  produce, provide, requite, revenue,
  succumb 9. acquiesce, surrender
  10. capitulate, relinquish
  11. acknowledge
yielding . . . 4. meek, soft 6. pliant,
  supple 7. bearing 8. flexible
  9. compliant, deference, producing,
  tractable 10. compliance,
  manageable, submissive
Yigdal . . . 4. poem (Jew Relig)
yill–caup . . . 6. ale cup
vin . . . 4. dark, evil (opp of yang)
Ymir, Ymer (pert to) . . .
blood of . . 3. sea
bones of . . 9. mountains
brains of . . 6. clouds
flesh of . . 5. earth
killed by . . 2. Ve 4. Odin, Vili
Norse Myth . . 3. God 13. rime–cold
  giant (body–shaped world)
yodel, yodle . . . 4. call, sing (falsetto)
  5. carol, shout 6. warble
yoga (pert to) . . .
follower of . . 4. yogi (yogin) 5. fakir
  7. ascetic 9. occultist
objective . . 16. mental discipline
stages . . 5. jnana, karma 6. bhakti
trance . . 6. dhyana 7. dharana
  samadhi
yoke . . . 3. two 4. join, link, pair, span,
  team 5. frame, marry 6. cangue,
  couple, inspan 7. bondage, enclave,
  harness, oppress, pillory, shackle,
  slavery 9. associate, servitude
yoked . . . 6. united 7. coupled
  9. conjugate
yokel . . . 3. oaf 4. boor, clod, hick,
  lout, rube 6. rustic 7. bumpkin,
  hayseed, plowboy 8. Abderite (anc),
  gullible 9. simpleton 10. countryman,
  slow–witted
yokemate . . . 4. mate 6. fellow, spouse
  7. partner 9. companion
yolked (egg) . . . 6. yellow 8. lecithal,
  vitellus
Yom Kippur (Jew) . . . 7. fast day
  14. Day of Atonement
Yom Teruah (Jew) . . . 15. Feast of
  Trumpets
Yom Tob, or Tov (Jew) . . . 8. festival
yon, yonder . . . 4. away 6. beyond
  7. distant, thither 11. at a distance
yore . . . 5. of old, olden 6. before 9. in
  old time, long since
young . . . 3. fry, new 4. tyro 5. brood,
  fresh, green 6. litter, novice, tender
  7. pliable 8. childish, immature,
  juvenile, youthful 9. offspring,
  succulent 13. inexperienced
young (pert to) . . .
bear, fox . . 3. cub

birds .. 5. brood
calf (motherless) .. 5. dogie
hare .. 7. leveret
herring .. 4. brit
horse .. 4. colt, foal
oyster .. 4. spat
pigeon .. 5. piper
youngling ... 5. youth 6. novice
  8. beginner, neophyte
youngster ... 3. boy, kid, lad, pup, tad
  4. baby, lass, tike 5. child, youth
  6. filius, shaver, urchin 7. Aladdin
  (Arab Nights) 8. teenager 9. fledgling,
  stripling
younker ... 5. child, youth 6. knight
  7. gallant 8. nobleman 9. stripling
youth goddess ... 4. Hebe
yo–yo ... 3. top, toy
Ypres, Belgium ...
  famed for .. 7. Battles (WWI)
  lace .. 12. Valenciennes
  province of .. 8. Flanders
  ruins rebuilt .. 9. Cloth Hall 15. Gothic
  Cathedral (St Martin)
ypsiliform, shape of ... 7. letter T (Gr)
yu (Chin) ... 4. jade
Yucatan, Cent America ...
  anc domain of .. 5. Mayas
  capital .. 6. Mérida
  city .. 5. Sisal
  peninsula of .. 6. Mexico
yucca (pert to) ...
  called .. 11. Adam's needle
  family .. 9. Liliaceae
  native of .. 7. America
  species .. 9. bear grass

State flower of .. 9. New Mexico
Yugoslavia ...
  capital .. 8. Belgrade
  city .. 5. Senta 7. Skoplje
  former leader .. 4. Tito (Communist)
  lead works (among world's largest) ...
  6. Trepca
  natives .. 5. Serbs 6. Croats
  8. Slovenes
  river .. 5. Drava, Drina 6. Danube
  sea .. 8. Adriatic
  seaport .. 6. Rijeka
yukkel ... 7. flicker 10. woodpecker
Yukon ...
  famed for .. 4. gold (mining)
  ocean .. 6. Arctic
  river .. 5. Lewes, Yukon
  territory of .. 6. Canada
  town .. 10. Whitehorse
Yule ... 4. Noel 8. Nativity (Feast of
  the), yuletide 9. Christmas
  13. Christmastide
Yule (pert to) ...
  plant .. 5. holly 9. mistletoe
  good cheer .. 11. wassail bowl
Yuma (Ariz) ... 4. city 9. Talkepaia
  (Indian)
yun ... 9. Laos tribe (tattooed)
Yunca ... 6. Indian (Peru)
Yurma ... 6. Indian (Brazil)
Yurok ... 6. Indian (Calif)
yurt, yurta ... 4. tent (Siberia)
Yuruk ... 10. Turkish rug
yutu ... 7. tinamou
Yuzen birodo ... 6. velvet (designed)

Z

Z ... 3. end, zed, zee 5. omega
  6. izzard, letter (26th)
zac ... 4. ibex
zacate ... 7. herbage 9. rice grass
Zacchaeus, Zaccheus ... 4. pure
  8. innocent, publican (Bib)
Zachariah, Zacharias (Bib) ...
  father .. 9. Barachias
  father of .. 14. John the Baptist
  literally .. 21. Jehovah hath
  remembered
Zadkiel (Jew) ... 5. angel (of planet
  Jupiter)
zaftig ... 5. buxom 7. shapely
Zagreus ... 3. god 8. Dionysus
  (identified with)
Zaire, Africa ...
  capital .. 8. Kinshasa
  formerly .. 12. Belgian Congo
  river .. 5. Kasai, Zaire (Congo)
zaman, zamang ... 8. rain tree
Zambia, Africa ...
  capital .. 6. Lusaka
  formerly .. 16. Northern Rhodesia

  wealth .. 6. copper (3rd largest)
Zamenhof, inventor of ...
  9. Esperanto
zampogna ... 7. bagpipe, panpipe
zanja ... 5. canal, gully 6. arroyo
zany ... 3. wag, wit 4. dolt, fool
  5. clown, crazy, goofy, kooky, nutty
  6. madcap, sawney 7. acrobat,
  bonkers, buffoon, idiotic 8. clownish
  9. simpleton 10. lieutenant,
  mountebank 11. merry–andrew
Zanzibar, Africa ... see Tanzania
zap ... 4. slay, stun 5. smite 6. strike
zapatero ... 7. boxwood, cobbler,
  dogwood
zarf ... 9. cup holder (Levant)
zati ... 6. monkey (bonnet)
zeal ... 5. ardor, piety 6. desire, fervor
  7. passion 8. devotion 9. eagerness
  10. enthusiasm, fanaticism
zealot ... 4. sect 5. bigot, freak (sl)
  6. votary 7. devotee, faddist, fanatic,
  pietist 8. partisan 10. enthusiast
zealous ... 5. eager, pious 6. ardent,

fervid 7. devoted, fervent
9. phrenetic 11. industrious
zebra (pert to)...
ally.. 6. quagga
Burchell's.. 4. dauw (nonstriped legs)
hybrid.. 8. zebrinny
insect.. 9. butterfly
ref to.. 7. zebrine, zebroid
zebrawood... 5. shrub 7. araroba
10. marblewood
zebu... 2. ox 5. zebus (group)
6. cattle 12. Brahmany bull (sacred)
zecchino... 6. sequin (chequeen)
Zechariah (Bib)... 7. prophet 12. King
of Israel
zed... 7. letter Z (Brit)
zeekoe... 12. hippopotamus
zeism... 8. pellagra 11. morbid state
zemi... 4. holy (Peru) 5. huaca (huaco)
6. fetish, sacred, spirit (magic)
Zemzem... 10. sacred well (Mecca)
Zen... 12. Buddhist sect
zenana... 5. harem, serai 7. mission
8. seraglio
Zenda, Prisoner of... 9. Ruritania
Zend–Avesta... 10. sacred text
(Zoroastrian)
zenith... 3. top 4. acme, apex, blue,
peak 6. apogee, climax, summit,
vertex 11. culmination 14. greatest
height (opp of nadir)
Zeno... 5. Stoic 11. philosopher (Gr)
zenography, study of... 7. Jupiter
(planet)
zenu... 5. sheep
zephyr... 5. shawl 6. breath, breeze
zero... 3. nil 4. hour 5. zilch
6. cipher, nought (naught) 7. nothing,
nullity 11. temperature
zest... 4. tang 5. gusto, savor
6. flavor, relish 8. membrane (fruit),
piquancy, pungency 9. eagerness
10. enthusiasm
Zeus (pert to)...
attendant.. 4. Nike
consort.. 6. Europa
brother of.. 5. Hades 8. Poseidon
deity.. 7. supreme 12. father of gods
father.. 6. Cronus
games in his honor.. 6. Nemean
8. Olympian
messenger.. 4. Iris 6. Hermes
mother.. 4. Rhea
oracle.. 6. Dodona
Roman.. 7. Jupiter
sister.. 4. Hera
son.. 4. Ares 5. Argus 6. Apollo,
Hermes 7. Perseus 8. Dionysus,
Hercules, Tantalus
temple (Athens).. 8. Olympium
ziara, ziarat... 4. tomb (Moslem saint)
6. shrine
zibet, zibeth... 5. civet
ziganka... 5. dance (rustic)
zigeuner... 5. gypsy 7. czigany,
Zincalo, zingaro
ziggurat... 11. temple tower
12. Tower of Babel (Bib)
zigzag... 5. turns 6. angles 7. stagger
8. flexuous, wavering 9. alternate
zillion... 4. many 9. countless

Zimbabwe...
capital.. 6. Harare
Falls.. 8. Victoria
Falls discoverer.. 11. Livingstone
(1855)
formerly.. 8. Rhodesia
tribe.. 5. Bantu
zinc (pert to)...
alloy.. 5. bidri 7. paktong
alloy with copper.. 6. oroide
crude.. 7. tutenag (tutenague)
slabs.. 6. solder 7. spelter
symbol.. 2. Zn
zing... 3. pep, vim, zip 5. vigor
6. energy, spirit, thrill 10. enthusiasm
zingaresca (gypsy)... 4. song 5. dance
zingaro... 5. gypsy
Zion (pert to)... 4. hill (Jerusalem)
10. Israelites 12. chosen people
zip... 4. zing 5. close, speed
6. energy 8. pungency 10. sibilation
zizith... 7. fringes (Bib), tassels
zoanthropy... 9. monomania
15. changed to animal (belief)
zobo... 6. hybrid 10. zebu and yak
zodiac... 4. belt, zone 5. stars
7. circuit
zodiac signs (twelve)... 3. Leo
5. Aries, Libra, Virgo 6. Cancer,
Gemini, Pisces, Taurus 7. Scorpio
8. Aquarius 9. Capricorn
11. Capricornus, Sagittarius
zoetic... 5. vital 6. living 7. organic
zombi, zombie... 5. corpse 6. voodoo
zone... 4. area, band, belt, isle, path
5. Canal, clime, girth, tract 6. assise,
circle, course, Frigid, region, Torrid
7. stratum 8. cincture, latitude
9. Temperate
zoo... 9. menagerie 10. collection
12. animal garden
zoo, zō (comb form)... 6. animal
zoologist... 9. biologist, scientist
zoology, science of... 7. animals
zoology branches... 8. taxonomy
9. bionomics, phylogeny
10. embryology, entomology
11. herpetology, ornithology
zoom... 4. lens, rise 5. climb
zoopathology, science of...
8. diseases (animal) 11. zoonosology
zoophilist... 11. animal lover
zoophobia... 11. fear of animals
zoophyte... 5. coral 6. sponge
10. sea anemone
zootomy... 13. animal anatomy
16. animal dissection
zootrophy... 13. animal rearing
zoril, zorillo... 5. skunk 7. polecat
Zoroaster, Zarathustra... 7. Persian
8. reformer (Relig)
Zoroastrianism (pert to)...
adherence to.. 5. Parse (Parsee)
doctrine.. 7. dualism 11. good and
evil
evil spirit.. 4. deva 7. Ahriman
fire worshiper.. 6. Gheber
founder.. 9. Zoroaster
literature.. 6. Avesta
lord of creation.. 6. Ormazd
religion of.. 6. Persia (anc)

zoster... 4. zona 6. girdle 8. shingles
(Med) 12. herpes zoster
Zouave... 4. Zu–Zu 8. chasseur
11. infantryman
Zu (Bab Myth)... 8. storm god (evil)
9. blackbird (symbol)
Zuider Zee (pert to)...
gulf.. 8. North Sea
Netherlands.. 4. dike 7. highway
present name.. 9. Ijsel Lake, Ijselmeer
zuisin... 7. widgeon
Zulu (pert to)...
army.. 4. impi 7. Kaffirs
boy.. 6. umfaan
conference.. 6. indaba
marauders.. 4. Viti
people.. 6. Santus 7. Kaffirs
spear.. 7. assagai (assegai)

Zululand capital... 6. Eshowe
Zuñi (pert to)...
famed for.. 19. Seven Cities of Cibola
(Myth)
Indian.. 4. Hopi 6. Ashivi
kingdom of Cibola.. 16. gold–paved
streets (Myth)
zwieback... 4. rusk 7. biscuit (toasted)
Zwinger... 6. palace (Dresden)
zygal... 7. H–shaped
zygodactyl (zygodactyle)...
8. yoke–toed 10. paired toes
zygon... 5. bench 6. thwart 9. brain
part
zygous... 5. yoked 6. paired
zymology *(science of)*...
12. fermentation
zymosis... 12. fermentation
zythum... 4. beer (anc Egypt)